THE ST. MARTIN'S PRESS DICTIONARY OF BIOGRAPHY

THE ST. MARTIN'S PRESS DICTIONARY OF BIOGRAPHY

BARRY JONES
AND M. V. DIXON

ST. MARTIN'S PRESS
NEW YORK

First published in Australia by The Macmillan Company of Australia Pty. Ltd.
Printed in Hong Kong
First U.S. Edition
10 9 8 7 6 5 4 3 2 1

Library of Congress Cataloging-in-Publication Data

Jones, Barry O.
St. Martin's Press dictionary of biography.

Rev. ed. of: The Macmillan dictionary of biography. 1981.
Includes bibliographies.
1. Biography — Dictionaries. I. Dixon, M. V. (Meredith Vibart), 1898–1967. II. Jones, Barry O. Macmillan dictionary of biography. III. St. Martin's Press. IV. Title. V. Saint Martin's Press dictionary of biography. VI. Title: Dictionary of biography.
CT103.J693 1986 920.'02 [B] 85-30393
ISBN 0-312-69733-3

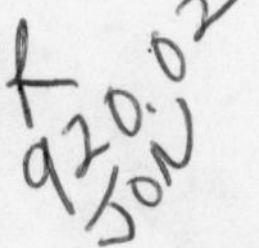

A

Aalto, Alvar (1898–1976). Finnish architect and designer. Finnish pavilions at international exhibitions in Paris (1937) and New York (1939) were his first major successes outside Finland. There he had long been known for his imaginatively functional buildings, public, industrial and domestic; in the first category the library at Viipuri is among the most notable. A feature of his work is his combination of wood with brickwork, glass, copper and cement. After the war Aalto lectured at the Massachusetts Institute of Technology, for which he designed a students' hostel. In 1957 he received the gold medal of the Royal Institute of British Architects.

Aalto also developed functional plywood furniture, mass-produced in his own factory. Until her death in 1949 his wife, Aino, collaborated with him in all his work.

Aaron. In the Bible story, with his brother Moses, he led the Israelites from Egypt to Canaan (Palestine) and became their first high priest, but while Moses was receiving the ten commandments on Mount Sinai he made a golden calf for the people to worship (Ex. xxiii).

Abbas (566–652). Uncle of Mohammed and ancestor of the Abbasid dynasty which held the caliphate of Baghdad from 750 to 1258.

Abbas II (Abbas Hilmi) (1874–1944). Khedive (viceroy) of Egypt 1892–1914. When Turkey entered World War I in 1914 he was deposed by the British. He was succeeded by his uncle, Hussein with the title of Sultan and went into exile in Switzerland.

Abbas, Ferhat (1899–). Leader of the Algerian National Liberation Front (F.L.N.) from 1956 until the granting of independence in July 1962. In September he was chosen to preside over the newly elected constituent assembly, but was forced to resign the following year when a new constitution was promulgated without consultation, his rival Ben Bella becoming first president of independent Algeria.

Abboud, Ibrahim (1900–1983). Sudanese soldier and political leader. His military service was mostly spent with the Sudan Defence Force, with which he served on the side of the Allies in World War II. He became commander-in-chief of the army of independent Sudan in 1956 and two years later assumed political control to end anarchy. He was removed from the presidency in a bloodless revolution in 1964.

Abd al Krim (1882–1963). Moroccan leader. For years from 1920 he maintained an active nationalist resistance in the Rif mountains (after which the war was called) until in 1926 he was finally overcome by a combined Franco-Spanish army. Exiled to the island of Réunion, he remained there till 1948, after which he went to Egypt, where he spent the rest of his life.
Furneaux, R., *Abdel Krim: Emir of the Rif*. 1967

Abdul Aziz ibn Saud *see* **Ibn Sa'ud**

Abdul-Hamid II (1842–1918). Sultan of Turkey. In 1876 he began a disastrous reign, marked by personal incompetence and military failure, as a result of which much of

Turkey's Balkan empire was lost. He lived in seclusion in his palace, the Yildiz Kiosk, surrounded by favourite astrologers and the apparatus of despotism. The Young Turk revolution of 1908 forced constitutional concessions and his abdication the following year.

Abdullah (1882–1951). Emir (1921–46) and king (1946–51) of Transjordan, renamed Jordan in 1949. He was the son of Emir Hussein of the Hejaz and brother of Faisal I of Iraq. With the rest of his family he gave active help to Britain in World War I and was made emir of Transjordan as a reward, the title of king being assumed when the country became fully independent in 1946. He annexed parts of Arab Palestine in 1948 when Israel was formed. Abdullah, a wise and cautious ruler, was assassinated by an Arab fanatic.

Abdul Rahman Putra, Tunku (1903–). Malayan prince (tunku) and politician. Educated in England at Cambridge University, he was called to the bar, and joined the public prosecutor's department of his state of Kedah in 1949. In 1952 he was nominated to the federal executive and legislative councils, became chief minister (1955) and then the first prime minister of the Malayan federation (1957–70). He retained this office when, as the result of an idea of his own, the federation was enlarged (1964) under the name of Malaysia to include Sabah (British North Borneo) and Sarawak.

Abelard, Peter (1079–1142). French philosopher and theologian of a noble Breton family. He became a lecturer in Paris and seduced and married a 17-year-old pupil, Héloïse, whose uncle, Fulbert, canon of Notre Dame, eventually had him castrated. She became a nun and he a monk. Later his retreat at Nogent-sur-Seine, known as Le Paraclet, was visited by scores of disciples. Convicted of heresy, he was eventually absolved by the pope. His own account of his life and his correspondence with Héloïse have perpetuated one of the most famous love stories of the world. In 1817 the two were laid together in one tomb in the Père-Lachaise cemetery in Paris.

His contribution to the philosophical problem of universals was that a general word (e.g. 'pink') does not have meaning by standing for a single quality (e.g. pinkness) that somehow exists, but rather by being tied to a mental concept we acquire by noticing similarities between different things (e.g. pink ones). He extolled the use of reason in religion while giving a place to faith. One of his best known works is *Sic et non* (*Yes and No*), which revealed the contradictions in the works of the early Christian fathers.

Gibson, E., *Héloïse and Abelard.* 1953. Sikes, J. G., *Peter Abailard.* 1932

Abercrombie, Lascelles (1881–1938). English poet associated with the 'Georgian' group. His most mature work was a poetic drama, *The Sale of St. Thomas* (1931). His prose works are mainly concerned with theories of poetry and prosody. He was professor of English at Bedford College, London University (1929–35).

Abercrombie, Sir (Leslie) Patrick (1879–1957). British town planner. He first practised as an architect in Manchester and was professor of civil design at Liverpool 1915–35. During these years plans for preserving Stratford-on-Avon and other English towns made him well known in his particular field. He was professor of town planning at University College, London (1935–46), and the 'Greater London Plan' (1943) crowned his life's work.

Abercromby, Sir Ralph (1734–1801). Scottish soldier. After being trained for the law he was commissioned in the 3rd Dragoon Guards in 1756, and fought with distinction in the Seven Years War and the French wars at the close of the century. He was knighted in 1795 and, as leader of the West Indies campaign which immediately followed, received fresh acclaim. While commander-in-chief of British forces in the Mediterranean he made (June 1801) a successful landing at Aboukir Bay, Alexandria. The French counter-attack was repulsed but Abercromby himself died of wounds.

Dunfermline, Lord, *Sir Ralph Abercromby.* 1861

Aberdeen, George Hamilton Gordon, 4th Earl of (1784–1860). Scottish nobleman, who succeeded to his title in 1801. After being ambassador in Vienna and in 1814 signing in Paris the treaty which was intended to bring the Napoleonic wars to a final end, he entered politics. Foreign secretary (1828–30) under Wellington, he later became a close supporter

of Robert Peel. He served in the ministry of 1834–35 as war and colonial secretary and was again foreign secretary (1841–46). Having succeeded as leader of the Peelite group, he was prime minister (1852–55), resigning after criticism of his feeble handling of the Crimean War.
Balfour, Lady F., *Life of George, Fourth Earl of Aberdeen*. 1923. Stanmore, Lord, *The Earl of Aberdeen*. 1893

Aberhart, William (1878–1943). Premier of Alberta in Canada (1935–43). He was remarkable for his attempt to transplant in Canada the Social Credit policies of Major C. H. * Douglas. His scope of action was however limited by the overriding authority of the federal government. In earlier life Aberhart had been a clergyman and a schoolmaster.

Abraham (or Abram) (*c.* 2100–*c.* 2000 B.C.). Traditional ancestor of the Israelites. According to the biblical account (Gen. xi, 26 ff.) he was born in Ur of the Chaldees (in Mesopotamia), went to Canaan and thence, at the call of God, migrated with Sarah his wife and his whole household to Canaan (Palestine). His faith was tested when God commanded him to sacrifice his son Isaac. It was only at the last moment that he was told to substitute a ram.

Abu-Bekr (573–634). Father of Ayesha, one of Mohammed's wives. In 632, on his son-in-law's death, he became the first caliph (*khalifa*, 'successor'). His claim was disputed by Mohammed's son-in-law * Ali, whose followers became known as Shi'ites.

Acheson, Dean Gooderham (1893–1971). American secretary of state (1949–53) under President Truman. He was especially associated with the Truman doctrine of aid to countries under threat of aggression. He was born in Connecticut, educated at Yale and Harvard and had gained a reputation as an international lawyer before becoming an assistant secretary of state in 1941. His *Present at the Creation*, an account of his time at the Department of State, won the Pulitzer prize for history in 1970.

Ackermann, Rudolph (1764–1834). German-born lithographer. He published and sold from his shop in the Strand (opened 1795) illustrated books and periodicals containing prints by Rowlandson, Pugin and other well known artists of his day.

Acton, John Emerich Edward Dalberg Acton, 1st Baron (1834–1902). English historian, born in the Kingdom of Naples where his grandfather was prime minister in Napoleonic times. He was brought up in the household of the 2nd Earl * Granville, who married his widowed mother, and his later education took place in Germany where he acquired his mastery of historical method. He was a Liberal M.P. (1859–65) but reached his greatest fame as professor of modern history at Cambridge (1895–1902), where he planned the original *Cambridge Modern History*. Though he was a Roman Catholic, his liberalism made him strongly oppose the dogma of papal infallibility (1870). To him is attributed the maxim 'Power tends to corrupt and absolute power corrupts absolutely'.
Mathew, D., *Lord Acton and his Times*. 1968; *Acton: The Formative Years*. 1972

Adam, Adolphe Charles (1803–1856). French composer. A professor at the Paris Conservatoire from 1848, his best known work is the ballet *Giselle* (1841), but he also wrote several operas.

Adam, Robert (1728–1792) and **James** (1730–1794). The two best known of a family of Scottish architects, James acting mainly as his brother's assistant. As a young man Robert, who was brought up on the family estate in Kinross-shire, was sent by his father (himself an architect of distinction in the Palladian tradition) to Italy, where, without neglecting the Renaissance masters, he made a special study of the antiquities of Rome, Pompeii and Herculaneum. Across the Adriatic the ruins of Diocletian's palace at Spalato (Split), much more complete than they are today, provided a theme for a book, fully illustrated by his own drawings, published in 1764. They also strongly influenced his designs for the Adelphi (i.e. The Brothers) Terrace, an unfortunate financial speculation but an artistic triumph (destroyed in our own time).

Out of his studies gradually emerged the so-called Adam style, based on the principle that exterior, interior and furnishings should form a harmonious whole. Details were largely elegant adaptations of Roman and Greek models. Outstanding among the many Adam

country houses are Harewood in Yorkshire, Kedleston in Derbyshire and Syon and Osterley near London. The famous town houses were a later phase. Robert, who was unmarried, was buried in Westminster Abbey.
Bolton, A. T., *The Architecture of R. and J. Adam*. 1922

Adams, Sir Grantley Herbert (1898–1971). First and only prime minister of the West Indian federation (1958–62). He was educated at Oxford University, and became a successful lawyer in Barbados, for which he played cricket. He was premier of Barbados (1954–58).

Adams, Henry Brooks (1838–1918). American historian. Grandson of John Quincy * Adams and son of Charles Francis Adams. American ambassador in Great Britain during the Civil War, Henry must have gained from experience as his father's secretary during this period. From 1870 to 1877 he was teaching history at Harvard, where he had been educated, but then moved to Washington for the preparation of his great *History of the U.S.A. During the Administrations of Thomas Jefferson and James Madison* (9 volumes, 1889–91), which set a standard in documentation. Lesser historical work followed but in later life Adams turned to general literature, having already written *Democracy* (1880), a slashing satirical novel of Washington society. *Mont-Saint-Michel and Chartres* is a study of the unifying forces of medievalism symbolized by these great buildings. *The Education of Henry Adams*, an ironical autobiography, is concerned by contrast with the centrifugal forces of modern life. Both (first printed privately in 1904 and 1906 respectively) have become American classics.
Levenson, J. C., *The Mind and Art of Henry Adams*. 1957. Samuels, E., *The Young Henry Adams*. 1948; *Henry Adams: The Middle Years*. 1958; *Henry Adams: The Major Phase*. 1964

Adams, John (1735–1826). Second president of the U.S. (1797–1801). Born in Braintree (Quincy), Massachusetts, and educated at Harvard College. He was cousin of Samuel * Adams. He became a leading lawyer and politically a strong supporter of the colonial cause, relying upon the argument 'No taxation without representation', but revealed his fairness by defending British soldiers who had fired upon and killed some of a group of Boston citizens who had been baiting a sentry. He was prominent in the Continental Congresses, and signed the Declaration of Independence (1776) which he had helped to draft. He was appointed diplomatic representative to France (1778) and Holland (1781) and with Franklin and Jay negotiated the treaty of Versailles (1783), which brought the War of Independence to an end. After serving as the first U.S. minister to Great Britain (1785–88), he returned home and as leading member of Washington's Federalist party became the first vice-president of the U.S.A. (1789–97), bewailing the lack of power of 'this most insignificant office'. When Washington announced his retirement in 1796 he was elected president of the U.S.A. but in 1800 was defeated by Jefferson when he stood for re-election. He returned to his home at Quincy, wrote several books analysing the machinery of American government, and died on the 50th anniversary of the signing of the Declaration of Independence.
Smith, P., *John Adams*. 1962

Adams, John Couch (1819–1892). English astronomer. In 1845 he predicted the existence of the planet Neptune from calculations on irregularities in the orbit of Uranus. Delay in publication resulted in his sharing credit for discovery of the planet with * Leverrier who, working independently, presented similar calculations to the Académie Française in 1846. Other notable work by Adams included researches on the moon's motion. He was professor of astronomy at Cambridge from 1859 until his death.

Adams, John Quincy (1767–1848). Eldest son of John * Adams and sixth president of the U.S. (1825–29). His natural precocity was increased by accompanying his father on diplomatic missions. At the age of 14 he was secretary to the American ambassador in St Petersburg and at 16 to his father, ambassador in Paris. He graduated at Harvard in 1787, started work as a lawyer, but was soon recalled to diplomacy. He was minister to Holland (1794–96), to Portugal (1796) and to Prussia (1797–1801). Back in America he was elected senator for Massachusetts in 1803 but disagreed with the Federalist party in such matters as voting for the Louisiana Purchase, and was soon back to diplomacy as minister to

Russia (1809–14). He was appointed a justice of the United States Supreme Court in 1811 but declined this office. He negotiated the peace treaty of Ghent with England in 1814, and was minister to Great Britain (1815–17). As secretary of state under President * Monroe (1817–25) he was responsible for formulating and applying the 'Monroe Doctrine'. No candidate gained a clear majority at the presidential election of 1824, and the situation was referred to the House of Representatives, which chose Adams. Embittered by slander and defeat by Jackson in the presidential election of 1828 he retired to Quincy only to show his resilience by securing election to the House of Representatives. Here from 1831 until his death he was known for his vehement attacks on slavery. He died in the House after a vigorous speech.
Lipsky, G. A., *John Quincy Adams: His Theory and Ideas*. 1950

Adams, Samuel (1722–1803). American politician. Born in Boston. The first distinguished member of the Massachusetts family which played such an important part in American history, Adams squandered his inheritance, mismanaged his post as a tax collector, but showed great talent as a political agitator and fiery propagandist. By fomenting and publishing the grievances of the American colonists as a radical leader in the state House of Representatives, he played a decisive part in the contrivance of events, such as the Boston Tea Party (1773), that led up to the Declaration of Independence, of which he was a signatory.
Miller, J. C., *Sam Adams: Pioneer in Propaganda*. 1936

Adams, William (1564–1620). English sailor. The first Englishman to settle in Japan (1600), he became the principal adviser on shipbuilding and trade: because of his usefulness he was not allowed to leave. He established a post there for the East India Company.
Purnell, C. J., *Log-Book of William Adams*. 1916. Sladen, D., and Lorimer, N., *More Queer Things about Japan and the Letters of William Adams*. 1904

Addams, Jane (1860–1935). American social reformer, born at Cedarville, Illinois. She founded (1889) the Hull House social settlement in Chicago and worked for female suffrage, social justice and the cause of peace. She shared the Nobel Peace Prize in 1931.
Tims, M., *Jane Addams of Hull House*. 1961

Addington, Henry, 1st Viscount Sidmouth (1757–1844). English politician. He entered parliament in 1784, was speaker of the House of Commons (1789–1801) and prime minister during Pitt's temporary retirement (1801–04). His incompetence was revealed when war broke out again; Pitt turned against him but after reconciliation took him into his own ministry. Thereafter he was almost continuously in office until his opposition to Canning's policy of recognizing the independence of the Spanish colonies in South America led to his final retirement. As home secretary (1812–21) he was responsible for many repressive measures and incurred odium as a result of the 'Peterloo Massacre' of 1819. As a Tory he was opposed to Roman Catholic emancipation and parliamentary reform. He received his peerage in 1805.
Zeigler, P., *Addington*. 1962

Addison, Joseph (1672–1719). English essayist, chiefly remembered as the founder of and chief contributor to the *Spectator* (first appeared 1711). A sickly precocious child, he was educated at Charterhouse and Oxford. His poem *The Campaign* (1704), written to celebrate Marlborough's victory at Blenheim, won him a post as commissioner of excise; similar posts maintained him in comfort for the rest of his life. He became the main contributor to the *Tatler*, founded (1709) by his boyhood friend Steele, and Steele later joined him on the *Spectator*. The declared aim of both men was to 'enliven morality with wit and to temper wit with morality', and it is likely that the influence of both on English manners in the 18th century was more profound than the elegance and sober good sense of the papers would suggest. Addison's tragedy *Cato* (1713) was highly successful in its day.
Smithers, P., *The Life of Joseph Addison*. 1954

Addison, Thomas (1793–1860). English physician and pioneer endocrinologist. His early work was on the action of poisons on the human body, and in his *Elements of the practice of medicine* (1839) he printed an important account of appendicitis. But he is mostly remembered for his researches into the glands, and for his pioneering work on anaemia. On the basis of autopsies, he sug-

gested in 1849 a connexion between anaemia and diseases of the suprarenals. This work was extended in his book *On the Constitutional and Local Effects of Disease of the Supra-Renal Capsules* (1855), in which he identified 'idiopathic' anaemia (later known as Addisonian anaemia). He also identified what became known as 'Addison's disease', a condition of the suprarenal capsules which produced weakness, a bronze pigmentation of the skin, and fatality in the patient.
Singer, C. and Underwood, E. A. *Short history of medicine*. 1962

Adelaide (1792–1849). The daughter of the Duke of Saxe-Coburg Meiningen, she married (1818) the Duke of Clarence, later * William IV of Great Britain. The capital of South Australia is named after her.
Hopkirk, M., *Queen Adelaide*. 1946

Adenauer, Konrad (1876–1967). The first chancellor (prime minister) and main architect of the West German federal republic. He first came into prominence as mayor of Cologne, a post which he held from 1917 until he was removed by the Nazis (1933). During the remaining years of Hitler's supremacy he was twice imprisoned. After the Allied victory (1945) he resumed office in Cologne and in the same year founded the Christian Democratic party, which included both Roman Catholics and Protestants. This became the basis of his power when (1949) he became the first chancellor of the new West German state. His political good sense combined with stubbornness won him respect and authority in Germany and enabled him to re-establish the position of his country within the community of nations, and to pursue a policy of economic rehabilitation which came to be known as the German 'economic miracle'. He negotiated West Germany's entry into NATO, the Common Market and other international bodies, and in particular established a personal rapprochement with President de Gaulle. He resigned the chancellorship in 1963 and was succeeded by his economics minister Ludwig * Erhard. Adenauer, however, retained the chairmanship of the party.
Weymar, P., *Konrad Adenauer*, Eng. trans. 1957. Wighton, K. C., *Adenauer: Democratic Dictator*. 1963

Adler, Alfred (1870–1937). Austrian psychologist. He was an eye specialist before taking up psychiatry and working with Freud, from whom however he finally broke away in 1911 (mainly through disagreement with what he regarded as Freud's undue emphasis on infantile sexuality), and established his own system. He stressed the link between hereditary physical defects and psychological states but is best known for the importance he ascribed to the will to dominate and its frustration. The popular use of the phrase 'inferiority complex' is derived from his teaching.
Bottome, P., *Alfred Adler: Apostle of Freedom*. 3rd ed. 1957

Adler, Felix (1851–1933). American sociologist. German-born son of a rabbi, he established the first child-study group and the first free kindergarten in the U.S.A. He was a pioneer of the Ethical Culture movement, aimed at providing ethical and moral teaching outside the churches.

Adrian IV (Nicholas Breakspear) (*c*. 1100–1159). The only Englishman ever to become pope (1154). Born near St Albans, he became a canon of a monastery at Avignon in France and was cardinal-bishop of Albano in Italy (1146–54). As pope he reasserted papal power (* Arnold of Brescia), crowned Frederick I (Barbarossa) emperor in 1155, but later opposed him on the basis of his theories of papal supremacy.
Mann, H. K., *Nicholas Breakspear*. 1914

Adrian VI (Adriaan Dedel), (1459–1523). Pope (1522–23). He was born in Utrecht and grew up to become a distinguished theologian. As tutor to the young Charles of Burgundy and the Low Countries (later king of Spain and emperor Charles V), he attained political and ecclesiastical preferment. Inquisitor-general of Aragon in 1516, cardinal in 1517, he became (1522) the last non-Italian pope until John Paul II. Zeal for reform within the church combined with opposition to all doctrinal change won him enemies both in Rome and among Luther's adherents: moreover his inability to prevent the Turkish seizure (1522) of Rhodes from the Knights of St John marked his political failure.
Hock, E., *Der Letzte deutsche Papst, Adrian VI*. 1939

Adrian, Edgar Douglas Adrian, 1st Baron (1889–1977). English physiologist. He was born in London, educated at Westminster and Trinity College, Cambridge, and trained for medicine at St Bartholomew's Hospital, London. Most of his career was spent at Cambridge, where he was professor of physiology (1937–51) and master of Trinity. He achieved fame for his work on the transmission, by nerve impulses, of sensation and muscular control: his later work was on the electrical activity of the brain itself. Among the many honours received for his neurological research were a Nobel Prize for Medicine and Physiology (shared with Sir Charles Sherrington) in 1932, the O.M. (1942), and his peerage (1955). He retired as master of Trinity in 1965 and was succeeded by R. A. Butler.

A. E. (pen name of George William Russell) *see* **Russell**

Aelfric (*c.* 955–*c.* 1020). The best known Anglo-Saxon scholar and writer of his time. He wrote homilies, sermons, a colloquy between the teacher, the pupil and such characters as ploughman, hunter, etc., a paraphrase of the early books of the Old Testament and some lives of saints, e.g. St Oswald and St Edmund.

Aeschines (389–314 B.C.). Athenian orator and great rival of Demosthenes. One famous speech (against Ctesiphon) and two others alone survive, but his importance lies in the fact that he was chief spokesman of the party of appeasement in the face of the encroachments of Philip II of Macedon and so delayed the resistance advocated by Demosthenes until too late.

Aeschylus (*c.* 525–456/5 B.C.). The earliest of the Athenian dramatists whose works have survived. Of ninety plays (which began to appear 499–496) only seven survive. *The Persians* deals with the historic struggle of the Greeks against Xerxes, the remainder are inspired by ancient legends of gods and heroes. Comprising the great trilogy of the *Oresteia* are the *Agamemnon*, telling of the king's murder on his return from Troy by his wife Clytemnestra and her lover Aegisthus, the *Choephoroe*, in which Orestes and his sister Electra avenge their father, and the *Eumenides*, which relates the pursuit of Orestes by 'Furies', his trial and final acquittal by the goddess Athena. Other surviving plays are *The Suppliants, Seven Against Thebes* and *Prometheus Unbound.* All deal with the expiation of sin. The plays of Aeschylus were the first to have two actors (in addition to chorus); in the *Oresteia* there are three.

Murray, G. G. A., *Aeschylus the Creator of Tragedy*. 1940

Aesop. The name of the traditional author of Greek beast-fables. He is supposed to have lived in the 6th century B.C. but even his existence is uncertain. The first collection of Greek fables, now lost, was made in the 4th century B.C. by Demetrius of Phaleron; a metrical collection by Babrius (probably 2nd century A.D.) contains the first Greek fables to survive. Clearly the fables ascribed to Aesop originated in many countries and were the work of many hands.

Aga Khan. Hereditary title held by the spiritual head of the Ismaeli sect of Moslems, who claims descent from Fatima, daughter of the prophet Mohammed. The first Aga Khan, **Hasum Ali Shah** (1800–81), fled from Persia to India, where his services to the British won him recognition and the title 'His Highness'. His grandson, **Aga Khan III** (1877–1957), though best known to British people as a racing enthusiast (he won the Derby five times), was also a statesman of distinction and in 1937 became president of the League of Nations after having represented India in the assembly for several years. He was succeeded by his grandson Karim.

Agassiz, Jean Louis Rodolphe (1807–1873). Biologist. Born in Switzerland, he graduated in medicine (1830), worked in Paris and in 1832 accepted a professorship at Neuchâtel. His early work on fossil fishes was followed by a systematic study of glaciers. In 1846 he went to America and in 1848 became professor of natural history at Harvard. Though a strong opponent of Darwin he proved himself one of the most influential (and most loved) teachers of science of his age. His *A Journey in Brazil* resulted from a scientific expedition to that country, but of his *Contributions to the Natural History of the United States* only four volumes were issued before his death, which took place while he was organizing a unique summer school at Penikese island on the Massachusetts coast. His son **Alexander Agassiz** (1835–1910) who became curator of the Harvard Museum on his father's death,

wrote much on oceanography, coral formations and the embryology of starfishes, etc.
Marcou, J., *Life, Letters and Works of Louis Agassiz*. 1972

Agesilaus (*c*. 444–360 B.C.). King of Sparta, famous for his military skill. His early successes were against the Persians in Ionia, but it was in the long war against an alliance of the other Greek states that he won his most famous victory, that of Coronea (394). In the Theban war, though defeated by Epaminondas at Mantinea (362), he maintained his country's defence.

Agnew, Spiro Theodore (1918–). US politician. Son of a Greek migrant (the family name was Anagnostopoulos), he served in the forces, then became a supermarket manager. County executive in Baltimore 1962–67, he had a meteoric rise to become Governor of Maryland 1967–69 and Richard * Nixon's vice president 1969–73 and seemed a likely nominee for president in 1976. When the Justice Department prosecuted him for receiving 'kickbacks' from Maryland contractors, he pleaded 'no contest' in court, was fined, placed on probation and resigned (October 1973) as vice president. He then joined an international real estate investment firm.

Agoult, Comtesse d' (née Catherine Sophie de Flavigny) (1805–1876). French novelist. Her novel *Nélida* (1846), written under the pen-name Daniel Stern, depicted her relations with the musician Franz Liszt. One of her daughters by Liszt, Cosima, married Richard Wagner.

Agricola, Georgius (Georg Bauer) (1494–1555). German physician and mineralogist. His great work *De re metallica*, written in Venice (1533–53), has caused him to be regarded as the founder of systematic metallurgy.

Agricola, Gnaeus Julius (*c*. 40–93). Roman soldier and administrator. He became governor of Britain in 77 or 78. He consolidated the Roman hold on Wales and pushed the frontier northward into Scotland, but shortly after defeating the Caledonians at Mons Graupius was recalled by the jealous emperor Domitian. His biography, written by his son-in-law Tacitus, survives.

Agrippa, Heinrich Cornelius (1486–1535) (known as Agrippa von Nettesheim). Agrippa enrolled at the University of Cologne (his birthplace) in 1499. He spent the next eleven years alternating studies with service in the army of the Emperor Maximilian I, before the turning-point of his life, his meeting with Johannes Trithemius. Trithemius confirmed Agrippa's life-long interest in magic, occult philosophy, and Hermeticism. He spent the rest of his life as an itinerant, occasionally patronized at the court of Francis I (where he was physician to the queen mother and court astrologer), but also persecuted for his writings. He died in poverty. His major work, the *De Occulta Philosophia* (1531) establishes his vision of the three God-created worlds of the elements, the stars, and the angels, each suffused with spirit, and comprehensible to man who is the microcosm. Through occult knowledge man can control the hidden powers, but only if he is moved by a true love of God. In his *De Incertitudine* (1531) Agrippa expounds the finite nature of man as a created being. Human understanding must always be limited because mundane knowledge can never aspire to the certainty of the word of God. Agrippa was important in the sixteenth century for uniting a magical with a scientific view of the universe. He has been considered as the prototype for Goethe's Faust.
Morley, M. H., *The Life of Henry Cornelius Agrippa von Nettesheim*. 1856

Agrippa, Marcus Vipsanius (63–12 B.C.). Roman commander, famous for his victory over the fleets of Antony and Cleopatra off Actium, a promontory on the west coast of Greece. This victory enabled Octavian, later known as Augustus, to become undisputed master of the Roman world; he showed his gratitude to Agrippa by giving him his widowed daughter Julia in marriage. Their two sons predeceased their grandfather Augustus and their daughter * Agrippina continued the imperial line. He was also a notable engineer: his Pantheon (25 B.C.) still stands in Rome.

Agrippina (died 33). Daughter of * Julia and * Agrippa, she became wife of Germanicus, nephew of Augustus's successor, Tiberius, whom she wrongly blamed for her husband's death. She died in exile. Of her children Gaius, nicknamed * Caligula, became emperor; her daughter, the younger **Agrippina** (died 59), was the mother of the emperor Nero by her first husband and probably poisoned her third, the emperor Claudius. Notorious for her cruelty and depravity, she was eventually put to death by her son Nero.

Ahab (reigned *c.* 875–852 B.C.). King of Israel, whose confiscation of Naboth's vineyard earned him the wrath of the prophet Elisha. His evil genius was his wife Jezebel who persuaded him to introduce the worship of Baal. He was killed in battle with the Syrians by a man who 'drew his bow at a venture'. See I Kings xvi, 29–xxii, 40.

Ahasuerus. The biblical name of several Persian kings. The one who made Esther his queen has been questionably identified with Xerxes I (reigned 485–464 B.C.). The name Ahasuerus was also attributed to the legendary Wandering Jew.

Ahmed Khan, Sir Sayyid (1817–1898). Indian Moslem educator and jurist. He worked in the judicial department of the East India Co. (1841–76), was a major influence in the revival of Urdu as a literary language, and reformed the organisation of Moslem education. In 1875 he opened the Anglo-Oriental College, later called the Aligarh Moslem University.
Graham, G. F. I., *Life and Work of Sir Syed Ahmed Khan*. 1909

Ahmed Shah (1723–1773). Afghan king. At first a successful general in the services of Nadir Shah, on the latter's death he conquered extensive territories of which Afghanistan was the central part. This survived the collapse of his wider empire on his death and he is thus regarded as the founder of modern Afghanistan.

Aidan, St (died 651). Irish monk. Summoned by King Oswald to become bishop of Northumbria, he left Iona in 635 and founded the monastery and see at the island of Lindisfarne. Thence his missionary journeys restored Christianity in northern England.

Aiken, Conard (Potter) (1889–1973). American poet, critic and novelist. He was born in Georgia but lived in England for many years. His *Selected Poems* (1929) won the Pulitzer Prize for Poetry (1930). His novels include *Great Circle* (1933).
Hoffman, F. J., *Conrad Aiken*. 1963

Ainsworth, William Harrison (1805–1882). English novelist. Born in Manchester, articled to a solicitor and for a short time a publisher, he edited *Ainsworth's Magazine* (1842–53) and wrote over forty historical novels, including *The Tower of London* (1840), *Guy Fawkes* (1841) and *Old St Paul's* (1841).
Locke, H., *A Bibliographical Catalogue of the Published Novels and Ballads of William Harrison Ainsworth*. 1925

Airy, Sir George Biddell (1801–1892). English astronomer. He was born at Alnwick, Northumberland, and educated at Trinity College, Cambridge, where he distinguished himself as a mathematician. In 1828 he became Plumian professor of astronomy at Cambridge and director of the new observatory there. As astronomer royal (1835–81) he reorganized Greenwich observatory, designed improved instruments and started meteorological and magnetic observations as well as solar photography and spectroscopy. He was elected F.R.S. in 1836 and was knighted in 1872.

Akbar the Great (Jalal-ud-Din Mohammed) (1542–1605). Third Mogul emperor. He succeeded his father in 1556 and having gained the allegiance of the warlike Rajputs extended his rule over most of India, Fatehpur Sikri, his wonderful new capital of red sandstone, symbolizing the new era. He divided the country into provinces, each under a viceroy to secure law and order, promote trade and collect taxes, but Akbar himself maintained absolute central control. One of his aims was to establish a new religion containing all that was best in existing faiths and so abolishing the strife between the various sects. Among the religious leaders summoned for this purpose were Jesuit missionaries from Goa.
Smith, V., *Akbar the Great Mogul, 1542–1605*. 2nd ed. 1919

à Kempis, Thomas *see* **Thomas à Kempis**

Akenside, Mark (1721–1770). English physician and poet. He was born in Newcastle upon Tyne, studied medicine at Edinburgh and eventually gained such distinction in his profession that he became (1761) physician to the Queen. His learned poem *The Pleasures of Imagination* appeared in 1744.
Houpt, C. T., *Akenside: A Biographical and Critical Study*. 1944

Akhmatova, Anna (pseudonym of Anna Andreyevna Gorenko) (1889–1966). Russian poet. Her poems, in the style of Pushkin, were extremely popular and collections included *The Rosary* (1914) and *The Willow Tree* (1940). She was a leader of the Acmeist movement which was led by her husband Nikolai Gumilov and included * Mandelstam. Gumilov was executed in 1921 and Akhmatova was placed under ban 1923–40 and 1946–56. Her long *Poem without a hero* (1940–62) achieved international recognition and she is regarded as Russia's greatest woman poet.

Akhnaton ('Glory of the Sun-disk'). The name adopted by the 18th dynasty pharaoh Amenophis or Amenhotep IV (14th century B.C.) when he abandoned the traditional religion in favour of a monotheistic cult of the god Aton. At the same time he moved the capital from Thebes to a new city of his own foundation (now Tell el-Amarna). A sculptured head of his beautiful wife Nefertiti is now in Berlin.
Aldred, C., *Akhenaten: Pharaoh of Egypt*. 1972

Aksakov, Sergei Timofeivich (1791–1859). Russian novelist. After retiring from the civil service he wrote a notable autobiographical trilogy of Russian family life, *Family Chronicle* (1856), *Years of Childhood* (1858) and *Reminiscences* (1856).

Alanbrooke, Alan Francis Brooke, 1st Viscount (1883–1963). British field-marshal. During the years 1941 to 1946 he was chief of the Imperial General Staff, an office to which he brought great strategic knowledge and a firmness of character which enabled him sometimes to withstand as well as admire the inspirations of his formidable political chief Sir Winston Churchill. In the early part of the war he commanded the 2nd Corps in France and showed great skill in extricating his troops. After Dunkirk he became commander-in-chief of the Home Forces and at the end of 1941 he succeeded Sir John Dill as Chief of Imperial General Staff.

Alarcón y Mendoza, Juan Ruiz de (?1581–1639). Spanish dramatist. He was born in Mexico but subsequently came to Spain and moved in the circle of Lope de Vega. He is best known for his comedies of manners but also wrote heroic dramas. Interest in his work revived in modern times after a period of neglect.

Alaric (*c.* 370–410). King of the Visigoths, who, in the reign of the Emperor Theodosius I, commanded Gothic auxiliaries in the Roman army, but on the death of the emperor in 395 broke with Rome and invaded Greece. The eastern emperor * Arcadius tried to win him over by appointing him governor of Illyricum (396–400). He invaded Upper Italy on behalf of the emperor but in 402 was defeated by Stilicho, the general of the western emperor Honorius. After another defeat (403) he changed sides but the bribe of huge sums of gold made by Stilicho was not paid by the emperor, and when two advances upon Rome (408 and 409) had failed to secure a satisfactory settlement, Alaric entered the city as a conqueror and gave it over to pillage (410), though as an Arian Christian he forbade the desecration of religious buildings. A plan to reach Africa by way of Sicily to find a home for his people was foiled by his death in southern Italy.

Alba, Fernando Alvarez de Toledo, Duke of (1507–1582). Spanish soldier and administrator. Alba had already gained a military reputation with the armies of the emperor Charles V in Italy, Tunisia, France and against Lutheran princes in Germany, but had equally incurred odium for intolerance and pride when (1567) Charles's son, Philip II of Spain, sent him as governor general to the Netherlands to crush the independence movement and stamp out Protestantism. In the first task he began successfully by forcing William the Silent (of Orange) to disband his army and take refuge in Germany, but his subsequent cruelty (in five years 18,000 people were executed by his Council of Blood and 100,000 forced into exile) stirred up the antagonism that inspired William the Silent's subsequent leadership and led to the emergence of Holland as a separate state. Meanwhile in 1573, ill and exhausted, Alba had asked to be recalled.

Alban, St (died *c.* 300). Roman soldier, reputed to be the first Christian martyr in Britain. He was supposed to have been beheaded at Verulamium (St Albans) for sheltering the Christian priest who converted him.

Albéniz, Isaac (1860–1909). Spanish composer. At first a prodigy pianist who studied under Liszt, he became a composer of large output, which included a number of operas with English libretti, written during a long and successful stay in London. His colourful suites *Iberia* (1907) and *Catalonia* (1899) show the influence of Debussy and of Spanish folk music.

Alberoni, Giulio (1664–1752). Son of an Italian gardener, he subsequently became a cardinal and first minister of Spain, to which country he went as secretary to the Duc de Vendôme. He soon gained ascendancy at court, which was strengthened when he brought about the marriage of Philip V with Elizabeth (or Isabella) Farnese, whose ambition to endow her sons with Spain's lost Italian duchies Alberoni (first minister 1714, cardinal 1717) fostered. The policy, which involved war (1718) with the Quadruple Alliance (Great Britain, France, Austria, Holland), was a complete failure and despite his sound internal administration Alberoni was dismissed.
Harcourt-Smith, S., *Alberoni*. 1963

Albert I (1875–1934). King of the Belgians (from 1909). He succeeded his uncle Leopold II. He gained world-wide admiration for his defiance of Germany's aggression in World War I and for leading the remains of the army throughout. He died in a mountaineering accident in the Ardennes.
Cammaerts, E., *Albert of Belgium*. 1935

Albert, Prince (1819–1861). Prince Consort of Britain (title granted 1857). The second son of the Duke of Saxe-Coburg-Gotha, he married Queen Victoria, his first cousin, in 1840. He took a keen interest in education, arts and science, but his political influence over his wife sometimes aroused mistrust. The Great Exhibition in London (1851) was a project he made particularly his own. The Queen was devoted to him, and after his death from typhoid fever she lived in seclusion for many years.
Fulford, R., *Prince Consort*. 1949

Albert of Magdeburg (1490–1545). Son of the elector of Brandenburg, archbishop of Magdeburg (1513–14), archbishop and elector of Mainz (1514–45), primate of Germany and cardinal. His extravagance became notorious and it was his sale of indulgences, by permission of Pope Leo X, that stirred * Luther to publish his ninety-five theses.

Alberti, Leon Battista (1404–1472). Italian humanist and architect. Born in Genoa, the son of an exiled Florentine nobleman, he was one of the most versatile figures of the Italian Renaissance. His ten-volume treatise on architecture, *De re aedificatoria* (1485), was the first printed book on architecture and encouraged interest in classical forms. His buildings include churches at Mantua and the Rucellai palace at Florence. His plays, educational and moral treatises, and essays on law, politics and science reflect the extent of his interests.
Gadol, J., *Leon Battista Alberti*. 1969

Albertus Magnus, St (Albert, Count of Bollstädt) (?1193–1280). German philosopher renowned for the depth and breadth of his knowledge. He proved himself a great teacher of the Dominican order, his most famous pupil being St Thomas * Aquinas, with whom he contributed to the infusion of Aristotelianism into medieval theology. His work in natural science drew on many sources and he introduced the notion of affinity into chemistry. His work in these scientific fields gave him a reputation as a magician. He was bishop of Regensburg (1260–62). He was canonized in 1931.
Scheeben, H. C., *Albertus Magnus*. 1932

Albuquerque, Afonso de (1453–1515). Portuguese soldier. Having been brought up at the court of King Afonso V, he led an adventurous life, which included fighting against the Turks, before going to the East, where he succeeded (1507) Almeida as viceroy. Goa, captured in 1510, became his capital and he gradually asserted control over Malabar, Ceylon, Malacca and some of the Indonesian islands. Intrigues at home led to his dismissal and he died on the way home.

Alcaeus (620–after 580 B.C.). Greek poet. He lived and worked in the island of Lesbos. Of his work, mainly battle songs, love songs and hymns, only fragments survive, but his Alcaic metre was used by others and especially by the Roman poet * Horace.
Page, D., *Sappho and Alcaeus*. 1955

Alcibiades (*c*. 450–404 B.C.). Athenian leader. He was brought up in the household of

* Pericles and became a brilliant but wayward member of the group of talented young men who found inspiration in discussions with Socrates. In the Peloponnesian War between Athens and Sparta which opened in 431 Alcibiades planned and jointly led the disastrous expedition to Syracuse. On the eve of departure all the statues of the god Hermes were mutilated. For this Alcibiades was blamed and to avoid prosecution took refuge with the Spartans, whom he helped by stirring up revolts among the allies of Athens in Asia Minor. Failing, however, to retain Spartan confidence he fled to the Persian satrap Tissaphernes, whom he tried to win over to the Athenian side in the hope of obtaining his own recall. He failed with Tissaphernes, but, chosen by the Athenian forces in Samos to lead them, he was so successful in the Hellespont (Dardanelles) that he returned home in triumph. But his command was not renewed and he withdrew to Thrace, where he was murdered.
Hatzfeld, J., *Alcibiade.* (in French) 1940

Alcock, Sir John William (1892–1919). English aviator. With Arthur Whitten Brown, he made the first aeroplane crossing of the Atlantic (14 June 1919) in a Vickers-Vimy, travelling about 1,960 miles from Newfoundland to Clifden in Ireland in 16 hours 12 minutes. He died after an air accident in France.

Alcott, Louisa May (1832–1888). American novelist. Her stories of family life in America, especially *Little Women* (1868), had phenomenal sales. She served as a nurse in the American Civil War.
Stern, M., *Louisa May Alcott.* 1971

Alcuin (735–804). English scholar and poet. Born of a noble Anglo-Saxon family, he acquired his great learning at the Cloister School of his birthplace, York. In 782 he accepted an invitation from Charlemagne to foster the revival of Latin language and literature throughout his empire. He spent much of the rest of his life at the imperial court at Aachen. He taught among many others the young princes, and even the emperor himself sometimes attended the classes. He was Charlemagne's adviser in all matters concerning education. From 796 he lived and taught at Tours, where he had become an abbot.
Buxton, E. M. W., *Alcuin.* 1922

Aldanov, M. A. (pseudonym of Mark Alexandrovich Landau) (1886–1957). Russian novelist. He left Russia in 1919 and wrote a series of books on the French Revolutionary period. Later (in *The Key* etc.) he turned to the Soviet revolution and in *The Fifth Seal* (1939) depicted the decline in revolutionary idealism that followed it. He lived in the U.S.A. from 1941.

Aldington, Richard (1892–1962). English poet, novelist and biographer. He wrote several volumes of Imagist and other poetry, the disillusioned war novel *Death of a Hero* (1929), and lively, controversial biographies of D. H. Lawrence (*Portrait of a Genius, but . . .*, 1950) and T. E. Lawrence (*Lawrence of Arabia, a Biographical Enquiry*, 1954). He married (1913) the American poetess Hilda Doolittle.

Aldrovandi, Ulisse (1522–1605). Italian naturalist. Of good family, after studying medicine at Bologna University and travelling he became professor in 1560 and later first director of the botanical garden. Like many Renaissance scholars, Aldrovandi's interests were wide-ranging, and included archaeological remains and medicine. But his main passion was for natural history, and especially the branches of botany, ornithology, embryology and the study of monsters. He observed the development of chicks by opening their eggs successively on each day of the incubation period, confirming that Aristotle was correct in stating that the heart is formed in the embryo prior to the liver. Aldrovandi's work had lasting interest chiefly through his pioneer collecting activities. His museum of natural history was amongst the largest in Europe. He planned to catalogue his collections in fourteen volumes, but lived to complete only four – one on insects, and three on birds. He bequeathed his collections and manuscripts to Bologna.
Bodenheimer, F. S., *History of Biology.* 1958

Aldus Manutius (Aldo Pio Manuzio) (1450–1515). Italian scholar and printer. He founded (1490) the press in Venice now known as the Aldine, and he was the first to print and publish the works of such classical authors as Aristotle, Sophocles, Plato and Xenophon. He devised italic printing and designed the first fount of Greek type. Manutius was a friend of Erasmus and other enthusiasts for the 'new learning'. His work was continued by his son **Paul Manutius** (1512–1574) and grandson **Aldus Manutius the Younger** (1547–1597).

Aleichem, Shalom *see* **Shalom Aleichem**

Alekhine, Alexander Alexandrovich (1892–1946). Russian chess master. He became a French citizen and was world chess champion from 1927, when he defeated Capablanca, to 1935 and again from 1937 until his death.
Alekhine, A., *My Best Games of Chess, 1924–1937*. 1939

Alemán, Mateo (1547–*c.* 1616). Spanish novelist. Born in Seville, he was famous for his *Guzmán de Alfarache* (translated into English in 1622 as *The Rogue*), a vigorous story, with moralizing digressions, of a boy who ran away from home and became involved with much sordid crime and vice before eventually being condemned to the galleys. Alemán himself, though a university student and for a short time in government service, spent much of his life in poverty, was more than once in prison and in 1608 went to Mexico where he died.

Alembert, Jean Le Rond d' (1717–1783). French mathematician and philosopher, best known as the associate of Diderot in the production of the great *Encyclopédie*. He was an illegitimate child, brought up by the wife of a glazier; his father, Chevalier Destouches, however, gave him a good education in many fields of study. He expounded a positivist philosophy but it was in mathematics that his genius lay. He wrote a notable study of dynamics and threw light on the precession of the equinoxes. He gained a great reputation for wit and wisdom in the Paris salons, but refused important offers from Frederick the Great of Prussia and Empress Catherine of Russia. He was admitted to the Académie Française in 1754.
Grimsey, R., *Jean d'Alembert*. 1963

Alexander (known as 'the Great') (356–323 B.C.). King of Macedon (from 337), son of Philip II. He was educated by Aristotle, who had great influence over his mind and character. He first distinguished himself at the battle of Chaeronea (338) against the Thebans, while his father was still king, and he was only 19 when his father was murdered and he succeeded to the throne. He had still to put down rebellions in his own kingdom, and secure his rear in Greece before he could cross the Hellespont (334) to begin the war against Persia for which his father had long prepared by creating a magnificent army based on the supremacy of the Macedonian line of battle known as the phalanx. Alexander won his first victory on the River Granicus, and in 333 marched through Phrygia to Issus, where he defeated King Darius III and captured his family and treasures. He now conquered Syria and Phoenicia and rejecting offers of peace reached Egypt (332) where the inhabitants, tired of the harsh Persian rule, welcomed him; in the following year he founded Alexandria. Returning north-eastwards he fought Darius once more (331) near Arbela on the upper Tigris and inflicted on him an even heavier defeat than at Issus; from Arbela he marched to Babylon, Susa and Persepolis, all of which surrendered. Pursuit of Darius, whom he was too late to save from a rebellious satrap but whom he buried with full honours, took him north-eastwards to the furthest corners of the empire in Sogdiana (Bukhara and Samarkand). It was on this campaign that he captured and married the beautiful Princess Roxana. In 327, starting from Balkh in Bactria, Alexander began his conquest of India. He crossed the Indus near Attock, and defeated Porus near the Hydaspes (it was here that he lost his famous charger, Bucephalus) and then went on through the Punjab. His troops, greatly depleted, would go no further; he returned to the ocean and having ordered one division to embark and sail to the Persian Gulf, he himself with the others marched back through Baluchistan and finally reached Persia in 325. At Susa he took a second wife, Barsine, daughter of Darius, and then remained in Babylon, ruling in great pomp until his death. Hailed as divine by many of his followers, he had already shown signs of megalomania. His judgement suffered and excesses had lost him the friendship of Clitus, whom he killed in a drunken brawl. But his achievement remains tremendous. With an army which probably never exceeded 35,000 fighting men he came to rule an empire stretching from Italy to India, and although it was soon divided among his generals, through them the civilizing influence of late Greek culture, known as Hellenism, spread and left enduring effects.
Fox, R. L., *Alexander the Great*. 1973. Green,

P., *Alexander the Great*. 1970; *Alexander of Macedon*. 1974

Alexander (1876–1903). King of Serbia (from 1889). A member of the Obreonović dynasty, he became king after the abdication of his father King Milan. An unpopular marriage to Draga Mashin, a lady of the court, and his own pro-Austrian policy provoked a revolution during which he and his wife were murdered by a group of army officers. Peter I of the rival Karageorgević dynasty was set upon the throne.

Alexander (1893–1920). King of Greece (from 1917), chosen by the Allies to replace his father * Constantine, who had been forced to abdicate because of his pro-German attitude in World War I. He died of blood-poisoning after a bite from his pet monkey.

Alexander I (1077–1124). King of Scots (from 1107), a son of Malcolm III (Canmore). He succeeded his brother Edgar. He ruled only north of the Forth and Clyde, his brother and successor David I governing the country to the south.

Alexander I (1777–1825). Tsar of Russia (from 1801). He came to the throne after the murder of his father Paul I. His education in humanitarian but abstract principles was directed by his grandmother, Catherine the Great, but though he was at first liberal in outlook and ordered the preparation of elaborate schemes of reform he shrank from putting all but a very small part into effect. He joined the coalition against Napoleon, but was forced to conclude the treaty of Tilsit (1807). There the two emperors met and Alexander conceived a hero-worship for the conqueror which postponed a further clash for five years. However, in 1812 Napoleon made the disastrous invasion into Russia which brought about his downfall. Alexander, the hero of the hour, was thus a leading figure at the Congress of Vienna (1814–15). With Austria and Prussia he formed the 'Holy Alliance', intended to preserve the *status quo*, but under the influence of * Metternich became increasingly reactionary, though he gave Russian Poland a constitution under his sovereignty. He was succeeded by his brother, Nicholas I.
Palmer, A., *Alexander I*. 1974

Alexander I (1888–1934). The first king of Yugoslavia (from 1929). As regent for his father Peter I of Serbia, who had become infirm, he led his nation through the trials of World War I to the final triumph when all the Slav lands under Austrian or Hungarian rule were linked with Serbia in a single state. When his father died (1921), Alexander was proclaimed 'King of the Serbs, Croats and Slovenes'. In 1929 this state took the name of Yugoslavia. As a result of rivalry between Serbs and Croats Alexander found himself compelled to suspend parliament and ruled as a dictator from 1929. He was assassinated by Croatian terrorists at Marseilles with Barthou, the French foreign minister.

Alexander II (1198–1249). King of Scots (from 1214). He succeeded his father William the Lion and was almost immediately excommunicated for helping the barons against the English King John. Two years later the sentence was lifted and the liberties of the Scottish church confirmed, while peace with England was secured by his marriage to a sister of Henry III. Alexander extended his rule over much of the western Highlands but died while seeking to win the Hebrides from Norway.

Alexander II (known as 'the Liberator') (1818–1881). Tsar of Russia (from 1855). He succeeded his father Nicholas I during the Crimean War. Defeat created the atmosphere for reforms, the greatest of which was the emancipation of 10,000,000 serfs and their families. Creation of provincial and district councils was another big step forward but before he could proceed with plans for a central constitution he was assassinated.
Mosse, W. E., *Alexander II and the Modernization of Russia*. 1958

Alexander III (1241–1286). King of Scots (from 1249). He was still a boy when he succeeded his father, Alexander II. He resumed his father's conflict with the Norwegians and by a decisive victory at Largs (1263) the Scots acquired the Hebrides and the Isle of Man. Alexander's children all died before him and his heiress was Margaret (Maid of Norway), whose mother, Alexander's daughter, had married Eric II of Norway.
Fergusson, J., *Alexander III*. 1937

Alexander III (1845–1894). Tsar of Russia (from 1881). He succeeded his father,

Alexander II. Though his manifesto pronouncing his 'faith in the principle of autocracy' struck the keynote of his policy, he was an honest ruler who encouraged his ministers to help the peasants and press forward with railway extension and currency reform. He promoted Russian colonization in central Asia and formed an alliance with France.

Alexander VI (Rodrigo de Borja or Borgia) (1431–1503). Pope (from 1492). One of the most infamous figures in papal history, he reached the highest office through nepotism and bribery. Born in Valencia, Spain, he rose through the influence of his uncle Pope Calixtus III and in a series of offices (he became a cardinal in 1476) he gained some reputation as an efficient financial administrator. But he was far more notorious for his profligacy, for his many mistresses, and for the complete lack of scruple with which he advanced the careers and fortunes of his numerous children, of whom the best known are * Cesare and * Lucrezia Borgia. The Florentine reformer, * Savonarola, who denounced such evils was excommunicated and executed (1498). Politically Alexander made it his principal purpose to build up a strong, unified papal state in central Italy, making use of Cesare's military skill and not hesitating to invite help from Charles VIII and Louis XII of France. His patronage of the arts, especially by inviting Bramante to the Vatican and commissioning Pintoricchio to decorate the Borgia apartments there, has at least proved of benefit to mankind. He died probably of a fever but, according to tradition, of poison intended for his guests at dinner.
Matthew, A. H., *Life and Times of Rodrigo Borgia, Pope Alexander VI.* 1912

Alexander, Samuel (1859–1938). Australian-born philosopher. Elected (1882) to a fellowship at Lincoln College, Oxford, he became the first Jewish fellow at Oxford or Cambridge. From 1893 to 1924 he was professor of philosophy at Manchester. His theory of 'emergent evolution' was that everything evolved, first things and then minds, from a beginning of pure motion or space-time. God, he held, is being evolved but does not actually exist. His *Space, Time and Deity* (1920) is one of the most ambitious and complete works of its kind. Alexander was awarded the O.M. in 1930.

Alexander Nevsky (1220–1263). Russian hero who gained his surname after defeating the Swedes on the River Neva (1240). In 1242 he overcame the Teutonic knights on the frozen Lake Peipus (on the Estonian border). Alexander, who ruled as grand prince in Novgorod (1236–52) and from 1252 in Vladimir, was canonized after his death. A knightly order named after him was founded by Peter the Great and revived by Soviet Russia in 1942 for deeds of valour.

Alexander of Tunis, Harold Rupert Leofric George Alexander, 1st Earl (1891–1969). British field-marshal. One of the most successful generals in World War II and the third son of the 4th Earl of Caledon, he joined the Irish Guards, served with distinction (M.C. and D.S.O.) in World War I and (1934–38) on the Indian frontier. He commanded the 1st Division in France in World War II and was left in command on the beaches after Lord Gort had been recalled. When Japan entered the war Alexander was sent to Burma and conducted the retreat with such skill that when Rommel's victories (1942) threatened Egypt he was chosen for the supreme command in the Middle East and was thus in general charge of Montgomery's brilliant campaign which started at Alamein. Later he was Eisenhower's deputy (and successor) in the campaign which cleared North Africa, Sicily and eventually Italy of the enemy. He served as governor general of Canada (1946–52) and minister of defence in Churchill's government (1952–54). He was created viscount at the end of the war and an earl when he left Canada.
Jackson, W. G. F., *Alexander of Tunis.* 1971. Nicolson, N., *Alex: The Life of Field Marshal Earl Alexander of Tunis.* 1973

Alexander Severus (208–235). Roman emperor (from 222). He succeeded his cousin Elegabalus. Weak, amiable and popular he lacked the forcefulness necessary for imperial rule. A campaign against the Persians (231–233) had failed to achieve decisive results when he was forced to return to the west by German attacks. Here his caution and indecisiveness provoked an army mutiny and his own murder.

Alexandra (1844–1925). Daughter of Christian IX of Denmark. She came to England to marry the future King Edward VII in 1863. She was famous for her beauty and held in great affection. Alexandra Rose Day, on which she used to drive through London, still serves its charitable purpose to help the hospitals.

Battiscombe, G., *Queen Alexandra*. 1972

Alexandra Fyodorovna (1872–1918). Born a princess of Hess-Darmstadt, and a granddaughter of Queen Victoria, she married Nicholas II of Russia (1894). Belief in the power of Rasputin to cure the young tsarevich of haemophilia brought her under his disastrous domination and led her to exert nefarious political influence. After the 1917 revolution she was murdered with her husband and children.

Massie, R. K., *Nicholas and Alexandra*. 1969

Alexis Mikhailovich (1629–1676). Tsar, son of Michael, first Romanov tsar; he succeeded him in 1645. Known as the 'quiet one' he gave Russia a new code of laws in 1649, and this remained in force until the early 19th century; it favoured the landowners and confirmed serfdom. He approved the church reforms of Metropolitan Nikon which led to the dangerous schism in the Orthodox church. He fought wars against Poland (1654–67) and Sweden (1656–61), and won the Ukraine for Russia. A serious revolt by cossacks under Stenka Razin was quelled in 1671.

Alfieri, Vittorio, Count (1749–1803). Italian dramatist. He inherited a fortune and his early life was occupied with travel and love affairs until the success of his first play, *Cleopatra* (1775), encouraged him to undertake a period of study. In Florence he fell in love with the Countess of Albany, wife of Charles Edward Stuart (Bonnie Prince Charlie), and lived with her after the prince's death (1788) for the rest of his life. He wrote over twenty plays by which he hoped to arouse Italy's nationalist spirit and a hatred of tyranny.

Alfonśin, Raúl (1926–). Argentinian politician. A lawyer, he served as councillor and congressman, opposed both Peronism and military rule and became leader of the Radical Civil Union in 1982. Elected president of Argentina (in the first free election for a decade) in 1983, he began to curb the military, normalized foreign relations, reformed trade unions and restored civil liberties.

Alfonso (or Alphonso). The name of two kings of Spain and of many kings of the constituent kingdoms of Aragon, Leon and Castile. For the kings of Portugal the form Afonso is used.

Alfonso X (known as 'the Wise') (1221–1284). King of Castile and Leon (from 1252). He engaged Arab and Jewish astronomers to prepare the 'Alfonsine Tables' of planetary movements and he codified the law by his *fuero real* (*c.* 1254). A notable poet himself, he made his court a great cultural centre, and by sponsoring works of learning (among them a general history and a history of Spain) written in Castilian (rather than Latin) he ensured that it became the literary language of Spain. Both his day-to-day administration and his foreign policy, however, suffered from a diffusion of energy. He had some success in bringing much of Moorish Spain under Castilian rule but had not the strength to pursue claims in Gascony, Portugal and Navarre to a successful conclusion. Most wasteful in money and energy as well as unwise was a vain attempt to obtain the imperial throne. The raising of money for all these ventures absorbed much of the economic strength created by other reforms.

Proctor, E. S., *Alfonso X of Castile*. 1951

Alfonso XIII (1886–1941). King of Spain (from 1886): as a posthumous child of Alfonso XII, he may be said to have been king before he was born. From the time that he took over the reins of government in 1902 his rule was threatened by revolutionary movements, but it was the fall in 1930 of Primo de Rivera's dictatorship, with which the king was associated in the public mind, that brought about his deposition and exile. In 1906 Alfonso married Victoria Eugénie, niece of King Edward VII.

Alfred (known as 'the Great') (849–900). King of Wessex (from 871). Born at Wantage, he twice visited Rome before succeeding his brother Ethelred. His reign began disastrously with invasions of armies from the Midlands which Alfred was forced to cut off. This won him only brief respite and early in 878 he was driven back into the Somerset marshes (it is to this period that the legend of his letting the cakes burn belongs). However, he won a decisive battle (almost certainly at Edington in Wiltshire) in May of that year and was able to impose the treaty of Wedmore by which Guthrum, the Danish king, accepted baptism and a division of the country between himself and the Wessex king. He acknowledged Alfred's supremacy in East Anglia, much of Mercia and all England south of the Thames. London, too, was gained in 886. Having made his kingdom secure, partly by a network of forts (*burhs*), partly by building war vessels, he turned to the tasks of peace. New codes of law and a fair, efficient administration restored stability after the wars, but Alfred's great love was education. He drew scholars to his court from other parts of England and from the continent but, even more importantly, initiated a programme of education far ahead of its time. To ensure the spread of the vernacular as a literary language he set his scholars to translating from Latin many religious, philosophical and historical works; he himself translated e.g. Orosius, Boethius and probaby Bede. As warrior, administrator and educator Alfred excelled.

Alger, Horatio (1834–1899). American author of boys' books. He wrote over 100, all on the theme that, by hard work and honesty, adversities can be overcome and honour and riches won. His books had an astonishing popularity and influenced a generation of American youth. His first story was *Ragged Dick* (1867).

Alhazen (abu-Ali al-Hasan ibn al-Haytham) (*c*. 965–*c*. 1038). Arab scientist, who was born in Basra and spent most of his life in Egypt. His work on optics was remarkably percipient, including discussions of the propagation, reflection and refraction of light and the phenomena of colour. This treatise was translated into Latin in the 13th century and published (1572) as *Opticae Thesaurus Alhazeni*. Alhazen opposed the theory of Euclid that the eye sends out visual rays and was the first to suggest that rays of light pass from an object to the eye.

Ali (*c*. 600–661). Fourth caliph of Baghdad (from 656). He was the son of Mohammed's uncle Abu Talib and husband of his daughter Fatima. On Mohammed's death (632) he contested the succession with * Abu-Bekr, the first caliph. He became the fourth caliph on Othman's death. He was assassinated in the interests of Moawiya, the first caliph of the Omayyad dynasty. Those who supported the claims of Ali's descendants became known as Shi'ites, who, in rivalry with the Sunnites, still form one of the great divisions of the Moslem faith.

Ali, Muhammad (Cassius Clay) (1942–). U.S. heavyweight boxer. After winning the light-heavyweight gold medal at the Rome Olympics (1960) he turned professional, and in 1964 took the world heavyweight title from Sonny Liston. Following success he changed his name to Muhammad Ali and became a Black Muslim. In 1967 he refused to join the U.S. army pleading conscientious objection and was convicted and deprived of his title. This decision was reversed on appeal (1971) and in 1974 he regained his pre-eminence, taking the title for the second time, on this occasion from George Foreman. Finally, having lost his title to Leon Spinks (February 1978) he made history when he became world heavyweight champion for the third time in September 1978.

Ali Pasha (known as 'the Lion') (1741–1822). Albanian ruler. Although nominally in the service of Turkey he came to exert despotic rule over most of Albania and Epirus and by 1820 was clearly intending to create an independent state. The sultan then ordered that he should be deposed and executed. His court at Yanina was visited by Byron, who described it in *Childe Harold*.

Allbutt, Sir Thomas Clifford (1836–1925). English physician and medical historian. Born at Dewsbury, he was educated at Cambridge and St George's Hospital, London. While a consultant in Leeds (1861–89) he introduced (1867) the clinical thermometer. He became Regius professor of medicine at Cambridge (1892–1925). His work on the use of the ophthalmoscope for nerve diseases and his *Diseases of the Arteries* (1915) are of lasting importance. He was knighted in 1907.

Allen, Ethan (1738–1789). American patriot of the Revolution. A flamboyant personality, he raised a private army, 'The Green Mountain Boys', and captured Ticonderoga from the British. He was later taken prisoner on a rash expedition against Montreal. Vermont at this stage declared its independence. Allen engaged in devious negotiations with the British regarding its status, which was still unsettled when he died in 1789.

Allen, Hervey (1889–1949). American novelist who achieved a great popular success with *Anthony Adverse* (1933), a monumental adventure story from which a successful film was made.

Allen, Sir Hugh Percy (1869–1946). English musician, professor of music at Oxford (1918–46) who succeeded Parry as director of the Royal College of Music (1918–37).

Allen, William (1532–1594). The English Roman Catholic priest who founded the English college at Douai, where the Douai Bible, the official Roman Catholic translation into English, was produced under his direction. Earlier (1556–60) he had been principal of St Mary's Hall, Oxford. Almost all the rest of his life was spent on the continent and he lost the sympathy of most Roman Catholics in England by supporting the project of the Spanish Armada. He was created cardinal in 1587.

Allen, Woody (Heywood) (1935–). United States writer, actor and director, born in New York City. At high school he began writing jokes and scripts for television. He directed and wrote the films *Bananas* (1971), *Everything You Always Wanted to Know About Sex But Were Afraid To Ask* (1972), *Sleeper* (1973), *Love and Death* (1975), *Annie Hall* (Academy Award for Best Film 1977), *Interiors* (1978), *Manhattan* (1980) and *Zelig* (1983), acting in most of them.

Allenby, Edmund Henry Hynman Allenby, 1st Viscount (1861–1936). British general. He commanded the 3rd Army in France (1915–17) and was then given command of the expeditionary force based on Egypt to fight the Turks. In the last great cavalry campaign in modern warfare he captured Jerusalem and Damascus, freeing Syria and Palestine from Ottoman rule. Made a viscount, he was then appointed (1919) British high commissioner in Egypt, a post which he filled with firmness and discretion until 1925.

Allende (Gossens), Salvador (1908–1973). Chilean socialist politician and physician. President of Chile 1970–73, he was the first Marxist elected in a free election in the western hemisphere, but lacked majority support in the electorate or in the Congress. On taking office he attempted to restructure Chile on socialist lines. Following considerable unrest mostly fomented from outside, the military demanded his resignation and in 1973 an attack was made on the presidential palace and his private residence. He died, according to some accounts, by his own hand. A ruthless military dictatorship succeeded him.

Alleyn, Edward (1566–1626). English actor and founder of Dulwich College, London (1619). He was associated with Philip * Henslowe in the management of several theatres. As an actor he was famous for his tragic roles. He retired (1604) with a considerable fortune.

Almagro, Diego (1464 or 1475–1538). Spanish conquistadore in South America. He served with Pizarro in Peru and obtained a large share of the plunder. In 1535 he organized the expedition which discovered Chile but was disappointed by failure to find any precious metals. Back in Peru he attempted to seize the country, but was defeated, captured and strangled by Pizarro. He was avenged by the second Diego (his son born of an Indian mother), whose followers stormed Pizarro's palace and murdered him.

Alma-Tadema, Sir Lawrence (1836–1912). Dutch painter who lived in England from 1869 and became an R.A. His pictures interpret classical subject matter in a highly finished academic manner evocative of the Victorian epoch in which he lived.

Almeida Garrett, João Baptista da Silva Leitão de (1799–1854). Portuguese writer. He is renowned for his epic *Camoes* (1825). A staunch liberal, as a young man he spent some years in exile in France and England. He returned with the liberal army supporting King Pedro in 1832, and in 1852, having been ennobled, became minister of foreign affairs.

Al-Rāzī *see* **Razi, Al-**

Altdorfer, Albrecht (*c.* 1480–1538). German painter, architect and engraver, born at Regensburg, the leader of the 'Danube school'. A meticulous draughtsman and engraver, he was the first great landscape painter, in the sense that in his later works the landscape ceases to be merely a background to human figures and is granted an importance never before given to it. Major works include the *St Florian Altar* (Linz) and *Alexander's Victory* (Munich).

Altgeld, John Peter (1847–1902). U.S. Democratic politician. Born in Germany, he went to America with his very poor immigrant family as a child. He became a lawyer and served as governor of Illinois (1893–97). A champion of the poor and trade unionism he pardoned the anarchists who had been, on scanty evidence, convicted of taking part in the Chicago Haymarket riots (1886). He also opposed the use of federal troops in the Pullman strike (1894).

Altman, Robert (1925–). American film director. Trained as an engineer, he was a pilot, documentary and feature producer and writer for television, then secured critical success with some major films, e.g. *M*A*S*H* (1970), *Nashville* (1975), *A Wedding* (1978) and *Health* (1979).

Alvarado, Pedro de (1485–1541). One of the most cruel of the Spanish conquistadores. Left in command during the absence of Cortes, by treacherously attacking the Mexicans he provoked an uprising which forced the Spaniards to retire from the city with disastrous losses. He became (1527) the first governor of Guatemala, eventually meeting his death when again fighting in Mexico.

Alvarez Quintero, Serafin (1871–1938) and **Joaquín** (1873–1944). Spanish dramatists who for forty years achieved success after success with light comedies mostly concerned with Andalusian life. Some, e.g. *Pueblo de las mujeres* (*The Women have their Way*) and *El centenario* (*A Hundred Years Old*), were delightfully translated into English by Harley and Helen Granville-Barker.

Amadeus (1845–1890). King of Spain (1870–73). The second son of King Victor-Emmanuel II of Italy, he accepted election as king by the Spanish Cortes after the 1868 revolution had forced Queen Isabella II into exile. A liberal constitution had been drawn up but after further revolts he abdicated.

Amalrik, Andrei Alekseevich (1938–1980). Author, who was expelled from Moscow University in 1963 for political reasons and in 1965 was sentenced to 21 years' exile for 'parasitism'. His experiences there formed the subject of his book *Involuntary Journey to Siberia* (1970). He also wrote *Will the Soviet Union Survive until 1984?* (1970).

Amanullah (1892–1960). Ruler of Afghanistan (1919–29). He lost his throne because he tried to modernize his backward state too quickly, his attempt to emancipate women being one of the most decisive causes of the revolution by which he was overthrown. Immediately on his succession after the assassination of his father, Habibullah, Amanullah provoked a war with British India and sustained defeat. From subsequent negotiations, however, Afghanistan emerged as a sovereign state with Amanullah as king. He lived in exile after his dethronement, and died in Rome.

Amati. A family of violin-makers living at Cremona, Italy. The most outstanding was **Nicolo Amati** (1596–1684), master of Stradivari and Guarneri. Others were **Andrea Amati**, (*c.* 1511–*c.* 1580) and his sons **Antonio** (*c.* 1540–1638) and **Girolamo**, Nicola's father (1561–1635). Another **Girolamo** (1649–1740) was Nicolo's son.

Ambrose, St (*c.* 339–397). Roman official and Christian prelate. He was governor of Liguria (in northern Italy) when (371) the bishop of Milan died. Rival factions being unable to agree on a successor, Ambrose was himself elected even though not yet baptized. As bishop he proved himself a brilliant administrator and a courageous opponent of Arianism which the Emperor Theodosius supported. He held that the church alone was guardian of moral and religious truth and even went so far as to excommunicate the emperor for his massacre of the Thessalonians. He wrote many hymns and introduced the 'Ambrosian chant' and much ritual into church services. The Ambrosian library at Milan is named after him.

Amenhotep. The name of four Egyptian kings of the 18th dynasty; Amenhotep III built the avenue of ram-headed sphinxes at Thebes (Luxor). For Amenhotep IV *see* * Akhnaton.

Amery, Leopold Charles Maurice Stennett (1873–1955). British politician born in India. A member of *The Times* staff 1899–1909. Conservative member of Parliament (1911–45). He held many senior posts in government including that of Colonial Secretary (1924–

29) and Secretary of State for India and Burma (1940–45). He was a strong advocate of the Empire/Commonwealth and of Imperial Preference. His rousing speech in Parliament in 1940 helped to hasten the resignation of Neville Chamberlain.

Amherst, Jeffrey Amherst, 1st Baron (1717–1797). British soldier who was chosen (1758) by Pitt to command the force sent against the French in Canada. The spectacular capture of Quebec by * Wolfe has somewhat obscured Amherst's achievement in securing all Canada for Britain in the space of two years. His nephew and successor **William Pitt Amherst** (1773–1857), the 1st Earl, was promoted to the peerage in 1826 for his success in the first Burma war. He had become governor general of India in 1823 and has previously gained notoriety by his refusal to 'kowtow' to the Emperor while on an embassy to China.

Amin Dada, Idi (1925–). Ugandan soldier and politician. He joined the British army in 1946, served in Kenya against the Mau Mau, and became commander of the Ugandan army in 1964. In 1971 the army overthrew President Milton Obote and Idi Amin became president. An economic nationalist, he expelled Uganda's Asian minority, violently suppressed his opponents and identified himself with the Arab cause. In 1979 he fled from the country following the invasion of Uganda by Ugandan exiles backed by Tanzania.

Amis, Kingsley (1922–). English novelist. After lecturing in English at the University College of Swansea, he became a fellow of Peterhouse, Cambridge. He married the novelist Elizabeth Jane Howard (1965). His first novel, *Lucky Jim* (1954), established his reputation as a comic-ironic observer of contemporary provincial life. He is also a poet and a staunch advocate of science fiction. Later novels include *That Uncertain Feeling* (1955), *I Like It Here* (1958), *Jake's Thing* (1979) and *Stanley and the Women* (1984). He also edited *The Oxford Book of Light Verse* (1978).

Amos. One of the prophetic writers in the Bible. Originally a shepherd or sheep-farmer. His denunciations of the Israelites for immorality and greed and oppression of the poor contain the implication that Jahweh (Jehovah) was not the God of Israel alone but of the whole world. The last part of the book of Amos, with its optimistic promises, is probably by another hand.

Ampère, André Marie (1775–1836). French mathematical physicist. Regarded as the founder of electrodynamics, by investigating the interaction of magnets and current-carrying conductors, he established the relationship between electricity and magnetism. After professorial appointments at Bourg (1801), Lyons (1804) and the Paris polytechnic (1809), Ampère was professor of physics at the Collège de France from 1824 until his death. He is commemorated by the name, the ampère, given to the unit of electric current.

Amundsen, Roald (1872–1928). Norwegian Arctic explorer, the first to reach the South Pole. He commanded (1903–06) the *Gjöa*, which was the first ship to navigate the Northwest Passage. In 1910, in rivalry with the British expedition, which he informed of his intention, he set out for the Antarctic and in December 1911 he reached the Pole – one month before Captain Scott. In 1926 he flew over the North Pole in a dirigible with the Italian explorer * Nobile. In an air search for Nobile, two years later, he lost his life.

Huntford, R., *Scott and Amundsen*. 1979.
Partridge, B., *Amundsen*. 1953

Anacreon (6th century B.C.). Greek lyric poet whose work reflects the voluptuous refinement of Ionian life. Few poems survive and he is best remembered by the Anacreontic metre to which his name is attached and in which many imitations of his style, known as *Anacreontea*, were written from the 2nd century A.D.

Anastasia (1901–1918). Daughter of Tsar * Nicholas II. It was assumed that she had been murdered with the rest of the Russian Royal family at Ekaterinburg until in 1929 a German citizen named Anna Anderson claimed to be Anastasia. Her claim provoked long-lasting controversy. She died in 1983.

Anaxagoras (*c.* 500–428 B.C.). Greek philosopher. He was born in Asia Minor but lived in Athens. He originated the idea that all things are composed of small particles, 'seeds' or atoms, the rearrangement of which was the cause of change and discovered the true cause of eclipses. He also believed that the world was flat and that the sun was a hot and glowing stone. He was prosecuted for the latter affront to the belief in the divinity of the heavenly bodies. The universe of 'seeds', he claimed, was organized into its apparent form by an all-pervading mind, *nous*. He taught Pericles, Euripides and other illustrious Greeks.

Anaximander (early 6th century B.C.). Greek philosopher (of Miletus in Asia Minor). Known for his elaborate system of cosmology, he conceived the universe as a boundless mass separated into hot and cold masses from which land, sea and air were ultimately formed. Apertures in misty substances enveloping parts of the hot mass appear as sun, moon and stars. From a misunderstanding of his belief that the first human beings were born from huge fishes he has been credited with anticipating the theory of evolution.

Anaximenes (fl. *c.* 546 B.C.). Greek philosopher. He was probably a follower of * Anaximander, and came from Miletus. He addressed himself to the question of the original nature of all things. He believed that origin to be air, for by processes of condensation and rarefaction air could be transformed into all other things. Condensation of air produces water, and eventually earth; rarefaction of air produced fire. * Plutarch tells us that Anaximenes demonstrated this truth by experiment. If we expel air from our mouths, it becomes cold if we exhale under pressure, whereas if we open our mouths wide, it is hot. Anaximenes probably thought of air as made up of small, separate particles. He believed in the infinity of worlds, and thought that each was formed by processes of condensation and rarefaction. He thought the earth was at the centre of things, and that both the sun and moon had been formed out of fire.
Burnet, J., *Early Greek Philosophy*. 1930

Anders, Wladislaw (1892–1970). Polish general. Captured by the Russians in their invasion of Poland during the early stages of World War II, he later formed an army from the Polish prisoners in Russia to fight the common enemy. In 1943 he took command of the Polish troops in Italy. In 1946 he was deprived of his nationality by the Polish Communist government and remained in Britain as a leader of the Free Polish community.

Andersen, Hans Christian (1805–1875). Danish author. He was born at Odense in Denmark, the son of a poor shoemaker. While still a boy he went to Copenhagen to seek his fortune but failed as an actor and through lack of education was equally unsuccessful as a playwright. At this juncture he was fortunate to come under the influence and patronage of a state councillor called Collin, who sent him to school and later to the University of Copenhagen. His first important literary work was published in 1828–29. From 1835 to 1857 came that flow of stories whose titles have become household words all over the world – *The Ugly Duckling, The Emperor's New Clothes, The Tinder Box, Thumbelina, The Red Shoes*, about 160 in all. After 1840 he travelled in Europe and became a friend of Charles Dickens. He never married, and failed to win the love of the great singer Jenny Lind.
Böök, F., *Hans Christian Andersen: A Biography*. 1962. Bredsdorff, E., *Hans Christian Andersen*. 1975

Anderson, Carl David (1905–). American physicist specializing in the study of the cosmic rays first observed (1911–12) by V. F. * Hess. In 1932 Anderson discovered the positron (a positively charged particle of the same mass as the negatively charged electron), the existence of which had been predicted by P. A. M. * Dirac. In 1937 he established the existence of mesons (particles of mass between those of the electron and the proton), predicted in 1935 by H. * Yukawa. Anderson, jointly with Hess, was awarded the Nobel Prize for Physics in 1936. He became professor of physics at the California Institute of Technology in 1939.

Anderson, Elizabeth (née Garrett) (1836–1917). English physician, the first woman to practise medicine in England. She passed her examinations in 1865. The hospital where she worked, now called the Elizabeth Garrett Anderson Hospital, survives though is now threatened with closure. Her efforts to obtain the admission of women into the medical profession were rewarded by the founding of the London School of Medicine for Women in 1874.
Bell, E. M., *Storming the Citadel*. 1953

Anderson, Marian (1902–). American contralto. A famed interpreter of Brahms and Sibelius and of Negro spirituals, she was the first black woman to sing at the Metropolitan

Opera, New York. She was U.S. delegate to the U.N. in 1958.
Anderson, M., *My Lord, What a Morning*. 1957

Anderson, Maxwell (1888–1959). American dramatist. Son of a Baptist minister, born in Pennsylvania but brought up in the Middle West, his first successful play, *What Price Glory?* (with Laurence Stallings, 1924), was concerned with front-line life in World War I. Other plays, many of which are in blank verse, include *Saturday's Children* (1927), *Both Your Houses* (Pulitzer Prize-winner, 1932), *Winterset* (1935) and *High Tor* (1937).

Anderson, Sherwood (1876–1941). American writer. He held executive positions in advertising and in the paint industry, which he abandoned abruptly to devote himself to literature. His works reveal his disenchantment with the complexities of modern industrialized society; they include the short-story collection *Winesburg, Ohio* (1919) and the novels *Poor White* (1920) and *Beyond Desire* (1926).

Andrássy, Count Julius (1823–1890). Hungarian nobleman. He gained great influence with the emperor Francis Joseph and was foreign minister of Austria-Hungary during the critical years 1871–79: these included the Congress of Berlin (1878), one clause of which gave Austria the administration of Bosnia and Hercegovina, thus adding to the number of Slavs within the empire. It was the fear that Russia might at some time intervene to liberate these Slavs which guided Andrássy's entire policy. He put aside therefore all thoughts of avenging the humiliating defeat of 1866 and did everything possible to build up and strengthen the German alliance. He did much therefore to create the political pattern that led to the 1914 war.

André, John (1751–1780). British officer. In America during the War of Independence, he was caught while negotiating with Benedict * Arnold for the betrayal of West Point, and hanged as a spy. In 1821 his grave was opened and his remains were later reinterred in Westminster Abbey.
Sargent, W., *Life and Career of Major John André*. 1902

Andrea del Sarto (1486–1531). Florentine painter of the High Renaissance period. Some of his best work is to be found in the frescoes in the churches of the Annunciation and St Salvi in Florence. A fine example of his portraiture, *A Sculptor*, is in the National Gallery, London. Influenced by Michelangelo, Fra Bartolommeo and others, he had his own colour values and achieved striking effects by diffusion of light. The accuracy of his crayon drawings earned him the name of 'the faultless painter'. In 1518 he accepted an invitation to visit Francis I in Paris and was commissioned to buy pictures in Italy. However, having squandered the money, he dared not return. He died of the plague. Robert Browning's poem 'Andrea del Sarto' tells of his unhappy marriage with Lucrezia del Fede.

Andrée, Salomon Auguste (1854–1897). Swedish engineer and Polar explorer. In 1897 his second attempt (the first had been abandoned) to reach the North Pole by balloon failed. The finding of his body and those of his two companions in 1930, with diaries, revealed that the balloon had come down on the ice and that the men had reached White Island on foot.

Andrew, St. (died *c.* 60–70 A.D.). One of the twelve apostles of Jesus Christ. With his brother Peter he was working as a fisherman on the Sea of Galilee when he received his call. According to tradition he preached in Scythia after Christ's death and was crucified on an X-shaped cross, in Achaia. He is patron saint of Scotland and Russia. His feast day is 30 November.

Andrewes, Lancelot (1555–1626). A favourite preacher of James I of England and one of the translators of the Authorized Version of the Bible. After being appointed bishop of Chichester (1605) and Ely (1609) he held the see of Winchester from 1618. He was the leading theologian of the High Church party, and his *Preces privatae* (*Private Prayers*) witnesses his personal holiness. T. S. Eliot drew attention to the remarkable originality and fine prose of his sermons.
Welsby, P. A., *Lancelot Andrewes*. 1958

Andrews, Thomas (1813–1885). Irish physical chemist. He studied in Glasgow and Paris, graduated in medicine at Edinburgh but spent most of his life at his birthplace, Belfast, where he was professor of chemistry at Queen's University, from 1849 to 1879. His most important discovery was that every gas has a 'critical' temperature below which it must be cooled if it is to be liquefied by applying pressure. This discovery opened the way to the ready liquefaction of gases such as oxygen, nitrogen and hydrogen.

Andreyev, Leonid Nikolaivich (1871–1919). Russian short-story writer and dramatist. Originally a lawyer, he became a journalist, and was befriended by Maxim Gorky, by whom his style was influenced. Most of his works reveal his obsession with death, madness and sex, although he was capable of an almost surrealistic humour. His best known works are ***Anathema, The Red Laugh, Seven Who Were Hanged*** and ***He Who Gets Slapped.*** He fled to Finland after the Russian revolution (1917) and died in poverty.
Newcombe, J., *Leonid Andreyev*. 1972. Woodward, J. B., *Leonid Andreyev*. 1969

Andrić, Ivo (1892–1975). Yugoslav author, winner of the Nobel Prize for Literature in 1961. He took to writing, in Serbo-Croat, during World War II. He served in many European countries as a diplomat but his works are dominated by his love of Bosnia. His best-known work is the trilogy *The Bridge on the Drina, Bosnian Story* and *Young Miss*, published 1945.

Andropov, Yuri Vladimirovich (1914–1984). Russian Communist politician, born in Stavropol. The son of a railway worker, he was a Volga boatman briefly, rose through the Komsomol and joined the CPSU in 1939 to become a party functionary in Karelia and Moscow. He was ambassador to Hungary 1953–57 (helping to suppress the 1956 revolt), chairman of the KGB 1967–82, and a member of the Politburo 1973–84. On * Brezhnev's death (November 1982) he succeeded him as first secretary of the CPSU and president of the USSR. However, illness forced him into seclusion and he died in January 1984.

Angelico, Fra (born Guido di Pietri) (*c*. 1387–1455). Italian painter. He was a Dominican friar (known as Giovanni da Fiesole) throughout his life and all his paintings, which are in a simple direct style, are of religious subjects. In 1443 he was summoned by the Pope to work in the Vatican. The name by which he is now known comes from the unearthly beauty of his angelic figures. The largest collection is in the Museo di San Marco, Florence (his own convent).
Pope-Hennessy, J., *Fra Angelico*. 2nd ed. 1974

Angell, Sir Norman (1874–1967). English journalist and politician. His book *The Great Illusion* (1910), which showed that war was as disastrous for the victor as the conquered, had an enormous influence, his work for peace eventually bringing him a Nobel Prize (1933). He was a founder of the Union of Democratic Control (1914) and a Labour M.P. (1929–31).
Angell, N., *After All*. 1951

Angerstein, John Julius (1735–1823). London merchant and philanthropist of Russian descent. On his death thirty-eight of his pictures were acquired, through the encouragement of George IV, for the nation. They formed the nucleus of the National Gallery collection.

Ångström, Anders Jonas (1814–1874). Swedish physicist. He studied, lectured and in 1858 became professor of physics at Uppsala University. He made extensive studies of the spectra of the sun's light and of the Aurora Borealis. In this work he expressed wavelengths of light in a unit equal to one hundred millionth of a centimetre. This unit, now called the 'ångström', has been generally adopted for spectroscopic measurements.

Anna Ivanovna (1693–1740). Empress of Russia (from 1730). She was a niece of Peter the Great, and became empress on the death of Peter II. Having been a neglected and unloved child, she grew up to be a coarse and ignorant woman. On ascending the throne she gave herself up entirely to pleasure, leaving affairs of state to her lover, Biron, who was detested by her subjects.
Longworth, P., *Three Empresses*. 1972

Anne (1665–1714). Queen of Great Britain and Ireland (from 1702) and the first to rule over the United Kingdom of Great Britain, created by the Act of Union (with Scotland) in 1707. The second daughter of James II by his first wife Anne Hyde, she married Prince George of Denmark (1683), by whom she had seventeen children, only one of whom survived infancy; he died while still a boy. The earlier

years of her reign were influenced by her favourite, the Duchess of Marlborough (Sarah Jennings), and these years, under Whig rule, were made glorious by the great series of victories won by the Duke of * Marlborough. This period ended when Anne quarrelled with the Marlboroughs in 1709 and appointed as political leader the Tory Robert Harley, the kinsman of her new favourite Mrs Masham. The last part of the reign was troubled by the question of the succession. The queen herself and some of the Tories favoured the natural heir, James, the son of James II, but he was a Roman Catholic, and in the event the crown went to George of Hanover, a great-grandson of James I through the female line. Anne was an emotional and rather foolish woman but her reign was a time of intellectual brilliance and was distinguished by such writers as Pope, Addison, Swift and Defoe.
Connell, N., *Queen Anne*. 1937. Trevelyan, G. M., *England under Queen Anne*. 3 vols, 1930–1934

Anne (Boleyn) (1507–1536). A relation of the Duke of Norfolk, she became the second wife of Henry VIII of England in 1533 and was the mother of Elizabeth I. Henry had her beheaded for adultery, once he had determined to marry Jane Seymour. Several men, including her brother, who were held by a secret commission to have been associated with her in guilt were also executed, but the alleged facts remain suspect.
Chapman, H., *Anne Boleyn*. 1974

Anne of Austria (1601–1666). Daughter of Philip III of Spain, she was married to Louis XIII of France. After her husband's death she became regent for her son Louis XIV but allowed all power to rest in the hands of her lover or even husband * Mazarin. Dumas in his *The Three Musketeers* tells the story of the alleged romance between her and George Villiers, Duke of Buckingham.
Freer, M. W., *The Regency of Anne of Austria*. 2 vols, 1866

Anne of Cleves (1515–1557). Her father ruled the German duchy of Cleves. She became the fourth wife of Henry VIII of England in 1540. The king had been guided by political reasons and encouraged by a flattering portrait, but Henry found her less than attractive and within a few months the marriage was annulled. Thomas Cromwell, who had negotiated the match, was disgraced but Anne herself was allowed to live in England in comfortable seclusion.

Annigoni, Pietro (1910–). Italian artist. His delicately flattering portraits of Queen Elizabeth and others won him an important niche in British social life. This partly obscures work in other styles which can be seen, e.g., in the Modern Art Gallery in Milan. In his work he has revived Renaissance techniques.

Annunzio, Gabriele d' *see* **Gabriele D'Annunzio**

Anouilh, Jean (1910–). French dramatist, born in Bordeaux. His plays vary from historical reconstruction – e.g. *L'Alouette* (1953; *The Lark*), his version of the Joan of Arc theme, and *Becket* (1959) – to comedy or farce, e.g. *L'Invitation au Château* (1947; translated by Christopher Fry as *Ring Round the Moon*) and *The Waltz of the Toreadors* (1952). In 1949 his film *M. Vincent* was awarded the Grand Prix du Cinéma Français. Anouilh, whose witty, sophisticated and elegant manner conceals a deep underlying pessimism, handles ingenious plots with a superb sense of stagecraft.
Marsh, E. G., *Jean Anouilh*, 1953. Pronco, L. C., *The World of Jean Anouilh*. 1961

Anselm, St (*c.* 1033–1109). Archbishop of Canterbury. He was born at Aosta in northern Italy, but as his father objected to his becoming a monk it was not until *c.* 1059 that he reached Lanfranc's abbey at Bec, in Normandy, of which in 1078 he eventually became abbot. Lanfranc, who had become archbishop of Canterbury, died in 1089, and the see was left vacant until Anselm was appointed in 1093; his opposition to William Rufus's depradations of the church led to his exile in 1097. He returned at the request of Henry I in 1100 but while on the continent he had become a convinced opponent of lay investiture, and refused to do homage to Henry for his bishopric. This led to a further period of exile, but eventually in 1107 a compromise was reached. Anselm, the leading theologian of his age, put forward the theory that faith and reason are not incompatible; he also advanced the 'ontological argument' that the very fact that man can conceive the existence of a supreme omnipotent Being must mean that such a Being exists. He was canonized in 1494.

Ansermet, Ernest (1883–1969). Swiss musician. At first a lecturer in mathematics, he became a conductor and a noted interpreter of modern composers such as Stravinsky, Ravel and Debussy. He founded (1918) the Orchestre de la Suisse Romande in Geneva.

Anson, George Anson, 1st Baron (1697–1762). English sailor. On the outbreak of war with Spain (1740) he was sent in command of six ships, with orders to inflict as much damage on Spanish trade and colonies as possible. Nearly four years later he returned with only one ship but £500,000 of treasure, having sailed round the world. He received his peerage during the war of Austrian succession for a great victory (1747) over the French off Cape Finisterre. Coin worth £300,000 was found aboard the six prizes taken.
Anson, W.V., *The Life of Admiral Lord Anson, 1697–1762*. 1912. Barrow, Sir John, *Life of Lord Anson*. 1839

Anstey, F. (pen-name of Thomas Anstey Guthrie) (1856–1934). British humorous writer. Two of his plays, *Vice Versa* (1882) and *The Man from Blankley's* (1893), are still remembered, as is his novel *The Brass Bottle* (1900), an amusing story on the Aladdin theme.
Anstey, F., *A Long Retrospect*. 1936. Turner, M. J., *Bibliography of the Works of F. Anstey*. 1931

Antiochus. The name of thirteen members of a dynasty which began with Seleucus, a general of Alexander the Great, and which ruled in Syria from 312 to 64 B.C. **Antiochus III** (237–187) came into conflict with Rome, sheltered Hannibal but was eventually forced to accept onerous terms. His son **Antiochus IV**, 'Epiphanes' (175–164), by attempting to substitute the Greek gods for Judaism, kindled the patriotic rising of the Maccabees (* Maccabaeus). By defeating **Antiochus XIII** (69–65) Pompey was enabled to make Syria a Roman province.

Antonello da Messina (*c*. 1430–1479). Sicilian painter. Born in Messina, he was greatly influenced by the techniques of the Flemish painters, especially the van Eycks. His surviving paintings are mostly portraits distinguished by a virtuoso style. His works influenced the Venetians, notably Giovanni Bellini.

Antonescu, Ion (1882–1946). Romanian general and politician. After King Carol II had been forced to abdicate (1940), he assumed dictatorial powers. Under his rule Romania fought as Germany's ally against Russia in World War II with the result that after the Russian victory he was overthrown and two years later excuted.

Antoninus Pius (86–161). Roman emperor (from 138). He succeeded Hadrian, who had adopted him as his heir. He governed with ability and his reign was remarkably happy and peaceful. Duuing his reign Roman control in Britain was extended northwards and the Antonine wall was constructed from the Forth to the Clyde. The Emperor's daughter, Faustina, married * Marcus Aurelius.

Antonioni, Michelangelo (1912–). Italian film director, born in Ferrara. He studied economics in Bologna, became a journalist, film critic, script writer and documentary film maker. His feature films include *L'Avventura* (1960), *Blow-up* (1967), *Zabriskie Point* (1969) and *The Passenger* (1974).
Cameron, I. and Word, R., *Antonioni*. 1970

Antony, St (*c*. 251–356). Born of a Christian family in Upper Egypt and renowned as a hermit. For twenty years he lived an ascetic life in the desert and is said to have been tormented by temptation, as depicted by Hieronymus * Bosch and others. Many anchorites followed his example and in this sense he may be said to have initiated the monastic system. In the great theological controversy of the time he opposed Arianism.

Antony, Mark (Marcus Antonius) (*c*. 82–30 B.C.). Roman soldier and statesman. An early suiporter of Caesar, he fought under him with distinction in Gaul and against Pompey, but it was after Caesar's death that by exploiting the popular indignation he was able to rise to greatness. With Caesar's heir Octavian and Lepidus, a figure of comparatively minor importance, he formed a ruling triumvirate and it was mainly due to Antony's skill that the assassins, Brutus and Cassius, and their supporters, who had been forced to leave Italy, were decisively defeated at Philippi

in Macedonia (42). After some dissension Octavian and Antony, Lepidus being tacitly ignored, agreed to separate their spheres of power, Octavian to rule Italy and the west, Antony over Asia and Africa, which included Egypt, where Cleopatra ruled in alliance with Rome. To cement the agreement Antony left Cleopatra to marry Octavian's sister Octavia. Unfortunately this marriage did not last. Egypt's resources were necessary for a war against Parthia and so, with self-interest and affection in convenient accord, Antony became openly the lover of Cleopatra and after the failure of the Parthian war lived with her in the state and style of an independent oriental monarch. His divorce of Octavia (32) immediately brought on the clash with Octavian which was in any case inevitable. A year of shapeless and indecisive struggle ended with the complete destruction of the fleets of Antony and Cleopatra at Actium (31). In the following year Octavian invaded Egypt. Defeated oudside Alexandria, Antony committed suicide and Cleopatra, after the failure of negotiations, followed his example. The triumphant Octavian was to become the emperor * Augustus.
Tarn, W. and Charlesworth, M., *Octavian, Antony and Cleopatra*. 1965

Antony of Padua, St (1195–1231). One of the most famous preachers of the Middle Ages, he was a Franciscan friar born in Lisbon but spent most of his working life in Italy. It was said that he preached to the fishes when man refused to listen. Miracles at his tomb at Padua caused immediate canonization. In art he often appears with a lily and the Christ-child in his arms.

Apollinaire, Guillaume (Wilhelm Apollinaris de Kostrowitsky) (1880–1918). French poet, born in Rome of a Polish mother. He died of wounds in World War I. A leader of the avant-garde, he helped to define Cubism, joined the Dadaists, and is said to have invented the term Surrealism. His volumes of poems *Alcools* (1913) and *Calligrammes* (1918), his play *Les Mamelles de Tirésias* (1918) and his novel *Le Poète assassiné* are among his best known works.
Adéma, M., *Guillaume Apollinaire*. 2nd ed. 1968. Bates, S., *Guillaume Apollinaire*. 1967

Apollodorus of Damascus (died *c*. 149). Chief architect and engineer of the Roman emperor, Trajan, for whom he built the Odeum, Gymnasium and Forum in Rome. Trajan's Column, with its banded relief sculptures, was an architectural novelty planned by him. His bluntness of speech in professional matters is said to have led to his banishment and execution by Trajan's successor, Hadrian.

Apollonius of Perga (born second half of third century B.C.; died early second century B.C.) Probably born at Perga, in Asia Minor; almost nothing is known of his life. Apollonius was the greatest student of Conics in antiquity, and several of his works in that area survive. One of his main concerns was with generating curves. He pioneered new modes of generating curves which had the advantage of rendering it easier to solve traditional conic problems (e.g. calculating areas) by geometrical means. His work in this field became canonical. Apollonius also wrote a tract on applied optics and was apparently famous for his astronomical studies, where he used his rigorous geometrical approach to solve the problem of the motions of the planets. He may have produced solar and lunar tables, and seems to have calculated that the moon lies about 600,000 miles distant from the earth.
Heath, T. L., *Apollonius of Perga*. 1896

Appia, Adolphe (1862–1928). Swiss musician and theorist of scenic design. While studying music at Bayreuth he was struck by the disparity between the music and the stage settings. In his book *Music and Staging* (1899) he attacked the conventional painted scenery and suggested three-dimensional sets based on linear constructions, e.g. staircase, ramp, etc. His theories and productions based on them (e.g. *Tristan und Isolde* at La Scala, Milan, in 1923) have, with those of Gordon * Craig, had a revolutionary effect on theatrical design.

Appleton, Sir Edward Victor (1892–1965). English physicist. He specialized in the study of long-distance radio waves and their reflections in the upper atmosphere. An ionized region which could cause this reflection had been predicted by * Heaviside, and in 1924 Appleton demonstrated the existence of such a region (the Heaviside Layer) at a height of about 60 miles. A higher reflecting region discovered later is called the Appleton Layer. Appleton was educated at and became a fellow of St John's College, Cambridge. He worked there in the Cavendish Laboratory and later was secretary to the Department of Scientific and Industrial Research from 1939 to 1949, when he went to Edinburgh University as principal and vice-chancellor. Among his many honours were F.R.S. (1927), K.C.B. (1941) and G.B.E. (1946). In 1947 he was awarded the Nobel Prize for Physics.

Apuleius, Lucius (fl. *c.* 160). African-born Latin author. Educated at Carthage and Athens, he travelled widely in his youth and was able to put his experiences to good account in the most famous of his works, the scandalous and amusing novel *The Golden Ass*. The main theme concerns a young man turned into an ass for witchcraft, and among the episodes are the legend of Cupid and Psyche. The youth is restored to human shape by the Egyptian goddess, Isis, whose initiate Apuleius had probably become. In the light of his novel it is interesting that Apuleius himself was accused by the family of his wealthy wife, Pudentilla, of influencing her by magic. His successful defence (*De magia*) survives.

Aquaviva, Claudio (1543–1615). Italian cleric. As fifth general of the Society of Jesus (from 1581) he composed the *Ratio studiorum*, the basis of Jesuit education. He showed great diplomatic finesse especially in relation to the French Huguenots.

Aquinas, St Thomas (*c.* 1225–1274). German–Sicilian theologian and philosopher. Born near Aquino in Italy, he became a Dominican, and despite family opposition left Italy to study theology in Paris and later under * Albertus Magnus at Cologne. Although nicknamed by fellow students 'The Dumb Ox', he is now considered to have been the greatest systematic theologian of the Catholic church. Except for study in Italy (1259–68) he worked and taught in Paris (1252–72). Influenced by the philosophy of Aristotle, he based his vast and clearly argued theology, now known as Thomism, upon it. He defended human reason as a source of knowledge of the natural world and also attempted to reconcile reason and faith. He opposed the claim that a belief could be philosophically false but theologically true, and set out five proofs of the existence of God. After his death his work was decried by the Franciscans for its debt to pagan Aristotle, but it remains today an enthusiastically studied theology. Aquinas died on his way to the Council of Lyons and was proclaimed a saint in 1323 and a doctor of the church in 1567. Of his many writings *Summa theologia* is much the most comprehensive exposition of his system.

Foster, K. (ed.), *The Life of St Thomas Aquinas*. 1959. Taylor, A. E., *St Thomas Aquinas as a Philosopher*. 1924

Arafat, Yasser (1929–). Egyptian–Palestinian politician. Educated at Cairo University, he became chairman of the Palestine Student Federation, and in Kuwait trained Palestinian commandos. He rose to the leadership of the Al Fatah commando group and in 1968 was elected chairman of the Palestine Liberation Organisation, claiming credit for later acts of terrorism against Israel.

Arago, Dominique François Jean (1786–1853). French physicist and politician, born at Perpignan. He was educated at Toulouse and Paris, where he became (1804) secretary to the Observatory. Sent in 1806 to measure an arc of the meridian between Barcelona and the Balearics, he was arrested as a spy when war broke out between France and Spain. On his release he became a member of and later secretary of the Académie des Sciences and (1830–50) was director of the Observatory. He helped to confirm the wave theory of light and discovered several important electromagnetic effects. In politics he was a man of the left and took part in the revolution that deposed Charles X in 1830. He was a deputy (1830–51) and was minister of war in the government that in 1848 abolished slavery in the French empire. In 1852 he refused to take the oath of allegiance to Napoleon III.

Aragon, Louis (1897–1982). French poet, novelist and essayist. An early Dadaist and later a Surrealist he turned to political activities and joined the Communist Party (1930). He was decorated for war service (1940). Among the best known of his works are *Les Beaux Quartiers* (1936), for which he was awarded the Prix Renaudet, and *Les Voyageurs de l'Impériale* (1943), published in English as *Passengers of Destiny*. He also wrote some notable war poems.

Juin, H., *Aragon*. 1960. Roy, C., *Aragon*. 1945

Aram, Eugene (1704–1759). English philologist and Yorkshire schoolmaster. Notorious as the murderer of Daniel Clarke, a shoemaker, he was hanged in 1759. This murder and its discovery were the subject of Hood's poem *The Dream of Eugene Aram* and Bulwer Lytton's novel *Eugene Aram*.

Arbuthnot, John (1667–1735). Scottish physician and author, who after an Oxford education became an M.D. at St Andrew's (1696). Settling in London he became an F.R.S. in 1704. An urgent summons to attend the prince consort, George of Denmark, resulted in his becoming physician to Queen Anne herself. With literary as well as scientific tastes he became a close friend of Pope and Swift, was the chief author of the *Memoirs of Martinus Scriblerus*, and wrote the *History of John Bull* (1712).
Beattie, L. M., *John Arbuthnot, Mathematician and Satirist*. 1935

Arcadius (377–408). Son of the emperor Theodosius I, he inherited the eastern portion of the empire, while the western part was assigned to his younger brother Honorius. His reign at Constantinople marks the permanent separation of the two parts of the Roman world and so the beginning of what came to be known as the Byzantine Empire.

Arch, Joseph (1826–1919). English social reformer. A farm labourer, he formed the National Agricultural Labourers' Union in 1872; later he helped obtain the franchise for agricultural workers. A firm supporter of Gladstone, he was the first English working man to serve as a Member of Parliament (1885–86, 1892–1902).
Horn, P., *Joseph Arch*. 1971

Archer, Frederick (Fred) **James** (1857–1886). English jockey. He became almost legendary in the history of English racing. Champion jockey from 1873 to 1885, he won 2,748 races, including the Derby five times, out of a total of 8,084 in which he rode.

Archer, William (1856–1924). British journalist, critic and dramatist. He was born in Scotland at Perth and educated at Edinburgh University but worked in London, where he won fame as the champion and translator of Ibsen's plays. His own play, *The Green Goddess* (1921), an exciting melodrama, proved a great success.
Archer, C., *William Archer*. 1931

Archimedes (287–212 B.C.). Greek mathematician and physicist born in Syracuse, Sicily. He studied in Alexandria and made many discoveries, notably in mechanics and hydrostatics. He deduced the laws of levers, devised the compound pulley, and invented the Archimedian Screw still widely used by primitive peoples for raising water. He is best known however for his statement of the principle (Archimedes' Principle) that a body immersed in a fluid appears to lose weight equal to the weight of the liquid it displaces. He thus discovered the property known as specific gravity. In mathematics he calculated the value of π to a close approximation and discovered the correct formula for the area of a parabola. His ingenious war machines enabled his city of Syracuse to hold out for three years against the Roman besiegers but on its fall (212) Archimedes was slain, in spite of orders by the Roman general that he should be spared.
Dijksterhuis, E. J., *Archimedes*. 1956

Archipenko, Alexander (1887–1964). Russian sculptor. His technique followed the same trends as those set by the Cubist painters. A gradual simplification of human contours brought him to the point of expressing the nude figure entirely in geometrical shapes.
Archipenko, A., *Archipenko: Fifty Creative Years, 1908–1958*. 1960. Karshan, D. H. (ed.), *Archipenko: International Visionary*. 1970

Ardashir *see* **Artaxerxes**

Arensky, Anton Stepanovich (1861–1906). Russian composer and pianist. He is now mainly remembered for his Trio in D minor and *Variations on a Theme of Tchaikovsky*.

Aretino, Pietro (1492–1556). Italian writer and wit. Born at Arezzo and later living in Rome and Venice, he became known as 'the scourge of princes', and by a mixture of flattery and literary blackmail won patronage from such formidable characters as Francis I of France and the emperor Charles V. His vivacious and satiric dialogues, plays and verses are of great value to the social historian.
Hutton, E., *Pietro Aretino: The Scourge of Princes*. 1922

Argyll, Earls and Dukes of. Heads of a noble Scottish family descended from the 13th-century Sir Colin Campbell of Lochow and thereafter prominent in Scottish history, especially as supporters of the Covenant and the Protestant succession. The 1st Earl was created in 1457; the second was killed at Flodden (1513); the fourth (died 1558) established a family pattern by being the first Scottish noble to accept the Reformed faith. **Archibald** (1607–1661), **8th Earl**, found himself at constant odds with his beliefs as a Covenanter and his loyalty to his king. He fought and was defeated (1645) by the royalist Duke of Montrose, but he crowned Charles II at Scone (1651), only to be executed after the Restoration for subsequently yielding to Cromwell. His son **Archibald** (1629–1685), **9th Earl**, who raised a rebellion, was also executed.

With the coming of William of Orange the Argylls could support the crown with a clear conscience and with hope of reward; the 10th Earl became 1st Duke in 1701. **John** (1680–1743), **2nd Duke**, played an important part in securing the Hanoverian succession and in 1715 led the Government troops against the Jacobites at Sherrifmuir. The **9th Duke, John Douglas Sutherland** (1845–1914), who married Queen Victoria's daughter Princess Louise, was governor general of Canada (1878–83).

Ariosto, Lodovico (1474–1533). Italian epic poet. He came of a good family of Ferrara and was intended for the law, but gained little from five years at the city's university. His father now secured employment for him with the d'Este family then ruling Ferrara. He served Cardinal Ippolito from 1503 to 1517 and his brother Duke Alfonso from 1518. Here he found the literary background which helped the inspiration of his great epic *Orlando furioso*. Orlando is the Roland of the Charlemagne legends and in form the work is the continuation of (but far superior to) Boiardo's *Orlando innamorato*. Ariosto's poem continues the story of Angelica, the beautiful princess of Cathay who has been carried off to the court of Charlemagne, then engaged in a war with the Saracens. In the new poem Angelica escapes; Orlando, who is in love with her, forgets his duties and pursues, but discovers her married to a Moorish youth, with whom she is idyllically in love. He becomes a raving madman (*furioso*) but eventually returns to sanity and duty and overcomes and kills the Saracen king. Nothing else of Ariosto's work compares with this great epic. Late in life he loved and married Alessandra Benucci and his last years were spent happily with her and in revising his poems.

Aristarchus of Samos (*c.* 310–230 B.C.). Greek astronomer. He taught at Alexandria and held the then unacceptable view that the earth and other planets revolve around the sun. Aristarchus was the first astronomer on record to estimate (crudely) the relative sizes of the sun and moon and their distance from earth.

Aristides (known as 'the Just') (*c.* 530–468 B.C.). Athenian leader. He distinguished himself against the Persians at the battle of Marathon (490) but was exiled by his fellow citizens (one of whom was alleged to have said that he was tired of hearing him called 'the Just'), probably for opposing the bold naval policy of * Themistocles. He was allowed to return, held a command at Salamis (480), and led the Athenians to victory against the Persians at Plataea (479). He played a major part in the formation of the Delian league for united action against the Persians.

Aristophanes (*c.* 448–*c.* 388 B.C.). Athenian dramatist. One of the greatest writers of comedy of all time, his plays have remained popular and are still frequently revived. Little is known of his life and of his character only that which can be deduced from the plays. He was clearly a conservative, which then meant that he favoured the interests of the agricultural rather than the commercial classes, and, since it was the countryside that suffered from the annual incursions of the Spartans, he wanted peace in the apparently never ending Peloponnesian War.

The earliest of his eleven plays to survive is *The Acharnians* (425), which tells of the efforts of the villagers of Acharnae to make a separate peace, and enables Aristophanes to ridicule the war party. In *The Knights* (424) a satiric presentation of the demagogic fire-eater Cleon provides a principal theme. *The Clouds* (423) is a skit on Socrates. In *The Wasps* (422) the law is the target, and when a juryman is persuaded to try cases in his own home great fun is provided by the trial of a dog. *The Birds* (414) tells of how the birds in contest with the gods build Cloud-Cuckoo Land between earth and heaven, and starve the enemy into submission by preventing the smoke of sacrifice from reaching them. *The Frogs* (405), where the god Dionysus is asked to decide the rival merits of

Aeschylus and Euripides, provides abundant opportunity for parody. Perhaps the most amusing to a modern audience is *Lysistrata* (411), where the women refuse intercourse with their husbands until peace is declared. The plays are written in verse and in style are comparable with the greatest of the Greek tragedies.

Murray, G., *Aristophanes*. New ed. 1966

Aristotle (384–322 B.C.). Greek philosopher. He was born in Stagira in northern Greece, the son of a court doctor. He learned biology from his father and studied at the academy of * Plato from the age of 17 until Plato died, twenty years later. He then became tutor of Alexander, later Alexander the Great. He came back to Athens and in 335 established his own school, the Lyceum. His followers became known as peripatetics after the *peripatos* (covered walk), where – perhaps pacing up and down – he taught. In 323, after the death of Alexander deprived him of the protection of his former pupil, Aristotle left Athens and took refuge on the island of Euboea, where he died. His work, known as Aristotelianism, covers many subjects, including philosophy, several sciences, poetry and drama. His influence on western civilization has been immense. In the Middle Ages his doctrines were combined with Christian theology, notably by St Thomas * Aquinas. In his philosophy, he set out a system of categories or basic classifications into which all things fall. Some things, for example, are classed as substances: those entities, if they are such, which are the foundations or possessors of each ordinary thing's various properties but not properties themselves. In his *Metaphysics* (merely meaning that which comes after *physics*), he also elaborated doctrines on the distinction between form and matter, on the development of potentialities into actualities, and on various kinds of cause. At the bottom of an ascending scale was 'prime matter', with potentiality but no 'form' or function other than existence and therefore incomprehensible. At the top and equally incomprehensible was the equivalent of God, with potentiality fully realized and therefore no potency, but to be regarded as 'pure act' (in these terms the 'soul' is regarded as the 'act' of the body). In between the terms 'form' and 'matter' may be sometimes interchangeable. A familiar example is that brick is 'form' when related to the clay of which it is made but 'matter' in relation to the building of which it forms a part. In logic Aristotle claimed to be the first to work out the theory of reasoning by syllogisms, arguments of a particular form whose conclusions follow necessarily or certainly from their premisses. Aristotle's *Ethics* contains the doctrine that virtue consists in a mean between excess and deficiency, and in his *Politics* he argues for a form of government which is an oligarchy of merit, preferably with the consent of the governed. Of Aristotle's science, his biology is by far the most impressive. It is systematic and based closely upon observation. His view of the universe, involving the older view that the sun rotates round the earth, which is fixed in space, was one of a number of doctrines that were taken as unquestionable in the Middle Ages and had the effect of delaying scientific advance. His views on drama, contained in his *Poetics*, led to the 'rules' of the Renaissance, including those of the unities of time and place.

Downey, G., *Aristotle*. 1965. Green, M., *A Portrait of Aristotle*. 1963. Ross, W. D., *Aristotle*. 1964

Arius (died 335). Greek theologian. He gave his name to the great Arian controversy, which rent Christendom during the 4th century. It related to the status of the members of the Trinity, whether God the Father was co-equal with God the Son or in some sense (as Arius maintained) his superior. At the council of Nicaea (325) the dispute was dramatized as the battle of the iota (i), whether the Father and Son were of the same substance (*homoousioi*) or of like substance (*homoiousioi*). The decision (formulated in the Nicene Creed) was against Arius, whose doctrines became heretical. Arius was born in Libya, studied in Asia Minor and returned to Alexandria to work and teach. Alexander, the bishop there, was a principal opponent. After Nicaea Arius was exiled to the Danube and died excommunicated, but the Arian controversy lived on.

Arkwright, Sir Richard (1732–1792). English inventor. Born at Preston, he was originally a barber. By the late 1760s he was devoting his attention exclusively to improving cotton-spinning processes and invented the water-driven spinning-frame in Preston in 1768. To escape Luddite antagonism he migrated to Nottingham and built (1771), in partnership with Jedediah Strutt, a factory with water power in Cromford, Derbyshire. His various inventions were copied, litigation went against him, and one of his factories was destroyed by a mob. However, his work was recognized by a knighthood (1786).

Arlen, Michael (Dikran Kouyoumdjian) (1895–1956). British novelist and short-story writer of Armenian extraction. He became a British citizen in 1922, but spent most of his later life in New York, where he died. In an elegant but artificial style he portrayed in such novels as *The Green Hat* and *These Charming People* the sophisticated, amoral but highly decorative young people of the English upper classes and their gay (or sometimes tragic) lives in the years immediately following World War I.

Arlington, Henry Bennet, 1st Earl of (1618–1685). English politician. One of the 'Cabal' (the clique that advised Charles II in the early years of his reign); he was impeached (1674) as an evil and corrupt counsellor but was acquitted.

Arminius (*c.* 18 B.C.–*c.* A.D. 19). Famous Germanic chief. Under his leadership his tribe, the Cherusci, annihilated a Roman army under Varus in A.D. 9, a defeat which led to the withdrawal of the imperial boundary to the Rhine. He was eventually killed in a feud with his own kinsmen.

Arminius, Jacobus (Jakob Hermandzoon), (1560–1609). Dutch theologian. Originally a Calvinist, he turned violently against Calvin's doctrine of predestination and taught that any person who repents of his sins and accepts Christ as saviour is granted forgiveness by God and eternal life. These doctrines were violently assailed by Calvinists and in 1608 he asked that a synod should be convoked to decide the issue. However, worn out by anxiety and illness, he died before it was held. The controversy continued after his death but with decreasing bitterness as his views, with some modification, gained wider and wider acceptance notably by Wesley and his Methodists.

Armstrong, Edwin Howard (1890–1954). American electrical engineer. Educated at Columbia University, he used Lee * De Forest's triode vacuum tube to develop a regenerative or 'feedback' circuit which enabled (1912) radio signals to be amplified × 1000 or more. (This led to unsuccessful litigation with De Forest.) In 1916 he invented the 'superheterodyne' circuit, still the basis of television and radio equipment. In 1933 he patented 'frequency modulation' (FM) as a means of overcoming natural static and set up the first FM transmitter in 1939. He committed suicide.

Armstrong, Louis (1900–1971). American jazz trumpeter and singer, born in New Orleans and popularly known as 'Satchmo'. He moved to Chicago to join King Oliver in 1922 and later formed the 'Hot Five' and the 'Hot Seven'. Apart from a period in the 1930s when he deserted ensemble playing to pursue a career as a virtuoso soloist, he and the groups he led remained in the forefront of the New Orleans style.

Jones, M. and Chilton, J., *Louis*. 1971

Armstrong, Neil Alden (1930–). U.S. astronaut, the first man to set foot on the moon. A licensed pilot from the age of 16, he studied aeronautics at Purdue University. He was active in the Korean war and in 1962 joined the U.S. National Aerospace Program, and was commander of *Gemini 8* in which he completed the first manual space-docking manoeuvre.

In July 1969 he lifted off from Cape Kennedy U.S. with Edwin Aldrin and Michael Collins in *Apollo 2* and 4 days later landed on the moon. As he stepped on to its surface he said 'That's one small step for man, one giant leap for mankind'.

Armstrong, N. A., *Change in the Space Age*. 1973

Armstrong, William George Armstrong, 1st Baron (1810–1900). English inventor. Born at Newcastle upon Tyne, he turned from the law to engineering and devised a steam-jet electric engine followed by a hydraulic crane and a hydraulic accumulator (1845–50). The Elswick works were built to make civil-engineering machinery, but soon became better known for military guns, particularly heavy artillery. His first rifled gun was manufactured in 1854. The wire-wound barrel was another of Armstrong's improvements. Armstrong, whose firm, Armstrong-Whitworth (later Vickers-Armstrong), was active in shipbuilding as well as ordnance, was raised to the peerage in 1887.

Arnau of Villanova (1240–1311). Catalan physician and astronomer. In the 1280s he was physician to Peter III of Aragon, and from 1291 taught medicine at Montpellier University. He seems to have been a successful medical practitioner – curing Pope Boniface VIII of the stone – but was chiefly important for his attempt to integrate empirical medicine with the medical philosophy of the Greeks and Arabs. Being familiar with Arabic, he translated works of Galen and Avicenna into Latin. Much of his medical teaching consisted in exposition of the works of Hippocrates and Galen, and this pioneering approach was taken up and became the basis of fourteenth century medical education. Arnau's chief theoretical medical interest was the attempt to conceptualize the body as being in a state of equilibrium between opposed forces (primarily those of hot and cold), which determines the resultant condition of health. Towards the end of his life, his interests took a more philosophical, mystical and theological turn. He investigated the occult world, wrote on astrology, and made a prophecy that the world would end in 1378. His theological heterodoxy involved him in difficulties with the Paris theologians.

Arnaud, Yvonne (1895–1958). French-born actress who spent her life in England. Ben Travers's *Cuckoo in the Nest* was among the first of the many farces and comedies in which she gained success. The Yvonne Arnaud Theatre at Guildford (opened 1965) was named after her.

Arne, Thomas Augustine (1710–1778). English composer, educated at Eton and working in a lawyer's office when he turned to music. He wrote *Rule, Britannia* (which comes from his masque *Alfred* and which Constant * Lambert called 'the best written of all national songs'), incidental music for plays (e.g. Shakespeare's *Where the Bee Sucks . . .*) and many other songs in addition to oratorios, light operas and the serious opera *Comus*, based on the poem by John * Milton.
Langley, H., *Doctor Arne*. 1938

Arnim, Countess von (née Elizabeth Mary Beauchamp) (1866–1941). English novelist, born in Australia. A cousin of Katherine * Mansfield, in 1890 she married Count Henning von Arnim and went to live in Germany where she wrote *Elizabeth and Her German Garden* (1898), a book of gentle irony and delicate charm which was one of the big successes of the period. She lived in England after her husband's death and in 1916 she married the 2nd Earl Russell. Her other books include *The Enchanted April* (1922) and *Mr Skeffington* (1940).

Arno, Peter (Curtis Arnoux Peters) (1904–1968). American cartoonist. One of the earliest recruits to the *New Yorker* magazine, on whose staff he continued to work, his clever linear characterization combined with metropolitan humour helped to establish the magazine's reputation.

Arnold, Benedict (1741–1801). American soldier. Eventually a traitor during the American War of Independence, he fought with gallantry first with Ethan Allen's 'Green Mountain Boys', in Canada, and under Washington, and was an excellent officer. The Senate, ignoring Washington's recommendations, promoted several other officers ahead of him but he was soon breveted major-general and fought with distinction at Saratoga, where he received wounds which limited him to less active commands. In 1780, as commander of West Point, he seemed embittered by lack of recognition and conspired with the British Major * André to surrender the post. The plot was discovered but Arnold escaped to the British, by whom he was given command of British troops. He lived in England after the war.
Sherwin, O., *Benedict Arnold*. 1931.

Arnold, Henry Harley (1886–1950). American soldier and airman. He reached the climax of his career by being commanding general of the United States Army Air Force (1942–46) during World War II.

Arnold, Malcolm (1921–). English composer. He was a trumpet player in the London Philharmonic and B.B.C. Symphony Orchestras who wrote many orchestral compositions, including the ballet *Homage to the Queen*, *English Dances* (1953) and four symphonies. He received an Oscar for music for the film *Bridge on the River Kwai* (1957).

Arnold, Matthew (1822–1888). English critic, educationist and poet, born at Laleham on Thames. Educated at Rugby under his father Thomas * Arnold, and at Balliol College,

Oxford, he became a disciple of Wordsworth. As an inspector of schools 1851–86, he was an important liberal influence in enriching the curriculum and pointing to the need for educating the working class. He became professor of poetry at Oxford 1857–67 and set high standards in his lectures on Homer and his collected *Essays in Criticism* (1865) which emphasised the social function of the critic. His own poetry was criticised for its harshness, gloom and difficulty but his *Dover Beach* (1867, set to music by Samuel * Barber) is deeply moving. He attacked middle-class cultural values as 'philistine' (his own coinage) in *Culture and Anarchy* (1869). In his later years he was deeply troubled by his own spiritual restlessness and a fear of anarchy.
Rowse, A. L., *Matthew Arnold*. 1976

Arnold, Thomas (1795–1842). English educator. Headmaster of Rugby School (1828–41). He created the educational pattern, followed by other British public schools, which encouraged the emergence of a class of capable and devoted administrators to meet the needs of the growing empire. To give older boys responsibility and self-discipline he introduced a prefectorial system while his own sermons and strict religious instruction supplied a moral background. The educational structure, based upon the classical form-master, had obvious limitations. A glowing picture of Rugby under Arnold is presented by Thomas Hughes in *Tom Brown's Schooldays*.
Bamford, T. W., *Thomas Arnold in Education*. 1970.

Arnold of Brescia (*c.* 1100–1155). Italian religious revolutionary. After studying under * Abelard in France he returned to his birthplace, Brescia, where he entered an Augustinian monastery and eventually became abbot. An embroilment with his bishop led to a period of exile, during which, after a quarrel with St Bernard, he was banished from France. Meanwhile a revolution in Rome had suppressed the power of the pope and created a republic on the lines of that of ancient Rome. Returned from exile, Arnold threw himself into the fray (*c.* 1147) as a violent supporter of the new régime and denouncer of the pope's temporal power. He accordingly had to flee when the new pope, * Adrian IV, brought about the republic's collapse. Arnold fell into the hands of the emperor Frederick Barbarossa, was delivered over to the papal prefect and hanged.
Greenaway, G. W., *Arnold of Brescia*. 1931

Arnolfo di Cambio (Arnolfo di Lapo) (*c.* 1232–1302). Italian architect and sculptor. A pupil of Pisano, he designed Florence Cathedral (from 1296) and, also at Florence, built the Franciscan church of S. Croce (1294 ff.) and the Palazzo Vecchio (also called the Palazzo della Signoria, 1298 ff.).
Mariani, V., *Arnolfo di Cambio*. 1943

Arp, Jean (Hans) (1887–1966). French artist. He was a founder of the Dadaist movement, which proved the forerunner of Surrealism. His versatility was immense, but he was known primarily as a sculptor, whose forms, though deriving largely from Surrealism, had an abstract purity of surface and contour. He also produced collages and wood-reliefs as well as works in more traditional media, and wrote poetry.
Arp on Arp: Problems, Essays, Memories. 1972

Arrhenius, Svante August (1859–1927). Swedish physical chemist. He was best known for his work, completed in 1887, of evolving a satisfactory theory of electrolytic dissociation from the many electrochemical observations of the nineteenth century. He put forward the idea, which is the basis of present-day 'Ionic Theory', that when salts are dissolved in water they split up almost completely into particles, which * Faraday had previously named 'ions'. Arrhenius was awarded the Nobel Prize for Chemistry in 1903. Much of his early work was done in Germany but he returned to Sweden in 1891 and served as director of the Nobel Institute at Stockholm from 1905 until his death.

Artaxerxes. The name of several Persian kings, **Artaxerxes I** (reigned 464–425 B.C.) brought the war with Greece to an end with the loss of Thrace and parts of Asia Minor. **Artaxerxes II** (died 358 B.C.) defeated his rebellious brother * Cyrus and gained the Greek cities of Asia Minor. A much later **Artaxerxes** or **Ardashir** (died A.D. 242) overthrew the last of the Parthian kings (A.D. 226), conquered Media, and as founder of the Sassanian dynasty restored the Persian monarchy.

Artemisia. Famous warrior queen of Halicarnassus, who fought with the Persians against the Greeks in the naval Battle of Salamis (480 B.C.).

Artemisia (Queen of Caria) *see* **Mausolus**

Arthur. Hero of many myths and legnds, he may represent the folk memory of one or more Romanized British chieftains who, after the departure of the legions, put up a heroic resistance to the invading Anglo-Saxons, in their westward advance. This would explain the number of places, from Astolat (Guildford) to the extreme Cornish west, associated with his name.

The hero of romantic legend is first mentioned by the ninth-century Nennius, but the first long account was given (*c.* 1135) by Geoffrey of Monmouth. The legends were embellished by such medieval writers as Chrétien de * Troyes, and a great number of the stories were woven together by Sir Thomas Malory in his vast *Morte D'Arthur*, printed by Caxton in 1485. Tennyson (*Idylls of the King* etc.) and others took up the tale and even in our own day the musical play *Camelot* is a reminder that the legends are still alive. Costume, armour and codes of conduct in the Arthurian stories are mainly those of the 12th–14th centuries.

Barber, R., *King Arthur in Legend and History*. 1973. White, T. H., *The Once and Future King*. 1958

Arthur, Chester Alan (1830–1886). Twenty-first president of the U.S. The son of a Vermont clergyman and a lawyer by profession, he held the lucrative post of collector of customs at the Port of New York (1871–78). During this period he became involved in the controversy within the Republican party over the use of patronage (i.e. the allocation of offices etc. to gain political support) and in opposition to President Hayes, a purist in such matters, who dismissed him for abuse of his official position. However, at the 1880 convention the choice of Garfield for the presidential nomination was offset by that of Arthur, as a prominent supporter of patronage, for the vice-presidency. The Republicans won the 1880 election, and after Garfield's assassination Arthur became president (1881–85), but to the dismay of his former associates proved himself a determined enemy of the corruption of patronage.

Reeves, T. C., *Gentleman Boss: Chester Allen Arthur*. 1975

Arthur of Brittany (1187–1203). A grandson of Henry II of England. Since his dead father, Geoffrey, was John's elder brother, Arthur had on Richard I's death a claim to the throne which was supported by Philip II of France. The story of his imprisonment by his uncle and of his death is told with much poignancy (but considerable historical distortion) in Shakespeare's *King John*.

Asbury, Francis (1745–1816). American prelate. The first Methodist bishop consecrated (1784) in America. John Wesley sent him from England and in the course of his missionary journeys he is said to have travelled 270,000 miles.

Asch, Sholem (1880–1957). Polish–Jewish Yiddish writer, born in Poland. His first novel, an admitted masterpiece, *Dos Shtete* (*The Township*) was published in 1904, but it was Max Reinhardt's Berlin production (1907) of his play *The God of Vengeance* that brought him fame. From 1910 he lived in America. Among his books are *The Mother, Mottke the Thief*, and *East River*.

Rosenberg, S., *Sholem Asch at Close Quarters*. 1959

Ascham, Roger (1515–1568). English scholar, born near Thirsk, in Yorkshire. He received his early education in the family of Sir Anthony Wingfield, who sent him to Cambridge University, where he became reader in Greek at St John's College (*c.* 1538). His *Toxophilus* (1545), an agreeable dialogue on archery, dedicated to Henry VIII, as well as his growing reputation as a teacher, brought him wider recognition and in 1548 he became tutor to Princess Elizabeth. After returning from a diplomatic mission (1550–53) he became Latin secretary to Edward VI, an office which, though a Protestant, he was prudent enough to retain under Mary. He was still in office under Elizabeth when he died. *The Scholemaster*, published posthumously, is a humanist and humane treatise on education.

Ryan, L. V., *Roger Ascham*. 1963

Ashcroft, Dame Peggy (1907–). English stage actress. She made her London debut in 1926 and played with outstanding success in Ibsen, Shakespeare and Chekhov. She was created D.B.E. in 1956.

Ashfield, Albert Henry Stanley, 1st Baron

(1874–1948). British transport expert. Though born in Derby, he received his education and early business experience in the U.S.A. His greatest achievement was the building up of the bus and underground railway combination known as the London Passenger Transport Board (nationalized as London Transport), of which he was chairman.

Ashford, Daisy (pen-name of Margaret Mary Devlin) (1881–1972). English writer. She gained sudden and perhaps immortal fame by the publication in 1919, under Sir James Barrie's sponsorship, of her book *The Young Visiters*, a remarkable and hilarious example of literary precocity, said to have been written when she was 9.

Ashmole, Elias (1617–1692). English antiquarian. His name is perpetuated by the Ashmolean Museum at Oxford. Born at Lichfield he started work as a solicitor, joined the excise, but soon retired to studies extending from botany to alchemy. His book on the Order of the Garter revealed his antiquarian interest. The nucleus of the Ashmolean collection was formed by ethnological objects from America, African and the South Seas bequeathed to him by his friend John Tradescant.
Josten, C. H. (ed.), *Elias Ashmole, 1617–92*. 5 vols., 1967

Ashton, Sir Frederick William Mallandine (1904–). English choreographer and dancer. After gaining prominence in creating ballets for and dancing with the Carmargo Society and the Rambert company he became in 1935 choreographer, and later associate director, of the Sadler's Wells Ballet (known as the Royal Ballet from 1956). He succeeded Ninette * de Valois as director in 1963. His best known ballets are *Cinderella* (in which he took the role of one of the ugly sisters), *Ondine, Daphnis and Chloë, La Fille mal gardée, Façade* and *Symphonic Variations*. Ashton was knighted in 1962 and received C.H. (1970) and O.M. (1977).

Ashur-Bani-Pal (669–626 B.C.). A great-grandson of Sargon and the last of the great kings of Assyria. His palace and the temples at Nineveh contained some of the finest of ancient sculpture (see the panels in the British Museum) and a remarkable library of cuneiform tablets. The prosperity was deceptive, however; within a few years of Ashur-Bani-Pal's death the whole empire was in revolt and Assyria became a Median and later a Persian province.

Aske, Robert (died 1537). A lawyer who led the rising in the north of England known as the 'Pilgrimage of Grace' (1536) in protest against the dissolution of the monasteries by Henry VIII. Having received assurances, including a promise of his personal safety, he persuaded the rebels to disperse, but was immediately arrested, convicted of treason and hanged.
Prescott, H. F. M., *The Man on the Donkey*. 1952

Asoka (reigned 273–232 B.C.). Indian emperor, grandson of the conquering Chandragupta Maurya. He became ruler of all India except the extreme South. Repentance for the bloodshed effected a conversion to Buddhism so violent and complete that (from *c.* 257) the whole machinery of government was used as a propaganda machine for spreading the Buddhist faith, by such means as texts carved on walls (many of which survive) and officers sent out to ensure that the rules of piety were observed. His ambassadors became missionaries and so compelling was the impetus set in motion that within twenty years of his death the faith had reached China, whence it spread to Japan and Korea and elsewhere. Asoka sent his own son to Ceylon, which has been a stronghold of Buddhism ever since. The unfortunate result of these pious and peaceful exercises was that the country, having abandoned its means of self-defence, was quickly overrun after Asoka's death.
Moorkerji, R. K., *Asoka*. 3rd ed. 1962

Aspasia *see* **Pericles**

Asquith, Herbert Henry, 1st Earl of Oxford and Asquith (1858–1928). British Liberal prime minister. Born at Morley in Yorkshire he was educated at the City of London School and Balliol College, Oxford, where impressive academic successes included the Craven Scholarship.

He became a successful barrister (Q.C. 1890) and first entered parliament in 1886 as Liberal member for East Fife, serving (1892–95) as home secretary under Gladstone and Lord Rosebery. During the long spell of Conservative rule that followed, Asquith's standing so greatly increased that when at last the Liberals returned triumphantly in 1905 he became chancellor of the exchequer in Campbell-Bannerman's government and, in 1908, when his leader retired through ill health, prime minister. His ministry, which contained such men as Lloyd George, Winston Churchill and Sir Edward Grey, put through a great programme of reform including old age pensions, Welsh church disestablishment and National Insurance, but the greatest parliamentary battles (in the course of which Asquith was confirmed in power by the two elections of 1910) were over a bill depriving the House of Lords of a final veto and over Irish home rule.

The outbreak of war in 1914 united the country behind the government, but early defeats and disappointments shook the faith of many in Asquith as a director of the war effort, brilliant though his peace-time administration had been. The formation of a coalition government in 1915 was temporarily reassuring, but in 1916 popular unease and political intrigue brought about his displacement by Lloyd George. From this rift neither Asquith nor the Liberal party (of which he remained the official leader) ever recovered. He lost his seat at East Fife in 1918 but though re-elected as Paisley (1920) he was never able to bring his party back to a position of strength. He accepted a peerage in 1925. Asquith enjoyed great happiness in both his marriages. His children by the first, all of whom gained distinction in different fields, included Baroness Asquith (Lady Violet * Bonham Carter), who inherited much of her father's political talent. His second wife was the brilliant, witty Margot Tennant, whose son Anthony Asquith became a distinguished film director.

Jenkins, R. H., *Asquith*. 1964

Astaire, Fred (Frederick Austerlitz) (1899–). American dancer. He performed in a number of musical comedies in London and New York with his sister Adèle (1898–1981) (who later married Lord Charles Cavendish), and subsequently made a series of highly successful films, in several of which he was partnered by Ginger Rogers.

Aston, Francis William (1877–1945). English physicist. He extended the work of J. J. * Thomson on isotopes and developed the instrument known as the mass spectrograph to study them. Aston showed that almost all the natural elements consist of mixtures of isotopes. For this work he received the Nobel Prize for Chemistry in 1922. His original mass spectrograph is preserved in the Science Museum, London.

Astor. A family with important social and business connections in Britain and America. **John Jacob Astor** (1763–1848), son of a German butcher of Waldorf near Heidelberg, arrived in America in 1784 and made a vast fortune in the fur trade and in property speculation in New York. A great-grandson, **William Waldorf Astor** (1848–1919), was active in American politics and diplomacy before settling in England. In 1917 he was created Viscount Astor. The wife of the 2nd Viscount, **Nancy Witcher Astor**, née Langhorne (1879–1964) was a Conservative MP 1919–45 and the first woman actually to sit in the Commons: she received the CH in 1937. Her brother-in-law, **John Jacob Astor** (1886–1971), was created Baron Astor of Hever in 1956. Among family interests were (elder branch) the *Observer* and (younger branch) *The Times* newspapers. Cliveden, with its social and political associations, was the family seat.

Porter, K. W., *John Jacob Astor*. 2 vols., 1931. Sykes, C., *Nancy: Life of Lady Astor*. 1972

Atahualpa (1500–1533). Last independent inca of Peru. On his father's death he became king of Quito (his mother's heritage) while his half-brother Huascar received the rest of the Inca empire. Shortly before the arrival of the Spaniards under Pizarro he defeated and imprisoned Huascar and made himself inca. Captured by the Spaniards in a sudden and treacherous attack he proffered a roomful of gold as ransom. Having accepted the gold the Spaniards convicted and hanged him for the alleged murder of Huascar.

Atatürk, Kemal *see* **Kemal Atatürk**

Athanasius, St (*c.* 293–373). Alexandrine theologian and one of the strongest opponents of the doctrines of * Arius at the council of Nicaea (the Athanasian creed, though it expresses his orthodox views, was not in fact written by him). Athanasius succeeded to the see of Alexandria in 328 but was beset by controversy. Despite the presence of the emperor Constantine at Nicaea, the Arian

cause gained increasing imperial support. Athanasius was forced five times into exile and in 356 a price was set on his head. In the last years of his life, however, he remained in peaceful occupation of his see. His early book *On the Incarnation* is the best known of his many works.
Goss, F. L., *The Study of St Athanasius*. 1945

Athelstan (895–939). English king (from 924). He was the son of Edward the Elder, and grandson of Alfred the Great, and continued and extended their policy of unification by bringing the north of England and much of Wales under his rule. The marriages arranged for his sisters with the royal houses of France and Germany confirmed his position as one of the great medieval kings. He ruled England firmly but also addressed his efforts to the liberation of slaves, care of the destitute and improvement of the coinage. At the end of his reign (937) he defeated a confederacy of Scots, Welsh and Danes in a desperate encounter at Brunanburh (Bourne in Lincolnshire).

Athlone, Alexander Augustus Frederick George Cambridge, 1st Earl of (1874–1957). British soldier, a brother of George V's consort, Queen Mary, and husband of Princess Alice, daughter of Queen Victoria's third son, Leopold, Duke of Albany. He fought in the South African war and was governor general of South Africa (1923–31) and of Canada (1940–45).

Atkinson, Sir Harry Albert (1831–1892). New Zealand politician, born in England. He migrated to New Zealand in 1853, held several ministries and was prime minister 1876–77, 1883–84 and 1887–91. He took a leading role in abolishing the provincial governments. He was a convinced social reformer but was forced to make financial stability his first concern.

Atterbury, Francis (1663–1732). English churchman. He rose to become bishop of Rochester (1713). On the death of Queen Anne he became involved in various Jacobite plots, was deprived of his offices and banished (1722). He died in Paris. Pope, Swift and Bolingbroke were among his friends.
Bennett, G. V., *Tory Crisis in Church and State, 1688–1730: Career of Francis Atterbury, Bishop of Rochester*. 1976

Attila (*c.* 406–453). King of the Huns (from 433), and known as 'the Scourge of God'. He became king, at first jointly with his brother, whom he murdered (445), of vast hordes living in lands from the Caspian to the Danube. He several times invaded the eastern empire and in 447 he devastated the Balkans as far as Constantinople and Thermopylae, forcing the emperor Theodosius to yield and pay tribute. In 451 he invaded Gaul and reached Orléans but was forced to return by Aëtius, the Roman commander, who had opportunely won over Theodoric, king of the Visigoths. Attila's enormous army was decisively defeated near Châlons-sur-Marne, but though forced to retire into Hungary in 452 he invaded Italy and sacked Aquileia, Milan and Pavia. An advance to Rome was stayed only after a personal interview between the conqueror and Pope Leo I, although shortage of provisions in his army and plague in northern Italy may have suggested the same course. He was preparing a further invasion of the Balkans when he died of a heart attack on the night of his marriage to the lovely Ildico. His empire collapsed with his death. Attila is the Etzel of German legend, where, as in the *Nibelungenlied*, he appears as a just ruler and not merely a ruthless conqueror.
Thompson, E. A., *A History of Attila and the Huns*. 1948

Attlee, Clement Richard Attlee, 1st Earl (1883–1969). British Labour politician. The son of a London solicitor and educated at Haileybury and Oxford University, he was converted to socialism by his work in the East End of London, where he was secretary of the Toynbee Hall centre (1910–13). Army service during World War I in Gallipoli and Mesopotamia as well as in France brought him the rank of major. After the war he was mayor of Stepney (1919–20) and entered parliament as member for Limehouse in 1922. He held office in both of Ramsay MacDonald's Labour governments but went into opposition with several of his colleagues when, during the financial crisis of 1931, MacDonald formed a coalition. He was elected George Lansbury's deputy leader of the Labour opposition in the House of Commons and in 1935 he himself became leader. His reluctance to commit the party to rearmament was not calculated to disturb Conservative passivity and contributed to the failure to stand up to Hitler's threats. Attlee was

Churchill's loyal and efficient deputy in the war-time coalition and after the 1945 election became prime minister at the head of a triumphant majority. The speedy granting of independence to Burma, India, Pakistan and Ceylon, the series of measures which provided the basis of the welfare state, and fulfilment of national obligations at the time of the Korean War are associated with Attlee's period of office. The Labour majority dwindled to almost nothing in the 1950 election and the Conservatives were returned in 1951. Attlee received his earldom on retirement from the Labour party leadership in 1955. He was succeeded by Hugh * Gaitskell.
Harris, K., *Atlee*. 1982

Auber, Daniel François Esprit (1782–1871). French composer, born at Caen. He wrote several vigorous 'comic operas', including *Fra Diavolo* and *Les Diamants de la couronne*. His *Masaniello* (*La Muette de Portici*) is a grand opera. He directed the Paris Conservatoire from 1842 to 1857.

Aubrey, John (1626–1697). English antiquary. Having lost through litigation his inherited estates in Wiltshire, Herefordshire and Wales, he had to depend upon the patronage of friends such as * Hobbes and * Ashmole. He published a quaint collection of ghost stories and folk lore in *Miscellanies* (1696), but is best known for his incisive but somewhat malicious profiles of his contemporaries, collected after his death and edited as *Brief Lives* by Andrew Clark in 1898. The 'Aubrey holes' at Stonehenge were discovered by and are named after him.
Powell, A., *John Aubrey and his Friends*. rev. ed. 1963

Auchinleck, Sir Claude John Eyre (1884–1981). British field-marshal (1946). His service, except for a short interlude (1940) in World War II, when he commanded the ill-fated British force landing at Narvik in Norway, was spent almost entirely in the east. He was in the Middle East during World War I, and afterwards with the Indian army on the north-west frontier he won a great reputation in mountain warfare. After Norway he returned to India as commander-in-chief but in 1941 was appointed to succeed Wavell in the Middle East command. He was a most effective bulwark against Rommel in North Africa. Back in his former post in India he provided the administrative skill which made possible the final success of the Burma campaign.
Connell, J., *Auchinleck*. 1959

Auden, Wystan Hugh (1907–1973). Anglo-American poet born and educated in England, but from 1939 a citizen of the U.S.A. While still at Christ Church, Oxford, he edited *Oxford Poetry*, and his own *Poems* appeared in 1930. Thereafter he became the most influential poet of his generation and one of the most prolific. He had strong left-wing sympathies and took part as an ambulance driver in the Spanish Civil War. His works include *The Orators* (1932), *The Dance of Death* (1933), *Look, Stranger* (1935) and *Another Time* (1940). *The Dog Beneath the Skin* (1935) and *The Ascent of F.6* (1936; with Christopher Isherwood) are verse plays, *The Rake's Progress* a libretto for a Stravinsky opera (1951). He edited *The Oxford Book of Light Verse* (1938). Auden was professor of poetry at Oxford (1956–61). He married Erika, daughter of the novelist, Thomas Mann, although he was a professed homosexual.
Hoggart, R., *Auden: An Introductory Essay*. 1951. Spender, S. (ed.), *W. H. Auden: A Tribute*. 1975

Audubon, John James (1785?–1851). American ornithologist and artist. Of French descent, born either near New Orleans or in Haiti and educated in France, where he studied painting under David, he spent most of his later life in Kentucky and on the Hudson devoting his time to the observation of birds. Between 1827 and 1838 he published *Birds of America*, with 435 remarkable coloured engravings. *The Quadrupeds of North America* was completed by his sons in 1854. The legend that he was the dauphin (Louis XVII), son of Louis XVI, has no substance.
Herrick, F. H., *Audubon the Naturalist*. 1968

Augustine, St (Aurelius Augustinus) (354–430). Latin father of the church, born at Tagaste, Numidia. His mother, St Monica, brought him up as a Christian, but for a time he was attracted to Manichaeism. It was not indeed until 387 that he was baptized by St * Ambrose, bishop of Milan, to which city he had been appointed professor of rhetoric three years before. Returning to Tagaste, he lived a monastic life until in 391 he was chosen as priest of the Christians at Hippo. He became bishop *c.* 395 and spent the rest of his life there;

he died during the siege of Hippo by the Vandals. His influence on Christian theology is incalculable. His *Confessions* (*c.* 397) is the story of the spiritual pilgrimage that led to his conversion. *De civitate Dei* (*The City of God*, written after 412) is his view of society, and especially, at a time when the fall of the Roman Empire was attributed to its abandonment of its pagan gods, of the relationship between church and state. *On the Trinity* is purely dogmatic, and a systematization of the Christian doctine on the subject. He also wrote energetically against the Donatist and Pelagian heresies and in doing so clarified and expounded his own convictions: that God's grace is offered independently of merit to those predestined for salvation and that it cannot be refused when offered; that man suffers from the burden of Adam's original sin unless through baptism he gains the redemption secured by Christ's passion; that only by the liberation of his will by God's grace from the enslavement of evil desires can man enjoy the vision and love of God. From his writings, which the above sentences summarize in barest outline, not only medieval Catholics but Calvin and Jansen derived their teaching on predestination. Indeed Augustine's thoughts as they developed over the years, contained inconsistencies, some of which were corrected in *Retractationes* (428). His feast is on 28 August.

Brown, P., *Augustine of Hippo*. 1967

Augustine (or Austin), **St** (died 604). First archbishop of Canterbury. He was prior of a monastery at Rome until in 596 Pope Gregory entrusted him with the mission to convert the English. With forty priests he landed in Kent, and was received favourably by King Ethelbert, whose wife Bertha, a Frankish princess, was already a Christian. Augustine was given land on which to build a church at Canterbury, and had soon converted and baptized the king. Before the end of 597 he was raised to episcopal rank. Early successes among the East Saxons were not maintained and Essex reverted to paganism. In 601 Augustine was given authority over the British by Pope Gregory, but they refused to recognize him as archbishop. This may have been due to his own haughty temperament as well as to resentment at foreign interference. Augustine's mission was therefore only a partial success, but he must be recognized as a great missionary pioneer whose successors ensured the primacy of the Canterbury see.

Deansley, M., *Augustine of Canterbury*. 1964

Augustulus, Romulus *see* **Romulus Augustulus**

Augustus (Gaius Julius Caesar Octavianus) (63 B.C.–A.D. 14). First Roman emperor (from 27 B.C.). A grandson of Julius Caesar's sister, and Caesar's adopted son and heir, he was known as Octavian before becoming supreme ruler. After Caesar's murder and the defeat of his assassins he shared power with * Antony and Lepidus, but with Antony's death he became sole ruler of the Roman world. The word emperor implies a status to which he himself did not pretend; he was *princeps* or chief citizen, but in theory his power merely rested upon his possession of old republican offices, e.g. consul, tribune, *pontifex maximus*. Even the title Augustus (the month Sextilis was renamed in his honour) merely means 'revered'. As *imperator* he was commander-in-chief. He at once set about the social, economic, political and military reforms which together created the imperial system of the next 400 years. In Italy and the older provinces he ruled through the Senate to which he left much of its dignity and at least some of its power. The outlying provinces were kept under his direct control through an agent (procurator) and here was kept the bulk of the army, with veterans settled in colonies near the frontiers to act as a first line of defence. His military policy was cautious: he did little to extend the limits of the empire except by advancing the frontier in the Danube area, which he held from Bavaria to the Black Sea. The loss of three legions which advanced in A.D. 9 fortified his cautious policy. It was a source of great pride to him that during his reign the doors of the temple of Janus were closed, indicating that the empire was everywhere at peace. Economic progress followed; the construction of roads, aqueducts and fine buildings all witnessed to a steadily advancing prosperity. He also patronized the arts and in the 'Augustan Age' Virgil, Ovid, Livy and Horace all flourished.

Only in his domestic life was Augustus unfortunate. His own marriages were unhappy and his dissolute daughter * Julia gave him little satisfaction. All her three sons died young and it was her stepson Tiberius, son of her third husband, who became heir to Augustus.

Grant, M., *Augustus to Constantine*. 1971. Hamond, M., *The Augustan Principate*. 1968

Augustus II (known as 'the Strong') (1670–1733). Elector of Saxony (as Frederick Augustus I) from 1694 and chosen as king of Poland in 1697. War against Charles XII of Sweden cost him his throne (1706) but he regained it in 1709 after the Russian victory at Poltava. Augustus, whose political schemes exceeded his power to achieve them, was far more successful in the artistic field, and under his inspiration his two capitals, Dresden and Warsaw, achieved a spectacular baroque magnificence. Augustus's nickname 'the Strong' referred to sexual rather than military powers. He was famed for the number of his mistresses and illegitimate children, of whom the best known was the French marshal, Maurice de Saxe.

Aurangzeb (1618–1707). Mogul emperor in India (from 1658). He gained the throne by imprisoning his father Shah Jehan and overcoming the rivalry of his brothers by defeating them one by one and having them put to death. Throughout his reign his bigoted Mohammedanism roused antagonism and revolt. Sikhs and Rajputs were alienated and the building up of the hostile Mahratta confederacy was hastened. Hopes of a strong united empire based on tolerance and justice were thus shattered and the way was opened for foreign intervention.
Sarkar, J., *A Short History of Aurangzeb, 1618–1707*. 1962

Aurelian (Lucius Domitius Aurelianus) (212–275). Roman emperor (from 270). Originally a common soldier, he was elected emperor by the Danube army and consolidated the provinces in that area by evacuating Dacia. In Syria he overcame (271–272) the famous queen* Zenobia. In the west he brought Gaul back to its allegiance by inducing the 'independent' ruler Tetricus to renounce his claims, by this and other successes fully deserving the title 'restorer of the Roman Empire'.

Aurelius, Marcus *see* **Marcus Aurelius**

Auric, Georges (1899–1984). French composer, one of the modernist group known as 'Les Six'. Much influenced by Satie and Stravinsky, he is best known for his colourful dramatic music for ballet (e.g. *Les Matelots*) and films (e.g. René Clair's *A Nous la liberté* and Shaw's *Caesar and Cleopatra*).

Auriol, Vincent (1884–1966). First president (1947–54) of the French Republic after World War II. A Socialist leader, he had filled a number of official posts from 1925, was imprisoned by the Vichy government during the war, but escaped to England and joined the Free French.

Aurobindo, Sri (Sri Aurobindo Ghose) (1872–1950). Indian mystic and poet. Educated at Cambridge, he took an active part in the revival of political nationalism but after a term of imprisonment, withdrew to Pondicherry in 1910. Here he set up an ashram devoted to his concept of a divine evolutionary force which would expand human capacity and lead to utopia. He was an active promoter of 'Integral Yoga' and a prolific writer.

Austen, Jane (1775–1817). English novelist. She was born at Steventon in Hampshire, where her father, George Austen, held a family living. She had one sister, Cassandra, who like herself remained unmarried, and five brothers. The quiet happy family life was varied by dancing, visiting and play-acting in the barn; in composing material for this last diversion Jane found early opportunities for exercising her talents. Retiring in 1801 George Austen took his family to Bath where they lived until his death in 1805. Four uncomfortable years at Southampton followed before the sisters found themselves installed at Chawton Cottage near Alton, Hampshire, now open to the public. Here, with routine enlivened by visits from a growing number of nephews and nieces, Jane lived for all but the last few months of her life. The order of publication of her novels is not always that of composition. *First Impressions*, refused by a publisher in 1797, was rewritten as *Pride* and *Prejudice* and published in 1813, after *Sense* and *Sensibility* (1811). *Northanger Abbey*, which began as a satire on the Gothic novel, was completed in 1803 but not published until 1818. *Mansfield Park* (1814), *Emma* (1816) and *Persuasion* (1818) followed. *Lady Susan, The Watsons* and *Sanditon* were unfinished when she died. Her novels, published anonymously, gradually gained a wide popularity after Sir Walter Scott and other well known writers had praised them. They are remarkable for the

beautifully poised irony with which she presents the tensions between individual ambition and social necessity among the 'middling classes' in English country towns in the late 18th and early 19th centuries. Outer events, such as the Napoleonic Wars then raging round her, have little or no place in her absorbing but limited themes.
Cecil, D., *Portrait of Jane Austen*. 1978.

Austin, Herbert, 1st Baron Austin of Longbridge (1866–1941). English motor car poineer. Born in Buckinghamshire, he started his career in Australia, where he managed various engineering enterprises. Back in England with the Wolseley Company, he brought out his first car. He founded his own Austin Motor Company in 1905; his highly successful 7 h.p. 'baby' Austin was the first of a line of small cars which revolutionized the pattern of car manufacture and ownership throughout Europe. He was created a baron in 1936.

Austin, John (1790–1859). English legal philosopher. 'The founder of the analytical school of jurisprudence in England', he was born at Creeting Mill in Suffolk, became a barrister and was first professor of jurisprudence (1826–32) at the new University College, London. Much of his middle life he spent in Germany, often in bad health, and his last years (from 1848), at Weybridge, Surrey. Sound and subtle reasoning, which discerned errors in the traditional phraseology of legal writers, is a main characteristic of his work, much of which is summarized in his *Province of Jurisprudence Determined* (1832) and the posthumously published *Lectures on Jurisprudence* (1861–63).

Austin, John Langshaw (1911–1960). British philosopher. His influence, exercised through lectures and essays rather than by any major work, was mainly directed at stressing the need for a clear and precise understanding of the language of thought. Austin was appointed White's professor of moral philosophy at Oxford in 1952 and had been a fellow of Magdalen College for many years. He served in the army with great distinction in World War II.

Austin, Stephen Fuller (1793–1836). American pioneer. In 1823 he received permission to settle 200 American families in Texas (then in Mexican possession). The colony prospered, but friction developed with the Mexican government and for a time Austin was imprisoned. After the revolution of 1835 caused by Mexico's abrogation of all states' rights, Austin served until his death as secretary of state in the provisional government of an independent Texas.

Avebury, John Lubbock, 1st Baron (1834–1913). British scientist, banker and social reformer. His title, taken from the stone circles at Avebury, reveals his predominant interest in archaeology (it was he who proposed the division of the Stone Age into Palaeolithic and Neolithic stages). His other scientific interests included geology, anthropology, botany and zoology. He was M.P. from 1870 to 1890 and is remembered also for the act (1871) which made statutory the general holidays in the U.K. known as Bank Holidays.
Grant Duff, A., *The Life-Work of Lord Avebury*. 1924

Averroës (1126–1198). Arabic philosopher, jurist and medical writer. Born at Cordova in Spain, where he later became 'cadi', as also of Seville, he is best known for his commentaries on the works of * Aristotle, which were widely influential in the Middle Ages. He attempted to reconcile the Mohammedan religion and Aristotelianism and so caused many Moslem heresies, and wrote an encyclopedia of medicine which was widely diffused in Latin translations.

Avicenna (980–1037). Arabic philosopher, theologian and physician, born near Bukhara. His great *Qanun* (Canon), which codified medical knowledge, rivalled in importance the works of Galen. He translated Euclid and also wrote on mathematics, alchemy, music and science. In his philosophical writings, which influenced St Thomas * Aquinas, he attempted a synthesis of Islamic religious teaching and the work of Plato and Aristotle: he accepted the view that matter has always existed and opposed the more orthodox belief that the universe was created from nothing.
Afnan, S. M., *Avicenna, his Life and Works*. 1958

Avogadro, Amedeo (1776–1856). Italian physicist. A doctor of law, he taught physics in Turin from 1806, eventually becoming professor of mathematical physics there. He is best known for the statement (Avogadro's hypothesis or law) that, under the same conditions, equal volumes of all gases contain an equal number of molecules. Although it was put forward in 1811, the importance of this hypothesis was not realized until 1858 when * Cannizzaro pointed out that it could be used to determine atomic weight. Thereafter it played a part in bringing order to chemical classification.

Avon, Earl of *see* **Eden, Anthony**

Ayer, Sir Alfred (Jules) (1910–). British philosopher. Educated at Eton and Oxford, he was originally known as an expounder of logical positivism. He was Grote professor of the philosophy of mind and logic at London University (1946–59), and in 1959 became Wykeham professor of logic at Oxford. His books include *Language, Truth and Logic* (1936) and *The Problem of Knowledge* (1956). In the former he expounds the theory that philosophic argument must be based on linguistic analysis; in the latter, he examines the nature of philosophical scepticism and such problems as perception and memory. He was knighted in 1970.

Aylmer, Sir Felix (1889–1979). English actor. He successfully played upper-class type-cast characters. He was Polonius in * Olivier's *Hamlet* (1947). He was knighted after a long and successful career ending in the mid-1970s.

Ayres, Ruby Mildred (1883–1955). English popular author. Her romantic novels, mostly serialized, achieved enormous sales especially in the World War I period. *Richard Chatterton V.C.* is a well known example.

Ayub Khan, Muhammad (1908–1974). Pakistani soldier and president. He entered the Indian army from the British military college at Sandhurst, served in Burma in World War II and became commander-in-chief of the Pakistani army (1951). He was defence minister (1954–55) and in 1958 succeeded President Mirza in the highest office. To mitigate corruption and faction he abolished the 1947 constitution and used authoritarian methods, but prepared for a return to democracy by creating a large number of local councils known as Basic Democracy Units. In 1965 he won the presidential election against Fatima Jinnah, sister of Pakistan's creator, but resigned in 1969 after crop failures and political riots. Ayub's party was obliterated in the 1970 elections.

Azaña y Diáz, Manuel de (1880–1940). Spanish left-wing politician. He was the first prime minister (1931–33) of the newly formed republic after the fall of * Alfonso XIII. He was president (1936–39) during the Spanish Civil War but exiled after Franco's victory.

Azikiwe, Nnamdi (1904–). President of Nigeria (1963–66) often nicknamed 'Zik'. After an American education, followed by a period as lecturer at Lincoln University, Pennsylvania, he returned to Nigeria, where he acquired large banking and newspaper interests. Prime minister of the Eastern region 1954–59, he was governor general in 1960–63 and, after Nigeria became a republic, the first president.

B

Baader, Andreas (1943–1977) and **Meinhoff, Ulrike** (1934–1976). Leaders of the Baader–Meinhoff gang, politically most active in the 1970s, of West German extreme left wing terrorists.

Babbage, Charles (1792–1871). English mathematician and computer pioneer, born in Teignmouth, Devon. Educated at Cambridge and elected FRS in 1816 (at the age of 24), he became a co-founder of the Analytical Society (1812), the Astronomical Society (1820) and the Statistical Society (1834). He held the Lucasian chair of mathematics at Cambridge 1828–39, but delivered no lectures. In *On the Economy of Machinery and Manufactures* (1832) he extended Adam * Smith's work on the 'division of labour' and proposed theories that F. W. * Taylor later called 'scientific management'. As early as 1823 he had suggested a machine for tabulating mathematical calculations for up to 20 decimal places. In 1834–35 he began twenty years work on the first analytical computer (called the 'analytical engine'), a machine fed by sets of * Jacquard punch cards read by mechanical 'feelers', which incorporated memory storage and anticipated modern computer techniques, such as 'conditional transfer', where intermediate calculations automatically direct the machine to modify its own program. The machine placed excessive demands on existing engineering precision and after 1854 the British government refused further funding. A small Swedish version of Babbage's machine appeared in 1855. He also invented the speedometer and the cowcatcher for trains.
Mosley, M., *Irascible Genius*. 1964.

Bab ed-Din (1821–1850). The name (Arabic: 'gate of faith') given to Mirza Ali Mohammed of Shiraz, who was recognized by one of the Shi'ite sects as a new prophet. The new religion he preached, Babism, was compounded from Sufism, Gnosticism and the Koran. He and his followers were persecuted and after an ineffectual rebellion in Tabriz the Bab was executed. His disciples took refuge in Turkey and Palestine and from the latter a new leader, Baha Ullah, emerged.

Babeuf, François Noel (1760–1797). French socialist and journalist. He found his original occupation as a collector of feudal dues highly distasteful and on the outbreak of the Revolution he immediately gave it enthusiastic support with popular and inflammatory articles. With the advent of the Directory his influence with the leaders waned. He believed strongly in economic as well as political equality and advocated a form of communism, i.e. the equal distribution of the products of labour. His paper and organization were proscribed. His plan for an insurrection was betrayed and he and thirty of his followers were executed. His theories (known as Babeufism) inspired several later egalitarian movements.
Thomson, D., *The Babeuf Plot: The Making of a Republican Legend*. 1947

Babington, Anthony (1561–1586). English conspirator. A wealthy Roman Catholic landowner in Derbyshire, he entered into a conspiracy to murder Elizabeth I, free Mary and make her queen. But cipher correspondence was discovered by * Walsingham: Babington fled, and was caught and executed.
Pollen J. H., *Mary, Queen of Scots and the Babington Plot*. 1922

Babur (Baber) (full name Zahir ud Din Mohammed) (1483–1530). The first of the mogul emperors in India. A descendant of Timur the Lame (Tamerlane) he became ruler of Turkestan at the age of 12 but, troubled by constant revolts, he aimed at conquests to the south. After exploratory raids resulting in the occupation of much of Afghanistan he crossed the Indus in 1525 and in 1526 gained a decisive victory at Panipat over the Afghan emperor of Delhi, confirmed by defeating the Rajputs the following year. In his short period of rule in northern India he improved communications and consolidated the administration of his realm.

Talbot, F. G., *Memoirs of Babar*. 1968

Bach, Johann Sebastian (1685–1750). German composer, born at Eisenach. His family had been connected with music since the early 16th century: about fifty of his relatives became church or town musicians in Thuringia and neighbouring provinces. He was the youngest son of Johann Ambrosius Bach (1645–1695), who taught him the violin. After his father's death, Johann Sebastian Bach lived with his eldest brother Johann Christoph Bach (1671–1721), from whom he learned organ and clavier playing. He sang in several church choirs, studied intensely and walked long distances to hear notable organists, including Buxtehude, who may have given him lessons. He composed his first instrumental works about 1703. He was a violinist in the orchestra of Prince Johann-Ernst of Weimar (1703), and organist at the Lutheran churches at Arnstadt (1703–07) and Mühlhausen (1707–08). During this period he wrote many complex organ works, revealing his absolute mastery of counterpoint: these include the Passacaglia and fugue in C minor and the Toccata and fugue in D minor. In 1707 he married his cousin, Maria Barbara Bach, who bore him seven children before her death in 1720. Bach had won much admiration as an organist and spent the years from 1708 to 1717 as court organist to the Duke of Weimar. Whilst director for Prince Leopold of Cöthen (1717–23) Bach composed much vivacious instrumental and orchestral music, including the six 'Brandenburg' concertos for orchestra with various combinations of solo instruments (1720–21), four orchestral suites, six cello suites, six violin sonatas and partitas, and concertos for violin and clavier. In 1722 he married Anna Magdalena Wilcken by whom he had thirteen children. After two other musicians (including Telemann) had refused the position, Bach became Cantor (musical director) and director of the Choir School at St Thomas's Church, Leipzig, in 1723 and held the post until his death. In order to strengthen his position in the many disputes over administration which broke out within the church, he sought, and gained, the honorary title of court composer to the Elector of Saxony (1736). At Leipzig he wrote 295 church cantatas, of which 202 survive, a few of them not definitely genuine. His greatest religious works are the magnificent *Passion according to St John* (1724), *Magnificat* (1723), *Passion according to St Matthew* (1727), Mass in B minor (1733), *Christmas Oratorio* (1733) and *Easter Oratorio* (1735). Most of this religious music was composed at great speed in order to provide variety for the church choir and congregation and the uniformly high quality of his huge output is amazing. He also wrote about thirty 'secular cantatas', cheerful works usually commemorating birthdays, weddings or ceremonies. Deeply concerned with improving standards of performance on keyboard instruments, in order to demonstrate the advantages of equal temperament (a tuning system which divides the octave into twelve equal semitones) he wrote the forty-eight preludes and fugues of *The Well-tempered Clavier* (1722–42). Bach was the greatest master of polyphonic form but he also experimented with rich chordal harmonies in *The Goldberg Variations* (1742) and in many of his organ works. *The Musical Offering*, a set of variations based on a theme given to Bach by Frederick the Great (1747), is an encyclopedia of instrumental counterpoint. In 1749 he became blind and an operation on his eyes proved unsuccessful; he died of a stroke in the following year. Bach enjoyed a modest fame as a composer during his lifetime, but his music soon became unfashionable and was seldom performed. In 1829 Mendelssohn revived the *St Matthew Passion* in Berlin, and the Bach Gesellschaft was founded in 1850. This body discovered many of his works previously thought lost and there followed a great revival of interest in his life and work. Many critics venerate him as the greatest of all composers. Three of his sons were noted musicians (contemporaries ranked them higher than their father): **Wilhelm Friedemann Bach** (1710–1784) was the greatest organist of his day, and composed sonatas, concertos and fantasias for organ and clavier. **Carl Philipp Emanuel Bach** (1714–1788) was a brilliant keyboard virtuoso who helped to establish sonata form and wrote several symphonies. **Johann Christian Bach** (1735–1782) lived in England for twenty years and is known as 'the London Bach'. He helped to develop symphonic form and influenced the young Mozart.

Bachelard, Gaston (1884–1962). French historian and philosopher of science, born at Bar-sur-Aube. Some of his early work, such as *La Formation de L'Esprit Scientifique* (1938) was concerned with the obstacles which had traditionally hampered scientific thinking: metaphysics, anthropomorphism. He wanted to apply Freud's work to understand the factors that had repressed scientific intelligence. Thus he saw alchemy as the projection of inner desires, whereas chemistry developed a body of formal experimental practices which took it out of the field of the subjective into the scientific. Bachelard also pioneered a 'structuralist' understanding of scientific thought. He tried to uncover the – often hidden – affinities which linked certain concepts. He believed that science progressed not by gradual evolution, but by sudden leaps from one framework of reference to another.
Dagognet, F., *Gaston Bachelard.* 1965

Bacon, Sir Francis, Baron Verulam, Viscount St Alban (1561–1626). English lawyer, scientist, essayist and philosopher. His father, Sir Nicholas Bacon (1509–1579), was Keeper of the Great Seal to Queen Elizabeth, his mother an aunt of William Cecil, Lord Burghley. He was educated at Cambridge, spent a few years in diplomacy and in 1586 became a bencher of Gray's Inn: he was a member of parliament (1584–1617). He became a protégé of the Earl of Essex but did not scruple to appear for the prosecution when Essex was tried for treason in 1601. Under James I Bacon advanced steadily: in 1613 he became attorney-general and in 1618 lord chancellor with the title Baron Verulam. In 1621 he became Viscount St Albans but in the same year was charged with bribery and corruption. He insisted that gifts received had not affected his judgments, but he was imprisoned briefly and banished from court and parliament. Side by side with his public life he followed his literary, scientific and philosophic pursuits. His *Essays* on such subjects as truth, adversity and death were first published in 1597 and issued in final form in 1625. His philosophic and scientific work was intended to summarize the state of knowledge so far attained and outline a method by which this knowledge could be renewed and advanced. The latter purpose is the theme of *Novum Organum*, written in Latin, published in 1620 and intended to be part of a great all-embracing work *The Great Instauration.* His method was a kind of tabular analysis of affinities and deviations by which he supposed scientific definition could be reached. The definition of heat arrived at by his method – 'Heat is an expansive motion restrained and striving to exert itself in the smallest particles' – is near the truth but the method in general has not proved useful to later scientists. His great significance in the history of science lies in the stress he gave to the value of experiment and to the failure of scholastic methods to arrive at a true understanding of nature. Other literary work includes *The Advancement of Learning* (1605) and *The New Atlantis* (1626), inspired by Sir Thomas More's *Utopia.*

The theory that Bacon was the real author of the Shakespearian plays was first put forward in 1769 and has been the subject of a vast literature since. It rests, however, on unsatisfactory and insufficient evidence.

Pope's description of Bacon 'as the wisest, brightest, meanest of mankind' is probably unfair, but it is certain that a lack of moral fibre prevented him in times of crisis from living up to his best intentions.
Anderson, F. H., *Francis Bacon: His Career and His Thought.* 1962

Bacon, Francis (1909–). British painter, born in Dublin. His formal art education was limited but he had the help and encouragement of Graham * Sutherland. He mainly works from photographs or other paintings. Some of his work (e.g. in the *Velasquez 'Popes'* series) has a disturbing effect upon the beholder. His work displays human figures caged in artificial space, their bodies and features wrenched and squeezed into horrifying distortions. Purchases of his paintings were made by the Tate Gallery, London. He held a large retrospective exhibition in London in 1962.
Rothenstein, J. and Alley, R., *Francis Bacon.* 1964

Bacon, Roger (*c.* 1214–1292). English scientific philosopher, born according to one tradition near Ilchester, Somerset, and according to another at Bisley in Gloucestershire. Though he was probably educated in Oxford the first certain date in his career seems to be 1236 when he was studying in Paris. In or after 1251 he returned for a time to England and it may have been then that he joined the Franciscans. For ten years from 1256 he seems to have been in France suffering from ill health and writing little. The last years of his life were spent at Oxford.

Roger Bacon was a man of great learning and wrote much (e.g. the vast *Opus Maius*, 1267–68), on many subjects, but as a systematizer rather than an originator. In philosophy Aristotle provided the basis of his philosophical studies as he did for those of all medieval philosophers. His probings into more arcane subjects such as alchemy were in line with the thought of his time. Some of his opinions and speculations evidently incurred the disapproval of his superiors but of his actual imprisonment the evidence is insubstantial. His popular image was, however, that of a necromancer. It is in experimental science that he produced real achievement, especially in optics. He remains, however, one of the greatest expounders of medieval knowledge and thought.

Crowley, T., *Roger Bacon*. 1950

Baddeley, Robert (*c.* 1732–1794). English actor. Famous for his bequest of £3 per annum to be distributed in cake and wine in the Green Room at Drury Lane, the custom is still observed. Baddeley played comedy parts and was making up for 'Moses' in *The School for Scandal* when he died. His wife Sophia Baddeley was a well known actress and singer.

Baden-Powell, Robert Stephenson Smyth Baden-Powell, 1st Baron (1857–1941). British soldier, and creator and world leader of the Boy Scout and Girl Guide movements. The former was founded in 1908, the latter with the help of his sister in 1911. He was helped by his fame as the defender of Mafeking during the South African War, when he was besieged (1899–1900) with 1,200 men for 215 days. Scenes of earlier campaigns included Afghanistan (1880–81), Zululand (1888) and Ashanti (1895–96). He wrote *Scouting For Boys* (1908) and about thirty other books, all illustrated by himself. He was awarded a baronetcy in 1922 and raised to the peerage in 1929.

Wade, E. K., *The Chief: The Life Story of Robert Baden-Powell*. 1975

Bader, Sir Douglas (1910–1982). British airman and hero of World War II. Despite losing both legs in a flying accident in 1931 he rejoined the RAF, led a Canadian fighter squadron in the Battle of Britain, and had already brought down fifteen opponents when (August 1941) after a collision with a German aircraft in France he was captured and held as a prisoner of war.

Brickhill, P., *Reach for the Sky*. 1954.

Badoglio, Pietro (1871–1956). Italian soldier. After distinguished service in World War I he was governor of Libya (1928–33) and was in command of the assault on Abyssinia in 1936. At the opening of World War II he was chief of staff but resigned in 1940 after Italian defeats in Albania. He was recalled from retirement after Mussolini's fall to lead an anti-Fascist government which at once negotiated an armistice with the Allies. He resigned in 1944.

Baedeker, Karl (1801–1859). German publisher. He was the son of an Essen printer and bookseller but established his own business in Coblenz. From 1827 he published the famous Baedeker guide-books. His son transferred the business to Leipzig.

Baekeland, Leo Hendrik (1863–1944). Belgian-born American chemist (he emigrated in 1889), a pioneer of the plastics industry. He discovered the first thermosetting resin of practical importance named Bakelite. He was elected an honorary professor of Columbia University.

Baer, Karl Ernst von (1792–1876). German zoologist, born in Estonia. He studied medicine and anatomy and in 1817 went to Königsberg where shortly afterwards he became professor of zoology. In 1834 he became professor of zoology at St Petersburg (Leningrad). By being the first to isolate and observe the mammalian ovum he was the virtual founder of the science of embryology.

Raikov, B. E., *Karl Ernst von Baer*. 1968

Baeyer, Adolf Johann Friedrich Wilhelm von (1835–1917). German organic chemist. Born in Berlin into a military family, Baeyer studied chemistry with Bunsen at Heidelberg, and later with Kekulé. He took up teaching positions at the Berlin technical institute and military academy, and then became professor of chemistry at Strasbourg and subsequently Munich. A superb experimenter in the field of organic chemistry, Baeyer devoted most of his life to solving problems of structure. After early work on uric acid, he investigated the carboxylic acids of benzene, and hoped to discover the structure of benzene itself. His main work, begun in 1865, was upon the synthesis of indigo. He successfully prepared indigo from other reagents, and by 1883 had unravelled the formula of its structure. He declined, however, to collaborate with the synthetic dye industry in making commercial use of his analysis. He turned his attention elsewhere, to studying polyacetylenes and other explosive compounds, and experimenting with oxonium compounds. Baeyer was chiefly an empirical chemist, but his work was of some theoretical interest in underlining the strength of ring structures, and investigating the direction of valence bonds. He was awarded the Nobel Prize for Chemistry in 1905.

Baffin, William (1584–1622). English Arctic explorer. A voyage to Greenland (1612) and whaling off Spitsbergen (1613–14) provided the experience for two vain attempts to find the North-west Passage. In the second (1616) he discovered and named Smith's Sound and Lancaster Sound and explored what is now Baffin Bay and the shores of Baffin Island. In 1617 he abandoned the Arctic for the East and it was while helping the Shah of Persia at the siege of Ormuz that he was killed. He wrote accounts of several of his voyages.

Bagehot, Walter (1826–1877). English economist, born at Langport, Somerset. After leaving London University he worked in his father's banking firm and, having married a daughter of its founder, James Wilson, was editor of the *Economist* (1860–77). He applied great scientific acumen to his rigorous analysis of 19th century economics and politics. His books include *The English Constitution* (1867), still a standard work, *Lombard Street* (1873), *Physics and Politics* (1875), and *Literary Studies* (1879).
St John-Stevas, N., *Walter Bagehot*. 1959; *Collected Works of Walter Bagehot*. 1966.

Bagnold, Enid (1889–1981). English author. She was best known for her novel *National Velvet*, about a young girl who won the Grand National, and her play *The Chalk Garden* (1954). She married Sir Roderick Jones, long the head of Reuter's agency.
Bagnold, E., *Enid Bagnold's Autobiography*. 1969

Bagration, Peter Ivanovich, Prince (1765–1812). Russian general of Georgian and Armenian descent. He served against the French revolutionary and Napoleonic armies in Italy, Switzerland and Austria and against Turkey in 1809. He commanded an army against Napoleon during the advance to Moscow in 1812, and was killed at Borodino.

Bahadur Shah II, Mohammed (1775–1862). Last Mogul emperor in India (1837–57). He was completely under the control of the British East India Company, but during the Mutiny of 1857 an abortive attempt was made to restore him to power. He died in exile in Burma.

Baha-Ullah *see under* **Bab ed-Din**

Bailey, Sir Donald Coleman (1901–). British engineer. His invention of a type of bridge which could be carried in sections and quickly erected solved many problems of military transport in World War II and was later adapted for civilian use.

Bailly, Jean Sylvain (1736–1793). French astronomer and politician. He became president of the National Assembly in the opening stages of the Revolution and was mayor of Paris (1789–91), but retired into private life when blamed for allowing the National Guard to fire on a mob demonstrating against the king. He was later denounced, condemned and guillotined. His great *Histoire d'astronomie* appeared in five volumes (1775–87).

Bain, Alexander (1818–1903). Scottish mental philosopher, born and educated in Aberdeen, where he was professor of logic (1860–81). His writings, e.g. *The Senses and the Intellect* (1855), *The Emotions and the Will* (1859), *Mind and Body* (1873), cover the borderland territory between physiology, psychology, and philosophy. He also wrote textbooks on grammar and logic and a study of James and John Stuart Mill (1882).

Baird, Sir David (1757–1829). Scottish soldier. He went with a Highland regiment to

India (1778) and almost at once became involved in war against * Haidar Ali of Mysore. One of the few survivors of an ambush, he was captured and kept for four years in a dungeon at Seringapatam. Back again in India after a visit home he had the satisfaction in 1799 of playing a leading part in the storming of the city where he had been confined. In 1805–06 he commanded the force that captured the Cape of Good Hope from the Dutch. In the Peninsular War he aided and, after his death at Corunna (1809), succeeded Sir John * Moore in command. He was knighted in 1804.
Wilkin, W. H., *Life of Sir David Baird*. 1912

Baird, John Logie (1888–1946). Scottish electrical engineer. A pioneer of television, he was dogged by ill health and his early inventions failed, but from 1922 he devoted himself to studying the transmission of pictures by wireless waves. In 1924, at a house in Soho, he first transmitted a televised image over several feet, using a mechanical scanning device. This apparatus (now in the Science Museum, London) was publicly demonstrated in 1926 and Baird's system was given a prolonged test by the B.B.C. Electronic scanning was, however, eventually chosen for television systems. Later researches enabled Baird to produce three-dimensional and coloured images (1944). In 1927 he also invented a method of direction-finding in total darkness by means of infra-red rays. He gave the first ultra-short wave radio transmissions.

Bajazet *see* **Bayezid**

Baker, Sir Benjamin (1840–1907). British engineer. His long association with John Fowler as consultant showed a record of remarkable achievement. Most spectacular was the Forth railway bridge (opened 1890), for which both were knighted, but they were also responsible for the construction of London's Metropolitan Railway and Victoria Station. Later Baker designed the Central London and other sections of underground railway. He was consultant for the Aswan dam in Egypt (completed 1902).

Baker, Sir Herbert (1862–1946). English architect, born in Kent. A pupil of Ernest George, while still a young man he secured the patronage of Cecil Rhodes and a number of commissions for the design of South African houses, churches and public buildings, of which the Union Buildings at Pretoria are the most grandiose and impressive example. His appointment (1912) as joint architect for the government buildings in New Delhi provided an even wider opportunity for him to display his talent for the magnificent. In London his best known works are the Bank of England and Church House, Westminster. Knighted in 1926, he became an R.A. in 1932.
Baker, H., *Architecture and Personalities*. 1944

Baker, Dame Janet (1933–). English mezzo-soprano, born in Yorkshire. In 1956 she won the *Daily Mail* Kathleen Ferrier Award; and in same year made her stage debut at Oxford in Smetana's *The Secret*. She sang throughout Europe and U.S.A. in recital, oratorio and opera, appearing at Covent Garden and Glyndebourne. She was particularly admired for stylish performances of Handel, Monteverdi and Mozart, as well as for being a fine interpreter of Berlioz and Britten. She was made an honorary fellow of St Anne's College, Oxford in 1975.
Blyth, A., *Janet Baker*. 1973

Baker, Josephine (1905–1975). American Negro dancer and singer at the Folies Bergère, Paris, who became in the 1920s and 1930s something of a symbol of the exotic sophistication of that city. She became a French citizen after World War II as a protest against racial discrimination in the USA.

Baker, Sir Samuel White (1821–1893). British sportsman, traveller and writer. He explored tributaries of the Nile (1861–62) and discovered Lake Albert, Nyasa. He was governor for four years of the Equatorial Nile basin and given the rank of Pasha. He sought to stamp out the internal slave trade. He wrote *Rifle and Hound in Ceylon* (1853); other works include *Ismailia* (1874).

Bakewell, Robert (1725–1795). English agriculturalist born at Dishley, Leicestershire, where he spent his farming life. A pioneer of systematic breeding, he greatly improved the standard of cattle, sheep and draught horses. He was best known for his breeding and improvement of Leicester sheep and Dishley cattle.
Pawson, H. C., *Robert Bakewell: Pioneer Livestock Breeder*. 1957

Bakst, Leon (1866–1924). Russian artist of Jewish extraction. He lived in Paris from 1906 and his fame rests mainly on the sumptuous sets and costumes he designed for Diaghilev's Russian ballet.
Levinson, A., *Bakst*. 1923

Bakunin, Mikhail (1814–1876). Russian anarchist. An aristocrat by birth and for a short time in the army, he left Russia in 1840, and was condemned in his absence. After taking part in a rising at Dresden during the revolutionary year of 1848 he was handed over to the Russian authorities and imprisoned. Later he was exiled to Siberia, but escaped and reached England in 1861. Most of the rest of his life was spent in a struggle with Karl * Marx to decide the form which socialist doctrine should take: Bakunin's anarchism or Marx's communism. Bakunin, defeated, was expelled from the International in 1872. His book *God and the State*, in which he called for militant atheism and the destruction of the state, had a great influence on the nihilist movement especially in Spain and Italy.
Carr, E. H., *Michael Bakunin*. 1937

Balakirev, Mili Alexeyevich (1836–1910) Russian composer and pianist born at Nizhny Novgorod. A pupil of Glinka, he was a successful pianist, and later taught Mussorgsky and Cui. He became a leading member of 'The Five' (Cui, Mussorgsky, Borodin, Rimsky-Korsakov and Balakirev), a group which did much to revive the nationalist tradition in Russian music. Balakirev, who had to support himself as a civil servant, wrote two symphonies, piano music, many songs and the symphonic poems *Tamara* (1882) and *Russia* (1884).
Garden, E., *Balakirev*. 1967

Balanchine, George Melitonovich (1904–1983). Russian-born choreographer. He left Russia in 1924 and was ballet master for * Diaghilev (1925–29). Later he went to the U.S.A. and there founded the School of American Ballet (1934) and the New York City Ballet (1948). Among the more than one hundred ballets he created are *Serenade*, *Orpheus* and *Ballet Imperial*.
Taber, B., *Balanchine*. 1975

Balbo, Italo (1896–1940). Italian airman. A leading Fascist, he became a popular hero as leader of a number of spectacular formation flights culminating in one to Rio de Janeiro (January 1931). In 1929 he had become air minister and in 1931 a marshal. His popularity now made him appear as a rival to Mussolini. He was accordingly sent as governor to Libya, where in 1940 during World War II he was accidentally shot down by anti-aircraft fire from his own side.

Balboa, Vasco Nūñez de (*c*. 1475–?1519). Spanish conquistador. In 1513 he became the first European to sight the Pacific when, having ousted his predecessor and made himself governor of Darien, he made an epic march across the isthmus of Panama. Meanwhile complaints at the Spanish court about his seizure of power had led to his being replaced by Pedro Arias de Avilla, who accused him of conspiracy and eventually had him beheaded.
Anderson, C. L. G., *Life and Letters of Vasco Nūñez de Balboa*. 1941

Baldwin. Name of five kings of Jerusalem. **Baldwin I** (1058–1118) accompanied his elder brother * Godfrey de Bouillon on the first crusade and on his brother's death in 1100 succeeded him as 'defender of the holy sepulchre', immediately taking the title of king and so establishing the Latin kingdom of Jerusalem. He gradually asserted his authority over most of the coastal area of Palestine and Syria. His cousin **Baldwin II** (died 1131) was lord of Edessa when chosen to succeed him in 1118; he spent most of his reign defending the northern parts of the realm. His son-in-law Fulk of Anjou succeeded him and his grandson, Fulk's heir, became **Baldwin III** (reigned 1143–62). At the beginning of his reign the second crusade, launched to retake Edessa, was defeated in Asia Minor, but Baldwin was an able ruler who by expelling the Egyptians from Ascalon secured his kingdom in the south. **Baldwin IV** (reigned 1173–85), 'the Leper', and his successor and nephew **Baldwin V** were both incompetent rulers.

Baldwin, James (1924–). American Negro writer. Born and educated in New York, his novels, e.g. *Go Tell it on the Mountain* (1954) and *Another Country* (1963), are concerned with the position of Negroes in American society, and his non-fiction works, e.g. *Notes of a Native Son* (1955) and *Nobody Knows my Name* (1961), contain several of the essays which brought him fame in America.

Baldwin, Stanley, 1st Earl Baldwin of Bewdley (1867–1947). British Conservative politician. The son of a rich steel manufacturer, born at Bewdley and educated at Harrow and Cambridge, he joined the family firm and it was not until 1908 that he entered parliament. After holding junior offices he was president of the Board of Trade when in 1922 leading members of the Conservative party forced the resignation of Lloyd George's coalition. Since most leading Conservatives refused office because of loyalty of Lloyd George, Baldwin gained rapid promotion as chancellor of the exchequer (1922–23) under Bonar Law. When fatal illness forced Law to retire, George V chose Baldwin as prime minister in preference to * Curzon. He was prime minister three times (1923–24; 1924–29; 1935–37) and was the all-powerful deputy to Ramsay * MacDonald in the 'National' government. At that time he showed great skill in handling people and situations. The potentially disruptive General Strike of 1926 and Edward VIII's abdication crisis of 1936 he overcame without leaving a trail of bitterness. Though aware of the threat from Hitler he shirked advocating a rearmament programme that would risk electoral defeat. It is true that he knew that the Labour party was even less ready than he to face the military and political problems caused by the resurgence of Germany but as the man in power he must be held largely responsible for the years of appeasement and their bitter consequences. Baldwin was a cousin of Rudyard Kipling and his own tastes were contemplative and literary. For many years he was held to be the epitome of the true-blue middle class Englishman.
Young, K., *Baldwin*. 1976

Balfe, Michael William (1808–1870). Dublin-born composer who lived and worked in England. His opera *The Bohemian Girl* (1843) remains well known, although the rest of his large output has been forgotten. Balfe started his career in the orchestra at Drury Lane Theatre and in 1827 was chosen by Rossini for the part of Figaro in his Paris production of *The Barber of Seville*.

Balfour, Arthur James, 1st Earl of Balfour (1848–1930). British Conservative politician. Born of an ancient Scottish family and educated at Eton and Trinity College, Cambridge, he was an M.P. 1874–1906 and 1906–22. At the opening of his career he was private secretary at the Berlin Conference of 1878 to his maternal uncle, Robert Cecil, 3rd Marquess of * Salisbury, and subsequently his promotion was rapid (whence the phrase 'Bob's your uncle!'). He was a strong and successful chief secretary for Ireland (1887) and, as Salisbury the prime minister was in the House of Lords, was leader of the House of Commons 1891–92, 1895–1902. When Salisbury retired in 1902 Balfour became prime minister, but his graceful balancing act between the factions of his party failed to convince the electorate of his ability to rule. He lost his seat when the government was defeated in the general election of 1906. He resigned the party leadership in 1911 and was succeeded by Bonar Law. The coalitions of World War I restored him to office. He was first lord of the Admiralty in Asquith's coalition, and foreign minister (1916–19) under Lloyd George. In 1917 he issued the 'Balfour Declaration', promising British support for a Jewish national home in Palestine. Balfour's mind was too detached, said his detractors, and his charm too great for a successful politician: he could see both sides of a question too clearly to be decisive in action. This view of his character was reinforced by the title of his first book and a misconception of its contents: *A Defence of Philosophic Doubt* (1879). Later books were *The Foundations of Belief* (1900) and *Theism and Humanism* (1915). He was created Earl of Balfour in 1922, and was president of the British Academy (1921–30).
Zebel, S. H., *Balfour: A Political Biography*. 1974

Ball, John (died 1381). English rebel and priest. He preached social equality and his famous sermon at Blackheath on the theme 'When Adam delved and Eve span, Who was then a gentleman?' helped to provoke the Peasants' Revolt of 1381. He was subsequently executed at St Albans.
Morris, W., *A Dream of John Ball*. 1888

Ballantyne, James (1772–1833), and **John** (1774–1821). Scottish printers. They were close friends of Sir Walter Scott and printed his works; from 1805 he was a secret partner in the firm which, expanding into publishing and bookselling, was known from 1808 as James Ballantyne & Co. The firm's bankruptcy

(1826) involved Scott in a liability of £130,000 and to pay it off he made a heroic writing effort that hastened his death.
History of the Ballantyne Press. 1871

Ballantyne, Robert Michael (1825–1894). Scottish author. From 1856 he wrote about eighty adventure books for boys, including *Martin Rattler, The Dog Crusoe* and *Coral Island.* As a young man he served in Canada in the Hudson Bay Company.
Quayle, E., *Ballantyne the Brave.* 1967

Balliol, John de (1249–1315). King of Scotland (1292–96). He was the son of the founder of Balliol College, Oxford, whose ancestors came from Bailleul in Normandy; but his claim to the Scottish throne came through his mother, Devorgilla, who was descended from King David I. In 1292 Balliol was chosen by Edward I of England from thirteen contestants to reign as a vassal king, but in 1296 he threw off his fealty. Edward immediately invaded his kingdom and forced him to surrender. After three years' imprisonment he was permitted to go to Normandy, where he died. His son Edward was crowned at Scone in 1332 but could only maintain himself with English help and in 1356, after years of intermittent rule, surrendered all his claims to Edward III.

Baltimore, George Calvert, 1st Baron (1580–1632). English colonizer. He was secretary of state from 1619 until 1625, when he announced himself a Catholic and on resigning received his Irish peerage. In 1627 he visited a colony which he had founded (1621) in Newfoundland, but after two years he decided to seek a warmer climate for his permanent home. He died while in England to obtain a grant for the selected territory. The grant passed to his son, the 2nd Lord Baltimore, who governed the colony, now called Maryland, from England.

Balzac, Honoré de (1799–1850). French novelist. Author of the great novel-sequence *La Comédie humaine*, he was born in Tours, the son of an eccentric civil servant. His unhappy schooldays are described in the autobiographical *Louis Lambert* (1832). An attempt to turn him into a lawyer failed, and from 1820 he was in Paris trying to make a living as a writer. An unfortunate speculation in a printing firm involved him in debt which took years to settle. His industry, both in research and in the writing of his novels, was enormous: his eventual earnings equally so. In total his output amounted to about 100 novels, six plays, many pamphlets and a huge amount of correpondence. His first successful novel, *Les Chouans* (1829), describes in the Romantic manner of Sir Walter Scott a rising in Brittany during the French Revolution. His Rabelaisian *Contes drolatiques* (1832–37) are medieval tales written in a pseudo-16th-century idiom. His vast conception of linking under a single title, *La Comédie humaine*, all the novels he had already written and those he planned to write, dates from 1842, his idea being to present an integrated picture of nineteenth-century France, with scenes of life in Paris, the country, the army, the family. The novels thus linked contain over 2,000 characters. He said of himself 'I penetrate the soul without neglecting the body', and this claim was vindicated by his genius for delineation of character, made possible by extraordinary powers of observation and imagination. Of the individual novels, the best known include *Eugénie Grandet* (1833), *Le Pére Goriot* (1834), *César Birotteau* (1837), *La Cousine Bette* (1846). His *Lettres à l'Étrangére*, published after his death, were written to a rich Polish countess, Evelina Hanska, who first wrote to him in 1832 and was soon promising marriage after her husband's death. This occurred in 1841 and thereafter they met regularly, but they were not married until 1850, only five months before Balzac's death, which was hastened by travel in the bitter cold of an East European winter.
Pritchett, V. S., *Balzac.* 1973

Bancroft, George (1800–1891). American historian and diplomat. He studied history at Göttingen University and on his return started a school where he began writing his monumental *History of the United States* (10 volumes, 1834–74). Services to the Democratic party were rewarded with official posts ending with that of minister to Great Britain (1846–49). The Whigs then returned to power but after the assassination of Lincoln he was sent as minister in Berlin (1867–74).
Wolfe Howe, M. de, *Life and Letters of George Bancroft.* 1971

Banda, Hastings Kamazu (1906–). Life president of Malawi. Educated at a mission school he emigrated to the U.S.A., where, after fifteen years' work, his savings allowed him to take degrees in philosophy and medicine. Coming to Britain he became an L.R.C.P. at Edinburgh and thereafter practised in England until 1953. From 1958 he led the independence movement in Nyasaland and headed the Malawi Congress party founded in 1959, being imprisoned for a time by the British. When the country attained self-government in 1963 Banda became prime minister, an office which he retained when in July 1964 Malawi became independent. During a cabinet crisis in the following September Banda dismissed or forced the resignation of most of his ministers, which greatly increased his personal power.

Bandaranaike, Solomon West Ridgeway Dias (1899–1959). Sri Lankan politician. Educated at Oxford University, he became a lawyer and after Ceylon's independence was minister of health (1947–51) in D. S. Senanayake's government. He resigned to form the Sri Lanka Freedom party, the basis of the People's United Front, the victory of which in the election of 1956 resulted in his becoming prime minister. He was assassinated by a Buddhist monk in 1959 but his policy of socialism at home (accompanied by expropriation of foreign interests) and neutralism abroad was continued by his widow **Sirimavo Bandaranaike** (1916–), who became the first woman prime minister. Her period of office was one of mounting financial difficulty, communal troubles and administrative chaos, some of it due to forces outside her control. She resigned after electoral defeat in 1965, but again became prime minister, 1970–77.

Bandello, Matteo (*c.* 1485–1561). Italian author, born in Piedmont. A Dominican friar, a diplomatist and (1550–54) bishop of Agen in France, he wrote about 250 short stories (*novelle*), some of which were used as the basis of works by Shakespeare (*Romeo and Juliet*), Lope de Vega, Byron etc.
Petrocchi, G., *Matteo Bandello*. 1949

Bankhead, Tallulah Brockman (1903–1968). American actress, famous in the 1920s and 1930s. The hysterical adulation aroused by her husky voice and vibrant personality was even more exuberantly expressed in London than in New York. She continued a successful career in America after World War II.
Gill, B., *Tallulah Bankhead*. 1973

Banks, Sir Joseph, 1st Bart. (1743–1820). British botanist. His wealth enabled him to be a munificent patron of research and exploration for the advancement of botany. He accompanied and later wrote about Captain Cook's great voyage on the *Endeavour* (1768–71) and thereby became recognized throughout Europe as an authority on Australia. He made other voyages of scientific exploration and from 1778 until his death was president of the Royal Society, of which he had been a fellow since 1766.
Cameron, H. C., *Sir Joseph Banks*. 1952

Bannister, Sir Roger Gilbert (1929–). English athlete. He won fame by being the first to achieve a four-minute mile (6 May 1954). He was knighted in 1979.

Banting, Sir Frederick Grant (1891–1941). Canadian physiologist. With C. H. * Best, he first succeeded in preparing the hormone insulin used to treat diabetes. Banting was born at Alliston, Ontario, and graduated in medicine at Toronto University. He served with the Canadian Army Medical Corps in World War I and after returning to Canada began the research which brought him and his colleagues fame. In 1923 he shared the Nobel Prize for Medicine, with J. J. R. Macleod, in whose laboratory he and Best had been working. Banting divided his share of the prize equally with Best. In 1930 he became director of the newly founded Banting Institute for Medical Research, Toronto, and it was while doing research on aviation medicine that he died in an air accident.

Bantock, Sir Granville (1868–1946). English composer. He started his career as a conductor and from 1908 to 1934 was professor of music at Birmingham University. His works include a setting for chorus and orchestra of Fitzgerald's *Omar Khayyám*, and *Fifine at the Fair*, an orchestral work based on a poem of Browning. He was knighted in 1930.

Banville, Théodore Faullin de (1832–1891). French poet and critic. He was an ingenious verse technician particularly in his use of medieval verse forms, which he revived. His works, including *Les Cariatides* (1941), *Odes funambulesques* (1857) and *Les Exilés* (1867), won him the admiration of his fellow poets and the title 'roi des rimes'. Baudelaire described him as the 'poet of the happy hours of life', Swinburne as 'the French Tennyson'.

Bao Dai (1911–). Last emperor of Annam (from 1932) and (1949–55) first head of state of Vietnam, part of which had composed his former realm. In 1954, after the Geneva Conference which followed the French defeat in Indo-China, North Vietnam split off to form a separate communist state. Bao Dai was still the nominal ruler in the south but showed little inclination for his task and spent much time on the French Riviera. He was deposed in 1955 in favour of Ngo Dinh Diem.

Barabbas. A robber mentioned in the New Testament as having been freed in response to the acclamation of the mob by Pontius Pilate during the trial of Jesus Christ. Pilate had hoped to save one whom he recognized as innocent by taking advantage of a supposed custom that a criminal, chosen by the people, should be released at the time of the Passover.

Barbarossa *see* **Frederick I (Barbarossa)**

Barbarossa, Uruj (*c.* 1482–1518), and **Khaireddin** (*c.* 1482–1546). Turkish corsairs, brothers of Greek parentage, whose name inspired terror in the Mediterranean area. Uruj, having treacherously murdered the amir, seized Algiers but was soon captured and beheaded. Khaireddin, succeeding him in Algiers, for about thirty years preyed upon Mediterranean shipping and the almost defenceless coasts. He died in Constantinople where he had eventually returned with over 1,000 captives and laden with spoils.

Barber, Samuel (1910–1981). American composer. He was born at West Chester, Pennsylvania, and studied at the Curtis Institute in Philadelphia. He wrote some of the most popular of modern orchestral works, including Adagio for strings (1936), Essay for orchestra No.1 (1937), Symphony No. 1 (1936), Cello concerto (1945), and Symphony No. 2 (1944). Himself an accomplished singer, he composed a setting of Matthew Arnold's *Dover Beach* for voice and string quartet. His first full-size opera, *Vanessa*, was performed at Salzburg in 1958. Later works include *Anthony and Cleopatra* (opera, 1960) and *The Lovers* (1971).

Barbey d'Aurevilly, Jules Amédée (1808–1889). French novelist, author of *La vieille Maîtresse* (1851), *L'Ensorcelée* (1854) and *Les Diaboliques* (1874), which, despite the author's diatribes against the realists, do in fact recall Flaubert in their psychological realism. Barbey d'Aurevilly was an ultra-romantic and a monarchist; his output of polemics against democracy and materialism was enormous.
Canu, J., *Barbey d'Aurevilly*. 1945

Barbirolli, Sir John (1899–1970). British orchestral conductor, of Italian descent. He was cellist in major string quartets for many years and conducted the British National Opera Company (1926–36). He succeeded Toscanini as conductor of the New York Philharmonic in 1936 and returned to England as conductor of the Hallé Orchestra (Manchester) in 1943.
Rigby, C., *John Barbirolli: A Biographical Sketch*. 1948

Barbour, John (?1320–1395). Scotland's first national poet. He travelled and studied in England and France and held court appointments in Scotland under Robert II. His only surviving work, the *Brus*, contains about 13,000 lines of eight-syllable couplets and tells the life-story of Scotland's hero-king Robert Bruce. It not only contains many vivid episodes but is now considered an accurate historical source.
Neilson, G., *John Barbour, Poet and Translator*. 1900

Barbusse, Henri (1874–1935). French journalist and novelist. His novels are strongly reminiscent of Zola's, but contain elements of existentialist thought; they include *L'Enfer* (1908) and *Le Feu* (1916), a grim study of life in the trenches during World War I, in which he served as a volunteer. Barbusse became a communist sympathizer and a propagandist of internationalist ideas. He died in Moscow.

Barclay, Alexander (*c.* 1476–1552). Scottish poet. He was chaplain of Ottery St Mary, Devon, and later became a monk. He wrote *The Ship of Fools* (1509), a long satirical poem based on a German original (Brant's *Narrenschiff*).

Barclay de Tolly, Mikhail, Prince (1761–1818). Russian soldier, of Scottish descent. He commanded the Russian forces resisting Napoleon's march to Moscow (1812). The unpopularity of his policy of continuous retreat into the heart of Russia caused him at last to make a stand and his defeat at Smolensk led to his being replaced by Kutuzov. On Kutuzov's death in 1813, Barclay de Tolly again became commander-in-chief. In the earlier part of his career he had lost an arm at Eylau in 1807 and in the same year had led the army which invaded Finland and forced the Swedes to sue for peace.

Bardeen, John (1908–). American physicist. Working mainly in the Bell Telephone Laboratories, he investigated super-conductivity in metals at very low temperature, and was co-inventor of the germanium transistor. He shared the Nobel Prize for Physics (1956) with W. H. Brattain and W. B. Shockley and in 1972 shared a second prize with Leon Cooper and John Schrieffer for a theory explaining super-conductivity.

Bardot, Brigitte (1934–). French actress, born in Paris. She started her career as a model and appeared as a 'cover girl' for the magazine *Elle*, but it was as a self-revealing star in such films as *Et Dieu créa la femme* and *Babette s'en va en guerre* that she became the symbolic 'sex kitten' of the 1950s–60s. She married Roger Vadim, the film director, in 1952 and Jacques Charrier, the actor, in 1959.

Barebone, Praise-God (1596–1679). English clergyman. His odd name was applied in derision to the parliament set up by Cromwell (1653), of which he was a member. A London leather merchant, he became a noted preacher and a leader of the Fifth Monarchy Sect.

Barenboim, Daniel (1942–). Israeli pianist and conductor, born in Argentina. He toured internationally from 1954, recorded all the Mozart piano concertos, and became a successful conductor as well. In 1967 he married the cellist Jacqueline du Pré.

Barents, Willem (died 1597). Dutch navigator and explorer. He led three expeditions (1594–97) in an unsuccessful search for a north-east sea passage to Asia, reaching Novaya Zemlya on the first two. On the third he accidentally discovered Spitsbergen and rounded the north point of Novaya Zemlya, but the expedition was caught in the ice and forced to winter there. In the following June he and his crew escaped in small boats but Barents died on the way. In 1871 his winter quarters were discovered undisturbed.

Barère (de Vieuzac), Bertrand (1755–1841). French revolutionary politician, known for his eloquence as the 'Anacreon of the guillotine'. He attached himself to Robespierre in the Convention and was a member of the Committee of Public Safety (1793–94). Under Napoleon he became a secret-service agent.

Barham, Richard Harris (1788–1845). English writer. A clergyman who became a minor canon at St Paul's, London, he wrote a series of burlesque verse tales under the pen-name Thomas Ingoldsby, many of them based on medieval legends. They were published collectively as *The Ingoldsby Legends* (1840).

Baring. A British family of merchant bankers, whose business was founded (1770) by the brothers John and Francis Baring, sons of a German immigrant. Titles borne by members of the family who have been successful not only in their own field are Ashburton, Northbrook, Revelstoke and * Cromer.

Baring, Maurice (1874–1945). English man of letters, fourth son of the 1st Baron Revelstoke. Educated at Eton and Cambridge, he left the diplomatic service in 1904 to become a journalist. He covered the Russo-Japanese War for the *Morning Post*, and the Balkan War of 1912 for *The Times*. He did intelligence work in World War I and later joined the R.F.C. After the war, novels, e.g. *Cat's Cradle* (1925), essays, plays and poems (he was also a skilled parodist) revealed a witty, well-informed mind. Chesterton and Belloc were among his many literary friends.

Lovat, L., *Maurice Baring: A Postscript*. 1948. Smyth, E., *Maurice Baring*. 1938

Baring-Gould, Sabine (1834–1924). English clergyman and writer. He was born of a well-known Devonshire family and held a quiet Devonshire living for most of his life, which allowed plenty of time for a large literary output. He is better remembered for his books on medieval lore and legends, e.g. *The Book of Werewolves* (1865), than for his many novels. 'Onward Christian Soldiers' is the best known of his hymns.

Dickinson, B. H. C., *Baring-Gould, Writer and Folklorist*. 1970. Purcell, W., *Onward Christian Soldiers*. 1957

Barker, Sir Herbert Atkinson (1869–1950). British manipulative surgeon. He had no medical qualifications, but his great success, the granting of his knighthood, and popular indignation at the medical authorities' denial of his right to the services of an anaesthetist did much to enhance the prestige of manipulative methods within and without the medical profession.

Barmecides. A Persian family of predominant influence at the court of the Abbasid caliphs at Baghdad. Their power was ended in 803 by the execution of one and the dismissal of the rest by * Harun al-Rashid. The term 'Barmecides feast' is derived from a story in the *Arabian Nights* telling of a practical joke which consisted in serving a dinner of elaborately named but empty dishes to a starving beggar. He, however, entered into the spirit of the occasion and was rewarded with real food.

Barnabas, St. According to the Acts of the Apostles he introduced Paul to the Christian community in Jerusalem and later accompanied him on a missionary journey until differences of opinion led to a parting of the ways. Barnabas went to Cyprus but accounts of his later movements and supposed martyrdom are apocryphal.

Barnard, Christiaan (Neethling) (1922–). South African surgeon who performed the first human heart transplant operation in 1967, born in Beaufort West, Cape Province. He was educated at the Universities of Cape Town and Minnesota, in 1958 was appointed director of surgical research at the University of Cape Town and since 1961 has been head of the cardiothoracic surgical unit at the Groote Schuur Hospital in Cape Town.

Barnard introduced open-heart surgery to the Republic of South Africa, designed artificial heart valves and has published much on congenital intestinal atresia.

Barnard, C. and Pepper, C. B., *Christiaan Barnard: One Life*. 1970. Barnard, C., *Heart Attack: You Don't Have to Die*. 1972

Barnardo, Thomas John (1845–1905). British social reformer. Physician and founder of the children's homes named after him, he was born in Dublin, and when only 17 did evangelizing work in the slums there. He went to London to study medicine and at Stepney founded the first of a number of homes for destitute boys. A home for girls at Barkingside followed in 1876 and by the time of his death more than 60,000 children had passed through his hands. In the intervening years the scope and scale of the work has vastly increased.

Wymer, N., *Father of Nobody's Children*. 1954

Barnato, Barnett (originally Barnett (Barney) Isaacs) (1852–1897). South African financier. Born in London of Jewish parentage, he arrived in South Africa in 1873, made a fortune by buying up abandoned diamond mines and eventually linked his interests with those of his rival Cecil Rhodes by joining the control of the De Beers Mining Companies. He became a member of the Cape Colony legislature (1888–97). He committed suicide at sea after suffering heavy financial losses.

Barnes, Ernest William (1874–1953). English ecclesiastic. As Bishop of Birmingham (1924–52) (after being Master of the Temple 1905–19 and then canon of Westminster) he was the centre of violent controversy caused by his attempts to reconcile beliefs fostered by religion with his mathematical and scientific conclusions (he became F.R.S. in 1919). In particular the rejection of the miraculous in his *Rise of Christianity* (1947) evoked official censure.

Barnes, J., *Ahead of His Age*. 1979

Barnes, Thomas (1785–1841). English journalist. He was educated at Christ's Hospital and in his early years contributed to periodicals edited by his school-fellow Leigh Hunt. He joined *The Times* (1809) as dramatic critic and in 1817 was appointed editor. During his twenty-five years of control *The Times* was the most formidable organ of opinion in Britain and Barnes, who was independent of any political party, was the most powerful journalistic influence.

Hudson, D., *Thomas Barnes of 'The Times'*. 1943

Barnes, William (1801–1886). English clergyman and poet. Having made a detailed study of local speech he became widely known as the author of three series (1844, 1859, 1862) of idyllic and pastoral poetry in the Dorset dialect, collected as *Poems of Rural Life in Dorset Dialect* (1879). His *Outline of English Speechcraft* (1878) was an odd attempt to teach English by using only words of native origin.

Dugdale, G., *William Barnes of Dorset*. 1953

Barnum, Phineas Taylor (1810–1891). American showman, famed for his flamboyant publicity. In 1834 he entered show business as the exhibitor of curiosities such as a Negro slave whom he claimed to be the nurse of George Washington and, later, the midget 'General Tom Thumb'. In 1847 he managed Jenny Lind's American tour. His circus, 'The Greatest Show on Earth', was founded in 1871, being merged with that of his chief competitor, J. A. Bailey in 1881. It soon became an American institution and continued for a generation after his death.

Baroja y Nessi, Pio (1872–1956). Spanish novelist. He was born in Navarre and his books, often picaresque in character, frequently have a Basque setting. As a young man he practised as a doctor. He wrote a number of trilogies, notable for their forceful, rather bare style and their undertone of social discontent. The best known is *La Lucha por la vida (The Struggle For Existence)*. Hemingway hailed his *Memoirs of a Man of Action* (1931), concerned with the 19th-century Carlist wars, as a masterpiece.

Barras, Paul François Jean Nicolas (1755–1829). French aristocrat and revolutionary politician. He wasted his inheritance and seized the opportunity of the Revolution to restore his fortunes. He was a member of the National Assembly, joined the Jacobins, and in the Convention voted for the execution of Louis XVI. He earned a reputation for cruelty at Toulon whither he had been sent after its capture by Bonaparte. However, he was wise enough to see when the people tired of bloodshed and, with Fouché and Tallien, organized Robespierre's overthrow in 1794. A leader of the Directory (the succeeding government) he exercised his power against a background of luxury and extravagance. He retired after Bonaparte's *coup d'état* in 1799.

Barrault, Jean Louis (1910–). French actor and stage director. After training at a drama school and service in World War II he was producer-director at the Comédie Française (1940–46). In the latter year he formed with his wife, Madeleine Renaud, a company, le Troupe Marigny, which by its Paris productions and tours and visits abroad (including London, 1956 and 1965, and Edinburgh festivals) gained wide renown. His own acting was influenced by his talents as a mime, demonstrated in his best known film *Les Enfants du Paradis*.
Memories for Tomorrow (Memoirs). 1971

Barrès, Maurice (1862–1923). French politician. An extreme nationalist, he acquired notoriety by the fervour of his articles in *L' Echo de Paris* during World War I. His literary talents were admired even by those who deplored his politics. Among his best known works are *Les Déracinés* (1897) and *Les Amitiés Françaises* (1903).

Barrie, Sir James Matthew, 1st Bart (1860–1937). Scottish playwright and novelist. He was born in Kirriemuir (the 'Thrums' of the novels) and educated at Edinburgh University. He left Scotland in 1883 and worked as a journalist on the Nottingham *Daily Journal* before coming to London in 1885. He began writing with novels (e.g. *A Window in Thrums*, 1889, *The Little Minister*, 1891), but from 1890 he turned to the theatre and achieved wealth and fame with *Quality Street* (1902), *The Admirable Crichton* (1902), *Peter Pan* (1904), *Dear Brutus* (1917), *Mary Rose* (1920), the problem 'first act', *Shall We Join the Ladies?* (1922), and the curious but moving *The Boy David* (1936), with the title role written for the actress Elizabeth Bergner. Barrie was chancellor of Edinburgh University from 1930. He received his baronetcy in 1913 and the O.M. in 1922. The whimsical humour of his works gradually lost much of its appeal, but *Peter Pan*, the royalties of which by his bequest go to a children's hospital, is revived annually.
Dunbar, J., *J. M. Barrie*. 1970

Barrow, Isaac (1630–1677). English mathematician. Son of a London merchant, Barrow studied at Trinity College, Cambridge, where he became a fellow in 1652. His royalist sympathies made life uncomfortable for him, and he left in 1655 for a five-year tour of the Continent. Returning at the Restoration in 1660, he became Professor of Greek in Cambridge. He took the Lucasian Chair of Mathematics in Cambridge in 1663. Barrow was a first class teacher. He produced editions of Euclid's *Elements* (1655) and *Data* (1657) and versions of works by Archimedes, Apollonius and Theodosius. He gave import-

ant optical lectures concerning a new method for finding the point construction of the diacaustic of a spherical interface. His geometrical lectures were not original, but did digest modern continental writers such as Descartes, Huygens and Pascal to his audiences. Isaac * Newton was a student at Trinity during this period, and it is possible that Barrow's work made some impression on him. Newton was Barrow's successor as Lucasian Professor of Mathematics.
Osmond, H., *Isaac Barrow, His Life and Times*. 1944

Barry, Sir Charles (1795–1860). English architect. He won the commission to design the new Houses of Parliament (erected from 1839) to replace the old buildings destroyed by fire in 1834. It was stipulated that the work should be in Gothic style, and Barry, who was essentially a classic architect, therefore obtained some assistance in Gothic detail from A. W. * Pugin. The Travellers' Club (1829–31) and the Reform Club (1837) in London are good examples of his work in the Italian renaissance style.

Barrymore. American family of actors. The best known, **Lionel Barrymore** (1878–1954), like his younger brother, John, was successful both on stage and screen but it was in character rather than romantic parts that he excelled. He became paralysed in 1940 but continued to act from a wheelchair. Their sister **Ethel** (1879–1959) was perhaps the most talented of the trio and in 1928 opened the New York theatre bearing her name. She is especially remembered for parts in plays by Ibsen and Shaw; she, too, later acted in films, especially *The Corn is Green* (1940–42). **John** (1882–1942) was the matinee idol of his time, achieving his greatest fame as a Shakespearian actor, particularly in *Hamlet* and *Richard III*. From 1925 onwards he was occupied almost exclusively with the cinema, in which he played romantic and dramatic roles in films such as *Don Juan* and *Dr Jekyll and Mr Hyde*. In his later years he was incapacitated by alcoholism.

Bart, Jean (1651–1702). French sailor. A hero of the French navy and a fisherman's son, he rose to command a squadron. He first served with the Dutch navy, and it was only after he had left that service and had achieved fame as a privateer that he was appointed lieutenant of a French man-of-war. In the War of the Grand Alliance his exploits were a constant menace to the English and Dutch by whom France was opposed. A raid was made near Newcastle, many ships were sunk and on one occasion he captured a whole flotilla of Dutch corn ships. In 1697 he was received personally by Louis XIV and given command of a squadron.

Bart, Lionel (1930–). English composer and song writer. His particular flair resulted in several successful musical plays. Amongst the most popular were *Lock Up Your Daughters*, *Fings Ain't Wot They Used t'Be*, *Oliver!*, and *Maggie May*.

Barth, Karl (1886–1968). Swiss Calvinist theologian, born in Basle. He was professor of theology at Göttingen (1923–25), at Münster (1925–30) and then at Bonn, until he was dismissed in 1934 for opposition to Hitler. He was appointed to a theological professorship at Basle in 1935, retiring in 1962. Barth's teaching insists that the word of God as revealed by Jesus Christ is the sole source of religious truth, and that consequently man is unable to solve his own problems by reason and is completely dependent on divine grace and the workings of the Holy Spirit within him. Barth's theology is systematically set out in his many-volumed work *Church Dogmatics*, publication of which began in 1932.
Hartwell, H., *The Theology of Karl Barth*. 1964

Barthes, Roland Gérard (1915–1980). French writer and critic. He developed and updated the ideas of the Swiss linguist Ferdinand de Saussure in promoting 'semiotics' (the sociology of signs, symbols and representations) and analysed the impact of film, radio, television and advertising in changing language, fashion and cultural iconography. His books include *S/Z* (1970), *The Pleasure of the Text* (1973) and *A Lover's Discourse* (1977). He held a chair at the Collège de France.

Bartholdi, Frédéric Auguste (1834–1904). French monumental sculptor, best known for his *Statue of Liberty* presented to the U.S.A. by the French government in 1886 and set up on Bedloe's Island, New York harbour.

Bartholomew, St. One of Christ's twelve apostles, sometimes identified with Nathaniel. Almost nothing is known of him but traditions tell of missionary journeys in Asia Minor, Armenia and India and of martyrdom by flaying and crucifixion.

Bartholomew, John George (1860–1920). Scottish cartographer and map and atlas publisher. He improved standards of British cartography and introduced into Great Britain use of contours and systematic colour layering to show relief. His father was Edinburgh map publisher **John Bartholomew** (1831–1893).

He published important atlases of Scotland (1895), England and Wales (1903), an *Atlas of Meteorology* (1899) and *Atlas of Zoogeography* (1911), the first 2 volumes of a major physical atlas. He began work on *The Times Survey Atlas of the World*, published 1921 by his son, **John Bartholomew** (1909–1962), also editor of the new *Times Atlas of the World* (1955).

Gardiner, L., *Bartholomew 150 Years*. 1976

Barthou, Jean Louis Firmin (1862–1934). French politician. He entered politics in 1889 and held a wide variety of ministerial posts. As foreign minister in 1934, he was assassinated with King * Alexander of Yugoslavia in Marseilles. He wrote biographies of Mirabeau (1913) and Lamartine (1916) and in 1918 was elected to the Académie Française.

Aubert, O., *Louis Barthou*. 1935

Bartók, Béla (1881–1945). Hungarian composer and pianist, born in Nagyszentmiklós (now part of Romania). He was taught music by his mother, then studied under László Erkel before entering the Budapest Academy of Music in 1899, and in 1901 he won the Liszt scholarship. His early works were influenced by Liszt, Brahms, Wagner and Richard Strauss. In 1905 he began to collect and publish Magyar folk-songs with Kodály which had an important influence on his own compositions. In 1907 he became piano professor at the Academy. Of his earliest mature works, his ballet *The Wooden Prince* (1917) and opera *Bluebeard's Castle* (1918) were most successful. By 1923 his importance was recognized and he was commissioned to write an orchestral work for the fiftieth anniversary of the union of Buda and Pest (the *Dance Suite*). After visits to the U.S.A. (1927) and the U.S.S.R. (1929) he resigned the Academy post (1934) and returned to collecting folk-songs for the Hungarian Academy of Arts and Sciences. In 1940 he emigrated to the U.S.A. and became a research assistant in music at Columbia University, continuing his work on folk music. There he published several important collections, including a study of Romanian folk music (3 volumes 1967). Unable through ill health to get more profitable employment, he died in penury in New York.

He combined the essential characteristics of Hungarian folk music with traditional music and developed a nationalistic, yet individual, style.

Stevens, H., *The Life and Music of Béla Bartók*. 2nd ed. 1964.

Bartolommeo, Fra (*c.* 1472–1517). Italian painter. The son of a muleteer, he early found work in a Florentine studio, but under the influence of * Savonarola, whose portrait he painted, he burnt his drawings of nudes and in 1500 joined the Dominican order. Thenceforth all his work was of a religious character, and it was to reflect in turn the influences of Raphael and Michelangelo. But his treatment of figures and draperies and his grand static compositions assert his own instincts.

Bartolozzi, Francesco (*c.* 1727–1815). Italian engraver. One of the most famous exponents of the art, in 1764 he settled in England, where George III was to be among his patrons; he became an original member of the Royal Academy, for which he engraved, from Cipriani's design, the diploma used ever since. His book plates, to be seen in many libraries of the period, were a pleasing sideline. He spent the last ten years of his life in Portugal, as director of the National Academy, Lisbon.

Barton, Clara (1821–1912). American social worker. Originally a schoolteacher, she served as a nurse in the American Civil War and the Franco-Prussian Wars. In 1877 she founded the American National Committee which later became the American Red Cross, of which she was president from 1882 to 1904.

Barton, Sir Edmund (1849–1920). First Australian prime minister (1901–03). This was the climax of a career in which he had done much to promote the cause of federation, first in his native New South Wales, where he had entered the legislature in 1879, and finally when he was leader of a delegation to London which persuaded the British government to

adopt the proposed Australian constitution (1900). A lawyer by profession, he became, on retirement from politics, a justice of the High Court of Australia (1903–20).
Reynolds, J., *Edmund Barton*. 1948.

Barton, Elizabeth (*c*. 1506–1534). English mystic, known as 'the Maid of Kent'. She was a domestic servant who after a period of illness began to fall periodically into trance states, during which she uttered prophecies which were taken to be divinely inspired. Unfortunately the monk, Edward Bocking, sent by Archbishop Warham of Canterbury to examine her, tried to make use of her for political ends. In particular she was impelled to prophesy Henry VIII's death if he married Anne Boleyn. Eventually she was arraigned before Cranmer, confessed her imposture and was executed, with Bocking and others.

Bartram, William (1739–1823). American naturalist and traveller. A Quaker who wrote a well-regarded account of *Travels through North and South Carolina* (1791). Wordsworth and Coleridge admired his descriptive powers.

Baruch, Bernard Mannes (1870–1965). American financier. He made a fortune by speculation by the age of 30 and became a friend and economic advisor to Woodrow * Wilson and Franklin D. * Roosevelt during World Wars I and II. He was also a close friend of Winston * Churchill. As US representative to the UN Atomic Energy Commission 1946–47 he devised the 'Baruch plan' for the international control of atomic energy.

Bashkirtsev, Maria Constantinovna (1860–1884). Russian diarist. Her correspondence (e.g. with de Maupassant) is of great psychological interest but most remarkable are her diaries (published in 1885), a self-study undertaken with a conscious effort to attain exact truth and as a revelation of the exultations and despairs of a talented and precocious girl. She lived in France from early childhood, studied painting, in which she achieved a limited success, and died of tuberculosis.
Creston, D., *Life of Marie Bashkirtseff*. 1943

Basil. The name of two Byzantine emperors. **Basil I** (reigned 867–886), called 'the Macedonian' and founder of the Macedonian dynasty, gained the throne by murdering his patron Michael III, but raised the empire to the height of its magnificence. **Basil II** (958–1025) began his reign in 963 and emerged from his minority as a soldier-emperor whose successes against the Bulgarians (986–1018) earned him the name Bulgaroctonus ('killer of Bulgars'). He shared rule with his brother Constantine VIII but was always dominant. He protected the peasants from encroachments by the nobles.

Basil, St (*c*. 329–379). Cappadocian father of the church. He was born of a noble family at Caesarea and was a brother of St Gregory of Nyssa. Ordained in 364 and appointed bishop of Caesarea in 370, he succeeded * Athanasius as one of the main upholders of Nicene orthodoxy over which he conflicted with emperor Valens. Monastic rules set out by him are still used with little alteration by communities within the Greek Orthodox church.
Prestige, G. L., *St Basil Great and Apollinaris*. 1956

Baskerville, John (1706–1775). English typographer born in Worcestershire. Footman, writing master, manager of a Birmingham japanning business – these were the steps by which he rose to be one of the most influential designers of type in the history of printing. His editions of Virgil (1757) and Milton (1758) followed years of experiments. As printer to Cambridge University (from 1758) he produced many magnificent editions, including the Bible and the Greek New Testament.
Gaskell, P., *John Baskerville: A Bibliography*. 1959

Bateman. An American theatrical family with many links with the English stage. **Hezekiah Linthicum Bateman** (1812–1875) took the Lyceum Theatre, London, in 1871, when his presentation of Henry Irving's *The Bells* achieved a notable success. His wife, a dramatist as well as an actress, managed Sadler's Wells for a time after his death, and all four of their daughters went on the stage. The best known of them, **Kate Josephine** (1842–1917), began at the age of 8 with a still younger sister. In later life, playing with Irving, she proved a notable Lady Macbeth. Another sister, **Virginia** (1853–1940), married Edward Compton, the actor; their children were Sir Compton Mackenzie and the actress Fay Compton.

Bates, Herbert Ernest (1905–1974). English writer. After starting his career in journalism and serving with the RAF in World War II, he produced a constant flow of novels and short stories, which enjoyed great popularity; he is regarded as a master of the short-story form in particular. Among his best known novels are *Fair Stood the Wind for France* (1944), *The Jacaranda Tree* (1949) and *The Darling Buds of May* (1958), which was filmed as *The Mating Game*. Television versions of some of his stories and novels are much admired.

Bathsheba. Wife of King David and mother of Solomon. The Bible story tells how David, having seduced Bathsheba, contrived the death of her husband, Uriah the Hittite, by placing him in the forefront of battle.

Batista y Zaldivar, Fulgencio (1901–1973). Cuban dictator. As an army sergeant he organized a 'sergeants' revolt' (1933) against the ruling oligarchy, became commander-in-chief of the Cuban forces 1933–40 and *de facto* ruler, serving as president 1940–44. He retired to Florida with his wealth after a period of stability, reform and corruption. He seized power again in 1952 and as president ruled as a dictator until his overthrow by Fidel Castro (December 1958). Thereafter he lived in the Dominican Republic, then Madeira and finally Portugal.

Battenberg. The family name used by descendants of Prince Alexander of Hesse's morganatic marriage; to disguise its German flavour it was changed to Mountbatten during World War I. Two sons, **Louis** (1854–1921) and **Henry** (1858–1896), married into the British royal family, the former to a grand daughter of Queen Victoria, the latter to a daughter (Princess Beatrice). Louis, 1st Marquess of Milford Haven, was a distinguished naval officer who became first sea lord in 1912. His son was Earl * Mountbatten of Burma; one of his daughters became Princess Andrew of Greece, mother of the Duke of Edinburgh; another was to become queen of Sweden. Henry's eldest son became 1st Marquess of Carisbrooke; Victoria Eugénie, a daughter, married * Alfonso XIII of Spain.

Baudelaire, Charles Pierre (1821–1867). French poet. Born in Paris, he was the cherished son of an elderly father, to whom he owed his artistic appreciation, and a young mother, whose second marriage, while he was still a boy, he never forgave. Educated in Lyons and Paris, he was sent to India but stopped off at Mauritius (1841–42). On his return to France he soon spent half his small fortune and though the remainder was tied up he had a constant struggle with poverty throughout his life. He frequented the artistic circle of his friend Delacroix, and had become known as an original critic before his attraction to the works of Edgar Allen Poe induced him to spend years on their translation into French. In 1857 he published a collection of poems, *Les Fleurs du mal (Flowers of Evil)*, an extraordinary mixture of morbidity, eroticism, mysticism, and acute aesthetic perception, for which author, printer and publisher were prosecuted on grounds of impropriety in 1864. Much of the reputation acquired by his works for immorality and decadence was due to misunderstanding. The unity of all art as a manifestation of the divine essence is one of his most important themes. There is to him unity, too, as well as contrast, between the beautiful and the ugly and evil; man should not shrink from the poor, the wicked or the tortured. He is indeed almost obessed with human suffering. But above all he is an artist in words who evokes, rather than describes, colours, scents, sensations, sounds, using a glowing imagination and a mastery of poetic symbolism. Other works by Baudelaire include *Petits Poèmes en prose* and studies of Balzac, Flaubert and Gautier. In later life he became addicted to opium and alcohol. Paralysis with aphasia attacked him in 1866 and his condition progressively worsened until his death.
Leakey, F. W., *Baudelaire and Nature*. 1968

Baum, Lyman Frank (1856–1919). American author. His *The Wonderful Wizard of Oz* (1900), the popular children's story, later achieved a great success on stage (1901) and screen (1939).

Baum, Vicki (1896–1960). Austrian novelist. She spent most of her life in the U.S.A. Her *Grand Hotel*, which used the accidental isolation of a group of people in an artificial setting as the basis of the plot, set a pattern followed by many other novelists. Its immense success, reinforced by a film version, was never quite achieved by her many later works.

Baur, Ferdinand Christian (1792–1860). German theologian. Professor of theology

(1826–60) at Tübingen University and the leading Protestant historian of religious dogma, he adopted much of Hegel's dialectical method and subjected the New Testament and church tradition to a rigorous analysis. His followers became known as the 'Tübingen school'.

Bax, Sir Arnold Edward Trevor (1883–1953). English composer, born in London. He composed the symphonic poems *In Faery Hills* (1909) and *Tintagel* (1917), in addition to seven symphonies, many songs and piano pieces. His richly romantic style is a musical reflection of the 'Celtic Twilight' movement in literature. Bax, who was knighted in 1937, was Master of the King's Musick (1942–53).
Scott-Sutherland, C., *Arnold Bax*. 1973

Baxter, James Keir (1926–1972). New Zealand poet. His parents were radical pacifists, and after an unhappy schooling in the South Island and England, he published his first volume of poetry, *Beyond the Palisade*, at 18 (1944). After a sporadic education at three universities, he worked as a postman, teacher and public servant, and became a Catholic (1958). He struggled with alcoholism, was tormented by his linking of sexuality and death, and torn between radical and conservative instincts. His poetry collections included *Pig Island Letters* (1966), *Jerusalem Sonnets* (1970) and *Autumn Testament* (1972). He set up an unsuccessful commune for juvenile drug-addicts, and malnutrition contributed to his early death.

Baxter, Richard (1615–1691). English Puritan divine, born in Shropshire. In 1638 he was ordained in the Church of England but never became a strong adherent of any particular denomination, though his pastoral work at Kidderminster (from 1641) is said to have 'transformed the town'. He was a chaplain in the Parliamentary army in the Civil War but opposed the King's execution and worked for the restoration of Charles II. Forced to leave the church because he rejected episcopacy, he was persecuted as a dissenter and was imprisoned (1685–86) after a brutal trial before Judge Jeffreys. He was a prolific writer. His best known works are *The Saints' Everlasting Rest* (1650) and an autobiography, *Reliquiae Baxterianae*.

Bayard, Pierre du Terrail, Seigneur de (*c*. 1473–1524). French soldier, known as 'le chevalier sans peur et sans reproche'. When only 20 years old he went with Charles VIII to Italy and in battle after battle he was to be found wherever danger was greatest. His reputation for humanity and piety grew with the fame won by his courage. In the wars of Louis XII and Francis I his exploits continued, but while returning from Italy in 1524 he was mortally wounded by an arquebus shot.

Bayezid (or Bajazet) (reigned 1389–1402). Ruler of the Ottoman Turks. He succeeded Murad I, greatly extended his dominions in Anatolia and invested Constantinople. The threat to Europe provoked a crusade against him by the emperor Sigismund, but by his victory at Nicopolis on the Danube Bayezid was able to move into northern Greece. Meanwhile a threat was developing in his rear from the Mongol leader Timur the Lame (Tamerlane) who entered Anatolia in 1400. Bayezid was defeated and captured at Ankara (1402); he died in captivity. He is a character in Marlowe's *Tamburlaine the Great*.

Bayle, Pierre (1647–1706). French philosopher. The son of a Calvinist minister, he became a Catholic and then reverted to Protestantism. He was professor of philosophy at Sedan (1675–81), of philosophy and history at Rotterdam University (1681–93), and wrote a famous *Dictionnaire historique et critique*. This acute and urbane work questioned many of the precepts of orthodox religious teaching and influenced Voltaire, Diderot and the French Encyclopedists.

Baylis, Lilian Mary (1874–1937). English theatrical manager. The benevolent autocrat of the 'Old Vic' off the Waterloo Road, London, she converted this music-hall into a national institution known all over the world. A musician by training, who had managed the music-hall for her aunt, Emma Cons, she took it over completely on her aunt's death in 1912 and two years later started the series of Shakesperian productions which made the theatre famous. Opera and ballet, which were also produced there, were transferred to Sadler's Wells, which after its rebuilding in 1931, she managed for a time. She was awarded the C.H. in 1929.
Findlater, R., *The Lady of the Old Vic*. 1975

Bazaine, Achille François (1811–1888).

French marshal. Having gained distinction in the Crimean War and against the Austrians in the Italian unification campaign, he was sent to Mexico, where from 1863 he was in supreme command and the main prop of Napoleon III's protége, the ill-fated emperor * Maximilian. In the Franco-Prussian War, he was forced to take refuge in the fortress of Metz after the defeat at Gravelotte. His surrender with over 150,000 men (October 1870) was a decisive disaster. In 1873 he was court-martialled for failure of duty, and given a death-sentence (commuted to twenty years' imprisonment). In the following year he escaped and managed to reach Spain, where he died.

Beaconsfield, 1st Earl *see* **Disraeli, Benjamin**

Beadle, George Wells (1903–). American geneticist. Professor of the California Institute of Technology, he shared the Nobel Prize for Medicine (1958) with Dr. E. L. Tatum of the Rockefeller Institute, for discovering that genes act by regulating definite chemical events.

Beaglehole, John Cawte (1901–1971). New Zealand historian. After a slow climb up the academic ladder, he became Professor of Commonwealth History at the Victoria University, Wellington 1963–66 and received the O.M. (1970) in the Cook Bicentennial Year for his scholarly work, including editing the four-volume *Journals of Captain James Cook* (1955–67).

Beale, Dorothea (1831–1906). English pioneer of women's education. She was principal of Cheltenham Ladies' College from 1858 for nearly fifty years and her success set an example which was widely followed. St Hilda's College, Oxford, was sponsored by her (1894), and in later life she supported the cause of votes for women.

Beardsley, Aubrey (1872–1898). English illustrator, born in Brighton, closely associated with the English Aesthetic movement, which his work typifies. He early developed a highly individual two-dimensional style, characterized by contrasts of fine richly detailed line-work and solid blacks, and by all the preoccupations and morbid tendencies of the Decadents. Among his most famous illustrations are those to Wilde's *Salome*, Pope's *Rape of the Lock* and his own work *Under the Hill* (1904). He became a Roman Catholic shortly before his early death from tuberculosis.
Symons, A., *Aubrey Beardsley*. 1972

Beatles, The (1962–1970). British pop group. The group comprised John Lennon (1940–1980), George Harrison (1943–), Paul McCartney (1942–) and Ringo Starr (1940–). All came from Liverpool and they first became cult figures in Germany. From 1963–67 'Beatlemania' was the dominant feature of world pop culture. Lennon and McCartney composed much of the Beatles most successful material which revealed a strong lyrical gift, and a yearning for new ideas (e.g. 'flower power', eastern religions). Lennon married the Japanese artist Yoko Ono and was shot dead in New York.

Beaton, Sir Cecil Walter Hardy (1904–1980). English photographer and designer. Long known mainly for his pictorial studies of people of fashionable society, he extended his range to include designs of sets and costumes for theatre and films. His costumes for the film *Gigi*, and his colour compositions for the musical success *My Fair Lady* in both its stage and screen versions, were widely acclaimed.
Vickers, H., *Cecil Beaton*. 1985

Beaton (or Bethune), **David** (1494–1546). Scotish prelate and statesman. Equipped for the church by studies at the universities of Glasgow, St Andrews and Paris, and qualified as a statesman by skilful diplomacy for James V, he was created a cardinal in 1538 and became archbishop of St Andrews and therefore primate of Sctoland. After the death of James V, when his widow Mary of Guise headed the regency for her young daughter, Mary Queen of Scots, Cardinal Beaton, though he had to contend with the Protestant faction and other rivals, attained almost supreme power, which he used in the Roman Catholic and French interest. He was murdered by Protestant conspirators in revenge for the execution of George Wishart, a Calvinist preacher. Beaton was a typical Renaissance figure, cultivated, able, brave, intensely individual but largely amoral.

Beatty, David Beatty, 1st Earl (1871–1936). British admiral. Born in Co. Wexford, Ireland, he joined the navy in 1884, served

with Nile gunboats in the Sudan (1896–98), played a fearless part in shore as well as sea operations during the Chinese Boxer rebellion (1900) and was in command of the battle cruisers at the beginning of World War I. He commanded successful naval actions at Heligoland Bight (1914) and Dogger Bank (1915). At the Battle of Jutland (1916), he lost two of his ships, but escaped the criticism encountered by Jellicoe. He succeeded Jellicoe as commander-in-chief of the Grand Fleet and as such received the surrender of the German fleet in 1918. For seven years from 1919 he served as first sea lord. Beatty, who in every capacity proved himself a born leader, received an earldom, the O.M. and a grant of £100,000 for his many services.
Chalmers, W. S., *The Life and Letters of David, Earl Beatty*. 1951.

Beaufort. The name taken by the children of John of * Gaunt and Catherine * Swynford when they were legitimized (1397). One of them, **Cardinal Beaufort** (1377–1447), bishop of Winchester, was the chief rival of his nephew Humphrey, Duke of Gloucester, for control of the government of England during the early years of Henry VI. The cardinal's brother, John, Duke of Somerset, was grandfather of **Margaret Beaufort,** mother of Henry VII, who through her inherited the claims to the throne of the Lancastrian house.

Beaufort, Sir Francis (1774–1857). British naval hydrographer. In 1805 he devised a scale of numbers (the Beaufort Scale) for expressing wind force. Originally the numbers ran from 0 (calm) to 12 (hurricane that no canvas can withstand) but they have now been given precise values in knots and the scale has been extended to Force 17. Beaufort also devised a system of letters, still in use, for denoting weather phenomena.

Beauharnais. A French family, which attained distinction during the Revolutionary and Napoleonic periods. **Alexandre, Vicomte de Beauharnais** (1760–1794), served in the American War of Independence and supported the Revolutionary cause in France, but was executed during the Terror. His widow, * **Josephine**, became the first wife of Napoleon Bonaparte. His son, **Eugène de Beauharnais** (1781–1824), was with Napoleon in Italy and the East and was an able and popular viceroy of Italy (1805–14). He was one of the few to gain fresh laurels during the Moscow campaign of 1812, and returned to hold Italy loyally to the last. After Napoleon's downfall he lived in Munich as duke of Leuchtenberg.

Beaumarchais, Pierre Augustin Caron de (1732–1799). French playwright, born in Paris, the son of a watch-maker called Caron. As a young man he invented an improved watch escapement and taught the harp to the daughters of Louis XV. He made a fortune from investment, took the name Beaumarchais from the first of two wealthy widows whom he married, went on secret missions in the king's service, and supplied arms to the insurgents in the American War of Independence. As a comic playwright he is regarded as second only to Molière. His plays *The Barber of Seville* (1775) and *The Marriage of Figaro* (1784) were sensationally successful and were used as operatic libertti by Rossini and Mozart respectively.

Beaumont, Francis (1584–1616). English playwright, born in Leicestershire. The son of a judge, he studied law but from 1603 devoted himself to literature. From 1606 until his marriage to Ursula Isley in 1613, Beaumont lived with his collaborator and friend John * Fletcher. Beaumont's part was predominant in *The Knight of the Burning Pestle* (1609), but the partners can share equal credit for *Philaster* (1611) and *The Maid's Tragedy* (1611). Altogether Beaumont is believed to have had a hand in about ten of the ingenious and sophisticated tragedies and tragicomodies attributed to the joint authorship.
Macaulay, G. C., *Francis Beaumont: A Critical Study*. 1972

Beaumont, William (1785–1853). American physiologist. Beaumont's great work lay in careful observation and experimentation upon the operations of the human stomach. Son of a farmer in Connecticut, Beaumont became a village schoolmaster, and began teaching himself medicine. After an apprenticeship with a practitioner, he became an assistant surgeon in the American Army. He retired from the army in 1839, and took up practice in St Louis, having two years earlier become Professor of Surgery at St Louis University. Beaumont's interest in the stomach arose from treating a fur trapper who had been very badly wounded in the stomach by a shotgun accident. Beaumont tended the man for some ten years and took the opportunity to make extensive experimental investigations into the operation of his gastric juices, which were published in his classic work of 1833, *Experiments and Observations on the Gastric Juice*. Beaumont established the presence of free hydrochloric acid in the juice, thus confirming that its action was primarily chemical in nature. Beaumont noted that gastric juices were not to be found in the stomach in the absence of food, and that psychological factors could influence their secretion. He also carefully investigated the digestibility of different aspects of diet, and studied the action of stimulants, such as coffee and alcohol, on the workings of the digestive system. His work was highly influential, especially in Germany. Miller, G., *William Beaumont's Formative Years*. 1946

Beauregard, Pierre Gustave Toutant (1818–1893). American soldier, born in New Orleans, and a confederate general during the Civil War. On joining the Confederate Army in 1861 he was appointed to a command at Charleston in South Carolina, and it was his order to fire on Fort Sumter that marked the opening of the war, throughout which he held high command with varying success.

Beauvoir, Simone Lucie Ernestine Maria Bertrand de (1908–). French author. Educated at the Sorbonne, she taught philosophy in various cities (1931–54) and became an intimate of Jean Paul Sartre, and a student of existentialism. Her works include *The Second Sex* (1949–50), an encyclopedic study of the human female; *The Mandarins* (1954), a novel about Parisian literary circles which won the Prix Goncourt; *The Long March* (1958), a study of modern China; and the autobiographical *Memoirs of a Dutiful Daughter* (1959), *The Prime of Life* (1963), *Force of Circumstance* (1965), *A Very Easy Death* (1966) and *All Said and Done* (1972).

Beaverbrook, William Maxwell Aitken, 1st Baron (1879–1964). Canadian-born British newspaper proprietor and politician. A millionaire when he came to England (1910), he entered Parliament as conservative member for Ashton-under-Lyne and became a friend of Bonar Law. Beaverbrook was Britain's first minister of information (1918), and was appointed minister of aircraft production (1940), an office which he filled with energy and considerable success.

But it was the *Daily Express*, bought in 1919, when it was almost derelict, that was his real life work. It became in a sense an enlargement of his own personality, energetic, exciting, entertaining, mischievous and sometimes brash. Subsequently he founded the *Sunday Express* and the *Evening Standard* was taken over in 1929. Beaverbrook's active interest in every detail and department of his newspaper was maintained throughout his life. His great collection of political papers, as well as providing valuable source material for historians, helped him with the writing of *Men and Power, 1917–18* (1956) and *The Decline and Fall of Lloyd George* (1963).

Bebel, (Ferdinand) August (1840–1913). German socialist politician. One of the founders of the German Social Democratic Party, he was a member of the federal German legislature (Reichstag) 1871–81, 1883–1913, was prominent in his opposition to Germany's nationalist policies, and was several times imprisoned. He belonged to the Marxist wing of his party and with Wilhelm Liebknecht founded the political journal *Vorwärts (Forward)*.

Beccaria, Cesare, Marchese de Beccaria-Bonesana (1738–1794). Italian legal reformer, born in Milan. In his work on crimes and punishments (*Dei delitti e delle pene*) published in 1764 he advocated that capital punishment and torture be abolished and drew attention to the part to be played by education in lessening crime. This work attracted the interest of Leopold of Tuscany (later the Emperor Leopold II), who put some of his penal theory into practice, and inspired all work on the reform of criminal law for the next century. His writings on economics were also important and in some ways anticipate both Adam Smith and Malthus.

Becket, St Thomas (1118–1170). English martyr, son of a rich London merchant of Norman descent. Having been given a knightly training and studied theology in Paris, he entered the household of Theobald, archbishop of Canterbury, who sent him abroad to study canon law. He became archdeacon of Canterbury in 1154 and in 1155 chancellor under Henry II, whose confidant and chief minister he became, offending many by his ostentation and pride. One of Henry's main preoccupations was to prevent what he regarded as the encroachments of church courts upon secular jurisdiction. To achieve this object he decided in 1162 that the ideal successor as archbishop of Canterbury would be his presumably compliant friend Thomas Becket. He was bitterly disappointed. From the moment of his appointment as archbishop Becket showed his talent for playing the role of the moment, not necessarily insincerely, to the full. He now became as vigorous a champion of the church as he had been of the king. Henry was furious, and to escape persecution Becket took refuge abroad. The quarrel was patched up and Becket returned, but again his actions were deliberately provocative. Henry reacted with the fatal words wishing for deliverance from the turbulent priest. Four of those listening were only too ready to take him at his word, and Becket was murdered in Canterbury Cathedral. Becket, the dead martyr, was far more powerful than the living priest. He was canonized in 1172 and Henry did public penance at his tomb.

Beckett, Samuel (1906–). Irish dramatist and novelist, born near Dublin. Educated at Trinity College, Dublin, he lectured in English at Paris (1928–30) and in French at Dublin (1930–31). He lived mainly in France from 1932 and became James Joyce's secretary (1935–37). As a writer he was equally at home in English and French. His major works included *Murphy* (1938), *Molloy* (1951; Eng. tr. 1955), *Malone meurt* (1951; *Malone dies* 1956), *En Attendant Godot* (1952; *Waiting for Godot* 1955), *Watt* (1953), *L'Innommable* (1953; *The Unnameable* 1958), *Fin de Partie* (1957; *End Game* 1958), *All that Fall* (1957), *Krapp's Last Tape* (1959), *Comment c'est* (1961), and a study of Proust (1931). His major preoccupations were with failures of communication between people and the tragic pointlessness of life. He was awarded the Nobel Prize for Literature in 1969.

Bair, D., *Samuel Beckett*. 1978

Beckford, William Thomas (1760–1844). English writer and collector. A large inherited fortune enabled him to lead an easy cultured life as a man of letters. His novel *Vathek*, a tragi-comic oriental fantasy, was begun in 1782 and first written in French. 'Episodes' intended to be interpolated were not published until 1912. From 1785 to 1798, partly as the result of a scandal, he spent most of his time in France, Switzerland, Spain and Portugal. His *Recollections of an Excursion to the Monasteries of Alcobaça and Batalha* (1835), esteemed his best book, recalls a Portuguese visit made in 1795. Much of his time was, however, spent in building up collections of books and pictures which were eventually housed at Fonthill, a Gothic extravaganza which he commissioned * Wyatt to build for him in Wiltshire (1796–1807), and where he lived in hermit-like seclusion.

Becquerel. A family of French scientists, of which the most famous, who belonged to the third generation, made discoveries that led to the isolation of radium. **Antoine César Becquerel** (1788–1878) served as an engineer in the Peninsular War and in 1837 became professor of physics (working on animal heat, electrochemistry, etc.) at the Musée d'Histoire Naturelle. In this post he was succeeded by his son **Alexandre Edmond** (1820–1891), whose principal field of study was optics. The same chair was held by Alexandre's son **Antoine Henri** (1852–1908), who held it for three years before becoming professor of physics (1895) at the École Polytechnique. In 1896, while investigating the fluorescence produced by exposing uranium salts to X-rays, Becquerel discovered that radiation was given off by the uranium salts even when they had not been exposed to X-rays. This 'radioactivity' he showed to be a fundamental property of salts of uranium, thorium and other heavy elements. His suggestion that the Curies should investigate radioactivity in pitchblende led them to isolate the element radium. Becquerel and the Curies were jointly awarded the Nobel Prize for Physics in 1903.

Beddoes, Thomas Lovell (1803–1849). English poet. The son of a physician, he studied at Oxford (1820–24) and spent the rest of his life as a doctor in Germany and Switzerland with occasional visits to England. From 1825 he worked on his most important work, a drama called *Death's Jest Book, or the Fool's Tragedy*, which was published posthumously after his suicide in Basle. His morbidity and obsession with death (he described himself as a 'creeper into worm holes'), is reminiscent of the Jacobean dramatists; but occasionally his lyrics display a delicate and moving poignancy. His collected poems first appeared posthumously in 1851.

Bede (or Baeda) (*c.* 673–735). English historian and theologian known as the 'Venerable Bede'. He spent most of his life as a Benedictine monk at Jarrow, Co. Durham, and became the greatest scholar in the English church and a European figure, writing works on grammer, theology and history with standards of scholarship unusual for his time. His chronological studies did much to establish the practice of dating events from the birth of Christ. His main work was *The Ecclesiastical History of the English Nation*, still an essential source for the period 597 to 731. He died immediately after completing a vernacular translation of St John's Gospel. His influence on the school at York was transmitted by * Alcuin to the court of Charlemagne.

Bedford, John of Lancaster, Duke of (1389–1435). On the death (1422) of his brother, Henry V of England, Bedford was regent in France for the boy king Henry VI. He proved himself able both as a soldier and administrator but found himself confronted by the French national spirit revived by Joan of Arc.

Beebe, Charles William (1877–1962). American ornithologist and explorer. In 1934 he reached a record depth of 3,028 feet in the sea off Bermuda in a bathysphere, a diving bell of his own design, in order to study marine life at intense pressures. He described the experience in *Half Mile Down* (1934).

Beecham, Sir Thomas, 2nd Bart (1879–1961). English conductor, born in St Helens, Lancashire, son of a millionaire patent medicine manufacturer. Educated at Rossall School, Fleetwood, and Oxford, he made his London debut in 1905. In 1906 he founded the New Symphony Orchestra and in 1910 initiated a series of opera seasons at Covent Garden. The following year he introduced Ballets Russes to England. He strove to establish opera permanently in Britain and to improve operatic and orchestral performances, using his own funds. Admired for the verve and elegance of his interpretations, he was associated particularly with music by Haydn, Mozart, Delius, Sibelius and Richard Strauss. He founded the London Philharmonic Orchestra in 1932 and the Royal Philharmonic Orchestra in 1946, was artistic director at Convent Garden 1932–39, and lived in the U.S. 1940–44. In 1916 he was knighted, succeeded to his father's baronetcy in the same year, and received a CH in 1957.
Cardus, N., *Sir Thomas Beecham*. 1961

Beecher, Henry Ward (1813–1887). American preacher. The brother of Harriet Beecher Stowe, the author of *Uncle Tom's Cabin*, as a Congregational minister he attracted 3,000 to Plymouth Church, Brooklyn (1847–87), where he won fame as a preacher of great eloquence and power. He denounced Negro slavery and advocated temperance and women's suffrage. A visit to Britain (1863) proved a triumph. In 1874 he was charged with having committed adultery with Mrs Theodore Tilton, the wife of a prominent journalist, but after a long trial the jury was unable to agree on a verdict.

Beeching, Richard, Baron Beeching (1913–). English manager. Having studied physics at the Imperial College of Science and Technology, London, he worked mainly for the Ministry of Supply in World War II. After a progressively successful career he became technical director of Imperial Chemical Industries in 1957, chairman of the British Transport Commission (1961) and of the British Railways Board (1963). The drastic closures of recommended lines in his report roused much opposition among those affected. Beeching returned to I.C.I. in 1965 and was created a life peer in the same year.

Beethoven, Ludwig van (1770–1827). German composer, born in Bonn, of Flemish descent. His father **Johann** (*c.* 1740–1792), a tenor in the Electoral choir, was Beethoven's first teacher and took him from school at the age of 11 to exploit his musical talents. Beethoven studied composition with the organist Christian Neefe (1781–87), who stimulated his interest in Bach. On a journey to Vienna (1787) he played for Mozart and perhaps had a few lessons from him. He was assistant conductor at the Electoral court (1784–88) and also played the viola in the Bonn opera orchestra. With the financial support of the Elector Maximilian Franz and Count Ferdinand Waldstein, Beethoven was sent to Vienna where he studied with Haydn, J. G. Albrechtsberger and Salieri. Apart from short visits to Berlin and Budapest, Beethoven remained in Vienna until his death and his acceptance by the highest social circles showed the revolutionary change in the status of composers since Haydn and Mozart, who had been patronized. The Archduke Rudolph, Prince Lichnowsky, Prince Kinsky and Prince Lobkowitz were not only his patrons but also his friends: they subscribed to a large annuity to keep Beethoven in Vienna, despite his rude manners, outbursts of temper and rough appearance.

His works are often classified into three periods, although these classifications cannot be applied arbitrarily. Beethoven's early music shows the extent of his debt to the Classical masters, especially Haydn and Mozart, with its restraint, balance, subtle emotion and strict observance of form. To this period belong the first two symphonies (1800, 1802); the first two piano concertos (1797, 1795–98); the first 12 piano sonatas; the first six string quartets and many trios. By 1796 he was becoming deaf and five years later he contracted liver trouble.

Between 1802–21 (the second period) Beethoven broke away from Classical tradition and created the new 'romantic' style, which had been hinted at in the late works of Haydn and Mozart. His symphonies and sonatas were longer than their Classical forebears, more vigorous, with a much greater range of dynamics, tempos, rhythms, key changes, syncopation and harmony. The music was much less predictable and much more emotional in both form and content. Beethoven's symphonies substituted the scherzo for the traditional minuet and trio movement and are scored for a substantially larger orchestra than Mozart's. An ardent democrat and republican, Beethoven originally dedicated his Third Symphony (1804) to Napoleon, but, disillusioned when Napoleon became Emperor, he changed the dedication and renamed it 'Eroica'. Other works of this period include the Piano Concertos Nos. 3 (1800), 4 (1806), 5 (1809, nicknamed 'The Emperor'); his Fourth Symphony (1806); 15 piano sonatas; the 'Kreutzer' (1803) and 'Spring' (1805) violin sonatas; five string quartets; the Violin Concerto (1806); several sets of variations; much chamber music; and the opera *Fidelio*. Originally titled *Leonora*, after the heroine, *Fidelio* was a failure when first performed in 1805, and it succeeded in 1814 only after drastic revisions had been made. Four more symphonies also were composed during this period: No. 5 (1807) – probably the most performed in the repertoire; No. 6 (1808, 'Pastoral'); No. 7 (1812, described by Wagner as 'the apotheosis of the dance'); No. 8 (1813).

The music of the third period (1821–27) includes his last five piano sonatas (although the 'Hammerklavier' was actually composed in 1818); the *Missa solemnis* (1823); the *Diabelli Variations* (1823); the Ninth Symphony (1823, also known as the 'Choral Symphony'); the last five quartets and the *Grosse Fuge* (1824–27).

Beethoven's musical innovations changed the entire course of music history and greatly influenced all the major nineteenth-century composers. The great and abiding popularity of his music shows that he is probably the most admired composer in the history of western music.

Arnold, D. and Fortune, N. (eds.), *The Beethoven Companion*. 1971

Beeton, Isabella Mary (née Mayson) (1836–1865. English author. Mrs Beeton's name has been a household word in British kitchens for over a century. Educated in Heidelberg and trained as a pianist, she married a publisher and began writing on cookery in his *Englishwoman's Domestic Magazine*. Her famous *Book of Household Management* (1861) originally appeared in three parts during 1859–60.

Begin, Menachem (1913–). Israeli politician, born in Poland. After working as a Jewish youth organiser in Poland he was deported to Siberia by the Russians, released and sent to Palestine. In 1943 he became leader of Irgun Zvai Leumi which adopted more militant tactics against the British than David Ben-Gurion's Zionists. He led the Likud party in the Knesset and defeated the Mapai to become Prime Minister (1977–83). He welcomed the visit of Egypt's President Sadat to Jerusalem (November 1977) and in 1978, with assistance from U.S. President Jimmy Carter, concluded an Israeli-Egyptian peace treaty at Camp David, Maryland. Begin and Sadat shared the 1978 Nobel Peace Prize.

Behan, Brendan (1923–1964). Irish playwright. The son of a Dublin house painter, he was arrested in Liverpool for terrorist activities on behalf of the Irish Republican Army in the early days of World War II. His subsequent years in an institution were described in *Borstal Boy* (1958). His fame rests on two plays *The Quare Fellow* (1956) and *The Hostage* (1958), both owing much to Joan Littlewood's production at the Theatre

Workshop in East London, and his notorious conviviality and outspokenness.
O'Connor, V., *Brendan Behan*. 1970

Behn, Aphra (1640–1689). English woman writer; the first to be a professional author. Her father's name was John Amis and she was brought up in Surinam before returning to England and marrying a merchant called Behn. An adventurous interlude as a spy in Holland followed her husband's death, and it was only then, after imprisonment for debt, that she took to writing as a career. She wrote twenty-two plays and fourteen novels, including *Oroonoko, or the Royal Slave*, which anticipates Rousseau's 'noble savage'.
Hahn, H., *Aphra Behn*. 1951

Behrens, Peter (1868–1940). German architect, born at Hamburg. He worked as an industrial designer in Munich before being appointed professor of architecture at Darmstadt in 1900. He became the principal architect of the Deutscher Werkbund, founded in 1907, an association of architects and designers formed to meet the needs of and take advantage of the new opportunities provided by industrial building and design. Among the earliest and best known of Behren's functional buildings was his turbine factory (1909) in Berlin, built for the great electrical combine A.E.G., for whom he designed other major buildings and a number of industrial products. Both his architecture and his design are characterized by functional expression and geometric simplicity. Le Corbusier, Gropius and Mies van der Rohe were influenced by his work.

Behring, Emil Adolf von (1854–1917). German bacteriologist. He graduated at Berlin and joined the Army Medical Corps, which he left (1888) to work on immunization at Koch's Institute for Infectious Diseases. He discovered (1890) an anti-diphtheria serum (used at once for animals but not until 1913 on human beings), for which he won the first Nobel Prize for Medicine in 1901. With Kitasato he also produced tetanus anti-toxin. In 1895, he went as a professor to Marburg, where he set up his own laboratories for the manufacture of anti-toxins.
Engelhardt, A., *Emil von Behring*. 1940.

Beiderbecke, Bix (Leon Bismarck Beidebecke) (1903–1931). American cornetist, pianist and composer. Born in Davenport, Iowa, he was the first to attempt to incorporate concert hall harmonies into jazz improvisation, and the first white musician to be acknowledged an important innovator by Negro contemporaries.

He worked with various musicians, including Frank Trumbauer and Jean Goldkette, but died in comparative obscurity. His posthumous reputation grew and he was remembered for the purity of tone of his cornet style, and the impressionistic influences shown in his piano playing. A Beiderbecke cult was initiated with the publicity of Dorothy Baker's novel *Young Man with a Horn* (1938).

Béjart family. A family of French actors closely associated with the playwright Molière.

Joseph Béjart (*c.* 1617–1659) was a strolling player and he joined the Illustre Théâtre and created the parts of Lélie and Eraste in Molière's *L'Étourdi* and *Dépit amoureux*.

Louis Béjart (*c.* 1630–1678), brother of Joseph, also a member of the Illustre Théâtre, created the parts of Valère in *Dépit amoureux*, Dubois in *Le Misanthrope*, Alcantor in *Le Mariage forcé* and others.

Madeleine Béjart (1618–1672) was head of a company of strolling players to which her sister Geneviève and brothers, Joseph and Louis, originally belonged. It is said she persuaded Molière to enter upon a theatrical career, and her acting boosted the company's morale in their periods of financial difficulty. She was particularly convincing in the parts of soubrettes (coquettish maids or frivolous young women), several written specially for her by Molière, including Dorine in *Tartuffe*. Her sister Geneviève was more successful as a tragedienne.

Armande Béjart (1642–1700), Madeleine's sister or daughter, joined the company at Lyons in 1653 and married Molière in 1662. In 1663 made her debut as Élise in *La Critique de l'École des femmes*. In 1665 she and Molière were parted, but were later reconciled (1671). She played many important Molière roles including Célimène (modelled on herself) in *Le Misanthrope* and Angélique in *Le Malade imaginaire*. Following Molière's death in 1673 she kept the company together, and in 1679 it secured Marie Champmesle, an outstanding tragedienne, and subsequently became the Comédie Française, the French national theatre. In 1667 she married Issac-François

Guérin d'Etriché, a leading actor who headed the Comédie Française.

Belasco, David (1853–1931). American dramatist and theatre manager. His career began in San Francisco and took him to New York, where he became an independent producer in 1895. Some of the scores of plays written or adapted by him, e.g. *Madame Butterfly* and *The Girl of the Golden West*, are still remembered, but it is for his realistic and lavish production methods that he is best remembered. His own Belasco Theatre in New York became a notable school of players.

Belisarius (*c.* 505–565). A brilliant and successful general in the service of the Byzantine emperor Justinian. His most successful campaigns were fought when he was trying to win back the former territories of the Roman Empire in Africa and Italy. He defeated the Vandals in Africa (533–534) and in 535 occupied Sicily, whence he proceeded to his main task of expelling the Ostrogoths from Italy. Rome was triumphantly reoccupied in 536 but this was only a beginning and it was not until 540 that the Ostrogoths' capital at Ravenna was taken. Recalled to repel Persian attacks in the East, he returned to Italy (544) when the Ostrogoths had renewed the struggle. Mainly through lack of support by the emperor, he failed to achieve decisive results and in 549 he was again recalled. Justinian, indeed, found it difficult not to suspect the loyalty of so successful and popular a general and though in the case of Belisarius they were quite groundless these suspicions continually hampered his career. Indeed in 562 he was even imprisoned for a short time, though only three years earlier the Huns had been driven back from the outskirts of Constantinople by his skill and courage. However, the legend that he was blinded and died a beggar is untrue.

Graves, R., *Count Belisarius*. 1938

Bell, Alexander Graham (1847–1922). American inventor, born in Edinburgh. Educated at Edinburgh and London Universities, he worked with his father as a teacher of the deaf 1868–70, migrated to Canada for his health (1870), then went to Boston where he taught deaf mutes and became professor of vocal physiology at Boston University (1873). (He married a deaf student in 1877 and Helen * Keller was one of his later protégés.) Preoccupied with the mechanical transmission of sound vibrations by wire, he invented the telephone in 1876, patenting it only a few hours before Elisha Gray. The telephone was an instant success at the Philadelphia Centennial Exposition (1876) and the Bell Telephone Company was founded in 1877. * Edison's carbon microphone (1878) improved performance greatly. In return he improved Edison's phonograph (1880). Bell became a co-founder of the magazines *Science* (1880) and the *National Geographic* (1898), supported experimentation in aviation, became a US citizen in 1882, and invented the tetrahedral kite. He also studied eugenics, the hereditary basis of deafness and sonar detection. He died in Nova Scotia. The name of his father **Alexander Melville Bell** (1819–1905), who also went to America and settled in Washington, D.C., in 1881, is even more closely associated with deaf mutes. He invented 'visible speech', his methods combining 'phonetic signs and graphs of the organs and motions of speech'.

Bruce, R. V., *Alexander Graham Bell and the Conquest of Solitude*. 1973

Bell, Andrew *see* **Lancaster, Joseph**

Bell, Clive Arthur Howard (1881–1964). English art and literary critic. He did much by his critical works, e.g. *Art* (1914) and *Since Cézanne* (1922), to explain and popularize the Post-Impressionists and Fauves. Other works include *Civilisation* (1928) and *Proust* (1929). A member of the Bloomsbury group, Bell married Vanessa, daughter of Sir Leslie * Stephen, and sister of Virginia Woolf.

Bell, Gertrude Margaret Lowthian (1868–1926). English traveller and author. Her travels from 1892 in almost every part of the Middle East were of great importance to the British government when these lands became battlefields or the objects of political contention during and after World War I. When Iraq was established she became assistant political officer at Baghdad and worked with T. E. Lawrence.

Bell, Patrick (1801–1869). Scottish inventor. He was born on a farm in Angus, and his agricultural machinery derived from a practical understanding of a farmer's needs rather than from specialized training. He invented the first practical reaper for cereal crops and machines for grinding oats and making wheat-flour, and devised equipment for extracting the sugar from sugar beet. He later became a minister in the Kirk.

Bellamy, Edward (1850–1898). American novelist and political writer. His most famous work was *Looking Backward* (1888), a Utopian romance which influenced socialist ideas of economic organization and became a best-seller. Other romances with similar aims were *Equality* (1897) and *The Duke of Stockbridge* (1900).
Morgan, A. E., *Life of Edward Bellamy*. 1944

Bellarmine, St Robert Francis Romulus (1542–1621). Italian cardinal and theologian. He entered the Jesuit order in 1560 and was ordained, after studying at Louvain and Padua, in 1570 and spent the rest of his life either teaching theology (at Louvain until 1576 and then in Rome) or engaged in theological controversy. Though he was among the most convincing supporters of the papacy and was obliged to denounce the teaching of * Galileo Galilei, he was regarded as moderating influence and praised for his tolerance and learning. Against his wishes, he was made a cardinal in 1599 and in 1602 archbishop of Capua. He avoided election to the papacy on the death (1605) of Clement VIII but was given high office at the Vatican. He was canonized in 1930.
Brodnick, J., *Robert Bellarmine: Saint and Scholar*. 1961

Bellini. A family of Venetian painters: **Jacopo Bellini** (*c.* 1400–1470) and his sons **Gentile** (*c.* 1429–1507) and **Giovanni** (*c.* 1430–1516). Few of Jacopo's paintings survive but his many drawings show his work covered a wide range of religious and secular themes and provided a link between the old Venetian style and its Byzantine traditions and the art of the High Renaissance.

Both sons were probably trained in their father's studio. Gentile, the lesser of the two, won success as a portrait painter, and in his narrative works (e.g. *The Procession in the Piazza of San Mario*) showed a taste for spectacular display. An interlude in Constantinople (1479–81) in response to a request by Sultan Mohammed II resulted in a number of paintings with an oriental flavour, including a portrait of the Sultan himself (National Gallery, London).

Giovanni, the greatest of the Bellini family, is justly regarded as the father of Venetian High Renaissance style, the most important influence on his work being clearly that of his brother-in-law Mantegna. His paintings are characterized by a sense of tragic pathos, quiet dignity and compassion: his masterpiece *St Francis in Ecstasy* (c. 1480) hangs in the Frick Collection, New York. Although mostly a painter of religious subjects, Bellini also executed mythological works such as the famous *Feast of the Gods*, later completed by Titian. As the teacher of Titian and Giorgione, Bellini's influence upon the next generation was profound. In many of his paintings we see in embryo the mood, the pastoral setting and the soft, warm colours which were to typify the work of his pupils. The well-known *Doge Leonardo Loredano* (National Gallery, London) is one of several fine portraits.
Robertson, G., *Giovanni Bellini*. 1968

Bellini, Vincenzo (1801–1835). Italian operatic composer. He was born at Catania in Sicily and studied in Naples. His operas, distinguished by their melodic charm, include *La sonnambula* (1831), *Norma* (1832) and *I Puritani* (1834), performed with great success in Milan and Paris. His music had an important influence on * Verdi.

Belloc, (Joseph) Hilaire (Pierre) (1870–1953). Anglo-French writer born near Paris, son of a French barrister and his English wife. He was educated at Oxford, became a Liberal M.P. (1906–10) and first gained fame with his nonsense verse in *The Bad Child's Book of Beasts* (1896), followed later by *Cautionary Tales* (1907). Versatile and prolific, he wrote essays, innumerable discursive travel books, historical studies, e.g. *Marie Antoinette* (1910), *Richelieu* (1929) and *Napoleon* (1932), fantastic or satirical novels, e.g. *Mr Clutterbuck's Election*, and serious political works such as *The Servile State* (1912). In World War I he gained a short-lived reputation as a military critic. He shared with his friend G. K. Chesterton his Roman Catholic religion, a hatred of the manipulations of finance, a gift for friendship and a romantic nostalgia for the Middle Ages. His sister (Marie Adelaide) **Mrs Belloc Lowndes** (1868–1947), wrote many detective stories and thrillers including *The Lodger* (1913 and later filmed), an imaginary reconstruction of the Jack the Ripper murders.
Haynes, R., *Hilaire Belloc*. 1958

Bellow, Saul (1915–). American novelist, born in Quebec of Russian-Jewish parents. His novels, some of which were filmed, include *The Adventures of Augie March* (1953), *Henderson the Rain King* (1959), *Herzog* (1964) and *Humboldt's Gift* (1975). He won the 1976 Nobel Prize for Literature.

Belshazzar (or Balthasar) (6th century B.C.). Regent in Babylon for his father King Nabonidus when the city fell to Cyrus of Persia (538). The Book of Daniel tells how the words 'mene, mene, tekel, upharsim' (that he had been 'weighed in the balance and found wanting') appeared on the walls of the banqueting room and were taken for a warning of the approaching disaster. Belshazzar seems to have been killed that night or shortly afterwards.

Belzoni, Giovanni Battista (1778–1823). Italian traveller and archaelogist. Of humble origins, he was gifted with enormous size and strength, which he exploited as a 'strong man' when he came to England in 1803. He also devised a hydraulic engine. A visit to Egypt (1815) stirred his interest in archaeology, or rather, in tomb robbing. He discovered the sepulchre of Seti I at Thebes (1817), cleared the rock temple of Abu Simbel and opened up the second pyramid at Giza. His clumsy practice and the adventurous circumstances of his Egyptian explorations are described in his *Narrative of the Operations and Recent Discoveries within the Pyramids, Temples, Tombs, and Excavations in Egypt and Nubia* (1820).
Mayes, S., *The Great Belzoni*. 1959.

Bem, Josef (1795–1850). Polish general and nationalist leader. He led the Hungarian nationalist forces against the Russians and Austrians during the revolution of 1848–49. On its failure, he fled to Turkey, became a Mohammedan and was given a command. Though able to report on early success over the *ban* (viceroy) Jellačić in the famous dispatch '*Bem Ban Bum*' ('Bem has beaten the Ban') he was eventually defeated.

Bembo, Pietro (1470–1547). Italian poet and cardinal (1539). He held a commanding position in Italian literature during his lifetime and was mainly instrumental in establishing Petrarch's versification and Tuscan vocabulary as standard poetical practice. His dialogue *Gil Asolani* (1505), which discusses platonic love, and his letters are well known. He was appointed historian to the republic of Venice in 1530.

Benavente y Martinez, Jacinto (1866–1954). Spanish dramatist. The son of a physician, he abandoned the study of law to become an actor and playwright. His very large output includes plays of many different styles and moods – satirical, romantic or fantastic. The best known of them is perhaps *Los intereses creados* (*Vested Interests*: 1907). Others well known in translation include *Saturday Night* (1903) and *Rose of Autumn* (1905). He won the Nobel Prize for Literature in 1922.

Ben Bella, Ahmed (1916–). Algerian statesman. A former sergeant major in the French Army, he was among the early workers for Algerian independence from France and became the leader of the Algerian nationalists in exile. In 1956 an aeroplane in which he was travelling was brought down by the French and he remained in confinement until the cease-fire conference at Évian in 1962. His advance to power in Algeria now became rapid; he displaced Ben Khedda to become prime minister in September of the same year. A year later (1963) the president Ferhat Abbas was also removed and, under a new constitution confirmed in a referendum by an overwhelming majority, Ben Bella occupied both offices. He was overthrown in a *coup* by his second-in-command, * Boumédienne, in 1965.
Merle, R., *Ahmed Ben Bella*. 1967.

Benbow, John (1653–1702). British sailor. He first entered the navy (1678) as master's mate and had risen to be rear-admiral at the time of his last and most famous exploit. This took place in August 1702 when he kept up a running fight for four days with a French squadron off St Marta in the West Indies. Virtually deserted by most of his squadron, probably because of his bullying temperament, he fought alone. With his leg smashed by a chain shot he still directed operations. In the following November he died of his wound.

Benda, Julien (1867–1956). French author and philosopher. The work for which he is chiefly remembered is *La Trahison des clercs* (1927), published in England as *The Great Betrayal*. The treachery referred to is the

introduction of love or prejudice or practical considerations into the search for truth. Other works are the novel *The Yoke of Pity* (1912) and *La Jeunesse d'un clerc* (1936), an intellectual autobiography.
Niess, R. J., *Julien Benda*. 1956

Benedict, St (*c*. 480–547). The founder of Western monasticism, born at Nursia near Spoleto. As a boy of 14 he withdrew from the world, and lived alone in a cave near Subiaco; he became famous for his piety and was soon surrounded by a number of disciples. He founded twelve small monasteries from the most devout of these followers and in *c*. 529 founded a monastery at Monte Cassino, between Rome and Naples, which later became one of the richest and most famous monasteries in Europe. His *Regula Monachorum* in addition to the usual spiritual exercises directs that the monks shall do manual labour by working in the fields, teaching the young and copying manuscripts, following the principle that 'to work is to pray' ('*laborare est orare*'). St Benedict did not found a particular order and the name Benedictines was applied to all who followed his rule.

Benedict XIV (Prospero Lambertini) (1675–1758). Pope (from 1740). He was one of the wisest and most conciliatory of popes and proved himself one of the most successful at reconciling the interests of the church with those of the European sovereigns. Thus he came to terms with Frederick the Great of Prussia concerning the Catholic minority, showed a tolerant attitude to the Jansenists in France, assented to nominations by the Spanish crown to nearly all benefices, and made concordats with Naples and Sardinia.

Benedict XV (Giacomo della Chiesa) (1854–1922). Pope (from 1914). He served in the papal diplomatic service for many years and was archbishop of Bologna (1907–14), being appointed a cardinal only a few months before his election to the papacy. His attempts to settle World War I by negotiation failed but he did much to alleviate the lot of prisoners of war and other sufferers.

Beneš, Eduard (1884–1948). Czechoslovak scholar and statesman. Of peasant origin, he built up his position solely by his own abilities. Educated in Prague and Paris (where he supported himself by journalism) he returned to become professor of sociology in Prague. During World War I he worked abroad with his political mentor * Masaryk to secure recognition by the Allies of Czechoslovakia's right to nationhood. So successful were these efforts that the Allied victory in 1918 was followed by the creation of Czechoslovakia as a separate state with Masaryk president and Beneš foreign minister. During his tenure of office he was the main architect of the Little Entente (Czechoslovakia, Romania and Yugoslavia), which in alliance with France was intended to sustain the post-war settlement. He was also one of the strongest upholders of the League of Nations and was president of the Assembly in 1935, the year in which he succeeded Masaryk as president of his own country. Meanwhile Hitler had come to power and was supporting with threats the nationalistic claims of the Sudeten Germans in Czechoslovakian border areas. Beneš remained firm until the betrayal and partition of Czechoslovakia by the Munich settlement of 1938 caused him to resign. In World War II he was president in London (1942–45) of the Czech government in exile. After the war he was again president of his liberated country but resigned in June 1948, after the Communists had seized power, and died soon after.
Beneš, E., *Memoirs*. 1954

Benét, Stephen Vincent (1898–1943). American writer. He won the Pulitzer Prize for Poetry in 1929 for *John Brown's Body*, a ballad-epic of the Civil War and in 1944 for his narrative poem *Western Star*. In prose *The Devil and Daniel Webster* (1937) is an example of the way in which he re-interpreted American legends. His brother **Willam Rose Benét** (1886–1950) won the 1942 Pultizer Prize for Poetry for his verse-novel *The Dust Which is God*.

Ben-Gurion, David (1886–1973). Israeli politician. Born in Poland, he first went to Palestine in 1906. In World War I, having been expelled by the Turks as a Zionist, he helped to organize, and served with, a Jewish force under Allenby. An organizer of the Jewish Mapai (socialist) party, he became the first prime minister when Israel was established in 1948. He resigned in 1963 having been prime minister except for one short interval since 1948. It was he who sanctioned the attack on Egypt in 1956.
Avi-Hai, A., *Ben-Gurion: State-Builder*. 1974.

Benjamin. Youngest son of the biblical patriarch Jacob. The tribe named after him, with the tribe of Judah, remained loyal to the house of David when, in the reign of Rehoboam, son of Solomon, the other ten tribes broke away to form a separate kingdom.

Benn, Tony (Anthony Neil Wedgwood) (1925–). British Labour politician. Educated at Oxford, he worked for the BBC, was a Labour MP 1950–60, but had to leave the House of Commons when he became 2nd Viscount Stansgate on the death of his father. He refused to use the title and campaigned for the right to disclaim inherited peerages: this led to passage of the Peerage Act (1963). Elected MP 1963–83; 1983– , he served as post-master general (1964–66), minister of technology (1966–70), secretary of state for industry (1974–75) and energy (1975–79). In opposition he emerged as leader of Labour's left and wrote *Arguments for Socialism* (1979).

Bennett, (Enoch) Arnold (1867–1931). English novelist, born near Hanley, Staffordshire, one of the 'Five Towns' of the potteries, which inspired so many of his novels. He completed his education at London University and he subsequently spent most of his working life in London, but the years (1902–10) which he spent in France provided him with a French wife, introduced him to European culture and awakened a taste for fine living.

His novels belong to two groups: the first and most lastingly important gives a vivid and naturalistic account of life in the industrial society in which he was brought up; it includes *Anna of the Five Towns* (1902), *The Old Wives' Tale* (1908), *Clayhanger* (1910), and *The Card* (1911); to this genre, though with a different setting (Clerkenwell, London), belongs also *Riceyman Steps* (1923); the second group is more concerned with entertainment than with character study and social comment; to it belong e.g. *The Grand Babylon Hotel* (1902) and *Buried Alive* (1908), successfully dramatized (1913) as *The Great Adventure*. With Edward Knoblock he wrote the play *Milestones* (1912), which also proved popular. In his later years Bennett achieved a new reputation as literary critic on the London *Evening Standard*.

Drabble, M., *Arnold Bennett*. 1974

Bennett, James Gordon (1795–1872). Scottish-born journalist. He emigrated to America and founded the *New York Herald*, which first appeared in 1835 and was both successful and revolutionary. His son (1841–1918), namesake and successor was among the most famous pioneers of modern journalism. He commissioned H. M. * Stanley to head the expedition which found Livingstone, and shared with the London *Daily Telegraph* the financing of Stanley's great journey in central Africa (1874–77). He established the *New York Herald's* reputation as one of the great newspapers of the world, with a brilliant team of reporters.

Bennett, Richard Bedford Bennett, 1st Viscount (1870–1947). Canadian politician, born in New Brunswick. He was elected a Canadian M.P. in 1911, became a leader of the Conservative party in 1927 and in 1930 became prime minister. His 'new deal'(1935) to combat the great depression was declared unconstitutional. The Ottawa conference of 1932, summoned by him, did however succeed in creating a system of preferential tariffs in the British Empire. After his government's defeat (1935) he became leader of the opposition until 1938, when he retired to Great Britain. He received a peerage in 1941.

Benois, Alexandre (1870–1960). Russian artist of French extraction. His conception of a decor integrated with the dancing and music added a third dimension to ballet. With * Bakst he put these ideas into practice, and did much to contribute to Diaghilev's glittering artistic success. *Sheherazade* and *Le Coq d'or* are examples of works which owed almost everything to his inspiration. He parted with Diaghilev after World War I and worked with Rubinstein and others. In 1957 he designed for a production of *The Nutcracker* by the Festival Ballet of London.

Benson, Edward White (1829–1896). English ecclesiastic, born in Birmingham. First a schoolmaster (Rugby; headmaster of Wellington) then the first bishop of Truro (1877) and archbishop of Canterbury (1882). His sons: **Arthur Christopher** (1862–1925), an Eton schoolmaster and later master of Magdalene College, Cambridge, was an essayist and critic of distinction (*Upton Letters*, etc.); **Edward Frederic** (1867–1940) wrote elegant novels, once considered daring, such as *Dodo* and *David Blaize*; **Robert Hugh**

(1871–1914), a Roman Catholic priest, wrote many historical novels, with more than a hint of Catholic bias, such as *Come Rack! Come Rope!*, which is concerned with the Catholic martyrs of Queen Elizabeth's reign.

Benson, Sir Frank Robert (1858–1939). English actor. His Shakespearian company, in its prolonged tours, and his management of the festivals at Stratford-on-Avon provided the chief means by which the plays were kept alive and familiar outside London. He was knighted by George V on Drury Lane stage during a Shakespeare tercentenary matinee (1916).
Trewin, J. C., *Benson and the Bensonians*. 1960

Bentham, Jeremy (1748–1832). English utilitarian philosopher. Born in London, the son of a solicitor, he was a precocious and prodigious student. After graduating from Oxford in 1763, he studied law under Blackstone but was dismayed by its anomalies and illogicalities and thus abandoned the idea of going into practice. The publication of his *Fragment on Government* in 1776 brought him to the friendly notice of Lord Shelburne, at whose house, by meeting people from the social and political worlds, he was able to gain self-confidence. In 1789, after four fruitful years of travel in Russia and elsewhere, he published *An Introduction to the Principles of Morals and Legislation*, which argues that all laws should work for the greatest happiness of the greatest number of people, and sets out a general doctrine of Utilitarianism, which inspired J. S.* Mill and others. He believed that all men seek only their own pleasure, and combined this psychological claim with the moral view that the right action is that one which seems likely to produce more happiness (pleasure or absence of pain) than any other possible action. Utilitarianism, modified and developed by his followers, was the source of much social investigation and reform in the nineteenth century. In 1785–88, Bentham spent much money and time on a plan for a model prison, the 'Panopticon', in which all prisoners could be observed from a single point. Reform and codification of the law to accord with his utilitarian principles remained his chief interest, but in later life he campaigned for a number of specific reforms: the secret ballot, universal suffrage, abolition of capital and corporal punishment, a national system for registering births, deaths and marriages, the ending of transportation of criminals and imprisonment for debt, and the setting up of an international authority to prevent the outbreak of wars. He founded the *Westminster Review* in 1823, and was also a founder of University College, London, where at his own wish his skeleton stands dressed in his clothes and with a model head.
Mack, M., *Jeremy Bentham 1748–1792*. 1963

Bentinck, Lord William Cavendish (1774–1839). English Whig politician. The son of the third Duke of Portland, he was an M.P. (1796–1803), governor of Madras (1803–07) and served under Wellington in the Peninsular War. He became governor general of Bengal in 1827 and by statutory conferment became the first holder of the title Governor-General of India (1833–35). He abolished *suttee* (the religious custom of widow-burning), suppressed the Thugs (a group of religious assassins), and introduced English as the language of higher education.

Bentley, Edmund Clerihew (1875–1956). English novelist and journalist. He originated the 'clerihew' a four-line humorous verse form, and wrote what is regarded as the first of the modern type of realistic detective novel, *Trent's Last Case* (1913). His verse form can here be exemplified by:

> The Art of Biography
> Is different from Geography;
> Geography is about maps,
> But Biography is about chaps.

Bentley, E. C., *Those Days: An Autobiography*. 1940

Bentley, Richard (1662–1742). English classical scholar, educated at Wakefield Grammar School and at Cambridge, where he was master of Trinity College from 1700 until his death. He established his reputation with the *Dissertation upon the Epistles of Phalaris* (1699), a brilliant contribution to a controversy concerning their authorship. This was followed by editions of Horace, Terence, etc.; he was a master of textual emendation. He was noted for his pedantic, quarrelsome and arrogant nature, but has maintained his reputation as one of the greatest of English classical scholars.
White, R. J., *Dr Bentley*. 1965

Benz, Karl (1844–1929). German motor car

pioneer. He produced (1885) a three-wheeled, chain-driven vehicle with a water-cooled internal-combustion engine using coal gas as fuel. It travelled at a maximum speed of 15 m.p.h.

Berchtold (von und zu Ungarschitz), Count Leopold von (1863–1942). Austrian diplomat. He served as ambassador in Paris 1894–99, London 1899–1906 and St Petersburg 1906–12 before his appointment as imperial foreign minister 1912–15. Largely responsible for escalating the assassination of * Franz Ferdinand (1914) into a world war, Berchtold was not a war criminal but a vacillating lightweight: the wrong man in the wrong job at the wrong time.

Berdyaev, Nikolai (1874–1948). Russian religious and social thinker. Born in Russia and expelled in 1922 although he had earlier been in sympathy with the revolution, he established the Academy of the Philosophy of Religion at Clamart near Paris. He insisted in his books, e.g. *The Destiny of Man* (Eng. tr. 1937) and *Spirit and Reality* (1939), that history is subject to the control of God, and looked forward to a Christian society, by which term he designated a way of life rather than outward observance.
Vallon, M., *Apostle of Freedom*. 1960

Berengario da Carpi, Giacomo (1460–1530). Italian anatomist. Born in Capri, Italy, he attended Bologna University and received his degree in 1489. He was appointed to the faculty in 1502. He became consultant to famous men, and his attendance upon Lorenzo de' Medici in 1517, who had received a gunshot wound and a fracture of the skull, led to his book on the subject in 1518. Partly because of its first-hand discussion of the different lesions, grouped according to symptoms, Berengario's book is a classic of neurosurgery. His interest in anatomy grew, and after performing several hundred dissections, he distilled his knowledge into his *Commentaria* (1521). His accounts of the reproductive organs were particularly important, as also of the greater capacity of the female pelvis. He described the pituitary and pineal glands and noted the corpus striatum. He could find no sign of * Galen's *rete mirabile* (the supposed source of animal spirit) – though he was traditionalist enough not to dismiss the idea of animal spirit itself. Berengario's importance lies in his pioneering careful anatomizing of the human body, and attempting to correlate his own observations with classical medical opinion. In this – as in his use of medical illustrations – he was engaged in similar work to * Vesalius.
Lind, L. R., *Berengario: A Short Introduction to Anatomy*. 1959

Berenson, Bernard (1865–1959). American art critic. A great authority on the art of the Italian Renaissance, Berenson lived in Italy from 1900, and as art adviser to the dealer Lord Duveen enjoyed a position of unparalleled eminence in matters of attribution and connoisseurship. He left his art collection and library to Harvard University. His best known work is *Italian Painters of the Renaissance* (1932).

Beresford, Charles Carr Beresford, 1st Viscount (1768–1854). British field marshal. An illegitimate son of the 1st Marquess of Waterford, he played an adventurous part in the French Revolutionary and Napoleonic Wars. After distinguished service in Toulon and Corsica, in Baird's desert march from the Red Sea to Egypt (1801), at the Cape of Good Hope (1806), and at Buenos Aires (1807), he eventually found permanent fame as the successful organizer and commander of the Portuguese army in the Peninsular War. His later life was troubled by controversy over his generalship at Albower. He bore the Spanish title of Duke of Elvas, and the Portuguese title of Conde de Trancoso and was master general of ordnance in Wellington's cabinet when he died.

Beresford, Charles William de la Poer Beresford, 1st Baron (1846–1919). British admiral. Son of the 4th Marquess of Waterford, he served with distinction in the navy but was best known as the leader of the naval faction opposed to Admiral * Fisher's reforms in the years preceding World War I.

Berg, Alban (1885–1935). Austrian composer, born in Vienna. As a boy he composed many songs which reveal his deeply romantic temperament, but after studying composition with Arnold Schönberg (1904–10) he developed his own modification of Schönberg's atonal or 'twelve-tone' system. His music is notable for its lyricism and dramatic intensity,

especially the operas *Wozzeck* (completed 1921) and *Lulu* (unfinished). Among his other works are the *Lyric Suite* for string quartet (1926) and *Violin Concerto* (1935).
Reich, W., *The Life and Work of Alban Berg*. 1965

Berger, Hans (1873–1941). German physiologist. His early work concentrated mainly on the effect blood supply and pressure had upon brain action, taking into account the influence of the heartbeat, respiration, and stimulants (e.g. caffeine, cocaine). He then moved on to the brain's electrical activity. Building on crude nineteenth century recordings of electrical activity in animal brains, Berger pioneered the technique of planting needle electrodes under the scalp of patients. He pioneered the use of the electroencephalogram as a tool of diagnosis. His work was negelected in his native Germany, and shortly after his retirement he committed suicide in a fit of depression.
E. Adrian and B. Matthews, 'The Berger Rhythm', *Brain*, 57 (1934), 355–385.

Bergerac, (Savinien) Cyrano de (1619–1655). French soldier, satirical poet and dramatist, famous also as a duellist and for his enormously long nose. He is best remembered as the hero of a play by Edmond * Rostand. His best known works are two fantastic romances (translated by Richard Aldington as *Voyages to the Moon and the Sun*), which influenced Swift and Voltaire.

Bergman, (Ernst) Ingmar (1918–). Swedish film and stage director and playwright, one of the major influences on the art of the cinema in the period after World War II. His taste for the grotesque and effective use of symbolism are shown in such films as *Smiles of a Summer Night* (1955), *The Seventh Seal* (1956), *Wild Strawberries* (1957), *The Devil's Eye* (1961), *The Silence* (1963), *Shame* (1968) and *Face to Face* (1976), all written by himself. In 1963 he became director of the Royal Dramatic Theatre, Stockholm. He has won many international film awards.
Wood, R., *Ingmar Bergman*. 1969.

Bergman, Ingrid (1915–1982). Swedish-born actress. Her first big success came in 1939 with *Intermezzo* (*Escape to Happiness*) in a Hollywood period which included *Casablanca* (1942), *For Whom the Bell Tolls* (1943) and her Academy-award picture *Gaslight* (1944), but ended with estrangement with the making of *Stromboli* (1949) in Italy and her affair and later marriage with Roberto * Rossellini, its director. The healing of the breach was marked by another Academy award (1957) for her part in *Anastasia* followed by *The Visit* (1963). Her few stage performances include a notable interpretation of the name part in *Hedda Gabler*. She was awarded three Oscars and has appeared in opera (*Joan of Arc at the Stake*, 1954) and television.

Bergson, Henri Louis (1859–1941). French philosopher. Born and educated in Paris and eventually professor at the Collège de France, he is best known for the theory set out in *Time and Freewill* (1889) and *Creative Evolution* (1907), which enjoyed considerable popularity despite its lack of clarity. It is opposed to the view that life evolves in a mechanical way, subject to physical laws and thus towards ends that are already fixed. Evolution, rather, results from a life-force ('*élan vital*') which is creative and unpredictable in its effects. This life-force, not adequately specified, is in conflict with 'matter', by which Bergson appeared to mean the regularity and repetitiveness of the natural world. This latter aspect of the universe is known by what Bergson calls Intelligence, which classifies reality into separate items and kinds, and tends to look upon natural change as a series of different fixed states. The faculty of Intuition, on the other hand, is related to the life-force and gives us knowledge of the kind of change which characterizes it: a development not made up of separable stages but one in which past and present run together in an unbroken stream or flux. This was called duration ('*la durée*'). Other important works include *Laughter* (1900) and *The Two Sources of Morality and Religion* (1932). Bergson was a member of the Académie Française. He was awarded the Nobel Prize for literature in 1927.
Jankelevitch, V., *Henri Bergson*. 1959

Beria, Lavrenty Pavlovich (1899–1953). Soviet commissar of Georgian peasant origins. He became notorious as chief of the secret police (from 1938) under Stalin on whose death (1953) he was (with Malenkov and Molotov) one of the triumvirate which assumed power. Almost immediately, however, he was accused of treason, tried and shot. He was mistrusted because he aimed at

making his security organization the ultimate power.
Williams, A., *Beria Papers*. 1973

Bering, Vitus Jonassen (1681–1741). Danish navigator. He joined the Russian navy in 1704 and in 1725 was commissioned by Peter the Great to explore the eastern extremity of Siberia. In 1728 he sailed through the Strait (separating Asia from North America) later named after him but did not then recognize its importance. On a later expedition he reached Alaska. He died after his ship was wrecked on what is now called Bering Island. The naturalist G. W. Steller, who escaped in a boat, wrote an account of the voyage.

Berio, Luciano (1925–). Italian composer, conductor and teacher. He was a leading serial (i.e. using 'tone-rows' like * Schönberg or * Berg) composer, also writing for electronic instruments and tape recorders, and produced some 'indeterminate' or 'aleatory' music in which the players themselves determine in what order they play the notes. His best known work was 'Sinfonia' (1968–69).

Berkeley, George (1685–1753). Irish philosopher and Anglican bishop of Cloyne, born in Kilkenny, educated at Trinity Cllege, Dublin. He spent several years in London, where he knew Swift, Pope and Addison, and in 1728–31 he taught at Rhode Island in preparation for the carrying out of his ill-fated plan to found a missionary college in Bermuda, a government grant for which was later withdrawn. In 1734 he accepted the bishopric of Cloyne in Southern Ireland: there he lived until 1752 when he retired through ill health and went to Oxford, where he died. Berkeley's philosophy of idealism is centrally a denial of the existence of matter, in the ordinary sense of the word. Locke had argued that the world of material objects gives rise to 'ideas' or subjective sense-impressions in our minds. We are directly aware of only these impressions. Berkeley held that there is no reason to suppose that anything lies behind these impressions: objects depend for their actuality on being perceived (*esse est percipi* – 'to be is to be perceived'). This doctrine can be easily misunderstood and ridiculed as it appears to violate common sense, but Berkeley is leading the argument to the point that since such impressions must be had by someone if they are to exist at all, and since it is accepted that material objects continue to exist when unperceived by men, their existence must depend upon perception by reason and ultimately by that of Supreme Reason or God. His doctrine, he claimed therefore, refuted scepticism. This is a vast over-simplification of the difficult series of arguments presented in his *Principles of Human Knowledge* (1710) and *Three Dialogues between Mylas and Philonus* (1713). On his return from Rhode Island he published *Alciphron* (1732), using the American background as a setting for more dialogues, Platonic in form.
Ritchie, A. D., *George Berkeley: A Reappraisal*. 1967

Berkeley, Sir Lennox (Randal) (1903–). English composer. Born at Oxford and educated at the University there, he studied under Nadia Boulanger in Paris and shows the influence of such French composers as Bizet and Chabrier. Among his better known works are many songs, the *Stabat Mater* (1946), the operas *Nelson* (1954) and *Ruth* (1956). He tried most musical forms including incidental music for films, cantatas and works for unaccompanied choirs. He was President of the Composers' Guild and the Performing Right Society.

Berlichingen, Götz von (1480–1562). German (Swabian) knight and adventurer. He lost his right hand in battle and wore an iron one. He was one of the discontented nobles who led the rebellious peasants in the Peasants' War (1524–26) and later fought against the French and the Turks. His life is the basis of plays by Goethe (*Götz von Berlichingen*), Sartre (*Le Diable et le Bon Dieu*) and John Arden (*Ironhand*).

Berlin, Irving (1888–). American songwriter, born in Russia. He wrote more than 1,000 popular songs including *Alexander's Ragtime Band* (1911) and *White Christmas*, and scores for several musicals (e.g. *Annie Get Your Gun*, 1946) and revues.

Berlin, Sir Isaiah (1909–). British scholar. Born in Riga, he went to England with his parents after the Russian revolution, gained a double first at Oxford and has remained there ever since, except during World War II (when he was attached to the British Embassy in Washington). In 1957 he succeeded G. D. H. Cole as Chichele professor of political theory and was knighted in the same year. His works include *Karl Marx* (1939), *The Hedgehog and the Fox* (a study of Tolstoy's theory of history, 1953), *Historical Inevitability* (1954), *Four Essays on Liberty* (1969) and *Vico and Herder* (1976). He was president of the British Academy 1975–78.

Berliner, Emile (1851–1929). American inventor, born in Germany, best known for his invention of the disc record for the gramophone, a word which he is said to have brought into use.

Berlioz, (Louis) **Hector** (1803–1869). French composer, born near Grenoble. The son of a physician, he studied medicine in Paris for some years but loathed it and, after a violent quarrel with his family, began to study music under Lesueur and entered the Paris Conservatoire in 1826. But again his emotional temperament brought him into conflict with his teachers. While a student he fell in love with the Irish actress Harriet Smithson, whom he married in 1833. The marriage was unsuccessful and they separated in 1842. Despite his genius for orchestration, Berlioz never completed his formal studies and was a poor instrumentalist, mastering only the guitar and flageolet. In 1830 his cantata *Sardanapale* won the Prix de Rome and then he studied in Italy for about a year. He won his first public success in 1832 with a performance of his *Symphonie fantastique* (1830; subtitled 'An episode in the life of an artist'), an extraordinarily vivid work describing five scenes (supposed to have been dreamt by Berlioz) in which the artist seeks out his beloved, kills her, is executed and then descends to hell. Berlioz composed most of his orchestral works to a definite literary programme and most contemporary critics attacked his addiction to 'programme music'. His later symphonies were *Harold in Italy* (1834; based on Byron's *Childe Harold*), *Romeo and Juliet* (1838; employing soloists and chorus) and *Symphonie funèbre et triomphale* (1840; written to commemorate the victims of the 1830 Revolution). He also composed the concert overtures *Waverley* (1827), *King Lear* (1831), *Le Carnaval romain* (1844) and *The Corsair* (1855), the operas *Benvenuto Cellini* (1838), *Beatrice and Benedict* (1862; based on Shakespeare's *Much Ado About Nothing*), and *The Trojans* (1862), an enormous work which Berlioz regarded as his masterpiece, rarely performed because of its great length and the cost of production; its first full production in England – by Sir John Gielgud at Covent Garden – took place in 1957. Among other works were the song cycle *Nuits d'été* (1842), the oratorio *L'Enfance du Christ* (1852) and the operatic cantata *The Damnation of Faust* (1846). He wrote a great *Treatise on instrumentation* (1844) and *Memoirs* (1865). He was a vigorous and vivacious music critic and his writings on his own music did much to attract attention to his genius. Paganini, Liszt, and, to a lesser degree, Schumann were among the few of his contemporaries to acknowledge his place in 19th-century music. His second wife was the singer Marie Recio (died 1862). He travelled widely, giving concerts in England and in Russia. He was appointed librarian of the Paris Conservatoire from 1852 and a member of the French Institute from 1856. Although controversy still rages as to the intrinsic merit of his compositions, the colour and originality of his orchestration have never been in dispute.

Elliot, J. N., *Berlioz*. 1967

Bernadette, St (1844–1879). French visionary. Daughter of François Soubirous, a miller of Lourdes, in 1858 she claimed to have experienced a vision in which she saw and spoke with the Virgin Mary. The grotto at Lourdes where the vision occurred has become the chief place of pilgrimage for Roman Catholics seeking relief from pain and disease. There has been much controversy at the time and since concerning the event, its interpretation and the subsequent cures, and religious, national and local politics have been at various times involved; but no one has questioned the sincerity and purity of the girl herself. She became a nun, served as a nurse in the Franco-Prussian War and died of tuberculosis. She was canonized in 1933.

Bernadotte, Folke, Count (1895–1948). Swedish diplomat. A nephew of King Gustav V of Sweden. In World War II he acted for the Swedish Red Cross in the exchange of wounded prisoners and was an intermediary in conveying an offer of surrender from Himmler to the U.S. and British authorities. While serving as United Nations mediator between Jews and Arabs he was murdered by Jewish terrorists.

Bernadotte, Jean Baptiste Jules (1763–1844). French field marshal and Swedish king (as Charles XIV). He was the son of a lawyer at Pau, enlisted when 17, was a sergeant when the Revolution broke out and seizing his chance rose (1792–94) from lieutenant to brigadier. He entered the Bonaparte family circle by marrying Désirée Clary, Napoleon's first fiancée and a sister of Joseph Bonaparte's wife. He took part in several of Napoleon's campaigns and was prominent in Austerlitz, but it was his governorship of the Hanseatic cities (1807–09) that made him known and liked in northern Europe and explains why in 1810 he was invited by the childless Charles XIII of Sweden to become his crown prince and *de facto* ruler. Napoleon accepted on his behalf in the hope of having a faithful ally but Bernadotte put the needs of his adopted country first and made an alliance with Russia. Accordingly, he was allowed to retain his position when Napoleon fell. As a reward for his services, Norway (acquired from the Danes in 1814) was confirmed by the Congress of Vienna as being in union with Sweden. In 1818 Bernadotte duly succeeded as Charles XIV to the joint heritage and proved himself a popular and successful ruler.

Bernanos, Georges (1888–1948). French writer. He was born in Paris and became one of the best known of the group of Catholic novelists who have been of major importance in modern French literature. Among his best known works are *Sous le soleil de Satan* (1926; translated into English as *The Star of Satan,* 1940) and *Journal d'un curé de campagne* (1936; English version: *The Diary of a Country Priest*, 1940). His *Les Grands Cimetières sous la lune* (1938) contains an unusually strong criticism (for a Roman Catholic) of Franco's rule in Spain. During World War II he was in South America, where he wrote *Lettre aux anglais* (1940–42).
Speaight, R., *Georges Bernanos.* 1973

Bernard, Claude (1813–1878). French physiologist. He was born near Villefranche, and worked in a Lyons pharmacy before studying medicine in Paris. He graduated in 1843 and worked for several years with F. Magendie, professor of medicine at the Collège de France, to whose chair he succeeded in 1855. Among his many other offices was that of president of the Royal Academy of Sciences (1869). He is best known for his work on the function of the pancreas in digestion, and for the inference which he drew from his experiments that the production of sugar in the liver is controlled by the nervous system: he named the sugar-producing substance, which he succeeded in isolating, 'glycogen'.
Holmes, F. L., *Claude Bernard and Animal Chemistry.* 1974

Bernard of Clairvaux, St (1090–1153). French theologian and reformer, born of a noble family near Dijon. In 1113 he entered the Cistercian monastery at Cîteaux, and in 1115 became the first abbot of the newly founded monastery at Clairvaux, in Champagne. Clairvaux remained the centre of his activities for the rest of his life and during his tenure of office its numbers rose from twelve to 700. From there he made the famous journeys which led to the foundation of about seventy more Cistercian houses, and his reputation as the second founder of the order. His ascetic and studious life made him one of the most influential men of his time. His stirring eloquence won him the name of 'Mellifluous Doctor', and his emphasis on spirituality and devotion still influences Catholicism. His practical achievements were also considerable. In 1131, by securing recognition for Pope Innocent II, he averted a schism, and his preaching from 1146 stirred the French to support the Second Crusade. He condemned the teachings of his great enemy, Peter * Abelard.

Bernard of Menthon, St (923–1008). Founder of the Augustinian hospice near the crest of the Great St Bernard pass, which bears his name, and patron of mountaineers.

Bernhard (1911–). Prince of the Netherlands. A prince of Lippe-Biesterfeld he married (1937) the future queen of the Netherlands, Princess * Juliana. He had many scientific, business and sporting interests.

Bernhardi, Friedrich von (1849–1930). German general and military writer. His book *Germany and the Next War* (1912) advocated that, where necessary for victory or survival, treaties should be disregarded and battles fought without regard for humanitarian principles. His book, translated in cheap editions, did much to exacerbate anti-German feeling in Allied countries during World War I.

Bernhardt, Sarah (1844–1923). French actress. Born in Paris of a Dutch–Jewish mother, she became known as 'the divine Sarah', a description which gives an idea of the emotions inspired by her art. More than once she joined the company of the Comédie Française, but the restrictions of the national theatre irked her and she finally left in 1880, formed her own company and from 1899 controlled her own theatre (Théâtre Sarah-Bernhardt). She toured frequently and was as warmly acclaimed in London, America and elsewhere as in her own country. She triumphed in the great classical parts, such as in Racine's *Phèdre*, and equally in a romantic and tearful melodrama such as the younger Dumas's *La Dame aux camélias*. Sardou provided her with several parts: she could exploit a delicious comedy sense in Molière. She even achieved male impersonations as Hamlet or in the title part (Napoleon I's young son) in Rostand's *L'Aiglon*. Despite the loss of a leg in 1915 she continued to act.
Skinner, C. O., *Madame Sarah*. 1967

Bernini, Giovanni Lorenzo (1598–1680). Italian architect and sculptor. The great master of the Italian baroque, he was born in Naples and went as a child to Rome, where his youthful skill, fostered and trained by his father, attracted the attention of Cardinal Scipione Borghese. The immense eccentric skill and psychological subtlety of the work (*Apollo and Daphne, Rape of Persephone* etc.) carried out for this patron brought him to the notice of the Vatican, and in 1629 he was appointed architect to St Peter's by Pope Urban VIII. He did much work there during the next decades, notably the great bronze baldacchino (1663) and the decoration of *Cathedra Petri* (1666), but it was not until 1656 that he embarked on his most ambitious and spectacular achievement, the enormous double colonnade which enclosed the piazza in front of the basilica: this consists of 640 columns, each four and a half feet in diameter, so arranged that the enclosed space acts as an enormous stage in which pilgrims congregate to receive the papal blessing. In 1665 Bernini was invited to France by Louis XIV where he worked on projects for the Louvre and executed a magnificent bust of the king.
Hibbard, H. *Bernini*. 1965

Bernouilli. A remarkable family of mathematicians, who originally came from Antwerp but are completely identified with Basle in Switzerland where they lived and worked (though not exclusively) during their period of fame. They include **Jakob Bernouilli I** (1645–1705), who wrote about the possibilities of the newly invented calculus; his brother **Johann I** (1667–1748), much of whose work was concerned with the mathematics of curves; **Daniel** (1700–1782), a son of Johann who contributed much to the study of hydronamics, though before becoming professor of physics at Basle he had been professor of anatomy and botany. He solved the differential equation now known as Bernouilli's equation. Less famous members of the family were **Nicolaus I** (1687–1759) nephew of Jakob and Johann; **Nicolaus II** (1695–1726), a son of Johann; **Johann II** (1710–1790), Johann I's youngest son; **Johann III** (1744–1807) and **Jakob II** (1759–1789) both sons of Johann II. All were concerned with the teaching of mathematics.

Bernstein, Eduard (1850–1932). German socialist. During years of exile in London he became a close friend of Friedrich * Engels. Bernstein argued that the teaching of Marx and Engels needed drastic revision in view of the increasing wealth and size of the middle class and slowly improving working class conditions, concluding that class war was not inevitable. Known as the father of 'revisionism', he served broken terms in the Reichstag 1902–28 and as a pacifist opposed World War I.

Bernstein, Henri (1876–1953). French dramatist, of Jewish extraction. He became a prolific playwright and theatrical manager in Paris and scored an enormous success with *Israel* (1906), *Le Voleur* (1906), *Le Secret* (1913) and *Judith* (1922).

Bernstein, Leonard (1918–). American musician. He composed the ballet *Fancy Free* (1944), the symphony *Jeremiah* (1943) and the musicals *Candide* (1956) and *West Side Story* (1957). He succeeded Dimitri Mitropoulos as conductor of the New York Philharmonic Orchestra in 1958 (until 1969). He wrote several books on enjoying music, notably *The Joy of Music* (1959).
Gradenwitz, P., *Leonard Bernstein*. 1949

Berry, Charles Ferdinand, Duc de (1778–1820). Younger son of the Comte d'Artois (later Charles X of France). He returned to

France in 1814 and was assassinated in 1820. His son, born posthumously, was the Comte de Chambord. His wife Caroline, a princess of Naples, attempted to raise a revolt in favour of her son, who was recognized by French royalists as Henry V. In 1832 she reached the Vendée, but was captured at Nantes and for a time imprisoned. She died at Palermo in 1870.

Berthelot, Pierre Eugène Marcellin (1827–1907). French chemist. He became Professor at the Ecole Supérieure de Pharmacie in 1859 and at the Collège de France in 1864 where he taught till his death. His career in chemistry was chiefly devoted to synthesis. Beginning with alcohol, he moved on to the synthesis of benzene, acetylene, and compounds of coal tar. He believed that organic compounds of great complexity could be built up out of simple elements and simple carbon compounds. Acetylene seemed to be the starting point in the investigation of hydrocarbons, since from it one could obtain ethylene, methane and benzene. The field of fatty acids interested him equally. Many of his experiments of the 1850s investigated the production of compounds of glycerin through heating it with hydrochloric acid and various fatty acids. These researches, together with similar analysis of sugars, led to studies of fermentation and the preparation of alcohol from ethylene. The work of Berthelot was of extreme importance in demonstrating the intimate links between organic and inorganic chemistry. Berthelot was a public servant of some prominence, being a Senator in 1881, Minister of Public Instruction in 1886 and Foreign Minister in 1895. He carried out important researches on explosives following the French defeat by Germany in the war of 1870. A man of the political Left, he attacked the influence of the Church, particularly in education.
Virtanen, R., *Marcellin Berthelot*. 1965

Berthier, Louis Alexandre, Prince of Neuchâtel (1753–1815). French marshal. A soldier's son, he enlisted in 1770, fought against the British in the war of American Independence and rose to be chief of staff of the French army in Italy (1795). He was a friend of Napoleon Bonaparte, both before and after he became emperor, and acted as his chief of staff throughout his wars, as well as being minister for war (1800–06). In 1814 he submitted to Louis XVIII, showed irresolution when he heard of Napoleon's return from Elba, and, as the Russian armies entered France after Waterloo, committed suicide.

Berthollet, Comte Claude Louis (1748–1822). French applied chemist. He studied medicine at the University of Turin, graduating in 1768. He then studied chemistry in Paris under Macquer. During the Revolutionary period in particular he was deeply involved in practical chemistry, seeking improvements in soap, explosives and metals. His theoretical researches into chlorine led to his pioneering its use for bleaching purposes. Berthollet was one of the earliest supporters of Lavoisier's antiphlogiston chemistry. His understanding of oxygen helped in his analysis of ammonia, and in other researches in the chemistry of gases. In later life he became more involved in theoretical issues. In his *Essai de Statique Chimique* he claimed that the forces of chemical affinity were proportional to the masses of the reacting substances, a view seemingly undermined by Dalton's law of definite proportions. Berthollet was a public figure in Revolutionary France. He taught at the Ecole Polytechnique, was a friend of Napoleon, and became a Senator in 1804. At Napoleon's request he travelled to Egypt in 1796 to collect art treasures and help found the Institute of Egypt.
Crosland, M., *The Society of Arcueil*

Bertillon, Alphonse (1853–1914). French criminologist. The scientific son of an anthropologist, he introduced a system of identifying criminals by a series of body measurements (anthropometry). In 1892 nearly 700 French criminals were identified by this method, later replaced by that of fingerprint comparison.

Bertolucci, Bernardo (1940–). Italian film director, born in Parma. He gained international recognition with his films *The Spider's Strategy* (1970), *The Conformist* (1970), *Last Tango in Paris* (1972) and *1900* (1975) which combined powerful, violent or sensual subjects with rich lyricism and elegant imagery.

Bertrand, Henri Gratien, Count (1773–1844). French general. He entered the army as an engineer and in that capacity fortified Alexandria in the Egyptian campaign. He was prominent at Austerlitz and his bridge-building skill helped to save the army at Aspern. He then became Napoleon's adjutant, shared his exile both at Elba and St Helena, and only after his master's death returned to France where a death sentence was repealed by Louis XVIII. In 1840 he accompanied the expedition which brought back Napoleon's remains to France.

Berwick, James Fitz-James, 1st Duke of (1670–1734). Illegitimate son of James II and Arabella Churchill, the sister of the Duke of Marlborough. He received his title in 1687 from his father, whom he later accompanied into exile. Joining the French army he served with distinction under Marshal Luxembourg. In 1706 he himself was created a marshal and by his victory at Almansa established Louis XIV's grandson Philip V on the throne of Spain. During the War of the Polish Succession he was killed at the siege of Philippsburg.

Berzelius, Baron Jöns Jakob (1779–1848). Swedish chemist. He discovered selenium, thorium and cerium, and first isolated silicon, titanium and zirconium. He was born and educated at Uppsala, where he was later a professor, until in 1815 he became professor of chemistry at the new Chirurgico Medical Institute in Stockholm. By consolidating and extending J. Dalton's work on the atom and compiling the first accurate table of atomic weights he did much to make the advances of modern chemistry possible. He first suggested the modern system of chemical symbols (e.g. H_2O for water, indicating that there are two atoms of hydrogen and one of oxygen in a molecule of water).

Besant, Annie (née Wood) (1847–1933). British theosophist. After separating from her husband, a clergyman, she became an active free-thinker closely associated with Charles * Bradlaugh, with whom she was tried for immorality after reprinting a pamphlet on birth control, and then an ardent propagandist for socialism. G. B. Shaw considered her the finest orator he had heard. In 1889 she met Madame * Blavatsky and turned to theosophy; she lived in India from 1895, interested herself in the education of women and having taken up nationalism became president of the Indian National Congress in 1917. In later life, she identified a young Indian, Jiddu Krishnamurti, as a new messiah.

Bessel, Friedrich Willhelm (1784–1846). German astronomer and mathematician. By studying astronomy in his spare time as a merchant's clerk and at sea he eventually became director of Königsberg Observatory, a post which he held from 1810 to 1846. In 1804 he recalculated the orbit of Halley's Comet from observations that had been made in 1607, and in 1838 he made the first accurate measurement of the distance of a star (61 Cygni). His theory that irregularities in the motion of Sirius and Procyon were due to gravitational pull was confirmed when, as he predicted, 'dark' companion stars were subsequently discovered. At the time of his death Bessel was investigating the irregularities in the motion of Uranus that later enabled * Adams and * Leverrier to discover the existence of Neptune. His chief mathematical work was on the functions now known as Bessel functions.

Bessemer, Sir Henry (1813–1898). English metallurgist. In 1856 he invented the 'Bessemer Converter', in which some types of pig iron can be directly and economically converted into high grade steel by oxidizing the impurities. This was originally achieved by passing air into the converter, but oxygen alone is now used. Bessemer also helped Young and Delcambre to develop the first composing machine known to be used in a printing office (1840). He was one of the founders of the Iron and Steel Institute in 1869. He was knighted in 1879.
Bessemer, H., *Autobiography*. 1905

Best, Charles Herbert (1899–1978). Canadian physiologist. With F. G. * Banting, he first succeeded in preparing insulin for the treatment of diabetes. He received many international awards, including the U.S. Legion of Merit (1947) and the C.H. (1971).

Betancourt, Romulo (1908–1981). Left-wing Venezuelan politician. He was driven into exile under the dictatorship of Juan Vicente Gomez, and again in 1939 for his underground activities. On his return he organized the *Acción Democratica* and was largely responsible for the revolution of 1945 which resulted in his becoming provisional president. In 1948 a military *coup d'état* once more forced him into exile, and this time he had to wait ten years for the tide of fortune to turn and enable him to return in 1958. He became president in

1959 and proceeded with his programme of social and economic reform.

Bethmann-Hollweg, Theobald von (1856–1921). German politician. He was Imperial Chancellor 1909–17, having been Prussian minister of the interior (1905–07) and then secretary of state. He was alleged to be shocked and dismayed that Britain should enter the war just for a 'scrap of paper' (the treaty with Belgium), but he was considered too moderate by the militarists and dismissed in 1917.

Betjeman, Sir John (1906–1984). English poet and journalist, educated at Marlborough and Oxford. He wrote several architectural guidebooks, championed Victorian and Edwardian taste, and gained wide recognition for his light verse, mild satire and nostalgic descriptive pieces. His blank verse autobiography, *Summoned by Bells* (1960), was a popular success. His *Collected Poems* appeared in 1958. He was appointed Poet Laureate in 1972.

Betterton, Thomas (*c.* 1635–1710). English actor. Despite disadvantages of face, voice and figure, he was esteemed by Pepys to be the best actor in the world. All, including Addison and Dryden, speak well of him as an actor and man, and when speculation proved his undoing a public benefit was arranged on his behalf. In 1705 he moved his company from his theatre in Lincoln's Inn Fields to the new Haymarket Theatre, designed for him by Vanbrugh.
Gildon, C., *Life of Mister Thomas Betterton, The Late Eminent Tragedian.* 1970

Betti, Ugo (1892–1953). Italian poet and playwright. He was a lawyer by profession, and rose to be a judge. He is better known for his plays, some of which, notably *The Queen and the Rebels*, were translated into English and performed with success. Most of his themes are concerned with questions of justice.
Rizzo, G., *Ugo Betti: Three Plays.* 1966

Bevan, Aneurin (1897–1960). British Labour politician. One of the great orators in the history of parliament, born at Tredegar in Monmouthshire (now Gwent), he was the son of a miner and himself a miner as a boy. He had early experience of trade union organization in the South Wales Miners Federation and gained a knowledge of politics and economics at the Central Labour College. He was elected M.P. for Ebbw Vale in 1929 and held the seat for the rest of his life. In World War II he often carried on a one-man opposition to the Winston Churchill coalition government and afterwards in Attlee's post-war Labour governments he was the life and soul of the left wing. As minister of health (1945–51) he gave the final shape to the National Health Service and secured the passing of the Act. His resignation in 1951 over what he regarded as excessive rearmament was soon followed by the Conservative return to office. In opposition his hostile attitude to the nuclear deterrent was almost as much an embarrassment to his own party leaders as to his opponents. However, as time went on, Bevan's views and those of his leader, Gaitskell, tended to converge and Bevan had become deputy leader of the party when he died. He married Jenny Lee in 1934. She too was a well-known politician and a member of Harold Wilson's Labour government in 1964. *Tribune*, a publication founded by Bevan, survived his death.
Foot, M., *Aneurin Bevan.* 2 vols. 1962 and 1973

Beveridge, William Henry Beveridge, 1st Baron (1879–1963). British economist, born in Bengal. He is famous for the so-called 'Beveridge Report' which, produced during World War II, was a series of detailed suggestions for social security and became the basis of the 'welfare state' legislation of post-war years. Beveridge had been director of the London School of Economics (1919–37) and master of University College, Oxford (1937–45). He was Liberal M.P. for Berwick-upon-Tweed (1944–45). Knighted in 1919, he received his peerage in 1946.
Beveridge, W. H., *Power and Influence.* 1953

Bevin, Ernest (1881–1951). British trade union leader and Labour politician. Though he was the son of an agricultural labourer and his early jobs were those of van boy and driver he soon entered and made progress in the trade union movement. At the age of 30 he was an official of the dockers' union, and the skill with which he put their case earned him the nickname of 'the dockers' K.C.'. But his greatest achievement and monument was the uniting (1922) of thirty-two separate unions into the huge Transport and General Work-

ers Union. In 1940 he entered Winston Churchill's wartime coalition as minister of labour and proved an outstanding success in keeping industry going and meeting the demands of the services. When Attlee formed his post-war Labour government it seemed a strange decision to place Bevin in the foreign office, but his vigorous common sense soon won the respect of those brought up in a more cultured tradition. Among the foremost architects of the Brussels treaty of 1948 (Western European Union) and NATO (1949), he was criticized for his pro-Arab outlook, and lack of sympathy towards Israel.
Bullock, A., *The Life and Times of Ernest Bevin*. 2 vols. 1960 and 1967

Bewick, Thomas (1753–1828). British wood engraver. Born in Northumberland, he was apprenticed to a Newcastle engraver, Ralph Beilby, with whom he afterwards entered into partnership. The highest quality of his work is seen in his *History of Quadrupeds* (1790) and even more so in the two volumes of his *History of British Birds* (1797 and 1804).
Bain, I., *Thomas Bewick*. 1975

Beza (or de Bèze), **Theodore** (1519–1605). French theologian. As a young man he led a dissipated life in Paris, but after a serious illness he changed his ways, and joined *Calvin at Geneva. He was professor of Greek at Lausanne (1549–54) and, returning to Geneva (1559) to take up a theological professorship, he worked closely with Calvin, proving his skill as a diplomat by obtaining Henry of Navarre's help for the Huguenots. On Calvin's death (1564) much of the burden of leadership fell upon Beza and he presided at the Huguenot Synods at La Rochelle (1571) and at Nîmes (1572). He was also an important biblical scholar.

Bhutto, Zulfiqar Ali (1928–1979). Pakistani politician. Born to a wealthy Sind family of Hindu origin, he studied at the University of California (Berkeley) and Oxford and became a barrister (1953). Minister of commerce 1958–60 and foreign minister 1963–66, he founded the Pakistan Peoples' Party (PPP) in 1967 and described himself as a democratic socialist. Imprisoned 1968–69 by Ayub Khan's government, he won an election victory in West Pakistan in December 1970. Following the war of December 1971 which resulted in the secession of East Pakistan (Bengal) and the creation of Bangladesh, Bhutto became president of Pakistan 1971–73. After the adoption of a parliamentary constitution, Bhutto stepped down to become prime minister 1973–77 until his overthrow by a military coup. In 1978 he was sentenced to death for conspiracy to murder and was executed in 1979.
Taseer, S., *Bhutto: A Political Biography*. 1979

Bichat, Marie François Xavier (1771–1802). French physician. His work on body tissues (called by him membranes) earned him the distinction of being 'virtually the founder of morbid histology'. Bichat was born in the Jura, studied at Lyons and Paris and in 1797 began giving courses of instruction in anatomy and physiology. He gained his practical experience in some 600 post-mortems.

Bickerstaffe, Isaac (*c*. 1735–1812). Irish playwright. He became an officer of marines but had to flee abroad in 1772 on a capital charge. The best known of his plays include *Love in a Village* (1762), *The Maid of the Mill* (1765) and *Lionel and Clarissa* (1768). The name 'Isaac Bickerstaff' was used as a penname by both Swift and Steele.

Bidault, Georges (1899–1983). French politician and journalist. He was a leader of the resistance movement during World War II. After the liberation he was appointed foreign minister by de Gaulle, and, as founder and leader of the Mouvement Républicain Populaire (Catholic Socialist party), he held that office or that of prime minister almost continuously until 1953. In 1962 he became head of the National Resistance Council, violently opposed to the independence of Algeria. Deprived of parliamentary immunity, Bidault had to operate from abroad, in association with the OAS. He returned to France in 1968.
Bidault, G., *Résistance* (political autobiography). 1967

Bierce, Ambrose Gwinnett (1842–1914?). American writer, born in Ohio. Apart from journalism, he was the author of cynical, sardonic, often macabre short stories, published in collections such as *Can Such Things Be?* (1893) and *In the Midst of Life* (1898), a reissue of *Tales of Soldiers and Civilians* (1891). He compiled *The Cynic's Word Book* (1906), later republished under the title of *The Devil's*

Dictionary. He disappeared while on a journalistic assignment in Mexico to join the rebel leader * Villa.
O'Connor, R., *Ambrose Bierce: A Biography*.

Billroth, (Christian Albert) Theodor (1829–1894). Austrian surgeon. He combined a career in pathological anatomy with brilliant innovations in practical surgery. Born into a well-connected North German clerical family, Billroth pursued extensive medical studies at Göttingen and Berlin, receiving his doctorate in 1852. He obtained a post at Berlin University in 1856, and then became director of the Zurich surgical hospital in 1860, eventually moving to Vienna. He made extensive studies of wound fever (especially the chemical poisons that produced it). He pioneered the use of antisepsis on the Continent, and developed important surgical techniques. He was the first to resect the esophagus (1872) and in 1873 he performed a total laryngectomy. He was especially skilled in plastic surgery. Billroth was a man of great culture. An expert violin and viola player, he was a friend of Brahms, who dedicated two string quartets to him. He developed ideas on the physiological basis of musical talent, which he wrote up in *Wer ist Musikalisch?*, published after his death by the music critic, Hanslick.
Fischer, I., *Billroth und seine Zeitgenossen*. 1929

Binyon, Laurence (1869–1943). English poet, dramatist and art critic. During World War I he wrote the elegiac poem 'For the Fallen', which became enormously popular, especially for war memorials. His *Collected Poems* were published in 1931. His plays included *Arthur* (1923) and *The Young King* (1935). He joined the British Museum staff in 1893 and was ultimately keeper of prints and drawings with a special interest in Chinese and Japanese art. He was professor of poetry at Harvard (1933–34).
Southworth, J. G., *Sowing the Field*. 1940

Birdseye, Clarence (1886–1956). American businessman and inventor, born in New York. His first employment was as a fur trader in Labrador, where he observed the method used of freezing food in winter when fresh supplies were unobtainable. Returning to the USA, he began experiments. In 1924 he was co-founder of the General Seafoods Co. and developed a highly profitable and efficient method of freezing which aimed at preserving original taste.

Birdwood, William Riddell Birdwood, 1st Baron (1865–1951). British soldier. He commanded the Australian and New Zealand Army Corps (ANZAC) in World War I, leading them at the Gallipoli landing and after the evacuation (when he was in command of all troops) in France. He was promoted to command the 5th Army in 1918 in time to lead it to the final victory. Except during the South African War, when he was on Kitchener's staff, Birdwood's earlier service had mainly been in India, where he returned in 1925 as commander-in-chief, being appointed field marshal in the same year. After his return in 1930 he held the office of master of Peterhouse, Cambridge, until 1938, when he received his peerage.
Birdwood, W. R., *Khaki and Gown*. 1941

Birkbeck, George (1776–1841). English educationist. Birkbeck College, London University, founded in 1824, was originally one of the Mechanics Institutes for the education of the working classes, in the establishment of which Birkbeck played a leading part. He was born in Settle, Yorkshire, and studied medicine at Leeds and Edinburgh.
Kelly, T., *George Birkbeck, Pioneer of Adult Education*. 1957

Birkenhead, Frederick Edwin Smith, 1st Earl of (1872–1930). English lawyer and Conservative politician, born in Birkenhead. Educated at Oxford, he became a barrister in 1899 and soon acquired an enormous practice. As M.P. (1906–19) his wit and audacity soon marked him out, but as Carson's chief lieutenant ('Galloper Smith' was his derisive nickname) he also won a reputation for reckless partisanship in support of the Ulster cause. It says much for the generosity and wisdom of his maturer years that he was a chief architect of the Irish settlement of 1921. In World War I coalitions he served as solicitor-general (1915) and attorney-general (1915–19); in the latter office he conducted the prosecution in the trial of Sir Roger Casement. As lord chancellor (1919) he was responsible for revising the Law of Property Act (1922). He was created earl in 1922. On the break-up of the coalition Birkenhead left office with Lloyd George, but joined the second Baldwin government in 1924 as secretary of state for India until his retirement in 1928. His books include *International*

Law (4th ed., 1911) *Famous Trials of History* (1927) and *Law, Life and Letters* (1927). Campbell, J., *F. E. Smith.* 1983

Birkett, (William) Norman Birkett, 1st Baron (1883–1962). English lawyer. Called to the bar in 1913, and a K.C. from 1924, he became notable as defence counsel in several important murder trials. At the Nuremberg Trials he was the British alternate judge to Lord Justice Lawrence. He was a Liberal M.P. for Nottingham East (1923–24 and 1929–31), a judge of the King's Bench (1941–50), and then a Lord Justice of Appeal until his retirement in 1957.

Biron (Bühren), **Ernst Johann** (1690–1772). German courtier. Son of a groom, he became Duke of Courland as the lover of Anna Ivanovna, empress of Russia. He was hated for his insolence and greed, and Anna's death (1740) brought exile in Siberia and temporary eclipse. He was recalled by Peter III in 1762 and restored to his dukedom by Catherine the Great.

Birrell, Augustine (1850–1933). British Liberal politician and writer. He was an MP, 1889–1900; 1906–18, but his gentle, scholarly nature was ill suited to the office of chief secretary for Ireland, to which he was appointed after the great Liberal electoral victory of 1906. He resigned after the Easter rebellion of 1916. He wrote many works of literary biography and criticism, but is best known for his *Obiter Dicta* (1884; 1887; 1924), urbane and charming critical essays. The verb 'to birrell' was coined to describe his gift of kindly but ironic comment.

Bismarck, Otto Edvard Leopold von, Prince Bismarck, Duke of Lauenburg (1815–1898). German statesman, born into a Junker family in Schönhausen (Brandenburg). He was deeply influenced as a boy by his mother, who encouraged him to study law at Göttingen with a view to public service. At the university he gained repute for skill in such traditional student rites as duelling and drinking bouts. He entered the Prussian civil service in 1835, disliked his duties and was disapproved of in turn for his unpunctuality and the excessive demands of his social life. Resignation (1839) and a post as an estate manager followed. During this time he engaged in country pursuits, read and corresponded much and entered into a happy marriage (1847) with Johanna von Puttkamer. His support for the monarchy, the army and the Lutheran church determined his strongly conservative political beliefs. Even though in 1847 he was a member of the Prussian Diet and an elected member for Brandenburg, in 1849 he objected to the constitution of which these Diets were the outcome and to the lack of authoritative measures for dealing with the liberal risings of 1848–49. It was as a somewhat crude advocate of royal absolutism that he went as Prussian ambassador to the German Diet at Frankfurt (1851–59) but he quickly acquired the arts of a diplomat and saw how assemblies of this kind could be used for his own ends, which more and more became clarified as the unity of Germany under Prussian leadership, with the exclusion of Austria. After serving as ambassador to Russia (1859–62) and to France (1862), appointments which enabled him to gain the confidence of one emperor (Alexander II) and to study the weaknesses of another (Napoleon III), Bismarck was called to head the Prussian government in order to overcome parliamentary opposition to King William I's army plans. He achieved this by the dissolution of parliament over a legal quibble and at once proceeded with his plans to unify Germany. A war with Denmark (over the Schleswig-Holstein duchies) was provoked and Austria's enlistment as a junior partner made Prussia, not Austria, appear as Germany's natural leader. Next Bismarck provoked war with Austria over the control of the former Danish provinces: in seven weeks Austria had surrendered (1866) but a generous settlement avoided the dangers of extreme bitterness and antagonizing Germany's southern states. The North German Confederation was then set up and Bismarck became chancellor (1867–71). His next step was to anticipate any possible resistance to his plans by France. By a series of adroit manoeuvres, such as support for the candidature of Prince Leopold of Hohenzollern for the vacant Spanish throne, and finally by 'editing' a telegram from Napoleon III to King William he created a situation which practically forced Napoleon to declare war in July 1870. Once more Bismarck had judged the military situation correctly: by August Napoleon's armies had been smashed at Sedan and he himself had been taken prisoner. In January 1871, in Versailles, William I was proclaimed sovereign of the new German empire, and

Bismarck became first chancellor. For the next twenty years the history of Bismarck was the history of Germany. His foreign policy was based on a friendly alliance between the three emperors of Germany, Austria and Russia, and he was able to assert Germany's leadership in 1878 by getting Berlin chosen as the venue of a conference which successfully settled the Balkan problems created by the Russo-Turkish war. At home he tempered his conservatism with an opportunism which often shocked his friends as it disarmed his opponents. He accepted manhood suffrage and initiated such reforms as the Sickness Insurance Law, the Accident Insurance Law (both subsidized by the employers) and the Old-Age and Invalidity Insurance Law (subsidized by the state). But his dictatorial methods could not be otherwise than irksome to the young prince who in 1888 became the emperor William II (the Kaiser of World War I), who wished to make his own mark. In 1890 Bismarck was dismissed. In retirement he was a constant and bitter critic of the policy of the Emperor, e.g. in his memoirs *Reflections and Reminiscences* (1898).
Taylor, A. J. P., *Bismarck: The Man and the Statesman.* 1955

Bizet, Georges (properly Alexandre César Léopold) (1838–1875). French composer. Born in Paris, and a pupil of Gounod, he showed early brilliance but received late recognition. He won the Prix de Rome in 1857 and spent three years studying in Italy. His operas include *The Pearl Fishers* (1863), *The Fair Maid of Perth* (1867) and *Carmen* (1875), his last and greatest work, based on a story by Prosper Mérimée. This was Bizet's first real success: he died a few months after its first performance. Another well known work is the incidental music to *L'Arlésienne*.
Dean, W., *Bizet.* 1965

Björnson, Björnstjerne (1832–1910). Norwegian poet, novelist and dramatist. The son of a Lutheran pastor, he was educated at Molde, Christiania and Copenhagen. He managed theatres in Bergen (1857–59), Christiania (1865–67), lived in Italy (1860–62) and travelled widely throughout Europe, while working as a newspaper editor and taking an active part in politics as an advocate of Norwegian nationalism and republicanism. His marriage to Karoline Reimers in 1858 was followed by one of his most creative periods to which belong the historical dramas *King Sverre* (1861) and the trilogy *Sigurd the Bastard* (1862) as well as the peasant novels *Arne* (1859) and *A Happy Boy* (1862). In 1874, influenced by his friend Ibsen, he wrote the first of his modern plays, *The Editor*, followed by the successful *A Bankruptcy* (1875) and a political play called *The King* (1877) which caused considerable offence. *The New System* (1879) contrasted the honest quest for truth by the younger generation with the hypocrisy of the old. As the years went by Björnson continued to combine political agitation (the liberal victory of 1882 owed much to him) with writing. *A Gauntlet* (1883) advocated sex equality and two plays under the title *Beyond Our Power* (1889) also dealt with such controversial topics as miracles and a strike. Also noted as a lyric poet, Björnson wrote 'Yes, we love this land' adopted as the Norwegian national anthem. With Ibsen he was one of the great figures of the Scandinavian literary renaissance. He won the Nobel Prize for Literature in 1903.

Black, Joseph (1728–1799). Scottish physician-chemist, born in Bordeaux. Educated in Belfast and at Glasgow University he took a medical degree at Edinburgh in 1754. He realized that carbon dioxide is chemically distinct from air, and was the first to show the difference between mild and caustic alkalis. Black also propounded the theories of specific and latent heat (the latter was applied by James * Watt to the steam engine with historic consequences) and laid the foundations of calorimetry. He became lecturer in chemistry at Glasgow University in 1756 and was also professor of medicine there. From 1766 until his death he was professor of chemistry at Edinburgh University.
Ramsay, W., *Life and Letters of J. Black*. 1918

Black Prince *see* **Edward, the Black Prince**

Blackett, Patrick Maynard Stewart, Baron Blackett (1897–1974). English phyśicist. He studied under Rutherford at Cambridge and developed the use of C. T. R. Wilson's cloud chamber in the studyof atomic structure and cosmic rays; in his cosmic-ray studies with Occhialinc in 1933 he confirmed the existence of the positron previously discovered by C. D. Anderson. He also made important contributions to the study of rock magnetism. Blackett was professor of physics at Birkbeck

College, University of London (1933–37), Manchester University (1937–53) and Imperial College, London (1953–74). In 1948 he was awarded the Nobel Prize for Physics and received an O.M., a C.H. and a peerage.

Blackmore, Richard Doddridge (1825–1900). English novelist. Educated at Blundell's School, Tiverton, and at Exeter College, Oxford, he gave up the law because of poor health and took up writing. Of his fifteen novels *Lorna Doone* (1869) is best known. The story is set in Exmoor, with Monmouth's rebellion against James II as one of its episodes. The heroine herself and John Ridd, who rescues her from the Doone clan of robbers and murderers, are among the most romantic characters of fiction.

Blackstone, Sir William (1723–1780). English jurist. His *Commentaries on the Laws of England* (1765–69), a lucid exposition of the whole of English law, exercised an immense influence upon succeeding generations of lawyers, and remains a standard work of reference. Son of a silk mercer and educated at Charterhouse and Oxford, he practised at the bar until 1758, when he became the first Vinerian professor of Law at Oxford. In this post he inaugurated courses in English Law (only Roman Law having been studied there until then). Blackstone was a Tory M.P. from 1761 to 1770, in which year he was knighted and made a judge.

Blackwell, Elizabeth (1821–1910). British woman doctor. Born in Bristol, she was taken to America as a child, studied in New York and in 1849 became the first woman medical graduate. Having then come to London to study at St Bartholomew's Hospital she later (1859) became the first woman on the British medical register. Back in America she organized nursing services during the Civil War. In 1869 she settled in England, and in 1875 she became a professor at the London School of Medicine for Women, which she had helped to establish.

Fancourt, M. St J., *They Dared to be Doctors: Elizabeth Blackwell and Elizabeth Garrett Anderson*. 1966

Blackwood, Algernon Henry (1869–1951). English author. After an adventurous career in Canada as a prospector he was a reporter in New York and finally won fame by his novels and short stories about ghostly or supernatural happenings, including *John Silence* (1908), *The Lost Valley* (1910) and *Tales of the Uncanny and Supernatural* (1949).

Blackwood, A. H., *Episodes before Thirty*. 1923

Blackwood, William (1776–1834). Scottish publisher. He came to prominence by publishing the first series of Sir Walter Scott's *Tales of My Landlord*. Later writers whose books bore the Blackwood imprint included George Eliot, Trollope and Charles Reade. In 1817 Blackwood founded *Blackwood's Magazine* as a Tory rival to the *Edinburgh Review*. Under his descendants it grew to be a national institution.

Blaine, James Gillespie (1830–1893). American Republican politician, born in Pennsylvania. After working as a schoolteacher, lawyer and journalist he entered the Maine legislature and in 1863 the U.S. House of Representatives, serving as speaker from 1869 to 1875. Allegations of corruption were responsible for his loss of the presidential nomination in 1876 and 1880, but he was U.S. senator (1876–81) and served as U.S. secretary of state under Garfield (1881) and (1889–92) under Harrison. In 1884 he was narrowly beaten for the presidency by Grover Cleveland.

Blake, Robert (1599–1657). English admiral. Son of a merchant of Bridgwater, Somerset, and educated at Oxford, he spent his early years at home occupied by business or country pursuits. Election to parliament in 1640 marked his entry into public life and during the Civil War he served with great distinction in the Parliamentary land forces, his defence of Taunton for a year winning him great renown. In 1649 he was appointed to command (with two others) the Commonwealth navy. Although he had little naval training he managed to destroy Prince Rupert's fleet (1650) and to establish Britain's naval supremacy in the North Sea and English Channel after a series of encounters with the famous Dutch admirals Tromp and de Ruyter. In 1654 he sailed to the Mediterranean and destroyed the power of the Tunisian and Algerian pirates. In 1657, having heard of the arrival of the Spanish West Indian Fleet at Vera Cruz, Tenerife, he immediately set sail and destroyed all sixteen ships, but as his ship entered

Plymouth harbour on its return Blake himself died.

Curtis, C. D., *Blake, Captain at Sea*. 1934; Beadon, R., *Robert Blake*. 1935

Blake, William (1757–1827). English poet, artist and mystic, born in London. His father, a hosier, was a follower of Emanuel * Swedenborg. From the very first he was a highly imaginative child who claimed to see angelic visions. Apprenticed to an engraver (1771–78), he studied briefly with the Royal Academy School and then set up shop in 1784 as a printseller and engraver. His first book of poems, *Poetical Sketches* (1783), was followed by *Songs of Innocence* (1789) and *Songs of Experience*, which includes *The Tyger* (1794), illustrated like all his later books with his own hand-painted engravings. Poems such as *The French Revolution* (1791) and *America* (1793) express a temporary political fervour which he did not retain as his views became more and more imbued with mysticism. His mystical and prophetic works include *The Marriage of Heaven and Hell* (1791), *The Book of Urizen* (1794), *The Book of Los* (1795) and many others, printed from his own copper plates and illustrated with his visionary designs. Nearly all his works have a highly individual symbolism, but while his early poems are notable for their simple language and serene brightness, his later works, with their symbolic characters – Urizen, the author of restrictive moral law, Orc in rebellion against him and Los, the captive champion of light – create an atmosphere of gloom and mystery. However, despair is set aside and mutual love and forgiveness of sin offer revived hope of salvation in the epics *The Four Zoas* (1796–1804), *Milton* (1804–08) and *Jerusalem* (1804–20). Some of Blake's finest artistic work went into the illustrations for the Book of Job (1820–26) and for Dante's *Divine Comedy* (left unfinished at his death). His paintings were ignored by the public but he enjoyed the unfailing support and belief of his wife, the friendship and sometimes the financial help of other artists such as Flaxman and Samuel Palmer and he remained serenely happy until his death. Most modern critics have acknowledged him as a lyrical poet and visionary artist of supreme power.

Raine, K., *Blake*. 1970

Blamey, Sir Thomas Albert (1884–1951). Australian soldier. He served as chief of staff to * Monash in World War I, commanded Australian troops in the Middle East and Greece 1940–41, and was commander-in-chief of Allied land forces in the south-west Pacific area 1924–45 under General Douglas * MacArthur. In 1950 he became the first Australian field-marshal.

Hetherington, J., *Blamey: Controversial Soldier*. 1974.

Blanc, (Jean Joseph Charles) **Louis** (1811–1882). French socialist politician and author, born in Madrid. After studying law he became a journalist and was attracted to socialism by the utopian schemes of * Saint-Simon and * Fourier. In his *Organisation du Travail* (1840) he advocated the nationalization of property and the institution of co-operative workshops to be run by the workers themselves. He became a member of the revolutionary government formed in 1848 and when this collapsed took refuge first in Belgium and then in England. On returning to France after the fall of Napoleon III (1871), he condemned the Commune, but served for the rest of his life as a leading deputy of the extreme left. He wrote a twelve-volume *Histoire de la Révolution francaise* while in exile (1847–64).

Vidalenc, J., *Louis Blanc, 1811–1882*. 1948

Blanqui, (Louis) Auguste (1805–1881). French revolutionary socialist. He took an active part in the political risings of 1830, 1839 and 1848 and was exiled and imprisoned for sedition for much of his life. He first used the phrase 'dictatorship of the proletariat' and organized several secret political societies in an attempt to gain power by force. He was released in 1879 from a life sentence imposed after the Commune and elected a deputy for Bordeaux.

Bernstein, S., *Auguste Blanqui and the Art of Insurrection*. 1971.

Blasco Ibáñez, Vicente (1867–1928). Spanish novelist and active anti-monarchist, born in Valencia. His early novels deal realistically with provincial life and social change; later he achieved world fame with *Blood and Sand* (1908), about a bull-fighter's life, and *The Four Horsemen of the Apocalypse* (1916), a sensational novel of World War I, both successfully filmed.

Cardwell, R. A., *Blasco Ibáñez' 'La Barraca'*. 1973

Blatchford, Robert (1851–1943). English journalist. A socialist and agnostic, he became a lively and prolific pamphleteer writing under the pen-name 'Numquam'. His paper, the *Clarion*, and his books, e.g. *Merrie England* (1894), had a strong influence on British socialism.

Blavatsky, Helena Petrovna (née Hahn) (1831–1891). Russian-born theosophist. Little is known of her early life but she seems to have travelled widely in the East and even to have penetrated Tibet. She became a keen spiritualist and while living in New York (1873–78) founded, in 1875, the Theosophical Society. From New York she moved to India where the tenets of her mystical creed were said to have evolved. Despite the fact that her psychic powers failed to satisfy the Society for Psychical Research she had about 100,000 followers at the time of her death. *Isis Unveiled* (1877) was the first of several books. She was succeeded by Annie * Besant as leader of the Theosophists.
Symonds, J., *Madame Blavatsky*. 1959

Blériot, Louis (1872–1936). French aviator and engineer. He devoted his personal fortune to the construction of monoplanes and in 1909 made the first aeroplane flight across the English Channel (Calais to Dover in 37 minutes), winning a prize of £1,000 offered by Lord Northcliffe's *Daily Mail*.

Blessington, Marguerite Gardiner (née Power), **Countess of** (1789–1849). Irish writer. After a first marriage at the age of 14, forced upon her by her father, a small Irish landowner, she married in 1818 the 1st Earl of Blessington. Their house in London became a social and literary centre: Byron was among the guests, and in 1834 she published *A Journal of Conversations with Lord Byron*. Another friend was the notorious Count * d'Orsay, who was her lover for twelve years and with whom she fled to France in 1849 to avoid imprisonment for debt. The Countess's writings included travel books and many forgotten novels.
Sadleir, M., *Blessington-D'Orsay: A Masquerade*. 1933

Bligh, William (1754–1817). English sailor. Having accompanied Cook on his third voyage (1776), he commanded H.M.S. *Bounty* on an expedition to Tahiti to collect bread-fruit plants (1789), with the object of introducing them into the West Indies. On the return journey the ship's crew, led by Fletcher Christian, mutinied and cast Bligh and eighteen of his men adrift in an open boat. The act was probably motivated more by the thought of 'wives' left behind in Tahiti than Bligh's alleged harshness of discipline. Despite his lack of navigational aids, Bligh sailed more than 4,000 miles until picked up at Timor. After distinguished service in the French wars, Bligh arrived as governor of New South Wales in 1806, clashed with the New South Wales Corps, largely over his attempt to control the traffic in rum, and in 1808 was imprisoned by mutineers. He was made a rear-admiral in 1811 and a vice-admiral in 1814.
Hough, R., *Captain Bligh and Mr Christian*. 1972

Bliss, Sir Arthur (1891–1975). English composer. Educated at Rugby and Cambridge, he served in the army during World War I and, after holding several teaching positions, was director of music for the BBC from 1942 to 1944. Among his vivid, but somewhat astringent, works are *A Colour Symphony* (1922), Clarinet Quintet (1932), the music for H. G. Wells's film *Things To Come* (1935), *Music for Strings* (1935), the ballets *Checkmate* (1937), *Miracle in the Gorbals* (1944), and *Adam Zero* (1946), Piano Concerto (1939) and Violin Concerto (1955). He was knighted in 1950 and was appointed Master of the Queen's Musick in 1953.
Bliss, A., *As I Remember*. 1970

Bloch, Ernest (1880–1959). American composer, born of Swiss–Jewish parents in Geneva. Educated in Switzerland and Germany, he studied the violin under Eugène Ysaÿe, and became a teacher and conductor in Geneva. His opera *Macbeth* was produced in Paris in 1910. He lived in the USA from 1916, teaching music in Cleveland (1920–25) and San Francisco (1925–30). He was back in Switzerland for most of the 1930s but when war threatened he returned to America, where he was associated with the University of California at Berkeley. His works include the *Israel Symphony* (1916) and *Schelomo* ('Solomon'), a rhapsody for cello and orchestra (1936). He composed religious works and a large quantity of chamber music, reviving the Handelian form of the *concerto grosso*. Bloch was a thoughtful composer who never

aimed at, or achieved, wide popularity. Many of his compositions have a Hebraic quality, while his Violin Concerto (1938) uses Red Indian themes.
Strassburg, R., *Ernest Bloch*. 1977

Blok, Alexander Alexandrovich (1880–1921). Russian symbolist poet. Mysticism and romanticism distinguish his earlier poems, such as the cycle *Verses about the Lady Beautiful* (1904). He applauded the revolution of 1917, about which his poem *The Twelve* (1918) became famous. Subsequently his hopes of the new régime were disappointed. He died in poverty.
Kisch, C., *Alexander Blok: Prophet of Revolution*. 1960

Blondel de Nesle (fl. *c*. 1200). French troubadour. Tradition relates that when, in 1192, Richard Cœur de Lion, returning from the first crusade, was imprisoned by Leopold of Austria, Blondel discovered his whereabouts – and so enabled his release to be secured – by hearing the king responding to his song.

Blondin, Charles (1824–1897). French acrobat. In 1859 he crossed Niagara Falls on a tight rope, varying the act by being blindfolded, pushing a man in a wheelbarrow etc.

Blood, Thomas (*c*. 1618–1680). British adventurer, famous for a daring attempt to steal the crown jewels. In 1671, dressed as a clergyman, he disabled the keeper and actually managed to escape with the crown under his arm while an accomplice carried off the orb. They were pursued, caught and imprisoned but later pardoned by Charles II.

Bloom, Claire (1931–). English actress. Born in London, she studied at the Guildhall School of Music and Drama, London and after working for the BBC, played Ophelia in *Hamlet*, Blanche in *King John* and Perdita in *A Winter's Tale* at Stratford on Avon in 1948. In 1952 she co-starred with Charles Chaplin in the film *Limelight* and was highly praised. She then concentrated on stage and was noted for moving portrayals of Shakespearian heroines. She has also acted in many films including *Look Back in Anger, Alexander the Great, The Spy Who Came in From the Cold, A Severed Head*, and in television series, *A Legacy* and *Brideshead Revisited*.

Bloomer, Amelia (née Jenks) (1818–1894). American feminist. Born at Homer, New York, she was remembered for her introduction of the 'rational' style of dressing for women – originally a loose skirt and loose trousers gathered at the ankles. This costume and its later modifications came to bear her name. She was an ardent campaigner for temperance and female suffrage.

Blow, John (1648–1708). English musician. He composed the masque *Venus and Adonis*, in which Venus was played by Mary Davies before Charles II. He also wrote anthems and songs. For a time he was organist at Westminster Abbey. One of his pupils was * Purcell.
Clarke, H. L., *John Blow: A Tercentenary Survey*. 1949

Blücher, Gebhard Leberecht von, Prince of Wahlstadt (1742–1819). Prussian general. He was born at Rostock in Mecklenburg Schwerin, joined the Swedish army in the Seven Years War (1757), but having been immediately taken prisoner by the Prussians joined the army of his captors. Having resigned in 1772 he rejoined in 1793 to oppose the French revolutionary armies. In the ensuing campaigns he gained renown as a cavalry leader. In 1806, by then a lieutenant-general, he was captured after the battle of Auerstadt, but was exchanged a fortnight later for the French general Victor. When Prussia reentered the war in 1813 he cleared Silesia and played an important part in Napoleon's decisive defeat at Leipzig. Having fought his way through northern France in 1814 he entered Paris on 31 March. When Napoleon escaped from Elba Blücher again took the field, was defeated at Ligny (16 June 1815), but was able to rally his troops and arrive at the decisive moment to complete Wellington's victory at Waterloo.

Blum, Léon (1872–1950). French lawyer and socialist politician of Jewish descent. A Deputy from 1919, he was the main architect of the Popular Front of left-wing parties, including the Communists, between the wars and was prime minister for two short periods (1936–38). For most of World War II he was interned in Germany but in 1946 was once again briefly prime minister pending the election of the first post-war president.

Blumenbach, Johann Friedrich (1752–1840). German physiologist. One of the founders of physical anthropology and comparative anatomy, on the basis of measuring cranial angles and capacity he proposed the division of *homo sapiens* into five groups: Caucasian, Mongolian, Malayan, Ethiopian and American.

Blunden, Edmund Charles (1896–1974). English poet and critic. Author of the novel *Undertones of War* (1928), based on his experiences in the Royal Sussex Regiment in World War I, his poetry, at first mainly pastoral, was issued in collected editions in 1930 and 1940. He also wrote an excellent biography of Leigh Hunt and discovered and issued hitherto unpublished works of John Clare. He was professor of English literature at Tokyo (1924–27) and was appointed emeritus professor of English at the University of Hong Kong in 1953 and elected professor of poetry at Oxford in 1966.
Hardie, A. M., *Blunden*. 1958; Thorpe, M., *The Poetry of Blunden*. 1971

Blunt, Wilfred Scawen (1840–1922). English poet and traveller. He served in the diplomatic service (1859–70) but it is as a romantic figure that his memory survives: travelling in the Middle East, espousing the cause of Egyptian, Indian or Irish nationalism and writing passionate political verse or tender love poems. He married a granddaughter of Byron (Baroness Wentworth). His *Diaries* appeared in 1922.
Lytton, E., *Wilfred Scawen Blunt: A Memoir*. 1961

Boabdil (Abu Abdullah) (died *c.* 1533). The last ruler of the Moorish kingdom of Granada in Spain before its capture (1492) by the troops of Ferdinand and Isabella.

Boadicea (or Boudicca) (died 62). Queen of the Iceni, a British tribe in East Anglia. On her husband's death (*c.* 60) her territory was occupied by the Romans and, so it was said, her daughters ravished. In revenge she gathered an army, destroyed the Roman camp at Colchester and took St Albans and London before being defeated by the Roman governor, Suetonius Paulinus. She then committed suicide to avoid capture.
Dundley, D. R. and Webster, G., *The Rebellion of Boudicca*. 1962

Boccaccio, Giovanni (1313–1375). Italian poet and author of the *Decameron*, the famous collection of amusing amatory and sometimes bawdy tales. The illegitimate son of a Florentine merchant, Boccaccio was sent for further study to Naples, where he began his literary career. The prose-work *Il Filicolo* was followed by the verse romances *Filostrato* and *Teseida* (on the legends of Theseus, Palamon and Arcite), on which Chaucer based his *Troilus and Criseyde* and his *Knight's Tale* respectively. It was in Naples, too, that he fell in love with Maria d'Aquino, an illegitimate daughter of King Robert. The title of his novel *Faimetta* hides her identity. News of his father's threatened ruin brought him back to Florence in 1340 and there he became close friends with * Petrarch and * Dante, whose biography he wrote and whose poetry he expounded in his later years. The stories of the *Decameron* (finished in 1358) were ostensibly told by a group of young Florentines sheltering in the country during the plague of 1348. Apart from its intrinsic interest, the *Decameron* was a stylistic model for future Italian writing, a source for countless other European writers, and a milestone in European literature, representing as it does a move towards realism and wholeheartedly secular themes. Boccaccio was restrained by Petrarch in 1362 from destroying his works during a spiritual crisis but thenceforward limited his writing mainly to works of learning.
MacManus, F., *Boccaccio*. 1947

Boccherini, Luigi (1743–1805). Italian composer of chamber music. He was born in Lucca, studied in Rome and later obtained positions at the Spanish and Prussian courts. He was extraordinarily prolific, writing several hundred string quartets and quintets. One, his Quintet Op. 13 No. 4, remains well known.
Rothschild, G. de, *Luigi Boccherini*. 1965

Bodin, Jean (*c.* 1530–1596). French political philosopher. Trained as a lawyer and appointed king's attorney by Henry III, he accompanied the Duke of Alençon on his journey to England to request Elizabeth I's hand in marriage. His books reveal views in advance of his time. In one, *Les six livres de la république* (1576), he introduces the idea of progress in history and anticipates * Hobbes in his statement of the need for a monarchy limited only by the laws of God and nature.

His economic theories called in question much of the mercantilist doctrine.
Franklin, J. H., *Jean Bodin and the Rise of Absolutist Theory*. 1973

Bodley, Sir Thomas (1545–1613). English bibliophile. Born in Exeter and brought up in Geneva, he became a fellow of Merton College, Oxford. On retirement from diplomatic work, which took him on several missions abroad, he offered to restore and re-equip Duke Humphrey of Gloucester's library at Oxford University. The change of name to the Bodleian Library is evidence of his enthusiasm for the task, in carrying out which he bought books all over Europe. He increased his benefaction by endowment and bequeathed the rest of his fortune to the University.

Boece, Hector (*c.* 1465–1536). Scottish historian. Born at Dundee, he completed his education at Paris University, where he met Erasmus and other humanist scholars. He was chosen (*c.* 1500) to preside over the new university at Aberdeen. His vast and famous *History of Scotland* (written in Latin) appeared in 1527. Though it harbours a fair amount of fiction, the author makes some attempt to apply critical standards.

Boehme, Jakob (1575–1624). German mystic, born in Lusatia of peasant parents. He became a cobbler, but spent much of his time in meditation and profound biblical study. His major works are *Aurora, De signatura rerum* and *Mysterium magnum*. In his theory, obscured by cloudy mystical language, all things come into existence by the separation of the original oneness, which is God, the nothing and the all, into discrete elements. Evil, in nature or in man, results from the efforts of single elements to become the whole. Boehme's works were studied in Holland and England (e.g. by Isaac * Newton) as well as in Germany, and interest in his work was revived in the 19th century, e.g. by * Schelling, * Hegel and * Schopenhauer.
Grunsky, H., *Jacob Boehme*. 1956

Boeing, William Edward (1881–1956). US industrialist. A timber merchant in Seattle, he became an airmail contracter between Seattle and British Columbia and founded the Boeing Airplane Co. in 1917. He retired before the planes bearing his name—e.g. B-17 (Flying Fortress) and B-29 (Super Fortress)—became famous.

Boerhaave, Herman (1668–1738). Dutch physician. At Leiden University he studied the whole range of natural sciences, but then specialized in medicine, taking the chair of medicine and botany in 1709. He was additionally made professor of physics in 1714 and professor of chemistry in 1718. He was easily the most prestigious medical and chemical teacher of the eighteenth century, and drew legions of students. The substance of his medical lectures appeared as the *Institutiones medicae* (1708), but his most important work was his *Elementae chemiae* (1732). Brought up in the rationalist tradition of * Descartes, Boerhaave was influential in introducing the English science of * Boyle and * Newton to the Continent. He accepted a corpuscular view of matter, and was deeply committed to the ideal of extensive experimentation, and strict quantification. The core of his system of medical ideas remained the mechanical theories of the seventeenth century, with their emphasis upon the body as a system of hydraulics, pumps, physical pressures and devices such as levers and valves. But the nature of vital heat also preoccupied him, and his teachings on the nervous system look forward to the physiology developed by scientists like * Haller later in the century.
King, L. S., *The medical world of the eighteenth century*. 1958

Boethius, Anicius Manlius Severinus (480–525). Roman theologian and philosopher. Born into one of the more eminent families of the Roman aristocracy, not much is known of his life before his imprisonment in 522 and his execution, on a false charge of treason, in 525. Boethius wrote extensively upon the *corpus* of Classical Greek texts, producing translations, commentaries, and fresh treatises in their own right. He was interested in * Aristotle's logical writings, and was a student of the Neo-Platonists. Most of his writings seem to be didactic in intention, and it is possible that he aimed to provide an encyclopaedic coverage of traditional learning. Boethius produced two works of philosophical theology, on the Trinity, and on the nature of Christ. He used Greek logic to overcome the apparent paradox of the Trinity in which three persons were also one. Easily his most famous work is the *Consolation of Philosophy* written while in prison. This sets out, within a Neo-Platonic context, to prove that unaided reason can have certainty about the existence of an omnipotent God. He seeks to show that human free will is not incompatible with Divine foresight. It was one of the most popular books in the Middle Ages, and was translated into almost all the European languages. His treatise *De Musica* was also for many centuries an authoritative work.

Barret, H. M., *Boethius: Some Aspects of his Times and Work* (1940)

Bogart, Humphrey (de Forest) (1899–1957). American film and stage actor. His first big success came, after several years of playing minor parts, when he acted with Leslie Howard and Bette Davis as the gangster in *The Petrified Forest* (1934). This led to a long series of tough dramatic and romantic parts in such well known films as *Casablanca, The Maltese Falcon, The Big Sleep, The Treasure of Sierra Madre, The African Queen, The Caine Mutiny, Sabrina Fair* etc. In 1947 he married the actress Lauren Bacall.

Bohr, Niels Henrik David (1885–1962). Danish physicist. He studied at Cambridge and was lecturer in physics at Manchester University (1914–16), where he worked with * Rutherford. In 1916 he became professor of physics at the University of Copenhagen, transfering to the Institute for Theoretical Physics when this was founded in Copenhagen (1922). During World War II he escaped dramatically from Denmark and worked in the USA on the research that led to the atom bomb. Bohr also helped to develop the quantum theory, applying it to the theory of atomic structure (1913), and he put forward the first theory of nuclear structure (1936). He won the Nobel Prize for Physics (1922). His son, **Aage Bohr** (1922–   ), was director of the Niels Bohr Institute for Theoretical Physics in Copenhagen and shared the 1975 Nobel Prize for Physics for work on investigating motion inside nuclei.

Moore, R. E., *Niels Bohr: The Man and the Scientist*. 1967

Boileau, Nicolas (1636–1711). French poet and critic. In his satires and burlesques he gives a realistic first-hand portrayal of bourgeois life in the reign of Louis XIV. He was the friend of many well known writers and especially of * Racine, with whom he shared the honour of being made historiographer royal. His verse treatise *L'Art poétique* (1674) won great contemporary esteem for its statement of classical literary principles. He was renowned in his lifetime as the 'law-giver of Parnassus', but his reputation did not survive the era of Romanticism, to which his views were anathema.

Brody, J., *Boileau and Longinus*. 1958

Boito, Arrigo (1842–1918). Italian poet and composer, born in Padua. He studied in Milan. He composed his first important opera, *Mefistofele*, in 1868. Among the libretti he wrote were those for Verdi's *Otello* and *Falstaff*.

Boleyn, Anne *see* **Anne Boleyn**

Bolingbroke, Henry St John, 1st Viscount (1678–1751). English Tory politician. Entering parliament in 1701 as member for the family borough of Wootton Bassett, Wiltshire, he attached himself to Robert * Harley and intrigued skilfully for the Tory cause. In the Tory ministry which began in 1710 he became a secretary of state and conducted the negotiations which led to the Treaty of Utrecht (1713). He became Viscount Bolingbroke in 1712 and, as Harley's power declined, rose to leadership. He had tried secretly to secure the succession of the Old Pretender (James III) and had openly dismissed Whig officers, replacing them with Tories. When George I became king on the death of Queen Anne, he fled to Paris, where he helped to plan the Jacobite rising of 1715. In 1723 he was allowed to return. * Walpole denied him the right to sit in the House of Lords, but Bolingbroke led the opposition to him, particularly with the brilliant letters published in the *Craftsman*. In his later years he wrote the *Idea of a Patriot King* (1749), in which he envisaged the king standing above and removed from party faction and serving the interests of the nation as a whole. George III's attempt to put these ideas into practice disastrously failed. Bolingbroke is remembered as a brilliant orator, a profligate, and a skilful if unscrupulous intriguer and propagandist.

Dickinson, H. T., *Bolingbroke*. 1970

Bolívar, Simón (1783–1830). South American revolutionary soldier, known as 'the Liberator'. He was born in Caracas of an ancient Basque family which had lived in Venezuela for 200 years. A tour of Europe during the early years of Napoleon's power awakened a mind already inspired by the writings of * Voltaire and * Rousseau to an interest in public affairs. It is said that it was in Rome (1805) that he determined to liberate South America from Spanish domination. He took part, under Miranda's leadership, in the formation of the first Venezuelan republic and when that was overthrown was allowed to leave the country unharmed. Eventually in New Granada (Colombia) he was in 1813 put in command of a force of 600 men and defeated the isolated Spanish detachments one by one to reoccupy Venezuela's capital at Caracas. But again the Spaniards rallied and restored the situation. Undismayed Bolívar collected a new army, secured Angostura in 1816 and by a daring winter march over the Andes drove the Spanish viceroy from Bogota (Colombia). Venezuela was finally gained after the battle of Carabobo in 1821: the liberation of Ecuador followed almost at once. This was linked with the republic of Great Colombia (Colombia and Venezuela), already formed under Bolívar's presidency. Meanwhile General José de * San Martin had liberated the South with Chile and had entered Peru, which was Bolívar's next objective, but all possibility of clash was avoided by San Martin's unselfish resignation in Bolívar's favour. Victories at Junin (August 1824) and the final triumph of Ayacucho (December) ended Spain's era of domination, and Upper Peru was named Bolivia in honour of its liberator. But faction and jealousy prevented his dream of a South American federation and the same influences turned against himself so that he was forced to resort to dictatorial methods which provoked hatred. He resigned from the presidency shortly before his death. But time has reinstated him as the greatest of South American heroes.

Masur, G., *Simón Bolívar*. 1969; Bushnell, D., *The Liberator: Simón Bolívar*. 1970

Böll, Heinrich Theodor (1917–1985). German novelist, born in Cologne. He served in the German forces during World War II and became a full-time writer in 1947. His works, pre-occupied with the implications of German war guilt, attack all forms of authoritarianism and bureaucracy and include *The Unguarded House* (1954), *Billiards at Half-Past Nine* (1961), *The Clowns* (1963), *Group Portrait of a Lady* (1973) and *The Lost Honour of Katharina Blum* (1974). He received the 1972 Nobel Prize for Literature, and was President of International PEN, 1971–74.

Reid, J. H., *Heinrich Böll*. 1973

Bolt, Robert Oxton (1924–). English dramatist (formerly schoolmaster), born in Manchester. Educated at Manchester Grammar School and Manchester University. *Flowering Cherry* (1957) was his first play to meet with success, a 'Chekhovian study of failure and self-deception'. His third and greatest play *A Man for All Seasons* (1960) was also made into a film (1966). Other plays include *The Tiger and the Horse* (1960), *Gentle Jack* (1963), *Vivat! Vivat! Regina!* (1970). He is also a talented scriptwriter of such films as *Lawrence of Arabia, Doctor Zhivago, Ryan's Daughter* and *Lady Caroline Lamb* (which he directed).

Boltzmann, Ludwig Eduard (1844–1906). Austrian physicist, born in Vienna. He taught at Graz, Vienna, Munich and Leipzig, worked (independently from * Maxwell) on the kinetic theory of gases and devised the 'Boltzmann constant' (the ratio of the mean total energy of a molecule to its absolute temperature). He modified the second law of thermodynamics to introduce the concept of probability: this led to statistical mechanics. Boltzmann hanged himself.

Bonaparte (Buonaparte). A family which migrated from Italy to Corsica in the 16th century and was made famous by * Napoleon I. His father, **Carlo Buonaparte** (1746–1785), was a lawyer, his mother, Letizia Ramolino (1750–1836), came of an old Corsican family: she was the **Madame Mère** of imperial history, a strong personality in her own right, who, however, eschewed political power. The fortunes of her other children were dependent upon their famous brother. **Joseph** (1768–1844), who married Julie Clary (* Bernadotte), was made king of Naples in 1806 and transferred to the throne of Spain in 1808. He was a competent administrator but the Peninsular War prevented effective rule. He abdicated in 1813. After Waterloo he farmed in the U.S.A. until 1832 and finally settled in Florence. **Lucien** (1775–1840) played a decisive part in the *coup d'état* which brought Napoleon to power. A republican by conviction he dissociated himself from his brother's policies but gained a large fortune by speculation. He was captured by the English army on the way to America in 1810 and imprisoned for the rest of the war. **Louis** (1778–1846), King of Holland (1806–10), was the father of Napoleon II (* Duke of Reichstadt). The youngest of the brothers, **Jerome** (1784–1860), married Elizabeth Patterson while in America as a young man. Later, as King of Westphalia (1806–13), he was forced to marry Princess Catherine of Württemberg, and it was their descendants who maintained the Bonapartist claims. Jerome returned to influence and office under his nephew Napoleon III. Of the sisters of this imperial brotherhood, **Eliza** (1777–1820) became Grand Duchess of Tuscany; the fascinating, frivolous **Pauline** (1780–1825) became by her second marriage Princess Borghese; **Caroline** (1782–1839) married Murat, Napoleon's dashing cavalry general who became king of Naples.

Markham, F., *The Bonapartes*. 1975

Bonaventura, St (John of Fidenza) (1221–1274). Italian theologian, born near Orvieto. He studied in Paris and entered (1243) the Franciscan order of friars of which he finally became general (1256). In 1274 he was appointed cardinal and bishop of Albano. He died during the Council of Lyons, and was canonized in 1482. His mystical philosophy earned him the name 'seraphic doctor'. As general he did much by tact and personality to reconcile the differences between those who demanded strict adherence to the order of absolute poverty laid down by St Francis and those who pointed out the impracticability of such rigour, as well as the evils of mendicancy. Bonaventura adopted a middle way: he enjoined the strictest simplicity of life but allowed certain departures from the letter of the rule, e.g. by defending the friars' right to receive offerings. In disputes between friars and regular clergy he strongly defended the friars' rights, e.g., to hear confession and preach without clerical permission. Bonaventura's theological writings remain important.

Bondfield, Margaret Grace (1873–1953). British Labour politician. She became an organiser with the shop assistants' union, was a Member of Parliament 1923–24 and 1926–31 and the first British woman cabinet member as Minister of Labour 1929–31. She became a privy counsellor (1929) and a Companion of Honour (1948).

Bonham-Carter, Lady Violet, Baroness Asquith of Yarnbury (1887–1969). British politician, daughter of Lord Oxford and * Asquith and wife of Sir Maurice Bonham-Carter. In 1945 and 1951 she stood unsuccessfully for Parliament as a Liberal candidate and was prominent in Liberal politics throughout her life. She was created a D.B.E. in 1953 and a life peer in 1964. She wrote the highly successful *Winston Churchill as I Knew Him* (1965) and other memoirs.

Bonhoeffer, Dietrich (1906–1945). German Protestant pastor and theologian. Born in Breslau, Prussia (now Wroclaw, Poland). He studied at the universities of Tübingen, Rome and Berlin (1923–27) and was then ordained a Lutheran minister.

After working in Barcelona, New York and Britain, he became a lecturer at the University of Berlin in 1931, and from 1933 spoke for the German Protestant opposition to the Nazis. He left Germany in 1933 but returned in 1935 as head of the seminary at Finkenwalk, and as a member of the Military Intelligence Department worked secretly with the resistance, for which he was sent to Buchenwald where he spent 2 years before his execution in 1945. A radical theologian, he rejected much of the apparatus of traditional Christianity. His published works include *Letters and Papers from Prison*, 1953 and *Act and Being*, 1962.

Bethge, E., *Dietrich Bonhoeffer*. 1970

Boniface, St (*c.* 675–754). The 'apostle of Germany'. His original name was Wynfrith and he was born in Anglo-Saxon England, in Wessex, and was educated in Benedictine monasteries at Exeter and Nursling, becoming abbot of the latter in 717. A preliminary missionary journey had failed but in 718 he went to Rome and was commissioned by Pope Gregory II to resume his task of converting the heathen. His method was to follow up his preaching by building churches and monasteries and planting little colonies of monks and nuns. Successes in Hesse and Thuringia led to his appointment as bishop of a new German church east of the Rhine, which, having become an archbishop (*c.* 732), he divided into the dioceses of Salzburg, Freising, Regensburg and Passau. Reorganization of the Frankish church followed and he is reputed to have

anointed * Pepin as king. In 753 Boniface resumed his missionary work in Friesland, but in the following year he and fifty of his followers were killed in a pagan attack. He was buried at Fulda abbey in Hesse, a future centre of learning which he had founded. His feast day is 5 June.
Reuter, T. A. (ed.), *The Greatest Englishman*. 1980

Boniface VIII (Benedetto Caetani) (1235–1303). Pope (from 1294). Trained in law and experienced in papal diplomacy he succeeded Celestine V, whose resignation he helped to bring about. Despite his ability and energy he failed to maintain the temporal supremacy of the papacy against Edward I of England and Philip IV of France.

Bonington, Richard Parkes (1801–1828). English painter in France. He grew up in France, devoted himself to water colours until 1824, then turned to oils. A friend of * Delacroix, he greatly admired * Constable and his seascapes, landscapes and travel scenes were popular in London and Paris.

Bonnard, Pierre (1867–1947). French painter. From about 1890 to 1899 he belonged with Vuillard and others to a Symbolist group of Post-impressionist painters called the 'Nabis' (after a Hebrew word for prophet), of which * Gauguin was the main inspirer. Bonnard's particular circle were known as 'Intimists'. After 1900 Bonnard developed an individual style, not working, like the Impressionists, direct from nature but from memory. Subtle light and colour effects provide the main theme of subjects such as landscapes, gardens, sailing boats, and nudes in various outdoor and indoor settings.
Ferminger, A., *Pierre Bonnard*. 1969

Bonnet, Georges (1889–1973). French Radical politician. He served as a deputy 1924–40 and 1956–68. As foreign minister 1938–39, he took part in the Munich conference and was a strong supporter of 'appeasement'.

Boole, George (1815–1864). English mathematician and logician. The son of a shoemaker, he was largely self-educated, became a school-teacher and professor of mathematics at Queen's College, Cork 1849–64. Boole pioneered modern symbolic logic and his 'algebra of logic' is one of the basic principles used in modern computer design, especially in 'binary switching', where quantities can be expressed by using only two symbols (0 and 1). 'Binary logic' led to the creation of the NOT, AND and OR gates in computers.

Boone, Daniel (1735–1820). American pioneer. He was born in Pennsylvania but in 1750 the family moved to the frontier of North Carolina. He gained his first experiences of frontier wars as blacksmith and teamster in General Braddock's campaign of 1755, but the heroic legends that have attached themselves to his name date from when he first entered Kentucky in 1767 and subsequently colonized and opened up the country, hunting, exploring and fighting Indians the while.
Bakeless, J., *Master of the Wilderness: Daniel Boone*. 1939

Boot, Jesse, 1st Baron Trent (1850–1931). English pharmacist and manufacturer. He worked in his mother's herb shop in Nottingham from the age of 13 until 1877 when he opened his own shop. This became a limited company in 1888, which subsequently developed into a chain of chemist shops, over 1,300 in 1960. His success was due to his realization of the advantages of selling large quantities of goods at low prices. His gifts and bequests to Nottingham were worth nearly £2m. and included a 150 acre park and land and buildings for the university. He was created a peer in 1929.

Booth, John Wilkes (1838–1865). The unstable American actor who assassinated President Lincoln at Ford's Theater, Washington. He regarded it as an act of revenge for the Confederate cause, which he had taken deeply to heart. He escaped to Virginia, where he was shot by troops.

His father, **Junius Brutus Booth** (1796–1852), was an actor who, having made successes in Shakespearian parts, especially Richard III, emigrated to America in 1821 and there enjoyed a successful career, but owing to alcoholism and melancholia died insane.

Edwin Thomas Booth (1833–1893), the assassin's brother, acted with his father for some years. The success of his Hamlet in New York in 1864 marked him out as one of the foremost actors of the day. During a European tour (1880–82) his Othello, played

to Irving's Iago, was enthusiastically received.
Stern, P. van D., *The Man who Killed Lincoln.* 1939

Booth, William (1829–1912). English-born founder of the Salvation Army. Born in Nottingham, he was an evangelist with the Methodist New Connexion for many years. Having left them to act independently, he founded, in 1865, a mission in Whitechapel, London, which proved to be the forerunner of the Salvation Army, established in 1878. In this he introduced military methods, uniform and discipline into evangelizing work, 'General' Booth himself being in supreme command. The organization, which spread over the world, became known for the rousing music of its open-air services, its shelters for the down-and-out and the courage with which its members penetrated the most degraded districts of the great cities. Booth's son, **Bramwell,** and his daughter, **Evangeline,** were among his successors (1912–29 and 1934–39 respectively).
Collier, R., *The General next to God.* 1965

Borden, Lizzie Andrew (1860–1927). 'Heroine' of one of the most famous of American trials and of a rhyme commemorating it. In 1892 her stepmother and father were hacked to death with an axe at their home at Fall River, Massachusetts; she was tried for their murder and acquitted.

Borden, Sir Robert Laird (1854–1937). Canadian politician. He was born in Nova Scotia and became prominent as a lawyer before his election to the Canadian parliament in 1896. By 1901 he was leader of the Conservative party. He won the election of 1911, and as prime minister guided the country through World War I. By insisting upon Canada's signing the treaty of Versailles separately from Great Britain he confirmed its status as a sovereign independent state. He resigned in 1920.
Wilson, H. A., *The Imperial Policy of Sir Robert Borden.* 1966

Bordet, Jules (1870–1961). Belgian bacteriologist. He won the Nobel Prize for Medicine (1919) for discovering the bacillus of whooping cough.

Borelli, Giovanni Alfonso (1608–1679). Italian scientist. In his early career he was chiefly a mathematician, becoming professor of mathematics at Messina in 1640 and professor at Pisa in 1656. He examined the mechanical basis of respiration, circulation, nerves, and above all muscular activities. He closely studied the processes whereby the brain communicated physical impulses to muscles *via* the nervous system, and tried to calculate the quantity of force involved. He was interested in the physical force required to pump blood round the body, and studied digestive processes (which he believed were chiefly mechanical rather than chemical). He made accurate observations of Jupiter's satellites and studied volcanic eruptions on Etna.

Borges, Jorge Luis (1899–). Argentinian poet, critic, short story writer and essayist, born in Buenos Aires. Regarded as the most important modern Latin American writer, educated in Switzerland, he lived for a time in Spain where he became associated with the *ultraísmo* movement in poetry, which he brought back with him to Argentina. His volumes of poetry include *Ferver de Buenos Aires* (1923) and *Luna de enfrente* (1925). His tales, revealing a baroque imagination, a taste for the arcane and an interest in metaphysical problems, appear in such collections as *Ficciones* (1944). Other important works include *El Aleph* (1949), *Extraordinary Tales* (1955), *Labyrinths* (1962) and *The Book of Imaginary Beings* (1967).

Borghese. A famous Italian family. **Camillo Borghese** became Pope Paul V (1605–1621), for whose nephew, Cardinal Scipione Borghese, the Villa Borghese (rebuilt 1782 and later known as the Villa Umberto I) was built at the beginning of the 17th century to house his treasures. The existing collection (now state property) was mainly brought together by **Prince Camillo Borghese** (1775–1832), husband of Napoleon's sister, Pauline. The Borghese palace is one of the most magnificent in Rome.

Borgia, Cesare (1476–1507). Son of Pope * Alexander VI. As a youth he was made a cardinal by his father but he gave up the office five years later. A mission to France in 1498 carrying papal dispensation for Louis XII to marry Anne of Brittany was rewarded with the duchy of Valentinois and the promise of help in the Romagna, which it was Alexander VI's policy to unite and rule. This aim was achieved

by Cesare in three campaigns in which guile and military skill were artfully combined. His father's death in 1503 caught him ill and unprepared to meet his enemies. Arrested in Neapolitan territory he escaped from a prison to die fighting at last in the cause of his brother-in-law, the king of Navarre. His political tactics – often treacherous – were described with admiration in Machiavelli's *The Prince*.
Sacerdote, G., *Cesare Borgia*. 1950

Borgia, Lucrezia, Duchess of Ferrara (1480–1519). Italian noblewoman. Born in Rome, daughter of the Spanish cardinal Rodrigo Borgia, later Pope Alexander VI, and sister of Cesare, she married first Giovanni Sforza, second the Duke of Biscelgie, and third the Duke of Ferrara. She was often accused of complicity in her family's crimes and moral excesses, though there is no evidence to support her active participation. In fact, she left a reputation for learning, beauty and charity, and was said to have enjoyed the respect of her subjects. In 1501 she appeared with the mysterious Roman Infant, Giovanni, her supposed natural son; two papal bulls recognized him first as Cesare's illegitimate son, then Alexander's. The latter was probably the true father. This and Lucrezia's attendance at an infamous orgy held at the Vatican led to rumours of incest. On Alexander's death in 1503 Lucrezia ceased to be a political pawn and led a more normal life at the court of Ferrara which became a cultural centre of the Italian Renaissance.
Belonci, M., *Lucrezia Borgia*. 1939

Borg Olivier, Giorgio (1911–1980). Maltese Nationalist politician. The political history of Malta in the years preceding independence (September 1964) were largely struggles for power between Borg Olivier's party, with strong clerical backing, and Dom * Mintoff's Labour party. He was prime minister 1950–55 (under British rule) and 1962–71.

Boris I (died 907). Prince of Bulgaria (853–888), who came to be regarded as a national saint. He succeeded his father, and was baptized (865) into the Greek church, to which he confirmed his allegiance in 870, though in the intervening year he had addressed a questionnaire to Pope Nicholas II, obviously with a view to change. He abdicated in favour of his son Vladimir (888), but four years later left the monastery to which he had withdrawn to blind and depose the new king and substitute his second son, Symeon.

Boris III (1894–1943). Tsar of Bulgaria (from 1918). He succeeded his father Ferdinand, who had been forced to abdicate after World War I, and despite a strange passion for engine driving was generally regarded as a well-meaning monarch with considerable skill at balancing opposing factions. Willingly or unwillingly he became Hitler's ally in World War II but is said to have refused to send his troops against Russia. He died mysteriously after a visit to Hitler in 1943. After the Communists had seized power his son Symeon (born 1937) became heir to his dynastic claims.

Bormann, Martin (1900–?1945). Nazi leader and, after the defection of * Hess, Hitler's deputy. He was with * Hitler to the end but there is no certain evidence of his death and at Nuremburg he was tried and condemned in his absence.
Trevor-Roper, H. (ed.), *Bormann Letters*. 1954

Borodin, Alexander Porfirievich (1833–1887). Russian composer, born at St Petersburg. He first trained as a chemist and his musical studies began in 1862 under * Balakirev. His works include three symphonies (one unfinished), the unfinished opera, *Prince Igor* and *In the Steppes of Central Asia*.
Dianin, S., *Borodin*. 1963

Borotra, Jean (1898–). French tennis player known as 'the Bounding Basque'. He won the men's singles at Wimbledon in 1924 and 1926 and the men's doubles with J. Brugnon in 1932 and 1933. Borotra, Cochet and Lacoste, who dominated French lawn tennis for many years, were known as 'the Three Musketeers'.

Borromeo, St Carlo (1538–1584). Italian prelate. Born of a noble Milanese family, and a nephew of Pope Pius IV, he was made a cardinal before he was a priest. His ordination took place in 1563 and enabled him to become archbishop of the see of Milan, of which he had so far been only the administrator. Meanwhile as papal secretary of state he was attending the final sessions (1563–64) of the

Council of Trent and took the leading part in its success by formulating the decisions by which the Roman church put its house in order and was so enabled to resist the spread of Protestantism. Later in his own diocese he put the reforms into practice, himself setting an example by his austere and simple life. He was canonized in 1610. His biography was written by Pope John XXIII. A kinsman, **Federico Borromeo** (1564–1631), who was also cardinal-archbishop of Milan, founded the Ambrosian Library there.

Borrow, George (Henry) (1803–1881). English author and traveller. The son of a Cornish army captain he was educated at the Royal Grammar School, Norwich, but later spent much of the time during which he was supposed to be studying law in acquiring languages. Coming to London he helped compile the *Newgate Calendar* but soon left (1825) to take up a wandering life, either alone or with gypsies, whose manner of life he later described in *Lavengro* (1851) and *Romany Rye* (1857). Meanwhile (1832–40) he was working and travelling for the British and Foreign Bible Society in Russia and Spain. *The Bible in Spain* (1843) describes experiences in the latter country, and Spanish gypsies are the theme of *The Zincali* (1841). *Wild Wales* appeared in 1862 and in 1874 *Romano Lavo-Lil*, a much criticized book on the gypsy language.
Myers, R. R., *George Borrow*. 1966

Bosanquet, Bernard (1848–1923). English philosopher, born near Alnwick, Northumberland. As a fellow of University College he taught philosophy at Oxford until (1880) an inheritance enabled him to live in London, where he combined writing with charitable work. For a few years (1903–08) he was a professor at St Andrews. His works cover a wide field but he is now best known for his *Logic: or the Morphology of Knowledge* (1888), setting out his theories of 'philosophic logic' based on the idea that if a universal essence could be logically analysed from all objects known to the various sciences a philosophy would result. He is generally considered to be 'the last great representative of British Hegelianism'.

Boscawen, Edward (1711–1761). British admiral. Known as 'Old Dreadnought' for his grit and courage, he was the third son of Viscount Falmouth and played a leading part in many engagements during the War of Austrian Succession and the Seven Years War: in 1757 he was second-in-command to Lord * Hawke, whom he later succeeded in command of the Channel fleet. In August 1759, as his career approached its end, he took five French ships in the Bay of Lagos.

Bosch, Hieronymus (originally van Aeken) (*c.* 1450–1516). Dutch painter, born probably at 's Hertogenbosch, where he spent his life and whence he took his adopted name. His paintings, strongly imbued with the fantastic and full of bizarre composite figures and grotesques, are perhaps the most extreme expression of the haunted mood of the late Middle Ages; the significance of his symbolism is now largely lost. Among the best known of his works are the *Seven Deadly Sins, The Hay Wain, The Earthly Paradise* and *The Temptation of St Anthony*. He was regarded by the Surrealists as an important precursor. His earlier work (e.g. *The Adoration of the Kings*) follows the tradition of Flemish religious art.
Combe, J., *Bosch*. 1957

Bose, Subhas Chandra (1897–1945). Indian nationalist leader. He opposed Gandhi's policy of non-violent resistance to the British. In World War II he escaped to Germany and later became head of a provisional government of India under Japanese sponsorship. He is said to have met his death in an air crash.

Bossuet, Jacques Bénigne (1627–1704). French prelate and historian. Born at Dijon, he showed his remarkable precocity by taking the tonsure as a small boy and at the age of 15 preaching in Madame de Rambouillet's Paris salon 'until nearly midnight'. His fame as a preacher steadily increased and his many famous orations included one at the funeral (1669) of Charles I's widow, Henrietta Maria. In 1670, the year in which he became bishop of Condom, he was appointed tutor to the dauphin, a position, held for ten years, which gave him great influence at court. For him he wrote his history of ancient peoples, *Discours sur l'histoire universelle* (1681). In 1681 he became bishop of Meaux. He did not dissent from the revocation (1685) of the edict of Nantes but did his best to mitigate its effects and bring Huguenots back to Catholicism. He obtained Rome's condemnation of * Fénelon's doctrine of quietism (interior inspiration).
Calvet, J., *Bossuet*. 1968

Boswell, James (1740–1795). Scottish author and biographer of Samuel * Johnson. The son of Lord Auchinleck, a judge, he was called to the bar but found his main interest in literature. In 1760 he went to London and lived as a conscious libertine. In 1763 he first met Dr Johnson, and until the latter died in 1784 he took notes of the conversations and opinions of the famous lexicographer. Between 1764 and 1766 he toured the continent, introduced himself to * Voltaire and * Rousseau and had numerous love affairs. His *Account of Corsica* (1768) commemorated a visit to the island hero Pasquale de * Paoli. In 1773 he took Johnson on the journey to the Hebrides immortalized in *Journal of a Tour of the Hebrides* (1785). In 1791 he published the *Life of Samuel Johnson*, which has become the most famous biography in the English language; it was the product of careful research as well as eyewitness – it has been calculated that Boswell met Johnson on 276 occasions. In recent years Boswell's private papers and journals have been discovered, assembled, and published by Yale University. His letters to his great friend William Johnson Temple are also a rich mine of biographical detail covering nearly forty years.
Pottle, F. A., *The Literary Career of James Boswell*. 1966; *James Boswell, the Earlier Years*. 1966

Botha, Louis (1862–1919). South African general and politician, born in Natal. Though an opponent of * Kruger's Uitlander policies he joined the Transvaal forces as a volunteer in the Boer War, and it was he who captured Winston * Churchill. Later, having been given command, he defeated the British at Colenso and Spion Kop. After the peace of Vereeniging (1902) he bore no bitterness and when Transvaal was given a constitution in 1906 he became first prime minister, as he also was of the Union of South Africa when it was formed in 1910. Throughout his premiership, which lasted until his death, his main object was to bring about harmony between South Africans of British and Dutch descent. Thus when war broke out in 1914 he immediately brought in South Africa on the side of the British, defeated a rebellion of extremists under De Wet and led the troops who in 1915 conquered German South West Africa.

Botha, Pieter Willem (1916–). South African Nationalist politician. He served as minister of defence (1965–78) and succeeded B. J. * Vorster as prime minister of South Africa 1978–84. He became the first executive state president under the new constitution 1984–.

Bothwell, James Hepburn, 4th Earl of (*c.* 1535–1578). Scottish nobleman. After the murder of Rizzio (1566), he became one of the chief advisers of Mary Queen of Scots, who had probably first met him when he came to France on a mission to ask help for her mother and regent, Mary of Guise, widow of James V. When Darnley, the Queen's second husband, was killed in an explosion (1567), Bothwell was charged with the murder and acquitted, although most historians believe him to have been guilty (and probably Queen Mary also). Bothwell then abducted the queen (almost certainly with her connivance) and married her, after divorcing his wife. The nobles rose in revolt, and the queen was captured and deposed. Bothwell escaped to Norway; he later became the prisoner of the king of Denmark and died in captivity, insane. The popular belief that Bothwell was a boorish, unmannered brute is not borne out by fact; he was reckless, pitiless and unscrupulous but he had the graces of a courtier and was fond of poetry as well as of dancing and dress.
Gore-Brown, R., *Lord Bothwell*. 1937

Botticelli, Sandro (Alessandro di Mariano dei Filipepi) (*c.* 1445–1510). Florentine painter. A pupil of Fra Filippo Lippi, he was patronized by the Medici family. His early works (e.g. his *Birth of Venus, Primavera* and *Mars and Venus*) have a great delicacy, freshness and poignancy coupled with a rare linear subtlety of design; the iconography of the major mythological pieces is highly complex. Although a product of Renaissance humanism as regards content, his painting represents, in its essentially linear manner, the persistence of a 'Gothic' tradition which was in slightly archaic contrast to the strongly plastic High Renaissance style evolved by Leonardo, Raphael and Michelangelo, and he declined in popularity after about 1500. Most of his work was done in Florence but in 1481 he was in Rome helping to decorate the Sistine Chapel for Pope Sixtus IV. After 1497 he became a follower of Savonarola and most of his later works are religious, ecstatic and anti-naturalistic, like *The Adoration of the Magi*

and *The Coronation of the Virgin.* He also illustrated Dante's *Divine Comedy* with sensitive outline drawings (1492–97). His work was much loved (and extensively forged) in the 19th century.
Argan, G. C., *Botticelli.* 1957

Bottomley, Gordon (1874–1948). English 'Georgian' poet. Much of his reputation rested on plays such as *King Lear's Wife* (1915), *Gruach and Britain's Daughter* (1921). *Poems of Thirty Years* (1925) contains the best of his work.

Bottomley, Horatio William (1860–1933). English journalist and criminal. He was editor of the *Financial Times* (1898–1900), but his most conspicuous journalistic achievement was the creating and editing of the vigorously sensational *John Bull*, which made itself loved and feared in defence of private rights and the exposure of alleged public wrongs. Throughout his career he found himself constantly in the courts, usually defending his activities in the promotion of dubious companies or suing his detractors for libel. He conducted his own cases so successfully that he began to think of himself as being above the law. Despite bankruptcies he contrived to live like a prince. He was an independent M.P. for South Hackney 1906–12 and, helped by the popularity engendered by his speeches during World War I, was again elected in 1918. His downfall came soon afterwards when an elaborate scheme launched through *John Bull* for attracting investment in government bonds was exposed as a fraud designed to divert much of the money to his own use. In 1922 he received a seven-year sentence.

Botvinnik, Mikhail (1911–). Russian chess player. He was world champion 1948–57; 1958–60; 1961–63.

Boucher, François (1703–1770). French artist. The most typical of the rococo decorators, he was a protégé of Madame de Pompadour (Louis XV's favourite) and was noted for tapestry designs, panelled interiors and gay, slightly improper mythological paintings. Fine examples of his work can be seen in the Wallace Collection, London.

Boucher de Perthes, Jacques (1788–1868). French prehistorian. He was a customs official at Abbeville who became an amateur archaeologist and was one of the first to declare that man had existed in the Pleistocene epoch. In 1837 he began collecting roughly worked flints in the Somme gravels and declared them to be of 'antediluvian' origin because of their association with extinct Ice-age animals. At first his theories were received with scepticism, but they began to win acceptance after John Evans pronounced in their favour before the Royal Society in 1859.

Bougainville, Louis Antoine de (1729–1811). French navigator and scientist. After the end of the Seven Years War, during which he served with Montcalm in Canada, he joined the navy and established a French colony in the Falkland Islands. He sailed round the world (1766–79) and rediscovered the Solomon Islands, one of which is named after him. He served with distinction in the War of American Independence but then occupied himself entirely with science. Bougainville was an expert mathematician and a friend of * Diderot and * Rousseau. His membership of the Légion d'honneur was one of several distinctions conferred on him by Napoleon.

Boughton, Rutland (1878–1960). English composer. He is remembered chiefly for his opera *The Immortal Hour* (1916), which reproduced the literary mood of the 'Celtic Twilight' and was popular when produced in London. He also composed a cycle of musical dramas based on the Arthurian legends.
Hurd, M., *Rutland Boughton.* 1962

Boulanger, Georges Ernest Jean Marie (1837–1891). French general. After much service elsewhere he helped to defend Paris in the Franco-Prussian War. In 1884 he commanded in Tunisia, and was minister of war (1886–87), attaining immense popularity by his jingoistic policy and unwavering attitude to Germany over an incident involving a frontier arrest. Fears, perhaps exaggerated, of a *coup d'état*, caused the removal of his name from the army list. This enabled him to seek election. With a somewhat vague programme of parliamentary dissolution and constitutional revision he drew support not only from militarists and monarchists but also from radicals. However, the government and its supporters reacted strongly. Boulanger was defeated in the Marne election (1888) and fearing arrest for treason he went to Brussels, where after the death of his mistress he committed suicide.

The term '*boulangisme*' was later used to decry any such movement towards military dictatorship.

Boulanger, Nadia (1887–1979). French teacher, conductor, composer and pianist. She worked in France and the U.S., took a leading role in the revival of * Monteverdi and her pupils included Lennox * Berkeley, Aaron * Copland, Jean Françaix, Igor Markevitch, Dinu Lipatti and her sister Lili Boulanger (1893–1918), an able composer.

Boulez, Pierre (1925–). French composer and conductor, born in Montbrison. He studied mathematics, engineering and music at Lyons. He studied with Oliver * Messiaen (1944–45) at the Paris Conservatoire, and then under René Leibowitz. In 1947 became musical director of a theatrical company, the Marigny; in 1954 he founded the Concerts Marigny, avant-garde concerts later known as Domaine Musical. By the 1960s he had an international reputation as a composer and conductor, and in 1971 was appointed musical director of the New York Philharmonic, successor to Leonard Bernstein. His works include *Flute Sonatina* (1946); *Le Visage Nuptial* (1946–52). He was also influenced by Debussy and Stravinsky. His *Structures* (1952 and 1961) for 2 pianos were a turning point in his musical development. His work has produced interesting and sometimes violent criticism and is considered difficult to perform. His *Pli selon pli* composed between 1958 and 1962 has become a modern classic.

Boulle (or Buhl), **André Charles** (1642–1732). French cabinet-maker. His elaborate marquetried furniture was in great demand in the reign of Louis XIV. The description 'boulle' is often applied not only to his own work and that of his sons, who worked with him, but to the many imitations of later years. There are examples in the Louvre, in Windsor Castle and the Wallace Collection, London.

Boult, Sir Adrian Cedric (1889–1983). English conductor. He was born in Chester and received his musical training at Oxford and Leipzig. He conducted the Birmingham Municipal Orchestra from 1924 to 1930 but it was as conductor of the B.B.C. Symphony Orchestra (1930–50) that his name became a household word. He conducted the London Philharmonic (1950–57) and resumed his connexion with Birmingham when he became conductor of the City orchestra 1959–60.
Boult, A., *My Own Trumpet*. 1973

Boulton, Matthew (1728–1809). English engineer best known for his partnership with James * Watt for the construction of steam engines. His main interest lay in the provision of power for the factory near his birthplace, Birmingham, where a variety of metal articles, useful or artistic, were produced. Later Boulton applied steam power to the manufacture of coins. Many scientists and writers (e.g. Boswell) were among his friends. He was a founder of the Lunar Society (* Darwin, Erasmus) and an F.R.S.
Dickinson, H. W., *Matthew Boulton*.

Boumédienne, Houari (Mohammed Boukharraba) (1927–1978). Algerian politician. Born near Bône, of a poor peasant family, he became a schoolteacher. He joined the National Liberal Front (1954) and became friend and confidant of * Ben Bella whom he supported in becoming the first president of independent Algeria. In 1965 he organized a *coup* which deposed Ben Bella and he became the new president. He died in office in December 1978.

Bourbon. Name of a noble family which provided dynasties for France, Spain, Naples and Parma. The line, named after a village in central France, was founded when in 1276 Robert de Clermont, a son of King * Louis IX, married Beatrice de Bourbon. The direct line died out but the name and title passed in 1527 to Charles, Duke of Vendôme, whose son married Jeanne d'Albret, queen of Navarre; their son Henry IV became the first of the Bourbon kings. The last of the senior line was * Charles X, though Louis Philippe of a younger branch reigned from 1830 to 1848, and it is his descendants who are the present pretenders. The Spanish Bourbons replaced the Habsburgs after Charles II had died childless and left his kingdom to Louis XIV's grandson * Philip V. Members of the dynasty continued to reign until Alfonso XIII left the country in 1930. The Neapolitan Bourbons and the Parma branch stemmed from the Spanish line.

Bourgeois, Léon Victor Auguste (1851–1925). French Radical politician. He defeated * Boulanger in the Marne election of 1888 and subsequently held a long series of ministerial posts. He was prominent in the international field at The Hague conferences and in the League of Nations which he helped to found. He won the Nobel Peace Prize in 1920.

Bourget, Paul (1852–1935). French writer. His novels at first concentrated upon the psychological analysis of characters but after his conversion to Catholicism in 1901 they tended to become vehicles for the transmission of traditionalist views. *L'Etape* (1902) marks the culmination of the first period, during which his best known books include *L'Irréparable* (1884), *Un Crime d'amour* (1886) and *André Cornélis* (1887). *Le Démon de Midi* (1914) is typical of the later period.
Austin, L. J., *Paul Bourget*. 1940

Bourguiba, Habib (1903–). First president of Tunisia. The son of an officer, born and educated in Tunis and trained as a lawyer in Paris, he founded the Néo-Destour party in 1934. In 1938 he was arrested for anti-French agitation but released under the German occupation of France during World War II. After the war he continued his agitation against the French protectorate. When independence was finally gained in 1956 he was the Bey's first prime minister and himself became president after the Bey's deposition a year later. Once he had secured the evacuation of the bases at Bizerta, Bourguiba showed wisdom and moderation in his dealings with the French.

Bowen, Elizabeth Dorothea Cole (1899–1973). Anglo-Irish novelist and short-story writer. She was one of the most sensitive of modern writers to the shades of mood in people and nature. In her handling of emotional interplay she had a rare and delicate touch. Her novels include *The Death of the Heart* (1938) and *The Heat of the Day* (1949). She was created a C.B.E. in 1948.

Bowman, Sir William, 1st Bart (1816–1892). English surgeon. The son of a banker with scientific interests, he studied at King's College, London, toured European universities in 1838, and became a member of the Royal College of Surgeons in 1839. He taught anatomy at King's College, London, and became assistant surgeon at King's College Hospital, rising in 1856 to full surgeon. He was knighted in 1884. Bowman's major scientific work lay in histology, the study of minute bodily tissues, such as skin, muscle, and cartilage, by means of the microscope. His *The Physiological Anatomy and Physiology of Man* (1843) presented a wealth of careful and original studies of the structure and function of muscles, nerves and sense organs. He became an eminent practising surgeon, pioneering the use of the ophthalmoscope and adopted the operation of iridectomy in treating glaucoma. He developed the instrument – still used – for examining obstructed lacrymal ducts known as 'Bowman's Probes'. In 1880 he was founder-president of the Ophthalmological Society.

Boyce, William (1710–1779). English composer and organist, who was Master of the King's Musick from 1735 to 1779. He also wrote church music, stage music, chamber and orchestral works and several songs, including 'Hearts of Oak'. He made a compilation of church music under the title *Cathedral Music* (1760–78).

Boycott, Charles Cunningham (1832–1897). English land agent. As agent for Lord Erne in Co. Mayo, Ireland his refusal to lower rents in times of hardship was punished (1880) by complete social and business isolation. This form of intimidation, invented by the Irish Land League, came to be known as a 'boycott'.

Boyd-Orr, John Boyd Orr, 1st Baron (1880–1971). Scottish agricultural scientist and dietetic expert. Educated at Glasgow University, he was director of the Rowett Research Institute (1914–45) and discovered many of the causes (e.g. lack of minerals) of nutritional deficiency in animals and human beings: these he subsequently expounded before many national and international bodies. He was director general of the U.N. Food and Agricultural Organization (1945–48) and received the Nobel Prize for Peace in 1949, in which year he was made a peer. He became chancellor of Glasgow University in 1946.

Boyer, Charles (1899–1978). French actor, in the U.S. from 1934. He played romantic leads with such actresses as Greta Garbo, Marlene Dietrich and Ingrid Bergman, later gaining a second reputation as a skilful character actor e.g. in *Stavisky* (1972).

Boyle, Robert (1627–1691). Irish chemist: often called the father of modern chemistry. He was born at Lismore Castle, Ireland, seventh son of the 1st Earl of Cork. The description cited he owes to the fact that his career and discoveries ensured that chemistry should become a separate branch of science rather than a mere adjunct of medicine and alchemy: he was an original member of the Royal Society (founded in 1660). He was the first clearly to define an element in the terms we accept today (i.e. as a substance that cannot be split into simpler substances by chemical analysis), and explained that all matter consists of atoms or combinations of atoms in motion. His widely ranging studies included pneumatics and crystallography. He is probably best known for his statement of the law (now known as Boyle's Law) that, at constant temperature, the volume of a gas varies inversely with the pressure. He founded a series of lectures to prove the existence of God.
Maddison, R. E. W., *Life of the Honourable Robert Boyle*. 1969

Bracegirdle, Ann (*c.* 1674–1748). English actress. Renowned alike for her professional skill and her virtue. At Drury Lane she played famous Shakespearian parts (Portia, Desdemona, etc.), and created many roles for her close friend William * Congreve.

Bracken, Brendan Bracken, 1st Viscount (1901–1958). British politician. Educated at Sedbergh, he entered publishing and helped to build up the group of periodicals which centred on the *Financial News*. In 1929 he became a Conservative M.P., closely associated with Winston Churchill; he succeeded Duff Cooper as minister of information in 1941 and was briefly first lord of the admiralty in Churchill's caretaker ministry of 1945.
Boyle, A., *Poor, Dear Brendan*. 1974. Lysaght, C. E., *Brendan Bracken*. 1979

Bracton, Henry de (died 1268). English ecclesiastic and lawyer. He was an itinerant justice, who eventually became chancellor of Exeter Cathedral, but his fame arises from his great treatise *On the Laws and Customs of England*, the first printed edition of which appeared in 1569.

Bradlaugh, Charles (1833–1891). English radical politician. After a legal training he wrote, under the pen-name 'Iconoclast', many propagandist pamphlets in favour of republicanism and freedom of thought, but is best remembered for the incidents that followed his election as M.P. for Northampton in 1880, when he asked, as a free-thinker, to make affirmation of allegiance instead of taking the oath. This was refused and he agreed to take the oath, questioning its validity in a letter to *The Times*. Because of this the oath was refused him, but he was allowed to affirm and took his seat. A common informer, Henry Clarke, however, invoked the penalties for voting without taking the oath, and Bradlaugh was expelled from the House. Each session thereafter he administered the oath to himself but was not allowed to take his seat, although his constituency re-elected him three times. At last, in 1886, the new speaker, Peel, permitted him to take the oath, and he took his seat. In 1888 he secured the passage of the Affirmation Act, by which affirmation could, for unbelievers, take the place of the oath.
Gilmour, J., *Charles Bradlaugh*. 1933

Bradley, Andrew Cecil (1851–1935). English literary critic. Brother of F. H. * Bradley, he was professor of poetry at Oxford (1901–06) and his *Shakespearian Tragedy* (1904) and *Oxford Lectures on Poetry* (1909) did much to guide the taste and stimulate the appreciation of students of his generation.

Bradley, Francis Herbert (1846–1924). English philosopher. A research fellow of Merton College, Oxford, his philosophy of idealism was inspired by Hegel and yet quite individual. In *Appearance and Reality* (1893), he argued that the ordinary world of qualities, relations, space, time and selves is in some sense 'unreal' and only 'appearance'. True reality is The Absolute, which is all-encompassing and mental or spiritual in nature. Bradley was a vigorous critic of utilitarianism and his best known writing in ethics is an essay called 'My Station and Its Duties', contained in his *Ethical Studies* (1876). *Essays on Truth and Reality* appeared in 1914. He received the O.M. in 1924.
Wollheim, R., *F. H. Bradley*. 1959

Bradley, James (1693–1762). English astronomer. Born at Sherborne, Dorset, and educated at Oxford he became vicar of Bridstow in 1719. Even earlier a remarkable talent for astronomy and mathematics had led to his election as F.R.S. (1718). He was a professor of astronomy at Oxford from 1721 until he became astronomer royal in 1742. While attempting to measure stellar parallax he discovered the aberration of light, thus providing the first confirmation by observation of the theory that the earth moved round the sun (* Copernicus). Bradley also discovered nutation (oscillation of the earth's axis about its mean position).

Bradley, Omar Nelson (1893–1981). American general. After having won distinction as a corps commander in North Africa he commanded an army group in the campaign for the liberation of France and directed operations from the first landing in the Cherbourg peninsula to final victory. He was Eisenhower's successor as chairman of the joint chiefs of staff (1949–53).
Bradley, O. N., *A Soldier's Story*. 1951

Bradman, Sir Donald George (1908–). Australian cricketer. Perhaps the most brilliant and consistent batsman ever known, he first played for New South Wales in 1927 and for Australia in 1928, making the record score for first-class cricket of 452 runs, not out, in a state match against Queensland in 1930. He was Australian cricket captain (1936–49), being knighted in 1949.
Bradman, D. G., *Farewell to Cricket*. 1950

Bradshaw, John (1602–1659). English lawyer and regicide. The culmination of his career came when he was selected to preside over the trial of King Charles I, on whom he passed sentence of death in 1649. After the Restoration, his body, buried in Westminster Abbey, was disinterred and hanged.

Bradstreet, Anne (*c.* 1612–1672). American poet. She emigrated to Massachusetts in 1630. Her *The Tenth Muse Lately Sprung up in America* was published in London in 1650 (second ed., Boston 1678). Her poems represent the first work of literary value to have been produced in New England. She left her *Meditations* in manuscript.

Bradwardine, Thomas (born about 1290/1300–1349). English mathematician. He pursued a career at Oxford University, being a fellow of Balliol in 1321 and of Merton in 1323. He was later chaplain to Edward III. He died of the plague. Bradwardine is remembered for his philosophical and mathematical works, which were probably all composed while he was in Oxford. The range of problems which occupied him concerned the physical and mathematical understanding of motion. He was searching for some general formula for understanding speed of motion in terms of the forces which produced and hindered it. His conclusion was that the ratio of speeds of motions follows the ratio of the motive powers to the resistive powers. In some ways, this is a confused notion, but his attempt to study speed in its own right was an important influence upon later medieval writers on physics such as Richard Swineshead and Nicole Oresme. Bradwardine also wrote on theological subjects. He was concerned to reduce the role of human free will in favour of the Divine Will. In his view, God was free to create whatever kind of world He wished, including one of infinite space.
Obermann, H. A., *Thomas Bradwardine*. 1958

Braga, (Joaquim) **Teofilo Fernandes** (1843–1924). First president of the Portuguese republic. Though he was a leader of the anticlericals in politics, it was as a poet, collector of folk lore and author of a monumental history of Portuguese literature that he was better known when he became president on the deposition of King Manuel (1910). He held another short term in 1915.

Bragg, Sir William Henry (1862–1942). British physicist born in Cumberland, educated on the Isle of Man and at Cambridge. He developed the X-ray spectrometer and used it to determine the molecular structure of cystalline substances. Bragg held professorships at Adelaide, Leeds and London and from 1923 until his death was director and professor of chemistry at the Royal Institution. He was knighted in 1920 and was president of the Royal Society (1935–40). Much of his work was done in association with his son, **Sir (William) Lawrence Bragg** (1890–1971), who shared with him the Nobel Prize for Physics in 1915. The younger Bragg, born in Adelaide, Australia, after being technical adviser on sound ranging at British G.H.Q. France in World War I, held a series of academic posts culminating in appointments as Cavendish professor of experimental physics at Cambridge and as director of the Royal Institution (1954–66). He was knighted in 1941.

Brahe, Tycho (1546–1601). Danish astronomer. Attracted to the study of the stars by an eclipse that occurred during his student days at Copenhagen University, he later established, under the patronage of King Frederick II, a large and well equipped observatory on the island of Hveen. There he made a series of astronomical observations more comprehensive and accurate than any previously recorded. Brahe did not accept in full the astronomical system of * Copernicus, for though he believed that the five known planets revolved around the sun he still affirmed that the sun itself, as well as the moon, revolved around the earth. So accurate were his observations, however, that * Kepler was later able to deduce the laws of planetary motion from them. King Frederick's death in 1588 exposed Tycho Brahe to the hostility of his fellow nobles, prejudiced against him because of his work and the king's favour. He went to Prague, where the emperor Rudolf II provided an observatory for him, and Kepler joined him as an assistant.

Brahms, Johannes (1833–1897). German composer, born in Hamburg. He was taught first by his father, a double bass player in the Hamburg State Theatre orchestra, and then studied in Hamburg under Marxsen. From the age of 15 he appeared in public as a pianist until 1853 when he accompanied Reményi, the Hungarian violinist, on a concert tour, after which he became friendly with Robert * Schumann. Largely because of Schumann's efforts to promote his music, Brahms began to gain recognition, and in 1857 was appointed musician-in-residence at the court of Detmold. His Piano Concerto No. 1 in D Minor (1858), conceived on a heroic scale, was initially a failure, later popularized by Clara Schumann. Brahms remained a close friend of Clara's: though he was in love with her, they did not marry, even after Schumann's death in 1856.

Brahms settled in Vienna in 1863, where he directed two musical groups. He composed his *German Requiem* there (1868). The great works of his full maturity include the four symphonies (1877; 1878, 1884; 1886), the Violin Concerto in D (1878), the Piano Concerto No. 2 in B Flat (1881), the Double Concerto for Violin and 'Cello (1887), the Clarinet Quintet (1891), many songs and piano music.

Brahms preserved the great musical traditions of the past in a period in which such composers as Liszt and Wagner were advocating 'revolution and progress' in art; he had a long feud with Wagner on this account. Notwithstanding, the highly personal style he created was influenced by the Romanticism of the time, as in many of his *Lieder* where he combined lyricism and nostalgia with a striking simplicity.

James, B., *Brahms: A Critical Study*. 1972

Braid, James (1870–1950). Scottish golfer, born in Fife. He was five times winner of the British open championship (1901–10) and French champion in 1910. He, Vardon and Taylor were known among golfers as 'the great triumvirate'.

Braille, Louis (1809–1852). French teacher of the blind. He became blind after an accident at the age of 3. He spent most of his life, as pupil and professor, at the Paris Institution des Jeunes Aveugles. From 1825 he developed the system of 'raised point' writing, which is named after him.

Bramah, Joseph (1748–1814). English inventor, born in Yorkshire. He became a carpenter and cabinet-maker and moved to London, where he invented or perfected many useful devices. His hydraulic press and security lock were of great value, but his water closet, beer-pump and machine for printing serial numbers on bank notes also bear witness to his ingenious and versatile mind.

Bramante, Donato (*c.* 1444–1514). Italian architect. Usually esteemed the greatest architect of the High Renaissance, he is lastingly famous as the designer of the initial, centralized, plan for St Peter's Basilica, Rome. His plan, which was commissioned by Pope Julius II and upon which work began in 1506, was somewhat altered by * Michelangelo and * Raphael, but the original conception remains Bramante's (except for the nave, which was an extension by Maderna). Other work in Rome includes the Tempietto in the courtyard of S. Pietro in Montorio as well as parts of the Vatican palace (notably the Belvedere). Before he went to Rome in 1499, Bramante, who was humbly born, had worked mostly in Milan, as a painter. His architectural work there includes the chancel of S. Satiro and the domed church of Santa Maria delle Grazie (1492–

98). Bramante's mature work is in a severe, pure Roman–classical style.
Foster, O., *Bramante*. 1956

Brancusi, Constantin (1876–1957). Romanian sculptor. Having been trained in art in Bucharest he went in 1904 to Paris, where he lived for the rest of his life. His work has been described as abstract, but his sculptures are rather symbolic reductions of objects to their essential form, as in his *Egg* (called by him *The Beginning of the World*) and *Seal*. The Musée de l'Art Moderne, Paris, has good examples of his work and a reproduction of his studio. Brancusi has been one of the most important influences on modern sculpture.
Geist, S., *Brancusi*. 1968

Brand, Sir Jan Hendrik (1826–1888). President of the Orange Free State, South Africa (1864–88). A barrister by profession, he was elected to succeed A. W. Pretorius as president in 1864. His chief aim being to maintain the state's independence, he refused all British attempts at federation. The Basutos were defeated by him (1865–66) but their territory was safeguarded (at their request) by British annexation. Brand's rule was popular and the £90,000 received from Britain for the diamond fields increased the country's prosperity.

Brandeis, Louis Dembitz (1856–1941). American lawyer and judge. Woodrow * Wilson appointed him as a Justice of the U.S. Supreme Court 1916–39, and this generated controversy: he was the first Jewish member of the Court and had been a radical advocate of unpopular causes, such as civil liberties and rights for unions, a line he maintained on the bench.

Brandes, Georg Morris Cohen (1842–1927). Danish literary critic. After a tour of Europe, on which he met Taine, Renan and J. S. Mill, he wrote *Main Currents in Nineteenth-century Literature* (6 volumes, 1872–90), which proclaimed him as a leading supporter of realistic literature, in which problems of everyday life should be discussed. Such views and his belief in free thought roused opposition which affected his career. Later he came to know * Nietzsche, whose influence can be seen in his studies of Shakespeare (1896), Goethe (1915) and Voltaire (1916) and others. In 1925 he wrote *Jesus, a Myth*.

Brando, Marlon (1924–). American actor. His naturalistic style of acting, acquired largely at Lee Strasberg's Actor's Studio, achieved great popular success in the play and film of Tennessee William's *A Streetcar Named Desire* and such films as *Julius Caesar* (where he played Antony), *On the Waterfront* (for which he obtained an Academy award in 1954), *The Young Lions, The Ugly American, Last Tango in Paris* and *The Godfather*.

Brandt, Willy (Herbert Frahm) (1913–). German politician. He was educated at Lübeck and early made his mark as a socialist propagandist. After Hitler came to power he went to Norway to become a Norwegian citizen, and during the German occupation in World War II worked with the Norwegian underground movement. After the war he re-entered German politics and became a member of the Bundestag (house of commons) in 1949. In 1957 he became Oberbürgermeister (lord mayor) of West Berlin and in 1960 succeeded Erich Ollenhauer as leader of the West German Social Democratic party. In 1969 he became Chancellor retaining this office after the elections of 1972. Following the arrest of one of his secretaries as a Communist spy he resigned as Chancellor in 1974. During his time as Chancellor he improved relations with Eastern Europe and was awarded the Nobel Peace Prize in 1971. His numerous writings include *The Ordeal of Co-existence* (1963) and *Reflections and Letters* (1971).
Harprecht, K., *W. Brandt: Portrait and Self-Portrait*. 1972

Brangwyn, Sir Frank (1867–1956). Welsh artist. Born in Bruges, Belgium, where a Brangwyn Museum was opened in 1936, as a boy he was apprenticed to William * Morris, ran away to sea at the age of 17, and exhibited at the Royal Academy the following year. It was in mural paintings of great size and rich colouring that he finally achieved his greatest success. Among the finest examples are those in the Skinners' Hall, London, and the parliament buildings, Winnipeg, Canada. Among other forms of art in which Brangwyn excelled were tapestry and furniture design. He was knighted in 1941.

Branting, Hjalmar (1860–1925). Swedish politician. The virtual creator of the Swedish Social Democratic party. In the parliament of

1896 he was its only member and though it never attained an independent majority in his lifetime Branting was able to form the first socialist government in 1920 and was prime minister in 1920, 1921–23 and 1924–25. He had been a strong supporter of the Allies in World War I and as prime minister he represented his country at the League of Nations, of which he was a vigorous upholder. He won the 1921 Nobel Prize for Peace.

Brantôme, Pierre de Bourdeille, Seigneur and Abbé de (*c.* 1534–1614). French writer and courtier. He accompanied Mary Stuart to Scotland and took part in military expeditions throughout Europe and in Africa. His works, particularly the *Vies de dames galantes*, are collections of anecdotes, mainly scandalous, which reflect the gay and immoral life of the Valois court.

Braque, Georges (1882–1963). French painter. The son of a decorator, he joined the group known as the 'Fauves' ('wild beasts') in 1905, then in 1908 began an association with Pablo * Picasso which was to lead first to a monumental, brutal 'African' phase (Braque's *Nude*, 1908) and then to the development (about 1910) of the analytical style known as Cubism. In subsequent still lifes Braque introduced elements of 'reality' into a pictorial context – newsprint, stencilled letters etc. After World War I he developed a less revolutionary but highly personal two-dimensional semi-abstract style, mainly in a still-life idiom, to which he brought a remarkable sense of design and significant shape. He also designed ballet settings and jewellery.
Mullins, E. B., *Braque*. 1969

Brasidas (died 422 B.C.). Spartan commander in the Peloponnesian War. By a brilliant diversionary campaign in Thrace (424 B.C.) he may have saved his country from defeat. In 422 B.C. he overtook and defeated the Athenians withdrawing from Amphipolis but both he and his opponent Cleon were killed.

Bratby, John (1928–). English painter. A vigorous and colourful artist, his concern is with the immediate environment of daily life, into which he has projected both religious and mundane themes. His pictures gained wider recognition after being used in the film of Joyce Cary's book *The Horse's Mouth* (1958). His writings include novels, a play and a study of Stanley Spencer (1969).

Bratianu, Ion Constantin (1821–1891). Romanian politician. After the failure of the revolutionary movement of 1848, in which he had been a leading spirit, he lived in exile in Paris but continued to work underground for the unity of the Romanian principalities. He returned to Romania in 1856 and was mainly instrumental in securing the throne for Prince Charles of Hohenzollern (* Carol I). From 1876 to 1888, as leader of the Liberal party he was seldom out of office. His son, **I. C. Bratianu** (1864–1927), his party successor, held a comparable position in Romanian politics and was largely responsible for bringing Romania into World War I on the Allied side. A grandson, **Constantin (Dinu) Bratianu** (1889–?1950), led the liberal opposition to Ion * Antonescu before World War II and, briefly, to the communist régime which followed it.

Brattain, Walter Houser (1902–). American physicist, born in China. From 1929 he worked in the Bell Telephone Laboratories and in 1956 shared the Nobel Prize for Physics with J. Bardeen and W. B. Shockley for their investigations on semi-conductors and development of the transistor.

Brauchitsch, Walther von (1881–1948). German field-marshal. Supreme commander during the first and most successful part of World War II, he was dismissed for the failure of the attack on Moscow in 1941, undertaken against his advice. He was succeeded by Hitler himself and was never again given an active command. His death saved him from trial as a war criminal.

Braudel, Fernand (1902–). French historian. Educated at the Sorbonne, he taught in Algeria and Brazil, was a prisoner of war (1940–45), held a chair at the Collège de France 1949–72, and edited the periodical *Annales* 1957–68. Often described as the greatest modern historian (although not in Britain), his major works include *The Mediterranean and the Mediterranean World in the Age of Philip II* (1949) and *Civilization and Capitalism 15th–18th Century* (3 vols, 1967–79). He was elected to the French Academy in 1984.

Braun, Eva (died 1945). Adolf Hitler's mistress and finally his wife. After some years as a model for Hitler's friend and photographer, Heinrich Hoffman, she became Hitler's mistress. They were married in the moment of defeat in the bunker headquarters of Hitler in Berlin, on 29 April 1945, and both committed suicide, probably the next day.

Braun, Wernher Magnus Maximilian von (1912–1977). German rocket specialist. From 1937 to 1945 he was technical director of the missile establishment at Peenemunde and took a major part in the development during World War II of the V2 rocket weapon. From 1950 he worked in the U.S. on rockets for launching missiles and satellites.
Goodrum, J. C., *Wernher von Braun: Space Pioneer*. 1969

Brazil, Angela (1868–1947). English writer. As the most popular writer of school stories for girls of her generation she was the perpetuator of the athletic, mischievous, but golden-hearted middle- and upper-class schoolgirl who has been the delight of caricaturists of a later and more sophisticated age.
Freeman, G., *The Schoolgirl Ethic: The Life and Work of Angela Brazil*. 1976

Breakspear, Nicholas *see* **Adrian IV**

Breasted, James Henry (1865–1935). American historian and archaeologist. He was professor of Egyptology at Chicago University (1905–33) and directed several important archaeological expeditions to Egypt and Mesopotamia. His general works include *The Development of Religion and Thought in Ancient Egypt* (1912) and *The Dawn of Conscience* (1933). His *History of Egypt* (rev. ed. 1928) and *Ancient Records of Egypt* (translations of Egyptian texts, 1906–27) are still valued.

Brecht, Bertolt (1898–1956). German dramatist, poet and director, born in Augsburg of middle-class parents. In 1916 he went to Munich University to study medicine, but his studies were interrupted by World War I, in which he served as a medical orderly. His first play, *Baal*, was written in 1918 and was shortly followed by *Drums in the Night*. In 1921 he became *Dramaturg* (resident playwright and adviser) in a Munich theatre; his first plays were produced and brought their author immediate recognition as a powerful new presence in the German theatre. From the first the special character of the Brechtian theatre began to emerge: Brecht demanded, and tried to achieve, both by his writing and by the styles of acting and direction that he developed, a theatre which would deny its audience the satisfaction of emotional involvement; instead they were to be fully aware that they were in a theatre, alert, conscious and 'ready for action'. In 1924 Brecht went to Berlin, where, under the influence of Erwin Piscator's revolutionary epic theatre, his work became even more directly propagandist; he was by now a confirmed, if highly independent, Marxist, as he was to remain for the rest of his life. In 1926 he published the first major collection of his poems (*Taschenpostille*) and met the composer Kurt Weill, who was to collaborate with him in his most famous musical works; *The Threepenny Opera* (1928), *Rise and Fall of the City of Mahagonny* (1930) and *Happy End* (1929). At the same time, he was writing a series of didactic plays, the *Lehrstücke*, aimed at educating the social attitudes of his audience; *St Joan of the Stockyards* (1929–30) stands out in this period. In 1933 Hitler came to power and Brecht, now a prominent writer in Germany, went into exile and semi-oblivion with his wife, the actress Helene Weigel. Living mainly in Denmark, Brecht produced some anti-Nazi propaganda plays, *The Threepenny Novel*, and some of his finest poetry. Then, between 1938 and 1941, he wrote the great and mature works for which he is mainly remembered: *The Life of Galilei* (1938–39), *Mother Courage and Her Children* (1939), *The Trial of Lucullus* (1939), *The Good Woman of Setzuan* (1938–40), *Herr Puntila and his Man Matti* (1940–41) and *The Resistible Rise of Arturo Ui* (1941). In 1941 he went to the U.S.A. and settled in Hollywood. There he wrote *Schweik in the Second World War* (1941–44) and *The Caucasian Chalk Circle* (1944–45), but failed properly to re-establish himself as a dramatist. In 1947 he was summoned to appear before the Committee on Un-American Activities, which was investigating Communist infiltration of the film industry. Adopting the Schweikian philosophy of self-interest and survival, Brecht denied his Marxist sympathies and emerged unscathed. He was in fact never a member of the Communist Party. Soon after, however, he left the U.S.A., and went to Switzerland, where he wrote his last complete play, *The Days of the Commune* (1948–49). In 1949 he

returned to East Germany and settled in Berlin. His relations with the East German authorities went not altogether happy, but his reputation was immense, and he was granted almost unlimited facilities for the production of plays. With these he created the Berliner Ensemble, a theatre company which could at last put into practice the dramatic theories which he had spent a lifetime in developing. At the time of his death he was beginning to be recognized in western countries as one of the major figures in the 20th-century theatre.
Esslin, M., *Brecht: The Man and His Work*. 1971

Brentano, Franz (1838–1917). Austrian philosopher. Known as 'the Austrian Socrates' because his influence depended more upon the spoken than the written word, he taught at Würzburg and Vienna from 1866–80; one of the great men who came under his influence was Masaryk, the future president of Czechoslovakia. Through inability to accept papal infallibility he gave up his priesthood in 1873. Much of his work consisted in reviewing and revising Aristotle's conceptions of logic and psychology. Parallels between right thinking and right living are discussed in *Origin of the Knowledge of Right and Wrong* (Eng. tr. 1902).
Kastil, A., *Die Philosophie Franz Brentano*. 1951

Breuer, Josef (1842–1925). German–Jewish physician, born in Vienna. A formative influence upon the development of psychoanalysis, he undertook medical studies at the University of Vienna. He kept up contacts with the university, but made a living through private practice. Breuer's main early scientific research lay in the field of physiology, but his fame chiefly rests upon his studies of hysteria, particularly one of his patients, 'Anna O'. She suffered from severe classic hysteria, including paralysis and aphasia. But Breuer found that, over a long period, by getting her to talk about her distant past, particularly when under hypnosis, a state of catharsis was induced and the symptoms gradually ceased. Thus Breuer had hit upon the 'talking cure' which became central to Freudian analytic therapy. * Freud and Breuer collaborated closely in the 1880s on a technique of curing by bringing into consciousness repressed phobias and wishes long consigned to the unconscious. After a series of quarrels their relationship ended in 1896, when Breuer refused to accept Freud's belief that infantile sexuality was a product of seduction by adults (Freud himself later abandoned that belief).
Sulloway, F., *Sigmund Freud, Beyond the Psycho-analytic Myth*. 1979

Breuer, Marcel Lajos (1902–1981). American architect, born in Hungary. He studied at the Bauhaus in Germany and designed the first tubular steel chair in 1925. In 1937 he went to the U.S. to teach at Harvard, where * Gropius, the German architect, whose pupil he had been, also came to work; they carried out some schemes in partnership. Breuer was a co-architect of the UNESCO building in Paris (1953–59).

Breughel, Pieter *see* **Bruegel, Pieter**

Breuil, Henri Edouard Prosper (1877–1961). French abbé and archaeologist. He was ordained in 1900 but from the first devoted himself to the study of prehistory and became recognized especially as the greatest authority on cave art. He studied and traced the figures of animals etc., in the caves of northern Spain (Altamira etc.) and France (the Dordogne and elsewhere), and by assigning them to the upper Palaeolithic enabled them to be dated approximately between 25,000 and 10,000 B.C. Breuil was professor of prehistory at the Collège de France (1929–47) and wrote many books, including *Four Hundred Centuries of Cave Art* (1952) and *The Painted Rocks of the Sahara* (1955).
Brodrick, A. H., *The Abbé Breuil*. 1963

Brewer, Ebenezer Cobham (1810–1897). English schoolmaster remembered for his *Dictionary of Phrase and Fable* (1870), still in general use.

Brewster, Sir David (1781–1868). Scottish physicist, born at Jedburgh. He worked mainly in the field of physical optics, and discovered the law (now known as Brewster's Law) that when polarization occurs in a reflected beam of light, the tangent of the angle of polarization is equal to the refractive index of the reflecting medium. Brewster invented the kaleidoscope, improved the stereoscope and devised a polyzonal lens still used in lighthouses. He helped to found the British Association for the Advancement of Science in 1831, in which year he was knighted. He wrote an authoritative life of Newton and many encyclopedia articles.

Brezhnev, Leonid Ilyich (1906–1982). Soviet politician. His official career began in the Ukraine and Moldavia; in 1933–34 he held appointments connected with the army and defence. In 1955 he became a member of the Kazakh presidium and in 1957 a full member of the supreme presidium and of the Central Committee. He succeeded Marshal * Voroshilov as chairman of the presidium of the Supreme Soviet (i.e. president of the USSR) 1960–64 and held that office again 1977–82. When * Khrushchev fell from power (1964) Brezhnev succeeded him as first secretary of the Central Committee of the Communist party, and so with * Kosygin became one of the two most powerful men in the government. He was awarded the Lenin Peace Prize in 1972, became a Marshal of the Soviet Union in 1976 and his resumption of the Soviet presidency in 1977, an office which he held with the party secretaryship, was regarded as the end of an era of collegiate leadership.
Dornberg, J., *Brezhnev*. 1974

Brian Boru (or Bóroimhe) (died 1014). Irish king. Having succeeded his brother as king of Munster in 976, he disputed the authority of Malachy II, the high king, gained supremacy over southern Ireland (997) and eventually (1002) expelled Malachy and usurped his power. The end came when in 1014 he found himself confronted with an alliance between the king of Leinster and the Vikings then holding Dublin. At Clontarf Brian Boru won a complete victory but was himself murdered after the battle. The many O'Briens perpetuate his name.

Briand, Aristide (1862–1932). French radical politician, born at Nantes. He became an advocate, co-founder of *L'Humanité* with his friend Jean * Jaurès and a Deputy 1902–32. He was premier of France for six periods (1909–11; 1913; 1915–17; 1921–22; 1925–26; 1929) and foreign minister four times (1915–17; 1921–22; 1925; 1926–32). After World War I he advocated reconciliation with Germany and after the Locarno Treaty of 1925 he shared the Nobel Peace Prize (1926) with Gustav * Stresemann and Austen * Chamberlain. The Briand–Kellogg Pact outlawing war followed in 1928. He was defeated in a bid for the presidency in 1931.
Hesse, R., *Aristide Briand*. 1939

Bridge, Frank (1879–1941). English composer. At the Royal College of Music under Sir Charles Stanford, he gained some distinction as a viola player. He was chiefly a composer of chamber music, but he also wrote a symphonic suite *The Sea* (1912) and a tone poem *Summer* (1916). His style, at first romantic, became recondite and radical in his later years in such works as the second and third String Quartets (1920, 1937) and *Phantasia* for piano and orchestra (1931). Among his pupils in composition was Benjamin * Britten.
Bray, T., *Frank Bridge*. 1977

Bridges, Robert Seymour (1844–1930). English poet, born at Walmer, educated at Eton and Oxford. He became a physician in London but was rich enough to be able to retire in 1882. Three volumes of graceful lyrics had already won him recognition as a poet. Later he wrote several plays and the narrative poem *Eros and Psyche*, now largely forgotten. A collected edition of 1912, followed by a more complete collection in 1936, introduced him as a major poet to a wider world. Bridges was a great friend of Gerard Manley * Hopkins, whose poems he collected, and published posthumously in 1918. The two shared a great interest in metrical and rhythmic experiments. Bridges also wrote critical studies of Keats and Milton and succeeded Alfred Austin as Poet Laureate in 1913. He expressed his philosophical and aesthetic ideas in his last long poem *The Testament of Beauty* (1929). He was given the O.M. in 1929.
Sparrow, J., *Bridges*. 1962

Bridget (or Brigid or Bride), *St* (*c*. 450–*c*. 523). Patron saint of Leinster, Ireland. She was active in the early 6th century but almost nothing is known of her life except that she founded a convent at Kildare, and that reports of her many miracles spread her cult widely over Europe.

Bridget, St (*c*. 1303–1373). Swedish visionary. Born of an aristocratic family, she became absorbed in religion only after the death (1344) of her husband, by whom she had had eight children. For the rest of her life she was seeing and recording visions, her revelations concerned not only spiritual matters but also political questions. In 1349 she left Sweden after a disagreement with the king and settled in Rome. In 1370, with papal consent, she founded the Augustinian order of Bridgettines.

Bridgewater, Francis Egerton, 3rd Duke of (1736–1803). English nobleman. Responsible for the first canal in England, he commissioned James * Brindley to build a canal from his Worsley coalmines to Manchester. This, later extended to join the Mersey at Runcorn, and subsequent canals forestalled the railways in providing cheap transport for heavy industrial loads. Bridgewater died unmarried and the dukedom became extinct.

Bridgman, Percy Williams (1882–1961). American physicist. He held professorships at Harvard from 1926 to 1954. In 1946 he was awarded the Nobel Prize for Physics for his pioneering studies in the physics of very high pressures. He also made valuable contributions to the philosophy of science.

Bridie, James (Osborne Henry Mayor) (1888–1951). Scottish playwright. A physician in Glasgow for many years, he achieved great success with his plays, some whimsical, some pleasantly macabre. They included *Tobias and the Angel* (1930), *The anatomist* (1931), *Mr Bolfry* (1943), *Dr Angelus* (1947) and *Daphne Laureola* (1949). He was one of the founders of the Glasgow Citizens' Theatre.
Luyben, H. L., *James Bridie: Clown and Philosopher*. 1965

Brieux, Eugène (1858–1932). French dramatist. Originally a journalist, he wrote many didactic plays aimed at the exposure of social evils and middle-class hypocrisy. His works include the well known play *Les Avariés* (*Damaged Goods*, 1901), dealing with venereal disease.
Thomas, P. V., *The Plays of Eugène Brieux*. 1913

Briggs, Henry (1561–1630). English mathematician, born in Halifax. His life was spent in the academic world and his fame rests on his simplification of logarithms (invented by Napier in 1614) and his extension of their use. He originated the use of 10 as the most practical base for tables and in his *Arithmetica Logarithmica* (1624) published logarithms for 30,000 natural numbers, calculated to 14 decimal places. In his *Trigonometria Britannica* (1633) he gave tables of logarithms of sines and tangents to a hundredth of a degree, calculated to 15 decimal places.

Bright, John (1811–1889). English Radical and Quaker politician, born in Rochdale, Lancashire, the son of a cotton manufacturer. He left school at 16 to enter the family business but had already made a reputation for speaking on such subjects as temperance when in 1841 he joined the Anti-Corn Law League and with his lifelong friend Richard * Cobden campaigned ardently for the repeal of taxes on imported grain. The Corn Laws were in fact repealed under Sir Robert * Peel in 1846. Bright's parliamentary career began in 1843 when he was elected for Durham, and he represented this and later constituencies, Manchester and Birmingham, almost continuously for the rest of his life. He campaigned for electoral reform, opposed * Palmerston's aggressive foreign policy, especially the Crimean War ('The angel of death has been abroad throughout the land; you may almost hear the beating of his wings'), and despite Lancashire's cotton interests supported the Union cause in the American Civil War. He served under * Gladstone as president of the Board of Trade (1868–70) and chancellor of the Duchy of Lancaster (1873–74, 1880–82), but resigned over the government's Egyptian policy and finally broke with Gladstone in 1885–86 on the issue of home rule for Ireland. He was one of the greatest modern orators and the most sincere of men.
Ausbel, H., *John Bright: Victorian Reformer*. 1966

Bright, Richard (1789–1858). English physician, whose name is perpetuated by the term Bright's disease, which is still applied collectively to a number of kidney disorders. He was born in Bristol and in 1812 graduated in Edinburgh after studying at Guy's Hospital in London. He became a leading London consultant and on the accession of Queen Victoria became her 'physician-extraordinary'.

Brillat-Savarin, Anthelme (1755–1826). French lawyer. Famous for his *La Physiologie du Goût* (1825), a witty treatise on gastronomy, he was mayor of his native Belley near Chambéry in 1793, but then took refuge from revolutionary excesses in Switzerland and America. On his return (1796) he became a member of the court of appeal.

Brindley, James (1716–1772). English engineer, born in Thornsett, Derbyshire. He was apprenticed to a millwright, set up on his own at Leek (1742) but was still almost illiterate when he was commissioned to design and supervise important canal systems by the Duke of * Bridgewater. Brindley built about 350 miles of canals, the longest one being the Grand Trunk Canal linking the Mersey with the Potteries, Derby and Birmingham.

Brinvilliers, Marguérite d'Aubray, Marquise de (*c.* 1630–1676). French murderess. She and her lover, Godin de Sainte-Croix, poisoned her husband and all his family to obtain their fortune and avenge her lover's imprisonment. The crime remained undiscovered until after Sainte-Croix's death, when incriminating papers were discovered. The marquise was arrested and beheaded.

Brisbane, Sir Thomas Makdougall 1st Bart. (1773–1860). Scottish administrator and astronomer. After distinguished army service he held the appointment (1821–25) of governor of New South Wales. During his term of office the penal code was reformed and a constitution given to the colony. The Brisbane river, discovered in 1823, and the city which was built on its banks were named after him. While in Australia he catalogued over 7,000 stars, for which he was awarded the Copley Medal of the Royal Society. In 1836 he was made a baronet, and in 1837 a G.C.B.

Brissot, Jacques Pierre (known as de Warville) (1754–1793). French revolutionary politician. Born at Chartres, the son of an innkeeper, he became a lawyer and campaigned for penal reform, abolition of slavery and other liberal causes. In the revolutionary period he was a member of the Legislative Assembly (1791–92) and of the Convention (1792–93) and became a leader of the Girondists, the more moderate faction which was overcome and destroyed by Robespierre's extremist Jacobins. Brissot attempted to flee but was caught and guillotined.

Britten, (Edward) Benjamin Baron Britten of Aldeburgh (1913–1976). English composer, born in Lowestoft and educated at Gresham's School, Holt. From the age of 12 he studied under Frank * Bridge, then at the Royal College of Music, London where he composed the set of choral variations *A Boy Was Born* (1933). After composing for radio, theatre and cinema, and working in the USA from 1939–42, he returned to Suffolk, England, where he devoted himself to composition.

His first stage work, the operetta *Paul Bunyan*, was performed in 1941, and *Peter Grimes*, premiered in 1945, confirmed him as one of the foremost twentieth century opera composers. Other operas include *The Rape of Lucretia* (1946), *Billy Budd* (1951), *The Turn of the Screw* (1954), *A Midsummer Night's Dream* (1960), *Death in Venice* (1973).

In 1948 he founded the Aldeburgh Festival, which became the centre of his musical activities. He was an excellent pianist and conductor, as well as a composer. His most important works include his song cycles, e.g. the *Seven Sonnets of Michelangelo* (1940), written for tenor Peter * Pears, for whom he composed many of his vocal works and operatic tenor roles; his *War Requiem* (1962), his best known choral work; the *Variations on a Theme of Frank Bridge* (1937) which first won him international acclaim; *The Young Person's Guide to the Orchestra* (1945) and the *Symphony in D Major for Cello and Orchestra*, written for the cellist Mstislav * Rostropovich.

He received the Aspen Award in 1964. He became a CH in 1952, a member of the OM in 1965, and a life peer (the first musician to be so honoured) in 1976.

White, E. W., *Benjamin Britten: His Life and Operas*. 1970

Broad, Charlie Dunbar (1887–1971). English philosopher. Knightsbridge professor of moral philosophy at Cambridge (1933–53), he was best known for his inquiry into the relation between mind and matter, called *The Mind and Its Place in Nature*, and for a three-volume examination of the work of * M'Taggart.

Brockhaus, Friedrich Arnold (1772–1823). German publisher. Founder of the firm in Leipzig which has borne his name, he published the encyclopedic *Konversations-Lexikon* (completed 1811), which has been followed by many encyclopedias during the history of the family firm.

Hübschner, A., *150 Jahre F. A. Brockhaus*. 1955

Broglie, Maurice, Duc de (1875–1960). French physicist. As a young man and again in World War I he served in the French navy, but it is for his work on the ionization of gases, radioactivity and X-rays, of which he obtained the first spectra, that he is known. His younger brother **Louis Victor** (1892–1960), who was trained by him and subsequently became a professor of physics at Paris University, laid the foundations of wave mechanics. His prediction of the diffraction of electrons was confirmed by experiments in America in 1927. His publications include *New Perspectives in Physics* (1962). He was awarded a Nobel Prize in 1929.

Bromfield, Louis (1896–1956). American novelist and short-story writer. He won the Pulitzer Prize for 1926 with *Early Autumn*; his other novels include *The Rains Came* (1937), *Night in Bombay* (1940), *Mrs Parkington* (1943).
Brown, M., *Louis Bromfield and His Books*. 1956

Brontë (originally Brunty or Prunty). A literary family of Irish descent, resident in England at the Parsonage at Haworth near Bradford, Yorkshire. **Patrick Brontë** (1777–1861), the father of the family, was educated at Cambridge, ordained in 1806 and came to Haworth as rector in 1820. Maria Branwell, whom he had married in 1812, died in 1821, and her sister Elizabeth came to take kindly charge of the orphans. Two girls died in childhood but of those who survived all developed amazing literary talent, the growth of which was encouraged by an aloof, sometimes eccentric, but understanding father, by strong mutual affections and shared tastes, and a semi-isolation imposed by moorland surroundings of great beauty and only occasional bleakness. Their circumstances, though poor, were not impoverished (they kept a maid). They found great happiness in sharing in the creation of plays and endless epics (*Gondal* or *Angria*) which they continued into adulthood.

Their literary careers started when in 1846 the sisters, Charlotte, Emily and Anne, published their poems under the names of Currer, Ellis and Acton Bell, a volume of which it is said that only two copies were sold!

Charlotte Brontë (1816–1855) went with her sisters to a hated school at Cowan Bridge (the Lowood of *Jane Eyre*) but found compensation (1831–32) at Miss Wooler's school at Roehead where she afterwards taught (1835–38). She also taught as a private governess and (1842–43) at the Héger Pensionnat in Brussels. All Charlotte's novels are in part autobiographical. Her schooldays were recalled in *Jane Eyre* (1847), a melodramatic masterpiece, and the Monsieur Paul of *Villette* (1853) is Professor Héger of Brussels. Her other novels were *Shirley* (1849) and *The Professor*, which though written first was not published until 1857. Charlotte married A. B. Nicholls (died 1906), a clergyman. She died a few months later. On a visit to London she had met * Thackeray and Elizabeth * Gaskell, her future biographer.

(Patrick) Branwell Brontë (1817–1848) shared the literary gifts of his family and may even have helped with the early chapters of Emily's *Wuthering Heights*, but he was too wayward and unstable to remain in regular work. Addiction to alcohol and opium precipitated his death from tuberculosis.

Emily Jane Brontë (1818–1848) was perhaps the most gifted of the family; she was certainly the most commandingly beautiful. Her poetry is of a much higher quality than that of her sisters and her only novel, *Wuthering Heights* (1847), is a work of great passion and power conveying a strong impression of the elemental force of nature and suggesting the frustration of her emotional life. She died unmarried.

Anne Brontë (1820–1849), a gentle and submissive character, seems colourless in comparison with her sisters; her novels *Agnes Grey* (1847) and *The Tenant of Wildfell Hall* (1848) are less esteemed.
Winnifreth, T., *The Brontës*. 1973

Brook, Peter Stephen Paul (1925–). English stage producer and film director. His particular talent in his field was exemplified by such productions as *Titus Andronicus* and *King Lear* for the Memorial Theatre, Stratford, and *Salome*, when he was director of productions (1947–50) at Covent Garden, or by less official productions such as *Ring Round The Moon* (1950), *The Little Hut* (1953), and *Irma la Douce* (1958). In 1962 he was appointed co-director of the Royal Shakespeare Company (Stratford and London). He also worked in Paris, in the U.S.A. and West Africa. Among his best known films were *The Beggar's Opera, The Lord of the Flies, King Lear, A Midsummer Night's Dream*, and *Marat/Sade*.
Brook, P. S. P., *The Empty Space*. 1968

Brooke, Sir Alan Francis *see* **Alanbrooke**

Brooke, Basil Stanlake *see* **Brookeborough**

Brooke, Sir James (1803–1868). First rajah of Sarawak, in Borneo (now part of Malaysia). Inheriting £30,000 from his father, a Bengal civil servant, he sailed his yacht to the East Indies on a voyage of study and exploration. He reached Sarawak in 1839 to thank the provincial governor, Hassim, a nephew of the ruling sultan of Brunei, for services to some wrecked British seamen. He found a revolt in progress and at Hassim's request returned the following year to restore order and mediate. His appointment as rajah of Sarawak, a sign of the sultan's gratitude for his success, was welcomed by the people, as was his subsequent just and paternal rule, conducted through a council with a native majority. In 1863 he handed over his government to his nephew, **Sir Charles Brooke**, who reigned for forty-nine years, but his son **Sir Charles Vyner Brooke** was the last ruler of his line as, after its liberation from the Japanese occupation at the end of World War II, the British government annexed the territory.
Payne, R., *The White Rajahs of Sarawak*. 1960

Brooke, Rupert Chawner (1887–1915). English poet. Born at Rugby, where his father was a master, he was educated there and at King's College, Cambridge. After travelling in Germany, the U.S.A. and the Pacific he was commissioned in the Royal Naval Division in the early days of World War I and died of blood poisoning in Skyros on his way to the Dardanelles. He was the 'gifted and golden youth', the poignancy of whose early death typified the tragedy of his generation.

If I should die think only this of me
That there's some corner of a foreign field
That is for ever England. . . .

are perhaps the most famous lines from his two slim volumes of poetry (1911 and 1915).
Hassal, C., *Rupert Brooke: A Biography*. 1972

Brookeborough, Basil Stanlake Brooke, 1st Viscount (1888–1970). Northern Ireland politician. A nephew of Lord Alanbrooke, he became a member of the Northern Ireland parliament in 1929 and after filling a series of ministerial offices from 1933 became prime minister in 1943 in succession to J. M. Andrews. Created a viscount in 1952, he was compelled by ill-health to retire in 1963.

Brooks, Van Wyck (1886–1963). American essayist, literary critic and translator. He wrote much on the influence of Puritanism on American culture, e.g. in *America's Coming-of-Age* (1915). Other works include notable biographies of Henry James (1925) and Emerson (1932) and *The Flowering of New England* (Pulitzer Prize for History, 1936).

Brougham and Vaux, Henry Peter Brougham, 1st Baron (1778–1868). British lawyer and politician. Born and educated in Edinburgh, he was admitted to the Scottish bar and was also active in journalism, helping to found the *Edinburgh Review* (1802). In 1805 he moved to London and in 1808 was called to the English bar; he was a Whig M.P. (1810–12 and again from 1816 to 1830), but it was as Queen Caroline's successful counsel in the bill of divorce brought against her in 1820 on behalf of George IV that he won popularity and fame. While in parliamentary opposition he interested himself in education and was a founder (1828) of London University. When the Whigs returned to office (1830) he became lord chancellor and was prominent in the Reform Bill debates. His eccentricities became so marked that after the defeat of the government (1834) he was never given office again. Much of his most lasting, if least known, work was in the field of law reform, where he was guided by the principles of Jeremy * Bentham. A carriage specially built for him became the prototype of the familiar brougham. A prolific writer, he formed the Society for the Diffusion of Useful Knowledge.
New, C. W., *The Life of Henry Brougham*. 1961

Brouwer (Brauwer), **Adriaen** (1606–1638). Flemish painter, born at Oudenaarde. He was a pupil of Frans * Hals. His pictures of brawls and taverns, in which he displays a strong sense of character, reflect the dissipation of his own life. He died of the plague in Antwerp.
Bode, W., *Adriaen Brouwer*. 1924

Brown, Sir Arthur Whitten (1886–1948). British engineer and aviator. He was navigator to Sir John William * Alcock on the first non-stop Atlantic flight. He was knighted in 1919.

Brown, Ford Madox (1821–1893). English painter, born in Calais. Though closely as-

sociated with the Pre-Raphaelite Brotherhood by style and personal contact he never became a member. *Christ Washing St Peter's Feet*, in the National Gallery, London, is a fine example of his mature style, but more characteristic are pictures of historical subjects, such as the murals for Manchester Town Hall which occupied the last years of his life.
Hilton, T., *The Pre-Raphaelites*. 1970

Brown, George Alfred, Baron George-Brown, (1914–). British politician. He became a local official of the Transport and General Workers Union and was elected as Labour M.P. for Belper in 1945. In the faction fights of the Labour opposition period he was a loyal supporter of * Gaitskell's defence policy and in 1960 was elected as deputy leader of the parliamentary party, an office for which he was again chosen when defeated for the leadership by Harold * Wilson after Gaitskell's death (1963). In Wilson's government, formed after the Labour electoral victory of 1964, Brown, still deputy leader, was given the new post of minister of economic affairs, and set out to achieve a working policy for incomes and prices. He became foreign secretary in 1966. He was created a life peer in 1970 and later left the Labour Party.
Brown, G. A., *In My Way*. 1971

Brown, John (1800–1859). American abolitionist, born in Connecticut. Attempts to gain a living by cattle trading and land speculation in Kansas proved largely abortive, but as the years went by he developed a fanatical belief in his personal mission to carry out, by force if necessary, the liberation of slaves. For this object he collected considerable sums from well-meaning sympathizers. His plan was to establish places of refuge first in one state and then in another where slaves would gather or be brought, in the belief that such insurrections would force anti-slavery legislation. Virginia was his first choice, but his raid on an arsenal and rifle factory at Harper's Ferry proved a fiasco. No one rose in his favour and all twenty members of his tiny force were killed or captured. Brown himself was condemned for treason and hanged. The emotional fires lit by this futile attempt did much to precipitate the Civil War, during which the song 'John Brown's Body' became a marching song of the Northern troops.
Oates, S. B., *'To Purge this Land of Blood': Biography of John Brown*. 1972

Brown, John (died 1883). Scottish servant. Queen Victoria's faithful retainer at her Scottish estate of Balmoral was not only a servant but a privileged friend whose pungent remarks to the sovereign herself and her visitors became legendary.
Cullen, T., *The Empress Brown*. 1969

Brown, Lancelot ('Capability') (1716–1783). English landscape gardener. His nickname referred to his custom of assessing the 'capabilities' of a landscape. As a gardener at Stowe he learnt much from William Kent, then at work there. Kent's ideas, improved upon by Brown, involved the abandonment of the formal symmetrical beds and walks of earlier gardens and the laying out of garden and park by adapting or simulating the natural features of a landscape. The surroundings of many great country houses, e.g. Harewood and Blenheim, bear witness to his skill. He also designed houses himself, mainly in the Palladian style.
Stroud, D., *Capability Brown*. 1957

Brown, Robert (1773–1858). Scottish botanist. Born at Montrose and educated at Edinburgh University, he collected many specimens while surveying the Australian coasts for the * Flinders expedition (from 1801), and eventually held the post of keeper of the botanical department at the British Museum from 1827 until his death. The behaviour of pollen grains in water led him to discover and investigate a random movement to which particles in suspension are subjected. This movement, now known to be caused by molecular bombardment, is called Brownian movement after its discoverer.

Browne, Hablot Knight (known as 'Phiz') (1815–1882). English artist. He is best known for his illustrations to *Pickwick Papers* (in succession to Seymour and Bass) and several of Dickens's later works. He also illustrated books by Lever, Harrison Ainsworth and Surtees.
Kitton, F. G., *Phiz*. 1882

Browne, Robert (1550?–1633). English religious leader. He gave his name to the Brownists, afterwards known as 'independents' and 'Congregationalists'. He was related to Queen Elizabeth's minister * Burghley, who obtained his release when he was imprisoned for his views. Later he moved with his congregation to Middleburg in Holland but his quarrelsome nature brought disruption, as it did wherever he went. Eventually he accepted Anglican orders but as a rector of Achurch from 1589–1631 he seems to have organized his church on Congregational lines. He died in Northampton gaol where he was incarcerated for an assault.

Browne, Sir Thomas (1605–1682). English scholar, physician and author. Born in London, educated at Winchester and Oxford, he studied medicine at Montpellier, Padua and Leyden Universities, and settled as a physician in Norwich. His famous *Religio Medici* (published 1642–43) is self-revealing but leaves his actual religion in doubt. In his *Pseudoxia Epidemica* or *Vulgar Errors* (1646) he speculates widely on new and old beliefs. His *Hydrotaphia* or *Urn Burial* (1658), with which was printed *The Garden of Cyrus*, was inspired by the discovery of some sepulchral urns in Norfolk. All of his works display vast and curious learning and are couched in a rhythmic, exotic style, rich in imagery.
Keynes, G., *A Bibliography of Sir Thomas Browne*. 1968

Browning, Elizabeth Barrett (1806–1861). English poet. Her father, Edward Moulton of Coxhoe Hall, Durham, where she was born, took the name Barrett on inheriting estates in Jamaica. Most of her childhood was spent among the Malvern Hills, but, injured by a fall from a horse at the age of 15, she became a semi-invalid. After her mother's death (1832) the family moved more than once until in 1838 Elizabeth was living in seclusion with her father in Wimpole Street, London. She had been a precocious child and her poems had long been published and known when, in 1846, Robert * Browning rescued her by an elopement and secret marriage from her father's jealous affection and from an invalidism continued through habit and nerves. She and Robert lived in great happiness in Florence where their only child, Robert (died 1912), was born. Her works published after her marriage included *Sonnets from the Portuguese* (1850) – misleading title as they are her own – and *Aurora Leigh* (1856), a verse-novel. Her elopement is the theme of a play, *The Barretts of Wimpole Street*, by Rudolf Besier (1930).
Hayter, A., *Elizabeth Barrett Browning*. 1965

Browning, Robert (1812–1889). English poet. Education by private tutors and a background of taste and learning provided by cultured and sufficiently wealthy parents offered the opportunity and inducement to a life of travel and poetry. He visited Russia and Italy, a country which thenceforth dominated his imagination and in which he spent his married life with Elizabeth Barrett * Browning.

His first important publication, *Paracelsus* (1835) brought him the friendship of Landor, Dickens and other literary men; but though *Men and Women* (1855) attracted wider attention, for renown he had to await the issue of his masterpiece *The Ring and the Book* (1868–1869), based on a murder story of Renaissance Italy. Other works included *Strafford* (1837) and other verse plays now largely forgotten, *Sordello* (1840), a narrative poem of the Guelph and Ghibelline feuds but described by Browning himself as the 'development of a soul'; and several dramatic monologues (*My Last Duchess, Andrea del Sarto, The Bishop Orders his Tomb*) for which he is now particularly remembered. Of his narrative poems, *Pippa Passes, How They Carried the Good News From Ghent to Aix* and *The Pied Piper of Hamelin* are among the best known. Browning obtained much of his story material from books, but his characterization was based on a close observation of ordinary people moving round him or doing their ordinary work and he approached moral questions unprejudiced by preconceived Victorian ideas. His verse has not the limpid flow or musical rhythm of that of some of his contemporaries, his idioms are sometimes obscure, and his eye often seems more widely open to the grotesque than to the beautiful but these qualities emphasize an individuality which, with his mastery of verse forms, has ensured the survival and enjoyment of his work. He is buried in Westminster Abbey.
Griffin, W. H., *The Life of Robert Browning*. 1966

Bruce, Sir David (1855–1931). British parasitologist born in Melbourne, Australia. Having graduated at Edinburgh he became a British army surgeon but his most important work was to be in discovering the causative agents of Malta (undulant) fever, and the part played by the tsetse flies of tropical Africa in spreading human sleeping-sickness and a destructive cattle disease called *nagana*. *Brucellosis* is named for him.

Bruce, James (1730–1794). Scottish explorer. Having originally studied law, he became a wine merchant, entered the consular service and acquired enough medical knowledge to enable him to travel as a physician in North Africa and the Middle East. In 1768 he went to Egypt, whence he set out on his famous journey to Abyssinia (Ethiopia); he arrived at Gondar, then the capital, early in 1770; in November he reached the source of the Blue Nile, then considered the main stream. Back in Scotland he married Mary Dundas (1776). It was not until 1790 that his 5-volume account of his journey appeared.

Bruce, Robert (1274–1329). King of Scotland as Robert I (from 1306), and a national hero. He was the grandson of the Robert Bruce who was a candidate for the throne in 1291, when John de * Balliol was ultimately chosen. It was his murder of the Red (John) Comyn in the Greyfriars Church, Dumfries, an act for which he was ex-communicated, that brought him into the open as national leader against England. He was crowned in 1306 at Scone and was fortunate that England's warrior King Edward I died the following year, for though Bruce still had to face some years of varying fortune he gradually asserted his mastery over the country and by his great victory over the English at Bannockburn (1314) assured Scotland's independence (finally recognized in 1328). He was succeeded by his son (by his first wife) * David II. From his daughter Marjorie (by his second wife) was descended the Stewart (Stuart) dynasty. His brother **Edward Bruce** crossed with a Scottish force to Ulster in 1315 and succeeded in having himself crowned King of Ireland. He failed, however, to maintain his power, was driven back into Ulster and was killed in 1318 near Dundalk.
Barrow, G. W. S., *Robert Bruce*. 1965

Bruce of Melbourne, Stanley Melbourne Bruce, 1st Viscount (1883–1967). Australian politician. He was born in Melbourne but graduated in England from Trinity Hall, Cambridge. In World War I he served with the British army, winning the M.C. and *Croix de guerre avec palme*. He entered the Australian parliament in 1918 and rose so quickly that by 1923 he was prime minister at the head of a Nationalist-Country-Party coalition; but in 1929 was defeated over a proposal that the states should in future control industrial arbitration. From 1932 he was in London either as resident minister or high commissioner, in which capacity he represented Australia in Britain's war cabinet. He was raised to the peerage in 1947.

Bruch, Max (1838–1920). German composer, born in Cologne. He conducted and taught composition in Germany and in England where he was conductor of the Liverpool Philharmonic Society (1880–83). He became the friend of Brahms and is best remembered for his romantic Violin Concerto in G minor (1886) and the *Kol Nidrei* variations for cello and orchestra (1880).
Gysi, M., *Max Bruch*. 1922

Bruckner, Anton (1824–1896). Composer. Born at Ansfelden, in Upper Austria, he studied Bach's organ works intensively and in 1856 became organist at Linz Cathedral. He came to be highly regarded as an organist, giving concert performances in Paris (1868) and London (1871). In Vienna, where he settled in 1868, he became organist at St Stephen's Cathedral and was for many years a revered teacher at the Conservatoire. He never married. In his early life, Bruckner's musical idols had been Bach and Beethoven; at Vienna he became a devotee of Wagner. He was painfully naïve and often ridiculed by his more sophisticated musical contemporaries, but his piety and sincerity emerge from his music. His best known symphonies are No. 3, dedicated to Wagner (1873), No. 4, the *Romantic* (1874), No. 5 (1877), No. 6 (1881), No. 7 (1883) – the best known of the series; its slow movement, intended to commemorate Wagner's death, incorporates an inversion of themes from *Tannhäuser* – No. 8 (1886) and No. 9 (1894), dedicated to 'Our dear God', and left unfinished.
Watson, D., *Bruckner*. 1975

Bruegel (or Brueghel or Breughel), **Pieter** (*c.* 1526–1569). Flemish painter. He studied at the Antwerp Guild and in 1552–53 travelled through France, Switzerland and Italy making scores of landscape drawings, ancestral to the landscapes of his mature work. In fact, the influence of the Alpine landscape was of infinitely greater significance than that of Italian art, even in the time of Michelangelo and Titian. Bruegel's early grotesque fantasies such as *The Fall of The Rebel Angels* clearly display the influence of Hieronymus * Bosch,

but in his mature works Bruegel shows himself a painter of greater subtlety and humanity than Bosch. Ugly, squat, puppet-like, Bruegel's tragi-comic characters constitute a teeming and toil-ridden humanity in uneasy truce with their natural environment, but at the same time give a fascinating representation of the peasant life and lore of his time (as in *The Peasant Wedding* and *Children's Games*). The cosmic perspective of Bruegel's landscapes, the villages crouched at the bottom or teetering on the slopes of huge mountain formations, are a comment on the human condition which contrasts with the anthropocentric world of Italian painting. Bruegel moved from Antwerp to Brussels in 1563 and there spent the rest of his life. His work was well received by his contemporaries and is still greatly admired. Most of his finest works are in Vienna; they include the superb landscape sequence known as *The Seasons*. Two of his sons achieved a lesser reputation. **Pieter II** (*c.* 1564–1636/8) became known as 'Hell Bruegel' for his nightmare scenes; **Jan** (1568–1625), known as 'Velvet Bruegel', became a court painter at Brussels and was a friend of * Rubens with whom he collaborated. He is best known for his artificial landscapes and flower pictures.
Grossmann, F. (ed.), *Pieter Brueghel: Complete Paintings*. 1973

Brummell, George Bryan (known as 'Beau Brummell') (1778–1840). English wit and dandy. Educated at Eton and Oxford, he became an intimate of the Prince of Wales (later George IV) and the leader of fashion in London. He quarrelled with the Prince, lost his fortune through gambling and fled to France in 1816 to escape his creditors. He died in madness and poverty.
Franzero, C. M., *The Life and Times of Beau Brummell*. 1958

Brunel, Isambard Kingdom (1805–1859). British engineer. Born in Portsmouth, son of Sir Marc Isambard * Brunel, he studied at Collège Henri Quatre, Paris and in 1823 entered his father's firm. His plans for the Clifton suspension bridge were adopted in 1831. He directed work on it, but owing to insufficient funds the bridge was not completed until after his death. Brunel had previously been chief engineer on the Thames tunnel project, also unfinished through lack of money.

From 1833 to 1846 he was chief engineer of the Great Western Railway and was responsible for construction of over 1,000 miles of track and many canals, and introduction of the broadgauge railway. In 1837 he designed the first transatlantic steamer, the *Great Western*, and later he improved on this design with the *Great Britain* (1843) and the *Great Eastern* (1858), each the largest in the world at time of launching. The *Great Britain* was the first large vessel driven by a screw propeller, the *Great Eastern* the first to have a double iron hull. The latter was also notable as the ship responsible for the laying of the first successful transatlantic cable.

In addition to his work, Brunel also carried out extensive improvements at docks throughout the country, including Bristol and Plymouth, and worked on large guns, designing a floating armoured barge that was used during the Crimean War.

He was an F.R.S., and hon. D.C.L. of Oxford.
Rolt, L. T. C., *Isambard Kingdom Brunel*. 1974

Brunel, Sir Marc Isambard (1769–1849). British engineer, born in France. During the Revolution he took refuge in America, worked there as an engineer and came to England in 1799. He had gained a great reputation for constructional work in dockyards etc. before embarking on his most ambitious and anxious task, the building of the Thames tunnel (1825–43). His son, Isambard Kingdom * Brunel, who worked with his father on the tunnel, became even more famous as the chief engineer of the New Great Western Railway.
Noble, C. B., *The Brunels: Father and Son*. 1938

Brunelleschi, Filippo (1377–1446). Italian Renaissance architect, born in Florence. Originally a sculptor, he turned to architecture after * Ghiberti's design for the bronze doors of the Florence baptistery was preferred to his own. He studied the classical buildings still existing in Rome. His theories of perspective were influential in Renaissance art. In the Ospedale degli Innocenti (begun in 1419) he introduced the device of supporting arches on the top of columns, a practice subsequently much imitated. His most spectacular achievement was the construction of the remarkable octagonal dome surmounting the Cathedral in Florence. Built as a double-shelled cupola, the

dome was erected entirely without scaffolding. He also built the churches of S. Lorenzo and S. Spirito.
Manetti, A., *Brunelleschi.* Eng. trans. 1970

Brunhilda (died 613). Visigoth princess who married Sigbert I, ruler of the Frankish kingdom of Austria in 566. As regent for her grandchildren (from 595) she exercised power until she was expelled in 599 and finally defeated and captured in 613. She was put to death by being dragged at the heels of a wild horse. She is often confused with the legendary Brunhilde whose story is told in Wagner's opera-cycle *The Ring*.

Brüning, Heinrich (1885–1970). German politician. A member of the Centre party who had become well known as a financial expert, he became chancellor of a coalition government in 1930, but was defeated in the same year over his stringent proposals to bring about stability. The general election which followed left him powerless in face of a voting combination of Nazis and Communists. Forced to govern by decree he had to rely upon the support of President * Hindenburg, which was withdrawn in 1932. Escaping murder attempts by Nazis he took refuge abroad and was a professor at Harvard (1937–52). After returning to Germany he held the chair of political science at Cologne (1952–55) but never entered politics again.

Brunner, (Heinrich) Emil (1889–1966). Swiss theologian. After pastoral work as a minister in the Swiss Reformed church he eventually became (1924) professor of theology at Zurich University. His views were formed in close association with Karl * Barth, with whom, however, he was in controversy (from 1933) concerning the nature of man. His pamphlet *Nature and Grace* gives his side of the argument. Among his many other works are *Revelation and Reason* (Eng. tr. 1943) and *Communism, Capitalism and Christianity* (1949).
Kegley, C., *The Theology of Emil Brunner.* 1962

Bruno, St (*c.* 1030–1101). Founder of the Carthusian order of monks. Born and educated in Cologne, he later became rector of the cathedral schools at Rheims. In 1084 he withdrew to found an austere religious order at Chartreuse (Cartusia) in the French Alps. He died in Calabria where he had founded a second monastery. London's Charterhouse, on the site of a Carthusian monastery, recalls the name of St Bruno's original foundation.

Bruno, Giordano (1548–1600). Italian philosopher. He became a Dominican monk in 1565, but was expelled for scepticism. Put on trial, he fled and led the life of a wandering teacher until in 1581 he obtained protection from Henry III of France. By 1586, after a vain attempt to obtain employment at Oxford, he was on the move again, and after finding temporary refuge in Wittenberg and Prague returned in 1591 to Italy, where he was handed over to the papal authorities, condemned after a seven-year trial by the Inquisition for his heretical pantheism and burned at the stake. As well as books on philosophy, he wrote poetry and a play. His philosophy had a profound effect on later thinkers, especially Spinoza and Leibniz.
Aquilecchia, G., *Giordano Bruno.* 1971

Brusilov, Alexei Alexeyevich (1856–1926). Russian general. In World War I his great drives through Galicia achieved spectacular if temporary success, but the last, undertaken in 1917 when he was commander-in-chief under the revolutionary provisional government, was halted by desertions of his troops. In 1920 he joined the Red Army in the war against Poland.

Brutus, Lucius Junius (fl. 509 B.C.). Roman consul. He is said to have led the revolt which after the rape of Lucrece caused the expulsion of the last king of Rome, Tarquinius Superbus, and so was honoured as a founder of the republic. Another legend (for even his existence has been doubted) relates how he sentenced his two sons to death for trying to restore the monarchy.

Brutus, Marcus Junius (85?–42 B.C.). Roman soldier and conspirator. Though his interest in philosophy had implanted a distaste for public life, he supported Pompey in the struggle for power which resulted in Caesar's victory at Pharsalus (48), but was pardoned, made governor of Cisalpine Gaul in 46 and praetor of the city of Rome in 44. Persuaded that Caesar planned to make himself king, Brutus reluctantly led the conspirators who murdered him (44). Later he fled from Rome to Macedonia and committed suicide, after his army was defeated at Philippi. (* Antony; * Augustus.)

Bryan, William Jennings (1860–1925). American Democratic politician, born in Illinois. He became a lawyer in Nebraska, and was a member of the House of Representatives (1891–95), identifying himself with the 'free silver' policy. A famous speech ('You shall not crucify mankind upon a cross of gold') won him the Democratic nomination for president at the Chicago convention of 1896, but in the election, as again in 1900 and 1908, he was crushingly defeated. Secretary of state under Woodrow Wilson (1913–15), he resigned during World War I because of his pacifist views. In religion he was an extreme fundamentalist, and his last public activity was to prosecute John T. Scopes, who was charged with teaching the theory of evolution in Tennessee schools in the famous 'Monkey Trial'.

Koenig, L. W., *Bryan: A Political Biography*. 1971

Bryant, Sir Arthur Wynne Morgan (1899–1985). British popular historian. His many books include a series covering from a British viewpoint the Napoleonic and Regency periods: *The Years of Endurance; The Years of Victory; The Age of Elegance*. *Restoration England* takes the story further back and the field is widened still further by *Makers of the Realm* and *The Age of Chivalry*. Subjects of his biographies include Pepys, Baldwin, Nelson and George V. *The Turn of the Tide* (1957) and *Triumph in the West* (1959) are based on the diaries of Lord * Alanbrooke.

Bryant, William Cullen (1794–1878). American poet and journalist. While practising at the bar he became editor of the New York *Evening Post* (1829–78), in which capacity he supported liberal causes, including the abolition of slavery, and helped to promote Lincoln's election to the presidency. His poetry consists mainly of meditations on nature in the manner of Wordsworth, but includes also translations of the *Iliad* and *Odyssey*. His best known poem is 'Thanatopsis' (1817).

McLean, A. F., *William Cullen Bryant*. 1965

Bryce, James Bryce, 1st Viscount (1838–1922). British historian and Liberal politician. Educated at Glasgow and Oxford Universities he was Regius professor of civil law at Oxford (1870–93) and an M.P. (1880–1907). After having held minor offices (1886; 1892–95) he was, as a strong home-ruler, a popular chief secretary for Ireland (1905–07). His most important political role was as ambassador to the USA (1907–13). After World War I he headed a commission to inquire into German atrocities. He was a staunch supporter of the League of Nations. His many works include *The Holy Roman Empire* (1864), *The American Commonwealth* (1888) and *Modern Democracies* (1921). He received the OM in 1907.

Fisher, H. A. L., *James Bryce*. 1927

Buber, Martin (1878–1965). Jewish philosopher. He was born in Vienna, lived in Lemberg (L'vov) as a youth and later attended German universities. He joined the Zionist movement in 1898 and during World War I organized the Jewish National Council in Berlin. From 1924 to 1933 he held a professorship at Frankfurt-am-Main and in 1938 became professor of social philosophy at the Hebrew University, Jerusalem. Much of his philosophical teaching is summed up by his concept *I and Thou* (the title of one of his most important books), in which religious faith is perceived as a continuing dialogue between God and man, in which man, 'addressed' by God, tries to respond. The history of Israel, as recorded in the Bible, appears as a similar dialogue between God and the nation and here Buber found inspiration for his insistence that the aim of Zionism should be to create a society in direct relationship with God. Among Buber's many other works was a German translation of the Hebrew Bible made in conjunction with Franz Rosenzweig.

Kohn, H., *Martin Buber*. 1961

Bucer (or Butzer), **Martin** (1491–1551). German religious reformer, born in Alsace. He became a Dominican friar at the age of 14, but, influenced by Luther and Erasmus, left the order (1521), married a former nun and settled in Strasbourg, where he became a powerful influence among those preaching reform. He took a middle course in the disputes between Luther and Zwingli, but found himself unable to sign the Augsburg Confession of 1530. Attempts to reach agreement between the groups of reformers continued with varying success, but Bucer finally found his position in Germany so irksome that in 1549 he accepted Cranmer's invitation and

went to England; he lectured in theology at Cambridge, where he died.
Hopf, C., *Martin Bucer and the English Reformation*. 1946

Buchan, John, 1st Baron Tweedsmuir (1875–1940). Scottish author and administrator. The son of a minister of the church, he was born in Perth and educated at Oxford. He became one of Lord Milner's assistants in South Africa and, before he crowned his career in 1935 with a peerage and the governor generalship of Canada, he held staff and administrative posts in World War I, was Conservative M.P. (1927–35), and directed the publishing firm of Thomas Nelson for many years. He wrote some fifty books, including biographies (e.g. of Sir Walter Scott, Julius Caesar, and Oliver Cromwell), and novels, of which the most famous, *The Thirty-Nine Steps* (1915), *Greenmantle* (1916) and *The Three Hostages* (1924), relate to the spy-hunting exploits of Captain Richard Hannay.
Smith, J., *John Buchan*. 1965

Buchanan, George (1506–1582). Scottish humanist and Latin poet, educated at Paris University. His *Franciscanus*, a religious satire on the friars, caused his arrest by Cardinal Beaton and imprisonment at St Andrews. He escaped in 1539 and taught Latin in Bordeaux, where Montaigne was among his pupils, and Coimbra (Portugal), where he was imprisoned for a time by the Inquisition. He returned to Scotland in 1561 and became a leading member of the reformed church. Though he had been for a time tutor to Mary Queen of Scots, his *Detectio Mariae Reginae* (1571) exposed her allegedly guilty part in Darnley's death. For the last years of his life he was tutor to James VI. Among many other Latin works was a history of Scotland (1582).
Aitken, J. M., *The Trial of George Buchanan*. 1939

Buchanan, James (1791–1868). Fifteenth president of the U.S., born in Pennsylvania. He was a lawyer, served as a Democratic member of Congress (1821–31), and as a minister to Russia (1832–34). Elected a senator in 1834, his efforts to obtain nomination for the presidency in 1844, 1848 and 1852 failed. However, having in the meantime been secretary of state (1845–49) and minister to Great Britain (1853–56), he gained the nomination in 1856 and was subsequently elected since his absence made him one of the few figures who remained uncommitted on the slavery question. As president (1857–61) he adopted a weak conciliatory policy and went out of office at the commencement of the Civil War, in which he supported the Union cause.
Klein, P. S., *President James Buchanan, A Biography*. 1962

Buchman, Frank Nathan Daniel (1878–1961). American evangelist. He was noted as the founder of the Oxford Group and its development, Moral Rearmament. Born in Pennsburg, Pa., he entered the Lutheran ministry in 1902, but his life work really began when in 1921 he visited England and began to preach his doctrine of 'world-changing through life-changing', mainly among undergraduates. This accounts for the movement's somewhat misleading name, the Oxford Group. One method for helping the achievement of these aims was through gatherings, such as house parties, where young men and women were encouraged publicly to confess their difficulties and misdemeanours (often sexual). In 1938 he gave his campaign the name of 'Moral Rearmament'.
Driberg, T., *The Mystery of Moral Rearmament*. 1964

Buchner, Eduard (1860–1917). German organic chemist. Buchner's major discovery was the reality of cell-free fermentation, which he demonstrated by obtaining supplies of cell-fluid through a complicated process of pulverising yeast. This extract, he showed, would ferment sucrose to ethanol. He attributed this property to a hypothetical enzyme which he termed 'zymase'. The importance of Buchner's researches was to show that living cells are not necessary for fermentation. He thus opened up the modern field of enzyme chemistry. Buchner worked on the fermentation processes of many micro-organisms – e.g. citrous fermentation and acetous fermentation. The general tendency of his work was to show that key life phenomena can be explained in terms of enzyme-catalyzed chemical reactions. A strong Bismarckian patriot, he volunteered for service in World War I and died of a shrapnel wound on the front in Romania.
Delbrück, M. and Schrohe, A., *Hefe, Gärung und Fäulnis*. (1904)

Büchner, Georg (1813–1837). German dramatist. His work has been newly recog-

nized and revived. Alban * Berg's opera *Wozzeck* (1923) is based on Büchner's play of 1837 and *Danton's Death* (1835) has been translated by Stephen Spender and was revived in the 1950s by Bertolt Brecht.
Mayer, H., *Georg Büchner und seine Zeit*. 1946

Buck, Pearl S(ydenstricker) (1892–1973). American novelist. The daughter of Presbyterian missionaries in China, she drew on her long experience of that country to write many novels, several of which, e.g. *The Good Earth* (1931) and *Dragon Seed* (1942), became very popular. She won the Nobel Prize for Literature in 1938.
Buck, P., *My Several Worlds*. 1955

Buckingham, George Villiers, 1st Duke of (1592–1628). English courtier, the son of a Leicestershire knight. He was for many years the favourite ('Steenie') of James I, and wealth was showered upon him. When a Spanish marriage was proposed for the future Charles I, Buckingham took the prince on the much ridiculed and unsuccessful visit to Madrid to woo the lady in person. When Charles came to the throne (1625), Buckingham remained in power but became increasingly unpopular; after the failure of his expedition to Cadiz only Charles's dissolution of parliament (1626) saved him from the consequences of impeachment. Attempts to aid the French Huguenots proved equally futile and it was when he was about to embark at Portsmouth on a second expedition to La Rochelle that he was killed by a discontented soldier, John Felton. His son, **George Villiers, 2nd Duke of Buckingham** (1628–1687), was brought up with the royal family after his father's death; he became the intimate friend of Charles II, fought at the Battle of Worcester (1648) and after the Restoration was a member of the ministerial group known as the Cabal (Clifford, Arlington, Buckingham, Ashley, Lauderdale). Parliament denounced him for improper use of government funds and for his open liaison with the Countess of Shrewsbury (who had witnessed the duel in which Buckingham killed her husband), and he was out of favour with the king from 1674 until 1684, when he retired from politics. He is remembered as a debauchee and a wit, but was one of the most brilliant of the men of the Restoration. He was part-author of the celebrated satire *The Rehearsal* (1671) and is the 'Zimri' of Dryden's *Absalom and Achitophel*.
Williamson, H. R., *George Villiers*. 1940

Buckle, Henry Thomas (1821–1862). English historian. He wrote two volumes of his *History of Civilisation in England* (1857–61) intended to be introductory to a much larger work. His new scientific method of history concentrated on mankind as a whole rather than 'great' individuals and linked the activities of man with natural conditions such as climate and soil, and had considerable influence on later historians.

Buddha, the (i.e. 'the enlightened one'. His personal name was Siddharta and his family name Gautama) (*c.* 560–480 B.C.). Indian religious teacher. He was born in northern India near Nepal, the son of Prince Suddhodana of Kappilavastu and a member of the Sakya clan. He was brought up amid the luxury and dissipations of an eastern court but his father, already fearing that his contemplative nature might lead him to renounce the world, arranged for him to marry young. But what the father had feared took place some years later. He left his wife and son, Rahula, and became a wandering seeker after truth. Six years of extreme asceticism, which he came to regard as futile, were followed by a mystical experience known as 'the enlightenment', said to have come to him while sitting under a Bo or Bode (pipal or wild fig) tree. It was borne in upon him that sorrow and suffering resulted from the craving for life and it was only by abolishing this craving that the cycle of birth and rebirth (i.e. reincarnation) could be broken and a state of *nirvana* (usually understood as a complete cessation of suffering and craving) attained. Buddha, as he was henceforth called, began the task of spreading the new faith in Benares. Five men who had been his original disciples but had left him were first converted; others soon followed and formed a mendicant order of brethren. Three months each year were spent with the brethren in a monastery in contemplation and discussion, the remainder of the year in wandering about the country, begging bowl in hand, gathering adherents. To attain the cessation of craving eight 'steps' were prescribed: (1) understanding, (2) intention, (3) speech, (4) action, and rightness of morals, (5) livelihood, (6) mental control, (7) clearness of thought, (8) concentration. Buddha died after about forty-five years of such missionary work. After the 4th century A.D. Buddhism gradually declined in

India but spread as far as China, Korea and Japan. It is still predominant or important in Tibet, Nepal, Sri Lanka, Burma, Thailand and Indo-China where its adherents run into hundreds of millions. It also has many Western devotees.
Brewster, E. W., *The Life of Gotama the Buddha*. 1956

'Buffalo Bill' *see* **Cody, William Frederick**

Buffet, Bernard (1928–). French artist. He suffered poverty and sickness in his youth but since 1948, when he shared the Grand Prix de La Critique, he has won success and fame. His pictures are often carried out in a gaunt linear style depicting human misery, but he has also achieved success with murals, book illustrations and stage decor.

Buffon, Georges Louis Leclerc, Comte de (1707–1788). French naturalist. Born in Burgundy and educated at the Jesuit college at Dijon, he spent his early manhood in travel and scientific writings; in 1739 he was appointed director of the Jardin du Roi in Paris (now the Jardin des Plantes, which houses the Zoo). From 1749 onwards he was engaged in publishing a vast *Histoire naturelle*. In some of his conjectures on the development of animal species he anticipated Darwin's theories. His speech on admission to the Académie Française included the famous phrase 'le style est l'homme'.
Dimier, L., *Buffon*. 1919

Bugatti, Ettore (1882–1947). Italian engineer, famous for the racing cars built at his Milan factory.

Buhl *see* **Boulle, André Charles**

Buick, David Dunbar (1855–1929). American manufacturer of automobiles. His Detroit company was taken over by General Motors in 1906 and he died in poverty.

Bukharin, Nikolai Ivanovich (1888–1938). Russian Bolshevik. Exiled before the Russian revolution, he returned to become editor of *Pravda* (1917–29) and a member of the Politburo (1924–29). Later he was for a time editor of *Izvestia* but, as a prominent member of the 'right opposition', became one of the victims of Stalin's purge and was convicted and shot.
Cohen, S., *Bukharin and the Bolshevik Revolution*. 1973

Bulgakov, Mikhail Afanasievich (1891–1940). Russian playwright, novelist and short-story writer, born in Kiev. He graduated as a doctor from the University of Kiev in 1916, but left medicine for writing.

His first comedies were staged in 1919, but he did not become really successful until the publication of his two satirical stories *Deviltry* (1923) and *The Fatal Eggs* (1924). His humour and penetrating satire are also much in evidence in the two comedies *Zoyka's Apartment* (1920) and *The Crimson Island* (1927). In 1925 he published his most successful novel *White Guards*, later dramatised as *Days of the Turbins*. Realistic and humorous, his works were extremely popular but his plea for artistic freedom expressed in later works, especially in *The Master and Margarita*, begun in 1928 but not published until 1966, led to government prohibition from publishing in 1930. This official disapproval ensured twenty-five years' neglect of his work after his death in relative obscurity. Publication of his works was resumed in the Soviet Union and abroad in the late 1960s.

Bulganin, Nikolai Alexandrovich (1895–1975). Soviet politician. He made his reputation as a military organizer during World War II when he was deputy commissioner of defence. In 1947 he was appointed a deputy prime minister and minister of the Soviet armed forces. After the death of Stalin (1953) and the subsequent displacement of Malenkov and Beria, Bulganin as premier (1955–58) shared power with Khrushchev and with him paid several visits abroad (e.g. to Britain in 1956). When Khrushchev replaced him Bulganin retired to obscurity as chairman of the state bank.

Bull, John (1562/3–1628). English composer and organist. He was organist of the Chapel Royal, London (1591–1607), left England in 1613 after a mysterious scandal and was organist of Antwerp Cathedral from 1617 to the end of his life. He is regarded highly as a brilliant technical innovator and as one of the founders of the English keyboard repertory; one of his pieces for virginals may be the source of *God Save the Queen*.
Caldwell, J., *English Keyboard Music*. 1973

Buller, Sir Redvers Henry (1839–1908). English soldier. He had great experience of warfare in China, Egypt and elsewhere overseas (including Zululand, where he won the V.C.) before being appointed to the British command in the Boer War. He raised the siege of Ladysmith in February 1900, but was held responsible for earlier defeats, was replaced by Lord Roberts and soon recalled home.
Symons, J., *Buller's Campaign*. 1974

Bülow, Prince Bernhard von (1849–1929). German politician and diplomat. A distinguished diplomatic career culminated in his serving as foreign minister (1897–1900) and chancellor (1900–09), his wit, culture and charm winning the support and friendship of Kaiser William II more effectually than his political skill. His ill-judged threats (e.g. to France in the Morocco crisis of 1905) exacerbated the international situation, and his denial that he had read an indiscreet interview given in 1908 by the emperor to the *Daily Telegraph* (though it had in fact been submitted to the German foreign office) lost him his ruler's support. His *Memoirs* (published 1932) are full of interest, but are basically an attempt at justifying his policies and denying responsibility for failure.

Bülow, Hans Guido von (1830–1894). German musician. The first husband of Liszt's daughter Cosima, who later married Wagner, he was noted alike as pianist and conductor. He gave first performances of works by Wagner, Tchaikovsky and Brahms. Part of his fame as a pianist was for the size of his repertoire, due to a prodigious memory.

Bultmann, Rudolf Karl (1884–1976). German Lutheran theologian. Professor of New Testament studies at Marburg University (1921–51), he was the most influential pioneer of 'form criticism' applied to the Gospels. Much of his work involved 'demythologising' traditional teachings. He emphasised what he called the 'existential' elements in Christ's teaching.

Bunche, Ralph Johnson (1904–1971). American United Nations official. Formerly a lecturer in political science at Howard University, Washington, he became the first black to be a division head at the State Department in 1945. In 1946 he became director of the U.N. Trusteeship Division. He succeeded Count * Bernadotte as U.N. mediator in Palestine in 1948 and for his work won the Nobel Prize for Peace in 1950. Later, he did much valuable work for the United Nations in the Congo and elsewhere.

Bunin, Ivan Alexeyevich (1870–1953). Russian writer. Born of an old but impoverished family, he first worked in an Odessa bookshop then travelled widely in Europe and the East, eventually settling down for three years with Maxim Gorky in Capri. After the Russian revolution he lived in France. He won the Nobel Prize for Literature in 1933. Of his novels the best known is *The Village* (1910) which gives a gloomy picture of Russian peasant life. However, his short stories—'The Gentleman from San Francisco' (1915), 'Mitya's Love' (1925) and 'The Well of Days' (1930)—provide more scope for the lyric vitality of his style.

Bunsen, Robert Wilhelm (1811–1899). German chemist. Born in Göttingen, he was professor of chemistry at Heidelberg from 1852 to 1889. In collaboration with * Kirchhoff he developed the new science of spectrum analysis by which elements can be identified from the spectra they emit when heated. This led to the discovery of caesium in 1860 and rubidium in 1861. Bunsen invented several scientific instruments but is best remembered for the simple laboratory burner which bears his name.
Ostwald, F. W., *R. W. Bunsen*. 1905

Buñuel, Luis (1900–1983). Spanish film director. Noted for the 'black' character of his work, his films include the surrealist work *Un Chien Andalou* (1928), in which Salvador Dali was his associate, *L'Age d'Or* (1930), *Los Olvidados* (1951), *Viridiana* (1961), *Belle de Jour* (1966) and *The Discreet Charm of the Bourgeoisie* (1972).
Buache, F., *The Cinema of Luis Buñuel*. 1973

Bunyan, John (1628–1688). English preacher and author of *The Pilgrim's Progress*. He was born near Bedford, the son of a tinker, became a tinker himself, and served in the parliamentary army in the Civil War. After his marriage (about 1649) he began to undergo profound spiritual experiences and a deep sense of guilt. He was converted, joined the Puritan community of John Gifford ('Evangelist' in *Pilgrim's Progress*) in 1653 and

became an active preacher. After the Restoration he was arrested for preaching without a licence, refused to give up his activities and was imprisoned at Bedford (1660–72). During his not very arduous confinement – he was even allowed to visit London – he wrote his autobiography *Grace Abounding*, and several other works. Release followed the Declaration of Indulgence in 1672 but he was again in prison for two years from 1675, during which time he wrote the first part of *The Pilgrim's Progress. The Life and Death of Mr Badman* and *The Holy War* followed in 1680 and 1682. Bunyan's considerable gifts as a realistic story-teller in plain but vigorous prose reveal themselves almost in spite of the narrow religious doctrines expressed. The second part of *Pilgrim's Progress* (published 1678) is the most serene and humane of his works. *The Pilgrim's Progress* enjoyed contemporary popularity but had to await the Victorian age for universal esteem.
Sharrock, R., *John Bunyan*. 1968

Buonaparte *see* **Bonaparte**

Burbage, Richard (*c.* 1567–1619). English actor. He won early fame on the stage but his period of greatest achievement began when he inherited from his actor father a share in the Blackfriars and Shoreditch Theatres. The latter was pulled down and replaced by the famous Globe Theatre. In this enterprise Shakespeare was one of Burbage's partners and provided him with several of his most popular parts (e.g. Hamlet, Lear and Richard III).
Stopes, C., *Burbage and Shakespeare's Stage*. 1973

Burbank, Luther (1849–1926). American horticulturist, who carried out many experiments in plant breeding. He was the son of a Massachusetts farmer and his early successes were achieved in that area. Later he moved to Santa Rosa in California. By grafting and cross-pollination he produced many improved varieties of plants such as the potato and tomato. He also produced new nectarines (a peach-plum cross) and the spineless cactus which can be used to feed cattle in desert areas.

Burckhardt, Jacob Christoph (1818–1897). Swiss historian. After studying history at the University of Berlin, he was subsequently a professor of history at Basle University (1844–93, with a short break). His particular interest was in the Renaissance, which he interpreted in terms of political and cultural developments (*Die Kultur der Renaissance in Italien*, 1869, is his major work). He also wrote on art. His cultural approach influenced other historians, in particular his friend Nietzsche.
Ferguson, W. K., *The Renaissance in Historical Thought*. 1948; *Jacob Burckhardt and the Renaissance, 100 Years After*. 1960

Burger, Warren Earl (1907–). US judge. Educated at the University of Minnesota, he became assistant attorney-general 1953–56 and a judge of the US Court of Appeals 1956–69. President * Nixon appointed him as chief justice of the Supreme Court 1969– . He attempted to curb the liberal tendencies established in the Court by his predecessor, Earl * Warren.

Burgess and Maclean. Guy Burgess (1911–1965) and Donald Maclean (1913–1983) were officials in the British Foreign Office, but secretly long-standing members of the Communist Party. In 1951 they defected to the USSR having been warned by a 'third man', later identified as Kim * Philby, that they faced arrest. This episode led to an intense security hunt for the 'third', 'fourth' and 'fifth' men involved in their activities. Philby revealed himself as a KGB officer in 1963 and the 'fourth man' was identified in 1979 as the art historian (Sir) Anthony Blunt who then lost his knighthood and position as art advisor to Elizabeth II.
Boyle, A., *The Climate of Treason*. 1979

Burgess, Anthony (John Anthony Burgess Wilson) (1917–). British novelist and critic, born in Manchester. He taught in England and Malaya, but his work as a serious writer only began in 1959 after he was diagnosed as incurably ill: he then wrote five novels in twelve months. His books include *Clockwork Orange* (1962—also filmed), *Shakespeare* (1970), *Napoleon Symphony* (1974), *1985* (1978), and *Earthly Powers* (1980).

Burghley, William Cecil, 1st Baron (1520–1598). English statesman, grandson of the favourite of Henry VII who raised the family to prominence. Educated at Cambridge and Gray's Inn, he held legal office under Henry VIII; in Edward VI's reign he became sec-

retary to the Lord Protector Somerset, on whose overthrow he was briefly imprisoned, but emerged to become secretary of state (1550–53). Under Mary he nominally conformed to Roman Catholicism but was without office. On her death, however, he drafted the proclamation of the accession of Elizabeth, with whom he had maintained secret contact. As secretary of state (1558–72) and Lord High Treasurer he guided the queen's affairs with prudence, loyalty, wisdom and courage for the rest of his life. He became a baron in 1571. Only when he anticipated Elizabeth's secret wishes by hastening the execution of Mary Queen of Scots, in 1587, did he suffer the full force of her venomous (but politic) rage. Burghley was incorruptible, but the various emoluments and perquisites of office enabled him to build and maintain great houses, where he proved a generous host to his many friends and clients. He was succeeded as chief adviser to the queen by his second son, Robert Cecil, later * Earl of Salisbury.
Read, C., *Mr Secretary Cecil and Queen Elizabeth*. 1955; *Lord Burghley and Queen Elizabeth*. 1960

Burgoyne, John (1722–1797). English soldier and dramatist. In the American War of Independence, when he was sent to lead an army from Canada against the rebels of the south, he was severely censured for his surrender at Saratoga (1777). He wrote several successful plays including *The Maid of the Oaks* (1775) and *The Heiress* (1786). He appears in G. B. Shaw's *The Devil's Disciple*.
Paire, L., *Gentleman Johnny*. 1973

Buridan, Jean (1295–1358). French philosopher. He studied at Paris University, obtained his M.A. soon after 1320, and became a teacher, and twice Rector, there. His death in 1358 was probably due to plague. Most of the works of his which survive comprise his lecture notes. His writings defend the autonomy of natural philosophy (= science) as a field of study, independent of metaphysics or theology. Buridan saw the characteristic method of science as being that of establishing empirically well-founded generalizations (rather than necessary truths). He did not believe that truths about the physical word could be shown to be rationally necessary, since thereby God's own infinite freedom would be at risk. Many of his writings about physics are a set of queries around the work of Aristotle. He gave particular attention to the problem of why projectiles continued in motion after they had ceased to be in contact with a source of motion such as a thrower. He formulated a concept that the projectile possessed 'impetus' in proportion to the quantity of matter it contained. Such an idea contains within it the seeds of the modern concept of inertia. Buridan speculated upon the possibility of the motion of the earth, believing that for the earth to move might be a simpler explanation of our observations of the heavens, than believing that all other bodies rotated round the earth.

Burke, Edmund (1729–1797). British politician and writer. He was born and educated in Dublin, came to London to study law but was mainly occupied by literature. He published *A Vindication of Natural Society* (1756) and *The Sublime and Beautiful* (1757) and was an intimate of Dr Johnson. His political career began in earnest when in 1765 he became secretary to the Whig leader Lord * Rockingham, whose government fell, however, a year later. Burke (who had been M.P. for Wendover from 1765, and was returned for Bristol in 1774) became the chief organizer of the Whig opposition and in 1770 produced his famous *Thoughts on the Cause of the Present Discontents*, an attack on the 'King's friends' and a defence of party government. His speeches in favour of conciliating the American colonists were also published and are among the finest examples of his oratory. Denunciation of discrimination against Roman Catholics and of the slave trade gave further evidence of his liberal and generous mind. Indian affairs absorbed him for a time and he moved the impeachment of Warren * Hastings, but in this case his hatred of tyranny led to a misjudgement of the man.

A turning point in Burke's political life came with the publication (1790) of his *Reflections on the Revolution in France*. Here, urging the necessity of political continuity, he found himself revolted by the excesses of violent change. Equally was he estranged from the progressive Whigs, and especially Charles James * Fox, with whom he had been so closely allied. He crossed the floor of the house and sat next to his old opponent Pitt. Thus his political life ended in sorrow and disillusion, but the inspiration of his wonderful eloquence, more effective in the written than the spoken word, survives. 'Magnanimity in politics is not seldom the

truest wisdom; and a great empire and little minds go ill together.'
O'Gorman, F., *Edmund Burke: His Political Philosophy*. 1973

Burke, Robert O'Hara (1820–1861). Australian explorer, born in Co. Galway, Ireland. Early episodes in his life included periods of service in the Austrian army and the Irish constabulary before he emigrated (1853) to Australia, where he became an inspector of police. In 1860 he set out as leader of an expedition to cross Australia from south to north. He succeeded in his purpose by reaching the estuary of the Flinders river with W. J. Wills but both men died of starvation on the way back. The expedition was elaborately equipped, but mismanagement and confusion of purpose in the rear, and Burke's impetuous character, which induced him to press forward without adequate attention to his chain of supplies, brought about disaster.
Wilcox, D., *Explorers*. 1975

Burke, William (1792–1829). Irish labourer. With another Irishman, William Hare, found an easy way of making a living by enticing the unwary to enter their Edinburgh lodging house, suffocating them and selling their bodies for dissection. The unsuspecting doctor, Robert Knox, had paid from £8 to £14 each for fifteen corpses before inquisitive neighbours summoned the police. Hare saved himself by turning King's Evidence but Burke was duly hanged.
Doyle, H., *Burke and Hare: The True Story*. 1973

Burlington, Richard Boyle, 3rd Earl of, and 4th Earl of Cork (1695–1753). British art patron. His influence was largely employed to further the use of the Palladian style in architecture, of which he had become a great admirer while travelling in Italy as a young man. He himself often acted as architect, e.g. for his own villa at Chiswick. Burlington House, London, the home of the Royal Academy, stands on the site of his former town house.

Burne-Jones, Sir Edward, 1st Bart (1833–1898). English-born painter of Welsh descent. Born in Birmingham, he formed a friendship with William Morris at Exeter College, Oxford, and with him, when both decided to take up art, was attracted to Rossetti and the Pre-Raphaelites. His subjects are mainly legendary or mythological scenes such as *King Cophetua and the Beggar-maid* (Tate Gallery, London) and episodes from the Arthurian cycle. Fine draughtsmanship, brilliant colours and romantic treatment are characteristics of his style. With William Morris he also designed stained-glass windows and tapestries.
Harrison, M. and Waters, B., *Burne-Jones*. 1973

Burnet, Gilbert (1643–1715). Scottish-born prelate and historian. Born in Edinburgh and educated at Marishal College, Aberdeen, he was professor of divinity at Glasgow from 1669 to 1674, when he came to London to take up a royal chaplaincy. In 1683, having earned disfavour by his condemnation of King Charles II's immorality and by his staunch Whiggery, he went to Holland, where he became friend and adviser of the Prince of Orange and chaplain to his wife. When the couple became William III and Mary II of Great Britain, he became bishop of Salisbury. The consummation of his life work was his great *History of My Own Time*, which appeared posthumously (1724–34), and in which his tolerance, enthusiasm and innocent indiscretions are revealed.
Clarke, T. E. S. and Foxcroft, H. C., *Life of Gilbert Burnet*. 1907

Burnet, Sir (Frank) Macfarlane (1889–1985). Australian medical scientist. Educated at Geelong College and Melbourne University, he became, through research at the Lister Institute, London, and elsewhere, an authority on virus diseases and was director of the Walter and Eliza Hall Institute, Melbourne (1944–65). He shared with P. B. * Medawar the 1960 Nobel Prize for Physiology and Medicine for their work on 'acquired immunological tolerance'. He was knighted in 1951 and made a member of the O.M. in 1958.

Burnett, Frances Eliza Hodgson (1849–1924). English-born writer, who emigrated to America in her youth, remembered for *Little Lord Fauntleroy* (1886) and *The Secret Garden* (1911).
Thwaite, A., *Waiting for the Party: A life of Frances Hodgson Burnett*. 1974

Burney, Fanny (or Frances; later Madame d'Arblay) (1752–1840). English novelist and diarist. She married a French officer and

lived in Paris (1802–15), then returned to England. Her husband died in 1818. She began to write quite early in life. *Evelina*, the story of a young girl's entry into society, had to be published under a pseudonym (1778). It was enormously popular; on her authorship being disclosed she became friend of Dr Johnson. Her second novel, *Cecilia* (1782), was also a success, but her later works did not prove popular. Her *Letters and Diaries* (published posthumously) give lively accounts of Dr Johnson, Garrick and their circle, and of her life at court.
White, E., *Fanny Burney, Novelist*. 1960

Burns, John (1858–1943). English politican, the first working man to become a British cabinet minister. His early reputation was that of strike agitator and political demonstrator, but he became more moderate with age and in 1906 joined Campbell-Bannerman's Liberal government as president of the Local Government Board; he had become an M.P. in 1892. Asquith promoted him to be president of the Board of Trade in 1914, but his pacifism compelled his resignation on the outbreak of World War I. He never joined the Labour party.
Kent, W., *John Burns: Labour's Lost Leader*. 1950

Burns, Robert (1759–1796). Scotland's national poet. He was born near Alloway, Ayrshire, the son of a self-educated tenant farmer who gave him his first lessons and inspired a love of reading encouraged later by John Murdoch, a village schoolmaster. From the age of 14 Burns wrote poems in dialect, but it was only while he and his brother were farming unsuccessfully at Mossgiel (1784–88) that, to obtain money for contemplated emigration to Jamaica, he listened to suggestions for publication. In the meantime he continued a life of hard work, varied by wide reading, and bouts of dissipation, and complicated by his many love affairs. The first edition of his poems (the Kilmarnock edition) appeared in 1786 and its immediate success caused him to be lionized in Edinburgh, where he won popularity by his modesty, intelligence and charm. But he soon tired of patronage and flattery, and having acquired £500 from a second edition he was encouraged to settle on a small farm at Ellisland and marry Jean Armour, one of his many loves. The failure of the farm caused him to accept a post as exciseman at Dumfries. His first generous sympathy with the French Revolution might have threatened this government post, but he was quickly disillusioned and in 1794 on a patriotic impulse joined the Dumfriesshire Volunteers. Over-work, alcohol and (probably) endocarditis induced by rheumatic fever combined to bring about his early death. The last years of his life as a writer were mainly spent in composing, collecting and adapting song-lyrics. In Edinburgh he had met James Johnson, collector and publisher of Scottish songs, and it is to Burns's cooperation with him (and others) that we owe that wonderful abundance of songs which immortalize his name. They include *Auld Lang Syne, My love is like a red red rose, Comin 'Thro' the Rye, John Anderson my Jo, Ye Banks and Braes o' Bonny Doon* and many just as famous.

Burns also achieved success with such masterly satires as *Holy Willie's Prayer* and *The Holy Fair*, and long narrative poems such as *The Jolly Beggars, Death and Dr Hornbrook* and *Tam o'Shanter*, all except for the last named belonging to the earlier part of his life. Burns is unique among the great poets (except Shakespeare) in having a universal and enduring appeal. He is much admired in the U.S.S.R.
Daiches, D., *Robert Burns and His World*. 1971

Burr, Aaron (1756–1836). American politician. He served in the War of Independence, then became a successful lawyer and in 1791 was elected to the Senate. He tied with * Jefferson in the presidential election of 1800 and became his vice-president 1801–05. In 1804 Burr killed Alexander Hamilton, his long-standing political adversary, in a duel. He fled and tried to set up an independent state comprising the south-western states and part of Mexico. A small expedition was equipped and sailed down the Mississippi but Burr was arrested, tried for treason (1807) and acquitted, mainly on technical grounds. He continued his intrigues abroad (1808–12), but later resumed his law practice in New York City.
Schachner, W., *Aaron Burr*. 1937

Burroughs, Edgar Rice (1875–1950). American author. He survives by the creation of a single character, 'Tarzan', the white man who was brought up by apes and whose adventures are recorded in many books, nearly all subsequently filmed.

Burton, Decimus (1800–1881). English architect. The son of a builder and trained by his father, Burton was not only a good architect but had a special talent for placing buildings in a landscape. In London his work included the Ionic screen and triumphal arch for Hyde Park Corner.

Burton, Richard (1925–1984). British stage and film actor, born in Pontrhydfen, South Wales. Educated at Port Talbot Secondary school and Exeter College, Oxford. He made his first stage appearance in 1943 as Glan in *Druid's Rest*, Liverpool. After serving with the R.A.F. he acted many times with the Old Vic Company and in New York; particularly noted for his Hamlet and Henry V. Films include *Exorcist II, The Heretic, Equus, Alexander the Great, Cleopatra, Look Back in Anger, Where Eagles Dare, Becket, Who's Afraid of Virginia Woolf?* He produced a highly praised film version of Dylan Thomas's *Under Milk Wood* in the early 1970s. He married four times, including Elizabeth Taylor, the actress, twice.
Cottrell, J. and Cashin, F., *Richard Burton*. 1971

Burton, Sir Richard Francis (1821–1890). English explorer and writer. While in the Indian army (1843–49), he served with Napier in Sind. In 1853 he became the first white man to visit the holy places of Mecca when he went on a pilgrimage there disguised as a Pathan Moslem. After exploring Somaliland he discovered Lake Tanganyika with J. H. Speke in 1858. Speke's discovery of Lake Nyanza and his claim that it was the main source of the Nile led to a prolonged controversy with Burton, only settled when H. M. * Stanley proved Speke right. Subsequently Burton held consular posts in Africa, Brazil, Syria, Damascus and finally Trieste (from 1872). He described his travels in a long series of vividly written books, but by far his greatest literary achievement, both in size and fame, was his translation of *The Arabian Nights* (1885–88). He is said to have mastered more than thirty languages.
Wright, T., *The Life of Sir Richard Burton*. 2 vols, 1968

Burton, Robert (1577–1640). English clergyman, famed as the author of *The Anatomy of Melancholy*. He spent nearly all his life at Christ Church, Oxford, first as a student and then, having taken orders, as tutor. The work upon which his fame entirely rests first appeared in 1621. The name 'Democritus Junior' which appeared on the title page was a reference to Democritus, 'the laughing philosopher' of the ancient Greeks. The book is in form a whimsical and immensely learned analysis of the various types of melancholia but contains the stories of most of the celebrated lovers and is illustrated by quotations from almost all the classical and medieval authors then known.

Bury, John Bagnell (1861–1927). British historian. Educated and later a professor at Trinity College, Dublin, he became professor of modern history at Cambridge in 1902 and was one of the editors of the *Cambridge Ancient History*. He wrote much on the history of the later Roman empire and his *History of Greece* (1900) remains a standard work.
Baynes, N. H., *Bibliography of J. B. Bury, with Memoir*. 1929

Busby, Richard (1606–1695). English educator. Headmaster of Westminster School, London (1640–95), he was equally famous for his scholarship and his use of the birch. Among his well known pupils were Dryden and Locke.
Barker, G. F. R., *Memoir of R. Busby*. 1895

Bush, George (1924–). US Republican politician. Son of a US senator, he was educated in Massachusetts, served in World War II, founded an oil company in Texas, and then entered politics. He served as a congressman (1967–70), Ambassador to the UN (1970–73), head of the US liaison office to Peking (1974–75), and Director of the Central Intelligence Agency (1975–76). He became vice president of the US under Ronald Reagan in 1981.

Bush, Vannevar (1890–1974). American electrical engineer. Educated at Tufts and the Massachusetts Institute of Technology, he taught at M.I.T. 1919–38 and in 1925 devised the first analogue computer, used in solving differential equations. Director of the U.S. Office of Scientific Research and Development 1941–46, he took ultimate responsibility for the atomic bomb project.

Busoni, Ferruccio Benvenuto (1866–1924). Italian musician. A child prodigy, he came to be regarded as one of the greatest of pianists. His greatest work, the opera *Doktor Faust*, left unfinished at his death and completed by a pupil, is rarely performed.
Dent, E. J., *Busoni*. 1933

Buss, Frances Mary (1827–1894). English educator. She worked with Dorothea * Beale to improve the opportunities of women to obtain higher education. When her mother's private school was converted into the North London Collegiate School (1850) she became its headmistress. The Girls' Public Day School Trust resulted from her handing over (1870) this school to a trust.
Burstall, S. A., *Frances Mary Buss: An Educational Pioneer*. 1938

Bustamente, Sir (William) Alexander (1884–1977). Jamaican politician. Of mixed birth, he spent some time abroad before returning to Jamaica in 1932. In 1934 he founded the Labour party, having left the People's National party led by his cousin Norman Manley. From 1953 to 1955 he was chief minister. After the formation of the West Indian Federation in 1958 he worked for the secession of Jamaica and was supported by a referendum held in 1961 and subsequent elections: Jamaica accordingly withdrew and in 1962 Bustamente became first prime minister of his newly independent country.

Bute, John Stuart, 3rd Earl of (1713–1792). British politician. Educated at Leiden University, Holland, he subsequently divided his time between London and his Scottish estates. He was a close friend of Frederick, Prince of Wales, and his wife, the Princess. The friendship with the family survived the prince's death in 1751. Bute gained a position in the household and became virtually the tutor of the young prince, the future George III, whose warm affection he won. Unfortunately he instilled into him the doctrines of * Bolingbroke's *Patriot King* which claimed for the sovereign a much more active part than George's abilities could sustain or recent constitutional practice could allow. The test came when George II died. Bute was brought into the government in 1761, manoeuvred Newcastle and Pitt out of office and became head of the administration in 1762. During his year of office he ended the Seven Years War, but what were considered the weaknesses of the settlement, his own personal unpopularity and his lack of a political following forced him to resign in 1763. But for several years the influence of the 'minister behind the curtain' banefully survived.
McKelvey, J. L., *George III and Lord Bute*. 1973

Butler, Josephine Elizabeth (1828–1906). English social reformer. She was a fervent supporter of education for women, but most of her work was done for the more unfortunate of her sex. Between 1883 and 1886, working with Florence Nightingale, Harriet Martineau and others, she secured the repeal of acts which bore hardly upon prostitutes. She also established a pioneer organization for suppression of the 'white slave trade'.
Bell, E. M., *Josephine Butler*. 1963

Butler, Nicholas Murray (1862–1947). American educationist. After graduating at Columbia University he studied further in Berlin and Paris. He returned to become professor of education at Columbia University of which he was president (1902–45). From 1907 onwards he worked incessantly for international goodwill, was president (1925–45) of the Carnegie Endowment for International Peace and in 1931 shared with Jane Addams the Nobel Prize for Peace. His many books include *The Meaning of Education* (1898 and 1915), *Scholarship and Service* (1921) and *The Path to Peace* (1930).
Butler, N. M., *Across the Busy Years*. 1939

Butler, Reg (Reginald Cotterell) (1910–1981). British sculptor. He made his name by his linear wrought-iron sculpture, such as his *Unknown Political Prisoner*, which won first prize in an international competition held in London in 1953. He then resumed his interest in modelling. He wrote on *Creative Development* (1962).

Butler, Richard Austen, Baron Butler of Saffron Walden (1902–1982). British politician, son of Sir Montague Butler, a famous head of Pembroke College, Cambridge. Born in India and educated at Marlborough and Cambridge, Butler became Conservative M.P. for Saffron Walden in 1929 and in the pre-war governments he was under-secretary of state for India (1932–37) and for foreign affairs (1938–41). During World War II he was minister of education (1941–45) and chief begetter of the famous act (1944) on which future educational policy was based. During the Labour party's periods of office it was as a result of Butler's hard work and inspiration at the Conservative research department that his party acquired forward-looking policies that helped it regain office. He served as Chancellor of the Exchequer (1951–55), Home Secretary (1957–62) and Foreign Secretary (1963–64), all with great distinction, and was deputy prime minister to Eden, Macmillan and Home, but the highest post of all – that of prime minister – always eluded him. In 1965, a few months after the Conservative electoral defeat, he became a life peer and master of Trinity College, Cambridge.

Butler, Samuel (1612–1680). English poet. He wrote the long satirical poem *Hudibras* (1663–78), which was much admired by Charles II, who is said to have kept it always at his side. Butler, however, was only meagerly rewarded for his work. *Hudibras* strings together into a connected whole, burlesques of hypocritical and more or less disreputable, Puritan characters of the Civil War period. Butler was the son of a Worcestershire farmer. He acted as clerk to several of the land-owning gentry before he became, in 1661, secretary to Lord Carbery, who appointed him steward of Ludlow castle.
Jack, I., *Augustan Satire*. 1952

Butler, Samuel (1835–1902). English author. The son of a Nottinghamshire clergyman he was educated at Shrewsbury (where his grandfather had been a great headmaster) and Cambridge. He refused to enter the church because of religious doubts, and became a successful sheep farmer in New Zealand (1860–64) instead. On his return to England, he lived alone in London, devoting himself to painting, writing and music; one of his paintings hangs in the Tate Gallery. In 1872 he published the Utopian satire *Erewhon*. 'Erewhon' (an anagram of 'nowhere') is a land of paradox where, for example, crime is regarded as an illness and illness as a crime. A sequel, *Erewhon Revisited*, appeared in 1901. *Erewhon* was followed by a number of semi-scientific works in which he examined the theories of Darwin, accepting evolution, while giving the credit for it to Darwin's predecessors, and rejecting natural selection. In its place he offered his own creative view of evolution. In *Unconscious Memory* (1880) he anticipated the theories of C. G. Jung. In his later years he became absorbed by Homer. He translated the *Iliad* (1898) and the *Odyssey* (1900) while *The Humour of Homer* (1892) is a notable piece of literary criticism. *The Authoress of the Odyssey* makes almost plausible an ingenious theory that the *Odyssey* was written by a Sicilian woman from Trapani. Possibly his best known work, however, is *The Way of All Flesh* (published in 1903 but written much earlier), an autobiographical novel in which, through a thinly disguised portrait of his own childhood and youth, he demonstrates the conflict of the generations and the deleterious effects of a typical Victorian upbringing.
Harkness, S. B., *The Career of Butler: A Bibliography*. 1955

Butterfield, William (1814–1900). English architect, one of the leading practitioners of the revived Gothic style. Of his many churches in a brilliant polychrome style, perhaps the best known is All Saints, Margaret Street, London (1849–59); Keble College, Oxford (1867–75), was one of his later works.
Thompson, P., *William Butterfield*. 1971

Butterworth, George Sainton Kaye (1885–1916). English composer, who collected and was strongly influenced by English folk songs. He composed two song cycles based on poems from Housman's *A Shropshire Lad* (embodying themes from the Housman lyrics) and *The Banks of Green Willow*. He was killed on the Somme in World War I after gaining an MC.

Buxtehude, Dietrich (or Diderik) (1637–1707). Danish musician, organist at Lübeck from 1668. J. S. Bach considered him to be the greatest organist of his era and once walked 200 miles to hear him play; Handel also came to hear his celebrated evening concerts. As a composer he is renowned for his church tatas and his imaginative works for the organ.
Starl, W., *Franz Tunder und Dietrich Buxtehude*. 1926

Buxton, Sir Thomas Fowell (1786–1845). English reformer. On election to parliament he instituted a private inquiry into the administration of prisons, which led to the formation of a prison reform society. He was also an opponent of the slave trade and as leader of the abolitionist group in succession to Wilberforce was instrumental in securing the passage of the 1833 act for the ending of slavery in British possessions.

Mottram, R. H., *Buxton the Liberator*. 1946

Byng, John (1704–1757). English admiral. At the beginning of the Seven Years War (1756) he was sent to relieve Minorca, blockaded by the French. After his van had been mauled and the rear, under his personal command, had fallen into some confusion, he decided after a council of war to abandon the project and withdraw to Gibraltar. For this possible error of judgement he was condemned to death and, despite a strong recommendation to mercy disregarded by George II, shot – 'pour encourager les autres', as Voltaire aptly put it.

Pope, D., *At Twelve Mr Byng was Shot*. 1962

Byng of Vimy, Julian Hedworth Byng, 1st Viscount (1862–1935). English field marshal. He was commander of the British 3rd Army in France in World War I, and his name is particularly associated with the capture of Vimy ridge and the Cambrai offensive. In the final victorious operations his army captured 67,000 Germans. Earlier in the war he had commanded the 9th Corps at the Dardanelles, and the Canadian Corps. Byng was governor general of Canada (1921–26) and commissioner of the London Metropolitan Police (1928–31).

Byrd, Richard Evelyn (1888–1957). American Arctic and Antarctic explorer. He was the first to fly over the North Pole (1926) and the South Pole (1929), the latter as leader of an expedition (1928–30) in the course of which Marie Byrd Land and other areas were discovered. He led further expeditions to the Antarctic in 1933–35, 1946–47 and 1955–56. Byrd, who was a naval officer, became a rear-admiral in 1930.

Montague, R., *Oceans, Poles and Airmen*. 1971

Byrd, William (1534–1623). English composer. He was born in Lincolnshire and became a pupil of Thomas Tallis. Though he was a Roman Catholic he accepted positions in the Anglican church as organist of Lincoln Cathedral (1563–75), and joint organist (with Tallis) of the Chapel Royal (1575–1623). He also shared with Tallis a monopoly for the printing and selling of music and was often engaged in litigation, much of it concerned with a disputed estate. He composed masses and motets for the Catholic church as well as music for the Anglican liturgy, in addition to his great output of madrigals and instrumental pieces (mainly for the virginal). The power of his music and the extraordinary skill of his contrapuntal writing gained him great fame in Europe during his lifetime.

Andrews, H. K., *The Technique of Byrd*. 1966

Byrnes, James Francis (1879–1972). American lawyer and politician. He represented South Carolina as a Democratic congressman (1911–25) and US senator (1931–41), and was a supreme court justice (1941–42). At first he supported but later became increasingly critical of Roosevelt's New Deal. This cost him the vice-presidential nomination in 1944. It was in the last stages of his career that, as President Truman's secretary of state (1945–47), he set the scene for the Cold War. He was also governor of South Carolina 1951–55.

Byrnes, J. F., *Speaking Frankly*. 1947

Byron, George Gordon Noel, 6th Baron (1788–1824). English poet. He was born in London, but spent his first ten years in Aberdeen lodging with his mother, whose fortune had been frittered away by her husband, 'mad Jack' Byron. Much of his childhood was made unhappy by unsuccessful attempts to cure a lame foot, of which he remained painfully conscious. He inherited the title in 1798 and went to live in the family home, Newstead Abbey, Nottinghamshire. At Harrow and Trinity College, Cambridge, he not only read eagerly but took pride in overcoming his lameness by boxing, playing cricket and becoming a powerful swimmer. In 1807 he published *Hours of Idleness*, which was savagely criticized in the *Edinburgh Review*. He withdrew it and replied with the satire *English Bards and Scotch Reviewers*. After leaving Cambridge he travelled to Greece and Albania with his friend J. C. Hobhouse (he swam the Hellespont in May 1810), and his tour was described in the first two cantos of the semi-autobiographical *Childe Harold's Pilgrimage* (published 1812). *The Giaour* (1813), *The Bride of Abydos* (1813) and *Lara* (1814) also reflect the romantic moods inspired by his travels. He had become famous overnight, was lionized in society, made a few radical speeches in the House of Lords, and engaged in a series of love affairs, not always by his own choice. The half-mad

Byron, George Gordon Noel, 6th Baron

Lady Caroline Lamb, for example, fell in love with him and pestered him almost to distraction. In 1815, he married an heiress, Annabella Milbanke, but the marriage was unhappy from the start; conjectures about his incestuous relationship with his half-sister Augusta Leigh, combined with his wife's complaints of his dark moods of cruelty and despair, made separation inevitable. Ostracized by many of his former admirers, Byron left England for good in 1816 and moved to Switzerland, where he spent happy weeks with the Shelleys. From a life of dissipation and promiscuous love affairs in Venice (1817–19) Byron was rescued by Teresa, Countess Guiccioli, a woman of cultivated tastes who became his mistress. In this Italian period he finished *Childe Harold* and among other writings produced the drama *Manfred* (1817), *Beppo* (1818) and *A Vision of Judgement* (1822). He also began *Don Juan* (1819–24), that extraordinary medley of satire, adventure and self-revelation which remained unfinished at his death. Byron's interest in the cause of freeing Greece from Turkish rule led him to join the liberation committee in 1823. He set out for Greece later in the year: the following April he died of fever at Missolonghi. For much of the 19th century he was regarded as the epitome of the romantic hero, a noble, melancholy wanderer and a passionate lover of freedom, but this judgement, based on his early poems, is largely the creation of his admirers (and in some moods of himself). The truer Byron, repressed in youth and always aware of his deformity, was much more of a satirist in the tradition of Voltaire, an ironical realist as little blind to his own failings as to those of others, as aware of the savagery, squalor and tedium of life as of its beauty and glory.

Marchand, L. A., *Byron: A Biography*. 3 vols. 1957; *Byron: A Portrait*. 1970

C

Caballero, Francisco Largo *see* **Largo Caballero, Francisco**

Cabell, James Branch (1879–1958). American novelist. Originally a teacher, then a journalist, he made his name with the novel *Jurgen* (1919). This, like most of his other works, was written in an elaborate, archaic style and set in the imaginary medieval country of Poictesme. In such books as *Beyond Life* (1919) and *Some of Us* (1930), he propounded the critical theory that allegory, not realism, can truly interpret life.

Cabot, John (Giovanni Caboto) (*c.* 1450–*c.* 1498). Italian navigator believed to have been born in Genoa, though later he became a Venetian citizen. Between 1484 and 1490 he came to England and lived in Bristol. Commissioned by Henry VII in 1497 he sailed westward with two ships and discovered what was probably Newfoundland or Nova Scotia but which he took to be Asia. He made a second voyage in 1498 from which he never returned.

His son, **Sebastian Cabot** (?1476–1557), was born in Venice. He probably accompanied his father on the 1497 voyage and later became map-maker to Henry VIII and Ferdinand V (of Spain). An attempt to find the North-west Passage (1509) failed owing to a mutiny of the crew. In 1518 he was appointed pilot-major by the emperor Charles V (Charles I of Spain). He led an expedition which explored the coast of South America (1526–30), seeking a passage to the Pacific. In 1548 he returned to England and founded a company of merchant venturers, for which he organized an expedition (1553) under Willoughby and Chancellor to search for a north-east passage from the Arctic ocean to the China coast. In 1544 Cabot published a map showing his own and his father's discoveries.

Williamson, J. A. (ed.), *Cabot Voyages and Bristol Discovery under Henry VII*. 1962

Cabral, Pedro Alvarez (*c.* 1460–*c.* 1520). Portuguese navigator. In 1500 he was made leader of an expedition to the East Indies with thirteen ships, but while on the way he was forced westward by adverse currents (some say he deliberately altered course) and landed on the north-east coast of Brazil, of which he formally took possession on behalf of Portugal. During his resumed voyage to the east he lost seven ships with their crews (including the famous navigator Bartolomeo Diaz) before reaching Mozambique and eventually Calient (near Madras) in India. Having made the first commercial treaty between India and Portugal, he returned to Lisbon in July 1501 with much booty.

Amado, J. C., *Pedro Alvares Cabral*. 1968

Cabrini, Francesca Xavier (1850–1917). Italian born nun who lived in the U.S.A. from 1889. She founded the Missionary Sisters of the Sacred Heart, and schools, hospitals and orphanages. She became the first saint of the U.S.A. when Pope Pius XII canonized her in 1946.

Cadbury, George (1839–1922). English manufacturer and social reformer. With his brother Richard (1835–1899) he assumed control of his father's Birmingham cocoa business in 1867, and when it expanded in 1879 he transferred the enterprise to Bournville. Being greatly interested in housing he integrated the factory in a planned housing project and so organized the first modern 'model' village. A Quaker and a Liberal, George Cadbury owned two London newspapers, the *Daily News* and the *Star*, which were active in all campaigns for social reform.

Cade, Jack (died 1450). English leader of the Kentish rebellion of 1450 during the reign of Henry VI. Misgovernment and financial oppression were the main causes of the rising which soon became formidable. Cade headed and managed to keep together a host which swelled to many thousands as it moved towards London, overcoming such resistance as it met on the way. Once they had reached the city the authorities induced them to disperse, partly by a show of force but mainly by concessions and promises. Cade was hunted down and killed at Heathfield in Sussex while resisting arrest.
Clayton, J., *The True Story of Jack Cade*. 1910

Cadillac, Antoine de la Mothe, Sieur (1656–1730). French administrator and soldier. He settled a colony on the site of modern Detroit (1701) and later governed Louisiana (1713–16), before retiring to Gascony.

Cadogan, William Cadogan, 1st Earl (1675–1726). British soldier. He was the Duke of * Marlborough's most trusted subordinate in the campaigns of the War of the Spanish Succession and was known as his 'maid of work' from the variety of tasks he undertook. At Oudenarde (1708) he commanded the Allied vanguard. He was ennobled for his success in suppressing the Jacobite rising of 1715.
Churchill, W. S., *Marlborough*. 1933–38

Cadorna, Count Luigi (1850–1928). Italian soldier. He was commander-in-chief of the Italian armies in World War I from 1915 to November 1917 when after the disaster at Caporetto he was replaced by Diaz.

Cadwallon (d. 634). King of the isles of Anglesey and Man. In revenge for his expulsion from his kingdom by * Edwin, he is said to have joined Penda, king of Mercia, and taken part in the battle in which Edwin was killed. Two years later he was defeated and killed by Edwin's successor * Oswald.

Caedmon (died *c.* 680). One of the earliest poets in England. According to * Bede he was a herdsman who was granted a vision and received the gift of song. Of his poems, most of which were said to be metrical paraphrases of the Bible, only a single hymn quoted by Bede is regarded as an authentic survival. Caedmon spent the last years of his life as a lay brother in Whitby Abbey, Yorkshire.

Caesar, Caius Julius (*c.* 101–44 B.C.). Roman soldier and statesman. Though born into one of the oldest and noblest Roman families he supported the democratic faction of Marius (who had married his aunt) against the senatorial oligarchy under Sulla. Sulla's triumph in 81 threatened his life and forced him to live abroad until 78, when, Sulla having died, he returned to Rome and resumed his political career as a leader of the democratic party, greatly increasing his popularity by lavish expenditure during his year (65) as aedile (organizer of games and festivals). A new political situation was now taking shape. Caesar, back from a year's campaigning in Spain, had formed a political association with * Marcus Crassus, an ambitious intriguer and the richest man in Rome; * Pompey had returned a national hero and was seeking political support for the terms of his settlement of Asia and especially for the provision of land for his returning veterans. The possibility of a bargain was evident, and in 60 the first 'triumvirate' between the three men was formed. It was in effect an unofficial division of spoils. Caesar, as consul in 59, was able to meet Pompey's demands and obtained what he most wanted for himself – a great military command in Gaul covering north Italy and the conquered lands beyond the Alps. During the next eight years (58–50) Caesar in a series of brilliant campaigns conquered much of Gaul, raided Britain twice (55 and 54) and advanced the Roman frontiers to the Rhine.

Meanwhile a rift between Crassus and Pompey threatened not only stability in Rome but the survival of the triumvirate. Caesar made a hasty return in 56 to meet his partners at Luca; he patched up the quarrel and renewed the triumvirate on fresh terms. This time each was to have a military command. Pompey's – which in fact he exercised from Rome through deputies – was in Spain; Crassus was to go to the east (he started a war against the Parthians and was killed in battle in 53); and Caesar was to have his command in Gaul prolonged. The arrangements were carried out but it soon became clear that relations between Caesar and Pompey were becoming increasingly strained. Caesar managed to postpone an open quarrel until he could safely leave Gaul, but in 49, instead of obeying orders from Rome to disband the legions, he led his troops across the Rubicon, the frontier stream, so indicating that he was making war upon the republic. Pompey, having few troops in Italy to oppose him, withdrew with the government to Epirus (Albania). This gave Caesar time to enforce the surrender of Pompey's troops in Spain and consolidate his own position in Rome, before crossing the Adriatic, luring Pompey out of his entrenched camp by marching into Thessaly and finally deciding the issue by his great victory at Pharsalus (48). Pompey fled to Egypt and was murdered on landing. Caesar followed him to Egypt and in 47 confirmed Cleopatra, whom he had made his mistress and by whom he had a son, on the disputed throne.

In 46 Caesar was in north Africa, where he crushed the remaining Pompeian leaders at Thapsus. He returned to Rome, now dictator and tribune for life, to celebrate four triumphs and distribute gifts. In 44 he declined the title of king. He had already proposed or carried out many practical and liberal reforms (improvements to the calendar, extension of the citizenship etc.) and was at the peak of success when he was assassinated on the Ides (15th) of March 44, by conspirators headed by Brutus and Cassius, his erstwhile friends. His will left all he possessed to his grand-nephew Octavian, later to become Augustus.

Though motivated by great personal ambition, Caesar was more than a self-seeking demagogue. He succeeded in winning stability for Rome and the provinces, and his dictatorship represented the crushing of an oligarchy and paved the way for the empire. He was among the greatest generals of history, a superb military narrator and commentator (his *De bello Gallico* stands supreme), a statesman of liberal thought and instantaneous and perfectly executed action, and a man of great personal charm.

Gelzer, M., *Caesar: Politician and Statesman*. 1968

Caesarion (47–30 B.C.). Nickname of the son of Cleopatra and Julius Caesar, who ruled in association with his mother as Ptolemy XIV. After Cleopatra's death he was lured from refuge in India by agents of Octavian (* Augustus) and put to death.

Caesarius, St (*c.* 470–543). Bishop of Arles (now in Provence), France (from 502). At a time when Visigoths, Ostrogoths and Franks were contending for mastery of the old Roman province he gained a great reputation not only for his sermons and for his staunch support of orthodox doctrines but for the statesman-like qualities which enabled him to safeguard the communities of monks and nuns under his care.

Cage, John (1912–). American composer, proponent of the principle of 'indeterminism' in music. He studied with * Schönberg and Varèse, and began to experiment in composition in the late 1930s. He used sounds of indeterminate notation and duration, produced by a variety of means (including but not limited to musical instruments). He aimed to encourage audience response to all sound; he did not intend to present a selected musical structure as a personal expression.

Cagliostro, Count Alessandro di (1743–1795). Italian adventurer (possibly Giuseppe Balsamo of Palermo). He travelled widely in the east, picked up some knowledge of chemistry and occult science. He claimed to be able to transmute base metals into gold and made a fortune in Europe selling love philtres and elixirs of youth. In 1776 he came to England. In Paris he was involved (1784–85) in the affair of the diamond necklace (* Marie Antoinette) and briefly imprisoned in the Bastille. Throughout this period his reputation as a man of mystery who could foretell the future (e.g. the execution of Louis XVI) was immense. He was condemned by the Inquisition and died in a Roman prison while serving a life sentence for founding a masonic lodge.

Caillaux, Joseph (1863–1944). French radical politician, who gained a high reputation by several successful terms (from 1899) as minister of finance. As premier in 1911 he negotiated with Germany a settlement of the Moroccan crisis, but his political life was abruptly interrupted when in 1913 his wife shot and killed (she was later acquitted of murder) Gaston Calmette, editor of *Le Figaro*, who had made various accusations against her husband. Caillaux favoured the ending of World War I by a peace of negotiation, and in 1918 he was imprisoned after being convicted

of corresponding with the Germans. Reprieved in 1924 he played an important part in war-debt negotiations.
Caillaux, J., *Mémoires*. 1942–48

Cain, James M(allahan) (1892–1977). American author and journalist. He achieved great success with his novels *The Postman Always Rings Twice* (1934) and *Mildred Pierce* (1946), both of which were filmed.

Caine, Sir (Thomas Henry) Hall (1853–1931). English novelist, best known for a series of romantic, religious and melodramatic novels, one of which, *The Deemster* (1887), sold over 1,000,000 copies. Others include *The Bondman* (1890), *The Manxman* (1894), *The Prodigal Son* (1904) and *The Woman Thou Gavest Me* (1913). His *Recollections of Rossetti* (1882) was inspired by a friendship with the poet from 1881 until his death (1882).

Caitanya (1485–1533). Hindu mystic, also called Gauranga, whose worship of Krishna in ecstatic dancing and singing inspired a form of Hinduism named after him. In 1510 he was initiated as an ascetic and afterwards settled in Puri, where a school of disciples grew up around him. His ecstatic trances and frenzies are thought to have undermined his health and hastened his death. His followers continued to follow his practices until the present day. They held that pure religious ecstasy was superior to all other forms of worship. An articulate theology, never established by Caitanya himself, who was not a teacher and did not intentionally establish an organized sect, was worked out by six of his disciples.

Caius (or Keys), **John** (1510–1573). English physician. He obtained his medical doctorate at Padua, returning in 1544 to England, where he lectured on anatomy in London; he became a fellow of the College of Physicians in 1547 and later was nine times president. He was in turn physician to Edward VI, Mary and Elizabeth and in 1557 endowed and enlarged Gonville Hall, Cambridge, where he had been a student, renaming it Gonville and Caius (pronounced 'Keys') College. He published *A Boke of Counseill against the Sweating Sickness* (1552) and wrote on a range of medical, scientific and antiquarian topics.

Calas, Jean (1698–1762). Victim of a notorious French miscarriage of justice exposed by Voltaire. Calas was a cloth merchant of Toulouse whom rumour accused of having hanged one of his sons – who had in fact committed suicide – to prevent his conversion to Roman Catholicism. The father was tried, tortured and executed, but Voltaire, suspecting priestly and official prejudice, took up the case and at last in 1765 the verdict was reversed.

Caldecott, Randolph (1846–1886). English book-illustrator. His series of picture books (from 1878) – among them *John Gilpin* and *The House That Jack Built* – are of increasing value. He died in Florida.

Calder, Alexander (1898–1976). American sculptor. Trained as an engineer, he invented a form of sculpture which he called 'stabiles' and 'mobiles', the former first exhibited in Paris, where he was then living, in 1928. Both consist of abstract shapes of metal, plastic or wood; the 'mobiles', being connected by wires, swing or rotate in a current of air.
Calder, A., *An Autobiography with Pictures*. 1966

Calderón de la Barca, Pedro (1600–1681). Spanish dramatist and poet, born in Madrid. He was educated at Alcalá and Salamanca Universities, and was soon writing plays so successfully that after the death of Lope de * Vega in 1635 his position as leading dramatist was undisputed. He was made a knight of the Order of St James in 1636. After a period of distinguished army service (1640–42) he took holy orders (1651) on the command of King Philip IV, but he continued to write religious plays. He wrote in verse and, like Shakespeare, with whom he has been compared, wrote both comedies and tragedies. His plays were concerned with themes of marital honour and with religious and philosophical ideas. They suffer, however, from the stylized conventions of the period, and are seldom now produced outside Spain. Over a hundred have survived, one of the best known, *El mágico prodigioso* (*The Prodigious Magician*), in some respects anticipating Goethe's *Faust*; others are *El alcalde de Zalamea* (*The Mayor of Zalamea*), *La vida es sueño* (*Life is A Dream*) and *El gran teatro del mundo* (*The Great Theatre of the World*). In addition there are some seventy of the so-called *autos sacramentales*, a special form of religious drama concerned with the mysteries of the Holy Eucharist.

Parker, A. A., *The Allegorical Drama of Calderón*. Repr. 1968

Caldwell, Erskine Preston (1903–). American novelist and screenwriter. His *Tobacco Road* (1932) and *God's Little Acre* (1933) are the two best known of a series in which the degraded conditions of 'poor whites' in the southern states are described with humour and indignation; both were successfully filmed. He has also written works of autobiography, criticism and travel.

Calhoun, John Caldwell (1782–1850). American politician. Born in South Carolina he became a lawyer, but from the time that he first joined Congress in 1811 he was almost wholly involved in politics. He was at first strongly nationalistic and a vigorous supporter of the war of 1812 and protective tariffs, but gradually his judgement of national measures became more and more influenced by their effect upon the southern states, and he finally emerged as the most eloquent advocate of states' rights, including the rights to nullify protective tariffs and to maintain slavery. In the meantime he had been secretary of war (1817–25) and then vice-president, an office which he resigned within eight years in order to oppose Andrew * Jackson more effectively. He is considered one of the greatest of American orators.

Current, J. C., *John C. Calhoun*. 1963

Caligula (Caius Caesar Augustus Germanicus) (12–41). Roman emperor (37–41). The son of Germanicus Caesar and * Agrippina, he owed his nickname Caligula (Little Boots) to his popularity as a child with his father's soldiers. At first he ruled with moderation but a serious illness, possibly epilepsy, a few months after his accession is believed to have affected his sanity. Thenceforth he behaved as an increasingly bloodthirsty and vicious tyrant. The story that he made his horse 'Incitatus' a consul is typical of many anecdotes indicating his irresponsibility. After only four years' rule, and having declared himself a god, a palace conspiracy brought about his assassination.

Callaghan, (Leonard) James (1912–). British Labour politician. The son of a naval chief petty officer, he joined the Inland Revenue in 1929. He served in the navy in World War II, became M.P. for South Cardiff, was parliamentary secretary in the Ministry of Transport (1947–50) and parliamentary and financial secretary to the Admiralty (1950–51). He was chancellor of the exchequer (1964–67) and home secretary (1967–70). In * Wilson's 1974 government he was foreign and commonwealth secretary. When Wilson retired he was elected leader of the Labour Party, defeating Michael * Foot in the third ballot. He became prime minister (1976–79). His small majority depended on continuous support from the Liberals and the minority groups. He lost the election of 1979 to the Conservatives, but continued as leader of the Labour Party until 1980.

Callas, Maria Meneghini (Maria Kalogeropoulos) (1923–1977). Greek-American dramatic soprano, born in New York. She sang for the first time at La Scala, Milan, in 1950, at Covent Garden in 1952 and at the Metropolitan Opera, New York, in 1956. Among her most famous roles are Bellini's *Norma*, and Amina in his *La Sonnambula*, while her magnetic stage presence and great gifts as an operatic actress yielded memorable portrayals of Violetta in Verdi's *La Traviata* and of Puccini's *Tosca*.

Calles, Plutarco Elias (1877–1945). Mexican soldier and politician. He took an active part in the revolution which in 1911 overthrew President Diaz, and subsequently served under Carranza and Obrégon. He was himself president (1924–28), and then controlled events from behind the scenes until in 1936 President Cárdenas asserted himself and had him deported. By the vigour with which he carried out the policy of land distribution and other reforms Calles did much to benefit the peasants, and his attacks on the church and the oil companies were in line with revolutionary tradition, but as his rule proceeded he became increasingly dictatorial and conservative. He thus alienated many of his former supporters, and his deposition had wide popular support.

Callimachus of Cyrene (*c.* 310–240 B.C.). Greek poet and scholar of Alexandria in the time of the Ptolemies. His most important work, *Aetia* (*Causes*), which survives in fragmentary form, tells a series of episodes purporting to reveal the origins of ancient customs. He also wrote hymns, elegant epigrams and scholarly works, of which only fragments remain.

Callisthenes (*c.* 360–327 B.C.). Greek historian. He was said to have been a nephew of Aristotle. He accompanied Alexander the Great on his campaigns but was put to death for being involved – so it was alleged – in a plot. It is said that the real reason was his opposition to Alexander's assumption of divine honours. Only fragments of his writings survive.

Calmette, Albert Léon Charles (1863–1933). French bacteriologist. With Alphonse Guérin he developed the BCG (Bacillus Calmette-Guérin) vaccine for the prevention of tuberculosis.

Calonne, Charles Alexandre de (1734–1802). French financier. An administrator of wide experience, he was one of the ablest of those who, in the hectic years of unrest before the French Revolution, were called in by Louis XVI to try to rescue French finances from the chaos that threatened disaster. Appointed controller-general of finance in 1783, he was at first successful in raising loans to meet immediate needs, but his proposals for taxing the privileged classes put before the Assembly of Notables in 1787 roused such indignation among those affected that Louis felt himself forced to dismiss his adviser. Calonne spent the revolutionary years in England as finance minister to the émigré government. He returned to France, poverty-stricken, in the year of his death.

Calvé, Emma (Rosa Calvet) (1858?–1942). French operatic soprano. She performed with great success in France, England and America. Her greatest role was Carmen in Bizet's opera.

Calverley, Charles Stuart (1831–1884). English poet, known for his witty verses and parodies collected in *Verses and Translations* (1862) and *Fly Leaves* (1866). His defiant *Ode to Tobacco* has a still topical theme. He was also a brilliant classical scholar who rendered Theocritus into English verse (1869).

Calvin, John (Jean Cauvin) (1509–1564). French religious reformer, born at Noyon in Picardy. The son of an ecclesiastical lawyer he went at the age of 14 to Paris University. He was intended originally for the priesthood, but was attracted by the new humanism; acting on his father's advice he began a legal training at Orléans, and later at Bourges. His aptitude proving greater than his interest, in 1531, after his father's death, he returned to Paris and devoted himself to classical scholarship, also beginning Hebrew. Already sympathetic to the attacks made on traditional theology by * Luther and * Bucer, Calvin experienced what he called 'sudden conversion' about 1533. Under threat of arrest as a Protestant, he spent the next two years constantly on the move, but at last took refuge in Basle, Switzerland, where he continued his Hebrew studies and worked on *The Institutes of the Christian Religion*, completed in 1536 with a prefatory letter to King Francis I of France in which he foresaw the destruction of any kingdom 'not ruled by the sceptre of God'. This, his greatest work, bears the imprint of St Augustine's teaching, especially in its emphasis on the doctrine of predestination and the supreme sovereignty of God. Calvin taught that certain souls ('the elect') are predestined for eternal life and the remainder are damned, salvation being the free gift of God and good works being the sign of salvation, not its cause. Whether Christ's death was an act of atonement for the benefit of all or only of the elect is not always clear and was a subject of much controversy in the Reformed churches. When passing through Geneva in 1536 Calvin accepted what was virtually a challenge from Guillaume Farel to take over his work of directing the religious and political life of the city and he used his organizing ability to create a system of theocratic government. He prescribed a profession of faith, banned all public entertainment, emphasized the need for unbending puritanism in private life and even issued regulations on dress. Such austerity soon proved unpopular, and Calvin was expelled from the city in 1538 after riots organized by a faction called the Libertines. The three years which elapsed before he was recalled were spent mainly at Strasbourg where he entered upon a brief but happy marriage (his wife died in 1549, their son having already died in infancy), continued his studies and renewed contact with Bucer and other reformers. Back in Geneva he resumed where he had left off and organized a presbyterian system of government, extending the intolerance which he showed in religious matters – exemplified by the burning of Servetus –

to any lapse from the code of social discipline and puritan morality which he imposed. The régime lasted during his lifetime and at least the hard work, thrift and sobriety enjoined brought trade and wealth to the city. The college which later became Geneva University was founded to supply the need for an educated clergy. Calvinism spread before and after its founder's death and shared with Lutheranism the allegiance of the greatest part of the Protestant world. It provided a pattern for presbyterian churches in Scotland and elsewhere; it was the faith of the Huguenots in France, of the Dutch Reformed Church and of several German states. The relationship (if any) of Calvinism to the rise of capitalism has been a matter of considerable historical controversy, as has the suggestion that Calvinism encouraged rebellion.
Wendel, F., *Calvin: The Origin and Development of his Religious Thought*. 1963; Parker, T. M., *Calvin*. 1976

Calvino, Italo (1923–1985). Italian writer, born in Cuba. He began work in Turin, on the magazine *L'Unita*; from 1959 he was co-editor of *Il Menabò di letteratura*. He began to write realistic stories of the Italian Resistance (in which he had served), but during the 1950s turned to fantasy, some of it allegorical. He gained a wide reputation with *Il visconte dimezzato* (1952), *Il barone rampante* (1957), and *Il cavaliere inesistente* (1959). All his work shows a concern with what he considers to be the dehumanising influence of contemporary society. His *If on a winter's night a traveller*. . . (1979) was widely acclaimed in translation.
Woodhouse, J. R., *Italo Calvino: A Reappraisal and an Appreciation of the Trilogy*. 1968

Calwell, Arthur Augustus (1896–1973). Australian politician. He succeeded H. V. * Evatt as leader of the Labor opposition in 1960. As minister of immigration (1945–49) he initiated a scheme which brought 1,000,000 Europeans to Australia within a decade.

Camargo, Marie Anne de Cupis de (1710–1770). French dancer. Born in Brussels, she was one of the most famous figures in the early history of ballet. She came of a well connected family and received early encouragement, and her whole career from her first appearance in Paris in 1726 to her retirement in 1751 was a series of triumphs. She appeared in about eighty ballets and her fame was perpetuated by the celebrated artists and writers (including Voltaire) of her time. She is said to have introduced the characteristic short ballet skirt. The Camargo Society was named after her.

Cambacérès, Jean Jacques Régis de, Duke of Parma (1753–1824). French politician, best known as Second Consul in the government set up after the *coup d'état* of 1799 had brought Napoleon Bonaparte (First Consul) to power. He received his dukedom in 1806.

Under the empire he was high chancellor and so again held the second place in the state hierarchy. In the violent stages of the Revolution he had played a placatory role. His great interest was jurisprudence and he played a prominent part in creating the Code Napoléon. After the restoration of Louis XVIII he was expelled but in 1818 allowed to return.
Ponteil, F., *Napoleon 1er et l'organisation autoritaire de la France*. 2nd ed. 1966

Cambon, Pierre Paul (1843–1924). French diplomat. As ambassador to Great Britain (1898–1921) he did much to bring about the Entente Cordiale between Britain and France, and at the same time, with the active help of his brother **Jules** (1845–1935), the ambassador in Berlin, to frustrate the aims of the German war party.

Cambyses, Kambusiya (died 522 B.C.). King of Persia (from 529). A son of Cyrus the Great, he added Phoenicia, Cyprus, and Egypt to the Persian empire but his subsequent expeditions to the south (Nubia) and west were partial or total failures, as a result of which, according to a tradition related by Herodotus, Cambyses became a cruel, drunken and capricious tyrant. He died while returning to Persia to deal with a usurper who claimed to be his murdered brother.
Olmstead, A. T., *History of the Persian Empire*. 1948

Camden, Charles Pratt, 1st Earl (1713–1794). English judge. As chief justice of the Common Pleas (1762–66) he pronounced against the legality of 'general warrants' in the case of John Wilkes and became extraordinarily popular. He became lord chancellor in 1766, but his support of Wilkes and opposition to the government's unyielding American policy caused him to resign in 1770.

He served under Rockingham and Pitt as lord president of the Council (1782–94) and was created an earl in 1786.

Camden, William (1551–1623). English antiquarian, historian and schoolmaster. Educated at Christ's Hospital, St Paul's School and Oxford, he became a master at Westminster in 1575 and was headmaster (1593–97). His professional occupation allowed him time to travel up and down England and collect material for his great antiquarian survey *Britannia*, the original Latin version of which appeared in 1586. His *Annals* of Queen Elizabeth's reign were published posthumously. Most of his many works, which include an account of the trial of the Gunpowder Plotters (* Fawkes) are in Latin. His name is commemorated by the Camden professorship at Oxford.
Trevor-Roper, H., *Queen Elizabeth's First Historian*. 1971

Cameron, Verney Lovett (1844–1894). British naval officer and explorer. Much of his service was spent in African waters in the suppression of the slave trade. Sent in 1873 to relieve * Livingstone he met the party carrying his body to the coast; proceeding westwards, he found some of Livingstone's papers and then surveyed Lake Tanganyika, arriving at the correct conclusion that its outlet flowed to the Congo. He himself eventually reached Portuguese Benguela (1875) and so was the first European to cross equatorial Africa from east to west. He wrote accounts of his travels and adventure stories for boys.
Cameron, V. L., *Across Africa*. 1877

Cammaerts, Émile (1878–1953). Belgian poet, author and scholar. He settled in England in 1908 and as first professor of Belgian studies at London University made translations of Ruskin and Chesterton into French. Apart from poems about World War I he published a history of Belgium (1920) and a biography of Rubens (1931). *The Flowers of Grass* (1944) is a personal record of his own conversion to the Christian faith.

Camões (or Camoens), **Luis de** (1524–1580). The greatest of Portuguese poets. Born of a poor family of the minor nobility, he received his education at Coimbra University and gained early recognition for his gifts as a lyric poet and dramatist. After he left the university it is surmised that he had many love affairs and that he was exiled from Lisbon as a result of one of these (supposedly with Caterina de Ataide, a lady of the court). He served in the army in North Africa (1547–49) and lost his right eye there, returned to Lisbon, was again exiled and went to Goa in India, where he served with military expeditions in the Far East. After further adventures and misadventures he left Goa in 1567 for Mozambique, but it was not until 1570, after his debts and passage money had been paid by friends, that he reached home. He lived in poverty on a small pension from the king until he died in hospital of the plague. While in the East he worked on his masterpiece, *As Lusiadas* (*The Lusiads* i.e. the Portuguese), a national epic, broadly modelled on Virgil's *Aeneid*, and largely inspired by the discoveries and heroic exploits of da Gama and his fellow navigators and soldiers in the East. The work was published in 1572 and was an immediate success, with thirty-six editions published between 1580 and 1640. Camões also wrote three verse comedies, many lyric poems of great poignancy (some to a favourite Chinese slave girl) and philosophical sonnets.
Bell, A. F., *Luis de Camões*. 1923. Salgado, A. (ed.), *Obra Completa de Luis de Camões*. 1963

Campanella, Tommaso (1568–1639). Italian astronomer and philosopher, born at Stilo in Calabria, Campanella entered the Dominican order. Early intellectual influences on him included the writings of Telesio (who advanced atomistic views of nature). In 1592 he was denounced to the Inquisition for heresy; between then and 1629 he spent much of his time in internment. He passed his last few years in safety in France. Campanella was one of the foremost champions of the Copernican view that the sun was the centre of the planetary system. He may have held such views because of his independent conviction of the truth of natural magic and astrology, which led him to see the sun as the source of great spiritual powers. Throughout his life he defended the right of philosophers and scientists to speculate freely in matters relating to the natural world. In his view, Scripture did not pronounce on such matters and the Church should not dogmatize. Campanella is of importance, also, as a political utopian. He conceived of a perfect state (the Civitas solis, the Commonwealth of the Sun) in which work and wealth were equally shared, and men perfected themselves by coming to a spiritual understanding of God through His Creation.

Campbell. Noble family of Western Scotland, the heads of which have been Earls (from 1457) and Dukes (from 1701) of * Argyll.

Campbell, Alexander (1788–1866). American religious leader, born in Ireland. He was a Presbyterian then a Baptist preacher, before forming his own group, which, merged with others, became the 'Disciples of Christ', a body with over 1,000,000 members in the U.S.A. Campbell, who founded Bethany College in 1840, believed that Christianity should rest solely on biblical authority and that forms of worship should resume the simplicity of New Testament times. He produced his own translation of the New Testament and was a prolific writer.

Campbell, Colin, 1st Baron Clyde (1792–1863). British commander-in-chief during the Indian Mutiny (1857–58). The son of a carpenter named Maclivery, he adopted his mother's family name, and as a young man served in the Peninsular War. Fame, knighthood (K.C.B.) and experience of Indian conditions came in the second Sikh War (1848–49), followed by much frontier fighting. In the Crimea (at Alma and Balaclava) he proved himself the most effective of the British generals and when the Indian Mutiny broke out (1857) he was the obvious choice for command. His relief of Lucknow was only the most spectacular of many successes and of much patient organization which firmly re-established British rule. For his services he was created Lord Clyde and made a field-marshal.

Campbell, Sir Malcolm (1885–1948). British sportsman. In 1935 his famous car *Bluebird* reached 301 m.p.h. on Bonneville Flats, Utah, U.S.A. In 1939 he captured the world water-speed record on Coniston Water, in the English Lake District, by reaching 141.7 m.p.h. in his motor boat, also named *Bluebird.* His son, **Donald Malcolm Campbell** (1921–1967), broke the world water-speed record again at Coniston in 1955 by travelling at 202 m.p.h., a speed which he had raised to 260 m.p.h. by 1959. In 1964 he also established a land-speed record of 403 m.p.h. at Lake Eyre, Australia. His boats and cars were likewise named *Bluebird.* In an attempt to attain a water speed of 300 m.p.h. his boat disintegrated and he was killed.

Campbell, Mrs Patrick (née Beatrice Stella Tanner) (1865–1940). English actress. She created the role of Eliza in Shaw's *Pygmalion* (1912) and was earlier successful in the plays of Pinero (notably in the title role of *The Second Mrs Tanqueray*), and Ibsen. Her close friendship with Bernard Shaw led to a lively and fascinating correspondence, later published.
Dent, A., *Mrs Patrick Campbell.* 1961

Campbell, (Ignatius) Roy (Dunnachie) (1901–1957). South African poet, born in Durban. His poems have a vigorous 'outdoor' quality, often mixed with sharp satire, and reflect the interests of Campbell himself, who was accomplished at bull-tossing, jousting and steer throwing. He fought for General Franco in the Spanish Civil War. His poetic works include *The Flaming Terrapin* (1924), *Wayzgoose* (1928), *Adamaster* (1930) and *Flowering Rifle* (1939), which was inspired by his experiences in the Spanish war. *Light on a Dark Horse* (1951) is autobiographical. He was killed in a motor accident in Portugal, where he had lived since 1947.

Campbell, Thomas (1777–1844). Scottish poet. He is now only remembered for his war songs such as *Ye Mariners of England* and for poems as familiar as *The Soldier's Dream* and *Lord Ullin's Daughter*, but he was held in high repute in his own day. He also edited the *New Monthly Magazine* (1820–30), and was one of the founders of University College, London, and lord rector of Glasgow University (1827–29). He is buried in Westminster Abbey.
Campbell, T. (ed.), Robertson, L., *Poems.* 1908

Campbell-Bannerman, Sir Henry (1836–1908). British Liberal politician. Son of a lord provost of Glasgow, he was educated at Glasgow and Cambridge Universities and was an M.P. from 1868. His early ministerial appointments were at the War Office, where he managed to secure the removal of the almost irremovable Duke of Cambridge. He was a strong supporter of Gladstone's Irish policy, and became chief secretary for Ireland (1884–85). He succeeded Sir William Harcourt as party leader in 1898. Campbell-Bannerman's ministry of 1905 included Asquith, Grey,

Haldane and Lloyd George, and was one of the most brilliant in history. The prime minister himself was responsible for one of its most generous acts, the granting of self-government to the defeated Boer republics, the Transvaal and the Orange Free State, from which stemmed the Union of South Africa. He was forced to resign as a result of ill health and died 17 days later.
Spender, J. A., *The Life of the Right Hon. Sir Henry Campbell-Bannerman*. 1923

Campion, Edmund (*c*. 1540–1581). English priest, born in London. He was educated at Christ's Hosital and Oxford, and later studied for the Roman Catholic priesthood at Douai and Rome. He joined the Jesuits (1573) and in 1580 returned to England on a mission to revive the spirit of the Roman Catholics suffering under Queen Elizabeth's Anglican rule. With his eloquence and the qualities of a brilliant mind he was proving most successful when within a year he was captured. Despite torture he refused to recant and argued persuasively with his accusers. Nevertheless he was condemned on charges of sedition and hanged, drawn and quartered. Campion was beatified in 1886.
Waugh, E., *Edmund Campion*. 1936

Campion, Thomas (1567–1620). English poet and musician. By profession a physician, he is best known for his books of 'ayres' containing lyrics, some set to music (for the lute) by himself; he also wrote masques for court performances and a treatise on harmony. In his *Observations in the Art of Poesie* (1602) he attacked the practice of rhyming.

Camrose, William Ewart Berry, 1st Viscount (1879–1954). British newspaper proprietor. He founded the *Advertising World* in 1901 and with his brother, **James Gomer Berry** (later Viscount Kemsley) he gained control of many London and provincial newspapers and magazines. The two brothers divided their interests in 1937, Camrose retaining the *Daily Telegraph*, of which he was editor in chief and which still remains with the Berry family. He was made a viscount in 1941.

Camus, Albert (1913–1960). French writer, born in Algeria. He became a journalist and an actor and (1935–38) managed a theatrical company. He went to Paris in 1939. Towards the end of World War II he worked for the resistance movement and was co-editor with * Sartre of the left-wing newspaper *Combat* (1944–48). For a time he belonged to the Communist party, but became disillusioned, and after breaking with Sartre abandoned public activities. In his later works he revealed himself as a humanist, discouraged by the failure of contemporary civilization to cope with major moral issues, and unable to accept the existence of God, but constantly trying to find significant values in a meaningless world. Most of his thought is centred on the concept of the 'absurd' – that man's predicament in the world is absurd. He is often termed an existentialist – to which he himself laid no claim. Among his works are the philosophical essays in *Le Mythe de Sisyphe* (1942); *L'Homme révolté* (1951), a declaration of his own attitude to life; novels such as *L'Étranger* (1942) and *La Peste* (1947), short stories, as *L'Exil et la Royaume* (1957), and plays such as *Le Malentendu* (1944). He won the Nobel Prize for Literature in 1957. He was killed in a motor accident.
Rhein, P. H., *Albert Camus*. 1969

Canaletto (Giovanni Antonio Canale) (1697–1768). Italian painter, famous for his pictures of Venice. He received his first training at Venice from his father, a scene-painter, but later studied in Rome. His best pictures combine exact topographical detail with a remarkably subtle feeling for light. An English connoisseur, Joseph Smith, whose collection of over fifty Canalettos was bought by George III, persuaded him to come to England, where he lived between 1746 and 1756; but though some of his London scenes are as skilful as the Venetian ones in reproducing detail and conveying atmosphere, it is upon the latter that his reputation finally rests.
Constable, W. G., *Canaletto*. 1962

Candolle, Augustin Pyrame de (1778–1841). French botanist, born at Geneva. After working in Paris he was professor at Montpellier from 1807 to 1816, when he returned to Geneva. He is best known for his system for classifying plants in natural categories rather than in what he held to be the artificial ones in the system of Linnaeus.
Candolle, A. de (ed.), *Mémoires d'Augustin Candolle*. 1862

Canetti, Elias (1905–). German–Jewish writer. Born in Bulgaria to a Sephardic family, he was educated in Manchester, Vienna, Zürich and Frankfurt, and became a British subject in 1935. He was awarded the 1981 Nobel Prize for Literature for a lifetime's work, including the novel *Die Blendung* (1935—translated as *Auto da Fé*), *Crowds and Power* (1960) and two volumes of autobiography.

Canning, Charles John Canning, 1st Earl (1812–1862). English administrator. Son of George * Canning, his fame rests on his tenure of the post of governor general (from 1855) and (from 1858) first viceroy of India. His skill and moderation in dealing with the Indian Mutiny (1857) and its aftermath – which earned him the nickname 'Clemency Canning' – are much more widely recognized today than they were at the time.

Canning, George (1770–1827). English politician, born in London. After his father died (1771), leaving his mother in poverty, Canning was brought up by relatives, who sent him to Eton and Oxford, where his brilliance soon attracted attention; in 1793 Pitt found him a seat in parliament. In 1797 he founded the satirical *Anti-Jacobin*, in which Tories less extreme than himself, especially Pitt's successor, Addington, were violently attacked. The other side of his political nature was shown when, after holding minor office, he first became foreign secretary, in the Portland administration of 1807. Expert and liberal statesmanship abroad and reactionary politics at home were characteristics of his policies. In his first term as foreign secretary his promptness in obtaining control of the Danish and Portuguese fleets after Napoleon's reconciliation with Tsar Alexander at Tilsit and his support for the Spanish insurgents against Joseph Bonaparte's rule had decisive effects in the struggle against Napoleon. A duel with his rival * Castlereagh in 1809 caused a long interruption in his political career, during which he occupied important posts (ambassador to Portugal, 1814–16; president of the Indian Board of Control 1816–21). He was recalled to the government after Castlereagh's suicide (1822), and became foreign secretary once more. It was during this second term that his recognition and support of the South American colonists in revolt against Spanish rule evoked the phrase 'I called the New World into existence, to redress the balance of the Old'. His support for the Greek independence movement also proved decisive. In 1827, the year in which he had succeeded Liverpool as prime minister, he died in office.

Petrie, C., *George Canning*. 2nd ed. 1946.
Hinde, W., *George Canning*. 1973

Cannizzaro, Stanislao (1826–1910). Italian chemist. He was appointed to academic posts at Genoa (1855), Palermo (1861), and Rome (1870). He was the first to appreciate the importance of the hypothesis of * Avogadro as a means of introducing order into chemical classification, and brought it to general attention in his *Sketch of a Course of Chemical Philosophy* (1858). Cannizzaro also did important work in organic chemistry. The reaction of benzaldehyde with potassium hydroxide to form benzylalcohol was discovered by him and is often referred to as 'Cannizzaro's reaction'.

Cannon, Walter Bradford (1871–1945). American physiologist. The son of a poor railroad worker, he gained admission to Harvard, and graduated in 1896. He had already developed interests in neurology and psychology, and proceeded to study at Harvard Medical School. From 1902–42 he was in the Harvard Physiology Department. Cannon's early research was on digestion. He made pioneer use of X-rays to examine gastro-intestinal action and the mechanisms of swallowing. He then directed his research to a study of the sympathetic nervous system, and developed the notion that the autonomic nervous system aims to keep the internal environment of the body in a state of constant equilibrium (homeostasis). These views he expounded in his *Wisdom of the Body* (1932). His later work on digestion shared many similarities with the researches of * Pavlov in Russia. During World War I he had made deep studies of the new phenomenon of shell shock. All the ways in which the nervous system operated to some degree autonomously from mental consciousness were of deep interest to him. Cannon was a man of strong civic and political convictions; he was sympathetic to the social experiment of early Bolshevik Russia, and was active in campaigning for the Republican cause in the Spanish Civil War.

Cano, Juan Sebastian del (died 1526). Spanish navigator. He commanded one of the five ships in * Magellan's great expedition of 1519, and when Magellan was killed in the Philippines (1521) Cano took command. On returning to Spain (1522) he was acclaimed as the first man to circumnavigate the world.

Canova, Antonio (1757–1822). Italian sculptor. He was leader of the Italian neo-classical movement, famous for his idealized and sometimes sentimentalized representations of the human form. Born near Venice, he was trained as a sculptor as a boy and was still only 24 when he settled in Rome, where Vatican patronage soon made him prominent. His monuments to Popes Clement XIII and XIV belong to this period. Later he was patronized by the Bonaparte family and especially Napoleon's sister, Pauline, who became the wife of Prince Borghese and whose portrait he made. In 1815 he was sent to Paris to negotiate for the return of works of art looted by Napoleon. Among his best known classical works are several versions of *Cupid and Psyche* and the *Perseus* of the Vatican.
Munoz, A., *Canova*. 1597

Canrobert, (François) Certain (1809–1895). Marshal of France. After long and distinguished service in Algeria he succeeded Marshal St Arnaud as French commander-in-chief in the Crimean War. In 1859 he commanded a division against the Austrians at Magenta and Solferino in the war for Italian independence. In the Franco-Prussian War of 1870 he was taken prisoner with his troops when Metz surrendered.

Cantor, Georg (Ferdinand Ludwig Philipp) (1845–1918). German mathematician, born in Russia. He developed an arithmetic of the infinite. He became a lecturer at the University of Halle in 1869, and professor in 1879. His work was summarized in *Contributions to the Founding of the Theory of Transfinite Numbers* (English translation, 1915).
Bell, E. T., *Development of Mathematics*. 1945

Capablanca y Granperra, José Raoul (1888–1942). Cuban chess master. A diplomat by profession, he was the world chess champion from 1921, when he defeated Lasker, until he lost the title in 1927 to Alekhine.

Čapek, Karel (1890–1938). Czech playwright and novelist. He was best known as the author of the very successful satirical plays *R.U.R.* (*Rossum's Universal Robots*) (1920) – which gave the word 'robot' to the languages of the world – and (with his brother Joseph) *The Insect Play* (1921), a terrifying satire on a hedonistic, acquisitive and regimented society. His novels include the satires on misused science *Krakatit* (1924) and *War With the Newts* (1938). He also wrote books on travel, on gardening, many essays and a biography of President Masaryk (1928).
Harkins, W. E., *Karel Čapek*. 1962

Capet. Dynastic name of kings of France from 987 to 1328.

Capet, Hugh (938–996). King of France (from 987). The surname was not used during his lifetime. Hugh's election to the throne ended the long unsettled period which followed the breakup of the Carolingian empire. One of his first acts was to make his son joint king and so secure the succession of his dynasty, which ruled by direct descent until 1328. Even before his accession, members of the family from which Hugh was sprung had been elected rulers from time to time.
Fautier, R., *The Capetian Kings of France*. 1960

Capodistrias, Ioannes, Count (1776–1831). Greek politician, born in Corfu. After service in the administration of the Ionian Islands, he went to Russia, where eventually he became foreign minister (1815–18). He returned to Greece in 1822 to devote himself to the national cause, and after independence from Turkey had been won was elected first president of Greece (1827); but his autocratic measures were unpopular, and he was murdered.

Capone, Al (Alphonso) (1898–1947). American criminal, born in Naples. He became a New York gangster, and in 1920 went to Chicago, where, during the Prohibition years, he became the head of a gang controlling the gambling, vice and supply of illegal liquor of Cook County. The gang's earnings were estimated to be in the region of $105,000,000. He was responsible for numerous brutal murders, but avoided prosecution by bribery and coercion of Chicago law officers. He was eventually prosecuted by Federal authorities, but could be convicted only of tax evasion (1931). He was released in 1939 after a mental collapse.

Capote, Truman (Truman Streckfuss Persons) (1924–1984). American novelist, born in New Orleans. He wrote much about social decay in the southern states of the U.S. and his novels include *Other Voices, Other Rooms* (1948), *The Grass Harp* (1951) and *Breakfast at Tiffany's* (1958). He wrote the dialogue for the film *Beat the Devil* (1953).

His *In Cold Blood* (1964) was a detailed sociological and psychological account of murders, and subsequent executions, in Kansas. It was his last major work but collected essays appeared in *Music for Chameleons* (1980). He conducted bitter and protracted literary feuds with Norman * Mailer and Gore * Vidal.

Capra, Frank (1897–). American film producer and director, of Italian parentage. Among his many successes were *It Happened One Night* (1934), *Mr Deeds Goes To Town* (1936) and *Lost Horizon* (1937).
Capra, F., *Frank Capra: The Name Above the Title*. 1971

Caprivi, Georg Leo, Graf Von (1831–1899). German soldier and politician, born in Berlin. A successful chief of staff in the Franco-Prussian War (1870–71), he then directed the administration of the German navy (1883–88) until William II appointed him chancellor and foreign minister (1890–94), after the dismissal of * Bismarck. He negotiated the treaty with Britain (1890) under which German claims in Zanzibar were abandoned in return for the cession of Heligoland. He was dismissed in 1894 after negotiating a commercial treaty with Russia.

Caracalla (Marcus Aurelius Severus Antoninus) (188–217). Roman emperor (from 211). He was given the nickname Caracalla from the long-hooded Gaulish tunic he wore. On the death of his father, the emperor Septimius Severus, he and his brother Geta became joint rulers but Caracalla seized power by murdering Geta and his supporters. He secured his popularity with the troops by a 50-per-cent increase in pay. His reign was one of cruelty, assassination and extravagance. He pacified the German frontiers and was unsuccessfully attempting to emulate the achievements of Alexander the Great in the East when his assassination was contrived by the prefect of his praetorian guards. During his reign Roman citizenship was extended to all free men in the empire (probably to increase the number of taxpaying citizens) and the famous baths of Caracalla were constructed at Rome.
Mackenzie, D. C., *The Reign of Caracalla*. 1949

Caratacus (known also as Caractacus or Caradoc) (died *c.* 54). British chieftain, the son of * Cunobellinus. After fighting bravely against the Romans, he was defeated and in 51 handed over by Cartismandua, queen of the Brigantes, and taken to Rome, where his gallant mien before the emperor Claudius secured him honourable treatment.

Caravaggio, Michelangelo Merisi da (1573–1610). Italian artist. His break with the conventions of the Mannerists created a resurgence of art in the 17th century and exercised enormous influence on, e.g., Rubens, Velasquez and Rembrandt. A revolutionary technique was the setting of brightly lit figures against a dark background (e.g. in his St Matthew series). Moreover he offended against accepted convention in his sacred pictures by depicting ordinary people in everyday surroundings. Another innovation was the introduction of 'still life' as a separate branch of painting.

The dramatic nature of his painting may have reflected the violence of his own life. In 1606 he was banished from Rome after killing a man in a fight. From Naples he reached Malta, where he insulted a knight, was imprisoned but escaped to Sicily. When disembarking in Italy on his way to Naples he was arrested in error but on release found that his boat with all his belongings had sailed away. He died shortly afterwards, a sick and hopeless wanderer.
Berenson, B., *Caravaggio: His Incongruity and his Fame*. 1953. Jullian, R., *Caravage*. 1961

Cardano, Geronimo (also known as Jerome Cardan or Hieronymus Cardanus) (1501–1576). Italian mathematician and physician. Although professor of medicine at Pavia (1543–59) and Bologna (1562–70), he is best known for his work in mathematics, particularly algebra. His *Ars Magna* (1545) was the first algebraic text to be printed. His academic career at Bologna ended with imprisonment for heresy (astrology was one of his interests). He spent his last years in Rome and is said to have starved himself to death to prove the accuracy of a prediction. He was a prolific writer in science, history, music and was, indeed, a polymath.

Cardenas, Lazaro (1895–1970). Mexican general and president (1934–40). He was a follower of * Calles and though he broke with him on becoming president he continued the revolutionary policy of breaking up large estates and redistributing the land among the peasants. A temporary breach with the U.S.A and Great Britain was caused by his nationalization of the oilfields in 1938. Of mixed Spanish and Indian descent he was greatly beloved both of the Indians and of the Mexican working class.
Scott, R. E., *Mexican Government in Transition.* Rev. ed. 1964

Cardigan, James Thomas Brudenell, 7th Earl of (1797–1868). British soldier, leader and survivor of the famous charge of the Light Brigade at the Battle of Balaclava (October 1854) during the Crimean War.
Woodham-Smith, C. *The Reason Why.* 1953

Cardin, Pierre (1922–). French courtier, born in Italy. He worked with Christian * Dior, established his own fashion house in 1949, extending his brand name to men's and women's clothing and shoes. He bought Maxim's and established it as a worldwide restaurant chain.

Cardozo, Benjamin Nathan (1870–1938). American judge, born in New York of Jewish parents. The culminating point of a highly successful career as advocate and judge was his appointment in 1932 by President Hoover to succeed Mr Justice Holmes as a member of the U.S. Supreme Court. In that office, by his liberal opinions he did much to facilitate the carrying out of Roosevelt's New Deal legislation and his views on law as a force in effecting social changes were highly influential. As well as several authoritative legal works Cardozo wrote *Law and Literature and Other Essays* (1931).

Carducci, Giosuè (1835–1907). Italian poet. Son of a physician, he was educated at Pisa University, was a schoolmaster for a time, and in 1860 was appointed professor of Italian literature at Bologna. In 1876 he was returned to the Italian parliament as a Republican and in 1890 he became a senator. His poems, representing a reaction from Romanticism, were written in strict classical form in a style and language of great distinction. His main works include *Rime* (1857), *Nuove poesie* (1873) and *Rime e ritmi* (1898). He won the Nobel Prize for Literature in 1906.

Cardwell, Edward Cardwell, 1st Viscount (1813–1886). British politician. An M.P. from 1842 to 1874, he is remembered for the army reforms carried out while he was secretary of state for war (1869–74) under Gladstone. These included the abolition of the purchase of commissions (1870), the reorganization of the regiments of the line on a county basis, and the system by which one battalion of a regiment served abroad while the other remained in support and reserve at home. He also established the supremacy of the minister over the commander-in-chief.

Carew, Thomas (*c.* 1594–1639). English poet. Having left Oxford without a degree, he accompanied diplomatic missions abroad. On his return his wit and pleasant manner made him a favourite of Charles I, before whom his masque *Coelum Britannicum* was produced in 1633. A friend and admirer of Donne and Jonson, he also wrote short, polished lyrics in the Cavalier tradition, the well known *Elegy on the Death of Dr Donne*, and *The Rapture*.

Carey, Henry (*c.* 1690–1743). English poet and musician. He wrote the burlesque tragedy *Chrononhotonthologos* and the comic opera *The Dragon of Wantley*, but with all his great output of poems, songs, plays etc., he is now little remembered except as the author and composer of the song *Sally in Our Alley* and for the nickname 'Namby-Pamby' he invented for the poet Ambrose Philips. He committed suicide.

Carey, William (1761–1834). English Baptist missionary and scholar. One of the first Baptist missionaries to go to India (1793), he began, almost at once, the translation of the Bible into Bengali. In 1799 he set up at Serampore not only a church and school but also an establishment for printing and publishing the Bible and other educational books in many Indian languages. In 1801 he became professor of Indian languages at Fort William College, and produced dictionaries of Sanskrit, Bengali, Marathi etc.
Smith, G., *William Carey.* 1884

Carleton, Guy, 1st Baron Dorchester (1724–1808). British soldier and administrator. He was first appointed to a command in America in 1758 where he served in the French and Indian Wars. As governor of Quebec (1766–77) he worked for the Quebec Act (1774) to better relations between English and French Canadians. He successfully defended Canada against American attacks during the American Revolution; he was briefly in command (1782) of the British forces towards the end of the fighting and was skilful in helping Loyalists to withdraw safely to Canada. He had a second term as governor of Quebec (1786–96).
Bradley, A. G., *Makers of Canada*. 1907

Carlile, Richard (1790–1843). English freethinker and publicist, originally a tinker. He was a disciple of Thomas Paine and his championship of the freedom of the press resulted in his spending more than nine years in prison for publishing radical and anti-religious literature.

Carlile, Wilson (1847–1942). English clergyman. His main life's work was the foundation (1882) and leadership of the Church Army to work, like the Salvation Army, for the very poorest members of the community. In 1906 he became a prebendary of St Paul's Cathedral, London and was made C.H. in 1926.
Dark, S., *Wilson Carlile*. 1944

Carlos (1863–1908). King of Portugal (from 1889). His suspension of the constitution provoked civil disturbances and led to the assassination of himself and his son while driving in Lisbon. The abdication of his younger son Manuel II in 1910 initiated the Portuguese republic.

Carlos, Don (1545–1568). Spanish prince, eldest son of Philip II of Spain and Mary of Portugal. Suspected of treason he was imprisoned by his father and shortly after died in prison. Carlos showed signs of insanity and was clearly an inadequate heir to the vast Spanish empire, but there is no real evidence for the legend that Philip II had him murdered. He is the subject of a tragedy by * Schiller.

Carlos, Don (1788–1855). Spanish prince, the son of King Charles IV. He was deprived of the right of succession to the throne when the Salic Law was revoked in 1833 and Isabella, the daughter of his brother Ferdinand VII, became queen. The first Carlist War then broke out and lasted until 1840. A second Carlist revolt (1873–76) was equally unsuccessful and the last pretender in the direct line died in 1936.

Carlota (1840–1927). Belgian princess, wife of the Mexican Emperor * Maximilian. After her husband's execution in 1867 she went mad.

Carlson, Chester Floyd (1906–1968). American inventor. A patent attorney, he invented the process of dry photocopying known as xerography (1938). The first copier was not marketed until 1959.

Carlstadt (or Karlstadt) (Andreas Rudolf Bodenstein) (*c.* 1480–1541). German religious reformer. A professor at Wittenberg University, he became an adherent of* Luther (1517), but, as the years passed, alienated him by his adoption of extremist views. Accused of being involved in the Peasants' War, he fled to Switzerland and from 1534 preached and taught in Basle.

Carlyle, Thomas (1795–1881). Scottish essayist and historian. He was the son of a stonemason of Ecclefechan, Dumfriesshire, and at the age of 15 went to Edinburgh University, intending to be a clergyman. Religious doubts ended this ambition, and after some years as a schoolmaster and private tutor (during which time he formed a close friendship with and was much influenced by Edward Irving, later the founder of the Irvingite sect) his true vocation had become manifest. His earliest works stemmed from his interest in German literature – a *Life of Schiller* (1825), and a translation of Goethe's *Wilhelm Meister* (1824), which won the author's praise. In 1826 he married Jane Welsh, whose wit could wound as well as delight, and whose letters still sparkle as brightly as when they were written. Her strong personality and her husband's produced one of the strangest love stories, a blend of irritation and mutual dependence, in literary history.

In 1828 the Carlyles withdrew to Craigenputtock where he set to work on *Sartor Resartus* (*The tailor retailored*), which appeared in *Fraser's Magazine* in 1833–34. It purports to reveal the philosophical speculations of a Professor Teufelsdröckh, and

concludes that all institutions, political, religious etc., are in fact clothes constantly in need of repair and renewal. The life of the Professor, which forms the second part, is based on that of Carlyle himself. He had already begun his most famous work, *The History of the French Revolution*, when he and his wife moved in 1834 to Cheyne Row, Chelsea, their permanent home. Disaster came when the manuscript was accidentally burnt in the flat of his friend J. S. * Mill – 'we must try and hide from him how very serious this business is' was Carlyle's generous comment. He rewrote the book and it was published in 1837. It is not strictly factual history but an inspired interpretation: its rhetorical style is highly eccentric but the sheer dynamism of the work is inescapable and the character descriptions (e.g. the 'seagreen incorruptible' Robespierre) memorable. From the point of view of Carlyle's development it is interesting that he, who believed himself a radical and welcomed revolutionaries such as Mazzini to his home, was beginning to feel and see history in terms of the hero or superman. In the *French Revolution* the chief characters, Danton especially, are already larger than life, and in *On Heroes, Hero-Worship and the Heroic in History* (1841) he expands the theme, which is implicit also in *Oliver Cromwell's Letters and Speeches* (1845) and his great biography of Frederick the Great (1858–65). He appears to disregard the corruption of character by power. *Past and Present* (1843) contrasts the ordered society of feudalism with the unordered confusion of modern times. The death of his wife in 1865 virtually ended his creative period. His influence on contemporary thought in many fields – religious and political especially – was immense. Carlyle should be seen as more of a prophet than a historian or commentator.
Froude, J. A., *Thomas Carlyle*. 1882–84

Carman, (William) Bliss (1861–1929). Canadian poet. A Bohemian claiming the freedoms demanded by writers and artists of the *fin de siècle*, he collaborated with the American poet Richard Hovey in publishing the series *Songs from Vagabonnia* (1912). Other collections of his poems appeared at intervals, between *Low Tide on Grand Pré* (1893) and *Wild Garden* (1929).

Carmen Sylva (1843–1916). Pen-name of Elizabeth, wife of King Carol I of Romania. She wrote songs, poems, stories etc., in French, German, English and Romanian, much of her work inspired by Romanian folk lore. Her *Pensées d'une reine* appeared in 1882 and *From Memory's Shrine: Reminiscences* in 1911.

Carmichael, Hoagy (1899–1981). American song-writer, singer and actor. Originally a lawyer, his many songs include *Stardust* (1931) and he appeared in several films, generally playing himself.

Carmona, Antonio Oscar de Fragoso (1869–1951). Portuguese president. A general with distinguished military service, he had almost no political experience when called upon in 1926 to join the ruling triumvirate. Shortly afterwards he became head of state, retaining office until his death, though all power rested with the dictator * Salazar.

Carnap, Rudolf (1891–1970). German-born philosopher, resident in the U.S.A. since 1936. He was an original member of the circle at Vienna which expounded and developed logical positivism, and he concerned himself with such problems as the structure and meaning of utterances and the nature of statements of probability.
Schilpp, P. A., (ed.), *The Philosophy of Rudolf Carnap*. 1963

Carnarvon, George Edward Stanhope Molyneux Herbert, 5th Earl of (1866–1923). English Egyptologist. With Howard * Carter he conducted excavations in the Valley of Kings near Thebes, which culminated in Carter's discovery of the tomb of Tutankhamen (1922).

Carné, Marcel (1909–). French film director, the most famous of whose many successes was *Les Enfants du Paradis* (1943), hailed as a cinematic masterpiece. Other films include *Quai des Brumes* and *Le Jour se lève*, both typical of the romantic pessimism of French cinema in the late 1930s; the latter, probably his best film, had a strong influence on Hollywood direction in the 1940s.

Carnegie, Andrew (1835–1918). American industrialist and philanthropist, born in Dunfermline, Scotland. The family emigrated to Pittsburgh in 1848 and the boy began work in a cotton mill and later acquired positions of

responsibility on the Pennsylvania Railway. He started to invest in oil in 1864 and a year later entered the iron and steel industry. By the judicious merging of companies, he gradually built up a chain of interests not as a financier but as an industrialist mainly concerned with steel (but also with coal and iron fields, rail and steamship lines). In 1901 he sold his vast interests to the U.S. Steel Corporation for $250 million. His remaining years, most of which were spent in Scotland in retirement, he devoted to philanthropic ends to which he gave more than $300 million, e.g. the Carnegie Endowment for International Peace, the endowment of libraries in Britain and the U.S.A., and gifts to Scottish and American universities. He considered that all rich men were merely trustees for their wealth which must be distributed for beneficial ends.
Carnegie, A., *Autobiography*. 1920. Wall, J. F., *Andrew Carnegie*. 1971

Carnot, Lazare Nicolas Marguerite (1753–1823). French military engineer and politician, born in Burgundy. An army captain in 1789, he was elected to the Legislative Assembly 1791–92 and the National Convention 1792–95, becoming one of the twelve members of the Committee of Public Safety 1793–95. As *de facto* minister of war 1793–95 he received the title 'Organizer of Victories' for his achievement in raising, clothing, feeding, and training fourteen armies—more than 1,100,000 men—to defend revolutionary France against intervention by foreign troops, also proving a resourceful and original strategist. (Claude-Antoine Prieur de la Côte-d'Or shares credit for producing the armaments.) He served on the Directory 1795–97 after * Robespierre's overthrow, fleeing to Nuremberg in 1797 under an accusation of royalist sympathies. He returned after * Bonaparte's seizure of power and as minister of war 1799–1800 provided the organizational skill necessary for the success of the Italian and Rhineland campaigns. He remained, however, a sincere republican, and retired when he understood Napoleon's aims. The disasters that followed the retreat from Moscow induced him to offer his services once more. Napoleon made him governor of Antwerp in 1814 and he defended it bravely against Allied attack; he was minister of the interior during the Hundred Days. He ended his days in exile and died at Magdeburg. He wrote mathematical treatises as well as *The Defence of Fortified Places* (1810). His son **(Nicolas Leonard) Sadi Carnot** (1796–1832), named in honour of a Persian poet, was born and educated in Paris, became an army officer and after 1819 devoted himself to the study of the steam engine. Regarded as the founder of thermodynamics, his book *Reflections on the Motive Power of Fire* (1824) first stated the principle that the efficiency of a heat-engine in operating a thermal cycle depended on the relative temperature of its hottest and coldest parts. This led to the formulation of the Second Law of Thermodynamics by * Clausius and * Kelvin nearly twenty years after he died of cholera. **Lazare Hippolyte Carnot** (1801–1888), his brother, was a journalist and radical politician, a consistent opponent of Napoleon III; his son (grandson of the Revolutionary leader), **(Marie François) Sadi Carnot** (1837–1894), was an engineer and local administrator before being elected deputy in 1871. After periods of office (1880–86) as minister of public works and finance he was elected president of the republic in 1887 but was assassinated by an Italian anarchist in the last year of his seven-year term.

Carol I (1839–1914). First king of Romania (from 1881). A member of the Hohenzollern family, he was invited by the powers in 1866 to become ruler of the United Principalities of Moldavia and Wallachia still under the nominal suzerainty of Turkey. The Congress of Berlin (1878) made these territories independent (1881) under the name of Romania. In 1869 he married Princess Elizabeth of Wied, who under the pen-name * Carmen Sylva became a well known writer. He was succeeded by his nephew * Ferdinand I (1865–1927).

Carol II (1893–1953). King of Romania (1930–1940), son of * Ferdinand I. An earlier marriage to Zizi Lambrino having been dissolved, in 1921 he married Princess Helen of Greece, who became the mother of his son and heir Michael. Subsequently scandal caused by his association with Magda Lupescu forced him to renounce his right to the throne and on King Ferdinand's death (1927) it was Michael who succeeded. Carol, however, was recalled in 1930 after a promise, soon broken, that he would give up his mistress. During World War II he tried to appease first Russia (by ceding Bessarabia and Bukovina) and then Germany but was forced in 1940 to abdicate by Ion

Antonescu, leader of the Fascist 'Iron Guard'. He lived in Mexico with Madame Lupescu, whom he married in 1947, and subsequently in Portugal where he died.

Caroline (1683–1737). Daughter of the Margrave of Brandenburg-Anspach, queen consort of George II of England. Her skill in managing an often obstinate king was a factor in maintaining Sir Robert* Walpole in power. She befriended the literary men of her time (e.g. Pope and Chesterfield) and took a keen interest in ecclesiastical patronage.

Caroline (1768–1821). Daughter of the Duke of Brunswick and wife of the future George IV of England, whom she married in 1795. After the birth of Princess Charlotte (1796) he deserted her and went to live with Mrs Fitzherbert. Caroline's indiscretions and eccentricities in Italy provided George with an excuse to seek divorce as soon as he became king, but when, in 1820, a bill was introduced into the House of Lords, a brilliant defence by the queen's counsel Henry (later Lord) Brougham caused the bill to be dropped. Her forcible exclusion from Westminster Abbey at the coronation (1821) caused much resentment among the populace of London, and when she died a month later her funeral procession was accompanied by rioting in the London streets.

Carothers, Wallace Hume (1896–1937). American polymer chemist, the discoverer of nylon. After long research, in 1929 he found that adipic acid and hexamethylene diamine would condense together to form a tough polymer which could be drawn into a fibre. This plastic, which was called nylon, could be made into tough fabrics, cords and mouldings. There is now a family of nylons derived from slightly different starting materials. He committed suicide.

Carpaccio, Vittore (fl. 1450–1523). Italian painter, born in Venice, and a follower of Gentile* Bellini. His subtle treatment of light and the warm humanity of his interpretations anticipate the work of the major painters of the Venetian High Renaissance. He is a painter of pageantry, of architectural vistas and of details of contemporary life. His major achievement is the illustration of the story of St Ursula in a series of large, teeming and charmingly decorative compositions. Another cycle illustrates the lives of St George and St Jerome. *The Presentation in the Temple* is his outstanding altar-piece. All the above are in Venice.

Carpentier y Valmont, Alejo (1904–1980). Cuban novelist, of French descent. He was an architect, journalist, professor of literature and composer, whose passionate novels include *The Lost Steps* (1953), *Explosion in a Cathedral* (1962), and *Reasons of State* (1974).

Carpentier, Georges (1894–1975). French boxer. He was light-heavyweight champion of the world (1919–22), and in 1921 an unsuccessful contender with Jack Dempsey for the world heavyweight title.

Carpini, Giovanni de Piano (*c.* 1182–? 1252). Italian friar, born in Perugia, who entered the Franciscan order, taught in Germany for many years and was sent by Pope Innocent IV as missionary and explorer to the Mongols. He set out from Lyons in April 1245, reaching Karakoram in July 1246. On his return, he wrote an account of the journey, *Liber Tartarorum*.

Carracci, Ludovico (1555–1619). Italian painter. His work, with that of his cousins **Agostino** (1557–1602) and **Annibale** (1560–1609) **Carracci** represented a reaction from the Mannerist painters of his time. They held that by a study of the great Renaissance masters, Michelangelo, Raphael, Titian etc., and by combining together their several outstanding characteristics, the art of painting could make a great step forward. After decorating several palaces in Bologna, where they founded an academy, they carried out decorations in the Farnese palace in Rome, Annibale being the leading spirit. The ceiling of the great gallery, with its mythological scenes (in settings painted to imitate architectural or sculptured work), became famous throughout Europe and greatly influenced the development of the Baroque decorative style.

Carranza, Venustiano (1859–1920). Mexican president. His access to power came as a result of the confused situation which followed the long dictatorship (1876–1911) of Porfirio Díaz. Madero, his supplanter, having been murdered by Huerta, the so-called 'constitutionalists', headed by Carranza, Obregón and Villa, rose in revolt and by 1914 were in control. With the support of Obregón, Carranza became president and the opposition of Villa and the popular leader Zapata was eventually crushed after American intervention.

During Carranza's presidency some social reform took place and in 1917 a new constitution was introduced, but in 1920 Obregón successfully rebelled and Carranza was murdered while in flight to the coast.

Carrel, Alexis (1873–1944). French biologist, born near Lyons. He worked in the USA (1905–39), at the Rockefeller Institute for Medical Research, New York, from 1912. He won the 1912 Nobel Prize for Medicine for his work on the surgery of blood vessels and his techniques for transplanting arteries and suturing (i.e. joining) veins which during World War I reduced the number of amputations. Carrel devised equipment for keeping animal organs alive outside the body and he was able to keep a chicken heart alive for thirty-two years. Later he devoted himself to cancer research. He wrote *Man the Unknown* (1935), *The Culture of Organs* (1938), with Charles A. Lindbergh, and *Reflections of Life* (1943).

Carrington, Peter Alexander Rupert Carington, 6th Baron (1919–). British Conservative politician. Educated at Eton and Sandhurst, he served as high commissioner to Australia 1956–59, First Lord of the Admiralty 1959–63, secretary of state for defence 1970–74 and foreign secretary 1979–82, resigning over criticism that the Foreign Office had not anticipated the invasion of the Falkland Islands by Argentina. He was chairman of General Electric 1983–84 and secretary-general of NATO 1984–

Carroll, Lewis (pen-name of Charles Lutwidge Dodgson) (1832–1898). English author and mathematician, born in Daresbury, Cheshire, the son of a clergyman. He was educated at Rugby and Oxford, and lectured in mathematics at Oxford (1855–81). His life was generally uneventful and he never married. His most famous children's books *Alice's Adventures In Wonderland* (1865) and *Through the Looking Glass* (1872) – both written for Alice Liddell, the daughter of Carroll's friend, the dean of Christ Church – are full of subtle and almost surrealist humour, and the many fantastic characters have become familiar to millions of readers. Both books were illustrated by Tenniel. Other favourites were *The Hunting of the Snark* (1876) and *Sylvie and Bruno* (1889 and 1893). Among his mathematical studies (written under his real name) was *Euclid and His Modern Rivals* (1879). He was also a skilful photographer.

Carson, Edward Henry Carson, 1st Baron (1854–1935). Anglo-Irish lawyer and Conservative politician, educated in Dublin. He became a barrister and won fame as the defender of the Marquess of Queensberry in the action for criminal libel brought by Oscar Wilde. In parliament, where he sat as Unionist M.P. (1892–1918) he bitterly fought Liberal proposals to grant Irish home rule and organized the Ulster Volunteers, a military group which planned to oppose home rule by force and was diverted from this by the outbreak of World War I during which Carson was attorney-general in the first coalition and in Lloyd George's war cabinet was First Lord of the Admiralty (1916–17) and minister without portfolio (1917–18). He was a Lord of Appeal in Ordinary (1921–29).

Carson, Kit (Christopher) (1809–1868). American trapper, guide and scout, born in Kentucky. He acted as a guide for J. C. Fremont (1842–44) and helped to settle and explore California (1845–46). Although almost illiterate, he became a prominent and effective Indian agent (1853–61) and served as a brigadier of volunteers in the American Civil War.

Carte, Richard D'Oyly (1844–1901). English impresario. He won fame by staging the Gilbert and Sullivan operas. His background was a family music-publishing and instrument-making business, from which he progressed to become a concert agent and impresario. His success with Gilbert and Sullivan's *Trial by Jury* in 1875 inspired him to form a syndicate for the performance of future productions. In 1881 he built the Savoy Theatre for this purpose. His later venture, the building of the Palace Theatre for serious opera, was not a success. The rights of the D'Oyly Carte family over the Gilbert and Sullivan operas ended only in 1961, when the libretto contract expired.

Carter, Howard (1873–1939). English Egyptologist. A pupil of Sir Flinders Petrie, he worked in Egypt for many years, and in 1922, when working with Lord Carnarvon, found near Luxor the tomb of * Tutankhamen.

Carter, Jimmy (James Earl Carter Jr) (1924–). Thirty-ninth president of the U.S. He was born in Plains, Georgia and educated at public schools and Georgia South-western College. He graduated from the U.S. Naval Academy in Annapolis (1946) and served as an electronics instructor and engineering officer in Hyman Rickover's atomic submarine project. In 1953 he left the navy and returned home to manage the family peanut business. He became actively involved in community and church affairs and was elected to the Georgia State Senate (1963–67). In 1970 he won the Democratic primary for Governor as a moderate conservative by defeating the liberal ex-Governor Carl Sanders. As Governor of Georgia (1971–75) Carter introduced 'zero base budgeting', urged reforms in environmental controls, schools and prisons and tried to ease racial tensions. In July 1976 he won the Democratic presidential nomination and was elected president in November. During his term of office he failed to work with his Democratic Congress and his only significant success was in negotiating the Egyptian-Israeli accord between * Sadat and * Begin. His inability to secure the release of 52 U.S. hostages in Iran (kept for 444 days until he left office) damaged his political image and he was heavily defeated in the 1980 presidential election by Ronald * Reagan.

Carteret, John *see* **Granville, John Carteret**

Cartier, Jacques (1491–1557). French explorer, born at St Malo, Brittany. He made three voyages to North America in search of a north-west passage linking the Atlantic to the Pacific. On his first voyage (1534) he explored and claimed for France the coasts of Newfoundland and Labrador and the gulf of the St Lawrence; on his second (1535) he ascended that river (hoping it was a passage to China) and reached the site of Montreal. The third voyage (1541), also to the St Lawrence, provided much information but brought no new discoveries.
Biggar, H. P. ed., *The Voyages of Jacques Cartier*. 1924

Cartwright, Edmund (1743–1823). English inventor. Educated at Wakefield Grammar School and Oxford, he became a clergyman but having married a rich woman was able to give time and money to his inventions. In 1785 he invented a power loom which became the parent of the modern loom. He also invented rope-making and wool-combing machinery. In 1793, having been forced by debt to sell a mill he had set up in Doncaster, he went to London and worked with Robert Fulton on steam engines. His money troubles were eased when in 1809, in response to a petition to the prime minister from fifty firms which had benefited by his inventions, he was awarded £10,000.

Caruso, Enrico (1873–1921). Italian operatic singer, acclaimed as the finest tenor of his time. He was born in Naples, and after becoming famous in Italy he first appeared in London in 1902 and in New York a year later. He sang most of the great tenor roles in French and Italian opera (Verdi, Puccini, Bizet etc.) and was one of the first opera stars to have his fame perpetuated by gramophone record.
Caruso, E., *Enrico Caruso*. 1945

Carver, George Washington (1864–1943). American agriculturalist, born of Negro slave parents. He obtained a doctorate in science at Simpson College, and from 1876 taught at Tuskegee Institute, Alabama, where he directed agricultural research. Among his most successful achievements was the use of the peanut (groundnut) both as food, in various forms, and as an industrial raw material (for fibres etc.).
Holt, R., *George Washington Carver: An American Biography*. Rev. ed. 1963

Carver, John (*c.* 1576–1621). English merchant who organized the London contingent of the Pilgrim Fathers. He was born in Nottinghamshire and acquired wealth in London before emigrating to Holland for religious reasons. His preparations for the voyage to America included the hiring of the *Mayflower*, on which he sailed in 1620 with his wife and members of his household. He was chosen as governor of the Plymouth plantation but died the following year.

Cary, (Arthur) Joyce (Lunel) (1888–1957). British novelist, born in Ireland. Educated at Oxford, he fought in the Balkan Wars (1912–13) and World War I and was for a time in the colonial service in Africa, where he found

inspiration for *Mr Johnson* (1939). His best known novel, *The Horse's Mouth* (1944), which was successfully filmed in 1958, is part of a trilogy with *Herself Surprised* (1941) and *To be a Pilgrim* (1942). Rich characterization and feeling for the complexities of human emotions distinguish his work.
Wright, A., *Joyce Cary*. 1958

Casabianca, Louis (1762–1798). Corsican-French sailor. As commander of the French ship *Orient*, he was burnt to death when his ship was destroyed at the Battle of the Nile. The heroism of his young son, who perished with him, is the theme of a poem by Mrs Felicia Hemans ('Casabianca').

Casadesus, Robert (1899–1972). French pianist. He was one of the great Mozart stylists and often appeared in concerts with his wife Gaby and son Jean.

Casals, Pablo (or Pau) (1876–1973). Spanish cellist and conductor. The son of an organist, he studied music at Barcelona and Madrid, and made his concert debut as a cellist in Paris in 1899. He revived interest in Bach's works for unaccompanied cello, and developed improved cello techniques, gaining great popularity for this instrument with concert audiences. Active in his support of the government in the Spanish Civil War, he left Spain after Franco's victory (1939). From 1950 he organized a series of music festivals at Prades, in the French Pyrenees, and he continued these from 1956 at San Juan in Puerto Rico.

Casanova de Seingalt, Giovanni Giacomo (1725–1798). Italian adventurer, born in Venice. He spent most of his life travelling through Europe in the varying capacities of preacher, gambler, journalist, violinist, lottery director, police spy, alchemist and cabbalist, and met most of the famous men and women of his time. He was a man of intelligence and learning; his famous *Memoirs* – twelve volumes written in the last years of his life, when (from 1785) he was secretary and librarian to Count Waldstein in Bohemia – though largely concerned with his love affairs, throw much light on the manners and morals of the time.

Casaubon, Isaac (1559–1614). French-Swiss scholar, born in Geneva. He became professor of Greek at Geneva (1581), at Montpellier (1596) and royal librarian in Paris (1604). As a Protestant he felt unsafe after the death of Henry IV and came to England, where he found himself in sympathy with the middle position of the established church and able to be of help in matters both of religion and scholarship. His religious writings display his tolerance, and his gifts as a classical commentator are shown by his editions of Aristotle, Theophrastus, Suetonius etc. His son, **Méric Casaubon** (1599–1671), also a classical scholar and controversialist, settled into a living in the Church of England.

Casella, Alfredo (1883–1947). Italian composer, conductor and music critic, born in Turin. A pupil of Fauré in Paris, he worked there until World War I when he went to Rome. In 1924 he joined d'Annunzio and others in founding a society to encourage contemporary Italian music, but he himself was a notable experimenter and retained an international outlook. His range of composition was wide and included two symphonies, concertos, songs, chamber music and lesser pieces.

Casement, (Sir) Roger David (1864–1916). Irish nationalist and colonial administrator. He joined the consular service and was knighted for his work in exposing the exploitation of natives in the Congo and in Peru. In Germany during World War I he attempted to form an 'Irish Brigade' of Irish prisoners of war which he hoped would invade Ireland and free it from British rule. On his return to Ireland by submarine (1916) he was captured by the British and tried for treason. He was convicted, deprived of his knighthood, and hanged at Pentonville. In 1960 his 'black diaries' revealing homosexual practices were made available for study in the Public Records Office in London. Casement's remains were restored to Ireland in 1965.
MacColl, R., *Roger Casement*. 1956

Casey, Richard Gardiner Casey, Baron (1890–1976). Australian Liberal politician. He was a member of the Australian House of Representatives (1931–40 and 1949–60), was commonwealth treasurer (1935–39) and first Australian minister to the U.S. (1940–42). Winston Churchill appointed him a minister of state (1942–45) in the Middle East during World War II, with a seat in the war cabinet; from 1944 to 1946 he was governor of Bengal. In Australia after the war he was minister of national development (1949–51) and for external affairs (1951–60). In the latter year he became the first Australian life peer. He was Governor-General (1965–69) and became the first Australian K.G. (1969).

Casimir III (the Great) (*c.* 1310–1370). King of Poland (from 1333). Knowing that his first task would be to unify Poland he learned western politics and secured help from his brother-in-law, Charles Robert, the Angevin king of Hungary, to whose son, Louis, he promised the Polish throne. He also came to terms with Bohemia and the Teutonic Knights. Subsequently he was able to enlarge his kingdom in the east and, thus secured, to concentrate upon internal reforms. Brigandage was suppressed, the liberty of the peasants protected and the nobles curbed. Jews were tolerated and encouraged to settle, and the new university that he founded helped to make Cracow not only an administrative and commercial centre but one of the great cultural centres of Europe.

Casimir IV (1427–1492). King of Poland (from 1447). He belonged to the Lithuanian * Jagiellon dynasty which, linked by marriage with the Polish royal family, had brought the two countries under one ruler. He therefore had the good fortune to reign during one of Poland's greatest periods. After failure against Turkey he turned against the old enemy, the Teutonic Knights in the north. After thirteen years of war he destroyed their power and in 1466 by the peace of Thorn (or Torun) he annexed Pomerania with Danzig and much of south and west Prussia. To achieve these successes Casimir conceded representative government to the lesser gentry and so a parliament (Sejm) came into being. He did much also to encourage the growth and influence of the university at Cracow, founded by his father.

Casimir-Perier, Jean-Paul-Pierre (1847–1907). French politician. He served as a deputy 1877–94, was president of the chamber 1893 and 1894, and premier 1893–94, being elected president of the Third Republic 1894 on the assassination of * Carnot. He resigned unexpectedly in 1895 and went into business.

Caslon, William (1692–1766). Famous English type-founder who worked in London. A broadsheet of 1734 gave examples of twelve different sizes of his roman and italic types, which at the time were recognized as the best in Europe. Caslon Old Face (1726), revived in 1840 after a temporary decline in fashion, remained among the most popular types in the first half of the 20th century, being favoured by printers because of its simplicity and legibility.

Cass, Lewis (1782–1866). American Democratic politician, born in New Hampshire. He became a lawyer, served in the 1812 war and as governor of Michigan Territory (1813–31) opened new territories in the west for settlement. He was U.S. secretary of war under President Jackson (1831–36), U.S. minister to France (1836–42), and a U.S. senator from 1845. He was Democratic candidate for the presidency in 1848, but was defeated by Zachary Taylor when he lost the support of the Free-Soil wing of his party. He resumed his work in the Senate, but was too old to be effective when secretary of state under President Buchanan (1857–60).

Cassatt, Mary (1845–1926). American artist. Whilst young she went to Paris, and under the influence of Degas, her teacher, and Manet, joined the Impressionists. Neglected at first in America, her pictures, which show the Impressionist techniques applied to domestic subjects such as mothers with children or ladies at the tea table, have won her posthumous fame.

Watson, F., *Mary Cassatt*. 1932

Cassel, Sir Ernest Joseph (1852–1921). German-born financier who settled in England. He raised state loans for China, Egypt and South American governments. From an immense fortune he gave away about £2,000,000 to hospitals, educational institutions etc. He became a friend of Edward VII, and his granddaughter, Edwina Ashley, married Lord Louis * Mountbatten.

Cassin, René (1887–1976). French jurist. He won the 1968 Nobel Prize for Peace, for his work as author of the U.N. Declaration of the Rights of Man, and as president of the European Court of Human Rights.

Cassiodorus, Flavius Magnus Aurelius (*c.* 477–570). Roman writer and administrator. Only about 20 years old when he joined the secretariat of the emperor * Theodoric, he rose to high office, in which he continued after Theodoric's death. In 540 he retired from the Ravenna court to a monastery he had built on the Calabrian coast, and there set himself the task of creating a compendium of learning, pagan and Christian alike, almost encyclopedic in its scope. This he achieved by getting his monks to copy and amend ancient manuscripts and by his own voluminous works on history, theology and grammar. His *Variae*, collections of edicts, documents, etc., issued during his period of office, are of great importance for the study of the history of the Ostrogothic empire.

Cassius (Gaius Cassius Longinus) (died 42 B.C.). Roman soldier and politician. An adherent of Pompey, he became reconciled to Caesar but was a principal in the conspiracy to assassinate him. He left Italy with Brutus and after their defeat by * Mark Antony at Philippi ordered one of his freedmen to kill Caesar.

Cassivellaunus (fl. 54 B.C.). Ancient British ruler. As chief of the Catuvellauni he offered the utmost resistance to Caesar's advance across the Thames during his second invasion (54). The loss of his capital (now Wheathampstead, Herts.), forced him to make peace. His subsequent history is unknown.

Casson, Sir Hugh Maxwell (1910–). English architect. One of the leading exponents in Britain of the contemporary style, he was chief designer (1951) for the Festival of Britain exhibition buildings on the south bank of the Thames in London. He was knighted in 1952. He wrote *Homes by the Million* (1947). He was president of the Royal Academy 1976–84 and was made a C.H. (1984).

Casson, Sir Lewis Thomas (1875–1969). English actor-manager and producer, noted for his productions of Shakespeare and Shaw. He married (1908) the actress Sybil * Thorndike, with whom he frequently appeared; he was knighted in 1945.

Castellani, Sir Aldo (1878–1971). English-Italian physician specializing in tropical diseases. He discovered the causes of sleeping-sickness and yaws, taught in Italy, England and the U.S.A., and became Mussolini's physician. He was knighted in 1928.

Castiglione, Baldassare, Count (1478–1529). Italian humanist writer, born near Mantua. The son of a nobleman, he served more than one Italian duke, but it was the court of Urbino that provided the background for his great book, the *Libro del cortegiano* (*The Courtier*: 1518), a prose dialogue defining the attributes of the 'perfect gentleman', and discussing etiquette, hunting, social problems, the significance of the arts and Platonic love. It was translated into English in 1561 and widely read in Europe.

Castle, Barbara Anne, Baroness Castle (1911–). English Labour politician. Married to a journalist, she was elected MP for Blackburn in 1945 and was a member of the national executive committee of the Labour Party 1950– . She was minister of overseas development 1964–65, of transport 1965–68 and secretary of state for employment and productivity 1968–70, and for social services 1974–76. She was elected a member of the European Parliament in 1979.

Castlemaine, Countess of *see* **Cleveland, Barbara Villiers, 1st Duchess of**

Castlereagh, Robert Stewart, Viscount (afterwards **2nd Marquess of Londonderry**) (1769–1822). Anglo-Irish politician, son of an Ulster landowner. He entered the Irish parliament (then separate) as a Whig (1790), but turned Tory in 1795. As chief secretary for Ireland (1799–1801), he was instrumental in securing the passage of the Act of Union of Ireland with England, which, as he realized, was likely to fail unless Catholic emancipation was granted. George III's veto on such concessions was crippling. He became secretary of state for war and the colonies (1805–06; 1807–09), being responsible for choosing Sir Arthur Wellesley, the future Duke of * Wellington, for the peninsular command. But equally he must take some responsibility for the selection of the incompetent Earl of Chatham for the disastrous Walcheren campaign. In 1809 Castlereagh fought a duel with and slightly wounded his political rival George * Canning, who had been intriguing against him. He left office but returned in 1812 to begin his great period as foreign secretary (1812–22), when he was responsible for forming and holding together the anti-French alliance in the late stages of the Napoleonic Wars; after the French defeat he represented England at the

Congress of Vienna and the signing of the Treaty of Paris (1815). He opposed vindictive peace terms and was instrumental in keeping Alsace-Lorraine French. Later he was opposed to the Holy Alliance being exploited as a means of suppressing all liberal movements in Europe. Little interested in domestic politics, he had to defend and bear censure for the government's repressive policies, and this, combined with strain and overwork, may have brought about his suicide. One of the greatest statesmen of his time and a man of character, he was far from deserving the great unpopularity of his last years, which was expressed in the cheering which broke out when he was buried in Westminster Abbey.
Montgomery Hyde, H., *The Rise of Castlereagh*. 1933

Castro Ruz, Fidel (1927–). Cuban politician. The son of a rich sugar planter, he studied law at Havana University and became a violent opponent of the repressive and dictatorial Batista régime. Sentenced to five years' imprisonment for an attack on an army barracks in 1953 he was released under an amnesty two years later and went into exile. He returned in 1956, landing secretly in the Oriente province, where he gradually built up a guerilla force which by the end of 1958 proved strong enough to overthrow the Batista régime. Castro emerged in the years that followed as a communist dictator but defeated all attempts by Cuban exiles in the U.S.A. and elsewhere to dislodge him. He turned increasingly to the U.S.S.R. for support and permitted the construction in Cuba of a Soviet-manned missile base; this led to a serious U.S.A.–Soviet crisis in 1962, when America secured the dismantling of the base. Castro's régime survived economic strains and diplomatic isolation, and had considerable impact upon developments in South and Central America and Africa.
Matthews, H. L., *Castro: A Political Biography*. 1969

Catesby, Robert (1573–1605). English conspirator. A Roman Catholic gentleman, embittered by a fine imposed for joining Essex's rebellion, he took a leading part in the gunpowder plot. After the arrest of Guy * Fawkes he fled to Warwickshire but was pursued and killed.

Cather, Willa Sibert (1876–1947). American novelist, born in Virginia, but more closely associated with the western state of Nebraska, to which she was taken at the age of 9, and whose pioneering history is the subject of some of her best books. After graduating at the University of Nebraska, she went to Pittsburgh as a teacher and journalist. In 1904 she moved to New York, where her career as a professional writer began. Her first major success was *O Pioneers* (1913). Other major works include *One of Ours* (Pulitzer Prize, 1922), *Death comes for the Archbishop* (1927) and *Shadows on the Rock* (1933).

Catherine (1401–1437). Daughter of Charles VI of France, who in 1420 married Henry V of England. After his death (1422) and the accession of their baby son Henry VI, she married Owen Tudor, a Welsh landowner, and her grandson, Henry Tudor, became King Henry VII in 1485.

Catherine II (known as 'the Great') (1729–1796). Empress of Russia (from 1762). Sophie Augusta Frederika (her original names), daughter of Prince Christian of Anhalt-Zerbst (in Prussia), was born in Stettin, joined the Orthodox Church in 1744 and married (1745) the future tsar, Peter III. Catherine hated her degenerate and feeble-minded husband but realized that marriage could be a path to power. Their only child, the future Paul I, was born in 1754. Peter became tsar in 1762 but six months later a military *coup* led by two of Catherine's many lovers, Count Grigory Orlov and Prince Grigory Potyomkin, deposed him, and he was murdered some days later. In taking the throne Catherine supplanted her own son. Though in her zeal for self-education she read and corresponded with Voltaire and others and practised and patronized art and literature, she ruled as an autocrat; an enlightened despot she may have been but a despot none the less, and she never forgot her political dependence on the nobility and gentry who had set her on the throne. Although she abolished capital punishment (except for political crimes), and prepared comprehensive schemes of educational, legal and administrative reform, little was actually accomplished. The number of serfs increased and the military and economic burdens on the peasantry grew worse. Following the revolt (1773–75) led by Emelian Pugachov, a pretender who claimed to be her dead husband Peter II, her domestic policy became increasingly repressive. She pursued an imperialist foreign policy and in two wars with Turkey (1768–72 and 1787–92) expanded her territories near the Black Sea and annexed the Crimea. The Ukraine was fully absorbed and when Poland was obliterated by the three partitions of 1772, 1793 and 1795 Russia took the largest share.

Grey, I., *Catherine the Great: Autocrat and Empress of all Russia*. 1961; Troyat, H., *Catherine the Great*. 1977

Catherine de'Medici (de Médicis) (1519–1589). French queen consort (1547–59), daughter of Lorenzo de'Medici, born in Florence. She married Henry II of France in 1533 and was the mother of three kings, Francis II (first husband of Mary, Queen of Scots), Charles IX and Henry III. She became regent in the reign of Charles IX; her aim was to increase the independence and power of the crown by maintaining a balance between the Roman Catholic extremists (under the Guises) and the Huguenots (Protestants). It was because the balance appeared to be endangered by the marriage of her daughter, Marguerite de Valois, to the Protestant leader Henry of Navarre that she obtained the agreement of Charles IX to the massacre (known as the massacre of St Bartholomew) of the Huguenot guests gathered in Paris for the wedding. Under Henry III Catherine's influence waned. She was much hated and traduced, but stood for a policy of moderation in general, in the interests of the survival of the monarchy – which she saw as the basis of French stability.

Romier, L., *Le Royaume de Catherine de Médicis*. 2nd ed. 1922.

Catherine (Howard) (1521–1542). Fifth wife of Henry VIII of England. A grand-daughter of the 2nd Duke of Norfolk and related to Anne Boleyn, she married the king in 1540 and less than two years later was beheaded for adultery with a young kinsman, Francis Dereham.

Catherine of Aragon (1485–1536). Daughter of Ferdinand and Isabella of Spain, and first wife of the English King Henry VIII. For this marriage (1509) a papal dispensation had to be obtained as she was the widow of Henry's elder brother, Arthur. Despite this dispensation and the fact that she had borne him six children (of whom only the future Mary I survived), Henry used this alleged irregularity as an excuse for getting the marriage annulled (though he had to break with Rome to do so) in order to marry Anne Boleyn. Catherine lived in seclusion until her death, devoting herself to religion and literature.

Mattingly, G., *Catherine of Aragon*. 1950

Catherine of Braganza (1638–1705). Daughter of John IV of Portugal and wife of Charles II of Great Britain, whom she married in 1662. She brought Bombay and Tangier to England as her dowry. They had no children, but though he was notoriously unfaithful Charles treated her with dignity and kindness. She finally returned to Portugal in 1692.

Catherine of Siena, St (*c*. 1347–1380). Italian nun, mystic and patron saint of the Dominican order, to which she belonged. She was influential in persuading Pope Gregory XI to return from Avignon to Rome. Later she became papal ambassador to Florence. Though illiterate, she dictated hundreds of letters and her famous *Dialogue* or *Treatise on Divine Providence*.

Catherine (Parr) (1512–1548). Sixth and last wife of Henry VIII. Daughter of a controller of the royal household, she had been widowed twice before marrying the king in 1544. After his death she married Lord Thomas Seymour, a brother of Jane Seymour, the mother of Edward VI. For a time she provided a home for the young Princess Elizabeth.

Catherine Swynford *see* **Swynford, Catherine**

Catiline (Lucius Sergius Catilina) (*c*. 108–62 B.C.). Roman conspirator. A supporter of Sulla as a young man, he later professed extreme democratic opinions to further his interests. The events which brought about his ruin originated from his belief that he was being unfairly deprived of the consulship, which he felt was his due. Thus his first conspiracy (65) was intended to help his own candidacy for 64. The plot was mismanaged and Catiline escaped conviction, but when he again sought election in 63, it was * Cicero, a man of lower rank than himself but with conservative backing, who was preferred. A second plot was then contrived to bring about the death of Cicero and other hostile senators. News of it had reached Cicero, who took emergency measures and in one of his most famous orations denounced Catiline in the Senate.

Catiline himself gained a short respite by flight, but in January 62, he was hunted down and killed, with many of his followers, at Pistoia, while those conspirators who had stayed in Rome were arrested and executed.

Cato, Marcus Porcius (known as Cato the Elder) (234–149 B.C.). Roman statesman. As a young man he served against the Carthaginians in the second Punic War. As consul (195) he fought in Spain, but it was as 'censor' (184) that he showed the zeal for moral reform by which he is best remembered. He denounced extravagance, tried to restore a sense of high moral values in public life, and strongly resisted Greek cultural influences, which he regarded as corrupting. His visit to Africa in 153 convinced him that Carthage could still be dangerous and for many years he ended every speech in the Senate with the words 'Carthage must be destroyed'. He wrote books on the history of Roman towns (*Origines*) and on farming.

His great-grandson, also named **Marcus Porcius Cato** (Cato the Younger) (95–46 B.C.), supported Pompey against Julius Caesar in the Civil Wars, and after Pompey's defeat at Pharsalus (48) escaped to Africa, where he defended Utica. When news of Caesar's victory at Thapsus (46) reached him he committed suicide. His daughter, Portia, married * Brutus. As a patron of the Stoic school of philosophers Cato was famed for his unbending rectitude. He was seen by his enemies as an obstructive, old-fashioned and inflexibly doctrinaire politician; his admirers saw him as upholding the ancient Roman virtues in a corrupt age.

Catullus, Gaius Valerius (*c.* 84–*c.* 54 B.C.). Roman lyric poet. Born in Verona, he lived mainly at Rome and at his villas at Tibur and Sirmio. His surviving works consist mainly of love poems, some passionate, some playful, and scurrilous, witty or satirical verses written probably in the last years of his short life. They show his command of lyric metres and ability to express the tenderest and most personal emotions.

Quinn, K., *Catullus: The Poems, edited with Commentary*. 1970. Wiseman, T. P., *Catullan Questions*. 1969

Cavaignac, Louis Eugène (1802–1857). French soldier and politician. He was the son of a revolutionary lawyer. When Louis Philippe was deposed (1848) he became minister of war in the provisional government, and armed with dictatorial powers suppressed an extremist rising in Paris with great loss of life. But for his republican principles he might have assumed supreme power; in fact he laid aside his dictatorship to become president of the council of ministers. A new constitution was promulgated under which Louis Napoleon (later Napoleon III) was elected president with about 5,500,000 votes, against less than 1,500,000 for Cavaignac. The latter after refusing to take the oath retired into private life.

Cavalcanti, Guido (*c.* 1255–1300). Florentine poet. He was a friend of Dante and his sonnets and other poems reveal a philosophic and introspective temperament. His active support of the Ghibelline (imperial) cause led to his exile in the last year of his life. English translations were made by Rossetti and Ezra Pound.

Cavalli, Francesco (Pietro Francesco Caletti-di Bruno) (1602–1676). Italian operatic composer. He was born at Crema, the son of Gian-Battista Caletti-di Bruno, and later took the name of his Venetian patron Federico Cavalli. At 15 he became a singer in the choir of St Mark's, Venice, where he was trained by Claudio * Monteverdi. He himself became *maestro di cappella* at St Mark's in 1668. He wrote 42 musical dramas, of which 27 survive. They use a small orchestra and show the beginnings of the use of recitative and aria; the music complemented extravagant sets and costumes.

Worsthorne, S. T., *Venetian Opera in the Seventeenth Century*. 1954

Cavallini, Pietro (*c.* 1250–*c.* 1330). Italian fresco painter and mosaic artist, working mainly in Rome. His first authenticated work is known to have been painted over a fifth-century Christian fresco in which the Roman classical tradition had survived. It is this tradition which seems to have influenced him in his departures from the contemporary Byzantine style. His paintings reject the stiffness of Byzantine art; they re-introduce sculptural modelling of figures and drapery, assisted by directed light. His best-known works are probably *The Last Judgment* (fresco) in Sta. Cecilia in Trastevere, Rome, and *The Life of the Virgin* (mosaic) in Sta. Maria. He had considerable influence on * Giotto.

Toesca, P., *Pietro Cavallini*. 1960

Cavell, Edith Louisa (1865–1915). English nurse. When Belgium was overrun by the Germans during World War I, she remained in Brussels to nurse the wounded of both sides and assisted over 200 Allied soldiers to escape into neutral Holland, for which she was condemned and shot by the Germans. Her statue in St Martin's Lane, London, carries her words: 'Patriotism is not enough. I must have no hatred or bitterness towards anyone'.
Hochling, A. A., *Edith Cavell*. 1958

Cavendish, Henry (1731–1810). English scientist. Born in Nice and educated at Cambridge, he was the younger brother of the 3rd Duke of Devonshire. Later he lived in London, either in Bloomsbury or at a villa at Clapham, in eccentric seclusion. His waking hours were devoted to scientific research. In 1766 he isolated hydrogen, realized that it was an element, and investigated many of its properties. He was the first accurately to determine the chemical composition of water and of air. Cavendish also conducted many experiments in heat and electricity, and measured the constant of gravitation, from which he was able to estimate the mean density of the earth (to within 1 per cent). The Cavendish Laboratory at Cambridge is named after him.
Berry, A. J., *Henry Cavendish: His Life and Scientific Work*. 1960

Cavour, Count Camillo Benso di (1810–1861). Italian politician. The main architect of Italian unity and independence, he was born in Turin, the son of a nobleman. He found army life alien to his liberal ideas and turned to scientific agriculture as a means of showing that to prepare a country for freedom practical improvements were more important than political agitation. His search for the newest techniques, which eventually brought him a fortune, took him abroad and introduced him to many influential people who shared his liberal views and moderate approach. In 1847 he founded *Il Risorgimento*, a liberal journal aimed at securing the political unification of Italy but at the same time advocating such steps as the construction of railways, free trade, democratic constitutions etc., which would tend to bring unity naturally about. Meanwhile, political events were helping him. In 1848 Charles Albert, the king of Sardinia (and ruler of Piedmont) went to war with Austria (which then held the rest of northern Italy), and though defeated was prepared to grant a democratic constitution, which provided a means by which Cavour could bring about his aims. In 1852 under the new king, Victor Emmanuel, he became premier of Piedmont-Sardinia. By reforms of the army and administration, expanding the economy and strengthening the financial situation by reducing debt, he steadily built up the idea in Europe that the supporters of Italian unification were no longer reckless revolutionaries but sober serious politicians. He gained further good-will by sending Sardinian troops to aid the British and French in the Crimea. Finally, in 1858, accord with * Garibaldi having already been reached, came the secret deal with Napoleon III by which Nice and the Savoy duchy were promised to France in return for French aid. When war broke out with Austria in 1859 the French victories at Magenta and Solferino secured northern Italy (except Venice). Garibaldi landed in Sicily in May 1860 and a few weeks later he and Victor Emmanuel rode through Naples together. In March 1861 Cavour became first prime minister of the almost united Italy. He died in June.
Mack Smith, D., *Cavour*. 1985.

Caxton, William (*c.* 1422–1491). English printer, born in Kent. He became a prosperous silk merchant, and was a prominent member of the English commercial community at Bruges (1463–69). From 1471 to 1476 he was attached to the court of Margaret, Duchess of Burgundy, sister of England's Edward IV. During this time he learned the art of printing, probably at Cologne, and began printing at Bruges, where he published the *Recuyell of the Historyes of Troye*, which he had translated from the French. This is the first known book to have been printed in the English language. In 1476 he set up the first English press at Westminster. His first publication there was *The Dictes or Sayengis of the Philosophers* (1477), a translation from the French by Earl Rivers. He also printed the works of Chaucer, Malory and Gower and was active until his death as translator and editor. His first illustrated work was the *Myrrour of the World* (1481) and his most elaborate the *Golden Legend*, lives of the saints illustrated with woodcuts. In all he published about 100 volumes, of which roughly one third survive.
Gordon Duff, E., *English Fifteenth-Century Books*. 1918

Cayley, Arthur (1821–1895). English mathematician. After being a senior wrangler at Cambridge he continued to devote himself to mathematics, was elected an F.R.S. when only 31 and in 1863 became first Sadleiran professor of mathematics at Cambridge. The honorary degrees and other distinctions which followed bear witness to the esteem in which he was held. He made important contributions to abstract geometry and theoretical dynamics, his best known book (his collected papers alone fill thirteen volumes) being *Elementary Treatise on Elliptic Functions* (1876).
Bell, E. T., *Men of Mathematics*. Repr. 1961

Cayley, Sir George, 6th Bart. (1773–1857). British aviation pioneer. As the first man to state in mathematical terms the problems of flying he originated the science of aerodynamics and so made subsequent development in aviation possible. He also constructed and flew a large glider, for which he claimed 'steadiness, safety and steerage'.

Ceaucescu, Nicolae (1918–). Romanian politician. When the first Communist government was installed in 1947 he was Minister of Agriculture until 1950 and deputy minister of the armed forces 1950–54. He became leader of the party on the death of the Stalinist Gheorghe Gheorghiu-Dej in 1965, and, in 1967, assumed the presidency of the state council and became head of state. While following a repressive, Stalin-style domestic policy, he won popularity by a nationalist approach and refused to allow Russian domination of Romania's internal affairs.

Cecchetti, Enrico (1850–1928). Italian ballet dancer and trainer. One of the strongest influences in the development of modern ballet, both his father and his mother were leading figures in ballet, and he himself, by a blend of vigour and precision with French grace, produced the style of male dancing which came to be known as Russian. In 1902 he became director of the Imperial School at Warsaw, but later took * Pavlova, at her special request, as his sole pupil. A long association with * Diaghilev followed, and in 1919 he started his own school in London, where Ninette * de Valois and Marie * Rambert were among his pupils.

Cecil. For distinguished members of this family other than those below, *see* * Salisbury, 3rd Marquess of, and * Salisbury, Robert Cecil.

Cecil, Lord (Edward Christian) David (Gascoyne) (1902–). English literary critic and biographer. Son of the 4th Marquess of Salisbury, he was professor of English literature at Oxford University (1948–69). He wrote biographies and studies of Walter Scott, Lord Melbourne, Jane Austen, William Cowper and Thomas Hardy, and a critical study, *Early Victorian Novelists* (1964).

Cecil, William, Lord Burghley (1520–1598). English administrator. Principal adviser to Queen Elizabeth I, he was appointed her sole Secretary of State in 1558. She valued him for his sound knowledge, his discretion and his ability. He is noted for his pragmatism and moderation which, although he could be ruthless in suppressing political Catholicism, achieved for England a period of relative calm in contrast to the violence and intrigue common elsewhere in Renaissance Europe. His second son, Robert Cecil, 1st Earl of * Salisbury (1563–1612) was secretary of state to Elizabeth I and James I, and Lord Treasurer (1608–12).
Beckingsale, B. W., *Burghley: Tudor Statesman, 1520–1598*. 1967

Cecil of Chelwood, Lord (Edgar Algernon) Robert Cecil, 1st Viscount (1864–1958). British politician. A son of the 3rd Marquess of Salisbury, he was a barrister by profession. After World War I, although he held office in the Baldwin government (1923–27), his main preoccupation was the League of Nations, where he was a British delegate for many years. He was also the mainstay and president of the League of Nations Union (1923–45) and subsequently of the United Nations Association. He was awarded the Nobel Peace Prize in 1937 and a C.H. in 1956.

Celestine V, St (Pietro di Morrone) (*c.* 1215–1296). Pope (1294). He lived for many years as a hermit in the Abruzzi and gathered round him an ascetic group, later known as the Celestines. After the death of Nicholas IV in 1292 the cardinals were unable to agree on a new pope, and after a two-year delay Celestine, now old and incompetent, was elected. Finding himself a political pawn he abdicated after five months, but was kept in captivity by his successor, Boniface VIII, to prevent him becoming a centre of faction. He was canonized in 1313, though * Dante sets him at the gateway of Hell.

Céline, Louis-Ferdinand (real name Louis-Ferdinand Destouches) (1894–1961). French novelist. His major novels, *Journey to the End of the Night* (1932) and *Death on the Instalment Plan* (1936), are autobiographical, describing his experiences during World War I, his work as a doctor in Paris slums, and his childhood and youth. Born a *petit bourgeois*, his writings reveal a pathological loathing for capitalist society and its products. Céline, assumed to be a leftist, was invited to the USSR in 1936 but hated what he saw. His visit made him first an anarchist and soon after a fascist. His anti-Semitism became so virulent that even the French fascist press rejected his writings. He fled to Denmark and went into hiding in 1945 and was sentenced to death in absentia. Broken in health, he was amnestied and returned to France in 1951.

Cellini, Benvenuto (1500–1571). Florentine artist. His life, according to himself, was as colourful as his work. His father was a musician and he himself studied music until the age of 15. Later he was apprenticed to a goldsmith, and it was during his apprenticeship that he was banished after fighting a duel. Making his way to Rome, he was employed by Pope Clement VII as a musician, but soon attracted notice by his gold and silver craftsmanship. He claimed, too, to have killed the Constable of Bourbon and the Prince of Orange during the sack of Rome by the imperial forces in 1527. After a short absence he was back in Rome in 1529, designing coins for the papal mint. Pardoned by Pope Paul III for the murder of a rival goldsmith, he was again in trouble in 1538 when he was charged (falsely it is said) with having stolen papal jewels during the sack. After escaping from prison he served Francis I of France until 1545, when he returned to Florence, where he enjoyed the patronage of Duke Cosimo for the rest of his life. Cellini's *Autobiography* (1558–62), a lively and boastful account of his adventurous life, also gives much valuable information about the goldsmith's craft. It is indeed for their intricate and ingenious craftsmanship rather than for their artistic sensibility that his works, such as his statue of Perseus in Florence, are most praised.

Ashbee, C. R., ed., *The Treatises Benvenuto Cellini on Goldsmithing and Sculpture*. Repr. 1967

Celsius, Anders (1701–1744). Swedish astronomer, nephew of **Olaf Celsius** (1670–1756), the botanist and patron of Linnaeus, and grandson of **Magnus Celsius** who deciphered the Helsing runes. He was professor of astronomy at the University of Uppsala (1730–44) and was a member of the expedition which in 1736 visited Lapland to measure an arc of the meridian and investigate the Aurora Borealis. In 1742 he introduced the Celsius or centigrade temperature scale.

Cenci, Beatrice (1577–1599). Italian noblewoman. To escape the cruelty and the incestuous attentions of her father, she arranged with her stepmother and brother to have him assassinated. Put on trial with her accomplices, she confessed under torture and was beheaded. Her story was the basis of Shelley's verse tragedy *The Cenci*.

Cerdic (died 534?). Founder of the West Saxon kingdom (Wessex), and so the first king of the line which included Egbert and Alfred the Great.

Cervantes Saavedra, Miguel de (1547–1616). Spanish novelist. He was born in Alacala, the fourth child of a surgeon-apothecary. Little is known of his childhood but he was an avid reader and a lover of the theatre. By 1569 he was in Rome and was an official in the household of Giulio Acquaviva, later cardinal, until 1570. In 1571 he served at the Battle of Lepanto, in which he received three gunshot wounds, one of them crippling his left hand. Afterwards he rejoined his regiment and served in Corfu and Tunis. Whilst returning to Spain with his brother Rodrigo his ship was captured by Moorish pirates and he was imprisoned as a slave in Algiers (1575–80). After several abortive attempts to escape he was finally ransomed. On returning to Madrid he tried to support himself by writing plays, poems, and a pastoral novel, *La Galatea* (1585). In 1584 he married Catalina de Palacios Salazar y Vozmediano (1565–1626); the marriage was unhappy and they had no children, though Cervantes had a daughter, Isabel, from an earlier liaison. He was employed (1587) in raising provisions for the Armada, was confirmed as a civil servant

(1588), but was finally dismissed (1597) and imprisoned for three months because of discrepancies in his accounts. He lived in Seville, in great poverty, from 1595 to 1603, and occupied himself with poetry, and with the first part of his masterpiece, *El ingenioso hidalgo Don Quixote de la Mancha* (*Don Quixote*), which recounts the adventures of an elderly and confused knight, who tours the countryside on his horse Rosinante, with Dulcinea del Toboso in his heart and his faithful squire Sancho Panza in his wake, 'to defend the oppressed and to undo wrongs'. This great novel, originally intended as a satire on medieval romances of chivalry, appeared in two parts: Part 1 was published in 1605, Part 2 in 1615. The first part secured an immediate success and was reprinted four times in the same year. But in that year, too, he was arrested on suspicion of conspiracy to murder, when the body of a well known rake believed to be a lover of his daughter, Isabel, was found in his house; the charge was, however, dropped. Isabel was again mixed up in some sort of mysterious imbroglio (1608–12). Fame seems however to have brought him some happiness though he remained poor. Among Cervantes's last works were some short plays, a collection of *Exemplary Novels* (1613) in the manner of * Boccaccio, and *The Trials and Peregrinations of Persiles and Sigismunda*, a linked series of about twenty short novels, published posthumously. He died in Madrid on 23 April 1616, the same day as Shakespeare.

Grismer, R. L., *Cervantes: a Bibliography*. 1946–1963

Cetewayo (*c*. 1(36–1884). Zulu king. After he had gained the throne by killing his brother his threatening attitude to the British settlers in Natal brought on the Zulu War of 1879. The results of early successes, including the victory of Isandhlwana, were wiped out by the decisive defeat of Ulundi. After imprisonment he was restored to part of his kingdom in 1883 but failed to secure the allegiance of his subjects, and was driven out.

Cézanne, Paul (1839–1906). French post-impressionist painter. He was the son of a rich banker of Aix-en-Provence, he wrote poetry, and had as one of his boyhood friends Emile * Zola, who persuaded him, against his father's wishes, to take up art in Paris. From 1863 he joined the group round Manet and his earliest works, influenced by Delacroix, were often erotic or mythological scenes executed with violent strokes of the palette knife. The Franco-Prussian War having broken up the group, Cézanne became more closely associated with the Impressionists, and through Camille Pissaro (1872–73) became friendly with Monet and Renoir; he soon developed an original and personal style. He saw natural objects as made up of basic geometrical forms, such as the cylinder, sphere or cone, and his aim was to represent them by colour alone without shadows or perspective, space being suggested by a series of receding planes. Cézanne achieved his effects with a limited colour range: blue, green and tan predominantly, and brushwork as distinctive as it is difficult to describe. From about 1876 he gave up small brush strokes and painted in masses. His subjects, repeated over and over again, were few: landscapes, still life (mainly fruit and flowers), a few local portraits (and some of himself) and groups of card players and bathers. The enormous prices now paid for his works make it hard to credit that until he was over 50 Cézanne's talent went almost unrecognized; he became embittered and eccentric, withdrew to Provence in 1878 and except for short intervals lived there in seclusion for the rest of his life. When his father died (1886), leaving him enough to live in comfort, he married Hortense Figuet, a model with whom he had previously lived, and his work of the next ten years is his most serene and assured. His last works are more violent and lyrical, e.g. the wonderful variants of *Le Château noir* and *Mont St Victoire*. In 1895 a leading art dealer, Vollard, showed his pictures in Paris and thereafter Cézanne enjoyed at least moderate fame. Cubism was the obvious development of his geometrical theories but his influence extended far more widely and his works led from the traditional schools to the revolutionary theories and techniques of today.

Rewald, J. (ed.), *Correspondence of Paul Cézanne*. 1941; *Paul Cézanne: a Biography*. 1948

Chabrier, (Alexis) **Emmanuel** (1841–1894). French composer. He was largely self-taught. At first a civil servant, he did not become a professional musician until 1880. His first successful work, the orchestral rhapsody *España* (1883), shows the gaiety and orchestral flair that characterize his music: other examples are the *Marche slave* and *Marche joyeuse*.

He also wrote the light operas *Gwendoline* (1886) and *Le Roi malgré lui* (1887). His influence on later French composers was notable, and his songs, piano music and the orchestral *Suite pastorale* were much admired by Ravel and Debussy.

Chabrol, Claude (1930–). French film director. Educated at the University of Paris, he became a critic, co-authored a book on Alfred * Hitchcock, and directed a series of films, many featuring his wife Stephane Audran, about crime, passion and family life among the bourgeoisie.

Chad, Saint (d. 672). Missionary and bishop born in Northumbria and educated at Lindisfarne. He succeeded his brother, **Saint Cedd,** as abbot of their joint foundation at Lastingham in 664. He was consecrated bishop of the Northumbrians with York as his see, but the appointment gave rise to a dispute and he resigned in 669 in favour of St Wilfrid. He was then made Bishop of Mercia, with his see at Lichfield, and is credited with the conversion of the Kingdom of Mercia. He died of the plague. His remains are in St Chad's Cathedral, Birmingham.

Chadwick, Sir Edwin (1801–1890). English social reformer. Originally a lawyer, he became a friend and disciple of Jeremy * Bentham. He worked (1832–46) for the Poor Law Commission and played an important part in the drafting of the Factory Act (1833) and the Poor Law Amendment Act (1834). He was the leading public-health reformer of the 19th century. He wrote *The Sanitary Condition of the Labouring Population* (1842) and advocated the introduction of comprehensive drainage and sewerage systems in English cities. This and other reports, e.g. that on *The Practice of Interment in Towns*, led to important reforms.

Chadwick, Sir James (1891–1974). English physicist. He studied at Manchester and under * Rutherford at Cambridge and was appointed professor of physics at Liverpool in 1935. Chadwick investigated highly-penetrating radiation which in 1930 had been observed by Bothe and Becker when certain light atoms, such as those of beryllium, were bombarded with alpha-particles. By analysing the masses and speeds of the particles involved, he showed in 1932 that neutrons, uncharged subatomic particles whose existence had been predicted by Rutherford, were being produced. Chadwick is thus generally credited with the discovery of the neutron, and was awarded the Nobel prize for Physics in 1935. He worked on atomic energy research during World War II and was knighted in 1945. He was master of Gonville and Caius College, Cambridge, from 1948 to 1958.

Chagall, Marc (1887–). Russian-Jewish artist, born in Vitebsk. He worked as a stage designer under * Bakst, lived in Paris (1910–14) and was there influenced by the Cubists. He returned to Russia, served in World War I and became a commissar of fine arts after the revolution. In 1922 he returned to Paris. During World War II he took refuge in America; later he lived in Vienna. His style, though it links up with that of the Surrealists, is highly personal. His dreamlike pictures are made up of Jewish and Russian folk fantasies and symbols and childhood memories: his first wife, Bella, appears in many of them. He also designed stained glass and ballet, e.g. *Firebird* (1945); illustrated a number of books, e.g. La Fontaine's *Fables*; and was responsible for the ceiling of the newly decorated Paris Opéra.
Alexander, S., *Marc Chagall*. 1979

Chain, Sir Ernest Boris (1906–1979). Anglo-German physiologist, born in Berlin. He lectured at Oxford from 1935 and with * Florey devised methods of producing penicillin in commercial quantities. He shared the 1945 Nobel Prize for Physiology with Florey and Fleming.

Chaliapin, Fyodor Ivanovich (1873–1938). Russian singer, born in Kazan. His family was desperately poor and he had little formal education, but after working at a variety of odd jobs he joined a touring opera company at the age of 17. His powerful bass voice and his great dramatic gifts soon brought him to St Petersburg and fame. The title roles in the operas *Boris Godunov* and *Ivan the Terrible* provided ideal opportunities for his talents. He also appeared in several films.

Challoner, Richard (1691–1781). English Roman Catholic Bishop and leader of the English Roman community. He was made apostolic vicar of the London Catholics in 1758, increased their numbers, strengthened their resistance to hostility and founded a

charitable institution for the poor and aged. He revised the Reims-Douai bible (an English translation of the Vulgate for Roman Catholic use) and wrote many devotional works.
Burton, E. H., *Life and Times of Bishop Challoner*. 1909

Chamberlain, Sir (Joseph) **Austen** (1863–1937). British politician, son of Joseph * Chamberlain by his first wife. He embarked early on a political career and was a Conservative M.P. from 1892 to 1937. He obtained office early and from 1903 until the fall of the Conservative government at the end of 1905 was chancellor of the exchequer. He held high office in the coalitions during and after World War I but by loyally adhering to Lloyd George in 1922 lost the opportunity of leading a Conservative government. Under Baldwin he was foreign minister (1924–29), and crowned his work for European conciliation by negotiating and signing the Locarno pact (1925) on which such high and such vain hopes were set, and for which he shared a Nobel Peace Prize with * Briand and * Stresemann.
Petrie, C., *Life and Letters of Sir Austen Chamberlain*. 1939

Chamberlain, Houston Stewart (1855–1927). British-born racial theorist. He was educated on the continent and eventually (1908) settled in Bayreuth and married a daughter of Richard * Wagner. He remained in Germany when World War I broke out and in 1916 became a German citizen. He wrote on Wagner and on aesthetic and philosophic themes, but the main work of his life, *The Foundations of the Nineteenth Century* (1899), was based on * Gobineau and expounded a racial theory of history which provided arguments for Aryan and German racial supremacy repeated by Hitler to justify anti-semitism.

Chamberlain, Joseph (1836–1914). British politician. The son of a London screw manufacturer, he studied at University College School, London, then, to further his father's interests, entered a firm of screw manufacturers at Birmingham with which city he remained closely identified. He retired from business in 1874, with a fortune of £100,000, and after service as mayor (1873–74) became M.P. for Birmingham in 1876. During his first years in parliament he was an advanced radical and even a republican; but after serving under Gladstone as president of the Board of Trade (1880–85) and president of the Local Government Board (1886), he disagreed with the proposal to grant Home Rule to Ireland and resigned to become a Liberal Unionist in alliance with the Conservatives. Always a staunch imperialist, he was colonial secretary (1895–1903) in the ministries of Salisbury and Balfour, and by many was held to have encouraged Rhodes and to have been partly responsible for the Boer War. His work for the creation of the federal Commonwealth of Australia proved, however, wholly beneficial, and he was enthusiastic for such measures of social reform as the Workmen's Compensation Act (1897). In 1903 he resigned to devote himself to the promotion of a scheme of tariff reform by way of 'imperial preference'. From 1906 a stroke kept him out of active politics. He was first chancellor of Birmingham University, whose development he did much to encourage.
Amery, J., and Garvin, J. L., *The Life of Joseph Chamberlain*. 6 vols, 1932–69

Chamberlain, (Arthur) **Neville** (1869–1940). British politician. Son of Joseph Chamberlain by his second wife and half-brother of Austen. It was not until he was appointed director of National Service (1916–17) during World War I that he became closely associated with national politics. Elected Conservative M.P. for the Ladywood division of Birmingham in 1918 he rose rapidly through a series of offices until his terms as chancellor of the exchequer (1923–24 and 1931–37) made him the natural successor to * Baldwin as prime minister in 1937. His government followed a policy of appeasement towards Hitler, for which he must bear the main responsibility, although the policy had wide political and popular support as the reception of the Munich Agreement of 1938 indicated. After Munich, Chamberlain turned to preparations for war, but lacked the powers of inspiration required of a political leader in time of war; there was general relief when in May 1940 he gave way to Winston * Churchill. In November he died of cancer.
Macleod, I., *Neville Chamberlain*. 1961

Chambers, Ephraim (*c.* 1680–1740). English editor. His two-volume *Cyclopaedia* (1728) was translated into French and provided the foundations for * Diderot's famous *Encyclopédie* (1751–80).

Chambers, Sir William (1726–1796). British architect born in Gothenberg. A voyage to China in his youth inspired his book *Designs of Chinese Buildings* (1757) and the pagoda at Kew Gardens. He designed Somerset House, London, in which he most successfully used and modified the English Palladian style. Chambers played an important part in the founding of the Royal Academy (1768) and did much to raise the status of the architectural profession.
Chambers, W., *A Treatise of Civil Architecture*. 1759

Chambers, William (1800–1883) and **Robert** (1802–1871). Scottish publishers. The brothers founded the Edinburgh firm of W. and R. Chambers. William Chambers started *Chambers's Journal* in 1832, and the well known *Chambers Encyclopaedia* (1859–68). Robert also wrote a number of books, including *Traditions of Edinburgh* (1824) and *The Vestiges of Creation* (1884), which foreshadowed some of * Darwin's theories.

Chamisso, Adelbert von (1781–1838). German writer, born in France. His parents fled to Germany during the French Revolution. He is remembered above all for his *Peter Schlemihls wundersame Geschicte* (1814), the story of how a man sold his shadow to the devil. This has assumed the rank of a legend. He also wrote on natural history, took part in a Russian round-the-world expedition and became keeper of the Berlin Botanical Gardens.

Champlain, Samuel de (1567–1635). French explorer. After an expedition to the West Indies (1599) he made three voyages (1603–08) to Canada and founded Quebec (1608). He was lieutenant-governor (1613–29) of New France (i.e. Canada), for the founding of which he was the prime mover. While holding that office he discovered (1615) and explored the Great Lakes, repelled Iroquois Indians and opened up the fur trade. In 1629 he was captured and taken to England but returned to Canada in 1613.
Bishop, M., *Champlain: the Life of Fortitude*. 1948

Champollion, Jean François (1790–1832). French scholar. He found the key to Egyptian hieroglyphics by deciphering the inscriptions on the Rosetta stone, a basalt slab discovered in 1799 during Napoleon's Egyptian expedition. Champollion was educated at Grenoble, where he was professor of history (1809–16), and was attracted to Egyptology at a very early age. He was still only 21 when he began publication of his *Egypt Under the Pharaohs*. In 1826 he became director of Egyptian antiquities at the Louvre, and a chair of Egyptology was founded for him at the Collège de France four years later.

Chancellor, Richard (died 1556). English navigator. In 1553 he commanded the *Edward Bonaventure* on the expedition of Sir Hugh Willoughby to find a north-east sea passage to China. Separated from his leader in a storm off the Lofoten Islands, he went alone into the White Sea, and travelled overland to Moscow, where he negotiated a trade with the tsar Ivan the Terrible. On his return to England his reports encouraged the foundation (1554) of the Muscovy Company. He went to Moscow again (1555–56) and lost his life in a shipwreck on the way home.

Chandler, Raymond Thornton (1888–1959). American detective-story writer. Educated in England at Dulwich College he followed a variety of occupations before winning fame as an author. He brought to the 'tough' school of thriller-writing a more sophisticated technique. His novels introduced the cynical, laconic private detective with moral standards, Philip Marlowe. Some of the best known were filmed, e.g. *The Big Sleep* (1939), *The Lady in the Lake* (1943) and *The Long Goodbye* (1953).

Chandos, Oliver Lyttelton, 1st Viscount (1893–1972). English administrator, politician and businessman. He was managing director of the British Metal Corporation and, on the out-break of World War II was made controller of Non Ferrous Metals and (1940) President of the Board of Trade. He was Colonial Secretary 1951–54, when he left political life and returned to business.
Lyttelton, O., *Memoirs*. 1962

Chandragupta Maurya (died 298 B.C.). Indian king (called Sandrocottus by the Greeks). At first an ally of Alexander the Great, he later founded a large empire in the north-west of India by driving out the garrisons left behind by Alexander. His spacious capital,

Pataliptura (Patna), was linked to the north-west frontier by a good road with rest houses.
Nilakanta Sastri, K. A., ed., *The Age of Nandas and Mauryas*. 1952

Chaney, Lon (1883–1930). American film actor. Well known for his horror roles (e.g. in *The Hunchback of Notre Dame*), it is said that his skill in miming originated with attempts to communicate with deaf-mute parents. His son, **Lon Chaney Jr**. (1906–1973) played Lennie in *Of Mice and Men* (1940).

Chang Tsu-Lin (1873–1928). Chinese war-lord. In the lawless period following the downfall of the Manchu empire Chang Tsu-Lin, with some aid from Japan, managed to carve out for himself in Manchuria almost a separate state and ruled in complete defiance of the central government. His power was, however, already waning when, while retreating before a government force, he was killed by a bomb.

Chantrey, Sir Francis Legatt (1781–1841). English sculptor. Having achieved fame and fortune by portrait busts of celebrities (George IV, Wordsworth, Wellington etc.), he was elected R.A. in 1818 and knighted in 1835. He bequeathed to the R.A. a sum the interest from which (£2,000–£3,000 p.a. – 'the Chantrey bequest') was to be spent on works of art executed in Great Britain by living artists or those recently dead. The collection, of mixed merit, is housed in the Tate Gallery, London.

Chaplin, Sir Charles Spencer ('Charlie') (1889–1977). British film actor, born of a poor family of music-hall artistes in Kennington, London. He went on the stage at a very early age but the crucial point in his fortunes came in 1913 when, having gone with one of Fred Karno's troupes to the U.S.A., he joined Mack Sennett's Keystone company, then producing farcical films in California. In his second film he adopted the famous costume, make-up and shuffling walk which he continued to use until 1940 (when he satirized Hitler in his sound film *The Great Dictator*). His earliest short films were mere slap-stick but in the later long films, as the character he had created developed and he himself took an increasing part in the writing and direction, pathos and satire became more pronounced, though the fun never flags. His best films belong to the silent-film period. They include *Shoulder Arms* (1918), *The Kid* (1921), *The Gold Rush* (1925), *City Lights* (1931), *Modern Times* (1936). He never took kindly to the use of speech in films, as his art was essentially that of mime. In 1919, with D. W. Griffiths, Douglas Fairbanks and Mary Pickford, he formed the United Artists Corporation. His left-wing views caused him to become out of sympathy with certain aspects of post-war American life and he left the U.S.A. in 1953, living thereafter mainly in Switzerland. Before this he had appeared in the unlikely role of a murderer in *Monsieur Verdoux* (1947). *A King in New York* (1957) was his first film made in Europe. He married Mildred Harris, Lita Grey (by whom he had two sons), Paulette Goddard, and Oona O'Neill (the playwright's daughter), by whom he had a large family.
Chaplin, C., *My Autobiography*. 1964. Chaplin, C., Jr., Rau, M., and Rau, N., *My Father, Charlie Chaplin*. 1960

Chapman, George (1559–1634). English poet and translator. A prolific and popular playwright, he was admired by Webster and Jonson, his best known plays being the comedy, written with Johnson and Marston, *Eastward Ho!* (1605), and the tragedy *Bussy d'Ambois* (1607), the story of a swashbuckling swordsman at the French court. But it is his translations of Homer that have ensured his immortality. The *Iliad* began to appear in 1598 and was continued under the patronage of Henry, Prince of Wales (1609–11). The *Odyssey* was completed in 1614, and *The Whole Works of Homer* (1616) comprised both epics. Though often inaccurate as a translation, since Chapman tended to expand the text to stress a moral issue, the work introduced Homer to many generations and so exercised enormous influence.
Ellis, H., *George Chapman*. 1934

Chapman, Sidney (1888–1970). British geophysicist. He was educated at Manchester and Cambridge Universities, at both of which he later taught. The most important of subsequent academic appointments was that of head of the mathematics department of Imperial College, London University, which he held until 1946. Subsequent years of travel combined with his mathematical and geomagnetic specialization equipped him for the presidency of the International Geophysical Year (1957–58).

Charcot, Jean-Martin (1825–1893). French neurologist. He studied medicine in Paris, and became an intern at the Salpetrière, Paris's largest hospital, in 1848. He became interested in the diseases of long-stay patients, such as arthritis, sclerosis, and other chronic nervous conditions. His medical interests ranged widely. He studied poliomyelitis and investigated liver and thyroid diseases. Later in his career he became more interested in the physiological roots of psychic behaviour. He supported the ideas of Hughlings Jackson who believed that specific aspects of behaviour were controlled from particular local centres of the brain. His lectures on hysteria attracted wide attention, since, partly through the use of hypnosis, he was able to control the behaviour of hysterics by gesture and suggestion. * Freud was one of many who were highly impressed by Charcot's demonstrations of hysteria, for they suggested a world of the unconscious beyond the rational control of the subject.
Guillain, G., *J. M. Charcot*. 1959

Chardin, Jean Baptiste Siméon (1699–1779). French painter. His still life pictures and domestic scenes follow the Dutch tradition and are notable for detail and simplicity and for the skill with which the natural appearance and texture of familiar objects, bread, fruit, an apron etc., are portrayed.
Rosenberg, P., *Chardin 1699–1779*. 1979

Chardonnet, Hilaire Bernigaud, Comte de (1839–1924). French industrial chemist who first developed rayon. He patented a cellulose nitrate-based fibre in 1884, and first exhibited rayon at the Paris Exposition of 1889.

Charlemagne (or Charles the Great) (742–814). King of the Franks (from 768) and emperor (from 800). He and his brother, Carloman, jointly succeeded their father, Pepin the Short. On his brother's death in 771. Charlemagne became sole ruler of the Franks and launched a vast expansion. Germany, Bavaria and Saxony had been conquered by 808 and Christianity forced upon the people. At the request of the pope he took his army over the Alps to Italy, conquered Lombardy (773–774) and established his son as king (781). His first expedition to Spain, however, ended in failure and the death of his commander Roland (the hero of romantic legend). But from 785 he systematically subdued north-east Spain and in 801 captured Barcelona. He accomplished the conquest and forced conversion (791–796) of Pannonia and the kingdom of the Avars (barbarian tribes in Hungary). By 800, Charlemagne was the supreme power in western Europe, and he and his counsellors, such as the English * Alcuin, wishing to emphasize an imaginary continuity between his empire and that of Rome, argued that the imperial throne was vacant owing to the crimes of the Beastorn (Byzantine) empress Irene. Having obtained the assent of Pope Leo III he went to Rome, and on Christmas Day 800, was crowned by the pope as emperor. This new empire associated the idea of ancient power with a Christian community; but while it thus created a focus of loyalty it soon led to a struggle between empire and papacy as well as conflicts between imperial claims and feudal states and thus eventually impeded the national development of Germany and Italy such as was gradually taking place elsewhere. To rule his vast empire Charlemagne retained the old system of local government – 'counties' governed by counts (*comtes*) – but exercised control and secured a degree of uniformity through the famous '*Missi Dominici*', palace officials sent on circuit, a system which became a feature of later medieval administration. Many legal reforms were effected by the issuing of ordinances, while the use of writing was encouraged to secure uniformity of administration. Although Charlemagne read little and never learned to write, he encouraged the foundation of monastic and episcopal schools, and from his court at Aachen (Aix) he stimulated the revival of arts and of letters known as the Carolingian Renaissance. His biographer, Einhard, gives a picture of a large, robust man, of great industry and natural talent. Though he lived simply he fully enjoyed the pleasures of the senses with a succession of three wives and many mistresses. His empire fell apart soon after his death and with it his dream of a united Europe.
Bullough, D. A., *The Age of Charlemagne*. 1965

Charles (1226–1285). Count of Anjou, and king of Sicily (from 1265). This ambitious ruler, the youngest son of Louis VIII of France, became Count of Anjou in 1246, acquired Provence by marriage, supported the papal party in Italy against the imperialists and by his victories was able to accept the throne of Sicily (1265). He was planning to invade the Balkan peninsula, with a view to reviving the Latin empire of Constantinople, when in 1282 his Sicilian subjects signalized their revolt by the massacre of Frenchmen known as the Sicilian Vespers and by offering the throne to Peter of Aragon. Charles failed to re-establish himself though his descendants remained kings of Naples until 1435.

Charles (known as 'the Bold') (1433–1477). Duke of Burgundy, son of Philip the Good. On his succession in 1467 he ruled extensive but scattered territories in France and the Low Countries and set out to unite them under a single form of rule. This brought him into collision with Louis XI, king of France, the feudal overlord of his French lands. Charles, having supported a baronial revolt against Louis, induced him (1468) to come to an interview, imprisoned him at Peronne and exacted a crippling treaty. He then annexed the prince bishopric of Liège, and by peaceful or war-like means extended his power in Guelders, Alsace and elsewhere. Meanwhile by subsidy and subtle diplomacy Louis XI continued to oppose him, especially by inflaming Swiss fears. War followed and in 1476 Charles was totally defeated at Granson on Lake Neuchâtel. In the following year the Burgundians were again defeated by the Swiss outside Nancy and Charles was killed. He left no male heir and the bulk of the Burgundian inheritance passed, through his daughter Mary, who had married the emperor Maximilian, to the Habsburgs.

Bartier, J., *Charles le Téméraire*. Rev. ed. 1970

Charles (Charles Philip Arthur George) (1948–). Eldest son of Queen Elizabeth II of Great Britain and her consort Prince Philip, Duke of Edinburgh. He was created Prince of Wales in 1958. He was educated at Gordonstoun School, Scotland, Geelong Grammar School, Australia, Trinity College, Cambridge, and the University of Wales. Subsequently he became a naval officer and aviator, and a very popular member of the royal family. He married Lady Diana Spencer in 1981 and they have two sons.

Charles I. King of Spain *see* * Charles V.

Charles I (1600–1649). King of Great Britain and Ireland (from 1625), son of James VI of Scotland (later James I of England) and Anne of Denmark. In 1616, on the death of his elder brother, Henry, he became Prince of Wales and heir to the throne. Charles, like his father, was firmly under the influence of the Duke of * Buckingham, with whom in 1623 he made an undignified and futile expedition to Madrid to woo a Spanish princess; after his accession he married Henrietta Maria, daughter of Henry IV of France, a union which introduced a Roman Catholic influence at court which alienated the growing body of Puritans. Buckingham's influence ended with his murder in 1628, but his last venture, an attempt to relieve the French Protestants in La Rochelle, was a fiasco which further discredited the king. Thus antagonized, Charles's first three parliaments failed to vote him adequate revenues and he had recourse to raise money by an intensive and dubious use of the royal prerogative. In 1628, however, in return for a promise of funds, he assented to parliament's 'Petition of Right', which denounced the levying of forced loans and illegal taxes. In 1629 Charles, still unable to work with parliament, dissolved it, and until 1640, ruled England with the help of Thomas Wentworth, Earl of * Strafford, an efficient but stern administrator, and of William * Laud, archbishop of Canterbury, whose attempt to impose a uniform liturgy roused even greater hostility than the forced exactions of the civil government. Indeed, it was the need to finance an unsuccessful war undertaken to impose a uniform prayer book on Presbyterian Scotland that forced Charles in 1640 to summon first the 'Short' and then the 'Long' parliaments. In an attempt at conciliation he even allowed the impeachment and execution of his loyal minister Strafford (1641), an act of treachery which brought him no respite. In January 1642, now desperate, he tried to arrest five of the leading opposition members in the House of Commons (Pym, Hampden, Holles, Strode and Haselrig). This act contributed to a complex situation which produced, in August 1642, a civil war. In the beginning the royalists (Cavaliers) had some successes but the possession of London by the parliamentarians (Roundheads) and the training of a New Model Army by * Cromwell turned the scales. After his last crushing defeat at Naseby, Charles surrendered to the Scots (1646) and in the following January was handed over by them to the English parliament, soon to fall into the hands of the army leaders. At first his

captivity was not strict and he was able to communicate with his friends abroad and even to negotiate a treaty with the Scots, which brought about the second Civil War. But the royalists' defeat strengthened the extremists, who brought the king before a court. Charles refused to recognize their jurisdiction and would not plead. His courage both then and at his execution (30 January 1649), as well as his stand against an illegality as great as any he had himself committed, caused him to be remembered as the 'martyr king'. Charles was the greatest collector and connoisseur of art ever to sit on the English throne.
Hibbert, C., *Charles I*. 1968

Charles I (Karl) (1887–1922). Last Emperor of Austria–Hungary (1916–18). He succeeded on the death of his great-uncle * Francis-Joseph, tried to secure a negotiated peace in 1917 and went into exile in Switzerland in 1919. After two unsuccessful bids to regain the Hungarian throne, he retired to Madeira and died there of tuberculosis.

Charles I and II (Kings of Romania) *see* **Carol I: Carol II**

Charles II (known as 'the Bald') (823–877). King of the west Franks (Francia, later France) and emperor (from 875). The death of his father, Louis I ('the Pious'), son and successor of * Charlemagne, was followed by a prolonged struggle for power with Charles's elder brother, Lothair, ended by the Treaty of Verdun (843), by which Charles became the ruler of the western part of the empire. On the death (875) of his nephew Louis II he invaded Italy and was crowned king and emperor by the pope. The disorders of his reign were increased by the Normans, who sacked Paris and Bordeaux.

Charles II (1630–1685). King of Great Britain and Ireland (from 1660), son of Charles I. He took some part in the Civil War but in 1646 made an adventurous escape first to Jersey and then to France. After his father's death he came to terms with the Scots and was crowned at Scone in 1651, but his invasion of England, with Scottish troops, was routed at Worcester by * Cromwell (1651). Charles, after hiding in an oak tree at Boscobel, escaped to the continent, and established a makeshift court first in France and then in the Low Countries. In 1658 Cromwell died and the protectorate soon collapsed. Early in 1660 General George Monck intervened from Scotland and eventually a convention parliament, called under his auspices, invited Charles to return to England on the basis of his Declaration of Breda. This offered assurances of a settlement generally acceptable to 'the political nation'. In May 1660 Charles landed at Dover and, to the joy of almost all, the monarchy was restored. Charles's main preoccupation was to retain the throne and 'never go on his travels again'. He never therefore pressed a point at issue to extremes and used his very considerable intelligence to evade a direct challenge. Thus he tried to thwart the 'Clarendon Code' (called somewhat erroneously after his chief minister Edward Hyde, Earl of * Clarendon), which imposed restrictions on dissenters and Protestants and was opposed to his natural tolerance, by a Declaration of Indulgence; this, however, he had to withdraw. But he welcomed the war with the Dutch (whom he disliked) by which the English acquired New Holland, including New York, and much trade. The plan of his next ministry, the Cabal (Clifford, Arlington, Buckingham, Ashley, Lauderdale), to create a Protestant alliance in northern Europe against the French, he evaded by a secret treaty (1670) with Louis XIV. In return for subsidies Charles helped France against Holland but failed to fulfil (until his deathbed) a clause that he should declare himself a Roman Catholic. This discretion was the more necessary because alarm was caused in the late 1670s by the 'discovery' by Titus * Oates of an alleged Roman Catholic plot. Having with patience and ingenuity discredited Oates, and defeating an attempt to have his Catholic brother and heir James, Duke of York (* James II) excluded from the throne, Charles came into calmer waters. The French subsidies had eased his financial necessities, but it was the proceeds of customs and excise granted by parliament and swollen by increasing trade that enabled him to rule without summoning parliament, which he had dissolved. Thus by tortuous methods Charles contrived to guide the country in the way he thought it should go, while at the same time encouraging science (the Royal Society dates from 1662) and interesting himself in the navy, the growth of the colonies and cultural activities. His main pursuit, however, was pleasure. His wife Catherine of Braganza, though she brought him as a dowry Tangier and Bombay, gave him no children, but in a

gay and licentious court he remedied the omission through a succession of colourful mistresses: Lucy Walters, mother of the Duke of Monmouth; Barbara Villiers, who became Lady Castlemaine and Duchess of * Cleveland; Nell Gwyn the actress; the fascinating intriguer Louise de Kérouaille, Duchess of Portsmouth, and many more. His intelligence, his wit and his amoral nature set the tone of the Restoration period as a whole.
Kenyon, J. P., *The Stuarts: a study in English Kingship*. 2nd ed. 1967. Fraser, A., *King Charles II*. 1979

Charles II (1661–1700). King of Spain (from 1665). An epileptic of weak intelligence, who succeeded his father Philip IV at the age of 4 and so spent the first years of his reign under his mother's regency. As he was childless he was induced to name in his will Philip, grandson of Louis XIV of France, as his successor. This provoked the War of the Spanish Succession (1700–13).

Charles III (1716–1788). King of Spain (from 1759), son of Philip V by his second wife Elizabeth (Isabella) Farnese, by whose intrigues he secured the throne (as Charles IV) of Naples and Sicily (1734). When he succeeded to the Spanish throne on the death of his half-brother, Ferdinand VI, he proclaimed a younger son (another Ferdinand) king of Naples and an elder one (the eldest was incompetent to rule) his heir in Spain. Charles was an able administrator and is considered the most successful Bourbon ruler of Spain.
Herr, R., *The Eighteenth-Century Revolution in Spain*. 1958

Charles IV (1748–1819). King of Spain (1788–1808). During most of his disastrous reign Charles was dominated by Manuel Godoy, lover and favourite of his queen. He was induced to abdicate (and was suitably pensioned) by Napoleon in 1808 and after four years in France spent the last years of his life in Rome.

Charles V (1338–1380). King of France (from 1364). He was regent from 1356 during the English captivity of his father, John II, and in 1358 suppressed the Jacquerie, a peasant revolt. By the reorganization of the army, the administration and finances, he was able to achieve his ambition of restoring his kingdom after its defeats by the English under Edward III. So successful were his military efforts that by the end of his reign the English had been driven out of all but a few fortresses and their ancient patrimony Guienne. His nickname was 'the Wise'.

Charles V (1500–1558). Holy Roman Emperor (1519–56) and (through his mother Juana, daughter of Ferdinand and Isabella) king of Spain (1516–56). He also inherited the Low Countries from his father Philip (died 1506), the son of the emperor Maximilian and Mary of Burgundy. He was brought up in the Netherlands under the care of his aunt, Maximilian's daughter, Margaret of Savoy. It was a happy boyhood during which he owed much to his tutor (afterwards Pope Adrian VI). Charles was declared of age in 1515, and on the death of Maximilian (1519) he was elected emperor and also acquired the Habsburg lands in Austria, Hungary and elsewhere, thus completing the vast inheritance which included not only the countries named but much of Italy and the new Spanish possessions in the New World. Charles's main rival was the young and equally brilliant Francis I of France, and though Charles was on the whole victorious, the final result (by the Treaty of Crepy, 1544, Burgundy remained in French hands while France relinquished its claims in Italy) was hardly worth nearly twenty-five years of struggle. A more vital matter with which Charles had to contend was the Reformation in Germany. Charles was a devout Catholic but in this matter his aim and interest was to come to some sort of terms with * Luther's movement to prevent the weakening of the empire by a prolonged religious struggle. The Peace of Augsburg (1555), though it satisfied neither side, was probably the best that could be obtained: it adopted the compromise formula *cuius regio eius religio* (i.e. each state was to adopt the religion of its ruler). After early difficulties Charles consolidated his rule in Spain and the conquests in the New World were among the many signs of the country's advance to greatness: to him in his last years it proved a place of refuge. In the autumn of 1555 he astonished all by announcing the abdication of his powers. The imperial crown and the Habsburg lands in east Europe were to pass to his brother Ferdinand, and the Netherlands and the Spanish throne to his son Philip, the husband of Queen Mary of England. He himself retired to a monastery at Yuste in the north of Spain.

Brandi, K., *The Emperor Charles V*. 1938

Charles VI (1368–1422). King of France (from 1380). His reign, during most of which he was either a minor or insane, saw a continuous struggle for power, at first in council and (from 1411) in the field, between factions (Burgundians and Armagnacs) headed by the royal dukes of Burgundy and Orléans. Henry V of England seized the opportunity to resume the Hundred Years War, won the Battle of Agincourt (1415), and in 1420 was able to secure the Treaty of Troyes, by which Charles's daughter * Catherine was to marry Henry V and their son was to succeed to the French throne. Meanwhile Henry was the virtual ruler of France.

Charles VI (1685–1740). Holy Roman Emperor (from 1711). Before succeeding his brother Joseph he was Austrian candidate for the Spanish throne, left vacant on the death of Charles II. During the War of the Spanish Succession (1700–13) he fought bravely in Spain. Ultimately the Bourbon Philip V was recognized as king. As emperor Charles became obsessed with securing (by means of the Pragmatic Sanction) the recognition by the European powers of the rights of his daughter Maria Theresa to succeed him as ruler of Austria and Hungary. Despite these efforts the War of the Austrian Succession followed his death.

Charles VII (1403–1461). King of France (from 1422). On the death of his father, * Charles VI, he had to contest the right to the throne with Henry VI of England, the legal successor under the Treaty of Troyes. He fought half-heartedly against the English in France from his own limited territory in the centre and south until the heroic efforts of Joan of Arc stirred him to greater action. After her capture of Orléans (1429) he was crowned at Reims and secured recognition as national leader. After the Burgundians joined Charles's cause in 1435, Paris was recaptured; by 1450 the English had been driven out of Normandy, and by 1453 nothing but Calais remained of their vast possessions in France. Charles was not a heroic figure, but for the thorough administrative reorganization which made these successes possible much credit was due to the king himself.

Beaucourt, G. du F. de, *Histoire de Charles VII*. 6 vols. 1881–91

Charles VIII (1470–1498). King of France (from 1483), the son of Louis XI. The reign began with the regency of his sister Anne of Beaujeu, who secured his marriage (1491) to Anne of Brittany to ensure the acquisition of that duchy. Charles revived the Anjou claim to Naples (* Charles, Count of Anjou) and, allied with the Sforzas of Milan, invaded Italy. Although he captured Naples easily he was forced to retreat to France after a few weeks by the forces of the League of Venice (the papacy, Venice, Spain and the empire) and died shortly after.

Charles IX (1550–1574). King of France (from 1560), the weak and indecisive son of Henry II and * Catherine de'Medici, the effective ruler throughout his reign, which was marked by a fierce religious struggle between the Roman Catholics and Huguenots which culminated in the massacre of the latter on St Bartholomew's Day, 1572.

Charles IX (1550–1611). King of Sweden (from 1600), brother of John II and uncle of his immediate predecessor John's son Sigismund, who had also been elected king of Poland. The accession of Charles, following a successful revolt against Sigismund, ended the union of the two crowns and so achieved Charles's aim of preventing Sweden from remaining under Roman Catholic rule, and prepared the way for the decisive part Sweden played under Charles's son * Gustavus II in the Thirty Years' War. Internally, having eliminated his enemies among the nobles at the 'Linköping blood bath', he efficiently developed the administration and economy of his country; he founded Göteborg (Gothenburg).

Charles X (1622–1660). King of Sweden (from 1654), nephew of King Gustavus Adolphus and cousin of Christina, on whose abdication he ascended the throne. A daring soldier, he revived the plan of trying to form a great Swedish empire on both sides of the Baltic to include east Prussia and the northern part of Poland. By 1656 he was nearly successful, but the defeated Poles rose against him, supported by both the Russians and the Dutch. Denmark, which also joined his opponents, became Charles's immediate target. After he had led his troops across the ice to attack Copenhagen, the Danes were forced to accept a harsh separate peace (1658). Later, as the Danes showed signs of wavering in the fulfilment of its terms, Charles attacked again but his sudden death brought a general peace.

Charles X (1757–1836). King of France (1824–30), the younger brother of Louis XVI and Louis XVIII. He left France in 1789 on the outbreak of the Revolution but returned to lead an abortive revolt in the Vendée in 1795. He then – until Napoleon's overthrow – lived almost continuously in England where he was known as the Comte d'Artois. After the Bourbon restoration he led the ultra-royalists and, becoming king on the death of Louis XVIII, tried to revive absolutism. The result was the revolution of 1830 after which he came once more to England, his cousin Louis Philippe succeeding him as French king. He died of cholera.

Charles XI (1655–1697). King of Sweden (from 1660), the son of Charles X. In 1672, when after a long minority he assumed power, Sweden was closely associated with Louis XIV of France and in 1675, as part of the general European conflict, found itself at war with Brandenburg and Denmark. Charles quickly reversed Denmark's early successes and by his victory of Lund (1676) reasserted Swedish power. His administrative reforms reduced the power of the aristocracy by depriving them of their official and feudal rights and powers exercised through the Riksdag (or council); and by raising lesser nobility into an official class dependent on royal favour, he created something much nearer to an absolute monarchy.

Charles XII (1682–1718). King of Sweden (from 1697). The son of Charles XI, he was a precocious child, and at once assumed full control. Immediately after his accession the old struggle for Baltic supremacy reopened and Charles found himself confronted with a coalition of Russia, Poland and Denmark. The Great Northern War broke out in 1699, and lasted intermittently until 1721. Charles invaded Denmark and forced its withdrawal from the coalition in 1700, then led his armies into Russia and defeated the forces of Peter the Great at Narva (1700). Poland was then conquered, Charles forced the abdication of the king, Augustus of Saxony, and secured the election of Stanislaus Leszcynski. In 1708 he again invaded Russia, gained initial successes but, forced to abandon his plan to seize Moscow, turned south to the Ukraine to link up with the rebel Cossack leader, Mazeppa. The winter of 1708–09 was, however, the most severe for a century and the Swedes, weakened and ill-supplied, were decisively defeated by Peter at Poltava (1709); Charles fled to Turkey. He persuaded the sultan to make war on Russia, which was soon concluded. The sultan then expelled Charles, and when he returned to Sweden he found the impoverished country on the verge of civil war. By drastic taxation and harsh measures he raised new armies and, after fruitless intrigues to divide his enemies, he attacked Norway in the hope of compensating himself for losses elsewhere, but in 1718 was killed by a sniper's bullet during the siege of Frederiksten. Charles had great military skill and amazing fortitude in adversity but his overweening ambition led to disaster and the decline of Sweden as a major power.

Hatton, R. M., *Charles XII of Sweden*. 1968

Charles XIV (King of Sweden) *see* **Bernadotte, Jean Baptiste Jules**

Charles, Jacques Alexandre César (1746–1823). French physicist. He gave public demonstrations of Franklin's electrical experiments and eventually became professor of physics at the Conservatoire des Arts et Métiers, Paris. Data obtained by him on the expansion of gases were added to by * Gay-Lussac, who devised the law (called Charles's Law) which states that the volume of gas at constant pressure is directly proportional to its absolute temperature. Charles was also the first to use hydrogen instead of hot air to lift balloons.

Charles Albert (1798–1849). King of Sardinia and ruler of Piedmont (1831–49). Charles Albert had supported liberal causes as a young man and was a believer in Italian unity, but he was no crusader; he shrank from Mazzini's extremism and harshly punished those of his followers who had taken part in a revolt. In 1848, 'the year of revolutions', however, having given the country a liberal constitution, he marched against the Austrians then ruling a large part of northern Italy. Defeated at Custozza and Novara he abdicated in favour of his son, Victor Emmanuel II; he died in Portugal.

Charles Edward Stuart *see* **Stuart**

Charles Martel (*c.* 688–741). Mayor of the palace under the decadent Merovingian kings, and so virtual ruler of the Franks. He extended his authority over lands now France, the Netherlands and the Rhineland and intervened in Bavaria. He gained his nickname Martel ('the hammer') by his great victory at Poitiers (732), the first decisive check to the Moslem advance into Europe. His rule marked the beginning of Carolingian power; his grandson was * Charlemagne.

Charlotte (1796–1817). British princess, wife of King * Leopold I of the Belgians. Her death in childbirth re-opened the question of succession to the English throne (she was the only child of George IV), and her unmarried uncles were persuaded to marry. Her uncle Edward, Duke of * Kent became the father of the future Queen Victoria.

Charpentier, Gustave (1860–1956). French composer. Encouraged by Massenet to take up composition he won the Prix de Rome in 1887. He is best known for his opera *Louise* (1900), for which he himself wrote the libretto, and the orchestral work *Impressions of Italy*.

Charteris, Leslie (Leslie Bowyer Yin) (1907–). British thriller-writer. He created 'the Saint', a charmingly ruthless detective called Simon Templar, the hero of most of his books and of film, television, radio and comic strip series based on them.

Chase, Salmon Portland (1808–1873). American lawyer and politician. He gained his reputation as an attorney for fugitive slaves, was U.S. senator from Ohio 1849–55 and 1861 and governor of Ohio 1855–59. He sought the 1860 Republican nomination for president, but was regarded as too extreme on the slavery issue and lost to * Lincoln. As U.S. Secretary of the Treasury 1861–64 he raised unprecedented taxes and established a national banking system. He resigned to pursue the presidency again, failed, and Lincoln made him chief justice of the U.S. Supreme Court 1864–73. He presided with notable fairness at Andrew * Johnson's impeachment (March–May 1868).

Chase, Stuart (1888–). American social scientist, educated at the Massachusetts Institute of Technology and at Harvard. He held various technical positions in government agencies as research economist. He wrote many books and articles on the 'economies of plenty' and was in a sense a precursor to Galbraith. Among his works are *The Economy of Abundance* (1934), *Live and Let Live* (1960) and *The Most Probable World* (1968).

Chastelard, Pierre de Boscosel de (1540–1564). French poet. Grandson of the chevalier Bayard. At the French court of Francis II he fell romantically in love with Mary, the future queen of Scots, and accompanied her to Scotland. Many of his poems were addressed to her. Found once hiding in her bedchamber, he was forgiven; later he repeated the offence and was hanged. The story was dramatized by Swinburne.

Chateaubriand, François René, Vicomte de (1768–1848). French author, soldier and diplomat, who exercised an outstanding influence on the French Romantics. He was born at St Malo and spent most of his lonely childhood in Brittany. He was a cavalry officer at the age of 18 and in 1791 went to North America which he described in his *Voyage en Amérique* (1827). Opposed to the Revolution he joined the emigrant army on the frontier, was wounded and lived in poverty in England (1794–99). He returned to France to hold minor diplomatic posts under Napoleon but soon became anti-Bonapartist. After the restoration of Louis XVIII he held ambassadorial posts in Berlin and London (1820–23) and was foreign minister (1823–24). After the revolution of 1830, which replaced the legitimate dynasty by Louis Philippe, he played little part in public life. About the time of his return to France he abandoned his scepticism and wrote his great apologia *Le Génie du Christianisme* (1802), which not only defended the religious aspects of Christianity but also its effects on art and architecture, literature and institutions. In advance he published with great success an episode intended for the book *Atala* (1801), a highly coloured story of a Red Indian girl convert and her tragic love. *René*, extracted from the great work and published separately (1805), presents a passionate, disillusioned, egotistical Byronic young man (in fact Chateaubriand himself), irresistible to those who initiated the French Romantic movement. Perhaps his greatest work was the autobiographical *Mémoires d'Outre-Tombe* (published in six volumes between 1848 and

1902). Madame Récamier was the best known of his many mistresses.

Chatham, William, Pitt, 1st Earl *see* **Pitt, William**

Chatterji, Bambin Chandza (1838–1894). Indian author. He revolutionized Indian literature by being the first to write novels following the European pattern devoted to Indian themes and in a native language (Bengali). The song *Bande Mataram*, originally a poem in his novel *Amanda Math* (1882), was adopted as the national anthem of the Republic of India.

Chatterton, Thomas (1752–1770). English poet, born in Bristol, the posthumous son of a schoolmaster. He read voraciously while a boy, began concocting pseudo-antique poetry, and at the age of 17 sent to Walpole manuscripts which purported to be the work of a 15th-century monk, Thomas Rowley. Walpole accepted them as genuine at first but later rejected them, and they are now known to have been entirely invented by Chatterton. In 1770 he went to London and in a few months produced an astonishing amount of work, including satires, political essays, and *The Balade of Charitie*. The death of his patron, Lord Mayor Beckford, and the increasingly frequent rejection of his manuscripts brought him to despair; at last, penniless and starving, he poisoned himself in his lodgings. The mock antique was regarded in that age not as forgery but as a semi-legitimate literary form (cf. Macpherson's Ossianic poems) and his rhythms and general approach to poetry were remarkably modern. The tragic boy poet became a literary hero romanticized by Keats, Wordsworth, Coleridge, Shelley and Rossetti, and controversy about the genuineness of the Rowley poems continued well into the nineteenth century.

Chaucer, Geoffrey (*c.* 1340–1400). English poet. He was born in London, the son of a rich vintner, entered the royal household of Edward III as a page, and later fought in the wars in France (1359–60), in which he was captured and ransomed. In 1366 he married one of the queen's ladies, Philippa de Roet, the daughter of a Flemish knight, and sister of Catherine Swynford who became John of Gaunt's third wife. Chaucer remained in the royal service for most of his life, travelled to France and Italy on seven diplomatic or commercial missions and may have met Boccaccio and Petrarch. He was a controller of customs (1374–84), a knight of the shire for Kent (1386) and clerk of works at the royal palaces (1389–91). On the accession of Henry IV he was granted a substantial pension and spent the remaining months of his life in comfort. Chaucer's works may be divided roughly into three periods: the first in which contemporary French influence was strong (*The Book of the Duchess*, and his part of the translation entitled *The Romaunt of the Rose*). In the second (*c.* 1372–86), the more realistic Italian influence of Dante and Boccaccio was apparent in his works (*Troilus and Criseyde, The Parlement of Foules, The Legend of Good Women* and *The House of Fame*). To the final period belongs his last and greatest work *The Canterbury Tales*, stories told by a party of thirty pilgrims, of all social classes – knight, miller, cook, wife of Bath, friar, merchant, doctor etc. – journeying to the tomb of St Thomas à Becket at Canterbury. 'Here is God's plenty', Dryden said of the work. Written in rhyming couplets, they present a vivid picture of life in the Middle Ages. A masterpiece by any standard, though incomplete, it is also the first major work written in vernacular English and one of the first to be printed. He is now regarded as one of the greatest of English poets.

Robinson, F. N. (ed), *Chaucer: Complete works*. 2nd ed. 1959. Rowland, B. (ed.), *Companion to Chaucer Studies*. 1698

Chausson, Ernest (1855–1899). French composer. Trained as a lawyer, he became a pupil of * Franck and * Massenet. His romantic but melancholy works include a symphony (1890), *Poeme* for violin and orchestra (1896), chamber works and songs. He was killed in a bicycle accident.

Chauvin, Nicolas (*c.* 1770–?1820). The French soldier whose exaggerated expressions of loyalty to Napoleon and vain-glorious patriotism resulted in the coining of the word 'chauvinism'.

Chávez, Carlos (1899–1978). Mexican composer, conductor and teacher, founder of the Mexican Symphony Orchestra (1928). His works include five symphonies and several operas. He was much influenced by Mexican folk music but also followed contemporary trends, e.g. abstract music. He was Norton professor of poetics at Harvard (1958–59).

Cheever, John (1912–1982). American novelist and short-story writer. Many of his stories appeared in *The New Yorker*, and his highly-praised novels include *The Wapshot Chronicle* (1958), *Bullet Park* (1969) and *Falconer* (1977).

Chekhov, Anton Pavlovich (1860–1904). Russian dramatist and short-story writer. Born at Taganrog he was the grandson of a liberated serf and son of a shop-keeper. He studied medicine at Moscow University (supporting himself by writing about 600 comic sketches), but later he practised little. Through the help of Suvorin, with whom he travelled in Italy, he achieved early success with his stories and in 1887 his first play *Ivanov* was produced. In 1892 he went to live with his family at Malikhovo near Moscow and helped in the cholera outbreak of 1892–93. In 1897, threatened by tuberculosis, he went to the Crimea, and from 1900 lived mostly at Yalta, where he became friends with Tolstoy and Gorky. After several false starts as a dramatist, he achieved great success with the revival by Stanislavsky of his play *The Seagull* (1898), which had previously failed. His masterpieces – *Uncle Vanya* (1901), *The Three Sisters* (1901) and *The Cherry orchard* (1904) – followed. In the last two, leading parts were played by Olga Knipper, whom he married in 1901. In his plays, as in his short stories, he used an impressionistic technique, eschewing the dramatic and the obvious and, while portraying the lives of ordinary people, hinting always at the tragedy and beauty of life. His heroes are almost always the gentle and the sensitive, at the mercy of forces which are too strong for them. His influence on European short-story writers has been immense.

Heifetz, A., *Chekhov in English: a List of Works By and About Him*. 1949. Yachnin, R., *The Chekhov Centennial Chekhov in English*. 1960. Valency, M., *The Breaking String*. 1966

Chelmsford, Frederic John Napier Thesiger, 1st Viscount (1868–1933). British administrator. He inherited the title of 3rd baron in 1905 and was created viscount in 1921. The culmination of a career mostly spent in imperial posts came when, as viceroy of India (1916–21), he became associated with the 'Montagu-Chelmsford' reforms under which dyarchy (i.e. a division of the functions and instruments of government between the centre and the provinces) was accepted as the basis of Indian constitutional advance. In 1924 he was first lord of the Admiralty in the first Labour government.

Chénier, André Marie de (1762–1794). French poet, born in Constantinople, the son of a diplomat. He hailed the French Revolution on its outbreak, but became disgusted with its excesses and in one ode extolled Charlotte Corday. He was arrested in 1794 and was guillotined on Robespierre's order only two days before the Terror was ended. His poems, *Élégies, Bucoliques, Odes, Hymnes* and *Iambes*, all follow classical models. Umberto Giordano wrote an opera based on his life.

His brother, **Marie Joseph Chénier** (1764–1811), was a poet and dramatist. Fully committed to the Revolution he obtained fame for his revolutionary poetry, especially the *Chant du départ*.

Cheops (the Greek form of Khufu) (reigned *c.* 2700 B.C.). King of ancient Egypt, a member of the 4th dynasty. He is famous as the builder of the largest of the pyramids at Giza just outside Cairo.

Ch'en Tu-hsiu (1879–1942). Chinese communist. In 1915 he became first editor of the periodical *New Youth* which launched a violent attack on traditional Chinese government and society, and promoted Western philosophies. He is regarded as the main inspiration of the May Fourth Movement, a social and intellectual revolution sparked off by a students' rising on 4 May 1919. He was imprisoned as a result. On his release, greatly impressed by the Soviet revolution in Russia, he became a Marxist. He founded the Chinese Communist Party in 1920 and became its first secretary-general. He was dismissed at the instigation of the international Comintern in 1927 (having failed to sustain a difficult alliance with the Nationalist Kuomintang) and expelled from the party in 1929. His influence came to an end, but he continued to teach a highly individual version of Marxism which incorporated some democratic ideas.

Tse-tsung, D., *The May Fourth Movement: Intellectual Revolution in Modern China*. 1960

Cherenkov, Pavel Alekseevich (1904–). Russian physicist. In 1958 he shared the Nobel Prize for Physics (with Tamm and Frank) for the discovery that light waves radiate from a charged particle passing through a transparent material at speeds greater than the speed of light through such material. This 'Cherenkov radiation' is used to detect charged particles and plot their course and speed.

Chernenko, Konstantin Ustinovich (1911–1985). Russian Communist politician. Son of a peasant, he joined the CPSU in 1931, became an official in Moldavia, worked for the Central Committee 1956–65 and for the presidium 1965–84. He was a Central Committee member 1971–85, joining the Politburo in 1978. On the death of Yuri* Andropov he was rapidly chosen to succeed him as First Secretary of the CPSU and President of the USSR 1984–85.

Cherubini, (Maria) Luigi Carlo Zenobio Salvatore (1760–1842). Italian composer. Born in Florence, he lived in Paris from 1788. He wrote much religious music in his early life and this, with chamber music, occupied him almost exclusively during his later years; but his main claim to fame rests upon his operatic work, which caused him to be regarded by Beethoven as the greatest of his contemporaries in this field. He wrote twenty-nine operas including *Médée* (1797) and *Anacréon* (1803). To the *opéra comique* he introduced a romantic interest and an exciting plot, though the music itself remained classical in form and rather austere. Cherubini was inspector general of the Paris Conservatoire from 1821, a post which brought most of the 19th-century French composers under his influence.
Deane, B., *Cherubini*. 1965

Cherwell, Frederick Alexander Lindemann, 1st Viscount (1886–1957). British scientist, friend and scientific adviser to Winston *Churchill. In World War I, as director of the experimental laboratory at Farnborough, he made a personal and practical test in the air of his theory of how to bring an aeroplane out of a spin. He became professor of experimental philosophy at Oxford in 1919. In World War II he advised the cabinet on scientific matters, while his close relationship with the prime minister made him a power behind the scenes. He was paymaster general (1942–45 and 1951–53) and was created viscount in 1956.

Cheshire, Geoffrey Leonard (1917–). British airman and social worker. In over 100 missions during World War II he proved himself one of the most daring and skilful bomber pilots of the war and was awarded the V.C. and many other decorations. In 1945 he was British official observer with one of the American planes that dropped an atomic bomb on Nagasaki. After his retirement in 1946 he devoted himself to the provision of homes for the sick and incurable. He was awarded the O.M. in 1981.
Braddon, R., *Cheshire V. C.*, 1954

Chesterfield, Philip Dormer Stanhope, 4th Earl of (1694–1773). English statesman and man of letters. As Lord Stanhope he was an M.P. (1715–23). After inheriting the earldom (1726) he was ambassador to the Netherlands (1728–32) and later held a succession of high offices. A friend of Pope, Swift, Bolingbroke and Voltaire, he took an active interest in scientific matters, but is best remembered for his letters to his illegitimate son **Philip Stanhope** (1732–1768): they are witty, elegant and cynical, and are marked by great shrewdness of observation, women, manners and education being the constantly recurring themes.
Dobree, B., ed., *Letters of Chesterfield.* 1932

Chesterton, Gilbert Keith (1874–1936). English writer, literary critic and author of the Father Brown detective stories. He was born in London and educated at St Paul's School before studying art at the Slade. But art was always secondary to letters. He wrote regular articles for many newspapers and magazines, took over the *New Witness* on the death of his brother, Cecil, in 1918 and revived it as *G.K.'s Weekly* in 1924. He was a man of much geniality but he had a strong antipathy for the squalor of industrialism and disliked both capitalism and socialism, yearning, like his great friend Hilaire Belloc (whose books he amusingly illustrated), for a return to the distributivist economics of the Middle Ages. All his work, which includes essays, poetry, novels, and literary, social and religious studies (he was converted to Roman Catholicism in 1922), reveals his tremendous energy, robust humour and mastery of paradox. He is probably best known as the creator of the detective-priest Father Ignatius Brown, who figured in several collections of semi-philosophical detective stories beginning with

The Innocence of Father Brown (1911). His novels, *The Napoleon of Notting Hill* (1904), *The Man Who Was Thursday* (1908) and *The Flying Inn* (1914), combine delightful fantasy with social comment. He also wrote biographies of Browning, Dickens and G. B. Shaw.
Barker, D., *G. K. Chesterton*. 1973

Chevalier, Albert (1861–1923). English song writer and famous comedian of the music-halls. Apart from his songs, of which *My Old Dutch* is a well known example, he wrote over 100 monologues, sketches and plays.

Chevalier, Maurice (1888–1972). French music-hall singer and film star. His engaging smile and charm won him fame not only in Paris music-halls (where he was long co-star with Mistinguett) but internationally. He appeared with some success in several films notably *Le Roi* (1949) and *Gigi* (1958).

Chevreul, Michel-Eugène (1786–1889). French chemist, born in Angers. He began a major study of the chemistry of oils and fats which led to soap-making becoming an exact science and to greatly improved candles. He was a director of the Gobelins tapestry works and became interested in the chemistry of dyes and in colour contrast: his ideas influenced neo-impressionist painters, e.g. * Seurat. He was the first to grasp the significance of sugar in the urine of diabetics. He was also a pioneer in gerontology and his 100th birthday was commemorated in the first photographic interview (by Felix Nadar).

Chevrolet, Louis (1879–1941). American manufacturer. In 1911 he founded his own automobile company but sold out to General Motors which retained his name for a popular model.

Cheyney, Peter (1896–1951). English thriller-writer. He achieved enormous popularity with his famous characters Lemmy Caution and Slim Calaghan.

Chiang Kai-shek (1887–1975). Chinese soldier and statesman, son of a Chekiang farmer. Whilst an officer cadet he became involved in the successful revolution (1911) against the last Manchu emperor and was from then onwards a loyal adherent of * Sun Yat-sen, who in 1921 established himself as president of the republican government centred on Canton. The north was still in the hands of self-appointed war-lords and after Sun's death in 1925 Chiang was chosen to command an expedition to bring them to heel. This was delayed by a split between the communist and nationalist wings of Sun's revolutionary party, the Kuomintang. Chiang Kai-shek was appointed leader of the nationalists and eliminated the rival communist government, adherents of which, however, made the 'Long March' and established themselves under a Soviet system in a remote and inaccessible part of central China; Chiang's preoccupation from 1931 with the Japanese War enabled them to survive there. Meanwhile the generalissimo had resumed the delayed northern drive and by 1928 had overcome the war-lords and occupied Peking.

The struggle with the Japanese opened when they occupied Manchuria in 1931. Chiang, unprepared, tried appeasement but in 1936 occurred a strange episode when he was kidnapped and forced to agree to a truce with the communists, to ensure national resistance to the Japanese. The Japanese reacted immediately, landed at Shanghai and forced the Chinese government to move from Nanking higher and higher up the Yangtze river until it found refuge above the rapids at Chungking. Pressure eased when in 1941 Japan entered World War II and in 1945 Chiang emerged as president of his stricken and impoverished country.

But immediately the old struggle with the communists broke out, and political manoeuvre was followed by civil war in which the communists finally triumphed. Chiang Kai-shek withdrew to Taiwan in 1950 and continued to lead a Kuomintang administration, which occupied the seat of China in the Security Council of the United Nations until 1971.

Chiang Kai-shek obtained help and encouragement at every stage of his career from his American-educated second wife **Soong Mei-ling** (1897–), sister of Sun Yat-sen's widow. His son **Chiang Ching-kuo** (1910–) was Premier of the 'Republic of China' (i.e. Taiwan) 1972–78 and President 1978– .
Boorman, H. L., and Howard, R., eds., *Biographical Dictionary of Republican China*. Vol. 1. 1967

Chichele, Henry (1362–1443). English prelate and patron of learning. Educated at

Winchester and New College, Oxford, he soon became prominent in church and state, and after serving on embassies abroad became bishop of St Davids in 1408 and archbishop of Canterbury in 1414. In the latter office he strongly supported the king's war policy in France and his resistance to the encroachments of papal power at home. In 1437 Chichele founded two colleges at Oxford: All Souls and that which became known as St John's.

Chicherin, Georgy Vasilyevich (1872–1936). Soviet diplomat. Born in the nobility he served in the Russian foreign office but resigned on joining the Social Democrat party; from 1904 he lived with revolutionaries abroad. In 1917 he was arrested in England and exchanged for Sir George Buchanan, British ambassador. He became Soviet foreign minister (1918) and signed the Brest-Litovsk Treaty which ended the German war. While attending the Genoa Conference (1922) he secretly negotiated the Rapallo Treaty, which secured recognition and trade agreements from Germany. Illness led to his resignation (1930).

Chichester, Sir Francis Charles (1901–1972). English aviator and yachtsman. In 1929–30 he made a solo flight from England to Australia in a Gipsy Moth bi-plane; in 1931 he made the first east–west flight between New Zealand and Australia. He began ocean sailing in 1953. In 1960 he won the first transatlantic race for solo yachtsmen. In 1966–67 he sailed round the world single-handed in *Gipsy Moth IV*.
Chichester, F., *The Lonely Sea and the Sky*. 1964

Chifley, Ben (Joseph Benedict) (1885–1951). Australian Labor politician. Originally a locomotive driver, he was a Member of the House of Representatives 1928–31 and 1940–51, and served as minister of defence 1931–32. He held the key position of commonwealth treasurer (1941–49) under Curtin when war with Japan broke out. He was prime minister (1945–49) in the post-war reconstruction period.

Chikamatsu Monzaemon (Sugimori Nobumori) (1653–1724). Japanese dramatist who wrote for the puppet theatre. He wrote over a hundred plays, and was the first playwright to introduce true drama to the puppet theatre, previously a display of virtuoso skill by the puppeteers. He wrote historical melodramas such as *The Battles of Coxinga* (1951) and realistic domestic tragedies such as *The Love Suicide at Amijima* (1720).

Childers, (Robert) Erskine (1870–1922). Irish author and nationalist. A clerk in the House of Commons, he won a sensational success with his novel, *The Riddle of the Sands* (1903), dealing with secret preparations for a German invasion of Britain. Later he became an extreme Irish nationalist. He was a leader of the Sinn Fein resistance to the Irish Free State and was condemned by an Irish military court and executed. His son **Erskine Childers** (1905–1974) was President of the Irish Republic 1973–74.

Chippendale, Thomas (*c.* 1718–1779). Famous English furniture maker and designer. The son of a Yorkshire joiner he moved from Worcestershire to London where by 1755 he and his firm were occupying three houses in St Martin's Lane. Furniture still surviving in Harewood House and elsewhere is mentioned in his accounts. His own best work, almost exclusively in mahogany, is in the neo-classical style, the association of his name with an anglicized rococo style (with Gothic and oriental variants) being due to the fact that it was to that particular style that the designs of his publication *The Director* (*The Gentleman and Cabinet Maker's Director*, 1754) were devoted. Much the greater part of the so-called Chippendale furniture was in fact the work of other craftsmen taken from *The Director* designs, inspired but not actually drawn by Chippendale himself.
Coleridge, A., *Chippendale Furniture*. 1968

Chirico, Giorgio De' (1888–1978). Italian painter, born in Greece. One of the most important precursors of surrealism, he painted objects and landscapes in unexpected juxtaposition with no regard to reality. Thus window dummies, plaster busts, abstract shapes or bits of machinery might be grouped against a background of classical architecture. From this he developed a style which came to be known as metaphysical painting in which there was a greater symbolic content. In the 1920s he abandoned his earlier style and turned to more conventional styles and subjects; but what the galleries of the world have

chosen to show are his earlier idosyncratic paintings.
Chirico, G. de', *Memorie della mia vita*. 1945

Chisholm, George Brock (1896–1971). Canadian psychiatrist. After a distinguished career he was director general of the World Health Organization (1948–53). His *Can People Learn to Learn?* (1958) was widely discussed.

Choiseul, Étienne François, Duc de (1719–1785). French diplomat. Through the patronage of Madame de Pompadour, he became ambassador to Rome and Vienna (1753–58), returning to take office as foreign minister (1758–70). He was thus at the heart of affairs during the Seven Years' War and signed the Treaty of Paris (1763), which confirmed the losses, e.g. in Canada and India, of the preceding years. He was also responsible for popular reforms in the services, supported the publication of the *Encyclopédie*, and assisted in the suppression of the Jesuits. Madame du Barry's party at court were responsible for his downfall (1770); he lived in retirement until his death.

Chomsky, (Avram) Noam (1928–). American educationist and linguist. Educated at Pennsylvania and Harvard Universities, he taught linguistics at the Massachusetts Institute of Technology from 1955 and was professor of modern languages there from 1961. His principle was first defined in *Syntactic Structures* (1957) and was developed further in *Aspects of the Theory of Syntax* (1965), *Language and Mind* (1968), *Reflections on Language* (1975) and *Essays on Form and Interpretation* (1977). He argued for the existence of a universal grammar which underlies all languages, and that the structural principles of language are innate, biologically determined and capable of genetic transmission.

Chopin, Frédéric François (1810–1849). Composer, born in Poland of a Polish mother and French father. From boyhood Chopin suffered from ill health, but early displayed musical gifts. His music teacher in Warsaw encouraged him to develop in his own way and by 21 Chopin was already an accomplished pianist and composer for the piano. He made his debut as a concert pianist in Vienna in 1829, and from 1831 he lived mainly in Paris and did not return to Poland. His piano recitals met with great success and he became the friend of Liszt, Berlioz, Schumann, Bellini (who may have influenced his melodic style) and Mendelssohn. His compositions established the piano as a solo concert instrument. No other composer has surpassed him in this field which he explored more fully than any of his predecessors. His individual lyric and harmonic sense and his innovations in the technique of playing the piano were profoundly influential. His fame rests upon the wide range of his piano compositions which include nocturnes, polonaises, waltzes, mazurkas, scherzos and ballades.

In Paris he fell in love with the woman novelist George * Sand; an affair which began in 1837, survived a horribly uncomfortable winter in Majorca (1838–39) to last ten years before ending in a quarrel. Chopin, who had long been consumptive and was at times so weak that he had to be carried to the piano, then made a musical tour in Great Britain. His health was rapidly deteriorating and he died in the following year in Paris.
Hedley, A., *Chopin*. 1947

Chou En-lai *see* **Zhou Enlai**

Chrétien de Troyes (fl. *c.* 1166, died *c.* 1190). French poet, author of several metrical romances based on the Arthurian legends; *Perceval*, left unfinished at his death, is the first in which the story of the Holy Grail is associated with Arthurian material. His claim that material for the epic *Guillaume d'Angleterre* was found at Bury St Edmunds suggests that he may have visited England. He was one of the most influential of medieval poets and many translations and imitations of his work appeared.

Christ, Jesus *see* **Jesus Christ**

Christian IX (1818–1906). King of Denmark from 1863. As Prince Christian of Glücksburg he had been recognized as heir of the childless Frederick VII to all parts of the Danish monarchy; but immediately after his accession he had to face war with Bismarck's Prussia and surrender the duchies of Schleswig-Holstein to overwhelming force. He ruled as a constitutional monarch but gained a special notoriety by the way in which he extended his family connexions. His children included his successor Frederick VIII, Alexandra, wife of Edward VII of Great Britain, George I of Greece, and Dagmar, wife of the Russian emperor Alexander III. In the next generation this dynastic network spread further still, and, not only through Queen Alexandra but through its Greek connexions, includes Prince Philip, Princess Marina and almost every other member of the British royal house.

Christian X (1870–1947). King of Denmark (from 1912). Son and successor of Frederick VIII, he proved himself a skilful and sympathetic constitutional monarch. He achieved great popularity by his courageous bearing and behaviour during the German occupation in World War II.

Christie, Dame Agatha Mary Clarissa (née Miller) (1890–1976). English writer of detective stories. Famous for her baffling plots, she wrote over fifty successful novels, most of them featuring the Belgian detective Hercule Poirot, or that homely sleuth of the countryside, Miss Marple. One of her many plays, *The Mouse Trap*, broke all records for a London run. She married the archaeologist M. E. Mallowan in 1930, after the break-down of her first marriage.

Christie, John (1882–1962). English schoolmaster and founder of the Glyndebourne Opera. After teaching science at Eton for many years, he inherited a fortune and with his wife, Audrey Mildmay (died 1953), a distinguished singer, he founded in 1934 the Glyndebourne Opera at his country home. He was made a C.H. in 1954.

Christie, John Reginald Halliday (1899–1953). English murderer. He was convicted and hanged for the murder of his wife but also confessed to the murder of five other women whose bodies were found at his home. Among those whom he claimed to have killed was the wife of Timothy Evans, an illiterate truck driver. When Evans was tried in 1950 for murdering his wife and daughter Christie had been the principal witness for the prosecution. Evans was hanged for the murder of the child but later received a posthumous pardon.

Christina (1626–1689). Queen of Sweden, daughter of Gustavus Adolphus, whom she succeeded in 1632. During her minority, which lasted until 1644, the country was effectively governed by the great chancellor Axel * Oxenstierna, but on assuming power she soon revealed her distrust of him and the ruling aristocracy. Able and capricious, she achieved at least two of her political aims, the early ending of the Thirty Years' War and the recognition as her heir of her cousin Charles, to whom she had previously been secretly engaged. But her main interests, apart from indulging her personal extravagances, were literature, art, philosophy and religion (Descartes came to Stockholm at her invitation). In 1651 she first announced her intention to abdicate, and though persuaded to postpone the decision, she left the country in 1654, became a Roman Catholic and went to live in Rome. On the death of Charles X (1660) and again in 1667, she attempted to regain her throne, but was refused because of her religion. Thereafter she was reconciled to life in Rome, where she ruled a brilliant artistic and literary circle until her death.

Weibull, C., *Christina of Sweden*. 1966

Christophe, Henri (1767–1820). King of Haiti (from 1811). Originally a Negro slave, he became Toussaint l'Ouverture's most successful general in his struggle against the French. After the death (1806) of * Dessalines he was elected president but, impatient of constitutional control, he set up an independent state in the north. After he was proclaimed king (1811), he built a palace on the model of St Cloud and created a nobility to provide a court. Though ruthless and capricious he showed an extraordinary willingness to learn and to introduce laws, educational methods, agricultural machinery – indeed anything he thought useful – from abroad. A stroke left him helpless in the face of a military revolt and he shot himself.

Christus (Cristus), **Petrus** (*c.* 1420–1473). Flemish painter, active in Bruges from 1444. He was strongly influenced by the van Eycks and is best known for his altarpieces. He may have been in Milan in 1457 and so carried Flemish techniques to Italy. As a portrait painter he is represented in the National Gallery, London.

Chrysler, Walter Percy (1875–1940). American motor manufacturer. He left the Buick company, of which he was president (1916–19), to form the firm which still bears his name.

Chrysostom, St John *see* **John Chrysostom, St**

Chu Hsi (1130–1200). Chinese philosopher.

He develoed a neo-Confucianism with a strong moral emphasis. He was a civil servant in T'ung-an (1151–58), Nan-k'ang (1179–81), Liang-che (1182), Chang-chou (1190–91) and, briefly, at the Imperial court in 1194. The rest of his life was devoted to teaching and writing in which he developed his philosophy, his ideas became the basis of Chinese intellectual life.
Fung Yu-Lan, *A History of Chinese Philosophy*. 2nd ed. Vol. 2. 1953. Wing-Tsit Chan, *An Outline and Annotated Bibliography of Chinese Philosophy*. Rev. ed. 1969

Church, Richard (1893–1972). English poet, critic and novelist. He was brought up in Battersea, London, where his father was in the postal service. He spent more than twenty years of his early life in the civil service, where he found the background for his novel *The Porch* (1937). His work, both prose and poetry, is characterized by a quiet, reflective quality and a receptiveness to beauty even in most unlikely surroundings. *Over the Bridge* (1955), *The Golden Sovereign* (1957) and *The Voyage Home* (1964) are autobiographical.

Churchill, Arabella (1648–1730). Siter of the great Duke of* Marlborough and mistress of James, Duke of York (later James II). Their son, the Duke of * Berwick, became a distinguished soldier in the French armies.

Churchill, Charles (1731–1764). English satirical poet. Ordained in 1756 he was briefly a curate but soon turned to writing satirical and political verse. He led a dissipated life, and left the church in 1763. He was a vigorous supporter of John * Wilkes and wrote much of his famous political polemic in *The North Briton*.
Laver, J., *Poems of Charles Churchill*. 1970

Churchill, Lord Randolph Henry Spencer (1849–1895). English politician. The third son of the 7th Duke of Marlborough, he was educated at Eton and Oxford and became a Conservative M.P. in 1874. He developed a policy of progressive conservatism, known as Tory Democracy, and attacked both Liberal and Conservative leaders. He was Secretary for India 1885–86 and Chancellor of the Exchequer 1886, resigning the latter office after six months as a protest against the excessive financial demands of the army and navy. He was then 37 and never held cabinet post again. He was crippled by paralysis in his later years. In 1874 he married Jenny Jerome (1854–1921), the daughter of a New York newspaper proprietor.
Churchill, W. L. S., *Lord Randolph Churchill*. Rev. ed. 1952

Churchill, Winston (1871–1947). American novelist, born in Missouri. Among his successful romantic novels were *Richard Carvel* (1899) and *The Crisis* (1901). Active in politics as a Progressive, he was sometimes confused with his namesake, the British politician.

Churchill, Sir Winston Leonard Spencer (1874–1965). English politician, soldier and author. Born at Blenheim Palace, the son of Lord Randolph * Churchill, he was educated at Harrow and Sandhurst. He served with the Spanish forces in Cuba (1895) then joined the British army in India, where he began to take an intense interest in history and literature. He was sent to the Sudan in 1898 and took part in the battle of Omdurman. A correspondent of the London *Morning Post* during the Boer War, he was captured by the Boers, escaped and returned to England as a hero. He published a novel, *Savrola*, in 1900 and in the same year was elected to the House of Commons, serving as a Member 1900–22 and 1924–64 (Conservative 1900–04, 1924–64; Liberal 1904–22).

In the Liberal ministry of Campbell-Bannerman he was Under Secretary for the Colonies 1906–08, President of the Board of Trade 1908–10, Home Secretary 1910–11 and First Lord of the Admiralty 1911–15. As First Lord he was responsible for the mobilisation of the fleet on the outbreak of World War I. He planned the Allied landing at Gallipoli (1915) and when this failed he was subject to severe criticism and resigned. In 1916 he served in France with the 6th Royal Scots Fusiliers, but when Lloyd George displaced Asquith he recalled Churchill to office as minister of Munitions in 1917. He was Secretary of State for War and for Air (1919–21) and Colonial Secretary 1921–22. When the war ended he was prominent in organising armies of intervention to overthrow the Soviet government in Russia. He saw the futility of continued violence in Ireland and supported the establishment of the Irish Free State. After the dissolution of the Turkish Empire he was responsible for creating the new states of Jordan and Iraq (he suggested the latter name himself as a substitute for Mesopotamia) which became British mandates.

He opposed the breaking-up of Lloyd George's coalition government and was defeated in the 1922 general election. In the 1924 election he won a seat and became Chancellor of the Exchequer in Stanley Baldwin's Conservative cabinet. He refused office in the National Governments of Baldwin and Ramsay MacDonald as he disagreed with the policy of advancing towards self-government for India. In 1935 he had denounced Mahatma * Gandhi as a 'seditious and half-naked fakir'. In 1936 he supported King Edward III over the question of his marriage. After * Chamberlain became Prime Minister (1937) he bitterly attacked the policy of appeasing Germany and, on the outbreak of World War II (1939), became First Lord of the Admiralty. Chamberlain resigned after widespread criticism of his wartime government, and in May 1940 Churchill was made Prime Minister. He told the nation: 'I have nothing to offer but blood, toil, tears and sweat.' As Prime Minister and Minister of Defence he led a coalition government with Labour and Liberal support. He worked in close co-operation with * Roosevelt and other world leaders including Joseph Stalin, General de Gaulle and Chiang Kai-Shek.

At the post-war general election of 1945 his party was heavily defeated; he continued as its leader and Leader of the Opposition. He led the Conservatives to a narrow victory in 1951 and resumed office as Prime Minister (1951–55) and Minister of Defence (1951–52). He maintained his close relations with the USA under Presidents Truman and Eisenhower. In April 1955, at the age of 81, he resigned from political life. He was replaced as Prime Minister by Anthony * Eden. He had declined a peerage several times, wishing to continue as a member of the House of Commons. Always a colourful and controversial figure, he earned the gratitude of the democratic world for his dynamic leadership in the wartime years.

A keen amateur painter, he was made an honorary Royal Academician in 1948. His literary work reflects the stylistic influence of Gibbon and Macaulay. Among his works were *Lord Randolph Churchill* (1906), *The World Crisis* (1923–29, a history of World War I), *My Early Life* (1930), *Life of the Duke of Marlborough* (1933–38), *Great Contemporaries* (1937). He published a six-volume history of World War II and *A History of the English Speaking Peoples* (1956–68). He was awarded the Nobel Prize for Literature in 1953 'for his mastery in historical and biographical presentation and for his brilliant oratory, in which he has always stood forth as the defender of eternal human values'.

He married Clementine Hozier (1885–1977) in 1908. Their son, **Randolph Frederick Edward Spencer Churchill** (1911–1968) was a writer and journalist. He served in the army in World War II and was a Conservative M.P. 1940–45. Among his books were *The Story of the Coronation* (1953) and *The Rise and Fall of Sir Anthony Eden* (1959).

Churchill, R. S., and Gilbert, M., *Winston S. Churchill*. Vols from 1966. Bonham-Carter, V., *Winston Churchill as I Knew Him*. 1965

Chu Teh *see* **Zhu De**

Ciano (di Cortellazzo), Count Galeazzo (1903–1944). Italian Fascist politician. The son of a naval hero who became a minister in the first Fascist government, he married * Mussolini's daughter Edda in 1930. He served as Minister for Foreign Affairs 1936–43 but voted for Mussolini's deposition at the Grand Council (1943). He was later captured by Mussolini's supporters, tried and shot as a traitor.

Cibber, Colley (1671–1757). English actor, playwright and poet. The author of about thirty plays, the best-known being *She Would and She Would Not*, he was denounced by Pope, Fielding and Johnson, and his appointment as Poet Laureate in 1730 was the subject of much derision. He achieved varying success on the London stage as an eccentric comedian.

Cibber, C., *Apology for the Life of Mr Colley Cibber, Comedian*. 1740.

Cicero, Marcus Tullius (106–43 B.C.). Roman orator, politician and philosopher, born in Arpinum. Educated in Rome, Rhodes and Athens, he achieved early fame as an orator, served as quaestor of Sicily (75) and praetor of Rome (66). Although he was not of noble birth his ability won him the support of the senatorial party. As Consul (63) he exposed and suppressed the conspiracy of * Catiline but was later exiled, and deprived of his property, for having illegally passed death sentences on some of the conspirators. He served as Governor of Cilicia 52–51. He supported Pompey against Caesar during the civil war (49–48) and only returned to Rome on Caesar's invitation in 47. He supported the conspiracy against Caesar but did not take part in his murder. He led the republicans in opposition to the Second Triumvirate (Mark Antony, Octavianus and Lepidus) and he was exiled and ultimately murdered on Antony's orders.

Vain but sincere, he proved an inept politician. He was regarded as the greatest of all Roman orators and 57 of his major speeches have survived. His vivacious letters and his books on law and philosophy (*On Oratory, On the Republic, On Old Age, On Friendship*) were of great historical significance and affected the development of Latin style. His writings were a major influence on the literature of the Renaissance, and Petrarch wrote commentaries on his works.
Stockton, D., *Cicero: a Political Biography*. 1971

Cid, El (Rodrigo Diaz de Vivar) (*c.* 1040–1099). Spanish soldier. The name 'El Cid' is Arabic: 'seyyid' means 'lord'. He was also called 'El Cid Campeador': 'the lord champion'. So many legends have been told about him that it is difficult to determine the truth. He seems to have been a soldier of fortune who sold his services from time to time to both the Christians and the Moors. Noted for his skill in guerilla warfare, he conquered and ruled Valencia 1094–99. Medieval legends incorrectly described him as a valiant champion of Christianity against the Moors.
Pidal, R. M., *La España del Cid*. 5th Ed. 1965

Cimabue, Giovanni (Cenni di Pepo) (*c.* 1240–1302). Italian painter born in Florence. Little has survived of his work apart from some mosaics in Pisa, and panel paintings and frescoes attributed to him in Florence and Assisi. His use of a golden background reveals the extent of Byzantine influence, but his figures are more natural than those of his predecessors. He was the teacher of * Giotto according to many commentators, but there is hardly any documentary evidence of his life and work. Dante, his contemporary, refers to him as enjoying a fame that was overtaken by that of Giotto.
Battisti, E., *Cimabue*. 1967

Cimarosa, Domenico (1749–1801). Italian composer, born in Naples. He wrote about sixty operas, few of which are still performed; the best-known is *The Secret Marriage* (1792), a comic opera. He became court conductor for Catherine the Great at St Petersburg. A popular oboe concerto was arranged by Sir John Barbirolli from Cimarosa's music.

Cincinnatus, Lucius Quinctius (519–435 B.C.). Roman politician and soldier. He was twice appointed dictator by the Senate in order to deal with invasions by the Aequians. On each occasion he returned to retirement in the country as soon as the military emergency was over. He was famous as a model of devotion to duty and the unselfish renunciation of power.

Cinna, Lucius Cornelius (*d.* 84 B.C.). Roman politician. A leader of the democratic party, he was Consul in 87 and in 86–84, and supported Marius in the civil war against Sulla. His daughter Cornelia became the second wife of Julius Caesar, whose ambitions Cinna encouraged. He was killed during a mutiny of his own troops. His son Lucius Cornelius Cinna (*d.* 44 B.C.) was one of Caesar's assassins.

Cipriani, Amilcare (1844–1918). Italian revolutionary politician. A friend of * Garibaldi, he fought for Italian unification, then served in the Paris Commune (1870–71). He spent many years in prison or in exile. He raised a battalion to fight for Greek independence from the Turks, and supported the Allied cause in World War I.

Citrine, Sir Walter McLennan Citrine, 1st Baron (1887–1983). English administrator and trade union leader. He became an official of the Electrical Trades Union, then served as General Secretary of the Trades Union Congress 1926–46, and Chairman of the Central Electricity Authority 1947–57. He wrote *British Trade Unions* (1942) and *In Russia Now* (1942).

Citroen, André Gustave (1878–1935). French motor-car manufacturer. After World War I he began to produce small, low-priced cars, but in 1934 he went bankrupt and lost control of the company which still carries his name.

Clair, René (1898–1981). French film director. Noted for developing a cinematic equivalent of the verbal cut and thrust stage comedy, and for his poetic originality, his best-known films are *The Italian Straw Hat, A Nous la Liberté* and *La Beauté du diable*. He became a member of the French Academy in 1960.
Clarensol, G., and Regent, R., *René Clair: un Maître du cinéma*. 1952.

Clare, John (1793–1864). English poet, called 'the Northamptonshire peasant poet'. He

became a farm-boy at the age of seven, then worked as a gardener until he joined the local militia. He was a vagrant for some years, lived with gipsies and, after an unhappy love-affair, became insane. He was confined in an asylum from 1837. His simple and direct lyrics have an unusual purity of style and he published *The Village Minstrel* (1821) and *Rural Muse* (1827) which were well received. His best-known lyric, written in the asylum, was: 'I am: yet what I am, who knows or cares?'.
Storey, F., *A Right to Song: The Life of John Clare*. 1982.

Clarence, George Plantagenet, Duke of (1449–1478). English prince, the son of Richard Duke of York and the brother of King Edward IV. He was also the son-in-law of the Earl of Warwick ('The Kingmaker'). A vacillating character, he first supported Warwick against Edward, then changed sides and was ultimately imprisoned in the Tower on a charge of necromancy. He died in the Tower, traditionally having been 'drowned in a butt of Malmsey', which may mean that he drank himself to death.

Clarence, William Henry, Duke of *see* **William IV**

Clarendon, Edward Hyde, 1st Earl of (1609–1674). English lawyer, politician and historian, born near Salisbury. The son of a squire, he was educated at Oxford, became a successful barrister and sat in the House of Commons 1640–42. Although he had criticised the practice of the monarchy of 'the personal government of Charles I', he joined the King before the outbreak of the Civil War (1642) and tried to exert a moderating influence on him. Chancellor of the Exchequer 1643–46, he was the chief adviser to the future Charles II from 1646. After the Restoration he served as Chancellor of the Exchequer (1660–61) and Lord High Chancellor (1660–67), being the effective head of Charles II's government. The Clarendon Code which aimed at maintaining supremacy for the Church of England and denied toleration to Catholics and Dissenters was somewhat erroneously ascribed to him. Charles II began unjustly to blame him for every failure of national policy and dismissed him in 1667, the 'Cabal' ministry then taking office. Clarendon was impeached and fled to France, where he remained for the rest of his life. He wrote an important *History of the Rebellion* which was published posthumously in 1704, with a perpetual copyright to the University of Oxford – the basis of the Clarendon Press. He also wrote against * Hobbes. He was Chancellor of Oxford University 1660–67. His daughter, Anne Hyde (1637 – 1671) was the first wife of James II.
Wormwald, B. H. G., *Clarendon: Politics, History and Religion, 1640–1660*. 1951

Clarendon, George Herbert Hyde Villiers, 6th Earl of (1887–1955). English peer. He was Chairman of the British Broadcasting Corporation 1927–30, Governor-General of South Africa 1931–37 and Lord Chamberlain 1938–52.

Clark, George Rogers (1752–1818). American surveyor, soldier and frontiersman. He led successful military expeditions defending Kentucky during the War of Independence. He attacked the Shawnee Indians as well as the British, his aim being the extension of American settlement. After the war he was appointed an Indian commissioner, and helped to negotiate a treaty with the Shawnee tribe in 1786. He lost his position as the result of intrigues, and in 1793 became involved with a mission to involve America in the war between England and France. He returned to Louisville on the Ohio River (which as Fort Nelson, had been one of his main war time bases) and lived in retirement.

Clark, Joe (Charles Joseph) (1939–). Canadian politician. A journalist and academic in Alberta, he was a Progressive Conservative MP 1972– , leader of the opposition 1976–79 and 1980–83, and prime minister 1979–80. He became foreign minister 1984– in the * Mulroney government.

Clark, Kenneth Mackenzie Clark, Baron (1903–1983). British art historian and critic. Educated at Oxford, he worked with Bernard * Berenson in Florence for two years, and became Director of the National Gallery, London, 1934–45. He was Slade Professor of Fine Arts at Oxford University 1946–50 and 1961–62. He was chairman of the Arts Council of Great Britain 1953–60 and chairman of the Independent Television Authority 1954–57. His books included *Leonardo da Vinci* (1939), *Landscape into Art* (1949), *Piero della Francesca* (1951), *The Nude* (1956) and

Rembrandt and the Italian Renaissance (1966). His television series and subsequent book *Civilisation* (1969) were widely popular. He received a KCB in 1938, the CH in 1959, a peerage in 1969 and the OM in 1976.
Secrest, M., *Kenneth Clark*. 1984

Clark, Mark Wayne (1896–   ). American soldier. He served in World War I and was wounded, and in World War II he became G.O.C. of the U.S. Fifth Army in the invasion of Italy (1943), later commanding all U.S. troops in Italy 1944–45 and Austria 1945–47. He succeeded General M. B. Ridgway as Supreme Commander of Allied Powers in the Far East and U.N. Commander-in-Chief in Korea 1952–53. He was in charge of the allied armies at the end of the Korean War. He wrote *From the Danube to the Yalu* (1954).

Clark, Thomas Campbell (1899–1977). American jurist. He served as Attorney-General of the U.S. 1945–49 and President Truman appointed him a Justice of the U.S. Supreme Court in 1949.

Clark, Sir Wilfred Edward Le Gros (1895–1971). English anatomist. Professor of Anatomy at Oxford University 1934–62, he wrote *History of the Primates* (1949) and *The Fossil Evidence of Human Evolution* (1955).

Clark, William (1770–1838). American explorer, born in Virginia. He joined the army in 1792 and fought against the Indians. With Meriwether * Lewis he went on an expedition to the north-west of the United States (1803–06): leaving from St Louis, they explored the Missouri River to its source, crossed the Rocky Mountains and followed the Columbia River to the Pacific. They returned to St Louis and published a valuable scientific record of their expedition. Clark was Governor of Missouri Territory 1813–20 and Superintendent of Indian Affairs 1822–38.

Clarke, Marcus Andrew Hislop (1846–1881). Australian novelist, born in London. He became a journalist in Melbourne and wrote a powerful novel about the convict settlement at Port Arthur (Tasmania), *For the Term of His Natural Life* (1874).

Claude, Georges (1870–1960). French chemist. He invented neon lighting and founded a company to exploit this invention. Among his other achievements was the invention of processes for the production of liquid air and of synthetic nitrates.

Claudel, Paul Louis Charles Marie (1868–1955). French poet, playwright and diplomat. He studied law, joined the diplomatic service in 1890 and spent most of his adult life abroad. He served as Minister to Brazil 1917–19, and Ambassador to Japan 1921–25, to the U.S. 1926–33, and to Belgium 1933–35. He called himself a follower of * Rimbaud and it was the influence of the Symbolists which turned him away from materialism and the acceptance of a mechanical universe: however he reacted against the decadence of the symbolists and his work reflects his devotion to Catholicism. His plays include *Break of Noon* (1908), *The Tidings Brought to Mary* (1916) and *The Book of Christopher Columbus* (1930). He was elected to the French Academy in 1946. He is important in the history of the theatre because of his use, in his later plays, of 'total theatre' stage presentation.
Fowlie, W., *Claudel*. 1958

Claudius I (10 B.C.–A.D. 54). Fourth Roman emperor; his full name was Tiberius Claudius Drusus Nero Germanicus. He was the son of Drusus, the brother of the Emperor * Tiberius. His supposed or assumed imbecility and physical incapacity saved him from the fate of many of his relatives, but he wrote and studied history although his works (in Latin and Greek) are now lost. He became emperor after * Caligula's assassination in 41. He built the Claudian aqueduct and commenced the conquest of Britain; he was present for part of the campaign. He appeared to condone the viciousness and profligacy of his wife * Messalina, but when she publicly married a lover he had her executed. His second wife Agrippina, who is believed to have poisoned him, was already the mother of the next emperor, * Nero.
Graves, R., *I Claudius*; *Claudius the God*. 1934

Claudius II (Marcus Aurelius Claudius Gothicus) (d. 270). Roman Emperor 268–270. Born in Illyria, he became a soldier, was governor of Illyria and received the Imperial title from his troops. He defeated the Goths at Naissus (269) and died of the plague.

Clausewitz, Karl von (1780–1831). Prussian soldier and military strategist, of Polish origin.

He served as a staff officer under Scharnhorst and Gneisenau, and directed the Prussian army school at Berlin 1818–30. His famous book *On War* (*Vom Kriege*, published posthumously by his widow in 1832–37) dealt with military strategy in an analytical manner and remained of major importance until World War I. He coined the aphorism 'War is the continuation of politics by other means'.
Parkinson, R., *Clausewitz*. 1971

Clausius, Rudolf Julius Emanuel (1822–1888). German mathematical physicist. Born in Pomerania (now in Poland), he was educated in Berlin and Halle, and became a professor of physics at the Artillery and Engineering School, Berlin 1850–55. In 1850 he enunciated the First and Second Laws of Thermodynamics ('Work and heat are equivalent'; 'Heat cannot of itself pass from a colder to a hotter body') precise formulations of discoveries by J. R. * Mayer, * Joule and * Helmholtz, and of Sadi * Carnot respectively, just anticipating * Kelvin with the Second Law. In 1857 Clausius provided explanations of how electrolysis works and the kinetic theory of gases. He held professorships at Zürich 1855–67, Würzburg 1867–69 and Bonn 1869–88. In 1865 he proposed the concept of 'entropy', the measure of unavailability of energy for work within a system: with any change in the system, entropy increases (from order to disorder).

Clay, Henry (1777–1852). American Whig politician, born in Virginia. He became a lawyer, lived in Kentucky from 1797, achieved great success as an advocate and served in the state legislature. He was a U.S. Senator 1806–07, 1810–11, 1831–42 and 1849–52; a member of the House of Representatives 1811–20 and 1823–25; and three times Speaker 1811–14, 1815–20 and 1823–25. He tried for the presidency in 1832 and 1844 but was defeated each time. He originated the phrase 'I would rather be right than President'. When no candidate secured a majority in the 1824 poll, he urged his supporters in the House of Representatives to vote for J. Q. Adams, rather than Andrew Jackson who had led on the popular vote. Adams was elected and appointed Clay as U.S. Secretary of State (1825–29). A great orator and magnetic personality, Clay was called 'The Great Pacificator' for his ability to effect compromises on issues which seemed likely to split the Union, e.g. the Tariff Bill of 1833, in which as an ardent protectionist he proposed that tariffs be lowered in order to appease the south. He also arranged the 1850 compromise, by which California was admitted to the Union as a non-slave state, and the Fugitive Slave Law was passed. His nephew **Cassius Marcellus Clay** (1810–1903) was an ardent abolitionist who edited an anti-slavery newspaper in Lexington.
van Deusen, G. G., *The Life of Henry Clay Repr.* 1967

Clay, Lucius DuBignon (1897–1978). American soldier. Military governor of the U.S. zone of Germany 1947–49, he served as assistant director of the U.S. Civil Defence Authority 1950–51. Later he entered business and was active in the 'Citizens for Eisenhower' campaign (1952).

Cleanthes (fl. *c.* 300 B.C.). Greek philosopher. A Stoic, he was the pupil of Zeno of Citium, and became a great teacher. St Paul quoted from one of his poems in *The Acts of the Apostles*.

Clemenceau, Georges Benjamin (1841–1929). French Radical politician, born in the Vendée. The son of a physician, he studied medicine in Paris, but went to the U.S. as a journalist (1865–68) and taught for a time at a school in Connecticut. He was Mayor of Montmartre 1870–71 and a Member of the Chamber of Deputies 1876–93. He founded a radical newspaper in Paris, *La Justice*, in 1880, and became a remorseless critic of ministerial ineptitude. He forced the resignation of President Grévy over an honours scandal (1887). He was defeated as a Deputy in 1893. The ferocity of his journalistic attacks earned him the soubriquet of 'The Tiger' and his revelations caused the fall of several ministries. He was a strong supporter of Captain Dreyfus who had been unjustly charged with espionage. A Senator 1902–20, he served as Minister of the Interior (1906), and Premier of France (1906–09), completing the separation of Church and State, but losing the support of the Socialists by using troops to break several strikes. During World War I he flayed government inefficiency in his newspapers, *L'Homme Libre* (suppressed by the censor in 1914) and *L'Homme Enchainé*. At a critical moment in the war, when French resistance was low (November 1917), President Poincaré appointed him as Premier and Minister of War, and

he held these posts 1917–20. He proved a vigorous leader, mobilised all available resources, and crushed defeatism, but ruled as a virtual dictator, ignoring the French legislature. He was responsible for the appointment of Marshal Foch as Allied Generalissimo in March 1918. After the war had been won he became President of the Paris Peace Conference (1919) and trenchantly criticised President * Wilson's proposals as impracticably idealistic. In 1920 the French legislature elected Paul Deschanel as President of the Republic in preference to Clemenceau: this was a left-handed compliment as his cynical advice at previous presidential elections had always been 'Vote for the stupidest'. He retired from public life, visited India and the U.S., and devoted himself to literature.
Monnerville, *G., Clemenceau.* 1968

Clemens, Samuel Langhorne *see* **Twain, Mark**

Clement I (St Clement of Rome) (*c.* 30–100? A.D.). Pope 90–?100. Thought to have been the fourth Bishop of Rome (i.e. Pope), assuming St Peter to have been the first; an old tradition claims that he was consecrated by St Peter himself. He wrote an Epistle to the Church of Corinth (*c.* 95) which has survived and demonstrates that the Roman see was exercising authority outside the boundaries of Italy. He is thought to have died in exile, perhaps in the Crimea.
Lowther Clarke, W. K., ed. *The First Epistle of Clement to the Corinthians.* 1937

Clement VII (Cardinal Giulio de' Medici) (1478–1534). Pope 1523–34. A cousin of Pope Leo X, he was Archbishop of Florence (1512–34). He proved an indecisive pope and failed to cope with the problems raised by the Reformation. In 1527 Rome was sacked by the Imperial troops of Charles V but by 1529 Clement had become reconciled with Charles, and begged him to solve the problem of Lutheranism. He refused Henry VIII's request for an annulment of his marriage to Catherine of Aragon, the aunt of Charles V (1534).
Crabitès, P., *Clement VII and Henry VIII.* 1936.

Clementi, Muzio (1752–1832). Italian pianist and composer. He lived in England 1766–80, 1782–1804, 1810–32, and achieved great fame, first as a pianist and composer, later as a publisher, teacher and piano manufacturer. He was one of the founders of the modern school of piano playing, and composed 70 sonatas and a famous collection of studies *Gradus ad Parnassum.*

Cleopatra (c. 69–30 B.C.). Queen of Egypt 51–30 B.C. She married her younger brother, Ptolemy Dionysus, in 51 but was forced into exile by her brother's guardian, Pothinus, in 53. From Syria she attracted the interest and attention of Julius * Caesar and after he conquered Egypt in 48 she was restored to power. She became Caesar's mistress, bore him a son (Caesarion, 47 B.C.) and lived with him in Rome 46–44. On returning to Egypt she married Ptolemy XIII, another of her brothers, but he was soon poisoned on her orders. In 42 she met Mark Antony; they lived together for 12 years and had three children. Cleopatra's union with Mark Antony cost him much support in Rome, and after his heavy defeat at the battle of Actium (31) he committed suicide. Cleopatra tried to win the love of the victorious Octavianus (Augustus) but failed, and killed herself (according to tradition) by applying an asp to her breast. Of Greek descent, she was intelligent and widely read but subject to an overmastering ambition and sensuality.
Volkmann, H., *Cleopatra.* 1958

Clerk Maxwell, James *see* **Maxwell, James Clerk.**

Cleveland, Barbara Villiers, 1st Duchess of (1641–1709). English noblewoman. The daughter of Viscount Grandison, she was the mistress of Charles II from 1660–74 and her sons became Duke of Cleveland, Duke of Grafton and Duke of Northumberland. She became a Roman Catholic and her influence over Charles contributed to the fall of * Clarendon. Among her other lovers was the future Duke of * Marlborough.

Cleveland, John (1613–1658). English poet. Champion of the Royalist cause during the Civil War, his best-known work is a series of political poems in heroic couplet: *Rupertismus, The Rebel Scot* and *The King's Disguise.*

Cleveland, (Stephen) Grover (1837–1908). 22nd and 24th president of the US, born at Caldwell, New Jersey. The son of a Presbyterian clergyman, he worked in a lawyer's office from the age of 17 and became an attorney in 1859. He served as assistant district attorney of Erie County, New York State, 1863, and sheriff of Erie County 1869–73, then returned to his law practice. In 1881 he began his extraordinary political career which took him in four years from a law office to the White House. As mayor of Buffalo 1881–82 he proved a notable reformer and gained the Democratic nomination for governor of New York State, serving in that Office 1883–85. He was Democratic candidate for the presidency 1884, 1888 and 1892. In the 1884 election he was narrowly elected and served as 22nd president 1885–89. In 1888, although he gained a majority of the popular vote, he was defeated in the electoral college by 233 votes to 168 and Benjamin Harrison succeeded him as president. He defeated Harrison in 1892 and became the only ex-president to return to the White House. He was extremely conservative on all economic questions and favoured a laissez-faire policy. He reformed the civil service, vetoed about 300 Civil War pension bills, urged a policy of free trade (believing that protection was 'pampering employers'), and instituted the Interstate Commerce Commission (1887). His second term was marked by an economic depression. He secured the repeal of the Sherman Silver Purchase Bill and was anxious to maintain the gold standard. He used Federal troops to suppress the Pullman strike in Illinois (1894), despite the protests of J. P. Altgeld, and invoked the Monroe Doctrine against Great Britain in a dispute over the Venezuelan border (1895). He was virtually repudiated by his party in 1896 when W. J. Bryan was nominated on a free-silver policy. He left politics a poor man, became a lecturer in political science at Princeton University 1904–06 and a Trustee of the Equitable Life Insurance Company, New York, 1905–08.

Clifford, Clark McAdams (1906–). American lawyer. He was an adviser to Presidents Truman, Kennedy and Johnson but held no public office until his brief term as secretary of defence (1968–69), during which the U.S. began to retract its military action in Vietnam.

Clifford of Chudleigh, Thomas Clifford, 1st Baron (1630–1673). English politician and courtier. Educated at Oxford, he was M.P. 1660–72, served on several diplomatic missions for Charles II, and became a member of the 'Cabal' (Clifford, Arlington, Buckingham, Ashley, Lauderdale) ministry, as Commissioner for the Treasury 1667–72 and Lord Treasurer 1672–73. He became a Roman Catholic about 1670. He was a sincere but ineffective minister.

Clinton, De Witt (1769–1828). American lawyer. Senator and governor of New York State (1817–23, 1825–28), he first put forward the idea of a canal linking the north-east coast with the Great Lakes through Lake Erie. The state legislature accepted a scheme in 1816 and Clinton supervised the project himself and opened the Erie Canal in 1825. He was also noted for his interest in education and the dissemination of the arts and sciences.

Clinton, George (1739–1812). American politician. He was Governor of New York 1777–95 and 1801–04, and Vice-President of the U.S. 1805–12.

Clinton, Sir Henry (*c.* 1738–1795). English soldier. A Member of Parliament 1772–84 and 1790–94, he was commander-in-chief of British Forces in North America 1778–81, and wrote a narrative of the campaign.

Clive, Sir Robert Clive, 1st Baron (1725–1774). English soldier and administrator, born near Market Drayton, Shropshire. The son of a squire, he was educated at the Merchant Taylors' School, became extremely unhappy there, and in 1743 joined the East India Company as a 'writer' (i.e. clerk-administrator). He worked in Madras 1743–46 but obtained an ensign's commission in the Indian army after fighting began with Dupleix' French troops. After training a large force of sepoys he defeated 10,000 French and Indian troops at Arcot in 1751 in a clash which resulted from a dispute over the control of the Carnatic. Lieutenant-governor of Fort St David 1755–57, he was sent in 1756 to punish the Nawab of Bengal and Calcutta, Suraj-ud-Dowlah, who had locked 146 British civilians in a small room, 123 of them dying of suffocation overnight in the 'Black Hole of Calcutta'. Clive defeated the Nawab at Plassey in 1757, thus placing the large state of Bengal under British Control. The Seven Years' War had begun in Europe and fighting between the British and French soon broke out in India. As

governor of Bengal 1757–60, he established the supremacy of British power throughout most of India. Returning to England in 1760 he was a Member of Parliament 1760–62. After being raised to the peerage, he returned to India as governor and commander-in-chief of Bengal 1764–67, making reforms in administration. He retired in 1767 because of ill-health, and after facing several charges of misgovernment and peculation, he was absolved of all blame. An opium addict, he committed suicide by cutting his throat.
Davies, A. M., *Clive of Plassey*. 1939

Clodius (Pulcher), Publius (*c*. 93–52 BC). Roman politician. A leader of the democratic party, he became a supporter of Caesar and an opponent of Pompey and Cicero. As Tribune of the People 59–57, he proved to be a capable demagogue, revived the guilds, ordered free gifts of corn for the people, and sent Cicero into exile. He organised street gangs to help him in his campaign for the Consulate but was killed by the rival gang of Milo.

Cloete, (Edward Fairly) Stuart (Graham) (1897–1976). South African novelist. His novels include *Turning Wheels* (1937), *The Hill of Doves* (1941), *The African Giant* (1955) and *The Mask* (1957). He became deeply concerned with the problem of the future of the whites in South Africa.
Cloete, S., *Victorian Son*. 1972

Clore, Sir Charles (1904–1979). British businessman and financier, noted as the chief practitioner of the take-over. The son of an immigrant Russian tailor who had become prosperous in the textile trade, he was an established dealer in businesses when he bought J. Sears and Co. in 1956, by going straight to the shareholders with an offer per share at well above market value. This method, now common, was then new. At the time of his death his fortune was estimated at £50m., and his companies were active in retailing, engineering, transport, shoe-making and book-making. He was committed to the Zionist cause, to which he gave generously, as he did to many charities. He was knighted in 1971.

Clough, Arthur Hugh (1819–1861). English poet. Brought up in the U.S.A., he was educated at Rugby and Oxford, and became the friend of Carlyle, Emerson and Matthew Arnold. A civil servant, he was a melancholy sceptic whose verse reveals his preoccupation with ethical questions. He revised Dryden's translation of Plutarch's *Lives*. His sister, **Anne Jemima Clough** (1820–1892) became the first Principal of Newnham College, Cambridge.
Chorley, K., *Arthur Hugh Clough*. 1962

Clovis I (466–511). King of the Franks. He led his army in a successful attack on France, which he attempted to weld into a unified kingdom, making Paris his capital. He became a convert to Christianity in 496.
Wallace-Hadrill, J. M., *The Long-Haired Kings*. 1962

Clyde, Sir Cohn Campbell, 1st Baron (1792–1863). Scottish field-marshal. During the Indian Mutiny of 1857–58 he was the British commander-in-chief and raised the siege of Lucknow (1857).

Clynes, John Robert (1869–1949). English Labour politician. Son of an Irish labourer, he worked in cotton mills from the age of 10, became a union organiser and a Labour M.P. (1906–31, 1935–45). He led the Labour Party 1921–22, during Ramsay MacDonald's absence from parliament, and was Lord Privy Seal (1924) and Home Secretary (1929–31).
Clynes, J. R., *Memoirs*. 1937

Coates, Albert (1882–1953). English conductor, born in Russia. He was famous for his interpretations of Wagner and the modern Russian composers.

Coates, Eric (1886–1957). English composer. His light music gained wide popularity and includes the *London Suite, London Again, The Three Elizabeths* and *The Three Bears Suite*.

Coates, Joseph Gordon (1878–1943). New Zealand politician. He was prime minister 1925–28, held ministerial office 1919–28 and 1931–35 and, as minister for finance (1933–35) attempted to bring New Zealand out of the Depression.

Cobb, John (1899–1952). English racing motorist. He broke the world land speed record, 1947, by travelling at 394.2 m.p.h in a Napier-Railton. He was killed in a motor-boat accident on Loch Ness, Scotland.

Cobbett, William (1763–1835). English pamphleteer and Radical politician. After service in the army in Canada 1783–91, he became a Tory propagandist, under the pen name of Peter Porcupine, and attacked all forms of radicalism and democracy. After 1804, he joined the radical cause, was imprisoned for denouncing flogging in the army and later acquitted on a charge of sedition. A Member in the first reformed Parliament (1832–35) he wrote many books on political and agricultural subjects, of which *Rural Rides* is regarded today as his greatest achievement.
Cole, G. D. H., *The Life of William Cobbett*. 3rd ed. 1947.

Cobbold, Cameron Fromanteel Cobbold, 1st Baron (1904–). English banker. Educated at Eton and Cambridge, he became Governor of the Bank of England in 1949 and Lord Chamberlain 1963–71.

Cobden, Richard (1804–1865). English Liberal politician. A Member of Parliament 1841–65, he was the co-founder, with John * Bright, of the Anti-Corn Law League and became known as 'The Apostle of Free Trade'. Prominent in opposing the Crimean War (which brought him much unpopularity), he was an active worker for international peace and disarmament. Although he regarded himself as a radical, he firmly believed in 'laissez-faire' and opposed trade-unions and factory legislation, which he thought were opposed to liberty of contract. He supported the North in the U.S. Civil War.
Hobson, J. A., *Richard Cobden*. 1918

Cobham, Sir Alan John (1894–1973). English aviator. After serving in the Royal Flying Corps during World War I, he entered civil aviation, took part in many notable long distance flights and won the Britannia Trophy in 1926 for his flight to Australia and back. He pioneered the London-Cape Town route and devised a system for re-fuelling planes in the air.

Cochrane, Thomas Cochrane, 10th Earl of Dundonald (1775–1860). Scottish sailor. After many brilliant exploits in which he captured over fifty French and Spanish ships, he became a Whig member of Parliament 1805–16. Deprived of his naval command in 1816, after being tried for fraud he was imprisoned for one year. On his release he went to South America, where the struggle against Spanish domination was in progress, and served as Commander of the Chilean Navy 1818–22, and of the Brazilian Navy 1823–25, contributing much to the success of the nationalist risings. On returning to Europe he became Commander of the Greek Navy 1827–28, but when the Whigs came to power in England he was reinstated in the British Navy (1832) and served as Commander-in-Chief of the North American Station 1848–51.

Cockcroft, Sir John Douglas (1897–1967). English physicist. In 1932, with E. T. S. Walton, he succeeded in splitting the nucleus of the atom. Professor of natural philosophy at Cambridge 1939–46, during the war he worked on the production of the atomic bomb in the U.S.A. He was director of the U.K. Atomic Energy Establishment at Harwell 1946–59 and first Master of Churchill College, Cambridge, 1959–67. He shared the Nobel Prize for Physics in 1951 with Professor Walton, received the OM in 1957, and won the Ford 'Atoms for Peace' Award of $75,000 in 1961.

Cockerell, Sir Christopher Sydney (1910–). English engineer. He was a pioneer of the amphibious hovercraft which can travel across a variety of surfaces on a cushion of air. The air is produced by jets. Cockerell was knighted in 1969, ten years after a prototype hovercraft crossed the English Channel.

Cocteau, Jean (1889–1963). French poet, ballet designer, novelist, playwright, actor, film producer and graphic artist, born near Paris. He published his first volume of poetry *La Lampe d'Aladin* in 1908, was associated with * Diaghilev's Ballets Russes and served as an ambulance driver in World War I. His ballets included *Parade* (1917), with music by Erik * Satie, sets by Pablo * Picasso and staged by Diaghilev, *Le Boeuf sur le toit* (1920: * Milhaud/* Dufy) and *Les Biches* (1924: * Poulenc). He wrote eight novels of which *Thomas l'imposteur* (1923) and *Les Enfants Terribles* (1929: filmed 1950) are the best known. His opera-oratorio *Oedipus-Rex* (1927) was set to music by * Stravinsky and remains in the repertoire. Several of his plays were filmed under his own direction e.g.

Orphée (1926: 1950), and *Les Parents terribles* (1938: 1948), while others were successful on television and radio e.g. *La Voix Humaine* (1930) and *La Machine à écrire* ('The Typewriter': 1941). His beautiful but obscure films were based on a private mythology not always shared with the audience: the best known were *Le Sang d'un poete* (1932), *L'Eternal retour* (1944) and *La Belle et la bête* (1945). In the 1950s he was active as a graphic artist and fresco painter. After decades as an '*enfant terrible*' and foe of artistic orthodoxy, Cocteau accepted immortalization by election to the French Academy (1955).

Cody, William Federick (1846–1917). American showman, known as 'Buffalo Bill'. Originally an Indian scout, he gained his title by supplying buffalo meat to railway workers. From 1883 he organized a 'Wild West Show' which stimulated wide interest in 'Cowboys and Indians'.

Coggan, (Frederick) Donald, Baron (1909–). English prelate. He was principal of the London School of Divinity 1944–56, Bishop of Bradford 1956–61 and Archbishop of York 1961–74. In 1974 he was appointed Archbishop of Canterbury, a post he held until 1980. His theology was Evangelical, and, although he was concerned with social issues, he stressed that a changed society can only come from the conversion of the individual to the service of God. His works include *Sinews of Faith* (1969) and *The Heart of the Christian Faith* (1978).

Cohan, George M(ichael) (1878–1942). American song-writer and performer. He composed the popular songs *Over There* and *I'm a Yankee Doodle Dandy*.

Coke, Sir Edward (1552–1634). English lawyer and politician. A Member of Parliament 1580–1606, he was Speaker of the House of Commons 1593–94 and Attorney General 1594–1606, proving to be a zealous supporter of the royal prerogative and being responsible for the prosecution of Essex, Raleigh and the Gunpowder Plot conspirators. However, on his appointment as Chief Justice of the Court of Common Pleas, in 1606, he became the champion of the Common Law in opposition to the exercise of the Crown's prerogative rights. In 1610 he decided that the King's proclamations could not override laws made by Parliament and that ecclesiastical causes must be subject to the jurisdiction of the secular courts. He was promoted to the office of Chief Justice of the King's Bench Division (1613–16) where it was hoped that he would prove less troublesome to James I and his advisers. His fearless defiance of those orders of the King which he regarded as illegal made the supporters of the Divine Right determined to secure his removal from office and in 1616 several trivial charges prepared by * Bacon, the Attorney General, were brought against him and he was dismissed. A leading Member of Parliament 1621–29, he denounced interference with the liberty of the House of Commons. In 1622 he was seized and imprisoned as a result of his attacks. He vigorously opposed the Duke of * Buckingham's monopoly of office and favour, describing him as 'the grievance of grievances'. Coke's law reports helped to systematise and consolidate the Common Law of England and his writings on jurisprudence, such as the four *Institutes* are well known, especially *Coke on Littleton*.
Holdsworth, W. S., *A History of English Law*. 2nd ed., vol. 5. 1937. Throne, S. E., *Sir Edward Coke*. 1957

Coke (of Holkham), Thomas William *see* **1st Earl of Leicester**

Colbert, Jean Baptiste (1619–1683). French administrator. After the death of Mazarin he became the Chief Minister of Louis XIV. As Controller General of Finance 1665–83, he repaid most of the national debt, re-organized the French Navy, established new colonies in Africa and America, encouraged ship-building and foreign trade and reformed the French administrative service. To finance these reforms he had to introduce higher taxation which made him unpopular.
Mongredien, G., *Colbert, 1619–1683*. 1963

Cole, George Douglas Howard (1889–1959). English economist. The author of *The Common People* (with Raymond Postgate) (1938) and *The Intelligent Man's Guide to the Post-War World* (1947), he became Professor of Social and Political Theory at Oxford University in 1944 and was active in the Labour Party and the Fabian Society. With his wife he wrote a number of detective stories.

Cole, Nat(haniel Adams) 'King' (1919–1965). American singer and jazz pianist, born in

Montgomery, Alabama. He first gained recognition as the leader of a jazz trio in the 1930s. Later he performed mainly as a singer. He had wide popular success with his more sentimental songs.

Coleridge, Samuel Taylor (1772–1834). English poet and philosopher. After leaving Cambridge University he became a friend of * Southey and * Wordsworth and with the latter he published *Lyrical Ballads* in 1798. This volume was a major contribution to the Romantic Revival in English literature. Coleridge's poems in this volume include *The Rime of the Ancient Mariner* and *The Nightingale*. He was keenly interested in religion and philosophy and, for several years, was a Unitarian preacher. At this time he wrote *Christabel* and his best-known poem *Kubla Khan*, which he claimed to be part of a longer poem that he heard in an opium dream. After 1800 he was completely addicted to opium and was dependent on the charity of friends. In his own time he was celebrated as a dazzling conversationalist but later, because of debt and increasing ill-health, he became a melancholic. His principles of literary criticism are to be found in his *Biographia Literaria* (1817) and he is regarded as the founder of the modern school of Shakespearian criticism. He was also interested in metaphysics and translated the works of several of the German idealist philosophers. Although most of his poetry is of uneven quality, at its best his work has mysterious and magical beauty which echoes the music of a visionary world.
Bate, W. J., *Coleridge*. 1968. Wilson Knight, G., *The Starlit Dome*. Repr. 1971

Coleridge-Taylor, Samuel (1875–1912). English composer, of West African descent. His cantata *Hiawatha* achieved great success and his *Little Concert Suite* is often performed.

Colet, John (1466–1519). English theologian. A friend of * Erasmus and Thomas * More, he revived the humanist tradition in the English Church and his liberal opinions influenced the Reformation in England. He was Dean of St Paul's Cathedral 1505–19, and founder of St Paul's School.

Colette, Sidonie Gabrielle Claudine (1873–1954). French novelist. She began her working life as a music hall actress. Her first husband Willy Gauthier-Villars discovered her talent for writing and, by keeping her prisoner, forced her to produce novels which he published under his pen-name of 'Willy'. After their divorce she continued to write and the semi-autobiographical 'Claudine' novels became very popular. A brilliant observer, she wrote always of love, with a masterly understanding of human motives. Her books include *The Vagrant* (1912), *Chéri* (1929), *Claudine in Paris* (1931), and *The Cat* (1936). *Gigi* (1951) was the basis of a highly successful musical film.
Richardson, J., *Colette*. 1982

Coligny, Gaspard de (1519–1572). French soldier, admiral and Huguenot leader, brother of a cardinal. Noted as a fearless leader, he was imprisoned in Spain 1557–59 and became converted to Protestantism during this time. From 1560 he was joint leader of the Huguenots with Louis I, Prince of Condé, and did much to assist the Protestant cause. Although he was a favourite of Charles IX, he was murdered by servants of the Duc de Guise at the St Bartholmew's Day massacre.

Colijn, Hendrikus (1869–1944). Dutch Christian Democratic politician. Prime Minister 1925–26 and 1933–39, he died in German captivity.

Collingwood, Sir Cuthbert Collingwood, 1st Baron (1750–1810). English sailor. After * Nelson's death he became Commander-in-Chief of the Mediterranean Fleet, 1805–10.

Collins, Michael (1890–1922). Irish politician and soldier. From 1916 he was imprisoned several times for his part in the Sinn Fein independence movement and became Minister of Finance under * de Valera 1919–22. In 1922, with Arthur Griffith, he was responsible for the treaty which established the Irish Free State. When de Valera demanded full independence and the formation of a Republic, civil war broke out between the two Irish factions and Collins commanded the Free State forces. On the death of Griffith, he became head of the Free State Government but only ten days later he was ambushed by soldiers of the Irish Republican Army and murdered.
Taylor, R., *Michael Collins*. 1958.

Collins, Norman (Richard) (1907–1982).

English novelist. He was Director of Associated Television Corporation and formerly an official of the BBC. His books include *Love in Our Time* (1938), *London Belongs to Me* (1945) and *Children of the Archbishop* (1951).

Collins, (William) Wilkie (1824–1889). English novelist. A close friend of * Dickens, whose literary technique he influenced, he is well known for his exciting but melodramatic novels. *The Woman in White* (1860) is based on a personal experience: while he was walking with Dickens one night a distraught young woman, dressed in white, begged him for help, claiming that her life was threatened. On this theme he wrote a dramatic story, featuring the memorable villian, Count Fosco. *The Moonstone* (1868) has been described by T. S. Eliot as 'the first, the longest and the best of modern English detective novels'.

Colman, Ronald (1891–1958). English actor, resident in Hollywood. He was well known for his romantic roles in films such as *Beau Geste, Random Harvest* and *The Prisoner of Zenda.*

Colombo, (?Matteo) Realdo (1510–1559). Italian anatomist. An apothecary's son from Cremona, Colombo studied medicine under * Vesalius at Padua. Colombo succeeded Vesalius in 1544, but in 1546 he moved to Pisa, and in 1549 under papal patronage he established himself in Rome, where he spent the rest of his life. His fame rests on his great skill and experience in dissection, vivisection and autopsy. In his only book, the *De Re Anatomica* (published posthumously in 1559) he offered excellent descriptions of the eye, the pleura, and the peritoneum. But he is best known for his discovery of the course of the passage of blood from the right cardiac ventricle to the left through the lungs ('the pulmonary circuit'). From this he drew the important conclusion that it is not in the heart, but in the lungs, that venous blood is mixed with air to become arterial blood. Colombo thus switched the focus of attention away from the heart to the lungs.

Colombo's vivisections also led him to major new views on the heartbeat. He emphasized the contraction of the heart, and the importance of its expulsion of materials. Such views were later taken up by * Harvey.

Colt, Samuel (1814–1862). American inventor. In 1835 he produced the famous revolver which is named after him, and which was adopted by the U.S. Army.

Coltrane, John (William) (1926–1967). American jazz saxophonist, born in North Carolina. He made his professional debut in 1945 and worked with Dizzy Gillespie (1949–51) and Miles Davis (1955–57). He was already regarded as a leader of modern jazz in the late 1950s. From then on he became increasingly interested in experimental jazz and free form.

Colum, Padraic (1881–1972). Irish playwright and poet. He helped to found the Abbey Theatre and wrote the plays *Land* and *The Betrayal*. He was also the author of several books of verse and stories for children.

Columba, St (521–597). Irish missionary. He established a monastery at Iona (563) and was responsible for the conversion of much of Scotland.

Colombus, Christopher (Cristobal Colon) (*c.* 1446–1506). Italian explorer, born in Genoa, resident in Spain. The son of a weaver, he was a sailor from the age of 14. He married a Portuguese wife and settled in Portugal where he became a map-maker. Believing that the earth was round, and that trade routes with Asia could be established by sailing westwards, he sought many times for a patron who would enable him to prove his point. John II of Portugal refused to finance him, but he ultimately gained the support of Ferdinand and Isabella of Spain. In August 1492, with 87 men and three ships (*Nina, Pinta* and *Santa Maria*) he set sail for the west. On 12 October 1492 he sighted land which he thought to be part of India; it was in fact Watling Island in the Bahamas. He then sailed by the north coast of Cuba and landed on Haiti, which he named Hispaniola. A party of men were left there to establish a fort. On his return to Spain in March 1493 his discoveries were acclaimed and he was made a duke. His second expedition (1493–96) consisted of 17 ships and 1,500 men. He discovered Dominica and Jamaica and established the first European town in the New World on Haiti, at Isabella. Because he was unable to secure financial advantage to Spain from his discoveries he had difficulty in gaining support for a third

expedition. However, in 1498 he sailed again, and discovered the mouth of the Orinoco. Colombus was a poor administrator and after clashes with the colonists he lost his position of Viceroy of the Indies. In 1499 he was arrested by his successor, Francesco de Bobadilla, and sent back to Spain in chains. He was soon released and, although still in disfavour, (especially as the Portuguese navigator, Vasco da * Gama, had discovered a lucrative trade route to India by way of the east) was finally reinstated to his former position of honour. In a fourth voyage (1502–04) he sailed along the coast of Honduras, Nicaragua and Panama but failed to find a western passage through which he hoped to travel to India. When he returned empty handed once more, his reputation was largely destroyed and he died in poverty and semi-disgrace. He never knew that he had discovered the New World of the west and it was not until many years later that the vast wealth of this area was realised.
Morison, S. E., *Christopher Columbus, Mariner*. 1955

Combes, (Justin Louis) Emile (1835–1921). French Radical-Socialist politician. He was trained for the priesthood but became a physician. A Senator from 1885, he became Minister of Education 1895–1906, and as Premier (1902–05) introduced anti-clerical legislation (1905) which ended the Concordat of 1801 and completed the separation of Church and State.

Comenius, Johannes Amos (Jan Amos Komensky) (1592–1670). Czech educationist. A pastor of the Moravian Church, he is famous for his innovations in the methods of teachings, especially of languages, and wrote the first pictorial text book for children *Orbis sensualism pictus* (1658). He was invited to England by the Parliament in 1641 to advise on education and also assisted in reforming education in Sweden and Hungary.
Spinka, M., *John Amos Comenius: that Incomparable Moravian*. 1943

Compton, Arthur Holly (1892–1962). American physicist. He shared the Nobel Prize for Physics in 1927 (with C. T. R. Wilson) because of his research on X-rays. He was Chancellor of Washington University 1945–53. His brother **Karl Taylor Compton** (1887–1954) was President of the Massachusetts Institute of Technology 1930–49. Both brothers were associated with the development of the atomic bomb.

Compton, Dennis Charles Scott (1918–). English sportsman. He was a noted Test Cricket batsman and a football player and wrote *The End of an Innings* (1958).

Compton-Burnett, Dame Ivy (1884–1969). English novelist, born in London. Her first two novels *Dolores* (1911) and *Pastors and Masters* (1925) were followed by a sequence of seventeen more, including *Men and Wives* (1931), *A House and its Head* (1935), *Parents and Children* (1941), *Mother and Son* (1955) and *A God and his Gifts* (1963) in which she examines the complexities of lives in middle-class families in the period around 1900. Her novels consist mostly of dialogue.
Baldanaza, F., *Ivy Compton-Burnett*. 1964

Comstock, Anthony (1844–1915). American reformer. Secretary of the Society for the Supression of Vice in New York 1873–1915, his name has been used in the word 'Comstockery', meaning prudery.

Comte, Auguste Isidore Marie François (1798–1857). French philosopher and mathematician. At first strongly influenced by Saint-Simon, he was a lecturer at the Ecole Polytechnique (1833–51) until periodic attacks of insanity compelled his retirement. He was financially assisted by J. S. Mill in his later years. In his *Positive Philosophy* (published in 6 volumes from 1830–42) he preached 'humanism' in its most extreme form, stating that mankind in general (and the individual also) passes through intellectual stages – the theological (dominant in Europe until the thirteenth century) and the Positive (which he hoped would dominate Europe in the future, science taking the place of theology and philosophy). He theorised that because nothing can be ascertained beyond physical facts, it is useless to enquire into the origin of physical phenomena. Human knowledge is relative and not absolute, therefore mankind must seek moral values not in God, who is unknowable, but in the perfecting of human society on a scientific basis. This system is known as Logical Positivism. There are small Positivist Churches in several countries and these follow 'The Religion of Humanity' by worshipping the personification of man as an ideal. Comte was finally excommunicated by

the Roman Catholic Church, and he died of cancer after a long illness.
Gould, F. J., *Auguste Comte*. 1920

Conant, James Bryant (1893–1978). American chemist, administrator and educationist. He was assistant professor 1919–27 and professor of organic chemistry 1928–33 at Harvard University, becoming president of the University 1933–53. After his retirement he served as high commissioner to West Germany 1953–55 and ambassador to West Germany 1955–57. On returning to America he undertook a survey of American secondary education. Among his books are *Organic Chemistry* (1942), *Education is a Divided World* (1948), *Education and Liberty* (1953), and *The American High School Today* (1958).

Condé, de. French noble family, members of which include **Louis I de Bourbon, Prince de Condé** (1530–1569). French soldier. He was, with Gaspard de * Coligny, a leader of the Huguenot faction in the religious struggle against the party of the duc de Guise. After his defeat at the battle of Jarnac he surrendered but was treacherously slain by a Catholic officer. **Louis II de Bourbon, Prince de Condé** (1621–1686), was the great grandson of the preceding. As duc d'Enghien he defeated the forces of the Spaniards and of the Holy Roman Empire in many notable battles, 1643–46. After a bitter dispute with Cardinal * Mazarin he defected to Spain and later led the Spanish forces in several battles against the French. However, in 1659, he returned to France where he was pardoned and later commanded the armies of Louis XIV in succession to Turenne. He is commonly known as the Great Condé.
Mongredien, G., *Le Grand Condé*. 1959

Condillac, Etienne Bonnot, Abbé de (1714–1780). French philosopher. Son of a Vicomte, he took orders essentially as a means of establishing a career and income; he became one of the leading Paris *philosophes* of the mid-eighteenth century, a friend of * Rousseau and * Diderot. One of his major undertakings was to make the empirical approach to epistemology developed by * Locke thoroughly familiar in France. Condillac however pursued a more reductionist analysis than Locke. Locke believed that all human information came into the mind through the senses, but that the mind possessed innate powers of reflection on those sense-data. Condillac argued that the powers of judgement themselves were associations which had been formed on the basis of previous sensations. In this regard, Condillac in particular insisted that language itself was not innate, but was learnt through individual experience. For this reason, he was an advocate of the reform and systematization of scientific language, in order to purify thought. This idea played an important role in Lavoisier's reforms of the language of chemistry.
Le Roy, G., *La Psychologie de Condillac*. 1937

Condorcet, Marie Jean Antoine Nicolas Caritat, Marquis de (1743–1794). French philosopher, mathematician and politician. Although an aristocrat he was a supporter of the French Revolution and a member of the National Convention 1792–94. He aroused the opposition of Robespierre and committed suicide after being sentenced to death under the Terror. As a political philosopher he was strongly anti-clerical and anti-Imperialist. He supported pacificism, birth control, legal equality for both sexes, and the establishment of a social service.
Cahen, L., *Condorcet et la Révolution Française*. 1904

Confucius (Latinised form of K'ung Fu-tzu: i.e. 'Master K'ung') (*c.* 551–479 B.C.). Chinese philosopher. Virtually nothing is known of his life with any certainty, but according to legend he was born in the state of Lu (modern Shantung), the son of a soldier who belonged to an impoverished noble family. His early years were spent in poverty and after some years of manual work he became an accountant and then a teacher (*c.* 531–517), wandering through the countryside discussing ethical problems. During his travels he is thought to have met * Lao-tzu, the founder of Taoism. He married at an early age but the marriage soon ended in divorce and women are seldom mentioned in the Confucian writings. During a period of civil war Confucius fled to the neighbouring province of Chi and his fame spread throughout China. Duke Ting of Lu made him governor of the city of Chung-tu. He was minister of works and justice (501–498) and prime minister of the province (498–495) until he was forced to resign by the pleasure-seeking duke. For thirteen years he was an itinerant teacher. In 482 a new duke of Lu invited him to return and his three remain-

ing years were devoted to collating and revising the ancient Chinese scriptures. He was buried with great ceremony at K'iuh-Fow where his grave still attracts pilgrims. While Confucianism has always been regarded as the major Chinese religion, Confucius was no more a religious teacher than Socrates or Plato: he was an ethical philosopher and none of his teachings deals with the nature of God or prospects of future life. He stressed that society depends on the observance of natural relationships of authority, obedience and mutual respect, both within the family and between ruler and subject, and urged strict observance of loyalty, submission and benevolence. Many of his sayings are included in the famous *Analects* copied down by his disciples: they include Confucius' 'golden rule': 'What you do not like when done to yourself do not do to others'. Although he was never deified he has been the object of prayers and sacrifices by the Chinese and ancestor worship is inextricably linked to his teachings. Confucius was an exact contemporary of the * Buddha. H. H. Kung, one of Chiang Kai-Shek's ministers, was a direct descendant of Confucius, in the 75th generation. Until World War II, knowledge of the Confucian scriptures (*The Five Kings, The Four Books,* and the *Analects*) was compulsory for university students and civil servants.
Creel, H. G., *Confucius and the Chinese Way*. 1960

Congreve, William (1670–1729). English dramatist. He was brought up in Ireland and originally intended to become a lawyer, but went to London in 1692, and became a novelist and playwright. His best-known play is *The Way of the World* (1700) which is regarded as one of the best comedies of manners in English drama. It was a failure at first and Congreve, disappointed, abandoned writing for the stage. His other plays, including *Double Dealer* (1694), and *Love for Love* (1695), show his mastery of construction and style. He was a friend of Dryden and Swift.
Lynch, K. M., *A Congreve Gallery*. 1951

Connaught and Strathearn, Prince Arthur William Patrick Albert, 1st Duke of (1850–1942). English soldier and prince. The son of Queen Victoria, he served for many years in the British Army and was Commander-in-Chief in the Mediterranean (1907–10). He was Governor General of Canada 1911–16. His son, **Prince Arthur of Connaught** (1883–1938), was Governor General of South Africa 1920–23.

Connelly, Marc(us Cook) (1890–1980). American playwright. He wrote the plays *The Wisdom Tooth* and *Green Pastures* and won the Pulitzer Prize in 1930.

Connolly, Cyril Vernon (1903–1974). English critic. He was the editor of *Horizon* 1939–50 and his books include *Enemies of Promise* (1938) and *Condemned Playground* (1944).

Connolly, James (1870–1916). Irish socialist politician. After joining the Sinn Fein movement, he became commander-in-chief of the Easter Rising in 1916. He was captured by the British and shot.

Conrad, Joseph (Jozef Teodor Konrad Nalecz Korzeniowski) (1857–1924). Polish-born novelist, resident in England. From 1874 he worked as a seaman on French ships, joining the British merchant marine in 1880. He sailed round the world and qualified as a master in 1886. He became a naturalised British subject in 1886, retired from sea life in 1894 and devoted himself to writing. His novels, which were all written in English, include *Almayer's Folly* (1895), *An Outcast of the Islands* (1896), *The Nigger of the Narcissus* (1898), *Lord Jim* (1900), *Victory* (1915), and *The Rover* (1923). His work shows a real mastery of narrative style and great psychological insight. There is also a strong sense of the mystery of nature, especially of the sea, and of the forces summoned up in human nature in order to fight it.
Baines, J., *Joseph Conrad: A Critical Biography*. 1960

Consalvi, Cardinal Ercole (1757–1824). Italian prelate and diplomat. As Papal Secretary of State 1800–23 he proved a masterly diplomat, took part in the Paris Peace Conference of 1814 and secured the restoration of the Papal States. He followed a relatively liberal domestic policy.

Constable, John (1776–1837). English painter. His landscape paintings have received world wide recognition for their spontaneity and freshness, and greatly influenced the techniques of many nineteenth century artists, notably the Barbizon school in France. He first exhibited at the Royal Academy in 1802, but he did not gain general recognition until about 1824, when his *View on the Stour* and *The Hay Wain* were exhibited in Paris, won gold medals and aroused great admiration. His work was rooted in a deep love of the East Anglian landscape, and characterised by his ability to convey atmosphere, weather and changing light. He is considered, with * Turner, the greatest English landscape painter.

Leslie, C. R. (ed)., *Memoirs of the Life of John Constable, Composed Chiefly of his Letters*. Rev. ed. 1951.

Constant de Rebecque, (Henri) Benjamin (1761–1830). French writer and politician. A member of the Tribunate 1799–1802, he later opposed Napoleon and was banished and after the Bourbon Restoration he supported constitutional liberalism. He published the psychological novel *Adolphe* in 1816 and later wrote the monumental study *On Religion*. In 1951 *Cécile*, another of his novels, was discovered and published.

Nicolson, H., *Benjamin Constant*. 1949

Constantine I (The Great) (Flavius Valerius Aurelius Constantinus) (*c.* 280–337 A.D.). Roman Emperor 306–337. The illegitimate son of Constantius Chlorus and Helena, he served as a soldier under Diocletian and Galerius, and in 305 accompanied his father to England. Constantius died at York (Eboracum) and Constantine was acclaimed as Caesar by his troops. There were several years of struggle before his authority was fully recognised throughout the empire. In 312 he finally defeated the general Maxentius (who had been proclaimed Emperor in Rome by his troops) at the battle of Milvian Bridge. At this battle he saw a vision of the cross in the Heavens accompanied by the words 'in hoc signo vinces' (In this sign shalt thou conquer). In the following year, by the Edict of Milan, he officially recognised Christianity as a legal religion. In 324 he became sole ruler of both the Eastern and Western Empires, and after gaining the support of the Christian Church for this administration, he established an absolute monarchy. Although he did not become a baptised Christian until shortly before his death, he took an active interest in Church affairs and was responsible for calling the Council of Nicaea (325) at which the Athanasian Creed was adopted. In 325 he chose Byzantium as the capital of the Roman Empire and in 330 it was renamed Constantinople in his honour. He then made Christianity the State religion and, before he died, improved the administration of the whole Empire. His son, Flavius Claudius Constantinus, ruled as **Constantine II** 337–340. He shared the government of the Empire with his brothers, taking Britain and Gaul as his personal responsibility. He was killed in a battle against his brother Constans.

Cambridge Medieval History. 2nd ed. Vol. 4. 1966

Constantine I (1868–1923). King of Greece 1913–17; 1920–22. The son of George I of Greece, he supported Germany during World War I and was forced to abdicate by the pro-British Prime Minister Eleutherios Venizelos. After the war he was recalled by a plebiscite but abdicated once more on the failure of the Greek campaign against the Turks in Asia Minor. He was the father of three Greek kings: **Alexander, George II** and **Paul I.**

Constantine XI Palaeologus (1404–1453). Byzantine Emperor 1448–53. He was the last Emperor of the East and was killed by the Turks after the capture of Constantinople.

Constantine XIII (1940–). King of Greece 1964–67. The son of Paul I, he grew up in South Africa and won an Olympic Gold Medal for yachting in 1960. Although his grandfather was Constantine I, he adopted the numeral XIII to stress his continuity with the Byzantine (Greek) emperors before 1453. Following a military coup in April 1967, the king attempted a counter-coup in December in order to restore his personal authority: this failed and Constantine retreated to exile.

Cook, Frederick Albert (1865–1940). American physician and explorer. In 1908 he claimed to have reached the North Pole but R. E. Peary challenged this and Cook was greatly discredited. To the end of his life he still maintained that he was the first man to reach the Pole. He died in poverty after having been jailed for five years for mail frauds.

Cook, James (1728–1779). English explorer, born in Yorkshire. The son of an agricultural labourer, he joined the Royal Navy in 1755 and received rapid promotion, largely because of his skill at navigation. In 1768 he was

appointed commander of the barque *Endeavour* which was to take an expedition of scientists, headed by Sir Joseph Banks, to observe the transit of Venus, at Tahiti. On his return he circumnavigated the two islands of New Zealand and discovered the eastern coast of Australia, landing at Botany Bay (south of Sydney) in 1770. He charted the whole of the eastern coastline, which he named New South Wales, and his discovery was acclaimed on his return to England in 1771. On a second expedition (1772–75), he explored New Zealand and the New Hebrides and discovered Antarctica. By scientific control of diet, he was able to eliminate scurvy in his crew and for this achievement he was awarded the Copley Medal of the Royal Society. On his third voyage to the Pacific (1776–79) he circumnavigated New Zealand, discovered the Hawaiian Islands (which he called the Sandwich Islands) and charted the Pacific coast of North America up to the Arctic regions in an unsuccessful attempt to find a passage around North America from the Pacific. On returning to Hawaii he was involved in a scuffle with natives over a stolen boat and was clubbed to death.
Beaglehole, J. C. (ed.), *The Journals of Captain James Cook*. 1955–67

Cook, Sir Joseph (1860–1947). Australian Nationalist politician, at first (until 1894) Labor. Originally a coalminer in Staffordshire, England, he emigrated to Australia in 1885 and served as a member of the New South Wales Legislative Assembly 1891–1901. He became a member of the Federal Parliament as a free-trader in 1901. He was Prime Minister 1913–14, Minister of the Navy 1917–20 and High Commissioner in England 1921–27.

Cook, Thomas (1808–1892). English tourist agent. His firm pioneered the organisation of international tourist services which greatly encouraged European travel.
Swinglehurst, E., *Romantic Journey: Story of Thomas Cook and Victorian Travel*. 1974

Coolidge, (John) Calvin (1872–1933). 30th President of the U.S. Originally a lawyer, he became active in local politics, served in the state legislature and was Lieutenant Governor of Massachusetts 1916–19. As Governor of Massachusetts 1919–21 he won fame by his firm handling of a police strike in Boston, 1919. In 1920 he was the successful Republican candidate for the Vice-Presidency and served in that office 1921–23. On the death of W. G. Harding, he succeeded to the Presidency. He served as President of the U.S. 1923–29 and, although he was re-elected overwhelmingly in 1924, he declined to stand again 1928. He believed 'That the best government is the least government', and exercised little executive authority as President. A cold, somewhat introverted personality, he was well known for his laconic utterances.
White, W. A., *A Puritan in Babylon*. 1938.

Cooper, (Alfred) Duff, 1st Viscount Norwich (1890–1954). English Conservative politician. A Member of Parliament 1924–29, 1931–45, he was Secretary of State for War 1935–37, First Lord of the Admiralty 1937–38 (resigning as a protest against Chamberlain's appeasement policy), Minister of Information 1940–41, and Ambassador to France 1944–47. A skilful author, he wrote biographies of Haig, Foch, and Talleyrand. In 1919 he married **Lady Diana Manners** (1896–), a daughter of the Duke of Rutland, a famous beauty and actress.
Cooper, D., *The Light of Common Day*. 1959; *Trumpets from the Steep*. 1960

Cooper, Gary (Frank James Cooper) (1901–1961). American film actor. He appeared in many films as a vigorous man of action. The best-known are *For Whom the Bell Tolls, Sergeant York* and *High Noon*.

Cooper, James Fenimore (1789–1851). American writer. His dramatic stories of the adventures of the pioneers with the American Indians include *The Last of the Mohicans* (1826), *The Pathfinder* (1840), and *The Deerslayer* (1841). His novels were very popular in France (where he lived for some years) and were praised by Victor Hugo and Balzac.
Grossman, J., *James Fenimore Cooper*. 1949

Coote, Sir Eyre (1726–1783). English soldier. He served under * Clive at the battle of Plassey; after the latter's death he became Commander-in-Chief in India 1779–83 and helped to complete the conquest of India.

Copernicus, Nicolaus (Mikolaj Koppernigk) (1473–1543). Polish astronomer, born in Thorn (Prussian Poland). He studied astronomy, mathematics and medicine and

was physician to his uncle, the Bishop of Ermeland, 1506–12. Although he was not in holy orders, his uncle appointed him to the office of Canon of Frauenburg in 1513 and he held this position until his death. For over thirty years he studied the theory, first enunciated by Pythagoras, that the earth is not the centre of the solar system, and his great work which lays down his final conclusions was not published until shortly before his death. In this book *De revolutionibus orbium coelestium*, he proved that the sun is the centre of the solar system and the earth rotates daily on its axis and that other planets also revolve around the sun in orbits. He is regarded as the founder of modern astronomy.
Rudnicki, J., *Nicholas Copernicus*. 1943

Copland, Aaron (1900–). American composer, born in New York. His parents came from Russia, where the family name was Kaplan. His works, mostly for orchestra, have great rhythmic vitality and many critics consider him the leading contemporary American composer. His music includes the ballets *El Salón Mexico, Appalachian Spring, Billy the Kid* and *The Tender Land* (an opera).
Smith, J., *Aaron Copland*. 1955

Copley, John Singleton (1738–1815). American portrait painter. Noted for his 'Boston portraits' of New England families, he moved to England in 1774 and extended his work into the genre of historical paintings. These were technically sophisticated but they lacked the vigour of his early work and his reputation suffered.

Coppola, Francis Ford (1939–). American film director and writer. The son of a musician, educated at UCLA, his extremely successful films included *The Godfather* (1972), *Godfather II* (1974), *The Conversation* (1974) and *Apocalypse Now* (1979).

Coquelin, Benoît-Constant (1841–1909). French actor. He made his debut at the Comédie Française in 1860, and became a full member of the company at 23. His range was exceptionally wide, and he excelled at the broadest comedy and most delicate pathos. He formed his own company in 1892. In 1895–97 he worked at the Renaissance Theatre, Paris. In 1897 he was a director of the Théâtre de la Porte-Saint-Martin, where he created the part of Cyrano de Bergerac in Rostand's play. In 1900 he toured with Sarah Bernhardt; he acted at her theatre during the last years of his career.
Coquelin, B.-C., *L'Art du Comédien*. 1894

Corbett, James J. (1866–1933). American pugilist, known as 'Gentleman Jim'. He was the World's Heavyweight Champion from 1892, when he beat Sullivan, to 1897 when he was defeated by Fitzsimmons.

Corbusier, Le *see* **Le Corbusier**

Corday, Charlotte (Marie Anne Charlotte Corday d'Armont) (1768–1793). French assassin and revolutionary. A member of an old Norman family, she supported the principles of the French Revolution, but, horrified by the Reign of Terror, she murdered one of the Jacobin leaders, Jean Paul * Marat, by stabbing him in his bath. She was guillotined four days later.

Corelli, Arcangelo (1653–1713). Italian composer and violinist. He toured throughout Europe, was hailed as a great virtuoso performer and is regarded as the creator of the Concerto Grosso. He wrote sixty of these and his well-constructed works influenced Bach and Handel.
Pincherle, M., *Corelli et son temps*. 1954

Corelli, Marie (Mary Mackay) (1855–1924). English novelist. Her books, which include *The Mighty Atom, The Sorrows of Satan* and *God's Good Man* were enormously popular, but are now regarded as too romantic and too ponderous in style for contemporary taste.

Cori, Carl Ferdinand (1896–). American biochemist, born in Czechoslovakia. Professor of Biochemistry at Washington University from 1931, he and his wife **Gerty Theresa Cori** (née Radnitz) (1896–1957) shared the Nobel Prize for Medicine in 1947 for their studies in carbohydrate metabolism.

Coriolanus, Gaius Marcius (fl. 490 B.C.). Roman hero. After being exiled from Rome he became Commander of the Volscian army, leading it against Rome. He stopped his forces outside the city in response to the pleas of his wife and mother, and was killed by the Volsces as a result. Shakespeare wrote a tragic play on this theme.

Corneille, Pierre (1606–1684). French playwright, born in Rouen of a middle-class family. Educated by the Jesuits, he became a lawyer and was crown counsel in Rouen until 1650. Between 1631 and 1635 he had written seven successful comedies, was awarded a pension by Cardinal Richelieu and became nationally famous with his drama *El Cid* (1637?) which led to an obscure quarrel over royalties and the loss of the Cardinal's favour. Corneille's later plays were mostly tragedies, dramatic rather than cathartic, written in Alexandrine verse, physically static but emotionally vigorous and brilliantly characterised, generally turning on the conflict between two duties, and mostly based on classical subjects. They include *Médée* (1637), *Horace* (1640), *Cinna* (1641), *Polyeucte* (1643), *Oedipe* (1659), *Othon* (1664) and *Suréna* (1674). He was greatly admired by Molière, Voltaire, Napoleon and Balzac. He became a member of the Académie Française in 1647. HIs brother **Thomas Corneille** (1625–1709) was the author of two very successful plays *Timocrate* (1656) and *Ariane* (1672).
Stegmann, A., ed., *Oeuvres complètes de Pierre Corneille*. 1963. Yarrow, P., *Corneille*. 1963

Cornforth, Sir John Warcup (1917–). Australian research scientist, born in Sydney. Educated at Sydney and Oxford Universities he worked for the UK Medical Research Council 1946–62, directed the Shell chemical enzyme laboratory 1962–75 and won the 1975 Nobel Prize for Chemistry.

Cornwall, Earl of *see* **Richard, Earl of Cornwall**

Cornwallis, General Charles Cornwallis, 1st Marquess (1738–1805). English soldier and politician. Educated at Eton and Cambridge, he was a Member of Parliament 1760–62, and served in British forces (under Howe and Clinton) in the American War of Independence from 1776, until forced to surrender at Yorktown in 1781. He was Governor-General of India 1786–93 and 1805, and Viceroy of Ireland 1798–1801.

Corot, Jean Baptist Camille (1796–1875). French painter. Most of his works are landscapes, noted for their sombre yet subtle tints, and he was one of the leaders of the Barbizon school.
Bazin, G., *Corot*. 1942

Correggio, Antonio Allegri da (*c*. 1494–1534). Italian painter. His works are mostly on religious subjects and show great mastery of the art of composition. One of the best-known is *The Ascension of the Virgin* in Parma Cathedral.
Bevilacqua, A., and Quintavalle, A. C., *L'opera completa del Correggio*. 1970.

Cortez, Hernando (1485–1547). Spanish explorer and administrator. In 1518 he led an army of 508 men which explored Mexico. In 1519 they entered Mexico City where they captured the Aztec Emperor, Montezuma II, holding him as a hostage. He died of wounds some days later and the Aztecs drove the Spaniards out. In 1521 Cortez returned with a larger army and conquered the whole country, which he ruled as Governor 1523–26. In 1536 he discovered lower California, but after his return to Spain he died in neglect.
Madariaga, S. de, *Hernán Cortéz, Conqueror of Mexico*. 1941

Cortot, Alfred (1877–1962). French pianist and conductor. For some years he devoted himself to the production of Wagner operas but later became famous as an interpreter of Chopin's piano works.

Corvo, Baron (Frederick William Rolfe) (1860–1913). English writer and eccentric. As a young man he trained for the Roman Catholic priesthood but was rejected. This disappointment soured his whole outlook. As a morose drifter, he embittered not only his own life but those of his friends. His books are generally on religious or philosophical subjects and include *Hadrian VII* and *Desire and Pursuit of the Whole*.
Woolf, C., and Sewell, B., eds., *New Quests for Corvo*. 1965

Cosgrave, William Thomas (1888–1965). Irish politician. Originally a grocer, he became active in the Irish Nationalist Movement and was a Member of the House of Commons (1918–22), although he did not take his seat. Following the sudden deaths of Arthur Griffith and Michael Collins, he became the first Prime Minister (President of the Executive Council) of the Irish Free State

1922–32. His son, **Liam Cosgrave** (1920–) was Minister for External Affairs 1954–57, and Prime Minister 1973–77.

Costa, Lúcio (1902–). Brazilian architect. He was appointed director of the School of Fine Arts in 1931. He was one of a team responsible for the Ministry of Education and Health building in Rio (1937–43) which is regarded as pioneering modern architecture in Brazil. He designed the plan for the city of Brasília in 1956.

Costello, John Aloysius (1891–1976). Irish politician. A barrister, he became Attorney-General under Cosgrave 1926–32 and was Prime Minister of Ireland 1948–51 and 1954–57. He was the leader of the Fine Gael Party, which opposed the Fianna Fael of Eamon* de Valera.

Cotman, John Sell (1782–1842). English landscape painter and etcher. With *Crome he is considered the leading member of the Norwich School. He had a deep interest in architecture, and painted landscapes with a strong structural form, emphasised by flat washes. His *Liber Studorium* of 1838 consists of 48 soft-ground etchings, and is considered a land-mark in etching technique.
Kitson, S. D., *The Life of John Sell Cotman*. 1937

Cotton, Charles (1630–1687). English poet. He was a country gentleman who wrote some beautiful short lyrics, admired by Wordsworth. He translated the *Essays* of Montaigne, and became the friend of Izaak Walton, to whose *Compleat Angler* he contributed. He wrote many parodies of the works of classical authors.

Coty, René Jules Gustave (1882–1962). French conservative politician. Originally a lawyer, he was active in local government and served as a Deputy 1923–35 and a Senator 1935–42. He took no part in politics during the war, but after the Liberation was re-elected as a Deputy (1945) and Senator (1948). He became Minister of Reconstruction (1947) and was Vice-President of the Senate 1949–53. In December 1953 on the thirteenth ballot he was elected as President of the Republic as a compromise candidate. In 1959 he retired from the Presidency in favour of General de Gaulle.

Coubertin, Pierre, Baron de (1863–1937). French publicist and educator. He was responsible for the revival of the Olympic Games and presided at the first modern Olympiad in Athens in 1896. He was President of the International Olympic Federation 1894–1925.

Coué, Emile (1857–1926). French psychotherapist. He believed that auto-suggestion has a powerful effect on sickness (even organic disease) and his slogan 'Every day, in every way, I am getting better and better' became extraordinarily popular in the 1920s.

Coughlin, Charles Edward (1891–1979). American priest, born in Canada. He began broadcasting from Detroit, Michigan, in the 1920s, originally in opposition to the Ku Klux Klan. In the period 1930–36 he had a weekly audience of more than 10 million. Originally a supporter of the New Deal, he turned strongly against Roosevelt and in 1935 formed the National Union of Social Justice which had anti-Semitic and pro-Fascist tendencies. In 1942 his broadcasts were banned and he quickly lost influence. Joseph P. Kennedy was a strong supporter of Father Coughlin.

Coulomb, Charles Augustin de (1736–1806). French physicist. Noted for his work on electricity and magnetism, he was a military engineer by profession, and invented a magnetoscope, a magnometer and a torsion balance. He proved that the force of attraction between two electrical charges is inversely proportional to the square of their distance: this is known as 'Coulomb's Law'. A 'coulomb' is the standard unit of electrical quantity, a current of one ampère per second. In 1802 Napoleon appointed him as inspector of schools.

Couperin, François (1668–1733). French composer, harpsichordist and organist, known as 'Couperin le Grand'. His family produced many notable musicians. He studied the works of Corelli and Lully, becoming a church organist at St Gervais in Paris (from 1683) and music-master at the Royal Court 1717–33. He was a great keyboard virtuoso and composed more than 300 vivacious and graceful harpsichord works which greatly influenced J. S. Bach and Handel. He also wrote chamber music, songs and religious works.

Mellers, W., *François Couperin and the French Classical Tradition*. 1950

Courbet, Gustave (1819–1877). French realist painter. Originally a student of theology, he taught himself painting by copying the works exhibited in the Louvre and ultimately became one of the most prolific of all French artists. His realism in painting made him the enemy of the traditionalists, and his original technique influenced later French schools. An atheist and socialist, he was active in the Paris Commune, sitting as a member of the revolutionary assembly (1871). He later served six months in jail, before he fled to Switzerland where he died. His best-known works include *Casseurs de Pierres, Baigneuses* and *Fileuses*.
Zahar, M., *Gustave Courbet*. 1950

Courtauld, Samuel (1876–1947). British industrialist and patron of the arts. As chairman of Courtauld's textile company he pioneered the commercial development of man-made fibres. His collection of French paintings became the nucleus of the collection at Home House, where he also set up the Courtauld Institute for the study of art history.

Courtneidge, Dame Cicely (1893–1980). English actress and impressionist, born in Sydney. A gifted comedienne, she appeared in plays and films and was a notable broadcaster. She married the actor Jack Hulbert. She was created a D.B.E. in 1972.

Cousin, Victor (1792–1867). French philosopher and educationist. A popular lecturer at the Sorbonne, he developed what he termed 'eclectic' philosophy, insisting that truth can be discerned by 'intuition'. As Minister of Education 1840–51, he introduced many reforms into French primary education, most of them derived from Germany. He translated Plato's works and wrote studies on Pascal and Kant.

Cousins, Frank (1904–). English trade union leader. He succeeded Arthur Deakin as Secretary of the Transport and General Workers' Union 1956–69. He was Labour Minister of Technology 1964–66, seconded for the post when he was T.G.W.U. Secretary. He was M.P. for Nuneaton (1965–66).
Stewart, M., *Frank Cousins*. 1968

Cousteau, Jacques-Yves (1910–). French author and marine explorer. He was one of the inventors of the aqualung (1936) and helped to make skin-diving popular. He has pioneered under-water exploration in specially-designed craft, producing notable colour-films of his descents.
Cousteau, J.-Y., *The Ocean World of Jacques Cousteau*. 20 vols. 1973

Couthon, Georges (1755–179). French revolutionary. A cripple, and trained as a lawyer, he was a member of the Legislative Assembly 1791–92, a member of the Convention 1792–94 and of the Committee of Public Safety 1793–94. He was guillotined with Robespierre.

Couve de Murville, Maurice (1907–). French diplomat and politician. He served as French Ambassador to Egypt 1950–54, to N.A.T.O. 1954–55, to the United States 1955–56 and to West Germany 1956–58. President de Gaulle appointed him Minister for Foreign Affairs 1958–68; in 1968 he was Minister of Finance and Economy (June and July) and then Prime Minister, 1968–69. He was Chairman of the Foreign Affairs Committee of the National Assembly from 1973.
Couve de Murville, M., *Une politique étrangére, 1958–1969*. 1973

Coverdale, Miles (1488–1569). English prelate and translator. Born in Yorkshire, he was educated at Cambridge and joined the Augustinian order, later becoming an ardent Protestant. In 1535 he published his own translation of the Bible, including the Apocrypha, based on German and Latin versions. This was the first complete translation to appear in English and, from 1539, he was in charge of the printing of 'The Great Bible'. He was a Puritan and, because of his extreme views, spent several years in European exile, mostly in Germany 1543–48 and 1555–59. A notable preacher, he was Bishop of Exeter 1551–53 but lost this office on the accession of Queen Mary.
Fry, F., *The Bible by Coverdale*. 1867

Coward, Sir Noël (Pierce) (1899–1973). English playwright, actor, producer and composer, born in Teddington. He made his stage debut as a boy and became a popular per-

former in light comedies. His first play *The Vortex* was a portrayal of decadence and caused a sensation when produced in London in 1923. It was followed by many sophisticated comedies including *Hay Fever* (1925), *Private Lives* (1930), *Blithe Spirit* (1931), *Present Laughter* (1943) and *Nude with Violin* (1956). He composed the music and wrote the dialogue for the musical comedies *Bitter Sweet* (1929) and *Words and Music* (1934). He wrote and produced the successful films *Cavalcade* (1938), *In Which We Serve* (1942), *This Happy Breed* (1944), *Blithe Spirit* (1945) and *Brief Encounter* (1947). Among his other works were several volumes of autobiography, e.g. *Future Indefinite* (1954) and a number of witty songs, e.g. 'Mad Dogs and Englishmen'. He was an accomplished actor who appeared in a number of films, e.g. *In Which We Serve* and *Our Man in Havana*. After World War II he lived in Bermuda. He was knighted in 1970.
Morley, S., *Noël Coward*. 1969

Cowley, Abraham (1618–1667). English essayist and metaphysical poet. Educated at Cambridge, he wrote a series of pastoral comedies as a young man but was expelled from university in 1643 on account of his Royalist sympathies during the Civil War. He lived on the Continent 1646–56 and undertook confidential missions for the Royal family. Later he became a physician and actively engaged in botanical experiments. His poems include *The Mistress* and *Pindaresque Odes*.

Cowper, William (1731–1800). English poet, trained as a lawyer. His verse was popular in his lifetime because of its directness and the natural sympathy he expressed towards everyday scenes and events. His life was characterized by evangelical religious fervour and periods of melancholia and mental instability. He collaborated with the great Evangelical divine John Newton in writing *Olney Hymns* (1779).
Ryscamp, C., *William Cowper*. 1959

Cox, James Middleton (1870–1957). U.S. newspaper publisher and politician. He was Governor of Ohio 1913–15 and 1917–21, and became Democratic candidate for President in 1920, running as a supporter of * Wilson's policies with F. D. * Roosevelt as his running mate. He was heavily defeated by Warren * Harding.

Cozens, Alexander (*c.* 1715–1786). English landscape painter. Born in Russia, he settled in England (1746) and from 1763 to 1768 was drawing master at Eton. His watercolour landscapes are mainly in monochrome and are sometimes almost impressionistic in technique. His son **John Robert Cozens** (1752–*c.* 1799), whom he taught, started to work in monochrome but later used a fuller range of colour.
Oppé, A. P., *Alexander and John Cozens*. 1954

Cozzens, James Gould (1903–1978). American author. His novels show a preoccupation with social problems and have been highly esteemed. They include *The S.S. San Pedro* (1931), *The Last Adam* (1933), *Men and Brethren* (1936), *The Just and the Unjust* (1943), *Guard of Honour* (1948) and *By Love Possessed* (1958). He won the Pulitzer Prize in 1949.

Crabbe, George (1754–1832). English poet. He was born at Aldeburgh, Suffolk, and went to London to seek success as a writer. Edmund Burke, to whom he had sent some poems, gave him encouragement, as did Dr Johnson. In *The Library* (1781), *The Village* (1783) and *The Newspaper* (1783), he showed that stark but vivid realism which is his predominant characteristic. He took holy orders and in the following years, when he was chaplain to the Duke of Rutland (1783–85) and then a parish priest, he published nothing further. In 1807 came *The Parish Register*, and *The Borough* in 1810. A tale in the latter inspired Benjamin Britten's opera *Peter Grimes*. His *Tales* (1812) and *Tales of the Hall* (1819) again show his realistic appreciation of character and somewhat grim sense of humour. Indeed his skill in telling a short story in verse is Crabbe's main contribution to the art of English poetry.
Blunden, E. (ed.), *The Complete Works of George Crabbe*. 1947

Craig, (Edward) Gordon (1872–1966). English theatrical designer, producer and actor. Son of Ellen * Terry, he acted on the London stage for some years, under Irving, but after 1900 he devoted himself to stage design and production. His first production (at the Hampstead Conservatoire, London) was followed by a few others (e.g. Ibsen's *Vikings* and Shakespeare's *Much Ado About Nothing*), but after 1904 he had no productions in London and only a few on the

continent (e.g. his notable *Hamlet* in Moscow in 1912). His outstanding influence upon modern stage production was conveyed through his books, *The Art of the Theatre* (1905), *Towards a New Theatre* (1913), *Scene* (1923) and his magazine *Mask*. By simplifying three-dimensional scenery with costumes and lighting effects in harmony, he conceived a production as a unified and complete work of art. He spent several years in Florence, where he started a school of stage design.
Craig, E. G., *Gordon Craig: The Story of his Life*. 1968

Craigavon, James Craig, 1st Viscount (1871–1940). Ulster politician. In the House of Commons (1906–21) he made his name as a bitter opponent of Home Rule for Ireland. After the partition of the country he was the first prime minister (1921–40) of Northern Ireland (Ulster).

Craik, Mrs Dinah Maria (née Mulock) (1826–1887). English writer. Famed for a single novel, *John Halifax, Gentleman* (1856), she wrote many other novels, essays and verse.

Cram, Ralph Adams (1863–1942). American architect. His work showed great skill and originality in adapting the Gothic style to modern needs. He was architect for the Cathedral of St John the Divine, New York, and his many churches include the Church of Calvary, Pittsburgh, and the Fourth Presbyterian Church, Chicago. Several of the buildings of Princeton University, including the chapel, are also his.

Cranach, Lucas (1472–1553). German painter and engraver. His name was derived from Kronach in Franconia, where he was born. His earlier work included religious subjects (e.g. *Rest on the Flight to Egypt*) with idyllic backgrounds and remarkable for their fresh colouring. He also executed many woodcuts. In 1505 he became a painter to the Saxon court at Wittenberg. He became an ardent Protestant and among his many portraits – in which he is inclined to over-concentrate on the accessories of dress – is one of Luther. Two of his sons were trained by him, **Lucas Cranach** (1515–1586), whose work is often indistinguishable from that of his father, and **Hans Cranach** (died 1537).
Thone, F., *Lukas Cranach der Ältere*. 1965

Crane, (Harold) **Hart** (1899–1932). American poet. After working as a reporter in New York, he drifted unhappily through a succession of odd jobs. Most of his poetry, which shows the influence of Rimbaud and Whitman, was published in two volumes, *White Buildings* (1926) and *The Bridge* (1930), which has been called 'a mystical interpretation of the past, present and future of America'. He jumped over the side of a ship in despair at his homosexuality and alcoholism.

Crane, Stephen (1871–1900). American writer and war correspondent. He wrote two novels, the stark and powerful *Maggie, A Girl of the Streets* (1892), ignored at the time of publication, and *The Red Badge of Courage* (1895), a sensitive account of heroism under fire in the American Civil War. Its success led to his appointment as war correspondent in the Greco-Turkish and Spanish–American Wars. He also wrote poetry and realistic short stories. From 1898 he lived in England and came to know Joseph Conrad, Henry James and other writers. He died of tuberculosis.
Stallman, R. W., *Stephen Crane: a Critical Bibliography*. 1972

Crane, Walter (1845–1915). English artist. He is best known as an illustrator (e.g. of the Toy-book series). Like William * Morris he sought to ally art to industry and everyday objects.

Cranmer, Thomas (1489–1556). English prelate. Born in Nottinghamshire, he was educated at Cambridge University, where later he became a fellow of Jesus College and lectured in divinity, though at the same time studying Luther's works. In 1529 he attracted the attention of Henry VIII by expressing his opinion that Henry's reasons for divorcing Catherine of Aragon were valid, and that views from European universities should be sought. Cranmer himself was sent on missions abroad to rally support and in 1530 arrived in Rome to present the case for annulment of the marriage to the pope. In January 1533 he was appointed archbishop of Canterbury. He declared the King's marriage null and void, just as later he again supported the king in the proceedings which led to Anne Boleyn's execution. He supported too, the Act of Supremacy (1534) which asserted the royal headship of the Church of England. He also encouraged the English translations of the

Bible but failed to reach doctrinal agreement with the German reformers, with the result that little change in doctrine was made in Henry's reign. The two prayer books of Edward VI's reign, the latter little different from the *Book of Common Prayer* (of Charles II's reign) still used, were, however, largely due to Cranmer's work and inspiration, and his gift for noble and sonorous expression is fully displayed. When Mary came to the throne his Protestantism, combined with his support for Lady Jane * Grey, made his fate inevitable. He tried to save his life by a recantation of his opinions, but this he afterwards withdrew and met his death at the stake at Oxford with the same courage as his fellow martyrs, * Ridley and * Latimer.
Pollard, A. F., *Thomas Cranmer and the English Reformation, 1489–1556*. 1966

Crashaw, Richard (1613–1649). English poet. The son of a Puritan clergyman, he was educated at Charterhouse and Cambridge University. While at Peterhouse, he became a Roman Catholic and in 1643 fled abroad. He eventually obtained a benefice at Loretto, where he died soon after his arrival. His gentle character made him much loved. He wrote secular and religious poems in both Latin and English; his fame mainly rests on those in which devotion and mystical experience are expressed in ardent, almost sensual terms.

Crassus, Marcus Licinius (*c.* 110–53 B.C.). Roman magnate. Considered to be the wealthiest Roman of his time, he used his money for political ends and so was able to form with * Caesar and * Pompey the first triumvirate which dominated Roman politics from 60 B.C. He held the office of consul twice (70 and 55) and as part of the bargain made with his associates at Luca became governor of Syria in 54. His campaign to subdue the Parthians (53) ended in disaster in Mesopotamia and his own death.

Crawford, Francis Marion (1845–1909). American author. The cosmopolitan settings of most of his novels result from many years of travel and living abroad. Many are historical and almost all have romantic appeal. Among them are *Zoroaster* (1885), *Paul Pattoff* (1887), *Sant'Ilario* (1889), *The Cigarette-Maker's Romance* (1890), *Via Crucis* (1898).

Crébillon, Claude Prosper Jolyot de (1707–1777). French novelist. A gay and witty man of the world, he chose elegant, sophisticated and licentious themes. In his most famous work, *Le Sopha* (1745), an oriental prince transformed into a sofa is titillated by overhearing the amorous conversations of those who choose him for a resting place. His father, **Prosper Jolyot de Crébillon** (1674–1762), a playwright, was regarded as a rival to Voltaire; his sensational tragedies, e.g. *Atrée et Thyeste* (1707), were based on unnatural crimes.

Creevy, Thomas (1768–1838). English diarist. His letters and journal, covering more than forty years, give a sometimes prejudiced but always vivid account of the political and social events and gossip of his time. He married a rich widow, was elected to parliament (1802) as an adherent of Charles James Fox, spent a year in minor office and the next twenty years in opposition with the Whigs.
Creevy, T., *Creevy Papers*. 1903

Crerar, Henry Duncan Graham (1888–1965). Canadian soldier. After having commanded the Canadians in Italy and the Mediterranean area (1943–44) he commanded the Canadian 1st Corps, which formed (1944–45) the left wing of the great Allied liberating drive from Normandy to the German frontier.

Cressent, Charles (1685–1768). French cabinet-maker. Considered the greatest in the Regency style and one of the greatest in the eighteenth century, he began his career in the studios of Boulle, and was appointed official cabinet maker to the Duke of Orleans, regent of France, in 1715. He was a skilled metal-worker, not only designing and making his pieces but casting and carving their characteristic gilded-bronze ornaments himself.
Verlet, P., *Les Meubles Français du XVIIIe siècle*. 1956

Crichton, James (1560–1582). Scottish scholar. Known as 'the Admirable Crichton' for his skill as a poet, linguist, mathematician and athlete, he graduated from St Andrew's University at the age of 15, left Scotland in 1577 and in the course of his continental travels gained fame by his ability to carry out disputations in many languages. He was killed in Mantua in a street brawl. (The play *The Admirable Crichton* by * Barrie is wholly unrelated.)

Crick, Francis Harry Compton (1916–). British molecular biologist, born in Northampton. Educated at Mill Hill School, he graduated in physics from University College, London and worked for the Admiralty developing magnetic mines during World War II. From 1947 he worked at Cambridge, first at the Strangeways research laboratory (1947–49), then at the Medical Research Council's molecular biology laboratory (1949–77). At the Cavendish laboratories he worked with J. D. * Watson on the molecular structure of DNA (deoxyribonucleic acid), partly basing their work on the X-ray diffraction studies of M. H. F. * Wilkins and Rosalind * Franklin. Crick and Watson published a joint paper in *Nature* (25 April 1953) explaining the double helical structure of DNA, the chemical bases joining the helixes (like steps on a staircase) and the replication mechanism. This was regarded as one of the greatest scientific discoveries in all biology, in the face of fierce competition e.g. from Linus * Pauling and many others. In 1962 Crick, Watson and Watkins shared the Nobel Prize for Physiology or Medicine. Crick was a fellow at the Salk Institute at San Diego 1962–73 and a research professor there 1977– . He proposed what he called the 'central dogma of molecular biology' (1970)—that DNA determines how cells will grow, that RNA acts as a transmission line, and 'information' is passed on to the protein which changes as directed. He wrote *Of Molecules and Men* (1966) and in the controversial *Life Itself* (1981) proposed the concept of 'directed panspermia'—that bacteria were introduced to earth from other planets.
Judson, H. F., *The Eighth Day of Creation*. 1979.

Crippen, Hawley Harvey (1865–1910). American-born murderer, resident in London. In 1910 he poisoned his wife, a music-hall actress known as Belle Elmore, and concealed her dismembered body beneath the floor of his house. With his mistress, Ethel Le Neve, who was dressed as a boy, 'Dr' Crippen sailed for America but was arrested on the ship as the result of a wireless signal – the first time this new invention had been used to bring a criminal to justice. Crippen was found guilty and hanged; Ethel Le Neve was acquitted.

Cripps, Sir (Richard) Stafford (1889–1952). British politician. Son of the ecclesiastical lawyer who became Lord Parmoor and served in the Labour government of 1924 and 1929. Cripps, who was educated at Winchester and London University, was already one of the most successful lawyers in the country when he became immersed in politics. First elected to parliament in 1931 after being appointed solicitor general to Ramsay MacDonald's second Labour government, he was expelled from the Labour party (1939) for supporting a 'Popular Front' with the Communists; but in World War II he was ambassador to Russia (1940–42), lord privy seal (1942) and minister for aircraft production (1942–45). In 1942 he failed in a mission to India to secure agreement among Indians on the terms on which a promise to give dominion status to India after the war could be fulfilled. In Attlee's post-war Labour government, Cripps, as president of the Board of Trade and chancellor of the exchequer, was especially associated with the austerity policy of rationing and controls. Illness forced him to retire in 1950.
Cripps, S., *Towards a Christian Democracy*. 1945

Crispi, Francesco (1819–1901). Italian politician, born in Sicily. A republican, inspired by * Mazzini, he took refuge in France after the collapse of the 1848 revolution. He landed in Sicily with * Garibaldi's Thousand in 1860. He accepted the monarchy of * Victor Emmanuel as a unifying force, and in the Chamber of Deputies gained a great reputation for independence and his support of a nationalism based on moral unity. As president of the Chamber from 1887 he abandoned Italy's traditional amity with France by strengthening the Triple Alliance with Germany and Austria. He also developed the Italian settlements in East Africa, Somalia and Eritrea. The crushing defeat of the Italians at Adowa (1896) obliged him to resign.

Cristofori, Bartoloméo (1655–1731). Italian harpsichord-maker. In about 1709 he invented a harpsichord that would produce a soft or loud note according to the pressure on the keys. This he did by introducing a hammer action in place of the former plucking of the strings. The instrument was the first 'pianoforte' ('soft-loud') and the forerunner of the present pianoforte.

Crivelli, Carlo (*c.* 1430–*c.* 1495). Venetian painter, mainly of altar-pieces and pictures illustrating the life of the Madonna. His *Annunciation* in the National Gallery, London, is remarkable for its background ornamentation (which includes a peacock, a hanging carpet and many other decorative objects) and the mathematical precision of its perspective.

Croce, Benedetto (1866–1952). Italian philosopher, historian and critic. He lost both parents and his sister in an earthquake at Ischia (1883) from which he narrowly escaped. He was minister of education in the Italian government (1920–21), but withdrew from politics when Mussolini came to power. He returned to head the liberal party after World War II. His philosophy, influenced by Hegel, is an idealism which holds that the only reality is mind or spirit. This is not a transcendent entity, however, but rather to be identified with human experience and includes works of art. Croce's discussion of this area, which in a rather wide sense of the word he calls aesthetics, has been the most influential part of his philosophy. Actual works of art, according to Croce, are expressions of sensuous insights of artists. The insights, it is claimed, are the 'real' works of art, and the actual paintings, for example, are merely means of communicating them to others. Croce's greatest work is the *Philosophy of the Spirit* (1902–17) but his views on aesthetics are also presented in *Aesthetic* (1902). Many early formulations of his views on literature, philosophy and history appeared in *La Critica*, which he founded in 1903.
Croce, B., *An Autobiography*. 1927

Crockett, David ('Davy') (1786–1836). American hero. This semi-legendary figure of the pioneer days ('cradled in a sap trough, clouted in a coonskin . . .') was in fact a lawyer who was active in the development of Tennessee, was a member of the House of Representatives for much of the period 1817–35, and was killed at the Battle of Alamo, fighting against the Mexicans.

Croesus (reigned 560–546 B.C.). Last king of Lydia (Asia Minor). He extended his kingdom eastwards but when opposed by Cyrus, the Persian king, he was quickly overthrown and his realm annexed. It is for his proverbial wealth that he is remembered. His help in the rebuilding of the temple at Ephesus is commemorated by a column inscribed with his name, now in the British Museum.

Croker, John Wilson (1780–1857). British literary critic and politician, born in Ireland. An MP 1807–52, he was a vitriolic opponent of parliamentary reform and coined the political name 'Conservative'. He was one of the founders of the Athenaeum Club. In 1809 he helped to found the *Quarterly Review*, in which appeared his attack on *Endymion* that, in Byron's words, 'killed John Keats'. Macaulay detested him 'more than cold boiled veal'.

Crome, John (1768–1821). English painter. A leading member (with * Cotman) of the Norwich School, he began as a sign painter and educated himself in art mainly by copying works owned by a friendly local collector. Most of his life was spent in and around Norwich (where he was a drawing master) and his pictures, e.g. *The Poringland Oak*, and *Mousehold Heath*, both in the National Gallery, London, which show the serenity and spatial quality of the Dutch landscapists, are mainly of local scenes. River and windmill, skies drenched in light, meadows and storm-wrecked trees are typical subjects.
Clifford, D., and Clifford, T., *John Crome*. 1968

Cromer, Evelyn Baring, 1st Earl of (1841–1917). English diplomat and administrator. A member of a rich banking family, he was privately educated and trained in international finance. He spent some years in the army, and was successful in a number of financial posts in Egypt and India: then came the great opportunity of his life when, nominally as agent and consul general but actually as minister, he played an all-important part in the creation of modern Egypt (1883–1907). Not only did he reform and regulate finances and bring order into the administration, but he promoted such vast schemes as the irrigation projects dependent on the first Aswan dam, he developed trade, helped to create a new army and at the same time did much – though in such a context the 'much' was all too little – to ease the burden borne by the *fellaheen* (peasantry). He received his earldom in 1901. His grandson, **George Rowland Stanley Baring** (1918–), 3rd Earl of Cromer, managing director of Baring Brothers (from 1947), headed the British

Treasury's delegation in the U.S.A. (1959–61), became a director of the International Monetary Fund and the World Bank, and was governor of the Bank of England (1961–66).

Crompton, Richmal (pen-name of Richmal Crompton Lamburn) (1890–1969). English writer. Originally a schoolmistress she became famous as the authoress of the overwhelmingly popular 'William' books about the mischievous but endearing boy of that name and his friends (and enemies). By 1977, nine million of her books had been sold.

Crompton, Samuel (1753–1827). English inventor, born near Bolton, Lancashire. He was working in a spinning mill when he invented the 'spinning mule', which combined the virtues of Hargreaves' 'spinning jenny' and Arkwright's waterframe. In 1812 Crompton received a grant of £5,000, but his business ventures failed and he died in poverty only mitigated by secret gifts from friends.

Cromwell, Oliver (1599–1658). English soldier, statesman and Lord Protector of the Commonwealth. Born at Huntingdon of yeoman stock and distantly connected with Thomas * Cromwell, he was educated at Cambridge University, studied law in London and in 1620 married Elizabeth Bourchier, the daughter of a London merchant. He represented Huntingdon in Parliament (1628–29), but during the eleven years of Charles I's absolute rule (1629–40) he was active only in local affairs, though he became a fervent but not bigoted Puritan. He was MP for Cambridge in the Short and Long Parliaments (1640). Soon after the Civil War broke out (1642) he was serving under * Essex and won distinction as a cavalry officer at Edgehill. His military skill became more and more evident, his tactics being especially effective at the great parliamentary victory (1644) at Marston Moor near York. He played a principal part in the creation of the New Model Army (known as the 'Ironsides'), who were subjected to rigid discipline and stern morality. Cromwell emerged as the leader of this body and it became devoted to his interests. He was helped too by the passing of the Self Denying Ordinance (1645) under which the parliamentary generals (Cromwell himself excepted) gave up their commands. This left Fairfax and Cromwell to lead the New Model Army to victory at Naseby. This was the beginning of the end: the west country and other royalist-held areas were gradually overrun, the towns were stormed or surrendered. Charles himself was harried and chased until at last he surrendered to the Scots near Newark, only to be handed over after a year of haggling to the English parliament. In 1647 parliament and army quarrelled, Charles was seized in the name of the army and thenceforth, Fairfax being in favour of conciliation and no longer able to influence events, Charles depended for his life on Cromwell's mercy. Probably the king's intrigues with the Scots, which brought them into a war against him, made Cromwell decide that he must die. Having crushed the Scots at Preston, he caused Charles to be brought to trial and his execution followed (January 1649).

With the formation of the Commonwealth, Cromwell's only official position was his army leadership, but he gradually gathered the executive reins into his hands. First a rising of the extremist 'Levellers' had to be suppressed (1649), then he went to Ireland, still in royalist hands, and achieved a conquest by cruelties, such as the massacres of the garrisons of Drogheda and Wexford, which provoked bitter memories that still survive. His settlement, based largely on dispossessing Roman Catholic Irish and replacing them by English ex-soldiers or land speculators, was equally disastrous. In contrast, after he had crushed, at Worcester, a Scottish invasion headed by Prince Charles (the future Charles II) he brought to Scotland the advantage of union and free trade with the more prosperous and advanced England.

Meanwhile he was in trouble with the surviving members of the old parliament, known as the Rump, who had little relish for a new autocrat. Cromwell dissolved them by a show of force and called a Puritan convention, nicknamed the 'Barebones Parliament'; this proved equally intractable and was also dismissed. Supreme power now rested with Cromwell and his officers. In 1653 under an 'Instrument of Government' he was declared Protector; a council of state assisted him in his executive functions and a single-chamber parliament dealt with legislation and taxation. His ordinances had the effect of law when parliament was not in session. The members varied from the sycophants to the querulous, but Cromwell never succeeded in working with assemblies and had to rule as a virtual dictator with 'major-generals' acting as regional administrators. He was offered the crown but would have forfeited the support of the army had he accepted.

Cromwell proved as good an administrator as he had been soldier. In his religious reforms he took measures to improve the quality of the ministry but showed tolerance to all denominations other than Roman Catholicism and Anglican episcopalianism. His legal ordinances aimed at the suppression of corrupt practices, swept away many barbarous punishments and provided relief for debtors. His foreign policy was designed to strengthen English trade. Although the 1651 Navigation Act precipitated the first Dutch War (1652–54), Van Tromp found a match in Blake, whose successes brought the Commonwealth much prestige. In the war with Spain (1655–58), in which Jamaica was won, Cromwell even managed to gain the alliance of Catholic France. He died on 3 September 1658, the anniversary of his victories at Dunbar and Worcester. His body was buried in Westminster Abbey, but after the Restoration was exhumed and hanged. Cromwell believed in, and found biblical justification for, all that he did and was unquestionably among the greatest of all English rulers: but that his system struck no deep roots was proved by the fact that within two years of his death the people were cheering the return of the monarchy. His third son, **Richard Cromwell** (1626–1712), succeeded him briefly as Lord Protector (1658–59), becoming virtually a prisoner of the army which deposed him. Known as 'Tumbledown Dick', he lived in exile in Paris until 1680.

Ashley, M., *The Greatness of Oliver Cromwell*. 1966. Fraser, A., *Cromwell: Our Chief of Men*. 1973

Cromwell, Thomas, 1st Earl of Essex (*c.* 1485–1540). English statesman. Born in Surrey, the son of a blacksmith and brewer, he left home after a family quarrel and led an adventurous life on the continent before becoming established (*c.* 1513) in London as a trader. He attached himself (1514) to * Wolsey and, though elected to Parliament (1523), continued to serve him as an assistant and secretary until his downfall. This he survived and was soon proving himself as useful to King Henry VIII as he had been to Wolsey. He became chancellor of the exchequer (1533), and secretary to the king (1534); after Henry's position as head of the church was secured by the Act of Supremacy (1534) he was given the title of vicar-general, in which capacity he carried out the dissolution of the monasteries and secured a large part of their revenues for the crown. He continued to support Henry's personal schemes – he was present at the execution of Anne Boleyn – and by centralizing the administration and making it more efficient added to his power. For his services he was loaded with honours, culminating with the earldom of Essex for arranging Henry's marriage with Anne of Cleves. It was this service that proved his undoing. He was widely unpopular for his ruthlessness and self-aggrandizement and so, when the marriage failed, Henry could vent his anger in the certainty of public approval. Cromwell was arrested, condemned by bill of attainder for heresy and treason, and executed.

Dickens, A. G., *Thomas Cromwell and the English Reformation*. 1959

Cronin, Archibald Joseph (1896–1981). Scottish novelist. Originally a physician, his books include *Hatter's Castle* (1931), *The Citadel* (1937), *The Green Years* (1944) and *The Spanish Gardener* (1950).

Cronje, Piet (1835–1911). South African soldier. He was a leading figure of the Transvaal army in the first and second Boer Wars. In the early stages of the latter he had a striking success at Magersfontein when he repulsed Lord Methuen's attempt to relieve Kimberley. In the following February, however, at Paardeberg he was forced to surrender with 4,000 men to Lord Roberts. He was confined at St Helena for the rest of the war.

Crookes, Sir William (1832–1919). English chemist and physicist. He discovered (1861) the element thallium from spectroscopic investigation of selenium residues from a sulphuric-acid plant. He also investigated the properties of cathode-ray tubes, and correctly concluded that they consisted of streams of particles, later called electrons. 'Crookes glass' was designed by him to protect the eyes of industrial workers from strong radiation and is now also widely used for protection against bright sunlight. He was also president of the Society of Psychical Research (1896–99), and of the Royal Society (1913–16); among his scores of awards and distinctions was his knighthood (1897) and the O.M. (1910).

Crosby, Bing (Harry Lillis) (1904–1977). American singer and actor. He began his career as a singer with dance bands and made his debut in films in 1931. His many films include *Pennies from Heaven, Road to Singapore* (one of a series with Bob Hope), *Going my Way* (Academy Award 1944), *The Bells of St Mary's* and *White Christmas.*

Crosland, (Charles) Anthony Raven (1918–1977). British politician. After war service in North Africa and Italy, he resumed his studies at Oxford and lectured in economics there (1947–50). He was a Labour MP 1950–77, serving under Harold * Wilson in a variety of ministries (1964–70), and as Minister for Environment (1974–76). He contested the party leadership in 1976, polling badly, but James * Callaghan appointed him foreign and commonwealth secretary, a post he held until his sudden death. Crosland will be best remembered for his writings on political philosophy, especially for his advocacy of democratic socialism in a mixed economy in *The Future of Socialism* (1956) and *The Conservative Enemy* (1962).
Crosland, S., *Tony Crosland.* 1982

Crossman, Richard Howard Stafford (1907–1974). British politician. Educated at Winchester and New College, Oxford, of which he became a fellow, he soon made his mark in Labour politics and journalism. In 1945 he was elected to parliament and as chairman (1956) of a Labour working party on superannuation he sponsored a comprehensive and controversial scheme for pensions. He became party chairman in 1960 and in Harold Wilson's Labour government (1964) was minister of housing and local government. His *Diaries*, published after his death, revealed much of the workings of the Labour party in power.

Crowley, Aleister (1875–1947). British charlatan, who liked to be known as 'the wickedest man in the world'. He devised a form of Satanism, which involved many obscure and repugnant rituals, and attracted a small number of eccentric disciples.

Crowther, Geoffrey Crowther, Baron (1907–). English economist, educated at Cambridge. He was editor of the *Economist* (1938–56). As chairman of the Central Advisory Council for Education (1956–60) he produced the 1959 report (the 'Crowther Report') on secondary education in Britain.

Cruden, Alexander (1701–1770). Scottish book-seller in London. He compiled the well known *Concordance of the Holy Scriptures* (1737). He became insane soon afterwards and was subsequently subject to periods of madness in which he called himself 'Alexander the Corrector'.

Cruikshank, George (1792–1878). English caricaturist. Both his father and his elder brother were caricaturists, and it was his caricatures, especially those ridiculing participants in Queen Caroline's trial, that first attracted notice. But he is now remembered best for his illustrations, especially those for Grimm's fairy tales, Dickens's *Oliver Twist* and some of Harrison Ainsworth's novels.

Cubitt, Thomas (1788–1855). English builder and developer, founder of the firm which bears his name. Belgravia and large parts of Bloomsbury, London, bear witness to his skill in planning and construction. He was the contractor for the 1845–57 extension to Buckingham Palace, and during the same period designed and built Osborne House, Queen Victoria's house on the Isle of Wight, later used as a naval college.
Hobhouse, H., *Thomas Cubitt: Master Builder*. 1971

Cudworth, Ralph (1617–1688). English philosopher. The best known of the group of philosophers generally called the 'Cambridge Platonists', he summed up his philosophy in his *The True Intellectual System of the Universe*, a rambling uncompleted work intended to counteract materialism by proving the existence of a supreme divine intelligence. The learning displayed was immense, the presentation of his opponents' case was so fair and their arguments against the existence of God so strongly put forward that Dryden could doubt whether he had successfully demolished them.
Passmore, J. A., *Ralph Cudworth*. 1950.

Cugnot, Nicolas-Joseph (1725–1804). French military engineer. In 1769–70 he designed and built two steam-propelled vehicles for hauling heavy guns. The vehicles had three wheels, the single front wheel steering and driving. Cugnot had not solved the problems of water supply and of maintaining steam pressure, but his invention pioneered steam traction vehicles.

Cui, Cesar Antonovich (1835–1918). Russian composer of French-Lithuanian origin. He was associated with the group of composers known as 'The Five' (* Balakirev), and composed operas, piano pieces and orchestral works. By profession he was a military engineer and became a lieutenant-general.

Culbertson, Ely (1891–1955). American bridge player. Himself a brilliant player, often partnered by his first wife, Josephine, he did more than anyone else to develop and popularize contract bridge. The card-showing conventions set out in his *Gold Book of Bidding and Play* (1941) and earlier works led the way to a vast literature on modern contract bridge.

Cumberland, Ernest Augustus, Duke of (1771–1851). Fifth son of the British King George III, who was also king of Hanover. On the death of William IV (1837) Cumberland inherited the Hanoverian throne (as Ernest I), because the Salic Law prevented the succession of Queen Victoria to this kingdom.

Cumberland, William Augustus, Duke of (1721–1765). Soldier son of George II of Great Britain, known as 'Butcher'. In the War of Austrian Succession he distinguished himself at the battles of Dettingen (1743) and Fontenoy (1745). He was then recalled to meet the threat of the Jacobite invasion from Scotland under Charles Edward Stuart (the Young Pretender). Having reached Derby the Scots retreated to their own country where Cumberland gained a decisive victory at Culloden (1746). It was his severity after this battle that earned him his nickname. He commanded the Hanoverian army in the Seven Years War but, hopelessly outnumbered by the French, was defeated at Hastenberg (1757) and signed the convention of Kloster Zeven (later repudiated by George II) which left Hanover and Westphalia in French hands.

cummings, e e (Edward Estlin) (1864–1962). American poet and painter, educated at Harvard. He was imprisoned for six months during World War I by the French who mistakenly believed him to be a spy; he wrote about this experience in *The Enormous Room* (1922). His volumes of poetry are notable for their unorthodox form and abandonment of punctuation and capital letters.

Cunard, Sir Samuel, 1st Bart (1745–1856). English ship-owner, born in Nova Scotia. Having acquired experience of coastal shipping by carrying the mails from Halifax to Boston he came to England in 1838 and in 1840, in association with Robert Napier and others, started a fortnightly trans-Atlantic service. The first vessel used was the *Britannia*, a wooden paddle steamer of 1,156 tons, but iron and screw propelled ships of much greater speed and tonnage were gradually introduced.

Cunningham of Hyndhope, Andrew Browne Cunningham, 1st Viscount (1883–1963). British sailor. In World War I he distinguished himself (D.S.O. with two bars) in the Dardanelles campaign and the Dover patrol. In May 1939 he was appointed commander-in-chief in the Mediterranean where he had to face the much more numerous enemy squadrons. In September 1940 a brilliantly planned and executed naval air attack on the ships in Taranto harbour crippled the Italian battle fleet. Three more cruisers and two destroyers were eliminated at the battle of Cape Matapan in the following March. Cunningham had to organize the evacuations from Greece and Crete, to contain and attack when possible the Italian fleet and above all to protect the passage of convoys to Malta and the armies in North Africa in the face of almost continuous German and Italian air attack. In 1943 he succeeded Sir Dudley Pound as first sea lord. Among his many honours he was a knight of the thistle and received the O.M. He was created a baronet in 1941 and viscount in 1946.

His brother, **Sir Alan Gordon Cunningham** (1887–1983), commanded the brilliant and successful attack from the south (1940) against the Italians in Ethiopia. His later appointment (1941) as commander of the 8th Army in the western desert ended when he was superseded while an offensive which he had launched was still in progress. He was later high commissioner in Palestine (1945–48).
Cunningham, A. M., *A Sailor's Odyssey*. 1951

Cunninghame-Graham, Robert Bontine (1852–1936). Scottish author and radical politician. He led a varied and adventurous life. As well as being a literary figure he was an M.P. (1886–92 and again in 1918), leader in a dock strike (1887), an anarchist and first president of the Scottish Nationalists. Much of his life was spent in travel in Morocco, Spain and South America, and his many travel books, essays and short stories reflect the strange countries and people he visited and lived among, as well as his own flamboyant personality.

Cunobellinus (died *c.* 40). Ancient British ruler at Verulamium (St Albans), who extended his power to cover most of south-east England. The legends preserved in Shakespeare's *Cymbeline* are of no historical value.

Curie, Marie (née Sklodowska) (1876–1934). Polish-born French physicist. She studied at Cracow, and went to Paris (1891), where she became the assistant of Pierre * Curie, whom she married (1895). Following Becquerel's discovery of radioactivity (1896), the Curies in 1898 discovered two new elements, polonium and radium, in pitchblende, and in 1902, after processing eight tons of pitchblende, isolated a gram of radium salts. On the death of her husband (1906), Marie Curie succeeded him as professor of physics in the University of Paris and held the post until 1919. She investigated the medical effects of radioactivity, and in 1910 isolated metallic radium. In 1911 she was awarded the Nobel Prize for Chemistry. From 1919 to 1934 she was professor of radiology at the University of Warsaw, continuing her intensive researches and also writing a biography of her husband (published in 1923). Of her daughters, **Irène Curie** (1897–1956), who worked with her mother, married another assistant, Jean Frédéric Joliot (later * Joliot-Curie), sharing the 1935 Nobel Prize for Chemistry with him; **Eve Curie** (1904–) wrote her mother's biography (1937) and *Journey among Warriors* (1943).
Cotton, E., *Les Curies.* 1963

Curie, Pierre (1859–1906). French physicist. In 1880, with his brother Jacques, he discovered piezoelectricity (electricity produced in certain crystals by pressure). He also investigated the magnetic properties of materials and established 'Curie's Law' which relates magnetic properties and temperature. He was director of the laboratories (1882–95) and professor of physics (1895–1906) at the University of Paris. In 1895 he married Marie Sklodowska (Marie * Curie) and thereafter they devoted themselves to the study of radioactive minerals. Jointly with his wife and Becquerel, he was awarded the Nobel Prize for Physics (1903).
Cotton, E., *Les Curies.* 1963

Cuomo, Mario Matthew (1932–). US Democratic politician. He served as secretary of state of New York 1975–79, lieutenant-governor 1979–82, and governor 1983– .

Curnow, Thomas Allen Munro (1911–). New Zealand poet. Some of his best poems have been collected in *At Dead Low Water and Sonnets* (1949), while his satiric verses, written under the pen-name 'Whim-Wham', have also proved popular. The much-praised *A Book of New Zealand Verse* (1946) was edited by him.

Currier and Ives. Nathaniel Currier (1813–1888) founded a lithographic and publishing business, engaging **James Merritt Ives** (1824–1895) as designer. The prints, which represent many aspects of the U.S.A. of their time – houses, coaches, railway and outdoor scenes in general – were popular in their day and have become valued collectors' pieces.

Curtin, John (Joseph Ambrose) (1885–1945). Australian politician. After being secretary of the Victorian timber-workers' union (1911–15) and editor of the *Westralian Worker* (1917–28), he was a Labor M.P. (1928–31 and 1934–45). He became leader of his party (1935) and from the opening of World War II advocated the fullest support of Britain in the struggle against Hitler. He became prime minister in 1941, and when Japan's successes in the East Indies and Pacific threatened Australia he appealed for American aid, with the result that a joint defence was set up under the supreme command of General * MacArthur. In the election of 1943 he obtained a massive majority. He died in office.

Curtis, Lionel George (1872–1955). British administrator and political theorist. He popularized the conception of the commonwealth of self-governing nations that is held today. Educated at Haileybury and Oxford, he was one of the brilliant team of young men who worked with and under the inspiration of Lord * Milner in South African administration. *Civitas Dei* (1934–37) is his best known work.

Curzon, Sir Clifford (Michael) (1907–1982). English pianist. He was noted as an exponent of Mozart, Beethoven and Brahms, and toured widely.

Curzon of Kedleston, George Nathaniel Curzon, 1st Marquess (1859–1925). British administrator and politician. He showed brilliance at Oxford, entered parliament (1886) and when the Conservatives came to power (1889) became under-secretary for foreign affairs, an office for which he had equipped himself by travel in Russia and the East, and much study. In 1899 he was appointed viceroy of India, where he effected substantial reforms in the administration; in 1904 his tenure was extended but in the following year an unfortunate quarrel with * Kitchener, as much a clash of two autocratic temperaments as a real difference concerning the relation between army and civil authority, led to his resignation. For the next few years he was occupied with the affairs of Oxford University of which he was chancellor (1907–25), but in World War I he was a member of Lloyd George's war cabinet and was foreign secretary from 1919. After the coalition had broken up (1922) he was bitterly disappointed when after Bonar Law's retirement Baldwin was preferred to him as prime minister. However, he continued to serve loyally under the new régime as foreign minister.

Curzon's temperament was as much his enemy as circumstances. His attempts to conceal his intense sensitivity, combined with a real love of pageantry, gave him a reputation for arrogance, *hauteur* and even bombast, which had a most damaging effect on his career.

Ronaldshay, *The Life of Lord Curzon*. 3 vols. 1928

Cushing, Harvey Williams (1869–1939). American surgeon. An early pioneer in brain surgery, he made valuable contributions both technical and as teacher and writer.

Custer, George Armstrong (1839–1876). American soldier. He was a dashing cavalry leader and saw service in the Civil War. He served in many campaigns against the Indians and is especially famous for 'Custer's last stand' (1876), when he led 200 cavalry into a Sioux Indian ambush in which they were all killed. This tragic exploit has made him the subject of much controversy.

Goble, P. and D., *Custer's Last Battle*. 1970

Cuvier, Léopold Chrétien Dagobert (usually known by his dead brother's name, **Georges,** which he assumed in youth) (1769–1832). French scientist. He was educated at Stuttgart, where he began his animal studies, and became a tutor near Caen, Normandy, where he could study fossils and the animal life of the seashore at first hand. His abilities were recognized by a visiting *savant* and he was invited to Paris, where eventually he became a professor at the Jardin des Plantes (zoological gardens). He pioneered the study of fossils and is regarded as the founder of comparative anatomy. Cuvier believed firmly in the fixity of species, and was strongly opposed to the evolutionist viewpoint. His *Le Règne animal* (1817) contained a systematic classification of all animal life, based on structural similarities, and these theories led him to modify the Linnean system of animal classification.

Coleman, W., *Georges Cuvier, Zoologist*. 1964

Cuyp, Aelbert (1620–1691). Dutch landscape painter. He was the son of **Jacob Cuyp** (1575–1649), also an artist, best known for animal subjects and military scenes. Aelbert, though he also painted portraits, military and hunting scenes, is famous for idyllic scenes near his native Dordrecht (e.g. *Landscape with Cattle* at the National Gallery, London) in tones warm and golden with sunshine. He had much influence on the English landscapists of succeeding generations.

Cymbeline *see* **Cunobellinus**

Cyprian, St (Thascius Caecilius Cyprianus) (*c.* 200–258). Christian bishop and martyr. Born in the Roman province of Africa he was trained as a rhetorician and had already reached middle life when (*c.* 246) he was converted to Christianity. As bishop of Carthage he proved to have great powers of organization, especially during the persecutions of the emperor Decius when he had to direct the affairs of the see from hiding; later he showed moderation and humanity in dealing with the *lapse*, those who for one reason or another had abandoned their faith. He himself was martyred during the persecutions of the emperor Valerian.

Benson, E. W., *Cyprian: His Life, His Times, His Work*. 1897

Cyril, St (827–869), and his brother **St Methodius** (?826–885) (known as the 'Apostles of the Slavs'). They were born in Thessalonica. In *c.* 860 Cyril went to preach among the Tartar Khazars to the north of the Black Sea. Meanwhile Methodius had been working among the Bulgarians but in *c.* 863 the two brothers went together to Moravia, where their knowledge of the Slav language of the people and their ability to transcribe the Bible and other liturgical works made them more influential than the missionaries already there who knew only Latin or German. Summoned to Rome, they received papal sanction for their use of the Slavonic language. Cyril died there (869) but Methodius, now bishop of Moravia, returned to complete their work. Cyril gave his name to the Cyrillic alphabet, a modification of the Greek with additional symbols for specifically Slavonic sounds.

Cyrus (died 401 B.C.). Persian prince. He was pardoned for conspiracy against his brother, King Artaxerxes II, and became sultan of Asia Minor; he then raised a rebel army, many of them Greeks, but was met, defeated and killed at Cunaxa in Babylonia. The epic homeward march of the Greeks, the dangers they encountered, including the snows of Asia Minor, is described in the *Anabasis* of * Xenophon, who was with them.

Cyrus (known as 'the Great') (died 529 B.C.). King of Persia (from *c.* 550 B.C.). He is regarded as the founder of the Persian empire from his conquest of Media, Lydia, where he overcame * Croesus, and Babylon, where, according to the biblical legend, Belshazzar saw (but too late) 'the writing on the wall'. At his death his kingdom spread from Afghanistan to the Bosphorus. He allowed the Jews to return from their captivity in Babylon and to rebuild the temple of Jerusalem.
Frye, R. N., *The Heritage of Persia.* 1963

Czerny, Karl (1791–1857). Austrian pianist and teacher. Noted for his studies and exercises designed to improve technique, he studied with * Beethoven, and * Liszt was among his pupils.

D

Dagobert (died 639). Merovingian king. He succeeded his father, Chlotar (Clotaire) II, in 629 and briefly reunited the whole kingdom of the Franks. St Eloi, a goldsmith and patron saint of craftsmen, was his treasurer.
Barroux, R., *Dagobert*. 1938

Daguerre, Louis-Jacques-Mandé (1787–1851). French painter and physicist, born at Cormeilles, Seine-et-Oise. He invented the daguerreotype, the first practical process of photography. He worked first as an officer for inland revenue, then as a scene painter for the opera. He opened the Diorama in Paris (1822), an exhibition of panoramic views, different effects achieved by changes in lighting. In the same year J.-N. Niepce produced the first permanent photograph, though it was of poor quality and required 8 hours exposure time. Learning of Daguerre's experiments in the same field, he joined him in 1829. After Niepce's death in 1833, Daguerre continued with their work and in 1839 was able to publish his daguerreotype process, which required only 20–30 minutes exposure time. By this process permanent pictures were produced on an iodised silver plate, called a daguerreotype. His publications include *Historie et description des procédés de daguerréotypie* (1839). He was made an officer of the Legion of Honour, and he and Niepce's heir were granted annuities in 1839.
Gernsheim, H. and A., *L. J. M. Daguerre*. Rev. ed. 1968

Daimler, Gottlieb (1834–1900). German pioneer of motor manufacture, born in Würtemberg. His success rested on his production (after earlier experiments with coal gas as a fuel) of a light, petrol-driven combustion engine, patented in 1883. He founded (1890) the Daimler car company at Cannstatt and in 1900 produced the first Mercédès cars (named after his daughter).

Daladier, Édouard (1884–1970). French politician. The son of a baker, he was born at Carpentras, Provence. He taught history at Grenoble and elsewhere before moving to Paris. After fighting in World War I, he was elected to the Chamber of Deputies (1919) and eventually succeeded Herriot as leader of the Radical Socialist party. He was prime minister (1934 and 1938–40) and negotiated the Munich agreement (1938) with Hitler, Neville Chamberlain and Mussolini. He was arrested (1940) by the Vichy government and interned by the Germans (1942–45).

Dalcroze, Émile Jaques *see* **Jaques-Dalcroze, Émile**

Dale, Sir Henry Hallett (1875–1968). English physiologist. He was secretary of the Royal Society (1925–35), director of the National Institute for Medical Research (1928–42), director of the Royal Institution, London (1942–46), and president of the Royal Society (1940–45). He shared the Nobel Prize for Medicine (1936) for his work on the chemical transmission of nerve impulses.

Dalen, Nils Gustav (1869–1937). Swedish physicist, born Stenstorp, Sweden. In 1906 he was appointed chief engineer of the Gas Accumulator company which marketed acetylene gas. He researched into gases and turbines, improved hot-air turbine engines and the Laval steam turbine. By 1909 he was appointed managing director, and invented

Agamassan, the substance which absorbs acetylene with no risk of explosion. In 1912 he won the Nobel Prize for Physics for his invention of the automatic sun valve 'Solventil'; this regulated a source of gaslight by the action of sunlight, turning it off and on according to intensity of light. It was widely used for buoys and unmanned lighthouses. He was blinded by an explosion during an experiment (1913) but continued his research until his death.

Dalhousie, James Andrew Broun-Ramsay, 1st Marquess of (1812–1860). Scottish administrator. After being president of the Board of Trade (1845–46), he became governor-general of India (1848–56). His first years were marked by the Second Burmese and the Sikh Wars; as a result more of Lower Burma and the Punjab were annexed, the latter being so wisely administered that it remained loyal in the Mutiny of 1857. The annexation of Oudh, however, was much criticized. Dalhousie initiated a system of primary education, introduced railways and the telegraph, developed roads, trade and the postal service, and inaugurated great irrigation schemes.

Dali, Salvador Felipe Jacinto (1904–). Spanish painter and sculptor. Through the influence of de Chirico and Max Ernst he became (from 1929) one of the principal exponents of Surrealism, a form of art which, it is claimed, springs wholly from the subconscious mind. Dali's paintings of nightmares or hallucinations often include figures drawn and painted with extreme realism. In addition to his paintings he has made films, designed ballets, and written an autobiography and other books. A 'retrospective' exhibition of his work was held in Paris in 1980.

Gerard, M., *Salvador Dali*. 1974

Dallapiccola, Luigi (1904–1975). Italian composer, born Pisino, Istria. Studied at the Florence Conservatoire 1921, and established a reputation as a teacher and pianist. First became known internationally at pre-war festivals of the International Society for Contemporary Music, with such compositions as *Songs of Captivity*, prompted by the fascist racial laws of 1938. In this work he used an original version of 12-tone technique; it is for this technique, which he combined with a warm and emotional expressiveness, that he is remembered.

His interest in 'protest music', concerning mental persecution, was continued in the opera *Il prigionero* (1944–48) and the *Songs of Liberty* (1951–55). Although Dallapiccola was an excellent orchestrator, his greatest achievement lies in his choral work, such as the oratorio *Job* (1950), *Goethe Lieder* (1953) and the opera *Ulysses* (1968). Influenced by Schoenberg, Busoni and Webern, he in turn had great influence on younger Italian composers such as his pupil, Luciano * Berio, a leading composer of electronic music.

Vlad, R., *Luigi Dallapiccola*. 1957

Dalton, Hugh Dalton, Baron (1887–1962). British politician. Educated at Eton and King's College Cambridge, he taught economics before becoming a Labour M.P. (1924). Except between 1935 and 1939 he was in parliament until 1959. He first held office in 1929 and in the coalition government of World War II was minister of economic warfare (1940–42) and president of the Board of Trade (1942–45). In 1945 he became chancellor of the exchequer in the post-war Labour government, but resigned (1947) after a leakage of his budget proposals. He was minister of town and country planning (1950–51), and in 1960 was made a life peer.

Dalton, John (1766–1844). English chemist, son of a Quaker weaver in Cumberland. He spent most of his adult life in Manchester as a teacher and private tutor. Earlier, while teaching at Kendal (from 1781), he began a series of 200,000 meteorological observations which he continued throughout his life. He revived the theory, originating in ancient Greece, that matter is not continuous but made up of atoms, and he showed that such an atomic theory is consistent with the observed laws of constant, multiple and reciprocal proportions. He published these ideas, with a table of atomic weights and a list of chemical symbols, in *A New System of Chemical Philosophy* (1808). In the physical field he did much research into the constitution of gases and their expansion when heated, and into the force of steam. Dalton and his brother were colour-blind, and he was the first to give a detailed description of this deficiency.

Thackray, A., *John Dalton: Critical Assessment of His Life and Science*. 1973

Daly, John Augustin (1839–1899). American theatrical impresario. He opened a theatre in New York in 1879 (demolished 1920) at which he presented Shakespearian and other comedies with great magnificence. Daly's theatre in London (opened in 1893 and demolished 1939) became the home of George Edwardes's sparkling musical comedies, e.g. Lehár's *The Merry Widow* (1907).

Damien, Father (Joseph de Veuster) (1840–1889). Belgian Catholic missionary. A member of the Picpus Society (Fathers of the Sacred Heart of Jesus and Mary), he went to the Hawaiian Islands in 1864 and from 1873 served at the leper colony at Molokai. After sixteen years of selfless devotion he contracted leprosy and died on the island.
Farrow, J., *Damien the Leper*. 1955

Damocles (4th century B.C.). Courtier of * Dionysius. He is said to have expressed envy of his master's wealth and happiness, whereupon Dionysius seated him at a banquet beneath a sword suspended by a single hair, thus demonstrating to him how uncertain is the tenure of power.

Damon and **Pythias** (5th century B.C.). Şyracusans who are remembered as exemplars of devotion between friends. When Pythias (more correctly Pinteas), condemned to death for plotting against * Dionysius, asked for temporary release to arrange his affairs, Damon provided surety by offering to be executed in his place should his friend not return. Pythias was indeed delayed but returned just in time to avert Damon's execution. Dionysius was so touched that he freed both and asked to be included in their bond of friendship.

Dampier, William (1652–1715). English navigator. Born in Somerset, he went early to sea and had taken part in several voyages before he became engaged (from 1679) in buccaneering along the South American coasts and further afield. On one such expedition (from 1683) he crossed the Pacific, touching on the Philippines, China and Australia. This brought him British government employment. In 1699 he explored the coasts of north-west Australia, New Guinea and New Britain. When wrecked off Ascension Island on the return voyage goats and turtles provided his diet for five weeks. He was soon at sea again, once more a privateer. The sailing master of one of his two ships was the prototype of Robinson Crusoe, Alexander * Selkirk, who was marooned (1704) on one of the islands of Juan Fernández; Dampier sailed with Woodes Rogers on the expedition that found and rescued him (1709). Dampier wrote vivid accounts of his voyages.
Wilkinson, C., *William Dampier*. 1929

Danby, Thomas Osborne, Earl of (later 1st Duke of Leeds) (1631–1712). English politician. He entered parliament (1665) and as a strong supporter of the king and the established church was quickly promoted. In 1674 he became chief minister to Charles II, but was impeached (1678) by the Commons on a number of charges, the worst of which were concerned with secret negotiations, on Charles's behalf, with Louis XIV and accepting bribes. The Commons rejected the king's immediate pardon, and Danby was imprisoned until 1684. After James II's accession his zeal for the established church led him to take an active part in promoting the revolution (1688) which placed William and Mary on the throne. He was virtually prime minister (1688–99) but lost his influence after being charged with bribery (1695) and retired in 1699.
Browning, A., *Danby*. 3 vols. 1944–51

Dance, George (?1695–1768). English architect. The son of a London merchant, he started his career as a mason and in 1735 became surveyor to the City of London. Among the buildings he designed were the Mansion House (1739–53), St Botolph's, Aldgate (1741–44), and the façade of Guy's Hospital (1764). His son, also **George Dance** (1741–1825), who succeeded his father as city surveyor, was responsible for many London buildings and churches, e.g. Newgate Prison (1770–78, demolished 1902), All Hallows, London Wall (1765–67), and the Royal College of Surgeons in Lincoln's Inn (1806–13, later reconstructed). As designer of country houses he was also in great vogue. He was an original member of the Royal Academy, where he became professor of architecture (1798).
Stroud, D., *George Dance, Architect*. 1971

Dandolo, Enrico (*c.* 1110–1205). Doge of Venice, elected in 1192, when he was blind and over 80. He provided transport for and accom-

panied the 4th Crusade, which he successfully diverted to the capture of Constantinople (1204). The islands and territories acquired by Venice were the foundations of its power in the Near East. Among the spoils were the four bronze horses which now surmount the doorway of St Mark's Cathedral (Venice).
Bravetta, E., *Enrico Dandolo*. 1929

Dane, Clemence (pen-name of Winifred Ashton) (1888–1965). English writer. Her first play, *A Bill of Divorcement* (1921), was her most successful and was later made into a film. Her novels include *Regiment of Women* (1917).

Daniel (6th century B.C.). Jewish exile in Babylon who gave his name to a book in the Bible. He is said to have won favour with King Nebuchadnezzar for his ability to foretell the future, for interpreting the words which presaged Belshazzar's doom and, finally, for his miraculous preservation when he was thrown into a lion's den for refusing to obey a royal decree which conflicted with his religion.

D'Annunzio, Gabriele (1863–1938). Italian poet, novelist, dramatist, political leader, born in Pescara, the son of an influential landowner, and educated at the University of Rome. His first poems, *Primo vere*, were published in 1879 and a prose continuation *Terra Vergine* appeared 1882, as did *Canto Nuovo*, followed in 1889 by an autobiographical novel *Il Piacere*. In 1892 he began reading Nietzsche who influenced his later works, several of which featured grasping, completely amoral Nietzschean heroes. He fought bravely during World War I; he advocated joining the Allies. After the war he occupied Fiume with a force of volunteers, ruled as dictator from 1919–21, and became a national hero. Later he became an ardent Fascist. He retired to Gardone Riviera and devoted himself to writing memoirs and confessions. His other important works include the two plays *La Figlia di lorio* (1904) and *Le Martyre de Saint Sébastien* (1911), the poetic works *Laudi del cielo del mare della terra e degli eroi* (1899) and *Alcyone* (1904) and the novel *Il trionfo della morte* (1894).

A prolific writer, he produced work of great passion and exuberance, and showed an individual and skilful use of language which influenced subsequent Italian literature. In his style of writing he broke away from the intellectualism of the nineteenth century, for which he was much criticized in his own time.
Julian, P., *D'Annunzio*. 1973

Dante Alighieri (1265–1321). Italian poet. He was born of a well-known Florentine family belonging to the Guelph or papal faction in politics. In his first principal work, *La Vita Nuova*, a sequence of love poems (1283–92), we are introduced to 'Beatrice', the love of his life. In the poems we are told that she was 9 years old when he first met her and fell under her enchantment; when she was 18 they met again and occasionally afterwards: her death (1299) left him utterly forlorn. Who she was has provided one of the most famous literary puzzles. The accepted version is that the 'glorious lady of his mind', as he describes her, was Bice Portinari, who married Simone de Bardi, a banker. Others suggest that the name merely masks an unknown lady, while a third theory supposes that she is the personification of his ideal of love.

In his sorrow he turned to theology and became interested in politics. In 1291 he married Gemma Donati, by whom he had three sons and two daughters. His ventures into politics proved unfortunate. Florence was a Guelph city but the party was divided into two factions, the moderate 'Whites' and the extreme papal faction, the 'Blacks'. Dante, a 'White', rose to be on the Supreme Council of One Hundred, but when the Blacks seized power he was accused on trumped-up charges and condemned (1302) to pay an impossible fine; when the fine remained unpaid he was sentenced to death, to escape which he lived in exile for the rest of his life, refusing a conditional pardon in 1315. Meanwhile he found employment on several diplomatic missions while in Forlì, Verona, Lunigiana and Ravenna (where he died).

In *c.* 1307 he began *La Divina Commedia*, the three parts of which describe the poet's journey through *Inferno, Purgatorio* and *Paradiso* (where Beatrice is found). To each he assigns, judging them on political as well as moral grounds, many personalities of his own and other times. Virgil, to whom the poet owes an acknowledged debt, is his guide through Hell and Purgatory. In a metaphorical sense, the epic, which was from the beginning recognized as a masterpiece and has been translated into almost every language, describes Dante's own spiritual development. Among his lesser works, the Latin *De Vulgari Eloquentia*

(1303–04) includes a classification of dialects and reveals his aim to secure a unified Italian tongue; the *Monarchia* (*c.* 1310) discusses the relations of emperor and pope and the concept of a universal empire. The *Convivio* (*Feast*; 1304–07), in which he discusses his moral and philosophic ideas, is the first important treatise written in Italian rather than Latin.
Moore, E., *Studies in Dante*. 1969

Danton, Georges Jacques (1759–1794). French revolutionary politician. Originally an advocate in Paris, after the revolution of 1789 he founded the Cordeliers' club and in 1792–93 played a leading part in the events which led to the deposition and execution of Louis XVI. He was minister of justice (but *de facto* minister of war) from August to October 1792 and president of the Jacobin club (1793) and the leading spirit in promoting resistance to the invading armies of the European monarchies. 'De l'audace . . . et toujours de l'audace' was one of his famous sayings. He was instrumental in removing the more moderate Girondists from power. He dominated the Committee of Public Safety from April to July 1793, but when his moderate policies failed he was displaced by the extremist leader * Robespierre, who had long been his rival. Danton and his friend Camille Desmoulins were denounced and guillotined. He was a great orator and was known as the 'the Mirabeau of the mob'.
Barthou, J. L., *Danton*. 1932

Da Ponte, Lorenzo (original name Emanuele Conegliano) (1749–1838). Jewish poet, born in Italy. He was converted to Roman Catholicism by the bishop of Cendea, whose name he took. He moved to Vienna (1780), became a friend of Mozart and wrote the libretti for his operas *The Marriage of Figaro, Don Giovanni* and *Così fan tutte*. He lived in London (1793–1805) and in 1805 moved to the U.S.A. where he became a store-keeper in New Jersey for a time. He was the first professor of Italian at Columbia University (1825–38).

Darby, Abraham (1677–1717). English ironmaster and inventor, born near Dudley, Worcestershire. He patented (1707) a method of casting iron pots in sand moulds. Having taken over a blast-furnace at Coalbrookdale, Shropshire, he brought about Britain's supremacy as an iron producing country by discovering (1709) a method of using coke instead of charcoal for the smelting of iron ore. A further development came when his son, the second **Abraham Darby** (1711–1763), successfully produced malleable iron from coke-smelted pig-iron. His son, the third **Abraham Darby** (1750–1791), helped to construct the cast-iron bridge over the Severn at Coalbrookdale – the first of its kind.
Raistrick, A., *Dynasty of Ironfounders*. 1953

Darius I (the Great) (548–486 B.C.). King of Persia (from 521 B.C.). The death (522 B.C.) of * Cambyses found Persia in the midst of civil war and Darius, who belonged to a junior branch of the royal line, had to fight hard for his throne. Gradually he restored order to the empire, continued the reorganization of the administration begun by Cyrus, and linked the provinces with the capital by highways of which the royal road from Sardis to Susa was the most famous. He was tolerant towards the Jews, who were permitted and assisted to rebuild the temple at Jerusalem. After successful invasions of north-west India, Thrace and Macedon, Darius sent three expeditions which failed to conquer Greece; in the second his armies were defeated by the Athenians at Marathon (490 B.C.), and the third was foiled by a rebellion in Egypt. He was succeeded by his son, Xerxes. Darius is mentioned in Daniel V, 31, and subsequently.

Darius III (died 330 B.C.). King of Persia (from 336 B.C.). His reign was marked by the conquest of his empire by * Alexander the Great, who inflicted on him a series of defeats, culminating with that at Arbela (331 B.C.) in the Tigris valley. Darius fled but was killed by a satrap who aspired to the throne. His daughter, Barsine, was taken by Alexander as a second wife.

Darlan, Jean Louis Xavier (1881–1942). French sailor and politician. A long and successful career had brought him, by the outbreak of World War II, to the position of commander-in-chief of the French naval forces. When France surrendered (1940) he joined the government of Marshal * Pétain as vice-premier. He was in Algiers when the Allies invaded North Africa (1942) and, having transferred his allegiance to them, was acknowledged – to secure a peaceful occupation – as chief of state in North Africa. This outraged the feelings of more ardent patriots, one of whom assassinated Darlan a few weeks later.

Darling, Grace (1815–1842). English heroine. When the steamship *Forfarshire* was wrecked in September 1838 she rowed with her father, lighthouse-keeper on the Farne Islands, off Northumberland, to the rescue of the few survivors, who were still clinging to the rocks. She became the object of great public admiration.
Smith, F., *The Ship Aground*. 1940

Darnley, Henry Stuart, Lord (1545–1567). Consort of Mary Queen of Scots. He was the son of the 4th Earl of Lennox, whose mother, Margaret, sister of England's Henry VIII, had married the Earl of Angus after the death of her husband James IV. Darnley was therefore a cousin of Mary, whose second husband he became in 1565; their son, the future James VI of Scotland (later James I of England), was born the following year. After the murder of her favourite * Rizzio, in which Darnley played a leading part, the queen came to hate her husband; but when he became ill there was an apparent reconciliation. He was brought from Glasgow to Edinburgh, but was almost immediately killed when the house where he was staying, at Kirk o'Field, was blown up with gunpowder. The Earl of Bothwell, already aspiring to take Darnley's position, was clearly guilty despite the show of a trial, at which he was acquitted. The strong probability of Mary's complicity has been the subject of continued controversy. Darnley was a man of cultivated tastes but was considered to be loose in morals and politically inept.

Darrow, Clarence Seward (1857–1938). American lawyer, who appeared for the defence in many controversial cases, notably for Eugene Debs in the railway strike case (1894), for Loeb and Leopold in the 'thrill-murder' case in Chicago (1924) and for John T. Scopes in the Dayton, Tennessee, 'Monkey Trial' (1925). He was a fervent opponent of capital punishment, and none of his clients was ever sentenced to death.

Darwin, Charles Robert (1809–1882). English naturalist, born in Shrewsbury. Famous for his theory of 'natural selection', he was the son of a well-known doctor, grandson of Erasmus * Darwin, and, through his mother, of the famous potter Josiah Wedgwood. After attending Shrewsbury Grammar School he studied medicine at Edinburgh and theology at Cambridge, but his inclinations turned him to botany and geology. He was appointed naturalist on a naval survey ship, H.M.S. *Beagle*, which was making a voyage round the world, and investigated (1831–36) the fauna, flora and geological formations of many areas, including South America, Australia and the Pacific Islands. He was secretary of the Geological Society (1838–41) and was elected F.R.S. (1839). In the same year he married his cousin Emma Wedgwood. For the rest of his life he lived and worked at his home at Down House, Kent, surrounded by a large and happy family, several of whom later attained distinction in academic life. In 1842 he published *The Structures and Distribution of Coral Reefs*, which contains the now generally accepted theory of the origin of coral formations. From observations made during the *Beagle* expedition, he had become convinced that instead of being immutable as was generally held – though the speculations and conclusions of ancient Greeks, Erasmus Darwin, * Lamarck and others suggested otherwise – the species had gradually evolved from earlier simpler species in an unbroken descent from monocellular life. Darwin's great achievement was to put forward a scientific explanation of how evolution takes place. The most important factor, he considered, was 'natural selection': because of slight differences (many of them heritable) in their characteristics, some members of a species are better fitted than others for survival under the conditions of their environment and are therefore the most likely to live long enough to reproduce; in this way the variations passed on to the next generation tend to be those which are favourable – the survival of the fittest. Although communicated privately to several colleagues, this theory remained unpublished until 1858 when A. R. * Wallace sent to Darwin from Malaya a manuscript putting forward a similar theory which he had worked out independently. Darwin then, in a paper before the Linnaean Society, announced their joint conclusions and in 1859 published his major work, *On the Origin of Species by Means of Natural Selection*. The work provoked furious opposition from clergy and others who saw it as an attack on the doctrine of the special creation of man, but with the support of Huxley and many other eminent scientists the theory of evolution gained widespread acceptance. In 1871 Darwin published *The Descent of Man*, which provoked fresh controversy by its insistence that man and the anthropoid apes must have a common ancestor.

Barlow, N. (ed.), *The Autobiography of Charles Darwin*. 1958

Darwin, Erasmus (1731–1802). English medical practitioner and philosopher of science, born at Elton Hall, Nottinghamshire. Best remembered as a forerunner of his grandson Charles * Darwin in developing evolutionary theories, his conclusions were essentially reached by philosophic speculation rather than scientific observation. He studied medicine at Edinburgh and took his degree at Cambridge. He practised as a doctor in Nottingham and with increasing success at Lichfield, when his fame even reached George III. The meetings of the Lunar Society in that town were attended by such men as Matthew * Boulton, James * Watt, Josiah * Wedgwood, and Joseph * Priestley. Darwin moved from this congenial environment to Derby (1802). *The Botanic Garden* (1789–91) is an odd work written in rhyming couplets and, among other eccentricities, personifying the forces of nature, but it contains, especially in the notes, a mass of miscellaneous information. Indeed the number of subjects to which Darwin turned his mind and pen is immense and includes sewerage, flying machines, temperance, canals, and female education in boarding schools. His *Zoonomia or the Laws of Organic Life* (1794–96) is the work which may be considered to anticipate the evolutionary theory; he envisages the possibility of an animal having the faculty of self-improvement and able to hand down 'those improvements by generation to its posterity world without end'.

Hele, D., *Erasmus Darwin*. 1963

Darwin, Sir George Howard (1845–1912). English astronomer, born in Down, Kent. The fifth child of Emma and Charles * Darwin, he studied law at Cambridge for six years, then returned to Trinity College to pursue his interests in mathematics and astronomy. He was elected to the Royal Society in 1879, and became Plumian Professor of Astronomy in 1883. Darwin was essentially a mathematical cosmogonist. His interests lay in applying detailed quantified analysis to cosmological and geological problems. He also carried out celebrated work on the origins of the moon. He believed it was the product of the fission of the parent earth, on account of instability caused by solar tides. He dated this event at atleast 50 million years ago, which he saw as being more compatible with the comparatively low estimate of the earth's age made by his friend, Lord Kelvin, than with his father's much longer time-span. By the early twentieth century, however, George Darwin recognized how the discovery of radio-activity overthrew Kelvin's calculations, and he became prepared to accept higher time-scales.

D'Aubigny, Charles François (1817–1878). French landscape painter, associated with the Barbizon school. After a residence of a few years in Italy he lived mainly near Paris (the last twenty years on a house-boat on the Seine). He is noted for his successful impression of atmosphere and half-light.

Daudet, Alphonse (1840–1897). French novelist, born at Nîmes. He went to Paris at the age of 17 and became a secretary to the Duc de Morny, publishing his first work, *Les Amoureuses*, a book of poems, in 1857. He confirmed his reputation with the collection of short stories *Lettres de mon moulin* (1866) and *Contes du lundi* (1873), and many novels which include *Le petit chose* (1868), with its memories of his own childhood. Best known of all is *Tartarin de Tarascon* (1872), first of a series centred upon this delightful Provençal character. Bizet wrote the music for his only play *L'Arlésienne* (1872). Daudet's ironic and sensitive work is notable for its realism. His son, **Léon Daudet** (1867–1942), editor of *L'Action Française*, was an unscrupulous but brilliant propagandist for the royalist cause.

Sachs, M., *The Career of Alphonse Daudet*. 1965

Daumier, Honoré (1808–1879). French painter and caricaturist, born of poor parents in Marseilles. In 1832 he drew a cartoon of King Louis Philippe which earned him six months' imprisonment. Throughout his life Daumier was victim of poverty and a savage critic of social injustice; he especially satirized the malpractices and foibles of lawyers and other members of the rich bourgeoisie, and the régime of Napoleon III provided some excellent targets. The effectiveness of his lithographs derives from bold silhouettes defined by an energetic line and strongly marked lights

and darks. In his paintings – whose near uniformity of style renders them difficult to date – Daumier made a still more imaginative play with strong shapes. His Don Quixote series constitutes a revolutionary reduction of form and narrative to the barest essentials. Daumier's paintings range between this extreme of modernism and a wholly romantic treatment of the commonplace (e.g. *Tireur de Bateau*).
Rey, R., *Daumier*. 1966

Davenant, Sir William (1606–1668). English poet and playwright, the son of an Oxford tavern-keeper. The gossip, repeated by John Aubrey, that he was Shakespeare's illegitimate son is unbacked by evidence. His first play *The Cruel Brother* was produced in 1627, and for the next eleven years he entertained the court of Charles I with a series of tragedies, comedies and masques; he became Poet Laureate in 1638. During the Civil War he was knighted (1643) by Charles for his military services. He followed Queen Henrietta Maria into exile and in 1650, while on the way to America, was captured by a parliamentary frigate and briefly imprisoned. His best known works are the tedious epic *Gondibert* (1651) and *The Siege of Rhodes* (1656), said to have been the first English opera. After the Restoration he was active in the London theatre, and collaborated with * Dryden on a new version of *The Tempest* (1667).
Nethercot, A. H., *Sir William D'Avenant: Poet Laureate and Playwright Manager*. 1967

David (11th–10th centuries B.C.). First king of a united Israel. According to the biblical story he was the son of Jesse, who farmed near Bethlehem; as a young minstrel he won the favour of King Saul by being able to assuage his melancholy, and became close friends with Saul's son, Jonathan. In the war against the Philistines David killed the giant, Goliath, but, having married Saul's daughter, soon roused his jealousy; he then lived as an outlaw until, after the death of Saul and Jonathan, he set up a court at Hebron and later built a new capital at Jerusalem, from which he ruled all Israel. Stories of his later life include the revolt of his favourite son Absalom, whose death he lamented so deeply; that his lust could lead him into wickedness was shown when, to take Bathsheba, the wife of Uriah the Hittite, he exposed her husband in the forefront of a battle, where as expected he met his death. That some at least of the psalms of David were of his own composition there is little doubt and the beautiful lament for Saul and Jonathan is almost certainly his own. The Messianic hopes of the Jews were fixed upon the royal line of David, a fact which explains the emphasis placed in the New Testament upon the genealogical links between him and Jesus Christ. David was succeeded by his son * Solomon.

David (or Dewi) (died *c.* 601). Patron saint of Wales, commemorated on 1 March. The details of his life are clouded by legend but he seems to have been a leading figure in the monastic revival in the Celtic countries of Europe during the 6th century. His bishopric of Menevia was renamed St David's (in Pembrokeshire) in his honour and his shrine was a famous place of pilgrimage in the Middle Ages (from *c.* 1000). He was canonized in 1120.
Rhys, E., *The Life of Saint David*. 1927

David I (*c.* 1080–1153). King of Scotland (from 1124). He was the younger son of Malcolm III and on his father's death (1093) he was sent for safety to the English court. Here he became friendly with the future Henry I who married his sister Matilda. He himself (*c.* 1113–14) married a daughter of Waltheof and so acquired the English earldoms of Huntingdon and Northumberland. Having succeeded his brother Alexander I in 1124 he supported Henry's daughter, the empress Matilda, against Stephen in her struggle for the English throne: though defeated at Northallerton he secured terms which allowed him to extend his kingdom to the Tees and Eden. He completed the alignment of the Scottish church with that of the rest of western Christendom by increasing the number of bishoprics and founding many monasteries, e.g. Holyrood and Melrose. During his reign he introduced important changes in law and administration.

David II (1324–1371). King of Scotland (from 1329). He succeeded his father, Robert Bruce, as a child, but owing to the confused state of his country was sent to France in 1334. Returning in 1341, he invaded England in 1346 but was captured at Neville's Cross (by Edward III's troops). After an imprisonment in England lasting eleven years, he was ransomed for a huge sum of which only half had been paid when he died childless.

David, Jacques Louis (1748–1825). French painter. He worked under Vien from 1765. After winning the first prize of the Académie des Beaux Arts he went to Italy, where he studied for some years. With the exhibition (1785) in Paris of his picture *The Oath of the Horatii* David became the leader of the neo-classical movement. It is a painting of great austerity and dramatic clarity with serious political undertones. During the Revolution David served as a member of the Convention (1792–95), and was briefly its president. From this period date some of his finest portraits and a haunting drawing of Marie Antoinette on the way to the guillotine. Under the Consulate and Empire David's paintings embraced stilted, antiquarian interpretations of classical subjects (*Leonidas at Thermopylae*), huge compositions of great occasions such as *The Coronation of Napoleon*, and excellent, if sometimes over-romanticized, portraiture (e.g. *Madame Récamier* and *Napoleon on Horseback*). With the return of the monarchy David lived as an exile in Brussels. From this period dates the wonderful, compassionate yet severely realistic portrait of *The Three Ladies of Ghent*. Conflicting trends appear in David's paintings – he moves from pure neo-classicism to freer use of light and colour, reverts to a stilted classicism albeit with a relaxation in its style. He exerted considerable influence as the teacher of, among others, Ingres, Gérard and Gros.
Hautecoeur, L., *Louis David*. 1954

Davies, Sir (Henry) Walford (1869–1941). British organist, broadcaster and composer, born Oswestry, Shropshire. From 1919–26 he was professor of music at the University of Wales, Aberystwyth and in 1934 succeeded * Elgar as Master of the King's Musick. A prolific composer he was best known for his *Solemn Melody* for organ and strings. Through his BBC radio series 'Music and the ordinary listener' (1926–30) he was an important force in musical education.

Davies, Sir John (1569–1626). English poet, lawyer, attorney general for Ireland and later Lord Chief Justice of England (though he died before he could take up office). His poetry is 'philosophical' in approach: *Orchestra* (1596) sees nature through a sustained metaphor of dancing and *Nosce Teipsum* (1599) considers the nature of man and his soul. His reputation as a wit is justified in *Hymns to Astraea* (1599), a series of nimble acrostics on the name Elizabeth Regina. He also wrote in prose on Irish history. His wife, Eleanor Audley, became a prophetess, foretold the death of Charles I and produced a series of cryptic pamphlets during the 1640s and early 1650s.

Davies, William Henry (1871–1940). British poet, born in Monmouthshire. He was for a time apprenticed to a picture-framer, but in his early twenties went to America. He lived as a tramp for many years, lost his right leg while jumping a train and returned to England. He described his early life in *Autobiography of a Super-tramp* (1908). The first volume of his poems, printed privately in 1905, attracted the attention of Bernard Shaw, who did much to help him.
Hockey, L., *W. H. Davies*. 1971

Davis, Bette (1908–). American film actress. Famous for the dramatic intensity with which she entered into her parts, her film career, which began in 1930, covered a great number of leading roles (for which she gained several Academy awards) in titles such as *The Petrified Forest, Jezebel, Dark Victory, All This and Heaven Too, The Little Foxes, All About Eve, Wedding Breakfast* and *Whatever Happened to Baby Jane?* Her autobiography, *The Lonely Life*, was published in 1963.

Davis, Dwight Filley (1879–1945). American donor of the Davis Cup. Competed for annually (except for twelve – mostly war – years) since 1900 by national lawn-tennis teams. It is a knock-out contest, victory going to the winners of the best of five matches, four singles and one doubles. Davis presented the cup while still an enthusiastic undergraduate; in later life he became a successful administrator as secretary of war (1925–29) and governor general of the Philippines (1929–32).

Davis, Jefferson (1808–1889). American politician, president of the Confederate states during the Civil War. Born in Kentucky, he lived in Mississippi from childhood, became an officer in the U.S. army, but resigned in 1835 after eloping with his commander's daughter. Returning to Mississippi, he became a cotton planter. He was elected to the U.S. House of Representatives in 1845, but resigned (1846) to serve in the Mexican War. Afterwards he returned to politics as a senator (1847–51, 1857–61), and was secretary of war (1853–57), under President Pierce. When Mississippi seceded from the Union (1861) Davis withdrew from the Senate, and in February was chosen by the Congress of seceding states as president of the Confederacy. In the ensuing Civil War (1861–65) Davis failed adequately to co-ordinate the civil and military administrations, and was regarded by many as unduly hesitant and moderate. At the end of the war treason charges against him were dropped: he returned home to live in obscurity and wrote *The Rise and Fall of the Confederate Government* (1878–81).

Davis, Joe (1901–). British professional billiards and snooker player. At the latter game his pre-eminence was almost unchallenged: in 1946 he had won all sixteen world championship contests for this game. He also won the world professional billiards championship ten times and held the U.K. championship from 1934 to 1946.

Davis, John William (1873–1955). U.S. lawyer. He was a congressman 1911–13, solicitor general 1913–18 and ambassador to U.K. 1918–21. At the 1924 Democratic convention the party was hopelessly deadlocked between Al Smith and W. G. McAdoo (a 'dry' supported by the Klan) and on the 103rd ballot Davis was chosen. In the following campaign against * Coolidge he seemed to avoid major issues (e.g. prohibition) and as a corporation lawyer for the Morgan banking interests he lost union voters, carrying only 12 states in the South. In 1953 he emerged from retirement to argue against the compulsory integration of Negro children in schools in the Deep South.

Davis, Sir Robert Henry (1871–1965). British inventor. Best known of his inventions is the Davis escape apparatus, used to save the lives of the crews of damaged submarines; of equal value is his 'submersible decompression chamber', used to enable divers to work in deep water and ascend without harmful results. He was knighted in 1932.

Davisson, Clinton Joseph (1881–1958). American physicist. In 1937 he shared, with Sir George Thomson, the Nobel Prize for Physics for his work on the diffraction of electrons by crystals; he showed that electrons reveal wavelike as well as corpuscular properties.

Davitt, Michael (1846–1906). Irish nationalist politician. He joined the Fenians in 1865 and served seven years in jail (1870–77) for his revolutionary activities. He became the co-founder, with C. S. * Parnell, of the Land League, and campaigned for reduced rents and peasant ownership of the land. The outlawing of the League brought him another year's imprisonment (1881–82). Thenceforward he advocated socialism and land nationalization for Ireland. This and Parnell's divorce led to a breach between the two men and it was as an anti-Parnellite that Davitt entered parliament (1882). He helped to start the United Irish League (1898). In 1903 he visited Russia, where he contacted revolutionary groups. He edited *Labour World* and was a collectivist and secularist as well as a nationalist.

Davout, Louis Nicolas, Duke of Auerstädt (later prince of Eckmühl) (1770–1823). French marshal. He was one of Napoleon's ablest commanders: he fought under him in Egypt, at Austerlitz (1805), Auerstädt (1806), after which he received his dukedom, and at Eckmühl and Wagram in 1809. He was a despotic governor of Warsaw (1807–10), accompanied Napoleon to Moscow and after the return from Elba was minister of war. He lost all his titles and rank after the Bourbon restoration, but was subsequently pardoned and, in 1819, made a peer of France.

Davy, Sir Humphry (1778–1829). English chemist. His name was given to the miners' safety lamp which he invented (1815) to meet the problem of fire-damp. Born in Penzance, he became apprentice to a surgeon apothecary, and having studied chemistry became superintendent (1798) of the laboratory in the Pneumatic Institution at Clifton, established to investigate the medicinal effects of inhaling gases. There he discovered (1799) the anaesthetic properties of nitrous oxide (laughing gas). From 1802 to 1813 he was professor of chemistry at the newly-established Royal Institution in London, and during this period he isolated sodium, potassium, calcium, magnesium, barium and strontium by using an electric current to decompose their fused salts.

He formulated a theory of the electrical nature of chemical affinity (not verified for more than a century) and analysed many substances such as metallic oxides and acids, suggesting what elements were responsible for their properties. He recognized chlorine and iodine as elements, although unable to isolate the former. President of the Royal Society 1820–27, he died after a life of extraordinary energy and diversity of interests.
Hartley, H., *Humphry Davy*. 1971

Dawes, Charles Gates (1865–1951). American general and banker. As director of the Allied Reparations Commission (1923–24) he proposed the 'Dawes Plan' for securing German repayment of war debts to the Allies. He was awarded the Nobel Peace Prize in 1925 and he was vice-president of the U.S. (1925–29) and U.S. Ambassador to Great Britain (1929–32).

Day Lewis, Cecil (1904–1972). British poet, born in Ireland. Regarded with W. H. * Auden and Stephen * Spender as one of the 'Thirties group' of poets he was Professor of Poetry at Oxford (1951–56). His work includes *A Hope of Poetry* (1934), *The Friendly Tree* (1936) and *Overtures to Death* (1938). He was created C.B.E. in 1950 and Poet Laureate in 1968. Under the pseudonym Nicholas blake he wrote several accomplished detective stories.
Collected Poems, 1954; *The Buried Day*, 1960 (autobiography)

Dayan, Moshe (1915–1981). Israeli soldier and statesman, born Deganya, Palestine (now Israel). In 1937 he was a member of the guerrilla force under British Captain Orde Wingate, organized to fight Arab rebels in Palestine and to form the nucleus of a Jewish army. Dayan formed the *Haganah* (Jewish militia) but the band was declared illegal and Dayan imprisoned 1939–41. Freed to serve in World War II, he led a Palestinian Jewish company against the Vichy French in Syria, and lost an eye: his black patch became his trademark.

He was commander of the Jerusalem area in the Israeli war of independence (1948), and later headed the delegation in armistice negotiations. From 1953–58 he was chief of staff and planned and led the 1956 invasion of Sinai Peninsula, which gained him the reputation of an outstanding military commander. In 1966 he published *Diary of the Sinai Campaign*. Retired as chief of staff, he was elected to the *Knesset* (parliament) as member of the Labour party. In 1959 he was appointed minister of agriculture by Prime Minister * Ben-Gurion, and served until 1964. In 1967 when war with the Arabs was imminent, Dayan was appointed minister of defence by popular demand; he directed the extremely successful attack on Egypt, Jordan and Syria in the 6-Day War.

A symbol of security to the Israelis, he played a large part in the post-war period in determining policy in Arab territory occupied by Israeli forces.
Teveth, S., *Moshe Dayan*. 1973

Deák, Ferencz (1802–1876). Hungarian politician. He entered parliament in 1833 and, though a progressive, gained a great reputation for moderation and wisdom. He was minister of justice during the ferment of 1848 but resigned when Kossuth seized power, and after his overthrow remained abroad for a few years. On Austria's defeat by Prussia (1866) he conducted the negotiations by which Hungary became an equal partner with Austria in the Habsburg Empire. Hungary was granted a constitution in 1867 and Deák was the leading figure in the Hungarian assembly until his death.
Király, B. K., *Ferencz Deák*. 1975

Deakin, Alfred (1856–1919). Australian politician. A barrister and a journalist, he first entered the parliament of Victoria in 1879 and soon became one of the leaders of the Liberal party. In 1883 he joined a coalition ministry, and as minister of public works and water supply won international repute for his irrigation plans. He then became one of the most persuasive advocates of Australian federation. He was attorney general in the first Commonwealth government (1901–03) and prime minister of three different political combinations (1903–04, 1905–08, 1909–10). He was in favour of imperial preference and compulsory military service.

Deakin, Arthur (1890–1955). English trade union official. As general secretary of the Transport and General Workers Union (1940–55) he became a figure of national importance during and after World War II. He used his power to maintain vigorous trade union opposition to the left-wing ideologies of the Labour party.

Dean, James (Byron) (1931–1955). American actor. Despite the brevity of his career, he was a spectacular screen success, embodying the restlessness of mid-50s American youth with his performance in *Rebel Without a Cause* (1955). His two other major films were *East of Eden* (1955) and *Giant* (released 1956). Since his death in a car accident, he has acquired international cult status.

Deborah. Prophetess and heroine in the Old Testament (Judges IV, V), wife of Lapidoth. Judge of Israel and the only woman to hold that office. *c.* 1125 B.C. she persuaded Barak to free her people from Canaanite oppression; with him she led an army against Sisera and the Canaanites, and soundly defeated them at the Battle of Esdraelon. A long period of peace ensued. Scholars generally accept the 'Song of Deborah' (Judges V) as a genuine contemporary document, and therefore one of the oldest Biblical records; it is one of the most brilliant poems in the Bible.

Debré, Michel Jean Pierre (1912–). French politician. A senator 1948–1958, he backed General de Gaulle's resumption of power (1958) and was appointed minister of justice. He drafted the new Constitution which was adopted by a referendum in December 1958, and in January 1959 he became the first premier of the Fifth French Republic until replaced by Georges * Pompidou. He served as minister for finance (1966–68), foreign affairs (1968–69) and defence (1969–73).

Debs, Eugene Victor (1855–1926). American union leader and Socialist. He was active in the organization of railway workers from 1875, and in 1893 became president of the American Railway Union. For his part in the Pullman strike (1894) he was imprisoned for contempt of court. He founded the U.S. Social Democratic Party (1897) and was Socialist candidate for the presidency regularly from 1900 to 1912 and in 1920. He was again imprisoned (1918–21) for alleged sedition in World War I. He was an advocate of organizing trade unions on an industry-wide basis.
Ginger, R., *The Bending Cross: A Biography of Eugene Victor Debs*. 1949

Debussy, Claude Achille (1862–1918). French composer, born at St-Germain-en-Laye. He entered the Paris Conservatoire when he was 10 and studied composition for a time under Massenet. He soon reacted against classical models and can be regarded as the founder of 'Impressionism' in music. In 1879 he visited Italy, Austria and Russia as the protégé of Madame von Meck, Tchaikovsky's patroness in the preceding generation. *L'Enfant prodigue* (1884) won for him the Prix de Rome. From 1892 to 1902 he was primarily occupied with the opera *Pelléas et Mélisande* (libretto by Maeterlinck) which, while it provoked much controversy, gave Debussy a position of indisputable importance in the musical world. The orchestral composition *Prélude à l'après-midi d'un faune* (1894), based on a poem by Mallarmé, was the first work of his maturity and was followed by *Printemps* (1896), *La Mer* (1903–05) and *Images* (1906–12), the last two showing that he had freed himself from the sensual influence of the 'decadents'. Debussy also wrote many songs, twenty-four preludes for piano, and three sonatas. Incidental music to D'Annunzio's *Le Martyre de St Sébastien* (1911) and music for the ballet *Jeux* (1912) were his last orchestral works. Debussy was at various times influenced by Javanese music, by an admiration for Wagner, and by the compositions of Berlioz, Mussorgsky and Fauré, as well as by the symbolist poets and the French Impressionist painters. In his later years he suffered from cancer, and was burdened by debts. He toured Europe giving concerts, and also composed some fine chamber music during World War I. He was a great innovator and experimenter, who enlarged the scope of music both by his introduction of medieval and oriental styles and by his progressive views about harmony.
Nichols, R., *Debussy*. 1972

Decatur, Stephen (1779–1820). American naval commander. During the war against Tripoli pirates in the Mediterranean (1801–1805), under fire from 141 guns he entered the harbour and boarded and burned the captured ship *Philadelphia*, a feat which Nelson described as the 'most daring of the age'. He captured the *Macedonian* in the 'war of 1812' against Britain but was forced to surrender in 1814. In 1815 he resumed the contest with the pirate régimes of Algeria, Tunis and Tripoli, defeated them and obtained indemnities. Violence pursued him to the last: he was killed in a duel. To Decatur Americans owe the toast 'May she be always in the right: but my country, right or wrong'.
Brody, C. T., *Stephen Decatur*. 1900

Dee, John (1527–1608). English astrologer, mathematician and reputed magician. He was educated at Cambridge and Louvain and travelled extensively. Although he was imprisoned by Mary Tudor under suspicion of arranging her death by magic, he impressed Elizabeth I with his scientific and occult skills. Many of his interests previously dismissed by historians and others as 'on the lunatic fringe' of learning and enquiry are now seriously investigated; Dee has been recognized as one of the most enterprising and intelligent, if still somewhat ambivalent, figures of the Elizabethan period.

Deeping, Warwick (1877–1950). English writer. His novels, some sixty in all, and especially *Sorrell and Son* (1925), achieved an enormous vogue.

Deffand, Marie de Vichy Chamrond, Marquise du (1697–1780). French literary hostess. Her *salons* were famous in 18th-century Paris. The witty and lively conversations there are recalled in her letters to Voltaire and Horace Walpole, with whom she developed a passionate friendship in her old age.

Defoe, Daniel (1660–1731). English writer. The creator of *Robinson Crusoe*, he was the son of a London tallow chandler named Foe, and the more impressive surname was adopted (*c.* 1700) by Daniel himself. He too was a business man for some years. By the turn of the century he was known as a vigorous political pamphleteer: the issue of an ironic pamphlet which purported to be an attack on the Dissenters but in reality was directed against the Anglican high church resulted (1703) in imprisonment, the pillory and bankruptcy. This crisis necessitated a *volte-face*. Though a Whig he started the *Review* with the aid and patronage of Harley, leader of the moderate Tories. When George I came to the throne he reversed the process by getting control of Tory periodicals and, gradually, without attracting attention, reconciling their policies.

At the age of 60 he started the new career as a prolific writer of fiction that brought him so much renown. In 1719 appeared *Robinson Crusoe*, based on the experiences of Alexander * Selkirk; *Moll Flanders* (1721) leads the story of a lady of easy virtue through many episodes to an ending of penitence and prosperity. Other works include *A Journal of the Plague Year* (1721), *Jack Sheppard* (1724) and *Roxana* (1724). *The History of Apparitions* (1727) is among the books which show the continuing interest in the supernatural revealed by *The Apparition of Mrs Veal* (1706). His *Tour Thro' the Whole Island of Great Britain* (3 vols. 1724–26) displays the author as a shrewd and observant traveller. He wrote a vast amount of hack-work, sometimes under pseudonyms, on economic, social, political and historical matters, all of it judged very competent and readable.

Sutherland, J. R., *Defoe*. 1954

De Forest, Lee (1873–1961). American physicist and engineer. He introduced the 'grid' into the thermionic valve and so made possible the large-scale amplification of radio signals. In 1916 De Forest was responsible for the transmission of the first radio programme, and in 1923 he invented a technique for recording sound on film. He later also devised a process whereby photographs could be transmitted by radio. See also E. H. * Armstrong.

De Forest, L., *Father of Radio*. 1950

Degas, (Hilaire Germain) Edgar (1834–1917). French painter. One of the greatest of the 19th century, he was a pupil of a follower of Ingres and although at first he seemed likely to become an academic painter, he developed into one of the great innovators of his time after coming to know Manet and his circle. In 1874 he took part in the first Impressionist Exhibition (he exhibited in seven of their eight exhibitions). He had private means and unlike many of the Impressionist painters did not depend on selling his pictures. After the Franco-Prussian War he turned in his painting to such unposed subjects as ballet girls and models in their off-duty moments, working girls and cabaret artists, showing a detached objectiveness of great power. He used a wide variety of media – oil, gouache, tempera, pastel – the latter increasingly as his eyesight failed. He was also a competent sculptor.

Rich, D., *Degas*. 1954

de Gaulle, Charles *see* **Gaulle, Charles de**

Degrelle, Léon Marie Joseph Ignace (1906–). Belgian Fascist politician. He led the Rexist party (from 1935) and collaborated with the Nazis during World War II, after which he took refuge in Spain.

De Havilland, Sir Geoffrey (1882–1965). English pioneer of aeroplane design. He built his first plane in 1908 but it never flew. He then joined the Army Aircraft Factory at Farnborough, where he produced the B.E.1, D.H.2, D.H.4, and D.H.9, which played an important part in World War I. He formed his own firm in 1920: perhaps the best known of his many commercial aircraft was the tiny Moth, which was priced within the reach of many hundreds of private flyers. In World War II the most successful of his achievements were the multi-purpose Mosquito and the Vampire jet; after the war came the Comet. Two of his three sons were lost in test flying. He received the O.M. in 1962.

Dekker, Thomas (*c.* 1572–1632). English dramatist, poet and pamphleteer. His plays are lively and realistic and are notable for their witty dialogue. His plays include *The Shoemaker's Holiday* (1600), *Old Fortunatus* (1600), *The Honest Whore* (1604, Part II 1630). Among the most interesting of his many pamphlets is *The Gull's Hornbook* (1609), a racy account of London's places of public resort. At various times he collaborated with (among others) Ben Jonson, Middleton, Massinger, John Ford, and Webster.

de Kooning, Willem (1904–). American painter. He was born in the Netherlands but settled in New York in 1926. His painting developed in the direction of abstract expressionism and by 1940 he was considered a leader in this field.
Rosenberg, H., *De Kooning Drawings*. 1967

De La Beche, Sir Henry Thomas (1796–1855). English amateur geologist. He travelled extensively in the 1820s through Britain and the Continent, and published widely in descriptive stratigraphy. He was a scrupulous fieldworker, stressing the primacy of facts and distrusting theories, as can be seen from his *Sections and Views Illustrative of Geological Phenomena* (1830) and *How to Observe* (1835). In the 1830s De La Beche conceived the idea of government-sponsored geological investigation of areas of Britain. He personally undertook a survey of Devon, for which he was paid £500. He then persuaded the government to formalize this arrangement, and in 1835 the Geological Survey was founded with De La Beche as Director. The Survey began work in Cornwall and on the South Wales coalfield, flourished and expanded. De La Beche's career reached its peak with the establishment of a Mines Record Office and then the opening in 1851, under the aegis of the Geological Survey, of the Museum of Practical Geology and the School of Mines in London.
McCartney, P., *H. T. De La Beche*. 1978

Delacroix, (Ferdinand Victor) Eugène (1798–1863). French painter. Probably the illegitimate son of * Talleyrand, he was the great leader of Romanticism in painting and the defender of colour (at the expense of draughtsmanship, though he drew admirably) and movement. He opposed Ingres's more static line and balance. He had been in Baron Gros's studio, knew the dying Géricault, studied Rubens and the Venetians, was a friend of Bonington and admired Constable's *Hay Wain* so much that he repainted parts of *The Massacre at Chios* (1824) just before it was exhibited. He admired English colour and freshness of handling. The exuberance both of his colours and of his subjects (mainly contemporary or exotic) was much attacked. His visit to North Africa (1832) provided many new subjects, e.g. scenes from Arab life and animals fighting. From the mid 1830s he undertook large-scale official decorations, e.g. the ceiling of the Salon d'Apollon in the Louvre (1849), works in the libraries of the Palais Bourbon and the Senate (1838–47) and the church of S. Sulpice. His *Journal* gives a remarkable picture of Parisian life and of the many celebrities who were his friends. His careful studies of colour and the prominence he gave to it had a great effect on later painters, notably * Renoir, * Degas and * Cézanne.
Jullian, P., *Delacroix*. 1963

de la Mare, Walter (1873–1956). English poet of Huguenot descent. He retired from his employment with the Anglo-Iranian Oil Company in 1908 to give his full time to writing, which included book reviewing as well as poetry. In his volumes of short poems – *Songs of Childhood* (1902), *The Listeners* (1912), *Peacock Pie* (1913) – he evoked a delicate and enchanting fantasy world. He also wrote short stories, children's books, and novels, e.g. *The Return* (1910) and *Memoirs of a Midget* (1921); the latter won the

Hawthornden and James Tate prizes. He received the O.M. in 1953.
Cecil, D., *Walter de la Mare*. 1973

Delane, John Thaddeus (1817–1879). English journalist. After working as a parliamentary reporter he was editor of *The Times* (1841–77), and his knowledge of world affairs, his innumerable sources of information, extraordinary flair for news and complete independence of judgement gave his paper a prestige and influence that extended far beyond his own country. His attacks during the Crimean War on the mismanagement responsible for shortages of food, warm clothing and ordinary necessities, revealed by the famous *Times* correspondent W. H. Russell, are an example of the way in which he could unseat a government.

De la Roche, Mazo (1885–1961). Canadian novelist. Her novel *Jalna* (1927) was the first of a series which told the story of the Whiteoaks family and achieved an enormous popular success.
De la Roche, M., *Ringing the Changes*. 1957

De la Warr, Thomas West, 12th Baron (1577–1618). English administrator. He was the first governor of Virginia (1610–11) and rescued the colony from ruin. The American state and river Delaware are named after him.

Delbruck, Max (1906–1981). German–American molecular biologist. He trained in physics under Niels * Bohr and biology with T. H. * Morgan and was a professor of biology at the California Institute of Technology 1947–81. His work on phage (a virus which attacks bacteria) and genetic recombination in bacteria laid the basis for molecular biology and he won the 1969 Nobel Prize for Medicine.

Delibes, (Clément Philibert) Léo (1836–1891). French composer. He studied at the Paris Conservatoire, and spent most of his life in Paris, where among his musical occupations were those of organist and chorus master with opera companies. His compositions include the very successful ballets *Coppélia* (1870) and *Sylvia* (1876) and the comic opera *Lakmé* (1883).

De L'Isle, William Philip Sidney, 1st Viscount (1909–). English politician, soldier and administrator, born in London. A descendant of Sir Philip Sidney, he was educated at Eton and Cambridge, served with the Grenadier Guards, rising to major, and won the Victoria Cross at Anzio (1944). A Conservative M.P. 1944–45, he was Parliamentary Secretary to the Ministry of Pensions 1945 and Secretary of State for Air 1951–55. He held directorships in banking and insurance and became the last U.K. resident to be appointed (1961) as Governor-General of Australia, serving until 1965.

Delius, Frederick (1862–1934). English composer of German extraction. As a young man he went to Florida to grow oranges, became a music teacher in Virginia, and, on returning to Europe, moved to Leipzig where he first made his mark as a composer. From 1890 he lived in France.

His music, rhythmic, rhapsodic, and harmonically luxuriant, was at first poorly received except in Germany. Its acceptance in England, where alone it has obtained a lasting hold, came largely through the efforts of Sir Thomas Beecham, whose performances were a model for other interpreters. Delius's works include operas, notably *A Village Romeo and Juliet* (composed 1900–01), a Violin Concerto (1916), the orchestral works *Brigg Fair* (1907), *A Song of the High Hills* (1911–12) and *Eventyr* (1917) and choral works *Appalachia* (1902), *Sea Drift* (1903), and *A Mass of Life* (1904–05). In his later years, blind and paralysed, he dictated his work to the musician Eric Fenby, who wrote a memoir of him.
Fenby, E., *Delius*. 1971

Deller, Alfred (George) (1912–1979). English counter-tenor. He worked in the furniture trade for thirteen years, sang professionally at Canterbury and St Paul's Cathedral (1941–61) and with the encouragement of Michael * Tippett revived the art of the counter-tenor (male alto), after 300 years of neglect. He made many recordings of works by Purcell, Bach, Handel and Gibbons.

Delorme, Marion (1613–?1650). French adventuress. Among her many lovers was said to be the English royal favourite, the Duke of Buckingham. She disappeared after her association with the Marquis de Cinq-Mars, who was executed for plotting with Spain, had brought her under the suspicious notice of Richelieu; she may have escaped to England.

She figures in works by Victor Hugo and de Vigny.

De Mille, Cecil Blount (1881–1959). American film director. He entered the film industry in 1913, founded the Paramount Company and pioneered the production of such lavish and spectacular films as *The Ten Commandments* (1923, 1957), *The Sign of the Cross* (1932), *The Greatest Show on Earth* (1952). His daughter **Agnes de Mille** (1908–), a dancer from 1928, won fame as choreographer for musical comedies such as *Oklahoma* (1943), *Brigadoon* (1947). She also devised her own ballets, e.g. *Fall River Legend* (1948), *The Rib of Eve* (1956).

Democritus (*c.* 460–370 B.C.). Greek philosopher. A citizen of Abdera in Thrace, he was known as the 'Laughing Philosopher' because of his amusement at the weaknesses of mankind. He is famous for an atomic theory which stimulated the thought of many future thinkers. The essence of it was that the only ultimate realities are (a) atoms, minute, solid, invisible and indestructible; (b) void. The atoms, whirling in the void, combine and coalesce in an infinite number of patterns and shapes which present 'images' to the senses. He is known to have left a vast quantity of writing on every aspect of human knowledge. Unfortunately only two or three hundred fragments survive and almost all that is known of his work is at second hand.

Demosthenes (*c.* 384–322 B.C.). Athenian orator and politician. Having studied law and oratory to regain his inheritance from fraudulent guardians, he became a speech writer for litigants in the courts. When 30 years old he entered politics. By two series of brilliant speeches known as the *Olynthiacs* and the *Philippics* he tried to convince the Athenians and their allies of the danger from Philip of Macedon. The Athenians did indeed go to war but failed to save Olynthus. From 346 to 340 Demosthenes was actively building up a coalition but it was decisively defeated by Philip at Chaeronea (338). Demosthenes vindicated himself in one of his greatest speeches, *On The Crown*, a reply to an attack by his great rival Aeschines on a proposal to award him a crown of honour. In 325, however, he went into exile after being charged (probably falsely) with embezzling money from the state treasury. He returned after Alexander the Great's death but an attempt to throw off the Macedonian yoke again met with disaster. Fleeing from the battlefield, Demosthenes was caught by the enemy and took poison.

Dempsey, Sir Miles Christopher (1896–1969). British soldier. A lieutenant-colonel at the beginning of World War I, he rose to command the British 2nd Army in the liberation campaign in western Europe (1944–45). Earlier he had won distinction in combined operations and had been a corps commander in the Mediterranean area. In 1945 he commanded in south-east Asia and in 1946 was commander-in-chief, Middle East.

Deng Xiaoping (Teng Hsaio-p'ing) (1904–). Chinese Communist politician, born in Sichuan province. After studing in France and Russia, he joined the CCP in 1924, served as an officer and political commissar in the Red Army in Shaanxi and Jiangxi and later in the Peoples' Liberation Army. He took part in the Long March 1934–36 and was political commissar of the PLA 2nd Field Army 1948–54. Elected to the CCP Central Committee in 1943, Deng was vice premier 1954–67, a Politburo member 1955–67 and general secretary of the CCP 1956–67. During the 'cultural revolution' he was denounced as a 'capitalist roader', forced from office and publicly humiliated, and he attempted suicide (1967). In April 1973 he was reinstated as a deputy premier and took charge of government operations during * Zhou Enlai's last illness, rejoined the Politburo and in 1975 became PLA chief of staff. In April 1976 he was dismissed from all posts, denounced as a 'capitalist roader' and subjected to a campaign of attack for months. In July 1977 he was restored as 1st deputy premier, vice chairman of the CCP, and PLA chief of staff and worked in conjunction with Chairman Hua Gofeng. In 1978 he visited Tokyo to conclude the China–Japan Friendship Treaty.

Denikin, Anton Ivanovich (1872–1947). Russian general of World War I. He rose from the ranks; after the Russian Revolution he was imprisoned for supporting Kornilov's attempted revolt against Kerensky's Socialist government but escaped to raise an army in the south. Meanwhile (November 1917) the Bolsheviks under Lenin had seized power and Denikin's 'White' army, with Allied support, occupied the Ukraine and northern Caucasus.

As Bolshevik power grew the 'Red' army gradually forced the 'Whites' back to the Crimea and in 1920 Denikin abandoned the struggle; he died in exile in France.

Denis (Dionysius), **St** (died *c.* 280). French patron saint. Sent from Rome (*c.* 250) to convert the Gauls, he won many converts in and around Paris, of which he became first bishop. During one of the periodical persecutions of Christians, Denis with two others was beheaded by order of the Roman governor. The Abbey of St Denis, founded (*c.* 630) by King Dagobert on the supposed site of his tomb, acquired great wealth and for long was the burial place of French kings.

Dennis, C(larence) J(ames) (1876–1938). Australian poet. After working as a journalist, he became a labourer at Broken Hill, where he gained the insight into human nature apparent in his poems. *Backblock Ballads and Other Verses* (1913) was his first collection, but it was his second, *The Songs of a Sentimental Bloke* (1915), which gave him an assured position in the ranks of popular poets.

De Quincey, Thomas (1785–1859). English writer. Son of a Manchester merchant, he was famous as the author of *Confessions of an English Opium Eater*. The experiences which gave rise to this book began at Worcester College, Oxford, where he went in 1803 after running away from Manchester Grammar School and a year's adventurous and hard wandering which had undermined his health. The *Confessions* first appeared in the *London Magazine* in 1821 and from then onwards he became one of the leading essayists of his day. In 1809 he went to live at Wordsworth's old home, Dove Cottage, Grasmere, and thus came to know well the Lakeland poets, Wordsworth himself, Coleridge and Southey, though his later brilliant accounts of them in his *Literary Reminiscences* (1834–40), published after his removal to Edinburgh in 1828, were waspish enough to cause offence. In 1816 he married Mary Simpson, daughter of a Lakeland farmer, who bore him a large family and did much to curb his addiction to opium. In all his writing de Quincey uses a beautiful and rhythmical, if sometimes intricate, prose. He had a genuine interest in German philosophy, to which he tried to direct English attention.

Hayter, A., *Opium and the Romantic Imagination*. 1968

Derain, André (1880–1954). French painter. He was one of the original 'Fauves' (a word meaning 'wild beasts' and referring to the sense of violence and heightened intensity imparted by strong colour and distortion) and much influenced by Vlaminck, Matisse and Cézanne. Before 1914 he used very bright colour and (often) a pointillist technique. His later works are more academic and mostly painted in browns and greens.

Sutton, D., *André Derain*. 1959

Derby, Edward Geoffrey Smith Stanley, 14th Earl of (1799–1869). English politician. He first entered the House of Commons (where his dash and brilliance won him the nickname the 'Rupert of debate') in 1820 as a Whig and supported the Reform Bill, but from 1834 he was a Conservative. (As colonial secretary he carried the act for the emancipation of West Indian slaves in 1833.) On his father's death (1844) he led the wing of his party in the Lords opposed to Peel's free-trade policy. Prime Minister for three short terms (1852, 1858–59, and 1866–68), he was, with Disraeli, responsible for the passing of the second Reform Bill (1867). He was a classical scholar who translated the *Iliad* (1864), a keen sportsman, and cared little for office (he declined to form a ministry in 1855).

Derwentwater, James Radcliffe, 3rd Earl of (1689–1716). English Jacobite. A Roman Catholic and linked by birth with the Stuart line (his mother was a daughter of Charles II by Moll Davis), he joined the Jacobite rebellion (1715). He was captured at Preston, attainted of treason and beheaded in London on Tower Hill – a savage sentence for a young hero, beloved by all.

Skeet, J. A., *Life of the Earl of Derwentwater*. 1929

Desai, Morarji Ranchhodji (1896–). Indian politician. A Gujerati, he became a public servant, a follower of Mahatma * Gandhi from 1930 and was imprisoned five times. He became chief minister of Bombay 1952–56, and served in the Union government as minister for commerce 1956–58, minister for finance 1958–63 and 1967–69, and deputy prime minister 1967–69. He contested the Congress leadership against Indira * Gandhi in 1966, supported by the traditionalists, founded the Janata Party, and became Prime Minister 1977–79 in a coalition united only by opposition to Mrs Gandhi.

Descartes, René (1596–1650). French philosopher, mathematician and scientist, born at La Haye, Touraine. Educated by the Jesuits, he was mainly impressed by the certainty of mathematical conclusions, which he tried to make the basis of his philosophical system. From 1628 he lived and worked in Holland for twenty years. In 1649 Queen Christina of Sweden invited him to live in Stockholm, but he died there after a few months. In his philosophy, he attempted to set out an account of the universe based on indubitable premisses from which all else could be rigorously deduced. Following the method which came to be known as 'Cartesian', he found that there was only one thing that he could not possibly doubt: since he did have certain thoughts, whether or not true, he must exist as a 'thinking substance' (*cogito ergo sum*: 'I think, therefore I exist'). He went on to establish the existence of his own body, of other 'extended substances' and hence of the material universe, and of God. A dualism of spirit and matter, so complete that the one cannot exercise influence upon the other without the intervention of God, was a fundamental part of his system, which provoked criticism by later psychologists. His work, set out in *Discourse de la Méthode* (1637), *Méditations de prima philosophia* (1641) and *Principia Philosophiae* (1644), was the first great philosophy written in French: it also established a literary style which has been of immense influence. In mathematics, he instituted a system of co-ordinate geometry, the application of algebra to geometrical problems, and although he mistakenly believed, at least initially, that scientific investigation should proceed by *a priori* deduction, he himself did important experimental work in optics. He is thought to have been a sincere Catholic and after Galileo had been condemned by the Inquisition he withdrew from publication an early work which advanced the Copernican system of the universe.
Vrooman, J. R., *René Descartes: A Biography*. 1970

Deschanel, Paul Eugène Louis (1856–1922). French politician. He was president of the Chamber of Deputies (1898–1902 and 1912–20) and was elected president of the Republic in February 1920 (defeating Georges Clemenceau), but had to resign in September after a temporary mental breakdown.

Desmoulins, Camille (1760–1794). French revolutionary politician. He was a lawyer and journalist in Paris, and despite his stammer helped to rouse the mobs at the storming of the Bastille (14 July 1789). He was a member of the National Assembly (1789–91) and of the National Convention (1792–94). In his newspaper, *Le Vieux Cordelier*, he attacked the terrorism of Robespierre and his party, and was guillotined with his friend * Danton.

De Soto, Hernando (*c.* 1500–1542). Spanish explorer. He was with Pizarro in the conquest of Peru, landed in Florida (1539), explored northwards as far as what are now the Carolinas, and then eastward to the Mississippi, which he discovered and crossed in 1541.

Desrochers, Alfred (1901–). French-Canadian poet. His collections *L'Offrande aux vierges* (1929) and *À l'Ombre de l'Orford* (1930) revealed his remarkable gift for evoking the way of life of the country people in the province of Quebec.

Dessalines, Jean Jacques (*c.* 1758–1806). Haitian adventurer. After taking part in the slave revolt (1791) he became a provincial governor under * Toussaint L'Ouverture. After the latter was captured he renewed the struggle, forced the French to surrender and in 1804 proclaimed Haitian independence. With British support he drove the French out of Haiti (1803), proclaimed himself as the emperor Jacques I (1804–06), but his cruelty and extortions led to his assassination.

Deterding, Sir Henri Wilhelm August (1865–1939). Dutch oil magnate. Born in Amsterdam, he was a bank clerk there until he went to the East Indies to seek his fortune. In 1896 he joined the Royal Dutch Oil Company, of which he had become director general by 1902. The merger with the British 'Shell' company in 1907 made the Royal Dutch–Shell group one of the strongest oil combines in the world. He was its director general until 1936.

Deutscher, Isaac (1907–1967). English writer born in Poland. He was a prominent Communist journalist in Poland, but was expelled from the party for his anti-Stalinist position. He fled to England (1939) and wrote for leading British periodicals. In addition to his journalistic work his biography of Stalin (1949) is regarded as a work of authoritative scholarship.

De Valera, Eamon (1882–1975). Irish politician of half-Spanish descent, born in New York. After graduating at the Royal University, Dublin, he became a mathematics teacher. He joined the nationalist Irish volunteers (1913) and was sentenced to death for his part in the Easter rebellion (1916), but was reprieved and, in 1917, released. He was elected Sinn Fein member of East Clare in 1917 but never took his seat. Another term of imprisonment (1918–19) was ended by a daring escape from Lincoln Jail. In 1919 he became head of the insurgent Irish government but did not accompany the negotiating team to London in 1921; he was bitterly opposed to concessions made by Arthur Griffith and Michael Collins and led the militant republicans in the ensuing civil war. In 1927 he finally abandoned his extremist attitude, formed a new political party, the Fianna Fail (soldiers of destiny), which he led in the Dail Eireann (parliament). After winning the election of 1932 he became president of the executive council (prime minister) and between 1932 and 1938 gradually snapped the links with Britain until, under a new constitution, Eire (as the Irish Free State became) was virtually independent and remained neutral during World War II. The final separation which took the Irish republic out of the Commonwealth came under John Costello, who succeeded him in 1948. De Valera regained office in 1951 and, except for a short interval (1954–56), retained it until he became president of the republic 1959–73.
Fitzgibbon, C. and Morrison, G., *The Life and Times of Eamon De Valera*. 1974

De Valois, Dame Ninette (Edris Stannus) (1898–). British ballerina and choreographer, born in Ireland. She danced under Diaghilev and from 1926 to 1930 was choreographer at the Old Vic Theatre, London. In 1931 she founded and became artistic director of the Sadler's Wells Ballet, now known as the Royal Ballet.
De Valois, N., *Come Dance with Me*. 1957

De Vries, Peter (1910–). American novelist, born in Chicago. The son of Dutch immigrants, he studied at Calvin College, became a freelance writer (1931), editor of *Poetry* (1942) and a staff writer on the *New Yorker*. His dead-pan, multi-punned humour exposes many aspects of life without individual responsibility in a commercialized mass society. His novels include: *No, But I saw the Movie* (1952), *Comfort Me with Apples* (1956), *The Mackerel Plaza* (1958), *The Blood of the Lamb* (1962), *The Cat's Pajamas and Witch's Milk* (1968), *Without a Stitch in Time* (1972), *The Glory of the Hummingbird* (1974), *I Hear America Swinging* (1976) and *Madder Music* (1977).

Dewar, Sir James (1842–1923). Scottish physical chemist. From 1875 he was Jacksonian professor of natural philosophy at Cambridge and also (from 1877) a chemistry professor of the Royal Institution. He is best known for his extensive researches into the properties of matter at very low temperatures. He invented the vacuum-jacketed flask, often referred to as a Dewar flask, the parent of the present-day vacuum flask. He showed that liquid oxygen and ozone are magnetic, and he was the first to prepare liquid and solid hydrogen. With Sir Frederick Abel he invented cordite.

De Wet, Christiaan Rudolph (1854–1922). Boer soldier and politician. He was a successful guerilla leader in the Boer War (1899–1902) and never accepted the political implications of defeat. Believing that the outbreak of World War I (1914) provided an opportunity to re-establish a Boer republic, he led a rising against the Botha government. He was captured and briefly imprisoned.
De Wet, C., *Three Years' War*. 1902

Dewey, George (1837–1917). American sailor. He led the U.S. fleet in the Spanish–American War (1898–99), destroyed the whole Spanish squadron and captured Manila (1898), and became a popular hero in the U.S.

Dewey, John (1859–1952). American philosopher. Important for his advancement of progressive education and Professor of philosophy at Michigan, Chicago and Columbia Universities, he was influenced by the pragmatism of Peirce and William James. He thought of philosophy as something relevant

to practical problems, his views being sometimes crudely summarized as 'truth is what works'. In fact his thoughts covered a much wider field, as such books as *Reconstruction in Philosophy* (1920) show: he also wrote on psychology, logic and ethics. His views on education, through the many translations of his *School and Society* (1900) and *Democracy and Education* (1916), achieved international influence. On the grounds that 'education *is* life, not a preparation for life' and that a 'school is a community in miniature' he held that children should be faced with practical concerns and real problems rather than given traditional instruction; he emphasized 'learning by doing'.
Berstein, R. J., *John Dewey*. 1966

Dewey, Melvil Louis Kossuth (1851–1931). American librarian. In 1876 he devised the 'Decimal Classification and Relative Index' for library books widely adopted in public libraries not only in the U.S. but in many other countries.

Dewey, Thomas Edmund (1902–1971). American lawyer and politician. As special prosecutor (1935–38) to investigate crime and vice in New York State, he won a national reputation for rooting out organized crime. He was governor of New York state 1942–54 and was chosen as a republican presidential candidate in 1944 (he lost to Roosevelt) and in 1948 when he again lost, by a narrow margin, to * Truman.
Hughes, R., *Thomas E. Dewey*. 1944

De Wint, Peter (1784–1849). English landscape painter. Son of a Staffordshire doctor of Dutch origin, he was particularly fond of Lincolnshire, where the broad expanses of flat country made the luminous washes in which he delighted particularly appropriate. As his work as a drawing master kept him in London for the early part of each year, many of his pictures show harvest scenes. A large collection is in the Victoria and Albert Museum, London.

De Witt, Johan (or Jan) (1625–1672). Dutch statesman. His father was burgomaster of Dordrecht and his family was traditionally opposed to the house of Orange: he himself took part in the administration of his native city until he became (1653) Grand Pensionary of Holland (an office which, as developed by him, made him the head of the largest of the Dutch provinces and predominant in the country as a whole). He connived with Cromwell that the peace treaty with England (1654) should stipulate that the house of Orange (which favoured the royalist cause in England) was to be excluded from all its offices. His foreign policy aimed at an alliance with France, so as to leave himself free to assert Dutch maritime power. Intervention in the Baltic proved profitable and some striking successes were achieved in an indecisive war with England (1666–67) but an unforeseen alliance between England and France created a crisis, in which the Dutch turned to their traditional saviours, the house of Orange. De Witt resigned in 1672 but a fortnight later, when visiting his brother Cornelius who had been imprisoned on a charge of conspiracy, he was killed by an angry mob of Orange partisans.

Diaghilev, Sergei Pavlovich (1872–1929). Russian ballet impresario, born in Novgorod. In pursuit of an idea of introducing Russian art to western Europe, he presented (1908) Chaliapin in a season of Russian opera in Paris. He followed this up with his famous 'Ballets Russes' presented in Paris (1909) and London (1911) in the conviction that in ballet he could form a union of all the arts. To this end he secured the services of dancers of outstanding skill – Pavlova, Nijinsky, Karsavina and Lopokova – and choreographers such as Fokine and Massine: he commissioned Benois, Bakst, Matisse, Picasso, Braque and others to design the decor and Debussy, Ravel, Stravinsky and Prokofiev to compose ballet scores. The Revolution broke his links with Russia, but with Paris as its headquarters his company continued to enjoy the highest reputation.
Percival, J., *The World of Diaghilev*. 1971

Diaz, Armando (1861–1928). Italian general of World War I. He succeeded Cadoma as commander-in-chief after the disaster at Caporetto (1917), retrieved the situation and by his decisive victory at Vittorio Veneto (October 1918) forced the Austrians to accept an armistice a few days later.

Diaz, Bartolomeo (*c*. 1450–1500). Portuguese navigator. Of noble birth, he became interested in geographical discoveries at the court of John II who sent him to explore the west African coast. In 1487, driven by a storm, he rounded the Cape of Good Hope, but, owing to the discontent of his crew, turned back without exploring the coast of east Arica. His discovery showed the route to India, but when he sailed with da Gama in 1497 he was sent back after a short distance. He was drowned in 1500 on a voyage to Brazil.

Díaz, Porfirio (1830–1915). Mexican soldier and president. Originally a supporter of the liberal president Juarez, he shared his triumph after the withdrawal of the French and the execution of their protégé, the emperor * Maximilian. Feeling himself inadequately rewarded, he twice vainly opposed Juarez for the presidency (1867 and 1872). In the latter year Juarez died and in 1876 Díaz took up arms to prevent his successor, Manuel Gonzales, from embarking upon a second term. Having achieved his object, Díaz ruled as a dictator for the next thirty-four years. By enforcing law and order and by proving himself the friend of big business in the development and modernization of the country, he greatly increased the state's revenues, but the discontents of nationalists, resentful of foreign control of their resources, of liberals, eager for democracy, and of the impoverished Indians and exploited peasants, accumulated. In 1911 Díaz was forced into exile by * Madero.

Beals, C., *Porfirio Díaz*. 1932

Dickens, Charles (1812–1870). English novelist, born near Portsmouth. Both his parents provided models for future characters: his father (a thrifter's clerk in the naval dockyard) for Mr Micawber; his mother for Mrs Nickleby. When his father was imprisoned (1824) for debt in the Marshalsea in London (see *Little Dorritt*, 1855–57) Charles, then twelve, worked for some months pasting on labels in a blacking factory, an experience that left much bitterness behind. After two more years at school he worked as a lawyer's clerk (1827–30) and then, having learned shorthand, became a parliamentary reporter, an apprenticeship in journalism which stood him in good stead. In 1833 he began to write, for the *Monthly Magazine* and other periodicals, a number of short sketches of places seen and personal encounters which were collected under the name of *Sketches by Boz* (1836) – Boz being his pen-name for some years. Its success led to a suggestion by the publishers Chapman and Hall that he should write the text to fit a series of plates by the well known artist Robert Seymour. Dickens's counter-proposal that the pictures should illustrate the text was accepted and his first great success *The Posthumous Papers of the Pickwick Club* began to appear, serialized in parts like many of the later novels, in 1836. Seymour, who died before the second part had appeared, was replaced by 'Phiz' (Hablôt K. Browne), Dickens's illustrator for over twenty years. The gallery of humorous eccentrics portrayed in this work, Pickwick himself, Sam Weller, Mr Winkle and the rest was to be constantly enlarged as the years went by; it is sometimes urged that the balance of the plot of the novels is upset by the intrusions of such characters as Pecksniff (*Martin Chuzzlewit*; 1843), Mr and Madame Mantalini (*Nicholas Nickleby*; 1839), Mr Boffin (*Our Mutual Friend*; 1865). A vein of autobiography occurs in many of the novels, especially in *David Copperfield* (1849–1850). London itself, the sprawling, vulgar, fog-bound, Cockney metropolis, is the setting of most of his novels, but sometimes he goes back into history for dramatic plots; the Gordon riots in *Barnaby Rudge* (1841) and the French Revolution (influenced by Carlyle's famous book) in *A Tale of Two Cities* (1859). Mystery and crime always attracted him, partly no doubt because of his great friendship with Wilkie * Collins, and are a feature especially of the more elaborately planned novels of his later period, e.g. *Bleak House* (1859), *Great Expectations* (1861), and the last, unfinished, *Edwin Drood* (1870), to which many distinguished writers such as G. K. Chesterton have tried to conjecture the solution. Especially when depicting children ill or doomed to die – Tiny Tim in *A Christmas Carol* (1843), Little Nell in *The Old Curiosity Shop* (1841) or Paul in *Dombey and Son* (1846) – Dickens can be over-sentimental. He is most effective as a satirist when he flays the *nouveaux riches*, the pompous and the hypocrites, or finds targets in the delays of the civil service ('Circumlocution Office') and the law. Any form of exploitation of the young or helpless by a schoolmaster, such as Wackford Squeers in *Nicholas Nickleby*, by a crook, such as Fagin in *Oliver Twist* (1838), or by a ruthless employer such as Gradgrind in *Hard Times* (1854) earns his abhorrence.

In addition to the novels mentioned Dickens wrote many short stories and sketches, *A Child's History of England* (1851–53), and *American Notes* (1842) and *Pictures from Italy* (1846), which illustrated his travels. He was first editor (1846) of the *Daily News*, he edited *Household Words* (1850–59) and *All The Year Round* (1859–70). From 1853 (at first for charity) he gave public readings from his novels in Britain and America, which enabled him to display his ability as an actor but exhausted him and hastened his death. Dickens was less than fortunate in his private life. An early love for Maria Beadnell (David Copperfield's Dora) was rejected. His marriage in 1836 to Katharine Hogarth was clouded a year later by the death of her dearly loved younger sister Mary (Little Nell); it finally was ended by separation twenty years later. Dickens is one of the few authors who has been continuously a best-seller for over a hundred years after the publication of his first success. Modern criticism has rediscovered the richness of his imagination, the depth of his insight, and the consummate skill with which he combines the many disparate strands of his works.

Collins, P., *A Dickens Bibliography*. 1970; *Dickens, the Critical Heritage*. 1971

Dickinson, Emily (1830–1886). American poetess. She was born and spent almost her whole life in Amherst, Massachusetts, where her father, a lawyer, was treasurer of the college. At the age of 23, possibly after an unhappy love affair, she became a recluse – seeing only her family and a very few intimates – and began writing poetry, intensely personal and daringly original in language and form. No one – not even her friends – recognized the merit of her poems, which were published after her death and won great acclaim. Her themes are those within her narrow experience, love, nature – the changing seasons, the birds, frogs and insects which inhabited her garden – and her feeling of intimate relationship with God.

Sewall, R. B., *The Life of Emily Dickinson*. 1974

Diderot, Denis (1713–1784). French encyclopedist. He was an important member of the group of scholars and sceptical thinkers known as *philosophes*, who created the climate of opinion (known as the 'enlightenment') critical of the *Ancien Régime*. In this his own great *Encyclopédie* played a most important part. Before embarking upon this enterprise Diderot had led a bohemian life and earned a precarious livelihood by writing plays, novels and art criticism, but the exuberance of his personality, his enthusiasm and wide knowledge gave him a secure place in intellectual society. The basis of the *Encyclopédie* (1751–72), for which he shared editorial responsibility with the mathematician d'Alembert, was the English *Cyclopaedia* of Ephraim Chambers, which he was asked to translate, but the conception was constantly enlarged until it became a vast work of seventeen volumes of text and eleven of plates. The intention of the work, which became the focus of the rationalism and anti-clericalism of the age, was to show the interconnexion of all branches of knowledge. Diderot wrote many articles himself on philosophical and mechanical subjects and gathered as contributors some of the greatest men of his time, including Voltaire, Rousseau (a great friend of Diderot, with whom he quarrelled in 1757), Montesquieu, Turgot and Buffon. Diderot, who had suffered imprisonment for his *Letter on the Blind* (1749), one of the many works in which he set out his materialistic philosophy, had some trouble with the censorship, but comparatively few articles were banned. Diderot's last years were made easier by a kindly gesture of Catherine the Great, who bought his library and appointed him its custodian. He went to St Petersburg (1774) and before returning had written for the benefit of his patroness a plan for a Russian university, a proof of the amazing industry and versatility that made him one of the most universal influences of his era.

Crocker, L. G., *Diderot, the Embattled Philosopher*. 1966

Diefenbaker, John George (1895–1979). Canadian politician. He was educated at the University of Saskatchewan and after service in World War I became a successful barrister; he also was a prominent member of the Progressive Conservative party which from 1956 he led in the Dominion parliament, to which he was first elected in 1940. In 1957 he became prime minister of Canada and at the election of 1958 won the greatest majority in Canadian history. In 1963 his opposition to a U.S. contention that nuclear warheads for Canadian missiles were a necessary part of North American defence led to a rift in his cabinet, his resignation and electoral defeat.

Diemen, Anthony van (1593–1645). Dutch administrator. As governor general of the

Dutch East Indies (1636–45) he commissioned Abel Tasman's voyages of exploration. The island off Australia named Van Diemen's Land was renamed Tasmania in 1853.

Diesel, Rudolf (1858–1913). German inventor. Born in Paris, he moved to England and studied engineering and thermodynamics in Germany. The engine which bears his name, an internal-combustion engine in which the fuel is ignited by heat following compression, was patented in 1892. After having been nearly killed in an explosion of an earlier model, he produced his first successful engine in 1897. He disappeared at sea.
Nitske, W. R. and Wilson, C. M., *Rudolf Diesel: Pioneer of the Age of Power*. 1965

Dietrich, Marlene (1904–). German film actress. After starring in her best known film, *The Blue Angel* (1930), in Germany, she went to Hollywood. She became an American citizen in 1937. She often played the part of an adventuress in films which included *The Flame of New Orleans* (directed by René Clair), *Destry Rides Again, Foreign Affair* and *Witness for the Prosecution*.

Dilke, Sir Charles Wentworth, 2nd Bart (1843–1911). English politician. After graduating at Cambridge, he travelled widely throughout the English-speaking world and in *Greater Britain* (2 vols., 1868) recorded the progressive views that he had formed, e.g. concerning trusteeship for backward peoples. In 1868 he was elected M.P. for Chelsea as a radical with republican leanings and soon became a prominent member of the Liberal party; after being under-secretary for foreign affairs (1880) he joined the cabinet in 1882 as president of the Local Government Board. Chairmanship of a royal commission on housing and work on parliamentary redistribution showed his interest in social conditions at home, while he closely associated himself with the imperial and colonial views of his (then) fellow radical Joseph Chamberlain. In 1885–86 came the event which at that time was calamitous for political progress; he was a co-respondent in a divorce case. Though he re-entered parliament (1892) and his brilliant books on foreign and colonial affairs were received with appropriate praise, he could never again aspire to high office. In his later years he did much to weld the Labour members into an organized party.
Jenkins, R., *Sir Charles Dilke*. 1958

Dill, Sir John Greer (1881–1944). British soldier. In his capacity as chief of the imperial general staff (1940–41), and as senior British representative on the combined chiefs of staff committee in Washington (1941–44) his professional knowledge, combined with power to persuade and charm, enabled him to make a unique contribution to the Allied victory. Earlier in his career he had held an important staff appointment in World War I, was commandant at the Staff College (1931–34) and director of military operations at the War Office from 1934 to 1939, when he commanded the first corps in France. He died in the U.S.A. and is buried in the Arlington Cemetery.

Dillinger, John (1903–1934). American gangster. After serving nine years of a sentence for robbery with violence he headed a gang of escaped convicts who terrorized the states of Indiana, Illinois, Ohio and Pennsylvania. He was eventually shot resisting arrest.

Dillon, (Clarence) **Douglas** (1909–). American administrator. In 1931 he joined the family firm of investment bankers, of which, after serving in the navy during World War II, he had risen to be chairman by 1953, when he was appointed by President Eisenhower as ambassador to France (1953–57). Although a Republican, he became secretary of the Treasury under Presidents Kennedy and Johnson (1961–65).

Dimitrov, Georgi (1882–1949). Bulgarian communist. He came into international prominence when in 1933 he was tried in Berlin and acquitted on a charge of setting fire to the Reichstag, a crime almost certainly committed by his Nazi accusers. He was secretary of the Communist International (Comintern) in Moscow (1934–43) and, after the war, premier of Bulgaria from 1946 until his death.

Dimitri (1581–1591). Russian prince, son of Ivan IV. When his elder brother Fyodor became tsar, he was removed from the court and died mysteriously. The regent, Boris Godunov, who reported that he had fallen on a knife during an attack of epilepsy, was accused by his enemies of murder. Subsequently several 'false' Dimitrys appeared, of whom one, after defeating Boris's troops, was crowned tsar in 1605, but was murdered by the nobles in the following year. Mussorgsky's opera *Boris Godunov* gives a version of the story. *See* **Dmitri, False.**

Dimitri Donskoy (died 1389). Grand prince of Moscow (from 1359), one of the heroes of Russian history. He asserted his dominance over rival princes but his real importance lies in the fact that, by his two victories over the Golden Horde at the River Vozha and more decisively at Kulikovo, near a crossing of the River Don (hence his additional name), he destroyed the legend of Tartar invincibility. Moreover, even though subsequently defeated, his prestige was so great that the princes of Moscow were thenceforth regarded as national rulers.

Dinesen, Isak (Baroness Karen Blixen) (1885–1962). Danish novelist, writing mostly in English. She lived in Kenya 1914–31, managing a coffee plantation, and her non-fiction works included *Out of Africa* (1937) and *Shadows on the Grass* (1960). She updated the Gothic novel with her *Seven Gothic Tales* (1934), *Winter's Tales* (1942) and *Anecdotes of Destiny* (1958).
Thurman, J., *Isak Dinesen*. 1982.

Dingaan (d. 1840). Zulu chief. After permitting them to settle in Natal he murdered (1837) a party of Boers under Piet Retief. The victory by which, in the following year, Andries Pretorius avenged their death is annually commemorated in South Africa on 16 December, 'Dingaan's Day'.

Dio, Cassius (Cassius Dio Cocceianus) (*c.* 155–235). Greek historian born in Bithynia. After a long period of distinguished public service under the emperor Commodus and his successors, he retired to write a comprehensive history of Rome in eighty books, of which Books 36–50 survive. His careful use of the best available sources give value to his record.
Millar, F., *A Study in Cassius Dio*. 1964

Diocletian (Gaius Valerius Aurelius Diocletanius) (245–313). Roman emperor (284–305). He was a Dalmatian by birth and was proclaimed emperor by the army after he had overcome a rival claimant. In order to rule and defend his vast empire, he took a co-emperor, Maximian, to whom the west was assigned, with Constantius Chlorus as junior colleague. Diocletian himself, though in general charge of the whole, operated chiefly in the east with Galerius as his junior. Diocletian's main concern was to maintain the great armies necessary to defend the empire and he introduced a tax system to enable him to do so. Sons of soldiers had to serve and landowners to provide recruits; a regular land tax was introduced, based on acreage, productivity and labour employed, but this had the effect of making taxation a hereditary responsibility and of tying the peasantry to the land. His attempt to curb inflation by price control under the edict of 301 failed. He tried to impress and overawe his eastern subjects by introducing elaborate court ceremonial and assuming semi-divine status, which led to violent persecution (from 303) of the Christians, to whom such practices were abhorrent. After twenty-one years as emperor, he abdicated and induced Maximian to do so also; the two junior emperors moved up and two more appointments were made. Apparently the scheme of succession had worked but confusion soon followed. The vast palace at Split (Yugoslavia) was built for his retirement.

Diogenes (*c.* 412–323 B.C.). Greek 'cynic' philosopher. He was born at Sinope on the Black Sea. His father was a magistrate convicted of 'defacing the currency'. Forced into poverty Diogenes found that it enabled him to lead a life in accordance with his belief in entire self-sufficiency and freedom from ordinary desires and conventions. He spent a wandering life begging his way and sleeping in the open or in such shelter as he could find – perhaps even in the proverbial tub. In Athens, where he was often to be found, he was called 'Cynic', a word much changed in meaning which then meant simply that he lived like a dog. He died, so legend goes, by eating raw cuttlefish in order to prove that cooking is unnecessary. Apparently he wrote plays and described an ideal republic where there were no armies or family life, but none of his work survives.

Dionysius (*c.* 430–367 B.C.). Tyrant of Syracuse (405–377 B.C.). He was able to seize and maintain power in Syracuse, a Greek colony in Sicily, by playing on the fears of his subjects of the Carthaginians who held a substantial part of the island. Much of his reign was occupied by this task, and varied by his own expeditions against the Greek colonies in southern Italy. Dionysius was a poet and a patron of letters.

His son **Dionysius II** (*c.* 390–344 B.C.) succeeded him and ruled despotically until he was ejected in 356 B.C. by a fleet sent from Greece under Dion, who temporarily restored the republic. Dionysius regained power in 347 B.C.

Dionysius Exiguus (died *c.* 556). Roman monk. He was born in Scythia and later became abbot of a monastery in Rome, where he died. He was among the most learned men of his time and collected canons and documents of the early Christian era. He introduced the system of dating events from the year (A.D. 1) of Christ's birth (the date he chose is a few years late: scholars estimate that Christ was born between 8 B.C. and 4 B.C.).

Dior, Christian Ernest (1905–1957). French fashion designer. After World War II he launched the 'New Look', which brought the period of wartime austerity in women's clothes to an end; he also revolutionized the world of *haute couture* by having simplified versions of his models reproduced for the mass market.

Dioscorides, Pedanius (fl. *c.* 60–77 A.D.) Greek physician, probably born in Anazarba, Cilicia. He pursued botanical studies, largely with a view to the use of herbs for pharmaceutical purposes. Several works survive which may be attributed to him, though the only one which is certainly genuine is his *De Materia Medica.* This became probably the most influential of all herbals, being used throughout the Middle Ages down to the seventeenth century. Dioscorides described each plant, gave its habitat, indicated for what diseases it was a specific, and gave an account of its preparation for medical use, and dosage. One of his claims was that his work was better organized than earlier herbals. Out of the five books the first dealt with aromatics and oils, the second with animals, pot herbs and sharp herbs, the third with roots, juices and seeds, the fourth was a continuation of the third, and the fifth covered wines and minerals. It is impossible now to know whether Dioscorides merely collected the pharmaceutical lore of his day, or made significant innovations.

Dirac, Paul Adrien Maurice (1902–1984). British physicist. A professor of mathematics at Cambridge from 1932, he was a pioneer of wave mechanics. In 1928 he predicted the existence of the positron, a positively-charged particle of the same mass as the negatively-charged electron; this was observed by * Anderson in 1932. Dirac was awarded, jointly with Schrödinger, the 1933 Nobel Prize for Physics and in 1939 and 1952 the Royal and Copley medals of the Royal Society. He was awarded the O.M. in 1973.

Disney, Walt (Walter Elias) (1901–1966). American producer of cartoon films. He devised the first successful film cartoon (*Oswald the Rabbit*) in 1923 and won immense popularity for the medium with his Mickey Mouse pictures and such favourite characters as Pluto and Donald Duck. Later he produced many full-length cartoon films in colour, e.g. *Snow White and the Seven Dwarfs* (1938), *Fantasia* (1940) and *Bambi* (1942). His nature films, e.g. *The Living Desert* (1953), won many Academy awards. In films such as *Treasure Island* (1950) he used living actors and combined live actors with cartoons in *Mary Poppins* (1965). He set up (1955) a vast amusement park in California called Disneyland.

Finch, C., *The Art of Walt Disney*. 1973

Disraeli, Benjamin, 1st Earl of Beaconsfield (1804–1881). British politician and author. He was born in London, son of Isaac D'Israeli (1766–1848), an Anglicized Jew whose literary talents (e.g. his *Curiosities of Literature*) won him the friendship of Byron, Scott and Southey. Benjamin was brought up as a Christian and studied law. His brilliant first novel, *Vivian Grey* (1826), won him immediate acclaim. After making the 'grand tour' of Europe he began (1831) the life of a man-about-town remarkable for his novels and brilliant attire. In 1837, at his fourth attempt, he won a seat in parliament, at first as a radical but later as Tory M.P. for Maidstone, which he held until he was raised to the Lords. In 1839 he married Mary Anne, the widow of his friend Wyndham Lewis; her wealth gave him financial independence and enabled him to buy Hughenden, Berkshire, later their home. The marriage though childless was a happy one (his wife died in 1872).

In parliament Disraeli addressed himself to advocating the ideas he later embodied in his political novels *Coningsby* (1844) and *Sybil* (1846). The Tory party as he envisaged it should no longer be representative merely of a small class of country gentlemen but should meet the needs of the growing electorate enfranchised by the Reform Act. Loyalty to the church, the crown and a vision of national greatness combined with material and social progress had, he thought, a greater appeal than the Liberal slogan of 'peace, retrenchment and reform'. He found an opportunity to make his mark when Sir Robert Peel's decision to repeal the Corn Laws split the Tory party. Disraeli became leader of the 'Young England' group of Tories who believed that protection for British agriculture was essential, and his biting attacks on the new policy led to Peel's political eclipse.

In the government of the Earl of Derby (1852) Disraeli was chancellor of the exchequer. Next year, however, the Tories fell and though they returned for a brief spell (1858–59) the Liberals were in office for the next seven years. Disraeli's comportment in opposition and his skill in parliamentary debate added to his reputation. The Tories were elected in 1866 and Disraeli piloted to success the Reform Bill of 1867, by which some two million voters (mostly factory workers) were added to the rolls. After Derby's retirement (1868) Disraeli became for the first time prime minister, but his hope that a wider electorate would rally to his support was disappointed. He resigned in 1868 and did not become prime minister again until 1874. From then until 1880 he led a government remarkable for the strange relationship with Queen Victoria – one of almost flirtatious affection. He bought for Britain a controlling interest in the Suez Canal, had the queen made Empress of India (1876), annexed the Transvaal (1877) and at the Congress of Berlin (1878) from which he brought back 'peace with honour', he did much to ensure that the Russo-Turkish conflict did not develop into a European war. Meanwhile his ambition to extend his party's interest in social welfare brought into being an act giving legal protection to trade unions, a great Factory Act, and a Public Health Act. He was created Earl of Beaconsfield in 1876. In the 1880 election, in response to higher taxes and a trade recession, the electorate returned an overwhelming Liberal majority. Disraeli died the following year.

Blake, R., *Disraeli.* 1966

Dixon, Sir Owen (1886–1972). Australian jurist. Educated at Melbourne University, he became a Justice of the High Court of Australia 1929–52, serving during World War II as Minister to the U.S. 1942–44, and Chief Justice 1952–64. He was awarded the O.M. in 1963.

Djilas, Milovan (1911–   ). Yugoslav politician and author. One of the most active of the partisans during World War II he was, when Tito came to power, at first the most trusted and certainly the most intellectually gifted of his lieutenants. He backed Tito in breaking with the Cominform but in 1954 he fell into disfavour for advocating greater democracy and in 1956 was imprisoned for supporting the Hungarian uprising. In 1957 he published *The New Class*, highly critical of communism in practice. He was subsequently imprisoned again for 'revealing official secrets' in his book *Conversations with Stalin* (published outside Yugoslavia in 1962).

Dmitri, False. Name given to three pretenders to the Muscovite throne during the Time of Troubles (1605–13). On the death of Fyodor I (1598), Boris Godunov succeeded and the First False Dmitri challenged his right to the throne and claimed to be Dmitri, the son of Ivan IV, who had died mysteriously in 1591 while still a boy. He is thought to have been, in fact, Yuri Otrepyev, a noble.

Threatened with exile he fled to Lithuania and in 1604 invaded Russia at the head of an army. In 1605 Boris died and Dmitri was proclaimed tsar, but soon alienated his supporters and was murdered in 1606.

Rumours that the First Dmitri had survived led to the appearance of a second pretender who quickly gained support and established his court at Tushino (1608). Initially very successful, he was ousted by Vasily Shuysky, the boyar who had murdered the first Dmitri and become tsar (1606), and assassinated by one of his own followers (1610).

In 1611 the Third False Dmitri, possibly a deacon named Sidorka, gained the allegiance of Cossacks who were ravaging Moscow's environs, but was betrayed in 1612 and executed in Moscow.

Dobson, (Henry) **Austin** (1840–1921). English poet and essayist. He worked in the civil service and published several volumes of poems, often in medieval French forms, and essays, all marked by a concern for graceful language and perfection of form. He excelled

as a biographer, with lives of Hogarth, Fielding, Steele, Horace Walpole and Fanny Burney.
Dobson, A. T. A., *Bibliography*. 1925

Dobson, Frank (1888–1963). British sculptor. With a simplified but naturalistic style, in sharp contrast with that of his more modernistic contemporaries, he achieved considerable success, notably with portrait busts (e.g. of Osbert Sitwell in polished brass) and nudes such as the bronze *Susannah* in the Tate Gallery, London.

Dodd, Charles Harold (1884–1973). English Congregational clergyman and biblical scholar. He was professor of divinity at Cambridge University (1935–49), and had the general direction of the work of translation required for the New English Bible (New Testament published 1961).

Dodgson, Charles Lutwidge *see* **Carroll, Lewis**

Dodsley, Robert (1703–1764). English publisher. While in service as a footman he was encouraged to write by Daniel Defoe. He published poems and plays, on the profits of the first of which, *The Toyshop* (1735), produced at Covent Garden, he established himself as a bookseller and publisher of (among others) Pope, Lord Chesterfield, Goldsmith, Gray and Dr Johnson, in whose *Dictionary* he had a share. In 1758, with Edmund Burke, he founded the *Annual Register*.

Doherty, Reginald Frank (1872–1911) and **Hugh Lawrence** (1876–1919). British lawn-tennis players. Between them (except for one year) they won the singles championships at Wimbledon from 1897 to 1906 (Reginald, 1897–1900; Hugh, 1901–06). In partnership they won the men's doubles from 1897 to 1905.

Dohnányi, Ernö (1877–1960). Hungarian composer, pianist and conductor, born in Pozsony. A friend and promoter of * Bartok, he was director of the Budapest Academy 1919 and 1934–41, and became musical director of Hungarian broadcasting 1931–34. His earlier works, notably the Rhapsodies for Piano and the Cello Sonata, were strongly influenced by Brahms. His most popular works are *Variations on a Nursery Song* (1919) and *Ruralia Hungarica* (1926). He lived in the U.S.A. from 1948.

Dolci, Danilo (1924–). Italian social worker. He studied architecture in Rome but from 1952 devoted himself to a campaign for better living conditions in Sicily. He not only denounced economic extortion by landlords and Mafia terrorists but showed by his own example, and that of his fellow workers, how the poor could improve their own lot by shaking off their fatalistic lethargy, by improving methods of work and by mutual help. He has survived many attempts upon his life.
Mangione, J., *World Around Danilo Dolci: A Passion for Sicilians*. 1973

Dolin, Sir Anton (real name Patrick Healey-Kay) (1904–1981). British ballet dancer, choreographer and writer. He studied ballet under Nijinsky and was *premier danseur* with the Old Vic–Sadler's Wells Company 1931–35. Later, with Alicia Markova, he formed the Markova–Dolin Ballet (1935–51).

Dollfuss, Engelbert (1892–1934). Austrian politician. He was known as the 'pocket chancellor' owing to his diminutive size. Of peasant origin but university-educated, he rose to prominence in the Christian Socialist party. When he became chancellor (1932) he found himself confronted with the rival hostility of Socialists and Nazis, both, by their resort to violence, providing him with justification for raising a private army and for dictatorial rule. His ruthless shelling (1934) of the flats of Viennese workers and his flouting of democratic sentiment deprived him of the help and sympathy of those who might have been his staunchest allies against the Nazis, by whom he was murdered, during an attempted *coup d'état*.
Brook-Shepherd, G., *Dollfuss*. 1961

Dolmetsch, (Eugene) **Arnold** (1858–1940). British musician and instrument maker, born in France. He was a great authority on early music and musical instruments, who settled (1917) with his family at Haslemere in Surrey, England, where he demonstrated his contention that composers' works could only be fully appreciated if played upon the instruments for which they were composed. His sons, of whom **Carl Dolmetsch** (1911–) was a noted performer on the recorder, continued his work.

Domagk, Gerhard (1895–1964). German biochemist. One of the pioneers of chemotherapy, in 1934 he discovered the antibacterial action of the red dye prontone, demonstrated that the effective agent was the sulphanilamide that prontone produced in the body, and thus showed the way for the application of a wide range of sulphanilamide drugs. He was awarded the Nobel Prize for Medicine (1939), but declined it on instructions from the Nazi government.

Domenichino (Domenico Zampieri) (1581–1641). Italian painter. He was born in Bologna and went to Rome (1602): there he assisted Annibale Carracci in the decoration of the Farnese Gallery but was soon accepting commissions on his own. For the many ceilings and murals which he carried out in Rome and Naples he used a style more severely classical than that of the Carraccis, whose traditions he carried on. The work which ranks as his most ambitious achievement was done (1624–28) for the choir of S. Andrea della Valle, Rome.

Dominic, St (*c.* 1170–1221). Spanish priest and founder of the Dominican Order. He was born in Old Castile, and became a canon of Osma Cathedral. In 1205 he adopted voluntary poverty, in his missionary journeys, to convert the Albigensian heretics of Languedoc, and he gathered a group of followers round him. Encouraged by success he attended (1215) the 4th Lateran Council and petitioned Pope Innocent III for permission to establish an Order of Preachers, for the conversion of heretics. Told that the order must follow an existing rule he chose that of St Augustine, but he soon adopted absolute poverty, so that in fact a new order of mendicant friars came into being. To equip the friars for their task of preaching, an elaborate educational system was evolved. Each 'house' contained a doctor of theology, each province contained one or more houses for advanced studies and selected students were sent to the universities. In 1220 a new constitution was drawn up. The priors, who ruled the 'houses', were grouped under provincial priors subject to a master general. The legislative and disciplinary bodies were 'chapters', mainly elected, the supreme body being the annual general chapter, for which a complicated system was created to ensure that it was efficient and representative. This departure from the authoritarian rule of former religious orders was unique. Dominic died at Bologna, and was canonized in 1234. He saw the Order as a body of learned and ascetic defenders of the faith, and was the first to put intellectual work as the first requirement of a friar.

Vicaire, M. H., *Saint Dominic and His Times.* 1964

Domitian (Titus Flavius Domitianus) (51–96). Roman emperor (from 81). He was a son of the emperor * Vespasian, a younger brother of * Titus, and the last of the Flavian dynasty. He fought defensively and on the whole successfully on the German and Danubian frontiers, and his administration of Italy and the provinces was efficient. As his reign progressed, however, he not only persecuted Jews and Christians but developed suspicions of any who seemed capable of aspiring to power. The employment of informers followed by murders and confiscations provoked a palace conspiracy in which he was assassinated.

Donald, William Henry (1875–1946). Australian journalist in China, known as 'Chinese Donald'. He was a proponent of modernization for China and became Secretary to * Sun Yat-sen. Later, as adviser to * Chiang Kai-shek, he greatly influenced Chinese policy.

Donatello (Donato de Niccolo) (1386/7–1466). Florentine sculptor, the greatest before Michelangelo: he also exerted great influence on the painters of the Paduan School and even on the Venetians. He introduced the 'heroic' style of sculpture – figures slightly larger than life infused with that feeling of determination and force so closely associated with the early Renaissance and first exemplified in his *St Mark* (1412). His relief of *St George killing the Dragon* (*c.* 1417) is the earliest datable example of the application of the new theory of perspective to sculpture; a further example is his very low relief in bronze of *Salome* (in Siena). His bronze *David* is one of the earliest free-standing nudes.

He was apprenticed to Ghiberti, whom he helped (1403) to carve the doors of the Baptistery, and shortly after was working on the Cathedral in Florence on which he continued to work intermittently for the next thirty years. He also worked at times in Rome and Padua. In his later years Donatello experimented with expressionistic and dramatic distortion, e.g. the *Magdalen* in carved wood (*c.* 1445) which inspired the tense and dramatic quality of Florentine painting of the period.

Dönitz, Karl (1891–1980). German sailor. He was a submarine commander in World War I, and as a firm adherent of Hitler he played an important part in the secret building of a submarine fleet in the years preceding World War II, in which he directed the submarine campaign with ruthlessness, administrative efficiency and tactical skill. In 1943 he became grand-admiral and succeeded Raeder as naval commander-in-chief. Hitler named him his successor and he was thus nominally head of state when Germany surrendered. He was condemned to ten years' imprisonment by the Nuremberg court for war crimes.
Dönitz, K., *Memoirs*. 1959

Donizetti, Gaetano (1797–1848). Italian opera composer, born at Bergamo. His early work reflected Rossini's influence but he developed a more personal style. His first big success was *Anna Bolena* (1830); his most famous is *Lucia di Lammermoor* (1835), and among the better known of the remaining sixty or so that he wrote are *Lucrezia Borgia* (1833), *La Favorita* (1840), *Don Pasquale* and *Maria di Rohan* (both 1843).
Ashbrook, W., *Donizetti*. 1965

Donne, John (1571–1631). English poet and cleric. The son of a merchant, and, through his mother, grandson of the dramatist John Heywood, he was brought up among adherents of Roman Catholicism, which he himself rejected in his twenties. He studied at both Oxford and Cambridge, and later at Lincoln's Inn, soon gaining a reputation as a man-about-town of profligacy, wit and much learning. He sailed with Essex against Cadiz in 1596 and again in 1597; in 1598 he became secretary to Lord Egerton, whose niece, the 16-year-old Ann More, he secretly married. With no dowry and a constant succession of children the couple lived in great poverty until, having become a fervent believer in Anglicanism, at last in 1615 he took holy orders. He now attained a new reputation as a great preacher, becoming dean of St Paul's in 1621.

His poetry is inspired by the phases of his life and is sensual, passionate, witty, subtle and deeply religious; the metrical form of the stanza is rough, the imagery vivid, if sometimes strained.

> Go and catch a falling star,
> Get with child a mandrake root. . . .

He is regarded as the greatest of the English metaphysical poets.
Keynes, G. L., *A Bibliography of Dr John Donne*. 1964

Donskoy, Mark Semyonovich (1901–1981). Russian film director. After studying medicine and law, he worked in film under * Eisenstein and became a director, achieving his greatest critical success with the trilogy based on Maxim * Gorky's autobiography: *The Childhood of Maxim Gorky* (1938), *My Apprenticeship* (1939) and *My Universities* (1940).

Doolittle, Hilda (1886–1961). American poetess (pen-name H.D.). One of the first, and most consistent, Imagist poets writing in English, she was a notable Greek scholar and the classicist influence is apparent in her work. She married Richard * Aldington in 1913 but they were later divorced.
Guest, B., *Herself Defined: The Poet H.D. and Her World*. 1985

Doolittle, James Harold (1896–). American airman. After service as a flying officer in World War I, he won renown by his victory in the Schneider Trophy of 1925: as a civilian (from 1930) he became known as a test pilot and for aerobatic feats. Recalled to the service in World War II, he led the first raid on Tokyo (April 1942), a spectacular achievement which brought a series of promotions, culminating with the appointment to command of the 8th U.S. Air Force (1944). After the war he was a businessman involved in insurance, oil and aeronautics.

Doppler, Christian Johann (1803–1853). Austrian mathematical physicist. He became professor of mathematics at Prague (1841) and professor of experimental physics at Vienna (1850). Although he wrote a number of mathematical works, his name is associated mainly with his contributions to physics. In 1842 he described in principle the phenomenon (later verified experimentally) now known as the 'Doppler effect' – the change that occurs in the pitch of sound or the colour of light when the hearer or observer is approaching or receding from the source.

Doré, Gustave (1832–1883). French artist. Famous for his book illustrations, early success came with his illustrations for Balzac's *Contes drolatiques.* Other works which he illustrated include Dante's *Inferno* and *Paradiso,* Cervantes' *Don Quixote* and Tennyson's *Idylls of the King.* In his Paris studios he employed at times as many as forty assistants working on his woodcuts. His style was often sensational and macabre. The drawings done for *London* (1871), which influenced Van Gogh, are held to be his best work.
Rose, M., *Gustave Doré.* 1945

Doria, Andrea (1468–1560). Genoese soldier and statesman. Born of a noble family he spent his early manhood as a mercenary in the service of the papacy, Naples, and other Italian states: he also restored Genoese rule in Corsica. After the expulsion of the French King Louis XII from Italy he restored the Genoese republic (1512), but himself entered French service (1522) when Francis I again imposed his suzerainty. A quarrel over Francis's treatment of Genoa caused Doria to change sides and put his services and the Genoese fleet at the disposal of Francis's rival for power in Italy, the emperor Charles V. Now the virtual autocrat in a restored Genoese republic, Doria was engaged for several years in fighting the Moslem pirates of the Barbary Coast, in the course of which he captured Tunis (1535).

Dornier, Claudius (1884–1969). German aircraft pioneer and builder, born at Kempten, now in the Federal Republic of Germany. Leaving Munich technical college he began work for Ferdinand Graf von Zeppelin, in his airship factory at Friedrichshafen (1910) and in 1911 designed the first all-metal aeroplane, after which Zeppelin allowed him to establish a separate factory, the Dornier aircraft works. After World War I during which wooden and metal fighter planes built to his design were used, Dornier was given complete control of his factory. During the 1920s he built very successful seaplanes. In 1929 he produced DOX, then the world's largest aircraft, although not a financial success, with 12 engines and a passenger capacity of 169. Dornier twin-engined bombers became standard Luftwaffe type in World War II. After the war Dornier moved to Spain because aircraft building was prohibited in Germany by the Allies; when the ban was lifted in 1955 he opened a factory near Munich which produced U.S. designed Starfighters.

Dos Passos, John Rodrigo (1896–1970). American novelist. *Three Soldiers* (1921) was a notable book about World War I, but his best known work is the powerful trilogy *U.S.A.*, consisting of *The 42nd Parallel* (1930), *Nineteen Nineteen* (1932) and *The Big Money* (1936). With a quickly moving, constantly switching technique of the cinema in these and later books he expresses his concern with the cultural, social and political developments of the 'American way of life'.
Wrenn, J. H., *John Dos Passos.* 1961

Dost Mohammed Khan (1793–1863). Amir of Afghanistan 1826–63, known as the 'Great Amir'. In 1839 he was overthrown by the British. Having regained power in 1842, he eventually (1855) made a treaty of friendship with the British, after they had defeated the Afghans' hereditary enemies, the Sikhs.

Dostoyevsky, Fyodor Mikhailovich (1821–1881). Russian novelist. His father, a Moscow doctor, was murdered (1839) by his serfs at his country home, an event which haunted Dostoyevsky all his life. He studied at the Military Engineering College at St Petersburg but resigned (1844) to take up a literary career. His first novel, *Poor Folk* (1846), achieved considerable success. Disaster overtook him when he was arrested (1849) on a charge of sedition (on the flimsiest of grounds) and condemned to be shot: he was already facing the firing squad when a reprieve arrived. He had to endure four years as a convict and two of exile in Siberia which undermined his health, an experience that he described in his *Memoirs from the House of the Dead* (1861). On his return from exile he engaged in journalistic enterprises which failed and left him deep in debt – a state aggravated by his passion for gambling. The unhappy marriage which he had contracted while in Siberia ended in 1863 on the death of his wife. In 1865 he travelled to Germany with a young woman, Polina Suslova, to retrieve his fortune by an 'infallible' method of winning at roulette which of course failed. On his return he set about writing a potboiler to satisfy his creditors (*The Gambler*). He engaged Anna Snitken as stenographer and shortly married her. They had again to go abroad to avoid creditors, a humilitating time for Dostoyevsky. His wife gradually restored order to his finances and they returned to Russia. In his later years he evolved a peculiar Slavophilism compounded of hatred for aristocrats and socialists alike, and of religious obsessions. However, even in his lifetime he won recognition both inside and outside Russia as a great novelist.

His best novels are *Crime and Punishment* (1866) and the unfinished *Brothers Karamazov* (1881): Freud has described the latter as 'the most magnificent novel ever written'. Dostoyevsky probed more deeply into the mind than any previous novelist, especially into the abnormal and criminal mind. His other novels include *Memoirs from the Underworld* (1864), *The Idiot* (1869) and *The Devils* (*The Possessed*), (1871–72).
Grossman, L., *Dostoevsky*. 1974

Doubleday, Abner (1819–1893). American general. For many years he was credited with inventing (1839) the game of baseball at Cooperstown, NY; revisionists now assert that the game is a variant of the English 'rounders' and that the modern rules were set in 1845 by Alexander Joy Cartwright. In the Civil War, Doubleday's troops fired the first shots at Fort Sumter, SC (1861) and he commanded a corps at Gettysburg.

Doughty, Charles Montagu (1843–1926). English author and traveller. To obtain the necessary information for his most famous work, *Travels in Arabia Deserta* (1888), he not only gained a mastery of Arabic but took the risk of living (1876–78) among the tribesmen, disguised as an Arab. The book is written in a consciously archaic style. He also wrote verse dramas and epic poems, e.g. *Adam Cast Forth* (1908) and *The Dawn in Britain* (1906).

Douglas, Lord Alfred Bruce (1870–1945). British poet, son of the 8th Marquess of Queensberry, chiefly remembered for his association with Oscar Wilde, which involved the latter in trial and imprisonment. He was a lyric poet of considerable attainment and a master of the sonnet form.
Croft Cooke, R., *Bosie*. 1963

Douglas, Clifford Hugh (1879–1952). British economist. An engineer by profession and known by his military rank of major, he published in 1919 his economic theory (Social Credit), intended to overcome the chronic shortage of purchasing power which he held to be the cause of economic depression. The method to be adopted was a carefully regulated distribution of money which he called a 'national dividend'. Douglas attracted many followers, especially in Canada, where (from 1935) a Social Credit government held office in Alberta for many years.

Douglas, Donald Wills (1892–1981). American aircraft manufacturer. In 1920 he founded the Douglas Aircraft Company, whose aeroplanes are well known under the names D.C.3, D.C.4 . . . D.C.8 etc. The 'Dakota', one of the safest and most widely used aircraft for military and civilian transport during and after World War II, was a development of the D.C.3.

Douglas, Gavin (*c*. 1475–1522). Scottish poet and prelate, third son of the 5th Earl of Angus. After the disaster at Flodden he joined the English faction and was appointed bishop of Dunkeld (1515), but after the French party had regained power (1520) he had to retire to England where he died of the plague. He wrote moral allegories (*The Palice of Honour* and *King Hart*), but his fame rests on his verse translation into Scots of Virgil's *Aeneid*, said to be the first rendering of a classical work into any form of English.

Douglas, (George) **Norman** (1868–1952). Scottish writer. After three years (from 1893) in the diplomatic service, he went to live in Italy and settled in the island of Capri, the 'Nepenthe' of his famous novel *South Wind* (1917), a witty, amoral story of the interplay of character in a small community. His travel books, e.g. *Old Calabria* (1919), are scholarly, while the author portrays himself in *Looking Back* (2 vols. 1933).
Greenlees, I., *Norman Douglas*. 1957

Douglas, Stephen Arnold (1813–1861). American politician. Born in Vermont he moved to Illinois. There he became a judge at the age of 27: but he chose politics as his career. From 1843 he was in Congress as a Democrat in the House of Representatives until 1847 and from then onwards as a senator. His interest in westward expansion made him demand that the Nebraska-Kansas region should be opened to settlement and that it should be left to the settlers to decide whether slaves should be introduced. This attitude cost him the Democratic nomination for the presi-

dency in 1852 and 1856 though he retained his seat as senator for Illinois in a contest with Lincoln (1858) and was nominated for the presidency in 1860. The Democratic party was split three ways and in the election Lincoln, the candidate put up by the wing opposed to the extension of slavery – which now became the new Republican party – won the day.
Johannsen, R. W., *Stephen A. Douglas*. 1973

Douglas, Thomas Clement (1904–). Canadian politician, born in Scotland. He became a Baptist minister in Saskatchewan and from 1935 represented Weyburn in that state in the Canadian House of Commons. In 1941 he became leader of the left-wing party, the Cooperative Commonwealth Federation. He became premier of Saskatchewan in 1944 and in 1961 he became first leader of the New-Democratic party formed by an amalgamation of the C.C.F. with other left-wing groups representing trade-union agricultural interests.

Douglas, William Orville (1898–1980). American jurist. Professor of law at Yale University (1931–39), he was a prominent supporter of civil rights and the New Deal. His appointment as a justice of the U.S. Supreme Court (1939) by President Roosevelt aroused considerable controversy. He served a record term, retiring in 1975 after a stroke.

Douglas of Kirtleside, William Sholto Douglas, 1st Baron (1893–1969). British airman. After proving himself a brilliant fighter pilot in World War I, during which he won the M.C. and D.S.O., he became a civilian test pilot but soon rejoined the R.A.F. When World War II began he was assistant chief of the air staff. He was commander-in-chief of Fighter Command (1940–42) and of Coastal Command (1944–45). He became a marshal of the Air Force in 1946. After commanding the British air forces in occupied Germany he became governor and commander-in-chief of the British zone of occupation (1946–47).

Douglas-Home, Sir Alexander Frederick *see* **Home of the Hirsel, Baron**

Douglass, Frederick (1817?–1895). American abolitionist. The son of a slave mother and a white father, he escaped from slavery (1838) and devoted himself to the anti-slavery movement. In the Civil War he organized Negro units to help the northern army and subsequently continued to try to secure equal civil rights for Negroes. He filled government posts in Washington, D.C., and was minister to Haiti (1889–91).
Douglass, F., *The Life and Times of Frederick Douglass*. 1947

Doumer, Paul (1857–1932). French radical politician. He was a deputy 1889–96 and 1902–12, and a senator 1912–31, serving as minister of finance (1895–96, 1921–22 and 1925–26). As governor-general of Indo-China (1897–1902) he set up a centralized administration which survived until 1945. President of the senate (1927–31), he became 13th President of the republic (1931–32), defeating * Briand. He was assassinated by a Russian anarchist, Paul Gorgulov.

Doumergue, Gaston (1863–1937). French politician. Elected as a radical socialist deputy in 1893, he moved steadily to the right, serving as premier (1913–14; 1934), president of the senate (1923–24), and president of the Republic (1924–31).

Dowding, Hugh Caswell Tremenheere Dowding, 1st Baron (1882–1970). British airman. His life as a pilot began in 1914 when as a young artillery officer he was attached to the Royal Flying Corps. In 1919 he became a group captain in the R.A.F. Thereafter he held important administrative posts until in 1936 he was appointed commander-in-chief of Fighter Command. He held this post until 1940, when his brilliantly successful direction of the Battle of Britain proved the efficiency of the plans he had already prepared. He received his barony in 1943.
Wright, R., *Dowding and the Battle of Britain*. 1969

Dowland, John (1563–1626). English lutenist and songwriter. His *First Booke of Songs or Ayres of Foure Partes with Tableture for the Lute* appeared in 1597, running to five editions by 1613. In 1598 he became lutenist to Christian IV of Denmark. His second and third books of airs appeared while he was abroad (1600, 1603). By 1605 he was back in London, and in that year appeared *Lachrymae*, accounted some of the finest instrumental consort music of the time. He is however now remembered chiefly for his songs, believed to be some of the most beautiful ever written.

Downing, Sir George (1623?–1684). English soldier and diplomat, after whom Downing Street in London is named. He served in Cromwell's army in Scotland and was prominent among those who offered Cromwell the crown. He was British resident at the Hague under Cromwell and Charles II. From the sale of estates left by his grandson, **Sir George Downing** (1684?–1749), Downing College, Cambridge, was founded.

Doxiadis, Constantinos Apostolos (1914–1978). Greek architect and city planner, born in Bulgaria. He became an architect in the 1930s, served in the Greek underground during World War II and was administrator of Marshall Plan aid in Greece (1947–51). A change of government and breakdown in health led Doxiadis to migrate to Australia where his architectural qualifications were not recognized. While working as a farmer in Western Australia (1951–52) he devised the principles of *ekistics* (the science of human settlements). After returning to Europe he won an international reputation for his prophetic work on the coming world city 'Ecumenopolis', needed to accommodate the population explosion. He was commissioned to design or restore many cities, e.g. Islamabad, Khartoum, Louisville (Ky.), and parts of Philadelphia and Washington, D.C. He founded his own university in Athens.

Doyle, Sir Arthur Conan (1859–1930). British novelist, the creator of Sherlock Holmes. He was born in Edinburgh, where he later graduated in medicine and encountered a Dr Joseph Bell, whose methods of deductive reasoning reappeared in Holmes. After practising medicine in Southsea (1882–90) he turned to authorship, and in *A Study in Scarlet* (1887) he introduced Holmes and his friend Dr Watson. The short stories of which the detective was the hero first appeared in the *Strand Magazine* and were collected as *The Adventures of Sherlock Holmes* (1891) and *The Memoirs of Sherlock Holmes* (1894). In the last tale Holmes (of whom his author was wearying) fell off a cliff but popular demand led Conan Doyle to retrieve him for *The Return of Sherlock Holmes* (1904), *His last Bow* (1918) and *The Case Book of Sherlock Holmes* (1928). Doyle himself regarded more highly his historical novels, e.g. *The White Company* (1891) and *Brigadier Gerard* (1896). In later life he became a convinced spiritualist and wrote a *History of Spiritualism* (1926).

Pearson, H., *Conan Doyle: His Life and Art*. 1961

Doyle, Richard (1824–1883). British caricaturist, painter and illustrator. Born in London, he was the son of **John Doyle** (1797–1868), a famous caricaturist. He was taught by his father, and at 15 published the *Eglington Tournament or The Days of Chivalry Revived.* From 1843 he was a regular contributor to *Punch*, for which he designed in 1849 the cover that was used for over a century. He drew a comic strip for *Punch* featuring Brown, Jones and Robinson, and much of his best work appeared in the publication including *Manners and Customs of ye Englyshe*, but he retired in 1850 because of the publication's anti-Catholic statements.

He illustrated many books, e.g. Thackeray's *The Newcomes* and Dickens's Christmas books, and painted landscapes; in particular, fantastic fairyland scenes, in water colour and oils, e.g. *In Fairyland*; *Pictures of the Elf-World.*

Hambourg, D., *Richard Doyle*. 1948

D'Oyly Carte, Richard *see* **Carte, Richard D'Oyly**

Draco (7th century B.C.). Athenian lawmaker, whose memory the word 'draconian' preserves. His code of laws (621 B.C.) was of such severity that even laziness was punishable by death.

Drake, Sir Francis (*c.* 1540–1596). English seaman and explorer. He was born in Tavistock, Devon, and from 1565 took part in expeditions organized and led by his kinsman, Sir John Hawkins, to carry slaves from West Africa to the West Indies. Later he was active in the unofficial sea war with Spain secretly encouraged by Queen Elizabeth, who shared in the plunder but denounced it as piracy if occasion demanded. On one such voyage he raided Spanish settlements on the Panama Isthmus (1572) and was the first Englishman to sight the Pacific. It was his aim to reach this ocean when he set out with four small ships in December 1577. Two were still with him when (August 1578) he entered the Magellan straits, but when at last after being driven south he was able to sail northward up the South

American coast he was, through the loss of one vessel and the return of the other, reduced to a single ship. After provisioning himself from coastal settlements and capturing a rich prize, he crossed the Pacific, eventually reached Java and headed for the Cape of Good Hope and home, which he reached in September 1580, having been the first Englishman to circumnavigate the globe. Despite Spanish protests, Elizabeth knighted him on board his ship. After another voyage to the Indies in search of plunder (1585–86), in the course of which he picked up and brought back 180 disillusioned colonists from Virginia, he turned to the task of forestalling the Armada by destroying as many Spanish ships as he could before they sailed. In 1587 he 'singed the King of Spain's beard' by entering Cadiz harbour and destroying, without loss, thirty-three enemy ships. When the Armada finally appeared (1588) Drake, who according to the familiar story was playing bowls at Plymouth, declared that there was time 'to win this game and to thrash the Spaniards too'. As vice-admiral he commanded a division of the English fleet, outfought the enemy in the Channel (he captured the *Rosario* off Portland) and later pursued them northwards up the east coast. The next few years were peaceful but in 1595 he left with Hawkins for the West Indies on a last unsuccessful voyage, during which both great captains died.
Williams, N., *Francis Drake*. 1973

Draper, Ruth (1884–1956). American actress. A stage phenomenon, year after year she filled theatres in New York and London with her monologues, gay, ironic or sad, performed with no scenery or stage properties and without change of costume.
Zabel, M. D., *The Art of Ruth Draper*. 1960

Drayton, Michael (1563–1631). English poet. He was born in Warwickshire, where he owed support and education to the patronage of Sir Henry Goodere, whose daughter Anne was named 'Idea' in his sonnets. Already as a child he was writing verse and in time attempted almost every kind of verse, eclogues in the manner of Spenser, pastorals, odes, sonnets (including the famous 'Since there's no help, come let us kiss and part'), historical poems (e.g. *Piers Gaveston*, *c.* 1593), imaginary exchanges of letters in verse between such famous lovers as Henry II and Fair Rosamund and finally the unique *Poly-olbion* (i.e. having many blessings; 1612–22), a poetic topographical survey of England.
Berthelot, J. A., *Drayton*. 1961

Dreiser, Theodore (1871–1945). American novelist. He was born in Indiana and was brought up in a poor and religiously strict family. His own sexual repression and his experience as a reporter of the sordid side of life in St Louis, Chicago, New York and other cities gave him an insight into the problems of sex and ambition which are the themes for his frank and realistic novels, which offended his contemporaries. His first novel, *Sister Carrie*, appeared in 1900 and was followed by e.g. *Jennie Gerhardt* (1911), *The Genius* (1915) and his best known work *An American Tragedy* (1925), which tells how obsession with sex and money leads a weak-willed boy to murder. He also wrote several autobiographical works, e.g. *A Book about Myself* (1922). Dreiser's later socialism inspired his *Tragic America* (1931).
Swanberg, W. A., *Dreiser*. 1965

Dreyfus, Alfred (1859–1935). French soldier. Victim of a famous miscarriage of justice, he was the son of a Jewish industrialist and at the time of the *affaire* (1894) was an army captain in the War Office in Paris. He was suspected of being the author of a letter (known as the *bordereau* and extracted from the German Embassy by a French agent) announcing the dispatch to the German military attaché of certain secret documents. On flimsy evidence based on similarity of handwriting Dreyfus was arrested, found guilty and sent to Devil's Island. In 1896 evidence was discovered by a Colonel Picquart indicating that the real culprit was a Major Esterhazy, but anti-Semitic prejudice in the army, combined with the effect on discipline of admitting the true facts, prevented the case being reopened. A massive counter-campaign, in the course of which * Zola wrote his famous open letter *J'accuse*, at last secured a retrial (1899); by the use of forged documents Dreyfus was again found guilty, but President Loubert at once ordered a pardon. In 1906 the sentence was finally quashed and Dreyfus was restored to his army rank. He took part in World War I. In 1930 the published papers of Colonel Schwarzkoppen, the German military attaché of the time, confirmed Esterhazy's guilt.
Chapman, G., *The Dreyfus Trials*. 1972

Drinkwater, John (1882–1937). English poet and dramatist. He was born in Birmingham and was associated from the first with Barry Jackson's theatrical enterprise which became the Birmingham Repertory Theatre. There was first produced (1918) his most famous play *Abraham Lincoln*, upon which his fame mainly rests. Its successors, e.g. *Mary Stuart* (1919), *Robert E. Lee* (1923), never achieved the same acclaim. Drinkwater's lyrical poems and critical 'lives' of literary figures are now almost forgotten.
Drinkwater, J., *Inheritance*. 1931; *Discovery*. 1932

Drummond, Sir (James) Eric, 16th Earl of Perth (1876–1951). British diplomat. After serving as private secretary to H. H. Asquith, Sir Edward Grey and A. J. Balfour (1913–19), he was the first secretary-general of the League of Nations (1919–33). He became U.K. ambassador to Italy (1933–39). He succeeded to his peerage in 1937.

Drummond, William (1585–1649). Scottish poet, known as 'Drummond of Hawthornden'. He studied at Edinburgh and abroad and succeeded his father as laird of Hawthornden in 1610. He was a Royalist and Episcopalian, though he played no active political part, and became the friend of Michael Drayton and Ben Johnson, whose visit to Hawthornden in the winter of 1618–19 is recalled in Drummond's lively *Conversations*. He wrote learned and ornate verses, religious, amatory and pastoral, in a style which belongs rather to the age of Spenser than to his own and which derives from his study of Petrarch and the Pléiade (* Ronsard). His best known prose work is *The Cypress Grove* (1623), a meditation on death. He also wrote a history of Scotland.
Fogle, F. R., *A Critical Study of William Drummond*. 1952

Dryden, John (1631–1700). English poet and dramatist. He came of a well established Northamptonshire family, was educated at Westminister, under the famous Dr Busby, and at Cambridge. He seems to have had some secretarial post in Cromwell's government but was quite ready to welcome Charles II (*Astraea Redux*, 1660) and was a consistent Tory for the rest of his life. His marriage (1663) to Lady Elizabeth Howard, daughter of the Earl of Berkshire and sister of his friend Sir Robert Howard, the dramatist, assured his place in the literary world. He retired to his father-in-law's house in the country in the plague year of 1665 and remained there to write *Annus Mirabilis* (1667), which relates the events of the Dutch War of 1665–66 and the Great Fire. In 1668 he became Poet Laureate. He had already written plays, but the success of *The Indian Emperor* (1667), a tragedy about the love of Montezuma's daughter for Cortez, the conqueror of Mexico, encouraged him to continue, and over twenty plays, tragedies, comedies and satires followed. The one best remembered is *All for Love* (1678), a version of the Antony and Cleopatra story. His earlier plays were written in rhyming couplets. This was his first in blank verse.

In 1679 he was attacked and beaten in the street as a result of another of his activities, political satire. His best known poem in this field is the allegorical mock-epic *Absalom and Achitophel* (1681), in which the title parts represent Monmouth and Shaftesbury. Charles II is David, Buckingham is Zimri and so on.

Many of Dryden's best lyrical poems appear as songs in his plays, but he also wrote odes, including *Alexander's Feast* (1679), which he thought the best of his poetry.

His *Hind and the Panther* (1678) indicated his conversion to Roman Catholicism which, after the expulsion of James II, cost him his laureateship. In his later years he was mainly active in translating Virgil and other classical writers. Much of his voluminous prose writing was on historical subjects or literary criticism; his *Essay on Dramatic Poesie* was published as early as 1668. His last major work was a collection of *Fables* (1699), of which the *Preface* is often cited as a fine example of late seventeenth-century prose. Dryden's greatness was fully acknowledged by the time of his death and he was buried in Westminster Abbey.
Myers, W., *Dryden*. 1973

Du Barry, Marie Jeanne Bécu, Countess (1743–1793). Mistress of Louis XV of France. She was a dressmaker's daughter who rose to fortune by her good looks and vivacity. Her association with the king lasted from 1769 until his death (1774) but she took no part in politics. On the outbreak of the Revolution (1789) she fled to England but rashly returned in 1793, when she was arrested and guillotined.

Laski, P. M., *Trial and Execution of Madame du Barry*. 1969

Dubček, Alexander (1921–). Czechoslovakian politician, born Uhrovec, Slovakia. Originally a factory worker, he joined the resistance movement in World War II and fought in the 1944–45 Slovak uprising against the Germans. After the war he associated with the Communist Party, becoming a member of the central committee of the Slovak Party in 1951. After studying law at Komensky University he became deputy in the Czechoslovak National Assembly (1951–55) and chief secretary of the Banská Bystrica regional party committee (1953–55). In 1955 he was sent to study at the Soviet Party's political college in Moscow; returning in 1958 he was elected to the central committees of the Slovak and Czechoslovak Communist Parties. In 1960 he was appointed industrial secretary of the Central Committee of the Communist Party of Czechoslovakia and in 1962 made a full member of the Presidium. He replaced Karol Bacílek as Slovak Communist Party leader in 1963 and from 1967–69 he was Czechoslovak party leader. In 1968 greater freedom of the press was granted and Stalin's political victims rehabilitated. On 9 April 1968 a reform programme entitled 'Czechoslovakia's Road to Socialism' was announced and these moves aroused concern in the U.S.S.R., which resulted in a Soviet invasion. Dubček was forced to make major concessions, and was replaced as secretary-general by Dr Gustav Husak. Serving briefly as ambassador to Turkey (1969–70) he was expelled from the Communist Party (1970).
Shawcross, W., *Dubcek*. 1970

Du Bellay, Joachim (1522–1560). French poet. He was born to a noble family, and became a leader of the group of poets called the Pléiade (* Ronsard). He wrote many ardent and melancholic Petrarchan love sonnets and an important literary treatise, *La Deffence et illustration de la langue françoyse* (1549), the manifesto of the Pléiade. He was the friend and fellow student of Ronsard.

Du Bois, W(illiam) E(dward) B(urghardt) (1868–1963). US scholar and black civil rights leader, born in Great Barrington, Massachusetts and educated at Fisk and Harvard Universities. He taught economics and history at Atlanta University (1897–1910). He devoted himself to sociological research into blacks in America. He published *Souls of Black Folk* (1903) in which he opposed Booker T. Washington's accommodation strategy and in 1905 founded the Niagara Movement, whose members, black intellectuals, agitated for Negro rights. This merged with the National Association for the Advancement of Colored People which he helped form; he was editor of its journal, *Crisis*, but resigned from the movement in 1934, to return to writing and teaching. However, he rejoined NAACP in 1944 as research director. His membership of the Communist party dated from 1961 and in 1962 he emigrated to Accra, Ghana, and renounced U.S. citizenship. Earlier he had advocated independence for African colonies.
Weinberg, M. (ed.), *W. E. B. Du Bois: A Reader*. 1970

Du Bois-Reymond, Emil Heinrich (1818–1896). German scientist. His early researches were into the well-known phenomenon of discharges from electric fish. He then moved on to investigate the presence of electrical charges in nervous impulses in general, particularly in muscle contractions. By devising ever more sensitive apparatus he was able to detect discharges in very localized muscle tissues; he laid the foundations for almost all subsequent work in electro-physiology. He had strongly-held views about scientific metaphysics. He condemned the vitalist beliefs that were prevalent in Germany in his day, and denied that Nature contained life-forces independent of matter. All force resided at some place in the material world.

Dubos, René (Jules) (1901–1982). French-American micro-biologist. He did much early research into the isolation of antibacterial substances from various soil micro-organisms, which led to the discovery of major antibiotics. Publications include *Bacterial and Mycotic Infections in Man* (1948), *Pasteur and Modern Medicine* (1960) and *Man, Medicine, and Environment* (1968). He was editor of the *Journal of Experimental Medicine*.

Duccio di Buoninsegna (*c.* 1255–*c.* 1319). Sienese painter. His influence on the Sienese school was comparable with that of Giotto in Florence. He has been called 'the last and greatest representative of the Byzantine tradition', but he imparted to his figures a liveliness and individuality quite unlike Byzantine portraiture. Duccio was a master of narrative, his finest work being the *Maestà*, painted for Siena Cathedral, consisting of twenty-six scenes from the Passion of Christ. He used much gold and surface pattern. An earlier work of his, the *Rucellai Madonna*, in Florence, was once ascribed to Cimabue.

Duchamp, Marcel (1887–1968). French painter. Associated with several modern movements including Futurism and Cubism, he became one of the leading Dadaists, the anti-aesthetics, anti-'art' protesters and precursors of Surrealism. In 1915 he went to New York and spent eight years working on *The Bride Stripped Bare by her Bachelors Even* (1915–23, Philadelphia), a famous and controversial ten-foot-high glass and metal composition. He became an American citizen in 1955.
Lebel, R., *Marcel Duchamp*. 1959

Dudley, Edmund (*c.* 1462–1510). English lawyer, one of the main instruments through whom Henry VII made his financial exactions. He was subsequently executed by Henry VIII. His son, John Dudley, became Duke of * Northumberland. John's elder son, Lord Guildford Dudley, married and shared the fate of Lady Jane * Grey: and his younger son became Elizabeth's favourite, the Earl of * Leicester.

Dufay, Guillaume (*c.* 1400–1474). Flemish composer and founder of the Burgundian School, born probably at Hainaut. A chorister at Cambrai cathedral (1409), *c.* 1420 he entered the service of Carlo Malatesta of Rimini, and in 1428 became a member of the Papal Choir at Rome. As a canon of Cambrai (from 1426), he supervised the cathedral music. The greatest composer of his time of church and secular music, he created the style which is characteristic of the Burgundian composers and links late medieval music with that of the Renaissance, and the later Franco-Flemish composers. His works include 87 motets, 59 French chansons and 7 masses.

Dufferin and Ava, Frederick Temple Hamilton-Temple-Blackwood, 1st Marquess of (1826–1902). British administrator. After holding political posts under Palmerston and Gladstone he was governor general of Canada (1872–78), ambassador to Russia (1879) and to Turkey (1881–84): while holding the latter post he went to Egypt to help in the reconstruction necessary after the defeat of Arabi Pasha's rebellion (1882). As viceroy of India he dealt diplomatically with the Russian threat through Afghanistan and was confronted with the quarrel with King Thibaw of Upper Burma, which led to that country's annexation. His career ended with two more ambassadorial posts, in Rome (1888–91) followed by Paris (to 1896). His last years were clouded by his loss of reputation as chairman of a finance corporation.

Dufy, Raoul (1877–1953). French painter. One of the original 'Fauves' (* Derain; * Matisse), Dufy was noted for his varied use of colour, lively subjects (e.g. race-meetings, regattas, flag-bedecked streets) and simplified form. He also designed wall decorations, textiles and ceramics. His drawing is swift and calligraphic.
Cogniat, R., *Raoul Dufy*. 1962

Du Gard, Roger Martin (1881–1958). French novelist and dramatist. He won the 1937 Nobel Prize for Literature for his long series of novels about middle-class life in France, *Les Thibault* (1922–40).

Du Gueselin, Bertrand (*c.* 1315–1380). French warrior of the Hundred Years War. He first achieved fame in Brittany, then defeated the English in a series of encounters which cleared them from the Seine valley; he was, however, captured at Auray (1364) and subsequently ransomed. He was made Constable of France by Charles V (1370) and gradually deprived the English of all their possessions there except for a few fortified towns.

Duhamel, Georges (1884–1966). French novelist. He studied medicine, and his *La Vie des Martyrs* (1917) describes his experiences as an army surgeon in World War I. Among his best known novels are those in the *Chronique des Pasquier* (10 vols., 1933–43), in which every character in the circle of the Pasquier family is portrayed with observation, humour and understanding. Duhamel was elected to the Académie Française in 1935.

Duhem, Pierre-Maurice-Marie (1861–1916). French scholar in the history and philosophy of science. His book *La Théorie Physique* (1906) argued that science could not expect to obtain a precise knowledge of the ultimate constituents of Nature. Nor should science attempt to picture Nature in visual terms (e.g. like a machine). Rather science proceeded best through attempting to explain more and more phenomena through deductions from a small number of mathematical laws.

Dukas, Paul Abraham (1865–1935). French composer. He studied and afterwards taught (1910–13; 1928–35) at the Paris Conservatoire. The orchestral piece *The Sorcerer's Apprentice* (1897) is perhaps his best known composition: but the opera *Ariadne and Bluebeard* (1907), based on Maeterlinck's play, and the dance-poem *La Péri* (1912) better reveal his special lyrical gifts.

Dulles, John Foster (1888–1959). American lawyer and diplomat. The son of a Presbyterian minister, he was born in Washington and educated at Princeton University and the Paris Sorbonne. He practised law in New York from 1911 but developed a keen interest in foreign affairs, in which, through a number of official and unofficial posts, he gradually became an acknowledged expert. Though a Republican he was employed (1950–51) by President Truman to negotiate the treaty with Japan, and when Eisenhower succeeded to the presidency (1953) he became secretary of state. His resistance to any concession to the communist countries, carried sometimes to the brink of war (hence the word 'brinkmanship' applied to his tactics) sometimes alarmed his allies, whose interests (e.g. at Suez) he did not appear to support with such fervour as they felt themselves entitled to expect. Ill health forced him to resign in 1959 and he died the same year.

His brother, **Allan Welsh Dulles** (1893–1969), was director of the Central Intelligence Agency (1953–61).

Hooper, T., *The Devil and John Foster Dulles*. 1973.

Dumas, Alexandre (1803–1870). French novelist, known as Dumas *père*. His father, illegitimate son of the Marquis de la Pailleterie, dropped this name for that of Dumas, the name of Alexandre's mother, a woman of Negro descent. His father was a general in the Revolutionary armies who, however, left his family in poverty. Alexandre came to Paris to seek his fortune, which he achieved with a number of long-forgotten historical melodramas. From 1836 he turned to historical romances and built up what amounted to a factory for their production. In a single year (1844) it is said that more than forty complete works were issued. 1500 novels were published under his name, most by hack-writers (his *nègres*). Dumas used his astonishing fertility of invention to supply plots, outline the sequence of events and write any purple passages that were required: a motley and changing collection of assistants did the rest. Nevertheless the best of his books have that remarkable gusto and vitality, which are Dumas's own special contribution. Foremost are *The Three Musketeers* (1844) with its sequels *Twenty Years After* (1845) and *The Viscount of Bragelonne* (1850). Of almost equal popularity are *The Count of Monte Cristo* (1845), *The Man in the Iron Mask* (1845), *The Queen's Necklace* and *Black Tulip* (both of 1848). His vitality spread to other fields; he travelled widely, made love prodigiously, and took part in the wars of Italian reunification (1859–60).

Craig Bell, A., *Alexandre Dumas*. 1950

Dumas, Alexandre (1824–1895). French playwright, known as Dumas *fils*, and the illegitimate son of the elder * Dumas. Of the many successful plays he wrote between 1852 and 1887, only one, the first (which began as a novel), *La Dame aux Camélias* (1852), is still remembered. It is the affecting love-story of a dying courtesan, and later provided a magnificent part for Sarah Bernhardt and other well known interpreters. Although, like his father, the younger Dumas led an irregular life all his plays point a moral, made abundantly clear (from 1867) in provocative prefaces. Dumas *fils* was elected to the Académie Française in 1875.

Du Maurier, Dame Daphne (1907–). English novelist and playwright. Born in London, she was the daughter of Sir Gerald Du Maurier. Her first novel, *The Loving Spirit* (1931), was the first of many successes, of which *Rebecca* (1938) is possibly her best known (filmed 1940). Her novels, usually stories with a Gothic or romantic flavour set on the coast of Cornwall, where her home is, include *Jamaica Inn* (1936), *Frenchman's Creek* (1942), *My Cousin Rachel* (1951) and *Rule Britannia* (1972). Collections of short stories include *The Breaking Point* (1959) and *Not after Midnight* (1971). Other works include several plays and *Vanishing Cornwall* (1967). She was created D.B.E. in 1969.

Du Maurier, George Louis Palmella Busson (1834–1896). Novelist and cartoonist, born in Paris, but a Londoner by adoption. He illustrated several books and became a cartoonist on *Punch*. He also wrote the novels *Peter Ibbotson* (1892) and *Trilby* (1894), the story of the hypnotist Svengali, later dramatized and filmed several times.

His son, **Sir Gerald du Maurier** (1873–1934), was a famous London theatrical manager and actor, knighted in 1923, and noted for his delicate understatement in comedies.
Ormond, L., *George du Maurier*. 1969

Dumouriez, Charles François (1739–1823). French soldier. He served with distinction in the Seven Years War, but it is as the general who saved Revolutionary France from the Prussians and Austrians that he is remembered. By skilful manoeuvres he stemmed the enemy onrush in Champagne and after he had successfully withstood the Prussian cannonade at Valmy (September 1792) he forced a retreat. He followed this up with a victory (November 1792) at Jemappes near Mons, which put the Austrian Netherlands (Belgium) in French power, but in the next year he was defeated near the Belgian village of Neerwinden and, in fear of the consequences, defected to the enemy; he settled in England in 1804.

Dunant, (Jean-) **Henri** (1828–1910) Swiss philanthropist. Founder of the Red Cross, he was born in Geneva. He organized emergency aid services for those wounded in the Battle of Solferino (1859), and proposed in *Un Souvenir de Solférino* (1862) the formation of voluntary relief societies in all countries. He also advocated an international agreement relating to war wounded. In 1864 he founded the Red Cross and in the same year the first national societies and the first Geneva Convention came into existence. He left Geneva because of financial difficulties (1867), and spent many years in poverty and obscurity; however he continued to argue for abolition of slavery, disarmament, international arbitration, fair treatment of prisoners of war and a Jewish homeland. Recognition of his work came in 1895 and he received many honours and annuities. In 1901 he was co-winner of the first Nobel Peace Prize.
Hart, E., *Man Born to Live*. 1953. Pandit, H. N., *The Red Cross and Henry Dunant*. 1969

Dunbar, William (*c*. 1460–*c*. 1530). Scottish poet. Little is known of his early life except what can be deduced from his poems. He was most probably a Franciscan friar whose wanderings as a mendicant friar took him to England and France. Later (*c*. 1500) as a secular priest he entered the service of James IV: in 1501 he accompanied the diplomatic mission to London which negotiated the king's marriage with Henry VII's daughter Margaret, whom in 1503 he welcomed to Scotland with the allegorical poem *The Thrissil and the Rois* (*The Thistle and the Rose*). An increase in his pension is mentioned in 1510 but after that nothing certain is known. *The Dance of the Seven Deadly Sins* is the best known of his other allegories. An elegy, *The Lament for the Makers* (i.e. poets), mourns the death of Chaucer and his successors. Dunbar was a metrical artist, who wrote with vigour, enjoyment and with humour, sometimes of a Rabelaisian kind.
Scott, T., *Dunbar*. 1966

Duncan I (died *c*. 1040). King of Scots. He succeeded (*c*. 1034) his grandfather, Malcolm II, but little is known of him except for his murder by Macbeth, which provided the theme of Shakespeare's tragedy.

Duncan, Isadora (1878–1927). American dancer. She lived in Europe from 1906 and her interpretative dancing, with bare feet and in flowing draperies, caused a sensation, as did her eccentric behaviour. She married the Russian poet Sergei Esenin (1922) but they separated in 1923. She died in an accident when her scarf was caught in the wheel of an open car.
Duncan, I., *Isadora*. 1968

Dundee, John Graham of Claverhouse, 1st Viscount (known as 'Bonnie Dundee') (1649–1689). Scottish soldier. He won the name 'Bonnie Dundee' when, after the revolution that brought William III and Mary to the throne, he raised the Highlanders in the cause of James II. At the battle fought in the pass of Killiecrankie, Perthshire, he outmanoeuvred and out-fought the enemy but was killed in the moment of victory. Earlier in his career the

Scottish Presbyterians, whom he harried by order of the royal government, had bestowed on him the sobriquet of 'Bloody Claverhouse', but in fact he does not seem to have shown exceptional cruelty by the standards of the time.

Taylor, A. S. H., *John Graham of Claverhouse*. 1939

Dundonald, 10th Earl *see* **Cochrane, Thomas**

Dunlop, John Boyd (1840–1921). Scottish inventor. Originally a veterinary surgeon, he invented (1887) the first successful pneumatic tyre, made of rubber tubing bound with linen tape, as a result of trying to improve one of his son's toys. The invention was patented in 1888 and in 1889 he was associated with Harvey du Gros (to whom he later assigned the patent) in setting up a factory in Dublin. Dunlop himself never made a large sum from his invention, nor was he closely associated with its development.

Dunne, John William (1875–1949). Irish-born philosopher and engineer. Though he played an important role in the design of the first British military aircraft, he is best known for the concept of 'serial time', set out in his books *An Experiment with Time* (1927) and *The Serial Universe* (1934), and for his theories about precognition and the analysis of dreams. His ideas influenced J. B. * Priestley in e.g. *Time and the Conways*.

Dunois, Jean d'Orléans, Comte de (1402–1468). Natural son of Louis, brother of Charles VI, and known as the 'Bastard of Orléans'. Comrade in arms of Joan of Arc, he was the most successful of the French leaders who fought the English in France; he defended Orléans until the French, inspired by Joan, forced the English to raise the siege; and in 1429 he won with her the Battle of Patay. After Joan's death he took Chartres, freed Paris, and had soon reduced the English hold on France to Normandy and Guienne: the former he regained in 1448–50, the latter in 1455.

Dunsany, Edward John Moreton Drax Plunkett, 18th Baron (1878–1958). Irish poet, dramatist and novelist, born in London. He served in the Boer War and World War I and became a professor of English literature at Athens. Many of his writings deal with 'the mysterious kingdoms where geography ends and fairyland begins', and include *Tales of Wonder* (1916), *Evil Kettle* (1926) and the plays *The Glittering Gates* (1909) and *The Gods of the Mountain* (1911).

Duns Scotus, Johannes (*c.* 1265–1308). Scottish theologian. Born near Roxburgh, he joined (*c.* 1280) the Franciscans at Dumfries and was ordained priest at Northampton in 1291. By this time he seems to have been studying at Oxford and spent almost all the rest of his life studying or teaching there and in Paris and, briefly, just before he died, at Cologne. His work consisted mainly of commentaries on the Bible, Aristotle and the *Sentences* of Peter Lombard. He gained an immense reputation for learning and owed his appellation *doctor subtilis* to the manner in which he criticized Thomas Aquinas's views concerning the harmony of faith and reason. He argued that assent to such concepts as the immortality of the soul cannot be attained by reason but must spring from a will to believe. In theology he was orthodox and gave the strongest support to the doctrine of the Virgin Mary's Immaculate Conception. Realism was the basis of his philosophy and he accepted the theory that a universal matter forms a common basis of everything that exists. His followers assailed the new learning of Renaissance humanists and in turn were attacked for pedantry and casuistry: the word 'dunce', derived from his name, thus unfairly came to mean a blockhead.

Dunstan, St (*c.* 924–988). English prelate and statesman, born at Glastonbury, where he was subsequently abbot for many years. After Athelstan's death (939), Dunstan's advice was constantly sought by his successors, but it was only when Edgar became king (959) that, as archbishop of Canterbury, he attained full power. A great scholar himself, he encouraged education, but his greatest achievements were the revival of monasticism and association of the monasteries with the life of the lay community. The peace and prosperity associated with Edgar's reign was largely due to Dunstan's influence.

Duckett, E. S., *Saint Dunstan of Canterbury*. 1955

Dupleix, Joseph François (1697–1763). French administrator. When he was 23 years old his father, a shareholder in the French East India Company, arranged for him to be given

a post on the Council at Pondicherry, the company's headquarters near Madras. He was so successful there, and later in Bengal, that in 1741 he was made governor general of all the French Indies. He now set about the fulfilment of his great ambition of creating a French empire in India. To this end he impressed the Indians by adopting oriental luxury, intervened in the local intrigues and supported, with diplomacy and troops, rulers in Hyderabad and the Carnatic upon whom he could rely. War between France and England, and Clive's military victories, transformed the situation and as Dupleix's difficulties increased his enemies in Paris became increasingly active until in 1754 he was recalled: he died in 1763 with reputation tarnished and fortune gone.
Dodwell, H. H., *Dupleix and Clive*. 1920

Du Pont, Eleuthère Irénée (1771–1834). American industrialist, founder of the chemical firm. His father, a French economist, **Pierre Samuel du Pont** (1739–1817), took him and the rest of his family to America in 1799. In 1801 Eleuthère started a gunpowder mill at Wilmington, Delaware, which grew into the vast industrial combine of E. I. Du Pont de Nemours, which now manufactures a great array of chemical and allied products ranging from explosives to paints, plastics, synthetic fibres, etc.

Dürer, Albrecht (1471–1528). German artist. Famous for his paintings, engravings, woodcuts and book illustrations, he was born in Nuremberg, the son of an immigrant Hungarian goldsmith, and was apprenticed to Wolgemut, a well known local painter and illustrator. He travelled widely in Germany from 1490 to 1494, returning to Nuremberg to marry Agnes Frey. The rest of his life was spent almost entirely in his native town except for visits to Venice (1494–95 and 1505–07), after which his paintings (e.g. the *Rosenkranz* altar-piece, and *The Ascension of the Virgin* and the later 'Four Apostles', now in Munich), show the marked influence of Venetian painters such as Giovanni Bellini. The best of his portraits suggest the simplicity of sculpture, and his characterization can at least be compared with that of Holbein.

In general Dürer stands between the Gothic and Renaissance periods, more interested in new techniques than new subjects. This is especially evident in his woodcuts and engravings, where the medieval preoccupation with the macabre is often combined with mathematical exactitude in reproducing the proportions of the human figure and a mastery of perspective. By a number of technical improvements he was able, too, to give a much greater flexibility to these branches of his art. His most important engravings include *The Knight, Death and the Devil* (1953), *Melancholia* and *St Jerome* (both of 1514). In woodcuts he abandons the colour of tradition and achieves contrast by making the figures stand out from a hatched background. He used the woodcut process even for pictures of great size. *The Triumphal Arch of the Emperor* contained 92 blocks and was over 11 ft. high. His output was enormous, with book-illustrating and designing for the fine arts to be added to his other works. In addition over 1,000 drawings exist in the great public collections of the world. His animal and plant studies in watercolour are the first known. He wrote treatises on artistic theory, and a diary.
Wölfflin, H., *The Art of Albrecht Dürer*. 1971

Durham, John George Lambton, 1st Earl of (1792–1840). British politician and administrator. He came of an old Durham family and was M.P. for the county from 1813 to 1828, when he was created a baron (the earldom came in 1833). 'Radical Jack', as he came to be called, was one of the most progressive members in the cabinet of his father-in-law, the Whig leader Lord Grey, and he took a prominent part in the drafting of the Reform Bill (1832). After a short spell as ambassador to Russia (1835–37), he was appointed governor general of the provinces of Canada with a mission to report and advise on the situation arising from the French-Canadian rebellion. The famous Durham Report (1839) recommended the union of Upper and Lower Canada, as a means of integrating the English and French, and local self-government for all the provinces. He also envisaged the federation of the provinces, which took place in 1867.
Cooper, L., *Radical Jack*. 1959

Durrell, Lawrence George (1912–). British novelist and poet. He spent part of his youth in Corfu, and during World War II was a press officer in several parts of the Middle East. This background helped him to write a highly successful series of novels 'The Alexandria Quartet' (1956–59) beginning with *Justine*, which gave a vivid and atmospheric portrayal of Alexandria, and some of the odder personalities among its inhabitants. His brother **Gerald** (1925–), author and naturalist, wrote *My Family and Other Animals* (1956) and similar books describing their life in Corfu. He founded the Jersey Wildlife Preservation Trust in 1963.

Duse, Eleonora (1859–1924). Italian actress. She came of a family of Venetian actors, appeared on the stage at the age of 4, played Juliet when she was 14, and at the age of 20 she was acclaimed as great. Thereafter, whether in Italy or in the capitals and great cities of the world, where she frequently toured, her fame was rivalled only by that of Sarah Bernhardt. She thought Ibsen the greatest dramatist of her time and played many of his parts; Maeterlinck's plays, too, attracted her, while her love for the poet Gabriele * d'Annunzio, the subject of his novel *Il Fuoco* (1900), made her the ideal interpreter of his dramatic poems.
Signorelli, O., *Eleonora Duse*. 1959

Duval, Claude (1643–1670). French highwayman. He went to England at the restoration of Charles II, and by the gallant manner and daring with which he carried out his robberies became a hero of ballad and legend. He was hanged at Tyburn.

Duvalier, François (1907–1971). Haitian politician. Known as 'Papa Doc', and a physician by profession, he did much good work in combating malaria before entering politics. Before becoming president (the sixth in ten months) in 1957 he had held the ministries of labour and public health. Once in power his personality seemed to change; he violated the constitution by extending his term of office, he became increasingly dictatorial in his methods and, unable to trust the army, he raised a force of brutal police known as the Tonton Macoute ('bogey-men'), to bolster his reign of terror. His son **Jean-Claude Duvalier** (1951–), known as 'Baby Doc', succeeded as president for life 1971– and moderated his father's excesses.
Diederich, B. and Burt, A., *Papa Doc! Haiti and its Dictator François Duvalier*. 1972

Duveen, Joseph, 1st Baron Duveen (1869–1939). English art dealer. The business of his father, **Sir Joseph Joel Duveen** (1843–1908), who had added a wing to the Tate gallery and presented many pictures to the nation, was greatly extended by the son, who achieved an almost legendary success in inducing European owners to sell and wealthy Americans subsequently to buy many of the most important pictures in the world still in private possession. He continued the family tradition of making munificent gifts to British public collections. He received his peerage in 1933.
Behrman, S. N., *Duveen*. 1952

Dvořák, Antonín (1841–1904). Czech (Bohemian) composer. He was born near Prague (then in the Austrian empire), the son of a butcher and innkeeper, and was familiar from boyhood with the folk music of the countryside. He showed early musical talent, was taught the organ, piano and viola by his schoolmaster, was accepted as a pupil at the Prague Organ School (later the Conservatoire), and at 21 became a viola player (under * Smetana) in the orchestra of the National Theatre. His overture to an opera *King and Collier*, conducted by Smetana, secured him his first public recognition. From 1880 he was a friend of Brahms, who admired his early works and helped to secure their publication. In his vigorous and warmly emotional music, Dvořák made much use of Czech folk dances. His *Slavonic Rhapsodies* became extremely popular and were performed throughout Europe and America. From 1884 he visited England seven times and wrote *The Spectral Bridge*, the *Requiem*, an oratorio, *St Ludmilla*, and his Symphony No. 8 in G Major especially for English audiences. In 1892–95 he was director of the New York National Conservatoire. To this period belong the best known of his nine symphonies No. 5 (now known as No. 9) in E Minor, *From the New World* (1893), contains reminiscences of Negro themes. He was director of the Prague Conservatoire from 1901 to 1904. His other works include operas, e.g. *Kate and the Devil* (1899) and *Rusalka* (1900), twelve String Quartets, many songs, e.g. *Songs my mother taught me*, religious music, e.g. *Stabat Mater* (1883), and a Cello Concerto (1895).
Hughes, G., *Dvořák: His Life and Music*. 1967

Dyck, Sir Anthony Van *see* **Van Dyck, Sir Anthony**

Dyer, Reginald Edward Harry (1864–1927). British officer. In 1919, as major-general, he

was responsible for the 'massacre' in Amritsar, the Sikh city of the Punjab, when he gave the order to fire on an Indian crowd, massed in defiance of orders. Nearly 400 people were killed and Dyer, after official censure, resigned from the army. His defenders claim that he was faced with a desperate choice and that his action averted a far greater catastrophe.
Colvin, I., *Life of General Dyer*. 1951

Dylan, Bob (real name Robert Zimmerman) (1941–). American singer and composer, born in Duluth, Minnesota. After a turbulent childhood, he travelled round the country, imitating the folk singer Woody Guthrie in his life and singing-style. He adopted his professional name from the poet Dylan Thomas. He first performed professionally in coffeehouses, but was not recognized as a musician of real talent until the release of his first record albums (1962–64); two of his songs 'Blowin' in the Wind' and 'The Times They are A-Changin' were adopted by the civil rights movement. His melodies and angry and sometimes cynical lyrics were tremendously popular and he became a cult figure; some of his songs were considered by critics to be serious poetry (e.g. in *Highway 61 Revisited*, 1965). In 1965 he adopted electronic instruments and a new musical form: folk rock. After a motorcycle accident he released an album *John Wesley Harding* (1968) which furthered his growing tendency to introspection and used country-and-western arrangements, as did his *Nashville Skyline* (1969). The seventies saw what some consider to be some of his finest mature work, e.g. in the albums *Blood on The Tracks* (1974) and *Desire* (1975). In 1979 Dylan, now divorced, professed himself to be a Christian.
Grey, M., *Song and Dance Man*. 1973

Dyson, Sir Frank Watson (1868–1939). English astronomer, educated at Cambridge. His contributions to astronomy were mainly concerned with the distribution and movement of the stars and with the structure of the universe. He was Astronomer Royal 1910–33 and was responsible for introducing into B.B.C. broadcasts the six-pip signals that were the first accurate time checks to be made available to the general public. In observing an eclipse of the sun in Brazil in 1919 he was able to test and confirm Einstein's theory of the effect of gravity on the path of light.

Dzerzhinsky, Felix Edmundovich (1877–1926). Russian Communist politician, of Polish noble descent. He was imprisoned for revolutionary activities several times, and was the first head of the post-revolutionary secret police (Cheka) 1917–24, and of its successors the O.G.P.U. and G.P.U.

E

Eakins, Thomas (1844–1916). American painter, photographer and sculptor, born Philadelphia, Pennsylvania. He studied art and anatomy, then went to Paris to study at the Ecole des Beaux-Arts under J. L. Gérôme, then under Léon Bonnat and the sculptor, Dumont. Later he visited Spain, where he was particularly influenced by Velasquez and Ribera.

Returning to the US, he was professor of and lecturer on anatomy and painting at Pennsylvania Academy. A 'realist', he was called 'the American Courbet'. His most famous picture, 'The Gross Clinic' provoked great revulsion, though his paintings are for the most part portraits of friends and depictions of outdoor sports. He was criticized for his teaching innovations which included working from live nude models, and his unwillingness to abandon the use of models resulted in his resignation in 1896. He assisted his pupil, Samuel Murray, in sculpting the Prophets on the Witherspoon Building, Philadelphia.

Earhart, Amelia (1898–1937). American aviator. The first woman to fly solo across the Atlantic (1932) and the Pacific (1935), she disappeared on an attempted flight round the world.
Putnam, G. P., *Soaring Wings*. 1939

Early, Jubal Anderson (1816–1894). American soldier. One of the Southern generals in the Civil War, he distinguished himself early in the war by his rapid advance down the Shenandoah Valley in July 1864, which threatened Washington; he continued to be valuable in several compaigns and proved a formidable opponent even when his forces were outnumbered.

Eastman, George (1854–1932). American inventor. His invention of the first practicable roll film (1884) and his development of cheap, mass-produced 'Kodak' cameras made photography a popular hobby. Experiments conducted jointly with * Edison did much to overcome the early difficulties of making motion pictures. He gave large sums (about $100 million) to educational institutions. He committed suicide.
Coe, B. W., *George Eastman and Early Photographers*. 1973

Ebert, Friedrich (1871–1925). German socialist, the first president of republican Germany after World War I. A saddler by trade, he became a trade union secretary, and by the outbreak of the war had become a member of the Reichstag and joint chairman of the Social Democratic party. As president of the republic from 1919 until his death, he dealt firmly with extremists of right and left and commanded respect by tact, prudence and common sense.
Peters, M., *Friedrich Ebert*. 1954

Eça de Queirós, José Maria de (1845–1900). Portuguese novelist, born Pavoa de Varzim. He graduated in law from Coimbra University (1866) and settled in Lisbon. He began a career in law but his real interest lay in literature. He wrote for the *Gazeta de Portugal* (1866–67) and contributed a satirical review to *As Farpas* (1871). By 1871 he was closely associated with the 'generation of '70', rebellious Portuguese intellectuals who advocated social and artistic reform. Joining the foreign service he was consul in Cuba (1872–76) and England (1874–79), when he wrote the novels for which he is best remembered, *O Crime do Padre Amaro* (1875), then *O Primo Basílio* (1878), stories of sexual misdeeds. In 1888 he wrote *Os Maias*, by which time he was designated the 'Portuguese Zola'. This novel was, like its predecessors, an attempt to bring about social reform by exposing the evils of contemporary society. His other novels show a change of style: *O Mandarim* (1880) is a fantasy, *A Relíquia* (1887) a satire and *A Cidade e as Serras* (1901) a picture of rural life, praising the beauty of the countryside. He was consul in Paris 1888–1900.

Of aristocratic temperament, he was contemptuous of the backwardness of Portugal, but his last novel expresses a sentimental feeling for the country. He introduced naturalism and realism in literature to Portugal and was a master of character analysis. He is considered by some to be Portugal's greatest novelist.

Simões, J. G., *Eça de Queirós, O Homen e o Artista*. 1945

Eccles, Sir John Carew (1903–). Australian physiologist. He was born in Melbourne and educated at Melbourne University. He undertook research at Oxford University (1925–37) where he gained his D.Phil. From 1944–51 he was professor of physiology at Otago Medical School, New Zealand and held the same chair at Australian National University, Canberra (1951–66). Here he discovered the chemical means by which signals are communicated or repressed by nerve cells, for which he was awarded the Nobel Prize in physiology and medicine in 1963 (with A. L. * Hodgkin and A. F. * Huxley). His work has had considerable influence on the medical treatment of nervous diseases, and research on the function of kidney, heart and brain. His publications include *Reflex Activity of the Spinal Cord* (1932) and *The Physiology of Nerve Cells* (1957).

Eckert, John Presper (1919–). U.S. inventor, born in Philadelphia. With J. W. Mauchly, a professor of electrical engineering, he improved computing equipment needed by the U.S. War Department to recompute artillery firing tables (1943). They also won a government contract to build a digital computer (completed 1946) and this first electronic computer, ENIAC (Electronic Numerical Integrator and Computer) was the prototype for most modern computers. In 1948 Eckert and Mauchly established a computer manufacturing firm and in 1949 produced Binac (Binary Automatic Computer) which stored information on magnetic tape rather than punch cards. Their third model, Univac I (Universal Automatic Computer) was widely used in the commercial world, and really began the computer boom.

Eckhart, Johannes (*c.* 1260–1327). German theologian, usually known as Meister Eckhart. He was one of the most profound medieval thinkers but the mystical and abstract nature of his speculations make them difficult to understand; they have been loosely described as Christian neoplatonism. He conceives an ultimate incomprehensible Godhead, of which the Father, Son and Holy Spirit are different manifestations. The soul of man also partakes of the essence of the Godhead and on reaching a stage of self-awareness is reabsorbed into the Godhead from which it came.

Eckhart's mysticism did not, however, take the form of trances, visions etc.; he was a powerful preacher and must have been a competent man of affairs. Two years after his death many of his teachings were condemned by the papacy. *Opus tripartitum* was his most important work.

Hustache, J. A., *Master Eckhart and the Rhineland Mystics*. 1958

Eco, Umberto (1932–). Italian writer. A historian and philosopher, he taught at Bologna University, became an expert on James * Joyce and semiotics (* Barthès) and wrote the best-selling novel, *The Name of the Rose* (1980).

Eddington, Sir Arthur Stanley (1882–1944). English astronomer. After being assistant at Greenwich Observatory (1906–13), he was a professor of astronomy and director of the observatory at Cambridge University for the rest of his life. In 1916 he began his work on the constitution of the stars, establishing their internal structure and bringing about a complete revision of ideas then current. He also made important contributions to relativity theory, particularly in relation to cosmology. He wrote a number of popular works expounding advances in physics: one of the

best known is *The Nature of the Physical World* (1928). He was knighted in 1930 and awarded the O.M. in 1938.
Douglas, A. V., *Arthur Stanley Eddington*. 1956

Eddy, Mary Baker (1821–1910). American founder of the Christian Science movement, born in New Hampshire. From childhood a devout Bible student, she was healed after a serious injury caused by a fall (1866) by applying the teaching of the healing of the palsied man in St Matthew's Gospel to her own condition. In 1875 she published *Science and Health* which asserted that matter was an illusion and that 'Spirit' (i.e. God) was everything. Thus all physical ailments could be overcome by prayer. In 1879 she founded the First Church of Christ, Scientist, in Boston and was pastor emeritus until her death. She founded a daily newspaper, the *Christian Science Monitor*, in 1908.
Peel, R., *Mary Baker Eddy* (3 vols, 1966, 1971, 1977).

Eden, (Robert) Anthony, 1st Earl of Avon (1897–1977). British Conservative politician. The second son of Sir William Eden, a Durham baronet, he was educated at Eton, won an M.C. in World War I and studied oriental languages at Oxford (1919–22). From 1922 to 1957 he represented Leamington as M.P.; from the first he specialized in foreign affairs and was parliamentary private secretary to Sir Austen Chamberlain (1926–29). In his subsequent posts his work at Geneva with the League of Nations gave him a great international reputation for sincerity and diplomatic skill. In 1935 he became foreign minister after the resignation of Sir Samuel Hoare (1st Viscount * Templewood). The attempts by the prime minister, Neville * Chamberlain, to bring about a *rapprochement* with Mussolini caused Eden to resign in 1938.

When * Churchill formed his coalition ministry in 1940 during World War II Eden was at first war minister but returned to the Foreign Office later that year. He was deputy leader of the Conservatives during the period of opposition after the war, and when they returned to power in 1951 was foreign secretary and deputy to Churchill, whom he succeeded as prime minister in 1955. His sponsorship in 1956 of the Anglo-French military intervention in Egypt after * Nasser had refused redress for seizing the Suez Canal provoked a violent controversy within and without his own party. The breakdown of his health forced his resignation in 1957. He accepted an earldom in 1961. Eden married as his second wife Clarissa Churchill, Winston Churchill's niece.
Churchill, R., *The Rise and Fall of Sir Anthony Eden*. 1959

Edgar (known as 'the Peaceful') (943–975). King of England (from 959). The first king for many years to be able to exercise undisputed rule over an undivided country, he was able to reform the administration, wisely allowing the Danes of eastern England to live under their own laws. His supremacy was symbolized by the legend that he was rowed on the Dee by eight subject kings. His chief adviser was * Dunstan, who enthusiastically supported his monastic reforms.

Edgar the Aetheling (*c.* 1055–after 1125). English prince. He was next in the royal line of descent when Edward the Confessor died and Harold became king. After the Norman conquest he submitted to William I but took refuge with his sister Margaret, who became the wife of Malcolm III of Scotland. After the northern rising of 1069–70, in which he took part, and wanderings in Europe, he made his peace with William. He was a crusader in 1099 and fought against Henry I at Tenchebrai (1106).

Edgeworth, Maria (1767–1849). Anglo-Irish writer. Her father, Richard Lovell Edgeworth (1774–1817), a landlord of Co. Longford, was a scientist, politician and educationist, with a score of children upon whom he could try out his theories. Maria, the eldest, co-operated with him as joint author of the Rousseauesque *Practical Education* (1798), and herself wrote *The Parent's Assistant* (1796–1801) and *Moral Tales* (1801). Better known are her realistic novels of Irish life: *Castle Rackrent* (1800), *The Absentee* (1812) and *Ormond* (1817). Excessive moralizing marred these and her other novels, e.g. *Belinda* (1801). She was a friend of Sir Walter * Scott.
Inglis-Jones, E., *The Great Maria: A Portrait of Maria Edgeworth*. 1959

Edinburgh, Prince Philip, Duke of (1921–). Consort of Queen Elizabeth II. He is the son of Prince Andrew of Greece: his mother, Princess Alice, was a sister of Earl

Mountbatten of Burma, with whom Philip lived while being educated at Gordonstoun School, Scotland, and whose surname he used before his marriage. He joined the Royal Navy in 1939 and served in the Pacific during World War II. He was created Duke of Edinburgh shortly before his marriage to Princess Elizabeth (November 1947). He has made many overseas journeys and takes a keen interest in science and sport. His 'Awards' scheme has achieved great popularity among young people.
Boothroyd, B., *Philip: An Informal Biography*. 1971

Edison, Thomas Alva (1847–1931). American inventor. He worked as a newsboy and later trained as a telegraph operator. While still a young man he invented and patented many improvements to telegraphic equipment, including the automatic repeater, the quadruplex telegraph, and a form of printing telegraph. With the fortune he made he was able in 1876 to set up a private experimental laboratory in Menlo Park, New Jersey. His interest lay in the practical application of science, not its principles. He made important inventions in many fields: the phonograph, the carbon microphone and an early form of incandescent lamp. In 1883 he discovered what became known as the 'Edison effect' – the passage of electricity, in a carbon filament lamp bulb, between the filament and a metal plate placed near it – which proved to be the forerunner of the radio valve. He also solved the problem of producing moving pictures on a screen. He was one of the most fertile of inventors and had over 1,300 patents to his credit.
Josephson, M., *Edison: A Biography*. 1959

Edmund (Rich), St (*c*. 1175–1240). English ecclesiastic, born in Abingdon. He studied at Oxford and in Paris. He lectured at Paris and Oxford (*c*. 1194–1200) and taught at Oxford after further theological studies at Paris (*c*. 1214–22). In 1222 he became canon of Salisbury Cathedral, and in 1227 preached for the 6th Crusade, at the request of Pope Gregory IX by whom he was appointed archbishop of Canterbury 1233. Outspoken, he clashed with Henry III, criticizing his reliance on favourites, and his foreign policies. Edmund averted civil war by bringing moral pressure to bear upon Henry but the threat of excommunication forced him to make concessions. Later, however, the papal legate, Otho, requested by Henry, undermined Edmund's authority, forcing him to leave England for Rome, to appeal to the Pope (1238). He died at Soissy en route to Poitigny to enter a monastery. Edmund's high ideals and virtue made him widely respected; he was canonised in 1247. Feast day: 16 Nov. His *Speculum ecclesiae* is considered a major contribution to medieval theology.
Lawrence, C. H., *St Edmund of Abingdon: A Study in Hagiography and History*. 1960

Edmund Ironside (980–1016). King of England (1016), son of Ethelred the Unready. He led the resistance to the Danish invaders under Cnut but after a long, and at first successful, struggle he was defeated at Ashington (1016) and had to divide his kingdom with Cnut, retaining the south for himself. After his death Cnut ruled over the whole kingdom.

Edmund the Martyr, St (*c*. 841–870). King of East Anglia (from 855–56). He was either slain in battle or martyred by the Danes – reputedly bound to a tree, scourged, shot with arrows and finally beheaded for refusing to renounce his Christian faith. His tomb at Bury St Edmunds, Suffolk, eventually became a shrine.

Edward (known as 'the Elder') (870–924). King of England (from 899). Before he succeeded his father, * Alfred the Great, he defeated the Danes repeatedly but on coming to the throne he immediately had to face a revolt by his cousin Aethelwald supported by the Danes of the east and north. Edward continued his victorious career and after the death of his sister and staunch ally Aethelflaed, the 'Lady of the Mercians' (918), he was lord of all England south of the Humber, and by 921 was overlord also of the north, Wales and parts of Scotland. He maintained his power by strategically placed fortresses, some of which survive. He was succeeded by his son * Athelstan.

Edward ('the Martyr') (*c*. 963–978). King of England (from 975), son of Edgar the Peaceful. His reign was disorderly and he was murdered at Corfe Castle, Dorset, probably at the instigation of his stepmother Aelfthryth, whose son * Ethelred the

Unready succeeded him. He was styled as martyr from *c.* 1001.

Edward (known as 'the Confessor') (1004–1066). King of the English (from 1043), canonized in 1161. He was a son of Ethelred the Unready by Emma, sister of the Duke of Normandy, at whose court he had, for safety's sake since England was in a state of turbulence, been brought up. Indeed when he came to the throne he had spent barely two years in England. It was natural therefore that he should surround himself with Norman friends but he also took to a life of pious practice and religious observance which later earned him the title of Saint (1161). Westminster Abbey, which he founded and where he is buried, is his finest memorial. Meanwhile power rested with his ambitious father-in-law Godwine, Earl of Wessex, and his son Harold. Edward had no liking for either but was unable to assert himself and eventually agreed that Harold should succeed to the throne. He acquired posthumously a reputation as a lawgiver.

Edward I (1239–1307). King of England (from 1272), son of Henry III. His nickname 'Longshanks' shows him to have been unusually tall. In 1254 he married * Eleanor of Castile, to whom he remained devotedly attached. During the Barons' War (1264–65) he led his father's army and defeated and killed Simon * de Montfort at Evesham (1265). He took a distinguished part in the Seventh Crusade (1270–73) and did not get back to England until two years after his father's death. He soon showed himself to be a great lawmaker. The first Statute of Westminster (1275) dealt with administrative abuses; that of *Quo Warranto*, by forcing the magnates to show warrant for the powers they claimed to exercise, was a protection against the usurpation of feudal power; the Statue of Mortmain prevented the handing over of land to the church except under licence. Edward believed in government by consent and that those who had to find the money for wars and other emergencies should be consulted as to amounts and the methods by which it should be raised. Therefore he extended de Montfort's experiments of adding new elements to the Great Council until there actually came into existence a body which began to be known as parliament and was somewhat akin to that which we know by that name. Outside England, Edward had to contend with the French king's provocations, designed to secure control of Edward's French inheritance, and was forced into a long, expensive and indecisive contest. In Wales a rising by the prince Llewelyn (1282) provided him with excuse and opportunity for a complete conquest secured by strategically placed castles, several of which still stand. His son, the future Edward II, was declared Prince of Wales (1301). In Scotland, where the death (1290) of the 3-year-old queen, Margaret, the Maid of Norway, had left a gap in the succession, he was less successful. Edward made three expeditions in support of his candidate John * de Balliol, but though he could usually win pitched battles and hold the fortified towns, though he could even bring the Coronation stone from Scone to Westminster (1296) and defeat and execute the patriot leader William * Wallace (1305), he could achieve no permanent conquest and was marching northwards to suppress yet another rising (under Robert Bruce) when he died. He was buried in Westminster Abbey. For his prowess as a soldier, for his great programme of legislation and above all for what he did towards the permanent establishment of a representative parliament, Edward I must be accounted one of the greatest of medieval kings.

Tout, T. F., *Edward the First.* 1920

Edward II (1284–1327). King of England (from 1307). Though he had the magnificent Plantagenet physique and was addicted to country sports and occupations (but not the jousting and tournaments of the nobility), he was always a weak and unstable king, strongly influenced by favourites, the first of whom, the Gascon Piers Gaveston, made Earl of Cornwall in 1307, so incited the hatred of the barons by his pride and extravagance that they had him murdered (1312). Edward's prestige was still further lowered when in an attempt to carry out his father's policy and bring Scotland to submission he marched northwards only to be decisively beaten by Robert * Bruce at Bannockburn (1314). For the next few years power was in the hands of a group of barons known as Lords Ordainers, under the leadership of the Earl of Lancaster. At last, in 1322, Edward regained control and secured Lancaster's execution; but, disastrously for himself, he fell once more under the domination of a favourite, Hugh Despenser, a Lord of the Welsh March. Once more rebellion was provoked, this time organized by Edward's

own wife Isabella of France and her lover Roger Mortimer. In 1326, Edward was forced to renounce the throne in favour of his son and was brutally murdered at Berkeley Castle.
Bingham, C., *The Life and Times of Edward II.* (1973)

Edward III (1312–1377). King of England (from 1327), son of Edward II and Isabella of France. In 1330 he obtained effective control by having his mother's lover Roger Mortimer seized and hanged (* Edward II). He resumed the Scottish War and by a major victory at Halidon Hill (1333) placed the son of John * de Balliol on the throne. He now turned his attention to France which provided him with all the justification he needed to gratify his love of chivalry and war (the Order of the Garter, founded by him in 1348, imitated the knighthood gathered at Arthur's Round Table). Not only were there the provocations of the last two reigns but there was his own claim through his mother to the French throne, from which he was only excluded by the Salic Law debarring succession through the female line. Thus in 1337 began what became the Hundred Years War, by no means a continuous conflict but a series of campaigns often separated by years and interrupted by treaties. In the first stages, marked by the victorious sea fight at Sluys (1340), which opened the way to the invaders, and the great battles of Crécy (1346) and Poitiers (1356), the English seemed invincible, Edward and his son, the Black Prince, achieved glory, but it was the dominance of the long bow over armoured knights that proved decisive. Calais was captured in 1347, its burghers spared, so the story goes, by the intercession of Edward's wife Queen Philippa. By the treaty of 1360 the English regained the duchy of Aquitaine while renouncing the claim to the French throne. But when the French renewed the war in 1369 the English were forced to give up all possessions except the district round Calais. At home Edward was not a great ruler; he maintained law and order, but in his reign parliament was considerably strengthened by its claim to grant or withold the funds necessary for the conduct of the war. In the king's last years he became senile and the government fell into the hands of his greedy mistress, Alice Perrers, and his son, * John of Gaunt, with the result that many difficulties awaited his successor and grandson, * Richard II. Ardent and chivalrous, with a strong taste for good living, Edward III was a more venturesome warrior but a much less able administrator than Edward I. By his marriage (1328) to Philippa, daughter of the Count of Hainaut in Flanders, he had five sons who reached maturity and five daughters.
Johnson, P., *The Life and Times of Edward III.* 1973

Edward IV (1441–1483). King of England (from 1461), first sovereign of the house of York. The son of Richard, Duke of York, he was the great-grandson of Edmund, fourth son of Edward III. During the Wars of the Roses he was, after the death of his father at Wakefield, the Yorkist candidate for the throne. After Henry VI's forces had been defeated in 1461 at the battles of Mortimer Cross and Towton, Edward was proclaimed king. His cousin, the Earl of Warwick, known as the 'kingmaker', sustained his rule but was later antagonized when Edward became increasingly influenced by the family of his wife, Elizabeth Woodville (m. 1464). In 1470, Warwick succeeded in deposing Edward, who fled to the Continent, and in restoring Henry VI. Having rallied support Edward returned the next year, defeated the Lancastrians at Barnet (where Warwick was killed) and Tewkesbury, and regained his throne, ensured by the murder of Henry VI. Though notorious for his indolence and love of pleasure, he proved a resourceful and capable ruler, encouraged trade and supported William * Caxton, who set up the first printing press in England.
Myers, A. R., *The Household of Edward IV.* 1959

Edward V (1470–1483). King of England (April–June 1483), one of the 'princes in the Tower'. On the death of his father, Edward IV, he was proclaimed king under the guardianship of his uncle, Richard, Duke of Gloucester. In June 1483 an assembly of peers and commoners deposed him on the grounds that Edward IV's marriage to Elizabeth Woodville was bigamous and the offspring illegitimate. Edward and his brother the Duke of York were taken to the Tower of London and there murdered, probably by their uncle, who became Richard III, or possibly by Henry VII (1485). The fate of the princes is a matter of continuing controversy.

Edward VI (1537–1553). King of England

(from 1547), son of Henry VIII, whom he succeeded, by his third wife Jane Seymour. He was precocious in his studies, interested in the reformed religion, but seems to have had a cold shrewdness, particularly unattractive in so young a boy. This was made apparent by the way in which he accepted and acquiesced in the execution of his uncle and first 'protector', Edward Seymour, Duke of Somerset. John Dudley, Duke of Northumberland, the new protector, persuaded Edward, on his deathbed, to nominate Lady Jane * Grey, Northumberland's daughter-in-law, as his successor, to the exclusion of his sisters Mary and Elizabeth. During his reign the church became steadily more national and protestant and a second, more stringent Act of Uniformity was passed. He died of tuberculosis.

Jordan, W. K., *Edward VI.* 2 vols. 1968 and 1971

Edward VII (1841–1910). King of Great Britain and Ireland (from 1901), eldest son of Queen Victoria and Prince Albert. Subjected to most extreme discipline and restraint upon his natural inclinations in his youth, as Prince of Wales he was excluded entirely by Queen Victoria from any share in, or indeed acquaintance with, affairs of state. He visited the U.S. (1860) and India (1861) and married the beautiful Princess Alexandra of Denmark in 1863. Reacting against his parents' rigid morality, he was renowned as a lover of wine, women and gambling. As king he came to terms with democracy and gained surprising popularity. He pushed the *entente-cordiale* with France (1905) and his nickname 'the Peacemaker' had some validity. His nephew, Kaiser William II, called him 'an old peacock'. His eldest son Albert Victor, Duke of Clarence, died in 1892 and his second son succeeded him as George V.

Magnus, P., *Edward VII.* 1967

Edward VIII (1894–1972). King of Great Britain (1936), later Duke of Windsor. Eldest son of George V and Queen Mary, he was created Prince of Wales in 1910, given a naval education at Dartmough College and proceeded to Magdalen College, Oxford. During World War I he served on the staff in France. From 1919 he toured the world constantly, winning adulation from vast crowds. He succeeded his father in January 1936. His long association with an American divorcee, Mrs Wallis Simpson (*née* Warfield), was suppressed by the British press and the BBC. He advised * Baldwin of his intention to Marry Mrs Simpson after her second divorce: the British and Dominion governments opposed her becoming queen and would not agree to legislation providing for a morganatic marriage. After 325 days, he abdicated in favour of his brother Albert, Duke of York, who became * George VI. Created Duke of Windsor, he married Mrs Simpson in France where they lived except for World War II (when he became Governor of the Bahamas 1940–45). His autobiography, *A King's Story*, appeared in 1947.

Donaldson, F., *Edward VIII.* 1974

Edward, the Black Prince (1330–1376). Eldest son of Edward III. Born at Woodstock, he won his spurs at Crécy (1346) and proved his ability as a commander at Poitiers (1356), where he captured the French king. He was less successful as ruler (from 1362) of his father's French possessions, Aquitaine and Gascony, but again showed his military prowess when he made a chivalrous incursion into Spain in aid of Pedro ('the Cruel') of Castile and won another great victory at Najara (1367). This was the end of his glory. He returned ill and despondent to England in 1371, having had to yield during the previous two years to rebellions among his subjects and encroachments from France, by which the English possessions were gradually whittled away. He died before his father, and his son, by his wife Joan, the 'Fair Maid of Kent', succeeded Edward III to the throne as Richard II. He was buried at Canterbury Cathedral where his armour can still be seen.

Edwards, Jonathan (1703–1758). American theologian and philosopher. He was born in Connecticut and became a pastor of Northampton, Mass., where his powerful preaching and writing kindled the religious revival known as the 'Great Awakening'. His doctrinal inspiration came from * Calvin and he was the last of the great New England Calvinists, advocating acceptance of the doctrine of predestination. For the last years of his life he worked as a missionary among the Indians, becoming president of the college of New Jersey (Princeton University) just before his death.

Miller, P., *Jonathan Edwards.* 1949

Edwin (Eadwine) (*c.* 585–633). King of Northumbria (from 616). He spent his youth in exile but in 616 made a victorious return. He gradually extended his powers until his kingdom stretched into Scotland (where he founded Edinburgh, named after him), and he was overlord of all the Anglo-Saxon kingdoms except Kent. He married Ethelburga, sister of Eadbald, King of Kent. It was through her and her confessor Paulinus (who is counted as the first archbishop of York) that Christianity came to Northumbria and Edwin himself was converted. He was killed in battle against an alliance of the Mercian king Penda and Cadwallon, king of North Wales.

Egalité, Philippe *see* **Orléans, Philippe, Duke of**

Egbert (died 839). King of the West Saxons (from 802). A descendant of Cerdic, the founder of the house of Wessex, he was an exile at the court of * Charlemagne as a young man. Though he returned to become king in 802, almost nothing is known of him until he defeated the kingdom of Mercia at the battle of Ellendun (825), a victory so decisive that it brought Mercian supremacy to an end and all south-east England under the control of Wessex. Egbert conquered Mercia in 829 and received Northumbria's submission in the same year. He could not hold his gains, however, and Mercia again had its own king the following year. But Egbert's reign pointed the way to the future destiny of the Wessex kings as rulers of all England.

Egk, Werner (1901–). German composer and conductor. He wrote the operas *Peer Gynt* (1938), *Columbus* (1948) and *Der Revisor* (1957), based on Gogol's *The Government Inspector*. Later compositions include the concertos *Moira* (1973) and *Temptation* (1977). He was President of the International Confederation of Authors and Composers (1976–78).

Egmont, Lamoral, Count of (1522–1568). Dutch soldier and statesman. One of the great lords of the century, he served the emperor * Charles V (who had acquired the Burgundian inheritance in the Netherlands) with great distinction, and in 1546 he was made a knight of the Golden Fleece. When * Philip II of Spain succeeded Charles (1555), the persecution of the Protestants by his minister in the Netherlands, Cardinal Granvella, so incensed * William the Silent, Egmont and Count Hoorn, that they went to Spain to try to get redress for their grievances from Philip himself. The extravagance of the language with which Egmont, on his return, expressed his anger at the failure of his mission gave Granvella's successor, the Duke of * Alba, an excuse to rid himself of such troublesome opponents. William had left the country but Egmont and Hoorn were publicly beheaded in Brussels. Their execution was a chief factor in sparking off open rebellion against Spanish rule.

Ehrenburg, Ilya Grigorevich (1891–1967). Russian writer. He was a war correspondent in World War I, supported the Russian revolution but spent most of his time between the wars in Paris (from 1934) as a correspondent for *Isvestia*. He was a most prolific writer of novels, of which *The Adventures of Julio Jurenito*, satirizing decadent western civilization, is among the best known. He won the Stalin Prize in 1947 with *The Storm*, a major novel about World War II. *The Thaw* (1954) commented on the oppressions of Stalin's régime.

Ehrlich, Paul (1854–1915). German physician and scientist. Born in Silesia, he graduated in medicine at Leipzig in 1878. After returning (1890) from treatment in Egypt for tuberculosis, he worked at the new Institute for Infectious Diseases in Berlin. In 1896 he became director of the State Institute for Serum Research and in 1906 of the Royal Institute for Experimental Therapy at Frankfurt-on-Main. He discovered 'salvarsan', an arsenical compound used in treating syphilis. The less toxic 'neosalvarsan' was produced in 1909. Much of his earlier work had dealt with blood cells and with immunity to infection. He won the Nobel Prize for Medicine in 1908.

Loewe, H., *Paul Ehrlich*. 1950

Eichmann, (Karl) Adolf (1906–1962). Austrian-born head of the German Gestapo's Jewish Extermination Department in World War II. After the war he was found living in Argentina under an assumed name, was kidnapped by Israeli agents (1960), tried in Israel, condemned and executed (1962) for crimes against the Jewish people and against humanity.

Arendt, H., *Eichmann in Jerusalem*. 1964

Eiffel, Alexandre Gustave (1832–1923). French engineer. He designated and built (1887–89) the famous 300 metre (*c.* 984 ft) high tower in Paris named after him. Earlier he had designed the structure for the New York *Statue of Liberty*. The collapse of locks he designed for the first Panama Canal scheme involved him in a scandal (1893) which brought a fine and imprisonment. Later he conducted pioneer researches in aerodynamics and the use of wind-tunnels.

Eijkman, Christian (1858–1930). Dutch physician. Professor of hygiene at Utrecht University (1898–1928), he was the co-discoverer, with Sir Frederick * Hopkins, of the vitamins which combat beriberi. He shared the Nobel Prize for Medicine (1929) with Hopkins.

Einstein, Albert (1879–1955). German-American mathematical physicist, born in Ulm, Germany. He moved with his family first to Italy and then to Switzerland, where he became naturalized. He was a specialist examiner at the patent office in Berne 1902–09, when a special professorship was created for him at the University of Zurich. In 1911 he went to Prague as professor of mathematics but returned to Zurich in 1912. He was director of the Kaiser Wilhelm Institute in Berlin 1913–33. His genius was first recognized in 1905 when he published three important papers on theoretical physics, one of which contained the principle of his Special Theory of Relativity. From this he developed his General Theory of Relativity, published in 1916. (He won the Nobel Prize for Physics in 1921). The relativity theory is based on the idea that the motion of a body can only be measured relatively (i.e., with respect to that of another body), since there is nothing which is at rest in any absolute sense. Measurement of space and time is also relative, because the motion of the measurer is involved. Einstein also deduced that energy and matter are interconvertible ($E=mc^2$, where E is energy, m is mass and c the speed of light), a principle which has had practical demonstration in the release of atomic energy. Einstein resumed his German nationality in 1918 but, as a Jew, was deprived of his post in 1933 and continued his work in the U.S., of which he became a citizen in 1940. He was made a life member of the Institute for Advanced Studies, Princeton and was a professor there 1933–45. At this period he was developing a form of unified field theory in which he expressed the basic laws of gravitation and electromagnetism in one set of equations. Horrified by the use of atomic power for war purposes, he actively campaigned after 1945 for international control of atomic weapons. He is generally regarded as the greatest mathematical physicist of all time. He declined the presidency of Israel in 1952.

Pais, A., *Subtle is the Lord* 1982

Eisenhower, Dwight David (1890–1969). American soldier and 34th president of the U.S. He was born at Denison, Texas, and graduated from West Point Military Academy in 1915. From 1935 to 1939 he was a lieutenant-colonel on General Macarthur's staff in the Philippines and subsequently gained rapid promotion. In 1942 he was appointed commander-in-chief of U.S. forces in Europe and later in that year, after the landings in North Africa, supreme Allied commander in the campaigns which cleared the Germans from Algeria, Tunisia, Sicily and Southern Italy. He came to England in 1943 to prepare for his task of supreme commander of the Allied forces engaged in the liberation of Western Europe. Eisenhower's strategy has been criticized and defended but his abilities in co-ordination and his skilful and conciliatory handling of a difficult Allied team have never been questioned. He returned to America as army chief of staff (1945–48) and in 1950 became supreme commander of the NATO forces in Europe, with headquarters near Paris. Chosen as Republican candidate for the presidency, he was returned with a triumphant majority over the Democratic candidate, Adlai Stevenson (1952), and was re-elected for a second term in 1956. During his terms of office (1953–61) he brought the fighting in Korea to an end and took a special interest in the rehabilitation of Europe and Asia by financial and other means.

Ambrose, S. E., *Eisenhower*. 2 vols. 1985

Eisenstein, Sergei Mikhailovich (1898–1948). Russian film director. He served as an engineer in the civil wars and subsequently was trained in Moscow as a stage designer and producer. He made his first film in 1924. He developed consummate skill in the direction of crowds and the dramatic use of cutting, notably in such films as *The Battleship Potemkin* (1925),

Alexander Nevsky (1938), his first talking picture, and *Ivan the Terrible* (1944–45).
Barna, K., *Eisenstein*. 1973

Eleanor of Aquitaine (*c.* 1122–1204). Queen of Henry II of England. She married Henry in 1152 after her earlier marriage (1137), to Louis VII of France, had been dissolved. As Duchess of Aquitaine she brought to the English crown much of south-western France, thus providing the cause of a struggle between the two countries which lasted, with intervals, for 300 years. A masterful woman, she supported her sons (the future Richard I and John) against her unfaithful husband, and after his death (1189) prevented them quarrelling. Her eldest son, Henry, died as a child; her third son was Geoffrey, who died before his father and whose son * Arthur of Brittany, was murdered in the Tower of London, probably on the instructions of John.
Pernoud, R., *Eleanor of Aquitaine*. 1967

Eleanor of Castile (died 1290). First wife of Edward I of England, whom she married in 1254. Before his accession (1272) she went with him on a crusade, but the story that she sucked poison from his wound is probably legendary. Edward showed his devotion to her memory by erecting crosses at each place where the funeral procession rested when her body was conveyed from Lincoln to Westminster. A replica of the final one stands at Charing Cross, London.

Elegabalus (or, less correctly, Heliogabalus) (*c.* 204–222). Roman emperor (from 218). The name by which he was known was that of the Syrian Sun God, of whom he was the hereditary high priest. He owed his elevation to the throne to the troops in Syria whom the intrigues of his grandmother (a sister of Julia, wife of the emperor * Septimus Severus) had suborned. The fame of the young emperor rests only on his depravity. The rites of the Sun God, whom he claimed to personify, were introduced by him to Rome and were so obscene that they scandalized the citizens. After an attempt to assassinate his cousin, Alexander Severus, whom he feared as a potential usurper, Elegabalus was himself murdered by the praetorian guard.

Elgar, Sir Edward (William), 1st Bart. (1857–1934). English composer. He was born in Broadheath, Worcestershire, and succeeded his father as organist of St George's Roman Catholic Church, Worcester. Apart from violin lessons, he was self-taught. Although he made no use of the folk-song tradition he was one of the pioneers of the English musical revival at the beginning of the 20th century, and was the first outstanding English composer since * Purcell. His earliest work, including pieces composed for the Worcester festivals, attracted little but local attention, but he won an international reputation almost overnight when Richard * Strauss acclaimed his *Variations on an original theme* (*Enigma*) for orchestra (1899). *The Dream of Gerontius* (1900), an oratorio based on Cardinal Newman's poem, was even more highly praised. *The Apostles* (1903) and *The Kingdom* (1906) belong to an uncompleted trilogy on the early Christian Church; other works include two symphonies, and the *Introduction and Allegro for strings* (1905). The violin concerto in B Minor was first performed by Kreisler (1910). His more popular works, such as the five *Pomp and Circumstance* marches (1901–07) and the concert overture *Cockaigne* (1901), are warmly extrovert and reflect something of the vitality of Edwardian England. After his wife died (1920) Elgar practically abandoned composition. He was professor of music at Birmingham University (1905–08) and Master of the King's Musick (1924–34). His knighthood had been bestowed in 1904, the O.M. in 1911 and a baronetcy in 1932.
Maire, B., *Elgar, His Life and Work*. 1973

Elgin and Kincardine, Thomas Bruce, 7th Earl of (1766–1841). Scottish soldier and diplomat. As ambassador to Turkey (1799–1802) he bought from the Sultan, and subsequently sold to the British Museum, the groups of statuary (the 'Elgin Marbles') from the frieze of the Parthenon at Athens. His son **James**, 8th Earl (1811–63), was governor general of Canada (1846–54), led a successful mission to China (1857–61) and was governor general of India (1862–63). **Victor Alexander**, 9th Earl (1849–1917), was a Liberal politician, viceroy of India (1894–98) and colonial secretary (1905–08).

Elijah (*c.* 870–840 B.C.). Prophet of Israel during the reigns of Ahab and Ahaziah. He denounced Ahab and his Phoenician wife Jezebel for trying to establish Baal worship, and for ordering the death of Naboth in order to secure his coveted vineyard. He appears in the Bible story as a worker of miracles and he himself is said to have been carried to heaven in a chariot of fire. The belief that he would return to earth, combined with the Messianic doctrine, led to his identification in the New Testament with John the Baptist, Christ's forerunner.

Eliot, George (pen-name of Mary Ann – from 1851 Marian – Evans) (1819–80). English novelist. Daughter of a Warwickshire estate agent she left school at the age of 16, when her mother died, and while looking after her father's household studied Latin, Greek, German and Italian under visiting teachers. She was brought up as a strict evangelical but at the age of 22 reacted violently against religion. After her father's death she went to London and became assistant editor (1851–53) of the *Westminster Review* under John Chapman, at whose home she lodged. While there she met Herbert * Spencer who introduced her to George Henry Lewes, a versatile literary journalist who had written a well known history of philosophy and was preparing a biography of Goethe. When she met him he was living apart from his wife but unable to obtain a divorce. Marian and he lived in happiness together from 1854 until his death (1878).

Hitherto her published literary work had been confined to translations from the German but the encouragement of Lewes, who had seen and liked her story 'Amos Barton', which appeared later with two others as *Scenes from Clerical Life* under her pseudonym George Eliot, decided her career. The novels which followed are considered among the greatest of their epoch. Social criticism and moral values are seldom lost sight of and her wide knowledge is a constant spur to the intellect; but it is the humour, compassion and understanding with which she builds up and probes her characters that give her novels their unique and lasting value. *Adam Bede* appeared in 1859, followed by *The Mill on the Floss* (1860), *Silas Marner* (1861), *Romola* (1863), set in Renaissance Florence, *Felix Holt* (1866), *Middlemarch* (1872) and, last and least successful, *Daniel Deronda* (1876). Minor works included a dramatic poem, *The Spanish Gipsy* (1868). In the year of her death she married John Walter Cross, an old friend of Lewes and herself.

Laski, M., *George Eliot and Her World*. 1973

Eliot, Sir John (1592–1632). English parliamentarian. He entered Parliament in 1614. Originally a protégé of the King's favourite, Buckingham; he later turned against him and took part in his impeachment. He opposed Charles I's forced loans and was instrumental in obtaining assent to the Petition of Right (1628). In 1629, with eight other members, he was sent to the Tower of London where he died. He left several manuscript works, including *The Monarchie of Man*, a defence of kingship.

Hulme, H., *The Life of Sir John Eliot*. 1957

Eliot, Thomas Stearns (1888–1965). Anglo-American poet, critic and playwright, born in St Louis, Missouri, and naturalized as British in 1927. He studied at Harvard, the Sorbonne in Paris, and at Oxford, philosophy being his main academic subject. In 1915 he married Vivien Haigh Wood and settled in London, where briefly he was employed at Lloyd's Bank. He then began to contribute to and take part in the editing of literary journals, and in 1927 he became editor of the *Criterion*. His early poetry, e.g., *The Love Song of J. Alfred Prufrock* (1917), is sometimes satirical and often appears flippant –

> When lovely woman stoops to folly and
> Paces about her room again, alone,
> She smoothes her hair with automatic hand,
> And puts a record on the gramophone
> (*The Waste Land*)

but there is an underlying pessimism as to the aesthetic and moral worth of society. This attitude, induced by the waste, disruption and upset of values caused by World War I, is most apparent in his longest poem *The Waste Land* (1922). Broadly based on the theme of the Holy Grail it is characterized by deep disillusion with contemporary spiritual blindness. The poem reveals great erudition (it is said to contain quotations from thirty-five authors in six languages) and academic precision in vocabulary. After the 1930s Eliot's poetry became increasingly metaphysical and the religious influences, especially in the case of Christian symbolism, are more apparent. Pessimism has been replaced by 'penitential hope' e.g., in *Ash-Wednesday* (1930) and *Four Quartets* (1943), philosophical poems which echo * Beethoven's final compositions. A poetic sedative of a most delightful kind is his *Old Possum's Book of Practical Cats* (1939).

Meanwhile as essayist and critic he had

gained a great and increasing influence especially in reviving interest in * Dryden and metaphysical poets such as * Donne. Lectures, as Charles Eliot, professor of poetry at Harvard, were reprinted as *The Use of Poetry and the Use of Criticism* (1933).

Yet a third reputation awaited him as a dramatist. *The Rock* (1934), written as the words of a church pageant, was followed by the verse drama *Murder in the Cathedral* (1935). After World War II he adapted verse drama to contemporary themes (with allegorical significance) in the very successful *The Cocktail Party* (1950), *The Confidential Clerk* (1954) and *The Elder Statesman* (1958).

In 1948 Eliot was awarded the O.M. and the Nobel Prize for Literature.

Ackroyd, P., *T. S. Eliot*. 1984

Elizabeth (1837–1898). Empress of Austria. A Bavarian princess of great beauty, she married the emperor * Francis Joseph in 1854, but her lively and wayward nature found the formality of court life in Vienna increasingly irksome. She spent much time abroad and built herself a palace on Corfu. She was assassinated by an anarchist at Geneva. In 1889 her only son, Rudolph, was found dead with his mistress, Marie Vetsera, in a shooting-box at Mayerling.

Elizabeth (1596–1662). Queen of Bohemia, daughter of James VI of Scotland (I of England). She provided the future link between the Stuart and Hanoverian dynasties. In 1613 she married Frederick V of the Palatinate, whose brief tenure of the throne of Bohemia (1619) gave her the title of the 'Winter Queen'. After their expulsion the family lived in Holland. Among her 13 children were the dashing Prince * Rupert and Sophia, who married Ernest Augustus, later elector of Hanover, and became the mother of Great Britain's * George I. Elizabeth, who returned to England after Charles II's restoration, was a vivacious fascinating creature who became known as the Queen of Hearts, the subject of a famous poem by Sir Henry Wotton.

Elizabeth (1709–1762). Empress of Russia (from 1741), daughter of * Peter the Great and his second wife, Empress Catherine I. She became empress after a group of guards officers had deposed the infant Ivan VI. She built the Winter Palace in St Petersburg and introduced French culture and language into court circles. When the Seven Years War broke out (1756) she joined the Franco-Austrian alliance against * Frederick the Great of Prussia, a policy reversed by her nephew and successor, Peter III. She never married.

Elizabeth (1900–). Queen consort of George VI, daughter of the 14th Earl of Strathmore. She was known as Lady Elizabeth Bowes-Lyon until her marriage (1923) to the then Duke of York. Of her two children the elder (born 1926) became Queen * Elizabeth II, the younger, Margaret Rose (born 1930), married Antony Armstrong-Jones, later Earl of Snowdon (marriage now dissolved).

Cathcart, H., *The Queen Mother*. 1965

Elizabeth (Queen of Romania) *see* **Carmen Sylva**

'Elizabeth' (author of *Elizabeth and her German Garden*) *see* **Arnim, Countess von**

Elizabeth I (1533–1603). Queen of England (from 1558), daughter of Henry VIII and Anne Boleyn. On her mother's execution Henry declared her illegitimate, but his will reinstated her in the line of succession. Before she came to the throne, either from compulsion or from prudence, she remained in studious retirement but she was for a time imprisoned in the Tower of London and later confined by Mary Tudor at Woodstock on suspicion of being involved in Wyatt's rebellion (1554). She was of notable intelligence and had good teachers (mainly exponents of the New Learning): she was proficient in Latin, Greek and the Romance languages. Basically indifferent in matters of religion, when she came to the throne she favoured a conciliatory religious policy: her aim was to be governor of a church whose doctrines would be acceptable to all but the most extreme. But she realized that to strengthen her position she must range herself with the Protestant rulers in Europe although her aim was to secure peace and prosperity and avoid foreign entanglement. Her Church Settlement was based on parliamentary statue (1559).

Within three days of her accession she made Lord Cecil, afterwards Lord * Burghley, her chief secretary, and though other favourites might come and go it was upon him and his sage judgement that she relied, until his death (1598). One crucial decision was expected of her – to choose a husband and to provide the country with an heir. Despite many suitors this she never did: her sister's widower * Philip II of Spain was an early suitor and well into her middle age others appeared, including two of Catherine de' Medici's sons. But none of these appealed to her. Her inclinations turned to Robert Dudley, Earl of Leicester, who remained at her side and served her at court and in the field, but she did not marry him. Virgin Queen as she was called, she nevertheless, from her teens to her fifties, was seldom unpreoccupied with some matrimonial scheme or affair of apparent passion.

Thus the actual heir to the throne was * Mary Queen of Scots, who, expelled from her own country, had taken refuge in England. Too dangerous to be left at large she was confined to a succession of country houses from 1568, the centre of many plots to kill Elizabeth which the indefatigable * Walsingham unravelled. Elizabeth under pressure from parliament and her council finally agreed to her execution (1587). Meanwhile captains Drake, Frobisher and Hawkins carried piracy and undeclared war against the merchant fleets and overseas possessions of Spain with the queen's tacit approval. In 1588 Philip of Spain organized a vast armada to overwhelm England (while the parsimonious Elizabeth delayed her own preparations) which her sea captains, with their superior gunnery and tactics, put to rout. The defeat of the Armada did not mean the end of the war with Spain, which became one of attrition, lasting until her successor * James I made peace (1604). Late in the 1590s there was an Irish uprising; in 1601 the Earl of Essex attempted an unsuccessful rebellion. But the period was also one distinguished by an unrivalled flowering of literature, especially drama.

Elizabeth said of herself that she had 'the heart and stomach of a king' – she had also feminine vanity and caprice, could be fickle and even callous. Yet she had a gift for holding the affection and esteem of her subjects and for choosing wise advisers.

Neale, J. E., *Queen Elizabeth I*. 1971

Elizabeth II (Elizabeth Alexandra Mary) (1926–). Queen of the United Kingdom and Head of the Commonwealth (since 1952). The elder daughter of the Duke and Duchess of York (later King George VI and Queen Elizabeth), she was educated privately and during World War II was commissioned in the A.T.S. In November 1947 she married Lt Philip Mountbatten R.N., * Duke of Edinburgh. Their children are Charles, Prince of Wales (born 1948), Anne (born 1950), Andrew (born 1960) and Edward (born 1964). Princess Elizabeth was on a visit to Kenya (1952) when in February she heard of the sudden death of her father and her own accession to the throne. She was crowned at Westminster in June 1953. In the course of her duties she has toured every part of the Commonwealth and has entertained many heads of state. Among her leisure interests horse-racing is prominent and as owner she has had much success. Her Silver Jubilee was enthusiastically celebrated in 1977.

Lacey, R., *Majesty*. 1977

Elizabeth, St (1207–1231). Daughter of Andrew II, king of Hungary. She was brought up at the court of the Landgrave of Thuringia, to whose son she was betrothed at the age of 4. Though the court at the Wartburg was famed for its gatherings of poets and minstrels, she gave herself up, from childhood, to religious austerity and charity. When 14 she married and, under her influence, her young husband went on a crusade but died on the way. Elizabeth, expelled from court for wasting the revenues on charity, went to Marburg where, encouraged in an overstrict asceticism by a harsh confessor, she soon died. She was canonized in 1235.

Elizabeth of York (1465–1503). Daughter of Edward IV of England, who by her marriage to Henry VII linked the dynasties of York and Lancaster. It is said she died of grief at the death of her elder son, Arthur.

Ellenborough, Edward Law, 1st Baron (1750–1818). English lawyer. He made a great name for himself by his defence of Warren * Hastings, and was Lord Chief Justice (1802–18). His son Edward Law, **1st Earl of Ellenborough** (1790–1871), held a number of political appointments both before and after being governor general of India (1841–44). He brought the Afghan War to a successful end, conquered Gwalior (1844), and annexed Sind (1842).

Ellet, Charles (1810–1862). U.S. engineer, born Penn's Manor, Penn. He worked for three years as a surveyor and assistant engineer, then studied at the Ecole Polytechnique, Paris, and travelled widely in Europe, returning to the U.S. in 1832. In 1842 he completed the first wire suspension bridge in U.S.A., at Fairmount, Pennsylvania, and between 1846–49 redesigned and built the world's first long-span wire cable suspension bridge, over the Ohio River at Wheeling. Central span 1,010 feet (308 metres). It failed in 1854 however owing to aerodynamic instability. He invented naval rams and in the U.S. Civil War he equipped nine Mississippi river steamboats as rams, which defeated a fleet of Confederate rams. He died in the battle.

Ellington, Duke (Edward Kennedy Ellington) (1899–1974). American composer and bandleader of partly black descent. One of the most skilled of jazz musicians, he produced numerous works which, though in the jazz idiom, are fully orchestrated throughout and allow no extemporization.
Lambert, G. E., *Duke Ellington*. 1959

Ellis, (Henry) **Havelock** (1859–1939). English writer whose work on the psychology of sex has had an immense influence on subsequent thought. After spending four years in Australia he studied medicine in London and turned his attention to a dispassionate study of sex, which resulted in his pioneering work, *Studies in the Psychology of Sex*, published from 1898 onwards. Among his other works were a series of books on science (1889–1914) and essays on Elizabethan and Jacobean drama.
Calder-Marshall, A., *Havelock Ellis: A Biography*. 1959

Ellsworth, Lincoln (1880–1951). American explorer. In 1926 he flew over the North Pole with Amundsen and Nobile in the airship *Norge*. He made a pioneering flight over Antarctica in 1935.

Elssler, Franjziske (or Fanny) (1810–1884). Austrian dancer. One of the most celebrated of 19th-century dancers, she was regarded as the chief rival of* Taglioni and, whether she was performing in London, Paris or America, was equally acclaimed. She was seen at her best in Spanish dances, which demanded the particular exuberance for which she was famed.
Gvest, I., *Fanny Elssler, The Pagan Ballerina*. 1970

Elyot, Sir Thomas (*c*. 1490–1546). English administrator and prose writer. A staunch advocate of the use of 'the English tongue' in all manner of subjects he was clerk to the Privy Council 1523–30, knighted in 1530 and English envoy to Emperor* Charles V in 1531. In 1531 he published *The Boke Named the Governour* which set out a system of popular education for the gentry stressing their social and political role. He was a translator and a coiner of new English words: he compiled a Latin-into-English dictionary (1536).

Elzevir, Louis (*c*. 1540–1617). Dutch printer, first of a family who became famous printers for many generations in Leyden. His son **Bonaventura Elzevir** (1583–1682), who took into partnership his nephew Abraham, produced (1634–36) beautiful editions of the classics; Caesar, Livy, Tacitus etc. Other members of the family established themselves in Amsterdam where they produced a famous French bible (1669).
Copinger, H. B., *The Elzevir Press*. 1927

Emerson, Ralph Waldo (1803–1882). American essayist and poet. He was born in Boston, one of the eight children of a Unitarian minister, after whose death (1811) he came under the care and guidance of an intellectual aunt. He was educated at Harvard and, like his father, joined the ministry but abandoned it in 1832. During a visit to Europe he came to England (1833) where he met Wordsworth, Coleridge and other writers, finding a kindred spirit and lasting friend in Carlyle. Back in America he married Lydia Jackson in 1835 and settled at Concord in the same year. In 1836 he published *Nature* in which he set down the philosophy at which he had arrived after years of thought and study. It was a form of Transcendentalism, influenced partly by the German philosophy of idealism and partly by his own Greek and Hindu studies. It centred upon doctrines of the immanence of the divine in the real world and thus was linked with pantheism. It was opposed to empiricism and materialism and celebrated individualism. His later works, e.g. *Representative Men* (1850), were often based on his notes for the long series of popular lectures for which he became famous. He regarded himself primarily as a poet but is

chiefly remembered for his essays on politics, religion and literature. He was also an active abolitionist. Among his other books, *The Conduct of Life* (1860) summarizes and clarifies, in a series of essays, his philosophic views on such subjects as worship, fate, power, etc. Later essays are contained in e.g. *Society and Solitude* (1870). His *Journals* were published in 1909–14.
Wagenknecht, C., *Ralph Waldo Emerson: Portrait of a Balanced Soul*. 1974

Eminence Grise *see* **Joseph, Père**

Emin Pasha. The name used by Edward Schnitzer (1840–1892), German doctor and explorer. He remained in the Equatorial province of Sudan after the death of * Gordon, whom he had served. He was eventually killed by Arabs about 100 miles east of Stanley Falls.

Emmet, Robert (1778–1803). Irish patriot. A protestant radical, he joined the United Irishmen while still at Trinity College, Dublin. Compelled to leave, he went to France but returned (1802) convinced that he would have French support for an Irish rising. This, when it took place (1803), was premature and ineffective. Fifty men were killed and Emmet himself betrayed, condemned and executed.
Landreth, H., *The Pursuit of Robert Emmet*. 1948

Empedocles (*c.* 493–433 B.C.). Greek philosopher, born in Sicily. In his theory of matter he postulates four indestructible elements, fire, air, water, and earth, of which, variously blended and compounded, all material substances are composed. He also worked out an important system of sense perception. His long poems, *On Nature* and *Purification*, in which his philosophic and religious theories were set out only survive in part. The legend ascribing his death to a fall or plunge into the crater of Mount Etna has attracted several writers; Milton, Meredith, and Matthew Arnold (*Empedocles on Etna*, 1852) refer variously to the theme.

Empson, Sir William (1906–1984). English literary critic and poet, born in Yorkshire. He was educated at Magdelene College and while still at Cambridge he began work on his first book *Seven Types of Ambiguity* (1930), one of the most influential critical works of the first half of the twentieth century. He taught English literature at Tokyo University (1931–34) and later at Peking University (1937–39, 1947–52). During World War II he was Chinese editor for the BBC, and in 1953 became professor of English literature at Sheffield University. Major critical works include *Some Versions of Pastoral* (1935), *The Structure of Complex Words* (1951), *Milton's God* (1961); he was notable in applying scientific method and matter in his criticism and poetry. He introduced the word and concept 'ambiguity'. His verse includes *Poems* (1930) and *The Gathering Storm* (1940); terse, witty, complex, yet conveying great emotion, his poetry had a strong influence on several poets of the 1950s, including John Wain and Kingsley * Amis.

Enders, John Franklin (1897-1985). American bacteriologist. His work (from 1942) as an associate professor and a professor at the Harvard Medical School, led to the eventual production of an anti-polio vaccine. In 1954 he shared the Nobel Prize for Physiology with T. H. Weller and F. C. Robbins for their discovery of the ability of the poliomyelitis virus to grow in cultures of different tissues.

Enescu, Georges (1881–1955). Romanian composer and violin virtuoso. One of the teachers of Yehudi * Menuhin, he composed three symphonies and a number of suites and sonatas. His later works, notably *Romanian Rhapsodies*, showed the strong influence of Romanian folk music.

Engels, Friedrich (1820–1895). German socialist. Son of a cotton manufacturer, he became (1842) the Manchester agent of his father's business and collected information for his *The Condition of the Working Classes in England* (1844). Meanwhile his life-long friendship with * Marx had begun. In 1845 he gave up his business to be with him and they jointly produced the famous *Communist Manifesto* (1848) in London. Thereafter he sustained Marx with constant financial support, even re-entering the business to do so, and when after his father's death he finally sold his partnership (1870) he joined Marx in London and stayed with him until he died (1883). The remaining years of his life were spent in editing and translating Marx's works.
Mayer, G., *Friedrich Engels*. 1969

Enghien, Louis Antoine Henri de Bourbon, Duc d' (1772–1804). Eldest son of the Prince de Condé and related to the French royal family, he left France in 1792 during the Revolution to join the *émigré* army. In 1804 * Napoleon, on the assumption or pretence that he was implicated in a conspiracy, sent agents to abduct him from neutral territory and had him tried and executed. The effect upon Napoleon's reputation proved it to be a blunder as well as a crime.

Ennius, Quintus (239–169 B.C.). One of the earliest of classical Latin poets. He wrote twenty-two tragedies, borrowing his themes mainly from Euripides, and his *Annals*, written in hexameters, which relate the history of Rome from earliest times. Only fragments of his works survive.

Ensor, James, Baron (1860–1949). Belgian painter. His father was English but he spent almost all his life at Ostend. His grotesque and satirical pictures, reminiscent of Brueghel and Bosch but painted in the technique of Manet or Courbet, gained recognition very slowly, but in 1929 he was created a baron. Among his best known pictures were *Christ's Entry into Brussels in 1889* (1888) and *Dangerous Cooks* (1896). He often painted masquerades and skeletons, and was a forerunner of Expressionism.
Tannenbaum, L., *James Ensor*. 1951

Enver Pasha (1881–1922). Turkish politician. As a leader of the 'Young Turks' he was prominent in the revolution of 1908 which restored the 1876 constitution. In 1913 he carried out a *coup d'état* which gave him, as war minister, effective power. He brought Turkey into World War I on the side of Germany, but after defeat fled to Russia. Sent to Turkestan to establish Bolshevik power, he raised a revolt in his own interest and was murdered by Soviet agents in Bokhara.

Epaminondas (died 362 B.C.). Theban soldier and statesman. But for his death at the moment of his final victory he might have achieved his statesman-like vision of a federation of all Greece. He had already destroyed Spartan supremacy by his victory at Leuctra (371) in Boeotia and subsequent march south. He built a fleet to keep that of the Athenians in check, and one more success against them would probably have enabled him to achieve his aims. Such victory was achieved (362) at Mantinea in the Peloponnese but at the cost of his life.

Epictetus of Hierapolis (*c.* 55–135 A.D.). Greek Stoic philosopher. A freed slave, born in Phrygia, he went to Rome to teach but was banished, with other philosophers, by Domitian and settled in Eporus. His moral view was that one ought to escape the slavery of desire and so become free to act in accord with divine providence. His maxims were collected by his pupil Arrian in the *Enchiridion* and in eight books of commentaries.

Epicurus (*c.* 342–270 B.C.). Greek philosopher, founder of the Epicurean system – the great rival of Stoicism in the Graeco-Roman world. Born in Samos, he first opened a school at Mytilene in 310 but moved it to Athens in 306. Epicureanism, in which the senses, the only arbiters of reality, are judged infallible, has been widely misunderstood since it equates 'pleasure' with moral good. Pleasure, however, Epicurus regards as absence of pain in matters concerned with ethics and morals, an untroubled mind, a state only to be reached through the practise of virtue. He both practised and preached moderation in physical pleasures. Epicurus adapted the atomic theory of * Democritus to the needs of his own system, e.g. by postulating that some soul-atoms may depart from strict mathematical precision and swerve in their paths, thus allowing for free will. Little remains of his writings, but his doctrines were presented by the Roman poet * Lucretius in the philosophical poem *De rerum natura*.

Epstein, Sir Jacob (1880–1959). Sculptor. He was born in New York of Russian-Polish parents but lived in England from 1905. His massive monumental pieces, in which distortion is used as a conscious technique for purposes of composition or emphasis, aroused at first much public protest. They include *Rima*, a memorial to W. H. Hudson in Hyde Park (1925), *Genesis*, a stone carving of a pregnant woman (1931), *Ecce Homo*, a controversial figure of Christ (1933), and *Adam* (1938–39). *Christ in Majesty*, for Llandaff Cathedral, was completed in 1957. In contrast are his vigorous and realistic bronze busts, in the manner of * Rodin, of such celebrities as Shaw, Einstein and Churchill.
Buckle, R., *Jacob Epstein, Sculptor*. 1963

Erasmus, Desiderius (1466?–1536). Dutch scholar and theologian, the illegitimate son of a clerk named Gerhard in whose home at Gouda he was brought up. After the death of his father (1484) he was induced by his guardians to enter an Augustinian monastery, an experience which left him with a deep dislike of monastic life. Later he became a secular priest and was engaged as secretary by the bishop of Cambrai, who sent him (1495) to the University of Paris where he acquired an unrivalled command of Latin. He remained in Paris to teach until invited by one of his pupils to visit England (1499–1500), where he first gained the friendship of Thomas * More and John * Colet; a second brief visit (1505–06) followed and after some years in Italy he was invited to return once more and became a Reader in Greek at Cambridge (1511–14). He spent the years 1514–21 mainly in Basle, and from 1517 was in Louvain where the introduction of the new humanist studies gained his approving encouragement. Already he had written his most notable work, *Adages*, a collection of classical proverbs (1500); *Praise of Folly* (1509), a witty and satirical attack on the corruption, ignorance and superstition of both society and the church; and *Colloquies* (1519), a collection of dialogues, which incidentally throw much light on his own life and convey a vivid and detailed picture of the times he lived in. In 1516 appeared his edition of the Greek text of the New Testament together with a Latin translation. After leaving Louvain he returned to Basle where he spent most of the rest of his life engaged in violent religious controversies, letter-writing and preparing critical editions of the works of early fathers of the church, such as St Jerome and St Augustine. He often attacked the shortcomings of the clergy and abuses within the church, but he refused to join * Luther's schismatic movement and constantly appealed for moderation. Erasmus, witty and provocative though he was, was not a creative thinker or writer, but his influence among the scholars and theologians of his day was immense and no one of his time was held in greater esteem.

Bainton, R. H., *Erasmus*. 1970

Erastus (or Leibler), **Thomas** (1524–1583). German-Swiss theologian and philosopher. He was a qualified physician and it was as professor of medicine that he went to Heidelberg University (1558), of which he became rector. A follower of the Protestant reformer * Zwingli, he denied that excommunication, whether the sentence was imposed by the pope or by, e.g., Presbyterian elders, was valid, claiming that the state has supreme authority over a church in matters (except those concerned with doctrines) arising within its boundaries. This tenet (known as Erastianism) was later used to justify complete subordination of ecclesiastical to secular authority.

Eratosthenes (*c.* 276–194 B.C.). Greek astronomer from Cyrene in North Africa, employed by Ptolemy III as librarian at Alexandria. He reasoned that the earth was a sphere, and made one of the first estimates of its circumference – by measuring the angle of the shadow cast by the sun at different points. His other contributions to science included a work on chronology and a treatise on geography which was used by * Strabo. Blind and tired of life, he is said to have starved himself to death.

Erckmann-Chatrian. Pen-name of the famous literary partnership of **Emile Erckmann** (1822–1899) and **Alexandre Chatrian** (1826–1890). They both came frm Lorraine, and some of their stories and novels reveal their local associations; others recall the macabre fantasies of Edgar Allan * Poe. The best known, e.g. *Histoire d'un conscrit* (1864) and *Waterloo* (1865), present a common soldier's attitude to the Revolutionary and Napoleonic wars.

Erhard, Ludwig (1897–1977). German economist and Christian Democratic politician. He was a teacher and later director of the Nuremberg Trade High School (1928–1942). Entering politics in 1945 he was Bavarian minister for economic affairs (1946), economic director in the American and British zone of occupation (from 1947) and became (1949) federal minister for economic affairs under Dr * Adenauer. He was an ardent advocate of competitive 'free market' economy and gained wide praise for his major contribution to the remarkable post-war recovery (the 'economic miracle') of West Germany. He succeeded Adenauer as chancellor of the German Federal Republic in 1963, and resigned in 1966.

Eric the Red (*c.* 950–*c.* 1003). Norse explorer. According to the Icelandic saga which bears his name, he was banished from Iceland (982) on a charge of homicide; then, again outlawed, he discovered and named Greenland, and spent three years (982–985) exploring the south-west coast. He established two colonies there which survived until the 14th century. His son **Leif** (*c.* 975–1020) discovered 'Vinland', perhaps Nova Scotia or Massachusetts, on the American coast.

Ericson, Leif *see* **Leif Ericson**

Ericsson, John (1803–1889). Swedish engineer and inventor. In order to exploit a hot-air engine which he had invented, he moved to England (1826) and remained there thirteen years. His locomotive *Novelty* competed (unsuccessfully) with Stephenson's *Rocket*. His outstanding contribution was his screw propeller for ships (patented 1836). In 1839 he went to the U.S.A. where he applied his propeller to merchant and war ships. He is particularly remembered for designing the *Monitor*, a new type of turreted ironclad war ship with very low free-board, which proved its worth in the Civil War. In his later years he constructed a sun-motor.

Erigena, Johannes Scotus (*c.* 810–890). Irish-born philosopher who became head of a school at the court of the Frankish king Charles the Bald. He was deeply versed in Platonism, whence he derived the doctrine that all that exists is an emanation from a divine source. His attempt to reconcile his Greek sources with the Bible and the works of the Christian fathers was later misunderstood and he was denounced by the Council of Paris (1210) and by Pope Honorius III (1225). Erigena's work prepared the way for medieval scholasticism.

Erlander, Tage Fritiof (1901–1985). Swedish Socialist politician. Originally a journalist, he edited an encyclopedia for some years, then entered the Riksdag in 1933. He initiated major educational reforms, and became prime minister of Sweden in 1946; he held that office through a period of great prosperity during the next two decades, to 1969.

Ernst, Max (1891–1976). German artist. He was born in the Rhineland and with * Arp brought Dadaism (1916–22) from Paris to Cologne. With Arp, too, he made the transition to Surrealism. In his earlier work he had made much use of *frottages*, i.e. rubbings taken from, e.g., floorboards or any surface that would create interesting patterns, and *collages*, pictures composed of pieces of paper, cloth, etc. stuck to a background, not so much for their plastic value as to combine disparate, anecdotal elements. For his later Surrealistic work he developed the techniques of painting. His paintings, more perhaps than those of any of his Surrealist contemporaries, evoke the emotional atmosphere of dreams.
Waldberg, P., *Max Ernst*. 1958

Erskine, John (1509–1591). Scottish religious reformer. He was a wealthy laird, and, returning from continental travels, brought the French scholar, Marsiliers, to teach Greek at Montrose School, an important encouragement to the new learning. He became a leading supporter of John * Knox, and tried to act as a conciliator between him and Queen Mary. Although a layman he served as moderator of the General Assembly of the Scottish Reformed Church for several years.

Erskine, Thomas Erskine, 1st Baron (1750–1823). British advocate, born in Edinburgh. He was called to the bar in 1778 and rapidly won a great reputation. In 1779 he successfully defended Admiral Keppel, charged with incompetence, and in 1781 he secured the acquittal of Lord George Gordon, who was charged with treason in connexion with the riots that bear his name. Some of his later defences of unpopular characters, such as Tom Paine, cost him temporary loss of court and official favour. In 1806 he became Lord Chancellor. He advocated the emancipation of negro slaves, and in the 1820s supported the Independence of Greece.
Lovat-Fraser, J. A., *Erskine*. 1932

Ervine, St John Greer (1883–1971). Irish playwright, critic and novelist, born in Belfast. In 1915 he joined the Abbey Theatre, Dublin, of which he was later manager. His earlier plays, 'problem dramas', include *Mixed Marriage* (1911), *Jane Clegg* (1913) and *John Ferguson* (1915). After World War I he settled in London and wrote conventional domestic comedies for performance in the West End. From 1919–23 and 1925–39 he was drama critic of *The Observer* and also of the *Morning Post* for a time. In 1929 he was guest drama critic for the New York *World*. His other works include several novels, essays and biographies, notably *Bernard Shaw: His Life, Work and Friends* (1956).

Esarhaddon (died 669 B.C.). King of Assyria (from 681). After succeeding his father Sennacherib he appeased the Babylonians by rebuilding their city and making it into a second capital. In 675 he attacked Egypt and annexed the Nile Delta. It was while advancing to put down a rebellion there that he died. His son Ashur-Baini-Pal was the last of the great Assyrian kings.

Esau. Old Testament character, son of Isaac and Rebecca, elder twin of Jacob, and ancestor of the Edomites according to Hebrew tradition. His name means 'hairy'. He became a nomadic hunter, and Jacob a shepherd. Jacob, though the younger, was the dominant character, and he persuaded Esau into selling him his birthright for some red pottage; he also took the father's blessing intended for the first born. He fled to escape the furious Esau, but on his return, 20 years later, Esau forgave him.

Escher, Maurits Cornelis (1898–1972). Dutch graphic artist. His lithographs, engravings and drawings explored visual paradoxes such as three-dimensional representation, the ambiguity of relations between substance and shadow or upper and lower planes on cubes, and the phenomenon of 'strange loops' (e.g. quasi-fugal forms such as the representation of two hands, each drawing the other, or a waterfall in which the source is lower than the base but where each isolated element of the design is logically consistent: only the totality is impossible). He achieved considerable posthumous fame.
Hofstadter, D. R., *Gödel, Escher, Bach: An Eternal Golden Braid.* 1980

Escoffier, Auguste (1846–1935). French master chef. After being chef on the staff of Napoleon III in the Franco-Prussian War, he came to London, where he gained an international reputation as chef at the Carlton and Savoy hotels. The latter was the place of origin of his famous *Pêche Melba*, invented for the great singer Dame Nellie * Melba.
Henboden, E., and Thalamas, P., *G. A. Escoffier*. 1955

Esenin, Sergei Alexandrovich (1895–1925). Russian poet. Regarded as the founder of the Imagist school of Russian poets, he was, stripped of his affectations, more truly a natural poet of the countryside, to which, being of peasant origin, he belonged. He celebrated the Revolution in verse but, having married the American dancer Isadora * Duncan and travelled with her abroad, he became disillusioned on his return to Russia and committed suicide.

Espartero, Baldomero Joaquin Fernandez (1793–1879). Spanish soldier and politician. He fought against and was captured (1826) by * Bolívar in the War of South American Liberation; he returned to Spain, fought with distinction (1833–39) against the Carlists (* Carlos, Don) and was created Duque de la Victoria (1839). Meanwhile he had become prime minister and made himself regent for the young queen * Isabella. From 1843 to 1848 he was exiled in London, but was again prime minister (1854–56). After Isabella's deposition (1868), he was offered the crown, but refused (1870).

Espronceda y Delgado, José de (1808–1842). Spanish poet and revolutionary. Often compared with * Byron, as a student he became involved in revolutionary societies and from 1827 to 1831 was an exile in London and Paris, where he came under the romantic influence of Scott, Byron and Hugo. He returned to Madrid (1833), where he became notorious as man-about-town, and his growing success as a poet modified his revolutionary sentiments. His two best known works, *El Estudiante de Salamanca* (1839) and *El Diablo Mundo* (1841), are based on the legends of Don Juan and Faust.

Essex, Robert Devereux, 2nd Earl of (1566–1601). English soldier and courtier. After distinguished service in the Netherlands under his stepfather, * Leicester, he returned to England (1587) and soon became a favourite of Queen Elizabeth I. He offended the queen by marrying Sir Philip Sidney's widow (1590) but regained her favour by his courage in the attack on Cadiz (1596). In 1598, during one of many quarrels with the queen, he burst out with the insolent remark that the conditions she imposed were as 'crooked as her carcass' and was never really forgiven. Sent to Ireland (1599) to fight the insurgents, he not only failed but returned to England without permission to find himself in disgrace. After some

months of house-arrest, early in 1601 he tried to organize a rising of the citizens of London to regain his position by force. The attempt was a hopeless failure and Essex was arrested, tried for high treason, convicted and beheaded. He was a patron of literature and himself a minor poet.
Lacey, R., *Robert, Earl of Essex, an Elizabethan Icarus*. 1971

Essex, Robert Devereux, 3rd Earl of (1591–1646). Son of the 2nd Earl of * Essex. Out of favour at court, he commanded the parliamentary army during the first Civil War, with varied success. He was compelled to resign in the moves which led to the formation of the New Model Army and died shortly afterwards. His first wife was the notorious Frances Howard, who was involved in the murder of Sir Thomas Overbury, go-between with her lover, James I's favourite Robert Carr, whom she later married.
Snow, V., *Essex the Rebel*. 1971

Esterhazy, (Marie Charles) **Ferdinand Walsin** (1847–1923). French soldier of Hungarian ancestry. He stole secret military papers and sold them to the Germans in order to pay his gambling debts. The need for a scapegoat and anti-Jewish feeling in the French army led to the wrongful arrest and conviction of * Dreyfus (1894). In 1899 Esterhazy confessed and went to live in England. He subsequently became a grocer in London.

Esther. Queen in the Bible whose name is given to an Old Testament book. She is said to be the wife of * Ahasuerus, King of Persia, but may be a fictional character.

Ethelbert (or Aethelberht) (died 616). King of Kent (from 560) and overlord of southern England. He married a Christian, the Frankish princess Bertha, which facilitated his own conversion (597) by * St Augustine; this link with the Franks probably stimulated him to issue a code of laws, the first known to have been written down in England.

Ethelred I (died 871). King of Wessex (from 866), brother and predecessor of * Alfred the Great. The brothers worked in perfect harmony in their efforts to keep the Danes at bay, and, though the devout king was still at his prayers when the Battle of Ashdown (871) began, the Danes sustained their first decisive defeat. He died soon afterwards at Merton.

Ethelred II (known as 'the Unready') (968–1016). King of England (from 987). The son of Edgar the Peaceful he succeeded his murdered half-brother * Edward the Martyr. He was called 'Unraed' (lacking in counsel or good sense) because of his vacillating policy towards the Danes, sometimes bribing, sometimes fighting them. His reign was one of unrest and treachery to which he himself contributed, for example by a general massacre of Danes on St Brice's Day 1002. The Danish leader, * Sweyn Forkbeard, responded with fierce reprisals, defeated Ethelred and compelled him to flee to the court of the Duke of Normandy, the brother of Emma, Ethelred's second wife and mother of Edward the Confessor. He returned to England in 1014.

Etherege, Sir George (1635–1691). English Restoration dramatist. While in a minor position in the embassy at Constantinople he married a rich widow and was sent to the imperial court at Ratisbon. On return to England he spent much time in a court circle of witty, amoral friends. He was influenced by * Molière, and his comedies, e.g. *She Would If She Could* (1667–68) and *The Man of Mode or Sir Fopling Flutter* (1676), anticipated * Congreve and * Sheridan. His early work, *The Comical Revenge or Love in a Tub* (1664) is held to be a prototype for Restoration Comedy and to have influenced Congreve and * Goldsmith.
Underwood, D., *Etherege and the Seventeenth Century Comedy of Manners*. 1959

Etty, William (1779–1849). English painter. He studied under Lawrence, but owed much to the Venetian colourists seen during visits to Italy. He became an A.R.A. in 1824 and an R.A. in 1828. He was admired by Delacroix, and is best known for luscious and voluptuous nudes and for large compositions, notable especially for their sense of design, on historical subjects or fanciful themes, e.g. *Youth at the Prow* and *Pleasure at the Helm* (National Gallery, London), *Cleopatra* and *Joan of Arc*.

Eucken, Rudolph Christian (1846–1926). German philosopher. His system influenced by the 'Idealist' school, expounds and examines oppositions, e.g. between the spiritual life and modern materialism, which Eucken strongly attacked. Professor of philosophy (1874–1920) at Jena, he won the Nobel Prize for Literature (1908).

Euclid (*c.* 330–260 B.C.). Greek mathematician. Little is known about him except that after studying in Athens he lived in Alexandria. The thirteen books of his *The Elements of Geometry* systematized existing knowledge of mathematics. The sections on geometry have remained the basis of standard textbooks for more than 2,000 years. He also wrote treatises on astronomy, optics and musical harmony, but most of his works are lost.

Eugène of Savoy, Prince (1663–1736). Austrian general. Born in Paris and brought up at the French court, he quarrelled with Louis XIV and joined the imperial forces in 1683. He fought with great distinction against Turkey and, having risen to the rank of field marshal, won the brilliant and decisive Battle of Zenta (1697), as a result of which the Turks were driven from Hungary and forced to sign the Treaty of Karlowitz (1699). In the War of the Spanish Succession he fought the French first in Italy and then on the Danube, where he invited * Marlborough to join him in resisting a French threat to Vienna. The result was the great victory of Blenheim (1704) by the combined armies. Another campaign in Italy followed, after which he joined Marlborough in Flanders in the Battles of Oudenarde (1708) and Malplaquet (1709). After Marlborough's recall he was supreme allied commander until the end of the war. In 1716 he was again fighting the Turks and after a victory at Petwordein he captured Belgrade. Much of the rest of his life was spent in the collection of books and pictures and the building of the Belvedere Palace in Vienna.

Eugénie (Marie Eugenie de Montijo de Guzman) (1826–1920). Spanish-born wife of the French emperor Napoleon III, whom she married in 1853. Famed for her beauty, she became a leader of fashion and maintained a gay and brilliant court. She was an ardent supporter of the papacy and it was through her influence that a French garrison preserved the pope's rule in Rome after the unification of the rest of Italy. When the emperor abdicated after defeat in the Franco-Prussian War she lived with him in England and remained there after his death. Their son, the Prince Imperial, was killed fighting for the British in the Zulu War (1879).

Sencourt, R. E., *The Life of the Empress Eugénie*. 1931

Euler, Leonhard (1707–1783). Swiss mathematician. Born at Basle, he became a pupil of Jean Bernouilli, and joined him (1727) at the newly opened Academy at St Petersburg; he held professorships there from 1730 to 1741. He then spent twenty-five years at the new Academy of Sciences at Berlin, returning (1766) to St Petersburg where, though blind, he continued to work for the rest of his life. To a great extent he laid the foundations of modern mathematics. His works include a survey of analytical mathematics, with important contributions to the theory of equations and the first complete textbook on the calculus. He also did notable work in astronomy and physics.

Euripides (*c.* 480–406 B.C.). Athenian dramatist. Younger than * Aeschylus and * Sophocles, he reveals a more 'modern' attitude to psychology, especially that of women, but his techniques are often inferior to those of Sophocles. He makes much use of the clumsy device known as *deus ex machina* by which a god is made to appear by a mechanical device to complete the dénouement. His use of a prologue to explain the legend and outline the play is in itself a confession that the action is not self-explanatory. Traditional elements of Greek tragedy, e.g. the chorus, whose singing, dancing, explaining and bewailing often hold up action, seem to irk him but he found nothing to take their place. * Aristophanes ridiculed him unmercifully and found his language often pretentious and obscure. But to English audiences (to whom Gilbert Murray's translations first made him familiar) he has always been the most acceptable Greek dramatist. Of more than eighty plays which he is said to have written only eighteen survive. Among the most popular is *Medea*, the story of Jason's wife who, afraid of being supplanted, poisoned her children to leave her husband childless. Phaedra's unrequited passion which brings violent death to her stepson Hippolytus is told in the play that bears his name. The legends of Agamemnon's kin are told again in *Iphigenia among the Taurians, Iphigenia at Aulis, Electra* and *Orestes*. The remainder include *Alcestis*

and *Ion* (founder of the Ionian race), *The Trojan Women* and *Hecuba* (both revealing the poet's detestation of war), *The Bacchae*, a horrifying portrayal of the orgiastic celebrations of Dionysian rites, and *The Cyclops*, a semi-burlesque. His first plays appeared in 455 and the last probably *c.* 408.
Murray, G., *Euripides and His Age*. 1965

Eusebius (*c.* 264–340). Historian and theologian. Bishop of Caesarea in Palestine (*c.* 313), he played a conciliatory part at the Council of Nicaea (325) but is best known for his *History of the Christian Church*, as a result of which he became known as the 'Father of Church History'. His *Life of Constantine* provides the original evidence that the emperor was actually baptized. His *Chronicle* is the basis of many dates accepted in Greek and Roman history.
Wallace-Hadrill, D. S., *Eusebius of Caesarea*. 1960

Eustachio, Bartolomeo (1520–1574). Italian anatomist. After being personal physician to the Duke of Urbino and others, he taught anatomy at the Collegia della Sapienza in Rome. He rediscovered the Eustachian canal (auditory tube) of the ear, and the Eustachian valve in the foetus. He also studied and described the thoracic duct, larynx, adrenal glands and kidneys.

Evans, Sir Arthur John (1851–1941). British archaeologist. Educated at Harrow and Oxford, he went to Ragusa (Dubrovnik) in 1871 as *Manchester Guardian* correspondent, but was expelled by the Austrians (1882) for implication in a South Slav rising. Meanwhile he had developed the interest in antiquities inherited from his father. From 1884 to 1908 he was keeper of the Ashmolean Museum, Oxford, where his interest in Minoan seals led to the negotiations which at last enabled him to start upon the excavations at Knossos, Crete, upon which his fame rests (1899–1907). Knowledge of the fascinating 'Minoan' civilization (named after the legendary King Minos), which lasted from *c.* 2500–*c.* 1100 B.C. and was as its peak *c.* 1550–*c.* 1400 B.C., was due almost entirely to the work of excavation and reconstruction carried out by Evans for many years from 1899. His results, published in *The Palace of Minos* (1921–35), created a sensation, although some doubts have been expressed about certain of his conclusions. He was among the founders of the British Academy (1902).
Evans, J., *Time and Chance*. 1943

Evans, Dame Edith Mary (1888–1976). British actress. Her first parts were the title roles in *Troilus and Cressida* (1924) and later *Romeo and Juliet* and *Cleopatra*. She was perhaps seen at her best in comedy, e.g. as Millamant in Congreve's *The Way of the World* (1924) and as Mrs Malaprop in Sheridan's *The Rivals* (1945–46). Modern plays in which she achieved striking successes were *The Dark is Light Enough* (1954) and *The Chalk Garden* (1956). She also made films, e.g. *The Queen of Spades* (1948). She was awarded the D.B.E. in 1946.

Evans, Edward Ratcliffe Garth Russell, 1st Baron Mountevans (known as 'Evans of the *Broke*') (1881–1957). British sailor. His nickname refers to an episode in World War I when his ship *Broke*, in company with *Swift*, defeated six German destroyers (1917). Earlier he had taken over command of the South Polar Expedition (1910–12) after the death of Captain * Scott. In World War II he was London regional commissioner for Civil Defence. He received his peerage in 1945.
Pound, R., *Evans of the Broke*. 1963

Evatt, Herbert Vere (1894–1965). Australian lawyer and Labor politician. A justice of the High Court (1930–40), he resigned to re-enter politics. Minister for external affairs and attorney general (1941–49), he represented Australia in the British war cabinet (1942–43). He was President of the U.N. General Assembly (1948–49) and from 1951 leader of the Federal opposition; but in 1955 a split in the Labor party developed between Evatt's majority section, primarily concerned with social reform, and the Roman Catholics, to whom the fight against Communism was the most urgent task. In 1960 Evatt gave up politics to become chief justice of the Supreme Court of New South Wales, retiring in 1962.

Evelyn, John (1620–1706). English diarist. He was born at the family estate at Wotton, Surrey. At heart a Royalist, he spent the years of the Civil War mostly abroad. When he returned to England he lived for nearly fifty years at Sayes Court, Deptford, spending the last years of his life at Wotton, which he inherited in 1696. His diary, discovered at

Wotton in 1817, remains an outstanding contribution to English letters; with that of * Pepys (though far less intimate), it provides an important, and delightful, record of the life of the period. Of his many other interests, garden-making and especially arboriculture are manifested in his *Sylva* (1664). He was secretary of the Royal Society (1671–80). The best edition of the *Diary* is edited by E. S. de Beer (1956).
Keynes, G. L., *Evelyn; A Study in Bibliophily and a Bibliography of His Writings*. 1968

Everest, Sir George (1790–1866). English surveyor. While he was surveyor-general of India (1830–43), the world's highest mountain was mapped and measured and named after him (1841).

Everett, Edward (1794–1865). American orator, scholar and administrator. He taught Greek at Harvard, but then his powers of oratory led him to public life: he was governor of Massachusetts (1835–39), minister to Great Britain (1841–45), president of Harvard University (1846–49), U.S. secretary of state under Fillmore (1852–53) and U.S. senator (1853–54).
Frothingham, P. R., *Edward Everett*. 1925

Ewing, Juliana Horatia Orr (née Gatty) (1841–1885). English writer of children's stories. Few have achieved such artistry or lasting popularity in her particular genre. Her best known book is *Jackanapes* (1884). She founded *Aunt Judy's Magazine* in 1856.
Avery, G., *Mrs Ewing*. 1961

Eyck, Hubert van (*c.* 1366–1426) and **Jan van** (*c.* 1390–1441). Flemish painters. There is ample historical record of Jan, who in 1425 became court painter to Philip, Duke of Burgundy, for whom he carried out several confidential missions abroad; there is evidence of his presence in Bruges up to the date of his burial (1441). There is little evidence about Hubert – so little that his very existence has been questioned. He is believed to have painted part of the great polyptych in the Ghent church of St Bavon on the theme of the *Adoration of the Lamb*, but recent art historians are inclined to attribute the work to Jan.

Jan was recognized in his own time as a great master. His works are characterized by uncompromising realism, rich and brilliant colouring (his development of a paint which had great lasting qualities was an ancillary accomplishment), acute sensitivity to surfaces and textures, and a miniaturist's passion for detail. He is at his greatest as a portraitist and his portraits of Albergati and the *Man in a Red Turban* are amongst the masterpieces of the northern Renaissance. Entirely unemotional, Jan's painting moves us by its absolute truth and attention to detail and its marvellous rendering of textural effects.
Baldass, L., *Van Eyck*. 1952

Eyre, Edward John (1815–1901). English explorer and administrator. He emigrated to Australia in 1833 and developed a taste for exploring. In 1840 his most famous expedition advanced northwards from Adelaide into the interior. When unable to proceed further he turned westward and reached the head of the Great Australian Bight. Having sent the expedition back he himself, with his overseer and three aborigines, set out for Albany, in the extreme south-west. He arrived there with a single native in July 1841 after great hardships. Publication of his experiences brought him a Royal Geographical Society medal and considerable fame. He subsequently served as lieutenant-governor of New Zealand (from 1846) and then as governor of Jamaica (1862–66), where he violently suppressed a rebellion in 1865, acquiring a reputation for cruelty. Attempts were made to have him tried for murder (1867, 1869) but he weathered the storm and lived on quietly in retirement.
Dutton, G., *The Hero as Murderer*. 1967

Ezekiel (*fl. c.* 590–610 B.C.). Hebrew prophet. Little is known of his life except that he was among those deported by Nebuchadnezzar to Babylon (597). The book of the Bible ascribed to him presents problems of authorship. The first twenty-five chapters, though apparently written in Babylon, predict the fall of Jerusalem, which actually took place in 586; this portion denounces neighbouring nations, while Chapters XXXIII–XXXIX predict the reunification of Israel and Judah under a king of the House of David. The last chapters paint an idealized picture of the restored state with its temple worship renewed and reformed. Much of this last section may well have been added later, though the earlier portions were probably written by Ezekiel himself, confusion being caused by an editor's attempt to weld together parts written at different times.

Ezra (5th century B.C.). Hebrew priest and scribe. He led a group of returning exiles from the court of the Persian king Artaxerxes I or II. He revived the Jews' conception of themselves as an exclusive and chosen people bound together by their unique religious observances. The Biblical book of Ezra is believed to be part of a larger whole containing also Chronicles and Nehemiah.

F

Fabergé, Peter Carl (1846–1920). Russian-born jeweller. He achieved fame by the ingenuity and extravagance of the jewelled objects (especially Easter eggs) he devised for the Russian nobility and the tsar in an age of ostentatious extravagance which ended on the outbreak of World War I.

Fabius, Laurent (1946–). French socialist politician. He was a Deputy 1978–81, Minister for Industry and Research 1983–84 and Premier of France 1984– .

Fabius Maximus Verrucosus, Quintus (known as *Cunctator*, 'delayer') (died 203 B.C.). Roman soldier. He served as dictator and commander of the army that held Hannibal's Carthaginian army in check during the Second Punic War. After the Roman defeat at Lake Trasimene (217), he pursued a policy of 'masterly inactivity' (hence his sobriquet), preferring to harass the enemy by cutting off his supplies and to avoid a direct battle. Hannibal remained in Italy fifteen years but, largely owing to Fabius's tactics, never gained decisive victory. The word Fabian has passed into the English language, e.g. The Fabian Society, dedicated to achieve socialism by gradual reforms.

His grandfather, **Quintus Fabius Maximus Rullianus** (died 315 B.C.), won several notable battles in the Samnite Wars.

Fabre, Jean Henri (1823–1915). French entomologist. He was a teacher for many years in Ajaccio, Corsica and (from 1852) at Avignon. In 1870 he retired to Sérignan, near Orange, and devoted almost all his time to studying insects, which he observed with the utmost patience and exactitude. His writings about them were published in many volumes as *Souvenirs entomologiques*, parts of which had been issued separately as, e.g., *The Life and Love of the Insect* (1911) and *Social Life in the Insect World* (1913).
Gordon, S., *Jean Henri Fabre*. 1971

Fabricius, Hieronymus (Girolamo Fabrizi) (1533–1619). Italian physician, born at Aquapendente, near Orvieto (hence the Latinized form of his name, Fabricius Ab Aquapendente). He studied medicine at Padua under the anatomist of the day, * Fallopio, whom he succeeded in 1562. He spent his academic career at Padua, and was actively concerned in the building of the university's magnificent anatomical theatre, which is preserved today. He acquired fame as a practising physician and surgeon, and made extensive contributions to many fields of physiology and medicine, through his energetic skills in dissection and experimentation. He wrote works on surgery, discussing treatments for different sorts of wounds, and a major series of embryological studies, illustrated by detailed engravings. His work on the formation of the foetus was especially important for its discussion of the provisions made by nature for the necessities of the foetus during its intrauterine life. The medical theory which he offered to explain the development of eggs and foetuses, however, was traditionally Galenic. Fabricius is best remembered for his detailed studies of the valves of the veins. He thought the function of these valves was to slow the flow of blood from the heart, thus ensuring a more even distribution through the body. His pupil, William * Harvey, drew on these studies in his work on the circulation of the blood.

Fadden, Sir Arthur William (1895–1974). Australian politician. He left school at 14 to join a sugar-cutting gang; later he became an accountant. He entered the Australian House of Representatives (1936) as a member of the Country Party, which he led 1940–58. He was prime minister August–October 1941 until * Curtin's Labor government took over. He kept his party in alliance with the Liberal party led by * Menzies. Fadden was federal treasurer from 1949 until he retired (1958).

Fadeyev, Aleksandr Aleksandrovich (Aleksandr Aleksandrovich Bulyga) (1901–1956). Russian novelist. He was born near Kalinin and educated in Vladivostock. After 1918 he fought against the White Russian army in Siberia, an experience which inspired his first important novel *The Nineteen* (1927). He was quickly recognised as a leader of a new, Soviet Communist, proletarian literature. He became a member of the board of the Union of Soviet Writers and was connected with the imposition of a stern party line, although in 1947 he suffered from official censure himself. His novel *The Young Guard* (1946) was criticised as failing to show the Party as dominant, and he re-wrote it. His later life was clouded by alcoholism and, after the official denunciation of Stalinism, he killed himself.

Fahrenheit, Gabriel Daniel (1686–1736). German physicist, born in Danzig and educated in Holland. He eventually settled in Amsterdam as a maker of meteorological instruments. He introduced (1715) mercury as the fluid in thermometers and devised the temperature scale that bears his name, with boiling point at 212° and freezing point at 32°.

Faidherbe, Louis Léon César (1818–1889). French soldier and colonial administrator. He began his military career with the corps of military engineers in 1840, and was given his first command, in Algeria, in 1849. In 1852 he went to Senegal as deputy director of engineers; he was made governor in 1854, serving till 1861 and again 1863–65. He established a strong military presence in Senegal based on the capital Dakar, which he founded. His achievements laid the foundations of the French West African colonies. He was recalled to fight in the Franco-Prussian war in 1870, and was defeated near St Quentin (1871).

Fairbanks, Douglas (1883–1939). American film actor, famous as the swashbuckling and romantic hero of such films as *The Three Musketeers* (1921), *The Thief of Baghdad* (1924) and *The Man in the Iron Mask* (1929). He formed the film making company United Artists with Charles Chaplin and Mary Pickford.

His son, **Sir Douglas Fairbanks Jr** (1908–), also an actor, settled in England in 1946 and was made honorary K.B.E. in 1949.

Fairfax, Thomas Fairfax, 3rd Baron (1612–1671). English soldier. He served as a volunteer in Holland (1629–37) and when the civil war broke out (1642) gained such distinction as a commander, especially at Marston Moor (1644), that when * Essex had to give up his post as commander-in-chief under the Self-denying Ordinance, Fairfax took his place. The Battle of Naseby (1645) was his greatest triumph. Thereafter he played a conciliatory role; he tried, but failed, to save the king's life and after refusing to march against the Scots (1650) was superseded by * Cromwell. In 1660 he went to The Hague to arrange for the return of Charles II.

Faisal (*c.* 1905–1975). King of Saudi Arabia (from 1964). A son of King Ibn Sa'ud, he was prime minister and foreign minister of Saudi Arabia (1953–60), and virtually ruled the kingdom (1958–60) until forced to resign by his half-brother King Sa'ud. Reconciliation took place early in 1964 and in November as a result of Sa'ud's continued ill health Faisal took his place as king. Murdered by a nephew, also called Faisal, he was succeeded by his brother Khalid.

Faisal I (1885–1933). First king of Iraq (from 1921). Son of Hussein, the sherif of Mecca, who made himself king of the Hejaz, he became, during World War I, a leader of the Arab revolt, in which T. E. * Lawrence was prominent. After the war he was made king first of Syria and then of the British mandated territory of Iraq, which became fully independent in 1932. Faisal, a man of statesmanlike vision and great courage, was succeeded by his only son Ghazi, who was killed in an accident (1939).

Faisal II (1935–1958). King of Iraq (from 1939), son of King Ghazi and grandson of Faisal I, educated at Harrow School in

England. The effective ruler until 1953 was the regent, his uncle Abdul Illah. The proclamation (1958) by Faisal and his cousin, King Hussein of Jordan, of a federation of their two kingdoms was followed almost immediately by a revolutionary *coup d'état* led by Brigadier Kassem, in the course of which Faisal and his prime minister, * Nuri es-Said, were murdered.

Falkenhayn, Erich von (1861–1922). German soldier. After a successful career in the Chinese Boxer rebellion and elsewhere, he came to prominence in World War I when he succeeded von Moltke as chief of the general staff after the defeat on the Marne. His attempt to redeem this by an outflanking movement failed, but he achieved great success against the Russians (1915) and destroyed the Serbian army (1915–16). Deprived of his staff post after failure at Verdun and on the Somme, he conducted a victorious offensive against Romania.

Falkland, Lucius Cary, 2nd Viscount (1610–1643). English courtier, soldier and scholar. Educated at Trinity College, Dublin (his father had served in Ireland as lord deputy), he succeeded to the peerage in 1633. To his Oxfordshire home flocked scholars from nearby Oxford, poets, wits and eager spirits with young ideals from London. As a member of the Long Parliament he opposed the authoritarian rule of Land and Straffod, but remained a keen Anglican. In a last effort to avert civil war he became secretary of state (1642). When the final tragic choice came he was loyal to the king, but it was known that at the Battle of Newbury he sought and welcomed death. He wrote poems and theological treatises, e.g. *Discourses of Infallibility*.

Falla, Manuel de (1876–1946). Spanish composer, born in Cadiz. He studied composition in Madrid. After his opera *La Vida Breve* (*Life Is Short*) had won him a national prize he continued his studies in Paris (1907–14), Debussy and Dukas being major influences. He developed, however, a strikingly original style which embodies much of the dramatic intensity, intricate rhythms and floridity of traditional Andalusian music. He was unusually fastidious and his total output is small. Among his best known works are the ballets *Love the Magician* (1915) and *The Three-cornered Hat* (1919), for which last Massine was the choreographer and Picasso the designer. Others include *Nights in the Gardens of Spain* (first performed 1921) for piano and orchestra, a Harpsichord Concerto (1926) and the song cycle *Seven Popular Spanish Songs*. He lived in Argentina from 1940.

Fallada, Hans (Rudolf Ditzen) (1893–1947). German noveliest. His most famous work, *Little Man, What Now?* (1932), expresses the dilemma and disillusionment which faced the middle classes in Germany in the years following World War I.
Schueler, H. J., *Hans Fallada*. 1970

Fallières, (Clement-) Armand (1841–1931). French politician. A lawyer, he served as a deputy 1876–90, premier briefly in 1883, a senator 1890–1906, president of the Senate 1899–1906 and president of the Third Republic 1906–13.

Fallopio (Fallopius), **Gabriele** (1523–1562). Italian anatomist, pupil and successor of Vesalius at Padua. He made a notable study of the organs of generation: the Fallopian tubes (ovarian ducts) and the Fallopian aqueduct for the facial nerve (which he first described) are named after him.

Fanfani, Amintore (1908–). Italian politician. An economist by profession, he succeeded * de Gasperi as secretary-general of the Christian Democratic party (1954). He was prime minister in 1954, 1958–59 and 1960–63. He also acquired a great reputation as a maker and breaker of governments.

Fangio, Juan Manuel (1911–). Argentinian racing driver, born in Buenos Aires. In 1934 he began racing in South America and met with considerable success. In 1949 he went to Europe and subsequently dominated motor racing competitions in the 1950s, becoming World Champion in 1951, 1954, 1955, 1956 and 1957. On his retirement in 1958 at the age of 47, he had won 24 Grands Prix, 16 of them World Championship.

Fanon, Frantz (1925–1961). French–African revolutionary theorist, born in Martinique. After army service, he studied in Paris, became a psychiatrist in Algiers and wrote *The Wretched of the Earth* (1961) which was used as a handbook by revolutionary and student movements in Africa and the U.S. He died of leukemia in Washington, D.C.

Fantin-Latour, Ignace Henri Jean Théodore (1836–1904). French painter. He studied under Courbet and first exhibited at the Salon in 1861. He was a friend of the Impressionists and painted their portraits, e.g. *Manet's Studio at Batignolles*. Fantasies suggested by the music of Wagner and Berlioz, and, above all, his exquisitely delicate flower pieces, are also well known.

Faraday, Michael (1791–1867). English chemist and physicist. He was the son of a Surrey blacksmith, and taught himself the rudiments of science while working as a bookbinder's apprentice. He attracted the attention of Sir Humphry * Davy with a bound set of notes he had taken at Davy's Royal Institution lectures in 1813, and was given a post as laboratory assistant under him. In 1827 he became director of the laboratory and was Fullerian professor of chemistry at the Institution (1833–67), where his lectures were highly popular. His most important work was in electricity and electrochemistry. He discovered (1831) electromagnetic induction and deduced the laws governing the relative movement of magnets and current-carrying conductors. These discoveries led directly to the generation of electricity and the development of the electric motor. His discovery (1832–33), of the laws of electrolysis (now known as Faraday's Laws) put this process on a sound quantitative basis. He also studied the liquefaction of gases and was the first to liquefy chlorine. He discovered benzene and was the first to prepare colloidal gold. The records of Faraday's researches are collected in his *Experimental Researches on Electricity*. The farad (unit of electrical capacity) is named after him. In 1845, having recovered from a mental illness, he began to work on magnetism again. He found that the plane of polarized light was rotated by a magnetic field and this led him to suggest a connexion between light and electricity; later he studied the properties of feeble magnetic materials. He was given a civil list pension in 1835 and in 1858 the house at Hampton Court where he died.

Pearce Williams, L., *Michael Faraday: A Biography*. 1965

Farel, Guillaume (1489–1565). French Protestant reformer. He was born of a noble family in the Dauphiné, and became a Protestant missionary, mainly in Switzerland. After being twice expelled from Geneva he was largely responsible for the town council's decision to proclaim the Reformation there (1535). He became the friend of * Calvin, who was, however, more closely concerned with administration, and shared with him a brief exile from Geneva (1538). Farel was pastor at Neuchâtel (1544–65). At the age of 69 he married a young wife, an action highly distasteful to the sterner Calvin.

Farinelli (professional name of Carlo Broschi) (1705–1782). Italian *castrato* or male soprano. He achieved remarkable success in London, Rome, Vienna, Paris, and finally Madrid, where he became court singer to King Philip V of Spain, over whom (from 1737) he exercised an extraordinary influence, even in affairs of state.

Farington, Joseph (1747–1821). English landscape painter and diarist. Though he became an R. A., his fame rests much more firmly on his diary (first published 1922–28), a vivid presentation of the people and events of his life from 1793 to the day of his death.

Farman, Henri (1874–1958). French aviator. With his brother Maurice he built their first biplane in 1907–08. During World War I the brothers manufactured many biplanes for the French army and in 1909 he became the first man to fly 100 miles.

Farnese. Italian ducal family, rulers of Parma from 1545 – when Pope Paul III (**Alessandro Farnese**) invested his illegitimate son **Pier Luigi** (1503–1547) with the duchy – until 1731. Alessandro's sister **Giulia** was mistress of Pope Alexander VI (Rodrigo Borgia). A grandson of Luigi, **Alessandro Farnese** (1546–1592), Duke of Parma, was the general of Philip II who (1578) became his governor in the Netherlands. **Elizabeth** (1692–1766), niece of the the last Farnese duke, married and dominated Philip V, her ambition to obtain the Parma duchy for her son being a constantly disruptive factor in European politics.

Farouk (1920–1965). King of Egypt (1936–1952). Son and successor of Faud I, he was educated in England. He followed a vacillating policy during World War II and, in the years that followed, proved himself unable to compete with political turmoil and administrative corruption; at the same time he incurred censure by the extravagance of the court and by much publicized episodes in his 'private' life. His exile followed an army revolt under General Neguib and Colonel Nasser and he was finally deposed in 1953 when a republic was proclaimed.

Farquhar, George (1678–1707). Anglo-Irish dramatist. He was an actor for a time in Dublin, but after wounding another actor in a stage duel went to London and achieved success with *Love and a Bottle* (1698), the first of his licentious but witty and amusing comedies. This, followed by *The Constant Couple* (1699), said to have run for 53 nights at Drury Lane, and other plays, brought him esteem with little reward; he managed to obtain an army commission and performed the duties of the title part in his play *The Recruiting Officer* (1706). Poverty forced him to sell his commission, but a gift from the actor Robert Wilks enabled him to write his last and best play *The Beaux' Stratagem* (1707). Farquhar's good nature and gift for satire are revealed in his plays, and by taking comedy out of the drawing room into a more realistic outside world he set a trend soon followed by * Goldsmith and others.

Farragut, David Glasgow (1801–1870). American admiral, born in Tennessee, the most successful naval commander of the Union in the Civil War. In spite of his long service, on the outbreak of the civil war he was at first suspected of Confederate sympathies. He was given a command in 1862 and distinguished himself in a number of daring actions, first at New Orleans where he ran the gauntlet of forts to destroy the Confederate fleet on the Mississipi, after which he was made senior rear admiral. In 1863 he won control of more of the Mississipi, which greatly helped Grant's Vicksburg campaign. In 1864 he achieved his most outstanding victory off Mobile to end blockade-running by the Confederates; on his famous signal 'Damn the torpedoes', his fleet steamed through a screen of mines (then called torpedoes) to overwhelm the Confederate flotilla. The rank of admiral was created for him in 1866.

Farrar, Frederick William (1831–1903). English clergyman, schoolmaster and author. Though important in his own day as headmaster of Marlborough, a friend of Queen Victoria, and dean of Canterbury (from 1895), he is now almost forgotton except as the author of the notorious schoolboy story *Eric, or Little by Little* (1858). He was the grandfather of Viscount * Montgomery of Alamein.

Farrell, James Thomas (1904–1979). American novelist. After a variety of occupations, Farrell achieved fame with his realistic trilogy (completed in 1935) of slum life in Chicago, *Studs Lonigan*. His later novels include *A World I Never Made* (1936) and *Bernard Clare* (1946).
Branch, E. M., *James T. Farrell*. 1963

Fastolf, Sir John (1378–1459). English soldier. Knighted for distinguished conduct at Agincourt and in other engagements, as landlord of huge estates in Norfolk, he is said to have been mean, rapacious and ill-tempered; but he was an educational benefactor and Magdalen College, Oxford, was eventually built from funds left by him. Shakespeare may have borrowed his name (but nothing else) for his character of Falstaff.

Fatima (*c*. 606–632). Daughter of Mohammed. She married her cousin * Ali. Long after her death Said Ibn Hussein, basing his claim on descent from Fatima, founded a powerful Shi'ite dynasty (the Fatimite).

Faulkner, William (1897–1962). American author, born in Mississippi. He served with the Canadian air force in World War I and worked at a succession of odd jobs while trying to sell his poetry and early novels, *Soldier's Pay* (1926), *Mosquitoes* (1927), *Sartoris* (1929). He gradually secured literary recognition with *The Sound and the Fury* (1929), *As I Lay Dying* (1930) and *Light in August* (1932), with their vigorous and powerful portrayal of upper-class whites, poor whites and Negroes in the South during a period of social conflict and disintegration; but he did not obtain wide popular responses until the publication of *Sanctuary*, a 'horror' story, employing the stream-of-consciousness technique, of a girl who becomes a nymphomaniac after rape. Later works include a comic trilogy (*The Hamlet* (1940), *The Town* (1956), *The Mansion* (1959)), *Intruder in the Dust* (1948), and *Requiem for a Nun* (1951), later dramatized. His many short stories include *A Rose for Emily* and the collection *Go Down, Moses* (1942). The film *Long Hot Summer* was based on one of Faulkner's stories. He won the

Nobel Prize for Literature in 1949 and in 1955 the Pulitzer Prize for *A Fable* (1954), an allegory of fighting in the trenches in France.
Volpe, E. L., *A Reader's Guide to William Faulkner*. 1965

Faure, François Félix (1841–1899). French politician. Originally a leather merchant and shipowner, he was a deputy (1881–95), minister of marine (1894–95) and president of the Republic (1895–99), dying in office. He cemented the Franco-Russian alliance by a visit to St Petersburg (1897), but the reopening of the * Dreyfus case clouded his presidential term.

Fauré, Gabriel Urbain (1845–1924). French composer. A pupil of Saint-Saëns, he became a well known organist in Paris, and succeeded (1896) Massenet as professor of composition at the Paris Conservatiore, of which he was director (1905–20). He encouraged and influenced a whole generation of younger composers including Ravel. His gentle, lyrical style, though unemphatic, is often harmonically audacious. He wrote a *Requiem* (1887–88), incidental music to Maeterlinck's *Pelléas et Mélisande* (1898) and a Ballade (1881) for piano and orchestra, but is at his best in chamber music (notably the two Cello Sonatas and two Piano Quartets), piano music and songs. He is second to none among French song composers and his *La Bonne Chanson* (1891–92), settings of Verlaine, is one of the world's great song cycles.
Orledge, R., *Gabriel Fauré*. 1979

Faust, Johann (or Georg) (*c.* 1480–*c.* 1540). German magician. The real man behind the Faust legends seems to have been a university student, an astrologer, magician, and debaucher, who travelled (or more probably was moved on) about the country, and who, after boasting that he had sold his soul to the devil, died mysteriously. Probably because his journeys made him so widely known legends soon gathered round him; in 1587 appeared a printed account of his life, and subsequently many differing versions were issued. Of the many dramatists who have used the theme Marlowe and Goethe are the most famous. Of the operas Gounod's is the best known.

Fawcett, Dame Millicent Garrett (1847–1930). English political reformer and campaigner for women's rights. She was born in Aldeburgh, Suffolk, the sister of Elizabeth Garrett * Anderson. In 1867 she married Henry Fawcett, a political economist who supported her work and was a leading social reformer. She made her first public speech advocating votes for women in 1868, and led the suffrage movement until 1918. She also advocated higher education for women, and was co-founder of Newnham College, Cambridge.
Fawcett, M. G., *Women's Suffrage*. 1912

Fawkes, Guy (or Guido) (1570–1606). English conspirator. He was a Roman Catholic convert of fanatical zeal and took part in the gunpowder plot to blow up the Houses of Parliament to kill King James I. Arrested in the cellars on 5 November 1605 he revealed, under torture, full details of the plot and was executed soon afterwards. His own role was actually to fire the barrels. November 5 has been commemorated ever since with bonfires burning his effigy and with fireworks.
Edwards, F., *Guy Fawkes*. 1962

Fechner, Gustav Theodor (1801–1887). German philosopher and physicist. He was professor of physics at Leipzig from 1834 to 1839, when a nervous breakdown forced him to resign. After recovery he spent the rest of his life in writing and lecturing. His most notable contribution was in the relationship of mind and body, but perhaps of greater interest to the layman is the pantheism expressed in such works as *Nanna* (1848), concerned with the soul of plants, and *Zendavesta* (1851), on star life.

Feisal (name of Arab rulers) *see* **Faisal**

Fellini, Federico (1920–). Italian film director. His films, for which he also prepares the scripts, include *La Strada* (*The Road*, 1957), *Cabiria* (the name of the Rome prostitute round whose life the film revolves, 1958), *La Dolce Vita* (*The Sweet Life*, 1960) and 8½ (1963). Other important works are *Clowns* (1970). *Roma* (1972), *Amarcord* (1974) and *Casanova* (1975). He received many national and international awards.

Fénelon, François de Salignac de la Mothe (1651–1715). French writer and cleric. He came of a distinguished Périgord family, was trained for the priesthood and ordained in 1675. In 1689 he was chosen as tutor to Louis

XIV's grandson, the Duke of Burgundy, for whose benefit he wrote Fables (published 1716), a series of imaginary dialogues between famous men in the manner of Lucian, and his best known work, *Les Aventures de Télémaque* (imaginary adventures of Odysseus's son). Published without his consent, with keys to the characters, this was a main cause of his withdrawal from court (1699) to his bishopric of Cambrai, to which he had been appointed in 1695. His *Explication des Maximes des saints sur la vie intérieure* (1697), a defence of quietism (i.e. 'interior inspiration,' opposed to the extreme dogmatism of Bossuet), was condemned by the pope, a verdict immediately accepted by Fénelon.

Feng Yu-shiang (1880–1940). Chinese warlord. The so-called 'Christian general', he contested (1920–26) the control of northern China with Chang Tsu-Lin and other warlords. Later he came to terms with the national government.

Fenton, Lavinia (1708–1769). English actress, famous in the part of Polly Peachum in *The Beggar's Opera*. After eloping with Charles Paulet, 3rd Duke of Bolton, she married him in 1751.

Ferber, Edna (1887–1968). American author. Of her many popular novels *Show Boat* (1926), like several of its successors, e.g. *Saratoga Trunk* (1941) and *Giant* (1953), was made into a film. She collaborated with G. S. Kaufman in writing the successful play *Dinner at Eight*. *A Kind of Magic* (1964) was autobiographical.

Ferdinand (1861–1948). Ruler of Bulgaria (1887–1918). A son of Prince Augustus of Saxe-Coburg-Gotha, he was chosen as prince of Blugaria, then still under Turkish suzerainty, after the abdication of Alexander of Battenberg. By adroit political manoeuvering, which afterwards earned him the epithet 'Foxy', he was able (1980) to declare his country's complete independence with himself as king. He was a leading spirit in the creation of the alliance which deprived Turkey of almost all of its European territory in the First Balkan War (1912), but Bulgaria's excessive demands provoked the Second Balkan War (1913), in which most of Bulgaria's gains were transferred to its former allies. Ferdinand aligned his country with Germany in World War I. After defeat he was forced to abdicate in favour of his son Boris.

Ferdinand I (1503–1564). Holy Roman Emperor (1558–64). He was the brother of the emperor * Charles V, who in 1521 handed over to him the Habsburg estates in Germany and made him president of the imperial executive. Having married Anna, sister of the king of Hungary and Bohemia, he was able to claim both thrones on his brother-in-law's death (1526). Bohemia he secured without difficulty but in Hungary a rival claimant with Turkish support was able to prevent him obtaining anything but the royal title, a strip of land in the west, and Croatia. Ferdinand played a conciliatory part in the struggle between Roman Catholics and Protestants and negotiated the compromise known as the Peace of Augsburg (1555). After Charles abdicated (1558) Ferdinand became emperor.

Ferdinand I (1751–1825). King (from 1759) of the Two Sicilies (Naples and Sicily). He became king as a minor when his father, of whom he was the third son, became Charles III of Spain (1759). In 1768 he married Maria Caroline, a sister of Marie Antoinette of France, and fell completely under her dominance and that of her favourite minister, the British Sir John Acton. Ferdinand was driven from Naples by the French revolutionary armies in 1798 and again in 1806 by Napoleon who made his brother Joseph, and later Murat, kings of Naples while Ferdinand ruled in Sicily under British protection. His restoration (1815) and, in 1816, the uniting of Naples and Sicily as the Kingdom of the Two Sicilies were followed by ruthless repression of all liberal opinion, and Ferdinand had to obtain Austrian support in order to retain his throne.

Ferdinand I (1865–1927). King of Romania (from 1914). In 1893 he married the English Princess Marie (1875–1938), a granddaughter of Queen Victoria, succeeding his uncle, * Carol I, in 1914. He led his country against the Germans in World War I (1916). Though the country was occupied by German troops (1917–18), the final Allied victory added Transylvania, the Banat, Bukovina and Bessarabia to its territories. Ferdinand was much distressed by the scandals involving his eldest son, who eventually became * Carol II.

Ferdinand II (known as 'the Catholic') (1452–1516). Spanish king, of Aragon and V of Castile and Leon. He succeeded to the throne of Aragon in 1479; his kingship of Castile he owed to his marriage (1469) to Isabella, sister of King Henry IV. Henry died in 1474 but it was only after a civil war that Isabella's position, with Ferdinand as consort, was secure (1479); Ferdinand's third throne, that of Naples, was gained by conquest (1504).

His main purpose was to achieve religious and national unity throughout Spain. He resumed the war against the Moors and by 1492 had forced Granada, the last Moorish kingdom, to surrender; he obtained the cession from France of Roussilon and Cerdagne (1493) and of Navarre (1512). To secure religious unity he expelled from his kingdoms all Jews and Moors unconverted to Christianity, thus depriving Spain of many of its ablest citizens; and to ensure Catholic orthodoxy he secured a Papal Bull setting up the Inquisition. Though Aragon and Castile retained their separate administrations he took every possible measure to centralize the government; the nobles were deprived of feudal privileges, and their castles were destroyed; royal magistrates supplanted elected officials in the towns; royal councils were set up to advise the ruler in both kingdoms and royal courts of justice were established. The power of the *Cortes* (parliament) steadily declined.

Ferdinand and Isabella sponsored * Columbus's voyage to America (1492) and from 1494, taking advantage of the pope's arbitrary division of the territories of the New World, they steadily enlarged Spain's colonial empire in Central and South America. The occupation of the Canary Islands in the Atlantic was completed by 1496. When Isabella died (1504), the throne of Castile passed to their daughter Juana (Joanna), known as 'the Mad', for whom her husband Philip of the Netherlands acted as regent. When Philip died (1506) Ferdinand assumed the regency and so was able to hand over to his grandson, the emperor * Charles V (Charles I of Spain), son of Philip and Jauna, a dynastically united country, second to none in wealth and power.

Ferdinand II (1578–1637). Holy Roman Emperor (from 1619), a grandson of Ferdinand I. He was educated by Jesuits and was chosen by the older archdukes as the most suitable person to head the dynasty and restore Roman Catholicism throughout the Habsburg lands. In 1617 he became king of Bohemia, in 1618 of Hungary and in 1619 he was chosen to succeed the emperor Matthias, who had died in that year. It was in Bohemia, where Protestantism was strong, that the accession of so rigid a Catholic caused most alarm; the nobles rebelled and invited Frederick V of the Palatinate (husband of the British princess Elizabeth, daughter of James I and VI) to be king. He ruled for a single winter before he was defeated at the White Mountain (1620) and expelled, but Ferdinand's measures were so repressive that other princes took alarm and war continued, to become the Thirty Years War (1616–48). Ferdinand did not live to see its end. In his own territories, however, Protestantism was effectively suppressed.

Ferdinand II (1810–1859). King (from 1830) of the Two Sicilies, son of Francis I of Sicily and grandson of Ferdinand I. His attempts to maintain autocratic rule in face of the political ferment that eventually produced the unification of Italy led him to every harsher measures of repression. His inhuman bombardment of rebellious cities while subduing the revolution of 1848–49 earned him the nickname 'Bomba'. His son **Francis II** (1836–1894) was driven out by * Garibaldi (1861).

Ferdinand VII (1784–1833). King of Spain (1808 and 1814–1833). After being Napoleon's tool in the manoeuvres by which his father Charles IV was induced to renounce his rights, he was himself enticed over the frontier and held in captivity while Napoleon's brother, Joseph Bonaparte, occupied the Spanish throne. After his restoration by the Allies (1814), he abrogated all constitutional reforms and enforced a policy of extreme reaction. A rebellion made him accept constitutional government for three years (1820–23); but then, having regained liberty of action with the aid of French troops sent in response to his appeal to the powers, he pursued a policy of reaction and vengeance until his death. The loss of the Spanish American colonies and his revocation of the Salic Law (which guaranteed male succession) for the benefit of his infant daughter * Isabella, were other features of his disastrous reign.

Fermat, Pierre de (1601–1665). French math-

ematician. A lawyer by profession, he was one of the founders of the modern theory of numbers; he developed a form of calculus which influenced Newton's investigations and anticipated Descartes's work on analytical geometry; and he deduced much of the mathematical theory of probability and the principles of permutations and combinations. He left no written works and his achievements can only be gathered from his correspondence with Descartes and others.
Mahoney, M. S., *The Mathematical Career of Pierre de Fermat*. 1973

Fermi, Enrico (1901–1954). Italian physicist. Specializing in nuclear and particle physics, he studied at Pisa, Göttingen and Leyden. He was awarded the Nobel Prize in 1938 for his work on radioactivity and in that year emigrated to the U.S.A. to escape Fascist anti-Semitism (which impinged on his wife). Professor of physics at Columbia University (1939–45), he built in Chicago (1942) the first 'atomic pile' for sustained and controlled nuclear fission, and co-operated in the research which resulted in the first atom bomb. Element 100 was named fermium in his honour.
Fermi, L., *Atoms in the Family*. 1954

Fernandel (Fernand Joseph Désiré Contandin) (1903–1971). French comedy actor. He is best known for his performances in such films as *Carnet de bal* (1937), *Coiffeur pour dames* (1953) and the series (1953 etc.) about Don Camillo, the ingenious and ingenuous Italian priest.
Rim, C., *Fernandel*. 1952

Fernel, Jean François (1497–1558). French physician and anatomist. An inn-keeper's son from Montdidier, Fernel pursued various studies in Paris in his early years, being particularly attracted to astronomy and astrology, philosophy and mathematics. One of his early works, the *Cosmotheoria*, contains a good estimate of the degree of meridian. For a career he took up medical studies, and received a licence to practise in 1530. He soon became one of the most sought-after physicians in France, especially after saving the life of the dauphin's mistress, Diane of Poitiers. His attempts to treat Francis I's syphilis without having recourse to mercury, however, met no success. Fernel published a number of works on the theory of medicine, which became influential texts for future teachers. His basic point of view was traditional and Galenic. His physiology depended upon a view that bodily conditions were the product of the interaction of humours, temperaments and innate spirits. He did however come to stress the importance of empiricism and personal observation, and to deny the role of astrological forces in disease. His *magnum opus*, the posthumously published *Universa Medicina*, contained some new observations, especially on the systole and diastole of the heart. He also gave a good description of appendicitis.
Sherrington, C. S., *Endeavour of Jean Fernel*. 1946

Ferranti, Sebastian Ziani de (1864–1930). English electrical engineer. He was born in Liverpool, and at 18 patented a dynamo; this was followed by a period of prolific designing of electrical plant and machinery. From a small generating station in Bond Street he supplied central London with electricity, and in 1890–91 he built and designed the equipment for the Deptford power station, which introduced the use of voltages far higher than previously possible. He was elected F.R.S. (1930). Succeeding members of the family have continued to direct the firm.

Ferrara, Andrea (fl. 1580). Italian swordsmith in Belluno. So famous were his blades that even in Scotland 16th- and 17th-century swordsmen spoke of their 'Andrea Ferraras'.

Ferrari, Enzo (1898–). Italian designer of racing cars. He was president of Ferrari Automobili SpA Sefac (1940–77).

Ferraro, Geraldine (1935–). American politician. Trained as a lawyer, she became a Democratic Member of the House of Representatives 1979–85, and became the first woman vice presidential candidate of a major party in 1984.

Ferrier, Kathleen Mary (1912–1953). English singer. First a telephonist, she did not take up singing professionally until she was 30, but from 1946, when she made her operatic debut in Britten's *Rape of Lucretia*, she was recognized as one of the greatest of modern contraltos. She died of cancer.
Rigby, C., *Kathleen Ferrier: A Biography*. 1956

Ferry, Jules François Camille (1832–1893). French politician. In 1870, during the Franco-Prussian War, he joined the 'Government of National Defence'; later he became a leader of the republican left and after several ministerial appointments was prime minister (1880–81 and 1883–85). As minister of public instruction he organized the modern educational system of France, based on free, compulsory, non-religious primary education. As prime minister he was also the principal builder of the French colonial empire in north Africa and Indo China. He was murdered by a religious fanatic.

Feuchtwanger, Leon (1884–1958). German author. Born at Munich, he sprang into European fame with his historical novels *The Ugly Duchess* (1923) and *Jew Süss* (1925), in which he employed a realistic technique unusual in books of his genre. He left Germany in 1933, was arrested in France by the Nazis in 1940, but made a daring escape to the U.S.A., which he then made his home.

Feuerbach, Ludwig Andreas (1804–1872). German philosopher. After studying theology at Heidelberg he was attracted by philosophy; but having gone to Berlin to work under Hegel he reacted against philosophical idealism. He argued that all religious feelings were projections of human needs or wish fulfilments, and that God was a deification of self. Later he tried to work out a philosophy (naturalistic materialism) which would be consonant with a programme of human betterment, and so in some measure he prepared the way for Marx. He coined the phrase 'Man is [ist] what he eats [isst]'. His *Essence of Christianity* (1841) was translated into English by George Eliot.

Kamenka, E., *The Philosophy of Ludwig Feuerbach*. 1970

Feydeau, Georges (1862–1921). French dramatist. His father, **Ernest Aimé Feydeau** (1821–1873), was the author of the novel *Fanny* (1858). He first won acclaim with his play *La Tailleur pour dames* (1887), which was followed, at approximately yearly intervals, by a series of light comedies, mostly in the tradition of bedroom farce, culminating with *La Dame de chez Maxim* (1899). Later with such plays as *La Main passe* (1904) he went deeper, to reveal the pathos and absurdity of marital relationships in disintegration. The fortune which he made from his plays he lost by speculation, and in later years his need for money spurred him to writing many one-act farces. Comparative oblivion followed his death, but recent reassessment, noting that he, like his characters, veered 'between extremes of happiness and depression', sees his plays as 'acted out fantasies'. Renewed interest in him was followed in 1966 by the revival in London of two of his plays *A Flea In Her Ear* and *The Birdwatcher*.

Feynman, Richard Philips (1918–). American physicist. Educated at MIT and Princeton, he worked on the 'Manhattan project' which produced the first atomic bomb, then taught at Cornell 1945–50 and the California Institute of Technology 1950– . He shared the 1965 Nobel Prize for Physics for his development of 'quantum electrodynamics'.

Fibonacci, Leonardo *see* **Leonardo da Pisa**

Fichte, Johann Gottlieb (1762–1814). German philosopher. He was an admirer of * Kant and after meeting him he wrote the *Kritik aller Offenbarung* (1792), which established his reputation in learned circles. He was appointed (1793) to a chair of philosophy at Jena, which he had to give up on being accused of atheism (1799). He continued to lecture in Berlin and in 1805 he was given a professorship at Erlangen. His *Addresses to the German Nation*, delivered in Berlin (1807–1808) after the humiliating defeat suffered by Prussia at the hands of Napoleon, did much to rekindle national spirit. However, it was an empire of reason based on a system of public education rather than military success that he saw as paving the way to revival. His philosophical system has been called 'transcendental realism': it propounds that all reality depends upon our personal, conscious egos and ultimately upon an entity which he calls the pure or infinite ego. In his ethics he stresses the importance of the individual conscience. His son **Immanuel Hermann von Fichte** (1797–1879) was also a well known moral philosopher and theist.

Field, John (1782–1837). Irish pianist and composer, born in Dublin. A child prodigy, he was a pupil of Clementi, for whom he worked (in his piano warehouse) for some years. After a tour with Clementi he made his name and settled in St Petersburg (1804) as a fashionable

teacher. It is as the creator of 'Nocturnes' (of which he left sixteen), a form later developed by Chopin, that he is best known.
Piggott, P., *The Life and Music of John Field.* 1973

Field, Marshall (1834–1906). American business man and philanthropist. He gradually built up the department store of Marshall Field & Co. (founded as such in 1881) and by virtue of his skill and innovations amassed a great fortune, much of which he devoted to educational purposes. He founded the Field Museum of Natural History and was the principal donor to the University of Chicago built on land which he gave in 1890.

His grandson **Marshall Field III** (1893–1956) abandoned commercial activities for newspaper publishing in 1936. He acquired the liberal New York paper *P.M.* and started the Chicago *Sun*, which supported Franklin D. Roosevelt.

Field, Winston Joseph (1904–1969). Rhodesian politician. He went to Southern Rhodesia from England in 1921 to grow tobacco, fought in World War II with the Rhodesian forces and took part in the D-day landings. He became a Rhodesian M.P. in 1957 and in 1958 became leader of the right-wing Dominion party. In 1962 he formed the Rhodesian Front, a coalition which, in December, achieved a great electoral victory after which he became prime minister. His demand for Rhodesian independence without any promise of African political advance produced a deadlock in his relations with Britain; he resigned in 1964 and was succeeded by Ian Smith.

Fielding, Henry (1707–1754). English novelist and dramatist. He was born in Somerest, and was educated at Eton and (having already produced a play in 1728) at Leyden University. In the next twenty years he wrote more than twenty plays, many of them dramatic burlesques of which the best known is *Tom Thumb* (1730). *Pasquin* (1736) and *The Historical Register for the Year 1736* (1737) were political and social satires; official reaction to them led to the passing of the Licensing Act. Thwarted in his dramatic aspirations, Fielding became a barrister (1740) and was a notable Westminster magistrate (1748–54). Meanwhile he had tried his hand at novels and political journalism. His novel *Joseph Andrews* (1742) was intended as a satire on Samuel Richardson's sentimental romance *Pamela* while *The History of the Life of the Late Mr Jonathan Wild the Great*, an ironic attack on the idea of popular heroes, describes the role of a gangleader in a manner curiously modern. This was the third volume of his *Miscellanies*, published in 1743, the first two containing essays, poems and plays. His greatest novel was *Tom Jones or the History of a Foundling* (1749). In it he carries out, in its most perfect form, his conception of the 'comic-epic' novel, so closely followed by Dickens. His last novel was *Amelia* (1751), concerned with the fortunes of one whom Dr Johnson described as 'the most pleasing heroine of all the romances'. Meanwhile Fielding had used his magistrate's position to wage war on the evils of society and his pamphlets show a wise and liberal mind. But his health was giving way: in 1754 he started on a voyage but died and was buried in Lisbon. His short trip is described in *The Journal of Voyage to Lisbon* (published in 1755). His sister **Sarah Fielding** (1710–1768) also wrote novels (e.g. *The Adventures of David Simple*, 1744) and translated from the Greek.
Rogers, P., *Henry Fielding: A Biography*. 1979

Fields, Dame Gracie (1898–1979). English musical star. Born in Rochdale, she first worked in a cotton mill; but after achieving her first important stage success in *Mr Tower of London* (1918–25) she became, through her wit, warmth of personality and fine singing voice, one of the most popular stars of music hall and musical comedy. She was created a DBE in 1979.

Fields, W. C. (William Claude Dukenfield) (1880–1946). American actor, born in Philadelphia. At the age of 11 he ran away from home and embarked upon a successful vaudeville juggling career. From 1915 to 1921 he had a comic juggling act of Broadway in the Ziegfeld Follies. In 1923 his first comic role on stage was in *Poppy* in which he created the grandiose fraud character type and his first important film was *Sally of the Sawdust* in 1925. By 1931 he was writing, directing and improvising action in Hollywood. Noted for his Mr Micawber in *David Copperfield* (1935) as well as for comic roles in such films as *The Bank Dick* (1940), *My Little Chickadee* (1940) and *Never Give a Sucker an Even Break* (1941).

He was one of America's greatest comedians. His style was pretension-pricking humour, characterized by wooden expression, nasal drawl etc. He played the cynic's role on and off the stage.

Fillmore, Millard (1800–1874). Thirteenth president of the U.S. (1850–1853). During twenty years in New York State and Federal politics he became a prominent member of the Whig party machine and, having been elected vice-president of the U.S. in 1848, he assumed the presidency on the death of Zachary Taylor (1850). He lost much support in the North because of his acceptance of a policy of compromise on the slavery issue and in 1852 was defeated for the Whig presidential nomination by General Winfield Scott; in the 1856 presidential election, fighting Republican and Democratic candidates, he carried only the State of Maryland.
Raybeck, R. J., *Millard Fillmore: Biography of a President*. 1959

Finsen, Niels Ryberg (1860–1904). Danish physician, of Icelandic parentage. He discovered that ultraviolet light has therapeutic properties, especially in the cure of *lupus vulgaris* (tuberculous infection of the skin) and smallpox, and in 1903 was awarded the Nobel Prize for Medicine.
de Kruif, P., *Men Against Death*. 1932

Firdausi (real name Abu'l Kasim Mansur) (*c.* 940–1020). Persian poet. For about 35 years he devoted himself to writing the *Shahnama* (*The Books of Kings*), an epic history, written in 60,000 rhyming couplets, of the Persian kings – both real and legendary – up to the Muslim conquest of 641. This work is the national epic of Iran and remains enormously popular. From it Matthew Arnold took the theme of his poem *Sohrab and Rustum*.

Firoz Shah (died 1388). Indian Moslem ruler, a most enlightened king of Delhi (from 1351). As well as building hospitals, mosques, educational establishments and public baths, he encouraged agriculture and commerce, and the poorest classes benefited from his reforms. Employment bureaux and dowries for the orphaned daughters of officers were further signs of his benevolent outlook.

Fischer, Bobby (Robert James) (1943–). U.S. chess champion, born in Chicago. He learned to play chess at the age of 6, and won the U.S. Junior Championship at 13. At 16 he left school and in 1958 became the youngest player ever to attain rank of grand master. In 1958 he also won the U.S. championship and in 1972 he defeated Boris Spassky to become World Chess Champion, the first American to hold the title officially. In 1975 he refused to meet Soviet challenger Anatoly Karpov and thus lost the crown by default. He is thought by some to be the finest player of all time.
Fischer, R. J., *My 60 Memorable Games*. 1969

Fischer, Emil Hermann (1852–1919). German chemist. He was one of the foremost organic chemists of the 19th century and elucidated the structure of many naturally-occurring substances, e.g. sugars, purines, amino-acids and polypeptides. This work opened the way for later investigations into the structure of the proteins. He was awarded the Nobel Prize for Chemistry (1902).

Fischer-Dieskau, Dietrich (1925–). German baritone. He had the largest repertoire of any singer of modern times, recording all of Schubert's 600 songs, appeared in operas of Mozart, Verdi and Wagner, and in sacred music by Bach and Brahms. He took up a second career as a conductor in the 1970s.

Fischer von Erlach, Johann Bernhard (*c.* 1656–1723). Austrian architect, trained in Italy, one of the great masters of Baroque. Oval cupolas and high transepts are characteristic of his heavily ornamented churches, of which the Collegiate Church at Salzburg (1694–1707) and that of St Charles Borromeo at Vienna (begun 1716) are among the finest. Among his secular buildings in Vienna are the Court Library, the Trautson Garden Palace and the town house of Prince Eugene (the last two having remarkable staircase halls).

Fish, Hamilton (1808–1893). American politician. Governor of New York (1849–50) and a U.S. senator (1851–57), he served in President Grant's Republican administration as a notably honest secretary of state (1869–77), and negotiated a settlement of the *Alabama* dispute with Britain (1871).

Fisher, Andrew (1862–1928). Australian Labor politician. He was born in Scotland, and worked as a coal miner from the age of 12 until 1885, when he emigrated to Queensland.

There he was a collier and engine-driver for a time before becoming a member of the Queensland legislature (1893) and of the federal House of Representatives (1901). He led the Labor party (from 1907), and was prime minister (1908–09, 1910–13 and 1914–15). In his last term, at the onset of World War I he promised aid to Great Britain 'to the last man and the last shilling'. He was Australian's high commissioner in London (1915–21).

Fisher, Geoffrey, Baron Fisher of Lambeth (1887–1972). English ecclesiastic. He was a school master (1911—32), when he was appointed Bishop of Chester. He became Bishop of London and dean of the chapels royal in 1939, and succeeded William Temple as Archbishop of Canterbury (1945–61). His church leadership was marked by a programme of reform of church law, and by increasing commitment to the Ecumenical movement. He was created a life peer on his retirement in 1961.

Fisher, Herbert Albert Laurens (1865–1940). English historian and politician. He was vice-chancellor of Sheffield University from 1912 until 1916, when he entered parliament as a Liberal. He became president of the Board of Education, where he was responsible for the 'Fisher Act' (1918), which extended the age of compulsory education to 14. For the last fifteen years of his life he was warden of New College, Oxford. His best known historical work is his *History of Europe* (3 volumes, 1935).

Ogg, D., *Herbert Fisher, 1865–1940*. 1947

Fisher, John (1469–1535). English churchman. He was a humanist and wanted to reform the church from within, but was strongly anti-Lutheran. As bishop of Rochester he was the only bishop who refused to support Henry VIII in getting his marriage with Catherine of Aragon annulled and in his subsequent quarrel with the pope. For refusing to take the oath required under the Act of Succession (1534), he was imprisoned with Sir Thomas More and in recognition Pope Paul III created him a cardinal. Incensed, Henry ordered him to be tried for denying the King's ecclesiastical supremacy, and he was hastily condemned and executed on Tower Hill.

Fisher, Irving (1867–1947). U.S. economist. Trained as a mathematician, he was Professor of Political Economy at Yale 1898–1935 and his influence on contemporary economic thinking was second only to J. M. * Keynes. He wrote *Mathematical Investigations in the Theory of Value and Prices* (1892), *Nature of Capital and Income* (1906) and *Theory of Interest* (1930) and developed the theory of index numbers as a measure of economic change and the modern theory of investment appraisal.

Fisher, John Arbuthnot Fisher, 1st Baron (1841–1920). English admiral. Famous as the sponsor of the *Dreadnought* battleships and for his collaboration (and quarrels) with Winston Churchill in World War I, he entered the navy in 1854 and was in service as early as the Crimean War. As first sea lord (1904–10) he made it his task to create a navy to meet the German threat. His great contribution to the problem was the abandonment of mixed armament, which was difficult to control, in favour of a single type of heavy gun. For these 12-in. monsters (which were followed later by 13.5-in. and even 15-in. guns), the new class of battleship named after the first *Dreadnought* was built and older ships were adapted with almost frantic speed. The fleet that dominated the seas in World War I may be said to be his creation.

Fitzgerald, Lord Edward (1763–1798). Irish nationalist. A younger son of the Duke of Leinster, he spent some years in America, and, while in Paris (1792), declared himself a supporter of the Revolution, renouncing his title. Back in his own country he joined the revolutionary United Irishmen; he again visited the continent to secure help and returned to prepare a rising. He was wounded in Dublin in May 1798, while resisting arrest, and died in the following month.

Pakenham, T., *The Year of Liberty*. 1969

Fitzgerald, Edward (1809–1883). English poet and translator, famous for his version of *The Rubáiyát* of Omar Khayyám. Educated at Cambridge, he lived quietly in Suffolk, and was the friend of Thackeray, Tennyson and Carlyle. He used his knowledge of Greek, Spanish and Persian to translate plays of Aeschylus, Sophocles and, with special success, those of the Spanish dramatist * Calderón. His method, which was to convey the spirit of the original rather than write an exact translation, was triumphantly displayed

in his *Rubáiyát*. Here the metre almost as much as the words suggests the languid, sensuous atmosphere of the Persian background. It appeared, anonymously, in 1859. After Swinburne and Rossetti praised it *The Rubáiyát* became phenomenally popular and much of that popularity remains.
Martin, R. B., *With Friends Possessed: A Life of Edward Fitzgerald*. 1985

Fitzgerald, Ella (1918–). American jazz and ballad singer, born in Virginia. She worked with orchestras and in cabaret from the 1930s but achieved her first wide acclaim in the 1950s as the star singer of Norman Granz's *Jazz at the Philharmonic* concerts. She recorded many albums, either solo or with jazz musicians such as Louis * Armstrong. Her voice was noted for its sweetness of tone and its range; her style has been widely copied.

Fitzgerald, F(rancis) Scott (1896–1940). American novelist, born in Minnesota. His novels vividly express the desperation and futility of a section of American life during the 'Jazz Age', his own term for the 1920s. His books include *The Beautiful and Damned* (1922), *The Great Gatsby* (1925), *All the Sad Young Men* (1926), *Tender Is The Night* (1934), his unfinished novel about Hollywood, *The Last Tycoon* (1941), and a posthumous collection, *The Crack-up* (1945). Despite popular success he fell into an inner despair and became an alcoholic. Several novels and films have been based on his life.
Miller, J., *F. Scott Fitzgerald*. 1966

Fitzgerald, George Francis (1851–1901). Irish physicist. Professor of natural philosophy at Dublin (1881–1901), he is best known for the hypothesis he put forward (1893) to explain the failure of the Michelson-Morley experiment to show the earth to be moving through the 'ether'. He suggested that because of its electrical structure all matter in motion contracts in the direction of motion. This 'Fitzgerald contraction' now forms an essential part of relativity theory. Fitzgerald was the first to suggest that the tail of a comet is formed by the pressure of solar radiation.

FitzGerald, Robert David (1902–). Australian poet, trained as a surveyor. He wrote lyrical verse in the 1920s while working as a surveyor, but in the late 1930s and after World War II he developed as a narrative poet with a strong leaning to philosophy. His best-known works are probably *Moonlight Acre* (1938), *Between Two Tides* (1952) and *Southmost Twelve* (1962).
FitzGerald, R. D., *Forty Years' Poems*. 1965

Fitzherbert, Maria Anne (née Smythe) (1756–1837). English morganatic wife. Twice widowed, she married George, Prince of Wales (later George IV), in 1785. This marriage, although canonically valid, contravened the Royal Marriages Act since the consent of the king had not been obtained; she was, moreover, a Roman Catholic. She continued to live with George until 1803 except for a short interval (1795) after he married Caroline of Brunswick.
Leslie, A., *Mrs Fitzherbert*. 1960

Fitzsimmons, Robert (Bob) Prometheus (1862–1917). English pugilist, born in Cornwall and brought up in New Zealand. He migrated to the U.S.A. (1890) and became world heavyweight boxing champion (1897), when he defeated Jim Corbett; in 1899 he lost the title to James J. Jeffries.
Odd, G., *The Fighting Blacksmith*. 1976

Flagstad, Kirsten Marie (1895–1962). Norwegian dramatic soprano. Both her parents, two brothers and a sister were all musicians. She herself made her operatic debut in 1913, but it was after she became known as a Wagnerian soprano in the early 1930s that she achieved her great success. She toured the world several times and made many recordings.

Flaherty, Robert Joseph (1884–1951). American film producer, of Irish descent. Explorations in the Canadian Arctic (1910–16) inspired *Nanook of the North* (1922) and so set the pattern of his career as the pioneer producer of documentary films; to their making he brought knowledge, sympathy and poetic imagination. Other successes include *Man of Aran* (1934), *Elephant Boy* (1935) and *The Louisiana Story* (1949).

Flambard, Rannulf (died 1128). One of the ablest administrators of the Norman kings of England. He entered royal service under William I and rose to greatness as justiciar and bishop of Durham (1089) under William II. Henry I deprived him of the wealth he had amassed by extortion and he was imprisoned in the Tower of London, but escaped to Normandy. He seems then to have become reconciled to Henry and returned to rule his see of Durham with his usual efficiency and rapacity.

Flammarion, Camille (1842–1925). French astronomer, whose many books and lectures did much to popularize the science. He erected a private observatory at Juvisy, near Paris, and made it available to amateur observers. His own work included the study of double and multiple stars and of the surface of the moon.

Flamsteed, John (1646–1719). English astronomer. He was appointed by Charles II the first Astronomer Royal at Greenwich Observatory (1674) and for over forty years he made stellar observations of an accuracy hitherto unknown; they were published with a catalogue of 300 stars (completed by Abraham Sharp) in *Historia Coelestis Britannica* (1712). In spite of meagre financial support Flamsteed made many improvements in observational technique but his conscientious methods led to long delays in responding to requests for observations and to consequent quarrels with Newton and Halley.

Flandin, Pierre Etienne (1889–1958). French politician. He was prime minister (1934–35) during the critical period of Hitler's rise to power, but as foreign minister (1936) was unable to secure British co-operation in resisting his military reoccupation of the Rhineland. During World War II he served in Pétain's government (1940–41).

Flaubert, Gustave (1821–1880). French novelist. Born at Rouen, the son of a prosperous physician, he went to Paris to study law, which he soon abandoned for writing (1844). Throughout adult life he was subject to hysterico-epileptic fits, the fear of which induced in him a profound pessimism. He was forced, in consequence, to leave Paris (1846) and thereafter lived quietly in the family home at Croisset, near Rouen. In 1846 he met the poetess Louis Colet and, though their love affair lasted till 1855, it seldom ran smoothly. It may have been syphilis, too, which induced the tendency, against which he struggled, to an excessive and almost frenzied romanticism of style. His masterpiece *Madame Bovary* (1857) was in fact a conscious effort, made on the advice of friends, to overcome this tendency by a deliberate exercise in realism. It was a carefully documented account of provincial middle-class dullness as background to a story of a woman's infidelity. Its (unsuccessful) prosecution for obscenity ensured the novel's success. For his next novel, *Salammbô* (1862), set in the highly-coloured background of Carthage and with a violent and romantic theme, he also applied the rigid discipline of exact documentation and even visited Tunis for the purpose, one of the very few occasions he left his country home. The partly autobiographical *L'Education sentimentale* (1869), though praised by critics, was not popular. It is lightened by the portrait of the heroine, Madame Arnoux, inspired by Madame Schlesinger, the object of Flaubert's early but unrequited love. *La Tentation de Saint Antoine* (1876) had begun in 1845 as a series of highly dramatized pen pictures of the temptations that might have beset the saint; the final version was a controlled and objective work. The unfinished novel *Bouvard et Pécuchet* was published posthumously in 1881. Flaubert also wrote some passionate and pessimistic short stories.

Stiegmuller, F., *Flaubert and Madame Bovary*. 1977

Flaxman, John (1755–1826). English sculptor. He was born in York and brought up in London. The influence of the classical revival is shown in the designs for pottery decoration which he did for Josiah Wedgwood (1775–85). He then spent seven years in Rome, to which period belong such ambitious works as *Cephalus and Aurora* (now at Port Sunlight). In 1793 his illustrations to Homer gave him an international reputation. Examples of statues by him are to be seen in Westminster Abbey and St Paul's Cathedral (e.g. *Nelson*). His work is remarkable for its purity of line and its cool style.

Constable, W. G., *Flaxman*. 1927

Flecker, James Elroy (1884–1915). English poet and dramatist. He joined the consular service, served in Constantinople, Smyrna and Beirut, and died in Switzerland of tuberculosis. His poetic works include *The Bridge of Fire* (1907), *Forty Two Poems* (1911) and, best known of all, *The Golden Journey to Samarkand* (1913). His play *Hassan* was produced with great success in London after his death.

Fleming, Sir Alexander (1881–1955). Scottish bacteriologist, the discoverer of penicillin. Born in Ayrshire, he studied at St Mary's Hospital, London, and while Hunterian professor at the Royal College of Surgeons (1919–28) devoted himself to the problem of discovering an effective antibiotic substance which would kill bacteria without harming cell tissue. In 1928 he discovered, accidentally, the germ-killing qualities of the mould *penicillium notatum*, but it was only under the pressure of war needs that a technique was worked out for large-scale manufacture. He was professor of bacteriology at London University (1928–48), was elected F.R.S. in 1943 and was president of the Society for Microbiology (1945–55). He shared the 1945 Nobel Prize for Medicine with * Florey and * Chain.

Macfarlane, R. G., *Alexander Fleming – the Man and the Myth*. 1984

Fleming, Ian Lancaster (1908–1963). British writer, creator of James Bond. Educated at Eton and abroad, he was a journalist and worked in the City of London before being engaged in naval intelligence in World War II. In 1953 he published *Casino Royale*, the first of his spy stories, featuring James Bond as hero and with a secret-service background and a mixture of heroic adventure, sex, mystery, and sadism. The James Bond series has sold by the million: among the best known books are *Moonraker, Dr No, From Russia With Love, Diamonds Are Forever*. Several have achieved even greater popularity as films, including the sensational *Goldfinger*, released just after his death.

His brother, **Peter Fleming** (1907–1971), achieved early success with his travel books *Brazilian Adventure* (1933), *News From Tartary* (1936); later works include a novel, *The Sixth Column* (1951), and *Invasion 1940* (1957) and *The Siege of Peking* (1959). He married the actress Celia Johnson.

Amis, K., *The James Bond Dossier*. 1965

Fleming, Sir (John) Ambrose (1849–1945). English physicist. His investigations into the 'Edison effect' led to his most important work, the development of the thermionic valve and its application to radio technology. He also did important work on the electrical resistance of materials at low temperatures, and on various forms of electric lamp. He was professor of electrical engineering at London University (1885–1926), received the Hughes Medal of the Royal Society in 1910 and was knighted in 1929.

Fletcher, John (1579–1625). English poet and dramatist, whose association with Francis *Beaumont produced one of the most interesting collaborations in literary history. He was born in Rye, son of a vicar who eventually became bishop of London. After studying at Cambridge University, he may have been an actor when (from about 1606) he began writing plays. Over fifty have survived of which Fletcher was at least part-author: the best known are those he wrote with Beaumont, e.g. *The Knight of the Burning Pestle* (1609), *Philaster* (1611) and *The Maid's Tragedy* (1611). He probably wrote about ten plays with Philip * Massinger (e.g. *The False One* and *The Spanish Curate*) and is supposed to have collaborated briefly with * Shakespeare, notably on *Henry VIII*. Works by Fletcher alone include *The Faithful Shepherdess, Valentinian, The Wild Goose Chase* and *The Island Princess*. He died of the plague.

Fleury, André Hercule de (1653–1743). French statesman. Having been almoner to Louis XIV and created bishop of Fréjus, he became (1726) a cardinal and the chief adviser of Louis XV, whose tutor he had been. Until his death he was virtually ruler of France. His great service was to restore order to the French economy, which had been practically ruined under Louis XIV. He consistently strove to maintain peace in Europe and ensured that France played a minimal part in the War of Polish Succession. He was, however, pushed by court intrigue into the War of the Austrian Succession (1741).

Flexner, Simon (1863–1946). American pathologist. While in the Philippines (1900) he established the bacillus that bears his name and causes one form of dysentery. He developed (1907) a serum to cure spinal meningitis, and showed (1909) that poliomyelitis is caused by a virus. He was director of the Rockefeller Institute for Medical Reserch, New York (1920–35).

Flinders, Matthew (1774–1814). English navigator who made one of the earliest and most complete investigations of the Australian coasts. He joined the navy in 1790, learning his seamanship under the notorious Captain * Bligh. He went to Australia in 1795 and on one of several voyages discovered the strait – named after George Bass, a surgeon who accompanied him – between Tasmania and the mainland. Almost immediately after his return to England (1800) he was appointed to command a scientific expedition (1801–03) which carefully mapped the south-west coast of Australia and the Great Barrier Reef. On the return voyage he was wrecked but regained Port Jackson after a voyage of 750 miles in a six-oared cutter. Several Australian places are named after him, e.g. the Flinders range (South Australia).

Flitcroft, Henry (1697–1769). English architect in the Palladian style. Originally a joiner, he advanced successfully under the patronage of Lord * Burlington. He served in the Board of Works, and was its controller from 1758. He built many churches and houses including St Giles-in-the-Fields and Chatham House in London, and the country mansions of Woburn Abbey and Wentworth Wodehouse, Yorkshire.

Flood, Henry (1732–1791). Anglo-Irish politician and orator. He entered the Irish parliament in 1759, and his powers as an outstanding orator brought him to prominence. He became leader of a reform group seeking ultimate independence. In 1775 he became vice-treasurer of Ireland under the British Viceroy. In 1779 he relinquished this post and returned to his efforts for legislative autonomy; in this (achieved 1782) he worked with Henry Grattan. He challenged Grattan's leadership of the patriotic reform movement in 1783, but his attempt to reform the Irish parliament failed in 1784, and he lost much of his support.

Flores, Juan José (1800–1864). First president of Ecuador. He rose to be a general under * Bolivar in the war of independence against the Spanish. When Greater Colombia began to disintegrate Flores led the secession of Ecuador and became its president (1830). He was a conservative and clericalist but came to terms with the liberals by arranging that their leader, Rocafuerte, should become president (1835), while he himself became head of the army. Flores was again president from 1839, but his constitutional amendment (1843) extending the presidential term to eight years was regarded as treacherous and he agreed to go into pensioned exile (1848). He regained power in 1860.

Florey, Howard Walter, Baron Florey (1898–1968). Australian pathologist. He was professor of pathology at Sheffield (1931–35) and then at Oxford (1935–68). During World War II, with Dr E. B. * Chain, he synthesized penicillin and developed techniques for its large-scale manufacture. He shared the 1945 Nobel Prize for Medicine with Chain and Sir Alexander * Fleming, became president of the Royal Society 1960–65 and received the O.M. (1965).

Fludd, Robert (1574–1637). English physician and philosopher. The son of a well-to-do family with court connexions, he studied at St John's College, Oxford. He then toured Europe, mainly pursuing medical studies. He was elected a fellow of the Royal College of Physicians in 1609, and built up a lucrative London practice. In middle age, he began to set down on paper a full system of natural philosophy, in which he was dismissive of the authority of Aristotle, Galen and the universities. Fludd himself sought to build up a new synthesis based on a mixture of personal observation, the truths of Scripture, and Neo-Platonic and Hermetic writings. He thought the universe was suffused with powers of sympathy and antipathy. Man was the microcosm. He was filled with spirit from the Divine principle, the Sun. Just as the earth circled around the sun, so in man, blood circulated round the body. Fludd denied the validity of Aristotle's four elements; he believed the bible revealed the three original elements to be light, darkness and water. Heat and cold were derivatives of light and dark.

Fludd stands at the cross-roads between magic and science. He believed in an occult universe, yet supported most of the new scientific discoveries of his day, seeing in them proof of his own magical explanations. Thus, for instance, Gilbert's magnetic researches proved the truth of universal attraction and repulsion.

Debus, A., *The Chemical Dream of the Renaissance*. 1968

Foch, Ferdinand (1851–1929). Marshal of France. Allied commander-in-chief in the late stages of World War I, he entered the army (1869) but saw no service in the Franco-Prussian War; the turning point in his career came when he was an instructor (1894–99) at the École de Guerre. In this post, through his book *Principles and Conduct of War* (1899), and later as the school's director (1907–11), he was able to impact his strategic doctrines and his views on the importance of the offensive to a whole generation of officers and military thinkers.

At the outbreak of World War I, as commander of the 9th Army he played a notable part in the victory of the Marne. In the next two years his main task lay in co-ordinating the French, British and Belgian roles on the Allied left flank. He retired with* Joffre (1916) but after the failure of Nivelle's offensive he became chief of staff (1917). When the Germans broke through (March 1918) the necessity for a unified Allied command was at last recognized and Foch was appointed generalissimo. His policy of husbanding his reserves until the enemy had fought to a standstill and then using them for a series of devastating attacks swept the Allied armies forward to their final victory. He accepted the German surrender in a railway carriage at Compiègne (November 1918). He subsequently supervised the carrying out of the military clauses of the peace treaty.
Marshall-Cornwall, J., *Foch*. 1972

Fokine, Michael (1880–1942). Russian dancer and choreographer. One of the founders of modern ballet, Isadora Duncan inspired him to free himself from the rigid classical discipline of the Imperial Ballet to create ballets in which dancing, music and scenery are combined in a related whole. *Le Cygne* (*The Dying Swan*, 1905) and *Chopiniana* (later known as *Les Sylphides*, 1906) were early works. His great period was with Diaghilev in Paris (from 1909) when he created *Petrushka, Scheherazade, The Firebird* and *Le Spectre de la rose*. He left Russia for France at the outbreak of the Revolution and during World War II moved to the U.S.
Beaumont, C. W., *Fokine and His Ballets*. 1935

Fokker, Anthony Herman Gerard (1890–1939). Dutch aircraft designer, born in Java. He set up a factory in Germany (1912) and it was Fokker fighters, with their forward-firing machine gun, that gave the Germans their air superiority in the early part of World War I. He also designed effective biplane and triplane bombers. After the war Fokker concentrated mainly on civil aircraft built in Holland. In 1924 he set up a factory in the U.S. and became an American citizen. He pioneered the use of light-weight metal fuselages in aircraft. He wrote an autobiography, *The Flying Dutchman* (1931).

Fontanne, Lynn (1887–1983). American actress, born in London. She had already made her name with such well known English players as Lewis Waller, Herbert Tree and Lena Ashwell before going to America. She married (1913) Alfred* Lunt, with whom her later successes were achieved.

Fontenelle, Bernard de Bouyer (1657–1757). French philosopher and scientist. He strongly championed the cause of the Moderns in the Battle of the Books, finding the science of the Greeks and the Scholastics nothing but empty words. He produced some original mathematical writings, trying to develop a general theory of the calculus. He became a great celebrity, and was accorded extensive public honours; elected to the French Academy in 1691, he became its perpetual secretary in 1699. For forty years he edited the publications of the Academy. He also took it upon himself to deliver lengthy funeral eulogies upon deceased French scientists, which expounded a view of the importance of science as true objective knowledge in an Enlightenment society, and subtly reinforced Cartesianism against English Newtonian science.

His most lasting work is the *Entretiens sur la Pluralité des Mondes* (1687). This work is a series of dialogues which popularize, for a general, educated audience, the superiority of modern, Copernican and Cartesian, systems of the Universe over those traditionally accepted. Fontenelle was even prepared to accept that there might be life on other systems in the Universe – evidence of his own mild religious heterodoxy.

Fonteyn, Dame Margot (née Margaret Hookham) (1919–). English ballerina. She made her debut (1934) with the Sadler's Wells Ballet and has subsequently been prima ballerina of the Royal Ballet, establishing a reputation as one of the most accomplished and sensitive interpreters of classical ballet. Her regular partner after his arrival in the West was Rudolf* Nureyev. In 1955 she married Dr Roberto Arias, then ambassador of Panama in London. She was created a D.B.E.

in 1956. She was Director of the Royal Academy for Dancing from 1954.
Money, K., *Fonteyn: The Making of a Legend.* 1973

Foot, Michael (1913–). British Labour politician. Member of a notable Cornish political family, he was educated at Oxford became a prolific polemical journalist, was MP 1945–55 and 1960– ; editor of *Tribune* (1948–52 and 1955–60) and biographer of Aneurin * Bevan. He was secretary of state for employment (1974–79), succeeding James * Callaghan as leader of the Labour party 1980–83.

Forbes-Robertson, Sir Johnston (1853–1937). English actor. Good looks, grace of movement and, above all, a beautiful speaking voice were amongst the gifts which helped to give him such prolonged success. In 1882 he became one of the leading Shakespearian actors in Irving's famous Lyceum company. When he went into management of his own he played with Mrs Patrick Campbell and achieved his greatest triumph with his Hamlet (1897), remembered by a generation of playgoers as the finest portrayal of the part. In later life he gained a new reputation and great financial success in a religious drama, *The Passing of the Third Floor Back* (1909). He married the actress Gertrude Elliot; his daughter Jean continued the stage tradition.

Ford, Ford Madox (formerly Ford Madox Hueffer) (1870–1939). English novelist, critic and poet. A grandson of the Pre-Raphaelite painter Ford Madox Brown, he helped Joseph Conrad to master English and collaborated with him in *The Inheritors* and *Romance*. The best known of Ford's sixty books are the quartet of novels dealing with the moral crisis of World War I, *Some Do Not, No More Parades, A Man Could Stand Up* and *The Last Post* (1924–28). He wrote studies of Henry James and Conrad and many critical essays and poems.
MacShane, F., *Life and Work of Ford Madox Ford.* 1965

Ford, Gerald Rudolph (1913–). U.S. Republican politician, born in Omaha, Nebraska. Originally Leslie Lynch King, he was renamed after his stepfather when his mother remarried. Educated at the University of Michigan and Yale Law School, he was a notable university footballer, graduated in law and served in the U.S. Navy 1942–46, practising law in Grand Rapids, Michigan 1946–49. As a Member of the U.S. House of Representatives 1949–73, he was a conservative moderate and internationalist. He sat on the Warren Commission of enquiry into the assassination of President Kennedy 1963–64 and became Minority Leader in the House of Representatives 1965–73. On the resignation of Spiro Agnew in 1973, President *Nixon used the provisions of the 25th Amendment of the U.S. Constitution for the first time to nominate Ford as 40th Vice-President. When Nixon resigned in 1974, Ford automatically succeeded him as 38th President of the U.S., nominating Nelson * Rockefeller as his Vice-President. The pardon he granted to Nixon was intended to bring a rapid end to the Watergate trauma, but aroused much controversy. He retained Henry * Kissinger as Secretary of State and continued Nixon's foreign policies. He survived two assassination attempts in 1975. In 1976 he sought election in his own right but was defeated by Jimmy * Carter.

Ford, Henry (1863–1947). American motor manufacturer. Born in Michigan, the son of an Irish immigrant farmer, he had already set up a machine shop on his father's farm and had constructed a gas engine and other appliances when he joined the Edison company in Detroit (1890). While still there he built his first petrol-driven car, capable of 25 m.p.h. In 1899 he established the Detroit Automobile Company which became (1903) the Ford Motor Company. The famous 'T' model (1909), the first mass-produced car, inaugurated the era of 'motoring for the million'. Ultimately more than 15,000,000 'flivvers' or 'tin Lizzies', as they were affectionately called, were produced when, in 1928, he turned to a new model, 'A', under the pressure of growing competition. Ford abominated banks and fought hard to keep his company free from their control; he was equally opposed to trade unions (though he paid high wages). In 1915 he chartered a 'peace ship' which he took to Europe with the fantastic idea of bringing World War I to a negotiated end. When America entered the war he became an important producer of munitions, motor transport and aircraft, and a similar part was played by the Ford factories in World War II. Ford himself was an isolationist. He set up (1936) the Ford

Foundation to stimulate scientific and industrial research. His son, **Edsel Ford** (1893–1943), and his grandson, a second **Henry Ford** (1917–), followed him as presidents to the firm.

Rae, J. B., *Henry Ford*. 1969

Ford, John (1586–*c*. 1640). English dramatist. Little is known of his life and many of his plays have been lost. In some of his best known works, e.g. *'Tis Pity She's a Whore* (*c*. 1626), a tragedy of incestuous passion, he explores some of the more devious paths of sexual psychology; in others he was evidently influenced by the publication (1621) of Burton's *Anatomie of Melancholie* to analyse the effects of despair. *Perkin Warbeck* (1634) is an example of his skill with a chronicle play. He also collaborated with Dekker, Rowley and Webster.

Ford, John (Sean O'Fearn) (1895–1974). American film director. Among his films were *The Informer* (1935), concerned with the Irish 'troubles', *Stage-Coach* (1939), *Wagonmaster* (1950), *The Searchers* (1956), and *The Man Who Shot Liberty Valance* (1962). *The Grapes of Wrath* (1940) and *Long Voyage Home* (1940) etc. dealt with serious themes, and amongst his several comedies was *Quiet Man*. Style and sense of period were among the merits which won him many awards.

McBride, J. and Wilmington, M., *John Ford*. 1975

Forester, Cecil Scott (1899–1966). English novelist. Best known for his stories of the adventures of Captain Horatio Hornblower, R. N., in the Napoleonic Wars, his first success was the novel *Payment Deferred* (1926), later dramatized. Among his other writings are historical biographies, e.g. of Louis XIV and Nelson, and the screenplay for the film *The African Queen*.

Forrest, Edwin (1806–1872). American actor. A notable Shakespearian, at his best in tragic parts such as Lear or Othello, he performed with great success in New York and in London (1836–37). His rivalry with W. C.* Macready led to a riot at the Astor Place Opera House, New York (1849), in which twenty people were killed.

Forrest, John Forrest, 1st Baron (1847–1918). Australian explorer and Liberal politician. He was born in Western Australia and as a member of its survey department explored vast areas of its interior. When responsible government was introduced, he was its first premier (1890–1901). He was a federal M.P. (1901–18) and served as treasurer of Australia (1905–07, 1909–10, 1913–14 and 1917–18). He was created the first Australian peer (1918). He described his journeyings in, e.g., *Exploration in Western Australia* (1876).

Forrest, Nathan Bedford (1821–1877). American soldier. Born in poverty in Tennessee, he made a fortune nd on the outbreak of the Civil War joined the Confederate army (1861). He raised a cavalry regiment and won fame for his daring, especially in raiding enemy communications in Tennessee, Mississippi and Alabama. After the war he was one of the founders of the Ku Klux Klan.

Forster, Edward Morgan (1879–1970). English writer. Educated at Tonbridge School (the 'Sawston' of two of his novels) and at King's College, Cambridge, he spent much of the years 1904–07 in Italy and Greece and he came to contrast the truth and passion of the Mediterranean world with conventional English life. During this time he wrote his first two novels, *Where Angels Fear to Tread* (1905) and *The Longest Journey* (1907), both of them remarkable for their sensitive analysis of the delicate balance in human relationships. The novel *A Room With A View* appeared in 1908 and *Howards End* in 1910, the latter's theme being the twofold struggle in which the middle-class characters were engaged, the outer one within the class structure and the inner one between the passionate and conventional sides of their natures. These and the collection of short stories, *The Celestial Omnibus* (1911), received critical rather than popular acclaim. He spent the years immediately preceding World War I in India and was again there in 1921 as secretary to the Maharajah of Dewas. While there he collected material for his final novel *A Passage to India* (1924), in which he faces sympathetically the difficulty of overcoming the artificial obstacles of race, class and nationality between individuals. Now at last came wider recognition; the book was awarded the Femina Vie Heureuse and James Tait Black Prizes, and henceforth Forster was regarded as a major figure in English literature. He also wrote three

volumes of essays, *Aspects of the Novel* (1927). *Abinger Harvest* (1936) and *Two Cheers for Democracy* (1951), and the libretto for Benjamin Britten's opera *Billy Budd* (1953). He was a resident fellow of King's College, Cambridge from 1927. He was made a C.H. in 1953 and O.M. in 1968. After his death his homosexuality was freely discussed and entered as a factor into critical revaluation; an early 'secret' novel, *Maurice*, on the theme, was published.
Kirkpatrick, B. J., *A Bibliography of Forster*. 1965

Forster, John (1812–1876). English man of letters. Best known as the friend and biographer of Charles * Dickens (3 volumes, 1872–74), he was early engaged in political journalism, succeeded Dickens as editor of the *Daily News*, and (1847–56) edited the *Examiner*. He wrote several historical studies of the struggle between Charles I and parliament, and biographies, in addition to that of Dickens, of Goldsmith, Landor and (unfinished) of Swift.
Renton, R., *John Forster and His Friendships*. 1912

Fortescue, Sir John William (1859–1933). English military writer, famous for his *History of the British Army* (13 volumes, 1899–1933). He was librarian at Windsor Castle (1905–26).

Foster, (Myles) **Birket** (1825–1899). English artist. In his own time he was as well known for his woodcuts and illustrations as for his paintings, but revived interest is concerned with his watercolours, mainly of rural scenes.

Foster, Stephen Collins (1826–1864). American song writer. Largely self-taught, he wrote about 200 songs (*Old Folks at Home, My Old Kentucky Home, De Camptown Races* etc.), performed and made famous by touring minstrel troupes. He had no financial acumen, and poverty and alcoholism led to his death in hospital.
Howard, J. T., *Stephen Foster, America's Troubadour*. 1953

Foucault, Jean Bernard Léon (1819–1868). French physicist. He demonstrated (1851), by means of a pendulum, the rotation of the earth, and invented (1852) the gyroscope. Between 1849 and 1862 he perfected a laboratory method of measuring the velocity of light using a rotating mirror. He also devised highly accurate methods of testing lenses for spherical and chromatic aberration.

Foucault, Michel (1926–1984). French philosopher. Professor of the History of Systems of Thought at the Collège de France 1970–84, he wrote extensively about the use of 'the conventional wisdom' as an instrument of power against cultural deviation e.g. in the treatment of insanity, criminality, sexuality (*Madness and Civilization* 1961, *Discipline and Punishment* 1975, *History of Sexuality* 1976–84).

Fouché, Joseph, Duke of Otranto (1759?–1820). French minister of police. He played a devious part in the politics of the Revolution, in the course of which he checked a rising in the Vendée and suppressed a revolt in Lyons with extreme ferocity. He became (1799) minister of police under the Directory and then under Napoleon Bonaparte, whom he had helped to power. While Napoleon was absent with his armies, Fouché maintained order at home with ruthless efficiency and in the course of his work amassed so many private secrets that he became a source of universal terror. Wealth and honours were showered upon him but by 1810 he was already intriguing with the royalist exiles as a precaution against Napoleon's downfall. He succeeded briefly in retaining office under the restored Bourbons (1815) but was exiled as a regicide and lived in exile at Trieste until his death.

Fouquier-Tinville, Antoine Quentin (1746–1795). French politician. Notorious for the ferocity with which he carried out his duties as public prosecutor during the Revolution, after the ending of the Terror he himself was executed.

Fourcroy, Antoine François de (1755–1809). French chemist. His father was a poor apothecary, who started his son in life as a copying clerk. Through the patronage of Vicq D'Azyr, young Fourcroy was enabled to study medicine. He became a doctor in 1780 and took to lecturing privately and at the Jardin du Roi, becoming professor there in 1784. He had a distinguished career in public life, becoming a member of the National Convention in 1793, a Professor at the Ecole Polytechnique in 1795, a Consul in 1801 and Minister for Public Instruction from 1802–08. He played a large part in the introduction of the metric system of weights and measures.

As a chemist, Fourcroy gave support to the oxygen chemistry of * Lavoisier. Most of his own research was on the chemical composition of various constituents of animal bodies. He analysed the composition of gall and kidney stones, trying to find effective solvents for them. He published extensive analyses of mineral waters and their medicinal properties. He carried out experiments on the constituents of muscle fibre, finding a high nitrogen content. He also pursued researches into herbal medicines, conducting analyses of cinchona bark.
Smeaton, W. A., *Fourcroy*. 1962

Fourier, François Marie Charles (1772–1837). French socialist reformer. He was the son of a prosperous draper of Besançon and spent much of his early life as a commercial traveller in Holland and Germany. Gradually he became convinced of the evils of a competitive society and the harm done to the individual by the suppression of natural passions by 'civilisation'. His ideas and theories, set out in three major books (1808–29), attracted little attention during his lifetime, except among his disciples, and he died poor and little known. His interests ranged over a wide religious and psychological field, but on the practical side he proposed that society should be based on life in communities (*phalanges*) of about 1800 people – enough to include most varieties of talent and temperament – in communal buildings, and entirely self-sufficient; each man would be allowed to change his occupation when he wished, and would be paid a minimum wage; the conventional idea of marriage was to be abandoned. Colonies set up on these lines in France rapidly failed; those established (notably by * Greeley) in the U.S.A. flourished for a time and then died out.
Maublanc, R., *Charles Fourier*. 1930

Fourier, Jean Baptiste Joseph (1768–1830). French mathematician. The son of a tailor, Fourier studied at a military school, and then subsequently taught there. During the Revolution, he became prominent in local politics. In 1795 he was appointed teacher at the Ecole Polytechnique. On Napoleon's fall he conformed to the new regime of Louis XVIII, and was rewarded in 1822 with the prestigious position of Perpetual Secretary to the Academy of Sciences. Fourier was a fertile thinker in the fields of mathematics and physics. He produced novel techniques in his theory of the functions of the real variable, which served as the starting point for more rigorous formulations from Riemann and Cantor. But his most important work lay in developing a mathematical approach to heat. Through much of the eighteenth century heat had been studied as part of chemistry. French science at the beginning of the nineteenth became far more concerned with the physics of heat. Fourier's contribution was to produce a series of equations to quantifying and theorizing about heat diffusion and heat flow. He also interested himself in problems of probability and the use of statistics.
Grattan-Guinness, I., and Ravetz, J., *Joseph Fourier 1768–1830*.

Fowler, Henry Watson (1858–1893) and **Francis George** (1871–1918). English lexicographers. They wrote *The King's English* (1906) and compiled the *Concise Oxford Dictionary* (1911–14). After his brother's death Francis Fowler wrote the *Dictionary of Modern English Usage* (published 1926).

Fowler, Sir John, 1st Bart. (1817–1898). British civil engineer, noted as the builder of the Firth of Forth railway bridge (1890), for which achievement he was made a baronet. He had previously worked for a number of small railway companies, designing track systems, and for the London Metropolitan Railway whose underground system he helped to build, and whose locomotives ('Fowler's Ghosts') he designed. He became president of the Insitution of Civil Engineers in 1866.

Fox, Charles James (1749–1806). English Whig politician. The son of Henry Fox, 1st Baron Holland, he first entered the Commons at the age of 19 and served almost continuously until his death. He was junior lord of the Treasury under Lord North (1770–74) until George III dismissed him because he opposed coercive measures against the American colonies. In opposition he campaigned violently for triennial parliaments and relief from legal disabilities for Roman Catholics and dissenters; he also attacked the royal influence in parliament. When North fell (1782), Fox became secretary of state under Rockingham, whose death a few months later caused him to resign. He now came to terms with North but the coalition ended when George III by personal intervention killed Fox's India Bill (1783). During the first years of William Pitt's ministry, which immediately followed, Fox led the opposition. He moved the impeachment of Warren Hastings (1788), strongly supported the French Revolution (breaking off his cherished friendship with Edmund Burke over this issue) and consistently opposed Pitt's foreign policy which he considered unduly sympathetic to European despotism. He especially denounced, too, Pitt's wartime suspension of habeas corpus (1794). In 1795 Fox married his mistress, Mrs Armistead, and after 1797 was seldom seen in parliament, but he returned in 1803 to try and prevent the rupture of the Peace of Amiens (1802) with France. On Pitt's death he became foreign secretary in the 'All-the-Talents' administration of Grenville (1806) but died of dropsy a few months later when he was about to introduce a bill for the abolition of the slave trade (eventually secured in 1807). Fox was a close friend of the Prince of Wales (later George IV), but as it became clear that the prince's opposition to his father was personal rather than political the intimacy lessened. Fox's fondness for drink and gambling (in 1793 his friends paid £70,000 to provide for him and clear his debts) won him a reputation which weakened his authority as a national leader. But he was a generous-minded and much loved friend and the principles he stood for were those of liberty – political and individual – tolerance and justice. * Burke characterised him as 'the greatest debater the world ever saw'.

Hobhouse, C., *Fox*. 1948

Fox, George (1624–1691). English religious leader. Founder of the Society of Friends ('Quakers'), he was the son of a weaver of Fenny Drayton, Leicestershire. At the age of 19 he heard an 'inner voice' and became an itinerant preacher. He disliked the outward ceremony of religion (for him the 'church' was the worshippers, not the building) and he often interrupted services to preach his own belief that everyone has direct access to God. He rejected the Calvinist doctrine that only the elect could escape predestined damnation: salvation, he held, was open to all who heard the inner voice of God. He believed in pacifism and was opposed to capital punishment. In about 1650 he founded the Society of Friends. He and his followers were constantly persecuted and Fox was imprisoned, at various times, for a total of six years. He and his supporters travelled widely in North America, the West Indies and the Continent; by 1660 their numbers had grown to 60,000. He married (1669) Margaret Fell, a widow of a judge at whose house the Friends had met as early as 1652. He was prolific writer and kept a valuable *Journal*.

Wildes, H. E., *The Voice of the Lord*. 1965

Foxe, John (1516–1587). English Protestant clergyman. Author of the book celebrated as *Foxe's Book of Martyrs*, this work, completed (in Latin) in 1559 and translated in 1563, contains (with much else) a prejudiced but valuable account of the persecution of Protestants under Mary I. He subscribed to and enhanced the belief that the English were 'an elect nation'. During Mary's reign Foxe had lived in Strasbourg and Basle but returned to England after Elizabeth's accession.

Mozley, T. F., *John Foxe and His Book*. 1948

Fracastoro, Girolamo (1477–1553). Italian scientist and poet. Born into a patrician Veronese family. Fracastoro studied philosophy and medicine at Padua University; from 1502 he taught medicine at Padua and perhaps served as a medical man in the Venetian army. He spent the bulk of his life cultivating his medical and general cultural interests with the literati of the day in Verona or on his estates near Monte Baldo. His interests ranged widely, from science to poetry, taking in mathematics, geography and astronomy. He is mainly famous for two books, one a poem on syphilis, and the other a book on contagion.

Fragonard, Jean Honoré (1732–1806). French painter and engraver. A master of the Rococo, a pupil of Chardin and especially of Boucher, he went to Italy having won the Prix de Rome. On his return he was commissioned to design a tapestry by Louis XV and subsequently became famous for his delicate pictures of the gay and graceful world in which he moved. *The Swing* (*c*. 1766), in the Wallace Collection, London, is characteristic of his style. He is ranked as one of the major painters of the 18th century.

Wildenstein, G., *The Paintings of Fragonard*. 1960

France, Anatole (Anatole François Thibault) (1844–1924). French writer. His father was a

Paris bookseller and he early devoted himself to writing. His philosophy, as expounded in, e.g. *Le Jardin d'Epicure* (1895), was tolerant and undogmatic – a person is born a believer or not, as he is born blond or brunette; beliefs are only personal opinions. Similar views appear in *La Rôtisserie de la Reine Pédauque* (1893), *Le Lys rouge* (1894), *Histoire comique* (1903) and *La Révolte des anges* (1914). Few writers display a more orderly arrangement of thought or have a clearer or simpler style. His earlier novels, e.g. *Le Crime de Sylvestre Bonnard* (1881), *Le Livre de mon ami* (1885) and *Thaïs* (1890), already show his tendency to criticize and ridicule what would be called today the 'establishment', and after his liaison with Madame de Caillavet his criticism became more biting. He was a strong partisan of Dreyfus and his sympathies are clearly expressed in *L'Affaire Crainquebille* (1902) and *L'Île des Pingouins* (1908), possibly the greatest of his works. He won the Nobel Prize for Literature in 1921.

Francesca, Piero della *see* **Piero della Francesca**

Francesca da Rimini (died 1285?). Heroine of one of the world's famous love stories. She was the daughter of the Lord of Ravenna, on Italy's Adriatic coast, and was given in marriage, in return for military services, to a son, said to be lame and ill-favoured, of Malatesta, Lord of Rimini. She fell in love with her brother-in-law, Paolo, and on discovery both were put to death by her husband. Dante relates a conversation with her in the *Inferno* and the story has been told by Leigh Hunt and other writers.

Francis I (1494–1547). King of France (from 1515). Descended from a younger branch of the Valois dynasty, he married (1514) the daughter of Louis XII, whom he succeeded in the following year. In 1519 despite heavy bribes he failed to secure election as Holy Roman Emperor. This began the long rivalry with the successful candidate, * Charles V, which was the central feature of his reign. At the Field of the Cloth of Gold (1520) he tried unsuccessfully to win the support of Henry VIII of England. In 1525 he was captured by imperial troops at Pavia in Italy and had to submit to a humiliating treaty. Fighting was resumed at intervals throughout the reign, but when peace was finally secured (1544) with the aid of the Sultan of Turkey little was gained by either side. Francis also began the persecution of Protestants which was to be an unhappy feature of French history for the succeeding century. On the positive side he established the nucleus of an efficient centralized administration; it was with his encouragement that * Cartier crossed the Atlantic and claimed the gulf of the St Lawrence for France. He was also a notable patron of the arts; during his reign the palace at Fontainebleau and the château of Chambord were altered or rebuilt; he summoned * Leonardo da Vinci to live at Amboise.

Seward, D., *Prince of the Renaissance: Life of François I*. 1973

Francis I (1708–1765). Holy Roman Emperor (from 1745). He succeeded his father as Duke of Lorraine (1729), but after the War of the Polish Succession he gave up Lorraine to Louis XV's father-in-law, Stanislas Leszcznski, ex-king of Poland, and accepted instead (1737) the grand duchy of Tuscany. In 1736 he married * Maria Theresa of Austria and in 1745 was elected emperor.

Francis II (1544–1560). King of France (from 1559). The son of Henry II and Catherine de' Medici, he married (1558) Mary Queen of Scots. During his brief reign his uncles (Francis and Charles de Guise) persecuted the Protestants.

Francis II (1768–1835). The last Holy Roman Emperor (1792–1806), son of the emperor Leopold II. He declared war on the French Revolutionary government in 1792, and his territory was whittled away in constant wars with France. In imitation of Napoleon, and to consolidate his rule over his remaining possessions, he declared himself (1804) emperor of Austria; and when Napoleon, having conquered most of Germany, set up (1806) the Confederation of the Rhine, Francis abandoned the empty title of Holy Roman Emperor, which was never revived. From 1809–13 he was, on the advice of * Metternich, Napoleon's unwilling ally; to cement the alliance his daughter * Marie Louise was married to the French emperor. After Napoleon's disastrous retreat from Russia Francis rejoined his former allies (1813) and took part in the campaign of liberation. Ater Napoleon's downfall he was, under Metternich's continuing guidance, a constant supporter of the reactionary régimes which followed.

Francis II (1836–1894). King (1859–1861) of the Two Sicilies (Naples and Sicily), successor of * Ferdinand II. The conquest of his kingdom by * Garibaldi and his enforced abdication ensured the unification of Italy. Francis then lived in exile in Austria.

Francis, Clare (1946–). British ocean sailor. She first crossed the Atlantic, sailing singlehanded, in 1973. Later she made a second trip and took part in the Round Britain Race of 1974 (placed 3rd) and the Round the World Race of 1977–78 (placed 5th).
Francis, C., *Come Wind or Weather*. 1978

Francis, Sir Philip (1740–1818). English administrator and politician. A civil servant by profession, he was appointed to the Council of Bengal, set up by the Regulating Act (1783). While in India he opposed Warren * Hastings, the governor, with a zeal amounting to malignancy, and it was he who later supplied most of the evidence upon which the impeachment of Hastings (1788) was based. Francis, having amassed a fortune in India, was knighted and entered parliament (1784). It has been asserted, but not proved, that he was the anonymous political pamphleteer 'Junius'. He was a supporter of the Prince Regent (* George IV) and was interested in political reform.

Francis Ferdinand (1863–1914). Archduke of Austria, nephew of the Emperor Francis Joseph, and (from 1896) heir to the throne. His assassination at Sarajevo by the Bosnian Serb Gavilo Princip (28 June 1914) precipitated World War I. Ironically, Francis Ferdinand favoured internal autonomy for the subject nationalities of Austria-Hungary.

Francis Joseph (Franz Joseph) (1830–1916). Emperor of Austria (from 1848) and king of Hungary (from 1867). He ascended the throne at the height of the revolutionary activities which had enforced the abdication of his uncle, Emperor Ferdinand, but soon managed to restore law and order. In 1851 he abolished the constitution and exercised personal rule until 1867. In that year, following the loss of Austrian territories in North Italy (1859–60) and defeat by Prussia (1866), he agreed to the establishment of a dual monarchy, Austria-Hungary, two semi-autonomous countries (though with one army and certain centralized institutions). Austria with a liberal and Hungary with an oligarchic constitution. The Slav provinces were grouped with one or the other. For the rest of his reign Francis Joseph struggled for peace abroad and a preservation of the *status quo* at home. In the process of time he became a revered institution, his subjects willing to await his death before change. His last days were darkened by the calamity of World War I. His life was marked by a series of personal tragedies, e.g. the suicide of his only son Rudolph at Mayerling (1889), the assassination of the Empress Elizabeth (1898) and of his nephew and heir Francis Ferdinand (1914). With his industry, grasp of detail and great sense of duty, Francis Joseph had the qualities of a distinguished civil servant but lacked the vision and inspiring leadership of a great ruler. His son **Charles (Carl) I** was the last Emperor of Austria and was forced to abdicate in November 1918.
Corti, E., *Vom Kind zum Kaiser*. 1950

Francis of Assisi, St (1182–1226). Italian friar, founder of the Franciscan Order, popularly associated with reverence for animals as part of God's creation. He was born in Assisi, the son of a merchant. In 1201 he was taken prisoner during war with Perugia; this experience together with serious illness, inspired him to a vow of poverty, prayer and care for the helpless. His father disowned him; he left his family and, with 11 disciples, went to Rome where he persuaded the Pope (Innocent III) to sanction a new order. The Franciscans were authorized in 1215; the order grew rapidly and sent missionaries to the neighbouring states, to France, Spain and Africa. In 1223 Francis himself went to Egypt where he persuaded the Sultan to grant his order the guardianship of the Church of the Holy Sepulchre in Jerusalem; he also obtained better treatment for Christian prisoners. Francis received the marks of the stigmata in 1224, and in 1226 he died. He was canonized in 1228.
Moorman, J. R. H., *Sources for the Life of Saint Francis of Assisi*. 1967

Francis of Sales, St (1567–1622). Roman Catholic bishop and religious writer. Born at the family château at Sales in Savoy, he was a law student in Padua before becoming a priest. His success in converting Swiss Calvinists led to his becoming bishop of Geneva (1602). He held this office until his death, living at near-by

Annecy in his native Savoy. His spiritual friendship with the Baronne de Chantal (afterwards canonized) led to their founding, jointly, the order of the Sisters of the Visitation. His *Introduction to the Devout Life* and the mystical *Treatise on the Love of God* are the best known of his religious works.

Franck, César Auguste (1822–1890). Belgian-French composer, born in Liège. When barely 11 he toured as a concert pianist. After his family had moved to Paris he entered the Conservatoire (1837) but was withdrawn by his father to resume his concert-playing career. Franck received little attention as a composer during his lifetime but attracted a circle of admiring disciples, including the composer d'Indy. His compositions are clearly influenced by the music of Beethoven and Liszt and his orchestration reveals his preoccupation with the sonorities and registration of the organ. The first of his works to win him real public recognition was his String Quartet, written in the year of his death; two other chamber works (the Violin Sonata and the Piano Quintet) are among his masterpieces. Others are the symphonic poem *Le Chasseur maudit* (1882), the *Symphonic Variations* for piano and orchestra (1885), and the Symphony in D minor (1885–88). He also wrote many pieces for organ and piano, several songs and much church music, including the oratorio *The Beatitudes* (1869). He died in a street accident.

Franco (y Bahamonde), Francisco Paulino Hermenegildo Teodulo (1892–1975). Spanish leader ('El Caudillo') and the head of State. An army general when the Spanish Civil War broke out, he left his post as military governor of the Canary Islands and flew to Morocco to organize the participation of the Foreign Legion (which he had formerly commanded) and Moorish troops in the insurgent army. In October 1936 he took the place of the insurgent commander-in-chief General Sanjujo, who had been killed in an air crash. In the course of the next three years he defeated, with Italian and German aid, the loyalist government and its supporters, and in 1939 he set up, under his leadership, a corporative state with a single party, the Falange, in a dominating but gradually diminishing role. During World War II he maintained a precarious neutrality – he refused Hitler permission to use Spanish territory for an attack on Gibraltar, but sent the 'Blue Division' to join the Germans on the Russian front. After the war, he maintained a stable government, and Spain progressed economically thanks to tourism and the leasing of bases to the U.S.A. From 1974 regional opposition to his political system grew. He arranged that the monarchy would be restored on his death under * Juan Carlos and major reforms, by implication critical of his regime, were soon implemented.

Gallo, M., *Spain under Franco*. 1973

Frank, Anne (1929–1945). German Jewish girl born in Frankfurt am Main. The family fled to Amsterdam to escape Nazi persecution; when Germany occupied Holland in 1941 they went into hiding, living in a back room and warehouse, supplied with food by Gentile neighbours. They were betrayed by Dutch informers in 1944 and were taken to a concentration camp where all but the father died. Returning to Holland, he found the diary kept by his daughter 1941–44. *The Diary of a Young Girl* was published in 1947 and established her as a symbol of Jewish suffering under Hitler.

Frank, Hans (1900–1946). German Nazi politician. During World War II as governor general of Poland he was responsible for the deportation and death in extermination camps of millions of Jews. He was sentenced at the Nuremberg war trials and hanged.

Frankfurter, Felix (1882–1965). American jurist. He was professor at Harvard Law School (1914–39) and in the early days of the New Deal was a valued adviser to his close friend, Franklin Roosevelt, who appointed him (1939–62) a judge of the Supreme Court, to which he brought strong liberal sympathies combined with respect for judicial procedure.

Franklin, Benjamin (1706–1790). American statesman and scientist. His father was a Boston tallow chandler whose children numbered seventeen in all; Benjamin was the fifteenth; the tenth by his second wife. His schooling was brief and he was largely self-educated, helped in this by being apprenticed, at the age of 12, to his half-brother James, a printer. Printing led to journalism and his career really started (though from 1724 he had already spent eighteen months in London) when by 1728 he was settled in Philadelphia as owner of the *Pennsylvania Gazette*. He also published (1732–57) *Poor Richard's Almanac*, which achieved enormous success; many of 'Poor Richard's' pithy aphorisms, some borrowed, some original, have become American proverbs. He was now becoming a prominent citizen; after starting a fire service (1736) and being postmaster (1737), he extended his interest in education by helping to found the American Philosophical Society (1743) and the Philadelphia Academy (1751), which developed into the University. Meanwhile he had become interested in electrical phenomena. With his famous kite experiment (1752) he proved that lightning is a form of electricity, produced a satisfactory explanation of the difference between positive and negative charges, and invented the lightning conductor, which brought him fame and election to the Royal Society in London. Political interests now began to dominate. He was a Radical member of the Pennsylvania Assembly (1751–64) and deputy postmaster for the American colonies (1753–74). As agent for the Assembly he visited England (1757–62) and was lionized in social and scientific circles. Again in England (1764–75), he played a conciliatory part in the quarrels between England and the American colonies and helped to secure the repeal of the Stamp Act (1766). When, however, a breach became inevitable, he returned to America to play a leading but always conciliatory part in the fight for independence. He helped to draw up the Declaration of Independence (1776) and in the same year went to Paris, serving first as the only successful one of the three commissioners sent to enlist French aid, and (from 1778) as sole minister. As such he helped to negotiate, and was one of the signatories of, the Treaty of Versailles (1783) by which American independence was finally secured. He was president of the Supreme Executive Council of Philadelphia (1785–88) and sat in the convention which drew up the U.S. constitution (1787–88).

It is ironical that his illegitimate son **William Franklin,** who was governor of New Jersey (1763–76), remained loyal to George III and subsequently withdrew to live in England.

His wisdom and moderation in politics and the breadth of his scientific and political achievements make Franklin one of the greatest figures of American history.

van Doren, C., *Benjamin Franklin*. 1948

Franklin, Sir John (1786–1847). English Arctic explorer. He joined the navy (1801), fought under Nelson at Trafalgar and, when peace came, made several voyages of Arctic exploration (from 1818). In 1836 he became lieutenant governor of Van Diemen's Land (Tasmania) where he was remembered for his humane treatment of the transported convicts. In 1845 with his two ships, the *Frebus* and *Terror* he began his last voyage, in search of the Northwest Passage, from which no survivor returned. After several expeditions had sought in vain, a full record was found in a cairn at Point Victoria; the party had been caught in the ice on the west side of King William Island and Franklin had died in June 1847; the others left the ships but succumbed to scurvy and starvation.

Lamb, G. F., *Franklin, Happy Voyager*. 1956

Franklin, Rosalind Elsie (1920–1958). British scientist. After early research on gas-phase chromatography, she pursued physical-chemical work on the structure of coals and carbonized coals. Between 1947 and 1950 she researched in Paris, using the techniques of X-ray diffraction to illuminate the study of carbons. From 1951 she worked at London University on the problems of virus structure. Her work up to this point had been concerned with developing models of carbon structure and investigating changes under high temperatures. Her work now concentrated upon X-ray diffraction pictures of DNA. Her experiments showed that the patterns of DNA crystallinity were compatible with a helical structure. She hoped to build up a picture of the structure using empirical means, while at the same time investigating various theoretical models (e.g. anti-parallel rods in pairs back-to-back). Her own attempts to find a satisfactory helical structure were pre-empted by * Crick and Watson's 'double helix' solution, which appeared in *Nature* for 25 April, 1953. Franklin had supplied Crick and Watson with vital X-ray data. She devoted the next few years to further research on coal, and to improving her earlier X-ray pictures.

Klug, A., 'Rosalind Franklin and the Discovery of the Structure of DNA', *Nature*, 219 (1968), 808, 844.

Franks, Oliver Shewell Franks, 1st Baron (1905–   ). British scholar and administrator. In World War II he left the academic world to join the Ministry of Supply, becoming (1945) its permanent secretary. He was ambassador to the U.S. (1948–52), and chairman of Lloyds Bank (1954–62). He became provost of Worcester College, Oxford, in 1962, the year in which he received his peerage. The Royal Commission (1964–66) on Oxford University, of which he was chairman, is referred to as the Franks Commission.

Franz *see* **Francis I** and **II**; **Francis Ferdinand**; *and* **Francis Joseph.**

Fraser, Peter (1884–1950). New Zealand politician, of Scottish birth. He emigrated in 1910, became a trade-union leader in Auckland and on the formation of the New Zealand Labour party (1916) became a committee member. He was elected to parliament (1918) and was eventually Labour prime minister (1940–49), and thus had to cope with the responsibilities and difficulties of World War II.

Fraser of North Cape, Bruce Austin Fraser, 1st Baron (1888–1981). British naval commander. At the beginning of World War II he was controller of the navy and so directed the vast expansion (including the construction of special ships for combined operations) of those years. He commanded the Home Fleet (1943–44) and organized the operation by which the battle-cruiser *Scharnhorst* was sunk. In 1945 and 1946 (when he was made a peer) he commanded the British fleet which cooperated with the Americans in the Pacific. He was first sea lord (1948–51).

Fraser, (John) Malcolm (1930–). Australian Liberal politician. A grazier's son, educated at Oxford, he became a member of the Australian parliament 1955–83, serving as a Minister 1966–71 and 1971–72, resigning in March 1971 after a clash with J. G. * Gorton. In March 1975 he became leader of the Liberal Party and pushed a hardline policy which led to the Senate deferring Supply to E. G. * Whitlam's Labor Government. Appointed Prime Minister (November 1975) on Whitlam's dismissal by the Governor-General, Sir John Kerr, he won the 1975 and 1977 elections, with massive majorities and 1980 more narrowly. Next to * Menzies he was the longest serving Prime Minister. In March 1983, he was defeated heavily by R. J. L. * Hawke and resigned the Liberal leadership.

Fraser, Simon (1776–1862). Canadian explorer. At 18 he joined the North West Company which sent him (1805) to extend the company's activities beyond the Rocky Mountains. The expedition proved to be difficult and dangerous. He discovered the river subsequently named after him (1808). He left an informative journal of his explorations.

Fraunhofer, Joseph von (1787–1826). German optical physicist. He was trained as a maker of optical instruments, and it was while working to perfect achromatic lenses that he was able to see more clearly the dark lines in the solar spectrum which (though previously observed) are now known as the Fraunhofer lines. He recorded over 500 of these lines, which were later (1859) explained by * Kirchhoff. In 1823 he became professor of physics at Munich.

Frazer, Sir James George (1854–1941). Scottish anthropologist. He was born in Glasgow, and was professor of social anthropology at Liverpool University (1907–1919). His greatest work, *The Golden Bough* (2 volumes, 1890, expanded into 12 volumes by 1915), is still greatly admired as a monumental source book for ritual beliefs throughout the world, although the interpretations he offered are no longer entirely accepted. His other major works are *Totemism and Exogamy* (1910) and *Folklore in the Old Testament* (1918).

Downie, A., *Frazer and the 'Golden Bough'*. 1970

Frederick III (1831–1888). German emperor and king of Prussia (1888). He reigned for only three months. In 1858 he married Princess Victoria of Great Britain and imbibed her political views, based on British political practice; he therefore found himself in opposition to his father, William I, and * Bismarck, between whom and himself there was a mutual dislike. He died of cancer and was succeeded by his son, William II.

Frederick I (known as Barbarossa) (*c.* 1122–1190). Holy Roman Emperor (from 1155) and German king (from 1152). He was the son of the Hohenstaufen Duke of Swabia, and was linked through his mother with the Guelph dynasty. After his election as German king (1152) he was in a position to end the long dynastic feud that had rent Germany. He

established his power in Northern Italy (1154) and was crowned emperor by Pope Adrian IV in Rome (1155). In 1158 his capture of Milan and enforcement of imperial claims in Lombardy produced a strained relationship between the papacy and empire, exacerbated when Alexander III succeeded Pope Adrian. The imperialists elected an anti-pope and Frederick was excommunicated. Time after time he returned to Italy to repair the damaging effects of his absence. He even captured Rome (1167) but was forced by the ravages of the plague to retire. In 1174 he found the Lombard cities again in revolt but, after a severe defeat at Legnano (1176), he made peace with the pope (1177) and eventually with the Lombards. Free now to deal with his Guelph cousin * Henry the Lion who had been causing trouble in Germany, he deprived him of his estates and drove him into exile (1180). On his way to Palestine for the 3rd Crusade, of which he was chosen leader, Frederick was drowned in a river in Asia Minor. He had an attractive personality and the qualities of a great ruler. There is a tradition that he is not dead, but sleeping, and one day will awake to defend Germany at a time of crisis.
Munz, P., *Frederick Barbarossa*. 1969

Frederick I (1657–1713). First king of Prussia (from 1701). He succeeded his father, Frederick William, the 'Great Elector', of Brandenburg in 1688 and assumed the title of king in 1701. He ranged himself against France in the War of the Spanish Succession and his policy throughout his reign was to sustain the Habsburg cause. He founded the Berlin Academy of Arts (1696) and Sciences (1707) and the University of Halle (1694); he was the patron of * Leibniz. An attempt to give peasants hereditary leases of his domains was foiled by the nobles.

Frederick II (1194–1250). Holy Roman Emperor (from 1220) and German king (from 1215). He was the grandson of * Emperor Frederick Barbarossa and the son of the emperor Henry VI, on whose death (1198) he inherited the throne of Sicily, where he was born. When orphaned at the age of 4 he was taken under the guardianship of Pope Innocent III. He received papal support during his struggle against Otto of Bavaria for recognition as German king, which ended with Frederick's coronation (1215) after Otto's defeat at Bouvines. He was crowned emperor (1220) in Rome, having promised, in return for the pope's aid, to give up the throne of Sicily to his son and lead a crusade. He delayed his start until 1227 and was excommunicated when, on the plea of illness, he almost immediately returned. He resumed his crusading activities, however, when having taken as his second wife the daughter of the King of Jerusalem he went to Palestine (1229), induced the Saracens to give up Jerusalem (where he was crowned king) and secured peace in the Holy Land for ten years. He reformed and centralized the government of Sicily but allowed the German princes yet more autonomy (1231), while his protracted struggle in Italy during the last twenty years of his reign failed to break the resistance of the papacy and the Lombard League. He suffered a severe defeat at Parma (1248) but was preparing a new campaign when he died. The conception of unified imperial rule over Italy and Germany had again proved impractical. Frederick was a brilliant but unstable figure, capable of both great cruelty and scientific detachment. His court at Palermo became a great artistic and cultural centre; he himself was fluent in six languages, was a legal reformer (his code for Sicily proved an enduring achievement), a natural historian (he wrote a textbook on ornithology) and a religious sceptic. Described by the English chronicler Matthew Paris as 'the wonder of the world' (*Stupor Mundi*) he fostered Greek, Jewish and Islamic cultural heritages and insisted on the use of Arabic numerals instead of Roman.
Masson, G., *Frederick II of Hohenstaufen*. 1973

Frederick II (known as 'the Great') (1712–1786). King of Prussia (from 1740). He was the son of Frederick William I and Sophia, daughter of King George I of Britain; his taste for music, poetry and philosophy and his predilection for French culture infuriated his boorish and tyrannical father, and the two lived in a state of mutual hatred. After an attempt by Frederick to escape to England had been foiled, he was imprisoned and forced to watch the execution of Katte, his friend and accomplice. After fifteen months he submitted to his father and was rewarded with the gift (1733) of a country estate, where he led the agreeable life of a dilettante, reading much, corresponding with Voltaire and other writers and conversing with the witty and the wise. His historical reading imbued him with a lust for fame, while his lifelong practice in concealing his thoughts and deeds from his father had left him with few scruples.

His accession coincided with the crisis caused by the death of the emperor Charles VI, who, lacking male heirs, had spent his last years in getting promises (the Pragmatic Sanction) from European rulers to support the transfer of his hereditary dominions to his daughter Maria Theresa. Frederick William had promised with the rest but Frederick, whose most valued inheritance was a fully trained and finely equipped army, revived an old claim to the duchy of Silesia which he invaded when it was denied. Frederick's victories at Mollwitz (1741) and Chotusitz (1742) decided Maria Theresa to yield Silesia by the Treaty of Breslau (1742); but Austrian successes against Bavaria and its French ally alarmed Frederick and in 1744 he again intervened; another series of victories enabled him to emerge from the War of Austrian Succession with his possession of Silesia confirmed. Maria Theresa, however, retained the Habsburg territories and her husband, Francis of Lorraine, was elected emperor.

The years of peace witnessed a diplomatic revolution. Maria Theresa, eager for revenge, came to terms with France (with the result that Britain was allied with Frederick in the ensuing Seven Years War) and gained the alliance of Empress Elizabeth of Russia. Frederick, after receiving no reply to a demand for a declaration of their intentions, invaded Saxony (1756). In 1757 the Austrians, who had invaded Silesia, had to withdraw after his great victories of Rossbach and Leuthen. But numbers began to tell, Frederick held his own in 1758, but in 1759 suffered a crushing defeat by Austrians and Prussians at Kunersdorf and spoke of suicide. He rallied in 1760 but ultimate defeat seemed certain when the Tsarina died (January 1762) and was succeeded by Frederick's admirer Peter II, who left the alliance. Frederick, thus saved, was glad to retain his position of 1756 by the Treaty of Hubertsburg (1763). The acquisition of West Prussia in the first partition of Poland with Austria and Russia (1772) enabled him to link East Prussia and Brandenburg. But from 1756 his time was mainly taken up with peaceful restoration of his country. The addition of Silesia had doubled the population of Prussia and his own efforts did much to increase its wealth. He played the role of benevolent despot, travelling constantly, remedying troubles as he went. A state bank, a state porcelain factory, and a silk industry were started; he bribed settlers to come in and cultivate reclaimed land. His personal extravagances were few. The small palace of Sans Souci, near Potsdam (1742–47), is perhaps the most notable of his buildings.

And yet he continued to dislike and despise the people for whom he did so much; when Voltaire was induced to settle in Berlin (1750) the two found that it was distance that had lent the enchantment, but Frederick remained true to his allegiance to French culture. He was a prolific writer in French and is usually counted among the 'enlightened despots'. His skill and acumen, both military and political, laid the foundations for Prussia's domination of the future Germany, but equally his aggressive policies and defiance of international obligations set a pattern which that Germany was to follow.

Horn, D. B., *Frederick the Great and the Rise of Prussia*. 1964

Frederick IX (1899–1972). King of Denmark (1947–72). He was the son of Christian X, and married Princess Ingrid of Sweden (1935). Lacking male heirs, he sponsored a constitutional amendment to enable his eldest daughter, now **Queen Margrethe II** (1940–), to succeed.

Frederick Henry, Prince of Orange (1584–1647). Dutch soldier and statesman, son of * William the Silent. He became regent for the princes of Orange on the death of his half-brother Maurice of Nassau. He was the first member of the House of Orange to assume quasi-monarchical powers in his fight to free the country of Spanish domination. His military successes, domestic policies and international diplomacy all paved the way for an honourable peace with Spain in 1648.

Frederick William (known as the 'Great Elector') (1620–1688). Elector of Brandenburg (from 1640). He built up his state, which had been enlarged though much weakened by the Thirty Years War (1618–48). To hold its scattered possessions together he managed by extreme frugality to build up a small standing army (about 30,000 men) which enabled him to pursue a foreign policy that varied in accordance with the amount of subsidy he could exact for the use of his troops. By

changing sides in the war between Sweden and Poland he was able to secure the independence (1657) of the Prussian duchy which he had formerly held as a Polish fief. Internally his rule was based on a compromise with the nobility. He established a centralized bureaucracy but allowed the nobles increased powers on their own estates and over their serfs. After the revocation of the Edict of Nantes by Louis XIV, Frederick William encouraged a large influx of Huguenot refugees, who helped the growth of industry. He founded libraries, introduced educational reforms and extended Berlin as the capital of his scattered dominions.
Schevill, F., *The Great Elector*. 1948

Frederick William I (1688–1740). King of Prussia and elector of Brandenburg (from 1713). His father, whom he succeeded, was Frederick I, his wife, Sophia Dorothea, daughter of George I of Great Britain. It was the centralized administration and the army which he perfected that enabled his son Frederick II to turn Prussia into a great power. Frederick William ruled as a complete autocrat and martinet; his court was like an officers' mess; anyone, such as his son, who opposed him he treated with savage intolerance, but despite his scorn for culture he introduced compulsory elementary education. His army was at once his pride and delight. To fill its ranks he compelled the peasants to enlist and the young nobles to become officer cadets; and he trained and equipped it to be the finest instrument of policy in all Europe. The collection of tall men for his personal guard was a favourite hobby, and kidnapping one of the methods used to indulge it. It was asserted that the forcible mating of its members with tall women was a way by which he hoped to secure future recruits. But he was reluctant to subject such a magnificent body of men to war and his foreign policy was to avoid conflict.

Frederick William II (1744–1797). King of Prussia (from 1786). He succeeded his uncle, Frederick the Great, but proved a feeble administrator, dependent on favourites. He joined Austria in an ineffective attempt to overthrow by force the French Revolutionary government (1792–95). During his reign Prussia gained territory by the partitions of Poland (1792 and 1795).

Frederick William III (1770–1840). King of Prussia (from 1797). The son of Frederick William II, he came to the throne shortly before Napoleon Bonaparte seized power; his vacillating character made him incapable of coping with events which precipitated him into war against France (1806), and he was heavily defeated at Jena. The humiliation of the Treaty of Tilsit impelled him to turn to Stein, Hardenburg, and Scharnhorst, whose reforms and administration braced Prussia for its part in the final overthrow of Napoleon, after which, as a member of the Holy Alliance, he grew more and more reactionary.

Frederick William IV (1795–1861). King of Prussia (from 1841). He succeeded his father, Frederick William III, after a long reactionary period, and his character, that of a romantic medievalist, was mistakenly thought by the liberal revolutionaries of 1848 to make him sympathetic to their own aspirations. He did indeed order the withdrawal of troops from Berlin, and though he refused to accept the throne of a united democratic Germany he did so with real or apparent reluctance. But soon his essential weakness was revealed: he yielded to the reactionaries around him, headed by his brother William, crushed the revolutionary forces and imposed a constitution (1850) that left the balance of political power virtually unchanged. In 1858 he became insane and his brother acted as regent.

Frege, Friedrich Ludwig Gottlob (1848–1925). German mathematician and philosopher. One of the pioneers of modern logic, he was particularly interested in the close connexion between logic and mathematics. His thinking exerted a recognizable influence on Bertrand Russell, who criticized, however, some of his propositions.

Frémont, John Charles (known as 'the Pathfinder') (1813–1890). American soldier and explorer. His surveys established various feasible overland routes from east to west in America. One of the first U.S. Senators elected from California (1850–51), he became the first Republican candidate for President in 1856, but lost to * Buchanan. He was major-general in charge of the Department of the West 1861–62 until forced to resign. During the California gold-rush he made a fortune which he then lost in railway speculations which involved a charge of fraud. He was governor of Arizona territory (1878–83).

Nevins, A., *Frémont: Pathfinder of the West.* 1955

French, Sir John *see* **Ypres, 1st Earl of**

Frescobaldi, Girolamo (1583–1643). Italian composer, organist of St Peter's, Rome from 1608. He is regarded as one of the first great masters of composition for the organ and, through his pupils, a strong influence on European baroque music.

Fresnel, Augustin Jean (1788–1827). French physicist. An engineer by profession, he became interested in physical optics and was the first to produce the optical effects now known as interference fringes. His discovery that these effects resulted from interference between two beams of light gave great support to the wave theory of light. He also gave a clear explanation of polarization and diffraction and invented the compound lighthouse lens. His many honours included the Rumford Medal of the British Royal Society.

Freud, Sigmund (1856–1939). Austrian neurologist, known for his development of psychoanalysis. Born in Moravia of Jewish parents, he spent most of his life in Vienna, which he left only in 1938 when Hitler took over Austria. He joined the medical faculty of the University of Vienna (1881) and specialized in neurology. In 1885 he studied for a time under * Charcot in Paris; but it was his association with Breuer that turned his attention to psychology and led to his examination of the cure for hysteria under hypnosis. He wrote *Studien über Hysterie* (1895). He adopted the use of 'free association' instead of hypnosis as the means to gain insight of the patient's subconscious memories and thus took the decisive step on the path to what is now conceived as psychoanalysis. In 1900 he published his *Interpretation of Dreams*; after working very much alone for many years he joined with * Jung and * Adler to found the International Psychoanalytic Association (1906) but they soon parted to found their own schools. The repressions which dominated the subconscious mind were held by Freud to be closely connected with infantile sexuality. To expound his system Freud invented a terminology: the 'id' is the subconscious drive to achieve basic desires, the 'ego' the conscious reasoning or executive force (often in conflict with the 'id'), and the 'superego' the largely subconscious directing force or conscience. Freud's theories have had immense influence not only in the field of psychology but also on art (e.g. Surrealism) and literature (e.g. James Joyce).

Jones, E., *Sigmund Freud: Life and Work.* 3 vols. 1953–57; Clark, R. W., *Freud: The Man and the Cause.* 1980

Freyberg, Bernard Cyril Freyberg, 1st Baron (1889–1963). New Zealand soldier. In World War I he won the V.C. and D.S.O. with two bars, and in World War II, he commanded the New Zealand forces in Greece, Crete, North Africa and Italy. He was governor general of New Zealand (1946–52).

Freyre, Gilberto de Mello (1900–). Brazilian scholar, born in Recife. He made a detailed studh of Brazilian social conditions. He visited many countries and his lectures and sociological writings won him an international reputation. His greatest work is *Casa Grande e Senzale* (*Masters and Slaves*, revised edition 1956), a penetrating study of Brazilian plantation life before the abolition of slavery. His other works include *Sobrados e Mucambos* (*Mansions and Shanties*) and (in English) *Brazil: an Interpretation* (1945).

Friedman, Milton (1912–). U.S. economist. The most influential of conservative American economists, he was a trenchant critic of Keynesian theories, advocating a monetarist position, i.e. that changes in money supply precede changes in economic activity rather than following on. A professor of economics at Chicago University 1948–76, he received the Nobel Prize for Economic Science in 1976.

Friese-Greene, William (1855–1921). English pioneer of cinematography. Originally a portrait photographer in Bristol, he took out (1889) the first patent for an apparatus involving the principle of intermittency of exposure of the film. He also worked on colour and stereoscopic films. But he lacked the finance necessary to exploit his discovery and died in poverty.

Frisch, Karl von (1886–1982). Austrian zoologist, born in Vienna. He studied in Munich, and later held chairs at Breslau, Munich and Graz. He conducted research on recognition and communication first in fish and later in bees. He demonstrated that fish had sharp hearing and could distinguish between colours and degrees of brightness. His most famous work established that honeybees orient themselves through the Sun and can recall patterns of polarization even when it is not visible and that they communicate with other bees by dancing movements: wagging dances for distant food, round dances when food is close. He shared the 1973 Nobel Prize for Medicine with his fellow ethologists Konrad * Lorenz and Nikolaas * Tinbergen.

Frisch, Max (1911–). Swiss novelist and playwright. Better known for his plays, he acknowledged the influence of both Brecht and Thornton Wilder, and his main concern is with man's destiny and the difficulties of realising it through the normal behaviour patterns of a modern society. His first play was *Nur Singen sie Wieder* (1945); the best-known is possibly *Andorra* (1962).
Weisstein, U., *Max Frisch*. 1967

Frisch, Otto Robert (1904–1979). British physicist, born in Austria. He was associated with the early work on nuclear fission in the 1930s; during World War II he worked in the U.S.A. on the production of the atomic bomb. In 1947 he became Jacksonian professor of natural philosophy at Cambridge and head of the nuclear physics section of the Cavendish Laboratory. He was elected an F.R.S. in 1948.

Frisch, Ragnar (1895–1973). Norwegian economist. Professor of Economics at Oslo 1931–65, he was editor of the journal *Econometrica* 1933–55 and pioneered the use of advanced statistical techniques in economic theory. He shared the first Nobel Prize in Economic Science in 1969 with Jan * Tinbergen.

Frith, William Powell (1819–1909). English painter. His huge paintings, notable for their almost photographic realism, are packed with incidents and reveal many details of historical interest about Victorian England. They include *The Great Exhibition* (1851), *Derby Day* (1858) and *The Railway Station* (1862). He became an R.A. in 1852.

Frobenius, Johannes (*c*. 1460–1527). German painter, born in Bavaria. By establishing himself (1491) at Basle he made the city the centre of the German book trade. He published a Latin Bible, a Greek New Testament and editions of several of the early fathers of the church; among those who prepared his publications for the press were Erasmus and Holbein.

Frobisher, Sir Martin (1535–1594). English sailor and explorer, born in Yorkshire. Originally, with Hawkins and others, a privateer in the Indies, he sailed (1576) with a small expedition in search of the North-west Passage. From Labrador he brought back some black earth believed to contain gold. Two other expeditions (1577 and 1578) brought further supplies but attempts to extract gold failed. He was knighted for his part in the Armada battles, after which he married and attempted to settle down. Soon he was at sea again on the look-out for Spanish treasure ships but was mortally wounded in an attack on Brest.

Froebel, Friedrich Wilhelm August (1782–1852). German educationist. Founder of the Froebel method for teaching small children, he worked with Pestalozzi in Switzerland (1807–09) and in several books developed his theories, based on the belief that children up to the age of 7 should grow naturally and spontaneously, like a plant or an animal, and that the development and co-ordination of mind and body should be helped by activities most calculated to achieve this purpose. Froebel opened (1837) his first *Kindergarten* ('children's garden') in Blankenburg, Thuringia; traditional schooling was replaced by methods involving the more spontaneous and creative activities he had advocated in his books. The rest of his life was spent in founding schools and training teachers.
Lilley, I. M., *Friedrich Froebel*. 1967

Froissart, Jean (*c*. 1333–1405). French chronicler. He observed, and wrote in vivid detail about, 14th-century life and events. He travelled widely in search of information for his *Chroniques*, and in England was received by Edward III and Queen Philippa, who, like himself, came from Hainaut. Although a chief source for the period in which he lived, his record is of the life of courts and chivalry and does not provide an authentic broad picture of the century of the Hundred Years War and its attendant misery. He also wrote verses in a wide range of forms, including a metrical romance about the Round Table.

Fromm, Erich (1900–1980). German-American social psychologist, born in Frankfurt. Educated at Heidelberg, he lived in the U.S. from 1922. His work attempted to link the teachings of * Freud and * Marx, applying psychoanalytical method to sociology. His books include *The Fear of Freedom* (1941) and *The Anatomy of Human Destructiveness* (1973).

Frondizi, Arturo (1908–). President of Argentina. The son of Italian immigrants, he made a name for himself as a lawyer by defending left-wing political prisoners, and as a politician (he became a deputy in 1946) by leading the opposition to Peron. In the first constitutional elections held after Peron's overthrow, Frondizi, leader of the left wing of the Radical party, was elected president (1957). He failed, however, to rally the country behind him and to cure the inherent economic ills and was deposed (March 1962).

Frontenac, Louis de Buade, Comte de (1620–1698). As governor of New France in North America (1672–82 and 1689–98), he constructed a chain of forts and trading stations from Quebec to the Gulf of Mexico, with the aims of linking the colonies, encouraging commerce and confining the English settlers to the coastal territories. His remarkable success in winning the confidence of the Indians enabled him to make them his allies against the English.
Le Sueur, W. D., *Count Frontenac*. 1964

Frost, Robert Lee (1874–1963). American poet, born in San Francisco. He studied briefly at Dartmouth College and Harvard, later working as carpenter, teacher (1905–12) and farmer. He lived in England (1912–15) and there published his first books of poetry, *A Boy's Will* (1913) and *North of Boston* (1914). Frost was professor of English at Amherst College for long spells between 1916 and 1938 and later gave lectures at Harvard. His later publications included *Mountain Interval* (1916), *New Hampshire* (1923), *From Snow to Snow* (1936), *A Witness ree* (1942) and *Steeple Bush* (1947). His *Complete Poems* was issued in 1951; *In the Clearing* appeared in 1962. He won the Pulitzer Prize for Poetry in 1924, 1931, 1937 and 1943. His poetry belongs in scene and character to rural New England, and extols self-reliance, self-knowledge and the simple life, conveying, moreover, by the subtlest means a hint of the mysterious or even the macabre to the most commonplace scene. He ranks among the greatest poets of the century.
Jennings, E., *Frost*. 1964

Froude, James Anthony (1818–1894). English historian. Son of a Devonshire clergyman, he was educated at Westminister School and Oxford and took deacon's orders, though because of increasing scepticism he never became a priest. His greatest work was *The History of England from the Fall of Wolsey to the Defeat of the Spanish Armada* (12 volumes, 1856–70). This was followed by *The English in Ireland in the Eighteenth Century* (3 volumes, 1871–74). Like Macaulay, he was a writer of history rather than a historian; his style is engaging but his use of historical evidence is careless (though not wilfully misleading). He was professor of modern history at Oxford (1892–94). He was the close friend, literary executor and biographer of Thomas * Carlyle.

Fry, Charles Burgess (1872–1956). English athlete. He was educated at Oxford, where he distinguished himself as both a scholar and an athlete of great versatility. He is best remembered as an outstanding cricketer for Sussex and for his captaincy of the England XI against Australia and South Africa (1912). His autobiography, *Life Worth Living*, was published in 1948.

Fry, Christopher (1907–). English dramatist. Though he had written *The Boy with a Cart* for a pageant in 1938, he spent many years first as a schoolmaster and then in directing repertory before he achieved his first major success with *The Lady's Not for Burning* (1948). Other plays included *Thor, with Angels* (1949), *Venus Observed* (1950) and *The Dark Is Light Enough* (1954). *Ring Round the Moon* (1950) was adapted from a play by Anouilh and *Tiger at the Gates* (1955) from Jean Giraudoux. Fantasy, lyricism and verbal facility almost give the effect of improvisation, making him one of the rare successful verse dramatists of the 20th century.

Fry, Elizabeth (née Gurney) (1780–1845). English Quaker and pioneer of prison reform. She interested herself early in social reform, and in 1813 she was appalled by the condition of women prisoners in Newgate: she gave them decent clothing, and read and explained the Bible to them. In 1817 she formed an association which extended its activity to prisons outside London and to convict ships.

Fry, Joseph (1728–1787). English Quaker, born in Wiltshire. First a doctor, he turned to manufacturing pottery in Bristol before founding (1764) the famous chocolate factory firm, basis of the family's fortunes. He also became famous as a type-founder. His son, Sir Edward Fry, achieved distinction as a jurist in international disputes and as a botanist; his grandson was Roger Elliot * Fry, painter and critic.

Fry, Roger Elliot (1866–1934). British painter and art critic. About 1907 he first saw works by Cézanne and then those by the Fauves; he introduced their works and those of other Impressionist artists to England and gradually succeeded in transforming their originally hostile reception into enthusiastic acceptance. His writings on art reflected an exact and formal approach to the exposition of aesthetic principles. His criticism appeared chiefly in essays, collected in *Vision and Design* (1921) and *Transformations* (1926). He maintained that the merits of a painting depended only on its form and that its content was unimportant.

Fuad I (1868–1936). King of Egypt (from 1922). Born in Cairo, he was the youngest son of * Ismail Pasha. He succeeded his brother Hussein as sultan of Egypt (1917) and became king (1922) when the British protectorate ended. His reign consisted mainly of a struggle between the king and the popularly elected Wafd party under its leaders Zaghlul Pasha and Nahas Pasha.

Fuchs, Klaus Emil Julius (1911–). German physicist. A communist, he fled to England from Nazi Germany (1933). On the outbreak of war he was interned in Canada (1939–41) but returned to England to help in research. Noted for his work on quantum physics, he played some part in the development of the first atomic bombs. He worked at the Harwell Atomic Energy Establishment from 1946 to 1950 when he pleaded guilty to having supplied secret information to the Russians, and was sentenced to fourteen years' imprisonment. Released in 1959, he took up a scientific position in East Germany.

Fuchs, Sir Vivian Ernest (1908–). British geologist and explorer. From undergraduate days at Cambridge he took part in many scientific expeditions. From 1947 he worked in the Falkland Islands Dependencies as leader of the survey and later director of the Scientific Bureau. He is best known as the leader of the Commonwealth Trans-antarctic Expedition (1957–58) in connexion with the International Geophysical Year. The crossing was successfully achieved when his party met Sir Edmund * Hillary coming from New Zealand by the South Pole. With Hillary he wrote *The Crossing of Antarctica* (1958).

Fugger. A South German (Swabian) merchant family which ultimately achieved immense wealth and influence as one of the earliest bankers of Europe. Three brothers, of whom **Jakob Fugger** (1459–1525) was the most important, developed a successful business centred on Augsburg, involved with trade, silver and copper mining and banking. Through loans to the emperor Maximilian and Charles V, Jakob, in addition to acquiring great riches, became a count and received grants of land. He built the first model town in Europe ('the Fuggerei' in Augsburg), which still exists. The family was staunchly Catholic and did much to support the Catholic cause during the Reformation.

Fulbright, James William (1905–). American Democratic politican. He was president of the University of Arkansas (1939–41), became a member of the House of Representatives (1943) and a Senator (1945–75). He initiated the Fulbright Scholarships for the interchange of teachers and students between the U.S.A. and foreign countries.

Fuller, (Richard) Buckminster (1895–1984). U.S. engineer, architect and inventor. Twice expelled from Harvard, he worked in industry for many years and gradually evolved construction techniques designed to maximize efficiency and minimize costs in producing houses and vehicles by devising interchangeable modular units. His 'Dymaxion' automobile, an omnidirectional vehicle with high safety and low operating cost, was ignored by the motor industry. In 1947 he invented the 'geodesic dome' which combined maximum strength with minimum structure and within 30 years 50,000 had been built. He lectured at several universities and his many books included *Operating Manual for Spaceship Earth* (1969).

Fuller, (Sarah) Margaret (1810–1850). American literary critic and feminist. She edited *The Dial* (1840–1842), the magazine of the 'New England Transcendentalists', and became the friend of Emerson and Thoreau. She wrote *Woman in the Nineteenth Century* (1845). In order to take part in the revolutionary movements of 1848 she went to Italy, where she married Marquis Ossoli. On the way back to America both were drowned in a shipwreck.

Fuller, Thomas (1608–1661). English writer and divine. He was author of the *Worthies of England* (1662), short biographical sketches of English notables; a history of the church; and numerous other works, e.g. *Good Thoughts in Bad Times* (1645), which remain readable not only for their quaint facts – of which he was an ardent collector – but because of his wit and homely commonsense. In the Civil War he was a chaplain of the Royalist armies but was unmolested during the Commonwealth.

Fulton, Robert (1765–1815). American pioneer of steam navigation. Born of poor Irish parents, almost uneducated and originally a painter, he showed his true talents in England (from 1786), where he invented machines for sawing marble and twisting rope and many devices for improving canal navigation. While living in France (1798–1806) he built a primitive type of submarine. In 1803 he experimented with a steamship on the Seine. Later, back in the U.S.A. he launched the *Clermont* which in tests on the Hudson River, New York State (1807), proved much more efficient than William Symington's earlier *Charlotte Dundas*. He built (1815) the first steam warship, the *Fulton*, of 38 tons.

Funk, Casimir (1884–1967). American biochemist of Polish birth. He studied the diseases caused by specific deficiences in diet and his paper (1912) on the subject aroused immediate interest. He coined the word vitamin for the critical food substances already identified by Sir F. G. Hopkins (1906) which he had called 'accessory food factors'.

Furtwängler, Wilhelm (1886–1954). German conductor. Noted for his romantic interpretations of the German masters, he was born in Berlin, and he was chief conductor of the Berlin Philharmonic (1922–27; 1938–50), the New York Philharmonic (1927–30) and the Vienna Philharmonic (1930–33). He remained in Germany during World War II and both before and afterwards conducted in London and many leading cities as well as at Bayreuth and Salzburg. In 1952 he was awarded the Grand Cross of Merit by the West German government.

Fuseli, Henry (1741–1825). Swiss painter. He modified his surname of Füssl to be more Italian-sounding. After a brief career as a minister of religion he went to Berlin to study art (1763), and later went to London where Reynolds encouraged him. His style with its range of imagination, movement and distortion is often in the same mood, but at a less elevated level, as the work of Blake.

Tomoroy, P. T., *The Life and Art of Henry Fuseli*. 1972

Fust, Johann (*c*. 1400–1466). German printer. He lent money to finance the printing of * Gutenberg's first books; but having sued him successfully for repayment he took over his equipment (1455) and in partnership with his son-in-law, Peter Schöffer, printed a number of fine editions.

G

Gable, Clark (1901–1960). American film star. His casual and debonair charm, edged sometimes with a cynical aplomb, brought him a host of admirers. Rhett Butler in *Gone with the Wind* (1939) and Fletcher Christian in *Mutiny on the Bounty* (1935) are two of his most memorable roles; for his light-hearted and amusing part in *It Happened One Night* (1934) he gained an Academy award.

Gabor, Dennis (1900–1979). Hungarian electrical engineer who invented holography. He worked as a research engineer for an electrical company in Berlin from 1927, left Germany in 1933 and moved to England. He first developed holography (three-dimensional photography) in 1947, but it did not become a commercial proposition until the invention of the laser (1960) provided the necessary intensity of light. He was elected F.R.S. (1956), made a C.B.E. (1970) and was awarded the Nobel Prize for Physics (1971) for his invention of holography. He wrote many books on scientific and social subjects including *Inventing the Future* (1963).

Gaboriau, Emile (1835–1873). French writer. Celebrated as a pioneer of the detective novel, *L'Affaire Lerouge* (1866) was his first great success.

Gabrieli Family (**Andrea,** *c.* 1520–1586; **Giovanni,** *c.* 1556–1612). Venetian organists and composers, uncle and nephew. Andrea was first singer and then organist at St Mark's; he studied composition with the cathedral's musical director Adriaan Willaert. He wrote madrigals, and ceremonial music for choir and instruments. Giovanni succeeded his uncle as second organist at St Mark's (Andrea having becoming first organist) in 1585. His two main publications were the *Sacrae Symphoniae* of 1597 and 1615. He is credited with introducing a new approach to orchestration, in that he directed, in detail, the specific instruments and types of voice to be used. Both composers are regarded as of great significance in Renaissance music.

Reese, G., *Music in the Renaissance*. 1954

Gadsden, James (1788–1858). American soldier. U.S. minister to Mexico who negotiated (1853) a treaty, known as the Gadsden Purchase, by which 45,500 square miles of territory, now part of Arizona and New Mexico, were acquired by the U.S.A.

Gagarin, Yuri Alexeyevich (1934–1968). Russian astronaut. A major in the Soviet air force, he was the first man to orbit the earth in a space capsule and return safely (April 1961).

Gagarin, V., *My Brother Yuri*. 1974

Gage, Thomas (1721–1787). English soldier. He was commander-in-chief of the British forces in America from 1763, and in 1774 was appointed governor of Massachusetts. His inflexibility precipitated the War of Independence. The first clash, at Lexington (1775), resulted from an expedition sent by him to seize arms stored at Concord. He was recalled three months later owing to the heavy losses incurred in forcing the colonists from their position on Bunker Hill.

Gainsborough, Thomas (1726–1788). English painter. Famous for both portraits and landscapes, and founder of the 'English School' of painting, he was born in Suffolk. Whilst living in London (from 1740), he married (1746) an illegitimate daughter of the Prince of Wales and in 1752 returned to Suffolk. It was not however until he moved to Bath (1759) that he gained a fashionable clientele. He became (1768) a foundation member of the R. A., and settled in London (1774), where he soon rivalled Reynolds as a painter of celebrities. His most important works were portraits (about 100 full-size, and many smaller ones), where the influence of Van Dyck is clear. Of simple and warm character, unlike Reynolds, he needed to feel sympathy with his subject to be at his best, when he achieves a freshness and vitality that is entrancing. He takes a special delight in materials and clothes, the sheen and creases of silk, the ripple of lace, the gleam of metal, e.g. in two of his best known works, the *Blue Boy* and the portrait of the actress *Mrs Siddons*. Despite the fashion set by * Poussin for idealized landscapes, Gainsborough, who loved the countryside, imparted much of the freshness of an observer's eye and can at least claim to anticipate Constable.

Corri, A., *The Search for Gainsborough*. 1984

Gaitskell, Hugh Todd Naylor (1906–1963). British politician. Educated at Winchester College and Oxford, and subsequently a lecturer in political economy at University College, London, he became a Labour M.P. in 1945. In Attlee's post-war government he became minister of fuel and power in 1947 and was chancellor of the exchequer (1950–51). In 1955 he succeeded Attlee as leader of the Labour party, by then in opposition. He refused to recognize as binding a resolution passed (1960) by the Labour party conference in favour of unilateral nuclear disarmament, and secured its reversal the following year. His sudden death deprived the Labour party of a widely respected leader of great promise.

McDermott, G., *Leader Lost: A Biography of Hugh Gaitskell*. 1972

Galbraith, John Kenneth (1908–). American economist, born in Canada. He became professor of economics at Harvard University in 1949. He was economics adviser to President Kennedy and subsequently U.S. ambassador in India. One of his books, *The Affluent Society* (1958), whose title became a popular phrase, directed attention to new phenomena occasioned by the post-war prosperity of America and Europe.

Galen (*c*. 130--201). Greek physician. He was born at Pergamum in Asia Minor, and studied at Pergamum, Corinth and Alexandria. In 157 he was appointed surgeon to the gladiators at Pergamum. He lived in Rome from *c*. 161 and became physician to Marcus Aurelius and several other emperors. He was a prolific writer and incorporated in his books the whole of Greek medical theory and practice; translated later into Arabic and Latin, they were accepted as authoritative for nearly 1,400 years.

Sarten, G., *Galen of Pergamon*. 1954

Galileo Galilei (1564–1642). Italian physicist and astronomer. He was born of a good Florentine family at Pisa, where (from 1581), at the university, he studied medicine before turning to mathematics and physics. When only 18 he made one of his most important discoveries while watching a swinging candelabrum in Pisa Cathedral, that identical time was taken by each oscillation whatever the distance covered by the swing. This discovery he used years later for the making of improved pendulum clocks. This led to his being appointed professor of mathematics at Pisa. A more startling discovery, traditionally demonstrated by dropping stones from the Leaning Tower of Pisa, was that objects fall with equal velocity irrespective of their size and weight. This theory contradicted Aristotle's teaching and provoked so much hostility that Galileo retired to Florence (1591); but in the next year he was appointed professor of mathematics at Padua, where he remained for eighteen years, attracting students from all over Europe. He devised the first thermometer (*c*. 1600) and constructed (1609) improved versions of the refracting telescope first produced by the Dutch Hans Lippershey about a year earlier. Galileo attained a magnifying power of × 32 and carried out (from 1610) numerous astronomical observations which convinced him that * Copernicus had been right in asserting that the earth rotates round the sun. He observed that the moon's light was reflected from that of the sun, and that its surface was covered by mountains and valleys; and that the Milky Way was composed for separate stars. He also discovered the existence of the four satellites of Jupiter; sunspots (from which he deduced the rotation of the sun); the 'rings' of Saturn; and the phases of Venus and Mars.

Meanwhile (1610) the Medici Grand Duke of Tuscany had invited him back to Florence

and appointed him his philosopher and mathematician extraordinary, a post with a satisfactory salary but no specific duties, which enabled him to continue his observations. In 1611 he was received with honour on a visit to Rome; but after the publication of a treatise on the sunspots (1613), in which he openly adhered to the Copernican theory, he became the object of ecclesiastical displeasure and was persuaded to promise (1616) not to 'hold, teach or defend' the new doctrines. After a long peaceful period his greatest work, *Dialogue on the Two Chief Systems of the World*, appeared (1632), and it was immediately evident that Galileo had not changed his views. The machinery of the Inquisition was turned against him and on the threat of torture he recanted; because of age and ill health he was allowed to return to Florence. In 1637 he became blind. Among his later discoveries were the parabolic trajectory of projectiles and the monthly and annual liberations of the moon. His misfortunes were due at least as much to his ironic and irascible nature as to the church's opposition to his theories.
Brecht, B., *Life of Galileo*. 1974

Gall Franz Joseph (1758–1828). German physiologist. Regarded as the founder of phrenology, he practised medicine in Vienna (until 1802) and later in Paris. He concluded that human character and abilities depend upon the development of particular areas of the brain and that these can be inferred from the shape of the skull. This inference, no longer accepted as scientific, has been exploited by many quacks.

Gallatin, Albert (1761–1849). American politician. A Geneva aristocrat by birth, he emigrated to America when 19 under the influence of Rousseau's idealism. He settled in Pennsylvania and gradually rose in state and national politics. He sat in the U.S. Congress (1795–1801), then as secretary to the Treasury under Jefferson and Madison (1801–14) he reduced the public debt by over $14,000,000. He was one of the negotiators of the Treaty of Ghent which brought the 'war of 1812' with England to an end; he was minister to France (1816–23) and to Britain (1826–27).

Galli-Curci, Amelita (1889–1963). Italian coloratura soprano, born in Milan. Largely selftaught, she achieved dazzling success in the operas of Verdi and Puccini and was a star of the Metropolitan Opera, New York (1920–30).

Gallieni, Joseph Simon (1849–1916). French soldier. After long and distinguished service, mainly in the colonies, he was military governor of Paris in 1914. By mobilizing Paris taxis to effect a quick concentration against the German right flank, he played a vital part in the Battle of the Marne. He was minister of war (1914–16) and was posthumously made a marshal (1921).

Gallup, George Horace (1901–1984). American statistician. He devised a method of predicting election results and measuring other public reactions by sampling cross-sections of the population. 'Gallup poll' became synonymous with public opinion polls.

Galsworthy, John (1867–1933). English writer. Educated at Harrow and Oxford, he entered, but soon abandoned, the legal profession and after some years of travel determined to become a writer. His first novel, *Jocelyn* (1898) attracted little attention but he continued with his chosen theme – the virtues, prejudices and way of life of the upper-middle-class society to which he himself belonged. His masterpieces were *The Forsyte Saga* (published 1906–21), a series of novels describing the family of Soames Forsyte (*The Man of Property, In Chancery, To Let*), and the novels collectively titled *A Modern Comedy* 1929). His many plays, usually regarded as humane rather than profound, were influenced by the social dramas of Ibsen and reflect a preoccupation with ethical considerations; they include *The Silver Box* (1906), *Joy* (1907), *Strife* (1909), *Justice* (1910), *The Skin Game* (1920), *Loyalties* (1922) and *Escape* (1926). He was the first president of International P.E.N. and was awarded the Order of Merit (1929) and the Nobel Prize for Literature (1932).
Dupre, C., *John Galsworthy: A Biography*. 1976

Galton, Sir Francis (1822–1911). English scientist. He was a cousin of Charles* Darwin and after studying medicine at Birmingham, King's College, London, and at Cambridge, he spent some years exploring in South-west Africa. His early scientific achievements were in meteorology; in 1863 he made the first

serious attempts to construct weather charts, and established the existence of, and named, anticyclones. He pioneered the application of statistical methods to the study of human heredity, about which he wrote extensively; he endowed a chair of eugenics at London University. He also devised a method of comparing fingerprints which is still used.
Forrest, D. W., *Francis Galton: The Life and Work of a Victorian Genius*. 1974

Galvani, Luigi (1737–1798). Italian physiologist, whose great contemporary reputation rested on his lectures on comparative anatomy at Bologna University. It is, however, through an electrical discovery that his name (e.g. in 'galvanize') has become incorporated in scientific language. He demonstrated (1791) that a frog's legs will twitch when placed in simultaneous contact with two different types of metal, but incorrectly interpreted the effect as being caused by 'animal' electricity, and not, as Volta afterwards showed, by an electric current flowing between the metals, as in cell.

Gama, Vasco da *see* **Vasco da Gama**

Gambetta, Léon Michel (1838–1882). French Radical politician. He became a lawyer and gained fame by his defence of opponents of Napoleon III's régime. After the capitulation at Sedan in the Franco-Prussian War he joined the Ministry of National Defence. Leaving besieged Pairs by balloon, he went to Tours to organize further resistance. After the war he succeeded in frustrating political attempts to restore the monarchy and headed a republican government (1881–82). He died after a pistol accident.
Bury, J. B., *Gambetta and the Making of the Third Republic*. 1973

Gamelin, Maurice Gustave (1872–1958). French soldier. In World War I he was on Joffre's staff in 1914 and drew up the orders for the Battlé of the Marne and subsequently proved an outstanding divisional commander. At the beginning of World War II he was commander-in-chief of all French and British troops in France. After the German breakthrough he was superseded by Weygand. He wrote, *Servir: Les Armées françaises de 1940*. (1946).

Gamow, George (1904–1968). American physicist, born in Odessa. Educated in Leningrad, he lived in the U.S. from 1934, teaching in Washington and Colorado. He worked on the evolution of stars and argued that nuclear fusion was increasing the sun's temperature. He supported * Lemaitre's theory of the expansion of the universe and coined the term 'big bang' (1948). Gamow also hypothesized a coding scheme for elements in genetic structures. He wrote more than thirty books popularizing science, including some for children.

Gance, Abel (1889–1981). French film director, born in Paris. After working in a lawyer's office he became an actor, script writer, theatrical producer and in 1911 directed the first of his 50 feature films, *La Digue*. He directed *La Folie du Docteur Tube* (1915: expressionist in style, using optical distortion which anticipated Robert Wiene's *The Cabinet of Dr. Caligari*), *J'Accuse!* (1918: remade in 1937), *La Roue* (1922), *Napoléon* (1927: an epic projected on a triple screen, converted to sound in 1934), *La Fin du Monde* (1931: his first talking film), *Un Grand Amour de Beethoven* (1936), *La Vénus Aveugle* (1940), *La Tour de Nesle* (1953: his first colour film), *Austerlitz* (1960) and *Bonaparte et la Révolution* (1971). He faced major problems in financing and distributing his films. They were notable for vigour, broad sweep and technical innovation, e.g. the use of wide-angle lens, wide-screen projection, stereophonic sound, split-screen images, hand-held cameras, low angled close-ups, and rapid, impressionistic editing, which anticipated many techniques in *cinéma-vérité*.

Gandhi, Indira (1917–1984). Indian politician. The daughter of Jawaharlal * Nehru, she was educated in Switzerland, Oxford and with Rabindranath * Tagore. In 1929 she founded a children's organization to help the movement for non-co-operation with British rule. In 1942 she married Feroze Gandhi (died 1960), a member of the Indian National Congress, which she joined the same year; she was its president (1959–60). From 1946 she acted as hostess for her father and she played an active part in politics, especially in matters relating to child welfare and social reform. After her father's death (1964) she was minister of information in Shastri's government, and became prime minister when Shastri also died (1969). She won a landslide election victory in 1971. In 1975 she declared a state of emergency and ruled by decree, eventually losing the elections of 1977 to a coalition led by Morarji * Desai. In 1980 her Congress (I) Party was returned to office and she again became Prime Minister. Sikh members of her bodyguard shot her in New Delhi (31 October 1984). Her son **Rajiv Gandhi** (1944–) succeeded as leader of Congress (I) and Prime Minister 1984– . Educated at Cambridge, he became a pilot for Indian Airlines and entered the Lok Sabha after his brother, **Sanjay Gandhi** (1946–1980), regarded as heir apparent to the Nehru dynasty, died in a plane crash. He won a record majority in the December 1984 election.

Masani, Z., *Indira Gandhi: A Political Biography*. 1975

Gandhi, Mohandas Karamchand (1869–1948). Indian religious and political leader known as *Mahatma* (in Sanskrit, *maha*: great, *atman*: soul), a title first conferred by Rabindranath * Tagore. Born in Porbander, in Kathiawar where his father had been chief minister, he was brought up as a member of a Hindu sect strictly opposed to taking life and therefore vegetarian. A quiet, studious boy, he was married at 13 to Kasturbai Nakanji (1869–1944) but continued his education. In 1888 he sailed to London where he was called to the bar (1891) and in 1893 went to Natal to represent an Indian firm, remaining in South Africa for twenty years (1893–1901; 1902–14). Jailed for refusing to register as an Indian alien, he urged his followers to burn their certificates—also organizing passive resistance campaigns. This ultimately compelled the Transvaal government to recognize the validity of monogamous marriages celebrated according to Indian rites. In 1913 he negotiated an agreement with J. C. * Smuts raising the status of Indian labourers. In South Africa he had become convinced that 'soul force' was the strongest power in the world and to maximize it in himself he must renounce sex, meat, tobacco, alcohol, and also threats, violence, coercion and other political weapons. Major influences on Gandhi included the Sermon on the Mount, the doctrine of 'non possession' in the *Bhagavad Gita*, and writings by * Thoreau, Ruskin and Tolstoy. He corresponded with Tolstoy and set up a Tolstoyan commune and school in Phoenix, Natal (1910).

He returned to India in January 1915 and with his followers withdrew to an *ashram* ('retreat') at Sabarmati, near Ahmadabad in Gujurat, where he campaigned on behalf of the 'untouchables' in the caste system. Britain's refusal to grant substantial self-government after the war persuaded Gandhi to lead a campaign for *Swaraj* ('self-rule'), employing the principles of *Satyagraha* ('soul-force'; literally 'firmness in the truth') which had proved successful in South Africa. He called for 'non-violent non cooperation' with government agencies and *hartal* (strikes with prayer and fasting) against economic regulation, and founded the influential journal *Young India*.

The *hartal* campaign led to the Amritsar massacre (R. E. H. * Dyer) in April 1919. He urged non-cooperation with the British in all forms: all government posts were to be given up; government schools were to be abandoned; in the place of foreign-made cloth, homespun only was to be used (hence Gandhi's familar appearance in a loin-cloth and homespun blanket and cape). He was opposed to violence in any form but was not always able to control his supporters. Such incidents as the burning of a police station with its inmates at Chauri Chaura (1922), in the United Provinces, forced the authorities to arrest Gandhi, who assumed responsibility. Sentenced to six years jail, he was released in 1922 on the grounds of ill-health. He became President of the Indian National Congress Party (1924–35), the only office he ever held, and in 1929 launched a new 'civil disobedience' campaign. In March 1930 Gandhi, with hundreds of followers, marched to the sea at Dandi to protest against the imposition of a tax on salt. After the 'Salt March' his followers formally broke the law by scooping up tax-free salt. Gandhi was jailed again (1930–31) but released (with 60,000 supporters) after the Salt Law was relaxed by the Viceroy, Lord Irwin (later Viscount * Halifax). A truce made during the abortive Round Table Conference in London (1931) was soon broken and he returned to jail, being released when he began a 'fast until death'. Winston Churchill was a scathing critic of 'this half-naked fakir, of a type well-known in the East'. Jailed for most of 1932 and again briefly in 1933, during the period 1935–41 Gandhi was in virtual retirement although publishing the weekly *Harijan* and campaigning on behalf of the untouchables. During World War II he gave moral support to Britain, but refused active cooperation on the grounds that Indian consent had

not been obtained. Following another civil-disobedience campaign (1942) he was interned until May 1944. Despite his alleged retirement from politics he played an active part behind the scenes in the negotiations which gave independence to India (1947) and the appointment of a Congress government under * Nehru. He opposed partition, mourning the massacres and forced displacement of Moslem and Hindu minorities. He toured Bengal, preaching unity between Hindus and Moslems. The impact of his renewed fasts alarmed Hindu extremists: at a prayer meeting (30 January 1948) he was assassinated by a Hindu fanatic, N. V. Godse. Combining a natural shrewdness with the character of a saint, Gandhi was one of the most influential and impressive figures of the 20th century.
Woodcock, G., *Gandhi* 1972.

Garbo, Greta (Greta Louisa Gustafsson) (1905–). Swedish film star. While working in a Stockholm department store, she studied dancing and acting and achieved great success in the film *The Atonement of Gösta Berling* (1924). She then went to Hollywood and, with her beauty, sincerity and elusive charm, achieved immediate stardom in silent films; her first talking part was in *Anna Christie* (1930), and she later added distinction to the title roles of e.g. *Queen Christina* (1933), *Anna Karenina* (1935), *Camille* (1936) and *Ninotchka* (1939). She disliked and avoided publicity and any intrusion into her private life, and retired from the screen in 1941 at the height of her fame.
Conway, M., *Films of Greta Garbo*. 1970

Garcia. Spanish family of singers. **Manuel del Populo Vicente Garcia** (1775–1832) was born in Seville and became a singer, actor, composer and conductor, creating the role of Almaviva in Rossini's *Barber of Seville* (Rome, 1816). He produced operas in New York and Mexico, composed 97 himself, and became a teacher in Paris where he died. His daughter, **Maria Felicita Garcia** (1808–36), became famous under her husband's name, **Malibran**, and had a contralto voice with an extraordinary range which made her a sensation in London, Paris and Italy. Another daughter, **Pauline Garcia** (1821–1910), known as **Viardot** (again, from her husband's name), was a mezzo-soprano and pianist who studied under her father and Franz * Liszt: she was renowned for her acting and became the mistress of * Turgenev. Their brother, **Manuel Patricio Rodriguez Garcia** (1805–1906), was a concert basso who became a teacher from 1829, first in Paris and (from 1848) in London. He wrote the first scientific text on the art of voice production, became the teacher of Jenny * Lind and Mathilde Marchesi, and was awarded the CVO on his 100th birthday.

García Márquez, Gabriel (1928–). Colombian novelist. His novels *One Hundred Years of Solitude* (1967) and *The Autumn of the Patriarch* (1975) are passionate epics of life in South America, full of powerful and hypnotic imagery, combining realism and fantasy. He won the 1982 Nobel Prize for Literature.

Gardiner, Samuel Rawson (1829–1902). English historian. The scale, scope and accuracy of his work on the early Stuarts, the Civil War and its aftermath make him an authority in this field. His books include *History of England 1603–1640* (10 volumes, 1883–84), *The Great Civil War* (3 volumes, 1886–91) and *The Commonwealth and the Protectorate* (3 volumes, 1895–1901).

Gardiner, Stephen (1483–1555). English ecclesiastic. He was Wolsey's secretary, and vainly negotiated on Henry VIII's behalf for the annulment of his marriage with Catherine of Aragon. He became bishop of Winchester (1531), and is remembered as the man mainly responsible for the persecution of the Protestants under Queen Mary (though he tried, vainly, to save Cranmer). Yet in 1535 he had accepted Henry VIII's royal supremacy and had even written a treatise in its support. He spent much of Edward VI's reign in prison.

Gardner, Erle Stanley (1899–1970). American detective-story writer. He practised as a lawyer in California for ten years but from 1930 devoted himself to writing. Most of his immensely popular stories end with a dramatic court scene of which the hero is the famous lawyer-detective, Perry Mason.

Garfield, James Abram (1831–1881). Twentieth president of the U.S. He was born on an Ohio farm, where he worked from the age of 10, but managed to enter and to graduate from Williams College; he then became a teacher, a lawyer, and a general in the American Civil War. From 1863 to 1880, the years of reconstruction and corruption that followed the war, Garfield sat in the House of Representatives – for the last four years as Republican leader. In 1880 he emerged as a compromise candidate for the presidency and was narrowly elected. In July 1881, four months after his inauguration, he was shot by a disappointed office-seeker and died in September.

Garibaldi, Giuseppe (1807–1882). Italian patriot. Born in Nice, the son of a fisherman, he became a sailor. Later he joined Mazzini's 'Young Italy' movement, but after taking part in an abortive attempt to seize Genoa (1834) he fled to South America. The part he played in the insurrection of Brazil's Rio Grande province and his other interventions in the troubled politics of the continent gave him experience of leading irregulars and a heroic reputation that followed him home. During this period he married Anita Ribera da Silva, who had accompanied his various expeditions and had borne him three children. Back in Italy in 1848 he led an irregular band against the Austrians after the defeat of the Sardinian regular army. Next he played a leading part (1849) in establishing a republican government in Rome after Pope Pius IX had been forced to flee, but papal authority was restored by French and Neapolitan intervention. His fortunes were now at their lowest; Anita had died from exhaustion and anxiety and he himself had to flee to New York. He returned (1854) and had settled as a farmer on the island of Caprera near Sardinia when in 1859 the renewed war between the Austrians and the Sardinians (now under King Victor Emmanuel and this time with French support) again called him to battle. Northern Italy was liberated and Garibaldi and his Alpine troops had played a gallant part. In 1860 began his greatest triumph. With his 1,000 'red-shirts' he landed in Sicily but met little serious resistance from the troops of King Francis II and within three months conquered the entire island. He then crossed to the Neapolitan mainland. Francis found himself abandoned and now the only danger lay in a clash between the two liberators, Garibaldi advancing on Naples from the south, Victor Emmanuel from the north. Good sense prevailed: Victor Emmanuel was proclaimed king of a united Italy (except Rome and Venice) and Garibaldi, seeking no reward, returned to his island farm. He and his red-shirts next appeared in 1866 in the brief campaign in which Italy, as Prussia's ally against Austria, gained Venice. But Rome remained his dream, and in 1867 he sailed from Caprera, gathered his volunteers and marched on the city. After a preliminary success he was overwhelmed by the French garrison left to protect the pope. It was the withdrawal of that garrison during the Franco-Prussian War (1870–71) that eventually enabled Rome to become the capital of the Italian state. In that war too Garibaldi had his last taste of battle; after the fall of his enemy, Napoleon III, he rallied to the side of the republican government and even achieved some success amid the general defeat. The rest of his life he spent (except for an occasional appearance in the Italian chamber, where he sat as a deputy) at Caprera crippled by illness. He wrote novels, he signed manifestos, but his strength was in action not the pen. He was a man who never wavered from a single fixed purpose, the unification of divided Italy under Italian rule, and though others planned more wisely for the same ideal it was Garibaldi, with his enthusiasm, his leadership and colourful exploits, that fired the hearts of men and more perhaps than any other single man brought it about.

Ridley, J., *Garibaldi.* 1975

Garland, Judy (Frances Gumm) (1922–1969). American film actress and singer. She began her stage career as part of a music-hall act, and began to make films in 1936. Throughout the following 14 years she played leading parts in musicals and comedy films and achieved a tremendous following. Her best-known films from this period are *The Wizard of Oz* (1939), a series in partnership with Mickey Rooney (1937–41), and musicals like *For Me and My Gal* (1942) and *Meet Me in St. Louis* (1944). She later turned to dramatic roles as in *A Star is Born* (1954), and to concert and cabaret tours. Her daughter **Liza Minnelli** (1946–) was acclaimed as an actress and singer, winning an Academy Award for her role in *Cabaret* (1972).

Garner, John Nance (1868–1967). U.S. Democratic politician, born in Texas. A Congressman 1903–33, he became Speaker of the House of Representatives 1931–33 and Vice President of the United States 1933–41.

Garnett, Edward (1868–1937). English writer and critic. He was the son of **Richard Garnett** (1835–1906), Carlyle's biographer. His work as literary adviser to the publishers Fisher Unwin, Heinemann, and Jonathan Cape brought him into touch with many authors, and his home became a sort of literary club where advice, kindness and help were always available. He gave much encouragement to Conrad, Galsworthy and D. H. Lawrence.

His wife, **Constance Garnett** (1862–1943), introduced a new world of Russian literature to English readers by her translations of Tolstoy, Dostoyevsky, Chekhov etc. Their son, **David Garnett** (1892–1981), won immediate literary success with his short fantasy *Lady Into Fox* (1922), which won the Hawthornden and James Tait Black Memorial Prizes; *A Man In The Zoo* (1924) won almost equal acclaim.

Garnier, Tony (1869–1948). French architect and planner. Over many years (from 1904) he elaborated his design (*Une Cité industrielle*, published 1917) for an integrated city for 35,000 people on original and revolutionary lines, some of which he was able to put into practice in Lyons, where he was city architect.

Garrick, David (1717–1779). English actor. As a youth in Lichfield he was briefly a pupil of Samuel * Johnson, whose close friend he later became. The two went to London together (1737), Garrick intending to study for the bar. In fact he joined his brother as a wine merchant before making his debut as an actor in 1741. His first part in London was Richard III; he was an immediate success and remained throughout his career the most popular actor of his age in both tragedy and comedy, Lear and Macbeth being among the most memorable of his Shakespearian parts. He was joint patentee and director of Drury Lane Theatre from 1747 to 1776 when he was succeeded by * Sheridan. He also wrote several plays (of little merit), and some excellent prologues and epilogues. He remained a member of Johnson's social group and he was portrayed by Hogarth, Gainborough and Reynolds.

Oman, C., *David Garrick*. 1958

Garrison, William Lloyd (1805–1879). American journalist and reformer, born in Massachusetts. He became editor of two New England newspapers, in which he vigorously attacked slavery; for one article he was briefly imprisoned for libel. The *Liberator*, in which for thirty-five years he campaigned for emancipation, first appeared in 1831. In 1833 he was a founder of the American Anti-slavery Society. With a violence and self-righteousness that often injured the causes for which he pleaded, he also supported female suffrage, the abolition of capital punishment, and prohibition.

Garvin, James Louis (1868–1947). English journalist. As editor (1908–42) of the *Observer* he exercised a strong political influence, his vast editorial pronouncements being accorded an almost oracular significance during World War I. He also edited (1926–29) the *Encyclopedia Britannica* (14th edition), and wrote a biography of his friend Joseph Chamberlain (3 volumes, 1932–34). He was made a C.H. in 1941.

Gaskell, Elizabeth Cleghorn (née Stevenson) (1810–1865). English novelist. She was born in Chelsea and brought up by an aunt in Knutsford, Cheshire, the scene of her best known novel *Cranford* (1853). In 1832 she married a Unitarian minister and moved to Manchester, which provided the background for *Mary Barton* (1848) and *North and South* (1855). She also wrote a notable life (1857) of Charlotte Brontë, the frankness of which provoked some criticism at the time.

Gérin, W., *Elizabeth Gaskell*. 1976

Gasperi, Alcide de (1881–1954). Italian politician. After his native province in the Austrian Tyrol was joined to Italy as a result of World War I, he served as parliamentary deputy until imprisoned by Mussolini (1926). After his release (1928) he withdrew from politics and worked in the Vatican library. He founded (1944) the Christian Democratic party which, like the pre-war Popular party that it replaced, had Vatican support. When Italy became a republic he was its first prime minister (1946–53). Under his leadership Italy joined NATO.

Gassendi, Pierre (1592–1655). French philosopher and scientist. He studied at Aix, and obtained a doctorate at Avignon, where he took holy orders. From an early age, studies in natural philosophy occupied his mind, and he became a partisan for the Moderns. His criticisms of Aristotelian philosophy were set out in his *Exercitationes Paradoxicae adversus Aristotelos*. He entered into deep study of * Epicurus, whose biography he wrote. In regard to philosophies of Nature, Gassendi was an eclectic. A pious Christian, he was aware that no man can penetrate to the heart of Nature's secrets. But he was a convinced supporter of the atomistic hypothesis of the composition of matter. Atoms were the first things created. Subsequently combinations of molecules formed by collision and complex bodies were built up. He believed that science could best proceed by the measurement of basic particles (weight, speed, acceleration, mass, density) rather than by inventing mythical 'virtues' such as 'powers', 'tendencies' and the other categories of Scholastic thought.

Gassendi was of importance as a defender of the autonomy of science in the age of * Galileo's persecution. He insisted that science was compatible with Christianity, so long as both sides knew their own place. Gassendi made few positive contributions to science in the technical sense. He did offer quite a good approximation of the speed of sound – 1,038 feet per second, and offered an accurate statement of the principle of inertia, seeing it not as a tendency to rest, but the tendency to resist change of state.

Gates, Horatio (*c.* 1728–1806). American soldier, British-born. He served with British forces in North America against the French (1754–63), returned to England but emigrated to West Virginia in 1772. Taking up the colonial cause, he was made adjutant general of the Continental Army in 1775 and became a general in 1777. He defeated British forces at Saratoga in that year and was considered by a group of officers as a replacement for General Washington, a scheme that came to nothing. He was defeated at the battle of Camden, South Cawling, in 1780. After the war he moved to New York and served a term in the state legislature.

Gaudi, Antonio (1852–1926). Spanish architect. He developed a highly idiosyncratic style, fantastic in design and construction, similar in spirit to Art Nouveau. He introduced colour, unusual materials and audacious technical innovations. His main works are around Barcelona, where the huge unfinished Church of the Holy Family is the greatest monument to his ingenuity and decorative virtuosity.

Sweeney, J. J., and Sert, J. L., *Antonio Gaudi*. 1970

Gauguin, Paul (1848–1903). French painter. Though successful as a stockbroker, he abandoned the profession in 1883, sent his wife with their five children to her parents in Denmark and devoted the rest of his life to art. Paris proving too expensive he settled in Brittany (1886). After a visit to Martinique and an acrimonious association with Van Gogh he went (1891) to the South Seas, first to Tahiti and (1901) to the Marquesas, where he died.

Originally influenced by the Impressionists, particularly by his friend Pissaro, he parted from them in 1887, dissociating himself from their techniques of breaking up colour. He himself evolved a decorative style using simplified drawing, and flat, strong, pure and not necessarily naturalistic colouring; outlines, as in cloisonné enamels, were often intensified by black lines. The brilliant colours of Tahiti provided ideal inspiration and he was also influenced by primitive sculpture, as is seen in some of his pictures of serene impassive islanders represented in attitudes of repose. Gauguin's paintings were a major influence on later non-representational art.

Goldwater, R., *Paul Gauguin*. 1957; Gaugin, P., *The Intimate Journals of Paul Gaugin*. 1985

Gaulle, Charles André Joseph Marie de (1890–1970). French soldier and statesman. He was born at Lille, and became an army officer. In World War I he was taken prisoner (1916) at Verdun. With Weygand (1921) he went to the aid of the Poles against the Russians. In 1924–25 he first formulated, at the École de Guerre, his ideas about tactics and especially the use of mechanized forces, which were published in France in 1932–34 and in English as *The Army of the Future* (1940). Little notice was taken in France but his basic ideas were adopted by the German general staff and later used in the 'Blitzkrieg' attacks of 1940. In June 1940, lately promoted a general, de Gaulle was appointed undersecretary of war, but France was already defeated and a few days before the French armistice he went to London, where he declared himself the leader of the Free French. The numbers of the troops at his disposal were few; and neither Roosevelt nor Churchill found him an easy colleague, but gradually he succeeded, by his personality and self-dedication, in creating, not only in his own mind but in the minds of millions of his fellow countrymen, an identification between himself and a new and glorious France, untarnished by defeat. In the later stages of the war, as leader of the Resistance movement he was associated with France's most active patriots and when the moment of victory came he was clearly the only man who could lead his country. In attempting to do this through a coalition of all parties, including the Communists, he failed; moreover the constitution of the Fourth Republic seemed to him no better than the old. His sense of frustration caused him to resign (1946) and found a new party, the 'Rally of French People' (R.P.F.), but despite its electoral success (40 per cent of the votes in 1947) he felt the curb of party ties and retired from its leadership in 1953. He was thus free of all party commitments when in 1958, after the failure of successive governments to defeat or conciliate the Algerian rebels, he accepted President Coty's invitation to form a government. Almost his first act was to bring in a new constitution, that of the Fifth Republic, passed by referendum; this gave de Gaulle, as president (1959–69), almost unlimited powers and while the legislature was still a forum for discussion and advice he deprived it of any decisive role. He faced the facts of the Algerian situation and gave the country full independence (1962), thus making himself a target for frequent attempts at assassination by aggrieved French colonists. He repeated this pattern throughout the French territories, all of which became free, held to France only by language, economic ties and the vague description of French communities.

Domestically de Gaulle was helped by the general prosperity of western Europe. He brought France into the European Economic Community, but maintained his support for it only so long as France's autonomy was unassailed and the needs of her agriculture served; and lest French hegemony be challenged he banned Britain's entry. In foreign affairs he saw western Europe as a third great power under Franco-German leadership; he welcomed the security of the American alliance but resented the curbs of NATO and asserted France's independence by manufacturing nuclear weapons and recognizing China. De Gaulle had great personal advantages; his height, his magnificent rhetoric, the clarity of his writing and thinking all marked him out as a great national leader. Moreover he had succeeded in the task to which he dedicated himself in 1940. His singleness of purpose, his obduracy and his prestige have, within a framework of his own devising, dispelled the disillusion and frustration of defeated and tortured France.

Crozier, B., *De Gaulle: The Warrior*. 1973. *De Gaulle: The Statesman*. 1974

Gaunt, John of *see* **John of Gaunt**

Gauss, Karl Freidrich (1777–1855). German mathematician and physicist. Educated at Göttingen University, he gave early proof of his great powers in both pure and applied mathematics, becoming a professor there and director of the observatory (1807). From celestial mechanics and geodesy he turned his attention in the 1830s to electromagnetic theory and research on terrestrial magnetism, establishing most of the important theory for the measurement of magnetic field strengths. Gauss was also, with Riemann and Lobachevsky, one of the pioneers of non-Euclidean geometry. The unit of magnetic flux density is named after him.

Dunnington, G. W., *Carl Friedrich Gauss, Titan of Science*. 1955

Gautama Buddha *see* **Buddha, The**

Gautier, Théophile (1811–1872). French poet and novelist. Prevented by short sight from being a painter, he began to write as a strong supporter of the Romantic movement, but was already mocking its excesses in his novel *Mademoiselle de Maupin* (1835); his volume of poems *Emaux et camées* (1852) was among the principal influences on the 'art for art's sake' movement, which stressed beauty of form and sound rather than significance. His daughter, **Judith Gautier** (1850–1917), also a novelist, married the poet Catulle * Mendès, and later Pierre * Loti.

Tennant, P., *Théophile Gautier*. 1973

Gaveston, Piers (died 1312). Created Earl of Cornwall, the favourite of Edward II of England. A noble of Gascon descent, he aroused the hatred of the barons by his swaggering display of power and mocking tongue. Twice they forced his banishment, and his second return led to civil war. Gaveston was forced to surrender, but three of his most popular opponents kidnapped him and had him beheaded.

Gay, John (1685–1732). English poet and dramatist. He was born in Devon, and after attending a local grammar school went to

London as a mercer's apprentice. His political satires and his amiable temperament won him much aristocratic patronage and the friendship of Pope. His early publications included *The Shepherd's Week* (1714) and *Trivia* (1716); the latter, with its humorous accounts of London life, became extremely popular. Having just dedicated his satiric *Fables* (1727) to the Duke of Cumberland, he had hoped, when the Duke's father succeeded to the throne as George II, for more than the sinecure offered. Thus gibes at * Walpole were included in his triumphant success *The Beggar's Opera* (1728), of which he wrote the libretto for an accompaniment of old tunes; its sequel *Polly* (1729), though banned from the stage, also brought its author a large sum on publication. His *Acis and Galatea* appeared as an opera with music by Handel in 1732.

Armes, S. M., *John Gay: Social Critic*. 1972

Gay-Lussac, Joseph Louis (1778–1850). French chemist. He was educated at and was later professor at the Ecole Polytechnique, Paris. For a time he worked at the government chemical works at Arcueil, at first mainly on physical properties of gases and liquids. In balloon ascents of up to 23,000 ft. he investigated the earth's magnetic field and atmospheric conditions. In 1808 he put forward his law of gas volumes which states that the volumes of gas (taking part and produced) in a chemical reaction are always in a simple proportion to one another (* Charles, Jacques). With Thénard he made discoveries in inorganic chemistry and also worked out the first satisfactory scheme of organic analysis. He investigated iodine and cyanogen compounds, and in 1815 was the first to isolate cyanogen itself. He also made important improvements in a number of industrial processes, e.g. for the manufacture of sulphuric acid by the Chamber process in which he introduced the so-called Gay-Lussac tower, first used in 1842.

Geddes, Sir Patrick (1854–1932). Scottish biologist, sociologist and pioneer in the development of town planning. He was chosen to design the buildings of the Hebrew University in Jerusalem. He wrote *City Development* (1904) and *Cities in Evolution* (1915).

Boardman, P., *Patrick Geddes: Maker of the Future*. 1957

Geiger, Hans (1882–1945). German physicist. He was best known for research on the alpha-particles given off from radioactive substances. For their detection he invented (1908), with * Rutherford, the device known as the Geiger counter. With Marsden he showed that alpha-particles passing through metal foil were occasionally deflected through large angles, and it was this observation that led Rutherford to formulate (1911) his nuclear model of the atom.

Geikie, Sir Archibald (1835–1924). Scottish geologist, born and educated in Edinburgh. He worked with the Geological Survey from 1855, became its director in Scotland in 1867 and was director general (1882–1901) for the whole of the U.K. He was professor of geology at Edinburgh University (1871–82) and president of the Royal Society (1908–13). His notable *Text-book of Geology* (1882) was one of his many books which included an autobiography, *A Long Life's Work*. (1924).

Gell-Mann, Murray (1929–). US physicist. Educated at Yale, MIT and Chicago (where he studied with * Fermi), he was a professor at the California Institute of Technology 1956– , working on subatomic particles. He proposed a systematic classification of particles which he called 'the Eightfold Way', now generally accepted, which led to his Nobel Prize for Physics in 1969. He also postulated the existence of 'quarks' as the basic building blocks for all matter.

Geminiani, Francesco (1687–1762). Italian composer and violinist. A pupil of Corelli, he lived in London for many years and composed works for violin and string orchestra. His book *The Art of Playing the Violin* (*c*. 1740), the earliest work of its kind, contains valuable information about the technique of his day.

Gênet, Jean (1910–). French writer. He lived in an orphanage as a child, then with a peasant family, followed by years in a reformatory and jail terms for theft and male prostitution. He began writing in jail with his *Our Lady of the Flowers* (1943) and was pardoned in 1948. His powerful plays included *The Balcony* (1956), *The Blacks* (1959) and *The Screens* (1961).

Geneviève, St (*c*. 422–*c*. 512). Patron saint of Paris. She is said to have been born at the nearby village of Nanterre and to have taken the veil at the age of 15. When her parents died she went to Paris, where she lived a life of great austerity and when Attila and the Huns invaded France (451) calmed the panic-stricken inhabitants by her absolute assurance, derived from her prayers and soon justified, that the enemy would pass the city by.

Genghis Khan (1162–1227). Mongol conqueror. He was born near Lake Bailal, and succeeded his father, Yesukei, who ruled the tribes in the steppes of central Asia from the Amur River to the Great Wall of China. He gradually extended his authority until in 1206 he took the title Genghis Khan ('mighty ruler'). In *c.* 1212 he followed up China's refusal to pay tribute by overrunning the country. Next he turned westwards and southwards, and even when he himself returned to Mongolia (1221) his captains continued the great conquering drives. Thus when he died, the Mongol empire stretched from the Yellow Sea to the Black Sea, and included Korea, Persia, Armenia, South-east Russia, Turkestan and parts of Siberia and China. His conquests aroused terror among Christian and Moslem nations alike and his massacres became legendary. But despite his brilliance as a soldier and ability as a ruler, he left no permanent institutions behind him, though important indirect results of the forces he set in motion were the entry of the Turks into Europe and the Mogul empire in India.
Fox, R., *Genghis Khan*. 1937

Gentile da Fabriano (*c.* 1370–1427). Italian painter in the late Gothic style. He worked on historical frescoes for the Doge's Palace at Venice (1409–19) and later in Florence, Siena and Rome. His *Adoration of the Magi* (in the Uffizi, Florence), with its richly caparisoned procession of kings and the clever foreshortening of the horses greatly influenced Florentine technique.
Harris, S. H., *The Social Philosophy of Giovanni Gentile*. 1960

Geoffrey (1113–1151). Count of Anjou. He was the second husband of Matilda, daughter of Henry I of England, and as father of Henry II founded the * Plantagenet dynasty.

Geoffrey of Monmouth (*c.* 1100–1154). British chronicler. He became bishop of St Asaph (Wales) in 1152 and wrote the *Historia Regum Britanniae*, in which he assembled much of the legendary history of King Arthur, giving it a 12th-century setting. His work influenced Wace and other medieval chroniclers.

Geoffroy Saint-Hilaire, Etienne (1772–1844). French anatomist had palaeontologist. He specialized in comparative anatomy, working out the principles which enable the scientist to deduce absent organic structures from surviving ones (in the case of defective extinct fossil creatures) and the principle of organic balance. Largely through contemplation of the palaeontological record, which seemed to show a historical succession from primitive to complex forms of life, from the invertebrates up to the mammals, he came to believe, like * Lamarck, in the reality of organic evolution. This he saw as proceeding by a series of big jumps, on the analogy of the embryological production of occasional monsters, when climatic and environmental conditions made survival of existing species precarious. He was bitterly attacked for his evolutionary views by his one-time collaborator, * Cuvier.

In his later years, he developed a broad-ranging, if somewhat mystical, view of the organic unity of all Nature.
Bourdier, F., 'Geoffroy Saint-Hilaire and his Struggle against Cuvier', in Schneer, C. J., (ed.), *Toward a History of Geology*. 1969

George I (1660–1727). King of Great Britain and Ireland (from 1714). He followed his father as elector of Hanover in 1698 as great-grandson of James I through a Protestant line of descent, and succeeded to the British throne by virtue of the Act of Settlement (1701), by which the Roman Catholic Stuarts were excluded. His reign marked the beginning of a long Whig supremacy, since the Tories were held to be tainted with complicity in the Jacobite rebellion of 1715. His long absences in Hanover and his lack of interest in British politics favoured the development of constitutional government. Having discovered (1694) an alleged liaison between his wife Sophia Dorothea and Count * Königsmark, he kept her confined until her death (1726), in spite of his own many and openly supported mistresses.

George I (1845–1913). King of the Hellenes (from 1864). Son of Christian IX of Denmark and brother of Britain's Queen Alexandra, he was chosen king after the abdication of Otho and proved to be the virtual creator of modern democratic Greece. His invitation (1909) to * Venizelos, the Cretan political leader, to head the government led to the formation of the Balkan alliance against Turkey, the successful Balkan Wars (1912–13) and the creation of a greater Greece. On the eve of a triumph which owed so much to him he was assassinated at Salonica.

George II (1683–1760). King of Great Britain and Ireland, and elector of Hanover (from 1727). Before he came to the throne he frequently deputized in England during the absences in Hanover of his father, George I, a resulting estrangement, due to jealousy, being ended by reconciliation in 1720. As king, he maintained * Walpole in office, encouraged to do so by his astute and able wife, Caroline of Ansbach, whom he had married in 1797; but though George openly expressed his preference for Hanover and his knowledge of English politics was limited, he was no puppet; he successfully played, without liking, his constitutional role and gave his ministers the full benefit of his knowledge of foreign affairs. After the death (1740) of the emperor Charles VI, George, despite Walpole's reluctance, fulfilled his obligations under the Pragmatic Sanction to secure the succession to the Austrian inheritance of Charles's daughter, Maria Theresa. At Dettingen (1743) he commanded his army in person, the last British sovereign to do so. Two years later * Charles Edward Stuart (Bonnie Prince Charlie) landed in Scotland and the Jacobite army came as far south as Derby before the danger passed and George could again feel secure. Walpole had fallen in 1742 and in the years that followed the Duke of Newcastle, that industrious purveyor of patronage, was the constant political factor, with Pitt, Carteret (Granville), and others giving intermittent support. The opposition centred upon the childish and disagreeable Frederick, Prince of Wales, who however predeceased his father. The reign ended in a blaze of glory; the success of the Seven Years War, which began in 1756, included the British conquest of French Canada and the destruction of French influence in India.

George II was brave, honest, quick-tempered but sometimes mean and vindictive; he was also promiscuous – after Queen Caroline's death (1737), the Hanoverian Amelia von Walmoden (Countess of Yarmouth) was the most conspicuous of the royal favourites.

George II (1890–1957). King of the Hellenes. He succeeded his father * Constantine I after his second abdication (1922), but was himself deposed when the republic was proclaimed (1924). He lived abroad, mostly in England, until he was restored (1935). Failing to end political strife he accepted the dictatorship of * Metaxas. In the World War II Greece successfully resisted the Italian attack of 1940 but was overwhelmed in 1941 when the Germans mounted a vigorous attack. King George withdrew to head a government in exile in England. He was recalled to his own country by a plebiscite (1946).

George III (1738–1820). King of Great Britain and Ireland, and elector (king from 1815) of Hanover (from 1760). He was the grandson and successor of George II. The difference between him and the two preceding Georges was underlined in his address to his first parliament 'Born and educated in this country I glory in the name of Briton'; in fact he never visited Hanover. His aim, derived from Bolingbroke's *Idea of a Patriot King*, was to choose the best men, irrespective of party, and to govern without 'influence' – an impossible ambition in the political conditions of the time. His first step to this end was to get rid of his grandfather's ministers Pitt and Newcastle and to install as chief minister his old tutor, the Earl of Bute, to whom he was devoted. This was a mistake, for Bute, already mistrusted as a Scot, a royal favourite and a totally inexperienced politician, earned more unpopularity by bringing the Seven Years War to an end on terms held to be disadvantageous to Britain, the victor. Bute found himself forced to resign (though he continued to advise until 1766) and there followed a period of frequent ministerial changes, complicated by the attacks of * Wilkes and his supporters, until George found Lord North, who by adroit use of patronage, considerable tactical skill and charm of manners managed to stay in office from 1770 to 1782. He could not survive the loss of the American colonies, but after another short period of frequent change (1782–83), George appointed the younger Pitt, who gradually weaned the control of government from the royal hands, George's refusal to violate his coronation oath by agreeing to any measure of Roman Catholic emancipation creating the only real impasse. The last part of the reign was almost totally dominated by the impact of the French Revolutionary and Napoleonic wars.

In 1761 George had married Princess Charlotte of Mecklenburg-Strelitz, by whom he had nine sons and six daughters; but faithful and devoted as he was, reaction against the atmosphere of happy and rather stuffy domesticity may have contributed to the extravagances of his eldest son (* George IV) who became regent in 1811, when his father – after earlier short periods of 'madness' (now known to have been caused by the disease porphyria) – became blind and incompetent. George's particular hobby, which earned him the nickname of 'Farmer George', was agriculture, and he set up a model farm at Windsor, which he made his permanent home. In his later years his high if confused idealism and his love and concern for England were recognized and his death, after the longest reign in British history to that time, was marked by widespread regret.

Clarke, J., *The Life and Times of George III*. 1972

George IV (1762–1830). King of Great Britain and Ireland and of Hanover (from 1820). Reacting against the restraints of a strict and pious father, on acquiring his own establishment he became notorious for extravagance and dissipation. He was however far from unintelligent, and the political friends he gathered round him – chosen from the Whig opposition as if further to spite and distress his father – were men like Charles James Fox and Sheridan, who, whatever their tastes in pleasure, were among the most brilliant and cultured men of the age. He secretly married (1785) a Roman Catholic widow, Maria * Fitzherbert, but the marriage, entered into without his father's consent, was illegal under the Royal Marriage Act (1722). In 1795 he agreed to marry Princess Caroline of Brunswick but they parted after the birth of Princess * Charlotte; his attempt to divorce her (1820) failed. When, after his father had become insane (1811), he became regent he failed to satisfy the hopes of his Whig friends and kept the Tories in office. The so-called Regency period in architecture, dress and decoration owed little to his direct encouragement, his own taste being more truly exemplified by the exuberant fantasy of the Brighton Pavilion. As king, George IV was prevented from effective action by languor and illness, but in the last years of his life, while opposing all reform at home, he strongly supported Canning's liberal policy abroad.

Hibbert, C., *George IV*. 2 vols. 1972–1973

George V (1865–1936). King of Great Britain and Ireland (from 1910). His elder brother, Albert Victor, having died in 1892, it was he who succeeded his father, Edward VII, as king. George was born at Marlborough House and was trained for the navy. He married (1893) Princess Mary of Teck, a great-granddaughter of George III, and in 1894 their eldest son, afterwards Edward VIII and Duke of Windsor, was born. Their other children were Albert, later George VI (1895–1952), Mary, Princess Royal (1897–1965), Henry, Duke of Gloucester (1900–1974), George, Duke of Kent (1902–1942), and John (1905–1919). It was a happy marriage but George was an intimidating father. As Prince of Wales he opened the first federal parliament in Australia; after his coronation in 1911 he went to India for the Durbar (1911). Shortly after, he was confronted with the political crises arising from the bill to curb the powers of the House of Lords and the Irish Home Rule Bill, and then with World War I. The political and social upheavals of the post-war period must have shocked the prejudices of the old-fashioned country gentleman that he was, but as the years went by he drew closer in thought and mood to his subjects and his Silver Jubilee (1935) was the occasion of a great demonstration of public esteem.

Rose, K., *King George V*. 1983

George VI (1895–1952). King of Great Britain, Ireland, the Commonwealth and Empire (from 1936), emperor of India (1936–47). Known as Prince Albert from boyhood and created Duke of York in 1920, he came to the throne on the abdication of his elder brother Edward VIII. Trained for the navy, he was present at the Battle of Jutland (1916). In 1920 he married Lady Elizabeth Bowes Lyon, a daughter of the Earl of Strathmore; their two children, the future Queen Elizabeth II and Margaret Rose (Countess of Snowdon), shared with them a happy and affectionate family life. His reign was overshadowed by World War II. He and the Queen remained in

London during the 'Blitz' and helped to create the feeling of solidarity among the people. He suffered all his life from diffidence, a stammer, and, in his later years from much illness, bravely borne.

Wheeler Bennett, J. W., *King George VI*. 1958

George, St (died *c.* 303). England's patron saint. It is difficult to distinguish legend from fact; a possible version of his life is that he was a military tribune in the Roman army in Palestine, who, having proclaimed his Christian faith during the persecutions inspired by Diocletian, was tortured and beheaded at Nicomedia, supposedly on 23 April. The story of St George and the dragon first appears in its present form in *The Golden Legend* (*c.* 1275). When a dragon appeared before Silence in Libya, its hunger was daily satisfied by a sheep. When sheep failed men and women were chosen by lot as substitutes; at last the lot fell upon the princess, but when, dressed as a bride, she faced her doom, St George, under the protection of the Cross, appeared and so wounded the dragon that it could be brought into the city and beheaded. A striking resemblance to the Greek story of Perseus and Andromeda is apparent. St George became popular in England during the Crusades, but supplanted Edward the Confessor as patron saint only in the reign of Edward III.

George, Henry (1839–1897). American economist, promoter of the doctrine of the 'Single Tax'. Born in Philadelphia, he went to California at the age of 19 and became, as journalist and editor, interested in current problems. *Our Land and Land Policy* (1870) was his first work on his chosen subject but it was in *Progress and Poverty* (1879) that his theory was clearly worked out. Faced with the anomaly that increase in productive power did not appear to lead to a rise in wages and general prosperity he concluded that the reason lay in the constant increase (as the demand – and with it speculation – grew) in land values and so in rent, which absorbed the surplus accruing from higher production. His remedy was to bring the increment in land values into public use by a single tax and abolish all others which fall upon industry or discourage thrift.

George, Stefan (1868–1933). German poet. He was the leader of an esoteric group of German poets over whom he exercised influence mainly through his literary journal *Blätter für die Kunst* (founded 1892). He in turn was clearly influenced by Baudelaire, Mallarmé and the French symbolists. His belief was that it was the form rather than the content of verse that was important; metre and word harmonies should create a mental picture irrespective of literal meaning. He left Germany when the Nazis seized power. His most famous disciple was * Rilke. George was also a gifted translator of English, French and Italian works.

Goldsmith, U. K., *Stefan George: A Study of His Early Work*. 1960

German, Sir Edward (1862–1936). British composer of songs and light operas, popular for their tuneful quality and national character. His best-known opera is probably *Merrie England*. He was knighted in 1928.

Gerry, Elbridge (1744–1814). American politician. He became prominent in Massachusetts politics and was a signatory of the Declaration of Independence. As governor of Massachusetts (1810–12), he rearranged the electoral areas in a way designed to benefit his own Republican party, a practice later known as 'gerry-mandering'.

Gershwin, George (1898–1937). American composer, born in Brooklyn. He wrote many popular songs and experimented with 'symphonic jazz' in his *Rhapsody in Blue* (1924) for piano and orchestra, and in the negro opera *Porgy and Bess* (1935). Other important works by Gershwin include the orchestral piece *An American in Paris* and the Piano Concerto in F.

Gesell, Arnold Lucius (1880–1961). American psychologist. As director of the Clinic of Child Development (1911–48) and professor of child hygiene at Yale, he acquired great authority on his subject; his best known books are *The Child from Five to Ten* (1946), *Youth: The Years from Ten to Sixteen* (1956).

Gesner, Konrad (1516–1565). Swiss naturalist. He produced encyclopedic surveys of several subjects, from botany to comparative philology. The best known is his *Historia animalium* (5 volumes, 1551–58), which surveyed all known forms of animals, and provided the foundation for much later work. He also produced bibliographies of all known Greek, Latin and Hebrew writers.

Getty, Jean Paul (1892–1976). American oil magnate. He took control of Pacific Western Oil in 1932, changed its name to Getty Oil and amassed a great fortune which he left to the J. Paul Getty Museum in Malibu, California.

Ghiberti, Lorenzo (1378–1455). Italian sculptor and goldsmith, born in Florence. In 1402 he won a competition for designing two bronze doors for the Baptistery of St John in Florence on the theme of Abraham and Isaac. Completed in 1424, these were followed by a second pair (1425–52), called the *Porta dei Paradiso*; Michelangelo is said to have remarked that they are 'worthy to be the gates of Paradise'. In these Ghiberti abandons the Gothic framework and the scenes are placed in rectangular compartments, the crowded figures in relief against backgrounds displaying his mastery and perspective. His output was small and nothing else he made equalled these famous doors, unsurpassed in their excellence.

Ghirlandaio, Domenico (1449–1494). Italian painter. He was born in Florence, and after an apprenticeship as goldsmith, started painting *c.* 1470. His many frescoes in Florence reveal not only the earnestness and dignity of his style but collectively provide a wonderful panorama of Florentine dress and ways of life. From 1481 to 1482 he worked in the Sistine Chapel in the Vatican for Pope Sixtus IV; he painted the fresco *The Calling of St Peter and St Andrew* as well as the figures of several popes. In addition to frescoes his work included mosaics in the cathedral at Florence and many fine altar-pieces. He employed many assistants, amongst whom was * Michelangelo.

Giacometti, Alberto (1901–1966). Swiss sculptor. After 1922 he worked mostly in Paris. He at first worked from nature, but under the influence of Cubism he became (1930–34) the most distinguished sculptor of the Surrealist group. From 1935 he returned to working from nature, developing his very personal style of figures, mostly standing or walking men and women, of exaggeratedly slender proportions.

Giap, Vo Nguyen (1912–). Vietnamese general, born in Annam. The son of a mandarin, he became a lawyer, teacher and journalist, and by 1939 was a leader of the Indochinese Communist Party. Imprisoned for some years, his sister was executed by the French and his wife died in jail. During World War II he led Vietminh guerrillas against the Japanese and worked with the Chinese. As Minister of Defence and Commander-in-Chief of the People's Army of Vietnam 1946–81 he defeated the French at Dien Bien Phu (1954) and led the long campaign against the South and the U.S.

Gibbon, Edward (1737–1794). English historian. He was born in Putney, educated at Westminster School and Magdalen College, Oxford, from which he was removed after fourteen months on his temporary conversion to Roman Catholicism. A 'cure' was effected by sending him to live with a Calvinist minister, with the result that he became a lifelong agnostic. While there he converted his pleasure in reading into a habit of serious study, and became engaged to Suzanne Curchod, the future Madame Necker, whom, with his usual pliancy, he gave up on his father's orders – 'I sighed as a lover, I obeyed as a son'. His first publication, *Essay on the Study of Literature* (1761), was written in French. In 1764, during a tour of Italy, occurred that most famous moment when 'musing amidst the ruins of the Capitol' he decided upon the great project which matured into *The Decline and Fall of the Roman Empire* (6 volumes, 1776–88), covering the period from Trajan and the Antonines to the Fall of Constantinople (1453). For its style, lucidity and completeness it has always been and is still considered one of the greatest masterpieces of historical writing. Even now its accuracy (except perhaps on the Byzantine period) and objectivity can seldom be impugned. Its treatment of the rise of Christianity has been criticized, and Gibbon's obsession with his own dogma that history is 'little more than the register of the crimes, follies, and misfortunes of mankind' may have led him to neglect other factors; nevertheless the book is a superb and lasting monument to the 'Age of Enlightenment'. Gibbon replied to his theological critics in *A Vindication* . . . (1779). Between 1774 and 1783 he served two spells in parliament, without distinction. He then retired to Lausanne and died on a visit to London. Gibbon cut a peculiar, if not ludicrous, figure in society, and the contrast between his

character and the excellence of his writing is extraordinary.
Swain, J. R., *Edward Gibbon the Historian*. 1966

Gibbons, Grinling (1648–1720/1721). English woodcarver and sculptor, born in Holland. His work attracted the attention of John Evelyn who introduced him to Wren. Gibbons entered the Board of Works and was 'master carver' under five British sovereigns. Much of his work, in which flower and fruit motifs predominate, was done for the royal palaces, Windsor Castle, Hampton Court etc.
Green, D., *Grinling Gibbons*. 1964

Gibbons, Orlando (1583–1625). English composer. In 1596 he became a chorister at King's College, Cambridge; he was appointed organist of the Chapel Royal (1604) and later of Westminster Abbey (1623). He wrote works for keyboard and viols and was a noted composer of church music (services and anthems such as *Lift Up Your Heads*) and of madrigals, e.g. *The Silver Swan*.
Fellowes, E. H., *Orlando Gibbons*. 1951

Gibbs, Josiah Willard (1839–1903). American mathematical physicist, born in New Haven, Connecticut. Son of a Yale professor, Gibbs studied mathematics and natural philosophy at Yale, and received a Ph.D. in 1863. He travelled widely in Europe in the 1860s, but then settled down at Yale for the rest of his life, as professor of mathematical physics from 1871. The field in which he excelled was thermodynamics. He made himself master of the concept of entropy recently developed by * Clausius, and accepted his belief (Second Law of Thermodynamics) that entropy tends to increase (i.e. the amount of usable energy in the world diminishes). As entropy increased, any material system tended towards an equilibrium. Gibbs was eager to develop a general theory of thermodynamics, and pursued theoretical researches into many forms of energy and heat exchange. He was also aware of the need to put thermodynamics on a statistical (rather than simply a mechanical) basis.

Gibbs exercised considerable influence on the work of Clerk * Maxwell in England, but had less impact on * Helmholtz and * Planck in Germany, who pursued their researches independently.
Wheeler, L. P., *Josiah Willard Gibbs*. 1970

Gibran, Khalil (1883–1931). Syrian–Lebanese poet and artist, in the US from 1895. His metaphysical prose poems, *The Prophet* (1923) and *Jesus, the Son of Man*, (1928), have been bestsellers for decades, their beauty of language being matched by extreme vagueness of thought.

Gibson, Althea (1927–). American tennis player. The first Negro to rise to great heights in the game, she played in the US (Forest Hills) championship in 1950, and at Wimbledon in 1951. She won the women's singles championships in the US and Great Britain in 1957 and 1958.

Gibson, Charles Dana (1867–1944). American black-and-white artist. His work for the New York periodicals became famous towards the close of the 19th century, and especially his society cartoons for which he created the type known as the 'Gibson girl'.

Gibson, Guy Penrose (1918–1944). British bomber pilot of World War II. He won the V.C. when leading the successful low-level bomb attack (1943) which breached the Möhne Dam. By attracting enemy anti-aircraft fire to his own plane he enabled others of the squadron to get through. He lost his life in a bomber raid in the following year.

Gide, André (1869–1951). French author. His parents were Protestants, but his mother's family were such recent converts that Gide felt himself born 'of two faiths'. His father, a distinguished professor of law, died when Gide was 11 and he was brought up by his strict and narrow-minded mother and her friend, Anne Shackleton. His education was interrupted by recurrent psychological troubles. Despite maternal disapproval Gide early determined to become a writer and through Pierre Louÿs he joined in the literary life of Paris; Mallarmé exerted considerable influence upon him. His mother died in 1895 leaving him a large fortune. Shortly after, he married his cousin Madeleine, whom he had long admired; but the marriage, though never broken up entirely, was unhappy, largely because of Gide's homosexuality. His social conscience led him to help refugees in World War I and in the Spanish Civil War, and later to protest at the treatment of Africans in the Congo. For a time inclined to support communism, he was disillusioned by a visit to

Russia (1936). He spent the last years of his life (his wife having died in 1938) in North Africa and Paris. He was awarded the Nobel Prize for Literature (1947).

His early works, though highly esteemed by fellow writers, made no impact on the public. It was not till Gide was 50, when general literary taste had evolved after World War I, that he received wide recognition; even then his works remained controversial and in particular repugnant to most Catholics. But increasingly his reputation as a writer grew to the extent of his becoming a major, if not the major, classic amongst modern French writers. His numerous works reflected, with the utmost sincerity, his innermost feelings and struggles, his search for 'authentic' experience, his rejection of the moral conventions of society. They are also, in a sense, a continuing autobiography. His early works, *Les Nourritures terrestres* (1897), *Saul* (1896), *L'Immoraliste* (1902), *La Porte étroite* (1909) and *Corydon* (1911), deal each in a different way with the struggle between the spiritual and sensual sides of his nature. *Si le Grain ne meurt* (1926) was his actual autobiography, supplemented by his extensive *Journal* (1889–1947). His later novels, *Les Caves du Vatican* (1914) and *Les Faux-Monnayeurs* (1925), were less intimately personal. He also played an important part in founding the *Nouvelle Revue Française* in which his own *Isabelle* and the work of many young writers appeared. Although recognition of Gide's powers was slow to come his very considerable writings exerted strong influence on 20th-century writers, both stylistically and because he never shrank from tackling the most difficult and intimate human doubts and problems.

Cordle, T., *André Gide*. 1976

Gielgud, Sir (Arthur) **John** (1904–). English actor. A great-nephew of Dame Ellen Terry, he made his debut at the Old Vic in 1921. He established himself as one of the greatest modern Shakespearian actors, notably as Hamlet in 1929–30, the longest run of the play since Irving. He also played in and produced the work of many other dramatists including Oscar Wilde, Congreve and Chekhov. To all his work he brought a fine intellect and a beautiful speaking voice. He wrote two volumes of autobiography, *Early Stages* (1938) and *Stage Directions* (1963).

Gierek, Edward (1913–). Polish politician. His father, a miner, was killed in a mining accident in Silesia; Gierek and his mother emigrated to France, where he joined the Communist Party in 1931. During World War II he was in Belgium. In 1948 he returned to Poland and became organiser of the party in Upper Silesia. He was made head of the government's heavy industry programme in 1954, and a member of the Politburo in 1956. He became First Secretary of the Central Committee after the food-price riots of 1970, promising a less austere economic policy and a modification of Russian communism to national needs. He was forced out of office in 1980.

Gigli, Beniamino (1890–1957). Italian singer. Considered one of the greatest operatic tenors of his age, he made his debut in 1914 at Rovigo, and later toured widely, making his New York debut in 1920 and his first London appearance in 1930. His voice combined lyricism with power and an apparently effortless production.

Gilbert, Sir Humphrey (1537/9–1583). English navigator. He was born in Devon, the half-brother of Sir Walter Raleigh. His conviction that there was a north-west sea route to China was set out in his *Discourse of a Discoverie for a New Passage to Cataia* (China), published in 1576, which inspired a series of English seamen to seek the 'North-west Passage'. His own explorations were unsuccessful. He was drowned when returning from an expedition in a very small vessel which capsized.

Gilbert, Walter (1932–). American molecular biologist. Educated at Harvard and Cambridge, he held a chair in molecular biology at Harvard 1968, shared a Nobel Prize for Chemistry in 1980 with Frederick * Sanger and became a leading figure in the commercialisation of biotechnological research.

Gilbert, William (1540–1603). English physician, known for his work on magnetism and electricity. Born in Colchester, he became president of the College of Physicians (1599) and physician to both Elizabeth I (1601) and after her death to James I. His *De Magnete* (1600) described the properties of magnets and explained his hypothesis that the earth itself acts as a large magnet. He also investigated frictional electricity, e.g. of amber and glass and tried to find a connexion between magnetism and electricity. The unit of magnetomotive force is named after him.

Gilbert, Sir William Schwenck (1836–1911). English humorist. Famous for operas written in collaboration with the composer Arthur * Sullivan. After some years in the civil service Gilbert was called to the bar (1864). As a writer he first attracted notice with his *Bab Ballads* (collected 1869–73). Between 1871 and 1890 he wrote the libretti for the highly successful comic operas, which (from *Iolanthe* onwards) were played at the Savoy Theatre built by Richard D'Oyly * Carte in 1881; these included *Trial by Jury* (1875), *H.M.S. Pinafore* (1878), *The Pirates of Penzance* (1880), *Patience* (1881), *Iolanthe* (1882), *The Mikado* (1885), *The Yeomen of the Guard* (1888) and *The Gondoliers* (1889). He quarrelled bitterly with Sullivan (1890) and the long partnership was dissolved. Two or three years later they resumed collaboration but never achieved the same success.

Gildas (*c.* 500–570). Roman-British writer. His *De Excidio et Conquestu Britanniae*, a highly coloured and obscene medley of events and castigations of contemporary vice, remains the only contemporary authority for the early period of the Anglo-Saxon invasions of Britain after the departure of the Romans. King Arthur is not mentioned.

Gilels, Emil Grigorevich (1916–1985). Russian pianist, born in Odessa. He achieved a national reputation for his wide repertoire which included bravura works (e.g. Tchaikovsky), Mozart, Beethoven and Brahms, and did not appear outside the USSR until 1953.

Gill, Eric (1882–1940). British sculptor and engraver. In 1904 he became a stone cutter and attracted notice by his beautifully carved inscriptions. An ultimate result of his interest in lettering were his now widely used typefaces, e.g. Perpetua and Gill Sans-Serif. From 1910 Gill began also to undertake the carving of stone figures, mainly of religious subjects, symbolic in style but not abstract; examples in London are the *Stations of the Cross* in Westminster Cathedral and the *Prospero and Ariel* sculpture on Broadcasting House.

Gillespie, Dizzy (John Birks) (1917–). American jazz trumpeter and composer. He became a professional musician in 1935, modelling himself on Roy Eldridge. In 1944 he joined Billy Eckstine's band and was recognized as a modern jazz innovator. He formed his own orchestra in 1945.

Gillray, James (1757–1815). English caricaturist. Though he continued the tradition of social satire in the manner of Hogarth, his most important targets were the courts of Napoleon and George III and the political world. He often used colour and achieved a huge output, of some 1,500 subjects, partly by dispensing with drawings and etching direct on copper. During his last four years he was insane.

Hill, D., *Mr Gillray, The Caricaturist*. 1965

Gil Robles, José Maria (1898–1980). Spanish politician. A journalist and leader of Catholic Action in the Cortes 1934–36, he was Minister of War (1935). Despite strong electoral support, he was kept out of power by * Franco and virtually exiled.

Giolitti, Giovanni (1842–1928). Italian politician. He first held office as finance minister in 1889. Thereafter he was an almost indispensable figure in all political combinations until Mussolini's accession to power (1922). He was a superb parliamentary manipulator and was premier five times between 1892 and 1921. He led Italy to victory in the war with Turkey (1911), by which Libya was gained. He did not support Italian entry in World War I, and opposed Mussolini after 1924.

Giorgione (Giorgio da Castelfranco) (1475/8–1510). Venetian painter of the High Renaissance. He was a pupil of Giovanni Bellini; very little is known about his career and life. A major difficulty lies in the fact that none of his works was signed or dated and that his high contemporary reputation caused him to be much imitated. The difficulties of attribution and dating are therefore particularly great. Those held most likely to be his include the *Judith* (Leningrad), *The Tempest* (Venice) and *The Three Philosophers* (Vienna), which X-ray photography has shown to have originally represented *The Three Magi*. The background of the famous *Dresden Venus* was almost certainly painted by Titian. A spiritual harmony between figures and background, well shown in the *Concert Champêtre* (Louvre) – if indeed it is his – distinguishes his landscapes;

he was indeed the first great romantic artist. In portraiture he shows the beginning of a psychological approach, and his claim to be an innovator is enhanced by a new type of small intimate easel picture for private collectors. He died of the plague, and several of his paintings were completed by others,
Pignatti, T., *Giorgione*. 1971

Giotto di Bondone (1266/7–1337). Italian painter. Famous for having freed his painting from the formalized traditions of Byzantine art, his figures acquire solidity and their faces, no longer restricted to the stereotyped expressions of the Byzantine style, show variety and individual character, Giotto owed much to * Cimabue, but for showing the way to Renaissance freedom he is rightly held to be a key figure in western art. His main surviving works are three famous sets of frescoes. The earliest, those in the church of St Francis at Assisi, present difficulties of attribution but the inspiration, if not in every case the execution, is certainly his. The frescoes in the Arena chapel at Padua (1304–06), illustrating the life and Passion of Christ, show Giotto's work in its full maturity. The third set of frescoes (*c*. 1317), which have lost much of their quality through repainting, are in chapels of the Santa Croce church in Florence. They relate the stories of St Francis and the two St Johns (the Baptist and the Evangelist). Of Giotto's other work one of the finest examples is the great altar-piece now in the Uffizi at Florence showing the Madonna in glory with the Child and angels. In 1334 Giotto became official architect in Florence where he is believed to have designed the Campanile of the Cathedral and almost certainly executed relief decorations on its ground floor.
Battisti, E., *Giotto*. 1966

Giraldus Cambrensis (Gerald of Wales) (*c*. 1146–1223). Norman–Welsh prelate and chronicler. He went with Prince John to Ireland (1185) and wrote extensively on the history and topography of that country; his descriptions of Wales are equally valuable. He also wrote lives of St David, St Hugh of Lincoln and others. His books contain much useful information about conditions in the reign of Henry II.
Jones, T., *Gerald of Wales*. 1947

Giraud, Henri Honoré (1879–1949). French soldier. He served in World War I with distinction and by the time of World War II he had risen to the rank of general and was in command of the 9th Division in 1940 when he was captured during the German onslaught. He escaped (1942) and reached Algiers after its capture by the Allies. He was made commander-in-chief of the French forces and (1943) co-president with de Gaulle of the liberation committee. De Gaulle, however, soon forced his retirement into private life.

Giraudoux, Jean (1882–1944). French writer. He wrote a number of novels, e.g. *Simon le pathétique* (1918) and *Bella* (1926), but is best known as the author of plays mainly based on classical themes treated satirically in modern terms. They include *Amphitryon 38* (1929), *Intermezzo* (1933), *La Guerre de Troie n'aura pas lieu* (1935) and *Électre* (1937; translated by Christopher Fry as *Tiger at the Gates*, 1955). During World War II he was head of the French Ministry of Information until the collapse of France.
Cohen, R., *Giraudoux: Three Faces of Destiny*. 1968

Girtin, Thomas (1775–1802). English painter and engraver. He was a pioneer and one of the finest exponents of watercolour painting, and revealed its full possibilities. He abandoned the concept of a watercolour as an outline drawing filled in with colour wash, and established a technique which turned it into a fully developed work of art. Much of his work was commissioned by publishers of books of engravings, e.g. of old monasteries and castles.

Giscard d'Estaing, Valéry (1926–). French politician. A former civil servant, he was employed by the Inspection des Finances 1952–54, and then became a member of the staff of the President of the Council. In 1956 he was elected Deputy for Puy de Dôme. He was made Secretary of State for Finance in 1959, and served as Minister for Finance and Economic Affairs 1962–66 and 1969–74. He was elected President of France in 1974 and defeated in his bid for re-election in 1981 by François Mitterrand.

Gissing, George Robert (1857–1903). English novelist, born in Yorkshire. His experience, as a young man in London and the U.S.A., of the depressing effects of poverty produced such powerful and pessimistic novels as *Demos* (1886) and *New Grub Street* (1891). His later

works include the literary study *Charles Dickens* (1898), and *The Private Papers of Henry Ryecroft* (1903), a fictional fulfilment of his own hopes for a serene old age. A historical novel, *Veranilda*, appeared after his death.
Tindall, G., *The Born Exile*. 1974

Giulio Romano (Giulio Pippi de'Giannuzzi) (*c.* 1499–1546). Italian painter and architect. A pupil and assistant of Raphael in Rome, he helped to finish the stucco ornamentation for the Loggia of the Vatican after the master's death. In his own work he exaggerated the tendencies of Raphael's later period and so came to be regarded as a founder of the Mannerist school. This exaggeration is especially apparent in *The Fall of the Giants* in the Palazzo del Tè at Mantua, where he went to work under the patronage of the ducal Gonzaga family (1524). His finest architectural work there was the reconstruction of the Cathedral and the Ducal Palace, while his drainage of the marshes showed his engineering skill. His method of combining stucco work with fresco panels was imitated all over Europe.

Gladstone, William Ewart (1809–1898). British politician, known in later life as the 'Grand Old Man'. Born in Liverpool, the son of a merchant of Scottish descent, he was educated at Eton and Oxford and at first intended to become an Anglican priest. Indeed, when he accepted an opportunity to enter the first reformed parliament (1832) as Tory member for Newark, it was at least partly in order to benefit the church. Described by Macaulay as 'the rising hope of those stern unbending Tories', the future Liberal prime minister was given several junior offices by Peel before becoming colonial secretary (1845). When the party split over Peel's decision to repeal the Corn Laws (1846) Gladstone followed his leader. The ensuing period out of office, which lasted until 1853, was to Gladstone years of indecision. A visit to Naples (1851), where savage reprisals against the revolution were in full swing, profoundly shook his faith in aristocratic government, but it was still as a Peelite that he joined Lord Aberdeen's ministry as chancellor of the exchequer (1852–55); but when he again held this office under Palmerston and Lord John Russell (1859–66) the transition to Liberalism was made. As chancellor Gladstone carried forward Peel's free-trade policy and accomplished the feat of reducing income tax to 4d. in the pound. The Post Office Savings Bank was introduced in 1861. When Russell became prime minister after Palmerston's death (1865), Gladstone was leader in the Commons, but a brief Conservative administration intervened before he was brought to power in a landslide election victory fought with the widened franchise of 1867. Gladstone, now almost 60 years old, formed his first administration. Showing how far he had moved from his early Anglican intolerance, he disestablished the church of Ireland (1869), abolished religious tests for universities, and passed an Education Act which *inter alia* enabled rates to be used for building non-denominational schools. The Irish Land Act (1870) was an attempt, which ultimately failed, to appease Irish grievances without constitutional change. The secret ballot for elections was introduced in 1872. To these measures must be added the great army reforms of Gladstone's war minister, Edward * Cardwell. Discontent was, however, aroused by weakness in foreign affairs and the Liberal attitude to trade unions; the ministry fell in 1874. Gladstone went into semi-retirement at Hawarden, the home that had come through his wife's family, and renewed his studies in theology and Homer. Apparent Conservative indifference to the 'Bulgarian atrocities', by which Turkey suppressed a Balkan rising, prompted him to return to office. By his famous whirlwind election campaign in Midlothian he led the Liberals to victory and was again prime minister (1880–85). New reforms included an act (1884) extending the franchise to farm labourers. But in this and his two final administrations (1885–86 and 1892–94) his main preoccupation was with Home Rule for Ireland and his relationship with the Irish party in parliament under * Parnell. The issue split the Liberal party and both Gladstone's Home Rule Bills (1886 and 1893) were defeated. He finally retired in 1894.

Queen Victoria disliked his pomposity and to many of the upper classes he was held up as a bogeyman; but few politicians have achieved so many lasting reforms or maintained the highest principles with such lofty eloquence. It is to him that the 'liberalism' of outlook which now permeates all political parties is largely due.

By his wife, Catherine Glyn, Gladstone had four sons, of whom **Herbert Gladstone** (1854–1930), raised to the peerage when he became

governor general of South Africa (1910), was prominent in Liberal politics.
Magnus, P., *Gladstone*. 1954

Glazunov, Alexander Constantinovich (1865–1936). Russian composer. His early works are romantic and reveal the influence of his teacher Rimsky-Korsakov, and of Tchaikovsky. Later he leaned more toward classical forms. He wrote eight symphonies, a series of popular *Concert Waltzes*, and violin concertos and ballet music (but no operas). Although honoured by the Soviet government, he emigrated (1928) to Paris, where he died.

Glendower, Owen (Owain Glyndur) (*c.* 1350–*c.* 1416). Welsh hero, and the last to assert the independence of Wales. Personal grievances for which he tried in vain to obtain redress from Henry IV led to incidents which provoked a general rising in Wales headed by Glendower, who was proclaimed Prince of Wales. Henry * Percy (Hotspur) was defeated by Henry IV at Shrewsbury (1403) on his way to join him, and from then onwards, though Glendower continued his efforts to consolidate a Welsh state, support gradually fell away and from 1410 nothing certain about him is known. He appears in Shakespeare's *Henry IV*.
Davies, J. D. G., *Owen Glyn Dŵr*. 1934

Glenn, John Hershel (1921–). American aviator. During World War II he received many decorations for his exploits as pilot in the Marine Corps. He was the first to fly across the U.S.A. faster than sound (1957) and the first American to orbit the earth in space (1962). He served as U.S. Senator from Ohio 1975–

Glière, Reinhold Moritzovich (1875–1956). Russian composer. A pupil of Taneyev and Ippolitov-Ivanov, he became professor of composition (1913) and director (1914) at the Kiev Conservatoire, and professor of composition at the Moscow Conservatoire (1920). He taught Prokofiev, Khachaturian and Miaskovsky. A prolific composer, Glière was highly honoured by the Soviet government. His works include several symphonies, of which the best known is No. 3, *Ilya Mourometz* (1909–11), the ballet *The Red Poppy* (1926–27) and a Cello Concerto.

Glinka, Mikhail Ivanovich (1804–1857). Russian composer. Rejecting the influence of the German or Italian composers, he turned to folk music for his inspiration. His *A Life for the Tsar* (1836) is the first important Russian opera and one of the first examples of nationalism in music. He also composed the opera *Russan and Ludmilla* (1841), after a poem of Pushkin.
Brown, D., *Mikhail Glinka*. 1974

Gloucester, Henry William Frederick Albert, Duke of (1900–1974). British prince, the third son of George V. He made his career in the army and was governor general of Australia (1945–47).

Gloucester, Humphrey, Duke of (1391–1447). Protector of the Realm during Henry VI's minority; while his brother John, Duke of Bedford, whom he kept ill-supplied, acted as regent in France. Greedy and factious, he was constantly embroiled with his uncle, Cardinal Beaufort, by whose adherents he was arrested (1447); he died in captivity. He was a patron of learning and his collection of books is still housed in 'Duke Humphrey's Library' at Oxford. The affabiliy of 'good Duke Humphrey' long lingered in popular memory.

Glubb, Sir John Bagot (1897–). British soldier, popularly known as Glubb Pasha. He organized the Arab Legion in Jordan, which he commanded from 1939 and which was the most effective Arab fighting force in the Middle East. In 1956, the pressures of Arab nationalism forced King Hussein to dismiss him.

Gluck, Christoph Willibald (von) (1714–1787). German composer. He was born in the Upper Palatinate and studied in Prague, where he earned his living as an organist and music teacher. He lived for a time in Italy and London (where he came to know Handel and Arne), but spent most of his life in Paris and Vienna where (1754–70) he was court musician to Maria Theresa. In his later operas he avoided excessive vocal display in the interests of dignity and simplicity. They include *Orpheus and Eurydice* (1762), *Alceste* (1768), *Iphigenia in Aulis* (1774) and *Iphigenia in Tauris* (1779). The last of these won him the final victory in the battle between the Gluckists and Piccinnists (the supporters of

Piccinni), representing respectively the French and Italian operatic styles.
Einstein, A., *Gluck*. 1964

Glyn, Elinor (1865–1943). English novelist. Her passionate novels, notably *Three Weeks* (1907), gained a reputation for 'naughtiness' and were enormously successful. The title of her novel *It* (1927) gave this pronoun a new significance. She wrote an autobiography, *Romantic Adventure* (1936).

Gneisenau, August Wilhelm Anton, Count Neithardt von (1760–1831). Prussian soldier. He was the principal reorganizer of the Prussian army after its crushing defeat by Napoleon at Jena. He was Blücher's chief of staff at Waterloo.

Gobineau, Joseph Arthur, Comte de (1816–1882). French diplomat and racial theorist. In his *Essay on the Inequality of Human Races* (1853–55) he maintained that the white races and especially those of the north are innately superior to all others and that they degenerate when they interbreed with others. This work had great influence in Germany, e.g. on Nietzsche and Wagner, and eventually was used to justify Nazi racial doctrines.

Goddard, Robert (1882–1945). American scientist. He was a pioneer in the design of high-altitude rockets (1919) and in the theory of rocket propulsion. His ideas and experiments in the U.S.A. attracted no government interest but were developed successfully in Germany.

Gödel, Kurt (1906–1978). Austrian–American mathematician, born in Brno (now in Czechoslovakia). Trained as an engineer at the University of Vienna, he published a paper, 'On Formal Theoretical Advances' (1931), which argued that not all mathematical problems are soluble and that any program for producing consistency in theory will ultimately break down, i.e. that mathematics contains unresolvable paradoxes. Gödel's 'incompleteness (or undecidability) theorem' had an impact comparable to * Heisenberg's 'uncertainty principle' in physics. Gödel lived in the U.S. from 1938 and became a professor at the Institute of Advanced Study, Princeton, from 1953.
Hofstadter, Douglas R., *Gödel, Escher, Bach: An Eternal Golden Braid*. (1980)

Goderich, 1st Viscount *see* **Ripon, 1st Earl of**

Godfrey de Bouillon (*c.* 1060–1100). Duke of Lower Lorraine and a leader of the 1st Crusade. With a force of *c.* 15,000 Germans he was prominent in the capture (1099) of Jerusalem, of which he became the first Christian ruler with the title of 'defender of the Holy Sepulchre'. After his death his brother Baldwin became first king.

Godiva, Lady (*c.* 1040–1085). Wife of Leofric, Earl of Mercia. According to legend, her husband promised to remit a tax he had imposed on the citizens of Coventry if she rode naked through the streets of the city. This she did. The only citizen to look through the shuttered windows was nicknamed 'Peeping Tom'.

Godolphin, Sidney Godolphin, 1st Earl of (1645–1712). English statesman. He was an M.P. from 1668 and held office as secretary of state (1684) and mainly in the Treasury, of which he was a commissioner under James II, to whom 'he remained faithful until the last respectable moment'. William III restored him to office but dropped him after discovering his correspondence with Jacobites. As lord high treasurer (1702–10) under Queen Anne, he maintained a favourable political background for * Marlborough's exploits on the continent and made available the necessary supplies. Their friendship was cemented by the marriage of Godolphin's son to Marlborough's daughter, and both fell from favour together.

Godoy, Manuel de, Duke of Alcuida (1767–1851). Spanish royal favourite, known as 'Prince of Peace'. While serving in the royal bodyguard, he became the lover of Queen Maria Louisa. Through her he exercised a dominant influence on King Charles IV, and was his chief minister (1792–97 and 1801–08). He was not without shrewdness but he was completely outfought in a battle of wits with Napoleon, who used the hatred inspired by Godoy's subservience and relations with the court to facilitate the manoeuvres by which King Charles was induced to abdicate (1808). Godoy accompanied the royal family into exile.

Godunov, Boris Fyodorovich (*c.* 1551–1605). Tsar of Russia (from 1598). He rose to importance under * Ivan the Terrible, and married a sister of Ivan's heir, the feeble-minded Fyodor. During Fyodor's reign (1584–98) Boris acted as regent, and after his death became tsar. He was an able but tyrannical ruler. He was suspected of the murder of Fyodor's younger brother, * Dimitry, who had died mysteriously (1591). Boris was killed in suppressing a revolt stirred up by a pretender claiming to be Dimitry. His life is the theme of Mussorgsky's well known opera *Boris Godunov*.

Grey, I., *Boris Godunov: The Tragic Tsar*. 1973

Godwin, William (1756–1836). English author and political thinker. The son of a nonconformist minister, he became an atheist and advocated an ideal society of universal benevolence in which the compulsory restraints of religion, marriage and centralized government should be abolished. His *Political Justice* (1793) greatly influenced English radicalism and was much admired by Coleridge, Wordsworth and Shelley; but, though it preached anarchy, it also deplored violence, and so its author escaped prosecution. The purpose of his novel *The Adventures of Caleb Williams* (1794) was to expose the domestic and unrecorded despotisms by which human beings destroy each other. **Mary * Wollstonecraft** (1759–1797) who, in *A Vindication of the Rights of Woman* (1792), demanded equality of the sexes became, despite their theories, his first wife when a child was expected. Their child, **Mary Godwin,** eloped with (1814) and later married * Shelley, who was for a time a disciple of Godwin and helped him in his incessant financial difficulties. Godwin's second wife was, by her first husband, the mother of Byron's mistress Claire Clairmont.

Locke, D., *The Life and Thought of William Godwin, 1756–1836*. 1980

Godwine (died 1053). Earl of Wessex. Though probably a Saxon, he was an adviser to King Canute and supported his sons. Edward the Confessor, though married to Godwine's daughter, Edith, resented his domination and banished him (1051), but was forced to submit when he returned with an invading force. On Godwine's death his power passed to his son Harold, afterwards king.

Goebbels, Joseph (1897–1945). German Nazi propagandist. He was prevented by a clubfoot from serving in World War I; he was among the first recruits to the National Socialist party and was party chief in Berlin (1926–30). It was, however, as minister of propaganda (from 1933) in Hitler's government that he won fame. He was adept at all the devices of whipping up mob hysteria and his evil power within Nazi Germany was immense. He was also a master at staging impressive demonstrations of loyalty to the régime. He remained loyal to his leader to the end, and poisoned himself and his family after Hitler's suicide.

Lochner, L. (ed.), *The Goebbels Diaries*. 1965

Goering, Hermann Wilhelm (1893–1946). Nazi politician. Born in Bavaria, he was a noted fighter pilot in World War I. He joined the Nazis (1922), was the first leader of the 'Storm Troops', and was elected (1928) to the Reichstag, of which he was president (1932–33). Hitler, once in power, rewarded him with a number of posts including minister president of Prussia, where he founded (1933) the Gestapo, air minister and head of the Luftwaffe (air force), and minister in charge of the economic preparations for war. He was made a general in 1933 and a field marshal in 1938; the rank of reich marshal was invented for him in 1940. In the early stages of World War II he was named Hitler's deputy and successor; but with the defeat of the Luftwaffe in the Battle of Britain and the subsequent revelation of Germany's inadequate air defence he steadily lost influence. In the last days of the régime he plotted to oust Hitler and was already disgraced when he was captured by the Americans. Condemned to death in the Nuremberg trials, he committed suicide in prison. His apparent geniality, to which his corpulence and pomposity gave a touch of the ridiculous, masked a greed and brutality equal to that of any of his colleagues.

Butler, E., and Young, G., *Marshal without Glory: Hermann Wilhelm Goering*. 1973

Goes, Hugo van der (died 1482). Flemish painter. He worked in Ghent (probably his birthplace) and in *c.* 1475 executed the Portinari Altarpiece which went to Florence where it aroused great admiration. He entered a monastery as a lay brother shortly afterwards, but continued to paint and to travel. He became insane and died young. He ranks as one of the best of the early Netherlands painters, distinguished by a highly perfected technique.

Goethe, Johann Wolfgang von (1749–1832). German poet and dramatist. The son of a prosperous businessman of Frankfurt-am-Main, he owed his love of learning to his father and his gaiety and imaginative gifts to his vivacious mother. Before going to Leipzig University to study law – which he never seriously practised – he already knew much Latin, Greek, French, Italian, English and had studied music. After two years at home, during which he became interested in mysticism and the supernatural, he resumed his legal studies at Strasbourg, where he came under the influence of Herder, who stimulated his interest in folk-music, Gothic architecture, Rousseau and above all the works of Shakespeare. Goethe was prominent in the *Sturm und Drang* literary movement. In this Strasbourg period, he first became obsessed with the Faust legend, inspired by a sense of guilt over a love affair. He wrote a version down two to three years later, but it was discovered and published (as *Urfaust*) only in 1887. His play *Götz von Berlichingen* (1771/3), based on the life of a medieval knight, was a response to Herder's demand for a national drama to match what Shakespeare had done for the English stage. Back in Frankfurt more love affairs provided an autobiographical basis for the novel, *The Sorrows of Young Werther* (1774), written in letter form, which ends with the hero's suicide.

Among his many admirers at this time was the young duke Charles Augustus of Saxe Weimar who invited him to settle at Weimar. Goethe accepted the move readily as it provided him with an opportunity to break his engagement with Lili Schonemann, his accomplished and patrician fiancée. In Weimar from 1775 he became the duke's chief adviser and filled a series of ministerial posts with a distinction which revealed his practical abilities and growing sense of responsibility. Another aspect of his many-sided genius now began to be revealed. To science he made the approach of the ancient or medieval polymath, the importance of the part resting, in his view, on its relationship to the whole. Thus he preferred an imaginative synthesis based on imagination and study to a mathematical analysis such as Newton's. His most important discoveries, revealed in several books, were in biology and some seemed to anticipate Darwin's theories; he found in the jaw of man traces of an intermaxillary bone such as apes possess; the leaf, he discovered, was the primary form of the plant. His observation that the skull of vertebrates is a modification of the bones of the spine led him to believe in the basic principle of metamorphosis. In optics, his distrust of the mathematical approach played him false and his conclusions were erroneous.

His literary work was inevitably retarded by his other activities, but under the influence of a new lover (Frau von Stein) he continued to write tender lyrics (Beethoven set a few, Schubert many, to music), and acquired a new social grace. But he began to feel himself a prisoner of public life and in 1786 he took refuge for two years in Italy; here he finished the verse plays *Egmont*, and *Iphigenie* begun years before; additions were made to *Faust*, the legend of the old magician * Dr Faust which had been taking shape in his head and intermittently on paper since the Strasbourg days; he mused over the specimens in the botanical gardens at Palermo, he studied classical art, made hundreds of drawings, and inevitably on his return to Weimar was found to have a new love, Christiane Vulpius, who came to live with him, who bore him several children and whom he at last married (1806). The Italian visit, too, marked the definite end of the *Sturm und Drang* period.

Almost immediately after his return the French Revolution broke out; Goethe, sympathetic at first, was alienated by its excesses, and attended and advised his duke on the 1892 campaign, so inglorious for the Germans, to restore the monarchy. Later, however, he came to admire Napoleon who in turn honoured him when he came (1808) to Weimar as conqueror. This was the year in which the first part of *Faust* was at last published; the second was not to appear until 1832. The story tells of Faust's pact to sell his soul to the devil (Mephistopheles), in return for pleasure, knowledge and power, of the seduction and death of Marguerite and of his final redemption. The second part is more classical in form and largely metaphysical in content. Gounod's famous operatic version ends with Mephistopheles claiming his soul. From 1791 to 1813 Goethe directed the state theatre at Weimar aided by * Schiller, with whom he wrote ballads in rivalry and maintained a fascinating correspondence on aesthetic subjects.

In 1796 appeared the first part (begun ten years before) of his novel *Wilhelm Meister*, telling of the wanderings of a stage-struck

youth with a theatrical troupe which included Mignon (of operatic fame). In the second part, which did not appear until 1830, Goethe is much more concerned with the educational and sociological impact of the travels than with the travels themselves. He continued to write on many subjects, and his lyrics, inspired as before by his transient loves, lost none of their intensity and beauty. He believed in life, in accepting it and in living it to the full; that was the essence of his philosophy. He practised it to the end.
Friedenthal, R., *Goethe: His Life and Times*. 1965

Gogarty, Oliver St John (1878–1957). Irish author and wit. By profession a surgeon in Dublin, he is chiefly remembered for the literary reminiscences of *As I was Going Down Sackville Street* (1937) and as 'Buck Mulligan' in Joyce's *Ulysses*. He also wrote several volumes of poetry and was an Irish senator (1922–36).
O'Connor, U., *Oliver St John Gogarty*. 1964

Gogh, Vincent van (1853–1890). Dutch painter. Son of a Calvinist preacher in Holland, he joined an art-dealer's firm when he left school, and tried without success several occupations, including that of an evangelist on the Belgian coalfields, before turning finally to art (1880). His early pictures, e.g. *The Potato Eaters*, are sombre in tone and subject, a change coming in 1886, when in Paris he came to know the work of the Impressionists. But though he painted some 200 pictures at this time, the Impressionist techniques did not satisfy him and he did not reach his full maturity until he went (1888) to Arles in Provence. Here in the blaze of southern sunshine, he expressed the hidden turbulence of his nature in pictures vibrant with power and cascading with colour. Primary colours, reds, yellows, blues, were squeezed straight from tube to canvas and spread with broad curving brush-strokes. Landscapes, interiors, sunflowers, café scenes, self-portraits – the subjects were repeated over and over again during this last period of astonishing productivity. But, though this is seldom discernible in his pictures, his mind was already giving way. As an act of remorse he cut off his ear with the razor with which he had threatened * Gauguin. In 1889 he went to a local asylum and in May 1890 put himself under the care of a doctor near Paris at whose house he committed suicide.

Only one of van Gogh's pictures was sold in his lifetime, and only the understanding help of his brother Theo, to whom he wrote most movingly of his sufferings, saved him from complete destitution and enabled him to struggle on in poverty and unceasing despair till finally tragedy overtook him.
Schapiro, M., *Vincent van Gogh*. 1950

Gogol, Nikolai Vasilyevich (1809–1852). Russian author. Born into a Ukrainian family of landed gentry, he went to St Petersburg where, after an unsuccessful attempt to be an actor, he (from 1831) gained literary success with several volumes of short stories and a romantic novel, *Taras Bulba* (1885), about a Cossack chief. He is best known for the play *The Government Inspector*, produced in 1836, satirizing the bureaucracy. Much of the rest of his life was spent in Rome where he wrote the first part of *Dead Souls* (1837), a satirical novel in which Chichikov, an adventurer, buys up serfs who have died since the last census – but are ostensibly alive since their owners still pay tax on them – and uses them as security for loans. He destroyed a draft of the second volume in the mood of religious melancholy into which he fell in his later years. Among his best known stories are *The Nose*, a fantasy about a severed nose which gained a government job on its own merits and the nightmarish *The Overcoat*. In portraying character, Gogol lacks psychological subtlety, but for sheer imaginative power and caricature he has few equals.
Troyat, H., *Gogol: The Biography of a Divided Soul*. 1971

Golding, William (1911–). English novelist. Educated at Marlborough and Oxford, he was a schoolmaster for many years, his novels, which have strong allegorical or symbolic undertones, include *Lord of the Flies* (1954), *Pincher Martin* (1956), *Free Fall* (1959), *The Spire* (1964), *Rites of Passage* (1980) and *The Paper Men* (1983). He received the 1983 Nobel Prize for Literature.

Goldmark, Karl (1830–1915). Hungarian-Jewish composer. He lived mostly in Vienna working as a violinist, music teacher and critic. His works included the popular *Rustic Wedding* symphony, and operas, e.g. *The*

Queen of Sheba (1875) and one based on Dickens's *The Cricket on the Hearth*.

Goldmark, Peter Carl (1906–1977). U.S. engineer, born in Budapest. From 1936 he worked for the Columbia Broadcasting System (CBS) laboratories, devising an early form of colour television and perfecting the microgroove record, electronic video recording (EVR), and electronic scanners used in space probes. He proposed decentralized wired cities to provide for greater access to more services at substantially lower cost.

Goldoni, Carlo (1707–1793). Italian dramatist. Born in Venice, he began his career as a lawyer but from 1734 turned to writing plays. In 1761 he accepted an invitation to go to France where he received a pension from the king. This ended with the Revolution and he died in poverty. He is said to have written altogether some 250 plays in French, Italian and in dialect. He was much influenced by Molière; his plays are well constructed, his characters are real, they behave naturally in comic situations and his satire is seldom unkind.

Goldschmidt, Hans (1861–1923). German chemist. He invented the thermite process, whereby certain metals, e.g. iron, chromium and manganese, can be extracted from their oxides by reduction with powdered aluminium. Great heat is given off during the reaction and a temperature of about 2500°C. is attained. This reaction is used in some types of incendiary bomb, and also in welding.

Goldsmith, Oliver (1728–1774). Anglo-Irish writer. Son of an Anglican Irish clergyman, he was educated at Trinity College, Dublin. After wandering about Europe he went to London where he failed as a doctor and barely supported himself as a hack writer on almost every conceivable subject. In 1761 he was introduced to Dr Johnson and thenceforth was a regular member of his 'club'. His poem *The Deserted Village* (1770), showing the Industrial Revolution's effect on the idyllic village of Auburn, earned an immediate acclaim. Equally famous are his novel *The Vicar of Wakefield* (1776) and the amusing play *She Stoops to Conquer* (1773), still frequently revived. Boswell represents Goldsmith as absurd, blundering and vain, but Johnson himself regarded him highly.

Rousseau, G. S., *Oliver Goldsmith*. 1974

Goldwater, Barry Morris (1909–). American businessman and politician. Born in Phoenix, Arizona, he was a pilot in World War II and Senator for Arizona 1953–65 and 1969– . From this background he emerged as an extreme conservative and strongly anti-communist and a staunch supporter of Joseph * McCarthy. His selection as the Republican candidate for the presidency (1964) antagonized many party supporters and led to the decisive Democratic victory of President Johnson.

Goldwyn, Samuel (1882–1974). American film producer, born in Warsaw. He entered the film industry in 1910 and was a co-founder of Metro-Goldwyn-Mayer. Notable productions included *Wuthering Heights* (1938), *The Secret Life of Walter Mitty* (1946) and *Guys and Dolls* (1955).

Gollancz, Sir Victor (1893–1967). English publisher. He set up his own company in 1928, founded the Left Book Club (1936) and was an active worker for humanitarian causes. He was knighted in 1965.

Gómez, Juan Vicente (1864–1936). Venezuelan dictator. A man of little education, brought up in a remote mountainous province (hence his nickname, 'tyrant of the Andes'), he joined Cipriano Castro's revolutionary movement and became the chief military support of his régime. He supplanted Castro (1908) and maintained an almost unchallenged dictatorship until his death. The beginning of oil-drilling (1918) enabled him to run the country like a vast and successful business enterprise, and with the aid of the money accruing from the oil exploitation Venezuela presented the appearance of an orderly, stable and well-run state. Behind the façade Gómez maintained his power by one of the most bloodthirsty and unscrupulous tyrannies in South American history, the full extent of which only became known after his death.

Gompers, Samuel (1850–1924). American labour leader. He was born in London of Dutch-Jewish origins, and went to America with his family (1863). In his father's cigar factory he came to pity the poverty and insecurity of unprotected workers, and devoted his life to trade union organization. He founded the American Federation of Labor and was its first president (1885–1924). He concentrated on economic issues, wages, hours, conditions, etc., and avoided all political affiliations. His Federation secured great advances for American workers. His autobiography *Seventy Years of Life and Labor* was published in 1925.

Gomulka, Wladyslaw (1905–1982). Polish politician. He joined the Communist party at an early age and for much of the period preceding World War II was imprisoned for revolutionary activities. During the German occupation of Warsaw he joined the resistance movement and was secretary general of the Polish Communist party until 1948, when he was accused of deviationism for advocating a 'Polish way to Socialism'. In 1951 he was imprisoned. In the turmoil created by anti-Stalinism (1956) Gomulka was released and obtained Soviet consent to a more relaxed régime. Some of the concessions then granted were later repeated, but Gomulka asserted a measure of Polish independence within the Communist bloc.

Goncharov, Ivan Alexandrovich (1812–1891). Russian novelist, a public servant for most of his working life. His greatest work was the novel *Oblomov* (1848–58), an acute psychological study of an indolent and indecisive Russian gentleman of the 19th century.

Goncourt, Edmond Louis Antoine Huot de (1822–1896) and **Jules Alfred Huot de** (1830–1870). French writers and critics. The brothers Goncourt were inseparable, and collaborated throughout their lives. The taste and sensuality of the 18th century especially appealed to them and they pictured its way of life in a fascinating series of 'histories' and 'lives'. They applied the same technique in their realistic novels of contemporary life. They shocked public and critics alike by choosing to describe characters such as a prostitute and nymphomaniac and writing novels such as *Soeur Philomène* (1861) *Renée Mauperin* (1864) and *Madame Gervaisais* (1869) in a style of vivid impressionism which tended to disdain grammar. They were notable critics of 18th-century art and letters and Edmond encouraged European interest in Japanese art, especially by his study of Hokusai. The brothers kept (from 1851) a notable *Journal des Goncourt*, of which Edmond published nine volumes (1887–95). The annual Prix Goncourt commemorates them.

Grant, R. B., *The Goncourt Brothers*. 1972

Gonsalvo di Cordova (Gonzalo Hernandez di Aguilar) (1442–1515). Spanish soldier, known as 'El Gran Capitan'. Having fought with distinction against the Moors, he achieved brilliant successes for King * Ferdinand II by expelling the French from Naples and eventually from the whole of Italy (1498). In the renewed war which followed the partition of Granada (1500), he once more occupied Naples and southern Italy and in November 1503 won the most spectacular victory of his career by crossing the Garigliano near Minturno with all the conditions, including the weather, in favour of the enemy. (The British achieved a similar feat there 440 years later.) He ended his career as viceroy of Naples.

Gonzaga. Italian ruling family. In 1328 Luigi Gonzaga was elected Captain-general of Mantua, and from that date until 1707, when the emperor deposed Ferdinando Carlo, members of the family ruled in the tiny state as marquis (from 1403) and as duke (from 1530).

Gooch, George Peabody (1873–1968). English historian. Of independent means, he was a Liberal MP (1906–10) and editor of the *Contemporary Review* (1911–60). The volume of his work and his skill in marshalling material have made him one of the most impressive historians of our time. Among his greatest achievements are *History and Historians of the Nineteenth Century* (1913), *Germany and the French Revolution* (1920). With Harold Temperley he showed immense skill and industry in documenting the origins of World War I. After World War II he reached a wider public with lives of Frederick the Great, Louis XV, Maria Theresa and Catherine the Great. He was awarded the O.M. in 1963.

Goodyear, Charles (1800–1860). American inventor. After many years of experimentation he discovered (1839) the process for vulcanizing (i.e. elasticizing and strengthening) crude rubber by mixing it with sulphur and heating it.

Goons, The (1949–60). British comedy group on BBC radio. Its members were Spike

(Terence Alan) Milligan (1918–), Sir Harry (Donald) Secombe (1921–) and Peter (Richard Henry) Sellers (1925–80). Milligan, the principal writer, performed several roles, acted in many films and was also a prolific novelist, poet and playwright (e.g. *The Bed Sitting Room* 1973). Secombe ('Neddy Seagoon') was a powerful tenor who became a popular concert and nightclub artist. Sellers, a gifted character actor, became an international superstar with his performance in many films (e.g. *Lolita, Dr Strangelove, Being There* and the Inspector Clouseau series). The Goons worked in the tradition of surrealist verbal humour which began with Lewis * Carroll.

Goossens Family. Sir Eugene Goossens (1893–1962), his brother **Leon** (1897–), his sisters **Marie** (1894–) and **Sidonie** (1899–). Noted English musical family. Their father and grandfather were both orchestral conductors. Sir Eugene Goossens, composer and conductor, formed an orchestra in 1921 and moved to America in 1923, where he became director of the Rochester Philharmonic Orchestra (until 1931) and of the Cincinnati Symphony Orchestra (1931–46). In 1947 he moved to Australia, conducting and teaching in Sydney. He was knighted in 1955. Leon Goossens was a distinguished solo oboist who did much to restore the instrument in public interest. His sisters, Marie and Sidonie, were harpists.

Goossens, E., *Overture and Beginners*. 1951

Gorbachev, Mikhail Sergeyevich (1931–). Russian Communist politician. He was a combine-harvester driver, worked as a party organiser in Stavropol until 1978, became a member of the Central Committee of the CPSU (1971–), secretary of the party agriculture committee (1978–85) and a Politburo member (1980–). On the death of K. U. * Chernenko (March 1985) he was speedily elected to succeed him as first secretary of the CPSU.

Gorchakov, Prince Mikhail (1792–1861). Russian soldier. Having served with distinction from the Napoleonic campaigns of 1812–14 onwards, he gained fame by his gallant and skilful defence of Sevastopol (1854–55).

Gordon, Charles George (1833–1885). British soldier, of Highland Scottish origins. He served in the Crimea, but the start of the adventurous career which made him famous came when, as a captain in the Royal Engineers, he was sent to China (1859). Here circumstances provided him with the extraordinary task, as head of the mercenary 'Ever Victorious Army', of saving the imperial régime from the fanatical revolutionaries. He returned to England (1865) with a reputation for courage and initative and the sobriquet 'Chinese Gordon'.

In 1874 he was invited to enter the service of the Khedive of Egypt and was made governor of the equatorial province. Fighting the slave trade almost single-handed, opening up the country – he brought steamers past the cataracts and swamps of the Nile and launched them on Lake Albert – contending with disease and corruption, he performed a marvellous feat, in the course of which he gained immense personal influence over the inhabitants. After an absence of four years he returned to Egypt (1884) with British government instructions to evacuate European and Egyptian citizens from the Sudan, which was being overrun by the followers of the fanatical zealot known as * 'El Mahdi'. This he achieved but could not bring himself to desert the loyal Sudanese. With his tiny force he was soon shut up in Khartoum, and after a ten months' siege and incredible hardship the city fell and Gordon and his men were killed. Two days later a British relief expedition arrived; its delays and their tragic consequences were attributed to Gladstone's government and helped to bring about its fall. Gordon was a man of high Christian principles, of great courage and devotion.

Garrett, R., *General Gordon*. 1974

Gordon, Lord George (1751–1793). British agitator. Son of the 3rd Duke of Gordon, he entered parliament in 1774. The passing of the Catholic Relief Act (1778) caused him to become president of the Protestant Association and instigate protests which culminated in the Gordon, or 'No Popery', riots (1780). Gordon himself marched to parliament to present a petition at the head of a mob of hooligans which later raged through the city, pillaging, burning and, if opposition was met, killing. Newgate Prison was among many buildings destroyed. After the riots (vividly described in Dickens's *Barnaby Rudge*) had been suppressed by troops, it was estimated

that over 400 had been killed. Gordon, acquitted of high treason because of insanity, later became a Jew.
Hibbert, C., *King Mob*. 1958

Gordon, Patrick (1635–1699). Scottish soldier. As a boy of 16 he sailed to the Baltic and took part, on both sides in turn, in the Swedish-Polish Wars. He joined the Russian army (1661), attained high rank and became friend and adviser of Peter the Great.

Gore, Charles (1853–1932). English ecclesiastic. A distinguished Anglo-Catholic theologian of liberal outlook, he was appointed bishop of Worcester (1902), Birmingham (1905) and Oxford (1911). He retired (1919) to a life of writing and teaching. He founded (1892) the Community of the Resurrection.
Carpenter, J., *Gore: A Study in Liberal Catholic Thought*. 1960

Gorky, Maxim (Alexei Maximovich Peshkov) (1868–1936). Russian writer. His pen-name *Gorky* is the Russian word for 'bitter'. He was born at Nizhny Novgorod (now named Gorky in his honour). Orphaned at the age of 5, he was brought up by his grandmother, whose immense fund of Russian folk tales gave him a bent for literature. At 12 he ran away to lead a roving and penurious existence in contact with the poorest strata of society. He began to write, and achieved success with *Sketches and Stories* (1898). His social novels which followed are concerned with the lives of the poor and outcast, and are remarkable for their stark realism. He was involved in revolutionary activities and after the failure of the 1905 revolution left Russia, not to return until 1914, when he engaged in revolutionary propaganda and got to know most of the Bolshevik leaders. He left Russia in 1922 for health reasons and lived in Capri until 1928. When he went back he was received with enthusiasm and hailed as the outstanding Communist novelist, the promoter of 'social realism' in Soviet literature.

Among his many works the autobiographical trilogy – *My Childhood* (1913), *My Apprenticeship* (1916) and *My Universities* (1923) – is considered his best.

Gort, John Standish Surtees Prendergast Vereker, 6th Viscount (1886–1946). British soldier. He joined the Grenadier Guards (1905) and in World War I, during which he won a V.C., his courage became almost a legend. Between the wars he gained quick promotion and after being appointed commandant of the staff college (1936), and chief of the imperial general staff (1937), he was chosen (1939) to lead the British Expeditionary Force to France, where in 1940 he had to meet the German thrusts which forced retreat to Dunkirk. He faced further ordeals, in which his courage and military skill were again proved, as governor of Malta (1942–44) and high commissioner for Palestine (1944–45).

Gorton, Sir John Grey (1911–). Australian politician. Educated at Oxford, he became an orchardist, a pilot in World War II, and a Liberal Senator from Victoria 1950–68. A minister from 1958, he was responsible for science 1962–68 and education 1963–68. On Harold * Holt's sudden death, Gorton was unexpectedly elected Liberal leader and became Prime Minister in a Liberal-Country party coalition 1968–71, the first from the Senate. He transferred to the House of Representatives 1968–75. His innovations, attempts to increase Commonwealth power at the expense of the states, caused resentment in his own party and he lost a vote of confidence on his own casting vote. He left the Liberal Party in 1975.

Gosse, Sir Edmund William (1849–1928). English poet and critic. He was son of the zoologist **Philip Gosse** (1810–1888), a Plymouth Brother, of whom he wrote a critical but compassionate account in *Father and Son* (1907). Apart from his poems and numerous critical works he wrote several biographical studies e.g. of Donne, Ibsen and Swinburne. His collected poems appeared in 1911 and his essays in 1912–27. He did much to encourage younger writers and was a great friend of Henry James; he was librarian to the House of Lords (1904–14), and was knighted in 1925.

Gottwald, Klement (1896–1953). Czechoslovak president. Born in Moravia, he was conscripted during World War I with the Austrian army, from which he deserted after Russia's collapse. He was an early member of the Communist party in the independent Czechoslovakia and in 1929, having meanwhile become its secretary-general, entered parliament. In 1938, after violently opposing the Munich agreement, he went to Moscow whence he returned after the war to become prime minister of a coalition. On its collapse in 1948 he succeeded * Beneš as president.

Gough, Sir Hubert de la Poer (1870–1963). British soldier. After fighting in South Africa, he was a leader of the officers stationed at the Curragh in Ireland who preferred resignation to the coercion of Ulster. In World War I he commanded a cavalry division in 1914, and in 1918 was in command of the 5th Army when in March the Germans achieved their spectacular breakthrough, for which Gough was unjustly blamed and recalled. In fact he showed great skill in extricating his army from a situation resulting from misguided deployment of forces by strategists at home. His autobiography, *Soldiering On*, was published in 1954.

Gould, Glenn (Herbert) (1932–1982). Canadian pianist, born Toronto. A juvenile prodigy, he gained an international reputation as a recording artist, especially for his interpretations of J. S. Bach, but also as an isolate and eccentric who withdrew from concert giving in 1964. However, he continued to record and made radio and television documentaries.

Gould, Jay (1836–1892). American speculator. A surveyor by profession, he began his speculation in tanning but soon turned to railways. Having overcome * Vanderbilt to gain control of the Erie Railway he was forced to resign (1872) for issuing fraudulent stock. A spectacular attempt, with the collaboration of Jim Fisk, to corner gold caused the 'Black Friday' panic (24 September 1869). Railway finance continued to be his main activity and he controlled at one time more than half the track in the south-west. He died worth about $70,000,000. His son, George Jay, continued in the same railroad tradition, but eventually was completely ruined.

Gould, Nat (1857–1919). English novelist. He achieved spectacular but brief popularity with some 130 books, nearly all relating to the turf.

Gould, Stephen Jay (1941–). American paleobiologist. He taught geology, biology and the history of science at Harvard and became internationally known with his books *Ever Since Darwin* (1977), *The Panda's Thumb* (1980) and *The Mismeasure of Man* (1981).

Gounod, Charles François (1818–1893). French composer, born in Paris, the son of a painter. He became an organist and choir conductor in Paris, closely studied the church music of Palestrina and Bach, and first won attention with a *Solemn Mass* performed in London (1851). He wrote eight operas of which only two are often performed: *Faust* (1859), for many years, partly owing to its dramatic story, partly to the melodic idiom for which Gounod was distinguished, the most popular work in the French operatic repertoire, and *Romeo and Juliet* (1867). He lived in England during the Franco-Prussian War and returned to sacred music with the oratorios *The Redemption* (1882) and *Mors et Vita* (*Death and Life*; 1885).

Gower, John (*c.* 1330–1408). English poet. He wrote three long poems; the didactic *Speculum Meditantis*, a satire in old French, telling of the struggle of seven virtues and seven vices for the possession of man; the Latin *Vox Clamantis* about the Peasants' Revolt of 1381; and, most important, *Confessio Amantis* in old English, in which stories in the Chaucerian manner take the form of the confessions of a lover weary of life. Gower was a friend of Chaucer and like him did much to develop English as a language.

Gowers, Sir Ernest Arthur (1880–1966). English civil servant. He campaigned for the writing of good English and wrote several books designed to reduce 'officialese' in official documents including *Plain Words* (1948) and *ABC of Plain Words* (1951). As chairman of the Royal Commission on Capital Punishment (1949–53) he became a convinced opponent of hanging and wrote *A Life for a Life?* (1956).

Goya y Lucientes, Francisco de (1746–1828). Spanish painter, engraver and etcher, born at Fuendetodos, near Saragossa, the son of a poor farmer. Very little is known of his early life but he apparently studied in Madrid and in Rome (1771) and was commissioned to paint frescoes at Saragossa Cathedral which he executed in the fashionable Tiepolo style (1771–81). In 1775 he began working on a series of cartoons for the royal tapestry factory and continued until 1792. His first, neo-classical, period ended in 1778 when he was commissioned to make a series of engravings of * Velazquez' paintings, previously confined to the royal collection. These masterworks made a profound impression on Goya and the engravings soon spread the fame of both Goya and Velazquez. In 1775 Goya married into a painter's family and moved up the patronage ladder, becoming a court painter in 1786, director of the royal academy from 1795 and chief painter to the royal family in 1799: he received the patronage of Manuel * Godoy, the Duchess of Osuna and the Duchess of Alba (immortalized in the 'Naked Maja', one of the rare nudes in Spanish painting). In 1792 a mysterious illness made him paralysed, deaf and subject to hallucinations; this marked the beginning of his third period. His later works flayed the corruption of Church and State and aspects of cruelty and servility in Spanish life. It is astonishing that his portraits *Charles IV and his Family* and *Queen Maria Luisa* (both 1800) or *Ferdinand VII* (1814), revealing his royal sitters as imbeciles or degenerates, did not lead to his dismissal or arrest. After the French invasion he supported Joseph Bonaparte's regime and remained court painter, continuing under the restored Bourbons.

The Prado in Madrid exhibits 103 Goya paintings and 485 etchings and sketches. His most famous series of etchings were *Caprices* (1799), scathing illustrations of proverbs, popular sayings and grotesqueries, *The Disasters of War* (1810), *Bullfights* and *Proverbs* (both 1814–19). His sketches are piercing, nightmarish visions of horrors and death made sometimes by working thick, gummy ink-blots with the fingers on small pieces of buff paper. The most famous of his wartime paintings was *Execution of the Defenders of Madrid* (*3rd May 1808*: painted 1814), with its penetrating tableaux of the horror and futility of violence. Other late paintings include *Colossus* (1809), *Senora Subasa Garica* (1808), *The Balloon* (1818), *The Witches' Sabbath* (1820), and *Saturn Devouring one of his Children* (1823). He left Spain in 1824 and died in Bordeaux at the age of 82. His fantastic later works look towards the expressionism of 20th-century painters.

Graaff, Sir de Villiers, 2nd Bart (1913–). South African politican. Descended from an old Cape family, he was educated at Oxford, called to the English bar and taken prisoner in World War II. In 1948 he entered the South African parliament and was leader of the United Party opposition 1956–77.

Gracchi. Roman brothers: **Tiberius Sempronius Gracchus** (163–133 B.C.) and **Gaius Sempronius Gracchus** (*c.* 159–121 B.C.), both statesmen and reformers. Their mother Cornelia – the daughter of * Scipio Africanus – was a woman of great character and a devoted citizen of Rome. Tiberius won recognition as a soldier and returned to Rome to press for reforms to alleviate the misery of the peasantry, who were being crushed by the concentration of land and power in the hands of a few. He was elected tribune (133) and proposed a land reform *Lex Sempronia Agraria*); to obtain its passage he resorted to methods technically unconstitutional in the face of the opposition of the senate who promoted a riot on the next election day, in which he was killed. In 123 Gaius decided to try to carry out similar reforms and introduced laws which benefited small landowners; he also won the support of the Roman wealthy class of *equites* by a legal reform. The senate was again firmly opposed; Gaius failed to secure re-election (121) and in disturbances which then broke out, opportunity to kill him was taken. The reform effort of the Gracchi was thus ended and the reactionary policy of the senate led to the social and political wars which ruined the Republic (* Marius; Sulla).

Grace, Princess *see* **Kelly, Grace**

Grace, William Gilbert (1848–1915). English cricketer of legendary fame. A physician by profession, he played for Gloucestershire from 1864 and continued playing first-class cricket until 1908 by which time he was known as the 'grand old man' (G.O.M.) of the game. He toured frequently and captained the English team in Australia (1873–74 and 1891–92). He is said to have scored 54,896 runs and to have made 126 centuries in first-class cricket (on pitches that were frequently ill-prepared) and also to have taken 2,876 wickets.

Weston, G. N., *W. G. Grace: The Great Cricketer*. 1973

Grafton, Augustus Henry Fitzroy, 3rd Duke of (1735–1811). English politician. His grandfather, the 1st Duke, was a son of Charles II and Barbara Villiers, Duchess of * Cleveland. Grafton was a familiar political figure in the early years of George III's reign. He became important after Pitt's resignation (1768) as head of the government; he applied the disastrous policy of coercion to the American colonies. He was one of the main targets of the *Letters of Junius*, and resigned in 1770.

Graham, Billy (William Franklin) (1918–) American evangelist. He was ordained (1939) in the Baptist ministry and from 1946 conducted a series of 'Crusades' throughout the U.S.A., Europe, India, Australia and Africa.

Graham, Martha (1894–). American dancer and choreographer, predominant influence on modern dance. She created about 150 ballets, all developing the art of body-movement as a means of emotional expression and theatrical narrative. She was trained by Ruth St Denis and Ted Shawn in a tradition that drew on a world-wide variety of dance forms. She went to the Eastman School of Music in Rochester, New York, as a teacher in 1924 and made her debut as a professional solo artist in 1926. She developed a unique repertoire of body movements to reveal 'the inner man'; their performance depended on vigorous physical discipline and tremendous virtuosity. Her best-known works are probably *Appalachian Spring* (1944) and *Clytemnestra* (1958).
Leatherman, L., *Martha Graham*. 1966

Graham, Thomas (1805–1869). Scottish chemist. He was born in Glasgow, and was professor of Chemistry at Anderson's College, Glasgow (1830–37), and at University College, London (1837–55). From 1855 until his death he was Master of the Mint. He worked mainly on the absorption and diffusion of gases and on osmosis. His discovery that the rates of diffusion of two gases are inversely proportional to the square roots of their densities is now known as Graham's law. He also investigated the properties of substances in the state between suspension and solution, and it was he who named such substances 'colloids'.

Grahame, Kenneth (1859–1932). British writer. Author of the children's classic *The Wind in the Willows* (1908), he was orphaned in childhood and, on leaving school, joined the Bank of England where he worked until 1907. His stories are a celebration of a child's world, and of an idyllic countryside. A. A. * Milne dramatized *The Wind in the Willows* in 1930, as *Toad of Toad Hall.*
Green, P., *Kenneth Grahame*. 1959

Grahame-White, Claude (1879–1959). British pioneer of aviation. In 1909, the year in which he started a flying school at Pau in France, he became the first Englishman to gain a proficiency certificate in aviation. He won the Gordon Bennett Cup (1910), and organized the first commercial airfield in England in the same year.

Grainger, Percy Aldridge (1882–1961). Australian composer. Noted for his interest in the English national tradition and in folk song, he settled in America in 1914 and became head of the music department at New York University. He was also interested in the traditions of his native country. He founded the Grainger Museum of Australian Music in Melbourne (1935).
Dreyfus, K. (ed.), *The Farthest North of Humanness: Letters of Percy Grainger 1901–14*. 1985

Gramsci, Antonio (1891–1937). Italian Communist writer. A Sardinian of Albanian descent, he was a hunchback, crippled by ill-health. Educated at Turin University, he became a journalist and a foundation member of the Italian Communist Party (1921) which he led from 1923. A Deputy 1924–26, he was imprisoned 1926–33, but wrote prodigiously in jail. He proposed polycentrism—the idea that Communist parties should adapt to local circumstances and ideas instead of following a rigid line imposed by Moscow. He was rejected the cruder forms of historical materialism and originated the concept of 'hegemony'.

Granados (y Campina), Enrique (1867–1916). Spanish composer and pianist. He studied in Barcelona and Paris and wrote many works for piano, of which the best known were *Goyescas* (1911–13), poetic evocations of Goya's art, including the beautiful 'Lover and the Nightingale'. His opera *Goyescas* was premiered in New York in 1916. On their return to Europe the composer and his wife drowned when the *Sussex* was sunk by a German submarine.

Granby, John Manners, Marquess of (1721–1770). British soldier, eldest son of the 3rd

Duke of Rutland. He first served under Cumberland in the Jacobite rebellion (1745) and was second in command (from 1758 in command) of the British forces in Germany in the Seven Years War. A gallant cavalry change at the Battle of Warburg was one of the explains that gave him a hero's reputation. Several of the veterans who went into innkeeping named the inns after him and the Marquis of Granby remains a familiar inn sign.

Grandi, Dino (1895–). Italian count and diplomat. He joined Mussolini's Fascist party (1922) and soon rose to a position of power; he was foreign minister (1929–32), and as ambassador to London (1932–39) during the Italian conquest of Ethiopia, the Spanish war, and the successive crises immediately preceding World War II, he so persuasively presented the case for Mussolini's ultimate good intentions and his possible detachment from Hitler that he disarmed effective opposition to his master's plans. In 1943 he moved the decisive vote in the Fascist Grand Council which brought about Mussolini's fall.

Grant, Cary (Archibald Alexander Leach) (1904–). American film actor, born in Bristol; in the U.S. from 1920. He made 73 films between 1932 and 1966, including *The Philadelphia Story* (1941), *Arsenic and Old Lace* (1944), *To Catch a Thief* (1955), and *North by Northwest* (1959). He combined good looks, elegance and a gift for comedy.

Grant, Ulysses Simpson (1822–1885). Eighteenth president of the U.S. The son of an Ohio merchant, he was trained as an army officer at West Point; disliking the tedium of army life he retired (1854) but in civil life he was incompetent. Recommissioned as a colonel when the Civil War came, his first major success was early in 1862 when he captured two important forts on the Tennessee and Cumberland Rivers. He followed this up by the capture of Vicksburg (1863) on the Mississippi, which resulted in cutting the Confederate states in two. Further successes in eastern Tennessee persuaded President Lincoln to make him (1864) commander of the Union armies. As such he devised the strategy – Sherman's army to march through Georgia and approach the Confederate capital (Richmond, Virginia) from one side, while Grant himself made a direct attack – which brought the war to an end with the Confederate surrender (1865) at Appomattox. Grant's reputation as the hero of the war secured his nomination as the Republican party's presidential candidate (1868). He was elected and served two terms, marred by poor administration, financial scandals and official corruption. Honest himself, though naïve enough to accept gifts from wealthy place-seekers, he was exploited and deluded by men whom he had appointed. The *Alabama* dispute with Great Britain was settled during his tenure of office by his excellent secretary of state, Hamilton Fish. After his presidency he proved his honesty by taking personal responsibility for the debts when a bank in which he was a partner failed. To relieve his poverty he wrote his *Memoirs*, the dictation of which he completed in agony while dying of cancer.

Granville, John Carteret, 1st Earl (1690–1763). British diplomat and politician. Inheriting his father's title of Baron Carteret at the age of 5, he entered the House of Lords when he came of age. As ambassador to Sweden (1619), he negotiated a series of agreements which paved the way to lasting peace in the Baltic area. On his return he was appointed a secretary of state but * Walpole, jealous of his success, soon transferred him to Ireland as lord lieutenant. Intended as political exile, his term of office (1724–30) proved happy and fruitful and enabled him not only to pacify the country but to enjoy the friendship of Dean Swift. Convinced of Walpole's hostility, he led the opposition to him from 1733 until his fall (1742). As secretary of state for the northern department in the new ministry, Carteret had charge of Great Britain's part in the War of the Austrian Succession then taking place on the continent. The use of British troops on Hanover's behalf was so unpopular that Henry * Pelham and his brother the Duke of * Newcastle found themselves able to manoeuvre the too brilliant Carteret out of office. In the same year he had inherited the earldom of Granville from his mother, countess in her own right. In 1751 the Pelhams brought Granville back into the cabinet as lord president of the Council and as a much esteemed elder statesman he stayed in office until he died.

Pemberton, N. W. B., *Carteret*. 1936

Granville-Barker, Harley (1877–1946). English playwright, actor and producer. As actor and producer for the London Stage Society, he introduced many of the plays of Shaw. His own plays include *The Voysey Inheritance* (1905) and *Waste* (1907). He also wrote the interesting *Prefaces to Shakespeare* (published in four series 1927–45) which examine Shakespeare's plays from an actor's and producer's viewpoint.

Grass, Günter (1927–). German novelist, poet and playwright. His allegorical writing, on the condition of Germany during and after the Third Reich, began with the novel *Die Blechtrommel* (*The Tin Drum*), 1959. This was followed by *Katz und Maus*, 1963, and *Hundejahre* (*Dog Years*), 1965.

Gratian (Flavius Gratianus Augustus) (359–383). Roman co-emperor (from 375) with his half-brother, Valentinian II. Though a civilized man and a moderate ruler, he alienated many by his attempts to suppress paganism in Rome by force. When the rebel Maximus crossed from Britain to Gaul, Gratian – faced with a mutiny of his troops – fled, and was killed at Lugdunum (Lyons).

Grattan, Henry (1746–1820). Irish politician. In 1775 he entered the Irish parliament, which under Poyning's Law was virtually subservient to the Privy Council. Grattan, a brilliant orator, fought for and secured the right of the Irish parliament to initiate laws. He advocated the emancipation of Catholics and won for them the right to vote (1793). George III vetoed their admission as members of the Irish parliament and Grattan resigned. He was bitterly opposed to (though unable to prevent) the linking of Ireland with Great Britain by the Act of Union, by which Pitt hoped (vainly as it turned out) to secure Catholic emancipation without political domination. Grattan spent most of his remaining years in promoting the cause of emancipation (achieved in 1829).

Graves, Robert Ranke (1895–). English poet, novelist and critic. He was born in London, the son of **Alfred Perceval Graves** (1846–1931), Irish poet and folk-song collector. He was educated at Charterhouse and Oxford, served in the army during World War I and became known as a poet. (His poetical works were collected in 1959). Since 1929 he has lived mainly in Majorca. His autobiography *Goodbye to All That* appeared in 1929. Later he wrote a series of vivid, scholarly historical novels, notably *I, Claudius* (1934), and its sequel *Claudius the God* (1934), *Count Belisarius* (1938) and *Wife to Mr Milton* (1943). He also wrote several works attempting to place Christianity in a mythological context, e.g. *King Jesus* (1946). He translated *The Golden Ass* of Apuleius (1949) and other classics and published *Greek Myths* (1955). His biography of his friend * Lawrence of Arabia appeared in 1938. He succeeded W. H. * Auden as professor of poetry at Oxford University (1961–66).
Seymour-Smith, M., *Robert Graves*. 1982

Gray, Thomas (1716–1771). English poet. Born in London and educated at Eton and Cambridge, he was the life-long friend of Horace * Walpole, with whom he toured the continent (1739–41). His poetical output was small, but his best poems, e.g. *Ode on a Distant Prospect of Eton College, Elegy written in a Country Churchyard, The Progress of Poesy* and *Ode on the Death of a Favourite Cat* (i.e. Walpole's), are among the finest products of the 18th-century reflective tradition, combining sensibility with an Augustan discipline and conciseness of expression. He declined the laureateship in 1757. Apart from visits to Scotland and the Lake District the whole of his adult life was spent in scholarly quiet in Cambridge, where he was professor of modern history (1768–71). Though esteemed the most learned man in England in this and other fields, he never delivered a lecture, had a pupil or published anything except his poetry. His letters reveal his character to a remarkable degree. His grave in the country churchyard at Stoke Poges, Bucks, believed to be that of the poem, is still a point of pilgrimage.
Golden, M., *Thomas Gray*. 1964

Graziani, Rudolfo (1882–1955). Italian soldier. In Ethiopia (1935–1936) he successfully led the invasion from the south and remained in the conquered country as viceroy until 1938. In World War II he was utterly defeated by * Wavell in Libya (1940–41). He was minister of defence (1943–44) in Mussolini's puppet government in North Italy, set up after his rescue by the Germans from the captivity that followed his fall from power. Graziani was imprisoned (1945–50).

Greco, El (Domenikos Theotokopoulos) (1541–1614). Painter, born in Crete, hence called in Italy El Grequa and later in Spain El

Greco. Few details of his life are known. He was in Venice by 1570 (he probably studied under the then aged Titian); when he went to Spain is uncertain; his earliest known painting there was done in 1577 in Toledo, where he spent the rest of his life. His early work, reflecting his origin, shows the influence of Byzantine icons, but the Italian influence in Venice of Titian, Tintoretto and Bassano was pronounced. From this he progressed to his extraordinary, very personal religious style expressive both of Spanish fanaticism and his own spiritual ecstasy. His works are finished with passion and power. An other-wordly quality is suggested by the elongated bodies, the bold, almost phosphorescent, colours with sharp contrasts of blue, yellow and green. The emotional rather than the actual content of the subject became increasingly stressed as the Mannerism of his earlier style is modified by a baroque conception of space and movement. Among his masterpieces are *The Burial of Count Orgaz* (Toledo); *The Scourging of Christ* (Madrid) and *The Disrobing of Christ* (Munich).
Wethey, H., *El Greco and His School*. 1973

Greeley, Horace (1811–1872). American journalist. His interest in political questions led him to found (1834) a newspaper, which, after he became a friend of * Seward, changed its name to *Tribune*, which, for thirty years, exerted tremendous influence. He campaigned for social reform. His advice 'Go West, young man' became proverbial. He was strongly anti-slavery and finally became a supporter of Lincoln – somewhat lukewarm as he was at heart a pacifist. He sought nomination as presidential candidate (for the Liberal Republican Party) in 1872 but was unsuccessful. He died shortly after, unhinged in mind by disappointment and the death of his wife. (* Fourier, François Marie Charles).

Green, Henry (Henry Vincent Yorke) (1905–73). English novelist. Educated at Eton and Oxford, he became managing director of H. Pontifex & Co., a family engineering works in Birmingham. He wrote a series of highly praised short novels, remarkable for their laconic style and keen social insights, including *Blindness* (1926), *Living* (1929), *Party Going* (1939), *Loving* (1945) and *Doting* (1962). His admirers included W. H. * Auden, Rebecca * West, Angus * Wilson and John * Updike.

Green, John Richard (1837–1883). English historian. Born at Oxford and educated there, both at school and university, he became a clergyman in London's East End. Forced by tuberculosis to retire (1865) he wrote his famous *Short History of the English People* (1874). It achieved such immense success that he enlarged it and republished it in four volumes (1877–81). As its title implies, it is a social rather than a political history and it takes special account of geographical factors and antiquarian relics. It remains historically valuable and survives also as a work of literature.
Addison, W. G., *J. R. Green*. 1946

Green, Julien (Hartridge) (1900–). Franco-American novelist. He was born in Paris of American parents, lived mostly in France and wrote almost entirely in French. His novels, while notable for psychological insight, painted a sombre and puritanical picture of French provincial life. They included *Adrienne Mesurat* (1927), *Christine* (1928), *Le Visionnaire* (1934). He was elected to the French Academy in 1971.
Burre, G. S., *Julien Green*. 1972

Green, William (1873–1952). American trade union leader. After working as a miner in Ohio he took up trade union organization and (1913–24) was secretary and treasurer of the United Mine Workers of America. He succeeded Samuel * Gompers as president of the American Federation of Labor (1924–52).

Greenaway, Kate (1846–1901). English illustrator. The pictures in her many children's books, e.g. *The Kate Greenaway Birthday Book*, recalled the charming fashions of the early years of the 19th century and were so popular that they provoked a widespread revival in her own time. The books are now highly prized by collectors.

Greene, (Henry) Graham (1904–). English novelist and playwright, born at Berkhamsted. Educated at Berkhamsted School (where his father was headmaster) and Balliol College, Oxford, he was a sub-editor on *The Times* 1926–30, film critic of the *Spectator* 1935–39, worked in the Foreign Office 1941–44 and later as a publisher. His reputation was first made by *Brighton Rock* (1938), a thriller of contemporary violence but with some social impact. His conversion to

Roman Catholicism introduced a religious element, but serious purpose was always subordinate to swiftly moving narrative. His novels include *The Power and the Glory* (1940; Hawthornden prize-winner), *The Heart of the Matter* (1948), *The End of the Affair* (1951), *The Quiet American* (1955), the satirical *Our Man in Havana* (1958), *The Burnt Out Case* (1961), *The Comedians* (1966), *The Honorary Consul* (1973), *The Human Factor* (1978) and *Dr Fischer of Geneva* (1980). His plays include *The Living Room* (1953), *The Potting Shed* (1957), *The Complaisant Lover* (1959), *The Return of A. J. Raffles* (1975) and *Yes & No* (1980). He received the CH in 1966 and many international awards, but the Nobel Prize for Literature eluded him, to the anger of his supporters. His brother, **Sir Hugh Carleton Greene** (1910–   ), was director general of the B.B.C. (1960–69).

Greene, Robert (1558–1592). English poet, playwright, pamphleteer and wit. Autobiographical pamphlets tell of his acquaintance with London's rogues and swindlers, an aspect of his life also reflected in *Groatsworth of Wit Bought with a Million of Repentance* (1592). His poems and romances, in which Shakespeare dipped more than once for a plot, contain passages of lyric beauty, but they and his plays are now mainly of academic interest; Greene probably shared in the composition of Shakespeare's *Henry VI*. He is said to have died from a 'surfeit of pickled herrings and Rhenish wine'.

Greenwood, Arthur (1880–1954). English Labour politician. An M.P. from 1922, he served under Ramsay MacDonald as minister of health (1929–31), and without portfolio in Churchill's wartime cabinet (1940–42). He was lord privy seal (1945–47) in Attlee's post-war Labour government.

Gregory I (known as 'the Great') (540–604). Pope (from 590) and saint. A Roman patrician, he was prefect of Rome (*c.* 573) but soon resigned to become a Benedictine monk, and was later summoned to represent the pope at Constantinople. As pope, he extended the area of papal primacy through missions, e.g. that of St * Augustine of Canterbury, and by skilled diplomacy. He did much, too, to spread the rule of St Benedict among the devotees of monastic life. Many of his letters survive to indicate his constant activities as well as his austere piety. The Gregorian chant is named after him, but it is doubtful whether all or any of the liturgical changes attributed to him were really his.

Gregory VII (Hildebrand) (*c.* 1020–1085). Pope (from 1073). He is among the best known of medieval popes for his success in opposing the custom by which lay rulers, in investing bishops with their lands etc., used words that seemed to imply a claim to spiritual as well as temporal authority. Gregory forced the Holy Roman Emperor * Henry IV to do penace at Canossa (January 1077) in the snow. The tables were turned when (1080) imperial troops compelled Gregory to leave Rome and end his life in exile at Salerno. Before becoming pope, Hildebrand, a Benedictine monk, had as papal envoy (from 1048) and as archdeacon of the Roman church (from 1058) exercised a strong influence over several earlier pontiffs, not only in the matter of investiture but also as a learned and enlightened reformer of canon law. He was canonized after his death.

Gregory XIII (Ugo Buoncompagni) (1505–1585). Pope (from 1572). As a violent proponent of the counter-reformation he inspired rebellion against Queen Elizabeth in Ireland and Jesuit activities in England; he also caused a medal to be struck to celebrate the massacre of St Bartholomew. He introduced the Gregorian calendar (1582).

Gregory, Isabella Augusta, Lady (née Persse) (1852–1932). Irish playwright. Author of the comedy *Rising of the Moon* (1907), she was a friend of W. B. Yeats and with him founded the Irish National Theatre Society and became a director of the Abbey Theatre, Dublin, opened in 1904. She believed that the literary revival, of which she was a leader, would further the cause of Irish national independence.

Kohfeldt, M. L., *Lady Gregory: The Woman Behind the Irish Renaissance*. 1985

Grenfell, Julian Henry Francis (1888–1915). English poet. The son of Lord Desborough, he was one of the young men who entered World War I in crusading spirit. He was killed before disillusion set in. His *Into Battle* is magnificently evocative of the time and mood.

Grenfell, Sir Wilfred Thomason (1865–1940). English medical missionary. He equipped the

first hospital ship for the North Sea fisheries. From 1892 he worked in Labrador and Newfoundland and established hospitals, orphanages, schools and agricultural centres for the Eskimos and the fishing communities.
Kerr, J. L., *Wilfred Grenfell, His Life and Work*. 1959

Grenville, George (1712–1770). English politician. He entered parliament in 1741. While he was prime minister (1763–65) the imprudent Stamp Act, which inflamed the anger of the American colonists, was passed; he also became unpopular by prosecuting * Wilkes.

Grenville, Sir Richard (1541–1591). English sea hero, of Cornish descent. He carried Raleigh's first colonists to Virginia (1585) and took an active part in the undeclared sea war against the Spaniards. The incident which won him fame occurred when (1591) Lord Thomas Howard's squadron of fourteen vessels encountered fifty-three Spanish ships off Flores, an island in the Azores; while the rest of the squadron escaped, Grenville disobeyed orders and stayed to fight it out. From 3 p.m. and all through the following night his ship *Revenge*, as Tennyson's poem dramatically relates, beat off fifteen Spanish ships in turn, of which four were sunk or foundered. In the morning Grenville, with his ship a wreck and ammunition gone, was forced to surrender and died of his wounds on a Spanish ship. A less charitable view portrays Grenville as ambitious, cruel and obstinate, and the episode as a useless expenditure of lives.

Gresham, Sir Thomas (1519–1579). English financier, founder of the Royal Exchange (1568). Much of his life was spent as adviser to Queen Elizabeth and financial agent of the crown. Gresham's law, which can be summarized as 'bad money drives out good', says that when two coins are of equal legal exchange value but one is of great intrinsic value, the latter will be hoarded while the one of lower intrinsic values remains in circulation. Revenue from shops in the Royal Exchange building was used to found Gresham's College (rebuilt 1841).
Salter, F. R., *Sir Thomas Gresham*. 1925

Greville, Charles Cavendish Fulke (1794–1865). English writer of memoirs. As clerk of Council in Ordinary (1821–59) he had a unique opportunity for observing and recording, with great psychological insight, the public and private lives of the celebrities whom he met. His famous *Memoirs* appeared (with tactful suppressions) in 1874–87.

Greville, Fulke, 1st Baron Brooke (1554–1628). English writer and courtier. He held office under Elizabeth – of whom he was a favourite – and James I, but is mainly remembered for his life of his friend Sir Philip Sidney (published posthumously in 1652), which contains vivid contemporary portraits.

Grey, Beryl (1927–). English ballerina. She made her first solo appearance at Sadler's Wells as Sabrina, in *Comus*, in 1941. She danced with the Sadler's Wells company 1942–57, and has appeared for seasons with the Bolshoi Ballet (1957–58) and Chinese Ballet (1964).

Grey, Charles Grey, 2nd Earl (1764–1845). British politician who secured the passage of the Reform Bill (1832). He entered parliament in 1786, joined the opposition and attacked Pitt for his foreign policy, his repressive legislation at home and the Union with Ireland. By 1792 he was already thinking of parliamentary reform and formed the Friends of the People club with that aim. He joined the Whig ministry (1806) and on Fox's death became foreign secretary and leader of the Commons. After he inherited his father's earldom (1807) he receded from politics but after the 1830 election he returned to lead the Whig party and head the new government. To secure the passage of the Reform Bill he persuaded William IV to threaten to create a sufficient number of peers to outvote opposition in the Lords. His ministry also passed (1833) the historic measure, proposed by * Wilberforce, abolishing slavery throughout the empire. After a split in the cabinet (1834) concerning the Irish church reform Grey resigned and thereafter lived in retirement.

Grey, Sir George Edward (1812–1898). English colonial administrator. He explored in Western Australia (1837–39), and became governor of South Australia (1841) and then of New Zealand (1845–53). There he ended the war with the Maoris, to whom he was sympathetic. After a spell as governor of Cape Colony (1854–61), during which he vainly urged South African federation, he returned to New Zealand as governor but became involved in a quarrel concerning the conduct of the renewed Maori War, and was recalled (1867). He returned to enter New Zealand politics and was Liberal prime minister (1877–79).

Grey, Lady Jane (1537–1554). Claimant to the English crown. She was the daughter of Henry Grey, Marquess of Dorset (afterwards Duke of Suffolk), and was linked with the royal family through a grandmother, a sister of Henry VIII. Jane married (1553) Lord Guildford Dudley, son of the Duke of Northumberland who as protector of the realm persuaded the dying boy-king Edward VI to name Jane as his successor (1553). On his death she was proclaimed queen, but Mary, the late king's sister, quickly rallied support; Jane was taken and imprisoned in the Tower of London. Her father joined Sir Thomas Wyatt's rebellion and this led to the execution of Jane together with her husband and her father. She had beauty, intelligence – she read five languages, including Greek and Hebrew – and piety.
Chapman, H., *Lady Jane Grey*. 1962

Grey Eminence *see* **Joseph, Père**

Grey of Fallodon, Edward Grey, 1st Viscount (1862–1933). English politician. Educated at Winchester and Balliol College, Oxford, he entered parliament (1885), and was under-secretary for foreign affairs in Gladstone's last administration (1892–95), when the 'Grey declaration' warned the French off the Sudan. He was foreign secretary (1905–16) in the Liberal administration of * Campbell-Bannerman and * Asquith. During that time he cemented the Triple Entente with France and Russia to counter the threat from Germany and its allies; in the Morocco crisis (1911) his support of France averted war; it was, also, largely through his influence that the Balkan Wars (1912–13) were localized. His efforts to avert war in 1914 were unsuccessful. He retired from politics in 1916, but was British ambassador in Washington (1919–20). He was made K.G. (1916) and received a peerage (1922).
Trevelyan, G. M., *Grey of Fallodon*. 1937

Grieg, Edvard Hagerup (1843–1907). Norwegian composer and leader of a new national school. He studied in Leipzig from 1858, and he was influenced by Mendelssohn and Schumann. In 1863 he went to Denmark where, in Copenhagen, he met the Norwegian composer Nordraak and through him discovered his own folk tradition. His own music was based on this tradition, refined by his own natural lyricism. His best-known works are his piano concerto, the *Holberg* suite and the incidental music to Ibsen's *Peer Gynt*.
Horton, J., *Grieg*. 1972

Griffith, Arthur (1872–1922). Irish politician. As a journalist he had great influence upon Irish nationalist opinion; he founded (1905) 'Sinn Fein' and edited a newspaper of the same name (1906–14), during which time the movement gradually adopted republicanism. He was imprisoned several times (1916–20). From 1919, when the republic was declared, he was de Valera's deputy. With Michael Collins he led the Irish delegation which signed the treaty (1921) setting up the Irish Free State, and, after de Valera had refused co-operation, for the last seven months of his life headed its provisional government.

Griffith, David Wark (1875–1948). American film director and producer, originally a journalist and actor. He entered the film industry in 1908 but it was only after years of experiment in short films that he made his great contribution to the history of the cinema with the first great American spectacular films: *The Birth of a Nation* (1915), and *Intolerance* (1916). He introduced 'close-ups', 'flash-backs', 'fade-outs' and other now familiar techniques.

Grimaldi, Joseph (1779–1837). Most famous of English pantomime clowns. He made his debut at Sadler's Wells at the age of 3 and soon became a legend. He retired (1828) worn out by hard work (often at two theatres nightly). His memoirs, edited by Charles Dickens, were published in 1838.

Grimm, Jakob Ludwig Karl (1785–1863) and **Wilhelm Karl** (1786–1859). German brothers, philologists and collectors of fairy tales and myths. The development of Germanic languages, law, folk lore, sagas and songs was to them a single composite study which one or both pursued down many avenues and recorded in numerous learned books. Jakob was particularly interested in language: 'Grimm's law' concerns the sound shifts which produced

the German language from its Indo-European origins.
Michaelis-Jena, R., *The Brothers Grimm*. 1970

Grimond, Joseph (1913–). English Liberal politician. Educated at Eton and Oxford, he was called to the bar (1937) and served in World War II. Since 1950 he has been M.P. for the Orkney and Shetland constituency. He succeeded Clement Davies as Liberal leader (1956). In the 1964 election the party vote was almost double that of the previous election at over 3,000,000. He resigned as head of the Liberal Party in 1967.

Grivas, Georgios (1898?–1974). Greek soldier, born in Cyprus. During World War II, under the *nom de guerre* 'Dighennis', he led guerrilla bands against the Germans and the rival Communist underground. In 1951 he returned to Cyprus to direct the EOKA terrorist forces in support of the Enosis movement for union of Cyprus with Greece. After the settlement (1959) he withdrew, but returned (1964) to command the Greek Cypriot troops.

Grock (Adrien Wettach) (1880–1959). Swiss musical clown. A master of miming, he captivated audiences of all nationalities without uttering a word; the most famous of his acts displayed him in his clown's make-up in a state of complete bewilderment when confronted with an array of musical instruments whose eccentricities he appeared unable to master, until with a sudden change of mood he revealed himself as a virtuoso performer.

Grocyn, William (*c.* 1446–1519). One of the great English humanist scholars of his time. He was educated at Winchester and New College, Oxford, and subsequently held a number of scholastic and ecclesiastical preferments before finally becoming (1506) master of the collegiate church of All Hallows, Maidstone, where he was buried. He was held in great respect by Erasmus, Sir Thomas More and Colet, and is important as one of the very first to teach Greek publicly in England.

Gromyko, Andrei Andreyevich (1909–). Soviet diplomat. He became ambassador to the U.S.A. in 1943, serving (1946–48) as Soviet representative on the U.N. Security Council. After a short time as ambassador to Great Britain (1952–53), he was deputy minister for foreign affairs (1947–57). As foreign minister (1957—), he signed (1963) the partial nuclear test ban agreement and played a key role in the détente conferences of the 1970s, and became a Politburo member 1973– .

Gröner, Wilhelm (1867–1939). German general. In World War I he was officer in charge of railways, personnel and supplies, succeeding * Ludendorff as Quartermaster-General (October 1918). With * Hindenburg he engineered the Kaiser's abdication, then worked with * Ebert against the communists. He became a conservative deputy in the Reichstag 1920–33, was a Minister and a strong opponent of the Nazis.

Gropius, Walter Adolf (1883–1969). German architect. A pioneer of 'functional' architecture, of which his early industrial buildings are fine examples, glass and concrete are the chief materials used. He founded the Bauhaus School (1919) and was its director until 1928, first in Weimar and (from 1926) in Dessau, where his design for the new premises was hailed as a landmark. He left Germany in 1933 and settled in the U.S.A. after three years in England. He was professor of architecture at Harvard (1937–52).
Fitch, J. M., *Gropius*. 1960

Grosseteste, Robert (1168–1253). English scholar. Little is known of Grosseteste's origins, though he probably came from a poor family. He studied at Oxford where he taught, before taking his mastership in theology, probably in Paris. Between 1214 and 1221 he was chancellor of Oxford University. In the 1230s he lectured to the Franciscans in Oxford on theology, before being appointed Bishop of Oxford in 1235.

Grosseteste produced numerous editions and commentaries on Aristotle's works, which show a familiarity with Arab contributions. His commentary on Aristotle's *Posterior Analytics* was much used in succeeding centuries.

His own approach to the natural world was somewhat eclectic. He emphasized the importance of experience, but was also aware of the role of mathematics in providing explanations. He saw study of Nature as revealing and reflecting aspects of God. Many of his studies were of light, which he regarded not just in a physical sense, but as a spiritual emanation. He studied the phenomenon of refraction, and showed how progress in optics depended upon the sister science of geometry, just as the science of sound was dependent on arithmetic.

Grosseteste's most original works included his treatises on the calendar. Recognizing that the moon was never full when the calendar indicated it should be, he planned reforms, for which exact knowledge of the length of the solar year and the lunar month would be required. This work was taken up by Roger * Bacon.

Crombie, A. C., *Robert Grosseteste and the Origins of Experimental Science*. 1953

Grossmith, George (1847–1912). English actor and author. Though he achieved great success on the stage, notably in Gilbert and Sullivan operas at the Savoy, and wrote hundreds of songs and sketches, it is as the author (with his brother Weedon) of *The Diary of a Nobody* (1892) that he is remembered.

Grosz, George (1893–1959). German satirical artist. He began his career as a savage caricaturist, and after World War I, e.g. in his series *Faces of the Ruling Class*, he venomously assailed militarists, bureaucrats and capitalists. From 1933 he worked in the U.S.A. and in World War II he painted anti-war pictures, whose power lay in their macabre and horrifying symbolism.

Bittner, H., *George Grosz*. 1965

Grote, George (1794–1871). English historian and politician. He is best known for his *History of Greece* (begun in 1822 and published in 10 vols. 1846–56), a work of great scholarship infused with a deep and understanding love of Greek civilization. He actively participated in the founding of University College, London, and was vice-chancellor of London University from 1862. He refused a peerage (1869).

Clarke, M. L., *George Grote, a Biography*. 1962

Grotewohl, Otto (1894–1964). East German politician. After some years as a printer he turned to politics and became prominent as a Social Democratic member of the Reichstag (1925–33). He was twice imprisoned by the Nazis. After World War II, as leader of his party in East Germany when it merged with the Communists, he became the first minister president (i.e. premier) of the German Democratic Republic 1949–64. He became a virtual figurehead as real power passed to his deputy Walther * Ulbricht.

Grotius, Hugo (Huig van Gruit) (1583–1645). Dutch international jurist. Born at Delft, he went to Leyden University at the age of 11, and at 15 accompanied a diplomatic mission to Henry IV of France. On his return he began to practise law at The Hague and soon gained public appointments. He became involved, however, in the violent religious disputes of the time, and was under sentence of death when his wife managed to get him carried out of prison in a chest. He escaped to Paris, was pensioned by Louis XIII and produced his *De Jure Belli et Pacis* (1625), the first great work on international law. Beyond its legal aspects it was a plea for more human conduct in the pursuit of war. He also devoted himself unsuccessfully to reconciling the Roman church and sects of a divided Christendom. In 1634 he was taken into Swedish service as their ambassador in Paris.

Grouchy, Emmanuel, Marquis de (1766–1847). Marshal of France. He joined the Revolutionary armies and is said to have been wounded fourteen times before he was captured at the Battle of Novi (1799). He fought with Napoleon's Grand Army from 1805, was prominent during the retreat from Moscow, rejoined the emperor after his escape from Elba and was made a marshal (1815). He was much criticized, perhaps unjustly, for failing to prevent Blücher's junction with Wellington at Waterloo.

Grove, Sir George (1820–1900). English engineer, musicologist and editor. He built the first cast-iron lighthouse (in the West Indies) and was secretary of the Crystal Palace Company (1852–73). In his other spheres of activity he edited *Macmillan's Magazine* and was a large contributor to *Smith's Dictionary of the Bible*; he is best known as editor (1878–90) of the standard work: *A Dictionary of Music and Musicians* (new edition 1980). He was knighted in 1883.

Young, P. M., *George Grove, 1820–1900*. 1980

Grünewald, Matthias (Mathis Nithardt, also called Gothardt) (*c.* 1470/1480–1528). German painter. He was probably born at Würzburg. He worked for the see of Mainz and eventually was court painter (1515–25) to its cardinal archbishop Albert of Brandenburg. His mysticism and extreme piety are discernible in all his work, and in his portrayals of the crucifixion he reveals the depth of his compassion. The great Isenheim altar-piece at Colmar shows tremendous emotional power, vividly expressive colouring, and magnificence of design. Changes of taste and style, coinciding with the coming of the Reformation, account for his neglect until recent times.

Guardi, Francesco de (1712–1793). Venetian painter. His teacher was Canaletto, who for long was esteemed above Guardi, whose paintings, most of Venice, though superficially similar to those of Canaletto, are in fact far different in their more sensitive treatment of light and colour. Whilst Canaletto is concerned with architectural precision Guardi takes delight in the fleeting moment, catching the interplay of light and shadow on water, the atmospheric effects on the lagoon and using a technique approaching that of the Impressionists.
Shaw, J. B., *The Drawings of Francesco Guardi*. 1951

Guarneri (or Guanieri). Family of Italian violin-makers in Cremona, of whom the chief were: **Andrea** (*c.* 1626–1698), taught by Nicolo * Amati; his sons **Pietro** (1655–1720), who lived in Mantua, and **Giuseppe** (1666–*c.* 1739); another **Pietro**, known as Peter of Venice (*c.* 1698–1732), a nephew of Pietro of Mantua, and lastly – perhaps the most famous of all – Giuseppe's son, known as **Giuseppe del Gesú** (1698–1744), because his violins were signed IHS, the first three letters of the name Jesus (in Greek), familiar in religious ornamentation.

Guderian, Hans (1888–1954). German general. An expert in mechanized warfare, he planned several of the great German armoured thrusts. He commanded a Panzer corps in the Polish campaign (1939) and the Panzer army in Russia (1941). In 1944, having become chief of army staff, he was virtually commander-in-chief against Russia. He retired because of ill health in 1945.

Guelph (Guelf or Welf). German dynasty, originating (like the * Hohenstaufens and the * Hohenzollerns) from Swabia. The Guelphs were allies of the papacy and contenders for the imperial throne in the twelfth and thirteenth centuries; their traditional rivalry with the Ghibellines (who opposed secular papal power) lead to constant instability in Italy. The Guelphs formed dynastic links with the d'Estes of Ferrara and became rulers of Bavaria (to 1180), Brunswick and Hanover; the name of Britain's royal family from 1714 to 1901 was Guelph-d'Este.

Guericke, Otto von (1602–1686). German physicist. Born at Magdeburg, he was noted for his investigations into pneumatics. He invented the air pump when carrying out experiments to produce a vacuum. His most famous experiment was that of the 'Magdeburg hemispheres', in which two hollow copper hemispheres were placed together to form a globe and emptied of air. Teams of eight horses pulling in opposite directions failed to separate them. He also studied electrical attraction and repulsion, obtaining his electricity by friction on a globe of sulphur.

Guevara (de la Serna), 'Che' (Ernesto) (1928–1967). Argentinian revolutionist. The son of an architect, he studied medicine, became a determined opponent of the Peron regime and left Argentina in 1952. He served in the Popular Front government of Guatemala until it was overthrown in June 1954. In 1956 he met Fidel * Castro in Mexico and accompanied his guerrillas to the Sierra Maestra as physician, and soon emerged as Castro's closest aide. In the Cuban revolutionary government he was president of the national bank (1959) and minister for industry (1959–65). He left the Cuban government in 1965 and disappeared. He visited the Congo and North Vietnam, reappearing in 1967 at the head of a guerrilla organization in Bolivia. In October he was captured and killed by the Bolivian army. His fascinating *Diaries* were published in 1968.

Guggenheim, Meyer (1829–1905). American industrialist. Born in Switzerland, he went to the U.S.A. (1847) and eventually with his sons succeeded in establishing vast enterprises for the mining and processing of metals. His sons created the well-known Guggenheim Foundations: that of **Daniel** (1856–1930) was 'to promote the well-being of mankind'; that of **Simon** (1867–1941) to help scholars, artists and writers.

Guicciardini, Francesco (1483–1540). Italian historian of the Renaissance. For much of his life he held distinguished diplomatic and administrative posts in the service of the Medicis, whether in the government of Florence, where he was born, or under the Medici popes Leo X and Clement VII. His greatest work *The History of Italy*, covering the period 1492–1534, is detailed, accurate and shrewd in its judgement of affairs and men.

Guido d'Arezzo (Guido Aretino) (*c.* 990–*c.* 1050). Italian Benedictine monk and musical theorist. He invented two devices of great practical help to musicians: (i) the names 'ut', 're', 'mi' etc. to indicate where in the hexachord scale then used the notes were placed (the origin of the subsequent tonic sol-fa); (ii) the mnemonic device of giving the tips and joints of the fingers names of the various notes.

Guido, Reni *see* **Reni, Guido**

Guillotin, Joseph Ignace (1738–1814). French doctor, member of the Revolutionary Convention. He recommended the use of, but did not invent, the instrument of execution introduced in 1792 and named after him.

Guinness, Sir Alec (1914–). English actor. He has appeared on the London and New York stage since 1933, in leading roles in, e.g., *The Rivals* (1938), *An Inspector Calls* (1948), *The Cocktail Party* (1949), *Ross* (1960), and in many films, e.g., *Great Expectations, Oliver Twist, Kind Hearts and Coronets, The Lavender Hill Mob, Tunes of Glory* and *Lawrence of Arabia*. In 1958 he won the Academy award for his role as Major Nicolson in *The Bridge on the River Kwai*. The intelligence, wit and versatility which have enabled him to impersonate such a wide range of characters are his main theatrical characteristics. He was knighted in 1959.

Guinness, Sir Benjamin Lee (1798–1868). Irish brewer. He enlarged the Dublin brewery of his father, Arthur Guinness, until it became a vast enterprise, and its product, Dublin stout, a household word. His eldest son, **Arthur Edward Guinness** (1840–1915), became Lord Ardilaun; his third son, **Edward Cecil Guinness** (1847–1927), who became (1919) 1st Earl of Iveagh, having amassed a great fortune through the business, endowed a trust for slum clearance and rebuilding in Dublin and London and gave to the nation Kenwood, the family mansion on Hampstead Heath, with a fine collection of pictures.

Guiscard, Robert (*c.* 1015–1085). Norman adventurer in Italy. With his brothers he carved out a territory for himself in Calabria and Apulia, with which he was invested by Pope Nicholas II in 1059. With the aid of his brother, * Roger I, Sicily was conquered and added to the family possessions. Robert conceived the idea of seizing Constantinople on behalf of his daughter's father-in-law, the deposed emperor, Michael VII, but after capturing Durazzo (1082), he returned to support Pope * Gregory VII against the emperor Henry IV. On his way to resume his Byzantine enterprise he died.

Guise. Noble French family of Lorraine. The first duke was **Claude** (1496–1550), whose daughter **Mary** (1515–1560) married James V of Scotland and became regent for their infant daughter, Mary Queen of Scots. Claude's son, **Francis** (1519–1563), second duke, helped by his brother, **Charles** (1525–1574), archbishop of Rheims and cardinal, led the extreme Catholic party which fought the Huguenots in the religious wars; he was assassinated. The third duke, **Henry** (1550–1588), was mainly responsible for the massacre of St Bartholomew (1572), for which the connivance of the queen mother, * Catherine de' Medici, had been with difficulty obtained. She subsequently was forced to come to terms favourable to the Huguenots. Guise in protest formed the Catholic League, and a triangular contest developed between the League, the Huguenots, and the crown, worn since 1574 by the vacillating * Henry III. Henry at last cut the Gordian knot by arranging for the treacherous murder of Guise at Blois (1588). After Henry's own assassination (1589) and the succession and conversion to Catholicism of the Protestant leader Henry of Navarre, the power of the Guises steadily declined.

Guitry, Sacha (1885–1957). French actor and playwright. With his father **Lucien Guitry** (1860–1925) and Yvonne Printemps, second of Sacha's five wives and the delightful heroine of many of his plays, he formed an incomparable trio, 'the Guitrys', who played a dominant role in French theatrical life for a generation. In addition to being a leading actor, producer and manager, he wrote over

100 plays, mainly light comedies, and in later life achieved new success as a film director (e.g. *Les Perles de la couronne*, 1938). Lucien played opposite Sarah * Bernhardt in many of his favourite parts, e.g. as Armand to her Marguerite Gautier in *La Dame aux camélias*.

Guizot, François Pierre Guillaume (1787–1874). French politician and historian. He was born of a Protestant family at Nîmes, and was professor of modern history at the Sorbonne (1812–22). Turning to politics, he supported the revolution (1830) against Charles X, but under King Louis Philippe he headed the right-centre in the chamber, his chief rival being * Thiers. When minister for public instruction (1823–37), he organized primary education; he also restricted the freedom of the press. After briefly being ambassador in London (1840), he became foreign minister and virtually controlled the government of which he eventually became the actual head. His refusal to concede any reform caused the downfall of the régime. His extensive historical works, several on English history, e.g. *Histoire de la révolution en Angleterre* (1826–56), earned him high respect as a historian.

Gulbenkian, Calouste Sarkis (1869–1955). Oil magnate of Armenian descent, born in Istanbul. His wealth and his nickname. 'Mr Five-percent', were originally based on a holding of one twentieth of the shares of the Anglo-Iranian Petroleum Company. He accumulated a fine collection of pictures in his lifetime and left most of a huge fortune (estimated at £300,000,000) to an international trust for educational, artistic and charitable purposes. His son, **Nubar Gulbenkian** (1896–), became a colourful figure on the British social scene.

Gunn, Thom(son William) (1929–). English poet who settled in the U.S.A. and became an important spokesman for modern urban society. His first volume of poems was *Fighting Terms* (1954), followed by *The Sense of Movement* (1957); both were written during his years of contact with Stanford University, California. He afterwards taught at Berkeley until 1966, then returned to England to write *Positives* (about Londoners).

Gürsel, Cemal (1895–1966). Turkish soldier and politician. After serving with distinction in World War I and under Kemal Atatürk, he became commander-in-chief in 1958. When replaced (1960), he led a military revolt against the unpopular prime minister Menderes, and became head of state.

Gustavus I (Gustavus Vasa) (1496–1560). King of Sweden (from 1523). Of a leading noble family, he led a successful revolt against the rule in Sweden of Christian II of Denmark. By confiscating church lands he later established a national Protestant church. He brought under his own direct control some of the lands held by the nobles, and encouraged trade and industry (partly by using a keen business sense to direct many concerns himself), thus bringing about financial stability and economic progress. Risings provoked by his policies were quickly suppressed. In alliance with Denmark he destroyed the domination of the Hanseatic towns and finally obtained from parliament a declaration that his dynasty should be hereditary.

Gustavus II (Gustavus Adolphus) (1594–1632). King of Sweden (from 1611). The son of Charles IX by his second wife, he was preferred as king to a cousin with a better hereditary claim. Aided by his chancellor * Oxenstierna, his adviser throughout the reign, he reorganized the administration by defining the spheres of local and central governments with a proper apportionment of finance. Finding himself at war with three countries, he came to terms with Denmark, led a successful campaign against Russia (1617), and then turned against Poland with whom he concluded an armistice on favourable terms (1629). His object throughout was Swedish domination of the Baltic with command of the river mouths and therefore control of trade. In the hopes of achieving this through a Swedish-controlled league of Protestant German states, in 1631 he took part, in agreement with the French, in the Thirty Years War. He marched victoriously through Germany and at Breitenfeld in Saxony met and defeated the imperial general Tilly, who was again defeated and mortally wounded at the passage of the Lech (1632). After overrunning much of Germany, Gustavus abandoned an attack on Austria to meet a threat to his rear by * Wallenstein, the result being the Swedish victory of Lutzen near Leipzig, in which Gustavus was killed. Gustavus's military innovations swept away the last medieval aspects of warfare from his campaigns. He introduced regimental uni-

forms, better discipline and also insisted on attention to the welfare of his troops. He provided them with lighter and more effective fire-arms and the consequent increase in mobility and fire power were the main contributions to his military success.
Roberts, M., *Gustavus Adolphus: A History of Sweden 1611–1632.* 2 Vols. 1953–1958

Gustavus III (1746–92). King of Sweden 1771–92. One of the most remarkable 18th-century 'enlightened despots', he seized power from the parliamentary factions, the 'Hats' (pro-French and anti-Russian) and the 'Caps' (pro-Russian and anti-French), dissolved the Riksdag in 1772, granted freedom of the press, abolished torture, guaranteed religious toleration, provided poor relief, reorganized administration and taxation, simplified trade laws and was a great patron of the arts. He founded the Swedish Academy (1786) and the Royal Opera, wrote and acted in plays, and was a great orator and conversationist. In February 1789, just before the French Revolution, he used the support of the commons to crush the remaining powers of the nobility. However, this did not endear him to constitutional liberals. Recognizing that the French Revolution had made enlightened despotism obsolete, he tried to organize an army of intervention and his agent Count Fersen stagemanaged the tragi-comic flight of Louis XVI and Marie Antoinette to Varennes. Many plots against Gustavus were laid by competing groups and on 16 March 1792, at a masked ball at his own opera house, he was shot in the back by Captain J. J. Anckarstroem and died 13 days later. This incident was the basis of * Verdi's opera *The Masked Ball* (1859), although censorship required its setting to be changed to Boston.

Gustavus VI (Gustavus Adolf) (1882–1973). King of Sweden (from 1950), the son and successor of Gustavus V. Ingrid, his daughter by his first wife, the English Princess Margaret of Connaught (died 1920), married Frederick IX of Denmark; his second wife was Lady Louise Mountbatten.

Gutenberg, Johann (*c.* 1400–1468). German printer, the first European to print from movable types. Born in Mainz he worked in Strasbourg for several years on the possibility of achieving this. In *c.* 1448 he retuned to Mainz where a rich goldsmith Johann Fust financed his printing shop. After a quarrel (1455) and an action to recover his money, Fust acquired the press and conducted it with the aid of his son-in-law, Peter Schöffer. Meanwhile Gutenberg received support that enabled him to set up another press. These events and the absence of dates, names or colophons on works printed at Mainz make ascription difficult, but it is fairly certain that Gutenberg printed the 32-line Mazarin Bible and twenty editions of Donatus's Latin school grammar.

Guthrie, Sir (William) **Tyrone** (1900–1971). British theatre director. He began as an actor and assistant stage manager with the Oxford Repertory Company in 1923. He then worked for the B.B.C., where he did much to realize the full potential of radio drama. He was director of the Festival Theatre, Cambridge, 1929–30. His production of James Bridie's *The Anatomist* in London, 1931, was successful and was followed by Pirandello's *Six Characters in Search of an Author* (1932). He achieved wide recognition for his fresh approach to traditional plays with his work for the Old Vic Company and at Sadler's Wells Theatre. His original productions of Shakespeare did much to revive audience perception of familiar plays.
Guthrie, T., *A Life in the Theatre.* 1960

Guy, Thomas (*c.* 1644–1724). English philanthropist. He was a bookseller in London from 1668, and printer to Oxford university (1679–92). Successful speculation in South Sea shares enabled him to multiply the fortune made by trade and economical living and so to build and endow the hospital in London that bears his name.

Guzman Blanco, Antonio (1829–1899). Venezuelan dictator. He was leader of the 'Yellow' (liberal faction in the civil wars of the 1860s). During this time he was vice-president or temporarily president and when his party was overthrown (1868) he staged a revolution which led to his election as president (1870). During the next twenty years he ruled as a despot – improving the economic basis of the country but doing nothing to help the Venezuelan peasants who remained little better than serfs. He himself grew immensely rich. He frequently made long trips abroad leaving men of straw to rule in his absence. He was in

Paris when in 1889 one of these was overthrown by a revolution and he stayed on in Paris until his death.

Gwyn (or Gwynne), **Nell** (1650–1687). English courtesan. She is said to have started her career as an orange seller at Drury Lane, where she later acted. 'Pretty, Witty Nell' was the liveliest and most popular of Charles II's mistresses: he is alleged to have said on his deathbed 'Let not poor Nelly starve'. She bore him two sons, Charles and James Beauclerk, the former of whom became Duke of St Albans. It is said that she persuaded the king to found Chelsea Hospital for veteran soldiers.

Bevan, B., *Nell Gwynn*. 1969

H

Haakon VII (1872–1957). King of Norway (from 1905). He was Prince Carl, second son of Frederick VIII of Denmark, and took the name Haakon when he was chosen (1905) to be king of the newly independent Norway after its union with Sweden had been dissolved. In 1940 he led the resistance of his country to German aggression, at home and later from England. His British wife, Queen Maud (died 1938), was a daughter of Edward VII. Their son, * Olaf V, succeeded to the throne.

Habsburg (or Hapsburg). The European dynasty which, deriving its name from a castle in Switzerland, gradually extended and consolidated its territories until the head of the house became Archduke of Austria, King of Hungary and Bohemia, with many outlying territories besides. From the time of Frederick III (German king 1440–93) the imperial title was held almost continuously by members of the Habsburg house until the end of the Holy Roman Empire (1806). The then holder assumed the title of Emperor of Austria which remained with the dynasty until the last emperor, * Charles, was deposed after World War I. His son Otto became the pretender.

From 1516 Spain also became subject to Habsburg rule under Charles, who had already acquired his father's Burgundian heritage in the Low Countries and who in 1519, in succession to his grandfather * Maximilian, became the emperor * Charles V. The partition after his abdication left the imperial title and the Central European lands to his brother * Ferdinand; Spain with its overseas possessions and the Low Countries to his son * Philip II. The Bourbons succeeded the Habsburgs in Spain when * Charles II died in 1700. The Habsburgs made a fine art of dynastic marriages and to this they mainly owed their immense success.
Taylor, A. J. P., *The Hapsburgs*. 1948

Hadrian (Publius Aclius Hadrianus) (76–138). Roman emperor. He was born into an Italian colonist family settled in Italica near Seville, Spain; the family were well-connected and Hadrian himself was possibly born in Rome and certainly educated there. He gained advancement through his father's cousin, the future emperor Trajan. He became tribune of the plebs in 105 and praetor in 106. He was made a provincial governor, on the Danube, in 107 and a consul in 108. This rapid rise was largely due to the favour of the politician Lucius Licinius Sura. Sura died shortly afterwards and Hadrian's advancement seemed at an end, but in 117 the Emperor Trajan adopted him, thus assuring his succession when Trajan died in August 117. As emperor he made lengthy tours of the Empire, 121–125 and 128–*c*. 133. A philhelene, he preferred the eastern provinces and did much for the arts and for religious and public life in Greece. His tours in the rest of the Empire, however, had lasting results in the form of defence systems (such as Hadrian's Wall in Britain) and both military and civil administrative reform. His periods of rule in Rome also produced judicial reforms of great importance. In 134 he made a last journey to Judaea to quell an uprising (partly caused by his own ban on circumcision which he considered inhumane). He died in 138, naming Antoninus as his successor.
Yourcenar, M., *Memoirs of Hadrian*. 1954

Haeckel, Ernst (1834–1919). German zoologist. In 1861 he became lecturer in Medicine at Jena, in 1862 Professor of Zoology and in 1865 Director of the Zoological Institute. Although medically qualified, he had no desire to practise medicine clinically. Zoology was his first love, and much of his scientific career was occupied in work in comparative anatomy and morphology. The publication of Charles Darwin's *Origin of species* (1859) made an enormous impact on him. He accepted evolution readily. Thereafter his detailed zoological work was increasingly concerned with evaluating structure in terms of evolutionary adaptation. He was above all interested in the way in which the embryonic development of each individual creature showed (as he claimed) its own evolutionary history; or, as he put it 'ontogeny recapitulates phylogeny'.

Unable to accept either traditional Christianity or dogmatic materialism, Haeckel developed his own philosophy of Nature, 'monism', a form of pantheism which celebrated the progressive emergence of ever higher forms in Nature. Partly as a result of this, Haeckel gradually swung over to more Lamarckian forms of evolutionary theory, emphasizing the participation of Will in the evolutionary process.

Hemleben, J., *Ernst Haeckel*. 1964

Háfiz (pseud. of **Shams ed-Dín Muhammed** (died *c.* 1388). Persian lyrical poet. He lived at Shíráz; his poetry was held to be so sweet that he was called 'Chagarlab' (sugarlip). He was a Súfi, one of the mystic philosphical sect of Islam, and while his poetry superficially deals with sensuous delight and beauty and may be seen simply as love songs, it yet possesses a deeper esoteric significance. His tomb is a shrine and is visited by pilgrims from all parts of Persia.

Arberry, A. J., *The Ghazals of Háfiz*. 1947

Hagen, Walter C. (1892–1969). American golfer. Hagen, who played a notable part in the history of American golf, won the American open championship twice, the British four times and took part six times in the competition for the Ryder Cup (once as a non-playing captain).

Haggard, Sir Henry Rider (1856–1925). English author. Before settling in England after marrying a Norfolk heiress, he held official posts (1875–79) in South Africa, which provided the background for his popular novels of adventure, e.g. *King Solomon's Mines* (1885), *She* (1887), *Allan Quatermain* (1887) and *Ayesha or The Return of She* (1905).

Higgins, D. S. (ed.), *The Private Diaries of Sir Henry Rider Haggard*. 1980

Hahn, Otto (1879–1968). German physical chemist. In 1918, with Lise * Meitner, he discovered the radio-active element No. 91 (protactinium = Pa.) and in 1935 found evidence of four other elements corresponding to the atomic numbers 93, 94, 95, 96. In 1938 he succeeded in splitting the uranium atom and this basic discovery, as developed by Meitner and O. R. * Frisch led to the production of the atomic bomb: paradoxically scientists expelled from Germany realized the implications of Hahn's discovery before Hahn himself. He remained in Germany through World War II as director of the Kaiser Wilhelm Institute for chemistry in Berlin-Dahlem (1928–46), won the 1944 Nobel Prize for Chemistry, and was president of the Max Planck institute at Göttingen (from 1946).

Hahnemann, Christian Friedrich Samuel (1755–1843). German physician and founder of homoeopathic medicine. He studied medicine at Leipzig, Vienna and Erlangen where he graduated in 1779. He practised in Saxony, and settled in Dresden. He cultivated interests in medical chemistry, and published on related subjects, including the treatment of venereal diseases with mercurous oxide. From 1796 onwards he developed his own medical views, to be known as homoeopathy, spelt out in *Organon der rationellen Heilkunde* (*Organon of Rational Healing*) (1810). He had been persistently worried about harm caused by drugs ordinarily used. Hence he recommended testing out drugs on healthy persons, and ensuring the absolute purity of drugs, which were to be administered to patients in very small quantities. He believed that a drug which produced in a healthy body identical primary symptoms to those produced by a disease, was likely to be efficacious in curing the disease, since it would set up reactions in the body.

Hahnemann's fame grew (although he caught the anger of apothecaries since he prepared all drugs himself, and refused to administer more than one drug to patients at a time). In 1835 he remarried and set up in Paris, where he managed a large practice till the age of 88. Doctors were soon practising the homoeopathic system in almost every European country; in the U.S.A. Konstantin Hering

(1800–80) was commissioned to attack it, was converted and devoted his life to further research.
Dudgeon, R. E., *Hahnemann, the founder of scientific therapeutics* (1882); Hobhouse, R. W., *Christian Samuel Hahnemann.* 1961

Haidar Ali (1728–1782). Indian ruler. He served as a soldier under the maharaja of Mysore, whom he virtually displaced as ruler. He fought successfully against the Mahrattas and also the British, with whom, however, he formed an alliance. When help under this alliance was refused in a renewed war against the Mahrattas he allied himself with the French, and ravaged the Carnatic to within forty miles of Madras. He was ultimately defeated by Sir Eyre Coote. His son was * Tippoo Sahib.

Haig, Alexander Meigs, Jr (1924–). US soldier and administrator. Educated at West Point and Georgetown University, he was deputy to Henry * Kissinger in the National Security Administration 1970–73, vice chief of staff in the US Army 1973, and, as White House chief of staff and assistant to the President 1973–74, took a critical role in the resignation of Richard * Nixon and the transition to Gerald * Ford. He was commander-in-chief of US and NATO forces in Europe 1974–79 and became secretary of state under Ronald * Reagan 1981–82.

Haig, Douglas, 1st Earl Haig (1861–1928). British soldier. He was inspector general of cavalry in India (1903–06), and was again there (1909–11) as chief of the general staff. Meanwhile he had been director of military training at the War Office in London. During World War I he took the 1st Corps to France (1914), commanded the 1st Army (1915) and after Sir John French's recall was commander-in-chief on the Western Front from 1915 until the end of the war. He was thus responsible for the Battle of the Somme (1916), the Passendale campaign (1917) and the final victorious offensive (1918), undertaken in co-operation with Marshal Foch. He was granted an earldom and voted £100,000 in 1919. He retained the confidence of the British public throughout the war despite his bitter quarrels with the prime minister, Lloyd George; but in recent years his handling of the British armies has been severely criticized, especially since the publication (1952) of his private papers. He was devoted to the welfare of ex-servicemen and the creation of the British Legion was largely his work.
Sixsmith, E. K. G., *Douglas Haig.* 1976

Haile Selassie (1891–1975). Emperor of Ethiopia (from 1930). Before coming to the throne he was known as Ras Tafari, his father (Ras Makonnen) being cousin of the emperor * Menelik. He led the revolt against Menelik's grandson * Lij Yasu and acted as regent for Menelik's daughter Zauditu from 1917 until her death (1930), when he succeeded her on the throne. The Italian conquest of his country forced him to take refuge in England (1936) but in World War I the British drove the Italians from Ethiopia and restored him to his throne (1941). Despite his attempts at social and economic reform, such as abolishing the slave trade and setting up a parliament, his country remained one of the most backward in Africa and he was deposed in 1974.
Kapuściński, R., *The Emperor.* 1983

Hailsham of St Marylebone, Quintin McGarel Hogg, Baron (1907–). British politician. A barrister by profession, he entered the House of Commons in 1938, but the death (1950) of his father, the 1st Viscount Hailsham (who as Sir Douglas Hogg was a prominent Conservative attorney-general between the wars) took him reluctantly as the 2nd Viscount to the House of Lords. In successive Conservative governments he held posts of increasing importance including that of minister of science and technology (1959). He was one of the candidates for party leadership after * Macmillan's resignation (1963): he renounced his title, under new legislation which made this possible, and continued to serve under Sir Alec Douglas-Home in the Commons. In 1970 he was made a life peer and was Lord Chancellor (1970–74; 1979–). Hogg's grandfather, also **Quintin Hogg,** founded (1880) the Polytechnic in Regent Street, London.

Hakluyt, Richard (1552–1616). English geographer. He may have acquired his passionate interest in geography from a cousin, who was a lawyer to the Muscovy Company. At Oxford he was a student and lecturer (1570–*c.* 1588). He was ordained but became more and more absorbed in reading about and discussing the great exploratory voyages of his time. By 1582 he had gained the friendship of Drake,

Gilbert, Raleigh and other great seamen and had written a book on the American discoveries. In 1583 an appointment as chaplain to the British Embassy in Paris gave him the opportunity to gather information about explorers of other countries. His greatest work, *Principal Navigations, Voyages and Discoveries of the English Nation*, appeared in 1589 (enlarged edition 1598–1600). After being appointed rector of Wetheringsett, Suffolk (1590), he worked hard as a propagandist for further American colonization. In 1602 he became a canon of Westminster Abbey where he is buried. The Hakluyt Society was formed in 1846.

Haldane, John Burdon Sanderson (1892–1964). English scientist, the son of the eminent Oxford physiologist John Scott Haldane. He pursued research in genetics and went to Cambridge as Reader in Biochemistry in 1923. In 1933 he became Professor of Genetics at University College, London, emigrating to India in 1957. Haldane's major area of scientific work lay in relating evolutionary biology to the development of studies of heredity. He did important research on the genetic origins of colour blindness and haemophilia. He was also concerned with populational studies in evolutionary biology. During World War II he worked for the Admiralty investigating the physiological aspects of life in, and escape from, midget submarines and similar underwater work. Throughout his life he submitted himself – and his friends – to much self-experimentation.

Haldane was a dedicated popularizer of science in such books as *Daedalus, or Science and the Future*. A committed Marxist, he saw a future in which socialism and science marched forward together to provide better living conditions and a more rational society for everyone. He helped the Republican government in Spain during the Civil War, and broke with the Communist party on the * Lysenko issue.

Clark, R. W., *J. B. S.: The Life and Work of J. B. S. Haldane*. 1968

Haldane, Robert Burdon, 1st Viscount Haldane of Cloan (1856–1928). Scottish lawyer and politician, born in Edinburgh. Educated in Germany, he became a barrister, QC (1890), and Liberal MP (1885–1911). As secretary of war (1905–12), he carried through major reforms in the armed forces, then became Lord Chancellor (1912–15) until forced from office by anti-German hysteria: he was given the OM as a consolation prize. He joined the Labour party after the war, became its leader in the Lords and was Lord Chancellor again (1924). A distinguished amateur scientist and neo-Hegelian philosopher, he became FRS in 1906. He was the brother of **John Scott Haldane** (1860–1936), an experimental physiologist who worked on the problem of gas exchanges in the blood e.g. why divers suffer from 'the bends' and how poor ventilation in mines causes death. John Haldane's son was J. B. S * Haldane.

Hale, Sir Matthew (1609–1676). English judge. He became a judge in the Court of Common Pleas in 1653. In 1660, after the Restoration, he was made chief baron of the exchequer, knighted and became lord chief justice (1671–76). For a short while (1655) he sat in parliament. His works include *History of the Common Law of England.*

Hales, Stephen (1677–1761). English scientist. He became an undergraduate at Corpus Christi College, Cambridge in 1696, decided upon a career in the Church, and became curate of Teddington in 1709, remaining there for the rest of his life, much of which he gave over to scientific research. He was a convinced adherent of Newtonian natural philosophy, accepting the particulate nature of matter and a largely mechanistic set of explanations (he always preferred physics to chemistry). Like Robert * Boyle, he excelled in detailed experiments in which accurate weighing, measuring and recording were all important. Much of his work concerned experiments on plants, written up in his *Vegetable Staticks* (1727). He studied the rise of sap, measuring its pressure, and the variations of that pressure according to time of year, climatic conditions etc. He carried out impressive experiments upon transpiration.

The pressure of blood in animal arteries also drew his attention. He performed experiments to gauge its force in horses, oxen, dogs etc. He conducted important experiments on air. Although he did not recognize that air is made up of a mixture of gases, he did collect the vapours severally given off by different substances, in some cases as a result of burning – to collect these he invented the pneumatic trough. The ill effect of bad air in spreading disease concerned him, and led him to invent

systems of ventilators which could be used on ships, in prisons etc.
Clark-Kennedy, A. E., *Stephen Hales*. 1909

Halifax, Charles Montague, 1st Earl of (1661–1715). English Whig politician. As William III's chancellor of the exchequer (1694–97), he was responsible for the establishment of the National Debt by issuing the first government loan to which the general public could subscribe. He moved the bill which established the Bank of England (1694) and gave it power to issue paper currency. He came into literary prominence as an author with Matthew Prior of a parody of Dryden's *Hind and the Panther* and later was a patron of Addison and Congreve. He was created Earl of Halifax in 1714.

Halifax, Edward Frederick Lindley Wood, 1st Earl of (new creation) (1881–1959). English politician. Made Baron Irwin on his appointment as viceroy of India (1926–31), he tried to guide India towards dominion status by conciliatory policies and became a friend of Gandhi, but continued agitation forced him to take repressive measures. Back in England, he returned to the Ministry of Agriculture (1932) and held other senior posts before succeeding (1938) Eden as foreign secretary. He was thus the instrument through whom Neville Chamberlain's appeasement policy was carried out. When Churchill's government was formed in World War II he proved a most successful ambassador to the U.S.A. (1940–46). Halifax was noted for his High Anglican religious views.
Birkenhead, Lord, *Lord Halifax*. 1965

Halifax, George Savile, 1st Marquess of (1633–1695). English politician and author. He was a member of parliament (1660–1685), and was instrumental in securing the rejection of the bill for the exclusion of Charles II's brother James, Duke of York, from the succession (1681). For this he was made Marquess of Halifax (1682), and when the Duke became king as James II, Halifax was made lord president of the Council, but was soon dismissed for opposing the repeal of the Test Acts and the Habeas Corpus Act. Later he was one of the committee of peers which negotiated with William of Orange the taking over of the government. Known as 'the Trimmer', he attempted to vindicate his policies in *The Character of a Trimmer* (1688). He was in fact a loyal and wise statesman whose advice, had it been taken, would have saved James's throne.

Hall, Asaph (1829–1907). American astronomer. From 1862–91 he worked at the naval observatory at Washington. In 1877 he discovered the two satellites of Mars.

Hall, Charles Martin (1863–1914). American chemist. In 1886 he discovered the first economic method of electrically obtaining aluminium from bauxite. In 1890 he became vice-president of the Aluminium Company of America, which he helped to found.

Hall, (Marguerite) Radclyffe (1886–1943). English author. She wrote several interesting novels including *Adam's Breed* (1924) before achieving a *succès de scandale* with *Well of Loneliness* (1926), a sympathetic study of Lesbian characters.

Hallam, Arthur Henry (1811–1833). A friend of Tennyson. *In Memoriam* was inspired by his early death. His father, **Henry Hallam** (1777–1859), presented careful, accurate and well documented accounts of medieval and English constitutional history from a Whig viewpoint. He also wrote a history of European literature (4 volumes, 1837–39).

Hallé, Sir Charles (1819–1895). German-born conductor, pianist and teacher who settled in Manchester in 1848 and founded (1857) the Hallé Orchestra. He was the first principal of the Royal Manchester College of Music. He was knighted in 1888.

Haller, Albrecht (1708–1777). German physiologist, a wide-ranging biological and medical scientist of great distinction. He studied medicine under Boerhaave at Leiden, received his M.D. in 1727, and in 1736 became Professor of Anatomy, Botany and Medicine at the newly-founded University of Göttingen. In 1744 he returned to his native Bern, where he spent the rest of his life in research and writing. His major work lay in physiology. He studied the operation of muscle fibres, and defined as irritability their action of contracting when under external stimulus (mechanical, thermal, chemical, or electrical). He recognized that the nerves as such played no part in this process. By contrast sensibility was a property of tissues imbued with nerves. His studies of irritability and sensibility helped bring a major reorientation of human physiology in the latter part of the eighteenth century, away from the notion that the body was essentially mechanical in its operation, emphasizing instead that the key to bodily function lay in the nervous system.

Haller also pursued researches on the circulation of the blood and the automatic actions of the heart. Having become addicted to opium (taken to relieve pain from gout and constant stomach disorders), Haller recorded his own observations upon its actions. He was an all-round man. Pious in religion, he wrote large quantities of verse, and was a pioneer bibliographer.

D'Irsay, S., *Albrecht Haller*. 1930

Halley, Edmond (1656–1742). English astronomer. He went at the age of 20 to St Helena to make the first map of the stars of the southern hemisphere, and from there he observed (1677) the transit of Mercury across the sun. By collecting observations of 24 bright comets between 1337 and 1658 he predicted the appearance of the great comet of 1758 ('Halley's Comet') on the grounds that it was the same comet as those of 1531, 1606 and 1682. He similarly predicted its later appearances. His observations on comets were collected in his *Astronomiae Cometicae Synopsis* (1705) which put forward theories of their motion based on the work of * Newton. Halley discovered the 'proper motions' of the so-called fixed stars. He also compiled charts of magnetic deviation, published the earliest wind map (1688) and was the first to use a barometer to reckon heights. Halley was professor of geometry at Oxford (1700–03) and succeeded (1721) Flamsteed to become the second astronomer royal.

Ronan, C. A., *Edmund Halley: Genius in Eclipse*. 1970

Hals, Frans (1581/5–1666). Dutch painter, of Flemish extraction, living in Haarlem. His first important painting was the life-size group portrait *The Banquet of the Officers of the St George Militia Company*, which is outstanding and unprecedented in its strong characterization. His group portraits culminated in *The Regents* and *The Regentesses of the Old Men's Alms House* (1664). In Dutch portrait-painting, they assure him a position next to Rembrandt. Hals also painted genre scenes with dramatic chiaroscuro, and vigorous single portraits of which *The Laughing Cavalier* (1624) is the best-known.

Trivas, N. S., *The Paintings of Frans Hals*. 1941

Halsey, William Frederick (1882–1959). American sailor. He served with destroyers in World War I and by 1938, as rear admiral, commanded a carrier division. During World War II he proved himself one of the great fighting admirals in command of the aircraft battle force (1940–42), and then as commander-in-chief of the South Pacific area when he conducted the great sweep northwards in support of the army's island-hopping offensive by which the Japanese conquests were regained.

Hamilton, Alexander (1757?–1804). American statesman. Born in the West Indies, the illegitimate son of a Scottish merchant, he showed such precocity that he was sent to New York for further study. During the War of American Independence he was *aide* and confidential secretary to Washington (1779–81) and later commanded in the field. His marriage (1780) to Elizabeth Schuyler assured him of a favourable social background. After the war he established a successful law practice in New York and attended (1787) the constitutional convention at Philadelphia. Though he would have preferred a more centralized and oligarchic form of government, he defended what emerged (as the best obtainable) in a brilliant series of articles in which he co-operated with James Madison in the *Federalist*. His appointment by Washington (1789) as his first secretary of the Treasury made him one of the most important of the personages moulding the new state. He consolidated the state debts into a funded national debt, he advocated excise and tariffs as the principal source of revenue and created the first National Bank, opposition to these measures resting on the fact that they placed financial power in federal rather than state hands. Hamilton returned to his law practice in 1795 but remained an important figure behind the scenes in the councils of the Federalist party. This involved him in a bitter quarrel with his rival Aaron * Burr; a duel resulted in which Hamilton was mortally wounded.

Hamilton, Sir William, 9th Bart (1788–1856). Scottish philosopher. Educated at Glasgow and Balliol College, Oxford, he gained a reputation for vast erudition; he was professor of history at Edinburgh from 1821 to 1836, when he acquired the more suitable chair of logic and metaphysics. His main interest was to show that human knowledge is relative and is attained only in relation to known properties. J. S. Mill wrote an extensive examination of his philosophy.

Hamilton, Sir William Rowan (1805–65). Irish mathematician and astronomer, born in Dublin. The son of a solicitor and a child prodigy, he was self-educated. He could speak 13 languages at the age of 12, made notable mathematical discoveries by 17, was made professor of mathematics at Trinity College, Dublin, at 22 and received a knighthood at 30. In 1824 he discovered various peculiarities of conical refraction and in 1843 invented the calculus of 'quaternions', a three-dimensional algebra or geometry, which led ultimately to the basis for quantum mechanics. He drank himself to death.

Hammarskjöld, Dag Hjalmar Agne Carl (1905–1961). Swedish administrator and (from 1953) secretary general of the United Nations. He was the son of a Conservative prime minister of Sweden and had served his country in general administrative posts before succeeding Trygve Lie at the U.N. He did much to extend the executive powers of the secretariat, especially by his organization and utilization of U.N. forces in the Congo (1961). While flying to Ndola in Northern Rhodesia on a truce-making mission he was killed in an air crash. He was posthumously awarded the Nobel Peace Prize.
Lash, J. P., *Dag Hammarskjöld*. 1962

Hammer, Armand (1898–). American businessman. The son of a physician, he was named for the emblems of the Socialist Labor Party. He became a doctor himself and in 1920 established personal links with Lenin, leading to trade (wheat for furs, caviar and asbestos). He became a major producer of coal, sulphur and—after 1956—oil and gas (Occidental Petroleum). Hammer was a great art collector and a generous donor.

Hammerstein, Oscar II (1895–1960). American song-writer, author of the libretti of many immensely successful musicals. He enjoyed a particularly good working partnership with the composer Richard * Rodgers. His best-known musicals are probably *Rose Marie* (1924), *The Desert Song* (1926), *Oklahoma!* (1943), *Carmen Jones* (1943), *South Pacific* (1949), *The King and I* (1951) and *The Sound of Music* (1959).

Hammett, Dashiell (1894–1961). American author. As a young man he worked for the Pinkerton Detective Agency in New York, and gained the experience which helped him become the first U.S. writer of 'private eye' crime fiction. His best-known works are *The Maltese Falcon* (1930) and *The Thin Man* (1934).

Hammurabi (18th cent. B.C.). Babylonian king, credited with the formulation of one of the first known legal codes; a tablet inscribed with it is in the Louvre.

Hampden, John (1594–1643). English parliamentary leader. He was born and lived in Buckinghamshire. He entered parliament in 1621; he was imprisoned (1627) for refusing to pay a forced loan; he played a prominent part in drawing up the Petition of Right (1628), aimed at curbing Charles I's illegal practices; and in 1636 he refused to pay 'ship money', a levy previously confined to ports. In 1637 he was prosecuted before the Court of Exchequer; the prosecution made Hampden a champion of liberties and the most popular man in England. When parliament again met (1640) he was active in the impeachment of Strafford and was one of the five members whom Charles tried to arrest in 1643. When war broke out he joined the parliamentary army, fought bravely at Edgehill but died as the result of a wound received in the skirmish of Chalgrove Field.
Adair, J., *A Life of John Hampden, The Patriot*. 1976

Hamsun, Knut (Pederson) (1859–1952). Norwegian novelist and dramatist, born at Lom in northern Norway of poor farming stock. In the 1880s he spent two periods in the United States, where he worked as a dairy-farmer, coal-miner, shop-assistant, fisherman and Chicago tram-conductor. Back in Norway he was a school teacher. Deeply influenced by Nietzsche and Strindberg, he became passionately concerned with the individual's role *against* his environment (in distinction to Ibsen who, in Hamsun's view, wrote merely of men struggling *within* a partly alien society). His novel *Hunger* (1890), largely autobiographical, later became an outstanding film. Other works were *Pan* (1894), *Victoria* (1898), *Look Back on Happiness* (1912), *The Growth of the Soil* (1917) and *The Women at the Pump* (1920). He won the Nobel Prize for Literature in 1920. His profound hatred of modern capitalism made him a sympathiser with the Nazis: he collaborated with German occupation forces (1940) and met Hitler. After the war treason charges were dropped on account of his age but he was fined Kr. 500,000 and his reputation suffered for a generation.

Hancock, Winfield Scott (1824–1886). American soldier. He fought in the Mexican War (1846–48) but his fame rests on his success in the Civil War and especially at Gettysburg (1863) where in command of the 2nd Corps he chose the position that stood firm against all General Lee's attacks. He ran unsuccessfully as Democratic candidate for the presidency against Garfield (1880).

Hand, Learned (1872–1961). US jurist. Educated at Harvard, he was a Federal district court judge (1909–24) and a Federal circuit court appeals judge (1924–51), establishing a lasting reputation for the breadth and humanity of his judgments.

Handel, George Frederick (1685–1759). English composer. Born in Halle, Saxony, he was the son of a barber-surgeon. He was a child protegy and from the age of eight was playing the organ, violin and klavier and composing. His teacher, F. W. Zachau, was the organist of Halle Cathedral. After studying law at Halle University (1702), Handel worked as a violinist and conductor at the Hamburg opera (1703–06) where his first two operas *Almira* and *Nero* (both 1705) were performed. In 1707 Handel went to Italy where he wrote much music and earned international fame but failed to gain a permanent appointment. In 1710 he was appointed *Kapellmeister* to the Elector of Hanover, who succeeded to the English throne as George I (1719). Handel went to London for the production of his opera *Rinaldo* (1711), and after a brief return to Hanover to resign his appointment, took up permanent residence in England (1712). He was pensioned by Queen Anne for his *Birthday Ode* (1713) and received the patronage of the Earl of Burlington and the Duke of Chandos (1712–15; 1718–20). He composed 40 operas in England of which the best known are *Giulio Cesare* (1724), *Rodelinda* (1725), *Alcina* (1735), *Berenice* (1737), *Serse* (*Xerxes*; 1738). In 1719 Handel's patrons founded the Royal Academy of Music as a joint stock company for the promotion of Italian opera and Handel was made director of the project. He also managed the King's Theatre (1728–34).

After 1735 Handel devoted himself to the composition of oratorio and produced a series of spacious, vigorous dramatic works including *Alexander's Feast* (1736), *Saul* (1738), *Israel in Egypt* (1738), *Messiah* (1742), *Samson* (1744), *Relshazzar* (1745), *Judas Maccabaeus* (1745) and *Jeptha* (1751). His instrumental works include the suites *Water Music* (1717) and *Music for the Royal Fireworks* (1749); 16 concertos for organ and orchestra (1738–40); 18 *Concerto grossi* for orchestra (1734–39); 16 harpsichord suites; and solo works for a variety of instruments.

Handel's health began to fail in 1745 and in 1751 he became partially blind, losing his sight completely by 1753. After his death he left £20,000 to charity; he was buried in Westminster Abbey. He was an internationally famous cosmopolitan whose religious works were essentially designed for the theatre and concert hall. Beethoven considered him the greatest of all composers, and he is still regarded as one of the outstanding musical figures of the eighteenth century.

Lang, P. H., *George Frederick Handel*. 1966

Hannibal (247–152 B.C.). Cathaginian soldier, the son of Hamilcar Barca. From 221 he commanded in Spain and by 219 had won the whole of southern Spain as far as the Ebro, with the exception of Roman-supported Saguntum. Its fall (218), by removing the threat to his rear, enabled him to launch the Second Punic War. From Spain he skirted the Pyrenees (with a force that included elephants), reached the Rhône, defeated the Gallic tribes which barred his way, and after almost insuperable difficulties crossed the Alps. At the first great battle on the River Trebbia, he scattered the Roman army and, marching on towards Rome, defeated Flaminius at Lake Trasimene (217). Skilful delaying tactics by * Fabius gave the Romans time to recover but in 216 Hannibal crushed another Roman army under less cautious generals at Cannae. Though not strong enough to take Rome,

Hannibal maintained himself in southern Italy and although through the years his army dwindled and he could not get reinforcements he still managed, by his masterly skill, to win several pitched battles. At last in 207 his brother Hasdrubal marched from Spain in a daring effort to relieve him but before junction could be made was defeated and killed at the Battle of Metaurus river. In 203 Hannibal was finally recalled to Carthage to meet a Roman invasion and in 202 his first defeat was inflicted on him by * Scipio at Zama, and the war was ended. Hannibal became the head of the Carthaginian government but political opposition to his reforms and Roman pressure drove him (196) into exile at the courts of kings in Asia Minor hostile to Rome. When he saw that demands for his surrender could no longer be resisted, he took poison.
Toynbee, A. J., *Hannibal's Legacy*. 1965

Han Suyin (1917–). Chinese novelist writing in English, born Elisabeth Chow in Peking. She trained as a doctor in Peking, in Brussels and in London, and practised in Hong Kong. The colony was the setting for her best-known novel *A Many Splendoured Thing* (1952).

Harcourt, Sir William George Granville Venables Vernon (1827–1904). British Liberal politician. In the same year that he was appointed professor of international law at Cambridge he entered parliament (1868); he was chancellor of the exchequer (1886 and 1892–95). Death duties in their present form were his creation and it is for this that he is mainly remembered. He succeeded Lord Rosebery as leader of the Liberal party (1896) but proved an unpopular choice and resigned (1898).

Hardenburg, Karl August von, Prince (1750–1822). Prussian politician. He was minister of foreign affairs from 1804 to 1806, and briefly in 1807 until Napoleon who had conquered the country in the previous year demanded his dismissal. Re-appointed chancellor (1810) he secured some remarkable reforms, including the emancipation of the Jews and the abolition of serfdom. He was created a prince in 1814 and in the negotiations that followed Napoleon's downfall he achieved the aggrandizement of his country, especially in the Rhineland. He stayed in office until his death but became increasingly bureaucratic in old age.

Hardicanute *see* **Harold I**

Hardie, (James) Keir (1856–1915). First British Labour M.P. Born in Lanarkshire, he worked as errand boy and in a mine before taking to journalism (1882–1887). He became secretary of the newly formed Scottish Miners Federation (1886). He was elected (1892) to parliament for West Ham, as the first and then only Labour member; he lost the 1895 election but after one or two more failures, caused partly by his opposition to the Boer War, he was elected consistently by Merthyr Tydfil. Meanwhile the Independent Labour Party had been formed with Keir Hardie as chairman (1893–1900). From 1901 to 1911 he was the first and most revered leader of the parliamentary party, devoting most of his energies to the cause of the unemployed. A lifelong pacifist, he was dissillusioned by the failure of international socialism to stop World War I.
Morgan, K. O., *Keir Hardie*. 1975

Harding, John, 1st Baron Harding of Petherton (1896–). British soldier. He began his army career as a subaltern in World War I, and rose to Chief of Staff, Allied Army in Italy, 1944. In 1955–57 he was governor-general of Cyprus; he was responsible for reorganizing military and civil resources to combat terrorism, introduced martial law and banished Archbishop * Makarios. He was made a baron in 1958.

Harding, Warren Gamaliel (1865–1923). Twenty-ninth president of the US (1921–23). He was editor and owner of a small newspaper in his native Ohio when he entered politics, first as state senator and from 1915 as a Republican senator in the US Congress. He opposed ratification of the Versailles Treaty; and it was those Republicans who favoured an ineffective president who secured his nomination for the presidency. In office he proved an easy prey for corrupt and selfish advisers and his administration was a scandal.
Murray, R., *The Harding Era: Warren G. Harding and His Administration*. 1969

Hardwicke, Sir Cedric Webster (1893–1964). English actor. He first came to prominence with the Birmingham Repertory Company, where he played in Shaw and in *The Barratts of Wimpole Street* (1934). He was knighted in 1934.

Hardwicke, C., and Brough, J., *A Victorian in Orbit*. 1962

Hardy, Thomas (1840–1928). English novelist and poet. He was born in Dorset, and the West Country as 'Wessex' was the background of his novels and of his whole life. He was articled to an architect and did some work as a restorer of churches before turning to literature. He married (1874) Emma Louisa Gifford; they lived at Max Gate, near Dorchester, built to his own design. His first novel, *Desperate Remedies* (1871), could be described as a 'thriller' and though he became more and more interested in character he never disdained a strong plot or a melodramatic situation. Of the novels that immediately followed the best known are *Under the Greenwood Tree* (1872), *Far from the Madding Crowd* (1874), *The Return of the Native* (1878), *The Mayor of Casterbridge* (1886), and *The Woodlanders* (1886–87). Hardy was by then widely read and esteemed, but *Tess of the D'Urbervilles* (1891), one of the greatest novels in English, was bitterly assailed by conventional moralists for condoning the immoralities of its tragic heroine. This attitude and similar attacks on *Jude the Obscure* (1895) so disturbed Hardy that after the publication of *The Well Beloved* (1897) he wrote no more novels, but found a new reputation as a poet with the publication of *Wessex Poems* (1898) and *Poems Past and Present* (1901). He considered the highest pinnacle of his literary achievement was *The Dynasts* (1904–08), a colossal epic-drama, written in blank verse, of the Napoleonic wars. It embodies, with a classical fatalism, his view of man as a weak creature struggling against the inexorable forces of nature and the gods, but its inflated style alienated many readers.

Hardy continued to write, mainly poetry, into old age. In 1913 his wife died, and he married Florence Dugdale in 1914. In 1910 he was awarded the O.M.

Gittings, R., *The Young Thomas Hardy*. 1975. *The Older Thomas Hardy*. 1978

Hardy, Sir Thomas Masterman, 1st Bart. (1769–1839). English sailor. He served under Nelson as flag-captain of the *Victory* (1803–05) and at Trafalgar. It was to him that Nelson, as he died, addressed the (disputed) words 'Kiss me, Hardy'. He became first sea lord (1830) and a vice-admiral (1837).

Hare, Robertson (1891–1979). English actor. He became famous playing farce at the Aldwych Theatre in the 1920s. He specialized in the meek, hen-pecked 'little man' character whose function was to be generally humiliated by the rest of the cast. He continued to work in television comedy until shortly before his death.

Hargreaves, James (died 1778). English inventor, born near Accrington, Lancashire. He was working in the calico mills of Robert Peel (the statesman's grandfather) when, between 1764 and 1767, he invented a 'spinning jenny' capable of spinning eight threads at once. He had to move to Nottingham (1768) when fellow workers broke into his house and destroyed the frame; later he became a partner in a small cotton mill. Delay in patenting (1770) prevented him gaining a great fortune, but he died comfortably circumstanced.

Harington, Sir John (1561–1612). English poet and inventor. A godson of Queen Elizabeth, his wit gave him privileges at court although he was sent to the country for a time for fear that his verses might corrupt the ladies-in-waiting. This gave him time to write a complete translation of Ariosto's *Orlando Furioso* (1591) but he had returned by 1596, when he published anonymously *Metamorphosis of Ajax*, in which he playfully advocated the earliest design for a type of flush water-closet, apparently of his own invention. He was knighted by his friend, the 2nd Earl of* Essex during his ill-fated Irish compaign.

Rich, T., *Harington and Ariosto*. 1940

Harley, Robert, 1st Earl of Oxford and Mortimer (1661–1724). English politician. Of no strong political convictions he was elected as a Whig (1689) and was Speaker of the House of Commons (1701–05). He intrigued with the Tories, shifted his allegiance to that party and became head of a Tory government in 1710. An attempt by a French spy to assassinate him made him suddenly popular; he received an earldom from Queen Anne, was made a K.G. and the last lord high treasurer. His government ended the War of Spanish Succession by the Treaty of Utrecht (1713). When George I succeeded (1714) Harley was impeached, imprisoned in the Tower, but eventually acquitted by the peers. He spent the rest of his life outside politics and cultivated literary acquaintances. He founded the Harleian Collection of books and MSS. in the British Museum.

Harmsworth. A journalistic and publishing dynasty, initiated by **Alfred Harmsworth,** who became Lord * Northcliffe, and his brother **Harold** (1st Lord * Rothermere) when together they started (1888) the weekly periodical *Answers*. Harmsworth also published a number of Sunday magazine papers and in 1896 revolutionised English newspapers with the American-style *Daily Mail*. In 1903 the brothers pioneered the first newspaper for women, the *Daily Mirror*. Among their dynastic successors is Northcliffe's nephew, **Cecil King** (1901–), who in the 1950s and 1960s came to hold an increasingly powerful position in the newspaper and periodical fields, and then fell from office.

Harold I (known as Harefoot) (died 1040) and **Hardicanute** (or Harthacnut) (died 1042). Kings of England 1035–40 and 1040–42 respectively. They were half-brothers, and succeeded in turn their father Cnut. On Hardicanute's death the Saxon royal line was restored with Edward the Confessor.

Harold II (*c*. 1022–1066). King of England (1066). The last of the Saxon rulers, he succeeded (1053) his father, Godwine, as Earl of Wessex and was virtual ruler under Edward the Confessor, on whose death (1066) he took the crown. Some three years previously, forced to land in Normandy, Harold had given his oath of loyalty (which he retracted once back in England) to William of Normandy, who on Edward the Confessor's death at once set sail to invade England. Harold found himself faced with enemies in both north and south and met the twofold threat with almost incredible energy. He crushed his rebel brother Tostig, who was aided by Hardrada of Norway, at Stamford Bridge, Yorkshire, on 25 September and hurried south to fight William of Normandy at Senlac, near Hastings on 14 October. Here despite gallant resistance he was defeated and died, shot by an arrow.

Compton, P., *Harold the King*. 1961

Harriman, (William) Averell (1891–). American diplomat and Democratic politician. He worked with Franklin Roosevelt on his New Deal and in World War II came to Britain as Lend-Lease administrator (1942–43). Subsequently, as ambassador to the U.S.S.R. (1943–46) and to Britain (1946), and in several other official and unofficial roles, he played an important part in the diplomatic history of the war and post-war years. He was governor of New York State (1955–58), but failed to secure nomination as Democratic presidential candidate in 1952 and 1956. His published works include *Peace with Russia?* (1960) and *Special Envoy* (1975).

Harrington, James (1611–1677). English political theorist. He attended Charles I personally, by order of parliament, both before and at his execution. After the King's death he retired to write *Oceana*, a political romance in which, recognizing that political power is dependent on economic circumstances, he propounded a more equal distribution of land, leading to government by a senate debating and proposing, the people deciding the legislation, and a magistracy (chosen on a principle of rotation by popular suffrage by the ballot) executing the laws. His theories influenced the doctrines of both the American and French Revolutions.

Russel-Smith, H. F., *Harrington and the 'Oceana'*. 1971

Harris, Sir Arthur Travers (1892–1984). British airman, marshal of the R.A.F. Known as 'Bomber Harris', he was commander-in-chief of Bomber Command (1942–45) in charge of the bombing raids on Germany during World War II.

Harris, Joel Chandler (1848–1908). American author. After a varied career he achieved fame with his *Uncle Remus* (written 1880–83), the immortal folk-stories in Negro dialect, of Brer Fox, Brer Rabbit etc.

Cousins, P. M., *Joel Chandler Harris: A Biography*. 1968

Harrison, Benjamin (1833–1901). Twenty-third president of the U.S. The grandson of W. H. * Harrison, he made the law his profession, and was an officer in the Civil War. After serving as U.S. senator (1881–87) he succeeded, as a compromise Republican candidate, in defeating Grover Cleveland in the 1888 presidential election. He was a capable administrator but his high tariff legislation

caused distress and he had none of the gifts that command popularity; his attempt to secure a second term met overwhelming defeat. The Sherman Anti-trust Law and the Silver Purchase Acts were passed during his term of office.
Wallace, L., *Benjamin Harrison*. 1888

Harrison, Rex Carey (1908–). British actor. He first appeared on the stage at the Liverpool Repertory Theatre (1924). He has performed in Britain and the U.S.A. and appeared in many films including *My Fair Lady, Blithe Spirit* and *Doctor Doolittle*.

Harrison, William Henry (1773–1841). Ninth president of the U.S. Son of a Virginia planter who was one of the signatories of the Declaration of Independence, he became a soldier and, as governor of the newly formed territory of Indiana (1800–12), he won a renowned victory over the Indian chieftain Tecumseh at Tippecanoe River (1811); he was a general in the war of 1812 against the British. It was probably more his reputation as a hero than his skill as a Whig politician that won his election to the presidency (1840). He died within a month of his inauguration.

Harte, Francis Bret (1836–1902). American author. Born in Albany, New York, he went to California as a youth and won fame by his stories, e.g. *The Luck of Roaring Camp* (1868) and *The Outcasts of Poker Flat* (1870). From 1885 he lived in London.

Hartley, David (1705–1757). English physician and pioneer psychologist. Born into the family of a poor Yorkshire clergyman, Hartley attended Jesus College, Cambridge, receiving his B.A. in 1726 and his M.A. in 1729. Though a religious man, Hartley had scruples about signing the 39 Articles, and so took up a career in medicine. He practised in London and later in Bath. His major book was the two volume *Observations on Man, his Frame, His Duty, and his Expectations* (1749). In this he attempted to prove that there is no knowledge innate in the mind, nor any innate moral disposition. All our knowledge and ideas are built up by patterns of associations formed in the mind from the data which come in from our senses. Such patterns of associations are themselves determined by our disposition to pursue pleasure and shun pain. Such a sensationalist psychology and associationist epistemology was not in itself totally original: much is to be found in * Locke. Hartley's originality lay in giving these a physiological basis. He saw the associations literally as vibrations and pathways of particles in the brain. Hartley was thus the first materialist psychologist in England. He believed his cause-and-effect psychology was compatible with Newtonianism, and also with his Christianity (man's psychology became part of predestination). It was enormously influential in the development during the next century of a more scientific psychological theory.
Halévy, E., *The growth of Philosophic Radicalism*. 1952

Hartmann, Karl Robert Eduard von (1842–1906). German philosopher, known for his synthesis of Hegel and Schopenhauer. His reputation for pessimism arises from a mistaken interpretation of his belief that the amount of pleasure in the world is exceeded by the amount of pain. His chief work *Philosophy of the Unconscious* (1869) was translated into English (1884).

Hartnell, Sir Norman (1901–1979). English couturier. He founded his own business in 1923 and was dressmaker to the Queen by 1940. He designed the wedding and coronation dresses of Queen Elizabeth II. He was created a K.C.V.O. in 1977.

Harty, Sir (Herbert) Hamilton (1880–1941). Conductor and composer born at Hillsborough, County Down. He was conductor of the Hallé Orchestra 1920–33, and was known for his arrangements of baroque music for modern orchestra.

Harun al-Rashid (763–809). The most famous of the Abbasid caliphs of Baghdad (from 786). His fame as a ruler induced even the distant Charlemagne to send gifts, and word of his generous patronage attracted to his magnificent court artists and scholars from many lands. An underlying cruelty was shown when, from jealously or fear of conspiracy, he ordered (803) the extermination of the Barmecides, a family which for fifty years and more had dominated the administration. Legend, as recorded in the *Arabian Nights* and elsewhere, relates how he walked in disguise through the city to seek adventure and learn the grievances of his subjects.
Philby, H. St. J. B., *Harun al-Rashid*. 1933

Harvard, John (1607–1638). English clergyman. In 1637 he went as a preacher to Charlestown, Mass., where he died of consumption. He bequeathed £779 and the basis of a library to the proposed college which took his name.

Harvey, William (1578–1657). English physician. Famous for his discovery of the circulation of the blood, after graduating at Cambridge (1597), he studied under the great anatomist Fabricius in Padua. Elected F.R.C.P. (1607), he became physician to St Bartholomew's Hospital (1609), to King James I (1618) and to Charles I (1640). His strong royalist sympathies led him to attend Charles I through the Civil War. He retired from professional life after the triumph of the parliamentary forces and occupied himself entirely with research. As early as 1628 he had published *An Anatomical Exercise on the Motion of the Heart and the Blood in Animals* in which he wrote that 'the blood performs a kind of circular motion' through the bodies of men and animals. Until then physicians knew of the existence of arteries and veins but did not understand that the function of the latter was to enable the blood to return to the heart; they regarded the inexplicable arterial movement as being in the nature of an irrigation of the body. Harvey demonstrated (after actually viewing it in animals) that the heart is a muscle, that it functions as a pump and that it effects the movement of the blood through the body via the lungs by means of the arteries, the blood then returning to the heart through the veins. He pointed out the difference between venous and arterial blood. Harvey's notable *Essays on Generation of Animals* (1651) comprise his researches in embryology. The doctrine that every living thing has its origin in an egg was affirmed by him.
Keynes, G., *The Life of William Harvey*. 1966

Harwood, Sir Henry (1880–1950). British sailor. In World War II he commanded the British cruisers *Exeter, Ajax* and *Achilles* at the Battle of the River Plate (December 1939) in which the German battleship *Graf Spee* was damaged and forced to take refuge in Montevideo. When she emerged she was scuttled to avoid destruction by the waiting British ships. Harwood was admiral in command of the British Mediterranean Fleet (1942–45).

Hasluck, Sir Paul Meernaa Caedwalla (1905–). Australian Liberal politician. An academic, diplomat and war historian, he was a Federal MP 1949–69, a minister from 1951, Foreign Minister 1964–69 and Governor General of Australia 1969–74.

Hastings, Warren (1732–1818). British Indian administrator. He became governor (1772) and then first governor general (1774) of Bengal (i.e. of nearly all British India). He reformed the whole system of administration, set up a board of revenue and established regular law courts for which he had old Hindu law books specially translated; he abolished private trading by the servants of the Company, and moreover successfully held the Mahrattas at bay. Unfortunately three of the four members of his Governor General's Council opposed and hampered his every action, one of them, Sir Philip * Francis, with the malignancy of personal enmity. When Hastings retired (1785) Francis instigated Fox, Sheridan and others to impeach him for oppression, maladministration and corruption. From 1788 the case dragged on over six years during which his every doubtful action or misdemeanour was exaggerated into a major crime. Hastings was acquitted on all charges, and though his whole fortune had gone he could live quietly on a pension provided by the Company. Though perhaps the ablest of the great administrators of British India he was almost the least rewarded, becoming Privy Counsellor in 1814.

Hathaway, Anne (1556–1623). Wife of William * Shakespeare, whom she married in 1582; she bore him a daughter, Susanna, and the twins Judith and Hamnet (or Hamlet). In his will Shakespeare left her the furniture and his 'second-best bed'.

Hatta, Mohammed (1902–1980). Indonesian politician. Trained as an economist in Europe and imprisoned by the Dutch (1935–42), he worked for the Japanese during World War II and during the * Soekarno era was prime minister (1948–50) and vice-president (1950–56).

Hatton, Sir Christopher (1540–1591). English lawyer and courtier. He was a great favourite of Queen Elizabeth, who knighted him and gave him large estates in Dorset including the historic Corfe Castle. He was often her spokesman in parliament and was active in the prosecution of Anthony

* Babington and Mary Queen of Scots. He became lord chancellor (1587).
Brooks, E. St J., *Sir Christopher Hatton*. 1946

Hauptmann, Gerhardt (1862–1946). German dramatist and novelist. He was born in Silesia and had been an art student before going to Berlin (1885) and turning to literature. His early plays, social dramas influenced by Ibsen, roused opposition by their 'naturalism', a technique which he applies, as in *Die Weber* (1892), to comparatively recent events (e.g. the revolt of the Silesian weavers in 1844) and even to remoter history, e.g. in *Florian Geyer* (1896) on the Peasant's War. A transition to fantasy is marked by *Hanneles Himmelfahrt* (*Hannele's Journey to Heaven*; 1893), in which a child's vision and sordid realism are successfully blended, and the popular *Die Versunkene Glocke* (*The Sunken Bell*; 1896). His later plays range through many styles from the realistic to the mystical and classical. Of his novels the best known are the psychological *The Fool in Christ: Emanuel Quint* (1910), and the classical *Atlantis* (1912). The verse epic *Till Eulenspiegel* (1928) symbolically portrayed Germany after World War I. Hauptmann won the Nobel Prize for Literature (1912).
Knight, K. G., and Norman, F. (eds), *Hauptmann Centenary Lectures*. 1964

Haushofer, Karl (1869–1946). German soldier and political theorist. After serving in the Bavarian army (1887–1918) and becoming a general, he was appointed (1921) professor of political geography at Munich University. On the basis of Mackinder's theory of Eurasian 'heartland', he built up a spurious science of geopolitics to justify a special role for Germany.

Haussmann, Georges Eugène, Baron (1809–1891). French administrator. Under Napoleon III, he tore down much of old Paris, created many boulevardes, parks and a new sewerage system.

Haüy, René-Just (1743–1822). French scientist, born at St Just-en-Chaussée, Oise. He entered the priesthood. Teaching in Paris, he became interested in mineralogy and crystallography. In 1802 he became Professor of Mineralogy at the Museum of Natural History, moving to a chair at the Sorbonne in 1809. His two major works are the *Treatise of Mineralogy* (1801), and the *Treatise of Crystallography* (1822). Haüy's importance lay in effectively redefining the questions to be posed in the study of crystals. The regular forms of crystals had drawn throughout the seventeenth and eighteenth centuries a plethora of causal explanations, in terms of shaping forces – some chemical, some physical, some atomistic – but none satisfactory. Haüy's approach was not to explain the causes of the regularly varied forms of crystals, but to try to classify those forms in terms of geometry – and above all, he hoped, through the geometry of simple relationships between integers. He envisaged crystals as structured assemblages of secondary bodies (integrant molecules: a concept deriving from Buffon) which grouped themselves according to regular geometric laws. He proposed six types of primary forms: parallelpiped, rhombic dodecahedron, hexagonal dipyramid, right hexagonal prism, octahedron and tetrahedron, and spent much of his career elaborating on this typology of forms.

His approach won strong supporters, but also met many detractors, who believed that physical questions were being neglected in this purely structural, geometrical approach.
Burke, J. G., *Origins of the science of crystals*. 1966

Havelock, Sir Henry (1795–1857). British soldier, hero of the Indian Mutiny. He went to India in 1823 and fought with distinction in Burma, Afghanistan, Gwalior and the Punjab. In the Indian mutiny (1857) he was sent to the relief of Cawnpore and Lucknow. Having reached Cawnpore only to find that on news of his coming all the European women and children had been killed, he fought his way through to Lucknow and so enabled the city to hold out until it was finally relieved by Sir Colin Campbell. Havelock died of dysentery within a month.

Hawke, Edward Hawke, 1st Baron (1705–1781). English sailor. After much distinguished service he became a full admiral in 1855 when he superseded * Byng in the Mediterranean. After two years he was back in the English Channel. His victory at Quiberon Bay (1759) was one of the greatest in British naval history. Hawke had been lying outside Brest watching the French fleet designed to cover an invasion of England, but in November a gale forced the British to withdraw and so allowed the French, under

Admiral de Couflans, to escape. Anticipating rightly that the aim was to join a sister fleet at Rochefort, Hawke intercepted the enemy fleet at Quiberon Bay and despite the gale and a menacing ice shore forced action and destroyed it. He was the first lord of the Admiralty (1766–71).
MacKay, R. F., *Admiral Hawke*. 1965

Hawke, Robert James Lee (1929–). Australian Labor politician, born in South Australia. Educated at Perth, he became a Rhodes Scholar at Oxford, returning to become an industrial advocate for the Australian Council of Trade Unions (ACTU). As president of the ACTU 1970–80, he was highly visible and gained immense popularity in resolving industrial disputes, and was also president of the Australian Labor Party 1973–78. He entered the Australian Parliament in 1980, took the Labor leadership from W. G. * Hayden in a bloodless coup in February 1983 and a month later defeated Malcolm * Fraser massively to become prime minister.
D'Alpuget, B., *Robert J. Hawke*. 1982

Hawking, Stephen William (1942–). British theoretical physicist and mathematician. Educated at Oxford, he worked at Cambridge from 1968, becoming a professor of mathematics in 1977 and Lucasian professor (a chair which Newton had held) in 1979. His work helped to confirm the 'big bang' theory of creation but his best known research is on the nature of 'black holes' and their relationship with the laws of thermodynamics. Hawking was grossly handicapped with multiple sclerosis which prevented him from moving or writing without assistance.

Hawkins, Sir John (1532–1595). English sailor. He was the first Englishman to traffic in African slaves, a venture which ended (1573) when his fleet was destroyed by storms on his third voyage across the Atlantic. As treasurer of the navy (from 1573) he did much to equip the fleet and turn it into an efficient fighting force; for his services against the Spanish Armada (1588) he was knighted. He harassed the Spanish West India trade for many years and died off Puerto Rico while commanding an expedition to the Spanish Main with his cousin, Sir Francis Drake.
Williamson, J. A., *Hawkins of Plymouth*. 2nd ed. 1969

Hawthorne, Nathaniel (1804–1864). American novelist. He was born of a Puritan family at Salem, Massachusetts. He developed a taste for solitude and as a young man lived for twelve years the life of a recluse in a single room at Salem, where he wrote the stories collected in two series as *Twice-Told Tales* (1837, 1842) Marriage (1842) to Sara Peabody, as a preliminary to which he had taken a position in the Boston Customs House, restored him to normal life. The couple lived in Concord with Emerson and Thoreau among their neighbours. He returned to Salem as surveyor of customs but was dismissed and took up writing again. The result was his masterpiece, the novel *The Scarlet Letter* (1850), which against a Puritan New England background paints a tragic picture of the cumulative effects of prejudice, guilt and sin. Among other works of this productive period were *The House of the Seven Gables* (1851), the satirical *The Blitheswood Romance* (1852), and the famous children's book *Tanglewood Tales* (1852). In 1853 he went to England as U.S. consul in Liverpool. His last work of importance, inspired by an Italian visit, was *The Marble Fawn* (1860).
Crowley, J. D. (ed.), *Hawthorne: The Critical Heritage*. 1970

Hay, Ian (Major General John Hay Beith) (1876–1952). Scottish playwright and novelist. He wrote light novels such as *Pip* (1907) and *A Knight on Wheels* (1914), and then came books based on his military service in World War I: *The First Hundred Thousand* (1915) and *Carrying On* (1917).

Hay, John Milton (1838–1905). American diplomat and author. At the request of John G. Nicolay, private secretary (1861–65) to President Lincoln, Hay was appointed his assistant, and the two friends wrote the enormous *Abraham Lincoln* (10 volumes, 1886–90). In later life Hay was U.S. ambassador to Great Britain (1897–98) and secretary of state (1898–1905). He enunciated the 'Open Door' policy in China and negotiated the Hay-Paunce-fote Treaty (1901) with Britain which enabled the U.S.A. to build the Panama Canal.

Hayden, William George (1933–). Australian Labor politician. After ten years as a Queensland policeman, he was a member of the Australian Parliament 1961–

, Minister for Social Welfare 1972–75 and Treasurer (1975) under E. G. * Whitlam. Leader of the Labor Party 1977–83, he was displaced by R. J. L. * Hawke but served as Hawke's Foreign Minister 1983–
Murphy, J. D., *Hayden*. 1980

Haydn, (Franz) Joseph (1732–1809). Austrian composer. Born at Rohrau, he was the second of 12 children. He studied at the St Stephan's Cathedral choir school, Vienna (1740–49) until his voice broke. In the next eight years he taught himself the fundamentals of composition (studying the works of C. P. E. * Bach), working as a valet to the Italian composer Niccolo Porpora (who instructed him in writing for the voice), and coaching pupils in the klavier and singing. In 1760 he became assistant *Kapellmeister* to Prince Esterházy at Eisenstadt and *Kapellmeister* at the castle at Esterháza (1766), remaining there until 1790. By 1790 he had written more than 70 symphonies, 50 piano sonatas, 125 works for baryton, 60 string quartets, nearly 20 operas and much church music. Gradually he acquired a European reputation and his status rose with the Esterházys. From 1781 he was the friend and mentor of * Mozart, who learnt much about symphonic form from Haydn. In December 1790 he left for England at the invitation of the London impresario J. P. Salomon and stayed there for three years. He wrote 12 symphonies for Salomon (Nos. 93–104) and six string quartets. Haydn was immensely popular in England and received an honorary Mus.D. from Oxford (1791). In 1792 he taught Beethoven for a short time, although without mutual benefit.

Haydn's two greatest oratorios, *The Creation* (1798) and *The Seasons* (1801) (texts by Baron Gottfried van Swieten) were written when he was close to 70, as were the six great masses (1796–1802) composed in his last period in Esterházy service. The dramatic Mass in D minor 'The Nelson' (1798) is arguably his greatest single work. Haydn virtually established the form of the modern symphony and string quartet, and his concertos have never left the repertoire.
Robbins Landon, H. C., *Haydn*. 1981

Hayek, Friedrich August von (1899–). Austrian–British economist, born in Vienna. He taught in Austria, Britain (where he was naturalised in 1938) and the U.S., became a strong opponent of * Keynes and the welfare state, and wrote *The Road to Serfdom* (1944). A passionate advocate of the free market, he won the 1974 Nobel Prize for Economics, became a major influence on Margaret * Thatcher and received a C.H. in 1983.

Hayes, Rutherford Birchard (1822–1893). Nineteenth president of the U.S. Born at Delaware, Ohio, he practised law at Cincinnati and rose to be a major-general in the Civil War. He was a member of the U.S. House of Representatives (1864–67), and became governor of Ohio (1867–71 and 1875–77). He was elected Republican president (1876) only after a disputed decision. He finally achieved acceptance by withdrawing the army from the southern states and so removing the pressures that had precluded a Democratic vote. This act did much to heal the wounds of the Civil War.
Davison, K. E., *The Presidency of Rutherford B. Hayes*. 1972

Hazlitt, William (1778–1830). English essayist and critic, born in Maidstone, the son of a Unitarian minister. He was employed on the *Morning Chronicle* and *Examiner* in London in 1812, and contributed to the *Edinburgh Review* 1814–30. Collections of his essays were published in *Round Table, Table Talk* and *Plain Speaker*. He wrote a series of contemporary portraits in *Spirit of the Age* (1825) and a life of Napoleon (1828–30).

Healey, Denis Winston (1917–). British Labour politician. Educated at Oxford, he was a major in the Commandos during World War II, became MP 1952– , serving as minister of defence (1964–70), and chancellor of the exchequer (1974–79). He contested the leadership of the Labour party in 1976 and 1980, but was deputy leader under * Callaghan and * Foot (1976–83).

Hearst, William Randolph (1863–1951). American newspaper proprietor, born in San Francisco. The son of a millionaire mine owner, he took charge of his father's paper, the San Francisco *Examiner*, in 1887, bought the New York *Journal* in 1895, and by 1925 owned 25 newspapers in 17 cities. His introduction of the 'the yellow press', characterized by banner headlines, sensationalism and lavish illustration, revolutionized journalism. A Congressman 1903–07, he ran as a

Democratic candidate for Governor of New York State in 1906. After supporting F. D. * Roosevelt in 1932 he became an extreme isolationist and Anglophobe. Orson * Welles's film *Citizen Kane* (1940) was largely based on his life (with some elements from the *Chicago Tribune*'s R. R. McCormick).

Heath, Edward Richard George (1916–). British Conservative leader. He first entered parliament in 1950, was appointed minister of labour (1959) and lord privy seal (1960). When, following his electoral defeat (1964), Sir Alec Douglas-* Home resigned, Heath, the first to be elected under a new procedure, was chosen to succeed him as leader of the party and the Opposition (1965). He was prime Minister (1970–74) and vigorously pursued entry to the European Community. In an effort to restore the economy and contain industrial strife he called an election in February 1974, was defeated and was replaced as leader by Margaret * Thatcher. He is a gifted organist, conductor and yachtsman. He won the Sydney–Hobart yacht race in 1970.
Laing, M., *Edward Heath: Prime Minister*. 1972

Heaviside, Oliver (1850–1925). English physicist. Though he had little formal education he made important contributions to the knowledge of how radio waves are propagated. He put forward the theory that an ionized layer in the atmosphere, about 50 miles above the earth's surface, is responsible for the reflection of medium-wave radio signals, and this layer is now named after him. He found difficulty in communicating his findings to others, was often engaged in academic controversies and for the latter part of his life lived as a recluse in Devonshire. He was elected F.R.S. in 1891 and in 1896 was awarded a Civil List pension.

Hébert, Jacques René (1757–1794). French revolutionary. A journalist, he was one of the most extreme members of the political faction, the Cordeliers. He was one of the prominent founders of the atheistic cult of Reason. His popularity with the Paris Commune earned him * Robespierre's animosity and after planning an abortive insurrection he was arrested and executed (1794).

Hedayat, Sadeq (1903–1951). Iranian novelist and playwright, considered the most important of the twentieth century. In his youth he was greatly influenced by nineteenth-century writers – Maupassant, Edgar Allan Poe, Chekhov and Dostoyevsky – and by Franz Kafka. All these he had discovered during a period in France and Belgium, but in 1930 he returned to Iran and became interested in the Iranian folk tradition. Most of his work is melancholy and deeply pessimistic; most human effort seemed to him absurd. He committed suicide in Paris. His best-known works are probably *Buried Alive* (1930), *Neyrangestan* (1932) and *The Blind Owl* (1937).
Kamshad, H., *Modern Persian Prose Literature*. 1966

Hedin, Sven Anders von (1865–1952). Swedish explorer and geographer. In 1885 he began a series of expeditions to Central Asia and mapped areas formerly unrecorded. In 1908 he made the first detailed map of Tibet.
Hedin, S. A. von, *My Life as Explorer*. 1925

Hegel, Georg Wilhelm Friedrich (1770–1831). German philosopher. Born in Stuttgart, he studied theology at Tübingen and in his early life was a critic of accepted Christian thought. He then turned to philosophy and, after working at Jena and elsewhere and achieving a growing reputation by his writings, was appointed (1818) to succeed to the chair formerly occupied by J. G. * Fichte as professor of philosophy at the University of Berlin. His views and those of his followers (known as Hegelianism) greatly influenced subsequent philosophy, sometimes indirectly, sometimes by reaction. Marxism, according to Marx, is Hegelianism turned right side up, and existentialism owes something to Hegel's thought. There were also outgrowths of Hegelian idealism in British and American philosophy. Essentially, Hegelianism makes the claim that spirit, sometimes conceived as the human spirit, more often as something transcendental and all-encompassing, is the true reality, and all else is dependent upon it. Spirit passes through various stages of development consisting of the attainment of a synthesis, when an antithesis is brought into antagonism with a thesis; this triadic process Hegel described as dialectical. Human history displays this development, as does philosophy itself. Hegel regarded his own philosophy as the furthest point to which philosophy had yet advanced. The chief

works published during his lifetime were *The Phenomenology of Mind* (1807), *The Science of Logic* (1812–16), *Encyclopedia of Philosophical Sciences* (1817) and *The Philosophy of Right* (1821); much more of his writing was published posthumously. It has been criticized or disdained by many philosophers for its extravagant claims to be setting out a train of necessary truths.
Taylor, C., *Hegel*. 1975

Heidegger, Martin (1889–1976). German philosopher, considered a leading exponent of existentialism despite his objection to being called an existentialist. He learnt much from * Husserl, whose phenomenological methods he used for his study of human existence; his best known book *Sein und Zeit* (*Being and Time*) (1962) is an approach to the examination of a wider and more difficult concept, that of Being. His support for Nazism cut him off from Husserl, but his influence can be seen in the work of * Sartre.
Blackham, H. J., *Six Existentialist Thinkers*. 1952

Heifetz, Jascha (1901–). Russian–American violinist, born in Vilna. A child prodigy, he performed the Mendelssohn Violin Concerto at the age of 5, made his St Petersburg debut in 1911 and left Russia in 1917. Regarded as the most brilliant virtuoso performer since Paganini, Heifetz was in great demand as a concert and recording artist, where his deadly accuracy in bowing and fingering and the extraordinary breathing quality of his tone produced a style of playing which was immediately recognizable. Heifetz devoted himself to teaching in Los Angeles and directing a chamber music group from the 1960s.

Heine, Heinrich (1797–1856). German poet, born in Düsseldorf to the poor branch of a rich Jewish family. He grew up under the French occupation and became an admirer of Napoleon. An uncle set him up in his own business (Harry Heine & Co.) in Hamburg which soon failed. He then studied law in Bonn, literature in Göttingen (under Schlegel) and philosophy in Berlin (under Hegel and Wolf). Several love affairs disturbed him, Goethe snubbed him, and to avoid the civil disabilities aimed at Jews he unhappily accepted Christian baptism in 1825, the year he took out his doctorate in law. He published *Reisebilder* ('Pictures of Travel', 1826) in which he proclaimed his revolutionary sympathies, and *Buch der Lieder* ('Book of Songs', 1827) which established him as Germany's greatest lyric poet after (or perhaps even ahead of) Goethe. From 1831 his political opinions obliged him to live in Paris where he became an ardent disciple of * Saint-Simon. He worked as a journalist, secretly accepted a pension from the French government (secured by his admirer * Thiers), had several more unhappy love affairs and became friendly with the brilliant French Romantics including Hugo, George Sand, Chopin, de Musset and Berlioz. In 1841 he married Mathilde Eugenie Mirat, a shallow-minded Parisian *grisette* with whom he had lived since 1835. Heine was torn by many conflicts and he was the *Doppelganger* of his own poem: the baptised Jew, the expatriate German, the unhappy lover, the unconvinced radical, the bittersweet poet. The pure classical form of his poetry combines exquisitive sensitivity and pessimism, marred at times by bitter cynicism, malicious satire and sentimentality. He has been called the 'poetic psychologist of love' and his later works, including *Romancero* (1851) and *Last Songs and Thoughts* (1853; 1854), were dubbed 'the swan song of romanticism'. From 1848 he was bed-ridden with spinal paralysis and suffered acute pain until his death. As a young man he called himself a 'soldier in the war of the liberation of mankind' but later he wrote, 'When I was young I loved truth, justice and liberty, and now that I am older I love truth, justice, liberty and crabmeat'. Heine wrote in both French and German and strove to make both nations aware of their mutual artistic and intellectual achievements. In his penetrating political essays he predicted the rise of Nazism; his works were suppressed in Germany (1933–45) and the Nazis insisted that his most famous poem, *The Lorelei*, was anonymous. Many of Heine's lyrics were set to music by Schubert, Schumann, Brahms and Hugo Wolf.
Kaufmann, H. (ed.), *Heinrich Heine: Werke und Briefe*. 10 vols. 1961–64

Heinemann, Gustav (1899–1976). German statesman. A founder member of the Christian Democratic Party, he was President of the Federal Republic of Germany 1969–74.

Heinkel, Ernst Heinrich (1888–1958). German aircraft engineer. He was chief designer for the Albatros Aircraft Company in Berlin before World War I. In 1922 he founded Ernst Heinkel Flugzeugwerke where he built a number of aircraft which were successful in World War II, the He III and He 162, and the first rocket-powered aircraft.

Heinz, Henry John (1844–1919). American food manufacturer of German descent, born in Pittsburgh. He sold produce from the family garden as a child and in 1876 he and his cousin founded F. and J. Heinz, which became H. J. Heinz Co. in 1888. He applied himself particularly to high standards of hygiene and quality.
Potter, S., *The Magic Number 57*. 1959

Heisenberg, Werner Karl (1901–1976). German physicist. A pupil of Arnold Sommerfeld, he was professor of physics at Leipzig university (1927–42), then directed the Max Planck Institutes at Berlin (1942–45), Göttingen (1946–58) and Munich (1958–70). He gained rapid recognition for his work on the general quantum theory in atomic physics, investigation of atomic structure and of the * Zeeman effect. He won the 1932 Nobel Prize for physics for his development of quantum mechanics based on the principle of 'indeterminacy', sometimes called the 'uncertainty principle', i.e. that the position and momentum of any body (or particle) cannot be simultaneously determined: the more precise the determination of one, the less precise is the other. Thus it is safer to refer to statistical probabilities than to formulate general laws. His 'uncertainty principle' is increasingly applied, by analogy, to philosophy and biology. During World War II he was in charge of German research on atomic weapons.

Helena, St (*c.* 250–330). Mother of the Roman emperor * Constantine. She apparently became a Christian early but was not baptized until after the defeat of Maxentius in 312. Tradition has it that on a pilgrimage to Jerusalem she there discovered the site of the Holy Sepulchre and the True Cross.

Helmholtz, Hermann von (1821–1894). German physiologist. In 1849 he was appointed to the chair of Physiology at Königsberg, from whence he moved to Bonn, to Heidelberg and finally to Berlin in 1871. In 1887 he became Director of the new Physico-Technical Institute at Berlin Charlottenberg. His early researches on animal heat, and on the body system as a balance of inputs and outputs led him to his fundamental memoir of 1847 'On the Conservation of Force', where he set out the mathematical principles of the conservation of energy. In the 1850s he pursued physiological researches on the eye, making early use of the ophthalmoscope. He moved on to studies of the relationships between the ear, the nervous system and the psychology of hearing.

Helmholtz wished to free science from old-fashioned religious and metaphysical constraints. He saw scientific investigation and mechanical and mathematical explanations as the essential source of truth about all phenomena, physical and psychological. He believed in the unity of nature, and devoted himself to searching out those great forces which operated throughout it, above all, energy.
Koenigsberger, L., *Hermann von Helmholtz*. 1902

Helmont, Johannes Baptista van (1579–1644). Flemish physician and chemist. He travelled widely and continued his medical studies, deeply dissatisfied with the academic orthodoxies he found. Frequently during the 1620s and 1630s he found himself summoned before ecclesiastical authorities for his heterodox medical and philosophical opinions. In his medical approach he was attracted towards an emphasis upon chemical cures (iatrochemistry) – though he treated the mysticism and alchemical leanings of much post-Paracelsan chemical medicine with scepticism. He performed accurate chemical analysis on materia medica, stressing the need for testing by fire for purity, and scrupulous attention to exact weights. He was well aware of acid as a digestive agent in the stomach. Of central importance to him were aeriform substances – 'gas' – for he saw living substances composed of spiritous matter and body, which could by chemical processes be separated. He also reserved a special role for water as the original principle of all things (a view partly taken from the account of Creation in the Book of Genesis). He undertook to demonstrate – by an experiment with a willow tree – that plants take all their nourishment out of water and not out of the soil. Helmont is a figure of great importance because he marks the emergence of scientific chemical medicine out of its various alchemical and magical predecessors.
Debus, A. G., *The English Paracelsans*. 1965

Héloïse (*c.* 1098–1164). Abbess of Paraclete, Nogent-sur-Seine, famous as the mistress and wife of the scholar Peter * Abelard. Her uncle Fulbert appointed Abelard her tutor; they fell in love and fled to Brittany where Héloïse bore a son; she was later married to Abelard. Fulbert, in revenge, arranged that Abelard should be attacked and castrated. Héloïse entered the convent of Argenteuil and was later given Abelard's own foundation of the Community of the Paraclete.

Helpmann, Sir Robert (Murray) (1909–). Australian dancer, choreographer and actor. He made his debut in Australia in 1923, toured with Anna Pavlova's company and went to England to join the then Vic-Wells ballet in 1933. He became their leading male dancer in 1934 and danced with Sadler's Wells until 1950. His dancing and choreography were always strongly dramatic, and he was also involved in theatrical production. In 1965 he became artistic co-director of the Australian Ballet. He was knighted in 1968. He was particularly well-known for his performances in *Checkmate* (1937), *The Rake's Progress* and *Hamlet* (1942).

Helvétius, Claude Adrien (1715–1771). French philosopher. Born in Paris, he was trained in finance, became chamberlain to the queen's household (1749) but was forced to resign public office when his book *De l'Esprit* (1758) was published. His materialism involved the claim that all thought is derived from sensations, and he argued that self-interest is the motive of all human action. Men, he thought, are originally equal in mental endowment and are made unequal by the influence of environment. His work influenced * Bentham's utilitarianism.

Hemans, Felicia Dorothea (née Browne). (1793–1835). English poetess. Her work was very popular in its time, and that she should be best remembered by *Casabianca* ('The boy stood on the burning deck . . . ') does less than justice to her merits.

Hemingway, Ernest (Miller) (1899–1961). American writer, born in Illinois. During World War I he served as a volunteer in an American ambulance unit and with the Italian army. Between the wars he was prominent among literary expatriates in Paris; he took an active part on the government side in the Spanish Civil War. These and other experiences provide backgrounds for his novels, e.g. *The Sun Also Rises* (1926), *Men Without Women* (1927), *A Farewell to Arms* (1929), *For Whom the Bell Tolls* (1940). Hemingway was awarded a Pulitzer Prize for *The Old Man of the Sea* (1952) and the Nobel Prize for Literature (1954). Both his novels and his numerous short stories are written in the harsh unsentimental style of his period.

Baker, C., *Ernest Hemingway*. 1972

Henderson, Alexander (1583–1646). Scottish ecclesiastic. Early in his career he began to oppose English control of the church in Scotland and in 1638 he was elected moderator of the General Assembly of the Covenanters, which established Scottish Presbyterianism despite the declared opposition of Charles I. He is reckoned as second only to John * Knox in the history of the Church of Scotland.

Henderson, Arthur (1863–1935). British politician, born in Glasgow. As an iron moulder in Newcastle he was active from his early youth in the trade union movement. He played an important part in building up the Labour Party whose chairman he became (1914–17; 1931–32). During World War I he served in the coalition government. In Ramsay MacDonald's two Labour governments (1924 and 1929–31) he was home secretary and foreign secretary respectively. In the latter capacity he worked vigorously for international disarmament and was awarded the Nobel Peace Prize (1934).

Hamilton, M. A., *Arthur Henderson*. 1938

Hengest (died *c.* 488) and **Horsa** (died *c.* 455). Warriors from Jutland, forerunners of the Anglo-Saxon invasion of Britain. According to the chroniclers they were invited by a British king, Vortigern, to help against the Picts, landed at Ebbsfleet (*c.* 449) and were given the Isle of Thanet as a home. They are said to have turned against their hosts; though Horsa was soon killed, Hengest, who according to another legend married Vortigern's daughter Rowena, is said to have conquered Kent.

Henlein, Konrad (1898–1945). German politician. He led the Sudeten German Youth Movement from 1923 and, when Hitler seized the Sudetenland from Czechoslovakia in 1938, he became Gauleiter (1938–39) and commissioner for Bohemia (1939–45). He committed suicide after capture by the Americans.

Henley, William Ernest (1849–1903). English poet. He was crippled by tuberculosis as a young man and spent many months in hospital where he produced his *A Book of Verses* (1888). He collaborated with his great friend R. L. * Stevenson in writing *Deacon Brodie* and other plays. As editor and critic in London he won the fear and respect of younger authors by his trenchant reviews. In his poems he often uses a declamatory style with great effect, e.g. (from *Invictus*):

It matters not how strait the gate,
How charged with punishments the scroll,
I am the master of my fate:
I am the captain of my soul.

Connell, J., *Henley*. 1949

Henrietta Maria (1609–1669). Queen-consort of Charles I of England. Daughter of Henry IV of France, she married Charles in 1625 and became very unpopular by maintaining a French and Roman Catholic entourage at court. Though she was a devoted wife and mother, she encouraged Charles's absolutist tendencies and incurred further odium by going to France (1642) to raise money for armed resistance to parliament. She finally left England (1644) returning only for short visits after the Restoration.

Oman, C., *Henrietta Maria*. 1936

Henry I (known as 'the Fowler') (876–936). German king (from 919). A man of strong character, he built a strong army and fortified his eastern frontier. He regained Lorraine and in the east extended the German influence over the Slavs beyond the Elbe, enforced the submission (929) of Wenceslas, Duke of Bohemia, and defeated the Magyars in battle (933) at Riade. Attacks from the Danes in the north were also repulsed.

Henry I (1068–1135). King of England (from 1100). Fourth and youngest son of William the Conqueror, he secured election to the English crown while his elder brother Robert was returning from a crusade. He defeated Robert, who retained possession of Normandy, at Tinchebrai (1106) and held him captive for the rest of his life. He gained the support of the Saxons by a charter restoring the laws of Edward the Confessor, and by a politic marriage to Matilda, daughter of Malcolm III of Scotland. The archbishop of Canterbury, * Anselm, was recalled, and a compromise agreed on the investiture dispute (1106). Henry created an efficient administrative machine, controlled the barons and ruled with severity but in accordance with the laws: his appellation 'the lion of justice' was well earned. His only legitimate son was drowned in the *White Ship* (1120). His daughter * Matilda thus became his natural heir. Henry was posthumously called 'Beauclerc' or the Scholar, as a tribute to his learning, which was considerable for a king at his time.

Henry II (1133–1189). King of England (from 1154). Son of Matilda (daughter of Henry I) and Geoffrey Plantagenet, he inherited Normandy through his mother and Anjou through his father; his marriage (1152) to Eleanor of Aquitaine added Poitou and Guienne to his dominions. He curbed the baronial power, confirming the laws of Henry I, raised a militia and organized juries, itinerant judges, assizes, and a central court of justice. His attempt to limit the church's independence and especially the power of the church courts by the Constitutions of Clarendon (1164) led to his quarrel with his old friend and chancellor * Becket, whom he had appointed archbishop of Canterbury, and ended in the latter's murder. In 1174 the king did penance at Becket's tomb but managed to avoid major concessions. He warred with Louis VII of France, invaded Wales and crushed the power of the Norman nobles in Ireland (1171–72). He obtained the overlordship of Scotland by the Treaty of Falaise (1174). Henry was a man of extraordinary ability and energy but with his own family he failed. His many liaisons – the partly legendary story of Fair Rosamond (Rosamond Clifford) is well known – antagonized his high-spirited wife and she in turn influenced his sons against him; he died while endeavouring to suppress a rebellion led by Richard and John, aided by King Philip II of France.

Henry II (1519–1559). King of France (from 1547). He was the son and successor of Francis I, whose policy of strengthening the power of the monarchy he continued. He persecuted his Protestant subjects, the Huguenots, on both religious and political grounds since he feared their disruptive influence. In alliance with

Scotland he carried on a war against England notable mainly for the capture of Calais (1558), which had been in English hands for 210 years. He also continued the struggle against the emperor Charles V and won the frontier bishoprics of Metz, Toul and Verdun. He married (1533) * Catherine de' Medici; their three sons became kings of France.

Henry III (1207–1272). King of England (from 1216). He succeeded his father King John, and declared himself of age in 1227. Five years later he deprived the regent, Hubert de Burgh, of all offices and took over the administration himself. His favouritism towards the relatives of his wife, Eleanor of Provence (married 1236), financial chaos caused by his acceptance from the papacy of the crown of Sicily for his son, and his inefficiency antagonized the barons and the people alike. Under Simon de Montfort, the nobles compelled him to assent to the 'Provisions of Oxford' (1258) which transferred power to a commission of barons. His subsequent repudiation of this (with support from Louis IX of France) resulted in the Barons' War, the defeat and capture of Henry at Lewes (1264) and his enforced acceptance of humiliating terms of surrender. De Montfort then summoned the first 'parliament' (January 1265). The military skill of his son Edward I and a split among the barons turned the scale: de Montfort was defeated and killed at Evesham (1265) and Henry spent the rest of his reign in peace. Westminster Abbey, a large part of which was built in his reign, is a monument to his artistic taste.

Henry III (1551–1589). The last Valois king of France (from 1574). The third son of Henry II and Catherine de' Medici, he succeeded his brother, Charles IX. As Duke of Anjou he had been a candidate for the hand of England's Queen Elizabeth, was credited with the victory of Jarnac and other successes in the religious wars and helped to organize the massacre of St Bartholomew (1572). Elected king of Poland in 1573, he resigned on his accession to the French throne. As king he tried to hold a balance between the extreme Roman Catholic faction under the Duke of Guise and the Protestants under Henry of Navarre, his natural heir. Fearful above all of an attempt by Guise to usurp the crown, he organized his murder (1588) and that of his brother, the cardinal of Lorraine, in the château of Blois. He himself was assassinated a year later. Surrounded by his pampered favourites ('*les mignons*'), Henry was a despised and sometime ludicrous figure but he had a certain astuteness that enabled him to retain some semblance of royal authority in faction-ridden France.

Henry IV (1050–1106). German king and Holy Roman Emperor (from 1056). When he came of age (1065) he spent some years in recovering the royal domains in Saxony. He then tried to assert his position in Italy, which led to a quarrel with Pope * Gregory VII whom he declared deposed. The pope excommunicated Henry in reply and forced him to make humble submission at Canossa (1077). Meanwhile in Germany Rudolf of Swabia had been set up as a rival king and in 1080 won papal support. Once more the emperor declared the pope deposed, once more he in turn was excommunicated; Rudolf having died in battle, Henry invaded Italy (1081), entered Rome (1083) and was crowned emperor by the anti-pope Clement III. In his absence Germany was again in arms with rival kings in the field and as soon as Henry had restored some sort of order more rebellions occurred, this time aided by the treachery of his sons. In the last years of his life Henry lost his power in both Germany and Italy and died a broken man. He had the vision to see what was needed and to pursue it, but he lacked the power to persuade or conciliate, and the diplomatic skill to divide his enemies.

Henry IV (1367–1413). The first Lancastrian king of England (from 1399). Known as Bolingbroke from his birthplace, he was the son of John of Gaunt and Blanche of Lancaster. He distinguished himself abroad as a soldier and returned to play an important part in the reign of his cousin Richard II. At first he sided with the king's baronial enemies but became reconciled with Richard and was created Duke of Hereford (1397); but in the following year Richard, whose rule was now unchallenged, found an excuse to banish his former rival and when John of Gaunt died seized the Lancaster estates. Henry's reaction was to land in Yorkshire and head the forces of discontent. Richard on his return from Ireland found himself confronted with overwhelming strength: he surrendered and was imprisoned in Pontefract Castle from which he never reappeared. The vacant throne was

seized by Henry but his usurpation was not uncontested. He had to overcome the Welsh under Owen Glendower (1399), the Scottish under Douglas (1402), and Hotspur, with the adherents of the Percy family, at Shrewsbury (1403) before he could feel himself secure. In order to win support Henry had to make concessions to his parliaments and council and to the church, introducing a law for the burning of heretics and the persecution of the Lollards. Illness in later life made him secretive and suspicious, but he was also devout, and the patron of Chaucer, Gower and other poets.
Kirby, J. L., *Henry IV of England*. 1970

Henry IV (known as Henry of Navarre) (1553–1610). The first Bourbon king of France (from 1589). He inherited the sovereignty of Navarre from his mother, Jeanne d'Albret. He was a Protestant, and in 1572 some 4,000 Huguenots who had gathered in Paris to celebrate his marriage with Marguerite de Valois, sister of King Charles IX, were killed in the massacre of St Bartholomew. Henry escaped by renouncing his faith but was virtually a prisoner until 1576, when he assumed the Protestant leadership. In 1588 he was in alliance with * Henry III of France against the Catholic League; Henry III was assassinated, but a four-year struggle, which included his great victory at Ivry (1590), followed before Henry IV could make his throne secure. Even then it was only by accepting the Catholic faith – 'Paris is worth a mass', he is supposed to have remarked – that he could gain entry (1594) to his capital. Having made peace with Spain (1596), and by the Edict of Nantes (1598) guaranteed religious freedom for the Protestants, he set himself to restore the country after thirty years of civil war. With the help of his great minister * Sully he reorganized finances, repaired and extended roads and canals, developed agriculture and manufactures (e.g. the silk industry), while at the same time centralizing the machinery of government and strengthening the monarchy. His first marriage having been dissolved, he married (1600) Marie de' Medici who became the mother of his successor Louis XIII. Of his mistresses (the number of whom won him the nickname *Le Vert Galant*), the best remembered is Gabrielle d'Estrées (died 1599). Henry was assassinated by a fanatic named Ravaillac, probably of the extreme Catholic faction.

Henry V (1082–1125). German king and Holy Roman Emperor (from 1106). He continued Henry IV's struggle with the papacy on the question of investiture until a compromise was reached at the Concordat of Worms (1122). He married Matilda, the daughter of Henry I of England.

Henry V (1387–1422). King of England (from 1413). He was born at Monmouth, the eldest son of Henry IV. He distinguished himself as a soldier at the Battle of Shrewsbury (1403) and during his father's last years of illness proved his ability as an administrator; it is thus probable that the stories of his wild youth were much exaggerated. As king he aimed to restore the Percys and others to favour, but rallied his countrymen behind him by renewing Edward III's claim to the French throne. He invaded France (1415), won the Battle of Agincourt against seemingly insuperable odds and in a few years so asserted his supremacy that in 1420 he was able to conclude the 'perpetual peace' of Troyes. By this he married Catherine of Valois, Charles VI's daughter, and was recognized as regent and 'heir of France'. His death at Vincennes two years later cut short the career of an outstandingly able, devout and successful soldier and administrator.
Earle, P., *The Life and Times of Henry V*. 1972

Henry VI (1165–1197). Holy Roman Emperor (from 1190). He was elected German king (1169) while his father, the Hohenstaufen emperor Frederick I (Barbarossa), was still alive. Immediately after his accession as emperor he went to Italy to secure the kingdom of Sicily, the heritage of his wife Constance. The Sicilians, however, chose Tancred of Lecce, and Henry had to return to Germany to face a rebellion by * Henry the Lion. By making skilful use of the bargaining power which the chance capture of England's Richard I, returning from the crusade, put in his hands, he obtained peace. Thus freed, he had little difficulty in mastering Sicily and was crowned at Palermo (1194). Able but ruthless, Henry left a sinister reputation behind him.

Henry VI (1421–1471). King of England (1422–61 and 1470–71). Born at Windsor, he succeeded his father Henry V in infancy, the administration being carried on by his uncles Humphrey, * Duke of Gloucester, and John, * Duke of Bedford, in England and France respectively. Henry grew

up to be gentle, scholarly and quite unsuitable to rule. In France, where by the Treaty of Troyes (* Henry V) he had been nominally king since the death (1422) of Charles VI, national resistance, fired by Joan of Arc, had steadily increased; none the less Henry's peace policy was felt to be a betrayal of his own father and the nation. This and his obvious incapacity, made further evident by his subservience to his wife Margaret of Anjou (married 1445), kindled the hopes of Richard, Duke of York, that he might successfully assert his hereditary claim to the throne – a better one than that of the Lancastrian line. Thus the Wars of the Roses began. Throughout the conflict, Henry, insane from 1453, was a puppet in the hands of others. His armies were defeated (1461) and he himself deposed by Edward IV (son of the dead Richard of York); he was restored briefly by * Warwick the King-maker (1470) but in 1471 after defeat at Barnet he was captured and imprisoned in the Tower of London, where he was murdered. Henry's most lasting achievements were his two foundations of Eton College (1440) and King's College, Cambridge (1441), in which he took great interest and pride. His only son, Edward, was killed at the Battle of Tewkesbury (1471).
Christie, M. E., *Henry VI*. 1922

Henry VII (1457–1509). First Tudor king of England (from 1485). His father, Edmund Tudor, was the son of Henry V's widow, Catherine of Valois; his mother, Margaret Beaufort, was descended from John of Gaunt. He was born at Pembroke Castle, but from 1471 lived abroad, as after the death of Henry VI and his son he was recognized as Lancastrian leader. In 1485 he landed at Milford Haven and won the Battle of Bosworth Field, Leicestershire, where Richard III was killed; Henry was recognized as king. To unite the rival houses of Lancaster and York he married Elizabeth, daughter of Edward IV, but still had to overcome two pretenders, Lambert * Simnel and Perkin * Warbeck. The main purpose of his reign, to restore law and order and build up a strong and efficient administrative system after the chaos of the Wars of the Roses, he successfully achieved. He weakened the nobles by enforcing laws against liveried retainers and inaugurating the Star Chamber, a special court intended to curb the overmighty subject. Through his notorious agents, Empson and Dudley, and many dubious expedients he collected fines and forfeits. In his way and by the strictest economy he gave the monarchy the added strength of a full treasury, an achievement helped by a cautious and peaceful policy abroad.
Chrimes, S. B., *Henry VII*. 1972

Henry VIII (1491–1547). King of England (from 1509). He was the son of Henry VII and heir to the throne after the death of his elder brother, Arthur. He fulfilled his father's dynastic purposes by marrying, within two months of his accession, Arthur's widow, * Catherine of Aragon. Henry, with Francis I of France, and the emperor Charles V (also king of Spain), was one of the three talented, ambitious rulers who came to power almost at the same time and between them controlled the destinies of Europe. Enabled by his father's parsimony to pursue an active policy, Henry aimed, with the help of his great minister * Wolsey, to maintian a balance between France and Spain. At the outset of his reign he invaded France and won the Battle of the Spurs, while his army of the north won the Battle of Flodden Field (1513) at which France's ally, James IV of Scotland, was defeated and killed. Francis I now tried to win Henry to his side but though he staged a spectacular meeting at the Field of the Cloth of Gold (1520) failed in his purpose. Henry, an orthodox Catholic, who had received from the pope the title of Defender of the Faith for a book on the Sacraments (1521), began to profess doubts about the legitimacy of his marriage to his brother's widow. Moreover, Catherine was older than he and plain, while of all the children she had borne him only one, Mary, had survived. He was determined to marry Anne Boleyn but Wolsey failed to get a papal annulment of the marriage and was disgraced (1530). In 1533, after * Cranmer, archbishop of Canterbury, had declared his former marriage invalid, Henry secretly married Anne; in 1534 his obedient parliament confirmed the invalidity of the marriage with Catherine, severed all links with the papacy and declared Henry supreme head of the church. This was the most important single event of his reign. A very few, e.g. Henry's old friend and chancellor, Sir Thomas * More, refused to accept this and were executed, but resistance was surprisingly small. Henry now set about making the change profitable by suppressing first the lesser then the greater monasteries and confiscating their property, some of which was used for educational purposes. This action, of which Thomas Cromwell was the instrument, provoked a rising in the north, the Pilgrimage of Grace (1537), which was crushed with great harshness.

In 1536 Anne (mother of Elizabeth I) was beheaded for adultery; Henry immediately married one of her ladies-in-waiting, Jane Seymour, who died giving birth to the future Edward VI (1537). Cromwell's intention in furthering the fourth marriage, with Anne of Cleves, was to gain alliance with the German Protestants, but when the lady failed to exhibit the charms of her portraits she was divorced and pensioned. Henry's next wife, Catherine Howard, shared Anne Boleyn's fate, and his last, Catherine Parr (married 1543), survived him. Despite the fact that he had at different times denied the legitimacy of his daughters, he prescribed in his will the order of succession, which was in fact carried out: Edward, Mary, Elizabeth.

Henry was a man of many parts, scholar, poet and musician, as well as a ruler of great strength and political skill. In his last years he became more and more tyrannical; his suspicions increased and the number of judicial murders – for example, that of the young Earl of * Surrey (1546) – mounted, but the memories of handsome talented, pleasure-loving 'Bluff King Hal' remained in the minds of the people and he retained his popularity to the end.

Scarisbrick, J. J., *Henry VIII*. 1968

Henry, Joseph (1797–1878). American physicist. The son of a labourer, he was largely self-educated, like his contemporary * Faraday. He became a watchmaker's apprentice, then taught mathematics in country schools. He discovered how to make more powerful electromagnets with improved insulation and by 1832 could lift a ton of iron. He anticipated * Morse's invention of the telegraph by using relays, and discovered the principle of induction (transferring a current or signal from one coil to another) independently of Faraday. His greatest achievement was the invention of the first practical electric motor (1831), but its widespread adoption depended on the development of a reliable power supply. Henry was professor of physics at Princeton 1832–46, first secretary of the Smithsonian Institution 1846–78 and virtual founder of the U.S. Weather Bureau.

Henry, O. (William Sydney Porter) (1862–1910). American short-story writer. His stories, written in an ironic, pungent, epigrammatic style, and usually ending with a sardonic unexpected twist, mainly relate some small but fateful incident in the lives of those, even the humblest, who together form New York. Among his books are *Cabbages and Kings* (1904). *The Four Million* (1906), *The Heart of the West* (1907), *The Voice of the City* (1908).

Williams, W. W., *O. Henry*. 1936

Henry, Patrick (1736–1799). American politician, born in Virginia. Though largely self-taught he quickly established himself as a successful lawyer. He was elected to the Virginia House of Burgesses (1765), and it was the eloquence and vigour of his speeches which inspired the agitation against the Stamp Act. He quickly became the leader in Virginian politics and summoned the Continental Congress. In the course of a speech urging military readiness he shouted the famous words 'give me liberty or give me death'. He took part in the events which led to the Declaration of Independence and was governor of Virginia (1776–79 and 1784–86), but a quarrel with Jefferson stultified his later activities. He fought bitterly against the constitution on the grounds that liberty had been betrayed, and delayed its ratification by Virginia for twenty-three days. He refused all invitations by Washington to serve in his administration.

Henry the Lion (1129–1195). Duke of Saxony and Bavaria. He was the head of the powerful Guelph family and played a dominant role in German history for many years, extending his power in the Baltic area and crusading against the Slavs beyong the Elbe. In later years he was in rebellion against the emperors * Frederick I and * Henry VI and suffered temporary banishment and loss of estates. His second wife, Matilda, was a daughter of England's Henry II.

Henry the Navigator (1394–1460). Son of King John I of Portugal and a grandson of John of Gaunt. An expedition to North Africa, which resulted in the fall of Ceuta (1415) and in which he played a distinguished part, fired his interest in exploration. Though

he made no voyages himself he planned, charted and sent out more than thirty expeditions to sail south along the Atlantic coast of Africa. His sailors went farther and farther south and at last reached Sierra Leone. Henry also sent explorers overland and they reached Senegal and the Sudan. He financed these expeditions in part by granting licences to merchants, who soon discovered the profits to be won from trade in slaves. He sent out settlers to the uninhabited islands of Madeira and the Azores and established trading posts on the African coast.
Major, R. H., *Life of Prince Henry of Portugal*. 1967

Henryson, Robert (*c.* 1425–*c.* 1508). Scottish poet, possibly a schoolmaster of Dunfermline. His works include the *Testament of Cresseid* and *Morall Fabels of Esope*, a metrical version of 13 fables.
Harvey Wood, H. (ed.), *Collected Poems and Fables of Robert Henryson*. 1958

Henty, George Alfred (1832–1902). English writer. A war correspondent during Garibaldi's 1866 campaign and at the siege of Paris (1870), he was, with some eighty books, e.g. *Under Drake's Flag, With Clive in India*, the principal purveyor of vicarious adventure to two generations of English schoolboys.

Hepburn, Katharine (1909–). American stage and film actress. Distinguished by a combination of elegance and eccentricity, she was born in Connecticut, educated at Bryn Mawr, and made her debut on the stage in 1928. Her first film was *A Bill of Divorcement* (1932); many of her best and most successful films were made with Spencer Tracy. She received Academy Awards for three films: *Morning Glory* (1933), *Guess Who's Coming to Dinner* (1967) and *The Lion in Winter* (1968).

Hepplewhite, George (d. 1786). English cabinet-maker and furniture designer. After his death his widow published a book of some 300 designs, called *The Cabinet-Maker and Upholsterer's Guide*. It is unknown whether the designs were Hepplewhite's own; they epitomized the taste of his time and have since been identified by his name.
Edwards, R., *Hepplewhite Furniture Designs*. 1948

Hepworth, Dame Barbara (1903–1975). English sculptress. Of international repute, the techniques of her abstract or semi-abstract work include pierced shapes and stringed figures and above all exhibit feeling for smooth form and texture. At the Venice *Biennale* (1950) a retrospective exhibition of her work was given. Her second husband was the artist Ben * Nicholson.

Heraclitus of Ephesus (fl. *c.* 500 B.C.). Greek natural philosopher. He wrote a book, *On Nature*, fragments of which survive as quotations and opinions in the writings of others, from which his views can be gauged. Heraclitus seems to have seen the world in terms of the tensions between pairs of opposites (an instance being a bow string, pulled in different directions). Plenty and hunger, sickness and health, life and death, hot and cold, are some of Heraclitus's pairs. Yet he also asserts that the two figures in each pair are essentially one, that they contain each other in a dialectical way. From this Heraclitus draws the conclusion that the universe is a Oneness, but continually in a state of flux. It is probable that Heraclitus was not so much arguing that, because everything changed, nothing could be known; but rather that, although everything changes, these changes are governed by some sort of order and natural law. It is possible that Heraclitus believed that the universe originated out of fire, and that it would at times be restored by cosmic conflagrations.
Kirk, G. S. and Raven, J. E., *The Pre-Socratic Philosophers*. 1957

Herbart, Johann Friedrich (1776–1841). German philosopher and educationist. A pupil of J. G. * Fichte, with whom he disagreed, he became professor of philosophy at Göttingen and Königsberg. He developed the philosophy of* Kant by stressing the existence of a world of real things behind the world of appearances, and he made an attempt to make psychology a mathematical science. In education, he stressed what are known as the 'Herbartian steps': preparation, presentation, comparison or association, generalization, application.
Dunkel, H. B., *Herbart and Herbartianism*. 1970

Herbert, Sir Alan Patrick (1890–1971). English writer and parliamentarian. A regular contributor to *Punch* from 1910, he wrote with equal facility light verse collected (e.g.) as *She Shanties*, or prose: e.g. *Holy Deadlock*. As a novelist he achieved a great success with *Water Gypsies* (1930), and proved equally accomplished as a librettist for musical comedy. He sat as independent M.P. for Oxford University (1935–50) and was responsible for the Matrimonial Causes Act (1938). His satirical novel *Holy Deadlock* (1934) helped to influence opinion. In later life he crusaded for obtaining royalties for authors on books loaned by public libraries. *Independent Member* (1950) is autobiographical.

Herbert, George (1593–1633). English metaphysical and religious poet. He was the younger brother of Lord * Herbert of Cherbury, and was already making his mark at court, when (1625) he turned against a worldly career and entered the priesthood. In 1630 he became vicar of Bemerton, Wiltshire, where he remained until he died of tuberculosis. His poems, almost all contained in *The Temple* (1633), constitute an emblematic survey, for the most part serene, of the interaction of the soul with God. Strikingly homely imagery sometimes contrasts with extravagant conceits and even puns. His chief prose work *A Priest to the Temple* (1652) was described by Izaak Walton as 'plain prudent useful rules for the country parson'.
Gardner, H. (ed.), *George Herbert Selected Works*. 1961; Leishman, J. B., *The Metaphysical Poets*. 1934

Herbert of Cherbury, Edward Herbert, 1st Baron (1583–1648). English soldier, diplomat and poet. After fighting in the Low Countries and spending some years in travel, he was ambassador to France (1619–24). A royalist at the outbreak of the Civil War, he came to terms with parliament and was left undisturbed. In *Of Truth* (1624) he propounded an anti-empirical theory of knowledge: his *Of the Religion of the Gentiles* (1663), in which he found satisfactory common factors in all religions, provided a basis for English 'Deism'. His *Autobiography* (to 1624), a notable picture of the man and his period, departs from accuracy when it conflicts with his conceit. His poetry, in Latin and English, belongs to the metaphysical school of * Donne.
Howarth, R. G., *Minor Poets of the Seventeenth Century*. 1931

Hereward the Wake (fl. 1070). English patriot. After plundering Peterborough with Danish help, he held out for many months against William the Conqueror in the marshes of the Isle of Ely and was defeated only with difficulty in 1071. Many legends grew up around his name.
Kingsley, C., *Hereward the Wake*. 1886

Hernández, José (1834–1886). Argentinian poet. His chief works, two poems on *Martin Fierro* (1872 and 1879), glorify the life of the *gauchos* (mounted herdsmen) of the pampas. The *gaucho* poetry of Argentina corresponds to the folk songs of other lands.

Herod. The name borne by several members of a dynasty which ruled in Judaea before and after the beginning of the Christian era. **Herod the Great** (*c.* 72–4 B.C.) was the second son of Antipater, appointed by Julius Caesar procurator of Judaea. Mark Anthony made Herod tetrarch of Judaea in 40, and in 31 Augustus granted him the title of king. The friendship of Rome enabled him to rule in peace and his taste for the magnificent in architecture caused him to rebuild Caesarea and restore Samaria: in 20 he began the reconstruction of the Great Temple at Jerusalem, but his fears and jealousies led to gross cruelties and wholesale butcheries. Every member of the rival Hasmonean dynasty was killed and several even of his own family; the 'Massacre of the Innocents' at Bethlehem, although not recorded by Josephus, would be in keeping with his character. Herod, who is said to have had ten wives, left his kingdom to be divided among three of his sons – Philip, Archelaus and Herod Antipas.

Herod Antipas (died *c.* A.D. 40) was tetrarch of Galilee and Peraea (4 B.C.–A.D. 39). John the Baptist was executed for protesting against his marriage with Herodias, the wife of his half-brother Philip. It was to this Herod that Pontius Pilate, in an effort to evade responsibility, sent Jesus for examination after discovering that he was a Galilean, but Herod refused to exercise jurisdiction. Herod travelled to Rome (38) to seek recognition as king, but failed through the intrigues of his nephew Herod Agrippa and was banished to Lugdunum (Lyons) where he died.

Herod Agrippa I (10 B.C.–A.D. 44), who succeeded his deposed uncle, had been brought up luxuriously in Rome. He suffered an eclipse under the emperor Tiberius but became a favourite of Caligula and later of Claudius. As a result he gradually acquired

(37–41) a larger territory than that of his grandfather Herod the Great and the coveted title of king. In the Acts of the Apostles it is related that he had the apostle St James put to death, that he imprisoned St Peter and that he died at Caesarea, being 'eaten by worms'. His devotion to Jewish observances and national interests won the affection of his subjects.

His son **Herod Agrippa II** (A.D. 27–100) was only 17 and was living in Rome when his father died. Claudius, therefore, took the opportunity of reconverting the kingdom into a Roman province. Herod held family prestige and possessions but no political authority; thus the Roman procurator Festus was present, according to the Acts, when St Paul made his defence at Caesarea.

Herodotus (*c.* 485–425 B.C.). Greek historian. His history of the Graeco-Persian wars is the first important history of ancient Greece and Asia Minor. He was born in Asia Minor, at Helicarnassus, but is said to have become unpopular for political reasons and forced into exile. His rational and scientific approach to writing history (as opposed to chronicles which attempt no explanation of events) was unique in the Greek world, and reflects the influences of Asian philosophy and Athenian experience on the growth of his mind.
Myres, J. L., *Herodotus: Father of History*. 1953

Hero of Alexandria (fl. 1st century). Greek mathematician, remembered mainly for his mechanical inventions. Some of the best known are described in his *Pneumatics*; they include a simple form of steam turbine, a fire-engine pump, a fountain in which the jet is sustained by air compressed by a column of water, and a water-organ. He wrote also on the principles of mechanics and their practical applications.

Herophilus (*c.* 4th century B.C.). Little is known of the life of Herophilus. He was a native of Chalcedon, in Asia Minor, and later taught and practised medicine at Alexandria. An expert in dissection, Herophilus laid the foundations of modern anatomy and physiology. He carried out important anatomical investigations of the brain, eye, genital organs and vascular system. He argued that it was the brain which was the centre of intelligence and control in the body. He recognized that it was through the nerves that the brain exercised its powers over the extremities of the body. In the brain he distinguished the cerebellum from the cerebrum, and understood the difference in function between sensory and motor nerves. He stressed the distinction between arteries and veins, and (contrary to common opinion) held that the arteries contain blood, not *pneuma* (spirit). His work on the heart stressed that the pulse was purely involuntary, and caused by the contraction and dilation of the arteries. As a clinician, Herophilus seems to have been particularly interested in gynaecology. He wrote a treatise on midwifery in which he offered accurate descriptions of the ovaries, the cervix and the uterus. He was probably also interested in menstruation, and its relation to general health.

Herrick, Robert (1591–1674). English poet. He was apprenticed to his father, a London goldsmith, studied at Cambridge, and on returning to London became friends with Ben Jonson and his literary set. Before 1627 he had taken holy orders and he was rector of Dean Priory, Devonshire (1629–47 and 1662–74), being dismissed during the Puritan supremacy. He was a prolific writer of exquisite love lyrics, *Hesperides* (1647) containing some 1,200 poems, many in the manner of* Horace, on the general theme of the transience of beauty:

> Gather ye rosebuds while ye may.
> Old Time is still a-flying.

Noble Numbers (1647) contains his religious poems.
Scott, G. W., *Robert Herrick*. 1974

Herriot, Edouard (1872–1957). French politician. As a senator (1912–19), a deputy (1919–42), and a leader of the Radical Socialist Party, he was a prominent member of many left-centre coalition ministries between the wars: on three occasions (1924–25, 1926 and 1932) he briefly combined the offices of prime minister and foreign minister. Meanwhile he was the almost perpetual mayor of Lyons (1905–47). He was interned in Germany for part of World War II and afterwards was president of the National Assembly (1947–54).

Herschel, Sir John Frederick William, 1st Bart. (1792–1871). British astronomer. Son of William * Herschel, he attended St John's College, Cambridge. He began to study law,

but was persuaded to follow his father into science. In the 1810s he helped his father with his astronomical observations, developed skill in the manufacture of telescopes, and made some useful discoveries in optics. His major work lay in providing a full star map of the Southern Hemisphere. He moved to the Cape of Good Hope in 1834, set up an observatory, and stayed four years, producing the massive and definitive *Results of Astronomical Observations Made During the Years 1834–1838 at the Cape of Good Hope*. Thereafter Herschel became one of the great public figures of Victorian science, becoming in 1850 Master of the Mint, and having been knighted in 1831. He interested himself in geophysics, and also the young art of photography, where he developed the use of sensitized paper and of hypo as a fixing agent. He served on the Royal Commission investigating the studies of Oxford and Cambridge Universities and was also on the Committee of the Great Exhibition of 1851. His writings on the philosophy of science – in which he stressed that the goal of science was the discovery of Law throughout Nature – were highly influential in his time.
Buttmann, G., *The Shadow of the Telescope*. 1970

Herschel, Sir William (1738–1822). British astronomer. The son of a poor Hanoverian military bandsman, he took early to mathematical and scientific studies, but followed his father into becoming a military musician. He left Hanover for England in 1757, settling in Bath in 1766 as an organist, concert-master, composer and music teacher, and building up an income sufficient to enable him to pursue his love of astronomy. Much of his time in the 1760s and 1770s was occupied with the construction of larger and larger telescopes. By 1774 he had constructed his own 51-inch reflector. He began making systematic sweeps of the heavens, and in 1781 discovered a hitherto undescribed object which he first took for a comet, but quickly recognized to be a planet (Uranus). For this discovery he was rewarded by George III with a pension of £200 per annum. Together with his sister, Caroline, he undertook massive surveys of the skies, producing numerous catalogues. In particular he sought out nebulae, raising the known total from a few hundred to over 2500. He speculated whether nebulae were very distant clusters of stars, or swirling clouds of gaseous material (which might one day coalesce into stars), and also upon the possibility that the whole heavens might have developed out of such nebulae. Amongst his other speculative ideas was a belief that life existed on the moon. He was also one of the discoverers of infra-red radiation in the light of the sun.
Hoskin, M. A., *William Herschel and the Construction of the Heavens*. 1964

Hertz, Heinrich Rudolf (1857–1894). German physicist. He was an assistant of * Helmholtz at the University of Berlin (1880–85), and later became professor of physics at Karlsruhe (1885–89) and Bonn (1889–94). His researches on the relation between light and electricity verified Maxwell's theory that light is a form of electromagnetic radiation, and he discovered the existence of electromagnetic waves which behave in all respects like light. These radiations, since called 'Hertzian waves', were used by * Marconi (1896) for sending his first wireless signals through space. Hertz also studied the behaviour of electrical discharges in rarefied gases.

Hertzog, James Barry Munnik (1866–1942). South African soldier and politician. A lawyer by training, and a well known commando leader in the Boer War (1899–1902), he was engaged in Orange Free State politics before becoming (1910) minister of Justice in * Botha's national administration. Excluded (1912) for his anti-British views, he formed the Nationalist party aiming at absolute equality, linguistically and otherwise, between Afrikaaners and English. After bitterly opposing South Africa's entry into World War I he became prime minister after the 1924 election, but in 1932 entered into a coalition with * Smuts, which ended with his resignation when he demanded neutrality during World War II.
Neame, L. E., *General Hertzog*. 1930

Herzen, Aleksandr Ivanovich (1812–1870). Russian writer and political philosopher. The illegitimate son of a rich nobleman who made him his heir, he became a civil servant and was exiled from Moscow (1834–42) for his espousal of radical causes. He evolved a 'left Hegelian' philosophy and supported the Westernizers against the Slavophils. He left Russia in 1847 and never returned, living mostly in Paris (where he died) and London. His weekly journal *Kolokol* ('The Bell') was widely circulated in Russia 1857–67. Herzen became disillusioned with the West and developed sympathy with the Slavophils, arguing that peasant communes could be the base for a revolutionary state. Drawn by elements in Mazzini, Proudhon, Bakunin and Marx, he failed to develop a coherent position of his own or a political machine. His memoirs, *My Past and Thoughts* (1852–55), were a major literary achievement.

Herzl, Theodor (1806–1904). Hungarian Zionist leader. Trained as a lawyer and journalist, his experience of French anti-Semitism, particularly as expressed in the * Dreyfus case, led him to propose (in *Judenstaat*, 1896) a separate Jewish state. He convened the first Zionist Congress in 1897 and became first president of the World Zionist Organisation. He spent the rest of his life in unsuccessful negotiations with various powers in order to acquire land for the new state.
Bein, A., *Theodor Herzl*. 1957

Heseltine, Philip *see* **Warlock, Peter**

Hess, Germain Henri (1802–1850). Swiss physical chemist. Professor of chemistry at St Petersburg, he made an important advance in thermochemistry when (1840) he showed that the heat change in a chemical reaction is always the same, irrespective of whether the reaction is performed directly or in stages. This is now known as Hess's Law. It put thermochemistry on a quantitative basis and made it possible to calculate the heat change in reactions where it could not be measured.

Hess, Dame Myra (1890–1965). English pianist. Outstandingly successful from her first appearance (1907) and a noted interpreter of Bach, she is remembered for the series of lunch-time concerts which she organized (in the National Gallery, London) during World War II. She was made D.B.E. in 1941.

Hess, Rudolf (1894–). German Nazi politician. He was with Hitler from the movement's beginnings, took part in the Munich *Putsch* (1923), and by 1933 had become deputy leader. During World War II, in May 1941 (on the eve of Germany's attack on Russia), he flew solo to Scotland, a mysterious and never satisfactorily explained exploit, undertaken apparently with the unauthorized aim of offering a compromise peace. While a prisoner he showed signs of mental instability but was tried by the international court at Nuremberg after the war and sentenced to life imprisonment.

Hess, Victor Franz (1883–1964). Austrian-born physicist. He held appointments at Graz, Vienna and Innsbruck Universities before becoming (1921) head of the research department of the U.S. Radium Corporation: he was professor of physics at Fordham University, New York (1938–56). For his work on cosmic radiation he shared with Carl D. Anderson the Nobel Prize for Physics (1936). Observations on balloon ascents (1911) convinced him that the radiation now known as cosmic was of extraterrestrial origin, a fact not hitherto established.

Hesse, Hermann (1877–1962). German novelist and poet. He dealt in vivid, sensuous language, with the problems of divided personality and the individual's need for harmonious self-fulfilment and integration. His novels include *Peter Camenzind* (1904; tr. 1961), *Demian* (1919; tr. 1958), *Steppenwolf* (1927; tr. 1965) and *Das Glasperlenspiel* (1943; tr. as *Magister Ludi*, 1949; *The Glass Bead Game*, 1970). In 1946 he won the Nobel Prize for Literature.

Heuss, Theodore (1884–1963). German politician. He was a lecturer in history in Berlin, and a member of the Reichstag (1924–28) and (1930–33), but was forced out of public life under the Nazi régime. He founded (1948) the Free Democratic party and was first president of the Federal Republic of Germany (1949–59).

Hevelius, Johannes (1611–1687). German astronomer, born and educated in Danzig. He built up what was probably the world's finest observatory (destroyed by fire in 1679 but subsequently rebuilt), made extensive observations and published them regularly. His maps of the moon were of the highest quality, and traced a whole range of hitherto undescribed mountains and craters. He also made masterly observations of comets, publishing them in his *Cometographia* of 1668. He thought that comets were exhalations from planets, and believed that they might be the material cause of sunspots. Hevelius's theoretical notions in science were of much less importance than his skill as an instrument maker, and as an astronomical observer. His magnum opus was the *Prodromus astronomiae* (1690) which listed 1,564 stars arranged alphabetically under constellation and stellar magnitude. This star catalogue was greatly used during the eighteenth century.

Hewish, Antony (1924–). British radio-astronomer. In 1968 he was a co-discoverer (with Jocelyn Bell) of pulsars, shared the 1974 Nobel Prize for Physics with Sir Martin * Ryle and became a professor of radioastronomy at Cambridge 1974– .

Heydrich, Reinhard (1904–1942). German politician. As the Nazi deputy protector of Bohemia and Moravia (Czechoslovakia) during World War II he became notorious for his brutal suppression of the Resistance movement. As a reprisal for his assassination (1942) the village of Lidice was destroyed and its male inhabitants massacred.

Heyerdahl, Thor (1914–). Norwegian anthropologist, noted for his trans-oceanic scientific expeditions in primitive craft. The voyage of the raft *Kon-Tiki* in 1947 was intended to demonstrate that Polynesians could have travelled to their islands from South America. He made two similar journeys, one in a reed boat from Morocco to Central America and a third in a reed boat from Mesopotamia along the ancient trade routes of the Indian Ocean.
Heyerdahl, T., *Kon-Tiki Expedition*. 1948; *The Ra Expeditions*. 1971

Heywood, John (1497?–1580). English musician, playwright and epigrammatist. As a singer and player on the virginals he won favour at court. His 'interludes' (i.e. plays or dialogues given not in theatres but in the halls of the nobility, colleges, etc.) included *The Play of the Wether* (1533) and *A Play of Love* (1534). Later he published a collection of proverbs and epigrams, in which many familiar phrases, e.g. 'The fat is in the fire' first appeared in print. In late life he retired abroad in search of religious freedom. He was the grandfather of John * Donne.

Heywood, Thomas (*c.* 1574–1641). English dramatist. Very little is known of his life though he appears to have joined Philip Henslowe as actor and dramatist soon after leaving Cambridge. He claimed to have written over 200 plays. The first to be published under his own name was *A Woman Killed with Kindness* (1603, published 1607), and others include *The Rape of Lucrece* (1608), *The English Traveller* (printed 1633), *A Maidenhead Well Lost* (1634). Apart from plays his works included *An Apology for Actors* (1612), much verse, and a miscellany (1624) which might have been called an apology for women.
Clark, A. M., *Thomas Heywood: Playwright and Miscellanist*. 1967

Hickok, 'Wild Bill' (James Butler) (1837–1876). American crack marksman, scout and marshal, born in Illinois. He worked for a stage-coach company and, in 1861, defeated single-handed an attack on Rock-Creek stage-coach station by the McCanles gang. He was a Federal Scout (1861–65) and U.S. Marshal for the district around Fort Riley, Kansas, after 1865. He was shot in the back during a poker game in 1876.

Hideyoshi Toyotomi (1536–1598). Japanese soldier. Having conquered the island of Shikoku he rose from the ranks to be a general, and finally dictator. He succeeded in unifying Japan, carried out useful administrative reforms but established a rigid class structure. He at first welcomed, but later expelled, Christian missionaries.

Hilbert, David (1862–1943). German mathematician, born in Königsberg. Professor of mathematics at Göttingen 1895–1930, he was a major contributor to mathematical logic, on the theory of numbers, the theory of invariants and integral equations. In *Foundations of Geometry* (1899) he tried to establish formal proof of axioms, moving from intuition (assumptions made without varification) to logic. However, his assertion that all mathematical problems were essentially decidable was overturned by the work of * Gödel and * Turing.

Hill, Octavia (1838–1912). English reformer, pioneer of the movement for public open space and improved housing, both inspired originally by her concern for the living conditions of the poor. She was a founder of the National Trust (1895) and established her first housing project in St Marylebone, London, in 1864; in the latter she was helped by John * Ruskin.
Hill, O., *Homes of the London Poor*. 1875; *Our Common Land*. 1878

Hill, Sir Rowland (1795–1879). English educationist and administrator, originator of the penny post and regarded as the father of modern postal systems. He suggested that a low postage rate would lead to an increased volume of mail and, therefore, greater income therefrom; that there should be a flat rate to cut out administrative costs; that letters should be pre-paid. To achieve this last objective he developed a franking system which was the forerunner of the postage stamp. He was made Secretary to the Postmaster General in 1846. He was knighted in 1860.

Hillary, Sir Edmund (1919–). New Zealand mountaineer. He was one of the party which made a reconnaissance of Mt Everest (1951); and as a member of Hunt's expedition (1953) he and the Sherpa Tensing were the first to reach the summit: for this feat he was knighted. He served under Sir Vivian Fuchs in the Commonwealth Trans-antarctic Expedition; in 1958, approaching from opposite directions the two leaders met at the South Pole. He became New Zealand High Commissioner to India 1984– .

Hillel (*c.* 65 B.C.–9 A.D.). Jewish rabbi, born in Babylonia. He became a leader of the Pharisees, president of the Sanhedrin in Jerusalem, an important innovator in scriptural analysis, and a liberal interpreter of the law. His grandson Gamaliel was the teacher of St Paul.

Hilliard, Nicholas (*c.* 1547–1619). English miniature painter, trained as a jeweller. He was the leading English miniaturist 1580–1600, and enjoyed a high reputation also in France, which he visited *c.* 1577. His work was noted for its grace and delicacy, and for his technique of modelling features with flesh-tones.
Auerbach, E., *Nicholas Hilliard.* 1961

Hilton, Conrad (1887–1979). American hotelier. Born in San Antonio, New Mexico, he was originally involved in local businesses including his father's hotel which he helped to establish. He began buying hotels after his father's death (1918) and expanded worldwide.

Hilton, James (1900–1954). British writer famous for popular novels including *Lost Horizon* (1933), *Goodbye, Mr Chips* (1934) and *Random Harvest* (1941).

Himmler, Heinrich (1900–1945). German Nazi politician. Having been leader of the S.S. (from 1929), he became, after Hitler's accession to power, head of the secret police, the Gestapo (from 1934), and of all police forces in Germany (from 1936). This quiet, sinister man, originally a schoolmaster, was thus ultimately responsible for the annihilation of the Jews, the deportations and forced labour, and for tortures and murders on a scale unparalleled in history. In 1944 he was made a commander of the home army, and on the eve of Germany's final defeat in the following year attempted vainly to come to terms with the Allies. When captured by British soldiers he killed himself by taking poison.
Manvell, R. and Fraenkel, H., *Himmler.* 1969

Hindemith, Paul (1895–1963). German composer. He was leader of the Frankfurt Opera Orchestra 1915–25, later playing the viola with the Amar-Hindemith quartet. Always a leader of contemporary music, he wrote works reflecting expressionist ideas in the 1920s, including 5 operas, which nevertheless used traditional form and tonality. He wrote altogether some 40 major works and a number of sonatas for chamber groups and solo instruments. His later work was based on a theory of tonality expressed in his book *The Craft of Musical Composition* (1937–39).
Kemp, I., *Hindemith.* 1971

Hindenburg, Paul von (Beneckendorff und von) (1847–1934). German soldier and president. He joined the Prussian war army (1858) and served in the Franco Prussian War (1870–71) and was a retired general when he was recalled at the beginning of World War I and given command of the army in East Prussia with * Ludendorff as his chief of staff. The great victory over the Russians at Tannenberg (August 1914) made him a national hero and he remained an immensely popular father figure throughout the war. The combination of Hindenburg (made a field-marshal) and Ludendorff – the former providing the dignity and prestige, the latter the strategic skill – lasted throughout the war. Victories on the eastern front (1915–16) were followed, when Hindenburg had been made chief of general staff (1916) with Ludendorff as his assistant, by the stalemate in the west from which the Germans sought to emerge by their great breakthrough in March 1918. When the allied counter-attack brought disaster Hindenburg secured an armistice which enabled him to lead the armies back intact to the frontiers, and so create a myth of an undefeated Germany.

He returned to public life when he succeeded Ebert as president of republican Germany (1925–34). Though his faculties were weakened by old age he tried by every means to delay * Hitler's accession to power but at last gave way and in 1933 appointed him chancellor.

Wheeler-Bennett, J. W., *Hindenburg: The Wooden Titan*. 1967

Hinshelwood, Sir Cyril Norman (1897–1967). English chemist. He became professor of chemistry at Oxford in 1937, and was president of the Chemical Society (1946–48) and of the Royal Society (1955–60). He was an authority on the kinetics of chemical reactions, especially of those involved in the growth of bacterial cells. He shared with * Semenov the Nobel Prize for Chemistry (1956). His works include *Kinetics of Chemical Change in Gaseous Systems* (1926).

Hipparchus (*c.* 180–125 B.C.). Greek astronomer, born in Nicaea (Bithynia). He catalogued the positions of some 1,080 fixed stars. He erected an observatory at Rhodes where he discovered *inter alia* some of the irregularities in the moon's motion and showed the existence of the precession of the equinoxes, a circular swing of the earth's axis so slow that it takes 25,000 years to complete each circle. The method of fixing the position of a place on the earth's surface by giving its latitude and longitude was devised by Hipparchus, and he improved the methods of predicting eclipses and calculated the length of the year to within six minutes. He was also the inventor of trigonometry.

Hippocrates (*c.* 460–*c.* 375 B.C.). Greek physician. Regarded as the 'Father of Medicine', he was the first to insist that the art of healing depended on scientific method and clinical observation. He was probably born on the island of Cos, where there was some sort of medical school linked with the cult of Aesculapius. There he is said to have taught under the traditional plane tree. The so-called Hippocratic collection, which almost certainly comprises not only his own work but that of pupils and followers, consists of more than seventy books on medicine, of which the *Aphorisms* and the *Airs, Waters and Places* are among the most important; the section on epidemics is of great interest as are the clinical descriptions, e.g. of pneumonia, malaria and mumps. Knowledge of anatomy was very limited and disease was defined as disharmony of the 'four humours' (a doctrine that survived into the 18th century); in the consideration of epidemics, however, the importance of diet, environment and climate is recognized. Descriptions of the ancient instruments are an interesting part of the surgical writings. Hippocrates prescribed a code of medical ethics for his disciples, summarized in the traditional Hippocratic Oath (though the exact wording may not be his), still administered to physicians on qualification.

Hippolytus (*c.* 160–*c.* 236). Greek theologian and anti-pope, who lived in Rome. His defence of the doctrine of the *Logos*, which implied that the Son, Jesus Christ, incarnate on earth had a pre-existence as the word (*Logos*) or creative power of God (cf. St John's Gospel), brought him into conflict with Callistus, who became pope in 217, and he seems to have received consecration as an anti-pope. He submitted, however, to Callistus's successor Pontianus when (235) both leaders were sent as convicts to the Sardinian mines and subsequently martyred. A work entitled *Philosophumena*, a refutation of heresy, found (1842) at Mt Athos, can almost certainly be attributed to Hippolytus. Hippolytus's *Commentary on Daniel* (202) is the earliest Christian work of its kind extant.

Hirohito (1901–). Emperor of Japan 1926– . Son of the emperor Yoshihito, he was the first crown prince to visit Europe (1921–22) and became regent after his father's mental collapse. After a comparatively brief liberal period, Japanese politics deteriorated in the 1930s. Military cliques and secret societies imposed their wills on ministers and Hirohito appeared unable or unwilling to intervene. Japan invaded Manchuria (1932) and China (1937) and attacked US bases (1941). After the dropping of the atomic bombs on Hiroshima and Nagasaki, Hirohito intervened, making an unprecedented broadcast in support of unconditional surrender, ceding power to General Douglas * MacArthur (1945). A gifted poet and marine biologist, his regnal name was 'Showa'.

Hiroshige Ando (1797–1858). Japanese graphic artist. The son of a fireman, he trained in the *Ukiyo-e* ('floating world') tradition of contemporary urban life, publishing his first prints in 1818. His greatest works are landscapes and seascapes, more lyrical than those of his contemporary * Hokusai, produced before 1844. They include the series *Fifty-Three Stages of the Tokaido Highway*. His work influenced the French Impressionists.
Robinson, B. W., *Hiroshige*. 1964.

Hiss, Alger (1904–). American administrator. He joined the U.S. State Department in 1936 and, among other important assignments, was secretary to the Dumbarton Oaks Conference (1944), accompanied President * Roosevelt to Yalta 1945 and was Secretary General of UNCIO (United Nations Conference on International Organization) at San Francisco 1945–46. In 1947 he became president of the Carnegie Endowment for International Peace. Accused (1949) by Whitaker Chambers (a self-confessed former communist) of having been a member of the Communist party in the 1930s and of having betrayed secret information, he denied the charge on oath but was tried and condemned to five years' imprisonment for perjury. Hiss himself and a large body of opinion continued to maintain his innocence.

Hitchcock, Sir Alfred Joseph (1899–1980). English film and television director resident in the U.S.A. since 1940. He directed many suspense thrillers including *The Thirty-Nine Steps* (1935), *The Lady Vanishes, Strangers on a Train, Rear Window, Dial M for Murder* and *Psycho*.
Durgnat, R., *The Strange Case of Alfred Hitchcock*. 1974

Hitchens, Ivon (1893–1979). English painter of landscapes and flower pieces; he carried on the English lyrical tradition into a semi-abstract discipline, relying on an interplay of rich colours. He was appointed a C.B.E. in 1958.

Hitler, Adolf (1889–1945). German political leader. He was born in Braunau, Austria, the son of a minor customs official originally named Schickelgruber. He had ambitions to become an artist but failed to win an art scholarship and became an architect's draftsman. In World War I he was a lance corporal in the Bavarian Army and won the Iron Cross. After the war he joined the German Workers' party in Munich, which he transformed into the National Socialist (Nazi) party, the instrument of his political advancement. After the failure of a *Putsch* organized by him with the aid of General * Ludendorff (1923) he spent nine months in prison where he dictated to his companion Rudolf * Hess his book *Mein Kampf* (*My Struggle*). From 1925 he reorganized his shattered party helped financially by industrialists who saw in him, with his anti-Semitism, anti-Marxism and extreme nationalism, a barrier against liberals and communists. Thus aided Hitler asserted an unchallenged despotism within the party and was able to create a vast propaganda machine, including a chain of newspapers, to further his cause. He organized strong-arm gangs of supporters (Brown Shirts) and others into an elite guard (S.S.). The prevailing world-wide depression made his economic theories plausible and acceptable and led numbers of unemployed to join him. In the 1930 election the number of Nazis in the Reichstag rose from 12 to 104 and in July 1932 to 230; though subsequently there was a decline * Hindenburg summoned Hitler to the chancellorship. The burning of the Reichstag, attributed by the Nazis to the communists, gave him the excuse to assume dictatorial powers. He proceeded to turn Germany into a one-party state; and to secure his own pre-eminence in the party purged it of all possible rivals in a night of murder in which his old ally Röhm, head of the S.A., and many others were slaughtered by the S.S., which then became the sole uniformed party organization. On Hindenburg's death (1934) Hitler became president – though he preferred the title Der Führer – and while indulging his own phobias by a reign of terror against Jews and communists he carried away the majority of his countrymen by frenzied eloquence, elaborate propaganda and by his spectacular success in the field of foreign policy. In startling succession came rearmament, military reoccupation of the Rhineland (1936), the Rome-Berlin Axis (1936), annexation of Austria (spring 1938) and in the autumn of that year the Munich Agreement, which gave him the Sudetenland. He seized the remainder of Czechoslovakia in spring 1939 and concluded a non-aggression pact with the Soviets. France and Britain failed to co-operate, their statesmen seduced by hopes of appeasing Hitler, their people divided between those who saw him as a barrier to communism and those who, whilst realizing the threat he was, clung to dreams of disarmament. Finally Britain and France reacted to his invasion of Poland (1939), where, however, they were impotent to help. In the spring of 1940 German armies quickly crushed the Allied forces and after the collapse of France only Britain still held out. Although Hitler's decision to attack Russia was to prove a fatal error, the run of success lasted into 1942. Then the joint strength of Britain and Russia, joined by the U.S.A., inexorably broke Hitler's boasted 'Thousand Years Reich' in its 'Fortress Europa'. He ordered a 'final solution' (i.e. extermination) for Europe's Jews and about 6 million died, 75 per cent of them in concentration camps. Millions of Slavs were also killed in the camps. The total death toll in Hitler's war was about 38 million, of which 7 million were German and 22 million Russian. Only a small minority of Germans raised the slightest opposition to Hitler and there was only one serious conspiracy when he narrowly escaped death at Rastenberg, East Prussia (July 1944), from a bomb planted by a staff officer Col. Klaus von Stauffenberg. When defeat finally came Hitler and Goebbels were in a bomb-proof bunker in besieged Berlin. There he married his mistress Eva Braun, and there, on 30 April 1945, she took poison and he shot himself. Like Goethe's Mephistopheles, Hitler was 'the spirit that denies', the supreme sceptic, 'a rationalist and realist' (in Alan Bullock's words) who rejected Christianity, despised attempts to revive the old Teutonic religion and in his political testament turned even against patriotism, declaring that Germany and its army were 'not worthy of him'. Only Stalin, 'a beast, but a great beast', won his admiration in the end.

Bullock, A. L. C., *Hitler:A Study in Tyranny*. 1969; Trevor-Roper, H., *The Last Days of Hitler*. 4th ed. 1971; Fest, J. C., *Hitler*. 1974

Hoare, Samuel *see* **Templewood, 1st Viscount**

Hobbes, Thomas (1588–1679). English philosopher. The son of a clergyman, he was born at Malmesbury and educated at Oxford, after which he was employed for most of his life by the Cavendish family as tutor and secretary. This career left him with much leisure for study of both classical authors and contemporary thinkers. Some of the latter, such as Galileo and Descartes, he was able to meet while visiting the continent; in England he came to know Bacon and others distinguished in the arts and letters. His own philosophical writing seems to have stemmed from a chance discovery of Euclid's geometry. This was a natural step to the 'mechanical philosophies' then current (which regarded the universe in motion, rather than the universe at rest, as the natural state of things); from these matured his own distinctive contribution to human thought.

Meanwhile the Civil War had broken out in England and when the royalist cause faced defeat Hobbes, who in 1640 had written in defence of the royal prerogative, took refuge on the continent and for a time (1647) was mathematics tutor to Prince Charles (Charles II). He was allowed to return in 1651, the year of the publication of *Leviathan*, the greatest of the works in which his political philosophy is expounded. He was in disfavour after the Restoration and his sketch of the Civil Wars, *Behemoth* (1680), was suppressed. In his extreme old age he wrote verse translations of the *Iliad* and *Odyssey*. In his ethics, rejecting as he did the supernatural and also any religious basis for morality he regarded human action as directed solely by egoistic motives which if given free play as in the natural state would make man's life 'nasty, brutish and short'. Self-interest therefore leads men to what he calls a 'social contract' whereby they give up their natural rights of aggression in return for the security of a society controlled by a 'sovereign', who may be an individual or a republic. Should he fail in his side of the contract the sovereign may be deposed. Although Hobbes held the rationalist view that philosophy ought to be a matter of rigid deduction from premises, his own work is empirical in nature and its acute semantic analysis sometimes foreshadows the philosophy of the present age.

Warrender, H., *The Political Philosophy of Thomas Hobbes*. 1957

Hobbs, Sir John (Jack) **Berry** (1882–1963). English cricketer. He was one of the greatest batsman of his time and the first cricketer to be knighted (1953) for his services to the game. During his first-class career with Surrey (1905–34) and England (1907–30) he scored a record total of 61,237 runs with 197 centuries. It was not only his play but his personality that endeared Hobbs to the crowd.

Ho Chi Minh (1890–1969). Vietnamese Communist leader, born in Annam. (His real name was Nguyen That Thanh, later changed to Nguyen Ai Quoc. Ho Chi Minh means 'he who enlightens'.) Son of a mandarin, he left Annam in 1911, worked as a merchant seaman (in the US 1915–16), assistant pastry cook to * Escoffier in London and a photographic retoucher in Paris. A foundation member of the French Communist Party (1920), he lived in Moscow, Bangkok, Canton, Hong Kong and Shanghai 1923–30. He founded the Indochinese Communist Party in Hong Kong (1930) and, on his return after thirty years (1941), the Vietnamese Independence League (Vietminh). In March 1945 the Japanese proclaimed Vietnamese independence with Ho as president of the Democratic Republic (DRV), and they withdrew leaving him in control in September. He retained office until he died. The French soon tried to reimpose their rule and established a puppet state in the South under * Bao Dai. War with France continued until 1954, then a temporary partition at the 17th Parallel was followed by war between North and South in which the Americans played an increasingly dominant role from 1963 (rising to a peak in 1969). Ho formed the Lao Dong ('Workers Party') in 1951. Like Mao he was an able strategist, poet and patriotic hero.
Lacouture, J., *Ho Chi Minh*. 1968.

Hodgkin, Sir Alan Lloyd (1914–). British physiologist. In 1963 he shared (with Sir Andrew Huxley and Sir John Eccles) the Nobel Prize for Physiology or Medicine, for his discovery of the chemical processes by which impulses travel along individual nerve fibres. He was president of the Royal Society (1970–75) and received the O.M. (1973). He became Master of Trinity College, Cambridge in 1978.

Hodgkin, Dorothy Crowfoot (née Crowfoot) (1910–). English biochemist. She became Wolfson research professor of the Royal Society and professorial fellow of Somerville College, Oxford. She has been specially distinguished for her use of X-ray techniques in the determination of the structures of biochemical compounds, notably penicillin and vitamin B 12, the latter essential to combat pernicious anaemia. She was awarded the Nobel Prize for Chemistry (1964), and in 1965 received the O.M., the first woman to be so honoured since Florence Nightingale.

Hodgson, Ralph (1871–1962). English poet. He was one of the 'Georgian' group of English poets. Simplicity, metrical facility and delicate irony distinguish his work. Some of his poems, e.g. *Time, You Old Gypsy Man*, attained wide popularity.

Hodson, William Stephen Raikes (1821–1858). British soldier. He joined the Indian Army in 1845. During the Indian Mutiny (1857), at the head of an irregular body of cavalry known as Hodson's Horse, he took part in the siege of Delhi and after its fall discovered the last Mogul emperor and his two sons. The controversy roused by his shooting the sons with his own hands would have been greater had not Hodson himself been mortally wounded during the assault on the palace at Lucknow in the following March.

Hofer, Andreas (1767–1810). Austrian innkeeper and patriot. He had fought against Napoleon (1796–1805) and when his native Tirol was transferred by the emperor from Austria to Bavaria, he organized and led a local rising (1809). Twice in that year he drove out the Franco-Bavarian troops, twice Austrian submission to the French terms brought them back. In October 1809 he roused the country once again but this time the enemy were in overwhelming force. He was forced into hiding, betrayed and shot.

Hoff, Jacobus Henricus van't (1852–1911). Dutch physical chemist. One of the founders of this branch of science in its modern form, he held professorships at Amsterdam (1877–87), Leipzig (1887–94) and Berlin (1895–1911), but even earlier (1874) he had put forward the theory that the four valencies of the carbon atom are directed to the corners of a regular tetrahedron, thus establishing the field of chemical structure now called stereochemistry. In 1887 he established his theory of solutions, which is the basis of present-day knowledge of the subject. He showed that the osmotic pressure of a dilute solution is equal to the pressure which the dissolved substance would exert if it were a gas occupying the same volume at the same temperature and pressure. Other studies included reaction velocity and thermodynamics. Van't Hoff was awarded the first Nobel Prize for Chemistry (1901).

Hofmann, August Wilhelm von (1818–1892). German chemist. After working with * Liebig, he went to London (1845) to be superintendent of the newly founded Royal College of Chemistry. He was chemist at the Royal Mint from 1856 until 1865, when he returned to Germany as professor of chemistry at Berlin. Organic chemistry was the main field of his research and his production of aniline from coal products led to the development of the great synthetic-dye industry in Germany.

Hofmannsthal, Hugo von (1874–1929). Austrian poet and dramatist, born in Vienna. His poems, written for the most part in early life, mainly display a nostalgic melancholy over a civilization in decay, a mood evident, but less so, in his plays, which he first began writing in his teens. The best, however, date from his later life when he took themes mainly from the Middle Ages or classical antiquity, as in *Elektra* (1903) and the morality play *Jedermann* (*Everyman*) of 1912. He also wrote the libretti for Richard Strauss's operas *Der Rosenkavalier* (1911), *Ariadne auf Naxos* (1912), etc. With Strauss and Reinhardt he founded the Salzburg Festival.
Kobel, E., *Hugo von Hofmannsthal*. 1970

Hofmeyr, Jan Hendrik (1845–1909). South African politician. A member of the Cape parliament from 1879, he worked to promote the political interests of the Dutch through the Afrikaner Bond. He distrusted Kruger's extreme nationalistic policy in the Transvaal, but broke with Cecil * Rhodes (with whom he had hitherto worked closely) over his part in organizing the Jameson Raid (1895). Hofmeyr was in Germany during the Boer War but afterwards was prominent in the negotiations which led to the union of South Africa.

His nephew **Jan Hendrik Hofmeyr** (1894–1948), noted for his liberal attitude towards the coloured population, was Smuts's deputy prime minister before his electoral defeat in 1948.

Hogarth, William (1697–1764). English artist. At 15 he was apprenticed to a silver engraver, and was an independent engraver by 1720, painting being then a spare-time study. From 1730 he painted his moral series of narrative pictures: *A Harlot's Progress* (*c.* 1731), *A Rake's Progress* (*c.* 1735) and *Marriage à la Mode* (*c.* 1742–44). These were painted to be later engraved, and the engravings sold widely. They are today regarded as unique, but of lesser quality as paintings than his more spontaneous work, portraits such as *The Shrimp Girl* and *Hogarth's Servants*. He published his theories in *An Analysis of Beauty* in 1753.
Antal, F., *Hogarth and His Place in European Art*. 1962

Hogg, James (1770–1835). Scottish poet, known because of his calling and the Lowland district where he practised it as the 'Ettrick Shepherd'. He was still almost illiterate when Sir Walter Scott, whom he helped with his collection of border ballads, discerned his talent. He went to Edinburgh (1810) and was introduced to the literary world. *The Mountain Bard* (1807) contained his early ballads. *The Queen's Wake* (1813), in which seventeen bards competed before Mary Queen of Scots, includes his best known poem, *Kilmeny*.
Mack, D., *James Hogg*. 1972

Hohenstaufen. German dynasty, deriving its name from an ancestral castle in Swabia. Members of it were German kings and Holy Roman Emperors from 1238 to 1254. The most important were * Frederick I, * Henry VI, and * Frederick II.

Hohenzollern. German dynastic family, deriving its name from a castle in Swabia. The family's prominence began when Count Hohenzollern was made elector and margrave of Brandenburg (1415). A later Hohenzollern, Albert of Brandenburg, grandmaster of the Teutonic Knights, dissolved that order and became first Duke of Prussia (1525). Brandenburg and Prussia subsequently became a kingdom under Hohenzollern rule, and its ruler (then William I) became the first emperor of the united Germany formed in 1871 after the Franco-Prussian War. The dynasty thus ruled as electors of Brandenburg (1415–1701), kings of Prussia (1701–1918) and German emperors (1871–1918).

Hokusai Katsushika (1760–1849). Japanese graphic artist, born at Edo (Tokyo). Brought up by the affluent Nakajima family, he worked in a bookshop and was apprenticed first to a wood-block engraver, then to the artist

Katsukawa Shunsho. His first published works (1780) are in the *Ukiyo-e* ('floating world') tradition, depicting contemporary urban life: street scenes, actors, love-making, processions. He moved frequently (about 90 times) and changed his name (about 20 times) so the complete range of his activity is not known. He concentrated on drawing, painting and print-making of innumerable studies of landscapes and seascapes, animals, birds, many of them published in book form or as illustrations of novels and poems. His *Thirty Six Views of Mt Fuji* (1826–33) are regarded as his greatest achievement and the summit of Japanese graphic art: this series includes the famous 'The Breaking Wave off Kanagawa'. He wrote an autobiography *Once Hokusai, Today the Old Man Mad about Drawing* (1835). His *Manga* (or *Ten Thousand Sketches*) appeared in 15 volumes (1812–75). From about 1890 his work was known and admired in Europe.

Holbein, Hans (1497/8–1543). German painter, born in Augsburg. His father **Hans Holbein the Elder** was a painter in the city. He settled in Basel *c.* 1514, at first working as a printer's designer. His paintings changed after 1526, becoming softer and richer in colouring; it is possible (although there is no evidence) that he had visited Italy and seen work of the Italian renaissance. His *Madonna of Burgomaster Meyer* (1526) combines this Italian richness with northern realism. In 1526 he came to England with an introduction (from Erasmus) to Sir Thomas More. His outstanding group portrait of More's family was the main work of this visit. He came back to England in 1532 and stayed for some years at the court of Henry VIII. In 1537 he painted a mural at Whitehall (only the cartoon survives) showing the king with his third queen, Jane Seymour, and his parents; his famous study of Henry VIII was for this mural, and was copied after the destruction of Whitehall Palace in 1698. Later royal portraits, although beautiful in technique, were impersonal compared with this strongly-characterized piece.
Chamberlain, A. B., *Hans Holbein the Younger*. 2 vols. 1913

Hölderlin, (Johann Christian) Friedrich (1770–1843). German poet. Trained for the Lutheran ministry, he fell in love with Greek mythology and his employer's wife and became a schizophrenic (from 1806). His lyric poetry was largely unrecognised until the 20th century.

Holinshed, Raphael (died *c.* 1580). English chronicler. He was commissioned by a London printer, Reginald Wolfe, to compile the *Chronicles of England, Scotland and Ireland* (2 volumes, 1577). Holinshed himself wrote the history of England; others contributed the Scottish and Irish sections. The *Chronicles* were much used by Shakespeare, especially for *Macbeth, King Lear* and *Cymbeline*.

Holland, Henry Richard Fox, 3rd Baron (1773–1840). English politician. His ideas were formed by his uncle Charles James * Fox. He served as lord privy seal (1806–07) and as chancellor of the Duchy of Lancaster twice (1830–34, 1835–40). He supported enlightened initiatives to abolish the slave trade and the Test Act, and was influential through his hospitality at Holland House in London to the leading personalities, political and literary, of his day.

Holland, Sir Sidney George (1893–1961). New Zealand politician. An engineer by profession, he entered parliament in 1935 and by 1940 was leader of the National party in opposition. From 1949 until his retirement (1957) he was prime minister.

Holmes, Oliver Wendell (1809–1894). American author and physician. He was born at Cambridge, Massachusetts. He spent most of his life in or near Boston and was among the last and best known of that traditional and exclusive group that gave Boston its cultural ascendancy. He studied in Paris (1833–35) and gained a Harvard M.D. (1836); as a professor at Dartmouth College (1839–41) and at Harvard (1847–82) he gave popular and important lectures on anatomy. He is best known, however, for his humorous and genial essays and verses, contributed to the *Atlantic Monthly*. Some of these were collected in *The Autocrat of the Breakfast Table* (1858), *The Professor at the Breakfast Table* (1860), *The Poet at the Breakfast Table* (1872). He also wrote novels, and memoirs of his friend Ralph Waldo Emerson.

His son, **Oliver Wendell Holmes** (1841–1935), after fighting in the American Civil War took a degree in law at Harvard (1866). He achieved international legal fame as a result

of his Lowell lectures (published 1881). Theodore Roosevelt appointed him to the U.S. Supreme Court (1902). He ranks as one of the greatest of all Supreme Court justices and as a great liberal. At a time when a majority of his colleagues declared social legislation controlling wages and other labour matters unconstitutional he disagreed with their conservative attitude and earned himself the title of 'The Great Dissenter'.
Tilton, E. M., *Amiable Autocrat*. 1947

Holst, Gustav (Theodore) (1874–1934). English composer of part-Swedish descent, born in Cheltenham. He began his career as an organist and choirmaster, and studied at the Royal College of Music under Sir Charles Stanford. He worked as an orchestral musician and as a teacher; in 1906 he became director of music at St Paul's Girls' School and also taught at Morley College, Lambeth. He was a highly original composer, rooted in but not limited by the English tradition. His best-known works are probably the suite *The Planets* and *The Perfect Fool.*
Holst, I., *Gustav Holst*. 1938

Holt, Harold Edward (1908–1967). Australian Liberal politician. A Member of the House of Representatives 1935–67, he was a minister under Sir Robert * Menzies 1940 and 1949–66, succeeding him as prime minister 1966–67. He was lost at sea while swimming.

Holyoake, Sir Keith Jacka (1904–1983). New Zealand Nationalist politician. He first entered parliament in 1932 and became deputy prime minister (1949). He succeeded Sir Sidney * Holland briefly (1957) and became prime minister and foreign minister (1960–72). He was governor-general 1977–80 and became the first New Zealand knight of the garter (KG) in 1980.

Home of the Hirsel, Alexander (Alec) Frederick Douglas-Home, Baron (1903–). British Conservative politician. Son of the 13th Earl of Home, he was educated at Eton and Oxford; and (as Lord Dunglass) he was M.P. for Lanark (1931–45 and 1950–51). He was parliamentary private secretary to Neville Chamberlain (1937–39). On his father's death (1951) he succeeded to the peerage in the year when the Conservatives were returned to power. He was secretary of state of commonwealth relations (1955–60) and foreign secretary (1955–60), a post he filled with skill. He succeeded Harold * Macmillan as prime minister (October 1963) unexpectedly, after the choice had wavered between several more favoured contenders. In order to sit in the Commons he renounced his peerage and was elected M.P. for Kinross and West Perthshire. He was called upon to lead his party at a moment when its fortunes were at a low ebb; his qualities of integrity and sincerity rallied all party factions around him and brought the Conservative party closer to success in the 1964 election than had been predicted. He remained leader of the opposition until July 1965 when he was succeeded by Edward * Heath as party leader under a revised procedure, sponsored by himself, for electing a successor.
Douglas-Home, A. F., *The Way the Wind Blows*. 1976

Homer (between the 11th and 7th century BC). Greek epic poet. Tradition has attributed to Homer the authorship of the *Iliad*, the story of the siege of Troy (or Ilium) and other events during the Trojan War, and the *Odyssey*, which described the wanderings of Odysseus after the war and his subsequent return to his home in Ithaca. Nothing certain is known about the date of Homer's birth, or the place, and at least seven Greek cities claim the honour of his birth. One tradition states that he was born near Smyrna, the illegitimate son of Maion, travelled extensively collecting material for his epics, becoming blind and spending the rest of his life as a wandering minstrel. Some legends say that he spent his last years as a blind beggar at the gates of Thebes, declaiming the ballads and stories which were later incorporated in the *Iliad* and the *Odyssey*. These works are notable for their vivid and accurate descriptions and deep insight into human nature. Homer's style is notable for his constant use of the fixed, or recurring, epithet, e.g. 'the wine-dark sea', 'the stalwart Odysseus' and 'the prudent Penelope'. Homer's works constitute the oldest surviving literature of antiquity, with the exception of the Pentateuch in the Old Testament, and their influence on western culture has been enormous. In the 18th and 19th centuries some literary critics concluded that Homer never existed and that the works attributed to him were merely anthologies of older ballads and legends, but the majority of critical opinion now supports Homer's authorship.

Kirk, G. S., *Homer and the Epic*. 1965

Honecker, Erich (1912–). German politician, life-long Communist imprisoned (1935–45) under the Third Reich. After the partition of Germany he became an assistant to Walter Ulbricht, first secretary of the Party in the German Democratic Republic, and succeeded him in office in 1971.

Honegger, Arthur (1892–1955). Swiss-French composer, born at Le Havre, one of the group of French composers known as 'Les Six'. Honegger was a prolific composer and an exponent of polytonality, although many of his works remained classical in form; they include the symphonic psalm *King David* (1923), the opera *Antigone* (1927), the ballet *Skating Rink* (1922), and orchestral works, e.g. *Pacific 231* (1924) and *Rugby* (1928).

Hooch, Pieter de (1629–1683). Dutch painter of interior and courtyard domestic scenes. His representations of figures in simple settings have come to symbolize the plain dignity of seventeenth-century Dutch burgher life. His later paintings, recording an over-padded, richer style of living, were far less successful.

Hood, Samuel Hood, 1st Viscount (1724–1816). British sailor. Having reached the rank of rear-admiral he was appointed (1786) to command a squadron in the West Indies, and under Rodney's command played a decisive part in the Battle of the Saints. He became a lord of the Admiralty in 1788. When the French Revolutionary wars opened (1793) he was given the Mediterranean command and conducted the operations which led to the occupation of Toulon, and those islands off the Corsican coast. Nelson, who served under him, paid high tribute to his skill as a tactician.

His younger brother, **Alexander Hood** (1737–1814), who became Baron Bridport (1796) and Viscount (1800), was also a distinguished naval officer and commanded a squadron at Howe's famous victory of the First of June (1794).

Rose, J. H., *Lord Hood and the Defence of Toulon*. 1922

Hood, Thomas (1799–1845). English poet and humorist. He was born in London. His father's death (1811) left him poor and he received no formal education. Having taken to writing for local newspapers while he was in Dundee (1815–17) he chose journalism as a profession when he returned to London. He became (1823) assistant editor of the *London Magazine* and came to know Charles Lamb and other writers. In 1829 he edited *The Gem*, for which he wrote his famous poem about the murderer Eugene * Aram. Most of his poems, collected, e.g., in *Whims and Oddities* (two series, 1826, 1827), were, however, humorous; but, relying so much on puns for their effect, they have been long outmoded. He is best remembered now for the indignation and compassion of, e.g., *The Song of the Shirt*, and *The Bridge of Sighs*, on a prostitute's suicide:

> Take her up tenderly,
> Lift her with care:
> Fashion'd so slenderly,
> Young, and so fair!

Hood's continued sufferings from poverty and tuberculosis were eased by the devotion of his wife and in his last two years by a civil list pension.

Reid, J. C., *Thomas Hood*. 1963

Hooke, Robert (1635–1703). English scientist. He studied originally for the church but turned to science and became assistant to * Boyle. He was curator of experiments to the Royal Society (1662–1703) and also (from 1665) professor of geometry at Gresham College. He stated, first as an anagram (1660) and later as a precisely expressed scientific law (1678), what is now known as Hooke's law, i.e. that the extension produced in an elastic body is proportional to the force applied to it. He worked on magnetism and on atmospheric pressure; he invented an improved form of escapement for pendulum clocks, and improved the microscope, which he used to examine a great number of minute bodies and processes. His *Micrographia* (1665) was the first extensive account, accurately and beautifully illustrated, of the microscopic world of animal and plant structure. Although he anticipated * Newton's statement of the 'law of inverse squares and universal gravity', he was unable to express his ideas in mathematical formulae.

Hooker, Joseph (1814–1879). American soldier. Having fought with distinction in the Mexican War (1846–48), he retired (1853) but offered his services to the Union government on the outbreak of the Civil War. As a divisional and corps commander he earned the title 'Fighting Joe' for the energy with which he sought out and attacked the enemy. At the beginning of 1863 he took over the command of the army of the Potomac but was superseded in June for having allowed himself to be surprised and outflanked near Chancellorsville and forced to retreat. In another exploit, known as the 'battle above the clouds', he stormed a summit at the Battle of Chattanooga (November 1863); he also took part with Sherman in the spectacular march through Georgia (1864).

Hooker, Sir Joseph Dalton (1817–1911). English botanist. He took a medical degree at Glasgow University; botany and plant geography became his life-long studies. He accompanied several expeditions, one of which is interestingly recorded in *Himalayan Journals* (1854). His most important work (written in collaboration with George Bentham) was *Genera Plantarum* (1862–83); his 'Flora' included *The Student's Flora of the British Isles* (1870) and *Flora of British India* (7 volumes, 1897). On the death of his father, **Sir William Jackson Hooker** (1785–1865), Hooker succeeded him as director of Kew Gardens.

Hoover, Herbert Clark (1874–1964). Thirty-first president of the US. He was born in Iowa and as a young man worked with great success as a mining engineer for a British firm in many parts of the world. During World War I he became well known for his organization of famine relief in Belgium and elsewhere, eventually becoming US food administrator. He entered political life as secretary for commerce under * Harding and * Coolidge. When the latter announced his retirement (1928) Hoover was the successful Republican candidate for the presidency. Unfortunately his term of office coincided with the financial collapse of 1929 and the ensuing depression and unemployment on an unparalleled scale. He believed in ultimate recovery through private enterprise, and the measures he initiated were ineffective. Despondency grew and the situation deteriorated; in 1932 he was defeated by Franklin D. * Roosevelt. After World War II, as chairman of the U.S. Commission of European Relief he was again in the forefront of relief activities.

Smith, G., *The Shattered Dream*. 1970

Hope, Anthony (Sir Anthony Hope Hawkins) (1863–1933). English author. He wrote the very successful romances *The Prisoner of Zenda* (1894) and the sequel *Rupert of Hentzau* (1898), both set in the imaginary state of Ruritania. The witty *Dolly Dialogues* (1894) was also very popular in his day. He was knighted in 1918.

Hope, Bob (Lester Townsend Hope) (1904–). American comedian, born in London. He became enormously successful (and rich) with a long series of films, many with his friend Bing * Crosby, radio and television programs and night-club performaces.

Hopkins, Sir Frederick Gowland (1861–1947). English biochemist, professor of biochemistry at Cambridge (1914–43). He proved by experiment (1912) the existence of 'accessory food factors' (now known as vitamins) and established their necessary place in a normal diet. He also helped discover the relationship between lactic acid and muscular contraction, and devised a method for the quantitative estimation of uric acid. Hopkins shared the Nobel Prize for Medicine (1929) with Eijkman, for pioneer research in 'accessory food factors'. He was president of the Royal Society (1930–35), and was awarded the O.M. (1935).

Hopkins, Gerard Manley (1844–1889). English poet. He was converted to Roman Catholicism. He spent his life teaching classics and from 1884 was professor of Greek at University College, Dublin. In publishing his poetry he accepted the guidance of his friend, Robert Bridges, with the result that only a few poems appeared in anthologies during his lifetime. Bridges published a complete edition in 1918, which gave rise to much controversy and it was only after the second edition (1930) in a different climate of literary appreciation that their quality was widely recognized. Hopkins's intense awareness of good and evil is, in itself, remarkable but even more so are the sensuous language and the rhythmic innovations with which his wide-ranging moods – exultant, contemplative, desolate – are expressed. He has had a major influence on 20th-century poetry.

Schneider, E. W., *The Dragon in the Gate*. 1968

Hopkins, Harry Lloyd (1890–1946). American administrator. A social worker, he became an adviser and one of the closest friends of Franklin Roosevelt; he was chosen to administer many of the operations of the New Deal. During World War II, as the president's special assistant he was constantly employed on confidential missions, in the course of which he won the affection and trust of Winston Churchill and other allied leaders.

Horace (Quintus Horatius Flaccus) (65–8 B.C.). Roman poet. The son of a freed-man, he studied at Athens University, served under Brutus in the Civil War and according to his own story ran away at Philippi. When Octavian (Augustus) came to power Horace came under the eye of that great patron of literature Maecenas and under his auspices became the friend of Virgil who introduced him to the emperor. Horace was given a small estate near Rome and lived in modest comfort until his death. In his *Epodes* and *Odes* (*Carmina*), he adapted to the demands of the Latin language the Greek metres of Archiloechus, Sappho, and Alcaeus. He is witty and urbane and possesses an almost uncanny genius for the right word and phrase. His subjects include love poems (graceful rather than passionate), appeals to patriotism, drinking songs and occasional and not very virulent attacks on his enemies. In the *Satires*, written in hexameters, are included episodes of everyday life (e.g. encounters and conversations in an inn) and humorously satirical poems on the vices and follies of mankind. In later life he produced a new literary form, letters (*Epistolae*) in verse. Those in the first volume are written to a variety of friends, acquaintances and servants; those in the second are more in the nature of essays, one of them, his famous *Ars Poetica*, containing much sensible advice (mainly on drama) to aspiring writers. More than most authors Horace had the gift of producing the quotable phrase, of which '*Dulce et decorum est pro patria mori*' is among the most famous.
Noyes, A., *Portrait of Horace*. 1947

Horowitz, Vladimir (1904–). Russian pianist. Resident in the United States since 1928, son-in-law of the conductor Arturo Toscanini, he first gained an international reputation in the 1920s but in later life his career was interrupted by long illness. He returned to the platform in 1965. Horowitz established his reputation as a virtuoso, romantic pianist, particularly in his interpretation of Chopin, Liszt and Rachmaninov.

Horthy de Nagybánya, Miklós (1868–1957). Hungarian admiral and regent. Commander-in-chief of the Austro-Hungarian navy in 1917, he was chosen (1920) to be regent of Hungary, acting according to the constitutional fiction of the time, as head of state on behalf of the absent king, Karl (Charles), the ex-emperor of Austria, after the expulsion of the communist faction under Béla * Kun. During World War II Hungary had joined the German alliance (1941) but in October 1944 Horthy proclaimed Hungary's withdrawal from the war and was imprisoned by the Germans. Released by the Allies he retired to Portugal.
Horthy, M., *Memoirs*. 1956

Hotspur, Harry *see* **Percy, Sir Henry**

Houdini, Harry (1874–1926). American showman of Hungarian extraction, famous for his sensational escapes from bondage. His ability to free himself from shackles, locked boxes, straitjackets, handcuffs and all kinds of sealed containers, brought him world-wide fame.
Kellock, H., *Houdini, His Life Story*. 1928

Houphouët-Boigny, Félix (1905–). African politician. First president of the Republic of the Ivory Coast, he was prominent in the Rallye Démocratique Africaine which later became the major political party in several French colonies. He was appointed (1957) a minister of state in France, the first African to reach such a position. When the Ivory Coast became independent (1959) he was first prime minister and then president (1960).

House, Edward Mandell (known as Colonel House) (1858–1938). American political adviser. Close friend and associate of President * Wilson, and on whose behalf during World War I he travelled about Europe on confidential missions, he helped to draft Wilson's 'Fourteen Points' and accompanied Wilson at the Paris Peace Conference (1919). After the president's illness later that year House's friendship with him came to an end. His *Intimate Papers* (1926–28) throw valuable light on the events of the war years.

Housman, Alfred Edward (1859–1936). English poet and scholar. A first-class in Classical Mods and a failure at 'Greats' at

Oxford was one of the many paradoxes that puzzled his contemporaries. Despite this failure he became – after a spell at the Patent Office – professor of Latin at London University (1892), and from 1911 for the rest of his life at Cambridge. The supreme paradox lay in the fact that this aloof, lonely scholar, held in awed reverence, was the author of *The Shropshire Lad* (1896), a collection of poems which for all their pessimism and nostalgia are among the most enchanting and exquisitely contrived of any in the language. Vaughan Williams with his song cycle *On Wenlock Edge* was not the only composer inspired to set them to music. Housman's *Last Poems* (1922) showed an even deeper pessimism.

His brother, **Laurence Housman** (1865–1959), was a writer and critic of distinction for many years before he achieved fame when his series of plays *Victoria Regina* (1935) were later welded into a single play and professionally performed. His earlier series *Little Plays of St Francis* (1922) originated the method of treatment.

Housman, L., *My Brother: A. E. Housman*. Repr. 1969

Houston, Samuel (1793–1863). American frontiersman and statesman. Born in Virginia, he lived much of his youth among the Cherokee Indians. After a popular political career in Tennessee he resigned governorship on the death of his wife and later moved to Texas, where, when it declared its independence of Mexico, he became commander-in-chief of the Texan forces. After the surrender of the Alamo (1836) to the Mexicans, Houston defeated them decisively at San Jacinto, and was elected first president of the new republic of Texas. On the admission of Texas to the Union (1845) Houston represented it in the U.S. Senate, and became governor of Texas in 1859. At the outbreak of the Civil War Houston, in defiance of general opinion, tried to prevent Texas from joining the Confederacy. His failure caused his withdrawal into private life.

Howard, Catherine *see* **Catherine Howard**

Howard of Effingham, Charles Howard, 2nd Baron (later 1st Earl of Nottingham) (1536–1624). English courtier and sailor. As lord high admiral of England (1585–1618) he commanded the English fleet which defeated the Spanish Armada (1588). With * Essex, whose rebellion (1601) he later put down, he led an expedition (1596) to destroy shipping at Cadiz. For this he received his earldom.

Howe, Julia Ward (née Ward) (1819–1910). American author and social reformer. She compaigned for the abolition of slavery, and wrote (1862) *The Battle Hymn of the Republic*. Later she was one of the leaders of the women's suffrage movement and first woman member of the American Academy of Arts and Sciences.

Howe, Richard Howe, 1st Earl (known as 'Black Dick') (1726–1799). English sailor. When only 20 he drove off two French ships coming to reinforce Prince Charles Edward in the Jacobite rebellion (1745); he gained successes in the Seven Years War, and in the American War of Independence he repelled the French fleet off Rhode Island. Meanwhile he had been a lord of the Admiralty (1763) and treasurer to the navy (1765). He was first lord of the Admiralty (1783–88), commanded the Channel fleet when the French Revolutionary war broke out (1793), and in 1794 off Ushant gained the greatest victory of his career (known as the Glorious First of June), in which seven enemy ships were destroyed and ten more dismasted. In 1797 he brought back to duty the mutineers at Spithead. Howe had inherited an Irish peerage (1758), received a U.K. viscounty (1782) and an earldom (1788).

His younger brother, **William Howe** (1729–1814), who succeeded him in the Irish viscounty, was one of the most successful British generals in the War of American Independence. Under Gage, whom he succeeded, he captured Bunker's Hill, and in the following year took New York and Washington, but failed to follow up his successes to decisive victory.

Howe, Sir (Richard Edward) Geoffrey (1926–). English politician. A barrister, he was a Conservative MP (1964–66 and 1970–), a junior minister under Edward * Heath (1970–74) and Margaret * Thatcher's Chancellor of the Exchequer (1979–83), given the task of implementing her Friedmanite 'free market' policies and Foreign Secretary (1983–).

Howel (known as 'the Good') (died 950). Welsh king. Through inheritance and marriage his rule gradually extended over south

Wales and from 943, when his cousin Idwal died, over north Wales as well. He is remembered as a law-maker; his code, probably quite a simple and uncomplicated affair, was expanded later until it developed into the full legal system of medieval Wales known as the Law of Howel the Good.

Hoxha, Enver (1908–). Albanian politician. He was a founder member of the Albanian Communist Party, and led the resistance movement against the Italians in World War II. He became prime minister when Albania was proclaimed a republic (1946) and also filled the posts of minister of foreign affairs and commander-in-chief. On the death of Stalin his close ties with the U.S.S.R. were replaced by adherence to the Peking line.
Halliday, J. (ed.), *The Artful Albanian: The Memoirs of Enver Hoxha*. 1985

Hoyle, Sir Fred (1915–). English mathematician, astronomer and science-fiction writer. Known as the proponent of the 'steady-state' theory of the universe, this theory held that matter is being created at a rate fast enough to keep an expanding universe at a constant mean density. He published this theory in 1948 when a mathematics lecturer at Cambridge. He went to the Mount Wilson and Palomar Observatories near Pasadena, California, in 1956, and in 1966 he returned to Cambridge as director of the Institute of Theoretical Astronomy.
Hoyle, F., *Of Men and Galaxies*. 1966

Hrdlicka, Aleš (1869–1943). American anthropologist, born in Bohemia. On appointment to the U.S. National Museum he organized (1903) a department of physical anthropology, of which he was curator (1910–42). He pursued his anthropological studies throughout the world and is especially known for his study of the route of migration of the American Indian.

Hua Gofeng (Hua Kuo-Feng) (1920–). Chinese communist politician, born in Sheni province. He joined the Communist Party of China in 1935 and served as an army officer for ten years. He acted as party secretary in Hsiang-T'an county (1953–58), promoting projects in Shaoshan, * Mao Zedong's birthplace. He became vice governor of Hunan province (1958–67), a member of the Central Committee of the Communist Party (1969), secretary of the Party in Hunan province (1970–71), administrator of the State Council Secretariat (1971–73), and a Politburo member (1973). Mao chose him as deputy premier and minister of public security (1975–76), and deputy chairman of the Party (April–October 1976) and wrote 'with you in charge I am at ease'. When * Zhou Enlai died Hua became acting premier (February–April 1976) and premier from April 1976. After Mao's death, Hua was elected chairman of the Communist Party (October 1976). With the trial of the 'Gang of Four' the Party distanced itself from Mao's legacy and Hua lost power to the pragmatic followers of Zhou, notably * Deng Xiaoping. Hua resigned as chairman on 30 June 1981 and was succeeded by * Hu Yaobang.

Hubble, Edwin Powell (1889–1953). American astronomer. He worked from 1919 at the Mount Wilson Observatory and became its director. Using its great 100-inch telescope he discovered (1923) that the great nebula in Andromeda contained Cepheid variable stars; he was thus able to prove that it was about 800,000 light-years from the earth, well outside our own galaxy, the Milky Way, and itself a galaxy of comparable size. He was soon able to show that there are millions of other galaxies, distributed throughout space. He helped to propound the theory of the expanding universe, and made (1929) the discovery (now known as Hubble's Law) that the velocities of receding galaxies are directly proportional to their distance from the solar system.

Huc, Evariste Régis (1813–1860). French missionary and explorer. In 1844 he set out on a mission which took him through nearly every province in China before, after many hardships, he reached Tibet. There he spent some time in a monastery where the lamas taught him the Tibetan language; he reached Lhasa but was quickly expelled.

Huddleston, Trevor (1913–). English missionary and bishop of the Anglican Church. He was ordained in 1937 and joined the Community of the Resurrection. In 1943 he went to South Africa. In 1956 he returned to the Community at Mirfield, Yorkshire, whence he was appointed Bishop of Masasi, Tanzania, in 1960. In 1956 he wrote *Naught for Your Comfort*, his beliefs on faith and apartheid.

Hudson, Henry (d. 1611). English navigator who tried to discover a route through the Arctic from Europe to Asia – the 'North West Passage'. After sailing round the north coast of Norway and exploring the Svalbard archipelago, he embarked on his voyage to North America in 1609. He discovered the bay, river and strait named after him, but failed to find a passage to the Pacific. He was deserted by his crew on a subsequent expedition and set adrift in Hudson Bay.

Hudson, William Henry (1841–1922). Writer, born in Argentina of American parents. He went to England in 1869. His books reflect his devotion to birds and animals. Rima, the bird-girl of his novel *Green Mansions* (1904), was the subject of Epstein's controversial sculpture in the bird sanctuary in Hyde Park, London. Tomalin, R., *W. H. Hudson*. 1954

Hueffer, Ford Madox *see* **Ford, Ford Madox**

Huerta, Victoriano de la (1856–1916). Mexican soldier and politician. He served under Díaz, and was commander-in-chief under * Madero, whom in 1913 he induced to resign to facilitate his murder. Huerta's reactionary reign as president (1913–14) was ended by U.S. intervention. He fled to Europe and subsequently settled in the U.S.A., where he was arrested for plotting against Mexico, and died in prison.

Huggins, Sir Godfrey Martin *see* **Malvern, 1st Viscount**

Huggins, Sir William (1824–1910). English astronomer. A pioneer of stellar spectroscopy, from a private observatory in Tulse Hill, London, he began the researches into the spectra of the stars and nebulae which marked the beginnings of astrophysics. With the stellar spectroscope which he and Millar invented (1856), he proved that some nebulae are composed of glowing gas out of which new star systems are being born. Huggins also demonstrated that the sun and the stars are similar in composition, and he used the Doppler effect to determine the velocity of some of the stars relative to earth. He was president of the Royal Society (1900–05).

Hughes, Charles Evans (1862–1948). US politician and jurist. Educated at Brown and Cornell Universities, he gained public attention as a vigorous investigator of corruption of public utilities in New York, defeated W. F. * Hearst to become governor of New York State 1907–10 until * Taft appointed him a justice of the US Supreme Court 1910–16. He resigned from the court (1916) to run as Republican candidate for president, losing narrowly to Woodrow * Wilson. He served under * Harding and * Coolidge as secretary of state 1921–25. He supported US entry to the League of Nations and the World Court, and isolationist opponents called him 'Wilson with whiskers'. He was chief justice of the United States 1930–41.

Hughes, David Edward (1831–1900). English physicist. He went to America as a child, taught music and physics there for some years, and returned to London (1867), where he contributued to the development of telecommunications; he introduced a printing telegraph instrument (patented 1855) a foreunner of the Telex machine. He was elected F.R.S. (1880); the Hughes Medal for physical discoveries (especially in electricity and magnetism) recalls his name.

Hughes, Howard (Robard) (1905–1976). American businessman, aviator and film producer. In 1923 he took over his father's company, Hughes Tool Company, in Houston, Texas. He went to Hollywood in 1926 and produced *Hell's Angels* (1930) and *Scarface* (1932). The profits from his Hughes Aircraft Company helped him to establish the Howard Hughes Medical Institute; he flew his own aircraft and broke three speed records. He held a controlling interest in T.W.A. until 1966, when he sold his shares for US$500,000,000. In 1950 he retreated into increasingly pathological seclusion which provoked international curiosity.

Hughes, Thomas (1822–1896). English author. He is famous for the novel *Tom Brown's Schooldays* (1857), which was prompted by memories of his own boyhood under Thomas * Arnold of Rugby School.

Hughes, William Morris (1862–1952). Australian politician. He emigrated to Australia (1884) and after a miscellany of jobs founded the Waterside Workers' Federation in Sydney (1893). Elected to the New South Wales Parliament in 1894, he had 58 continuous years as an M.P., transferring to the

Commonwealth Parliament (1901–52). A remarkable and quick-witted orator he led the Labor party when he became prime minister of Australia (1915); he left the party in 1917 over the issue of conscription for overseas service and continued in office as head of a Nationalist government. At the Paris Peace Conference (1919) he secured an Australian mandate for part of New Guinea and other German colonies in the Pacific. He resigned after the break-up of his coalition government (1923), but continued political activity. He was minister for external affairs 1937–39, attorney-general 1939–41 and leader of the United Australia Party 1941–43.

Hugo, Victor Marie (1802–1885). French writer. His father was an officer in Napoleon's army and his childhood was a series of moves from one military station to another in Italy, Spain and France. He won prizes for poetry from the age of 17, married at 20, published his first novel at 17 and in 1827 heralded with his play *Cromwell* the rise of Romantic drama. The long run of the tragedy *Hernani* (1830), which withstood the boos, hisses and even rioting of the classicists among its audiences, assured the victory of the Romantic movement and Hugo's own position. Among later plays were *Le Roi s'amuse* (1832), the basis of Verdi's *Rigoletto; Lucrèce Borgia* (1833) – in which a part was played by Juliette Drouet, his mistress for nearly fifty years, though he remained a devoted husband; and *Ruy Blas* (1838). Meanwhile his *Les Orientales* (1829), mainly on Grecian and Moorish themes, and *Les Feuilles d'Automne* (1931) confirmed his reputation as a great lyric poet. Also in 1831 appeared his great novel *Notre-Dame de Paris*, the story set in medieval times, of the hopeless love of the hunchbacked bell-ringer, Quasimodo, for Esmeralda.

Politics, in which he was a somewhat unpredictable liberal, began to play an increasing part in his life. King Louis-Philippe made him a peer, but during the dictatorship and empire of Napoleon III, whom Hugo attacked in verse and prose, he lived in exile in Brussels, Jersey, and from 1855 at Hauteville House, Guernsey, still preserved much as he left it. Much of his writing during exile was philosophic and historical (the first part of *La Légende des Siècles* was published in 1859), but it includes his greatest novel *Les Misérables* (1862), the story of the criminal Jean Valjean, and *Les Travailleurs de la mer* (1866), a wonderful evocation of a Guernsey fisherman's life. Hugo returned to France after the fall of Napoleon and was present at the siege of Paris; he sat in the Constituent Assembly (1870–71) and became a senator in 1874. Now a national institution, he continued to write novels – e.g. *Quatre-vingt-treize* (1874), concerned with the Revolutionary year of 1793 – and a verse drama, *Torquemada* (1882). Vast crowds attended his funeral at the Panthéon. Hugo wrote too much for too long and his work is, therefore, uneven; moreover Romanticism lost its vogue and he shared loss of favour with e.g. Sir Walter Scott. But few writers have produced so much that is first-rate, in so many different fields, and he does not deserve André Gide's taunt that 'France's greatest poet was Victor Hugo, alas'.

Hulagu Khan (1217–1265). Mongol ruler, grandson of Genghis Khan. He led a successful campaign against the Persians who were in revolt, captured Baghdad and advanced beyond Damascus until he was checked by the Mamelukes. He then retreated, and, having adopted Islam, founded the Il-Khan dynasty which lasted till 1335.

Hull, Cordell (1871–1955). American politician, born in Tennessee. A Congressman 1907–21 and 1923–31, and Senator 1931–33, he campaigned for an income tax and tariff reform. He was President Franklin Roosevelt's secretary of state (1933–44), and was thus the main instrument of American policy in the vital years preceding and during World War II. Among his achievements were the creation of a new friendly relationship between the USA and the South American states, and the promotion of more liberal trade and tariff policies. He was awarded the Nobel Peace Prize (1945).

Hull, C., *The Memoirs of Cordell Hull*. 1948

Humbert I and II (Kings of Italy) *see* **Umberto I and II**

Humboldt, Baron (Friedrich Heinrich) Alexander von (1769–1859). German naturalist and explorer, son of the chamberlain to the king of Prussia. While still a student at the universities of Göttingen, Frankfurt-on-Oder and Freiburg, and in the years following, he did field work locally on geology, mineralogy and botany, and made laboratory studies of the nervous systems of animals. In 1799 he sailed with his friend, A. Bonpland, on a five-year scientific expedition to Mexico, Cuba and the northern part of South America, especially regions in and adjacent to the Amazon and Orinoco valleys. The sorting, collating and describing of the vast amount of data and materials gathered on the journeys occupied most of the ensuing twenty years and resulted in a vast work of thirty volumes (1807–17) (*Voyage de Humboldt et Bonpland*) containing not only scientific sections on physical geography, geology, astronomical observations etc., but also a historical survey and abundant maps. At the request of Tsar Nicholas I, he made, with two friends, a similar expedition (1829) to the Urals and a large part of Asiatic Russia (where he located gold, platinum and diamonds); this was described in *Asia Central* (3 volumes, 1843). His famous work *Cosmos* (5 volumes, 1845–62) is a masterly attempt to give a comprehensive description of the physical universe as it was then known. Some of his own most valuable scientific work was in the fields of meteorology, climatology and earth magnetism.

His elder brother, **Baron** (Karl) **Wilhelm von Humboldt** (1767–1835), reformed the secondary and higher education of Prussia (1806) and later carried out many diplomatic missions before he retired (1818) in disgust at his country's reactionary policy and turned to philology. He made a complete study of the Basque language and identified the Malayo-Polynesian group. He was particularly interested in the philosophy of language on the grounds that it expresses the mind and culture of those that use it.

Kellner, K., *Alexander von Humboldt*. 1963

Hume, David (1711–1776). Scottish philosopher and historian, often regarded as the greatest of British empiricists. Born in Edinburgh, he attended the university there and began preparing his greatest work, *A Treatise of Human Nature*, before he was 20. Because of his notorious atheism his applications for the professorships of philosophy at Edinburgh and Glasgow were unsuccessful, and instead he served the insane Marquess of Annandale as tutor and went on military and diplomatic missions as secretary to General St Clair. In 1752 he became keeper of the Advocates' Library in Edinburgh, and was secretary to the British embassy in Paris (1763–65), where he moved in a literary circle and made a friendship with Rousseau which ended with the almost inevitable quarrel. In his own time he was much better known as a historian than as a philosopher and his *History of Great Britain* (1754–61) long remained a standard work; but it is by his earlier philosophical works that his name is now chiefly remembered. His *Treatise* (1739–40) sets out to establish empirically a science of the human faculties. He describes the mind as consisting of impressions and ideas – by 'impressions' he means first of all sense-impressions. There are simple ideas, which are reflections of impressions, and complex ideas, which are got by combining simple ideas. All thought is thus based on experience and we have no innate ideas. Reasoning is either the setting-out of necessary relations between ideas, as in the assertion of mathematical truths, or else based on empirical fact. There is no possibility of logically necessary reasoning about claims of fact; e.g. one cannot 'demonstrate' the existence of God. Reasoning about facts involves assertions of cause and effect. With respect to causation, Hume argued that we regard something as being the cause or effect of something else because the two always go together, not because there is such a thing as a necessary connexion between them in the world. In ethics he is important for his enunciation of the principle that one cannot deduce a moral judgement from any statement of fact, since the deduction of any deductive inference must be implicit in its premise. Moral judgements, in fact, are expressions of their maker's approval or disapproval. Hume's influence was considerable, notably on utilitarians, phenomenalists, and on Kant, who said he had been awakened by Hume from his dogmatic slumbers. Hume's other philosophical works include the *Enquiry Concerning Human Understanding* (a simplified version of the *Treatise*, published 1748), *The Enquiry Concerning the Principles of Morals* (1751), and *Dialogues Concerning Natural Religion* (1779).

Basson, A. H., *David Hume*. 1958

Humphrey, Hubert Horatio (1911–1978). American politician, born in South Dakota. As senator for Minnesota (1944–64 and 1971–78) he was one of the most outspoken liberals in the Democratic party. After being rejected for nomination as presidential candidate in 1960, he was Johnson's vice-president (1965–69) and Democratic presidential candidate 1968.

Solberg, C., *Hubert Humphrey, A Biography*. 1985

Hung Hsiu-ch'uän (1812–1864). Chinese leader of the Taiping rebellion, born near Canton. With messianic claims and a social and political programme not unlike communism, he claimed to be ruler of 'the great peaceful heavenly empire'. Taipings, as his followers came to be called, soon numbered tens of thousands; they marched from Kweichow in the south to the Yangtze, and by 1853 had seized Nanking, where a massacre took place which showed the underlying savagery of the leader. For eleven years Hung Hsiu-ch'uän in Nanking exercised an increasingly unpredictable despotism over some 20,000,000 people. At last in their helplessness the Chinese government enlisted the help of a British officer, Charles * Gordon, who trained 'the ever victorious army', the main factor in bringing about the defeat of the Taipings and the suicide of their leader.

Hunt, (James Henry) Leigh (1784–1859). English poet, critic and essayist. He edited the *Examiner*, a liberal journal (1808–21): here and in several other journals he came to edit he 'discovered', by publication or praise, Shelley, Keats, Tennyson, Browning, Dickens (who caricatured him in *Bleak House* as Harold Skimpole) and others. In 1812 he was sentenced to two years' jail and a fine for libelling the Prince Regent. He joined the Shelleys and Byron in Italy (1822) to edit a magazine *The Liberal* but the death of both poets wrecked the enterprise and he returned. Although some of his poems, e.g. *The Story of Rimini* (about Paolo and Francesca) and *Abou Ben Adhem* are still read, his importance was as a focus of literary life; his essays and his *Autobiography* (1850) provide valuable sketches of his friends, his opinions, and of events in his life.
Blainey, A., *Immortal Boy: A Portrait of Leigh Hunt*. 1985

Hunt, (Henry Cecil) John, Baron Hunt (1910–). British soldier and mountaineer. Much of his service was in India and he had considerable Himalayan experience before he led the Everest expedition (1953), two members of which * Hillary and the Sherpa Tensing were the first to reach the summit. He wrote *The Ascent of Everest* (1954). For his part in the achievement Hunt was knighted. In 1966 he was created a life peer.

Hunt, William Holman (1827–1910). English painter, one of the founders of the pre-Raphaelite movement in nineteenth-century art. He described the aims of the movement as: expressing serious ideas; direct study from nature; reconstruction of events according to realistic probability and not according to principles of design. His best-known pictures are religious – *The Scapegoat* and *The Light of the World*. The harshness and the sometimes crude colouring of his work are equalled by his intensity of purpose.
Hunt, W. H., *Pre-Raphaelitism and the Pre-Raphaelite Brotherhood*. 1905

Hunter, John (1728–1793). Scottish anatomist, physiologist and surgeon. After working as a cabinet-maker in Glasgow he came to London to assist dissecting at the school of anatomy directed by his elder brother William * Hunter. He also studied surgery and became surgeon-pupil (1754) and surgeon (1768) at St George's Hospital. Later (1776) he became surgeon-extraordinary to George III. He made numerous discoveries about human anatomy and has been recognized as the founder of scientific surgery. He was the first to apply methods of pressure (e.g. the ligature) to the main trunk blood arteries, and to succeed in grafting animal tissues. Meanwhile he was busy in biological and physiological research, for which he made extensive collections of specimens illustrating the living processes of plant and animal life. His museum, his finest memorial, was bought by the government (1799) and subsequently administered by the Royal College of Surgeons; it contained 13,600 preparations at the time of his death. His biological studies included work in hibernation, the habits of bees, silkworms etc., on the electric organs of fish, and egg incubation. His treatise on human teeth (1771–78) gave dentistry a scientific foundation.

Hunter, William (1718–1783). Scottish physician, elder brother of John * Hunter. Educated at Glasgow University, he studied medicine under William Cullen and the first Alexander Monro before moving to London where he soon acquired a high reputation as surgeon and lecturer on anatomy, later specializing in obstetrics.

Hunyadi, János (*c.* 1387–1456). Hungarian soldier, famed as a champion of Christendom against the Turks. In a series of brilliant campaigns he succeeded in clearing the Turks from most of the Balkans, but suffered a severe defeat at Varna (1444) when the Hungarian king was killed. As regent for the king's successor, Ladislas, Hunyadi continued to keep the Turks at bay, and was with the army when he died of the plague. His younger son was Matthias * Corvinus.

Hus, Jan (*c.* 1369–1415). Bohemian religious reformer, born in Husinec. He became a lecturer in philosophy at Prague University 1398–1401, dean of philosophy 1401–02 and rector 1402–03 and 1409–12. He entered the Catholic priesthood in 1400. Deeply influenced by the writings of John Wycliffe, he denounced the corruption of the papacy. His preaching was banned but he continued to preach, even after his excommunication in 1410. Despite his popularity in Prague, Hus had to leave the city and in virtual retirement he wrote *On the Church* (1413). In 1415 Hus was summoned to the Council of Constance under a promise of safe conduct from the Emperor Sigismund. He was arrested at the Council and charged with heresy because the Emperor insisted that heretics could not be given the benefit of an 'agreement of honour'. He refused to recant all his views and was burnt at the stake.

Huskisson, William (1770–1830). British politician. Converted from radicalism by observing the French Revolution at first-hand, he entered parliament (1796) and served under Pitt and in several later ministries. Canning thought him the best business man of his time, but as a convinced free-trader he was often in difficulties with his colleagues. It was only after his death that his admirer Peel, by repealing the Corn Laws, carried out his policies. He was accidentally killed at the opening of the Liverpool and Manchester Railway.

Hussein (1856–1931). King of the Hejaz (1916–24). As grand sherif of Mecca (1908–16) he supported the Arab uprising against the Turks, undertaken with British help (* Lawrence, T. E.) during World War I. He was rewarded by being made first king of the Hejaz but was expelled by the rival Arabian leader * Ibn Sa'ud and took refuge in Cyprus. His sons became King * Abdullah of Jordan and * Faisal I of Iraq.

Hussein (1935–). King of Jordan (from 1952). Great-grandson of King Hussein of the Hejaz, he succeeded his father, Talil, who was debarred by ill health, to the Jordan throne. He was educated in England, and as king showed considerable dexterity in maintaining himself in face of Egyptian intrigues, frontier incidents on his Israeli borders, and his own Arab extremists.
Snow, P., *Hussein: A Biography*. 1972

Husserl, Edmund Gustav Albrecht (1859–1938). German philosopher, born in Moravia, then part of the Austro-Hungarian empire. He studied at Leipzig, Berlin and Vienna; after coming under the influence of Franz Brentano at Vienna University, he made philosophy his career. He lectured at Halle from 1887 and from 1900 was professor at Göttingen and Freiburg. The system set out in his works he called phenomenology. Refuting the philosophical claims of logicians and natural scientists, he maintained that the approach should be made by analysing the experience of phenomena by self. This process, which Husserl called a 'phenomenological reduction', leads to the revelation of a 'transcendental self', the experiences of which it is the task of the researcher in this field to explore. His ideas led to 'Gestalt' psychology.

Hutcheson, Francis (1694–1747). Scottish philosopher, born in Ulster. He held a chair of philosophy at Glasgow from 1727, was outstanding as a moral philosopher and wrote on ideas of beauty and virtue or the nature and conduct of the passions. His most important work, *A System of Moral Philosophy*, was published posthumously (1755). Hutcheson denied that beneficence is motivated by selfishness and argued that ethical distinctions result from a 'moral sense'; the criterion is the tendency to promote the good of the greatest number – an anticipation of utilitarianism.

Hutten, Ulrich von (1488–1523). German poet and reformer. A man of puny stature but impetuous pride, he gave up monastic life, studied in Germany and Italy and then found employment at the court of the archbishop of Mainz. The anonymous and satirical *Letters of Obscure Men*, of which he was part-author, poured ridicule in dog-Latin on the doctrines, morals, follies, speech etc. of the monks and ecclesiastics of the time, and provided much of the intellectual tinder that Luther and others were to set aflame. Meanwhile he had been made (1517) Poet Laureate by the emperor Maximilian. He supported Luther at first from national sentiment against papal claims, but later became one of the most formidable religious propagandists. Forced to leave the archbishop's service he led a dangerous existence until with the help of * Zwingli he found an island refuge in Lake Zurich.

Hutton, James (1726–1797). Scottish geologist. After studying medicine at Edinburgh, Paris and Leyden he returned to Scotland to devote himself to agriculture, chemistry, and (from 1768 when he moved to Edinburgh) to geology. In his *Theory of the Earth* (1795) Hutton expounded his view that the continuing geological processes of erosion by rivers and seas result in the sedimentary deposit accumulating under great pressure on the sea bed and subsequently splitting into cracks and fissures, into which the flowing of molten mineral matter would produce granite and other igneous rocks in the earth's crust. Rain, he explained, was caused by condensation due to the mingling of two air strata of different temperatures.

Huxley, Aldous Leonard (1894–1963). English novelist and essayist, grandson of T. H. * Huxley. Defective vision – eventually much helped by the system he described in *The Art of Seeing* (1943) – prevented him from studying biology. He contributed essays and criticisms to several London journals before attracting attention with a series of satirical novels, *Crome Yellow* (1921), *Antic Hay* (1923), *Those Barren Leaves* (1925) and *Point Counter Point* (1928). Huxley became the mouthpiece of the disillusioned generation that followed World War I. In *Brave New World* (1932) he mockingly described a 'Utopia' in which human beings allowed themselves to be directed by an elite of planners who were able to satisfy emotional cravings by drugs. He returned to the theme in *Brave New World Revisited* (1958), and less pessimistically in *Island* (1962). Apart from *Grey Eminence* (1941), a brilliant biography of Richelieu's *alter ego*, and *Ape and Essence* (1949), a satirical appraisal of the results of atomic war, most of his later work was philosophic or mystical. He lived in Italy (1923–30), France (1930–38) and California (from 1938).

Huxley, J. (ed.), *Aldous Huxley 1894–1963*. 1965

Huxley, Sir Andrew Fielding (1917–). British physiologist. A half-brother of Aldous and Julian Huxley, he studied at Cambridge and was professor of physiology at London 1960–83. He shared the 1963 Nobel Prize for Medicine with J. C. * Eccles and A. L. * Hodgkin for their work on the transmission mechanism of nerve impulses. He was president of the Royal Society 1980-85, and received the OM in 1983.

Huxley, Sir Julian (1887–1975). English biologist, grandson of T. H. * Huxley. He was professor of zoology at King's College, London (1925–27), professor of physiology at the Royal Institution (1927–30), secretary of the Royal Zoological Society (1935–42), and first director-general of UNESCO (1946–48). His very numerous and important books on biological and sociological topics include *Scientific Research and Social Needs* (1934), *Essays of a Humanist* (1963) and *Evolution, the Modern Synthesis* (1942). He also devoted much energy to the conservation of wild life and the creation of nature reserves.

Huxley, Thomas Henry (1825–1895). English biologist. Having studied medicine, he sailed (1846) as assistant surgeon with H.M.S. *Rattlesnake* which had been commissioned to chart areas off the Australian Great Barrier Reef. He took the opportunity to collect, examine and compare some of the myriad marine organisms in those seas, from which he derived and published evidence which later lent support to * Darwin's evolutionary theory. Huxley's work was immediately appreciated and he was elected F.R.S. in 1850, the year of his return; in 1854 he became lecturer in natural history at the Royal School of Mines. Meanwhile he continued his studies of the invertebrates and when Darwin published *Origin of Species* (1859) Huxley was one of his warmest supporters; faced with the criticism that the human brain had no counterpart in the animal kingdom he used the recent discovery of Neanderthal Man and his own anthropological studies to make a reply which forms the substance of his book of essays *Man's Place in Nature* (1863). Huxley is said to have introduced the word 'agnostic' to define his own philosophical viewpoint, which is set out in his *Science and Morals* (1886). He retained his position at the School of Mines until his health gave way (1885); meanwhile he had held other academic or honorary appointments, e.g. Fullerian professor at the Royal Institution (1863–67), secretary (1871–80), and president (1880–85) of the Royal Society. His great interest in education was recognized by his seat on the first London School Board (1870–72); the first biological laboratory in Britain was opened through his inspiration, and his *Science and Education* (1899) contains many of his papers on this theme. Many of his public lectures, among the most popular of the period, appeared in *Lay Sermons, Addresses and Reviews* (1870). In moulding opinion in the great controversies of his own and succeeding generations on the relationship of religion and science and the place of science in a general education, Huxley's role was of outstanding importance.

Bibby, C., *Scientist Extraordinary: T. H. Huxley*. 1972

Hu Yaobang (1915–). Chinese Communist politician. A veteran of the Long March, close associate of * Deng Xiaoping, he was twice purged in the Cultural Revolution. He became general secretary of the CCP 1980–81 and succeeded * Hua Guofeng as party chairman 1981–

Huygens, Christiaan (1629–1695). Dutch astronomer-physicist, who lived for long periods in England and France. He developed the art of grinding lenses, and designed an eyepiece which greatly reduced spherical aberration. With a powerful telescope of his own making he investigated and explained the 'rings' of Saturn. He built (1656) the first clock to be regulated by a compound pendulum, and also applied the balance wheel to the same purpose. In 1673 he published *Horologium Oscillatorium*, his great work on pendulum clocks, and in 1690 his *Traité de la Lumière*, a partially satisfactory wave theory of light.

Huysmans, Joris Karl (1848–1907). French writer, of Dutch descent. His first novels, e.g. *Marthe* (1876), were in the naturalistic and often sordid pattern set by Emile * Zola. His best known novel *A Rebours* (1884), however, in revolt from this style, tells of a sensualist's search for new experience through perverse and deliberate derangement of the senses. The writing of *Là-bas* (1891), a life of the Satanist Gilles de Rais, had the paradoxical effect of converting him to Catholicism, *En Route* (1895) describing the journey which took him to this goal.

Hyde, Douglas (1890–1949). Irish writer and philologist. Mainly concerned with the survival of the Gaelic language and its use in literature, he founded (1893) the Gaelic League. As a non-party man he was, by unanimous election, first president (1938–45) of Eire under the 1937 constitution.

Daly, D., *The Young Douglas Hyde*. 1974

Hyde, Edward and Anne *see* **Clarendon, 1st Earl of**

Hyder, Ali *see* **Haidar Ali**

I

Ibáñez, Vicente Blasco *see* **Blasco Ibáñez, Vicente**

Ibn Battutah (1304–?1369). Arab explorer, born in Tangier. He trained as a judge. From 1325 he travelled extensively in North Africa, Syria, Arabia, Mesopotamia and Persia, going to India (after 1332) by crossing the Black Sea and journeying through Central Asia. In Delhi he was employed by the Sultan Muhammad ibn Tuqhluq, who sent him as an envoy to China in 1342; he reached the Chinese imperial court only after many adventures in S.E. Asia. After his return to Morocco in 1349 he visited Granada and western Sudan. In 1353–54 he dictated an account of his travels and his experience of different rulers and societies.
Ibn Battuta, *Travels in Asia and Africa 1325–1354*. 1983

Ibn-Khaldun (1332–1406). Arab historian. He was born at Tunis and served as a diplomat and administrator in N. Africa, Spain and Egypt. After his pilgrimage to Mecca (1382–87) he spent the rest of his life in Cairo. His history of Islam has a valuable account of the Berbers, prefaced by a treatise on the philosophy of history, of which he was one of the earliest exponents.
Muhsin Mahdi, *Ibn-Khaldun's Philosophy of History*. 1957

Ibn Sa'ud, Abdul 'Aziz (*c*. 1880–1953). King of Saudi Arabia (from 1932). He spent his early years in exile but in 1902 seized Riad, home of the Sa'ud family, and made it the base for a revival of the Wahabis, a puritanical Mohammedan sect dating from the 18th century. During World War I he declined to join the Arab revolt organized by T. E. * Lawrence but used the opportunity to throw off Turkish suzerainty and greatly expanded his territories. Recognized from 1921 as the sultan of Nejd, he came into conflict with * Hussein, king of Hejaz, whom he dethroned and whose kingdom he annexed (1926), thus acquiring Mecca, with the prestige and wealth attached to its possession; in 1932 he assumed the title king of Saudi Arabia. The discovery of oil (1933) and the lucrative concession to the Americans provided him with great wealth, which he used personally or by distributing to the tribal sheikhs – mainly his relatives. Ibn Sa'ud was a great Arab warrior of the traditional type, who proved his potency by the number of his wives and children as much as by his physical prowess in war; but, shrewd and often harsh as he was, and although he avoided any close international alignment, he was loyal to principles and obligations.
Howarth, D. A., *The Desert King*. 1964

Ibrahim Pasha (1789–1848). Egyptian soldier. Son or stepson of * Mehemet Ali, the Turkish viceroy of Egypt, as a Turkish general Ibrahim achieved military success against the Wahabis (* Ibn Sa'ud) in Arabia (1818) and the Greek insurgents (1824) during the Greek War of Independence. After his father broke away from the Ottoman sultan he was made governor of Syria, where he became involved in hostilities against the Turks. He succeeded in conquering much of Asia Minor but British and Austrian intervention forced him to withdraw (1841). In the last year of his life, when his father became insane, he was regent in Egypt.

Ibsen, Henrik (Johan) (1828–1906). Norwegian dramatist. He was born in Skien;

his father, ruined by speculation, apprenticed him to an apothecary. His first play was rejected but he became a stage manager at Bergen and later was artistic director of the Norwegian Theatre in Christiania (Oslo). During this time he was writing plays, at first in the conventional romantic mould and later inspired by the old sagas. The historical drama *The Pretenders* (1864) already showed much psychological insight. Angered that Sweden and his own Norway should leave the Danes to fight alone against Prussia (1864), he lived mainly in Italy and Germany for many years. The first fruits of his disillusion, the lyrical dramas *Brand* (1867) and *Peer Gynt* (1867), were both intended to display the timidity and irresolution of which he accused his countrymen. He returned to a historical subject with *The Emperor and the Galilean* (1873) about the struggle of Christianity with paganism under Julian the Apostate; and then at last, when he was already middle-aged, came the series of prose dramas that revolutionized the European theatre. By relating the character of individuals to their social environment, by relying for drama on psychological development rather than external events, by substituting realism for romanticism, and by revealing the passions, the deprivations and the rebellions of women, he made the theatre a reflection of the contemporary world outside. Without Ibsen, Shaw, Hauptmann, Brieux and many others could hardly have written as they did. The plays that brought about this remarkable change were *Pillars of the Community* (*The Pillars of Society*) (1874), *A Doll's House* (1879), *Ghosts* (1881), which dealt frankly with hereditary disease, *A Public Enemy* (*An Enemy of the People*) (1882), *The Wild Duck* (1884), *Rosmersholm* (1886), *The Lady from the Sea* (1888), *Hedda Gabler* (1890), *The Master Builder* (1892), perhaps marking the highest point of his technique, *Little Eyolf* (1894), *John Gabriel Borkman* (1896) and *When We Dead Awaken* (1900).
Koht, H., *Life of Ibsen*. 1971; McFarlane, J., ed., *Henrik Ibsen: Penguin Critical Anthology*. 1970; Meyer, M., *Henrik Ibsen*. 1967–71

Idris I (Mohammed Idris of Senussi) 1890–1983). King of Libya 1951–1969. As chief of the Senussi tribesmen he led resistance to the Italians, who after defeating Turkey (1911–1912) occupied Tripolitania and Cyrenaica. Italy's defeat in World War II provided an opportunity for Idris, exiled in Egypt, to return. From 1945 he was emir of Cyrenaica and in 1951, when the United Nations established the new kingdom of Libya, Idris was chosen as first king. He was deposed by a military *coup d'état* in September 1969.

Ieyasu Tokugawa (1542–1616). Japanese soldier and statesman. He assisted Nobunaga (died 1582) and * Hideyoshi in overcoming the feudal nobility, and after the latter's death (1598) succeeded in establishing in his own Tokugawa family a hereditary *Shogunate* (nominally subject to the emperor), which lasted until 1867. At first he tolerated the Christians, but, hearing how in other lands the entry of Jesuit missionaries had led to Spanish and Portuguese conquest, he expelled them. For foreign trade he relied on the English and Dutch, and kept William * Adams at his court as adviser on shipbuilding and navigation.

Ignatius Loyola, St *see* **Loyola, St Ignatius**

Ignatius of Antioch, St (*c.* 35–107). Apostolic father of the church. Probably second bishop of Antioch, according to Eusebius he was executed in Rome under Trajan. His seven 'epistles', which seem to have been written on the journey from Antioch to Rome for his execution, contain valuable information about the early church. There is a legend that he was the child taken up in his arms by Christ (Mark ix. 36).
Chadwick, H., *The Early Church*. 1967

Ii Naosuké (1815–1860). Japanese nobleman and statesman. He favoured developing relations with the West, an issue raised when the U.S.A. sent a fleet to Japan in 1853 to bring about the end of Japanese isolation. The Japanese government, which was not in a position to repel the fleet, began on his advice to negotiate new relations and trade. This exacerbated disagreements between factions in Japan, already divided over the succession to the *Shogunate* (military dictatorship). Ii Naosuké took direct control as chief councillor in 1858, settled the question of succession and forced acceptance of a Japanese-American treaty. He was murdered by an opposing faction.
Shunkichi Akimoto, *Lord Ii Naosuké and the New Japan*. 1909

Ikeda Hayato (1899–1965). Japanese politician. After serving many years in the

Ministry of Finance, he was elected to the Diet (1949) as a Liberal Democrat and held several offices in connexion with finance and trade before becoming prime minister (1960). He retired through ill health (1964), having earned much credit for Japan's spectacular economic advance during his term in office.

Illich, Ivan Denisovich (1926–) Austrian–American social theorist. Educated in Rome and Salzburg, he became a priest, moved to the U.S. in 1951 and later worked in Puerto Rico and Mexico. His 'subversive' books applied lateral thinking to question fundamental assumptions about social structures and demystify professionalism e.g. *Deschooling Society* (1971), *Energy and Equity* (1973), *Medical Nemesis* (1974) and *The Right to Useful Unemployment* (1979).

Ilyushin, Sergei Vladimirovich (1894–1977). Russian aircraft designer. A lieutenant-general in the Red Army, he designed the Soviet military and civilian aircraft which bore his name.

Imhotep (fl. *c.* 2800 B.C.). Egyptian sage, traditionally versed in alchemy and astrology as well as medicine. Some accounts say that he designed the step pyramid of Saqqara for King Zoser, whose chief minister he was. In Ptolemaic times he was identified with Asclepios (Aesculapius), the Greek god of healing.

Ingenhousz, Jan (1730–1799). Dutch physician. He practised medicine in Holland, Austria and England, at the same time carrying out scientific studies of considerable interest. In 1779 he published his *Experiments Upon Vegetables* in which he described the respiration of plants and drew attention to the importance of the process in relation to animal life.

Ingres, Jean Auguste Dominique (1780–1867). French classical painter. The son of a sculptor, he was born at Montauban and went to Paris (1797) to study under * David, whose influence is marked in the brilliant portraits (1805: now in the Louvre) of the Rivière family. He won the first Prix de Rome (1802) with the *Ambassadors of Agamemnon* but did not go to Italy (where he remained many years) until 1806. He was greatly impressed by 15th-century Italian painting and became more and more convinced that the highest effects in painting were to be achieved by line and form, emphasized by the cold jewel-like brilliance of his colour. He now came under the spell of Raphael – who remained a major influence on his style – and it was perhaps some consequent softening of his line that won his *Vow of Louis XIII* such instant acclaim at the Salon (1824). Many success followed, his works including portraits, mythological scenes and nudes (e.g. *Odalisque* in the Louvre), but his main interest is always in the essential line: his drawings, most of which he bequeathed to his native Montauban, are by some more admired than his pictures.
Wildenstein, G., *Ingres*. 1954; Rosenblum, R., *Jean-Auguste-Dominique Ingres*. 1967.

Innocent III (Lotario de'Conti de Segni) (1161–1216). Pope from 1198. The son of a noble family, he was still young and in full vigour when he became pope; though his interventions were as often as not ill-advised, he was one of the most successful medieval popes in exercising the papal right of intervening in temporal affairs. He deposed the emperor Otto IV; he ex-communicated King John of England, but attacked Magna Carta; he promoted the 4th Crusade (diverted to the conquest of Constantinople), and the bloody crusade that crushed the Albigenses in France. He presided at the Fourth Lateran Council (1215).
Tillman, H., *Papst Innocenz III*. 1954

Innocent XI (Benedetto Odescalchi) (1611–1689). Pope (from 1676). He was a man of great piety but became involved in a bitter struggle with Louis XIV of France over the rights of the Gallican church, and especially Louis's claim to administer and collect the revenue of vacant bishoprics. More fruitful was the part he played in bringing about and sustaining the alliance between the emperor Leopold I and King John Sobieski, king of Poland, which relieved Vienna from the Turkish threat (1683).

Inönü, Ismet (1884–1973). Turkish soldier and politician. He was the comrade-in-arms of Mustafa * Kemal (Atatürk) and fought in the Balkan Wars and World War I; he was his leader's chief of staff in the subsequent campaigns (1919–23) which ended in the expulsion of the Greeks from Asia Minor. He signed the Treaty of Lausanne (1923) on behalf of

Turkey, and was the first prime minister of the new republic from 1923 almost continuously until, on Atatürk's death (1938), he succeeded him as president. Defeated in 1950, he led the Republican People's party opposition to Bayar and Menderes. Following the military *coup* (1960) he was again prime minister from 1961 to 1965, when he resigned after his government had been defeated in the Assembly.
Frey, F. W., *The Turkish Political Elite*, 1965

Ionesco, Eugène (1912–). French playwright. Born in Romania, he spent his childhood in Paris and adolescence in Bucharest, settling permanently in France in 1942. His first play *The Bald Prima Donna* (1950) established him as the most important writer in the 'theatre of the absurd'. Since then he has written numerous plays, mostly translated into English and successfully performed in England and the U.S.A. They include *The Lesson* (1951), *Rhinoceros* (1960), *Exit the King* (1962) and *Hunger and Thirst* (1965). His ballet, *The Triumph of Death*, was first performed in Copenhagen (1972). He was made a member of the Académie Française (1970) and Légion d'Honneur (1970).

Iqbal, Sir Muhammad (1876–1938). Indian poet and philosopher. He taught philosophy in Lahore, before visiting Europe at the age of 30. His poetry, written in Persian and Urdu under the name of 'Iqbal', at first dealt mainly with general themes – grief and love and their philosophic implications – but became increasingly a means of awakening the social consciousness of the Moslems of India, whose poverty and passivity he considered unworthy of their ancestors. He was originally a believer in Hindu–Moslem unity, but, although never a narrow nationalist, he gradually came to advocate a separate Moslem state and was President of the Muslim League (1930).
Schimmel, M., *Gabriel's Wing*. 1963

Ireland, John (1879–1962). English composer, born in Cheshire. His music was often inspired by ancient traditions and sites, e.g. his orchestral prelude *The Forgotten Rite* (composed 1913) by the Channel Islands and the rhapsody *Mai-Dun* (1920–21) by Maiden Castle, Dorset. Other works include song settings of poems by, e.g. Hardy, Housman and Masefield (*I have twelve oxen, Sea fever* etc.), and much music for piano.
Longmire, J., *John Ireland*. 1969

Ireland, William Henry (1777–1835). English forger. Son of an engraver, he became a forger of 'Shakespearian' manuscripts, including the plays *Vortigern and Rowena* and *Henry II*, which he was able to impose even on acknowledged experts. Sheridan produced *Vortigern* at Drury Lane. Ireland eventually confessed he was a fraud.

Ireton, Henry (1611–1651). English soldier, the son-in-law of Oliver Cromwell. He was taken prisoner at Naseby (1645) but was soon rescued by Cromwell's cavalry charge. He was prominent in Army politics between 1647 and 1649, notably at the Army Council discussions with the Levellers at Putney ('The Putney Debates' Oct. 1647) and was one of the instigators of Pride's Purge (Dec. 1648). He took a part in the trial of Charles I, and signed his death warrant. He was second in command to Cromwell in Ireland, became lord-deputy (1650) and died of the plague after the fall of Limerick. He had a clear mind, a ready tongue and had a considerable influence with Oliver Cromwell.
Ramsey, R. W., *Henry Ireton*. 1949

Irigoyen, Hipóleto (1850–1933). President of Argentina. A teacher by profession, he became (1896) leader of the Radical Civic Union party and in 1905 unsuccessfully attempted a revolution. After a change in the corrupt electoral system he was elected president; though splitting the party by his autocratic rule (1916–22), he carried through considerable social reform. He maintained the neutrality of his country in World War I. In 1928 he was again elected president, but the ineffectiveness of his administration provoked a military *coup* and his deposition (1930).

Ironside, William Edmund Ironside, 1st Baron (1880–1959). British soldier. He was chief of the Imperial General Staff at the outbreak of World War II but after the withdrawal from Dunkirk he assumed command of the home forces and was made a field-marshal. In his earlier years he had an adventurous career, serving against the Bolsheviks in the Archangel campaign (1918–19) and in Persia (1921).
Ironside, W. E., *Archangel, 1918–19*. 1953

Irvine, William (1741–1801). American soldier and member of the Continental Congress. Irish in origin, he settled in Pennsylvania; he advocated the purchase of 'The Triangle', a tract of land giving the State access to Lake Erie.

Irving, Sir Henry (John Henry Broadribb) (1838–1905). English actor and manager. He was born in Somerset, made his debut in Sunderland (1856) and first appeared in London in 1859. His first appearance as Matthias in *The Bells* (1871), a play that was to prove such a stand-by in the years to come, marked a stage on his road to popularity, and his *Hamlet* which ran for 200 nights (1874–75) established him as a tragic actor of the highest rank. In 1878 began his tenure, as lessee manager, of the Lyceum Theatre, London, where in memorable association with Ellen * Terry he directed and acted in a series of Shakespearian and other plays that made theatrical history. He was the first actor to be knighted (1895) and was buried in Westminster Abbey.
Irving, L., *Henry Irving, the Actor and his World.* 1951

Irving, Washington (1783–1859). American author and diplomat. The son of an English immigrant merchant, he was born in New York and spent many years in Europe, where he made many literary friendships, e.g. with Scott at Abbotsford. He held occasional diplomatic appointments, and is remembered for his success, while a member of the American embassy in Madrid, in rescuing the Alhambra from falling into ruins. He made his reputation as a writer with his good-humoured satire *History of New York . . . by Diedrich Knickerbocker* (1809); but his lasting popularity depends upon the short pieces in his *Sketch Book* (1819–20), containing *Rip Van Winkle, Bracebridge Hall* (1822) and *Tales of a Traveller* (1825).
Hedges, W. L., *Washington Irving.* 1974

Irwin, 1st Baron *see* **Halifax, Edward Frederick Lindley Wood, 1st Earl of**

Isaac. Biblical patriarch. According to Genesis xxi–xxviii, Abraham was preparing to obey a divine command to sacrifice his son Isaac when at the last moment God substituted a ram for the boy. By his wife Rebecca, Isaac was the father of Jacob and Esau.

Isaacs, Sir Isaac Alfred (1855–1948). Australian lawyer. Having been attorney-general (1905–06), a judge (from 1906) and chief justice of Australia (1930–31) he was the first Australian-born governor-general (1931–36).

Isaacs, Rufus Daniel *see* **Reading, 1st Marquess of**

Isabella (known as 'the Catholic') (1451–1504). Queen of Castile (from 1474). Daughter of John II of Castile, she married (1469) the prince who, already king of Sicily, became Ferdinand II of Aragon in 1479. She herself had succeeded her brother Henry IV on the throne of Castile in 1474, so that she and her husband were joint rulers of the whole of Spain, which became a united country under their successors. For the main events of the reign *see* * Ferdinand II.
Mariéjol, H., trans. Keen, B., *The Spain of Ferdinand and Isabella.* 1961

Isabella II (1830–1904). Queen of Spain (1833–70). With her mother as regent, she succeeded her father * Ferdinand VII, who had induced the *Cortes* to repeal the Salic Law against female succession. In what came to be known as the First Carlist War (1833–39), her uncle Don Carlos, who disputed her title, was defeated; a liberal rising which followed her abolition of the *Cortes* – one of her first acts after being declared of age (1843) – was put down. She proved herself an unreliable and wilful intriguer, and her government was inefficient and corrupt. The so-called Glorious Revolution (1870) forced her to abdicate in favour of her son Alfonso XII. She lived abroad, mostly in France, for the rest of her life.

Isaiah (8th century B.C.). Major Hebrew prophet. He received his call in the temple in the year of King Uzziah's death (*c.* 727) and seems to have acted as adviser, both in spiritual and temporal affairs, to Kings Jotham, Ahaz and Hezekiah. The interpretation of the biblical Book of Isaiah has always been difficult as so many of his prophecies may equally well refer to contemporary as to future events. He foresees the survival of a national remnant (referring either to those who returned from Babylonian exile or to those who maintained their religious identity after the great dispersal) and looked forward to the coming of a Messiah. Almost all scholars are now agreed that Chapters xl–lxvi are by a later hand, since

the background events belong to the 6th rather than the 8th century B.C.
Kissane, E. J., *The Book of Isaiah*. Rev. ed. 1960

Isherwood, Christopher William Bradshaw (1904–). British author, American by naturalization. The period he spent in Berlin (1923–33) before the Nazis came to power provided the material for his best known novels, *Mr Norris Changes Trains* (1935), *Goodbye to Berlin* (1939), and for his play (and film) *I am a Camera*, on which was based the musical *Cabaret*. He later wrote plays, e.g. *The Ascent of F. 6* (1936), in collaboration with his friend W. H. * Auden. He settled in America in 1939, and wrote for films. His interest in Indian religion led him to translate, *inter alia, The Bhagavad-Gita* (1944).
Isherwood, C., *Christopher and his Kind*. 1977

Ishmael. The son of Abraham and Hagar (the Egyptian handmaid of Abraham's wife Sarah). According to Genesis xvi, xvii and xxi, he and his mother were driven into the desert as a result of Sarah's jealousy. He is said to be the ancestor of twelve Bedouin tribes.

Isidore of Seville (*c.* 560–636). Spanish prelate and scholar, bishop of Seville (from *c.* 600). He was prominent at the councils of Seville (619) and Toledo (633), but is best known as a writer on religion, science (astronomy etc.) and history (e.g. of the Goths, Vandals and Sueves). His most important work is his *Etymologies*, a kind of encyclopedia which as an early medieval reference book transmitted much classical knowledge. It was one of the earliest books printed and was much consulted until the seventeenth century.

Ismail (8th century). Son of Jafar, the sixth imam of the line stemming from Ali, Mohammed's son-in-law. This line, according to the Shi'ite sect, is that of the true succession. When Jafar died the majority of the Shi'ites passed over Ismail and chose his younger brother Musa as imam. A minority recognized Ismail and formed a separate sect; the movement eventually spread to India where the * Aga Khan became its spiritual leader.
Lewis, B., *The Origins of Ismailism*. 1940

Ismail Pasha (1830–1895). Khedive of Egypt. He pursued the forward-looking policy of his grandfather * Mehemet Ali and was able to obtain large credits owing to the rise in the value of the cotton crop when American shipments dwindled in the Civil War. He embarked on an extravagant development programme: much of Alexandria and Cairo was rebuilt and the construction of the Suez Canal put in hand. But his plans were too grandiose for his means and some of the money was squandered. Crippled by interest payment, he sold his Suez Canal shares to Britain, but despite temporary relief he was forced to accept Anglo-French financial control (1876) and to abdicate (1879) in favour of his son Tewfik.

Ismay, Hastings Lionel Ismay, 1st Baron (1887–1965). British general. As military secretary to the war cabinet (1940–45) he was one of Winston Churchill's closest companions and advisers during World War II. He was * Mountbatten's chief of staff in India 1947–48, Secretary for Commonwealth Relations 1951–52 and Secretary General to NATO 1952–57. Knighted in 1940, he was made a C.H. in 1945 and received a peerage in 1947.

Israel *see* **Jacob**

Ito Hirobumi, Prince (1841–1909). Japanese statesman. After the fall (1867) of the shogunate (* Ieyasu) and the restoration to active rule of the emperor Mutsuhito under the title of Meiji, Ito led the group of able politicians who set about bringing Japan out of isolation and turning it into a powerful modern state. He was four times prime minister (1885–88; 1892–96; 1898; 1900–01) and a principal architect of the Anglo-Japanese alliance (1902), which enabled Japan to wage victorious war against Russia (1904–05) without fear of outside intervention. Ito was special adviser to the emperor during the war; in 1906 was appointed resident general in Korea (by then a virtual protectorate of Japan); he was assassinated by a Korean, and Korea was then annexed.
Akita, G., *Foundations of Constitutional Government in Modern Japan, 1868–1900*. 1967

Itúrbide, Augustin de (1783–1824). Emperor of Mexico (1822–23). Having fought in the Spanish royalist army (1810), he led revolution (1821) promising to establish representative government under a monarchy. Most of the country supported him and the new Spanish viceroy handed over Mexico City to him. When the constituent assembly proved far from submissive, Itúrbide's followers proclaimed him emperor and for a few months he ruled as an imitation Napoleon, bestowing titles lavishly upon his family and friends. Early in 1823 the army revolted, Itúrbide abdicated and fled, but was arrested and later shot on his return.

Ivan III (known as 'the Great') (1440–1505). Grand prince of Moscow (Muscovy). He drove out the Tartar rulers, conquered and annexed a great part of Novgorod and brought the scattered provinces and principalities of his realm under central rule. His marriage to Sophia Palaeologus, a niece of the last Byzantine emperor, gave him imperial ideas; he styled himself tsar of all Russia. He was a patron of the arts and brought in foreigners to beautify Moscow with churches, palaces and works of art.
Fennell, J. L. I., *Ivan the Great of Moscow*. 1961

Ivan IV (known as 'the Terrible') (1530–1584). Tsar (from 1547) of Russia (Muscovy). He was the son of Vasily III and grandson of Ivan III, and was crowned at the age of 17. His minority spent at the mercy of boyars (nobles) competing for power had implanted in him a bitter hatred of the whole class. In the early part of his reign he carried out many legal and social reforms; but from about 1564 his behaviour, always harsh, rapidly deteriorated and his fear and suspicion developed. He instituted a secret police (*oprichnina*), and torture, execution and imprisonment became the everyday instruments of a neurotic sadism. In a fit of rage he killed his son Ivan (1580): he spent the rest of his life in penance. Despite or because of these methods his personal power was greater than that of any previous Russian ruler and he established firmly the autocratic tsarist tradition. He conquered the Tatars Khanates of Kazan and Astrakhan and extended his territory to the Caspian; he formed links also with the west and offered to Queen Elizabeth of England a trade treaty and even his hand in marriage. He was the subject of a remarkable film by Sergei * Eisenstein.
Payne, R., and Romanoff, N., *Ivan the Terrible*. 1975

Iveagh, Edward Cecil Guinness, 1st Earl of *see under* **Guinness, Sir Benjamin Lee**

Ives, Charles Edward (1874–1954). American composer. A bold experimenter, he was noted for his use of polytonality and complex rhythms. He wrote the orchestral *Three Places in New England* (1903–14), four symphonies, over 100 songs, and much chamber music.
Cowell, H. and S., *Charles Ives and his Music*. 2nd ed. 1966

Iwakura Tomomi, Prince (1825–1883). Japanese nobleman and politician, born in Kyoto. Anti-foreign at the time of American penetration of Japan, he was a key figure in organizing the restoration of imperial rule in 1868 (* Mutsuhito). In 1871–73 he led a mission of 50 officials to investigate modern administration in the US and Europe, and favoured the adoption of a Prussian model. He was chief minister 1873–83.

J

Jabotinsky, Vladimir Evgenyevich (1880–1940). Russian Zionist. He worked for the establishment of a Jewish state on both banks of the River Jordan. He was born in Russia, where he advocated organised Jewish defence against pogroms. He later went to Palestine, where he opposed British policy and formed Jewish self-defence units against Arab attack; he founded the Zionist Revisionist organisation in 1925 and was working for the establishment of a Jewish army when he died.
Schechtman, J. B., *Vladimir Jabotinsky*. 1956–61

Jackson, Andrew (1767–1845). Seventh president of the U.S. (1829–37). Born in South Carolina, he fought as a boy in the American War of Independence. Later as a lawyer in Tennessee he entered local politics and became a general in the militia. His defence of New Orleans in the war of 1812 against the British, and subsequent exploits against the Indians in Florida (of which he became military governor in 1821) made him a national hero. He had already served briefly in Congress (1796–98) as representative and senator and now his political friends decided to exploit his popularity by putting him up for the presidency (1824), but a combination of his assorted opponents defeated him. In 1828 he easily defeated John Quincy * Adams. Jackson was hailed as the friend of the people, and stood for what later came to be known as the common man. In encouraging the 'spoils system', by which political service was rewarded by official positions, he saddled the Democratic party and indirectly the whole of American public life with this lasting incubus. His attitude to the issues which confronted him was distinctively personal. He supported a strong federal government against states' rights; he struck a blow at the power of money by vetoing the rechartering bill for the Bank of the United States, which he later crippled by removing federal deposits; he overcame what might have developed into a disruptive refusal to accept a new tariff bill by accepting compromise under which the tariff was imposed on condition that it was steadily reduced. In his second term he tried to purchase Texas from Mexico and would have annexed it when it revolted had he not been prevented by the opponents of slavery (it finally joined the Union in 1845). He was succeeded by his nominee Martin * Van Buren and continued to dominate Democratic politics.

Though there was much of the simple frontiersman – indicated by the nickname 'Old Hickory' – in Andrew Jackson, he had an imaginative perception of the popular will and an astute and logical mind to interpret it, together with a deep sense of loyalty to the people.
Bassett, J. S., *The Life of Andrew Jackson*. 1911

Jackson, John Hughlings (1835–1911). British neurophysiologist. He was preoccupied throughout his life with the neurological explanation of physical and mental disorders. After early work on the nerves of the eyes, Jackson occupied himself with epilepsy, seeing the epileptic's convulsions as the product of some kind of nervous discharge onto muscle. He was concerned to classify the different modes of epilepsy, and to describe its varied automatic symptoms (such as involuntary chewing). Jackson is best remembered for his work on the localization of brain function. There was still great debate in mid-century as to whether bodily movements were controlled by the brain as a whole, or by different sectors of the brain for each function. Partly on the basis of studies of patients with injured, diseased, or deficient brains, he proposed a localization model. His insights were confirmed by the electrical experiments of Fritsch and Hitzig, and David Ferrier. After 1863 Jackson spent most of his life practising at the London Hospital and at the National Hospital for the Paralysed and Epileptic.

Jackson, Thomas Jonathan (known as 'Stonewall Jackson') (1812–1863). American soldier. He served in the Mexican War (1846–48) and taught at the Virginia Military Institute (1851–61). His stand at the Battle of Bull Run (1861) in command of the Confederate forces in the Civil War earned him his nickname. In 1862, as commander in the Shenandoah Valley, by successively defeating his opponents and constantly threatening Washington he relieved the Confederate capital, Richmond, of much of the pressure upon it. Later in the year he joined Lee at Richmond and played an important part in the invasion of Maryland. At Chancellorsville (May 1863), when returning from a reconnaissance, he was mistaken for the enemy and shot by one of his own men. His firmness of character, sustained by rigid Calvinism, made him a strict disciplinarian but his masterly tactics, based on those of Napoleon, and his personal idiosyncracies gave him popularity with his troops.

Freeman, D. S., *Lee's Lieutenants: A Study in Command*. 1942–1946

Jack the Ripper. Unidentified London criminal who stabbed and mutilated a number of prostitutes in the Aldgate and Whitechapel areas of East London in 1888. He was never caught; public alarm at his escape brought pressure to bear on the police and produced reforms in detection methods. There have been numerous ingenious attempts to identify him.

Jacob (later called Israel). Biblical patriarch, second son of Abraham and Sarah. According to Genesis xxv ff., he tricked his elder brother Esau out of his birthright; by his two wives Leah and Rachel (for each of whom he had to serve their father Laban seven years) he had twelve sons, from whom were descended the twelve tribes of Israel: Reuben, Simeon, Levi, Judah, Zebulon, Issachar, Dan, Gad, Asher, Naphtali, Joseph and Benjamin.

Jacobs, William Wymark (1863–1943). English short-story writer. Most of his stories were humorous tales about seafaring men, e.g. *Many Cargoes*; but he also wrote some macabre narratives, e.g. *The Monkey's Paw.*

Jacobsen, Arne (1902–1971). Danish architect. He was among the most prominent of those who in the 1930s introduced 'functionalism' into Danish architecture. He designed (sometimes in collaboration) many civic and industrial buildings in Denmark, e.g. Aalborg Town Hall (1938–42), the Massey-Harris building, Glostrup (1953) and the Copenhagen air terminal (1958–59), and his influence soon spread. He was chosen to design the new building for St Catherine's College, Oxford (completed 1965). He also turned his attention to applied art and designed furniture, lighting appliances, textiles etc.

Jacquard, Joseph Marie (1752–1834). French inventor. After many years of experimenting with textile machinery he devised a successful loom for the mechanical weaving of complicated patterns (1801). This was bought by the French government (1806), but Jacquard received a royalty on all machines sold. The Jacquard loom has played a major role in the development of patterned textiles for 150 years. His use of punched cards on which details of patterns were recorded was adopted by * Babbage in his calculating machine. Jacquard's cards remained indispensable until the electronic era.

Jadwiga (1374–1399). Queen of Poland (from 1384). She was the daughter of Louis I of Hungary; her marriage to the future Ladislaus II of Lithuania led to the union of that country with Poland, where she is considered as a saint.

Jagiellon. A medieval dynasty which reigned in Lithuania, Poland, Hungary and Bohemia. It is named after Jagiello, who became grand-duke of Lithuania in 1381 and in 1386, having married Jadwiga, heiress to the Polish throne, became king of that country as Wladislaw (Ladislas) II. Six kings of his dynasty reigned in Poland until 1572. Another Wladislaw, son of * Casimir IV, was elected king of Bohemia

(1471) and became (1490) king of Hungary also; but the defeat and death of his son Louis at the Battle of Mohacz (1526) ended the Jagiellon dynasty in both those countries. Reddaway, W. F., et al., ed., *The Cambridge History of Poland*. 1941–50

Jahangir (1569–1627). Third Mogul emperor, son of Akbar the Great. He was cruel, idle, and self-indulgent, but artistic; he left the administration to his wife, the strong-minded Nur Jahan ('light of the world'), who is said to have varied her governmental duties 'by polo-playing and shooting tigers'. Jahangir's reign saw the arrival of the first Englishmen ever to visit the Mogul's court; one of them, William Hawkins, who brought a letter from James I, was favourably received and given leave to start a trading port at Surat. Jahangir laid out the Shalimar gardens in Kashmir and erected several magnificent buildings in Lahore and elsewhere.

James I (1208–1276). King of Aragon and Catalonia (from 1213), known as 'the Conqueror' for his victories over the Moors. Majorca was conquered by Catalans (1229–32) and the Moorish kingdom of Valencia by the Aragonese in 1245. By relinquishing fiefs on the French side of the Pyrenees by the Treaty of Corbell (1258) he made Catalonia a purely Spanish kingdom. He initiated many legal reforms and the first maritime code.

James I (1394–1437). King of Scotland (from 1406), son of Robert III. While at sea on the way to be educated in France, he was captured and detained in England for twenty-one years, during which time he was honourably treated at court and was made a Knight of the Garter. Ransomed in 1424, he returned to Scotland where his energetic attempt to introduce a parliament on the English model failed; his personal foibles lost him general support and the antagonism of the nobles led to his assassination. James is credited with having written *The Kingis Quair*, a fanciful poem about his love for Joan Beaufort, whom he married in 1424. His son, **James II** (1430–60), and his grandson, **James III** (1452–80), succeeded in turn. The reigns of both began with long minorities, both had to contend with a discontented and factious nobility, and both met violent deaths, the former killed at the siege of Roxburgh, the latter found murdered near the battlefield of Sauchieburn.

James I (1566–1625). King of England (from 1603), king of Scotland, as James VI (from 1567). He was the only child of * Mary Queen of Scots and Henry, Lord * Darnley, and as a baby succeeded his mother after her enforced abdication, in a Scotland torn by rival political and religious factions, for whom possession of his person and the powers of regency that went with it were valuable prizes to be won. He grew up nervous, awkward and pedantic, with a great fund of knowledge and little common sense – 'the wisest fool in Christendom' he was to be called. However, when he came to rule he managed with some astuteness to keep Roman Catholic and Presbyterian factions at bay by favouring each in turn and seeking a middle way. He was helped to do this by the Treaty of Berwick (1586) under which, in return for subsides, he pledged himself to be England's ally. Meanwhile his mother, whom he could not remember and whose folly had brought such misfortune, was a prisoner in Elizabeth's hands. He interceded on her behalf but was careful not to jeopardize his own hopes of accession, based on descent from Margaret, daughter of Henry VII and wife of Scotland's James IV.

These hopes, with the collaboration of Elizabeth's chief minister, Robert Cecil, were attained in 1603. One of his earliest acts was the summoning of the Hampton Court Conference to discuss the grievances of the Puritans in the Church of England. This broke down but at least one of its projects was implemented, the 'Authorized Version' of the Bible which was completed in 1611 and sponsored by James. Despite their shared escape when Roman Catholic malcontents planned the Gunpowder Plot (* Fawkes) to blow up the king in parliament, the relations between James, a firm believer in the 'divine right' of kings, and his legislature were sometimes strained. From 1611 to 1621 he ruled without summoning parliament (apart from the 'Addled Parliament' in 1614 which lasted six weeks), raising troops for Ireland by creating baronetcies – a title introduced by him and carrying this obligation – and money by selling monopolies, benevolences etc.

The Roman Catholic conspiracy did not prevent James from reversing Elizabethan policy towards Spain, but by assenting to Raleigh's execution and by his attempt – which ended in fiasco – to arrange a Spanish marriage for Prince Charles, he only added to his own unpopularity. In 1589 James had

married Anne of Denmark. Henry, the elder son, predeceased his father; the younger succeeded as Charles I; and from his daughter * Elizabeth, the 'Winter Queen' of Bohemia, was descended the house of Hanover. For much of his reign James was under the sway of two unworthy favourites, Robert Carr, whom he created Earl of Somerset, and George Villiers, Duke of Buckingham. In addition to several books on politics he wrote *A Counterblast to Tobacco* (1604), and issued *The Book of Sports* (1617) defining the amusements (e.g. archery, dancing, but *not* bowls) permissible on Sundays. Historians have tended to stress James' deficiencies, but they can be over-stressed. The reign saw a continuance of the literary effulgence of the Elizabethans, justifying the coinage 'Jacobean'.
Willson, D. H., *King James VI and I.* 1956; Russell, C., *Parliaments and English Politics 1621–1629.* 1979

James II (1633–1701). King of England and of Scotland, as James VII (1685–88). He was the second son of Charles I. Before returning to England after the restoration of his brother, Charles II, he had fought with courage in the armies of France and Spain. As lord high admiral (1669–73) he did much to restore the efficiency of the navy and was a successful general against the Dutch (1664–67). His conversion to Roman Catholicism (1670) meant that after the passing of the Test Act (1673) he had to resign his command. The 'Popish Plot' (Titus * Oates), it was alleged, was designed to place him prematurely on the throne; but after the failure of two Exclusion Bills, he succeeded Charles II with parliamentary and general consent. A rising in the West Country under Charles's illegitimate son * Monmouth was quickly and cruelly suppressed, but James's precipitate attempts to advance the Roman Catholic cause quickly aroused antagonism. He used 'dispensing power' (i.e. from the provisions of the Test Act) to promote Catholics to office, he raised a standing army, stationed on Hounslow Heath with obvious intent to overawe the capital. In 1687 he issued a Declaration of Indulgence giving toleration to dissenters, Catholic and Protestant alike. A second Declaration in 1688 was ordered to be read in all churches; the acquittal of 'the Seven Bishops' for seditious libel in petitioning not to have to do so was greeted with popular enthusiasm. Leading Anglican politicians invited James's cousin and son-in-law, William of Orange, to intervene in England. William's landing in England (1688) found James with an army uncertain in its loyalty and with no strong body of support. James fled, leaving the way clear for William to take the throne jointly with his wife Mary. These events are commonly labelled the Glorious Revolution. James attempted to regain his kingdom from Ireland, but his cause was finally lost when he was defeated at the Battle of the Boyne. For the rest of his life he lived in France. By his first wife Anne Hyde, daughter of the Earl of Clarendon, he had two daughters: Mary II, wife of William III, and Anne, afterwards queen; by his second wife, Mary of Modena, he was the father of James Edward Stuart, the 'Old Pretender'.
Turner, F. C., *James II.* 1948; Miller, J., *James II.* 1978

James IV (1473–1513). King of Scotland (from 1488), son of James III. He took part in the nobles' rebellion which led to his father's death but soon asserted his mastery over them. By strengthening the administration of justice he restored confidence in law and order. His court became renowned for pageantry, tournaments and sport. He renewed the traditional alliance with France but at the same time came to terms with England, and in 1503 made the marriage with Henry VII's daughter Margaret which eventually united the Scottish and English crowns. When Henry VIII, in response to the pope's appeal, attacked France, James, torn by conflicting loyalties, took (1513) the fateful decision of invading England, but when the armies met at Flodden Field James was killed and the Scots routed with great slaughter.

James V (1512–1542). King of Scotland (from 1513). He was only 17 months old when he succeeded his father, James IV. During his minority the English faction, headed by his mother and her second husband Archibald Douglas, Earl of Angus, competed for power with the French faction led by the Duke of Albany. Albany ruled until 1524 when, by declaring the 12-year-old king capable of rule, his mother and Angus began to exercise authority in his name. In 1528 James asserted his independence, quelled his turbulent subjects and with political and matrimonial alliances to offer was immediately courted by the rulers of Europe. France gained the day and he married (1538) Mary of Guise. The consequences were persecution of the Protestants and a war with England. The humiliation of the defeat at Solway Moss (1542) coupled with the strain of maintaining an efficient administration in a country so difficult to rule was too much for a highly strung temperament; he died three weeks later, only a few days after his daughter Mary, the future Queen of Scots was born.

James VI and James VII (of Scotland) *see* **James I and James II** (of Great Britain)

James, St (d.c. 44 A.D.). Apostle of Jesus Christ. Son of Zebedee and brother of * St John, he was prominent among the apostles and after the Resurrection became a leader of the church in Jerusalem. Put to death on the orders of Herod Agrippa, he was the first of the apostles to suffer martyrdom. According to legend his body was taken to Spain, where in 835 the bones were found at Santiago (St James) da Compostella, which became and remains a great centre of pilgrimage. James became Spain's patron saint.

Another apostle, identified as James the son of Alphaeus or 'James the Less' plays no distinctive part in the New Testament story.

James, St (d.c. 62 A.D.). The leader of the church in Jerusalem after the Resurrection. The Authorized Version of the Bible describes him as the brother of Jesus, but Roman Catholics and others translate the Greek word *adelphos* as 'kinsman'. At the council (Acts xv) held to decide whether Gentile converts should be bound to accept the Jewish rite of circumcision, St James persuasively argued that no unnecessary obligation should be laid upon them. According to accounts repeated and confirmed by Josephus, James was stoned to death by the Jews after being hurled down from the pinnacle of the Temple.

James, Henry (1843–1916). American novelist. Born in New York, he was named after his father, a well known philosopher whose other son, William * James, became famous in the same field. His education, much of it in Europe but finishing at Harvard, succeeded in its purpose of making him cosmopolitan, and he was already a mature intellectual when (1865) he began writing essays and reviews for the *Atlantic Monthly*. But it was only in the more sophisticated circles in Europe that he was happy. He left America (1869) and from 1876 made England his home.

His work is usually divided into three periods. The predominant theme of the first is the impact of European culture on American life, e.g. in his first important novel *Roderick Hudson* (1875); *Daisy Miller* (1879), one of his rare popular successes; *The Portrait of a Lady* (1881) and in the same year *Washington Square* (dramatized and filmed long after his death as *The Heiress*); *The Aspern Papers* (1888), also later dramatized. The second period, distinguished as the English one, shows the shrewdness with which this cosmopolitan American could assess national character, e.g. in *The Tragic Muse* (1890), *The Awkward Age* (1899). The last period, in which he returns to the contrast between Americans and Europeans, contains three of his greatest novels: *The Wings of the Dove* (1902), *The Ambassadors* (1903) and *The Golden Bowl* (1904). In addition he wrote over 100 short stories, many of them long short stories or *nouvelles*, a genre of which he was a master. *The Turn of the Screw*, equally successful as a play, is a fascinating study in the macabre. Among his many miscellaneous writings is a biography of Nathaniel Hawthorne. His *Notebooks* remained unpublished until 1948. James's style has been interminably discussed; some find it tortuous and over-elaborate but he has many admirers who take delight in the minuteness of observation, the meticulous care with which he selects a phrase, always using an appropriate vocabulary for each differing character, the patience with which he follows the labyrinths of the human mind. As a gesture of sympathy for the Allied cause in World War I, James assumed British citizenship in 1915. In 1916 he was awarded the O.M.
Edel, L., *The Life of Henry James*. 1953–72

James, Montague Rhodes (1862–1936). English scholar and author. During an academic career culminating in his appointment as provost of King's College, Cambridge (1905–18), and of Eton College (1918–36), he found relaxation in writing ghost stories with an antiquarian flavour. These were collected as *Ghost Stories of an Antiquary* (1905), *More Ghost Stories* (1911) etc. His scholarly books include *The Apocryphal New Testament* (1924). He received the O.M. in 1930.

James, William (1842–1910). American philosopher and psychologist. A brother of Henry

* James the novelist, he studied art, chemistry and medicine before turning to his real interests, psychology and philosophy. Meanwhile he had been incapacitated by melancholia for several years. After teaching physiology at Harvard he held professorships there in philosophy and psychology (1885–1897). His *Varieties of Religious Experience* (1902) reveals the direction of much of his psychological work; he is also known for the disputed James-Lange theory which equates emotion with the perception of bodily change. In *Pragmatism* (1907) – the word was originally used in this sense by Charles * Peirce – he expounds the doctrine that the validity of human ideas and principles can only be tested by an examination of their practical results. James's influence was wide (* Dewey, John).
Dooley, P. K., *William James*. 1974

James Edward Stuart *see* **Stuart, James Edward**

Jameson, Sir Leander Starr, 1st Bart (1853–1917). Scottish physician and South African politician. Born in Edinburgh, he went to South Africa for reasons of health and established a medical practice in the diamond town of Kimberley, where he became a friend of Cecil Rhodes. He took part in the negotiations with the Matabele chief * Lobengula from which stemmed the creation of Rhodesia, and it was from there that he led, with Rhodes's connivance, the famous Jameson Raid (1896) into the Transvaal, then a Boer republic. The intention was that it should coincide with a rising of the *Uitlanders*, the British and other settlers in Johannesburg and its neighbourhood, to whom civil rights were denied. It was hoped either to seize the country or to force President Kruger to agree to advantageous terms. The raid was a fiasco; there was no rising and Jameson was arrested and handed over to the British who sentenced him to eighteen months' imprisonment. Afterwards, until Rhodes died (1902), he was his close companion, and was prime minister of Cape Colony (1904–07).

Janáček, Leoš (1854–1928). Czech composer. Son of a village schoolmaster, he was choirmaster at Brno in Moravia before studying in Prague and Leipzig. He produced a large volume of compositions of strongly national character including many operas: *Jenufa* (composed 1896–1903), *Katya Kabanova* (1919–21), *The Cunning Little Vixen* (1921–23), and *The Makropulos Case* (1923–25); the orchestral works *Taras Bulba* and *Sinfonietta*, the song cycle *The Diary of One Who Vanished* and two string quartets. His powerful and original works were rarely heard outside his native country until after 1945, but he came to be recognized as one of the few outstanding twentieth-century operatic composers.
Vogel, J., *Janácek dramatik*. 1948

Jane, Frederick Thomas (1870–1916). English naval writer and artist. He founded and edited *Jane's Fighting Ships* in 1898 and *All the World's Aircraft* in 1909; the series is still regarded internationally as the most authoritative independent catalogues.

Jane (Seymour) (1509–1537). Third wife of * Henry VIII of England, the sister of the Duke of * Somerset. She married the king in 1536 and died twelve days after giving birth to a son, afterwards * Edward VI.

Jansen, Cornelius (1585–1638). Dutch Roman Catholic theologian. After teaching in school and college he became a professor at Louvain (1630) and bishop of Ypres (1636). In his book *Augustinus* (published 1642) he claimed that the Jesuit teaching on the freedom of the will (i.e. that man's power to choose between good and evil is a matter for his own free choice and not necessarily dependent on divine grace) was identical with the heretical doctrine of the Pelagians condemned by St Augustine; the book attracted many Roman Catholics, especially in France, but aroused much controversy. Jansenism, whose best known proponent was * Pascal, found a stronghold among scholars and theologians of Port-Royal-les-Champs in Paris; but it was condemned as heretical by the papacy and harshly repressed by Louis XIV.
Escholier, M., *Port-Royal*. 1968

Jansky, Karl Guthe (1905–1950). American radio engineer. He worked for the Bell Telephone Laboratories and concluded (1932) that one source of communications static were waves from beyond the solar system. This was the beginning of radioastronomy, but Jansky took no further part in its development.

Jaques-Dalcroze, Émile (1865–1950). Swiss music teacher. He originated the system, now known as eurhythmics, by which musical appreciation is taught through physical movement. Graded exercises, musically accompanied, enable different rhythms to be expressed by movements of head, arms and legs.

Jarry, Alfred (1873–1907). French dramatist. His farce *Ubu roi* (1896), a parody of *Macbeth*, was a subversive work which anticipated surrealist theatre and set design in the late 20th century. The play was revived in Europe and the U.S. in the 1950s.

Jaspers, Karl (1883–1969). German philosopher. He was regarded as an existentialist (* Sartre) although he himself differentiated his views from theirs. Though he wrote many books, some vast, he had little influence outside a limited circle. He emphasized the uselessness of philosophies in ultimate situations such as failure and death. His works include *Psychologie der Weltanschaungen* (1919), *Existenzphilosophie* (1938).
Schilpp, P. A., *The Philosophy of Karl Jaspers*. 1957

Jaurès, (Auguste Marie Joseph) Jean (1859–1914). French socialist. He was a member of the Chamber of Deputies from 1885 to 1889 and from 1893 almost continuously until the end of his life. In the socialist newspaper *L' Humanité*, which he founded, he fought strenuously on behalf of * Dreyfus. By 1905 he was leader of a united Socialist party. He was a democratic socialist, not a Marxist. His efforts to avert World War I by organizing a general strike of French and German workers provoked his assassination by a nationalist fanatic, Raoul Villain. His *Socialist History of France* (1st volume, 1900) is notable for its treatment of the French Revolution.

Jay, John (1745–1829). American lawyer and politician. He belonged to the revolutionary party in New York and later helped to draw up the state's constitution and became its first chief justice. Meanwhile he had been a delegate to the first and second Continental Congresses, and later took part with * Hamilton and * Madison in the defence of the new U.S. constitution in the *Federalist*. In 1782–83 he was one of the commissioners who went to Paris and negotiated with Britain the Treaty of Versailles, by which American independence was recognized; he returned to be U.S. secretary of foreign affairs (1784–89). In 1790 he became the first U.S. chief justice and in 1794 went to England to negotiate outstanding questions. Concessions granted by him in the so-called Jay's Treaty provoked severe controversy. From 1795 to 1801 he was governor of New York State.
Combs, J. A., *Jay Treaty, Political Batteground of the Founding Fathers*. 1970

Jean Paul (Johann Paul Friedrich Richter) (1763–1826). German author. He was born in a remote mountainous region of Bavaria, the Fichtelgebirge, where he found the simple characters about whom he wrote with most success. His early books were little noticed but with the publication of *Hesperus* (1795) and *Siebenkäs* (1796) recognition came. He married in 1801 and lived for the rest of his life at Bayreuth. Among the best known of his later works were *Titan* (1803) and *Dr Katzenberger's Badereise* (i.e. visit to the spa) (1809). His books have no regular plots and he combines humour with sentiment somewhat in the manner of Sterne, one of his favourite authors.

Jeans, Sir James Hopwood (1877–1946). English mathematical physicist and astronomer, born at Ormskirk in Lancashire. From a lectureship at Cambridge he went (1905) to a chair in applied mathematics at Princeton, U.S.A. After his return in 1910 he spent most of his life in writing and research; he was secretary of the Royal Society (1919–29) and vice-president (1938–40). He gave the first complete picture of stellar evolution. From consideration of the physics of rotating masses, he suggested how the stars and spiral nebulae are formed, and attributed the origin of the planets of the solar system to the forces between two stars passing close to each other. Jeans was a prolific author of popular works, e.g. *The Mysterious Universe* (1930) and *Science and Music* (1937), which gave simple explanations of complex scientific discoveries. In 1939 he was appointed to the O.M.

Jebb, Sir Richard Claverhouse (1841–1905). Scottish classical scholar, born in Dundee. His distinguished academic career culminated in his appointment (1889) as Regius professor of Greek at Cambridge University. He wrote many books on classical subjects but his great edition of the plays of Sophocles (1883–96), with textual and critical commentary and prose translation, was his chief work. He helped to found the British School of

Archaeology at Athens, was M.P. for Cambridge University (from 1891) and received the OM (1905).

Jefferies, (John) Richard (1848–1887). English naturalist and author. Born in a Wiltshire farmhouse, he becan his career as a journalist specializing in rural subjects. In addition to, e.g., *The Amateur Poacher* (1879), *The Story of a Boy* (1882), he wrote the strange introspective autobiography *Story of My Heart* (1883) and the imaginative *After London, or Wild England* (1885).
Looker, S., and Porteus, C., *Richard Jefferies*. 1965

Jefferson, Thomas (1743–1826). Third president of the U.S. (1801–09). He was born at Shadwell, Virginia, his father being a well-known surveyor. He began to practise law in 1767; he was learned in many subjects, European as well as classical languages, literature, history and above all mathematics and the natural sciences. Turning to politics, he was a member of the Virginia House of Burgesses (1769–74) and immediately became a prominent supporter of colonial claims. He attended both continental congresses (1775, 1776) and played a principal part in drafting the Declaration of Independence. Once more a member of the Virginian legislature (from 1776), he was successful in obtaining the repeal of the Law of Entail, the passage of bills for religious freedom and prohibiting the import of more slaves (he would have enacted emancipation, had he been able) and a revision of the whole legal code; he was state governor (1779–81).

As a member of Congress (1783–84) he was responsible for the granting of free institutions to the new territories beyond the Ohio and for a report favouring decimal coinage. As minister to France (1784–89), he saw the beginnings of the Revolution there and gave its first leaders the benefit of American experience. He returned to be U.S. secretary of state (1790–93) in which office he pursued a policy of no 'entangling alliances'. With his political followers he formed, in opposition to Hamilton's centralizing policy, a new grouping called the Republican party (which despite its name was the ancestor of the Democratic party of today). Jefferson was second to John Adams in the presidential election of 1796 and, according to the consitutional provision of the time, became vice-president (and leader of the opposition). In 1800 he was elected to the presidency and won again easily in 1804; he was the first president to be inaugurated in Washington (which he had helped to plan).

The most important event of his presidency was the 'Louisiana Purchase' (1803) of the French territories in the Mississippi basin, made possible by Napoleon's difficulties in maintaining adequate communication and control. In internal affairs he followed a conciliatory policy and did not press his earlier campaign for states' rights. The slave trade was abolished (1808). In 1809 he retired to Monticello, the home of his own design; here he returned to the studies of his earlier years and in particular became absorbed in the work for the establishment of the University of Virginia, inaugurated (1825) at Charlottesville.

Jefferson envisaged the United States as a mainly agricultural community since industrialization, in his opinion, would put power in the hands of financial interests. His political doctrines were based on those of Locke and Rousseau; his practice proved him to be one of the great liberal statesmen of history.

He married (1772) a widow, Martha Skelton (née Wayles) who died in 1782; only two daughters survived infancy.
Malone, D., *Jefferson and his Time*. 1948

Jeffery, Francis, Lord Jeffrey (1773–1850). Scottish lawyer and editor. A lawyer by profession who rose to be a Scottish judge, he is better known as the co-founder (with Sydney Smith) of the *Edinburgh Review*. Jeffrey's bias against the Lakeland poets (especially Wordsworth) was as strong as his political leaning towards the Whigs.

Jeffreys, George Jeffreys, 1st Baron (1648–1689). English lawyer. He rose rapidly in his profession, partly through royal favour, in obtaining which he showed subservience and a talent for intrigue; he was knighted (1677), made a baronet (1681) and chief jusitce of the King's Bench (1683). His first trial resulted in the condemnation and execution of Algernon * Sidney, and he presided over the trial of Titus * Oates. Soon after the accession of James II he was given a peerage and earned the reputation for infamy that still clings to his name by his conduct of the 'Bloody Assize' which followed the defeat at Sedgemoor (1685) of the rebellious supporters of the Duke of Monmouth. During his progress through

Dorset and Somerest he condemned some 320 men to be hanged, more than 800 to be transported and even large numbers to be imprisoned and flogged. Jeffreys was appointed Lord Chancellor in October 1685 and served James II well. When in the autumn of 1688, faced with the invasion of William of Orange and the desertion of many of his friends, James contemplated flight, Jeffreys delivered up to him the Great Seal, which James dropped into the Thames. Jeffreys tried to escape, disguised as a sailor, but was taken at Wapping and lodged in the Tower of London, where he died. Jeffreys had many of the qualities of a good lawyer, but his reputation was marred by his brutality, irascibility (he suffered from the stone) and his patent support for royal claims.

Jellicoe, John Rushworth Jellicoe, 1st Earl (1859–1935). British sailor. He commanded the Allied expedition to relieve Peking during the Boxer Rising (1900). A strong supporter of Admiral * Fisher, he was on the committee which produced designs for the revolutionary first *Dreadnought*; and having been second sea lord (1912–14), commanded the Grand Fleet in World War I. His tactics at the Battle of Jutland (1916) were criticized at the time and only later did it appear from German documents how skilful and successful they had been; the German fleet never put to sea again. In 1919 he was made admiral of the fleet and became governor-general of New Zealand (1920–24).

Jenghiz Khan *see* **Genghis Khan**

Jeng Ho (also Cheng Ho, originally Ma Sanpao) (*c*. 1371–1433). Chinese admiral and diplomat. Born to a Mongol family, he became a eunuch in the Ming court and led seven great voyages of exploration for the emperor Yung-lo (1405 ff; 1409, 1411, 1413, 1417, 1421, 1433), visiting India, Ceylon, Persia, Java, Arabia and East Africa. His largest excursion involved 300 ships and 27,000 men.

Jenkins, Roy Harris (1920–). British politician. Born in Wales, the son of a miner who later became a union official and Labour MP, he was educated at Oxford, became an army captain in World War II, member of parliament for Central Southwark in 1948 and for Stetchford, Birmingham, in 1950; member of the executive committee of the Fabian Society 1949–61. Regarded as a liberal (or right-wing) socialist, he was Minister of Aviation in Harold * Wilson's cabinet 1964–65, Home Secretary 1965–67 and Chancellor of the Exchequer 1967–70. He was Home Secretary again in Wilson's second government 1974–76. His connection with European politics began in 1955 when he served as a delegate to the Council of Europe. He resigned from Parliament in 1976 to accept appointment as president of the European Commission (1976–80). In 1979 he had advocated the formation of a 'Middle Party' in British politics and in 1981 he established the Social Democratic Party (SDP) with the support of Shirley * Williams, David * Owen and Bill Rodgers ('The Gang of Four'). He won re-election to the House of Commons in a by-election (1982) and was first leader of the SDP until 1983. He wrote biographies of Attlee, Asquith and Dilke.

Jenner, Edward (1749–1823). English physician, renowned as the originator of vaccination. Born at Berkeley, Gloucestershire, he became a resident pupil of John Hunter in London and while there arranged the specimens brought back by Captain Cook from his first voyage. In 1773 he returned to his birthplace to practise medicine. During the next twenty years his observation of smallpox cases seemed to confirm the local belief that dairymaids who contracted cowpox (the milder bovine form of the disease) were immune. This led him to inoculate a boy of 8 with lymph taken from cowpox sores (1796). Jenner's account of this and subsequent successful vaccinations was published in his *Inquiry into the Causes and Effects of the Variolae Vaccinae* (1798). A number of leading physicians soon declared their acceptance of the idea and the opposition of the majority of other doctors was overcome when the number of deaths from smallpox fell by about two thirds in less than a decade. Parliament awarded him a grant of £30,000 for his discovery which was rapidly taken up throughout the world.
Fisk, D. M., *Jenner of Berkeley*. 1959; Rains, A. J. H., *Edward Jenner and Vaccination*. 1974

Jensen, Johannes Vilhelm (1873–1950). Danish novelist and lyric poet. His native Jutland provides a background for his *Himmeland Stories* (1898–1910). These and

his three-novel epic *The Long Journey* (1908–22), which traces the evolution of man from preglacial times up to the sixteenth century, are perhaps the best known works of this prolific author. He was awarded the Nobel Prize for Literature (1944).
Nedergaard, L., *Johannes V. Jensen*. 1968

Jeremiah (?650–*c*. 570 B.C.). Hebrew prophet, active from *c*. 626 B.C. during the reign of the Judaean kings Josiah (d. 609 B.C.) and Jehoiakim (d. 598 B.C.). He spoke against the contemporary worship of gods other than Jehovah which, he foretold, would bring divine retribution in the form of attack from the north. When these prophecies were fulfilled in the assault by the Babylonians, he urged submission to what he saw as a just punishment of the Jews by Jehovah; this view aroused great hostility and he was kidnapped and exiled to Egypt *c*. 586.
Blank, S. H., *Jeremiah, Man and Prophet*. 1961

Jerome, Jerome Klapka (1859–1927). English humorous writer and playwright. His best known works are *Three Men in a Boat* (1889), *Three Men on the Bummel* (1900), and the morality play *The Passing of the Third Floor Back* (1908), which provided one of Forbes-Robertson's most famous parts.

Jerome, St (Sophronius Eusebius Hieronymus) (*c*. 340–420). Latin doctor of the church. Born in Dalmatia, he was educated in Rome. After a period of travel and study he fell ill at Antioch and for a time lived as an ascetic in the desert. He was ordained priest in 379. In 382 he went to Rome, became the secretary of Pope Damasus and was commissioned to revise Latin translations of the Gospels and Psalms. On the death of the pope he again went to Antioch where he was joined by Paula, a wealthy Roman matron, and a party of female devotees with whom he visited sacred sites in Egypt and the Holy Land before settling at Bethlehem, where he founded a convent with Paula in charge of the women, he himself of the men. Here (from *c*. 385) he spent the rest of his life and made his famous Latin translation of the Hebrew Old Testament, which together with his New Testament revisions forms the vulgate translation still used by Roman Catholics. In addition he wrote biographies of well-known Christians, theological works, commentaries and letters. He is commemorated on 30th September.

Jerrold, Douglas William (1803–1857). English writer. Best known as one of the most regular contributors to *Punch* (where *Mrs Caudle's Curtain Lectures* won great popularity in 1845) from its second number (1841). Until his death Jerrold wrote dramas and farces for the old Coburg and Surrey Theatres, edited a succession of periodicals, e.g. *Douglas Jerrold's Weekly Newspaper* (1846–48) and found a home for his liberal opinions as editor of *Lloyd's Weekly Newspaper* (from 1852).

Jespersen, Jens Otto Harry (1860–1943). Danish philologist. Professor of English at Copenhagen University (1893–1920), and an outstanding phonetician, he wrote several studies of English grammar and originated (1928) the international language 'Novial'.

Jesus Christ (Greek name: Iesous Christos. Aramaic: Yeshu'a Mashiah. Also known as Jesus of Nazareth; to his contemporaries Jesus bar Joseph) (*c*. 8/4 B.C.–30 A.D.). Founder of Christianity. The main sources for the life of Jesus are the four Gospels, which cover barely 40 days, the Acts of the Apostles and the letters of St Paul, two brief references to the crucifixion in Suetonius and Tacitus and a disputed passage in Josephus. Archaeological research in Palestine and the discovery of the Dead Sea Scrolls have not shed any fresh light specifically relevant to Jesus and his followers.

The Gospel story, told with minor but interesting variations by the evangelists, Matthew, Mark, Luke and John, is as follows: Jesus was born, after the miraculous conception of his mother, Mary, at Bethlehem in Judaea, whither (as members of the royal house of David) **Joseph**, a carpenter of Nazareth in Galilee, and his wife (or his betrothed) Mary had come to pay a special tax decreed by the emperor Augustus. Soon after the birth of Jesus, Joseph and Mary took him for a short time to Egypt to escape the Massacre of the Innocents, ordered by King Herod, after whose death in 4 B.C. (a factor in dating these events) the family returned to Nazareth where Jesus was brought up. The exact relationship of those referred to in the New Testament as his brothers and sisters is a matter of theological dispute. Except for a visit to Jerusalem when he was 12 years old no other event is recorded until his baptism by John the Baptist when his career as preacher began, lasting two (perhaps three) years, though the actual order of events is not always clear. John's arrest by Herod Antipas may have determined when Jesus set out to preach in Galilee. After summoning the twelve disciples, who thereafter remained his close companions throughout, Jesus continued to preach, teach and heal, sometimes attracting large crowds (e.g. the Feeding of the Five Thousand). His popularity clearly dismayed the Jewish leaders, whose hypocrisy and formalism he attacked.

As Passover drew near Jesus and his disciples set out for Jerusalem; his approach caused great excitement in the city crowded with Jews gathered to celebrate the feast of Jewish independence. Jesus added to this by driving the money-lenders from the Temple. Those in power, thoroughly alarmed, bribed one of his disciples, Judas Iscariot, to betray Jesus. Then came the Last Supper, from which Judas Iscariot stole out to complete his betrayal, then the night of prayer in the garden of Gethsemane, the arrest, the trials before the Jewish authorities and the Roman governor, Pontius Pilate, each anxious to evade the final responsibility. The charge for which Pilate eventually condemned him to death was the misunderstood claim to Jewish kingship.

The Crucifixion took place immediately, on a Friday, at Golgotha (Calvary) outside Jerusalem. Permission was apparently given for the body to be taken to a private sepulchre, which, though it had been sealed was found to be empty on the morning of the third day (Easter Sunday). He appeared to the disciples and others on several occasions in different places until the time, forty days later when the Ascension into Heaven took place.

The date of Christ's birth has been taken as the base year for the Christian calendar. The calculation (made in the 6th century) was inexact and the date of his birth was almost certainly between 8 B.C. and 4 B.C.

Jevons, William Stanley (1835–1882). English economist. He worked in the Sydney Mint, and subsequently taught political economy at Manchester and London Universities. He was the proponent of the theory of utility – i.e. that the utility of materials and products determined their value. *The Theory of Political Economy* (1871) was his principal contribution to economic theory.

Jewett, Sarah Orne (1849–1909). US novelist, born in Maine. She located most of her stories in New England. Her best-known work is *The Country of the Pointed Firs* (1896).

Jezebel (*c.* 875–852 B.C.). Phoenician wife of Ahab of Israel. She introduced the worship of Baal and her name became a byword for wickedness or a painted wayward woman. She was eventually trampled to death by the horses of the successful rebel, Jehu, and reputedly eaten by dogs (II Kings ix, 32).

Jimenes *see* **Ximenes de Cisneros, Francisco**

Jiménez, Juan Ramón (1881–1958). Spanish poet. Though many of his poems are written in an evocative and melancholy mood he is a modernist in the sense that he constantly introduces new words, new sound-pictures and rhythms, e.g. those of jazz, from the modern world. He had much influence in Spain during the republican era but on the outbreak of the Spanish Civil War (1936) went to America and lived subsequently in Florida and Puerto Rico. He won the Nobel Prize for Literature (1956), the citation praising the 'high spiritual quality and artistic purity' of his lyrics.

Young, H. T., *Juan Ramón Jiménez*. 1968

Jinnah, Mohammed Ali (1876–1948). First governor general of Pakistan. A barrister by profession, he entered Indian politics in 1906 and became president of the Moslem League (1916). He tried at first to work in concert with the Indian National Congress, was present at the Round Table Conference (1930–31) and promised to try to make the 1935 constitution effective. Gradually, however, he became convinced that Hindus and Moslems could not work in harmony and from 1940 strenuously advocated the partition of India by the creation of a Moslem state to be known as Pakistan. All subsequent British attempts at compromise broke down; when the two dominions of India and Pakistan were established by a British Act of Parliament (August 1947), Jinnah became governor general of the new Moslem state.

Hodson, H. V., *The Great Divide*. 1969. McDonagh, S., *Mohammed Ali Jinnah, Maker of Modern Pakistan*. 1971

Joachim, Josef (1831–1907). Hungarian violinist and composer. He was a child prodigy, and as a virtuoso violinist at the age of 12 attracted the notice and encouragement of

Mendelssohn; when 13 he first appeared in England, where later he was a frequent and much honoured visitor. He became (1868) director of the Berlin Conservatoire (Hochschule) and founded (1869) the celebrated Joachim Quartet. His compositions for violin are now neglected.

Joan of Arc, St (Jeanne d'Arc) (*c.* 1412–1431). French heroine, known as the 'Maid of Orléans'. She was born of prosperous and devout peasant parentage in Domrémy, a village on the borders of Lorraine. At 13 she began to hear mysterious voices, which she claimed to be those of St Michael, St Margaret and St Catherine, and became convinced that she had been chosen by God to deliver France from the English. Receiving a specific call to rescue beleaguered Orléans she went, early in 1429, to Robert de Baudricourt, in command of the neighbouring castle of Vaucouleurs, and persuaded him to supply an escort to take her to the Dauphin (Charles VII) at Chinon. Having convinced him and the ecclesiastics who examined her of the genuineness of her call, she was allowed to join the army gathered for the relief of Orléans. Wearing armour, and with the shining confidence stemming from complete faith in her divine summons, she so inspired the troops that on 8 May 1429, within ten days of her coming, the siege of Orléans was raised. Joan's next move was to persuade Charles to be crowned. Accompanied by Joan and with an army of 12,000 men, he marched deep into enemy-held territory to Rheims, where in the cathedral, the traditional place for the crowning of French kings, the coronation was held. The event raised French morale to its highest point and Joan pressed for an immediate advance on Paris, but Charles dallied and before anything was achieved Joan had been captured (May 1430) while she was leading a sortie from Compiègne, threatened by Burgundian attack. The Burgundians sold Joan to their English allies. She was tried by an ecclesiastical court, presided over by Pierre Cauchon, bishop of Beauvais, which found her guilty of witchcraft and heresy. She had defended herself with great skill and superb courage, but now for the first time she weakened and made a recantation, almost immediately withdrawn: she was burned at the stake (30 May 1431) in the market place at Rouen. The judgement was reversed in 1456; Joan was canonized in 1920 by Pope Benedict XV. She was the subject of Voltaire's *La Pucelle*, and dramas by Schiller, Shaw and Anouilh.

Rankin, D. S., and Quintal, C., *The first Biography of Joan of Arc with the Chronicle Record of a Contemporary Account*. 1964; Sackville-West, V., *Joan of Arc*. 1973

Job. The hero of a book of that name in the Old Testament. The character of Job, according to the narrative, was tested and his spiritual pride cured by the loss of his property and family and by much illness and suffering, all of which he endured with exemplary patience; wealth and a long life were his eventual reward. The authority of both story and text is a matter of controversy.

Jodl, Alfred (1890–1946). German soldier. Described as the 'arch planner of the war', he was chief of staff to * Keitel in World War II. The great victories by which Europe and much of Russia were overrun were made possible by his strategic concepts and brilliant grasp of intricate detail. He was tried and sentenced to death at Nuremberg for having authorized the execution of commandos and prisoners of war.

Joffre, Joseph Jacques Césaire (1852–1931). French marshal. His early career as an engineer officer was spent mainly in the colonies, Tongking, French Sudan, Madagascar; during a successful rescue operation (1894) he captured Timbuktu. He became a divisional commander (1905) and chief of the general staff (1911), a post which made him automatically commander-in-chief of the French armies when World War I broke out. The original defence plans broke down, but the great victory of the Marne (September 1914), which halted and repelled the German advance on Paris, was largely due to his courage and decision. The prolonged stalemate which followed the stabilization of the line, coupled with the heavy losses incurred on the Somme and at Verdun, caused his replacement (December 1916) by Nivelle. He was made a marshal in 1916 (the first created since 1870), elected to the French Academy in 1918 and received the British O.M. in 1919.

Joffre, J. J. C., *Memoirs*. 1932

John (known as Don John of Austria) (1547–1578). Spanish prince, the illegitimate son of the emperor Charles V. He was brought up in Spain and given princely rank by his half-brother Philip II. His most notable exploit, when in command of the combined fleet, was to defeat the Turks at Lepanto (1571); in 1573 he captured Tunis. While viceroy of the Spanish Netherlands (from 1576) he died suddenly, thus provoking an unfounded suspicion that he had been poisoned by Philip's orders.

John (known as 'the Fearless') (1371–1419). Duke of Burgundy (from 1404). He earned the name 'Fearless' by his courage at the siege of Nicopolis (1396) while on crusade. A struggle with Louis, Duke of Orleans, for control of the insane king of France, Charles VI, ended when John had his rival murdered (1407). The heightened quarrel between the two factions, the Burgundians and the Orleanists (henceforward called Armagnacs, after Count Bernard of Armagnac, by whom they were reorganized), enabled Henry V of England to enter France and win the Battle of Agincourt (1415), from which Burgundy was pointedly absent. After the fall of Rouen (1419) Burgundy and the Dauphin (as head of the royalist or Armagnac faction) became ostensibly reconciled, but at a meeting on Montereau Bridge Burgundy was murdered by the Dauphin's followers in revenge for his assassination of the Duke of Orléans twelve years before.

John (1167–1216). King of England (from 1199). Youngest son of Henry II, he succeeded his brother Richard I, having already attempted to usurp the throne during Richard's absence on crusade. This and the murder (1204) of his nephew Arthur, a possible dynastic rival, show unscrupulous ambition, but he was not quite the ogre that early historians portrayed; his misfortunes at least matched his crimes. The barons reproached him for losing Normandy, Anjou, Maine and Touraine, but they had done little to help him resist Philip II, one of the ablest of all French kings. Moreover, in resisting the pope's claim to enforce his choice of Stephen Langton as archbishop of Canterbury, John was only making the same stand as the emperor and his fellow monarchs were making all over Europe. Again, John's failure to command the barons' loyalty left him powerless against a pope as strong and determined as * Innocent III. After England had been placed under an interdict and John himself excommunicated he made abject surrender, even accepting (1213) the pope as overlord. This won him papal support, but Langton, the new archbishop, now headed the barons' resistance to the king, who was compelled (June 1215) to accept Magna Carta at Runnymede beside the Thames. This famous document, though it aimed at preserving baronial privilege, proved ultimately to be a symbol of the achievement of popular liberties. John's very virtues as an administrator, with his extension of the power of the royal courts and his reform of the machinery of government, had roused the fears of the barons. By curbing the powers of the king they confirmed their own. John, still struggling against the barons, died at Newark in the following year.

Holt, J. C., *Magna Carta*. 1965. Warren, W., *King John*.

John. The name of six kings of Portugal. **John I** (1357–1433; succeeded 1385) married Philippa, daughter of * John of Gaunt. **John II** (1455–1495; succeeded 1481) gave encouragement and help to * Bartolomeo Diaz who rounded the Cape of Good Hope (1488). **John III** (1502–1557; succeeded 1521) was responsible for the introduction (1533) of the Inquisition into Portugal. **John IV** (1604–1656; succeeded 1640) was the first king of the house of Bragança (Braganza), his reign marking the end of sixty years' union with Spain. His daughter Catherine married Charles II of England. **John V** (1689–1750; succeeded 1707) was a great patron of learning. Fifty thousand men were employed for thirteen years on the palace and monastery of Mafra which he started. **John VI** (1769–1826; succeeded 1816) took refuge in Brazil during the Napoleonic Wars and remained there until 1821. In 1822 Brazil became independent with his son Pedro as first emperor.

Livermore, H. V., *A New History of Portugal*. 1969

John XXIII (Angelo Giuseppe Roncalli) (1881–1963). Pope (from 1958). Born near Bergamo, in northern Italy, the son of a peasant, he was ordained in 1904. As apostolic visitor or delegate (1925–44) to Bulgaria, Greece and Turkey and as papal nuncio to France after World War II, he acquired a knowledge of other lands and a breadth of vision that stood him in good stead later. In 1953 he became a cardinal and patriarch (archbishop) of Venice. As pope his greatest achievement was the summoning of the ecumenical council which met in Rome in 1963, one of whose main objects was the furtherance of Christian unity. Though by the simplicity and generosity of his character Pope John became one of the best loved figures of his generation, he was a firm and shrewd administrator and by no means subservient to the bureaucracy which surrounded him. He wrote an important biography of St Carlo Borromeo (5 volumes, 1936–52).

The title 'John XXIII' was also used by the Neopolitan 'anti-pope' Cossa. His election (1410) was recognized by France, England and some other countries but he was deposed by the council of Constance (1415) for his excesses.

John XXIII, Pope, *Journal of a Soul*. 1965

John, Augustus Edwin (1878–1961). British painter, born at Tenby, Wales. Gipsy life appealed to him and inspired such large and colourful pictures as *The Mumpers*, but it is as a portrait painter that he is best known. His own vigour, vitality and personality are reflected in, e.g., his *Bernard Shaw* (1914), the cellist *Madame Suggia* (1927), and *Dylan Thomas* (1937). John's paintings display few contemporary trends and owe almost everything to his own intuitive talent. He was elected A.R.A. in 1921, R.A. in 1928, and awarded the O.M. in 1942. His sister, **Gwen John** (1876–1939), was distinguished for her delicate, sensitive paintings. His sailor son, **Sir Caspar John** (1903–1984), was first sea lord at the Admiralty (1960–63).

Holroyd, M., *Augustus John*. 1975

John the Divine, St (also known as 'the Apostle' and 'the Evangelist') (*c.* 3 A.D.–100 A.D.?). Christian apostle; one of the four evangelists. He was a son of Zebedee and brother of * James and like him a Galilee fisherman. Jesus called them the 'Boanerges', sons of thunder, because they asked permission to call down fire from Heaven upon a Samaritan village. The identification of John with 'the disciple whom Jesus loved' of the fourth Gospel is traditional but disputed, but he was certainly in the inner ring of the apostles – he was present at the Transfiguration and the raising of Jairus's daughter and took part in preparing the Last Supper; he appears in the Acts as one of the leaders of the early church. Also traditional and also disputed are his exile to Patmos and death at Ephesus in extreme old age.

St John is the reputed author of the fourth Gospel, three Epistles and the Book of Revelation (the Apocalypse). The last has been the subject of endless discussion. Of the Epistles only the first can with any degree of certainty be ascribed on grounds of style to the author of the Gospel. From the 19th century, scriptural scholars assumed that John was the last written of the four canonical Gospels, composed in Greek and showing Hellenistic influence. However, Bishop John Robinson and others have argued a revisionist position: that the language used resembles that of the Dead Sea scrolls, that it was probably written in Aramaic and may predate Mark, Matthew and Luke. John denies that Christianity provides just another field for abstract speculation: 'The Word [*Logos*] became flesh'. Throughout there is a much more developed theology than in the three synoptic Gospels.

John Chrysostom, St (347–407). Patriarch of Constantinople. Born at Antioch, he was ordained priest there (386) and soon gained a great reputation as a preacher (*Chrysostom* = '*golden mouthed*'). In 398 the emperor Arcadius secured his appointment as patriarch of Constantinople. His outspoken preaching, however, which included attacks on the empress Eudoxia, earned the hostility of the court. He was temporarily exiled (403) and in 404 banished to Armenia. He died while on his way to a still more distant place of exile. Among his many works are *On the Priesthood*, an early treatise, and his *Homilies*, which give some idea of the eloquence for which he was famous. The liturgy of St Chrysostom has no authentic claim to the ascription.

John of Gaunt (1340–1399). English prince, called after Ghent, where he was born. He was the fourth son of Edward III and having acquired the vast Lancastrian estates through his first wife, Blanche, was created Duke of Lancaster in 1362. After his second marriage, to Constance of Castile, he assumed the title king of Castile (1372), but having failed to establish himself he abandoned his claim when his daughter married (1388) the Castilian heir. When Edward III's powers began to fail, John of Gaunt virtually ruled the kingdom and continued in power during part of Richard II's minority. In 1390 he was created Duke of

Aquitaine and again was unsuccessful in establishing control of an overseas territory. In 1396 he married his mistress Catherine Swynford, and obtained from Richard legitimization for her three sons, who took the name of Beaufort; a descendant, Margaret Beaufort, was the mother of Henry VII. John of Gaunt gave, for a time, powerful support to John * Wyclif with the political aim of combating church privilege; Chaucer too found in him a patron. (* Henry IV.)
Armitage-Smith, S., *John of Gaunt*. 1964

John of Leyden (Jan Beuckelzoon) (1509–1536). Dutch anabaptist. An innkeeper of Leiden, he became a wandering preacher and established (1533) in Münster a 'Kingdom of Zion' in which he instituted polygamy and community of goods. Within a year the city was captured by the bishop of Münster and John and his chief supporters were tortured and killed.

John of the Cross, St (San Juan de la Cruz) (1542–1591). Spanish mystic and monk. He joined St * Teresa in trying to restore a stricter discipline for the Carmelite monks and nuns. This involved him in much persecution and eventually led to a split between the reformed houses of 'discalced' (i.e. shoeless or barefoot) and 'calced' Carmelites. Throughout the many vagaries of fortune resulting from the quarrel John was writing, in language combining great beauty of expression with spiritual ecstasy, the three great poems, with commentaries on them, upon which his fame rests: *Dark Night of the Soul, The Spiritual Canticle* and *The Living Flame of Love*. Together they describe the full range and depth of the mystical experiences of a contemplative life. He was canonized in 1726.

John of Salisbury (d. 1180). Ecclesiastical politician and scholar. A pupil of Abelard, he spent a great part of his life in France, notably at Chartres. He wrote a life of * Becket, at whose murder he was present and for whose canonization he pressed. A prolific writer, he contributed significantly to what has been called 'the twelfth-century renaissance'.
Webb, C. C. J., *John of Salisbury*. 1932

John Paul I (Cardinal Albino Luciani) (1912–1978). Pope 1978. The son of poor parents, he was ordained a priest in 1935, became Bishop of Vittorio Venuto (1958–69), Patriarch of Venice (1969–78) and a Cardinal (1973). On the death of Paul VI, he was elected Pope on the fourth ballot. Regarded as a theological conservative, but with wide pastoral experience and great personal simplicity, he ended some of the Vatican's traditional pomp. He died unexpectedly after a reign of 33 days.

John Paul II (Cardinal Karol Wojtyla) (1920–). Pope from 1978. Born near Krakow, the son of an army sergeant, he received a secular high school education, worked in a quarry and chemical factory, was active in Poland's anti-Nazi resistance and studied theology in an underground seminary. Ordained in 1946, he became a student chaplain and university teacher, writing many books and articles. Archbishop of Krakow (1963–78) and a Cardinal (1967), he was elected Pope on the eighth ballot (24 Oct. 1978) after the sudden death of John Paul I, becoming the first non-Italian Pope since Adrian VI (elected 1523) and the youngest since Pius IX. He travelled extensively, visiting Ireland, Poland, Britain, the USA, Korea, Africa, Mexico and South America, where he reaffirmed to large and enthusiastic congregations basic Catholic principles.

John the Baptist, St. According to the account in St Luke's Gospel, an angel appeared to a priest called Zacharias to tell him that his prayers had been answered and that his wife Elizabeth, hitherto believed barren, would bear him a son. This son, John, appeared (*c.* A.D. 27) in the desert beyond the River Jordan giving warning of the judgement to come and 'preaching the baptism of repentance and the remission of sins'. Some asked him if he was the promised Messiah but this he denied saying that he was only the forerunner of a mightier one, 'the latchet of whose shoes I am not worthy to unloose'. John showed his fearlessness in denouncing sin when he rebuked Herod Antipas for marrying his brother Philip's wife Herodias. Cast into prison he was executed at the request (prompted by her mother Herodias) of Salome – unnamed in the Bible – who had pleased Herod by her dancing.

Johnson, Amy (1903–1941). English pioneer airwoman, born in Hull. She became (1930) the first to fly alone from London to Australia (in 19½ days), and she made record flights e.g. from London to Cape Town and back (1932 and 1936) and, with her husband, James A. Mollison (1905–59), from London to the U.S.A. (1933). During World War II she flew aircraft from factories to airfields and is believed to have drowned after parachuting into the Thames.

Johnson, Andrew (1808–1875). Seventeenth president of the U.S. (1865–69). Born in North Carolina, he was trained as a tailor and set up his own business in Greenville, Tennessee. He soon became active in local politics as the champion of the 'little man', and was eventually governor of Tennessee (1853) and U.S. Senator (1857–62). When the south seceded on the outbreak of the Civil War he declared for the Union, and after his appointment as a military governor (1862) even managed to bring his state back to its federal allegiance. In 1864 he was chosen vice-president of the U.S. and after Abraham Lincoln's assassination (1865) assumed the presidency. To him fell the difficult task of reconstruction, which he felt should be left to the southerners themselves, and he held that only those who had taken an active part against the Union should be penalized. This lenient policy incensed the Republican radicals: both houses of Congress, over the president's veto, passed a Reconstruction Bill, giving full civil rights, including the vote, to Negroes, and unleashed a campaign of vilification of unprecedented virulence against Johnson. His dismissal (1867) of Stanton, secretary for war, gave his enemies the final excuse they needed for the president's impeachment; he was acquitted by a single vote but did not seek re-election.
McKitrick, E., *Andrew Johnson, a Profile*. 1969

Johnson, Hewlett (1874–1966). English clergyman. Called 'The Red Dean', he was ordained in 1905 after work in engineering and social welfare; he became Dean of Manchester in 1924 and Dean of Canterbury in 1931. He first visited Russia in 1938 and thereafter became famous for his continuous praise of the Soviet system and of Marxist philosophy.
Johnson, H., *Searching for Light*. 1968

Johnson, Jack (John Arthur) (1878–1946). American boxer. By beating Tommy Burns (1908) in Sydney he became the first Negro world professional heavyweight champion; he lost the title to Jess Willard (1915).

Johnson, Lyndon Baines (1908–1973). Thirty-sixth president of the U.S. (1963–69). He was born in Texas, where he started his career as a teacher. He became director of the National Youth Administration of Texas (1935) and later became prominent in business and Democratic party politics. He was first elected to Congress in 1936 and after serving as a representative until 1949 was elected as senator. During World War II he served with distinction for a time in the navy and was Roosevelt's personal representative in Australia and New Zealand. As Democratic leader of the Senate from 1953 he showed remarkable skill in using constitutional procedures against the Republicans, and persuasiveness in gathering support. After failing to obtain nomination as Democratic candidate for the presidency (1960) he became vice-president to Kennedy, after whose assassination Johnson succeeded as president, and was returned in the 1964 election. At home he continued Kennedy's liberal policies, one of his greatest triumphs being the passage of the Civil Rights Bill (1964). In his most difficult and continuing foreign problem, the war in Vietnam, while expressing willingness to negotiate he greatly increased the scale of American military participation.
Caro, R. A., *The Years of Lyndon Johnson*. 1982; 1984; incomplete

Johnson, Philip Cortelyou (1906–). American architect, born in Ohio. Educated at Harvard, he directed the architecture department of New York's Museum of Modern Art 1930–36 and 1946–54, and became an influential critic, patron and propagandist of the 'International Style' of * Gropius and * Mies. As an architect he won rapid recognition with a 'glass house' built for himself at New Canaan, Conn. (1949); further buildings were added in his grounds (to 1965). Johnson's designs, vehemently attacked as 'frivolous' or 'neo-Fascist', emphasized elegance and style. He saw architecture as primarily an art form and rejected functionalism, with its strong social concern. Among his major public buildings were the IDS Centre at Minneapolis (1973), extensions to the Boston Public Library (1973), the twin towers at Pennzoil Place, Houston (1976) and the Avery Fisher Hall interior, New York (1976), all with John Burgee.

Johnson, Samuel (1709–1784). English man of letters. He was born at Lichfield, the son of a bookseller. As a boy he suffered from scrofula, the 'King's evil', for which he was taken to London to be 'touched' by Queen Anne. Having left Oxford University early because of poverty (he was later given an honorary LL.D.) he taught and wrote until his marriage with Elizabeth Porter, a widow twenty years older than himself, provided him with £800, with which he set up a small school near Lichfield. When this failed he set out (1731) with one of his pupils, David * Garrick, to seek his fortune in London. His first important poem *London* (1738) appeared anonymously and it was only after several years as a hack writer for the *Gentleman's Magazine*, to which he contributed poems, essays and parliamentary reports, that he achieved some degree of fame with his life of his friend, Richard * Savage (1744). The plan of his *Dictionary* appeared in 1749, addressed to Lord * Chesterfield, who received it coolly and was later suitably snubbed; this great work was eventually published in 1755 and an abridgement in 1756. Meanwhile an old play of Johnson's, *Irene*, was staged in 1749 at Drury Lane, through Garrick's kindness, but only ran for nine nights. In the same year came *The Vanity of Human Wishes*, a satire modelled on one by * Juvenal. Shortly afterwards he began to edit the *Rambler* (1750–52), which was followed by the *Idler* (1758–60). The contents of both periodicals were written almost entirely by himself and consisted mainly of essays on literary and social themes. To pay for his mother's funeral he also wrote, 'in the evenings of a single week' a most successful pot-boiler, *Rasselas, Prince of Abyssinia*, a novel of which the prince's vain journey in quest of happiness provides the theme. In 1763 Johnson escaped for the first time 'from the tyranny of writing for bread' by the grant of a crown pension of £300 a year, and was at last able to enjoy what to him was the greatest pleasure in life, the company and conversation of congenial friends. At this time that most brilliant and sympathetic of recorders, James * Boswell, entered his circle of friends – one of the happiest coincidences of literary history. Other members of the 'Club' included Reynolds, Burke, Goldsmith, Garrick and Boswell's rival biographer, Sir John Hawkins. Johnson's wife had died in 1752; in the last twenty years of his life he found great pleasure in the friendship of the lively Mrs Thrale, in whose home he was welcomed as an almost perpetual guest.

During these later years Johnson's literary works included a comprehensive edition of Shakespeare's plays (1765), a notable critical achievement; *A Journey to the Western Islands of Scotland* (1775), a parallel account to one made by Boswell, his companion on the tour; and finally the work which showed his full maturity as a critic, *Lives of the Poets* (1779–81). Few writers have so dominated the literary scene as did Johnson in later life and his burial at Westminster Abbey was tribute not only to his work but to a character which, however rugged, was generous-hearted, virtuous, just and marked by common-sense.

Boswell, J., *Life of Johnson*. 1791. Wain, J., *Samuel Johnson*. 1974

Johnson, William Eugene (known as 'Pussyfoot') (1862–1945). American temperance reformer. His nickname referred to his methods of suppressing illicit traffic in liquor in Indian territory where he served as a special officer (1908–11). He was the dominating figure of the Anti-Saloon League (1912–20). The passage of the 18th constitutional amendment (1920) made prohibition mandatory throughout the U.S.A. until it was repealed (1933).

Johnston, Sir Harry Hamilton (1858–1927). British colonial administrator. As a naturalist he led the Royal Society's expedition (1884) to Mount Kilimanjaro and afterwards held official posts in many parts of Africa. He was very largely responsible for the British acquisition of Nyasaland (Malawi) and large areas of Northern Rhodesia (Zambia).

Joliot-Curie, Jean Frédéric (1900–1957). French physicist. He added Curie to his name on his marriage (1926) to Irène, daughter of Pierre and Marie * Curie, whom he met at the Radium Institute, Paris. In 1933 he and his wife, by bombarding boron with accelerated alphaparticles, discovered that radioactivity could be artificially induced in non-radioactive substances. They later also discovered that there is a net emission of neutrons during nuclear fission. They were awarded the Nobel Prize for Chemistry (1935). Irène died (1956) of burns caused by radiation from radium.

Biquard, P. (trans. Strachan, G.), *Frédéric Joliot-Curie: The Man and his Theories*. 1965

Jolson, Al (1886–1950). American popular singer and entertainer. He was born in Russia

as Asa Yoelson and emigrated to America *c.* 1895. He began his career in the New York variety theatre in 1899 and became successful by bringing a powerful voice and melodramatic style to sentimental songs. His film *The Jazz Singer* (1927) was the first to use sound so that the plot could progress through dialogue.
Freedland, M., *Jolson.* 1972

Jonah. Jewish prophet and missionary. The Book of Jonah (Old Testament) relates how he was summoned by God to go to Nineveh, the capital of Assyria, to preach repentance. To evade this mission he sailed for Tarshish, but a storm convinced the crew that a bearer of ill luck was among them; they established, by casting lots, that this was Jonah and threw him overboard. He was swallowed by a great fish which spewed him up three days later, alive, and he went to Nineveh, whose citizens he induced to repent.

Jones, David (1895–1974). English poet and artist. His major work *In Parenthesis* (1937) records in a melange of blank verse and prose his experiences and feelings during World War I.

Jones, Henry Arthur (1851–1929). English playwright. He wrote a long series of plays, some of which by their realistic treatment of social problems resembled the work of his more talented Norwegian contemporary, Ibsen. *The Silver King* (1882), *Saints and Sinners* (1884) and *Mrs Dane's Defence* (1900) were among the best known.
Jones, J. D., ed., *Life and Letters.* 1930

Jones, Inigo (1573–1652). English architect. He studied in Italy and was deeply impressed by the buildings of * Palladio, whose style, with its classical features, he introduced to England. Of his works his finest is held to be the Banqueting House at Whitehall (1619–22), the only part of the palace to survive. The elaborate plans which he made (*c.* 1638) for rebuilding the rest of the palace were never executed. Another masterpiece is the Queen's House, Greenwich, which reveals his liking for centrally planned cubic buildings, a characteristic of his work elsewhere; the famous double-cube room at Wilton is his design. In addition to his architectural work he planned the layout of Lincoln's Inn Fields and Covent Garden. He was surveyor general of works (1615–43), but both James I and Charles I employed him to design elaborate sets for court masques as much as for building. As a theatrical designer he is said to have introduced the proscenium arch and movable scenery. Inigo Jones was the first in England to make a full time profession of architecture.
Orgel, S., and Strong, R., *Inigo Jones.* 1973

Jones, (John) Paul (1747–1792). American sailor, born in Scotland. His name was John Paul until he changed it, probably in 1773. Paul Jones, who had served in a slaver for five years, had already visited America several times before offering his services to the American colonists who, to aid their bid for independence, were in 1775 fitting out a small fleet. In 1778 in a brig of eighteen guns he made several raids on the Scottish coast; he fired a ship and spiked thirty-six guns at Whitehaven in Cumberland and captured a sloop in Belfast Lough. In the following year, in command of a small French squadron in American service, he captured two British men-of-war in a fierce encounter off Flamborough Head, Yorkshire. For this he was awarded a congressional medal. In 1788 he served for a year in the Black Sea as a rear-admiral in Catherine the Great's navy, then at war with the Turks. He died in Paris, but in 1905 his remains were taken to the U.S.A., where he is regarded as a national hero.
Morrison, S. E., *John Paul Jones.* 1960

Jones, Robert (Bobby) **Tyre** (1902–1971). American amateur golfter. He competed in the U.S. amateur championship at the age of 14 and later won the U.S. open championship four times and the British open championship thirteen times; he was the outstanding golfer of the 1920–30 decade.

Jonson, Ben (1573–1637). English dramatist and poet. He had a good education at Westminster School, but was bricklayer, soldier and actor before taking to writing. Eighteen of about thirty of his plays survive. *Every Man in his Humour* (1598) was his first success (the word 'humour', as always in that period having a physical as well as a psychological connotation). In the same year he was imprisoned and his goods confiscated for killing an actor in a duel. *The Poetaster* (1601), though set in ancient Rome, was an attack on Dekker and Marston which caused offence. His first tragedy *Sejanus* was acted by Shakespeare's company in 1603, but neither this nor a later tragedy from Roman history, *Catiline* (1611), achieved much success. In collaboration with Chapman and Marston he wrote *Eastward Ho!* (1605), for which he was briefly imprisoned for disparaging the Scots. His masterpieces are *Volpone or The Fox* (1606), a savage attack on human greed; *The Alchemist* (1610), a lively study of gullibility; and one of his greatest successes, *Bartholomew Fair* (1614), notable for its vivid picture of low life in London. From 1603 he was also busily employed in writing masques for the court of James I, some staged by Inigo * Jones; they include *The Masque of Beauty* (1608), *The Masque of Queens* (1609). In 1616 he was given a pension and his literary pre-eminence was fully acclaimed. His many beautiful lyrics include *Drink to me only with thine eyes*. Jonson was forthright and quick-tempered, but his generosity and sincerity endeared him to a wide circle of friends, including Donne, Bacon and Shakespeare and to his patrons, the Sidneys.

Herford, C. H., and Simpson, P. and E. (eds.), *Works*. II vols., 1925–1951; Chute, M., *Ben Jonson of Westminster*. 1953

Jordaens, Jakob (1593–1678). Flemish painter. He lived and worked in Antwerp at the same time as Rubens, whom he admired and assisted, and van Dyck. He did not equal these masters by reason of a certain harshness or crudity of his colour and technique. He peopled even religious and mythological paintings with the earthy, vigorous bourgeois or peasant types he encountered in everyday life.

Joseph. Hebrew patriarch. The elder son of * Jacob and Rachel, he was his father's favourite, and his jealous brothers sold him into slavery in Egypt. There he gained a position of trust in the household of his master Potiphar. Resisting the blandishments of Potiphar's wife he won the pharaoh's favour and rose to be chief administrator, established a great granary and when his brothers came to Egypt to buy grain in the years of famine forgave them and secured a home for the family in the land of Goshen. His sons Ephraim and Manasseh became the ancestors of two of the tribes of Israel.

Joseph, St *see* **Jesus Christ**

Joseph II (1741–1790). Holy Roman Emperor (from 1765–90), Archduke of Austria (from 1780). He followed his father Francis I as emperor and at the same time began to rule the Habsburg possessions jointly with his mother * Maria Theresa, though as long as she lived she limited his authority to military and foreign affairs. After her death (1780) he showed himself to belong to the 'age of enlightenment' by attacking the power of the church – he reduced the clergy from 63,000 to 27,000 and issued an edict (1781) granting complete religious toleration – and by abolishing serfdom, greatly extending the facilities for general and scientific education, hospital treatment, care of orphans, the insane etc., and by reforming taxation. He also tried to establish German as a common language throughout his dominions. To achieve these measures he centralized government in Vienna and extended in every direction the powers of the state, for which, however, he made it clear that he alone was entitled to speak. By this mixture of radicalism and despotism he antagonized many of his subjects, not only clergy, nobles and local administrators but all the inhabitants of the non-German lands. In 1788 there were widespread revolts. He died a disillusioned and disappointed man.

Joseph, Père (François Leclerc du Tremblay; known as 'Eminence Grise', 'Grey Eminence') (1577–1638). French Capuchin friar, adviser and confidant of Cardinal * Richelieu. This position led to his nickname (from the colour of his habit), now applied to any unofficial power behind the throne. Richelieu used him from 1612 in all the most difficult negotiations of a critical period which included the Thirty Years War. Aldous Huxley's *Grey Eminence* gives a fascinating account of his somewhat mysterious personage.

Joseph, Sir Keith Sinjohn, 2nd Bart. (1918–). English politician. A Fellow of All Souls, Oxford, he was a Conservative MP (1956–), minister for health and social services (1970–74), secretary of state for industry (1979–81), and for education and science (1981–). A strong 'free marketeer' he drew inspiration from Adam * Smith and Milton * Friedman and supported Margaret * Thatcher.

Joseph of Arimathea. Legendary owner of the tomb in which Jesus Christ was laid, and founder of Glastonbury as a Christian shrine (where he is reputedly buried). The Glastonbury thorn which flowered at Christmas was believed to be his staff plunged into the ground.

Josephine (Marie Josèphe Rose Tascher de la Pagerie) (1763–1814). Empress of the French (1804–09). The daughter of a planter in Martinique, she married (1779) the Vicomte de Beauharnais, who was guillotined in 1794. After his death Josephine became one of the liveliest members of the gay society that came to the surface after the ending of the Terror. A member of the Directory, Barras, whose mistress she had been, introduced her to Napoleon Bonaparte; she married him in 1796 and during the Consulate and Empire she was the centre of his court. As she bore him no children she frustrated his dynastic ambitions; he divorced her (1809) to marry the Austrian archduchess Marie Louise. Josephine retired to Malmaison. Of her children by her first marriage, Eugène became Napoleon's viceroy in Italy, and Hortense married his brother Louis Bonaparte and so became queen of Holland and mother of Napoleon III.

Josephson, Brian David (1940–). British physicist. He shared the 1973 Nobel Prize for Physics for his work on superconductivity in metals leading to the 'Josephson effect'—a flow of current between two pieces of superconducting material separated by a thin layer of insulation. He was a professor of physics at Cambridge 1974–

Josephus, Flavius (*c.* 37–*c.* 100). Jewish priest, soldier and historian, descended from a royal and priestly line. He at first took an active part in the Jewish revolt against the Romans (66) and was made governor of Galilee. He fought valiantly but after being captured he sought and won the favour of Vespasian, and was with Titus at the siege of Jerusalem. When the revolt was crushed he was rewarded by a grant of confiscated land, but spent the rest of his life in Rome. There he wrote in halting Greek his *History of the Jewish War*, the main authority for the events of Jewish history in the first century A.D. and of the Jewish war (66–70), and *The Antiquities of the Jews* (written in 93), a history of the Jews from the Creation up to the period covered by his earlier work. His *Autobiography* is mainly concerned to refute criticism of his own activities before and during the revolt. His knowledge of the country, its religion, politics and people, give the books a particular value except where self-defence demands a biased account.
Williamson, G. A., *The World of Josephus*. 1964

Joshua. Hebrew leader, after whom a book of the Old Testament is named. Son of Nun of the tribe of Ephraim, he succeeded Moses as leader of Israel. The book describes the various episodes of the conquest of Canaan.

Josquin des Prés (*c.* 1450–1521). Flemish composer. Born at Condé, he trained under Okeghem, contemporary master of contrapuntal technique. He is known to have been attached to ducal courts it Italy in the 1470s, and worked at the Sistine chapel in Rome 1486–94. He was choirmaster in Cambrai cathedral 1495–99 and served Louis XII of France until 1516, when he returned to Condé as a canon of the collegiate church of St Quentin. His published work includes 17 masses, at least 100 motets and a number of secular songs. In his lifetime he was regarded as a genius in counterpoint and expressive melody. He was forgotten during the seventeenth century and re-discovered through Charles Burney's *History of Music* 1776–80.
Ambros, A. W., ed. Kade, O., *History of Music, Vol. 3*. 1893; Blume, F., *Josquin des Prés*. 1939

Joubert, Petrus Jacobus (1834–1900). South African soldier. As commandant-general of the forces of the Transvaal, he defeated the British in the war of 1880–81 and * Jameson in the Raid of 1896. After directing the siege of Ladysmith in the Boer War he fell ill and died.

Jouhaux, Léon (1879–1954). French trade-union leader. As general secretary (1909–47) of the French General Confederation of Labour (C.G.T.), he played the leading role in promoting the trade-union movement in France. He was imprisoned by the Germans in World War II. He won the Nobel Peace Prize (1951).

Joule, James Prescott (1818–1889). English physicist. The son of a Salford brewer, he had little formal training but was tutored by * Dalton and showed exceptional aptitude for experimental work. He investigated the transformation of heat into other forms of energy and was one of the first to establish the principle of the conservation of energy. He established (1840) the law concerning the relationship between the heat developed in an electrical circuit and the strength of the current and resistance. He discovered (1843) a method for measuring the mechanical equivalent of heat, and published (1851) the first calculation of the average velocity of a gas molecule. His theories were initially rejected by the Royal Society but in 1850 he was elected a Fellow and was awarded the Society's Royal and Copley Medals. He is commemorated by the name joule, given to the unit of energy.

Jowett, Benjamin (1817–1893). English classical scholar. A famous master (1870–93) of Balliol College, Oxford, of which he had been fellow since 1838, he managed to attract and influence a succession of brilliant undergraduates who, for a generation and more, came to exercise an intellectual domination in the academic and political worlds. His own reputation as a possessor of universal knowledge depended as much upon his personality as upon his excellent, but at times inexact, translations of Plato, Thucydides and Aristotle.
Faber, G., *Jowett: A Portrait with a Background.* 2nd ed. 1958

Jowitt, William Allen Jowitt, 1st Earl (1885–1957). English lawyer and Labour politician. In his profession he became known as a brilliant advocate and cross-examiner. He first entered parliament in 1922 and in the course of an intermittent career there he was attorney general (1929–32), solicitor general (1940–42), first minister of National Insurance (1944–45) and finally lord chancellor under Attlee (1945–51).

Joyce, James (1882–1941). Irish novelist. Born in Dublin, one of a civil servant's family of fifteen, and educated in Jesuit schools and at University College, Dublin, he developed great talents as a linguist. In 1904, having returned after two years in Paris studying medicine he met Nora Barnacle (1883–1951) with whom he lived for the rest of his life, marrying her in 1931. From 1905, except for short intervals, he lived in Vienna, Trieste, Zurich and from 1920 in Paris. For most of his life he had to struggle with poverty and severe eye disease.

In his first novel, the autobiographical *A Portrait of the Artist as a Young Man* (1916), he is already preoccupied with the sordid realities of life – a preoccupation carried further in his famous *Ulysses* (1922), which describes eighteen hours in the lives of a group of Dublin residents in minute detail and with a hitherto unknown realism. Such shape as there is to this enormous work is given by a parallel between the eighteen episodes and those of the *Odyssey* and between the central characters, Leopold Bloom, his wife Molly and their friend Dedalus, with Homer's Ulysses, Penelope and Telemachus. One method of composition used has come to be known as 'stream of consciousness', words and sentences following one another by an automatic process of mental association; some of these associations, such as similarity of sound (e.g. rhymes and puns) are fairly obvious; some derive from telescoping one or more words or ideas; others, springing from the width and depth of the author's knowledge, are so recondite as to be unintelligible to the ordinary reader. *Ulysses* was banned in America until 1933 and until 1934 in England. Seventeen years went to the making of *Finnegans Wake* (1939), a work recording the dreams experienced in a single night by H. C. Earwicker, a Dublin hotelier. T. S. Eliot called Joyce 'the greatest master of the English language since Milton'.
Ellman, R., *James Joyce.* 1959

Joyce, William (known as 'Lord Haw-Haw') (1906–1946). American-born Nazi propagandist of Irish parentage. After being a speaker and 'storm trooper' in Fascist organizations in the East End of London, he went to Germany (August 1939) and became the principal Nazi broadcaster in English during World War II; he owed his nickname to his unpleasant sneering voice. After the war he was captured, being held subject to British jurisdiction by reason of the fact that he used a British passport, tried, and executed for treason.

Juan Carlos (1938–). King of Spain 1975– . Grandson of * Alfonso XIII, he was born in Rome. General * Franco nominated him as his successor in 1969.

Juarez, Benito Pablo (1806–1872). Mexican president. A Zapotec Indian, he came as a servant to Oaxaca where, having married his employer's daughter and graduated in law, he eventually rose to be state governor (1847–52). As minister of justice in a radical government he attempted to curb the power of the church and the army. In 1857 the liberals declared him president but the conservatives rose against him and forced him to retire to Vera Cruz. He re-entered Mexico City in 1860 and was confirmed as president by the election of 1861. Suspension of interest payments led to a French invasion and the establishment of * Maximilian of Austria as emperor. After Maximilian's execution (1867) Juarez was again elected president and resumed his programme of reform, but when he was re-elected (1871) he failed to quell a revolt by an unsuccessful candidate, Porfirio * Díaz, and shortly afterwards died.

Roeder, R., *Juarez and his Mexico*. 1947

Judah. Fourth son of * Jacob and Leah. He became the ancestor of the tribe that bears his name, to which the royal house of David belonged. The area in the south of Palestine occupied by the tribe and that of Benjamin became, after the death of Solomon, the separate kingdom of Judah.

Judas Iscariot. The betrayer of Jesus Christ. He was the treasurer of the apostles, and though no motive for his treachery is given in the Gospels it has been surmised that it was due to disappointment that Jesus had no plans to establish an earthly kingdom. After betraying his master for thirty pieces of silver he committed suicide.

Judas Maccabeus *see* **Maccabaeus**

Jugurtha (reigned 118–104 B.C.). King of Numidia (roughly modern Algeria). Having secured undisputed possession of the whole kingdom by the murder of two co-rulers, he provoked the intervention of Rome by a massacre of Roman merchants. By going himself to Rome, he gained a respite, but war was soon resumed. Despite early success Jugurtha was forced to adopt guerrilla tactics by the systematic occupation of his bases by Metellus and * Marius; finally he was betrayed by his ally, Bocchus of Mauritania, and died in prison at Rome.

Hawthorn, J. R., *Rome and Jugurtha*. 1969

Juin, Alphonse Pierre (1888–1967). French soldier. Having previously fought in World War I and in Morocco, he was taken prisoner during the battle for France (1940) of World War II. Released by the Germans, he was appointed by Pétain's Vichy Government to command the French forces in North Africa. He continued in command under Giraud and de Gaulle, and subsequently commanded French troops in Italy. He was then successively chief of the French general staff (1944–47) and resident general in Morocco (1947–51). From 1951 he filled important posts in NATO and was in command of Allied forces in central Europe (1953–56). He opposed de Gaulle's policy of granting independence to Algeria. When appointed marshal (1952), he was the only living Frenchman to hold that distinction.

Julia (39 B.C.–A.D. 14). Only child of the Roman emperor Augustus. She was married to Marcellus (25 B.C.), Agrippa (21 B.C.), and the future emperor Tiberius (12 B.C.). Her daughter by Agrippa was * Agrippina, mother of the emperor * Caligula. Julia's last marriage gave her no happiness; she gave way to profligacy and in 2 B.C. was banished for adultery and scandalous behaviour. Eventually she starved herself to death.

Julian (Flavius Claudius Julianus; known as 'the Apostate') (*c.* 331–363). Roman emperor (from 361). He was born in Constantinople, the nephew of Constantine I. He and his half-brother Gallus were the only males of the Flavian line spared in the general massacre which took place (337) on Constantine's death; his education in philosophy in Nicomedia, Constantinople and Athens turned him away from Christianity and he secretly adopted paganism (351). In 335 he was given command on the Rhine by his cousin the emperor Constantius and in the next five years succeeded in restoring the frontiers and purging the provincial government of dishonesty and corruption. He became highly popular with the army, and when the emperor sought to transfer his troops to the East to restore the situation there, they mutinied and proclaimed him emperor (360); in the same year he openly announced his paganism. He then moved eastwards, but Constantius's death (361) forestalled a conflict. Julian spent a year in Constantinople, introducing a number of reforms; though he himself worshipped the pagan gods and deprived the Christian church of its privileges, he exercised a wide tolerance. In 363 he began a war against Persia and was mortally wounded in a skirmish. Julian was one of the most accomplished of the emperors,

and his writings – some philosophical and self-justificatory, some satires on the lives of his predecessors – are distinguished by the purity of their Greek.
Vidal, G., *Julian*. 1972

Juliana (1909–). Queen of the Netherlands (1948–80). She succeeded on the abdication of her mother, Queen Wilhelmina, and proved a conscientious and popular constitutional monarch. In 1937 she married Prince Bernhard of Lippe-Biesterfeld by whom she had four daughters: Beatrix, Irene, Margriet and Maria. The marriages of both the elder princesses aroused criticism and controversy: that of Beatrix because Claus von Amsberg was a German; that of Irene because her husband, Don Carlos, was a pretender to the Spanish throne, a circumstance which led to the princess's surrender of her rights of succession in the Netherlands. In the 1970s Juliana's husband was accused of involvement in illicit financial dealings with American companies. She abdicated in 1980 in favour of her daughter Beatrix.

Julius II (Giuliano della Rovere) (1443–1513). Pope (from 1503). One of the great popes of the Renaissance, he was made a cardinal (1479) by his uncle Sixtus IV. When his arch-enemy Alexander VI (Rodrigo Borgia) was pope, Cardinal della Rovere went to France and induced Charles VIII to invade Italy with a view to his deposition. The expedition failed but after the death of Alexander (1503) only the brief interlude of Pius III's reign delayed his accession as pope. Julius's two main aims were to unite all papal territories under his personal rule and to expel all foreigners from Italy. He forced Cesare * Borgia to give up his conquests, took Perugia and Bologna, and through the League of Cambrai forced Venice to come to terms. By 1512 he had succeeded in expelling the French (now under Louis XII) from Italy by means of the Holy League, of which Henry VIII of England was a not very active member. Meanwhile Julius was engaged in beautifying Rome. He laid the foundation stone of Bramante's St Peter's Basilica in 1506, employed * Michelangelo and * Raphael to adorn the Vatican and patronized the arts and letters in every field.

Jung, Carl Gustav (1875–1961). Swiss psychiatrist. He became a physician at the psychiatric clinic in Zurich (1900) and a university lecturer there (1905). He coined the word 'complex' to describe memories or emotions which, though repressed by the conscious mind, still influence behaviour and may cause neuroses. He met * Freud in 1907 and worked closely with him in Vienna for several years; they quarrelled (1912–13) largely because of disagreement over the extent of the contribution of sexuality to the life force. Jung returned to academic appointments at Zurich and Basle. His own system, called 'analytical psychology', was an attempt to effect classification by psychological analysis; he divided people into two main types, 'introverts' and 'extraverts'. Another concept of his work is the 'collective unconscious' which is assumed to spring from atavistic experiences of society itself rather than of individuals. Jung's attitude to religious experience was less negative than that of Freud. Jung's books include *The Psychology of the Unconscious* (1921), *Modern Man in Search of a Soul* (1933), *Answer to Job* (1954).
Fordham, F., *An Introduction to Jung's Psychology*. 3rd ed. 1966

Justin, St (known as 'the Martyr') (*c.* 100–*c.* 165). Greek theologian. Born in Samaria, he studied philosophy and was converted (*c.* 134) to Christianity. He spent a wandering life preaching the Gospel. He founded a school of Christian philosophy at Rome, where with some of his proselytes he was martyred. In his *Apologies* (*c.* 155) he tried to reconcile Greek philosophy, especially that of Plato, with the teaching of Christ. *The Dialogue with the Jew Trypho* is the only other work indisputably his.

Justinian I (Flavius Anicius Justinianus) (*c.* 482–565). Byzantine (or east Roman) emperor (from 527). He was born in Illyria, the son of a Macedonian peasant; his uncle, an imperial guardsman who made himself the emperor Justin I, had him educated in Constantinople, and eventually made him co-emperor and heir. Justinian's wife, * Theodora, a former actress and courtesan, was a talented and courageous woman who was a constant source of strength. As emperor, Justinian's military aim was to restore the Roman empire to its ancient limits; with the help of his generals Belisarius and Narses he nearly succeeded in the west by the reconquest of North Africa, most of Italy and part of Spain. In two wars against Persia he more than held his own. On other frontiers, especially in the north where raids from Slavs and Huns were a constant menace, he strengthened and renewed the old lines of fortifications. In Constantinople the perpetual feud between the supporters of the 'Blues' and 'Greens', rival teams in the chariot races in the hippodrome, had spread into the streets. Gang warfare became political faction until at last, with insurgents threatening the throne, troops were called in and a massacre followed in which it was said more than 35,000 people were killed. Justinian's political reforms were directed at removing corruption and at centralizing the régime by breaking up the large self-governing departments and making more ministers directly responsible to himself. He was a strictly orthodox Christian and worked hard to bring unity both of doctrine and discipline into church affairs; he built St Sophia in Constantinople and many other churches. It is, however, as a great codifier of Roman law that Justinian is best remembered. This work, in which his minister Tribonius was his principal assistant, resulted in a revision, known as the *Codex Justinianus* (529, revised 435) of the Theodosian code of 438; the *Pandectae* or *Digesta* (533) gave a selection from the writings of earlier jurists. The *Institutiones* provided elementary instruction mainly for use in schools. New laws made from time to time were known as *Novellae*, and these, with the *Institutiones, Digesta* and *Codex*, make up the *Corpus Juris Civilis*, the Roman civil law that provided the pattern for many later codes.

Browning, R., *Justinian and Theodora*. 1971

Juvenal (Decimus Junius Juvenalis) (*c.* 60–*c.* 130). Roman satirical poet. Little is known of his life except that he lived most of it in poverty, the client of mean though wealthy men. He wrote sixteen surviving satires in which he denounced the vicious Roman society of the time of Trajan and Hadrian and aired his venomous views of Jews and women. He is regarded as one of the greatest masters of the 'satire of indignation'; Dryden and Johnson (in *London* and *The Vanity of Human Wishes*) wrote versions of some of his works. The title 'The English Juvenal' has been accorded to both George Crabbe and John Oldham.

Highet, G., *Juvenal the Satirist*. 1962

K

Kadar, Janos (1912–). Hungarian politician. He joined the Communist party, then illegal, in 1932. In 1948 when the party took control he became minister for home affairs. After three years imprisonment, accused of Titoism, he became prime Minister and first secretary of the party in 1956. In the revolution of October 1956 he at first joined the anti-Stalinist revolutionaries; then in November he set up an opposing, pro-Soviet government and with Soviet military help crushed the revolt. He has since followed pro-Moscow policies while allowing some liberal measures at home.
Zinner, P. E., *Revolution in Hungary*. 1962

Kafka, Franz (1883–1924). Czech–Jewish novelist, writing in German, born in Prague. The son of a merchant, he gained a doctorate in law and worked for the Workers' Accident Insurance Institute in Prague 1908–22. Little of his work was published before his early death from tuberculosis but he is now recognized as a leading and influential literary figure. His introspective and symbolic novels are marked by a discomforting sense of spiritual oppression and frustration, their strange events seeming the more uncanny because of the clarity of the author's style. That a hidden theme is man's vain struggle to establish a relationship with God is an interpretation put forward by some. His works include three unfinished novels, *The Trial* (*Der Prozess*; 1925), *The Castle* (*Der Schloss*; 1926) and *Amerika* (1927), essays, and several short stories, e.g. *Metamorphosis*.
Anders, G., *Kafka*. 1960. Brod, M., *Franz Kafka*. 2nd ed. 1960

Kaiser, Georg (1878–1945). German dramatist, born at Magdeburg. He is known as the playwright of Expressionism, because his style in some of his best known plays, e.g. *The Burghers of Calais* (1914), *From Morning to Midnight* (1916), and *Gas* (1918), was analogous to that of the Expressionists in art; but his range of subjects was wide enough to include social comedies, problem plays and to take up many other themes to each of which he appropriately adapted his style.
Kenworthy, B., *George Kaiser*. 1957

Kalecki, Michal (1889–1970). Polish economist. Trained as an engineer, he worked as a journalist and economic analyst, and in 1933 published (in Polish) *Essays in Business Cycle Theory* which largely anticipated J. M. * Keynes' theories on demand management and employment. (His priority was not recognized until after Keynes' death.) He worked in England 1936–45, then with the U.N. 1946–55, returning to Poland in 1955 in an attempt to provide a theoretical framework for growth in a socialist economy.

Kalinin, Mikhail Ivanovich (1875–1946). Russian Communist politician. A sheet-metal worker, he joined the RSDLP in 1897, adhered to the Bolsheviks after 1905 and was a candidate member 1919–25, then a full member of the Politburo of the CPSU 1925–46. As chairman of the Executive Committee of the Russian Soviet Socialist Republic, he succeeded * Sverdlov as head of state (1919) and retained this position until his death, in later years as chairman of the Presidium of the Supreme Soviet. * Stalin imprisoned his wife 1937–46.

Kamehameha. Five kings of Hawaii. **Kamehameha I** (1758–1819) became king of

Hawaii *c.* 1790 and subjected the various warring islands to his sole rule. He was friendly towards traders and encouraged western influences. **Kamehameha II** succeeded his father in 1819 and continued his policies. He was succeeded by his brother **Kamehameha III** (1814–54; reigned from 1825) who developed the islands into a modern monarchy of a constitutional kind, and obtained recognition of their independence by France, Britain and the U.S.A. **Kamehameha V** (1831–1872) succeeded his brother in 1863, abrogated the constitution and tried to restore tribalism and monarchical rule. However, he died without heir and the Kamehameha dynasty ended.

Daws, A. G., *Shoal of Time: A History of the Hawaiian Islands.* 1968

Kamenev (originally Rosenfeld), **Lev Borisovich** (1883–1936). Russian politician. He adhered to the Bolshevik wing of the Social Democratic Party. Banished to Siberia (1915) he became a member of the first Communist Politburo (1917), and, when * Lenin died, he, * Stalin and * Zinoviev formed the triumvirate opposed to * Trotsky (1924). Outmanoeuvred by Stalin (1925) he rallied to Trotsky and was expelled from the Communist party (1927). In 1936 he was tried in the first big 'purge trial' and executed for treason.

Kamerlingh Onnes, Heike (1853–1926). Dutch physicist. Professor of physics at the University of Leyden (1882–1926), and a pioneer of low-temperature research, he was the first to achieve temperatures within 1° of absolute zero and to liquefy hydrogen (1906) and helium (1908). During his studies of the properties of materials at low temperatures, Onnes discovered the phenomenon of superconductivity, the disappearance of electrical resistance of some metals (e.g. lead) at temperatures near absolute zero. He won the Nobel Prize for Physics (1913).

Kandinsky, Wassily (1866–1944). Russian artist, born in Moscow. He was already 30 years old and had been a lawyer and economist before taking up art. He studied in Munich where he and Franz Marc formed (1911) a group which came to be called (after one of Kandinsky's pictures) the *Blaue Reiter* (Blue Rider), pioneers of abstract painting and theory. Kandinsky had painted his first abstract picture in 1910 and had begun to write *Concerning the Spiritual in Art* (1912). From 1914 to 1921 he was in Russia, where he played a part in re-establishing the arts after the revolution. He left to join the Bauhaus, a school of design and architecture at Weimar in Germany and from 1933 he lived in Paris. Features of his painting which have attracted particular attention have been the calligraphic brush strokes of his earlier period and afterwards his use of geometric symbols; his later pictures reveal a softening of mood and with it a less severe use of geometric forms.

Overy, P., *Kandinsky: The Language of the Eye.* 1969

Kant, Immanuel (1724–1804). German philosopher. Son of a saddler, born in Königsberg where he was educated and eventually became professor of philosophy, he travelled hardly at all and did not marry. He was little more than five feet high but his health was good and his brilliant conversation enlivened prolonged luncheons with friends and the social gatherings of his younger days. He was interested in politics, approving both the French and American revolutions, but he lived a quiet life devoted to philosophy, the course of which he greatly influenced. He was also a student of physics and mathematics, and is known for the Kant–Laplace theory of the origin of the solar system. In his philosophy, Kant argues that human knowledge is the result of our own ordering of sense experience, which by itself would be unintelligible. In the *Critique of Pure Reason* (1781), he sets out the *a priori* categories which we impose upon experience, e.g. the categories of space, time and relation. They are, it is sometimes said, the spectacles through which we are always looking. Without them, he claims, there could be no understanding of our experience. Since knowledge derives from and depends upon both experience and categories, there can be no knowledge of that which is beyond our experience. Kant thus denies the possibility of metaphysics, when conceived as the study of any reality beyond our actual experience. He thus also denies the possibility of proof of the existence of God, which remains a matter of faith. Supplementary to this great work were his *Critique of Practical Reason* (1788) and *Critique of Judgement* (1790), the latter containing his widely influential views on taste. In his writings on ethics, he enunciates as the supreme moral principle what he calls the

Categorical Imperative. It has several formulations, of which the final one is that the will is completely autonomous in laying down laws that are to be applied universally and in accordance with which it is its duty to act.
Korner, S., *Kant*. 1955

Kapitza, Pyotr Leonidovich (1894–1984). Russian physicist. Educated at Leningrad and at Cambridge (under Rutherford), he was assistant director of research in magnetism at the Cavendish Laboratory (1924–32) and Messel research professor at the Royal Society's Mond Laboratory (1932–35). He did important work on the magnetic and electrical properties of substances at low temperatures, and also designed improved plant for the liquefaction of hydrogen and helium. Kapitza was detained in the U.S.S.R. in 1935, and later became director of the Institute for Physical Problems at the Academy of Sciences, Moscow. He was awarded the Stalin prize for Physics (1941 and 1943), held the Order of Lenin, many foreign honours and the 1978 Nobel Prize for Physics.
Collected Papers, 3 vols. 1964–1967

Kapteyn, Jacobus Cornelius (1851–1922). Dutch astronomer. While professor of astronomy at the University of Groningen (1878–1921), he established that there are two streams of stars moving in opposite directions in the plane of the Milky Way, and made considerable contributions to the knowledge of star distribution and the structure of the universe. He also pioneered the use of photographic methods for determining stellar parallax.

Karageorgević. Serbian dynasty founded by **Kara** ('black') **George Petrović** (1766–1817), a patriot who led the 1804 revolt against the Turks. For ten years he waged guerrilla warfare, striking terror in the Turks and gaining adherents amongst the Serbs by his gigantic size, ruthless discipline and immense courage. In 1808 the Serbs swore allegiance to him as their hereditary leader. Defeated at last, he took refuge in Austria but returned (1817) only to be assassinated by a member of the rival * Obreonović dynasty. Kara George's son **Alexander** (1806–1885) succeeded (1842) Michael Obreonović and reigned as prince of Serbia until deposed (1858). After the murder (1903) of Alexander (Obreonović), the dynasty returned to power under Alexander's son, * Peter I, who was succeeded by his son, * Alexander I (of Yugoslavia), and his grandson, Peter II (* Peter I).

Karajan, Herbert von (1908–). Austrian conductor, born in Salzburg. He was an opera conductor at Ulm 1927–33, Aachen 1933–40 and Berlin 1938–42. A member of the Nazi Party for some years, he received * Goebbels' patronage and was promoted as a rival to * Furtwängler. He gained an international reputation after the war, conducted at La Scala 1948–52 and in London with the Philharmonia, and directed the Vienna State Opera 1956–64 and 1976– , the Berlin Philharmonic Orchestra 1958– , and the Salzburg Festival 1964– . He made many recordings and several films.

Karamanlis, Konstantinos (1907–). Greek politician. He entered the legislature in 1936, served as a minister 1946–55, succeeding Papagos as premier 1955–63, and went into exile in Paris (1963) when the military took power. He returned after Greece's military failure in Cyprus and was premier again 1974–80, becoming president 1980–85.

Karl I *see* **Charles I**

Karlfeldt, Erik Axel (1864–1931). Swedish lyric poet. He worked as a schoolteacher and librarian; his themes are drawn from the countryside, its moods and seasons, and the loves, lives and deaths of country people. He declined a Nobel Prize for Literature, but it was awarded to him posthumously (1931).

Karloff, Boris (1887–1969). English film actor working in Hollywood. Born in Dulwich as William Pratt, he began as a character actor and became famous playing grotesque roles in early horror films, notably *Frankenstein* (1931).

Karsavina, Tamara (1885–1978). Russian ballet dancer. After being prima ballerina of the Mariinsky Theatre, St Petersburg, from 1902, she starred (1909–22) in Diaghilev's Ballets Russes. She scored a particular triumph with Nijinsky in the *Spectre de la Rose*.
Karsavina, T., *Theatre Street*. 1930

Kasavubu, Joseph (*c.* 1910–1969). First president of the republic of Congo. A member of the Bakongo tribe, he was a teacher and a civil servant under the Belgian administration. In the struggle for power that followed independence (1960) Kasavubu obtained U.N. recognition and, in the civil war that followed, his supporters gained ascendancy over his main rival, Patrice * Lumumba. Throughout the disturbances of the following years Kasavubu retained office until deposed (1965) by General Mobutu, the commander-in-chief.

Kassem, Abdul Karim ('Abd al-Karim al-Qasim) (1914–1963). Iraqi soldier and politician. Having led the revolt during which King Faisal was murdered (1958), he made himself president and commander-in-chief of the new republic. The failure of his attempt to establish an Iraqi claim (1961) to Kuwait lowered his prestige and he was assassinated during a *coup d'état* organized against him.

Kästner, Erich (1899–1974). German novelist and journalist. He wrote many humorous and satirical books, including the delightful children's book, *Emil and the Detectives* (1929), which was translated into many languages.

Katherine. For entries under this name *see* **Catherine**

Kauffman, Angelica (1741–1807). Swiss painter. Having gained a reputation as a child artist in Rome she spent the years 1766–81 in England, where she was befriended by * Reynolds and achieved success with portraits and mythological scenes; she was an original member of the Royal Academy (1768). She undertook decorative paintings for several houses designed by the * Adam brothers, e.g. Syon House, Harewood House etc.
Smythe, C. *Angelica Kauffman*. 1972

Kaunda, (David) Kenneth (1924–). First president of Zambia. He entered politics in Northern Rhodesia (now Zambia) in 1948. He founded (1958) the Zambia African National Congress, which was re-formed (1961) after being banned, Kaunda meanwhile having spent a short time in prison. When his party came to power (1964) – after the first election to be held under a system of universal adult suffrage – he became prime minister, and later that year, when independence was achieved, first president of the new republic of Zambia. He was chairman of the Organisation of Africa Unity in 1970.
Hall, R. S., *The High Price of Principles: Kaunda and the White South*. 1969. Mulford, D. C., *Zambia: the Politics of Independence, 1957–1964*. 1967

Kaunitz-Rietberg, Wenzel Anton, Prince of (1711–1794). Austrian diplomat. He gained a reputation for statesmanship as a negotiator of the Treaty of Aix-la-Chapelle (1748), by which the War of the Austrian Succession was brought to an end. Afterwards he convinced his sovereign, Maria Theresa, that as Prussia had become the real enemy the traditional hostility to France had become an anachronism. He was thus able, as ambassador to Paris (1751–53) and then as state chancellor (1753–92), to bring about the famous 'diplomatic revolution', as a result of which France entered (1756) the Seven Years War as Austria's ally against Frederick the Great. Kaunitz controlled Austria's foreign policy for forty years.

Kautsky, Karl (1854–1938). German socialist. He was a supporter of * Marx and worked closely with * Engels in London (1881–83). He is best known for his violent controversies with * Lenin over the interpretation of Marxist doctrines. Eventually the opinions of Lenin held the field and after the Russian revolution Kautsky refused to join the German Communist party. Shortly after the end of World War I he settled in Vienna, where he rejoined the Social Democrats. After Hitler's annexation of Vienna he fled to Amsterdam.

Kawabata Yasunari (1899–1972). Japanese novelist, born in Osaka. He was influenced by traditional Japanese and modern French styles, and wrote lyrical, impressionistic novels dominated by the beauty of nature and the struggle to accept death. His works include *Snow Country* (1956) and *Thousand Cranes* (1959). He received the Nobel prize for literature in 1968 and committed suicide four years later.
Nakamura, M., *Contemporary Japanese Fiction*. 1969

Kay, John (1704–?1778). English inventor. He was born near Bury, Lancashire, where his trade as a clockmaker brought him into contact with the cotton-weaving industry. The most important of his inventions, the flying shuttle (patented 1733), greatly increased speed of manufacture and possible widths of finished fabric. His invention was hated as a threat to unemployment; he was attacked and his model destroyed. For ten years from 1747 he lived in France, where he introduced his invention. On his return to England lawsuits to protect his patents seem to have brought about his ruin, and it is thought that he went back to France (1774) and there in 1778 received a pension. The date of his death is uncertain.

Kaye, Danny (1913–). American comedian. Born Daniel Kaminsky in New York, he began work on the variety stage but achieved his main popularity in films, of which the most successful was *The Secret Life of Walter Mitty* (1946). His early success arose from a talent for clowning, a direct contrast to the sophisticated situation comedy prevalent in Hollywood at the time. Later films include *Five Pennies* (1959) and *The Madwoman of Chaillot* (1968). He was ambassador-at-large for UNICEF.

Kay-Shuttleworth, Sir James Phillips, 1st Bart (1804–1877). English educationist. As a medical practitioner in Manchester and as an assistant poor-law commissioner in East Anglia, he became acutely aware of the educational needs of the poor. He introduced teachers into workhouses, where he developed what was to become the pupil-teacher system of teacher training. He became (1839) secretary of the government committee for education and introduced the system of school inspection with the aim, not of control, but of seeing that knowledge of improved methods was spread as widely as possible. Having failed to obtain a state grant for a teachers' training college, he founded one on his own initiative (later called St John's College, Battersea). On his retirement (1848) he received a baronetcy. He was a member of various social and scientific commissions and wrote extensively on educational issues.

Kazantzakis, Nikos (1885–1957). Greek novelist and poet, born in Crete. He studied philosophy with * Bergson in Paris, and served briefly as a minister of state in 1945. Among his best known works are *The Odyssey* (a poetic continuation, 33,333 lines long, of Homer's epic; published in 1951); *Freedom and Death* (1947), *Zorba the Greek* (1952; also a film) and *The Greek Passion* (1953; filmed as *He Who Must Die*). *Christ Recrucified*, his last novel, was published posthumously in 1960.

Kean, Edmund (1789–1833). English actor. He learnt his craft as a strolling player before making his debut (1814) as Shylock at Drury Lane. His success was immediate and his fame steadily increased; he was one of the greatest tragic and emotional actors in the history of the English stage. Coleridge remarked that to see Kean 'was like reading Shakespeare by flashes of lightning'. Macbeth and Richard III were among his greatest parts. He collapsed while playing Othello and died a few weeks later. He was a heavy drinker, extravagant and over-generous. His son, **Charles Kean** (1811–1868), also a leading actor, was playing Iago on this occasion. Edmund Kean's private life was as tempestuous as his stage appearances. Jealous, passionate and violently intemperate, he shocked London by his excesses and was almost forced to retire when his involvement with an alderman's wife led to a *cause célèbre*. Edmund's wife, **Ellen Kean** (1805–1830), also excelled in Shakespearian roles, notably Viola and Gertrude.

Playfair, G. W., *Kean*. 1950

Keaton, Buster (1895–1966). American film actor. Born Joseph Francis Keaton in Piqua, Kansas, he worked mainly in silent comedy playing the small, frail protagonist against overwhelming odds, which he defeated single-handed without the smallest change of expression. He is considered one of the greatest comedians of American silent film. His films include *The Navigator* (1924), *The General* (1926) and *Steamboat Bill Junior* (1927).

Beesh, R., *Keaton*. 1966

Keats, John (1795–1821). English poet. Son of a well-to-do London livery-stable keeper, he went to Clarke's School, Enfield, then well known, where, though athletic and pugnacious, he was already remarked upon for his sensitivity and tenderness. When his father died, John, then aged 16, became the ward of a merchant named Richard Abbey, by whom he was apprenticed to an apothecary at Edmonton. Being near Enfield he was able to keep in touch with his former headmaster, who lent him books (Spenser's *Faerie Queene* particularly inspired him) and eventually introduced him to the circle of Leigh * Hunt.

Thus he came to know Haydon, Reynolds, Shelley, and others as well as Charles Brown, a retired merchant, who enjoyed helping young men of promise; with him he shared a double house in Hampstead, now a Keats museum. Meanwhile he had passed his examination at the Apothecaries Hall and had 'walked' the hospitals; but by 1817 he had recoiled from surgery (without anaesthetics) and abandoned the profession.

His first book of poems (1817), which included the famous sonnet *On First Looking into Chapman's Homer*, created little stir, but already he was working on *Endymion* (1819), with its familiar opening line 'A thing of beauty is a joy for ever'. A great but uneven poem in four books, it provoked savage criticism and some discerning praise.

In 1818 he had lost both his dearly loved brothers; George emigrated to America, Tom died of tuberculosis. To the period that immediately followed belong some of his finest poems, which appeared in *Lamia and Other Poems* (1820). This included *Lamia*, the odes *To a Nightingale, To Psyche, To Autumn, On Melancholy* and *On a Grecian Urn; The Eve of St Agnes; La Belle Dame Sans Merci*; and the unfinished *Hyperion*. To the same period belongs his love for Fanny Brawne, lively, kind and loyal, who tended him when ill – but with little understanding of the poet's emotional needs. Early in 1820 with the coughing up of blood came signs of serious illness; he steadily got worse and became dependent on the charity of friends. In September he went to Italy with the artist Joseph Severn, who has left a faithful record of the last days. In the following February he died in Rome, the words 'Here lies one whose name was writ in water' inscribed (at his own request) on the nameless grave. Shelley's *Adonais* was written in lament for his friend.

Gittings, R., *John Keats*. 1968; ed., *Letters of John Keats*. 1970

Keble, John (1792–1866). English clergyman and poet. He was elected to a fellowship at Oriel College, Oxford (1811), and became tutor (1817), but from 1823 spent some years in parish work. His very popular book of poems *The Christian Year* appeared in 1827, and he was professor of poetry at Oxford (1831–41). His sermon on National Apostasy (1833) was afterwards held to have initiated the Tractarian (or Oxford) Movement in the Church of England which advocated the restoration of some of the forms of worship and practices, e.g. use of incense, vestments, intoning, which had fallen into disuse since the Reformation. He wrote seven of the *Tracts for the Times* but unlike * Newman remained loyal to the Anglican church. He left Oxford (1836) after his marriage and later translated parts of the early Christian fathers and wrote or edited several religious works. Keble College, Oxford, was built in his memory (1870).

Battiscombe, G., *John Keble*. 1964

Keene, Charles Samuel (1823–1891). English artist. Best known for his work for *Punch*, he was also one of the most popular illustrators of the period (e.g. of *The Cloister and the Hearth*). A masterly economy of line is one of his outstanding qualities.

Keitel, Wilhelm (1882–1946). German soldier. An artillery officer during World War I, he became a devoted Nazi; his appointment (1938) as chief of staff of the Supreme Command signalized the army's subservience to * Hitler. During World War II he was virtually Hitler's second in command and executive officer. A courtier as much as a soldier, he showed skill in converting Hitler's occasionally brilliant strategic conceptions into practicable operations, but lacked the strength to combat his master's military follies. He was condemned for war crimes at Nuremberg and executed.

Keith, Sir Arthur (1866–1955). Scottish anthropologist, born near Aberdeen. He qualified in medicine and was known for his anatomical research; he was also a recognized authority on morphology and evolution. He became Hunterian professor at the Royal College of Surgeons (1908), and president of the British Association (1927); in his presidential address he propounded some revisions of Darwinian theories which have since become generally accepted. His books include *Antiquity of Man* (1915) and *New Theory of Human Evolution* (1948).

Keith, Sir A., *Autobiography*. 1950

Keith, James Francis Edward (1696–1758). Scottish soldier of fortune. Known, because of an office hereditary in his family, as Marshal Keith, after taking part in the Jacobite rising (1715) he became a colonel in the Spanish army; in 1728 he was made a general when serving for Russia and made a name for himself in the Turkish and Swedish wars. In 1747 he left the Russian service and was immediately employed as field-marshal by Frederick the Great of Prussia; he fought for him in the Seven Years War during which he was killed.

Kekkonen, Urho Kaleva (1900–). President of Finland 1956–81. A lawyer and popular athlete, he fought with the Whites during the civil war (1919) and joined the Agrarian party. He was legal counsellor of the Agrarian party and an administrative secretary of the Agriculture Department (1932–36) when he entered parliament in 1936. He served as minister of justice (1936–37; 1944–46), minister of the interior (1937–39; 1950–51), chairman of the Finnish Olympic Games Committee (1938–46), chief of the bureau of displaced persons (1940–43) and speaker of the parliament (1948–50). In 1944 he assisted J. K. * Paasikivi in negotiating peace with the USSR and devoted his career to maintaining the 'Paasikivi line' (neutrality, no anti-Soviet policies, but no Russian domestic intervention). Prime minister (1950–53; 1954–56), he was defeated for the presidency by Paasikivi in 1950 but elected in 1956, holding office for a record term, retiring in 1981.
Jakobsen, M., *Finnish Neutrality*. 1968. Kekkonon, U., *Neutrality, the Finnish Position*. 1970

Kekulé von Stradonitz, Friedrich August (1829–1896). German chemist. Professor of chemistry at Ghent (1858–67) and Bonn (1867–96), he laid the foundations of structural organic chemistry with his discovery (1858) of the quadrivalence of carbon and of the ability of carbon atoms to link with one another in chains. He was thus able to systematize the chemistry of the aliphatic compounds. He did the same for aromatic compounds when he devised (1865) the now familiar ring formula for benzene: the resolution of this problem came in a dream as he was dozing on a bus and he saw the elements dancing. He convened the First International Chemical Congress at Karlsruhe in 1860.

Keller, Gottfried (1819–1890). Swiss author. He went to Munich to study art but soon turned to literature, remaining in Germany, latterly in Berlin, until 1855, when he returned to Switzerland. His long, vivid and partly autobiographical novel, *Der Grüne Heinrich* (1854), achieved little popularity until it was revised and given a happy ending. He achieved most success with his humorous short stories of Swiss life; on one of them Delius's opera *A Village Romeo and Juliet* was based.
Lindsay, J. M., *Gottfried Keller: Life and Works*. 1969

Keller, Helen Adams (1880–1968). American author and lecturer. She became blind and deaf at 19 months of age, after scarlet fever, but later learned to read Braille, to write and speak. She became a symbol of human determination to overcome physical handicaps and an inspiration for all similarly handicapped. In 1904 she graduated from Radcliffe College, Cambridge, Mass. She toured the world lecturing and wrote several books. e.g. *The Story of My Life* (1902), *The World I Live In* (1908) and *Let Us Have Faith* (1940).
Tribble, J. W. and A., *Helen Keller*. 1973

Kellogg, Frank Billings (1856–1937). American politician. Having become known as a corporation lawyer, he served as U.S. senator (1917–23), and was U.S. ambassador in Great Britain (1924–25) and secretary of state (1925–29). He worked for the pact of Paris (Briand-Kellogg Pact; 1928) by which fifteen nations renounced war as an instrument of policy. He was awarded the Nobel Peace Prize (1929).
Ellis, L. E., *Frank B. Kellogg and American Foreign Relations, 1925–1929*. 1961

Kellogg, Will Keith (1860–1951). American manufacturer. In 1894 he developed the first breakfast cereal (wheat flakes) as a health food for an Adventist sanitorium at Battle Creek, Michigan, run by his brother John Harvey Kellogg. Corn flakes soon followed. Kellogg's principal rival, General Foods, was founded by C. W. Post who also produced Postum (a coffee substitute), Grape-Nuts and Post Toasties at Battle Creek.

Kelly, Grace (Princess Grace of Monaco) (1929–1982). American actress. The daughter of a Philadelphia industrialist, she made eleven films in her brief film career (1951–56) and good looks, sexual elegance and cool style brought her international acclaim. She married Rainier III, Prince of Monaco, in 1956 and had three children. She died after a car accident.

Kelly, Ned (1855–1880). Australian bushranger. The son of a transported Irish convict, he took to the hills with his brother Dan and two other mates after several clashes with the law. He killed three policemen in a shootout (October 1878) and was captured at Glenrowan after 18 months of flamboyant outlawry. He was tried and hanged in Melbourne. Kelly has become a central figure in Australian mythology, the subject of books, films and paintings (Sidney * Nolan).

Kelvin of Largs, William Thomson, 1st Baron (1824–1907). Scottish mathematician and physicist. Born in Belfast, where his father was professor of mathematics, after showing brilliance in mathematics at Cambridge he became, when only 22, professor of natural philosophy at the University of Glasgow, a position he held 1846–99. In 1848 he proposed the adoption of an absolute temperature scale (later named for him) in which absolute zero (– 273°C) is 0°K (or Kelvin), and the boiling point of water (100°C) is 373°K. One of the founders of thermodynamics, he expanded * Joule's findings and enunciated the Second Law of Thermodynamics in 1851, just after * Clausius. Kelvin invented many instruments, mainly electrical, e.g. the mirror galvanometer, a magnetically-shielded ship's compass, the dynamometer, tide gauges, and the quadrant electrometer. He was consultant to the company which laid the first transatlantic cable (1858). Kelvin, who was president of the Royal Society (1890–94), was knighted in 1866, received his barony in 1892, and in 1902 became one of the original members of the Order of Merit. After 1880 he became increasingly rigid in his attitudes and rejected new discoveries in physics e.g. radioactivity, atomic structure and X-rays.
MacDonald, D. K. C., *Faraday, Maxwell and Kelvin.* 1965

Kemal Atatürk (Mustafa Kemal) (1881–1938). First Turkish president. He was born in Salonika, the son of a customs official. He joined the Young Turk reform movement. He gained an army commission and won rapid promotion; he fought against the Italians in Tripoli (1911) and in World War I saved the situation at a critical moment in the Gallipoli campaign; he later served in the Caucasus and Syria. After the Turkish defeat, when Constantinople (Istanbul) was in Allied occupation (1919) and the sultan, Mohammed VI, was supine and powerless, he was in Anatolia and led the great movement of national resistance stirred by the Greek invasion. He threw off allegiance to the Sultan, and established a provisional government at Ankara (April 1920). He himself led the Turks to victory in the War of Independence, which resulted, with eventual Allied acquiescence, in the expulsion of the Greeks, the deposition (1922) of the sultan, and the establishment (1923) of a republic with Kemal as first president. He made no attempt to regain the Arab lands lost in the war and concentrated his activities upon creating a strong modern state in the Turkish homelands of Anatolia and what remained of Turkey in Europe; Ankara became the new capital. The outward signs of his modernization – e.g. the unveiling and emancipation of women, the replacing of the fez by western headgear, the adoption of surnames, the introduction of the Gregorian calendar and of Latin script – signalled a reawakening of a people dormant for centuries under corrupt and often oppressive rule. That these changes had taken place so quickly and with so little disturbance was due to the patriotic fervour, the military skill, the driving energy, the shrewd judgement and occasional restlessness of Mustafa Kemal, who auspiciously took the surname 'Father Turk' (Atatürk).
Kinross, J. P. D., *Atatürk: The Rebirth of a Nation.* 1964

Kemble, John Philip (1757–1823). English actor. Leading member of a famous English stage family, after some years in the provinces, he was given the chance to come to London through the success of his sister Sarah * Siddons. Hamlet (1783) was the first of many tragic roles that he played with great distinction at Drury Lane. In keeping with his character, his approach was intellectual; in contrast with his successor Edmund * Kean, he was at his best in parts requiring dignity and nobility, Brutus and Coriolanus providing outstanding examples. He was appointed manager of Drury Lane by * Sheridan (1788), but in 1802 he bought a share in Covent Garden Theatre, which he managed and where he thenceforth performed. The theatre was burnt down (1808); the price of seats in the rebuilt theatre (1809) caused disturbances directed against the Kemble family. Kemble retired (1817) to live in Lausanne.

Kemble's brother, **Charles Kemble** (1775–1854), whose grace and charm fitted him more especially for comedy, was the father of **Fanny Kemble** (1809–1893) who unwillingly followed the family tradition and in 1829 made a triumphant debut as Juliet at Covent Garden. Baker, H., *J. P. Kemble: the Actor in his Theatre.* 1942

Kempe, Margery (b. 1364). English mystic. *The Booke of Margery Kempe* narrates her spiritual and physical travels (she went to Italy, Compostella and the Holy Land). She was illiterate and dictated her work; it was printed in part by Wynkyn de Worde *c.* 1501.

Kempis, Thomas à *see* **Thomas à Kempis**

Ken, Thomas (1637–1711). English prelate and hymn writer. He was appointed bishop of Bath and Wells (1684) despite the fact that in the previous year he had refused to accommodate Nell Gwyn during Charles II's visit to Winchester. In the next reign he was one of the seven bishops who refused to sign the Declaration of Indulgence (* James II), but on the other hand lost his bishopric (1691) for refusing to take an oath of allegiance to Willian and Mary. Later he was given a pension by Queen Anne and lived at Longleat until his death. His hymns include *Praise God, from whom all blessings flow* and *Awake, my soul.*

Kendrew, Sir John Cowdery (1917–). British biochemist. A Fellow of Peterhouse College, Cambridge 1947– , he shared the 1962 Nobel Prize for Chemistry with Max * Perutz for working out the protein structure in the molecules of horse hemoglobin.

Kennan, George Frost (1904–). American historian, diplomat and foreign policy theorist. He served as a diplomat in Moscow (1933–38; 1945–46; 1952–53) and devised the policy of 'containment' of the USSR adopted by * Truman after World War II. He was the BBC's Reith Lecturer (1957), a professor at the Institute for Advanced Study at Princeton (1956–74), ambassador to Yugoslavia (1961–63), and won the Pulitzer prize (1968) for his *Memoirs.*

Kennedy Family. Massachusetts family of Irish descent active in American politics. **Joseph Patrick Kennedy** (1888–1969) became a bank president, businessman, stock-market investor and millionaire, contributing largely to the funds of the Democratic party. He was appointed ambassador to Britain in 1937 and resigned in 1940, believing Nazi victory to be imminent. He supported isolationism for the United States.

Kennedy, John Fitzgerald (1917–63). Thirty-fifth president of U.S. The first Roman Catholic president, he was born in Boston, son of Joseph * Kennedy. John interrupted his Harvard course to accompany his father in his London embassy but graduated in 1940. During World War II he served in the U.S. Navy and was decorated for heroic rescues of his crew members after his PT boat 109 was rammed off the Solomons. This aggravated an acute spinal injury which caused him great pain and led to near-fatal operations (1954–55) and to Addison's disease. He served in the U.S. Congress 1947–53 and as a Senator from Massachusetts 1953–60. In 1957 he won the Pulitzer Prize for history with his (ghost-written) *Profiles in Courage*, accounts of courageous Senators. After failing to secure the Democratic vice-presidential nomination in 1956, he began his campaign for the presidency in 1957. In 1960 he defeated Richard M. * Nixon in the closest race since 1916: Lyndon B. * Johnson became vice-president. He served as president 1961–63, pursuing the liberal policies to which he had pledged himself, civil rights for Negroes, aid for underdeveloped countries and many measures of social reform. Much of his proposed legislation was blocked by Congress. His handling of foreign policy did not escape criticism, but he won great admiration in the confrontation over Cuba with * Khrushchev, who was obliged to dismantle missile bases the Russians had set up. On 22 November 1963, while on a ceremonial visit to Dallas, Texas, he was shot and died in hospital immediately afterwards. The assassination caused widespread grief and shock, abroad as well as within the US and has excited a considerable historical controversy.

In his social life and behind the scenes Kennedy owed much to his beautiful and talented wife Jacqueline Lee Bouvier (married 1953), who later married the Greek shipping magnate Aristotle * Onassis.

Two of his younger brothers gained distinction in politics: * Robert and **Edward Kennedy** (1932–), a U.S. senator, who campaigned for the presidency in 1980.

Latham, E., ed., *J. F. Kennedy and Presidential Power*. 1972. White, T. H., *The Making of the President, 1960*. 1961

Kennedy, Robert Francis (1925–68). American politician, younger brother of President John Fitzgerald * Kennedy. Educated at Harvard and the University of Virginia Law School, he became counsel to a Senate sub-committee in 1953, and, from 1957, gained recognition by exposing corruption in the Teamsters Union. He became Attorney General in his brother's cabinet in 1961, with a special interest in civil rights. He resigned in 1964 and was elected Senator for New York, becoming a popular critic of President * Johnson's Vietnam policy. In 1968 he announced his candidacy for the presidency, but died on 6 June after being shot by Sirhan Sirhan.

Kenny, Elizabeth (1886–1952). Australian nurse. She developed the 'Kenny method' of treating poliomyelitis by stimulating the muscles; although it was denounced by many physicians, some clinics using the treatment were established in Australia and U.S.A.

Kent, George Edward Alexander Edmund, Duke of (1902–1942). British prince, fourth son of George V. He married (1934) Princess Marina of Greece and was killed in an air crash while on service duty in World War II. An earlier **Edward, Duke of Kent** (1769–1820), was the fourth son of * George III and father of Queen Victoria. He pursued a military career, becoming field-marshal in 1805. He was the first army commander to dispense with flogging.

Kent, William (1685–1748). English architect, interior decorator and landscapist. Born in Yorkshire and apprenticed to a coach-builder, he was helped by rich wellwishers to go to Rome to study painting, at which however he never excelled. In Rome he met (1719) * Lord Burlington, whose enthusiasm for Palladian architecture he shared. Back in England he decorated a suite for Kensington Palace (1723); he turned to architecture after 1730 and designed the Horse Guards (1750–58), the Treasury (1734) and several London houses. In the country, where Holkham Hall and Stowe were among his creations, he was a pioneer in the art of treating buildings and their surroundings as a single artistic conception, temples and pavilions in the grounds for example taking their appropriate place in a composition which included the house and gardens. This art of landscaping was carried further by his pupil, Capability * Brown.

Kenyatta, Jomo (1893–1978). First president of Kenya. A member of the predominant Kikuyu tribe, he went (1931) to the London School of Economics to study anthropology, and returned to Kenya finally in 1946 after having studied in Russia and spent the war years in England. He was imprisoned in 1953 for his part in the Mau Mau rebellion; within two months of his release (1961) he was re-elected president of the Kenya African National Union (KANU). Two years later he became prime minister of a coalition government, but the two parties merged; and in 1964 he became first president of a single-party republic. He wrote several books about Kenya, notably *Facing Mount Kenya*.
Delf, G., *Jomo Kenyatta*. 1961; Murray-Brown, J., *Kenyatta*. 1972

Kenyon, Dame Kathleen Mary (1906–1978). British archaeologist. She lectured at the Institute of Archaeology, London University (1948–62), specializing in Palestinian archaeology. She directed the British School of Archaeology in Jerusalem 1951–63, working herself at Jericho and Jerusalem. She was principal of St Hugh's College, Oxford 1962–73. Her numerous works include *Archaeology in the Holy Land*, 3rd ed. 1970, and *Digging up Jerusalem*, 1974.

Kepler, Johann (1571–1630). German astronomer. At the University of Tübingen he first studied for the Lutheran ministry but became absorbed in scientific studies and in 1594 was appointed professor of mathematics at Graz. In 1600 he went to Prague and became assistant to Tycho * Brahe. After Brahe's death Kepler succeeded him as astronomer and mathematician (1601–30) to the emperor Rudolf II, and inherited his valuable papers and records. As he received no salary he suffered great poverty. In 1612 he obtained a mathematical appointment at Linz and in 1627 became astrologer to Wallenstein, the imperial general in the Thirty Years War. Kepler was an adherent of the Copernican system and is regarded as one of the founders of modern astronomy. He enunciated the three fundamental laws of planetary motion

now known as Kepler's Laws, which half a century later helped * Newton to formulate his universal law of gravitation. Kepler also suggested that tides are caused by the moon's gravitational pull on large bodies of water. His *Rudolphine Tables* (1627) giving the positions of sun, moon and planets, remained standard for about a century. The principle of the astronomical telescope that bears his name was envisaged by him.
Koestler, A., *The Sleepwalkers.* 1959

Kerensky, Alexander Fyodorovich (1881–1970). Russian lawyer and politician. He made his name as a brave and eloquent opponent of the tsarist government in the *Duma* of 1912; and during World War I, after the revolution (March 1917), Kerensky, as a leader of the Social Revolutionary party, became minister of justice, then minister of war, and in July head of the provisional government. His decision to pursue the war against Germany undermined his popularity and in November he was overthrown by the Bolsheviks. Thenceforward he spent a life of exile and propaganda in Paris and, from 1940, in the U.S.A.
Browder, R., and Kerensky, F., eds., *The Russian Provisional Government, 1917.* Kerensky, A., *Russia and History's Turning Point.* 1965

Kern, Jerome David (1885–1945). American composer. He wrote many successful musical comedies including *Showboat* (1927), with its very popular song 'Old Man River'.

Kerouac, Jack (1922–69). American author. Exemplar of the lifestyle and discontents of the 'beat' generation, his best-known novel, *On the Road* (1957), is written in a spontaneous, discursive idiom and embodies the attitudes and alienation of the '50s 'beatnik' youth. Later novels include *The Subterraneans* (1958) and *Big Sur* (1962).
Charters, A., *Kerouac.* 1974

Kéroualle, Louise de *see* **Portsmouth, Duchess of**

Kerr, Sir John Robert (1914–). Australian lawyer, born in Sydney. He became an industrial court judge, chief justice of New South Wales (1972–74) and governor-general of Australia (1974–77) on the nomination of E. G. * Whitlam. In November 1975 he dismissed the Whitlam Labor government in an unprecedented use of the governor-general's reserve powers, after the Liberal-dominated Senate deferred passage of Supply, and appointed J. M. * Fraser as Prime Minister. Kerr became the centre of bitter controversy and resigned from his post in 1977 before the expiry of his five-year term. He left Australia and subsequently wrote his memoirs *Matters for Judgment* (1978).

Kesselring, Albert (1885–1960). German soldier and airman. Having transferred (1935) from the artillery to the *Luftwaffe* (air force) he commanded air fleets in the early offensives of World War II, including the Battle of Britain. He became supreme commander of the Axis forces in Italy (1943) and conducted a series of delaying actions with remarkable skill. In April 1945, when all was already lost, he superseded von Rundstedt as commander-in-chief on the western front. He received a death sentence (commuted to life imprisonment) for war crimes in 1947 but was released in 1952.

Kettering, Charles Franklin (1876–1968). American engineer and inventor. His inventions included the electric cash register (1908), the electric self-starter for cars (1912), quick drying lacquer and anti-knock petrol. He was vice-president and director of research at General Motors 1920–47. The Sloan-Kettering Institute for cancer research in New York was named for him and Alfred P. Sloan, chairman of GM.

Key, Francis Scott (1779–1843). American lawyer and poet, remembered as the author of *The Star-Spangled Banner*, which became the American national anthem by an act of Congress (1931).

Keyes, Roger John Brownlow Keyes, 1st Baron (1872–1945). British sailor. He gained distinction in China (1900) and in World War I proved himself an inspiring leader as vice-admiral in command at Dover and responsible for the famous Dover patrol. On St George's Day 1918 he commanded the operations against the German-held submarine bases at Zeebrugge and Ostend, which, though only partially successful, ranked with the most heroic exploits of the war. In World War II he served as liaison officer with the Belgian King Leopold III, whose much criticized conduct he warmly defended; subsequently he was director of combined operations (1940–41).

Keyes was a Conservative M.P. (1934–43) before being raised to the peerage.
Keyes, R. J. B., *Naval Memoirs*. 1935

Keynes, John Maynard Keynes, 1st Baron (1883–1946). British economist. Fellow and lecturer at King's College, Cambridge, from 1909, he worked during World War I at the Treasury, of which he was the principal representative at the negotiations preparatory to the Treaty of Versailles. Having shown, by his resignation, disapproval of the financial proposals, especially those relating to reparations, he predicted trenchantly, in *The Economic Consequences of the Peace* (1919), the results of imposing obligations which a defeated Germany would be unable to meet. The book made Keynes the centre of immediate controversy and ensured his fame when his worst fears were realized. He was equally critical of Britain's return to the gold standard (1925) and predicted the rapid increase in unemployment that would arise from its deflationary effects. The direction in which his mind was working was shown by the proposals he made for dealing with unemployment in the 1929 election manifesto of the Liberal party (to which he belonged), as large programme of public works being among the chief recommendations. His matured ideas for regulating the economy as well as his new conclusions on monetary theory were elaborated with great skill and persuasive power in *The General Theory of Employment, Interest, and Money* (1936). The general acceptance of its main tenets in many countries after World War II constituted what is known as the Keynesian revolution. It marked the end of the classical economists' belief in the self-regulating economy: aggregate demand was to be adjusted to available supply, consciously using such financial techniques as enlarging or reducing the credit base or varying the rates of interest; government expenditure, too, should be adjusted as necessary so as either to stimulate or to discourage public demand. Keynes himself modified some of his prescriptions in later years; it is clear from the 'stop-go' tactics enforced upon governments in Britain and elsewhere that the full answers have not been found; but the great overall post-war rise in prosperity in the developed countries and the absence of catastrophic unemployment is largely due to Keynes.

He was one of the few theoretical economists who had the opportunity or skill to bring his ideas into practice. In World War II he was adviser to the chancellor of the exchequer, having become (1940) a peer and a member of the Court of the Bank of England. The years from 1943 on were mainly spent on financial missions to America. He was the chief British delegate at the Bretton Woods Conference (1944), and it was his plan, welded with similar American proposals, that became the basis of discussion and agreement there on the foundation of the International Monetary Fund and the World Bank. Keynes was a lover and patron of several arts, and built and endowed the Cambridge Arts Theatre; he married (1925) the Russian ballerina, Lydia Lopokova (1892–1981).
Dillard, D. D., *The Economics of John Maynard Keynes*. 1948. Skidelsky, R., *John Maynard Keynes*. 1983

Khachaturyan, Aram Ilyich (1903–1978). Russian composer. Born of poor parents in Tiflis, Georgia, he studied at the Mosco Conservatoire (1923–34). His compositions were influenced by the Armenian, Georgian and other folk tunes which he collected. He wrote three virtuoso concertos (for piano, cello and violin) in addition to three symphonies, the popular ballet suites *Gayaneh* and *Masquerade*, a number of songs (some of them for the Red Army), and incidental music for films and plays. He composed the National Anthem of Soviet Armenia (1945). He was awarded the Order of Lenin (1939).

Khama, Sir Seretse (1921–1980). African politician. A hereditary tribal chief of Bechuanaland, he was educated at Balliol College, Oxford. His marriage (1950) to an Englishwoman, Ruth Williams, led to a period of exile but he returned to Bechuanaland in 1956. He was first prime minister of Bechuanaland 1965–66 and first president of Botswana 1966–80.

Khomeini, Rohallah (1900–). Iranian ayatollah and political leader. A Shi-ite Moslem, he opposed attempts to westernize and secularize Iran by Shah * Mohammed Reza Pahlevi and was exiled in Turkey, Iraq and France 1964–79. In February 1979 he returned to Iran, the Shah's government collapsed and Khomeini nominated a new ministry. He became virtual head of state with the support of his Islamic Revolution party.

Under the new constitution accepted by plebiscite Iran returned to a strict observance of Moslem principles and traditions.

Khrushchev, Nikita Sergeyevich (1894–1971). Russian politician, born in Kalinkova, Kursk Province. The son of a miner and shepherd, he first worked on a farm, then became a plumber and a locksmith. He joined the Communist party in 1918 and after training began his career as party organizer at the age of 35. He was a member of the Central Committee of the party (1934); Secretary of the Moscow District Party Committee (1934–38); General Secretary of the Ukraine (1938–46, 1947–53); and held the rank of lieutenant-general when the Ukraine was occupied by Germany. He was premier of the Ukraine (1944–47) and purged the anti-Stalinists there after the war. He was elected to the Politburo in 1939 and was also secretary of the Moscow Province Communist Party (1949–53). On Stalin's death he acted as a liaison man between the 'collective leadership' (Malenkov, Molotov, Beria) and the Party machine. He was first secretary of the Communist party (March 1953–October 1964) during which time he steadily eliminated the top echelon of leadership. He replaced his own nominee N. A. * Bulganin, as premier (1958–64). He visited the U.S. in 1959, India and China in 1960. He was forced out of office in October 1964 and passed into obscure retirement. A volume of autobiography, *Khrushchev Remembers*, was published in the West in 1970; although he denied its authorship it appears that the basic materials are authentic but possibly compiled without his consent.

Kidd, William (1645–1701). Scottish privateer. After successful operations against the French, he was provided (1696) by London merchants with a ship of thirty guns to destroy pirates in the Indian Ocean. In 1698 rumours began to trickle through that Kidd had turned pirate himself. Two years later he returned to American waters but when he landed at Boston, which had been his home for some years, he was arrested, despite a half-promise of a safe conduct. He was sent to London, tried, condemned and hanged. Hoards of treasure said to have been his were found in Long Island and elsewhere, but the exploits which have made him notorious as a pirate chief are mostly legendary and he may even have been innocent, as he claimed to the end.

Kierkegaard, Sören Aabye (1813–1855). Danish philosopher and theologian. Though influenced strongly by the philosophy of * Hegel, he then reacted against the Hegelian notion that through the ultimate reality, the Absolute, nature exists rationally and systematically. In his revolt against reason he stressed that the great problems of men, which he identified chiefly as dread (Angst) and anxiety, could only be resolved by an individual search for God, whom he saw as infinitely different in quality from man. He rejected, therefore, all conventional, communal and ethical religion and indeed the Christian dogma of an historical incarnation. His major works include *Either/Or* (1843), *Concluding Unscientific Postscript* (1846) and his *Journals*. His theme that 'truth is subjectivity' and his anti-Hegelian 'existential dialectic', at first scarcely known outside Denmark, profoundly influenced twentieth-century thought and led directly to existentialism.

Rohde, P., *Sören Kierkegaard: An Introduction to his Life and Philosophy*. 1963

Kildare, Earls of. From 1316 the earldom of Kildare was the title held by the head of the Irish family of Fitzgerald. **Gerald, 8th Earl of Kildare** (or 'Great') (died 1513), took advantage of English pre-occupation with the Wars of the Roses to build, by marriage alliances and conquest, an all but independent domain; though he supported the pretender Lambert * Simnel he managed to effect a reconciliation with Henry VII. His son **Gerald, 9th Earl** (1487–1534), for some time maintained much of his power in face of Henry VIII's centralizing policy, but he was forced to obey a summons to London where he was imprisoned. A false report of his execution provoked a rebellion by his son Silken Thomas, who was defeated and put to death (1537). Queen Mary re-instated as earl his brother **Gerald** (1525–1585). The title is now held by the Duke of Leinster.

Kilvert, Francis (1840–1879). English cleric and diarist. His *Diary* was discovered in 1937 and edited by William Plomer in three volumes, 1938–40. It describes his life and environment in graphic and sometimes humorous detail and is an important document of social history.

Kim Il Sung (1912–). Korean Communist politician and soldier. Son of a school teacher, he probably studied in China. He founded the Fatherland Restoration Association (1936), led guerilla forces against Japan in Manchuria and may have served as a colonel at Stalingrad. After Korea's partitioning in 1945, Russian troops occupied the North and Kim, secretary-general of the Korean Workers' Party, became chairman of the provisional government. On the Russian withdrawal, the Democratic Peoples' Republic of Korea was founded and Kim was premier 1948–72 and president 1972– . During the Korean war (1950–53) he commanded the armed forces of the North and became a marshal. The DPRK attempted an ambitious industrialization program after the war and Kim's philosophy of 'Juche' had the force of law.

King, Cecil *see* **Harmsworth**

King, Ernest Joseph (1878–1958). American sailor. Having served in the Spanish American War and World War I, he had risen to be (1938–39) vice-admiral commanding aircraft battle force, an experience of great value for the air–sea battles of World War II, when he was commander-in-chief of the U.S. fleet and (from 1942) director of naval operations. By his mastery of the problems of strategy and supply he was, more than any other single man, responsible for Japan's defeat.

King, Martin Luther (1929–1968). American Negro leader. A Baptist minister by profession, he was one of the most successful and determined leaders of American Negroes in their campaign for civil rights. Though he led and organized many demonstrations, he was a consistent opponent of violence and was awarded the Nobel Peace Prize (1964). He was assassinated in Memphis, Tennessee on 4 April 1968.

Lewis, D. L., *King: A Critical Biography*. 1970

King, Sir (Frederick) **Truby** (1858–1938). New Zealand physician. He founded many 'mothercraft' and infant welfare clinics and helped to make New Zealand's infant mortality rate the lowest in the world.

King, W(illiam) L(yon) Mackenzie (1874–1950). Canadian Liberal politician. Grandson of William Lyon * Mackenzie, he gained a PhD in industrial sociology at Harvard, was deputy minister of labour 1900–08 and a member of the Canadian House of Commons 1908–11 and 1919–48. On Sir Wilfred * Laurier's death in 1919, King (then out of parliament) was elected Liberal party leader. Prime minister of Canada for a record period, over three terms (1921–26, 1926–30 and 1935–48) and also foreign minister 1926–30 and 1935–46, he secured a degree of national unity by persuading French Canadians that the Liberal party would protect their interests. However, his free trade policies led to the increasing dominance of the Canadian economy by US commercial interests, creating many social and political problems. His view that the relationship between each dominion and Britain should be completely equal were embodied in the Statute of Westminster (1931), based on the 1926 Westminster Conference where he had played a leading role. Externally he insisted on Canada's complete freedom of action and shunned all alliances; nevertheless he brought Canada into World War II on the side of Britain. On his retirement (1948) Louis * St Laurent became prime minister and Liberal leader, and King received the OM. He was unmarried and an introverted mystic.

Pickersgill, J. W., and Forster, D. F., *The Mackenzie King Record*. 1960–70.

Kinglake, Alexander William (1808–1891). English historian. He wrote an account of his travels in the east in *Eothen* (1844). In 1854 he followed the British army to the Crimea and wrote *History of the War in the Crimea* (8 volumes, 1863–87), a brilliant and detailed narrative based upon the papers of the commander-in-chief, Lord * Raglan. He was a Liberal M.P. (1857–68).

Kingsley, Charles (1819–1875). English clergyman and author, one of the founders of the Christian Socialist movement. He became rector (1844) of Eversley, Hampshire, a living he held for the rest of his life. His social doctrines are most clearly expressed in his novels *Yeast* (1850), *Alton Locke* (1851) and *Two Years Ago* (1857). His historical romances include *Westward Ho!* (1855), *Hypatia* (1853) and *Hereward the Wake* (1866), and he also wrote the children's books *The Heroes* (1856; stories from Greek mythology) and *The Water Babies* (1863). He was professor of modern history at Cambridge 1860–69. His brother, **Henry Kingsley** (1830–1876), also a novelist, is best remembered for *Ravenshoe*

(1861); his niece **Mary Kingsley** (1862–1900), wrote with unusual insight about native problems in West Africa, where she travelled extensively.
Kingsley, C., *Letters and Memories.* 1877, repr. 1973

Kinnock, Neil Gordon (1942–). British Labour politician. The son of a labourer and a nurse, he was educated in Wales, lectured in Cardiff, worked for the Workers' Educational Association and became MP for Bedwellty 1970– . He served as shadow minister for education 1979–83 and succeeded Michael * Foot as leader of the opposition 1983– .

Kinsey, Alfred Charles (1894–1956). American zoologist and social scientist. The publication of his *Sexual Behaviour of the Human Male* (1948) and *Sexual Behaviour of the Human Female* (1953) roused considerable controversy, caused partly by the nature of the theme but more particularly because his conclusions were reached mainly from answers (not necessarily truthful) to standard questionnaires.

Kipling, (Joseph) Rudyard (1865–1936). English writer. He was the son of **John Lockwood Kipling** (1837–1911), author-artist of *Beast and Man in India* (1892). Rudyard Kipling was born in Bombay and educated in England, returning to India to become (1882) assistant editor of the *Civil and Military Gazette*, Lahore. He first achieved fame with *Departmental Ditties* (1886) and two books of short stories (1888), *Soldiers Three* and *Plain Tales from the Hills*. He returned to England (1889) and published a novel, *The Light that Failed* (1890). Collaboration with the American Wolcot Balestier on *The Naulahka* (1892) led to his marriage to Balestier's sister, Caroline. After living in America for a time the Kiplings returned to England in 1899. The intervening years had produced *Barrack-Room Ballads* (1892), another book of poems, more short stories and a novel *Captains Courageous* (1897). In the two *Jungle Books* (1894–95) his skill as a writer for children was revealed, to be shown again in *Just-So Stories* (1902), *Puck of Pook's Hill* (1906) and *Rewards and Fairies* (1910). *Stalky and Co.* (1899) recalls his schooldays in the form of a novel, but even more popular is *Kim* (1901), the story of the vagabond boy who grows to adventurous manhood in India, which, in all its variety and detail, magnificence and squalor, he vividly and lovingly recalls. He settled in Sussex after the Boer War and concentrated on poems and short stories, some of the best of which appeared in e.g. *Actions and Reactions* (1909). He was the first English winner of the Nobel Prize for Literature (1907).

Kipling's belief in the imperial mission of his countrymen to protect, serve and administer the subject multitudes with devotion, altruism and justice gave him a not fully deserved reputation for jingoism. His attitude towards the British Empire was to stress, not the rewards it offered, but the duties it imposed:

> The tumult and the shouting dies:
> The Captains and the Kings depart:
> Still stands Thine ancient sacrifice,
> An humble and a contrite heart.

The centenary of his birth saw a revival of interest in Kipling and a more favourable assessment of his work.
Dobree, B., *Rudyard Kipling: Realist and Fabulist*. 1967. Wilson, A., *The Strange Ride of Rudyard Kipling*. 1977

Kirchhoff, Gustav Robert (1824–1887). German physicist, born and educated at Königsberg. He became professor of physics at Breslau (1850), Heidelberg (1854) and Berlin (1857). Working with * Bunsen, he developed the spectroscope and the technique of spectrum analysis by which they discovered caesium (1860) and rubidium (1861). Kirchhoff enunciated two basic laws (Kirchhoff's Laws of Electricity) that are used to calculate current and voltage in complex electrical circuits, and a law of radiation (Kirchhoff's Law of Thermodynamics) that relates emissive and absorptive power. He was the first to explain the Fraunhofer lines in the solar spectrum (1859).

Kirov, Sergey Mironovich (1888–1934). Soviet politician. He was a close associate of * Stalin and, from 1926, secretary of the Communist party in the Leningrad area and a Politburo member 1930–34. His assassination was followed by a witch-hunt and the judicial execution of over 100 suspected opponents of Stalin's régime.

Kishi Nobusuke (1896–). Japanese politician. An elder brother of * Sato Eisaku and nephew of Matsuoko Yosuka, he was adopted by an uncle's family, became a civil servant and directed Japanese economic investment in Manchuria (Manchukuo) 1936–39. He served under General * Tojo as a Vice-Minister and Minister of State 1943–44, was held as a war criminal 1945–48 but never tried. A Member of the Diet 1942–45; 1953– , he was Foreign Minister 1956–57 and Prime Minister 1957–60, seeking close economic ties with the U.S. and the right to re-arm. He remained a powerful conservative force in the Liberal Democratic Party.

Kissinger, Henry Alfred (1923–). American statesman. Born in Germany, he emigrated to the U.S.A. in 1938. He established a reputation as an expert on international relations and defence, and in 1969 was appointed President * Nixon's assistant responsible for national security. He became Secretary of State in 1973. He negotiated the cease-fire between the U.S.A. and North Vietnam in 1973 and was also instrumental in achieving a cease-fire between Egypt and Israel. He continued in office under President Ford (1974–77) and negotiated a settlement between hostile factions in Rhodesia which was accepted by the Rhodesian government but not by the Patriotic Front guerrilla movement. He was awarded the Nobel Peace Prize in 1973. In 1977 he returned to academic life as Professor of Diplomacy at Georgetown University. A prolific writer, he published his memoirs in 1979.

Kitasato Shibasaburo (1852–1931). Japanese bacteriologist. A pupil of * Koch, he was noted for his independent discoveries of the bacilli of anthrax (1889), diphtheria (1890) and bubonic plague (1894).

Kitchener of Khartoum, Herbert Horatio Kitchener, 1st Earl (1850–1916). British soldier. While still a cadet at the Royal Military Academy, he served with the French army in the Franco-Prussian War. As an engineer officer, with a knowledge of Arabic and Hebrew, he proved his ability in Palestine survey work, in Cyprus, and (from 1882) in Egypt. He was deeply involved in the events leading up to and following the death of * Gordon and as a result of the skill and thoroughness with which he performed all the tasks assigned him, he was made (1890) sirdar (i.e. Egyptian commander-in-chief). He spent the following years in training men and building up resources to avenge Gordon and rescue the Sudanese from the fanatical rule of the khalifa and his dervishes. When ready, he moved up the Nile and won the decisive Battle of Omdurman (1898), for which he was created a baron and made governor general of the Sudan, in which office he planned the modern city of Khartoum. In the Boer War he was appointed (1900) chief of staff to Lord * Roberts, whom he succeeded as commander-in-chief in the same year. He was rewarded by being one of the original members of the Order of Merit. His tenure of the post of commander-in-chief in India (1902–09) was famous for his quarrel with the viceroy, Lord * Curzon, concerning spheres of authority, but it was also notable for many reforms, e.g. hygiene, sanitation. In 1911, Kitchener, by then a field-marshal, returned to Egypt as British agent and was still holding that position when on the outbreak of war (1914), having earlier received an earldom, he became secretary of state for war. His administration of that office has been criticized, and it is certain that he found delegation difficult and that the faults of over-centralization became apparent; but the amount he actually achieved was prodigious and his final judgement was seldom at fault. As a result of his immense prestige, 3,000,000 men (Kitchener's Army) responded voluntarily to his call to arms, and some seventy infantry divisions were formed. In June 1916 H.M.S. *Hampshire*, carrying Kitchener on an urgent visit to Russia, was mined and sank off the Orkneys. The news of his death struck the public as such an unbelievable calamity that for many months legends circulated that he had been seen alive engaged on this or that secret duty. A national memorial fund of over £500,000 was raised for higher education for boys, and a medical school at Khartoum.

Cross-eyed, huge, moustachioed and unmarried, Kitchener was an enigmatic figure, a master of colonial warfare but with vivid insights into the nature of World War I.

Magnus, P., *Kitchener*. 1958

Kléber, Jean Baptiste (1753–1800). French soldier, born in Alsace. Having fought with distinction in the French Revolutionary campaigns, he went (1798) to Egypt as a divisional commander under * Napoleon. He was left in command in 1799 when Napoleon returned to Paris. On the refusal by the higher British authorities to ratify an agreement with the local commander, Sidney Smith, for the evacuation of his troops, he reopened hostilities, defeated the Turks at Heliopolis but was assassinated by a fanatic in Cairo shortly afterwards.

Klee, Paul (1879–1940). Swiss painter. Undecided at first whether to pursue art or music, he eventually went to Munich to study and joined the *Blaue Reiter* group (* Kandinsky). His eyes were opened to the use of colour during a tour in Tunis (1914), and henceforth his colour harmonies and contrasts were as much a feature of his work as his brilliant draughtsmanship. In 1920 he joined the Bauhaus in Weimar, but soon after Hitler came to power he was dismissed (1933) from an appointment at the Düsseldorf Academy, on the grounds that his art was decadent, and settled in Switzerland. As Klee has been one of the most important influences on modern art, his methods of composition are significant. Instead of consciously deciding upon a subject for a picture, his starting point would be splashes of colour intuitively conceived, which by the processes of association and suggestion, modified by his acquired knowledge of composition, set up a train of 'pictorial thinking' which he would follow until a picture was achieved. The naming of the picture was the final act.
Grohmann, W., *Paul Klee*. 1956

Kleist, Heinrich von (1777–1811). German writer. For a short time he followed the traditions of his family by entering the Prussian army but soon left it to become absorbed in study, travel and writing. Much of his writing was inspired by a misinterpretation of * Kant, whom he believed to say that human beings are marionettes helplessly and hopelessly in the toils of inscrutable powers. His masterpiece, the drama *Prinz Friedrich von Homburg* (1811) is, however, in lighter vein. As well as novels and plays he also wrote poems and short stories – e.g. *Michael Kohlhaas* (1808) – of originality and power. That his pessimism was of pathological as well as intellectual origin is shown by the manner of his death; he shot his mistress, Henriette Vogel, and then himself.
Maass, J., *Kleist: A Biography*. 1983

Klemperer, Otto (1885–1973). German conductor. A protegé of Gustav * Mahler, he was an early champion of modern composers. He held various posts, mainly as operatic conductor, in Germany and then directed the Los Angeles Philharmonic orchestra (1933–39). Thereafter he appeared widely as guest conductor and from 1954 conducted regularly in England, where he was known chiefly as an interpreter of the German classics; in 1955 he was appointed principal conductor of the Philharmonia Orchestra, and after its disbandment became president of the New Philharmonia Orchestra and Chorus.

Klimt, Gustav (1862–1918). Austrian painter. A co-founder of the Vienna Sezessionist school (1897), he was a leader in the Art Nouveau (Jugendstil) movement. His sumptuous and erotic style concealed a deep pessimism. He died in an influenza epidemic.

Klopstock, Friedrich Gottlieb (1724–1803). German poet. While still at school he read a translation of Milton's *Paradise Lost* and determined to create a German epic on an even more magnificent theme. *The Messiah*, resulting from this decision, took over twenty years to write (1746–73); it is an epic on the grand scale, written in hexameters, in twenty books, and its admirers and detractors have waged literary war over the years. For most, Klopstock is more accessible through his shorter poems. By using the lyric as a means of self-revelation and by his adaptation of the classical metres based on 'quantity' to a language like German based on stress, he influenced many later writers, even * Goethe himself.
Stahl, E. L., and Yuill, W. E., *German Literature of the Eighteenth and Nineteenth Centuries*. 1970

Kluck, Alexander von (1846–1934). German soldier. As commander of the German 1st Army at the outbreak of World War I he directed the drive through Belgium and France; but in September 1914 Joffre counterattacked at the Marne and gained a crucial victory.

Kneller, Sir Godfrey, 1st Bart. (1646–1723). German-born painter. Already well known as a portraitist on the continent before he settled in England, he was appointed (1678) principal painter by Charles II, and reached the height of his fame as a court painter under William and Mary and Queen Anne. He received a knighthood in 1692 and in 1715 a baronetcy from George I. His portraits, which provide a magnificent series of illustrations for the book of fame, are of greater social than artistic interest, but his best pictures achieve their effect not only by assured technique and dignity of treatment but also by colour subtlety and psychological insight. His most famous pictures include the great equestrian portrait of William III and striking likenesses of Louis XIV and Peter the Great; other well known portraits are the *Beauties* at Hampton Court, the Kit Cat club series in the National Portrait Gallery and the *Admirals* at Greenwich. His brother, **John Zacharias Kneller** (1644–1702), was also a painter. He, too, settled in England and painted portraits and architectural scenes.

Killanin, Lord, *Sir Godfrey Kneller and His Times, 1646–1723.* 1948

Knox, John (1513?–1572). Scottish religious reformer, born in East Lothian. Though from 1530 he had been a Roman Catholic priest, he became a close friend of the reformer George Wishart who was burned at the stake for heresy (1546). Knox then joined the reforming party, but was captured (1548) by French troops (serving the cause of Mary of Guise, Scotland's queen dowager) in St Andrews' Castle, the refuge of many reformers fearing reprisals of the murder of Cardinal * Beaton. Knox was taken to France and toiled as a galley-slave, until released at the request of England's Edward VI, who made him a royal chaplain. On Mary's accession he fled to Geneva where he worked for three years with * Calvin. He briefly returned to Scotland (1555–56), a visit during which the oppression suffered by his co-religionists at the hands of Mary of Guise, acting as regent for her daughter Mary Queen of Scots, inspired his famous *First Blast of the Trumpet Against the Monstrous Regiment* (i.e. 'regimen' or rule) *of Women* (1558), which offended Queen Elizabeth, at whom it was not aimed. Knox returned to Scotland again (1559) after the lords of the congregation (the leading lay reformers) had established an organized 'kirk' with churches in Dundee and elsewhere and ministers assisted by elders. Despite the regent's retaliatory ban Knox rallied the reformers by his preaching, and secured acceptance of the doctrine that 'the regent's commands must be disobeyed if contrary to God's'. With civil war imminent, the English government intervened by sending troops to occupy Edinburgh. This marked the triumph of the Protestant cause. The Scottish parliament abolished papal authority, voted for reform, and later approved the *Confessions of Faith* prepared by Knox and five others. The General Assembly of the church first met in 1560 and adopted the *Book of Common Order* (sometimes called Knox's Liturgy), thus ensuring that the Church of Scotland, based on Calvin's teaching, should develop as a presbyterian community. When Mary Queen of Scots returned (1561) from France with the idea of restoring Catholicism, she tried in vain to dazzle and charm Knox, and the murder of Darnley, her flight with Bothwell, and finally her imprisonment in England (from 1567) soon removed her from the scene. Knox, who had become minister of St Giles, Edinburgh's largest church, remained in the forefront of events except in the year 1566–67 when he withdrew into seclusion to complete his *History of the Reformation in Scotland.* That the Church of Scotland took the form it did was due almost entirely to the work of Knox. From his two marriages Knox had two sons and three daughters, but his many public activities left little time for family life.

Ridley, J. G., *John Knox.* 1968

Knox, Ronald Arbuthnot (1888–1957). English scholar and priest. The son of an Anglican bishop, he became a Roman Catholic (1917) and entered the priesthood. Previously he had been an Anglican chaplain at Oxford University, with which he was associated all his life. From 1939 he devoted himself to the great task of retranslating the Vulgate (which finally appeared complete in 1954). He also engaged in theological controversy and wrote essays and novels. He was one of the wittiest men of his generation.

His brother, **Edmund Valpy Knox** (1881–1971), better known under his *nom de plume* 'Evoe', was a regular contributor to *Punch*, of which he was editor (1933–49).

Waugh, E., *The Life of Ronald Knox.* 1959

Koch, Robert (1843–1910). German bacteriologist, born near Hanover. Having qualified at Göttingen and served as a surgeon in the Franco-Prussian War, he became a medical officer at Wollstein, where he devoted himself to the microscopic study of bacteria. He isolated (1876) the anthrax bacillus and perfected the method of inoculation against it;

two years later his studies of wound infection appeared. In 1880 he moved to Berlin where he was successively a member of the imperial Health Office, a professor of hygiene at the university and director of the Institute for Infectious Diseases. He discovered (1882) the bacillus causing tuberculosis; the discovery of the one causing cholera followed his appointment (1883) to preside over a commission to study this disease in Egypt and India. During the decade 1897–1906 visits to New Guinea, South Africa, India and Uganda enabled him to do valuable work on malaria, rinderpest, bubonic plague and trypanosomiasis (sleeping sickness). He received the Nobel Prize for Medicine (1905).
Moellers, B., *Robert Koch: Persönlichkeit und Lebenswerk, 1843–1910.* 1950

Kodály, Zoltán (1882–1967). Hungarian composer. He studied under Hans Koessler at the Budapest Conservatoire, where he later became professor. With * Bartók he started to collect and study Hungarian folk music. His best known works are the suite from his comic opera *Háry János* (1926), and the choral works *Psalmus Hungaricus* (1923) and *Te Deum* (1936).
Eösze, L., *Z. Kodály, his Life and Work*. 1962

Koestler, Arthur (1905–1983). British–Hungarian author, born in Budapest. After a scientific education he went as an enthusiastic Zionist to work on a collective farm in Palestine, then worked as a reporter for a German newspaper and travelled in the Soviet Union. Later while reporting the Spanish Civil War for an English newspaper he was sentenced to death as a spy by Franco's forces, but was released and went to France; here he was arrested and imprisoned after the fall of France but escaped to England. In 1938 he left the Communist party – his disillusionment is described in *The God That Failed* (1950). Koestler first wrote in Hungarian but for his later writing mastered German, French and English. His first novel in England was *Arrival and Departure* (1943); *Darkness at Noon* (1941), regarded as his masterpiece, is a great political novel. He has written many works, e.g. the autobiographical *Arrow in the Blue* (1952) and *The Yogi and the Commissar* (1945). *The Sleep-walkers* (1959), *The Act of Creation* (1964) and *The Roots of Coincidence* (1972) are of considerable scientific interest. Koestler, an advocate of euthanasia, committed suicide with his wife Cynthia after long suffering from Parkinson's disease.
Frazier, T., and Merrill, R., *Arthur Koestler, an International Bibliography*. 1979

Kohl, Helmut (1930–). German politician. Educated at Frankfurt and Heidelberg universities, he was a member of the Rhineland–Palatinate legislature 1959–76 and premier 1969–76. He became chairman of the National Christian Democratic Union in 1976 and defeated Helmut Schmidt to become chancellor 1982– .

Kohlrausch, Friedrich Wilhelm Georg (1840–1910). German physicist. He was best known for the accurate measuring methods he introduced into many branches of physics and for his pioneer investigations into the conductivity of electrolytes. His improved techniques and his statement of the principle now known as Kohlrausch's Law put the measurement of conductivity on a sound quantitative basis for the first time.

Koivisto, Mauno Henrik (1923–). Finnish politician. A dock-worker who gained a doctorate in economics, he led the Social Democrats and was prime minister 1968–70 and 1979–82, succeeding U.K. * Kekkonen as president of Finland 1982– .

Kokoschka, Oskar (1886–1980). Austrian painter. In 1919 he became a professor at Dresden, then lived in Vienna (1931–34), Prague (1934–38), London (1938–53) and Switzerland. He developed a very personal and imaginative Expressionist style; vivid colouring is combined with a sense of movement in the town scenes, landscapes and portraits for which – apart from his stage-settings – he was best known. Unlike many of his contemporaries, he maintained traditional links with the old masters and preserved with penetrating insight the individual characteristics of the scenery and personalities he portrayed. His draughtsmanship, developed separately, is seen at its best in his portrait lithographs. He wrote several plays.
Goldscheider, L., *Kokoschka*. 3rd ed. 1967

Kolchak, Alexander Vasilyevich (1874?–1920). Russian sailor. He reorganized the navy after the Russo-Japanese War (1904–05), in which he had taken part. In World War I he commanded the Black Sea fleet from 1916, and after the Bolsheviks seized power (1917) headed a counter-revolutionary government in Siberia. Despite early successes on his westward march he was checked by the Bolsheviks and forced to retreat. Eventually he fell into their hands and was shot.

Kollwitz, Käthe (1867–1945). German graphic artist. Born in East Prussia, she lived from 1891 in Berlin where both her life and art were a constant protest against poverty and oppression. Her artistic protest was made through representations of historic scenes, e.g. *The Peasants' Revolt*, realistic studies of working-class life, and illustrations to books, e.g. Zola's *Germinal*, that expressed compassion for and indignation at the miseries of the poor. Her versatility allowed her to be expert at all the graphic arts, and even as a sculptor she managed by a rough-hewn technique to convey the same message as in her other works.
Kollwitz, K. S., ed. Zigrosser, C., *Prints and Drawings*. 2nd ed. 1969

Konev, Ivan Stepanovich (1895–1973). Russian soldier. After serving as a private in World War I he rose rapidly under the Soviet régime. He distinguished himself in World War II as an army commander in the 1941 counter-offensive to the north-west of Moscow, and later in command of an army group during the Ukrainian campaigns, and the subsequent great offensive that ended with his advance to Berlin in March 1945; in May he liberated Prague. He was made a marshal and commanded (1955–60) the armies of the signatories of the Warsaw Pact.

Kondratiev, Nikolai Dimitrievich (1892–1931?). Russian economist. After examining statistics of prices, wages, interest and consumption in Europe and North America since the 1780s, Kondratiev identified 'long waves of cyclical character' which bear his name. If his cycles are extended to the future (which he did not attempt) 1970–95 would be an era of downswing. He was purged under Stalin and never rehabilitated.

Königsmark, Philipp Christoph, Count of (1665–1694). Swedish adventurer. While in the service of Ernest Augustus of Hanover he became aware of the unhappy plight of Dorothea, wife of Elector George Louis (later George I of Great Britain). Whether he was her lover or whether his motives were those of pure chivalry, he tried and failed to aid her to escape. He was arrested, disappeared and was almost certainly put to death; the unfortunate Dorothea was secluded at Ahlden Castle for the rest of her life.

Korda, Sir Alexander (1893–1956). British film producer and director, born in Hungary. He produced films in Budapest, Vienna, Berlin and Paris and founded London Film Productions in England in 1932. His films, notably *The Private Life of Henry VIII* (1933), *Catherine the Great* (1934) and *Rembrandt* (1936) stimulated a revival of feature films at a time when British cinema was dominated by documentaries.

Kornilov, Lavr Georgyevich (1870–1918). Russian soldier. He served in the Russo-Japanese War (1904–05), and in World War I as a divisional commander in Galicia, when, captured by the Austrians, he made a sensational escape. After the revolution (March 1917) he was appointed commander-in-chief but *Kerensky's refusal to satisfy his demands for the restoration of army discipline provoked him to a vain attempt to establish a military dictatorship. Kerensky had him arrested, but when he fell Kornilov escaped to join *Denikin's anti-Bolshevik army on the Don, where he was killed in action.

Kościuszko, Tadeusz Andrzej (1746–1817). Polish patriot. He received a military training in France; being devoted to the cause of national freedom, he offered his services to the revolutionary forces in America (1777), and served with distinction in the War of Independence. In 1786 he returned to Poland, which had made a remarkable recovery from the effects of the first partition between Russia, Prussia and Austria; but his attempts to introduce democratic government as a means of reviving the national spirit frightened the nobles; after a second partition (1793) Kościuszko inspired a national uprising against the tsar. At first he achieved striking success and freed Warsaw, but with the Prussians threatening in the rear he was defeated and captured. Released two years later by the tsar he went to Paris. Though he continued to work for the national cause, he refused overtures made (1806) by Napoleon, whom he distrusted, to cooperate with him in the achievement of Polish freedom. He attended the Congress of Vienna (1814) and vainly pleaded his country's cause with the tsar Alexander. He died after a riding accident in Switzerland. He was buried in Cracow and is revered as one of the greatest Polish patriots.

Kossuth, Lajos (Louis) (1802–1894). Hungarian revolutionary leader. He became a lawyer and first sat in the Hungarian Diet from 1825 to 1827, but it was as a journalist that he won fame and popularity by his newspaper campaigns to free Hungary from Austrian control. For these attacks upon the Habsburg régime he suffered two terms of imprisonment, but he weakened his cause by insisting on Magyar supremacy and so alienating the Slav peoples, Slovenes, Croats, etc., who had come under Hungarian rule. He sat again in the Diet (1832–36 and 1847–49) and in 1848, the 'year of revolutions' throughout Europe, he was mainly instrumental in passing the 'March laws' which abolished the privileges of the nobles, freed the peasants, and created a ministry responsible to the legislature, in which he became minister of finance. In 1849 the final step was taken: the Hungarian parliament declared Hungary independent, and Kossuth became provisional governor and ruled as virtual dictator. The Russians now intervened to support the Austrian government; the combined Austrian and Russian forces were too strong for the Hungarian army and the short-lived republic was overcome. Kossuth fled to Turkey and lived subsequently in England and (from 1870) Italy.
Kossuth, L., *Memories of my exile*. 1880

Koster (or Coster), **Laurens Janszoon** (*c.* 1370–1440). Dutch craftsman. Some authorities credit him with the invention of printing with movable type (using first wooden and then tin letters). He is said to have gone to Mainz, the presumption being that Gutenberg learned from him, thus not deserving the credit that posterity has bestowed.

Kosygin, Alexey Nikolayevich (1904–1980). Soviet politician, born in Leningrad. He joined the Communist party in 1923, and having been trained at the Textile Institute became (1939) commissar of the textile industry, the first of several posts which brought him (1946) to the Politburo. He became chairman of the State Economic Planning Commission (1959) and a first deputy prime minister (1960). When * Khrushchev fell from power Kosygin succeeded him as chairman of the Council of Ministers (i.e. prime minister) 1964–80. He received the Order of Lenin six times and was twice entitled Hero of Socialist Labour.

Kotelewala, Sir John Lionel (1893–1980). Ceylonese politician. He played an important part in politics during the first years of Ceylon's independence after World War II and was prime minister (1952–56). He was a prominent participant in the Asian prime ministers' conference at Colombo (1954) and the Afro-Asian conference (1955) at Bandung, Indonesia.

Kotzebue, August Friedrich Ferdinand von (1761–1819). German dramatist. As a young man he held various offices in the Russian civil service; in Estonia where he was posted (1785–95) he established an amateur theatre for which he wrote *Menschenhass und Reue* (1789). Its fame rapidly spread; * Sheridan produced it (1789) at Covent Garden as *The Stranger*; in the same year Sheridan produced *Kind der Liebe* as *Lovers' Vows* and in 1799 *Der Spanier in Peru* as *Pizarro*. All in all, Kotzebue wrote some 200 plays as well as tales, historical works and satires. In the last years of his life he was the tsar's representative at Weimar, where a new German constitution was being elaborated. There he was stabbed to death on political grounds by a member of a nationalist student society.
Bonford, W. H., *Theatre, Drama and Audience in Goethe's Germany*. 1950

Koussevitzky, Sergei Alexandrovich (1874–1951). Russian conductor. Earlier a double-bass virtuoso, in 1910 he founded a symphony orchestra with which he toured Russia. After visiting most of the countries of Europe, he settled in the U.S.A. as conductor of the Boston Symphony Orchestra (1924–49).

Kraepelin, Emil (1856–1926). German psychiatrist. Having studied medicine, he filled a number of clinical and academic posts before holding professorships of psychiatry at Heidelberg (1890–1903), and Munich (1904–22). He claimed that the basic cause of mental disorders was physiological and that many problems of insanity would be solved by clinical observations made throughout the patient's lifetime. A research institute was founded (1917) in accordance with his plans. His *Textbook of Psychiatry* (first published 1883) was enlarged and modified in successive editions. He visited India, the East Indies and Mexico to pursue comparative psychology.

Krafft-Ebing, Baron Richard von (1840–1902). German neurologist. He held several chairs of psychiatry in Germany and Austria. His case studies *Psychopathia Sexualis* (1886) were a notable contribution to the study of sexual perversion.

Kraft (Krafft), **Adam** (*c.* 1455–1508/9). German sculptor. One of the most prolific and popular of the Nuremberg sculptors, his development makes him a link between the Gothic and Renaissance styles. His most famous work is the 62-inch-high tabernacle in St Laurence's, Nuremberg, especially remarkable for its tracery and reliefs and for the remarkable self-portrait statue on one knee before it.

Kreisky, Bruno (1911–). Austrian politician. Of Jewish origin, he held a doctorate in law from Vienna University, and after Hitler annexed Austria in 1938, Kreisky lived in Sweden until 1951. He was a socialist member of parliament (1956–), foreign minister (1959–66) and chancellor (1970–83).

Kreisler, Fritz (1875–1962). Austrian violinist and composer. Born in Vienna, he studied both there and in Paris under Massart. His performances though often flawless were variable in quality, and it was chiefly for his warm and sensuous tone that he became one of the most popular virtuoso performers in Europe and in the U.S.A., where he lived from 1920. In 1935 he revealed that he himself had composed some pieces which he had previously performed as the works of little-known seventeenth- and eighteenth-century composers.
Lochner, L. P., *Fritz Kreisler*. 1950

Kreuger, Ivar (1880–1932). Swedish financier. Using his family firm of Kreuger and Toll as a base for his operations, he became head of the Swedish Match Company, which he developed into a vast international trust and financial agency by lending money to a dozen or more countries impoverished by World War I, in return for match monopolies and contracts. When he committed suicide in Paris, it was discovered to the surprise and consternation of the financial world that he had tried to avert the collapse of his enterprises by a huge and complex conspiracy of forgery and falsification.
Shaplen, R., *Kreuger, Genius and Swindler*. 1960

Krishna Menon, Vengalil Krishnan (1897–1974). Indian politician and diplomat. He lived in England from 1924, studied at the London School of Economics, became a lawyer, was a St Pancras borough councillor 1934–47 and the first editor of Pelican Books (1936). A left-wing member of the Indian National Congress, he was strongly anti-British. After India gained independence (1947), he became first high commissioner in Great Britain. From 1952 to 1956 he was India's representative at the United Nations and a strong advocate of non-alignment. Back in Indian politics, he represented the left wing in * Nehru's Congress government. In 1957 he was appointed defence minister; he was forced to resign when the Chinese aggression (1962) revealed the inadequacy of India's military preparedness. In the elections of 1966 he was defeated.

Krishnamurti, Jiddu (1897–). Indian mystic, born near Madras. Sponsored by the theosophist Annie * Besant, who believed him a messiah, he was proclaimed by devotees as leader of the Order of the Star of the East (1911); he himself disbanded the order in 1929.
Lutyens, M., *Krishnamurti: The Years of Awakening*. 1975

Kropotkin, Prince Peter Alexeyevich (1842–1921). Russian explorer and anarchist. Having made a name by geographical and geological exploration in Siberia, Manchuria and Scandinavia, he became attracted to anarchism and renounced his title. After two years' imprisonment in Russia (1874–76) for his iconoclastic opinions, he escaped to England, Switzerland (from which he was expelled in 1881) and France, where he was imprisoned (1881–86). He then lived in England (twice visiting the U.S.A.) where the publication of his ideas (e.g. in *Nineteenth Century* and *Atlantic Monthly*) aroused no resentment. He returned to Russia after the revolution (1917). Though opposed to communism he was held

in high esteem. The moral basis for his anarchistic conclusion is set out in his *Ethics* (1924).
Arakumovic, I., and Woodcock, G., *Anarchist Prince*. 1971

Kruger, (Stephanus Johannes) Paulus (1825–1904). Boer politician. The northward Great Trek took him as a child with his parents to the Transvaal, the new territory outside the sphere of British rule. There he grew up to be prominent as farmer, politician and soldier. After the British annexation of the Transvaal (1877), Kruger was one of the leaders of the revolt (1880) by which independence was regained. Kruger was elected president (1883) and had to face the political and social problems raised by the influx of *Uitlanders* (non-Boer settlers) after the discovery of gold in the Rand. His refusal to grant the newcomers civil rights (for fear that they might come to dominate the country), coupled with the provocation of the * Jameson Raid were basic causes of the Boer War. Kruger took some part in the early phase of the war but in 1900 sailed to Europe on a Dutch warship in the vain hope of obtaining support for the Boers. He did not return to Africa and died in Switzerland. Kruger, who belonged to a puritanical sect known as Doppers, had honesty, shrewdness and common sense, but lacked any adaptability for conciliation. Known to his fellows as 'Oom [Uncle] Paul' he was revered as the exemplar of resistance to the British.
Kruger, D. W., *Paul Kruger*. 1961–63

Krupp, Alfried (1812–1887). German steel and armament manufacturer. After taking over his father's metal foundry at Essen (1848) he developed a process for making cast steel, and introduced (1862) the Bessemer steel process. The manufacture of guns started in 1861 and Bismarck's frequent wars hastened a vast expansion. Coal and iron mines were added in 1876. His paternalistic relationship to his large labour force became traditional in the firm and he offered the best wages and welfare conditions of any in Germany. Under his son **Friedrich Alfried Krupp** (1854–1902), who added armour plating (1890) and shipbuilding (1902), expansion continued and the number of employees had risen to 43,000 when the firm was taken over by his daughter **Bertha** (1886–1957). On her marriage (1906) she transferred administrative power to her husband, **Gustav von Bohlen und Halbach** (1870–1950) known as Krupp von Bohlen. Under his régime gun manufacture reached a culmination in World War I with the vast 17-in. howitzers that smashed the Belgian forts, and with 'Big Bertha' which shelled Paris at a range of seventy miles. German defeat meant a temporary decline in Krupp's fortunes and a switch to the manufacture of locomotives and agricultural machinery, but an even greater degree of prosperity was attained when Hitler, whom Krupp partly financed, began rearmament. Von Bohlen was senile at the end of World War II but his son **Alfried Krupp** (1907–67) was tried at Nuremberg and condemned to twelve years' imprisonment. He was released in 1951, however, and was soon back in control of his vast industrial empire.

In 1968 the company became a public corporation and the family relinquished control.
Klass, G. von, *Krupps: The Story of an Industrial Empire*. 1954. Manchester, W., *The Arms of Krupp*. 1968

Krupskaya, Nadezhda Konstantinovna (1869–1939). Russian revolutionary. She married V. I. * Lenin in 1898, shared his exile and became a powerful influence in education after the Revolution.

Krylov, Ivan Andreyevich (1768–1844). Russian writer. Though he also edited satirical journals and wrote plays, his fame rests on his racy and humorous fables. He had translated * La Fontaine, but drew his material largely from peasants met during his years (1793–1806) of wandering through Russia. He has been called 'the Russian La Fontaine'.

Kubelík, Jan (1880–1940). Czech violinist and composer. He began his platform career in Vienna in 1898 and gained international success through his virtuosity and dramatic style. His son **Rafael Kubelík** (1914–) was a conductor and composer.

Kublai Khan (1216–1294). First Mongol emperor of China, the grandson of * Genghis Khan. When he became (1259) great khan he gained at least nominal suzerainty over a territory stretching from the Black Sea to the Pacific. But it was China that stirred his imagination and absorbed his energies. He proclaimed himself emperor of China to become the first of a new Yüan dynasty, and established a splendid capital at Cambaluc

(Peking), described by * Marco Polo, who visited his court. Hangchow, the capital of the Chinese Sung dynasty, was taken in 1276 but another fifteen years elapsed before all China was conquered. During his reign he also sent expeditions to Tibet; further south he subdued Burma but failed to achieve success against Japan. Unlike his ferocious ancestors, Kublai Khan was a liberal-minded ruler; he welcomed foreigners and fostered the arts and commerce; he established lamaistic Buddhism as the state religion but was tolerant of other faiths. He improved the civil service, and many great public works were carried out during his reign.
Saunders, J. J., *The History of the Mongol Conquests*. 1971

Kubrick, Stanley (1928–). American film director, born in New York. Originally a magazine photographer, he made low-budget documentaries then a series of powerful films, including *Paths of Glory* (1957), *Lolita* (1962), *Dr Strangelove or How I learned to Stop Worrying and Love the Bomb* (1964), *2001: A Space Odyssey* (1968), *A Clockwork Orange* (1971) and *Barry Lyndon* (1975).

Kun, Béla (1886–1939). Hungarian politician of Jewish origin. He was captured by the Russians in World War I and returned to set up a short-lived Soviet republic in Hungary (March–August 1919). After the counter-revolution he escaped to Vienna and thence to Russia, where he died or was put to death.
Tokes, R. L., *Bela Kun and the Hungarian Soviet Republic*. 1967

Kundera, Milan (1929–). Czech writer, resident in France. He worked at the Prague film school, left Czechoslovakia in 1969 and became a professor at Rennes 1975–80 and Paris 1980– . His novels include *The Joke* (1967), *Life is Elsewhere* (1973) and *The Book of Laughter and Forgetting* (1979).

Kurosawa Akira (1910–). Japanese film director. One of the best known of those directors whose artistry, especially in the use of colour, has, within two decades, given Japanese films a high reputation. His first film was *Sugata Sanshino* (1943) followed by, e.g., *Rashomon* (1951), *The Seven Samurai* (1954), *Throne of Blood* (1956) and *Red Beard* (1965).

Other leading directors who have taken part in this Japanese cinema renaissance include Misoguchi (died 1956) – *Sansho Daiu* etc.; Masaki Kobayishi – *Hara Kiri, Kivaidan*; and Kon Ishikawa, whose film of the Tokyo Olympics turned a great sports event into an artistic sensation.
Richie, D., *The Films of Akira Kurosawa*. 1965

Kutuzov, Mikhail Ilarionovich (1745–1813). Russian soldier. He served with distinction against the Turks (1788–91), and as commander of the Russian troops at Austerlitz (1805), when he had advised against risking battle. In the event Napoleon won a most spectacular victory against the Russian and Austrian armies. When Napoleon invaded Russia (1812) Kutuzov replaced * Barclay de Tolly as commander-in-chief; he at first continued Tolly's strategy in avoiding a pitched battle until just before Moscow, at Borodino where, after fearful carnage on both sides, the Russians withdrew. Napoleon occupied Moscow but the advent of winter and the threat of Kutuzov's undestroyed army decided him to begin his disastrous retreat. Kutuzov won a great victory over Davout and Ney at Smolensk and harassed the Grand Army continuously as it straggled homewards. He is held in high esteem by the Russians as one of their greatest generals.

Kyd, Thomas (1558–1594). English dramatist. Little is known of his life except that he was educated at Merchant Taylors' School, that he was an associate of * Marlowe and died intestate. His fame rests on a single play *The Spanish Tragedy* (presented 1585–89 and printed before 1594). It tells of a father driven almost mad by the murder of his son, a situation exactly opposite to that in *Hamlet*, of which Kyd is believed to have written an earlier version. Of other attributions to Kyd none is certain except *Cornelia* (1594), a play of no special interest translated from the French.
Freeman, A., *Thomas Kyd*. 1967

L

Labouchère, Henry (1831–1912). English journalist and politician. As Radical M.P. for Northampton 1880–1906 he used his biting wit to campaign for many radical reforms, and as founder-editor (1877–1910) of *Truth*, he devoted himself to the exposure of fraud and other abuses. He was well known in society and though his fearless tongue and pen made enemies, his personality won him many friends.

La Bruyère, Jean de (1645–1696). French essayist and moralist. He studied law but disliked it and eventually (1684) became tutor to Louis de Bourbon, grandson of the Prince de Condé. In 1688 appeared the work for which he is renowned: *Les Caractères ou les Mœurs de ce Siècle*, containing disguised and satirical pen-portraits of contemporaries, accompanied by moral maxims. Originally a pendant to a translation of the *Characters* of Theophrastus, it gradually developed as a separate work and the number of 'Characters' steadily increased with each edition. The fitting of the right cap to the right anonymous head became a social relaxation and several 'keys' were published, the authenticity of all being denied by the author. The 'maxims' are scathing about not only human wickedness and folly but also the inequalities and harshness of the social system; yet La Bruyère was no revolutionary and seems to have accepted in a disillusioned spirit the inevitability of human ills.

Richard, P., *Bruyère*. 1946

La Condamine, Charles Marie de (1701–1774). French geographer. Sent to Peru on an expedition (1735–43) to measure the meridional arc there, he took advantage of the opportunity to explore the Amazon. He obtained positive evidence concerning india-rubber and brought back the poisonous plant curare. His full journal of the expedition was published in 1751.

Lacoste, René (1905–). French lawn-tennis player. With Borotra and Cochet he was one of the famous 'Three Musketeers' who monopolized the Wimbledon singles championship from 1924 to 1929, Lacoste himself winning in 1925 and 1928.

Ladislaus (Polish Wladislaw). Four Polish kings. **Ladislaus I** (known as the 'the Short') (1260–1333; reigned from 1320) was instrumental in restoring the kingdom. **Ladislaus II (Jagiello)** (1350–1434; reigned from 1386), a grand duke of Lithuania, married the Polish queen Jadwiga. He checked the power of the Teutonic knights and agreed to the conversion of the Lithuanian subjects to Christianity, **Ladislaus III** (1424–1444; king of Poland from 1434 and of Hungary from 1440) led two crusades against the Turks. The reign of **Ladislaus IV** (1595–1648; reigned from 1632) was one of internal turmoil and external wars.

Laënnec, René Théophile Hyacinthe (1781–1826). French physician, born in Brittany. As a hospital physician he made important contributions to research on tuberculosis, peritonitis, parasitic complaints etc.; his greatest contribution was to devise the stethoscope and the method of ausculation for diagnosis of diseases of the chest. He developed the disease from which he died (probably tuberculosis) four years after becoming professor of medicine at the Collège de France.

Lafayette, Marie Joseph Paul Yves Roch Gilbert du Motier, Marquis de (1757–1834). French soldier and politician. A liberal-minded member of an aristocratic family, he went to America (1777) to fight for its independence, became a friend of Washington and returned to France to urge his country to go to war with Great Britain on America's behalf. Successful in this he was back in America in time to take part in the events that led to the capitulation of Yorktown (1781). With a hero's reputation and his liberal principles he was elected to the States-General of 1789 and became commander of the National Guard. A constitutionalist rather than a violent revolutionary, he tried to restrain mob rule in Paris and, after the failure of Louis XVI's flight to Varennes, to protect the king. Forced to give up his post in Paris he became commander of the army of the east, but a final effort (1792) to avert the danger to the king's life by a march on Paris failed. Lafayette sought refuge across the Rhine and was held in prison until the peace of 1797. Under Napoleon he lived quietly, but after the emperor's fall he served in the Chamber of Deputies and was active in the revolution (1830) by which Charles X was displaced by Louis Philippe. He made a triumphant visit (1824–25) to America, where he has since been regarded as a symbol of the revolutionary bond between the United States and France.

La Fayette, Marie Madeleine Pioche de la Vergne, Comtesse de (1634–1693). French novelist. She was the first French writer to publish a novel of psychological insight and sincere observation; *La Princesse de Clèves* (1678) deals with a married woman's renunciation of a love affair – a theme probably inspired by her own unsatisfactory marriage. In 1667 she became an intimate of the Duc de la * Rochefoucauld – an attachment which lasted till his death in 1680 – who may have helped her with her novels.
Ashton, H., *Madame de la Fayette, sa vie et ses oeuvres*. 1922

La Follette, Robert Marion (1855–1925). American politician. He played a notable part in the politics of his native state, Wisconsin, of which he was governor (1901–06), and carried out a programme of reform (the Wisconsin idea) which gained him a national reputation. As U.S. Senator (from 1906) he continued to fight for progressive causes and in 1924 stood as an independent Progressive candidate for the presidency. He failed – which is almost inevitable for a third candidate under the American system – but polled over 5,000,000 votes.

La Fontaine, Jean de (1621–1695). French poet. His marriage was early dissolved and he later frequented numerous patrons, including Madame de la Salière and Fouquet. He wrote a variety of forms of poetry but his enduring masterpiece was his twelve books of Fables (1668–94) (some 230 in all), mainly adaptations of Aesop's fables, often concealing under their childish appeal a biting satire of the foibles and weaknesses of French society in particular and human nature in general.
Clarac, P., *La Fontaine*. Rev. ed. 1959

Lagerkvist, Pär (Fabian) (1891–1974). Swedish writer. He was concerned with destructive forces in society. Two poems in expressionist style, *Angest* and *Kaos*, were written during World War I to emphasize its horrors. He later widened his scope to attack all political and social extremism and its destructive power. He won the Nobel Prize for Literature for the novel *Barabbas* (1951).
Spector, R. D., *Pär Lagerkvist*. 1973

Lagerlöf, Selma Ottiniana Lovisa (1858–1940). Swedish novelist and poet. Crippled from girlhood, she was a school-teacher for many years and wrote a series of popular children's stories, e.g. *The Wonderful Adventures of Nils* (1907), and religious stories, e.g. *Legends of Christ* (1904). Her greatest work was the romantic story of peasant life in Sweden, *Gosta Berlings Saga* (1891). She was the first woman to win the Nobel Prize for Literature (1909) and to be elected to the Swedish Academy.

Lagrange, Joseph Louis, Comte (1736–1813). French mathematician. His family had long lived in Italy; he became (1755) professor of mathematics at Turin Artillery School. Before he was 20 he had won a place in the front ranks of mathematicians as the result of a memoir he sent to Euler, in the course of which he developed the calculus of variations, one of his most important contributions to mathematics. He helped to develop the theory of sound and, with Laplace, carried out investigations which led to the formulation of the law governing the eccentricity and stability of the solar system. He was director of the Berlin Academy of Sciences (1766–87) and then settled in France, where he headed the commission appointed during the Revolution to draw up the new system of weights and measures; he also introduced the system of decimal coinage. His greatest work was his *Mécanique Analytique* (1788).

La Guardia, Fiorello Henrico (1882–1947). American Republican politician. Though he spent some years in the US House of Representatives (1917–21, 1923–33), he is remembered as an immensely popular mayor of New York City (1933–45). Here he initiated housing and labour schemes, was civil defence director and an early opponent of Hitler's anti-Semitic policies. He was the first director-general of the UN Relief and Rehabilitation Administration (UNNRA) (1946).
Mann, A., *La Guardia, 1882–1933*. 1959

Lalande, Joseph Jerome Le Français de (1732–1807). French astronomer. He was professor of astronomy in the Collége de France (1762–1807) and (from 1768) director of the Paris Observatory. His *Histoire céleste* (1801) gave the positions of nearly 50,000 stars. His *Traité d'Astronomie* (1764) was his principal work. The Lalande Prize was instituted by him (1802) for the most important observation or book of the year.

Lamarck, Jean Baptiste Pierre Antoine de Monet, Chevalier de (1744–1829). French naturalist. After three years in the army, he took up banking but soon turned to natural history; he published a French *Flora* (1778) and in 1779 was put in charge of the royal garden, which became the nucleus of the later Jardin des Plantes in Paris where he gave lectures over many years on the invertebrates until 1818, when failing eyesight forced him to retire. He put forward the theory, often called Lamarckism, which explains variations in species as being primarily due to environment and which concludes that such adaptive variants are hereditary. He introduced the term 'biology', which he made into a science with his system of classification, and is regarded as the founder of invertebrate palaeontology. In his own time he was regarded as something of an eccentric; later his evolutionary theories aroused considerable scientific interest. His ideas concerning the inheritance of acquired characteristics are now discredited, though the Soviet biologist * Lysenko attempted to establish their validity.
Cannon, H. G., *Lamarck and Modern Genetics*. 1960.

Lamartine, Alphonse Marie Louis de (1790–1869). French poet and politician. He achieved his first great poetic success with the Romantic *Médiations poétiques* (1820) in which the influence of Byron is evident. He had minor diplomatic appointments in Italy until 1828 where in 1820 he married an English woman Maria-Ann Birch. His religious orthodoxy was given lyrical expression in his *Harmonies poétiques et religieuses*. Later works include the epic in fifteen visions *La Chute d'un Ange* (1838) and *La Vigne et la Maison* (1856), which has been described as 'his finest individual poem'. As a politician Lamartine was a moderate and he won a great reputation as an orator in the parliaments of Louis Philippe; after the latter's fall he was briefly foreign minister but the election of his rival Louis Napoleon (later Napoleon III) as president closed his political career. Later he wrote historical and autobiographical works in a vain effort to pay off a vast accumulation of debt.
Whitehouse, H. R., *Life of Lamartine*. 2 vols. Repr. 1969

Lamb, Lady Caroline (1785–1828). English writer. Daughter of Frederick Ponsonby, 3rd Earl of Bessborough, the scandal caused by her passionate pursuit of * Byron (1812–13) made her ridiculous and embarrassed him. After their rupture she caricatured him in *Glenarvon*, published anonymously in 1816; this, the first of three not very distinguished novels, was republished (1865) as *The Fatal Passion*. In 1805 Lady Caroline married William Lamb, later Lord * Melbourne; he bore kindly with her eccentricities, which turned to insanity when (1824) she happened to witness Byron's funeral procession.
Jenkins, E., *Lady Caroline Lamb*. 1932

Lamb, Charles (1775–1834). English essayist, known as 'Elia'. He was educated at Christ's Hospital, London, where he formed a lifelong friendship with S. T. * Coleridge. At the age of 17 he went to work as a clerk at the London office of the East India Company, where he remained for thirty-three years. In 1796 his sister Mary killed their mother in one of the fits

of recurring insanity to which she was subject; Lamb declared himself her guardian and devoted his life to her care, which was repaid with deep affection. Together they wrote *Tales from Shakespeare* (1807) and *Poetry for children* (1809). During the next decade Charles wrote little of importance except the criticism which appeared (from 1812) in Leigh Hunt's paper the *Reflector*; but in 1820 he began the famous series of essays in the *London Magazine* under the pen-name 'Elia'. A considerable depth of thought, concealed by a style of infinitely varied harmonies and a persuasively whimsical charm have made these essays (collected 1823 and 1833) one of the most abidingly popular books in the field of belles-lettres. All the qualities which give delight in his essays are present, though less formally presented, in his letters, published in several collections after his death; he also wrote poetry throughout his life. Despite his circumstances Lamb was a man of many friends, deeply loved for his genial companionship, generosity and courage. His sister Mary survived him for thirteen years.
Lucas, E. V., *The Life of Lamb*. 1921

Lambert, Constant (1905–1951). English composer and conductor. His versatility was directed into a particular channel when Diaghilev commissioned the ballet *Romeo and Juliet* (1926). Later ballets included *Pomona* (1927) and *Horoscope* (1938); he was musical director of the Sadler's Wells Ballet (1938–47). His works in other fields include *The Rio Grande* (1929), a successful jazz concert piece with words by Sacheverell Sitwell, which effectively included jazz idioms; *Music for Orchestra* (1931); and the choral *Summer's Last Will and Testament* (1936).

Lambert, John (1619–1684). English soldier. During the Civil War he fought with distinction under Fairfax at Marston Moor, and under Cromwell at Preston, Dunbar and Worcester. He played no part in King Charles's trial and was resolutely opposed to Cromwell's becoming king though he helped to make him protector. After Cromwell's death he put down a rising in Cheshire (1659), expelled the parliamentary 'Rump' and became virtual dictator. But any future plans he may have had were frustrated by the Restoration, secretly organized and carried out by * Monk who brought him to trial for treason. Convicted (1662), Lambert was imprisoned for life.

Lamennais, Hugues Félicité Robert de (1782–1854). French political theorist. He was a Roman Catholic priest who, in his chief work *Essay on Religious Indifference* (1818–24), presented an untraditional view of Christianity. Although he also argued that the evils of the time could only be overcome by a universal Christian society in which kings and peoples were subject to the pope, his unorthodox views were condemned by the papacy. In 1840, one of his books earned him a year's imprisonment. He was for a short time after the revolution of 1848 a member of the Constituent Assembly.

Lamerie, Paul de (*c.* 1688–1751). Dutch silversmith, who worked in England. He was apprenticed to a London goldsmith in 1703 and was his own master from 1712. He became one of the most famous craftsmen of the century and his work is correspondingly valued. His earlier work shows a simplicity and delicacy lacking in the rococo elegance of his later productions.
Phillips, P. A. S., *Paul de Lamerie*. 1935

La Mettrie, Julien Offray de (1709–1751). French physician and philosopher. He published his first important work, *Histoire naturelle de l'âme* in 1745. Its belief in a materialistic theory of mind offended the Church and the medical establishment, and from then till his death, La Mettrie was involved in a running war with both. His major work was *L'Homme machine* of 1748 which expounded both materialism and atheism quite openly. La Mettrie saw the body as nothing other than a machine. Mental states, such as love, hunger, illness, ideas, all had physiological roots. Man was superior to the animals simply because he possessed a bigger brain. He was fascinated by the close interaction of brain and body to produce delicate feelings and purposive bodily behaviour, and explored the possible interface between medicine and morals, the relationship between sin and sickness. La Mettrie also wrote four medical treatises, on venereal disease, vertigo, dysentry and asthma. His *Observations de médecine pratique* (1743) indicates his clinical practice, in which he gives a specially important place to autopsies.

Lampedusa, Giuseppe Tomasi, Prince of (1897–1957). Italian novelist. His novel, *Il*

Gattopardo (*The Leopard*), appeared posthumously (1958) and was widely praised for its description of social and political change in Sicily in the mid-19th century.
Buzzi, G., *Tomasi di Lampedusa*. 1973

Lancaster, House of. Branch of the Plantagenet dynasty stemming from * John of Gaunt, fourth son of Edward III, created Duke of Lancaster after the death of the 1st Duke, whose daughter and heiress he had married. The Lancastrian kings were John of Gaunt's son Henry IV, followed by his son Henry V and grandson Henry VI.
Storey, R. L. *The End of the House of Lancaster*. 1966

Lancaster, Joseph (1778–1838). English educationist. He is remembered for the monitorial system, which is described in his *Improvement in Education* (1803); it was similar to one introduced in Madras by **Andrew Bell** (1753–1832). Lancaster first opened a school for the poor in Southwark in 1798, whereby the system of teaching by monitors a hundred pupils could be taught under the supervision of a single master. Lancaster's supporters included * Brougham, * Wilberforce and * Mill, but in time he quarrelled with his backers, quit their organization (the Royal Lancasterian Society) and went to America (1818).

Lancaster, Sir Osbert (1908–). British cartoonist, author and theatrical designer. He was a cartoonist at the *Daily Express* from 1939, wrote satirical books on architecture, an autobiography and designed many opera and ballet sets.

Lanchester, Frederick William (1868–1946). British engineer and physicist. A pioneer of the motor industry, he designed the Lanchester car (1899) and during the next thirty years was consultant to the Daimler and other companies. He was equally well known for his research in aeronautics, on which subject he wrote several books. In 1922 he was elected F.R.S.

Lancret, Nicolas (1690–1745). French painter. Under Watteau's influence he painted *fêtes galantes* and other gay court occasions. Despite the artificial nature of his subjects and the fastidious elegance of his style his keen observation gave life and realism both to characters and the background details in his scenes.
Wildenstein, G., *Lancret: biographie et catalogue critiques*. 1924

Land, Edwin Herbert (1909–). U.S. inventor. He dropped out of Harvard to work on inventions including the Polaroid – a plastic sheet incorporating many tiny crystals which polarized light. This was used in Polaroid sunglasses and the Polaroid Land camera.

Landon, Alfred Mossman (1887–). US politician and businessman. An oil producer in Kansas, he later acquired radio and TV interests. He was governor of Kansas 1933–37 and Republican presidential candidate in 1936, suffering an overwhelming defeat by Franklin D. * Roosevelt. A rural progressive, he was a strong supporter of the United Nations and urged recognition of Mao's China. His daughter, **Nancy Landon Kassebaum** (1932–), was a US Senator from Kansas 1979– .

Landor, Walter Savage (1775–1864). English writer. The consequences of an irascible nature, which caused him to be removed from Rugby and rusticated from Oxford, pursued Landor throughout his life; although he was impressive both physically and intellectually, his life was a series of quarrels and lonely wanderings. From 1815 to 1835, the year in which they had their decisive quarrel, he lived in Italy with his wife. Despite his pugnacity his impulses were nearly always generous. Much of his inherited wealth was used to equip volunteers for the Peninsular War, more went into a scheme of agricultural and social reform at Llanthony; he turned over his property to his children only to be rewarded by ingratitude and he would have died in extreme poverty had not Robert and Elizabeth Browning rallied his brothers to his support and enabled him to spend his last years in Florence in a comparative tranquillity. Except by a few his literary work was never highly esteemed: his best known book is *Imaginary Conversations* (1824–29).
Elwin, M., *Savage Landor*. 1942

Landowska, Wanda (1877–1959). Polish pianist, harpsichordist and musicologist. She lived in France (1919–40) and in the U.S.A. from 1940 onwards, becoming famous for her scholarly interpretations of Bach, Handel and other 17th- and 18th-century composers. She was responsible for the modern revival of the harpsichord and Falla's Harpsichord Concerto was written for her.

Landseer, Sir Edwin Henry (1802–1873). English painter. He gained immense popularity by his animal pictures, especially of deer and dogs, which, in the excellent engravings made by his brother, appeared in countless Victorian homes. Despite a certain sentimentality of subject, his animals are natural and realistic, and his drawings reveal a much wider and less conventional talent. The lions of Trafalgar Square, London, were modelled by him.

Landsteiner, Karl (1868–1943). Austrian pathologist, resident in the U.S.A. from 1922. He was famous for his discovery (1901) of the four main human blood groups. He also discovered (1940), in collaboration with A. S. Wiener, the Rh factor, so called because it was first found in the Rhesus monkey. He won the Nobel Prize for Medicine (1930).

Lane, Sir Allen (Williams) (1902–1970). English publisher. He founded Penguin Books, which grew from modest beginnings (1935) into one of Britain's major publishing houses within a few years. His father **John Lane** (1854–1925), of the Bodley Head, published the famous *Yellow Book*, the art quarterly which with Aubrey Beardsley's illustrations was a *succès de scandale* in the 1890s.
Monpurgo, J., *Allen Lane: King Penguin*. 1979

Lane, Sir Hugh (1875–1915). Irish art connoisseur. He intended to bequeath his collection of pictures to Dublin, but the city refused to build a gallery to house them, and he left them instead to the British National Gallery. After a quarrel with the latter about the hanging of his pictures he changed his decision once more, but before a codicil to this effect was signed he was drowned when the *Lusitania* was torpedoed. Eventually it was agreed that this collection should be exhibited alternately in the National Gallery and Dublin.

Lanfranc (1005?–1089). Italian-born prelate. He left Italy (*c.* 1039) and founded a law school at Avranches which became famous. Later he became prior (1045) of the abbey of Bec in Normandy; he came to the notice of Duke William, whose gratitude he earned by obtaining papal dispensation for his marriage. Thus when William conquered England, Lanfranc was rewarded (1070) with the archbishopric of Canterbury. He reorganized the English church to meet the changes caused by the conquest and showed his legal talent and diplomatic skill in the reconciling the demands of a reforming pope (Gregory VII) and an autocratic king.

Lang, Cosmo Gordon Lang, 1st Baron (1864–1945). Scottish prelate. Originally a Presbyterian he became an Anglican priest in 1890. He made his mark by his demeanour, eloquence and social work; he became archbishop of York (1908) and archbishop of Canterbury (1928–42). His opposition to Edward VIII's marriage to Mrs Simpson on ecclesiastical grounds was probably not a decisive factor in Edward's abdication.
Lockhart, J. G., *Cosmo Gordon Lang*. 1949

Lang, Fritz (1890–1976). German film director, born in Vienna. Originally an architect, his early films were important examples of Expressionism, including *Dr Mabuse, the gambler* (1922), *Metropolis* (1926) and *M* (1932). He worked in the U.S. 1933–58, directing a variety of films including Westerns, thrillers and psychological dramas.

Lang, John Thomas (1876–1975). Australian Labor politician. As ALP leader in New South Wales 1923–39, he was state premier 1925–27 and 1930–32, introducing welfare state measures and promoting construction of the Sydney Harbour Bridge. During the Depression he adopted reflationary policies later advocated by J. M. * Keynes, repudiating payments on foreign debts and to the Commonwealth Government. The semi-fascist 'New Guard' was formed (1930) to work for his overthrow and in 1932 the New South Wales Governor, Sir Philip Game, dismissed him. He left the ALP in 1939 and formed the Lang Labor Party.

Lange, David Russell (1942–). New Zealand Labour politician. A lawyer, he was leader of the Labour Party 1983– , and defeated Sir Robert * Muldoon in July 1984 to become prime minister.

Langland, William (*c.* 1330–*c.* 1400). English poet. All that is known of his life is deduced

from his work. He was probably born in or near Worcestershire and educated at a monastery at Great Malvern; later he went to London and seems to have acquired some knowledge of law. He is now remembered only as the author of the *Vision of Piers Plowman*, an allegorical and didactic poem in alliterative verse. The survival of fifty manuscripts shows its popularity in medieval times but its later influence was small. The fact that the poem survives in three versions (*c.* 1362, 1377 and 1393–98), the two later ones being nearly three times as long as the first, has suggested multiple authorship but critical opinion has veered to the acceptance of the first two, at least, as the work of a single hand. The subject of the poem is the salvation of souls; its chief interest for modern readers lies in its descriptions of the scenes (roads, inns, law courts, etc.) and characters of medieval life.
Goodridge, J. F., (ed. and trans.), *Langland; Piers the Ploughman*. 1970. Vasta, E., (ed.), *Interpretations of Piers Plowman*. 1969

Langley, Samuel Pierpont (1834–1906). American astronomer and physicist. He was professor of the observatory at the Western University of Pennsylvania (now Pittsburgh University) from 1867, and from 1887 until his death was secretary of the Smithsonian Institution, Washington. He made important studies of solar radiation and with the aid of a sensitive instrument called a bolometer mapped the infra-red region of the solar spectrum. He also constructed a steam-powered model aeroplane (length 16 ft, wing-span *c.* 13 ft) which was successfully flown, but a full-size machine built to the same design disappointingly failed.

Langmuir, Irving (1881–1957). American physical chemist. He joined the General Electric Company (1909) and was its director of research (1932–50). He was much concerned with the handling of high vacua and developed a number of inventions, e.g. the gas-filled tungsten lamp, the mercury vapour lamp and the atomic hydrogen welding torch. In the course of his work on surface chemistry he derived the equation (now known as the Langmuir absorption isotherm) relating the pressure to the extent of absorption of a gas on a solid surface at constant temperature; for this he won the Nobel Prize for Chemistry (1932).

Langton, Stephen (*c.* 1150–1228). English prelate. A fellow student in Paris of the future Pope Innocent III, he was later given a place in the papal household and (1206) was made a cardinal. King John's refusal (1207) to accept him as archbishop of Canterbury led to a prolonged struggle between the king and the papacy and Langton was not able to enter his see until after John's submission to the pope (1213). Langton sided with the barons in their struggle with the king, and played an important part in drafting Magna Carta.
Cheney, C. R., *From Becket to Langton*. 1956

Langtry, Lillie (née Emilie Charlotte Le Breton) (1852–1929). British actress, born in Jersey. She was famed for her beauty and was at one time the mistress of Edward VII. After Edward Langtry's death she married (1899) Sir Hugo de Bathe.
Sichel, P., *The Jersey Lily*. 1958

Lanier, Sidney (1842–1881). American poet, born in Georgia. He fought with the Confederate army in the American Civil War, which was the subject of his novel *Tiger Lilies* (1867). Later he became a flautist in a symphony orchestra in Baltimore; in a series of lectures at Johns Hopkins University, he advocated a scientific approach to poetry, which he regarded as a kind of verbal music. Such a definition permitted the discarding of metrical restrictions, replaced by more flexible musical rhythms. The best of his own poems include *Corn, The Symphony* and *The Song of the Chattahoochee*.
Starke, A. H., *Sidney Lanier: a biographical and critical study*. 1933

Lansbury, George (1859–1940). British Labour politician. A pacifist and supporter of women's rights, he was on the Poplar Borough Council (from 1903), M.P. for Bromley and Bow (1910–12 and from 1922) and editor (1912–22) of the *Daily Herald*, the organ of the Labour Party. He led the Labour opposition from 1931 but resigned during the Abyssinian crisis (1935), feeling unable as a pacifist to support a policy of sanctions against Italy that might lead to war.

Lansdowne, 1st Marquess of *see* **Shelburne, 2nd Earl of**

Landsdowne, Henry Charles Keith Petty-Fitzmaurice, 5th Marquess of (1845–1927).

English politician. He was governor general of Canada (1883–88) and viceroy of India (1888–93). He was foreign secretary (1900–05) and was responsible for the negotiations leading to the Anglo-Japanese Alliance (1904) and the Anglo-French Entente (1910). A minister briefly in World War I, he was out of office when he wrote the famous 'Lansdowne letter' (1917) to the *Daily Telegraph* advocating a negotiated peace with Germany.

Lansing, Robert (1864–1928). American administrator. As a specialist in international law he was chosen by Woodrow* Wilson to be his secretary of state; during his term of office (1915–20) he was the principal executant of U.S. foreign policy during World War I. He was a leading delegate at the Paris Peace Conference (1919), but disagreements with the president forced him to resign.

Lanson, Gustave (1857–1934). French critic and literary historian. He became a professor at the Sorbonne in Paris in 1900. His *Historie de la littérature française* (1894) showed remarkable critical acumen and is a model of its kind. He was a pioneer of the historical approach to works of literature, placing them against their historical background and achieving a far fuller and more sophisticated appreciation than literary criticism had previously attained.

Lao-tzu (or Lao-tse) (fl. *c.* 604 B.C.). Semi-legendary Chinese philosopher. He is said to have been born in Honan, to have held office at court and to have been visited by Confucius. Lao-tzu is the traditional author of *Tao te ching*, which sets out the ideas and practice which came to be known as Taoism. A unity (*tao*) underlying the apparently conflicting phenomena of the universe is perceived; the attitude to the fundamental laws of the universe should be unconditional acceptance, the achievement of such acceptance being helped by quietist techniques: complete relaxation, 'sitting with a blank mind' (*tso wang*) etc. The other book of early Taoism, *Chuang Tzu*, may have been written by some-one of that name, a conjectural pupil of Lao-tzu.
Waley, A., *Lao-Tzu: The Way and the Power*. Repr. 1956

La Pérouse, Jean François de Galaup, Comte de (1741–1788). French sailor and explorer. He was put in command (1785) of an expedition of exploration, and from the north-west coast of America crossed the Pacific with two ships. He explored the north-east coasts of Asia and in particular, while sailing to investigate the possibility of a north-east passage, found the strait (named after him) between Sakhalin and Hokkaido (Yezo), thus proving both to be islands. By 1788 he was in Australia and in February his two ships sailed from Botany Bay, never to be seen again. They foundered on a coral reef to the north of the New Hebrides.

Laplace, Pierre Simon, Marquis de (1749–1827). French astronomer and mathematician, the son of a farm labourer. His ability attracted the attention of * d'Alembert, who secured his appointment at the Ecole Militaire, Paris (1771–97). After being an associate of the Académie des Sciences from 1773 he became a member (1785). He made an important contribution to the theory of capillarity and devised a correct equation for the velocity of sound in a gas, correcting Newton's equation. He added to the calculus, which he applied to the theory of gravitation, and he developed a calculus of probabilities. His major work was in astronomy. In his *Exposition du système du monde* (1796) he put forward his well known 'nebular hypothesis' suggesting that the solar system originated from the gradual contraction of a rotating sphere of nebulous material. Although this theory has now been superseded, it acted as a powerful stimulant to 19th-century astronomical thought. In his greatest work, the five-volume *Mécanique céleste* (1799–1825), Laplace worked out a generalized statement of the laws governing movement throughout the whole solar system. In addition to his academic work he took part in public life. After Bonaparte's *coup d'état* (1799), he was briefly minister of the interior, and in the same year became a senator; under the Empire he was made a count and eventually, under Louis XVIII a marquess. In 1817 he became president of the Académie Française.

Lardner, Ring (Ringold Wilmer Lardner) (1885–1933). American author. He was a sports writer for many years but became famous for his short stories, which displayed remarkable powers in the use of colloquial dialogue and a bitter contempt for average Americans, especially those connected with sport and the theatre, with which he was well acquainted. His *How to Write Short Stories* (1924) is typical of several volumes in this vein.

Largo Caballero, Francisco (1869–1964). Spanish politician. He was prime minister (1936–37) during part of the Civil War. As Madrid was threatened by the nationalist insurgents, his government operated first from Valencia, then from Barcelona. He was succeeded by Juan Negrin. Caballero was arrested by the Germans in 1940 and held until 1945.

Larkin, James (1876–1947). Irish labour leader, born in Liverpool. He formed (1909) the Irish Transport and General Workers Union in Dublin and became famous when a lock-out (1913) of his members by employers was followed by an eight-month strike ending in a partial victory for Larkin. From 1914 to 1923, when he was deported for communist activities, he was in the U.S.A. In 1924 he was expelled from his former union and founded the more extremist Workers Union of Ireland.

La Rochefoucauld, François, Duc de (1613–1680). French writer. A political opponent of Richelieu, he later quarrelled with Mazarin and partly because of his passion for Condé's sister, the Duchesse de Longueville, joined the Fronde; but after being wounded he retired (1652) to write his memoirs. Even though he was forgiven by the court he devoted himself thenceforth to a literary life; he attended the *salons* of, amongst others, Mademoiselle de Scudéry and the Marquise de Sablé, and was a friend of * Corneille, * Molière and * La Fontaine. He later set up house with Madame de * La Fayette. In his *Maxims* (*Réflexions on Sentences et Maximes morales*; 1665 etc.) he made no attempt to preach but set out objectively his own cynical view of human nature, to which he ascribed self-love as the mainspring.
Moore, W. G., *La Rochefoucauld: his Mind and Art*. 1969

La Salle, René Robert Cavelier, Sieur de (1643–1687). French explorer. He settled in Canada (1666) and in 1670 began the descent of the Ohio River, which he believed to flow into the Pacific. Having found out his mistake he decided to follow the Mississippi, of which the Ohio is a tributary, down to the sea, a voyage which lasted several years and entailed many hardships. The vast area of the Mississippi Basin he named Louisiana in honour of the French king. In 1684 he led an expedition from France to establish a permanent settlement but failed to find the Mississippi from the seaward side. Having entered Matagorda Bay (Texas) in mistake for one of the mouths of the Mississippi he and his men landed and spent two years in a vain search for the great river. The hardships endured provoked a mutiny amongst his men in which La Salle was murdered.

Las Casas, Bartolomé de (1476–1566). Spanish colonial reformer. He went (1502) to the West Indies, where he became a priest (*c.* 1510) and started to work to improve the position of all Indians under Spanish rule, in particular to abolish the system by which grants of Indian serfs were made to settlers. Visits to Spain won him the support of King Ferdinand and his successor Charles I (the emperor Charles V) but having failed to make the reforms effective he assented to a proposal to introduce African labour, a decision he bitterly regretted as it encouraged the growth of the slave trade. Another disappointment came when a settlement, which he had started (1520) in Venezuela to prove the advantages of free colonization over slave-run estates, was destroyed by the Indians, who distrusted all Spaniards. Before the conquest of Peru (1531) he again visited Spain and returned with royal instructions for the protection of the Indians. He became bishop of Chiapas in Mexico (1542) and continued to struggle for the enforcement of the laws against Indian serfdom. In 1547 he finally returned to Spain. His books bear witness to his compassion and zeal.
Hanke, L., *Bartolome de las Casas: An Interpretation of his Life and Writings*. 1951

Lasker, Emanuel (1868–1941). German chess master and mathematician. He was world chess champion from 1894 until 1921, when Capablanca defeated him in a great contest at Havana.

Laski, Harold Joseph (1893–1950). British socialist. Born in Manchester, he was a lecturer at Yale University in the U.S.A. and McGill University in Canada before joining (1920) the London School of Economics, where he was professor of political science (1926–50). He was chairman of the British Labour party (1945–46); through his lectures

and books, e.g. *Parliamentary Government in England* (1938) and *Reflections on the Revolution of Our Time* (1943), he exercised considerable influence over the intellectuals of his party, but his academic Marxism did not attract the rank and file.
Martin, K., *Harold Laski*. 1953

Laski, Marghanita (1915–). English writer, critic and broadcaster. Her first novel, *Love on the Supertax*, appeared in 1944. She wrote extensively for newspapers and magazines and broadcast regularly as a critic. Her best known novel was probably *The Victorian Chaise-Longue* (1953), a time-travel fantasy in which Victorian repressive attitudes are equated with death.

Lassalle, Ferdinand (1825–1864). German socialist. Son of a rich Jewish silk merchant, he abandoned his religion while still a young man and devoted several years at the universities to the study of Hegel. He gained notoriety by conducting a protracted law suit (1846–57) on behalf of the Countess Sophie von Hatzfeldt, whose estate had been seized by her estranged husband; gratitude and an annuity were the rewards of his success. He was imprisoned for six months during the revolution of 1848, by which time he was a confirmed socialist. He came to know Karl Marx, but differed from him in his nationalist approach and in advocating state intervention rather than revolution to secure social reform; later, when Marx was living in poverty in London, Lassalle gave him generous help. When Bismarck came to power (1862) Lassalle, as a rationalist, gave him reluctant admiration. He founded (1863) the General Workingmen's Association, which later developed into the Social Democratic party; the main feature of its programme was universal suffrage, which Lassalle thought would place the power of the state at the service of the working population. He died from wounds received in a duel for the hand of Helene von Dönniges, which he fought outside Geneva with a rival favoured by her parents.
Mayer, G., *Bismarck und Lassalle*. 1928

Lasso, Orlando di (Orlandus Lassus) (1532–1594). Flemish composer, born in Mons (now in Belgium). He became choirmaster at St John Lateran in Rome but for most of his life was court composer of the Duke of Bavaria (1556–94). His works (reputed to number 1,183) include masses, motets, psalms (especially the *Seven Penitential Psalms)* and hymns, in addition to many secular pieces. His madrigals and songs, set to German, Italian and French words, are still highly regarded for their melodic beauty. His work is more varied and adventurous, if less profound, than that of Palestrina, with whom he is often compared.

Latimer, Hugh (1485–1555). English Protestant martyr. Born a yeoman's son near Leicester, he was educated at Cambridge University and there became a university preacher. For his support of the annulment of Henry VIII's marriage to Catherine of Aragon he was taken into royal favour and became (1535) bishop of Worcester but resigned (1539) when it was clear that his reforming zeal had outpaced that of the king, and he was in prison for most of the remainder of Henry's reign. After Edward VI's accession (1547) Latimer's influence as a preacher denouncing the evils of the day reached its zenith, but under Queen Mary persecution of Protestants was resumed. Latimer was taken to Oxford and there, after confrontation with Roman Catholic divines had failed to induce him to recant, he was burned at the stake. His last words, to his fellow martyr Bishop * Ridley, were 'We shall this day light such a candle by God's grace in England as I trust shall never be put out'.

La Tour, Georges de (1593–1652). French painter. Little is known of his life except that he lived in Lorraine; his work, forgotten after his death, was rediscovered and favourably reappraised in the 20th century. The influence of Caravaggio is especially noticeable in his groups of figures by candlelight. In his use of colour, especially of crimson and lilac, he shows marked individuality. His *Nativity with Shepherds* in the Louvre is a fine example of his work.
Bloch, V., *Georges de la Tour*. 1950

Lattre de Tassigny, Jean de (1889–1952). French soldier. He was the outstanding general of the Free French forces in World War II and signed the instrument of surrender at Berlin (1945) on behalf of France. He commanded the French armies in Indochina (1947–52) and was posthumously created a marshal.
Salisbury-Jones, G., *So Full of Glory*. 1954

Laud, William (1573–1645). English prelate. Born at Reading, the son of a wealthy clothier, he was educated at Oxford and ordained in 1601. Despite, or because of, his opposition to the prevalent Puritanism, his industry, administrative ability and religious sincerity won him powerful patrons. He became bishop of Bath and Wells (1626), of London (1628) and archbishop of Canterbury (1633). In the period which followed the murder of Buckingham (1628) he tried, with * Strafford and King Charles I himself, to impose authoritarian rule on church and state alike. Laud was determined to free England of Calvinism and Scotland of Presbyterianism. Many English Puritans were deprived of their livings, ritual was reintroduced, the doctrine of the Real Presence reasserted and, among other contentious measures, the Communion table was removed from the centre of the church to the east end. His attempt to anglicize the Church of Scotland, however, led to riots, to the signing of the Covenant, to the 'Bishops' War' between the two countries, and eventually (to meet the costs of the war) to the summoning of the Long Parliament, which impeached Laud of high treason. He was found guilty by the House of Lords on several counts, none of which, however, amounted to treason and it was on a bill of attainder that he was beheaded on Tower Hill.
Trevor-Roper, H., *Archbishop Laud 1573–1645*. 2nd ed. 1962.

Lauder, Sir Harry (Harold MacLennan) (1870–1950). Scottish singer. With such famous songs as 'Roamin' in the Gloamin', 'I Love a Lassie' and 'A Wee Deoch-an-doris', he was for two generations one of the most famous and popular of music-hall stars. He was knighted (1919) for services in World War I.

Lauderdale, John Maitland, 1st Duke of (1616–1682). Scottish politician. During the Civil War he acted as the agent of Scottish Presbyterians at the court of Charles I and later established a similar connexion with the exiled Prince Charles, of whom he became a close friend. When Charles crossed to Scotland to make a bid for the crown, Lauderdale went with him but was captured at Worcester. The Restoration brought release and he was placed in charge of Scottish affairs (1660–68). From 1667 to 1673 he was the 'L' of the famous 'CABAL' ministry. In Scotland he tried to work in harmony with the Presbyterians but this became increasingly difficult. Disillusion, combined with the corruption of power, made him harsh and intractable; in suppressing the revolt of the Covenanters (1666–79) he incurred an odium bitter indeed for the humane scholar it was his nature to be. He inherited the earldom of Lauderdale (1645); he was created duke in 1672 and was dismissed from all offices in 1680.

Laue, Max von (1879–1960). German physicist. Director of the Institute for Theoretical Physics, Berlin (1919–50), he was a pioneer in X-ray analysis, using the pattern of diffracted X-rays to determine crystal structure. He won the Nobel Prize for Physics (1914).

Laughton, Charles (1899–1962). English-born actor. He portrayed, at first on the London stage and after 1932 in films, many characters of ruthless and overbearing personality. Film parts such as the king in *The Private Life of Henry VIII* and Captain Bligh in *Mutiny on the Bounty* revealed him at his powerful best. He married (1929) the actress Elsa Lanchester, and became a naturalized American (1950).

Laurel, Stan (Arthur Stanley Jefferson) (1890–1965) and **Hardy, Oliver** (1892–1957). Film comedians. Stan Laurel, born in Lancashire, began work in circuses and music-halls as a slapstick comedian. In 1926 he joined the American Oliver Hardy who had begun his career in vaudeville but who had worked in silent film comedy since 1913. Together they made over 200 films in which they combined slapstick with clashes of personality: Laurel the bumbling innocent, Hardy the would-be sophisticate.

Laurier, Sir Wilfred (1841–1919). The first French-Canadian prime minister of Canada. He was born in Quebec province, made his name as a lawyer and entered the provincial legislature in 1871 and the Canadian parliament in 1873. In 1887 he became leader of the Liberals and in 1896 prime minister. His period of office was one of prosperity and expansion, especially in the wheat-growing provinces in the west. The issue on which he finally fell, in the election of 1911, was his support for commercial reciprocity with the

USA. He led the anti-conscriptionist wing of his party in World War I.
Schull, J., *Laurier*. 1966

Lautrec, Henri Toulouse *see* **Toulouse-Lautrec, Henri**

Laval, Pierre (1883–1945). French politician. Born in the Auvergne, he was largely self-educated but obtained academic degrees and became (1907) a lawyer in Paris. He was a member of the Chamber of Deputies (1914–19 and from 1924). At first he was a Socialist but from 1927, when he became a senator, was party-free. After holding a succession of ministries he was prime minister from 1931 to 1932 and again from 1935–36, when he negotiated the Hoare-Laval Pact (1935). He advocated friendship with Italy and Germany. After the collapse of France (1940) he took a leading part in the establishment of Marshal Pétain's Vichy Régime. In 1942 he became prime minister in active collaboration with the Germans: he set up the notorious French militia with its Gestapo-like activities and supplied conscript labour for German factories. After the liberation of France he fled to Germany and then to Spain; he was repatriated. He was tried, condemned and executed for treason. Laval was ambitious, persuasive and subtle. Whether, in his own mind at least, he was a traitor remains in doubt. He probably convinced himself that by his appeasement he preserved the last remnants of liberty for conquered France.
Cole, H., *Laval*. 1963

La Vallière, Louise Françoise de la Beaume le Blanc, Duchesse de (1644–1710). Mistress of Louis XIV of France. She was only 17 when Louis first saw her and fell in love. By her sweetness and sincerity, coupled with a lack of ambition or greed, she won – to everyone's surprise – the admiration of the court. When, supplanted by Madame de Montespan (1674), she departed without rancour to the Carmelite convent where she spent the rest of her life. Only one of her three children by Louis survived her.

Lavoisier, Antoine Laurent (1743–1794). French chemist, born in Paris. He became a 'farmer general' (responsible for the collection of taxes) to enable him to pursue scientific research. He was elected to the Académie des Sciences (1768) and was director of the Gunpowder Office (1776–91). He also made practical use of his scientific knowledge in agriculture and acquired an estate for experimental purposes. After the Revolution he played a leading part in the establishment of the metric system. He was a liberal constitutionalist, believed in social reform, and played his part in the various Revolutionary assemblies; but this was not enough to appease the terrorists and his previous occupation as tax collector provided a pretext for his execution. Lavoisier has been called the founder of modern chemistry because he was mainly responsible for systematizing it by introducing a new nomenclature (1787), still in use, and by constructing the first table of elements (1780). By his experimental work he not only made many new discoveries but disproved the long-held belief that water could be converted into earth and the theory then current that the existence of an invisible, inflammable gas, phlogiston, explained many of the problems of combustion. His own experiments showed that air was composed of two gases, which he called oxygen and 'azote' (later known as nitrogen), and that oxygen played an essential role in the respiration of animals and plants. His law of the 'conservation of mass', arrived at by burning objects in a sealed chamber and finding that matter is neither created nor destroyed in a chemical reaction, established that combustion was accompanied by the chemical combination of oxygen with the substance burned (such combinations being later known as oxides). In 1783, almost simultaneously with Cavendish and Priestly, he announced that water is a combination of hydrogen and oxygen. Among the most important of Lavoisier's publications (apart from the new nomenclature) was *Opuscules physiques et chymiques* (1774).
McKie, D., *Antoine Lavoisier: Scientist, Economist, Social Reformer*. 1952

Law, Andrew Bonar (1858–1923). British Conservative politician, born in Canada. He had already achieved success as an iron merchant in Glasgow when he entered parliament (1900) at the age of 42. He was parliamentary secretary to the Board of Trade (1902–06) when the Liberals returned to office. When Liberal successes in the two elections of 1910 seemed to call for more vigorous tactics he was elected (as a compromise candidate) to succeed Balfour as leader of the Opposition, the Liberal Home Rule Bill being his principal target. When World War I broke out (1914) he supported the government and in 1915 served as colonial secretary in the coalition formed by * Asquith. When, as a result of the movement to dislodge Asquith – in which Law's close friend Max Aitken (Lord * Beaverbrook) played a behind-the-scenes part –* Lloyd George became premier, Bonar Law was his chancellor of the exchequer (1916–18) and was then lord privy seal in the first years of peace; he resigned (1921) through ill health. In October 1922 a Conservative revolt ended the coalition, Lloyd George had to resign and Bonar Law succeeded as prime minister for six months until inoperable cancer forced his resignation (May 1923): he died in October. He had a mastery of detail and could deliver long, intricate speeches without notes.

Blake, R., *The Unknown Prime Minister*. 1955

Law, William (1686–1761). English clergyman. Forced to give up his Cambridge fellowship for refusing to swear an oath of allegiance to George I, he spent most of his life in controversial and devotional writings, which, however, sparkle with epigrammatic wit. His books, especially *A Serious Call to a Devout Way of Life* (1729), in which he asserted that Christianity is not mere obedience to a moral code but a complete pattern of life, had great influence on Dr Johnson and, amongst others, the Wesleys, and thus on the whole Evangelical movement.

Walker, A.K., *William Law: HIs life and Work*. 1973

Lawes, Sir John Bennet, 1st Bart. (1814–1900). English agricultural chemist. He was born at, and later inherited, Rothamsted Manor, Harpenden, Herts., where he founded (1843) the famous Rothamsted Experimental Station. In 1837 he began experimenting with manures and discovered that by treating bones, then popular as a fertilizer, with sulphuric acid and calcium phosphate he could achieve better and quicker results; the next stage was the discovery that mineral rock phosphate treated with sulphuric acid would make an efficient substitute. The manufacture and sale of 'superphosphate of lime', as he called it, marked the begining of the great artificial fertilizer industry. He remained, however, primarily interested in research and collaborated for over fifty years (from 1843) with the chemist (Sir) Joseph Henry Gilbert in building up Rothamsted to be one of the world's greatest agricultural research stations (covering botany, chemistry, meteorology, plant and animal physiology etc.).

Lawrence, St (died 258). Christian martyr. He was one of seven deacons of Pope Sixtus II, who were beheaded in Rome during the persecution in the reign of the emperor Valerian. The tradition that he was tortured on a gridiron is not accepted by scholars, though it has formed the subject of many classical paintings.

Lawrence, David Herbert (1885–1930). English author. Son of a Nottinghamshire miner, he was educated at the High School and University College at Nottingham. His youth was troubled by an obsessive relationship with his mother and by tuberculosis symptoms which made him increasingly irritable. The publication of *The White Peacock* (1911) pointed to his future career; it was followed by the semi-autobiographical *Sons and Lovers* (1913). Meanwhile he had fallen in love and eloped with Frieda von * Richthofen, the German wife of an English scholar, whom he married in 1914. Such a marriage in wartime, added to his bitter class-consciousness, heightened the persecution mania from which he had always suffered. Expelled from Cornwall in 1917 as a suspected German spy, he became a restless traveller after the war, living in Italy, Germany, Ceylon, Australia, the US (New Mexico) and Mexico; books from this period include *Sea and Sardinia* (1921), *Kangaroo* (1923) and *Mornings in Mexico* (1927). He finally settled on the French Riviera and died near Nice. The novels reflect the often contradictory emotional and intellectual impulses stirred by the circumstances of his life and the theories which he formed in an attempt to build up a personal philosophy that would enable him to cope with them. Thus the mother–son relationship becomes the basis of a theory that the instincts of the blood are superior to the reasonings of the mind; he wrote: 'My religion is in the blood, the flesh, as being wiser than the intellect'. In rebellion against his Puritan background he stands for sexual freedom and frankness, but though in the long-banned *Lady Chatterley's Lover* (1928) the language of the gamekeeper-lover is wilfully coarse, the main impression left by the lovemaking scenes is one of deep tenderness. To be set against this attitude to sex is his vision of woman as an inert consumer of man's vitality, keeping him earth bound and preventing his spirit and intellect from taking wing. Yet the very fact that Lawrence was torn and almost destroyed by these inner conflicts showed his essential nobility.

Among his other novels were *Women in Love* (1921), *Aaron's Rod* (1922), *The Plumed Serpent* (1927). His short stories, in such collections as *The Woman Who Rode Away* (1928), range over many countries and many themes, including the macabre; his poetry (collected 1932) is vivid and sensitive. He remains one of the most important and controversial influences in 20th-century literature.
Nehls, E., (ed), *D. H. Lawrence, A Composite Biography*. 3 vols. 1957–1959

Lawrence, Ernest Orlando (1901–1958). American physicist. Professor of physics at the University of California from 1928 until his death, in 1930 he put forward the idea of a machine that could accelerate atomic particles to enormous speeds and then use them to bombard atoms. He constructed (1931) the first model of such a machine, which he called the cyclotron, and used it to carry out transmutation of elements and to produce artificial radioactivity. He was awarded the Nobel Prize for Physics (1939).

Lawrence, John Laird Mair Lawrence, 1st Baron (1811–1879). British administrator. He joined the Indian civil service and became famous for his work (1852–59) in the newly annexed Punjab as commissioner and lieutenant governor. By curbing the chiefs, introducing a new system of land tenure, and many other reforms and above all by his firm and just rule, he gained such esteem that at the time of the Indian Mutiny (1857) he was able to disarm any disloyal soldiers in his area and at the same time raise an army of nearly 60,000 men, with which he made possible the capture of Delhi. Back in England he received a baronetcy and other honours. He returned to India (1863) as governor general and provided a much needed period of tranquillity and reconstruction after the Mutiny. On his retirement (1869) he was made a peer.

His brother, **Sir Henry Montgomery Lawrence** (1806–1857), joined the Bengal artillery and served in the First Burmese War. He later joined the political department (1841), accompanied the march to Kabul in Afghanistan, was in Nepal (1843), took part in the Punjab Wars and subsequently became head of the administrative board, but was transferred after disagreement with his brother and the viceroy. In the Indian Mutiny he was defeated and mortally wounded at the Battle of Chinhut.

Lawrence, Sir Thomas (1769–1830). English painter. Son of a Bristol innkeeper, he entered the Royal Academy Schools in 1787 and in 1789 achieved instant fame with a picture of Queen Charlotte (now in the National Gallery, London); he became A.R.A. (1791), court painter (1792), R.A. (1794), and president of the R.A. (1820). He was the most prolific and fashionable portrait painter of his time; and, though with so large an output he is often slick and over-facile, a masterly sense of character is shown in many of his portraits of royalty and celebrities, especially notable being those at Windsor Castle of the delegates to the Congress of Vienna (1814–15). His portraits of children, e.g. the famous *Red Boy* in the National Gallery, are often oversentimental.
Garlick, K., *Sir Thomas Lawrence*. 1954

Lawrence, Thomas Edward (known as 'Lawrence of Arabia') (1888–1935). English scholar, writer and soldier, leader of the Arab Revolt. The son of Sir Thomas Chapman, Bart, he became interested in medieval studies at Oxford and visited (1910) Palestine and Syria to study the castles of the crusaders, which he subsequently vividly described. From 1911 to 1914 he was in Syria engaged in archaeology and surveying. When Turkey entered World War I, Lawrence, with his intimate knowledge of Arabs and their language, was sent by Military Intelligence in Egypt to organize Arab resistance behind the Turkish lines; in this, he worked closely with the emir * Faisal, later king of Iraq, whose close friend he became. He later described his exploits and experiences in *The Seven Pillars of Wisdom* (1926) and its shortened form *Revolt in the Desert* (1927). At the Paris Peace Conference (1919) he championed the Arab claim to independence; he regarded its refusal as a betrayal, and in consequence, after brief service in the Colonial Office (1921–22), he sought anonymity in the R.A.F. as Aircraftsman Ross. Publicity caused him to disappear once more but he was again in the Air Force – this time under the name of Shaw – when he was killed in a motor-cycling accident. The complex character of this scholar-hero has

been a constant subject of speculation and controversy in books, plays and films.
Brent, P., *T. E. Lawrence*. 1975

Lawson, Henry (Hertzberg) (1867–1922). Australian writer. Of Norwegian descent, he spent his boyhood moving from job to job throughout Australia. His first verses appeared (1887) in the *Sydney Bulletin*, and thereafter, though his travels continued, he gave his life to authorship and became one of the most important figures in the Australian literary tradition. His books of prose and verse, e.g. *While the Billy Boils* (1896), *On the Track and Over the Sliprails* (1900), provide an episodic panorama, humorous, sentimental or tragic, of Australian life in city and bush.

Layard, Sir Austen Henry (1817–1894). British archaeologist. He was born and educated on the continent. He set out (1837) to travel overland to Ceylon but after adventures among Persian tribesmen he changed plans and finished up in Constantinople, where the British ambassador employed him as a political agent and also sent him to make archaeological investigations of Assyrian sites. At Nineveh (Mosul) and Babylon (1845–47 and 1849–51) he unearthed a great mass of sculptured material and cuneiform tablets (now in the British Museum), from which the history of Assyria has been largely deduced. Later he entered parliament, held political and diplomatic appointments, was knighted (1877) and became ambassador to Turkey.

Leach, Bernard Howell (1887–1979). British potter. The main influence on twentieth-century ceramics in Britain, from 1909 he studied as a potter in Japan, and also visited artist potters in Korea and China. In 1920 he returned to England and, with Shoji Hamada, founded the Leach Pottery at St Ives. He subsequently practised and taught the Japanese tradition, bringing back into English ceramics a close relationship between artist and raw material, which had almost been lost. He received the C.H. in 1973.
Leach, B. H., *A Potter's Work*. 1973

Leacock, Stephen Butler (1869–1944). Canadian humorist and economist, born in England. He was professor of economics at McGill University, Montreal (1908–36), but is best remembered for his humorous essays and stories, e.g. *Literary Lapses* (1910), *Nonsense Novels* (1911), *Sunshine Sketches of a Little Town* (1912). It was a fresh vein of humour that he discovered and one that brought him sudden and immense popularity. Later he turned to more general literature, e.g. *My Discovery of England* (1922).
Davies, R., *Stephen Leacock*. 1960

Leakey, Louis Seymour Bazett (1903–1972). English archaeologist. Son of a Kenya missionary, Leakey went to England to study at Cambridge, taking a Ph.D. in African prehistory. He was much influenced by the anthropologist A. C. Haddon. In 1924 he took part in an archaeological research expedition to Tanganyika (Tanzania) and from 1926 led his own expeditions to East Africa. Palaeontological work with his wife **Mary Douglas,** née Nicol (1913–), on the Miocene deposits of western Kenya led him to discover the skull of *Proconsul Africanus*, the earliest ape skull then found. His archaeological investigations led him to the Acheulian site of Olduvai, in the Rift Valley, where the skull of *Australopithecus boisei*, and the first remains of *Homo habilis*, a hominid dated at some 1.7 million years, were found.

Other skulls have since been discovered of the founders of Acheulian culture at Olduvai, dubbed *Homo erectus*. Leakey's son **Richard Erskine** (1944-) discovered hominid remains in tufas dating back perhaps two and a half million years. Leakey's archaeological work on the early hominids was set out in many books, of which the most important are *The Stone Age Cultures of Kenya* (1931) and *The Miocene Hominidae of East Africa* (1951).

Lear, Edward (1812–1888). English artist and humorist. He worked for the Zoological Society making ornithological drawings, and was then engaged by the Earl of Derby to provide plates for *The Knowsley Menagerie* (1846). It was for his grandchildren that he wrote the immortal *Book of Nonsense* (1846) which contains the ever-popular 'The Owl and the Pussy-Cat went to sea In a beautiful pea-green boat'. His travels in Greece, Italy and elsewhere are described in books illustrated by his own delightful line and tone drawings.
Noakes, V., Edward Lear. 1968

Leavis, Frank Raymond (1895–1978). English literary critic. Editor of *Scrutiny* (1932–53) he was regarded as a formidable critic and controversialist. His wife **Queenie**

Dorothy Leavis (1906–81) was also a critic of some note.

Lebrun, Albert (1871–1950). French politician. After a long political career (Left Republican party) he was elected to the presidency in 1932 and re-elected in 1939. On France's collapse (1940) in World War II he was unable to assert any authority and was dismissed by Marshal Pétain.

Lebrun, Charles (1619–1690). French artist. He first studied in Rome and was much influenced by Poussin. With the support of Colbert he became something akin to an artistic dictator in the reign of Louis XIV. He was a leading light in the newly founded Académie Royale and was appointed director of the tapestry factory of Les Gobelins. With these positions he was able to direct and combine the works of artists in different fields into a single decorative scheme; he can be regarded as the virtual creator of the Louis XIV style and it is against this setting that his vast and rather overpowering pictures must be judged. Much of his work is in the Palace of Versailles, where he decorated the state apartments (1679–84).

Le Brun, Marie Elisabeth Louise (usually known as Vigée Le Brun) (1755–1842). The daughter of an artist named Vigée, who trained her, she was commissioned (1799) to paint Marie Antoinette and quickly established a reputation. She also became successful outside France when she travelled in many European countries to avoid the dangers of the French Revolution. She excelled in portraying women and children.
Shelley, G., trans., *The Memoirs of Madame Elisabeth Louise Vigée-Le Brun*. 1926.

Lecky, William Edward Hartpole (1838–1903). Anglo-Irish historian. He wrote *Rationalism in Europe* (1865) and *A History of European Morals* (1869), but his great work was *A History of England in the Eighteenth Century* (8 volumes, 1878–1890), in which ideas and institutions are given as much prominence as political events. He was Unionist M.P. for Trinity College, Dublin (1895–1903) and received the O.M. (1902).

Leclerc de Hautecloque, Philippe François Marie (1902–1947). French soldier. He dropped the title Vicomte when after the collapse of France (1940) he joined the Free French forces under de Gaulle. He showed his brilliance when (1942) he led an expeditionary force from the Chad for 1,500 miles across the Sahara to join the British in the Western desert. Later he was a divisional commander in Tunisia (1943) and in the campaign (1944) for the liberation of France. He was commander-in-chief in Indochina (1945–46); he was killed in an air crash a year later. He was posthumously created a marshal.

Leconte de Lisle, Charles Marie (1818–1894). French poet. He was the son of a planter in the island of Réunion (Indian Ocean). He went to Brittany (1837) to study law, which he abandoned for literature: his family recalled him, but by 1845 he was again in France struggling to make a living by journalism. He took part in the revolution of 1848 but, disillusioned by its result, abandoned politics. His first work *Poèmes antiques* appeared in 1852; his *Poésies barbares* (1862) attracted more attention. He became the recognized leader of the Parnassian group of poets who in a reaction from Romanticism and subjective emotionalism, sought objectivity and perfect form. De Lisle also produced, e.g., adaptations of the Greek dramatists, and translations of classical authors from Homer to Horace; his *Poèmes tragiques* was published in 1884. But de Lisle was moved as much by hatred of the present as by love of the past. In his disillusion he saw history as a series of stands, in which one by one the upholders of strength and beauty perished. Apart from his poetry he published historical works anonymously or as 'Pierre Gosset'. In 1886 he was elected to the Académie Française.

Le Corbusier (Charles Edouard Jeanneret) (1887–1965). Swiss-born architect. The son of a craftsman in enamel, he was trained at a local art school and had tried his hand at Art Nouveau before, after visits to Italy and Vienna, he went in 1908 to Paris, where he achieved some success among the modern artists who followed Cézanne. From 1916, however, he turned almost exclusively to architecture, his aim, expressed in print in *Towards a New Architecture* (1922), being to make use of engineering techniques (steel frameworks, concrete etc.) not merely functionally but to give artistic freedom to the architect in his endeavour to provide brighter living in terms of air, sunlight and space;

rooms leading into one another with movable partitions were among his methods for achieving this. He designed many interesting buildings in France and elsewhere but perhaps the most impressive illustration of his ideas is the Unité d'Habitation (1952) at Marseille, a great block of two-storey maisonettes with shops, recreation facilities etc., making a complete community – vertical living as it was called. Though much of the work of his imitators is merely monumental, in Le Corbusier himself the artist is always uppermost. His Swiss House (1932) in the Cité Universitaire, Paris, has been described as 'a precise and monumental interplay of form within light', and the church at Ronchamp, France (1954) as a 'tense dynamic rhythm of plastic forms'. Le Corbusier was chosen to design (1951–56) Chandigarh, the new capital of the Punjab. Through his writings and his drawings as much as by his comparatively few finished works he was one of the most important influences on modern architecture.
Le Corbusier, *My Work*. 1960

Lederberg, Joshua (1925–). U.S. geneticist. Educated at Columbia and Yale, he shared the 1958 Nobel Prize for Medicine with G. W. Beadle and E. L. Tatum for their work on the sexual recombination of bacteria.

Lee, Robert Edward (1807–1870). American soldier. Born in Virgina, he was the son of **General Harry Lee** (1756–1818), a brilliant cavalry commander of the War of Independence. Robert E. Lee became prominent in the Mexican War (1846–48) as a chief engineer and gained rapid promotion. He was superintendent (1852–55) of the military school at West Point, and in 1859 led the force which suppressed John Brown's anti-slavery rising at Harper's Ferry. When the Civil War broke out (1861) he adhered, as a Virginian, to the Confederacy, and in 1862 was given supreme command in Virgina. Though in the Richmond campaign of that year he was outnumbered, he manoeuvred to gain local superiority at decisive points and thus discomfited McClellan, the Union commander. Having disposed of Pope by a threat to his rear, he boldly invaded Maryland; though he had a narrow escape at Sharpsburg was able to retire almost without loss. In 1862 and 1863 the tactical and strategical skill which enabled him to foresee the enemy's move was nearly always apparent, but at Gettysburg (July 1863), where both sides fought to the point of exhaustion, he is said to have lost an opportunity on the second day. By 1864 the disparity in numbers was having its effect but Lee still held his opponent, * Grant, at bay by a clever use of field fortifications. It was only in 1865 that the long postponement of the inevitable ended with the surrender at Appomattox. Lee, with his modesty, generosity and superb skill, has become almost a legendary hero to southerners and northerners alike.
Dowdey, C., *Lee*. 1965

Lee, Sir Sidney (1859–1926). English editor. He succeeded Sir Leslie Stephen and was editor-in-chief (1891–1917) of the *Dictionary of National Biography*. His own numerous books included biographies of Shakespeare, Queen Victoria and Edward VII.

Leech, John (1817–1864). English artist. He is best known for his long association with *Punch*, for which he drew many political cartoons, from 1841 until his death. Among the many books and journals illustrated by Leech were Dickens's Christmas books; his woodcuts were of the highest order.
Rose, J., *The Drawings of John Leech*. 1950

Leeds, 1st Duke of *see* **Danby, Thomas Osborne, Earl of**

Lee Kuan Yew (1923–). Singapore politician. Born into a Chinese family, he read law at Cambridge University and was called to the bar in 1950, returning to Singapore as legal adviser to the postal union. He continued to work for this and other trade unions, forming a socialist and communist political group, The People's Action Party. In 1955 the number of elected seats on the Legislative Council was increased; his party won three, of which he held one. He was a delegate to the London conferences on independence in 1956, 1957 and 1958; ultimate success increased his standing at home and his party won the election of 1959. As Prime Minister he followed a moderate and progressive domestic policy, favourable to industrial growth. His left-wing associates broke away shortly after his appointment, but their efforts against him were defeated by a referendum in 1962. His one serious mistake was to take Singapore into the new Federation of Malaysia in 1963; he underestimated the strength of Malay–Chinese hostility and was forced to withdraw in 1965.
Josey, A., *Lee Kuan Yew*. 1968

Leeuwenhoek, Antony van (1632–1723). Dutch naturalist, born at Delft. Apprenticed to a draper, he often used a lens to examine the texture of cloth and developed a method of grinding optical lenses to give greater magnification. He made many simple microscopes and became a self-taught student of anatomy and biology. He demonstrated the blood circulation through the capillaries, was the first to describe blood corpuscles accurately and made important observations of the structure of muscle, hair, teeth, skin and eye. His equally valuable zoological work revealed the Infusoria and Rotifera and disproved the idea of spontaneous generation.
Dobell, C., *Antony van Leeuwenhoek and his 'Little Animals'*. 1932

Le Fanu, Joseph Sheridan (1814–1873). Irish novelist. Great-nephew of the dramatist Sheridan, he wrote stories of mystery and terror, e.g. *The House by the Churchyard* (1863) and *Uncle Silas* (1864).
Bignal, M. H., *Joseph Sheridan Le Fanu*. 1971

Legendre, Adrien Marie (1752–1833). French mathematician. Through the influence of * d' Alembert he became (1777) professor of mathematics at the Ecole Militaire, Paris, transferring (1795) to the Ecole Normale. He carried out important researches on the theory of elliptical function, and wrote a treatise on the theory of numbers.

Léger, Fernand (1881–1955). French painter. The son of a Normandy farmer, he went to Paris (1905) to follow art. Influenced at first by Impressionism and Cézanne, he began to develop his individual style from the time (1910) he met Picasso and Braque and joined in the first Cubist exhibition. Service in World War I drew his attention to the possibilities inherent in mechanical contrivances of all kinds, wheels, cogs, shining surfaces etc., which he introduced into his paintings with their broad planes and bright colours. As his art developed his pictures became warmer and more human, acrobats began to appear, boys with bicycles, and suggestions of landscape. His versatility was shown in murals, tapestries, stained-glass windows (at Audincourt) and mosaics.
Delevoy, R., *Léger*. 1962

Léger, Paul Emile (1904–). Canadian cardinal. After service in France and Japan he became Archbishop of Montreal 1950–67, resigning to work as a missionary to lepers in Africa. His brother, **Jules Léger** (1913–1980) was an academic, diplomat and administrator, Ambassador to Italy 1962–64, to France 1964–68, Under Secretary for Foreign Affairs 1968–73 and Governor-General of Canada 1974–79.

Lehár, Franz (Ferenc) (1870–1948). Hungarian composer. After studying music he went to Vienna as a conductor of military bands. He then turned to composing operettas which won great popularity, e.g. *The Merry Widow* (1905).

Leibniz, Gottfried Wilhelm, Baron von (1646–1716). German philosopher and mathematician. The son of a professor at Leipzig University, he studied law and philosophy there, and then entered the service of the archbishop-elector of Mainz. A diplomatic mission to Paris gave him the opportunity of four years' (1672–76) intensive study and contact with other leading scientists. He then became librarian to the Duke of Brunswick, on his return journey visiting England, where he was made a member of the Royal Society for his invention of a calculating machine.

One of Leibniz's fundamental beliefs was that the search for truth should be the common task of men of all nations; to this end he tried to invent a universal language and at the same time worked upon a system of symbols, like those of algebra, to be used in logic so as to give it a mathematical basis. It was this work which led to his discoveries relating to the differential and integral calculus, for which he invented the notation still used. The accusation that his system was stolen from * Newton was completely unfounded.

As a philosopher Leibniz was influenced by Descartes and also by Spinoza, whom he met. His metaphysical system, which has interested later philosophers (notably Bertrand Russell), grew out of a dissatisfaction with existing doctrines, including the atomic view of the universe. He argued that everything consists of certain substances (monads) which are immaterial, have no extension whatever in space and do not interact in any way. To explain the fact that these independent monads do seem to act in unison – go together to make up things – he supposed that God had instituted what he called 'a pre-established

harmony'; i.e., monads move in accordance with a built-in plan which gives rise to the world as we know it. Leibniz, whose versatility extended to religion (an attempt to reunite the churches), history (publication of documents relating to the house of Brunswick), and codification of law, was satirized by Voltaire in *Candide* as Dr Pangloss, who believed that 'everything happens for the best in the best of all possible worlds'. A serious doctrine of optimism is central to Leibniz's belief and is the subject matter of theodicy (***Eassais de Theodicée sur la bonté de Dieu, la liberté de l'homme et l' origine du mal***, 1710).
Haase, C., and Totok, W., *Leibniz: sein Leben, sein Werken, seine Welt*. 1966

Leicester, Robert Dudley, Earl of (1532?–1588). English courtier. He was the son of the Duke of * Northumberland, with whom he was sentenced to death for his part in the attempt to secure the crown for Lady Jane Grey. Pardoned and freed (1554) he came into court favour with the accession of Queen Elizabeth, his childhood friend at Henry VIII's court. Offices and emoluments were lavished upon him, and when (1560) his wife, Amy Robsart (married 1550), was found dead at the foot of the stairs at Cumnor Place near Abingdon, where she lived in seclusion, it was rumoured that Leicester (with or without Elizabeth's complicity) had contrived her death in order to be free to marry the Queen. But though Elizabeth stood by him and in 1564 created him Earl of Leicester, the prospect of their marriage became increasingly remote. His famous reception of her (1575) at Kenilworth (described in Scott's novel of that name) marked their reconciliation after her anger at the news of his secret marriage to the dowager Lady Sheffield. A bigamous union (1578) with Lettice, the widowed Countess of Essex, was his last essay in matrimony. In 1585 he was given command of an English army to support the Dutch in their struggle for independence with the Spaniards; and, despite the military incapacity he then displayed, he was chosen in the Armada year (1588) to command the forces gathered at Tilbury to prevent a Spanish landing. The celebrations for her fleet's victory were in October clouded for Elizabeth by news of her favourite's death.
Jenkins, E., *Elizabeth and Leicester*. 1972

Leicester, Thomas William Coke, 1st Earl of (1752–1842). English agricultural innovator. He represented Norfolk in parliament almost continuously from 1776 to 1832, but is much better known for the many farming improvements he introduced on his Norfolk estate of Holkham. By the use of bone meal and fertilizers, by sowing seeds in drills, by planting sainfoin and clover to enable larger numbers of livestock to be maintained, by many other new or improved methods, he so increased the value of his estate that in the forty years from 1776 the rents are said to have risen from about £2,000 to £20,000. His example led to a general improvement in British farming.

Leichhardt, Friedrich Wilhelm Ludwig (1813–1848). Prussian explorer. He arrived in Sydney in 1841, and led an expedition (1843–45) from Moreton Bay near Brisbane to the Gulf of Carpentaria. In November 1847 he again started from Moreton Bay in an attempt to cross the continent from east to west, but, last heard of in the following April, he disappeared without trace.

Leif Ericson (Eirikson) (fl. *c*. 1000). Reputedly the first European to discover the American continent. Son of Eric the Red, first colonizer of Greenland, he sailed along the American coast and after passing 'Helluland' and 'Markland' (probably Labrador and Newfoundland or Nova Scotia) he landed at 'Vinland' (almost certainly Nova Scotia or Massachusetts). A subsequent attempt to settle 'Vinland' failed.

Leighton, Frederic Leighton, 1st Baron (1830–1896). English painter. After spending most of his early life in Italy, he studied in Dresden and Paris and became the leading neo-classical painter of the Victorian era. His nudes, refined almost to the point of sexlessness and elegantly posed in Grecian architectural settings, became immensely popular. He was president of the Royal Academy 1878–96. The first British artist to be made a peer, he died on the day his elevation was announced.

Lely, Sir Peter (Pieter van der Faes) (1618–1680). Dutch painter. He lived in England (from 1641) and became painter at court in succession to Van Dyck. Although after the parliamentary victory in the Civil War he managed to adapt his style to the demands of his new patrons, he was happier at the

Restoration to revert to court paintings. His most famous pictures are the *Beauties* of King Charles II's entourage (now at Hampton Court) and the more remarkable series, because more expressive of character, (now at Greenwich) of the twelve British admirals in the Second Dutch War. Despite his large output, Lely, who amassed fame, property and a knighthood (1680), seldom became perfunctory.
Beckett, R. B., *Lely*. 1951

Lemaître, Georges Edouard (1894–1966). Belgian astronomer. Trained as an engineer, he studied physics in Britain and the US, became a priest and was a professor at Louvain from 1927. He originated the theory (later called the 'big bang' by George * Gamow) that the universe began with a small 'cosmic egg' which has been expanding ever since.

Lemnitzer, Lyman Louis (1899–). American soldier. He served with distinction in World War II: in 1942 he accompanied Mark * Clark on his daring landing from a submarine in North Africa to prepare for Allied invasion. In the Korean War (from 1950) he led the U.S. forces in the fighting zone. Finally, having already commanded American armies in the Far East and in Europe, he succeeded (1963) General Norstad as supreme Allied commander of NATO forces in Europe.

Lemon, Mark (1809–1870). English author and journalist. He wrote many plays, novels and children's stories, but is best remembered as the founder, with Henry Mayhew, of *Punch*, of which he was sole editor from 1843 until his death.

Lenard, Philipp Eduard Anton (1862–1947). German physicist, born in Hungary. For most of his working life he held professorships at Kiel and Heidelberg universities. He was a pioneer in the field of cathode rays; in 1894 he first obtained cathode rays outside a tube, by allowing them to pass from the tube through a window of aluminium foil; such rays became known as Lenard rays. His observations helped to prepare the way for Rutherford's first atomic model in 1911 – he had suggested a model of the structure of the atom as early as 1903. He also studied the ejection of electrons from metals by the action of ultraviolet light, and found that the energy of the emitted electrons is independent of the intensity of the incident radiation, and depends only upon its wavelength. He won the Nobel Prize for Physics in 1905.

Lenclos, Anne (called Ninon de Lenclos) (1620–1705). French courtesan. She was a woman of intelligence and great beauty: amongst her many lovers (and friends) were distinguished men such as La Rochefoucauld. Her salon in Paris was a meeting place for literary figures. In her last years she took a special interest in her lawyer Arouet's son, who afterwards took the name * Voltaire.
Magne, E., *Ninon de Lenclos*. 1948

L'Enfant, Pierre Charles (1754–1825). French architect. An engineer in the French army, he served on the American side in the War of Independence. He was commissioned (1791) by George Washington to prepare the original plans for Washington, the new capital city. The central feature of his grandiose plan was the dome-surmounted Capitol, built upon a small hill and approached by four great converging avenues, thus dominating the city. The plans, which were clearly influenced by Versailles, were discarded as far too extravagant and he was dismissed (1792); his designs were later restudied and the existing city, built up over the years, follows fairly closely his original plan.

Lenglen, Suzanne (1899–1938). French lawn tennis player. She dominated women's lawn tennis in the years following World War I and raised the standard of women's play to a height far beyond any previously reached. She was women's singles champion at Wimbledon from 1919 to 1923 and again in 1925. In the following year she turned professional.

Lenin, Vladimir Ilyich (V. I. Ulyanov) (1870–1924). Russian revolutionary and creator of the Soviet state. He was born at Simbirsk (later renamed Ulyanovsk) where his father was a school inspector. His mother was the daughter of a doctor and from this middle-class family sprang two revolutionary sons: the elder, Alexander, took part in a conspiracy to assassinate Tsar Alexander III and was hanged in 1887. The younger, who was to take the name Lenin, studied law and was expelled from Kazan University for subversive activity. He abandoned the legal profession and after having studied Marx intensively went to St Petersburg (Leningrad) where he organized the illegal League for the Liberation of the Working Class. Arrested in 1897 he was exiled for three years in Siberia, where he married a fellow revolutionary, Nadezhda * Krupskaya; he then left Russia to pursue his revolutionary activities abroad. At a conference (1903) in London the Russian Social Democratic Labour party split into two factions – the Mensheviks ('minority') and the more extreme Bolshevik ('majority') dominated by Lenin. He was clandestinely in Russia for the abortive risings of 1905 but fled to Switzerland in 1907. From there and other places in Europe he continued, through his political writings and underground organization, to control the revolutionary movement in Russia. In 1912 the Bolsheviks became in fact (though not formally until 1917) a separate party upon the expulsion of the Mensheviks from the R.S.D.L.P. During World War I Lenin stayed in Switzerland to await a chance to lead a revolution in Russia. On the outbreak of the first Russian Revolution (March 1917) the Germans, with the object of weakening Russian war efforts, smuggled Lenin into St Petersburg (in a train which passed sealed through Sweden), and he set about overthrowing the provisional government of * Kerensky. Under the slogan 'All power to the Soviets' he seized power in a second revolution in November. He was president of the Council of People's Commissar's (in fact premier) 1917–24. He agreed to the severe terms of the Treaty of Brest-Litovsk to secure peace with Germany but the Red Army had to struggle until 1921 to overcome the various counter-revolutionary movements of the 'white' Russian leaders * Denikin and * Kolchak, who had some support from the Western Allies. Meanwhile as chairman of the Communist party Lenin became a virtual dictator. In 1919 he had established the Comintern or Communist International to foster world revolution. In the chaotic economic conditions then prevailing it was impossible to carry through his projected communist revolution (War Communism); there was a temporary retreat into the New Economic Policy, which was a partial return to private enterprise. His health deteriorated rapidly after a gunshot wound (1918) and he was incapacitated by a stroke in 1922. Shortly before his death Lenin wrote a warning that Stalin should be removed from his post as secretary general of the Communist party. This was suppressed, and in the struggle for power after Lenin's death between his chief lieutenants, Trotsky and Stalin, it was the latter who triumphed. Although in his writings Lenin was the chief theoretician of Marxism he was most important as a skilful revolutionary and a master of political and party organization.

Lenin's embalmed body lies in a mausoleum in Red Square, Moscow, which has become a national shrine visited by thousands daily; his statue finds a place in every Soviet town of any size. St Petersburg was renamed Leningrad in his honour five days after he died. Though for a time Stalin enjoyed an equal place with him before the Russian public, Lenin has been restored to a position of primacy since Khrushchev denounced the 'personality cult' of Stalin.

Shub, D., *Lenin*. Rev. ed. 1966

Leno, Dan (George Galvin) (1860–1904). English actor. He achieved almost legendary fame in theatrical history for his virtual creation of pantomime dames, of whom Widow Twankey is the classic personification. He played in the Drury Lane pantomime every Christmas from 1888 to 1903.

Le Nôtre, André (1613–1700). French landscape architect. He succeeded his father as chief of the royal gardens: later (1657) he became 'controller' of the royal buildings as a result of the impression he created by the park and grounds (1656–61) laid out at Vaux-le-Vicomte for Nicolas Fouquet. Among his other parks were those of St Germain, St Cloud and Chantilly. His greatest achievement was the gardens of Versailles (1662–90).

Fox, H. M., *André le Nôtre, Garden Architect to Kings*. 1962

Lenthall, William (1591–1662). English politician. He was speaker of the House of Commons 1640–53, 1654 and 1659–60, famous for refusing Charles I access to the Commons (1642) when he sought to arrest five members, and for being dragged from the chair when Cromwell forcibly dissolved the Long Parliament (1653).

Leo I (known as 'the Great') (died 461). Pope (from 440) and saint. A man of noble character and a theologian of distinction, he did much to establish the primacy of Rome. His exposition of the divine and human natures of Christ was accepted by the council of Chalcedon (451). His resolute bearing persuaded Attila the Hun to spare Rome but he could not save the city from sack by the Vandals (455).

Leo III (known as 'the Isaurian') (*c.* 680–740). Byzantine emperor (from 717). He was a successful general who rebelled against the feeble Theodosius and usurped the throne. After saving Constantinople from the Saracens he stabilized Asia Minor, strengthening the administration by subdividing the Asiatic provinces. He is chiefly remembered for the pronouncement (726) by which he tried to suppress the use of religious pictures and images (icons) and so started the great iconoclast controversy.

Leo X (Giovanni de' Medici) (1475–1521). Pope (from 1513). The second son of Lorenzo the Magnificent of Florence, he was made a cardinal at the age of 13. He led a graceful, cultured life and used the opportunities provided by his position as pope to become, in the tradition of the Medicis, a munificent patron of the arts; the tapestries of the Sistine Chapel of the Vatican were executed by Raphael on his orders and he invited Leonardo da Vinci to Rome. He proved his skill in diplomacy by maintaining a balance in Italy between Francis I of France and the emperor Charles V. However he underrated the influence of Luther and took no active steps to forestall him by initiating the necessary reforms.

Leo XIII (Gioacchino Pecci) (1810–1903). Pope (from 1878). The son of a nobleman, he studied law but became a priest in 1883 and was bishop of Perugia from 1845. Much of the credit for the modernization of the papacy can be ascribed to him. In many public letters he expounded his church's attitude to the social and political ideas of his day. He denounced both materialism and socialism; but in his famous *Rerum Novarum* (1891) he analysed the conditions and problems of the working classes with generosity, understanding and realism, and in this and other letters restated the Christian ideas in relation to the changing patterns of social life. In theology he asserted the pre-eminence of St Thomas Aquinas and directed that Thomism should be the basis of all priestly training. His attitude to primitive peoples was liberal and constructive and he encouraged a great increase of missionary activity. He achieved an important diplomatic success by bringing to an end the German *Kulturkampf*, Bismarck's great campaign to remove Catholic influence from education. In 1883 he opened the Vatican archives to scholars of all faiths and encouraged the study of astronomy and natural science. He published 86 encyclicals and is regarded as the most brilliant pope of recent times: he was also the oldest (dying at 93).

Gargan, E. T., (ed.), *Leo XIII and the Modern World*. 1961

Leonardo da Pisa (Leonardo Fibonacci) (*c.* 1170–1240). Italian mathematician. The son of a merchant, he was one of the greatest early writers on arithmetic and algebra. In his *Liber abaci* (*c.* 1202) he introduced the Arabic system of numerals into Europe; in later works he made highly original applications of algebra to geometry.

Gies, J., and Gies, F., *Leonardo of Pisa and the New Mathematics of the Middle Ages*. 1969

Leonardo da Vinci (1452–1519). Florentine artist. Unique in the history of art because of the exceptional scope of his intellect, his powers of observation and the versatility and strength of his technique, his interest in natural science was sustained by a conviction that 'knowing how to see' is the basis of understanding nature. His diverse talents led him to attempt an enormous variety of work; much of it was never completed.

He was born in Vinci, near Empoli, the illegitimate son of a peasant woman and a Florentine notary who, being otherwise childless until 1476, brought him up and treated him as a legitimate son. When he was 15 he was apprenticed to the Florentine painter and sculptor * Verrocchio, in whose workshops he worked until 1481, having been accepted into the painters' guild of Florence in 1472.

In 1482 he went to the court of Ludovico Sforza, Duke of Milan, as painter, sculptor, designer of court entertainments and technical adviser on military buildings and engineering. During his stay in Milan he painted 'The Last Supper' and a version of 'The Virgin of the Rocks'. He also began to write down his own theories of art, and to record his scientific observations in books of drawings and explanatory text. By the time of his death his notebooks covered painting, architecture, mechanics and natural science.

In 1499/1500 he returned to Florence, leaving again in 1502 to work for a year as military adviser to Cesare Borgia. In 1503 he began work on the mural painting 'The Battle of the Anghiari', which he never finished; before returning to Milan in 1506 he had also begun three paintings which he worked on in subsequent years – 'Leda', 'The Virgin and Child with St Anne' and 'Mona Lisa'.

Sforza had been overthrown by the king of France in 1499, but Leonardo nevertheless returned to Milan as the king's adviser on architecture and engineering. In 1513 he went to Rome, possibly expecting Papal commissions which he did not receive, and in 1516 left Italy for France, appointed painter, architect and mechanic to Francis I. Most of the rest of his life was devoted to finishing 'St John the Baptist' and to editing his scientific studies.

His surviving work consists of 17 paintings definitely attributable, studies for two ambitious monuments which he never completed, and extensive writings. Notes and diagrams are all that survive of his varied and sometimes enormous civic engineering schemes.

Clark, K., *Leonardo da Vinci: an Account of his development as an Artist*. 2nd ed. 1952. Richter, J. P., *The Literary Works of Leonardo da Vinci*. 2 vols. 3rd ed. 1970

Leoncavallo, Ruggiero (1858–1919). Italian operatic composer. He achieved fame and wealth with *Pagliacci* (1892), one of the most widey performed of all operas. His other works included *La Bohème* (1897), which has been overshadowed by Puccini's more successful work, and *Zaz* (1900). He wrote his own librettos.

Leonidas (died 480 B.C.). King of Sparta and national hero of Greece. With only 300 Spartans he held the pass of Thermopylae, north of Athens, against the invading army of the Persian king, Xerxes, but after two days of heroic resistance, a path leading to his rear was betrayed to the enemy. Fighting to the end, Leonidas and every one of his men were killed.

Leontieff, Wassily Wassilief (1906–). U.S. economist, born in Russia. Educated in Leningard and Berlin, he taught at Harvard from 1931. He won the 1973 Nobel Prize for Economics for his development of input-output analysis, a study of the relationship within an economy between total inputs (raw materials, labour, manufacturing and related services) and total demands for final goods and services.

Leopardi, Count Giacomo (1798–1837). Italian poet. Described by critics as the greatest Italian lyricist since the 14th century, he suffered greatly from constant ill health. His parents distrusted his liberal ideas and he fled as soon as he could from the reactionary atmosphere of his home. He prepared an edition of Cicero's works for a Milan publisher, settled later in Florence and spent his last years in Naples. Apart from his works of scholarship and philosophy, he found in lyric poetry an instrument which proved sensitive to all his moods, mainly of disillusion with life as he had found it. The main collection of his poems, *I Canti* (1836), has been translated into English several times.

Leopold I (1640–1705). Holy Roman Emperor (from 1658) and ruler of Austria, Hungary and Bohemia. Most of his reign was spent in a prolonged struggle with the Turks; in 1683 Vienna was saved only by the intervention of the Poles under John Sobieski. In 1701 he joined the coalition against France to secure the Spanish throne for his son Charles in whose favour he had renounced his own rights (* Philip V of Spain).

Leopold I (1790–1865). King of the Belgians (from 1831). Son of Francis, Duke of Saxe-Coburg-Saalfeld, he fought with the Russian armies in the later stages of the Napoleonic Wars. He married (1816) Charlotte, daughter of the British prince-regent (George IV), but she died in childbirth a year later; his connexion with England gave him an insight into its political system which he used to good effect. In 1830 he refused the Greek throne, but in the following year was chosen as the first king of the Belgians. He ruled with such constitutional prudence that his country escaped the revolutionary turmoils of 1848. Leopold was a trusted adviser of his niece Queen Victoria, who married one of his nephews, Albert.

Leopold II (1747–1792). Holy Roman Emperor (from 1790), the third son of the empress Maria Theresa and brother and successor of Joseph II. As grand-duke of Tuscany (from 1765) he had, among other reforms, abolished torture, but as emperor he had no time to display his qualities and died before he could give effective aid to his sister Marie Antoinette in Revolutionary France.

Leopold II (1835–1909). King of the Belgians (from 1865). During his reign Belgium's industrial and colonial activities expanded greatly. In 1876, in collaboration with H. M. * Stanley, he founded (in his private capacity, not as king) an association to explore and civilize the Congo; in 1884 a European International Congress on African affairs sanctioned the establishment, under Leopold's personal control, of a 'Congo Free State', from which he gained an immense fortune. Forced labour and other inhumane practices used by the administrators caused a scandal, following which Leopold transferred the Congo to the Belgian government. At home industrialization proceeded rapidly and the attendant deterioration in social conditions led to labour troubles and political unrest. Energetic, rapacious and hypocritical, his personal life was disapproved by his conservative Catholic subjects. He was succeeded by his nephew * Albert I.

Leopold III (1901–1983). King of the Belgians 1934–51. The son of Albert I, he married Princess Astrid of Sweden (1926) who has killed in a car accident near Lucerne (1935). During World War II, he surrendered to the Germans (1940), despite the opposition of his cabinet. In 1941 he married Marie-Liliane Baels morganatically; she was created Princesse de Rethy. Both actions aroused intense hostility. After liberation a regency was created under his brother Charles and Leopold remained in Switzerland. In 1950 a plebiscite voted 57 per cent in favour of his return but following strikes and demonstrations he abdicated in favour of his son Baudouin I.

Lepidus, Marcus Aemillius (died 13 B.C.). Roman leader. He was a strong supporter of Julius Caesar, after whose murder he joined with Mark Antony and Octavian (Augustus) in forming (43) the Second Triumvirate. In 36 Lepidus, who had been assigned Africa as his sphere of command, left there to seize Sicily: Augustus then deprived him of office.

Lermontov, Mikhail Yuryevich (1814–1841). Russian poet of Scottish descent. He became a cavalry officer (1832) but was exiled to the Caucasus for a year for publishing a revolutionary poem on the death of Pushkin (1837). He was again banished in 1840 for fighting a duel, and in another duel in the following year he was killed. His poems reveal him as a true romantic; they consist mainly of lyrics, many inspired by the wild beauties of the Caucasus. *The Demon* (1839), a supernatural narrative poem, shows Byronic influence (indeed Lermontov has been compared with Byron both for his passionate praise of freedom and for his impulsive character). In another vein is *The Song of the Merchant Kalashnikov*, which is imbued with the spirit of Russian folk lore. *Masquerade* is the best known of his verse plays; his finest work was the short novel *A Hero of Our Times* (1840) an isolated masterpiece, but the first of the long line of Russian psychological novels.
L'Ami, C. E., and Welikotny, A., *Michael Lermontov: Biography and Translation.* 1967

Le Roy Ladurie, Emmanuel Bernard (1929–). French historian. A pupil of Fernand * Braudel, he taught at the Collège de France. He worked within the *Annales* tradition but made effective use of econometrics and anthropology e.g. in *Montaillou* (1978), the story of a French village 1294–1324, which became an international best seller.

Lerroux, Alejandro (1864–1949). Spanish politician. Originally an ardent republican, he was exiled several times before 1931 but served as Foreign Minister (1931–33 and 1934–36) and prime minister (1933–34, 1935). His opponents denounced him as an opportunist.

Lesage (Le Sage), **Alain René** (1668–1747). French dramatist and novelist, born in Brittany. He started his literary career with translations from Latin, Greek and Spanish. His early plays too, were adapted from the Spanish and it was not until 1707 that his first original work appeared. *Turcaret*, a satirical comedy about financiers and considered the best work of its kind since Molière, was produced at the Comédie Française in 1708. Lesage gained a greater reputation as a novelist with *Le Diable boîteux* (*The Devil on Two Sticks*), published in 1707. This was followed by a picaresque novel, *Gill Blas de Santillane* (1715–35), in which the hero climbs the ladder of success from robber's servant to a ministerial post and encounters on the way a wonderful array of characters in almost every class of Spanish society. This great work, which influenced Smollett (who translated it) and Fielding, marked the peak of Lesage's achievement. He married in 1694 and lived quietly and happily with his wife and three sons.

Leskov, Nikolai Semyonovich (1831–1895). Russian writer. Having visited many parts of Russia and met people of all classes, he was able to cover a wider range of Russian society than his contemporaries Turgenev and Dostoyevsky. He was clever at catching individual oddities of appearance and speech, but though he often writes with irony, optimism is the keynote of his mood. The best known of his novels is *The Cathedral Folk* (1872) about the provincial clergy.

Lesseps, Ferdinand Marie, Vicomte de (1805–1894). French engineer. After resigning from the diplomatic service (1849), he revived his interest in the project he had conceived, during a visit to Egypt (1832), of constructing a canal across the isthmus of Suez. His opportunity came in 1854, when an old friend, Mohammed Said, became khedive. Funds were raised by loan and in 1860 work began. On the canal's completion (1869) international honours were showered upon de Lesseps, the hero of the hour. A grandiose plan to repeat his success, this time at Panama, was launched in 1879. Work on a sea-level canal without locks began in 1881, but fever and the difficulties of the task exhausted the funds, and so caused the financial jugglery that brought disaster to the scheme and disgrace to de Lesseps. Though his sentence of five years' imprisonment for fraud was quashed on technical grounds, he was a ruined man.
Bonnet, G. E., *Ferdinand de Lesseps*. 2 vols. 1951 and 1959

Lessing, Doris May (1919–). British writer. Born in Iran, she was brought up in southern Africa, the background of many of her books. She has written novels and short stories, mainly in a forthright, colloquial style, which express her socialism and her interest in feminine psychology. Her best known novels are probably *The Grass is Singing* (1950) and *The Golden Notebook* (1962).
Thorpe, M., *Doris Lessing*. 1973

Lessing, Gotthold Ephraim (1729–1781). German dramatist and critic. Born in Saxony, he studied theology at Leipzig University, went to Berlin (1748) and with a friend started a theatrical journal to which he contributed several articles including one on Plautus. A second journal of the same type followed (1754–58), and he resumed university studies in Wittenberg. Back in Berlin he formed a close friendship with the philosopher Moses Mendelssohn; in discussion and correspondence at this time he formulated his ideas that the natural drama of Shakespeare and his English successors was to be greatly preferred to the classical tragedies of Corneille, against which he waged incessant critical warfare. His own *Miss Sara Sampson* (1755), a tragedy of common life – a new type in Germany – exemplified his viewpoint, as does his second tragedy *Emilia Galotti* (1772). In between came one of the best German comedies, *Minna von Barnhelm* (1767), in which the influence of English writers is clear. In *Laokoon* (1776), an influential work on aesthetics, he assigns limitations to the various arts (unacceptable nowadays), e.g. that only static treatment of subjects should be attempted by the plastic arts. Lessing was secretary to the governor of Breslau (1760–65) and was then (until 1769) occupied at Hamburg with another journal of theatrical criticism and comment. Eventually (1770) he settled permanently in Wolfenbüttel. Lessing was a great fighter for intellectual liberty and religious toleration to which subject his poem *Nathan der Weise* (1779) was devoted.
Garland, H. B., *Lessing, the founder of Modern German Literature*. 2nd ed. 1962.

Leszczynski, Stanislas (1667–1766). King of Poland (1704–09 and 1733–35). He was elected as king by the Diet, but had to surrender the throne when the Russians defeated Charles XII of Sweden, whose protégé he was. In 1725 his daughter Marie was married to Louis XV of France; but his son-in-law gave him little effective support in the War of the Polish Succession, which followed the second election (1733) of Stanislas as king of Poland, and he once more lost his throne. He was compensated with the duchy of Lorraine and Bar, and proved an enlightened ruler. His treatises on government etc. reveal his advanced political thought.

Le Tellier, François Michel *see* **Louvois, François Michel le Tellier, Marquis de**

Lettow-Vorbeck, Paul Emil von (1870–1964). German soldier. During World War I he defended German East Africa (Tanganyika etc.) against General Smuts in one of the most brilliant campaigns of colonial military history.

Lever, Charles James (1806–1872). Irish novelist. He won great popularity with his stories, e.g. *Charles O'Malley* (1840), of the rollicking military and foxhunting cliques in the Irish society of his time.

Leverhulme, William Hesketh Lever, 1st Viscount (1851–1925). British industrialist. He began his business career in his father's grocery at Bolton, Lancs. In partnership with his brother he started the manufacture of soap from vegetable oils (instead of tallow). This product – Sunlight soap – proved to be the starting-point of one of the greatest industrial enterprises of the century. Port Sunlight on the Mersey (begun in 1888) was among the first factory centres to combine the needs of industry with model housing for the workers. By mergers aad purchase the business continued to expand and, linked with its Dutch counterparts, came to form the great international combination, Unilever. Lever, who became a baronet (1911), a baron (1917) and a viscount (1922), devoted much of his wealth to public and private benefactions.

Leverrier, Urbain Jean Joseph (1811–1877). French astronomer. He taught astronomy at the Ecole Polytechnique from 1839 and in 1846 was admitted to the Academy. In the turmoil that followed the revolution of 1848 he played a political role and was made a senator by Louis Napoleon (Napoleon III) in 1852; he subsequently became director of the Paris Observatory. From his study of the irregularities of the motions of the planet Uranus he was able to predict the position (independently predicted by J. C. Adams) of the previously unidentified planet Neptune. Later he found the theoretical solutions that permitted him to construct more accurate tables of the movements of the sun and the more important planets.
Grosser, M., *The Discovery of Neptune*. 1962

Lévesque, René (1922–). Canadian politician. He was a journalist, foreign correspondent and broadcaster and a Liberal M.P. in the Quebec legislature from 1960 until 1970 when he founded the *Parti Québecois*. In 1976 he became Premier of Quebec, retiring in 1985.

Levi ben Gershom (Levi Gersonides of Avignon, also known as Ralbag) (*c.* 1228–1344). Jewish philosopher, astronomer and Biblical commentator. His chief work, *Wars of the Lord*, deals with the immortality of the soul, the nature of prophecy, God's omniscience, divine providence, the nature of the celestial sphere and the eternity of matter. He wrote a notable commentary on Euclid.

Lévi-Strauss, Claude (1908–). French social anthropologist and writer, noted as the exponent of 'structuralism' – his method of analysing cultural systems. He began his career at the University of São Paulo, Brazil, and worked also in New York at the New School for Social Research. He was Director of Studies at the École Pratique des Hautes Études, Paris, 1950–74.
Lévi-Strauss, C., *A World on the Wane*. 1961

Lewes, George Henry (1817–1878). English writer. He was editor of the *Fortnightly Review* 1865–66) and wrote many popular philosophical works and a biography of Goethe, but is better known for his association with Mary Ann Evans (George * Eliot).
Lewis, G. H., *Problems of Life and Mind*. 5 vols. 1873–1879

Lewis, Cecil Day *see* **Day Lewis, Cecil**

Lewis, Clive Staples (1898–1963). English scholar and writer. He wrote on medieval courtly love in *The Allegory of Love* (1936) and on Christian belief in a number of popular works, especially the well known *Screwtape Letters* (1942). He also wrote science-fiction allegories, e.g. *Out of the Silent Planet* (1938), and children's books, *The Chronicles of Narnia*.
Green, R. L. and Hooper, W., *C. S. Lewis*. 1974

Lewis, Gilbert Newton (1875–1946). American scientist. He became in 1912 Dean of the College of Chemistry at Berkeley, California and turned the department into one of the leading centres for chemistry in the United States. Lewis's career was a series of endeavours to unite chemistry and physics, theoretical and experimental approaches. He first worked in the field of thermodynamics, attempting to apply Gibbs's and Duhem's ideas of free energy to chemistry via the concept of the 'escaping tendency' (or 'fugacity') of gases – the tendency of a substance to pass from one chemical stage to another. He was however more successful with his work on valence theory. In 1916 he proposed his theory that the chemical bond was a pair of electrons shared jointly by two atoms. This idea was successfully taken by Irving Langmuir, who took most of the credit. In his later years, Lewis did important work in photochemistry. In the late 1930s and early 1940s he produced important experimental papers on fluorescence and phosphorescence spectra.

Lewis, John Llewellyn (1880–1969). American trade-union leader. Having worked as a miner from the age of 12, he became (1920) president of the United Mineworkers of America, an office he held until 1960. In 1935 he broke away from the American Federation of Labor (A.F.L.) and formed the Congress of Industrial Organizations (C.I.O.), a more political and aggressive body of which he became president. In 1942 he led his union out of the C.I.O. It rejoined the C.I.O. in 1946, but withdrew once more in 1947. Lewis was successful in obtaining better conditions and wages for coalminers; he accepted mechanization with the inevitable consequence of massive reductions in the numbers of coalminers employed.
Alinksy, S., *John L. Lewis*. 1949

Lewis, Matthew Gregory (1775–1818). English novelist. His sobriquet 'Monk' Lewis derived from his famous 'Gothic' romance, *Ambrosia, or the Monk* (1795), a tale of horror which won him the friendship of Sir Walter Scott, Byron and the Prince Regent himself. Other novels and poems followed in the same vein. Yellow fever, caught during a visit to the West Indies to improve the lot of the slaves on estates he had inherited, caused his death.
Peck, L. F., *Life of Matthew G. Lewis*. 1961

Lewis, Meriwether (1774–1809). American explorer. With William * Clark, he made an expedition to the north-west of the U.S.A. (1803–06).
Dillon, R. H., *Meriwether Lewis: A Biography*. 1965

Lewis, (Percy) Wyndham (1884–1957). English painter and novelist. Born in New York and trained in art at the Slade School, London, he was a pioneer of modernism in English art. The Vorticist group, which he led and of whose periodical *Blast* he was co-editor with Ezra Pound, derived some of its ideas from Futurism and Cubism, but in his own paintings Wyndham Lewis never restricted himself to a single style; he was a founder member of the London Group. Outside his art he had a separate reputation as a satirical novelist, his works including *Time and the Western Man* (1918), and *The Apes of God* (1930). *Rude Assignment* (1950) is his autobiography.
Handley-Read, C., ed., *The Art of Wyndham Lewis*. 1951

Lewis, Sinclair (1885–1951). American novelist. Born in Sauk Center, Minnesota, the son of a doctor, he became a journalist and wrote several minor works before beginning, at 35, the series of penetrating social satires on American life for which he is now remembered. In *Main Street* (1920) he pilloried the narrowmindedness of small-town life in the Midwest; *Babbitt* (1922) described the spiritual vulgarity of the business classes; *Arrowsmith* (1925) dealt with the fight of an honest physician against the inroads of commercialism; *Elmer Gantry* (1927) was an attack on a hypocritical evangelist. In 1930 Lewis became the first American to win the Nobel Prize for Literature. His later novels include *It Can't Happen Here* (1935), an attack on Nazism, *Cass Timberlane* (1945), and *Kingsblood Royal* (1947), a study of racial problems.

Ley, Robert (1890–1945). German politician. A chemist by profession, he joined the Nazi Party in 1924 and was notorious for his anti-Semitism in the Rhineland district. Ley was the head of the German labour front (1933–45) and had the tasks of suppressing the trade unions and recruiting slave labourers. He committed suicide during the Nuremberg trials.

Liang Qichao (1873–1929). Chinese teacher and publicist. He founded the first Chinese newspaper in Peking (1898) and was associated with Kang You-wei in the 'Hundred Days of Reform' and fled to Japan when the movement was crushed. He supported attempts to set up a constitutional monarchy but then collaborated with Sun Yat-sen and held several government administrative and diplomatic posts. He translated and popularised Darwin and Spencer, and became Mao Zedong's favourite author.

Liaquat Ali Khan (1895–1951). Pakistani politician. He was deputy leader under * Jinnah, of the Moslem League (1940–47), and in 1947 became Pakistan's first prime minister. He was assassinated.

Libby, Willard Frank (1908–1980). American chemist. He worked on the atomic bomb during World War II, then taught at Chicago and UCLA, winning the 1960 Nobel Prize in Chemistry for developing a technique using the radioactive isotope carbon-14 to date materials such as trees, parchments and fabrics. This has been an indispensable tool in archaeology and earth science.

Liddell, Henry George (1811–1898). English scholar. After a distinguished academic career, including nine years (1846–55) as headmaster of Westminster School, he returned, as dean, to Christ Church, Oxford, where he had been educated. *The Greek Lexicon*, which he undertook in collaboration with Robert Scott, has made his name familiar to generations of English schoolboys. His daughter, Alice, was the child for whom Lewis * Carroll wrote *Alice's Adventures in Wonderland* and *Through the Looking Glass*.

Liddell Hart, Sir Basil Henry (1895–1970). British military expert. He served in World War I and retired from the army (1927) to become military correspondent for *The Times* and the *Telegraph*. He was a believer in mechanized forces and a strategy of movement. His theories were closely studied in Germany and greatly influenced the organization of the rejuvenated German army under Hitler. He wrote many books on the history of strategy and tactics and on military leaders, e.g. *The Future of Infantry* (1933), *The German Generals Talk* (1948), *The Tanks* (1959).
Liddell Hart, B. H., *Memoirs*. 2 vols. 1965–1966

Lidgett, John Scott (1854–1953). English clergyman. He lead the successful campaign for the uniting of the separated branches of the Methodist Church in Britain and he was first president of the United Church (1932–33). Lidgett became vice-chancellor of London University (1930–32).

Lie, Trygve Halvdan (1896–1968). Norwegian lawyer, politician, and first secretary general of the United Nations (1946–53). After being legal adviser to the Norwegian trade unions he was minister of justice (1935–39) and then minister of trade. He became (1940) foreign minister and was a member of the Norwegian government in exile in World War II. He presided over the commission that drafted the UN Charter (1945). After resigning his UN post he wrote several books including *In the Cause of Peace* (1954), and later returned to Norwegian political life.

Liebermann, Max (1847–1935). German painter. He studied in Weimar and (1872–79) in Paris, where he came under the influence of Millet and Courbet. His early pictures were realistic, many of them genre scenes (e.g. *Women Plucking Geese*) but after moving to Berlin (1884) he painted from a much brighter palette and from 1890, under the influence of the French Impressionists, his subjects, e.g. bathing scenes on the Wannsee, became full of light. He became leader (1899) of the newly founded Berlin movement known as the *Sezession*.
Scheffler, K., *Max Liebermann*. 1953

Liebig, Justus, Baron von (1803–1873). German chemist. He first studied under * Gay-Lussac in Paris, and was later professor of chemistry at Giessen (1834–52) and Munich (1852–73). He was an important contributor to organic chemistry and its application to agriculture; he especially studied plant and animal nutrition processes. He also first isolated chloroform (1832).

Liebknecht, Karl (1871–1919). German politician. A member of the extremist left wing of the Social Democratic party in the Reichstag (1912–16), he assailed his party's acquiescent attitudes to World War I and was imprisoned (1916–18) for incitement to treason. He formed, with Rosa * Luxemburg, the Communist body known as Spartacists and in 1919 led their rising in Berlin. Arrested after its defeat, he was killed while being taken to prison.
Meyer, K. W., *Karl Liebknecht: Man without a Country*. 1957

Li Hung-Chang (1823–1901). Chinese minister and mandarin, born in Anhwei. He supported General * Gordon and the 'Ever Victorious Army' in suppressing the Tai-ping revolt (1864) and became Viceroy of Chihli (1870–94; 1900–01) under the Manchus. He tried to introduce reforms along more modest lines than those of the Meiji restoration in Japan but found the Manchu dynasty and the Confucian system were resistant to change. Chinese influence in Vietnam was replaced by France (1883–85) and China was beaten in the Japanese war (1894–95) and humiliated in the Boxer rebellion (1900–01). He tried to urge reform on the Dowager Empress * Tz'u-hsi. The first railway was built and the services were reformed during his term as prime minister (1895–98). He was often called 'the Asian Bismarck'.

Lij Yasu (1896–1935?) Emperor of Ethiopia (1913–16). In 1916 he was converted from Christianity to Islam, whereupon the Ethiopian nobles, led by his cousin the future * Haile Selassie, revolted. Lij Yasu was deposed and imprisoned.

Lilburne, John (*c.* 1614–1657). English political agitator. Having already been imprisoned as an anti-church pamphleteer, he rose during the Civil War to be a lieutenant-colonel in the parliamentary army, and there became leader of a Puritan and republican sect whose adherents were known as Levellers, since their demands included extreme egalitarian social reforms. Cromwell, whose arbitrary methods they had denounced, easily defeated a mutiny in 1649 and the movement and its leader who suffered temporary exile soon lost importance.
Gregg, P., *Free-Born John.* 1961

Lilienthal, David Eli (1899–1981). American administrator. He was a director (from 1931) and chairman (1941–46) of the Tennessee Valley Authority (T.V.A.) and later first chairman of the atomic energy commission (1946–50).

Lilienthal, Otto (1848–1896). German engineer, a pioneer in aeronautics. A keen student of the flight of birds, he designed successful gliders and he made more than 2,000 flights before he was killed in a glider accident.

Li Li-san (1896?–1967?). Chinese Communist politician. Educated in France, he founded a French branch of the Chinese Communist Party in 1921 and led the party in China from 1929 until the failure of his policy of trying to organize a proletarian revolution in the cities. He retreated to Moscow in 1931 and was imprisoned there as a Trotskyist in 1936, returning to China in 1945. He served under Mao as minister of labour (1949–54) and for a time was a political adviser to * Lin Biao until he confessed to 'leftist opportunism' in September 1956. While unseen by the public, his name remained on several important party committees until 1967.

Liliuokalani (1838–1917). Queen of Hawaii, the last sovereign and only reigning queen. In 1891 she succeeded her brother **David Kalakaua,** a moderately liberal ruler, and tried to impose an older style of autocratic monarchy. In 1893 she stepped down at the request of the Missionary Party, but appealed to the U.S.A. to reinstate her. When their efforts to do so failed she finally abdicated in 1895. When the U.S.A. proposed annexation in 1898 she opposed it bitterly and supported a nationalistic independence movement. She wrote the popular song 'Aloha Oe' in 1898.

Lillie, Beatrice (1898–). British revue artist and comedienne, born in Canada. She began as a straight ballad singer, with little success, and turned to comic singing in 1914. During the 1920s she achieved international fame as a singer and comedienne in revue.

Linacre, Thomas (1460?–1524). English humanist and physician. After becoming a fellow of All Souls, Oxford (1484), he travelled in Italy and felt the invigorating impact of the new learning upon continental scholarship. He obtained degrees in medicine at Padua and at Oxford. He became Greek tutor to Erasmus and More, and from 1509 was one of the royal physicians; he founded the Royal College of Physicians (1518) but abandoned the practice of medicine on becoming a priest (1520). He wrote a Latin grammar for Princess Mary (1523), followed by a much larger work on the same subject. He also made Latin translations from the Greek medical works of Galen and parts of Aristotle.

Lin Biao (1907–1971). Chinese soldier and politician. He was born in Hubei and joined the Socialist Youth League in 1925, the year in which he began his military career at the

Huangpu Academy. He took part in * Chiang Kai-shek's Nationalist uprising but, when the Communist and Socialist groups abandoned Chiang Kai-shek in 1927, he went with the Communists and joined * Mao Ze-dong in Jiangxi Province. He became a commander with Mao's Red Army in 1928 and a corps commander in 1934. As such he helped to lead the 'Long March' north when Jiangxi was over-run by Nationalist Forces.

In 1937–38 (when the civil war in China was halted in order to fight the Japanese) he served as a divisional commander. He was in Russia for medical treatment 1939–42. The civil war began again in 1946, when Lin Biao's victories in Manchuria were largely responsible for the fall of Chiang Kai-shek. In the People's Republic (established in 1949) he became vice premier of the State Council in 1954 and minister of defence in 1959. His reorganization of the army, combining military skill with political consciousness, was the main spur to the Great Cultural Revolution of 1966–69. He became vice-chairman of the party in 1969 and Mao's designated successor. However, in September 1971 he appears to have led an abortive coup against Mao and tried to reach Moscow, but his plane crashed in Mongolia.

Lincoln, Abraham (1809–1865). Sixteenth president of the U.S. (1861–65). He was born in a log cabin near Hidgenville, Kentucky, the son of **Thomas Lincoln** (1778–1851), a farmer of restless temperament from Virginia who moved on first to Indiana and, when Abraham was 21, to Illinois. In 1819, a year after his first wife's death, Thomas married Sarah Bush Johnston, a widow with three children who brought order into the household and introduced her stepson to the delights of reading with such books as *Pilgrim's Progress* and *Robinson Crusoe*, so providing the spur to a remarkable feat of self-education. Meanwhile Abraham helped the family income with odd jobs such as operating a ferry on the Ohio river. It was a river journey to New Orleans (1828) that gave the awkward, lanky youth, 6 ft 4 in in height, his first view of the greater world and the shock of seeing slavery in action. Soon afterwards he left home; he worked in New Salem, Illinois, as clerk, store-keeper and (in 1833) postmaster, and was captain of the local volunteers, becoming well known for his racy anecdotes and home-spun humour. He was elected to the Illinois state legislature in 1834, serving until 1841. His romance with Anne Rutledge who died of fever in August 1835 has passed into American folk-lore but rests on very slender foundations. In 1837, the year he moved to Springfield, he was admitted to the bar after having virtually taught himself law. His marriage (1842) to Mary Todd (1818–1882) to whom he was temperamentally unsuited probably led him to pursue his political interests more single-mindedly. The Lincolns had four sons: two died before 1865. Lincoln was a very successful advocate who acted in many railroad and criminal cases. He was a Whig member of the U.S. House of Representatives (1847–49) where he took an unpopular stand against the Mexican War and began to campaign against the extension of Negro slavery to the northwestern territories. His reputation was still largely local: he failed to secure appointment as U.S. Commissioner for Lands in Illinois (1849), declining an offer of the secretaryship of the Oregon Territory in the same year. In 1854 the Kansas-Nebraska Act, promoted by Stephen A. * Douglas, had abolished the 'Missouri Compromise' of 1820 which had prohibited slavery north of 36° 30′, and left the issue of slavery to the vote of settlers in each new state. When 'bleeding Kansas' became a battle-ground over slavery this led to the formation of the Republican Party (1854): Lincoln did not join until 1856 but soon became a leading member, although he failed to win nomination for the Senate or as vice-president. He was not an abolitionist – he saw slavery as an economic question which threatened the status of white labourers in the new states and territories of the west, and his moral objections to the 'peculiar institution' only developed later. In 1858 he campaigned for election against Douglas for U.S. Senator and in seven great debates (published in book form soon after) the rivals argued the implications of the slavery issue: he declared '"A house divided against itself cannot stand". I believe this government cannot endure permanently, half slave and half free'. He won the debates and the popular vote but lost the election which was decided by the Illinois legislature. At the Republican Convention held at Chicago in May 1860 he gained the presidential nomination on the third ballot, defeating his better known rivals W. H. * Seward and S. P. Chase. In November be won the election with 39 per cent of the votes because the Democrats were split between three candidates (Douglas, Breckinridge of

Kentucky, Bell of Tennessee). Six weeks later South Carolina led a secession from the Union of the Southern slave-owning states;' in February 1861 the Southern Confederacy was formed and in April an attack on the federal Fort Sumter at Charleston, S. C., sparked off the Civil War on the issue, not only of slavery but of the right to secede. (Many Southerners referred to the War of Southern Independence.) It was not until 1863 that a proclamation emancipating slaves (but only in the states in arms against the Union) was issued. Lincoln had to contend with a divided cabinet and blundering and miscalculation in the conduct of the war. But his firmness and wisdom enabled the weight of numbers, equipment and wealth, which lay with the North, to have decisive effect. But Lincoln saw beyond the struggle. Re-elected president by defeating General * McClellan (1864), in his second inaugural address he proposed a policy of conciliation: 'With malice toward none; with charity for all . . . let us strive on to finish the work we are in; to bind up the nation's wounds . . . to do all which may achieve a just and lasting peace . . . '. Only Lincoln, perhaps, was brave, generous and strong enough to give reality to his own vision and to him the opportunity was denied. Five days after Lee's surrender (April 1865) at Appomattox had brought the Civil War to an end, Lincoln was shot in Ford's Theatre, Washington, by the fanatical actor John Wilkes * Booth. It is perhaps true that no nobler, more discerning or humane man ever guided a great nation in a supreme crisis of its destiny. His words in the dedicatory speech at Gettysburg (1863), defining democracy as 'government of the people, by the people, and for the people', still point the way for the nations of the world. Superficially he seemed a simple and straightforward character – but closer examination reveals his great depth and complexity. Underlying his cheerful whimsy was a vein of deep mysticism and melancholy, intensified by his unhappy marriage. His law partner and biographer W. H. Herndon wrote, 'That man who thinks that Lincoln calmly gathered his robes about him, waiting for the people to call him, has a very erroneous knowledge of Lincoln. He was always calculating and planning ahead. His ambition was a little engine that knew no rest'. Not a great administrator but an outstanding moulder of public opinion, he was devout in the manner of an 18th-century deist and had little sympathy for the religion of the churches. Lincoln had a high-pitched metallic voice, awkward hands and movements, and his feet hurt. He left an estate of $90,000. American historians have voted him overwhelmingly as the greatest of all U.S. presidents. His son **Robert Todd Lincoln** (1843–1926) was secretary of war under Garfield and Arthur (1881–85), ambassador to London (1889–93) and president of the Pullman railway company (1897–1911).
Thomas, B. P., *Abraham Lincoln*. 1952

Lind, Jenny (Johanna Maria Lind-Goldschmidt) (1820–1887). Swedish soprano, long resident in Britain. Famed for her brilliant coloratura singing, she was known as the 'Swedish nightingale'; she performed until 1849 mainly in opera, and later in concerts and oratorios. She married the German conductor and composer Otto Goldschmidt; her kindness and generosity added to her popularity.

Lindbergh, Charles Augustus (1902–1974). American aviator. He achieved fame when (May 1927) he flew the monoplane *The Spirit of St Louis* on the first solo transatlantic flight from New York to Paris (3,610 miles, $33\frac{1}{2}$ hrs). Later Lindbergh worked on physiological experiments with Dr Alexis Carrel for some years. In 1938 he inspected European air forces and expressed his views about German military superiority; he favoured U.S. isolationism. His marriage to Anne Morrow, daughter of a U.S. senator, was clouded by tragedy when their infant son was kidnapped and murdered (1932). His wife was the author of several books, some about aviation, others of poetic prose and poetry.
Ross, W. S., *The Last Hero*. 1967

Lindemann, Frederick Alexander *see* **Cherwell, 1st Viscount**

Lindsay, Norman (1879–1969). Australian artist and author. He joined the *Sydney Bulletin* in 1901 and became its chief cartoonist. His style as an illustrator (e.g. of Boccaccio) resembled that of Aubrey Beardsley. His novels, e.g. *Redheap* (1931), and short stories have also been popular.

Linklater, Eric (1889–1974). Scottish author. The best known of his humorous novels include *Poet's Pub* (1929), *Juan in America* (1931), *Juan in China* (1937) and *Private Angelo* (1946).

Linnaeus, Carolus (Carl von Linné) (1707–1778). Swedish naturalist. He studied medicine at Lund and then at Uppsala, where he turned to natural history, and became assistant professor and, from 1742, professor of botany. He had already, during a 4,000-mile scientific journey in Lapland, discovered and classified many new plants. He evolved a system (published in his *Systema Naturae*, first drafted in 1735) of classifying plants by generic and specific names, with accurate definitions of the species, and applied this system also to zoology and mineralogy; although subsequently modified, it brought order to scientific nomenclature. After Linnaeus's death, his collection of books and plants passed to the care of a newly formed English biological association which came to be known as the Linnaean Society.
Blunt, W., *The Compleat Naturalist: A Life of Linnaeus*. 1971

Lin Piao – *see* **Lin Biao**

Linlithgow, John Adrian Louis Hope, 1st Marquess of (1860–1908). Scottish nobleman. As 7th Earl of Hopetoun, he was a youthful governor of Victoria 1889–95. Appointed first governor-general of the Commonwealth of Australia 1900–02, he blundered in nominating the New South Wales premier, W. J. Lyne, as first prime minister (1901) instead of Edmund * Barton, leader of the federation campaign. His son, **Victor Alexander John Hope**, 2nd Marquess of Linlithgow (1887–1952), was unexpectedly appointed viceroy of India 1936–43, facing growing civil disobedience, the war and Gandhi's 'Quit India' campaign (1942).

Linus (d. *c.* 79 A.D.). Bishop of Rome (i.e. Pope) after St Peter (from 67?). Some Protestants regard him as the first Roman bishop and he is thought to be the Linus referred to in II Timothy iv, 21.

Lin Yutang (1895–1976). Chinese author and teacher. Educated in the U.S. and Europe, he became a professor at the Peking National University and wrote many works on history and philosophy, including *My Country and My People* (1935), *The Wisdom of Confucius* (1938), *The Wisdom of China and India* (1942), and *The Importance of Understanding* (1960). He left China in 1936.

Lipatti, Dinu (Constantin) (1917–1950). Romanian pianist. He studied in Bucharest, then in Paris with * Cortot, * Boulanger and * Dukas. In his brief career he acquired a unique reputation as virtuoso and poetic interpreter. He died of leukemia, leaving a legacy of magnificent recordings.

Lipchitz, Jacques (1891–1973). French sculptor, born in Latvia of Polish–Jewish parentage. He worked in Paris from 1909 and was the first sculptor to produce Cubist sculpture. Later works were based on Biblical or mythological themes.

Li Po (Li T'ai-po) (*c.* 700–762). Chinese poet of the T'ang dynasty. Whenever he was not wandering in disgrace because of his dissipated life, Li Po appears to have lived at the emperor's court. His 2,000-odd surviving poems – seldom more than twelve lines long – treat of the pleasures of life, and are famous for their delicate imagery and lyrical quality. Li Po is said to have been drowned while trying (in a drunken state) to embrace the reflection of the moon. Arthur Waley translated many of his verses into English.

Lipperschey, Hans (*c.* 1570–1619). Dutch inventor. A spectacle maker in Middelburg, he is usually credited with inventing the first telescope (*c.* 1608), traditionally after inadvertently watching a child playing with a lens. * Galileo soon improved Lipperschey's crude instrument.

Lippi, Filippino (1457–1504). Italian painter, son of Filippo * Lippi. He was a pupil of Botticelli whose influence (as well as that of his father) is reflected in his works. He skilfully finished (1484–85) Masaccio's frescoes in the Brancacci Chapel, Florence, and most of his subsequent work was done in Florence or Rome. At his best he can be compared with the greatest, but some of his work is pretentious, fussy and even vulgar. Among his best known pictures are the *Madonna kneeling before the Child* (Uffizi, Florence) and the *Madonna and Child with St Jerome and St Francis* (National Gallery, London).
Scharf, A., *Filippino Lippi*. 1935

Lippi, Fra Filippo (*c.* 1406–1469). Italian painter. He was sent to a Carmelite monastery (1421) but in 1431 was allowed to leave the cloister. Some of the romantic incidents of his career are probably exaggerated or even invented. Whether he was captured by pirates is uncertain, but he seems to have been accused of forgery (1450) and to have abducted a nun who became the mother of Filippino * Lippi. His earlier work was strongly influenced by Masaccio, but later he freed himself and developed a more lively and dramatic style. Like Fra Angelico he painted mostly Madonnas and angels, but despite the radiance of their innocence he portrayed them with a closer approach to realism. His frescoes at Prato and Spoleto are considered his finest work.

Pittalugu, M., *Filippo Lippi*. 1949

Lippmann, Gabriel (1845–1921). French physicist. He held the chair of physics at the Sorbonne (from 1882) and in 1891 devised a method for photographing in colour, producing a faithful picture of the spectrum. He was awarded the 1908 Nobel Prize for Physics. Lippmann also predicted the nature of the 'piezo-electric' effect later discovered by Pierre Curie. During World War I he worked out a primitive type of radar which was used for detecting the presence of submarines.

Lippmann, Walter (1899–1974). American editor and author. His articles on political affairs, which appeared in the New York *Herald Tribune* (1931–66), were syndicated throughout the world. They were influential in the formation of public opinion in the U.S. He coined the phrase 'cold war' and acquired an enormous reputation as a pundit with a sound grasp of U.S. and European affairs, but showed little interest in the 'third world'.

Lipton, Sir Thomas Johnstone, 1st Bart (1850–1931). British merchant and sportsman, born of Irish parents in Glasgow. After spending five years in various jobs in America he returned to Glasgow and in 1871 opened his first small grocery. Gradually, he built up a chain of shops throughout Great Britain, supplied by the tea, coffee and cocoa plantations he had acquired overseas. As his wealth grew Lipton became a friend of Edward VII and a noted yachtsman; his five attempts (1899–1930) to win the America's Cup in *Shamrock* and its similarly named successors made him one of the best known sportsmen of his time.

Lister, Joseph Lister, 1st Baron (1827–1912). English surgeon. Born in Essex, he was the son of **Joseph Jackson Lister** (1786–1869) a Quaker wine merchant and amateur microscopist whose researches on the structure of red corpuscles gained him an F.R.S. The young Joseph studied medicine at London University and, having become M.D. and F.R.C.S. (1852), joined the famous Edinburgh surgeon, James Syme (whose daughter he married), as assistant. From 1855, when he was appointed assistant surgeon at the Edinburgh Royal Infirmary, and especially after his appointment as professor of surgery at Glasgow University (1860) and as surgeon to the Glasgow Royal Infirmary (1861), his reputation steadily mounted not only for his surgical skill but for his investigations, which shed important new light on the involuntary muscles of eye and skin, on the causes of inflammation, on pigmentation and on coagulation of the blood.

The major problem in surgery at the time was the high rate (25–60 per cent) of deaths from post-operative sepsis (partly a result of the introduction of anaesthesia, which had greatly increased the number of major operations performed, and had also lessened the need for speed). In the light of * Pasteur's discoveries Lister rejected the theory that the introduction of air was harmful; he concluded that the blood-poisoning and suppuration which occur in a wound surgically or otherwise inflicted are due to micro-organisms (loosely called germs). To destroy these he used a spray of carbolic acid with such success that in his wards the postoperative mortality rate fell almost at once from 43 to 15 per cent. He found means to overcome the difficulty that carbolic acid is itself a tissue-irritant. He also introduced catgut, which is absorbed by the body, for ligatures instead of silk or hemp, the removal of which often caused renewed haemorrhage.

He was greater as a teacher and innovator than surgeon, designed special operating tables and surgical tools, introduced the use of white operating costumes instead of street dress, emphasised *aseptic* (excluding germs) rather than *antiseptic* (killing germs) measures, and used drainage tubes for wounds and incisions. Lister's successes were followed by further distinctions; he became a professor of surgery at Edinburgh (1869) and at King's College, London (1879), and was president (1895–1900) of the Royal Society. A baronetcy was bestowed in 1883, in 1897 a peerage and in 1902 the O.M. The Lister Institute of

Preventive Medicine (founded 1903) preserves his name.
Godlee, R. J., *Lord Lister*. 1917

Liszt, Franz (Ferencz) (1811–1886). Hungarian composer and pianist. He was the son of a steward on Prince Esterházy's estate, studied music under his father, himself a keen amateur, and gave his first public performance as a pianist at the age of 9. With money provided by a group of Hungarian noblemen, he went to Vienna, where he studied under Czerny and Salieri, and won praise from Beethoven. From 1823 his tours, which included three visits to England, won him widespread admiration but after the death (1827) of his father, who had accompanied him, Liszt taught in Paris and came under the musical influence of Berlioz, Paganini (whose works he transcribed for the piano) and Chopin. His thought and way of life were affected by a friendship with the romantic novelist George * Sand, coincident (from 1833) with a love affair with the Comtesse d'Agoult, who bore him a son and two daughters, the younger of whom, Cosima, became the second wife of Richard Wagner. Liszt parted from his mistress in 1839 and spent the next eight years making concert tours throughout Europe, in the course of which he reached the pinnacle of his fame as a virtuoso pianist. In 1847 he met the Princess Caroline zu Sayn-Wittgenstein, with whom he lived until 1865, when he entered the Franciscan Order and was known as 'Abbé Liszt'. Liszt became conductor of the ducal opera at Weimar in 1848 and thereafter ceased to play the piano professionally; in his new post he was a generous patron of many artists, producing several operas by Wagner, whom he supported financially, and helping Berlioz and Schumann. After his resignation (1858) he spent his remaining years mainly in teaching at Weimar, Budapest and Rome. He composed about 1,300 works. Most of these are transcriptions; the finest of the 400 original compositions include the symphonic poems *Tasso, Orpheus, Mazeppa* and *Prometheus*, two Piano Concertos (1857 and 1863), the *Dante Symphony* (1856), the *Faust Symphony* (1853–56) and the Piano Sonata (1854). He wrote many 'Transcendental Studies' for piano, transcribed many songs and violin works as display pieces, and composed organ pieces and several major religious works including the oratorio *Christus* (1866).

Liszt was one of the most important pioneers of the Romantic school in music. His invention of the one-movement symphonic poem influenced composers such as Tchaikovsky and Richard Strauss, while Wagner learned from his principle of thematic transformation. His bold harmonic innovations affected composers even in the 20th century. Contemporary critics considered Liszt the greatest virtuoso pianist of all time: by giving a complete solo recital for the first time and playing a whole programme from memory he gave the concert pianist a status he had never before enjoyed; moreover, through his pupils, many of whom he taught without payment, his new pianoforte techniques shaped those of future generations.
Walker, A., *Liszt*. 1971

Littleton, Sir Thomas (1402–1481). English jurist. He was recorder of Coventry (1450), king's sergeant (from 1455) and a judge of common pleas (from 1466). He wrote a notable textbook on land tenure (originally in legal French), on which Sir Edward * Coke later published a famous commentary, *Coke upon Littleton* (1628).

Littlewood, Joan (1914–　). British theatrical producer. With her repertory company, founded in 1945 and established (1953) at the Theatre Royal, Stratford, in east London, she became known for advanced ideas and techniques which included much improvisation and, in the manner of * Brecht, audience participation. Among the young playwrights who achieved success under her auspices were Brendan Behan (*The Quare Fellow*) and Sheelagh Delaney (*A Taste of Honey*). *Oh What a Lovely War*, produced in 1963 after a short retirement, was an original and controversial treatment of World War I.

Litvinov, Maxim Maximovich (real name M. M. Vallakh) (1876–1951). Soviet diplomat. An early Bolshevik and friend of Lenin, he worked in London from 1907, married an English woman, and was appointed diplomatic agent to Britain after the 1917 Revolution. As deputy foreign commissar (1921–30; 1939–46) and foreign commissar (1930–39) he had little authority in directing foreign poicy, but attempted to make it more palatable. By leading Russia into the League of Nations (1934) and championing the cause of collective security, especially against Nazi

Germany, he made Soviet policies more generally acceptable.

Liu Shaoqi (*c.* 1898–1969?). Chinese Communist politician, born in Hunan. Little is known of his early life, but he apparently studied in Moscow, became a spy at Kuomintang headquarters and was an official in the Communist government of Jiangxi (1932–35). He suffered from tuberculosis and did not take part in the Long March – a significant omission. Regarded as one of the leading theoreticians of the Chinese Communist Party, he wrote the pamphlets *How to be a good Communist* and *On the Party Struggle*. He was Deputy Premier (1949–59) and succeeded Mao as President of China (1959–68) until his expulsion from the party and denunciation as 'China's Khrushchev . . . a lackey of imperialism, modern revisionism and Kuomintang reactionaries . . . a Renegade, Traitor and Scab'. Liu stood for a scientifically controlled urban industrial China against Mao's vision of 'revolutionary romanticism' and the spontaneity of the masses. His death was reported several times but in 1978 it was hinted that he had survived.

Liverpool, Robert Banks Jenkinson, 2nd Earl of (1770–1828). British politician. Son of Charles Jenkinson, leader of the 'King's friends', he entered parliament (1790) as a Tory. He was first given office (1793) by Pitt, and under his successor Addington was, as foreign secretary, responsible for the Treaty of Amiens (1802). In 1803 he was created Lord Hawkesbury. He became home secretary (1804); on * Pitt's death he declined to become prime minister but resumed his former post as home secretary, 1808–09. In 1808 he succeeded his father as Earl of Liverpool. In the most critical stage of the Peninsular War he was secretary of state for war and the colonies (1809–12) under Spencer-Perceval, after whose assassination he at last became prime minister. Despite only moderate ability he retained that office for nearly fifteen years, making full use of the brilliant attainments of Castlereagh, Canning and others, and keeping difficult teams together by tact, experience and common sense. He guided his country through the last stages of the Napoleonic wars, the period of repression that followed and its more liberal aftermath.

Livingstone, David (1813–1873). Scottish missionary and explorer. Born at Blantyre, Lanarkshire, he worked for fourteen years from the age of 10 in a local cotton mill. He read the missionary journals which his devout father received and also learnt Latin at an evening class. Having joined the London Missionary Society he was sent (1840) to the settlement in Bechuanaland created by Robert Moffatt, whose daughter Mary he later married. After some years he decided to explore, and carry the Christian message northwards. He discovered Lake Ngami (1849) and in 1852, having sent his wife and children to England, he started from Cape Town on a journey across Central Africa which ended (1856) at Quilimane at the mouth of the Zambezi River, on which he had made the thrilling discovery of the Victoria Falls (1855). On his return and after the publication of his *Missionary Travels* (1857), he was acclaimed by the public, but the London Missionary Society felt that he spent too much of his time in exploration; his next expedition (1858–64) was sponsored by the government. During this period he lost his wife and many helpers; he explored Lake Shirwa and much of the Lake Nyasa area, which he thought suitable for a mission and commercial centre, but the steamers sent out to him proved defective; and he found, to his indignant horror, that slave traders were using his discoveries to extend their activities. He published *The Zambezi and its Tributaries* (1865) on his return, and in March 1866 set out again, hoping to combine missionary work with settling the dispute concerning the sources of the Nile. He discovered Lakes Moero and Bangweulu (1867–68) and, after returning for rest to Ujiji, again struck westward and reached the River Lualaba, uncertain whether it was the Nile or, as it afterwards proved, the Congo. Meanwhile nothing had been heard of him at home until in 1871 he was discovered ('Dr Livingstone, I presume'), once more in Ujiji, by H. M. * Stanley at the head of a relief expedition. Together they proved that Lake Tanganyika had no northern outlet; but, though ill, Livingstone refused to return with Stanley until he had made one more attempt to solve the Nile problem. He went back to Lake Bangweulu, but having reached the village of Chief Chetambo, was found dead one morning by his followers, who despite all dangers brought his embalmed body to the coast whence it was taken for burial in Westminster Abbey.

Seaver, G., *David Livingstone: his Life and Letters*. 1957

Livy (Titus Livius) (59 B.C.–A.D. 17). Roman historian. He was born in Padua and became a member of the literary circle of the emperor Augustus. His greatest work, which took forty years, was a history of the Roman people in 142 books; thirty-five of these survive, Books 1–10 (to 293 B.C.) and Books 21–45 (218–167 B.C.), which include the struggle with Hannibal in the Second Punic War, Livy wrote with the patriotic purpose of glorifying Rome; he consulted the earlier annalists and the Greek historian Polybius but though he does not wilfully distort, he does not bring to bear any critical faculty. His narrative, however, seldom flags and his reputation as a writer has been maintained.
Walsh, P. G., *Livy: His Historical Aims and Methods*. 1961

Li Xiannian (1905–). Chinese Communist politician. He joined the CP in 1927, was a veteran of the Long March and served as vice premier and finance minister 1954–76. He was appointed president of the Peoples' Republic 1983– after the office had been left vacant for 15 years.

Li Yuan-Hung (1864–1928). Chinese general and politician. He was president of the Chinese Republic (1916–17; 1922–23).

Llewellyn, Richard (Richard Dafydd Vivian Llewellyn Lloyd) (1907–1983). Welsh novelist, born in Pembrokeshire, writing in English. His novel *How Green Was My Valley* (1939), a romantic chronicle of a nineteenth century mining community, was an immediate success. Later books, moderately successful, did not have the background of the mining valleys with their strong character and were not so popular.

Llewelyn (Llywelyn) **ap Iorwerth** (known as 'the Great') (died 1240). Welsh noble. By first consolidating his ancestral lordships in North Wales and then gradually extending his power over rival princes to the south, he did more than any other single man to create the possibility of a Welsh national state; moreover, by taking advantage of the difficulties of the English king John, whose daughter he married, he was able to stem further Anglo-Norman aggression.

Llewelyn ap Gruffydd (died 1282), trying to emulate his grandfather's achievements, overcame his brothers and exacted homage from other princes; he even obtained from Henry III, fully occupied with his problems in England, recognition (1267) as Prince of Wales, but he overreached himself by refusing homage on Edward I's accession (1272). War followed (1277) in which Llewelyn lost his title and all lands except Anglesey and Snowdonia. In 1281 he was goaded again into rebellion. His death in a skirmish in the following year facilitated Edward's conquest of Wales.

Lloyd, John Selwyn Brooke, Baron Selwyn-Lloyd (1904–1978). British Conservative politician. A barrister by profession, he rose to be a brigadier in World War II and in 1945 entered parliament. He served in a succession of Conservative governments from 1951: as Eden's foreign secretary (1955–60), he was the principal defender of the Suez campaign; he was chancellor of the exchequer (1960–62). He was speaker of the House of Commons 1971–76.

Lloyd George, David, 1st Earl Lloyd George of Dwyfor (1863–1945). British politician. He was born in Manchester but when his father, a schoolmaster, died, David, who was not yet 2, was brought up by his mother and her brother, Richard Lloyd, at Criccieth, Caernarvonshire, a place with which he remained associated for the rest of his life. He became a solicitor in 1880 and in 1890 won a by-election at Caernarvon Boroughs, a seat he held for fifty-five years. His Welsh nationalism and links with the dissenters cast him for the role of a Radical leader, and his reputation as pro-Boer in the South African War (1899–1902), though it brought him great unpopularity confirmed his position on the left wing of the Liberal party. When at last the Liberals came to power (1906), Campbell-Bannerman made him president of the Board of Trade (in which capacity he introduced the bill by which the Port of London was formed); but it was not until * Asquith succeeded as prime minister (1908) that Lloyd George got his great opportunity as chancellor of the exchequer. With the full support of his chief he was the main-spring of a great programme of social reform which laid the foundations of the later 'welfare state'; the best known measures were the Old Age Pensions Act (1908) and the National Insurance Act (1911). His budget of 1909, with its provision of a graded income tax, was rejected by the House of Lords and led to a constitutional crisis and the Parliament Act of 1911, which reduced the power of the Lords to delaying, but not blocking, legislation. Meanwhile, Lloyd George was taking a wider view of international affairs. His speech at the Mansion House (1911) provided a stern warning to Germany over the Agadir crisis, and from the moment that Germany invaded Belgium at the beginning of World War I there was no keener war leader than he. When Asquith's coalition government was formed (1915) he became minister of munitions and after Kitchener's death (1916) minister of war. For some time there had been a growing body of opinion that Asquith lacked the powers of leadership necessary in wartime and in December of that year he was overthrown, but the manoeuvres by which this was brought about, and which resulted in Lloyd George taking the place of the leader to whom he owed so much, created enduring bitterness and a rift in the Liberal party from the effects of which it never recovered. He remained prime minister from 1916–22.

Lloyd George proved an inspiring war leader and never failed in courage, though his relations with his military commanders were too often based on mutual distrust. When the war ended and the Treaty of Versailles, in the negotiation of which he fully displayed his nimbleness of mind, was duly signed, he was at the pinnacle of his power. After the 'khaki' election, however, which immediately followed the war, he was dependent on Conservative votes in parliament. In 1922 Tory MPs voted, by a majority, to withdraw from the coalition, and Lloyd George was forced to resign. His leading Conservative colleagues stood by him but Bonar * Law, whose illness had previously forced him to retire, returned to lead a Conservative administration. In opposition Lloyd George tried hard to re-unite the Liberal party but distrust of him was too deep for more than formal success. This pointed, indeed, to a fatal flaw in the character of a man so brilliant and otherwise so great. Where his emotions were involved, e.g. the compassion for the underdog that inspired his social reforms, or later his patriotic fervour, sincerity gave power to his eloquence, but there was nevertheless, in both his public and his private life, a total lack of principle, the consequences of which neither he himself nor those closest to him could escape. He married (1888) Margaret Owen of Criccieth, who became a GBE and died in 1941, and secondly (1943) Frances Louise Stevenson, his secretary for many years. He was a remarkable orator, whose eloquence on social issues, especially in earlier life, was probably sincere. He was known as 'the Welsh wizard'. He published *War Memoirs* (1933–36) and *The Truth about the Peace Treaty* (1938). He was awarded the OM in 1919 and an earldom in 1945. His second son **Gwilym** (1894–1967) was first elected as a Liberal M.P., then became a Conservative, rising to be home secretary and minister for Welsh Affairs (1954–57), becoming Viscount Tenby in 1957. His daughter **Lady Megan** (1902–1966) was a Liberal MP (1929–51), then transferred her allegiance and was elected as a Labour MP (1955–66).

Grigg, J., *Lloyd George*. 1973; 1978; 1984; incomplete

Lobachevsky, Nikolai Ivanóvich (1793–1856). Russian mathematician. Professor of mathematics at the University of Kazan (born 1814), he put forward, in *Principles of Geometry* (1829–30), the first complete system of non-Euclidean geometry.

Bonola, R., *Non-Euclidean Geometry*. Repr. 1955

Lobengula (died 1894). Chief (from 1870) of the Matabeles. A section of the Zulu people, escaping (*c.* 1820) from the tyranny of King Chaka, had subdued the Mashonas and settled in what became known as Matabeleland. Here Lobengula was chief when he was persuaded (1888) to grant Cecil * Rhodes mining rights in his territory (which later became part of Rhodesia). He died a fugitive after being defeated by white settlers with whom he came into conflict.

Locke, John (1632–1704). English philosopher. The son of a Somerset lawyer, he was educated at Westminster School and Christ Church, Oxford, where he was later a tutor, he also became interested in science and began to practise medicine. Through his practice he met Lord Ashley, later 1st Earl of Shaftesbury (with whose political ideas he was closely in tune), and became his secretary. After Shaftesbury's final disgrace (1682) Locke lived for five years in Holland. He returned to England after the accession of William and Mary and eventually became eminent as the provider of a philosophical basis for Whig doctrine. His greatest work, the starting point for empirical theories of philosophy, was his *Essay Concerning Human Understanding* (1690). All knowledge, he claims, derives from sense-experience. Every mind is initially a *tabula rasa* or blank slate upon which the lessons of sense-experience are subsequently written. This experience, in Locke's language, is of ideas, both those that result from sense-impressions or sense-data, and those introspective ones that refer to the operation of the mind. The world, indeed, which gives rise to these ideas does not, in fact, reflect them in every way, some ideas (those of primary qualities, e.g. solidity and extension) having counterparts in the actual world, but others (those of secondary qualities, e.g. colour and taste) being dependent on our own perceptual equipment and not existing in the actual world. Locke's theory of knowledge and metaphysics, as has been pointed out, is in essence the 17th-century scientific view. His political ideas, as set out particularly in his treatise *Civil Government* (1690), are similarly tied to his age. He argues that the ruler of a state is to be regarded as one party to a contract, the other party being those over whom he rules. If the ruler breaks his contract by not serving the good end of society he may be deposed. Locke's contemporary influence was enormous and he became known throughout Europe as the philosopher of freedom. From 1691 Locke, already in ill health, found a home and tranquillity (except for four years from 1696 as commissioner of the Board of Trade) with Sir Francis and Lady Masham at their house near Epping. His literary activity was mainly concerned with successive editions of his *Essay* and replies to criticism. In the anonymous *Reasonableness of Christianity* (1695) he brought to religion the same spirit of tolerance that he had already brought to politics, and sought to recall the churches to scriptural simplicity from their obsession with dogma.

Cranston, M. W., *John Locke: A Biography*. 1957

Lockhart, John Gibson (1794–1854). Scottish writer and editor. He was editor of the *Quarterly Review* (1825–53) and wrote several novels and biographies. His life of his father-in-law, Sir Walter Scott (7 volumes, 1837–38), is considered one of the greatest books of its kind.

Lockyer, Sir (Joseph) **Norman** (1836–1920). English astronomer and pioneer astrophysicist. Until 1875 he was an official in the War Office but also an enthusiastic amateur astronomer. He later became director of the Solar Physics Laboratory at the Royal College of Science. He pioneered the use of the spectroscope for analysing the chemical composition of the sun, and he gave the name 'helium' to the new element which was discovered (1868) in the solar spectrum as a result of observations made independently by Lockyer and Janssen. He founded (1869) and edited the scientific periodical *Nature*, was knighted in 1897 and in 1903 was president of the British Association.

Lodge, Henry Cabot (1850–1924). American politician. He took part in politics from 1878 and as a republican senator (1893–1924) became renowned for his isolationist views, and in particular for his fight against U.S. membership of the League of Nations. His grandson, **Henry Cabot Lodge, Jr** (1902–1985) was U.S. Senator from Massachusetts (1937–44; 1947–53), Ambassador to the United Nations (1953–60), Republican Vice-Presidential candidate (1960), and Ambassador to South Vietnam (1963–64; 1965–67). In 1969 he became U.S. delegate to the Paris peace talks.

Garraty, J. A., *Henry Cabot Lodge, a Biography*. 1953

Lodge, Sir Oliver Joseph (1851–1940). English physicist. After helping in his father's business as a boy, he gained an exhibition at the Royal College of Science and was later a demonstrator at University College, London. In 1881 he became professor of physics at Liverpool University and was principal of Birmingham University (1900–19). He did pioneer work on wireless telegraphy, and invented the coherer, a tube loosely filled with iron filings, which could be used as a simple detector for electromagnetic signals. Later he devised the system of radio 'tuning' which became generally used. In later life Lodge became a convinced spiritualist and wrote widely on the subject. He was knighted in 1902; among many academic and professional honours he was awarded (1887) the Rumford Medal of the Royal Society.

Lodge, Thomas (1558?–1625). English writer, son of a lord mayor of London. He is best

known as the author of a romance *Rosalynde* (1590), the source of Shakespeare's *As You Like It*, but he combined with a versatile literary career the study of law and medicine, freebooting expeditions to the Canaries (1588) and South America (1591). In addition to *Rosalynde* he wrote amorous sonnets, imitations of Horace, translations from Josephus, and historical romances. With Robert Greene he wrote the play *A Looking Glasse for London and England* (1594) which exposed contemporary vice and demanded reform.
Tenrey, E. A., *Thomas Lodge*. 1969

Loeb, Jacques (1859–1924). German-born biologist. His early work was concerned with the localization of the brain's visual functions, but in 1891 he went to America, where his principal studies were connected with instinct and free will, leading to the investigation of behaviour and regeneration in the lower animals. Among the best known of his experiments was one in which he achieved a kind of artificial parthenogenesis, initiating, by chemical means, the development of a sea urchin's unfertilized egg. From 1910 he worked with the Rockefeller Institute for Medical Research.

Loewi, Otto (1873–1961). German pharmacologist. Professor of pharmacology at Graz University (1909–38) and New York University (1940–45), he shared the Nobel Prize for physiology in 1936 with Sir Henry Dale for his discoveries on the chemical transmission of nerve impulses.

Lombard, Peter (*c*. 1100–1160). Italian theologian. He studied at Bologna and in Paris, where he eventually became bishop (1159). He was known as the 'master of sentences' from his four books, in which sentences culled from Augustine and other early Christian fathers were accompanied by comments from other religious writers, the whole providing a systematic discussion of various aspects of Christian faith.

Lombroso, Cesare (1836–1909). Italian criminologist. After studying mental diseases he became professor of forensic medicine at Turin. He evolved the theories, set out in his books *The Delinquent Man* (1876) and *The Man of Genius* (1888), that criminals belong to a distinct anthropological type and that genius springs from some form of physical or mental illness. His theories have been largely rejected, but his vast collection of anthropometric data on criminals was of the greatest value to * Bertillon and other criminologists. His observation that when in the course of interrogation a person tells a lie his blood pressure changes significantly anticipated the modern lie-detector.

Lomonosov, Mikhail Vasileivich (1711–1765). Russian scientist. Born in Archangel, the son of a shipowner, Lomonosov studied in many places, including Kiev, St Petersburg, Moscow, and Marburg (with Christian Wolff). He first showed most talents as a linguist and philosopher, but increasingly inclined towards chemistry and mathematics. Mining and mineralogy then caught his interest, and he studied at Freiberg under Henckel. Lomonosov returned to St Petersburg in 1741, and spent the rest of his life there. Much of his work in physics consisted of attempts to find, within the framework of corpuscularian matter theory, adequate theoretical explanations of heat, gravity and weight. He also performed mineralogical experiments, attempted to provide a theory of electricity, and kept tables of the weather. He was the first to lecture about science in Russian. He took keen interest in the mineral resources of Russia, wrote about Russian geography, and speculated on the Arctic regions. A man of great culture, he wrote a large body of poetry, much of it religious, and made compilations of Russian history and antiquities.
de Lur-Saluces, M., *Lomonossoff*. 1933

London, Jack (John Griffith) (1876–1916). American novelist. Born in San Francisco and largely self-educated, he gathered material for his highly successful adventure stories from his early experiences as (among other occupations) a sailor, a gold prospector and a tramp. His novels, several of which are set in Alaska, include *The Call of the Wild* (1903), *The Sea-Wolf* (1904) and *The Iron Heel* (1907). *Martin Eden* (1909) and *John Barleycorn* (1913) are autobiographical. He also wrote socialist tracts and never lost his revolutionary fervour. He committed suicide during a bout of depression. His works are widely read in the USSR.

Long, Crawford Williamson (1815–1878). American surgeon. In 1842 he used ether while removing a tumour from a boy's neck; but as this and subsequent cases were unpublicized for many years, he had no effect on the development of anaesthesia.

Long, Huey Pierce (1893–1935). American politician. A farmer's son, and a lawyer by profession, he gained control of the Democratic party machine in his native Louisiana and built it up to sustain his personal power. He was elected governor of the state in 1928 and from 1931 was a U.S. senator. His 'Share the Wealth' campaign, which he pursued with all the arts of a demagogue, gained him considerable popularity and the nickname 'the Kingfish', derived from his slogan 'Every man a king'. He also became famous for the prolonged 'filibusters' by which he held up the business of the Senate. In Louisiana his dictatorial rule, secured by intimidation and falsification of election results, ended only with his assassination. His son **Russell Billiu Long** (1918–) was U.S. Senator from 1948 (elected at the minimum constitutional age of 30). Huey's brother **Earl Kemp Long** (1895–1960) was Governor of Louisiana (1939–40; 1948–52; 1956–60). Towards the end of his third term he was abducted, taken to Texas and certified insane: however he soon escaped and resumed the governorship, claiming that he had been victimised by extreme segregationists.

Longfellow, Henry Wadsworth (1807–1882). American poet, born at Portland, Maine. He was educated at Bowdoin College, where he became (1829) professor of modern languages. From 1836 to 1854 he held a similar chair at Harvard University. Craigie House, his home, is preserved as a literary shrine.

Longfellow was at his best in long narrative poems, e.g. *Evangeline* (1847), *Hiawatha* (1855) – an Indian epic later set to music by Samuel Coleridge-Taylor – and *The Courtship of Miles Standish* (1863). *Tales of a Wayside Inn* (1863, with a further series in 1872) contained such poems as *Paul Revere's Ride*. In an earlier collection (1842) had appeared *The Wreck of the Hesperus, The Village Blacksmith* and *Excelsior*. Longfellow himself took special pride in the *Christmas* trilogy, an attempt to reconcile religion with modern thought; the first part, *The Golden Legend* (1851), is a particularly successful reconstruction of a medieval story. Longfellow's enormous reputation has declined; much of his poetry is now seen to be superficial, but the rhythms and cadences of his (if sometimes monotonous) verse are always pleasing.

Longfellow was twice widowed. His prose romance *Hyperion* (1836) expressed his grief at the death of his first wife; his second wife Frances Elizabeth Appleton, by whom he had six children, was tragically burned to death.

Wagenknecht, E. C., *Henry Wadsworth Longfellow: Portrait of an American Humanist*. 1966

Longman, Thomas (1699–1755). English bookseller and publisher, founder of Longmans. The son of a merchant from Bristol, he bought a bookseller's shop in Paternoster Row, London, in 1724. One of his best-known projects was a share in the publication of Samuel Johnson's *Dictionary*. He was followed by a nephew, also Thomas (1730–1797), and then by Thomas Norton Longman (1771–1842) and his son Thomas (1804–1879). The company published work by * Wordsworth, * Southey, * Coleridge, * Scott and * Macaulay.

Longstreet, James (1821–1904). American soldier. One of the leading confederate generals, he fought at the battle of Bull Run, Antietam, and Gettysburg. Later he supported the U.S. Government during the 'Reconstruction' period and became minister to Turkey (1880–81).

Lonsdale, Frederick (1881–1954). English playwright. The son of a tobacconist, he wrote witty and fast-moving comedies of upper class life, with a swift repartee in the tradition perfected later by Noel Coward. His best known plays are *The Last of Mrs Cheyney* (1925) and *On Approval* (1927).

Donaldson, F., *Freddy Lonsdale*. 1957

Lonsdale, Hugh Cecil Lowther, 5th Earl of (1857–1944). English sportsman. The Lonsdale Belts presented to British professional boxing champions since 1909 recall his patronage of the sport.

Loos, Adolf (1870–1933). Austrian architect, born at Brno. He studied in Germany and the U.S. and became an admirer of the American architect Louis Sullivan, returning to Europe to lead the attack on 'Art Nouveau' and excessive decoration, designing buildings of uncompromising severity. His ideas were published in his *Ornament and Crime* (1908). He pioneered the use of reinforced concrete in building municipal housing in Vienna. In 1923 he settled in Paris.

Loos, Anita (1888–1981). American writer. Her two books, *Gentlemen Prefer Blondes* (1925) and its sequel *But Gentlemen Marry Brunettes* (1928), with their new style of sophisticated humour, achieved tremendous success.

Lope de Vega *see* **Vega Carpio, Lope Félix de**

Lorca, Federico Garcia (1899–1936). Spanish poet. He was born near Granada, a fact of importance since much of his poetry was inspired by the cave-dwelling gypsies of that area. This is at once apparent in his *Poema de Cante Jondo* (1931), his first important work, and in *Romancero Gitano*, which fully established his fame; here he sees the endless fight of the gypsy against the world around him as a kind of symbolic struggle. The poem *Oda del Rey de Harlem* with its suggestion of jazz rhythms is one of several recalling a visit to America (1929–31). On his return he made a new reputation as a playwright with *Blood Wedding, Yerma* and *The House of Bernarda Alba*. Though he belonged to no political party Lorca was shot by the Falangists at the outbreak of the Civil War.
Brown, G. G., *A Literary History of Spain*. Vol. 6. 1972

Lord, Thomas (1755–1832). English sportsman born in Yorkshire; noted as the founder of Lord's cricket ground in St John's Wood, which has been the home of the Marylebone Cricket Club since 1787.

Lorentz, Hendrik Antoon (1853–1928). Dutch physicist. Professor of mathematical physics at Leyden from 1877, he was an authority on Planck's quantum theory, to which he made important contributions. His studies on the application to moving bodies of Maxwell's theory of electromagnetism helped to prepare the way for Einstein's formulation of the theory of relativity. Lorentz attempted to unify the mathematical treatment of light, electricity and magnetism; one of the results of his work was his explanation of the Zeeman effect. He shared with * Zeeman the Nobel Prize for Physics (1902).

Lorenzo the Magnificent *see* **Medici**

Lothair I (799?–855). Emperor (from 840) of the Franks, son of the emperor Louis I, and grandson of Charlemagne. He was made co-emperor in 817 but his father's arrangements in the following year for the partition of the Frankish empire between his sons after his death was followed by feuds and fighting between the members of his family which continued almost without intermission for the rest of the reign. Lothair's claim to be sole emperor on his father's death (840) was followed by renewed fighting only ended by the partition Treaty of Verdun (843), by which Lothair retained the imperial title but only that portion of imperial territory bounded by the rivers Rhine, Meuse, Saône and Rhône. This area, named Lotharingia after him and steadily reduced by the encroachment of its neighbours, was the Lorraine of future history. This partition in fact marked the end of the Carolingian empire.

Loti, Pierre (pseudonym of Louis Marie Julien Viaud) (1850–1923). French writer. He served as a naval officer for most of his adult life and spent some years in the South Seas, Indochina, Japan and China during the Boxer Rising; he retired as captain in 1910 but returned to fight in World War I. He wrote memoirs, descriptions of his voyages, and a number of very popular novels which are notable for their sensuous descriptions, their vein of romantic melancholy and their power of evoking the exotic places and peoples among whom he had lived so long. His novels include *Pêcheur d'Islande* (1886), *Madame Chrysanthème* (1887), *Ramuntcho* (1897) and *Désenchantées* (1906). He was a member of the Académie Française from 1891.

Lotka, Alfred James (1880–1949). American mathematician. After years of teaching and government work, he became an actuary with the Metropolitan Life Insurance Co. and published major studies on the mathematical implications of biological and societal change, e.g. ageing, population growth and distribution, and demographic movements.

Loubert, Emile François (1838–1929). French Radical politician. He served as a senator (1885–99), premier (1892), and president of the Senate (1896–99). His term as president of France (1899–1906) was marked by the 'Entente-Cordiale' with England (1904), the separation of Church and State (1905), and the conclusion of the Dreyfus case.

Louis (Kings of Bavaria) *see* **Ludwig I**

Louis I (known as 'the Pious') (778–840). Carolingian emperor (from 814). He was made co-emperor by his father Charlemagne in 813 and succeeded to the throne the following year. In 816 the pope went to Rheims and placed the crown upon his head, an assertion of papal supremacy which pointed to the controversies of the future. Louis's first acts were aimed at cleansing the court of profligacy; even his own sisters were sent to convents. As a ruler, however, he was quite inadequate and his attempts (818) to arrange for the partition of the empire after his death between his three sons, * Lothair, Pepin and Louis (the German) opened a period of strife which outlasted his reign. Matters became worse when his second wife, Judith, gave birth (823) to a son who was later known as * Charles the Bald; her ambitions to secure an appanage for her son, and her character, which enabled her to dominate her husband, introduced new and even more disruptive elements into the family struggle, which was still raging when Louis died, worn out and broken-hearted.

Louis VIII (1187–1226). King of France (from 1223), son and successor of * Philip II. Before he came to the throne he was offered the English crown by a group of barons who wished to depose King John. He arrived in England (1216) and was proclaimed king, but was forced to withdraw when John's death deprived him of baronial support. As king Louis took over the campaign against the Albigensian heretics and made important gains in Languedoc.

Louis IX (1214–1270). King of France (from 1226), canonized (1297) as St Louis. During his minority, his mother, Queen Blanche, widow of Louis VIII and a remarkable woman in her own right, was regent and brought the Albigensian war to an end, ensuring a tranquil opening to his period of personal rule. The first disturbance resulted from his investment (1241) of his brother with the government of Poitou. The feudatories rose in rebellion and invoked the aid of Henry III of England, who crossed to France in their support. Louis's victory enabled him to acquire the north of Aquitaine at English expense. In 1244 he fell ill, and was inspired by gratitude for his apparently miraculous recovery to lead the 6th Crusade (1248–54) against Egypt, where he was captured by the Saracens (1250). When ransomed, he spent two years in the Holy Land, to return (1254) on the death of his mother, whom he had left as regent. Back in France, Louis ruled with wisdom and firmness, improving the administration of law and taxes. Architecture flourished in his reign during which the cathedrals of Chartres, Amiens and Beauvais took shape and the beautiful Sainte Chapelle in Paris was built on his personal orders. He was regarded as the ideal medieval king, religious but not bigoted nor unduly subservient to the church, simple in habits, friendly and popular. In 1270 he embarked upon another crusade but the odd decision to go to Tunis exposed his army to a pestilence to which he himself succumbed.
Pernond, R., (ed.), *Le Siècle de Saint Louis*. 1970

Louis XI (1423–1483). King of France (1461–83). Even as a young man he showed his untrustworthy nature and was twice exiled for rebelling against his father, Charles VII. As king he saw as his main task the strengthening of the monarchy, a course which brought conflict with the great feudal lords. The chief of these was Charles the Bold, from 1467 Duke of Burgundy, and the struggle between these two and the combinations of power allied with each lasted throughout his reign. Louis's principal weapons – dissimulation, corruption, treachery and intrigue – account for his sinister reputation, but his cause was no more selfish and far less harmful to the country than that of his opponents. On one occasion, Louis, relying upon his wits to outmatch those of Charles, overreached himself: almost unguarded he visited (1468) the Duke at Peronne; his arrival coincided with the news of an uprising at Liège (then part of the Burgundian heritage), thought to be fomented by Louis. Confronted with Charles's rage, he barely escaped with his life after making the most humiliating concessions. The English Wars of the Roses provided another occasion for the rivals to take different sides, Louis favouring Lancaster, Burgundy York, but when the triumphant Yorkist, Edward IV, invaded France, Louis found a wedge to split the alliance and bribed him to depart. The final account was settled only when (1477)

Charles, embroiled with the Swiss and with René of Lorraine, both heavily subsidized by Louis, was defeated and killed. Louis seized the opportunity to annex the provinces of Burgundy and Artois, and Charles's heiress Mary managed to save her inheritance in the Netherlands only by marrying Maximilian of Austria. By the time of his death Louis, by contrivance or accident, had gained in addition Maine and Provence, Roussillon and Cerdagne, Anjou and Guienne, and had rid himself of nearly all the nobles who had taken sides against him. It was thus an immeasurably strengthened monarchy he left to his son, Charles VIII. His advisers (rather than ministers) were masters of corruption and intrigue, such as the barber Olivier le Dain, his notorious 'gossip' Tristan l'Hermite and the equally notorious Cardinal La Balue, who was caged on the walls of Loches for betraying his master's secrets. Louis's character is vividly presented in Scott's novel *Quentin Durward* (though the events are fictionalized).

Kendall, P. M., *Louis XI, the universal Spider*. 1970

Louis XII (1462–1515). King of France (from 1498). He succeeded his brother-in-law, Charles VIII, and his first aim was to retain Brittany by marrying Charles's widow Anne, who would otherwise inherit. The obstacle, his own wife Jeanne, daughter of Louis XI, was removed by dissolution of the marriage with the pope's connivance gained by the bestowal of a dukedom and a pension upon the latter's son Cesare * Borgia. Married to Anne, Louis pursued his dynastic claims in Italy; he succeeded in ousting Lodovico Sforza from Milan, and, by coming to a bargain with his rival, Ferdinand of Spain, was able to expel the king of Naples and share the spoils. The unnatural partners soon fell out and a catastrophic French defeat on the Garigliano led to the expulsion of the French. Louis's subsequent attempts to maintain and enlarge his hold on northern Italy led to a bewildering series of shifting alliances and even more confusing campaigns, but by the end of his reign French power in Italy was broken. Despite his disastrous foreign policy, Louis was popular in France and the country was prosperous. On the death (1514) of Anne, he married the English princess Mary, sister of Henry VIII, but almost immediately the accompanying festivities brought about the death of the ailing king.

Louis XIII (1601–1643). King of France (from 1610). He was the son and successor of Henry IV. His personal part in the events of his reign was small. Under the regency of his mother Marie de Médicis the early years saw the Huguenots in rebellion and the nobles competing for power. When he was 16 Louis tried to assert himself by entrusting power to his favourite, de Luynes, whose incompetence and unpopularity provoked renewed civil war; fortunately his death (1621) paved the way for the rise to power of * Richelieu who entered the council in 1622 and from 1624 exercised almost supreme power. The years of his rule were marked by France's skilful intervention in the Thirty Years War, the prelude to a long period of greatness. Not the least of Richelieu's triumphs was the reconciliation, after a long estrangement, of Louis and his wife Anne of Austria, with the result that in 1638 a dauphin, who was to be Louis XIV, was born.

Louis XIV (known as '*le Grand Monarque*' or '*le Roi Soleil*') (1638–1715). King of France (from 1643). Under the will of his father, Louis XIII, his mother Anne of Austria became regent for the boy king, but the substance of power she confided to Richelieu's successor Cardinal * Mazarin. The Thirty Years War, ended triumphantly for France by the Treaty of Westphalia (1648), was followed by the civil war known as the Fronde (after the *frondeurs* or stone-slingers in Paris street brawls). This began as a constitutional struggle by the Paris *parlement* and developed into an attempt to gain power by sections of the nobility, mortified at Mazarin's exclusion of them from the tasks and perquisites of office. The insurrection failed, helped though it was by Spain, which in 1659 came to terms cemented by Louis's marriage (1660) with Maria Theresa, daughter of Philip IV. It was thus a peaceful and united country over which, on the cardinal's death (1661), Louis began his personal rule. From the first he was determined that neither an over-powerful minister nor factions of the nobility should share in the function of government; he became his own prime minister and with unremitting industry and unfailing regularity presided over the daily meetings of his council. He chose his ministers carefully and they were seldom changed; the best known were * Colbert, who restored financial stability, encouraged industry and created a strong navy, and * Louvois, who was responsible for creating the strongest army in Europe. The main weakness of a system by which every aspect of government centred on the king and his small ministerial entourage was that as the king grew older the machinery of government also slowed down. Ministers were replaced by lesser men and the brilliant successes of the early years were later dimmed by setbacks.

Since the monarchy was the centre of power Louis proceeded to glamorize it; thus the great palace of Versailles and its lesser counterparts not only reflect the king's love of grandeur but were deliberately intended to impress men with the greatness of the monarchy and the glory of France. Thus he gathered round him at Versailles not only ministers, functionaries and courtiers but men of every kind of genius, e.g. Molière, Racine, Poussin, Lully, Pascal: this was indeed a 'Golden Age'.

Louis's foreign policy matched his grandiose taste in architecture. His first efforts to seize the Netherlands and the Franche Comté (on behalf of his wife after the death of Philip IV of Spain) were partially foiled; but as his diplomatic skill and the strength of the army grew so did his ambitions. He failed to subdue Holland in the long war which opened in 1672, but gained considerable successes over his Habsburg opponents, the emperor and the king of Spain, and the peace of Nijmegan (1678) left France with the Franche Comté and the frontier towns of Flanders, turned by * Vauban into almost impregnable fortresses. Louis at once used these gains as bases for further encroachments but Europe was now fully alarmed. William of Orange, infinitely strengthened when (1689) he became William III of Great Britain, patiently built up coalitions against Louis, resulting in the War of the League of Augsburg (1689–97), which marked a decline in French power, for though Louis lost only minor territories (chiefly Luxembourg) he had to disown James II and recognize William III.

France might have suffered only temporary exhaustion had not Louis been unable to resist the temptation to accept, on behalf of his grandson Philip, the legacy of Spain bequeathed by the childless Charles II. In the War of the Spanish Succession (1702–13), of which * Marlborough was the hero, he met with a series of defeats; he lost, thanks to diplomacy, little territory, and that mainly colonial, and Philip V continued to rule in Spain, but Louis's glory was irretrievably tarnished and the country's finances were in ruins.

During this long period of fighting, the Edict of Nantes, which gave security and privileges to the Huguenots, was repealed (1685). Louis's motives were partly religious but mainly sprang from his desire for administrative unity. The consequent emigration of many of the most skilled workers and merchants was a great loss. The king's private life seldom interfered with his task of kingship. His three important mistresses were Louise de la Vallière, Madame de Montespan, and Madame de Maintenon, the last of whom he secretly married after the death (1683) of Maria Theresa. In the latter part of his reign public misfortunes were matched by private grief. One after another members of the royal family died and it was his great-grandson who succeeded as Louis XV.

Louis XV (1710–1774). King of France (from 1715). When, at the age of 5, Louis succeeded his great-grandfather Louis XIV, France was ruled by a regency for the third successive time; but neither the regent, the indolent, dissolute Duke of Orléans, nor his creator, the infamous Dubois, showed talent for government; the main events were a useless war against Spain and the financial scandal caused by William * Law. Louis came of age in 1723 and in 1725 married Marie, daughter of Stanislas * Leszczynski, the deposed king of Poland. In 1726 the government came into the capable hands of Cardinal Fleury and there followed a long period of tranquillity (broken only by the War of Polish Succession), in which France was at last able to rebuild its shattered economy and regain prosperity. Fleury died soon after the opening of the War of Austrian Succession (1741–48), to which he had reluctantly assented. In this war France supported Frederick the Great of Prussia against Austria and England; but a change of alliances was organized by the Marquise de Pompadour, the mistress now in control of the king's will, and her chosen minister, the duc de Choiseul, and in the Seven Years War (1756–63) France was allied against England and Prussia. The expense of these two wars, in which Canada and many other colonial possessions were lost by France, accelerated the coming of the Revolution. At Versailles, the king, intelligent and good-natured, with his mistresses (la Pompadour, la du Barry and many more), lived amidst an extravagant court.

Gooch, G. P., *Louis XV: The Monarchy in Decline*. 1956

Louis XVI (1754–1793). King of France (from 1774). The grandson of his predecessor Louis XV, he was 20 when crowned and had already been married for four years to Marie Antoinette, youngest daughter of Maria Theresa. To her he remained devoted for the rest of his life, but her frivolity and extravagance and her ingrained opposition to political changes were constantly harmful to her husband's popularity.

The early part of the reign witnessed valiant efforts by ministers such as Turgot and Necker to sort out the financial tangles; but as soon as a serious attempt was made to tax the nobles and the privileged classes the court party, encouraged by the queen, forced their dismissal. Matters had become worse owing to France's intervention on the American side in the War of Independence for, though the result assuaged French pride after the losses of the Seven Years War, it increased the burden of debt and popularized the ideas of constitutional liberty favoured by the colonists. Financial controllers, Calonne and Brienne, failed in turn and at last in 1788 * Necker, recalled, demanded the summoning of the states-general. In May 1789, at Versailles, this body met for the first time since 1614. The tiers-état (third estate or commons), representing the merchant classes and more liberal elements, decided to sit as a 'national assembly', in which members of the other estates – the nobility and the clergy – could (though in fact few did) take part. This was the first revolutionary act. In July the Bastille was taken by the Paris mob and in October the royal family was brought by a triumphant crowd to Paris. Louis, well-meaning but slow-witted, became progressively less able to control events. In April 1781, * Mirabeau, who might have guided him to constitutional safety, died; in June the royal family, under the queen's influence, made a rather ludicrous attempt to flee the country but were caught at Varennes and ignominiously brought back. The king was soon at loggerheads with his legislative assembly; at the queen's instigation, he and she wrote secretly to their fellow monarchs for aid. By 1792 France was at war with Prussia and Austria. The king's part was suspected and in August the Tuileries palace was stormed by the mob. The royal family, which had taken refuge in the Assembly, was imprisoned. In September the Assembly became the republican National Convention. Louis was brought to trial, sentenced on 20 January and guillotined the following day – a brave, bewildered, unfortunate man.

His son, proclaimed by the monarchists as Louis XVII, was said to have died in prison in June 1795 at the age of 11, but there was enough uncertainty to enable several pretenders to come forward. Louis XVI's other child lived to be Duchess of Angoulême, a figure of some importance in the days of the revived monarchy after Napoleon's fall.

Padover, S. K., *Life and Death of Louis XVI*. Rev. ed. 1963

Louis XVIII (1755–1824). King of France (from 1814), younger brother of Louis XVI. During the Revolution he fled from France (1791). He spent the following years moving about Europe, maintaining links between the various groups of monarchist exiles, but it was not until Napoleon fell (1814) that he was able to return to France and take up his kingship. Napoleon's escape from Elba forced him to withdraw to Ghent but after Waterloo he resumed his throne. He himself hoped to achieve national conciliation by mild constitutional rule, but he had neither the strength of will nor the ability to prevent the government passing into the hands of the ultra-royalists, led by his brother, the future * Charles X.

Louis, Joe (Joseph Louis Barrow) (1914–1981). American Negro boxer. He won the world heavyweight boxing championship in 1937 and retained it until 1949, when he retired undefeated, having defended the title twenty-five times. He returned to the ring in 1950 and lost his title to Ezzard Charles. He then won eight more fights before being knocked out by Marciano in 1951.

Louis Philippe (1773–1850). King of the French (1830–48). Like his father, the Duke of * Orléans, who became known as Philippe Egalité, he supported the Revolution of 1789 during its early stages but later withdrew to live abroad, mainly in England. After Waterloo he was looked upon with suspicion by the restored Louis XVIII but was allowed to return (1817) to France, where he wisely remained in the background until, after the revolution of 1830, he was chosen king to

replace the deposed Charles X. Known as the 'citizen king' because of the informal bourgeois manners he adopted, he was at first very popular but he came to rely more and more on the conservative Guizot and the *nouveaux riches* of the upper bourgeoisie, a change in the national mood being shown by several attempts on the king's life. As hopes for reform by constitutional means dwindled, the republican strength increased, but the revolution of 1848 was unexpected, and resulted from an almost accidental chain of circumstances. Louis Philippe took refuge in England and the eventual heir to the revolution was * Napoleon III. The most important external event of the reign was the French conquest of Algeria.
Haworth, T. E. B., *Citizen King*. 1961

Louvois, François Michel le Tellier, Marquis de (1641–1691). French minister. He succeeded his father – from whom he learned how to organize an efficient army – as minister of war (1677–91) under Louis XIV. The introduction of better weapons, a quarter-master organization and a professional approach made the French army a highly effective force. Louvois aided and encouraged Louis in his aggressive ambitions.
André, L., *Michel le Tellier et Louvois*. 1942

Louÿs, Pierre (1870–1925). French writer, born in Ghent. He started (1891) a literary review, *La Conque*, which supported the Parnassian school. His lyric poetry (e.g. *Astarté*, 1891), based on Greek forms, is stylistically much admired. His novel *Aphrodite* (1896) was extremely successful.

Lovat, Simon Fraser, 11th Baron (*c.* 1665–1747). Scottish chieftain and intriguer. To escape the consequences of his failure to carry off the child heiress of the previous Lord Lovat, followed by his forcible marriage to her mother, he took refuge in France. He returned to Scotland as a double agent, helping to prepare for a Jacobite invasion but communicating the plans to the British government. After a period of imprisonment in France he was in Scotland again to offer his services to the government in the 1715 rising. In the later rising (1745) he sent his son to lead his clansmen in support of the Jacobites, while he himself stayed at home expressing loyalty to King George. After Prince Charles Edward's defeat at Culloden, Lovat was taken to London and beheaded – the last peer to suffer execution for treason.

Lovelace, Richard (1618–1658). English Cavalier poet, heir to large estates in Kent. In 1649, the year of Charles I's execution, he published the collection *Lucasta*, which includes his most famous poems: *To Althea, From Prison* ('Stone walls do not a prison make/Nor iron bars a cage') and *To Lucasta, going to the Wars* ('I could not love thee (Dear) so much,/Lov'd I not honour more'). Both reflect episodes in his career, the first a term of imprisonment (1642) after he had presented a 'Kentish Petition' to parliament; the second (probably) his departure to join the French army at Dunkirk, where he was wounded (1646). Back in England he was again in prison (1648–49) and died in poverty.
Weidhorn, M., *Richard Lovelace*. 1970

Lovell, Sir Bernard (1913–). English astronomer. As professor of radio astronomy at Manchester University (from 1951), he directed the Jodrell Bank (Cheshire) Radio Telescope, with which some of the principal advances in radio-astronomy have been made. The telescope has also provided valuable service in the tracking of space vehicles.
Lovell, B., *Story of Jodrell Bank*. 1968

Lovett, William (1800–1877). English Chartist. He went penniless (1821) to London, where he worked as a cabinet-maker and educated himself. In 1836 he became one of the founders and secretary of the London Working Men's Association, which put forward the People's Charter (with six points including manhood suffrage and voting by ballot), the starting point of the Chartist movement. It was incongruous that a man so averse to violence should spend a year in prison because of riots during the convention at Birmingham (1839), but it gave him time to write (with John Collins) *Chartism: a New Organization of the People* (1840). The stress on moral rather than political action alienated his more extreme colleagues and he gradually lost influence. In later life his main interest was in education for the working classes.

Low, Sir David (1891–1963). British cartoonist, born in New Zealand. He made his reputation in Sydney, and worked in England from 1919 as cartoonist for the London *Star* (1919–27), *Evening Standard* (1927–50), *Daily*

Herald (1950–53) and finally for the *Manchester Guardian*. Though his viewpoint was in general anti-Conservative (especially during the appeasement era), pretentious stupidity, rather than party affiliation, was his real target. Some of the most effective of his cartoons featured 'Colonel Blimp'.

Lowe, Sir Hudson (1769–1844). British soldier. He became a lieutenant general in the French wars and after Waterloo was made governor of St Helena. He was accused of undue severity towards Napoleon, especially by * O'Meara, the latter's surgeon, yet the truth seems to be that though his manner was stiff and though he refused to address his prisoner by his imperial rank, his conduct was formally correct. He was commander-in-chief in Ceylon (1824–31).

Lowell, James Russell (1819–1891). American writer, editor and diplomat. He came of a distinguished Massachusetts family and was grandson of **John Lowell** (1743–1802), a noted judge. J. R. Lowell himself abandoned law for a literary career; he was first editor (1857–61) of the *Atlantic Monthly* and joint editor (1864–72) of the *North American Review*, and had succeeded (1855) Longfellow as professor of modern languages at Harvard. Gradually his poetry, essays and critical studies won him a position as unchallenged king of the literary realm. His best known verse was contained in the satirical *Biglow Papers* (1848), written to oppose the Mexican War and the annexation of Texas. Of his later prose works *Among My Books* (1870–76) and *My Study Windows* (1871) are well known. Lowell's unique position was recognized by his appointments as minister to Spain (1877–80) and to Great Britain (1880–85).

Among other members of the great Lowell clan were: **Percival Lowell** (1855–1916), the astronomer after whom the observatory at Flagstaff, Arizona, is named, and who was one of the main proponents of the theory that Mars is inhabited; **Amy Lowell** (1874–1925) was a poetess who succeeded Ezra Pound as leader of the Imagist group: her collections of poems include *Pictures of the Floating World* (1919), and she also wrote critical essays and a biography of Keats (1925); **Robert Traill Spence Lowell** (1917–1977). American poet. Educated at Harvard, he became a Catholic in 1940 and served a short jail sentence during World War II as a conscientious objector. His first book of poetry was *The Land of Unlikeness* (1944) and he won the Pulitzer Prize for poetry with his second *Lord Weary's Castle* (1957). Other volumes include *The Mills of the Kavanaughs* (1952), *The Old Glory* (1964), *For the Union Dead* (1965) and *Near the Ocean* (1967). He became a leader in the anti-Vietnam movement in the U.S. In addition to his powerful and pessimistic verse, he published much-praised translations, e.g. of Aeschylus's *Prometheus Bound* (1967) and of Baudelaire.

Duberman, M., *James Russell Lowell*. 1967

Lowry, Laurence Stephen (1887–1976). English painter, born in Manchester. He slowly gained recognition for his spare, deceptively simple, industrial landscapes (peopled by matchstick figures) and seaside scenes and was elected R.A. in 1962.

Rohde, S., *Private View of L. S. Lowry*. 1979

Lowry, (Clarence) Malcolm (1909–1957). British novelist. Educated at Cambridge, he became an alcoholic whose life was marked by a long series of personal disasters and constant movement (Mexico, Canada, Haiti, the US). His masterpiece is *Under the Volcano* (1947), a richly textured account of cultural and personal tensions in Mexico in the 1930s. All his other works were published posthumously.

Loyola, St Ignatius (of) (Inigo de Onez Loyola) (1491/5–1556). Spanish-Basque founder of the Jesuit order. When fighting against the French he was wounded (1521) at the siege of Pamplona in Navarre. During his long convalescence he underwent a conversion and at Manresa spent a year (1522–23) in prayer, in religious austerity and in service to the sick and poor. There, too, he probably wrote most of *Spiritual Exercises*, a book of rules and meditations designed to overcome passions, make sin abhorrent and bring the soul closer to God. After making pilgrimages to Rome and to Jerusalem he studied for several years in Spanish universities and in Paris. In 1534 with a handful of companions, including * St Francis Xavier, Ignatius took vows which were the basis for the Society of Jesus but it was not until 1540, Ignatius having in the meantime (1537) been ordained priest, that the Society was officially established, with Ignatius as first general, by a Bull of Pope Paul III. With its founder's insistence on strict discipline and devotion, and complete obedience to the Pope, the order although not designed as such, became almost at once the spearhead of the Counter-Reformation; at all times it has concentrated on education and missionary work. Ignatius was canonized in 1622.

Dudon, P., *St. Ignace de Loyola.* 1949

Lübke, Heinrich (1894–1972). German statesman. He was not active in public life during the Third Reich and so was considered a suitable worker for the re-organized Christian Democrats of Westphalia after 1945. He served as a member of the North Rhine-Westphalia *Landtag* 1946–52, and was *Land* minister for food, agriculture and forestry from 1947. He sat in the Federal Bundestag 1949–50 and 1953–59; in 1953 Chancellor Adenauer appointed him federal minister for food, agriculture and forestry. He was elected President of the Federal Republic in 1959, was re-elected in 1964 and retired in 1969. He was noted for his tact and his ability to work constructively with Adenauer.

Lucan (Marcus Annaeus Lucanus) (39–65). Roman poet. A nephew of * Seneca, he was born in Spain and educated in Rome and Athens. He was a favourite of Nero for some years, but later joined in a conspiracy against him, was betrayed and committed suicide. His greatest work is the epic *Pharsalia* (10 books of which survive), describing the civil war between Caesar and Pompey. It is factually unreliable, being especially unfair to Caesar, and revels in gruesome details of the battle scenes; but it is eminently readable and was long popular.

Housman, A. E., *Lucan.* Repr. 1950

Lucan, George Charles Bingham, 3rd Earl of (1800–1888). British soldier. He was in command of the cavalry in the Crimean War when the jealous hostility between him and his subordinate, the Earl of Cardigan, commander of the Light Brigade, caused the misunderstanding that resulted in the famous and heroic charge up the 'valley of death' at Balaclava from which less than 300 out of nearly 700 men returned. He became a field marshal in 1887.

Luce, Henry Robinson (1898–1967). American journalist and publisher. In 1923 he founded and edited the weekly news magazine *Time*, followed by *Fortune* (1930), a business magazine, and *Life* (1936). His wife, **Clare Booth Luce** (1903–), wrote successful plays, e.g. *The Women* (1937) and was a Republican member of the House of Representatives (1943–47) and U.S. ambassador to Italy (1953–56).

Lucian (*c.* 120–*c.* 190). Greek satirical writer. He was born in Syria, and after being a rhetorician in Antioch, he travelled in Italy, Greece and Gaul. He was already about 40 when he studied in Athens and learned enough about philosophy to be able to satirize the dogmas of almost every school, including Christianity. Later he held a government post in Egypt. All his writing shows his talent for satire and parody. In verse there are mock-tragedies such as *Tragoedopodagra* (*Tragic Gout*); in prose such amusing works as *True History*, a parody of travellers' tales, which is said to have influenced Rabelais, Swift and Voltaire. He uses the savagery of his wit in *Dialogues of the Dead* and his powers of burlesque in *Dialogues of the Gods. Zeus Cross-examined* is a title which suggests its contents.

Allinson, F. G., *Lucian, Satirist and Artist.* 1926

Lucretius (Titus Lucretius Carus) (99–55 B.C.). Roman philosophical poet. Almost nothing is known of his life. His fame rests on his great work *De rerum natura* (*The Nature of the Universe*), one of the greatest of all didactic poems. It is an epic in six books, written in hexameters, and contains the clearest exposition that we have of the philosophic system of * Epicurus. Books 1 and 2 describe the atomic system of Democritus as adapted by Epicurus; Book 3 deals with the nature of the soul; Book 4 with the doctrine of perception and with sexual emotions; Book 5 is devoted to the theories of Epicurus concerning the evolutionary development of mankind, the earth and the universe; Book 6 covers a variety of topics and includes a description of the great plague of Athens. He denounced all forms of religion and superstition and considered that since death means annihilation it should present no terrors.

Lucullus, Lucius Licinius (*c.* 110–*c.* 57 B.C.). Roman soldier and administrator. Of noble birth, he first became prominent under Sulla in the war (88–85) against Mithridates, king of

Pontus in Asia Minor. His later campaigns (from 74) were also waged against Mithridates and his ally Tigranes of Armenia, but though Lucullus gained many successes and did much, by his financial measures, to restore prosperity to the Asian province, he was unable to bring the wars to a decisive conclusion before he was superseded by Pompey. After his return to Italy his great wealth enabled him to lead a life of luxury in Rome, where his gardens were renowned, or in his villas at Naples and Tusculum; the banquets for which he was famous were distinguished for the conversation as well as for their splendour.

Ludendorff, Erich (1865–1937). German soldier. Son of a railway official, he had a staff officer's training; the deployment of the armies at the outbreak of World War I was largely due to his planning. When the Russians achieved their early successes in East Prussia, Ludendorff and * Hindenburg, to whom he was appointed chief of staff, turned the tide by the Battle of Tannenberg and other victories. This partnership – Ludendorff, the brains, and Hindenburg, the character, personality and prestige – remained in being until the end of the war. Transferred to the Western Front in 1916, they restored the German line's stability, shaken by the Battle of the Somme, and planned the great offensive of spring 1918 which so nearly achieved a complete breakthrough. Ludendorff's defects of character showed, however, when the situation was once more reversed and the Allies again pressed forward; he lost his nerve and left it to Hindenburg, whom he despised, to bring the army back to Germany. After the defeat of Germany he fled to Sweden and did not return to Germany until 1920; eccentric and given to fantastic notions, he marched with Hitler's followers in their abortive Munich *Putsch* (1923), but founded an unsuccessful party of his own in 1925.
Goodspeed, D. J., *Ludendorff*. 1966

Ludwig I (1786–1868). King of Bavaria (1825–45). His artistic taste led him to enrich Munich, his capital, with many buildings and paintings. The cost of these extravagances, and the money Ludwig lavished upon the object of his infatuation, the dancer Lola Montez, exacerbated the indignation caused by his increasingly arbitrary rule; he was forced to abdicate (1848).

His tastes were shared in an exaggerated form and to the point of eventual madness, by **Ludwig II** (1845–1886) who succeeded to the throne in 1864. He was the patron of Wagner, for whom he built the theatre at Bayreuth. His mania for fantastic castles endowed Bavaria with buildings which have become tourist attractions. In 1886 he was declared insane, and shortly after was found drowned in Lake Stainberg.

Ludwig, Karl Friedrich Wilhelm (1816–1895). German physiologist. In 1865 he helped to establish a famous institute of physiology in Leipzig. Throughout his career Ludwig was embattled to establish physiology more securely as a science. He was a thorough teacher, who invented a number of important instruments, such as the mercurial blood pump (1859) and the stream gauge (1867) for measuring circulation. His own research concentrated mainly on the kidneys and their secretions. The problem of how secretion takes place through membranes was a lifelong preoccupation. The secretion of the saliva via the glandular nerves was another field in which he worked. The circulation of the blood also attracted his attention. He investigated how blood pressure related to heart activity, and the role of muscles in the fluidity of the blood.

Lugard, Frederick John Dealtry Lugard, 1st Baron (1858–1945). British colonial administrator. He had a varied career as soldier and administrator in India, Burma, the Sudan, Central and West Africa before he was appointed (1900) the first high commissioner of Northern Nigeria. Here he put into practice his principles of 'indirect rule' through native rulers and institutions, for which he became famous. He left Africa (1906) to become governor of Hong Kong (1907–12) but returned to govern North and South Nigeria (amalgamated 1914). His views are expressed in *The Dual Mandate in British Tropical Africa* (1922). His peerage was bestowed in 1928.
Perham, M., *Lugard, the Years of Authority*. 1960

Lukács, Georg (Gyorgy Szegedy von Lukács) (1885–1971). Hungarian philosopher and literary critic. The most influential of 20th century Marxist scholars, he revived interest in the Hegelian background of Marx's work and emphasised the concepts of 'alienation' and 'reification'. He took an active, but not always consistent, role in politics and served as minister of culture in two revolutionary governments (1919 and 1956). He was an advocate of 'cultural realism', opposing both Modernism and * Brecht, and appears as Naphta in Thomas * Mann's *The Magic Mountain*.

Luke, St (died *c.* 90 A.D.). Traditional author of the third Gospel and of the Acts of the Apostles. The only known facts of his life are contained in three passages in the epistles of St Paul, which describe him as a Gentile, a physician and a close associate of St Paul, and his companion in imprisonment in Rome.

The strong tradition that he was the author of the Gospel attributed to him and of the Acts dates from the late 2nd century and there seems little reason to dispute it. Critical examination of the texts suggests that the two books were almost certainly by one hand and it is clear that much of the Acts must have been written by someone in the closest touch with St Paul. The Gospel was probably written for Greek-speaking Christians at Antioch close to the siege and fall of Jerusalem (A.D. 70); it is clear that the author consulted St Mark's Gospel and had access, as did the author of St Matthew's Gospel, to the source known as 'Q'. Other sources must have also been available as there are discrepancies in detail and some incidents not found elsewhere. For example the incidents concerning the Virgin Mary are elaborated, and several women are mentioned who are not referred to elsewhere.

Lully, Jean Baptiste (Giovanni Battiste Lulli) (1632–1687). French composer, of Italian parentage. As a child he was taken to France and when his musical talents were discovered he was a scullion in the service of a cousin of the king. An appointment in the royal orchestra quickly followed and soon he was presiding over his own players and composing ballets (some of them as *divertissements* in Molière's plays) in which Louis XIV himself liked to dance. Both in ballet and in opera (from 1652) he so transformed the musical techniques as almost to create a new art, and he defined the form of the French overture. He also introduced female dancers to the stage. Among his fifteen operas are *Alceste* (1674), *Atys* (1676) and *Acis et Galathée* (1686). He died from blood poisoning resulting from striking his foot with a heavy baton while keeping time during a performance of his *Te Deum*.

Lully, Raymond (Ramón Lull) (1232/5–1315). Spanish theologian and mystic, born in Majorca. After a life of ease in his youth, he was converted by a vision and fired with the desire to convert all Moslems to Christianity. He became an Arabic scholar and also wrote *Ars Generalis sive Magna*, which was to be the intellectual instrument of his mission. Having spent some thirty years in travelling Europe in the hope of getting support for his plan, he himself made a direct attempt to convert the Moslems of Tunis (1292) and Bougie (1306). Imprisonment and banishment were the only results. In a third mission he was stoned, and died on shipboard in sight of his native Majorca. In *Llibre de Contemplació*, which reveals the mystical side of his complex personality, he was a pioneer in the use of the Catalan language for serious works of this kind.

Lumière, Louis Jean (1864–1948). French industrial chemist and pioneer photographer. With his brother **Auguste Lumière** (1862–1954) he constructed (1895) a practical motion-picture camera and a projector which incorporated what have since become the standard devices for photographing and projecting motion pictures.

Lumumba, Patrice (1925–1961). Congolese politician, born in the province of Kasai. He was a post-office clerk before setting up in business in Leopoldville. In 1958 he founded the Mouvement National Congolais, and when independence came (June 1960) he was the first prime minister of the Congo republic. His anti-Belgian extremism led to a breakdown of authority and by September he had lost control of the central government, though he still governed in Stanleyville, with communist support. In December he was arrested by troops sent by the central government and flown to Katanga, where he mysteriously died. Part of the University of Moscow – reserved for African students – has been named after him.

Lunacharski, Anatoli Vasilievich (1875–1933). Russian educationalist and communist politician. A brilliant orator and propagandist, he supported the Bolsheviks from 1903 and lived in Italy until the October Revolution of 1917 brought Lenin to power in Russia. He became commissar for education (1917–29) and introduced many important reforms in public education. He wrote 14 plays and much literary and artistic criticism.

Lunt, Alfred (1893–1977). American actor and producer. With his wife, Lynn * Fontanne, he appeared in many plays, e.g. *Amphitryon 38, Love in Idleness* etc., in the U.S.A. and Britain, and was also a successful producer.

Lupescu, Magda (1904?–1977). Mistress and (from 1947) wife of * Carol II of Rumania, whose exile she shared. She was given the title of Princess Helena.

Lurçat, Jean (1892–1966). French artist. His great contribution is as a tapestry designer, of striking designs and flamboyant colour which have given a new lease of life to the tapestry industry of France.

Luther, Martin (1483–1546). German Protestant leader. He was born in Eisleben, Saxony, of a modest family; after schooling in Magdeburg and Eisenach he went to Erfurt University, where he studied law. The death of a friend turned him towards religion; he became an Augustinian monk and was ordained priest (1507). In 1508 he moved to Wittenberg in Saxony to teach philosophy and theology at the university. On a mission to Rome (1511) he was shocked by the luxury and corruption of the papal court, but for several years he remained faithful to the church, attracting thousands by his lectures and sermons and working out a personal theology based on the Augustinian doctrines of faith and grace and the study of St Paul, rather than on the writings of Erasmus and the humanists.

The arrival (1517) of Tetzel, a Dominican friar sent by the archbishop of Mainz to raise money for the rebuilding of St Peter's, Rome, by the sale of indulgences (i.e. remission of the penalties of sin), a practice against which Luther had already preached, caused him to take the momentous step of fixing to the church door an announcement of ninety-five theses attacking the sale of indulgences. Luther refused to withdraw his theses before a papal legate at Augsburg (1518) and in disputations – especially in one with the theologian Johann Eck (1519) – he was goaded to take a more extreme position and even challenged the condemnation of Jan Huss as a heretic. Luther next published his address *To the Christian Nobility of Germany* (a call to resistance and reform), *The Liberty of a Christian Man* (on the doctrine of justification by faith alone, not by good works), and *The Babylonish Captivity of the Church* (on the Sacraments, especially rejecting transubstantiation). To these attacks on the church the Pope replied by a Bull of excommunication, which Luther burned publicly. An attempt at conciliation was made by the emperor * Charles V who summoned Luther, under safe conduct, to the Diet of Worms (1521), but Luther withdrew nothing ('Here I stand, I can do no other, so help me, God'). He was allowed to depart but, with the issue of an imperial ban, the Elector of Saxony placed him under protection in the Castle of Wartburg. He risked leaving his security (1522), however, as his deputies were unable to control the fast growing movement. Luther still hoped that separation from Rome would be only temporary but the issue of the *Augsburg Confession* (1530), mainly the work of * Melanchthon, and still the basic statement of Lutheran belief, was tantamount to creating a new church. Meanwhile in 1525 Luther had married (a decisive step for a former priest) Katharina von Bora, herself a former Cistercian nun, and she bore him 3 sons and 2 daughters. Their happy home became a meeting place for his friends and admirers.

The Peasants Revolt (1523–25) – partly the result of the example set by his own rebellion – and the ensuing violence, so shocked Luther that he urged its repression with extreme ferocity but the political result was that the Reformation ceased to be a largely popular movement and came to rely on the support of the princes. The compromise finally established by the religious peace of Augsburg (1555) – *cujus regio, ejus religio* (i.e. that the religion of the state should follow that of the ruler) – set a limit upon the extent of the Lutheran reformation. Luther was extremely intolerant of other Protestant groups: he despised the English reformers and Catholic moderates such as Erasmus, joined with the Catholic Bishop of Münster in suppressing the Anabaptists, and quarrelled bitterly with * Zwingli and * Carlstadt over the doctrine of the Lord's supper. He was deeply pessimistic, superstitious (firmly believing in demon possession) and anti-Jewish. He insisted that Scripture is 'the sole rule of faith alone', believing mankind to be totally depraved and vehemently rejecting reason.

Luther's greatest literary achievement was the translation of the Bible, started at the Wartburg and completed in 1532, but throughout his life he was engaged in writing and expanding his theories – controversies with such contrasting opponents as Henry VIII and Erasmus were innumerable – and his sermons, letters and theses all show the vigour and clarity of his mind.

Todd, J. M., *Martin Luther*. 1964

Lutoslawski, Witold (1913–). Polish composer. He was educated in Warsaw. His works include two symphonies, several concertos, compositions for films, theatre, radio and children's groups, and he received many international awards.

Lutuli (Luthuli), **Albert John** (1898–1967). South African (Zulu) chieftain and politician, born in Natal. The son of an African Christian missionary, he was educated by American missionaries at the Adams College and later taught there for 15 years. He was elected by tribal elders to succeed his uncle as Chief of the Abasemakholweni Zulu tribe at the Umvoti Mission Reserve (1935–52), until dismissed by the South African Government for refusing to resign as president-general of the African National Congress, an office he held (1952–67). He was arrested on a charge of treason in 1959 but released in 1960, although banned from leaving his village at Groutville without permission. He burned his pass in public after the police shot blacks at Sharpeville. Lutuli repeatedly urged that South Africa become a multi-racial society but adopted Gandhi's policy of passive resistance. He was awarded the 1960 Nobel Prize for Peace.

Lutyens, Sir Edwin Landseer (1869–1944). English architect. His earlier country houses, of which he built, enlarged or restored over forty between 1899 and 1909, showed the 'picturesque' influence of William Morris but later he turned with equal success to the Renaissance style. In 1908 he was architect to the Garden Suburb scheme in Hampstead, where he built the church and other buildings. His public buildings and especially the architectural scheme for New Delhi (the Viceroy's house and other official buildings) designed in collaboration (from 1912) with Sir Herbert Baker, revealed his talent for the grandiose. Other works included the Cenotaph in Whitehall, London (1918), the British Embassy at Washington (1926) and plans for the Roman Catholic Cathedral at Liverpool, for which he was acclaimed by some as the greatest English architect since Wren. Lutyens was president of the Royal Academy (1938–44) and received the O.M. (1942).

Hussey, C., *Sir Edwin Landseer Lutyens*. 1950

Luxembourg, François Henri de Montmorency-Bouteville, Duc de (1628–1695). French soldier. His aunt was the mother of the great Condé whom he supported against the crown in the wars of the Fronde. Subsequently pardoned by Louis XIV, he became one of his most brilliant generals and was in charge of the French armies in the Netherlands in 1672. He was made a marshal in 1675 but having quarrelled with the minister of war, Louvois, he was out of favour for twelve years. He then returned to achieve his most famous victories: over William III in Flanders in the Battles of Fleurus (1690), Steinkerk (1692) and Neerwinden (1693), none of which, however, was fully exploited.

Luxemburg, Rosa (1870–1919). German revolutionary leader, born in Russian Poland. She was imprisoned (1915–18) for opposing World War I, but after the German defeat she founded, with Karl * Liebknecht, the communist group known as Spartacists, whose revolt in January 1919 she organized. She was a brilliant orator and political writer and is regarded by communists as one of their great heroes. Both she and Liebknecht were murdered by officers who arrested them.

Nettl, J. P., *Rosa Luxemburg*. 1966

Lu Xun (real name Chou Shu-jen) (1881–1936). Chinese author. Trained as a physician, his sardonic and incisive short stories and essays, e.g. *The True Story of Ah Q* (1921) and *Call to Arms* (1923), were derisive of Chinese traditionalism and fatalism. He refused to join the Communist Party but was an active fellow traveller, hailed as a revolutionary hero by Mao Ze-dong. He is the most widely read author in modern China.

Lvov, Prince Georg Yevgenyevich (1861–1925). Russian statesman. A prominent member of the Duma (1905–17) of liberal views, he was prominent in developing a system of local government (zemstvo). As chairman of the all-Russian Union of zemstvos it devolved upon him to head the provisional government in the first months of the Russian Revolution (1917). His moderation and dislike of violence made him unsuited for a revolutionary situation and he resigned later in the year in favour of * Kerensky. When the Bolsheviks came to power he escaped to France.

Lyadov, Anatoly Konstantinovich (1855–1914). Russian composer. One of the most brilliant of Rimsky-Korsakov's pupils, he wrote a number of symphonic poems, national in spirit, including *The Enchanted Lake*, *Kikimora* and *Baba-Yaga*.

Lyautey, Louis Hubert Gonzalve (1854–1934). French soldier and administrator. He was the virtual creator of modern Morocco, where after earlier service in Indo-China and Madagascar he was resident-general almost continuously from 1912 to 1925. He had to contend for years with the leader of the Rifs, * Abd al Krim, whom he finally defeated. Elected to the French Academy 1912, he became Marshal of France in 1921.
Maurois, A., *Lyautey*. 1935

Lycurgus (?9th century B.C.). Spartan lawgiver. Traditionally he was the author of the rigid Social Code by which the Spartiate aristocracy was kept apart from the other inhabitants, and of the system of military education by which from the ages of 6 to 20 the strictest obedience, self-discipline and rigorous training were imposed on all Spartan boys. (These institutions almost certainly belong to a later date and the very existence of Lycurgus may be mythical.)

Lydgate, John (*c.* 1370–*c.* 1450). English poet, he was almost certainly born at and called after Lydgate in Suffolk, and was a monk of Bury St Edmunds. He produced long narrative poems, mostly adapted or translated, e.g. *Troy-Book* (from a Latin work), *The Falls of Princes* (from Boccaccio), *The Siege of Thebes* (intended to be a supplement to *The Canterbury Tales* by Chaucer, his acknowledged master), and a drearily prolix allegory *The Pilgrimage of Man* (translated from the French). The satirical *London Lickpenny*, a shorter poem, gives a lively picture of the contemporary scene.
Pearsall, D. A., *John Lydgate*. 1970

Lyell, Sir Charles, 1st Bart. (1797–1875). Scottish geologist. He was a barrister by profession but from 1827 devoted himself to geology. After investigatory tours in Europe (1824 and 1828–30), he published *Principles of Geology* (3 volumes, 1830–33), which had immense influence on the development of the science. Equally important was *The Geological Evidences of the Antiquity of Man* (1863) which gave unbiased support, from the evidence of a different science, to Darwin's evolutionary theories. Further publications (1845 and 1849) resulted from travels in North America. Lyell was briefly (1832–33) professor of geology at King's College, London, twice (1836 and 1850) president of the Geological Society and (1864) president of the British Association.

Lyly, John (1553–1606). English dramatist and novelist. His best known work is *Euphues*, a romantic 'novel' in two parts (1578 and 1580). It is written in an amusing but rather affected ('euphuistic') style, which Shakespeare both adopted and parodied in several of his plays. His comedies were mostly written for troupes of boy players and probably for this reason have more delicacy and a gentler wit than others of the time.

Lyons, Joseph Aloysius (1879–1939). Australian politician. He was born in Tasmania, the son of Irish immigrants, became a teacher, then a Tasmanian MP (1909–29) and premier of Tasmania 1923–28. Elected to the Commonwealth Parliament in 1929, he was postmaster-general and minister for works (1929–31) in the Labor government of J. H. * Scullin. He broke with Labor in 1931 following personal clashes and policy differences on methods of combatting the depression and formed the United Australia Party, serving as prime minister of Australia 1932–39. His wife, **Dame Enid Muriel Lyons** (1897–1981), was the first woman member of the Commonwealth Parliament (1943–51) and the first woman minister (1949–51).

Lysander (died 395 B.C.). Spartan leader. He won a crushing victory over the Athenian fleet at Aegospotami (405), and in 404 took Athens, thus ending the Peloponnesian War. By imposing oligarchic régimes in the Greek city states, he secured Spartan domination throughout Greece. He died fighting in Boeotia, which had become restive under the assertion of Spartan power.

Lysenko, Trofim Denisovich (1898–1976). Russian biologist. He claimed that his experiments showed that acquired characteristics could be inherited and bolstered his presentation with 'Marxist' argument and hoodwinked both Stalin and Khrushchev. His theory is at variance with the views of * Mendel, and it never found support outside the Soviet Union; even there it was discredited after 1953, with some revival 1957–64.
Joravsky, D., *The Lysenko Affair*. 1971

Lytton, Edward George Bulwer-Lytton, 1st Baron (1803–1873). English author and politician. He began writing novels when he was 23, and produced some thirty in all; they include *Eugene Aram* (1832), named after the schoolmaster murderer, and several – considered his best – on historical themes, e.g. *The Last Days of Pompeii* (1834), *The Last of the Barons* (1843). He also wrote plays and poetry, and combined this large literary output with a career as a politician. He was created a baronet (1837) and a peer (1859).

His only son, **Edward Robert Bulwer-Lytton, 1st Earl of Lytton** (1831–1891), was viceroy of India from 1876 to 1880, a period when the unpopular Afghan War led to the defeat of the Conservative government and his own resignation. He was also ambassador to Paris (1887–91) and wrote much lyrical poetry under the pen-name 'Owen Meredith'.

M

Mabuse (Gossaert), **Jan** (*c.* 1478–1533/5). Flemish painter. His early work was done in Antwerp where he became a master in 1503. A visit to Rome in 1508, though it has labelled him as a 'Flemish Romanist', had little effect on his style except perhaps in his use of light, the influence of Dürer (not only on his woodcuts and engravings) being much more apparent, e.g. the nudes *Hercules and Deianira* at Birmingham. This and *Neptune and Amphitrite* at Berlin may have been painted (1516–17) as part of a project by Philip, prince bishop of Utrecht, to decorate his castle of Souberg. The earlier *Adoration of the Kings* in the National Gallery, London, is more typically Flemish.

Macadam, John Loudon (1756–1836). Scottish engineer and road-maker. Born at Ayr, he went to New York at the age of 14 and returned to Britain in 1783 with a fortune made in commerce. From 1810 his interest in road-making became dominant and the building of experimental stretches of road absorbed most of his fortune. The method of surfacing called after him consisted of a layer, 6–10 inches thick, of shaped granite pieces, each of about 4 ounces, covered by gravel and rubble. In 1827 he received a government grant of £10,000 and was appointed surveyor-general of metropolitan roads.

McAdoo, William Gibbs (1863–1941). American politician. As U.S. secretary of the Treasury (1913–18) under President Wilson (whose daughter he married in 1914), he introduced the Federal Reserve system. Subsequently he became an unsuccessful contender for the Democratic nomination for president (1920 and 1924) and a U.S. Senator for California (1933–39).

MacArthur, Douglas (1880–1964). American soldier. He served as a young officer in the Philippines and as A.D.C. to his father, a military attaché in Japan. In World War I he won a brilliant reputation as a divisional commander, became superintendent of the West Point Military Academy (1919–22) and saw further service in the Philippines. For five years before retirement (1935) General MacArthur was US chief of staff. He was then appointed to prepare a scheme for the defence of the Philippines; when (1941) the Japanese attacked he was given command of the US forces in the Far East. Ironically, his scheme for defending the Philippines proved to be the occasion of the greatest American military defeat of all time. He fought skilful delaying actions at Bataan and Corregidor and was then sent to Australia as supreme Allied commander in the S.W. Pacific. Working in close conjunction with the US navy and Australian command, he checked the Japanese advance in New Guinea and devised the island-hopping campaign which led back by stages to the Philippines once more; he was preparing the final attack on Japan when the atom bombs on Hiroshima and Nagasaki ended the war. MacArthur accepted the surrender and showed wisdom and moderation while supervising the transformation of Japan into a democratic state. When South Korea was invaded from the north (1950), he became supreme commander of the UN armies which checked the onslaught and but for Chinese intervention would have gained a complete victory. His plan to break the stalemate by air attack upon the Chinese bases in Manchuria

was not accepted by President Truman, who recalled MacArthur and deprived him of his command (April 1951). MacArthur was given a hero's welcome when he returned to the US for the first time since 1935 but an attempt to launch him politically received little support and he withdrew into retirement. An impressive and dominating personality combined with long-sighted strategic perception and a mastery of the military art place him among history's greatest commanders.
Clayton James, D., *The Years of MacArthur*. 3 vols. 1970

Macarthur, John (1767–1834). Australian pioneer. Born in England near Plymouth, he joined the army and in 1789 was posted to the New South Wales Corps. By breeding sheep for wool rather than meat he pioneered the industry that has been an Australian mainstay.
Ellis, M. H., *John Macarthur*. 1955

Macaulay, Dame Rose (1881–1958). English novelist. She first won success with *Potterism* (1920); among the best known of her many novels were *Orphan Island* (1924) and, almost at the end of her life, *The Towers of Trebizond* (1956) for which she was awarded the James Tait Black Memorial Prize. Her astringent and ironic style gave much pleasure to connoisseurs. In 1958 she was made a D.B.E.

Macaulay, Thomas Babington Macaulay, 1st Baron (1800–1859). English historian, poet and politician. A precocious child with a prodigious memory, he abandoned law for literature and politics soon after leaving Cambridge. His essays began to appear in the *Edinburgh Review* in 1825; their pretext was always a recently published book but in reality they were Macaulay's own assessments of the subject. First collected in 1843 they give a magnificent impression of brilliance sustained over nearly twenty years; those on Chatham and Clive are among the best, that on Warren Hastings among the most unfair. As a Whig M.P. (1830–34, 1839–47 and 1852–56), Macaulay displayed his talent in parliament in oratory rather than debate. He went to India (1834) as legal adviser to the supreme council; there he wrote a famous 'minute' on education and played the leading part in drawing up a new criminal code. On his return he was secretary for war (1839–41) and paymaster general (1846–47). In 1848 appeared the first two volumes of his *History of England, from the Accession of James II*, which proved an immense popular success, and some 25,000 copies of the third and fourth volumes (1855) were sold in ten weeks. The work was uncompleted when he died. The period covered is that of James II and William III and the Whig bias is obvious; more important is the lack of imagination, which prevented him from recalling to life the people and events from the point of view of their period rather than of his own. Thus despite Macaulay's knowledge and research it can never be a great history; it has endured because few can resist the vigour and eloquence of the style and the narrative skill. *The Lays of Ancient Rome* (1842) which contains the poem on Horatius is still read.
Trevelyan, G. O., *The Life and Letters of Macaulay*. 1876

Macbeth (died 1057). King of Scotland (from 1040). The son of the ruler of Moray, he killed King Duncan, seized his throne and ruled until defeated and killed in battle by Duncan's son * Malcolm III. His reign seems to have been relatively prosperous. He is said to have made a pilgrimage to Rome (1150). Shakespeare's tragedy is based on the account in Holinshed's *Chronicle* but the characters are largely fictional.

Maccabaeus, Mattathias (died *c.* 166 B.C.). The founder of the Jewish Hasmonean dynasty, the first members of which were known as the Maccabees. Mattathias was a Jewish priest who led the revolt against King Antiochus of Syria. It is said that after rejecting all promises made to him to induce him to abandon his faith he himself killed the first Jew to approach the heathen altar. This was the signal for rebellion. Mattathias gathered an increasing number of followers in the wilderness whence they raided the towns and villages, attacked Syrians and reconverted Jews. After his death his son **Judas** (Judah) **Maccabaeus** took command, reconquered Jerusalem and purified the temple (165–164 B.C.). He made an alliance with the Romans but was killed in battle (160 B.C.). His brother **Jonathan,** who became high priest, was treacherously executed by the Syrians. Another brother, **Simon,** who also gained Roman recognition and support, completely re-established the independence of the nation (141 B.C.) and ruled with wisdom and justice until he was murdered by his son-in-law (135

B.C.). The Hasmonean dynasty was continued by Simon's son **Johanan Hyrcanus,** whose son Aristobulus took the title of King. Eventually it was superseded by the Idumaean dynasty to which * Herod the Great belonged.

MacCarthy, Sir Desmond (1878–1952). British writer and critic. He became literary editor of the *New Statesman* in 1920 after periods on *New Quarterly* and *Eye Witness.* He wrote much as a journalist, reviewer and critic, and broadcast frequently. He was knighted in 1951.
MacCarthy, D., *Memories.* 1953

McCarthy, Eugene Joseph (1916–). American politician, born in Minnesota. He studied for the priesthood, but became a social science teacher, first at high schools, then at colleges in Minnesota. He was a U.S. Congressman (1949–59) and a Senator from Minnesota (1959–71). He became closely identified with the political cause of Adlai Stevenson and was recognized as a witty and fastidious man with a distaste for the vulgarities of the political routine. In 1968 he campaigned against President Johnson's renomination and fought for the nomination against Hubert Humphrey and Robert Kennedy.

McCarthy, Joseph Raymond (1909–1957). American Republican politician. Senator for Wisconsin (1947–57), as chairman of a senatorial committee on subversion, his hectoring inquisitorial methods, hysteria-raising, and a technique of charging people with 'guilt by association' constituted a smear campaign which provoked mounting national and international criticism. In 1954 the Senate passed a vote of censure on him for breach of constitutional privilege and thereafter his influence rapidly declined. Truman described him as a 'pathological character assassin'.
Rorty, J. and Decker, M., *McCarthy and the Communists.* 1972

McCarthy, Justin (1830–1912). Irish journalist, politician and man of letters. From being a parliamentary reporter he rose to be editor of the *Morning Star* and later joined the *Daily News.* He was M.P. (1879–96) and became leader of the anti-Parnellites of the Irish Home Rule party. Of his historical works *A History of Our Own Time* (4 volumes, 1879–80) was the most important. *Dear Lady Disdain* (1875) is a typical example of his many novels; biographies include *George Sand* (1870) and *Sir Robert Peel* (1891). His best known work was *If I Were King* (1901), later staged as the musical *The Vagabond King.*

McCarthy, Mary (1912–). American novelist and critic. A satirist of the intellectual's attempts to come to terms with modern urban life and human relationships, she is best known for *Memories of a Catholic Girlhood* (1957), *The Groves of Academe* (1952) and *The Group* (1963), the last taken from her own education at Vassar College.

McClellan, George Brinton (1826–1885). American soldier. He served as an engineer in the Mexican War (1846–48) and in 1855 was sent as an observer to the Crimean War. He was recalled from retirement when the Civil War broke out (1861) to reorganize the army of the Potomac, of which he was made commander-in-chief. Government impatience forced a premature offensive directed towards Richmond, the Confederate capital; but he skilfully extricated himself and in 1862 fought a brilliant campaign to repulse a Confederate invasion of Maryland. He followed up his advantage by moving into Virginia but the pace was too slow to satisfy the impatient cabinet at Washington and he was dismissed. In the 1864 election he unsuccessfully opposed Lincoln for the presidency. He then became a railroad executive and governor of New Jersey (1877–81).

McClintock, Barbara (1902–). US geneticist. Educated at Cornell University, she devoted herself to plant breeding, working at the Cold Spring Harbour laboratory of the Carnegie Institute 1942– . Her decades of work on maize led to the identification of 'jumping genes', mobile elements in chromosomes which helped to explain mutability in hereditary traits in some plants. The importance of her research was not recognized until after the revolution in molecular biology promoted by F. H. C. * Crick and J. D. * Watson. She won the 1983 Nobel Prize for Medicine.

McCormack, John (1884–1945). Irish-born tenor. He sang in opera for a time but later specialized in the concert singing and recording of simple, sentimental songs. He became

an American citizen in 1919 and a papal count in 1928.
Strong, L. A. G., *John McCormack*. 1949

McCormick, Cyrus Hall (1809–1884). American inventor. He was the son of **Robert McCormick,** a Virginian farmer, who invented (1809) a successful but crude reaping machine. A greatly improved model was patented by young McCormick in 1839 and in 1848 he was able to arrange for the manufacture of a more advanced version in Chicago. It was exhibited at the Hyde Park Exhibition in London (1851) and when he was elected (1879) to the French Académie des Sciences McCormick was acclaimed as having done 'more for science than any living man'. Under the presidency of his son and namesake (1859–1936) his firm became the International Harvester Company, one of the greatest firms in the U.S.A.
McCormick, C. H., *The Century of the Reaper*. 1931

McCullers, Carson (1917–1967). American novelist. She achieved consistent success with her novels several of which were filmed, including *The Heart is a Lonely Hunter* (1940), *The Member of the Wedding* (1946) and *Clock without Hands* (1961).

McDiarmid, Hugh (pen-name of Christopher Murray Grieve) (1892–1978). Scottish nationalist leader and poet. Written mostly in Scots the best of his poems give lyrical expression to his feelings for his native land. He became both a Communist and a Scots Nationalist, and his later works, reflecting his social and philosophical concerns which could not be adequately written in Scots, were published in English.
Buthlay, K., *Hugh MacDiarmid*. 1964

Macdonald, Flora (1722–1790). Scottish heroine. After the defeat at Culloden had ended the Jacobite rising (1745–46) she aided the escape of Charles Edward * Stuart (Bonnie Prince Charlie) by bringing him, disguised as her maid, safely to the island of Skye. Captured ten days later, she was released in 1747. She married a few years later and after living in America for a time with her husband (also a Macdonald) she eventually died in Skye leaving many descendants to hand down the story.
Linklater, E., *The Prince in the Heather*. 1965

MacDonald, George (1824–1905). Scottish writer. He is best remembered for his fairy stories, e.g. *The Princess and the Goblin* (1872) and *The Princess and Curdie* (1883), which became classics of their kind. He also wrote novels, including *David Elginbrod* (1862) and *Robert Falconer* (1868), in which a vein of mysticism blends with realistic and sympathetic portrayals of country people. His poems have charm but sometimes suffer from sentimentality.

MacDonald, J(ames) Ramsay (1866–1937). British Labour politician. Born at Lossiemouth, he was educated at the village school where he later became a pupil teacher. He went to London (1884) but after a breakdown of health abandoned his studies in science for political journalism. He was a determined propagandist for socialism; he joined the Independent Labour party (1893) and became secretary (1900) of the newly formed Labour party. Elected MP for Leicester (1906), he became leader of the party in the House of Commons (1911). His pacifist attitude during World War I, however, cost him the leadership of the party in 1914 and his seat in parliament in the 1918 election.

After the 1922 election he was again MP and chosen to lead the parliamentary opposition of 140 Labour members. In a snap election (December 1923) called by * Baldwin on the protection issue, Labour and the Liberals won a majority for free trade: MacDonald became the first Labour prime minister (and foreign minister) January–November 1924, with Liberal support. The * Zinoviev letter incident led to press allegations of Communist influence on Labour. The Liberals withdrew their support and the elections of November 1924 resulted in a Conservative victory. (The heaviest losers were the Liberals.) MacDonald was Labour prime minister again 1929–31 but lacked any clear idea of how to deal with the Great Depression and his chancellor, * Snowden, was ultracautious, rejecting * Mosley's alternative program. When a majority of Labour ministers refused to accept Budget cuts, MacDonald resigned, then formed a National Government (1931–35) with the Conservatives and some Liberals, and was expelled from the Labour Party. He came under increasing Conservative domination and in declining health, became vague and forgetful. He served as Lord President of the

Council under Baldwin 1935–37 and died on a holiday voyage to South America.
Marquand, D., *Ramsay MacDonald.* 1976

Macdonald, Sir John Alexander (1815–1891). First prime minister of the dominion of Canada. He was born in Glasgow and emigrated with his parents to Canada when he was 5. In 1844 he became a Conservative member of the legislature of Upper Canada and from 1847 held cabinet offices; from 1856, as leader of the government, he played the principal part in the discussions and negotiations leading to the formation of the dominion of Canada, of which he became (1867) first prime minister. One of the great benefits he conferred upon Canada was the encouragement of the building of railways, which he looked upon as a means of linking the widely separated areas of the vast country and so providing a secure basis for unity. He also introduced tariff protection of industry. Except for a short interval (1873–78) after his government had been defeated on charges of financial irregularity, he retained his office for the rest of his life.
Creighton, D., *Sir John A. Macdonald.* 2 Vols. 1952–1955

MacDonald, Malcolm John (1901–1981). British administrator. Son of the former prime minister James Ramsay * MacDonald, he sat in Parliament as an MP (National Government) and was appointed colonial secretary in 1935 and again 1938–40. In 1941 he went to Canada as high commissioner and stayed until 1946, when he became governor-general of Malaya and Borneo. In 1948 he was appointed commissioner-general for south east Asia, and became British high commissioner in India (1955–60). From 1963–65 he served in Kenya, first as governor-general (1963–64) and then as high commissioner. He was awarded the OM in 1969.

McDougall, William (1871–1938). British psychologist. After holding academic appointments in England he went to America, where he was professor of psychology at Harvard (1920–27) and then at Duke University, N. Carolina. His Championship of Lamarck's theory of biological inheritance was based on laboratory work, which though valuable was not conclusive: his reputation is mainly based on his *Introduction to Social Psychology* (1908). He also became interested in psychical research or 'parapsychology' as he termed it.

MacDowell, Edward Alexander (1861–1908). American composer and pianist. He studied in Germany where, with the encouragement of Liszt, he stayed until 1888. He was the first professor of music at Columbia University (1896–1904) and his work provided a refreshing contrast to the academicism then in fashion. The best of his music is to be found in comparatively short piano pieces, e.g. *Woodland Sketches, Sea Pieces, To a Wild Rose* etc., in which his sense of harmony and his lyrical gift could be given full play. He also wrote two Piano Concertos; his *Indian Suite* for orchestra showed his sensitivity to folk themes.

McEwen, Sir John (1900–1980). Australian politician and farmer. A soldier settler after World War I, he entered parliament in 1934 and became leader of the Country Party (1958–71) and deputy prime minister. Long recognized as the strong man of the commonwealth government, he was prime minister briefly (December 1967–January 1968) on the disappearance of Harold * Holt and became a CH in 1969.

McGovern, George Stanley (1922–). US politician. The son of a clergyman, he was trained for the Methodist ministry, served as a bomber pilot in World War II, then took a PhD in history. He served as a congressman from South Dakota 1957–61, foundation director of the Peace Corps 1961–62 and US Senator 1963–81. In 1972 he won the Democratic nomination for president as an anti-war candidate, losing heavily to Richard * Nixon.

McGuffey, William Holmes (1800–1873). American educator, born in Pennsylvania. He taught in Ohio after picking up a sporadic education and was appointed to the chair of mental and moral philosophy at the university of Virginia in 1845. His name was immortalised by his five volumes known as *McGuffey's Eclectic Readers* (1836–44) of which 122,000,000 copies were sold between 1836 and 1920. These became the model for school readers throughout the world and had an extraordinary influence in the U.S., especially where reading material was scarce. They contained extracts from the Bible,

Shakespeare, Dr Johnson and Dickens and proclaimed a philosophy based on Alexander Hamilton's concept of democracy, Calvin's theology, and Blackstone's view of property.

Mach, Ernst (1838–1916). Austrian physicist and philosopher. He was professor of mathematics at Graz (1864–67), of physics at Prague (1867–95) and at Vienna (1895–1901). He investigated the behaviour of projectiles at high speeds and thus provided valuable data on the phenomena of supersonic flight; the ratio of the airspeed on an aircraft to the speed of sound was named, after him, the 'Mach number'. His theoretical studies of mechanics and thermodynamics led him to a reassessment of Newtonian concepts and influenced Einstein in his development of the relativity theory. As a philosopher Mach held that the laws of physics should be divorced from metaphysical speculation and should be pure descriptions of observed data. In that sense he can be described as a phenomenalist.

Machiavelli, Niccolò (1469–1527). Italian diplomat and writer. Born in Florence, the son of a lawyer, he held office as secretary of the Council of Ten in charge of Florentine foreign affairs from 1498 until 1512 when the republic fell and the Medici regained power. During those years he was sent on diplomatic missions to Louis XII of France and the emperor Maximilian, and while in attendance upon Cesare* Borgia was able to study the practices and motives of the ambitious prince. Back in Florence he organized the citizen army which captured Pisa (1509). When the Medici returned Machiavelli was imprisoned for a time and had to retire from public life. He occupied himself by writing not only to instruct but to amuse as in the lively, satirical and bawdy play *La Mandragola*. His serious works include *Discourses on Livy, The Art of War*, a *History of Florence* and the book upon which his fame and his sinister reputation rest, *Il Principe* (*The Prince*; 1513), largely based on his observations of Cesare Borgia. Originally dedicated to the younger Lorenzo de' Medici (1492–1519), grandson of 'the Magnificent', by whom Machiavelli may have hoped that Italy might be saved from foreign intervention and united under a single rule, the book was not actually published until 1532. *Il Principe* set out to give precise and practical information concerning the qualities and practices necessary for a prince to achieve these worthy ends in a corrupt age. It is thus a work not of moral precept but of practical instruction, and in so far as it is held to reflect Machiavelli's personal character it defames him. The view of Spinoza and Rousseau is now generally accepted: that *The Prince* is a savage satire against tyranny by a man of profoundly pessimistic insight who recognized that the methods he detested (and scrupulously refrained from in his own life) were likelier to be successful than policies of restraint and conciliation. He bases the argument of *The Prince* on the contention that in an age where everyone is self-seeking the only hope lies in a single ruler whose sole interest would be his people's welfare; but that in order to obtain that position and achieve that aim it is necessary to rule despotically, to cast all moral principles aside and concentrate entirely on the end in view. The cynical dictum 'the end justifies the means' had long been approved in practice: the odium that was attached to Machiavelli's name was due to the fact that he seemed to give it theoretical justification. In Elizabethan and Jacobean England, Machiavelli and their perception of machiavellian politics were so execrated that his works and possibly his name (Old Nick) became synonymous with the devil. Machiavelli returned to public life in his later years and performed some services for Pope Clement VII.

Hale, J. R., *Machiavelli and Renaissance History*.

Mackail, John William (1859–1945). Scottish classicist. Originally a civil servant with the board of education (1884–1919), Mackail became professor of poetry at Oxford (1901–11) and professor of ancient literature at the Royal Academy (1924–45). He wrote a life of William Morris, translated the *Odyssey* and the *Aeneid*, and edited anthologies. He was awarded the O.M. in 1935. His daughter was the novelist Angela * Thirkell.

McKell, Sir William John (1891–1985). Australian Labor politician. Originally a boiler-maker, he entered the New South Wales State parliament in 1917, studied law and became a KC and was premier (1941–47), retiring on his controversial appointment as the second native-born governor-general of Australia (1947–53).

Mackensen, Anton Ludwig Friedrich August von (1849–1945). German field-marshal. He was one of the most successful commanders of World War I. He drove the Russians from Galicia and overran Serbia (1915), and conquered Rumania (1916–17).

Mackenzie, Sir Alexander (1764–1820). Scottish explorer of Canada. His interest in a fur-trading company provided opportunities for journeys of exploration. He reached (1789) the mouth of what is now called the Mackenzie River and (1792–93) made the first expedition across the Rockies to the Pacific. He was knighted in 1802.

Mackenzie, Alexander (1822–1892). Canadian politician. Born in Scotland, he emigrated (1842) to Canada and led the Liberal opposition to Sir John * Macdonald in the dominion parliament from 1867 until 1873, when he became the first Liberal prime minister. Defeated in 1878 he headed the opposition for two more years.

Mackenzie, Sir Compton (1883–1972). British novelist, son of Edward Compton, the actor, and brother of Fay Compton, the actress. His earlier novels, included *The Passionate Elopement* (1911), *Carnival* (1912), *Sinister Street* (1913–14) – perhaps his greatest achievement – and *Sylvia Scarlett* (1918). During World War I he served in the Gallipoli campaign and in military intelligence in the Near East. In 1923 he founded *The Gramophone*, the first magazine of its type, and remained its editor until 1961. An ardent Scottish nationalist, he was elected as Lord Rector of Glasgow University (1931–34) and in 1938 published *The Windsor Tapestry*, a study of Edward VIII's abdication. *Four Kinds of Love* (1937–45), a somewhat pretentious novel about the inter-war years, followed. After World War II he became occupied with humorous trifles, e.g. *Whisky Galore* (1947), which were turned into successful films. Mackenzie, knighted in 1952, also succeeded as poet, essayist, journalist, and television lecturer. His autobiography *My Life and Times* appeared, in eight 'octaves' between 1963–69.

Mackenzie, William Lyon (1795–1861). Canadian politician. An emigrant from Scotland (1820) he founded in York (now Toronto) a newspaper, the *Colonial Advocate*, in which he demanded self-government for Upper Canada. Several times he was elected to the assembly and as often expelled. In 1837 he led an armed rebellion, which proved a complete fiasco. MacKenzie took refuge in the U.S.A. but returned (1849) under an amnesty and served (1850–58) in the legislature. His main achievement was to bring home to the British government the urgency of constitutional reform. His grandson was W. L. Mackenzie * King.

Mackinder, Sir Halford John (1861–1947). English geographer. His appointment as reader in geography at Oxford (1887) marked the belated achievement of academic status by that subject in England. Later he was director of the London School of Economics (1903–08) and professor of geography at London University (1908–15); he was also a Conservative M.P. (1910–22). His methods of using geographical considerations in the study of political questions were borrowed by Karl * Haushofer, associated with the Eurasian 'Heartland' theory. MacKinder's books include *Britain and the British Seas* (1902). In 1899 he made the first recorded ascent of Mt Kenya.

Gilbert, E. W., *Sir Halford MacKinder 1861–1947*. 1963

McKinley, William (1843–1901). Twenty-fifth president of the U.S. (1897–1901). He served in the Union army during the Civil War, studied law and was first elected as a Republican representative to Congress in 1876. Throughout his political career he supported the high tariff policy of the industrialists and it was with their support that, after serving as governor of Ohio (1892–96), he was elected president (1896), defeating William Jennings * Bryan. His administration was made notable by the successful Spanish American War by which the U.S.A. gained control of the Philippines and Cuba. McKinley, re-elected (1900) as a champion of imperialism, was shot by an anarchist in the first year of his second administration and died shortly afterwards.

Leech, M. K., *In the Days of McKinley*. 1959

Mackintosh, Charles Rennie (1868–1928). Scottish architect, a poineer of the 'Modern Movement'. Discarding historicism in his buildings, Mackintosh became the centre of a group in Glasgow which, having aroused Continental interest, was asked to exhibit in Vienna (1901) and Turin (1902). His Glasgow

School of Art (1896–99), designed when he was 28, is, with its great area of window glass, remarkably advanced for its time.
Howarth, T., *Charles Rennie Mackintosh and the Modern Movement*. 1952

MacLeish, Archibald (1892–1982). American poet and dramatist. In his earlier lyrics, e.g. *Frescoes for Mr Rockefeller's City* (1933), he showed himself to be a social critic but is better known for his long poem, *Conquistador*, which won the Pulitzer Prize (1932). He lived in France for many years and his poetry was deeply influenced by Eliot and Pound. As Librarian of Congres 1939–44 and assistant secretary of state 1944–45, he took an active role in preparing war propaganda and was a founder of UNESCO (1945). He won a second Pulitzer Prize (1953) for his *Collected Poems*; his play, *J. B.*, a religious parable based on the story of Job, was produced in 1958 and won a third Pulitzer.

Macleod, Fiona *see* **Sharp, William**

MacLeod, George Fielden, Baron MacLeod (1895–). Scottish clergyman. Educated at Oxford, he won an M.C. in World War I and in 1938 founded the Iona Community which attracted international interest. He was Moderator of the Church of Scotland 1957–58. A notable broadcaster and preacher, he called himself 'an uncomfortable socialist and a reluctant pacifist'. He inherited a baronetcy but refused to use the title.

Macleod, Iain Norman (1913–1970). English Conservative politician. He was leader of the House of Commons (1961–63). When * Macmillan resigned (1963) he declined to serve under * Home and became editor of the *Spectator* (1963–65). On * Heath's succession as party leader Macleod was chosen for the shadow cabinet and soon afterwards resigned his editorship. He was chancellor of the exchequer in the 1970 Conservative government for four weeks before his death.

McLuhan, (Herbert) Marshall (1911–1980). Canadian media analyst, born in Alberta. Educated at Manitoba and Cambridge, he taught in the U.S. and Canada, directing the centre for culture and technology at Toronto University (1964–76). His work examined the impact of mass media and advertising. His controversial books included *The Mechanical Bride* (1951), *The Gutenberg Galaxy* (1962) *Understanding Media* (1964), *The Medium is the Massage* (1967), *War and Peace in the Global Village* (1968), *Take Today: Executive as Drop-Out* (1972) and *City as Classroom* (1977). He defined 'media' as extensions of human capacity and included electric light, vehicles and tools as well as newspapers, telephones, radio and television. He described television as a 'cool' (low definition) medium aimed at group (or family) viewing, favouring low intensity subjects or events (e.g. J. F. Kennedy not R. M. Nixon, sports programmes not war reportage, variety not intensity), while 'hot' (high definition) media such as film or radio were better suited for propaganda aimed at an isolated individual. He argued that 'the medium is the message (or massage)' – i.e. communication environments influence total response rather than specific programme content: literacy or television availability alters life style more than individual books or programmes.

MacMahon, Marie Edmé Patrice Maurice de (1808–1893). French marshal of Irish descent. He served in the Crimea, was made a marshal and given the title Duke of Magenta for his part in the North Italian campaign (1859), and was governor general of Algeria (1864–70). In the Franco-Prussian War he commanded the 1st Army Corps and was captured at Sedan. In 1871 he suppressed the revolt of the Paris commune. In 1873, though a monarchist, he was elected president of the republic but in 1879 resigned.

McMahon, Sir William (1908–). Australian Liberal politician. A solicitor, he was a Member of the Commonwealth Parliament 1949–82, Treasurer 1966–69, Foreign Minister 1969–71 and Prime Minister 1971–72, until his defeat by E. G. * Whitlam.

Macmillan, Daniel (1813–1896), and **Alexander** (1818–1896). British publishers. Sons of a Scottish crofter, they made their way to England, had a small bookshop in Aldersgate St, London, and borrowed money to buy a larger one in Cambridge (1844). Here they came to know Charles Kingsley, Dean Stanley and many others who were to be useful to them later on. Among their most successful early publications were Kingsley's *Westward Ho!*, an *Tom Brown's Schooldays* by Thomas Hughes. A London branch (1858) was the next step to success and soon the firm was based in London.

Macmillan, (Maurice) Harold, 1st Earl of Stockton (1894–). British Conservative politician. A member of the famous publishing family, he was educated at Eton and Oxford, and served with distinction in World War I. From 1924 he combined membership of parliament with publishing and gained a considerable reputation as an independent-minded politician with much sympathy for the unemployed. During World War II he held several offices, including that of minister resident in North Africa (1942–45), which brought him the friendship of General de Gaulle. He was active in opposition after the war until the return of Churchill's Conservative administration gave him the opportunity as minister of housing (1951–54) to fulfil a party promise to bring up the total number of houses built to 300,000 per annum. He was minister of defence (1954–55), then succeeded Anthony Eden as foreign minister (April–December 1955) and became chancellor of the exchequer (1955–57). When Eden resigned because of ill-health (January 1957), Macmillan was appointed prime minister. He served until October 1963, the longest single term since Asquith. He rapidly restored the party image blurred by the Egyptian adventure and for a time (marked by his election triumph in 1959) seemed to have the magic touch which brought prosperity and success. But as the years went by the administration seemed to lose momentum and the government's popularity began to decline. Macmillan drastically reconstructed his government in 1962; in January 1963 de Gaulle's refusal to admit Britain to the Common Market and later the Profumo affair were further embarrassments. Macmillan's future resolved itself when in October illness forced him to resign. He was succeeded by Lord * Home (Sir Alec Douglas-Home). Macmillan married (1920) Lady Dorothy Cavendish, daughter of the 9th Duke of Devonshire. He was awarded an O.M. in 1976 and received an earldom on his 90th birthday. His son, **Maurice Victor Macmillan** (1921–84) followed his father into publishing and into politics as a Conservative M.P. and was chief secretary of the treasury (1970–72), secretary of state for employment (1972–73) and Paymaster-General (1973–74).
Hutchinson, G., *The Last Edwardian at No 10*. 1980. Macmillan, H., *Autobiography in 5 volumes*, 1967–1973.

McMillan, Margaret (1861–1931). Scottish educationist. Her special interest and that of her sister Rachel was the physical education and health of schoolchildren. She founded several clinics on her own initiative, that at Deptford (1910) being the largest. To protect the health of younger children she founded (1910) the first nursery school. She became a C.H. in 1927.
Mansbridge, A., *Margaret McMillan, Prophet and Pioneer*. 1932

MacNamara, Robert Strange (1916–). American administrator. After serving in World War II with the air force he joined the Ford Motor Company (1945) and became its managing director (1955) and president (1960). He served as U.S. secretary of defence (1961–68) under Kennedy and Johnson. Originally a 'hawk' on Vietnam, he became disillusioned. He was president of the World Bank (1969–80).

McNaughton, Andrew George Latta (1897–1966). Canadian soldier. After serving as an artillery officer in World War I he was Canada's chief of the general staff (1921–35) and commanded the Canadian forces in Britain in World War II. He was minister of defence (1944–45), Canadian delegate to the UN (1946–49) and chairman of the Atomic Energy Control Board (1946–48). He was appointed C.H. in 1946.

MacNeice, Louis (1907–1963). Poet and critic born in northern Ireland. He was a classics lecturer in Birmingham and London, and in 1941 he began to work for the B.B.C. As a poet in the 1930s he was associated by critics with Auden, Day Lewis and Spender but his astringent style is strongly individual and his imagery is such that he can liken the lights of approaching buses at night to the glory of chrysanthemums. His *Collected Poems* appeared in 1949. Apart from translations from the Greek and critical works, e.g. on Yeats (1941), he wrote *Christopher Columbus* (1944), one of several radio plays, and *The Dark Tower* (1947), a collection of scripts.
Press, J., *Louis MacNeice*. 1966

McPherson, Aimée Semple (née Aimée Elizabeth Kennedy) (1890–1944). American

Christian revivalist. She toured in the U.S.A., China and Europe, and was the founder of the Angelus Temple in Los Angeles (1921) and the International Church of the Four Square Gospel (1930), which soon had several hundred churches in America and many missions abroad. Three marriages and a claim to have been kidnapped (1926) were among the episodes of her colourful career.
McPherson, A. S., *The Story of My Life*. 1951

Macpherson, James (1736–1796). Scottish author. From 1760 he published a series of poems which he claimed were translations from the Gaelic of a bard named Ossian. These poems were widely admired, by Goethe and others, and were an important influence behind the Romantic revival. But their genuineness was soon suspect, with Dr Johnson conspicuous among the doubters. Challenged to produce his sources, Macpherson fabricated Gaelic originals. After his death a commission considered that the works (*Fingal*, an epic in six books, is the best known) were free adaptations, with passages of Macpherson's own inserted, of traditional Gaelic poems. This is still the general view. He was London agent to the nabob of Arcot and an M.P. 1780–96.

Macquarie, Lachlan (1761–1824). Scottish soldier. Army service took him to Canada, India, the East Indies and Egypt before he went to Australia as governor (1810–21) of New South Wales. By encouraging the construction of roads, bridges and public buildings, by founding the first bank (1817) he changed a penal settlement into a flourishing embryo colony. He believed that ex-prisoners should have the chance to become settlers. He met opposition on this and resigned (1821).
Ellis, M. H., *Lachlan Macquarie: His Life, Adventures and Time*. 1947

Macready, William Charles (1793–1873). British actor. He came of a theatrical family and made his debut in Birmingham in 1816. After the death (1833) of * Kean, Macready became the leading actor of his time and his management (1837–43) at Covent Garden and Drury Lane, during which he was both producer and actor, was famous. During a visit to New York (1849), twenty lives were lost when a mob incited by an envious American actor, Forrest, tried to break into the theatre where Macready was performing. His most famous parts included Macbeth, Lear, Iago and King John and it is said that he tried 'to combine the dignity of the Kembles with the naturalness of Kean'.
Trewin, J. C., *Mr. Macready, a 19th Century Tragedian and his Theatre*. 1955

MacSwiney, Terence (1880–1920). Irish nationalist. He took part in the Easter Rising (1916) and after subsequent revolutionary activity in the Irish Republican Army became lord mayor of Cork in 1920. In August he was arrested on a sedition charge and his death in October after a 74-day hunger strike provoked world-wide sympathy and protest.

M'Taggart, John Ellis (1866–1925). English philosopher. Fellow of Trinity College, Cambridge, he was one of the foremost English exponents of Hegel and his own philosophical idealism was deeply influential. In his monumental *Nature of Existence* (2 volumes, 1921, 1927) he argued with unusual clarity to the conclusion that conscious selves were the only ultimate existence and that the society of these eternal spiritual entities is a sufficient explanation of final reality without need to introduce theism.

Madariaga y Rojo, Don Salvador (1886–1978). Spanish author. He served as director of disarmament for the League of Nations (1922–27). He was professor of Spanish studies at Oxford University (1928–31) and, after the establishment of the Republic, Ambassador to the U.S. (1931–32) and to France (1932–36). He stood aloof from the Spanish Civil War but in England after 1950 he was a frequent and outspoken critic of the Franco régime. Amongst his extensive literary works are books on Bolívar, Columbus, Don Quixote, Hamlet and Shelley, and he also wrote on historical and political topics.

Madero, Francisco (1873–1913). Mexican president (1911–13). He was educated abroad and returned with liberal and humanitarian ideas to become (1909) the principal opponent of the re-election of the dictatorial President * Díaz. When Díaz declared himself re-elected, a local rising in response to Madero's agitation caused the administration suddenly to collapse and Díaz fled (May 1911). Madero was elected with popular acclaim but, when his incompetence provoked rebellions, he was induced to resign and then murdered by his own commander-in-chief, General Huerta.

Madison, James (1751–1836). Fourth president of the U.S. (1809–17). The son of a landowner, he belonged to a prominent Virginia family, studied at New Jersey College (later Princeton University) and at a precocious age helped to draft the Virginia state constitution (1776), serving in the Continental Congress (1780–83) and the Virginia legislature (1784–86). At the Federal Constitutional Convention (1787) held at Philadelphia he was, despite his youth, the major intellectual force in shaping the U.S. Constitution (although Gouverneur * Morris was the principal draftsman). He contributed to the *Federalist Papers* (1787–88) with * Hamilton and * Jay, showing remarkable prescience about the problems of large government, the development of factions, information flow and oligopoly. As a member of the US House of Representatives (1789–97) he campaigned for adoption of the Bill of Rights and against Hamilton's financial policies. He was * Jefferson's secretary of state (1801–09), arranged the 'Louisiana purchase' from France, and succeeded as leader of the Democratic–Republicans. Elected as president in 1808 and 1812, his second term was marked by the unpopular war with Britain (1812–14), known as 'Madison's war', in which Washington was captured and the White House burned. His wife Dolley Madison (née Payne) (1768–1849) was White House hostess for Jefferson (a widower) and himself. He was rector of the university of Virginia 1826–36 and died at his home in Montpelier.

Brant, I., *The Fourth President*. 1970

Maecenas, Gaius Cilnius (*c.* 70–8 B.C.). Friend and counsellor of the Roman emperor Augustus. Though without specific office, he acted as the emperor's chief minister and had great influence over him. He was renowned for his wealth and luxury and for his patronage of writers, e.g. Virgil and Horace.

Maeterlinck, Count Maurice (1862–1949). Belgian poet and dramatist. He studied law at Ghent but went to Paris (1887) and soon came under the influence of the French 'symbolists' as seen, notably, in his metaphysical dramas, e.g. *Pelleas and Melisande* (1892), later the basis of an opera by Debussy, and *The Bluebird* (1909), a children's favourite despite its mysticism. Maeterlinck also wrote a series of popular works on natural history, e.g. *The Life of the Bee* (1901), and *The Intelligence of Flowers* (1907). In 1911 he won the Nobel Prize for Literature and in 1932 was created a count.

Halls, W. D., *Maurice Maeterlinck*. 1960

Magellan (Magalhães), **Ferdinand** (*c.* 1480–1521). Portuguese explorer. While on service in Morocco he was accused of theft and made an unauthorized return to Portugal to appeal against the charge; unable to gain satisfaction, he offered his services to Spain and obtained acceptance of a scheme to sail to the Moluccas (East Indies) from the west. He sailed (1519) with five ships and rounded South America through the straits that now bear his name into the Pacific (the name of which was suggested to him by the fine weather he encountered there). He reached the Philippines where he was killed in a skirmish with natives. His ship was sailed back to Spain by his second-in-command, Sebastian del Cano, who thus completed (1522) the first circumnavigation of the world, which also established that the Americas were a separate continent.

Guillemard, F. H. H., *The Life of Ferdinand Magellan and the first Circumnavigation of the Globe 1480–1521*. Repr. 1971

Magendie, François (1783–1855). French physician. Considered a founder of experimental physiology, he investigated the relationship of the nervous system with the spinal chord and the effects and uses of strychnine, iodine, morphine and various other drugs. He demonstrated the stomach's passive role in vomiting and studied emetics. He did much work on the nerves of the skull and a canal leading from the fourth ventricle is named after him the 'foramen of Magendie'. He was elected a member of the Académie des Sciences (1821) and was its president (1837). In 1831 he became professor of medicine at the Collège de France.

Maginot, André (1877–1932). French politician. As minister of war (1922–24 and 1929–32), he ordered the construction of the 'Maginot line', a series of immense fortifications, concealed weapons, underground storehouses and living quarters on the Franco-German frontier. In World War II it was outflanked by the German advance through

Belgium and its defensive strength was never put to the test.

Magritte, René François Ghislain (1898–1967). Belgian artist. Important member of the Surrealist movement, he trained at the Brussels Academy from 1916 and began his career as a wallpaper designer. He became a full-time painter in 1926 and held his first one-man exhibition ten years later. His pictures are realistic, even mundane, but they are put together in composite images which are bizarre, sinister, comic or nightmarish.
Nadeau, M., *The History of Surrealism*. 1965

Magsaysay, Ramon (1907–1957). Philippine politician. A mechanic by trade, he became famous for his exploits in the anti-Japanese underground movement. Afterwards he was equally successful against the revolutionary Communists. He was secretary of national defence from 1950 until 1953 when he became president. He was killed in an air crash.

Mahan, Alfred Thayer (1840–1914). American naval historian. He served in the navy (1856–96) and retired with the rank of captain, which was raised to that of rear-admiral in 1906. His great work, *The Influence of Sea Power upon History, 1660–1783* (1890), proved a powerful stimulant to political thought on this subject, its thesis based on, and strikingly confirmed by, British imperial growth. He also wrote a life of Nelson (1897).

Mahdi, El. The title used by Moslems for the spiritual and military deliverer whom traditionally they are led to expect; it was especially claimed by Mohammed Ahmed (1848–1885) in order to rouse the fanatical tribesmen against the Egyptian occupation of the Sudan. He had already gained complete ascendancy when (1885) General * Gordon, sent to evacuate Europeans, Egyptians and Sudanese, lost his life after the fall of Khartoum. The Mahdists remained in control until their final defeat by * Kitchener at Omdurman (1898).
Holt, P. M., *The Mahdist State in the Sudan*. 2nd ed. 1970

Mahler, Gustav (1860–1911). Austrian composer and conductor. He was born in Bohemia; of Jewish origin, he was converted to Catholicism as a young man. He studied at the Vienna Conservatoire, where he attended Anton * Bruckner's classes in theory. Regarded as the greatest conductor of his era, he directed the Budapest Opera (1888–91), the Hamburg Opera (1891–97), the Vienna Imperial Opera (1897–1907), the Metropolitan Opera, New York (1907) and the New York Philharmonic Society (1908–11). His symphonies Nos. 2, 3 and 4 (first performed 1895, 1896 and 1901) include movements for solo voice, or soli and chorus, with orchestra; and No. 8 (1910) consists of two movements for chorus (the second with soli) and orchestra. The unfinished tenth symphony was performed in 1964 in a version partly reconstructed from Mahler's notes by Deryck Cooke. Other important works are three song cycles for voice and orchestra, *The Song of the Earth* (*Das Lied von der Erde*; 1908–09), *Songs on the Death of Children* (*Kindertotenlieder*; 1904) and *Des Knaben Wunderhorn* (1892–96). Mahler's music, in its prolixity (most of the works, including all the symphonies, are unusually long), its emotionalism, its sudden and extreme changes of mood, its programmatic content and its use of large orchestral and vocal forces, represents in many ways the culmination of the Romantic movement in music. The fluctuating quality of the musical material and the uncertainty of taste which are the obverse of its positive qualities have led to critical division as to its worth, but Mahler's originality and inventiveness have been widely recognized and have influenced * Shostakovich and (notably in his use of the orchestral song cycle) * Britten. His widow **Alma Maria Mahler**, née Schindler (1879–1964), later married Walter * Gropius and Franz * Werfel; her lovers included Oskar * Kokoschka. She lived in the US from 1940.
Kennedy, M., *Mahler*. 1974

Mahomet *see* **Mohammed**

Mailer, Norman (1923–). American writer. Service in the Pacific during World War II provided the documentation for that 'nightmarish piece of realism' *The Naked and the Dead* (1948). Later writings include *The White Negro* (1958), *Advertisements for Myself* (1959), *An American Dream* (1966), *The Armies of the Night* (1968 – Pulitzer Prize), *A Fire on the Moon* (1971), *Marilyn* (1973), *The Executioner's Song* (1979) and *Ancient Evenings* (1983).

Maillol, Aristide (1861–1944). French sculp-

tor. He turned from painting to tapestry designing and then, owing to failing sight, to monumental sculpture (*c.* 1900). Nearly all his works are nudes, realistic in conception but idealized to some extent in execution. He made a special study of the proper use of his materials, clay, bronze and marble.
George, W., *Aristide Maillol.* 1965

Maimonides, Rabbi Moses Ben Maimon (1135–1204). Jewish philosopher, born in Córdoba, Spain. Maimonides left with his family on the Muslim invasion and settled in Morocco. He received orthodox Jewish training, and in addition studied philosophy and law. In 1166 he settled in Egypt, where he became head of the Jewish community and court physician. His mind ranged widely. He wrote works of popular Jewish religious devotion, a major codification of the Jewish law, a philosophical–religious work, called *The Guide for the Perplexed*, and a number of medical works. He is the leading exponent of the school of Jewish Aristotelianism. Like Aristotle Maimonides asserts the rationality of God, and man's duty through the use of his reason to comprehend the Divine Mind. But Maimonides also emphasized the limits of human reason, which was unable to know the Divine attributes directly and positively. This secured a place for faith, and for positive revelation, both of which played central roles in Maimonides's beliefs. This religious vision informed his scientific studies. He did not believe that science had achieved certain knowledge of nature. As a medical man, Maimonides was a close follower of * Galen, though he accused Galen of ignorance in theological matters. Maimonides's writings became canonical for Jewish philosophy for the next few centuries, and also exercised considerable influence over Thomas * Aquinas and other Scholastics.
Baron, S. (ed.), *Essays on Maimonides.* 1941; Minkin, J. S., *The World of Moses Maimonides.* 1958

Maine, Sir Henry James Sumner (1822–1888). English legal historian. After showing academic brilliance he became Regius professor of civil law at Cambridge University (1847–1854), being called to the bar in 1850. The remainder of his career was divided between academic legal appointments and positions in India and the Indian Office at home, which enabled him to reform and shape the legal system of that country. He is most famous, however, for his classic studies of the evolution of legal and social institutions, e.g. *Ancient Law* (1861), *Early History of Institutions* (1875) and *Early Law and Custom* (1883).

Maintenon, Françoise d'Aubigné, Marquise de (1635–1719). Second but unacknowledged wife of Louis XIV of France. She lived in Martinique with her Huguenot father until his death, when she returned to France, was converted to Roman Catholicism and was in great poverty when she married the poet * Scarron (1652). In 1669, by then a widow, she was chosen as governess to the king's sons by Madame de Montespan, whom she succeeded in the king's affections (1680); in 1684 the king married her secretly. She was an intelligent and attractive woman, who behaved with complete discretion and exercised little influence on politics. The king bestowed upon her the château of Maintenon and the title of marquise.
Langlois, M. (ed.), *Lettres de Madame de Maintenon.* 1935–39

Maitland, Frederick William (1850–1906). English legal historian. After spending fifteen years at the bar he devoted the rest of his life to his historical work. In 1888 he became professor of English law at Cambridge. The breadth and profundity of his research, his imaginative power of recalling the past and his brilliance of style combine to make his *History of the English Law* (up to Edward I), written in collaboration with Sir Frederick Pollock, one of the great classic works in this field. His other works include a constitutional history (from Edward I) published posthumously.

Makarios III (1913–1977). Cypriot archbishop and president. As archbishop of the Orthodox church of Cyprus (from 1950), he was political leader of the *Enosis* movement which demanded the end of British rule and union with Greece. He was exiled to the Seychelles (1956) but returned to Cyprus (1957) and became its first president (1959) after the conclusion of an agreement between Britain, Greece and Turkey for an independent Cyprus. There were several assassination attempts and in 1974 he was deposed as president for a few days and escaped after an attempt on his life. He returned to Cyprus as president in December 1974. His presidency was marred by a failure to weld Cyprus into a single sovereign state.

Malan, Daniel François (1874–1959). South African Nationalist politician. Born in Cape Colony (now Cape Province), he was a preacher and journalist before entering political life, at first in the legislative assembly at the Cape and later in that of the Union. Between 1924 and 1933 he held several ministerial posts and worked hard for African education. In 1936 he became leader of the opposition. He favoured neutrality in World War II and was prime minister (1948–54) after the defeat of * Smuts. He instituted (1948) the much criticized policy of apartheid.

Malaparte, Curzio (real name Kurt Erich Suckert) (1898–1957). Italian journalist, playwright and novelist. After war service, he was an enthusiastic propagandist not only for Fascism but also for *avante garde* literature, and wrote on revolutionary violence in his *Coup d'etat* (1932). In the 1940s the Fascists expelled him. He wrote two powerful war novels, *Kaputt* (1944) and *The Skin* (1949).

Malatesta, Sigismondo Pandolfo (1417–1468). Italian soldier, who succeeded his uncle as lord of Rimini in 1432. Though he was a *condottiere* or mercenary captain – cruel, profligate, and described by Pope Pius II as 'the enemy of God and man' – he was a scholar and friend of scholars: on his orders the cathedral of Rimini was converted into a temple of the arts.

Malcolm III (died 1093). King of Scotland. When his father, King Duncan, was killed and his throne usurped by * Macbeth he took refuge in England. In 1054, with the help of his uncle Siward, Earl of Northumbria, he recovered southern Scotland and in 1057 he defeated and killed Macbeth in battle. After the Norman conquest of England he supported the claims of Edgar the Aetheling (brother of his wife, * St Margaret) but was forced by William I to pay tribute. When William Rufus succeeded, Malcolm was trapped and killed during a raid on Northumbria.

Malcolm X (assumed name of Malcolm Little) (died 1965). Leader of the Black Moslems, an extremist movement of Negroes in the U.S.A. After expulsion he formed his own group, but was murdered in Haarlem by even more extreme rivals.
Malcolm X., *Autobiography*. 1965

Malebranche, Nicolas (1638–1715). French philosopher, whose philosophical ideas brought him a contemporary esteem second only to that of Descartes, many of whose views he shared. Dismissing the information provided by the senses as confused, Malebranche taught that truth could only be apprehended through what he termed 'clear ideas' and that the seat of such 'clear ideas' (though not in a locational sense) was God. He denied that there was a direct causal relation between mind and matter; sensation on the one hand and the physical activity that follows an act of willing on the other he explained as occasional acts of God in creating new mental images to correspond with items in the physical order or in creating new physical conditions to correspond with a mental picture. His *De la Recherche de la vérité* (1674) contains the best exposition of his philosophy. Apart from philosophy Malebranche was well known as a physicist, especially for his work in optics.

Malenkov, Georgi Maximilianovich (1902–). Soviet politician. He rose quickly in the Communist party organization and as head of the party secret service was closely associated with the purges of 1936–39. During World War II he reorganized industrial production and railway transport. As deputy premier 1946–53 and a Politburo member 1946–55, he was Stalin's closest associate and on his death (March 1953) succeeded him as premier and (for eight days, until he lost that position to * Khrushchev) general secretary of the CPSU. Forced out as premier in 1955 in favour of Khrushchev's nominee * Bulganin, he became minister for electric power stations 1955–57.

Malherbe, François de (1555–1628). French poet and grammarian. His early life was spent mostly in Provence but in 1605 he obtained a post at court and the patronage of Henry IV, Louis XIII and Cardinal Richelieu. His importance lay not so much in his own verse, which consisted mainly of conventional accounts of noble deeds or adaptations of poems by ancient or contemporary writers, as in his achievements as a grammarian. He was largely responsible for creating a clear and easily understandable literary language free of the archaisms, pedantries and foreign influences

that had made the work of his predecessors obscure. Moreover he laid down firm rules for the various verse forms and showed how to combine euphony with sense.
Fromilhagne, R., *Malherbe*. 1954

Malik, Jacob Alexandrovich (1906–). Soviet politician. Born in the Ukraine, he rose to high office under Stalin. After serving as ambassador to Japan (1942–45) he became deputy foreign minister in 1946 and Soviet spokesman at the U.N. in 1948. From 1953, the year of Stalin's death, he served as ambassador to Britain, but his career survived the official denunciation of Stalin's policies and he was re-appointed to government office by * Khrushchev in 1960.

Malinovsky, Rodion Yakovlevich (1898–1967). Russian marshal. He served with the French army in World War I; in World War II he was one of the most successful Russian commanders. After a fighting retreat in the Ukraine (1941) he commanded one of the armies which in 1942 surrounded and enforced the surrender of General Paulus at Stalingrad. Thenceforward on the offensive, he retook Odessa (April 1944) and by the end of that year was advancing through Romania and Hungary. In the next year he liberated Czechoslovakia. He succeeded * Zhukov as minister of defence 1957–67.

Malinowski, Bronislaw Kaspar (1884–1942). Polish anthropologist resident in England. In 1914 he accompanied an anthropological expedition to New Guinea and continued to Australia. On his return he joined the teaching staff at London University and became (1927) professor in social anthropology. He introduced the method of investigation by functional comparison of the activities of different peoples. Among his books were *Crime and Custom in Savage Society* (1926) and *Sex and Repression in Savage Society* (1927).
Firth, R. W., (ed.), *Man and Culture: an Evaluation of the Work of Bronislaw Malinowski*. 1957

Malipiero, Gian Francesco (1882–1973). Italian composer. Musicologist, teacher and (from 1934) director of the Liceo Marcello at Venice, he edited the works of Monteverdi and Vivaldi, and composed songs, orchestral and choral works, and operas, e.g. *Julius Caesar* (1936) and *Antony and Cleopatra* (1938).

Mallarmé, Stéphane (1842–1898). French 'symbolist' poet, born in Paris. Having decided to learn English in order to read and translate Edgar Allan Poe, he was in London for that purpose (1862–63) and spent the rest of his active life teaching English in various French towns and eventually in Paris. There he came to admire the Impressionists and especially Manet, whose close friend he became. He tried to bring light and movement into his creations with words as the Impressionists had done with paint; thus the sound and rhythm of the words, as in music, conveyed their meaning directly to the senses of the reader. Moreover, as a follower of Baudelaire, he gave to certain key words the quality of symbols which evoke picture-patterns in the mind that go far beyond a purely linguistic interpretation. Mallarmé was not prolific and was at his best in short pieces such as *L'Après-midi d'un faune* (1875), which inspired Debussy's prelude. Mallarmé also had a talent for gay, witty – but, alas, unrecorded – talk, and the gatherings on his 'Tuesday evenings' became famous.
Mondor, H., *Vie de Mallarmé*. 1941–42

Malmesbury, William of *see* **William of Malmesbury**

Malone, Edmund (1741–1812). Irish editor and critic. He abandoned the law for literature and moved to London, where he became a friend of Samuel Johnson. His great edition of Shakespeare appeared in 1790, and the revised edition published after his death in 1821 was by far the best up to that time. He also exposed the literary forgeries of William Henry Ireland and Thomas * Chatterton. He is commemorated by the Malone Society (founded 1907) which prints texts and documents relating to the study of Elizabethan drama.
Prior, J., *Life of Edmund Malone*. 1860

Malory, Sir Thomas (died *c*. 1470). English writer of Arthurian romances. Little is known with certainty about his life; the most probable identification is with a Warwickshire knight in the service of the Earl of Beauchamp. If so, most of his writing must have been done in prison, where he spent a large part of his life charged with a number of violent crimes. His eight Arthurian romances were published by Caxton in 1485 (though the text found at Winchester College in 1934 is held to be more authentic). The work consists almost entirely of adaptations from the French 13th-century versions, written to idealize the medieval code of chivalry. Malory, writing two centuries later in English prose, is no nearer than his originals to creating a realistic historical picture. Arthur is no Romano-British chieftain, and both he and his companions dress as 12th-century knights and their exploits are those about which the troubadours sang; but Malory's approach to character is more realistic and he writes with directness and vigour. Two main themes compose the story that runs through the eight romances: (a) the tragic end of Arthur's reign and the break-up of the knightly brotherhood that gathered at the Round Table; (b) Launcelot's failure, through sin, to find the Holy Grail (the cup used at the Last Supper) and Galahad's success. Almost all later versions of the legends (e.g. Tennyson's *Idylls of the King*) are based on Malory. * Geoffrey of Monmouth.

Reiss, E., *Sir Thomas Malory*. 1966

Malpighi, Marcello (1628–1694). Italian anatomist and microscopist. He studied and (from 1666) was a professor at Bologna University. Malpighi virtually founded histology (including that of plants) and is noted for his studies of the structure of the brain, lungs, glands and liver and especially for extending * Harvey's work on the circulation of the blood, by discovering the capillaries. He also investigated muscular cells and wrote a treatise on the silkworm.

Adelmann, H., *Marcello Malpighi and the Evolution of Embryology*. 5 vols. 1966

Malraux, André (1901–1976). French writer and politician. Having studied oriental languages he accompanied an archaeological expedition to Indo-China (1923–25), where, as a Communist, he played an important part in Chinese politics (1925–27). He utilized his varied experiences in his novels, e.g. *Les Conquérants* (1928) and *La Condition humaine* (1933, winner of the Prix Goncourt) and *L'Espoir* (1937). He also wrote on the psychology of art. He fought against Franco in the Spanish Civil War, and during World War II he became a leader of the French resistance movement. As a friend and admirer of de Gaulle he proved himself an energetic and imaginative minister of cultural affairs (1958–69).

Suarès, G., *Malraux: Past, Present and Future*. 1974

Malthus, Thomas Robert (1766–1834). English population theorist. Born near Dorking, he distinguished himself in mathematics at Cambridge, where he became (1797) a fellow of Jesus College. Meanwhile he had taken holy orders and led a county clergyman's life in Surrey until (1805) he became a teacher at Haileybury College, where he worked for the rest of his life. In his famous *Essay on the Principle of Population* (published anonymously in 1798 and revised in 1803) he showed that population tends to increase faster than the means of subsistence. This applies to animals and humans alike, but only man can impose a reasoned check by moral restraint or 'vicious practices' (by which he presumably meant birth control, to which he was opposed). That the disastrous over-population which he foresaw had not already taken place he attributed to celibacy, infanticide, war, famine and disease. He also noted that the rate of population increase tends to be greatest in countries and classes where the standard of living is low. This pessimism, in striking contrast to * Rousseau's glowing belief in the perfectibility of man, was bitterly assailed; but his analysis remains incontrovertible although industrial development and the effect on food production of fertilizers and improved agricultural methods have so far postponed the ultimate crisis.

Bonar, J., *Malthus and His Work*. 1966

Malvern, Godfrey Martin Huggins, 1st Viscount (1883–1971). Rhodesian politician. British-born, he practised as a doctor in Rhodesia from 1911, both before and after his service in the R.A.M.C. during World War I, and became a member of the legislative assembly of Southern Rhodesia in 1923. He was prime minister of Southern Rhodesia (1933–53) and then of the newly formed Federation of Rhodesia and Nyasaland (1953–56).

Mamum (Abul Abbas Abdallah al Mamum) (786–833). Seventh caliph of Baghdad, the son of * Harun al-Rashid. Politically his reign was troubled, but it was a time of great intellectual distinction as Mamum encouraged learning, especially the study of Greek science. Many Greek works were preserved through their translation into Arabic in his 'House of Wisdom', (founded 830), where he gathered together the leading scholars of his day.

Mandelstam, Osip Emilyevich (1891–1938).

Russian poet, born in Warsaw. Educated in the West, he became a leader of the Acmeist (* Akhmatova) movement. He saw poetry as an instinctive recognition of cultural order and continuity in contrast to the chaos and fragmentation of man in nature, and published the collections *Kamen* (1913) and *Tristiya* (1922). In 1934 he was exiled and later died in a labour camp. Forgotten until the 1960s, he is now regarded as a poet of the first rank.

Mandeville, Sir John (born late 13th century). Ostensible author of one of the most popular medieval books of travels. In the preface the alleged author claims to have been born at St Albans and in the epilogue states that the memoirs were written in 1357 and that his journeys had begun thirty-five years previously. The earliest MS, which probably contains the original text, is the French (translations into English and many other languages exist) and dates from 1371. The first part, which takes the reader to the Holy Land and neighbouring countries, is possibly the genuine record of some traveller, but the second part describing journeys in Asia extending to China is merely a compilation from other writers.
Letts, M., *Sir John Mandeville: The Man and His Book*. 1949

Manet, Edouard (1832–1883). French painter. He was born in Paris to a well-off bourgeois family and so was enabled to pursue his vocation and enjoy travel without hardship. Among early influences were Goya and Velasquez, and even in later life his paintings reflect what he had learnt from their work; the period which later made him recognized as a forerunner of the Impressionists began when (1863) his *Déjeuner sur l'herbe* was rejected by the Salon. The subject, in which two women – one naked and one half-naked – are at a picnic with two fully dressed men, was an assertion in paint that the only point of view that should count is the pictorial one. But though to some such an explanation only added to the offence, the young men (Monet, Renoir, Pissaro etc.) who were later to be dubbed 'Impressionists' found inspiration in the picture. His *Olympia* (1865) was attacked as indecent with even more venom. Like the Impressionists Manet began (1870) to paint in the open air, but he was less concerned with landscape and the effects of sunlight than with the portrayal of the gay and lively scenes around him e.g. racecourse scenes (1872) and at the end of his life famous *Bar aux Folies Bergère* (1882; National Gallery, London). Some of his portraits, e.g. that of Zola, are important.
Tabarant, A., *Manet et ses oeuvres*. 1947

Mani (*c*. 216–*c*. 276). Persian mystic, founder of the Manichean sect. He spent the last thirty years of his life on missionary journeys throughout the Persian empire and even reached the borderlands of India and China. He was put to death at the instigation of the Zoroastrian priesthood. In his teaching Mani speaks of the two 'roots', God and matter, equated with good and evil, light and darkness. Mani's teaching was intended to produce a synthesis of Christianity, Zoroastrianism and Buddhism; at first the sect grew rapidly but wilted under persecution, and by the 10th century was virtually extinct. Traces of its teaching, however, survived among the Albigenses of medieval France and the Bogomili of the Balkans.

Manin, Daniele (1804–1857). Italian lawyer and politician, born in Venice. An ardent liberal and nationalist, he was imprisoned for his outspoken denunciation of Austrian rule in northern Italy but was released by the populace during the 1848 revolts and was subsequently elected president of the new Venetian republic. When the Austrians besieged the city he inspired a heroic defence (April–August 1849) ending in capitulation enforced by starvation and disease. Manin, excluded from an amnesty, died in Paris.

Mankowitz, (Cyril) Wolf (1924–). British writer resident in Ireland. He was born in Bethnal Green and wrote novels and plays on Jewish East End life, notably *A Kid for Two Farthings* (1953) and *The Bespoke Overcoat* (1954). He was also editor of the *Concise Encyclopaedia of English Pottery and Porcelain* (1957) and a specialist in the study of * Wedgwood.

Mann, (Luis) Heinrich (1871–1950). German novelist. After an early period as a romantic monarchist, he was attracted by French liberal philosophy and adopted a utopian progressivism, breaking with his younger brother Thomas * Mann because of his passionate opposition to World War I. His books included *Professor Unrat* (1905), filmed by Fritz * Lang as *The Blue Angel* (1928), *Der Untertan*

('The Man of Straw', 1918), and the *Henri Quatre* novels (1935; 1938). He left Germany in 1933, lived in France until 1940, then in the US. He was recognized as leader of the German literary left.

Mann, Thomas (1875–1955). German novelist and critic. He was born in Lübeck of an old Hansa family and was working in an insurance office at Munich when he wrote his first novel *Buddenbrooks* (1901). In this and other works he illustrates the opposition between the extrovert life of the ordinary bourgeois and that of the intellectual and artist; it is the emergence of the traits of the latter that he regards as a sign of decay, remarking, too, on the affinity of genius with disease and the 'fascination of death'. Mann described himself as 'primarily a humorist' but it is with such psychological problems that he is most deeply concerned and in probing them he reveals the particular influence of Schopenhauer and Wagner. The short novels *Death in Venice* (1912), *Tristan* (1913) and *Tonio Kröger* (1914) were all successful but because of World War I, during which he wrote *Reflections of a Non-political Man* (1916), it was not until 1924 that his next major work, *The Magic Mountain* (*Der Zauberberg*), appeared. Here life in a tuberculosis sanatorium symbolizes the disintegrating civilization of Europe. Later works include *Children and Fools* (1928), *Mario and the Magician* (1930) and the biblical tetralogy (1934–44) on Joseph and his brethren, in which he stresses the mutual dependence of God and man. He won the Nobel Prize for Literature (1929) but left Germany when Hitler came to power and eventually (1938) settled in the U.S.A., of which he became a citizen in 1944. Among novels of his last period were *Dr Faustus* (1948), *The Black Swan* (1955) and the posthumously published comic novel *The Confessions of Felix Krull*. He also wrote many essays on literary subjects and contemporary themes. His daughter, **Erika Mann** (1905–69), an actress and author, married the actor–director Gustaf Gründgens (1899–1963) and later (1935) the poet W. H. * Auden, but never lived with him. Of his sons, **Klaus Mann** (1906–49), a novelist, essayist and playwright, wrote the novel *Mephisto* (1936), based on Gründgens' political accommodation with the Nazis (later an acclaimed film (1981) by István Szabó), became a US citizen and committed suicide; while **Golo Mann** (1909–), a historian, taught in the US, Germany and Switzerland, and wrote many books.

Buergin, H., and Mayer, H.-O., *Thomas Mann: A Chronicle of His Life*. 1969

Mannerheim, Baron Carl Gustav Emil von (1867–1951). Finnish marshal and president. When during World War I Finland declared its independence of Russia after the Bolshevik revolution, Mannerheim left the Russian army, returned to Finland and in the ensuing civil war commanded the 'white' Finnish troops against the communist ('red') Finns and, their Russian Bolshevik allies, whom he defeated with German aid. When the Russians attacked Finland in the winter of 1939–40 he again took command and, with the aid of the 'Mannerheim line' across the Karelian isthmus and brilliant defensive operations in the snow-covered forests of the north, greatly delayed the inevitable Russian victory. When at last he was elected president (1944) he was universally admired national hero; he resigned in 1946.

Warner, O., *Marshal Mannerheim and the Finns*. 1967

Manning, Henry Edward (1808–1892). English cardinal. After a distinguished academic career at Oxford he was ordained (1832) an Anglican clergyman and became archdeacon of Chichester (1841). In 1851 he became a Roman Catholic priest and soon rose to prominence. He established (1857) the congregation of St Charles (Borromeo) in London and in 1865 after being provost of the metropolitan chapter of Westminster succeeded Cardinal Wiseman as archbishop; he was created cardinal in 1875. He was a strong supporter of the dogma of papal infallibility as defined at the Oecumenical Council (1870) and in social affairs was closely identified with prison reform, education and help for the poor.

Manoel I (known as 'the Fortunate') (1469–1521). King of Portugal (from 1495). He succeeded his elder brother, John II, who was assassinated. His nickname was due more to events and circumstances than to his own abilities. He did, however, encourage the great revival of arts and letters that marked his reign and the term 'Manoeline style' applied to the architecture of the period was not merely an empty compliment. Moreover the 'Manoeline Ordinances' were an important revision of the

first systematic collection of laws made by Alfonso V. Manoel's reign, marred by the expulsion of Moors and Jews, saw the rounding of the Cape of Good Hope by * Diaz, the voyage of * Vasco da Gama to India, the discovery of Brazil and finally the start of * Magellan on his last and greatest voyage.
Sanceau, E., *The Reign of the Fortunate King 1495–1521*. 1969

Manoel II (1889–1932). Last king of Portugal (1908–10). He became king when his father, King Carlos, and his elder brother were assassinated, but abdicated on the outbreak of the 1910 revolution. He lived in England from 1910 and became known as an antiquarian and bibliophile.

Mansart, Jules Hardouin (1646–1708). French architect. A life-long favourite of Louis XIV, he rose in a short time to the position of architect to the king (1675) and became surveyor of the royal works in 1699. He was responsible for the Grand Trianon and other buildings at Versailles and for the Dôme des Invalides (1716), Paris. As a town planner, he created in Paris the Place des Victoires (1684–86) and the Place Vendôme (1699). His surname was originally Hardouin, but he added Mansart after his great-uncle François Mansart (1598–1666), a famous architect of the previous reign, who popularized the mansard (attic) roof named after him.

Mansfeld, Peter Ernst, Count von (*c.* 1580–1626). German military commander. In the early stages of the Thirty Years War (from 1618) he played a leading part in securing Frederick's position as king of Bohemia. After Frederick's expulsion he waged an independent campaign against the Emperor Frederick II. In 1624 with the aid of French and English subsidies he again took the field, but in 1626 he was defeated by the imperialists under * Wallenstein at Dessau and died in the same year.

Mansfield, Katherine (Katherine Mansfield Beauchamp) (1888–1923). British short-story writer, born in Wellington, New Zealand. She arrived in London at the age of 20 and wrote a series of sensitive and sometimes ironic short stories which soon proved her meticulous craftsmanship and mastery of that difficult form. Her volumes include *In a German Pension* (1911), written while recovering in Bavaria from the birth of a still-born baby; *Bliss and Other Stories* (1920), which established her fame; and *The Garden Party* (1922) containing 'The Daughters of the Late Colonel' and 'The Voyage'. She married (1918) John Middleton * Murry and died of tuberculosis in France.
Gordon, I. A., *Katherine Mansfield*. 1954

Mansfield, William Murray, 1st Earl of (1705–1793). British lawyer. Born in Scotland, fourth son of David, Viscount Stormont, he was called to the bar (1731) and after ten years of successful practice he entered parliament; he became attorney-general in 1754 and was lord chief justice (1756–88). He was raised to the peerage (1756) as Baron Mansfield and contrary to precedent continued in politics not only as a member of the House of Lords but also of the Cabinet. This link with an unpopular administration caused him to be virulently assailed by the pamphleteer 'Junius' and during the Gordon riots (1780) his house was burt down. In fact, as a judge, he was tolerant and impartial. He received his earldom in 1776.
Fifoot, C., *Lord Mansfield*. 1936

Manson, Sir Patrick (1844–1922). Scottish physician. Son of a wealthy Aberdeenshire family, he graduated M.D. from Aberdeen University in 1866. After a year working in an asylum in Durham, he took a series of medical posts abroad, beginning as medical officer for Formosa in the Chinese Imperial Maritime Customs. He stayed there till 1871, making careful notes on such diseases as elephantiasis, leprosy and a heart disease which he later identified as beriberi. He moved to Amoy on the mainland and developed a private practice, specializing in elephantiasis, and concluding that the means of transmission of elephantiasis was via the mosquito. His researches suggested that the worm which caused the disease developed in the common brown mosquito. Manson's understanding of the role of the mosquito as parasite became fundamental for the diagnosis and treatment of a host of tropical illnesses. Manson, however, was mistaken in some of his ideas. He thought that mosquitos bit only once, and that man became infected by ingesting the worm larvae in water. Manson later pioneered the understanding of the transmission of malaria by mosquitos. By 1898 he had developed a sophisticated understanding of the life cycle of the parasite, and

had grasped the importance of protecting humans against mosquitos at night. He was largely instrumental in setting up the London School of Tropical Medicine in 1899, and was a tireless teacher.
Manson-Bahr, P., *Patrick Manson, the Father of Tropical Medicine*. 1962

Manstein, Fritz von (1887–1973). German soldier. After serving as chief of staff in Poland and France in the early stages of World War II he held commands on the Russian front. In the great southern campaigns he showed, both in advance and retreat, superb skill in co-ordinating the movements of military formations of the largest scale, and was generally considered the ablest of German generals during the war. He was ordered to retire in 1944 by Hitler, whose policy of clinging to untenable positions until they were overwhelmed he resolutely opposed. Sentenced in 1949 to eighteen years' imprisonment for war crimes, he was freed in 1953.
von Manstein, F. E., *Lost Victories*. 1959

Mantegna, Andrea (*c.* 1431–1506). Italian painter of the Paduan school. The founder of that school, Francesco Squarcione, adopted him when he was orphaned, but by 1458 when he painted a series of frescoes on the life of St James (destroyed in World War II) he was working independently. The most important influence on his work was derived from his study of archaeology, stimulated by the drawings of his father-in-law Jacopo Bellini; he went to Rome to study classical buildings and was himself a collector of coins and fragments. Even in biblical subjects, e.g. the *Agony in the Garden* (National Gallery, London), he betrays his zeal to introduce classical details into his composition. His knowledge of perspective was profound and he used it, e.g. in the *Lamentation of the Dead Christ* (at Milan), in an astonishingly bold manner. In the early 1460s Mantegna was called to Mantua to decorate the Camera degli Sposi in the palace with scenes from the lives of the Gonzagas, the ruling house, with which he remained, with intervals, for the rest of his life. While there he painted the pictures representing the *Triumph of Julius Caesar* (*c.* 1486–94), bought by Charles I of England and now, much damaged and restored, at Hampton Court.
Tietze-Courat, E. ed., *Mantegna: Paintings, Drawings, Engravings*. 1955

Mantoux, Charles (1877–1947). French physician. He devised the Mantoux test for tuberculosis and investigated the formation of tubercular cavities in the lungs.

Manutius (Manuzio) *see* **Aldus Manutius**

Manzoni, Alessandro (1785–1873). Italian writer. Though he belonged to noble Milanese family he spent his early manhood in Paris where he was influenced by the prevailing scepticism; he was, however, reconverted to Catholicism (*c.* 1810) soon after his first marriage and all his work shows a liberal outlook and deep moral purpose. He worked very slowly; the two well known odes on the death of Napoleon and the Piedmontese rising (1821) against the Austrians, together with a few hymns, comprise almost his entire poetic output. Two tragedies with stories derived from the early Middle Ages reflect a mood of pessimism caused by the failure of liberal movements in the early 1820s; finally in 1827 came his great and only novel *I Promessi Sposi* (*The Betrothed*). This historical romance set in 17th-century Lombardy under Spanish rule (the Spanish representing the Austrians of his own day), was at once hailed as a masterpiece and is still held to be among the greatest of Italian novels; it took six years to write and was constantly revised, but marked the end of his creative period, except for a number of critical essays on various themes. In his later years he took part in the struggle for Italian unification and served as a senator of the new kingdom of Italy. He did important work for national unity by helping to establish the Florentine dialect as the linguistic standard for the whole of Italy. The deaths of both his wives and several of his children were saddening influences in his life.
Croce, B., *Alessandro Manzoni*. 1930

Mao Ze-dong (also Mao Tse-tung) (1893–1976). Chinese Communist leader, born in Shao-shangch'ung, Hunan province. The son of a small landowner, he returned to school after a brief child marriage, and became a voracious reader (Darwin, Spencer, Mill and Rousseau), later turning to Marx. He served in Sun's revolutionary army (1911) and studied at Changsha teachers' training school. Unlike * Li Li-san, * Zhu De and * Zhou Enlai, he did not study abroad. Mao worked as a laundryman in Shanghai (1919), then as a teacher, trade union secretary and library assistant at

Peking National University. He was one of the twelve foundation members of the Chinese Communist Party in Shanghai (July 1921). As CP secretary in Hunan 1921–25, he organized trades unions and worked closely with the Guomintang. He set up more than 50 peasant unions 1925–27. After the risings of 1927 were defeated in the cities, he founded a workers' and peasants' army in Hunan with Zhu De and was a political commissar of the Red Army 1930–31. In 1930 his second wife Yang Kaihui and his sister were executed by a Guomintang war-lord. Ultimately he won major support from the Central Committee for his view that revolution must be based on the peasantry rather than the proletariat which barely existed in China. Mao was chairman of the Soviet republic in Jiangxi province 1931–34. Chairman of the Chinese Communist Party 1935–76 he was only recognized as the dominant leader after the 'Long March' (October 1934–October 1935, with the rear guard arriving in January 1936). After repeated Guomintang attacks, 80,000 people walked 9,650 kilometres, fighting fifteen major battles on the way, from Jiangxi to the caves in Yan'an, Shaanxi province: only 20,000 survived and Mao's three children were lost on the way. From 1937 to 1945 Mao collaborated with * Chiang Kai-shek against the Japanese. By 1945 the Red Army had 1,000,000 soldiers and controlled the north-west: civil war resumed in 1946. On the Guomintang's defeat and withdrawal to Taiwan, Mao proclaimed the foundation of the Chinese Peoples' Republic (1 October 1949) and served as chairman (i.e. president) 1949–59, retiring as head of state to devote himself on party organization and ideological formation. He visited Moscow in 1950 (his first journey abroad), in 1953 (for Stalin's funeral) and in 1960. Mao's Communism was highly moralistic, decentralized and ostensibly anti-bureaucratic. Unlike the Soviet CP, Mao used rival forces (e.g. the army, Red Guards) to discipline the party organization. He wrote many works on ideology and strategy and was a gifted lyric poet. His precepts ('Mao Zedong thought'), as contained in the 'little red book', had the force of moral law—however, after the failure of the Cultural Revolution and the defection of his chosen successor * Lin Biao in 1971, Mao's direct power declined. He was embalmed and placed on permanent exhibition in Beijing. His fourth wife **Jiang Q'ing** (1910–   ), formerly called Lan-P'ing, was a movie actress before her marriage in 1939. In 1966 she emerged as a public figure, took a leading role in the Cultural Revolution, rose to fourth place in the Politburo and was a fierce opponent of Zhou. Demoted at the 1973 Congress, she was denounced as one of the 'Gang of Four' and given a suspended death sentence in 1981 after a show trial.

Marat, Jean Paul (1743–1793). French revolutionary journalist. A physician by profession, especially interested in optics, he had travelled much and spent many years in England before returning to France and becoming physician to the Duke of Artois's household troops. After the outbreak of the Revolution he founded (1789) an extremist newspaper *L'Ami du peuple* which in 1793 played a considerable part in rousing public opinion against the Girondists. Charlotte * Corday, a member of that party, came from Normandy to assassinate him, found him in his bath where, as a sufferer from a skin disease, he transacted much business, and stabbed him to death.

Marchand, Jean Baptiste (1863–1934). French soldier and explorer. Having successfully led an expedition from Senegal to the sources of the Niger he was ordered to extend the area of French interest by an advance across Central Africa. When he reached Fashoda in the southern Sudan (1898) he refused the demands of * Kitchener to evacuate that area and thus caused such tension between France and Britain that a threat of war was averted only by the French Government's order to Captain Marchand to withdraw.

Marconi, Guglielmo (1874–1937). Italian physicist and inventor. After studying at the University of Bologna, he experimented with primitive wireless equipment based on the work of * Hertz and * Maxwell and is credited with the first practical system using radio for signalling, though several others, particularly the Russian scientist Professor A. S. Popov, had anticipated him to some degree. By 1895 he could transmit signals between points a mile apart, and two years later, having in the meantime enlisted the interest and support of the British Post Office, had increased the distance to nine miles. By 1898 he could send messages from England to France, and in 1901 successfully transmitted across the Atlantic

from Cornwall to Newfoundland. The Marconi Telegraph Company which he founded in 1897 played a major part in the development of radio, television and electronics. Marconi shared the Nobel Prize for Physics with Braun in 1909. He was an Italian senator (1915–37) and an Italian delegate to the Paris Peace Conference (1919). He was created a marquis (*marchese*) in 1929.
Baker, W. J., *A History of the Marconi Company*. 1970

Marco Polo *see* **Polo, Marco**

Marcos, Ferdinand Edralin (1917–). Filipino politician. He was the most highly decorated Filipino war hero, became a lawyer and a Congressman 1949–65, serving as president of the Philippines 1966– . The constitution was changed to allow him to rule for a record term and martial law imposed 1973–81. His wife **Imelda Romualdez Marcos** (1931–) was appointed governor of Manila 1975– , and secretary of the department of ecology and human settlements 1978– .

Marcus Aurelius (121–180). Roman emperor (from 161). He took the additional name Antoninus when he was adopted (138) by Antoninus Pius, whom Hadrian chose as his successor and whose daughter, Faustina, Marcus married (145). When Marcus succeeded Antoninus as emperor, he shared the government with Lucius Aurelius Verus, adopted by Antoninus at the same time as himself. From 162 to 165 the armies of Verus (who died in 169) fought the Parthians successfully in Armenia, where a puppet ruler was installed, and in Mesopotamia where Ctesiphon was taken by Avidius Cassius, whose subsequent rebellion (175) Marcus easily overcame. Meanwhile the Germanic tribes, the Marcomanni and Quadi, had broken through the northern frontiers and were threatening Italy and the Balkans. Marcus had fought two successful campaigns against them when he died. A successful general, a wise and patient ruler, Marcus Aurelius is perhaps best known as a Stoic philosopher and his introspective *Meditations*, written in Greek, has been one of the most influential books ever composed by a ruler. He reveals himself, without arrogance, as an instrument used for a time by providence to guide the Roman empire towards its destiny of becoming part of a dimly perceived world order. The virtues he espoused were those usually regarded as Christian, but he saw Christianity as an emotional, intolerant and disruptive sect, which sought the empire's protection while refusing or avoiding military service and other duties. Such persecution as he practised was on public not religious grounds. His reign was looked back on by later Romans as a Golden Age.
Birley, A., *Marcus Aurelius*. 1966

Marcuse, Herbert (1899–1979). German-American philosopher, born in Berlin. Educated at Freiburg, he became Martin Heidegger's assistant, left Germany in 1933 and worked in the US for the State Department and the Office of Strategic Services, later holding professorships at Brandeis University (from 1954) and the University of California at San Diego (1958). His books became enormously influential with the 'New Left' and the students in revolt during the late 1960s. Although deeply influenced by Marx and Freud, Marcuse was primarily a disciple of Hegel and advanced a complete body of philosophical doctrine, being sharply critical of logical positivism, scientific attitudes or analysis. He denounced the 'hell of the affluent society', argued that sexual freedom was an anti-revolutionary device and (in his *Critique of Pure Tolerance*, 1966) contended that tolerance was outmoded when it served subtle enslavement through fraudulent democracy in the industrial state. He called for 'selective intolerance' and 'counter-indoctrination' where necessary. His books include *Eros and Civilization* (1955), *One-Dimensional Man* (1964) and *Reason and Revolution* (1941).

Margaret (known as 'the Maid of Norway') (1283–1290). Daughter of Eric II of Norway and grand-daughter of the Scottish king Alexander III whose death (1286) left her as sole heir to the throne. Edward I of England intended that she should marry his son (afterwards Edward II) and so effect the union of the two crowns; but the scheme came to nothing as the child died aboard the ship which was carrying her to Scotland, and union came only several centuries later.

Margaret (1353–1412). Queen of Norway. Daughter of Kind Valdemar of Denmark and wife of Haakon VI of Norway she became on her father's death (1376) regent for her son Olaf, infant king of Denmark and (1380) of Norway. A tribute to her qualities was paid when on Olaf's sudden death (1387) she was permitted to continue her rule of both countries. In 1389 at the request of dissident nobles in Sweden she defeated King Albrecht and added that country (nominally on behalf of her grand-nephew, Eric of Pomerania) to the area under her control. By the Union of Kalmar (1397) Eric became king of all three countries but Margaret maintained her strong personal rule until her death.

Margaret (1489–1541). Queen consort of James IV, king of Scotland. A daughter of Henry VII of England, she provided by her marriage the link between the Tudor and Stewart (Stuart) dynasties, upon which depended the union of the crowns of the two countries under James VI and I, the first king of Great Britain. After her husband's death at Flodden, she married Archibald Douglas, 6th Earl of Angus, who headed the English faction at the Scottish court.

Margaret of Anjou (1430–1482). Queen consort of Henry VI of England, whom she married in 1445. Her French birth (she was a cousin of the French king and daughter of René, Duke of Anjou, titular king of Sicily and Jerusalem) made her very unpopular in England. When the Wars of the Roses broke out and her saintly husband began to show mental incapacity, she was, with her courage and strength of character, the life and soul of the Lancastrian cause. She was finally captured after the Battle of Tewksbury (1471), where her son Edward was killed, and she was imprisoned until ransomed by Louis XI of France.
Bagley, J. J., *Margaret of Anjou, Queen of England*. 1948

Margaret of Navarre (1492–1549). French authoress of the *Heptameron*. She was a sister of Francis I of France, and through her marriage to Henry II of Navarre she became the grand-mother of Henry IV of France and the ancestress of the Bourbon kings. She was learned and pious but also gay and tolerant; her courts became centres of humanist culture and places of refuge for persecuted scholars. In the *Heptameron*, following the pattern set by Boccaccio's *Decameron*, five gentlemen and ladies held up by the floods beguile the time with stories; but though ribaldry is far from absent in her stories, Margaret, unlike Boccaccio, treats love as a serious and often tragic passion.

Margaret Rose (1930–). British princess. The younger daughter of King George VI and the sister of Queen Elizabeth II, she was born at Glamis Castle in Scotland, the seat of her mother's family. She married (1960) Anthony Armstrong-Jones, a London photographer, afterwards created Earl of Snowdon; they divorced in 1970.

Maria Theresa (1717–1780). Archduchess of Austria, queen of Hungary and Bohemia (from 1740). She was daughter and heiress of the emperor Charles VI and herself gained the title empress when her husband Francis of Lorraine (married 1736) was elected emperor (1745). By the Pragmatic Sanction Charles VI had sought to guarantee his daughter's succession to all Habsburg lands but on his death (1740) Frederick the Great of Prussia invaded Silesia and provoked the War of the Austrian Succession, as a result of which he retained the province but recognized the Pragmatic Sanction in other respects. By making an alliance with France, Maria Theresa hoped to regain Silesia but failed to achieve her purpose in the Seven Years War (1756–63). She was an unwilling partner in the partition of Poland (1772), from which she acquired Galicia. In the administration of her many territories Maria Theresa proved herself a wise and prudent practitioner of the system of paternal government then in vogue. She freed the peasants from many feudal burdens, abolished torture and did much to foster education trade and industry and to reform the legal and taxation systems. She associated her son * Joseph II with herself as ruler when on his father's death (1765) he became emperor. Of her many other children, Leopold followed his brother as emperor and * Marie Antoinette became queen of France.
Pick, R., *Empress Maria Theresa*. 1966

Marie Antoinette (1755–1793). Queen of France. A daughter of Maria Theresa of Austria, she married the future Louis XVI of France in 1770, four years before he ascended the throne. She retained his complete devotion throughout his life. Her frivolity and extravagance made her unpopular but she was not unkind. She was further discredited by an

obscure confidence trick by which Cardinal de Rohan was induced to promise payment for a diamond necklace of great value allegedly for the queen. Marie Antoinette was in fact almost certainly ignorant of the entire affair. In the Revolution Marie Antoinette inspired the court partly by her firmness and courage but her course of action, e.g. the mismanaged flight of the royal family to Varennes (1791) and her secret correspondence (especially with her brother the emperor Leopold II) asking for intervention, did much to bring about the deposition of her husband (1792), his death on the guillotine (January 1793) and her own in the following October. Her son (Louis XVII) died in prison. Her daughter lived to be Duchess of Angoulême.
Cronin, V., *Louis XVI and Marie Antoinette*. 1974

Marie de Médicis (1573–1642). Queen of France. She was the daughter of Grandduke Francis I of Tuscany and became (1600) the second wife of Henry IV of France. As regent after his assassination (1610), she dismissed the experienced minister * Sully and squandered wealth on her favourite Concini. Her son Louis XIII had Concini murdered but was content to let power pass to * Richelieu. Marie de Médicis, having failed to displace him, retired to live in exile, mainly in the Low Countries.

Marie Louise (1791–1847). Empress of the French. Daughter of Francis, last Holy Roman emperor and first emperor of Austria, she married (1810) Napoleon I, and became the mother of his son (1811), known later as the Duke of * Reichstadt, who after his father's abdication was brought up by his Austrian grandfather; Marie Louise, who refused to accompany her husband into exile, was given the duchies of Parma, Piacenza and Guastalla. She became the mistress of the Austrian general Neipperg, whom she secretly married after Napoleon's death.
Turnbull, P., *Napoleon's Second Empress: Marie Louise*. 1971

Marin, John (1870–1953). American painter. He was born in New Jersey and most of his paintings depict scenes on the coasts of Maine. His composition shows the influence of Cézanne, and he used expressionist and abstract painting techniques to achieve representational results. He is best known for his watercolours but used oils more freely in later life.
Williams, W. C., *John Marin*. 1956

Marinetti, Filippo Tommaso (1876–1944). Italian writer, born in Alexandria. After studying in France he developed his theory of 'Futurism', which rejected the past and exalted present and future, glorifying machinery and war (seen as a cleansing mechanism). He joined the Fascists, hailed * Mussolini as an embodiment of Futurist aims and was a prolific writer of poetry, plays and novels.

Maritain, Jacques (1882–1973). French philosopher. After being a pupil of Bergson, he was converted to Catholicism (1906) and became an exponent of the philosophy of * St Thomas Aquinas, seeing in it a solution of modern problems of the mind, of society and of culture. He became a professor of the Institut Catholique in Paris and from 1933 taught at Toronto. After World War II he was French ambassador to the Vatican (1945–48) and then professor at Princeton, N.J. (1948–52).

Marius, Gaius (157–86 B.C.). Roman soldier and politician, who was seven times elected consul. His first campaign was in Spain (134–133) where he subsequently served as propraetor. He took part (109–108) in the war in Numidia against * Jugurtha under Metellus to whose command he succeeded (107). As consul in that year he abolished the property qualification for military service and thus founded a virtually professional and more efficient army. He brought the war in Africa to an end (107–105), though it was actually * Sulla, soon to be his deadly rival, who captured Jugurtha himself. He was again elected consul for the five successive years 104 to 100, during which he trained his army and eventually crushed the Teutoni (at Aquae Sextiae in 102) and the Cimbri (at Vercellae in 101), who were invading Italy from the north. These successes were followed by a period of eclipse after he had let himself become the tool of the demagogue Saturnius during is consulship of 100. He took part in the Social War (91–88) which was followed by enfranchisement of the Italians as Roman citizens, but in 88 the new electors were organized to vote for the supersession of the consul Sulla by Marius in the war against Mithridates. Sulla retorted by marching his legions back to Rome, getting the legislation repealed and Marius exiled. But as soon as Sulla was in the East the new consul Cinna brought Marius back and for Sulla's supporters there followed a reign of terror (87), for which Sulla's vengeance only came after Marius's death. Meanwhile it had been shown how easily a successful general could usurp civil power – an example which was to inspire many similar events.

Carney, T. F., *A Biography of Gaius Marius.* 1970

Mark, St (also called John Mark; Johanan to the Jews, Marcus to the Romans) (*c.* 10–70 A.D.). Christian apostle; one of the four evangelists. The earliest Christians met at the house of his mother, Mary, and he met * Paul through his cousin * Barnabas. Mark accompanied them on their first missionary journey, but at Perga left them to return to Jerusalem, which led Paul to refuse to take him on his second journey. The result was a split, with Barnabas taking Mark to his native Cyprus. The friendly references in Paul's Epistles indicate a reconciliation and Mark is mentioned as sharing Paul's imprisonment, probably in Rome. He then worked closely with * Peter ('my son Mark', 1 Peter v: 13) and, according to Papias and Irenaeus, his Gospel was written after the martyrdom of Peter and Paul but probably before the destruction of Jerusalem.

St Mark's Gospel is the shortest of the synoptics, with a dramatic, abrupt narrative and was long thought to be the earliest. Written in Greek, it is addressed to a Roman audience, somewhat anti-Jewish in tone and with a shaky grasp of Palestinian geography (curious in a work thought to embody Peter's recollections). According to tradition Mark became the first bishop of Alexandria and died there, but his remains were later transferred to Venice.

Markova, Dame Alicia (1910–). English ballerina. She joined the Diaghilev company in 1924, her work with them being the strongest influence on her future career. She danced with the Sadler's Wells Ballet (1933–35), Ballet Russe de Monte Carlo and, during World War II, the Opera Ballet of the New York Metropolitan Opera. She was prima ballerina of the newly-formed London Festival Ballet 1950–52. Her dancing, particularly in partnership with Anton Dolin, was probably the nearest English approximation to the Russian tradition. She did much to raise technical and artistic standards and was made D.B.E. in 1963.

Marlborough, John Churchill, 1st Duke of (1650–1722). English soldier. He was the son of Sir Winston Churchill, royalist who, forced to sell his property to pay a fine for his part in the Civil War, was recalled in 1663 to court. John was sent to St Paul's School; his sister Arabella became the mistress of the Duke of York (later James II), who obtained for her brother a commission in the guards. Churchill served in Tangiers (1668–70) and in the third Dutch War, at first with the fleet (1672) and then (from 1673) with a British contingent under the French commander * Turenne, from whom he learnt much of the art of war. In the winter of 1677–78 he married one of the Duchess of York's ladies-in-waiting, the dominating and ambitious Sarah Jennings (1660–1744), who commanded his life-long devotion and did much to steer his fortunes.

Under James II Churchill played a leading part against * Monmouth at Sedgemoor, but joined William of Orange when he landed (1688) and was created Earl of Marlborough. He was commander-in-chief in England during William's absence in Ireland (1690), but in 1692 he was suddenly dismissed from all his posts and for a time imprisoned in the Tower of London on forged evidence that he was plotting to restore James. He was restored to favour in 1698 and when the War of the Spanish Succession broke out (1701) he was appointed to command the British forces in Holland. On the accession of Anne (1702), over whom the influence of Marlborough's wife Sarah was complete, he was made captain-general of all British forces at home and abroad, and with Dutch consent, supreme commander of all allied forces against France. Further to safeguard his power, his friend * Godolphin, whose son was married to Marlborough's daughter, was lord treasurer. Marlborough's first great victory at Blenheim (1704) resulted from a march to the Danube and the effective support of the imperial commander Prince Eugene: the chain of victories was continued by Ramillies (1706), Oudenarde (1708), which led to the fall of Lille, and Malplaquet (1709) which opened the way (1710–11) to the capture, one by one, of the great fortresses protecting the French frontier. But at home, from Marlborough's point of view, catastrophe had occurred. His wife was replaced in the royal affections by

Mrs Masham, and as head of the government the Whig Godolphin was succeeded by the Tory, * Harley. In the autumn of 1711 Marlborough was dismissed from all his offices and the war was hurried to a close (1713). After Anne's death (1714) Marlborough was reinstated by George I, and he had, to console him, the ducal title (1702) and the parliamentary vote, earned by his first great victory, which resulted in the construction of Vanbrugh's magnificent Blenheim Palace. Sarah, his duchess, fruitfully spent the twenty-two years by which she survived him in embellishing the mighty domain and haggling over the necessary funds: she left £3,000,000. Marlborough was among the greatest captains of his own or any time; he was avaricious and his political loyalties sometimes wavered, but his care for the welfare of his troops won their love and he had a generosity of mind and a greatness of spirit that matched his deeds.
Rowse, A. L., *The Early Churchills*. 1956

Marlowe, Christopher (1564–1593). English dramatist and poet. The son of a shoemaker, he went to King's School, Canterbury, and graduated at Cambridge. After he went to London (*c*. 1586) he seems to have lived, despite his almost immediate fame as a playwright, a dangerous underworld existence linked in some sort of way with secret-service work. He was killed in a tavern-brawl at Deptford. The subject of his first play *Tamburlaine the Great* (1587) is the life of the great Mongol conqueror * Timur the Lame. It was followed by *The Tragical History of Dr Faustus* (1588), relating the story of the German necromancer who sold his soul to the devil, *The Jew of Malta* (1589), an almost fantastic tale of revenge and murder, and *Edward II* (1592). Lesser works are *The Massacre of Paris* (1593) and *Dido Queen of Carthage* (*c*. 1593, written in collaboration with Thomas Nash).

Marlowe was the first to realize the full potentialities (both rhetorical and dramatic) of blank verse for tragedy and thus paved the way for * Shakespeare, with whom he may have collaborated in the writing of *Titus Andronicus* and *Henry VI*. He also introduced the tragedy of character (e.g. the effects of power) as opposed to the tragedy of events, though he does this with less subtlety than Shakespeare and his minor characters are often sketchily drawn. In addition to his dramatic work Marlowe translated from Ovid and Lucan and wrote much poetry; *Hero and Leander* (1598), completed by George Chapman, is his best known poem. The song *Come live with me and be my love* was published in *The Passionate Pilgrim* (1599).
Boas, F. S., *Christopher Marlowe*. 1940

Marot, Clément (*c*. 1496–1544). French poet. At the court of Francis I and his sister Margaret of Navarre, Marot gained favour by graceful and witty satires, elegies, rondeaux and ballads. His translation of the Psalms, however, brought upon him the objurgations of the Sorbonne; and his life brought several alternations of fortune and he died as an exile in Turin. In literary history he stands at the junction point of medieval and Renaissance styles.
Mayer, C. A., *Clément Marot*. 1972

Marquand, John Phillips (1893–1960). American novelist. He became popular with a series of stories about the Japanese detective, Mr Moto, but later wrote a series of sharp-edged satires on society in New England, e.g. *The Late George Apley* (1937), which won the Pulitzer Prize, and *H.M. Pulham Esq*. (1941).

Marquis, Don (Donald Robert Perry) (1878–1937). American journalist and humorist. In *Archy and Mehitabel* (1927) he published the stories of Mehitabel the cat and her friend Archy the Cockroach. Earlier he had worked with Joel Chandler Harris, the creator of Uncle Remus.
Anthony, E., *O Rare Don Marquis*. 1962

Marryat, Frederick (1792–1848). English sailor and novelist. After many years in the navy, during which he fought in the Napoleonic Wars and in Burma, he retired to write popular adventure stories, e.g. *Peter Simple* (1834), *Mr Midshipman Easy* (1836), *Masterman Ready* (1841) and the delightful story for children *The Children of the New Forest* (1847).
Warner, O., *Captain Marryat*. 1953

Marsh, Dame (Edith) Ngaio (1899–1982). New Zealand novelist. She was second only to Agatha * Christie as a prolific writer of detective stories and superior as a stylist.

Marsh, George Perkins (1801–1882). American writer, born in Woodstock, Vermont. He was a lawyer, philologist, congressman and diplomat (Minister to Italy 1861–82) whose book *Man and Nature* (1864; revised and retitled in 1874 as *The Earth as Modified by Human Action*) developed the concepts of resource management and anticipated ecology as a major study.

Marshal, William, 1st Earl of Pembroke (*c.* 1141–1219). English soldier and administrator. His marriage to a daughter of Strongbow (Earl of* Pembroke) brought him wealth and an earldom and later he became prominent in the royal service. He was joint-marshal and justiciar to Richard I and was consistently faithful to King John. After John's death he expelled the French invaders, secured the accession of Henry III and became regent for the boy king.

Marshall, Alfred (1842–1924). English economist. From the time he became an undergraduate at Cambridge his whole life was spent in academic circles. After resigning (1881) for health reasons as principal of the new University College at Bristol he returned to Cambridge as professor of political economy (1885–1908). He is the last of the line of the great classical economists and his *Principles of Economics* (1890) became a standard work used by many generations of students; and though some of its conclusions are now disputed or outmoded it remains a basic work. He also wrote *Industry and Trade* (1919) and *Money, Credit and Commerce* (1923).

Marshall, George Catlett (1880–1959). American soldier. He entered the army in 1901 and served in the Philippines and the France during World War I. Between the wars he had instructional, administrative and staff experience and in 1939 he was given the rank of general and promoted over the heads of many seniors to be chief of the general staff. After American intervention he was therefore the focal point of the Allied military leadership, and he not only presided over the vast expansion of the American forces but was the chief professional spokesman at the conferences of Casablanca, Cairo, Yalta etc. His support, therefore, for the policy of defeating Hitler first was of the utmost importance. After Japan's defeat he became (1945) U.S. ambassador to China but failed to avert * Chiang Kai-shek's collapse. As U.S. secretary of state (1947–49) he put forward the European Recovery Programme (Marshall Aid) for channelling American assistance to the war-stricken areas which accelerated the recovery of Europe. He was U.S. secretary of defence (1950–51) and won the Nobel Peace Prize in 1953.

Mosley, L., *Marshall: Organizer of Victory*. 1982

Marshall, John (1755–1835). American lawyer. He served in the War of Independence, was called to the bar and from 1783 practised in Richmond where he soon rose to be head of the Virginian bar. He served in the state legislature (1782–88 and 1795–97) and led the Federalist party in Virginia. Wider fame came when he was sent to Paris to negotiate with the Directory. The exposure in the famous X.Y.Z. letters of * Talleyrand's unsuccessful attempt to bribe the delegates made Marshall a popular hero. He was elected to U.S. Congress in 1799 and in 1800 President Adams made him secretary of state and in the next year chief justice of the Supreme Court. Marshall used his powers of interpreting the constitution to strengthen the federal government and issued several judgements invalidating acts of state legislatures which aimed at or tended to nullify acts of Congress. On the other hand he tried to protect the individual from state oppression.

Marsiglio of Padua (1275/80–?). Italian scholar. He was the author (or co-author) of *Defensor Pacis*, an exposition of political ideas, based on the constitutions of some of the city states of northern Italy, that (a) the source of political power should be the people (i.e. all adult citizens), but (b) executive action should be delegated either to a council or to a single despot, and (c) the church should be a solely spiritual body and papal supremacy was unjustified. These views were immediately condemned as heretical (1327) and Marsiglio fled to Paris. Later he was to see his persecutor, Pope John XXII, deposed, and an emperor elected by an assembly in Roman; though this development proved ephemeral, *Defensor Pacis* guided much subsequent political thinking.

Marston, John (1576–1634). English dramatist. He wrote coarse, vigorous satire and a number of tragedies, some of them in collaboration with other dramatists. He started the campaign of mutual satire (1599–1601), the 'war of the theatres', with Ben * Jonson, but later became his friend and collaborator. His most interesting plays include *The Malcontent* (1604; with additions by Webster), *Eastward Ho!* (1605; with Ben Jonson and George Chapman) and *The Dutch Courtesan* (1605).

Martel, Charles *see* **Charles Martel**

Marti, José (1853–1895). Cuban writer and patriot. He was equally distinguished as a writer of prose and poetry and as leader of the Cuban struggle for independence from Spain. When only 16 he was exiled for political activity and for many years he was obliged to live abroad – in Mexico, Guatemala, Spain and the U.S.A. While in the U.S.A. he organized the Cuban revolutionary party of which he was an outstanding leader. The Cuban rising against the Spaniards began in 1895 and Marti was killed in the opening stages at the Battle of Dos Rios.

Martial (Marcus Valerius Martialis) (*c.* 40–*c.* 104). Latin poet and epigrammatist, born in Spain. He went to Rome where the wit and topicality of his verses won the approval of the emperors Titus and Domitian and widespread support. He wrote fifteen books, containing several hundred epigrams, polished, cunningly twisted and frequently indecent, which became the models for the epigram in post-Renaissance Europe. He spent his last years at his native Bilbilis.
Carrington, A. G., *Aspects of Martial's Epigrams*. 1960

Martin, John (1789–1854). English painter of the Romantic school. For a time hailed as a rival to Turner, his vast canvases, e.g. *Belshazzar's Feast* (1821) and *The Deluge* (1826), teem with people and incident and brought him a great, but transient, popularity.
Balston, T., *John Martin 1789–1854 – His Life and Works*. 1947

Martin, (Basil) Kingsley (1897–1969). English journalist. During his editorship of the *New Statesman* (1913–62), which he exercised with independence and skill until his retirement, he secured a commanding influence over the left-wing intellectuals of the Labour party.
Rolph, C. H., *Kingsley: Life, Letters and Diaries of Kingsley Martin*. 1973

Martin du Gard, Roger (1881–1958). French novelist. His work went unrecognized until his novel *Jean Barois* (1913) – a telling description of the France of the * Dreyfus era. His eight-part novel *The World of the Thibaults* won for him the Nobel Prize for Literature (1937).
Schalk, D. C., *Roger Martin du Gard, the Novelist and History*. 1967

Martineau, Harriet (1802–1876). English writer, daughter of a Norwich manufacturer. In her time her books were very popular; they included *Illustrations of Political Economy* (1832–34), *Poor Law and Paupers Illustrated* (1833), *Society in America* (1837), written after a visit to America, and *Letters on Mesmerism* (1845), a result of her belief that she owed recovery from serious illness to hypnotic treatment. Her aim in each case was to present a simplification (sometimes in fictional disguise) of serious themes. Her other work, historical, philosophic and autobiographical, much of it quite ephemeral, included a novel, *Deerbrook* (1839), and books for children.
Webb, R. K., *Harriet Martineau, a Radical Victorian*. 1960

Martinet, Jean (died 1672). French military engineer. His severe system of drill made his name a synonym for a harsh disciplinarian.

Martini, Simone (*c.* 1284–1344). Italian painter of the late Gothic period, regarded as second only to * Giotto. He was born in Siena and returned there (1321) after working at Naples for the Angevin court, at Orvieto and at Pisa. Except for intervals at Assisi to work on the scenes from the life of St Martin in the lower church of St Francis, he stayed at Siena until 1339, when on the summons of Pope Benedict XII he went to Avignon, where his work included the small panel (now at Liverpool) of the Holy Family, and where he died. Of his work at Siena, the fresco (1328) of Guidoriccio da Fogliano, destined for the council chamber, and the altar-piece of the Annunciation for the cathedral (now in the Uffizi, Florence) are among the best known. The two saints at the outside of the latter are probably the work of Lippo Memmi, but the work as a whole, with its graceful figures harmoniously posed against a gold background shows his treatment of his subjects at its best.
Paccagninni, G., *Simone Martini*. 1957

Martin of Tours, St (*c.* 316–397). Bishop of Tours (from *c.* 371). He was born in Pannonia and as the son of a military tribune had to serve in the Roman army. Converted to Christianity, he studied under Hilary of Poitiers. He founded a convent near Poitiers (*c.* 360), where he shared with the monks a life of seclusion and great austerity. In his bishopric of Tours, to avoid the distraction of the crowds attracted by his reputation for saintliness and miracles, he founded and lived in the monastery of Marmoutier. His feast day (11 November) became associated with a period of warm weather which often occurs about that time known as a St Martin's summer.

Marvell, Andrew (1621–1678). English poet. He was the son of a Yorkshire clergyman, and held a number of posts as tutor, notably to Fairfax's daughter at Nunappleton, where some of his best work, poems of wit and grace in praise of gardens and country life, was written. Later he became a secretary in government service and went with an embassy to Russia (1663–65). From 1659 he was M.P. for Hull. Politically a follower of Cromwell he could not withhold admiration for Charles I's bearing on the scaffold:

He nothing common did or mean
Upon that memorable scene.

Marvell did not marry and his love poems seldom carry conviction, though occasional lines such as

But at my back I always hear
Time's wingèd Chariot hurrying near

have earned immortality. In later life he became a satirist of an arbitrary government which he deplored.

Legouis, P., *Andrew Marvell, Poet, Puritan, Patriot*. 2nd ed. 1968

Marx, Karl Heinrich (1818–1883). German political philosopher. The son of a Jewish lawyer, and born at Trier, he was educated at the universities of Bonn and Berlin, abandoning the law for history and philosophy. He was editor of the *Rheinische Zeitung* from 1842 to 1843, when the Prussian government suppressed it for its radicalism. In 1843 he married Jenny von Westphalen (1814–1881) and moved to Paris, where he came to know * Engels. Expelled from France (1845), he moved to Brussels where with Engels he reorganized the Communist League, for which they wrote the famous *Communist Manifesto* (1848). This, though it contained a preformulation of the views later worked out in detail, was essentially a call to revolutionary action, ending with the exhortation 'The proletarians have nothing to lose but their chains. They have a world to gain. Workers of the world unite'. Marx took part in the revolutionary risings in the Rhineland in 1848 and after their failure settled (1849) in London for the rest of his life. After 15 years of research he wrote *Grundrisse* ('Outlines') at great speed in 1857–58; this was the framework of a vast incomplete work of which *Das Kapital* was only a part. *Grundrisse* included material on alienation, the impact of technology, the economies of time and his utopian vision. * Kautsky published excerpts in 1903, but the complete work did not appear until 1939–41 in Moscow, and in English translation until 1973.

He resumed active political work as founder and secretary of the International Working Mens' Association (later known as the First International) 1864–72. Here he had to contend with the views of rival leaders, especially the anarchist * Bakunin, whose withdrawal he forced in 1869. After the death of * Lassalle, Marx's influence became predominant in the German Social Democratic Party, and Marxist parties were founded in France and Russia during his lifetime. For more than 12 hours each day he worked in the reading room of the British Museum on *Das Kapital*. Volume I was published in Hamburg in 1867 (in Russian translation in 1872, French 1872–75 and English 1887). Volume II edited by Engels, appeared in 1885 and Volume III, completed by Engels from Marx' notes and private papers, in 1894. Marx was often in extreme poverty and from 1868 depended on an annual allowance of £350 from Engels. He died in London in March 1883 and is buried in Highgate Cemetry.

Marx' philosophical basis is an adaptation of * Hegel's dialectical system. With Marx it becomes dialectical materialism: historical stages succeed one another by way of conflict: the economic basis of one phase provokes its antithesis and the two then merge into a third. Thus the bourgeoisie displaced feudal society and the stage was then set for the final struggle between the bourgeoisie and the working classes. On the theoretical economic side Marx followed the classical economists in their concept of the labour theory of value. A capitalist society depended, in his view, on 'surplus value', i.e. that part of the amount received for the product of labour in excess of the amount paid for labour. Moreover, as the larger capitalist devoured the smaller, so its members would become fewer and richer, while the proletariat, its bargaining power reduced as the means by which labour can be employed (land, factories, machines etc.) became concentrated in fewer and fewer hands, would become relatively poorer. That being so, a clash was inevitable and the communist's part therefore must be to educate the proletariat in the role it must play both to hasten events and to bring about the desired future, in which production would be carried out for the good of all in a classless society. Since a capitalist state is the instrument by which the exploitation of the proletariat is carried out political action must be revolutionary: if successful, the next stage (from which no communist state has yet emerged) must, as Marx foresaw, be a dictatorship of the proletariat, necessary to prevent counter-revolution. This would be eventually followed by the third stage, the withering away of the state and the emergence of a classless society living and working in the perfectionist conditions referred to above. Marx developed his theories against the background of capitalist development as it existed in England in the middle of the 19th century. The influence of Marx's writings, though often misinterpreted, has been immense. His theories form the intellectual basis of almost all socialist parties, irrespective of the means they envisage to put them into effect. Even in his own time Marx could say 'I am not a Marxist'.

McLellan, D., *Karl Marx*. 1973; Singer, P., *Marx*. 1980; Kamenka, E. (ed), *The Portable Karl Marx*. 1983

Marx Brothers. A family of Jewish–American comedians. Four of them, 'Groucho' (Julius; 1895–1977), 'Chico' (Leonard; 1891–1961), 'Harpo' (Arthur; 1893–1964) and, until his withdrawal (1935), 'Zeppo' (Herbert; 1901–1979), became famous in vaudeville and developed a surrealistic humour of their own in a series of successful films (after 1935) including *Duck Soup, At the Circus, A Night at the Opera* and *A Day at the Races*.

Mary (Hebrew Miriam). The mother of Jesus Christ, known also as the Blessed Virgin. According to apocryphal gospels she was the daughter of St Anne. The narratives of the Annunciation, the miraculous Conception and the birth of Jesus Christ at Bethlehem are told with varying details in the Gospels of St Matthew and St Luke, where also it is recorded that her husband Joseph was a craftsman of Nazareth in Galilee. The most important of the very few other biblical references is the one in St John's Gospel where it is related that she stood by the cross at the Crucifixion and that Jesus entrusted her to the care of that unnamed 'beloved disciple', who took her to his own home.

The traditions and dogmas that are connected with the name of Mary, and especially her Perpetual Virginity and the exceptional degree of veneration bestowed upon her by the Roman Catholic church belong to the realm of theology rather than biography. Among the important church festivals associated with the events of her life are the Annunciation (25 March), known as Lady Day, and the Purification (2 February) or Candlemas.

Mary (1542–1587). Queen of Scots 1542–67. Daughter of James V of Scotland and Mary of Guise, and heiress to the English throne through her grandmother Margaret Tudor, she became queen when her father died six days after her birth. To keep her out of the hands of the Protestant or 'English' party who wished her to marry the future Edward VI, she was sent to France, her mother remaining in Scotland as regent. On her return in 1560, while remaining a Catholic, she was able to negotiate a political-religious settlement with the nobility and supporters of John * Knox. She married three times: (1) in 1558 to the French dauphin who became * Francis II and died in 1560; (2) in 1565 to her cousin, Henry Stuart, Lord * Darnley, who fathered her only child * James VI of Scotland (and I of England), murdered her confidante David * Rizzio and was blown up in February 1567; and (3) in May 1567 to James Hepburn, Earl of * Bothwell, who had murdered Darnley. Her last marriage was politically disastrous and she lost all support: the army deserted, Bothwell fled to Denmark and in June 1567 she was deposed in favour of her son. After an attempt to regain power failed in June 1568, she sought asylum in England. * Elizabeth kept her as a prisoner until her death because she was a rallying point for English Catholics.

Elizabeth believed that she was part of a series of conspiracies (the evidence is not completely convincing) and after the * Babington plot, Mary was tried for treason at Fotheringay Castle (October 1586), convicted and beheaded (February 1587). On Elizabeth's death in 1603, Mary's son James succeeded as King of England. She was a romantic figure, the subject of books, plays, films and Verdi's opera *Maria Stuarda*.
Fraser, A., *Mary Queen of Scots*. 1969.

Mary (1658–1718). Queen consort of James II of Great Britain, known, after her father's Italian duchy, as Mary of Modena. She married the then Duke of York in 1673. The birth (1688) of a son, James Edward * Stuart, an event which seemed likely to perpetuate a Roman Catholic dynasty, was one of the causes of the revolution by which James was deposed. The story that the baby was not hers but had been smuggled into the palace in a warming pan may be discarded.

Mary (1867–1953). Queen consort of George V of Great Britain. She was the daughter of Francis, Duke of Teck, and a great-granddaughter of George III. In 1889 she became engaged to the Duke of Clarence, elder son of the future Edward VII, but a year after his death (1892) she married his younger brother, the Duke of York, who ascended the throne (1910) as George V. The grace and dignity as well as the unwearying thoroughness with which she performed her royal duties and the particular interest she showed in the work of women's organizations won wide popularity. In the pursuit of her main hobby, the collection of antiques, she showed enthusiasm and flair.
Pope-Hennessy, J., *Mary: Consort of George V*. 1960

Mary (1897–1965). British princess. Only daughter of George V, she was known from 1932 as the Princess Royal. In 1922 she married Viscount Lascelles, who succeeded (1929) as 6th Earl of Harewood. Her elder son, **George Henry Hubert Lascelles, 7th Earl of Harewood** (1923–), became known for his interest in opera and was artistic director of the Edinburgh Festival (1961–65).

Mary I (1516–1558). Queen of England (from 1553). She was the daughter of Henry VIII by his first wife * Catherine of Aragon. Mary's prospects were at first brilliant and negotiations for marriage were pressed forward with royal suitors (including the emperor Charles V) from her childhood days. But all was changed when King Henry and her mother became estranged and the marriage was annulled (1533). Mary had to live in retirement and even acknowledged herself to be illegitimate. She was restored to the line of succession by her father's will but her way of life was hardly changed while her Protestant brother Edward VI was on the throne. On his death, however, she foiled with general public support the Duke of Northumberland's bold attempt to transfer the crown to his own family by establishing the claim of his daughter-in-law Lady Jane * Grey. Unfortunately Mary, who began her reign with the avowed aim of restoring the supremacy of the Roman Catholic church, was already a frustrated and embittered woman, and though she at first acted with caution her proposed marriage to Philip (later Philip II) of Spain deprived her of much of her popularity and provoked a rebellion by Sir Thomas * Wyatt. This was suppressed but the marriage (1554) brought her no joy, as Philip, who left the country in 1555, could not conceal his indifference and the false pregnancy which deluded her into making all preparations for an expected child deprived him of his political hopes.

Meanwhile Roman supremacy was restored (1554) and Cardinal * Pole, the papal legate and later archbishop of Canterbury, became Mary's chief adviser. The persecutions which were to make the queen remembered as 'Bloody Mary' began in 1555. The first to die were * Ridley and * Latimer, and * Cranmer (1556) and some hundreds more followed. Whatever allowances are made for her unhappiness and the pressures that her religion laid upon her, Mary, who was not naturally cruel, must bear the main responsibility. In 1557 the English were dragged into the Spanish war against France, the only result being the loss (1558) of their last continental possession, Calais, the name said to be written on Mary's heart when, tormented in mind and body and almost unlamented, she died. She was succeeded by her half-sister Elizabeth.

Mary II (1662–1694). Queen of Great Britain (from 1689). The elder daughter of James, Duke of York (James II), by his first wife Anne Hyde, she married (1677) her first cousin

William, Prince of Orange (later * William III). After her father's deposition, she and her husband were invited to become joint sovereigns. Mary was much loved and after her early death, from smallpox, deeply mourned.
Van Der See, B. and H. A., *William and Mary*. 1973

Mary Magdalene (or Mary of Magdala), **St.** The Gospel stories relate that Jesus cast out seven devils from her, that she became a devoted disciple and that she was the first to whom Jesus appeared after the Resurrection. Tradition links her with a penitent sinner mentioned by St Luke. Her name has thus come to symbolize the harlot restored to purity by faith and penitence.

Masaccio (nickname 'clumsy' of Tommaso Guidi) (1401–?1428). Florentine painter. He lived and worked mostly in Florence until he went (1427) to Rome where he died. He probably derived from his contemporary * Brunelleschi much of the knowledge of perspective and space revealed in his pictures. In particular he masterd tonal perspective, by which an appearance of depth is achieved by gradations of colour; he is also said to have been the first to light his pictures at a constant angle from a single point of origin. The figures are solidly and realistically conceived and belong naturally to their surroundings. His finest work is generally held to be the frescoes in the Brancacci Chapel of the Carmelite Church, Florence, but the fact that he worked in collaboration with Masolino has caused an acute artistic controversy as to the part played by each. The finest of Masaccio's undisputed works include the *Expulsion from Paradise* and *Tribute to Caesar*. Masaccio is ranked as one of the greatest figures in Renaissance art between Giotto and Leonardo da Vinci.
Salmi, M., *Masaccio*. 1948

Masaryk, Thomas Garrigue (1850–1937). First president of Czechoslovakia. The son of a Slovak coachman, he studied sociology and philosophy at Vienna University. This enabled him to take up a professorship at the re-established Czech University at Prague, and write several books on philosophy, sociology and Slav nationalism. Meanwhile he had married (1878) an American girl, Charlotte Garrigue. In 1891 he was first elected to the Austrian parliament and though he resigned in 1893 he gradually became recognized as the spokesman of all the Slav minorities in the Austro-Hungarian empire. He was re-elected to parliament in 1912 but when World War I broke out (1914) he at once saw it as an opportunity to obtain independence for the subject peoples. In December 1914 he escaped to Italy and in one country after another, Switzerland, France, Britain, Russia and the U.S.A., pressed his cause. He organized a Czech national council in Paris (1916) and in May 1917 went to Russia to build up a Czech Legion (mainly from prisoners of war). After the Bolshevik Revolution the Legion reached the Pacific via Siberia and reached America where Masaryk awaited it. At last (June 1918) the governments of Great Britain, France and the U.S.A. recognized Czechoslovakia as an independent ally, with Masaryk as the government's provisional head. In December with the Austro-Hungarian régime collapsed around him Masaryk returned triumphantly as president–liberator of the new state of Czechoslovakia. During his tenure of office, which lasted until his resignation (1935), his wisdom and liberality of mind inspired the growth of Czechoslovakia as the most prosperous and progressive country of the new Europe.

The shadow of Hitler was already looming when he died but it was upon his son **Jan Masaryk** (1886–1948) that the darkness fell. He was Czechoslovak minister in London from 1925 until 1938, when he resigned after the Munich agreement. In World War II he was foreign minister in the goverment in exile established in England and was still holding that office when after Germany's defeat (1945) the government returned to France. A fortnight after the Communists (February 1948) seized control Jan Masaryk allegedly committed suicide in a fall from a window of the Foreign Office.
Birley, R., *Thomas Masaryk*. 1951

Mascagni, Pietro (1863–1945). Italian composer. After abandoning law he became famous with the one-act opera *Cavalleria Rusticana* (1890). This, a brutal and melodramatic treatment of a subject drawn from working-class life, established the style of Italian opera known as *verismo*. None of his later operas, e.g. *L'Amico Fritz* (1891) and *La Maschera* (1901), won the same celebrity.

Masefield, John Edward (1878–1967). English poet and novelist. He worked as a merchant seaman (1889–97), and many of his finest poems and stories are concerned with the sea. His first volume of poetry was *Salt Water Ballads* (1902). Other volumes include the long narrative poem *The Everlasting Mercy* (1911), *Reynard the Fox* (1919) and *Right Royal* (1920). In the first of these the fastidious complained that the sordid scenes of violence were unsuited to poetry while the others delighted those to whom hunting and racing are even more important than verse. *Dauber* (1913) reveals to the full his sense of the beauty of ships and the sea. In his poetry it is the combination of realistic language with lilting rhythm which produces some of his most striking effects:

Dirty British coaster with a salt-caked smoke stack.
Butting through the Channel in the mad March days,
With a cargo of Tyne coal,
Road-rail, pig-lead,
Firewood, iron-ware, and cheap tin trays.

His prose works include a memoir of the Gallipoli campaign, several novels, e.g. *Sard Harker* (1924), literary studies etc. He succeeded (1930) Robert Bridges as Poet Laureate and became a member of the O.M. (1935).

Spark, M., *John Masefield*. 1953

Masinissa (Massinissa) (*c.* 238–149 B.C.). King of Numidia (roughly modern Algeria), a vassal state of Carthage. He transferred his allegiance to Rome during the Second Punic War (206) and his cavalry carried out the decisive charge at the Battle of Zama when Hannibal was defeated. His kingdom grew strong and prosperous. In 150 a Carthaginian attack on Numidia – then the ally of Rome – led to the Third Punic War.

Maslow, Abraham Harold (1908–1970). American psychologist and educator. His text book *Motivation and Personality* (1954) identified a 'hierarchy of needs' in human development and has been influential in sociology.

Masolino da Panicale (*c.* 1383–1447). Italian painter. He assisted Ghiberti and may have taught * Masaccio, with whom he collaborated and by whose techniques he was much influenced. His most important works are the frescoes rediscovered (1843) under whitewash at Castiglione d'Olona. The frescoes in San Clemente at Rome have also been attributed to him.

Micheletti, E., *Masolino da Panicale*. 1959

Mason, Charles (1730–1787). American surveyor. Employed with Jeremiah Dixon to mark out (1763–67) the boundary between the American colonies Pennsylvania and Maryland, this Mason-Dixon line came to be regarded as the frontier between North and South in the U.S.A.

Maspero, Gaston Camille Charles (1846–1916). French Egyptologist. While in Egypt (1880–86) as director of excavations and curator of the museum at Cairo, he discovered the royal mummies at Deir el Bahri. He returned (1886) to Paris to take up a professorship, but was appointed (1889) director of the Department of Antiquities in Egypt, which he reorganized with an efficiency that earned him a K.C.M.G.

Maspero, G. C. C., *New Light on Ancient Egypt*. 1908

Masséna, André, Duke of Rivoli, Prince of Essling (1758–1817). French marshal. He was born in Nice (then in the kingdom of Sardinia) and became a soldier, but during the Revolution he volunteered for the French army and by the end of 1793 was a divisional general. He made a name for himself in the Italian campaigns against the Austrians – where the Rivoli (1797), from which he took his title, was his most striking success – and against the Russian General Suvoroff in Switzerland (1799). Thereafter he fought in nearly all Napoleon's campaigns in central Europe and won his princely title by his heroic covering of the Danube crossing (1809) at Aspen or Essling. Sent to Spain in 1810 he drove Wellington right back to the lines of Torres Vedras, but on finding the position impregnable extricated himself by a masterly retreat. Napoleon chose to make him a scapegoat, refused to employ him on his Russian campaign and himself received no reply when he called for Masséna's aid after the escape from Elba.

Massenet, Jules Emile Frédéric (1842–1912). French composer. He taught (1878–96) at the Paris Conservatoire, where he had been a student, and after winning the Prix de Rome produced his first opera (1867) soon after his return to France. It is his twenty-three operas,

deeply romantic, unfailingly melodious and characteristically accomplished, that form his main achievement, notably *Manon* (1881) and *Thaïs* (1894). He also wrote songs and orchestral, choral and piano works.
Massenet, J. E. F., *My Recollections*. 1919

Massey, William Ferguson (1856–1925). New Zealand politician. He emigrated from Ireland (1870) and worked on first his father's then his farm. He was elected to the House of Representatives (1894), became leader of the conservative (Reform party) opposition (1903) and, after a government defeat, prime minister. During his tenure of office (1912–25) he led his country successfully through World War I and attended the Paris Peace Conference on its behalf.

Massine, Léonide (1896–1979). Russian ballet dancer and choreographer. He was principal dancer (1914–20) of Diaghilev's Ballets Russes in Paris and was chief choreographer (from 1915). He created several new ballets including *La Boutique Fantasque* (music by Rossini) and *Le Sacre du printemps* (music by Stravisnky). He worked with the Ballets Russes de Monte Carlo (1932–41). His autobiography *My Life in Ballet* was published in 1968.

Massinger, Philip (1583–1639/40). English dramatist, born at Salisbury. He collaborated with other dramatists, notably John * Fletcher and Thomas * Dekker; plays which are probably independent include dramas, often on religious and political themes, which to his audience suggested contemporary parallels. Among them are *The Duke of Milan* (1623), *The Maid of Honour* (*c*. 1625) and *The Roman Actor* (1626). He is better known for his satirical comedies, *The City Madam* (acted 1632) and *A New Way to Pay Old Debts* (published 1633). Psychological interest and constructive power are Massinger's main assets.

Massys, Quentin *see* **Matsys, Quentin**

Masters, Edgar Lee (1869–1950). American author and poet. His collection of poems, *Spoon River Anthology* (1915), contains what purport to be confessions of and revelations about those lying in a mid-western cemetery. He also wrote biographies of Lincoln, Walt Whitman and Mark Twain.
Master, E. L., *Across Spoon River*. 1936

Mata Hari (Margarete Gertrude Zelle) (1871–1917). Dutch-born spy of World War I. She was a dancer in Paris who by consorting with officers was able to obtain information which she passed on to the Germans; for this she was tried and shot, though some allege she was a double agent.

Matanzima (*c*. 1917–). South African politician. Chief of the Xhosa people and a qualified lawyer, he was elected (1963) by his fellow chiefs to head the government of the Transkei, the first of the self-governing 'Bantustan' areas, reserved for Africans, set up under the apartheid policy.

Mather, Increase (1639–1723). American Congregationalist minister. After taking his degree at Harvard, he spent some time preaching in England and Guernsey before returning to America as minister of the Second Church, Boston (1664–1723). In 1685 he became president of Harvard. He did much to allay the panic caused by the Salem witch trials and wrote *Causes of Conscience concerning Witchcraft* (1693).

His son, **Cotton Mather** (1662–1727), a theologian, was responsible above others for fanning the flames of the Salem witchcraft mania by his many books on the subject of possession by evil spirits.
Murdock, K. B., *Increase Mather: the foremost American Puritan*. Repr. 1966

Mathew, Theobald (1790–1856). Irish friar. His work amongst the poor in Cork (1812–38) convinced him that drink aggravated their misery and he led a great temperance crusade which had astonishing success. In 1848 he went to America, where he achieved similar results. On his return to Ireland (1851) he declined a bishopric. Temperance advocates still hold Father Mathew festivals.

Matilda (1102–1167). Daughter of Henry I of England. At the age of 10 she married the Holy Roman Emperor Henry V (died 1125). By her second husband Geoffrey, Count of Anjou (* Plantagenet), she became the mother of the future Henry II. When Henry I died (1135) many of the barons, despite oaths to the late king, refused to recognize her as queen, and her cousin * Stephen of Blois seized the throne. Civil war ensued, but though Stephen was captured (1141) Matilda's arrogance soon alienated support and she eventually gave up her claim in favour of her son, whom Stephen accepted as his heir.

Matisse, Henri (1869–1954). French painter. He studied art in Paris, copied pictures in the Louvre and succumbed to the influence of the Impressionists, Cézanne and Gauguin. In 1905 he became the leader of a revolutionary group of artists, labelled by critics 'Les Fauves' ('wild beasts'). To them colour was end in itself and its use was unconnected with the colour of the subject portrayed. Matisse covered large unbroken areas with colour, disregarding perspective and the distortion its absence produced, but discovering new decorative effects by the vibrancy and luminosity of the colour itself; yet though the effect of his work was to hasten the arrival of abstract art, he himself was not an abstract painter; similarly though his colour patterns often took geometrical shapes he was never a cubist. In fact as the years went by he reduced the element of violence and 'balance, purity and moderation' became his aims; just as fruit and flowers supplied him with decorative themes so did women; his *Odalisques* adorn and delight but convey no sensual message. After a period in which his pictures became smaller and less spontaneous, he was again, in the 1930s, seeking bolder effects; a commission for the Burnes Foundation (U.S.A.) provided him with an opportunity to undertake murals. The last few years of his life were mainly devoted to designing and decorating with murals and stained glass a Dominican chapel at Vence near Nice, but even when he was over 80 he showed his versatility in a new way by using decorative collages (paper cut-outs) as an art form.
Escholier, R., *Matisse, from the Life*. 1960

Matsushita Konosuke (1896–). Japanese industrialist, born in a peasant family near Osaka. He started (1918) a manufacturing firm on a very small scale for the production of electrical appliances. World War II gave a tremendous impetus to his business and he emerged from the war period as a leader in the field of electronic equipment and quickly became the undisputed giant. His mass production of electrical household accessories eased and simplified the traditional domestic duties of Japanese women.

Matsys (or Massys), **Quentin** (*c.* 1465–1530). Flemish painter. His early altar pieces followed the tradition of the Van Eycks, though with almost life-sized figures; but his later religious pictures, e.g. the *Magdalen* at Antwerp, reveal a softer modelling and a sweetness of expression reminiscent of the work of Leonardo da Vinci, by which he may have been influenced. He is also known for gently satirical genre pictures and portraits.

Matteotti, Giacomo (1885–1924). Italian politician. A leader of the socialist party, he was a courageous opponent of Fascism. He was kidnapped and murdered by a gang of Fascists who went virtually unpunished, after which there was no effective opposition to Mussolini and the last vestiges of political liberty disappeared.

Matthew, St (*c.* 5–85 A.D.). Christian apostle; one of the four evangelists. Nothing certain is known about him except that at the time he was called upon to be a disciple he was a publican (tax-gatherer) and therefore despised and hated for his profitable association with Roman rule. He was probably identical with Levi, mentioned in St Mark's and St Luke's gospels in which the name of Matthew does not appear. There is continuing controversy about the priority of the Gospels of Mark and Matthew. The Jerusalem Bible's editors argue that the Gospel bearing Matthew's name may have appeared in two versions, first in primitive Aramaic, perhaps as early as 40–50 and known to Mark (augmented by a collection of *Sayings* attributed to Matthew), then a Greek version produced 70–80 which in turn was influenced by Mark. Matthew's Gospel is longer and more systematic than Mark, with a strong emphasis on Jesus' Messiahship, on teaching and on his fulfilment of Old Testament prophecies. It was essentially aimed at a Jewish audience: the Sermon on the Mount only appears in Matthew (v–vii). There are three separate traditions about Matthew's martyrdom.

Matthews, Sir Stanley (1915–). English professional footballer. He played in league football from 1931 until 1965, when he was knighted, the first professional footballer to be so honoured. The first of his fifty-six appearances for England was in 1934.

Matthias Corvinus (1440–1490). King of Hungary (from 1458). Second son of * János Hunyadi. Having successfully continued his

father's struggle against the Turks, he was able to add Moravia and Silesia to his dominions, conquer Carinthia and Styria and capture Vienna, which he made his capital. His vigour and justice as a ruler were matched by his fame as a scholar, a sign of which was the magnificent library he founded. He died without legitimate heirs at the height of his power.
Malyusz, E., *Matthias Corvinus in Menschen die Geschichte machten*. Vol. 2, 1931

Maude, Sir Frederick Stanley (1864–1917). British soldier, conqueror of Baghdad in World War I. After service in the Sudan and South Africa he was a colonel when the war broke out; he fought in France and Gallipoli before being sent to Mesopotamia (Iraq). He was made commander-in-chief of that area (September 1916) and in one of the most brilliantly conceived and executed campaigns of the war he captured Baghdad (March 1917). His series of successes was still unbroken when in November he died of cholera.

Maudling, Reginald (1917–1979). British Conservative politician. He was called to the bar (1940), served in the R.A.F. during World War II and entered parliament in 1950. In 1955 he became minister of supply, the first of a number of ministerial appointments culminating in that of chancellor of the exchequer (1962). He retained this post when (1963) Macmillan was replaced by Douglas-Home. When Home resigned the leadership of the Conservative party a few months after the Labour victory of 1964, Maudling was one of the chief contestants to succeed but his parliamentary colleagues (in the first election for a party leader) chose Edward * Heath. He became deputy leader and served as home secretary (1970–72).
Maudling, R., *Maudling's Memoirs*. 1978

Maudsley, Henry (1835–1918). English psychiatrist. Born in Yorkshire, he settled in London and exercised important influence on the treatment of mental illness, notably through his book *The Pathology of Mind* (1867). Believing that insanity was a disease of the brain, he stressed the need for treating it as such and not merely controlling the symptoms; he gave special attention to hereditary factors. In the hope of securing systematic research into mental disease and early treatment for sufferers he gave a large sum to the London County Council for a psychiatric hospital to be linked with London University. The result was the Maudsley Hospital, opened shortly after his death.

Maugham, W(illiam) Somerset (1874–1965). British author. Trained in medicine, he drew on his experience as a physician in the London slums in his first novel, *Liza of Lambeth* (1903). But it was as playwright that he first attained fame and wealth in the years preceding World War I a succession of plays with a sharp flavour and astringent wit, e.g. *Lady Frederick*, filled the theatres; after the war the plays became more sophisticated and satirical, e.g. *The Circle* (1921), *Our Betters* (1923) and *The Letter* (1927). In the war itself he did secret-service work, reflected in the spy stories in *Ashenden* (1928). Meanwhile he had continued writing novels; *Of Human Bondage* (1915) is discursive and partly autobiographical; the character of Strickland in *The Moon and Sixpence* (1919) is based on that of Gauguin; *Cakes and Ale* (1930) contains thinly veiled portraits (not always kind) of literary friends, e.g. Hugh Walpole. Maugham was, however, at his best as a writer of short stories, material for many of which he found during travels in Malaysia and the East. Though the plots were often melodramatic, his gift for economy of phrase, his scepticism and his narrative skill found their most effective use in this genre. In the story *Rain*, set in the South Seas and later made into a play and a film, he displays something of a quality often lacking in his work – warmth. Several other stories were filmed with an introduction by himself, e.g. *Quartet* (1948). Light is thrown on his style in general by *A Writer's Notebook* (1949); he also wrote critical essays and autobiographical works, e.g. *Strictly Personal* (1941). He lived in the south of France from 1928.
Raphael, F., *Somerset Maugham and His World*. 1976

Maupassant, Guy de (1850–1893). French author. He was born and brought up in Normandy, his father a profligate aristocrat, his mother artistic and sensitive. All these traits were visible in their son. He served briefly in the army during the Fanco-Prussian War and then became a civil servant. In the following years he was a friend, protégé and pupil of Flaubert, who introduced him to Zola. The immediate success of the well known story *Boule de Suif*, Maupassant's contribution to an anthology edited by Zola

(1880), decided him to devote his whole time to writing; in the remaining years of his short life he wrote six naturalistic novels, e.g. *Une Vie* (1883) and *Bel Ami* (1885), travel books inspired by frequent journeys for his health (which had begun to deteriorate in 1876), and some 300 short stories upon which his fame rests. He writes as an observer not an analyst, letting his characters be judged by their actions, not their thoughts and feelings; and the actions he observes are those of sensual, self-seeking but never spiritual human beings. He views the consequences of these actions not without pity but he neither condemns, condones nor even examines their cause. For this limited end he mastered, with the guidance of Flaubert, a superb technique; his style is taut and his economy of phrase exactly suits the brevity of his tales; his construction is seldom at fault and he uses without abuse the trick of the surprise ending. In the last years Maupassant's illness developed into insanity and he died after eighteen months in an institution.
Lanoux, A., *Maupassant le 'Bel-Ami'.* 1967

Maupertuis, Pierre Louis Moreau de (1698–1759). French mathematician and astronomer. He led an expedition to Lapland to measure the length of a degree of the meridian and as a result was able to confirm Newton's assertion that the earth is slightly flattened at the poles. He published his conclusions in *Sur la Figure de la Terre* (1738). He entered (1740) the service of Frederick the Great of Prussia and became (1745) president of the Academy at Berlin.

Mauriac, François (1885–1970). French novelist and dramatist. An ardent Roman Catholic, he was preoccupied with the conflict of Christian morality with human passions and temptations. His novels include *Le Baiser au lépreux, Le Désert de l'amour, Thérèse Desquefroux, Le Nœud de vipères* written between 1922 and 1932, and *La Pharisienne* (1941). His most successful plays were *Asmoldée* (1937) and *Les Mal-Aimés* (written 1939; first performed 1945). Mauriac was elected to the Académie Française (1933) and won the Nobel Prize for Literature (1952).
Mauriac, F., *Mémoires.* 3 vols. 1959–67

Maurice, Sir Frederick Barton (1871–1951). British soldier. In World War I he was director of military operations on the Imperial General Staff (1915–18). A sensation was caused when in a letter he charged Lloyd George with wrongfully blaming the British army commanders for the success of the German spring offensive in 1918. Asquith took up his case in an exciting debate in the House of Commons, but Maurice had to retire for his breach of discipline. He was later professor of military studies at London University.

Maurice, (John) Frederick Denison (1805–1872). Anglican clergyman and theologian. He held a succession of professorships at King's College, London (1840–53), and became professor of moral theology at Cambridge in 1866. He played a leading part in the foundation of Queen's College for Women (1848) and the Working Men's College (1854). He wrote several theological works but his great significance was as the leading spirit of the Christian Socialist movement.
Vidler, A. R., *F. D. Maurice and Company.* 1966

Maurice, Prince of Orange, Count of Nassau (1567–1625). Stadholder of Holland. After the assassination (1584) of his father * William the Silent he continued (with the help for a time of the Earl of * Leicester and an English contingent) the struggle against the Spaniards; as a result of his series of brilliant successes the United Provinces were recognized (1609) by Spain as a free republic. In the following years. Maurice and the Orange party were involved in a quarrel with domestic opponents, but he emerged victorious and renewed the war with Spain (1621).

Maurois, André (pen-name of Emile Herzog) (1885–1967). French writer. His first book, *Les Silences du Colonel Bramble* (1918), draws on his experience as a liaison officer with the British army in World War I; his preoccupation with the English is shown in the list of his biographies, which includes Shelley (*Ariel*; 1923), Disraeli, Byron and Dickens as well as such French writers as Voltaire, Proust and George Sand (*Lélia*; 1952). He also wrote novels, essays etc, and histories of England (1937) and the U.S.A. (1947). His autobiography, *I Remember, I Remember*, was published in 1942. He was elected (1938) to the Académie Française.
Le Maître, G., *André Maurios.* 1968

Maurras, Charles (1868–1952). French writer. An early distrust of republicanism, fostered by his study of the philosophy of Auguste Comte, and his disgust at the influence of foreigners revealed by the * Dreyfus case turned him into an ardent monarchist. From the turn of the century his views were violently expressed in several books and in the journal *Action Française*, in the direction of which he played an important part. More than once he was in prison for his bitter attacks and his election to the Académie Française (1938) was widely assailed. He supported the Vichy government in 1940 and was sentenced (1945) to life imprisonment but was released just before he died.

Mauser, Paul von (1838–1914). German inventor (with his brother Wilhelm) and gunsmith. The Mauser pistol was named from him; he also developed an improved needle-gun, a breech-loading cannon and (in 1897) the first magazine rifle.

Mausolus (reigned 377–356 B.C.). Persian satrap of Caria in Asia Minor. He was commemorated by the magnificent memorial (one of the Seven Wonders of the ancient world) erected by his widow Artemesia at Halicarnassus, which gave rise to the word mausoleum.

Mawson, Sir Douglas (1882–1958). Australian geologist and Antarctic explorer. Born in England, he went to Australia as a child and after geological work in the New Hebrides (1903) joined the staff of Adelaide University (1905) where he was professor of geology (1921–52). In 1907 he was among the members of Shackleton's expedition which reached the South Magnetic Pole. He led an Australian expedition (1911–14) in which much of the coast of Queen Mary Land was explored; after a 600-mile sledge journey he returned ill and alone after losing his two companions. Coasts east of Enderby Land were similarly mapped by his British, Australian and New Zealand expedition (1929–31). Mawson was knighted in 1914.
Mawson, P., *Mawson of the Antarctic*. 1964

Maxim, Sir Hiram Stevens (1840–1916). American-born inventor. He settled in England in 1883, became naturalized in 1884 and was knighted in 1901. The best known of his many inventors – he took out over 100 patents – is the Maxim (recoil-operated) machine gun (1884), later lightened and simplified as the 'Vickers', which continued to prove its outstanding merits in both world wars. 'Maximite', a smokeless powder, was among his other inventions.

Maximian (Marcus Aurelius Valerius Maximianus) (died 310). Roman emperor (286–305). He was chosen by * Diocletian to be co-emperor (i.e. Augustus) with himself, with two junior emperors (Caesars) under them. Maximian, in charge of the West, pacified Gaul and drove back the Germanic tribesmen on the Rhine frontiers until in 305, by arrangement with Diocletian, both senior emperors retired in favour of Constantius (West) and Galerius (East) with two new Caesars. On the death of Constantius (306), however, his son * Constantine and Maximian's son Maxentius, notorious for cruelty and greed, combined to dethrone Severus, the new western emperor. Maximian emerged from retirement to help his son, but they soon fell out and Maximian went to Gaul to the court of Constantine I (son of Constantius) whose father-in-law he had become; but, unable to endure a subordinate role, he took advantage of Constantine's absence on campaign by seizing power. Constantine's vengeance was swift and Maximian found himself besieged in Marseilles. He was handed over by the citizens and committed suicide. Two years later, at the Milvian Bridge near Rome, Constantine defeated Maxentius, who was drowned trying to escape.

Maximilian I (1459–1519). Holy Roman Emperor (from 1493). The son of Emperor Frederick III, he added greatly to his inheritance by marrying Mary, the heiress of Charles the Bold of Burgundy, though in fact he found it is necessary to relinquish the French provinces while retaining the Netherlands for his son Philip. His policy of consolidating the Habsburg dominions by marriage and conquest was on the whole successful, though it involved a number of indecisive wars in France and Italy; but his dream, in accordance with medieval thought, of reviving a universal empire in the west (he even conceived the idea of also becoming pope) inevitably failed. The administrative reforms he achieved were minor, but the enforced acceptance of a committee of princes as a supreme executive would have rendered him impotent had he not succeeded in finding means to frustrate its efforts. Maximilian had the courage and many of the virtues of a medieval knight; he was a patron and connoisseur of arts and letters, and won wide popularity with a gracious and conciliatory manner. He was succeeded by his grandson * Charles V.

Waas, G. E., *The Legendary Character of Kaiser Maximilian I.* 1941

Maximilian (1832–1867). Emperor of Mexico (from 1864). He was the younger brother of the Emperor Francis Joseph of Austria and was married to * Carlota, daughter of Leopold I of the Belgians. This liberal-minded, well-meaning man, whose short experience of administration (1857–59) had been as governor of the Austrian-controlled Lombardo-Venetian territory in Italy, acceded to Napoleon III's request to found a new kingdom in Mexico. After defeating the conservatives in the war of 1857–60, the Mexican 'liberals' under Benito Juarez had found themselves unable to meet foreign debts. France being a principal creditor, Napoleon decided to send a French army primarily to collect debts. His forces soon held most of the country and the enthronement of Maximilian was the French emperor's solution to the problem of what to do next. While Maximilian was planning freedom for Indians, education and social justice for all, the republican forces were gathering strength, and when the French (on US insistence) departed, Maximilian was helpless. Defeated and betrayed, he was given a pretence of trial and shot. The empress Carlota, who had returned to Europe on a vain quest for help, became insane.

Maxton, James (1885–1946). Scottish Socialist politician. He was imprisoned during World War I for inciting munition workers to strike. From 1922 he represented the Independent Labour party in parliament and in 1926 became the party's chairman. He was affectionately regarded by supporters and opponents alike.

McNair, J., *James Maxton, the Beloved Rebel.* 1955

Maxwell, James Clerk (1831–1879). Scottish physicist. He was educated at the Edinburgh Academy and at the Universities of Edinburgh and Cambridge, and while still a schoolboy of 15 communicated his first paper to the Royal Society of Edinburgh. He was a professor at Aberdeen (1856–60) and King's College, London (1860–65), and was the first Cavendish professor of experimental physics at Cambridge (1871–79). Maxwell showed (1859), on mechanical principles, that the rings of Saturn could consist only of separate small particles revolving like satellites. Later he worked on the kinetic theory of gases and deduced many of the laws governing their behaviour. His major work, however, was on electricity and magnetism. He evolved the electromagnetic theory of light and showed that there should be electromagnetic waves travelling at the speed of light; these were observed (1887) by * Hertz. Maxwell redetermined the speed of light with great precision and pointed out the fundamental nature of this natural constant; he also evolved many of the theoretical relationships which contributed to the development of electricity. His books include *Treatise on Electricity and Magnetism* (1873) and *Matter in Motion* (1876).

Campbell, L., and Garnett, W., *The Life of James Clerk Maxwell.* Repr. 1969

May, Phil (1864–1903). English humorous draughtsman. After early struggles he went to Australia (1884) and worked on the *Sydney Bulletin.* On his return (1892) he began to work for *Punch* and later, as a regular member of the staff, became one of the best known humorous artists with a great economy of line and special aptitude for presenting East End types.

Mayakovsky, Vladimir Vladimirovich (1894–1930). Russian futurist poet. He came to prominence as the poet of the 1917 revolution with such works as *150,000,000* (1920), in which President Wilson personifies capitalism. He also wrote satirical plays, of which *The Bed Bug* (1921) is the best known. Mayakovsky later fell from official favour and committed suicide. Much of his work is crudely propagandist but it has pathos and sincerity and shows original ideas.

Brown, E. J., *Mayakovsky: A Poet in the Revolution.* 1973

Mayer, Julius Robert von (1814–1878). German physicist and physician. After serving as a ship's doctor, he carried out research on the transfer of heat energy by working horses, which led to the first hypothesis (1842) of the law of the conservation of energy. Credit was given to * Joule and * Helmholtz who independently provided (1847) more detailed proofs. A forgotten figure who spent years in an asylum and was assumed dead, Mayer received belated recognition, including ennoblement and the Copley Medal of the Royal Society (1871).

Mayer, Louis Burt (1885–1957). American film producer, born in Minsk. He merged his production company with Sam * Goldwyn's in 1924 to form MGM (Metro-Goldwyn-Mayer).

Mayo, Charles Horace (1865–1939). American surgeon. With his father and brother he founded (1889) the Mayo Clinic at Rochester, Minnesota. His researches into goitre cut the U.S. death rate from this disease by 50 per cent.
Clapesattle, H. B., *The Doctors Mayo*. 2nd ed. 1954

Mazarin, Jules (Giulio Mazarini) (1602–1661). French statesman and cardinal. Born in Italy, he was educated by the Jesuits in Rome and Spain and entered the church. He was papal nuncio in France (1634–36) and in 1639 assumed French nationality. Meanwhile he had come to the notice of Cardinal Richelieu, who took him as his assistant and, having secured his cardinalate (1641), recommended him as his successor to Louis XIII. Mazarin retained his power when the boy–king Louis XIV came to the throne, largely through the affection of the widowed queen, now regent, Anne of Austria, to whom Mazarin may have been secretly married. Mazarin brought the Thirty Years War to a successful end (1648) with the acquisition for France of Alsace and the bishoprics of Toul, Metz and Verdun, but was immediately involved in the civil wars of the Fronde, a last attempt by the nobles and legalists to avert a centralized autocracy. Again successful he made an advantageous peace with Spain (1659) and prepared France for its great role under Louis XIV. In other respects he was less admirable. He amassed a vast fortune with part of which he provided large dowries to enable his several pretty nieces to marry well; his valuable collection of books and manuscripts was left to the royal library.
Hassall, A., *Mazarin*. 1973

Mazeppa, Ivan Stepanovich (*c*. 1645–1709). Cossack leader. After an adventurous early life he was elected hetman (military leader) of the Cossacks (1688), served Peter the Great as soldier and diplomat but later, in the hope of acquiring a semi-independent kingdom in the Ukraine, joined the invading army of Charles XII of Sweden. After Charles's defeat at Poltava (1709) Mazeppa took refuge in Turkey. Byron's poem *Mazeppa* relates how, detected in a love affair with a magnate's wife, the Cossack hero was bound naked to a wild horse which was lashed to madness and galloped across country from Poland to the Ukraine before dropping dead.

Mazzini, Giuseppe (1805–1872). Italian patriot. He was born in Genoa and, deeply moved by the absorption (1815) of the Genoese republic into the kingdom of Sardinia, he joined the revolutionary elements among the university students and in 1829 became a member of the Carbonari, a secret republican society. He soon abandoned it, however, disliking its elaborate ritual and formed at Marseilles (1832) his own society, 'Young Italy', for which he edited a periodical of the same name, his aims being a united, free, republican Italy. After a first ineffective invasion (1834) he lived as an exile in Switzerland and in England (1836–48). His writing and correspondence kept him in touch with revolutionary movements abroad and in England he formed a warm friendship with Thomas * Carlyle and his wife. The year of revolutions, 1848, created the conditions for his return to Italy, where he was greeted as a hero. But by 1849 Austrian power had asserted itself and only the republics of Venice and Rome, whence the pope had fled, survived. Mazzini became a triumvir of the republic of Rome but after the intervention of French troops had to return to London. When the liberation and unity of Italy were finally achieved (1859–60) it was carried out by statesmen such as Cavour and men of action such as Garibaldi, but it might never have happened at all had not the ferment been started by Mazzini, the political idealist and persistent propagandist whose hopes in the end were but half fulfilled.
Griffith, G. O., *Mazzini: Prophet of Modern Europe*. 1932

Mboya, Tom (1930–1969). Kenya trade unionist and politician. From 1953 he was secretary of the Kenya Local Government Workers Union (later the Federation of Labour). He was among the first African members to be elected (1957) to the Kenya legislative council and became one of the most important members of the Kenya African National Union (KANU), the leading political party before and after independence. From 1962, when he entered the coalition government, his influence incrased. He was minister of economic planning and development (1964–69). He was assassinated in 1969.

Mead, Margaret (1901–1978). American anthropologist and social psychologist. She worked in Samoa and New Guinea and made an intensive study of tribal customs and marriage laws. She notes the difficulty which exceptional characters find in primitive societies closely regulated by custom in coming to terms with the norm. Her books include *Coming of Age in Samoa* (1928), *Growing up in new Guinea* (1930) and *Male and Female* (1949).
Freedman, D., *Margaret Mead and Samoa*. 1983

Meade, George Gordon (1815–1872). American soldier. As an engineer officer he fought in the Mexican War (1848) and was then employed on survey and construction duties until the outbreak of the Civil War. Having distinguished himself as a divisional commander he was given command of the army of the Potomac (1863–65) almost at once winning the great victory over Lee at Gettysburg, the turning point of the war.

Meany, George (1894–1980). American trade union official. A plumber by trade he made his career in the trade union movement and as president (1952–55) of the American Federation of Labor (A.F.L.) he was in office at the time of its amalgamation with the Congress of Industrial Organizations (C.I.O.); he thus became (1955) the first president of the combined union retiring in 1979.

Mechnikov, Ilya (1845–1916). Russian biologist. After studying in Germany he became (1870) professor of zoology at Odessa University, worked with Pasteur in Paris (from 1888) and became (1904) deputy director of the Pasteur Institute. In a study of the digestion processes of invertebrates he discovered phagocytosis (the engulfing of solid particles by amoeboid cells). Later he showed that the white blood corpuscles of vertebrates play a part in defence against disease by engulfing bacteria in the blood stream. He won the Nobel Prize for Medicine (1908) for his work in developing vaccines.

Medawar, Sir Peter Brian (1915–). British biologist, born in Rio de Janeiro, of Lebanese descent. Educated at Oxford where he worked with * Florey, he was professor of zoology at Birmingham 1947–51 and professor of zoology and comparative anatomy at University College, London 1951–62, then worked for the Medical Research Council. He gave the BBC Reith Lectures (1959) on *The Future of Man*. He shared the Nobel Prize for Physiology and Medicine (1960) with Sir Macfarlane * Burnet for their studies of 'acquired immunological tolerance'. He also wrote *The Uniqueness of the Individual* (1957), *The Hope of Progress* (1972) and *Advice to a Young Scientist* (1979). He was knighted in 1965, received the CH in 1972 and the OM in 1981. He was seriously disabled by a stroke in 1969. He published several volumes of literacy and scientific essays, brilliantly and scathingly written, including *Pluto's Republic* (1982).

Medici. Florentine ruling family. The power of the family was founded upon the huge fortune amassed as a banker by **Giovanni de'Medici** (1360–1429). His son **Cosimo** (1389–1464) was exiled as a popular rival by the ruling oligarchy but returned (1434) and, though preserving republican forms succeeded in suppressing faction and was virtual ruler for the rest of his life; he was the generous patron of Brunelleschi, Ghiberti, Donatello, Filippo Lippi, Fra Angelico etc. Cosimo was succeeded in power by his son **Piero** (1416–1469) and his grandson **Lorenzo** (1449–1492), known as 'the Magnificent'. The failure of a conspiracy in which his brother **Giuliano** (1453–1478) was killed enhanced Lorenzo's popularity and enabled him to increase his powers; like his grandfather he patronized artists and beautified the city. After his death the invasion of Italy by Charles VIII of France in search of a Neapolitan crown led to the temporary exile of the Medici and though they came back (1512), power was mainly exercised from Rome where Leo X, a grandson of Lorenzo, was pope. When the Medici were again deposed (1527) a second Medici pope * **Clement VII** once more brought back the family (1530), but it was a collateral **Cosimo** (1519–1574) who restored it to greatness.

Having been granted Siena by the emperor, he was created (1569) the first grand-duke of Tuscany by the pope and thus started a line which did not become extinct until the death of the seventh grand-duke (1737), when the duchy passed to the house of Lorraine. * Catherine de'Medici; * Marie de Médicis.
Brion, M., *The Medici: A Great Florentine Family*. 1969

Medina Sidonia, Alonzo Perez de Guzman, Duke of (1550–1615). Spanish commander. Owing to the sudden death of Admiral Santa Cruz, a last-minute decision was taken to give the command of the Armada against England (1588) to Medina Sidonia, who was a good organizer but had little experience of the sea. It cannot be held, however, that his mistakes brought about the ensuing disaster.

Mee, Arthur (1875–1943). English journalist and educator. At the age of 20 he was already editor of the *Nottingham Evening News* and in 1903 he became literary editor of the *Daily Mail*. As editor of educational works issued in fortnightly parts and above all of the *Children's Encyclopaedia*, which first appeared 1908–12, he brilliantly awakened the minds of generations of children to the delights of knowledge.

Meegeren, Hans van (1889–1947). Dutch artist. One of the most famous 'fakers' in art history, having failed to find a regular market for pictures under his own name, he started painting in the style of Vermeer and sold the pictures as genuine works of the master. His career reached a fantastic climax during World War II when he succeeded in selling them at inflated prices to the German occupation authorities and even to Marshal Goering himself. He was tried after the war and sentenced to a year's imprisonment but died soon afterwards.

Mehemet Ali (Mohammed Ali) (1769–1849). Viceroy of Egypt (from 1805). Born in Albania, he was orphaned early and was brought up in the household of an officer of janissaries, with whom he gained some military experience. After fighting with Turkish troops in Egypt against the French army of occupation, he remained there in command of Albanian troops and emerged (1805) from a confused struggle for power as pasha or viceroy, but was still confronted by the Mamluk beys, descendants of the Mamluk sultans who though conquered by the Turks in 1517 still retained semi-independence. By organizing their treacherous massacre (1811) Mehemet became supreme and though nominally under Turkish suzerainty built up Egypt into a virtually independent state. Immediately after the massacre he invaded Arabia where an extremist Mohammedan sect, the Wahabis (* Ibn Sa'ud), had seized the holy cities of Mecca and Medina. The war was ended (1818) by Mehemet's son * Ibrahim, and the Wahabi prince Abdullah was sent to Constantinople for execution.

Mehemet now proceeded to create a modern state, deriving revenues from monopolies for the sale of agricultural produce and from new industries which he established. He was thus able to raise new armies with which he conquered the Sudan (1820–30) and aided the Turks against the Greek independence movement (1824–27). The Turks were, however, made restive by the increasing power of their overgrown subject and when Ibrahim conquered Syria enlisted British aid to make him withdraw – a major setback for Mehemet who was, however, compensated by having his office made hereditary and was thus enabled to found the khedival dynasty. In 1848 Mehemet became insane; Ibrahim, who succeeded, died in the same year.

Meiji. Regal name of the Japanese emperor * Mutsuhito.

Meir, Golda (1898–1978). Israeli politician. Born Goldie Mabovitch in Kiev, Ukraine, she was educated in the USA. She emigrated to Palestine in 1921 to work on a collective farm; she had already been involved in Zionism in America and she became active in local political life in 1928, through the Labour movement. She served on the Executive and Secretariat of the Federation of Labour 1929–46. She sat on the War Economic Advisory Council from 1939 and, after the war, became head of the Political Department of the Jewish Agency for Palestine. After independence her first cabinet appointment in the Knesset was as Minister of Labour and Social Insurance (1949–56), then Foreign Minister (1956–66) and Prime Minister (1969–74). She worked for support from USA and from the non-aligned countries, particularly in Africa. She was the founder of the Israeli Labour Party which was formed in 1967.
Meir, G., *My Life*. 1975

Meissonier, Jean Louis Ernest (1815–1891). French artist. His historical pictures, especially those relating to the Napoleonic campaigns, realized large prices in his life-time and are still familiar in reproduction.

Meitner, Lise (1878–1968). Austrian physicist. Until she emigrated to Denmark (1938) she carried out research in radio-chemistry and nuclear physics at Berlin University and the Kaiser Wilhelm Institute for Chemistry. In 1939, with Hahn and Frisch, she played an important part in the discovery of the nuclear fission process for the liberation of atomic energy. She settled in Sweden (1940), became a Swedish citizen (1949) and retired to England in 1960.

Melanchthon (a Greek translation of his German name Schwarzerde, 'black earth'), **Philipp** (1497–1560). German Protestant reformer and scholar. From 1518 he was professor of Greek at Wittenberg University, where he became an early adherent of * Luther, helping him also with his translation of the New Testament from the Greek. He issued the first systematic formulation of the Protestant dogma (1521) and the *Augsburg Confession* (1530). He was much more tolerant and conciliatory than Luther, and when he succeeded to the leadership he lost the confidence of many Protestants by the concessions he made to the Catholics in his quest for peace.

Melba, Dame Nellie (Helen Porter Mitchell) (1859–1931). Australian soprano, born in Melbourne. After a brilliant operatic debut in Brussels (1887) she became prima donna at Covent Garden (1888) and sang throughout Europe and America until her retirement (1926). Her greatest successes were in lyric and coloratura roles in the operas of Verdi and Puccini. She was created DBE in 1918. Pêche Melba, the sweet dish invented in her honour, is evidence of her contemporary reputation.

Melbourne, William Lamb, 2nd Viscount (1779–1848). English politician. He was called to the bar (1804) but entered parliament (1806) as a follower of Charles James * Fox. In the previous year he had married the eccentric Lady Caroline * Lamb, who became notorious for her infatuation with * Byron. He was defeated in the election of 1812 but returned to parliament in 1816. Though a Whig he was an admirer of Canning and served in the coalition as chief secretary for Ireland (1827–28). He succeeded as 2nd Lord Melbourne in the same year. As a supporter of parliamentary reform he was home secretary (1830–34) in Earl Grey's administration: his harsh treatment of the agricultural rioters of 1830 mars the record of a humane man. He succeeded Grey as prime minister (1834); his ministry was almost immediately dismissed by William IV but an election brought him back to power in 1835. He was thus prime minister on the accession of Queen Victoria, whose warm affection he won by his kindly and paternal guidance in the arts of constitutional government. He resigned after a vote of censure (1841) and stricken with paralysis (1842) played no further significant role. A sensation was caused during his premiership when he was cited as co-respondent in a divorce case (1836) brought by George Norton against his lively and intelligent wife, Caroline. Though he had spent pleasant evenings in her company, the association was shown to be entirely innocent.
Cecil, D., *The Young Melbourne*. 1939; *Lord M*. 1954

Melchett, 1st Baron *see* **Mond, Ludwig**

Melchior, Lauritz (1890–1973). Danish heroic tenor. Originally trained as a baritone, he became the greatest of all Wagnerian *heldentenors*, singing at the Metropolitan Opera, New York, 1926–50. He also appeared in a number of films.

Mellon, Andrew William (1855–1937). American financier and politician. He accumulated a huge fortune through a complex of financial and industrial interests, notably the Mellon National Bank of Pittsburgh and the Aluminium Corporation. Turning to politics he served under Presidents Harding, Coolidge and Hoover as secretary to the Treasury (1921–31) and ambassador to Great Britain (1931–33). He was among the greatest of all American art collectors and a considerable part of his wealth was used to construct and endow the National Gallery of Art in Washington D.C.

Melville, Herman (1819–1891). American novelist. Forced to leave school at the age of 15 by his father's bankruptcy, he worked as a bank clerk and taught at country school before working his passage to Europe (1839). In 1841 he joined the whaler *Acushnet* bound for the Pacific; because of harsh treatment he deserted the ship and lived for some months among the cannibals of the Maquesas Islands (1842). After being rescued by an Australian whaler, he was delayed in Tahiti by a mutiny and was eventually shipped home in a U.S. frigate (1844). On his return Melville began a series of novels, based on his adventures, e.g. *Typee* (1846), *Omoo* (1947) and *White Jacket* (1850), the first two especially popular for their exuberant descriptions of native life. After his marriage to Elizabeth Shaw (1847) he bought a farm in Massachusetts where among his neighbours was Nathaniel* Hawthorne to whom Melville dedicated his masterpiece, *Moby Dick or the White Whale* (1851). *Moby Dick* is the story of the fatal voyage of the *Pequod* under Captain Ahab whose obsession it is to track down and kill 'the great white whale' which had crippled him in a previous encounter. Although Melville denied that *Moby Dick* was an allegory, critics have regarded the book as expressing man's struggle with nature or even with God. Even more puzzling to critics was *Pierre* (1852), a strange and morbid story about incestuous passion. The harsh welcome it received is said to have induced the melancholia into which Melville sank; however, he continued to write, e.g. *The Confidence Man* (1857). *Billy Budd*, the novel on which Benjamin Britten's opera (1951) is based, was left unfinished and not published until 1924.

Melville's style is rhetorical, his vocabulary eccentric, rich and varied, but the note of 'oddity' bewildered the critics and for a time repelled the public; he was almost forgotten until revival and reassessment in the 1920s gave him a very exalted position among American writers.

Humphreys, A. R., *Melville*. 1962

Memling, Hans (*c.* 1440–1494). Flemish painter. He was almost certainly a pupil of Roger van der Weyden and from 1465 lived in Bruges. His pictures, nearly all religious, are not inventive, but calm, deeply sincere and often warm in colouring, with an obvious delight in jewels and shining fabrics. His principal religious works include the *Donne Triptych* (?1468; once at Chatsworth and now at the National Gallery, London), *The Betrothal of St Catherine* (1479; for an altar at Bruges) and *The Legend of St Ursula* (1489; Bruges). His portraits show originality and he is said to have introduced the practice of setting a three-quarter bust against a scenic background.

Baldass, L. von, *Hans Memling*. 1942

Menander (*c.* 343–291 B.C.). Athenian poet. The principal dramatist of the 'New Comedy', his innovations included the disappearance of the chorus (except as a 'turn' between the acts) and the presentation of humorous situations of everyday life (in contrast to the fantasies of Aristophanes). Here are the slave or servant with a taste for intrigue, the jealous husband, lover, wife or mistress, the long-lost child suddenly restored, the shrew, the cheat – all to reappear in the Latin plays of Plautus and Terence, and in Shakespeare, Molière and many lesser writers. Until large portions of several of Menander's plays were discovered in the 20th century, it was thought that only fragments of his work had survived.

Sandbach, F. H., *Menander: A Commentary*. 1973

Mencius (fl. second half of 4th century B.C.). Chinese philosopher. He founded a school devoted to the study of the works of Confucius. After wandering through China for over twenty years attempting to persuade princes and administrators to rule in a moral rather than opportunist way, he retired to teach and write.

Legge, J., ed., *The Chinese Classics. Vol. 2: Mencius*. 3rd ed. 1960

Mencken, Henry Louis (1880–1956). American author and critic. He was on the staff of the Baltimore *Sun* (1906–1941) and his greatest work is the monumental *The American Language* (4 volumes, 1919–1948). As editor of the *American Mercury* (1925–1933) he helped to gain public recognition for Theodore Dreiser and Sinclair Lewis. He was an outspoken critic who denounced religion, intellectuals, politicians, sentimentalists and foreigners. Although violently prejudiced, his attacks on complacency and conformity did much to raise the standards of U.S. writing. He also wrote books on Shaw, Nietzsche and Ibsen.

Stenerson, D. C., *H. L. Mencken: Iconoclast from Baltimore*. 1971

Mendel, Gregor Johann (1822–1884). Austrian biologist. Discoverer of the Mendelian laws of inheritance, he became a monk at Brunn (Brno) and was ordained in

1847. His scientific studies at Vienna University were encouraged and paid for by the monastery, of which he later became abbot (1869). Many of his experiments on the breeding and hybridization of plants were carried out in the garden there. He kept (1857–68) systematic records of the pedigrees of many generations of plants, closely examining the effects of heredity on the characteristics of individual plants and discovering the statistical laws governing the transmission from parent to offspring of unit hereditary factors (now called genes). His results were published (1866 and 1896) in a local journal only, so that his work was not appreciated until its rediscovery *c.* 1900. Complicating factors have since been discovered but Mendel's fundamental principles remain undisturbed by later research.

Stern, C., and Sherwood, E. R., eds., *The Origin of Genetics: A Mendel Source Book*. 1967

Mendeleyev, Dimitry Ivanovich (1834–1907). Russian chemist. Professor of chemistry at St Petersburg (1867–90), he published (1869) a statement of his periodic law, the first complete expression of the relation between the properties and the atomic weights of the chemical elements. His classification of the elements in the periodic table enabled him to predict correctly the existence and properties of several elements, later discovered, for which there were gaps in the table.

Mendelsohn, Erich (1887–1953). German architect. An exponent of expressionism, his early work is characterized by an exuberant plasticity which was first realized in his Einstein Tower (Potsdam Observatory). He became a leading architect in Germany, but was forced to leave (1933) on the advent of Nazism. After a short stay in England, he spent some years in practice in Palestine before finally settling in the U.S.A. He specialized in factories and department stores but his designs were less purely functional than those of, e.g. * Gropius.

Whittick, A., *Erich Mendelsohn*. 2nd ed. 1956

Mendelssohn (-Bartholdy), (Jakob Ludwig) Felix (1809–1847). German composer. He was born at Hamburg, the son of a rich banker and the grandson of Moses Mendelssohn, the Jewish philosopher. The family adopted the double name Mendelssohn-Bartholdy on conversion to Christianity. He began to compose when only about 10 years old, and between the ages of 16 and 21 reached the height of his powers. The overture to *A Midsummer Night's Dream* was written in 1826 (the incidental music, which included the famous *Wedding March*, followed seventeen years later). The overture *The Hebrides* (1829; also known as *Fingal's Cave*) was inspired by a visit to Fingal's Cave on the island of Staffa during a study tour, organized by his father, to Britain (1829) – the first of many visits – and Italy. Similarly Holyrood Palace, Edinburgh, inspired the *Scotch Symphony*, and in Rome (1831) the *Italian Symphony* was begun. Another of his major achievements was a revival of public interest in Bach, especially in his choral music; Mendelssohn conducted the first performances outside Leipzig of the *St Matthew Passion*. His own compositions, e.g. *Seven Characteristic Pieces* for piano (1827), show Bach's influence.

He married (1837) Cecile Jeanrenaud and, with his family wealth, escaped the struggles and hardships with which so many artists have had to contend.

Werner, E., *Mendelssohn*. 1963

Mendelssohn, Moses (1729–1786). German–Jewish philosopher. The grandfather of Felix * Mendelssohn-Bartholdy, he was a noted propagandist for the social and legal emancipation of the Jewish people and at the same time tried to break down the prejudiced isolation of the Jews from those who did not share their faith. He was a close friend of the writer and critic * Lessing and collaborated with him on a book on the philosophy of Pope. He also wrote popular explanations of the sensations and metaphysics. In the dialogue *Phaedon* (1767) he discusses in Socratic manner the immortality of the soul; in *Jerusalem* (1783) he defends Judaism as a religion.

Attman, A., *Moses Mendelssohn*. 1973

Menderes, Adnan (1899–1961). Turkish politician. He helped to found (1945) the Democratic party, led it in opposition and, when it came to power (1950), became prime minister. He brought Turkey into full membership of NATO (1951) and helped to bring about the Baghdad Pact (1955). He was reelected in 1957, but the extravagance of his social and economic policies and the allegedly corrupt practices of his administration provoked (1960) a successful military revolt. In May 1961 Menderes, found guilty of a number of personal and political offences, was executed.

Mendès, Catulle (1831–1909). French writer. He was born in Bordeaux but went to Paris in 1859. As co-founder of *Le Parnasse contemporain* (1866) he helped to give cohesion to the Parnassian group led by * Leconte de Lisle. He wrote a history of the movement (1884); his own poems owed more to facility of expression than to literary distinction.

Mendès France, Pierre (1907–1982). French Radical Socialist politician. A lawyer by profession, he gained a reputation through his books as a financial analyst before becoming a deputy (1932). He joined the air force in World War II, and eventually reached Algiers, later joining de Gaulle and becoming commissioner of finance in the provisional government (1943–44). He was minister of national economy (1944–45) and as prime minister (1954–55) played a leading part in bringing the war in Indo-China to an end. He became a powerful opponent of de Gaulle during the Fifth Republic. His autobiography, *Pursuit of Freedom*, was published in 1955.

Menelik II (1843–1913). Emperor (from 1889) of Ethiopia (Abyssinia). For some twenty years, he was king of the province of Shua and, though nominally subject to the emperor John IV, greatly extended his dominions; having subdued his rivals he was able to succeed when the emperor died. His relations with the Italians, who invaded Eritrea in 1885 and whose interests were extensive throughout the country, were at first friendly but difficulties of the interpretation of the Treaty of Ucciali (1889) led to war and Italy's calamitous defeat at Adowa (1896). Thus fortified, Menelik did much to modernize the administration and, by skilful bargaining with European powers, increased Ethiopia's economic strength. His son, Lij Yasu, proved a worthless successor (* Haile Selassie).
Marcus, H., *The Life and Times of Menelik II of Ethiopia 1844–1913*. 1975

Mengelberg, (Josef) Willem (1871–1951). Dutch conductor. As conductor of the Amsterdam Concertgebouw Orchestra 1895–1945 he raised this ensemble to the first rank in Europe. His intensely romantic interpretations of Mahler, Richard Strauss, Tchaikovsky and Beethoven were successfully recorded. He was co-conductor of the New York Philharmonic 1921–29. He collaborated with the Germans during World War II and died in Switzerland.

Menken, Adah Isaacs (Dolores Adios Fuertes) (1835–1868). American actress and dancer. She created a sensation in London when she appeared (1864) bound and scantily clothed on a horse in a stage version of Byron's *Mazeppa*. She was the 'Dolores' of Swinburne's poem:

O splendid and sterile Dolores,
Our Lady of Pain.

Menno Simons (1492–1559). Dutch religious leader. After the suppression of the Anabaptists he organized the less fanatical remnants into a religious group known as Mennonites. From Holland and north Germany colonies were introduced by Catherine the Great into Russia, but when in 1871 their privileges, including exemption from military service, were withdrawn, many emigrated to America where colonies had been established from 1683. Mennonites are more concerned with a Christian life than with dogma; among their tenets are adult baptism and refusal to bear arms, to take oaths or to serve in public office.
Dyck, C. J., *A Legacy of Faith: The Heritage of Menno Simons*. 1962

Menon, V. K. Krishna *see* **Krishna Menon, V. K.**

Menotti, Gian Carlo (1911–). Italian composer, who settled (1928) in the U.S.A. He composed and wrote the libretti for a number of short incisive operas, e.g. *The Consul* (1950), an effective treatment of a modern theme which achieved great success, *The Medium* (1946), *Amahl and the Night Visitors* (1951; first performed on television) and *The Saint of Bleecker Street* (1955).
Trecoire, R., *Gian Carlo Menotti*. 1966

Menshikov, Prince Alexander Danilovich (*c.* 1660–1729). Russian soldier and politician. The son of a groom, he was a guardsman in attendance on Peter the Great and became his close friend and adviser. He served with distinction against Sweden, and after the victory of Poltava (1709) was made a field-marshal. On Peter's death (1725) Menshikov placed his widow Catherine I (his own former mistress whom he had introduced to the tsar) on the throne and during her brief reign of two years virtually ruled the kingdom. His last days were spent in exile.

Menuhin, Yehudi (1916–). American violinist. Born in New York of Russian-Jewish parents, he first performed as a child. His precocious talent was shared by his pianist sister **Hephzibah** (1922–1981). He developed into a brilliant virtuoso and a thoughtful interpreter of the concertos of Bach, Brahms, Beethoven, Elgar and Bartok. He toured the world with a triumphant success for many years but lived mainly in England, where he founded (1959) a music festival at Bath and became an honorary K.B.E. (1965).

Menzies, Sir Robert Gordon (1894–1978). Australian Liberal politician. Educated at Melbourne University, he became a barrister and KC (1929), served in the Victorian Parliament 1928–34 and was deputy premier 1932–34. A member of the Commonwealth House of Representatives 1934–66 and Attorney-General 1934–39, on the death of J. A. * Lyons he succeeded as leader of the United Australia Party and (after a brief interregnum) prime minister 1939–41. Bitter political divisions led to Menzies' resignation, the UAP broke up and he created a new anti-Labor coalition, the Liberal Party, which he led 1944–66. Prime minister again 1949–66, for a record term, he maintained a strong political commitment to the British connection and to closer economic and military alliance with the US. His political dominance was assisted by the split in the Labor Party over attitudes towards Communism. A persuasive orator, he succeeded Winston * Churchill as Lord Warden of the Cinque Ports 1965–78.
Perkins, K., *Menzies: Last of the Queen's Men*.

Mercator, Gerhardus (Gerhard Kremer) (1512–1594). Flemish geographer and map-maker. For his world chart of 1569 (18 sheets) he first used his famous map projection in which the meridians are drawn parallel to each other. Since in fact they converge towards the poles, the degree of distortion in the polar regions is enormous; the projection does however facilitate sailing by dead reckoning and became lastingly popular. He also constructed globes. Two parts of his great atlas (107 maps in all) were published in 1585 and 1589; his son published the third part (1595) after his death.
Averdunk, H., and Mueller-Reinhard, J., *Gerhard Mercator*. 1914

Mercer, John (1791–1866). English calico printer. He discovered that cotton fibres could be made stronger and more receptive to dyes if treated with a solution of caustic alkali. This process is called 'mercerizing'.

Meredith, George (1828–1909). English novelist and poet, born in Portsmouth. He contributed to periodicals, published much poetry and wrote an oriental fantasy *The Shaving of Shagpat* (1856) before the appearance of his first novel, *The Ordeal of Richard Feverel* (1859). He shared rooms with Swinburne and Rossetti from 1861 to 1862, in which year he published his tragic poem *Modern Love* and became a reader (which he remained until 1894) to the publishers Chapman & Hall. In 1876 he settled at Flint Cottage, Box Hill, Surrey, his home for the rest of his life. Among his best known novels are *Rhoda Fleming* (1865), *Beauchamp's Career* (1876), *The Egoist* (1879), *The Tragic Comedians* (1880), based on the love story of Ferdinand * Lassalle, and *Diana of the Crossways* (1885), the only one to achieve real popularity. Meredith combined intellectual clarity, a hatred of the commonplace and an impressionistic technique; from this union emerged a style so difficult and convoluted that Oscar Wilde is quoted as having said 'As a writer he mastered everything but language'. Meredith was twice married, in 1849 to a daughter of Thomas Love * Peacock, who left him in 1858 and died in 1861, and (1864) to Marie Vulliamy (died 1885), who lived with him at Box Hill. He received the O.M. in 1905.
Stevenson, L., *The Ordeal of George Meredith*. 1953

Mérimée, Prosper (1803–1870). French novelist. Born in Paris, he studied law but became specially interested in archaeology and other learned pursuits. During travels in Spain he came to know the family of the future Empress Eugénie, and so ensured a subsequent welcome at the court of Napoleon III. The collapse of the Second Empire, under which he was a senator and academician, in

the Franco-Prussian War is said to have hastened his death. His first successes as a writer were achieved with historical novels in which he brings a detached observer's eye and a deceptively simple style to the recording of violent and exotic scenes. His gifts were more suited to the short stories, e.g. the superb *Mateo Falcone*, that brought him fame, but even better known are the *nouvelles* (longer stories) *Colomba* (1840) and *Carmen* (1845), which was the basis of Bizet's opera.
Raitt, A. W., *Mérimée*. 1970

Merriman, Henry Seton (pen-name of Hugh Stowell Scott) (1863–1903). English novelist. He was a business man who took to writing novels with exciting plots, exotic settings and characters including memorable 'strong, silent men'. The best of his books include *With Edged Tools* (1894), *The Sowers* (1896) and *In Kedar's Tents* (1897).

Mersenne, Marin (1588–1648). French scientist. Educated by the Jesuits, in 1611 he joined the Minim Order, and lived at the Minim Convent in Paris till his death. Mersenne's major contribution to European intellectual life lay in his vast correspondence. He acted as a kind of clearing house for all the great contemporary intellects in the fields of philosophy and science. He supported the modern, mechanical philosophy against the science of the Ancients, and defended the right to pursue scientific knowledge against theological bigots. But he was also violently opposed to what he saw as 'atheistic' and 'materialistic' currents in the thinking of Bruno, Campanella, and Fludd. Mersenne's own scientific research was largely concerned with the physics of sound. He experimented with pitch and harmonies counting the vibrations of long strings against time: he succeeded in formulating quantified explanations of consonance, resonance and dissonance. He was interested in the effect of music on the human emotions, which he sought to attribute to entirely rational and mechanical forces. Mersenne emphasized that languages were merely combinations of signs invented by men for the sake of convenience in communication. Like many seventeenth century scholars he was eager to develop a perfect, universal language, based on scientific principles. Mersenne dedicated himself to scientific explanations. His dying wish was an autopsy to discover the cause of his own death.
Lenoble, R., *Mersenne*. 1943

Mesmer, Franz Anton (1734–1815). Austrian physician. The word 'mesmerism' is derived from his name. His theories concerning the influence of planets on the human body and the existence of an all-pervasive 'magnetic fluid' that affected the nervous system naturally did not commend themselves to the medical profession, which was even less attracted by the healing sessions in Paris in which he appeared dressed in purple silk with an iron rod in his hand. A commission set up by the Académie des Sciences rejected (1784) his magnetic theories and thereafter his popularity waned. He owed his successes partly to the effects of his mumbo jumbo upon the imaginations of his patients, partly to amelioration produced by hypnotism which he had the power to induce without being able to comprehend it.

Messager, André Charles Prosper (1853–1929). French composer. He was a pupil of Saint-Saëns and first won wide acclaim with a comic opera, *La Basoche* (1890). He was artistic director (1901–06) of Covent Garden opera in London. *Monsieur Beaucaire* (1919) is perhaps the best known of his many operettas.
Ferrier, H., *André Messager*. 1948

Messalina, Valeria (A.D. 24–48). Wife of the Roman emperor * Claudius. She was only 15 when she married, and as the beautiful young mother of his son Britannicus held Claudius completely enthralled, though she was notorious in Rome for her lasciviousness, amorality and the murders she instigated. What finally brought about her downfall and execution was her 'marriage' in public to her favourite lover, Silius.

Messerschmitt, Willy (1898–1978). German aircraft designer and manufacturer. He produced his first aeroplane in 1916 and a few years later founded his own firm for their manufacture. His fighters and fighter bombers, Me. 109, 110, 210 and 410, were among the most successful German aircraft of World War II.

Messiaen, Olivier (Eugène Prosper Charles) (1908–). French composer, born in Avïgnon. Son of a professor of English and a poetess, he taught himself the piano, then studied organ with Marcel * Dupré and composition with Paul * Dukas. From 1931 he was organist at the Trinité church, Paris, taught at the Schola Cantorum 1935– , and was a professor of composition at the Sorbonne 1942– : Pierre * Boulez was a pupil. After army service, he was a prisoner of war at Görlitz (1940–41). Primarily a melodist, he used innovative tone-colouring influenced by his studies of Greek chants, Hindu ragas, bird songs, plainsong and microtonality. He wrote on musical theory and his philosophy was imbued with his Catholic faith. His major works include *La Nativité du Seigneur* (1935, organ solo), *Quatuor pour la fin du temps* (1941, quartet), *Vingt Regards sur l'Enfant-Jesus* (1944, piano), *Turangalîla-Symphonie* (1946–8, a luxuriantly romantic work, probably his most accessible), *Chronochromie* (1960; 'The Colour of Time' for large orchestra), *Couleurs de la Cité Celeste* (1963) and *Et Exspecto Resurrectionem Mortuorum* (1964).

Mestrovic, Ivan (1883–1962). Yugoslav sculptor, who became a U.S. citizen in 1954. Born in Dalmatia, he studied in Vienna and Paris. Between the two World Wars he became widely known for the vigorous monumental style and emotional intensity which he applied to the many war memorials for which he was commissioned. In his own country the best known works include the great Yugoslav national temple at Kossovo and the immense statue of Bishop Gregory outside the walls of Split.

Metaxas, Ioannis (1870–1941). Greek soldier and dictator. He was assistant chief of staff in the Balkan Wars but opposed co-operation with the Allies in World War I and was exiled by * Venizelos. After the war he was an ultra-royalist and several times held office. After George II was restored (1935) Metaxas was first minister of war and then prime minister (1936–41). On the dissolution of parliament in 1936 he ruled as dictator until his death. He organized the successful defence against the Italian attack (1940–41).

Methodius, St *see* **Cyril, St**

Metsu, Gabriel (*c.* 1630–1667). Dutch painter. He was born at Leyden and from 1657 lived at Amsterdam. His pictures, which now command high prices and may be compared with those of Vermeer, mainly portray quiet domestic scenes with three or four figures. Rich garments as well as the effects of sunlight give the opportunity to display his skill in handling a variety of colour tones. There are works by him in London at the National Gallery and the Wallace Collection.

Metternich (-Winneburg), Clemens Wenzel Lothar, Prince (1773–1859). Austrian statesman. Some experience of revolutionary methods gained as a student at Strasbourg University is said to have implanted his hatred of democracy; but as son of a diplomat and as a creator and expositor of Habsburg policy all his life he could hardly have been otherwise. His diplomatic heritage was enlarged and his social and material standing greatly increased when he married the granddaughter and heiress of the Prince of * Kaunitz-Rietberg. He became Austrian minister to Saxony in 1801, and after an ambassadorial career which included Prussia and Napoleon's France (1806–09), he became Austrian chancellor and foreign minister. His task was to provide a breathing space in which Austria could recover from successive defeats at the hands of the French; to achieve this he played a double game with great caution and skill. He negotiated the marriage of the Austrian archduchess Marie Louise with Napoleon, and when the latter quarrelled with Russia provided him with a small Austrian contingent while secretly informing the tsar that he had nothing more to fear. Thus though he expected a French victory he was well placed to steer Austria to the winning side after the Moscow retreat of 1812 and as the princely host (his title was conferred in 1814) at the Congress of Vienna to play a dominating part in the reshaping of Europe after Napoleon's fall. The final settlement, for which Metternich found allies in * Castlereagh for Britain and * Talleyrand, now acting for the restored monarchy of France, was a cleverly contrived balance of power, with Austria left at the head of a confederation of sovereign German states. Sustained by the 'Holy Alliance' of the rulers of Russia, Prussia and Austria, 'Metternich's Europe' survived for some thirty years. He himself controlled Austria throughout; not so blind to the need for reforms as is often supposed but so underrating the forces of nationalism that the revolutions of 1848 took him by surprise. He was forced to resign and after spending eighteen months of the intervening period in England returned to

Vienna in 1851 after the revolution had been suppressed.

Cecil, A., *Metternich, 1773–1859.* 1933

Meyer, Julius Lothar (1830–1895). German chemist. Professor of chemistry (1868–76) at Karlsruhe Polytechnic and then at Tübingen University, in *Die modernen Theorien der Chemie* (1864) he discussed the relation between the atomic weights and the properties, in particular the atomic volumes, of the chemical elements. In 1870 he put forward a periodic classification of the elements independently of and a little later than * Mendeleyev; but he did not see the important consequences of this relationship as clearly as Mendeleyev.

Meyerbeer, Giacomo (Jakob Liebmann Beer) (1791–1864). German-Jewish composer. Originally a boy pianist he studied opera in Italy and there composed several works now forgotten. Once settled in Paris he developed a grandiloquent style, to which Wagner, whom he befriended, owed much; this he successfully applied to such operas as *Robert le Diable* (1831), *Les Huguenots* (1836) and *L'Africaine* (produced 1865). Meyerbeer was immensely self-critical and rewrote many passages time after time. He was known especially for his magnificent stage effects and choral climaxes.

Meynell, Alice (née Thompson) (1847–1922). English poet and essayist. The home she shared with Wilfred Meynell, whom she married in 1877, became a gathering place for young writers – above all Francis * Thompson to whom they gave encouragement and help. Her own writings, collections of essays, e.g. *The Rhythm of Life* (1893), and poems, reflect the mysticism which was an important part of her character. Her sister, Elizabeth, Lady Butler, was a well known painter of battle scenes.

Tuell, A. K., *Mrs Meynell and Her Literary Generation.* 1925

Miaskovsky, Nikolai Yakovlevich (1881–1950). Russian composer, pupil of Glière and Rimsky-Korsakov. He wrote twenty-seven symphonies, other orchestral works, and chamber and piano music.

Michael (1921–). King of Romania (1927–30 and 1940–47). He succeeded his grandfather, Ferdinand, as king, his father (later Carol II) having renounced his rights. Carol seized power in 1930 but in 1940 was again forced to abdicate. Michael, once more king, attempted to resist German encroachments in World War II and organized (1944) the *coup d'état* which took his country out of the war. In 1947 he was forced by communist pressure to abdicate. A year later he married Princess Anne of Bourbon-Parma.

Michelangeli, Arturo Benedetti (1920–). Italian pianist, born in Brescia. Although he rarely gave concerts or recorded, Michelangeli acquired a legendary reputation for his performances of Bach, Beethoven, Chopin, Debussy and Ravel.

Michelangelo Buonarroti (1475–1564). Italian painter, sculptor, artist and poet. He was born near Florence at Caprese, where his father was an official. As a boy of 13 he was apprenticed to * Ghirlandaio in Florence. In 1489 he came to the notice of * Lorenzo de' Medici who admitted him to his sculpture school in the Medici Gardens and took him into his house, where he met and imbibed the wisdom of the poet Politian and many humanist scholars. The *Madonna of the Steps* (in low relief) and the *Battle of the Centaurs* (in high relief and already showing the strength and energy of his maturity) belong to this period. In the confused years following Lorenzo's death (1492), Michelangelo left Florence (1494–95) and in 1496 went to Rome, where the *Bacchus* (now in Florence) and the *Pietà* in St Peter's, showing the crucified Christ lying in the Virgin's arms, were created. On his return to Florence (1501) he executed the colossal marble statue *David* (now in the Academia), a nude which shows the sculptor's conception of the perfect male form. Michelangelo returned to Rome (1505) commissioned by Pope Julius II to design and work on his tomb. The scheme was constantly reduced by the pope and his heirs and Michelangelo completed only after years of intermittent work the great statue of Moses and the figures of four slaves now in St Pietro in Vincoli. From 1508 to 1512 Michelangelo was again in Rome occupied with one of his greatest tasks, the decoration of the ceiling of the Sistine Chapel. To him was allotted that part of the biblical story which preceded the giving of the law to Moses; his scenes portray the Creation, the Fall of Man and the story of Noah. Technically the work presented immense difficulties partly of perspective, partly because the painting had to be done in a recumbent position. The figures here depicted, e.g. those in the Creation of Adam and the nudes surrounding the main panels, illustrate the neoplatonist theory that the beauty of the human body symbolizes divine beauty. This idea, derived from his studies and colloquies with the scholars in Lorenzo's garden, permeates all Michelangelo's work.

Fourteen years from 1521 were occupied (with interruptions) by the Medici chapel in the church of St Lorenzo, Florence. The wall decorations and the tombs of Lorenzo and Giuliano de' Medici were complete or nearly so, as were the reclining figures of *Day, Night, Dusk* and *Dawn*. The chapel wall – an architectural experiment much imitated – is solely designed to provide a sculptured setting for the figures. But the project as a whole was left unfinished. Intermittently until 1559 the library of St Lorenzo at Florence was also constructed to Michelangelo's designs. Here manneristic techniques (e.g. pillars set in niches to conceal their function) begin to appear. In 1534 the Medici pope * Clement VII summoned him to Rome to paint a fresco of the Last Judgement for the altar wall of the Sistine Chapel. The work, carried out (1536–41) under Paul III, is one of the most awesome pictures ever painted, with Christ, the stern judge, the elect, observant and fearful, and the crowd of struggling nudes representing the damned; it provoked controversy from the first, though the magic of the draughtsman's skill and overwhelming power of the picture's message could not be denied. The same mood of tragedy provoked by the sufferings of the world he lived in is visible in his last great pictorial works, the frescoes in the Pauline Chapel of the Vatican – the *Conversion of St Paul* and the *Crucifixion of St Peter*.

Michelangelo devoted his last twenty years mainly to architecture. In reconstructing the Capitol in Rome he designed the first planned square of modern times; he made additions to the Palazzo Farnese; but most important he was chosen (1546) to succeed Sangallo as chief architect of St Peter's. Here he modified Bramante's original plans for transepts and choir and designed the new higher, lantern-topped dome which towers over the building. Michelangelo never married and his longest sustained friendship was for the poetess Vittoria Colonna, to whom he wrote some of the 100 or so sonnets which place him high among the poets of his time. In his last years he spent much time in solitary religious and mystical contemplation, between moods of ecstasy and despair and conscious of the dark abyss beneath the thin layer of civilization.

Michelangelo was primarily a sculptor and his pictures have been described as sculptures in paint; but just as his works are monumental so he himself is a colossus dominating all the fine arts, painting, sculpture and architecture alike during the Renaissance.

Goldschieder, L., *Michelangelo: Paintings, Sculptures, Architecture*. 1953; *Michelangelo: Drawings*. 1966

Michelet, Jules (1798–1874). French historian. Professor of history at the Collège de France, Paris (1838–53), he conceived his greatest work, the *Histoire de France* (24 volumes 1833–67) as a biography of the nation and brought to it the emotions, prejudices and lively interest that he would to the life of an individual. This coupled with a wealth of picturesque episodes makes it one of the most readable historical works of the 19th century. His evocation of the medieval period is especially valuable.

Viallaneix, P., *La Voie royale*. 1959

Michelson, Albert Abraham (1852–1931). Polish-born American physicist. Early in his career he was an instructor in physics and chemistry at the U.S. Naval Academy; later he studied in Europe and on his return held two professorships before he was appointed (1893) chief professor at the Ryerson Physical Laboratory, Chicago. Much of his success was due to his extreme skill in designing optical instruments, e.g. the interferometer with which he carried out, with Morley, the famous Michelson-Morley experiment to determine the speed and direction of the earth through the ether. The basis of this experiment was to determine, with great accuracy, the velocity of light in two directions at right angles to each other. The two velocities were found to be exactly equal, this surprising result leading * Einstein to the formulation of his theory of relativity. Michelson made many determinations of the speed of light, the most accurate of which were made in 1924 and 1925. He was awarded the Nobel Prize for Physics (1907).

Jaffe, B., *Michelson and the Speed of Light*. 1960

Michurin, Ivan Vladimirovich (1855–1935). Russian horticulturist. He revived

* Lamarck's thesis that even genetically inferior plants can be altered over generations if the environment is improved sufficiently. His views were enthusiastically promoted by his disciple T. D. * Lysenko.

Mickiewicz, Adam (1798–1855). Polish poet, born in Lithuania. The founder of the Romantic movement in Poland, he is regarded as among the greatest poets of that country. During a period of exile he met Pushkin; from 1829 he lived abroad, mostly in Paris. His poems are nearly all devoted to the exaltation of the Polish nation in one or other of its aspects. They include *Ballads and Romances* (1822); short epics, e.g. *Konrad Wallenrod* (1825–28), about the medieval struggles with the Teutonic knights; and above all his masterpiece, *Pan Tadeusz* (1834), an epic in twelve books describing the life of the Polish gentry and their decay in the years 1811–12. Mickiewicz died at Constantinople, where he was trying to form a Polish legion to fight the Russians in the Crimean War.
Lednicki, W. (ed.), *Adam Mickiewicz in World Literature*. 1956

Mies van der Rohe, Ludwig (1886–1969). German-born architect, resident in the U.S. from 1933. Trained (like Gropius and Le Corbusier) by Peter Behrens, his architecture is notable for its use of glass walls, subtlety of proportion and refinement of detail. He attracted international attention in 1921 with an all-glass skyscraper. In 1927 he was put in charge of a housing development in Stuttgart where steel construction was first applied to domestic building. In the USA his well-known works include the Farnsworth house and the IBM building in Chicago and the Seagram Building in New York. In 1946 he became director of the Illinois Institute of Technology's School of architecture, retiring in 1958.
Blaser, W., *Mies van der Rohe: The Art of Structure*. 1965

Mifune Toshiro (1920–). Japanese actor, born in China. The greatest Japanese screen actor, he achieved international recognition in * Kurosawa's films *Rashomon* (1950), *Seven Samurai* (1954) and *The Lower Depths* (1957). He later appeared in U.S. and British films.

Mihailovich, Draga (1893–1946). Yugoslav soldier. In World War II, after the collapse of Yugoslav resistance of the German attack (1941), Mihailovich organized a resistance movement under the direction of the Yugoslav royal government in London. He was accused by * Tito, the communist leader, of acting with more vigour against his rival partisans than against the Germans. After the war Mihailovich was charged with collaboration and shot.

Mikoyan, Anastas Ivanovich (1895–1978). Soviet politician of Armenian descent. After fighting in the revolutionary wars he rose quickly in the communist ranks and from 1926, when he became Stalin's commissar of trade, showed an extraordinary ability to survive all political upheavals. Most of his appointments were connected with internal and external trade; he was a Politburo member (1935–66), first deputy premier (1955–64), and the first non-Russian president of the U.S.S.R. (1964–65).

Miles, Bernard Miles, Baron (1907–). English actor and director. A successful character actor (e.g. as Joe Gargery in the film *Great Expectations*), he founded the Mermaid Theatre in 1950, producing operas, repertory and musicals. He was knighted in 1969 and created a life peer in 1979.

Milford Haven, 1st Marquess of *see* **Battenberg**

Milhaud, Darius (1892–1974). French composer. One of 'Les Six', a group of French modernists who were active after World War I, and associated with important literary figures, e.g. Claudel and Cocteau, he was both prolific and versatile, his works including the ballets *Protée* (1913–19), *Le Boeuf sur le toit* (1919), and *La Création du monde* (1923), in which he uses jazz techniques; the operas *Bolivar* (1943) and *Christophe Colombe* (1928); the suite *Scaramouche* (1939) for two pianos; much chamber music and many symphonies, some of them only a few minutes long. Milhaud was professor of music at Mills College, California (1940–47), and then returned to Paris to teach at the Conservatoire. He published *Notes sans Musique* (1952).
Roy, J., *Darius Milhaud*. 1969

Mill, James (1773–1836). Scottish philosopher and political scientist, son of a shoemaker and father of John Stuart * Mill.

Intended for the ministry he studied Greek and philosophy at Edinburgh University, but went to London (1802) and became a close friend of Jeremy * Bentham, by whom he was considerably influenced. For some time he was editor of the *Literary Journal* and contributed articles to various other periodicals. In 1806 he began work on his *History of British India*; its publication (1817–18) secured him a post at the London offices of the East India Company. He continued to write articles on political and economic subjects; his *Elements of Political Economy* (1821–22) was written primarily for the benefit of his son's education; it was followed in 1829 by his *Analysis of the Human Mind.*

Mill, John Stuart (1806–1873). British philosopher and economist. He was rigorously educated by his father James * Mill and at the age of 3 had begun to learn Greek. That he should be equipped as rapidly as possible to carry further his father's philosophic and economic studies seems to have been the purpose for which he was made to sacrifice all the normal pleasures of childhood. The analogy between the two careers became closer when (1823) the young Mill joined his father at India House, where he remained until 1858, when the government of India was transferred to the Crown. Mill also adopted his father's philosophical and political views, for which he revived the name utilitarianism (used and discarded by Bentham). He became the acknowledged head of a utilitarian group of thinkers but in 1826–27 he endured a mental crisis from which he emerged to see that 'happiness' in its utilitarian sense was an inadequate standard of human well-being; that the inward nature of the individual was as important as his outward circumstances; and that therefore training for right thought and action was necessary to the attainment of true happiness, which should not be regarded as an end in itself but should be sought by the pursuit of some altruistic or even perhaps artistic ideal. This line of thought led him not only to widen his cultural interests (he reviewed Tennyson's poems in 1837 and Carlyle's *French Revolution* in 1840) but also to modify some of the constitutional doctrines of the utilitarian school. Thus he retained his faith in representative government, but in his famous essay *On Liberty* (1859) his concern for the freedom of individual thought and action made him keenly sensitive to the danger of tyranny by the majority and suspicious of machinery such as universal and equal suffrage that might bring it about. Even in his *Principles of Political Economy* (1848), though he adheres in general to the principles of * Ricardo and the classical economists, he is becoming aware of the danger of forcing human activities and social institutions into too rigid a theoretical mould. Mill is best known to many philosophers for his *A System of Logic, Ratiocinative and Inductive* (1843), which contains a doctrine of meaning that suggests that many terms have two kinds of meaning. They have denotations, in that they pick out or denote particular things, and they have connotations, in that they suggest that the things picked out have certain common properties. Proper names, on the other hand, have only denotations. Mill's view of the public world was a version of phenomenalism and is known for his definition of a material thing as a permanent possibility of sensation. Much of Mill's inspiration for his later work came from Mrs Harriet Taylor, the one romance of his life, whom he came to know well from 1830 and married in 1851. Mill was M.P. for Westminister (1865–68) and during the debates on the Reform Bill of 1867 strongly supported women's suffrage. His *Autobiography* (1873) was published after his death.
Britton, K. W., *John Stuart Mill: His Life and Philosophy*. 2nd ed. 1969

Millais, Sir John Everett, 1st Bart (1829–1896). British painter. He was born at Southampton into a family of Jersey origins and exhibited at the Royal Academy at the age of 17. In 1848 he joined with his friends Holman * Hunt and * Rossetti in the foundation of the Pre-Raphaelite Brotherhood. His first picture in the Brotherhood's detailed manner, *Christ in the House of his Parents* (1850), caused controversy but such pictures as *Ophelia, The Blind Girl* and *Autumn Leaves* show the Pre-Raphaelites' preoccupation with colour, detail and design combined with the artist's own poetic vision. With the end (*c.* 1859) of his Pre-Raphaelite period Millais lapsed into conventional sentimentality with such pictures as *The Boyhood of Raleigh* and the notorious *Bubbles*, a portrait of his grandson (Admiral Sir William James), which was bought as an advertisement for Pears' Soap, one of the earliest examples of a picture by a famous artist being used for such a purpose.

He married (1854) * Ruskin's former wife, Euphemia (Effie) Gray.
Millais, J. G., *The Life and Letters of Sir John Everett Millais*. 1899

Millay, Edna St Vincent (Mrs E. J. Boissevain) (1892–1950). American poet. Her verses, often in sonnet form, are intensely lyrical and derive in spirit and technique from the Elizabethans. She also wrote short stories and plays, e.g. *The Murder of Lidice* (1942), and translated Baudelaire's *Flowers of Evil*.

Miller, Arthur (1915–). American author of a number of powerful plays, some of which were filmed; they include *All My Sons* (1947); *Death of a Salesman* (which won the 1949 Pulitzer Prize); *The Crucible* (1953), a satire on McCarthyism (* McCarthy) filmed by a French company as *Les Sorcières de Salem*; and *A View from the Bridge* (1955). He also wrote the novel *Focus* (1945). He married (1956) the film actress Marilyn * Monroe and after her death wrote *After the Fall*.
Nelson, B., *Arthur Miller, Portrait of a Playwright*. 1970

Miller, Glenn (1904–1944). American dance-band leader, trombonist and composer. He formed his own band in 1938 and became world famous for a sweet orchestral sound, mainly saxophones, which was unique. He was made leader of the U.S. Air Force Band in Europe during World War II and disappeared on a flight from England to France. His posthumous popularity was if anything greater than that during his lifetime. His style and sound have been widely imitated and reproduced.

Miller, Henry (1891–1980). American writer. Born in New York, he lived in Paris (1930–39) and later settled in California. His works are largely a passionate indictment of modern, especially American, civilization, and an equally passionate affirmation of what is called the Bohemian life. His novels (largely works of heightened personal reminiscence) include *Tropic of Cancer* (1934) and *Tropic of Capricorn* (1938); other works include *The Colossus of Maroussi* (1941), describing travels in Greece, and *The Air-Conditioned Nightmare* (1945). The early novels, first published in Paris, were for many years banned as obscene in Britain and the USA.
Gordon, W. A., *The Mind and Art of Henry Miller*. 1968

Miller, Joaquin (Cincinnatus Heine Miller) (1841?–1913). American poet. His adventurous life among the Indians is reflected in his *Songs of the Sierras* (1871).
Marberry, M., *Splendid Poseur*. 1953

Miller, Stanley Lloyd (1930–). American chemist. Educated at Chicago, he was a student of * Urey and became a professor at the University of California. He found that by creating a 'primordial' atmosphere of hydrogen, ammonia and methane, mixing this with distilled water, and exposing the combination to repeated electrical discharges simple amino acids could be produced, suggesting a likely explanation for the development of life forms on Earth. *See* A. I. * Oparin.

Millerand, (Etienne) Alexandre (1859–1943). French politician and president. A lawyer by profession he entered (1885) the Chamber of Deputies as a member of the extreme left and tried to unify the Socialist groups. From 1899 he held several ministerial offices including the ministry of war at the beginning of World War I. After the war he reorganized the administration of Alsace and Lorraine, regained from the Germans. Elected president in 1920, he was forced to resign (1924) after the 'left' victory in the parliamentary elections.

Millet, Jean François (1814–1875). French painter. The son of a Normandy peasant, he idealized the life of the labourer in such pictures as *The Angelus* and *The Man With a Hoe*, painted with a deep religious sense but with a sentimentality which has alienated later generations. He lived for many years (from 1849) at Barbizon, a small town near Fontainebleau which gave its name to the 'school' of landscape painters gathered there.

Millikan, Robert Andrews (1868–1953). American physicist. In a brilliant academic career he was professor of physics at the University of Chicago (1910–21) and then became director of the Norman Bridge Laboratory, Pasadena, and chairman of the California Institute of Technology. He carried out much research into atomic structure and cosmic rays, but is best known for his accurate determinations (1909) of the charge on the electron from measurements of the charge picked up by oil drops exposed to X-rays. He won the Nobel Prize for Physics (1923).

Millin, Sarah Gertrude (1889–1968). South African writer. She wrote a number of novels, e.g. *God's Stepchildren* (1924), biographies of Cecil Rhodes (1933) and Smuts (1936), and works, e.g. *The South Africans* (1926), dealing with the problems of her country.
Millin, S. G., *The Measure of my Days*. 1955

Mills, Bertram (1873–1935). British circus proprietor. Originally a coachbuilder and horse expert, he produced a circus at Olympia, London, in 1920, which became an annual Christmas event. It was continued by his sons until 1965. In 1930 Mills started a touring circus which toured Great Britain in the summer months.

Milne, A(lan) A(lexander) (1882–1956). British author, born in Scotland. He was assistant editor of *Punch* (1906–14) and later wrote successful comedies, e.g. *Wurzel Flummery* (1917), *Mr Pim Passes By* (1919), and *The Dover Road* (1922); but he is best known as the author of children's books written originally for his son Christopher Robin: *When We Were Very Young* (1924), *Winnie the Pooh* (1926), *Now We Are Six* (1927) and *The House at Pooh Corner* (1928). He dramatized Kenneth Grahame's *Wind in the Willows* as *Toad of Toad Hall*.
Milne, A. A., *It's Too Late Now*. 1939

Milne, George Francis Milne, 1st Baron (1866–1948). British soldier, remembered for his command of the British troops at Salonica in World War I. He had earlier served in the Sudan and South Africa; he was chief of the Imperial General Staff from 1926 to 1933, when he was made a field-marshal and a baron.

Milner, Alfred Milner, 1st Viscount (1854–1923). British administrator and politician. After a brilliant career at Oxford, he was a journalist for a time before entering public life. Successful service in Egypt (1889–92) as under-secretary of finance paved the way for chairmanship of the Board of Inland Revenue (1892–97). His career reached its peak when he was British high commissioner for South Africa (1897–1905), with governorships of the separate colonies. His activities on behalf of the *Uitlanders* (immigrants attracted to the goldfields, but denied political rights) of the Transvaal were interpreted by some as provocations that led to the Boer War, but no-one disputed the clarity of Milner's mind or the inspiration he gave to the brilliant group of young men he gathered round him (his 'kindergarten' which included Lionel Curtis, who first propounded the commonwealth ideal). Milner's own conception, modified later, was of an organic empire with a prescribed constitution. Despite his diehard resistance (1909) to the abolition of the House of Lords veto, he was one of the most useful members of Lloyd George's war cabinet (from 1916). In the post-war years he became an ardent advocate of imperial preference in a system of protectionist tariffs.
Halperin, V., *Lord M. and the Empire*. 1952

Milnes, Richard Monckton, 1st Baron Houghton (1784–1858). British politician and literary patron. Having spent much of his early life in travel, he was MP (1837–63) for Pontefract (where he lived the life of a cultural dilettante at Fryston Hall), sponsoring such liberal causes as slave emancipation and women's rights. Through his support his friend Tennyson became Poet Laureate, and he early perceived Swinburne's genius; he himself wrote poetry and travel books which recorded such adventures as his penetration of an eastern harem. Disraeli depicted him in *Tancred* as Mr Vavasour.

Milosz, Czeslaw (1911–). Polish poet, novelist and essayist, born in Lithuania. He fought in the Resistance but left Poland in 1951, becoming a US resident in 1960 and a professor of Slavic literature at Berkeley 1960–78. He won the 1980 Nobel Prize for Literature.

Miltiades (died *c.* 488 B.C.). Athenian general, famous for his great victory over the Persians at Marathon (490). It was through his persuasion that the outnumbered Athenian army left the doubtful protection of the city walls and met the enemy near their landing place. By strengthening his flanks at the expense of his centre he achieved an encircling movement, from which few of the enemy escaped. The news of the victory was taken to Athens (22 miles) by the runner Phidippides, a feat commemorated by the Marathon race at the Olympic Games.

Milton, John (1608–1674). English poet. He was born in London, the son of a scrivener (i.e. one who drew up legal documents); he was a precocious scholar at St Paul's School, London, and spent seven years at Cambridge University. On graduation (1632) he spent six years at his father's country house at Horton, Buckinghamshire, and in this Anglican and Puritan household studied in preparation for his poetic vocation. There and at Cambridge he wrote many of his earliest works, e.g. the *Hymn on the Morning of Christ's Nativity* (1629), *Il Penseroso* and *L'Allegro* (both 1632), the masque *Comus* (1634), and the great pastoral elegy *Lycidas* (1637), written in memory of his friend Edward King, drowned in the Irish Sea. Milton travelled (1638–1639) in Italy, where he met Galileo in prison; after returning to England he virtually gave up writing poetry for twenty years (except sonnets, e.g. the one *On the late Massacre in Piedmont*), and devoted himself to parliamentary cause, writing pamphlets against episcopacy, e.g. *The Reason of Church Government* (1642). He married (1642) Mary Powell, who left him after a few months and did not return until 1645; during her absence Milton wrote *The Doctrine and Discipline of Divorce*, which advocated the dissolution of unhappy marriages. Two other famous pamphlets are *Tractate on Education* and *Areopagitica* (both published 1644), the latter championing the liberty of the Press. A pamphlet defending the execution of Charles I was published in 1649, the year in which Milton was appointed Latin (i.e. foreign) secretary to the State Council. His eyes began to deteriorate in 1644 and from 1651 he was blind but continued his duties with assistance. His first wife having died (1652), he married Catherine Woodcock in 1656, her death two years later prompting the famous sonnet *On His Deceased Wife*. In 1662 he married Elizabeth Minshull, who survived him.

After the restoration of Charles II Milton went into hiding but was soon pardoned. He immediately began *Paradise Lost* (published 1667), his great epic in blank verse, which tells the story of Satan's rebellion against God, of the subsequent scenes in Eden and of the fall of Man. In 1671 the twelve books of *Paradise Lost* were followed by the four of *Paradise Regained*, which recounts Christ's victory over Satan after the temptation in the wilderness; it is an allegory on a much less ambitious scale, less highly coloured in style and language but with a distinctive subtlety of its own. *Samson Agonistes* (1671), constructed like a Greek tragedy, gives the biblical theme a pathos and inspirational power transcending the original. Milton's later prose works, e.g. the tract *Of True Religion* (1673), are of less interest.

Because of the majesty and sublimity of his language Milton has generally been placed next to Shakespeare, but he has never moved the hearts of the masses; critics have even contended that he was a bad influence, especially on 18th-century poets, who imitated his solemn and sonorous verse without matching the grandeur and intensity of his thought.

Tillyard, E. M. W., *Milton*. Rev. ed. 1966

Mindszenty, József (1892–1975). Hungarian prelate. He was imprisoned (1944) by the Nazis, but after World War II ended (1945) he was appointed archbishop and primate of Hungary. He became a cardinal in 1946. An ardent upholder of the church's rights and of the national cause, he was imprisoned by the Communists (1949). During the revolt of 1956 he was released but, when the Russians restored Communist power, he was forced to take refuge in the US Embassy and lived there for 15 years. The pope retired him in 1974, against his will. His *Memoris* were published in 1975.

Minto, Gilbert John Elliot-Murray-Kynynmound, 4th Earl of (1845–1914). British administrator. After an adventurous early career as soldier and war correspondent in many parts of the world (he also rode in the Grand National five times), he inherited the earldom (1891) and was governor general of Canada (1898–1904) in the Klondyke gold rush period. As viceroy of India (1905–10) he initiated the Minto–Morley reforms which increased the numbers and powers of the central and provincial executive and legislative councils and introduced more Indians at all government levels. He also banned the export of opium. His great-grandfather, the identically named **1st Earl** (1751–1814), took part in the impeachment of Warren* Hastings and was governor general of India (1806–13). He captured Mauritius and Batavia during the Napoleonic Wars.

Buchan, J., *Lord Minto*. 1924

Mintoff, Dom(inic) (1916–). Maltese politician. He trained as an architect and civil engineer, practising in Britain 1941–43 and later in Malta. He helped to reorganize the Maltese Labour Party in 1944. In 1945 he became a member of the Council of

Government and Executive Council. He was elected to the Legislative Assembly in 1947, becoming at the same time deputy prime minister responsible for works and reconstruction. He became prime minister in 1955, but resigned in 1958 in order to work for complete independence of British rule and the governor assumed direct rule. Mintoff became prime minister again 1971–84.

Minton, Thomas (1765–1836). English potter. After working for Josiah Spode he started his own factory (1796), produced earthenware and bone china, and became well known for his decorated vases and 'Parian' figures and groups. He was also a noted engraver.

Mirabeau, Honoré Gabriel Victor Riqueti, Comte de (1749–1791). French revolutionary. He was so wild and dissipated as a young man and so constantly in debt that his father had him imprisoned several times. From 1785, when his pamphlet *On Despotism* appeared, his serious interest in politics increased. In 1786 he went to Berlin where several interviews with Frederick the Great bore fruit in a critical study of the Prussian monarchy, published in 1788. His great opportunity came when (1789) Louis XVI summoned the Estates-General, the step which proved the starting point of the Revolution; Mirabeau was elected for the third estate and by his oratory and personality soon asserted his dominance. He initiated the steps by which the Estates-General was converted into the National Assembly. The phase that followed the fall of the Bastille and the transference of the Royal family (October 1789) from Versailles to Paris saw Mirabeau at the height of his power. On the one hand he led the Assembly in its debate on a new constitution, on the other he was acting as secret adviser to Louis XVI and accepting bribes for his help in preserving as much as he could of the royal prerogative. That he would have performed in the same way without bribes (for, despite the violence of his oratory, he was a cautious and moderate constitutionalist) is likely but irrevelant to the moral issue. Unfortunately neither Louis nor Marie Antoinette (whom Mirabeau met only once) could overcome their aversion to his reputed character, and they withheld the trust which would have enabled Mirabeau to act with confidence on their behalf. After his sudden death at 42 there was no one to protect them from their own weakness and folly.
De la Croix, R., *Mirabeau: ou, l'échec du destin*. 1960

Miranda, Francisco de (1750–1816). Spanish American soldier. He was born in Venezuela, and served in the Spanish army against the British in Florida. Suspected of disloyalty to the Spanish crown he spent many years in the U.S.A. and Europe (and fought for a time as a general in the French Revolutionary armies), trying to enlist support for freeing Venezuela from Spanish rule. He returned to London (1798) and finally gained British and American support for an expedition which sailed (1806) from New York. The result was a fiasco; but when a junta seized power in Venezuela (1810), he again left England to lend support. Eventually he became commander-in-chief of the Venezuelan forces but was forced to capitulate (1812); he died in prison.

Miró, Joan (1893–1983). Spanish painter. He worked with the French Dadaists for a time, later joined André Breton's Surrealist group and designed settings and costumes for Diaghilev's ballets. The style for which in the 1940s he ultimately became famous had its origins in the work of primitive peoples, e.g. the Eskimoes and the Indians of North America. It was an art of hieroglyphs and symbols painted with strokes and spots in primary colours, red, blue, yellow, usually against a green or black background. He preferred to work on a large scale, as in his notable murals for the UNESCO building in Paris. He also produced ceramics and lithography.
Bonnetoy, Y., *Miro*. 1967

Mishima Yukio (1925–1970). Japanese novelist, born in Tokyo. The son of a civil servant, he was rejected for war service, studied law and worked in the finance ministry. He devoted himself to writing after the success of his autobiographical *Confessions of a Mask* (1948). His novels included *The Temple of the Golden Pavilion* (1959) and *The Sea of Fertility* (1970). He also directed and starred in the film *Yukoku* (1966). Obsessed with the disappearance of the *bushido* tradition, he formed a small private army, attempted a coup and died by hara-kiri in the traditional manner.

Mistinguett (Jeanne-Marie Bourgeois) (1875–1956). One of the great stars of the Paris music-halls. She appeared in revue from about 1899 and in the 1920s her partnership with Maurice Chevalier at the Folies Bergère and elsewhere made her world famous.

Mistral, Frédéric (1830–1914). French poet. He was born and spent his life near Avignon in Provence, and the Provençal language was both the object of his study and the instrument of his creative work. The rural epic *Miréio* (1859) was the most popular of his books but with *Nerto* (1883), a novel in verse about Avignon in the years of papal residence, he achieved almost equal success in another field. In his longer works he showed narrative skill and a great sense of character, while his lyrics are often exquisite. Mistral won the Nobel Prize for Literature (1904).

Mitchell, Margaret (1900–1949). American novelist, born in Georgia. In 1936 she published *Gone with the Wind*, which won her the Pulitzer Prize (1937), sold eight million copies and was equally popular when made into a film.
Edwards, A., *The Road to Tara*. 1983.

Mitchell, William Lendrum (1879–1936). American soldier and airman. After World War I, in which he rose to be chief of air operations, he carried out a vigorous campaign against official failure to realize the importance of air power. When he attacked a superior for 'almost treasonable incompetence', he was court-martialled and had to resign. In one of his many books on air warfare he predicted the Japanese attack on Pearl Harbor. Nine years after his death he was vindicated by Congress, posthumously promoted to the rank of major-general and awarded the Medal of Honour.
Mitchell, R., *My Brother Bill, the Life of General 'Billy' Mitchell*. 1953

Mitford, Nancy (1904–1973) English novelist and biographer. Her romantic comedies of upper class manners were widely popular and her historical biographies well regarded. In 1956 she edited *Noblesse Oblige*, a catalogue of class mannerisms which defined behaviour as 'U' (Upper class) or 'Non-U'. Her best known novels are probably *The Pursuit of Love* (1945) and *Love in a Cold Climate* (1949). Her biographies included *The Sun King* (a study of Louis XIV, 1966).

Mithridates VI (known as 'the Great') (*c*. 120–63 B.C.). King of Pontus (from *c*. 132), a country bordering the Black Sea. When he occupied Bithynia and Cappadocia he clashed with Rome and in 92 he was forced by * Sulla to withdraw and pay a large indemnity. When Rome became involved in civil war Mithridates felt it safe to refuse to pay and so provoked the First Mithridatic War (89–84). He began it by overrunning Asia Minor and sending troops to Greece to raise that country against Rome. Sulla, victorious in the political struggle at home, went to Greece where he defeated Mithridates at Chaeronea and Orchomenos. Having crossed to Asia Minor he found that the Roman army sent by his opponents was already victorious, and was thus able to impose a settlement by which Mithridates renounced his conquests. The Second Mithridatic War (83–81), a minor affair provoked by an irresponsible act of aggression by the Roman legate left in command, made Mithridates angry and suspicious and he began to make preparations for a renewal of the struggle by forming alliances with Egypt, Cyprus and Roman malcontents. To anticipate him, Rome declared war (74). Mithridates won an early naval victory, but the Roman commander Lucullus forced him to the defensive, and he took refuge with his son-in-law Tigranes of Armenia. A mutiny among the Roman troops allowed him to return to Pontus (67), but * Pompey completely defeated him. Mithridates, rejected by subjects and allies alike, poisoned his wives and children and killed himself.

Mitscherlich, Eilhard (1794–1863). German chemist. He was already known for researches covering a wide field when he became a professor (1822) at Berlin University, where he remained for the rest of his life. He is best known for his work on crystallography. He recognized isomorphism, dimorphism, and stated (1819) the law of isomorphism which bears his name, i.e. that substances which crystallize in the same crystal form have similar chemical compositions. This law was of great value during the early 19th century in fixing the formulae of newly discovered compounds.

Mitterrand, François Maurice (1916–). French socialist politician. He worked in the

Resistance during World War II. He was a deputy (1946–58, 1962–81) and a senator (1959–62). He held a variety of ministries briefly under the Fourth Republic. He was a Socialist candidate for the presidency in 1965 and 1974 defeating Valéry* Giscard d'Estaing in 1981.

Mobutu Sese Seko (1930–). Zaïre politician. He was employed in the Belgian Congo *Force Publique* 1949–56, became a member of *Mouvement National Congolaise*, and was a delegate to the Brussels conferences on independence, 1959–60. Following independence he became secretary of state for National Defence in the Cabinet of Patrice * Lumumba in 1960; he was also commander-in-chief of the army. In September 1960 Lumumba was overthrown and Mobutu took power. He became President of Zaïre in 1965.

Modigliani, Amedeo (1884–1920). Italian artist. After an artistic education based on study of the old masters, he went to Paris (1906) and met several of the 'Fauves' group. He lived in great poverty and died of tuberculosis, the effects of which were heightened by drink. His portraits and melancholy nudes – which now command high prices – show the influence of Cézanne and primitive African sculptors, but the melody of line produced by subtle linear distortion expresses his own individual genius.
Werner, A., *Modigliani*. 1967

Mohammed (Muhammad) (*c.* 570–632). Founder of Islam. He was born in Mecca, was orphaned early in life and later adopted by an uncle, Abu Talib. When about 25 he was engaged by Khadija, a wealthy older woman, to accompany one of her caravans and he subsequently married her. Despite the disparity in age the marriage was a happy one. By her Mohammed had two sons and four daughters, one of whom, Fatima, married his cousin Ali – a union from which all the direct descendants of the prophet sprang.

In 610, when he was 40, Mohammed had a vision of Archangel Gabriel. The faith Mohammed preached was one of the strictest monotheism: while he accepted that Jew and Christian also worship the same god he felt that they had strayed from the strict monotheistic path. He denounced idols, proclaimed a single God, Allah, and promised true believers physical resurrection in Heaven. He preached complete submission to the will of God (this is the meaning of 'Islam') and the equality of all men of every race. Christians and Jews he classed not as pagans but as Ahl al Kitab (people of the book), towards whom he extended toleration. At first only his wife believed in him and in the first ten years he made less than a hundred converts; but this was enough to alarm the citizens of Mecca who had a vested interest in preserving the image of their city as a religious centre of all Arabs with the Kaaba and its many idols: to escape their animosity Mohammed and his followers moved unobtrusively (622) to Yathrib (renamed Medinah) some 250 miles away, which offered them security. This was the Hegira (Flight) from which the Moslem era dates. Here he had greater success in winning adherents than in Mecca and he became the revered law-giver and ruler of the city. His followers organized attacks on caravans from Mecca and his fame spread and attracted support. In 623 the Moslems won a signal victory over the Meccans at Badr and in 630 Mohammed marched on Mecca, which surrendered. The Kaaba was cleared of its idols and became the shrine of Islam. Mohammed was recognized as a prophet and the new faith spread rapidly throughout Arabia. He returned to Medinah, where he died. After his first wife's death (*c.* 620) Mohammed took several wives, of whom his favourite was Ayesha; it was her father, Abu Bekr, who became Mohammed's successor and who caused to be recorded the prophet's revelations and sayings which form the *Qu'ran* (*Koran*).

There is little about Mohammed's life to explain those undoubted qualities which inspired such devotion among his followers – an inspiration which founded a great new world religion and carried the hitherto backward peoples of Arabia to the conquest of an empire which, at its peak, was greater in extent than that of the Romans, and to a flowering of arts and sciences which shone all the more brightly against the background of the Dark Ages in Europe.
Watt, W. M., *Mohammed: Prophet and Statesman*. 1961

Mohammed II (known as 'the Conqueror') (1430–1481). Turkish sultan (from 1451). At the time of his accession the Ottoman empire already included most of Asia Minor and much of the Balkans, but he conquered (1453) the Byzantine city of Constantinople', a feat which transformed the history of Europe. He conquered a large part of the Balkan peninsula, including Greece, and a war with Venice (1463–79) added to his possessions in the Adriatic and Aegean. He was the effective founder of the Ottoman Empire.

Mohammed V (Sidi Mohammed ben Yussuf) (1910–1961). King of Morocco (from 1956). He succeeded as sultan under French protection (1927) but in 1953 he put himself at the head of the nationalist movement and was deposed and exiled by the French. He was restored in 1955 and when Morocco gained its independence (1956) he was its first king, abandoning (1957) the title sultan. He was succeeded by his son Hassan II.

Mohammed VI (1861–1926). Last sultan of Turkey (1918–22). The defeat of Turkey in World War I left him a helpless pawn in the hands of the Allies and he was unable to contend with the nationalist rising under Mustafa Kemal (* Kemal Atatürk). He was deposed and retired to the Italian Riviera, where he died.

Mohammed Ali *see* **Mehemet Ali**

Mohammed Reza (1919–1980). Shahanshah of Iran (1941–79). He succeeded his father * Reza Shah, who was forced to abdicate by the Allies in World War II. He made efforts to modernize his country, to reform economic inequalities but scorned western liberalism. From the 1970s onwards he was under increasing pressure from religious leaders of Islam and in January 1979 he left Iran with his family and stayed in Morocco, Mexico, the USA and Panama. The religious leaders demanded his return to Iran to answer charges of corruption. In early 1980, he left Panama for Egypt where he died.

Moiseiwitsch, Benno (1890–1963). British pianist, born in Russia. He won the Rubinstein prize at 9 and later studied at the Imperial Academy of Music in Odessa. He first appeared in Britain in 1908. He was noted as an interpreter of the romantic composers.

Moissan, Ferdinand Frederic Henry (1852–1907). French chemist, best known for his success in isolating the elusive element fluorine (1886), and for his development of the electric arc furnace, with which he studied high-temperature reactions, preparing new compounds, e.g. the metal carbides and nitrides. He became (1889) a professor of chemistry in Paris and won the Nobel Prize for Chemistry (1906).

Molière (Jean Baptiste Poquelin) (1622–1673). French playwright and actor. The son of the upholsterer to the king, he received his education at a Jesuit college in Paris but more serious studies were abandoned when he formed a theatrical company (1643), adopting the stage-name Molière. After touring the provinces for many years his company returned to Paris (1658) and gained the patronage of the king's brother and eventually (1665) of Louis XIV himself. He was thus able to provide court entertainments though in fact most of his greatest plays were performed at his own theatre at the Palais Royal. These plays, in most of which he himself played the leading part, range from slapstick farce to philosophical satires and many of them reveal the extent of his debt to Plautus, Terence and Lope de Vega. Molière's motto was 'No truth without comedy and no comedy without truth', and in his works he poked fun at hypocrites, quacks, extremists and all those 'enslaved by a ruling passion'. He achieved his first big success with *Les Précieuses ridicules* (1659), followed by a series of masterpieces, e.g. *L'Ecole des femmes* (1662), *Tartuffe* (1665), an attack on religious hypocrisy which was banned for four years, *Le Misanthrope* (1666), *Le Bourgeois gentilhomme* (1671) and *Les Femmes savantes* (1672). His last play was *Le Malade imaginaire* (1673); while acting in it he suffered a haemorrhage and died later the same night. After his death his company joined with another to form the Comédie Française, where the traditions of the original performances are observed.

Bray, R., *Molière, homme de théâtre*. Rev. ed. 1963

Mollet, Guy (1905–1975). French politician. A teacher by profession and an active Socialist, he joined the army in World War II, was a prisoner of war (1940–42) and was later active in the Resistance movement. He entered (1945) the Constituent Assembly and became (1946) secretary general of the Socialist party. After a number of ministerial appointments he was prime minister (1956–57) and so directed French participation in the Suez attacks

(November 1956). He supported de Gaulle's return to power (1958) and served in his ministry until 1959.

Mollison, Amy and James *see* **Johnson, Amy**

Molnár, Ferenc (1878–1952). Hungarian playwright, who settled in the USA in 1910. He was a war correspondent in World War I, and both before and after wrote popular and successful comedies, e.g. *The Guardsman* (1910), *Liliom* (1924), *The Glass Slipper* (1924) and *The Good Fairy* (1937).

Molotov (Scriabin), Vyacheslav Mikhailovich (1890–). Russian Communist politician. Born to a middle-class family, he was a cousin of the composer Alexander * Scriabin. He joined the Bolsheviks in 1906 and later adopted the name Molotov ('hammer'). He was a candidate member of the Politburo 1921–25, general secretary of the Communist Party 1921–22, and a full Politburo member 1925–57, working closely with * Stalin. Premier 1930–41, he displaced * Litvinov as foreign minister when in 1939 Stalin made the volte-face which led to the Nazi-Soviet pact. In this office he came to symbolize a negative attitude towards any attempt to seek real harmony between Soviet Russia and its western allies during and after World War II. He was a deputy premier 1941–57 and again foreign minister 1953–57. After Stalin's death (1953) he was, with Beria and Malenkov, one of the ruling triumvirate, but the struggle for power which brought Khrushchev to the front ended Molotov's long ascendancy. He was ambassador to Mongolia 1957–60, then to the International Atomic Energy Agency, Vienna 1960–62. In 1964 the CPSU expelled him.

Moltke, Helmuth, Count von (1800–1891). German soldier. He entered the Prussian service (1822) and was appointed (1832) to the general staff. He remodelled the Turkish army (1835–39), and became chief of the Prussian general staff (1858), reorganized the army and planned the successful lightning campaigns against Denmark (1864), Austria (1866) and France (1870–71). He was one of the first generals to base his strategy on the use of railways for the rapid assembly and movement of troops. With the formation of the German empire (1871) his position, which he retained until 1888, became that of chief of the Imperial General Staff.
Kessel, E., *Moltke*. 1957

Mommsen, Theodor (1817–1903). German historian. He reached the climax of a successful academic career when he went to Berlin University (1858) as professor of ancient history, a post he retained for the rest of his life. The *History of Rome* (3 volumes, 1854–56) for which he is famous ends with the fall of the republic and reveals the author's hero-worship of Julius Caesar. A supplementary volume on the imperial provinces appeared in 1885. In addition Mommsen wrote specialized works touching Roman history at many points, on coinage, chronology, constitutional law etc. His great *Corpus* of Latin inscriptions was a remarkable editorial feat. He received the Nobel Prize for Literature in 1902.
Wickert, L., *Theodor Mommsen; eine Biographie*. 1959

Monash, Sir John (1865–1931). Australian general. An eminent civil engineer and citizen soldier, in World War I he fought at Gallipoli and later, after commanding the 3rd Australian Division in France, became (1918) commander-in-chief of the Australian Corps. He became chairman of the Victorian State Electricity Commission 1920–31 and vice chancellor of Melbourne University 1923–31.
Serle, A. G., *John Monash*. 1982.

Mond, Ludwig (1839–1909). German chemist. A pupil of * Bunsen at Heidelberg, he invented processes for recovering sulphur from alkali waste, and ammonia from nitrogenous substances. He settled in England (1867) and formed (1873), with (Sir) John Brunner, the firm of Brunner, Mond & Co. (later merged with Imperial Chemicals) to produce soda from common salt by the Solvay process. One of Mond's most valuable discoveries was the carbonyl process for extracting nickel from its ores. His son Alfred became 1st Baron Melchett.

Mondale, Walter Frederick (1928–). American politician and lawyer, born in Minnesota. A protégé of Hubert * Humphrey, he was state attorney general 1960–64, US Senator from Minnesota 1964–77 and vice president under Jimmy * Carter 1977–81. In 1984 he became the Democratic nominee for president, losing heavily to * Reagan.

Mondrian, Piet (1872–1944). Dutch painter. His earliest work was in landscape in the Dutch Romantic and Impressionist tradition. In Paris (1912–14) he was influenced by the 'Fauves'. He went back to Holland (1914) and began his search for a formal purity without 'content' or reference and by 1922 his paintings had become geometric, rectilinear, in primary colours against a grey or ochre background. With Theo van Doesburg, Mondrian founded (1917) the magazine *De Stijl*, a name also given to the 'school' of painting which followed his lead. He himself called his work 'Neo-plasticism' and in the USA (to which he emigrated in 1944 after living in Paris and London) it was held to be the purest, least literary expression of the age of technology. Some modification of the earlier stark severity was admitted in his last works.
Elgar, F., *Mondrian*. 1968

Monet, Claude (1840–1926). French Impressionist painter. Born in Paris, he grew up at Le Havre and acquired an early love for the Seine with its reflections of trees, buildings, boats and its scenic effects. He studied painting with Boudin. When in 1862 he settled in Paris he met Cézanne, Renoir, Sisley and others who were later to become the Impressionists – a name mockingly bestowed by a critic of Monet's picture *Impression, Soleil levant*, shown at an exhibition organized by Monet, Berthe Morisot and Sisley in 1874. The group's greatest innovation was to take painting out of the studio into the open air. With Renoir, at first at Argenteuil on the Seine, Monet tried to achieve greater naturalism by exact analysis of tone and colour and to render the play of light on the surface of objects, using a flickering touch and paint applied in small bright dabs in a high key and with a lack of outline. His pictures were mostly landscapes, many with water or snow; he would paint the same objects, e.g. haystacks or cathedrals, at different times of the day to get different light effects, but in his later works the light patterns began to be used mainly for their decorative effect rather than as a means to describe form.
Seitz, W. C., *Claude Monet*. 1960

Monge, Gaspard (1746–1818). French scientist. His early work was concerned with improving teaching methods in military engineering. He made systematic advances in descriptive geometry; modern engineering drawing owes much to him. While continuing his military studies (he was much concerned with logistic problems of moving materials for use in fortifications) he developed interests in fields of applied and pure mathematics. He developed new techniques for applying the calculus to curves and faces in three dimensions. After his election to the Academy in 1780 Monge spent more time in Paris, and his interests moved towards physics and chemistry. He aided Lavoisier in the analysis and synthesis of water, and carried out experiments on the composition of iron, steel, and carbon dioxide. In the Revolutionary period, Monge played increasingly prominent roles in public life. He became minister for the navy in 1792, and then in 1795 Director of the newly-founded Ecole Polytechnique. He was closely involved in establishing the metric system of weights and measures. Monge's substantial publications, including his *Géometrie descriptive* (1795) and *Traité élémentaire de statique* (1810) became key teaching texts.

Moniz, Antonio Caetano de Abreu Freire Egas (1874–1955). Portuguese neurologist. He held chairs at Coimbra and Lisbon, served as a deputy 1903–17 and foreign minister 1918. He shared the 1949 Nobel Prize for Medicine for his work on prefrontal leucotomy (a technique no longer in fashion).

Monk (Monck), George, 1st Duke of Albemarle (1608–1670). English soldier. He gained military experience in the Thirty Years War; in the English Civil War he at first served with the Royalists, was captured, and gained Cromwell's confidence. As a commander he distinguished himself at Dunbar and (at sea) with* Blake. In 1654 Cromwell appointed him governor of Scotland where he successfully restored order. Cromwell's death gave him the opportunity to exercise his skill in political matters. On New Year's Day 1660 he entered England with 6,000 men, reached London unopposed, reinstated the Long Parliament and secured a new election. He worked skilfully to reconcile the army to the growing public desire for a restoration of the monarchy. Charles II, from whom he had obtained pledges of constitutional rule before inviting him to return, made him a duke on Dover beach.

Monmouth, James, Duke of (1649–1685). Son of Charles II of Great Britain and his mistress Lucy Walters. He came to England from Holland after the Restoration and was created (1663) Duke of Monmouth. On marrying Anne, Countess of Buccleuch, he adopted her surname, Scott, and was made Duke of Buccleuch. Spoilt by his father and the adulation of the people, he was a ready tool of Shaftesbury and those who put him forward as a candidate for succession to the throne to the exclusion of the Duke of York (James II). It was even said that proofs of his legitimacy were contained in a mysterious black box. The discovery of the extremist Rye House plot to hasten Monmouth's accession by assassinating King Charles forced him to flee to Holland (1683), but on James II's accession (1685) he landed at Lyme Regis and claimed the throne. His little army, mostly peasants, was quickly defeated at Sedgemoor and Monmouth himself was captured and executed.

Chevenix-Trench, C., *The Western Rising*. 1969

Monnet, Jean (1888–1979). French politician. Pioneer of European unity and recognized as a founder of the European Community, he was the first deputy secretary-general of the League of Nations. After World War II he originated the French Modernization Plan and, later, the Schuman Plan for organizing European resources. This led to the formation of the European Coal and Steel Community of which he was president 1952–55. He was chairman of an action committee for a United States of Europe. He was awarded the Charlemagne Prize in 1953, the Schuman Prize (1966) and the title 'Honorary Citizen of Europe' (1976).

Monnet, J., *Mémoires*. 1976

Monod, Jacques Lucien (1910–1976). French biochemist. Educated at the Univeristy of Paris and the California Institute of Technology, he was a colonel in the Resistance during World War II and worked at the Pasteur Institute 1945–76. He shared the 1965 Nobel Prize for Medicine with André Lwoff and François Jacob for work on the regulatory action of genes. Monod was a brilliant controversialist and debater, an excellent writer on the philosophy of science (*Chance and Necessity* 1970) and a gifted 'cellist.

Judson, H. F., *The Eighth Day of Creation*. 1979

Monroe, James (1758–1831). Fifth president of the US (1817–25). Born of a well known Virginian family, his education was cut short by the War of Independence in which he served with distinction. He entered Virginia politics (1782) and opposed the ratification of the US constitution on the grounds that it would lead to excessive federal control of the individual states. He was elected (1790) to the US Senate as a strong supporter of his friend * Jefferson, then secretary of state, by whom he was employed as minister to France (1794–96). He was governor of Virginia (1799–1802 and 1809–11). When Jefferson became president Monroe was sent to Europe on a series of diplomatic missions (from 1803), on the first of which he helped to negotiate the purchase from Napoleon of a vast area of the Mississippi basin (the Louisiana Purchase). He was secretary of state under * Madison and was his natural successor as president, being elected in 1816 and 1820. He is best remembered for his promulgation of the Monroe Doctrine, which banned further European colonization of the Americas and European interference with independent governments in those continents.

Cresson, W. P., *James Monroe*. 1946

Monroe, Marilyn (Norma Jean Martenson) (1926–1962). American actress. After a hard upbringing she achieved enormous popular success in a series of comedy films, e.g. *Seven Year Itch* (1955), *The Prince and the Showgirl* (1957, with Laurence Olivier) and *Some Like it Hot* (1959). Evidence that the role of 'sex symbol', for which beatuty, talent and the circumstances of her life and cast her, left her unsatisfied was provided by her frequently expressed cultural ambitions and her unfortunate third marriage with the playwright Arthur Miller. She committed suicide.

Mailer, N., *Marilyn Monroe*. 1973

Monsarrat, Nicholas John Turney (1910–1979). British author. He began writing novels in 1934 but it was his war-time experience in the Royal Navy that inspired his instantly successful *The Cruel Sea* (1951). He subsequently wrote other popular sea novels. He lived in Johannesberg as Director of the U.K. Information Office 1946–53, and, in the same capacity, in Ottawa 1953–56. His autobiography in two volumes, *Life is a Four-Letter Word*, was published 1966 and 1970.

Montagu, Lady Mary Wortley (1689–1762). English letter writer. She was a daughter of Evelyn Pierrepoint, who eventually became 1st Duke of Kingston. She accompanied her husband, Edward Wortley Montagu, on a diplomatic mission (1716–18) to Constantinople, whence she introduced the practice of vaccination into England. She had acquired considerable education and this combined with her own lively intelligence enabled her, on her return, to become the centre of a fashionable group of artists, writers and wits. From 1739 she lived mainly in Italy. Her letters, covering the years 1709–62, are her real claim to fame. In them she gives vivid descriptions of places, people and events, revealing herself as a woman of much worldly wisdom, of warm and compassionate affection and an engaging wit, not unspiced with malice.
Halsband, R., ed., *Complete Letters of Lady Mary Wortley Montagu.* 1965–1967

Montaigne, Michel Eyquem, Seigneur de (1533–1592). French essayist. He was born at the Château de Montaigne in Périgord, but it was on Bordeaux, where his father was at one time mayor, that his life centred: his mother was a Protestant of Jewish origin. He himself served as a 'counsellor' of the Bordeaux *parlement* and eventually became mayor (1581–85). After his father's death (1568) and that of his elder brothers he inherited the family estate. From 1571 he devoted most of his time to travel and to the writing of the famous *Essais*: Books I and II appeared in 1580, Book III was included in an enlarged edition (1588), and a further edition was published (1595) after his death. His perpetual question was 'What do I know?' and in his writings he discusses in a detached, sceptical fashion philosophical, religious and moral questions with a tolerant awareness of the fallibility of reason. In some he seems to be engaged in self-preparation for disease and death, with which he was much obsessed in later years. His essays, first translated into English by John Florio (1603), influenced many English writers from Shakespeare and Bacon onwards.
Frame, D. M., *Montaigne*. 1965

Montefeltro, Federigo Ubaldi da, Duke of Urbino (*c*. 1420–1482). Italian nobleman. The last of the great condottieri, he ruled as Duke of Urbino 1444–82 and, because he often held the balance of power in northern Italy, was able to increase his duchy threefold. The pupil of Vittorino da Feltre, and a model for Castiglione's *The Courtier*, he owned the greatest library in Italy, patronized humanist scholars, never lost a battle, was considered the greatest soldier of his era, became an honorary Knight of the Garter and the subject of a memorable portrait by * Piero della Francesca.

Montefiore, Sir Moses Haim, 1st Bart. (1784–1885). Jewish philanthropist of Italian birth. He settled in England (1805), made a fortune on the London Stock Exchange and retired (1824) to devote his energies to philanthropic work to help Jews. He also negotiated agreements with Russia, Turkey and Egypt by which persecution in Poland, Syria and elsewhere was mitigated. He was knighted in 1837 and created a baronet in 1846.

Montespan, Françoise Athenaise Rochechouart, Marquise de (1641–1707). Mistress of Louis XIV of France. She was of high birth, gay, sophisticated and witty, in contrast to the shyly devoted Louise de la Vallière who finally left the court in 1674 having watched for some years her rival's gradual ascent. Madame de Montespan bore the king seven children, but her increasing haughtiness and bouts of jealousy (not unjustified) had already shaken her position when in 1680 her name was mentioned with those by many others during secret investigations into charges of poisoning and witchcraft. Her share (if it existed) in the matter was hushed up, but though she remained at court the liaison was ended. Her successor was her children's governess, Madame de * Maintenon.

Montesquieu, Charles Louis de Secondat, Baron de la Brède et de (1689–1755). French political philosopher. Charles de la Brède studied law and in 1716 became president of the *parlement* of Bordeaux in succession to his uncle, whose wealth he inherited on condition that he also assumed his name, de Montesquieu. For a time he was interested in science but abandoned it for letters and with the publication of his *Letters persanes* (1721) he became famous. The book purports to contain the letters of two Persians visiting Paris to each other and to their friends at home. Witty and frivolous comment is mingled with serious observations on the social

and political institutions and the various influences (climate, religion etc.) on the people. In 1726 he gave up his official position at Bordeaux and settled in Paris with interludes of travel. He visited England (1729–31) and studied its constitutional procedures. In his next major work, *Considérations sur les causes de la grandeur des Romains et de leur décadence* (1734) he tried to explain the greatness and the decline of the Roman empire by giving full weight to economic, cultural, climatic and racial factors – the first time that historic processes had been submitted to such a scientific examination. The monumental *De l'Esprit des lois* (2 volumes, 1748) occupied him for twenty years and summarized his life's work. By the 'spirit' of the laws he meant the social and natural (e.g. climatic) conditions which have brought laws and constitutions into being. The English system of constitutional government is, e.g., analysed in detail and the respective functions of legislature and executive art accurately assessed and presented for admiration and imitation. The rulers of France failed to heed the book's message in time to avert revolution but its influence was profound in shaping the intellectual background to political life there and elsewhere.
Shackleton, R., *Montesquieu: A Critical Biography*. 1961

Montessori, Maria (1870–1952). Italian educationist. She worked as a doctor in a Rome asylum teaching mentally handicapped children and applied this experience to the education of normal pupils. From 1911 she lectured throughout the world on the 'Montessori method', which emphasized that young children learn best through spontaneous activity and under minimal constraint.
Standing, E. M., *Maria Montessori, her Life and Work*. 1957

Monteux, Pierre (1875–1964). French conductor. He was conductor of Diaghilev's Ballets Russes (1911–14), directing the first performances of Stravinsky's *Firebird, Petrushka* and *The Rite of Spring* and Ravel's *Daphnis and Chloe*. He was conductor of the Boston Symphony Orchestra (1919–24), founder of the Orchestre de Paris (1929–38), and directed the London Symphony Orchestra (1961–64).

Monteverdi, Claudio (1567–1643). Italian composer, born at Cremona. Little is known of his early years but he won fame by his nine books of madrigals, the first of which appeared in 1587 and the second in 1590, the year he joined as a player of the viol the service of Vincenzo Gonzaga of Mantua, with whom he stayed until the duke's death (1612). In 1613 he became choirmaster of St Mark's, Venice, then the most important musical post in Italy. In 1632 he was ordained. His first opera, *La Favola d'Orfeo* (*The Legend of Orpheus*), was produced at Mantua for the carnival of 1607. In this work, the first opera of importance, Monteverdi consolidated the experiments of the earliest opera composers, the far less accomplished Jacopo Peri and Giulio Caccini. He was the first composer to employ an orchestra and in his moving vocal music revealed the psychological possibilities of the operatic medium. Of the many other operas and ballets of this period the best is *Arianna* (1608). The operas of his Venetian period were destroyed during the sack of Mantua (1630) but two later works, *The Return of Ulysses* (1640) and *The Coronation of Poppaea* (1642) remain. As the pioneer of opera (he also introduced opera techniques into church music) and composer alike he is among the greatest figures in musical history.
Arnold, D., *Monteverdi*. 1975

Montez, Lola (Maria Dolores Eliza Rosanna Gilbert) (1818–1861). Irish-born dancer of partly Spanish descent. She made her debut in London (1842) and subsequently toured Europe until (1846) she reached Munich, where the eccentric King Ludwig I of Bavaria became so enthralled that he made her a countess and in every aspect of his political and social life submitted his judgement to her whims. The scandal helped to bring about the revolution of 1848 which enforced his abdication. She died in New York after several years of renewed wandering.

Montezuma II (or Moctezuma) (1466–1520). Last of the Aztec emperors of Mexico (1503–20). He was not by nature warlike and the landing of the Spanish leader * Cortez in circumstances suggesting that he might be a divine visitant persuaded him to send propitiatory gifts. These only whetted the Spanish appetite for plunder and when repeated embassies and an ambush also failed to stop Cortez he decided to give him a ceremonial welcome at Tenochlitlan, his lake-encompassed capital. Cortez managed to seize him as hostage but on returning from a temporary absence, found that his men in sudden panic had started a massacre and were now besieged with Montezuma. Whilst trying to appeal to his own nobles from the walls the emperor was struck by a stone and killed.

Montfort, Simon de, Earl of Leicester (*c.* 1208–1265). Anglo-French baron. He was the son of Simon de Montfort who led the crusade against the Albigensian heretics. He married (1238) a sister of the English king Henry III against whom, ironically, he was to lead the baronial revolt. He was Henry's capable deputy in Gascony (1248–63), but a grievance that he had not been given royal support when his actions had been called in question made him readier to side with his fellow nobles in their efforts for government reform. By the Provisions of Oxford (1258) and of Westminster (1259) it was held that the king should govern through a council of fifteen magnates, but de Montfort's contention that the barons themselves should be subject to the council caused a split in their ranks which enabled the king and his son Edward to repudiate the Provisions. Civil war followed, decided by de Montfort's victory at Lewes (1264) which left him in command of the country with Henry and Edward prisoners in his hands. To regularize proceedings he summoned (1265) a 'parliament' (*parlement* or session of the magnates). The difference from earlier sessions was that to strengthen his position, since many hostile barons did not respond to the summons, he summoned also knights of the shire (i.e. the country gentry). By adding a more representative element (likely to give him support), the association of de Montfort's name with the first English parliament (in the modern sense) can somewhat dubiously be justified. In the same year Prince Edward escaped from surveillance, rallied the royalist supporters and gained the decisive victory of Evesham, where de Montfort was killed.
Labarge, M. W., *Simon de Montfort*. 1962

Montgolfier, (Jacques) Etienne (1745–1799) and **Joseph Michel** (1740–1810). French inventors of a man-carrying balloon. The brothers, paper-makers by profession, experimented first by filling paper bags with hot air, and later used a bag of silk with an open bottom under which paper was burnt to heat the air to lift the balloon. After an experiment with animals (September 1783) and captive flights, the first free manned ascent was made on 21 November when a balloon 48 ft in diameter and 75 ft high travelled for nearly six miles across Paris at a height of 300 ft.
Gillispie, C.C., *The Montgolfier Brothers and the Invention of Aviation*. 1983

Montgomery of Alamein, Bernard Law Montgomery, 1st Viscount (1887–1976). British general. He joined the Royal Warwickshire Regiment (1908) and fought on the western front throughout World War I. At the beginning of World War II he led the 3rd Division in France, his corps commander being the future Lord * Alanbrooke. After Dunkirk he served in England and was G.O.C. South-eastern Command when (August 1942) he was sent to Egypt to take over the 8th Army, which had already checked * Rommel on the Alamein position guarding Alexandria. After defeating a strong German attack (31 August) he planned, and the 8th Army achieved, a decisive breakthrough (October). The chase continued westwards across Africa: the 8th Army joined the American and British forces in Tunisia where early in 1943 the last German forces surrendered. Montgomery remained with the 8th Army for the invasions of Sicily and Italy but at the end of 1943 left to prepare for the liberation of France. He was in command of all Anglo-American troops in the landing operations and later of the army group forming the left wing. Once the break out had been achieved the advance to the Dutch frontier was amazingly fast. After the German surrender (April 1945), Montgomery commanded the British Military Zone; he was chief of Imperial General Staff (1946–48) and chairman of the NATO forces in Europe. The publication (1958) of his autobiography caused a sensation by its criticisms of his commander-in-chief * Eisenhower, for overruling his 1944 plan for a swift thrust on a narrow front direct to the Ruhr in favour of a slower and more systematic advance along the whole front. One of Montgomery's most striking assets was his supreme self-confidence which he managed to transmit to his men.
Chalfont, A., *Montgomery of Alamein*. 1976

Montherlant, Henry Millon de (1896–1972). French novelist, poet and playwright. An aristocrat by birth, he was wounded in World War I, was a bullfighter in Spain for a time and lived in the Sahara (1925–32). His

forceful and cynical novels, e.g. *Les Bestiaires* (1925), *Les Célibataires* (1934) and *Les Jeunes Filles* (1939), reveal his contempt for bourgeois values. After World War II he wrote successful plays, including *Le Maître de Santiago* (1947). Elected to the Académie Française in 1960, he committed suicide, fearing the onset of blindness.
Cruickshank, J., *Montherlant*. 1964

Montpensier, Anne Marie Louise d'Orléans, Duchesse de (1627–1693). French princess. For her heroic conduct in support of * Condé during the French civil war called the Fronde, she became known as 'la Grande Mademoiselle'.

Montrose, James Graham, 1st Marquess of (1612–1650). Scottish leader. After returning from continental travels he joined the anti-royalists and helped to draw up the National Covenant; but, disgusted by the extremism of the Covenanters, he abandoned their party and was appointed (1644) lieutenant general in Scotland by Charles I. With an army mainly of Highlanders, he achieved an astonishing series of victories which made him virtually master of the country. In 1645, however, he was surprised at Philiphaugh and forced (1646) to take refuge in Holland. In 1650, determined to avenge Charles's death, he invaded the north of Scotland from the Orkneys, but he found no support, was defeated at Invercarron, betrayed and hanged at Edinburgh. He was a chivalrous, romantic leader and gifted poet.
Wedgwood, C. V., *Montrose*. 1952

Moody, Dwight Lyman (1837–1899). American evangelist. After being a Boston salesman, he went to Chicago (1856) and began the missionary work for which he became famous. With the singer and hymn writer **Ira David Sankey** (1840–1904), he made remarkably successful revivalist tours of the U.S.A. and Great Britain.
Pollock, J. C., *Moody without Sankey*. 1964

Moody, Helen *see* **Wills, Helen**

Moore, George (1852–1933). Irish writer. Life in Ireland, where his father was a landlord and racehorse owner, made little appeal to Moore as a youth. He went to London, joined a bohemian set and when, aged 18, he inherited the family estate he went to Paris and studied art, with no great success. He returned to Ireland (1879) with an enthusiasm for the French Impressionists and the novelist Zola, who became his model for a series of realistic novels culminating in *Esther Waters* (1894), in which the humiliations and hardships which follow surrender to passion are, as in his other novels, the prevailing theme. Meanwhile Moore's life was spent between Ireland and London, where he finally settled (1911). A new phase of his literary life, an autobiographical one, began in 1888 with the publication of *Confessions of a Young Man* followed at intervals by portrayals of himself in later years, all written in an easy conversational style quite unlike that of his other works. In his final group of books the aesthete in George Moore predominates, the style, smooth and flowing, is everything, and human warmth is almost lacking. He uses this style for the reconstruction of old stories and legends, e.g. *The Brook Kerith* (1916), *Héloise and Abelard* (1921) and *Aphrodite in Aulis* (1930).

Moore, George Edward (1873–1958). English philosopher. Until his retirement (1939) his life was academic and almost entirely associated with Cambridge – as winner of a Craven scholarship and a prize fellowship, as lecturer, and finally (from 1925) as professor of philosophy. He was editor (1921–47) of *Mind*. Moore, who made a distinction between knowing and analysing, asserted that what is commonly understood (appreciated by common sense) to be the meaning of a term was frequently at variance with the results achieved by those who analysed its meaning. He therefore used analysis not for demonstrating meaning but as a tool for discovering the component parts of a concept and its relationship to other concepts. Much of his work was in the field of ethics, and his principal books were *Principia Ethica* (1903) and *Philosophical Studies* (1922).

Moore, Henry Spencer (1898–). British sculptor. He was the son of a Yorkshire coal miner and after studying at Leeds School of Art and the Royal College of Art won a travelling scholarship (1925). His style verges on the abstract but he is concerned with the aesthetic problems of the human figure, a major aim being the relation of sculpture to natural environment. Thus the anatomy of his 'reclining figures' is so disposed as to reflect natural landscape forms. Early influences

were African, Mexican and Polynesian sculptures but any borrowings were adapted to suit his own aims. Moore shows a deep understanding of the nature of his material – the importance of the grain in his wood sculptures providing a striking example. Generally regarded as the most important sculptor since * Rodin (and possibly since Michelangelo), Moore's works were prominently displayed in public places in Britain, the US, Canada, Germany, Israel, Japan and Australia. He was awarded the CH in 1955 and the OM in 1963.
Read, H., *Henry Moore*. 1965.

Moore, Sir John (1761–1809). British general. After serving in many parts of the world, including Corsica, St Lucia in the West Indies, the Helder campaign in Holland, and in Egypt, he won new fame at Shorncliffe Camp, Kent, where he proved himself (1803) one of the most remarkable trainers of troops in British army history. The rapidly moving light infantry regiments were his creation and his new drill system was a major factor in later British successes. In 1808 he was given command in the Peninsula and despite Spanish defeats he concealed his whereabouts from Napoleon and made a diversionary movement which delayed and disconcerted Soult while allowing time for the Spaniards to raise new armies. So much achieved, he retreated rapidly to the coast at Corunna, and his troops had already begun to embark when Soult attacked. He was repulsed with heavy loss but Moore was killed. His burial on the ramparts of Corunna was the subject of a famous poem by Charles Wolfe; 'Not a drum was heard, not a funeral note . . . '
Oman, C., *Sir John Moore*. 1953

Moore, Marianne Craig (1887–1972). American poetess. She contributed to the imagist poetry magazine *Egoist* and edited the *Dial* (1925–29). Her urbane and precise poetry first appeared in book form in *Poems* (1921), later followed by e.g. *Observations* (1924).

Moore, Thomas (1779–1825). Irish poet. He published several collections of graceful songs and verses, notably *Irish Melodies* (10 parts, 1808–34), for some of which he also wrote the tunes: among the most familiar of the lyrics are *'Tis the Last Rose of Summer*, *The Minstrel Boy*, and *The Harp that Once through Tara's Halls*. He gained a European reputation with *Lalla Rookh* (1817), a series of oriental verse-tales linked by a prose narrative. From the time of his marriage (1811) to Bessy Dyke, an actress, he lived mostly at Sloperton Cottage, Wiltshire.

Moravia, Alberto (Alberto Pincherle) (1907–). Italian novelist. His books deal with the frustrations of love in the modern world; they include *The Woman of Rome* (1947) and *The Empty Canvas* (1960).
Moravia, A., *Man as an End*. 1966

Moray, James Stewart, 1st Earl of (1531–1570). Scots nobleman. Illegitimate son of James V of Scotland and half-brother of * Mary Queen of Scots, he was a Protestant and in the early part of her reign gave Mary prudent advice about her dealings with the Reformed church and other matters. Alienated by her follies, he turned against her but returned from France to act as regent after her abdication (1568). When she escaped he defeated her forces at Langside and subsequently maintained order – not without creating enemies among rival factions – until his assassination.

More, Hannah (1745–1833). English writer. Born near Bristol, where her sister kept a boarding school at which she was educated, after publishing a pastoral play (1773) she went to London (1774) where she became a friend of Garrick, Burke, Reynolds, Horace Walpole and Dr Johnson and was prominent at the gatherings of intellectual women known as 'Blue Stockings' (she herself wrote a poem called *Bas Bleu*). *Percy*, the first of two tragedies, was produced successfully (1777) by Garrick but after his death her writings were nearly all concerned with religious and humanitarian subjects, her tracts being so successful that they led to the formation of the Religious Tract Society. Her novel *Coelebs in Search of a Wife* (1809) was popular at the time.

More, Henry (1614–1687). English philosopher. He cultivated interest in science, philosophy and theology, and was deeply concerned with their interconnexion. He became Doctor of Divinity in 1660, and a fellow of the Royal Society in 1664. In science, his early inclinations were towards the approach of * Descartes. He approved and helped to popularize the 'New Philosophy'; Descartes's attempted demonstration of the reality of the world of the spirit, of the existence of God, and of the separate existence of an immaterial mind from the body all underpinned More's attack upon the materialistic philosophy of * Hobbes, in his *Antidote against Atheisme* (1652). More later worried, however, that Descartes's philosophy itself was too materialistic, and he helped develop a new approach to natural philosophy, known as Cambridge Platonism. This emphasized the reality of a wide range of spiritual, and non-material forces which helped to sustain nature. Witches and magical manifestations were evidence of this. He held that science and piety were compatible.

Lichtenstein, A., *Henry More*. 1962

More, Sir Thomas (1478–1535). English scholar, writer, lawyer and saint (canonized 1935). At Oxford he worked for such scholars as Grocyn and Linacre, and became a close friend of Colet and Erasmus. He practised law with great success and in 1504 entered parliament. In the same year he married Jane Colt, and made a home at the 'Old Barge' in London, where he lived for twenty years, becoming under-sheriff (1510). In 1515 he accompanied a trading mission to Flanders: Antwerp provided him with a setting for the introductory scene of *Utopia* (1516), the meeting with Raphael Hythlodaye, who had discovered the island of Utopia, the ideally tolerant state, where possessions are shared and an education is available for men and women alike. The book, written in Latin, at once became popular and was widely translated (into English in 1551). Earlier More had written *Praise of Folly* (1510) and his *History of Richard III* (1513), the main authority for the story of the Princes in the Tower. So brilliant a man could not escape the notice of Henry VIII: More was present at the Field of the Cloth of Gold (1520), he became a privy councillor and was given a number of offices of growing importance until, after Wolsey's downfall (1529), he unwillingly became lord chancellor. Meanwhile he was living in his new house built (1524) at Chelsea; his daughter Margaret and her husband, William Roper, his future biographer, were living under the same roof, his other daughters married (1525); there are several accounts of a happy, devoted highly intellectual family group with many friends coming and going, of discussions both serious and gay and something of the atmosphere of a school under a wise, witty and tolerant master.

Henry turned confidently to More to arrange for the dissolution of his marriage with Catherine of Aragon, but More justly feared this would lead to a schism within the church and offended the king by resigning his chancellorship (1532). In 1534 the Act of Supremacy was passed by which Henry was declared head of the church in England. Though as an intellectual and humanist he saw the need for church reform, More could not accept a denial of papal supremacy; he was arrested and after a year's imprisonment was convicted of treason and executed.

Reynolds, E. E., *The Field is Won: The Life and Death of St Thomas More*. 1968

Moreau, Jean Victor Marie (1761–1813). French soldier. He was the most brilliant leader of the Revolutionary armies, and had he had political ambitions he might have forestalled Napoleon. After becoming a divisional general under Dumouriez in Belgium (1794), he succeeded Pichegru on the Rhine (1796) and drove the Austrians back to the Danube. In 1798 he was given the command in Italy and saved the French army from destruction. After Jourdan's defeat at Novi he brought the army safely home to France. He supported Bonaparte's coup of 18 Brumaire (9 November 1799) and in 1800 gained a succession of victories over the Austrians, culminating in the decisive triumph of Hohenlinden. With Bonaparte's jealousy rapidly mounting, Moreau was given no further opportunities. Instead he was accused of connivance with plotters against Bonaparte's life (1804) and a two-year sentence of imprisonment was commuted to banishment. He lived in America until after Napoleon's retreat from Russia he set out (1813) to join the Allied armies. He died of wounds while with the Russian army at Dresden.

Morgagni, Giovanni Battista (1682–1771). Italian anatomist. In 1711 he obtained a chair of medicine at Padua, where he stayed for the rest of his life. Morgagni devoted himself to the study of the mechanisms of the body. His investigations of the glands of the trachea, of the male urethra and of the female genitals broke new ground. Above all, he pioneered the study of morbid anatomy. He himself undertook 640 post mortems, and was careful to relate the diseased organs which he dissected

to the patient's own life history and symptoms. Morgagni regarded each organ of the body as a complex of minute mechanisms, and the life of the whole was an index of its balanced functioning. His pioneering work in morbid anatomy was made specially valuable to later clinicians on account of his highly detailed case notes which he published in his *De sedibus et causis morborum per anatomen indagatis* (1761).
Fiorentini, C., *Giovanni Battista Morgagni*. 1930

Morgan, Charles Langbridge (1894–1958). English novelist and playwright. He was trained as a naval officer and served in World War I. From 1926 he was for many years dramatic critic of *The Times*. His polished and thoughtful novels include *The Fountain* (1932), *Sparkenbrooke* (1936) and *The River Line* (1937), later successfully dramatized. Among his other plays were *The Flashing Stream* (1938) and *The Burning Glass* (1953). His literary essays were collected as *Reflections in a Mirror*.

Morgan, Sir Henry (*c.* 1635–1688). Welsh buccaneer. He was the most famous of the piratical adventurers who, like their Elizabethan prototypes, carried on a private and profitable war against the Spanish empire in the West Indies and South America. Among his most daring exploits was his march (1681) across the isthmus of Panama to capture and plunder the city of that name. For the buccaneers this opened the way to the Pacific, which was to become one of their richest hunting grounds. In later life Morgan made peace with authority; he was knighted by Charles II and was deputy governor of Jamaica (1674–83).
Forbes, R. T., *Henry Morgan, Pirate*. 1946

Morgan, John Pierpont (1837–1913). American financier. Son of Junius Spencer Morgan, who had built up a reputation and a fortune in international finance, J. P. Morgan expanded his financial interests into the industrial field, at first in partnerships with others and later through his own firm, J. P. Morgan & Co. (founded 1895). He had meanwhile taken over the London interests of George Peabody, whose firm eventually became (1910) Morgan, Grenfell & Co. Much of Morgan's money was made by great industrial mergers especially of railway and shipping companies, for which the financial crisis of 1873 provided many opportunities. Even the US government, faced with a run on gold (1895), turned to Morgan for help. His most spectacular achievement took place when he formed (1900) the United States Corporation. Although in 1912 his affairs were carefully scrutinized as a result of anti-trust legislation, no charge against him could be brought. Like so many American millionaires he was a great collector; most of his pictures and works of art were eventually presented to the Metropolitan Museum of Art, New York; his library, containing many rare books and MSS, was endowed and made available to the public by his son, **John Pierpont Morgan Jr** (1867–1943), who played a great part in World War I, acting as purchasing agent in the USA in the financing of the Allied war effort for the British and French governments.

Morgan, Lewis Henry (1818–1881). American anthropologist. He lived among the Iroquois Indians for many years and wrote some important studies on kinship and the development of primitive societies. The classificatory system which he deduced is contained in his *Systems of Consanguinity in the Human Family* (1869).

Morgan, Thomas Hunt (1866–1945). American geneticist and embryologist, born in Kentucky. One of the founders of modern genetics, he was educated in Kentucky and Johns Hopkins, and taught at Bryn Mawr and Columbia. His academic career culminated in his becoming Professor of Biology at the California Institute of Technology from 1928. Morgan experimented on breeding mice and rats, and then fruit-flies (*drosophila*), tracing patterns of variation over many generations of breeding, and demonstrating that particular characteristics (e.g. eye colour) were inherited through the transmission of genetic material. He termed the particles which conveyed the messages for these characteristics in the chromosome 'genes'. Morgan's work proved that heredity could be treated rigorously. His laboratory became the training ground for a generation of Mendelian geneticists – Bridges, * Müller, Dobzhansky and * Monod. Morgan himself attempted to summarize his work in his 1934 volume, *Embryology and Genetics*, which argued that because inherited characteristics were genetically coded, they produced the quite sharp variations needed by Darwin's

theory of evolution by natural selection. Thus modern genetics have come to lend support to Darwin. He received the 1933 Nobel Prize for Medicine.
Dunn, L. C , *Short History of Genetics*. 1965

Morison, Stanley (1889–1967). British typographer. He was typographical adviser to Cambridge University Press (1923–44 and 1947–59) and to the Monotype Corporation. He designed Times New Roman typeface which was introduced in 1932. He wrote extensively on typography and calligraphy, edited *The Times Literary Supplement* (1945–47) and the *History of the Times* (1935–52).
Barker, N., *Stanley Morison*. 1972

Morland, George (1763–1804). English painter. His paintings, influenced by Dutch genre pictures, present homely subjects, e.g. *Interior of a Stable* and *The Alehouse Door* (both in the National Gallery, London). Popular, too, were his drawings for engravings on moral subjects, e.g. *The Effects of Extravagance and Idleness*. Drink and dissipation accelerated his death.
Williamson, G. C., *George Morland*. 1904

Morley, Edward Williams (1838–1923). American chemist and physicist. He became (1869) a professor at the Western Reserve College, Hudson, with which he remained when it moved to Cleveland and became a university: he retired in 1906. He joined * Michelson in carrying out the Michelson-Morley experiment (1881): he is also known for his accurate determination (1895) of the ratio of combination by weight of hydrogen and oxygen (1:7·9395), which allowed the atomic weight of oxygen to be accurately fixed on the hydrogen scale.

Morley of Blackburn, John Morley, 1st Viscount (1839–1923). English politician and writer. As editor of the *Fortnightly Review* (1867–82) he provided a rationalistic and anti-imperialist philosophy that convinced a large section of the Liberal party. He entered parliament (1883) and after only three years was appointed chief secretary for Ireland by Gladstone. His party's Home Rule policy was, however, rejected by the electorate and during his years in opposition he was able to complete his greatest literary achievement, the *Life of Gladstone* (1903). His earlier biographies, e.g. of Burke, Voltaire, Rousseau, Cobden and Cromwell, form a guide to his political thought. Morley held office whenever the Liberals were in power until the outbreak of World War I: he was again Irish chief secretary (1892–95), and secretary of state for India (1905–10), and lord president of the Council (1910–14).

Morley, Thomas (*c.* 1557–1607/8). English composer. He was a pupil of William Byrd, and the organist of St Paul's, London (from 1592), and a member of the Chapel Royal. He was one of the greatest of English madrigal composers, set a number of Shakespeare's songs (e.g. *It was a lover and his lass*) for voice and lute, composed church music and works for viols and for virginals, and wrote the textbook *A Plaine and Easie Introduction to Practicall Musick*.

Moro, Aldo (1916–1978). Italian politician. A Christian Democrat, he served as prime minister (1963–68, 1974–76) and foreign minister (1970–72). In 1978 he was kidnapped and murdered by the Red Brigade.

Moroni, Giovanni Battista (*c.* 1525–1578). Italian painter. His portraits of noblemen and tradesmen in and around Bergamo reveal skill and observation of character and they shed light on Italian provincial life in the 16th century. *The Tailor* in the National Gallery, London, is an excellent example of his work.

Morris, Gouverneur (1752–1816). American politician of partly Huguenot descent. After becoming prominent in New York politics, he was a conservative at the Federal Constitutional Convention (1787), argued for a strong central government and became principal draftsman of the U.S. Constitution (although * Madison and * Franklin contributed more substance). He was minister to France (1792–94) at the time of the revolutionary 'Terror', of which his *Diary* gives a graphic first-hand account. He spent some years in travel before returning to the U.S. A Senator from New York (1800–03), he retired to view with aristocratic disdain the increasing egalitarianism of the times.

Morris, William (1834–1896). English artist, writer, craftsman and socialist. The son of a prosperous bill-broker in the city of London, he lived during his boyhood in a large house on the borders of Epping Forest. As a pupil at

Marlborough he already showed his architectural interests and at Oxford became friends with Burne-Jones and later Rossetti and the other Pre-Raphaelites: Ruskin's books guided his architectural taste at this time. After graduating he trained as an architect, first in Oxford and then in London, where he shared rooms with Burne-Jones. His marriage (1859) to the lovely Jane Burden (immortalized by Rossetti), and the building for them of the famous Red House by Philip Webb provided the incentive to found (1861) the firm of Morris, Marshall & Faulkner (later Morris & Co.) for the manufacture of carpets, wallpaper, furniture etc. This enterprise, of which his friends Ford Madox Brown, Rossetti, Burne-Jones and Webb were all original members, enabled Morris to express his hatred of industrial civilization and love of the medieval past reflected also in his poetic works *The Defence of Guinevere* (1858) and *The Earthly Paradise* (1868–70). The Morris designs are now being restored to favour but it has been argued that the vogue for 'handicrafts' that they heralded delayed the evolution of good industrial design.

Morris's wish to revive the dignity and joy of work led him to a romantic form of socialism. He joined (1883) Hyndman's Social Democratic Federation and founded (1884) the Socialist League. In *The Dream of John Bull* (1888) and *News from Nowhere* (1891) he presented his vision of a more human and joyful society. The last years of his life were occupied in the writing of prose romances partly inspired by his study of Icelandic sagas, and in founding the Kelmscott Press, which by reviving and improving the old standards of book binding and type design had an important influence on the history of printing.

Henderson, P. P., *William Morris, His Life and Friends*. 1967

Morrison of Lambeth, Herbert Stanley Morrison, Baron (1888–1965). British Labour politician. The son of a policeman, he was born in South London and worked as an errand boy, shop-assistant and for a newspaper. As a member of the Labour party he rose to be leader of the Labour group in the London County Council (1933–40), where he gained a great reputation as an organizer. He was an M.P. 1923–24, 1929–31 and 1935–59. Minister of transport (1929) in Ramsay MacDonald's government, during World War II he was a very successful home secretary in Churchill's coalition. In Attlee's Labour government he was deputy prime minister and Lord President of the Council 1945–51, and foreign secretary 1951. When Attlee retired as party leader in 1955, Morrison lost the succession to * Gaitskell.

Donoughue, B. and Jones, G. W., *Herbert Morrison*. 1973

Morse, Samuel Finley Breese (1791–1872). American inventor. Educated at Yale, he studied art in England and became a successful portrait painter in the U.S.A. From 1832 he experimented with means of transmitting messages using either electricity or a system of flashing lights. He devised the 'Morse Code' and patented (1837) an electric telegraph: in 1844 he sent a telegraphic message from Washington, D.C. to Baltimore.

Mortimer, Roger, 1st Earl of March (1287–1330). English nobleman, who played a conspicuous part in the struggle for power in the reign of Edward II. He allied himself with Queen Isabella, whose lover he became, in the conspiracy by which her husband was deposed (1327) in favour of her son, the boy-king Edward III. Three years later the hatred inspired by Mortimer's rule encouraged Edward to have him seized and later hanged.

Another **Roger Mortimer** (1374–1398), his descendant, became heir presumptive to Richard II and (through the marriage of his daughter, Anne) the source of the Yorkist claim to the throne.

Morton, James Douglas, 4th Earl of (*c.* 1516–1581). Regent of Scotland (1572–78 and 1578–80). A Protestant, he was (from 1557) at the centre of the plots and intrigues against * Mary Queen of Scots. He took part in Rizzio's murder and was almost certainly privy to that of Darnley. It was he who discovered the 'casket letter' which, if genuine, implicated Mary. After the death of * Moray he was regent for James VI and did his best to restore tranquility to a land torn by religious dissension and war. A party of the nobles plotted to secure his dismissal. He seized Stirling Castle and the young king, but a further plot resulted in his execution for the murder of Darnley.

Morton, John (1423–1500). English ecclesiastic and lawyer. After various turns of fortune during the Wars of the Roses he became Henry VII's most trusted adviser: he was archbishop of Canterbury (1486–1500), lord chancellor (1487–1500), and became a cardinal (1493). It is said (through the story is probably apocryphal) that he assisted the king's extortions by impaling potential victims on the horns of a dilemma known as Morton's Fork; but he certainly used his visits to nobles to assess their wealth: if they had a costly retinue, he concluded they were rich and able to pay heavy taxes: if modest, that they were avaricious and equally able to pay.

Morton, William Thomas Green (1819–1868). American dentist. Famous for introducing ether as an anaesthetic, he used it (1846) at Massachusetts General Hospital, Boston, in the first successful major operation for which general anaesthesia was used.
Keys, T. E., *The History of Surgical Anaesthesia*. 1945

Moseley, Henry Gwynn-Jeffreys (1887–1915). English physicist. Lecturer in physics at Manchester University under Rutherford, he studied the X-ray spectra of many elements and discovered (1913) that the frequency of the characteristic line in each spectrum increases in regular sequence from one element to the next in the periodic table. He thus showed the fundamental importance of the atomic number of an element, which defines the element and is directly related to its atomic structure. He was killed at Gallipoli.

Moses (*c.* 15th century B.C.). Hebrew leader and law-giver. According to the Pentateuch he was born in Egypt, was brought up by Pharaoh's daughter, and having killed an Egyptian overseer, took refuge with the Midianites. After many years he received in a vision a order from Jehovah to lead the Jewish people from their captivity in Egypt to Palestine. The ten plagues which afflicted Egypt are reputed to have been among the reasons why Pharaoh allowed them to depart. Moses and his brother Aaron led them to Mount Sinai where the 'Ten Commandments' were received. Moses led his people for many years in the wilderness but died when in sight of the 'Promised Land' of Palestine, which he never reached. It has been a matter of critical discussion how far the Mosaic Law can be attributed to Moses himself.

Moses, Grandma (Anna Mary Robertson) (1860–1961). American painter. A farmer's wife, she took up painting at the age of 77 and won fame for her gay and spontaneous pictures of rural scenes.

Mosley, Sir Oswald Ernald, 6th Bart. (1896–1980). British politician and through his first wife, Cynthia, a son-in-law of Lord * Curzon. He became a Conservative M.P. (1918) but joined the Labour party (1924) and was a member of Ramsay Macdonald's government (1929–30): he resigned because of its failure to cope with unemployment. He formed the New Party (1931) and founded (1932) the British Union of Fascists. The violence of his followers was a feature of pre-war politics: in World War II he was detained under defence regulations. In 1948 he started a new Union movement.
Mosley, N., *Rules of the Game: Sir Oswald and Lady Cynthia Mosley, 1896–1933*. 1982.
Mosley, N., *Beyond the Pale: Sir Oswald Mosley 1933–1980*. 1983

Mostel, Zero (1915–1977). American actor. A masterful mime, skilled in drama and comedy, he starred in *Ulysses in Nighttown* (1958), Ionesco's *Rhinoceros* (1961; stage and film) and created the role of Tevye in *Fiddler on the Roof* (1964).

Mountbatten of Burma, Louis Francis Mountbatten, 1st Earl (1900–1979). British sailor. Son of the 1st Marquess of Milford Haven (* Battenberg), he was closely related to the British and other royal families, and was an uncle of Prince Philip, Duke of Edinburgh. In World War II, after distinguishing himself as a destroyer leader, he was appointed (1942) chief of combined operations: he organized several successful commando raids and the techniques and equipment divised under his leadership were successfully used in the Allied landings (1944). As supreme commander in south-east Asia (from 1943) he was responsible for the defence of India and the campaigns by which the Japanese were expelled from Burma. He was the last viceroy of India (1947) and, after the transfer of power, first governor general of the new dominion of India (1947–48): he then returned to naval duties and was commander-in-chief of NATO naval forces in the Mediterranean (1953–54), first sea lord at the Admiralty (1955–59) and chief of the combined defence staffs (1959–64). While on holiday in 1979 in the Republic of

Ireland his boat was blown up and he was killed.
Zeigler, P., *Mountbatten*. 1985

Mozart, Wolfgang Amadeus (Johann Chrysostom) (1756–1791). Austrian composer. Born in Salzburg, he was the son of the distinguished violinist and composer **Leopold Mozart** (1719–1787), director of the Archbishop of Salzburg's orchestra. The most precocious genius in the history of music, Mozart began to play the harpsichord at the age of three, composed an *Andante and Allegro* and gave his first public performance when he was five (by which time he had mastered the violin), and at the age of six played at the court of the Empress Maria Theresa. By 1763 he was an accomplished alto singer and organist and amazed the French Court with his skill. In 1764 he visited London, played for George III, met J. C. Bach and was the subject of a report to the Royal Society. He composed his first symphony (1764–65) and a motet, *God is our Refuge*, in 1765. In 1768 he composed the opera, *La finta semplice*, for Joseph II of Austria and made his début as a conductor with his *Missa Solemnis*. He toured Italy at 13, was made a Knight of the Golden Spur by Pope Clement XIV and gave a series of extraordinary concerts at which he demonstrated his astounding improvisatory skills.

In 1782 he married Constanze Weber (1763–1842). The couple had six children of whom only two survived infancy: Karl (d. 1858) and Franz (d. 1844). Soon after his marriage Mozart met Haydn who helped him greatly, especially with the string quartets, and remained a loyal friend. After a series of successful concerts in Prague (1787), Mozart was appointed Imperial and Royal Chamber Composer at Vienna by Joseph II, but his salary was grossly inadequate and he fell heavily into debt. He borrowed money, taught piano, played violin and piano at frequent concerts and arranged dance music and salon pieces in order to survive. He declined two lucrative offers to live in London (1790). As a result of strain and overwork his health gave way and he died of rheumatic inflammatory fever shortly before completing the *Requiem*. He was buried in an unmarked communal grave in the St Marx cemetery, Vienna, in conformity with the burial laws of Joseph II.

Over 630 of Mozart's compositions have survived: these were catalogued in chronological order by Ludwig von Köchel. His output includes over 50 symphonies, the most notable of which are Nos. 28, 31 ('Paris'), 35 ('Haffner'), 36 ('Linz'), 38 ('Prague'), 39, 40 and 41 ('Jupiter'); the last three were composed in six weeks (1788). He wrote 27 piano concertos, and may be regarded as the pioneer of this form; 6 violin concertos; and 8 concertos for solo wind instruments. He wrote 17 masses including the great *Requiem* (1791), his last work. Among his chamber works are the serenade for strings (*Eine kleine Nachtsmusik*, 1787); 26 string quartets; 6 string quintets; 7 piano trios and a clarinet quintet. Of his 22 operas, the best loved and most often performed are: *Die Entführung aus dem Serail* (a German opera usually known by its Italian name *Il seraglio*, 1782); *Le nozze di Figaro* (based on Beaumarchais' comedy, 1786); *Don Giovanni* (1787); *Cosi fan tutte* (1790); and *Die Zauberflöte* (1791).

Mozart brought the Viennese classical style to its height. He excelled in every medium of his time, and is considered the most universal composer in the history of western music.
Deutsch, O. E., *Mozart: A documentary Biography*. 2nd ed. 1966

Mubarak, Muhammad Hosni (1929–). Egyptian politician. Trained as a pilot, he was commander-in-chief of the air force 1972–75 and launched air attacks on Israel in the 1973 war. He was vice-president 1975–81 and on the assassination of* Sadat succeeded him as president 1981– .

Mugabe, Robert Gabriel (1925–). First prime minister of independent Zimbabwe (1980–). After training he went to Northern Rhodesia (now Zambia) to teach and from there to Ghana in 1958. Later he became secretary-general of the Zimbabwe African National Union (ZANU). After ten year's detention he left Rhodesia for Mozambique in 1974 and his party became guerrilla-based. It was this party that he led to the Lancaster House negotiations. His party having won 57 of the seats in the February 1980 elections he was invited by the governor-general of Rhodesia to form a government.

Muggeridge, Malcolm (1903–). English journalist. Service as a foreign correspondent and much subsequent travel gave him a comprehensive insight into the problems of many parts of the world including Russia, India, America and many parts of the Middle East.

This he was able later to use with great effect as a wise, witty and versatile television commentator. He was editor of *Punch* (1953–57).

Muir, Edwin (1887–1959). Scottish poet, born in Orkney. After working as a clerk in Glasgow, he became involved in left-wing politics. He married Willa Anderson (1919) and went to Prague, where, with his wife, he translated the works of Kafka and began to publish his own poetry. He worked for the British Council from 1942 until 1950, when he became warden of Newbattle Abbey College. His *Collected Poems* appeared in 1952. His prose works include a study of John Knox and his *Autobiography* (1954).

Mujibur Rahman, Sheikh (1920–1975). Bangladeshi politician. A lawyer, he was secretary of the Awami League 1950–71 and campaigned for the succession of East Pakistan (Bengal). In 1970 the League won 151 of 153 Bengali seats. In March 1971 Mujibur proclaimed an independent Republic of Bangladesh with Indian support, while China backed Pakistan. Pakistan was defeated in open war (December 1971), Mujibur became prime minister (1972–75), and in 1975 'president for life'. With the Bangladesh economy facing collapse, he established a one-party state, provoked violent opposition from the army and was soon assassinated.

Muldoon, Sir Robert David (1921–). New Zealand politician. Trained as a cost-accountant, he entered parliament as member for Tamaki, for the National Party, in 1960. He was parliamentary under-secretary to the minister of finance 1964–66, and minister of finance 1967–72. He became leader of the opposition in 1974 and prime minister 1975–84.

Muller, Hermann Joseph (1890–1967). American geneticist. Educated at Columbia University, and a student of T. H. * Morgan, he worked on the genetics of the fruit fly. In 1926 he produced an experimental induction of mutations by the use of X-rays and received the Nobel Prize for Medicine in 1946 for this work. He taught at the University of Texas 1920–32, in the USSR 1933–37 (leaving over a dispute with * Lysenko), Edinburgh 1937–40, Boston 1941–45 and Indiana from 1945. He was among the first scientists to warn of the dangers of X-rays and nuclear fall-out.

Müller, Johannes Peter (1801–1858). German physiologist. In 1833 he took the chair of physiology at Berlin University. His early researches were chiefly in two fields, embryology and the nervous system as it relates to vision. He experimented to determine whether the foetus breathes in the womb. He was also concerned to ascertain the relations between the kidneys and the genitals. In optics, he investigated the capacity of the eye to respond not just to external but also to internal stimuli (whether organic malfunction, or simply the play of imagination). Müller's physiological work was summarized in his *Handbuch der Physiologie* (1830–40). He argued that life was animated by some kind of life-force not reducible to the body, and that there was a soul separable from the body – ideas rejected by the next generation of German physiologists.

Müller, Paul Hermann (1899–1965). Swiss chemist. He synthetized (1939) DDT (dichloro diphenyl trichlorethane) and discovered its great power as an insecticide. He won the Nobel Prize for Medicine (1948).

Mulroney, (Martin) Brian (1939–). Canadian lawyer and politician, born in Quebec. He worked as an electrician, graduated in law from Université Laval, became a labour lawyer and gained a national reputation as president of the Iron Ore Co. 1976–83. He was elected as leader of the Progressive Conservative Party 1983– , the first leader from Quebec for 90 years and the first recruited directly from industry. He became prime minister in September 1984.

Multatuli (pen name of Eduard Douwes Dekker) (1820–1887). Dutch novelist. He worked in Java 1838–57 in the colonial service and his novel, *Max Havelaar* (1860), an exposure of imperialism, is regarded as a masterpiece. It was made into a powerful film by Fons Rademakers in 1976.

Mumford, Lewis (1895–). American town planner and social philosopher. His lectures and books are mainly concerned with the growth or creation of a social environment best suited to meet all the needs of a city's population: shelter, work, leisure, religion, culture – the whole complicated organization of modern urban living. His works include *Technics and Civilization* (1934), *The Culture*

of the Cities (1938), *The City in History* (1961), *The Myth of the Machine* (1967) and *The Pentagon of Power* (1970).
Mumford, L., *The Letters of Lewis Mumford and Frederick J. Osborne: a transatlantic Dialogue, 1938–70*. 1972

Munch, Edvard (1863–1944). Norwegian painter. The misfortunes and miseries which surrounded him as he grew up seem to have embittered his attitude to life and left him with a feeling of the malignancy of fate. Having been much influenced in Paris by the work of Van Gogh and Gauguin, and by the ideas of Ibsen and Strindberg he held an exhibition in Berlin (1892) which caused an immediate scandal but paved the way for the German Expressionist movement. In later work he depicted emotional states by colour and form alone – thus the 'Threat' in the picture of that name is conveyed by the black treetops. From 1899 to 1908 he worked mainly in Paris, thereafter mainly in Norway. A nervous breakdown (1908) was followed by a happier period during which he painted murals at Oslo University (1909–15) and found solace in the serene Norwegian landscape. He did much, too, to revitalize the woodcut and other graphic arts.
Benesch, O., *Edvard Munch*. 1960

Münchausen, Hieronymus Karl Friedrich, Baron von (1720–1797). Hanoverian soldier. The real bearer of this name seems to have fought in the Russian army against the Turks and to have become notorious for his exaggerated accounts of his own exploits. His name was attached, therefore, to a collection of apocryphal and fantastic tales, published in English as *Baron Münchausen's Narrative of his Marvellous Travels and Campaigns in Russia* (1785), by Rudolf Erich Raspe (1737–94), a German friend who had fled to England to escape prosecution for theft.

Munnings, Sir Alfred James (1878–1959). English artist. His love of country life led him to specialize in pictures of horses, to which he adapted some of the Impressionist techniques he acquired while studying art in Paris. For these, especially for pictures of famous racehorses, he commanded exceptionally high prices, well maintained after his death. As president of the Royal Academy (1944–49) he was an outspoken critic of non-representational art. Three volumes of autobiography were published between 1950 and 1952: *An Artist's Life, The Second Burst* and *The Finish*. He was knighted in 1944.

Munro, Hector Hugo *see* **Saki**

Munthe, Axel (1857–1949). Swedish physician and author. After a successful professional career, for part of which he was physician to the Swedish royal family, he retired to the Italian island of Capri where he wrote the semi-autobiographical bestseller *The Story of San Michele* (1929) and where, largely through his influence, a sanctuary for migrating birds was established.
Munthe, G. and Vexkull, G., *The Story of Axel Munthe*. 1953

Münzer, Thomas (*c.* 1490–1525). German Anabaptist leader. He toured Germany preaching his communistic doctrines and eventually settled at Mühlhausen (1525): there he set up a communist theocracy which, despite Luther's denunciations, won the support of large numbers of the peasantry. The movement was crushed by Philip of Hesse and Münzer himself captured and executed.

Murasaki Shikibu (usually called Lady Murasaki) (978?–1026?). Japanese novelist. A member of the Fujiwara clan, she was a court lady in Kyoto to the Empress Akiko during the Heian period of Japanese history. She wrote the long romance *Genji Monogatari* (Tale of Genji), generally regarded as the world's oldest surviving novel, a subtle and complex picture of aristocratic life built around the life of Prince Genji Hiraku. Translated by Arthur Waley, *Genji Monogatari* has often been compared to *In Search of Lost Time* by Marcel Proust.

Murat, Joachim (1767–1815). French marshal, later king of Naples. The son of an innkeeper, he rose to prominence during the Revolutionary Wars, being noted for his courage and brilliance as a cavalry leader. He served in Italy and Egypt with Napoleon, whose sister Caroline he married (1800). His fighting career continued, Austerlitz being one of the many battlefields where he won renown. He was made a marshal of France (1804) and was appointed (1808) to succeed Joseph Bonaparte as king of Naples, where he proved himself capable and popular. He accompanied Napoleon to Moscow (1812) and commanded the retreating armies after the emperor had returned to France: he then resumed his kingship and after Napoleon's escape from Elba made a vain attempt to raise Italy on his behalf. Defeated, he took refuge in Corsica, where he made a last attempt to win back Naples but was captured and shot.

Murchison, Sir Roderick Impey, 1st Bart (1792–1871). Scottish 'gentleman' geologist. He spent a generation in the field, surveying strata according to clear interpretative principles. He believed in a near universal order of deposition, indicated by fossils rather than purely lithological features. Fossils themselves would show a clear progression in complexity from 'azoic' items (i.e. pre-life) to invertebrates, and only up to vertebrate forms, man being created last. This progression was aligned to the earth's cooling. The great triumph of these principles, and his own fieldworking, was to unravel the 'Silurian System' (i.e. those strata beneath the Old Red Sandstone). For Murchison the Silurian contained remains of the earliest life (though no fossils of vertebrates or land plants were to be expected). Controversy over the younger end of the Silurian led to him introducing with Sedgwick the fruitful concept of the Devonian, which incorporated the Old Red Sandstone. He then, however, quarrelled with Sedgwick over the lower limits of the Silurian, erroneously denying there were fossiliferous systems underlying it. Later in life he became highly dogmatic and an opponent of Darwinian evolution.

Murdoch, (Jean) Iris (1919–). Anglo-Irish novelist, born in Dublin. Educated at Oxford, she was a civil servant in the Treasury 1942–44, an administrative officer with UNRRA in Europe 1944–46 and a Fellow and tutor in philosophy at St Anne's College, Oxford 1948– . She turned from writing philosophy and a study of J. P. Sartre (1953) to a series of novels notable for wit and black humour, starting with *Under the Net* (1954), including *The Bell* (1958), *An Unofficial Rose* (1962), *The Nice and the Good* (1967) and *The Sacred and Profane Love Machine* (1974). Murdoch's characters are complex, often caught in a prism of irreconcilable conflicts, in which the search for truth and self-knowledge appears from time to time as inevitable, painful, selfish or irrelevant, and guilt punishes those it is intended to protect. She also wrote plays, *The Servants and the Snow* (1970) and *The Three Arrows* (1972), and a study of Plato (*The Fire and the Sun*). She married Prof. John Bayley, scholar and critic.

Murdoch, (Keith) Rupert (1931–). Australian newspaper publisher. Chief executive and managing director of News Ltd. Group and associated companies, his papers included *The Times*, *Sun* and *News of the World* (London), the *New York Post*, *Chicago Sun* and the *Australian*. He exerted a powerful political influence in Britain, the U.S. and Australia. He also owned an airline and television stations in Australia.

Murdock, William (1754–1839). Scottish inventor. He joined the Birmingham engineering firm of Boulton and Watt (1777), helped Watt with the development of his steam engine and invented a practical slide-valve (1799). His experiments with the production of gas from coal enabled the factory to be lit up with gas to celebrate the Treaty of Amiens (1802), a development which led to the widespread adoption of gas for internal and external lighting.

Murger, Henri (1822–1861). French novelist. His life in Paris among poverty-stricken artists provided the background for his famous *Scènes de la vie de Bohème*, which appeared serially (1847–49), was dramatized (1849) was published in book form (1851). It inspired Puccini's well known opera *La Bohème*. His later novels are of small account.

Murillo, Bartolomé Estebán (1617–1662). Spanish painter. Like Velazquez, whom he knew well, he was born in Seville, but unlike the older painter he spent almost all his life there. He was primarily a painter of religious subjects but his style, which at first displayed a rather hard naturalism, gradually became warmer and more charming and eventually over-sweet, tender and glamorized. He is best known for his representations of the Virgin, among the most famous being the *Immaculate Conception* (now in the Louvre). Perhaps even more appealing to modern taste are his realistic genre pictures of young fruit-sellers and beggar-boys.

Murray, (George) Gilbert Aimé (1886–1957). British classical scholar, born in Australia. While Regius professor of Greek at Oxford (1908–36) he became well known for his translations of the Greek dramatists, especially Euripides, which were used in many notable performances. He also did much to interpret the spirit of ancient Greece to the modern world by a series of books, exemplified by his last great work *Hellenism and the Ancient World* (1953). He was a keen Liberal and between the wars was chairman of the League of Nations Union for fifteen years. He was awarded the OM (1941).

Murray, Sir James Augustus Henry (1837–1915). British lexicographer. He was a schoolmaster until 1885 when he moved to Oxford to work on the editorship of the *New English Dictionary on Historical Principles* and planned and outlined the whole project, and personally edited letters A–D, H–K, O, P and T. He also wrote on Scots literature and language. He was knighted in 1908.

Murray, K. M. E., *Caught in the Web of Words*. 1977

Murray, John (1745–1793). British publisher, born in Edinburgh. Changing his name from MacMurray to Murray, he bought a small publishing business in London which continued to expand under his dynastic successors in the 19th and 20th centuries. **John Murray II** (1778–1843) founded the *Quarterly Review* and established links with Scott and other famous authors, including Byron, whose unpublished memories he burned after the poet's death. Darwin's *Origin of Species* (1859) was published by **John Murray III** (1808–1892).

Murray, Philip (1886–1952). American trade union leader of Scottish birth. He was president (1940–52) of the Congress of Industrial Organizations (CIO), one of the two great trade union confederations, which were later amalgamated (1955).

Murry, John Middleton (1889–1957). English writer and critic. As editor of various journals, including *The Athenaeum* (1919–21), and *The Adelphi* (1923–30) he had considerable influence on English intellectual life in the 1920s. He was a friend of D. H. Lawrence, and married (1913) Katherine * Mansfield, whose biography he wrote (1932). His books include studies of Blake, Keats, Shakespeare and Dostoyevsky.

Murry, J. M., *Between Two Worlds*. 1935

Musil, Robert, Edler von (1880–1942). Austrian novelist, born at Klagenfurt. He trained to be a soldier (his *Young Törless* (1906) gives an unforgettable picture of the military academy), then qualified as an engineer and took a PhD in Berlin (1908) for a study of the philosophy of Ernst * Mach. He worked as a librarian in Vienna so that he could devote himself to writing, served with the Austrian army during World War I, then spent some years in Berlin and acquired a modest reputation as a freelance writer. He returned to Vienna in 1933 and moved from there to Switzerland in 1938. His masterwork was *The Man Without Qualities* (*Der Mann ohne Eigenschaften*), a colossal work begun in 1920 and left incomplete at his death, worthy of ranking with Joyce and Proust. The central character Ulrich (a self-portrait), a man of scientific training unable to commit himself passionately to any aspect of life, is given the post of secretary (in 1913) of a committee charged with commemorating Franz Josef's 70th anniversary as emperor by making 1918 'the Austrian year'. The novel has been brilliantly translated into English by Eithne Wilkins and Ernst Kaiser; it was not published in English until 1953.

Muskie, Edmund Sixtus (1914–). American Democratic politician. The son of a Polish immigrant (the family name was Marciszewski) and educated at Cornell, he served in the navy during World War II, was governor of Maine 1953–59 and a US Senator 1959–80. He ran for vice-president in 1968 with Hubert * Humphrey, sought the presidential nomination in 1972 and served as Jimmy * Carter's secretary of state 1980–81.

Mussadiq, Mohammed (1876–1967). Persian politician. During the earlier part of his career he was minister of finance and of justice. He became prime minister in 1951, and almost his first act was the nationalization of the oil industry in defiance of the 1933 convention with the Anglo-Iranian Oil Company. He rejected any compromise settlement, and this led to the evacuation of the Abadan refinery and the breaking off of Anglo-Persian relations. His government fell in 1953 when General Zahedi led a royalist uprising. On the Shah's return Mussadiq was tried and imprisoned. He was released in 1956.

Musset, Alfred de (1810–1857). French poet and dramatist. He was born in Paris, and dabbled in law and medicine; he published, at the age of 18, a translation of de Quincey's *Confessions of an English Opium Eater*. As an aristocratic dandy he frequented the literary circle of Victor Hugo, who praised his poems, *Contes d'Espagne et d'Italie* (1830). The influence of Hugo's Romanticism is evident in *La Nuit vénitienne* (1830), Musset's first play: its failure decided him to write plays for reading only. The hero who agreeably combined charm with debauchery, and the flirtatious but tender heroine were popular at this period and *A quoi rêvent les jeunes filles* (1831) was a typical and revealing title. In 1833, the year in which appeared the witty and emotional prose plays *André del Sarto* and *Les Caprices de Marianne*, began his stormy love affair with George * Sand, described after its break-up in his series of poems, *Les Nuits* (1835–37): the autobiographical *Confession d'un Enfant du siècle* (1836) also reflects the pessimism induced by his sufferings. The play *On ne badine pas avec l'amour* ends tragically but *Le Chandelier* (1836) shows something of the old sparkle. *Un Caprice* (1837), had such success that his later plays were frequently played at the Comédie Française. Musset was elected to the Académie Française in 1852.

Mussolini, Benito (1883–1945). Italian dictator. He was born near Forli and early absorbed the socialist and revolutionary views of his blacksmith father. He started his career as a teacher (1901) but a year later went to Switzerland, where he lived as a revolutionary exile until 1904. In 1908 he served his first prison sentence for revolutionary activity and thereafter took to journalism. Having joined a socialist paper at Trento (then in Austria) he became fired with nationalist zeal for recovering the lost provinces. Another term of imprisonment brought him increased prestige in his own party and secured him the editorship of the national socialist newspaper, *Avanti* (1912). World War I caused him to split with the socialists, who favoured neutrality: Mussolini saw that only by joining the Allies could Italy regain from Austria the unredeemed provinces: and in November 1914 he was editing his own paper *Popolo d'Italia*, a powerful voice in favour of intervention. When Italy entered the war (May 1915), he joined the army, but after being wounded (February 1917) he returned to his paper. After the war, with the socialist party closed to him and communism threatening disruption, he founded (1919) the first *Fascio di Combattimento*, nominally to serve the cause of the neglected ex-servicemen. This proved the starting point of 'Fascism': Mussolini took over the nationalist theme and the theatrical equipment (black shirts, banners etc.) from * d'Annunzio and was quick to realize that by turning his gangs against the communists he would win government toleration and much outside support. In 1921 Mussolini, already called Il Duce ('the leader') by his followers, was elected to the Chamber of Deputies and in 1922 he organized the celebrated 'march on Rome.' There was no resistance, for Mussolini had already come to a tacit understanding with the prime minister, Giolitti: the armed forces, whose cause Mussolini had so consistently espoused, stood inactively by, and the ordinary citizen, weary of the anarchy of faction, favoured strong rule. King Victor Emmanuel decided therefore to put a constitutional gloss on the accomplished fact by making Mussolini prime minister. Thenceforward his dictatorship was virtually unchallenged until the end. The economics of Fascism were based on the syndicalism of Georges * Sorel, its political institutions merely a background to Il Duce's personal rule. With his overbearing personality and bombastic oratory Mussolini deceived the Italians, deceived Europe and even deceived himself. In spite of the completion of grandiose public works and road-building, in terms of real wages the Italians were worse off after ten years of his rule than before. Even such military successes as he achieved, the conquest of Ethiopia, the overrunning of Albania and support for Franco in Spain, involved quarrelling with all his natural allies and becoming entirely dependent on Nazi Germany. World War II revealed his weakness: though he delayed entry into the war until it seemed that Germany's victory was certain, Italy's war record was calamitous. Italian forces were everywhere defeated until German backing was received: Ethiopia, Eritrea and Somalia were lost. Mussolini was a puppet in Hitler's hands: when (July 1943), after the Allied landings in Sicily, the Fascist grand council turned against him, he was swept aside without a struggle. He was dramatically rescued from captivity by German paratroops and, already a pathetic figure without will or purpose, briefly headed a puppet government in northern Italy. When the Allied victory was achieved he tried, with his mistress Clara

Petacci, to reach safety in Switzerland, but both were caught and summarily executed.

Of his five children by his wife Rachele, Edda, the eldest of the two girls, married Count * Ciano, Mussolini's foreign secretary for many years.

Mack Smith, D., *Mussolini*. 1982

Mussorgsky, Modest Petrovich (1839–1881). Russian composer, born in the Ukraine. After army service till he was 20, he spent the rest of a chaotic and rambling life between the capital and the countryside, where his sympathetic study of the peasants introduced him to the folk idioms that appear in his music. Frenzied spells of composing alternated with drinking bouts, by which his health and character were gradually destroyed. His musical reputation depends on one outstanding dramatic masterpiece, *Boris Godunov* (1874). In this, as in his other works, he ignores much musical convention so as to create a distinctive national style. Thus, though he belonged to the 'national' school of Borodin, Rimsky-Korsakov etc. (* Balakirev), he so far departed from contemporary musical standards that Rimsky-Korsakov, who was his friend, produced a more conventional version of *Boris* which was formerly used instead of either of Mussorgsky's original versions. The same stylistic peculiarities occur in his operatic fragments, *The Marriage, Khovanshchina* and *Sorochintsy Fair*. Among his other works are *Pictures at an Exhibition* (1874), written for the piano but usually played in Ravel's orchestral version, and several song cycles, in which his style more nearly matches his themes; but he remains one of the most tragic 'might have beens' of musical history,

Hofmann, M., *La Vie de Mussorgsky*. 1964

Mustafa Kemal *see* **Kemal Atatürk**

Mutesa II, Sir Edward (1924–1969). Kabaka of Buganda and first president of Uganda. He inherited (1939) the sovereignty of Buganda (which formed part of the protectorate of Uganda). In 1953 the British withdrew recognition because of his demand for Buganda's independence from Uganda, and he was deported. He returned (1955) under a new constitution; when Uganda achieved independence he became (1963) its first president. In 1966 he was ousted in a *coup* led by Milton Obote; he escaped to Britain and died in exile.

Mutsuhito (1852–1912). Emperor of Japan 1867–1912. His reign is known as 'Meiji' ('enlightened reign'). The term 'Meiji Restoration' refers to the period which began with the abdication of the last hereditary *shogun* of the * Tokugawa clan, Keiki, in January 1868, the transfer of his powers to the emperor and the imperial court's move from Kyoto to Tokyo. His advisers, mostly young and able samurai, investigated reforms in Europe and the US and, within a few years, primary schools were developed on American lines and a variation of the Code Napoleon and some elements of the British parliamentary system were adopted. Feudal land tenure and the samurai class were abolished. Railways and the telegraph, the Gregorian calendar and western dress were quickly adopted. Mutsuhito's reign was marked by suppression of the Satsuma revolt (1877), successful wars against China (1894–95), Russia (1904–05) and the annexation of Korea. Intelligent and sympathetic to reform, he took little direct part in administration. He was an amateur painter and poet, and modelled his uniform, hair and bearing on Napoleon III. * Hirohito was his grandson.

Muybridge, Eadweard (originally Edward John Muggeridge) (1830–1904). English photographer, in the U.S. 1865–1900. His studies of 'animal locomotion' led to recognition of the phenomenon of persistence of vision. His 'Zoöpraxiscope' which showed human and animal movement was a direct forerunner of the cinema. In 1874 he was acquitted of murdering his wife's lover.

Myers, Frederic William Henry (1843–1901). English writer. Well known in his own day as a literary critic (e.g. of Wordsworth and Virgil), he is remembered as a pioneer in applying the methods of science to the investigation of apparently supernatural phenomena. A founder member of the Society for Psychical Research, he wrote *Human Personality and its Survival of Bodily Death* (1903).

Myrdal, (Karl) Gunnar (1898–). Swedish economist. One of the first economists to write on population pressure and world poverty, he was minister for commerce 1945–47, held chairs in Sweden and the US, wrote many books including *The Asian Dilemma* (1968) and *The Challenge of World Poverty* (1970), and received the 1974 Nobel Prize for Economics. His wife **Alva Myrdal**, née Reimer

(1902–), worked for UNESCO and the ILO, conducted research into 'futures' scenarios and disarmament, and became minister for disarmament 1967–73. She was awarded the 1982 Nobel Prize for Peace.

Mytens, Daniel (*c.* 1590–*c.* 1642). Dutch artist. Possibly studied under Rubens before coming to England, where he was settled by 1618. He worked for James I, and under Charles I (whose portrait by him is in the National Portrait Gallery) he had a court appointment. His portraits are mostly of members of the nobility, e.g. the *1st Duke of Hamilton* (now in the National Gallery), in a natural, informal style.

N

Nabokov, Vladimir Vladimirovich (1899–1977). Russian-born novelist, resident from 1940 in the U.S.A., where he became professor of Russian literature at Cornell University in 1948. He translated *Alice in Wonderland* into Russian (1923) and had already made a name for himself by a brilliant series of novels in Russian (*Mashenka; King, Queen, Knave; Invitation to a Beheading* etc.), before publishing his first English novels *The Real Life of Sebastian Knight* (1938) and *Bend Sinister* (1947). *Lolita*, a story of the infatuation of a middle-aged intellectual for a 12-year-old girl, was published in Britain in 1959. Subsequent novels included *Pale Fire* (1962). His memoirs, *Speak, Memory* were published in 1967.

Dembo, L. S., *Nabokov: The Man and His Work*. 1968

Nader, Ralph (1934–). American lawyer born in Connecticut of Lebanese parentage. Educated at Harvard, he wrote *Unsafe at Any Speed* (1965), an attack on General Motors' Corvair: GM had to pay him $300,000 damages for personal harassment. Nader formed 'citizens action' groups to carry out research, raise levels of community awareness and put pressure on governments to strengthen laws on consumer protection, car and highway safety, pollution, pure food and access to information.

Nadir Khan (or Nadir Shah) (*c.* 1880–1933). King of Afghanistan (from 1929). He was descended from a brother of * Dost Mohammed and as King Amanullah's commander-in-chief was prominent in the Third Afghan War with British India (1919). Having fallen into disfavour in 1924 he lived in exile in France, which he left in 1929 to make his successful bid for the Afghan throne. Assassination ended a brief reign in which he showed personal integrity as well as skill and moderation as an administrative reformer.

Nadir Shah (1688–1747). Shah of Persia (from 1736). By origin a Turcoman tribesman, he emerged as dominant figure from the period of confused fighting following the break-up of the Safavid dynasty. Soon after his proclamation as shah he made a pretext to invade India, marched through India to the plains below and met his first serious resistance only 100 miles from Delhi. Here he completely defeated the forces of the Mogul emperor, who accompanied his conqueror to Delhi. A false report of Nadir's death provoked a rising in the city, which he punished with one of the most terrible massacres in history. Loaded with plunder, including the famous peacock throne, he returned home having annexed large areas west of the Indus. Nadir continued to fight with success against internal revolt, external enemies (especially the Ottoman Turks), but assassination, caused by disgust at his atrocities, brought his career to an end.

Nägeli, Karl Wilhelm von (1817–1891). Swiss botanist. Son of a physician, he chose to specialize in botanical studies, and took up the study of cells. Between 1845 and 1858 he was involved in brilliant researches into the formation of tissues in the roots and stems of vascular plants, particularly from the point of view of cell division, for which he hoped to find quasi-mathematical laws. He correctly observed the distinction between formative tissues (ones multiplying) and structural tissues (those no longer multiplying). Later in his career, he became increasingly interested in the building blocks of plant life, especially starches and cellulose. But though this work took a more chemical turn, Nägeli always held to the somewhat teleological approach which his early training in *Naturphilosophie* had given him. He accepted organic evolution, but saw it as the fulfilment of an internal organic drive. He rejected * Mendel's work out of hand.

Nahas Pasha, Mustafa (1876–1965). Egyptian politician. He succeeded (1927) Zaghlul Pasha as leader of the Wafd, a nationalist party. In 1936 he led a delegation to London and negotiated a treaty of perpetual alliance with Britian by which, *inter alia*, British forces could be stationed in the Suez Canal zone for twenty years and the Egyptian position in the Sudan was restored. This was followed (May 1937) by a convention by which capitulations (special discriminatory arrangements favouring foreigners) were abolished. In December Nahas was dismissed by King Farouk but during World War II the British forced his recall (1942) when the German threat to Egypt was at its greatest. Again dismissed in 1944 Nahas played no active part in the events leading to the revolution of 1952.

Naipaul, V(idiadhar) S(urajprasad) (1932–). British writer, born in Trinidad of Indian descent. His masterpiece *A House for Mr Biswas* was published in 1961. Other much acclaimed works include *The Mimic Men* (1967), *In a Free State* (1971) and *Guerrillas* (1975). He has received many literary prizes including the Booker Prize (1971). Later works include *India: A Wounded Civilization* (1977), *A Bend in the River* (1979), *The Return of Eva Peron* (1980) and *Among the Believers* (1981). His brother **Shiva Naipaul** (1945–1985), also a writer, wrote *North of South* (1978) and *Black on White* (1980).
White, L., *Naipaul: A Critical Introduction*. 1975

Nakasone Yasuhiro (1918–). Japanese politician. Trained as a lawyer, he served in the Japanese navy, was a Diet member 1947– , and held several portfolios, also rising rapidly through the Liberal Democratic Party machine. He was prime minister of Japan 1982–

Namier, Sir Lewis Bernstein (1888–1960). British historian of Polish origin. Professor of modern history (1931–53) at Manchester University, he threw entirely new light on 18th-century political affiliations in his *The Structure of Politics on the Accession of George III* (1929). By probing the life, background and opinions as well as the voting records of individual M.P.s he showed how often personal considerations outweighed those of party alignment. He was political secretary (1929–31) of the Jewish Agency for Palestine, the Zionist organization.
Namier, J., *Lewis Namier: A Biography*. 1971

Nana Sahib (born *c.* 1820). Indian rebel. Adopted son of the last of the Mahratta 'peshwas', and swayed by a personal grievance about his pension he committed one of the most atrocious crimes of Indian history. During the Mutiny (1857) the isolated British garrison of Cawnpore capitulated on terms safeguarding the lives of the men and their dependants. Despite this pledge Nana Sahib ordered a general massacre of men, women and children alike. After the defeat of the mutineers Nana Sahib fled; his subsequent history is unknown.

Nanak (1469–1538). Indian *guru* ('preacher'), founder (*c.* 1505) of the Sikhs. He preached a puritanic, monotheistic, tolerant form of Hinduism, rejecting the caste system and the quest for power. Later under persecution the Sikhs became a militant sect.

Nansen, Fridtjof (1861–1930). Norwegian explorer, scientist and humanitarian. In 1888 he crossed Greenland on skis and in 1893–97 carried out a daring project of forcing the *Fram*, a ship specially built to withstand ice-pressure, into the pack-ice and letting it drift with the great north-west current. Entering the ice near the New Siberian Islands in the eastern Arctic, the *Fram* drifted with the current and reached Spitsbergen in just under three years. Meanwhile Nansen (with F. H. Johansen) had left the ship (March 1895) and on foot had reached a latitude of 86° 14′. They wintered in Franz Josef Land, where they were picked up in the spring. Nansen was professor of oceanography at Oslo University (1908–30); after Norway's independence (1905) he was its first ambassador to Great Britain. After World War I he worked for the repatriation of prisoners of war, for famine relief in

Russia, and (on behalf of the League of Nations) for refugees to whom the issue of a 'Nansen passport' often meant a new life. Nansen won the Nobel Prize for Peace (1922). Shackleton, E., *Nansen the Explorer*. 1959

Napier, Sir Charles James (1782–1853). British soldier, chiefly remembered for his conquest and subsequent governorship of Sind in India. His career is vividly recorded in his own dispatches and his brother's histories. He was an impetuous, autocratic soldier, a hero to his own men but also a maker of enemies, who even declared that he had created the situation in Sind to justify its annexation.

Napier, John (1550–1617). Scottish mathematician and engineer. By introducing the comma (where we now use the 'decimal point'), he simplified the notation of the decimal system. His most important contribution to mathematics was his invention (1594) of the number ratios which he called logarithms. He spent almost twenty years calculating the necessary tables, which he published in his *Mirifici Logarithmorum Canonis Descriptio* (1614). He also devised a simple calculating system made of rods (Napier's bones), which he described in his *Rabdologiae* (1617). As an engineer he invented a hydraulic screw for pumping water, and other devices. He was also interested in millenarianism and wrote a commentary on the Revelation of St John the Divine.

Napier of Magdala, Robert Cornelis Napier, 1st Baron (1810–1890). British soldier. He commanded (1868) the expedition against King Theodore of Abyssinia, his march from the coast to the final storming of Magdala showing a remarkable combination of organizational, engineering and military skills. For this he was awarded a peerage and an annuity. He was afterwards commander-in-chief in India 1870–76 and governor of Gibraltar 1876–82.

Napoleon I (1769–1821). Emperor of the French (1804–14 and 1815). He was born at Ajaccio in Corsica, the son of Carlo Buonaparte (* Bonaparte) and his wife Letizia. Napoleon left the island (1778) to learn French at Autun and to attend military schools at Brienne (1779–84) and at Paris (1784–86). He emerged as a lieutenant of artillery who gave much time to study. On the outbreak of the Revolution he went to Corsica and took a leading part in overthrowing the royalist government; but when a quarrel developed between the followers of the veteran for Corsican independence, * Paoli, and those, including the Bonapartes, who favoured union with revolutionary France, the whole family moved to the mainland. In 1793 Napoleon was in charge of the artillery in the French republican army besieging Toulon, which had been seized by the British, and he was largely responsible for the city's capture. For this he was made a brigadier general by * Robespierre but on the latter's fall he was imprisoned briefly. His rise to power was resumed when Barras, who was shortly to become the leading figure in the Directory, appointed him as his second-in-command to suppress the Paris rising (1795). Napoleon's quick success, which showed his promise, brought him into the new-rich society of the moment where he met, fell in love with and married (1796) Josephine de * Beauharnais, a fascinating widow six years older than himself. Almost immediately afterwards he was given command of the army in Italy, where he conducted a whirlwind campaign against the Austrians, culminating in the brilliant victories of Arcola and Rivoli and the capture of Mantua.

Back in France, Napoleon secured consent for an ambitious plan for the conquest of Egypt. In May 1788 a fleet carrying 36,000 troops slipped out of Toulon. Napoleon received the surrender of Malta on the way and avoiding Nelson's fleet reached Egypt. After winning the Battle of the Pyramids outside Cairo he quickly conquered the country (while the accompanying scientists practically instituted Egyptology) but when Nelson destroyed the French fleet at the Battle of the Nile the army was cut off from France. Afraid of losing political opportunities and checked at Acre in Syria Napoleon left the army, reached France after again avoiding the British in a fast frigate, and engineered the *coup d'état* of 18 Brumaire (9 November 1799) which overturned the unpopular Directory and made him the first of three consuls and virtual ruler of France. At once he proved himself a great administrator: local government was centralized through prefects; the civil code of law (Code Napoléon) was issued; the Bank of France was created; and, with military needs in mind, roads (e.g. Mont Cenis pass), bridges etc. were built and ports re-equipped. Meanwhile victories over Austria (again at war) at Marengo and Hohenlinden (* Moreau) enabled peace to be made with them at Lunéville (1801) and at Amiens with Britain (1802), the latter enabling the army of Egypt to return. In 1804 a docile Senate proclaimed the conqueror emperor of the French and in December the pope was brought to Paris for the coronation in Notre Dame. A court formed from some returned émigrés and a new aristocracy of talent achieved a somewhat artificial splendour. But by this time France was again at war. Napoleon broke the treaties by further encroachments, and coalitions were again formed against him. In 1805 he decided to move the army, assembled at Boulogne for the invasion of England, into central Europe; Austerlitz (1805), Jena (1806) and Friedland (1807) were the most important of the victories by which the coalition of Austria, Prussia and Russia was subdued. After the Treaty of Tilsit (1807) Russia became his firm ally. A major purpose of his reorganization of the continent was to weaken Britain by shutting it off from European trade. During the next few years he made his brother Louis king of Holland and created the Confederation of the Rhine (later the kingdom of Westphalia), for his brother Jerome; he himself became king of Italy while his brother Joseph (succeeded later by his brother-in-law * Murat) was made king of Naples. His greatest mistake was to invade Spain (1808), where he transferred Joseph as king, and Portugal, thus opening up a battleground for the British (the Peninsular War) where Wellington's army was a constant drain on his resources. Austria again took up arms (1809) but after the Battle of Wagram had to sue for peace. To satisfy his pride and prolong his dynasty Napoleon divorced Josephine (1809) and married (1810) Marie Louise, daughter of the emperor of Austria (a new title assumed by the Habsburg ruler after the dissolution of the Holy Roman Empire in 1806). Their son, the future Duke of * Reichstadt was born in 1811. Restiveness at the restrictions on trade caused by Napoleon's Continental System, directed against Britain, was the prime cause of the tsar's estrangement, which led to Napoleon's invasion of Russia (1812). The catastrophic winter retreat from Moscow after the burning of the city virtually destroyed the Grand Army, and though Napoleon raced ahead of his exhausted troops and raised new armies they were never of the quality of the old. In 1813 all his old enemies resumed the struggle, Napoleon's hold on Germany was lost and after his decisive defeat at the 'Battle of the Nations' at Leipzig in October he had to withdraw across the Rhine. In 1814, with Wellington's army advancing from Spain and the Allies breaking into France from Germany, Napoleon's skill could only delay the end. He abdicated at Fountainebleau in April and was granted sovereignty of the Italian island of Elba. From there, in March 1815, to the victors haggling over terms at the Congress of Vienna came the electrifying news that Napoleon had escaped to France. As though by magic the country rallied to his side, his old marshals, troops, the country at large. King Louis fled and for a hundred days Napoleon was emperor once again. But Europe had had enough. The Prussians and British were first in the field; and though for a time it looked as if by dividing and defeating his opponents in turn Napoleon might achieve yet another miracle his final defeat at Waterloo (18 June) ended the story. He abdicated once again and surrendered to the British. He was sent to the Atlantic island of St Helena where he spent his last years in creating, through his self-justificatory *Mémorial*, the Napoleonic legend, with such effect that in 1840 his body was reburied with pomp and splendour in Paris at the behest of Louis Philippe, a member of the royal line to which Napoleon had been consistently opposed.

Napoleon's greatness as a commander and administrator none will contest and few men have had a greater gift for inspiring devotion. His legal codes and his centralized administrative system have endured in France, and several other countries of Europe. By sweeping away the feudal hotch-potch of the Holy Roman empire he enabled a new Germany to be born; he showed that a united Italy could be more than a dream. But he was ambitious beyond measure, cynical, unscrupulous and sometimes ruthless.

Cronin, V., *Napoleon*. 1973

Napoleon II *see* **Reichstadt, Duke of**

Napoleon III (Charles Louis Napoleon Bonaparte) (1808–1873). Emperor of the French (1852–70). His father, Louis, was the brother of Napoleon I, who had made him king of Holland; his mother, Hortense de Beauharnais, was a daughter of the empress

Josephine. Brought up in Germany and Switzerland, he was fired as a young man by liberal causes; he took part in a rising in the Romagna against the pope's temporal power and organized revolts against the French monarchy, including one at Strasbourg (1836) for which he was deported. In England (where he lived 1839–40) he published *Idées Napoléoniennes*, which interpreted his uncle's political thought and showed where his own ideas were leading. In 1840 he was sentenced to life imprisonment for trying to stir the troops in Boulogne to revolt, but after six years escaped from the castle of Ham and fled to London. After the deposition of King Louis Philippe (1848) he was elected to the National Assembly, at once returned to Paris and in December was elected President of the new republic. As the result of a *coup d'état* (December 1851) he proclaimed himself emperor; though his action was approved by plebiscite and he imitated his uncle's institutions, he tried to forestall future opposition by creating prosperity at home and pursuing a liberal policy abroad. Thus he opened up the country with railways, encouraged the formation of banks, created and protected new industries and, through Haussman, rebuilt and beautified the capital. Great exhibitions (1855 and 1867) displayed French achievements to the world. He avoided his uncle's mistake of quarrelling with Britain, whose ally he became in the Crimean War (1854–56). Without his help and the French victories over the Austrians (1859) at Magenta and Solferino the unification of Italy would have been impossible; but he lost much of the credit by exacting Savoy and Nice as the price of his support, and by using a French garrison to maintain papal rule in Rome and so keeping the Italians out of their natural capital. In doing this he was partly influenced by his beautiful Spanish wife, Eugénie de Montijo (married 1853), an active supporter of the papal cause. A much worse loss of prestige resulted from sending an army into Mexico on a debt-collecting mission. Having gained control of the country and installed * Maximilian, an Austrian archduke as emperor, he withdrew his troops under American pressure, leaving the unfortunate Maximilian to his fate.

Meanwhile republican opposition had been growing and the emperor had only half-hearted support when he allowed himself to be manoeuvred by Bismarck into the France-Prussian War. In the military débâcle which followed Napoleon was captured at Sedan (1870) and two days later a republic was declared. After the war Napoleon spent the last two years of his life in England, at Chislehurst in Kent. His only son, the prince imperial, was killed (1879) fighting for Britain in the Zulu War.

Ridley, J., *Napoleon and Eugenie*. 1979

Narses (*c.* 478–*c.* 573). Byzantine administrator and general. He was a eunuch who rose to high office in the imperial household at Constantinople and proved his usefulness to the emperor * Justinian by suppressing (532) an insurrection in the city. He was sent to Italy (538) to assist (and perhaps spy upon) * Belisarius and to gain experience of command. He was soon brought back to Constantinople but after the Goths had taken advantage of the recall of Belisarius (548) to conquer most of the country, Narses was sent to Italy (552) with a large army to retrieve the situation. To the surprise of all he showed great military skill, defeated the Gothic leader Tortila in a decisive battle, recaptured Rome and by 554 had driven Tortila's Frankish allies from northern Italy. He governed Italy until his recall in 567, after which date little certain about him is known.

Nash, John (1752–1835). English architect. Having developed his professional skill while employed by Sir Robert Taylor, he used money inherited from an uncle for speculative building, a venture which led to bankruptcy. He then moved to Wales where he practised with success and formed a partnership with the landscape gardener Humphry * Repton, who may have brought him to the notice of the Prince of Wales (George IV). The connexion brought him many commissions for country houses and when the prince became regent (1811), it was to Nash that he turned for the realization of his ambitious scheme for developing London's West End. Regent Street (now rebuilt) began the approach to the redesigned Marylebone Park (now Regent's Park), round part of which were built the famous 'Nash terraces' of stucco houses that still survive. The planning of Trafalgar Square and its relationship to a re-developed St James's Park area were all part of the general scheme; and Buckingham House was reconstructed as Buckingham Palace. Nash also created the Brighton pavilion for his royal

patron (1818–21). As a town planner he had few equals; as an architect he popularized the Regency style of stucco-covered houses in the classical idiom which, despite technical defects, had much dignity and charm and set the pattern (followed with little taste and understanding) for the monotonous Victorian developments of the next decades.
Davis, T., *The Prince Regent's Architect*. 1973

Nash, Ogden (1902–1971). American poet. His humorous verse, featured in the *New Yorker*, is notable for lines of irregular length and unconventional rhymes. Several collections have been published, e.g. *The Private Dining Room* (1953), *You Can't Get There from Here* (1957) and *The Untold Adventures of Santa Claus*. 1965

Nash, Paul (1889–1946). English painter. Trained at the Chelsea Polytechnic, he was a regular exhibitor at the New English Art Club and became known mainly for landscapes in a simplified geometric style influenced by Cubism. He was an official artist in both World Wars and was adept at investing with symbolism the debris of a battlefield. Some of the most striking of his war pictures are in the Imperial War Museum. From 1927 he introduced a note of surrealism and exhibited at the London surrealist exhibition (1936). He also designed, especially in his earlier career, textiles, book illustrations and stage settings. His brother, **John Nash** (1893–1977), was also well known as a landscape painter.
Eates, M., *Paul Nash*. 1973

Nash, Richard (known as 'Beau Nash') (1674–1762). English dandy. He lived by his wits and by gaming until (1705) he went to Bath, where he soon became the master of ceremonies and undisputed 'king', with autocratic powers over dress and behaviour in the assembly rooms and other places of resort. He introduced gambling, duelling, and a dance band from London; road improvements and even street lighting came under his control; and Bath became the most fashionable of English spas.

Nash (or Nashe), **Thomas** (1567–1601). English pamphleteer and dramatist. Educated at Cambridge, he became one of the group of playwrights and pamphleteers known as 'university wits'. *The Anatomy of Absurdities* (1589) and *Pierce Penilesse* (1592) were satirical exposures of the evils of society in his day. He wrote the first picaresque novel in English, *The Unfortunate Traveller* (1594); his play *The Isle of Dogs* (1597), which attacked abuses of state power with such freedom that he was imprisoned, is lost.
Hibbard, G. R., *Thomas Nash*. 1962

Nash, Sir Walter (1882–1968). New Zealand politician. He emigrated from England (1909) and became a Labour M. P. in 1929; from 1935 until the party was defeated (1949) he was minister of finance. He succeeded Peter Fraser as party leader (1950) and after success in the 1957 election was prime minister until the election of 1960 brought the Nationalists back to power. His writings included *New Zealand: A Working Democracy* (1943).

Nasmyth, James (1808–1890). Scottish engineer. He invented the first successful steam hammer, which he patented in 1842. That the first one to be built was constructed in France was probably due to the pirating of his design. The hammer permitted the production of metal forgings of better quality and much greater size. He also invented the stop-valve and a steam pile-driver. The success of his foundry, established (1834) at Bridgewater, near Manchester, enabled him to retire with a fortune at the age of 48. His autobiography was edited by Samuel * Smiles (1883).

Nasser, Gamal Abdel (1918–1970). President of Egypt (1956–58) and then the United Arab Republic (1958–70). He had a successful military career and emerged with credit from the war with Israel (1948–49). He was the chief organizer of the revolt (1952) which under General * Neguib deposed King Farouk. Having supplanted Neguib in 1954 he eventually became president of Egypt in 1956. In the same year he nationalized the Suez canal which provoked Anglo-French intervention. In 1958 he became president of the United Arab Republic formed by the union of Egypt and Syria, but the union proved short-lived and Nasser's subsequent efforts to form an Arab federation under Egyptian leadership were constantly foiled. He obtained much economic and military aid from Russia but remained doctrinally 'neutralist'.
Lacouture, J., *Nasser: A Biography*. 1973

Nathan, George Jean (1882–1958). American editor and dramatic critic. With H. L.

Mencken he edited *Smart Set* (1914–23) and founded the *American Mercury* (1924). He was for many years the leading American dramatic critic. His collection of criticisms included *The House of Satan* and *The Morning after the First Knight*.

Nebuchadnezzar (or Nebuchadrezzar) **II** (died 562 B.C.). King of Babylonia (from 605). He recovered many of the lost provinces of the empire and added more. In 597 he took Jerusalem and in 586, after a revolt, destroyed the city and took most of the people into captivity in Babylonia. He rebuilt the city of Babylon, where at his palace he constructed the famous 'hanging gardens', regarded as one of the wonders of the ancient world.

Necker, Jacques (1732–1804). Swiss-born financier. Having made a large fortune as a banker he represented Geneva in Paris, where his wife's *salon* attracted literary celebrities as well as businessmen. As French director-general of finance (1777–81), Necker made such an impression by his integrity and was so successful with his administrative economies that he was able to raise money without difficulty for the War of American Independence. Those who had suffered from his measures forced his retirement (1781) and he was not recalled until 1788, when France was on the brink of the Revolution. He advised Louis XVI to summon the States General but the consequence of this step lost him the king's confidence. He was dismissed (July 1789), only to be reinstated a few days later when the Bastille fell. Disillusioned by events, he finally retired to Switzerland in 1790. His daughter became famous as Madame de * Staël.
Chapuisat, E., *Necker 1732–1804*. 1938

Needham, Joseph (1900–). British biochemist and historian. Educated at Cambridge, where he worked all his life, he produced the encyclopedic *Chemical Embryology* (1931). A Christian Marxist, he visited China 1942–46 as head of a scientific mission, then devoted the rest of his career to a massive study of *Science and Civilisation in China* (1954 ff: still incomplete).
Werskey, G., *The Visible College*. 1978.

Nefertiti (14th century B.C.). Wife of * Akhnaton, king of Egypt. Her beautiful sculptured head, now in Berlin, is one of the most famous examples of ancient Egyptian art.

Negrin, Juan (1891–1956). Spanish politician. Whilst a professor at the University of Madrid he played an active role in the socialist party. On the outbreak of the Spanish Civil War Negrin's resolution singled him out as a leader and he was premier (1937–39). He took refuge in France and England on the defeat of the Republicans.

Neguib, Mohammed (1901–1984). Egyptian general. With * Nasser as his deputy, he led the revolt (1952) by which King Farouk was dethroned. After being prime minister and then president he was forced into retirement (1954) by Nasser.

Nehru, Jawaharlal (1889–1964). Indian politician. He was a Kashmiri Brahmin by descent and the son of **Motilal Nehru,** a rich and distinguished lawyer who had been leader of the *Swaraj* or Home Rule party. Jawaharlal Nehru was educated in England at Harrow and Cambridge and studied law in India, but from the moment he met * Gandhi his life was given to politics. He joined the Indian National Congress (1918) and was president in 1929 and four times subsequently. He was not a pacifist like Gandhi and did not share his economic views but his personal devotion was intense, and while agitation and propaganda were the main activities their differences lacked practical importance. Several terms of imprisonment for political activities only increased Nehru's influence. Complete independence was always his aim for India and after the failure of the Cripps mission he was interned for his rebellious attitude. After the war, when the subcontinent was partitioned between India and Pakistan Nehru's prestige made him the inevitable prime minister of India (1947). Owing to the immense difficulties of his task his success was only partial. He kept his country within the Commonwealth, achieved some success with industrialization and maintained democratic forms of government, with stability and order. But the Kashmir problem remained unsolved and he shocked world opinion by invading Goa. His policy of non-alignment with the eastern or western power blocs did not prevent the Chinese invasion of 1962. Nevertheless when he died the consensus was that a great influence for good had gone from the world. His daughter

Indira * Gandhi became prime minister in 1966. He wrote an autobiography (1936) and several historical works including *Glimpses of World History* (1939) which is more Asian than Eurocentred .

Gopal, S., *Jawaharlal Nehru*. 2 vols. 1975 and 1979

Neill, Alexander Sutherland (1883–1973). English educationist. His libertarian views on education were fully exemplified in the best known of his schools, Summerhill in Suffolk. Many of his methods, which before World War II made him a centre of controversy, have later won wide acceptance.

Niell, A. S., *Summerhill*. 1962

Nelson, Horatio Nelson, 1st Viscount (1758–1805). English sailor. The son of a Norfolk clergyman, he joined the navy (1770), served at sea in the Arctic, the East and West Indies, and in 1781 commanded a converted French prize, newly commissioned as HMS *Albemarle*. In this ship he joined Lord Hood's squadron in North American waters during the American War of Independence. From 1783 to 1787 he commanded a frigate, *Boreas*, in the West Indies, where he married Frances, widow of Dr Josiah Nisbet of the island of Nevis. After five unemployed years with his wife in Norfolk he was appointed, war with France being again imminent, to the *Agamemnon* and went with Hood to the Mediterranean. While commanding the naval brigade in Corsica he lost the sight of his right eye. Spain having come into the war on the French side, it was the British task to prevent the Spanish fleet joining the French ships at Brest. This was achieved by the great victory off Cape St Vincent (1797) won by Sir John Jervis with Nelson, who boarded and captured two ships, as his commodore. Later in the year Nelson lost his right arm in an attack on Santa Cruz in Tenerife which ended in an exchange of courtesies but no success. After a period of recuperation in England he hoisted his flag (1798) on the *Vanguard* and sailed again for the Mediterranean to watch the movements of the French fleet in Toulon; it took advantage of a storm to slip out (20 May) carrying Napoleon's army to Egypt. At length in August Nelson caught up with the French fleet drawn up and anchored in Aboukir Bay, near Alexandria. Though inferior in numbers Nelson boldly took an inshore course and completely destroyed the fleet, thus cutting Bonaparte off from France. Back in Naples he fell under the spell of Emma * Hamilton, whose husband was ambassador there, and the liaison started which lasted until his death. Meanwhile the hero of the Battle of the Nile received a peerage and a pension and the King of Naples gave him the title of Duke of Bronte. When the French invaded Naples he conveyed the royal family to Sicily; but his long stay with Lady Hamilton there brought admiralty censure; he returned by a long overland journey with the Hamiltons to arrive in England in January 1801.

The Danes having espoused the French cause, he was immediately sent to the Baltic as second-in-command and was in charge of the attack upon Copenhagen. Having destroyed the enemy ships in a fierce action during which he raised his glass to his blind eye and 'failed to see' the signal for retreat, he was able to avert the bombardment of the city by arranging an armistice. He now succeeded to Sir Hyde Parker's Baltic command but he became ill and returned to England in July. The peace of Amiens now intervened to give him eighteen months ashore, mainly spent with the Hamiltons; Sir William died in April 1803, in Emma's arms and with Nelson holding his hand. In May war was resumed and Nelson was given the Mediterranean command and resumed the watch on Toulon. On 29 March 1805 Admiral Villeneuve slipped out, passed through the straits of Gibraltar and reinforced by Spanish ships sailed for the West Indies. This was part of Napoleon's master plan; that Nelson should be lured in pursuit, that Villeneuve should then double back, link up with the Brest fleet and the Spaniards and gain command of the Channel for long enough for the troop carriers to convey the great army mustered at Boulogne to England. The first part was successful; Nelson heard on 8 April that Villeneuve had reached the Atlantic; he at once pursued but so outsailed his opponent that on the return journey he reached European waters first. When it was realized that Villeneuve, despite orders, had gone to Cadiz, Nelson, by then back in England, was ordered to follow. Frightened by the thought of Napoleon's anger, Villeneuve sailed on 19 October and on the 21st the two fleets met. Collingwood broke into the rear of the enemy line, Nelson, assumed that their van could not intervene, attacked the centre and his flagship, the *Victory*, came under heavy musketry fire; while talking to Captain Hardy, Nelson fell

mortally wounded in the spine and died three hours later. Mourned as one of the nation's greatest heroes he is commemorated in London by the monument in Trafalgar Square. He was beloved by his men for his humanity and admired for his memorable courage.
Warner, O., *Nelson*. 1975

Nenni, Pietro (1891–1980). Italian Socialist politician. He was exiled by Mussolini (1926) and fought for the loyalists in the Spanish Civil War. After Mussolini's fall (1943) he was able to resume political life in Italy and became president of the Socialist party. In the post-war coalitions he was a deputy prime minister (1945–46) and foreign minister (1946–47). His close association with the Communists caused a party split (1947) and a breakaway, under Saragat, of the Socialist right wing. He rejoined the government in 1963; in successive coalitions under Moro he was vice-president of the council.

Nennius (8th/9th centuries). Early medieval British historian. His Latin work *Historia Britonum* is an uncritical compilation of facts and legends from various unknown sources and is not therefore trustworthy. It contains the first brief references to King Arthur and his twelve victories, but not all of them, e.g. the one recording that no two measurements of his son's tomb ever coincided, reinforce his credibility.

Nepos, Cornelius (*c*. 100–25 B.C.). Roman historian. Of his lives of the famous (*De Viris Illustribus*) some twenty-five survive. His lost writings include a universal history and letters to his friend Cicero.

Neri, St Philip *see* **Philip Neri, St**

Nernst, Walther Hermann (1864–1941). German physical chemist, a professor at Göttingen (1891–1905) and Berlin (1905–33). His many important contributions to structural chemistry included his 'solution pressure' theory (1889) to explain the production of electromotive force in electrical cells; the concept of solubility product (1889), which governs the precipitation of solids from solution; and the 'Nernst heat theorem' (1906) which later became known as the Third Law of Thermodynamics. He won the Nobel Prize for Chemistry (1920).

Nero (Nero Claudius Drusus Germanicus) (37–68). Roman emperor (from 54). Proclaimed emperor at the instigation of his mother Agrippina (a sister of * Caligula) on the death of her husband the emperor Claudius, he began his reign with his tutor Seneca, timid but wise, to guide his inexperience. Only too soon, however, his character showed itself. Claudius's son Britannicus, the rival claimant, was poisoned; Agrippina and Nero's own wife, Octavia, were also put to death. Nero instituted a fierce persecution of the Christians to provide scapegoats who could be blamed for the great fire (64) which destroyed much of Rome, for which he himself was the obvious suspect. His grandiose plans for rebuilding work, including his 'golden palace' on the Palatine Hill, demanded money that could only be obtained by exactions of every kind. Plots, real or imaginary, yielded victims such as Seneca, Lucan and a host of rich, distinguished men, whose property could be confiscated. Meanwhile the emperor's vanity led him to appear in public as a musician or charioteer; passion and cruelty caused him – one crime of many – to kick his wife Poppaea to death. Finally the legions of Gaul and Spain proclaimed Galba emperor in his place, the praetorian guards and senate also turned against him, and Nero, in desperate flight and already hearing the sounds of pursuit, nerved himself to take his own life. External events of the reign included Boadicea's revolt in Britain.

Neruda, Pablo (1904–1973). South American poet, born Neftali Ricardo Reyes in Chile. Considered one of the most original poets writing in Spanish, he began publishing his verse in Chile in 1923. He met the Spanish poet Federico Garcia * Lorca in 1933 and his work was introduced to Spain. Much of his strongest realist poetry was written in reaction to the Spanish Civil War and the outbreak of World War II. After the war he entered political life in Chile as a communist. He was forced out of political life in 1948, when he went into hiding and wrote *Canto general*, an epic poem. He returned to Chile in 1952. He was awarded the 1971 Nobel Prize for Literature.
Aguirre, M. (ed.), *Obras completas de Pablo Neruda*. 2nd edn 1968

Nerva, Marcus Cocceius (*c*. 30–98). Roman emperor (from 96). He proved a humane and tolerant ruler when raised to the purple by the senate after the assassination of * Domitian. He was, in fact, only a stop-gap and assured a vigorous successor by selecting Trajan as his heir.

Nerval, Gérard de (Gérard Labrunie) (1808–1855). French Romantic writer. He published a translation of Goethe's *Faust* (1827) and moved for a time in the orbit of Victor Hugo and collaborated in writing plays with Alexandre Dumas. While living a self-consciously bohemian life in Paris (he is said to have led a lobster on a ribbon-lead), he wrote essays, poems – including the beautiful mysterious sonnets known as the *Chimères* (1854) – and travel sketches, resulting from his searches in Europe and the East for exotic backgrounds. The ecstasies and agonies of his love affair with Jenny Colon are told in *Sylvie*, one of his many short stories, which became increasingly fantastic in later years. After a mental breakdown (1838) and further attacks his power to distinguish reality from dream became more and more intermittent and eventually he committed suicide.

Nervi, Pier Luigi (1891–1979). Italian engineer. He was a pioneer in the application of 20th-century engineering techniques to the construction of large buildings, especially the use of steel mesh subsequently clad with concrete and of prefabricated components. This enabled him to design and build vast and often intricate structures. Outstanding are the Exhibition Halls at Turin (1949–50) and his buildings for the Olympic Games in Rome (1956–59).

Nesbit, Edith (1858–1924). English writer of children's stories, noted for their cheerful realism. *Five Children and It* (1902) and *The Railway Children* (1906) are still popular. She was a founder-member of the Fabian Society, married to Hubert Bland.

Nestlé, Henri (1814–1890). Swiss manufacturer, born in Germany. An artisan and inventor, he experimented with supplementary milk products for babies and established a plant in Vevey for making condensed milk. He sold out his interest in 1875 but the name was retained. The Nestlé company did not enter the chocolate market until 1904; now it is the world's largest manufacturer.

Nestorius (died after 451). Christian theologian. A member of a community of monks near Antioch he was chosen (428) to be patriarch of Constantinople by the emperor Theodosius II. His interpretation of the doctrines concerning the Godhead and Manhood of Jesus Christ were held to be heretical by the ecumenical synod of Ephesus (431) and Nestorius was deposed and (436) exiled to Egypt. The Nestorian church came into being (*c.* 500) under Persian protection, but it shrank under constant Mongol and Turkish persecution and only a remnant, now known as Assyrians', survives in Iraq.

Neumann, John von (1903–1957). Hungarian–American mathematician, born in Budapest. He studied chemistry in Zürich, received a PhD in mathematics from Budapest, published a classic definition of ordinal numbers at the age of 20, and taught at Göttingen. He migrated to the U.S. in 1930, became a professor at Princeton University 1930–33 and at the Institute for Advanced Study (Princeton) 1933–57. He wrote more than 150 papers on quantum theory, pure mathematics, logic, meteorology, games theory and computer programming. During World War II he worked on designing the atomic bomb and later was a 'Cold War' hardliner. He turned * Turing's concept of a 'universal computing machine' into reality. His Electronic Discrete Variable Automatic Computer (EDVAC), operational from 1947, was the first fully electronic computer, using binary notation and stored internal programming. Conventional computers are sometimes called 'von Neumann machines'. He was a member of the U.S. Atomic Energy Commission 1955–57.

Neurath, Baron Konstantin von (1873–1956). German diplomat and administrator under the Third Reich. He was ambassador to Italy in 1921 and to Britain in 1930. In 1932 he became foreign minister and remained so, under Hilter, until 1938. He was appointed Protector of Bohemia and Moravia in 1939. He was sentenced at Nuremberg to 15 years, but was released in 1954.

Newbolt, Sir Henry John (1862–1938). English poet. He is best known for his vigorous ballads, e.g. *Drake's Drum* and *The Fighting Temeraire* (1914); his posthumously published *A Perpetual Memory* (1939) turns to themes of tenderness and fantasy. He was knighted in 1915 and in 1923 appointed official naval historian.

Newcastle, Thomas Pelham Holles, 1st Duke of (1693–1768). English politican. He was a son of the 1st Lord Pelham and added the name Holles when, as adopted heir, he inherited the estates of his uncle, Duke of Newcastle-upon-Tyne of an earlier creation. Thus richly endowed and having married a daughter of Lord Godolphin he began his political career with every advantage. He proved a superb party manager and an adroit and indefatigable wielder of patronage, with the result that no Whig administration, for more than forty years from 1717, could exist long without him. He was, for example, the nominal head of Pitt's great ministry which won many successes in the Seven Years War (1756–63). He worked closely with his brother Henry * Pelham.

Newcomb, Simon (1835–1909). American astronomer. He held an appointment at the Washington Naval Observatory and from 1884 a professorship of Johns Hopkins University. He studied the motions of the sun, moon and planets and tabulated those of the sun, Mercury, Mars and Venus. He also worked with A. A. Michelson in determining the velocity of light. His popular books included *Astronomy for Everybody* (1903); he also edited the U.S. *Nautical Almanac*.

Newcomen, Thomas (1663–1729). English inventor, born in Devon. He invented the first practical steam engine, which he erected in 1712 after ten years of experiment. Its main purpose was to pump water from mine shafts (e.g. of the tin mines of his native country). Its principles were later modified to achieve greater efficiency for wider use (* Watt). Owing to patenting difficulties Newcomen made little or no financial profit from his invention.

Newman, Ernest William Roberts (1868–1959). English music critic. For fifty years his comments in well known newspapers, especially the *Sunday Times*, on current performances and more general articles did much to guide British musical appreciation. He wrote a definitive life of Wagner (4 volumes, 1933–46), an authoritative monograph on Hugo Wolf and studies of Beethoven, Liszt and Richard Strauss.

Newman, V., *Ernest Newman: A Memoir*. 1963

Newman, John Henry (1801–1890). English theologian and cardinal. He became a fellow of Oriel College, Oxford (1822), and as rector of St Mary's Oxford (1828–43), and in spiritual charge at Littlemore won an immense reputation as a preacher. In 1833 he heard a sermon on 'National Apostasy' by * Keble which he regarded as the starting point of the Tractarian (or Oxford) Movement, in which he played so pre-eminent a role. Its purpose was to reinvigorate the Anglican church and, by turning back to the early Christian fathers (of whose works Newman had made a profound study) as the custodians of doctrine, to reconcile the beliefs of the Roman and Anglican branches of the Catholic church. Newman wrote many of the *Tracts for the Times*, but the same logic which made many of the movement's supporters turn to the Roman church led Newman eventually (1845) to take the same step. He was ordained priest in 1847 and shortly afterwards founded an Oratory (a brotherhood of secular priests without vows * Philip Neri, St) in England. Its branch in London came to be known as Brompton Oratory; the main body was at Edgbaston, Birmingham. Here Newman lived in seclusion, partly because of an estrangement between him and the more ultramontane Cardinal * Manning. Any suspicion of Vatican disapproval was, however, removed when Pope Leo XIII made Newman a cardinal (1879). As a writer Newman was a supreme stylist as can be seen in his *Apologia Pro Vita Sua* (1864), a vivid and moving spiritual autobiography written in reply to Charles * Kingsley, who had challenged his integrity. His other works include *The Dream of Gerontius* (1866), a dramatic poem on the flight of the soul from the body, later set to music by Elgar. *The Idea of a University Defined* (1876) contained an earlier work on the subject, which preceded his tenure (1854–58) of the office of rector of the new Catholic university of Dublin, and a later series of lectures. *Lead, Kindly Light*, written before his conversion, is the best known of his many hymns.

In the last years of his life Newman was revered by people of all denominations and his influence did much to encourage the progressive tolerance which has made possible the

present-day search for a basic for church reunion.
Coulson, J., *Newman, A Portrait Restored.* 1965

Newton, Sir Isaac (1642–1727). English mathematician and physicist. He was the posthumous son of a small landowner at Woolsthorpe, Lincolnshire, and was brought up there, after his mother's remarriage (1645), by his maternal grandmother. Already as a schoolboy he had a reputation for making sundials and water clocks; he went in 1661 to Trinity College, Cambridge, where he graduated in 1665. When the college closed during the plague he was back at Woolsthorpe (1665–66) where at the age of 23 he worked out practically the whole of his universal law of gravitation. He built upon the work of Galileo, but it was his genius to supply a generalized set of principles and provide a new and infinitely challenging conception of the universe. Moreover he devised the tools with which to give his concept mathematical expressions: by 1665 he had evolved the binomial theorem and divised the elements of the differential calculus, which he called fluxions. He also developed the integral calculus (inverse fluxions). Because of his inherent dislike of publications, these discoveries were not published until 1685 and this caused a bitter 'priority' controversy with * Leibniz. Yet another major discovery was made by this astonishing young man; he found (1666) that so-called white light is composed of many colours, which may be separated by a prism and then combined into white light again. Having returned to Cambridge in 1667 he was from 1669 to 1695 professor of mathematics there. He constructed (1668) the first reflecting (Newtonian) telescope, in which he used a parabolic mirror to reflect and magnify the object observed. In 1672 he became a fellow of the Royal Society but more than twelve years elapsed before he published his findings, and even then it was only through the eager encouragement and help of the astronomer * Halley that his great *Philosophiae Naturalis Principia Mathematica* (1687), known as the *Principia*, appeared. In this he sought to explain all physical phenomena by a few generalized laws. The laws of motion and a systematized study of mechanics provide a starting point and he goes on to explain the action of the tides and the orbits of the planets. He ends by showing the philosophical conclusions to be deduced from the earlier sections of the work. In 1704 he published his *Optics* in which he advanced the corpuscular theory of light, later disproved by Young. Newton was also a student of alchemy and biological chronology, to which he appears to have attached as much significance as to his scientific work.

Newton was elected president of the Royal Society in 1703 and was annually re-elected until 1727. He was M.P. for Cambridge University (1689–90 and 1701–02) and was knighted in 1705. His reports on the coinage (1717 and 1718) resulted from his appointment (1699) as Master of the Mint. He is buried in Westminister Abbey and is universally recognized as one of the greatest thinkers of all time.
Manuel, F. E., *A Portrait of Isaac Newton.* 1968

Ney, Michel (1769–1815). French marshal. Called by Napoleon 'the bravest of the brave', he was a non-commissioned officer when the Revolution broke out. He rose quickly and by 1796 was general of a brigade. He was given the title Duke of Elchingen by Napoleon for the heroism with which he stormed the entrenchments in that engagement (1805). He won further distinction at Jena, Eylau and especially Friedland; and for the part he played at Smolensk and Borodin during the advance into Russia (1812) he was created prince of Moscow. As leader of the rearguard during the disastrous retreat he saved the remnants of the Grand Army from annihilation. When Napoleon abdicated (1814) Ney was allowed by Louis XVIII to retain a command but when the emperor again landed (1815) his marshal joined him with his troops. Ney showed his courage once more in the Waterloo campaign but was caught when trying to reach Switzerland after the defeat and despite efforts by Wellington and others to save him, he was shot as a traitor.
Morton, J. B., *Marshal Ney.* 1958

Ngo Dinh Diem (1901–1963). Vietnamese politician, born in Annam. Son of a mandarin, and a Roman Catholic, he became a civil servant and minister of the interior from 1933. He refused to co-operate with the Japanese, * Ho Chi Minh or * Bao Dai, and lived abroad as a virtual recluse 1950–54. He was prime minister of the 'State of Vietnam' (i.e. the South) 1954–55, engineered Bao's deposition, succeeding him as president 1955–63, during the period of open war with the North. He was a bachelor but his family aroused great hostility, especially his brother Ngo Dinh Nhu and his wife. Although utterly dependent on US support he refused advice, launched a campaign against the militant Buddhists and was murdered by army officers, together with Nhu (November 1963).

Nicholas I (1796–1855). Tsar of Russia (from 1825). After the assassination of his brother Alexander I he came to the throne in place of his elder brother Constantine, who had renounced the succession but whose name was invoked by the so-called 'Decembrist' plotters who were demanding reforms. The movement was easily suppressed; and though Nicholas appointed a committee to investigate the state of the country it was clear that he would permit no reform not emanating from himself. A codification of the law was, however, a definite achievement of the reign. Meanwhile Nicholas maintained his autocracy with the aid of censorhip and secret police, cruelly suppressed a Polish rising (1830–31) and in 1849 sent an army to help the emperor of Austria in quelling the Hungarian revolt. His readiness, however, to champion Turkey's Christian subjects against the sultan involved him in the humiliations of the Crimean War, during which he died.

Nicholas II (1868–1918). The last tsar of Russia (1894–1917). The eldest son of Alexander III, he was an amiable weak man; he failed to support any liberal movement and accepted the advice of reactionary ministers. The aftermath of the humiliating Russian defeat in the war with Japan (1904–05) forced him to accept an elected *duma* (parliament) but he quickly acquiesced in rendering it ineffectual. Socialist and revolutionary movements were driven underground, and, though for a time war with Germany temporarily relieved internal difficulties, defeats and governmental incompetence fanned discontent into open rebellion. Distrust of the tsarina, moreover, lost him the support of many of the aristocracy, his natural allies, Nicholas had married (1894) Princess Alix of Hesse Darmstadt. Of the five children of this happy marriage, only the youngest was a boy, who suffered from haemophilia. A charlatan monk * Rasputin, who seemed to have the power of relieving the boy's illness, gained such complete power over the tsarina (and through her the tsar) that they were suspected of such treasonable acts as correspondence with the enemy. Thus when the Revolution broke out (March 1917) the tsar, lacking the determination or support to contest the issue, abdicated. In August with his wife and children he was taken to Siberia and in the following July the whole family was supposedly murdered by the Bolsheviks (* Anastasia). Nicholas was a kindly, well-meaning man but he had neither the strength, ability nor ruthlessness to be a successful autocrat.

Massie, R. K., *Nicholas and Alexandra*. 1969

Nicholas, St This semi-legendary figure, the 'Santa Claus' of nursery lore, seems to have derived his legends from two historical bishops of Lycia in Asia Minor: Nicholas of Myra (4th century) was venerated for miraculously saving three generals condemned to death by Constantine; Nicholas of Sion (died 564) was revered throughout the Byzantine empire and his cult spread to Russia, of which he became the patron saint. Whatever his origin the cult of St Nicholas spread rapidly in the west. Bari, where his alleged bones – rescued it is said from the Seljuk Turks – were brought from Myra, became one of the most important places of medieval pilgrimage. As well as being the patron saint of children and the bringer of gifts on the day of his festival (6 December) – his identification with 'Father Christmas' came later – he was impartially the patron of judges and murderers, pawnbrokers, merchants and thieves and especially scholars and sailors.

Nicholas of Cusa (1401–1464). German theologian, mathematician and philosopher. The son of a Moselle boatman, he was nevertheless able to study at Heidelberg and Padua Universities and presented to the Council of Basle (1413) his ideas (contained in *On Catholic Concord* but afterwards abandoned) on reforming the church by giving a general council supremacy over the pope. He also presented calendar reforms derived from his mathematical studies, which he pursued with the aim of arriving at exact truth. He did not, as scholars once claimed, anticipate * Copernicus's conclusion that the earth revolves round the sun. After acting as papal legate in Germany (1440–47) he was made a cardinal (1448).

Bett, H., *Nicholas of Cusa*. 1932

Nicholson, Ben (1894–1982). British abstract artist. Husband of the sculptor Barbara * Hepworth and son of Sir William * Nicholson, in the 1930s he was a member of the Unit One Group of British artists seeking a 'truly contemporary' approach, and he developed a style allied to constructivism. His work was first exhibited at the Venice Beinnale in 1934, after which he exhibited widely and gained an international reputation. He was awarded the OM in 1968.

Nicholson, John (1821–1857). British soldier. He gained a great reputation as an administrator in the Punjab; he even attracted the worship of a section of the people. The Indian Mutiny (1857) brought him a hero's fame. He organized and inspired the assault on Delhi but was killed while leading the attack.
Pearson, H., *John Nicholson.* 1939

Nicholson, Sir William (1872–1949). English painter and engraver. He won an international reputation with the posters executed (in collaboration with James Pryde) under the pseudonym 'The Beggarstaff Brothers'. He designed the first stage settings for *Peter Pan.*

Nicias (died 414 B.C.). Athenian politician and general. Cautious, conservative and virtuous, he was, after the death of * Pericles, the most important of the 'generals' (popularly elected commanders) left to carry on the Peloponnesian War against Sparta. His efforts for peace and pleas for prudence were constantly thwarted by the demagogue Cleon and by the headstrong * Alcibiades, who with Lamachus was appointed to share with Nicias the command of an attack upon Syracuse in Sicily, then a Spartan colony. When Alcibiades was recalled for impiety and Lamachus killed, Nicias was left in sole command of an expedition in which he did not believe. In the event he delayed evacuation too long; the Athenians were all killed or captured and Nicias himself was taken and put to death.

Nicolle, Charles Jules Henri (1866–1936). French bacteriologist. Director of the Pasteur Institute at Tunis, he discovered (1909) that the body louse transmits typhus fever, and he also claimed success for immunization against trachoma. He won the Nobel Prize for Medicine (1928).

Nicolson, Sir Harold George (1886–1968). British man of letters. He was a diplomat, an independent MP 1935–45, wrote lives of Byron, Curzon and the official biography of George V (1952) for which he received a KCVO. Other books included *Some People* (1927), *Public Faces* (1932) and *Good Behaviour* (1955). He married the poet Vita * Sackville-West.

Niebuhr, Barthold Georg (1776–1831). German historian. After many years spent in public service, culminating with a term as Prussian ambassador in Rome (1816–1823), he lectured at Bonn on ancient history. His great *History of Rome* (3 volumes, 1811, 1812, 1832) set new standards of scholarship by his critical examination of original sources. Many of his conclusions remain unchallenged.

Niebuhr, Reinhold (1892–1971). American theologian. Educated at Yale, he taught at the Union Theological Seminary, New York (1928–60) and wrote many books, including *The Nature and Destiny of Man* (1941–43), which promoted the concept of a 'social gospel' with a heavy political emphasis.

Nielsen, Carl August (1865–1931). Danish composer. His first Symphony (1892–1894) shows the influence of Brahms, but other works of the 1890s illustrate the tendency towards combining contradictory keys which, first prominently asserted in the second Symphony (1902), was to lead Nielsen far on the road to polytonality. In 1915 he became director of the Copenhagen Conservatoire. His works include six Symphonies, a Violin Concerto and the comic opera *Masquerade* (1906).

Niemeyer (Soares Filho), **Oscar** (1907–). Brazilian architect. Strongly influenced by Le Corbusier's functional architecture, he designed many strikingly original buildings in Rio de Janiero and São Paulo and was commissioned to design (1956) the principal buildings for the city of Brasilia, the new capital of Brazil. He was awarded the Lenin Peace Prize in 1963.

Niemöller, Martin (1892–1984). German Lutheran pastor. After being a submarine commander in World War I he was ordained in 1924. He at first supported but later actively opposed the Nazi régime and was held in a concentration camp from 1937 until the end of

World War II. He was president of the World Council of Churches (1961–68).
Schmidt, D., *Pastor Niemöller*. 1959

Nietzsche, Friedrich Wilhelm (1844–1900). German philosopher. He was the son of a pastor, studied classical philology at Bonn and Leipzig and showed such ability that in 1869 – even before graduation – he was appointed to a professorship at Basle University. He served in the Franco-Prussian War (1870) and contracted a disease which kept him in pain for much of his life and led to insanity in the last eleven years. His earliest work, *The Birth of Tragedy* . . . (1871), was dedicated to Wagner whose operas he clearly regarded as being in the line of descent from Greek dramas. The influence of Wagner again and of Schopenhauer is apparent and acknowledged in a group of essays published 1873–76, in one of which he enunciates the principle, elaborated in his later work, that it is not the movements of masses which are historically significant but the deeds of the great. Here in fact is the genesis of the superman. He admired 'paganism' and the Renaissance and considered Christianity to be 'slave morality' and democracy ('a mania for counting noses'), the machinery by which quantity (i.e. of the weak and the mediocre) is made to prevail over quality.

Following this line of thought he developed the idea of the superman 'beyond good and evil' – and yet with virtues of his own, courage, self-reliance, pride in his strength and superiority, an enthusiastic or defiant acceptance of everything, good fortune or ill, that life has to offer. Such are the themes presented in *Thus Spake Zarathustra* (1883–85), his major work, in which his thoughts are attuned to the rhythms of an eastern prophet, and in *Beyond Good and Evil* (1886) and *Towards a Genealogy of Morals* (1887). Although some of his ideas were adapted and adopted by the Nazis, Nietzsche despised nationalism and racialism alike. In summarizing the last 2,000 years of history as a conflict between Rome and Judaea he was using these nations primarily as symbols for his two contrasting types, the hero and the weakling slave. None the less the works of Nietzsche have provided justificatory texts for nationalists and socialists in many countries.
Hollingdale, R. J., *Neitzsche: The Man and His Philosophy*. 1965

Nightingale, Florence (1820–1910). English nurse. She was the daughter of a wealthy Hampshire landowner, and was named after the Italian city where she was born. Moved by a sense of vocation, she gradually wore down parental opposition to her taking up nursing; she visited and compared many hospitals at home and abroad and gained some nursing experience with the deaconesses of Kaiserswerth in Germany (1851–52) and training with nursing sisters in a convent in Paris. In 1853 she became superintendent of the London Hospital for Invalid Gentlewomen. On the outbreak of the Crimean War (1854) she agreed to take thirty-eight nurses to Constantinople and run the military hospital at Scutari. She was involved in a continuous battle against officialdom, medical jealousy, incompetence and inertia, but at last she managed to overcome the chaos and introduce cleanliness and sanitation, organize the provision of food as well as maintain the standards of nursing. She used her own money and influence unsparingly and at last the appalling death-rate began to shrink to comparatively negligible proportions. A similar task was attempted at the hospitals at Balaclava in the Crimea. The troops idolized her and as news of her work reached England she became an almost legendary heroine as 'the Lady of the Lamp'. She returned in 1856 and with £50,000 raised by public subscription she founded (1861) a nurses' training school at St Thomas's Hospital. A uniform for nurses and competitive examinations were among her other reforms which gave the nursing profession an entirely new status. She was an invalid 1858–80, but had a new burst of energy until 1896. Among the many other tasks to which she devoted herself were reform of the conditions under which soldiers lived in India, and this led her on to the much vaster problems of India itself. She gave much time in later life to religious study. From 1896 ill health confined her to her room, and very gradually her faculties began to fail. In 1907 she became the first woman to be awarded OM.
Woodham-Smith, C., *Florence Nightingale*. 1969

Nijinsky, Vaclav (1890–1950). Russian ballet dancer and choreographer. Trained at the Imperial school at St Petersburg (Leningrad) he was the leading dancer in Diaghilev's

Ballets Russes in Paris (1909), where he enjoyed enormous popularity, especially in *Le Spectre de la rose (1911)*. Later he created the leading roles in *Petrushka, Scheherazade* etc. His work as a choreographer, e.g. for Debussy's *L'Après-midi d'un faune* (1912), provoked both controversy and scandal. His health was undermined by a period of internment in Hungary during World War I and from 1917 he was insane. He is remembered as one of the greatest male dancers of all time and especially for the agility, lightness and grace of his prodigious leaps. Moreover his technical skill was matched by his interpretative powers and dramatic sense. His sister, **Bronislava Nijinska** (1891–), made a name for herself as a choreographer with such works as *Les Noces* (1923), *Les Biches* (1924) and *Le Train bleu* (1924).
Buckle, R., *Nijinsky*. 1971

Nimitz, Chester William (1885–1966). American sailor. Before and during World War I he served mainly in submarines. Between the wars he held a variety of operational and staff appointments and at the outbreak of World War II was the admiral at the head of the Bureau of Navigation of the Pacific fleet. As a result, when Japan attacked Pearl Harbor and entered the war (1941), it fell to him to organize and direct the Pacific counter-attack. The vast American and smaller Allied fleets which he successfully operated and supplied gave him a task greater than any previous commanders had faced. In 1949 he went as United Nations mediator to Kashmir.

Ninian, St (*c.* 360–432). First Scottish evangelizer. While on a pilgrimage to Rome he was consecrated bishop (*c.* 395) and, having visited St Martin at Tours on the way back, named after him the church of Whithorn in Galloway, which he founded. He succeeded in making many converts among the southern Picts.

Nithsdale, Winifred, Countess of (died 1749). Scottish heroine. During the Jacobite rebellion of 1715 her husband, the 5th Earl, was captured at Preston and subsequently condemned to death. On the eve of his execution she smuggled him, dressed as a woman, out of the Tower of London and enabled him to reach the continent, where she afterwards joined him.

Nivelle, Robert Georges (1858–1924). French general. He succeeded * Joffre as commander-in-chief of the French army in December 1916 and was dismissed in May 1917 when his major offensive failed to break through German lines.

Nixon, Richard Milhous (1913–). 37th President of the US (1969–74). Briefly a lawyer, he served in the US Navy in World War II and then entered politics. As a Republican Congressman (1947–51) he gained prominence for his zeal on the notorious House Committee on Un-American Activities, and especially in his pursuit of Alger * Hiss. Elected as a Senator from California 1951–53, he served as Eisenhower's vice president 1953–61, playing an active role (unusual in the holders of that office), and travelled widely, e.g. to Russia in 1959. He won the Republican nomination to succeed Eisenhower in 1960 but lost narrowly to John F. * Kennedy, partly due to a series of television debates which appeared to put him at a disadvantage. He lost a contest for governor of California in 1962, moved to New York as a lawyer, and did not seek presidential nomination in 1964. In 1968, with Democrats in disarray over Vietnam, he defeated Hubert * Humphrey narrowly and was president 1969–74. He visited China in 1972 (to the discomfort of his traditional supporters), began to ease the US out of Vietnam and attempted detente with the Soviet leadership. He won a landslide victory in 1972 over George * McGovern. However, his excessive anxiety about another possible close result led to connivance in illegal acts by his staff, notably an attempt to burglarise Democratic headquarters at the Watergate Hotel. This led to indictment for conspiracy of his seven close associates and a strenuous attempt to cover up the scandal. A grand jury found Nixon was an 'un-indicted co-conspirator' and a House Committee recommended impeachment. Nixon became the first US president to resign (August 1974) and Gerald * Ford succeeded him. He published his *Memoirs* in 1978.
Evans, R. and Novak, R. D., *Nixon in the White House*. 1971

Nkrumah, Kwame (1909–1972). Ghanaian politician. He was educated at Achimota College and from 1935 studied theology and philosophy in the U.S.A.; in 1945 he attended the London School of Economics. Two years

after his return to the Gold Coast (1947) he founded the Convention People's party and spent two years in prison (1949–51) for political agitation. In 1951 he was appointed first prime minister of the Gold Coast (Ghana from 1957) and became the first president of the republic in 1960. He established authoritarian rule in a single-party state, and increasing vanity led him to self-glorification (e.g. he took the title of Redeemer) and to extravagant projects which had all but ruined the country's economy when during his absence in Moscow, he was deposed by a military *coup* (1966). His ambitious plan to unite the emergent African states in a federation under his leadership met with constant rebuffs.
Bretton, H. L., *The Rise and Fall of Kwame Nkrumah*. 1967

Nobel, Alfred Bernhard (1833–1896). Swedish chemist. His main interest, the development of explosives, was inspired by his father, a manufacturer of explosives at St Petersburg (Leningrad), where he was brought up. From 1859 he studied the subject in Stockholm; and while seeking an effective means of making nitroglycerine safe to handle he invented (1867) dynamite, in which the introglycerine was dispersed in an earthy material called Kieselguhr. He left most of the large fortune he had made from the manufacture of explosives (about £2,000,000) for the establishment of five prizes to be awarded annually for literature, medicine (or physiology), physics, chemistry and the promotion of peace. The first Nobel Prizes were awarded in 1901.
Bergengren, E., *Alfred Nobel: The Man and His Work*. 1962; *Nobel the Man and His Prizes*. 1972

Nobile, Umberto (1885–1978). Italian airman and explorer. Having risen to the rank of general, he took the airship *Norge* (with * Amundsen) across the North Pole (1926). He was severely censured for the crash (1928) of his airship *Italia* from which he was rescued after forty days on the ice, but cleared in 1945. Meanwhile he had served as an aeronautical consultant in the USSR and USA, returning to Italy after Mussolini's fall.

Noel-Baker, Philip John, Baron Noel-Baker (1889–1982). British Labour politician and peace advocate. Educated at Cambridge, he was an athlete in the 1912 and 1920 Olympic Games. A professor of international relations at London University, 1924–29, he became a Labour MP 1929–31 and 1936–70, and served as a minister under Attlee 1945–51. He won the 1959 Nobel Peace Prize for his book *The Arms Race* (1958).

Nolan, Sir Sidney Robert (1917–). Australian painter, born in Melbourne. Many of his paintings develop themes from Australian history e.g. the series on Ned * Kelly, the explorers * Burke and Wills, and Gallipoli, as well as flora, fauna, China, Africa, and scenic designs for ballet and opera. He received the OM in 1983.

Nollekens, Joseph (1737–1823). English sculptor of Dutch extraction. He worked (1760–70) in Rome, where he did busts of Garrick and Steine; on his return to London he quickly achieved success and became A.R.A. (1771) and R.A. (1772). Though he was commissioned to do many public monuments, often adorned with mythological groups, his busts (e.g. of George III, Dr Johnson, Fox and Pitt) are his most significant achievement.

Nollet, Jean Antoine (1700–1770). French abbé and physicist. Professor of physics in the University of Paris, he was the first clearly to describe (1748) osmosis (the passage of a solvent through a semi-permeable membrane separating a weaker from a stronger solution).

Norman, Montagu Collet Norman, 1st Baron (1871–1950). British banker. His policies as governor of the Bank of England (1920–44) during the inter-war period and the most vital years of World War II have been the subject of continuous controversy, especially the deflationary return to the gold standard (1925) and the devaluation of the pound (1931). Norman had much influence with the governments of the period; his reputation as an *éminence grise* was enhanced by his habit of crossing the Atlantic under the easily penetrable disguise of an assumed name.
Clay, H., *Lord Norman*. 1957

Norodom Sihanouk (1922–). Cambodian prince. He succeeded his grandfather as king of Cambodia 1941–55, abdicating in favour of his parents to enter party politics. He founded the Popular Socialist Community Party in 1955 and was premier 1955–60 and chief of state 1960–70 until deposed by military *coup*. He lived in Beijing 1970–75 until restored briefly as chief of state, lacking real power. He wrote and directed his own films and composed.

Norstad, Lauris (1907–). American soldier and airman. He became a pilot in 1931 and in World War II was appointed (December 1943) director of operations of the Allied air forces in the Mediterranean. He also directed bombing offensives against Japan. In 1950 General Norstad became commander-in-chief of US air forces in Europe, and succeeded General Gruenther as supreme Allied commander in Europe (1956–62). He retired in 1963.

North, Frederick North, Lord (1732–1792). English politician. Known as Lord North until he succeeded (1790) his father as Earl of Guildford, he was able, idle and well liked and George III, who retained him as prime minister from 1770 to 1782, found him an excellent instrument through whom, while maintaining a parliamentary majority by royal patronage, he could exercise his influence over the government. Most of his term of office was occupied by the American colonies' struggle for independence: North's attempts at conciliation were constantly thwarted by royal obduracy. He remained in office only out of loyalty and gladly resigned in 1782; he returned briefly (1783) in coalition with Fox. Important legislation passed during his term of office included the Royal Marriage Act, an act submitting the East India Company's policies to parliamentary control, and the Quebec Act (1774), which guaranteed to French Canadians their traditional religion and laws.
Butterfield, H., *George III, Lord North and the People*. 1949

North, Sir Thomas (1535?–1602). English translator. His fame rests on his English version (1579) of Plutarch's *Lives*, translated not from the original Greek but from the French rendering (1559) by Jacques Amyot, bishop of Auxerre, whom North may have met when accompanying a diplomatic mission to Henry III of France. Shakespeare borrowed freely from it for his classical dramas, sometimes using the actual words as well as reconstructing the scenes.

Northcliffe, Alfred Charles William Harmsworth, 1st Viscount (1865–1922). British journalist and newspaper proprietor. He began his journalistic career (1880) on the *Hampstead and Highgate Gazette*; the step which led to his future greatness was the launching (1888), with his brother Harold * Harmsworth, of *Answers*, a weekly magazine in which snippets of information and competitions with lavish prizes procured a success which enabled them to buy (1894) the London *Evening News*. Two years later they launched the *Daily Mail*, which sold at 1d, and with its bold headlines and brightly written features provided a quickly copied pattern for popular newspapers. In 1908 he acquired control of *The Times*, but though he greatly increased its circulation and even at one time reduced the price to 1d., his touch was never of the surest when handling what was in effect a national institution. In World War I his papers helped to expose the shell shortage and attacked Haldane, Asquith and Kitchener with a venom which paid no attention to fairness. He headed a war mission to the USA (1917) and in 1918 was director of propaganda in enemy countries. Progressive illness produced signs of megalomania in his last years. He was made a baronet in 1903, became Baron Northcliffe in 1905, and a viscount in 1917.
Greewall, H. J., *Northcliffe: Napoleon of Fleet Street*. 1957

Northumberland, John Dudley, 1st Duke of (1502–1553). Lord protector of England (1552–53). He was the son of Edmund * Dudley, Henry VII's minister, grew to importance under Henry VIII and was an executor of his will. He was made Earl of Warwick in recognition of his support of Edward Seymour, Duke of * Somerset, as lord protector during Edward VI's minority but at once intrigued against him. He succeeded him (1552) and secured his execution. He tried to prolong his power by inducing the sickly Edward to exclude his sisters from the succession, and so leave the way clear for Lady Jane * Grey (whom he married to his son Guildford Dudley) to ascend the throne. The scheme failed when on Edward's death (1553) the country rallied to Queen Mary. Northumberland was taken and executed. For his son Robert, Elizabeth's favourite, *see* Earl of * Leicester.

Nostradamus (Michel de Nôtre Dame) (1503–1566). French astrologer and physician of

Jewish descent, born in Provence. With university qualifications in medicine, he gained much esteem for his devotion to duty during times of plague. In 1555 appeared his collection of rhymed prophecies called *Centuries* because of their arrangement in 100-year periods. A second edition covering ten centuries instead of seven was published in 1558. The fame of these enigmatic predictions was so great that Catherine de'Medici invited him to court and he became physician to Charles IX.

Novalis (Baron Friedrich von Hardenberg) (1772–1801). German lyric poet and novelist. His poetic works include *Hymns to the Night* (1800), inspired by his grief at the death of Sophie von Kuhn, with whom he was in love. His novel *Heinrich van Ofterdingen* (1802), the story of the development of a young poet, ranks high among the achievements of the German Romantic movement.

Novello, Ivor (Ivor Novello Davies) (1893–1951). Welsh actor and composer. Son of Clara Novello Davies, a well-known singer and teacher of singing, he achieved early success during World War I with his song *Keep the Home Fires Burning*. Later he acted in and wrote sophisticated comedies but his greatest triumphs, as actor and as composer, were achieved with romantic musical plays, e.g. *Glamorous Night* (1935), *The Dancing Years* (1939) and *King's Rhapsody* (1949).
Noble, P., *Ivor Novello*. 1951

Noverre, Jean Georges (1727–1809). French choreographer. In 1747 he became *maître de ballet* at the Opéra Comique in Paris and in 1754 gained fame as a choreographer with *Fêtes chinoises* and *La Fontaine de Jouvence* for which * Boucher did the décor. The outbreak of the Seven Years War (1756) interrupted a London season which he had undertaken for * Garrick, who called him 'the Shakespeare of the dance'. His *Lettres sur la danse et sur les ballets* (1759–60) established an aesthetic tradition which still influences choreography.

Noyes, Alfred (1880–1958). English poet. His poetry is firmly traditional in manner, but in his most ambitious work *The Torchbearers* (3 volumes, 1922–30), which tells of those who carried the light of scientific knowledge through the centuries, he strikes an original theme. He was a professor of literature at Princeton, U.S.A. (1914–23).

Nuffield, William Richard Morris, 1st Viscount (1877–1963). English manufacturer and philanthropist. Originally owner of a bicycle shop in Oxford, he started (1912), in an improvised works at Cowley just outside the city, to build motor cycles and then the first Morris Oxford and Morris Cowley cars. World War I intervened, but his 1925 output of 53,000 cars achieved a European record. A series of mergers (with Wolseley, Riley etc.), culminating with amalgamation (1952) with the Austin Motor Company, led to the formation of the vast British Motor Corporation under Nuffield's presidency. He was equally well known as a philanthropist, especially for the foundation of Nuffield College, Oxford (1937), and the Nuffield Foundation (1943), a charitable trust endowed with stock in Morris Motors Ltd valued at £10,000,000. Morris, who received a peerage (1934) and became a viscount (1938), was an unassuming man who led an unpublicized and unostentatious life.
Andrews, P. W. and Brunner, E., *Life of Lord Nuffield*. 1955

Nureyev, Rudolf (1939–). Russian ballet dancer. Having risen to become a leading dancer of the Russian Kirov ballet he defected while the company was in Paris (May 1961) and later came to England. There he won new fame in the Royal Ballet, especially when partnered by Margot * Fonteyn in e.g. *Le Corsair, Marguérite and Armand, Giselle* and *Swan Lake*. Of some ballets (e.g. *Raymonda*) he revised the choreography to satisfy the demands of his technical skill and the agility and strength which won him great acclaim. In 1977 he took the leading role in the film *Valentino*.

Nuri es-Said (1888–1958). Iraqi soldier, born in Baghdad. He served in the Ottoman army against the British, was captured in 1916, then joined the Sharifian army revolt against the Turks. On Iraq's creation in 1921, Nuri became a comitted supporter of the Hashemite regime of * Faisal I and a permanent alliance with Britain. Between 1930 and 1958 he served as prime minister of Iraq fourteen times and became first prime minister of the Arab Federation (Iraq and Jordan) May–July 1958. His pro-western views were increasingly unpopular with Iraqis and he was murdered with * Faisal II.

Nurmi, Paavo (1897–1973). Athlete known from his nationality as 'the flying Finn'. After winning the 10,000-metres race in the 1920 Olympics he was the dominant figure in long-distance running for the next ten years and for a time held world records at distances from 1,500 metres to 10,000 metres and the cross country events.

Nyerere, Julius Kambarage (1921–). Tanzanian politician. The son of a chief, he studied at Makerere College in Uganda and at Edinburgh University. In 1954 he founded the Tanganyika African National Union with a policy aimed at independence. In his successful pursuit of this aim he was successively chief minister (1960) of Tanganyika, prime minister when independence was granted (1961), and president (1962) when a republic was proclaimed. When Zanzibar, after the revolution of 1964, became linked with Tanganyika, Nyerere became president of the combined country, known thereafter as Tanzania. His publications include a Swahili translation of *The Merchant of Venice* (1969).

O

Oates, Lawrence Edward Grace (1880–1912). English soldier and exlorer. He joined * Scott's Antarctic expedition in 1910; during the arduous return from the South Pole in 1912 he became convinced that with his frostbite injuries he would handicap his companions and lessen their chances of survival. He accordingly left camp and walked to his death in the bizzard.
Bernacchi, L. A., *A Very Gallant Gentleman*. 1933

Oates, Titus (*c.* 1649–1705). English conspirator. After being dismissed as a naval chaplain, he claimed to have spent some time in the guise of a convert in Jesuit seminaries abroad in order to discover their secrets. In 1678 he reappeared in London and made a declaration on oath before Sir Edmund Berry Godfrey concerning an alleged 'Popish plot' for the murder of Charles II and the massacre of Protestants. When Sir Edmund was found dead in a ditch (possibly murdered by Oates or his followers) the story of the plot, hitherto ridiculed, seemed to acquire some plausibility. Mass hysteria, fanned by * Shaftesbury for political reasons, followed; Oates poured forth his denunciations and some thirty-five Roman Catholics were executed for treason. Meanwhile the king was manipulating opinion in favour of sanity. A reaction set in and in 1685 Oates was found guilty of perjury and imprisoned for life. The revolution which expelled James II brought him release and a pension, but he died destitute.
Lane, J., *Titus Oates*. 1949

Obregón, Alvaro (1880–1928). President of Mexico (1920–24 and 1928). He joined forces with * Carranza and * Villa against * Huerta, but when the two fell out he supported Carranza and by his military skill overcame Villa. Obregón temporarily retired but, after the revolution in which Carranza was murdered while in flight, became president. He achieved valuable reforms on behalf of organized labour and assisted education. By arrangement with his successor Calles he was again candidate in 1928 but was assassinated shortly after re-election.

Obreonović. Serbian dynasty in hereditary feud with the Karageorgević line. The feud started when **Milos** (1761–1860), a guerrilla leader, allegedly murdered (1817) Kara George, under whom he served. His son **Michael**, prince of Serbia, was murdered by a member of the Karageorgević clan (1868). The latter's adopted son **Milan** proclaimed himself king of Serbia (1882) but abdicated (1889) as a result of domestic scandals. His son **Alexander** succeeded, but, with his notorious wife, Draga, was murdered by a group of officers (1903); Peter Karageorgević, the father and grandfather of the future Yugoslav kings, succeeded.

O'Brien, Flann (Brian O'Nolan) (1911–1966). Irish novelist. He was a civil servant and wrote a weekly satirical column in the *Irish Times* under the name Myles na Gopaleen. His masterpiece *At Swim-Two-Birds* failed on its first publication in September 1939, although praised by James Joyce, and was recognized as a work of genius only in the 1960s. Other works include *The Third Policeman* (1940), *The Hard Life* (1960) and *The Dalkey Archive* (1965).

O'Casey, Sean (1884–1964). Irish playwright, born in Dublin and educated, so he said,

in its streets. After working as a labourer he became active in politics and literature. His first plays, produced at the Abbey Theatre, Dublin, were *The Shadow of a Gunman* (1923), *Juno and the Paycock* (1924) and *The Plough and the Stars* (1926). Their harsh realism contrasted strongly with the mythological drama of Yeats; their language was often poetic, but this stemmed mainly from effective use of the Dublin vernacular. His next play, *The Silver Tassie*, rejected by the Abbey, was produced in London (1929). Thereafter, O'Casey was a voluntary exile from Ireland and criticized the oppressiveness of Irish life in some of his later plays, e.g. *Red Roses for Me* (1943), *Cock-a-Doodle Dandy* (1949), *The Bishop's Bonfire* (1955) and *The Drums of Father Ned* (1958). His six volumes of autobiography, beginning with *I Knock at the Door* (1939), contain many vivid and acid descriptions of his life and times.
Fallon, G., *Sean O'Casey*. 1965

Occam (Ockham or Ocham), **William of** (*c.* 1290–?1349). English philosopher, probably born at Ockham in Surrey. He early joined the Franciscans and studied at Oxford. Summoned to Avignon by Pope John XXII on a charge of heresy (1326), he was confined to a friary until 1328 when, after siding against the pope in a Franciscan dispute concerning poverty, he fled to live under the protection of the emperor Louis IV at Pisa and Munich, where he wrote vigorously in support of the emperor's political supremacy and in opposition to the pope's claim to authority in temporal affairs. He sought reconciliation with the church in 1349. Occam's political writings were only part of his general attack on the medieval scholastic system and the secular order it sustained; his system (known as nominalism), which included a denial that universals exist outside the mind, led to a philosophic scepticism which in some measure provided an intellectual preparation for the Reformation. 'Occam's razor' is the principle that in explaining anything 'entities are not to be multiplied without necessity' (i.e. the simplest possible explanation is always to be preferred). He was known variously as 'Venerabilis Inceptor' and 'Doctor Invincipilis'.
Duncan, D., *Occam's Razor*. 1958

Occleve (or Hoccleve). **Thoman** (*c.* 1370–*c.* 1450). English poet. He wrote in the Chaucerian tradition but his main work *De Regimine Principum*, an English version (addressed to the future Henry V) of a Latin treatise on the duties of a ruler, is less interesting for the advice given than for irrelevant insertions about Occleve's own troubles. More autobiography, often unflattering, is contained in *La Male Règle* (1406).

Ockham (or Ocham) *see* **Occam, William of**

O'Connell, Daniel (1775–1847). Irish patriot. He was born in County Kerry, was educated in Catholic institutions abroad and was called to the Irish bar (1798). He later started an agitation in favour of the repeal of the Act of Union with England, demanding complete Roman Catholic emancipation. By his energy, organizing ability and his emotional oratory he roused the country and transformed the conservative Catholic Association into a mass movement (1823). Its success caused its suppression (1825); but O'Connell, elected M.P. for Clare (1828), continued his agitation and Roman Catholic emancipation was obtained (1829). After 1832 he headed a group of forty-five Irish M.P.s in the English parliament; he launched (1840) a new mass movement for the repeal of the Act of Union. This involved him in a trial for sedition (1844); his sentence was quashed by the House of Lords but his refusal to adopt revolutionary methods and his conservative attitude to social questions militated against his success. He died in Genoa.
Gwynn, D., *Daniel O'Connell*. 1930

O'Connor, Feargus Edward (1794–1855). Irish Chartist leader. He became an M.P. (1833) as a follower of * O'Connell but quarrelled with his leader over his attitude to social conditions; he denounced the new Poor Law and the factory system and was obliged to resign. He was the principal leader of the Chartist movement (whose six demands included universal suffrage and voting by ballot); having been re-elected to parliament in 1837, he presented the Chartist 'monster petition' to parliament (1848). The subsequent collapse of the movement unbalanced his mind and in 1852 he became insane.

O'Connor, Thomas Power (1848–1929). Irish journalist and radical politician. After working on the London *Daily Telegraph* and other papers, he was elected M.P. for Galway in 1880 and from 85 represented the Scotland division of Liverpool, eventually becoming the 'father of the House'. He founded (1887) the London evening *Star* and among his other journalistic enterprises was *T.P.'s Weekly* (from 1902).

Octavian(us) *see* **Augustus**

Odets, Clifford (1906–1963). American playwright. Originally an actor, he wrote several socio-political dramas, e.g. *Waiting for Lefty* (1935), *Awake and Sing* (1935) and, probably his best-known play, *The Golden Boy* (1937). Much of his work was produced by the Group Theatre, New York, of which he was a founder.

Odo (*c.* 1036–1097). Bishop of Bayeux (from 1048). He ruled England as regent during the absence of his half-brother, William the Conqueror. He lost all his English possessions for joining a revolt against William II and died at Palermo on the way to the 1st Crusade. He was a patron of scholarship.

Odovacar (or Odoacer) (died 493). Germanic chieftain. After the abdication of Romulus Augustulus, last of the Roman emperors of the west, was proclaimed king of Italy by his troops (476). After four years he gained full control of Italy and later proved his ability to defend and extend the area he had won. Alarmed by his growing power, the Byzantine emperor Zeno encouraged Theodoric, king of the Ostrogoths, to invade Italy (488). After three defeats (489–490) Odovacar retired to Ravenna, where he was besieged until he was forced by famine to yield (493). Shortly afterwards, it is said, he was stabbed to death by Theodoric at a feast.

Oersted, Hans Christian (1777–1851). Danish physicist. Professor of physics at the University of Copenhagen (1806–29) and director of the Polytechnic Institute, Copenhagen (1829–51), he discovered (1820) the magnetic field created by an electric current, showing for the first time that electricity and magnetism are connected. The unit of magnetic field strength, the oersted, is named after him.

Offa (died 796). King of Mercia (from 757), one of the greatest Anglo-Saxon kings. By conquest or marriage ties he controlled all England south of the Humber and protected his subjects from Welsh raiders by the mighty earthwork known as Offa's Dyke, which stretched from the estuary of the Dee to that of the Wye. He was a patron of monasticism and a lawmaker.

Offenbach, Jacques (Jakob Levy Eberst) (1819–1880). German–Jewish composer. He was born in Cologne and lived in Paris from 1833. He wrote many successful operettas and *opéras bouffes*, e.g. *Orpheus in the Underworld* (1858) and *La Belle Hélène* (1865). The opera on which he worked for many years, *The Tales of Hoffmann*, was produced posthumously (1881).
Brindejontbach, J., *Offenbach mon grand-père*. 1940.

Ogden, Charles Kay (1889–1957). English educationist. With I. A. Richards of Harvard University, he made the researches necessary for the production of 'Basic English', a simplified form of the language by which most ordinary concepts could be expressed with a vocabulary of some 850 key words and a minimum of verbs.

Oglethorpe, James Edward (1696–1785). English soldier, colonist, philanthropist and founder of Georgia, USA. After service with Prince * Eugène of Savoy against the Turks (1717), he returned to England where as an M.P. (1722–54) he roused public opinion against the press gang, prison conditions and imprisonment for debt. He obtained a charter to found the colony of Georgia, which he peopled mainly with English debtors and refugee Austrian Protestants. He himself accompanied the first contingent (1733) and raised a regiment with which he successfully defended the colony against the Spaniards. In 1743 he returned to England to answer charges of incompetence and was later court-martialled for his conduct of operations in the Jacobite rebellion (1745). Both times he was acquitted, but his military career was ended and in 1754 he was not re-elected to parliament. Among the many friends of this colourful general were Johnson, Boswell and Burke.

O'Higgins, Bernardo (1776–1842).Chilean liberator. His father Ambrosio rose in the Spanish service in South America to be governor of Chile. Bernardo went to England at the age of 15 and joined a group of men plotting to free South America from Spanish rule. He returned to Chile (1802) and after playing a prominent part in the revolution of 1810–11 became commander-in-chief of the Chilean forces. After military setbacks he fled to join * San Martin, who gave him a command in the army about to cross the Andes to liberate Chile. When he returned with the victorious army O'Higgins was appointed (1817) director of Chile, proclaiming its independence in 1818; but his rule proved so unpopular that he was forced to resign and retire to Peru (1823). Kinsbruner, J., *Bernardo O'Higgins*. 1968

Ohm, Georg Simon (1787–1854). German physicist. He did fundamental work on the mathematical treatment of electric currents and published (1827) the law stating that the current flowing in a conductor is directly proportional to the potential differences between its ends (Ohm's law). He also did important work on acoustics. The unit of electrical resistance, the ohm, is named after him. His most important work was done while he was a teacher at the Cologne Gymnasium. Later he was a professor of physics at Nuremberg (1833–49) and Munich (1849–54).

Oistrakh, David (Fyodorovich) (1908–1974). Russian violinist. He was born in Odessa and graduated from Odessa Conservatory in 1926. He made his debut in Moscow in 1933, but for many years was known in western Europe only from recordings. He began extensive tours after 1951. His son **Igor Davidovich** (1931–) was also an outstanding player.

O'Kelly, Seán Thomas (1882–1966). Irish president. He was closely associated with Sinn Fein and other nationalist organizations and took part in the Easter Rising (1916). He opposed the Irish Free State and became prominent in de Valera's Fianna Fail party. When de Valera came to power (1932), O'Kelly was his deputy on the executive council. He served two terms as President of the Irish republic (1945–59).

Olaf II (St Olaf) (995–1030). King of Norway (1015–28). He propagated Christianity in his country but with such severity that he was forced to take refuge in Russia (1028). Returning (1030), he was defeated and killed in battle against King Cnut (Canute) of Denmark, thus becoming the symbol of Norwegian resistance to Danish domination. He became the hero of legend and saga and came to be considered patron saint of Norway. He is commemorated in England by several churches (St Olave's) and Tooley Street, London (a corruption of his name).

Olaf V (1903–). King of Norway (since 1957), son and successor of Haakon VII. Through his mother, originally Princess Maud, daughter of Edward VII, he is closely connected with the British royal family. His son **Prince Harald** (1937–) is heir presumptive to the throne.

Oldcastle, Sir John (*c.* 1377–1417). English Lollard. He took the title of Lord Cobham through his third wife. He was condemned as a heretic (1413) but escaped from prison and led a Lollard rising (1414). After its failure he remained in hiding for three years but was recaptured and exected. He is sometimes thought to have been the original of Shakespeare's Sir John Falstaff: the character was, indeed, originally called 'Oldcastle' but the name was changed on the objection of the Lord Cobham of the day; it is also true that the real Oldcastle was a friend of Henry V when he was Prince of Wales. He was regarded as a martyr by Tudor protestant reformers and was extolled by Bale, Foxe and Weever.

Oldenbarnevelt, Johan van (1547–1619). Dutch statesman. Prominent in the estates (parliament) of Holland, he became a leading figure in the struggle for independence from Spain. After the death of William the Silent he offered the throne to the English Queen Elizabeth, effected the appointment of Prince Maurice of Orange as stadtholder of Holland and Zeeland, and as the most important member of the republican government did everything possible to support and finance the war. Alliances were made with England and France (1596) and eventually a twelve-year truce with Spain (1609). The religious conflict, however, between Remonstrants and Counter-remonstrants, brought about a breach between him and Maurice. Oldenbarnevelt was accused of corruption and treason and Maurice had him arrested, tried and executed.

Oldenburg, Henry (1618–1677). German scientist. One of the most important figures in seventeenth century scientific communications, he went to England in 1653, joined the

Royal Society in 1661 and soon became its secretary. He devoted the rest of his life to the administration of the Royal Society, and was one of the chief reasons for its early success. Oldenburg helped launch the *Philosophical Transactions* (1665), the first modern scientific journal, which published scientific findings, news, book reviews and correspondence. He was an ideal secretary for the Society, since he had a particularly extensive body of foreign contacts. There was evidently some danger in keeping up correspondence with enemy nations: he was temporarily put in the Tower in 1667 during the Anglo-Dutch War. Oldenburg made no scientific contributions of his own, but passionately supported the Baconian, empirical, utilitarian approach to science.

Oliphant, Sir Marcus Laurence Elwin (1901–). Australian physicist born in Adelaide. He studied under * Rutherford in Cambridge and became a professor in Birmingham and Canberra. He worked on development of the atomic bomb and his studies on hydrogen-isotope interactions contributed to the development of the hydrogen bomb. He was Governor of South Australia (1971–76). He was elected F.R.S. in 1937 and made K.B.E. in 1959.

Olivares, Gaspar de Guzmán, Count-Duke of (1587–1645). Spanish statesman. He entered the service of Philip IV of Spain (1615) and so completely dominated his master that he was chief minister and virtual ruler of the country from 1621 until 1643, when he was dismissed. During those years, wholly occupied by the Thirty Years War, Spain's hold on Holland was irretrievably lost, Portugal resumed its independence and in Catalonia there was a dangerous revolt.

Elliott, J. H., *The Revolt of the Catalans*. 1963

Olivier, Laurence Kerr, Baron Olivier (1907–). English actor. His professional skill matured under Sir Barry Jackson's management and with the Old Vic, but he only emerged into full stardom during the famous seasons (1944–47) of the Old Vic Company at the New Theatre, with Richard III and Lear among his most notable interpretations. He both produced and acted in the films *Henry V* (1944), *Hamlet* (1948) and *Richard III* (1956). His talent however, was seen to equal advantage in e.g. Sheridan and Chekhov, as well as in contemporary plays, e.g. Osborne's *The Entertainer* (1957) and Ionesco's *Rhinoceros* (1960). In 1962 he became first director of Chichester Festival Theatre and was appointed (1963) first director of the National Theatre, for which, pending the construction of new buildings, he arranged several seasons at the Old Vic. He married Vivien Leigh (1940) and Joan Plowright (1961), both well known actresses. Knighted in 1947, he was created a life peer in 1970 and given the OM in 1981.

Ollenhauer, Erich (1901–1963). German Socialist politician. He fled to Czechoslovakia when Hitler came to power in Germany, and was in England during World War II. He succeeded Schumacher as leader of the West German Social Democratic party (1952) and opposed * Adenauer's policy of joining the western alliance. He was superseded (1960) by Willy * Brandt.

Omar I (*c.* 581–644). Second caliph of Islam (from 634). He succeeded Abu-Bekr, and maintained the discipline and control of his armies as they advanced to the conquest of Syria, Mesopotamia (Iraq) and Egypt. He was the first caliph to be known as Commander of the Faithful. His descendant **Omar II**, ninth Omayyad caliph, who ruled (717–720) from Damascus, imposed the 'ordinances of Omar' by which restrictions (e.g. of dress) were placed upon Jews and Christians.

Omar Khayyám (*c.* 1050–1132). Persian poet and mathematician. Long famous in his own and adjacent countries, his *Rubáiyát* (i.e. 'quatrains') first became widely popular in the west in the English verse paraphrases of Edward * Fitzgerald, and were later translated more accurately into many languages. The *Rubáiyát* (Omar's exact part in which has been the subject of prolonged controversy) is a collection of epigrammatic verses recommending enjoyment of wine, poetry and love while professing a gentle scepticism about the future, whether expressed in human hopes or divine plans. His mathematical work produced improvements in algebra, the calendar and the compilation of astronomical tables.

Dashti, A., *In Search of Omar Khayyám*. 1971

O'Meara, Barry Edward (1786–1836). The Irish-born surgeon of H.M.S. *Bellerophon*, which conveyed Napoleon to St Helena. At the fallen emperor's request he stayed to attend him on the island and became his ardent partisan in his quarrels with Sir Hudson * Lowe. Having been sent home (1818) for this, he suggested that Napoleon's life was in danger in the governor's hands. He was dismissed and wrote *Napoleon in Exile* (1822), a sensational but one-sided account of the events.

Onassis, Aristotle Socrates (1906–1975). Greek millionaire and ship-owner, born in Smyrna. He bought his first ships in 1932 and gradually built up one of the largest independent fleets. He was one of the first owners to develop the 'super-tanker' for bulk liquid cargo. In 1968 he married, as his second wife, Jacqueline, the widow of President John * Kennedy.

O'Neill, Eugene Gladstone (1888–1953). American playwright. The son of James O'Neill, an actor, he worked, during an adventurous early life, as a gold prospector in Central America, an actor and a newspaper reporter. He joined (1915) the Provincetown Players and not only acted for them but wrote and produced a number of short plays. He won the Pulitzer Prize for his first full-length play, *Beyond the Horizon* (1920), and also for *Anna Christie* (1921), a realistic drama of the waterfront and the regenerating influence of the sea upon the heroine. *The Emperor Jones* (1920) shows how a Negro adventurer reverts from ruler to savage; the title of *The Hairy Ape* (1922) refers to a powerful stoker on a liner, whose vain attempt to overcome his handicaps provides the theme. *All God's Chillun got Wings* (1924) deals with the problem of a black-white liaison in which the white woman is of low mentality, with which the black tries to contend. The much discussed *Desire under the Elms* (1924), dealing with a father-son conflict, was followed by *The Great God Brown* (1926), in which masks were used to symbolize characters. In *Strange Interlude* (1928), which lasts five hours, O'Neill tried another experiment with the 'stream of consciousness' technique. *Mourning Becomes Electra* (1931) is an attempt to place the Oresteian trilogy in a modern context. From 1934 there was a gap until *The Icemen Cometh* (1946); the 'iceman' symbolizes death and the play handles the theme of the effect of the touch of death on a group of waterfront characters. The posthumously published *Long Day's Journey into Night* (1957) is mainly autobiographical. These plays are perhaps the most important of a long series which has caused O'Neill to be regarded, almost without question, as America's greatest dramatist. He won the Nobel Prize for Literature (1936).

Sheaffer, L., *O'Neill, Son and Playwright*. 1969

O'Neill, Hugh, 2nd Earl of Tyrone (*c.* 1550–1616). Last member of the great Irish O'Neill family to exercise independent rule. Grandson of the O'Neill who, having submitted to the English King Henry VIII, was created (1543) the 1st Earl, Hugh O'Neill had an English education; he remained on good terms with England until he had had his earldom recognized and made his position secure in Ireland, where he aspired to rule all Ulster. This aim brought him into conflict with Elizabeth I and after a long struggle (1593–1603) he was forced to submit, though allowed to retain his personal estates. Finding English supervision intolerable he left Ireland (1607), and travelled throughout Europe, finally settling in Rome from 1608 to his death. The O'Neills had ruled turbulently in Ireland, with constant quarrels between branches of their own line and rival families, e.g. the O'Donnells, ever since the days of **Niall of the Nine Hostages** (died 405), from whom they claimed descent.

Onnes, Heike Kamerlingh *see* **Kamerlingh Onnes, Heike**

Onsager, Lars (1903–1976). American chemist, born in Norway. He taught at Yale from 1935, developed the gas-diffraction method of separating U 235 from U 238 and won the 1968 Nobel Prize for Chemistry. His discovery of reciprocal relations in irreversable chemical processes has been called 'the Fourth Law of Thermodynamics' (* Nernst).

Oparin, Aleksandr Ivanovich (1894–). Russian biochemist. A professor at Moscow University (from 1929), he wrote *The Origin of Life on Earth* (1936) which proposed that the interaction of sunlight on a methane/ammonia atmosphere could have led to the development of amino acids and — ultimately — cellular life, a thesis later confirmed by S. L. * Miller.

Oppenheim, Edward Phillips (1866–1946). British author. He was one of the most prolific and popular novelists in the thriller and spy tradition, producing some 150 books.

Oppenheim, E. P., *The Pool of Memory*. 1941

Oppenheimer, Sir Ernest (1880–1957). South African businessman, born in Germany. He lived in South Africa from 1902, formed the Anglo American Corporation of South Africa, Ltd, in 1917 (with the backing of J. P. Morgan) and began to exploit the Witwatersrand goldfield. He formed Consolidated Diamond Mines of South West Africa, Ltd, in 1919. Through the success of this company he was able to gain control of De Beers, the predominant diamond company. He also mined Rhodesian copper through his Rhodesian Anglo American Corporation. He was mayor of Kimberley 1912–15, received a knighthood in 1921 and became a Unionist MP 1924–38. His son, **Harry Frederick Oppenheimer** (1908–), was a Unionist MP 1947–58, chairman of over 60 companies, a notable art collector and a racial liberal.

Oppenheimer, (James) Robert (1904–1967). American physicist. Professor of physics at the University of California (1936–47) and director of the Institute for Advanced Studies at Princeton (from 1947), he was an authority on nuclear disintegration, cosmic rays and relativity, and as director of the Los Alamos Laboratory (1943–45) led the team which constructed the first atomic bombs; he was adviser (1946–53) of the U.S. Atomic Energy Commission. A sensation was caused when (1953) secret information was withheld from him on the grounds of alleged past association with communists; he was subsequently cleared of any suspicion of disloyalty.

Orczy, Baroness Emmuska (1865–1947). English writer of Hungarian birth. She won immediate success when she turned her rejected novel *The Scarlet Pimpernel* (1905) into a play. Fred Terry as Sir Percy Blakeney, the heroic rescuer of French aristocrats doomed to the guillotine, and Julia Neilson, his real and stage wife, performed their roles for four years in London and then made it the mainstay of their provincial repertoire for the rest of their lives. In addition to this book and its sequels Baroness Orczy wrote other romances, some detective stories collected as *The Old Man in the Corner*, and an autobiography, *Links in the Chain of Life* (1947).

Oresme, Nicole (1320–1382). Norman-French philosopher. He seems to have been particularly interested in the notion of the universe operating as if by clockwork, and yet he made no break with the Aristotelian idea of intelligences being directly responsible for motion in nature. He pondered over the problem of the possibility of the plurality of worlds. He believed that science was against such a view, but stressed that God undoubtedly possessed the free will to have created such a state of affairs. Oresme denied the validity of astrological forces on both physical and theological grounds. Some of his most prescient thinking in physics relates to his studies of falling bodies. His emphasis that acceleration depends upon time of fall, rather than distance fallen, contains an idea to be developed later by * Galileo.

Clagett, M., *The science of mechanics in the Middle Ages*. 1959

Orff, Carl (1895–1982). German composer, born in Munich. Reacting against the complexity of much 20th-century music he developed a style with direct appeal and a prevalence of strongly marked rhythms. The scenic cantata *Carmina Burana* (1937), a series of medieval Latin and German verses set for soloists and chorus with accompaniments of dancing and mime, was designed for stage performance like its inferior successor *Catulli Carmina* (1943). Among his other works are the operas *Die Kluge* (1942), *Antigone* (1949) and incidental music to *A Midsummer Night's Dream* (1939).

Orford, Robert Walpole, 1st Earl of *see* **Walpole, Sir Robert**

Origen (Origenes Adamantius) (*c.* 185–*c.* 253) Christian theologian and biblical scholar, born at Alexandria. He accepted the orthodox Christian doctrines as revealed in the Bible but held it to be the right and the duty of individual Christians to seek for themselves answers to unanswered questions (e.g. the nature of the soul) in philosophical writings, even those of pagans on the ground that there were 'Christians before Christ'. As his reputation grew, his Alexandrian friends and followers encouraged him to publish his views and he wrote *De Principiis* (*On First Principles*) one of the most influential books of early Christian philosophy. He was ordained in Palestine (230) but Demetrius, his bishop, regarded such ordination as irregular and exiled him. He settled at Caesarea, and there produced his *Hexapla*, a revised version of the Septuagint (the Greek text of the Old

Testament) and other versions and the Hebrew original set out in parallel columns. During the persecutions of the emperor Decius Origen was imprisoned and tortured, which led to his death. The official ecclesiastical view continued to be hostile to Origen; * Justinian condemned the study of his voluminous works with the result that the greater part is lost.
Daniélou, J., *Origen*. 1955

Orlando, Vittorio Emmanuele (1860–1952). Italian politician. First elected to the Chamber of Deputies in 1897, he held ministerial offices and in the last years of World War I was prime minister (1917–19). As Italy's chief representative at the Paris Peace Conference (1919) he was one of the 'Big Four' and had frequent clashes with President Wilson in his attempt (largely successful) to obtain implementation of the secret Treaty of London, by which Italy had been induced to enter the war on the side of the Allies.

Orléans, Philippe, Duke of (1674–1723). Regent of France for Louis XV. A nephew of Louis XIV, he set aside (1715) the late king's will and made himself sole regent, an act which encouraged suspicions that the numerous recent deaths in the royal family were caused by poison on his orders. Such suspicions (based on his dissolute character, rather than on evidence) were almost certainly unfounded. Orléans, guided by his old tutor, Abbé Dubois, shrewd and energetic but as dissolute as his master and entirely corrupt, made a special effort to put the finances in order; but an inquisition, extending back over more than twenty years to discover any moneys that might be owed to the state by tax-gatherers and others, was abandoned because of its unpopularity; nor was his involvement with the banker John * Law much more fortunate. He completely reversed Louis XIV's foreign policy by allying France with its former enemies, England, Holland and Austria, against his dynastic rival Philip V of Spain. He retired when Louis XV came of age.

His grandson **Louis Philippe Joseph, Duke of Orléans** (1747–1793) was an atheist and equally debauched. Perhaps hoping for the crown, he espoused the Revolutionary cause, adopted the nickname 'Philippe Egalité' and voted for Louis XVI's death. This did not save him, however, and he was condemned and executed. His son became * Louis Philippe, King of the French. The present French 'pretender' belongs to the Orléanist line.

Orlov, Gregory Grigoryevich (1734–1783). Russian noble. He was prominent in the revolution which replaced * Peter III by his wife, * Catherine II (Catherine the Great). He was already Catherine's lover and even when he ceased to be so remained her principal adviser.

Ormandy, Eugene (1899–1985). American conductor, born in Hungary. A juvenile prodigy as violinist, he lived in the US from 1921, became conductor of the Minneapolis Orchestra 1931–36 and succeeded Leopold * Stokowski at the Philadelphia Orchestra 1936–80.

Orsay, Alfred Guillaume Gabriel de Grimaud, Comte d' (1801–1852). French dandy. Son of a general, he resigned from Louis XVIII's bodyguard (1822) to attach himself to Lord and Lady Blessington, whom he had met in England and who were touring Europe. His marriage (1827) with the Blessingtons' 15-year-old daughter soon ended in separation, and in 1831 Lady Blessington (whose husband had died two years before) returned to London with d'Orsay. For the next twenty years the pair dominated the fashionable world, d'Orsay proving his accomplishment as a gentleman not only by his style in clothes but by practising painting and sculpture. In 1849 they fled from their creditors to France, where Louis Napoleon (Napoleon III) made the count director of fine arts.

Orsini, Felice (1819–1858). Italian conspirator. Having already served in the galleys for plots against the papacy, he took part in many conspiracies designed to further the cause of Italian unification. Considering * Napoleon III, who maintained a garrison in Rome, as the greatest single obstacle, he threw three bombs at the imperial carriage outside the Paris Opéra. The emperor and empress were unhurt but ten bystanders were killed and 156 injured. Orsini was captured; before he was guillotined he wrote to Napoleon urging him to free Italy and, admiring his courage, the emperor published his last letter.

Ortega y Gasset, José (1883–1955). Spanish writer and philosopher. Born in Madrid, he

became professor of metaphysics in the Central University. He supported the 1931 revolution, became civil governor of Madrid, and lived abroad after Franco seized power. His philosophy shows the influence of * Kant but he is best known for his essays on modern civilization, which he regarded as being destroyed by totalitarianism. His works include *Meditations of Quixote* (1914), a symbolic framework for a comparison of the Spanish spirit with that of other nations; *Invertebrate Spain* (1923), an analysis of the historical development of the national character; *The Revolt of the Masses* (1930), which looks forward prophetically to the Civil War, and studies of Kant, Goethe and Mirabeau.
Mora, J. F., *Ortega y Gasset: An Outline of His Philosophy*. 1956

Orwell, George (Eric Blair) (1930–1950). English essayist and novelist. His early life with the police in Burma (1922–27) and subsequently in poverty in Europe is described in *Burmese Days* (1935) and *Down and Out in Paris and London* (1933). He fought for the Republicans in the Spanish Civil War and was wounded; he then wrote *Homage to Catalonia* (1938). *The Road to Wigan Pier* (1937) is an angry portrait of working-class life and an attack on middle-class socialists; *Animal Farm* (1946) is a satire, in the form of a farmyard fable, on the degeneration of idealistic revolt into tyranny; *1984* (1949), his last book, is a terrifying vision of a totalitarian state. His volumes of essays include *Inside the Whale* (1940), *Shooting an Elephant and Other Essays* (1950), and *England, Your England* (1953).
Williams, R., *Orwell*. 1970

Osborne, Dorothy (1627–1695). English letter writer. Her love letters to Sir William Temple, whom she married (1655) after a long courtship, reveal the writer's gay and intelligent mind and paint a delightful picture of 17th-century English life. They were first published in 1888. Nearly all the letters are now in the British Museum.
Cecil, D., *Two Quiet Lives*. 1947

Osborne, John James (1929–). English playwright. He became an actor (1948) and began to work at the Royal Court Theatre, where his play *Look Back in Anger* was first produced (1956); its hero (or anti-hero), Jimmy Porter, came to be regarded as a representative figure of a new classless generation. Sir Laurence * Olivier played the lead in his next play, *The Entertainer* (1957). *Epitaph for George Dillon*, an earlier play written in collaboration with Anthony Creighton, was produced in 1957. Later plays include *The World of Paul Slickey* (1959), a musical, an historical drama *Luther* (1961), *West of Suez* (1971) and *Sense of Detachment* (1972).
Trussier, S., *The Plays of John Osborne*. 1969

Osbourne, Lloyd (1868–1947). American author. He wrote three novels in collaboration with his stepfather, Robert Louis * Stevenson: *The Wrong Box, The Wrecker* and *The Ebb Tide*.

Oscar I (1799–1859). King of Sweden and Norway (from 1844). His father, Marshal * Bernadotte, had become king of Sweden during the Napoleonic Wars. Oscar was a moderate liberal and furthered reforms, e.g. freedom of the press.

Oscar II (1829–1907). King of Sweden (from 1872). The second son of Oscar I and the brother of Charles XV, he was also king of Norway until 1905, when he accepted without rancour the decision of that country to establish a dynasty of its own.

O'Shea, Katherine (Kitty) *see* **Parnell, Charles Stewart**

Osler, Sir William, 1st Bart (1849–1919). Canadian-born physician. He graduated and later taught at McGill University and was elected (1882) a fellow of the Royal College of Physicians. He was professor of clinical medicine (1889–1904) at the new Johns Hopkins University, where the medical unit became famous under his direction. After leaving Baltimore he went to England to take up a Regius professorship at Oxford University; he was created a baronet in 1911. The most important of his many works is *The Principles and Practice of Medicine* (1892).
Belt, W. R., *Osler*. 1952

Osman *see* **Othman**

Osman Pasha (1832–1900). Turkish soldier. After distinguishing himself in the Crimean War, he gained an international reputation for the skill and courage with which he defended Plevna in Bulgaria for five months against the Russians (1877).

Ossian *see* **Macpherson, James**

Ostade, Adriaen van (1610–1684). Dutch painter. Though he was a pupil of Frans * Hals, little of his teacher's influence is seen in his genre scenes in which topers, fiddlers, dancers, often performing in country inns, play a conspicuous part. His brother, **Isaack van Ostade** (1621–1649), at first chose similar subjects but later turned to the streets and countryside (especially in winter) for inspiration.

Ostrovsky, Alexander Nikolayevich (1823–1886). Russian dramatist. He had close associations with the Maly Theatre in Moscow, where he became noted for realistic plays mostly concerned with the middle classes, merchants, officials etc. There is much more poetic force, however, in *The Storm* (1860), usually considered his masterpiece.

Ostwald, Wilhelm Friedrich (1853–1932). German physical chemist, professor of chemistry at Riga (1881–87), and at Leipzig (1887–1916) where he adopted and advocated the electrolytic dissociation theory of * Arrhenius, applied the laws of mass action to obtain what is now known as Ostwald's dilution law, and discovered the process for the catalytic oxidation of ammonia into nitric acid by which most nitric acid is now made. He won the Nobel Prize for Chemistry (1909).

Oswald (604–642). King of Northumbria (from 633). A son of King Aethefrith of Bernicia, he returned from exile to succeed King * Edwin. At the time * Cadwallon was ravaging Northumbria, but Oswald defeated him at Hexham (634) and was able to consolidate and extend his rule until he was overlord of nearly all England. He revived Christianity in Northumbria by inviting Aidan and monks from Iona to found a monastery at Lindisfarne. Oswald was killed in battle against King Penda of Mercia and received almost immediate recognition as a saint.

Oswald, Lee Harvey (1939–63). American assassin. After joining the US Marines in 1954, he defected to the USSR in 1959, married there and returned to the US, apparently disillusioned, in 1962, and worked in Texas for Communist-fringe organizations. On 22 November 1963 he assassinated President John F. * Kennedy by shooting him twice as he drove in an open car through the streets of Dallas. Oswald also wounded Governor John Connally of Texas and killed a policeman. Two days later Oswald was shot by Jack Ruby, a nightclub owner, as he was being transferred from one jail to another. Oswald's record indicated him to be a psychopathic isolate, and despite his political associations the President's murder was generally thought to have a psychological rather than a political significance, although speculation about conspiracies continued for two decades.

Othman (or Osman) **I** (died 1326). Turkish ruler. He is regarded as the founder of the Ottoman empire, because the descendants of those who under his leadership made extensive conquests in N.W. Asia Minor became known as Ottoman or Osmanli Turks; they pursued their victorious march westward, captured Constantinople (1453) and made it the centre of the great empire that bore their name.

Otho, Marcus Salvius (32–69). One of four Roman emperors in a single year (69). While governor of Lusitania (Portugal) he joined Galba (68) against Nero; but, disappointed in his hopes of the succession, he was proclaimed emperor by his troops in the Roman forum and had Galba put to death. Meanwhile the troops in Germany had proclaimed Vitellius, and he defeated Otho in north Italy. Otho then committed suicide.

Otto I (known as 'the Great') (912–973). German king (from 936). He was crowned emperor at Rome (962) and because of the extension of his power into Italy and close relations with the papacy he is usually held to be the founder of the Holy Roman empire. In Germany he centralized the administration, controlled the Slavs and repelled the Magyars. In Italy he became king of the Lombards, mastered Rome and the country to the south as far as Capua. His first wife was a daughter of Edward the Elder of England. His son, **Otto II** (955–983), crowned German king in 961, while his father was still alive, and subsequently emperor, was defeated by the Saracens in southern Italy and in consequence lost control of the Slavs in Germany. An attempt by his son, **Otto III** (980–1002), to establish an empire on the Byzantine pattern centred on Rome failed and was resented by his German subjects. **Otto IV** (*c.* 1175–1218), a son of * Henry the Lion was crowned German king (1198) but his title of emperor was constantly in dispute. In alliance with the English King John he was completely defeated at Bouvines (1214) by Philip II of France.

Otto, Nikolaus August (1832–1891). German inventor. He was co-inventor (1867) of a successful internal combustion engine and patented (1884) the four-stroke 'Otto engine'. Gottlieb * Daimler was the chief engineer of the company formed to exploit the patent.

Otway, Thomas (1652–1685). English Restoration dramatist. He left Oxford without taking a degree and went to London, where, after failing as an actor, he produced his first successful play, *Don Carlos* (1676). Adaptations from Racine's *Bérénice* and Molière's *Les Fourberies de Scapin* followed (1677); he is chiefly remembered for the blank-verse tragedy *The Orphan* (1680) and his masterpiece *Venice Preserved* (1682). After a breach with his patron, the Earl of Rochester, he died in poverty.
Ham, R. G., *Otway and Lee*. 1969

Oudinot, Charles Nicolas (1767–1847). French marshal. His 'grenadiers Oudinot' won fame at Austerlitz (1805), and after the Battle of Wagram (1809) he was created Prince of Reggio. With * Ney he covered the crossing of the Beresina River in the heroic rearguard action which saved the remnants of the Grand Army retreating from Moscow. He remained aloof during the Waterloo campaign. He later gained distinction in the royal service.

Ouida (pen-name of Marie Louise de la Ramée) (1839–1908). English novelist. Her pseudonym was a childish mispronunciation of her own name. Her romances, about fifty in number, show a reaction from the moralistic novels of her time. The heroes may be too handsome to be true, and the 'pasts' that rise to haunt some of the ladies that decorate her pages may seem less lurid now than once they did, but the stories, e.g. *Under Two Flags* (1867), *Two Little Wooden Shoes* (1874), are told with such gusto and narrative skill that they retain something of their former glamour.
Bigland, E., *Ouida: The Passionate Victorian*. 1950

Outram, Sir James, 1st Bart (1803–1863). British soldier and political officer. He joined the Bombay army and his career was similar to, and at times overlapped, that of Sir Charles * Napier. During the First Afghan War he made an adventurous journey through the country in disguise. He was a political officer in Sind, where he became involved in controversy with Napier over the treatment of the Mirs (Amirs). Among other appointments he was political resident in Baroda and Oudh and in the Indian Mutiny served under Havelock in the first relief of Lucknow, where he was left in command of the garrison. For these services he was awarded a baronetcy. His chivalrous nature won him the title of the 'Bayard of India'.

Overbury, Sir Thomas (1581–1613). English poet and courtier. In the reign of James I of England he was the go-between of the beautiful Frances Howard, Countess of Essex, and her lover Robert Carr, the king's favourite, afterwards Earl of Somerset. Overbury's remark to Carr during a discussion about divorce, that the Countess was all right for a mistress but not for a wife, seems to have been repeated and so angered the lady that she contrived a pretext on which Overbury was confined to the Tower of London, where he was found dead from poison. Four minor participants in the crime were later hanged and afterwards the Countess of Somerset (as she had become) admitted her guilt but was pardoned by the king, as was her husband.
McElwee, W., *The Murder of Sir Thomas Overbury*. 1952

Ovid (Publius Ovidius Naso) (43 B.C.–A.D. 17). Latin poet. Among his earliest poems were the *Amores*, written to an imaginary mistress, Corinna. Equally imaginary are the letters in the *Heroides*, allegedly written by legendary heroines, to their husbands or lovers (e.g. Penelope to Ulysses). In the *Art of Love*, often regarded as his masterpiece, the poet tells a lover how to gain a courtesan's favour and advises a girl on how to win and hold a lover. The *Metamorphoses* contains myths where change of shape provides the central theme. Having written this Ovid was suddenly and mysteriously banished by Augustus (perhaps because he had become involved in one of the intrigues of the emperor's daughter Julia) to Tomi (now Constanta) on the Black Sea.

Tristia, his laments for the misfortune, was already started while he was on the way. While in exile, from which he was never recalled, he also revised the *Fasti*, a month-by-month description of the festivals of the Roman year. Only six of these survive and perhaps no more were written. Ovid had an astonishing facility for turning almost any subject into hexameters and pentameters without metrical blemish, and provided themes and examples for many writers, e.g. Shakespeare and Pope; but through lack of deep thought and feeling he has provided tasks for the schoolroom rather than inspiration to the world outside.
Rand, E. K., *Ovid and His Influence*. 1925

Owen, David Anthony Llewellyn (1938–). British politician. Educated at Cambridge, he became a neurologist and Labour MP 1966–81, serving as foreign secretary 1977–79. He left Labour to become a co-founder of the Social Democratic Party in 1981 and in 1983 succeeded Roy * Jenkins as SDP leader. He published *Face the Future* (1981).

Owen, Sir Richard (1804–1892). Scottish palaeontologist. His early career was marked by a phenomenal quantity of zoological identification and classification in the style of Cuvier, culminating in his *On the Anatomy and Physiology of Vertebrates* (1859–1868) and his *Descriptive and Illustrative Catalogue of the Physiological Series of Comparative Anatomy* of the Royal College of Surgeon's museum.

Owen became progressively more interested in palaeontology. His work on the reconstruction of the New Zealand Moa and the Archaeopteryx (an English Jurassic bird) were classics of their kind. He published an important History of *British Fossils Reptiles* (1849–84) and a popular text-book, *Palaeontology* (1860).

Owen came into collision with the Darwinians on two important issues: firstly, he made Man into the single example of a special subclass of Mammalia. * Huxley in reply showed plausibly that the anatomical grounds for this classification were illusory. Owen also fiercely attacked * Darwin's natural selection mechanism for evolution.
Owen, R., *The Life of Sir Richard Owen*. 1894

Owen, Robert (1771–1858). Welsh social reformer, born in Montgomeryshire. After being a draper's assistant in Manchester, he became a master spinner and took over (1800), with partners, the New Lanark mills, originally started by * Arkwright and David Thale, whose daughter Owen married. Here he improved working conditions and housing, shortened hours and for the children introduced a new educational system (visual methods etc.) designed to bring out the special aptitudes of each particular child. Some of his improvements were incorporated in the Factory Act (1819). In the industrial depression that followed the Napoleonic Wars, Owen proposed as a substitute for the poor-relief system 'villages of co-operation' in which each member was expected to work according to his ability for the good of the whole. The few experimental settlements all failed, for though New Harmony (1825) in Indiana, U.S.A. survived, the co-operative principle was soon abandoned.

As early as 1813 Owen had, in *A New View of Society*, propounded the view that man's character was formed by his environment and he denounced the churches for holding people responsible for sins resulting from capitalism and other social evils. He also held that such evils could be swept away if only the 'industrial classes' would combine to overthrow them. With this in view he took the lead in the foundation (1833) of the 'Grand National Consolidated Trades Union', but this collapsed within a year. Undeterred, he and his followers, now called 'Socialists', founded a new settlement, Queenwood in Hampshire, but this too only survived a few years.
Cole, G. D. H., *Life of Robert Owen*. 1965

Owen, Wilfred (1893–1918). English poet. A teacher by profession, he served in World War I and was killed a week before the armistice. His war poems, written with irony, pity and ruthless honesty, were published after his death by his friend Siegfried * Sassoon. Some of them were set to music by Benjamin * Britten in his *War Requiem* (1962).
Stallworthy, J., *Wilfred Owen: A Biography*. 1974

Owens, Jesse (1913–1980). American Negro athlete. At the 1936 Olympic games at Berlin, watched by Hitler, he won five gold medals, including one for a record long jump of 26ft $8\frac{1}{4}$ ins., which was not surpassed until 1960. Such feats, performed in Berlin by a Negro at a time when the Nazis were proclaiming their theories of Nordic racial superiority, were widely commented on.

Oxenstierna, Axel (1583–1654). Swedish statesman. Of aristocratic birth, he was instrumental in securing a settlement between the nobles and * Gustavus II, whose chancellor he became (1612). The diplomatic preparations which left Gustavus free to sweep into Germany as the Protestant hero of the Thirty Years War were in Oxenstierna's hands and, after his master's death at Lützen (1632), it was he, as regent for Gustavus's daughter * Christina, who kept the war going and made sure that Sweden was adequately rewarded by territorial gains. Meanwhile he had made notable administrative reforms, but after the war a faction of the nobility asserted itself; Queen Christina was lukewarm in his support and finally, despite his persuasions, abdicated. Soon after this final disappointment Oxenstierna died.

Oxford, Robert Harley, Earl of *see* **Harley Robert.**

Oxford and Asquith, 1st Earl of *see* **Asquith, Herbert Henry**

P

Paasikivi, Juho Kusti (1870–1956). Finnish politician. He was the first prime minister of Finland (1918) after the declaration of independence, and again (1944–46) at the end of World War II, serving as president (1946–56). With U. K. * Kekkonen he negotiated peace with the USSR and Finland's neutralist policy is known as 'the Paasikivi line'.

Pachmann, Vladimir de (1848–1933). Russian pianist. He was one of the most popular and accomplished (though often eccentric) concert performers of his generation, his technique being seen to best advantage in his interpretations of Chopin.

Paderewski, Ignace Jan (1860–1941). Polish pianist, composer and politician. He studied under Leschetizky (1884–87) before specializing as a virtuoso pianist, and touring Europe and America with enormous success. He wrote two operas, a symphony, two concertos and much piano music, including the famous Minuet in G. His international reputation and his efforts for his country in raising relief funds and in nationalist propaganda during World War I caused him to be chosen prime minister of the new independent Polish republic after the war. As such he took part in the Paris Peace Conference and signed the Treaty of Versailles (1919). In December he retired and returned to his music but in 1939, after Poland had been overrun in World War II, he reappeared briefly in political life as chairman of the Polish national council in exile.
Gronowicz, A., *Paderewski.* 1943

Páez, Juan Antonio (1790–1873). Venezuelan liberator. He fought against the Spanish with varying success until he joined (1818) * Bolívar and shared with him in the victory of Carabobo (1821) by which Colombia and Venezuela were liberated. When Bolívar went to Ecuador, Páez stayed in Venezuela and when Venezuela seceded from Colombia he became first president (1831), dominating the country, either in office himself or through nominees, until he was defeated by a rival (1850) and forced into exile. In 1858 he returned to power but in 1863 was again expelled; he died in New York.

Paganini, Niccolò (1782–1840). Italian violinist and composer, born in Genoa. He toured Europe repeatedly and wrote many virtuoso pieces, useful as students' exercises, e.g. his Twenty-four Caprices and the Concerto in D. His technique was regarded as phenomenal and he enlarged the range of the violin by introducing left-hand pizzicatos and double harmonics. His tempestuous career and odd appearance made him a popular idol. He early recognized Beethoven's greatness.
Pulver, J., *Paganini.* 1936

Page, Sir Earle Christmas Grafton (1880–1961). Australian politician. A surgeon by profession, he entered the federal House of Representatives (1919) and became co-founder and leader of the Australian Country party. Among the many offices he held was that of prime minister (briefly in 1939). As minister for health (1949–56) he introduced a national health scheme.

Page, Sir Frederick Handley (1885–1962). British aeronautical engineer and pioneer of flying. He founded Handley Page Limited in 1909 and during World War I designed and

built his twin-engined 0/400, one of the earliest heavy bombers. He established a civil air service between England and the continent in 1919 and continued to build aircraft, notably the Heracles airliner. During World War II Handley Page Limited built transport planes and bombers, notably the Halifax. He was president of the Royal Aeronautical Society 1945–47 and received the Society's Gold Medal in 1960. His company closed down in 1970.
Gibbs-Smith, C. H., *Aviation: an Historical Survey from its Origins to the end of World War II*. 1970

Pagnol, Marcel (1895–1974). French author, playwright and film director. His plays include *Catulle* (1922), *Topaze* (1928) and the trilogy *Marius, Fanny, César* (1929–36). He directed or produced several films, e.g. *César* (1936), *Le Regain* (*Harvest*; 1937) and *La Femme du boulanger* (1938). Among his novels are *Le Château de ma mère, Le Temps des Secrets*.

Paine, Thomas (1737–1809). English political writer. Having tried several occupations including that of excise officer, he went on the advice of Benjamin * Franklin to America, where he published *Common Sense* (1776), a pamphlet demanding complete independence from Britain, and *The Crisis* (1776–83), a series of pamphlets advocating the same end. Meanwhile he had fought in the colonial armies and had been administratively concerned with the framing of the constitution. In 1791 he returned to England, but publication of his greatest work, *The Rights of Man* (1791–92), a reply to Edmund * Burke's *Reflections on the Revolution in France*, forced him to go to France to avoid prosecution. There he was elected to the Convention but after opposing the execution of Louis XVI he was for a time in prison, where he began *The Age of Reason* (1794–96), a work defending deism (i.e. a belief in God which is divorced from Christianity or any other 'enslaving' religion). He returned to America in 1802, where he came into conflict with the Federalists. He died in New York. Paine's writings continued to inspire radicals in the century after his death.
Williamson, A., *Thomas Paine: His Life, Work and Times*. 1973

Palaeologus. Byzantine dynasty. The family was famous in the history of Constantinople from the 11th century, but its first emperor was *Michael VIII* (reigned 1258–82). His successors ruled the empire until *Constantine XI* (reigned 1443–53) died while vainly trying to defend Constantinople against the Turks.
Nicol, D. M., *The Last Centuries of Byzantium, 1261–1453*. 1972

Palafox (y Melci), José, Duke of Saragossa (1776–1847). Spanish patriot. In the early stages of the Peninsular War he was a leader of those Spaniards who, with British aid, resisted the invasion of Napoleon's armies. He became famous for his heroic defence of Saragossa but after its final capitulation (February 1809) he was imprisoned by the French until 1813. He was created duke in 1834.

Palamas, Kostas (1859–1943). Greek writer. His epics, e.g. *The King's Flute* (1910), concerned with the Byzantine period, reawakened Greek pride and sorrow in the events of their great history: liberty and justice were his constant themes. In addition to poetry, lyric and philosophical as well as epic, he wrote stories, essays and a tragedy. His use of the 'Demotic', the language of contemporary Greece, did much to enhance its literary status.

Palestrina, Giovanni Pierluigi da (1525?–1594). Italian composer. He was born at Palestrina (Praeneste), and at the cathedral there became organist and choirmaster (1544). In 1551 Pope Julius III (who as bishop of Palestrina had been the composer's master) appointed him a member of the Julian choir, St Peter's. In 1555 Palestrina was briefly a member of the pontifical choir until he was forced to resign, by the reformist pope Paul IV. He remained in Rome as musical director of the church of St John Lateran (1555–60) and of S. Maria Maggiore (1561–67), returning to St Peter's (1570) as master of the Julian choir, a post which he held until his death. Palestrina's output was enormous and included motets, litanies, magnificats and ninety-four masses. (The legend that his famous *Missa Papae Marcelli* had the effect of dissuading the Council of Trent from burning polyphonic church music is unfounded.) His work represents the culminating point of development in polyphonic vocal music, but the new ideals inaugurated by his immediate successors led to its neglect until the late 19th century, since when it has remained, at least

in technique, the chief model for liturgical composers.
Coates, H., *Palestrina*. 1938

Paley, William (1743–1805). English clergyman and theologian. He held a number of livings and diocesan appointments but is chiefly remembered for his *View of the Evidences of Christianity* (1794), one of the most convincing and influential books of its kind.

Palladio, Andrea (1508–1580). Italian architect, born in Padua. His ability was first noticed, while he was working as a stonemason at Vicenza, by Trissino, who enabled him to study and make drawings of classical antiquities in Rome (1545–47). In and around Vicenza he built, in a distinctive classical style which became known as 'Palladian', the famous Basilica (1549), with two arcaded storeys round an older hall; town palaces and country villas; and his last important work, the Teatro Olimpico (begun 1580). The churches of S. Giorgio Maggiore (1566) and Il Redentore (1576), both in Venice, have remarkable facades. Through his *Quattro libri dell'architettura* (1570), which contained many of his designs, his influence spread widely; in England his style was introduced by Inigo * Jones and later popularized by Lord * Burlington. He was also copied in eighteenth-century America.
Ackerman, J. S., *Palladio*. 1966

Palme, (Sven) Olof Joachim (1927–). Swedish Social Democrat politician. Partly educated in the US, he was a prominent youth leader and a Riksdag member 1957– , succeeding Tag * Erlander (whose secretary he had been) as prime minister of Sweden 1969–76 and 1982–

Palmer, Samuel (1805–1881). English painter and engraver. The son of a bookseller, he was largely self-educated as an artist but exhibited at the Royal Academy as early as 1819. His most original work was done when he lived at Shoreham (1826–35), where with George Richmond and others he formed a group (known as 'The Ancients'), of admirers of William * Blake, whom Palmer had first met in 1824. Thus inspired, Palmer produced landscapes that showed a vision and fire almost entirely missing from his later work. He worked much in water-colour.
Peacock, C., *Samuel Palmer: Shoreham and After*. 1968

Palmerston, Henry Temple, 3rd Viscount (1784–1865). British Liberal politician. As an Irish peer, he was eligible to be elected to the House of Commons, and sat as an MP 1807–65. Originally a Tory, he broke with the party (1828) and henceforth as a Whig or Liberal favoured a policy of nonalignment with European powers and support for national movements. Thus when he became foreign secretary (1830) he supported Belgian independence and the constitutionalists in Spain and Portugal, and saved the decaying Turkish empire from domination by Russia. After a period in opposition (1841–46) he was again foreign minister (1846–51) and in 1848 he supported the nationalist uprisings, especially those against Austria; and when Louis Philippe was deposed in France he recognized the republic and later, without consulting his colleagues, the *coup d'état* (1851) of Louis Napoleon (Napoleon III). Lord John Russell forced his resignation over this but he returned (1853) as home secretary in Lord Aberdeen's coalition. He was prime minister 1855–58 and 1859–65, and died in office. He brought the Crimean War to a satisfactory end and acted vigorously in response to the Indian Mutiny (1857). Depite his liberalism his methods were often domineering and his judgement was often faulty, especially in his later years (e.g. over the American Civil War). He was extremely popular with the British public, but Queen Victoria and his colleagues sometimes found his readiness to take forceful action very trying.
Ridley, J., *Lord Palmerston*. 1970

Paneth, Friedrich Adolf (1887–1958). Austrian chemist. Professor of chemistry at Prague, Berlin and Durham, and (from 1953) director of the Planck Institute for Chemistry, Mainz, his most important work was on the use of radio-isotopes in chemical research, and he devised techniques for measuring the minute quantities of helium produced in rocks by radioactive decay, and thus provided a method of finding the age of rocks.

Panhard, René (1841–1908). French engineer and motoring pioneer. Founder of the Panhard company, in 1886 he formed a partnership with Émil Lavassor. They acquired the French and Belgian rights to use * Otto's internal combustion engine and pioneered the building of true cars with the engine mounted on a chassis.

Georgano, G. N. (ed.), *The Complete Encyclopaedia of Motorcars 1885–1968*. 1968

Pankhurst, Emmeline (née Goulden) (1858–1928). British militant suffragette. She worked with her husband, **Richard Marsden Pankhurst** (1839–1898), on behalf of many radical causes, but after his death concentrated upon votes for women. The dramatic methods by which she, her daughters and the militants of the Women's Social and Political Union (founded by her in 1903) pursued their ends included chaining themselves to lampposts, slashing pictures, assaulting the police, hunger strikes in prison (Mrs Pankhurst was confined eight times). Many less extreme supporters were estranged, but World War I, in which women proved their ability in almost every occupation, broke down opposition. In 1918 women over 30 acquired the vote and in 1928 they attained equality of franchise with men. Two of Mrs Pankhurst's daughters were especially identified with her work: **Dame Christobel Pankhurst** (1880–1958), who was even more extreme, later took up revivalism in the U.S.A.; **Sylvia Pankhurst** (1882–1960), who was also active in the early days, became a keen socialist after World War I and later devoted herself to the cause of Ethiopia (Abyssinia) when it was overrun by the Italians. She lived in Addis Ababa from 1956.

Pankhurst, S., *The Life of Emmeline Pankhurst*. 1935

Paoli, Pasquale de (1725–1807). Corsican patriot. After many years in exile (1739–55) for opposing the Genoese, he was chosen as president of Corsica. When the Genoese sold Corsica to France he opposed the French authority but after a valiant resistance was defeated and fled to England, where * Boswell befriended him. In 1791 he was appointed governor of Corsica by the French Revolutionary government, and when accused (1793) of being a counter-revolutionary, he proclaimed Corsica independent. With the help of the British Navy he defeated the French and the island was declared a British protectorate. After he was recalled to England (1795) the pro-French islanders drove the British from Corsica.

Paolo and Francesca *see* **Francesca da Rimini**

Papagos, Alexander (1883–1955). Greek field marshal. Having distinguished himself in both Balkan Wars, in World War I and in the Turkish War that followed, he was commander-in-chief against the Italians in World War II. Despite inferiority of numbers and equipment he gained a series of remarkable victories until German intervention made further resistance impossible. After the war he resumed his post as commander-in-chief (1949) and quickly defeated the communists. Entering politics, he formed (1951) a new party, the Greek Rally, at the head of which he gained (1952) a great electoral victory. As prime minister (1952–55) he did much to restore political and economic stability.

Papen, Franz Joseph Hermann Michael Maria von (1879–1969). German politician and diplomat. When military attaché in the USA during World War I he was expelled (1915) for promoting sabotage. He was elected to the Prussian Diet (1921) and subsequently used his friendship with President * Hindenburg's son, Oskar, to secure advancement. Finally (June 1932) he was appointed chancellor. His first attempt to bring * Hitler into his government failed, but after another election (November 1932) and Papen's resignation the two came to terms; Hitler became chancellor and Papen vice-chancellor, with a secret assignment from Hindenburg to curb Nazi excesses. Papen soon became critical of his new ally and narrowly escaped death in Hitler's blood purge (1934). The warning was enough. He accepted the post of ambassador in Vienna and prepared the ground for the Nazi occupation of Austria. During World War II he was sent to Turkey, where his embassy became the centre of a spy network. After the war he was acquitted at Nuremberg, and was released after serving two years of a nine-year sentence imposed by a German denazification court.

Papen, F. von, *Memoirs*. 1952

Papin, Denis (1647–*c*. 1712). French phycisist. He assisted * Huygens and (from 1675) Robert * Boyle in work on air pumps. Among his inventions were the double-stroke air pump, the condensing pump and the autoclave (then known as the 'digester'), a pressure vessel in which temperatures above the boiling point of water may be attained. He was also a pioneer of the steam engine. He was elected a member of the Royal Society (1680).

Papineau, Louis Joseph (1786–1871). French-Canadian politician, born in Montreal. He was elected (1808) to the Quebec legislative assembly, of which he was later speaker (1815–37). His bitter oratory gave fervent support to the cause of French-Canadian self-government and after the defeat of the 1837 rebellion he took refuge in the U.S.A. and then France. He returned to Canada in 1845, was elected to the lower house 1848–54, then retired from politics.

Pappus of Alexandria (fl. A.D. 300–350). Greek geometer. His treatise, the *Synagoge*, is particularly valuable as a source of information about earlier Greek mathematicians and geometers. When giving proofs from earlier figures, Pappus frequently offers alternative solutions, or his own improvements. He offers full discussions of many of the classic problems of Greek mathematics, such as squaring the circle or the trisection of an angle. Pappus also evidently had interests in geography; he is known to have composed a geographical work, which has not survived. He wrote commentaries on Euclid and Ptolemy's *Almagest*.
Heath, T. L., *A History of Greek Mathematics*. 1921

Paracelsus (Theophrastus Bombastus von Hohenheim) (*c.* 1493–1541). Swiss physician and alchemist. He travelled widely in Europe, lecturing and practising medicine, and won considerable renown. Although he practised alchemy and the occult sciences, he did not accept demonological explanations for insanity, and many of his medical views were advanced for his time: he attacked the traditional belief that diseases were caused by 'humours' in the body and taught the use of specific remedies. He introduced opium, laudanum, mercury, sulphur, iron and arsenic as medicines. Of his numerous works, the *Paragranum* gives the best exposition of his medical views. Robert Browning's dramatic poem *Paracelsus* (1835) is based on his life.
Pachter, H. M., *Paracelsus: Magic into Science*. 1951. Stoddart, A., *The Life of Paracelsus*. 1911

Paré, Ambroise (1510–1591). French army surgeon. Known especially for introducing more humane methods in surgery, he abandoned the boiling-oil treatment of wounds in favour of dressings with egg yolk, attar of roses and turpentine, and used ligatures to seal blood vessels after amputations instead of cauterization. He was surgeon to all French kings from Francis I to Charles IX. He has been called the father of modern surgery. He always stressed the importance of proper nursing, and was much concerned about the treatment of women in childbirth. His *Apology* is a vivid autobiography.
Hamby, W. B., *The Case Reports and Autopsy Records of Ambroise Paré*. 1960

Parini, Giuseppe (1729–1799). Italian poet. His work was modelled on Latin poets, especially Horace, but he abandoned the artificialities of the preceding period and wrote creatively with elegance and feeling. His most famous poem, *Il Giorno* (*The Day*, begun 1763), gives an ironic and lively account of a day in the life of a young nobleman in a corrupt age.
Petronio, G., *Parini e l'illuminismo lombardo*. 1961

Paris, Matthew (1200?–1259). English monk and chronicler. He entered (1217) the monastery of St Albans, where he acquired skill not only as a writer and illuminator but in gold and silverwork. He continued Roger of Wendover's *Major Chronicles* from 1235 to 1259, enlarging their scope to include foreign events. His *Minor History* is a summary of events from 1200 to 1250. He was favoured by Henry III, and his chronicles, apart from their historic value, are vigorous and vivid and not without critical comment on contemporary trends and developments.

Park Chung Hee (1917–1979). Korean soldier and politician. In 1961 he led a military coup in the Republic of Korea, served as president (1963–79) and promoted rapid growth and technological adaptation until his assassination by the head of Korea's Central Intelligence Agency.

Park, Mungo (1771–1806). Scottish explorer in Africa, a surgeon by profession. In 1795 he went to Africa to explore the course of the river Niger and find its exit to the sea. After much hardship he joined the Niger at Segou, followed it downstream and, before being forced by obstructions to return, proved that it had an eastward flow at this point: the problem of its point of exit remained unsolved. His *Travels in the Interior of Africa* (1799) proved a

popular success, and in 1805 he made another journey but of his forty-five companions only seven reached the Niger. They struggled on as far as Boussa (Basa), where the canoe was wrecked and Park and four remaining Europeans were attacked by natives and drowned while trying to escape.
Schiffers, H., *The Quest for Africa*. 1957

Parker, Dorothy (née Rothschild) (1893–1967). American writer, well known for short stories, collected in, e.g., *Laments for the Living* (1930) and *Her Lies* (1939), and for her mordantly humorous poems, sayings and book reviews contributed to *The New Yorker*.
Keats, J., *You Might As Well Live: The Life and Times of Dorothy Parker*. 1970

Parker, Matthew (1504–1575). English prelate. He was a moderate churchman, interested in church history, and though he became a Protestant and supported Lady Jane Grey, he was merely deprived of his office as dean of Lincoln by Queen Mary and was not made to suffer martyrdom. Queen Elizabeth appointed him (1559) her first archbishop of Canterbury, and to him are largely due the prayer book of 1559 and the Thirty-nine Articles of 1562, both modelled on the corresponding publications of Edward VI's reign. One of the Parker's main problems was that the clergy who returned from exile demanded the much more drastic Protestantism which they had met on the continent. It was they who reinforced the growing body of 'Puritans' and were opposed to Parker's course of compromise. He was a great contributor and benefactor to Anglo-Saxon studies.
Dickens, A. G., *The English Reformation*. 1964

Parkes, Sir Henry (1815–1896). Australian Liberal politician, born in England. He reached New South Wales in 1839 and there founded a newspaper (1850) and became a prominent opponent of convict transportation. He entered the legislature (1854): in five broken terms he was premier of New South Wales (1872–75; 1877; 1878–83; 1887–89; 1889–91), state education being among the many reforms he introduced. His restrictions on Chinese immigration were first steps towards the White Australia policy. His most statesmanlike contribution was in raising the federation issue (1889–90) and afterwards devoting all his energy to its promotion. He received the KCMG (1877) and the GCMG (1888). He wrote on Australian politics and history and published some poetry.
Martin, A. W., *Henry Parkes*. 1980

Parkinson, C(yril) Northcote (1909–). British writer, historian and political scientist. He was the propounder of Parkinson's Law, a serio-comic analysis of the growth of bureaucracy, e.g., work expands in order to fill the time available for its completion.
Parkinson, C. N., *Parkinson's Law, the Pursuit of Progress*. 1958

Parmenides (fl. *c*. 475 B.C.). Greek philosopher. Born at Elea in southern Italy, he was the founder of the Eleatic school. His views, presented in a poem and containing ideas on 'being', had much influence on later philosophers, e.g. Plato and Aristotle (who held that 'atomism' was derived from Eleatic teaching). Unlike * Heraclitus, who held that everything is in a state of flux, Parmenides taught that the universe is a single, unchanging whole, indivisible, immobile and indestructible, and that any appearances to the contrary are delusions of the senses. As well as being a philosopher, Parmenides played an active part in the political life of his native city.
Guthrie, W. K. C., *A History of Greek Philosophy*. 1965

Parnell, Charles Stewart (1846–1891). Irish nationalist politician. He came of a Protestant landowning family and was educated in England; he was elected M.P. for County Meath (1875) as a home-ruler. As a speaker he was cold and sardonic but as a tactician he was superb, making especially skilful use of all the parliamentary rules that help obstruction.

After becoming leader of the party (1880) he handled his colleagues autocratically. He became president (1879) of the Land League and inaugurated (1880) the policy of the boycott, which resulted in a large increase of agrarian crime. Parnell himself was imprisoned but was released (1882) after promising to fight crime if the government would provide relief for rent arrears. Such bargaining was soon ended by the murder of the chief secretary, Lord Frederick Cavendish, in Phoenix Park, Dublin, but in 1885 Parnell, with the Irish votes holding a balance of power, provided the pressure behind the introduction of * Gladstone's Irish Home Rule Bill of 1886 which split the Liberal party and brought the

Conservatives back to office. In 1887 *The Times* published allegations, based on documents forged by Richard Pigott, that Parnell had condoned political murders. Pigott was exposed but in 1889 Parnell was successfully cited as co-respondent by a colleague, Captain O'Shea, with whose wife, Catherine (Kitty), he was alleged to have committed adultery. Parnell refused to resign his leadership, but Gladstone and half the party, backed by the Roman Catholic hierarchy, turned against him: his political career was foundering when shortly after marrying Kitty he suddenly died. His outstanding achievement was to make, in his eleven years of leadership, home rule for Ireland the main item of the programme of one of the great English parties.
Lyons, F. S. L., Parnell. 1963

Parr, Catherine *see* **Catherine Parr**

Parry, Sir Charles Hubert Hastings, 1st Bart. (1848–1918). English composer. He became professor of the Royal College of Music on its foundation (1883) and was its director from 1894. He was a prolific composer, especially of choral and orchestral music: his best known works are the choral ode *Blest Pair of Sirens* (1887) and his setting of Blake's *Jerusalem* (1916), inspired by World War I. He was made a baronet in 1902. Like his contemporary * Stanford, Parry is important less for the quality of his own works than as a pioneer of the revival of English music which began at the end of the 19th century. Among his pupils was * Vaughan Williams.
Graves, C. L., *Hubert Parry, His Life and Works*. 1926

Parry, Sir William Edward (1795–1855). British Arctic explorer. In the second of two attempts to find the North-west Passage to the Pacific (1819), he almost succeeded by reaching Melville Island; he failed again in 1824–25. He discovered (1821–22) the Hecla and Fury Straits, which he named after his ships. His last (1827) expedition, an attempt to reach the pole by boat and sledge from Spitzbergen, was unsuccessful (though he reached latitude 82° 43′ N.).
Parry, A., *Parry of the Arctic*. 1963

Parsons, Sir Charles Algernon (1854–1931). Irish engineer. He developed the steam turbine named after him which revolutionized marine propulsion. The *Turbinia* (1897), the first turbine-powered ship, achieved the unprecedented speed of 36 knots. He was also concerned with optics and manufactured 34- and 76-inch reflecting telescopes. He received the K.C.B. (1911) and the O.M. (1927).

Parsons (or Persons), **Robert** (1546–1610). English priest. After leaving Oxford University he became a Roman Catholic convert, went to Rome and became (1575) a Jesuit. He returned to England (1580) to minister to Roman Catholics and eluded capture for a whole year. After the arrest of Edmund * Campion he returned to the continent, where he intrigued with Philip of Spain to invade England. He died in Rome as Rector of the English College there. He was the author of a large number of controversial pamphlets.

Pascal, Blaise (1623–1662). French theologian and scientist, born at Clermont-Ferrand. He owed much to his father, an exchequer official of great mathematical ability. He was a precocious youth and at 16 wrote a treatise on conic sections, greeted with admiration by * Descartes (who did not believe it was Blaise's own work). The experiments which he conducted with his father, and in 1647 described, on the problems of a vacuum and the effects of air pressure on tubes of mercury, led to the construction of barometers. To facilitate his father's work he also invented a calculating machine (patented 1647). Later in life he did basic work on the mathematical theory of probability, and laid the foundation for the invention of differential calculus.

Two years after his father's death (1651) his sister, Jacqueline, became a nun at Port-Royal, near Versailles, a headquarters of the Jansenists, whose doctrines, later declared heretical, stressed those parts of St * Augustine's teaching which appear to support predestination and redemption solely through grace. In 1654 Pascal too went to live there, though he took no vows, and wrote his *Lettres provinciales* (1656–57), a defence of the Jansenists combined with a brilliant, if unfair, attack on the casuistry of their main adversaries, the Jesuits. His more personal views on religion and philosophy as well as his most brilliant writing are, however, contained in his *Pensées*, notes for a projected apology for the Christian religion, collected and published in 1669, after his death. The foundation of all his religious thought is devotion to Christ, the

Saviour: 'I lay all my actions before God who shall judge them and to whom I have consecrated them'.
Menhard, J., *Pascal: His Life and Works*. 1952

Pasmore, (Edwin John) Victor (1908–). British painter and graphic artist. Largely self-taught, he passed through naturalism and post-impressionism to evolve a personal style, of which his three dimensional abstractions and relief paintings are best known. He received the CH in 1981.

Passfield, 1st Baron *see* **Webb, Sidney**

Pasternak, Boris Leonidovich (1890–1960). Russian writer. His father was an artist and friend of * Tolstoy, and he himself studied law, art and music before turning to literature. He was well known within the Soviet Union as a poet, original story writer and a translator of Shakespeare. He was refused permission to publish his wide-ranging novel *Doctor Zhivago* (completed 1957) about Russia in the years 1903–29. It was smuggled out of the Soviet Union and published abroad (in Italy 1957). It immediately attracted international acclaim and won for Pasternak the Nobel Prize for Literature in 1958. It was attacked in the U.S.S.R. for its lack of enthusiasm for revolutionary values, and Pasternak declined under pressure the Nobel award. He made a conventional apology for errors as the price for remaining in Russia. He also wrote the autobiographical *Safe Conduct* (1931) and *Essay in Autobiography* (1959) in addition to much poetry.

Pasteur, Louis (1822–1895). French bacteriologist, born at Dôle in the Jura. His father, a tanner, had been a sergeant-major during the Napoleonic Wars. His education led him to the Ecole Normale in Paris where he eventually became (1857–63) director of scientific studies, having earlier taught at Dijon, at Strasbourg (where he married Marie Laurent, daughter of the university rector) and as professor of chemistry at Lille. His early researches were on crystallography and the polarization of light. In 1857 he began to study why fermentation in wine vats produced lactic acid which caused the wine to go sour. He proved conclusively (and his success was said to have saved France more money than was paid in reparations after the Franco-Prussian War) that this fermentation was caused by bacteria in the air. This verified the 'germ theory' of disease and demolished the old idea of spontaneous generation; these conclusions (published 1864) were of basic importance in * Lister's development of antiseptic surgery. In 1865 Pasteur discovered, and found how to cure, a disease which was attacking silk worms and threatened the whole French silk industry. He devised (1870) the process known as pasteurization for killing bacteria in milk, and developed vaccines against the cattle disease anthrax (1877; later successfully extended to hydrophobia, or rabies) and chicken cholera (1880). He was elected to the Académie Française in 1881 and the first Pasteur Institute was founded in his honour in 1885. Pasteur's work ranks him as one of the greatest of all benefactors of the human race, and in effect the founder of bacteriology.
Nicolle, J., *Louis Pasteur: a Master of Scientific Enquriy*. 1961; *Louis Pasteur: the Story of his Major Discoveries*. 1961

Patch, Alexander McCarrell (1889–1945). American general of World War II. Among his outstanding achievements in the Pacific campaign was the recapture of Guadalcanal from the Japanese (1942). During the campaign for the liberation of Europe (1944) he commanded the 7th Army, which invaded France from the south.

Patel, Vallabhbhai (1875–1950). Indian politician. After being called to the bar in England, he became a member of the Indian National Congress and was one of * Gandhi's most active supporters. For his part in the civil disobedience campaign he was several times imprisoned but became (1947) * Nehru's deputy prime minister in the government of the newly independent India.

Pater, Walter Horatio (1839–1894). English essayist and critic. Born in London, he spent most of his life at Oxford as a fellow of Brasenose. A journey to Italy (1865) and the works of Ruskin and Winckelmann influenced his thought, but his polished and poetic style, first known to the public through the essays collected as *Studies in the History of the Renaisance* (1873), is highly individual. His belief that the cultivation of beauty should be an end in itself, irrespective of its relationship to life, provided academic justification for the aesthetic movement, then blossoming into

fame. His best known book is the philosophical romance *Marius the Epicurean* (1885), set in the time of Marcus Aurelius and concerned with the intellectual and spiritual processes by which a young Roman moves towards Christianity. Other works include *Imaginary Portraits* (1887) and the unfinished romance *Gaston de Latour* (1896).
Charlesworth, B., *Dark Passages*. 1965

Paton, Alan Stewart (1903–). South African writer. His famous novel, *Cry the Beloved Country* (1948), presents with compassion rather than bitterness the psychological problems besetting the coloured man in South Africa, where the environment is created for and by the white. He was president of the South African Liberal Party (made illegal in 1968).

Patrick, St (*c.* 385–461). Patron saint of Ireland. He was probably a Romanized Briton, born in South Wales. Kidnapped by Irish marauders when about 16 years old, he worked as a slave (traditionally in County Antrim) for about six years before he escaped to Gaul (France) and thence back to Britain. He then seems to have had a vision summoning him to convert the Irish, for which he did not rapidly obtain sanction, but at last he was ordained bishop and started his Irish mission (432 is the traditional date). Christianity had already penetrated parts of the country, but he was the first missionary in the more remote areas. His method was to convert the princes and through them the common people (hence the story of his preaching before the 'high king' at Tara). He organized the Irish church on a territorial basis and became the first bishop of Armagh (444?). He describes his life and work in his *Confessio*. St Patrick's Day is 17 March.
Bieler, L., *Works of St. Patrick*. 1953. Hanson, R. P. C., *Saint Patrick: his Origins and Career*. 1968

Patti, Adelina (Adela Juana Maria Patti) (1843–1919). Italian soprano, born in Madrid. She sang in New York at the age of 7, and made her operatic debut there in 1859. She was noted for her brilliant execution of coloratura roles.

Patton, George Smith (1885–1945). American soldier. He rose to be one of the most successful and colourful generals of World War II. In 1940 he was in command of an armoured division, and he led the landing forces in North Africa and in Sicily but was temporarily relieved of his command for striking a soldier whom he suspected of malingering. He returned to lead the 3rd Army in the European liberation campaign (1944) exploiting its breakout of the Cotentin peninsula (south of Cherbourg) with a triumphant drive across France, outflanking the Germans in Normandy, taking Paris and reaching the Moselle. He died the following year after a car accident.
Whiting, C., *Patton*. 1973

Paul I (1754–1801). Tsar of Russia (from 1796). He succeeded his mother Catherine the Great; having been kept from the throne by her for thirty-four years, he established a law of primogeniture. He broke his alliance with England to come to terms with Napoleon and planned to invade India. His rule as a capricious tyrant provoked a military plot and he was strangled by officers.

Paul I (1901–64). King of the Hellenes (1947–64). Son of * Constantine I, he was exiled in England 1923–35, served in the Greek army during World War II and in 1947 succeeded his brother * George II as king. He attempted to popularise the monarchy, but his wife, Frederika of Brunswick, was disliked because of her alleged pro-Nazi sympathies. He was the father of * Constantine II (XIII).

Paul III (Alessandro Farnese) (1468–1549). Pope (from 1534). Born of a noble family, he combined the roles of zealous church reformer and Renaissance potentate. He confirmed the first Jesuit constitution (1540), established the Inquisition in Rome (1542) and initiated the Council of Trent. A great patron of the arts, he commissioned * Michelangelo to design the dome of St Peter's and paint the fresco of the Last Judgement for the Sistine Chapel.
Pastor, L., *The History of the Popes from the Close of the Middle Ages*. Vols. 11–12. 1923

Paul IV (Gian Pietro Carafa) (1476–1559). Pope (from 1555). Born of an aristocratic Neapolitan family, he was made a cardinal by Paul III and was recognized as leader of the Counter-Reformation long before becoming pope at the age of 70. A strict and ruthless moralist, he introduced the Index of prohibited books and increased the range of the Inquisition and the severity of its sentences. After his death a mob destroyed his statue and burned the prisons of the Inquisition.

Paul VI (Giovanni Battista Montini) (1897–1978). Pope from 1963. Ordained in 1920, he was immediately selected for a post with the Secretariat of State and spent almost the whole of his career at the Vatican until becoming archbishop of Milan (1955); he was made a cardinal in 1958. As pope he continued the work of adapting the teaching and practices of the Catholic church to modern needs through the ecumenical council summoned by his predecessor * John XXIII. He took a number of unprecedented initiatives, e.g. his pilgrimage to Jerusalem (1964) and his visit to a session of the United Nations in New York.
Gonzalez, J. L., and Perez, T., trans. Heston, E. L., *Paul VI*. 1964

Paul, St (died ?64/5). Christian apostle. Born in Tarsus, he was a Jew and a Roman citizen. Before his conversion he was known as Saul. His life can be only partially reconstructed from the Acts of the Apostles and some of his Epistles. A tent-maker by trade, he was a zealous Pharisee and took part in the persecution of Christians; but while on his way to Damascus (33?) to bring back some Christians for trial he was temporarily blinded by a sudden vision and was suddenly and miraculously converted. After some time spent in meditation in the desert he went to preach at Jerusalem, but, though supported by Barnabas, he was regarded with suspicion and returned to Tarsus where he remained for ten years before Barnabas sought him out and took him to Antioch. A year later the two friends, with Mark as assistant, set out on their first missionary journey through Cyprus and many cities of Asia Minor. They made many converts but sooner or later were nearly always stoned and turned out by bands of fanatical Jews.

When Paul and Barnabas (Mark having left them) returned to Antioch, they were faced with controversy concerning the need for Gentile converts to accept circumcision and other observances prescribed by Jewish law. Paul and Barnabas supported the liberal view exempting Gentiles from such requirements and the eventual compromise by which these were reduced to a minimum enabled him then to continue their work. A second missionary journey was now begun but in Cyprus a dispute as to whether Mark should again be taken led to a parting, Paul choosing Silas as his companion, Barnabas taking Mark. For part of the way Paul retraced his steps in Asia Minor but after a dream in which he was begged to come over to Macedonia and help he crossed to Greece. From Thessalonica Jewish rancour drove them out, and in Athens, the home of philosophy, they had little success, but in Corinth (from *c.* 51) Paul found a home for eighteen months before returning to Antioch. After again visiting churches in Asia Minor (it was his habit to organize a congregation of believers in as many as possible of the places he passed through) he made Ephesus the focal point of his third journey. There he stayed nearly three years and from there wrote the first Epistle to the Corinthians. Then once more he went to Macedonia and again to Corinth, whence his letter to the Romans was written to prepare them for a visit. First, however, he returned to Jerusalem, where his old enemies roused the mob against him. Only the intervention of the commandant saved him, but the Roman governor Felix and his successor Festus kept him imprisoned for two years until at last Paul, as a Roman citizen, exercised his right to appeal to Caesar. Wrecked at Malta on the way, Paul eventually reached Rome and there was held in custody (though with considerable liberty) for about two years, and from there certainly wrote letters, of which some survive, to the churches he had founded. The Biblical narrative ends here but there is a strong tradition that he perished in the Neronian persecutions. His Epistles were almost certainly written before the gospels and inspired a great part of Christian theology. St Paul – the Apostle of the Gentiles – was above all instrumental in transforming Christianity from a Jewish sectarian creed to a universal religion.
Glover, T. R., *Paul of Tarsus*. 1925.

Pauli, Wolfgang (1900–1958). Austrian physicist. He became (1928) professor of physics at Zurich but later worked in the U.S.A. at Princeton. A pioneer in the application of the quantum theory to atomic structure, his most notable contribution was the 'exclusion principle' stating that two electrons cannot occupy the same quantum mechanical state at the same time. He suggested (1931) the

existence of the neutrino, an uncharged particle of almost zero mass. Pauli won the Nobel Prize for Physics (1945).
Kronig, R., and Weisskopf, V. F., eds., *Collected Scientific Papers*. 1964

Pauling, Linus Carl (1901–). American chemist. Professor of chemistry at the California Institute of Technology from 1927, he is best known for his work on molecular structure and valency. He introduced (1931) the concept of resonance, the rapid alternation of a pair of structures to produce a median structure or resonance hybrid, and this idea made it easier to elucidate the structure of several compounds that had previously offered great difficulties. He won the Nobel Prize for Chemistry (1954) and the Nobel Prize for Peace (1962).

Pausanias (2nd century A.D.). Greek geographer. He travelled through Greece, Italy and parts of Asia Minor and Africa, and may be regarded as the first writer of guide books, since his *Itinerary* of Greece gives the history of and legends connected with all the places he visited as well as details of all the works of art he saw there. It has thus inestimable value for the historian, geographer, archaeologist and mythologist.

Pausanias (fl. 5th century B.C.). Greek soldier. A regent of Sparta, he was the general who led the Greek army to victory over the Persians at Plataea (479 B.C.). Later he adopted Persian clothes and manners and seems to have entered into treacherous relations with the enemy. When finally he tried to gain power in Sparta by raising the serfs in revolt he was starved to death in the temple to which he had fled.

Pavlov, Ivan Petrovich (1849–1936). Russian physiologist. He took a medical degree (1883) and from 1891 was director of the physiology department of the Institute of Experimental Medicine at St Petersburg. He won the Nobel Prize for Medicine (1904) for his study of gastric secretions in the digestive glands. The experiments on dogs undertaken in the course of this work and the studies which developed from it won him world-wide notice. In his best known experiment Pavlov rang a bell before giving food to dogs, whose glands would begin to secrete saliva at the sight of food; after repetition the dogs salivated when they heard the bell even if no food was forthcoming. Such experiments revealed the 'conditioned reflexes' and led to a study of their effect on human behaviour and so to the behaviourist theories in modern psychology.
Babkin, B. P., *Pavlov: A Biography*. 1949

Pavlova, Anna Pavlovna (1882–1931). Russian ballerina. Born in St Petersburg, she was educated at the Imperial Ballet School. She quickly won renown and after a single season (1909) in Paris with * Diaghilev she formed her own company, with which she toured the chief cities of the world for the rest of her life. She was most famous for her solo performances in *divertissements*, e.g. *The Dying Swan* (music by Saint-Saëns), but she was also acclaimed for her roles in such ballets as *Don Quixote, Chopiniana* and *Autumn Leaves* (the last her own creation).
Franks, A. H., ed., *Pavlova*. 1956

Paxton, Sir Joseph (1806–1865). English gardener and architect. As superintendent of the Duke of Devonshire's gardens at Chatsworth he gained experience in the construction of large conservatories, which led to his commission to design the Crystal Palace for the Great Exhibition (1851), a landmark in the development of structural steel architecture. He was knighted for this work.
Chadwick, C. F., *The Works of Sir Joseph Paxton*. 1966

Peabody, George (1795–1869). American philanthropist. Having made a fortune as a wholesaler in the U.S.A., he settled in London (1837) as a merchant banker. His benefactions included over £1,000,000 for educational purposes in the U.S.A. and £500,000 for working-class flats in London. He refused honours, but on his death a British battleship conveyed his body to America where the name of his birthplace, Danvers, Massachusetts, was changed to Peabody.

Peace, Charles (1832–1879). Notorious English murderer. By day he made picture-frames; by night he was a burglar. In 1876 (as he confessed just before his execution) he shot and killed a Manchester policeman who appeared to be following him; in the same year, when observed loitering outside a house near Sheffield, he shot a Mr Dyson. Two years later, when living under an assumed name in London, he was disturbed while trying to enter a house at Blackheath: again he shot at the police but this time he was arrested, tried and found guilty of attempted murder. Meanwhile the link with his past had been established; he was taken to Sheffield, convicted of the murder of Dyson and hanged at Leeds.

Peacock, Andrew Sharp (1939–). Australian Liberal politician. A lawyer, he was a member of the House of Representatives 1966– , a minister 1969–72, 1975–81 and 1982–83, foreign minister 1975–80, and leader of the Liberal opposition 1983–85, following Malcolm * Fraser's defeat by Labor.

Peacock, Thomas Love (1785–1866). English novelist and poet, an employee of the East India Company from 1819. His conversational novels, interspersed with lyrics, satirize contemporary writers, philosophers and literary fashions. They include *Headlong Hall* (1816), *Melincourt* (1817), *Nightmare Abbey* (1818), *Crotchet Castle* (1831) and *Gryll Grange*, which did not appear until 1860; he also wrote two romances, *Maid Marian* (1822) and *The Misfortunes of Elphin* (1829). Peacock was a close friend of * Shelley (from 1814) and was his executor. His *Memorials of Shelley*, edited by H. Brett Smith, appeared in 1909. One of Peacock's four daughters was George * Meredith's first wife.
Mills, H., *Peacock*. 1969

Pears, Sir Peter (1910–). English concert and opera singer (tenor). Noted for his interpretation of works by Benjamin * Britten, he made his stage debut in 1942 and subsequently sang at Covent Garden, at Sadler's Wells and with the English Opera Group. He was (with Britten) co-founder of the Aldeburgh Festival (1948). He has created principal roles in 13 of Britten's operas, of which the best known is *Peter Grimes* (1945). He was knighted in 1978.

Pearse, Patrick (Padraic) **Henry** (1879–1916). Irish republican leader. He combined enthusiasm for the revival of Gaelic with a political extremism which induced him to join the Irish Republican Brotherhood and the nationalist Irish Volunteers (1913–16). He was chosen as president of the provisional republican government proclaimed during the Easter Rising (1916), and after its suppression was court-martialled and shot. He was a man of the highest ability and integrity.

Pearse, Richard William (1877–1953). New Zealand pioneer aviator. A self-educated farmer, he built a monoplane at Waitohi, South Island, and it is almost certain that he succeeded in a short manned flight on 31 March 1903, some 8 months before the * Wright Brothers. He was derided as a crank and became easily discouraged, concluding that the Wrights would have much easier access to finance and engineering support. He abandoned aviation and later became a recluse.
Ogilvie, G., *The Riddle of Richard Pearse*. 1973

Pearson, Sir Cyril Arthur, 1st Bart. (1866–1921). British newspaper proprietor and journalist. Founder of St Dunstan's charity for blinded servicemen, he began his editorial career on the magazine *Tit-Bits*, and during the 1890s founded his own *Pearson's Weekly*, followed by *Home Notes* and five others. He founded the *Daily Express* in 1900 and gained control of the *Standard* and *St James's Gazette* in 1905. His sight failed from 1910 and from then on he worked for the welfare of the blind.
Pearson, Sir C. A., *Victory over Blindness*. 1919

Pearson, Karl (1857–1936). British scientist. A man of wide interests and prolific talent, he was deeply involved in issues of social policy, science and religion and the popularization of science. Much of his life was given over to applying mathematical techniques – above all, statistics and probability – to the understanding of genetics and inheritance. Pearson was an ardent evolutionist. He believed evolution was a gradual and smooth process, involving shifts in characteristics across whole populations of creatures. These could in principle be traced statistically. This new approach he called 'biometrics'. It was opposed to the more orthodox Darwinism of men such as Bateson, who saw evolution as involving rather more discrete variations. The rediscovery of * Mendel's genetic work lent more support to Bateson.

During the last years of his life, Pearson became steadily more convinced of the crucial role of race in determining nationhood and civilization. He became a prominent eugenicist (he was the first Galton Professor of Eugenics at London University 1911–33), though within a framework of political thinking akin to Fabian socialism.
Pearson, E. S., *Karl Pearson*. 1938

Pearson, Lester Bowles (1897–1972). Canadian politician. After lecturing in history at Toronto University he entered the Department of External Affairs, was ambassador in Washington (1945–46) and became (1948) secretary of state for external affairs. He was president of the United Nations General Assembly (1952–53), and after a period (1958–63) as leader of the Liberal opposition became prime minister 1963–68. His diplomatic work, especially his attempts to settle the Suez crisis (1956), won him the Nobel Prize for Peace (1957). He received the OM in 1968.
Pearson, L. B., *The Four Faces of Peace*. 1964

Peary, Robert Edwin (1856–1920). American Arctic explorer. He joined the U.S. navy (1881) and an expedition to Greenland roused his interest in the problem of reaching the North Pole; in 1891–92 he crossed the Greenland ice pack from west to east and discovered what is now Peary Land. Subsequently (on leave from the navy) he made repeated expeditions with his aim always in view, and finally on 6 April 1909, accompanied by a Negro servant and after a dangerous sledge journey, he became the first explorer to reach the Pole. His book *The North Pole* (1910) describes the achievement. He was promoted to rear-admiral in 1911.

Peckinpah, Sam (1926–1984). U.S. film director. His major films include *The Wild Bunch* (1969) and *Straw Dogs* (1971) which have aroused considerable controversy over their explicit violence.

Pedro I (known as 'the Cruel') (1334–1369). King of Castile and Leon (from 1350). He was the only legitimate son of Alfonso XI, but he had to contend with the implacable enmity of his illegitimate half-brothers. Three were disposed of by assassination, but the most important, Henry of Trastamara, who had taken refuge in France, returned with a mercenary army. Pedro fled to Gascony and enlisted the support of the English Black Prince, who won a great victory at Najera but retired in disgust at Pedro's vengeful atrocities. Once more Henry invaded Castile, and after his victory at Montiel (1369), the two half-brothers met in single combat and Pedro was killed.

Pedro I (1798–1834). Emperor of Brazil (1822–31), and, as Pedro IV, king of Portugal. During the Peninsular War, when Portugal was invaded by Napoleon's armies, his father, John VI, and other members of the royal family took refuge in the Portuguese colony of Brazil. When John returned to Europe (1821) Pedro was left as regent, but when Brazil resisted Portuguese efforts to reimpose a colonial relationship Pedro put himself at the head of the independence party, and a declaration, the 'Grito do Ipiranga' (1822), gave independence to Brazil with himself as first emperor. He granted a constitution (1826) and in the same year on his father's death he also became king of Portugal. Shortly after, however, he renounced the Portuguese crown in favour of his daughter Maria. His involvement in the affairs of Portugal brought him unpopularity in Brazil and in 1831 he abdicated in favour of his son Pedro II. He then returned to Europe and in 1832 with the help of the English naval forces defeated the Miguelist faction in Portugal which had driven out Maria and re-established her as queen.
Haring, C. H., *Empire in Brazil: a New World Experiment with Monarchy*. 1958

Pedro II (1825–1890). Emperor of Brazil (1831–89). Though only 16 when he assumed power after a period of troubled regency, Pedro proved himself a liberal-minded constitutional ruler and showed skill in reconciling the political disputes of the various parties. In 1870 a long war with Paraguay ended successfully but the heavy Brazilian losses caused recriminations. The army's support for the régime weakened and a republican party appeared. The landed gentry, the emperor's strongest supporters, were offended by extensions of the franchise, and his position became untenable in 1888 when during his absence on a trip to Europe his daughter freed the slaves without compensating the owners. After a bloodless revolution Pedro retired to Europe (1889).

Peel, Sir Robert, 2nd Bart. (1788–1850). English politician. The son of a rich Lancashire cotton manufacturer, he was a friend of * Byron at Harrow and distinguished himself at Oxford. He was a Tory MP (1809–50), being first elected at 21, and was still only 24 when he became secretary for Ireland, where * O'Connell, the Roman Catholic leader, was his powerful opponent. He became (1822) home secretary, his term of office made famous by the creation of the Metropolitan police force (whose members were nicknamed after him 'peelers' or 'bobbies'). Though he had worked in harmony with * Canning, he resigned with the Duke of * Wellington (1827) as a protest against Roman Catholic emancipation, which however they both accepted and passed through parliament when they returned to office in the same year after Canning's death. By the election following George IV's death the Whigs returned to power and passed the famous parliamentary Reform Act (1832) against Peel's opposition. When * Melbourne resigned (May 1839) Peel's return to office was delayed by Queen Victoria's refusal to part with her ladies of the bedchamber (all Whigs). After the election of 1841 Peel became prime minister with a useful majority, and in defiance of his Tory supporters gradually became a convert to free trade. His first step was to introduce a sliding scale by which the duty on corn varied in accordance with the price at home, the lost revenue being replaced by an income tax of 7d. in the pound. But when the potato blight in Ireland, followed by famine, made the cheapest possible corn an urgent necessity in Peel's opinion, he introduced (1846) his measure for Corn Law repeal. A party split was the inevitable result and though Peel pushed the act through with Whig support, he was forced to resign. He was never again in office but his prestige in the House of Commons and his popularity in the country remained undiminished. He died as a result of being thrown from his horse on Constitution Hill. In public life Peel appeared cold and austere, and though highly competent was never a good party man. In private he led an ideally happy domestic life with his wife (née Julia Floyd) and seven children, and he was a genial and generous friend.

Gash, N., *Sir Robert Peel*. 1972

Péguy, Charles (Pierre) (1873–1914). French poet and publisher. He combined active socialism with Catholicism and sincere patriotism, revealed in the drama *Jeanne d'Arc* (1897), which he wrote in pseudonymous collaboration with his friend Marcel Baudouin. He founded (1900) the journal *Cahiers de la Quinzaine*, in which he published his own works and those of other writers, several of whom, e.g. Romain Rolland, subsequently became important. Péguy's later works include *Le Mystère de la charité de Jeanne d'Arc* (1910) and *La Tapisserie de Notre Dame* (1913). He was killed in World War I.

Wilson, N., *Charles Péguy*. 1965

Pei, I(eoh) M(ing) (1917–). American architect, born in Canton. In the US from 1935, he taught at Harvard and won international recognition with a series of important buildings in Boston—the Christian Science Church Centre, the east wing of the Museum of Fine Arts, the Kennedy Memorial Library (Harvard), and (with Henry Cobb) the John Hancock Tower. He designed the east wing of the National Gallery in Washington and the Place Ville-Marie in Montreal.

Peirce, Charles Sanders (1839–1914). American philosopher. The son of a well known mathematician, he studied mathematics, physics and chemistry, spending much of his life in the U.S. Government Coast and Geodetic Survey. Because of his unconventionality he obtained no proper academic recognition, and most of his writing became available only after his death. He is best known for his view of the meaning of concepts: our idea of something is made up of notions of that thing's effects. William * James and others turned this 'pragmatic maxim' into the dubious theory ('pragmatism') that the test of a statement's truth is whether or not it has (good) effects, but this extension was disdained by Peirce. His own theory of truth, which he named 'pragmaticism' to distinguish it from James's version, involved the verification of hypotheses by the scientific community.

Murphey, G. M., *The Development of Peirce's Philosophy*. 1961

Peisistratus (*c.* 600–528 B.C.). Tyrant of Athens. He fought successfully against Megara; then by claiming that his wife was threatened he obtained a bodyguard, with which (*c.* 560) he seized the Acropolis. He was twice expelled but as the owner of gold and silver mines he was able to hire mercenaries to ensure his victory over his opponents. He ruled with wisdom and success and by using his own fortune and money confiscated from his adversaries helped the farmers, and did much to assist the poor, as well as fortifying and beautifying Athens. He is traditionally held to have been the first to collect Homer's

poems. He was succeeded by his sons Hippias and Hipparchus.
Andrewes, A., *The Greek Tyrants.* 1956

Pelagius (born *c.* 370). Early Christian monk, born either in Britain or Brittany. With his disciple Coelestius he settled in Rome (*c.* 400); when the Goths threatened the city the two withdrew to Carthage (409). From there Pelagius made a pilgrimage to Jerusalem, while the impetuous Coelestius, still in Carthage, attacked St * Augustine's doctrines on predestination and original sin, thus opening the Pelagian controversy. Pelagius objected to the doctrine of original sin and affirmed that Adam would have died whether or not he had sinned, and that each of his descendants is born as innocent as he. He further held that it is at least theoretically possible for a man to live without sin, solely by his own free will, a doctrine which seemed to diminish the need for God's grace. Pelagianism was first officially condemned in 416 and more formally at the Councils of Carthage and Ephesus (418 and 431). Pelagius was banished from Rome (418); it is not known where, when or how he died.
Evans, R. F., *Pelagius.* 1968

Pelé (real name Edson Arantes do Nascimento) (1940–). Brazilian soccer player. He played for the Santos Football Club (from 1955) as inside centre left in 1,114 games and was often regarded as the greatest player in the history of football. He appeared in the film *Escape to Victory* (1981).

Pelham, Henry (1696–1754). English Whig politician, member of Parliament 1717–54, and prime minister 1743–46 and (after a three-day resignation) 1746–54. He held several important offices under * Walpole but after his fall (1742) joined his own elder brother, the Duke of * Newcastle in building up such a successful system of patronage that no administration could exist without them. Henry, the cleverer of the two, became head of the government (1743) and having shed the brilliant Carteret (Lord * Granville), whose continental policy he distrusted, was able to enjoy a decade of efficient and unspectacular rule. He maintained his parliamentary influence, however, as much by systematic corruption as by his political and financial abilities.
Owen, J. B., *Rise of the Pelhams.* 1971

Pembroke, Richard de Clare, 2nd Earl of (known as 'Strongbow') (*c.* 1130–1176). Anglo-Norman adventurer. He led an expedition into Ireland (1169) and married Eva, the daughter of the deposed King Dermot of Leinster, whose kingdom he recovered. On his father-in-law's death (1171) he himself ruled the kingdom, for which he paid homage to Henry II of England, thus inaugurating the long and unhappy period of English rule in Ireland.

Penda (died 655). Anglo-Saxon king of Mercia (from 633). He gradually built up the strength of his kingdom and finally (633) allied himself with the Christian Welsh king Cadwallon to defeat and kill Edwin of Northumbria and so make Mercia independent. For a time Penda was the most powerful king in England, but Northumbria reasserted its power when Oswald's brother Oswy (Oswiu) defeated and killed Penda in a battle near Leeds.

Penderecki, Krzysztof (1933–). Polish composer. He won international recognition with his *St Luke Passion* (1966), an eclectic work showing the influence of Monteverdi and Bach, but using an atonal style. He composed two symphonies and a violin concerto.

Penfield, Wilder Graves (1891–1976). Canadian neurosurgeon, born in the US. A Rhodes scholar at Oxford, he studied under * Osler and * Sherrington, and lived in Montreal from 1926. His operations on epileptics led to his 'mapping' brain areas responsible for memory, sensory and motor functions. He was a prolific writer on the mechanism of the brain and received the OM in 1953.

Penn, William (1644–1718). English Quaker and founder of Pennsylvania, U.S.A. The son of a distinguished admiral of the Commonwealth period, he adopted the beliefs of the Quakers which he expounded in, e.g., *The Sandy Foundation Shaken* (1668), for which he was confined in the Tower of London, and *No Cross, No Crown* (1669). His belief in toleration and the need for it in the members of the Society of Friends (Quakers) brought him into touch with James, Duke of York (later James II), who suggested emigration and helped Penn to secure the lease of a large territory,

named Pennsylvania after its founder, to the west of the Delaware River. Here he set up a colony of Quakers: its religious tolerance also attracted English, Dutch and German settlers of other sects. Philadelphia ('city of brotherly love') was founded in 1682. Penn, who visited the colony twice (1682–84 and 1699–1701), drew up for it a constitution that was remarkably liberal: e.g. the governor (at first Penn himself) could rule only by consent, the legislature was chosen by ballot and, most important of all, toleration was enjoined for all forms of religion compatible with Christianity. Penn's later years were clouded by religious disputes and financial difficulties, but he remains one of the most practical idealists of his time. He wrote extensively on theological matters and from time to time was an itinerant preacher.
Dunn, M. D., *William Penn: Politics and Conscience*. 1967

Penney, William George, Baron Penney (1909–). British scientist. After teaching mathematics at the Imperial College of Science and Technology, London (1935–44), he directed armament research in the ministry of supply (1946–52). In 1953 he superintended the testing at Woomera, Australia, of the second British atomic bomb, was awarded the KBE, and became director of the nuclear weapons establishment at Aldermaston, Berks. He was chairman of the United Kingdom Atomic Energy Authority 1964–67 and received the OM in 1969.

Penzias, Arno Allan (1933–). American radioastronomer, born in Germany. He worked for the Bell Telephone Laboratories 1961– and with Robert W. Wilson (1936–) continued research, which Karl * Jansky had begun, into the origins of background interference to radio signals. After all specific sources had been eliminated, a weak, evenly spread signal was detected which they concluded came from the universe at large and was decisive evidence for the 'big bang' theory. Penzias and Wilson shared the 1978 Nobel Prize for Physics with Peter * Kapitza.

Pepin. The name of several members of a Frankish family who served the Merovingian kings and were the ancestors of Charlemagne and, the later Carolingians. **Pepin I** (died 640) and his grandson **Pepin II** (died 714) were executive leaders with the title 'mayor of the palace'. **Pepin III** (714/715–768) took the decisive step of deposing the Merovingian king Childeric and assuming the royal title. By helping the pope to regain the papal territories he obtained consecration, and his victories over the Arabs in France enabled him to hand over an enlarged and strengthened kingdom to his son * Charlemagne.
Wallace-Hadrill, J. M., *The Barbarian West 400–1000*. 3rd ed. 1967

Pepys, Samuel (1633–1703). English diarist and government servant. In the Admiralty he rose to be secretary to the Commission (1673–79 and 1684–89), where he worked with great industry and efficiency. During the Dutch War (1664–67), when his duties were mainly concerned with supply, he waged a continuous struggle with corrupt officials and dishonest contractors. He served as MP 1673–79; 1679; 1685–87. Pepys was one of the many falsely accused (1679) in the Popish plot (Titus * Oates); he was briefly imprisoned in the Tower of London, and was not restored to his post until 1684. A friend of * Wren, * Newton and * Dryden, Pepys was president of the Royal Society (1684–86).

His famous diary covers the years 1660–69. The gossip and scandal of Charles II's court, theatrical life, and public events (e.g. the Plague, the sailing up the Thames by the enemy Dutch fleet and the Great Fire) are all vividly recorded. The diary also describes his own domestic life with his lively French wife, Elizabeth de Saint-Michel, who was only 15 when he married her (1655). Throughout his constant philanderings, their mutual jealousies and ardent reconciliations he and his wife, 'poor wretch', never ceased to be in love. The diary (written in cipher) came into the hands of Magdalene College, Cambridge, but was left undeciphered until the 19th century and was first published in 1825. It was republished in eleven volumes, 1970–83.
Ollard, R., *Pepys*. 1974

Perceval, Spencer (1762–1812). British Tory politician and barrister. He entered parliament in 1796 and with the support of * Pitt had risen to be attorney general when Pitt died (1806). He served as chancellor of the exchequer under Portland (1807–09) and succeeded him as prime minister (1809). He was killed by a lunatic, John Bellingham, in the lobby of the House of Commons, the only British prime minister ever assassinated.

Percy, Sir Henry (known as 'Hotspur') (1364–1403). English nobleman. He was one of the most distinguished members of the family which has for centuries been associated with the earldom and dukedom of Northumberland. The son of the 1st Earl, he had already gained renown as hero of the Battle of Otterburn (1388) against the Scots when supporting his father in his quarrel with Henry IV, he joined a conspiracy to replace the king by a rival claimant, Edmund Earl of March. He was intercepted on his way to join the Welsh rebel leader Owen * Glendower and was killed in the battle of Shrewsbury.

Perelman, S(idney) J(oseph) (1904–1979). US humorist, born in New York. He wrote scripts for the * Marx Brothers' films *Monkey Business* and *Horse Feathers*, was a regular contributor to *The New Yorker* from 1931 until his death, produced several travel books and won a 1956 Academy Award for his *Around the World in 80 Days*. He had a genius for parody and a mastery of language comparable to * Joyce and * Nabokov.

Peres, Shimon (1923–). Israeli Labour politician, born in Poland. He migrated to Palestine in 1934 and studied in the US (NYU and Harvard). He served in the Knesset 1959– , and was minister of defence 1974–77, Labour leader 1977– , and prime minister in a 'national unity' coalition 1984– .

Perez de Cuellar, Javier (1920–). Peruvian diplomat. He was permanent delegate to the United Nations 1971–75, under-secretary general 1979–81 and succeeded Kurt * Waldheim as secretary general 1981– .

Pérez Galdós, Benito (1843–1920). Spanish writer, born in the Canary Islands. He is considered the greatest Spanish novelist since * Cervantes. In his forty-six *Episodios nacionales* (1873–1912) he followed a plan of relating important historical events to ordinary lives. In his extensive series of *Novelas españolas contemporáneos* he throws into dramatic relief the incompatibles of 19th-century life and thought, e.g. liberalism and absolutism, science and imagination, progress and tradition; in others (e.g. the Torquemada series) he dramatizes the parallel conflicts in the individual conscience. Many of his plays are dramatized versions of his novels.
Varey, J. E., ed., *Galdós Studies*. 1970

Pergolesi, Giovanni Battista (1710–1736). Italian composer. He produced religious music (e.g. the famous *Stabat Mater* for female voices and strings), instrumental pieces and operas (serious and comic) but is best known for the enormously successful *La Serva Padrona* (1733), which though it came to be performed as a comic opera was initially a series of *intermezzi* between the acts of his serious opera *Il Prigionier superbo*. Tuberculosis and personal disappointments clouded his short life.
Giraldi, R., *Giovanni Battista Pergolesi*. 1936

Pericles (*c.* 490–429 B.C.). Athenian statesman. He came of a noble family and was educated by leading thinkers, e.g. Anaxagoras; though he was aloof in manner and never courted popularity, politically he was a radical and opposed the ruling oligarchy headed by the commander-in-chief Cimon and backed by the Spartans. A rift between the latter and Cimon enabled Pericles to reorient the constitution by depriving the Areopagus (the conservative council of ex-magistrates) of its power (426) and securing the ostracism of Cimon (461). A change in foreign policy followed; Athens and Sparta parted company and thereafter were either at war or enjoying uneasy peace. Peace too was made with Persia, and most of the states which comprised the Delian League against Persia were gradually converted under the guidance of Pericles, who dominated the Athenian assembly until his death, into a maritime empire under Athenian control. He even secured the acceptance of a proposal that the League funds collected for the war should be used not only for policing the seas but for rebuilding and beautifying Athens, which had suffered much during the Persian invasion. Under his guidance, and through his patronage of such artists as the great * Phidias Athens grew in a few years into the most beautiful city in the world, the Parthenon, the Propylaea and the Odeum being among the buildings constructed at this time. Meanwhile there was mounting jealousy of Athens' growing strength. Some of the allies, including Samos (which was decisively crushed), revolted; and the Spartans invaded Attica (446) but were bribed by Pericles to withdraw and renew the truce. The crisis was thus delayed until 433 when Pericles, feeling that the time was ripe for a final trial of strength, induced the assembly to accept the plea of Corcyra (Corfu) for an alliance against

Sparta's ally Corinth; this provoked the Peloponnesian War with Sparta (which lasted with intervals from 431 to 404 and eventually brought about the Athenian empire's downfall). Pericles' death was caused by the great plague of 430, during which a quarter of the population died. His domestic life was dominated by his mistress, the beautiful and talented Aspasia.

Burn, A. R., *Pericles and Athens.* 1970

Perkin, Sir William Henry (1838–1907). English chemist. While attempting to synthesize quinine when he was only 18, he discovered the first aniline dye, which he named 'mauve'. The commercial application of his discovery was pursued much more intensively in Germany than in Britain, which had no sizeable synthetic dye industry till after World War I. Perkin made a number of discoveries in organic chemistry, the most important of which was probably the 'Perkin synthesis' (1867) for the preparation of unsaturated aromatic acids. He was knighted in 1906. His son, also **William Henry Perkin** (1860–1929), was an organic chemist who worked on the formation of rings of carbon atoms and berberine, and made important contributions to the organization and extension of chemical studies and facilities at Oxford.

Perón, Juan Domingo (1895–1974). Argentine president. One of a group of discontented officers in the 1930s, he led a revolt (1943) against President Castillo and became vice-president and war minister under General Farell. He curried favour with labour unions by decrees which granted social welfare benefits. Briefly imprisoned in 1946 he was released following labour demonstrations largely organized by his wife Eva, and in the general election of 1946 was elected president by an overwhelming majority. For the next nine years (he was re-elected in 1951) he ruled as a dictator backed by the militant support of the industrial workers who were delighted with his policy ('peronismo'), which was in essence to favour the workers at the expense of other classes and fiscal stability. From 1952 Perón had increasing difficulty in managing the country and was foolish enough to provoke the antagonism of the Roman Catholic church. This, together with the chaos caused by inflation, provoked the revolt of the army and navy (1955) which led to his exile. He remained in exile for 18 years but in 1973 he returned to Argentina and assumed the presidency. At his death the country was in political chaos.

His wife, **Eva Maria Duarte de Perón** (1919–1952), was originally a popular actress; she threw her vast energy and ambition on the side of Perón whom she married in 1945. She skilfully wooed the support of Argentine women especially through the Eva Perón Social Aid Foundation for dispensing help to the poor. His second wife, **Isabelita Martinez Perón** (1931–), was a folk and cabaret dancer when he married her in 1961. Elected as vice president in 1973, she succeeded as president on his death (1974) until deposed by the military (1976).

Ferns, H. S., *Argentina.* 1969. Rock, D., ed., *Argentina in the Twentieth Century.* 1975

Perrault, Charles (1628–1703). French civil servant and writer. The son of a lawyer, he became adviser on art to * Colbert and was elected (1671) to the Académie Française. In his own time he was known in France for his part in the 'quarrel of the ancients and the moderns' in which he championed the moderns in a lengthy controversy with * Boileau. His greater fame comes from his *Histoires ou Contes du temps passé* (1697), a collection of eight traditional fairy stories, among them 'Sleeping Beauty', 'Red Riding Hood', 'Blue Beard', 'Puss in Boots' and 'Cinderella', to which he gave a definitive shape of lasting popularity. They are sometimes called 'Mother Goose's Tales' after the secondary title *Contes de ma mère l'Oye* on the frontispiece of the original edition.

Perry, Matthew Calbraith (1794–1858). American sailor. As commodore of a US squadron he was sent to Japan (1853) to conclude a trade agreement; he succeeded on his second attempt in the following year, when he negotiated a treaty which ended Japan's 250 years of isolation from the west. This began the process by which Japan became one of the most powerful and technologically advanced nations of the world.

Perry, M. C., *Narrative of the Expedition of an American Squadron to the China Seas and Japan.* 1856

Perse, Saint-John (pen-name of Marie René Auguste Alexis Saint-Léger Léger) (1887–1975). French poet and diplomat, born near

Guadeloupe. He was permanent secretary for foreign affairs and was consistently opposed to appeasement. He escaped from Vichy France to the USA (1940) where he became an adviser on French affairs to the administration. His best known poem, *Anabase* (1924), was translated into English by T. S. * Eliot (1930). Later volumes of poetry include *Exil* (1942), *Vents* (1946), *Amers* (1957) and *Chroniques* (1960). He won the Nobel Prize for Literature (1960) for 'the soaring flight and evocative imagery of his poetry, which in visionary fashion reflects the condition of our times'.
Little, J. R., *Saint-John Perse*. 1973

Pershing, John Joseph (1860–1948). American general. He commanded the US troops in France in World War I and accomplished a remarkable feat of organization in building up an army of thirty-eight divisions which in 1918 played a vital part in the final victorious campaign. Earlier, Pershing had served in Cuba, the Philippines and Mexico.
Pershing, J. J., *My Experience in the World War*. 1931

Perugino, Il (Pietro Vannucci) (*c.* 1445–1523). Italian painter. After woking in Florence and Rome he settled at Perugia, where some of his best work remains. His art is characterized by clearly articulated composition; he is traditionally regarded as the teacher of * Raphael, and certainly Raphael's early works bear striking Peruginesque qualities. Perugino executed (1481) part of the decorative programme in the Sistine Chapel at the Vatican (e.g. the the fresco of Christ giving the keys to Peter). He is represented in the National Gallery, London, by a characteristic triptych, originally at Pavia.
Castellanata, C., *Pietro Vannucci Perugino*. 1969

Perutz, Max Ferdinand (1914–). British biochemist, born in Vienna. He left Austria in 1936, worked at Cambridge but was interned during World War II as an enemy alien. He directed research into molecular biology at Cambridge 1947–73 and won the 1962 Nobel Prize for Chemistry (with J. C. * Kendrew) for their use of X-ray diffraction in working out the structure of protein molecules.

Pestalozzi, Johann Heinrich (1746–1827). Swiss educational reformer. Under the influence of * Rousseau he believed that primary education for the masses (and especially for destitute children) would best achieve its aim of creating useful and virtuous people in the natural surroundings and occupations of agricultural life; he therefore started his first educational experiment in a farm at Neuhof, but lack of practical ability led to its failure (1780). He then gave up for a time his educational experiments to think out a system derived from his experience. His books, especially the social novel *How Gertrude Teaches her Children* (1801), propound his basic theory that education should develop and train all the faculties, not merely the intellect. In 1798 he again opened an orphan school at Stanz but within eight months it was ruined by peasant bigotry. Finally (1805) he established himself at Yverdon, but, though he had many admirers and followers, the attempt to extend his methods to secondary education was one of several mistakes which caused him to die a disappointed man.

Pétain, Henri Philippe Omer (1856–1951). French Marshal. In World War I he became famous for his defence of Verdun and he succeeded (1917) General * Nivelle as commander-in-chief of the French armies in the field. He restored discipline and morale and under Foch's supreme command conducted the final victorious offensives. On Armistice Day he was made a marshal. He restored order in Morocco (1926–28) after Abd al Krim's revolt and among other posts was ambassador to Franco's government in Spain (1939–40). He was recalled to be vice-premier in Reynaud's government. After the French defeat he became prime minister with a policy of surrender and after the armistice the national assembly at Vichy appointed him head of state (i.e. of the unoccupied portion, which became known as Vichy France). Within the limits enjoined by collaboration with the Germans he probably maintained such dignity and independence as the situation allowed, making use of such ministers as * Darlan, * Flandin and * Laval, but when the Allied armies of liberation landed (1944) he was removed to Germany. On his return to France (1945) he was tried and condemned to death but * de Gaulle commuted the sentence to life imprisonment.
Griffith, R. M., *Pétain*. 1970

Peter I (known as 'the Great') (1672–1725). Tsar (emperor) of Russia (from 1682). He was the only son of Tsar Alexis by his second wife, and succeeded Fyodor II, but, after a revolt engineered by his half-sister Sophia, he shared the throne (under her regency) with his feeble-minded half-brother Ivan. When the latter died (1696) Peter assumed full power. Much of his education, mainly in mechanics, navigation, military science etc., he had acquired from young foreigners in Moscow whom he made his companions. Two expeditions (1695 and 1696) against the Turks, by which Russia acquired the fortress of Azov and so gained access to the Black Sea from the Don, gave him his first experience of leadership. While travelling abroad (1696–98) he spent much of his time in the shipyards of Holland and England (where he worked for a time at Deptford) working with his own hands and learning shipbuilding and navigation. He also engaged skilled men to go to Russia as instructors. With the aim of modernizing Russia he started schools, arranged for textbooks to be translated, edited the first Russian newspaper, opened the first museum; he brought the church entirely under state control by abolishing the patriarchate and substituting a Holy Synod; and, without abandoning any of his autocratic powers, he turned the administration into an efficient machine, but the poll-tax and other impositions to provide revenue were not popular. Peter's most spectacular undertaking, designed to make the country look west-wards, was to build an entirely new capital on swampy ground won from Sweden at the point where the Neva joins the Baltic Sea. Thousands of peasants, many of whom died in the unhealthy conditions, were forcibly enrolled for the task; government offices and palaces sprang up, nobles and wealthy men were compelled to build houses in the new capital; so, through the emperor's initiative and genius for planning, the city of St Petersburg (later Petrograd and now Leningrad) came into being as one of the most beautiful cities of the world.

Peter's foreign policy was in line with his westernizing policy. In the course of a prolonged war with Sweden (1700–21), defeat after defeat was finally reversed by a great victory over Charles XII at Poltava (1709) which enabled him to annex parts of Finland, Estonia and Livonia and secure for Russia a commanding influence in the Baltic.

Peter's domestic life was unhappy. Under the influence of his first wife, his son Alexis joined the faction opposed to his policies and died mysteriously during the investigation into their intrigues. After divorce, Peter married Catherine, his peasant mistress and ultimate successor, whom he had taken over from his friend and collaborator * Menshikov. She bore him twelve children, but Peter died without naming an heir.

Kliuchevskii, V., *Peter the Great*. 1965. Anderson, M. S., *Peter the Great*. 1978. De Jorge, A., *Fire and Water*. 1979

Peter I (1844–1921). King of Serbia (from 1903) and of Yugoslavia (from 1918). As a member of the * Karageorgević dynasty, he lived in exile until the assassination (1903) of King Alexander of the rival Obreonovic dynasty brought him to the Serbian throne. He secured great territorial advantages for his country at the expense of Turkey and Bulgaria in the two Balkan Wars (1912–13). Meanwhile he had reversed his predecessor's policy by aligning Serbia with Russia instead of Austria, and it was a Serb patriot who murdered the Austrian Archduke Francis Ferdinand, sparking off World War I. Peter remained steadfast while his country was overrun and after the final victory, which united the Austro-Hungarian South Slav territories with his own, he was declared king of the Serbs, Croats and Slovenes (Yugoslavia). He was succeeded by his son * Alexander I; his grandson, **Peter II** (1923–   ), became king in 1934 and was declared of age (1941) when his uncle Paul was deposed from the regency during World War II for failing to stand up against Hitler's demands. When Yugoslavia was overrun Peter went into exile (1940), from which, after the Allied victory, Marshal * Tito did not allow him to return.

Temperley, H. W. V., *History of Serbia*. 1917

Peter II (1715–1730). Tsar of Russia (from 1727). As the son of Alexis, Peter the Great's dead son, he would have been his grandfather's natural successor had not * Menshikov secured the proclamation of the emperor's widow as Catherine I. On her death Peter II inherited peacefully, but died from smallpox within three years.

Peter III (1728–1762). Tsar of Russia (1761–62). He succeeded his aunt, the empress * Elizabeth, and made his single contribution to European history when he immediately withdrew Russia from the coalition which at that stage of the Seven Years War was threatening * Frederick the Great with disaster. He was one of Frederick's most uncritical admirers, and one of his more harmless hobbies was drilling soldiers dressed in Prussian style. Vain, obstinate and feeble-minded, Peter was soon seen to be unfit to rule. A plot was formed by the guards regiment and successfully carried out by which his wife was to be proclaimed empress as * Catherine II. Peter abdicated and was killed a week later, allegedly in a drunken brawl.

Peter, St (died *c.* A.D. 67). Apostle of Jesus Christ. The name Peter (from the Greek *petra*, the equivalent of the Aramaic *cepha*, 'rock') is the anglicized form of the name given by Jesus to the most prominent of his disciples, Simon, son of Jonah. The interpretation of the sentence 'Thou art Peter and upon this rock I will build my church' (Matthew 16, 18) has long been the subject of controversy between Roman Catholics and Protestants, the former using it to support their claim for the supremacy of St Peter's church of Rome.

Peter, a fisherman on the sea of Galilee, lived with his wife at Capernaum. One of the first apostles, he was regarded by Jesus with special affection. He was the first to hail Jesus as Messiah, but just before the Crucifixion, he denied three times that he had any connexion with Jesus. Peter was the first to enter the sepulchre and the first to see Jesus after the Resurrection. He became the acknowledged leader of the earliest Christian community, as is shown by the several references to him in Acts 1–12, e.g. the episodes of Ananias and Sapphira and of Simon Magus, of Peter's arrest by Herod and his miraculous release. In the controversy concerning the observance of Jewish practices by Gentile converts Peter appears to have supported the compromise view eventually adopted (* Paul, St). The first and second Epistles of St Peter seem to be by different hands: the first, early in date and simple in doctrine, is usually accepted as Peter's work. That Peter visited Rome and there became 'bishop', that he was martyred during Nero's persecutions, as St Paul is supposed to have been, are assumptions based on strong tradition. Peter is often represented in art holdings keys, as the gate-keeper of Heaven. St Peter's is the metropolitan church of the bishopric of Rome, begun in 1506 and situated near the presumed site of his martyrdom. Excavations in this century have uncovered a tomb which is believed by many to be Peter's.

Peter the Hermit (*c.* 1050–*c.* 1115). French monk, one of the many preachers in Germany and France who aroused enthusiasm for the 1st Crusade. In 1096 he led a group of fanatical peasants across Hungary into Asia Minor, but by then they had become so unruly that he left them to almost inevitable slaughter at the hands of the Turks. He himself returned to Constantinople and joined the main body of crusaders who in 1099 captured Jerusalem. On his return he founded a monastery at Huy in the Low Countries, where he died.

Peterborough, Charles Mordaunt, 3rd Earl of (1658?–1735). English adventurer. After naval service in the Mediterranean he was able to render such help to William III in his bid for the throne that he received high office and rewards. Under Queen Anne he was given joint command (1705), with Sir Clowdisley * Shovell, of an expedition sent to Spain during the War of the Spanish Succession; he captured Barcelona and made a spectacular victorious march through Catalonia, quarrelling constantly, however, with his associates or allies. Ambassadorial appointments followed, each ended by some irregular or impetuous action. His appointment (1714) as governor of Minorca was terminated when Queen Anne died in the same year. This closed his official career though he continued to tour Europe as a self-appointed and self-accredited envoy. He was a friend of Pope and Swift.

Petipa, Marius (1822–1910). French dancer and choreographer. He performed at the Comédie Française and soon became well known throughout France and in Spain. He went to Russia (1847) where he was immediately acclaimed, and he is regarded as one of the founders of the Russian ballet. His best remembered works were produced in association with * Tchaikovsky, e.g. *The Sleeping Beauty* (1890) and *Swan Lake* (1895).

Petit, Roland (1924–). French dancer and choreographer. He worked as a boy with the Paris Opéra ballet, and in 1948 formed his own company which appeared at the Théâtre Marigny. He created many new ballets, e.g. *Le Loup*, *Ballabille* (for the London Royal Ballet) and *Cyrano de Bergerac* (1959), his first full-length ballet. In 1965 he created and danced in

Notre Dame de Paris, suggesting the hunchback's deformity without padding.

Petrarch (Francesco Petrarca) (1304–1374). Italian poet and scholar, born at Arrezzo. His father moved (1311) to Avignon, then the seat of the papacy, and Francesco later returned there after three years' uncongenial study of civil law at Bologna; he then took minor orders. He first saw Laura (plausibly identified as the wife of Hugues de Sade) in church at Avignon at Eastertide in 1327; worshipped from a distance, she remained the love of his life until and even after her death (1348) and was the inspiration of his famous love poems (*Rime* or *Canzoniere*). Petrarch did not invent the fourteen-line sonnet form, in which nearly 300 of them were written, but his fame inspired the many imitators (e.g. Sir Thomas Wyatt) and so justifies the name Petrarchan sonnet.

By his contemporaries, however, Petrarch was acclaimed for scholarship. He was among the first to revive interest in the language and literature of classical Rome. He took advantage of his travels to search for and discover old MSS., including an interesting batch of Cicero's letters. Through the patronage of the Colonna family, in Avignon and Rome he came to know the learned and great and even to correspond with rulers on political affairs. Evidence of his fame came after he had settled (1337) in retirement at Vaucluse in Provence and had started his epic *Africa* on the life of Scipio Africanus. Invitations came to him simultaneously from the university of Paris and the Roman senate to accept the tribute of a laurel crown.

Back in Vaucluse he must have begun to question his own motives, for in the imaginary dialogues of *De Contemptu Mundi* (1343) he finds himself confronted with * St Augustine's censure for his attachment to Laura and to fame. Laura's death and the failure of the attempt (1347) by his friend * Cola di Rienzi to establish a republic in Rome seem to have stirred in him a deep pessimism about the state of Italy. From Rome, where he met and won the admiration of * Boccaccio, he went to Padua and then to Venice, where he advocated peace with Genoa. He returned to France (1351), but after further travels in Italy he settled at Arqua in the hills near Padua and there he was found dead with his head resting on a book. Petrarch is commonly regarded as the Father of Italian Humanism.

Wilkins, E. H., *Life of Petrarch*. 1961

Petrie, Sir (William Matthew) Flinders (1853–1942). English archaeologist. Even as a boy he collected Roman coins, and he published a book on Stonehenge in 1880. He first went to Egypt in 1881, and there surveyed the pyramids of Giza and established standards of excavation procedure that entitle him to be regarded as the founder of scientific archaeological methods. In particular he saw the value of stratification (i.e. uncovering a horizontal layer in which all objects found will be of the same date). This combined with systematic recording enabled a particular stage of a civilization to be accurately assessed for the first time. He spent nearly his whole life in excavations of this kind in Egypt and adjacent countries. He also wrote many books on the history, religion, arts and crafts and social life of ancient Egypt. Among the many interesting sites examined was the Greek city of Naucratis in the Nile delta. He was a professor of Egyptology at London University (1893–1935) and he established (1894) what later became the British school of Archaeology in Egypt. He was knighted in 1923.

Marek, W. K., *Gods, Graves and Scholars*. 2nd ed. 1967

Petronius (Arbiter) (d. 66). Probably the Gaius Petronius who was 'Arbiter elegantiae' at the court of Nero, directing the emperor's lavish entertainments, his only surviving works are fragments of the *Saturae* (wrongly known as *Satyricon*), a prose extravaganza interspersed with verse, parodying the sentimental Greek romances of the day. Among episodes relating the obscene adventures of three rascals in *Dinner with Trimalchio*, a banquet in the house of a typical *nouveau riche*. To avoid execution by Nero, Petronius staged an elaborate suicide to the accompaniment of a witty discourse, delaying his death by continually rebandaging the opened veins.

Sullivan, J. P., *The Satyricon of Petronius*. 1968

Peugeot, Armand (1849–1915). French automobile maker. His family ran weaving, dying and steelmaking firms. After a career as a bicycle-maker, Peugeot produced a steam car in 1889, a petrol car in 1891 and the popular 'Bébé Peugeot' in 1911.

Pheidippides (5th century B.C.). Greek runner. He carried the news of the Persian invasion and a request for help from Athens to Sparta

(490 B.C.), covering the distance of 150 miles in two days. Some versions of the story name him also as the runner who fell dead after conveying news of victory from the battlefield of Marathon to Athens. This exploit is commemorated in the modern Olympic games by the marathon race (26 miles, 385 yds).

Phelps, Samuel (1804–1878). English actor and theatre manager. After touring in the provinces he made a successful London debut (1837) as Shylock at the Haymarket Theatre. His years as manager of Sadler's Wells (1844–62) made theatrical history: in an extraordinarily wide range of productions he presented thirty-one Shakespeare plays. He was best known as a tragedian but his interpretations of comedy parts, e.g. Malvolio and Bottom, were also famous.

Phidias (*c.* 490–*c.* 430 B.C.). Athenian sculptor. He was the principal artist employed by * Pericles to carry out the beautification of Athens, which he had planned. The frieze of the Parthenon was probably carved from his designs, but none of his actual work survives: representations of the two works for which he was most famous in the ancient world – the ivory and gold statues of Athena Parthenos in Athens and of Zeus at Olympia – can be seen on coins etc. Accusations of theft and sacrilege, made by the enemies of Pericles, caused Phidias to leave Athens (432).
Richter, G., *A Handbook of Greek Art.* 1969

Philby, Kim (Harold Adrian Russell) (1912–). British journalist and KGB agent. Educated at Cambridge, he entered the British foreign service in 1941 and was first secretary at the British embassy in Washington 1949–51. After the defection to Moscow of * Burgess and Maclean, his friendship with Guy Burgess led to an investigation and although nothing was proved against him he was forced to resign, largely because of his Communist associations in the 1930s. He went to the Middle East as an *Observer* correspondent until he disappeared from Beirut in January 1963. He soon surfaced in Moscow as a KGB major-general and confirmed that he had been 'the third man' in the Burgess and Maclean case.
Seale, P., and McCouville, M., *Philby, the Long Road to Moscow.* 1972

Philidor, François André Danican (1726–1795). French musician and chess-player. He composed many operas; and through his *Analyse du jeu des échecs* (1749) he became one of the most famous names in the early history of chess. His 'Philidor's Defence' is an example of his tactical mastery of the game.

Philip (known as 'the Good') (1396–1467). Duke of Burgundy (from 1419). To avenge the murder of his father, John the Fearless, by adherents of the Dauphin (afterwards Charles VII), he negotiated the Treaty of Troyes (1420) with the English king * Henry V. This treaty disinherited the Dauphin in favour of any child that Henry might have by Princess Catherine of France. Philip therefore supported the cause of Henry VI in the wars in which * Joan of Arc played a notable part, but he was reconciled with Charles in 1435. Most of his energies were devoted to the extension of his inheritance in the Netherlands, almost all of which he brought under his control, suppressing a rebellion (1454) with great bloodshed. He founded (1430) the Order of the Golden Fleece and made his court one of the most magnificent of medieval Europe.
Vaughan, R., *Philip the Good.* 1970

Philip I (1504–1567). Landgrave of Hesse; he assumed power in 1518 after succeeding his father in 1509. He became one of the most prominent supporters of the Protestant cause: he initiated the Reformation in Hesse (1526) and founded (1527) the first Protestant university at Marburg, where in 1529 he tried to reconcile * Luther and * Zwingli. A far-sighted plan to reform the constitution of the Holy Roman empire and at the same time overcome the dominance of the Habsburg emperors was frustrated when the League of Schmalkalden formed for that purpose was defeated (1547). Philip's bigamy, agreed to by his first wife and (reluctantly) by Luther, was a lively scandal of the time.

Philip II (382–336 B.C.). King of Macedonia (from 356), and father of * Alexander the Great. He was chosen to take the place of his nephew Amyntas, for whom he had acted as regent from 359. His kingdom when he began to rule was poor and backward; when he died he had made it by war and diplomacy the dominant power in Greece and had created an army with which his son achieved his great victories. An early success (356) which made the others possible was his occupation of Grenides (Philippi) to gain control of the vital gold and silver deposits. Another stage was his occupation of Thessaly. To Thebes he readily gave help against Phocis, thus bringing both states into his power-orbit. Roused by the warnings of Demosthenes (in the famous *Philippics*), Athens at last saw her danger, but it was too late and after Philip's great victory at Chaeronea (338) all Greece except Sparta lay at his mercy. He now showed his statesmanship by creating the League of Corinth, a confederacy in which every state but Sparta had votes to accord with its military strength, Philip himself being its supreme head. Now all was ready for the trial of strength with Persia, which Philip had long planned, but as the first Macedonian troops moved into Asia Minor he was assassinated.

Hogarth, D. G., *Philip and Alexander of Macedon*. 1897

Philip II (known as 'Philip Augustus') (1165–1223). King of France (from 1180). He was more successful than any other French medieval king in asserting his suzerainty over the feudal nobles, winning his greatest triumph over the most powerful of all his feudatories, the English king. He quickly returned from the 3rd Crusade and was able to take advantage of the captivity of * Richard I to despoil him of his possessions. Interrupted briefly by Richard's return, he was soon able to exploit John's difficulties and eventually gained Normandy, Anjou and parts of Poitou. At Bouvines, between Lille and Tournai, Philip gained his greatest victory (1214) over a coalition of the court of Flanders, the emperor Otto IV and King John. By his success Philip established the strength and prestige of the French monarchy for a century and more.

Painter, S., and Tierney, B., *Western Europe in the Middle Ages 1300–1475*. 1970

Philip II (Felipe) (1527–1598). King of Spain (from 1556). He succeeded on the abdication of his father, Charles I (the emperor * Charles V), and acquired the whole of the western part of the Habsburg heritage, Spain and Spanish America, the Low Countries, Naples and Milan. He conquered Portugal (1580); but his hope of adding England peacefully to his dominions ended when his second wife, Mary Queen of England, failed to provide him with an heir. With immense industry but little wisdom the proud and lonely king ruled his vast inheritance. Moreover he considered himself the military arm of the Counter-Reformation, destined to bring all Europe back into the Roman Catholic fold, though he was frequently in conflict with the Papacy on political issues. He thus provoked a long struggle in the Netherlands and so deprived himself of much of the trade and wealth of Europe's richest land; even before the defeat of the Armada (1588) the English privateers had sapped his overseas trade and naval strength. In addition he carried a long dynastic war with France and felt it his duty to hold the Turks at bay. Meanwhile at home the over-centralized governmental machine creaked ominously; agriculture and industry were ruined by the inflationary flow of gold from Mexico and Peru; the Inquisition produced, indeed, an enforced unity, but the country lost much of its vigour through the imprisonment or expulsion of many of the most industrious citizens (especially those of Moorish descent). Philip lived aloof in the monastic palace of the Escurial. He was suspected (unfairly) of murdering his eldest son, the unstable Don * Carlos. Although he married four times only one son survived to succeed him: **Philip III** (1578–1621). Pious and benevolent in his private life, he was indifferent to public affairs which he left to his favourite the Duke of Lerma. Under Philip III Spanish culture was at its height.

Merriman, R. B., *The Rise of the Spanish Empire in the Old World and the New*. Vol. 4 1934. Parker, G., *Philip II*. 1979

Philip IV (known as 'the Fair') (1268–1314). King of France (from 1285). A strong ruler, he was determined to extend the royal power; this led him into quarrels with Edward I of England, the Flemish burghers, his own nobles and above all with Pope Boniface VIII, this last settled only by the pope's death, when Philip secured the election of a Frenchman, Clement V, and the removal of the papacy from Rome to Avignon. He further asserted his strength by forcing the pope to disband the Order of the Templars. The monarchy's power was also increased by developing centralized institutions, e.g. the *Parlement* of Paris.

Glotz, G., *Histoire générale, histoire du moyen âge*. Vol. 6, 1940

Philip V (1683–1746). The first Bourbon king of Spain (1700–24; 1724–46). A grandson of * Louis XIV of France, he was named by the childless Charles II of Spain as his successor.

By permitting Philip to accept, Louis provoked the War of the Spanish Succession. By the Treaty of Utrecht (1713) Spain ceded the Spanish Netherlands to Austria and some possessions, including Gibraltar, to Britain, but Philip was able to retain his Spanish throne. He was much under the influence of two women: the Princesse des Ursins, his first wife's maid of honour, and his second wife, Isabella (Elizabeth) Farnese, whose ambitions for her children moulded the foreign policy of the reign. His acute melancholia was soothed each night by the singing of * Farinelli.

Philip, Prince *see* **Edinburgh, Duke of**

Philip, St. One of the twelve apostles of Jesus Christ. He plays no conspicuous part in the Gospel story and his later life is unknown, though he is traditionally associated with Ethiopia.

Philip Neri, St (1515–1595). Christian reformer. Born in Florence, he went to Rome (1533) as a tutor but from 1538 led an ascetic life, sleeping in the catacombs, visiting the sick and instructing the poor. He was ordained (1551) and while continuing his work among the poor he found a new vocation in making religion attractive to the young by holding informal meetings which combined religious instruction and discussion with social and musical entertainment. In 1575 he founded with papal consent the first Oratory in Rome, a brotherhood of secular priests, which to some extent formalized his earlier work. He is remembered as one of the most vivacious, human and lovable of all saints. He was canonized in 1622.

Philippa (1314?–1369). Daughter of Count William of Hainaut (in Flanders) and wife of Edward III of England, to whom she bore seven sons and five daughters. It was her pleas that resulted in the sparing of six prominent burghers of Calais, whose lives Edward III, incensed by his year-long siege, had demanded as his price for not sacking the city. She appointed the chronicler * Froissart as her secretary. She is buried at Windsor.

Philips, Anton Frederik (1874–1951). Dutch industrialist. The son of a banker, with his elder brother Gerard he founded a factory at Eindhoven in 1892 for the manufacture of electrical light bulbs. The company became the largest European manufacturer of radios and television, with subsidiaries throughout the world.

Phillip, Arthur (1738–1814). English sailor and administrator. As first governor (1788–1792) of the penal settlement in New South Wales, he showed firmness and courage and clearly foresaw the colony's future greatness. He chose the site on which Sydney was to be built.

Phillpotts, Eden (1862–1960). English novelist and playwright. He achieved great popularity with his regional novels, e.g. *Children of the Mist* (1898) and *Widecombe Fair* (1913), in which Devonshire characters are convincingly and lovingly portrayed: he is best remembered perhaps for his long-running play *The Farmer's Wife* (published 1916).

Philo Judaeus (*c.* 20 B.C.–*c* A.D. 45). Jewish philosopher, born in Alexandria. He made a wide study of Greek philosophy and literature, but remained a Jew and accepted the Old Testament without reservations. He conceived his task as the integration of Greek philosophy, based on reason, with Jewish religion, based on revelation and faith. The *logos* (God's divine message) he regarded as supreme, but he recognized that it can reach mankind through the lips of Greek philosophers such as Plato. This thought was taken up by the neoplatonists, both Christian and pagan, and is at the root of nearly all medieval philosophy.
Sandmel, S., *Philo's Place in Judaism*. 1956

'Phiz' *see* **Browne, Hablot K.**

Phryne (4th century B.C.). Greek courtesan, traditional model for a picture by Apelles of Aphrodite (Venus) rising from the waves and for the *Aphrodite of Cnidos*, a famous statue by Praxiteles. Accused of profaning the Eleusinian mysteries, she was acquitted after her robe was cast aside to reveal to the judges her naked beauty.

Piaget, Jean (1896–1980). Swiss psychologist. Educated in Neuchâtel, Zurich and Paris, he was professor of child psychology at Geneva 1929–71 and wrote over fifty books, many on the intellectual developmental stages in children, such as concept formation, classification and ordering. He argued that classroom teaching is inappropriate when it attempts to impose adult reasoning on children who are not yet genetically programmed to receive it.

Picasso, Pablo Ruiz y (1881–1973). Spanish artist. Born at Malaga, he studied art in Barcelona and was so precocious that in his early teens his work, then in the style of the old masters, was of exhibition standard. Soon after the turn of the century he settled permanently in Paris, where the work of * Toulouse-Lautrec was among the most powerful of the influences to which he was exposed. In his 'Blue Period' (1901–04) the colour provided symbolic backgrounds for pictures, sometimes satirical, sometimes anguished, of the poor and lonely. In the 'Pink Period' (1905–06) circus figures and young nudes, strangely pathetic against their rose and terracotta backgrounds, predominated. An abrupt change of style (*c.* 1907) derived from a study of Negro masks, from which he learnt the forcefulness that a work of art can gain from simplification and distortion. *Les Demoiselles d'Avignon*, painted in 1907, was a decisive step on the road upon which he was travelling with * Braque, towards Cubism; though his shapes, now in subdued greys and browns, were not entirely abstract and retained some relationship to actual objects. The impact of World War I revived his interest in colour and decoration and led to his Classical Period (1920–25) during which, e.g. in *Mother and Child* and *Woman Bathers*, the influence of * Ingres is immediately apparent. But this did not endure: the increasing tensions and the prospect of chaos in Europe drew him towards Surrealism and no picture reflects the agonies of the time more cogently than his *Guernica* (1936), commemorating one of the most barbarous episodes of the Spanish Civil War. After World War II Picasso moved from Paris to the South of France; though he was a professed communist, his art was regarded as decadent in the USSR. He spent much of his creative energy in these years on lithographs, ceramics and sculptures (especially of animals and birds), many of his pictures showing the importance that his children and their mother now had in his life. He is often regarded as the greatest artist of the twentieth century.

Barr, A. H., ed., *Picasso: Fifty Years of his Art*. 1946. Penrose, R., *Picasso*. 1971

Piccard, Auguste (1884–1962). Swiss physicist. Best known as a pioneer explorer of the stratosphere and the deep oceans, he was professor of physics at the Free University of Brussels (1922–54) and a close associate of * Einstein. With his twin brother Jean-Felix (1884–1963), a pioneer in studying cosmic radiation, he took up ballooning and finally (1932), in an airtight gondola designed by himself, reached a height of 54,150 ft. After World War II he turned to investigating the ocean depths and designed a special steel diving capsule or 'bathyscaphe'. With his son **Jacques** (1922–   ) he descended to a record depth of 10,335 ft off the island of Capri (1953) and Jacques, with a U.S. naval officer, reached a depth of 37,800 ft off the Pacific island of Guam (1960).

De Latil, P., and Rivoire, J., *Man and the Underwater World*. 1956

Pichegru, Charles (1761–1804). French soldier. He gained rapid promotion in the revolutionary armies; in 1793 as commander-in-chief of the Rhine army he thrust back the Austrians and overran the Palatinate. In the following year he was given the command in Flanders and in January 1795 entered Amsterdam. After this triumph he returned to the Rhine, but was soon in active correspondence with the Bourbons. Arrested in Paris (1797), he was sentenced to banishment in Cayenne but managed to escape. He returned to France (1804) with another conspirator against the life of Napoleon but was arrested and shortly after found strangled in prison.

Pickford, Mary (Gladys Smith) (1893–1979). American film star, born in Canada. Having first appeared on the stage at the age of 5, she started to act in films in 1909 and through her child-like sentimental parts soon became known as 'the world's sweetheart'. With her second husband, Douglas Fairbanks, she was one of the founders (1919) of the cinema company United Artists. Among the most popular of her films were *Poor Little Rich Girl* (1916) and *Daddy Long Legs* (1919). She has been described as the founder of the Hollywood 'star system'.

Pico della Mirandola, Giovanni (1463–1494). Italian philosopher. Having settled in Florence (1484), he applied his immense industry and powers of memory to the search for Christian truths in the works of Pythagoras, Moses and Zoroaster. Subsequently he offered to defend 900 theses at

public disputations, but thirteen of the theses were condemned (1487) by Pope Innocent VIII and Pico went into exile in France, where he was briefly imprisoned. His book *De Hominis Dignitate*, with its stress on the spiritual freedom of humanity, provided a philosophic justification for the proudly individualistic outlook of Renaissance man. His writings influenced Sir Thomas * More (who translated some) and John * Colet.
Kristeller, P. O., *The Renaissance Concept of Man*. 1973

Pierce, Franklin (1804–1869). Fourteenth president of the US (1853–57). Son of a governor of New Hampshire, where he was born, he became prominent in state politics and later served as a US Congressman (1833–37) and Senator (1837–42). He fought with distinction in the Mexican War (1846–48), and was elected president (1852) as Democratic candidate. By the Gadsden Purchase he secured from Mexico some 45,000 square miles of valuable territory (now in Arizona or New Mexico), but the unpopularity of his Kansas-Nebraska Act, which left the question of slavery there to the decision of the inhabitants and so provoked a competing rush of partisan immigrants, prevented him from standing for re-election.

Piero della Francesca (*c.* 1420–1492). Italian Renaissance painter of the Umbrian school. He was born at Borgo San Sepolcro, south of Urbino, and studied in Florence under Domenico Veneziano, whose methods of revealing form by light he learned and improved upon. During his career his patrons included Sigismondo Malatesta of Rimini, the Duke of Urbino, and Pope Pius II. He studied mathematics and wrote treatises on geometry and perspective which he hoped would influence later artists, and his composition followed a geometric pattern. Most of his works are frescoes based on religious themes, e.g. his most ambitious work, *The Story of the True Cross* in Arezzo (1452–66). Modern critics hold his work in high esteem. Amongst his outstanding paintings are *The Baptism* (National Gallery, London) and *The Flagellation of Christ* (Urbino).
Clark, K. M. *Piero della Francesca*. 1951

Pigott, Richard (1828?–1889). Irish journalist. He forged documents purporting to implicate * Parnell in the murders (1882) of Lord Frederick Cavendish and T. H. Burke (the Irish chief secretary and his under-secretary) in Phoenix Park, Dublin. The publication of these documents in *The Times* (April 1887) caused a political sensation which was not abated until a commission of inquiry (1888–89) proved them to be forged. Pigott, having confessed, escaped to Madrid where he shot himself.

Pilate, Pontius. Roman procurator of Judaea and Samaria (26–36). He sentenced Jesus to be crucified, and later was recalled to Rome to answer charges made against him. He seems to have been well-meaning but ignorant of the Jewish character and prejudices. His later career is unknown. Among many legends is one that he became a Christian; his wife Claudia Procula, said to have been converted, even became a saint in the Orthodox church. He is remembered for his question 'What is truth?', put to Jesus at his trial.

Pilsudski, Józef (1867–1935). Polish soldier and politician. He was born in Vilna and spent the first part of his life in two overlapping causes, revolutionary socialism and freeing what was then Russian Poland from tsarist rule. He was sent to Siberia (1887–92) and on release founded the Polish Socialist party. He was arrested again (1900) but after pretending to be insane escaped abroad. He soon returned and from 1907 began to create units of Polish riflemen on Austrian territory. With these he fought for Austria against Russia in World War I but finding himself exploited for German aims disbanded his forces and was imprisoned (1917) at Magdeburg. After the Allied victory he was hailed as head of state (1919) and played a prominent part in the battles, political as well as military, by which Poland's frontiers were determined. Having refused the presidency (1922), he lived in retirement until in 1926 he carried out a *coup d'état* as a result of which he exercised almost dictatorial power ('on or behind the throne') for the rest of his life.
Reddaway, W. F., *Marshal Pilsudski*. 1939

Pinckney, Charles Cotesworth (1746–1825). American soldier and politician. He was educated in England, practised as a lawyer in Charleston, S. Carolina, and was active in the first Continental Congress; this precipitated the War of Independence, during which he was A.D.C. to * Washington and rose to be a brigadier-general. At the Constitutional Convention (1787) he introduced the clause forbidding religious tests. He was the unsuccessful Federalist candidate for the presidency (1804 and 1808).

Pindar (*c.* 522–*c.* 440 B.C.). Greek lyric poet, born near Thebes. He wrote numerous ceremonial odes, hymns, convivial songs etc. for rulers and cities throughout Greece. From 476 to 474 he was at the court of Hicron king of Syracuse and other rulers in Sicily. Of the seventeen book rolls of his poetry only four survive almost entire, i.e. those celebrating victories in the Olympic, Nemean, Pythian and Isthmian games. Into these he introduced myths and other apparent irrelevances which give colour and variety to what might seem a monotonous theme, though to the Greeks themselves the games were religious festivals and victory symbolized divine favour as well as conferring prestige on the athletes and their cities. The poems are choral odes to be accompanied by dancing, but owing to their early date and linguistic problems they are hard to translate and their merits difficult to assess. The Greeks, however, counted Pindar among their greatest poets. * Dryden's *Alexander's Feast* is an imitation of a Pindaric ode.
Bowra, C. M., *Pindar*. 1964

Pinel, Philippe (1745–1826). French physician. Born in Languedoc, he qualified at Toulouse and went to Paris (1778); in 1787 he began to write about insanity, of which he had made a first-hand study. Both at the Bicêtre, of which he became head in 1793, and later at the Salpêtrière he introduced more humane treatment of the insane (e.g. removal of chains by which they were restrained) and as far as possible substituted empirical and psychological treatment for the then customary drugs, bleeding etc. He paved the way for future improvements by establishing the custom of keeping case histories and records for research.

Pinkerton, Allan (1819–1884). American detective. Born in Scotland, he emigrated to the U.S.A. (1842) and founded in Chicago the private detective agency which became the best known in the world. During the American Civil War he did secret service work and in 1861 frustrated a plot against Lincoln's life. The agency was continued and enlarged by his sons.

Pinter, Harold (1930–). British playwright and producer. He was an actor in repertory before turning to writing. He attracted attention with *The Dumb Waiter* (1957) and *The Caretaker* (1960), plays written in ostensibly colloquial, 'ordinary' speech, and concerned with problems of communication between individuals. His screen plays include *The Servant* (1962), *The Go-Between* (1969), *The Last Tycoon* (1974) and *Betrayal* (1983). He became associate director of the National Theatre in 1973.

Piper, John (1903–). English painter. His vivid and effective use of bold, vigorous draughtsmanship and dramatic colour contrasts is seen at its best in architectural themes (e.g. the pictures of bombed buildings for which he became known in World War II). He has designed stage sets, and engraved glass, e.g. in Coventry cathedral. Piper has also written poetry and architectural and topographical guides.
Woods, J., *John Piper*. 1955

Pirandello, Luigi (1867–1936). Italian writer. He was born in Sicily, the scene of most of his early stories. His novels include *Si Gira* (1916) which introduces the reader to film stars and photographers. During World War I he began to write plays of a slightly surrealistic nature: among the best known of about forty are *Six Characters in Search of an Author* (1921), in which a rehearsal stage is invaded by a group of characters seeking to take part in a play, and *Henry IV*, where the theme of madness is treated in an original way. He won the Nobel Prize for Literature (1934).
Starkie, W., *Luigi Pirandello, 1867–1936*. 4th ed. 1967

Piranesi, Giambattista (1720–1778). Italian draftsman and etcher. His powerful series *Carceri d'invenzione* ('Imaginary Prisons', 1745) were precursors of Romantic art and his Roman scenes were conceived on the grand scale.

Pisano, Nicola (*c.* 1225–*c.* 1278). Italian sculptor, founder of the Pisan school. He had made a study of classical sculpture, and though he applied the knowledge that he had gained to essentially Gothic structures he has a claim to be regarded as the first Renaissance sculptor. For example, on the pulpit of the baptistery at Pisa, for the characteristically

Gothic line of figures against a flat background he substitutes groups, each member of which is expressively natural in pose, dress and expression and so carved as to give an impression of depth. Among the best known of his other works are the pulpit at Siena cathedral and the fountain in the Market Place, Perugia. In much of his work Nicola was helped by his son **Giovanni Pisano** (*c.* 1250–1330) who won an independent reputation both as architect and as sculptor and was praised by * Michelangelo. The sculptor **Andrea Pisano** (*c.* 1290–1348) worked with * Giotto on the campanile of Florence cathedral.
Pope-Hennessy, J., *Italian Gothic Sculpture.* 1955

Pissarro, Camille (1830–1903). French painter, born in the West Indies. His early pictures show the influence of * Corot, but after meeting * Manet (1866) he worked closely with the Impressionist group, of which he was the oldest member. For a time (1884–88) he adopted * Seurat's pointillist techniques; in the last years of his life he painted figure studies of peasants etc. and pictures of warmly sunlit Paris streets.
Rewald, J., *Camille Pissarro.* 1963

Pitman, Sir Isaac (1813–1879). English inventor. His shorthand system based on phonetic principles gained worldwide popularity. He also devised a simplified spelling of English but for this he won little support.

Pitt, William, 1st Earl of Chatham (known as 'Pitt the Elder' and 'the Great Commoner') (1708–1778). English orator and statesman. He was the grandson of 'Diamond Pitt', who had made a fortune in India, and his elder brother's marriage to a Lyttelton provided a link with the 'cousinhood' of Lytteltons, Grenvilles and Temples which was of great importance to his political career and was further strengthened when Pitt himself married Lady Hester Grenville, a sister of Lord Temple. He accepted an army commission (1731) but in 1735 entered parliament as member for the rotten borough of Old Sarum. As M.P. he added the artillery of his oratory to the sniping attact upon * Walpole directed by the 'boy patriots' of the cousinhood. While nominally moving a congratulatory address to the king (1736) on the marriage of Frederick, Prince of Wales (the object of his father's active dislike), Pitt made such barbed references, masquerading as compliments, to Walpole and his royal master that he was deprived of his commission – and appointed groom of the bedchamber by the prince.

Until his resignation (1742) Walpole continued to be the object of attack. Then it was Carteret (Lord * Granville) whose pro-Hanoverian policy in the War of the Austrian Succession Pitt assailed. Carteret survived until 1744 when his resignation gave Henry * Pelham, the prime minister, an opportunity to disarm with office the now formidable Pitt (who however was absent for a year with manic depression, a hereditary scourge which tormented him at several critical junctures of his career). He became paymaster-general to the forces (1746) and not only showed administrative skill but set a new standard of public morality by refusing to take advantage of the lucrative perquisites of his office. He felt free, however, to attack the government of which he was a member; and for a famous speech (1755) denouncing subsidies for Hanoverian defence he was dismissed. The government itself, led now by the Duke of * Newcastle, was forced to resign a year later as a result of the disasters (including the loss of Minorca) with which the Seven Years War opened. Pitt's conviction of his ability to guide the country ('I know that I can save this country and that no one else can') began to be shared by all. In an interim ministry (1756–57) and in Newcastle's great war ministry (formed in June 1757), Pitt, though he left political management to others, was the driving force which carried the country to victory. His was the strategic design by which a holding action was fought in Europe while Britain's main strength was used to build up a great colonial empire overseas. The result ensured British supremacy in India, the conquest Canada by Amherst and Wolfe, and of many rich islands in the West Indies and elsewhere. When George II died (1760) the war seemed to have reached a stalemate, likely to be broken by Spain's entering the war on France's side. Pitt wished to forestall the event by attacking Spain; Newcastle refused and Pitt resigned, with the title of Earl of Chatham. This enabled the young king, eager to test his strength, to manoeuvre the replacement of Newcastle by * Bute, his political mentor and friend. Peace was made in 1763 and though more than once asked by the king to form a ministry Pitt remained on the sidelines.

In 1765 he made one of the most magnificent speeches of parliamentary history against the Stamp Act, a measure to tax the American colonies, introduced by the ministry of his cousin George Grenville, from whom he was now estranged. The Act was repealed (1766) and at last Chatham was persuaded to head a government, but having no regular following he was obliged to form it from family connexions and ill-assorted individuals. Within a few months Chatham, again a victim of his old malady, withdrew into absolute seclusion and even had to refuse a visit from King George. In his absence Charles Townshend, the chancellor of the exchequer, imposed new colonial taxations. Learning of this on his recovery Chatham immediately resigned (October 1768). In the years that followed, between bouts of depression and the agonies of gout, he went to the House of Lords to deliver impassioned orations pleading for policies of generosity and conciliation in the American dispute. His last speech, after which he collapsed and died, was a fervent protest against final withdrawal.

Plumb, J. H., *Chatham*. 1965

Pitt, William (known as 'Pitt the Younger') (1759–1806). English statesman, second son of William Pitt the Elder. He was always destined by his father for a political career to match his own, but ill health prevented him from going to school and, though he showed a precocious talent for classical scholarship, segregation from his contemporaries increased the reserve and aloofness which were part of his character. He entered parliament (1780) during the closing years of Lord * North's ministry and attached himself to Lord * Shelburne, leader of a surviving opposition remnant which had followed Pitt's father. North's government fell (1782) and Pitt declined a junior post in the succeeding coalition, but when Rockingham, the new prime minister died in the same year Shelburne formed an administration with Pitt as chancellor of the exchequer. The unpopularity of the Treaty of Versailles (1783) by which American independence was recognized caused this government's downfall; and after an even briefer coalition of the old enemies Fox and North Pitt was called by King George III to be prime minister at the age of 25. The political wiseacres gave the ministry two to three weeks; it lasted seventeen years. Until the election of 1784 gave him a majority he disregarded adverse votes and carried on. Combining his office as prime minister with that of chancellor of the exchequer he first put the finances into order. Then came his India Act (1784) by which through a Board of Control the East India Company shared its responsibilities with the Crown. (This Act endured until 1858.) Among other reforms, he abolished public hangings at Tyburn and admitted Roman Catholics to the army and the bar. On the other hand he failed to achieve parliamentary reform.

The outbreak of the French Revolution, the subsequent reign of terror and the emergence of the republic as a strong and aggressive power markedly changed Pitt's viewpoint; he became increasingly conscious of the need for national security, internal as well as external, and believed that vigilance and firmness – and occasional ruthlessness – were necessary if England was not to go the way of France. As a war minister he has been criticized for using the slender military resources in small and scattered enterprises, but against this must be set the courage which flinched at no disaster and made England the inspiration and focal point of all resistance to the enemy.

In 1800 Pitt secured the passage of the Act by which Ireland, like Scotland nearly a century earlier, became part of the United Kingdom, its own parliament being dissolved. To achieve this he had so nearly promised Roman Catholic emancipation that when the king refused concurrence he felt his honour involved and resigned. He returned (1804) to meet the rising danger from * Napoleon, and before he died, unmarried and only 46, he had the satisfaction of hearing the news of the victory at Trafalgar (October 1805). In his last Guildhall speech he proclaimed 'Europe is not to be saved by any single man: England has saved herself by her exertions and will, as I trust, save Europe by her example'.

Ehrman, J., *The Younger Pitt*. 2 vols., 1969, 1983

Pitt-Rivers, Augustus Henry Lane-Fox (1827–1900). British archaeologist and army officer. He began his career in the army in 1845 and rose to Lieut.-General. In 1880 he succeeded to the Rivers estate in Dorset, where he pioneered scientific, properly recorded archaeological digs. His work in Dorset is preserved in the Pitt-Rivers museum at Farnham. His personal ethnological and archaeological collection formed the Pitt-Rivers

Museum at Oxford University; he was also the first Inspector of Ancient Monuments (1882). Pitt-Rivers, A. H., *Excavations in Cranborne Chase*. 1887–98

Pius II (Enea Silvio de Piccolomini) (1405–1464). Pope (from 1458). A generous patron of artists and writers, he was a diplomat, the author of poems, histories and a novel and strove for European unity against the Turks.

Pius VII (Barnabas Chiaramonti) (1742–1823). Pope (from 1800). He had the extraordinarily difficult task of facing the consequences of the French Revolution and * Napoleon's rise to power without offending Austria, the papacy's firmest ally. His first great achievement was the Concordat (1801) with France, whereby he recognized the republic and its factual consequences in return for the withdrawal of all anti-Catholic laws. Later he went to Paris to anoint Napoleon at his coronation. He refused, however, to take part in the French emperor's measures against England and in consequence the papal states were invaded and the pope held in captivity in France (1809–14). His reign is also remembered for his restoration (1814) of the Society of Jesus (Jesuits).

Pius IX (Giovanni Mastai-Ferretti) (1792–1878). Pope (from 1846). Bishop of Imola (1832–46), on his election he began as a liberal reformer of the constitution and government of the papal territories, but his failure (1848) to head the national movement against Catholic Austria caused an uprising in Rome, the murder of several members of the administration, the flight of the pope to Neapolitan territory and the establishment of a republic under * Garibaldi and Mazzini. Restored by a French army (1849) and his secular power maintained by a French garrison, the reformer became a conservative, his main preoccupation being to retain his political status. In the 'Syllabus of Errors' (1864) he denounced 80 elements relating to 'progress, liberalism and modern civilisation', including socialism, democracy, science and freedom of conscience. During the Franco-Prussian War (1870) the French withdrew and Rome became the capital of unified Italy. Pius responded by refusing to recognize these events and henceforth remained in self-imposed imprisonment in the Vatican – an example followed by his successors until * Pius XI came to terms with the Italian state (1929). During his reign the doctrine of the Immaculate Conception was promulgated (1856), and at the Vatican Council of 1869–70 the dogma of papal infallibility in matters of faith and morals was defined. Pius IX was amiable, witty and of great charm, with no personal enemies.
Hales, E. E. Y., *Pio Nono*. 1954

Pius X (Giuseppe Sarto) (1835–1914). Pope (from 1903). He came from a very poor family and had spent his whole previous career in diocesan work; his talents were essentially practical. He was cardinal-patriarch of Venice from 1892 until his election to the papacy. A strong conservative, deeply opposed to 'modernism', he codified the canon law, reorganized the papal administration and rearranged the missal and the breviary. His refusal to accept secular control over the French church led to a twenty-year breach between the papacy and the French State. Much beloved for his simplicity and holiness, he was canonized in 1954.

Pius XI (Achille Ratti) 1857–1939). Pope (from 1922). A scholar of the first rank, he directed the Ambrosian and Vatican libraries, until at the age of 61 he was appointed nuncio to Poland (1918). After five months as archbishop of Milan (1921–22) he was unexpectedly elected pope. He showed great ability as a diplomat: his undisguised hostility to totalitarianism did not, however, deter him from signing the Lateran Treaty (1929) with * Mussolini, by which in return for recognition of his papal sovereignty within the Vatican City and of Roman Catholicism as the state religion of Italy, the papacy recognized the kingdom of Italy under the house of Savoy.

Pius XII (Eugenio Pacelli) (1876–1958). Pope (from 1939). Early in his career he joined the papal secretariat; he was papal nuncio to Bavaria during World War I and to Germany (1925–31) until he became Pius XI's secretary of state. Cardinal Pacelli had thus considerable diplomatic experience when on the eve of World War II he was elected pope. His main objective was to ensure that the Roman Catholic church survived with its independence and strength unimpaired, and he has

been criticized for not explicity denouncing Nazi atrocities.
Falconi, C., *The Popes in the Twentieth Century*. 1967

Pizarro, Francisco (*c*. 1478–1541). Spanish conqueror of Peru. Illegitimate and illiterate, he became a soldier and went to Darien (Panama) in 1509 and in 1522 made his first attempt, in association with Diego de Almagro, to conquer Peru. This failed but after returning to Spain and receiving authorization and the title of governor, he again set out (1531), from Panama, with his brothers Hernando, Juan and Gonzalo and a band of less than 200 men to conquer the Inca empire. By a combination of courage, craft and luck he seized Atahualpa, the Inca ruler (whom he later had murdered), and, with the heart of the resistance broken, spent the next nine years in overrunning the country and amassing a vast treasure from the Inca hoards. Lima was founded in 1535. A dispute with Almagro, his fellow conquistador, mainly concerned with the ownership of Cuzco, proved disastrous. Almagro occupied the city (1537) but was defeated by Hernando Pizarro, tried and strangled. In revenge Francisco Pizarro was attacked and killed in his own house by some of Almagro's men. He and the conquistadors wiped out the whole Inca nobility and virtually destroyed every trace of Inca culture.
Innes, H., *The Conquistadors*. 1969

Place, Francis (1771–1854). English reformer. Born in poverty, he achieved a remarkable feat of self-education and became a successful master tailor, while sponsoring practical causes such as the monitorial schools associated with the name of Joseph * Lancaster, and birth control. He retired from business in 1817 but the library behind his old shop in Charing Cross remained a centre for his political activities, in which he was associated with Jeremy * Bentham and other reformers. Although not an M.P. he became a master of parliamentary lobbying, his greatest achievement being to secure the repeal (1824) of the Combination Acts which made trade unions illegal. He was a leading figure in the agitation that led to the Reform Act (1832) and he helped William Lovett to draw up the People's Charter in 1838.
Thale, M., *Francis Place*. 1972

Planck, Max Ernst Ludwig (1858–1947). German mathematical physicist. He was the son of a professor at Kiel and at Berlin University attended the lectures of * Kirchhoff, whom he eventually succeeded as professor (1889). Planck originated (1900) the quantum theory stating that energy, like matter, is not continuous in nature but is radiated and absorbed in small portions called quanta. Planck won the Nobel Prize for Physics (1918), and in 1930 became president of the Kaiser Wilhelm Institute of Berlin. One of his sons was executed in World War II on suspicion of having taken part in the plot against Hitler's life.
Planck, M., *Scientific Autobiography and Other Papers*. 1949

Plantagenet. English dynasty sprung from Geoffrey, Count of Anjou, whose badge was a sprig of broom (*planta genista*). The first English Plantagenet king was Henry II, Geoffrey's son by * Matilda, daughter of Henry I: the last of the line was Richard III.
Harvey, J., *The Plantagenets, 1154–1485*. 1970

Plantin, Christophe (1514–1589). French printer, who settled in Antwerp. He is one of the best known of the early printers, and versions of the type which he designed for his *Biblia Polyglotta* and editions of the classics are still in use. He established branches for his sons-in-law in Paris and Leyden and his Antwerp office is now maintained by the city as a museum.

Plato (*c*. 427–347 B.C.). Athenian philosopher. Born of noble parents, he almost certainly studied under * Socrates. After Socrates was put to death by the restored democracy (399) Plato lived and travelled abroad for a number of years, visiting probably Egypt and certainly Sicily, where he won Dion to his philosophy. On his return (388) he set up a school at his house in Athens which became known as the Academy because it was near the grove of the mythical hero Academus. The students, mainly young aristocrats, devoted themselves to philosophy and mathematics and to practical studies in politics and administration.

After the death (368) of Dionysius I of Sicily Plato was invited by Dion, the tyrant's son-in-law, to return to Syracuse to train Dionysius II to become the philosopher–king of Plato's dreams. The young ruler soon tired of his studies; he quarrelled with Dion, and Plato had to depart. A later visit (*c.* 361), undertaken to reconcile Dionysius with Dion, was again unsuccessful. Plato is said to have died at a wedding feast.

Almost all Plato's work seems to have survived: most is in the shape of dialogue, a method of discussion known as dialectic. Socrates, the venerated teacher of his youth, is nearly always a participant: it is not clear therefore how much of the thought is that of the historic Socrates and how much Plato's own. The Socratic method was not to propound a philosophic scheme but by exposing a pupil's statements to a searching cross-examination to achieve precise definitions and so enable him to reach towards the truth for himself. Thus an approach to a general answer to such questions as 'What is beauty?' 'What is justice?' or 'What is knowledge?' is made by a series of questions leading to the elucidation of specific points. In the *Republic*, a discussion about the ideal state, a conclusion is reached favouring rule by a philosopher-king. Theories about the universe ascribed to * Pythagoras are expounded in the *Timaeus*, the dialogue which was regarded as essentially Platonic by those neoplatonists who helped to give Christian theology its Platonic character: the influence of Pythagoras is also apparent in the *Symposium*, from a literary point of view one of Plato's most attractive works. Here Socrates, Aristophanes, Alcibiades and others discuss the nature of love, the real background and real people here, as so often in Plato, adding to the charm and naturalness of the dialogue.

Perhaps the most important of Plato's own contributions to philosophic thought is his theory of 'ideas' (or more literally 'forms'). According to this theory the 'idea' of a thing is the unchanging and fundamental reality behind the superficial and mutable concepts produced by imagination or the senses. Highest of such 'ideas' is 'the good', knowledge of which is supreme virtue. But, since such complete knowledge is all but unattainable, for practical purposes man must act in accordance with his true nature under such guidance or constraint as the education implicit in the laws of the ideal state would provide.

Through his own writing and those of his most famous pupil, * Aristotle, Plato's influence has probably transcended that of any other writer in the philosophic field.

Taylor, A. E., *Plato, the Man and his Work*. 7th ed. 1960

Plautus, Titus Maccus (Maccius) (*c.* 250–184 B.C.). Roman writer of comedies. He began to write plays (*c.* 224) after failing in business, and continued to produce them with remarkable regularity for the rest of his life. Twenty-one comedies – those regarded by Varro as the only certainly genuine ones – survive complete. The plots of the plays were derived from Greek originals (e.g. Menander), as were the stock characters – the clever rascal of a servant, the long-lost daughter, the duped father, the interchangeable twins – and indeed they have served the turn of Shakespeare, Molière and many lesser men, but Plautus made the farce much broader than that of his Greek originals and introduced songs and sometimes a chorus. One of his best known plays is *Miles Gloriosus* (*The Boastful Soldier*), to whose chief character Falstaff bears some resemblance.

Duckworth, G. E., *The Nature of Roman Comedy*. 1952

Plekhanov, Georgi Valentinovich (1857–1918). Russian socialist and propagandist. Born to a noble family, he was an army officer, then joined the Populists, became a Marxist and was exiled, living in Geneva 1883–1917. Regarded as the founder of the Russian Social Democratic Labour Party (RSDLP), he founded *Iskra* ('The Spark') in 1900 but gradually active leadership passed to his disciple * Lenin. He became a Menshevik after 1904 and opposed Lenin's dictatorship after 1917. He was a prolific theoretical writer.

Plimsoll, Samuel (1824–1898). British politician. Known as the merchant seaman's friend, he was in the coal trade in London when he became interested in the condition of merchant ships and seamen. Overloading and undermanning and the deliberate sending out of unseaworthy ships in order to collect insurance after shipwreck were among the evils he fought against. To obtain reform he became an M.P. (1868) but it was not until 1876 that he got the Merchant Shipping Act passed. One provision was that ships should carry the 'Plimsoll mark', a disc with a horizontal line drawn through it to indicate the loading limit.

Pliny the Elder (Gaius Plinius Secundus) (A.D. 23–79). Roman official and writer. He was brought up as an accomplished, well-educated soldier, administrator and naval commander; he is known to have practised law. But he is chiefly remembered for his interest in natural history. His *Natural History* is the most comprehensive account of its kind written in antiquity. The first two books deal with astronomical and cosmological matters; Pliny then moves on to cover the geography of the globe and the nature of man. Books 8–11 treat of the animal world, and books 12–19 deal with plants, including long discussions of agriculture and the use of herbs for medical purposes. The last sections of the work discuss such topics as pharmaceuticals, metals, precious stones, the history of painting, magic and charms. Pliny's work is essentially a compilation; it is comprehensive, but Pliny was careless in his use of sources, and frequently credulous. He enjoyed the fabulous and the moralistic aspects of natural history, and retailed old wives' tales. Pliny's *Natural History* remained the standard encyclopaedic compilation covering the three kingdoms of nature down to the seventeenth century. He was killed while watching an eruption of Mount Vesuvius.

A figure of lesser stature was his nephew and adopted son **Pliny the Younger** (Gaius Plinius Caecilius Secundus) (61/2–*c*. 114), a notable orator and a diligent official under Trajan. His letters are factually interesting as they deal with the lives of ordinary respectable citizens in provincial towns, and his exchanges of letters with Trajan reveal how even the more enlightened men of his time regarded the early Christians, whom he found 'unboundedly superstitious' but not 'grossly immoral'.

Pliny, ed. and trans. Rackham, H., et al., *Natural History*. 10 vols. 1938–63

Plotinus (205–270). Roman philosopher, born in Egypt. Having studied philosophy in Alexandria, he joined a military expedition to the east in the hope of learning the philosophy of Persia and India and barely escaped with his life in Mesopotamia. In 244 he went to Rome, where he founded a school and lived for the rest of his life. As an old man he attempted to found in Campania a 'republic' on the pattern of Plato's ideal state. Relying on inward vision rather than reasoning, he effects in his writings an integration of all Greek philosophy in order to provide a philosophic basis for a renaissance of Greco-Roman civilization. He regards all souls as one with a world-soul, all intelligences as one with a world-mind, the source of both being the Light of God within us (variously described as the 'One' or the 'Good'). This pagan version of the Trinity was adapted by Christian neoplatonists to accord with their own creed.

Hadot, P., *Plotin, ou la simplicité du regard*. 1963

Plücker, Julius (1801–1868). German physicist and mathematician. Professor of mathematics (1836) of physics (from 1847) at Bonn, his investigations into electrical discharge in gases at low pressure led to his discovery (1859) of cathode rays, which formed the basis of later work on atomic structure and of many technical developments, including television.

Plumer, Herbert Charles Onslow Plumer, 1st Viscount (1857–1932). British field marshal. In command of the Rhodesian Frontier force in the Boer War, he was renowned for the rapidity with which he moved his forces. After succeeding (1915) * Smith-Dorrian in command of the 2nd Army he became one of the most popular and trusted generals of World War I. After the Italian defeat at Caporetto (1917) he went with a British force to bolster the Italians and helped to restore morale. He was later governor of Malta (1919–24) and high commissioner in Palestine (1925–28).

Plunket, St Oliver (1629–1681). Irish Roman Catholic Saint, bishop and martyr, primate of all Ireland from 1669. He was one of many victims of the Popish Plot campaigns of Titus * Oates, who accused him of plotting a foreign invasion of Ireland. He was tried and acquitted in Ireland, tried again in London, convicted and executed. He was canonized in 1975.

Curtayne, A., *The Trial of Oliver Plunket*. 1953

Plutarch (*c*. 46–126). Greek historian. He was educated in Athens and often visited Rome but spent most of his life in his native Boeotia. Best known of his works on history and philosophy is his *Lives*, containing parallel biographies of twenty-three Greek and twenty-three Roman figures notable in history. Distinguished by their literary excellence and narrative interest, the lives vary much in historical value owing to Plutarch's uncritical use of his sources. They became available to

Elizabethans through North's translation (1579) of Amyot's great French translation (1559) and Shakespeare used them for his Roman plays.
Barrow, R. H., *Plutarch and his Times*. 1967

Pocahontas (or Matoaka) (1595–1617). American Indian princess. When Captain John Smith, leader of the settlement of Jamestown, Virginia, was captured, Pocahontas, though only 11 years old, allegedly saved his life 'by taking his head in her arms'. Five years later, when she was held as a hostage in Jamestown, one of the settlers, John Rolfe, fell in love with her: they were married and in 1616 he took her (now baptized 'Rebecca') to England where she was received by the king and queen. She had one son.

Podgorny, Nikolai Viktorovich (1903–1983). Russian politician, born in the Ukraine. Originally a mechanic, he became a food technologist and a protégé of * Khrushchev, serving as secretary of the Ukraine CP 1957–63 and a Politburo member 1960–77. He was President of the USSR 1965–77.

Podiedrad, George (1420–1471). King of Bohemia (from 1458). As leader of the moderate Hussites he was elected king by the Diet although he had no blood ties with the former rulers. He quickly restored the country after the Hussite Wars and strengthened the power of the monarchy at the expense of the nobility, the Catholic members of which formed a league against him. This acted in concert with the invading army of Matthias Corvinus, king of Hungary, whose pretext was a mandate of deposition by the pope, by whom George had been excommunicated (1446). George, however, held his opponents at bay and fighting was still in progress when he died.

Poe, Edgar Allan (1809–1849). American poet and short-story writer, born in Boston. Both his parents were on the stage, and on his mother's death (1811) he was adopted by John Allan, a merchant who sent him to school in England and to the University of Virginia, from which he ran away after a quarrel over debts. A projected career as an army officer became financially impossible when Allan married again, and Poe had to manoeuvre his dismissal from West Point (1831). Meanwhile his first book *Tamerlane and Other Poems* (1827) had appeared, but like its two successors (1829 and 1831) attracted little notice. A prize-winning short story, *MS. Found in a Bottle* (1833), obtained for him the editorship of a paper in Richmond, Virginia, which he turned into a success. In 1836 he married his 13-year-old cousin Virginia Clemm and to better himself moved to New York and then Philadelphia. In 1840 he published *Tales of the Grotesque and Arabesque* (which included *The Fall of the House of Usher*) and in 1841 he joined George Graham for whom he edited *Graham's Magazine* the circulation of which he raised from 5,000 to 35,000, his own contributions including the famous detective story *The Murders in the Rue Morgue*. Recognition as a major poet came with the publication of *The Raven and Other Poems* (1845). After the death of his wife (1847) he had a nervous breakdown and he died in Baltimore two years later on his way to fetch his aunt, Mrs Clemm, to attend his second marriage to a boyhood sweetheart, Sarah Elmira Royster.

The commonly held view that Poe was a drug addict and an alcoholic is derived from a slanderous account in the preface to the collected edition written by his literary executor, Rufus W. Griswold, an old enemy with whom Poe believed himself reconciled. Every item has been refuted by his many loyal friends but the myth persists. He was in fact hard working and much loved. Few writers have equalled Poe in his presentation of the macabre and his tales of mystery and horror (e.g. *The Pit and the Pendulum, The Gold Bug* – a classical reference for the solution of ciphers – and *The Cask of Amontillado*) have been reprinted over and over again. His poems, e.g. *The Raven, Annabel Lee* and *The Bells*, show metrical mastery, haunting rhythms and resonances and undertones of melancholy which deeply influenced * Baudelaire and the French Symbolists.
Quinn, A. H., *Edgar Allan Poe: A Critical Biography*. 1969

Poincaré Jules Henri (1854–1912). French physical scientist and mathematician. He was originally trained as a mining engineer, but became a physics lecturer first at Caen University and then at the Paris Faculté des Sciences where he taught till his death. His major work was in the field of functions. He developed important techniques of probing their properties by partial differential equations (which he termed 'fuchsian' and 'kleinian' functions). In much of his mathematical work he was a follower of C. Hermite, especially in regard to the application of non-Euclidian geometry to the theory of quadratic forms. Another field of interest was an investigation of the properties of integral curves of differential equations. His long-standing concern for probability theory was expressed in his book of 1895, *Leçons sur le Calcul des Probabilités*.

By the turn of the century he was thinking more philosophically about the foundations of Newtonian physics, and becoming aware of some of the dimensions of relativity. He grasped how absolute motion was incapable of being observed (i.e. that for the observer, everything in nature must be relative to something else). One of Poincaré's legacies lay in penning clear descriptions of the processes of mathematical discovery and logic, capable of being understood by the layman.

Poincaré, Raymond Nicholas Landry (1860–1934). French politician. He first became a deputy in 1887 and held a number of government offices including two terms as finance minister (1894–95 and 1906). In 1912 he proved himself a firm and popular premier and was elected president of the republic for the term 1913–20; during World War I he did much to inspire and maintain confidence. As premier he insisted upon a stern reparations policy towards Germany and ordered the occupation of the Ruhr when German payments were in arrears (1923). Recalled to 'save the franc', he was premier for the last time 1926–29.

Poincaré, R. N. L., *Au Service de France*. 1926–1933

Poisson, Siméon Denis (1781–1840). French mathematician and scientist. Poisson adopted a two-fluid theory of electricity: like fluids repelled and unlike attracted. Their strengths were in proportion to the inverse square law. Poisson presupposed that the normal condition of any body was to possess equal quantities of both fluids. Bodies became electrically charged when they acquired a superfluity of one. Using Lagrangian methods, he attempted to render these ideas in mathematical terms.

Poitiers, Diane de (1499–1566). Mistress of Henry II of France. Although she was 48 when he came to the throne she long kept her beauty and used her power to counteract that of the Guises.

Pole, Reginald (1500–1558). English prelate. A son of the Countess of Salisbury, through whom he was connected with the royal family, he was educated at Oxford and abroad and grew up to be a distinguished humanist scholar and a friend of Henry VIII. Ecclesiastical preferment, including the archbishopric of York, was offered in the hope that he would approve the annulment of Henry's marriage with Catherine of Aragon. Unable to respond, Pole withdrew abroad and made public his disapproval of the divorce and of Henry's claim to supremacy of the English church in *De Unitate Ecclesiastica* (1536). Henry was even more enraged when (1536–37) Pope Paul III made Pole a cardinal and appointed him papal legate; he attainted him, arrested members of his family and later had his mother executed. Pole continued in papal employment and in 1545 was one of the three legates who presided over the opening of the Council of Trent. He remained abroad during Edward VI's reign, but on the accession of Queen Mary I, he returned as papal legate and was the principal instrument by which Roman Catholicism was reimposed; he must be held therefore at least partly responsible for the burnings of Protestant martyrs. He succeeded * Cranmer as archbishop of Canterbury (1556) but in 1558 his legateship was cancelled by Paul IV. He died on the same day as Queen Mary (17 November 1558).

Schenk, W., *Reginald Pole*. 1950

Politian (Angelo Poliziano) (1454–1494). Italian scholar and poet. He was educated in the Florence of Lorenzo * de'Medici, whose patronage he attracted by a Latin translation of Homer's *Iliad* which he began at the age of 17. His later works include translations of the great medical writers Hippocrates and Galen. In 1584 he became professor of Latin and Greek at Florence University. Some of his poetry (e.g. his Latin elegy on Lorenzo) shows much depth of feeling as well as metrical skill. His *Orfeo* was the first secular drama written in Italian.

Maïer, I., *Ange Politien*. 1966

Polk, James Knox (1795–1849). Eleventh president of the U.S. (1845–49). Born in N. Carolina, he became a lawyer in Tennessee. He entered the U.S. House of Representatives in

1825, was speaker (1835–39), and governor of Tennessee (1839–41). In 1844 he was the unexpected but successful Democratic candidate for the presidency. His term of office was notable for the settlement of the Oregon boundary dispute with Britain, the occupation of Texas and the ensuing war with Mexico by which California and New Mexico were acquired. He died soon after his term ended.

Quaife, M. M., ed., *The Diary of James K. Polk during his Presidency, 1845–49*. vols. 1910

Pollock, Jackson (1912–1956). American painter. The pioneer and leading exponent of New York Abstract-Expressionism, by spraying or dribbling paint on to an unstretched canvas tacked to floor or wall and being thus enabled to approach his picture from all sides, he claimed that he could achieve an intimacy with his subject otherwise unattainable. Using this method he created tense and intricate patterns of swirling lines and shapes into which representational elements were sometimes introduced. He had great influence among his contemporaries. His *Blue Poles* (1952), bought by the Australian National Gallery for $US 1.9 million in 1973, set a record for modern art prices.

Polo, Marco (1254–1324). Venetian traveller. The journeys which he vividly described resulted from an earlier expedition (1260–1269) by his two uncles to Mongol territory during which they were persuaded to visit the great khan, * Kublai, who as the result of Mongol conquests was also emperor of China. They set out (1271) on a second journey, taking Marco with them, and travelled overland from Acre through Persia, Turkestan and the Gobi desert, reaching Cambuluc (Peking) in 1275. Marco became a favourite of Kublai Khan, who employed him on missions which took him to the furthest parts of the country, and also appointed him governor of Yangchow. So high were the Polos in the khan's favour that it was not until 1292 that they were allowed to leave as part of the escort of a Mongolian princess on her way to Persia to marry a prince. The voyage took two years and the bridegroom had died meanwhile, but she married his brother, and the Polos eventually reached Venice in 1295. In 1296 Marco commanded a galley against the Genoese and was captured; while in prison he was allowed to send for his notes and with the help of a fellow prisoner, Rustichello (or Rusticiano), he composed from them a record of his adventures. The book was published in 1298 as *Divisament dou Monde* ('Description of the World') but was soon better known, because of the incredulity it provoked, as *Il milione*, and became the great best-seller of the pre-Gutenberg age. Although the book contains some legendary material, its descriptions of China are generally accurate.

Latham, R., ed. and trans., *The Travels of Marco Polo*. 1958

Pol Pot (also Tol Saut or Pol Porth) (1928–). Kampuchean (Cambodian) politician. A rubber worker, he was a leader of the Khmer Rouge which took power on the US withdrawal from Indo-China and became prime minister 1976–79, until overthrown by Vietnamese troops. Accused of genocide, he commanded guerrilla forces against the Vietnamese-backed Heng Samhrin government.

Polybius (*c.* 200–*c.* 120 B.C.). Greek historian. Sent to Rome (166) as a hostage, he became friendly with Scipio Aemilianus whom he accompanied when Carthage was destroyed (146). It was thanks to the encouragement of the Scipio family that he wrote his *Universal History*, one of the greatest historical works ever written. The first five books survive intact, but of the other thirty-five only fragments remain. The extant books mainly cover the period 221–168 B.C. and provide a careful and critical account of the Punic Wars.

Walbank, F. W., *Polybius*. 1973

Polycarp, St (*c.* 70–155/6). Bishop of Smyrna. His long life made him a link between the apostles and the fathers of the Church: Irenaeus relates that as a boy he had heard Polycarp speaking of his 'intercourse with John and others who had seen the Lord'. He was martyred in Smyrna. He wrote a notable epistle to the Church at Philippi. His feast day is 26 January.

Polyclitus (5th century B.C.). Greek sculptor, particularly in bronze, contemporary with * Phidias. * Pliny thought his *Doryphorus* perfect sculpture.

Polycrates (6th century B.C.). 'Tyrant' of Samos (*c.* 540–*c.* 524). Having built a large fleet he dominated the Aegean as a kind of pirate king. Enriched with spoils, he beautified Samos and made it temporarily the cultural centre of the Greek world, Anacreon being one of the many poets and artists attracted to his court. At last the Persian governor of Lydia, whose ships and ports had suffered most heavily, lured him to Magnesia where he had him assassinated. The famous legend of the ring and the fish relates to Polycrates: told to throw away something precious, lest his prosperity provoke the envy of the gods, he hurled a valuable ring into the sea. When the ring came back to him the next day in the belly of a fish, it was taken as a portent of his doom.

Pombal, Sebastian José de Carvalho e Mello, Marquis of (1699–1782). Portuguese statesman. He showed his outstanding ability as secretary of state (from 1750) and as prime minister (1755–77) under King Joseph. The skill with which he met the problems created by the earthquake which destroyed Lisbon (1755) gave him a reputation which enabled him to carry out important reforms and curb powers of the church which he thought excessive. Thus sentences passed by the Inquisition now required government approval; censorship passed to state control; he also expelled the Jesuits, whome he suspected of political intrigue. Facilities for education, hitherto almost entirely in church hands, were extended by building 800 schools and reforming the universities. He promoted the development of Brazil and decreed the liberation of the Indian slaves. Ruthlessness in carrying out his policies gradually built up opposition and when Maria I succeeded (1777) he was dismissed. Energy, honesty and vision made Pombal one of the greatest figures of Portuguese history.

Cheke, M., *Dictator of Portugal.* 1938

Pompadour, Jeanne Antoinette, Marquise de (1721–1764). Mistress of Louis XV of France. She was the daughter of a business man called Poisson and because a fortune-teller had predicted she would become a queen was nicknamed Reinette. Having grown up to be beautiful and accomplished she married Lenormant d'Etoiles, a man rich enough to enable her to entertain and be entertained. She became the king's mistress in 1745 and for the rest of her life maintained a hold over him even after her sexual attractions had ceased. As her beauty faded her extravagance increased, but she had good taste and her patronage of literature and the arts was wisely bestowed, e.g. on * Voltaire and * Boucher. She founded the porcelain factory at Sèvres and the Ecole Militaire. Her meddling in politics resulted in the diplomatic upheaval by which the hereditary enemies France and Austria fought as allies in the disastrous Seven Years War (1756–63). Her protégé the Duc de Choiseul became foreign minister in 1758.

Mitford, N., *Madame de Pompadour*. 1964

Pompey (Gnaeus Pompeius Magnus) (106–48 B.C.). Roman soldier and politician. He sided with Sulla against Marius in the Civil War and for his successes in Africa won the title *Magnus* ('the great'). After Sulla's death (78) he put down a revolt by Lepidus, and in Spain crushed the remaining faction of Marius. Back in Rome, his quest for office led him to break with the senatorial party, heal an old feud with Crassus and jointly with him hold the consulship of 70, gaining popularity by restoring the power of the tribunes. He received a special commission to clear the Mediterranean of pirates, which he accomplished in a single brilliant campaign (67): his next achievements were to finish off the war with Mithridates (66), annex Syria and capture Jerusalem (63). On his return to Rome (61) he found the timid and jealous Senate reluctant to concede his two reasonable demands, provision for his veterans and confirmation of his eastern settlement – which involved the creation of four new Roman provinces, Bithynia (with Pontus), Cilicia, Syria and Crete. He was thus almost forced into forming (60) the First Triumvirate with Caesar, whose daughter Julia he married, and Crassus. Caesar departed to pursue his conquests in Gaul and Crassus went east. Pompey began to be suspicious of the activities of Caesar's friends in Rome, and following the deaths of Julia (54) and Crassus (53) the friendship deteriorated. The death of Clodius followed by anarchy in Rome brought about the final breach. Pompey and the Senate, the only sources of law and order, were reconciled and in 52 Pompey was made sole consul. Caesar, seeing his prospects of renewed power and even his life endangered if he returned unarmed, took the symbolic step of crossing the Rubicon and entering Italy with his legions (49). Pompey with most of the senators withdrew to Greece to collect an army but when the rivals finally met at Pharsalus (48), Pompey was defeated; he himself fled to Egypt, where he was murdered.

Gelzer, M., *Pompeius.* 1959

Pompidou, Georges Jean Raymond (1911–1974). French politician. He was a teacher before World War II, during which he served with the Resistance movement. He was a member of the council of state from 1946 until he became director general of Rothschild's French banking house (1954). When * de Gaulle returned to power (1958) he chose Pompidou to head his personal staff and in 1962 appointed him prime minister in succession to Michel Debré. He was president of France 1969–74.

Poncelet, Jean Victor (1788–1867). French mathematician and engineer. He served in the Napoleonic army at Walcheren and in Russia, where he was wounded, and imprisoned. During his years of captivity (till 1814) he applied himself to the mathematical works of Monge, and wrote some important papers. He returned to Metz in 1814 and worked in the field of projective geometry, producing his *Traité des Propriétés Projectives des Figures* in 1822.

Poncelet's most fertile period in applied mechanics was between 1825 and 1840. He spent much time on the improvement of water wheels and turbines. He made some important advances in the field of fortifications, and wrote extensively about the theory of machines. His main influence, however, was a practical teacher. In 1848 he was made head of the Paris Ecole Polytechnique.

Tribout, H., *Un grand savant : le général Jean-Victor Poncelet* (1936)

Poniatowski, Jozef Antoni (1762–1813). Polish patriot and marshal of France. A nephew of Stanislas Augustus (1732–1798), the last king of Poland, in the struggle that preceded the final partition of the Polish kingdom (1793), he gained several victories over the Russians; in 1794 he commanded the division of Kosciuszko's patriot army which vainly defended Warsaw. When Napoleon formed the grand duchy of Warsaw Poniatowski became war minister and commander-in-chief. In 1812 he headed the large Polish contingent which fought its way with Napoleon to Moscow and, still with the French army after the retreat, he performed so gallantly at Leipzig (1813) that Napoleon created him marshal. He was drowned whilst covering the French retreat.

Ponti, Gio(vanni) (1891–1979). Italian architect, designer and craftsman. From 1923, when he appeared at the Triennale Exhibition as a ceramics designer, he designed furniture, industrial products, the interiors of liners, and stage costume and settings, as well as buildings throughout Europe and America. Of his modern commercial buildings the Pirelli tower (1957) in Milan is among the most striking. He founded (1928) the magazine *Domus* and became its editor.

Pontiac (*c.* 1720–1769). Chief of the Ottawa tribe of American Indians. He planned a large-scale concerted attack on the British colonists in which all the frontier forts from Canada to Virginia except Detroit and Pittsburgh were captured (1763). It was not until 1766 that Pontiac eventually came to terms.

Peckham, H. H., *Pontiac and the Indian Uprising*. 1947

Pope, Alexander (1688–1744). English poet. He was the son of a London linen merchant, but the family, to avoid persecution as Roman Catholics, left London (*c.* 1700) to live in Windsor Forest. Deprived of a normal education by life-long deformity caused by a tubercular spine, the boy Alexander educated himself, with his father's encouragement and help, by precocious reading and writing – he began an epic at the age of 12. His pastoral poems were the first to be published, followed by the *Essay on Criticism* (1711) and the mock-heroic *Rape of the Lock* (1712). With these works and other poems he was steadily building up a reputation when the publication of his Homeric translations, the *Iliad* (1715–20) and the *Odyssey* (1725–26), brought fame and enough fortune to enable him to rent a villa at Twickenham and lay out a five-acre garden in the romantic fashion of the time, with a temple, obelisk (in memory of his mother), 'sacred groves', an orangery and above all a grotto, where he could talk with his many and famous visiting friends.

His edition of Shakespeare (1725) produced much criticism, to which the *Dunciad* (1728), in which his opponents were satirized as pedants and dunces, was a reply. His *Essay on Man* (1733–34) is a popular exposition in verse of current philosophical beliefs, while his *Moral Essays* (1731–35) deal with the characters of men and women, the use of riches, and good taste. The fitting of names to the imaginary characters involved the author in several literary quarrels. The most famous of them was with Lady Mary Wortley * Montagu by whom Pope was at first dazzled but whose unkind cynicism soon disillusioned him. In his *Imitations of Horace*, perhaps the best of Pope's satirical works, she saw herself in the lines:

From furious Sappho scarce a milder fate.
Poxed by her love, or libelled by her hate.

But if Pope had a talent for making enemies, he had also a gift, much truer to his real character, of making friends – Swift, Gay, Bolingbroke, the kindly Dr Arbuthnot, his beloved Martha Blount and many more. Pope's 'heroic couplets' in which so much of his work is written would be monotonous were it not for the flexibility he introduced by variation of stress, turn of phrase and exact choice of word. The wit and wisdom is accompanied, too, by a poet's imaginative vision. In spite of his deficiencies of character, Pope is one of the great figures of English literature.
Mack, M., *Alexander Pope*. 1985

Popper, Sir Karl Raimund (1902–). Austrian-born philosopher. He left Europe in the period of Hitler's domination and was a lecturer in philosophy in New Zealand (1937–1945). He then held academic posts in America and England before his appointment (1949) to the chair of logic and scientific method at the London School of Economics. His books, e.g. *The Open Society and its Enemies* (1945), *The Logic of Scientific Discovery* (1963), and *Conjectures and Refutations* (1963), examine the conditions of scientific and social progress and elaborate his main theories that the confirmation of a theory can never be more than provisional, while its refutation will always be final; that ethical standards are 'autonomous' (i.e. are not derivative from facts); hence that individuals have the right to criticize authorities and institutions; finally that progress is made possible not by Utopian approach but by readiness to make the best of existing material resources.
Popper, K., *An Intellectual Autobiography*. 1976

Porsche, Ferdinand (1875–1951). German engineer and motor-car designer. He began work with * Daimler and Auto Union, and set up his own workshops in 1931. In 1934 he designed the revolutionary *Volkswagen*, a cheap, reliable people's car with a rear engine; it was intended for a mass market in the 1930s, but was not marketed until after 1945. The Porsche company continues to make distinguished sports cars.
Georgano, G. N., ed., *The Complete Encyclopaedia of Motorcars 1885–1968*. 1968

Porson, Richard (1759–1808). English classical scholar. The founder of scientific textual criticism, his editions of Euripides and those of Aeschylus and Aristophanes compiled from his notes set new standards of criticism. He was also a connoisseur of wine, and his correspondence reveals a mischievous sense of humour.

Portal of Hungerford, Charles Frederick Algernon Portal, 1st Viscount (1893–1971). British airman. A brilliant record (M.C., D.S.O. and bar) in World War I ensured him important administrative posts between the wars. As chief of the air staff during World War II he was largely responsible for operational strategy. He was created marshal of the Royal Air Force (1944) and was chairman (1946–51) of the U.K. Atomic Energy Commission. His barony (1945) was raised to a viscounty in 1946, when he also received the OM.

Porter, Cole (1893–1964). American composer of songs and lyrics. He developed an astringent sophisticated style in both media. Notable are the scores for *Nymph Errant* (1933), *Anything Goes* (1934) and *Kiss Me Kate* (1949) and such songs as *Begin the Beguine, Night and Day* and *In the Still of the Night*.

Portland, William Henry Cavendish-Bentinck, 3rd Duke of (1738–1809). British politician. He served twice as prime minister, in April–December 1783 as nominal head of the Fox–North coalition and 1807–09 in a government dominated by * Canning and * Castlereagh.

Portsmouth, Louise de Kéroualle, Duchess of (1649–1734). French-born mistress of Charles II of England, also acting as confidential agent of Louis XIV of France. Charles Lennox, her son by the king, was created Duke of Richmond and Gordon.

Post, Emily (1873–1960). American writer, born in Baltimore. After writing some novels on social themes she turned to becoming mentor to Americans in all matters of social behaviour and etiquette, broadcasting and writing newspaper articles on these subjects. Her book *Etiquette* (1922) was the foundation of her reputation.

Potemkin, Gregory Alexandrovich, Prince of Tauris (1739–1791). Russian soldier. He was one of the guards officers who conspired to put * Catherine the Great on the throne (1762); he became her lover (1769) and perhaps her secret husband (1774). He was of impressive physique and personality and showed his talents as an administrator when he was sent to colonize territory conquered from Turkey. He also created the Russian Black Sea fleet and founded the naval base of Sevastopol. He acquired his princely title and vast wealth from Catherine, but he was not merely the self-seeking rascal portrayed by those who invented the tale that to deceive the empress he had built cardboard villages to convey a false impression of the prosperity of the Crimea.

Potter, (Helen) Beatrix (1866–1943). English author and illustrator of many famous children's books, e.g. *The Tale of Peter Rabbit* (1900) and *Tailor of Gloucester* (1902). She lived in the Lake District for many years and left her extensive estate to the National Trust. Her books have been translated into many languages, modern and classical, and are still highly popular.
Lane, M., *The Tale of Beatrix Potter*. 1970

Poulenc, Francis (1899–1963). French composer and pianist. One of 'Les Six' (* Honegger), his output includes concertos, chamber music, piano pieces, e.g. *Mouvements Perpetuels* (1918), the ballet *Les Biches* (1923), the *Mass in G Minor* (1937), the cantata *La Figure Humaine* (witten 1943) and the operas *Les Mamelles de Tirésias* (1944) and *Dialogues des Carmélites* (1956). His characteristic blend of wit and sentiment are however perhaps best expressed in his songs, many of which are reminiscent in style of the café and music-hall.
Roy, J., *Francis Poulenc*. 1964

Pound, Sir (Alfred) Dudley (Pickman Rogers) (1877–1943). British sailor. He was a captain in World War I and after distinguishing himself at Jutland became director of operations at the Admiralty. Shortly before the outbreak of World War II he was appointed first sea lord at the Admiralty, which post he filled despite failing health during the most difficult war years. He was made an admiral of the fleet in 1939 and received the OM in 1943.

Pound, Ezra Loomis (1885–1972). American poet, born in Idaho. After spending the years 1906–07 in European travel he lived mainly in England. His early works, e.g. *Provenca* (1910), *Canzone* (1911) and *Ripostes* (1912), included adaptations of Latin, Provençal, Chinese and Japanese verses (the two latter based on literal translations). As a leader of the Imagist group (*c.* 1914), which attempted to transfer to poetry the modern movements in art, he was distinctive with his 'velvet coat . . . pointed beard . . . and fiery hair'. In pursuit of the same aim he was co-editor with Wyndham Lewis of *Blast*, the organ of Vorticism. He was also foreign correspondent of *Poetry* (Chicago) (1912–19) and the *Little Review* (1917–19). Among his best works were *Quia Paupera Amavi* (1919) and *Hugh Selwyn Mauberly* (1920). During this time he formed literary friendships with Robert * Frost, James * Joyce, Ernest * Hemingway and T. S. * Eliot (who wrote an introduction to his *Selected Poems*, 1928). Between the wars he lived mainly in Italy, working as secretary to W. B. * Yeats, while continuing his own *Cantos*, a vast obscure compilation appearing in sections from 1919, which made much use of 'free association' and distorted spellings and contained a sprawling medley of quotations ranging from ancient Greek and Chinese to modern slang. Meanwhile he had taken up in turn Social Credit and Fascism, for reasons deriving in part at least from his obsessive hatred of 'usura' as the basis of all the evils of modern life. For broadcasting for Italy during World War II he was taken to America at the end of the war and charged with treason. He was, however, declared insane and allowed to return to Italy (1958). He had a major influence upon modern poetry but critics are sharply divided as to his merits.
Pound, E., *Letters*. 1951. Stock, N., *The Life of Ezra Pound*. 1970

Pound, Roscoe (1870–1964). American jurist. Trained as a botanist, and without a law degree, he held a number of academic appointments, especially in his native Nebraska and in the Harvard Law School, where he was Story professor (1910–13), Carter professor of jurisprudence (1913–16) and then dean (1916–36), his influence in the development of modern jurisprudence was important in directing attention to social implications.

Poussin, Nicolas (1594–1665). French painter. Born in Normandy, he was trained in Paris then went to Rome (1624), where he remained for the rest of his life. The carefully planned compositions for which he is famous show historical, mythological and biblical scenes in settings where usually some statue or building exactly copied from the antique gives the necessary verisimilitude. His work is remarkably homogeneous but the passage of years is marked by the change from the warm colours of the Venetians, Titian and Tintoretto, to the cool, clear tones of the north. From about 1645 Poussin devoted more attention to landscapes, which he peopled with mythological figures. In these he achieves even more significantly than in other works the beauty that comes from perfect compositional balance. In 1640 Poussin accepted an invitation from Louis XIV to return to France and decorate the long gallery of the Louvre, but he found the work uncongenial and returned to Rome. Poussin's influence was strong during the classical revival of the following century.
Blunt, A., *Nicolas Poussin.* 1966–67

Powell, Anthony Dymoke (1905–). British novelist. His first novel was *Afternoon Men* (1931). In 1951 he wrote *A Question of Upbringing*, which was the first of a sequence called *A Dance to the Music of Time*, which he completed in 1975 with *Hearing Secret Harmonies*. The books have a single narrator, who records (somewhat satirically) his own life and circle in a prosperous, fashionable society from the 1920s. He also wrote *John Aubrey and His Friends* (1948).

Powell, (John) Enoch (1912–). English politician and classicist. Educated at Trinity College, Cambridge, he was professor of Greek at the University of Sydney, New South Wales 1937–39. During World War II he served in the army (general staff) and rose to the rank of brigadier. He became parliamentary secretary to the ministry of housing and local government in the Conservative government of 1955, financial secretary to the treasury 1957–58 and minister for health 1960. He became famous for his views on the dangers he saw attending coloured immigration and for his opposition to Britain's membership of the Common Market. He refused to stand as a Conservative in the general election of Feb. 1974 and was adopted as a United Ulster Unionist Council candidate at the elections of Oct. 1974; he was re-elected in 1979 and 1983.
Powell, J. E., *Wrestling with the Angel.* 1977

Powys, John Cowper (1872–1963). British writer. His works include the historical novels *A Glastonbury Romance* (1933) and *Owen Glendower* (1941); the epic poem *Lucifer* (written 1905); and literary criticism. e.g. *Dostoievsky* (1947) and *Rabelais* (1948). His brother **Llewelyn** (1884–1939) was also a novelist and essayist of distinction – e.g. *The Pathetic Fallacy* (1928) and *Love and Death* (1939) – as was his brother **Theodore Francis** (1875–1953). He wrote chiefly on rural and allegorical themes, notably *Mr Weston's Good Wine* (1927).
Graves, R. P., *The Powys Brothers.* 1983

Poynings, Sir Edward (1459–1521). English statesman. An opponent of Richard III, he fled to France to join the Earl of Richmond, who became king of England as Henry VII (1485). Poynings was later appointed (1494) the king's deputy in Ireland and his name is given to the law (1494) which laid down that the summoning of an Irish parliament and its legislative agenda were both dependent upon the consent of the English Privy Council and that all laws passed in Westminster were applicable in Ireland.

Prasad, Rajendra (1884–1963). Indian politician. A follower of * Gandhi, he was, between 1932 and 1948, three times president of the Indian National Congress, and like Gandhi was imprisoned for nationalist activities. When India after partition became a dominion he entered the government and when the republic was created (1950) became its first president, until 1962.

Pratt, Sir Charles *see* **Camden, 1st Earl**

Praxiteles (*c.* 390–330 B.C.). Greek sculptor. He excelled in portraying the grace and beauty of the female form, but the only surviving statue known with certainty to be his work is the famous one of Hermes carrying off the infant Dionysus. Of his many statues of

Aphrodite (Venus) one brought by Cridians can be appreciated from copies in the Vatican and at Munich.
Richter, G., *A Handbook of Greek Art.* 1969

Prescott, William Hickling (1796–1859). American historian. Though handicapped by near-blindness, he wrote dramatic but scholarly histories of Spain and the Spanish adventurers who conquered South America. First came *The History of Ferdinand and Isabella* (1838), followed by *The Conquest of Mexico* (1843), *The Conquest of Peru* (1847) and lastly the unfinished *History of Philip II.*
Gardner, C. H., *William Hickling Prescott.* 1970

Presley, Elvis Aron (1935–1977). American rock and roll singer and film actor. He became an international cult-figure for teenagers and succeeded in widening his appeal even after his early death.
Goldman, A., *Elvis.* 1981

Prester John. A legendary figure of medieval times, generally believed to be the Christian ruler of some distant Asian or (more usually) African kingdom of great wealth. Garbled reports of the Christian kingdom of Ethiopia may have lain behind this curiously persistent legend. The search for Prester John was not infrequently the motive for many voyages of exploration.
Slessarev, V., *Prester John: The Letter and the Legend.* 1959

Pretender, the Old and **the Young** *see* **Stuart, James Edward** and **Stuart, Charles Edward**

Pretorius, Andries Wilhelmus Jacobus (1799–1853). Boer leader. He became prominent during the Great Trek from the Cape to Natal, when by his victory over the Zulus (1838) he avenged the massacre of Piet Retief and his sixty followers by the Zulu chief, Dingaan. After the British occupation of Natal, Pretorius moved on to the Transvaal, the independence of which was secured by the Sands River Convention (1842). The capital Pretoria is named after him.

Prévost, l'Abbé (Antoine François Prévost d'Exiles) (1697–1763). French novelist. Having left his Jesuit college to serve as a soldier, he joined the Benedictines and became a priest. His vocation was real enough but often in conflict with the demands of his nature for passion and adventure. His life in consequence contained clashes with his church superiors (and even the police) as well as periods when he found it wise to live abroad, especially in England. The conflict was to some extent resolved by his writings in which he could enjoy by proxy some of the experiences otherwise denied. In the abbey of St Germain-des-Prés in Paris, he wrote the novel *Les Mémoires d'un homme de qualité* (1728–31), which includes the famous love story *Manon Lescaut*, of which the titular heroine was the *femme fatale* in the life of the chevalier Des Grieux, a young man closely resembling Prévost himself. He translated several of * Richardson's novels into French.
Roddier, H., *Prévost, l'homme et l'oeuvre.* 1955

Price, Richard (1723–1791). Welsh unitarian minister and thinker on moral and political problems and ideas. He advocated the reduction of the National Debt in 1771 and defended the policies and aspirations of the American Revolutionaries. A friend of Benjamin * Franklin, he was well regarded in America and was invited over by Congress in 1778, after his *Observations on Civil Liberty and the War with America* (1776).

Priestley, John Boynton (1894–1984). English novelist, playwright and essayist, born in Bradford. After making his name with critical studies of Meredith (1926) and Peacock (1927) he wrote the picaresque novel *The Good Companions* (1929), the most popular of all his works, followed by, e.g., *Angel Pavement* (1930), *Bright Day* (1946) and *Festival at Farbridge* (1951). The plays *Dangerous Corner* (1932) and *Laburnum Grove* (1933) showed his skill and originality in a new medium; three others – *Time and the Conways* (1937), *I Have Been Here Before* (1937) and *Music at Night* (1938) – have plots based on J. W. * Dunne's space-time concepts. He has been a prolific writer both of plays and novels and the above are only a fraction of his total work. He received the OM in 1977.

Priestley, Joseph (1733–1804). English clergyman and scientist. He made a hobby of chemical experiments as a relaxation. His religious and social views were unorthodox and became more radical as he grew older. Benjamin * Franklin, whom he met in

England, was interested in his scientific activities and encouraged him to write a *History of Electricity* (1767). In chemistry he is credited with having been the first to prepare several gases, e.g. ammonia, sulphur dioxide and the oxides of nitrogen. His experiments with carbon dioxide led to his invention of soda water (1772). Priestley is best known for his preparation (1774) of oxygen; he called it dephlogisticated air and it was named oxygen later by Lavoisier. That his religious views remained heterodox was shown by his *History of Early Opinion concerning Jesus Christ* (1786) which involved him in long controversy. He was a strong supporter of the French Revolution which led to his house in Birmingham being sacked by a mob (1791). Increasingly cold-shouldered for his opinions he emigrated to America (1794).
Gibbs, F. W., *Joseph Priestley: Adventurer in Science and Champion of Truth.* (1965)

Prigogine, Ilya (1917–). Russo-Belgian physicist, born in Russia. He held chairs in physics at Brussels 1951– , Chicago 1961–66, and the University of Texas (Austin) 1967– . He won the Nobel Prize for Chemistry in 1977 for his work on the thermodynamics of systems which are not in a state of equilibrium. His books include *From Being to Becoming* (1980).

Prim y Prats, Juan, Count of Reus, Marquis de los Castillejos (1814–1870). Spanish soldier and politician. He was a capable general and military administrator in several fields and also had a chequered but influential political career. He played a large part in the rivalries of Queen Isabella's reign and helped to overthrow * Espartero. Exiled for a time for complicity in a military plot he returned to Spain in 1850. Again exiled (1864–66) he was prominent in the revolution by which Isabella was deposed (1868) and in 1870, now prime minister, he took the unpopular step of offering the crown to Prince Amadeo of Savoy, which provoked his murder by an unknown assassin.

Primo de Rivera y Orbaneia, Miguel, Marquis of Estella (1870–1930). Spanish dictator. After a military career which took him to Morocco, Cuba and the Philippines, he held a number of administrative appointments; after a military *coup* (1923) he set up a dictatorship welcomed by King Alfonso XIII. He joined with France to crush * Abd al Krim in Morocco (1926) and improved Spain's material prosperity, but opposition to his authoritarian rule steadily grew and in 1930 he resigned and retired to Paris, where he died. His son **José Antonio Primo de Rivera** (1903–1936) who founded Falangism, was executed early in the Civil War.
Carr, R., *Spain 1808–1939*. 1966. Payne, S. G., *Falange*. 1961

Prior, Matthew (1664–1721). English poet and diplomat. He was the son of a Wimborne joiner but was educated under the patronage of Lord Dorset and sent to Holland as secretary to the British ambassador. There he was noticed by William of Orange (William III) and subsequently played so important a part in the Treaty of Utrecht (1713) that it was known as 'Matt's Peace'. The success of his *Poems on Several Occasions* (1718) relieved him of financial anxiety and, though the Whigs had no use for his political services, he led an agreeable life much courted for his wit. Much of his work was in the form of burlesques and he was a successful writer of light verse.
Eves, C. K., *Prior, Poet and Diplomatist*. 1939

Proclus (410–485). Greek philosopher. Born of wealthy parents in Constantinople, he studied rhetoric, grammar and law, and was a mathematician and astronomer as well as a philosopher. He is ranked with neoplatonists, and indeed he carries to an extreme their practice of forming a synthesis of all beliefs and philosophical systems, using not only the inner vision of * Plotinus but a Euclidian method of classification of gods, demons etc. derived from all the mythologies and theologies known to him. Using the method of dialectic, he also applied this system of subdivision to the Intellect (or Mind) and Soul, forming an elaborate chain of descent from the One. Having thus carried the neoplatonist process of integration to an extreme point, he could have no direct successors, though he influenced * Descartes and * Spinoza among others, and in a sense anticipated deism. He himself lived as an ascetic and, though like the other neoplatonists he interpreted * Plato as a theologian, he was himself an initiate of the pagan mysteries.
Proclus, trans. Dodds, E. R., *Elements of Theology*. 1932

Procopius (died *c.* 565). Byzantine historian. He accompanied Belisarius on his campaigns, and his books – one known as Procopius' History of his own time and an often scurrilous Secret History (*Historia arcana*) – provide valuable first-hand accounts of the wars against the Vandals and other events of Justinian's reign. His *De Edificiis*, a book describing the public buildings of his time, has great archaeological interest.

Prokhorov, Aleksandr Mikhailovich (1916–). Russian physicist, born in Queensland. With Nikolai Basov he worked out the theoretical basis of the maser, independent of C. H. * Townes' research: all three shared the 1964 Nobel Prize for Physics.

Prokofiev, Sergei Sergeyevich (1891–1953). Russian composer, born in the Ukraine. A brilliant pianist from his early childhood, he studied composition with Glière, Rimsky-Korsakov and Lyadov. Among his early works written before he left Russia in 1918 or during his sojourn abroad were his Classical Symphony (1916–17) the first and still perhaps the best known of seven symphonies, the opera *Love of Three Oranges* (1921) and ballet scores for * Diaghilev in Paris (1921–27). He returned to the U.S.S.R. in 1933. He was a prolific composer, his later works including two Violin Concertos, five Piano Concertos, the operas *The Flaming Angel* (1922–25) and *War and Peace* (1941–42), scores for * Eisenstein's films *Alexander Nevsky* and *Ivan the Terrible*, the ballets *Romeo* and *Juliet* (1935) and *Cinderella* (1941–44), the popular 'symphonic fairy tale' for children *Peter and the Wolf* (1936) and nine Piano Sonatas. His music is noted for its astringent, often satirical, tone.
Shlifstein, S., ed., *S. Prokofiev: Autobiography, Articles, Reminiscences.* 1960

Propertius, Sextus (*c.* 50–*c.* 15 B.C.). Roman poet. He spent most of his life in Rome. Almost all his poems are dedicated to his passion for 'Cynthia', the courtesan Hostia. His elegiacs lack the smooth perfection of * Ovid's but show much deeper feeling.
Luck, G., *The Latin Love Elegy*. 2nd ed. 1969

Protagoras (*c.* 485–*c.* 411 B.C.). Greek sophist from Abdera in Thrace. His religious scepticism was, he explained, due to ignorance of the existence of the gods, owing to 'the obscurity of the subject and the shortness of human life'. He is remembered for his maxim 'Man is the measure of all things, of the existence of the things that are and the non-existence of the things that are not'. Good (i.e. efficient) conduct, leading to success, was the target at which his teaching was aimed. He is portrayed in * Plato's dialogue that bears his name.
Guthrie, W. K. C., *A History of Greek Philosophy.* 1965

Proudhon, Pierre Joseph (1809–1865). French political theorist. Born in poverty, he was educated with the help of friends and later won a three-year bursary given by the Besançon Academy. He went to Paris where he published *Qu'est-ce que la propriété?* (1840), the answer to the question being 'property is theft'. The clearest exposition of his views is found in his *Système des Contradictions économiques* (1846). In the revolution of 1848 he was elected to the assembly but the violence of his opinions and writings led to more than one period of imprisonment and exile. His writings fill thirty-three volumes with another fourteen of correspondence. His statement that property is theft is based on the theory that owners of property whether in land or industry exact the produce of labour in the form of rent, interest, profit etc, without giving equivalent recompense. Another main thesis – that anarchy is the culmination of social progress – predicts that when man attains his full social development he will have acquired enough self-discipline to enable police and government restraints to be dispensed with. Much of Proudhon's thought has been adopted by others, but he died neglected.
Woodcock, G., *Pierre-Joseph Proudhon: His Life and Work.* 1972

Proust, Marcel (1871–1922). French novelist. He was born in Paris into a wealthy bourgeois family but his education was much interrupted by asthma and he abandoned his law studies at the Sorbonne. Until he was 35 he lived the life of a dilettante, ambitious to rise in society and haunting the literary salons. During this time he published only a few volumes of verse and translations of two of Ruskin's works, but he had become attracted to Bergson's philosophy and especially to his views on the subconscious, on the limitations placed on the intellect's ability to grasp and hold by the continuous process of time, and finally on the superiority of intuition over intellect in assessing reality. His mother's death (1905) brought a complete change; without her protective care and understanding the sensitive invalid withdrew into the seclusion of a soundproofed flat and devoted himself for the rest of his life to the writing of his immense series of novels which bear the collective title *A la Recherche du temps perdu* – a complete record of his perceptive observations as reflected by his peculiarly introspective mind. The dividing line between the real and the imaginary is often unclear. But this is no dream sequence; the characters are sharply and often ironically drawn and the book has even been described as a 'comic masterpiece'. In fact it defies definition and comparison and only in a superficial sense can it be described as a semi-autobiographical work giving a minutely observed account of decaying French society (1870–1914) as seen through the eyes of a social climber. The first novel was first completed in 1912 but was only accepted for publication at the author's expense; in 1913 the first volume, *Du côté de chez Swann*, appeared. World War I interrupted publication and meanwhile the author had changed and expanded his plan. A new publisher took over; a second volume, *A l'ombre des jeunes filles en fleur*, was awarded the Prix Goncourt (1919). The remaining volumes, including the notorious *Sodome et Gomorrhe* (3 volumes, 1922), continued to appear until his death and afterwards (1920–25).

Painter, G. D., *Marcel Proust*. 1959–65; Shattuck, R., *Proust*. 1974

Prout, William (1785–1850). English chemist and physician. He pioneered researches into organic chemistry, principally on the digestive system, and on urine. He recognized that the gastric juices of many animals contain hydrochloric acid, and experimented upon the chemical decomposition of foodstuffs (seeing them as combinations of water, fats, carbohydrates and proteins). Prout's main theoretical concept was the belief – based upon some experimental work – that the atomic weights of all elements were integral if the atomic weight of hydrogen was taken as unity. He had an underlying conception of hydrogen as a kind of primary matter from which all other matter might be formed. Prout's hypothesis turned out to be untrue, but it proved an important stimulus through the nineteenth century to the study of atomic weights, and to attempts to classify the elements.

Prynne, William (1600–1669). English Puritan politician and pamphleteer. Because his *Histriomastix* (1632), a huge work attacking the stage and its players, was alleged to defame Charles I and his queen Prynne was savagely sentenced by the Star Chamber to imprisonment in the Tower of London, a large fine and the loss of his ears. Three years later he was again fined, and branded 'S.L.' on his face for attacking Archbishop Laud in pamphlets. He was released in 1640, became an M.P. in the Long Parliament and a strong supporter of the parliamentary cause. In December 1648 he was expelled, following Pride's Purge. He wrote many pamphlets attacking the army and the developments of the 1650s. Under Cromwell he suffered imprisonment and became a vigorous propagandist for the Restoration, after which event he was rewarded by being appointed keeper of the records – at the Tower of London. He published valuable historical work.

Lamont, W. L. *Marginal Prynne*.

Ptolemy (Claudius Ptolemaeus) (*c.* 90–168). Greek astronomer and geographer, who lived in Alexandria. He wrote an astronomical treatise (known under its Arabic name *Almagest*) which is the source of almost all our knowledge of Greek astronomy and was a fundamental textbook until the discoveries of * Copernicus upset its basic theory that the earth is the centre of the universe. His *Guide to Geography*, with the accompanying maps, was equally influential. He conceived of the world as a sphere and he introduced the method of fixing locations by means of parallels of latitude and meridians of longitude. That he made mistakes of measurement is of small account when compared with the greatness of his achievement, to which the whole science of cartography owed its origin. It was due to Ptolemy's mismeasurement of the equator that * Columbus believed that he had reached Asia by a westward route when he discovered the West Indies.

Dreyer, J. L. E., *A History of Astronomy*. 1963. Thomson. J. O., *History of Ancient Geography*. 1948

Ptolemy I (*c.* 367–283 B.C.). Founder of an Egyptian dynasty. He was one of * Alexander the Great's Macedonian generals and became governor of Egypt when the Macedonian conquests were divided after the king's death. In 305 for his assistance to besieged Rhodes he was named Soter (Saviour), and in the same year assumed the title king of Egypt. He made Alexandria, his capital, a centre of commerce and Greek culture.

His son **Ptolemy II** (*c.* 308–?246 B.C.) founded the great Alexandrine library and raised Ptolemaic Egypt to its zenith. There followed a long line of which **Ptolemy XIV** (47–30 B.C.) was the last. **Ptolemy XII** was the brother of * Cleopatra.

Bevan, E. R., *The House of Ptolemy*. 1968

Puccini, Giacomo (1858–1924). Italian composer. He wrote some religious and instrumental music as a young man, but it was in opera that his melodic gift (genuine if limited in scope), resourceful musical craftsmanship and remarkable theatrical sense were combined with greatest success. His intensely romantic operas, e.g. *Manon Lescaut* (1893), *La Bohème* (1896), *Tosca* (1900), *Madama Butterfly* (1904), *The Girl of the Golden West* (1910), *Turandot* (unfinished at the time of Puccini's death but completed by Franco Alfano and first performed in 1926), brought him international fame.

Marek, G. R., *Puccini*. 1951

Pugachev, Emelian Ivanovich (1744?–1775). Russian imposter. He was a Cossack who posed (1773) as * Catherine the Great's dead husband Peter III. He managed to attract a large force, mainly of serfs whom he had enlisted with promises of freedom. Despite early successes he was defeated, betrayed into captivity, taken to Moscow in an iron cage and there executed.

Pugin, Augustus Welby Northmore (1812–1852). English architect and writer, protagonist of the Gothic Revival. Although he was responsible for over sixty churches (e.g. the Roman Catholic Cathedral, Birmingham) and many country houses, he exercised more influence through his writings, notably *The True Principles of Pointed or Christian Architecture* (1841), which became the textbook of Victorian Gothic. He worked under * Barry on the Houses of Parliament and much of the elaborate detail of ornament and fittings was designed by him. Pugin was no mere copyist but indicated how Gothic forms and structural principles were adaptable to modern buildings.

Stanton, P., *Pugin*. 1971

Pulitzer, Joseph (1847–1911). American newspaper proprietor, born in Hungary. Having fought in the Civil War he became a reporter, and later acquired the *St Louis Post-Despatch* (1877) and the *New York World* (1883), which he made the leading Democratic newspaper. In his will he established a fund for annual prizes for journalism, literature and music.

Pullman, George Mortimer (1831–1907). American industrialist. He invented and, in America, practically monopolized the manufacture of the railway sleeping-cars and luxury day-coaches that bear his name. The town of Pullman in Illinois was built for his employees.

Pulteney, William, 1st Earl of Bath (1684–1764). English politician and orator. He led the Tory opposition to * Walpole in the House of Commons from 1725 until he accepted a peerage in 1742.

Purcell, Henry (1659–1695). English composer. He came of a family of musicians and as a boy was a chorister of the Chapel Royal, London (1669?–73). After being a music copyist at Westminster Abbey he was appointed (1677) composer to the king's violin band. Two years later he became organist of Westminster Abbey, and from 1682 of the Chapel Royal. He composed much church music, over 200 songs, duets and catches, keyboard works, chamber music (some early string fantasies on the Elizabethan model and later works in the new Italian concerted style), nearly seventy anthems, many with orchestral accompaniment, and incidental music for plays. His six operas and semi-operas include *Dido and Aeneas* (1689?), *King Arthur* (1691), *The Fairy Queen* (1692) – an adaptation of Shakespeare's *Midsummer Night's Dream* – and *The Indian Queen* (1695) to words by Dryden. His occasional works included the ode for St Cecilia's Day *Hail, Bright Cecilia* (1692) and odes of welcome and birthday odes for the sovereign, e.g. *Come Ye sons of Art Away* (1694).

Westrup, J. A., *Purcell*. 7th ed. 1973

Purkyně, Jan Evangelista (1787–1869). Czech physiologist. His main work centred on the physiology of the senses. He experimented on vertigo, he was interested in the aberrations of the eyes and, performed interesting self-experimentation on the visual effects of applying pressure to the eyeball. The physiological basis of subjective visual effects had been examined but hitherto largely ignored in the German-speaking world, partly because of the assumption, made by * Goethe and other Romantics, that they were essentially products of the imagination. After 1830 much of Purkyně's work centred on cell observations, using compound microscopes; he described nerve fibres and cell division. He observed the 'fibres of Purkyně' in the heart ventricles. He was one of the earliest scientists to use the term 'protoplasm'.

Pusey, Edward Bouverie (1800–1882). English religious leader. After being ordained (1828) he was appointed to the Regius professorship of Hebrew at Oxford, which he held for the rest of his life. With * Newman and * Keble he was a leader of the Tractarian or Oxford Movement which started in 1833 with the publication of the first issues of *Tracts for the Times*, to which Pusey made notable contributions on the eucharist and baptism. The movement was designed to combat rationalism and by stressing the common heritage of the Roman Catholic and English Catholic churches it was hoped to pave the way for eventual reunion. But Pusey did not himself follow Newman's example of joining the Roman Catholic church and in his writings and sermons argued against such a course. He was responsible for many benefactions and worked in the East End of London during the cholera epidemic of 1866. Pusey House, Oxford, containing a library of which his own collection of books formed the nucleus, was opened in memory of him in 1884.

Pushkin, Alexander Sergeyevich (1799–1837). Russian writer. He came of a poor but noble family; there was an exotic strain in his ancestry – his maternal great-grandfather was an Abyssinian prince who became a general under Peter the Great. In St Petersburg as a young man he combined work at the Foreign Office with life as a poet and man about town; but many of his poems, e.g. the fiery *Ode to Liberty* (1820), were infected with the ideas which the French armies had carried with them through Europe and he was exiled to south Russia. There, under * Byron's influence, he began to replace the rigid classicism which Russia had borrowed from France by freer, romantic and more dramatic forms. In Odessa he began (1824) his verse novel *Eugene Onegin* suggested by Byron's *Don Juan* and later converted into an opera by * Tchaikovsky. A similar musical destiny awaited several of Pushkin's best known creations. *Ruslan and Lyudmila* (1820), his first major work, became an opera by * Glinka. The tragic drama *Boris Godunov* (1825) is even better known as * Mussorgsky's opera; *The Queen of Spades*, a remarkable short novel, had a future not only as an opera by Tchaikovsky but also as a film. Among Pushkin's other well known works was the narrative poem *The Bronze Horsemen* (1833); he also wrote folk and fairy stories and many beautiful lyrics, several of which have been turned into songs. Pushkin returned to St Petersburg after the accession of Tsar Nicholas I, and a visit to the Caucasus (1829) resulted in a finely descriptive prose work, *The Journey to Aryrum*. In 1831 he succeeded at last in making the beautiful but frivolous Nathalie Goncharova his wife, but the marriage was not a happy one and he died of wounds received in a duel with a French nobleman whom he suspected of being his wife's lover.

Toyat, H., *Pushkin*. 1974

Puvis de Chavannes, Pierre (1824–1898). French painter. He attempted with partial success to restore to wall paintings their significant place in art. Examples of his work are the paintings of the life of St Genevieve on the walls of the Pantheon, which occupied him from 1874 until his death.

Jullian, P., *Dreamers of Decadence*. 1971

Pu-yi, Henry (Hsüang Tung) (1906–1967). The last Manchu emperor of China (1908–12). A nephew of the murdered emperor Kuang-Hsü, he was appointed to the throne by the dowager empress * T'zu-Hsi at the age of 2. Deposed by * Sun Yat-sen's revolution (1912), he adopted his English pre-name as a tribute to Henry VIII. In July 1917 he was restored for one week. He lived in Japan from 1924 and, after the invasion of Manchuria, became puppet emperor of Manchukuo (1934–45). Jailed as a war criminal (1950–59), he declared himself as a supporter of the Peoples' Republic, worked as a gardener in

Shenyang, then as a research worker in Beijing. He wrote memoirs.

Pym, Barbara (1913–1980). English novelist. She published six novels between 1950 and 1961 with modest success, only gaining wider recognition after 1977 when critics in the *Times Literary Supplement* singled her out as one of the most under-rated writers of the century. Her books included *No Fond Return of Love* (1961), *Quartet in Autumn* (1977) and *The Sweet Dove Died* (1978).

Pym, John (1584–1643). English politician. He first entered parliament in 1614, but it was after the accession of Charles I that he became the crown's sternest and most effective opponent. He was prominent in the impeachment of * Buckingham and took an active part in promoting the Petition of Right (1628). After the eleven years during which Charles called no parliament (1629–40) he was foremost in pressing the proceedings against Strafford and Laud. In 1642 he was one of the five M.P.s whom Charles tried to arrest. Until his death in December 1643, he was the leader of the Commons. After the outbreak of the Civil War he devised the alliance with the Scots which eventually gave the parliamentarians the victory. Pym was certainly one of the outstanding exponents of the parliamentary arts.
Hexter, J. H., *The Reign of King Pym*. 1941

Pynchon, Thomas (1937–). U.S. novelist. He studied engineering at Cornell University, wrote several short stories and published the novels *V* (1963), *The Crying of Lot 49* (1966) and *Gravity's Rainbow* (1973) which were hailed by critics as works of major literary importance. He then stopped publishing.

Pyrrho of Elis (*c.* 310–270 B.C.). Greek philosopher. He taught an extreme form of scepticism, which held that it was impossible to understand the nature of things and that the best state of mind was obtained by suspending judgement rather than attempting to make decisions. He would admit that man could have a sensation of sweetness or pain but in the latter case would lessen its effect by not believing it to be evil. The term 'Pyrrhonian scepticism' passed into common speech. None of his writings survive.
Zeller, E., *Stoics, Epicureans and Skeptics*. 1962

Pyrrhus (319–272 B.C.). King of Epirus (roughly the equivalent of modern Albania). After the death of * Alexander the Great, to whom he was related, he tried to carve an empire for himself out of the Macedonian heritage. With the help of * Ptolemy I he became joint king of Epirus (*c.* 297). Seeking new conquests, he accepted an invitation (281) from Tarentum (Taranto), a Greek city in Italy, for help against Rome, and his army of 25,000 men with elephants (seen by the Romans for the first time) gained a hard fought victory near Heraclea with the loss of 4,000 men. Another victory near Asculum (279) brought such losses that the phrase 'Pyrrhic victory' gained immortal currency. After further campaigns he returned to Epirus (275); after an unsuccessful attack on Sparta, he retreated to Argos, where he was killed by a tile thrown by a woman.
Hammond, N. G. L., *Epirus*. 1967

Pythagoras (6th century B.C.). Greek philosopher and mathematician. He was born in Samos, but later established a school or brotherhood in Croton, a Greek colony of southern Italy. The brotherhood seems to have formed a mystical cult, to have led an ascetic life and to have practised purificatory rites. It seems also to have formed a ruling oligarchy, for after twenty years the people rose against it and forced it to leave Croton. Pythagoras himself withdrew to Megapontum, where he died; no writings of his have survived, and it is difficult therefore to separate his views from those of his followers.

Pythagoras adopted the belief in transmigration of souls, both from animal to man and from man to animal, the necessity for this being removed when purification, attained by ritual practices and spiritual contemplation, was complete. Pythagoras himself was however primarily a mathematician; he had a mathematical conception of the universe, that its order is due to the mathematical relationships of one component to another, both location and movement conforming to strict mathematical laws. This concept has been followed by many others, e.g. * Copernicus, * Galileo, * Newton and * Einstein. These laws he related to those of music – hence such terms as music (or harmony) of the spheres. To the rotation of the earth, which he is said to have discovered, he ascribed day and night. To his mathematic conception he gave philosophic point by asserting that by the contemplation of such harmonies man achieves virtue – that virtue is in fact a harmony of the soul just as health indicates a harmony of the body. Many of these ideas were adopted by * Plato and * Aristotle or critically examined by them, and in so far as Pythagoreanism, with its emphasis on discernible order in being , paved the way for rational metaphysical speculation as against a materialistic (or simply positive) classification and explanation of knowledge, it fathered most of the schools of philosophy that existed in the European tradition for the next two millennia.

Guthrie, W. K. C., *A History of Greek Philosophy*. 1962. Vogel, C. J. de, *Pythagoras and Early Pythagoreanism*. 1966

Pytheas (4th century B.C.). Greek navigator and geographer, born at Massilia (Marseilles). He sailed past the coasts of Brittany and reached Cornwall, where he traded in tin at an island believed to be St Michael's Mount. Eventually he reached 'Thule' (probably one of the Shetlands). His account, now lost, was received with incredulity in his own day but was used by * Strabo and seems to have been as accurate as possible with his limited resources.

Stefansson, V., *Ultima Thule*. 1944

Pythias *see* **Damon and Pythias**

Q

Qaddafi, Muammar al- (1942–   ). Libyan soldier and politician. A Bedouin, he led the *coup* which deposed King * Idris I in 1969 and as Chairman of the Revolutionary Command Council he became Prime Minister of Libya 1970–72 and President from 1972. Qaddafi directed a puritan Islamic and socialist regime close to the USSR and hostile to the Egyptian-Israeli detente.
First, R., *Libya: The Elusive Revolution*. 1974

Quarles, Francis (1592–1644). English metaphysical poet. He was the most successful verse-moralist of his day, *Divine Emblems* (1635) being the main source of his fame. Some of his epigrams are remembered, e.g. 'No man is born unto himself alone', 'He that begins to live, begins to die'. A royalist in the Civil War, he was plundered by the Roundheads.
Hasan, M., *Quarles: A Study of his Life and Poetry*. 1966

Quasimodo, Salvatore (1901–1968). Italian poet. He is considered the leading writer of the Italian Hermeticist movement which was inspired by a symbolical use of language. His later poems are much concerned with 'la poesia sociale', expressing a social conscience and a sense of history. He received the Nobel Prize for Literature in 1959.
Tondo, M., *Salvatore Quasimodo*. 1970

Queen, Ellery. Pen-name for Frederick Dannay (1905–1982) and Manfred B. Lee (1905–1971), American authors of a large number of well known detective stories. 'Ellery Queen' is the name not only of the author but also of the detective hero.

Queensberry, John Sholto Douglas, 8th Marquess of (1844–1900). Scottish peer. A keen patron of boxing, he devised the rules which bear his name (1865). In 1895 his insulting letter to Oscar * Wilde, whose close association with his son Lord Alfred * Douglas he disliked, provoked the litigation that led to the writer's downfall.

Queensberry, William Douglas, 4th Duke of (known as 'Old Q') (1725–1810). Scottish peer, notorious in his lifetime as an extreme example of worthless and dissolute aristocracy.

Quennell, Peter Courtney (1905–   ). English writer and critic. He edited the *Cornhill Magazine* (1944–51) and later became joint-editor of *History Today* (till 1979). His works include biographical and critical studies, notably of Lord Byron, John Ruskin, Shakespeare, Pope and Samuel Johnson. In his younger years he wrote poetry, e.g. *Inscription on a Fountain Head* (1929).
Quennell, P. C., *The Marble Foot*. 1976

Quesnay, François (1694–1774). French physician and economist. He was physician to Louis XV but is better known for his many books on economics and for his contributions, on agricultural and economic subjects, to the famous *Encyclopédie*. As the leader of the Physiocrats, he held that land was the ultimate source of all wealth and that to interfere with production or exchange must lead to disaster. His *Tableau économique* (1758) anticipates to a limited extent the tables of national income and expenditure of today.
Gooch, G. P., *Louix XV: The Monarchy in Decline*. 1956

Quetelet, Lambert-Adolphe-Jacques (1796–1864). Belgian statistician. Born in Ghent, he showed early mathematical talent. In 1815 he was appointed professor of mathematics at the collège de Ghent, and in 1819 he received a doctorate from the newly-founded University. In the 1820s he developed an interest in astronomy, and began to take a mathematical approach to meteorology. But the work for which he feted in his own day emerged in the 1830s. He began to develop the theory of mathematical statistics, devised careful tests for the validity of statistical information, and pioneered the use of social statics for the understanding of the 'average man'. Quetelet's belief that the regularities of human behaviour revealed by weight of data demonstrated that man, too, operated under natural law was not in itself original (political economists, for example, had always presupposed so). But much use was made of Quetelet's mathematical prestige in attempts to generate an empirical sociology or a theory of man as part of Nature. Quetelet pioneered the conception of the normal distribution curve, which became an important tool in later studies of criminal and deviant behaviour.
Hankins, F. H., *Adolphe Quetelet as Statistician*. 1908

Quevedo y Villegas, Francisco Gómez de (1580–1645). Spanish writer. He became secretary to Philip IV (1632) but after opposing * Olivares was imprisoned, which so injured his health that he died soon after release. His works both in poetry and prose display a striking contrast between those that are moral or religious in tone and the burlesques noted for their broad humour, puns, slang and exaggerated style. A picaresque novel, *La Vida del Buscón Pablos* (1626) is perhaps his best known work. His Sueños, translated as *Visions*, were popular in Stuart England.
Jones, R. O., *A Literary History of Spain*. 1971

Quezon y Molina, Manuel Luis (1878–1944). Filipino politician. He fought in the revolt against the Spaniards (1898), and later became leader of the nationalists in the Philippine Assembly (when the Islands were under U.S. control). He campaigned vigorously for independence both as commissioner to the U.S.A. (1909–16) and as president of the Philippine Senate (1916–35). When the Commonwealth of the Philippines was created (1935) he was elected the first president and he was a loyal supporter of the Americans against the Japanese. He took refuge in the U.S.A. when the Japanese invaded the country and headed a government in exile. Quezon City, the capital, was named after him.

Quiller-Couch, Sir Arthur Thomas (known as 'Q') (1863–1944). English scholar and writer. He came of an old Cornish family and made his reputation with a series of Cornish novels of which *Troy Town* (1888) and *Hetty Wesley* (1903) were among the best known. He edited *The Oxford Book of English Verse* (1900) which shared with Palgrave's *Golden Treasury* (1861 and 1896) the honour of introducing more readers to English poetry than any other works. In 1912 he became the first King Edward professor of English literature at Cambridge, an appointment he retained until his death. His vivid inspiring lectures were published as *On the Art of Writing* (1916), *On the Art of Reading* (1920) etc. He also completed Stevenson's unfinished novel *St Ives*. He was joint editor of the *New Cambridge* edition of Shakespeare.
Brittain, F., *Quiller-Couch: A Biographical Study of 'Q'*. 1947

Quilter, Roger (1877–1953). English composer. He wrote many delightful settings of songs by Shakespeare, Wordsworth and Herrick. His *Children's Overture* (1920) is well known.

Quincy, Josiah (1772–1864). American politician. Continuing the tradition of his father, the **Josiah Quincy** (1744–1775) who had been a prominent New England revolutionary, he played an important political role. He was elected to the House of Representatives in 1802 and became known as a staunch individualist, strongly opposed to slavery. He was a senator (1813–20) and having been an energetic and reforming mayor of Boston (1823–28) he became head of Harvard University, where his long presidency (1829–45) was marked by liberalism and progress. In 1854 he emerged from retirement to greet the new Republican party and welcome its denunciation of all compromise with slavery.

Quintilian (Marcus Fabius Quinitilianus) (*c.* 30–96). Latin writer on rhetoric. He became famous for his *Institutio Oratoria* (*The Training of an Orator*). The theme is wider than the title since it discusses what to say as well as how to say it; it not only advises the would-be orator on everything from dress to figures of speech but provides the basis of an elementary education, and lists authors whose style merits imitation. None of his own speeches, however, has survived. Little is known of his life except that he was born in Spain, and the date of his death is uncertain.

Butler, H. E., trans., *Institutiones Oratoriae*. 1920–1922. Clarke, M. L., *Rhetoric at Rome*. 1953

Quirino, Elpidio (1890–1956). Filipino politician. As a law clerk in the Philippine Senate he became friendly with * Quezon and was for years his close ally. He led the Filipino resistance to the Japanese and was first vice-president of the Independent Philippines (1946) and president (1948–53). Ramon Magsaysay defeated him in 1953 on the issue of government corruption.

Quiroga, Juan Facundo (1790–1835). Argentine *Caudillo* (army chieftain). He took part in the revolution of 1810 against Spain and subsequently established himself as *caudillo* of the Andean provinces. To ensure his local supremacy he was a strong advocate of a federal form of government, which was adopted in 1827. He was notorious for his pitiless suppression of a faction which favoured a unitary state and raised a rebellion. He was assassinated, probably at the instigation of Rosas, governor of the province of Buenos Aires.

Quisling, Vikdun (1887–1945). Norwegian traitor. After serving in the army and as consul abroad, he founded (1933) the National Unity party, a Norwegian version of Hitler's Nazi organization in Germany. After the German invasion (1940) he proclaimed himself head of the Norwegian government and though temporarily disowned by the Germans was reorganized by them (1942) as head of an administration under German control. After the German defeat he was sentenced to death by a criminal court and executed. His name has become a synonym for a traitor and renegade.

R

Rabelais, François (*c.* 1494–1553). French writer. He was born near Chinon in Touraine where his father was probably an advocate. He entered (*c.* 1520) the Franciscan order but transferred, with papal consent, to the Benedictines (*c.* 1524). He seems to have visited several universities and acquired a great range of learning before finally leaving the order to become a lay priest. In 1532 he graduated in medicine at Montpellier and afterwards practised at Lyons, where he wrote *Pantagruel* (1532) and *Gargantua* (1534) under the pseudonym Alcofri bas Nasier, an anagram of his own name. The giant Gargantua is Pantagruel's father and so in a sense the two books and those which followed are parts of a single work. A third book was published in 1546 and a fourth appeared complete in 1552. The authenticity of a fifth published after Rabelais's death is doubtful. The books were condemned at various times by the Sorbonne, though it was not the doctrines of the church that were satirized but the ignorance and obscurantism of monks and priests and the many abuses that had become established. Francis I refused to ban them and Rabelais himself was protected by Jean du Bellay, bishop of Paris (cardinal from 1536), whom he twice accompanied to Rome, probably as his physician. The details of Rabelais's later life are obscure. Most of the time must have been spent in medical practice: he seems to have again visited Rome more than once; after the condemnation of the third book (1545) he took refuge in Metz and finally received an appointment (which he seems never to have taken up) as *curé* of Meudon, a small town near Paris. The books, which achieved an astonishing contemporary success (by 1600 more than a hundred editions had appeared), tell of the travels of two giants Pantagruel and Gargantua with their companion Panurge. They are a compound of great learning, bawdy wit and satire, expressing in an extreme form and by unusual means the humanism not only of the author but of Renaissance culture generally. Sir Thomas Urquhart (1611–60) made a famous English translation (Books 1 and 2 published 1653, Book 3 1693) in language almost as exuberant as the author's own.

Plattard, Jean., *François Rabelais*. 1932

Rabi, Isidor Isaac (1898–   ). American physicist, born in Austria. In 1937 he became professor of physics at Columbia University in New York where he worked on the magnetic properties of atomic nuclei and perfected the molecular-beam resonance method. For this he was awarded the Nobel Prize for Physics (1944).

Rabi, I., *My Life and Times as a Physicist*. 1960

Rachel (Elisa Rachel Felix) (1821–1858). French actress of Swiss birth. From her first stage appearance in Paris (1837) her greatness as a *tragédienne* was recognized. As one by one she played the great parts of Corneille, Racine (above all as Phèdre) and Voltaire she won renewed acclaim. During the revolution of 1848 her public recital of *La Marseillaise* provoked a sensation. She had a reputation for avarice and amassed a huge fortune; through her liaison with Count Walewski, the emperor's natural son, she became the mother of a grandson of Napoleon I.

Agate, J., *Rachel*. 1928

Rachmaninov, Sergei Vasilyevich (1873–1943). Russian composer and pianist. He

studied first at St Petersburg and then (1885–92) at the Moscow Conservatoire, where he was the pupil of Arensky and Taneyiev and became a friend of * Tchaikovsky, whose music decisively influenced his own. At the age of 19 he wrote the Prelude in C sharp Minor which won him world-wide fame and eventually by its very popularity caused him to hate it. After a long concert tour in Russia he began teaching in Moscow in 1893, becoming director of the Imperial Opera four years later. After the Russian Revolution he lived in the U.S.A., continuing to travel widely in Europe and America giving piano recitals. As a pianist he was among the greatest of his period. As a composer, though he wrote symphonies, tone poems, operas, chamber music and songs, he is best known for his piano works, notably two sets of Preludes (1903–04; 1910) four Concertos (1890–91; 1901; 1909; 1927, revised 1938) and the *Rhapsody on a Theme of Paganini* (1934). These works have earned popularity by their strongly emotional content, at times seeming excessive, by the skill with which the composer deploys material that is not itself specially original, and the dazzling virtuosity of the writing for the piano.
Leyda, J., *Sergei Rachmaninov: A Lifetime in Music*. 1956

Racine, Jean (1639–1699). French dramatist. Born in Picardy, the son of a lawyer, he was educated at Port-Royal, where he was influenced by Jansenist teachings. In Paris, where he sought literary fame, he became a friend of * Molière, * La Fontaine and later * Boilèau, meanwhile winning the favour of Louis XIV with complimentary poems. Molière's company staged his first play, *La Thébaïde*, in 1664, but the production of the second, *Alexandre le Grand* (1665), led to the famous quarrel between the two playwrights. After a fortnight's run Racine, dissatisfied with the performance of Molière's company, transferred the production to that of his main rival, at the same time, it is said, stealing his mistress and star actress Mademoiselle du Parc. There were, indeed, many defamatory stories about Racine's life in Paris at this time, including one said to have been extracted under torture from a well known sorcerer that he had poisoned his mistress, but Racine had the art of making enemies as well as friends and much can be attributed to malice. With the production of his third play, *Andromaque* (1667), Racine entered his great period. In this play and those that followed he displayed the great human emotions of love, jealousy and hatred at their highest point of intensity with their consequences of crime, madness or death. Though he was bound by the same classical formulas as his predecessors, he achieved freshness by a remarkable simplification of design combined with a psychological subtlety hitherto unknown. Moreover, he was a great poet and the musical cadences of his lines are a delight in themselves.

The plot of *Andromaque* was taken from Euripides, as were those of *Iphigénie* (1674) and *Phèdre* (1677) – a grim tale of illicit passion and jealousy which provides one of the finest parts ever written for a tragic actress. *Bajazet* (1672), which with *Britannicus* (1669), *Bérénice* (1670) and *Mithridate* (1673) forms a historical group, has an uncharacteristically complicated plot and an atmosphere of oriental intrigue. His only comedy, *Les Plaideurs*, appeared in 1668. In 1677 the office of royal historiographer enabled him to leave the theatre in dignity and comfort. The event coincided with a 'conversion', inspired perhaps by the coming of middle age, the influence of Madame de Maintenon and Boileau and his own underlying piety inculcated at Port-Royal. To this period belong his last two plays, *Esther* (1689) and *Athalie* (1691), both on biblical themes and written for the Maison de Saint-Cyr, the school founded by Madame de Maintenon. With the possible exception of *Phèdre, Athalie* is considered Racine's greatest work. Its mighty theme concerned with God's anger and divine providence is enriched by stage effects and choruses of outstanding beauty.
Brereton, G., *Jean Racine: A Critical Biography*. 1951

Radcliffe, Ann (née Ward) (1764–1823). English novelist. She was the most important of the writers of the 'gothick romances', the fashion for which was set by Horace Walpole's *Castle of Otranto* (1765). The principal ingredients are romantic settings in which occur deeds of darkness, strange and mysterious events, and 'supernatural' happenings, afterwards rationally explained. Her best known work is *The Mysteries of Udolpho* (1794), set in a sombre castle in the Appenines. She influenced * Byron and * Scott, but Jane * Austen, in *Northanger Abbey*, ridiculed her inferior imitators.
Grant, A., *Ann Radcliffe*. 1952

Radek, Karl Bernardovich (real name K. B. Sobelsohn) (1885?–1940). Russian author and politician. Born in Poland of Jewish descent, he became a journalist and supported the German Social Democratic Party from 1904. He was imprisoned several times, fought in the Russian Revolution (1917) and tried to organize a communist revolution in Germany (1918–19). He was a member of the presidium of the Communist International (1919–1923) but his influence declined when the Comintern proved ineffective, and he became head of the Sun Yatsen University for Chinese Students in Moscow (1923–27) until being expelled from the Communist party (1927) on a charge of having supported Trotsky. Readmitted to favour he wrote for *Izvestia* and helped draft the 1936 constitution. In 1937 he was sentenced for treason to ten years, jail. He is thought to have died in prison.

Radetzky, Johann Joseph, Count (1766–1858). Austrian field-marshal. He fought against France throughout the Revolutionary and the Napoleonic Wars and was commander-in-chief in Austrian Italy from 1831. In the revolutionary year of 1848–49 he defeated the insurgents and their Sardinian allies at Custozza and Novara and forced the surrender of Venice. He held the country in firm control until his retirement (1857).

Radhakrishnan, Sarvepalli (1888–1975). Indian philosopher and (1962–1969) president of the republic of India. Born and educated at Madras, he held professorial appointments at several Indian universities before he was Spalding professor of eastern religions at Oxford (1936–52) and concurrently (1939–48) vice-chancellor of Benares University. Appointed ambassador to the Soviet Union in 1949, his appointment as president of the Indian republic followed a ten-year term (1952–62) as vice-president. Besides his *History of Indian Philosophy* (1923–27) his writings on eastern philosophies and religions include *The Hindu View of Life* (1927) and *An Idealist View of Life* (1932). He was made an Honorary OM in 1963.

Radishchev, Aleksandr Nikolayevich (1749–1802). Russian philosopher, poet and radical thinker. In 1790 he wrote *Journey from St Petersburg to Moscow*, which portrayed the miseries of serfdom and called for a social revolution. He was subsequently sentenced to death, the sentence being commuted to exile in Siberia. He was allowed to return home after the death of Catherine the Great in 1796. In 1801 he became a member of a law commission but, despairing of any progress towards abolishing serfdom, committed suicide. His writings influenced Russian reformers throughout the nineteenth century.
Lang, D. M., *The First Russian Radical*. 1959

Raeburn, Sir Henry (1756–1823). Scottish portrait-painter. After two years in Rome (1785–87) he became a fashionable portrait-painter in his birthplace, Edinburgh. A keen sense of character, combined with strong colour and vivid effects of light, make his portraits lively as well as realistic. Sir Walter Scott was among his many well known sitters, who are often presented in national costume or on horseback in parkland settings. He became president of the R.S.A. in 1812 and R.A. in 1815; his knighthood followed in 1822.
Dibdin, E. R., *Sir Henry Raeburn*. 1925

Raeder, Erich (1876–1960). German sailor. He was chief of staff (1912–18) to Admiral Hipper, who commanded the battle cruisers in World War I; and, having been appointed grand-admiral in 1939, was commander-in-chief during World War II until superseded by Admiral Dönitz (1943). He was condemned by the Nuremberg tribunal to life imprisonment for his part in planning the war and especially the invasion of Norway, but was released in 1955.

Raemaekers, Louis (1869–1956). Dutch cartoonist. The bitter irony of his cartoons attacking the Germans in the Amsterdam newspaper *De Telegraaf* had a remarkable effect on neutral opinion in World War I.

Raffles, Sir (Thomas) Stamford (1781–1826). English colonial administrator. Founder of Singapore, he was the son of a sea-captain and was born at sea. He joined the East India Company and went to Malaya (1805) as assistant secretary at Penang. In 1811 the British occupied Java (Holland then being under Napoleon's rule): as lieutenant-governor (1811–16) Raffles founded the magnificent botanical gardens at Bogor, began restoring Borobudur and wrote a monumental *History of Java*. On his personal initiative and despite official misgivings he founded (1819) Singapore, and so secured British control of

Malaya. In 1824 a fire on board the ship on which he was returning to England destroyed his botanical and zoological specimens but with such replacements as he could collect he founded the London Zoological Society, of which he became first president.

Wurtzburg, C. E., *Raffles of the Eastern Isles*. 1954

Raglan, Fitzroy James Henry Somerset, 1st Baron (1788–1855). British soldier. The eighth son of the 5th Duke of Beaufort, he was A.D.C. to the Duke of * Wellington and was present at all the great battles of the Peninsular War. He lost an arm at Waterloo and after serving for long periods afterwards on Wellington's staff – the duke was by then commander-in-chief – Raglan was appointed (1854) to command the British forces in the Crimea, where he died from dysentery. For his victory at Inkerman he was made a field-marshal but blame was attached to him for the misconstrued order that led to the fatal charge of the Light Brigade at Balaclava. Though an excellent tactician, he lacked the outstanding qualities demanded of a commander-in-chief. His barony was awarded in 1852.

Rahman, Tunku Abdul *see* **Abdul Rahman**

Raikes, Robert (1735–1811). English philanthropist. He was born at Gloucester, where his father was a printer and owner of a local newspaper which he inherited. Concern for the children whom he saw wandering in the streets on Sundays fired him to start a Sunday school (1780), where children might learn to read and repeat the catechism. Newspaper reports led to the scheme spreading to all parts of the country.

Rainier III (1923–   ). Prince of Monaco (since 1949). Head of the house of Grimaldi which has ruled in Monaco since medieval times, he succeeded his grandfather Louis II and married (1956) the film star Grace * Kelly. Much of the little state's revenue is derived from the casino at Monte Carlo.

Rais (or Retz), **Gilles de** (1404–1440). French soldier and murderer. After fighting with * Joan of Arc at Orléans and being made a marshal by Charles VII, this Breton nobleman took to necromancy and murder. Over 140 children are said to have been tortured and killed by him before he was taken and hanged. Breton tradition links him with the fairy-tale figure of Bluebeard.

Rajagopalachari, Chakravarti (1879–1972). Indian politician. A lawyer by profession, he joined * Gandhi's non-co-operation movement, but served as prime minister of Madras (1937–39). After partition and independence he was governor of West Bengal and was * Mountbatten's successor as governor-general (1948–50), the last to hold that post. He was * Nehru's deputy prime minister (1950–52).

Rákosi, Mátyás (1892–1971). Hungarian Communist politician, of Jewish descent. As a young man he worked in a London bank, became a minister under Bela * Kun (1919), and was jailed (1927–40) under * Horthy. As first secretary of the United Workers (i.e. Communist) party (1945–56) and prime minister (1952–53), he took a tough Stalinist line. He coined the phrase 'salami tactics'—dividing opponents ideologically and cutting them off piece by piece.

Raleigh (or Ralegh), **Sir Walter** (1552?–1618). English courtier, adventurer and writer, born in Devon. After accompanying his half-brother Sir Humphrey Gilbert on an unsuccessful colonizing expedition to the West Indies (1578), he served in Ireland (1580) and in 1582 went to court as a protégé of the Earl of * Leicester. He quickly won the favour of Elizabeth I by his good looks, his wit and his fine clothes, and he received estates, trading monopolies in wine and wool, and a knighthood (1585). His haughty impatient manner brought him, however, many bitter enemies. He used his wealth to finance privateering expeditions and colonizing schemes, but he was not lucky. Money for Sir Humphrey Gilbert's last and fatal voyage was found by him. The attempts (1585 and 1587) to found a colony of 'Virginia', named after the queen, failed. He did not accompany the expeditions, but by planting on his Irish estates the potatoes his men brought back, and by setting a persuasive example of smoking the tobacco, he popularized the use of both (though they had already been discovered by the Spanish and Portuguese). The rivalry of a new favourite, * Essex, and the discovery (1592) of Raleigh's liaison with Elizabeth Throckmorton, one of the queen's maids of honour (whom he later married), brought temporary disgrace. In 1595 he was again at sea bound for the Orinoco, but gold from the fabled 'El Dorado' eluded him, and his discoveries in Guiana stirred few. He shared with Howard and Essex the credit for the successful Cadiz raid (1596) but by taking no part in the intrigues which brought James I to the throne, he earned the new king's suspicious hostility. On trumped-up charges of conspiracy he was condemned to death (1603), and though finally reprieved he was confined in the Tower of London until 1616. Then at last he was allowed to lead another gold-hunting expedition to Guiana, on condition that he did no injury to Spanish interests (an impossible condition as Spain claimed all these lands). He returned unsuccessful, and to appease the Spanish was executed on the old charge. James had indeed exalted his enemy and by his shameful treatment had turned an unpopular court favourite into a national hero.

Like many of his contemporaries Raleigh wrote verse: his political thought, e.g. in *The Prerogative of Parliaments* (written 1615, published 1628), was liberal and progressive and his religious thought (which brought accusations of atheism) showed wide tolerance. His most famous achievement was his great *History of the World* (1614), written while in prison. The completed portion carries the story from the creation to the fall of Macedonia (130 B.C.); it has little historical value but is a fine example of Elizabethan prose style, and was much admired by Oliver Cromwell for its moral lessons.

Adamson, J. H., and Follard, H. F., *The Shepherd of the Ocean*. 1969

Rama V (Chulalongkorn) (1853–1910). King of Thailand (Siam) from 1868. He abolished slavery, introduced telephones and railways and was the subject of the book *Anna and the King of Siam* and the musical *The King and I*.

Ramakrishna (Gadadhar Chatterji) (1834–1886). Indian mystic. Son of a poor Brahman of Bengal, he lived as a wandering ascetic and in his meditations became convinced that the fundamental unity of Hinduism, Mohammedanism and Christianity could be attained by the practice of piety. His teachings were widely spread in America and Europe by his disciple **Svami Vivekananda** (1862–1902) who on his return to India founded (1897) the Ramakrishna mission for the destitute.

Raman, Sir Chandrasekhara Venkata (1888–1970). Indian physicist. He held a long series of academic posts culminating in the directorships of the Indian Institute of Science, Bangalore (1933–47), and of the Raman Research Institute (from 1947). He discovered (1928) that when a transparent substance is irradiated with monochromatic light of a given frequency the scattered light contains additional frequencies characteristic of the substance. This is known as the Raman effect, and study of the Raman spectra so produced gives valuable information about molecular structure. He won the Nobel Prize for Physics (1930) and was knighted in 1929.

Rambert, Dame Marie (1888–1982). English ballet teacher of Polish birth. She was trained by Cecchetti and worked with Diaghilev's company (1912–13) but has devoted most of her life to teaching. She launched (1931) the Ballet Rambert in London, and from it many important dancers and choreographers have emerged. Among her honours were the Légion d'honneur (1957) and the DBE (1962).

Clarke, M., *Dancers of Mercury*. 1962

Rambouillet, Catherine de Vivonne, Marquise de (1588–1665). French literary hostess. During the reign of Louis XIII she presided (in her 'blue room') over one of the most famous *salons* in French literary history, its guests from *c.* 1615 to 1650 including Richelieu, Malherbe, Mademoiselle Scudéry, La Rochefoucauld, Saint-Evremond, Madame de Sévigné, and Corneille, whose new plays were read there. The good conversation and refined manners set a highly civilized pattern in French social circles.

Rameau, Jean-Philippe (1683–1764). French composer, born at Dijon. After studying in Italy he became a church organist. In his important *Treatise on Harmony* (1722) he published the results of some years of study of the composition and progression of chords; in later theoretical works he improved the system he had advanced. He was a prolific composer of keyboard works, chamber music and church music. The first of more than twenty operas and ballets to achieve success was *Hippolyte et Aricie* (1733), from Racine's *Phèdre*. This was followed by *Les Indes galantes* (1735), *Castor et Pollux* (1737) and *Dardanus* (1739). Rameau was important as Lully's successor in the history of French

opera, and as a bold innovator in harmony and orchestration.
Girdlestone, C. M., *Jean Philippe Rameau. His Life and Work*. Rev. ed. 1969

Rameses (or Ramses). The name of eleven ancient Egyptian kings of the 19th and 20th Dynasties from Rameses I (died *c.* 1314 B.C.) to Rameses XI (died 1900 B.C.). Rameses II and Rameses III were both great warriors, the former engaged in a struggle with the Hittites, the latter with the Philistines and other sea powers of the eastern Mediterranean. Rameses III built a temple at Thebes, his capital, to house a record of his exploits. Rameses II founded the great temple of Abu Simbel, for the dismantling and re-erection of which (made necessary by the higher water level caused by the Aswan High Dam) an international fund was raised.
Gardiner, A. H., *Egypt of the Pharaohs*. 1961

Ramón y Cajal, Santiago (1852–1934). Spanish physiologist. Son of a poor barber-surgeon in Navarre, after a year as an army surgeon in Cuba (where he contracted malaria), he decided on an academic career in anatomy. In 1883 he became professor of anatomy at Valencia (having made himself, by self-teaching, an expert histologist and microscopist). He became professor of histology at Barcelona in 1887 and at Madrid in 1892, where he stayed till his retirement in 1922. He devoted the creative period of his life to the study of the fine structure of the nervous system, concerned above all to discover the functional pathways of the transmission of stimuli. He was acutely aware of the problem of understanding how neural information is passed across anatomical gaps. His researches were published in his massive and highly influential *Textura del Sistema Nervioso del Hombre y de los Vertebrados* (1904). For this work, he shared the Nobel Prize for Medicine (1906) with Camillo Golgi. His later work focused more on the degeneration and regeneration of nervous structures. His researches confirmed the correctness of the 'monogenesist' school which believed that the regeneration of fibres came from the sprouting of the cylinders of the central stump. One of very few internationally famous Spanish scientists, Ramón y Cajal devoted much of his energies to attempting to promote science within the Spanish educational and administrative systems.

Ramsay, Sir William (1852–1916). British chemist. Professor of chemistry at University College, Bristol, and later at University College, London, he is best known for his work on the inert gases: * Rayleigh had found (1892) that atmospheric nitrogen is heavier than nitrogen produced from compounds, and Ramsay's investigation of this led to the discovery of argon (announced 1894) and of neon, krypton and xenon (1898). Helium, discovered in the sun in 1868, was obtained by Ramsay from a uranium mineral in 1895. He won the Nobel Prize for Chemistry (1904).

Ramsey, Allan (1713–1784). Scottish painter. After studying in Italy he returned to Edinburgh but settled in London (*c.* 1862). He became painter to George III (1867); his portraits of the king and of Queen Charlotte are in the National Portrait Gallery, London. His intellectual interests made him a friend of Johnson and the correspondent of Hume, Rousseau and Voltaire.

Ramsey, Arthur Michael, Baron Ramsey of Canterbury (1904–). English prelate. Before succeeding as archbishop of Canterbury (1961–74) he had been bishop of Durham (1952–56) and then archbishop of York. Otherwise his work had been mainly in the academic field with professorships of divinity at Durham and Cambridge Universities extending from 1940 to 1952. A high churchman and a scholarly theologian of distinction, he wrote several books. As archbishop of Canterbury he worked hard to reconcile the differences between the various churches and in 1966 made the first official visit by an English archbishop to the pope since the Reformation. He was made a life peer on his retirement.
Ramsey, A. M., *Canterbury Pilgrim*. 1974

Ramus, Petrus (Pierre de la Ramée) (1515–1572). French scholar. The son of a charcoal burner, he was able to educate himself by taking advantage of his position as the servant of a wealthy scholar. His statement that 'all Aristotle said was false' was symptomatic of a life-long rebellion against scholastic authority. After some years of travel and exile he returned to France (1571) only to meet his death in the Massacre of St Bartholomew. As well as his explorations in philosophy and a new system of logic for which he became famous, he brought his rational and original mind to bear upon the study of Greek and Latin, mathematics, astronomy and almost every known subject. His followers, known as Ramists, exercised much educational influence, notably at Cambridge.

Ranjit Singh (1780–1839). Sikh ruler. One of the most remarkable men of his time, he succeeded his father as leader of his clan at the age of 12 and was only 19 when he seized Lahore from the Afghans and 22 when he drove them from Amritsar. Before he died he had welded together the warring tribes and made the Punjab India's most powerful state. He achieved this by adopting western methods of warfare and by establishing a relationship of trust with the British East India Company, the River Sutlej being their agreed boundary.
Singh, K., *Ranjit Singh, Maharajah of the Punjab*. 1962. Smith, A. V., ed. Spear, P., et al., *The Oxford History of India*. 1958

Ranjitsinhji, Kumar Shri, Maharajah Jam Saheb of Nawanagar (1872–1933). Indian prince and cricketer. Grace of action and exact timing were among the qualities which made him one of the greatest batsmen in cricket history as well as one of the game's most popular figures. After playing for Cambridge University he joined the Sussex county club for which (from 1895) he played for many years; he played for England against Australia fifteen times. He was the first cricketer to score over 3,000 runs in a year (1899) and repeated the feat in 1900 with an aggregate of 3,065. He proved an enlightened ruler when he came into inheritance (1906); he took part in World War I and afterwards represented India at the League of Nations.

Rank, J(oseph) Arthur Rank, 1st Baron (1888–1972). English financier. With a fortune derived from his family's flour milling interests he gradually gained, by purchase and amalgamation, a predominant position in the production and distribution of British films.

Ranke, Leopold von (1795–1886). German historian. He was noted as a pioneer in the application of modern critical methods to historical sources and for the thoroughness and objectivity with which he documented his narratives. In the preface to the first of his many books, a history of medieval and later Europe, he announced his purpose 'merely to relate what actually occurred'. His best known work is *The History of the Popes* (1840): though it is confined to the Counter-Reformation period and its author was denied access to the Vatican library, it is numbered among the world's historical masterpieces. Ranke was over 80 when he started on the world history of which nine volumes (to the 15th century) were complete when he died.
Gooch, G. P., *History and Historians in the Nineteenth Century*. 1952

Ransome, Arthur (1884–1967). English author. Realistic treatment and keen observation characterize his stories of children's adventures, several of which, e.g. *Swallows and Amazons* (1931), are concerned with the handling of small boats.
Hart Davis, R., ed., *The Autobiography of Arthur Ransome*. 1976

Raoult, François-Marie (1830–1901). French physical chemist, professor of chemistry at Grenoble (1870–1901). His chief work was the investigation of the changes that occur in the boiling point, freezing point, and vapour pressure of liquids when solids are dissolved in them. From these investigations he was able to deduce the fundamental law (Raoult's law) relating the vapour pressure of a solution to the concentration of the dissolved substance, and he thus laid the foundations on which Van't * Hoff built the modern theory of solutions.

Raphael Santi (Raffaello Sanzio) (1483–1520). Italian Renaissance painter, born at Urbino. He studied with Perugino and (*c.* 1504–*c.* 1510) in Florence, where he came under the influence of Leonardo da Vinci and Michelangelo (apparent, e.g., in *The Entombment* of 1507). The *Crucifixion* in the National Gallery, London, is among the pictures of this early period. The rest of his short life was spent in Rome, where his agreeable nature as well as his remarkable and pleasing talent ensured immediate success. For Pope Julius II, the subject of one of his greatest portraits, he painted the frescoes decorating the papal apartments (Le Stanze) at the Vatican; they include the *Disputa* and the *School of Athens*. After Bramante's death he was appointed architect in charge of the building of St Peter's and drew the cartoons for the tapestries in the Sistine Chapel (at the same time painting the mythological Galatea cycle for the Palazzo Farnese); he also produced many large and small altar-pieces as well as portraits. Raphael's output was large for so brief a life though in his last years he left the completion of his intentions more and more to his assistants (of whom Giulio Romano was the most gifted). He died of a sudden fever and was buried in the Pantheon at Rome.

Raphael's nature was receptive rather than dynamic and he was able to absorb ideas taken from Leonardo, Michelangelo, and ancient sculptures without destroying the unity of his own work. Few, if any, artists have excelled him in the facility with which he transferred to paint his intuitive ideas.

Fischel, O., *Raphael.* 1964

Rapp, Jean, Count (1772–1821). French soldier, born in Alsace. One of the bravest of the revolutionary soldiers, he gained distinction in Germany and Egypt before becoming A.D.C. to Napoleon. A brilliant charge at Austerlitz won him the rank of a divisional general and for further services he was made a count. He served throughout the Russian expedition, the plan of which he had opposed, and on his return held Danzig for nearly a year.

Rashi (formed from the initials of Rabbi Shelomo Yitzchaki, i.e. Solomon ben Isaac) (*c.* 1040–1105). Jewish exegete and grammarian. His commentary on the Pentateuch is believed to have been the first Hebrew book to be printed (1475). The Talmud is seldom printed without his commentary. Rashi was born in Troyes in France, where he also died after wanderings probably confined to Lorraine but greatly expanded by legend.

Liber, M., *Rashi.* 1906

Rasputin, Grigori Efimovich (1871/2–1916). Russian 'holy man'. Born in Siberia, he was an illiterate peasant, and he owed the name Rasputin ('debauchee') to the orgies resulting from his teaching that salvation – sin followed by repentance – could only be achieved by his followers by union of body and soul with himself, the bearer of a particle of divinity within himself. A chance encounter at Kiev with a lady of the court brought him to St Petersburg, where mystical religion was then fashionable. An introduction to the tsarina followed and his apparent success in alleviating her son's haemophilia gave him her complete devotion and confidence. The tsar's absence at the front during World War I enabled him to exploit his power for private gain and the political advancement of his friends. Changes in the ministries became so unpredictable that confusion, easily interpreted as treachery, grew. The loyalty of the tsarina and her complete innocence of any scandalous association with Rasputin are now known, but there was enough evidence of debauchery, in which ladies of the highest social status were involved, to make rumours plausible and to impel a group of patriotic nobles, headed by Prince Felix Yusupov, to remove his sinister influence. Rasputin was assassinated (30 December 1916) and his body thrown into the Neva.

Minney, R. J., *Rasputin.* 1972

Rathenau, Walther (1867–1922). German industrialist and politician of Jewish origin. His father was the virtual founder of the German electrical industry and he himself was president (1915–20) of the great electrical company abbreviated as AEG. In the republican government after World War I he was minister of reconstruction (1921) and in 1922, as foreign minister, signed the Russo-German Treaty at Rapallo. Soon afterwards he was assassinated by two young nationalist fanatics.

Rattigan, Sir Terence Mervyn (1911–1977). English playwright. He ranged from brilliant farce, e.g. *French Without Tears* (1936), to character studies in depth, e.g. that of Lawrence of Arabia in *Ross* (1960). *The Winslow Boy* (1946) reconstructs a well known factual episode and here as in *The Browning Version* (1948) Rattigan introduced poignant situations without sentimental overemphasis. Other plays include *The Deep Blue Sea* (1952) and *Separate Tables* (1954). He adapted some of his plays for the cinema.

Ravel, Maurice Joseph (1875–1937). French composer. Born in the Basque country, he studied in Paris under * Fauré and others. His life was uneventful. He joined the army in 1914 but was invalided out. So far he had lived chiefly in France but after World War I he frequently conducted his music abroad. Vaughan * Williams was one of his few pupils. Following a motor accident in October 1932, he suffered from a brain injury which affected his memory and he died after surgery. A fine pianist, he showed a perfect understanding of

the capabilities of this instrument in the early Sonatina (1903–05) and in the suites *Miroirs* (1905), *Gaspard de la nuit* (1908) and *Ma Mère l'oye* (duet, 1908). An equal mastery of orchestration was evident in *Daphnis et Chloé* (1909–11), a ballet written for * Diaghilev, his only large-scale work and probably his masterpiece. Other works were the String Quartet (1904), the Introduction and Allegro for harp, string quartet, flute and clarinet (1906), many songs, two one-act operas – *L'Heure espagnole* (1907), *L'Enfant et les sortilèges* (1924–25) – the suite for piano *Le Tombeau de Couperin* (1914–17), the choreographic poem *La Valse* (1920), the popular ballet score *Boléro* (1928) and two Piano Concertos, one for left hand (1930–31) – his last works. Ravel's music, which blends such disparate influences as Couperin, Mozart, Liszt and Rimsky-Korsakov, is outstanding in its technical brilliance and he was probably the most gifted orchestrator of all time. * Stravinsky called him 'a watchmaker among composers'. His music is less impressionistic and more classical in temper than that of * Debussy with which it is often linked.
Stuckenschmidt, H. H., *Maurice Ravel*. 1968

Rawlinson, Henry Seymour Rawlinson, 1st Baron (1864–1925). British soldier. A successful military career culminated in his appointment to the command of the 4th Army in World War I. His greatest success, a break through the Hindenburg Line near Amiens (August 1918), opened the way for the final advance.

His father, **Sir Henry Creswicke Rawlinson, 1st Bart** (1810–1895), who held many official appointments in India and the Middle East, was known – mainly for his work on cuneiform inscriptions – as 'the father of Assyriology'. His uncle, **George Rawlinson** (1812–1902) was Camden Professor of Ancient History at Oxford (1861–89) and author of a notable translation and commentary upon Herodotus (1858–60).

Rawsthorne, Alan (1905–1971). British composer. He taught during 1932–34, but afterwards worked exclusively at composition, establishing a reputation with *Symphonic Studies* which was performed at the Warsaw Festival in 1939. After World War II he wrote concertos for oboe, violin and piano. His music is atonal and his works small in scale.
Mellers, W., *Studies in Contemporary Music*. 1948

Ray, John (1627–1705). English naturalist. The son of an Essex blacksmith, he studied botany and zoology at Cambridge University. He spent the years 1658–66 in extensive travels, during which by observation and collection he gained a unique knowledge of European flora and fauna. He systematized and classified this vast amount of material in a series of volumes, a foundation on which * Linnaeus and others were to build. He was no mere compiler, however, as he proved and was the first to distinguish between monocotyledons and dicotyledons. Major works were *Methodus Plantarum Nova* (1682), *Historia Plantarum* (1686–1704) and *Synopsis Methodica Animalium* (1693). Ray was also a philologist and published *A Collection of English Proverbs* (1670).
Raven, C. E., *John Ray, Naturalist*. 1942

Ray, Satyajit (1921–). Indian film producer and film director since 1953. His films are highly regarded both for their visual beauty and realism. They include *Pather Panchali* (1956), *Apu Sansar* (1959), *The Coward and the Holy Man* (1965), *Days and Nights in the Forest* (1970) and *The Chessplayers* (1979). He composes the background music for his own films. In 1947, Ray founded the first Film Society in Calcutta.

Rayleigh, John William Strutt, 3rd Baron (1842–1919). English mathematical and experimental physicist. He was Cavendish professor of experimental physics at Cambridge (1879–84), professor of natural philosophy at the Royal Institution (1887–1905), and finally chancellor of the University of Cambridge (1908–19). His researches covered a wide range of subjects, e.g. sound and other aspects of vibratory motion, scattering of light and the colour of the sky, the theory of radiation. He discovered (1892) that atmospheric nitrogen is heavier than nitrogen from compounds, which led to * Ramsay's work on the inert gases. Rayleigh, who succeeded to his father's title in 1873, won the Nobel Prize for Physics (1904), was president of the Royal Society (1905–08) and was admitted to the Order of Merit when it was established in 1902.
Strutt, R. J., *Life of John William Strutt, Third Baron Rayleigh*. 1968

Raynouard, François Juste Marie (1761–1836). French poet and philologist. A prosperous Paris advocate, he entered the legislative assembly (1791), joined the Girondins, and was imprisoned. His poems and tragedies were successful, and in 1807 he was elected to the Académie Française, later becoming secretary (1817). He wrote on Provençal language and literature, notably his *Lexique Roman* (1838–44).

Razi, Abu Bakr Muhammad Ibn Zsksriyya Al- (known as Rhazes) (*c.* 854–925). Persian physician. His main scientific interests lay in alchemy with a strong empirical concern with descriptions of exact processes, closely related to a descriptive and clinical approach to medicine. Sceptical about * Galen's theories, he wrote many manuals and distinguished between smallpox and measles. In cosmology and natural philosophy, he took issue with * Aristotle, believing that the world had been created in time and that there were five eternal principles: Creator, soul, matter, time and space. Time was not—as for Aristotle—a measure of movement or process, but rather a boundary principle, existing independently of objects. In the Islamic world, Razi had a high reputation as an alchemist and medical writer, but his scepticism and pugnacious character led to religious and philosophical attack.

Razumovsky, Count Andrey Kyrillovich (1752–1836). Russian statesman, art collector, amateur violinist and patron of music. He was the Russian ambassador in Vienna (1792–1807). He was Russia's main representative at the Congress of Vienna in 1814 and for this he was subsequently made a prince. From 1808–14 he maintained the celebrated Razumovsky Quartet. Razumovsky's name was immortalized through the dedication to him of Beethoven's three string quartets, Op. 59, and (with Prince Lobkowitz) the Fifth and Sixth Symphonies. He was a munificent and prodigal patron of art: his enthusiasm for music had drawn him to Haydn; he knew Mozart personally and had close associations with Beethoven (1796–1816). However, after the destruction by fire of his Vienna palace, he was forced to discontinue his way of life, and lapsed into obscurity.

Read, Sir Herbert (1893–1968). English poet and critic. His emotions and experiences in the army during World War I (in which he won the MC and DSO) provided themes for his first book of poems, *Naked Warriors* (1919). His later poetry, with its more intellectual content, mainly attracted the connoisseur. In his literary criticism, as revealed in *Reason and Romanticism* (1926), he took a psychological approach to the work of his subjects (e.g. *In Defence of Shelley*, 1935). He wrote much, too, in support of new movements in art in, e.g., *Art Now* (1933) and *Contemporary British Art* (1951). He was professor of fine art at Edinburgh (1931–33) and edited (1933–39) the *Burlington Magazine*.
Woodcock, G., *Sir Herbert Read*. 1972

Reade, Charles (1814–1884). English novelist. He was called to the bar (1843) and began (*c.* 1850) writing plays. The most successful (written in collaboration with Tom Taylor) was *Masks and Faces* (1852); the rewriting of this in the form of a historical novel, *Peg Woffington* (1853), showed him the way to his future great success with realistic novels, mainly of social protest. His masterpiece, *The Cloister and the Hearth* (1861), is an imaginary reconstruction of the life of the unknown father of Erasmus. The element of social protest in this exciting, detailed and carefully documented account of medieval life is against enforced celibacy.
Burns, W., *Reade: A Study in Victorian Authorship*. 1961

Reading, Rufus Daniel Isaacs, 1st Marquess of (1860–1935). British lawyer and administrator. After establishing a reputation for skilful cross-examination at the bar, he became one of the highest paid KCs. He entered parliament as a Liberal (1904) and was solicitor-general in Asquith's government (1910) and attorney-general (1910–13). He was involved (1912) in the Marconi scandal (favour was alleged to have been shown to the company in return for an opportunity to make private profit), but after a parliamentary inquiry he and other ministers were absolved from blame. In 1913 he became lord chief justice (with a peerage): he was sent on financial missions to Washington in World War I and was ambassador there (1918–21). As viceroy of India 1921–26 he adopted a sympathetic attitude towards Congress moderates, but Gandhi's leadership was increasingly important. Created a marquess in 1926, he became chairman of ICI 1928–31 and

1931–35. He briefly returned to political life (1931) to become foreign secretary in Ramsay * MacDonald's coalition. He was Lord Warden of the Cinque Ports from 1934–35.

Reagan, Ronald Wilson (1911–). 40th president of the U.S. (1981–). Born in Tampico, Illinois, he graduated from Eureka College and became a radio sports announcer. Between 1937 and 1964 he acted in 54 films, mostly as a second lead: these included *Kings Row* (1942) and *The Hasty Heart* (1950). President of the Screen Actors Guild (1947–52 and 1959–60), he was originally a staunch liberal but became a hard-line conservative in the 1950s. For some years he was an effective spokesman for the General Electric Co. both on television and in public appearances. He supported Barry * Goldwater in 1964 and was governor of California 1967–74, defeating Edmund G. ('Pat') Brown who had beaten Richard * Nixon in 1962. In 1976 he challenged Gerald Ford in a close race for the Republican presidential nomination. He defeated Jimmy * Carter in 1980 by a 51–41 percentage of the popular vote. His robust anti-Communism, appeal to patriotism, support of traditional American values and gifts as a communicator led him to a second-term victory over Walter * Mondale (1984) in 49 states, with 59 per cent of the popular vote.

Réaumur, René Antoine Ferchault de (1683–1757). French scientist. His work for the Académie des Sciences, of which he became a member in 1708, led him into such diverse avenues of research as metallurgy, turquoise mines and the manufacture of opaque glass. The thermometer which bears his name has the boiling point of water at 80° and the freezing point at zero.

Récamier, Françoise Julie Adélaïde (née Bernard) (1777–1849). French beauty and wit. Her *salon* attracted some of the most notable literary and political personalities of the day. Among them were Madame de Staël, Benjamin Constant and Chateaubriand; her husband, a middle-aged banker, died in 1830. The painter David has perpetuated the charm of Madame Récamier as she reclines at ease.
Trouncer, M., *Madame Récamier*. 1949

Redgrave, Sir Michael Scudamore (1908–1985). English actor. He went to the stage after a brief career as a schoolmaster, and gained much of his early experience at London's Old Vic. He became outstanding as a Shakespearian actor and has returned again and again to the familiar parts, but he has also adapted his technique to suit the continental classics (e.g. *The Father, Uncle Vanya* and *A Month in the Country*) and to modern plays such as *The Aspern Papers*, where stylish acting combined with acute characterization is required. His film career, equally varied, included parts in *The Importance of Being Earnest, The Browning Version* and *The Dam Busters*. He was knighted in 1959. He married the actress Rachel Kempson and their three children were all successful performers. **Vanessa** (1937–) a stage and film actress won an Academy Award for her role in *Julia* (1977). She was a strong opponent of U.S. foreign policy and a PLO supporter. **Corin** (1939–) was an able character actor and **Lynn** (1943–) won an international reputation in *Georgy Girl* (1966).

Redmond, John Edward (1856–1918). Irish politician. He led the Parnellite wing (* Parnell) of the Irish National party in the British House of Commons (from 1891) and (from 1900) the reunited party. He accepted Asquith's Home Rule Bill (1912–14): but when Sir Edward * Carson raised a volunteer force in the north to resist it Redmond countered him with volunteers raised in the south. Civil war was imminent when the World War I broke out. Redmond's support of the war cost his party the confidence of the Irish electors but Redmond died before they were swept out of parliament by Sinn Fein.
Gwynn, D., *The Life of John Redmond*. 1932

Redon, Odilon (1840–1916). French Symbolist painter, lithographer and etcher. Influenced by Goya, he developed a style of fantastic and haunted imagery, which evokes the world of Poe and Mallarmé. His later works anticipated the psychedelic art of the 1970s.

Redouté, Pierre Joseph (1759–1840). French flower painter. Born in Liège, he went to Paris and there gained great fame in his specialized field. Both Marie Antoinette and the empress Josephine were among his pupils.

Reed, John (1887–1920). American Communist journalist, who went (1918) to the

U.S.S.R. His *Ten Days that Shook the World* (1919) is considered one of the best eye-witness accounts of the Bolshevik Revolution.

Reed, Walter (1851–1902). American surgeon and bacteriologist. He joined the U.S. army medical corps (1874) as an assistant surgeon and became (1893) professor of bacteriology at the Army Medical School. He headed a commission sent to Havana to study yellow fever (1900) and proved that the disease is caused by a variety of mosquito.

Reger, Max (1873–1916). German composer. During his short life he published a large number of works, few of which (apart from the organ music and songs) are now heard, owing partly to their great complexity and style. He became director of music in Leipzig University (1907) and professor (1908).
Bagier, G., *Max Reger*. 1923

Regiomontanus (Johann Müller) (1436–1476). German astronomer and mathematician. Born at Königsberg the son of a miller, he studied philosophy at Leipzig and astronomy and geometry under Peurbach at Vienna, from 1452. It was at this time that he came to recognize the inadequacy of the current astronomical tables (the Alfonsine). On Peurbach's death, Regiomontanus completed his work on * Ptolemy's *Almagest*, which finally appeared in 1496. This digest was a work of current scholarship in its own right. * Copernicus's careful study of it revealed to him some of Ptolemy's errors, and stimulated the development of his own system of astronomy. Regiomontanus learned Greek from Cardinal Bessarion, and spent much of the 1460s combing Italy for astronomical manuscripts. His concern was to purify the learning of antiquity. He discovered an important manuscript of the mathematician Diophantus, but did not live to edit it. Amongst his completed works however were lectures on astrology and important trigonometrical writings which gave tables of tangents and sines. He was more important as a publisher of astronomical data – he made early use of the printing press – than as a theorist in his own right.
Zinner, E., *Leben und Wirken des Johannes Müller*. 1968

Reichstadt, François Charles Joseph, Duke of (1811–1832). Son of Napoleon I and the empress Marie Louise, styled king of Rome (1811–14) and known to the Bonapartists as Napoleon II. After his father's abdication he was brought up at the court of his grandfather, Francis II of Austria, where he remained under strict supervision until his early death.

Reid, Sir George Houstoun (1845–1918). Australian politician. Born in Scotland, he went to Australia at the age of 7, was called to the bar (1879) and entered the New South Wales parliament (1880). There as minister of public instruction he introduced (1883–84) a public system of secondary education. He became leader of the opposition (1891) and was prime minister (1894–99). In addition to tax simplification and a factories act, he freed the civil service from political control. He became a strong supporter of federation and when the federal parliament was formed became leader of the opposition with a policy favouring free trade. After being prime minister (1904–05) he went to London (1910) as first federal high commissioner; in 1916 he was elected a British M.P.

Reid, Thomas (1710–1796). Scottish philosopher. After a number of academic appointments he succeeded * Adam Smith as professor of moral philosophy at Glasgow (1764–80). In his *Inquiry into the Human Mind on the Principles of Common Sense* (1764) he argued, against * Hume and others, that in perception we are directly aware of physical objects and not of sensations or 'ideas' which may be related to them. He believed that all knowledge is based on self-evident principles established in 'common sense', a term which came to be applied to his philosophy as a whole. His larger *Essays on the Intellectual Active Powers of Man* (1785) is in effect a theory of knowledge based on these principles, while in his *Essays on the Active Powers of the Human Mind* (1788) he discusses moral issues and arrives at the conclusion that 'moral approbation implies a real judgement'.
Grave, S. A., *The Scottish Philosophy of Common Sense*. 1960

Reiner, Fritz (1888–1963). Hungarian–American conductor, born in Budapest. He conducted the Dresden Royal Opera 1914–21, went to the U.S. in 1922 and directed the Pittsburgh Symphony 1938–48, the Metropolitan Opera 1948–53 and the Chicago Symphony 1953–62.

Reinhardt, Max (1873–1943). Austrian-born theatrical producer. He acted at the Deutsches Theater, Berlin (1894–1905), and then became its director and filled the next twenty-five years with a remarkable series of some 450 productions, which brought fame to the theatre and himself. As well as the ancient Greek and European classics he staged the works of such writers as Ibsen, Strindberg and Shaw; he was closely identified, too, with the Salzburg Festival. He specialized in spectacular productions, e.g. *The Miracle in London* (1911), which entailed the handling of crowds of performers and remarkable lighting effects. He left Hitler's Germany in 1933 and later became a naturalized citizen of the U.S.A.
Adler, G., *Max Reinhardt*. 1964

Reith of Stonehaven, John Charles Walsham Reith, 1st Baron (1889–1971). British administrator. An engineer by profession, he became the first general manager (1922) of the British Broadcasting Company and, after it had become a public corporation (1927), its first director-general. He implanted a tradition of complete integrity in the presentation of news and of educational and cultural zeal. After leaving the B.B.C. (1938) Reith was first chairman of BOAC (1939–40) and a minister (1940–42) before becoming chairman of the Colonial Development Board (1950). He received a knighthood in 1927 and his peerage in 1940. The B.B.C. instituted a yearly series of 'Reith Lectures' in honour of his great services to broadcasting.
Reith, J. C. W., *Into the Wind*. 1949

Reitz, Deneys (1882–1944). South African author and politician. The son of a president of the Orange Free State, he fought against the British in the Boer War, went into voluntary exile in Madagascar, but had cast off all bitterness when he returned in time to fight in World War I, at first under Smuts in East Africa and later in France. Colonel Reitz held ministerial posts in South Africa (1923–24 and 1933–39) and went to London as high commissioner (1943). The interweaving of his personal narrative with South Africa's story is brilliantly achieved in his books *On Commando* (1929), *Trekking On* (1933), *No Outspan* (1943).

Réjane (Réju), **Gabrielle Charlotte** (1856–1920). French comedy actress. She acquired a reputation comparable with that of Sarah * Bernhardt: wit, brilliant technique and subtlety of mood, rather than beauty of face or voice, were the qualities on which she relied for her success.

Remarque, Erich Maria (1897–1970). German-born author. He served in World War I and his novel *All Quiet on the Western Front* (1929) was one of the most realistic and effective war novels and enjoyed great popularity. It was made into an effective film. He lived in Switzerland (1932–39) and then the USA, of which country he became a citizen.

Rembrandt (Rembrandt Harmenszoon van Rijn) (1606–1669). Dutch painter. Born at Leyden, the son of a miller, he left university early (1621) to study painting. After three years' apprenticeship to a local artist he spent six months in Amsterdam with Pieter Lastman who had been to Italy and had become familiar with the work of * Carracci and others. Rembrandt seems to have been more influenced by the Dutch followers of * Caravaggio, who by directing the fall of light from a single direction could create emphasis by contrast and suggest sculptured form. From this technique was developed Rembrandt's famous chiaroscuro, with several illuminated points gradually fading into the golds and browns of deepening shadow. He returned to Leyden (1625) and soon acquired a considerable reputation and several pupils. Chiaroscuro effects are already to be seen in, e.g., *Simeon in the Temple*.

In 1631 Rembrandt moved to Amsterdam and quickly became a fashionable portrait-painter, and since his subjects were mostly rich burghers whom he did not have to flatter unduly, provided he gave them the dignity and trappings of wealth, he was free to display his great gift for interpreting human personality. The romantic side of his own character was shown (as indeed earlier at Leyden) by his delight in dressing his sitters in all sorts of fantastic finery, not only silks and satins but furs, turbans and even armour. To indulge this taste to the full he painted large numbers of self-portraits, thus arrayed. Biblical and classical subjects continued to attract him and he excelled in dramatic narrative. Group portraits, of which *The Anatomy of Dr Tulp* (1632) was among the first to achieve fame, were also popular and by their greater size provided scope for the stronger colours he now liked to employ. The year 1642 marked a turning point in his life. His wife, Saskia van Uylenburgh (married 1634), whose dowry combined with his own earnings had enabled him to lead the life of a substantial citizen, died in 1642, a year after the birth of Titus, their only child to survive infancy. In the same year the group portrait *The Night Watch* failed to attract, mainly because the background figures were not sufficiently individualized to please the vanity of the persons portrayed. In the years that followed Rembrandt's earning power steadily declined until (1656) his house and possessions were auctioned to pay his debts. But, ironically, the change in his circumstances marked no decline in the powers of the artist but the reverse. His increasing impatience with the artistic conventions of the time may have frightened off his patrons but it completed his emancipation as an artist. The rich burghers may have been less often seen in his studios, but that only left him freer to concentrate upon the intense inner life of those who took their place and who had no social importance that it was necessary to convey. Some of his most perceptive portraits are of his son Titus, of Hendrickje Stoffels (who became his mistress in 1645, bore him a daughter, Cornelia, and was his constant attendant in old age), and the continuing series of self-portraits reflecting alike the passing years and his changes of mood and style. As regards the latter Rembrandt was becoming increasingly interested in the texture of his works. He abandons the illusionist convention by which the activity of the paint is always concealed and discovers the emotive power of brush strokes left visible. He no longer pursues the search for the dramatic with its attendant contrasts of light and shade; the vivid colours of the middle years are subdued to the browns, russets and olive greens familiar in his later work. Biblical (and sometimes mythological) subjects recur more often but they are simpler and more serene. Among the most famous of the pictures of these later years are *Saul and David* and the group portrait of the *Syndics of the Clothmakers Guild*. He is said to have made in all some 700 paintings, 300 etchings and over 1,000 drawings.

Haak, B., *Rembrandt: his Life, his Work, his Time*. 1969. Houbraken, A., *De Groote Schouburgh der Nederlantsche Konst-schilders en Schilderessen*. 1718–1721

Renan, (Joseph) Ernest (1823–1892). French religious writer. He was brought up for the priesthood but after a long period of doubt abandoned his faith and turned to academic work, and achieved renown with the first volume of an immense work on the history of the origins of Christianity. This volume, the *Vie de Jésus* (1863), tells the life story of an 'incomparable man'. Under Napoleon III its anti-religious content cost him his professorship, restored after the Franco-Prussian War. He continued his great history and other works, was elected to the Académie Française (1878), and became (1883) administrator of the Collège de France, playing a notable part in the form of French education. The substance of his personal belief was that though God does not exist he is in the process of becoming, through man's struggle for perfection.

Chadbourne, R. M., *Ernest Renan*. 1968

Renault, Louis (1877–1944). French motorcar manufacturer. He collaborated with the Germans during World War II and is believed to have been murdered by members of the Resistance. His factories were taken over by the state.

Reni, Guido (1575–1642). Italian painter. He was born in Bologna and became one of the most prominent of the Baroque painters, the main influences on his style being Carracci, under whom he studied, and Caravaggio, whose contrasting effects of light and shade he adopted; in later years his colours became paler and cooler. His subjects are mainly mythological and Biblical, e.g. *Aurora*, a famous ceiling painting, and *Ecce Homo* and *Mater Dolorosa*.

Rennie, John (1761–1821). Scottish engineer and bridge builder. He constructed many docks and canals and is best known for the Southwark (1819) and old Waterloo (1817) bridges in London, and the great Plymouth breakwater.

Renoir, Jean (1894–1979). French film director. Son of the painter Pierre Auguste * Renoir, he began work as a director in 1924 and established a reputation by a unique blend of lyricism and realism. His films include *Nana* (1926), *Une Partie de Campagne* (1936), *La Grande Illusion* (1938), *Le Règle du Jeu* (1939) and *French Can-Can* (1956).

Renoir, J., *My Life and My Films*. 1974

Renoir, Pierre Auguste (1841–1919). French painter. One of the most important of the Impressionists, he was born at Limoges where as a boy he was employed as a painter on porcelain. At Gleyre's studio in Paris (1861) he met and became friends with * Monet and Sisley; with them he worked in the open air concentrating on the problems of sunlight and its reflection, for example, on water or human flesh. It was with the latter that Renoir showed his special skill and the exuberant delight that his painting gave him and which he always wished to impart. There is no exotic frailty about his nudes: their flesh is rosy and their limbs are muscular. For Renoir love of painting and a love of life were inseparable. A more sophisticated gaiety is seen in *La Loge, Les Parapluies* and *Au Théâtre: la Première Sortie*. He experimented briefly with pointillism but in general he was a more scholarly painter and more concerned with composition, e.g. his large paintings of *Bathers* in the 1880s, than many of his contemporary Impressionists. He spent most of his life between Paris and the French countryside and though his hands were crippled with arthritis continued to paint in his garden near Cagnes to the time of his death; he achieved a total of six thousand paintings. He was happily married.
Drucker, M., *Renoir*. 1944. Gaunt, W., ed., *Renoir: Paintings*. 1971

Repton, Humphry (1752–1818). English landscape-gardener. He began to design gardens *c.* 1790, working in partnership with the architect John * Nash on some of his designs. He restored a formal setting to country houses by planting the immediate surroundings of the house in a decorative and obviously artificial style. This was a departure from the carefully 'natural' parkland, unrelieved by planted beds, which was formerly prevalent.
Repton, H., *Observations on the Theory and Practice of Landscape Gardening*. 1794

Respighi, Ottorino (1879–1936). Italian composer and musicologist. He was noted for his skilful orchestration, e.g. of Rossini's piano pieces for the ballet *La Boutique Fantasque*, and composed several high-spirited 'pictorial' orchestral works, e.g. *The Fountains of Rome* (1917), *The Pines of Rome* (1924) and *Roman Festivals* (1929). His edition of Monteverdi's *Orfeo* (1935) exemplified his valuable work in reviving interest in early Italian music. Of his nine operas none achieved lasting success.

Reszke, Jean de (1850–1925). Polish tenor. He made his operatic debut at Venice (1874) as a baritone, but developed into one of the most famous tenors of his epoch, especially in Wagnerian roles.

Retz, Gilles de *see* **Rais, Gilles de**

Retz, Jean François de Gondi, Cardinal de (1613–79). French churchman and politician. A colourful character, famed as a young man for his duels, love affairs and wit, he played an important part in the wars and disturbances of the Fronde (1648–53). He was arrested (1652) but escaped from prison (1654) and reached Spain and Italy. In 1662 he conciliated Louis XIV by giving up his archbishopric (in return, however, for generous compensation elsewhere). His *Mémoires* (published 1717) show a lively talent for describing character and events.
Salmon, J. H. M., *Cardinal de Retz*. 1969

Reuchlin, Johann (1455–1522). German humanist. Having mastered Greek and Hebrew (the latter from a Jewish physician) he became the principal promoter of these two languages in Renaissance Germany. He protested successfully against the destruction of Jewish books and did much, by his writing and teaching, to encourage intellectual tolerance.
Brod, M., *Johannes Reuchlin und sein Kampf*. 1966

Reuter, Baron Paul Julius de (1816–1899). German-born founder of the news agency named after him. As a bank clerk at Göttingen he realized the importance for business of speedy information and organized (1849) the transmission of stock exchange prices between Aachen and Brussels by pigeon post. He moved to Paris and then London where he set up (1851) an office for the collection of not only share prices but also news items from the continent. From these small beginnings sprang the huge international news agency with still bears his name. Reuter himself became a naturalized British citizen and in 1871 was created baron by the Duke of Saxe-Coburg-Gotha.

Reuther, Walter Philip (1907–1970). American trade union leader. He began to organize workers in the motor industry in 1935. He became (1952) president of the Congress of Industrial Organization (C.I.O.), and when it merged (1955) with its rival, the American Federation of Labor (A.F.L.) he became vice-president of the combined organization.

Revere, Paul (1735–1818). American patriot, born in Boston of French Huguenot descent. He took part in the 'Boston Tea Party', the prelude to the War of Independence, but is remembered as the hero of a famous 'ride' from Charlestown, near Boston, to Lexington and Concord (April 1775). The story is told in a well known poem by * Longfellow but there were in fact two rides, the purpose of the first being to warn the insurgents to move their stores to Concord, and that of the second, two days later, to raise the alarm that British troops were on the move.
Green, M., *Paul Revere, Man Behind the Legend*. 1964

Reynaud, Paul (1878–1966). French politician. After a successful career as a barrister he entered the Chamber of Deputies (1919) and quickly acquired a reputation as a speaker, becoming leader of the nationalist groups. He distinguished himself in a variety of ministerial posts and in the early stages of World War II was Daladier's deputy prime minister. In March 1940 he took over the leadership, but after the German breakthrough and the crushing defeats that followed he lacked the force of character to inspire the French will to resist. In June Reynaud, unable to command a majority in his cabinet, retired in favour of Marshal * Pétain, and surrender followed. Reynaud was imprisoned by the Germans for the rest of the war but afterwards returned to political life.

Reynolds, Sir Joshua (1723–1792). English painter. Born at Plympton, Devon, the son of a schoolmaster, he began his art studies under Thomas Hudson (1740–43), and widened his range by practice and study: the turning point came with a visit to Italy (1749–53) during which he made an intensive study of the work and methods of the great masters, Raphael, Michelangelo, Correggio, Titian and the other Venetians. The rest of his life was spent in London where his record as a fashionable portrait-painter was one of continued and remarkable success. The versatility with which he could adapt his knowledge and technique to the changes of time and fashion amazed his contemporaries. He was equally successful with the formal or informal occasion, the latter often enhanced by a parkland or garden setting; he also shows something of van Dyck's pleasure in the texture and decorative value of fine clothes. He was one of the founders of the Royal Academy (1768) and was its first president, remaining in office for the rest of his life. His prize-giving *Discourses* retain their value for the student, and also give a valuable account of his own aims. He visited Flanders and Holland (1781) and a renewed study of * Rubens in particular brought fresh life into his later pictures. He painted almost every celebrity of his time (over 2,000 in all): *Lady Cockburn and her Children* and *Mrs Siddons as the Tragic Muse* are perhaps the best known of his works. Reynolds, sociable and good-natured, was a member of Dr * Johnson's circle, almost all of whom he painted.
Waterhouse, E. K., *Reynolds*. New ed. 1973

Reza Shah Pahlevi (1878–1944). Shah of Iran (1925–41). He was a man of unusual energy and untutored intelligence, who rose from the ranks in the army to become a distinguished officer. He led a military *coup* (1921), became military dictator, and deposed Ahmed Shah, the last of the Qajars (1925). As shah he adopted the dynastic name 'Pahlevi' to recall an early and famous Persian dynasty. He abolished the veil for women, broke the power of the mullahs (the Moslem clergy) and strove to modernize the country, whose name, he insisted, should be 'Iran'. His pro-German attitude during World War II led the Allies to occupy Persia and force him to abdicate (1941) in favour of his son * Mohammed Reza. He died in Johannesburg.
Avery, P., *Modern Iran*. 1965

Rhee, Syngman (1875–1965). Korean politician. He was educated at a Methodist school and while imprisoned for nationalist activities by the Japanese, then ruling Korea, he became a Christian. In 1904 he went to America. After the failure of the Korean rising of 1919 he was chairman of the Korean government in exile, and after World War II he became first president of liberated South Korea. When communists from North Korea invaded the south (1950) he invoked the aid of the United Nations; an international force, largely American and led by General MacArthur, helped the South Koreans in a long and costly war to restore the frontier. Syngman Rhee was re-elected in 1956 and 1960 but his dictatorial rule had become increasingly unpopular and after hostile demonstrations (April 1960) he resigned and lived abroad.

Rhine, Joseph Banks (1895–1980). American psychologist. As head of the laboratory of parapsychology at Duke University, N. Carolina, he investigated extra-sensory perception and tried to find scientific explanations for 'supernatural' occurrences, e.g. telepathy, clairvoyance, psychical phenomena (ghosts, poltergeists etc.). His numerous publications include *Extrasensory Perception* (1934) and *Frontier Science of the Mind* (1957).

Rhodes, Cecil John (1853–1902). South African politician and financier, born in England at Bishop's Stortford. The son of a clergyman, he went for health reasons to South Africa at the age of 17 and secured many valuable claims at the diamond diggings at Kimberley. Eventually he joined 'Barney' Barnato in forming (1888) the De Beers Consolidated Mines Company to unite their interests. Meanwhile he had been to Oxford University, gained a degree and became one of the youngest of self-made millionaries. Already his mind was busy with his dream of a British-controlled Africa from the Cape of Good Hope to Cairo. For this he needed the co-operation of the Cape Dutch and he secured it by promising their leader Jan * Hofmeyr support for the protection of Cape farmers in return for acquiescence in his northward advance. First he limited the expansion of the Dutch South African Republic (the Transvaal) by inducing the British to declare a protectorate over Bechuanaland; with the same motive he purchased from the Matabele chief Lobengula the mining rights in his territory. As a result the British South Africa Company was formed by royal charter (1889). The creation of Rhodesia soon followed. In 1890 Rhodes became prime minister of the Cape. Still in co-operation with Hofmeyr, he passed an act giving the coloured population a voice in their local government, while in pursuit of his expansionist policy he completed the Cape–Cairo telegraph and to overcome the most difficult obstacle he tried to negotiate a confederation with the South African Republic. In this he failed. The discovery of gold had reduced the need for the economic advantages that confederation would bring and President * Kruger stood firmly for independence, to maintain which he refused all political rights to the British and other foreigners (the Uitlanders) who had come to exploit the goldfields and upon whom the country's prosperity depended. Angry and impatient, Rhodes tried to synchronize an armed raid under * Jameson from the north with a rising of Uitlanders. Jameson came but the Uitlanders failed to rise and the whole episode was a fiasco. Rhodes was forced to resign when his part in it was discovered, and the divisions it created brought about the Boer War. Rhodes spent much of his remaining life in developing Rhodesia; he is buried there, a great if mistaken patriot, among the solitary Matopo hills. Of his huge fortune, all bequeathed for public purposes, he left a large sum for the foundation of Rhodes scholarships at Oxford University for students from the British Empire, the United States and Germany.

Lockhart, J. G. and Woodhouse, C. M., *Rhodes*. 1963

Rhondda, David Alfred Thomas, 1st Viscount (1856–1918). Welsh industrialist and politician. He developed the Rhondda Valley mining interests and became a leading British industrialist. He was Liberal M.P. for Merthyr Tydfil (1889–1910). In World War I he became Britain's first food controller (1917) and introduced an orderly and successful rationing scheme. His daughter, **Viscountess Rhondda** (1883–1958), owned and edited the journal *Time and Tide*.

Rhys, Ernest (1859–1946). Anglo-Welsh editor. He went to London (1886) and pursued a varied literary career until he was introduced by Edmund Gosse to J. M. Dent, for whom he produced the famous Everyman's Library of reprints, which brought great literature within the reach of millions. From 1906 when the first books were published (at a price of ls.) until Rhys's death, nearly 1,000 titles were issued and nearly 35,000,000 copies sold.

Ribbentrop, Joachim von (1893–1946). German diplomat. Originally a champagne salesman he joined the Nazi party (1933) and became Hitler's adviser on foreign affairs. He negotiated the Anglo-German naval treaty (1935) and after being ambassador in London (1936–38) he was recalled to become minister of foreign affairs. He was largely responsible for the Russo-German pact of 1939, the necessary prelude to World War II. He held office throughout the war, was subsequently sentenced by the Nuremberg tribunal and hanged.

Ribera, Jusepe (or José; known as Spagnoletto, 'little Spaniard') (1591–1656). Spanish painter. He studied in Spain and Italy, and eventually settled in Naples (1616) where he became court painter to the viceroys. He adopted * Caravaggio's style of the contrasts in lighting and painted such subjects as *The Massacre of St Bartholomew* with brutal realism.

Ricardo, David (1772–1823). English economist. He was born in London, the son of Dutch-Jewish immigrants, whom his marriage to a Quakeress estranged. He became a successful stockbroker, and added to his business experience the theoretical knowledge of economics acquired through his friendship with Jeremy * Bentham and James * Mill to produce the famous *Principles of Political Economy and Taxation* (1817). In his own words he gives an account 'of the natural course of rent, profit and wages'. The method of assessing value by the amount of labour put into the production of commodities was later abandoned by him (at least in its unmodified form) but was used by Karl * Marx and so achieved a lasting influence. Of greater importance was his theory that 'comparative costs' are the factor by which international exchange is determined. This pointed the way to Free Trade. Ricardo was M.P. for an Irish pocket borough 1819–23.
Hollander, J. H., *David Ricardo: A Centenary Estimate*. 1910

Ricci, Matteo (1552–1610). Italian Jesuit missionary. He learned Chinese and went to China (1583) but he was expelled from place after place until in 1601 he was allowed to settle in Pekin. Here he attracted interest by showing and explaining European clocks, maps etc., and soon made converts. His adaptation of Christian theology to accord with Chinese custom, however, aroused controversy and disapproval in Rome.
Spence, J., *The Memory Palace of Matteo Ricci*. 1985

Rice, Elmer (Elmer Reizenstein) (1892–1967). American playwright. He wrote farces, melodramas and novels, but it was by his presentation of social problems in such unusual plays as *The Adding Machine* (1922), *Street Scene* (1929) and *We, The People* (1933) that his great reputation was achieved.
Rice, E., *Minority Report*. 1964

Richard I (known as 'Cœur de Lion') (1157–1199). King of England (from 1189). He was the son and successor of Henry II and of his queen Eleanor of Aquitaine. At the time of his father's death Richard and his brothers, incited by their mother (by then separated from Henry), were in rebellion against him. Almost immediately after his succession Richard joined the 3rd Crusade provoked by the capture (1187) of Jerusalem by Saladin. He conquered Cyprus (where he married Berengaria of Navarre), proved his military skill by the capture of Acre, but having quarrelled with, and been deserted by, Philip II of France and Duke Leopold of Austria had to be content with only a sight of Jerusalem before making a truce (1192). On the way home he was wrecked in the Adriatic and while trying to return overland in disguise was caught by his enemy Duke Leopold and imprisoned for two years until a sufficient instalment of the vast ransom demanded had been paid. (The legend that the king's place of captivity was discovered by the troubadour Blondel de Nesle is unsubstantiated.) On his return he forgave his brother John, who had been in arms against him, and spent the rest of his reign defending his French dominions against Philip II. He was killed by a chance arrow-shot at the siege of Chaluz. He had spent only a few months in England during his reign, but his justiciars, William de Longchamp and Hurbert de Burgh ruled well and the ransom was ungrudgingly paid. Richard earned his nickname for his bravery and was generous and chivalrous.
Harvey, J. H., *The Plantagenets*. 1970

Richard II (1367–1400). King of England (1377–99). Born at Bordeaux, he was the son of Edward the Black Prince, and succeeded his grandfather, Edward III. During the crisis of the Peasants' Revolt (1381) Richard, though still under the regency of John of Gaunt, personally intervened and when their leader, Wat Tyler, was struck down he courageously took charge and promised to redress their grievances. From *c.* 1382 Richard tried to assert his kingship, but his aims were frustrated by the magnates in his council

(Lords Appellant) who objected to the favours bestowed upon members of the court party. Richard tried to resist, but from 1386 to 1389 the Lords Appellant were in complete control. Their divisions destroyed them: Richard regained the initiative and for the next eight years ruled constitutionally and well. But he foresaw danger: and for an expedition to Ireland (1394) he raised an army dependent only upon himself. Thus fortified, he struck back (1397) at his opponents. Execution or exile was their fate, and with parliament packed and submissive he established a despotism that became increasingly severe. He made the mistake, however, of quarrelling with and exiling his cousin Henry Bolingbroke, and more foolish still, sequestrating the Lancastrian estates when his uncle, John of Gaunt, died (1399). While Richard was absent in Ireland, Henry landed in Yorkshire and marched across England gathering adherents. The king returned and judging the position hopeless surrendered: he was taken to Pontefract Castle in Yorkshire from which he never emerged. He was married twice but died childless: Bolingbroke succeeded him as Henry IV. Richard encouraged the arts and his court became a centre for culture.

Barron, C. M., and du Boulay, F. R. H., *The Reign of Richard II*. 1971

Richard III (1452–1485). King of England (from 1483). The brother of * Edward IV, he was created Duke of Gloucester (1461) for his loyal services during the Wars of the Roses. When Edward IV died (1483) the boy–king Edward V succeeded and Richard, as protector, ruled. The events that followed arose directly from the hostility to him of the widowed queen and the swarm of her relations raised to wealth and power by Edward IV. Richard proceeded to isolate the king from his mother, to seize and kill the most prominent of the queen's relations and then to induce parliament to declare the queen's marriage invalid and the king a bastard, and consequently to dethrone him. Richard then accepted the crown as next in line of inheritance. Meanwhile, young Edward and his brother Richard were in the Tower of London, where they were killed in circumstances that have never been established: Sir Thomas More's narrative (followed by Shakespeare), which made Richard Crouchback the exemplar of all wicked uncles, may be exaggerated and certainly contains Tudor bias, but there remains a strong possibility that the boys were murdered by their uncle's orders or by someone who believed that he was fulfilling his unspoken wishes. Richard, a successful and just administrator and hitherto very popular, now began to lose adherents, a process accelerated when the Lancastrian claimant Henry Tudor (Henry VII) landed at Milford Haven, and Richard III was defeated and killed in the battle which ensued at Bosworth in Leicestershire. Richard's reputation has had several champions among the historians of this century, and he is certainly to some extent rehabilitated.

Cheetham, A., *The Life and Times of Richard III*. 1972

Richard, Duke of York (1411–1460). Leader of the Yorkist faction against Henry VI of England. He was a grandson of Edmund, a younger son of Edward III, but his claim to the throne came through his mother, Anne Mortimer, who was descended from an older son of Edward III. Soon after the outbreak of the Wars of the Roses he was killed at the Battle of Wakefield. Two of his sons became * Edward IV and * Richard III.

Richard, Earl of Cornwall (1209–1272). King of the Romans (from 1257). The brother of Henry III of England, he went on crusade (1240–41). His birth, wealth and integrity enabled him to take an important part in continental politics in the confused period following the death (1250) of the Holy Roman Emperor Frederick II. He refused the Sicilian crown offered (1253) by Pope Innocent IV but in 1257 was the successful candidate for the office of king of the Romans (i.e. emperor elect) and was crowned German king at Aachen; but he only gained partial recognition. In the baronial civil war in England he tried to mediate but finally sided with his brother, was captured at Lewes and held prisoner until after the royalist victory at Evesham.

Richards, Frank (Charles Hamilton) (1875–1961). English author of books for school-boys and, under other pseudonyms, for schoolgirls. He is best known for his serials on Tom Merry and Billy Bunter which appeared in the *Gem* and *Magnet* boys' magazines between 1906 and 1940. He was probably the most prolific author of all time.

Richards, F., *Autobiography*. 1952

Richards, Sir Gordon (1904–). English jockey. Having begun his career as a stable apprentice at the age of 15 he had become a leading jockey by the time he was 21. His total of 4,870 winners exceeded that of anyone hitherto known in racing history. He won the Derby on Pinza in 1953, the year of his knighthood. He retired (1954) to become a trainer.

Richardson, Henry Handel (pen name of Eliza Florence Richardson) (1870–1946). Australian novelist. After her marriage to Professor J. G. Robertson of London University, she gave up a musical career and took to writing, but though her first novel was published in 1908 it was not until the conclusion (1929) of a trilogy entitled *The Fortunes of Richard Mahony* that she achieved success and fame. In a detailed day-by-day account of a man's life in the harsh Australia of the 1850s and 1860s the author conveys the ruthless inevitability of great tragedy.
Kramer, L., *Henry Handel Richardson*. 1967

Richardson, Sir Ralph David (1902–1983). English actor. He first won fame by his Shakespearian performances with the Old Vic, and especially in the New Theatre season, immediately following World War II, during which he had done naval service. He has been even more successful in modern plays, and has played leading parts in, e.g., *Arms and the Man, The Heiress, Flowering Cherry*. From the 1930s he has been equally well known for his appearances in many famous films e.g. *South Riding, The Fallen Idol, Dr Zhivago*. He was knighted in 1947.

Richardson, Samuel (1689–1761). English novelist. The son of a cabinet-maker 'who understood architecture', he had a grammar-school education, after which he was apprenticed to a London printer, whose daughter he married (1721). He established (1724) his own business in Salisbury Square and managed it successfully for the rest of his life. He was already 50 when at the suggestion of two friends he wrote a book of specimen letters for various occasions for the benefit of those unable to express their own thoughts. From one of these letters, 'A Father to a Daughter in Service on hearing of her Master's attempting her Virtue', sprang *Pamela; or Virtue Rewarded* (1740), the first of three epistolary novels intended, since Richardson was primarily a moralist, 'to promote religion and virtue'. Often described as the first modern novel, *Pamela*, a hugely popular book, was followed by *Clarissa* (1747–48), a prodigious work in seven volumes where death appropriately follows a lapse from virtue. In *Sir Charles Grandison* (1753–54) the hero and heroine, their virtue proof against all trials and misfortunes, ultimately and happily unite. Richardson's influence was various and widespread. *Pamela* was parodied by Fielding in *Shamela* and *Joseph Andrews*, and Voltaire made use of it for one of his own plays; *Clarissa* was translated by the Abbé Prévost, and Diderot and Rousseau were among the author's fervent admirers.
Duncan Eaves, T. C., and Kimpel, B. D., *Samuel Richardson: a Biography*. 1971

Richelieu, Armand Jean du Plessis, Duc de (1585–1642). French statesman and cardinal. He was a younger son of François du Plessis, grand provost of France, and at the age of 21 was nominated bishop of Luçon. Representing the clergy at the states-general of 1614, he made contact with the court and in 1616 was appointed secretary of state as the protégé of Concini, favourite of the queen mother and regent Marie de Médicis. Concini's assassination (1617), consented to by Louis XIII to assert his independence, seemed likely to end Richelieu's career but by reconciling the king and his mother he made himself acceptable to both. Richelieu became a cardinal in 1622, chief minister in 1624 and from then until the end of his life was virtual ruler of France. He crushed the political power of the Huguenots (1625–29) by reducing the strongholds granted to them as places of refuge by Henry IV. La Rochelle, the most important, fell (1628) after heroically resisting a siege of fifteen months, Richelieu himself ensuring the result by building a huge dyke across the harbour and so preventing relief by the English fleet. Richelieu next had to contend with attempts by the feudal nobility, aided by the king's vain and foolish brother Gaston, Duke of Orléans, to undermine his power. Plot after plot Richelieu unveiled and punished, and even overcame a desperate attempt by Marie de Médicis, now turned against him, to have her former adherent removed from office. Having created the centralized autocracy of which Louis XIV was to be the beneficiary, Richelieu turned to foreign affairs. The Thirty Years War was raging and with the death of the Swedish king Gustavus Adolphus (1632) the Protestant cause might have foundered and France been at the mercy of Habsburg Austria had not Richelieu, Catholic cardinal though he was, stepped in with subsidy and armed forces to fill the gap. During the last two years of Richelieu's life (1640–42). Artois, Alsace and Roussillon were occupied by France. Though primarily a politician, Richelieu proved himself a discerning patron of the arts and learning, with the Académie Française, founded by him in 1635, as his most abiding memorial.

Richelieu's confidential agent was known as Eminence Grise (* Joseph, Père).
Buickhardt, C. J., *Richelieu and his Age*. 1940–1970

Richter, Hans (1843–1916). Hungarian-born conductor. An authority on Wagner, he had a strong influence upon British music of the period, first through his series of orchestral concerts in London (from 1879) and later when he conducted the Hallé Orchestra in Manchester (1900–11).

Richter, Johann Paul Friedrich *see* **Jean Paul**

Richthofen, Manfred, Baron von (1892–1918). German aviator. His exploits as a fighter pilot made him an almost legendary figure in World War I; he is said to have shot down eighty planes before being killed in action. Goering was a member of his squadron. His sister, Frieda von Richthofen (1881–1956), married (1914) D. H. * Lawrence.

Ridgway, Matthew Bunker (1895–). American soldier. Much of his early service was on the staff, but in World War II he commanded a division in Sicily and Italy (1942–44), and during the liberation campaign in northern Europe (1944–45) the 18th Airborne Corps was under his command. He was GOC the US 8th Army in Korea (1950–51) and succeeded (1951) * MacArthur in the supreme command. In 1952 he took over * Eisenhower's command in Europe. He was awarded (1955) an honorary KCB.
Ridgway, M. B., *Soldier*. 1956

Ridley, Nicholas (*c*. 1500–1555). English Protestant martyr. A strong but unbigoted supporter of the Reformed doctrines, he became bishop of Worcester (1547) and of London (1550). As long as Edward VI was alive he had a powerful influence in the church and helped Archbishop * Cranmer to prepare the Forty-two Articles. On the king's death he supported the cause of Lady Jane * Grey, but subsequently when Queen Mary I gained power he was arrested, tried for heresy at Oxford with Latimer and Cranmer, and burned at the stake.
Ridley, J. G., *Life of Nicholas Ridely*. 1957

Riebeek, Jan van (died 1670). Dutch administrator. With seventy Dutch burghers he was sent by the Dutch East India Company (1652) to found a settlement at the Cape of Good Hope which should act as revictualling station for ships bound for the East Indies. He remained for ten years, the settlement he started forming the nucleus of the South African republic of today.

Riefenstahl, Leni (Helene) (1902–). German actress, film maker and photographer, born in Berlin. She trained as a dancer, starred in several romantic 'ice' pictures in the 1920s and directed four important films: *The Blue Light* (1932), *Victory of Faith* (1933), *Triumph of the Will*, a powerful evocation of Germany's mood at the time of Hitler's accession in 1934, and *Olympia 1936* (1938). Barred from film making after 1945 because of her Nazi links, she turned to photography and published three dramatic books *The Last of the Nuba* (1973), *The People of Kau* (1976) and *Coral Gardens* (1978).

Riel, Louis (1844–1885). Canadian insurgent. He led a rebellion (1869) of his fellow halfbreeds in the Red River area against the introduction of settled government. The rising was easily suppressed but Riel, who had taken refuge in the U.S.A., returned (1885) to head another uprising. Once more suppression proved easy, but Riel was captured, tried and executed.
Davidson, W. M., *Louis Riel*. 1955

Riemann, Georg Friedrich Bernard (1826–1866). German mathematician. He studied under Gauss at Göttingen, where he returned to teach (1851) and was professor of mathematics (1857–66). He put forward (1854) a system of non-Euclidean geometry which includes the idea of a finite but unbounded space capable of any number of dimensions and which rejects many of the basic concepts of * Euclid, e.g. the notion that parallel lines meet only at infinity.

Rienzi, Cola di (1313–1354). Italian patriot, son of an innkeeper in Rome. Trained as a lawyer, he looked back to the glories of the ancient republic and convinced himself that it was his destiny to restore the squalid city of his own time to its former greatness. He headed a mission (1343) to Avignon, where the papacy was installed in voluntary exile, to secure constitutional reforms from Pope Clement VI. Returning empty-handed, he succeeded by his eloquence in obtaining popular support for the revival of the Roman republic and he was proclaimed tribune (1347). As long as he used his despotic power to mantain law and order all was well, but by stirring the people against the nobles he provoked fights and bloodshed and his pretensions to exercise the old Roman supremacy over the rest of Italy were resented. Seven months after assuming office he was forced to flee. He went to Prague (1349–50) to enlist the support of the emperor Charles IV in his plans for a revived Roman empire. Charles sent him captive to Avignon but in 1353 Pope Innocent IV, hoping to use him to restore papal power, sent him back to Rome, where he resumed despotic rule. But now the mob turned against him, stormed the Capitol and killed their former hero. His story is told in Bulwer Lytton's novel *Rienzi.*

Rikhter, Sviatoslav Teofilovich (1915–). Russian pianist. His recordings of Brahms, Schumann, Liszt, Rachmaninov, Bartok and Prokoviev in the great Romantic tradition were highly praised.

Riley, Bridget Louise (1931–). British painter, born in London. Educated at Goldsmiths' College and the Royal College of Art, she achieved international recognition from 1962. Her paintings were created within the 'Op' art tradition, depending on tension between contrasting colours in stripes and curves, leading to an instability of focus so that the canvas seems to be in motion.

Rilke, Rainer Maria (1875–1926). Austrian poet, born in Prague. His earliest work is largely composed of melancholy reveries but after visits to Russia and meetings with * Tolstoy he developed his mystical perceptions, and his poems of this period are concerned with the interrelationship of God (identified with Life), Man and Death. He married (1901) a pupil of the French sculptor * Rodin, and became his secretary and fervent admirer. Though his spiritual search continued he learnt from Rodin the importance of form; his poems thus lost much of their vague mysticism and as his vision became more objective he directed it to more concrete themes. His novel *The Notebook of Malte Laurids Brigge* (1910) is partly autobiographical. After further travels he settled in Switzerland (1919), and with the publication (1923) of the *Sonnets to Orpheus* and the *Duinese Elegies* he seems to have found in the cult of beauty a degree of tranquillity. There is much symbolism and medieval flavour in his very special type of poetry: his reputation has in recent years attained great proportions.
Holthusen, H. E., *Portrait of Rilke*. 1971

Rimbaud, (Jean Nicolas) Arthur (1854–1891). French poet. He reacted against the dominating puritanism of his mother and an unhappy home life by running away from home several times before settling in Paris (1870). His amazing precocity was shown in all his early pieces and especially in his *Le Bateau ivre* (1871) in which the rhythms and images already have the magical quality that appears in the work of the later symbolists. He lived with * Verlaine in Paris from 1871 but the association ended abruptly when Verlaine was sent to prison for firing two shots at Rimbaud who was theatening to leave. But it was Verlaine who made Rimbaud famous with an analysis of his poems in *Les Poètes maudits* (1884). Rimbaud never knew of this. All his poems were written before he was 20, many under the deliberate stimulation of drink, drugs, or debauchery: all the fragments, *Les Déserts de l'amous* (1871), *Les Illuminations* (1872–73), *Une Saison en enfer* (1873) are infinitely revealing of a genius in the making and the spoiling. After that he drifted round the world until in 1883 he reached Abyssinia, where he established a harem and set himself up in trade. His account of his travels there was published in 1928. He died in hospital at Marseilles after an amputation for a tumour on the knee.
Starkie, E., *Arthur Rimbaud*. 3rd ed. 1961

Rimsky-Korsakov, Nikolay Andreyevich (1844–1908). Russian composer. Though trained for the navy, he joined * Balakirev's group of 'nationalist' composers known as 'the Five' (the other three being Borodin, Mussorgsky and Cui), who made it their rule to introduce the themes and spirit of Russian folk music into all their compositions. His first symphony (1861–65), his second (1868; twice revised and eventually published as a symphonic suite, *Antar*, in 1903), and an opera *The Maid of Pskov* (1868–72) belong to this period. The group broke up *c.* 1870, but as all lacked academic training Rimsky-Korsakov was astonished to find himself appointed (1871) professor at the St Petersburg Conservatoire. He succeeded, none the less, in making himself a master of orchestration and contrapuntal technique, and though the effects upon his work were at first devitalizing he later achieved the brilliance of *Capriccio Espagnol* (1887) and *Scheherazade* (1888). From 1888 he turned to opera but only gave of his best when he had succeeded in shedding * Wagner's influence with 'such fairy-tale operas as *Sadko* (1894–96), *The Snow Maiden* (1880–81) and *The Golden Cockerel* (1906–07), his last work. Rimsky-Korsakov's work lacks depths of feeling and it is largely upon his supreme skill as an orchestrator that his fame finally rests. This skill was notably employed in revising and reorchestrating the works of other composers who lacked his technical versatility, especially Dargomyzhski's *Stone Guest*, Mussorgsky's *Boris Godunov* (here the original has more individuality) and Borodin's *Prince Igor*.

Abraham, G., *Rimsky-Korsakov: A Short Biography*. 1948

Ripon, Frederick John Robinson, 1st Earl of (1782–1859). English Tory politician. From 1809 to 1846 he held, whenever his party was in power, important ministerial posts, including that of chancellor of the exchequer (1823–27) and briefly, as Viscount Goderich, (1827–28) prime minister.

His son, **George Frederick Samuel Robinson, 1st Marquess of Ripon** (1827–1909), was a Liberal politician, who as viceroy of India (1880–84) was responsible for introducing local self-government. Ripon subsequently served in several Liberal governments at home, retiring as Lord Privy Seal in 1908: he served every Liberal government from Palmerston to Asquith. After four years as head of the English Freemasons he became a Catholic in 1874.

Jones, W. D., *Prosperity Robinson*. 1967

Rivera, Diego (1886–1957). Mexican painter. He studied in Paris where he came to know the principal Cubists and was influenced by * Gauguin. His best known works are large murals and frescoes for which he revived the encaustic methods of the ancient Maya sculptors. His themes were revolutionary episodes from history intended to promote the communist cause. His style was a composite of 'folk art', symbolism and Aztec undertones directed towards political ends. He was for a time obliged to leave Mexico. After his return (1935) he began to adopt surrealist techniques.

Wolfe, B. D., *The Fabulous Life of Diego Rivera*. 1963

Rivera, Primo de *see* **Primo de Rivera y Orbaneia, Miguel**

Rizal y Mercado Alonso, José Prolasio (1861–1896). Filipino writer and patriot. As a writer he aimed at fostering a desire for Filipino independence. His novels *Noli me Tangere* (1886) and *El Filibusterismo* (1891) were eloquent attacks on Spanish misrule. He founded a nationalist society, and was exiled from Manila. When the Filipino revolt of 1896 broke out Rizal was arrested (outside the Philippines), brought to Manila and executed. He is regarded as a national hero.

Rizzio, David (*c.* 1533–1566). Italian musician. He went to Scotland (1561) and he became the favourite and secretary of Mary Queen of Scots. His arrogant assumption of power and his personal relations with the queen roused such anger and jealousy that * Darnley, her husband, joined a group of nobles in a conspiracy to murder. The queen was having supper in her room with Darnley, Rizzio and Lady Argyll, when Lord Ruthven burst in and denounced the favourite. Other conspirators appeared and during the ensuing fracas the supper table was overturned. Rizzio was dragged from the room and immediately killed.

Robbia, Luca della (1400–1482). Florentine sculptor. A skilled worker in bronze and silver, he is best remembered for his terracotta sculptures to which, in the manner of the Moors in Spain, white and coloured enamels were applied. The Madonna and Child 'type', which he developed, perhaps influenced Raphael's Florentine Madonna series. Luca's first dated and justly celebrated major work was the Cantoria or Singing Gallery for Florence Cathedral (1431–38), known for its panels of singing and dancing boys. Luca's nephew, **Andrea della Robbia** (1435–1525), his partner and less accomplished successor, is remembered for the medallions of babes in swaddling clothes on the Foundling Hospital in Florence. His sons, including **Giovanni della Robbia** (1469–1529) and **Girolamo della Robbia** (1488–1566) carried on the family workshop.

Pope-Hennessey, J., *Italian Renaissance Sculpture*. 1971

Robert I *see* **Bruce, Robert**

Robert II (1316–1390). King of Scotland (from 1371). He was the son of Walter the Steward, whose hereditary office passed to him and so made him the first king of the Stewart (Stuart) dynasty. His claim to the throne came through his mother Marjorie Bruce, daughter of Robert I (Robert * Bruce) and sister of David II, for whom he acted as regent during his captivity in England.

Robert III (1340–1406). King of Scotland (from 1390), son and successor of Robert II. Injury from the kick of a horse made him incapable of rule, and power was exercised by his brother, the Duke of Albany. Robert was succeeded by his surviving son * James I.

Roberts, Sir Charles George Douglas (1860–1943). Canadian naturalist and poet, born in New Brunswick. Described as 'the doyen of Canadian literature' he became known for his stories of wild animals, e.g. *Feet of the Furtive* (1912) and *Eyes of the Wilderness* (1933) as well as for poetry.

Keith, W. J., *Sir Charles G. D. Roberts*. 1969

Roberts, Frederick Sleigh Roberts, 1st Earl (1832–1914). British soldier, born in India. As a young officer in the Bengal artillery he won the V.C. during the Mutiny (1858). He became a national hero in the Afghan wars, when in 1880, from Kabul he led an army of 10,000 men through the mountains to the relief of Kandahar, covering a distance of 300 miles in twenty-two days and then defeating the Afghans. In 1885 he was appointed commander-in-chief in India; he received a peerage (1893) and in 1895 was appointed to the chief command in Ireland and made a field-marshal. After the serious defeats with which the Boer War opened (December 1899) Roberts was sent out as commander-in-chief and quickly retrieved the situation. Pretoria was captured (June 1900) and, though guerrilla warfare continued, organized operations were at an end. Roberts returned to become commander-in-chief of the British army, a post abolished in 1904. From then on, with the threat from Germany in mind, he campaigned in vain for national military service.

Hannah, W. H., *Bobs: Kipling's General*. 1972

Robertson, Sir William Robert, 1st Bart (1860–1933). British soldier. He rose from private (1877) to become a field-marshal (1920). After long service in India, he was intelligence officer under Lord * Roberts in South Africa and subsequently held a succession of staff appointments until he became, on the outbreak of World War I, Q.M.G. to the British armies in France and (1915) chief of the Imperial General Staff. He commanded the armies on the Rhine (1919–20).

His son, **Sir Brian Hubert Robertson** (1896–1974), also had a distinguished military career. After World War II he commanded the British army of occupation in Germany, and he was commander-in-chief in the Middle East (1950–53). He gained a new reputation as chairman of the British Transport Commission from 1953 to 1961, when he was created Baron Robertson of Oakridge.

Robertson, W. R., *From Private to Field-marshal*. 1921

Robeson, Paul (Le Roy) (1898–1976). American singer and actor. He was trained for the law before he began a successful theatrical career in such plays as Eugene O'Neill's *The Emperor Jones* and *All God's Children Got Wings*; he was a notable Othello but achieved his most triumphant successes with the song *Ol' Man River* in *Showboat* and as Bosambo in *Sanders of the River*. He had a very fine bass voice. From the 1930s was attracted to left-wing political movements and championed Negro rights; from 1958 to 1963 he lived in England.

Hoyt, E. P., *Paul Robeson*. 1968. Robeson, P. *Here I Stand*. 1958

Robespierre, Maximilien François Marie Isidore de (1758–1794). French Revolutionary leader, born at Arras. Orphaned at 7 and brought up (with his brother Augustin) by maiden aunts, he was a leading lawyer, judge and *littérateur* in Arras until elected (1789) to the Estates-General, soon renamed the National Assembly. At first little known, he spoke 500 times in the National Assembly—nearly every sitting day. In 1791, having moved to Paris, he was elected to the Paris Commune and consolidated his great support among the Jacobin clubs. His rigidity and honesty earned him Marat's description as 'incorruptible' ('the seagreen Incorruptible' was Carlyle's famous phrase), but it was by his speeches and his gift for putting into words what others were feeling that he gradually gained ascendency in the Jacobin Club, the meeting place of the extreme republicans encouraged and supported by the Paris mob. As leader of the left Jacobins, he made 100 speeches in Paris between September 1791 and August 1792. He opposed declaration of war on Austria (April 1792) bitterly—and predicted its outcome. He was elected as the first of Paris' 24 delegates to the Convention in September 1792. He proposed and secured the passage of the 1793 Constitution, modelled along the ideas of his idol J.-J. * Rousseau. In July 1793 the murder of * Marat contributed to the proscription of the Gironde and the election of Robespierre to the Committee of Public Safety, where he served from 27 July 1793 to 26 July 1794. This was his first exercise of power, more as a resident conscience than a minister. He called for a regime based on 'virtue without which terror is baneful; terror without which virtue is powerless' and purged the Convention of 'ultra-revolutionaries' such as Hébert (March 1794) and moderate 'indulgents' led by Danton (April 1794). He introduced the 'Maximum', rigorous government control of the economy, and planned what was virtually a welfare state. He proposed a state cult based on Rousseau's 'civil religion', seeing this as a compromise between atheism and Catholicism. His great day of triumph, presiding at the 'Festival of the Supreme Being' (8 June), marked the beginning of a conspiracy against him by Tallien, Fouché and Barras, corrupt men who feared for their own lives as the Reign of Terror increased in intensity. The battle of Fleurus (June 1794) confirmed that the Committee of Public Safety had placed France militarily in the ascendant, thus removing the main justification of Terror. A scene was staged in the Convention 27 July (9 Thermidor in the Revolutionary calendar) during which Robespierre was denounced and arrested. Next day, after rescue and recapture he was guillotined without trial with twenty-one other leaders of the Terror. The historians Mathiez and Lefebvre have gone far towards rehabilitating his reputation as a sanctimonious butcher and Crane Brinton has suggested that he was best explained as essentially a religious figure, pledged to destroy corruption and error. Nevertheless he was a flawed character, cold, remote and inflexible.

Robey, Sir George (George Edward Wade) (1869–1954). English music-hall comedian, often called 'the prime minister of mirth'. He made his debut in 1891 and for twenty years delighted music-hall audiences as a curate whose blackened eyebrows rose in shocked surprise when his listeners seemed to detect some hidden meaning in his 'innocent' words. From 1916 when he first achieved a triumphant success in *The Bing Boys are Here*, the famous revue of the World War I, he found a new outlet for his talents, and in later life showed by his performances as Falstaff how good a classical comedian he might have been. He was knighted in 1954.

Robin Hood. Legendary English folk-hero, probably based on a bandit-rebel active during the reign of Richard I (1189–99). Robin, originally in all probability a hero of oral folktales, appears first 'formally' in the fourteenth-century poems *Piers Plowman*, but popularity was mainly stimulated by fifteenth-century ballads. These depict him living in Sherwood Forest as the leader of a gang of outlaws, an expert archer and champion of the poor, particularly active against the injustices and extortions of the Sheriff of Nottingham.
Oman, C., *Robin Hood*. 1973

Robinson, Edward Arlington (1869–1935). American poet. Born in Maine and educated at Harvard, he lived in poverty until Theodore Roosevelt gave him a post in the New York Custom House (1905). He published twenty-six volumes of epigrammatic and conversational verse in strict classical forms. His best known poem is *Minver Cheevy*, from *The Town Down the River* (1910). He sees man as a creature trapped between his animal and spiritual natures and in each he studies 'the small Satanic king': the poet is 'the modern man seeking light in a dark universe'. The same problems and the same pessimism appear in his great Arthurian trilogy, *Merlin* (1917), *Lancelot* (1920) and *Tristram* (1927). He won the Pulitzer Prize three times.

Robinson, (William) Heath (1872–1944). English illustrator and comic artist. He was best known for his drawings of weird elaborate machines for performing elementary operations.

Robinson, Henry Crabb (1775–1867). English diarist. He studied in Germany; and was correspondent for *The Times* in the Napoleonic Wars; he retired in 1828 to travel and to entertain at his home or at the Athenaeum club of which he was a founder. His diary and correspondence (1869: with additions and improved text, 1927) record conversations with Goethe, Wordsworth, Coleridge, Lamb etc.
Sadler, T., ed., *The Diary, Reminiscences and Correspondence of Crabb Robinson*. 1869

Robinson, Mary (1758–1800). English actress. Known as 'Perdita' from her role in Shakespeare's *The Winter's Tale*, she played at Drury Lane (1776–80) and became (1779) the mistress of the Prince of Wales (George IV). She wrote poetry, plays and novels, but despite a pension she died in poverty.

Robinson, Sir Robert (1886–1975). English chemist. Educated at Manchester, he was a professor there and at other universities: as Waynflete professor of organic chemistry at Oxford (1930–55), he headed a team investigating the chemistry of penicillin. His researches into organic chemistry have been mainly in the fields of the alkaloids, plant pigments and phenanthrene derivatives. He was knighted in 1939, was president of the Royal Society (1945–50), won the Nobel Prize for Chemistry (1947) and was admitted to the Order of Merit in 1949.

Rob Roy ('Robert the Red', i.e. Robert Macgregor) (1671–1734). Scottish outlaw. A grazier on the braes of Balquhidder (where he is buried) in S.W. Scotland, he maintained an armed band for the protection of his flocks and those of his neighbours as well as for purposes of his own. His exploits, real and legendary, earned him the reputation of a Scottish Robin Hood, robbing the rich for the benefit of the poor, while at the same time pursuing a personal vendetta against the Duke of Montrose.

Robsart, Amy (1532–1560). First wife of Robert Dudley, later Earl of * Leicester. Her mysterious death at Cumnor Place, Berkshire, roused suspicions that she had been killed on her husband's order (with or without Elizabeth's most improbable connivance), in order to enable him to pursue his ambition to marry the queen. Her story forms the basis for Sir Walter Scott's *Kenilworth*.

Robson, Dame Flora (1902–1984). English actress. She made her debut in 1921 and played her first season at the Old Vic Theatre, London, in 1934, after which she appeared frequently in London, on tour and in New York in an unusually wide variety of classical and contemporary plays. Her first film was Korda's *Catherine the Great* (1934). She was made DBE in 1960.
Dunbar, J., *Flora Robson*. 1960

Rochefoucauld, Duc de la *see* **La Rochefoucauld, Duc de**

Rochester, John Wilmot, 2nd Earl of (1647–1680). English poet and courtier. His father was a royalist general ennobled by Charles I; he himself was one of the profligate wits who attended the court of Charles II, of whom he wrote 'He never said a foolish thing. Nor ever did a wise one'. An exaggerated reputation of being a debauchee overshadowed his achievements as a poet. Some of his lyrics are exquisite expressions of tender feeling, and his *Satire Against Mankind* (1675) sparkles with devastating wit, though much of what he wrote is certainly pornographic. His death-bed repentance is described by Bishop * Burnet.
de Sola Pinto, V., ed., *Poems by John Wilmot, Earl of Rochester*. 1964

Rockefeller, John Davison, Sr (1839–1937). American industrialist and financer, born in Richford, New York. The son of a farmer and patent medicine salesman (who later disappeared), his family moved to Cleveland, Ohio in 1853 and he left school at 16. He progressed from book-keeper to oil-well owner in the young oil industry (1862) and in Ohio founded (1870) the Standard Oil Company. This, by 1878, controlled 98 per cent of the American oil industry. In 1892 the monopoly was broken by court order, but he continued to dominate the industry through a holding company (Standard Oil of New Jersey) until he retired in 1911. He gave over $550 million to charity, founded Chicago University and the Rockefeller Institute of Medical Research and was reputed to be the richest man in the world. He founded (1931) Rockefeller Center, New York, the largest non-governmental building so far built.

His son **John Davison Rockefeller Junior** (1874–1960) was an active philanthropist and gave the United Nations the site on which it stands (East River, New York).

His son, **Nelson Aldrich Rockefeller** (1908–1979), was assistant secretary of state for Latin American affairs (1944–45) and under-secretary of state for health and public welfare (1953–54). He was governor of New York (1959–73), being the only Republican to score a major victory in 1958, and vice-president of the US (1974–77) under Gerald Ford. He was an active patron and promoter of modern art.
Collier, P. and Horowitz, D., *The Rockefellers*. 1976

Rockingham, Charles Watson Wentworth, 2nd Marquess of (1730–1782). English politician. A member of the same family as Charles I's famous minister * Strafford, he led the main body of the Whigs after the retirement of Newcastle, but he had too many outside interests (including the turf) and too little force of character to be a great leader. He favoured the conciliation of the American colonists and led the government (1765–66) which repealed the Stamp Act. He was again briefly prime minister in the last months of life. He owed many of his political ideas to * Burke, his private secretary (1765).

Rodgers, Richard (1902–1979). American composer of musical comedies, in collaboration with the librettists Lorenz Hart (1919–1942) and Oscar Hammerstein (1942–1960). Among the many successes for which he wrote the music were *Pal Joey, Oklahoma, South Pacific* and *The King and I*.

Rodin, Auguste (1840–1917). French sculptor. He began his art training at the age of 14 but was slow to mature. During a visit to Italy (1875) he was influenced by Donatello and Michelangelo, while a tour of French cathedrals (1877), about which he wrote a book, led him to call himself a latter-day Gothic artist. This was true only in the sense that he eschewed the plastic smoothness of the antique and expressed spiritual and emotional stresses through the effect of light and shade on roughened surfaces. After his tour he settled at Meudon near Paris and lived there or in Paris itself for the rest of his life. His most famous works include *The Burghers of Calais* (1884–95), *Le Baiser* (1898) and *Le Penseur* (1904); the two latter were intended to be part of a vast work, *La porte d'enfer* (186 figures), inspired by Dante's *Divine Comedy*, which from 1880 occupied much of his time. In addition he did many sculptured portraits, e.g. of Balzac, Hugo, Clemenceau and Bernard Shaw. He presented some twenty pieces to the British nation in gratitude for its army in World War I. The remainder of his unsold works he gave to France and they are now housed in Paris in a special museum.
Chabrun, J. F. and Descharnes, R., *Auguste Rodin*. 1967

Rodney, George Brydges Rodney, 1st Baron (1719–1792). British sailor. He joined the navy as a boy and from 1742 served brilliantly as a captain under * Hawke, with an interval (1748–52) as governor and commander-in-chief in Newfoundland; he was promoted rear-admiral (1759) and his squadron destroyed in Le Havre the flat-bottomed boats assembled for an invasion of England. Two years later he captured Martinique, Grenada and St Lucia in the West Indies. He was governor of Greenwich Hospital (1765–71) and had two more spells of active service (1771–74 and 1779–82), in the second of which he captured a Spanish convoy on the way to the West Indies, and, by destroying seven out of eleven ships of a squadron sent against him, temporarily relieved Gibraltar. At the islands of Les Saintes he gained (1782) a great victory (the Battle of the Saints) over the French admiral de Grasse, whom he captured with his ship and six other vessels. Unfortunately he had been recalled before the news reached England and though he received a barony and a pension his career was over. Despite his brilliance Rodney's dominating character made him many enemies in the service and he was unpopular with his men.
Spinney, D., *Rodney*. 1969

Roebuck, John (1718–1794). English inventor. He devised (1749) the first commercially practicable method of producing sulphuric acid, and set up (1762) a factory for converting pig iron to malleable iron by means of a blast furnace. He collaborated with * Watt in producing the steam engine.

Roehm (or Röhm), **Ernst** (1887–1934). German politician and soldier. One of the original Nazis, he was Hitler's chief adviser (1931–34). He organized and was head of the Stormtroops, whose support made him a close rival to Hitler. He was murdered, on Hitler's orders, or with his connivance, on the night of the 'blood bath' in 1934, when a large number of prominent members of the Nazi party, suspected of less than complete loyalty to the Führer, were ruthlessly eliminated.

Roemer, Olaus (1644–1710). Danish astronomer. Born in Jutland, he went to Paris (1671) and, working with Picard at the Observatory there, achieved his best known discovery (1675), that the velocity of light is finite, which he deduced from the fact that the observed time of eclipses on one of the satellites of Jupiter varied with the planet's distance from earth. He returned to Denmark (1681) and was professor of astronomy at Copenhagen (1685–1710) and mayor of the city (1705–10).

Roentgen *see* **Röntgen, Wilhelm Konrad**

Roger I (1031–1101). Count of Sicily. He joined his brother the Norman adventurer, Robert * Guiscard, in an enterprise by which much of southern Italy as well as Sicily was conquered. Left to rule Sicily, he showed great administrative gifts which enabled him to leave his successor a united state. His second son, **Roger II** (1097–1154), who succeeded (1105) his brother, united the Norman conquests into a single kingdom of Sicily, Calabria and Apulia (with Naples and Capua also included). Though pope and emperor temporarily combined against him, he extended his absolute rule over Malta and the African coast from Tripoli to Tunis. His Sicilian capital, Palermo, embellished with buildings in a blend of Romanesque and Saracenic styles, became a great meeting place for scholars from the Greek and Arab worlds.
Norwich, J. J., *The Normans in the South*. 1967; *The Kingdom in the Sun 1130–94*. 1970

Rogers, Will (William Penn Adair) (1879–1935). American actor and humorist, born in Oklahoma of Indian descent. His cowboy act in vaudeville, with its shrewd and homely monologues filled with sharp criticisms of manners and politics, achieved enormous success. Films, newspapers and books, e.g. *Illiterate Digest* (1924), provided him with further outlets. He was killed in a plane crash.

Roget, Peter Mark (1779–1869). English physician, inventor and lexicographer. His work on the slide-rule earned him his F.R.S., and his investigations into 'persistence of vision' suggested the possibilities of cinematography, but he is best remembered for his *Thesaurus of English Words and Phrases* (1852).

Rogier van der Weyden *see* **Weyden, Rogier van der**

Röhm, Ernst *see* **Roehm, Ernst**

Rokitansky, Karl (1804–1878). Austrian pathologist. Born in Bohemia, Rokitansky studied medicine at Prague and later Vienna, where he graduated in 1828. From an early stage he was drawn to specialize in pathology; his first post was in the pathological department of the Vienna Hospital. He subsequently became associate and full professor (1834 and 1844) at the University. Together with a small number of assistants, Rokitansky devoted his time entirely to autopsies, insisted upon making the fullest case histories and claimed to have performed 30,000 autopsies between 1827 and 1866. The fruits of his labours were set down in his *Handbook of Pathological Anatomy* of 1846. This work revealed unrivalled knowledge of abnormalities. Rokitansky in particular worked out the various forms of pneumonia and enumerated their symptoms, studied the atrophy of the liver and was an expert on gastric diseases, and wrote a famous book on the diseases of the artery.
Long, E. R., *History of pathology*. 1928

Rokossovsky, Konstantin Konstantinovich (1896–1968). Russian marshal. He was a major in World War I and joined the Red Army (1919). In World War II a brilliant turning movement carried out before Moscow (1941) brought him immediate fame. He fought outside Stalingrad (Volgograd), in White Russia and in Poland, where his orders did not include aid to the Warsaw insurrection (1944). In the spring of 1945 he invaded East Prussia and, marching to the north of

Zhukov's Berlin army, met the British near Lübeck. After the war he went to Poland as minister of defence (1949–56).

Roland de la Platière, Jean Marie (1754–1793). French Revolutionary politician, a leader of the Girondin faction for the members of which his wife Jeanne Manon (1754–1793) presided over a famous *salon*. He was minister of the interior in 1792 but after a quarrel with * Robespierre he took refuge in Normandy. News of his wife's execution caused him to commit suicide.
Roland de la Platière, M. J. P. (ed. Perroud, C.), *Mémoires*. 1905

Rolfe, Frederick William *see* **Corvo, Baron**

Rolland, Romain Edmé Paul Émile (1866–1944). French writer. After studying archaeology and history in Rome he gained his doctorate (1895) at the Sorbonne in Paris with a thesis on the early history of music, and returned there to teach musical history (1904–10). His early plays, e.g. *Danton* (1900), lacked distinction, and he first achieved success with lives of Beethoven (1903), Michelangelo (1906) and Tolstoy (1911): his major work of this period was the huge novel *Jean Christophe* (10 volumes, 1904–12), which describes the life of a musical genius in a world of mediocrity. As a pacifist opponent of World War I he lived in Switzerland from 1914 where he wrote *Au dessus de la mêlée* (1915). Between the wars he wrote another long novel *L'Âme enchantée* (7 volumes, 1922–33) and showed a lively interest in the non-violent campaign in India by lives of Gandhi (1924) and Ramakrishna (1930). Growing communist sympathies took him to Russia, where he spent some months with his friend Maxim * Gorky, but he modified his pacifist attitude as the Fascist-Nazi threat developed. His later works included *Par la Révolution la paix* (1935). He returned to France in 1938 and offered his full support to the Allies. He won the Nobel Prize for Literature (1915).
Barrère, J.-B., *Romain Rolland. L'âme et l'art*. 1966

Rolls, Charles Stewart (1877–1910). English aviator and motor manufacturer. A son of Lord Llangattock, he was a pioneer of motoring and aviation. With F. H. * Royce he founded (1906) the Rolls-Royce Company. He made a two-way cross-channel flight (1910); he died in a flying accident.
Georgano, G. N., ed., *The Complete Encyclopaedia of Motorcars, 1885–1968*. 1968

Romains, Jules (pen-name of Louis Farigoule) (1885–1972). French writer. He taught philosophy in French universities, and wrote plays, e.g. *Knock* (1923), poetry and novels. He evolved the literary theory of 'unanisme' – an attempt to convey the collective spirit of a city or locality. His major work is the novel sequence known as *Les Hommes de bonne volonté* (27 volumes, 1932–47), a vivid panorama of French life in the first part of the 20th century and especially about World War I. Romains lived in the USA (1940–45) and was elected to the Académie Française in 1946.
Cuisenier, A., *Jules Romains et 'Les Hommes de bonne volonté'*. 1954

Romanes, George John (1848–1894). British physiological scientist and evolutionist. Much of Romanes's early work was on the nervous system of invertebrates, such as jelly-fish, trying to ascertain their place in the evolutionary chain of nervous organs. But from the 1880s he developed the researches for which he is best remembered, on animal intelligence, which he set out in three books, *Animal Intelligence* (1882), *Mental Evolution in Animals* (1883) and *Mental Evolution in Man* (1888). Following Herbert * Spencer, Romanes adapted the traditional British associationist account of thinking to an evolutionary scheme. He became embroiled in many of the controversies of the day concerning the adequacy of natural selection as an explanation for evolution. He tended to side with Spencer's view, that the inheritance of acquired charactristics had some role to play, and preferred a multi-cause to a single cause explanation. Following the work of John Thomas Gulick, Romanes became an enthusiastic supporter of the (Darwinian) idea of the importance of isolation as a factor in evolution.
Romanes, E., *The life and letters of George John Romanes*. 1896

Romano, Giulio *see* **Giulio Romano**

Romanov. The ruling dynasty of Russia from 1613, when Michael Romanov was chosen

tsar, to 1917 when Nicholas II was forced to abdicate.
Kluchevsky, V., *The Rise of the Romanovs*. 1970

Romberg, Sigmund (1887–1951). American composer, born in Hungary. He composed over seventy operettas including such great successes as *The Student Prince* (1924) and *The Desert Song* (1926).

Romilly, Sir Samuel (1757–1818). English lawyer. He had already achieved success at the bar, mainly in chancery practice, when an able pamphlet (1790) on the French Revolution brought him to wider notice. In 1806 he was appointed solicitor general and entered parliament. At once he put his whole heart into the reform of the criminal law and especially into reducing the number of offences, then some 200, punishable by death. Bill after bill he presented but the results of his perseverance were seen only after his death. He joined the anti-slavery movement and firmly opposed all arbitrary acts (e.g. suspension of Habeas Corpus) by the government. He committed suicide three days after his wife's death.
Oakes, C. G., *Sir Samuel Romilly*. 1935

Rommel, Erwin (1891–1944). German field-marshal. He gained the highest decoration for valour in World War I and in 1933 joined the Nazi party. In World War II he commanded an armoured division in France (1940) and in 1941 was given command of the Afrika Korps sent to rescue the Italians in Libya. This he built up with astonishing speed into a powerful instrument of attack and counter-attack, and in the ding-dong struggle of the following months he more than once turned defeat into victory; in the summer of 1942 he drove the British back into Egypt as far as Alamein. Here the British stood successfully until in late October Montgomery, strongly reinforced, opened the attack which eventually drove Rommel's forces westward across the continent into Tunisia, where the German armies finally surrendered. Before this Rommel had been recalled; later he fought in Italy and in 1944 was given command of an army group resisting the Allied invasion of northern France. In July he was seriously wounded in an air raid, and it is not certain whether he died in October from his injuries or (more probably) was ordered to commit suicide because of suspected complicity in the bomb attempt on Hitler's life.
Douglas-Home, C., *Rommel*. 1973

Romney, George (1734–1802). English portrait-painter. The son of a Lancashire carpenter, he learnt to draw mainly from copying, but when he went to London (1762) he soon achieved considerable success. He paid his first visit to Paris in 1764 and the delicacy and charm then fashionable there is evident in his work. After a time he ceased to exhibit his pictures and so never became an R.A.; but he had no difficulty in attracting sitters – especially women, to whose portraits his style with its clean brushwork and clear, light colouring was particularly adapted, whereas his drawing and composition were noticeably weak. In 1782 he met and became infatuated with Emma Hart, afterwards Lady Hamilton, of whom he painted portrait after portrait, many in the theatrical poses in which she took delight. In later life he developed melancholia and lived as a recluse. He was one of the most esteemed English portrait-painters of the eighteenth century, although artistically excelled by Gainsborough and Reynolds.

Romulus Augustulus (born *c.* 461). Sometimes called the last Roman emperor of the West (475–476), a description convenient for the historian, but which has no constitutional justification and would have surprised his contemporaries. Romulus was a usurper set upon the throne by his father, a rebel general, the patrician Orestes. Almost immediately the German mercenaries rose against him and their leader Odoacer (Odovacar) killed Orestes, contemptuously spared Romulus's life and proclaimed himself king of Italy. The Roman empire reverted to its original constitutional form with a single ruler, now resident in Constantinople; a century later * Justinian reasserted the imperial power.

Ronsard, Pierre de (1524–1585). French poet. He was the son of a courtier and his boyhood was spent as a page in the royal service. He accompanied James V and his bride, Marie de Lorraine, to Scotland where he stayed for three years. In 1540 illness and deafness forced him to give up his career at court and after his father's death (1544) he went to Paris; here he became the centre of a small group of poets (later called the Pléiade) whose aim was to improve French poetry by a close study of

Greek, Latin and Italian verse, and by the introduction of new words and forms, e.g. the Petrarchan sonnet. The final test should be, as for music, that of the ear. Five books of Ronsard's *Odes* were published in 1550–52, and the *Amours*, sonnets addressed to his mistresses, first appeared in 1552. Henry II made him court poet (1554), an office which he retained under Francis II and Charles IX. The first collected edition of his poems appeared in 1560, and was constantly enlarged until his death, that of 1578 containing the *Sonnets to Hélène de Surgères*. In addition he wrote political poems, e.g. *Remonstrance au peuple de France* (1562), which reveal his patriotism, and the ambitious, disappointing and unfinished epic *La Françiade* (1572). Ronsard has been described as the 'prince of poets and poet of Princes'.

Armstrong, E., *Ronsard and the Age of Gold*. 1968

Röntgen, Wilhelm Konrad (1845–1923). German physicist, discoverer of X-rays. He became professor of physics at Würzburg (1885) after having had similar posts at Strasbourg and Giesse. There he discovered (1895) that when a high-voltage direct current is applied to a discharge tube containing a rarefied gas the resulting stream of electrons from the cathode, if made to bombard a metal target amode, will produce invisible rays capable of passing through many opaque substances. He also made notable contributions to other branches of physics; he won the first Nobel Prize for Physics (1901).

Rooke, Sir George (1650–1709). English sailor. He played a distinguished part at Cape La Hogue (1692), the anchorage where twelve French warships taking refuge after their defeat off Cape Harfleur (as well as many troopships and storeships assembled for an invasion of England to restore James II to the throne) were destroyed; in reward Rooke was promoted to be vice-admiral and knighted. Among other important successes was his capture of Gibraltar (1704) in conjunction with Sir Clowdisley Shovell.

Roon, Albrecht Theodor Emil, Count von (1803–1879). German field-marshal. After long service on the staff he was Prussian minister of war (1859–71) and effected the military reorganization which enabled victory in the Austro-Prussian War (1866) and the Franco-Prussian War (1870–71) to be achieved with such remarkable speed and success.

Roosevelt, (Anna) Eleanor (1884–1962). American journalist, political writer and wife of President Franklin Delano * Roosevelt, her cousin. She remained a popular public figure after the death of her husband in 1945, and also retained some political influence. She attended the first United Nations Assembly as a US delegate, and served on the United Nations Commission on Human Rights 1946–53.

Lash, J., *Eleanor and Franklin Roosevelt*. 1974

Roosevelt, Franklin Delano (1882–1945). 32nd president of the US (1933–45). Born into one of the most distinguished families of the country, he had had every educational and social advantage when, having already married (1905) a distant cousin, Eleanor * Roosevelt, he joined a New York firm of lawyers. Unlike the other branch of his family, he was a Democrat but opposed the corrupt Democratic machine, Tammany Hall, which dominated New York politics. Under President * Wilson, to whom he gave firm support, he was assistant secretary of the navy in World War I. In 1920, when Governor * Cox was the Democratic presidential candidate, Roosevelt was nominated for the vice-presidency, but the overwhelming Republican victory was a grave set-back to his political hopes. In 1921 he was afflicted with poliomyelitis which left him partly paralysed for the rest of his life. His fight to regain a measure of mobility and the internal battle which he fought and won against self-pity and despair strengthened his will, sharpened his intellectual power and instilled a deep compassion for human suffering.

Roosevelt returned to his law work (1922) and in 1924 and again in 1928 he supported the nomination of his friend Al Smith – whose biography, *The Happy Warrior*, he wrote – as Democratic candidate for the presidency, but the Republicans won on both occasions. Meanwhile Roosevelt was elected governor of New York and, though the financial depression of 1929 prevented him from carrying out much of his policy of social reform, he was re-elected in 1930 with a much larger majority; and at the Democratic convention of 1932 he won the Presidential nomination on the fourth ballot. President * Hoover, baffled and overwhelmed by the financial avalanche of the Depression, subsequently suffered a humiliating defeat, with Roosevelt carrying 42 of the 48 states and a total majority of over 7,000,000 votes. The 'New Deal', the instrument by which Roosevelt fought the Depression, brought governmental intervention and subsidies into economic enterprises on an unprecedented scale. He gathered round him, mainly from the universities, a team of economic advisers, known as the 'Brain Trust'. Important agencies (e.g. the National Recovery Administration) were created, vast industrial and hydro-electric schemes (e.g. that of the Tennessee Valley Authority) were put in hand, while at the other end of the scale work was found for hosts of unemployed people. Some of the measures were ill-conceived, some were ruled out by the Supreme Court as being unconstitutional (Congress thwarted Roosevelt's attempt to reconstitute the Court), but the 'Labour Code' which enforced collective bargaining with the trade unions and many measures of social amelioration had lasting results. Meanwhile the psychological effect was immense – 'the only thing we have to fear', cried Roosevelt, 'is fear itself, unreasoning terror that paralyses the will' – and in speech after speech and in broadcast 'fireside chats' he enlisted the people's co-operation and drove his lessons home. His reward came in the 1936 election when he carried all states but two and had a lead of 11,000,000 in the popular vote.

In foreign affairs Roosevelt had originally been an isolationist. He had signed without demur the Neutrality Act of 1935 – an Act which he himself was later to circumvent and modify. Gradually he began to voice his opposition to the dictators of Europe but he refrained from giving a decided and positive lead to public opinion. Although he helped Britain with the device of Lend Lease and built up a vast war potential it was not Roosevelt who took America into the war but the Japanese attack on Pearl Harbor. Roosevelt participated less in the planning and conduct of campaigns than * Churchill, but he was the inspirational force behind the whole mighty American war effort. He attended the great inter-Allied conferences – Casablanca, Cairo and Tehran – where the way to victory was planned. Meanwhile he had been elected (1940 and 1944) to a third and fourth term, an unprecedented sequence. In 1944–45 he gave energy and enthusiasm to the task of bringing the United Nations to birth, and in February 1945 he attended his last international conference at Yalta in the Crimea. In an attempt to conciliate and win the confidence of * Stalin he kept aloof from Churchill and made concessions and allowed ambiguities to stand which were to have unhappy consequences. For this he has been much criticized; his powers were already affected by his fatal illness: two months later he died of a cerebral haemorrhage at Warm Springs. Few men have been more honoured and revered by the world at large, but in America itself the superb political tactician was to his out-manoeuvred opponents nothing but a trickster, 'a traitor to his class' and a dangerous revolutionary. If his approach to his ends was sometimes devious he had the cause of the 'under-dog' at heart, and poverty, oppression and injustice were enemies which had to be fought with the same courage and persistence as he had fought his own handicaps.

Leuchtenberg, W. E., *Franklin D. Roosevelt and the New Deal, 1932–1940*. 1963. Schlesinger, A. M., *The Age of Roosevelt*. 3 vols, 1957–60

Roosevelt, Theodore (1858–1919). 26th president of the U.S. (1901–09). Born in New York into a rich family that had emigrated in the 16th century from Holland, he was admitted to the New York bar in 1881. As a Republican member of his state legislature (1881–84) he took his stand against corruption, but after the death (1884) of his wife (née Alice Hathaway Lee of Boston) and a breakdown of health he became a rancher in North Dakota. In 1886 he married Edith Kermit Carow of New York and he abandoned the outdoor life of a typical Westerner to return to politics. Unsuccessful in his bid for election as mayor of New York, he was appointed (1889) by President Harrison to the Civil Service Commission, from which he resigned (1895) to become president of the board of the New York City police. His spectacular attempt to break the link of corruption between police and underworld made him well known, in 1897 he was appointed assistant secretary of the navy. He resigned on the outbreak of war with Spain (1898) to raise a mounted force known as 'Rough Riders' for the Cuban campaign. On his return as a national hero he was elected governor of New York State, and showed in his legislation (e.g. the laws for slum clearance etc.) a zeal for social reform. In 1900 he was elected vice-president of the U.S.A. so that on the assassination of * McKinley (September 1901) he became president. He used the presidential power more vigorously than any holder of the office since * Lincoln. His re-election in 1904 followed almost as a matter of course. He helped to settle the great coal strike of 1902, inspired the fight against monopolies ('trust-busting'), the passage of the pure food act (1906) and the enforcement of laws against child and female labour. His interventions in foreign affairs, e.g. when troops were sent to Venezuela (1902) and Dominica (1904) and the seizure of the Canal Zone to facilitate the building of the Panama canal, were characteristic of his belief in forceful policies, further illustrated by his mediation which brought the Russo-Japanese War to an end (Treaty of Portsmouth, U.S.A., 1905) for which he was awarded the Nobel Peace Prize (1906). In 1908 he virtually insisted on the nomination of his friend W. H. * Taft, who succeeded him as president. The next year he spent hunting in Africa and touring Europe; on his return Taft's increasing conservatism could no longer command his support. However, the conservative wing prevailed and secured the nomination in 1912 of Taft; Roosevelt thereupon stood as the candidate of a new Progressive party. This Republican split brought the Democrats under Woodrow * Wilson back to power. Roosevelt made one more vain attempt (1916) to obtain Republican nomination; he was a vigorous advocate of America's entry into World War I.

Mowry, G. E., *The Era of Theodore Roosevelt, 1900–1912.* 1958

Root, Elihu (1845–1937). American politician. A lawyer and district attorney, he became President McKinley's secretary of war (1904–05) and was secretary of state under Theodore Roosevelt (1905–09). He won the Nobel Peace Prize (1912) for his work as a judge on the International Court at The Hague.

Rootes, William Edward Rootes, 1st Baron (1894–1964). British industrialist. With his brother, **Sir Reginald Claud Rootes** (1896–   ), he formed a company for selling cars, and later gained control of companies manufacturing Hillman, Humber, Singer, Sunbeam etc. cars. In 1951 he became chairman of the Dollar Exports Council and did much to stimulate British exports to the U.S.A.

Roper, Margaret (1505–1544). Eldest daughter of Sir Thomas * More. Her husband was More's nephew and subsequent biographer. William Roper. She saved her father's letters and treatises written while he was imprisoned in the Tower of London.

Rosa, Carl August Nicolas (1842–1889). German-born conductor and opera director. While on a concert tour in America he formed his first opera company which in 1871 he moved to London. His season at the Princess's Theatre in 1875 led to the creation of the Carl Rosa Opera Company which, playing year after year in London and the provinces, familiarized generations of British music lovers with the continental masterpieces and provided an operatic training for hundreds of British singers.

Rosa, Salvator (1615–1673). Italian painter. He was born near Naples and became a pupil of Aniello Falcone, whose taste for battle scenes he acquired. He went to Rome in 1635 and in 1640 to Florence, where he received the patronage of the Medici. Back in Rome (1649) he became popular, not only for his energetic landscapes in which with his fine use of chiaroscuro he often produced eerie and fantastic effects, but also for his other accomplishments as musician, satirist and poet; *Babylon*, his satire on Rome, won particular acclaim.

Salerno, L., *Salvator Rosa.* 1963

Rosas, Juan Manuel de (1793–1877). Argentine dictator. After winning popularity as a leader of irregulars in frontier defence against the Indians, he served as governor of Buenos Aires province (1829–32). More successes against the Indians resulted in his returning (1835) with full dictatorial powers. For the first time since 1810 the country had stable government, but the methods of terrorism by which it was achieved undermined the popularity of Rosas, and a Franco-British blockade when he intervened in Uruguay weakened the country's economic strength. He was defeated and deposed by General Urquiza (1852) and died in exile in England.

Levene, R., ed., *Historia de la Nación Argentina.* 3rd ed. 1961

Roscius, Quintus (d. 62 B.C.). Roman actor, the greatest comedian of his age. He won the patronage of Sulla and taught oratory to Cicero, who defended him in a surviving speech when he was sued for debt.

A boy actor, **William Betty** (1791–1874), was called 'the young Roscius'. To enable M.P.s to see his Hamlet the House of Commons was adjourned by Pitt (1805).

Rose, Sir Alec (1908–). English yachtsman. Noted for his single-handed circumnavigation of the world in *Lively Lady* in 1968, he became president of the British Junior Exploration Society in 1969 and of the British Wildlife Society in 1970.
Rose, A., *My Lively Lady*. 1968

Rosebery, Archibald Philip Primrose, 5th Earl of (1847–1929). English politician. Destined by birth and talents for success in politics, he first entered a Liberal government in 1881. In 1886 he first became foreign secretary and later returned to that office (1892–94), allying himself with his party's imperialist wing. He succeeded Gladstone as prime minister (1894) but resigned (1895) after a disagreement with his colleagues. He never returned to office and pursued thereafter a more and more independent line: he opposed, for example, the entente with France on the grounds that it would provoke a German war and produced a plan of his own for the reform of the House of Lords. He was an excellent orator, first chairman of the L.C.C., and a racehorse owner who won the Derby in 1894, 1895 and 1905. His historical studies, e.g. *Pitt* (1891) and *Napoleon, the Last Phase* (1901), reveal a distinguished literary style.
James, R. R., *Rosebery*. 1963

Rosenberg, Alfred (1893–1946). German writer and politician. He joined the Nazi party (1920), became editor of their official newspaper, and by his *The Myth of the Twentieth Century* (1920) did more than anyone else to propagate Nazi racialist doctrines. During World War II as minister for occupied territories in eastern Europe he used his opportunities to put his theories into brutal practice. For these atrocities he was condemned by the Nuremberg court and hanged.

Rosenberg, Julius (1918–1953). American Communist. An electrical engineer, Rosenberg, with his wife Ethel, née Greenglass (1916–1953), was convicted in 1951 on a charge of 'conspiracy to commit espionage in wartime' for passing in early 1945 technical details of detonation devices in US atomic weapons to the USSR (then an ally). The trial was conducted in an atmosphere of Cold War hysteria and they were both electrocuted. Freedom of Information disclosures indicate there was a reasonable case against Julius (although the penalty is now thought grossly excessive) but the case against Ethel was threadbare, relying entirely on allegations by her brother, David.

Ross, Harold (Wallace) (1892–1951). American editor. Co-founder of the *New Yorker* (1925), which he edited until his death, the magazine had a major impact on writing and cartooning. Ross promoted the work of * Thurber, * Arno, * Perelman, * White, * De Vries, Edmund * Wilson and many others.

Ross, Sir James Clark (1800–1862). British polar explorer. He was the nephew of the arctic explorer **Sir John Ross** (1777–1862), under whose command he discovered (1829) the magnetic pole. While leading a scientific expedition (1839–43) to the Antarctic for the British government he discovered Mounts Erebus and Terror (named after his two ships) and the Ross Ice Barrier. He was knighted on his return. The purpose of his last polar expedition (1848–49) was to search for Sir John * Franklin.
Dodge, E. S., *The Polar Rosses*. 1973

Ross, Sir Ronald (1857–1932). British bacteriologist, born in India. After qualifying as a doctor (1881) he served in the Indian Medical Service until 1889; during this time he studied the causes of malaria and concluded that it was transmitted by the female *Anopheles* mosquito. This discovery won him the Nobel Prize for Medicine (1902). While professor of tropical medicine at Liverpool University (1902–12) he carried his studies further in many expeditions to the tropics. He went to King's College Hospital, London, as physician for tropical diseases (1912) and became (1926) director of the Ross Institute founded at London University in his honour. He was knighted in 1911.
Ross, Sir R., *Memoirs*. 1923

Rossellini, Roberto (1906–1977). Italian film director. The son of an architect, he made propagandist films during World War II, then became a leader of the neo-realist school. His *Open City* (1945) was the first internationally recognized European film after the war; followed by *Paisan* (1946), *Ways of Love* (1948) and *Stromboli* (1949). His affair with Ingrid * Bergman led to an unofficial boycott of their films and his career never recovered, although he continued to be a prolific producer, screenplay writer and operatic director.

Rossetti, Christina Georgina (1830–1894). English poet of Italian extraction, sister of Dante Gabriel * Rossetti. Her first published verse appeared in 1847. She continued to write poems which showed an exceptional sense of beauty combined with strong religious instincts. The best known collections are *Goblin Market* (1862) and *The Prince's Progress* (1866).
Packer, L. M., *Christina Rossetti*. 1963

Rossetti, Dante Gabriel (1828–1882). English painter and poet. Born in London, he was a son of **Gabriel Rossetti** (1783–1854), a political refugee from Naples. Dante Gabriel studied art at the Royal Academy School, then with Ford Madox Brown, an important influence, and with Holman Hunt, at whose house he and * Millais discussed their aim of returning to the principles of pre-Renaissance painting by imposing upon themselves the disciplines of a noble subject, truth to nature and meticulous detail. The result was the formation in 1848, the year after Rossetti had written his best known poem *The Blessed Damozel*, of the Pre-Raphaelite Brotherhood. The paintings produced (among which was Rossetti's *Ecce Ancilla Domini*, now in the National Gallery, London) were received with such abuse that he was discouraged and after 1850 produced no important oil painting for ten years. In 1860 he painted an altar-piece for Llandaff cathedral, followed by portraits and pictures in a highly individual imaginative style, with jewelled colouring and of a dream-like character. The first of the new-style portraits was an ethereal, idealized representation of his dead wife, Elizabeth Siddal. Only two years after their marriage (1860) she had died from an overdose of laudanum. In despair he buried his poems with her and only in 1870 were they retrieved and published, but were attacked for belonging to the 'fleshly school of poetry'. His *Ballads and Sonnets* appeared in 1881. Meanwhile he had continued to paint. His most frequent model was the beautiful wife of William * Morris, with whose ventures in the applied arts Rossetti was closely connected. Of his other pictures the large *Dante's Dream* (1870) and *The Blessed Damozel* (1875–76) are among the best known. Partial paralysis marked the onset of his final illness.
Grylls, R., *Portrait of Rossetti*. 1965

Rossini, Gioacchino Antonio (1792–1868). Italian composer. Born at Pesaro, he studied at Bologna, but claimed that he had been more influenced by the music of Haydn and Mozart than by his teachers. At 14, he was already working in local theatres, and by the age of 21 he had composed a dozen operas including *L'Italiana in Algeri* (1813). In all he wrote nearly forty operas, serious and comic. Most of the latter enjoyed outstanding contemporary success for their vivacity, humour and biosterous spirits; the best known include *the Barbar of Seville* (11816), based on Beaumarchais – probably his best and certainly his most popular work – *La Cenerentola* (1817), and *Le Comte Ory*, which were triumphantly acclaimed in Vienna, Paris and London. Suddenly, at the age of 37, he abandoned opera composition and apart from a mass (1864) his only subsequent major work was his *Stabat Mater* (1832–41). There were also a few songs and piano pieces, some of which were later orchestrated by Respighi for the ballet *La Boutique fantasque* and by Benjamin Britten (*Soirées musicales*).
Weinstock, H., *Rossini*. 1968

Rostand, Edmond (1868–1918). French dramatist and poet, born in Marseilles. An early volume of verse, *Les Musardises* (1890), was followed by a series of light poetic plays; *Les Romanesques* (1894), *La Princesse Lointaine* (1896) and *La Samaritaine* (1897). Fame came with the play *Cyrano de Bergerac* (1897), based on the life of a 17th-century soldier and poet disfigured by his grotesque nose. This was followed by *L'Aiglon* (1900) about the life of the son of Napoleon and Marie Louise at the Austrian court: Sarah * Bernhardt played the young prince. *Chantecler*, a farmyard fantasy in which Lucien Guitry appeared (1910), proved disappointing. Rostand was elected to the Académie Française in 1901.

Rostovtzeff, Michael Ivanovich (1870–1952). Russian historian. He was a professor at St

Petersburg (Leningrad) from 1898 but after the Revolution went to the USA, where he was professor of ancient history at Wisconsin (1920–25) and Yale (1925–44). His best known work *The Social and Economic History of the Roman World* (3 volumes, 1941), is important in being the first application of archaeological research to expand and illuminate ancient history.

Rostropovich, Mstislav Leopoldovich (1927–). Russian cellist, pianist and conductor. He made his debut in 1942, became a professor of the Moscow Conservatoire in 1957 and subsequently gained an international reputation as a solo cellist. Many works were written for him by * Shostakovich, * Prokoviev, * Britten and other composers. In 1955 he married the soprano Galina Vishnevskaya. He left the U.S.S.R. in 1974 and became director of the National Symphony Orchestra, Washington, in 1977.

Rothenstein, Sir William (1872–1945). English artist. He studied in London and Paris and joined the New English Art Club (1894). As principal of the Royal College of Art (1920–35) he exercised a progressive influence on the succeeding generation of artists. He is best known for his portrait drawings; he drew many of the most notable when he was an official war artist in World War I. His *Men and Memoirs* (1932) contains fine examples of his work. His son, **Sir John Rothenstein** (1901–), well known as a critic and for his studies of Manet, Turner etc., was director and keeper (1938–64) of the Tate Gallery, London. He played an important part in familiarizing the British public with modern art by arranging many exhibitions.

Rothermere, Harold Sidney Harmsworth, 1st Viscount (1868–1940). English newspaper proprietor. He worked closely with his brother, Lord * Northcliffe, in many enterprises, providing the business acumen to match the other's journalistic flair. He brought the *Daily Mirror* (1914) and founded (1915) the *Sunday Pictorial*. He took over Northcliffe's business interests on his death and in turn handed them on to his son. As air minister (1917–18) he helped to create the R.A.F. from the Flying Corps and the Naval Air Service. He was made a viscount in 1918.

Camrose, W., *British Newspapers and their Controllers*. 1948

Rothko, Mark (originally Marcus Rothkovich) (1903–1970). American painter, born in Latvia, of Russian–Jewish parentage. His family migrated to the US in 1913, he grew up in Oregon and later studied painting in New York. After 1948 he became a leading figure of the Abstract Expressionist movement and his huge, brooding canvasses rely on the use of colour alone for their emotional impact. He is strongly represented in major US galleries and at the Tate in London. He committed suicide and the 658 paintings left in his estate were the subject of bitter litigation between his heirs and his agents.

Rothschild, Meyer Amschel (1743–1812). German banker. During the Revolutionary and Napoleonic Wars he ensured the family fortunes (whatever the outcome of the wars) by sending his sons to operate in different European capitals. The eldest stayed with his father at Frankfurt-on-Main and the others went to London, Paris, Vienna and Naples. **Nathan Meyer Rothschild** (1777–1836), the London representative, made more than £1,000,000 by arranging to receive speedy news of the result of the Battle of Waterloo and being able to speculate on the basis of knowledge. His son, **Lionel Rothschild** (1808–1879), was three times elected M.P. for the city of London, but took his seat only when the act removing Jewish disabilities was passed (1858). It was he who arranged the £4,000,000 which enabled Disraeli to secure for the British government a controlling interest in the Suez Canal. The next in line, another **Nathan Meyer Rothschild** (1840–1915), made a baron in 1885, was the first Jew to sit in the House of Lords.

Morton, F., *The Rothschilds*. 1962

Rouault, Georges (1871–1958). French painter. He was first trained as a glass painter, a fact recalled by the broad black outlines by which he later emphasized the luminous colours in his pictures. His earliest paintings were of religious subjects in the manner of his teacher Gustave Moreau. Later, as his constitutional pessimism deepened, he painted in passionate and horrified protest scenes in brothels or other places where human misery abounds. In his later work the horror changes to pity; he returns to religious themes, but they are painted with the same passion and reveal the same distortions as his pictures of everyday life. These distortions are a reminder of his

link with the group known as the 'Fauves'; but though he joined them he was never truly of them; the conventions they used for decoration he used for emphasis; he was in fact an isolated figure in the world of art. His pessimism is seen also in his etchings, e.g. *Miserere* and *Guerre* (reminiscent of Goya).
Courthion, P., *Georges Rouault*. 1962

Roubiliac, Louis François (*c.* 1695–1762). French sculptor. He was trained in France but did nearly all his work in England, where he lived from 1727 as a Huguenot refugee. His reputation was established by a statue of Handel made (1737) for Vauxhall Gardens. Strong modelling and subtle characterization distinguish his works, among which one of the finest is the statue of Newton at Trinity College, Cambridge. His sepulchral work includes the monument of the Duke of Argyll at Westminster Abbey (1749).
Whinney, M. D., *Sculpture in Britain, 1530–1830*. 1970

Rouget de Lisle, Claude Joseph (1760–1836). French author and composer. He wrote *La Marseillaise* (1792), the French national anthem, while an engineer officer in the Revolutionary army: it was adopted as a marching song by a Marseilles battalion bound for Paris and its stirring words and music soon gave it national fame.

Rous, Francis Peyton (1879–1970). U.S. physician. Educated at Johns Hopkins, he worked at the Rockefeller Institute for Medical Research from 1909 and in 1911 identified the first tumour virus, known as the 'Rous chicken sarcoma virus'. In 1966 he shared the Nobel Prize for Medicine for his work on the chicken virus: at 87 he was the oldest recipient of the award and the gap between research and recognition is a record (55 years).

Rousseau, Henri (known as 'le Douanier') (1844–1910). French painter. His nickname derives from his position as a customs officer (1871–85). He was thus 41 when he went to Paris to devote his time to painting. He was a naïve and natural painter belonging to none of the contemporary groups, but he was able to transfer to canvas with a wonderful child-like assurance the pictures that his vision saw, his memory recalled or his rich imagination conceived; it was as natural to him to paint streets, landscapes, neighbours as the mysterious jungles where tigers prowl. Animals and birds, human beings, he paints them all as they pass before his inner or outer vision, the colour schemes seeming the more original because they are seldom schemed at all. Gauguin, Seurat, Signac and Pissarro were among his friends and in 1908 Picasso gave a memorable banquet in his honour.
Uhde, W., *Henri Rousseau*. 1914

Rousseau, Jean-Jacques (1712–1778). French writer and political philosopher, and inspirer of the Romantic movement. His father, a Geneva watch-maker, abandoned him to relatives; he was apprenticed to an engraver but ran away from his harsh treatment, crossed the frontier into Savoy and found a refuge, half servant, half lover, with Madame de Warans, a lady of loose morals and an affectionate heart. In the years of vagrancy that followed he would always be welcomed back to her home and in the domestic interludes found time to study music, literature, and philosophy. In 1744 he was settled in Paris making a living by copying music and writing comedies, and having as mistress a kitchenmaid named Thérèse Levasseur with whom he lived for twenty-five years. Each of the five children she bore him he deposited on the steps of a foundling hospital, an inconsistency between principle and practice of which he became increasingly ashamed. Meanwhile his opera *Les Muses galantes* (1747) had led to a correspondence with Voltaire and an acquaintance with Diderot, for whose great *Encyclopédie* he wrote articles on music and political economy. His winning (1749) of a prize for an essay in which he argued that the arts and sciences merely corrupted the natural goodness of man may have encouraged him to develop the theme of the 'noble savage' which pervades much of his work. His political thoughts spring from the same romantic origins. In their natural state men are free, equal and good; it is institutions that have made them otherwise. His *Discours sur l'origine de l'inégalité parmi less hommes* (1755) explains how this came about. Even more influential was his *Contrat social* (1762). The famous opening words, 'Man is born free, but everywhere is in chains', show the same romantic starting-point, the problem of political association being to enable the noble impulses of free man to find collective expression. Much of the book relates to the way in which there can emerge in a community a 'general will' in which the individual wills of each participant will find identification. Sovereignty lies with the people as a whole and is the exercise of the general will. There is an implied contract that each individual hands over all his personal rights to the community on the understanding that the precepts of the general will are observed. Sophistries abound in the book; it provides an intellectual preparation for the French Revolution, but has equally provided texts in support of the state despotisms of our own times.

In *Emile* (1762) Rousseau uses the form of a novel to give views on education which closely resemble those described as 'modern' today. Education should release and not inhibit natural tendencies; a child's natural curiosity should provide the incentive to learn; experience rather than book-learning is the key to knowledge. In lighter vein *La Nouvelle Héloïse* (1761), a novel in the form of letters, again takes up the theme of 'return to nature' in the context of sex and the family. After his death were published his *Confessions* (1781), where vanity and candour often compete. There are to be found episodes of his childhood and early manhood, his inner reveries and descriptions of the beauties of nature; and though there are many lapses of judgement and taste in this book, it contains, with its supplementary volume, *Rêveries d'un promeneur solitaire* (1762), some of the most exquisite passages of French literature. Since *Emile* had provoked a threat of arrest, Rousseau went to Switzerland and then, on David Hume's invitation, to England. Signs of delusional insanity began to appear here. (He imagined Hume was plotting against him.) He returned to France (1770) still suffering at times from insanity and died eventually of a heart attack. In 1794 his remains were buried in the Pantheon near those of Voltaire.

Guehenno, J., *Jean-Jacques Rosseau*. 1966

Rousseau, Théodore (1812–1867). French landscape painter. He painted in the Auvergne and Normandy before he became a leading figure of the Barbizon school, called after a village in the forest of Fontainebleau (* Millet). Groupings of trees, marshy patches, all the quiet details of an unspoilt countryside are the subjects in which he takes unwearying delight.

Huyghe, R., *Millet et Rousseau*. 1942

Roussel, Albert (1869–1937). French composer. Originally a naval officer, he devoted himself to music from 1893, studying (1898–1907) under Vincent D'Indy in Paris at the Schola Cantorum, where he was also professor of counterpoint (1902–14). From 1918 he was forced by ill health to live in the country. His orchestral works include four symphonies and the ballets *Le Festin de l'Araignée* (*The Spider's Banquet*, 1912) and *Bacchus and Ariadne* (1930). He also wrote piano and chamber music. His sturdily individual style blends French influence with that of Stravinsky.

Rowe, Nicholas (1674–1718). English poet and dramatist. Among the best known of his plays were *Tamerlane* (1702), *The Fair Penitent* (1703) and *Jane Shore* (1714), the last two of which provided excellent parts for Mrs * Siddons. He also published a translation (highly praised by Dr Johnson) of Lucan's *Pharsalia* and an edition of Shakespeare in which he divided the plays into acts and scenes. He became poet laureate in 1715.

Rowe, N., *Dramatic Works*. 1971

Rowland, Henry Augustus (1848–1901). American physicist. Professor of physics of Johns Hopkins University (1867–1901), he developed methods of producing better and larger diffraction gratings, and made (1882) the first concave grating. The Rowland circle, a circle having the radius of curvature of a diffraction grating, is named after him. He improved on the determinations of the mechanical equivalent of heat made by * Joule; he also investigated electromagnetic effects and made an accurate determination of the value of the ohm.

Rowlandson, Thomas (1756–1827). English draughtsman and caricaturist. Extravagant tastes, love of travel and a zest for life, combined with a determination to pay his way to make him one of the most industrious and prolific of artists. Wherever he went, he drew; he is best known for his book illustrations (e.g. *A Sentimental Journey*, by Sterne, and *Baron Münchausen's Travels*) and political cartoons and caricatures, the quality of which he and his contemporary * Gillray raised almost to the level of a new art.

George, D. M., *Hogarth to Cruikshank*. 1967

Rowntree, Joseph (1801–1859). English Quaker philanthropist and chocolate manufacturer. He founded the firm at York that still bears his name and helped to found the Friends' Education Society (1837) as well as schools in York and elsewhere. His son, **Benjamin Seebohm Rowntree** (1871–1954), also combined his duties as head of the family firm with social work. His *Poverty* (1900) and *Poverty and Progress* (1941) resulted from social surveys in York, which set a pattern for later surveys and led to the foundation of the Industrial Welfare Society and similar organizations, in several of which he had a hand.
Brigg, A., *Seebohm Rowntree*. 1961

Royce, Sir Frederick Henry, 1st Bart (1863–1933). British engineer. He was founder (with C. S. * Rolls), and for many years engineer-in-chief, of the famous Derby firm of Rolls-Royce.
Bennet, M., *Rolls Royce Story*. 1974

Rubbra, Edmund Duncan (1901–). English composer, pupil of Vaughan Williams and Holst. His compositions include seven symphonies, a *Sinfonia Concertante* for piano and orchestra, piano and viola concertos, choral works (including unaccompained settings of the mass) and chamber music. He became a lecturer at Oxford University in 1947. Influenced by the polyphonic composers of the late 16th and early 17th centuries and in the main unaffected by modern trends, his music is reflective in manner.

Rubens, Sir Peter Paul (1577–1640). Flemish painter. He was born in Westphalia, where his father, a burgomaster of Antwerp, was living in exile during the religious wars. Rubens returned with his mother (1587) after his father's death, was trained as a court page and was taught art in local studios: but, prolific as he was, art never absorbed the full talents of this great and versatile man, who studied antiquity, absorbed the classics, learnt six languages and became an accomplished diplomat. In 1600 he went to Italy as court painter to the Duke of Mantua and in frequent travels had the opportunity of studying the works of the great Renaissance masters, especially Titian and Tintoretto. He absorbed with a natural eclecticism the features of each necessary for the maturing of his own style, which, as he gradually shed the effects on his early Manneristic training, displayed the full exuberance of the Baroque. In 1608 he returned to Antwerp where he became court painter to the Spanish regents. From his studios came a continuous flow of religious pictures, battlepieces and mythological subjects, portraits both singly and in groups. In the first category the *Descent of the Cross* can be contrasted with the *Raising of the Cross* (1610, both in Antwerp cathedral), the latter (and earlier) showing a much greater sense of strain; in the second category, the *Rape of the Daughters of Leucippus* is well known; and the first Bacchanales, the nudes revelling in their unrestrained sensuality, bear witness to the intoxicating joy of life. Among the portraits one of the artist himself with his first wife Isabella Brant (died 1626) is of special interest. By 1621, the year in which he depicted for Marie de Médicis, the French queen, episodes of her life in a magnificent allegorical sequence, Rubens had reached full maturity. Movement is freer, composition and colour more dramatic, draughtsmanship (e.g. his daring foreshortenings) confident and secure.

The death of his first wife left him freer to undertake confidential missions for which he was well equipped by his artistic and diplomatic talents. Thus he negotiated and painted in France (1620–28), in Spain (1628) and in England (1629–30) with Charles I, to whom he presented *Allegory of the Blessings of Peace*, for whom he designed the ceiling panels for the Banqueting Hall at Whitehall and from whom he received a knighthood. Whenever he was at home the outflow of his pictures continued; for this purpose he maintained an elaborate organization of assistants, of whom * Van Dyck was among the chief, others being employed for painting, e.g., fruit and flowers (Jan * Brueghel) or animals.

Rubens abandoned court life in 1633 and retired to his estate at Steen with his young second wife Helena Fourment whom he had married in 1630 and who appears in the nude as *Andromeda* and in several fine portraits, e.g. *The Fur Coat*. His subjects are little changed but outlines are softer, shadows less opaque and the colours more delicate, often with a silvery tone. Some of his most famous pictures belong to this period, e.g. *The Rape of the Sabines* (1635), *The Judgement of Paris* (1638–40) and the 'martyrdoms' (1635–40) e.g. *Crucifixion of St Peter*. Rubens ranks among the greatest of the world's artists not only because of the brilliance of his painting techniques, his superb draughtsmanship, inventiveness and observation, but also because his buoyant satisfaction with his life, his success, and with his art communicates itself through his work.

Wedgwood, C. V., *The World of Rubens, 1577–1640*. 1967

Rubinstein, Anton Gregorovich (1829–1894). Russian composer and pianist, first director of the St Petersburg conservatoire. He toured Europe and the U.S.A. as a pianist, but his many compositions, including operas, symphonies, cantatas, and chamber and piano music, are now hardly remembered.

Rubinstein, Arthur (1887–1982). Polish-American pianist, born in Lodz. He first played in public at 4, studied in Warsaw and Berlin, making his US debut in 1906. After an early reputation as a virtuoso, he gained a more serious reputation after 1930 as an interpreter of Chopin, Mozart, Beethoven and Ravel. A prolific recording artist, he toured incessantly for more than 60 years, appeared frequently on film and television, wrote a lively autobiography and was a witty raconteur.

Rudolf (1858–1889). Austrian archduke, only son of the emperor Francis Joseph. He married (1881) Stephanie, a daughter of the king of the Belgians, but he is remembered only for the tragedy that ended his life. In January 1889 the bodies of the prince and Baroness Maria Vetsera, the girl he loved, were found dead at the shooting box at Mayerling. Suicide was announced and can be presumed, but since all state records were destroyed the details remain obscure.

Rudolf II (1552–1612). Holy Roman Emperor (from 1576). He was one of the most ineffective rulers of the Habsburg dynasty, and after a halfhearted attempt to stiffen the laws against Protestants he ceased to play an active part in government and withdrew into his palace at Prague where he practised astrology, alchemy and, so it was said, demonology. His interest in more normal science was shown when, on Tycho * Brahe's departure from Denmark (1597), he gave him a pension and established him, with * Kepler as his assistant, in an observatory near Prague. In 1608 the Habsburg archdukes transferred their allegiance from Rudolf to his brother Matthias to whom the emperor ceded Hungary, Austria and Moravia. Rudolf retained only Bohemia, but this too had to be yielded in 1611.

Ruisdael *see* **Ruysdael, Jacob van**

Rumford, Benjamin Thompson, Count (1753–1814). Anglo-American scientist and administrator. He was born at Woburn, Mass., and from 1770 was a schoolmaster in Rumford, New Hampshire. His Anglophile views in the events which led to American independence caused him to go to England where he worked for the Colonial Office. His experiments with gunpowder won him election as F.R.S. He returned to America (1782) as a British officer, but the coming of peace (1783) brought him back to England and he was knighted. The next phase of his career, resulting from a friendship with Prince Maximilian, was in Bavaria where, as minister of war and police and also grand chamberlain, he introduced army education, drained marshes and established workshops, and provided relief for the unemployed. In 1791 he was made a count of the Holy Roman Empire, choosing his title from his former American home. He finally left Bavaria in 1799 and eventually settled in France where he died. In 1805 he married * Lavoisier's widow. Meanwhile he had endowed Rumford medals for English and American scientists, had conducted researches and had written a paper (1798) for the Royal Society concerning the causes of heat, his conclusion being that heat was not a substance but a form of motion. On the practical plane he designed ovens, grates and chimneys to avoid loss of heat.

Larsen, E., *An American in Europe*. 1953

Runcie, Robert Alexander Kennedy (1921–). English prelate. Before succeeding as archbishop of Canterbury (1980–) he had been bishop of St Albans (1970–80).

Rundstedt, (Karl Rudolf) Gerd von (1875–1953). German field-marshal. Born into an old Junker family, he fought in France, Russia and Turkey in World War I but despite his seniority he was passed over in favour of Brauchitsch for chief command in World War II. He proved himself one of the greatest German generals. He commanded an army group in Poland (1939); he directed the drive across the Meuse (1940), which reached the Channel ports; he was in charge of the great sweep through southern Russia (1941) and in 1942 was transferred to the West to prepare for, and resist (1944), the Allied attack. He was briefly supplanted by von Kluge owing to strategical disputes, and on his return staged the last spectacular counter-attack in the Ardennes. After the war he was held prisoner in England for a time but, ill and old, he was never sent for trial to Nüremberg.

Runeberg, Johan Ludvig (1804–1877). The national poet of Finland. His works, written (as was then customary) in Swedish, include the long narrative poems *The Elk-hunters* (1832) and *The Tales of Ensign Stal* (1848), an old soldier's memories of the war with Russia of 1808, the opening poem of which has become Finland's national anthem; *King Fjaler* (1844) is a romance cycle of the Viking period. Many of Runeberg's ballads and lyrics were set to music by * Sibelius.
Viljanen, L., *Runeberg ja häuen runoutensa.* 1944–1948

Runyon, Damon (1884–1946). American writer. Originally a sports writer, he gained fame by his stories and sketches of New York characters set down in a racy continuously flowing style to which the constant use of the present tense gives an exciting immediacy. Among his creations are Harry the Horse, Ambrose Hammer, Little Dutch, Ropes McGonagle and many more. Many of his tales have made successful films, e.g. *Guys and Dolls* (written 1931).

Rupert, Prince (1619–1682). Son of the elector Palatine Frederick V, and of Elizabeth, daughter of James I of Great Britain. After fighting in the Thirty Years War he went to England (1642) to support the cause of his uncle Charles I. His brilliance as a cavalry officer won many successes in the early part of the conflict, though his reckless impetuosity sometimes led him to continue the pursuit instead of returning to consolidate victory. Criticism of his surrender of Bristol (1645) caused him to demand a court martial, which acquitted him. After Charles's defeat and imprisonment he went to France and subsequently commanded the royalist fleet. He returned to England after the Restoration and served as an admiral in the Dutch Wars. His military exploits were supplemented by his achievements as artist, scientist and inventor. He attended meetings of the newly formed Royal Society and introduced (but probably did not invent) the mezzotint process. In 1668 he spent the winter in the Arctic, and he helped to found the Hudson Bay Company (1670).
Ashley, M., *Rupert of the Rhine.* 1976

Rurik (died 879). The semi-legendary founder of Russia's medieval dynasties. It is said that he reached Novgorod (*c.* 862) from Scandinavia and that after his death his descendants formed principalities in Kiev, Moscow and elsewhere. Indeed, until the failure of the Muscovite line led to the ascendancy of the * Romanovs, a usurper in even a small principality had a diminutive hope of success were he not of Rurik's blood. Even in later times Rurik's descendants were automatically styled 'prince'.

Rush, Benjamin (1746–1813). American chemist and medical practitioner. He studied medicine at the College of New Jersey, and subsequently at Edinburgh under Cullen and Black. He received an Edinburgh M.D. in 1769, then became Professor of Chemistry at the College of Philadelphia; in 1789 he moved to the chair of the Theory and Practice of Physick. His chemical thinking closely followed that of Black, but he was more original in his medical outlook. Whereas Cullen had explained most diseases in terms of the nervous system, Rush thought the arterial system more important. Thinking that most diseases originated from excessive tension in the arterial system, he became an enthusiastic exponent of reducing that pressure by heroic quantities of bleeding. Later in his life, his interest turned chiefly towards mental illness, having been placed in charge of the insane at Pennsylvania Hospital in 1787. His *Medical Inquiries and Observations Upon the Diseases of the Mind* (1812) is the first American work of psychiatry. Rush was an ardent supporter of American Independence, being a signatory of the Declaration. He was opposed to slavery and capital punishment, and a promoter of women's education, being a founder of Dickinson College. He was a teacher of importance, and one of the inspirational figures of American medicine.
Goodman, N. G., *Benjamin Rush.* 1934

Rusk, Dean (1909–). American diplomat. After a professorship at Mills College, California, and army service (1940–46), he was deputy under-secretary of state under Truman (1946–52), president of the Rockefeller Foundation (1952–61) and secretary of state under Kennedy and Johnson (1961–69). He took a leading role in negotiating for the nuclear test ban treaty (1963) but was a prominent 'hawk' during the Vietnam war.

Ruskin, John (1819–1900). English author and critic. The son of a wealthy London wine merchant, he was brought up in a cultured and religious family, but his mother's over-protectiveness undoubtedly contributed to his later psychological troubles. On his frequent trips in Europe, he took an artist's and a poet's delight both in landscape and in works of art, especially medieval and Renaissance. His first great work, *Modern Painters* (5 volumes, 1843–60), began as a passionate defence of Turner's pictures, but became a study of the principles of art. In *The Seven Lamps of Architecture* (1849) and *The Stones of Venice* (1851) he similarly treated the fundamentals of architecture. These principles enabled him, incidentally, to appreciate and defend the Pre-Raphaelites, then the target of violent abuse. To Ruskin the relationship between art, morality and social justice was of paramount importance and he increasingly became preoccupied with social reform. His concern inspired, among others, William Morris and Arnold Toynbee, whilst in the practical field he founded the Working Men's College (1854) and backed with money the experiments of Octavia Hill in the management of house property. He advocated social reforms which later were adopted by all political parties – old age pensions, universal free education, better housing.

Gothic was for Ruskin the expression of an integrated and spiritual civilization; classicism represented paganism and corruption; the use of cast iron, and the increasing importance of function in architecture and engineering seemed to him a lamentable trend. He was Slade professor of art at Oxford (1870–79 and 1883–84). His later works, e.g. *Sesame and Lilies* (1865), *The Crown of Wild Olives* (1866) and *Fors Clavigera* (1871–1884), contain the programme of social reform in which he was so interested.

Ruskin married (1848) Euphemia (Effie) Gray (the child for whom he had written *The King of the Golden River*) but in 1854 the marriage was annulled and Effie later married Millais. Ruskin did not marry again, although on other occasions he fell in love with girls much younger than himself, and his last disappointment over Rose la Touche contributed to the mental breakdown which caused him to spend his last years in seclusion at Brantwood on Lake Coniston, where he wrote *Praeterita*, an unfinished account of his early life. Much of his wealth he devoted to the 'Guild of St George', which he founded, and other schemes of social welfare.

Rosenberg, J. D., *The Darkening Glass*. 1961; Hilton, T., *John Ruskin: The Early Years*. 1985

Russell. Family of the Dukes of Bedford. The family fortunes were founded by John Russell, favourite of Henry VIII, who created him Earl of Bedford and gave him Woburn Abbey and other church lands. Drainage of that part of the Fens known as the Bedford Level was begun by Francis, the 4th Earl. William, the 5th Earl (1613–1700), who had helped to restore Charles II, was created 1st Duke (1694) by William III. The names of the Bloomsbury squares (Russell, Bedford, Woburn) recall an enterprising piece of property development by the Russell family. (* Russell, Bertrand; * Russell, Lord John; * Russell, Lord William).

Russell, Bertrand Arthur William Russell, 3rd Earl (1872–1970). English philosopher and mathematician, grandson of Lord John * Russell. He studied mathematics at Trinity College, Cambridge, of which he became a fellow in 1895. Having also studied philosophy (his *Philosophy of Leibniz* appeared in 1900) he was particularly well equipped to write (in collaboration with Alfred North Whitehead) *Principia Mathematicia* (3 volumes, 1910–13), an attempt to show that the truths of mathematics are derivable from the basic truths of logic; this great work had immense influence. The appearance of *Problems of Philosophy* (1912) marked a gradual transference of interest to less purely abstract fields. He had already abandoned his early Hegelian idealism for a form of realism demanded by his faith in mathematical truth. He now offered a theory of knowledge which had at its centre not idealistic inferences from the unkown but logical constructions out of sense-data and other ascertainable phenomena.

In contrast with the austerity of Bertrand Russell's academic thought is his exuberant championing of the unorthodox view in public life. A characteristic essay explained why he was not a Christian; he defended sexual freedom, and from a study of his own children established a progressive 'school'; in World

War I he was fined and imprisoned for pacifism. A visit to Russia disillusioned him about Communism. He abandoned his pacifist views in World War II, but later became a notable supporter of the Campaign for Nuclear Disarmament and the Committee of 100. Among his many honours were the OM (1949) and the Nobel Prize for Literature (1950).
Russell, B., *Autobiography*. Vol. 1 1967, Vol. 2 1968; Clarke, R. W., *The Life of Bertrand Russell*. 1975

Russell, Charles Taze (1852–1916). American preacher, founder (1872) of the International Bible Students. In 1884 the movement was formed into the Watch Tower Bible and Tract Society, the members of which became known (1931) as Jehovah's Witnesses. They hold extreme pacifist views and believe in the imminence of a second armageddon and a period of a thousand years when sinners will be given a second chance to reform and repent.

Russell, George William (1867–1935). Irish writer. Better known under his pseudonyms AE, A E and A.E., he was closely linked with other leaders of the Irish literary renaissance, notably W. B. Yeats, with whom he was associated in the creation (1904) of the Abbey Theatre, Dublin. Russell's drama *Deirdre* had been produced only two years before. Earlier he had joined Horace Plunkett's Agricultural Organization designed to improve the lot of the Irish peasant; and he was editor (1923–30) of the *Irish Statesman*. Among his prose works are *Imaginations and Reveries* (1915) and *Song and its Fountains* (1932); his poems are mostly mystical in content.

Russell, Lord John, 1st Earl Russell (1792–1878). British politician. The third son of the 6th Duke of Bedford, he was an MP almost continuously from 1813 until his elevation to the peerage. His nickname 'Radical Jack' indicated his support for all measures of civil and religious liberty. He was a member of Earl Grey's ministry which carried the parliamentary Reform Act of 1832, which Russell had a principal part in framing. As home secretary in Lord Melbourne's second ministry he passed the Municipal Reform Act (1835) and the Tithes Commutation Act (1836) but a moderate attempt to secure freer trade caused the defeat and fall of the government. To prove that he had the support of the financial community Russell stood for and was elected by the City of London, which he represented thenceforth. When * Peel became prime minister, Lord John was leader of the opposition; he pronounced (1846) in favour of complete repeal of the Corn Laws. The government fell but Russell was unable to form a ministry; Peel returned and having secured the repeal with Whig support was immediately defeated and again resigned. Russell now became prime minister and proved his worth by coping with the Irish famine and the Chartist agitation; but friction with * Palmerston, his foreign secretary (whom he dismissed), broke up the ministry. Russell was foreign minister in Lord Aberdeen's coalition but criticisms of the conduct of the Crimean War caused him to resign (1855). The compromise he tried to agree with Russia as British delegate to the Vienna conference was rejected by the cabinet and Russell was without office until in 1859 he came to terms with Palmerston, and as his foreign minister (1859–65) and as prime minister (1865–66) supported the unification of Italy under King * Victor Emmanuel and maintained British neutrality in the American Civil War. He resigned after failing to secure the passage of a new Reform Bill.
Walpole, S., *The Life of Lord John Russell*. 1889

Russell, Lord William (1639–1683). English Whig politician, son of the 5th Earl (later 1st Duke) of Bedford. He was a vigorous opponent of the court party and was executed for alleged participation in the Rye House plot to assassinate Charles II on his way back from Newmarket. Of Russell's ignorance of this conspiracy there is no doubt, but it is equally certain that he, Algernon Sidney and the more violent Whigs were planning rebellion. Popular indignation aroused by the unmasking of the Rye House plotters spread to the others and enabled a charge of treason to be maintained.

Russell, Sir William Howard (1820–1907). Irish-born journalist. The first and one of the greatest war correspondents, he had gained experience of reporting the stormy politics of Ireland before being sent as war correspondent for *The Times* to the Crimea. As well as thrilling readers with accounts of the great battles (Balaclava, Inkerman etc.) he shocked them by revelations of appalling sufferings caused to the troops by the failures of the

supply and medical services, the latter leading to the dispatch of Florence Nightingale. Later he reported the Indian Mutiny (and by his articles stayed indiscriminate punishments), the Civil War in America (where his impartiality offended both sides), and finally the Austro-Prussian, Franco-Prussian and Zulu Wars. He founded (1860) the *Army and Navy Gazette*.
Russell, W. H., ed. Bentley, N., *Despatches from the Crimea, 1854–1856*. 1970

Ruth, George Herman (known as 'Babe') (1895–1948). American left-handed baseball player. The most famous player of the era 1914–35, he established many records, e.g. the most home runs secured in a season (60 in 1927). He played for the Baltimore Orioles, the Boston Red Sox (1914–20) and the New York Yankees (1920–34). After retirement he coached the Brooklyn Dodgers.

Rutherford, Dame Margaret (1892–1972). English actress and comedienne. Famous for portraying the elderly eccentric, she was originally a teacher of elocution, and made her stage debut in 1925. Her most famous roles were Madam Arcati in *Blithe Spirit* (1941) and Miss Whitechurch in *The Happiest Days of Your Life* (1948). Her film career included the character of Miss Marple in the filmed detective novels of Agatha Christie. She was made D.B.E. in 1967.

Rutherford, Mark (William Hale White) (1831–1913). English novelist. Trained for the congregational ministry, he developed unorthodox views and entered the civil service. He is remembered for *The Autobiography of Mark Rutherford* (1881) and its sequels, works of sincere spiritual self-revelation. He wrote novels as well as critical and ethical works.

Rutherford of Nelson, Ernest Rutherford, 1st Baron (1871–1937). British physicist, born in New Zealand. After winning a post graduate scholarship he went to England and at Cambridge began the long series of fundamental researches into radioactivity and the structure of the atom for which he became famous. His progress was marked by professorships of physics at McGill University, Montreal (1898–1907), Manchester (1907–19) and the Cavendish chair at Cambridge (1919–37). With Soddy, he put forward (1903) the radioactive transformation theory, which showed that radioactivity arises from spontaneous disintegration of atoms; he also deduced the laws governing the transformations producing radioactivity. He suggested (1911) that the atom consists of a minute nucleus around which electrons orbit, and his model of the nuclear atom became the basis of modern concepts of atomic structure. He realized that if the atom could be split artificially very large amounts of energy would be released. He succeeded in transforming nitrogen into an isotope of oxygen (1919) and thus, for the first time, achieved transmutation of elements. Apart from his own important discoveries, Rutherford was a great teacher and had as pupils many scientists who became famous, e.g. Bohr, Cockcroft, Walton, Hahn, Chadwick and Oliphant. He won the Nobel Prize for Chemistry (1908), was knighted in 1914, admitted to the Order of Merit in 1925, and created a baron in 1931. He was President of the Royal Society (1925–30). He was a great experimenter and for him the next step was nearly always the right one. He was not only one of the greatest figures in the history of science but had a warm, open nature and a kindly common sense for which he was loved by pupils and contemporaries alike.
Chadwick, J., ed., *The Collected Papers of Lord Rutherford of Nelson*. 1962–1965

Ruysdael (or Ruisdael), **Jacob van** (1628–1682). Dutch landscape painter, born at Haarlem, and probably trained by his uncle **Solomon van Ruysdael** (*c.* 1600–1670). His quiet pictures of dunes, marshes, rivers and woodlands, mostly in golden-brown tones, are inspired with strong feeling and had much influence on the German Romantics, the *Mill at Wijk* being among the best known. His Scandinavian landscapes are also notable.

Ruyter, Michael Adrianzoon de (1607–1676). Dutch sailor. He first went to sea as a cabin boy in a merchantman, but having transferred to the navy was a captain by 1635. In the first Dutch War (1652–53), fought during the Commonwealth, he and Tromp contended with varying fortunes against the English admiral Blake. In the second Dutch War (1664–67) against England he captured forts on the African coast, preyed upon shipping in the West Indies and fought (1666) a four-day battle against Prince Rupert and Monk off Dunkirk. In 1667 he made sensational raids up the Medway to Rochester and the Thames to

Gravesend, burning ships as he went. In 1676 – Holland and England having come to terms – he took his fleet into the Mediterranean to aid Spain, but died from wounds after a defeat by the French off Sicily.

Rykov, Alexei Ivanovich (1881–1938). Russian politician. Originally a Social Democrat, he joined the Bolsheviks in 1905. He was arrested and imprisoned several times. After the Revolution he was head of the Supreme Economic Council (1917–24) and succeeded Lenin as premier of the U.S.S.R. (1924–30). Stalin dismissed him, but in 1931 he re-entered the government when he recanted his opposition to Stalin's policies. Charged with complicity in a plot to murder Stalin (1936) he was tried and executed.
Schapiro, L., *The Communist Party of the Soviet Union*. 1960

Ryle, Gilbert (1900–1976). English philosopher. Grandson of **John Charles Ryle**, the first bishop of Liverpool, he became Waynflete professor of metaphysical philosophy at Oxford in 1945. His influential work on the analysis of concepts culminated in *The Concept of Mind* (1949), in which he concluded that many concepts that have been usually considered as reflections of the introspective mind are in fact referable to tendencies to act or behave in particular ways.

Ryle, Sir Martin (1918–1984). British radioastronomer. He worked on radar during World War II, and at Cambridge (from 1945) developed new techniques involving the use of radar devices and, later, computers, leading to the aperture synthesis interferometer. He directed the Mullard Radio Astronomy Laboratory 1957–84, was a professor of radioastronomy at Cambridge 1959–84 and Astronomer Royal 1972–84. Discoverer of the quasar, he shared the 1974 Nobel Prize for Physics with Antony * Hewish.

Rysbrack, John Michael (1693–1770). Dutch sculptor who worked in England from 1720. He first worked for James Gibbs and William Kent on figures for tombs in Westminster Abbey (e.g. Matthew Pryor, Newton). Later the family tomb (1733) erected for the Marlborough family at Blenheim and the bronze equestrian statue of William III at Bristol led to a steady flow of commissions. He executed the statue of George II at Greenwich Hospital and many fine portrait busts (e.g. Pope, Milton and Sir Robert Walpole).

S

Saarinen, Eero (1910–1961). American architect, born in Finland. Son of the architect **Eliel Saarinen** (1873–1950), the family lived in the US from 1923. His buildings include the General Motors technical centre at Detroit, the TWA terminal at Kennedy Airport, the US Embassy in London, and major buildings at MIT, Yale and Dulles Airport, Washington.
Temko, A., *Eero Saarinen*. 1962.

Sabatier, Paul (1854–1941). French chemist. Professor of chemistry at Nîmes, Bordeaux and Toulouse, he is best known for his discovery (1899), with Senderens, of the method of converting oils into fats by hydrogenation over a catalyst of finely divided nickel. This is the basis of present-day manufacture of margarine from materials such as palm oil and whale oil. He won the 1912 Nobel Prize for Chemistry.

Sabatini, Rafael (1875–1950). English novelist, born in Italy. His popular historical novels and adventure stories include *Scaramouche* (1921), *Captain Blood* (1922) and *The Black Swan* (1932).

Sabine, Sir Edward (1788–1883). British soldier and scientist. After being commissioned in the Royal Artillery he accompanied several voyages of exploration as an astronomer. He carried out much research on terrestrial magnetism and discovered the connexion between sun-spots and magnetic disturbances on the earth.

Sacco, Nicola (1891–1927), and **Bartolomeo Vanzetti** (1888–1927). Italian anarchists, resident in the U.S.A. They were sentenced to death (1921) on circumstantial evidence for the murder of a cashier in Dedham, Mass., but it was widely believed that they were the victims of political prejudice. An international public outcry followed but an appeal was refused and both were executed.
Russell, J., *Tragedy in Dedham*. 1971

Sacheverell, Henry (1672–1724). English clergyman. He shared rooms with * Addison at Oxford and subsequently became well known as a 'high-church' preacher. He preached at Derby and St Paul's, in 1709, sermons so violent in their denunciation of the Act of Toleration and the Whig ministry that he was impeached and, despite his skilful defence and the encouragement of a yelling crowd of supporters outside, was suspended from preaching for three years. At the end of this time the government had changed, Sacheverell was invited to speak before the House of Commons and was made rector of St Andrew's, Holborn, where he is buried. Quarrels with parishioners and Jacobite intrigues occupied his remaining years.
Madan, F., *Bibliography of Dr Sacheverell*. 1887

Sackville-West, Vita (Victoria) (1892–1962). English poet and novelist. In *Knole and the Sackvilles* (1922) she tells of her own family and its historic home. Her long poem *The Land* won the Hawthornden Prize (1927). Her best known novel is *The Edwardians* (1930). She married (1913) Sir Harold * Nicolson, and was the lover of Virginia * Woolf.

Sadat, Mohamed Anwar el (1918–1981). Egyptian statesman. President of Egypt from 1970, he began his career in the army, being commissioned in 1938 and rising to the rank of colonel. He took part in the army officers' coup of 1952 which deposed King Farouk. He was minister of state 1955–56, speaker of the United Arab Republic National Assembly 1961–69 and member of the Presidential Council 1962–64. Vice-president of Egypt 1964–66 and again in 1969, he was elected president in October 1970 and was particularly noted for his initiative in going to Israel for peace talks in November 1977. His action put an end to a long-standing policy of Israeli-Egyptian confrontation. A peace treaty was finally signed in 1979. He shared the Nobel Prize for Peace with Prime Minister Begin in 1978. He was assassinated by dissident officers.

Sadat, M. A. el, *In Search of Identity*. 1978

Sade, Donatien Alphonse François, Marquis de (1740–1814). French author. He fought in the Seven Years War, and was imprisoned many times for crimes of wanton cruelty (hence the word 'sadism'). To avoid a death penalty he lived for a time in Italy but returned (1777) and was again imprisoned. Released in 1791, he began to publish a number of 'novels' (e.g. *Justine*) which are in part sexual fantasy, in part pseudo-philosophical attempts to justify his vices. He also wrote a melodrama, *Otiern*. He was confined on the orders of Napoleon in a criminal lunatic asylum where he died.

Gorer, G., *The Life and Ideas of the Marquis de Sade*. 1963

Sa'di (Muslih ibn abd Allah) (*c*. 1184–1291). Persian poet. His many books are concerned with morals and ethics and his long poem *Bustan*, and *Gulistan*, a miscellany in verse and prose, are still highly regarded and used as models of style for Persian schoolboys.

Sagan, Françoise (1935–). French novelist. Her books, *Bonjour Tristesse* (1954) and *Aimez-vous Brahms*? (1959), probed with frankness and subtlety the sexual relationships of sophisticated youth in her social environment and achieved immense contemporary success. Later novels had less impact. She also wrote the plays *Château en Suede* (1960), *Les Violons, parfois* (1961) and *Un piano dans l'herbe* (1970).

Saigo Takamori (1827–1877). Japanese field marshal. A samurai from Satsuma, he was a notable warrior, famous for his bravery and height (1.8m), who led imperial troops in the final overthrow of the shogunate. He urged invasion of Korea (1873) and resigned in a fury when his plans were rejected. He led the Satsuma revolt (January–September 1877) against foreign influence and the adoption of western technologies during the Meiji restoration, but was defeated by a conscript peasant army. Wounded in battle, he asked a friend to behead him. Japanese militarists in the 1930s regarded him as a hero.

Morris, I., *The Nobility of Failure*. 1980.

Saint Arnaud, Jacques Leroy de (1796–1854). French soldier. After achieving a high reputation in Algeria, he was created a marshal for helping to effect the *coup d'état* by which Napoleon III became emperor. He commanded French troops co-operating with the British in the Crimean War and took part in the Battle of the Alma; he died nine days later.

Saint Arnaud, J. L. de, *Lettres*. 1864

Sainte-Beuve, Charles-Augustin (1804–1869). French critic. After studying medicine he took to journalism and joined the group of Romantic writers of whom Victor* Hugo was the centre. Successful neither with his own poems nor a self-analytical novel, *Volupté* (1835), he turned to criticism, an art form much more suited to his natural scepticism. In a long series of critical studies beginning with *Portraits littéraires* (1832–39) and *Portraits de femmes* (1844), he arrived at his literary verdicts by identifying himself with the writers concerned, aided in this by his medical knowledge, psychological insight and analytical mind. His thoroughness is shown in his vast *Histoire de Port Royal* (1840–60) which in order to explain the characters and background of the learned members of this headquarters of Jansenism includes a series of vivid portraits of such great contemporary figures as Corneille, Molière, Racine. After the revolution of 1848 Sainte-Beuve withdrew for a time to Belgium, but soon returned, became reconciled with the new régime, was given teaching posts at the Collège de France and the École Normale Supérieure and with a critical article produced regularly week after week, became one of the great literary figures of the Second Empire, and is considered one of the greatest of critics.

Lehmann, A. G., *Sainte-Beuve: a Portrait of the Critic 1804–1842*. 1962

Saint-Evremond, Charles de Saint-Denis de (1616–1703). French critic and essayist. Having offended * Mazarin by incautious criticism, he was imprisoned in the Bastille and later took refuge first in Holland and then in England where he spent the rest of his life except for a five-year interval following a flight from the plague of 1665. From 1675 he was in devoted attendance upon Hortense, Duchesse de Mazarin, who had also fled from her uncle's displeasure. He kept in close touch with Paris, and the essays and correspondence of this wise and witty observer of the literary and political scene long remained popular. He was buried in Westminster Abbey.

Saint-Exupéry, Antoine Marie Roger de (1900–1944). French aviator and writer. He became a pilot in 1926, pioneered several commercial air routes, and despite his age flew for the French Air Force in World War II; he disappeared on a reconnaissance flight over Italy. Flying had always fascinated him, and he conveyed the rare sense of exaltation he derived from flying in books such as *Vol de nuit* (1931) and *Pilote de guerre* (1942). In this way he inspired a whole generation of flyers. Thought and fantasy make a successful blend in his children's story *Le Petit Prince* (1943).

Saint-Just, Louis Antoine Léon de (1767–1794). French revolutionary. He was one of the most implacable of the extremist section, which voted for the death of Louis XVI, and later turned against the Girondins. He was a member of the Committee of Public Safety, and a follower and friend of * Robespierre, whose downfall he shared. He was executed two days after his leader.
Curtis, E. N., *Saint-Just, Colleague of Robespierre*. 1955. Soboul, A., *Proceedings de Saint-Just Symposium*. 1968

St Laurent, Louis Stephen (1882–1973). Canadian Liberal politician. After a distinguished career as a lawyer he was brought into politics (1942) as attorney-general by his friend Mackenzie * King, whom, after a spell as minister of external affairs (1946–48), he succeeded as prime minister (1948–57).

Saint-Saëns, (Charles) Camille (1835–1921). French composer, pianist and organist, born in Paris. An infant prodigy, he first attracted recognition as a pianist, playing all Mozart's concertos and Beethoven's sonatas. Liszt praised him, especially as an organist, and he served at the Madeleine church 1857–77. He studied composition with Halévy at the Paris Conservatoire and was also an accomplished writer, linguist and amateur scientist. He promoted the music of Bach, Mozart and Wagner, and toured extensively, visiting Russia, the U.S., Uruguay and Algeria. Of his thirteen operas only *Samson et Dalila* (1877) remains in the repertoire; of five symphonies (only three of them numbered), the 'Organ' symphony No. 3 (1886) is often played and recorded. His best known work, *Le carnaval des animaux* (1886), a brilliant set of parodies, was not performed until 1922, at his direction, except for 'The Swan'. He also composed five piano, three violin and two cello concertos, *Marche heroique* (1871), *Le rouet d'Omphale* (1872) and *Danse macabre* (1875). He taught * Fauré and was a contemptuous antagonist of * Debussy and * Stravinsky.
Saint-Saëns, C. C., *Au courant d la vie*. 1914

Saintsbury, George Edward Bateman (1845–1933). English critic. He exercised an immense influence over more than one literary generation as professor (1895–1915) of English literature at Edinburgh University and by his many volumes on the history of criticism. *Scrapbook* (1922–24) and its successors cover a much wider area of reminiscence, opinion, and study.

Saint-Simon, Claude Henri, Comte de (1760–1825). French social philosopher, belonging to the same family as the Duc de * Saint-Simon. He fought in the American War of Independence, but during the French Revolution was suspect as an aristocrat and briefly imprisoned though he resigned his title. His 'experiments in living', undertaken to prepare him for his task as a social philosopher, reduced him to poverty, but his self-confidence was unbounded, as was shown by his unsuccessful proposal to Madame de Staël on the grounds that the marriage of two such remarkable people would produce an even more remarkable child. His thought was revealed in such books as *Du Système industriel* (1821) and the more important *Nouveau Christianisme* (1825). The latter contained his fundamental precept, which was the Christian 'Love one another'; this was to be put into practice by reorganizing society so that it should be controlled by industrial chiefs instead of military or feudal leaders and by

scientists instead of priests. His ideas were, however, diffuse and vague and Saint-Simon can be described as the 'founder of socialism' only by virtue of the activities of his followers and his influence on such thinkers as * Comte.
Booth, A. J., *Saint-Simon and Saint-Simonism*. 1971

Saint-Simon, Louis de Rouvroy, Duc de (1677–1755). French writer of memoirs. Having resigned a commission in the King's Musketeers because of failure to gain promotion, he attended court and from 1710 to 1723 he lived at Versailles, an embittered observer of a way of life he shared but affected to despise. After the death of Louis XIV (1715) he was a member of the regency council but never played an effective political role. His fame rests on his posthumously published *Mémoires* which he began to write in their final form in 1740. With malice and prejudice but with unique powers of memory and observation he recalls quarrels, love affairs, intrigues, dress, mannerisms and personal foibles with an authenticity and minuteness of detail seldom if ever equalled in descriptions of court life.
Saint-Simon, L., duc de, *Mémoires*. 1752, ed., Boislise, M. A. de, in *Les Grands Ecrivains* (43 vols.). 1879–1930

Sakharov, Andrei Dimitrievich (1921–). Russian nuclear physicist. A pupil of Peter * Kapitza and Igor Tamm, he gained his PhD for work on cosmic rays and led research on hydrogen fusion, playing a decisive role in creating the hydrogen bomb (1953). After 1958 he campaigned against nuclear proliferation, calling for Soviet–American friendship and a convergence of capitalism and communism in his *Progress, Co-existence and Intellectual Freedom* (1968). In 1970 he founded the Committee for Human Rights. He was awarded the Nobel Prize for Peace in 1975. In 1980 he was exiled to Gorky and kept under police surveillance. Reports of his failing health led to international concern about his welfare.

Saki (pen-name of Hector Hugo Munro) (1870–1916). Scottish author. Born in Burma where his father was inspector general of police, about 1900 he started in journalism in London as a political satirist on the *Westminster Gazette* and was the *Morning Post* correspondent in Russia and France (1902–08). The first of the volumes of fantastic, elegant and witty short stories for which he became famous was published in 1904 under his pseudonym and in 1912 appeared his novel *The Unbearable Bassington*. Interest in his work was later revived by television versions of many of his stories and a collected edition of his works (1963). He was killed in France during World War I.

Sala, George Augustus (1828–1896). English writer. A leading journalist of the Victorian age, he was a regular contributor to *Household Words* among others. He was special correspondent of the *Daily Telegraph* for the American Civil War and the Franco-Prussian War. He also wrote novels and travel books. He died bankrupt.

Saladin (Salah-al Din Yusuf ibn Ayyub) (1137–1193). Sultan of Egypt and Syria (from 1174). Born in Mesopotamia of Kurdish origin, he succeeded his uncle as vizier of Egypt (1169). In 1171 the caliph of the Fatimid dynasty in Egypt died. No successor was appointed and in 1174 Saladin was confirmed as sultan of Egypt and Syria by the caliph of Baghdad. He consolidated his hold over Syria, and conquered Mesopotamia (1180). He ruled his new empire from Damascus and in 1187 invaded the Christian kingdom of Jerusalem. The fall of the city provoked the 3rd Crusade, during which * Richard Coeur de Lion won back the coastal towns from Acre to Jaffa. Saladin retained Jerusalem but allowed pilgrims access. His chivalry was much admired by the Crusaders and he was a just and efficient ruler as well as a fine soldier; he built many roads and canals.
Lane-Poole, S., *Saladin and the fall of the Kingdom of Jerusalem*. 1926, repr. 1964

Salazar, Antonio de Oliveira (1889–1970). Portuguese dictator. Originally trained for the church, he became professor of economics at Coimbra University (1916) and was General Carmona's minister of finance from 1928 until 1932 when he was appointed prime minister. Thereafter, having introduced a modified form of fascism, he ruled as virtual dictator and rescued the country from financial chaos. He was sternly repressive of opposition but avoided any spectacular display of power. He kept Portugal neutral in World War II while proving his loyalty to the ancient British alliance by granting facilities in the Azores. In

1968 he suffered a stroke and was unaware that he was no longer premier at the time of his death in 1970.

Salieri, Antonio (1750–1825). Italian composer. He composed 44 operas, all of which have disappeared from the repertoire, and much instrumental, orchestral and sacred music. He served as court composer to the Habsburg emperors from 1774–88 (when Mozart was a young rival) and music director 1788–1824. Suggestions that he poisoned Mozart were revived in Peter Shaffer's play *Amadeus* (1979): the poisoning was almost certainly metaphorical. Salieri was a friend of Haydn and teacher of Beethoven and Schubert.

Salinger, Jerome David (1919–). American writer. He won acclaim with his novel *The Catcher in the Rye* (1951), the acutely-observed story of a boy's teenage problems. *Franny and Zooey* (1961) and his short stories continued to deal with the subject of adolescents' ways of seeing and problems.
Grunwald (ed.), *Personal Portrait*. 1964

Salisbury, Robert Arthur Talbot Gascoigne Cecil, 3rd Marquess of (1830–1903). British Conservative politician. He entered parliament in 1853 and held office (as Viscount Cranbourne) first in 1866 as secretary of state for India in Lord Derby's government but resigned (1867) over Disraeli's Reform Bill, returning to the same office in 1874. He was foreign secretary for twelve years (1878–80; 1887–92; 1895–1900) and found this office very congenial. He went with * Disraeli to the Congress of Berlin where he revealed an independent mind unhampered by party shibboleths. He served three terms as prime minister (June 1885–January 1886; July 1886–August 1892; June 1895–July 1902), a total of nearly 14 years. He declined a dukedom in 1886. He was mainly concerned with agreements which secured peace in Egypt and the Mediterranean lands, and with the problems of African partition. He worked closely with * Bismarck but refused an alliance. He was a keen amateur botanist and astronomer, bored with politics. His successors in the marquessate and his younger sons, Robert (Viscount * Cecil of Chelwood) and Hugh (Lord Quickswood), were all politically prominent.
Kennedy, A. L., *Salisbury, 1830–1903: Portrait of a Statesman*. 1953

Salisbury, Robert Cecil, 1st Earl of (1563–1612). English secretary of state. Son of Lord * Burghley, he succeeded to much of his father's power when he was appointed (1596) secretary of state by Queen Elizabeth. He dealt successfully with the rebellion of * Essex but was increasingly occupied with the intrigues by which he secured the succession of the Scottish James VI as James I of England. Not unnaturally he was retained in office (as lord treasurer from 1608): he discovered the Gunpowder Plot and was largely responsible for the downfall of Sir Walter * Raleigh, whose bellicose attitude towards Spain conflicted with his own pacific policy. Salisbury showed wisdom and moderation as a ruler but lacked his father's personality and was extremely conscious of the spinal deformity which gave him a dwarf-life appearance. He was created Baron Cecil (1603), Viscount Cranbourne (1604) and Earl of Salisbury (1605). He devoted much time to the building and adorning of the palace known as Hatfield House, still the family seat.

Salk, Jonas Edward (1914–). American physiologist. During World War II he was a consultant on epidemic diseases and afterwards held a series of professorships at the University of Pittsburgh. He produced (1954) a successful vaccine against poliomyelitis. In 1963 he founded the Salk Institute for Biological Studies at La Jolla, California, which he directed until 1975. He married the painter Françoise Gilot, Picasso's widow.

Sallust (Gaius Sallustius Crispus) (86–35/6 B.C.). Roman historian. Having served under Caesar and enriched himself as a proconsul in north Africa, he bought Caesar's villa at Tivoli, there built the famous 'Sallustian gardens' and settled down to write histories of the Catiline conspiracy and the Jugurthine wars as well as the more general *Histories*, of which only fragments survive.
Syme, R., *Sallust*. 1964

Samson. The strong man of the Bible, one of the 'judges' of Israel and probably an authentic hero of the war against the Philistines. The Bible tells how he was charmed by the Philistine Delilah to reveal that the secret of his strength lay in the flowing locks on one who had taken the Nazarite vow. She cut off his hair, and thus weakened, he was captured, blinded and taken to Gaza, where with a last effort of renewed strength he pulled down the supporting pillars of the temple, killing both himself and his enemies. Milton's *Samson Agonistes* is a poetic reconstruction of the tale.

Samuel (fl. *c.* 1040 B.C.). Hebrew prophet. When the nation was hard pressed by the Philistines, inspired by God and yielding to the persuasions of the people, he anointed Saul as the first of the Israelite kings.
Hertzberg, H. W., *I and II Samuel: A Commentary*. 1964

Samuel, Herbert Louis Samuel, 1st Viscount (1870–1963). British politician and administrator. He became an M.P. in 1902 and held ministerial posts in the Liberal administrations of * Campbell-Bannerman and * Asquith. He was home secretary when he resigned in 1916. After World War I he was British high commissioner in Palestine (1922–25) and again home secretary (1931–32) in the national coalition. He wrote with distinction on philosophic and autobiographical themes, including *In Search of Reality*. 1957

Samuelson, Paul Anthony (1915–). American economist. Educated at Chicago and Harvard, he was a professor of economics at the Massachusetts Institute of Technology 1940– , was a proponent of * Keynes' ideas during wartime government work and wrote a standard text *Economics* (1948), which has remained in print. He advised the Kennedy and Johnson administrations and won the 1970 Nobel Prize for Economics.

Sancroft, William (1617–1693). English prelate. After living abroad during the Commonwealth period he returned at the Restoration and rose quickly in the church to become dean of York and (1664) of St Paul's, and (1678) archbishop of Canterbury. The same outspokenness which he is said to have used at Charles II's death-bed marked the dealings of this robust Tory High-churchman with later monarchs. He was the leader of the seven bishops tried by order of James II for presenting a petition against having to read out publicly the Declaration of Indulgence, their acquittal being regarded as the starting point of the Glorious Revolution. However, having taken an oath of allegiance to James, Sancroft refused one to William and Mary; he was therefore deprived of his see and was ejected from Lambeth Palace. He retired to the Suffolk village where he was born.

Sand, George (Aurore-Lucile Dupin) (1804–1876). French novelist. She was brought up by her grandmother, an illegitimate daughter of Marshal de Saxe, at the château de Nohant, in the province of Berry; it is now a museum maintained in her memory. She grew up with feminist views, an independent mind and romantic disposition. After an incompatible marriage to Baron Dudevant, she went to Paris (1831) where she lived with Jules Sandeau, from whose name her pseudonym was derived. Her novels tended to be linked with the circumstances of her life: *Indiana* (1832) glorifies free love, *Elle et lui* (1859) and *Lélia* (1833) relate to her love affair with * Musset; her socialism inspired other novels. Meanwhile her search for the perfect lover went on but she could offer only an excess of sentiment or maternal care for the passion demanded. Her love affair with the exiled and ill * Chopin (1838–47) was the nearest to her needs but even that progressed with bickering and ended with bitterness. The château at Nohant was her most constant and abiding love and there after 1848 she retired to write rustic novels, e.g. *La Mare au Diable* (1846), and to show in her *Histoire de ma vie* (20 volumes, 1855) and her *Correspondance* (1882 and 1904) that her own life and character were more interesting than anything she could invent.
Toesca, M., *The other George Sand*. 1947

Sandburg, Carl (1878–1967). American writer. He led a wandering life collecting folk songs and ballads, and writing his own poems in the idiom of the country people he met. His collecting produced, e.g., *The American Songbag* (1927); his own verse is in such books as *Smoke and Steel*. His most ambitious enterprise was a four-volume biography of Abraham Lincoln (1926–42) which won the 1940 Pulitzer Prize for history. His *Collected Poems* won the 1951 Pulitzer Prize for poetry.
West, R. (ed.), *Selected Poems of Carl Sandburg*. 1926

Sanderson, Frederick William (1857–1922). English schoolmaster. As headmaster of Oundle School (from 1892) he introduced large workshops and laboratories, and by providing facilities for practical instruction in technical and scientific subjects in addition to the academic curriculum of the time was a pioneer who greatly influenced modern education.

Sandow, Eugen (1867–1925). German 'strong man'. Born in East Prussia of Russian parents, he displayed feats of strength on the stage and set up a physical culture school in London. His name continued to symbolize extreme muscular development long after the man himself had been forgotten.

Sandwich, John Montagu, 4th Earl of (1718–1792). English politician. Despite notorious profligacy he held several ministerial posts during an undistinguished career, including more than one term as first lord of the Admiralty. The Sandwich islands (now Hawaii) were named after him by Captain * Cook. He is best known for inventing the sandwich to enable him to eat without interrupting his play at cards.

Sanger, Frederick (1918–). British biochemist. Educated at Cambridge, he worked for the Medical Research Council 1951–83. He won two Nobel Prizes in Chemistry: in 1958, for determining the first complete structure and the amino-acid sequencing of a protein (bovine insulin); in 1980, sharing the award for work on determining the chemical structures of elements in DNA. He became a CH in 1981.

San Martin, José de (1778–1850). South American liberator. Having returned to Spain with his parents from South America as a child, he served with the Spanish army in the Peninsular War but in 1812 again crossed the Atlantic and volunteered his services to the revolutionary government of Buenos Aires. In 1816 independence was declared with his support. Regarding the whole of Spanish America as a single country he enlarged the area of independence by a daring march over the Andes, by passes 12,000 ft high, into Chile; the Spaniards were defeated at Chacabuco, and Santiago occupied. Chileans and Argentineans, helped by a naval contingent under * Cochrane, now combined to liberate Peru. San Martin occupied Lima (1812) and declared himself 'protector', but the interior was still in Spanish hands while * Bolívar had reached Ecuador. The two 'liberators' met but, as they were unable to agree, San Martín with characteristic self-denial withdrew. He left South America (1824) and died in poverty and exile at Boulogne.

Santa Anna, Antonio López de (1797–1876). Mexican soldier and politician. Having helped to overthrow * Itúrbde he led a successful Liberal revolution in 1828. He forced the surrender of a Spanish expedition sent to recover Mexico and in 1832–33 became president. Two years later, having seized dictatorial powers, he resigned to lead a campaign to secure Texas but was defeated and captured. Victory over a French debt-collecting expedition (1838) made him again a popular hero; another period of dictatorship (1841–46) was followed by exile, but he returned to lead the Mexicans to defeat against the U.S.A. (1847–48). In 1853 he was again dictator, but was once more overthrown in 1855. After many years of exile, and an unsuccessful landing in 1867, he was allowed to return (1872) but never regained power.
Muñoz, R. F., *Santa Anna*. 1936

Santayana, George (1863–1952). Spanish-born philosopher and poet. Though he was brought up in the U.S.A. and was educated at Harvard, where he later had a long academic career, he continued to think of himself as a European and never became a U.S. citizen. In his philosophy he was sceptical about proving the existence of matter or indeed anything, and suggested that ordinary beliefs derive from 'animal faith'. His view of the world was thus a species of naturalism. He also accepted, in a somewhat poetic way, the existence of a realm of universals or essences similar to the 'forms' of * Plato. His philosophical ideas are contained in *The Life of Reason* (5 volumes, 1905–06), *Scepticism and Animal Faith* (1923) and the 'realm' series, *The Realm of Essence* (1927), . . . *of Matter* (1938) and . . . *of Spirit* (1940). His more general books include *Sense of Beauty* (1896), a novel, *The Last Puritan* (1936), two volumes of poetry and autobiographical works. All reveal the author's wisdom and cultivated wit.
Cory, D., *Santayana: The Later Years*. 1963. Howgate, G. W., *George Santayana*. 1938

Santos-Dumont, Alberto (1873–1932). Brazilian aviation pioneer. After building balloons and airships in France he experimented with aeroplanes and was the first man to fly one in France (1906). He committed suicide.

Sappho (born *c.* 600 B.C.). Greek poetess, born in Lesbos where she spent most of her life. Her poems, with one or two exceptions, survive only in fragments. Passionate, graceful and intensely personal, they are mostly addressed to a group of young women, perhaps fellow devotees of the love goddess Aphrodite. She was married and had at least one daughter. Enough remains of her work to support the belief of the ancients that she was the greatest poetess of their time.

Saragat, Giuseppe (1898–). Italian president. He led a minority group of Socialists which broke away from Nenni's leadership in protest against the alliance with the Communists, and he founded (1947) the Social Democratic party, which entered into coalition with the Christian Democrats. He was deputy premier (1947–49 and 1954–57) and was president from 1964 to 1971.

Sarasate (y Navascues), Pablo Martin Meliton (1844–1908). Spanish violinist and composer. A brilliant player in the * Paganini tradition, he wrote many works which have remained in the repertoire, including *Zigeunerweisen* (1878) and *The Carmen Fantasy* (1883).

Sarasvati, Dayanand (1820–1883). Indian religious reformer. He founded (1875) an association called the Arya-Samaj which claimed for all Hindu castes the right to study the Vedas. The many adherents of the society form one of the most progressive elements of modern Hinduism.

Sardou, Victorien (1831–1908). French writer. The most successful playwright of his day, for forty years from 1860, when he was first acclaimed, he produced success after success, the result not only of his superb technique but of his gift for creating parts specially adapted to the particular talents of the great players of his time. Thus the title roles of *Fedora* (1882), *La Tosca* (1887) and *Gismonda* (1894) were created by Sarah * Bernhardt and the comedy *Madame Sans-Gêne* (1893) was written for Réjane. He also wrote for Irving and others. His plays now seem artificial, and revivals are rare.

Sargent, John Singer (1856–1925). American artist. He was born in Florence and studied painting there and in Paris. He moved to England (1884) and soon won great success as a fashionable portrait-painter. If his work sometimes seems too facile, he showed at his best a brilliant technique (e.g. in evoking the shimmer of stain) modelled on that of * Velazquez, and an eye for character, which could at times be almost too penetrating (e.g. the Wertheimer portraits at the Tate Gallery, London) for the comfort of his sitters. In America he worked on a series of decorative paintings for public buildings, including the *Evolution of Religion* for Boston library.

Sargent, Sir Malcolm (1895–1967). English orchestral conductor. He became chief conductor of the Royal Choral Society in 1928, and built up a great popular reputation with the Hallé and Liverpool orchestras, showing particular skill in blending singers' voices with orchestral accompaniment. He conducted the B.B.C. Symphony Orchestra (1950–57).

Sargon I (3rd millennium B.C.). Mesopotamian king. After being a royal cupbearer he founded the Accadian dynasty and extended his kingdom from Syria to the Persian Gulf.

Sargon II (reigned 722–705 B.C.). King of Assyria. He inaugurated a period of great expansion by conquering Elam and Babylonia, subduing the Medes and extending his power from Anatolia to Egypt. He exiled whole nations of conquered peoples to the remoter reaches of his territories. The excavations of his palace at Khorsabad bear witness to his magnificence.

Saroyan, William (1908–1981). American author of Armenian descent. His first work was a volume of short stories, *The Daring Young Man on the Flying Trapeze* (1934). Since then he has written a number of novels and plays, including *The Time of Your Life* (1939) for which he was awarded (but did not accept) a Pulitzer Prize. *The Human Comedy* (1943) exemplifies the simplicity and optimism of much of his work.

Saroyan, W., *The Bicycle Rider in Beverly Hills*. 1952

Sartre, Jean Paul (1905–1980). French existentialist philosopher, playwright and novelist. A teacher of philosophy before World

War II, he was imprisoned by the Germans (1941) and after his release joined the French Resistance. His philosophy is sometimes summed up in the dictum that 'man's existence precedes his essence', by which is meant that a man's essence or essential being is determined by the facts of his nature. Standing alone in a godless world, man can, within the limits of these facts, determine and develop his own essence: thus men choose to make themselves what they become and they are therefore responsible for what they are. His major philosophical work is *L'Etre et le néant* (1943; *Being and Nothingness*) and an introduction to some of his views is contained in *L'Existentialisme est un humanisme* (1946). His literary works are largely vehicles for his ideas; they include the plays *Les Mouches* (1942; *The Files*), *Huis-clos* (1944; *In Camera*), *Le Diable et le bon Dieu* (1951; *Lucifer and the Lord*), *Nekrassov* (1956), and *Les Séquestrés d'Altona* (1959; *Altona*); the short stories in *Le Mur* (1939); and the novels *La Nausée* (1938; *Nausea*) and the series of novels *Les Chemins de la liberté* (1945). He lived for many years with the French feminist writer Simone de * Beauvoir. He was awarded, but declined, the 1964 Nobel Prize for Literature.
Belkird, A. J., *Jean-Paul Sartre*. 1970

Sassoon, Siegfried Lorraine (1886–1967). English poet. The disgust produced by his experiences in World War I produced the fierce satire of *Counter-attack* (1918) and *Satirical Poems* (1926). He also wrote a series of semi-autobiographical works including *Memoirs of a Fox-hunting Man*, which won the Hawthornden Prize (1929), *Memoirs of an Infantry Officer* (1930) and *Sherston's Progress* (1936). Other books more directly autobiographical followed, e.g. *The Old Century* (1938).
Sassoon, S. L., *Siegfried's Journey 1916–1920*. 1945

Satie, Erik Alfred Leslie (1866–1925). French composer. He lived in obscurity until, from 1910, he was hailed as leader of the younger, more advanced composers, notably of the groups 'L'Ecole d'Arcueil' and 'Les Six'. His work, harmonically advanced, also influenced Ravel and other contemporaries. He wrote limpid, beautiful piano works with eccentric titles (e.g. *Three Pear-shaped Pieces* and *Limp Preludes for a Dog*), ballets, e.g. *Parade* (1917), the more serious symphonic drama *Socrate* (1919), and a *Messe des pauvres* (1895).
Myers, R., *Erick Satie*. 1948

Sato Eisaku (1901–1975). Japanese politician. The younger brother of * Kishi Nobusuke, he gained a law degree at Tokyo Imperial University and became a railway administrator until he became a member of the Diet 1949–75. A follower of * Yoshida Shigeru, he was a major figure in forming the Liberal Democratic Party, served as finance minister 1957–60 under his brother, and minister of nuclear science, energy and technology 1960–64. As prime minister 1964–72, he was identified with Japan's rapid economic expansion and concluding the 1969 Sato-Nixon treaty with the US. The award to him of the Nobel Prize for Peace in 1974 was greeted with some international scepticism. Sato was a complex character—forceful and ruthless, but also a gifted calligrapher.

Sauckel, Fritz (1894–1946). German Nazi politician. During World War II he was in control of manpower in occupied territories and was responsible for the deportation of millions of slave labourers. He was hanged after condemnation by the Nuremberg court.

Saul (11th century B.C.). The first king of Israel. He was anointed by the prophet * Samuel in response to the need for a single warrior king to lead the Hebrew tribesmen in unity against the Philistines. Saul was at first successful, but his jealousy of David and the bitter quarrel that followed so weakened national unity that he was defeated by the Philistines and killed at the Battle of Mount Gilboa.

Saussure, Horace Benedict de (1740–1799). Swiss scientist. He was a professor at Geneva University and gained fame for his exhaustive studies of Alpine botany, geology and meteorology. He offered a prize won (1786) by two guides, for the first ascent of Mont Blanc; he himself made the climb in the following year. His *Voyage dans les Alpes* (1779–96) is a personal record of many expeditions.
Freshfield, D. W., *The Life of Saussure*. 1920

Savage, Michael Joseph (1872–1940). New Zealand politician. He arrived from Australia in 1907, entered parliament in 1919, and in 1935 became the first Labour prime minister of New Zealand. His pledge to Britain at the outbreak of World War II became historic; 'Where she goes we go – where she stands we stand'. He died in office.

Savage, Richard (1697?–1743). English poet. His biography by his friend Dr Johnson, which is chiefly responsible for his being remembered, is based on a now discredited story. He assails his supposed mother, Ann, Countess of Macclesfield in the poem *The Bastard* (1728). His other works include a poem in five cantos, *The Wanderer* (1728), described by Johnson as 'a heap of shining materials thrown together by accident', and the tragedy *Sir Thomas Overbury* (1723). He died in a debtors' prison. He is the subject of an eponymous novel by Gwyn Jones (1935).

Savery, Thomas (1650?–1715). English engineer. He patented (1798) a 'fire engine' which by direct steam pressure could raise water to a height of 40–50 ft. The patent did not expire until 1733 and was held to cover the very different engine of Thomas * Newcomen. Savery was elected F.R.S. in 1705.

Savonarola, Girolamo (1452–1498). Florentine preacher. In 1475 he became a Dominican friar; he was sent to the convent of S. Marco in Florence in 1481 and again in 1490, after which he gained enormous influence by his sermons denouncing corruption, sensuality and luxury. When the 'Scourge' constantly predicted by him came (1494) in the form of the French army, which drove out the Medici, he emerged as the dominating figure of the new republic. Many great works of art (as well as rich dresses and other signs of luxury) perished in the 'bonfire of vanities' on the grounds that they commemorated pagan cultures. Savonarola was blamed for the inefficient administration of the republic as well as for his adherence to the French alliance. He was excommunicated (1497) by Pope * Alexander VI who was building an alliance against the French; his opponents in Florence gained the upper hand and after a trial by papal commissioners for heresy, Savonarola with two companions was strangled and burned.

Ridolfi, R., *Life of Girolamo Savonarola*. 1959

Saxe, Maurice, Comte de (1696–1750). French soldier. Usually known as Marshal de Saxe, he was an illegitimate son of * Augustus II of Saxony and Countess Auora von Königsmarck. As a boy he ran away to join Marlborough's army in Flanders; in 1711 he was fighting with Russo-Polish forces, and next with Prince Eugène against the Turks. Made Duke of Courland, he had to withdraw in 1729 and thereafter fought only for France. In the War of the Austrian Succession he invaded Bohemia and took Prague (1741). He became a marshal in 1744, and defeated the Duke of * Cumberland at Fontenoy (1745), and again at Laffett (1747), where as on other occasions he lost the full benefit of victory by failure to pursue. He wrote a book on the art of war, *Mes Rêveries* (1757).

Saxo Grammaticus (late 12th century). Danish chronicler who wrote the Latin work *Gesta Danorum* (16 volumes). The early books relate episodes from the Danish and Norse legendary past (including the story of Hamlet); the last two record recent events of the years 1134–1185. The surname 'Grammaticus' was added in the 15th century to indicate his learning.

Say, Jean Baptiste (1767–1832). French economist. In preparation for a business career he spent some of his early years in England. On his return to Paris he became a journalist and wrote effectively about the new economic theories of Adam * Smith. He was the most influential economist in France: his chief work was *Traité d'économie politique* (1803). He later lectured on political economy at the Conservatoire des Arts et Métiers and (from 1831) at the Collège de France.

Sayers, Dorothy Leigh (1893–1958). English writer. She wrote many detective novels also valuable as literary works, e.g. *Busman's Holiday* (1933) and *The Nine Tailors* (1934), in which the hero is an aristocratic detective, Lord Peter Wimsey. Her religious works include the series of radio plays *The Man Born to be King* (1942), and she also translated Dante's *Inferno* (1949) and *Purgatorio* (1955).

Sayers, Tom (1826–1865). English prizefighter. A brutal bare-fisted fight (1860) between Sayers and the American J. C. Heenan, both of whom were injured, roused such indignation that the modern type of boxing contest under Queensberry rules (1865) was introduced.

Scaliger, Joseph Justus (1540–1609). French scholar of Italian descent. He was the son of the scholar **Julius Caesar Scaliger** (1484–1558), who was notorious for his scurrilous attacks on Erasmus. At the university in Paris he acquired a complete mastery of Greek and Latin and some Hebrew; he also became a Protestant. After travels in Italy and England he was professor (1570–72) at Calvin's academy at Geneva and then for twenty years lived in France with the Roche-Pozay family. During this time he produced the editions of Catullus, Tibullus and Propertius which made him famous, and above all his *De Emendatione Temporum* (1583) by which he is ranked as the founder of the modern science of chronology. He spent his last years at Leyden University preoccupied with controversies engendered by his arrogant disposition, which did not prevent his recognition as one of the greatest scholars of the age.

Scanderbeg *see* **Skanderbeg, George Castriota**

Scarlatti, Alessandro (*c.* 1659–1725). Italian composer, born at Palermo in Sicily. He was *maestro di cappella* (i.e. court or household musician) to the eccentric Queen * Christina of Sweden in Rome, to the viceroy of Naples, and to Cardinal Ottoboni. He wrote over 100 operas of which thirty-five survive, as well as about 600 cantatas for solo voices, and choral works. He is believed to have invented or introduced the *aria da capo* which was of fundamental importance in 18th-century opera. For the opera *Tigrane* (1715) horns were introduced into the orchestra.
Dent, E. J., *Alessandro Scarlatti.* 1960

Scarlatti, (Giuseppe) Domenico (1685–1757). Italian composer and harpsichordist, the son of Alessandro * Scarlatti. In Rome he wrote operas for the queen of Poland, and church music for St Peter's. He lived in Spain from 1729 and there wrote his famous harpsichord sonatas of which over 550 survive; they mark an important stage in the development of sonata form.
Kirkpatrick, R., *Domenico Scarlatti.* 1953

Scarron, Paul (1610–1660). French writer. He was known (from 1643) as a writer of burlesque verse, but equally successful was *Le Roman comique* (1651–57), a satiric novel about strolling players which provided an agreeable contrast to the artificial romances then in vogue. From 1638 he was half-paralysed; when a beautiful 15-year-old girl, Françoise d'Aubigné, was taken to visit him (1651) she wept in pity. The pity was mutual: it grieved him that so lovely a girl should be so poor; he offered to provide a dowry and when she refused he himself proposed marriage. They were married in 1652 and she showed her gratitude by watching over his health and his career for the rest of his life. She was later better known as Madame de * Maintenon.
Mazne, E., *Scarron et son millieu.* 1924

Schacht, Hjalmar Horace Greeley (1877–1970). German financier. He became president of the Reichsbank in 1923; under Hitler he alternated this appointment with ministerial posts in the economic field and was admired for the manoeuvres by which he enabled German rearmament to be financed. He claimed at the Nuremberg trials that he had never been a Nazi and was acquitted. A sentence of imprisonment by the German denazification court was quashed on appeal.
Schacht, H. H. G., *My First 76 Years.* 1955

Scharnhorst, Gerhard Johann David von (1756–1813). Prussian officer. After the Prussian defeats in the Napoleonic Wars he undertook (1817) the complete reorganization of the Prussian army, and forged the more efficient forces which won victories (e.g. Leipzig, 1813) against the French.

Scheel, Walter (1919–). Federal German politician. He served in the Luftwaffe during World War II, became a merchant banker and was a Bundestag member 1953–74 and leader of the Free Democratic Party 1968–74. He was Vice-Chancellor and Foreign Minister 1969–74, and President of the Federal Republic of Germany 1974–79.

Scheele, Karl Wilhelm (1742–1786). Swedish chemist. He made many important discoveries while working as an apothecary. He discovered oxygen in 1772 (two years before Joseph * Priestley did so independently) but did not publish his findings until 1777. He was the first to prepare chlorine, phosphorus, hydrogen sulphide, glycerine, and many organic acids. He also discovered the action of light upon silver salts, a reaction basic to photographic reproduction.
Zekert, O., *Life of Carl Wilhelm Scheele.* 1931

Scheer, Reinhold von (1863–1928). German sailor. During World War I he was appointed (1916) commander-in-chief of the high sea fleet and was in command at the Battle of Jutland (* Jellicoe).

Schelling, Friedrich Wilhelm Joseph (von) (1775–1854). German philosopher. He began teaching as J. G. Fichte's successor at Jena and ended his long academic career at Berlin, having been called there (1841) by Frederick William IV. Starting as a believer in Fichte's philosophy of the 'ego', Schelling, under the influence of * Spinoza and Boehme, arrived at a form of pantheism – in his view the Absolute unifies the subjective conscious self and the external natural world, both of which possess a spiritual value though the one is antithetical to the other.
Sandkuehler, A., *Friedrich Wilhelm Joseph Schelling*. 1970

Schiele, Egon (1890–1918). Austrian expressionist painter and designer. A follower of * Klimt, he developed a tight linear style and his figure drawings show great virtuosity. Also an important painter, he died of influenza, aged 28.

Schiller, Ferdinand Canning Scott (1864–1937). English philosopher. He taught at Corpus Christi College, Oxford (1897–1926) and later became a professor at the University of Southern California. His chief contribution to English philosophy was his part in the revival of the empirical tradition. Under the influence of William James, with whom he formed a friendship in early life, he emphasized that the primary cause of human thinking is the need to act; and indeed he looked on pragmatism as a form of philosophical humanism, which rejected, as secondary or unreal, metaphysical idealism and the formal logic that so often fortified it. He had a deep knowledge of the physical sciences, wrote on eugenics, and was an active member of the Society for Psychical Research. His more general works include *Studies in Humanism* (1907) and *Logic for Use* (1929).

Schiller, Johann Christoph Friedrich von (1759–1805). German poet and dramatist. He was born at Marbach near Stuttgart, his father being a captain in the service of the Duke of Württemberg, at whose instigation the promising boy became (1773) a pupil at the new academy for officers and public servants. He became an army surgeon but absented himself without leave to watch a performance of his first play *Die Räuber* (1782; *The Robbers*) at Mannheim. For a similar offence he was briefly imprisoned; he fled from the Duke's service and took refuge at Mannheim where after an interval he was appointed theatre poet. He continued to write plays but it was after a move (1785) to Leipzig and Dresden, on the invitation of admirers, that he completed his first dramatic masterpiece *Don Carlos* (1785), which, though involved with the fate of the unhappy son of Philip II of Spain, finely expressed the 18th-century ideals of political and religious liberty. His next moves were to Weimar and Jena where he held a historical professorship (1789–99) and published his *History of the Revolt of the Netherlands* (1788) and *History of the Thirty Years War* (1789–93). After an illness from which he was slow to recover, he studied * Kant's philosophy, especially those parts relating to aesthetics, and himself wrote essays on such subjects as the nature of tragedy, the meaning of beauty, and aesthetic education. His philosophic poems of this time reflect the same themes. From 1794 he was a close friend of * Goethe and in 1799 he settled at Weimar in order to be near him. To the last period of his life belong some of his greatest plays, *The Death of Wallenstein* (1799), *Mary Stuart* (1800), *The Maid of Orleans* (1881) and *William Tell* (1804). He is also well known for his lyrics and ballads (e.g. *Die Glocke*, in which the processes of casting a bell symbolize the events and influences that make up the life of man).
Mainland, W. F., *Schiller and the Changing Past*. 1957

Schirach, Baldur von (1907–1974). German Nazi politician. He was youth leader of the Nazi party (1936–40) and Gauleiter of Vienna (1940–45). He was sentenced to twenty years' imprisonment by the Nuremberg tribunal.

Schlegel, August Wilhelm von (1767–1845). German critic. In 1797 he became professor of literature at Jena, and his lectures there and at Berlin and Vienna provide a clear exposition of the romantic viewpoint. He is best known, however, for his translations of Shakespeare's plays (1798–1810) and of Dante, Calderón and Camões. His brother, **Friedrich von Schlegel** (1772–1829), is regarded as the finest critic produced by the Romantic movement and, with * Hegel, one of the most important influences on German thought of his period. He also wrote poetry and a novel, *Lucinde* (1799), based on his own love affair with a daughter of the philosopher Moses Mendelssohn. He was among the first in Germany to study Sanskrit.

Schleicher, Kurt von (1882–1934). German general and politician. He served on the general staff in World War I and became politically important in 1932 as defence minister in June and chancellor in December. His attempt to find a basis of power by alternately angling for the support of the Nazis and of the trade unions lost him the confidence of all. He resigned early in 1933 and was murdered during the Nazi purge of 1934.

Schleiden, Mathias Jacob (1804–1881). German botanist. Born at Hamburg, he studied law at Heidelberg and practised for a time in his home town. He proceeded to study botany at the Universities of Göttingen and Berlin, and became professor of botany at Jena. He retired in 1864. His life-long concern was to orientate botany away from the obsession with classification which had followed from the work of * Linnaeus. His interest was in plant physiology, with cellular structure and growth. With * Schwann he helped to formulate the notion of the cell structure of plants. He believed – wrongly – that cells formed out of a nucleus and then became encased in cell walls. Schleiden pursued a great variety of plant studies with the aid of the microscope. He was involved with the pathology of plants, and investigated fungoid infections which attacked plant roots. He was a famous teacher, and his text-book, *Die Pflanze und ihr Leben*, achieved great popularity.

Schlesinger, Arthur Meier, Jr (1917–). American historian. After being professor of history at Harvard (1954–61) he became special assistant to President Kennedy. His books include *The Age of Jackson* (Pulitzer Prize 1945) and *The Age of Roosevelt* (3 volumes, 1957–60).

Schlieffen, Alfred, Count von (1833–1913). German soldier. He was a staff officer in the Prussian Wars of 1866 and 1870. He later developed a strategic plan for future wars by which France would be attacked through Belgium whilst only a holding operation would be fought on the Russian front. This plan was more or less closely followed in both 1914 and 1940.

Schliemann, Heinrich (1822–1890). German archaeologist. The discoverer of the site of Troy, he was fascinated by Homer from childhood, and while in a variety of occupations he dreamed of proving that the Homeric stories had a historical basis. In 1846 he went for his firm to St Petersburg and as a contractor during the Crimean War he amassed a fortune, which enabled him to retire (1863) and devote himself to archaeology. Delays over permission to excavate kept him from Troy until 1872 but meanwhile he had discovered evidence of the Mycenaean civilization: by 1884 he had excavated not only Troy but Mycenae and Tiryns also. Plans to excavate Knossos and Ithaca were frustrated by his death. He wrote several books about his discoveries, including *Troia* (1884), written in collaboration W. Dörpfeld who had worked with him there and at Tiryns.
Poole, L and G., *One Passion, Two Loves*. 1966

Schmidt, Helmut (1918–). German statesman. He joined the Social Democratic Party in 1946 and became a member of the Bundestag in 1953, serving until 1962 and again from 1965. Chairman of the Social Democratic Party in the Bundestag 1967–69, he was appointed minister of defence 1969–72, minister of finance 1972–74 and federal chancellor 1974–82. He had been also active in Land politics in his native Hamburg as manager of transport administration 1949–53 and senator for domestic affairs 1961–65.
Schmidt, H., *Balance of Power*. 1970; *Als Christ in der Politischen Entscheidung*. 1976

Schnabel, Artur (1882–1951). German pianist, teacher and composer. Resident from 1939 in the U.S.A., he became famous throughout Europe and America for his interpretation of the German classics, notably Beethoven. His compositions are in Schönberg's manner.

Schnitzler, Arthur (1862–1931). Austrian physician, dramatist and novelist. His medical profession made him interested in psychological problems, usually erotic but sometimes morbid. He is at his best in cycles of short plays, e.g. *Anatol* (1893), *Reigen* (1900), in which one or more characters of one play are carried on into the next. (The French film *La Ronde* was based on his work.) Schnitzler was a Jew, and the theme of *Professor Bernhardi* (1912) is conflict between a Jewish doctor's sense of duty and Roman Catholic principles in an antisemitic country.

Schönberg, Arnold (1874–1951). Austrian composer. Largely self-taught, his early works, e.g. *Transfigured Night* (1899) for string sextet and the huge *Gurrelieder* (1901) for four soloists, four choruses and large orchestra, are in a romantic post-Wagnerian idiom. He then began a process of discarding traditional harmony that was completed in *The Book of the Hanging Gardens* (1908; settings of Stefan George) and the mono-drama *Erwartung* (1909). The works of this period are often called 'atonal' but Schönberg preferred the term 'atonic' since, though he had never abandoned the key system, he employed tonic centres. In *Pierrot Lunaire* (1912) a cycle for singer employing 'speech song' and instrumental accompaniment, he evolved the 'twelve-tone row'; according to this system a given composition is based throughout on the twelve notes of the chromatic scale arranged in a particular order. Almost all Schönberg's work from the *Serenade* (1921–23) onwards were composed according to this method, notably the Violin Concerto (1936), the String Quartets Nos. 3 and 4, the *Ode to Napoleon* (1943) and the opera *Moses and Aaron*, which was unfinished at his death. He lived in Vienna (apart from a few years in Berlin) until at 51 he became professor at the Prussian Academy of Arts in Berlin. He was dismissed by the Nazis in 1933 and after a brief stay in Paris he went to the U.S.A. where he taught in New York and Boston and then became a professor at the University of California.

Schönberg's 12-note row or serial system was one of the most important innovations in the history of music. His radical breakthrough with tradition gained even wider influence through his two great pupils, * Berg and * Webern, who died in his lifetime.

Reich, W., *Schoenberg: A Critical Biography*. 1971; Rosen, C., *Schoenberg*. 1975

Schopenhauer, Arthur (1788–1860). German philosopher of metaphysics. Best known for his view that will is the reality of the universe, he was a lecturer in philosophy at Berlin (1820–31) and suffered a dramatic reverse when he deliberately lectured at the same time as * Hegel and did not win away students. Influenced by eastern philosophy, he stressed the existence of human suffering and is sometimes called the philosopher of pessimism. His major work is *The World as Will and Idea*, the will being the active principle, a blind irrational impulse, a term which includes all active processes, even those of gravity or motivation. The 'idea' on the other hand was merely something received, a brain picture, a nothing of itself and with no exploratory function such as would be implied in such phrases as 'intellectual intuition'. Schopenhauer's ethical system rests on sympathy, which to him is much more than fellow-feeling – the actual identification of self with another. But asceticism he places even above sympathy, since through it is attained the subjection of the will to live and the intellect is freed to pierce the veil of illusion. Schopenhauer spent the last thirty years of his life in isolation at Frankfurt-on-Main. He gained little acceptance until old age and received few academic distinctions. His subsequent influence has been partly due to his emphasis on the irrational.

Gardiner, P., *Schopenhauer* 1963. Huebscher, A., *Schopenhauer: Gespräche*. 1971

Schreiner, Olive (1862–1922). South African novelist, now remembered only for *The Story of an African Farm* (1883), an outspoken story of life in a Boer homestead and of spiritual problems similar to her own. It showed a rebellious attitude to the subordination of women and caused much controversy at the time.

Schrödinger, Erwin (1887–1961). Austrian physicist. He was educated at Vienna University and held a series of academic appointments there and elsewhere before becoming (1940) professor of physics at the Insitute for Advanced Studies, Dublin. He has been largely responsible for the development of wave mechanics, for which he deduced the fundamental equation (Schrödinger's wave equation). This makes it possible to treat atomic structure on a more mathematical basis than is permitted by * Rutherford's mechanical model. With * Dirac, Schrödinger won the Nobel Prize for Physics (1933).

Scott, W. T., *Erwin Schrödinger*. 1967

Schubert, Franz Peter (1797–1828). Austrian composer, born in Vienna where he spent most of his life. He showed precocious musical talent, and from 1808 studied at the choir school which provided singers for the Imperial Court chapel. In 1813, the year he left school, he composed his first symphony; in 1814, when he went to teach at his father's school, he composed his first opera *The Devil's Pleasure Palace*, the first six masses and the first of his great settings of Goethe, *Gretchen at the Spinning Wheel*. In 1816 he gave up schoolteaching and henceforward led a more or less hand-to-mouth existence, sometimes becoming a private music master (e.g. in Count Esterházy's household) but more often giving lessons as opportunity arose and enjoying the companionship of his many friends. By 1822 when he reached full maturity he had written six of his nine symphonies, had tried and failed at opera, and had composed many hundreds of songs with which he gave poems of Goethe, Schiller, and other Romantics immortality. And yet it is to the last years of his life that some of his best work belongs, e.g. the song cycles *Die Schöne Müllerin* (1823) and *Die Winterreise* (1827); the famous eighth (*Unfinished*) Symphony (first performed 1865) and the ninth (the *Great* C Major; first performed in 1839); the String Quartets in A Minor, D Minor (*Death and the Maiden*), and G Major and the String Quintet in C Major. The misfortunes of his last years – ill health, financial difficulties, failure (1826) to obtain salaried posts – were offset by belated appreciation. Beethoven bestowed praise. Schubert was elected to the Vienna Philharmonic Society and then to others. In March 1828 his only public concert took place in Vienna, where in November he died.

Schubert was the first great Austrian composer to express the pleasure-loving, nostalgic and partly rustic atmosphere of Vienna (e.g. in the many songs and dances in which folk influence is discernible). In his orchestral works he imbued the Viennese classical tradition with qualities inherently romantic and above all with melodic fertility. His lyricism, which has never been surpassed, found its finest expression in his songs. He founded the 19th-century lieder and indeed the whole of the modern art of song.

Brown, M. J. E., *Schubert: A Critical Biography*. 1958

Schumacher, Ernst Friedrich (1911–1977). British economist, born in Germany. He lived in Britain from 1937, worked for the National Coal Board, then devoted himself to promoting 'intermediate' and alternative technology. His book, *Small is Beautiful* (1973), was a major best seller.

Schuman, Robert (1886–1963). French politician, born in Luxembourg. He first became a deputy in 1919, played an active part in the Resistance during World War II and after the war was a prominent member of the M.R.P. (Mouvement Républicain Populaire). He was prime minister (1947–48) and as foreign minister (1948–53) in ten administrations he proved himself a strong supporter of European integration; the so-called 'Schuman plan' led to the European Coal and Steel Community (ratified 1952). In 1958 he became the first president of the European Parliamentary Assembly.

Schumann, Elisabeth (1888–1952). German soprano. She sang opera and lieder, and was a member of the Vienna State Opera 1919–37. Much of her international success came from her recordings of songs by Schubert. She settled in New York in 1938.

Schumann, Robert Alexander (1810–1856). German composer, born in Zwickau in Saxony. He showed early musical ability but went as a law student to Leipzig, where he was unhappy, and to Heidelberg where law competed unsuccessfully with music and a gay and extravagant social life. Music carried the day when he became a piano pupil in the house of Wieck, the father of Clara Josephine (1819–96) whom Schumann married (1840). She became a brilliant concert pianist and made repeated tours in Europe. Meanwhile any hopes that Schumann had of being a virtuoso player were shattered by an injury to his right hand. He founded and edited *The New Journal of Music* (Leipzig, 1834–44) in which his vividly written criticisms did much to promote the reputations of * Chopin and * Berlioz. Of his compositions in this first period the set of piano pieces known as *Carnaval* were inspired by an early love affair, while his love for Clara is immortalized in the C Major Fantasia, the *Kreisleriana* and several other works for piano. In the year of his marriage he was absorbed by the romantic poems of Heine, many of which he turned into songs. In 1841 he turned to composition on a more extended scale; the Symphony No. 1 (*Spring*), the first version of the Symphony No. 4 and the first movement of the Piano Concerto (completed 1845) date from this year; in 1842 there followed three String Quartets and the piano Quartet and Quintet. His first large choral work, *Paradise and the Peri*, was finished in 1843. A move to Dresden with its opera house suggested experiment in the theatrical field (e.g. incidental music for Byron's *Manfred*). The directorship of the Düsseldorf Orchestra (1849–1853) proved too much for his health and mental stability, and despite the solace of the friendship of the young Brahms, he tried to drown himself (1854) and spent his last two years in an asylum at his own request.

Except for the Symphony No. 3 (*Rhenish*) and two Violin Sonatas, Schumann's many works in the last phase show a decline in creative power. With notable exceptions he was not at his best in the large instrumental works which demanded extended abstract musical thinking. He made his unique contribution in those miniature forms (the character piece for piano and the song) which he was able to fill at the prompting of a poet's idea. His *Dichterliebe* cycle and *Liederkreis* collection (both 1840) provide the perfect musical counterparts to the romantic poetry of Heine and Eichendorff respectively, and Schumann is ranked amongst the greatest of song composers.

Chissell, J., *Schumann*. 1967

Schumpeter, Joseph Alois (1883–1950). Austrian economist. He served as minister for finance (1919–20) in the first Austrian republican government, became professor of economics at Bonn in 1925 and in 1932 moved to the US where he held a Harvard chair until his death. His *Capitalism, Socialism and Democracy* (1942) and *History of Economic Analysis* (1950) were enormously influential. His wife, Elizabeth Boody, was an economic historian.

Schuschnigg, Kurt von (1897–1977). Austrian politician. He became a Christian Socialist deputy in 1927 and held a number of ministerial offices before becoming chancellor after the murder of * Dollfuss. On the arrival of Nazi troops (1938) he resigned to avoid bloodshed. During the German occupation of Austria he was imprisoned. He was freed by the Americans at the end of the war and afterwards lived in the U.S.A.

Schuschnigg, K. von, *Austrian Requiem*. Eng. ed. 1947

Schütz, (Saggitarius) Heinrich (1585–1672). German composer. He studied under Giovanni Gabrieli but spent most of his working life in Dresden. He wrote the first German opera, *Daphne* (1627: now lost), and much church music, including four *Passions*. His *Seven Words from the Cross* (1645) and *Resurrection* (1623) represent a link between the 16th-century polyphonic composers and the accompanied choral works of Bach and Handel.

Schuyler, Philip John (1733–1804). American politician. He was a member of the colonial assembly (from 1768) and delegate to the Continental congress (1775). As well as being Commissioner for Indian affairs, he sat in Congress between 1778–81 and was a Senator 1789–91, and 1797–98. He was a leader of the Federal party in New York and helped to prepare the State's Constitution.

Schwab, Charles Michael (1862–1939). American industrialist. He worked his way up from being a stake-driver to become first president of the United Steel Corporation (1901–03) and president of the Bethlehem Steel Corporation (from 1903).

Schwann, Theodor (1810–1882). German chemist. Professor of Anatomy at Louvain in 1838 and at Liège in 1847, his main work lay in the chemistry of life processes. He early devoted himself to the study of digestion, and discovered the enzyme 'pepsin'. He worked on the formation of sugar solutions and the role of yeast in ferments. His denials of spontaneous generation led to experiments on sterilization which * Pasteur was later to build upon. Schwann is perhaps best known for his contributions to cell theory in plants and animals. He was concerned to show the differentiation of cell structure in very different tissues (e.g. cartilage and bones). All aspects of animals and plants were either cells or their products. Cells had a physiological and chemical life of their own, which was however subordinate to the overall life of the organism.

Henle, J., *Theodor Schwann*. 1882

Schwarzkopf, Elisabeth (1915–). German soprano. Her career flourished after World War II with the encouragement of her husband Walter Legge, a record producer and founder of the Philharmonia Orchestra. Her enormous ability as singer and actress, combined with striking good looks, made her the most admired operatic and concert soprano of her time, and she made several films. She was a notable Countess in *Figaro* and Feldmarschallin in *Rosenkavalier*.

Schweitzer, Albert (1875–1965). French medical missionary, theologian and musician, born in Alsace. He studied theology and philosophy at the universities of Strasbourg, Paris and Berlin, but first became known as an interpreter of Bach, on whose music he wrote authoritatively. Of his theological work *The Quest of the Historical Jesus* (1901) aroused most interest. Fired by zeal for the welfare of the less fortunate, he began in 1905 to study medicine and when qualified went to French Equatorial Africa (1913), where he established a mission hospital at Lambaréné in Gabon. Apart from brief visits to Europe to obtain funds by organ recitals and one to America, he remained in Africa in selfless devotion to his work. He received some criticism for neglecting modern methods of hygiene, e.g. by letting wives and children accompany the patients to hospital and cook meals etc. in the hospital precincts. His answer was that his methods won the affection and trust of those for whom he worked and that the fear of hospital was removed. Improvements were, however, gradually introduced. He wrote many books concerning his fields of study, and a number of autobiographical works, e.g. *From my African Notebook* (1936). He received countless honours including the Nobel Prize for Peace (1953) and the British O.M. (1955).
Seaver, G., *Albert Schweitzer: The Man and His Mind*. 6th ed. 1969

Scipio, Publius Cornelius (surnamed Aemilianus) (185–129 B.C.). Roman soldier, the adopted son of Publius Scipio, the son of Scipio Africanus. He was elected consul (147), commanded the Roman forces in the Third Punic War and after a long siege took and utterly destroyed Carthage (146). Back in Rome, he became a leader of the conservative opposition to the reforms (especially the agrarian law) of his brother-in-law Tiberius Gracchus (* Gracchi). Scipio's death was generally believed to be a political murder.
Astin, A. E., *Scipio Aemilianus*. 1967

Scipio, Publius Cornelius (surnamed Africanus) (237–183 B.C.). Roman soldier, the conqueror of Carthage. Having gained self-confidence and public esteem in battle against * Hannibal in Italy, he was appointed, at the early age of 27, proconsul in Spain. One by one he reduced the Carthaginian strongholds and by 207 had conquered the whole country, thus depriving Hannibal of his base. He was elected consul (205) but instead of directing his forces against Hannibal, still in Italy, he conceived the plan, which he carried out against strong opposition, of going direct to Africa and by a threat to Carthage itself ensuring Hannibal's recall. So it transpired. Scipio was victorious on the plains outside Carthage and Hannibal's army on its return was surrounded and destroyed at Zama (202). For the next ten years Scipio's prestige gave him almost unlimited power, though his love of all things Greek and a policy to accord with it created a conservative opposition under * Marcus Porcius Cato. Scipio's campaign (190–189) against Antiochus of Syria provided an opportunity for his enemies. Lucius Scipio, Africanus's brother, was asked to account for using part of the indemnity received from Antiochus as a bonus to his troops. Africanus, who realized that he was the real target, was insulted by what he felt to be base ingratitutde and retired from public life. By his victories and breadth of vision he had ensured the future of Rome as a great imperial power.
Scullard, H. H., *Scipio Africanus: Soldier and Politician*. 1970

Scopes, John Thomas (1901–1970). American teacher. After being dismissed for teaching the Darwinian theory of evolution (forbidden by Tennessee law), he was the protagonist of the famous 'monkey' trial at Dayton, Ohio (1925). Defended by Clarence Darrow against a prosecution led by William Jennings * Bryan, he was fined $100 but the sentence was reversed on appeal.

Scott, Charles Prestwich (1846–1932). English newspaper editor. From 1872 he edited the *Manchester Guardian* which, under his guidance, became the most literary and authoritative newspaper outside London and a main support of the Liberal party. When the proprietor, J. E. Taylor, died (1905), Scott became governing director and he and his son edited the paper until his death. He was a Liberal M.P. (1895–1906).

Scott, Sir George Gilbert (1811–1878). English architect. After being articled to a London firm he gained a major success by winning (1844) an open competition for designing St Nicholas's Church, Hamburg. From then on he was constantly in demand for building new churches, mainly in the Gothic style, and restoring old ones, including Westminster Abbey and the cathedrals of Hereford, Salisbury, Chester, Ripon etc. Among his works were the Albert Memorial (1864) and the St Pancras Hotel (1865) in London.
Clark, K., *The Gothic Revival.* Repr. 1950

Scott, Sir Giles Gilbert (1880–1960). English architect. Grandson of Sir George Gilbert * Scott, he won a competition for designing the Anglican Cathedral for Liverpool (1902) and supervised its construction for many years. Among his other designs were those for the Cambridge University Library, the new Bodleian Library, Oxford, the new Waterloo Bridge, London, and the new chamber of the House of Commons after World War II (designed 1944, completed 1950).

Scott, Michael (1175–1234). Scottish scholar. He translated parts of Aristotle from Arabic and became official astrologer to the emperor Frederick II. His magical powers are referred to by Dante. Some of this works survive. He was buried at Melrose Abbey, where his grave is still marked.

Scott, Sir Peter Markham (1909–). British ornithologist and artist. Son of the explorer Capt. Robert Falcon * Scott, he worked for the conservation of endangered species partly through the World Wildlife Fund but principally through his own Wildfowl Trust at Slimbridge which he founded in 1946. He led ornithological expeditions to Iceland, the Galapagos Islands, the Antarctic etc.
Scott, P., *The Eye of the Wind.* 1961

Scott, Robert Falcon (1868–1912). English sailor and Antarctic explorer. He joined the navy (1881) and was promoted captain in 1906. He led two expeditions to the Antarctic: the first (1901–04) explored the Ross Sea area; in a second voyage (begun 1910) to the same area he commanded the *Terra Nova* and among his objectives, which included much scientific and exploratory work, was a sledge journey to the South Pole. When Scott and his four companions, E. A. Wilson, L. E. G. * Oates, H. R. Bowers and E. Evans reached their goal (17 January 1912) they found that the Norwegian explorer Roald * Amundsen had been there a month earlier. Disappointment became tragedy when, already delayed by bad weather and ill health, the party was forced by a blizzard to remain in their tent until provisions were exhausted. Scott himself recorded the last hours in his diary, later discovered and published.
Scott, R. F., ed. Huxley, L., *Scott's Last Expedition.* 1913

Scott, Sir Walter, 1st Bart. (1771–1832). Scottish writer. To please his father, an Edinburgh lawyer, he studied law and advanced in the profession, but medieval history and the Romantic literature becoming popular in Germany were his more fruitful regions of study. The collection *Minstrelsy of the Scottish Border* (1802–03) was followed by his own original *The Lay of the Last Minstrel* (1805), *Marmion* (1808) and several more ballads. Popular fame and wealth immediately ensued, the latter encouraging him to start building what was intended to be the ancestral home of Abbotsford on the Tweed near Melrose. He now turned from poetry to prose and *Waverley* (1814), published anonymously, introduced the great series of romantic and historical novels which their creator's thin disguise as 'the author of *Waverley*' caused to be known as the Waverley novels. The best known include *Guy Mannering* (1815), *Rob Roy* (1818), *The Heart of Midlothian* (1818), *The Bride of Lammermoor* (1819), which inspired Donizetti's opera, *Ivanhoe* (1819), *The Monastery* and its sequel *The Abbott* (both 1820), *Kenilworth* (1821), *Quentin Durward* (1823) and *The Talisman* (1825). Coincident with the publication of *Woodstock* (1826) came the disaster which shadowed Scott's last years. Partly to meet the cost of Abbotsford he had entered into partnership with his friend James Ballantyne, the publisher. The firm crashed; Scott with his delicate sense of honour refused bankruptcy and with immense courage and industry assumed the task of repaying in full a sum of £130,000 due to the creditors. This was eventually achieved by the sale of copyrights after his death, hastened by strain and exhaustion. The quality of his work inevitably declined but to this last period belong three more novels (e.g. *Anne of*

Geierstein), the collection of stories from Scottish history titled *Tales of a Grandfather* (1828–30), and his *Life of Napoleon* (1827). He had been created a baronet in 1820.

Scott's particular form of romanticism is out of fashion; his characterization was often poor, but some of his historical portraits, e.g. of Louis XI of France in *Quentin Durward*, are remarkable. He played an important part in the development of the historical novel.

Abbotsford passed eventually to Scott's grand-daughter (child of his daughter Sophie and J. G. Lockhart, whose biography of his father-in-law is among the greatest achievements in this field); it then passed to her descendants.

Johnson, E., *Sir Walter Scott: The Great Unknown*. 1970

Scott, Winfield (1786–1866). American soldier. He introduced French tactics into the American army, and showed his skill in the Mexican war (1847); after a series of victories he took Mexico City. Though a Virginian, he stayed loyal to the Union in the Civil War and remained nominally in command of the army until 1861. In 1852 he had been Whig candidate for the presidency, losing to Franklin * Pierce. His nick-name was 'Old Fuss and Feathers'.

Scriabin, Alexander Nikolayevich (1872–1915). Russian composer and pianist. A cousin of V. M. * Molotov, he was a contemporary of Rachmaninov at the Moscow Conservatoire, where he was professor of the pianoforte (1898–1904). His own early piano works were strongly influenced by Chopin. After leaving Moscow he devoted himself to composition and lived in Switzerland, Belgium and France. Later under the influence of theosophy he developed doctrines which attached religious significance to all forms of art, and in his compositions subordinated everything to the achievement of ecstasy for which purpose he used such effects as clanging bells, incantations and blaring trumpets. The orchestral works *Poem of Ecstasy* (1908) and *Prometheus* (1911) and the last five Piano Sonatas (Nos. 5–10) illustrate this development. In his later works he introduced a harmonic system based on a 'mystic' chord of ascending fourths.

Swan, A. J., *Scriabin*. 1923

Scribe, Augustin Eugène (1791–1861). French dramatist. He was a prolific writer of plays which entertain mainly by the skill of the plot and clever dénouements. He also wrote libretti for several operas. He believed that the function of the theatre was to amuse, not to be a true reflection of life or a means of instruction.

Arvin, N. C., *Eugène Scribe and the French Theatre 1815–1860*. 1924

Scullin, James Henry (1876–1953). Australian Labor politician, born near Ballarat. He was a grocer, journalist and union organiser, a member of the House of Representatives (1910–13; 1922–49) and leader of the Labor party (1928–35). His term as prime minister (1929–32) coincided with the onset of the Great Depression in which Australian was severely hurt. His party split and J. A. * Lyons won the 1931 election in a landslide.

Seaman, Sir Owen, 1st Bart. (1861–1936). English journalist. A professor of literature, he became famous as a contributor of *Punch* (from 1904), a member of its staff (from 1897) and its editor (1906–32). He was a brilliant parodist and published many collections of his work. He was knighted in 1913 and made a baronet in 1931.

Searle, Ronald (1920–). British artist and cartoonist. He published his first work in 1935 and joined *Punch* in 1956. He was also attached to *Life* from 1955 and to the *New Yorker* from 1966. He has published about thirty books of drawings and cartoons in a detailed, linear style, and first gained wide popular success with his grotesque schoolchildren, whom he drew as inky-fingered caricatures of juvenile delinquency. The most famous of these, the girls of St Trinian's, appeared in the early 1950s.

Sebastian (1554–?1578). King of Portugal (from 1557). A posthumous child, he succeeded his grandfather John III; he grew up with an antipathy to women and a fanatical sense of mission to lead a crusade against the Moslems of North Africa. He sailed to Morocco in 1578 but was defeated and never seen again. The mystery of his disappearance produced imposters and led to the growth of a legend that he would return to deliver Portugal in time of need.

Seddon, Richard John (1845–1906). New Zealand politician. Born in Lancashire, he emigrated to Australia in 1863 and then went to the Westland goldfields of New Zealand (1866). First elected to the House of Representatives in 1879, he became (1891) a minister in the Liberal government of John Ballance, whom he succeeded as prime minister in 1893. During his long term of office which lasted until his death, he straightened the affairs of the Bank of New Zealand, assisted Britain in the Boer War with New Zealand troops, introduced Imperial Preference (1903), and annexed the Cook Islands. He was no socialist but to control prices he introduced state coal-mining (1901), fire insurance (1903), and house-building (1905).

Sedgwick, Adam (1785–1873). British geologist. Son of the curate of Dent in Yorkshire, he went to Trinity College, Cambridge where he became fellow in 1810. Though knowing no geology he was appointed Professor in the subject in 1818, holding the chair for the next 55 years and becoming one of the foremost British geologists. He was an empirical geologist, with strong Christian sentiments. He did not approve of Lyell's Uniformitarianism, was suspicious of Glacial Theory, and rejected all theories of evolution, especially * Darwin's. He excelled in two fields. He was a great student of palaeontology, especially expert in palaeozoic fossils. He also contributed greatly to understanding the stratigraphy of the British Isles, using fossils as an index of relative time. His greatest work lay in the geology of Wales, bringing to birth the concept of the Cambrian System on which he eventually quarrelled with * Murchison. Together with Murchison he was a leading proponent of the Devonian system.
Clark, J. W. and Hughes, T. McK. *The life and letters of Adam Sedgwick*. 1890

Sedley, Sir Charles (1639–1701). English poet and dramatist. A member of the circle of wits and profligates which surrounded Buckingham and Rochester at the court of Charles II, he wrote charming lyrics, excellent translations of Virgil and Horace, and plays, e.g. the comedies *The Mulberry Garden* (1667), based on Molière's *L'Ecole des maris* and *Bellamira* (1687).
Sedley, Sir C., ed. de Sola Pinto, V., *Works*. 1928

Segovia, Andrés (1893–). Spanish classical guitarist. Regarded during his active period as the greatest in the world, he made his debut at 14 and established an international reputation mainly with Spanish music. He inspired contemporary Spanish work for the guitar, notably by Villa-Lobos and Castelnuovo-Tedesco. He also adapted pieces by Bach and Mozart.

Segrave, Sir Henry O'Neal Dehane (1896–1930). British racing motorist. After serving in the Royal Flying Corps in World War I he took up motor racing, and in 1929 at Daytona Beach, Florida, achieved a record speed of 236·36 m.p.h. He was killed in England on Lake Windermere on a trial run prior to an attempt on the world's water-speed record.

Segrè, Emilio Gino (1905–). Italian nuclear physicist. He was born in Italy and was professor of physics at the University of Palermo (1935–38); he then went to work in the U.S.A., where he became (1946) professor of physics at the University of California. He helped to prepare artificially the elements technetium and astatine, which are below uranium in atomic number but are nevertheless not found naturally on earth. Segrè was a pioneer in the investigation of anti-matter and discovered (1955) the anti-protòn. He won the Nobel Prize for Physics (1959). His publications include *Nuclei and Particles* (1964).

Selden, John (1584–1664). English jurist, parliamentarian and scholar. From 1621 he sat almost continuously in parliament. He helped to draw up the Petition of Right and (1629–31) was imprisoned in the Tower; but though he sat in the Long Parliament his refusal to vote for the attainder of Strafford made him suspect and he gradually withdrew from public life. His *Titles of Honour* (1614) and *History of Tithes* (1618) still have value, but most of his learned works are long forgotten and he is remembered mainly for his *Table Talk* (1689), a record collected by his secretary of his conversations and remarks during his last twenty years. He was also an orientalist whose collection of manuscripts came to the Bodleian Library, Oxford. The Selden Society (for legal publications) was founded in his honour.

Seleucus I Nicator (died 280 B.C.). Founder of the Seleucid dynasty of Syria. After the death of Alexander the Great (323) his conquests were divided among his generals. By 312

Seleucus, one of the ablest and most ambitious, had married a Persian princess and ruled Babylonia. He gradually enlarged his empire until it included much of Asia and extended from Syria to India. He was assassinated. Under his successors, known as the Seleucids, the eastern provinces were gradually lost and the power of the dynasty continued in Syria until 64 B.C., when the country was conquered by the Romans, though the Hellenistic culture introduced by the Seleucid dynasty survived.
Bevan, E. R., *The House of Seleucus I.* 1902, repr. 1966

Selfridge, Harry Gordon (1858?–1947). American-born businessman. He made his early career with the American firm of Field, Leiter & Co. (later Marshall Field), which he joined in 1879 and of which he became junior partner in 1892. He began a new career when (1909) he opened his store in Oxford Street, London. Its success enabled him to live in princely style in Lansdowne House. Later, difficulties arose; he relinquished all active participation in 1939 and the store passed into other hands.

Selkirk, Alexander (1676–1721). Scottish seaman. While serving under William * Dampier on a privateering expedition he was marooned (1704) – according to one account he was left at his own request – on one of the Juan Fernández Islands in the Pacific. He was rescued (1709) and his story is said to have inspired Defoe's *Robinson Crusoe*.

Sellers, Peter *see* **Goons, The**

Semenov, Nikolai Nikolayevich (1896–). Russian physical chemist. He was professor of physics at Leningrad Polytechnic Institute (1920–56) until he was appointed to the chair of physical chemistry at Moscow University. He was Director of the USSR Institute of Physics from 1931. He has carried out important researches in chemical kinetics. He shared the Nobel Prize for Chemistry (1956) with * Henshelwood for their important discoveries in this field.

Semmelweis, Ignaz Philipp (1818–1865). Hungarian obstetrician. Working in a Vienna hospital he discovered that the death rate from puerperal fever was far higher (10 per cent against 3 per cent) in the ward attended by doctors who had come straight from post-mortem rooms than in that attended by midwives. By insisting on adequate use of antiseptics he reduced the death rate from infection to 1 per cent. The value of his work was recognized after his death but provoked much controversy at the time.
Gortvay, G., and Zoltán, I., *Semmelweis, his Life and Work*. 1968

Senanayake, Don Stephen (1884–1952). Ceylonese politician. He led Ceylon's independence movement, and as minister of agriculture (1941–46) he achieved much by irrigation and land reclamation. He became (1948) the first prime minister of the newly created dominion; he died in office after a fall from a horse. He was succeeded as prime minister by his son, **Dudley Senanayake** (1911–1973), who resigned in 1953 and remained out of office (except briefly in 1960) until he again became prime minister 1965–70.

Seneca, Lucius Annaeus (*c.* 4 B.C.–A.D. 65). Roman advocate, philosopher, tragedian and statesman. His fame as an orator roused the jealousy of * Caligula and almost cost him his life. Under Claudius the favour of the emperor's sister brought the hostility of Messalina, the emperor's wife, and Seneca was banished to Corsica. He was recalled (A.D. 49) to be tutor to the young * Nero and when his pupil became emperor provided five years (the famous *quinquennium Neronis*) of model government. Later he became involved in a conspiracy and was forced to commit suicide. As a philosopher he inclined to modified Stoicism and wrote essays on such subjects as *Calm of Mind, Shortness of Life*; he is better known for his nine surviving verse tragedies, which elaborate the familiar classical stories (*Medea, Phaedra* etc.) with much melodrama, moralizing and horror; they influenced Elizabethan drama and Corneille and Racine. Though Seneca's private life was blameless, he lacked strength of character, became a time-serving flatterer and condoned vices he could not prevent. He even wrote the oration defending Nero's matricide of * Agrippina. Nevertheless, as his 124 *Moral Epistles* show, he was in his timid way a seeker after virtue.
Mendell, C. W., *Our Seneca*. 1941

Sennacherib (died 681 B.C.). King of Assyria (from 705 B.C.). He successfully maintained the empire of his grandfather, * Tiglath-Pileser III and his father Sargon. Babylon, constantly in

revolt, he destroyed, and he punished a revolt in Judaea (see 2 Kings) by laying waste part of the country and besieging Jerusalem. His greatest achievement was the building of a large part of the capital city of Nineveh (on the Tigris opposite Mosul), where magnificently carved reliefs illustrated his campaigns. He is the subject of Byron's *The Destruction of Sennacherib*.
Luckenbill, D. D., trans., *The Annals of Sennacherib*. 1924

Senussi (or Sanusi), **Mohammed ibn Ali as** (*c.* 1787–1859). Arab religious leader. He established an order or fraternity which aimed at a return to the pure and simple Islamic doctrines untainted by later 'reformers'. Forced to leave Arabia, Mohammed ibn Ali established himself and his followers in Cyrenaica, where the Senussi, whose numbers grew eventually to over 200,000, formed a semi-independent state under Mohammed ibn Ali and his dynastic successors. The Senussi proved the most tenacious opponents of the Italian régime which succeeded that of Turkey after the war of 1911–12; their leader Mohammed * Idris became the first king of Libya in 1951.

Septimus Severus (146–211). Roman emperor (from 193). He was governor of Upper Pannonia (parts of Austria and Hungary) when news of the murder of Pertinax reached his troops, who immediately proclaimed him emperor. He marched at once to Rome and having overcome his rivals turned against the Parthians and annexed northern Mesopotamia. He died at Eboracum (York) while defending Britain's northern frontier. He introduced a complicated administrative system involving strict delimitation of function under imperial control. By encouraging troops to live and marry in the frontier regions he increased the incentive to vigorous defence at the cost of mobility.

Sertorius, Quintus (123–72 B.C.). Roman soldier. In the civil war between * Sulla and * Marius, Sertorius was among the most successful of the latter's generals and after Sulla's victory withdrew to Spain of which he had obtained complete mastery by 77. He was assassinated by a disloyal adherent. He was described by Mommsen as 'one of the greatest men, if not the very greatest man, that Rome had hitherto produced'.

Servetus, Michael (Miguel Serveto) (1511–1553). Spanish theologian and physician. While studying law at Saragossa and Toulouse he became interested in theology, an interest heightened by visits to Italy and Germany, where he encountered Bucer and other reformers. An essay on the Trinity (1531), though not going so far as to express Unitarian views, was far from orthodox. In 1536 he went to Paris to study medicine and from 1541 practised at Vienna; he is famous for his demonstration of the pulmonary circulation of the blood. After secretly printing *Christianismi Restitutio* (1553) he was denounced to the Lyons inquisitor, but escaping from arrest he went to Geneva, where the fanatical Calvin held sway. Servetus, unfortunate in that his views were as antagonistic to the reformers at Geneva as to the Catholics, was again arrested and after a prolonged trial was burned alive.
Wilson, E. M., *A History of Unitarianism*. 1945

Service, Robert William (1874–1958). Canadian poet. Famous for his songs and ballads told in the rough idiom of the frontier country, one of his best known ballads, often used as a recitation, is the shooting of Dan McGrew. Titles of his verse collections include *Songs of a Sourdough* (1907) and *Rhymes of a Rolling Stone* (1912). He also wrote novels.

Seurat, Georges (1859–1891). French painter. At the Salon des Indépendants (1884) he exhibited *Une Baignade* (now in the Tate Gallery, London), the first of the huge pictures in which he excelled. With Signac and Pissaro he developed, under the influence of optical theorists, the 'pointillist' technique by which the canvas is covered with dots of unmixed colour ('confetti' according to the scoffers) which merge at a distance into the required tones. This technique was the hall-mark of the neo-Impressionists; more distinctive of Seurat himself was the nobility he gave to ordinary activities by strictly disciplined composition.
de Hauke, C., *Seurat et son oeuvre*. 1961

Severus. For Roman emperors of that dynasty *see* **Alexander Severus, Septimus Severus.**

Sévigné, Marie de Rabutin-Chantel, Marquise de (1626–1696). French noblewoman. After the death of her husband in a duel (1651) she went to Paris where she wrote to her daughter in Provence her famous letters, which record with wit and apparent spontaneity her impressions of society in Paris and the provinces at the time of Louis XIV.

Seward, William Henry (1801–1872). American politician. He was born in New York and as a Whig lawyer he became active in the politics of the state, of which he was governor (1839–43). In the U.S. Senate (1849–61) he was an active protagonist of slave emancipation and hoped to obtain Republican nomination for the presidency. Abraham * Lincoln, however, was the successful candidate (1860) and Seward was consoled with the secretaryship of state (1861–69). He drew up the Emancipation Proclamation (1863). After Lincoln's murder he continued to serve under Andrew Johnson and was statesman enough to foresee the advantage to be obtained by the purchase (1867) of Alaska from Russia.
Seward, W. H., *Autobiography*. 1877

Sewell, Anna (1820–1878). English author, remembered for a single book, *Black Beauty* (1877), the story of a horse.

Seymour, Edward *see* **Somerset, 1st Duke of**

Seymour, Jane *see* **Jane Seymour**

Seymour of Sudeley, Thomas Seymour, 1st Baron (1508?–1549). The brother of Edward Seymour, Duke of * Somerset, and of Jane * Seymour, third wife of Henry VIII and mother of Edward VI. He married Henry's widow Catherine Parr. In 1547 he was appointed Lord High Admiral but two years later was beheaded for intrigue against his brother, who had become protector of England during King Edward's minority.

Seyss-Inquart, Arthur von (1892–1946). Austrian Nazi politician. He became chancellor and governor of Austria after Hitler's annexation of the country, and for most of World War II (1940–44) he was German high commissioner in occupied Holland. For the brutality of his rule there he was sentenced to death by the Nuremberg tribunal after the war.

Sforza, Carlo, Count (1872–1952). Italian diplomat. After a period of successful foreign service and a short spell (1920–22) as foreign secretary, he resigned when Mussolini came to power. He lived in Belgium and (from 1940) in the U.S.A., where he became prominent for his anti-Fascist views. After Mussolini fell he helped to form the provisional government of 1944 and was foreign minister under de Gasperi (1947–51).
Sforza, C., *European Dictatorships*. 1931

Sforza, Lodovico (1451–1508). Ruler of Milan (1481–1499), known for his dark skin as Il Moro ('The Moor'). His father, **Francesco Sforza** (1404–1466), was a famous *condottiere* who fought on both sides in the struggle between Venice and Milan but whose allegiance was finally determined by his marriage to Bianca, an illegitimate daughter of the Visconti Duke of Milan. This enabled him to become duke in 1450. The duchy passed to his son, then to his grandson the 7-year-old **Gian Galeazzo Sforza** (1476–1494) whose authority was usurped by his uncle Lodovico, strongly suspected of hastening his death. The court of Lodovico and his brilliant wife Beatrice d'Este became a centre of Renaissance culture, * Leonardo da Vinci being the most famous of the artists he befriended and employed. Lodovico was expelled (1499) by Louis XII of France and after failing to regain his duchy was imprisoned at Loches on the Loire, where he died.
Santoro, C., *Gli Sforza*. 1968

Shackleton, Sir Ernest Henry (1874–1922). British Antarctic explorer, born in Ireland. He was with * Scott on his first voyage of exploration, and sailing in the *Nimrod* he led his first expedition (1907–09) during which the magnetic pole and a record southern latitude of 88° 23′ were reached. His second expedition (1914–16) was an attempt to cross Antarctica from the Weddell to the Ross Sea. After his ship, the *Endurance*, had been crushed by ice, Shackleton and five companions made a hazardous journey to bring relief. All were in fact saved. He helped to organise the northern expeditionary force intervening in the Russian Civil War (1918–19) and died in South Georgia while on a third voyage to Antarctica. He wrote about his expeditions in, e.g., *Heart of the Antarctic* (1909) and *South* (1919).
Huntford, R., *Shackleton*. 1985

Shadwell, Thomas (1642–1692). English poet and dramatist. His first play, *The Sullen Lovers* (1668), was followed by sixteen more, the best of them comedies and the majority successful. As plays were used for political propaganda, he was as a Whig unable to produce plays from 1681, when the party fell into disfavour until the revolution of 1688. In 1689 he replaced the Tory * Dryden as Poet Laureate. Shadwell's reputation for dullness is largely due to the brilliant but cruel lampoon of him in Dryden's *MacFlecknoe*; in fact he often presents a vivid and entertaining picture of contemporary life.

Shaffer, Peter Levin (1926–). British playwright. His plays included *Five Finger Exercise* (1958), *The Royal Hunt of the Sun* (1964), *Equus* (1973) and *Amadeus* (1979). All were successful in Britain and the U.S. and also as films. His twin brother **Anthony Shaffer** (1926–) wrote *Sleuth* (1972) and many film scripts.

Shaftesbury, Anthony Ashley Cooper, 1st Earl of (1621–1683). English politician. In the Civil War he first fought as a royalist, but in 1644 went over to the parliamentary side. He was a member of Cromwell's Council of State but by 1659 he was imprisoned as a suspected royalist. Thus at the Restoration he was favoured by Charles II. He was created Baron Ashley in 1661 and from then until 1672, when he was made Earl of Shaftesbury, he acted as chancellor of the exchequer (from 1667 as a member of the famous Cabal ministry). He was lord chancellor (1672–73) but, always disliked, he was then dismissed by Charles II and became the force behind the movement to exclude the Roman Catholic Duke of York (James II) from the succession, making use of the infamous Titus * Oates to 'expose' a Catholic plot. In the ensuing reaction Shaftesbury himself was acquitted of treason but took refuge in Amsterdam where he died. He was the most skilful politician of the day and was the virtual founder of the Whig party. His methods were devious, but, as is shown by his association with John * Locke and the part he played (1679) in amending the Habeas Corpus Act, he had liberal causes at heart. An envenomed satirical portrait of him is contained in Dryden's *Absalom and Achitophel.*
Haley, K. H. D., *The First Earl of Shaftesbury*. 1968

Shaftesbury, Anthony Ashley Cooper, 3rd Earl of (1671–1713). English philosopher. His chief work, *Characteristics of Men, Manners, Opinions, Times* (1711) discusses virtue, integrity, self-respect and the 'Affections' which he believed men had naturally for themselves, other men and even fellow living creatures. The good of society and the good of the individual in the nature of things run into one another. Men have a 'moral sense' – he introduced the term – which enables them to separate right from wrong.

Shaftesbury, Anthony Ashley Cooper, 7th Earl of (1801–1885). English philanthropist. As Lord Ashley he was an M.P. (1826–51) until he succeeded to the peerage; he took the lead in securing the passage of a succession of Factory Acts and the Coal Mines Act of 1842. Among the many improvements he secured were the appointment of factory inspectors to ensure that children under 9 were not employed in the mills and that women and children should not work underground in the mines. Another of his measures prohibited the employment of children (such as Tom in Kingsley's *Water Babies*) to climb and clean chimneys: he was closely associated with the 'Ragged Schools' movement, and legislation to provide lodging houses for the poor: he helped the work of Florence * Nightingale and numerous other good causes. Politically he was a strong Tory and in religion strictly evangelical. He is commemorated by the statue of Eros (Love) in Piccadilly Circus, London.

Shah Jahan (1592–1666), 5th Mogul emperor of Delhi (1627/8–58). He fought successfully against the Deccan princes but several attempts to recover Kandahar from Persia eventually failed. He was an able ruler and by skilful financial management maintained a court of the greatest magnificence (he constructed the 'peacock throne'). He built the palace and great mosque at Delhi, and at Agra the beautiful 'pearl mosque' and the Taj Mahal, the most famous of all his buildings, erected as a mausoleum for Mumtaz Mahal, his favourite wife. In 1658 he fell ill and his son Aurangzeb, successful in a struggle for the succession, deposed him and held him prisoner until his death. Dryden's *Aureng-Zebe* (1676), is based loosely on these events.

Shakespeare, William (1564–1616). English dramatist and poet, born at Stratford-on-Avon on St George's Day, 23 April. Very few of the traditional stories of his early life can stand up to serious examination. His father, John Shakespeare, was a prosperous glover and held prominent positions in civic life; later his fortunes declined. Shakespeare's mother, Mary Arden, was the daughter of a well-to-do farmer. The boy was no doubt educated at the Stratford free grammar school, where he would be well grounded in Latin. After his christening the next positive evidence of Shakespeare's existence is the licence to marry Anne Hathaway (1582). The christenings of their children are recorded, that of his elder daughter Susanna in May 1583, that of the twins Judith and Hamnet in February 1585. The boy Hamnet died aged 11 but Judith married and survived her father; his granddaughter Elizabeth (*d.* 1670), the daughter of Susanna, who had married John Hall, a Stratford physician, was his last known descendant. The next established fact in Shakespeare's life is that by 1592, when he is referred to disparagingly by the dramatist Greene, he was well established as an actor-playwright in London. What had happened in the previous ten years is unknown. A well known legend relates that he left Stratford (*c.* 1585) to avoid prosecution for poaching on the estate of Sir Thomas Lucy of Charlecote. According to a more likely story he was a schoolmaster in the country until he was drawn to London by the glamour of city life and a realization of his own talents. Circumstances favoured him: the first theatre (inn-yards had been previously used) was built in 1576 and others followed to meet an ever increasing demand for good plays. The collected edition of Shakespeare's plays, known as the First Folio, appeared in 1623, and the names of the editors, Heminge and Condell, friends and fellow-actors, vouch for its authenticity. But the plays are not dated and attempts to arrange them in chronological order have provoked endless controversy. It is reasonably certain that among the earliest are *The Comedy of Errors* (derived from Latin comedy), *Titus Andronicus* and *1 Henry VI.* Despite many virtues of plot and versification each in its different way has elements of crudity, and in the case of the tetralogy *1, 2* and *3 Henry VI* and *Richard III*, it is interesting to see the quality rise as the poet matures. When the later tetralogy (1594–99) – *Richard II, 1* and *2 Henry IV* and *Henry V* is considered with the first, it is clear that Shakespeare's purpose was to show that the original crime of the murder of Richard II was finally expiated only when the victory at Bosworth Field brought the Tudors to power. In comedy too, he was gaining an increased sureness of touch in combining farcical incident with subtle understanding of human nature. This is especially true of *The Taming of the Shrew*, which with *The Two Gentlemen of Verona* and *Love's Labour's Lost* was almost certainly written by 1594. To this period also belong the narrative poems *Venus and Adonis* (1593) and *The Rape of Lucrece* (1594) and most of the sonnets. The identity of 'Mr W. H.', the 'onlie begetter' of the sonnets, has caused much speculation: a favourite candidate has been Henry Wriothesley, the young Earl of Southampton, to whom the narrative poems were dedicated. Later sonnets were addressed to an equally mysterious 'dark lady'. To the next five years (1594–99) belong some of the most popular of Shakespeare's plays. First were *Romeo and Juliet* and *A Midsummer Night's Dream*, followed by *The Merchant of Venice* and *The Merry Wives of Windsor*, and another history play, *King John.* In 1599 Shakespeare's company acquired the Globe Theatre. He himself had become increasingly prosperous and in 1597 had bought 'New Place', the largest house in Stratford. As a playwright he now reached his zenith. *Julius Caesar* was followed by the still greater tragedies, *Hamlet, Othello, King Lear* and *Macbeth*, which are matched by the comedies *Much Ado About Nothing, Twelfth Night* and *As You Like It.* From the great climax there is some decline, not in quality (except in *Timon of Athens*) but in intensity: in the tragedies *Anthony and Cleopatra* and *Coriolanus* the author seems less personally involved, and in the comedies *Measure for Measure, All's Well that Ends Well* and *Troilus and Cressida* the boundary between comedy and tragedy is becoming blurred. Even in the last phase (from 1608) any falling off in quality is, at worst, intermittent. *Pericles* (only partly his) and *Cymbeline* still contain fine passages: even the pageant play *Henry VIII* (in which the extent of Shakespeare's participation is disputed) has some magnificent scenes. But *The Winter's Tale* is a masterpiece and his last completed day, *The Tempest*, shows his creative powers still at their highest. The last five years of Shakespeare's life were spent at Stratford, where he is buried. He died on his birthday, 23 April 1616, the same day as * Cervantes. His plays remained popular in his lifetime but as fashions changed he suffered some eclipse,

until Dryden proclaimed his pre-eminence, which has never been challenged since. In Shakespeare's hands blank verse became an instrument of great delicacy whether for dialogue, narrative, description or argument; adaptable equally to any plot or situation, tragic or comic. His works have been widely translated and his characters are household names: no writer has given more continuous delight or shown greater insight into the heart and mind of man.
Chambers, E. K., *William Shakespeare: A Study of Facts and Problems*. 1930. Tillyard, E. M. W., *The Elizabethan World Picture*. 1966

Shalmaneser III (reigned 859–824 B.C.). King of Assyria. Son and successor of Ashur-pasirpal, after regaining control of the Phoenician cities he achieved the great victory commemorated by the Black Obelisk in the British Museum, which shows the biblical king Jehu of the Israelites and other rulers bowing before him.

Shalom Aleichem ('Peace be upon you!': pseudonym of Shalom Rabinowitz) (1859–1916). Yiddish writer, born in the Ukraine. Originally a rabbi, he wrote first in Russian and Hebrew, devoting himself to Yiddish after 1883 and producing more than 40 volumes. His plays and stories describe life in small Jewish towns during the tsarist era. The story cycle, *Tevye and his Daughters*, was adapted by Joseph Stein for the play *Fiddler on the Roof*, later a successful film (1971). He moved to the U.S., became known as the 'Jewish Mark Twain' and died in New York.
Waife-Goldberg, M., *Shalom Aleichem*. Samuel, M., *The World of Shalom Aleichem*. 1943. Grafstein, M. (ed.), *Shalom Aleichem Panorama*. 1949

Shamir, Yitzhak (1915–). Israeli politician, born in Poland. Migrating to Palestine in 1935, he was an activist in the Stern Gang and imprisoned by the British during World War II. A Knesset member 1973– , he became speaker 1977–80, foreign minister 1983–83 and succeeded Menachem * Begin as prime minister 1983–84. In a 'national unity' coalition he became foreign minister again 1984– .

Shannon, Claude Elwood (1916–). American mathematician. He graduated from the Massachusetts Institute of Technology, then worked for the Bell Telephone labs and taught at MIT from 1967. His paper 'The Mathematical Theory of Communication' (with Warren Weaver, 1949) is regarded as the beginning of information theory: in it he equates 'information' with entropy.
Campbell, J., *Grammatical Man*. 1982

Sharp, Cecil James (1859–1924). English collector of folk songs and dances. He began collecting folk songs in 1903 and thereafter made it his life's work. It was largely through him that English folk music was saved from extinction, though he bowdlerized a good many songs. He wrote *English Folk Song – Some Conclusions* (1907) and founded (1911) the English Folk Dance Society. The London headquarters of the English Folk Dance and Song Society is named after him.

Sharp, William (1855–1905). Scottish author who also wrote under the name Fiona McLeod. Under his own name he wrote poetry and literary biographies, e.g. of Shelley (1887) and Browning (1890), but he is better known for the mystical Celtic stories written under his pen-name, and especially for his play *The Immortal Hour* (1900), which when set to music (1914) by Rutland Boughton and produced in London during the 1920s achieved great success.

Shastri, Lal Bahadur (1904–1966). Indian politician. Born in Uttar Pradesh, son of a schoolmaster, he became one of the most active workers for Congress and was several times imprisoned for civil disobedience. He first entered the Indian cabinet in 1952, and succeeded * Nehru as prime minister in 1964. Much of his brief term of office was occupied with disputes with Pakistan and the frontier war that followed. He had just reached an agreement for a cease-fire at a conference held under Soviet auspices at Tashkent when he died. He was a man of very small stature with a gentle and persuasive manner that commanded much affection.

Shaw, George Bernard (1856–1950). Anglo-Irish dramatist. He was born in Ireland, paid little attention to school subjects but acquired a cultural background at art-galleries, concerts etc. After five years in a Dublin land agent's office, he went to London (1876), where his mother, a singing teacher, supported him while he wrote unsuccessful novels and haunted the British Museum to improve his education. He was already a vegetarian, teetotaller, and non-smoker, and now, having studied Marx, became a socialist. He was among the first to join the Fabian Society (1884) and having overcome his shyness became a noted public speaker. His professional career began when as 'Corno di Bassetto' he was music critic on the *Star* (1888–90) and on *The World* (1890–94). He was a champion of Wagner, and equally warmly championed Ibsen when he was appointed dramatic critic of *The Saturday Review*, then under the editorship of Frank Harris. Since his defence of Ibsen was combined with attacks on Shakespeare, Shaw doubly shocked many of his readers, but others revelled in the flippant irreverence of his style and were stimulated by his paradoxes. Thus when his first play *Widowers' Houses* was produced (1892) he had at least a nucleus of fervent support to set against the general disapproval. Nevertheless, his next play, *The Philanderers* (1893), was rejected by managements and the third, *Mrs Warren's Profession* (1893), by the censor (until 1924). These 'unpleasant plays' were followed by 'pleasant' ones: *Arms and the Man* (1894), *Candida* (1894), *You Never Can Tell* (1895–96), and *The Devil's Disciple* (1896). After a serious illness (1898) Shaw gave up regular journalism and married Charlotte Payne-Townsend (died 1943). He was always grateful for the money she then brought although his own earnings were soon to become prodigious. To what extent his emotions were involved with women is questionable. He was probably too self-centred for love and was at his happiest when in flirtatious correspondence with women he admired, e.g. Ellen Terry or Mrs Patrick Campbell. For the former he wrote *Captain Brassbound's Conversion* (1899); he had already written *Caesar and Cleopatra* (1898–99), a delightfully modern conception of an historic theme, for Forbes-Robertson, his favourite actor. His views on creative evolution are expounded (1901–1903) in *Man and Superman* (and he returned to the theme in the epic *Back to Methuselah* of 1917–1920), a play which with *John Bull's Other Island, Major Barbara* and some of his earlier ones was produced under the management of Vedrenne and Granville-Barker at the famous repertory season at the Court Theatre, which finally brought the full recognition for which he had worked so long. To 1912 belong the successful comedy *Pygamalion* and the flippant play based on an old legend *Androcles and the Lion. Heartbreak House*, begun just before the First World War, during which Shaw's political views made him unpopular, analysed the breakdown of European society in a domestic setting evocative of Chekhov. The most financially successful of his plays was *St Joan* (1924) which was followed by the political satire *The Apple Cart* (1929). In 1925 he was awarded the Nobel Prize for Literature which he had previously declined. Among the non-dramatic works of his later period the best known are *The Intelligent Woman's Guide to Socialism and Capitalism* (1928) and *The Black Girl in search of God* (1932). In old age Shaw became obsessed with the idea of simplifying English spelling and left most of his money for that end. Shaw's wit has made his audiences laugh and his flippancy has often made them angry: but these reactions would not have displeased him for his purpose was, by goading, provoking, ridiculing or cajoling them to make them think.

Morgan, M., *The Shavian Playground*. 1972

Shaw, Richard Norman (1831–1912). English architect. Under the influence of William Morris he broke away from current Victorian Gothic and returned, in many London and country houses, to the classic principles of Georgian architecture and to traditional craftsmanship and use of materials. His London buildings included New Scotland Yard (1891), the Gaiety Theatre (1905), now demolished, and the Piccadilly Hotel (1905).

Shelburne, William Petty, 2nd Earl of (1st Marquess of Lansdowne) (1737–1805). English politician. After distinguished service in the Seven Years War he entered politics. After joining Grenville's ministry (1763) he became closely associated with Chatham (William * Pitt) both in office, as secretary of state (1766), and later in opposition to Lord North and his American policy. He was again secretary of state (1782) under Rockingham, after whose death in the same year he himself formed a government which was mainly notable for introducing the younger William * Pitt to high office as chancellor of the exchequer. Shelburne was a man of great ability and a natural Radical (favouring free trade, Roman Catholic emancipation and parliamentary reform) but the time was not ripe; his political shifts and turns to approach his objectives were misunderstood and secured him the nickname 'the Jesuit of Berkeley Square'. He was given his consolatory marquessate on retirement (1784). He was a patron of the arts and a collector of manuscripts (which were purchased for the British Museum in 1807).

Shelley, Mary Wollstonecraft (1797–1855). British novelist, daughter of the rationalist philosopher William Godwin and second wife of the poet Percy Bysshe * Shelley. She wrote *Frankenstein or the Modern Prometheus* in 1818, and three other novels.
Wollstonecraft Shelley, M., *Journals*. 1947

Shelley, Percy Bysshe (1792–1822). English poet. He was born near Horsham, Sussex, the grandson of a baronet. At Eton he read *Enquiry into Political Justice* by his future father-in-law William Godwin, a book which did much to encourage his desire to reform contemporary social systems. He was expelled from Oxford (1811) for writing *The Necessity for Atheism*. This led to a breach with his father which left the poet constantly short of money. Soon afterwards he married his sister's school friend, the beautiful 16-year-old Harriet Westbrook, childish even for her years. Even on the prolonged honeymoon Shelley needed the mental stimulus of his great friend Thomas Jefferson Hogg who committed the quickly forgiven indiscretion of falling in love with Harriet. In London Shelley joined the Radical Godwin circle: Shelley and Harriet were already estranged when he fell violently in love and (1814) eloped with Mary Godwin; they married two years later, when Harriet drowned herself. Shelley always refused to accept responsibility for her death, as he had never hidden his views about free love, but he was deeply wounded when the courts gave the care of his children by her into other hands. From 1818 the Shelleys lived in Italy where he, while composing some of the loveliest lyrics ever to be written in English, became involved in the tangled financial, emotional and political affairs of the Godwins, Byron and Leigh Hunt. In 1822 the Shelleys were living in a villa at Lerici on the Gulf of Spezia and on 8 July while Shelley, after a meeting with Byron, was sailing back from Leghorn (Livorno) his boat, the *Ariel*, was upset in a storm; he and his two companions were drowned.

Shelley had first revealed his greatness as a poet by long poems, e.g. *Queen Mab* (1813) and *Alastor* (1816); but with the exception of his verse plays, of which the greatest were *The Cenci* (1819), a grim tale of incestuous passion, and *Prometheus Unbound* (1820), it is by his songs and odes that he is best remembered. *Ode to a Skylark, Ode to the West Wind* and *Adonais* (1821), the great lament for the poet Keats, are among the many familiar titles. **Mary Shelley,** whose son by the poet inherited his grandfather's baronetcy, was the author of *Frankenstein* (1818), the story of the man who created a monster.
White, N. I., *Shelley*. 2nd ed. 1947; Shelley, P. B., *Letters* ed. F. L. Jones, 1964

Sheppard, Jack (1702–1724). English criminal. Whilst apprenticed to a London carpenter he took to crime (1720). In 1724 he was caught four times but always escaped, on one occasion forcing six of Newgate Prison's great doors. On the last occasion he was held and hanged at Tyburn before a vast and admiring crowd. He was the hero of many ballads and of a novel by Harrison Ainsworth.

Sheraton, Thomas (1751–1806). English furniture designer, born at Stockton-on-Tees. Before moving to London (*c.* 1790) he was a journeyman cabinet-maker and may later have supervised the manufacture of some furniture; but his style became influential through his illustrated design manuals, notably the *Cabinet-maker and Upholsterer's Drawing Book* (1791). Sheraton furniture is distinguished by lightness and simplicity, an emphasis on straight, vertical lines and a preference for inlay decoration.
Fastnedge, R., *Sheraton Furniture*. 1962

Sheridan, Philip Henry (1831–1888). American soldier. A captain when the Civil War began (1861), Grant soon gave him command of all the cavalry of the army of the Potomac and he became famous for his spectacular raids behind the enemy lines, in one of which he reached the outskirts of Richmond, the Confederate capital. Later as commander of the army in the Shenandoah Valley (1864–65) he at first showed unwonted caution but while he was absent his army suffered a severe setback at Cedar Creek: a dramatic ride back to the battlefield enabled him to reverse the situation with a counter-attack in which twenty-four guns were taken. Sheridan displayed his dash and brilliance to the full as Grant's principal lieutenant in the operations leading to the surrender at Appomattox. He was commander-in-chief of the U.S. army (1883–88).

Sheridan, Richard Brinsley (1751–1816). Irish dramatist and politician, born in Dublin, the son of an actor. His mother, Frances Sheridan (1724–1766), was a minor novelist and dramatist. Having fought two duels on behalf of Elizabeth Ann Linley with whom he eloped and (1773) married, he soon won fame with his three brilliant comedies, *The Rivals* (1775), *The School for Scandal* (1777) and *The Critic* (1779). *The Duenna* (1775) and others are much inferior. He bought * Garrick's share of the Drury Lane Theatre (1776), assumed the managership and built (1794) a new theatre, burnt down in 1809. Meanwhile he had become a Whig M.P., a friend of * Fox and the Prince of Wales, and was appointed successively under-secretary for foreign affairs (1782), secretary to the treasury (1783), and treasurer to the Navy (1806). He became renowned as an orator, especially for his speeches at the impeachment of Warren * Hastings. When fire destroyed Drury Lane Theatre (1809) Sheridan was financially crippled: he was arrested for debt (1816). He was buried in Westminster Abbey.
Moore, T., *Memoirs of the Life of the Rt. Hon. Richard Brinsley Sheridan*. 5th ed. 1827

Sherman, William Tecumseh (1820–1891). American soldier. When the Civil War broke out (1861) Sherman, who had abandoned his career as an officer, was a professor at the Louisiana military academy. He at once rejoined the Union army, commanded a brigade at Bull Run and 'saved the day' at Shiloh. Appointed by Grant to command in the south-west he captured Atlanta (September 1864). Unable to bring his opponent, Hood, to battle, he began in November the great march through Georgia which created a wide band of destruction from Atlanta to the port of Savannah. The march incurred lasting odium, and its military usefulness has been a matter of controversy ever since. It seems certain that then and on other occasions Sherman showed himself more adept at destroying communications than in coming to grips with the enemy. He was commander-in-chief of the U.S. army (1869–83).

His brother, **John Sherman** (1823–1900), a Republican politician, sponsored the Anti-Trust Act (1890) and was secretary of state (1897–98).

Sherriff, Robert Cedric (1896–1975). English dramatist. His play about World War I, *Journey's End* (1929), achieved an outstanding success not repeated by his later work.

Sherrington, Sir Charles Scott (1857–1952). English physiologist. He studied at St Thomas's Hospital, London, where later, after research into cholera in Spain and Italy, he became a lecturer in physiology. Later appointments included professorships at Liverpool University (1895–1913) and then at Oxford until his retirement (1935). His work on the nervous system was of great importance, especially that relating to the effects of reflex actions. With Lord * Adrian he was awarded the Nobel Prize for Medicine (1932) for their joint study of the neuron (nerve cell). He was elected F.R.S. (1893) and P.R.S. (1920–25) and won the Royal and Copley medals. He received the O.M. (1924). His books include *Integrative Action of the Nervous System* (1906) and *Man on his Nature* (1940).

Sherwood, Robert Emmet (1896–1957). American author. His successful plays include *Idiot's Delight* (1936), *Abe Lincoln in Illinois* (1939) and *There shall be no Night* (1941). He wrote some of President Roosevelt's speeches and won the Pulitzer Prize (1949) for *Roosevelt and Hopkins: an Intimate History*.

Shih Huang Ti ('First sovereign emperor': personal name Cheng Wang) (259–210 B.C.). Chinese emperor (221–210 B.C.), founder of the Ch'in dynasty. King of the state of Ch'in, based on Shen-xi in the north-west, through war and diplomacy he defeated six rival states to unify China under his rule. Assisted by his minister Li Ssu, he imposed an authoritarian regime from his capital Hsien-yang. Writing, weights and measures were standardised; he built the Great Wall with remarkable speed and efficiency, and imposed a rigorous censorship, burning manuscripts (except on farming and medicine). He made frequent journeys through his empire and died while travelling. His dynasty fell in 206 B.C. to the western Hans. Traditionally regarded as one of the arch villains of Chinese history, his reputation was restored under the People's Republic.

Shinwell, Emanuel, Baron Shinwell (1884–). English politician. He entered Parliament as Labour member for Linlithgow in 1922 and became financial secretary to the War Office in 1929. He was parliamentary secretary to the Department of Mines in 1924 and again 1930–31. In Attlee's government he was minister of fuel and power (1945–47), minister for war (1947–50) and of defence (1950–51).
Shinwell, E., *I've Lived Through It All*. 1973

Shirley, James (1596–1666). English dramatist. After leaving Oxford he became a Roman Catholic and took up teaching but soon began writing for the stage. He wrote over forty plays: the tragedies, e.g. *The Maid's Revenge* (*c.* 1626), *The Traitor* (1631) and *The Cardinal* (1641), are undistinguished, but the comedies, e.g. *The Gamester* (1633), later adapted by Garrick, and *The Lady of Pleasure* (1635), were revived after the return of Charles II (1660) and strongly influenced Restoration comedy. He died from stress and exposure during the Great Fire of London.

Shockley, William Bradford (1910–). American physicist. He lectured in physics at the Massachusetts Institute of Technology and later worked for the Bell Telephone laboratories. He was co-inventor with Brattain and Bardeen of the transistor and shared with them the Nobel Prize for Physics (1956).

Sholokhov, Mikhail Alexandrovich (1905–1983). Russian novelist. In his first major work, *And Quiet Flows the Don* and its sequel *The Don Flows Home to the Sea* (1928–40), he gave an account of the events leading up to and following the Revolution and Civil War (in which he fought in the Red army) and the effects on a Cossack village. His second epic, *Virgin Soil Upturned* (1932–33), dealt with the collectivization of agriculture. *They Fought for their Country* (from 1959) is an epic of World War II. He also published many short stories and won the Nobel Prize for Literature in 1965.

Shore, Jane (died 1527?). Mistress of Edward IV of England. She was the wife of a London goldsmith and famed for her beauty and wit; she was accused of sorcery and forced to do public penance by Richard III. Sir Thomas More writes of her, and her story is the theme of ballads and of a tragedy by Nicholas Rowe.

Shostakovich, Dimitri Dimitrievich (1906–1975). Russian composer. Born in St Petersburg (Leningrad), where he later studied at the Conservatoire, he won fame with his Symphony No. 1 (1926). Of its fourteen successors the second was dedicated to the *October Revolution* and the seventh called the *Leningrad* symphony because he began it during the German siege of that city in World War II. Two years after the production of his opera *Lady Macbeth of Mtsensk* (1934), Shostakovich was attacked in *Pravda* for the work's bourgeois formalism and other alleged shortcomings: he agreed he was in error and duly changed his style. In middle age he seemed to achieve a reconciliation between Soviet ideological demands and his own powers in three of his finest works: the Symphony No. 10 (1953) and the Concertos for Violin (1948 and 1967) and Cello (1959) and 1965). Other notable works are the Concerto for Piano and Trumpet (1933), the String Quartets (from 1938), Piano Quintet (1940), and Preludes for piano. Brooding seriousness and ironical gaiety are the dominant moods of Shostakovich's music, which (like that of Mahler who influenced it) embraces a wide range of feeling.

Shovell, Sir Clowdisley (*c.* 1650–1707). British sailor. He was a Norfolk village lad who ran away to sea, and from being a cabin boy rose by sheer ability to become a rear-admiral. When he was a lieutenant he burned four pirate ships in the Mediterranean (1674): he was knighted for his conduct at the Battle of Bantry Bay (1689). At La Hogue (1692), now a rear-admiral, he burned twenty enemy ships. He took part in the capture of Barcelona (1705) but failed at Toulon (1707). On the way home his ship struck a rock and sank off the Scilly Isles, and he and 800 aboard were lost. How his body came to be found in Cornwall is a mystery (was it washed ashore? or was he murdered after landing?). He was buried in Westminster Abbey.

Shrapnel, Henry (1761–1842). English soldier. He was an artillery officer in the Duke of York's army in Flanders (1793) and invented the spherical case-shell, first used in 1804 and later named after him. It explodes in the air at a fuse-controlled height and propels bullets in a forward cone. He became a lieutenant-general in 1837.

Shrewsbury, John Talbot, 1st Earl of (1388?–1453). English commander. His exploits in the period when Joan of Arc's death was followed by the decline of English power made his name one of odium and terror to the French. Among his successes were a victory over the Burgundians at Crotoy (1437) and the recapture of Harfleur (1440). A reckless and precipitate attack at Castillon (1453) brought defeat and death.

Shultz, George Pratt (1920–). US administrator. Educated at Princeton and the Massachusetts Institute of Technology, he taught economics in Chicago, serving as US Secretary of Labor 1969–70, director of the Office of Management and Budget 1970–72, and secretary of the Treasury 1972–74. He was president of the Bechtel Corporation, engineers, 1975–82 and US secretary of state 1982– .

Sibelius, Jean (Johan Julius Christian) (1865–1957). Finnish composer. Regarded as an embodiment of national culture, after abandoning law for music he studied in Helsinki, Berlin and Vienna (under Goldmark). His gifts were early recognized by the Finnish authorities with a grant for life which enabled him to devote himself to composition. Though not a conscious nationalist in music – he did not base his work on folk lore – he was interested in Finnish mythology. He first won international recognition with the tone poem *En Saga* (1892, revised 1902). The first movement of the Symphony No. 2 (1902) introduces Sibelius's individual approach to formal structure: the movement is built up not from two clearly defined groups of subjects as in classical sonata form, but from a number of short phrases that gradually fuse and develop organically. This method, apparent also in the last movement of the Symphony No. 3 (1907), was to dominate the rest of the series. The fourth (1911), remarkable for the compression of its material, economical orchestration and bitterness of mood, was followed by the glowing and expansive fifth (1915, revised 1916, 1919), the restrained sixth and the one-movement seventh (1924). Comparable with the symphonies in mood and sometimes in manner, are the tone poems *The Bard* (1913), *Luonnotar* (1910) for soprano and orchestra, *The Oceanides* (1914) and *Tapiola* (1926), the last of his important works. He also wrote incidental music for plays (e.g. Maeterlinck's *Pelléas et Mélisande* and Shakespeare's *The Tempest*) and songs. His idiom was unmistakably personal in its melodic, harmonic and orchestral expression. The comparative lack of lyricism in his music and its preoccupation with nature (especially its sinister aspect) must partly account for lack of appreciation outside Scandinavia and the English-speaking world. His structural changes have not been significantly adopted.
Blum, F., *Jean Sibelius. An International Bibliography* 1965; Layton, R., *Sibelius*. 1965

Sica, Vittorio de (1901–1974). Italian film director and actor. After a stage career which began in 1923 he made films such as *Bicycle Thieves* (1948), *Miracle in Milan* (1950) and *Umberto D.* (1951) in which pathos, whimsical humour and a keen sense of character are combined. As a character actor in such films as *Bread, Love and Dreams*, he also won high esteem.

Sickert, Walter Richard (1860–1942). British painter of Danish descent, born in Munich. He studied in London at the Slade School and under Whistler, and in Paris under Degas. In 1886 he began to exhibit at the New English Art Club which he helped to found, and lived mainly in London, Dieppe and Venice. After returning to London (1905) he headed a group of artists who formed (1911) the 'Camden Town Group', which later (1913) became part of the 'London group'. Under Degas's influence he painted scenes of theatre life but many of his subjects were the dark rooms and dismal streets familiar to him from his early London days, painted in the subdued colour schemes he had learnt from Whistler, using French Impressionist and post-Impressionist techniques. In later years he introduced colour and sunshine into his pictures using a fuller and richer palette. He became an A.R.A. in 1924 but having been elected R.A. in 1934 resigned a year later.
Sickert, W. R., *A Free House*. 1947

Sickingen, Franz von (1481–1523). German knight. After serving as a soldier of fortune under Francis I of France and the Emperor Charles V, he conducted on behalf of the Protestant reformers his own private war against the ecclesiastical princes. Placed under the ban of the Empire, he died of wounds while besieged in his own castle. His death symbolized the end of the independent power of German knighthood.

Siddons, Sarah Kemble (1755–1831). English tragic actress. She came of a famous stage family, the Kembles, and was a sister of John * Kemble. At the age of 17 she married a member of her father's company, and two years later made her debut (1775), under * Garrick's management at Drury Lane as Portia. She was not notably successful and for the next six years she toured the provinces. She made a triumphant return to London (1782) and until her retirement (1812) dominated the London stage. In tragic roles, above all as Lady Macbeth, perfection was claimed for her, beauty of face, form and voice being allied with vibrant emotional power. She is immortalized in paintings by Gainsborough and, as *The Tragic Muse*, by Reynolds.
ffrench, Y., *Mrs Siddons, Tragic Actress*. 1936

Sidgwick, Henry (1838–1900). English philosopher and economist. His academic life was centred on Cambridge where he eventually became Knightsbridge professor of moral philosophy (1883). The first book that made him known in a wider field was *Methods of Ethics* (1874) in which he not only regards his subject from a historical viewpoint but shows keen analytical power in his approach to such concepts as 'the good', and such classifications as 'hedonism'. This work was supplemented by his *Outlines of the History of Ethics* (1886). In his writings on economics he enlarges on * Mill's exceptions to his general *laissez-faire* principle and so points the way to the modern use of economic theory as an instrument to provide social welfare. His wife, Eleanor Mildred (1845–1936), a sister of A. J. Balfour, shared his intense interest in physical research. She became President of Newnham College in 1892, her husband having successfully worked for the admission of women to the university and its examinations in the 1880s.

Sidmouth, 1st Viscount *see* **Addington, Henry**

Sidney, Algernon (1622–1683). English radical. A son of the 2nd Earl of Leicester and a grandnephew of Sir Philip * Sidney, in the Civil War he fought for the parliamentary forces. Though he opposed Cromwell's Protectorship he was forced after the Restoration to live as an exile on the continent until 1677. After another visit to France (1679) during which it was alleged (without proof) that he was bribed by Louis XIV, he returned to England and was arrested after the discovery of the Rye House plot to murder Charles II on his way back from Newmarket. Tried by Judge Jeffreys, he was condemned on doubtful evidence for treason and beheaded. His name was officially cleared in 1689. His *Discourses Concerning Government*, attacking the patriarchalism of Filmer and advocating aristocratical republicanism, were printed in 1689.

Sidney, Sir Philip (1554–1586). English poet and soldier. Nephew of Robert Dudley, Earl of Leicester, travels as a young man enabled him to absorb continental and especially Italian culture, and on his return to Elizabeth I's court he seemed, with his looks, his birth, talents and chivalrous attitude to life, the English personification of the Renaissance ideal. There were numerous portraits (including miniatures) painted of him. Ill-timed advice to the queen against her proposed French marriage robbed him of her favour, but he returned to court in 1583 and was knighted. He married (1583) the daughter of Walsingham. After his death at Zutphen (where he was said to have passed a cup of water to a wounded soldier in even greater need) during Leicester's campaign to aid the Dutch against the Spaniards, he became a national hero. Over 200 poems were produced in commemoration of his death.

None of his works was published in his lifetime. *Arcadia*, a pastoral prose romance with poems interspersed, was begun in 1580 and published in 1590. The *Apologie for Poetrie* (called in a later edition *Defense of Poesie*) was written about the same time; it was the first application of Italian critical methods to English poetry. *Astrophel and Stella*, consisting of 108 Petrarchan sonnets and eleven songs, is believed to have been inspired by his love for Penelope Devereux, daughter of the 1st Earl of Essex, after she had been forced to marry against her will (1580).
Wallace, M. M., *The Life of Sir Philip Sidney*. 1915

Siemens, Sir William (Karl Wilhelm Siemens) (1823–1883). German-born engineer who became a naturalized British subject (1859). He first visited England in 1843 and 1844 to launch two of his own and his brother's processes and settled there to take advantage of the more favourable patent laws. His principal researches were on applications of heat and electricity. Among his many inventions

were a gas-fired regenerative furnace (1848) later used for open-hearth steel production, an early platinum resistance thermometer (1871), and the electric-arc steel furnace (1879). He also designed the steamship *Faraday*, which laid the first transatlantic cable (1874). Already an F.R.S. he was president of the British Association (1882) and was knighted in the following year. His elder brother **Ernst Werner von Siemens** (1816–1892) invented the self-excited dynamo and was a pioneer of telegraphy.
Scott, J. D., *The Siemens Brothers*. 1958

Sienkiewicz, Henryk (1846–1916). Polish novelist. His early novels belong to the idealistic school but in 1883 he published *Fire and Sword* which, with *The Deluge* (1884) and *Pan Michael* (1887), pictured the troubled scene of the 17th century in Poland. With *Quo Vadis* (1896), a story of Nero's persecution of Christians, he won an international reputation, later enhanced by *The Crusaders* (1900), which told of the Polish struggle against the Teutonic knights. He won the Nobel Prize for Literature (1905).

Sieyès, Emmanuel Joseph, Comte (1748–1836). French politician (often known by his pre-Revolutionary title, Abbé Sieyès). His pamphlet, *Qu'est-ce que le tiers état?*, written on the eve of the revolution and indicating the role the 'third estate' might take in bringing about constitutional change, had great influence. In the early days he was a prominent adherent of * Mirabeau in the National Assembly and helped to draw up the Constitution of 1791; but later, though he voted for the king's execution, he was cautiously inactive. 'I survived' was his answer when asked what part he had played in 'the Terror'. At first he refused to join the Directory but when it was re-formed under Barras's leadership (June 1799) he became a member. But he saw the need for further change: 'We must have a head and a sword', he said. For 'the head' he did not have to look far, for the 'sword' he chose the popular General Bonaparte and joined with him in staging the revolution of 18 Brumaire (9 November 1799). Unfortunately, Bonaparte was not content to be 'sword' alone. He emerged as First Consul and Sieyès's constitution was doctored to ensure Bonaparte's primacy. Disappointed, Sieyès refused to be Second Consul and was compensated by a seat in the Senate and a large estate. He was an exile in Brussels after Napoleon's fall until the revolution (1830) which brought Louis Philippe to the throne enabled him to return.

Sihanouk: *see* **Norodom Sihanouk**

Sikorski, Wladyslaw (1881–1943). Polish soldier and politician. In the Poland made independent by World War I he distinguished himself against the Russians (1920); he was prime minister (1922–23) and then minister of war, but soon resigned after opposing the dictatorship of * Pilsudski. After Poland as overrun at the beginning of World War II he became prime minister of the government in exile, at first in France and then in England, raising troops among the Polish miners in northern France and elsewhere. He was killed in an air crash.

Sikorsky, Igor Ivanovich (1889–1972). Russo-American engineer, born in Kiev and resident in the U.S.A. from 1919. He built (1913) the first multi-engined aeroplane (the four-engined Bolsche) and introduced (1940) practical single-rotor helicopters.
Sikorsky, I. I., *Recollections and Thoughts of a Pioneer*. 1964

Silhouette, Étienne de (1709–1767). French minister of finance (1759). He acquired such a reputation for parsimony that his name was given to likenesses obtained cheaply by tracing the shadow of a face in profile thrown by a lighted candle on to a sheet of paper and then blackening the enclosed space.

Sillanpäa, Frans Emil (1888–1964). Finnish novelist. The Finnish Civil War of 1918 provided the background of *Mark Heritage* (1919), by which he first became known. *The Maid Silja* (1931; *Fallen Asleep While Young*) brought international acclaim. He won the Nobel Prize for Literature (1939).

Silone, Ignazio (Secondo Tranquilli) (1900–1978). Italian novelist. Communist and socialist by turns, he was imprisoned several times by Mussolini before escaping to live in Switzerland (until 1944). His best known novel, *Fontamara* (1933), describes the effects of Fascism on an Italian village. Other works include *The School for Dictators* (1938), *The Secret of Lucca* (1958), and a play *The Story of a Humble Christian* (1969).

Simenon, Georges (Joseph) (1903–). French-Belgian novelist, born in Liège. He left school at 16, became a journalist and in 1922 went to Paris, where he wrote more than 200 short popular novels under 16 different pseudonyms. In 1930 he published the first of 80 detective novels featuring Inspector Maigret: some were translated into 30 languages, 50 were filmed and others used in a popular television series. Maigret's popularity diverted attention away from Simenon's penetrating psychological novels. As André Gide wrote to Simenon: 'You are living on a false reputation—just like Baudelaire or Chopin . . . You are much more important than is commonly supposed.' He lived in the U.S. 1945–55, then in Switzerland. Simenon published more than 200 novels in his own name and autobiographical studies, *When I was Old* (1972) and *Intimate Memoirs* (1981).

Simeon Stylites, St (*c.* 390–459). Early Christian ascetic. He was born in Cilicia and is said to have spent about thirty years in preaching and contemplation on the top of a tall pillar (Greek *stylos*, hence his name), near Antioch. This feat, which attracted many imitators, is the subject of a poem by Tennyson.

Simnel, Lambert (*c.* 1475–*c.* 1525). English pretender. A boy of humble birth, he was carefully coached by a priest, Roger Simon, to play the part of the Earl of Warwick, son of the Duke of Clarence and nephew of Edward IV. He was 'recognized' by Warwick's aunt, the Duchess of Burgundy, and was taken to Ireland (1486) and crowned in Dublin as Edward VI (1487). With a small Yorkist following and a few mercenaries sent from Burgundy, he then crossed to England, but was defeated and captured near Stoke-on-Trent. As a sign of contempt Henry VII employed him in the royal kitchen.

Simon, Herbert Alexander (1916–). American social scientist. He held chairs at the Carnegie-Mellon University, Pittsburgh, from 1949 and was professor of computer science and psychology 1965–81. He worked on the 'behavioural' theory of how firms work and on computer modelling. His books included *The Sciences of the Artificial* (1969) and *Human Problem Solving* (with Alan Newell; 1972). He won the 1978 Nobel Prize for Economics.

Simon, Sir John (1816–1904). British physician. He held the post of surgeon at St Thomas's Hospital, London, from 1847, and built up a reputation as a great teacher in pathology. In 1848 he became Medical Officer of Health for the City of London and thereafter devoted himself to sanitary improvement, writing a series of influential reports on water supply, cholera, vaccination etc. He was one of the leading proponents in England of compulsory smallpox vaccination. In public life, he insisted that the field of urban public health should be staffed by medical experts, rather than by bureaucrats. His own medical eminence gave him the ear of government. During his period of overseeing London's health enormous strides were made in improving the sanitation of the capital, including the development of the present system of mains sewage.

Lambert, R., *Sir John Simon*. 1962

Simon, John Allsebrook Simon, 1st Viscount (1873–1954). English lawyer and politician. Born in Manchester, the son of a Congregational minister, he was elected to a fellowship at All Souls College, Oxford, and was called to the bar in 1899. He had a brilliant legal career (K.C. in 1908) and having entered parliament as a Liberal (1906) was solicitor general (1910–13), attorney general (1913–15), and then home secretary. He resigned (1916) in opposition to conscription in World War I and after brief military service returned to the bar, where for a time his income was £50,000 a year. His expression of opinion in parliament that a general strike was illegal did much to end that of 1926. He headed the statutory commission on Indian constitutional reforms (1927–30). In 1931 he adhered to the coalition as leader of the National Liberals, and was foreign secretary (1931–35), chancellor of the exchequer (1937–40) and lord chancellor (1940–45). He was a distinguished lawyer but, despite the force and clarity of his intellect, lacked the human qualities that would have made him a great politician.

Simon, J. A., *Retrospect*. 1952

Simpson, Sir James Young, 1st Bart. (1811–1870). Scottish physician. He was professor of medicine and midwifery at Edinburgh University (1839–70), where he introduced the use of anaesthetics in childbirth (1847), using ether at first. He discovered (1847), the anaesthetic properties of chloroform previously used only as an antiseptic. The original antagonism to its use was overcome when it was given to Queen Victoria for the birth of Prince Leopold. In 1866 he was made a baronet. He anticipated the discovery of Röntgen rays.

Sinan ('the Great') (1489–1588). Turkish architect. Born of Christian parents, he worked for the sultanate as a military engineer, then as an architect, constructing 79 mosques, 34 palaces and many other public buildings. The mosques of Sultan Sulaiman I in Istanbul and Sultan Selim at Edirne are considered his masterpieces.

Sinatra, Frank (Francis Albert) (1915–). American popular singer and film actor. He began his career as a crooner with the Harry James and Tommy Dorsey bands in the 1930s, and made his first film in 1941. The most popular and successful of his early films were *Anchors Aweigh* (1945) and *On The Town* (1949). His first non-singing dramatic role was in *From Here to Eternity* (1953). He made over forty films and also gained an international audience as a singer (on record and in cabaret). His style changed from the romantic to the abrasive *c.* 1960, but he remained highly popular throughout the 1960s and 1970s.

Sinclair, Archibald Henry MacDonald, 1st Viscount Thurso (1890–1970). British Liberal politician. He led the independent Liberals (1935–45) and was air minister in Sir Winston Churchill's wartime coalition (1940–45).

Sinclair, Upton (Beall) (1878–1968). American novelist and socialist. He wrote over seventy novels, most of them dealing with social evils. They include *The Jungle* (1906), an exposure of conditions in Chicago stockyards, *The Moneychangers* (1908), *King Coal* (1917) and *Oil* (1927). With *World's End* (1940) he began a series of eleven novels about his hero Lanny Budd. It provides in the form of fiction a socialist view of contemporary history. He founded End Poverty in California (EPIC), ran as Democratic candidate for governor (1934) and was narrowly defeated.
Sinclair, U. B., *The Autobiography of Upton Sinclair*. 1962

Singer, Isaac Bashevis (1904–). American novelist and journalist, born in Poland. He emigrated to America in 1935 and joined the staff of the *Jewish Daily Forward.* He wrote novels and short stories of Jewish-American life and they include *The Slave* (1962), *The Manor* (1967) and *The Estate* (1969). He was awarded the Nobel Prize for Literature in 1978.

Singer, Isaac Merrit (1811–1875). American inventor. He patented (1851) a practical sewing machine. Although he lost a suit for infringement brought by Elias Howe, his company was already well established and soon took the lead in manufacturing sewing machines.

Sitting Bull (1834–1890). American Indian chief. He was head of the Dakota Sioux from 1875, led them in the war of 1876–77 and defeated Custer's U.S. army at the Battle of Little Big Horn (1876).

Sitwell, Dame Edith Louisa (1887–1964). **Sir Osbert, 5th Bart.** (1892–1969) and **Sir Sacheverell, 6th Bart.** (1897–). English writers, children of the eccentric **Sir George Revesby Sitwell, 4th Bart.** (1860–1943). It is probable that this formidable (though essentially kindly) personality was unconsciously instrumental in transforming his children into a closely-knit literary clan. Their actual work was, however, highly individual. Edith Sitwell, by using startling or grotesque images, odd epithets (e.g. 'periwigged green leaves') and many other arresting techniques, e.g. the adaptation of poetry to dance rhythms, escaped from the conventional constraints of the poetry of her time. A miscellany called *Wheels* (1916–21), funded by her brothers, friends and herself, helped to make her work more widely known. Her best known collection was *Façade* (1923), declaimed with great success to chamber accompaniment by William * Walton. Her *Collected Poems* were issued in 1930. Among her prose works are a perceptive biography of Pope (1930), *The English Eccentrics* (1933), and *The Queens and the Hive* (1962), in which are interwoven the stories of Elizabeth I and Mary Queen of Scots.

Osbert Sitwell's elegantly satirical verse and prose had long been familiar to the connoisseur before he reached a much wider public with his diverting and idiosyncratic autobiographical works, beginning with *Left Hand, Right Hand* (1945) and later including

The Secret Tree (1946) and *Laughter in the Next Room* (1949).

Sacheverell Sitwell's books were more specifically confined to the arts, especially of southern Europe; they revealed a fastidious taste, an alert eye for landscape and a curiosity ever ready to investigate the unknown. He wrote on Mozart (1932) and Liszt (1935), but more characteristic are, e.g., *Southern Baroque Art* (1931), *British Architects* and *Craftsmen* (1945) and *Gothic Europe* (1969). He has also published numerous small volumes of poetry.

Pearson, J., *Façades*. 1978

Sixtus IV (Francesco della Rovere) (1414–1484). Pope (from 1471). Famous as a patron of art and architecture, he embellished Rome with the Sistine Chapel, named after him, and many other buildings.

Sixtus V (Felice Peretti) (1521–1590). Pope (from 1585). During his short term of office he proved himself one of the most effective of the counter-Reformation popes. He suppressed banditry in the papal states, disciplined the factious Roman nobility, and finished the dome of St Peter's. He reformed the ecclesiastical administration by raising the number of cardinals in council to fifteen, each with a separate sphere of responsibility; he hastened the revision of the Vulgate. In foreign affairs, he prompted the Armada against England, but supported the compromise by which Henry IV became king of France.

Skanderbeg, George Castriota (1403–1468). Albanian national hero. He rose high in Turkish service, but when an attempt was made to conquer Albania he renounced Islam and in 1443 led a national rising of the Albanian and Montenegrin chiefs. With some support from Venice, Naples and the pope, he preserved Albanian independence for over twenty years. But as the years passed his followers dwindled and support from outside failed; his cause died with him.

Skelton, John (*c.* 1460–1529). English poet. Born probably in Norfolk, he became tutor to Prince Henry (Henry VIII). He was ordained (1498) and for the rest of his life he spent his time mostly in London, where he became notorious for his wild life, buffoonery and practical jokes. Eventually, having offended Wolsey by his satires on the clergy, e.g. *Colyn Cloute* (1522), he took sanctuary in Westminster Abbey where he remained till his death. One of his best known works, *The Tunnying of Elynour Rummyng*, describes a drunken woman's revels. His metrical lines (Skeltonics) have been described as 'voluble, breathless doggerel', but deserve a higher reputation. His one surviving morality play, *Magnyfycence*, was possibly written as a guide to good government for the young Henry.

Skinner, B(urrhus) F(rederic) (1904–). American experimental psychologist. He taught at Harvard from 1931 and was professor of psychology 1947–75. Skinner became the major proponent of 'behaviourism', an extension of the work of * Pavlov and J. B. Watson, which asserts that behaviour should only be examined empirically and objectively as a series of reactions to stimuli. Skinner's teachings aroused much controversy because they assumed a mechanistic view of human experience, with no recognition of 'inner states'. He wrote *Science and Human Behaviour* (1953), *Walden Two* (1948) and *Beyond Freedom and Dignity* (1971).

Skinner, Otis (1858–1942). American actor. He won a great reputation in Shakespearian parts (especially Falstaff) in London and New York, and in 1911 played in a two-year run of *Kismet*. His daughter, **Cornelia Otis Skinner** (1901–1979), a well-known actress and writer, wrote books of reminiscence, e.g. *Our Hearts were Young and Gay* (1942).

Skryabin, *see* **Scriabin, Alexander Nikolayevich**

Slade, Felix (1790–1868). English antiquary and collector. He left £350,000 to found art professorships at Oxford, Cambridge and London Universities. The Slade School of Art, London, is named after him.

Slater, Oscar (died 1946). Scottish convict, victim of a notorious miscarriage of justice. In 1909 he received a sentence of death (afterwards commuted) for the murder of an old woman at Glasgow. Sir Arthur Conan * Doyle, convinced that it was a case of mistaken identity, waged a strenuous campaign as a result of which Slater was finally released (1927).

Slim, William Joseph Slim, 1st Viscount (1891–1970). British soldier. In World War II

he commanded an Indian division in the Middle East and the 15th Corps in Burma before being appointed to commahd the 14th Army (1943–45). In this capacity he was responsible for halting the Japanese offensive in Burma and for directing the great campaign by which Mandalay, Rangoon and the rest of the country were eventually liberated. After the war he served as chief of the Imperial General Staff (1948–52) and governor general of Australia (1953–60). In 1949 he became a field-marshal.
Slim, W. J., *Unofficial History*. 1959

Sloane, Sir Hans, 1st Bart. (1660–1753). British physician. After studying medicine in France he made a journey to the West Indies from which he brought back (1689) some 800 species of plants. He then settled in practice in Bloomsbury, London. His undiminished interest in natural history was, however, shown by his book *A Voyage to the Islands of Madeira* (1707 and 1725). When the colony of Georgia was founded (1732–33) as a refuge for debtors, Sloane was one of the promoters. The great collection of books, manuscripts and curiosities which he handed over to the nation (1749) became the nucleus of the British Museum. He was made a baronet in 1716.

Smart, Christopher (1722–1771). English poet. Though a scholar of distinction, he was forced to leave Cambridge owing to debts, and his whole life was dogged by poverty. Most of his early work was trivial but after a serious illness followed by attacks of insanity he turned to religion, and besides a poetical version of the Psalms wrote his tender, imaginative masterpiece *A Song to David*. In similar vein is his *Rejoice in the Lamb*. He died in a debtors' prison.

Smeaton, John (1724–1792). English engineer. The son of a Leeds lawyer, he was intended to enter his father's firm, but from boyhood showed the keenest interest in mechanics and engineering. He was elected F.R.S. in 1753 and won fame when he rebuilt the Eddystone Lighthouse (1756–59) to a new and successful design. For his work on the mechanical laws governing the construction of wind- and water-mills he received the Royal Society's Copley Medal (1759).

Smetana, Bedřich (1824–1884). Czech composer. Founder of the Bohemian Nationalist school, he was born in south-east Bohemia, his father being the manager of a country brewery. He studied music in Prague and subsequently earned a living as a music master in a nobleman's family and then in a school of his own. In 1856 he went to Sweden as a conductor to the Philharmonic Society of Gothenburg and in the next few years he wrote some symphonic poems (e.g. *Wallenstein's Camp*) on non-Czech subjects. Back in Prague in 1861, he eventually became the chief conductor of the Provisional Theatre, where the Austrians allowed plays and operas to be given in Czech. Of his eight patriotic operas, *The Bartered Bride* (produced 1870), a gay peasant comedy, is the most popular. Apart from the operas his best known works are *Má Vlast* (*My Country*), a cycle of six symphonic poems (1874–79) and two String Quartets (1876 and 1882). From 1874 he struggled against the handicaps of deafness and mental illness by which he was finally incapacitated. * Dvořák and others maintained the nationalist tradition of Czech music created by him.
Clapham, J., *Smetana*. 1972

Smiles, Samuel (1812–1904). Scottish writer. After studying medicine at Edinburgh, and working as a surgeon in Leeds, an editor and a secretary to railway companies, he achieved enormous success with his *Self Help* (1857), translated into seventeen languages, a collection of lives of great or successful men held up as models to Victorian schoolchildren. This was followed by, e.g., *Thrift* (1875) and *Duty* (1880); he also wrote several biographies, e.g. *George Stephenson* (1857).

Smith, Adam (1723–1790). Scottish economist, born at Kirkcaldy, Fife, the posthumous child of a comptroller of customs. He studied at Oxford University for seven years before returning to Scotland where he was one of the brilliant intellectual circle of which David * Hume became the best known member. As professor of moral philosophy at Glasgow (1752–64) he gained fame as a lecturer and wrote *Theory of Moral Sentiments* (1759). He travelled in France (1764–66) as tutor to the young Earl of Buccleuch and in Paris met * Turgot and * Necker and discussed their economic ideas. In 1776 he settled in London where he joined Dr * Johnson's literary circle. In the same year he published his *Inquiry into the Nature and Causes of the Wealth of Nations*, the original source of most future writing on political economy. He was opposed to the monopolistic mercantilism (e.g. Navigation Acts, trading monopolies such as the East India Company etc.) that had dominated previous economic thinking, but neither was he an uncritical advocate of *laissez-faire*. He believed with Hume that enlightened self-interest would promote public welfare, but insisted in all his works on the maintenance of the link between individual freedom and such moral obligations as kindness, sympathy and justice. Individual freedom releases the energy that produces wealth, but the wealth can only fructify by the consumption of goods, not by being hoarded as gold. He also saw that unfettered individual enterprise must be combined with the division of labour (i.e. specialization) to maximize efficiency. Specialization entails the need for markets, which in turn need a common purchasing medium, a conclusion leading to considering methods of determining money values. Thus, one by one, he considered the many interlocking factors of political economy. Though some of Adam Smith's conclusions have been assailed or even overthrown, *The Wealth of Nations* has been one of the most influential books ever produced, and Smith has been considered the founder of the study of political economy as a separate discipline.

Rae, J., *Life of Adam Smith*. Repr. 1965

Smith, Al(fred Emanuel) (1873–1944). American Democratic politician, born in New York City. In 1928 he was the Democratic presidential candidate, the first Catholic nominee of a major party, but lost heavily to * Hoover. He was a 'wringing wet' opponent of prohibition, and campaigned against child labour and for state parks. In 1932 he contested the presidential nomination against F.D. * Roosevelt, failed and was a bitter loser.

Smith, George (1824–1901). English publisher. A founder of Smith & Elder (1846), he appointed * Thackeray as editor of his new *Cornhill* magazine (1860) and also started the *Pall Mall Gazette* (1880). Among the famous writers whose works he published were George Eliot, the Brownings, Mrs Gaskell and Anthony Trollope. The original edition of the *Dictionary of National Biography* (1885–1900) was his biggest publishing achievement.

Smith, George Joseph (1872–1915). English criminal. Convicted in the 'Brides in the Bath' case, a famous murder trial, he killed three wives in succession by drowning them in a bath in circumstances suggesting natural death. In this way he acquired from them some £3,500. Only the chance reading of similar reports in different parts of the country led to inquiries and his arrest.

Smith, Ian Douglas (1919–). Rhodesian (Zimbabwe) politician. After distinguished service as a pilot in the R.A.F. during World War II he played an increasingly important part in Southern Rhodesian and Federal politics. In 1961 he helped to found the Rhodesian Front, headed by Winston Field. When the party came into power in Southern Rhodesia (1962) Smith was deputy premier to Field, whom he succeeded in 1964. The policy of a Unilateral Declaration of Independence (UDI), based on the fear that Britain would hasten majority (i.e. African) rule of the country, was already in Smith's mind, but he delayed its implementation until the breakdown of negotiations with the British Government in 1965. After thirteen years of unconstitutional rule, Smith negotiated an agreement in 1978 with some of the black nationalist leaders, which was rejected by the Patriotic Front. When black majority rule was finally attained in 1980, Smith continued to represent the white minority.

Smith, John (1580–1631). English adventurer. He had already had an extraordinary career as a soldier of fortune – mainly in service against the Turks during which he escaped from slavery – and as a Mediterranean pirate when (1605) he joined the expedition to colonize Virginia. Captured by Indians, he was saved, it was said, by the young Princess * Pocahontas, whom he subsequently married. He wrote books about the colony as well as a highly coloured autobiography.

Smith, Joseph (1805–1844). American religious teacher. Founder of the Mormons, he was the son of a Vermont farmer and from boyhood claimed to have had visionary experiences. In 1830 he published the *Book of Mormon*, the original of which, inscribed on gold plates, was said to have come into his hands (with instructions for translation) as the result of an angelic visitation. The book purported to be supplementary to the Bible and to contain divine revelations to Mormon, a prophet of the era, concerning the history of a second 'chosen people' which came from Jerusalem and, before the Red Indians, inhabited America. The Church of Jesus Christ of Latter-Day Saints was founded in 1830 and attracted many converts as well as much ridicule and persecution, which forced the 'saints' to move several times before they found a permanent home. In 1843 Smith split the community, then settled in Illinois, by announcing a divine message favouring polygamy. More persecution followed; in 1844 he announced his intention to stand for the presidency. Smith and his brother Hyrum were arrested on charges of conspiracy and were murdered by a mob which broke into the jail.

Smith, Sir Matthew (1879–1959). English painter. Born at Halifax, Yorkshire, he studied art in Manchester, London and eventually Paris, where he joined the school of Matisse. His life thereafter was spent between France and England. His scale is large, his composition simplified and bold, and both are admirably suited to the luxuriance and translucence of his colours; for subjects he turned to flowers, fruits and nudes. He was knighted in 1954.

Smith, Stevie (Florence Margaret Smith) (1902–1971). British poet, born in Hull, Yorkshire. She published several collections of verse, three novels and two critical editions; one of T. S. Eliot's verse, one of children's poetry. She won the Queen's Gold Medal for Poetry (1969). There is a great sense of humour, even comedy, in her work, at the same time as a sense of isolation and blankness, and a preoccupation with death. Her *Collected Poems* appeared in 1975.
Dick, K., *Ivy Compton-Burnett and Stevie Smith*. 1971

Smith, Sydney (1771–1845). British clergyman, journalist and wit. He was born in Essex, educated at Winchester and Oxford, and having gone to Edinburgh as a private tutor planned the *Edinburgh Review* (1802), the first three numbers of which he edited. He remained a regular contributor; among the causes he supported were Roman Catholic emancipation (*The Letters of Peter Plymley*, 1807–08) and the Reform Bill. While in London his lectures and sermons were attended for their wit as much as their serious content: a consummate conversationalist, he was a *habitué* of the Whig salons at Holland House. In 1831 he became a canon of St Paul's.
Auden, W. H. (ed.), *Selected Writings of Sydney Smith*. 1957

Smith, Thomas Southwood (1788–1861). Scottish physician. He served on various government inquiries into living and working conditions, and in 1839 was a founder member of the 'Health of Towns' association. From 1847 he served on the General Board of Health and produced important reports on quarantine, cholera, yellow fever and sanitary improvement. Southwood Smith made few theoretical advances in the field of public health. His importance lay in combining medical competence with high ideals of public service and administrative capacity. He was in many respects a follower of Jeremy * Bentham.

Smith, William (1769–1839) ('Strata' Smith). British cartographer. Smith's achievement was actually to determine the succession of English strata from the coal measures up to the chalk in greater detail than previously and to establish their fossil specimens. But his greatest work lay in mapping. Smith rightly saw the map was the perfect medium for presenting stratigraphical knowledge. In developing a form of map which showed outcrops in block, he set the essential pattern for geological mapping throughout the nineteenth century.
Cox, L. R., *William Smith and the Birth of Stratigraphy*. 1948

Smith, William Henry (1792–1865). English newsagent. He built up a small firm inherited from his parents by creating a speedy country delivery service, using fast carts, coaches and eventually railways.

His son, also William Henry (1825–1891), secured contracts for most of the railway bookstalls, became a Conservative MP (1868–91) and was first lord of the admiralty (1877–80) and first lord of the treasury (1886–91). His widow was created Viscountess Hambledon.

Smith, William Robertson (1846–1894). Scottish theologian. As professor of Hebrew and Old Testament Exegis at the Free Church College, Aberdeen, he excited animosity with his 'heretical' articles in the 9th edition of the *Encyclopaedia Britannica*, and was deprived of his chair. He became Professor of Arabic at Cambridge in 1883.

Smith-Dorrian, Sir Horace Lockwood (1858–1930). British soldier. During a distinguished career he fought in the Zulu War (1879), in Egypt and the Sudan, and in the Boer War, during which he became major-general. In World War I he commanded the 2nd Corps of the B.E.F. and, from December 1914 to April 1915, the newly created 2nd Army. He was then dismissed for suggesting a slight withdrawal (which in fact proved inevitable) after the first German gas attack.

Smithson, James Macie (1765–1829). English scientist. Natural son of the 1st Duke of Northumberland, he studied chemistry and mineralogy. In 1826 the Royal Society rejected a paper he had written and in revenge he left the reversion of £105,000 to found an institution in Washington 'for the increase and diffusion of knowledge among men'. This was the basis of the great Smithsonian Institution.

Smollett, Tobias George (1721–1771). Scottish-born novelist. He received a medical training in Glasgow, went to London in 1739 and in 1740 sailed with the fleet to the West Indies as surgeon's mate. It was not until *The Adventures of Roderick Random* was published (1748) that he achieved literary success. *The Adventures of Peregrine Pickle* (1751) followed, and thus encouraged, Smollett started an intensive publishing career in Chelsea. Of the many works produced there by himself and his collaborators the best was *The Expedition of Humphry Clinker* (1771). His last years were mainly occupied by travels in search of health, injured by hard work and the worries due to the ease with which he gave and took offence. He died near Leghorn (Livorno). In construction and characterization his picaresque novels do not equal those of * Fielding, but he had a great gift for narrative and a very observant eye.

Knapp, L. M., *Tobias Smollett: Doctor of Men and Manners*. 1949

Smuts, Jan Christiaan (1870–1950). South African soldier and politician. He was born in Cape Colony and after attending Victoria College, in Stellenbosch, completed his education in England, at Christ's College, Cambridge, where he won high honours in law. He was admitted to the bar in Cape Colony (1895), entered politics but turned against * Rhodes after the Jameson Raid. Leaving the Cape for the Transvaal he became President * Kruger's attorney general. In the latter stages of the Boer War he proved himself one of the most successful guerrilla leaders, penetrating deep into Cape Colony with his raids. He played a leading part at the Peace Conference of Vereeniging (1902). In the following years he became a close political associate of General * Botha and together they built up the South African party. When the Union of South Africa was formed (1910) Botha was prime minister while Smuts held key posts as minister of the interior and defence. With Botha he was a strong supporter of Britain in the World War I and took over command against * Lettow-Vorbeck in East Africa. After Botha's death Smuts succeeded as prime minister (1919). He was defeated in 1924 but was minister of justice in Hertzog's coalition from 1933 until 1939 when he overcame Hertzog's policy of neutrality in the World War II by taking over the premiership. South Africa thus allied with the rest of the Commonwealth, but Smuts, who became a British field-marshal in 1941, lost ground to the Nationalists. He was defeated in the 1948 election.

Smuts had a fine brain and a subtle and agile intelligence which sometimes led outwitted opponents to charge him with duplicity. His finest and most enduring achievements were probably in the international field, especially in the formative stages of the League of Nations and the United Nations. In South Africa itself he did much to weld together the Europeans of British and Dutch descent, but despite his long term of office made no real attempt to tackle the racial problem. He was awarded the CH (1917) and OM (1947).

Hancock, W. K., *Smuts*. 2 vols. 1962 and 1968

Smyth, Dame Ethel Mary (1858–1944). British composer and feminist. She studied in Leipzig, and her early operas, the best known of which was *The Wreckers* (1906), were produced in Germany. A comic opera, *The Boatswain's Mate* (1916), was founded on a short story by W. W. Jacobs. She also wrote much chamber music and a Mass in D. She was imprisoned (1911) for her activities as a suffragette, for which movement she composed a marching song.

Snell, Willebrord van Roijen (1591–1626). Dutch mathematical physicist. He was professor of mathematics at Leyden from 1613 and is best known for the general law (1621), named after him, governing the refraction of light when it passes into a medium of different density. This law which had eluded * Kepler, was published in a slightly improved form (1637) by * Descartes, without acknowledgement to Snell.

Snorri Sturluson (1179–1241). Icelandic historian. He took part in and was killed during the bitter internal struggles by which Iceland was racked in his time. He was one of the most interesting medieval historians, and after visits to Norway wrote a great history of the Norwegian kings in which he showed critical abilities and much insight into character. His *Younger Edda* surveyed Norse mythology and traditions, with the aim of giving help and guidance to poets in search of a theme. His nephew, **Sturla Thordson,** was author of the *Sturlunga Saga.*

Snow, Charles Percy, Baron Snow (1905–1980). English novelist and scientist. As a scientist and a civil service commissioner he was much concerned with the cleavage between humane and scientific traditions of culture. His novels, e.g. *The Masters* (1951), *The Affair* (1959) and *Corridors of Power* (1964), explore the manipulations by which decisions are achieved in a university and in government. He was a member of the Labour government (October 1964) as parliamentary secretary to the new minister of technology, and resigned in March 1966.

Snowden, Philip Snowden, 1st Viscount (1864–1937). British politician. The son of a weaver, he became an excise-man (1886–1891); he entered politics, joined the Independent Labour Party (1894) and was elected M.P. for Blackburn (1906). He was the chancellor of exchequer in the Labour governments of 1924 and 1929 and was known for the rigid orthodoxy of his financial policies. In the coalition government that followed the crisis of 1931 he became lord privy seal but resigned in protest against the abandonment of Free Trade.
Snowden, P. S., *Autobiography.* 1934

Soane, Sir John (1753–1837). English architect, son of a builder. After working under George * Dance the younger, he won a Royal Academy Gold Medal and a travelling studentship (1776–80). On his return he evolved an austere, highly individual modification of the classical style. From 1788 he was architect to the Bank of England, the rebuilding of which occupied forty years. He built the Dulwich College picture gallery and the founder's mausoleum (1811–14), three London churches and among many houses one for himself in Lincoln's Inn Fields. Here he kept his collection of prints, drawings etc., and as a result of his endowment it became and survives as a museum.
Stroud, D., *The Architecture of Sir John Soane.* 1961

Sobieski, Jan (1624–1696). King of Poland as Jan III (from 1674). He was born in Galicia, became a soldier, and after being engaged in constant warfare with Turks and Tartars rose to be Polish commander-in-chief. A great victory over the Turks at Khotin (1673) made him a national hero and in the next year he was elected king. In 1683 he won European renown by putting the cause of Christendom before any considerations of national policy and marching to rescue Vienna from the Turks. Aristocratic faction and intrigue at home disturbed his reign.

Socinus, Faustus (Fausto Sozzini) (1539–1604). Italian theologian. He was known for his anti-Trinitarian doctrines adopted from his uncle **Laelius Socinus** (Lelio Sozzini) (1525–1562). He left Italy (1575) to pursue his theological studies; thence he went to Transylvania and in 1579 to Poland where he remained for the rest of his life. Reason was the test which he applied to doctrines and it was as an offence against reason that he condemned Trinitarianism, though he accepted the immortality of the spirit (but not of the body). He rejected the divinity of Christ, and the doctrine of Original Sin. Socinianism survived in Transylvania into the 20th century, and was influential elsewhere in the 16th and 17th centuries.

Socrates (*c.* 469–399 B.C.). Greek philosopher. The son of a sculptor, he left no writings and the only first-hand evidence concerning his life and thought comes from * Plato and * Xenophon; the former makes him the chief spokesman of his dialogues, but the ideas expressed may well be those of Plato though the method of eliciting them is almost certainly Socratic. The known facts are simple: Socrates served and showed courage in the Peloponnesian War; the rest of his life was spent in Athens where he frequented public places such as markets and gymnasia and talked with anyone who would listen but delighted especially in the company of young men of good mind and pleasing appearance. That these were most often to be found among the young aristocrats (Alcibiades, Critias etc.) may have helped to estrange him from the general populace. He himself was ugly, with thick lips, bulging eyes and flat nose; he walked barefoot, wore the simplest of garments and was indifferent to comfort; but he was no ascetic and could out-drink any of the other guests at a banquet. As it is clear from the caricature of him in *The Clouds* by Aristophanes he was regarded as a sophist, but though he knew, and probably disputed with, sophists he had no use for their verbal pedantries. Nor was he a follower of any school of philosophy. His interests did not extend to the workings of the universe; that each of his followers and friends should learn to know himself was the aim to which his dialectical method was applied. He was no propounder of truths, he only guided the search for truth, or that part of it which lay within the mind of each of his companions. His method was to feign ignorance and then by question and answer to get nearer and nearer to the heart of the matter without achieving a final solution. The achievement of knowledge, he argued, would be the achievement of virtue, for virtue is the knowledge, in its fullest philosophical sense, of what ought to be done, and vice is correspondingly ignorance.

A minor mystery about his character was his claim to be guided in emergencies by a *daimonion* (divine sign) which, since it was peculiar to himself, had more affinity with intuition than conscience. Whatever its exact nature, his talk of it may help to explain the charge of blasphemy which was coupled with that of corrupting the morals of young men when he was brought to trial by the restored democracy in 399. He was found guilty by a very slender majority and later condemned to death. He refused an opportunity of escape and after an interval of thirty days took hemlock, the customary alternative to execution. A moving account of his last day is contained in Plato's dialogue *Phaedo*, in which Phaedo describes him as 'the wisest and justest and best of all men I have ever known'.

Guthrie, W. K. C., *A History of Greek Philosophy*. Vol 3. 1969

Soddy, Frederick (1877–1956). English chemist. He was professor of chemistry at Glasgow (1904–14), Aberdeen (1914–19) and Oxford (1919–36). With * Rutherford he put forward (1903) the radioactive transformation theory showing that radioactivity arises from the spontaneous disintegration of atoms. Soddy's work led to the discovery that certain atomic species, which he called isotopes, could have the same atomic number but different atomic weight. He was elected F.R.S. in 1910 and won the Nobel Prize for Chemistry (1921). Among his important books are *Radioactive Elements* (2 volumes, 1912–14) and *Matter and Energy* (1912).

Soeharto (1921–). Indonesian soldier and politician; President of Indonesia from 1967. He was chief of army staff in 1965–68 when dissatisfaction with the government of President * Soekarno reached a climax. He assumed emergency executive powers in 1966 and became President when Soekarno was deposed in 1967.

Hughes, J., *Indonesian Upheaval*. 1967

Soekarno (or Sukarno; his personal name is given as Achmed or Koesnosoro) (1901–1970). First president of Indonesia 1945–67. Born in Surabaja, East Java, his father was a Javanese Moslem schoolteacher, his mother a Balinese Hindu. He graduated as an engineer in 1925 and in 1927, with D. M. Kasuma, became co-founder of the Indonesian Nationalist Party (PNI). He fought against Dutch colonial rule, being imprisoned (1930–31) and exiled to remote islands (1933–42). After the Japanese invaded the Netherlands East Indies, Soekarno worked with them, visited Japan in 1943, and was made president of the Java central council and of *Putera* ('Centre of Peoples' Power'), a nationalist Islamic Body. On Japan's sudden collapse in August 1945, he proclaimed Indonesian independence and with Mohammed * Hatta set up a provisional government. The British occupied Indonesia and supported the restoration of Dutch rule, at least on a temporary basis, and four years of conflict followed, in which the islands were partitioned in a Netherlands–Indonesian Union. In 1949 the Netherlands recognized Indonesia as a federal state and withdrew; by

1950 a unitary republic was proclaimed. He was prime minister 1959–66 and proclaimed 'President for Life' in 1963. He did much to stimulate a sense of national identity but his rule was marred by extravagance, corruption and caprice. For all his shortcomings as an administrator he was an extraordinary orator and master of communication. Following an abortive coup against the army by the Communist Party (PKI) in September 1965, probably with Soekarno's connivance, he lost power to General * Soeharto and was removed from the presidency in March 1967. Moslem puritans disapproved of his private life.

Solomon (*c.* 970–*c.* 932 B.C.). King of Israel, the son of * David and Bathsheba. Under him the kingdom reached its widest limits and his wealth and luxury became proverbial. He is known as a great builder and is credited with the construction of the great temple at Jerusalem that bore his name. Surrounded by his concubines he ruled as an oriental despot, and his way of life offended the austere nationalists led by the prophets, while heavy taxation alienated popular support. These causes, combined with tribal jealousies, brought about the partition of the country in the next reign. Solomon left behind him a tradition of great wisdom and supernatural powers. He may have written parts of the Biblical book of Proverbs, but the Song of Songs, Ecclesiastes and the apocryphal works attributed to him are much later. The royal dynasty of Ethiopia claims descent from Solomon and the Queen of Sheba.

Solon (*c.* 638–?559 B.C.). Athenian legislator and poet. It seems that he first gained popularity by using poetry to express political aims (e.g. the relief of economic distress). As archon (594–563) he was given unlimited power to make economic and constitutional reforms. He started with his revolutionary *Seisachtheia* (shaking off of burdens) by which all debts were cancelled, land forfeited for debt restored, and those who had pledged their persons as security for debt were freed from slavery: the acceptance of such pledges was in future forbidden. Currency reforms and encouragement of homegrown food (e.g. corn for wine) were among his other measures. He divided the citizens into classes by economic standards, rights and duties being prescribed accordingly. Though the people as a whole were more widely represented in the assembly and the courts, Athens was as yet far from being a democracy. After completing his reforms he refused the offered role of 'tyrant' and spent several years in travels about which many legends were told. He is numbered among the Seven Sages of Greece.
Linforth, I. M., *Solon the Athenian*. 1919

Solti, Sir Georg (1912–). Hungarian–British conductor. A pupil of * Bartok and * Kodaly, he was an excellent pianist, turning to conducting after World War II. He was musical director of the Covent Garden Opera Company 1961–71, the Chicago Symphony 1970– and the Orchestre de Paris 1971–75. He won many awards with his recordings, e.g. the first complete Wagner *Ring* cycle.

Solzhenitsyn, Aleksandr Isayevich (1918–). Russian author and dissident thinker, born in Rostov-on-Don. Son of an office worker, he studied mathematics at Rostov and Moscow Universities, served as an artillery officer and was decorated for bravery. He spent eight years (1945–53) in a forced labour camp in the Arctic for criticising Stalin obliquely in a letter: this was the basis for *One Day in the Life of Ivan Denisovich* (1962). During a three-year exile in Central Asia he was cured of cancer: he used this experience in *Cancer Ward* (1965). Officially rehabilitated in 1957, he became a teacher at Ryazan, and in 1962 during a period of thaw * Khrushchev allowed his first book to be published. *The First Circle* (1967), set in 1948, described Mavrino prison where skilled personnel worked on special KGB projects.

Expelled from the Soviet Writers' Union in 1969, he was awarded the 1970 Nobel Prize for Literature but was prevented from receiving the prize in Stockholm. Later books included *August 1914* (1972) and *The Gulag Archipelago* (1974), a study of a network of Soviet concentration camps, *Lenin in Zurich* (1975), and *The Oak and the Calf* (1980). In 1974 he was expelled from the USSR, settling first in Switzerland, then (1975) in Vermont, USA.
Scammel, M., *Solzhenitsyn: A Biography*. 1984

Somers, John Somers, 1st Baron (1652–1716). English Whig politician. He was a barrister by profession, defended the Seven Bishops put on trial by * James II, and played an important part in drafting the Bill of

Rights. As keeper of the Seal he presided over William III's informal cabinet councils and was one of the king's most trusted advisers. Impeached by his opponents he lost office in 1700 but was briefly restored to power (1708–10) under Queen Anne.

Somerset, Edward Seymour, 1st Duke of (1506?–1552). English nobleman. He became prominent on the marriage of his sister Jane Seymour to Henry VIII. Soon after the accession of his nephew, the boy-king * Edward VI, he was created Duke of Somerset and virtually ruled the country as lord protector. His rough wooing of Mary Queen of Scots on behalf of his master led to the victory of Pinkie (1547), after which Mary was sent to France for safety. In England he hastened the growth of Protestantism; his personal acquisitiveness, coupled with mildness, made him vulnerable to the intrigues of the Earl of Warwick (afterwards Duke of * Northumberland), who engineered his downfall and execution.

Somerville, Mary (*née* Fairfax) (1780–1872). Scottish mathematician and scientific writer. The daughter of Admiral Sir William Fairfax, she wrote *Celestial Mechanism* (1830) and a popular version of Laplace's work. Somerville College, Oxford, one of the first women's colleges, is named after her.
Somerville, M., *Autobiography*. 1873

Soong, T. V. (Tse-ven) (1891–1971). Chinese politician. Son of a well known industrialist, he held many offices in Kuomintang governments including that of prime minister (1944–47). One of his sisters married * Sun Yat-sen, the other * Chiang Kai-shek.

Sophia (1630–1714). Electress of Hanover. Her descent from James I of Great Britain accounted for the accession to the British throne of her son George I and the Hanoverian dynasty. Her parents were Frederick V of the Palatinate and * Elizabeth, daughter of James I. Sophia married (1658) Ernest Augustus, afterwards elector of Hanover. Under the British Act of Settlement (1701), which excluded Roman Catholics, the crown was to pass (on the assumption that Anne died childless) to Sophia; but as she had predeceased Queen Anne it was her son who succeeded.

Sophocles (*c.* 495–406 B.C.). Greek dramatist. Born near Athens into a prosperous family, he is said to have led a boys' choir which celebrated the naval victory of Salamis; later having failed as an actor owing to the weakness of his voice he devoted himself to writing plays. A mark of his success was that he won first prize at the great festival of the god Dionysus eighteen times. Of over 100 plays written by him only seven survive complete. *Ajax*, almost certainly the earliest, takes up the hero's story from the point when he is driven to suicide by anger and disappointment at not being awarded the arms of Achilles. Conflicts provoked by refusal to accord him honourable burial are the theme of the play, which ends with a change of decision by King Agamemnon. In *Antigone* the theme is similar, but the efforts of the Theban princess (the title role) to bury her brother Polynices result in a series of tragic events, including her own death. *Oedipus the King* (usually considered his masterpiece) and the sequel *Oedipus at Colonus* (the latest of the surviving plays) tell the terrible story of Oedipus, king of Thebes, who, having discovered that unknowingly he had killed his father and married his own mother, came in his last years, an old, blinded and impoverished exile, to seek his death. *Electra* is Sophocles's version of the events that followed the murder of the heroine's mother Clytaemnestra, the unfaithful wife of Agamemnon. The *Trachiniae* (*Maidens of Trachis*) tells of the death of Heracles at the hands of his wife Deianira who gives him poison in the belief that it is a love charm. *Philocteles* is the story of a Greek hero who, stricken by a loathsome disease, is abandoned by his companions on the way to Troy, but is at last induced to come to their aid with his magic bow. Sophocles, who first introduced a third actor, was the most technically accomplished of all Greek dramatists, both in construction and dramatic language. He is essentially interested in human character and the interplay of one character upon another. Matthew Arnold wrote that he 'saw life steadily and saw it whole'.
Kitto, H. D. F., *Greek Tragedy*. 3rd ed. 1961

Sordello (died *c.* 1270). Italian troubadour, born near Mantua. His love lyrics and other surviving poems are written in Provençal. He is mentioned several times in Dante's *Purgatorio* and is the hero of Robert Browning's *Sordello*.

Sorel, Georges (1847–1922). French civil engineer and social philosopher. Deeply influenced by Marx and Nietzsche, and profoundly pessimistic about the future of European civilization, he was bitterly opposed to bourgeois morality, parliamentarianism and utilitarianism, which he saw as cowardly evasions of history. He became successively a liberal conservative (1889), Marxist revisionist (1893), Dreyfusard (1897), revolutionary syndicalist (1902), supporter of *Action française* (1910), and Bolshevik sympathizer (1919). In *Reflections on Violence* (1908) he urged a 'myth' of a heroic view of man and urged the use of (psychological) violence against the force of the State: out of such a confrontation would come a new order. Both Mussolini and Trotsky admired him.

Sorensen, Soren Peter Lauritz (1868–1939). Danish bio-chemist. As director of the chemical section of the Carlsberg Laboratory, his chief researches were on amino-acids, proteins and enzymes; he is best known for his introduction of the pH scale for expressing acidity and alkalinity in terms of hydrogen-ion concentration. On this scale neutrality is represented by a pH value of 7; different degrees of acidity and alkalinity are represented by pH values respectively below and above 7.

Sothern, Edward Askew (1826–1881). English actor. He made theatrical history with the part of Lord Dundreary in Tom Taylor's *Our American Cousin*, first produced in New York in 1858, followed by a 400-night run in London. The vogue for 'Dundreary whiskers' provided a new form of embellishment for the Victorian male. Sothern was renowned as a practical joker.

Soult, Nicholas Jean de Dieu, Duke of Dalmatia (1769–1851). Marshal of France. After serving in the ranks he rose to become a general (1799) in the French Revolutionary armies and in 1802 was created a marshal. He played a decisive role at Austerlitz (1805) and commanded the right wing at Jena (1806). In 1807 he drove the British forces from Spain, and was made a duke in 1808. In the subsequent campaigns against Wellington in the Peninsula he fought with varying fortune but could never achieve a decisive success, and as Napoleon became less able to reinforce him was gradually driven back. In 1813 he was unable to prevent Wellington breaking through into France. Soult acted as chief of staff to Napoleon in the Waterloo campaign, after which he was banished. Recalled in 1820 he served under Louis Philippe as ambassador in London (1838), minister for foreign affairs (1839) and of war (1840).

Soult, N. J. de D., *Mémoires*. 1854

Sousa, John Philip (1854–1932). American bandmaster and composer, born in Washington. The son of a Portuguese father and a Bavarian mother, he was leader of the band of the U.S. marine corps (1880–92) and then formed his own band, with which he toured the world. He was a prolific composer of marches, including *The Stars and Stripes for Ever* and *The Washington Post*.

Soustelle, Jacques (1912–). French anthropologist and politician. He studied and wrote about Aztec culture in Mexico, turning to politics during World War II when he joined the Free French movement. After the war he was a firm supporter of de Gaulle; and hoping to ensure the continued association with France of Algeria – of which he had been governor general (1955–66) – he helped to organize the *coup* that brought de Gaulle back to power (1958). When there was an army revolt in Algiers (1960) against de Gaulle's policy of independence Soustelle was suspected of sympathizing with it and was dismissed from office. An order for his arrest was issued (1962) and he lived outside France until 1968 when a general amnesty was declared.

Southampton, Henry Wriothesley, 3rd Earl of (1573–1624). English nobleman. Best known as the man to whom * Shakespeare dedicated *Venus and Adonis* and *The Rape of Lucrece*, he may have been the 'Mr. W. H.' and the 'lovely boy' of Shakespeare's Sonnets. He lost the favour of Elizabeth I after his secret marriage to Elizabeth Vernon, and was imprisoned for his part in Essex's rebellion (1601). James I pardoned him (1603) and he took part in a number of commercial and colonial enterprises, including the expedition to Virginia (1605). He died of fever on an expedition to the Netherlands to help the Dutch.

Southcott, Joanna (1750–1814). English 'prophetess'. She was a domestic servant, born in Devonshire, who began in 1792 to claim divine inspiration for prophecies in prose and verse announcing the imminent 'second coming' of Jesus Christ. When 64 she claimed that she was about to give miraculous birth to a Prince of Peace, but her own death intervened. An intensive propaganda continues for the opening of a box or boxes left by her. A box was opened in 1927 but no documents or articles of importance were found.

Southey, Robert (1774–1843). English writer. A close friendship with S. T. * Coleridge marked his first years after leaving Oxford University. The two friends married sisters and in 1803 the two couples shared Greta Hall, Keswick. When Coleridge left Keswick that winter he entrusted his wife and family to Southey's care. Southey remained there for the rest of his life, one of the renowned Lakeland poets, with his friend Wordsworth near by. Landor, Lamb and Walter Scott were also among his friends, and the younger writers such as Carlyle and Charlotte Brontë were helped by his kindness. He was a mainstay of the Tory *Quarterly Review*. He was made Poet Laureate in 1813. Overwork brought about his mental breakdown in 1839. Time has dealt unkindly with his work and of his vast output of poetry and prose, which included epics such as *The Vision of Judgement* (1820) and a valuable *History of Brazil* (1810–1819). He is best remembered for his lives of Nelson and Wesley and the children's classic *The Three Bears*.
Simmons, J., *Southey*. 1945

Soyer, Alexis (1809–1858). French chef de cuisine. He fled to London from the 1830 revolution in France. He was chef to the Reform Club and became the most famous cook of his time. He was sent to the Crimea to reform the army's food commissariat, and introduced the 'Soyer Stove'. Soyer was the author of a variety of cookery books.
Morris, H., *Portrait of a Chef*. 1938

Spaak, Paul-Henri (1899–1972). Belgian socialist politician. He served as a deputy (1932–66), was foreign minister four times (1936–38; 1939–46; 1947–49; 1954–57) and prime minister twice (1938–39; 1947–49). A founding father of the United Nations and first president of the General Assembly (1946–47), he became secretary general of NATO (1957–61).

Spaatz, Carl Andrews (1891–1974). American airman. He joined the American Army air force in 1916; in 1941 he was sent to Britain to organize the 8th Air Force which worked in close association with the British Bomber Command. He commanded (1943) all Allied forces taking part in the North African campaign. He was head of the US Army Air Force (1946–48).

Spallanzani, Lazzaro (1729–1799). Italian zoologist. He studied law at Bologna and entered orders. In 1757 he became Professor of Mathematics and Physics at Reggio, moving on to Modena in 1763 and to the Chair of Natural History at Pavia in 1769, where he divided his time between zoological research and teaching, and natural history travelling. Spallanzani's reputation rests upon his skill as an experimenter in many fields of natural history. He carried out a notable series of experiments disproving spontaneous generation, by demonstrating that no life formed in sealed containers. He was a pioneer student of the chemical action of gastric juices in digesting foodstuffs. He hypothesized that this was due to the action of acids, but failed to locate these. In embryology Spallanzani was a staunch preformationist, believing that the new creature already existed in microscopic form complete in the embryo.
Needham, J., *History of embryology*. 1934

Spark, Muriel Sarah (1918–). British novelist, born in Edinburgh. Her first published novel was *The Comforters* (1957); she wrote also some verse and criticism and a play, *The Prime of Miss Jean Brodie* (1961). Her novel *The Mandelbaum Gate* (1965) won the James Tait Black Memorial Prize; like most of her work, it takes an ironic view of the results when personalities interact.

Sparks, Jared (1789–1866). American journalist, Unitarian minister and biographer. He edited the *North American Review* (1824–31) and began in 1832 his *Library of American Biography*. He was later president of Harvard (1849–53). He edited the writings of George Washington and Benjamin Franklin.

Spartacus (died 71 B.C.). Thracian gladiator who led a slave revolt against the Romans (73–71 B.C.). The insurrections began in Capua where seventy-three members of a school of gladiators broke out to become the nucleus of a slave army of nearly 100,000 men. Spartacus won several victories but was finally defeated and killed by the forces of Marcus Licinius Crassus; thousands died in the final battle or were later rounded up and executed.

Speer, Albert (1905–1981). German architect. His buildings attracted Hitler's interest and on the death of Fritz * Todt he became minister of armaments and munitions (1942–45), producing a record-breaking 3,031 fighter planes in the month September 1944. He prevented Hitler's scorched earth policy being fully implemented in March–April 1945 and urged the Führer to capitulate. He was sentenced to 20 years' jail at the Nuremberg trials for his use of slave labour. On his release he published the valuable memoirs *Inside the Third Reich* (1969).
Schmidt, M., *Albert Speer: The End of a Myth*. 1985

Speidel, Hans (1897–). German soldier. He was Rommel's chief of staff for a time in the World War II and was imprisoned (1944) for alleged participation in the attempt to assassinate Hitler. He was commander-in-chief of the new West German army (1955–1957); his appointment (1957) to command the NATO forces in Central Europe marked an important stage in the post-war history of the Federal Republic of Germany.

Speke, John Hanning (1827–1864). British explorer. After service in the Indian army he joined Richard * Burton to explore Somaliland (when he narrowly escaped with his life). Three years later (1857) the same two explorers were sent by the Royal Geographical Society to look for the great lakes of Central Africa. They reached Lake Tanganyika together but Speke was alone when he discovered Lake Nyanza and concluded (rightly) that it must be the source of the Nile. Burton disagreed and to settle the dispute Speke made another journey in 1860 (with Captain J. A. Grant) and followed the river emerging from the lake far enough to be sure that it was identical with the Nile. Burton still refused to be convinced; on the day before a public meeting to discuss the issue Speke accidentally shot himself.
Speke, J. H., *Journal of the Discovery of the Source of the Nile*. 1863

Spelman, Sir Henry (1562–1641). English antiquary. He made major contributions to the study of English mediaeval history, including writings on sacrilege and tithes and his *Glossarium Archaiologicum*, produced over nearly forty years. He is credited with the introduction of the term 'feudalism'. His son **Sir John Spelman,** was also a historian, and wrote a life of Alfred the Great.

Spence, Sir Basil Urwin (1907–1976). British architect, born in Bombay. He worked in the office of Sir Edwin * Lutyens for a year before World War II. After the war the originality of his architectural concepts distinguished him: he produced (1951) the winning design for the rebuilding of Coventry Cathedral, of which he became the architect. Among other appointments he was consultant architect to Edinburgh, Nottingham, Sussex and Southampton Universities and for Basildon new town. He was president of the R.I.B.A. (1958–60), knighted in 1960 and received the O.M. in 1962. He designed the 'Beehive' extension to the New Zealand Parliament in Wellington.

Spencer, Herbert (1820–1903). English philosopher. The son of a Derby schoolmaster, he became first a schoolmaster and then a railway engineer, and worked at this profession, with occasional incursions into journalism, until 1843 when he became sub-editor of the *Economist*. In his first book, *Social Status* (1850), he tried to show that social equilibrium would finally result from *laissez-faire* liberalism, if allowed to work unchecked. His subsequent defence on individual freedom against the encroaching power of the state, *The Man versus the State* (1854), was one of the most widely read books of the day. His next work, *The Principles of Psychology* (1855), propounded the theory that life is an 'adjustment of inner relations to outer relations' and went on to examine particular relations, e.g. association, reflex action, memory and reason. In 1860, only partly influenced by the publication (1859) of Darwin's *On the Origin of Species*, he launched his vast *Programme of a System of Synthetic Philosophy*, aimed at linking all fields of knowledge on the basis of a principle that evolution is a kind of progress from homogeneity to an organized heterogeneity, the whole being dependent on an unknowable force which sets the whole system in motion. The series of books issued to illustrate this theme included works on biology, sociology, psychology, education and ethics.

Peel, J. Y. D., *Herbert Spencer: The Evolution of a Sociologist*. 1971

Spencer, Sir Stanley (1891–1959). English painter. Except during his service in Macedonia in World War I, he lived and worked in his native village of Cookham, Berkshire. The murals (1927–32) in the memorial chapel at Burghclere, near Newbury, are his finest works. Equally impressive is the huge *Resurrection* in the Tate Gallery, London.
Rothenstein, W., *Stanley Spencer*. 1945

Spender, Sir Stephen (1909–). English poet and critic. At Oxford where he was educated, he became, with his friends Auden and Day Lewis, one of the group of young poets who contributed to *New Signatures* (1932). In 1930 his own first volume of poetry, *Twenty Poems* appeared. He fought in Spain with the Loyalists, and his *Poems from Spain* (1939) reflect this period. His *Collected Poems* appeared in 1954. He also wrote fiction and literary criticism, e.g. *The Destructive Element* (1935), and a poetic drama, *Trial of a Judge* (1938). From 1939 to 1941 he was co-editor, with Cyril Connolly, of the monthly *Horizon*, and in 1953 was co-editor of *Encounter*.
Spender, S., *World Within World*. 1951

Spengler, Oswald (1880–1936). German philosopher. After some years as a teacher he came into sensational prominence with the publication (1918) of the first volume of *Untergang des Abendlandes* (Volume II, 1922; Eng. trans. *The Decline of the West*, 1926–29). His theme was that civilizations are subject to the same laws of growth and decay as individuals.

Spenser, Edmund (*c.* 1552–1599). English poet, born in London. He left Cambridge University in 1576, and in 1580 became secretary to Lord Grey, lord deputy of Ireland. A year earlier he had published his first major work, *The Shepheardes Calendar*, dedicated to his friend Sir Philip Sidney. After leaving Lord Grey's service he remained in Ireland in official appointments, and living (from 1588) at Kilcolman Castle, Co. Cork, where he continued work on his great epic *The Faerie Queene*. In 1589 he went to London with Sir Walter Raleigh to arrange for the publication of its first three books. Disappointed in his hopes of preferment, he returned to Ireland (1591), where he described his recent visit in *Colin Clout's Come Home Again*. The next three books of *The Faerie Queene* were published in 1596. This famous epic, which he left unfinished at his death, is an allegory (modelled to some extent on Ariosto's *Orlando Furioso*) of the England of his time, in which Elizabeth appears as Gloriana, Queen of Fairyland. Much of the allegory is no longer easily comprehensible but the adventures of the knights can be enjoyed as separate episodes and there still remains the sensual delight of the poem's rich colouring and its metrical charm. It is written in what are now known as Spenserian stanzas. His other works include *Astrophel* (1586), an elegy on Sir Philip Sidney, and the sonnet sequence *Amoretti*, which immortalized his courtship of an Elizabeth (supposedly Elizabeth Boyle) whom he married in 1594; *Epithalamion* was probably written to celebrate the event, while the double wedding of the two daughters of the Earl of Worcester was commemorated by *Prothalamion* (1596). The prose work *View of the Present State of Ireland* (1596) was a defence of English policy. When Kilcolman was burnt by insurgents (1598), the last books of the *Faerie Queene* were probably destroyed. Spenser returned to London where he died in poverty; he was buried in Westminster Abbey.
Judson, A. C., *The Life of Edmund Spenser*. 1945

Speransky, Count Mikhail Mikhailovich (1772–1839). Russian minister of state. As Alexander I's adviser he devised a liberal constitutional system for Russia, but intrigues of his opponents drove him from office and stultified his work. Under Nicholas I he took a prominent part in the proceedings against the Decembrist conspirators and codified Russian law.

Sperry, Elmer Ambrose (1860–1930). American inventor. He designed and manufactured numerous devices incorporating the principle of the gyroscope, among them the gyroscopic compass and stabilizers for ships. He also made improvements in the manufacture of electrical machinery and introduced (1915) the high-intensity searchlight.

Spilsbury, Sir Bernard Henry (1877–1947). English physician, pathologist to the Home Office. He gave evidence at many famous murder trials (including that of* Crippen). He had a phenomenal memory and a passion for

detail and was particularly expert in toxicology: his pronouncements carried great weight.
Browne, D. G. and Tullett, E. V., *Bernard Spilsbury*. 1951

Spinoza, Benedict de (Baruch Despinoza) (1632–1677). Dutch philosopher of Jewish parentage, born in Amsterdam. Given a traditional Jewish education, he became lax in his observances, was estranged from his people, and was excommunicated (1656). While earning his living as a lens-grinder he learnt Latin and absorbed western culture. A version (1663) of Descartes's *Principles of Philosophy* was the only book published under his own name during his lifetime, but *Theological-Political Treatise* (1670) was generally recognized as his. While admitting that human passions necessitate strict obedience to the state, the book pleaded for liberty for the philosopher to express his ideas. Despite the uproar that it caused (difficult now to understand), he was offered (1673) a professorship by the Elector Palatine but preferred to devote himself to completing his greatest work, the posthumously published *Ethics* (1677). Beginning from the notion of substance, which may be roughly described as having properties or attributes but not being such itself, he proceeds by classically deductive argument to establish that nature is identical with God, the being who possesses infinite attributes but is not the personal God of Christianity. He sees man's mind as part of the divine one and for that reason incapable of exercising free will in an absolute sense. With the same integrating pantheistic vision he argues that man's highest good is his knowledge of his union with nature or intellectual love of God (*amor Dei intellectualis*). He died of a lung disease aggravated by the glass dust produced by lens-grinding.
Hampshire, S., *Spinoza*. 1956

Spock, Benjamin McLane (1903–). American physician. Millions of copies of his books on the care of children have been sold in America, Britain and many other countries. They include *A Baby's First Year* (1950) and *Feeding Your Baby and Child* (1955). He was appointed (1955) professor of child development at Western Reserve University, Ohio.

Spode, Josiah (1733–1797). English manufacturing potter. He learned to make earthenware from Thomas Whieldon of Fenton, and set up his own factory at Stoke on Trent in 1770. His successor, Josiah Spode II (1754–1827) is credited with perfecting a formula for bone china *c.* 1800 which has been the basis of the English table-ware industry ever since. He was potter to George III. The firm of Spode was bought by William Copeland in 1833 and amalgamated with Wedgwood in 1964.
Hayden, A., *Spode and his Successors*. 1925

Spofforth, Frederick Robert (1853–1926). Australian cricketer. Known as the 'demon bowler', in eighteen test matches (1876–86) against England he took 94 wickets, fourteen in Australia's first test victory (Oval, 1882). Later he settled in England and played for Derbyshire (1889, 1890).

Spohr, Ludwig (1784–1859). German violinist and composer. He was born in Brunswick and was aided in his studies by the Duke. After being musical director at theatres in Vienna and Frankfurt he was Kapellmeister at the Court of Hesse Kassell (1822–57). He composed many violin concertos, operas, oratorios, symphonies and chamber music. One oratorio, *Die Letzten Dingen* (1826), had a long vogue in England as *The Last Judgement*.

Spurgeon, Charles Haddon (1836–1892). English Baptist pastor. His preaching attracted vast congregations and the huge Metropolitan Tabernacle seating 6,000 was built to cope with these (it burnt down in 1898). He withdrew from the Baptist Union in 1887 on theological grounds. He was a prolific author, publishing weekly sermons.

Squire, Sir John Collings (1884–1958). English critic and poet. As editor of the *London Mercury* (1919–34) he did much to encourage young writers of his time. His own poems appeared in *A Face in Candlelight* (1932) and other volumes; he was pre-eminent as a parodist, e.g. in *Steps to Parnassus* (1913) and *Tricks of the Trade* (1917). He was knighted in 1933.
Squire, Sir J. C. *Water Music*. 1939

Stacpoole, Henry de Vere (1863–1951). English novelist. His famous best-seller *The Blue Lagoon* (1909) tells – with a frankness then regarded as daring – the story of a boy and girl, castaways from a wreck, who grow to maturity on a desert island.

Staël-Holstein, Anne Louise Germaine (née Necker; known as Madame de Staël) (1766–1817). French author. She was the daughter of the financier * Necker. She married (1785) the Swedish ambassador in Paris (who died in 1802). She was regarded as the most intellectual and cultured woman of her time and her *salons*, both in Paris and later at her Swiss home at Coppet, were attended by many of her most brilliant contemporaries. Her efforts to attract Bonaparte (who disliked clever women) failed; they became bitter enemies and in 1803 he ordered her to leave Paris. She went to Germany and there met Schiller, Goethe and August von Schlegel. A later visit resulted in *De l'Allemagne* (1810), which did much to introduce German Romanticism to France. It was suppressed by Napoleon; to escape his enmity she visited Vienna, Russia, Stockholm and England (where she was warmly welcomed). After the emperor's downfall she again presided over *salons* in Paris and Coppet. Her literary career had opened (1788) with a panegyric of Rousseau. In *De la littérature* (1800) she compared French literature unfavourably with German and English. Her two novels, *Delphine* (1802) and *Corinne* (1807), contain self-portraits and relate to her long liaison with Benjamin Constant. *Considérations sur la Révolution Française* and the autobiographical *Dix Années d'exil* appeared posthumously.
Herold, J. C., *Mistress to an Age: a Life of Madame de Staël.* 1958

Stafford, Sir Edward William (1819–1901). New Zealand politician, born in Edinburgh. He became a large sheep-owner in the Nelson settlement and a prominent New Zealand political figure. As prime minister (1856–61, 1865–69 and 1872) he pursued an unpopular policy of centralization, but as an administrator he showed much wisdom and capacity for rule. He returned to England in 1874 and was knighted in 1879.

Stahl, Georg Ernst (1660–1734). German scientist. Son of a Protestant minister, and inclined to Pietist views himself, Stahl studied medicine at Jena and taught there from 1683 till he was appointed professor at Halle in 1693. From 1716 he was personal physician to Frederick I of Prussia. His medical writings stressed that living bodies possess some sort of soul, or life-force, which cannot simply be reduced to the total of the separate mechanical organs. This was at bottom a religious conception, but it harmonized with his chemical interest in gases and his concern with heat. In chemistry he developed the concept of phlogiston, a substance contained within combustible bodies and given up when burnt. In smelting metals, phlogiston was assumed to be transferred from the charcoal to the ore. The idea of phlogiston tied together the chemistry of combustion in the eighteenth century until * Lavoisier's rethinking of the subject and the development of the concept of oxygen (taken out of the air on combustion).
Partington, J. R., *A History of Chemistry.* 1961

Ståhlberg, Kaarlo Juho (1865–1952). First president of Finland (1919–25). He was a lawyer, judge, professor and member of the Finnish diet who drafted the republican constitution of 1917 when Finland seized its independence during the Russian Revolution. In 1930 he was kidnapped by the pro-Fascist Lapua movement and lost the presidential elections of 1931 and 1937 by very narrow margins.

Stair, John Dalrymple, 1st Earl of (1648–1707). Scottish politician. His father was the first codifier of Scots law; on his death (1695) he became 2nd Viscount Stair. He too was eminent as a lawyer and was advocate-general under James II and William III, whose cause he strongly supported. As secretary of state at the time of the Massacre of Glencoe (1692) he was held chiefly responsible and was forced to resign. Later he played an important part in preparing the Act of Union (1707) and securing its passage through the Scottish parliament. On the morning after one of his most convincing speeches he was found dead.

Stakhanov, Alexei Grigorevich (1905–1977). Russian miner. He worked in coal mines from 1927, and in 1935 achieved notoriety by cutting twelve tons of coal per shift (seven being the norm). He was praised by Stalin who inaugurated the 'Stakhanovite movement', designed to raise production in Soviet industry.

Stalin (Djugashvili), **Joseph Vissarionovich** (1879–1953). Soviet politician, born near Tiflis in Georgia, the son of a shoemaker. Educated at a seminary, he was expelled for 'propagating Marxism' to his fellows. He continued his political work underground but was arrested and sent to Siberia whence he escaped (1904); rearrested, he made five similar escapes before World War I. Meanwhile he had organized a strike of oil workers, toured in Russia, attended conferences on * Lenin's instructions and had written books mainly concerned with the applications of Marxism to the nationalist minorities (e.g. his own Georgians). He was released from exile in Siberia when the Revolution occurred (1917), worked closely with Lenin and was especially active in the organization of the second (Bolshevik) revolution (October–November 1917); he made many personal interventions at critical points in the Civil War, to the annoyance of Trotsky, minister of war. From 1922, when he became general secretary of the Communist party, he used his position to undermine * Trotsky's power and when Lenin died (1924) he gradually eliminated him and his other rivals and became a virtual dictator armed with the unchallenged and ruthless power of the secret police. The main difference between Stalin and his opponents was that he believed that the best way to ensure Communist supremacy was to make Russia a powerful industrial state. Trotsky and his followers advocated the fomenting of proletarian revolution throughout the world. A series of five-year plans did much to stimulate Russia's economic growth; but the ruthless purges by which, in the years immediately before World War II, Stalin eliminated all leaders, military and political alike, whom he suspected (often on the slenderest of mistaken grounds) of possible opposition, weakened national unity and confidence. The Soviet-Nazi pact (1939) was a high mark of Stalinist opportunism. He refused to believe warnings of German plans to attack, but when Germany did so (1941) Stalin rallied the nation behind him; his great administrative ability, combined with strategic insight, was a major factor in securing victory. The enormous inflow of Allied aid he acknowledged in the most niggardly spirit or not at all. At the Tehran and Yalta conferences he bluffed or outwitted the Allied leaders and secured agreement for an eventual settlement that surrendered half the nations of Europe to Russian control. He died in Moscow and his body was enshrined alongside Lenin's in Red Square. At the Twentieth Party Congress (1956) * Khrushchev attacked his character, ability and 'encouragement of the personality cult' and the Twenty-second Party Congress (1961) voted for the removal of Stalin's body from the Lenin Mausoleum. Stalin was ruthless, cunning and determined. With his many conflicting qualities he remains a main architect of Soviet Russia.

Payne, R., *Rise and Fall of Stalin*. 1965. Ulam, A., *Stalin*. 1973

Stambolisky, Alexander (1879–1923). Bulgarian politician. He founded the Agrarian party and dreamed of a Balkan federation that would be part of a 'Green International' unifying the peasants of all Eastern Europe. Imprisoned for opposing King Ferdinand's pro-German policy in World War I, he became prime minister on his abdication (1918). He lost popularity by favouring the country people at the expense of the towns and by compromising with Yugoslavia on the Macedonian question. His régime was overthrown, and he himself assassinated.

Standish, Myles (*c.* 1584–1656). American colonist. He came of a Lancashire family and had made a career as a soldier of fortune when he was hired by the Pilgrim Fathers to accompany them on the *Mayflower* (1620). His skill in handling the Indians was indispensable to the safety of the colony in its early years and he remained one of its most important members for the rest of his life. He is the subject of poems by Longfellow and Lowell.

Stanford, Sir Charles Villiers (1852–1924). British composer, born in Dublin. He was organist at Trinity College, Cambridge (1873–1892), and also studied at Berlin and Leipzig. When the Royal College of Music was founded (1883) he became professor of composition. He wrote operas, e.g. the successful *Shamus O'Brien* (1896), and much orchestral and chamber music but was at his best in small forms. It was, however, as a teacher that he showed real genius and his influence was felt by a whole generation of British composers.

Green, H. P., *Stanford*. 1935

Stanhope, Lady Hester Lucy (1776–1839). English eccentric. Daughter of the 3rd Earl Stanhope, she kept house for her bachelor uncle, the younger Pitt, for the last three years of his life, which included his second premiership (1804–06). In 1810 she startled her aristocratic friends by going to the Levant, where on the slopes of Mount Lebanon she lived the life of an Oriental princess, entertaining friends, dispensing charity, and influencing the neighbouring tribes. Her prodigality exhausted her fortune and her last years were spent in poverty.

Stanhope, Philip *see* **Chesterfield, Philip Dormer Stanhope, 4th Earl of**

Stanislavsky, Konstantin (Konstantin Sergeyevich Alexeyev) (1863–1938). Russian actor and producer. As director of the Moscow Art Theatre (1898–1938) – of which he was co-founder – he devised the famous 'method' in which actors are trained to develop their own conception of their roles and to analyse and express emotion in an entirely natural manner. Stage settings have to be realistic. After the Russian Revolution it was discovered that his 'method' was in exact accord with the doctrine of 'socialist realism'. As actor and producer he was accorded the highest distinctions, including the Order of Lenin (1937). His house is preserved as a museum and the street in which he lived named after him.
Stanislavsky, K., *An Actor Prepares*. Eng. ed. 1980. Stanislavsky, K. S., *My Life in Art*. Repr. 1980

Stanley. The family name of the Earls of Derby from 1485, when Thomas Stanley was created Earl of Derby for the decisive contribution that he and his brother, Sir William Stanley, made to the victory of Henry VII at the Battle of Bosworth Field (1485). The sovereignty of the Isle of Man was held by the Stanley family from 1406 until it passed to the Dukes of Atholl in the 18th century. Among the Stanleys who made their name in politics were the 14th Earl of * Derby and the 17th Earl, whose 'Derby scheme' provided a means of recruitment in World War I before the introduction of full conscription.

Stanley, Sir Henry Morton (1841–1904). British explorer and journalist, born in Wales. An orphan (then known as John Rowlands), he ran away from the workhouse at the age of 15, sailed to America as a cabin boy and was adopted by a New Orleans merchant, whose name he assumed. After the Civil War (during which he served on both sides) he became a reporter and joined (1867) James Gordon Bennett's *New York Herald*. After assignments with Robert * Napier in Abyssinia, in Egypt (for the opening of the Suez Canal), and elsewhere in the East, he was sent (1869) to find David * Livingstone, then missing in Africa. The meeting made historic by Stanley's casual greeting – 'Dr Livingstone, I presume' – took place near Lake Tanganyika, but after exploring the Lake together they parted company, Stanley returning to Zanzibar and England while Livingstone, now re-equipped and reprovisioned, remained. The publication of Stanley's book *How I Found Livingstone* (1872) caused him to be fêted as a hero; and after an interlude with * Wolseley on the Ashanti campaign, he was jointly commissioned (1874) by the *New York Herald* and the London *Daily Telegraph* to make another African expedition, which succeeded in solving several geographical problems, including the exact course of the Congo. From 1879 he established on behalf of King * Leopold II of the Belgians the trading stations on the Congo that led to the foundation of the Congo Free State. On his last journey (1887–89) he overcame immense hardships to rescue * Emin Pasha, and discovered the Mountains of the Moon (Ruwenzori range). To complete an astonishing career he was a Unionist M.P. (1895–1900). A book followed each of his exploits, e.g. *Through the Dark Continent* (1878). He was knighted in 1899.
Farwell, B., *The Man Who Presumed*. 1957. Hird. F., *H. M. Stanley, the Authorised Life*. 1935

Starling, Ernest Henry (1866–1927). English scientist. His contributions to physiology are amongst the most important of the early twentieth century. Son of a barrister, Starling studied medicine at Guy's Hospital from 1882, qualifying M.B. in 1889. From 1887 he was demonstrator at Guy's and from 1890 was researching part-time with Schäfer at University College, London. Working with William Maddock Bayliss, Starling pioneered the study of hormones, the chemical messengers of the body produced by the endocrine glands. He then moved on to research on the heart, being interested in its response to stress in the body organism at large. Starling was a turbulent man of strong views. He campaigned for educational reform, demanding a larger place for science in the school curriculum and in national priorities.

Stas, Jean Servais (1813–1891). Belgian chemist. He studied organic chemistry under

Jean Baptiste André Dumas of Paris and later worked with him; he was professor of chemistry (1840–45) at the Ecole Royale Militaire, Brussels. He greatly improved methods for determining atomic weight and obtained much more accurate values for the common elements.

Stavisky, Serge Alexandre (1886?–1934). French speculator, born in Kiev. He promoted a series of fraudulent companies and as the scale of his operations grew he cultivated government and municipal officials, involving many of them in his transactions. His final and most ambitious plan was to obtain control of the issue of bonds, secured by goods pledged with the municipal pawnshops, and soon a flood of worthless bonds began to circulate. Though alerted the police delayed action until Stavisky had disappeared. When traced to a villa near Chamonix he committed suicide to avoid arrest. The scandal mounted as more and more well known people were suspected of being involved; demonstrations in Paris led to the fall of the government and the scandal did much to shake national confidence in the years before World War II.

Stead, William Thomas (1849–1912). English journalist. He edited the *Pall Mall Gazette* (1883–89) and the *Review of Reviews* (1890–1912). He was an advocate of social reform. He forced (1885) a strengthening of the laws against juvenile prostitution (he proved the inadequacy of the previous law by purchasing several girls aged 8–13 for £5 each, and since he committed a technical breach of the revised law he was sentenced to three months' imprisonment). He later became very interested in psychical research. He was drowned in the sinking of the *Titanic*.

Steel, David Martin Scott (1938–). British politician. First elected as Liberal M.P. for Roxburgh, Scotland in 1965, he became leader of the Liberal Party in 1976 succeeding Jeremy Thorpe. He was the first Liberal leader to be elected by a majority of Liberal supporters rather than by Liberal M.Ps.

Steele, Sir Richard (1672–1729). English essayist and dramatist, born in London. He was educated at Charterhouse and Oxford, joined the army, but soon took to writing. His first works were the plays *The Funeral* (1702), *The Lying Lovers* (1703) and *The Tender Husband* (1705). The second of these introduced 'sentimental comedy', which, in contrast with Restoration drama, treated lapses from virtue sentimentally rather than with ribaldry. He started (1709) the *Tatler*, on which he was soon joined by an old schoolfriend, Joseph * Addison. It contained a mixture of news, social comment, essays etc., and was intended to elevate morals and manners as well as to amuse. Steele himself wrote as 'Isaac Bickerstaff'. When the *Tatler* was succeeded by the *Spectator* (1711–12) the two friends again collaborated; the famous character Sir Roger de Coverley was invented by Steele and developed by Addison. Later, however, they became estranged by political quarrels. Steele's association with other papers never achieved the same success. He was a vigorous supporter of George I's succession, became a Whig M.P. (1714) and was knighted (1715). Soon after his last comedy, *The Conscious Lovers* (1722), was produced, he left London, and he died in Wales.

Loftis, J., *Steele at Drury Lane*. 1973. Winton, C., *Captain Steele*. 1964; *Sir Richard Steele*. 1970

Steen, Jan (*c.* 1626–1679). Dutch painter, born at Leyden. He is one of the gayest of the Dutch genre painters, and his *The Bean Feast* or *The Skittle Alley* (the latter in the National Gallery, London) show his pleasure in the company and occupations of his fellows. His satire, e.g. *The Lovesick Maiden*, is gentle, and the colour of such pictures as *The Lute Player* (Wallace Collection, London) is of rare delicacy.

Steer, (Philip) Wilson (1860–1942). English painter. After studying in London and Paris he was, with * Sickert, one of those who helped to found th New English Art Club. In 1893 he became a teacher at the Slade School. In his early landscapes, e.g. *The Beach of Walberswick* (1890), now in the Tate Gallery, London, he was influenced by Whistler; later he adhered more closely to the traditions of Gainsborough and Constable, using Impressionist techniques (especially those of Monet) though he was not a true Impressionist since he did not paint direct from nature. From *c.* 1900 some of his paintings recall * Boucher in his rococo period; in others, e.g. *The Muslin Dress* (1910), the exactitude of detail recalls the pre-Raphaelites. The water-colour revival (from

c. 1918) owed much to Steer's example. He was awarded the O.M. in 1931.
Ironside, R., *Philip Wilson Steer*. 1943; *Steer*. 1944

Stefan, Joseph (1835–1893). Austrian physicist. His most important work was on radiation, the kinetic theory and hydrodynamics. While professor of physics at Vienna University he discovered the fundamental law of radiation, known as Stefan's Law: that the rate of radiation of energy from a black body is proportional to the fourth power of its absolute temperature.

Stefansson, Vilhjalmur (1879–1962). Anthropologist and explorer, born in Canada of Icelandic parentage. He studied Eskimo life and habits (1908–12) and wrote *My Life with the Eskimo* (1913). Later he did valuable exploratory work in the Arctic and discovered several new islands. He made two attempts to resist a Russian claim to Wrangel Island by planting the Union Jack (1914 and – on behalf of Canada – 1921–22) but the Soviet government secured recognition of their sovereignty in 1924. His other books include *Unsolved Mysteries of the Arctic* (1939) and an autobiography, *Discovery* (1964).

Stein, Sir (Marc) **Aurel** (1862–1943). Hungarian-born archaeologist, naturalized as British in 1899. He explored much of central Asia and discovered evidence of cultural exchanges between the Chinese and the Greeks in the period of Alexander the Great. Among the regions he visited were China, Turkestan, Persia and Mesopotamia. He died exploring in Afghanistan. He was knighted in 1912.

Stein, Gertrude (1874–1946). American author. From 1905 she lived mainly in Paris, after having studied psychology under William James, and medicine at Johns Hopkins. The main elements in her poetic work include free association and repetition, as in her famous line 'A rose is a rose is a rose'. Her works include *Three Lives* (1909), *Tender Buttons* (1914, poetry), *The Autobiography of Alice B. Toklas* (1933), *Portraits and Prayers* (1939, art criticism), and *Everybody's Autobiography* (1937). She had much influence on modern art movements as well as on literature.
Sprigge, E. M. S., *Gertrude Stein*. 1957. Brinnin, J. M., *The Third Rose*. 1960

Stein, Karl, Baron von (1757–1831). German political reformer. His outspoken criticism of the backward political system caused his dismissal (1807) from the Prussian civil service, but he was soon recalled as chief minister by Frederick William III in the hope of reinvigorating the country after Napoleon's victories. He was unable to secure acceptance of representative government but he managed to introduce municipal self-government and abolish serfdom (1807–08). Eventually his opponents, now including the king, forced him to flee and in 1812 he entered Russian service. Tsar Alexander I sent him to administer East Prussia and to organize resistance to Napoleon but, still unable to carry out reforms, he withdrew into private life (1813).
von Ranmer, K., *Freiherr von Stein*. 1961

Steinbeck, John Ernest (1902–1968). American novelist, born in California. He first gained notice with the novel *Tortilla Flat* (1935), portraying the lives of Spanish-Californian peasants. His masterpiece, *The Grapes of Wrath* (1939) is the story of a typical family of poor farmers in the dust bowl of Oklahoma. In its graphic depiction of human dignity in the face of adversity, it exposed exploitation, hardship and social inequity, and led to reforms, while winning for its author the 1940 Pulitzer Prize. Other works include *Of Mice and Men* (1937), *The Moon is Down* (1942), *Cannery Row* (1943) and *The Wayward Bus* (1947). He received the Nobel Prize for Literature (1962).
Davis, R. M., *Steinbeck: A Collection of Critical Essays*. 1972

Steiner, George (1929–). English writer and critic. He taught at Cambridge and Geneva, and his books included *Tolstoy or Dostoevsky?* (1958), *After Babel* (1975) and *The Portage to San Cristobal of A.H.* (1981).

Steiner, Rudolf (1861–1925). German anthroposophist. First known as editor (1890–97) of Goethe's works on natural science, he was a prominent theosophist until he evolved a system of his own known as 'anthroposophy', to develop which he opened (1912) a school (the Goetheanum) near Basle in Switzerland. The system aimed at a restoration of human contact with spiritual reality, lost since the days of myth-making. The fields in which his aims were particularly applicable were medicine, agriculture and education. The

special schools which his followers set up were often successful, where other educational methods had failed, in preserving the spiritual essence of the subjects taught.
Steiner, R., *Mein Lebensgang*. 1925

Steinmetz, Charles Proteus (1865–1923). American electrical engineer. Forced to leave his native Germany because of his socialist beliefs (1888), he became chief engineer for the General Electric Company and also a professor at Union College, New York. Of his many contributions to electrical engineering the most important are his law of magnetic hysteresis, his notation for alternating-current circuits and his development of lighting arrestors for power transmission lines.
Hammond, J. W., *Charles Proteus Steinmetz: A Biography*. 1924

Steinway, Heinrich Engelhard (originally H. E. Steinweg) (1797–1871). German piano-manufacturer. He founded a factory in Brunswick but in 1851, leaving a son to run the German firm, he went to the U.S.A. to establish a new factory, where pianos were manufactured under the name of Steinway.

Stendhal (pen-name of Marie Henri Beyle) (1783–1842). French novelist. He served in Napoleon's Moscow campaign; afterwards he went to Milan, where he wrote travel sketches, books on the arts etc. and began his psychological analysis of love, *De l'Amour* (1822). He spent many years in Italy or in travel; after the revolution of 1830 he was appointed French consul in Italy. In 1830 he published the first of two masterpieces, *Le Rouge et le noir*, a remarkable picture of his times (the 'red' being the army, the 'black' the church) and a penetrating analysis of the character, successes and downfall of its hero, Jean Sorel. His second great novel, *La Chartreuse de Parme* (1839), amid a magnificent medley of politics, diplomacy, plots and counterplots, contains a vivid impression of the Battle of Waterloo, and of life in a small Italian state. His posthumously published works include the unfinished novel *Lucien Leuwen* (1894). Stendhal was little recognized before 1880, but from then his vogue steadily increased. He anticipated both the realism and the psychological approach of modern novelists.
Wood, M., *Stendhal*. 1971. Fowlie, W., *Stendhal*. 1969

Stephen (*c.* 1100–1154). King of England (from 1135). He was the son of the Count of Blois and of Adela, daughter of William the Conqueror. On the death (1135) of Henry I of England he was elected king despite the fact that he and the barons had sworn fealty to Henry's daughter Matilda. Most of the reign was marked by civil war and for a short time in 1141 he was a prisoner in Matilda's hands. After the death of his son (1152) a compromise was reached; he acknowledged Matilda's son, the future Henry II, as heir to the throne. He was a weak man, unable to control the barons upon whose support he relied.
Davies, R. H. C., *King Stephen*. 1967

Stephen, St (1st century). The first Christian martyr (Acts 6). Condemned by the Sanhedrin for his unorthodox doctrine, he was stoned to death in the presence of Paul (who had not yet been converted). St. Stephen's day is 26 December.

Stephen, St (*c.* 977–1038). First king of Hungary (from 1000). He came of a princely family and adopted the name of Stephen when he was baptized. After overcoming rival leaders he was recognized as king by Pope Sylvester II. With this prestige he united and converted the whole country, which he divided into counties and bishoprics. He was revered for his saintly life and was canonized in 1083. His feast day is 2 August.
Hóman, B., *Szent István*. 1938

Stephen, Sir Leslie (1832–1904). English man of letters. On becoming an agnostic he gave up his position as a Cambridge don and went to London (1864) to lead a literary life. He contributed to many journals, was editor of the *Cornhill Magazine* (1871–82) and eventually (1882–91) of the *Dictionary of National Biography*, a field in which his lives of Johnson (1878), Pope (1880), Swift (1882) etc. had shown his pre-eminence. Meanwhile he had also written his *History of English Thought in the Eighteenth Century* (1876). His main hobby was alpine climbing about which he wrote several books. His first wife was a daughter of Thackeray; his daughters by his second wife were Vanessa Bell (* Bell, Clive) and Virginia * Woolf.
Annan, N. G., *Leslie Stephen*. 1984

Stephens, Alexander Hamilton (1812–1883). American politician. Even though he supported slavery and was chosen as vice-president of the Confederate states, Stephens, who had been a member of the House of Representatives (1843–59), was against secession, and had strongly, but vainly, opposed that of his native state of Georgia. Later he was again in Congress (1873–82) and was governor of Georgia when he died. He wrote *Constitutional View of the Late War between the States* (1868–70).

Wilson, E., *Patriotic Gore*. 1962

Stephens, James (1882–1950). Irish writer, born in Dublin. He became known by *The Crock of Gold* (1912), *The Demi-Gods* (1914) and other prose fantasies in which fairies and mortals (e.g. policemen) meet on natural and familiar terms, the author's rhythmic style and happy use of Irish idiom adding a special charm. His collected poems appeared in 1921. Other books include *Deirdre* (1923) and *Etched in Moonlight* (1928).

Stephenson, George (1781–1848). English engineer. He started work in a colliery at the age of 7. As a young man he devised several improvements to pumping machines and in his spare time taught himself engineering and mathematics. He won a prize of £1,000 for inventing a miner's safety lamp (1815) and became involved in a controversy with Humphry Davy who had independently invented a similar lamp. A year earlier he had built his first colliery locomotive. He constructed (1825) the first public railway between Stockton and Darlington, Durham (on which, however, horses were still used for passenger trains). He surveyed and constructed the twenty-eight-mile railway line between Manchester and Liverpool, which was opened in 1830. His engine *The Rocket* won (1829) a prize of £500 for maintaining an average speed of 29 m.p.h.

At his works at Newcastle, managed from 1827 by his son, **Robert Stephenson** (1803–1859), most of the notable locomotives for the next generation were made and the two constructed many other railway lines in England and Scotland. Robert subsequently became famous as a bridge builder, his works including the well-known suspension bridges over the Menai Straits and at Conway in North Wales, as well as the Victoria Bridge over the St Lawrence at Montreal.

Rolt, L. T. C., *George Stephenson*. 1960

Stern, Isaac (1920–). American violinist, born in Russia. He toured internationally from 1947, and made many recordings and some films. He was identified with non-musical causes e.g. conservation and peace.

Sterne, Laurence (1713–1768). English novelist, born in Ireland. He came of a distinguished stock (his great-grandfather was an archbishop of York); his father was a brave but erratic ensign in the army, and Sterne's childhood was spent in camps and billets. At 17 when his father died he was left penniless. However, with a cousin's help he went to Cambridge and in 1737 entered the church. In 1737 he began his highly elaborate courtship of Elizabeth Lumley; even a handkerchief or a plate she had used called for a display of sensitivity, and through his letters he introduced the word 'sentimental' to her and to the world. They were married in 1741, but the marriage soon faltered. Elizabeth became cantankerous and even, at times, insane. This gave Sterne freedom to pay frequent visits to 'Crazy Castle', the home of an eccentric Cambridge friend, John Hall-Stevenson, where he found Rabelaisian conversation, much wine and a library filled with rare (often obscene) books. Stimulated by such influences and by an eager flirtation with Mademoiselle Fourmantelle (the 'dear, dear Jenny' of his forthcoming masterpiece), he started writing *The Life and Opinions of Tristram Shandy*, an extraordinary medley of reminiscence and opinion, narrative and digression, in which now famous characters – Walter Shandy (Tristram's father and obviously modelled on Sterne's father), 'my uncle Toby', and Corporal Trim – play the leading roles. The first two books, published in New York at his own expense, appeared in 1759 and were immediately acclaimed. Sterne went to London and was lionized by Lord Chesterfield, Garrick and others; his portrait was painted by Reynolds and more volumes were commissioned (volumes 3–6, 1761–62; volumes 7 and 8, 1765; volume 9, 1767). Success and dissipation increased his normal ill-health and from 1762 he spent much time in France, where he was welcomed by Diderot and others and joined by his wife and daughter. A tour of France and Italy began in 1764 provided material for *A Sentimental Journey* (1768), the other work by which he is remembered. He died during a visit to London to supervise the publication of Volume 9 of *Tristram Shandy*.

Cross, W. L., *Life and Times of Laurence Sterne*. 3rd ed. 1929. Howes, A. B., *Sterne: The Critical Heritage*. 1974

Stettinius, Edward Reilley, Jr. (1900–1949). American administrator. He resigned his presidency of the U.S. Steel Corporation to become Lend-Lease administrator (1941–43). After being under-secretary of state (1943–44) he succeeded Cordell Hull as secretary. In 1946 President Truman appointed him chief U.S. delegate to the United Nations; for the last year of his life he was rector of the University of Virginia.

Stevens, Thaddeus (1792–1868). American Republican politician. He served as a U.S. Congressman from Pennsylvania (1849–53; 1859–68) and developed a detestation of slavery. After the Civil War he was the leader of those who demanded a policy of harsh retribution towards the southern whites. He was the driving force behind the impeachment of President Andrew Johnson, who tried, however ineffectively, to carry out Lincoln's plans for reconciliation. Disappointment over Johnson's acquittal is said to have hastened Stevens's own death.

Stevens, Wallace (1879–1955). American poet. He was vice-president of a large insurance company. His first book, *Harmonium* (1923), was followed by a number of volumes, e.g. *Ideas of Order* (1935) and *The Man with the Blue Guitar* (1937). *The Necessary Angel* (1951) is a volume of essays. In his poems Stevens uses the technique of Impressionism to give highly coloured pictures of civilized decadence, his main theme. His *Collected Poems* (1954) won him the National Book Award (his second), and he won the Pulitzer prize in 1955.

Kermode, F., *Wallace Stevens*. 1960

Stevenson, Adlai Ewing (1900–1965). American politician. Born in Los Angeles, he practised (from 1926) as a lawyer in Chicago and became legal assistant to many agencies set up under the New Deal. He served Roosevelt's wartime administrations in various capacities; as governor of Illinois (1949–53) he carried out many reforms. He was Democratic candidate for the presidency in 1952 and 1956 but was easily defeated by General Eisenhower. His campaign speeches were published under the titles *Call to Greatness* (1954) and *What I Think* (1956); they were accounted 'egg-headed' and had a limited appeal to the general population. President Kennedy appointed him permanent representative at the United Nations, an office he retained under President Johnson. He was known for his liberal outlook and high intellectual integrity.

Busch, N. F., *Adlai Stevenson*. 1952

Stevenson, Robert (1772–1850). Scottish engineer. He succeeded his stepfather (1796) as first engineer to the Northern Lighthouse Commission and during his forty-seven years of office constructed twenty-three lighthouses round the Scottish coasts, including the famous Bell Rock (1807). He also invented the system of intermittently flashing lights which enable a particular lighthouse to be identified. He was the grandfather of Robert Louis * Stevenson.

Stevenson, Robert Louis Balfour (1850–1894). Scottish novelist, essayist and poet, born in Edinburgh. He suffered from tuberculosis, from which he died. He studied engineering and then law but abandoned both for writing. On a canal tour in France and Belgium, which provided the subject of his first book, *An Inland Voyage* (1878), he met Mrs Osbourne (Fanny van der Grift); they married in California (1880), and her son, Lloyd Osbourne, was later his companion and collaborator. Meanwhile *Travels with a Donkey in the Cevennes* (1879) had recalled another journey. Before embarking on the novels which made him famous he had written the essays collected as *Virginibus Puerisque* (1881) and *Familiar Studies of Men and Books* (1882), as well as the tales of fantasy in *The New Arabian Nights* (1882). In 1881 he started *Treasure Island* (1883), the first and most famous of his series of exciting and imaginative adventure stories, which combined Scott's historical method with the clarity and brevity of his own distinctive style. This was followed by *Kidnapped* (1886), *The Black Arrow* (1888), *The Master of Ballantrae* (1889) and *Catriona* (1893). Another immensely popular work was *The Strange Case of Dr Jekyll and Mr Hyde* (1886), in which the conflict of good and evil in a man's nature is symbolically treated in a macabre and exciting tale. Stevenson undertook a tour of the South Seas (1889) for the sake of his health and settled in Samoa with his wife and stepson. Three of his last books, *The Wrong Box* (1889), *The Wrecker* (1892) and *The Ebb Tide* (1894), were written in collaboration with Lloyd Osbourne; *St Ives* (1897, completed by Quiller-Couch) and *Weir of Hermiston* (1896), a masterpiece, were left unfinished. Of his poems the best remembered are contained in *A Child's Garden of Verses* (1885).

Cooper, L., *Robert Louis Stevenson*. 1947. Furnas, J. C., *Voyage to Windward: The Life of Robert Louis Stevenson*. 1951

Stevin (Stevinus), **Simon** (1548–1620). Flemish mathematician. He was born at Bruges and studied law at Leyden University. He contributed to the development of algebraic notation and of decimals. He put forward (1586) the law of equilibrium of a body on an inclined plane and a partial statement of the parallelogram of forces. He was also well known as a military engineer and for his work on land drainage.

Stewart. The name of the dynasty which ruled in Scotland from 1371 and in England from 1603, when James VI of Scotland became James I of England. It stemmed from the marriage of Walter, hereditary high steward (hence the family name) of Scotland, to Marjorie, daughter of Robert * Bruce. Their son * Robert II was the first Stewart king. From the time of Mary Queen of Scots, the French spelling Stuart became the commoner form of the name. The dynasty ceased to reign when George, elector of Hanover, succeeded Queen Anne (1714). The last of the Stewarts in the direct line was Henry, Cardinal York (died 1807), younger son of James Edward * Stuart.

Ashley, M., *The House of Stuart*. 1980

Stewart, Dugald (1753–1828). Scottish philosopher. Professor of moral philosophy at Edinburgh from 1785, a follower of Thomas * Reid, he was responsible for systematizing the doctrines of the 'Scottish school of commonsense'. His systematic work of *Elements of the Philosophy of the Human Mind* (3 volumes, 1792, 1814 and 1827) on the powers of the mind resulted in mental philosophy becoming a separate field of study.

Stikker, Dirk Uipko (1897–1979). Dutch politician and banker. He helped to finance the Resistance movement in World War II. He revived (1946) the liberal Freedom party, was foreign secretary in the coalition of 1948–52, ambassador to Great Britain (1952–58) and secretary general of NATO (1961–64).

Stilicho, Flavius (*c.* 365–408). Roman soldier, appointed by the emperor Theodosius I (whose niece he had married) to be guardian of his son and successor Honorius. For several years, in the east, in Greece, Africa and Italy he held back the waves of barbarians who were engulfing the empire; some of his most spectacular victories were gained (401–403) in northern Italy against Alaric, leader of the Visigoths. Stilicho was suspected of aspiring to become Emperor himself; he was killed in a military revolt. Shortly afterwards, Alaric's army reached Rome.

Stilwell, Joseph Warren (1883–1946) American soldier. He became known as an authority on China, where he was military attaché in the years preceding World War II. As deputy to * Chiang Kai-shek, he commanded a Chinese–American force in Burma which acted in co-operation with the forces based on India against the Japanese. He became (1945) deputy supreme commander of Allied forces in southeast Asia. He was no orthodox soldier and was difficult to work with – hence his nickname 'Vinegar Joe' – but of his courage and ability there is no doubt.

Stimson, Henry Lewis (1867–1950). American lawyer and administrator. A Republican, he twice served as U.S. Secretary of War, first under * Taft (1911–13), and during World War II (1940–45) under F. D. * Roosevelt and * Truman. He was Governor-General of the Philippines (1927–29) and as * Hoover's Secretary of State (1929–33) proposed the 'Stimson doctrine' in opposition to Japan's aggression in Manchuria. He took the ultimate responsibility in recommending use of the atomic bomb against Japan (1945).

Stinnes, Hugo (1870–1924). German industrialist. He inherited a large concern which he built up into a vast industrial empire, which made him an almost symbolic representative of acquisitive man. To river transport, coal-mining and distribution he added shipping and shipbuilding, electricity, oil, motor cars and newspapers; his tentacles spread into almost every trade and industry. In 1920 he became a member of the Reichstag.

Stockhausen, Karlheinz (1928–). German composer. He studied under Messiaen and was part of the *Musique Concrète* group in Paris, experimenting with compositions based on electronic sounds. He wrote choral, orchestral and instrumental works, sometimes combining electronic with normal sonorities, and *avant garde* piano compositions.

Stokes, Sir George Gabriel, 1st Bart. (1819–1903). Irish mathematician and physicist. After graduating with the highest honours at Cambridge University he became Lucasian professor of mathematics there (1849). He was elected (1851) a Fellow of the Royal Society and was its president (1885–90). He won the Rumford Medal (1853) and the Copley Medal (1893). He was a Tory M.P. (1887–92). He played a major part in the development of hydrodynamics and aerodynamics. His contributions to optics were also important, e.g. his work on spectrum analysis (1852) and his explanation of fluorescence and phosphorescence (1878).
Stokes, Sir G. G., *Memoir*. 1907

Stokowski, Leopold (1882–1977). American conductor, born in London of Polish–Irish parents. After studying at the Royal College of Music he went to the U.S.A. where he conducted the Philadelphia Orchestra (1912–36), the New York Philharmonic (1946–50) and the Houston Symphony Orchestra (1955–60). In 1962 he founded the American Symphony Orchestra, based in New York.

Stolypin, Piotr Arkadievich (1862–1911). Russian lawyer and politician. As prime minister of conservative tendencies (1906–11) he endeavoured to keep the Duma in being as an adjunct of government under strict control but not to suppress it. He combated revolutionary movements by severe repression accompanied by measures of social reform. He introduced changes in land tenure aimed at turning the peasants into satisfied and loyal small landholders; but these reforms, partly achieved, came too late to check the growing unrest. He opposed Rasputin, whom he sent briefly into exile in 1911. He himself was murdered by a secret agent.

Stopes, Marie Carmichael (1880–1958). English pioneer of women's rights. As the first female science lecturer, on palaeobotany, at Manchester University, she developed a passionate interest in eugenics and birth control, on which she wrote several books, e.g. *Married Love* (1918) which broke new and unconventional ground. She founded the first birth-control clinic in Britain (1921), a step which inspired similar clinics in other countries. She also wrote poetry and was deeply interested in drama.
Hall, R., *Marie Stopes*. 1977

Stoppard, Tom (1937–). English playwright, born in Czechoslovakia. He began his career in 1954 as a journalist. His first stage play was *Rosencrantz and Guildenstern are Dead* (1967). Later successes include *Jumpers* (1972) and *Travesties* (1974) and he also wrote radio and television plays. His humour is based on juggling with philosophical concepts and on brilliant word-play.

Stout, Rex Todhunter (1886–1975). American author. After a varied career he made enough money to retire from business in 1929 and devoted himself to writing. He created the fictional detective Nero Wolfe (loosely based on Mycroft Holmes).

Stow, John (*c*. 1525–1605). English chronicler and antiquarian. As well as doing original work he translated and summarized much of the work of earlier chroniclers. He is best known for *A Survey of London* (1598–1603), which gives valuable information about Elizabethan London and the customs and lives of its inhabitants.

Stowe, Harriet Elizabeth Beecher (1811–1896). American author. She was the sister of Henry Ward Beecher, the religious writer, and is remembered almost solely for her famous anti-slavery novel, *Uncle Tom's Cabin* (1851–52). In the years before the Civil War this book did much to solidify the movement in the north against slavery.
Wagenknecht, E., *Harriet Beecher Stowe*. 1965

Strabo (64 B.C.–A.D. 25). Greek geographer and geophysicist. Born in Amasia, Asia Minor, of wealthy parents, he was Greek by language and culture. He studied in Rome, specializing in geography, and became a convert to Stoicism. He travelled quite extensively, going up the Nile as far as Aswan and exploring the Ethiopian frontier. The only work of Strabo's which has survived is his *Geographica*. This was compiled more from reading than from personal observation, though he had travelled extensively as far East as Armenia and as far South as Ethiopia. Most of his sources were Greek and have been lost. He attempted a complete geography, which would tackle the questions of the globe from the mathematical, physical, topographical and political points of view. Strabo saw the known world as a single landmass comprising Africa, Asia and Europe, entirely North of the Equator, though he speculated on the existence of one or more Southern continents. He thought the known world was about 7,000 miles long, from East to West, and about 3,000 miles from North to South. He saw the Middle Territories of the Mediterranean as the cradle of civilization. His detailed accounts of Spain, Asia Minor and Egypt are of high quality; other parts he knew less well. Strabo showed some interest in geo-physics. He was aware of the role of earthquakes and volcanoes in changing the face of the globe; he thought the Mediterranean had perhaps been a lake which had overflowed through the Straits of Gibraltar. He also studied the development of river deltas. Amongst ancient geographers, Strabo is the leading physical geographer, whereas * Ptolemy excelled him as a mathematical geographer.

Tozer, H. F., *Selections from Strabo*. 1893

Strachey, (Giles) **Lytton** (1880–1932). English biographer. His *Eminent Victorians* (1918), in which with brilliant satire he amusingly but often unfairly dissected the lives and characters of some of the great figures in 19th-century history, created a literary sensation and started a fashion for 'debunking'. His other works include *Queen Victoria* (1921), *Elizabeth and Essex* (1928) and *Portraits in Miniature* (1931).

Stradivari (Stradivarius), **Antonio** (1644–1737). The best known member of a family of violin makers of Cremona. A pupil of * Nicolo Amati, he brought violin-making to its highest point of perfection. In later life he was helped by his sons, **Francesco Stradivari** (1671–1743) and **Omobono Stradivari** (1679–1742).

Strafford, Thomas Wentworth, 1st Earl of (1593–1641). English administrator. A member of a rich and distinguished Yorkshire family, he entered parliament in 1614 and became an opponent of Buckingham and the court party and supported the Petition of Right (1628). His opposition to the royal government was based on the grounds of inefficiency and petty illegality and he showed none of the political and religious ideals of his colleagues. He had an opportunity of putting into practice his plans for strong, honest, efficient government when he was appointed president of the Council of the North (1628) and still more so when as lord deputy in Ireland (1633–40) he demonstrated the method of government which he himself described as 'thorough'. If Charles I (who had made him Earl of Strafford in 1639) had followed his advice to bring troops from Ireland and overcome his Scottish and English opponents by force, history might have taken a different course, but Charles procrastinated; when at last the Scottish war forced him to call what became the Long Parliament Strafford was impeached unsuccessfully. An Act of Attainder was passed by both Houses. Partly to divert hostility from the queen, Charles finally gave the royal assent. His betrayal of Strafford haunted him throughout the coming years until he suffered similar execution.

Wedgwood, C. V., *Thomas Wentworth*. 1961

Stratford de Redcliffe, Stratford Canning, 1st Viscount (1786–1880). English diplomat. First cousin of George * Canning, most of his career was spent in Constantinople, where he came to exercise a predominant influence over Turkish policy. He first went there (1808) as first secretary and was minister plenipotentiary from 1810. During his last period there (1841–58) his influence over the Sultan became so great that for a time he practically controlled Turkey's foreign policy. He aimed to secure Turkey's independence of Russia without war, and though he failed to avert the Crimean War he obtained enough external support for Turkey to ensure Russia's defeat. He was also largely responsible for many internal reforms. Throughout his career he acted as a proconsul almost entirely independently of the British government.

Strathcona and Mount Royal, Donald Alexander Smith, 1st Baron (1820–1914). Canadian administrator, born in Scotland. He rose from clerk to governor of the Hudson Bay Company (1838–99) but his name is chiefly associated with the construction of the

Canadian Pacific Railway, the first to cross the country from coast to coast. He endowed McGill University and for service in the Boer War raised and equipped Strathcona's Horse.

Strato of Lampsacus (died *c.* 271/268 B.C). Greek philosopher, born on the Asian coast of the Hellespont. He moved to Athens to study at Aristotle's school under * Theophrastus. After spending some time in Alexandria as tutor to the future Ptolemy II, Strato returned to Athens to lead the Lyceum on the death of Theophrastus, a position he occupied between 287 and the time of his death about 268. None of Strato's writings has survived, but much is known about them from accounts in other authors. He set himself the task of teaching Aristotelian doctrine, and he seems throughout his life to have been an orthodox follower of the philosopher. But he was also concerned to shape an interpretation of * Aristotle in a particular direction, that is, to stress the purely naturalistic elements in Aristotle's thought. He stripped Aristotelianism of its religious and transcendental elements, and emphasized material causality. Strato thus underlined the difference between Aristotle's naturalism and * Plato's idealist views. He saw causality and force residing in natural objects themselves, rather than guiding them from above. He had no place for Aristotle's 'quintessence' preferring to see phenomena as the product of the mingling of the four elements, earth, air, fire and water. Strato was consistent in his discussion of man. He denied an immaterial soul. He thought intellect resided in the brain, and communicated itself to other parts of the body by some sort of 'air'. He was one of the most distinguished disciples of Aristotle, and of great influence in the ancient and mediaeval world.

Straus, Oscar (1870–1954). Austrian composer. He won fame by his Viennese operettas, especially *Waltz Dream* (1907) and *The Chocolate Soldier* (1908), based on Shaw's *Arms and the Man*.

Strauss, David Friedrich (1808–1874). German biblical critic. In his most celebrated work, *The Life of Jesus* (2 volumes, 1835–36; translated by George Eliot, 1846), he applied the methods of literary criticism to the Gospels in an attempt to sift historical truth from what he held to be myth. This departure in biblical cricitism was greeted with such hostility that his whole life was embittered and his academic career destroyed.

Strauss, Franz-Josef (1915–). West German politician. Already prominent in Bavarian politics, he entered the Federal government in 1949. There, as leader of the Christian Social Union (the Bavarian counterpart of the Christian Democrats), he soon became prominent as * Adenauer's minister of defence (1956–62). His arbitrary arrests (for alleged revelation of military secrets) of the proprietor and editorial staff of *Der Spiegel* (1962) forced his resignation, but he kept his popularity in Bavaria and with his party. He returned as finance minister (1966–69), served as premier of Bavaria (1978–), and was the unsuccessful candidate of the CDU–CSU coalition for chancellor (1980).

Strauss, Johann (1825–1899). Austrian composer. His father, **Johann Strauss the elder** (1804–1849), also wrote waltzes but is best known for his famous *Radetzky March* (1848). The younger Johann Strauss wrote over 400 waltzes, including *The Emperor, Voices of Spring, Tales from the Vienna Woods* and, most popular of all, *The Blue Danube* (1867). In later life he wrote sixteen operettas of which the best known is *Die Fledermaus* (*The Bat*, 1874). These works, like the waltzes, display the composer's melodic spontaneity and verve, his sense of style and his skill in orchestration.

Strauss, Richard (Georg) (1864–1949). German composer and conductor, born in Munich. The son of Franz-Josef Strauss (1822–1905), a virtuoso horn player who married into a brewing family, he was no relation to Johann * Strauss. Largely self-taught as a composer, his first major work was the Horn Concerto No. 1 (1882; No. 2 dates from 1942). As a protegé of Hans von * Bulow, he gained conducting experience (1885–96) at opera houses in Meiningen, Munich and Weimar, becoming chief conductor at the Munich Opera (1896–98) and the Berlin Royal Court Opera (1898–1910) and joint director of the Vienna State Opera (1919–24). Influenced by Liszt and Wagner, he wrote a series of dramatic symphonic poems, e.g. *Macbeth* (1888, revised 1891), *Don Juan* (1889), *Tod und Verklärung* (1889), *Till Eulenspiegel* (1895), *Also sprach Zarathustra* (1896), *Don Quixote* (1897) and *Ein*

Heldenleben (1898). While in his thirties he was recognised as the greatest German composer since Wagner and Brahms. He wrote almost 200 songs (many of his best in the 1890s), and a monologue for speaker and piano, *Enoch Arden* (1897, after Tennyson). Strauss wrote fifteen operas, and they include his finest music. *Salome* (1905), based on * Wilde's play, was attacked as lurid, salacious and blasphemous, but this only aided its success. *Elektra* (1909), which Hugo von * Hofmannsthal adapted from his own play, was denounced for its polytonality and extreme modernity. His masterpiece *Der Rosenkavalier* (1909–10), a neoclassical comedy of manners, with libretto by Hofmannsthal, set in Vienna of 1740, paid obvious homage to Mozart. It premiered in Dresden in January 1911. His other operas included *Ariadne auf Naxos* (1912), *Die ägyptische Helena* (1928) and *Arabella* (1933), all with Hofmannsthal's dialogue, and *Capriccio* (1941). In the 1930s Strauss' creative powers waned and he unwisely accepted appointment as president of the Reich Music Chamber under Hitler (1933); however, he was able to protect Jewish relatives by marriage. During 1942–48 he experienced a remarkable 'Indian summer': works of his last period include *Metamorphosen* (for 23 strings, 1945), an Oboe Concerto (1945) and the *Four Last Songs* (1948). Strauss was in Ravel's class as an orchestrator but his writing for voice was even finer, and only Mozart equalled him in setting the high soprano.

del Mar, N., *Richard Strauss*. 1972; Krause, E., *Richard Strauss, the Man and his Work*. 1964

Stravinsky, Igor Feodorovich (1882–1971). Russian composer, born in Oranienbaum, near St Petersburg. Son of a famous operatic bass, he studied law but devoted himself to music from 1902, and was for three years a pupil of * Rimsky-Korsakov in instrumentation. Reacting against Wagner's music, he evolved a strikingly original but emotionally neutral style, influenced by * Debussy and Russian folk music. For Sergei * Diaghilev's Ballets Russes he wrote three great scores which made him famous: *The Firebird* (*L'Oiseau de feu*; 1910), *Petrushka* (1911), and *The Rite of Spring* (*Le Sacre du Printemps*; 1913), the last a savage and mysterious evocation of primitive fertility dances which caused a riot at its premiere under Pierre * Monteux in Paris, the audience having to be ejected by police. Stravinsky lived in France 1910–14 and in Switzerland 1914–20, returning to France 1920–39. In the works of his second period (1914–20) he evolved a new style, abondoning the huge orchestra and blazing colour of *The Rite of Spring* for an austere preoccupation with line and structure; they include *The Soldier's Tale* (1918, for narrator, three actors and seven instruments), *The Wedding* (1923, vocalists, four pianos and percussion), *Symphonies of wind instruments* (1920) and songs. In a third, neo-classical, period (1920–32) he wrote the ballets *Pulcinella* (1920, after Pergolesi), *Apollo* (1928, for strings), and *The Fairy's Kiss* (1928, after Tchaikovsky), the opera-oratorio *Oedipus rex* (1927, set to * Cocteau's Latin text), the *Symphony of Psalms* (1930) and a Violin Concerto. His fourth period (1932–52) was both eclectic and prolific, marked by varied influences ranging from plainsong, Bach, Beethoven, Verdi, through jazz and swing; music included the ballets *The Card Party* (1936), and *Orpheus* (1947), Symphony in C (1940), Symphony in three movements (1945), a mass (1944), and the opera *The Rake's Progress* (1951, libretto by W. H. * Auden and Chester Kallman), based on Hogarth's drawings. Stravinsky became a French citizen in 1934, lived in the U.S. from 1939 and was naturalised in 1945. His fifth period (from 1952) was influenced by the serial techniques of * Schönberg and, especially, * Berg in such works as *In memoriam Dylan Thomas* (1954), the ballet *Agon* (1957), *Threni* (*Lamentations of Jeremiah*, 1958), two masses, a cantata, *Abraham and Issac* (1963, baritone and chamber orchestra) and *Requiem Canticles* (1966). He made many recordings and toured the world as a conductor of his own works, visiting Australia and Africa in 1961 and making a triumphant return to Russia in 1962. He published an autobiography in 1935 and collaborated with Robert Craft in two volumes of *Conversations* (1959; 1962). He had enormous intellectual curiosity about literature, mathematics and aesthetics, and for two generations was the greatest single figure in 20th century music. He died in New York and was buried in Venice.

Young, P. M., *Stravinsky*. 1966. White, E. W., *Stravinsky: The Composer and his Works*. 1966

Streicher, Julius (1885–1946). German Nazi

politician. Originally a primary schoolteacher, he founded the German Socialist Party which merged with the Nazis in 1923. His journal *Der Stürmer* ('The Stormtrooper') was so pornographic in its attacks on Jews that many Nazis regarded it as distasteful. He had fallen from the front rank by 1939, was Governor of Franconia 1940–44 and hanged for war crimes after the Nuremberg trials.

Stresemann, Gustav (1878–1929). German politician. A successful businessman, he entered the Reichstag (1907) and after World War I founded the German People's party; during a short period as chancellor (1923) he succeeded in checking inflation. From November 1923 until his death he was foreign minister in a succession of governments. He was a main architect of the pacts by which it was hoped to build a permanently peaceful Europe: he signed the Locarno and Kellogg-Briand Pacts and six years before the appointed date he secured the evacuation of the Rhineland by foreign troops. For much of the time he worked closely with * Briand and Austen * Chamberlain with whom he shared the Nobel Peace Prize (1926).
Gatzke, H. W., *Stresemann and the Rearmament of Germany*. 1969. Hirsch, E. F., *Gustav Stresemann: Patriot und Europäer*. 1964

Strijdom, Johannes Gerhardus (1893–1958). South African politician. Originally an ostrich farmer, he became a lawyer, entered the South African parliament in 1929, led the extremist Transvaal wing of the Nationalist party and succeeded Dr D. F. * Malan as prime minister (1954–58). He entrenched 'apartheid' even more harshly than his predecessor.

Strindberg, (Johan) August (1849–1912). Swedish dramatist. From the days of his childhood, which was spent in a depressing family home, his neurotic temperament was always at war with his surroundings. His three marriages were disastrous and were among the causes of his persecution mania, leading to periodic insanity and alcoholism. In the 1870s he began writing plays which reflected his radical views, and he gained a considerable reputation by his novel *The Red Room* (1879), a satirical and realistic account of artistic life in Stockholm. From 1883 to 1889 he lived abroad, returning in 1884 to defend himself successfully against a charge of blasphemy resulting from the publication of his collection of short stories *Giftas* (*Marriage*). Meanwhile he wrote poems on social and philosophical subjects, more plays, and the beginnings of his autobiography. To this middle period belong the three great plays by which he is best remembered, *The Father* (1887), *Miss Julie* (1888) and *The Dance of Death* (1901), all obsessed by family conflict in an atmosphere of foreboding. By this time Strindberg was falling under the influence of * Nietzsche and adopting the attitudes, including contempt for democracy, of his mentor. In his last years came a series of historical plays, novels, e.g. the trilogy *To Damascus* (1898–1904), and fairy plays, indicative of a growing interest in religious mysticism and the occult. He again went to live abroad in 1892 but returned finally in 1896. In 1907 he founded the Intimate Theatre for the production of what he called his 'chamber plays'.
Sprigge, E., *The Strange Life of August Strindberg*. 1972; Ollen, G., *August Strindberg*. 1984

Stringfellow, John (1799–1883). English inventor. A lace manufacturer of Chard, Somerset, until 1956 he was given credit for having built the first power-driven aircraft, but it was then shown that he was only trying to improve one of W. S. Henson's designs.

Stroheim, Erich von (1885–1957). Austrian-born film actor and director, subsequently naturalized American (1926). His first film role was in *Intolerance* (1916) and thereafter he tended to become typecast as a German officer. Among his most distinguished parts was that of a soldier in Renoir's *La Grande Illusion* (1938), as Rommel in *Five Graves to Cairo* and the butler in *Sunset Boutevard* (1950). The best known of the films he directed were *Foolish Wives* (1922), *Wedding March* (1928) and notably *Greed* (1923–24).
Quinn, T., *Von Stroheim*. 1973

Strongbow, Richard de Clare *see* **Pembroke, 2nd Earl of**

Stuart family *see* **Stewart**

Stuart, Charles Edward (known as 'Bonnie Prince Charlie' or 'the Young Pretender') (1720–1788). The eldest son of James Edward * Stuart, on whose behalf he led the Jacobite rebellion of 1745, he landed in Scotland with

only seven followers but was joined by an increasing number of Highlanders as he moved south. He captured Edinburgh and secured his position by defeating the government army at Prestonpans. Six weeks later he marched south into England. After capturing Carlisle and reaching Derby he began to withdraw. At Falkirk (17 January 1746) he won a last success before his army was overtaken and virtually annihilated by the Duke of * Cumberland, who here earned the name 'Butcher', at Culloden (16 April). Charles, with £30,000 offered for his capture, spent five months unscathed and unbetrayed among the hills and islands of western Scotland until, with the help of Flora * Macdonald, he was able to reach France. So far with his looks and charm he had been the true hero of romance, but the rest of the story is one of disappointment, disillusion and dissipation. Harried by English agents, he wandered about Europe seeking help for schemes by which he vainly hoped to regain his rights. He married (1772) Louisa of Stolberg, a childless and unhappy match. He finally settled in Italy and in his last years was looked after with devotion by a natural daughter.
Tayler, H., *Charles Edward Stuart*. 1945

Stuart, James (Francis) Edward (known as 'the Old Pretender') (1688–1766). Son of James II of Great Britain and Mary of Modena. He was brought up in France. On his father's death he was acclaimed by the 'Jacobites' as king and a number of risings were made on his behalf of which the best known were those of 1715 and 1745. For the former, ended by defeats at Sheriffmuir and Preston, James Edward was in Scotland for a few weeks; he spent the remainder of his life mainly in Rome; the latter was fought under the leadership of his son, Charles Edward * Stuart, born of his marriage to Clementina Sobieska of Poland. His second son, **Henry** (1725–1807), created Duke of * York by his father, became a cardinal in 1747.

Stubbs, George (1724–1806). English painter and engraver. In 1766 he published his *Anatomy of a Horse* based on the study of dead horses in his studio. The engravings created a revolution in animal painting and he was later able to use his anatomical knowledge to give his sporting pictures, e.g. *The Grosvenor Staghunt* a verisimilitude never before obtained. He had, moreover, a true artist's gifts and his pictures have strength, balance and charm. He was elected R.A. in 1781.

Stubbs, William (1825–1901). English historian and churchman. He devoted himself to the study and publication of medieval documents. His fame rests on two great works, *Select Charters and other Illustrations of English Constitutional History* (1870), and *The Constitutional History of England* (3 volumes, 1874–78). He became Regius professor of history at Oxford (1866), bishop of Chester (1884), and bishop of Oxford (1889).

Sturgeon, William (1783–1850). English electrical engineer. The son of a shoe-maker, he was self-educated. He built the first practical electromagnet, capable of lifting twenty times its own weight. He devised the first moving-coil galvanometer, and built, in accordance with the principles of Michael * Faraday, the first successful rotary electric motor.

Sucre, Antonio José de (1795–1830). South American leader, born in Venezuela. He served under * Bolívar in the War of South American Independence and became a general in 1819. His great victory near Guyaquil ensured the independence of the future Ecuador. With Bolívar he then won a long struggle for the independence of Peru and in 1826 was installed as first president of the newly created Bolivia, but his army mutinied and he was expelled. Two years later he was on his way through the mountains to rejoin Bolívar in Peru when he was killed by robbers.

Sudermann, Hermann (1857–1928). German playwright and novelist. His plays include *Die Ehre* (1889), *Sodoms Ende* (1891) and *Heimat* (1893). The last named, translated into English as *Magda*, provided a star role for Mrs Patrick Campbell and other well known actresses. His novels, of which *Frau Sorge* (1887) was the first and best known, are mostly set against a background of his native East Prussia.

Sue, Eugène (1804–1857). French novelist. He was among the most successful of writers at adapting his work to serial form. The best known example in an immense output of popular works was *The Wandering Jew* (1845). His socialist and republican views, shown in his novels by his idealization of the downtrodden and criminal classes, earned him the disfavour of Napoleon III and brought about his exile.

Suetonius (Gaius Suetonius Tranquillus) (fl. 117–138). Roman historian. His best known work, which has survived almost complete, contains the biographies of Julius Caesar and the first eleven emperors, Augustus to Domitian. His mixture of documented fact and gossip provides lively reading. Only part of another series on less exalted men (e.g. Virgil, Horace) survives.

Suger, Bernard (*c.* 1081–1151). French prelate. Abbot of the Benedictine monastery of St Denis, Paris (from 1122), he was employed as chief minister by Louis VI, and later virtually ruled the country while Louis VII was absent on crusade. The beautiful abbey church of St Denis, reconstructed to his design, is one of the earliest examples of the Gothic style. His histories of the kings he served provide an important record of contemporary events.

Suharto *see* **Soeharto.**

Sukarno *see* **Soekarno.**

Sulaiman (or Suleiman: known as 'the Magnificent') (1494–1566). Turkish sultan (from 1520). He was the son and successor of Selim I (reigned 1512–20) and under him the Ottoman empire reached its zenith. He captured Belgrade (1521) and Rhodes (1522); he crushed the Hungarians at Mohacz (1526) but failed to take Vienna in 1529 and eventually the emperor Ferdinand I, while retaining Austria, was left with only a small portion of Hungary. Meanwhile his fleet, under the celebrated corsair Khaireddin Barbarossa, was terrorizing the Mediterranean but it failed to capture Malta from the Knights of St John. Sulaiman won Baghdad (from Persia) and it remained in Turkish hands until 1917. He died during renewed war in Hungary. His legal reforms, mainly relating to land tenure, earned him the name *Kanuni* (the lawgiver) and he proved himself a lavish patron of the arts, employing the famous architect Selim Sinan to build the four magnificent mosques.
Merriman, R. B., *Suleiman the Magnificent 1520–1566*. Repr. 1966

Sulla, Lucius Cornelius (138–78 B.C.). Roman soldier and dictator. He fought under Marius against Jugurtha in Africa and against the Cimbri and Teutones, but their mutual antipathy soon developed into political rivalry, Marius siding with the turbulent popular party and Sulla with the more conservative groups. After his victories in the Social War (for the enfranchisement of the Italians as Roman citizens) Sulla gained his first consulship (88) but, angered by a proposal that the command in a war against Mithridates should be transferred to Marius, he led an army against Rome and captured the city. He obtained laws to legitimize his position and left for the east, but as soon as he had gone the Marians regained control. Meanwhile Sulla was expelling the armies of Mithridates from Greece and from the Roman province of Asia. He then returned with his army to Italy and after another victory over Sulla's supporters at the gates of Rome (82) he was appointed dictator. Massacres and proscriptions of his opponents followed. He then carried out a large constitutional and administrative programme, the main feature being the restoration of full power to the Senate. He retired voluntarily in 79 and died the following year.

Sullivan, Sir Arthur Seymour (1842–1900). English composer. After being a chorister at the Chapel Royal he studied music in London and Leipzig; he achieved successes with music for Shakespeare's *The Tempest* and for the famous comedy *Box and Cox* before he began his long collaboration with W. S. * Gilbert and the impresario Richard D'Oyly Carte in the popular 'Savoy Operas' (so-called from their production at that theatre from 1881). The best known are *Trial by Jury* (1875), *H.M.S. Pinafore* (1878), *The Pirates of Penzance* (1880), *Patience* (1881), *Iolanthe* (1882), *Princess Ida* (1884), *The Mikado* (1885), *Ruddigore* (1887), *The Yeomen of the Guard* (1888) and *The Gondoliers* (1889). Sullivan's melodic gift and deft and lively scoring admirably partnered the witty libretti; but the two men later had a business quarrel and abandoned the partnership. Neither collaborator achieved comparable success alone, though Sullivan's serious opera *Ivanhoe* (1891) and ballads such as *The Lost Chord* were popular for a time. He was knighted in 1883.
Young, P., *Sir Arthur Sullivan*. 1971

Sullivan, Louis Henri (1856–1924). American architect. After studying in Paris he joined a Chicago partnership and became the most important pioneer of modern steel frame construction. His Transportation building for the World's Columbian Exposition (1893) provided a striking illustration of the new technique. He was a strong advocate of the unity of form and function but did not favour stark austerity and introduced original types of decoration in conformity with his ideas. The Schiller Theatre and the Stock Exchange were among his Chicago buildings; there are many other fine examples of his work in St Louis, Buffalo and New York.

Morrison, H., *Louis Sullivan: Prophet of Modern Architecture*. 1935

Sully, Maximilien de Béthune, Duc de (1559–1641). French minister, son of a Huguenot, Baron de Rosny. He fought for Henry of Navarre (Henry IV of France) and became his chief friend and adviser. He approved Henry's adoption of Roman Catholicism in order to become king. His first task was to restore the finances and economy by removing abuses in the collection of taxes. He strictly controlled expenditure, reduced tax exemptions and re-established former taxes; he fostered agriculture and industry and the building of roads and canals. When he retired after Henry's assassination he had amassed a huge surplus in the treasury. He was made a duke for negotiating Henry's marriage with Marie de Médicis (1606).

Sully-Prudhomme, René François Armand (1839–1907). French poet. He studied science and philosophy in Paris; his earlier poems are permeated with melancholy. His later long poems are *La Justice* (1878) and *Le Bonheur* (1888), concerned with philosophic and scientific theories. In this he resembled the Roman poet Lucretius, whom he translated (1866). He also wrote in prose. He was elected to the Académie Française in 1881 and won the first Nobel Prize for Literature (1901), defeating Tolstoy, Ibsen and Henry James.

Summerskill, Edith Summerskill, Baroness (1901–1980). English physician and Labour politician. As an M.P. (from 1938) and life peeress (from 1961) she made a mark in public life as much by her very personal points of view as by her achievements. Among her posts was that of minister of national insurance (1950–51). She was chairman of the Labour Party 1954–55. Her daughter **Shirley Summerskill** (1931–), a physician, also held office under a Labour government.

Summerskill, E., *Letters to My Daughter*. 1957

Sumner, Charles (1811–1874). American Republican politician. A U.S. Senator from Massachusetts (1851–74), he was one of the most ardent and eloquent speakers against slavery. After the Civil War he was among the strongest advocates of punishment for the south and of harsh terms for aid in reconstruction.

Sunderland, Robert Spencer, 2nd Earl of (1640–1702). English politician. He became secretary of state of Charles II (1679) and negotiated the secret treaty under which, in return for an annual pension from Louis XIV, England was to become subservient to France. He was James II's closest adviser and secretly adhered to the Roman Catholic faith, but at the same time was negotiating with William of Orange, whose lord chamberlain he subsequently became. His son, **Charles Spencer, 3rd Earl of Sunderland** (1675–1722), was a Whig politician who became all-powerful under George I. His involvement in the South Sea Bubble, when he was accused of accepting a bribe of £50,000 of the company's stock, caused his resignation. Father and son shared the brilliance and lack of scruple of the age in which they lived.

Kenyon, J. P., *Robert Spencer, Earl of Sunderland*. 1958

Sun Yat-sen (1866–1925). Chinese revolutionary politician. He was born near Canton into a family of Christian peasants and became influenced by western ideas at a missionary school in Honolulu (1878–83). Afterwards he took a medical degree (1892) at Hong Kong and practised at Macao and in Canton. There he began his revolutionary activities, but the failure of the first of a series of plots forced him to live in exile in Japan, the U.S.A. and England. In London (1896) he was kidnapped and confined in the Chinese Embassy; he would in all probability have been murdered there had he not contrived to send a letter to a former English tutor. Many plots instigated by Sun from abroad failed, but finally a mutiny at Hankow (1911) spread so quickly that in 1912 the boy emperor, Hsuan T'ung, abdicated. Sun Yat-sen was briefly president of the new republic but had to retire in favour of * Yüan Shih-kai, the general who had the victorious army at his back, and rapidly assumed the role of dictator with ambitions to become emperor. In the year of

Yuan's death (1916), Sun returned from enforced exile to Canton where he became president of a new republic of the south, which had split from the militant north. There he tried to put into practice the *Three People's Principles* (lectures published in book form after his death). These were Nationalism (by which he meant the abolition of European exploitation and the unification of the many peoples of China); Democracy (a gradual approach under the guidance of a single party – the Kuomintang – to constitutional government); and Livelihood (the welfare of the masses was to be the first care of the state). He did not live to see the reunification of China, but in his last years he became increasingly ready to accept guidance and help from Communist Russia. This caused a split in the Kuomintang after his death. The communist cause was espoused even more strongly by his widow, Soong Ch'ing-ling (1893–1981), who became vice-president of the People's Republic 1949–81. All his successors, however, united in revering Sun as the founder of the republic.

Schriffrin, H. Z., *Sun Yat-sen and the Origins of the Chinese Revolution*. 1968. Sharman, L., *Sun Yat-sen: his Life and its Meaning*. 1934

Suppé, Franz von (1819–1895). Austrian composer, born in Dalmatia. A distant relative of * Donizetti, he lived in Vienna from 1835. He wrote music for ballet, chamber music and some sacred works, but his reputation was mainly based on his successful operettas, notably *Light Cavalry*.

Suraja Dowlah (died 1757). Nawab of Bengal. After his attack (1756) on the British settlement of Calcutta, his imprisonment of over 100 Europeans caused their death by suffocation in the notorious 'Black Hole'. Quick retribution came when his forces were routed by Robert * Clive at Plassey (1757).

Surrey, Henry Howard, Earl of (*c.* 1517–1547). English poet, the inventor of blank verse. He was in attendance on Henry VIII at the Field of the Cloth of Gold and long remained in favour at court, even after the execution of his cousin, Catherine Howard. Eventually, however, he was tried and executed on a trumped-up charge of treason. Blank verse, introduced by him for a translation of Virgil, was adaptation of one of Chaucer's metres. He can also share with * Wyatt the credit for bringing to England the Petrarchan sonnet. His poems were first printed, with those of Wyatt and others, in *Tottel's Miscellany* (1557). Many of his love poems were written to 'the fair Geraldine', a daughter of the ninth Earl of Kildare.

Chapman, H. W., *Two Tudor Portraits*. 1960

Surtees, Robert Smith (1805–1864). English sporting writer. He made a name by the magazine sketches collected as *Jorrocks' Jaunts and Jollities* (1838). After inheriting his father's estate (1838) he was able to live the life of a country gentleman while continuing to write. A series of sporting novels resulted, of which *Handley Cross* (1843) is the best known; nearly all were illustrated by either Leech or 'Phiz'.

Suslov, Mikhail Andreivich (1902–1982). Russian politician and theorist. A peasant's son, he joined the Communist Party in 1921, was active in Stalin's purges and became the leading Cominform propagandist. He served on the Politburo 1952–53 and 1955–82, and was regarded as the leading Soviet political theorist.

Sutherland, Graham Vivian (1903–1980). English painter. While an engineering apprentice he started art night classes in London. He first turned his talents to etching and engraving but from 1935 he devoted himself to painting. Influenced by Blake, Samuel Palmer and the surrealists, he produced Pembrokeshire landscapes in which fantastic and sinister-looking plant and insect forms dominate. After working as a war artist in World War II he painted vigorous and original portraits of Somerset Maugham, Lord Beaverbrook and Sir Winston Churchill (the last, disapproved of by Sir Winston, being destroyed by the Churchill family). He designed the altar tapestry, *Christ in Majesty*, for the new Coventry Cathedral. He received the O.M. in 1960.

Sutherland, Dame Joan (1926–). Australian soprano, born in Sydney. She made her debut at Covent Garden, London in the *Magic Flute* (1952). Her fame arose from her performance (1959) of *Lucia di Lammermoor* and from that time she sang in every major opera house of the world.

Suvorov, Alexander Vasilyevich (1730–1800). Russian soldier of Swedish descent.

Although sickly and small he fulfilled his ambition by starting service as a soldier in the ranks at the age of 15. After gaining distinction in the Seven Years War (1756–63) and the Polish War (1768–71), he fought against the Turks (1773), crushed a rising in the Caucasus (1780) and in a second Turkish War won a great victory at Focsani (1789). He crushed * Kościuszko's nationalist rising in Poland (1794) and in the French Revolutionary Wars was sent to help the Austrians in Italy (1799). After several successes against the French in Italy he was ordered to join Korsakov in Switzerland; the march over the Alps involved his troops in terrible hardships and losses and he arrived to find that Korsakov had already been defeated by Masséna. Suvorov extricated his troops with difficulty to Austria. He died soon after returning to St Petersburg. Never defeated in battle, he was known for his many eccentricities and beloved by his troops. His name is revered in Soviet Russia.

Suzuki, Daisetz Teitaro (1870–1966). Japanese Zen Buddhist. He was the leading modern authority on Buddhism, with a particular interest in the Zen form. He wrote over 100 books or major studies on religious topics in both Japanese and English.

Sverdlov, Yakov Mikhailovich (real name Y. M. Nakhamkes) (1885–1919). Russian communist politician. A professional revolutionary from the age of 17, he was exiled to the Arctic, escaped several times and became Lenin's closest collaborator. After the Revolution he held three important posts (1917–19): chairman of the All-Russian Executive Committee of Soviets and virtual head of state; general secretary of the Bolshevik Party; and commissar for internal security. He ordered the execution of the imperial family in Ekaterinburg (later renamed Sverdlovsk). He died of typhus.

Svevo, Italo (1861–1928). Italian author, born in Trieste of Jewish origin. His early novels based on personal experience – *A Life* (1892) and *As a Man Grows Older* (1898) – failed to attract and for many years Svevo abandoned writing. He resumed with his masterpiece *The Confessions of Zeno* (1923) which brought some appreciation, maintained by at least one critical study. He was a friend of James Joyce.

Swammerdam, Jan (1637–1680). Dutch biologist. One of his major areas of interest was animal physiology. Swammerdam adhered to the mechanical philosophy. He sought to apply Cartesian (* Descartes) models of explanation to the action of the lungs, the heart, the respiratory system. Experiments on dogs demonstrated the contractility of muscles, even when separated from the body. In these and other instances his work was aiming to demonstrate the purely mechanical nature of bodily action, independent of transcendental principles like 'spirits' or 'virtues'. Swammerdam's other field of expertise was in the microscopic study of lower animals. He was one of the first naturalists to find insects worthy of scientific study. He made detailed studies of the development of insects within the chrysalis, and showed the life history of the butterfly and the dragonfly. He sought to refute the view that insects generate spontaneously (the making of something out of nothing seemed to him both unscientific and also contrary to his religious belief in the order of the world).

Swan, Sir Joseph Wilson (1828–1914). English inventor. A manufacturing chemist by profession, he invented twenty years before * Edison (1860) an experimental carbon-filament electric lamp which however was not commercially in production until he improved it (1881). He patented (1883) a process for carbon-filament production which revolutionized the manufacture of electric lamps. He also made a number of inventions of great practical value in the field of photography. A fast gelatine emulsion, for example, confirmed the supremacy of the dry-plate technique. Many improvements in photographic printing were also due to him. He was elected F.R.S. in 1894 and knighted ten years later.

Swedenborg (originally Svedberg), **Emanuel** (1688–1772). Swedish scientist and theologian. At first employed by Charles XII as an assessor in the College of Mines, he gained a seat in the House of Nobles when his family was ennobled (1719). Meanwhile he wrote on all kinds of mathematical, mechanical and scientific subjects (sometimes anticipating later discoveries) on the calculus, on finding longitude at sea, on tides, decimal coinage and the planetary system, on the atom as a vortex of particles etc. His study of geology and palaeontology led him to a theory of creation, published in the *Opera Philosophica et Mineralia* (3 volumes, 1734). In other works, e.g. *The Animal Kingdom* (1745), he treats, among many other subjects, of anatomy, human and zoological, and eventually explores the relationship of body and soul. By this time his inquiries as a scientist were beginning to merge with his visionary speculations as a seer. He believed that in 1745 direct personal insight into the world of the spirit was conferred upon him to enable him to reveal the true sense of the Bible. In his *Heavenly Arcana* (8 volumes, 1749–56) he gives the first two books of the Bible an allegorical and symbolic meaning. In the following years he had further visions and published some forty theological books, including *The Christian Religion* (1771) which systematically presents the theology that had appeared piecemeal in earlier writings. The essence of Swedenborg's theology is his view of Jesus Christ whom he sees not as a Person of the Trinity but as a human possessed of a divine soul. He spent several of his last years in London where he died. He had organized no sect but the 'New Church' based on his doctrines was founded in London some fifteen years after his death, and still has many groups in Britain and elsewhere.

Sigtedt, C. O., *The Swedenborg Epic*. 1952. Jonsson, I., *Emanuel Swedenborg*. 1971

Sweyn I (known as 'Forkbeard') (*c.* 960–1014). King of Denmark (985–1014). In revenge for the death of his sister, who perished in the massacre of St Brice's Day (1002) organized by * Ethelred the Unready, he attacked and ravaged England repeatedly and just before his death was recognized as king but not crowned. He was succeeded by his son Cnut.

Swift, Jonathan (1667–1745). English author, born in Dublin after his father's death. At Trinity College, Dublin, he showed himself idle and undisciplined. After the revolution of 1689 he joined his mother in England and became secretary to her relative Sir William Temple at his Surrey home of Moor Park. He remained there with intervals (during one of which he took Anglican orders in Ireland) until Temple's death (1699). There he wrote *The Battle of the Books* (classics v. moderns), which was published (1704) with *A Tale of a Tub*, a satire on religious humbug and corruption which effectively barred him from the highest offices in the church. At Temple's house, too, he first met Esther Johnson, then a child of eight, to whom he later wrote the famous *Journal to Stella* (1710–13), which gives, mostly in childish language, an intimate account of his London life. The nature of the bond between them is one of those literary mysteries that many have probed: they may even have married though it seems clear that despite mutual dependence and devotion they had no sex relations. Similar doubts concern Hester Vanhomrigh, the heroine of *Cadenus* (anagram of *decanus*, 'dean') and *Vanessa*. She loved him passionately, but, having encouraged her, he rejected her and broke her heart. Meanwhile Swift had become known as the most formidable political satirist alive, at first for the Whigs and from 1710 on behalf of the Tories. He became dean of St Patrick's, Dublin (1713), and from 1714, except for occasional visits to London to see old friends (e.g. Pope and Gay), he lived in the Irish capital. Some of his best known tracts and treatises were written during this period, many, including *Drapier's Letters* (1724), protesting against the grievances under which Ireland suffered. The most famous of all his works, *Gulliver's Travels*, part fairy tale, part satire, appeared in 1726. From 1738 Swift's mind began to give way and his last years contained much suffering. Stella had already died (1728) and Swift was buried beside her in St Patrick's.

The clarity of his intellect and the pungency of his writing have seldom been equalled; he could give and demand devotion, and in the later years he won the love of the Irish among whom he lived. But he remained a frustrated and unhappy man and something of an enigma to his contemporaries and to later generations. Everything he wrote was published anonymously and except for *Gulliver* he received no payment.

Murry, J. M., *Jonathan Swift, a critical biography*. 1955. Stathis, J. J., *A bibliography of Swift Studies*. 1967

Swinburne, Algernon Charles (1837–1909). English poet and writer. A friend of Rossetti, Morris, George Meredith and Landor, in 1879 his health broke down under the strain of a dissipated life. His friend Theodore Watts-Dunton took him into his home at No. 2, The Pines, Putney, where the bohemian rebel quietly spent the rest of his life. The publication of his *Poems and Ballads* (1865), with their sensual rhythms, pagan spirit and contempt for conventional morality, had aroused both enthusiasm and violent criticism. *Songs Before Sunrise* (1871) was inspired by Mazzini's republicanism; *Tristram of Lyonesse* (1822) and *The Tale of Balen* (1892) are his contribution to Arthurian legend. He wrote poetic dramas, including *Atalanta in Calydon* (1865), his first work to attract attention, and, an ambitious trilogy on Mary Queen of Scots; his works of literary criticism, e.g. *Essays and Studies* (1875) and monographs on many individual writers, Shakespeare, Victor Hugo etc., display a characteristic over-emphasis but are written with imagination and perception. Few poets have surpassed Swinburne in the composition of verbal music, but though he can still disturb he no longer shocks.

Fuller, J. O., *Swinburne: A Critical Biography*. 1968

Swineshead, Richard (fl. *c.* 1340–1355). English mediaeval philosopher and physicist. It is probable that a Roger Swineshead was at Oxford and wrote logical treatises and a work in physics, the *De Motibus Naturalibus*, and that a Richard Swineshead was at Merton College in the 1340s and was author of the important *Liber Calculationum*, an exhaustive treatise which provides techniques for calculating physical variables and their changes. Swineshead devotes attention to variables such as density and rarity, action and reaction, constant speed and acceleration, forces and resistances. Questions of resistance in a medium are given prominence. His English 'calculatory' tradition exercised notable influence on the development of physical studies, especially on * Oresme.

Weisheipl, J. A., 'Roger Swyneshead', in *Oxford Studies Presented to Daniel Callus*. 1964

Swithin (or Swithun), **St** (died 862). English prelate. A man of great piety, he built many churches and for the last ten years of his life was bishop of Winchester. When his body was transferred from the churchyard to the cathedral itself (971), tradition says that heavy rain delayed the exhumation, which was to have taken place on 15 July; and to this happening can be traced the belief that rain on St Swithin's Day portends a long spell of rainy weather.

Swynford, Catherine (1350?–1403). Mistress and later wife of * John of Gaunt. Her sister Philippa was married to the poet Chaucer. After the death of her first husband, Sir Hugh Swynford, she became the mistress of John of Gaunt. They married in 1394, their children being legitimized under the name of * Beaufort.

Sydenham, Thomas (1624–1689). English physician. The founder of modern clinical medicine, his studies at Oxford were interrupted by service with the parliamentarian forces, but from 1655 (though he did not obtain a licence to do so until 1663) he practised as a physician in Westminster and was thus able to study the fevers arising from the marshes of St James's Park. The great plague (1665) provided another exacting test of his medical skill. As his fame grew he got to know John Locke, Robert Boyle and other scholars and scientists of the time. He recognized that the physician's task was to assist nature in its constant efforts to eliminate morbid matter or render it harmless. Thus his task was to study the disease in relation to the particular patient. Some of his descriptions (e.g. of gout, based on his own symptoms) are classics of medical literature; convulsions of children are still known as Sydenham's chorea. He was not afraid to do nothing if he felt that he could not render effective help, and his prescription of fresh air, few coverings and a light diet for fevers was almost revolutionary.

Sydney, Thomas Townshend, 1st Viscount (1733–1801). British politician. He is remembered because he was home secretary (1783–89) when the first settlers reached New Holland (Australia). In consequence the great city which grew around the cove where a first landing was made (1788) bears his name.

Syme, Sir Ronald (1903–). British historian, born in New Zealand. His *The Roman Revolution* (1939) was an important study of the age of Augustus. He became professor of ancient history at Oxford 1949–70 and was awarded the O.M. in 1976.

Symington, William (1763–1831). Scottish engineer. He made early experiments in applying steam power to ships and patented (1801) a horizontal direct-acting steam engine which he fitted to the tug *Charlotte Dundas* on the

Forth-Clyde canal. This was the first effective steam-boat but though it towed two coal barges 19 miles in 6 hours its adoption was rejected for spurious reasons; a further plan to introduce steam-powered tugs on the Bridgewater Canal ended in disappointment when the 3rd Duke of Bridgewater died (1803). Symington died in poverty.

Symonds, John Addington (1840–1893). English man of letters. His *Studies of the Greek Poets* (1873) was followed by the notable *The Renaissance in Italy* (1875–86). He translated Benvenuto Cellini's autobiography, and the sonnets of Michelangelo, whose biography he also wrote (2 volumes, 1893). He wrote several volumes of poetry, and studies of Ben Jonson, Shelley etc.

Symons, Albert James Alroy (1900–1941). English writer. He was remembered almost solely for an astonishing piece of literary detection, *The Quest for Corvo* (1934), which revived interest in the eccentric novelist Frederick Rolfe, Baron * Corvo.

Symons, Arthur William (1865–1945). British critic and poet. By his translations and studies of Baudelaire and by *The Symbolist Movement in Literature* (1899) he was largely responsible for introducing the work of this French literary school to English readers. His other books include *The Romantic Movement in English Poetry* (1909) and several volumes of essays and poems. In 1905 he suffered a mental collapse and never recovered.

Synge, John Millington (1871–1909). Irish playwright, born near Dublin. After some years in Paris (where he met Yeats) he returned to Ireland and made several visits to the Aran Islands, studying folk speech and culture. This study provided him with the setting for his plays, the first two of which, *In the Shadow of the Glen* (1903) and *Riders to the Sea* (1904), brought him into close association with the Abbey Theatre, Dublin. There followed *The Well of the Saints* (1905) and his great comedy *The Playboy of the Western World* (1907). His tragic verse-drama *Deirdre of the Sorrows* was unfinished when he died. His influence upon succeeding Irish playwrights was immense.

Skelton, R., *The Writings of J. M. Synge*. 1971

Syngman Rhee *see* **Rhee, Syngman**

Szell, George (1897–1970). Hungarian-American conductor, born in Budapest. A juvenile prodigy as a pianist, he made his début as a conductor in Berlin (1914) and became a protégé of Richard * Strauss and Arturo * Toscanini. Chief conductor of the Metropolitan Opera, New York, 1942–45, he directed the Cleveland Orchestra 1946–70 and raised it to the first rank, also making many recordings.

Szilard, Leo (1898–1964). Hungarian-American physicist, born in Budapest. He studied in Germany, lived in England from 1934 and the U.S. from 1937. He was the first to understand the technique of nuclear chain reaction. He worked with * Fermi in Chicago on the original 'atomic pile' and on developing the atomic bomb, although opposing its use against civilian targets. He was professor of biophysics at Chicago 1946–53.

Szymanowski, Karol Maciej (1882–1937). Polish composer. Director of the Warsaw Conservatoire (from 1926), his early works are individual for all their eclectic romantic blend of influences (Richard Strauss, Scriabin, Debussy). Later his study of Polish folk music strongly affected his compositions. His works include his three symphonies: piano and chamber works, e.g. *The Fountain of Arethusa* for violin and piano; operas, e.g. *King Roger* (1926); two violin concertos; *Stabat Mater* for soloists, chorus and orchestra.

T

Tacitus, Publius (or Gaius) **Cornelius** (*c*. 55–120). Roman historian. He was born in the reign of Nero and lived to be proconsul of Asia under Trajan and thus lived through seven of the reigns which he described. Of his undisputed works *Agricola* was a eulogistic account of his father-in-law, especially interesting for its account of Britain; *Germania* was a first hand account of the country and its people; *The Histories* (fourteen books, of which Nos. 1–4 and part of 5 survive) relate the events of his lifetime from the death of Nero (68) to that of Domitian (96). Even better were the *Annals* (sixteen books, with most of 1–6 and all of 11–16 extant), which cover the earlier period from the death of Augustus (A.D. 14). Tacitus was a shrewd psychologist but where his prejudices were involved (e.g. against Tiberius) he becomes unreliable and unfair. He aims to be an exact recorder of events, which however he sometimes misinterprets. In striking contrast with the rotundity of * Cicero's periods is Tacitus's terse, epigrammatic style which adds dramatic intensity to the episodes which he describes.
Syme, R., *Tacitus*. 1958

Taft, William Howard (1857–1930). Twenty-seventh president of the U.S. (1909–13). Born in Cincinnati and trained for the law, he held a number of local offices before becoming (1887) a judge of the Ohio Supreme Court, solicitor-general of the U.S. (1890) and a Circuit Court judge (1892). After the acquisition of the Philippines from defeated Spain, he was president (1900–01) of the commission sent to the islands and was their first governor general (1901–04). His friend Theodore Roosevelt appointed him secretary of war (1904–08) and secured his nomination as his successor. His conservativism and lack of initiative as president cost him re-election in 1912. Roosevelt, in his disappointment, ran as a third candidate against him and so ensured the success of Woodrow * Wilson, the Democratic nominee. Taft was subsequently professor of constitutional law at Yale (1913–21) and chief justice of the US. (1921–30).

His son, **Robert Alfonso Taft** (1889–1953), was a U.S. Senator from Ohio (1939–53). As conservative as his father, he sponsored the controversial Taft-Hartley Labor Act (1947) to curtail union power. He first sought the Republican nomination in 1944 and 1948; in 1952 he lost narrowly to * Eisenhower. The most effective conservative of his era, in 1957 he was voted by political scientists as one of the five greatest senators ever.

Taglioni, Marie (1804–1884). Italian ballerina. Her father, a *maître de ballet*, created for her *La Sylphide* (1832), which heralded a long period of romantic ballet. Taglioni, who taught dancing to members of the British royal family, is said to have introduced dancing on the points of the toes.

Tagore, Rabindranath (1861–1941). Indian writer. Born in Calcutta of a well known Bengali family belonging to an unorthodox Brahman community, which allowed a liberal attitude to religion and life, he studied in England, and founded (1901) at Bolpur in Bengal a school for the reconciliation of western and eastern educational thought; later at Santiniketan near by, he established an institution to guide the rehabilitation of village life and a seat of international culture. In his world-wide lecture tours on Indian philosophy and religion in Europe, America and

the Far East he continued to stress the international theme. He first became known as a poet outside India by *Gitanjali*, for which he was awarded the Nobel Prize for Literature (1913). Translations of several other volumes of his poems and of his other works followed; he also wrote many plays, novels and essays. In the natural beauties of earth and sky, the love of children and his mystical experiences (upon which rather than on theology his religion was based) he found the inspiration for his poems, into the original Indian versions of which he introduced much metrical experiment. He was no extreme nationalist but after the Amritsar massacre (1919, Reginald E. H. * Dyer) he resigned the knighthood bestowed upon him in 1915.
Bose, A., *Rabindranath Tagore*. 1958

Taine, Hippolyte Adolphe (1828–1893). French historian and critic who established the principle of applying scientific method to the analysis of history and literature. He first gained recognition with a study of * La Fontaine in 1853. His most famous work, which was still unfinished at his death, is *Origines de la France contemporaine*. He was made professor of aesthetics at the École des Beaux Arts in 1864. His studies of history revealed a pessimistic view of society and its development.
Devonshire, R. L., *The Life and Letters of Hippolyte Taine*. 1902

Talbot, John *see* **Shrewsbury, 1st Earl of**

Talbot, William Henry Fox (1880–1877). English physicist who was one of the pioneers of photography. He worked independently of * Daguerre, and in 1839 described his method of making negative prints by using paper impregnated with silver chloride. In 1841 he succeeded in making positive prints, and by 1850 had laid the foundations of modern photography by overcoming the need for long exposures. He also carried out useful investigations on spectra and showed how to distinguish certain elements by their spectral lines. He was also one of the ten first to decipher the Assyrian Cuneiform scripts from Nineveh. He was briefly an M.P. (1833–34).
Gernsheim, H. and A., *The History of Photography*. 1969

Talleyrand (-Périgord), Charles Maurice de, Prince of Benevento (1754–1838). French diplomat. Combining a dissolute life with theological studies, he became bishop of Autun in 1788. During the Revolution he was president of the Constituent Assembly (1709), supported the civil constitution of the clergy and resigned his bishopric. When the Directory came to power his friend * Barras made him foreign minister (1797) but this did not prevent him from scheming to bring about Napoleon Bonaparte's *coup d'état* or accepting the same office under the new leader. In the years that followed Talleyrand used his keen and subtle intelligence to consolidate by diplomacy the victories won in the field. Among the treaties which he negotiated were those of Lunéville (1801) with Austria, of Amiens (1802) with Great Britian and of Tilsit (1807) with Russia. Soon after Tilsit he resigned as foreign minister, apparently in disagreement with Napoleon's policies in Spain and Portugal. He remained, however, at the centre of events and accompanied Napoleon to the Congress of Erfurt (1808). Here, convinced that the policies of his master and the interests of France were increasingly divergent, and being by no means neglectful of personal advantage, he entered into secret relations with the Tsar Alexander and the Austrian statesman, * Metternich. Thereafter he played a double game. After Napoleon's fall (1814) he headed the French provisional government, and as Louis XVIII's foreign minister, at the Congress of Vienna defended French interests with consummate skill. His last important post was that of ambassador (1830–34) to Great Britain under Louis Philippe. In the negotiations about the future of the Netherlands his views in favour of creating a neutral, independent Belgium prevailed.
Orieux, J., *Talleyrand*. 1974

Tallien, Jean Lambert (1769–1820). French Revolutionary politician. He first became prominent as a printer of Jacobin broadsheets. As a member of the Committee of Public Safety he was sent to Bordeaux (1793) to institute the 'Terror'. There he met his future wife, whom he saved from the guillotine. Later she became known as 'Notre Dame de Thermidor' because of the prominent part she played with her husband during the rising of 9 Thermidor (28 July) which resulted in * Robespierre's downfall. Tallien's importance soon declined and he died forgotten.

Tallis, Thomas (*c.* 1505–1585). English composer. He was organist at Waltham Abbey

until its dissolution (1540); for the rest of his life he was joint organist, with Byrd, of the Chapel Royal. The two men further collaborated in obtaining (1575) a monopoly for printing and selling music and music paper and in publishing in that year a volume of motets, of which they were joint composers. Tallis's huge output consists almost entirely of liturgical music, including the *Lamentations* for five voices and the motet *Spem in Alium Nunquam Habui* for forty voices.
Doe, P., *Tallis*. 1968

Tamayo, Rufino (1899–). Mexican expressionist painter. Influenced by pre-Columbian and popular arts forms, as well as Picasso and Braque, he lived in the US and was recognized as the most important modern Mexican artist.

Tamerlane (or **Tamburlaine**) *see* **Timur the Lame**

Tammany (fl. 1685). American Indian chief who is said to have welcomed and come to terms with William * Penn. Named after him was Tammany Hall, founded (1789) as the Tammany Society of Columbian Order, a patriotic political club. Later, as the headquarters of the Democratic party organization in New York City, it won an evil reputation for the methods of corruption and intimidation by which it was alleged to secure votes.

Tanaka Kakuei (1918–). Japanese politician. Educated at a technical college, he began his own construction business at 19, became a member of the Diet 1947– and secretary general of the Liberal Democratic Party 1965–66 and 1968–71. As prime minister 1972–74 he initiated closer links with China and promoted proposals for remodelling the Japanese archipelago. Accused of taking bribes from the Lockheed Corporation, he resigned as prime minister and faced a lengthy trial from 1976. Convicted in 1983, he was sentenced to four years jail, fined $US 2.1 million, and then released on appeal.

Taney, Roger Brooke (1777–1864). American jurist. Andrew * Jackson appointed him attorney-general 1831–33, secretary of the treasury 1833–34 (the first presidential nomination ever rejected by the Senate) and chief justice of the Supreme Court 1836–64, being chosen over the objections of Clay, Calhoun and Webster. Taney broadly supported increasing Federal power at the expense of the states. However, he is best remembered for his decision in the Dred Scott case (1857) that Negroes had no right to sue in the courts and Congress could not exclude slavery from the territories. Taney, a devout Catholic, was personally opposed to slavery.

Tange Kenzo (1913–). Japanese architect. Educated at Tokyo University, where he became professor of architecture 1946–74, he designed buildings for the Tokyo Olympics 1964, Expo '70 at Osaka, the Hiroshima Peace Centre and major projects in Italy, Yugoslavia, Algeria, France and the US.

Tardieu, André Pierre Gabriel Amédée (1876–1945). French politician. A journalist who wrote mostly on foreign affairs, he became a deputy in 1914, fought in World War I and assisted * Clemenceau in the peace treaty negotiations. As founder and leader of the Republican Centre party he was almost continuously in ministerial office (1926–32) and was prime minister (1929, 1930 and 1932).

Tarkington, Booth (1869–1946). American popular novelist. He is mainly remembered for the novels of life in the Middle West which were dramatized into successful plays or films, e.g. *Monsieur Beaucaire* (1901) and *The Magnificent Ambersons* (1918).
Tarkington, B., *The World Does Move*. 1928

Tarquinius Superbus, Lucius (*c*. 564–505 B.C.), seventh and last of the semi-legendary kings of Rome. His reign (534–510) and that of his father **Lucius Tarquinius Priscus** (616–578) represented a period of Etruscan domination, interrupted possibly by the intervening reign of Servius Tullius (who may, however, have been an Etruscan also). Tradition assigns the cause of Tarquinius's expulsion from Rome to the anger caused by the rape of the beautiful Lucretia (Lucrece) by his son Sextus, but it was more probably due to the tyranny of his rule which was remembered so vividly that 'king' became a hated word and the title was never adopted even by the all-powerful rulers of later days. An attempt by Lars Porsena (* Horatius) to restore Etruscan supremacy failed.

Tartini, Giuseppe (1692–1770). Italian composer, mainly of violin music. The best known of his surviving compositions is the *Devil's*

Trill sonata, a memory, it is said, of music played to him by the devil in a dream. He wrote on acoustics and is known as the discoverer of 'resultant tones'. He was the greatest violinist of his time and founded (1728) his own school at Padua.

Tasman, Abel Janszoon (*c.* 1603–1659). Dutch navigator. He was sent on several voyages of exploration by van * Diemen, governor of the Dutch East Indies, he discovered Tasmania (1642), which he named Van Diemen's Land, and New Zealand, Tonga and Fiji (1643). On another voyage (1644) he entered the Gulf of Carpentaria (previously discovered) and went on to explore the north-west coast of Australia.

Tassigny, Jean de Lattre de *see* **Lattre de Tassigny, Jean de**

Tasso, Torquato (1544–1595). Italian poet, born at Sorrento. He was the son of **Bernardo Tasso** (1493–1569), author of *Amadigi di Gaula* and *Floridante*. He studied at Padua, where he wrote his epic *Rinaldo*. In 1565 he went to Ferrara where he served first Cardinal d'Este and then (from 1571) his brother Duke Alfonso II. In 1573 he published a pastoral play, *Aminta*, the sensuous atmosphere of which was repeated in his great epic of the 1st Crusade, *La Gerusalemme liberata* (1575). In the following year, partly because of objections to his epic by the Inquisition, he showed signs of persecution mania. For a scene of violence (1577) in the presence of the Duchess he was briefly imprisoned. Given a refuge in a Franciscan monastery he fled to his sister but in 1579 was back in Ferrara. After renewed outbursts of frenzy he was again imprisoned, this time for seven years; the legend repeated by Goethe and Byron that the sentence resulted from his love for the Duke's sister has no basis in fact. Released in 1586, he was received by the Gonzagas in Mantua but soon began a wandering life, working intermittently on *Gerusalemme conquistata*, a revision of his earlier epic, from which many of the loveliest passages were removed. Among his other works were his 'discourses' on poetry, his letters and an unsuccessful tragedy, *Torrismondo*.

Brand, C. P., *Torquato Tasso*. 1965

Tate, Sir Henry, 1st Bart. (1819–1899). English merchant and manufacturer born in Lancashire. As a young man employed in a sugar refinery in Liverpool he patented a device for compressing and cutting sugar into cubes; the profits from this enabled him to set up his own company, Henry Tate and Sons. In 1897 he established the Tate Gallery, to which he gave his own collection of paintings and £80,000.

Tate, Nahum (1652–1715). Irish-born poet. He wrote a metrical version of the Psalms (1696) and, almost certainly, the hymn *While Shepherds Watched Their Flocks By Night* (1702). He is best known for his version of *King Lear* which practically ousted Shakespeare's original until 1840. He was Poet Laureate from 1692. His best-known work is *Panacea, or a Poem on Tea* (1700).

Tauber, Richard (Ernst Seiffert) (1891–1948). Austrian tenor, naturalized (1940) British subject. He sang in opera and, increasingly from 1925, in light opera (e.g. *Lilac Time*) and films. He was also a noted exponent of Schubert's songs. He composed several songs and the musical comedy *Old Chelsea*.

Taverner, John (1495–1545). English composer. He composed his best music before 1530, while choirmaster at Cardinal College (Christ Church), Oxford. His masses (notably *Gloria tibi, Trinitas* and *O Western Wynde*) show him to have been a strongly gifted precursor of English polyphonic masters of the later 16th century. He played a fanatical and active part in the suppression of the monasteries instituted by Henry VIII.

Tawney, Richard Henry (1880–1962). English economic historian. Elected fellow of Balliol College, Oxford (1918). After a period as a social worker at Toynbee Hall in the East End of London, he became tutor and then president (1928–44) of the Workers' Educational Association. A Christian and a non-Marxist socialist, his studies of English economic history (particularly of the 16th and 17th centuries) include *The Acquisitive Society* (1926), *Religion and the Rise of Capitalism* (1926), *Equality* (1931) and *Business and Politics under James I* (1958). He was professor of Economic History at London (1931–49).

Taylor, A(lan) J(ohn) P(ercevale) (1906–). English historian born in Lancashire.

Educated at Oxford, he lectured at Manchester (from 1927) and Oxford, where he was a Fellow of Magdalen (from 1936). Taylor was a controversial figure, devastating in debate and with mastery of sources, incisive in style, witty and argumentative in manner, determinedly paradoxical in approach. His involvement in television lecturing and popular journalism aroused deep professional prejudice which often obscured the merit of his published work e.g. *The Habsburg Monarchy* (1941), *The Struggle for Mastery in Europe* (1954), *Bismarck* (1955), *The Origins of the Second World War* (1961), *English History 1914–45* (1965).

Taylor, Elizabeth (1932–). English film actress in the US. Famous as a child star (*National Velvet*, 1944), she was a celebrated beauty who appeared in many vapid romances, later gaining a reputation as a dramatic actress e.g. in *Cat on a Hot Tin Roof* (1958) and *Who's Afraid of Virginia Woolf?* (1966), for which she won an Academy Award. She married the film director Mike Todd, the singer Eddie Fisher, Richard * Burton (twice), a U.S. Senator and three others.

Taylor, Frederick Winslow (1856–1915). American industrial engineer. He wrote *Principles of Scientific Management* (1911) which applied technocratic modes to industrial practice, setting scientific standards, such as time-study and cost-benefit, to measure efficiency. Opponents of 'Taylorism' thought that his methods increased alienation and dehumanization in the workplace.

Taylor, Jeremy (1613–1667). English author and clergyman. He attracted attention as a preacher, became chaplain to Laud and Charles I and (1638) rector of Uppingham, Rutland. In the Civil War he was a chaplain with the royalist forces, was taken prisoner in Wales and took a post as chaplain to the Earl of Carbery (1645–57); later he was bishop of Down in Northern Ireland (1661–1667). His theological works, of which *The Liberty of Prophesying* (1646), *Holy Living* (1650) and *Holy Dying* (1651) were the most influential, were written in a style combining simplicity and splendour. They reveal him as a moderate and tolerant churchman ready to limit matters of faith to what is found in the Bible and the Apostles' Creed, leaving a large area in which a Christian was entitled to think for himself. Such teaching, which provided a basis of belief for later evangelical churchmen, was supplemented by *Ductor Dubitantium* (1660), a vast work on moral theology aimed at formulating distinctions between good and evil.
Gosse, E., *Life of Jeremy Taylor*. 1904

Taylor, Zachary (1784–1850). 12th president of the US (1849–50). Son of a Virginian planter who had settled in Kentucky, he joined the army and was prominent in the frontier fighting against the Indians. Sent to Texas (1844) to be ready to take over, he was present when an exchange of shots led to the Mexican War (1846–47). His victory at Buena Vista (1847) was the decisive and culminating episode of a successful campaign and ensured his success when he was nominated by the Whigs as their presidential candidate (1848). Though a slave-owner himself he took the common-sense view that California (acquired from Mexico) should, as she wished, enter the Union as a free state. He died in office.

Tchaikovsky, Piotr Ilyich (1840–1893). Russian composer, born at Kamsko-Votkinsk in the Urals. As a boy he was hypersensitive and abnormally dependent on his mother; her death when he was 14 affected him for the rest of his life. After being trained for the law, for which he was unfitted, he began at 21 to study music under Anton Rubinstein at the St Petersburg Conservatoire. In 1865 he became professor of harmony at the Moscow Conservatoire which had been founded the previous year by Rubinstein's brother Nicholas. In his early works, e.g. the first symphony (*Winter Dreams*, 1868) and the fantasy-overture *Romeo and Juliet* (1870, revised 1880), he was influenced by the ideals of the nationalist group of Russian composers of whom * Balakirev was the leader. The marked Russian flavour of Tchaikovsky's early music (often based on folk song) was now gradually superseded by a cosmopolitan idiom in which his preference for the French over the German masters became apparent. This increasing cosmopolitanism was partly due to his extensive journeys abroad, undertaken for health reasons and financed by a rich widow, Nadezhda von Meck, with whom he started an intimate correspondence in 1876; in 1877 she settled on him an annuity for life which released him from financial worries. The two never spoke; at their only two meetings they passed one another in embarrassed silence. Partly to quash rumours that he was homosexual he married (1877) an ex-pupil, Antonina Milyukova, despite their mutual lack of affection; he left after a fortnight, but the episode caused insomnia, hallucinations and a lasting worsening of his mental health. He died, allegedly of cholera, but probably by suicide, in St Petersburg.

The emotionalism and rhetoric which have accounted for much of the popularity of Tchaikovsky's music (while repelling many) are largely at odds with classical symphonic form in the Symphonies No. 4 (1877) and No. 5 (1888); in the fine No. 6 (*Pathetic*, 1893), his last finished work, these qualities do not submerge the structure. By comparison with them (and with the Piano Concerto No. 1) the first three symphonies have been (unjustly) neglected. Other notable orchestral works are the Violin Concerto (1878). *Variations on a Rococo Theme* (1876) and the symphonic fantasy *Francesca da Rimini* (1876); he also wrote chamber music, piano music and songs. Of his ten operas only *Eugene Onegin* (1878) and *The Queen of Spades* (1890), both based on Pushkin, have won acceptance outside Russia. Tchaikovsky's genius was probably best expressed in his ballet scores, e.g. *Swan Lake* (1876), *The Sleeping Beauty* (1889) and – less so – in *Nutcracker* (1891–92).

Weinstock, H., *Tchaikovsky*. 1943

Tcherepnin, Nicolai Nicolaievich (1873–1945). Russian composer. After studying under Rimsky-Korsakov he was attached to the Mariinsky Theatre as an orchestral conductor, moving on in 1908 to work with the Diaghilev ballet. He wrote music for Diaghilev until 1914 and in 1918 became principal of the Tiflis conservatoire. He wrote two operas, but was best known for his ballet music which showed a mixture of traditional Russian and modern French influences.

Tecumseh (1768?–1813). Chief of the Shawnee tribe of American Indians. Helped by his brother 'the Prophet', he enforced order and discipline, and, above all, forbade all intercourse with the white settlers or any cession of land without consent of the Indian peoples as a whole, He fought on the British side with the rank of brigadier-general in the 'war of 1812', among the causes of which were alleged British intrigues with the Indians on the U.S.–Canadian frontier. Near this frontier Tecumseh was killed at the Battle of the Thames (Ontario).

Tucker, G., *Tecumseh: Vision of Glory*. 1956

Tedder, Arthur William Tedder, 1st Baron (1890–1967). British airman. He joined the army in 1913 and after service with the infantry in World War I was seconded (1916) to the RFC and gained distinction as a pilot. At the beginning of World War II he was director general of research and development at the Air Ministry. In 1940 he was sent to Egypt and became (1941) air-officer-in-command Middle East and (1943) of all Allied air forces in the Mediterranean, his term of office ending with the clearance of all Germans from Africa. As * Eisenhower's deputy commander he played an even more important part in the closing stages of the war. He became a marshal of the RAF in 1945 and received his peerage in 1946.

Owen, R., *Tedder*. 1965

Teilhard de Chardin, Pierre (1881–1955). French geologist, palaeontologist, Jesuit priest and philosopher. He was closely involved in the 'discovery' of Piltdown man (1912–13). This may have been intended as a scientific joke rather than a serious hoax. After serving in World War I as a stretcher bearer, he became professor of geology at the Institute Catholique, Paris, in 1918. He lived in China 1923–46, made palaeontological expeditions into Central Asia and worked on the Peking man excavations (1929). In his writings he tried to reconcile Christian theology with science and developed the concept of 'cosmic evolution', leading to the ultimate 'Omega point' and the second coming of Christ. He lived in France 1946–51 and the U.S. from 1951; he died in New York. Forbidden to publish during his lifetime, he achieved great posthumous fame with his *The Phenomenon of Man* (1938–40, published 1959) but his reputation has declined as rapidly (and mysteriously) as it rose in the 1960s.

Chardin, T. de, *The Phenomenon of Man*, 1959. Cuénot, C., *Life of Teilhard de Chardin*. 1965

Telemann, Georg Philipp (1681–1767). German composer, born in Magdeburg. A self-taught musician, he abandoned the study of law to become director of the Leipzig Opera (1702) and later the Hamburg Opera (1722–

38). He declined the post of *Kantor* at the Thomaskirche, Leipzig, in favour of his lesser-known colleague J. S. Bach. Telemann was almost certainly the most prolific composer of all time, writing 40 operas, more than 600 orchestral suites, 44 passions, 12 complete sets of services, over 1000 cantatas and many chamber works and concertos. Bach and Handel admired his music and Handel, especially, borrowed heavily from it. His works have sometimes been dismissed as tuneful, ornamental and lacking in dynamic tension; however, with renewed interest in his music, the admiration of his contemporaries appears well-founded.

Telford, Thomas (1757–1834). Scottish engineer. He was born in Dumfriesshire, the son of an Eskdale shepherd, and worked for several years as journeyman mason, using all his spare time for engineering study. After superintending dockyard construction at Portsmouth (from 1784) he was appointed surveyor of public works in Shropshire and built his first bridges in 1792. Two of his greatest achievements in a career during which he built some 1,200 bridges and 1,000 miles of roads, were the London–Holyhead road (including the Menai Straits suspension bridge, 1826) and the Caledonian Canal (1803–47). He was elected F.R.S. in 1827 and was first president of the Institution of Civil Engineers.
Rolt, L.T.C., *Thomas Telford*. 1958

Teller, Edward (1908–). Hungarian-American physicist, born in Budapest. Educated at the Karlsruhe Technical Institute and the Universities of Munich and Leipzig, was professor of physics at George Washington University 1935–41, Columbia 1941–42, Chicago 1946–52 and California 1953–71. He worked on the atomic bomb during World War II and later as assistant director of Los Alamos Scientific Laboratory (1949–52), he made important contributions to physics by his work on, e.g., the structure of matter, cosmic rays and magnetohydrodynamics. Known as the 'father of the hydrogen bomb', first tested in 1952, he was a hardliner in the Cold War and an opponent of J. R. * Oppenheimer.
Jungk, R., *Brighter than a Thousand Suns*. 1958.

Tempest, Dame Marie Susan (1864–1942). English actress. At the age of 20 she was playing the lead in light operas but later gained a new reputation as a brilliant and talented *comédienne*. Noel Coward's *Hay Fever*, written specially for her, was among the best of the plays with which she continued to delight audiences into old age. She was made a D.B.E. in 1937.

Temple, William (1881–1944). Archbishop of Canterbury (from 1942). His career closely paralleled that of his father, **Frederick Temple** (1821–1892), headmaster of Rugby (1858–69), whose views were suspected of unorthodoxy; he became bishop of Exeter (1869), of London (1885), and archbishop of Canterbury (1897). William Temple was headmaster of Repton (1910–14) and became bishop of Manchester (1921), archbishop of York (1929) and of Canterbury (1942). He was much influenced by the ideas of Charles * Kingsley on Christian Socialism and worked for much of his life to link Christian thought with social and economic reconstruction. He was president of the Workers' Educational Association (1908–24) and became (1943) first president of the World Council of Churches.
Iremonger, F. A., *William Temple*. 1948

Templer, Sir Gerald Walter Robert (1898–1979). British field-marshal. As high commissioner in Malaya (1952–55) he became prominent for his decisive role in planning the methods by which the Communist rebels were eventually brought under control. He was chief of the Imperial General Staff (1955–59).

Templewood, Samuel John Gurney Hoare, 1st Viscount (1880–1959). British politician. He was a Conservative M.P. (1910–44) and he initiated, as secretary of state for India (1931–35), the act of 1935 by which provincial self-government was granted. Hoare became foreign secretary (1935) but was forced to resign by a storm of protest against the Hoare-Laval Pact which proposed a partition of Ethiopia and thus recognition of the Italian conquests so far achieved. He returned as a minister (1936–40) and served in the sensitive post of ambassador to Spain (1940–44), retiring with a peerage. He was an active opponent of capital punishment.

Teniers, David (1610–1690). Flemish painter. Like his father, **David Teniers the Elder** (1582–1649), by whom he was trained, and under the influence of Adriaen Brouwer, he

painted mostly genre pictures – tavern scenes with soldiers gambling or brawling, a village festival, alchemists, witches etc. He worked in Antwerp and later Brussels; he was court painter to the Archduke Leopold, and compiled an illustrated record of his collection of pictures.
Eekhoud, G., *Life of David Teniers*. 1926

Tenniel, Sir John (1820–1914). English draughtsman. He joined the staff of *Punch* in 1851 and in 1901 retired after fifty years as the leading political cartoonist. He became even better known as the illustrator of Lewis Carroll's *Alice in Wonderland* and *Through the Looking Glass*. He was knighted in 1893.
Monkhouse, C., *The Life and Works of Sir John Tenniel*. 1901

Tennyson, Alfred Tennyson 1st Baron (1809–1892). English poet, born at Somersby, Lincolnshire. At Cambridge University he met Arthur Hallam, who became his greatest friend and whose sudden death (1833) evoked his famous elegy *In Memoriam* (published anonymously in 1850). Some of his juvenilia had already appeared in print and a volume published in the same year as Hallam's death contained his first successes such as *Oenone, The Lotus-eaters* and *A Dream of Fair Women*. A further collection (1842), including *Morte d'Arthur* (the genesis of *Idylls of the King*), *Locksley Hall, Ulysses* and such famous lyrics as *Break, Break, Break*, confirmed his reputation. A state pension of £200 (1842) per annum relieved immediate financial anxiety but it was not until 1850, when he succeeded Wordsworth as Poet Laureate, that he felt free to marry Emily Sellwood, to whom he had been engaged for seventeen years. But now his poetry became a source of wealth. As Laureate he was able to create poems to match the greatness of the event they celebrated (e.g. *Ode on the Death of the Duke of Wellington, The Charge of the Light Brigade*). *Maud* (1855) was read or recited in every drawing room; of *Enoch Arden* (1864) 60,000 copies were at once sold. In 1854 Tennyson began to live at Farringford, his house at Freshwater in the Isle of Wight, and he began to build his second home near Haslemere in 1868. Meanwhile he had found inspiration in the legends of King Arthur and his *Idylls of the King* were appearing in steady sequence (1855–89). Of his verse plays the genius of * Irving managed to make something of *Becket* (1879), but the others, e.g. *Queen Mary* (1876) and *Harold* (1877), were among his least successful works. He received his peerage in 1884.

Tennyson was so prolific a writer and the demand from his public so great that much that is trite and second-rate appears in his *Collected Works*; his very skills, his complete mastery of versification and the lilting music of his lines, turned opinion against him when a later age equated roughness with sincerity. He was capable of deep emotion, as *In Memoriam* and many other poems show. His approach was not primarily intellectual but he brought to the problems and discoveries of his day a philosophic outlook and a somewhat scientific mind.
Tennyson, C., *Alfred Tennyson*. Repr. 1968

Tenzing Norgay (1914–). Nepalese mountaineer. He first climbed as a porter with an expedition to Everest in 1935. In 1952 he reached 28,215 ft and in 1953, on the then Col. John Hunt's expedition, he and Edmund * Hillary reached the summit. He was president of the Sherpa Association.
Ullman, J. R., *Man of Everest*. 1955

Terborch (or Terburg), **Gerard** (1617–1681). Dutch painter. He was able to spend much of his time as a young painter in travel. One of his finest pictures (now in the National Gallery, London) portrays the delegates to the peace congress at Münster which ended the Thirty Years War (1648). By 1650 he was back in Holland and perfected a type of genre picture, nearly always of small size, depicting scenes in which one or more figures, usually ladies, are reading, writing, playing music etc. in rooms appropriate to the elegance of their attire. Soft and delicate colour harmonies characterize his work.
Gudlaugsson, S. J., *Gerard ter Borch*. 1959

Terence (Publius Terentius Afer) (*c.* 190–160 B.C.). Roman comic playwright. Born in Carthage, he was taken to Rome as a slave but was educated and freed by his master; he achieved great success with *Andria* (166), the first of six plays all extant. His others were *Hecyra* (*The Mother-in-law*; 165), *Heauton Timorumenos* (*The Self-punisher*; 163), *Eunuchus* (161), on which the first English comedy, *Ralph Roister Doister*, was based, *Phormio* (161), *Adelphi* (*The Brothers*; 160). All were based on Greek originals, *Hecyra* and *Phormio* on plays by Apollodorus, the rest

derived from Menander. The stock situations and characters of ancient comedy were later again revived by Shakespeare, Molière etc. Terence was famed for his use of polite colloquial speech.
Beare, W., *The Roman Stage*. 3rd ed. 1965

Teresa, Mother (Agnes Gonxha Bojaxhiu) (1910–). Albanian Roman Catholic missionary. She joined the order of Sisters of Loretto in 1928. As principal of St Mary's High School, Calcutta, she founded Missionaries of Charity in 1950 and, through this organization, founded fifty orphanages and refuges for the destitute in India, notably the Pure Heart Home for Dying Destitutes. She was awarded the Pope John XXIII Peace Prize in 1971, the Nobel Prize for Peace in 1979, and the OM in 1983.
Muggeridge, M. *Something Beautiful for God*. 1971

Teresa of Jesus, St (Teresa de Cepeda y Ahumada) (1515–1582). Spanish nun. She entered a Carmelite convent in Avila (*c*. 1526) and had lived there over twenty years, much troubled by ill health, before she left to found, after considerable opposition, a convent governed by the original, stricter rule. St Joseph's Convent at Avila was the first of fifteen established during her lifetime for 'discalced' or barefooted Carmelites (a separate order from 1580), for men as well as women. Despite this immense practical activity her books are among the most famous examples of mystical literature. *The Life* (1562–65) is a spiritual autobiography, *The Way of Perfection* (1565) provides guidance for her nuns, *The Foundation* (from 1576) tells of her work in establishing the new convents, and *The Interior Castle* (1577), perhaps her most illuminating work, is an account, written with all the conviction of her rich experience, of a contemplative life. Minor works too and letters, vivid, witty and wise, help to reveal one of the most attractive personalities of religious history. She was canonized only forty years after her death.

Teresa of Lisieux *see* **Thérèse of Lisieux, St**

Terry, Dame Ellen (1847–1928). English actress. She achieved immense success as a Shakespearian actress and was Irving's leading lady (1878–1902). She married three times, first and disastrously to the painter G. F. * Watts (1864). The theatrical designer E. G. * Craig was her son by Edward Godwin, an architect. She had a long 'paper courtship' with G. B. * Shaw. Other members of her family won fame on the stage: her brother, Fred Terry (1863–1933), who created the part of Sir Percy Blakeney in *The Scarlet Pimpernel*, her grand-daughter Phyllis Neilson-Terry and her greatnephew John * Gielgud.
Manvell, R., *Ellen Terry*. 1968

Tertullian (Quintus Septimus Florens Tertullianus) (*c*. 155–*c*. 225). The first great Latin theological writer. He was a convert who became a presbyter of Carthage, but little is known of his life. Of his thirty-one surviving works one of the greatest was *Apologeticus* (197), written to defend Christianity against charges that it was immoral, useless and dangerous to the state; it warns Roman officials that the blood of martyrs provides the seeds of growth. A second series deals with practical subjects: attendances at theatres and games, idolatory and extravagance in dress etc. are condemned; chastity and fasting are among the virtues praised. In his theological works he claims that true doctrine is handed down through apostolic succession and cannot be assailed by argument. He further stresses the ascendancy of faith over reason by such paradoxical assertions as his saying that a subject of belief is 'certain because it is impossible'.
Barnes, T. D., *Tertullian*. 1971

Tesla, Nikola (1856–1943). American electrical engineer, born in Croatia, of Serbian family. The son of an Orthodox priest, he was educated at Graz and Prague and migrated to the U.S. in 1884. He worked briefly with Thomas * Edison and from 1885 with George * Westinghouse. Edison was deeply committed to the use of direct current (DC); Westinghouse and Tesla saw greater efficiency and economy with alternating current (AC). In 1888 Tesla invented the first AC electric motor, substantially in the form still in current use, and this was the most important single development in the electric revolution. He sold his patents to Westinghouse and set up his own laboratories. In 1891 he invented the Tesla coil, an air-core transformer used to produce high voltage in radio (and later television) equipment. He improved the transmission of AC over long distances and was the first to demonstrate that the earth is an electrical conductor. Tesla did not patent most of his inventions and died in poverty, bitterly disappointed not to have received a Nobel Prize.

Hunt, I., and Draper, W. W., *Lightning in his Hand: the Life Story of Nikola Tesla*. 1964

Tetrazzini, Luisa (1871–1940). Italian singer, born in Florence. She made a great name for herself as a coloratura soprano mainly in Italian opera and commanded huge audiences in virtuoso recitals in many cities of the world.

Thackeray, William Makepiece (1811–1863). English writer. He was born in Calcutta, but soon after the death of his father, an official in the East India Company, he went to England (1817) where he was subsequently looked after by his mother (later portrayed as Helen Pendennis) and his stepfather (afterwards transformed into Colonel Newcome). From Charterhouse ('Grey Friars') he went to Cambridge, where prospects of wealth encouraged idleness, travel (after failure to get a degree) and a half-hearted study of art and law. The disappearance of most of the money through the failure of a Calcutta agency (1833) forced him into activity. Unable to sell his pictures, he took to journalism in 1836, the year in which he married Isabella Shawe. In his first period of writing appeared *The Yellow-plush Papers* (1840) in which Thackeray in the guise of a footman called Yellow-plush dilated with good-humoured satire upon the social follies and foibles of his time. *Fraser's Magazine*, *The Times* and *Punch* were among the periodicals that accepted his work. In 1840 his wife showed signs of insanity. After trying to cope with an increasingly impossible situation he was forced to part from her and place her under control. She lived for another fifty years but never recovered. The effect upon his work was to soften its asperity and introduce a new note of pathos. *The Great Hoggarty Diamond* (1841) and the *Punch* series (1846–47) later published as *The Book of Snobs* are among the numerous writings which preceded the publication of his best novels. The first, *Vanity Fair* (published as was then the custom in monthly parts, 1848–50), tells of the manoeuvres of the clever adventuress Becky Sharp in the days of Waterloo. *Henry Esmond* (1852) is the story of a disputed inheritance in Ireland with a background of Marlborough's wars and Jacobite intrigue. Its sequel, *The Virginians* (1857–59), continues the hero's story in America; *Pendennis* (1848–50) returns to Thackeray's own time with several autobiographical passages. *The Newcomes* (1853–55), in that it purported to be written by Pendennis is aligned with the earlier book. The later novels show a marked decline. The best known of his miscellaneous writings include the delightful children's story, *The Rose and the Ring* (1854), and two series of lectures collected as *The English Humorists of the Eighteenth Century* (1853) and *The Four Georges* (1860). In 1860 he fulfilled an ambition by becoming editor of the *Cornhill* magazine. As a novelist Thackeray had the same taste for melodramatic plots as Dickens but his stories are more tightly constructed, while his characters move within a narrow range; his humour is more astringent than that of Dickens and his compassion less evident. This was partly due to the unhappiness of his domestic life, which made him as the years passed increasingly sensitive to personal slights.

Carey, J., *Thackeray: Prodigal Genius*. 1977

Thales (*c*. 640–*c*. 550 B.C.). Greek philosopher. A citizen of Miletus in Asia Minor and regarded as one of the 'seven wise men' of Greece, he was held to be the first of the philosophers because he sought to explain the universe rationally rather than by mythology. The tradition recorded by Aristotle that Thales believed that all things are made of water is probably based on an attempt by him to give a rational explanation of an ancient myth. It seems likely that he was a merchant and that in his travels in Babylonia and Egypt he acquired the mathematical knowledge that enabled him, e.g., to predict the solar eclipse of 585 B.C.

Thant, U (1909–1974). Burmese diplomat. After spending the years 1928–47 as a schoolmaster he entered the public service in Burma and became the trusted adviser of the prime minister of the time. In 1957 he became Burma's permanent representative at the United Nations, and on the death (1961) of Dag * Hammarskjöld was first acting secretary-general of the organization, and then secretary-general from 1962–71.

Thatcher, Margaret Hilda (1925–). British Conservative politician, born in

Grantham, Lincolnshire. Educated at grammar schools and at Oxford University, she worked as chemist 1947–51 and then studied law, being called to the bar, Lincoln's Inn, in 1953 and was Conservative MP for Finchley from 1959. She was Parliamentary Secretary to the Minister of Pensions and National Insurance 1961–64 and was appointed Secretary of State for Education in Edward Heath's cabinet, 1970–74. In February 1975 she was elected leader of the Conservative party and became Britain's first woman Prime Minister following the general election of May 1979, and was re-elected with a large majority in June 1983. The war with Argentina over the Falkland Islands (April–June 1982) was the most controversial act of her first term.

Theaetetus (417 B.C.–369 B.C.). Greek mathematician, who studied under Theodorus of Cyrene and at the Academy with Plato. None of his writings has survived, though we have adequate accounts of them from other sources. * Plato wrote a dialogue about him (the *Theaetetus*) and he is the principal character in *The Sophist*. One of Theaetetus's main contributions to mathematics was the development of a proper classification of irrationals (irrationals in mathematics had only recently been discovered). * Euclid also notes that he was the first mathematician to write upon the five regular solids. It is possible that he discovered the octahedron and the dodecahedron, though it is much more likely that these figures were earlier known to the Pythagoreans. What Theaetetus undoubtedly did was to set out the theory of the construction of the solids probably in much the form used by Euclid in book 13 of the *Elements*. Scholars have debated how far Euclid simply reported Theaetetus's work in several of the books of the Elements (e.g. Book 10). There is no way of knowing. Euclid himself attributes some of his theorems to Theaetetus.

Heath, T., *A history of Greek mathematics*. 1921

Themistocles (*c.* 523–*c.* 458 B.C.). Athenian soldier and statesman. During the Persian Wars he saw the importance of a navy for Athens; having secured the banishment of his rival Aristides he made use of the opening of a new seam in the silver mines at Laurium to raise the total number of ships from seventy to 200. When the Persians forced to pass of Thermopylae, the 'gateway' to Athens on the north, he persuaded the citizens to take refuge with the ships and himself directed the strategy by which the Persian fleet was destroyed at the Battle of Salamis (480). In the next year the Persians were forced to withdraw. Arrogance soon cost Themistocles his popularity, and his anti-Spartan policy threatened Greek unity. Banished from Athens, he went first to Argos and then, after accusations of intrigue with the enemy, to Persian territory, where he was generously received.

Theocritus (fl. *c.* 280 B.C.). Greek poet, born at Syracuse. He visited Cos and then Egypt where he attracted the notice of Ptolemy II Philadelphus. He perfected the type of poem which came to be known as an 'idyll' – a short sketch or scene in dramatic form usually taken from country or village (but sometimes from town) life. His poems were much imitated by later 'pastoral' poets and one provided a model for Milton's *Lycidas*.

Theodora (died 548). Byzantine empress. Said to have been the daughter of a bear-keeper at the hippodrome in Constantinople, she was an actress and courtesan before becoming the mistress of * Justinian I and in 523 his wife. She proved a valued adviser and her courage helped to save the throne during the faction fights of 532.

Browning, R., *Justinian and Theodora*. 1971

Theodore (Theodor, Baron von Neuhoff) (1694–1756). German adventurer, self-styled 'king' of Corsica. The son of a Westphalian nobleman, he led a life of adventure and political intrigue. In 1736 he landed in Corsica with instructions he had received from the Austrian government in 1729 to investigate the causes of a rebellion there. On his arrival he was crowned king and proceeded to issue coins and acquire a revenue by selling knighthoods in his 'Order of Deliverance'. This not proving enough, he left to seek foreign aid, but after two attempts to return had failed he settled in London, where he was imprisoned for debt and died in Soho.

Pirie, V., *His Majesty of Corsica*. 1939

Theodore (1816–1868). Emperor of Abyssinia (from 1855). Originally a brigand named Kassa, he fought his way to supremacy and showed considerable talents as a ruler though prone to unpredictable violence. Taking the absence of a reply to a letter sent by him to Queen Victoria as a slight, he seized the British consul and other Europeans. Eventually a British force was sent under Sir Robert * Napier. When Theodore's stronghold of Magdala was taken, he shot himself.

Theodoric (known as 'the Great') (*c.* 454–526). King of Italy (from 493). Son of the ruler of the Ostrogoths, he was educated in Constantinople and in 488 was urged by the emperor Zeno to lead his people to regain Italy from the German mercenary Odovacer who had made himself king. Theodoric succeeded, after four years of confused fighting, only by inspiring the treacherous murder of his opponent. Setting up his court at Ravenna and proffering only the most nominal allegiance to Zeno, he consolidated and enlarged his kingdom and entered into friendly relations with the Franks and other peoples of Europe. He showed unusual religious tolerance and, though he had to take large areas of land to provide settlements for his 200,000 Ostrogoths, he ruled with prudence, making use of many of the old Roman institutions and paying special attention to the preservation of the splendour and dignity of Rome.

Theodosius I (known as 'the Great') (*c.* 346–395). Roman emperor (from 379). A Spaniard by birth and son of the Count Theodosius who had protected Britain from raids from Scotland, he was summoned by * Gratian to be his co-emperor. In this role he restored law and order in the Balkans by providing the barbarians with land in return for their service in the Roman army. On the death of Gratian he maintained Valentinian II in power in Italy until his somewhat mysterious death (492). Despite his ability, Theodosius, who had been baptized (480) and condemned any who rejected the decisions of the Council of Nicaea, could be fiercely cruel. Having pardoned rioters in Antioch, he punished a similar outbreak in Thessalonica by a massacre (390) in which 7,000 perished, an act for which St * Ambrose successfully demanded that he make public atonement in Milan cathedral. He was succeeded by his sons Honorius and Arcadius.

Lippold, A., *Theodosius der Grosse und seine Zeit*. 1968

Theophrastus (368–373?–*c.* 287 B.C.) Greek naturalist and philosopher. He was taught by Plato and Aristotle, inherited the latter's library and manuscripts and carried on his school at Athens. Most of the 224 books he is said to have written are lost, including the series on zoology; but books on plants, stones and fire are among the survivors, which also include the *Characters*, a book on moral types which may not be wholly his work.

Thérèse of Lisieux, St (known as 'the Little Flower') (1873–1897). French nun. She was the daughter of a watch-maker named Louis Martin, and at the age of 15 first entered the Carmelite convent of Lisieux, where she spent the rest of her short life and, after a prolonged illness, died. *L'Histoire d'une âme* (1898), an account of her experiences, quickly established her cult throughout France. She was canonized in 1925.

Thiers, (Marie Joseph Louis) Adolphe (1797–1877). French politician and historian, born at Marseilles. He went to Paris (1821) and became known by his *Histoire de la Révolution* (1823–27) which revealed his opposition to Charles X's régime. He supported the revolution that brought Louis Philippe to the throne (1830), was elected a deputy and became minister of the interior (1832) and prime minister (1836). The king's refusal to intervene in the civil war in Spain soon forced his resignation; he returned in 1840 but his government fell when Great Britain and her allies thwarted his attempt to sustain the seizure of Syria from the Turks by * Mehemet Ali, the Egyptian viceroy. For the rest of Louis Philippe's reign he vigorously opposed Guizot's right-wing government, while writing his *Histoire du Consulate de l'Empire* (1845–62). He supported Louis Napoleon in the first stages of the revolution of 1848 but turned against him when he made himself emperor as Napoleon III (1851). He was expelled from the country and spent the next twelve years on his literary work. A deputy again 1863–70, he was the only major politician to oppose the Franco-Prussian war, and on France's defeat negotiated peace with Bismarck. Pending any decision to revive the monarchy he was elected (February 1871) 'Chief of the Executive Power' and suppressed the Paris Commune brutally. In August 1871, he was elected first president of the third French republic, resigning in 1873 in conflict with the ultra conservative legislature.

Christophe, R., *La Siècle de Monsieur Thiers*. 1966

Thirkell, Angela Margaret (1890–1961). English novelist, a daughter of Professor J. W. Mackail. Her novels (e.g. *The Brandon, Love Among the Ruins*), which gave her a limited but devoted following, told of melodramatic happenings in country-house settings. They were written in a highly individual style to which a type of dialogue spoken by all the characters, whatever their social status or occupation, gave a highly original flavour.

Thistlewood, Arthur (1770–1820). English conspirator. Having lived in America and France, where he imbibed revolutionary doctrines, he enlisted others to join him (1820) in an attempt to murder the members of the British cabinet while at dinner. The plan was betrayed and the plotters were arrested at a house in Cato Street (after which the conspiracy was named). Thistlewood and four others were subsequently hanged; five more were transported.

Thomas (of Canterbury), St *see* **Becket, St Thomas**

Thomas à Kempis (Thomas Hammerken) (1380–1471). German Augustinian monk and mystic, born at Kempen near Cologne. He seems to have spent his whole life at the monastery of Zwolle (now in the Netherlands) and there wrote in Latin *The Imitation of Christ*, which was published posthumously (1486) and in its many translations has proved probably the most popular of all devotional works. Its four books relate in simple and sincere language the progress of the Christian soul to perfection, its gradual dissociation from the human world and its eventual union with God. Its authorship has also been attributed to Jean Charlier de Gerson, a French theologian.

Thomas, Albert (1878–1932). French Socialist politician. From 1920–32 he was the foundation director of the International Labour Organization set up under the auspices of the League of Nations by the peace treaty of 1919.

Thomas, Dylan (1914–1953). Welsh poet, born in Swansea. He moved to London in 1932 and published *Eighteen Poems* in 1934, followed by *Twenty-five Poems* (1936) and *The Map of Love* (1939), the last containing prose as well as poetry. The *Collected Poems* appeared in 1952. His poetry, rich in vivid and highly original imagery, technically ingenious, frequently obscure, has been highly praised as part of a 20th-century neo-romanticism. He achieved immense successes with his radio play *Under Milk Wood* (1954), a brilliant evocation of a day in an imaginary Welsh village; it later proved successful on stage and screen. He also wrote the autobiographical sketches *Portrait of the Artist as a Young Dog* (1940), and an unfinished novel, *Adventures in the Skin Trade* (published 1955). His death, hastened by excessive drinking, occurred in New York during a lecture tour. His wife, Caitlin Thomas, wrote an autobiography of great poignancy, *Leftover Life to Kill* (1957).
Fitzgibbon, C., *The Life of Dylan Thomas*. 1965. Watkins, V. (ed.), *Letters to Vernon Watkins*. 1957

Thomas, James Henry (1874–1949). British trade union leader and politician. After being an engine driver he became engaged in trade union activities, and as general secretary of the National Union of Railwaymen (1918–24 and 1925) showed great organizing ability and skill in negotiation. He became a Labour M.P. in 1910 and served in both Labour governments between the wars and in the subsequent national coalition. He was colonial secretary (1924, 1931 and 1935–36), lord privy seal with responsibility for unemployment (1929–30) and dominions secretary (1931–35). He resigned after disclosure of budget secrets (1936).
Thomas, J. H., *My Story*. 1937

Thomas, St. One of the twelve apostles of Jesus Christ. From his reluctance to accept the fact of the resurrection without tangible evidence originated the phrase 'Doubting Thomas'. Tradition relates that he became a missionary in India. The 'Christians of St Thomas of Malabar' claim to have been founded by him and a shrine (rebuilt in 1547 by the Portuguese) near Madras is said to indicate his place of martyrdom. He is Portugal's patron saint.

Thomas Aquinas, St *see* **Aquinas, St Thomas**

Thompson, Francis (1859–1907). English poet, born at Preston, Lancashire. Having abandoned his medical studies he went to London, where he lived in direst poverty and misery – relieved by opium – until rescued by Wilfred and Alice * Meynell who sent him to hospital and subsequently watched over him through years of ill health. Of his works, which were preponderantly religious, *The Hound of Heaven*, contained in a collection of poems published in 1893, is best known. It tells how the poet in his flight from God is pursued and overtaken: its style is reminiscent of 17th-century poets, e.g. * Crashaw.

Meynell, E., ed., *Collected Works of Francis Thompson*. 1913

Thomson, James (1700–1748). Scottish poet. Intended for the ministry, he went to London to seek his literary fortune and achieved recognition by *The Seasons* (1730), originally published separately, beginning with *Winter* (1726), in Miltonic blank verse. His poem *Britannia* (1729) brought him political patronage and sinecure offices: Frederick, Prince of Wales, to whom he dedicated his poem *Liberty* (1734–36), granted him a pension. His tragedies, e.g. *Sophonisba* (1730) – with its famous line 'Oh! Sophonisba! Sophonisba! oh!' – and *Agamemnon* (1738), are long forgotten. His *Alfred, a Masque* (1740) contained the song *Rule, Britannia*. Thomson used the forms of the classical age to which he belonged but some of his rapturous descriptions of nature in *The Seasons* presaged Romanticism.

Thomson, James (1834–1882). Scottish-born poet. He was brought up in poverty and tried his hand at various careers, including that of an army schoolmaster from which he was dismissed in 1862. He went to London where he lived a lonely life, made worse by the use of stimulants and drugs to relieve illness and melancholy. Friendship with Charles * Bradlaugh enabled him to contribute to the *National Reformer*, for which he wrote his most famous poem, *The City of Dreadful Night* (1874), in which London is pictured as a city of despair. He wrote over the initials B. V. (Bysshe Vanolis).

Thomson, Sir Joseph John (1856–1940). English physicist. Cavendish professor of experimental physics at Cambridge (1884–1918) and master of Trinity College, Cambridge (1918–40), he discovered (1897) the electron and deduced that cathode rays consist of these subatomic particles. This work laid the foundations of modern atomic physics, He invented (1911) positive-ray analysis and showed that the naturally occurring elements are mixtures of isotopes. He won the Nobel Prize for Physics (1906), was admitted to the Order of Merit (1912), and was president of the Royal Society (1915–20).

His son, **Sir George Paget Thomson** (1892–1975), won the Nobel Prize for Physics (1927) – for discovering the diffraction of electrons by transmission through crystals – jointly with the American physicist C. J. Davisson who had made the same discovery by a different method. He was professor of physics at Aberdeen (1922–30) and at Imperial College, London (1930–52), and was knighted in 1943.

Thomson, G. P., *J. J. Thomson and the Cavendish Laboratory in his Day*. 1964.

Thomson, Virgil (1896–). American composer and critic. His works, notable for their economy and simplicity of style, include symphonies, sacred choral music and two operas with libretti by Gertrude Stein.

Thomson of Fleet, Roy Herbert Thomson, 1st Baron (1894–1976). Canadian-born newspaper proprietor who became a British citizen in 1963. After starting from small beginnings as a seller of radio equipment, he acquired radio stations and newspapers in Canada, breaking into the British market with the purchase of the *Scotsman* (1953). His greatest single enterprise was the acquisition of the Kemsley Newspaper groups (1959) which included the *Sunday Times*. In 1966 he gained control of *The Times*. He was raised to the peerage in 1964.

Thoreau, Henry David (1817–1862). American poet, essayist and mystic. His birthplace (Concord, Massachusetts) became the centre of his life: he returned there after graduating at Harvard, where he added a love of the classics, especially of Homer, to that of the English poets whom he already knew. His first book, *A Week on the Concord and Merrimack Rivers* (1849), intertwines philosophy and observation. From Concord he went into a two-year retreat in a cabin which he himself constructed at Walden Pond. The record of that experience, contained in his most famous book, *Walden* (1854), remains an American classic. It tells a story interesting in itself and is important as a study of nature, but its greatest significance is derived from the revelation of his own idealistic faith. Nor was

his faith a matter of theory only; he preferred prison to paying a poll tax to sustain the Mexican War. Essays such as *Civil Disobedience* (1849) provided texts for Gandhi and many other fighters for liberty. Much of his later life was spent in travel and nature study in Canada and the area round Cape Cod. He returned to Concord to die.
Harding, W., *The Days of Henry Thoreau*. 1965

Thorndike, Dame Sybil (1882–1976). English actress. Her early successes were won with Miss Horniman's repertory company at Manchester and at the Old Vic, London (1914–18); she received special acclaim for her performances of Medea and Hecuba in classical Greek plays. Among her later parts the best known was perhaps that of Joan of Arc in Bernard Shaw's *St Joan*. She continued to play into old age and achieved a great success in a revival of *Arsenic and Old Lace* (1966). She was awarded the D.B.E. in 1931.
Trewin, J. C., *Sybil Thorndike*. 1955

Thornhill, Sir James (1675–1734). English painter. He is best known for the decorative murals which he painted for Wren's hall at Greenwich, for the dome of St Paul's and for great baroque houses such as Blenheim. His portraits included one of the criminal Jack Sheppard. He was knighted in 1720 and was appointed history painter to the king in 1728. * Hogarth became his son-in-law (1729) and they collaborated in a conversation-piece of the House of Commons (1730).

Thorvaldsen, Bertel (1768/70–1844). Danish sculptor. He spent most of his life in Rome and came to be recognized as the chief exponent of neoclassicism after Canova. Modern taste has rebelled against the smooth perfection of his style but his contemporary success was immense; among his patrons was Napoleon, who commissioned a frieze of Alexander's campaigns. He left all his unsold works, religious and classical, to his country and they are collected, with casts of many other of his important works, in the Thorvaldsen Museum, Copenhagen.

Thrale (Piozzi), Hester Lynch (née Salusbury) (1741–1821). English writer. Born in North Wales, she had learning, vivacity and charm, but was unsuitably married to a wealthy Southwark brewer. She entertained at her country house at Streatham a lively, intellectual circle including Dr * Johnson. The house became his second home: he was outraged when, three years after her husband's death (1781), she announced her impending marriage to Gabriel Piozzi and subsequently lived happily with him in Wales. She published a book of anecdotes about Dr Johnson (1786) and his correspondence with her (1788).

Throckmorton, Francis (1554–1584). English conspirator. He became entangled in plots to restore Roman Catholicism in England and to bring Mary Queen of Scots to the English throne. Caught in the act of writing in cipher to Mary, he was tortured and executed. He came of a family long distinguished in public affairs; his uncle, **Sir Nicholas Throckmorton** (1515–1571), served Queen Elizabeth well as ambassador in France and Scotland. **Elizabeth Throckmorton,** daughter of Sir Nicholas, was lady-in-waiting to Queen Elizabeth but was disgraced for marrying * Sir Walter Raleigh.

Thucydides (*c*.470–400 B.C.). Athenian historian. He was naval commander in the Peloponnesian War; for his failure to capture Amphipolis (424) he was forced to live in exile for twenty years, during which time he wrote his famous unfinished history of the war which carries the story as far as 411. The first book is introductory and discloses his own methods of impartial record; the remainder contain in chronological sequence narratives of the summer campaigns alternating with accounts of diplomacy in the winter months. An exception to this method is the interpolation of speeches said to have been made by the characters concerned but in reality expressing the author's summing up of the situations. Lucid, impartial and often writing with restrained passion, Thucydides achieved the greatest historical work to be handed down from the ancient world.
Romilly, J. de, *Thucydides and Athenian Imperialism*. 1963

Thurber, James Grover (1894–1961). American humorist. He worked on the *New Yorker* for many years and won fame with his essays, stories and drawings, the last especially noted for the originality of their anarchic humour. Among his favourite subjects were dogs, dominating women and the pathetic little men whom they owned; sometimes his drawings accompanied his text, sometimes they stood alone. His publications include *My Life and Hard Times* (1933), *Men, Women and Dogs* (1943) and a later work, *The Years with Ross* (1959), * Ross being editor of the *New Yorker*. Thurber suffered from deteriorating sight, the result of an accident when a boy.

Tiberius (Tiberius Claudius Nero) 42 B.C.–A.D. 37). Roman emperor (from A.D. 14). He was brought up by his stepfather, the emperor Augustus, whom he eventually succeeded. As early as 15 B.C. he had shown his abilities as a soldier on the Alpine frontiers and later he achieved further successes in Germany, his troops by 9 B.C. having reached the Elbe. To further Augustus's dynastic scheme he was now forced to divorce his wife Agrippina, whom he loved, and marry the emperor's widowed daughter, Julia. Partly in anger, partly to conceal Julia's notorious profligacy, Tiberius withdrew to Rhodes. This act cost him the favour of the emperor by whom it was misunderstood. However, the sudden death of his two grandsons left Augustus no choice: Tiberius was recalled, adopted (A.D. 4) and acknowledged as his colleague and heir. During the first eight years of his reign he showed his old efficiency, though he also appeared pedantic, austere and suspicious. From 23, however, he fell more and more under the influence of the ambitious and unscrupulous Sejanus, prefect of the imperial guards. In 26 Tiberius retired to the island of Capri whence stories of unspeakable and improbable orgies – he was nearing 70 – drifted back to Rome, where Sejanus, now in undisputed control, exercised a corrupt tyranny. Tiberius roused himself in 31 to organize with his usual skill the downfall of Sejanus but in his last years showed the embitterment of disillusion. Outside Rome and in the provinces his reign was remembered as one of prosperity and enlightened rule.

Tibullus, Albius (*c.* 60–19 B.C.). Roman poet. A friend of * Horace, his love poems and those descriptive of the countryside have much tenderness and charm.

Tichborne, Sir Roger Charles, 10th Bart. (1829–1854). English baronet. Belonging to an old Hampshire family, he was presumed to have been lost at sea and was duly succeeded by his younger brother; but when this brother, the 11th Baronet, died (1866), Arthur Orton, a butcher from Wagga Wagga, Australia, claimed the inheritance on the grounds that he was the missing Sir Roger. The court proceedings that followed were among the longest, most sensational and most expensive in Victorian history. Orton's case eventually collapsed and at a subsequent trial he was sentenced to fourteen years' imprisonment for imposture.

Tiepolo, Giovanni Battista (1696–1770). Venetian decorative painter. The finest exponent of the late baroque or rococo styles in Italy, his pictures were often contrived to enhance architectural effects by being allowed, so to speak, to escape from their frames or the spaces to which they would be normally assigned. From 1733 to 1750 he flooded the palaces and churches of northern Italy with examples of his work, sometimes aided by assistants (including his sons), who, however, had no hand in the oil sketches from which pictures were worked up. Outstanding is the festive and theatrical *Banquet of Cleopatra* (*c.* 1749) in the Labia Palace, Venice. In 1750 he was commissioned to decorate Neumann's architectural masterpiece, the Würzburg Residenz in Germany, for which he produced some of his greatest work. His last years (from 1762) were spent in Spain (specially notable are the decorations done for the palaces of Madrid and Aranjuez) where the light and airy atmosphere of earlier work is carried to the point where his pictures seem to dissolve in light.

Morassi, A., *G. B. Tiepolo: His Life and Work*. 1955

Tiglath-Pileser III (reigned 745–727 B.C.). King of Assyria. Like his namesake **Tiglath-Pileser I** (1114–1076 B.C.), whose conquests, however, proved ephemeral, he overcame Babylon; and he became its king in 729. Many Syrian and Phoenician cities also fell into his hands.

Tilden, Samuel Jones (1814–1880). American politician. Having made a fortune as a railway lawyer, he resumed an early interest in politics at a time when the Democratic party, to which he belonged, was recovering after the Civil War. As governor of New York (1875–76) he made a successful stand against corruption and was Democratic candidate in the disputed presidential election of 1876. It was held that the majority of one held by his Republican opponent, Rutherford * Hayes, in the Electoral College resulted from fraudulent returns by the Negro-controlled states of South Carolina, Florida and Louisiana. A special commission (with a Republican majority) declared in favour of Hayes and it was said that Tilden was reconciled to the decision by some sort of promise by Hayes that support for the Negro states would be withdrawn.

Tilden, Bill (William Tatum) (1893–1953). American lawn tennis player. Distinguished by his great size, he was the leading amateur player of the early 1920s. He led the US Davis Cup team to seven straight victories (1920–26). After an intervening period of French domination (* Borotra) he again won (1930), at the age of 37, the singles title at Wimbledon: in the following year he turned professional. His career was destroyed by disclosure of his homosexuality.

Tillett, Ben(jamin) (1860–1943). English trade union leader and Labour politician. Having organized the Dockers Union (1887) he remained its general secretary until it amalgamated (1922) with the Transport and General Workers Union; he was closely associated with the famous strike of 1889. He was Labour M.P. for North Salford (1917–24 and 1929–31). His name is one of the most honoured in the history of the Labour movement.
Tillett, B., *Memories and Reflections*. 1931.

Tilley, Vesta (Matilda Powles) (1864–1952). English actress. She first appeared in London in 1878 and, always performing in male attire, became one of the greatest stars of the music-hall stage, then in its heyday. Having married Sir Walter de Frece she retired in 1920.

Tilly, Johann Tserklaes, Count of (1559–1632). Flemish soldier. Born in the castle of Tilly in Brabant, he had fought for Spain and against the Turks before entering the service of Maximilian, Duke of Bavaria (1610). On the outbreak of the Thirty Years War (1618) he commanded the armies of the Catholic League. He gained early successes at Prague and in the Palatinate and forced Denmark to come to terms by his victory at Lutter (1629). He succeeded * Wallenstein (1631) as commander-in-chief of the imperial armies and those of the League, but in 1632 was routed by * Gustavus II at Breitenfeld and in a second defeat was mortally wounded.

Timoshenko, Simeon Konstantinovich (1895–1970). Russian marshal. He was minister of defence in the early stages of World War II and later commanded in the south-west, where he organized the defence of Stalingrad and the recovery of the Caucasus.

Timothy (died *c.* 100). One of St Paul's companions in his missionary work. The Epistles to Timothy in the New Testament, with that supposed to be addressed to Titus, are called the 'pastoral Epistles'. On grounds of style and content, modern critics have rejected Pauline authorship, but the personal details suggest that they have a basis in letters written by St Paul, though probably enlarged and adapted for his own purposes by a later editor.

Timur the Lame (or Tamerlane) (1336–1405). Mongol conqueror. He is said to have been descended from Genghis Khan in the female line, and despite the fact that he was crippled from birth he took advantage of a period of Moslem anarchy to establish, by 1369, his rule in Samarkand and to assume the title of Great Khan. For the rest of his life he followed a career of conquest with extreme brutality in war but with firm, just rule over conquered territory and with an appreciation of the arts. By 1385 he was master of all central Asia; his armies had conquered Persia, Georgia and Armenia, had defeated the Tartars and marched as far north as Moscow. He invaded India (1398), sacked Delhi and founded a sultanate which later grew into the Moghul empire. After over-running Syria he smashed the Turkish army at Ankara (1402); he died while preparing to invade China. Among English plays inspired by his career are Marlowe's *Tamburlaine the Great* (1590) and Nicholas Rowe's *Tamerlane* (1702).

Tinbergen, Jan (1903–). Dutch economist. He served on the staff of the Central Bureau of Statistics at The Hague, 1929–36 and 1938–45; between 1936 and 1938 he was engaged in research on commerce for the League of Nations. He was director of the Central Planning Bureau at The Hague 1945–55, and professor of Development Planning at first Rotterdam and then Leiden universities until 1975. He shared the first Nobel Prize for

Economic Science in 1969 with Ragnar * Frisch for their work in developing econometrics. His brother, **Nikolaas Tinbergen** (1907–), an experimental zoologist, taught at Oxford from 1949 and was professor in animal behaviour 1966–74. He wrote *The Study of Instinct* (1951) and *Animal Behaviour* (1965) and shared the 1973 Nobel Prize for Medicine with Karl von * Frisch and Konrad * Lorenz for their pioneering work in ethology.

Tinbergen, J., *Developing Planning*. 1968

Tintoretto (Jacopo Robusti) (1518–1594). Venetian painter. He was the son of a dyer – hence the name by which he is known – and except for short visits he seems to have spent all his life in Venice. Here with his wife and children he lived happily, respected for his piety and increasingly renowned for his work.

His fellow Venetian, Titian, in whose studio he worked for a time, and Michelangelo, were the strongest influences on him but mainly he was self-taught. In his earlier works, many of them mythological, he continued the ideals of the High Renaissance but as the Counter-Reformation proceeded and he became more and more absorbed by religious themes he gradually became the most robust exponent of the style loosely called Mannerism. In his *St Mark* series (1548) the thunderous atmosphere, the glowing and insubstantial architecture, the perspective effects produced by design and lighting exemplify the vigour and inventiveness of Tintoretto's grand operatic manner. His greatest undertaking was the decoration of the Scuola de San Rocco in Venice. In the Doge's palace he executed an enormous *Paradise*, in which the milling overcrowded figures are manipulated with the control of a master choreographer. His portraits of the celebrities of his day are much less spectacular and rely upon characterization more than upon the splendour of the garments. His last pictures at San Giorgio Maggiore, especially *The Last Supper* (1591–94), show the final culmination of his colour techniques.

Bernari, C., and de Vecchi, P., *L'opera completa del Tintoretto*. 1970.

Tippett, Sir Michael Kemp (1905–). English composer. He studied at the Royal College of Music and was musical director of Morley College, London (1940–52). The Elizabethan composers and Purcell as well as later influences, e.g. Stravinsky, Hindemith and jazz, have all contributed to his highly individual idiom, notable for springy rhythms and for 'long-breathed' melodies that are woven into an elaborate contrapuntal texture. His works include four symphonies, a Concerto for Double String Orchestra (1939), a Piano Concerto (1956), String Quartets, operas to his own libretti – *The Midsummer Marriage* (1954) and *King Priam* (1962) – the oratorio *A Child of our Time* (1944), and the cantata *The Vision of St Augustine* (1966). In the Concerto for Orchestra (1963) he constructs the movements out of consecutive sections each associated with a certain group of instruments. He was knighted in 1966, given the CH in 1979 and the OM in 1983.

Kemp, I., (ed.), *Michael Tippett*. 1965

Tippoo Sahib (1749–1799). Indian ruler. Son of * Haidar Ali, from whose French officers he acquired his military skill, he became sultan of Mysore on his father's death (1782). The peace (1783) between Great Britain and France, to which he as France's ally adhered, gave him time to consolidate his rule, but in 1789, moved by an almost obsessional hatred of Britain, he invaded the protected territory Travancore and as a result of the retaliatory war by Britain lost half his territory (1792) and had to pay a huge indemnity. As he continued to intrigue, however, the war was renewed (1799); he was quickly driven back into his capital Seringapatam, and was killed when the city was stormed after two months' siege. Tippoo was fanatical and cruel, but as a ruler showed great industry and (e.g. by a new currency and calendar reform) interest in his country's welfare.

Tirpitz, Alfred von (1849–1930). German sailor. He had already been chief of staff with the Baltic and Asiatic fleets before being appointed secretary of state (1897) and becoming the driving force behind the successful campaign for a greater German navy. He was dismissed (March 1916) because his demand for ruthless submarine warfare – adopted later – was considered premature. He thus missed the Battle of Jutland.

Steinberg, J., *Yesterday's Deterrent*. 1965

Tiselius, Arne Wilhelm Kaurin (1902–1971). Swedish chemist. Appointed professor of biochemistry at Uppsala (1938), he became known for his application of electrophoresis to the analysis of proteins, especially serum proteins. He also adapted chromatographic techniques to the analysis of colourless substances. From its foundation (1946) he was president of Sweden's State Council for Research in Natural Sciences. He won the Nobel Prize for Chemistry (1948).

Titian (Tiziano Vercelli) (*c.* 1488–1576). Venetian painter. While still in his boyhood he entered the studio of Giovanni Bellini and later studied with Giorgione, by whom he was much influenced in his early work. An independent style is, however, already apparent in the first of his famous works, *Sacred and Profane Love* (*c.* 1515), a work, despite its allegorical subject, of human realism. From this time his technique steadily developed. Experiments are made with figures in action; pyramidal shapes and diagonals become the compositional bases of several of his works; and significance is given to the main figures by use of light and shade. From 1516 to 1530 the series of great religious pictures, including the *Assumption of the Virgin* (1516–18) and the *Madonna with Members of the Pesaro Family* (1519–26), are matched by equally great mythological paintings for Alfonso d'Este, Duke of Ferrara, e.g. *Bacchus and Ariadne* (1521; now in the National Gallery, London). By then the richness of his palette, with its bright reds, blues, greens and golden browns, sometimes used in contrast, sometimes to build up an almost sculptural effect, had established him as one of the boldest colourists so far known. In such works and in his portraits he is said to have 'liberated' colour, a further sign of freedom being the broad brush strokes with which it was applied. For much of the decade which followed (1530–40) he worked for the emperor, Charles V, portraits of whom and the members of the court kept him busily occupied. One of the best of the emperor himself (now in the Prado, Madrid) shows him full-length with a dog. Portraits of Pope Paul III and other members of the Farnese family reveal a growing power to probe the character of his subjects. From 1556, when Charles V abdicated, Titian's principal patron was his son, Philip II of Spain, for whom he painted a series of 'poesies' – *Diana and Actaeon, The Rape of Europa, Perseus and Andromeda* etc. – similar in subject to the earlier mythological pictures but painted with much softer, almost iridescent colours. Titian continued to paint to the end of his life, his last work being an unfinished *Pietà* intended for his own tomb.

Titian's painting is warmly emotional and sensual. He was no intellectual and attempted no superhuman scale of effect; his painting techniques were developed by Rembrandt, Rubens and Velazquez, with whose greatness his can be compared.

Crowe, J. A. and Cavalcaselle, G. B., *Life and Times of Titian*. 1887. Fosca, F., *Titian*. 1955

Tito, Josip Broz (1892–1980). Yugoslav leader and Marshal. The son of a Croatian locksmith, he was conscripted into the Austro-Hungarian army in World War I, was taken prisoner and remained in Russia to serve in the Red Army during the Civil War. Back in Yugoslavia he helped to form the Communist party and took the name 'Tito'. He was imprisoned (1928–34), was subsequently active in the interests of his party in Paris and Central Europe, recruiting for the Spanish Civil War. By 1939 he was back in Yugoslavia and in 1941, after the Germans had overrun the country, became a leader of partisans whose task was to harry the occupying forces. This brought him into conflict with a rival resistance leader, General Mihailovich, who was acting in the royalist interest. Eventually the Allies decided to give Tito, the more active of the two, full support. This enabled him, after the German defeat, to execute Mihailovich, to exclude King Peter and to establish a Communist state. He was prime minister 1945–53 and president 1953–80. In 1948 Yugoslavia was expelled from the Cominform for adopting nationalistic policies (i.e. for rejecting Russian dictatorship). Eventually relations became less strained and in the following years Tito maintained an independent communism at home, opened trading relations with the west and kept a clever balance between the rival groups of powers who dominated Europe.

Auty, P., *Tito*. 1970

Titus (Titus Flavius Vespasianus) (39–81). Roman emperor (from 79). The elder son of the emperor Vespasian, he was a brilliant soldier and after his father's elevation quickly brought the Jewish rebellion to an end by the capture of Jerusalem. He became virtual co-ruler with Vespasian and on his succession not only delighted the Roman populace by his magnificent displays but won esteem by firm, just rule and by his discouragement of flatterers and informers. His popularity was threatened only by his passion for the Jewish Berenice (the Bernice of Acts 25), whom he had brought to Rome but soon dismissed. He completed the Colosseum and did much to help the survivors of the tragic eruption of Vesuvius (79).

Tizard, Sir Henry Thomas (1885–1959). British scientist. After playing an important part in aeronautical research in and after World War I, he was rector of the Imperial College of Science and Technology (1929–42) and president of Magdalen College, Oxford (1942–46). During World War II and afterwards (1946–52) when he was chairman of the Advisory Council on Scientific Policy and of the Defence Research Policy Committee, he was in keen rivalry with Lord * Cherwell. His advice was of particular value on matters of aircraft construction and the use of radar.

Tocqueville, Alexis de (1805–1859). French political writer. He came of an aristocratic family, studied law, and in 1831 visited the U.S.A. to investigate the penal system there. Writing and an incursion into French politics occupied the rest of his life. He became a deputy (1839), was briefly foreign minister after the revolution of 1848 and in 1851 was imprisoned for opposing the *coup d'état* of Louis Napoleon (Napoleon III). In his two well known books *La Démocratie en Amérique* (1835–39) and *L'Ancien Régime et la Révolution* (1850), he arrived at the broad conclusion that by abolishing aristocracies (with their inborn protection of the rights and privileges of the different social classes) the peoples both of France and America had sacrificed liberty for equality; that demands for economic equality must necessarily follow those for social equality and that the final result must be authoritarian, centralized rule. His arguments were given point by the rule of Napoleon I and Napoleon III in his own epoch and his foresight justified by the centralizing tendencies of modern egalitarian governments.
Brogan, H., *Tocqueville*. 1973

Todd, Alexander Robertus Todd, Baron (1907–). British chemist. As professor of chemistry at Manchester (1938–44) and then professor of organic chemistry at Cambridge, he made notable contributions in the fields of vitamins and drugs, and particularly in the elucidation of nucleotide structure. From 1952 he was chairman of the Advisory Council on Scientific Policy; he won the Nobel Prize for Chemistry (1957); in 1961 he was made a life peer, becoming president of the Royal Society in 1975. He was awarded the O.M. (1977).

Todleben, Eduard Ivanovich (1818–1884). Russian soldier. He developed a genius for military engineering and won international fame for his defence of Sevastopol (1854–55) during the Crimean War. In the Russo-Turkish War (1877–78) he was put in charge of the siege of Plevna, which he eventually captured.

Todt, Fritz (1891–1942). German engineer. He shared with Hitler a taste for the grandiose, and undertook much of the constructional work under the Nazi régime (e.g. the autobahns) and the Siegfried line. During World War II squads of the Todt organization were most effective in keeping communications open and in bringing factories back into production after bombing attacks.

Togliatti, Palmiro (1893–1964). Italian Communist leader. While a student at Turin University he made a study of socialism. In 1926 he became secretary of the Italian Communist party (a post he retained until his death) and in that year went into exile and lived abroad, mostly in Moscow, for eighteen years (from 1935 as secretary of Comintern). He returned to Italy (1944) after Mussolini's fall, and joined Badoglio's cabinet. Subsequently he built up the Italian Communist party until it became the second largest party in the country and the largest Communist party in Western Europe. To secure support he compromised on communist doctrine to the extent of recognizing Roman Catholicism as the state religion and the Lateran Treaty by which the Vatican City became an independent state.

Togo Heihachiro, Count (1847–1934). Japanese sailor. In command of the fleet during the Russo-Japanese War (1904–05), he succeeded in bottling up the Russian pacific fleet in Port Arthur and then (May 1905) in annihilating (in the Tsushima Straits) a relieving fleet sent from Europe. He received the British O.M. in 1906.

Tojo Hideki (1884–1948). Japanese soldier and politician. After having served as chief of staff (1937–40) with Japanese occupation troops in China, General Tojo was minister of war (1937–40) and prime minister during the vital years 1941–44. Accused as largely responsible for Japan's entry into World War II he was hanged by the Allies as a war criminal.

Tokugawa. Name of the family which controlled the shogunate (hereditary military government) in Japan from * Ieyasu in 1603 to 1868, when the last shogun Keiki (1837–1913) resigned his powers to the emperor in the 'Meiji Restoration'.

Tolbukhin, Fyodor Ivanovich (1885–1949). Russian soldier. In World War II, having made his name as a general at Stalingrad, he became commander of the army which swept through the Ukraine (1943), and reconquered the Crimea, Romania and Bulgaria (1944) and finally (1945) Budapest and Vienna. He became a marshal in October 1944.

Tolkein, John Ronald Reuel (1892–1973). English writer and philologist. He was professor of Anglo-Saxon (1925–45) and of English Language and Literature (1945–59) at Oxford University. His academic work on early and medieval English texts was highly regarded, but he achieved popular success in fiction; his interest in language and mythology enabled him to create a world with its own cultures, languages and beliefs. *The Hobbit* appeared in 1937 and the more sophisticated *Lord of the Rings* in 1954–55. It speedily attracted a cult following which persisted into the 1980s.

Toller, Ernst (1893–1939). German playwright and poet, of Jewish origin. He was imprisoned for taking part in the Communist rising in Germany after World War I; his plays, e.g. *Man and the Masses* (1921) and *The Machine Wreckers* (1923), reflect his revolutionary opinions. He also wrote poetry and autobiographical works. He lived in exile after Hitler's rise to power, and committed suicide in New York.

Toller, E., *Ein Jugend in Deutschland.* 1933

Tolstoy, Alexey Nikolayevich (1882–1945). Russian writer. Unrelated to the famous Leo Tolstoy, he went abroad after the Revolution but returned (1922) and soon became well known for science fiction like that of H. G. Wells. His *The Road to Calvary* (1945), describing events before and during the Revolution, won a Stalin Prize. His patriotic play about Ivan the Terrible was a great success during World War II. His best work was an unfinished historical novel, *Peter I.*

Tolstoy, Count Leo Nikolayevich (1828–1910). Russian writer and thinker. He was born on the family estate of Yasnaya Polyana in the Tula province and after the early loss of both parents was privately educated until he went to Kazan University (1844–47) to study law and languages. A life of ease and mild dissipation followed but in 1851 he joined the army and from 1853 took part in the Crimean War. This inspired *The Sevastopol Stories* (1865) which, together with the autobiographical sequence *Childhood* (1852) and its two sequels, established him as a writer. Life in St Petersburg did not attract him, and he travelled over much of Europe. From 1862 he settled down with his young wife, Sophie Andreyevna Behrs, became the father of fifteen children, and applied himself to the management of his estates, establishing peasant schools on the pattern of those he had seen abroad, attending to the problems arising from the emancipation of serfs and filling the role of a humane and forward-looking landlord. To this happy period belong his two most famous novels. *War and Peace* (1865–68) gives an epic account of Russia's conflict with Napoleon and shows how the great historical happening affects the lives of a large group of characters and especially impinges upon the romance of the heroine, Natasha Rostov. Tolstoy's genius for reaching the heart of women is shown in the other great novel, *Anna Karenina* (1874–76) in which he reveals the inexorable social pressures which doomed Anna and Count Vronsky because they were too honest to disguise their love. These two works are supreme amongst Russian novels.

Tolstoy had always been troubled by inner conflict. His eager acceptance of life and his zestful response to the demands of the natural instincts conflicted (as is apparent in his books) with his reactions as moralist and reformer. About 1877 the conflict became acute and he emerged from the struggle as a kind of solitary prophet, revered even by those who disregarded him. His house at Yasnaya Polyana became a centre of pilgrimage for disciples from all over the world. His teaching was set out in a series of books. e.g. *What I Believe* (1883), and *What Then Must We Do?* (1886). His teaching amounted to a form of Christianity, stripped of theology. This brought him into conflict with the Orthodox Synod, by which he was excommunicated. He denounced all authority and all violence, even in resisting evil (Gandhi corresponded with him about this concept). To bring his own life into accord with his teaching he became a vegetarian, refused to exploit the service of others and tried (1895) to renounce all property rights in his estates and book royalties. Family quarrels resulted, of such intensity that they embittered his last years. Eventually with his youngest daughter he fled from the estate but caught a chill and for several days lay dying at the little railway station of Astapovo, still refusing to see his wife.

Among the novels of the last period were *The Death of Ivan Ilyich* (1886), *The Kreutzer Sonata* (1899) and *Resurrection* (1900); he also wrote plays, stories and critical essays. But it is upon the earlier novels that his claim to be one of the greatest literary masters finally rests.

Tolstoy, N., *The Tolstoys: Twenty Generations of Russian History 1353–1983*. 1983

Tompion, Thomas (1638–1713). English clock-maker. Both his father and grandfather were blacksmiths, which may have set his mind to working in metals but cannot account for the extraordinary skill and artistry which he brought to his craft. The first clocks for Greenwich Observatory were built by him (1676); for William III he made a clock that would strike the hours and quarters for a year without rewinding. Survivors of the 650 clocks made by him now fetch very high prices. In addition he made about 5,500 watches, including some of the earliest to be fitted with balance springs.

Tone, (Theobald) **Wolfe** (1763–1798). Irish politician. Having become convinced that only independence would bring about Roman Catholic emancipation and overcome the many injustices of British rule, he formed the Society of United Irishmen (1791) and in 1795 left the country to seek help in America and France. He accompanied the French invasion fleet (1796) and after its failure returned to Ireland with a small squadron to aid the rebellion of 1798. Defeated and captured by the British he killed himself in prison while awaiting execution. His journals show him to have been a man of good nature, gaiety and wit.

Tone, W., *Autobiography*. 1826

Tooke, John Horne (1736–1812). English politician. His father's name was Horne; he added the name Tooke (1782) at the request of a rich friend of that name. He became a clergyman as a young man but spent his life in political agitation, at first on behalf of John * Wilkes; but after a quarrel he formed (1771) the Constitutional Society to agitate for parliamentary and economic reform. In 1777 he was imprisoned for raising money for American troops 'murdered' at Lexington (in the War of American Independence). He filled the time by writing *The Diversions of Purley* (published 1786 and 1805), which amid much philological, metaphysical and political comment pointed to the need for studying Anglo-Saxon and Gothic. His attitude when the French War opened caused him to be tried for treason (1794), but he was acquitted. After two failures to enter parliament he was elected for Old Sarum in 1801.

Torquemada, Tomás de (1420–1498). Spanish inquisitor. He was a Dominican friar, who having become confessor to Queen Isabella easily persuaded her and King Ferdinand (who was jealous of the rich Moors and Jews of Castile) to ask the pope for the Inquisition to be established in Spain. In 1483 he became the first inquisitor-general and centralized and organized a campaign of torture hitherto unparalleled. He was largely instrumental in the expulsion of the Jews (1492).

Torricelli, Evangelista (1608–1647). Italian physicist and mathematician. He succeeded (1642) his former teacher * Galileo as professor of mathematics at the Florentine Academy. In experiments with a long glass tube of mercury inserted in a trough of the same liquid he discovered (1643) the principle of the mercurial barometer; he demonstrated that a vacuum (now called the Torricellian vacuum) was created above the mercury. He also discovered the law (now known as Torricelli's Law) governing the flow of liquids through small holes.

Torrigiano, Pietro (1472–1528). Florentine sculptor. He had to leave Florence after breaking Michelangelo's nose in a quarrel. He worked in the Netherlands (1509–10) and then went to England, where he did some of his best work, notably the tombs of Margaret Beaufort, Henry VII, and his wife, Elizabeth of York, in Westminster Abbey.

Toscanini, Arturo (1867–1957). Italian conductor. Trained as a cellist, he made his debut as a substitute conductor in Rio de Janeiro in 1886 and quickly rose to prominence. He was chief conductor at La Scala, Milan (1898–1903, 1906–08 and 1921–24), conductor at the Metropolitan Opera, New York (1908–15), and chief conductor of the New York Philharmonic Symphony Orchestra (1928–36). As a protest against fascism in Italy and Germany he left Europe in 1937 for the USA, where he conducted the N.B.C. Symphony Orchestra until his retirement (1954). His repertoire revealed a remarkable catholicity of taste and included not only the German and Italian classics but composers as different as Debussy, Elgar and Sibelius. This, combined with an astonishing musical memory, deep insight into a composer's meaning, scrupulous fidelity to the score and the driving energy of his interpretations, made him pre-eminent among the conductors of his time.
Sachs, H., *Toscanini*. 1981

Tosti, Sir Francesco Paolo (1846–1916). Italian musician. Resident in England from 1880, he became teacher of singing to the British royal family.

Toulouse-Lautrec, Henri (Marie Raymond) de (1864–1901). French painter and lithographer. He was descended from an ancient family of south-west France and was born at Albi, where a permanent exhibition of his work remains. A fall from a horse crippled him and he grew up to be such a stunted dwarf that he felt cut off from ordinary people. He sought refuge in art and went to Paris in 1882. There in the cafés and cabarets of Montmartre (e.g. the Moulin Rouge) he found the subjects for his pictures and drawings – dancers, singers and prostitutes, as well as circus and racecourse scenes. He shared the gay, grotesque, dissipated life of those he painted and developed a sympathetic insight into their character. The main influences on his style were Japanese woodcuts and the work of Degas. In the last decade of his life he mastered lithography and his work in that field had an important influence on the development of poster art.
Joyaut, M., *Henri de Toulouse-Lautrec*. Repr. 1968

Tourneur, Cyril (*c.* 1575–1626). English dramatist. His fame rests on two plays, *The Revenger's Tragedy* (printed 1607) and *The Atheist's Tragedy* (printed 1611). The greater is the first, a dark, tightly-woven intrigue of blood in which the Machiavellian protagonist becomes as corrupt as his opponents. It was very influential on the contemporary theatre.
Eliot, T. S., 'The Revenger's Tragedy' in *Selected Essays*. 1932

Tourville, Anne Hilarion de Colentin, Comte de (1642–1701). French sailor. Having made a name for himself against the Turks and the Algerian pirates, he fought the combined Dutch and Spanish fleets (1677); but his great triumph came (1690) when, commanding the French fleet that was aiding the exiled James II against William III, he won a dramatic victory over the Dutch and English near Beachy Head. For a time he commanded the Channel and anchored in Torbay. However, he suffered complete defeat when convoying the invasion fleet intended to bring back James II, with the loss of sixteen men-of-war in one of the longest naval battles of history (19–24 May 1692). Despite this he was made a marshal of France.

Toussaint l'Ouverture, Pierre Dominique (*c.* 1746–1803). Haitian leader. He was born a slave but managed to acquire enough education to read French works on Caesar's and Alexander's campaigns. The military and diplomatic lessons thus learned he was able to put to good account in the Negro rebellion of 1791 from which he emerged as the most important man in the island. When France, then in the throes of revolution, abolished slavery in her colony (1794) he returned there, held the Spanish and British at bay and made himself governor general for life under a new constitution (1801). He would have liked to come to terms with France but Napoleon Bonaparte, now in control, sent a force against him. Toussaint surrendered (1802) and was taken to France, where he died in prison – partly from the hardships inflicted on him. He was a remarkable man, a firm, just and usually humane ruler, though often sharp-tongued and a natural intriguer.
James, C. L. R., *The Black Jacobins: Toussaint L'Ouverture and the San Domingo Revolution*. 2nd ed. 1963

Tovey, Sir Donald Francis (1875–1940). English musician and musicologist. Reid professor of music at Edinburgh University (1914–40), he was acclaimed for his *Essays in Musical Analysis* (6 volumes 1935–37). He was also a pianist, and composed concertos for cello and piano, chamber music and an opera, *The Bride of Dionysus* (1929). He was knighted in 1935.
Grierson, M., *Donald Francis Tovey*. 1952

Tovey, John Cronyn Tovey, 1st Baron (1885–1971). English sailor. As commander-in-chief of the Home Fleet (1940–43) he directed the pursuit and sinking of the German battleship *Bismarck* (May 1941). He was raised to the peerage in 1946.

Townes, Charles Hard (1915–). American physicist. He won his PhD at the California Institute of Technology, then worked at the Bell Telephone Labs, and held chairs in physics at Columbia (1948–61), MIT (1961–67) and CalTech (1967–). In 1953 he built the first 'maser' (microwave amplification by stimulated emission of radiation) and by 1958 he had worked out the theoretical basis of an 'optical maser', using highly concentrated visible light; this was the 'laser' (light amplification by stimulated emission of radiation'). In 1964 he shared the Nobel Prize for Physics with A. M. * Prokhorov and N. G. Basov for work in quantum mechanics. Masers and lasers are now indispensible scientific, medical and industrial tools.

Townshend, Charles Townshend, 2nd Viscount (known as 'Turnip Townshend') (1674–1738). English diplomat, politician and agriculturist. He became, on George I's accession, secretary of state in the Whig ministry which crushed the Jacobite rebellion of 1715. In 1717 he was briefly lord lieutenant of Ireland, but soon was back in office in London and in 1721 was again secretary of state. His foreign policy, however, gave anxiety to * Walpole, the prime minister, as by its close alliance with France it tended to divide Europe into two potentially hostile leagues. Forced to resign (1730), Townshend spent his retirement studying and improving agricultural methods on his Norfolk estates. His introduction of the Norfolk 4-court crop rotation – wheat, turnips (or other roots), barley, grass and clover – gained him his nickname.

Townshend, Charles (1725–1767). British politician. One of the most brilliant and wayward of 18th-century parliamentarians, he was a thorn in the flesh of any ministry to which he was opposed and equally dangerous to any ministry he joined. He was in most of the Pitt–Newcastle combinations during the Seven Years War, joined and left * Bute, and assailed Grenville over the question of John * Wilkes. His greatest capacity for harm was seen when he became chancellor of the exchequer (1766) in the ministry nominally led by Pitt (by then Earl of Chatham), who was, however, so ill that he could only sporadically exercise authority. Thus able to ignore the known wishes of his leader, Townshend in his anxiety for revenue introduced a bill to tax all tea, glass, paper and several other products entering American ports. This measure precipitated the events which led to the American War of Independence.

Toynbee, Arnold (1852–1883). English economic historian. His great and influential work, *The Industrial Revolution in England* (published posthumously in 1884), was originally composed as a course of lectures at Oxford. Its title popularized the term 'industrial revolution' to describe the social and economic changes that transformed British life in the late 18th and early 19th centuries. He gave vigorous support to adult education and did much social work: Toynbee Hall in Whitechapel, London, was built in his memory.

His nephew, **Arnold Joseph Toynbee** (1889–1975), was a historian, the range and scope of whose work has rivalled that of Gibbon. His *A Study of History* (10 volumes, 1934–54) analyzes the growth and decay of past civilizations and contends that their survival depends on their response to internal and external challenges. He supports his arguments by a mass of illustrative material, fascinating in itself and indicative of the astonishing industry and receptivity of mind with which he has explored the roads and byroads of historical research. Some critics complained that he selects examples that support his argument but neglects those which appear to counter his main thesis.

Traherne, Thomas (1637?–1674). English religious poet. He was educated at Oxford; after some years as a country rector he spent the rest of his life as chaplain to Sir Orlando

Bridgeman, lord keeper of the seal. Most of his work appeared after his death and two books of poems were found and printed in 1903 and 1906. *Centuries of Meditations*, written in musical prose, was printed in 1906 and *Poems of Felicity* in 1910. His *Thanksgiving for the Body* showed that he had not the mystic's usual fear of the senses.
Margoliouth, H. M., ed., *Complete Works of Thomas Traherne*. 1958

Trajan (Marcus Ulpius Trajanus) (*c.* 53–117). Roman emperor (from 98). Born near Seville, he was a distinguished soldier who was consul under Domitian and eventually adopted as heir by the emperor Nerva. As emperor he overcame Dacia (approximately the modern Transylvania) in two campaigns (101–102 and 105–106) and made it a Roman province, but his Parthian conquests (113–117) proved ephemeral. His exploits are carved on the column that bears his name in Rome. He was a wise and moderate ruler, as is shown by his fair-minded letter to Pliny about the treatment of Christians.

Travers, Ben (1886–1980). English playwright. Noted for farce, he wrote originally for the actors Ralph Lynn, Robertson Hare and Tom Walls; *A Cuckoo in the Nest* was first produced in 1925, *Rookery Nook* in 1926, *Thark* in 1927 and *Plunder* in 1928. All have been regularly revived.

Tree, Sir Herbert Beerbohm (1853–1917). English actor-manager. The half-brother of Sir Max Beerbohm, he was lessee-manager of the Haymarket Theatre (1887–97), where he achieved one of his greatest successes, *Trilby* (1897). Profits enabled him to build Her Majesty's Theatre where for twenty years he provided lavish productions of Shakespeare and other plays.
Beerbohm, Sir M., ed., *Herbert Beerbohm Tree, some Memories of Him and his Art*. 1920

Treitschke, Heinrich von (1834–1896). German historian. Born in Saxony, he completed his education in the liberal atmosphere of Leipzig and Bonn Universities, but in the Austro-Prussian War (1866) he completely identified himself with Prussia; when a series of academic appointments had brought him (1874) to Berlin he shared Bismarck's vision of a united, nationalistic Germany under Prussian leadership. This bias permeates his great *History of Germany in the Nineteenth Century* (1915–1919) despite prolonged and accurate research, its literary brilliance, and its excellent chapters on the cultural and social achievements of the lesser states; the book provided an armoury of justification for the Prussian militarists who were planning for World War I. He wrote several other volumes of historical and political essays. His usefulness as a member of the Reichstag (1871–84) was much hampered by deafness.
Housrath, A. T., *Treitschke: his Life and Work*. Eng. ed. 1914

Trenchard, Hugh Montague Trenchard, 1st Viscount (1873–1956). British airman. He was a colonel in the Royal Scots Fusiliers and had fought in South Africa before taking up flying and joining the RFC. In World War I he commanded the British air forces in France and his persistent advocacy brought into being the Independent Air Force and the beginning of strategic bombing. He was chief of the air staff (1918–29) and became (1927) the first marshal of the RAF. The RAF was largely the creation of his strategic insight and organizational planning.
Boyle, A., *Trenchard*. 1962

Trevelyan, Sir George Otto, 2nd Bart. (1838–1928). British politician and historian. His father was an Indian civil servant, his mother, Harriet, a sister of Macaulay. He was a Liberal MP 1865–86 and 1887–97, and a minister. He is better known, however, as a writer, especially for *The Life and Letters of Lord Macaulay* (1876), *The Early History of Charles James Fox* (1880) and *The American Revolution* (1899–1914). He was awarded the O.M. in 1911.

His son, **George Macaulay Trevelyan** (1876–1962), was Regius professor of history at Cambridge (1927–40) and master of Trinity College (1940–51). His works include a remarkable trilogy on the life of Garibaldi (1907–11), *England under Queen Anne* (1930), and *English Social History* (1944), which achieved a great popular success. They rank as highly as works of literature as of history. He became an O.M. in 1930.

Trevithick, Richard (1771–1833). English engineer, born in Cornwall. Largely self-educated, he worked as a mining engineer and invented (1798) a pumping engine driven by water pressure; more important was the high-pressure steam engine (patented in 1802) which he applied to both road and rail transport. For the latter, to win a bet, he used the Penydaren tramway on which he gave several demonstrations. The engine was also used for a dredging machine when he was working on a tunnel under the Thames (1806). He went to Peru (1816) where his engine was introduced in the silver mines and for a time served as a military engineer under * Bolívar. When he returned after eleven years' absence he was almost forgotten, and when he died while working at Dartford he had to be buried at the expense of his fellow workers.

Dickinson, H. W., and Titley, A., *Richard Trevithick: The Engineer and the Man*. 1934

Trevor-Roper, Hugh Redwald, Baron Dacre (1914–). English historian. He studied at Christ Church, Oxford, and taught at the University from 1936, apart from his wartime service with military intelligence, which commissioned him to investigate the circumstances of Hitler's death, published in 1947 as *The Last Days of Hitler*. He wrote comparatively little but his books covered a very wide range and were highly praised, e.g. *The Gentry 1540–1640* (1953), *The Rise of Christian Europe* (1964) and *The Jesuits in Japan* (1968). He was best known as a critic and a devastating analyst of other historians' deficiencies. He became Regius professor of modern history at Oxford 1957–80. Trevor-Roper married a daughter of the 1st Earl * Haig.

Trollope, Anthony (1815–1882). English novelist. He had an unhappy childhood because of the harshness and extravagance of his irresponsible father. He became a clerk in the G.P.O., London (1834); but after a breakdown he was sent as a deputy postal surveyor to Ireland, where hunting, marriage and steady promotion made a new man of him and he began to write. (He is also credited with the invention of the red pillar box.) In 1859 he returned to England and settled at Waltham Abbey which he left (1871) for Montagu Square, London. With a happy domestic life, with his novels and with official journeys (e.g. to Australia, South Africa and America) to provide subjects for travel books, he was content. The more important of his novels fall within two series. The 'Barsetshire' series, which comprises chronologically *The Warden* (1855), *Barchester Towers* (1857), *Doctor Thorne* (1858), *Framley Parsonage* (1861), *The Small House at Allington* (1864) and *The Last Chronicle of Barset* (1867), is mainly concerned with clerical intrigue in the cathedral town of Barchester and reveals to the full his great gift of characterization (e.g. Mrs Proudie, the bishop's vulgar but masterful wife). For the second series, which is political, Trollope gained some first-hand experience when he stood unsuccessfully as parliamentary candidate for Beverley (1868). The books are concerned with the fortunes of Plantagenet Palliser (Duke of Omnium) and his wife Glencora, and once again the interplay of character and motive is enthralling. The best known of this sequence are *Phineas Finn* (1869), *Phineas Redux* (1874) and *The Prime Minister* (1876). Trollope's other novels include *The Claverings* (1867) and *The Eustace Diamonds* (1873).

His autobiography (1883) revealed the almost cold-blooded persistence with which he wrote his daily quota of 2500 words before breakfast; he admitted the strength of the money motive and recorded that by 1879 he made £68,939 17s. 5d from his books. Such methods and motives suggest lack of spontaneity and it is true that his style is at times pedestrian but the characters are so vividly brought to life that interest is sustained. This is proved by the fact that, after a period of neglect, Trollope has won new and prolonged popularity in recent years. He was the most prolific of all major English novelists (even more so than Samuel * Richardson) with 40 books to his credit.

Sadleir, M., *Trollope: A Commentary*. Rev. 1945

Tromp, Maarten Harpertszoon (1597–1653). Dutch sailor. He went to sea as a child and after capture by the English had to serve as a cabin boy for two years. His most famous achievements took place during the long and evenly matched struggle with Cromwell's soldier-admirals Blake and Monk for command of the narrow seas. From encounter to encounter (over a score in all), fortune veered; in May 1652 Blake, with only fifteen ships, had the best of a fight with forty ships under Tromp, but only six months later it was a triumphant Tromp who, according to legend, sailed down the Channel with a broom at his masthead to show that the English had been swept from the seas. Yet in February 1653, a three-day battle in which Tromp showed his

usual courage in defence of a large convoy cost the Dutch nine warships and thirty out of 200 merchantmen. In the last desperate encounter fought off the Dutch coast against the English under Monk, Tromp lost thirty warships and was himself killed.
Oudendijk, J. K., *Maarten Harpertszoon Tromp*. 2nd ed. 1952

Trotsky, Leon (Lev Davidovich Bronstein) (1879–1940). Russian revolutionary politician, of Jewish origin. Expelled from Odessa University for his political activities, he was exiled to Siberia (1900), but escaped abroad to take part in the 1903 congress of the Russian Social Democratic party. In 1905 he returned to Russia to become president of the first Soviet in St Petersburg (Leningrad) but he was again arrested, was once more sent to Siberia and repeated his successful escape. At the outbreak of World War I he went to Paris but, expelled (1916) for pacifist and revolutionary propaganda, eventually reached America. After the Revolution of March 1917 he returned to Russia and after being arrested by the provisional government joined the Bolsheviks and with Lenin organized the November revolution which brought them to power. In successive posts as commissar for foreign affairs and for war, he negotiated the Treaty of Brest-Litovsk (1918) with Germany and virtually created the Red Army. His policy of 'permanent revolution', based on the contention that Bolshevism could not survive in Russia unless revolutions were stirred up in the west, was not, however, accepted by the majority of the party and when Lenin died (1924) it was Stalin who took his place. Trotsky headed various opposition factions but was expelled from the party (1927) and was ordered to leave Russia (1929). From Turkey he travelled widely and at the same time built up dissident communist groups, some of which long survived his death. In the official Communist party 'Trotskyite' became a term of abuse applied to anyone whose loyalty to party decisions was in doubt. In 1937 Trotsky settled in Mexico. In August 1940 he was murdered with an ice-axe by Ramon Mercader, alias Jacques Mornand, alias Frank Jacson (1914–60?), a Spaniard whose mother was the mistress of a NKVD general. Released from jail in 1960, he flew to Prague and disappeared. Trotsky was a brilliant and prolific writer whose works include *The History of the Russian Revolution* (3 volumes, 1932–34) and *The Revolution Betrayed* (1937).
Howe, I., (ed.) *The Basic Writings of Trotsky*. 1963

Trudeau, Edward Livingston (1848–1915). American physician. As a sufferer from pulmonary tuberculosis he derived much benefit from the air of the Adirondacks and in consequence established there (1884) the Trudeau Sanatorium. He was the first in the U.S.A. to isolate and study the tubercle bacillus.

Trudeau, Pierre Elliott (1919–). Canadian politician and lawyer. Called to the bar in 1943, he was associate professor of law at the University of Montreal, 1961, and became a member of the House of Commons in 1965. He was parliamentary secretary to the prime minister 1966–67 and Attorney General 1967–68. He was elected leader of the Liberal party in 1968 and held office as prime minister 1968–79 and again 1980–84. One of his main preoccupations was to satisfy the aspirations of French-speaking Canada without destroying the federal system.
Trudeau, P. E., *Federalism and the French Canadians*. 1968

Truffaut, François (1932–1984). French film director, critic and publisher of *Cahiers du Cinéma* from 1954. He worked as an assistant director to Roberto Rossellini in 1956 and directed his own films from 1957. His study of childhood, *Les Quatre-cent Coups* won first prize at the Cannes Film Festival in 1959; he was thereafter recognised as the leader of the French 'New Wave' of realist cinema, which deliberately dispensed with accepted formulae in the structure of film stories.
Crisp, C. G., *François Truffaut*. 1972; Truffaut, F., *Les films de ma Vie*. 1975

Trujillo Molina, Rafael Leonidas (1891–1961). Dominican dictator. He graduated from the military academy in 1921; by 1928 he had risen to be chief of staff and in 1930 he became president. For the next thirty years, whether as president himself or acting through a nominee, he maintained dictatorial rule. While enriching his own family he pursued a conciliatory policy towards the U.S.A., and provided a firm administration which brought social and economic benefits. Within six months of his assassination the last of the

Trujillo clan had left the country. From 1936 to 1961 Santo Domingo, the capital, was known as Ciudad Trujillo.

Truman, Harry S. (1884–1972). 33rd president of the US (1945–53). The initial 'S' represents the names of his grandfathers but has no other significance. He was born on a Missouri farm. Despite bad eyesight which prevented his entry into West Point Military Academy, he served in World War I. After the war he was handicapped by the failure of a business venture in Kansas; he insisted on paying the creditors in full, an effort which took fifteen years. He studied law but did not qualify as a lawyer and entered politics as a Democrat; he presided (1926–34) over an administrative court in Jackson County for controlling expenditure on construction. As US senator (1935–45) he became well known through his chairmanship (1941–44) of the Committee for Investigation of the Defence Program. Elected vice-president in 1944, he succeeded to the presidency on Franklin Roosevelt's death (1945). He was responsible for dropping of the atomic bombs on Japan, news of which came when he was attending the Allied conference at Potsdam called to solve the problems of Germany's defeat. Despite predictions to the contrary he won a comfortable victory in the 1948 presidential election after a marathon electoral campaign. He took the decision that initiated the Korean War (1950) and showed great courage in dismissing General * Mac Arthur for his political interventions. His policy towards the communist powers was one of containment, to which end he encouraged the formation of NATO and signed the treaty (1949) which set it up. To counter Soviet influence and expansion in Europe he devised a policy of economic and military aid (the 'Truman Doctrine'). His home policy, aimed to promote racial harmony and help the under-privileged, was summarized by the term 'Fair Deal'. He declined to stand for re-election in 1952.
Phillips, C., *The Truman Presidency*. 1966; Truman, M., *Harry Truman*. 1973

Trumper, Victor Thomas (1877–1915). Australian cricketer. His batting achievements included 3,163 runs in test cricket, of which 2,263 were made against England. His greatest performance was 300 not out made in 1899 against Sussex at Hove.

Tshombe, Moïse Kapenda (1919–1969). Congolese politician. After the Belgian Congo had become an independent republic (1960) he declared the independence of Katanga, the copper-producing province of which he was president. United Nations troops were sent against him on the invitation of the Congo prime minister, Patrice * Lumumba, for whose mysterious death (1961) Tshombe was alleged by his enemies to have some responsibility. In 1963 having lost health and power he went into exile but in 1964 after a change of political climate he was recalled to be prime minister by President Kasavubu. In 1965 both president and prime minister had to give way to the military leader General * Mobutu. After fleeing abroad he was kidnapped and flown to Algiers (1967) where he died.

Tsiolkovsky, Konstantin Eduardovich (1857–1935). Russian physicist. Originally a schoolteacher (hampered by extreme deafness), he carried out fundamental research into aeronautics, constructed the first 'wind-tunnel' and by 1895 was writing about space travel. From 1898 he was predicting (with a high degree of accuracy) future space exploration in rockets using liquid fuel. The launching of Sputnik I (1957) was timed to coincide with his centenary.

Tswett, Mikhail Semenovich (1872–1919). Russian chemist and botanist. Inventor of the important chemical technique known as chromatography, he showed (1906) that plant pigments dissolved in petrol could be separated by means of their differential rates of absorption by powdered calcium carbonate in a vertical glass tube. This method of analysis has since been widely developed.

Tubman, William Vachanarat Shadrach (1895–1971). Liberian politician. A lawyer, judge and leader of the 'True Whig' party, he was elected president in 1944 and re-elected six times, dying in office. He attempted social, economic and educational reforms.

Tudor. Dynastic family of Welsh origin which ruled England from the accession of Henry VII (1485) to the death of Queen Elizabeth (1603). Its links with the English royal line were first forged by the marriage of Owen Tudor to Henry V's widow, Catherine of France. Henry VII's claim to the throne rested, however, upon the marriage of his father Edmund Tudor, son of Owen, to Margaret Beaufort, grand-daughter of John Beaufort, one of the legitimized children of * John of Gaunt and Catherine * Swynford.

Tukhachevsky, Mikhail Nikolaievich (1893–1937). Russian soldier. Of noble origin, he joined the army in 1911 and was a prisoner-of-war 1915–18. He supported the Bolsheviks in 1918, commanding the Red Army in the Caucasus during the civil war, and becoming chief of staff 1925–28 and deputy commissar of defence 1931–37. He was accused of treason and shot on the basis of evidence by the NKVD and the Gestapo. * Khrushchev rehabilitated him in 1958.

Tull, Jethro (1674–1741). English agriculturist. He was called to the bar (1699) but as a result of the enclosure system, which by bringing large acreages under direct control of landlords encouraged more scientific agriculture, he turned to farming. A prolonged tour of Europe enlarged his knowledge, among the things learnt being the value of the cultivator in aerating the soil and allowing access of water. His practices were explained in *Horse-hoeing Husbandry* (1733). He invented a seed-drill (1701), and his advocacy of planting cereals and turnips in rows instead of by broadcasting the seed was of the greatest importance in improving yields.

Tunney, James Joseph (known as 'Gene') (1898–1978). American boxer. By defeating Jack Dempsey, he became world heavyweight champion (1926) and retired undefeated (1928).

Tupolev, Andrey Nicoloyevich (1888–1972). Russian aeronautical engineer. Educated at the Moscow Higher Technical School, in 1922 he became director of the Central Aero-hydrodynamic Institute. He fell into disfavour with the authorities in 1938 but was reinstated in 1943. He was responsible for over 100 aircraft both civilian and military; the Tu-104 (1955) was the first jet transport to provide a regular commercial service for passengers.

Tupper, Martin Farquhar (1810–1889). English writer and inventor. Trained as a barrister, he emerged as a literary phenomenon whose extraordinary success – especially with his *Proverbial Philosophy* (1838–67), a book of trite sayings in rhythmical form – throws much light on the taste of his time. He wrote some forty books in all and also turned his ingenious mind to such inventions as safety horsehoes and glass screw-tops, which did not, however, meet with the same success.

Tupper, M. F., *My Life as Author*. 1886

Turenne, Henri de la Tour d'Auvergne, Vicomte de (1611–1675). French soldier. A grandson of * William the Silent (Prince of Orange), after his father's death he was brought up in Holland as a Protestant. He returned to France in 1630 and soon showed his military abilities during the Thirty Years War. In 1641 he was given the supreme command and in 1643 was rewarded for his conquest of Roussillon from the Spanish by being made a marshal of France. He ended the Thirty Years War with triumphant campaigns in Bavaria and Flanders. In the civil wars that ensued he at first joined the Fronde but later was reconciled with the regency government led by * Mazarin, and thus found himself opposed to his great military rival * Condé. From a period of confused fighting Turenne emerged victorious, while Condé, a declared traitor, crossed the frontier and took service with Spain. The contest between the two men continued with Condé leading the Spanish army, Turenne the French, and was only finally settled when Turenne, after overrunning much of the Spanish Netherlands, finally, with the help of a force of Cromwell's Ironsides, defeated Condé at the Battle of the Dunes (1658), which led to the surrender of Dunkirk. Peace followed (1659) and when hostilities were resumed (1667) Condé had been pardoned and taken into favour by Louis XIV. In 1668 Turenne turned Catholic. In the war (1672) with Holland, soon joined by the emperor Leopold and other allies, the two great commanders campaigned in concert. In the winter of 1674–75 Turenne fought his last and most brilliant campaign in Alsace but in the spring, while reconnoitring the imperialist position near the defile of Sassbach, he was struck by a cannon ball and killed.

Weygand, M., *Turenne: Marshal of France*. 1930

Turgenev, Ivan Sergeyevich (1818–1883). Russian novelist. He was brought up on the family estate in Oryol province but quarrelled with his masterful and neurotic mother about her treatment of the serfs. After a university education and a short time in the civil service he achieved his first popular success as a writer with *A Sportsman's Sketches* (1847–52), a series of delightful rural sketches. In 1843 he fell in love with Pauline Viardot, a famous singer then visiting Russia. She was married but, moved by a hopeless but enduring passion, he followed her around from place to place in Germany and France; he even maintained a friendship with her husband and collaborated with him in the French translations of his works, sometimes even sharing their home. This barren love affair may explain why so many of the men in Turgenev's books are such emotional weaklings. Turgenev was on bad terms with Dostoyevsky, Tolstoy and other Russian contemporaries; after 1856 he spent much time in Paris, where he was a friend of Flaubert, Zola, Daudet and the Goncourt brothers. He died near Paris.

His most important novels, among which are *A Nest of Gentlefolk* (1859), *Fathers and Sons* (1862), a story of political conflicts between the generations, and *Virgin Soil* (1876), belong to a series referring to social and historical developments in Russia between 1830 and 1870, which were criticized both by the progressives and the reactionaries although much admired outside Russia. Of equal or greater fascination are the short stories – love stories, tales of the countryside and of the supernatural. Here the fastidious elegance of his style can be appreciated at its best.

Schapiro, L., *Turgenev: His Life and Times*. 1978

Turgot, Anne Robert Jacques (1727–1781). French economist and administrator. Having abondoned the idea of a church career, he lived in Paris in the midst of the great intellectual ferment of which * Diderot's great *Encylopédie* was the symbol. Turgot's interests were mainly economic and in his writings on the subject, especially in his advocacy of freer trade, he anticipated the work of Adam * Smith. As intendant of Limoges (1761–64) he was able to put theory into practice; by substituting a money tax for the *corvée* (the compulsory road-labour of peasants dating from feudal times) he greatly improved communications; and by establishing free trade in corn, by stimulating the porcelain industry and encouraging new ones he transformed the Limousin from one of the poorest into one of the richest regions of France.

On the accession (1774) of Louis XVI he was called upon to do for the country what he had done for the region. As controller general with the watchwords 'no bankruptcies, no tax increase, no loans', he began by making stringent economies, including the suppression of some 32,000 government posts. The measures which followed – abolition of the *corvée*, free trade in corn (followed by bread riots), and a minor land tax on nobles and clergy etc. – produced such a selfish outcry from those adversely affected and the privileged classes in general that Louis lost his nerve and in 1776 Turgot had to resign. His delcared conviction that the alternative to far reaching reforms was revolution was soon borne out.

Tunkin, D., *Turgot and the Ancien Régime in France*. 1939

Turing, Alan Mathison (1912–1954). English computer scientist. Educated at King's College, Cambridge and Princeton, he published a paper 'On Computable Numbers . . .' (1936) which proposed a formal theory of how a universal computer would work, embodying the logic of all future computing machines. During World War II, he worked for the British Code and Cypher Unit and helped to build a large cryptographic decipherer called 'Colossus' (1943). He was reader in mathematics at Manchester University 1945–49 and worked on two computer projects. Elected FRS in 1951, he died by suicide after conviction for a homosexual offence.

Hodges, A., *Alan Turing: the enigma*. 1983

Turner, John Napier (1929–). Canadian politician and lawyer. Educated at the University of British Columbia, he was a Rhodes Scholar at Oxford, became a lawyer in Montreal and a Liberal MP 1962–75, serving as attorney-general 1968–72 and minister for finance 1972–75. In 1975 he resigned over policy differences with Pierre * Trudeau, became active in business, and was nominated to succeed him as party leader and prime minister of Canada June 1984; in September he was overwhelmingly defeated at the polls.

Turner, Joseph Mallord William (1775–1851). English painter. He was born in London where his father kept a barber's shop in Maiden Lane, Covent Garden. He was sent to the free school Brentford and in 1789 gained entrance to the Royal Academy school.

His first money was made by selling sketches in his father's shop and colouring engravings. With his savings he made sketching tours and also worked with Girtin, whose style in water-colours influenced him greatly. His first Academy exhibit was shown in 1791. His early oil paintings were influenced by Richard Wilson and Claude Lorrain but after going to the continent (1802) he came to admire Titian and Poussin. In the same year he was elected R.A., having been A.R.A. since 1799. By about 1810 he had fully developed the technique which made him famous, showing the subject of his picture, whether a natural phenomenon, mythological figures, or – in accordance with the romantic vogue of the time – an ancient building, through cascades and explosions of light and colour. The technique was more suited to water-colour than to oils, but he was successful in both. He painted sometimes direct from nature but usually in the studio, where an astonishing visual memory enabled him to reproduce almost exactly the original scene. Series such as those done for *Rivers of England* (1824), and a later one *Rivers of France*, were especially suited to his gifts. Of his more ambitious pictures *Ulysses Deriding Polyphemus* from his earlier period and *The Fighting Temeraire*, one of his later works, are among the best known. Despite prolonged attacks by the leading art critics of the time Turner was supported by the Royal Academy and, to his surprise, by John Ruskin and above all by Lord Egremont of Petworth, with whom Turner often stayed and where some of the best of his pictures are still exhibited. In his old age Turner lived as a recluse in Chelsea under an assumed name and there died. He left £140,000, more than 300 oils, 20,000 water colours and 19,000 drawings to the nation. Until the 20th century his works were more admired in Europe than in Britain.

Wilton, A., *The Life and Work of J. M. W. Turner*. 1979

Turpin, Dick (1706–1739). English criminal. Romanticized in Ainsworth's novel *Rookwood* (1834), he was in fact a brutal thief engaged in smuggling, housebreaking and highway robbery. He was hanged at York. The legend of his ride on 'Black Bess' seems to have been adapted from the story of 'Swift John Nevison', who is said to have established an alibi for a murder at Gadshill at 4 a.m. by arriving at 7.45 p.m. on the same day at York (1676).

Tussaud, Marie (née Grosholtz) (1760–1850). Swiss founder of the waxworks that bear her name. She learned modelling in Paris from her uncle, J. C. Curtius, whose wax museums she inherited (1793). She prepared death masks from heads severed by the guillotine. Having separated (1800) from her soldier husband she established her exhibition in London, first at the Lyceum Theatre and then (1835) in Baker Street. The move to Marylebone Road was made in 1884 after her death.

Tutankhamen (Tut-ankh-amen) (died *c.* 1340 B.C.). King of Egypt. He was son-in-law and successor of * Akhnaton, who had tried to impose a sort of monotheism with Amon as the one god. Popular and priestly opposition had rent the kingdom and under the young Pharaoh the country reverted to its former pantheon, with Amon as its presiding deity. As he was only 18 when he died after a reign of six years he had little opportunity to show his qualities. His tomb was found undisturbed by Lord Carnarvon and Howard Carter (1922). Its magnificent treasures are now displayed in the Cairo Museum.

Desroches-Noblecourt, C., *Tutankhamen*. 1963

Tutu, Desmond (1931–). South African bishop. Educated in England, he became a priest, then bishop (1976) of the Anglican church in South Africa and general secretary of the South African Council of Churches 1978– . He received the 1984 Nobel Prize for Peace.

Twain, Mark (pseudonym of Samuel Langhorne Clemens) (1835–1910). American author and humorist. His father was a Virginia lawyer who had moved west to seek a fortune by land speculation but died poor (1847). The boy, who had a casual upbringing in Hannibal, Missouri, where the river provided many scenes for his later books, became a journeyman printer. After some years of wandering he visited New Orleans and became a pilot on the Mississippi (1857–61). His later pseudonym was derived from the leadsman's cry indicating that the water was two fathoms deep. The Civil War ended this chapter; he joined his brother in Nevada to prospect for gold. But soon his early humorous writings began to appear. He was encouraged by Artemus * Ward and in his writings for the San Francisco papers by Bret * Harte. A

commission to visit and write about the Sandwich Islands was followed by a lecture tour in the east which proved a great success. A Mediterranean tour resulting in *Innocents Abroad* (1869) established his fame. Having married Olivia Langdon of New York State (1870) he settled down as editor of the Buffalo *Express* but was fortunately encouraged by friends to draw on his boyhood memories of life on the great rivers for *Tom Sawyer* (1876) and his masterpiece *Huckleberry Finn* (1884). In later life, as well as having to submit to much ceremonial and hero worship he dissipated his energies in foreign travel – *A Tramp Abroad* (1880) records a European walking tour – and business ventures which sometimes involved heavy losses. Meanwhile, and partly to recoup himself, he continued to write with industry and versatility. The burlesque *A Connecticut Yankee in King Arthur's Court* (1889) is sometimes very funny; *Personal Recollections of Joan of Arc* (1896) reveals a long-felt devotion to this historic heroine; others, e.g. *The Stolen White Elephant*, show his satirical gifts, but he will always be best remembered by the books which owe their inspiration, vigour and freshness to the river lands of his childhood.
Kaplan, J., *Mister Clemens and Mark Twain*. 1966

Tweedsmuir, 1st Baron *see* **Buchan, John**

Tyler, John (1790–1862). 10th president of the US (1841–45). Son of a governor of Virginia, he became a lawyer, governor and US Senator. Supporting States' rights he joined the new Whig party formed by president Jackson's opponents. In 1841 he became vice-president to W. H. Harrison, on whose death, a month after inauguration, he succeeded as president. His term of office was rendered largely ineffective by the party split created by the conflict between the national policies of Henry * Clay and the belief in States' rights favoured by the president. It was marked, however, by the annexation of Texas (1844), and the Webster-Ashburton Treaty (1843) by which difficulties with Great Britain were smoothed.

Tyler, Wat (or Walter) (died 1381). English rebel and popular leader. In the peasants' Revolt (1381) he led the Kentishmen, who with the men of Essex converged on London to present their demands of which the main one was the abolition of serfdom and the crippling poll-tax. Three days and nights of burning and looting had already occurred when, at a conference with * Richard II at Smithfield, Tyler, who was acting as spokesman, was struck down by Lord Mayor Walworth. He was killed in the subsequent scuffle; only Richard's courage in taking over the leadership of the peasants saved the situation. The gesture was a token one, however, and few of the rebels' grievances were met or their hardships lightened.

Tylor, Sir Edward Burnet (1832–1917). English anthropologist, professor of anthropology at Oxford (1896–1909). A journey through Mexico with the ethnologist Henry Christy, described in *Anahuac*, or *Mexico and the Mexicans* (1861), gained him a considerable reputation as an anthropologist. His later books included *Primitive Culture* (2 volumes, 1871), which quickly became a standard work, and an excellent introduction to the subject, *Anthropology* (1881).
Marrett, R. R., *Tylor*. 1936

Tyndale, William (*c.* 1494–1536). English Biblical translator. He graduated at Oxford, and later at Cambridge came under the influence of humanists such as Erasmus (one of whose works he translated) and the religious reformers. Having set his heart on Biblical translation but having failed to get patronage in London he went (1524) to Hamburg, to Wittenberg (where he met Luther) and to Cologne. Here he began printing his New Testament but, forbidden to proceed, fled to Worms. Of the edition there printed (1526) and smuggled into England, almost all copies were destroyed. His later works were published at Antwerp; they included translations of the Pentateuch (1530), Jonah (1531) and New Testament revisions. The section Joshua–II Chronicles was left in manuscript. Both in his marginal notes to the Biblical books and his many theological works he revealed his Lutheran doctrines and attacked papal supremacy. He lived secure at Antwerp, however, in the privileged house of the English merchants, until in May 1535 he was lured out on a pretext (by an English Roman Catholic) and after sixteen months' imprisonment in the state prison of the Low Countries was condemned for heresy and burned at the stake. His superb use of the words and rhythms of the English language is enshrined in the

Authorized Version of the Bible, of which his translations formed the basis.
Mozley, J. F., *Life of William Tyndale*. 1937

Tyndall, John (1820–1893). Irish-born physicist. After studying in Germany and a prolonged study of diamagnetism, he became (1853) professor of natural philosophy at the Royal Institution in London, where he later succeeded (1867) as superintendent * Faraday, whose biography he wrote. Interest in glaciers and meteorology turned him into a mountaineer: he was among the first to climb the Matterhorn, and made a first ascent of the Weisshorn (1861). His other researches concerned heat, sound (lighthouse sirens) and light (the 'Tyndall effect', the imitation of the blue of the sky by passing a beam of light through a cloud of very fine particles).

Tyson, Edward (1650–1708). English anatomist. Best known for his *Orang-Outang* of 1699, this described the anatomy of a primate (actually a chimpanzee) brought back from Malaya. Tyson saw the specimen as half way between a man and an ape, a link on the Great Chain of Being. Throughout the eighteenth century, there continued to be fierce debate as to whether such higher primates were really forms of men, or of monkey, and whether man gradually shaded into the primates, or whether there was a sharp distinction.
Ashley Montague, F. M., *Edward Tyson*. 1943

Tz'u Hsi (Tsu-Hsi) (1835–1908). Dowager empress of China. Daughter of an army officer, her personal name was Yehonala. A striking beauty who became the concubine of the weak and dissolute emperor Hsein Feng, she achieved personal domination over him, bore his only son, Tung Chih (1856) and became regent when he succeeded at the age of five. She was probably responsible for the death of Tung and his wife (1875). She gained a new term of regency by placing her sister's 4-year old son Kuang-hsu on the throne. When he came of age (1889), however, he joined the westernizing reformers; but the empress rallied the reactionaries, regained power, interned the emperor and continued to act in his name. Despite the dynastic difficulties Tz'u-hsi maintained authority at home and with considerable diplomatic skill had prevented further foreign encroachments, but the Chinese defeat in the Japanese War of 1894 and the still more disastrous effects of the reprisals for the anti-foreign Boxer Rebellion of 1904 (secretly encouraged by the empress) left the Manchu dynasty thoroughly discredited; when 'Old Buddha' finally died and only a 2-year-old child (* Pu'yi', or Hsuan T'ung) was left to succeed, the revolution was in sight. She liked to be designated 'Motherly Auspicious Orthodox Heaven-Blest Prosperous All Nourishing Brightly-Manifest Calm Sedate Perfect Long-Lived Respectful Reverend Worshipful Illustrious Exalted Empress Dowager'.

U

Uccello, Paolo (*c.* 1400–1475). Florentine painter. He worked as a boy in Ghiberti's studio, and was later in Venice and Padua as well as Florence. In most of his paintings he is preoccupied with problems of perspective which he worked out by mathematical means. This is evident in the well-known fresco *The Deluge* done for S. Maria Novella in Florence. He won contemporary fame for three panels of the *Battle of San Romano*, painted for the Medici palace in Florence, but now dispersed. He was one of the first to draw plants and birds from nature, a sign of the spirit of innovation that marked the Early Renaissance.
Pope-Hennessy, J., *Paolo Uccello*. 2nd ed. 1969

Udall, Nicholas (1505–1556). English playwright and scholar. He was headmaster of Eton from 1534 until dismissed and imprisoned for misconduct (1541). He translated a number of classical and scholarly works but is remembered as the author of the earliest extant English comedy, *Ralph Roister Doister* (*c.* 1553), inspired by Plautus and Terene and written in doggerel verse.

Ulanova, Galina Sergeyevna (1912–). Russian ballerina. She held an incomparable reputation in her own country, fully confirmed when she led the Bolshoi Ballet Company in London in 1956. On retirement from star dancing roles (1963) she became ballet mistress at the Bolshoi Theatre.

Ulbricht, Walter (1893–1973). German politician. He joined the Communist party in 1919 and was a member of the Reichstag 1928–33. In the latter year he went to Moscow; after the collapse of Germany in World War II he reappeared in Berlin and was Russia's principal agent in East Germany. In 1946 he became first secretary of the Socialist Unity party formed by the merger of the Communists and Social Democrats. On the formation (1949) of the German Democratic Republic (East Germany) Ulbricht was one of the three deputy premiers, but was in fact virtual ruler of the country. This was publicly acknowledged in 1960 when the presidency was abolished on the death of Wilhelm Pieck and Ulbricht became chairman of the Council of State. He retired in 1971.
Keller, J. W., *Germany: The Wall and Berlin*. 1964

Umberto I (also known as Humbert I) (1844–1900). King of Italy (from 1878). He was the son and successor of * Victor Emmanuel II. The events of his reign included the war with Ethiopia which ended with the disastrous Italian defeat at Adowa (1896). The king himself was widely popular and there was deep distress when, having escaped several earlier attempts on his life, he was assassinated at Monza by a foreign anarchist.

Umberto II (1904–1983). King of Italy (1946). The son of* Victor Emmanuel III and grandson of * Umberto I, he was briefly king after his father's abdication in May 1946, but in a referendum held a month later a majority voted in favour of a republic. Umberto left Italy 'temporarily' but in 1947 a ban was placed on his return or that of his descendants. He married (1930) Princess Marie José, a sister of King Leopold III of the Belgians.

Unamuno y Jugo, Miguel de (1864–1936). Spanish philosopher and writer. In 1892 he became professor of Greek at Salamanca University, where he was afterwards rector and spent most of his later life. In the sense that he tilted against dogmatism and hypocrisy he was a modern Don Quixote, the hero or anti-hero whom he came to regard as the symbol of the nobility and tragedy of man (see *Life of Don Quixote and Sancho*, 1927). Yet even such a generalization was alien to him; he propounded no general system, and was above all an analyst and critic. His longing for eternal life and his realization that reason and scientific thought stand as bars to the acceptance of immortality are the theme and substance of *The Tragic Sense of Life* (1913) and other of his numerous poems, essays and novels. His passionate love of Spain was shown not only in his books but in his political opinions and acts. He became known outside Spain for his opposition to the dictator * Primo de Rivera and the monarchy. He returned triumphantly from exile when the republic was formed but was soon as disillusioned with the new régime as with the old, though he strongly protested against foreign intervention in the Civil War.

Undset, Sigrid (1882–1949). Norwegian novelist. She was the daughter of a well-known antiquary who inspired her fascination with medieval Norway, the setting of several of her best novels culminating with *Kristin Lavransdatter* (3 volumes, 1920–22) and *Olav Audunssön* (1925–27), for which she was awarded the Nobel Prize for Literature (1928). Treating the characters and themes with modern realism she brought a remarkable sense of conviction to her picture of life in 14th-century Norway. Of her many contemporary novels, the tragedy *Jenny* (1911) is among the best known.

Updike, John Hoyer (1932–). American novelist, born in Pennsylvania. Educated at Harvard and Oxford, he was a staff writer (1955–57) on the *New Yorker*, which published many of his poems, short stories and essays. His novels, witty and inventive, explore human tensions arising from conflicts of flesh v. spirit, freedom v. responsibility, in a rapidly changing world of family life in the United States. His novels include *Rabbit, Run* (1960), *The Centaur* (1963), *Couples* (1968), *Bech: A Book* (1970), *Rabbit Redux* (1971), *A Month of Sundays* (1975), *Marry Me* (1976) and *The Coup* (1979). He won a Pulitzer Prize for *Rabbit is Rich* (1981).

Urban II (Odo) (1042?–1099). Pope (from 1088). In 1095 he proclaimed the 1st Crusade at the Council of Clermont. He followed this up with letters, sermons and exhortations, the result being the capture of Jerusalem (1099) and the establishment there of a feudal kingdom.

Urban VI (Bartholomeus Prignanus) (1318–1389). Pope (from 1378). In the same year that he was elected the College of Cardinals, claiming that they had chosen Urban under pressure from the Roman mob, chose Clement VII. The latter went to Avignon, where he was recognized by France and her political associates, while Urban remained at Rome. So started the Great Schism (1378–1417), with two rival popes competing for the allegiance of Christendom.

Urban VIII (Maffeo Barberini) (1568–1644). Pope (from 1623). As papal envoy to France he showed his diplomatic ability, and he was created cardinal in 1606. As pope he was led by fear of the Habsburgs to support * Richelieu and the German Protestants in the Thirty Years War. He befriended writers and scholars, and sanctioned only reluctantly the proceedings against * Galileo. The Barberini, the Florentine merchant family to which he belonged, rose to princely prominence with his support.

Urey, Harold Clayton (1893–1981). American chemist. Professor of chemistry at the University of Columbia (1934–45) and at Chicago (from 1945), he discovered (1931) deuterium, the heavy isotope of hydrogen, and this led almost at once to the commercial production of heavy water. He subsequently worked out methods for separating the heavy isotopes of carbon, oxygen, nitrogen and sulphur. As a recognized authority on the separation of isotopes, he took a large part in the research leading to the production of the atomic bomb. He won the Nobel Prize for Chemistry (1934).

Usher (or Ussher), **James** (1581–1656). Irish prelate and scholar, famous for his calculations of biblical chronology: he arrived at the long accepted date of 4004 B.C. for the Creation. He was ordained in 1601, and appointed professor of divinity in Dublin (1604), bishop of

Meath (1621) and archbishop of Armagh (1625).
Ball Wright, W., *The Ussher Memoirs*. 1889

Uspensky, Gleb Ivanovitch (1840–1902). Russian novelist. His themes are generally concerned with the impact of industrialisation on peasant life, treated realistically, as in *The Power of the Soil* (1887). Depressed by social conditions, he committed suicide.

Ustinov, Peter Alexander (1921–). English actor, producer and playwright of Russian descent. He first appeared on the stage in 1938 and soon became well known for his versatility and skill in a wide variety of roles both on the stage and in films. Among his plays two of the most successful were *The Love of Four Colonels* (1951) and *Romanoff and Juliet* (1959).
Ustinov, P. A., *Dear Me*. 1978

Utamaro Kitigawa (1753–1806). Japanese graphic artist. He was the first great artist of the *ukiyo-e* ('floating world') school, whose works illustrated everyday scenes in Japanese towns. His prints appeared in book form, e.g. *Insects, Types of Love* and *Book of Birds and Flowers*. His striking use of colour, especially red and gold, and his sensuous portraits of women were much admired by European collectors. He was followed by * Hokusai and * Hiroshige.

Utrillo, Maurice (1883–1955). French painter. He was the adopted son of Miguel Utrillo, a Spaniard; his mother, the French painter Suzanne Valadon, encouraged him to take up art, partly to combat the alcoholism of which he was a victim at an early age. The pictures which won him fame in the 1920s were much influenced in their colouring by the Impressionists, notably Pissarro, but his freshness of vision resulted from an almost naïve affection for his subjects, mostly the narrow streets of Montmartre and little French towns near Paris. Success and his way of life soon dimmed his powers and many of his later pictures display an exaggerated style almost like caricature. Collectors have been embarrassed by the frequent forgery of his works.
George, W., *Utrillo*. 1960

Utzon, Joern (1918–). Danish architect. A pupil of Alvar * Aalto, he won (1956) an international competition for designing the Sydney Opera House. Construction began in 1957. The external sail configuration was completed in 1967 (after a tenfold escalation in cost) and the opera house complex opened in 1973.

V

Valdivia, Pedro de (*c.* 1500–1559). Spanish *conquistador*. After taking part in the conquest of Venezuela and Peru, he was sent by * Pizzaro against Chile. At the head of 175 Spaniards and some Indians he set out in 1540, crossed the desert without loss and founded Santiago. Almost immediately the Indians rose in rebellion and the Spaniards had not only to defend themselves but to grow food to live on. When rescued two years later they were in pitiable plight but Valdivia carried on and then, with his appointment as governor of Chile confirmed, proceeded to the conquest of the south; soon after founding Concepcion, Valdivia and other towns, he was defeated and killed by the local Indians.
Prescott, W. H., *The Conquest of Peru*. 1847

Valens *see* **Valentinian and Valens**

Valentinian (321–375) and **Valens** (328–378). Roman emperors (from 364). After the death of Jovian, Valentinian, acclaimed by the troops, made his younger brother Valens co-emperor with responsibility for the Eastern provinces. Meanwhile Valentinian, having reorganized the administration, ruled with savage justice in the west, kept the German Alemanni at bay, restored Roman supremacy in Britain and Africa, and was campaigning in Hungary when he died from a burst blood vessel.

In the lower Danube, pressure from the Huns in their rear had caused the Goths to seek safety within the imperial territories. Weak and indecisive, Valens hesitated whether to welcome them as allies or resist them as foes. Eventually he turned against them and near Adrianople, in one of the most decisive battles of Roman history (378), was defeated and killed.

Valentino, Rudolf (Rudolfo Guglielmi di Valentia Antognollo) (1895–1926). Italian film actor. He went to the U.S.A. in 1913 and in such films as *The Sheik* and *Blood and Sand* became the romantic ideal of girls of the 1920s. He died at the height of his popularity and his funeral was the occasion for the display of mass grief and adoration. He wrote a book of poetry, *Daydreams*, in 1923.
Brownlow, K., and Kobal, J., *Hollywood – the Pioneers*. 1979

Valera, Eamon de *see* **De Valera, Eamon**

Valéry, Paul Ambroise (1871–1945). French writer, son of a Corsican father and Italian mother. He settled in Paris (1892) and wrote graceful pictorial poems which show the influence of his friend * Mallarmé. For nearly twenty years from 1898 he published no poems but devoted himself to mathematical and philosophic studies. When he resumed writing poetry it was in an entirely new style. *La jeune parque* (1917) is a harmonious but difficult poem dealing with feminine 'consciousness' in symbolic and philosophic terms. Valéry's prose works include *Soirée avec M. Teste* (1896), an analytical self-study of the inner workings of a human mind, and many essays on aesthetic themes, e.g. *Eupalinos* and *L'Âme et la danse* (both 1924). Valéry was elected to the Académie Française in 1925; in later life his lectures at the Collège de France became well known. He was working on a version of *Faust* when he died. He was buried at his native Sète (Cette), west of Marseilles.
Mackay, A. E., *The Universal Self: A Study of Paul Valéry*. 1961

Valla, Lorenzo (1406/7–1457). Italian humanist scholar. He was born and studied in Rome, but spent some years moving from university to university before settling in Naples under the protection of Alfonso V. A defence of Epicurus, in which he maintained that satisfaction of the appetites was the chief good, provided a warning of controversy to come. He went on to prove that a document 'discovered' in 1440 and purporting to be a transfer of the temporal power of the emperor to the papacy was a recent forgery. By similar critical methods – which became the basis of later historical research – he refuted the contention that the Apostles' Creed was in fact the joint work of the Apostles. Saved from the Inquisition by his protector Alfonso, he became (1447) secretary to the humanist pope Nicholas V.

Valois. The dynasty which ruled France from the accession of Philip VI (1328) to the death of Henry III (1589). The county of Valois was bestowed (1285) by Philip III on his third son Charles, who founded the family, which was thus a junior branch of the Capetian line. When the main dynastic line failed under the miscalled Salic Law by which the succession could not pass to or through females, the crown passed to the house of Valois.

Van Allen, James Alfred (1914–). American physicist. Professor of physics at Iowa State University from 1951, he was a pioneer of space research with rockets and artificial satellites, and investigated cosmic rays. He discovered (1960), from the results of the first communications satellite (*Echo I*) sent up by the U.S.A., a belt of radiation which surrounds the earth (and is now named after him).

Vanbrugh, Sir John (1664–1726). English dramatist and architect. Grandson of a Flemish refugee, on a visit to France (1690) he was arrested and imprisoned as a suspected spy. On his release (1692) he returned to England and quickly established a reputation as both playwright and architect. His first comedy *The Relapse* (1696) was followed by *The Provoked Wife* (1697). His third play *The Confederacy* was staged in 1705 at the New Opera House in the Haymarket, which he himself had built, and managed in partnership with * Congreve. Three years earlier he had produced grandiose designs for Castle Howard, the Earl of Carlisle's Yorkshire seat, and in 1705 was commissioned to build the even more spectacular Blenheim Palace for the Duke of Marlborough. Despite frequent quarrels with the Duchess, Sarah, over the plans and the enormous expense, he succeeded in creating the most splendid and by far the largest example of English baroque. He became comptroller of works in 1702 and was knighted by George I. His last play, *The Provoked Husband*, was unfinished at his death.

Whistler, L., *Sir John Vanbrugh: Architect and Dramatist*. 1938; Holland, N. N., *The First Modern Comedies*. 1959

Van Buren, Martin (1782–1862). 8th president of the U.S. (1837–41). Born near Albany, New York, he became a lawyer and was prominent in state politics, becoming a U.S. senator in 1821. When his friend Andrew Jackson became president he chose Van Buren to be his secretary of state (1829–31) and his vice-president (1833–37). Jackson's influence secured him the election to the presidency in 1836. As president he was confronted with a financial panic and though he tackled the situation not unskilfully it prevented his re-election to a second term. He emerged from his retirement (during which he had written an illuminating book on U.S. political parties) in 1848 to run unsuccessfully for the presidency as a 'Free Soil' candidate. Van Buren was a political manipulator of great skill but lacked the qualities that inspire devotion.

Lynch, D. T., *Epoch and a Man: Martin Van Buren and His Times*. 1971

Vance, Cyrus Roberts (1917–). American lawyer and politician. He began practising law in 1947, and in 1957 was appointed special counsel to a Senate sub-committee. He became General Counsel to the Department of Defence in 1961, Secretary of the Army in 1962 and Deputy Secretary of Defence 1964–67. He was the President's special envoy to negotiations for peace in Cyprus (1967) and Vietnam (1968). President Carter made him Secretary of State in 1977; he resigned over the Iranian crisis in 1980.

Vancouver, George (1758–1798). British naval explorer. As a youth he sailed with Captain * Cook on his second and third voyages (1772–80) and later he was commissioned to lead an expedition to north-west America, partly to settle a territorial dispute, partly to explore. On the voyage out he went by the Cape route to Australia, where he explored the south-west coast, and thence to Tasmania, New Zealand and Hawaii. He spent three years (1792–94) on the American coast, during which he circumnavigated Vancouver Island (named by the Spaniards after him) and made an accurate survey of the coasts of what are now California and British Columbia.

Vanderbilt, Cornelius (known as 'the Commodore') (1794–1877). American financier. As a boy he established a ferry service from State Island to New York which expanded until he controlled several shipping lines. He then turned to railways, and after a series of financial battles gained control of the New York Central Railway and many other lines. He amassed a vast fortune with part of which he founded the Vanderbilt University. His grand-daughter Consuelo Vanderbilt married the 9th Duke of Marlborough.
Howden Smith, A. D., *Cornelius Vanderbilt*. 1928

Van der Walls *see* **Waals, Johannes Diderik van der**

Van der Weyden *see* **Weyden, Rogier van der**

Van de Velde. A family of Dutch painters. **William van de Velde the Elder** (1611–1693) painted large pictures of ships and sea battles, usually drawn in black paint or Indian ink on a white ground. In 1672 he and his elder son, **William van de Velde (the Younger)** (1633–1707), were in London where they remained as official marine painters. Several hundred marine paintings are attributed to William the Younger, who is held to be among the greatest masters in this genre. Many of their paintings of sea fights were made from sketches done on the scene of action and sometimes under fire. **Adriaen van de Velde** (1636–1672), the younger son, painted gentle Dutch landscapes with figures and grazing cattle.

Van Druten, John William (1901–1957). English-born playwright. His exploration of adolescence, *Young Woodley* (1928), first made him known. His plays include *Bell, Book and Candle* (1950), and *I am a Camera* (1951), a picture of inter-war Berlin based on Christopher* Isherwood's stories. He became a U.S. citizen in 1944.

Van Dyck, Sir Anthony (1599–1641). Flemish painter, born in Antwerp and knighted in England. He was the son of a well-to-do silk merchant and seems to have been something of a prodigy in art, as by 1617 he was already one of the chief assistants of * Rubens with whose work, especially his portraits and religious subjects, Van Dyck's work has been often confused. Van Dyck was invited to England for the first time in 1620 but stayed only a few months and from 1621 to 1627 he was in Italy (Genoa, Rome, Sicily, Venice), and with * Titian as a strong influence perfected a style of aristocratic portraiture which remained fashionable for 150 years. After winning a great reputation among members of Genoese society he returned to Antwerp where, working in friendly competition with Rubens, he found an overwhelming demand for his portraits. In 1632 under pressure from Charles I he returned to England, where he remained for the rest of his life, and painted many portraits of the sad and solemn king, of his family and of the great men and ladies of the court. The glittering clothes, the texture of the materials, the perfumed hair, the jewelled accessories, the very dogs and horses combine to give a romantic effect; the draughtsmanship is sure and true (his etched heads are superb) and the characterization convincing. As a court painter he has had few, if any, equals.
Strong, R., *Sir Anthony Van Dyck*. 1972

Van Dyke, Henry (1852–1933). American clergyman and writer. Pastor of the Brick Presbyterian Church, New York, 1883–90, professor of English Literature at Princeton 1900–13, and American minister to the Netherlands 1913–16, his writings include *The Story of the Other Wise Man* (1896) which became a best-seller.

Vane, Sir Henry (1613–1662). English parliamentary leader. He entered the House of Commons in 1640, and by purloining a note made by his father, the secretary of the Privy Council, he played a vital part in bringing about the execution of* Strafford. For this act Vane was himself executed after Charles II's restoration. In the intervening years he had been, after Pym's death, Cromwell's principal parliamentary supporter, had taken part in the creation of the New Model Army (1644–45) and the settlement of Scotland (1652–53). Under the Commonwealth he was a member of the Council of State. Disagreement with Cromwell brought a temporary eclipse but after his leader's death he was again active. After the restoration he was the only man apart from the actual regicides to be executed.

Van Eyck *see* **Eyck, Hubert van and Jan van**

Van Gogh *see* **Gogh, Vincent van**

Vanier, George Philias (1888–1967). Canadian diplomat. Trained as a lawyer, he practised in Montreal; in World War I he won the D.S.O., M.C. and bar. Afterwards he held a number of official posts, culminating with that of minister to France (1939–40). He returned to Paris as Canadian ambassador (1944–53), the intervening years of World War II having been spent on the Defence Board at Ottawa and as minister to the Allied governments exiled in London. His appointment as governor general of Canada (1959–67) made him the first French-Canadian to hold the position. His son, **Jean Vanier** (1929–), established L'Arche, an international network of 67 communities for the intellectually disabled.

Van Loon, Hendrik Willem (1882–1944). Dutch–American historian and biographer, born in Rotterdam. He went to the U.S. as a child, studied at Harvard and Munich universities and, after a period as a war correspondent, wrote a series of books which aimed to explain the world and its complexities both to children and mystified adults, illustrated by himself. All were enormously successful: they included *The Story of Mankind* (1922), *The Story of the Bible* (1923), *The Story of America* (1927), *The Home of Mankind* (1923), *The Arts of Mankind* (1938), *Van Loon's Lives* (1943) and the autobiographical *Report to St Peter* (1944).

Vansittart, Sir Robert Gilbert Vansittart, 1st Baron (1881–1957). English diplomat. As permanent under-secretary for foreign affairs (1930–38) he expressed to his political superiors his misgivings about Hitler and his policies. These warnings went unheeded and he was given the less effective position of chief diplomatic adviser to the foreign secretary (1938–41). He retired in 1941.
Colvin, I., *Vansittart in Office*. 1965

Van't Hoff *see* **Hoff, Jacobus Henricus van't**

Vanzetti, Bartolomeo *see* **Sacco, Nicola**

Vardon, Harry (1870–1937). British golfer. He was one of the triumvirate who dominated British golf between 1890 and 1914, the others being J. H. Taylor and James Braid. Vardon won the British open championships in 1896, 1898, 1899, 1903, 1911 and 1914 and was U.S open champion in 1900.

Vargas, Getulio Dorneles (1883–1954). Brazilian politician. He first became a deputy in 1911 and was soon prominent in and out of office until the revolution of 1930 enabled him to become president with dictatorial powers. He took Brazil into World War II on the Allied side, but afterwards had to give way to constitutional demands; he resigned (1945) but remained leader of a re-formed Labour party. After a free election he again became president (1951), but the rise in the cost of living soon dimmed his popularity and when a group of officers gave him the choice of resignation or exile he shot himself.
Dulles, J. W. F., *Vargas of Brazil, a political biography*. 1967

Vasari, Giorgio (1511–1574). Italian art historian. Though he gained considerable contemporary reputation as an architect (e.g. of the Uffizi in Florence) and as a Mannerist painter (e.g. of overcrowded battle scenes in the Palazzo Vecchio), he is remembered for his book *The Lives of the Artists* (1550), containing the biographies of the Italian painters of the previous 300 years. Despite considerable inaccuracy and bias it is the only source for much of the material, is full of lively anecdotes and shrewd comment. A revised and enlarged edition appeared in 1568.
Vere, G. de (trans.) Vasari: *The Lives of the Artists*. 10 vols. 1912–1915

Vasco da Gama (*c.* 1469–1525). Portuguese navigator. He had already made a name for himself as a mariner when he was chosen by King Manuel the Fortunate to follow up the explorations of Bartolomeo Diaz, who had reached the Cape of Good Hope (1488). Vasco da Gama left Lisbon with four ships and 160 men in July 1497. Having rounded the Cape the fleet turned northward up the African coast and then sailed eastward across the Indian Ocean to land at Calicut (May 1498).

The Indians, at first friendly, turned hostile, and the Portuguese had to fight their way out, the fleet eventually reaching home in September 1499. A second expedition under Cabral founded a factory at Calicut but the forty men left behind to man it were all murdered. To avenge their death Vasco da Gama, supplied this time with twenty ships, sailed in 1502, and after founding the African colony of Mozambique again reached Calicut, destroyed twenty-nine of the Indian ships, secured an indemnity and returned with rich booty. After twenty years of comparative inactivity he was sent (1524), now as viceroy, to make Portugal's position secure again.

Vauban, Sebastian le Prestre de (1633–1707). French military engineer. Orphaned and destitute, he joined the army and served under * Conde; having gained (1655) an engineer's commission in the army of the king, he was primarily engaged in the taking and making of fortresses. In the Low Countries (1672–78) he conducted seventeen successful sieges, reducing Maastricht in thirteen days by an approach by parallels, a method he himself introduced. In the decade between the wars (1678–88) he constructed the magnificent series of frontier fortresses which were effective until they fell under the attack of German howitzers in World War I. Already a general he was appointed marshal of France in 1703.
Lazard, P., *Vauban, 1633–1707*. 1934

Vaughan, Henry (1622–1695). Welsh religious poet. In 1647 he bagan practising medicine in his native Brecknockshire. He began writing secular poetry (*Poems with the tenth Satyre of Juvenal Englished* 1646) but after a religious conversion (*c.* 1648) wrote only devotional verse and prose meditations. His religious poetry, the best of it in *Silex Scintillans* (1650) and *Thalia Rediviva* (1678), owes much to the influence of George * Herbert. In his natural descriptions and some of his thought (e.g. the nearness of a child to God, based in a belief of a life before birth) he seems to presage Wordsworth.
Durr, R. A., *The Mystical Poetry of Henry Vaughan*. 1962

Vaughan Williams, Ralph (1872–1958). English composer, born in Gloucestershire. The son of a clergyman, he studied at Cambridge (where in 1901 he took a MusDoc), the Royal College of Music under * Stanford and * Parry, in Berlin with * Bruch (1897–98) and in Paris with * Ravel (1909). However, the turning point came with his discovery of English folk-song (1905) and of the Tudor polyphonic tradition. His *Fantasia on a Theme of Thomas Tallis* (1909), probably his best work, shows both the influence of church music and Ravel's orchestration. His song cycle *On Wenlock Edge* (1909), to poems by A. E. * Housman, remains in the repertoire, as do many songs, hymn tunes and folk-song arrangements. He wrote nine symphonies between 1901 and 1958, of which No. 4 (1935), a stark and violent work, marks an abrupt change from his romantic and lyrical style. He wrote several operas, including *Hugh the Drover* (1914) and *The Pilgrim's Progress* (1951); many choral works; *The Lark Ascending* (rhapsody for violin, 1921); and the ballet *Job* (based on Blake's etchings, 1931). He received the O.M. in 1935 and continued composing until his death.

Veblen, Thorstein (1857–1929). American economist and sociologist, of Norwegian decent. He taught economics and social science at several universities before reaching a much wider audience through his books. *The Theory of the Leisure Class* (1899) is an analysis of the psychological motives for the business class in an acquisitive society. His style was astringent and witty; the concept of 'conspicuous waste' was one of his creations. Others works include *The Theory of Business Enterprise* (1904) and *The Engineers and the Price System* (1921).
Mitchell, W. C., *What Veblen Taught*. 1936

Vega Carpio, Lope Félix de (1562–1635). Spanish dramatist and poet. As a young man he took part in the Spanish expedition to the Azores (1583) and sailed with the Armada (1588); he was also secretary to the Duke of Alva, the Marquis of Malpica and the Marquis of Sarria. He had many love affairs, was twice married and had several illegitimate children; his sensuousness is reflected in his love-poems, and in this, and the religious poetry which was written in his periods of remorse and his charitable gifts to the church and poor, there is a dichotomy which makes his writing more immediate and personal than that of many of his contemporaries. He had great literary prestige during his lifetime, which was, however, marred by tragedy, including the death of two wives, the blindness and madness of a mistress, the abduction of a daughter and the deaths of two sons.

After 1588, his dramatic production was huge and generally sensational, and approximately 500 pieces (including *entremeses* and *autos*) survive of approximately 1500. He was the master of the *Comedia* in 3 acts, full of action and sentiment but not noted for individual characterisation or powerful situation. His plays are roughly (1) 'cloak and sword' plays – comedies of intrigue, complicated aristocratic love-stories such as *La discreta enamorata*, *Noche de San Juan*, and *Maestro de Danzar*, and (2) plays on Spanish history or legends, such as *Peribáñez*, *Fuenteovejuna* and *El ultimo godo*.

Lope de Vega is critically praised for his neatness and inventiveness of plot, his lyricism, his sympathetic and unpatronising portrayal of the peasant characters of his plays, and his charming lovers. He also wrote many poems, religious and secular, a pastoral novel *Arcadia* (1581) amongst others, prose, a mock epic about cats and an autobiographical novel *La Dorotea* (1632).

Veidt, Conrad (1893–1943). German actor. He made his stage debut in 1913 and appeared in films from 1917, notably as Cesare the somnambulist in *The Cabinet of Dr Caligari* (1919), *The Thief of Baghdad* (1940) and *Casablanca* (1943). He left Germany in 1933 and became a British subject.

Veil, Simone (1927–). French administrator. She served at the ministry of justice 1957–65, first as an attaché and later (from 1959) as an assistant. She was secretary general to the Conseil Supérieur de la Magistrature 1970–74 and a member of the French broadcasting administration 1972–74. She achieved wide popularity and recognition as minister of health (1974–77), minister of health and social security (1977–78) and minister of health and family affairs (1978–79); she was noted for her concern for women's rights in the family. She was president of the European Parliament at Strasbourg 1979–82.

Velazquez, Diego Rodriguez de Silva y (1599–1660). Spanish painter of Portuguese descent, born in Seville. At the age of 14 he began to study under Francisco Pacheco, an indifferent artist whose daughter he married. At first working closely from life, he painted genre scenes, such as kitchen interiors, with figures and objects in realistic detail. The strong contrasts of light and shade recall the chiaroscuro of * Caravaggio then becoming popular in Spain. In 1622 and 1623 Velazquez visited Madrid where he painted his first portrait of Philip IV, which led to his appointment as court painter and to other more or less honorific appointments as his reputation grew. Rubens visited Madrid in 1628 and his influence enabled Velazquez to go on a two-year visit to Italy (1629–31), which resulted in a softening of the harshness of his early style; colour began to show in the shadows; light and space became his preoccupations, whilst the range of subjects was enlarged. He resumed his position as royal painter on his return. In his royal portraits he avoids flattery but the *infantes* and *infantas* have freshness and charm despite their elaborate and formal clothes. In his only surviving battlepiece, the *Surrender of Breda* (1634–35), the chivalrous compassion depicted in the attitude of the victors to the defeated gives a humanity to the picture almost unknown in paintings of this kind. Where he is less inhibited by his subject, e.g. in his pictures of court jesters and buffoons, he is at his most effective in combining realism with interpretation of character. The loose brushwork of the views of the Medici Gardens, two of his rare landscapes, indicate a stylistic development to which his second visit to Italy (1648–51) may have contributed. To this last period belong the masterpieces *The Toilet of Venus* (*The Rokeby Venus*, painted while he was in Italy); *Maids of Honour* (*Las Meninas*, 1656), one of the finest group paintings known; *The Tapestry Weavers* (*Las Hilanderas*). Velazquez founded no school of painting and his genius was little appreciated outside Spain until the Impressionists revealed their debt to him.

Guidol, J., *Velázquez*. 1974; Lopez-Rey, J., *Velazquez: a catalogue raisonné of his oeuvre with an introductory study*. 1963

Venizelos, Eleutherios (1864–1936). Greek politician, born in Crete. He was prominent in the rising of 1896 against Turkish rule, and when as a result independence for Crete was obtained he became foreign minister. He continued the struggle for union with Greece. In 1909 he was summoned to Athens to become Greek prime minister, and having overcome a constitutional crisis he became the prime mover in building up the Balkan alliance which resulted in the wars of 1912–13 against

Turkey and Bulgaria. The aim of Venizelos' life since boyhood, the union of Crete with Greece, was now achieved. World War I led to a deep rift between King Constantine (who was married to the German emperor's sister) and his pro-Allied prime minister. Venizelos eventually felt himself obliged to set up a provisional government at Salonica (1916) and there were two governments in Greece until the Allies forced the deposition of Constantine (1917). Venizelos led the Greek delegation at the Paris Peace Conference (1919) but was defeated at the election of 1920 (in which year Constantine was recalled). After the Greek defeat by the Turks in Asia Minor (1921–22) the monarchy was suspended in 1923 but Venizelos remained (except briefly) out of office until 1928. Defeated in 1932 after a successful term during which he had done much for the economic reconstruction of the country, he returned to Crete, where he took part in an unsuccessful revolt against the restored monarchy (1935). Forced into exile, he died in Paris.

Ventris, Michael George Francis (1922–1956). British architect and scholar. While practising as an architect he pursued his self-imposed task of interpreting the ancient Mycenaean writing known as Linear Script B. His conclusion that it was an early form of Greek writing gradually gained general acceptance. In collaboration with John Chadwick of Cambridge University he wrote *Documents in Mycenaean Greek* (1956). He died after a motor accident.

Verdi, Giuseppe (1813–1901). Italian composer, born near Parma. The son of a village tradesman, he studied under the local organist. A friend and patron named Barezzi, a rich merchant (whose daughter he married in 1836), supported his early musical education. The Milan Conservatoire refused to admit Verdi (as he was over age for admission), and he continued his training in Milan with Lavigna, a repetiteur at La Scala. To his great grief his wife and children died in 1839–40 and for a time his enthusiasm for music failed; but in 1842 he gained his first major success, *Nabucco* (*Nebuchadnezzar*). *Ernani* (Venice, 1844) followed and then *Macbeth* (Florence, 1847), in which Verdi developed a strong melodic style ideally suited to the dramatic episodes of the plot. The achievement of dramatic 'truth', now Verdi's main aim, made such demands on acting ability that the virtuoso singers, so long the mainstay of opera, were deprived of their dominance. The first operas of Verdi's full maturity, *Rigoletto* (Venice, 1851), *Il Trovatore* (Rome, 1853) and *La Traviata* (Venice, 1853), reveal the further pursuit of his aims. Those that followed, including *I Vespri Siciliani* (Paris, 1867), *Un Ballo in Maschera* (Rome, 1859) and *Don Carlos* (Paris, 1867), were of unequal merit and success. Verdi's last and finest period opened with *Aida* (1871), commissioned for the opening of the Suez Canal. For his last operas, *Otello* (Milan, 1887) and *Falstaff* (Milan, 1893), Verdi was provided with texts by Arrigo Boito, by far the best of his librettists. After that time he composed little music. Among his last compositions were religious works, e.g. the *Requiem, Ave Maria* and *Stabat Mater* for chorus and orchestra. Much of his work reflected the contemporary Italian nationalist fervour, and represents the full flower of Italian operatic style.

Weaver, W., *Verdi*. 1977

Verlaine, Paul (1844–1896). French poet. At 17, after leaving the Lycée Condorcet, Paris, he became a clerk in the municipal service and was already writing poetry. Soon as a contributor to *Le Parnasse contemporain* he mixed with such poets as Leconte de Lisle, Catulle Mendès and Mallarmé. His first volume, *Poèmes Saturniens* (1860), won moderate praise; the next, *Fêtes galantes* (1869), was a more mature work evocative of the elegance of the 18th century in which it was set. His courtship of his 16-year-old bride Mathilde Mauté is recorded in *La Bonne Chanson* (1870), but in 1871, having met the young * Rimbaud, he left her and their infant son to spend a year of bohemian wandering with him in Belgium and England. In Brussels (1873), Rimbaud threatened to leave him. They quarrelled, Verlaine shot him in the wrist and he was later arrested and sentenced to two years' imprisonment. While in prison he wrote *Romances sans paroles*, in which the meaning is almost submerged by the music of the words. On his release he became a schoolmaster, and in a mood of religious penitence wrote *Sagesse* (published 1881). Back in France (1877) he continued to teach for a time; the poems in his *Amour* (1888) were inspired by grief at the death of a former pupil whom he had adopted

as a son. Despite growing fame he had difficulty in making a living; his works progressively deteriorated. His critical writings, e.g. *Poètes maudits* (1884), short stories and lecture tours were not remunerative. Alcoholism and illness brought him to poverty and squalor, though his friends and admirers, and even the state, rallied to his help at the end.
Le Dantec, Y. G. (ed.), *Verlaine; Œuvres poétiques complètes*. 1938; Richardson, J., *Verlaine*. 1971

Vermeer, Jan (1632–1675). Dutch painter. He was born and spent all his life at Delft where in 1653 he joined the Guild of St Luke as a master painter. Except for a famous *View of Delft* and a very few portraits and other pictures, he painted mainly interiors, where a single wall and a tiled floor provide backgrounds for the harmoniously composed figures in the soft serene light pouring through tall windows – lighting effects over which he gained a supreme mastery. The figures, mostly young women, appear singly or in very small groups and confirm by their attitudes and occupations the pictures' moods, e.g. *The Letter, A Lady Weighing Pearls, The Milkmaid.* Vermeer was popular in his own day but was then almost forgotten until the 19th century revival. He was a slow worker and only about forty of his pictures are known. Vermeer can be recognized by the monumental and spacious effect he gives to small rooms by sitting close to the model, by his characteristic dark blues and warm yellows or by the occurrence in picture after picture of the same small objects painted with the same meticulous detail. Such idiosyncrasies provided an opportunity for the forger van * Meegeren in World War II (although as Vermeer's work has become better known, it is hard to see how the forgeries could have fooled anybody). Vermeer cared little for commercialism; at his death his baker held two of his paintings for unpaid bills, and his wife, declared bankrupt, could not retrieve them.
Gowing, L., *Vermeer*. 2nd ed. 1970

Verne, Jules (1828–1905). French novelist, born at Nantes. Originator of 'scientific' romances, he wrote a long series beginning with *Five Weeks in a Balloon* (1863) and including *Twenty Thousand Leagues under the Sea* (1870) and *Around the World in Eighty Days* (1873). Their enormous success, based largely on their plausibility, inspired H. G. Wells and later writers of science fiction.
Evans, I. O., *Jules Verne and His Work*. 1965

Vernier, Pierre (*c*. 1580–1637). French mathematician and soldier. He spent much time in the Low Countries in the service of Spain and invented (1630) the auxiliary scale named after him. By using the vernier to subdivide the smallest divisions of an ordinary scale he greatly improved the accuracy of linear and angular measurements.

Vernon, Edward (known as 'Old Grog') (1684–1757). British sailor. As a vice-admiral he was in command at the storming (1739) of Portobello, Panama, in the war against Spain; but he is remembered by his nickname, which originally referred to the grosgrain trousers he habitually wore but was transferred to the mixture of rum and water which he served to his crews.

Veronese (Paolo Caliari) (1528–1588). Italian painter, born at Verona. Though the titles of his pictures, e.g., *Marriage of Cana* (1563), *Feast of the House of Levi* (1573) etc., are religious, the episodes depicted are removed in time and place to contemporary Venice. In architectural settings of unparalleled magnificence, emphasized sometimes by his experiments in false perspective, he sets the men and women of the aristocratic world in which he moved, brilliant in silk brocades and glittering with jewels. He had to appear before the Inquisition (1573) for introducing dwarfs and jesters into biblical scenes but he claimed the artistic privilege of a decorator. Though he was a contemporary of the Mannerists his work is nearer to that of the High Renaissance. Most of the paintings went to adorn the great palaces of Venice and Rome.
Orliac, A., *Veronese*. 1948

Veronica, St. According to tradition she was a woman of Jerusalem who offered her veil to Jesus to wipe the sweat from his face while he was carrying the cross to Calvary. His features, so it was said, were miraculously imprinted on the fabric and the picture survived and was eventually brought to Rome. A naturalistic explanation suggests that the name Veronica is a corruption of an anagram of *vera icon* ('the true image').

Verrocchio (Andrea di Cioni) (1435–1488). Florentine artist. He took the name by which

he is known from Giuliano Verrocchi, the goldsmith who was his first teacher, but like so many of the great Renaissance figures he worked with almost equal facility in all the arts and crafts. Not only was he a painter and sculptor but showed his skill as a metal-worker and wood-carver. He succeeded (1467) Donatello in the service of the Medici and among his many tasks were the making of tournament armour and carnival masks. There are notable differences between him and his predecessor; Donatello's statue *David* is an idealized naked youth; Verrocchio portrays him with sword and armour. Among his pupils was Leonardo da Vinci who is said to have painted the angel on the left of *The Baptism* (now in the Uffizi, Florence), one of Verrocchio's few known paintings. At the time of his death he was still working on the equestrain statue of Bartolomeo Colleoni, a magnificent portrayal of the great and arrogant Venetian mercenary.
Planiscig, L., *Andrea del Verrocchio*. 1941

Verwoerd, Hendrik Frensch (1901–1966). South African politician. Born in the Netherlands, he went to South Africa as a child. He was educated at Stellenbosch University, to which, after further study in Europe, he returned (1928) as head of the department of sociology and social services. From 1938 to 1948, when he became a senator, he edited *Die Transvaler*, a new Afrikaans daily. In 1950 he became minister of native affairs in the Nationalist government and strictly applied the apartheid policy of racial segregation. This he continued when he became prime minister (1958). In 1960 South Africa decided by referendum to become a republic, and the decision was put into effect (1961) when South Africa left the Commonwealth. An English settler had attempted to assassinate him in 1960, and in September 1966 he was stabbed to death in the House of Assembly at Cape Town.

Vesalius, Andreas (1514–1564). Flemish anatomist, born in Brussels. He studied in Paris and Louvain before becoming professor of surgery at Padua University, where he had just (1537) taken his degree. His publications were based on the works of * Galen, but by carrying out dissections (a revolutionary practice at that time) he was able to point out many errors. His greatest work, *De humani corporis fabrica* (1543), was enriched by superbly engraved illutrations. Upset by criticism, Vesalius burnt his books and became court physician to the emperor Charles V and his son Philip II of Spain. He died on the way back from a pilgrimage to Jerusalem.
O'Malley, C. D., *Andreas Vesalius of Brussels 1514–1564*. 1964

Vespasian (Titus Flavius Sabinius Vespasianus) (9–79). Roman emperor (from 69). He was born near Rome; with no particular social advantages he slowly climbed the military and official ladders until he had become consul (51) and a senator. He took part in the conquest of Britain (43) by the emperor Claudius, and at the time of Nero's suicide he was fighting the Jewish rebels in Palestine. While Galbo, Otho and Vitellius were contending for Nero's vacant throne he remained at his post; but when his legions proclaimed him emperor (July 69) he left his son Titus in Judaea and marched on Rome. When Vitellius died defeated, there was no further resistance and after he had suppressed a revolt on the Rhine the empire was at peace (71). His reign was one of prudent consolidation; he himself lived simply, he restored the empire's finances, patronized the arts and began the Colosseum. He was succeeded by his son Titus and thus initiated the Flavian dynasty.

Vespucci, Amerigo (1451–1512). Italian merchant-adventurer, after whom America was named. As agent of the Florentine Medici at Seville and a successful man of business, he was given the task of fitting up the royal fleets that sailed in Columbus's wake. He himself claimed to have made four voyages (1497–1504), the first two in the Spanish service, the others on behalf of the Portuguese. The first voyage was to the coasts of Mexico, Honduras and Florida, the second to Brazil; he also claimed to have explored the South American coast almost to the southern tip in the third voyage. These claims have been in part disputed; whatever the truth, the wide currency given to his accounts of his voyages (a German translator even mentions 'America' – i.e. South America – as being called after 'its descoverer Americus') ensured that it was his name, not that of Columbus, that was inscribed on the first maps of the New World.

Vian, Sir Philip (1894–1968). British sailor. He was famous for his exploits in World War

II, first rescuing 300 British merchant sailors from the German tanker *Altmark* within Norwegian waters. Later he commanded a destroyer squadron in the operations (1941) by which the *Bismarck* was hunted down and sunk.

Vickers, Thomas (1833–1915) and **Albert** (1838–1919). British industrialists. The two brothers entered a Sheffield steel-making firm, and gradually control passed into their hands. Decisive steps which led to their becoming ranked among the great armament makers in the world were the taking over (1897) of the Maxim, Nordenfelt Company (* Maxim) and the Naval Construction and Armament Company of Barrow-in-Furness. A wide variety of armament from machine-guns to battleships (and aeroplanes after the brothers' death) was made by the firm, known (from 1911) as Vickers Ltd.

Vico, Giambattista (1688–1744). Italian philosopher of history. A professor at the University of Naples and historiographer to Charles III of Naples, he was a pioneer in developing a theory of history (as against a mere recording of events) and of advocating serious historical research. He believed in a modified form in the cyclical nature of history, but not to the extent of believing that 'history repeats itself'. His major work is *Scienza Nuova* (1725; revised 1730, 1744).
Berlin, I., *Vico and Herder*. 1976; Bergen, T. G., and Fisch, M. H., trans., *The Autobiography of Giambattista Vico*. 1944

Victor Emmanuel I (1820–1878). King of Italy (from 1861), king of Sardinia, as Victor Emmanuel II (from 1849). He succeeded his father Charles Albert as king of Sardinia (and ruler of Savoy and Piedmont), and became the first king of united Italy. He showed military skill in the vain struggle against Austria (1848–49), and when his father abdicated in his favour continued by political and diplomatic means to support the cause of Italian unity. His chief instrument was the great minister * Cavour, with whom he often disputed but whom he always finally sustained, even when it meant the surrender of his historic Savoy territories to France to gain the support of Napoleon III in the coming struggle. His reward came when after the French victories (1859) of Magenta and Solferino only Venice was left to the Austrians (this came to Italy as a reward for alliance with Prussia in 1866). Victor Emmanuel, free to move south, was welcomed everywhere and having won the reluctant adherence of * Garibaldi was proclaimed king of Italy. Florence was his capital until the French garison, left to maintain papal rule in Rome, was withdrawn during the Franco-Prussian War (1870–71). Throughout his reign, both of Sardinia and of Italy, Victor Emmanuel observed the conditions of constitutional rule.
Forester, C. S., *Victor Emmanuel*. 1927

Victor Emmanuel III (1869–1947). King of Italy (1900–1946). He became king (as Victor Emmanuel III because the Sardinian numeral sequence was usually employed) after the assassination of his father Umberto I. He ruled as a constitutional monarch without serious problems (though he used his influence to ensure that Italy should join the Allies in World War I) until the rise of * Mussolini and the 'march on Rome' (1922) caused him to take the decision which eventually proved fatal to his dynasty; he chose (against parliamentary and military advice) to give a constitutional appearance to an unconstitutional act by inviting Mussolini to become his prime minister. This made the king an accomplice (even if at times an unwilling one) of the Fascist dictator. He gave active assistance in the conspiracy by which after the defeats of World War II Mussolini's downfall and arrest were achieved, but his countrymen could not forget the past. Victor Emmanuel retired from public life (1944) after appointing his son * **Umberto** lieutenant general of the realm and in 1946 abdicated. He died in exile in Egypt.

Victoria (1819–1901). Queen of Great Britain, Ireland and British territories overseas (from 1837), empress of India (from 1877). She was the only child of George III's fourth son, Edward, Duke of Kent, and of Victoria of Saxe-Coburg, sister of Leopold I, king of the Belgians, and she succeeded her uncle, William IV. As the succession laws of Hanover did not allow a woman to reign, her uncle the Duke of Cumberland became king of Hanover, and the link between the two countries was broken. During the first years of her reign the girl queen found a friend and a political mentor in her prime minister, Lord * Melbourne, but after her marriage (1840), her husband, * Albert of Saxe-Coburg, who was her cousin, became the dominant influence in her life. This was of special importance in foreign affairs, where his interventions – wise as they usually were and aimed at the liberalization of the European monarchies – sometimes provoked friction with her foreign ministers, especially * Palmerston. The network of royal relationship which played an important part in international affairs during the 19th century was greatly extended as their children reached marriageable age. The eldest, * Victoria, married a future emperor of Germany, Albert Edward (later Edward VII) married the beautiful Danish princess Alexandra, whose brother became king of Greece, and whose sister was empress of Russia. From Queen Victoria's third child, Alice, who married the Grand Duke of Hesse, were sprung the Mountbattens and the last Russian empress. The marriage of Alfred, her fourth child, brought another link with the Russian royal house and his daughter became queen of Romania. Following Helena and Louise came two more sons, Arthur, Duke of Connaught (whose daughter became queen of Sweden), and Leopold; the youngest child, Beatrice, became the mother of the queen of Spain. Victoria's relationships with her family were mostly happy, but her distrust of her eldest son and her long refusal to allow him any part in public affairs did serious damage to his character. The death of the Prince Consort (1861) darkened Queen Victoria's life. She retired into complete seclusion at Windsor which for a time eclipsed her popularity and it was only the tact and gentle flattery of * Disraeli that at last induced her to emerge. His success in having her proclaimed empress of India (1877) greatly pleased her. For the other great prime minister of her reign, * Gladstone, the queen had respect but little affection; 'he speaks to me as if I were a public meeting', she was known to say. In the last years of her life the queen became identified in the public mind with the nation's great achievements during her reign. The Jubilee (1887) and the Diamond Jubilee (1897) celebrations revealed the extent of her popularity and the veneration in which she was held. Although neither intellectually brilliant nor highly imaginative she had much shrewdness and common sense and despite her keen moral perceptions her judgements were usually charitable and kind. If her taste was no better than that of the majority of her subjects, it was certainly no worse. During her reign 'constitutional government' in the modern sense was fully developed; she did not conceal her opinions and often showed bias (especially towards conservatism in her old age) but she never 'acted' against advice. Under her the crown's prestige was fully restored and became a symbol of devoted public service and imperial unity. Few women have revealed themselves more fully than she did in her letters, many of which have been published.

Benson, A. C., and Esher, Viscount, eds., *Letters of Queen Victoria 1837–1861.* 1907; Buckle, G. E., ed., *Letters of Queen Victoria 1862–1885*, 1926–28; – *Letters of Queen Victoria 1886–1901.* 1930–32; Longford, E., *Queen Victoria.* 1964

Victoria Adelaide Mary (1840–1901). Empress of Germany. The eldest child of Queen Victoria and known in Great Britain as the Princess Royal, she was trained in politics by her father, Albert, the Prince Consort. Her marriage (1858) to the future Emperor Frederick of Germany, who shared her views, gave promise of a liberal empire, but he died of cancer (1888) within three months of his accession. Already unpopular for her English connexions and her insistence upon calling in an English doctor for her husband, she became estranged from her son, Kaiser * William II, and lost all influence.

Fulford, R., (ed.), *Dearest Child.* 1964; *Dearest Mama.* 1968

Victoria, Tomás Luis de (Tommaso Ludovico da Vittoria) (1548?–1611). Spanish composer. His output was entirely of religious music. The two settings of the Passion and nine Lamentation lessons contained in his *Holy Week Office* (1585) and his Requiem Mass for the empress Maria (published 1605) are of special importance. His work superficially resembles that of * Palestrina but he had a more pronounced sense of harmony and key relationship.

Vidal, Gore (1925–   ). American novelist. He grew up in a political family, served in World War II, ran for Congress and was an acidulous and penetrating critic. His novels include *Myra Breckinridge* (1968), *Burr* (1973), *1876* (1976) and *Lincoln* (1984). He also published several volumes of critical essays.

Vidocq, Eugène François (1775–1857). French criminal and detective. The son of a baker, he started his career by robbing the till of his father's shop. After a period as a circus acrobat and (as a supposed savage) a 'drinker of blood', he joined the army; but he was in Paris in 1796 and sentenced to eight years in the galleys for forgery. He escaped to join a gang of highway-men, whom he handed over to the police. Accepted now as a police informer he became (1809) head of the 'Brigade de Sûreté', which he may have founded himself. His success as a detective was regarded as marvellous until it was found that he himself organized many of the burglaries he 'discovered'. In 1825 he was dismissed; his memoirs (1828), possibly spurious, contain as much fiction as truth.

Viète, François (1540–1603). French mathematician. Probably the most significant figure in the development of modern algebra, son of an attorney, he himself studied law, and began his career as an advocate and a councillor in the *parlement* of Brittany. As a Huguenot, he was banished from court during the reign of Charles IX but restored to favour by Henri IV. One of his greatest political services lay in decoding enemy messages during the war against Spain. Viète was one of the first to advocate algebraic rather than geometrical constructions in mathematical proofs. He introduced many key technical terms into algebra, such as 'coefficient' and 'negative', and pioneered the technique of using letters of the alphabet to denote unknown quantities. He was principally concerned with algebra as a practical tool; most of his own work in the subject was geared to solving cosmological and astronomical problems. He involved himself deeply in calendar reform. When Pope Gregory XIII proposed a major reform of the calendar (by making 15 October 1582 follow immediately after 4 October) Viète was one of the sternest opponents of the new Gregorian calender (though in fact his own astronomical calculations were incorrect).

Vigée Le Brun *see* **Le Brun, Marie Elisabeth Louise**

Vigeland, Adolf Gustav (1869–1943). Norwegian sculptor. Under a unique agreement Vigeland was provided with a studio and a livelihood on condition that he handed over all his work to the Oslo municipality, which in turn promised to exhibit them in perpetuity. The result is an array of robust and realistic nudes in single figures or groups in a beautiful setting in the Frogneorpark at Oslo. The influence of Rodin is apparent but both the merits of the work and its symbolism (clearly linked with the life cycle) have provoked much controversy.

Vigny, Alfred Victor, Comte de (1797–1863). French Romantic writer. After serving in the army for twelve years, an experience which inspired *Servitude et grandeur militaires* (1835), he became one of the leading figures in the Romantic literary movement. His *Poèmes antiques et modernes* (1826) show the influence of Byron; the Scott-inspired *Cinq-Mars*, a novel of the reign of Louis XIII, appeared in the same year. *Chatterton* (1835), a play written for the actress Madame Dorval, for whom he cherished a jealous love for years, is considered his masterpiece. He had married (1828) Lydia Bunbury, an Englishwoman, but the marriage was not a success. He was no more fortunate in public life. His attempt to enter parliament (1848–49) was unsuccessful. These failures are reflected in the pessimism of his work. After his death the philosophic poems *Les Destinées* appeared in 1864; while *Daphne*, concerned with the struggle between Christianity and what he considered a new paganism, was published only in 1912.
De la Salle, B., *Alfred de Vigny*. Rev. ed. 1963

Villa, Francisco (1877–1923). Mexican bandit and revolutionary. After escaping from peonage he became a bandit and was nicknamed Pancho Villa. His aid in the revolution of 1910–11 helped Madero to overthrow Porfirio Díaz. Subsequently he came into conflict with his previous allies and Villa was obliged to flee to North Mexico where he operated as a rebel until 1920. An American punitive expedition under General Pershing was sent against him (1916) after the murder of several Americans but failed to take him and caused much ill feeling in Mexico. Villa, a daring and impulsive fighter for social justice, became a popular hero.

Villa-Lobos, Heitor (1887–1959). Brazilian composer. One of the first South American composers to win international recognition, he was largely self-taught. Most of his vast output, which includes operas, symphonies, chamber music and piano music, is influenced by the style of Brazilian folk song. The *Choros*, for various instrumental combinations, blend Brazilian, Indian and popular elements and the suites entitled *Bachianas Brasileiras* fuse Brazilian melody with the manner of Bach.

Villars, Claude Louis Hector, Duc de (1653–1734). French soldier. One of the most celebrated of Louis XIV's generals, in the opening stages of the War of the Spanish Succession his bold efforts against the Austrians were constantly foiled by the hesitant obstinancy of his ally, the elector of Bavaria. In 1705 he conducted a masterly defence of the north-eastern frontier of France against Marlborough, and, after forcing his retreat, captured the Allies' reserves of food, equipment and artillery in Alsace. He was equally successful against Prince Eugène (1708). He was wounded at Malplaquet (1709) but after Marlborough's recall he more than held his own until the Peace of Utrecht (1712) brought the war to an end.
De Vogüé, ed., *Mémoires du Duc de Villars.* 1884–1904

Villeneuve, Pierre Charles Jean Baptiste Sylvestre de (1763–1806). French sailor. One of * Nelson's leading antagonists in the Napoleonic Wars, he was a captain at the Battle of the Nile and managed to save his own ship and two frigates in that disaster (1798). Chosen by * Napoleon to play the leading part in the strategy to gain command of the Channel for long enough to enable him to invade England, Villeneuve slipped out of Toulon early in 1805 and, joined by a Spanish squadron from Cadiz, reached the West Indies in May. Nelson followed, Villeneuve doubled back, but after an encounter with the British off Ferrol decided that the remainder of the plan to rescue the ships blockaded at Brest and then enter the Channel was impractical; he turned south to Cadiz where Nelson found him. Anxious to redeem himself before a successor could arrive Villeneuve sought battle and at Trafalgar was defeated and captured. Released in 1806 he killed himself on the journey to Paris rather than face the emperor's anger.

Villiers, Barbara *see* **Cleveland, 1st Duchess of**

Villiers de l'Isle Adam, Auguste, Comte de (1838–1889). French writer. He dedicated an early volume of symbolist poetry, *Premières poésies*, to de Vigny, but is chiefly remembered for his prose works, late Romantic studies in the fantastic and the macabre. The best known are *Contes cruels* (1883), short stories in the manner of Poe, the novel *L'Ève future* (1886), and the play *Axël* (1885). Both his plays and novels suffered because they were used to display ideas rather than to represent the development of character.
Wilson, E., *Axel's Castle.* 1931

Villon, François (1431–*c.* 1470). French poet. Born in Paris of obscure parentage, he was brought up by Guillaume de Villon, a priest who lectured in canon law. After graduating in the Sorbonne he continued the irregular life of his student days. In 1455 he stabbed Philippe Chermoye, a priest, to death in a brawl, fled to the countryside, joined a band of criminals and learned the thieves' *argot* in which he later wrote ballads. He returned to Paris (1456) but continued his criminal life and took part in a robbery at the Collège de Navarre. In 1460 he was under sentence of death at Orléans for an unknown crime, but was released after an amnesty. Another amnesty, this time to mark a visit by the new king, Louis XI, saved him again in 1461. He returned to Paris (1462) only to be imprisoned once again for the old Navarre robbery. He was freed through the influence of Guillaume de Villon, but a street brawl, at the cost of another life, again brought a death sentence. This sentence was commuted to ten years' banishment from Paris. Nothing more is known of his life.

Villon used medieval verse forms but the individuality of the poet's voice, the intensity of his feeling, his perception, and surprisingly – if his life be considered – a strain of religious devotion, have given his work a permanent appeal. The poems are variously ribald, urbane, boisterous, and penitent, learned and coarse; they revel in life and are preoccupied with death. The major works, the *Lais* or *Petit Testament* (written 1456) and *Grand Testament* (1461), comprise poems interpersed with ballads. In addition (apart from ballads in *argot*) there is the grim *Ballade des pendus* (written under sentence of death) which ranks with the *Ballade des dames du temps jadis* with its famous refrain 'Mais où sont les neiges d'antan?' ('But where are the snows of yesteryear?').

Villon's work was first printed in 1489 and a critical edition appeared in 1533. A period of neglect intervened but in the 19th century

French scholars made serious studies, and several English poets, including Rossetti and Swinburne, chose pieces for translation.
Bonner, A., ed., *Complete Works of François Villon.* 1960

Vincent de Paul, St (1581?–1660). French priest. He was the son of a peasant in the Landes and was ordained in 1600. There are various versions of the story of his being captured by Moorish pirates and sold into slavery at Tunis. He escaped to Rome and the French ambassador there sent him on a confidential mission to Henry IV of France; he became chaplain (1610–12) to Marguerite de Valois, Henry's wife. Later as tutor to the family of the general in charge he had an opportunity to show his compassion for the convicts condemned to work in the galleys. By 1633 he had acquired enough influential friends to set up two charitable orders, the 'Priests of the Mission' (or 'Lazarists', after the Convent St Lazare in Paris where they were established) for men, and the 'Little Sisters of the Poor' for women. Hospices for the old, the poor (La Salpêtrière) and foundlings were also started and missionaries dispatched abroad. The lay Society of St Vincent de Paul, founded by students in Paris (1833), has spread through the world. He was canonized in 1737.

Vinogradoff, Sir Paul Gavrilovich (1854–1925). Russian–British historian. After settling in England (1901) he was appointed to a professorship in jurisprudence at Oxford. His outstanding contributions to medieval history included *Outlines of Historical Jurisprudence* (1920–22), *Villeinage in England* (1892) and *The Growth of the Manor* (1908).

Viollet-le-Duc, Eugène Emanuel (1814–1879). French architect. Talent as a draughtsman combined with a love of medieval architecture shaped his career. He was employed by the Commission des Monuments Historiques when he was a joint winner of a competition for the restoration of Nôtre Dame in Paris. He also restored the medieval fortress-city of Carcasonne. His works included a ten-volume dictionary of architecture and a six-volume dictionary of furniture.

Virchow, Rudolf (1821–1902). German pathologist. After being professor of pathology at Würzburg (1849–56) he held a corresponding post at Berlin for the rest of his life. His *Cellular Pathology* (1858) indicated a revolutionary approach to the subject.
Ackerknecht, E. H., *Rudolf Virchow: Doctor, Statesman, Anthropologist.* 1953

Virgil (Publius Vergilius Maro) (70–19 B.C.). Roman poet, born near Mantua. He was given the best education but did not take the usual course of entering public life. After some years in the country writing poetry, he went to Rome and attracted the friendship of * Maecenas. His earliest known works are the *Eclogues* or *Bucolics* (*c.* 37), pastoral poems modelled on those of * Theocritus. In the four books of the *Georgics* (completed 30) he uses graceful poetical techniques and verbal artistry in a series of didactic poems on agriculture – olive-growing and vine culture, stock-raising and bee-keeping. His greatest work is the *Aeneid*, published after his death, a national epic which tells the story of the flight of Aeneas (a minor prince in Homer) from defeated Troy, his stay at Carthage with Queen Dido, and his final settlement in Italy, where his descendants were to found the Roman nation. The *Aeneid* stems from Homer and uses Homeric mechanisms but differs completely in being the product of a sophisticated society rather than of the heroic semi-barbaric world of Homer. A main weakness is in the character of Aeneas himself. The fine poetry is there, the resonant verse, the romantic episode (e.g. that of Dido) but the hero remains something of a dull prig. From the first the *Aeneid* was used as an educational work and it was natural that this use should survive the change to Christianity. In the process Virgil emerges in the role of a prophet and in the Middle Ages passages of his works were held to contain prophecies of Christ's coming. In the *Divine Comedy* Virgil appears as Dante's guide through Inferno. From the 15th century until the 18th, the *Aeneid* was regarded as a model of epic form.
Glover, T. R., *Virgil.* (7th ed.) 1942

Visconti, Gian Galeazzo (1351–1402). Duke of Milan. He sprang from a family which from 1262 (when Ottone Visconti had been made archbishop) gradually assumed ascendancy in Milan. Gian Galeazzo, who had succeeded his father in Pavia (1378), and dispossessed his uncle in Milan (1385), concentrated the family power in his own hands. By uniting Milan with the neighbouring cities into a single powerful state, he gained the title of Duke from the emperor. He married his daughter Valentina to the Duke of Orléans, an alliance held to justify the future claims of French kings to the territories of Milan.

Visconti, Luchino, Duca di Mondrone (1906–1976). Italian film director, born in Milan. Member of a noble Milanese family, he worked with Jean * Renoir as an assistant director, then went to the U.S. His first film *Ossessione* (1942) was mutilated by Fascist censors but marks the beginning of the Italian neo-realist school. His sixteen films had varying success but the best were regarded as masterpieces: *Rocco and his Brothers* (1960), *The Leopard* (1963), *The Damned* (1969) and *Death in Venice* (1971). Visconti, also a successful operatic producer, was murdered by a young lover.
Servadio, G., *Luchino Visconti: A Biography*. 1982

Vitellius, Aulus (15–69). One of the four Roman emperors who ruled in 69. Sent by Galba to command on the lower Rhine he was proclaimed emperor by his troops, and after the defeat and death of Otho hastened to Rome. His gluttony, extravagance, cruelty and inertia in the face of Vespasian's army advancing from the north left him with no friends. When his enemies entered Rome he was killed by being dragged through the streets.

Vitruvius (Marcus Vitruvius Pollio) (early 1st century A.D.). Roman architect and engineer. His celebrated ten-book treatise, *De Architectura*, is virtually an encyclopedia, and, as it is the only Roman work of its kind to survive, Vitruvius had enormous influence on the architects of the classical revival from the late 15th century, when the work was first printed, to the 18th century.
Granger, F. (ed.), *Virtruvius: On Architecture*. 1931

Vittoria, Tommas *see* **Victoria, Tomás Luis de**

Vittorino da Feltre (1378–1446). Italian educationist. From 1425 he directed a school at Mantua under the patronage of Marquis Gian Francesco Gonzaga, whose children were among the pupils. By combining religious instruction with physical training and classical studies Vittorino aimed at producing the Renaissance ideal of a complete, balanced individual. The school provided a pattern followed by the many succeeding humanist educators.

Vivaldi, Antonio (*c.* 1675–1741). Italian composer and violinist, born in Venice. He was ordained (1703) but turned to music (1709). For many years he conducted the concerts at the Conservatorio dell'Ospedale della Pietà in Venice, a music school for orphan girls whose concerts enjoyed great prestige. He wrote operas and choral works but his fame rests on the large number of concertos which form the bulk of his output, for example the twelve concertos of *L'Estro Armonico* (1712). Many are for violin but he wrote examples for other instruments and for various instrumental combinations; several were transcribed by J. S. * Bach. Vivaldi was a great violin virtuoso and had considerable influence on violin technique and on the concerto.
Kolneder, W., *Antonio Vivaldi: his life and Work*. 1970

Vives, Juan Luis (Ludovicus Vives) (1492–1540). Spanish humanist. The dedication of his translation of St Augustine's *Civitas Dei* to Henry VIII brought an invitation to go to England as tutor to Princess Mary. His disapproval of the royal divorce was punished by imprisonment; from 1528 he lived and taught mostly in Bruges. His *De Disciplinis* (1531) became one of the best known books of guidance on humanist studies, and his psychological observations in a commentary (1528) on a work by Aristotle (*De Anima*) show a remarkably modern outlook.

Vlaminck, Maurice de (1876–1958). French landscape-painter of Belgian descent. An admirer of van Gogh, he became a friend of André Derain, with whom he joined the revolutionary group known, because of its violent use of strong colour, as the 'Fauves' ('wild beasts'). This period of his development lasted until 1907 when he came for a time under the influence of Cézanne. His later, more realistic, work lacks the earlier force. As a young man Vlaminck was well known as a racing cyclist.
Vlaminck, M. de, *Paysages et personnages*. 1953

Vogel, Sir Julius (1835–1899). New Zealand politician, born in London. He migrated to Victoria, then to New Zealand (1861) and in the same year founded the *Otago Daily Times*. He entered parliament in 1862 and as colonial treasurer he made bold proposals for the financing of immigration, railways and other public works by large loans. His policy as premier (1873–75 and 1876) led to the abolition of the provinces (1876).

Volstead, Andrew Joseph (1860–1947). American politician. A lawyer, he was a progressive Republic Congressman (1903–23) and supported liberal measures. He gained national attention as sponsor of the act (known as the Volstead Act) which made detailed legislative provisions for the enforcement of the 18th Amendment to the U.S. Constitution – the prohibition of the sale of alcohol. The act was passed in 1919 despite President Woodrow Wilson's veto; it was abrogated by the repeal of Prohibition (1933).

Volta, Alessandro, Count (1745–1827). Italian physicist. Professor of physics at Como (1774–79) and at Pavia (1779–1804), from 1815 he directed the philosophical faculty at Padua. He discovered that electrical effects could be brought about by contact between two dissimilar metals, and he invented the simple battery or 'voltaic pile'. He also investigated electrification by friction, and invented the electrophorus and the condensing electroscope. He is commemorated by the name volt given to the unit of electromotive force.

Voltaire (François Marie Arouet) (1694–1778). French writer; epitome and genius of the eighteenth century Enlightenment. The son of a Parisian lawyer, he was educated at a Jesuit school but soon found congenial company in a lively young set of sceptical aristocrats. He declined to study law and after a year spent in the country studying history he returned to Paris. Accused of lampooning the regent, the Duke of Orléans, he was sent to the Bastille where he changed his name to Voltaire (supposedly an anagram of his name, Arouet l(e) j(eune)) and revised his first tragedy, *Oedipe* (1718), a great success. Publication of an epic (*La Ligue*) was forbidden because it championed Henry IV's efforts to establish toleration, but it was secretly printed and later revised and reissued – as *L'Henriade* (1728) – in England to which country Voltaire had been allowed to go (1721) after further undeserved confinement in the Bastille. In England he was lionized by the fashionable and literary worlds (Bolingbroke, Walpole, Swift, Pope, Gay etc.) and came under the influence of Newton and Locke. After his return (1729) he wrote several more plays, and a history of the Swedish king Charles XII which (with a later one on the age of Louis XIV) initiated modern historical methods; most controversial were his *Lettres philosophiques* (1734) in which his praise for the constitution, tolerance, and scientific achievements of England implied a criticism of France. From the storm this raised he found shelter at the home of Émilie, Marquise du Châtelet, at Cirey-sur-Blaise near the Lorraine frontier. Here he stayed for ten years writing more plays (of which *Alzire*, 1736, is regarded as one of his best), two philosophical letters and other works. By 1736 Frederick the Great of Prussia was already trying to persuade the great literary lion of Europe to grace his court but it was not until after Émilie's death (1749) that he eventually succeeded. Voltaire reached Berlin in 1751 but the experiment was not a success. The vain writer and the authoritarian king were ill at ease together, and in 1753 Voltaire was again on the move. In 1755 he went to live near Geneva and finally (1760) he made a permanent home in France at Ferney, near the Swiss frontier. In 1755 his mock epic on Joan of Arc, *La Pucelle*, appeared and in 1760 his best known work, *Candide*, in which Candide travels in the company of futilely optimistic Dr Pangloss (a satire on * Leibniz) who, however great the injustice and intolerance encountered, can only reflect that everything is for the best in the best of all possible worlds. Diderot and d'Alembert persuaded Voltaire to write many articles for their encylopedia, author and book alike contributing to the great revolution of ideas which preceded the political upheaval. Not only was much of Voltaire's later work propagandist but took practical steps (e.g. in defence of Jean * Calas) to right injustice. His belief in tolerance is summed up in his phrase 'I may disapprove of what you say but I will defend to the death your right to say it'. In 1778 he was triumphantly received in Paris, but the excitement was too much for him at his age (84) and he died shortly afterwards.

Topazio, V. W., *Voltaire: A critical study of his major works*. 1967

Vonnegut, Jr, Kurt (1922–). American novelist. Educated in science at Cornell, he served in World War II and was a prisoner of war in Germany. His novels, written in a 'hip' humorous style, reminiscent of some science-fiction, deal with the threats to individuality in a technologically obsessed society and include *Player Piano* (1952), *Slaughterhouse Five* (1969), *Breakfast of Champions* (1973) and *Slapstick* (1976). He was also a prolific essayist.

Voronoff, Serge (1866–1951). Russian physiologist. Working in Switzerland, he gained considerable notoriety in the 1930s with experiments designed to prolong human life by grafting animal glands, especially those of monkeys, into the body.

Voroshilov, Klimenty Yefremovich (1881–1969). Russian political soldier. A sheetmetal worker, he joined the Bolsheviks in 1903, led Red Army guerrillas against the Germans 1918, defended Tsaritsyn (later Stalingrad, now Volgograd) in 1919 during the Civil War and worked closely with * Stalin. He became commissar for defence 1925–40, a Politburo member 1926–60 and marshal of the Soviet Union (1935). However, he failed during the war with Finland (1939–40) and the German encirclement of Leningrad (1941), and Stalin dismissed him. On Stalin's death he became president of the USSR 1953–60, but lost any influence after 1957 when his attempt to dislodge * Khrushchev failed.

Vorster, Balthazar Johannes (1915–1983). South African politician and lawyer. A founder of the pro-Axis Ossewa Brandwag ('Ox-wagon Guard'), he was interned 1942–44 for opposing the war effort. In 1953 he entered parliament as an extremist National Party member, becoming a deputy minister (education, arts and science, social welfare and pensions) in 1958. He was minister of justice 1961–66, and was noted for a stringent application of apartheid law and traditional Boer principles; this also characterized his term as prime minister (1966–78). In 1978 he resigned and was elected president; in 1979 disclosures concerning the involvement of a former cabinet minister, Connie Mulder, in improper use of public funds for party propaganda led to his resignation (1979). Despite his hard line on racial issues, he cultivated trade and diplomatic links with black African states.

Voysey, Charles Francis Annesley (1857–1941). English domestic architect. Like those of Norman Shaw, the small country houses to which he devoted his career and of which his own house, The Orchard at Chorley Wood, Hertfordshire, is a good example, anticipate the simplicity and comfort of modern trends. For interior decoration he was much influenced by the traditions established by William Morris.

Vries, Hugo de (1848–1935). Dutch botanist and plant geneticist. Born of a wealthy and long established Dutch Baptist family, his interests from the time he was at school tended towards natural history, and his early research work was on plant cells. He spent part of the 1870s working for the Prussian government preparing works on cultivated plants such as sugar beest potatoes and clover. In 1877 he obtained a post teaching plant physiology at Amsterdam University where he stayed until his retirement in 1918. He is best known for work from the 1890s on plant inheritance; how hereditary characteristics were passed down had been a source of immense debate within evolutionary theory. In his two major books, *Intracellular Pangenesis* (1899) and *Die Mutationstheorie* (1901) de Vries argued that inherited characteristics were quite separate individual units each of which had its own separate genetion bearer. De Vries called this bearer a 'pangene'. Pangenes combined in fixed ratios to breed either true or mutant forms – as de Vries showed with his own extensive experiments on hybridization. He made use of * Mendel's writings, and came to the conclusion that mutations could be preserved because the information for them was contained in fixed, transmissible genetic material. He believed that evolution occurred by quite large 'steps' (corresponding to mutant forms of pangene), though this notion won little favour with the scientific community.

Vries, Peter de *see* **De Vries, Peter**

Vyshinsky, Andrey Yanuarevich (1883–1954). Russian lawyer and politician. He became public prosecutor (1931) and was soon notorious for the rancour and vindictiveness with which he conducted state trials, notably in the 'purges' of 1936–37. From 1943 he became active in foreign affairs and was Molotov's successor as foreign minister (1949–53). As a delegate to the United Nations Organization he often attacked western policies with the same vigour as he had shown in the Soviet courts.

Waals, Johannes Diderik van der (1837–1923). Dutch chemist. Poverty delayed his progress so much that it was not until 1873 that his dissertation for a doctorate was published. In one of the most important papers of its kind ever published he pointed the way to all modern methods of gas liquefaction. As a result of immediate academic appreciation he became (1877) professor of physics at Amsterdam, where his prestige as a scientific leader added authority to his great reputation as a teacher. He won the Nobel Prize for Physics (1910).

Wagner, (Wilhelm) Richard (1813–1883). German composer, born at Leipzig. He was of unknown parentage though it is likely that his mother was an illegitimate daughter of Prince Constantin of Weimar and his father an actor named Geyer. He studied music chiefly at St Thomas's School, Leipzig. His musical career started unhappily with immature compositions and ill paid conductorships of small orchestras, e.g. at Königsberg and Riga. When he went to Paris (1839) he was forced to keep himself by hack-work while trying to gain support for the operas upon which he was engaged. At last he obtained a post as opera conductor at Dresden (1842) and there *Rienzi* (1842) was produced with considerable success. *The Flying Dutchman* (1843) and *Tannhäuser* (1845) were less well received. Wagner was now becoming involved in revolutionary politics; in consequence *Lohengrin*, which had been written in Paris, was refused by the authorities. When a revolution failed (1849) he was exiled (until 1862) from Saxony and took refuge in Switzerland; but * Liszt came to the rescue (1850) by staging *Lohengrin* at his small theatre at Weimar. In 1853 Wagner began work on the music of the cycle *The Ring of the Nibelungs*, comprising *Rhinegold, The Valkyrie, Siegfried* and *The Twilight of the Gods* (*Götterdämmerung*): as always he wrote the libretto himself (this time in short fluid lines without rhyme) and so secured the unity so often lacking between words and music. Having completed the first two operas and part of *Siegfried* he interrupted the enterprise to write *Tristan and Isolde*. Since *The Ring* would require a special theatre for its performance, he knew that production must in any case be distant; *Tristan and Isolde* was written therefore to fill the gap and improve his finances (he was always in debt). Even for this production, there were long and daunting delays before the enthusiasm of King * Ludwig of Bavaria enabled it to take place at Munich in 1865. It was followed by *The Mastersingers* (1868). These two operas were conducted by Hans von Bülow, with whose wife Cosima, an illegitimate daughter of Liszt, Wagner eloped. They were married in 1870 after having three children. Despite debts and difficulties Wagner now set about the construction of an opera house equipped by its size and mechanical arrangements to house the production of *The Ring*, with all the lavish scenic effects, aerial flights and elaborate transformations in which he took such delight. With the help of Nietzche and others he succeeded, and the Bayreuth Festival Theatre was opened in 1876 with the production of the whole *Ring cycle* (completed 1874). His last opera *Parsifal* was produced there in 1882; after his death the theatre passed to his wife, his son Siegfried (to celebrate whose birth he wrote the *Siegfried Idyll* for orchestra) and his descendants. He died at the Palazzo Vendramin-Calergi in Venice.

The literary influences on Wagner's work are clear: Greek tragedy (e.g. the Oedipus theme), Teutonic legend, the romances of Gottfried von Strassburg and Wolfram von Eschenbach, and the philosophy of Nietzsche and Schopenhauer. But by his own reforms and innovations he altered the course of operatic history. He conceived 'music drama' as a synthesis of all the art forms, with music, poetry, dancing, mime and scenic effects all of equal importance. He abolished the classical structure of opera with arias and recitative links and substituted a continuous dramatic narrative in which recurring themes (leitmotifs) register the presence of characters and ideas. By an extension of Weber's practice he also discarded tradition by concentrating the thematic material in the orchestral accompaniment, Beethoven being his model for the development of this material. He went far beyond his predecessors in the expansion of orchestral resources and development of chromatic harmony. Few composers have been so slow to gain contemporary recognition or have been the subject of such keen controversy. His character was fundamentally unattractive: he was egotistical and disloyal: he lived on friends, whom he often alienated by ingratitude: he was sybaritic and extravagant. He kept his first wife Minna Planer (married 1836, died 1866) in a torment of jealousy (e.g. of Mathilde Wesendonck, who inspired his Isolde). On the other hand his one comic opera, *The Mastersingers*, contains ample evidence of the humour, humanity and attractive high spirits to which contemporary accounts bear witness.

Newman, E., *The Life of Richard Wagner*. 4 vols., 1933–47

Wagner-Jauregg, Julius (1857–1940). Austrian neurologist. He graduated in medicine at Vienna University and quickly rose to become a professor at Graz (1889). His early work was largely concerned with thyroid deficiency; he also made the controversial proposal that to prevent cretinism iodine should be introduced compulsorily into the manufacture of common salt. His later work was concerned with the treatment of psychotic ailments by fevers artificially produced. Among the various fever-producing agents tested, tuberculin was used with success in the treatment of general paralysis of the insane. During World War I, however, he coped with this disease more effectively by inoculating patients with benign tertian malaria. For his researches in this field he won the Nobel Prize for Medicine (1927).

Wakefield, Edward Gibbon (1796–1862). English colonial reformer. After holding diplomatic posts in Turin and Paris, he was imprisoned in Newgate (1827–30) for abducting an heiress, and while there studied colonial government and outlined his views in *A Letter from Sydney* (1829). To test his theories the South Australia Association was formed to found a new colony in that area, but before this had taken place (1836) Wakefield ended his connexion with the promoters: he formed (1837) a similar Association (which became chartered company in 1841) for the colonization of New Zealand. In 1838 he went with Lord Durham to Canada to advise on the use of crown lands, and in 1839 he encouraged the dispatch of the first group of setters to New Zealand. In 1849 his book *A View of the Art of Colonization* appeared. Meanwhile settlements had been made in New Zealand under the auspices of the Company and in 1852, after a constitution had been enacted, he went there himself. He was a member of the first assembly of 1854.

Waksman, Selman Abraham (1888–1973). American microbiologist, born in Russia. A naturalized American from 1916, he was professor of microbiology at Rutgers University, New Jersey (1930–56). After examining a great many microscopic organisms from soil, he isolated two powerful antibiotics – the highly poisonous antimycin (1941) and the widely-used streptomycin (1943). He won the Nobel Prize for Physiology and Medicine (1952).

Waksman, S. A., *My Life with the Microbes*. 1954

Waldheim, Kurt (1918–). Austrian diplomat and U.N. official. He entered the Austrian foreign service after World War II and served as counsellor and head of the personnel division, ministry of foreign affairs, 1951–55. He was three times an observer or representative to the U.N.: 1955–56, 1964–68 and 1970–71. In 1960–64 he served as director general of political affairs at the Austrian foreign ministry, and was minister for foreign affairs (1968–70). He was secretary general of the United Nations 1972–81.

Waldo, Peter (or Pierre) (died 1210?). French religious reformer. A rich merchant of Lyons, he gave up his wealth and formed a band of itinerant preachers. His followers (known as 'the Poor Men of Lyons' or the Waldenses), rejected the sacramental claims of the priesthood and said that every man may exercise priestly functions if moved by the spirit. The sect was rigorously but intermittently persecuted by popes and rulers throughout history (e.g. in 1655, provoking Milton's sonnet 'Avenge, O Lord, thy slaughtered saints'), but it has survived in isolated parts of France and Italy.

Walesa, Lec (1943–). Polish trade union leader. A shipyard worker from Gdansk (formerly Danzig), a practising Catholic and Polish nationalist, Walesa was sacked in 1976 for his anti-government activity. He became a cofounder in 1978 of the Baltic Free Trade Unions, an underground movement. In 1980 he led a strike of shipyard workers in Gdansk which aroused massive public support and international sympathy, and led to the founding of the independent trade movement, Solidarity, which sought significant political concessions from the Polish government. The imposition of martial law in December 1981 led to Walesa's arrest and imprisonment for eleven months. He was awarded the 1983 Nobel Peace Prize.

Walewski, Alexandre Florian Joseph Colonna (1810–1868). French diplomat. The son of Napoleon I and his Polish mistress Marie Walewska, he came into prominence under his cousin Napoleon III as ambassador in London (1851–52), foreign minister (1855–60), minister of state (1860–63) and finally president of the legislative assembly (1865–68).

Waley, Arthur David (original name A. D. Schloss) (1889–1966). English orientalist and poet. Although he never visited China or Japan, he published outstanding translations of Chinese and Japanese classics, notably *The Tale of Genji* (1925–33) by * Murasaki Shikubu, and received the CH in 1956.

Wallace, Alfred Russel (1823–1913). English naturalist. Originally trained as a surveyor, he turned to natural history and explored with H. W. Bates the Amazon basin (1848–50); but his collections were destroyed by shipwreck on the way home. He investigated (1854–62) animal and plant life in the Malay archipelago. Independently of * Darwin, to whom he communicated his ideas, he developed the theory of natural selection. Their joint work was read to Royal Society in 1858. Their views were not, however, identical: Wallace did not believe, for example, that natural selection alone could explain such changes as the loss of human hair: he thought too that the male adornments required to provoke sexual selection by animals would conflict with other requirements for the 'survival of the fittest' by natural selection. Wallace also wrote the important treatise *The Geographical Distribution of Animals* (1876). He was the first Darwin medallist (1890) and received the O.M. in 1910.

George, W. B., *Biologist Philosopher*. 1964

Wallace, (Richard Horatio) **Edgar** (1875–1932). English author. An orphan, brought up in poverty, he joined the army and later became a sporting journalist. An immense literary output, mainly of thrillers, included novels as popular as *The Four Just Men* (1905) and *Sanders of the River* (1911), and successful plays, e.g. *The Ringer* and *On the Spot*.

Wallace, George Corley (1919–). US politician. He was an army sergeant in World War II, then took a law degree from Alabama University. As governer of Alabama 1963–67 and 1971–75, he became a notorious opponent of desegregation. Nominally a Democrat, he backed Barry * Goldwater for president in 1964. His wife Lurline Wallace succeeded him as governor (1967), but died in office (1968). As presidential candidate of the American Independent Party in 1968 he polled 13.5 per cent of the vote. In May 1972 he was shot in Washington, DC, by Arthur Bremer and paralysed but in 1982 he won election for a third term as governor of Alabama.

Wallace, Henry Agard (1888–1965). American politician, born in Iowa. His grandfather, also Henry Wallace (1836–1916), founded the journal *Wallaces' Farmer* (1895); his father, Henry Cantwell Wallace (1866–1924), succeeded as editor and served as U.S. secretary of agriculture 1921–24. He also edited *Wallaces' Farmer* (1924–33) and developed high-yielding strains of hybrid corn (maize). F. D. Roosevelt appointed him (1933) secretary of agriculture, an office which he held until 1941, when he became vice-president of the U.S. He was secretary of commerce (1945–48) until dismissed by President Truman for attacking the government's foreign policy. He ran unsuccessfully for the presidency (1948) as candidate for the Progressive party which in 1950 he denounced as a Communist front.

Wallace Lew(is) (1827–1905). American soldier and author. He served in the Civil War as a major-general, was governor of New Mexico (1878–81) and minister to Turkey (1881–85). He is remembered, however, as author of the novel *Ben Hur* (1880), set in the time of Christ. It was one of the most successful books ever published, and the basis of several lavish films.

Wallace, Sir William (*c.* 1274–1305). Scottish patriot. He emerged from obscurity as the leader of the Scottish national resistance to the pretensions of the English king, Edward I. After early successes he inflicted a major defeat on an English army at Stirling Bridge (1297) and, advancing rapidly, devastated England's border counties. Against this threat Edward moved in person and gained a decisive victory at Falkink (1298). For a short time Wallace maintained a guerrilla struggle before making his way to France, where he tried to enlist support, and possibly visiting Rome. He was back in Scotland in 1303 but was betrayed (1305) to the English by Sir John Menteith, taken to London and hanged, drawn and quartered.
Fergusson, J., *Wallace*. 1938

Wallenberg, Raoul (1912–?   ). Swedish diplomat. He served in Hungary from July 1944 and was responsible for saving the lives of 70,000 Jews. He was taken prisoner by the Russians in January 1945 and disappeared. Following reports that he was still alive, an international 'Free Wallenberg' campaign was mounted.
Bierman, J., *Righteous Gentile*. 1981.

Wallenstein (or Waldstein), **Albrecht Eusebius Wenzel von, Duke of Friedland and Mecklenburg and Prince of Sagan** (1583–1634). Bohemian soldier. He came of a noble Czech family, and added to his family wealth by marrying a rich widow. Converted from Protestanism to Catholicism, he raised troops privately in support of the cause of the emperor Ferdinand II in Bohemia against * Frederick of the Palatinate at the beginning of the Thirty Years War. From the land of the defeated Protestant nobles he added still further to his own estates until his duchy of Friedland (he became duke in 1623) became an almost independent state. In 1625 he was made imperial commander-in-chief, quickly restored the situation in Hungary and Silesia, and advanced to the altic, gaining the duchy of Mecklenburg as a reward. Held up, however, by the siege of Stralsund and unable to carry out his intention of building a fleet he made peace with the Danes. Meanwhile his arrogance and his pretensions to act as a separate ruler roused jealousy of the traditional Catholic nobility and in 1630 Ferdinand found himself compelled to dismiss him. Wallenstein retired to his duchy of Friedland; but the emperor, dismayed by the victorious campaign of * Gustavus II of Sweden, was forced to recall Wallenstein, who after preliminary success in Bohemia and Saxony was defeated by the Swedes at Lutzen (1632). Defeat was more than compensated for by the death of Gustavus, but in 1633 Wallenstein was strangely inactive; he was in fact negotiating with Catholics and Protestants alike, with the probable aim of imposing a peace which, under nominal imperial rule, would leave him supreme. Ferdinand, aware of these manoeuvres, had already signed an order of dismissal when Wallenstein was murdered by a group of officers.
Mann, G., *Wallenstein*. 1976

Waller, Edmund (1606–1687). English poet. He was related to John Hampden and Oliver Cromwell and his wealth, already considerable, was increased when he married an heiress (1631). After her death (1634) he courted without success Lady Dorothy Sidney (the 'Sacharissa' of his poems). He served in parliament from earliest manhood, but after joining the opposition veered in his allegiance and engineered the 'Waller plot' to enable Charles I to seize London (1643). For this he was banished, but in 1651 was reconciled with Cromwell, to whom he wrote a panegyric. He contrived to remain in favour under Charles II. As a poet he was important for the development of the heroic couplet but is better

remembered for such charming lyrics as *Go Lovely Rose*.
Chernaik, W. L., *The Poetry of Limitation: A Study of Waller*. 1968

Waller, Thomas 'Fats' (1904–1943). American jazz composer and pianist. He influenced much of jazz technique and of 'stride' piano playing. His best known numbers are 'Ain't Misbehavin', 'Honeysuckle Rose' and 'Squeeze Me'.
Kirkeby, E., *Ain't Misbehaving*. 1966

Waller, Sir William (*c.* 1597–1668). English soldier. He served in the Thirty Years War and fought for parliament in the English Civil War but after a series of successes in the south and west was defeated at Roundway Down (July 1643). Convinced that the latter was due to the unreliability of his troops, he helped to found the New Model army (* Cromwell), but as an M.P. surrendered his command (1645) under the Self-denying Ordinance. As a Presbyterian he opposed Cromwell and the army extremists: he favoured a settlement with Charles I, and later conspired for Charles II's return.
Adair, J., *Roundhead General*. 1969

Wallis, Sir Barnes Neville (1887–1979). British aeronautical engineer. He trained as a marine engineer and later became designer in the airship department of Vickers Ltd. He designed the airship R100 but is most remembered for the bouncing bombs used against the Möhne and Eder dams during World War II. At the time of his death he was working on a square-shaped aeroplane capable of 5,000 m.p.h. (8,000 k.p.h.).
Morpurgo, J. E., *Barnes Wallis: A Biography*. 1972

Wallis, John (1616–1703). English mathematician. Professor of geometry at Oxford (from 1648), his most important work is the *Arithmetica infinitorum* (1655) which paved the way for the introduction of calculus and the binomial theorem. He introduced negative indices and our present symbol for infinity. Among many other works he wrote *Treatise of Algebra* (1685). He was among the founders of the Royal Society.
Scott, J. F., *The Mathematical Work of John Wallis 1616–1703*. 1938

Walpole, Horace, 4th Earl of Orford (1717–1797). English man of letters. Fourth son of Sir Robert * Walpole, at Cambridge he became a friend of the poet Gray, with whom he made the 'grand tour' of Europe. He was an M.P. (1741–68), obtained several sinecure offices, but took no active part in politics. In 1747 he bought a house near Twickenham and devoted many years to transforming it into the fanciful 'little Gothic castle' of Strawberry Hill: he spent most of the rest of his life there, establishing a private press. His letters, witty, graceful and with an almost feminine love of gossip, are now regarded as his most important literary work; they provide a valuable first-hand account of polite society and of such events as the Gordon riots. Though clearly intended for publication they reveal none the less a warm and affectionate disposition. Of his other writings the most famous is *The Castle of Otranto* (1764), an early and influential 'Gothic novel'. In 1791 he inherited the earldom from his nephew. He invented the term 'serendipity'.
Lewis, W. S., *Horace Walpole*. 1961

Walpole, Sir Hugh Seymour (1884–1941). English novelist. He was born in New Zealand but was brought up and subsequently lived in Great Britain. His earliest success was *Mr Perrin and Mr Traill* (1911), a story of a schoolmaster's life. During World War I he served with the Russian Red Cross, and *The Dark Forest* (1916), which resulted from this experience, revealed his homosexuality. In *The Cathedral* (1922), however, which recalls Trollope (whose life he wrote), he is in his happiest vein. Among his later successes was the historical series beginning with *Rogue Herries* (1930), set in the Lake District, where Walpole made his home. He was knighted in 1937.
Hart-Davis, R., *Hugh Walpole: A Biography*. 1952

Walpole, Robert, 1st Earl of Orford (1676–1745). English politician. He was the third son of a Norfolk landowner and after the death of his brothers the inheritance came to him. He was an M.P. (1701–12; 1713–42) when he was created Earl of Orford. He held office as war secretary (1708–10) and treasurer to the navy (1710–11) in Queen Anne's Whig ministry but he resigned with his colleagues when the Tories came to power (1710) and he had to await the accession of George I before returning to office. From 1715 to 1717 he was first lord of the Treasury and chancellor of the exchequer but in the latter year a party split caused him to resign: in 1721 he returned to his former office and for the next twenty-one years was in all but name prime minister; it is little more than a legend that he was left to preside over the cabinet because of the king's inability to understand English. The truth was that Walpole was little interested in foreign affairs and left the handling of them to the king and Lord * Townshend while he concerned himself with the domestic situation. At the beginning of his period of office he dealt satisfactorily with the crisis of the South Sea Bubble and thereafter, in a long period of peace, built up British prosperity by retrenchment (involving a dangerous neglect of the armed services), by establishing a sinking fund and by lightening taxation. He kept control of parliament by the traditional method of bribery ('every man has his price'); the fact that he roused the envy of his opponents because he bestowed his favours monetary or otherwise with greater subtlety and skill need not be held against him. Less excusable was the jealousy which made him secure his own position by keeping potential rivals, e.g. Carteret, in the background. A cabinet of second-raters was the inevitable result.

In his later years war was held at bay only by a policy of appeasement and when hostilities broke out (the war of 'Jenkins' Ear' with Spain of 1739 merging in 1742 with the War of Austrian Succession) it was evident that so determined a man of peace as Walpole was not suitable in time of war. He resigned after a hostile vote (1742) and retired from politics. Even Macaulay, who praised his 'prudence, steadiness and vigilance' admitted that 'he was content to meet daily emergencies by daily expedients'.

Plumb, J. H., *Sir Robert Walpole*. Vol 1, 1956; Vol 2, 1961

Walpurga, St (died *c.* 780). English abbess of Eidenham in Germany. Her day is 1 May, the eve of which, Walpurgis night, is according to German legend a time when witches hold their sabbaths and sacrifice to the Devil.

Walsingham, Sir Francis (1530?–1590). English diplomat and secretary of state. He lived abroad to escape the troubles of Mary's reign but, when Elizabeth succeeded, his abilities were discovered by * Burghley and in 1570 he was sent as ambassador to Paris. After his return he was appointed a secretary of state (1573). His main task was to gain information of links between the powers on the continent and Roman Catholic conspirators in England, whose object was to murder or dethrone Elizabeth and replace her by * Mary Queen of Scots. To achieve this he maintained a body of spies which (though far from being comparable to a modern secret service) kept him closely informed of the comings and goings of conspirators. Letters were intercepted and decoded but subsequently delivered to give a feeling of false security to his victims which enabled him to arrest them at their most unguarded moments. The exposure of the Babington plot which clearly implicated Mary and led to her execution was among his notable successes. Walsingham was a patron of arts and letters and supported voyages of exploration and colonization but was so ill rewarded that he died in poverty.

Read, C., *Mr. Secretary Walsingham*. 1925.

Walter, Bruno (Bruno Walter Schlesinger) (1876–1962). German–American conductor, born in Berlin. Trained as a pianist, he conducted at the Vienna Imperial Opera (1901–12) as a protégé of Mahler whose *Das Lied von der Erde* (1911) and Symphony No. 9 (1912) he he premiered. General music director at the Munich Opera (1913–22) and the Gewandhaus Orchestra, Leipzig (1929–33), he left Nazi Germany for Austria, where he helped to shape the character of the Salzburg Festival and became artistic adviser to the Vienna State Opera. The overruning of Austria by the Germans (1938) caused him to seek refuge in Paris and then in the U.S.A., of which country he became a citizen in 1946. Walter's repertory was wide though he excelled notably in interpretations of Mozart and of his friend Mahler.

Walter, John (1739–1812). English publisher. Having acquired a printing office (1784) he founded the *Daily Universal Register* (1785) which he renamed (1788) *The Times*. Under his younger son, **John Walter II** (1776–1847), it developed into a great national newspaper. A third **John Walter** (1818–1894) continued the family association.

Walter the Penniless (died 1097). Burgundian knight. With Peter the Hermit, he led the march across Europe of the enthusiastic but undisciplined body which set out in advance of the organized armies for the 1st Crusade.

Having crossed the Bosphorus they were all but wiped out by the Turks at Nicaea.

Walther von der Vogelweide (*c.* 1170–1230). German minnesinger. The greatest of medieval German lyric poets, after several vicissitudes at the court of Vienna he became (*c.* 1215) court minstrel to the emperor Frederick II, who rewarded him with an estate. As well as songs, he wrote maxims which have a strong political flavour. He enriched the art of the troubadour by introducing into his songs not only the conventional gallantries of courtly love but the more natural affections of the less high-born.
Taylor, R. J., *The Art of the Minnesinger*. 1968

Walton, Izaak (1593–1683). English author. As the owner of a shop in Chancery Lane he came to know John * Donne, in whose parish it was. Thus brought into contact with ecclesiastical and literary circles, he was asked by Sir Henry * Wotton to collect material for a preface to a biography of Donne he proposed to write. This started him on a literary career which led to his writing biographies of Donne, Wotton, Hooker, Herbert and Bishop Sanderson. In 1644 Walton retired to rural Clerkenwell and there wrote *The Compleat Angler* (1653, enlarged 1655), a rhapsody on the joys of fishing (with concealed advice for living in troubled times), containing verses, ancedotes and pastoral descriptions.
Bottrall, M., *Izaak Walton*. 1955

Walton, Sir William Turner (1902–1983). English composer. As a chorister of Christ Church, Oxford, he received some formal training of his precocious talent. The early *Façade* (1923), a setting for reciter and chamber ensemble of poems by Edith * Sitwell, was suffused with a wit that dominates the overture *Portsmouth Point* (1926) and the outer movements of the Sinfonia Concertante (1928: revised 1943). In the Viola Concerto (1929), probably his masterpiece, the wit deepens into a violence that contrasts with a new vein of romantic melancholy, a change of mood that was to become characteristic. The cantata *Belshazzar's Feast* (1931) is notable for the savagely brilliant orchestration, representing the sufferings of the exiled Jews, and for choral writing of Handelian splendour. This was followed by the Symphony No. 1 (1935) and the Violin Concerto (1939). A String Quartet (1947) and a Violin Sonata (1950) preceded the opera *Troilus and Cressida* (1954), Symphony No. 2 (1960) and *Variations on a theme by Hindemith* (1963). He composed film music, e.g. *Henry V, Hamlet* and *Richard III* and music for coronations, *Crown Imperial* (1937) and *Te Deum* (1953). Later works include a comic opera *The Bear* (1967) and a *Magnificat* and *Nunc Dimittis*. He was knighted in 1951 and received the O.M. in 1968.

Wang Hung-Wen (1934?–). Chinese Communist politician. Of unknown background, he was apparently well-educated, became a textile worker and rose to power in Shanghai during the Cultural Revolution. As a protégé of * Mao Ze-dong he was a Politburo member (1973–76) and third in the Chinese Communist Party hierarchy. He was forced out in October 1976, attacked as one of the 'Gang of Four', tried in 1980 and sentenced to life imprisonment.

Warbeck, Perkin (*c.* 1474–1499). Pretender to the English throne. By birth a Fleming, he was persuaded by the Yorkists to claim that he was Richard, Duke of York, the younger of Edward IV's sons believed to have been murdered in the Tower of London. In 1492 he was 'recognized' by Edward IV's sister, Margaret, Duchess of Burgundy. After an unsuccessful landing at Deal, Kent (1495), he went to Ireland and then to the court of James IV of Scotland, where he was married to Catherine Gordon, the Earl of Huntley's daughter. He next sailed to Cornwall, failed to take Exeter by siege, fled and eventually surrendered to Henry VII. He was imprisoned in the Tower of London and after an attempt to escape and alleged involvement in a plot with the Earl of Warwick he was tried and executed.

Warburg, Emil Gabriel (1846–1913). German physicist. He carried out extensive experimental investigations of electrical conduction in solids, liquids and gases. His work on spark discharges in rarefied gases led on to the experiments by Franck and G. L. Hertz on electron collisions. He later moved in the direction of photochemical studies and confirmed the fundamental law of the quantum nature of light absorption formulated by Einstein. Warburg was a celebrated teacher. During his ten years at the Berlin Physics Institute he trained about a fifth of the productive German physicists of the next generation.

Ward, Artemus (pseudonym of Charles Farrar Browne) (1834–1867). American humorist. He was famous for his lectures in the U.S.A. and England, and for his contributions, quaint and misspelled, to American and English publications, including *Punch*. His humour was one of the classic American variety, the shrewd plain-speaking of the ostensibly 'simple' man.

Ward, Mrs Humphrey (née Mary Augusta Arnold) (1851–1920). English writer. She was born in Tasmania, but at the age of five returned to Britain with her father, a son of Arnold of Rugby, himself a scholar and writer who having been converted to Roman Catholicism became co-editor of the *Catholic Dictionary* (1883). His daughter, who married (1872) Thomas Humphrey Ward, an Oxford don and art critic, was also preoccupied with religion and the best known of her books, *Robert Elsmere* (1888), studies the hero's struggle with religious doubt.
Trevelyan, J. P., *Mrs. Humphrey Ward.* 1923

Ward, Sir Joseph George, 1st Bart. (1856–1930). New Zealand politician born near Melbourne. He was the last in the line of Liberal prime ministers who from 1870 brought New Zealand through its great period of social and economic development. His own term of office (1906–12) was ended by parliamentary defeat, but he returned (1915) to join his opponent, W. F. Massey, in a coalition which led their country to victory in World War I; both were present at the Paris Peace Conference (1919). Ward was again briefly prime minister (1928–30).

Warhol, Andy (1931–). American artist and film-maker. He was a leading exponent of Pop Art in the 1960s using household objects, such as soup cans. He also produced silk screen portraits of film stars including Marilyn Monroe. Later he turned to making 'underground' films, some of which lasted as long as twenty-five hours; these included *Chelsea Girls* (1966) and *Blue Movie* (1969). His New York based 'Factory' became a fashionable studio and centre for the artistic avant-garde and eccentrics of the sixties and early seventies.

Warlock, Peter (pseudonym of Philip Heseltine) (1894–1930). English composer. He wrote music criticism and edited music under his own name Heseltine. He wrote nearly 100 songs, in which the predominant moods are Elizabethan jollity (many were settings of Elizabethan poems) and sensuous melancholy, e.g. *The Curlew* (1923), a setting for tenor and chamber ensemble for poems by Yeats. He also wrote choral and orchestral works, e.g. the *Capriol Suite* for strings (1926).

Warner, Charles Dudley (1829–1900). American journalist. In 1884 he became editor of *Harper's Magazine*. He wrote works of travel and biographies and collaborated with Mark * Twain on *The Gilded Age* (1873).

Warner, Harry Morris (1881–1958). American film producer. With his brothers Samuel, Albert and Jack, he formed (1923) the motion-picture company Warner Brothers. He produced (1929) *The Jazz Singer*, the first talking picture. His parents, whose family name was Eichelbaum, went to the U.S.A. from Russia in 1890.

Warner, Sir Pelham Francis (1873–1963). English cricketer. As captain of Middlesex and England for many years and as one of the most attractive and informed writers on the game, he occupied an important place in the history of English cricket.
Warner, P. F., *Long Innings*. 1951

Warren, Earl (1891–1974). American lawyer and Republican politician. He served as attorney-general (1939–43) and governor (1943–53) of California until President * Eisenhower appointed him as chief justice of the U.S. Supreme Court (1953–69). His activist court made liberal decisions which changed the U.S. far more than Congress or the presidency by ruling against segregated schools (1954), securing legal protection for accused persons, redistributing state legislative districts, striking down censorship laws, and emphasizing civil liberties and the right to dissent. His commission of enquiry into President * Kennedy's assassination (1963–64) was attacked as inadequate and its conclusions criticised. Warren was a favourite whipping boy for right-wing extremists.
White, G. E., *Earl Warren*. 1982

Warren, Robert Penn (1905–). American poet, novelist and critic. Born in Kentucky, he studied at Berkeley, Yale and (as a Rhodes Scholar) Oxford. He won a Pulitzer Prize in 1947 for his novel, *All the King's Men* (1946), based on the life of Huey * Long, and made into an award-winning film. In 1958 he won a second Pulitzer Prize for *Promises: Poems 1954–56*.

Warwick, Richard Neville, Earl of (known as 'the King-maker') (1428–1471). English nobleman. He acquired the Warwick earldom (1449) through his wife's rights, while the earldom of Salisbury came to him on his father's death (1460). He thus owned so much land and wealth that he was able to hold the balance in the Wars of the Roses. At first he joined the Yorkist faction and after the death of its leader, Richard, Duke of York, was able (1461) to supplant Henry VI by Richard's son, Edward IV. Edward was not the man, however, to submit tamely to a power behind the throne, and when Warwick secretly married (1469) his daughter Isabel to the king's brother, the Duke of Clarence, Edward was strong enough to force Warwick and Clarence to take refuge in France, where a reconciliation took place with Margaret, Henry VI's queen. As champion of the Lancastrian cause Warwick now returned to England, compelled Edward in his turn to leave the country, and reinstated Henry VI. In March 1471 Edward landed in Yorkshire, was joined by his repentant brother Clarence, and met, defeated and killed Warwick at Barnet. Warwick's younger daughter Anne married Richard III.
Kendall, P. M., *Warwick the Kingmaker*. 1957

Washington, Booker Taliaferro (1856–1915). American Negro educationist. He was born in Virginia and by becoming (1872) a janitor at the Hampton Normal and Agricultural Institute he was able to work his way through the course and graduate (1875). He then began to teach and interested himself in educational methods. In 1881 he became principal of a school for Negroes at Tuskegee, Alabama, and made it a centre of Negro education. His writings, e.g. his autobiography *Up from Slavery* (1901), aimed to promote racial understanding.

Washington, George (1732–1799). First president of the U.S. (1789–97). He was born at Bridges Creek, Virginia, the eldest of his father's six children by his second wife, there being already four children in his first family. His father was the grandson of John Washington, whose family home was at Sulgrave, Northamptonshire, England, and who had emigrated (1656/7) to Virginia, where his domains had been enlarged by his successors. After his father's death (1743) George, then aged 11, came under the guardianship of his elder half-brother Lawrence, with whom he lived at Mount Vermon. Here he came to know Lord Fairfax and his brother, who was Lawrence's father-in-law. The brothers took George under their wing, encouraged him to educate himself in their large library, and by sending him to survey their own outlying land enabled him to become (1749) a public surveyor. The death of Lawrence (1751) and that of his daughter soon afterwards gave George the ownership of the Mount Vernon estate. In 1751 he had been appointed adjutant-general, with the rank of major, of the provincial militia, and in 1753 was sent on a dangerous mission (described in his *Journey to the Ohio*) to the French commander, 600 miles distant, to warn him against encroachments upon British territory. The warning being disregarded, Washington accompanied General Braddock on the disastrous expedition of 1755 and showed great skill in rallying the routed survivors. On his return he was given command of all the Virginian forces, but the subsequent fighting in which he took part was of only minor importance. In 1758 he was elected to the Virginia House of Burgesses, where his contributions to debate were marked by common sense rather than eloquence.

For most of the next few years, however, Washington was leading, at Mount Vernon, the ordinary life of a prosperous country gentleman, spending much time in riding, of which he was particularly fond, performing many public duties and steadily improving his estate. In his social activities he was greatly helped by the rich young widow, **Martha Dandridge Custis** (1732–1802), whom he married (1759). Washington accepted, without approving, the institution of slavery, and freed at his death the 100 or so slaves whom he owned.

The events which preceded the War of American Independence found Washington firmly on the side of the colonists. Despite the dissolution of their House by the British government for its support of the Boston resistance to taxation without representation, the burgesses continued to meet elsewhere and Washington was chosen as a delegate to the two continental congresses (1774 and 1775) summoned to decide on future action. The second was interrupted by the outbreak of hostilities, and Washington, one of the few with the necessary military experience, was made commander-in-chief of all revolutionary forces. Assuming the leadership just after the American defeat at Bunker Hill (June 1775), he began the enormous task of recruitment, training and equipment necessary to match his troops on equal terms with the British and German regulars. A new vigour and determination were soon apparent, but though the British were driven from Boston (1776) Washington's attempt to hold New York against * Howe failed and a year of varying fortunes (1777) culminated in the defeat at Brandywine. Having overcome a movement to deprive him of his command, Washington emerged from the hardships of wintering at Valley Forge (1777–78) with a hardened, better trained and much more efficient army, unitedly devoted to its leader. The tide finally turned when France entered the war and it was the surrender of Cornwallis at Yorktown (October 1781) to a combined attack by French ships and American troops that virtually ended the fighting, though formal acknowledgement of independence awaited the Treaty of Versailles (1783). Washington was no great strategist, but without the patience, courage and will-power of his formidable personality victory could have scarcely been achieved.

The war over, Washington returned to Mount Vernon but in 1787 was recalled to preside over the Constitutional Conference of Philadelphia, at which delegates from the twelve states hammered out the terms of their future association. On one point all were agreed, that Washington should be their leader and in 1789 he took office as first president of the U.S. He chose his first government from members of all factions and only his force of character could hold together, even temporarily, men of such different outlook as Thomas * Jefferson and Alexander * Hamilton. Jefferson eventually went into opposition and after his unanimous re-election (1792) Washington worked mainly with the Federalists. Among his most important decisions was that which kept America neutral in the war between England and France. He refused a third term of office. Henry Lee's words, contained in the Resolutions in the House of Representatives at the time of his death, remain his finest epitaph: 'First in war, first in peace, and first in the hearts of his fellow citizens'.

Freeman, D. S., *George Washington*. 6 vols. 1948–54; Knollenberg, B., *George Washington*. 1965.

Wassermann, August von (1866–1925). German bacteriologist. After practising as a physician for some years he became (1902) a professor at the Koch Institute for Infectious Diseases at Berlin and in 1913 was given the direction of a new institute of experimental therapy. He is best remembered for the reaction test for syphilis which bears his name, but he also worked to provide antitoxins for immunization against other diseases, e.g. diphtheria, cholera, tuberculosis.

Waterhouse, Alfred (1830–1905). English architect, born in Manchester. He designed several important London buildings, e.g. the Natural History Museum, St Paul's School and the Prudential building in Holborn.

Watson, James Dewey (1928–). American biologist. Educated at Indiana and Chicago Universities, he worked with F. H. C. * Crick in Cambridge on establishing the structure and function of DNA (deoxyribonucleic acid) and published the joint findings in 1953. In 1962 he shared the Nobel Prize for Medicine with Crick and M. F. H. * Wilkins. He wrote *The Double Helix* (1968), a lively account of the DNA discovery.

Watson, John Christian (1867–1941). Australian Labor politician, born in Valparaiso, Chile. After serving in the New South Wales Parliament (1894–1901), he was a foundation Member of the Commonwealth Parliament (1901–10), the first federal leader of the Australian Labor Party (1901–04) and the first Labor prime minister (1904). He left the ALP over conscription (1916) and went into business.

Watson-Watt, Sir Robert Alexander (1892–1973). Scottish physicist. He played the chief part in the introduction of radar. While superintendent of the Radio Department at the National Physical Laboratory, he convinced military and political leaders of the possibility of applying to the location of aircraft the known principle of range-finding by the reflection of radio waves (1935). In the following

years he led the team which developed this idea into an important defence weapon for World War II. He was elected F.R.S. in 1941 and knighted in 1942.
Watson-Watt, Sir R. A., *Three Steps to Victory*. 1958

Watt, James (1736–1819). Scottish engineer. The son of a merchant, he became, after an apprenticeship, instrument-maker to Glasgow University, where he had the use of a workshop for making engineering experiments. Here he devised (1765) means of improving the steam engine, notably by the addition of a separate condenser and a steam jacket. The reduction of wastage would, he estimated, cheapen steam power by about 75 per cent and thus make its use economic throughout industry. Delay in the construction of a full-size engine was overcome when Watt eventually obtained the backing of John Roebuck of the Carron Ironworks. Roebuck sold his interest to Matthew Boulton of Birmingham, and it was there that Watt successfully completed his engine (1775). Taken into partnership by Boulton he continued to make improvements. To transform the reciprocating (i.e. to-and-fro) motion into a rotary movement he devised a 'sun and planet' gear; he invented also the two-cylinder engine, the double-acting engine and a centrifugal governor for controlling speed. In another field he invented a copying press which by eliminating hand-made copies greatly reduced officework. The unit of electric power, the 'watt', was named after him.
Dickinson, H. W., *James Watt, Craftsman and Engineer*. 1936

Watteau, (Jean) **Antoine** (1684–1721). French painter. He was born at the border town of Valenciennes and so was in contact with the Flemish tradition. He went to study in Paris (1702) but continued to paint in the Flemish manner until he made his permanent home in Paris. While living there (1712–19) he introduced a new and highly sophisticated style in accord with the artificiality of court life. Subjects are the serenade, the dance, the whispered conversation, the picnic: shimmering gowns in a pastoral setting, a nostalgic transposition of the aura of the sweeter classical myth into the terms of Watteau's own day. Paintings like the *Embarkation for Cytherea* (1717) are among the masterpieces of baroque art. To these subjects he brought techniques derived from a study of Rubens's work and his own acute observation. In part, too, the pictures represent a dream-like escape from reality. He died of tuberculosis from which he had long suffered and for which a visit to England (1719) was a vain attempt to find a cure.
Adhémar, H., *Watteau: sa vie, son oeuvre*. 1950

Watts, George Frederic (1817–1904). English painter. He gained wide popularity, mainly through reproductions of allegorical pictures such as *Hope* and *Galahad*, but his best work is to be found in his portraits (most of which are in the National Portrait Gallery, London). His first marriage (1864) to the actress Ellen * Terry, then barely 17, was dissolved. He was an original member of the O.M. (1902).

Watts, Isaac (1674–1748). English hymn-writer. He was a nonconformist pastor in London, constantly handicapped by ill health; from 1712 he lived with and was cared for by Sir Thomas and Lady Abeny. He wrote a metrical version of the Psalms and was a most prolific writer of hymns, among the best known being *O God, our help in ages past, When I survey the wondrous cross* and *Jesus shall reign where'er the sun*.

Watts-Dunton, Theodore (1832–1914). English man of letters. He was the friend of many literary celebrities, e.g. William Morris, Tennyson, the Rossettis, but is remembered chiefly for having taken * Swinburne into his house on Putney Hill (1879) when he was in almost desperate plight; he tended and looked after him there until his death thirty years later. He was a constant contributor of essays and criticisms to the periodicals and as well as poetry wrote *Aylwin* (1898), an eerie novel about gipsies, and *The Old Familiar Faces* (1915), a book about his many friends.

Waugh, Evelyn Arthur St John (1903–1966). English novelist. Nearly all his works are characterized by great wit, cynicism and, in his later works, a firmly conservative view of life. The early novels include *Decline and Fall* (1928), *Vile Bodies* (1930), *Black Mischief* (1932), *A Handful of Dust* (1934) and *Scoop* (1938). He became a Roman Catholic convert (1930) and wrote a notable biography of Edmund Campion (1935). After World War II, in which he served and which provided the theme of some of his later novels, he wrote, e.g., *Brideshead Revisited* (1945), *The Loved One* (1948) – a satire on American funerary methods, *Men at Arms* (1952) and *Officers and Gentlemen* (1955). *The Ordeal of Gilbert Pinfold* (1957) was a remarkably percipient self-portrait in the form of a fantasy. His brother, **Alec Waugh** (1898–1981) won a precocious success with his school story *The Loom of Youth* (1917), but none of his later works, e.g. *Island in the Sun* (1956), achieved the same renown. His son, **Auberon Alexander Waugh** (1939–), is a prolific journalist, cultivating a cynical style.

Waugh, E. A. St. J., *A Little Learning*. 1983

Wavell, Archibald Percival Wavell, 1st Earl (1883–1950). British soldier. Just before the opening of World War II he became commander-in-chief Middle East. His brilliant campaign of December 1940 resulted in the conquest of Cyrenaica and the capture of 130,000 Italian prisoners. In July 1941 Wavell was sent to command in India and while there had the hopeless task of defending the East Indies against the Japanese. From 1943 to 1947 he was viceroy of India. Wavell, a soldier whose modesty matched his skill, achieved more with infinitely fewer resources than almost any of his successors. His charming anthology, *Other Men's Flowers* (1944), revealed his love of poetry.

Wavell, A. P., *Generals and Generalship*. 1941

Waynflete, William of (*c.* 1395–1486). English scholar and prelate. He had been headmaster of Winchester for eleven years when (1441) he was called upon by Henry VI to organize his new school at Eton, of which he became provost when it opened (1443). He became bishop of Winchester (1447) and founded Magdalen College, Oxford (1448).

Webb, Sir Aston (1849–1930). London-born architect. He is best known for the new east front of Buckingham Palace, as well as the Victoria Memorial and Admiralty Arch which distinguish its ceremonial approach. Large extensions to the Victoria and Albert Museum were designed by him (1909).

Webb, Mary (née Meredith) (1881–1927). English novelist, born in Shropshire. Her best known works are the novels *The Golden Arrow* (1916) and *Precious Bane* (1924), which won the Femina Vie-Heureuse Prize.

Webb, Sidney James, 1st Baron Passfield (1859–1947). English socialist. Though he worked for a time in the Civil Service his career was in fact a literary and political collaboration with his wife, **Beatrice Webb** (née Potter) (1858–1943), on behalf of socialism. Even before her marriage Beatrice had assisted Charles Booth on an investigation of London working-class conditions and had written *The Co-operative Movement in Great Britain* (1891). The Webbs helped to found the Fabian Society (1884) and Sidney became an early member of the L.C.C. (1892). They sat on many Royal Commissions, e.g. on trade union law, the coal mines, and the Poor Law (for which in 1909 Beatrice produced a notable Minority Report); they helped start the London School of Economics (1895) and the *New Statesman* (1913). Their works on social history were of great importance, e.g. *The History of Trade Unionism* (1894), *English Local Government* (10 volumes, 1906–29) and *The Decay of Capitalist Civilization* (1921). Sidney became an M.P. (1922) and held ministerial appointments (1924 and 1929–31) in both the early Labour Governments (in the second as Lord Passfield). After a visit to Russia (1932) the Webbs wrote *Soviet Communism* (1935), a thorough but excessively admiring account.

Cole, M., and Drake, B., (eds.), *Our Partnership*. 1948

Weber, Carl Maria Friedrich Ernst von (1786–1826). German composer. His father ran a travelling theatre. In the hope that he would become a youthful prodigy he was sent to study music under Michael Haydn (brother of Joseph). After his first post as conductor at Breslau he entered the service of the Duke of Württemberg, where he and his father were expelled for debt and dissipation. To his early period belong his only two symphonies (of little worth), two tuneful Concertos (and one Concertino) for clarinet and strings and the operas *Sylvana* (1810) and *Abu Hassan* (1811). In 1813 he was director of the Prague opera and in 1817 was given the newly created post (which he retained for the rest of life) of director of German opera at Dresden. Here he succeeded in checking the dominance of Italian opera and in establishing the school of German romantic opera with its emphasis on the supernatural. His own contribution comprised his three mature operas, *Der Freischütz* (1821), *Euryanthe* (1823) and *Oberon* (1826).

Only *Der Freischütz* has remained popular, but their colourful, dramatically apt orchestration, the occasional use of leitmotifs and a new structure of the overture (based solely on themes from the opera itself) influenced * Wagner profoundly. Weber died while in London for the production of *Oberon* at Covent Garden. Of his other works one remains outstandingly popular, his piano waltz *Invitation to the Dance* (1819), to which the orchestration by Berlioz and, later, by Weingartner gave a fresh brilliance.

Warrack, J., *Carl Maria von Weber*. 1968

Weber, Max (1864–1920). German sociologist. While holding a succession of university appointments he wrote voluminously on social subjects, some of his most valuable work being concerned with the categorizing of social groups. His best known work, *The Protestant Ethic and the Spirit of Capitalism* (1920), an attempt to explain the link between the two halves of his title, had much influence in England and America.

Bendix, R., *Max Weber: An Intellectual Portrait*. 1962

Webern, Anton von (1883–1945). Austrian composer. He studied composition with * Schönberg, whose methods he adapted to his own purposes. After holding several posts elsewhere, Webern settled in Vienna where he conducted concerts of modern music and became conductor of the Vienna Workers' Symphony Orchestra. The Nazis banned his works and forbade him to teach; after liberation he was accidentally shot dead by an American soldier. Webern's orchestral works include a Passacaglia and two symphonies. He also wrote songs and two cantatas dating from World War II. In his compositions (most of which are very short) Webern, who developed Schönberg's principle of serialism by dividing the series into small cells and extended the serial principle to instrumental timbre, has had important influence on post-war composition (including Stravinsky's late works).

Wildgans, F., *Anton Webern*. 1966

Webster, Daniel (1782–1852). American lawyer, orator and politician. He was born in New Hampshire and later practised law in his native state and in Boston, where legal skill combined with magnificent eloquence made famous many of the cases (some concerned with constitutional matters of great importance) in which he appeared. Meanwhile he had become interested in politics. He was a distinguished figure in Congress (1813–17) and under President * Adams he was the administration's principal spokesman (1823–27) in the House; he was a member of the Senate (1827–41; 1845–50). He was prominent in the formation of the new Whig party (1833) but never obtained the presidential nomination. His electoral support (1841) of President Harrison won for him the secretaryship of state (1841–43), the Webster–Ashburton agreement on the Maine boundary dispute with Britain being one of his principal achievements. He was strongly opposed to slavery but in the interests of the preservation of the Union became the main instrument by which the passage of the Compromise of 1850 was secured. He was secretary of state again 1850–52. Webster was the greatest of American orators. His speech on the bicentenary of the Pilgrim Fathers (1820), his two Bunker Hill orations (1825 and 1843), that on the supremacy of the Union (1830), and funeral orations (e.g. on the deaths of John Adams and Jefferson, 1826) are among the many that illustrate his mastery of phrase and superb gift of matching style with content.

Webster, John (*c.* 1580–*c.* 1625). English dramatist. Many of his plays were written in collaboration, notably with * Dekker and * Heywood; only three, in fact, of the surviving plays are known to be his independent work: *The White Devil* (1612), *The Duchess of Malfi* (*c.* 1614) and the much less important *The Devil's Law Case* (1623). The first two, based on Italiam originals, vie with Shakespeare's work in tragic intensity but the characterisation is cruder, the range of emotions narrower, and humour except in its grimmest form is lacking; Webster's poetry, however, occasionally touches greatness.

Bradbrooke, M. C., *Themes and Conventions of Elizabethan Tragedy*. 1935. Brooke, Rupert, *John Webster and the Elizabethan Drama*. 1916

Webster, Noah (1758–1843). American lexicographer. After spending some years as teacher, journalist and political writer, he took to writing dictionaries and grammatical works. In 1828 he published *An American Dictionary of the English Language*, which immediately became a standard work.

Shoemaker, E. C., *Noah Webster: Power of Learning*. 1936

Wedekind, Frank (1864–1918). German dramatist. He was a promoter, cabaret performer, poet, actor and director who wrote many expressionist plays which anticipate the work of Bertholt * Brecht. The best known are *Earth Spirit* (1895) and *Pandora's Box* (1904), in which the central character is the courtesan 'Lulu'. G. W. Pabst filmed *Pandora's Box* and Alban Berg composed the opera *Lulu*.

Wedgwood, Dame (Cicely) Veronica (1910–). English historian, educated at Oxford. Her books included *The Thirty Years War* (1938), *Oliver Cromwell* (1939), *William the Silent* (1944), *The Trial of Charles I* (1964) and *Milton and his World* (1969). In 1969 she received the O.M.

Wedgwood, Josiah (1730–1795). English potter. Descendant of a family of Staffordshire potters, in 1759 he started his own business in Burslem. He eventually succeeded in developing for large-scale manufacture the hard white earthenware already made in Staffordshire and possessing many of the qualities of porcelain. His improvements to body and glaze were made by introducing china-clay and china-stone, then recently discovered in Cornwall. Apart from this utilitarian product Wedgwood became famous for his 'jasper ware' generally pale blue or green and, to accord with the classical taste of the time, adorned with a frieze of Greek figures embossed on it in white. For these decorative pieces, made near by at his new works (1769) called Etruria he employed many artists, notably * Flaxman. Wedgwood was an enlightened employer who did much to improve education and living conditions of his men.
Mankowitz, W., *Wedgwood*. 1953

Weelkes, Thomas (*c.* 1575–1623). English composer. He wrote church music, music for keyboard and for viols, but is at his most original in madrigals, regarded as among the finest of the Elizabethan school.

Wegener, Alfred (1880–1930). German geologist, the most influential of the present century, because of his championing, and extension of the theory of Continental Drift. Born in Berlin in 1880, he studied at Heidelberg, Innsbruck and Berlin, and before World War I taught at Marburg. From 1924 till his death on his third expedition to Greenland he had a special chair at Graz in Austria. From 1910 he developed his theory of Continental Drift or Displacement. Empirical evidence for this seemed to be the close jigsaw fit between coastlines on both sides of the Atlantic, and palaeontological similarities between Brazil and Africa. But Wegener had strong convictions that geophysical and geodetical considerations would also support a theory of wandering continents. As to the cause of the displacement he looked to tidal forces and a 'flight from the poles'.

Wegener supposed that the Mesozoic had seen the existence of a united supercontinent, 'Pangaea'. This had split apart. During the Cretaceous, South America and North America had split, but not till the end of the Quaternary had North America and Europe finally divided, or South America split from Antarctica. Only since the rise of Plate Tectonics since World War II has Wegener's theory become accepted.
Georgi, J., 'Memories of Alfred Wegener', *Continental Drift*. 1962

Weill, Kurt (1900–1950). German–American composer. A pupil of Humperdinck and Busoni, his best known work is *Dreigroschenoper* (*The Threepenny Opera*, 1928), a modernized version of Gay's *Begger's Opera* with libretto by Brecht, who also collaborated with Weill in later works, equally harsh and satirical in character, e.g. *Happy End* and *The Rise and Fall of the City of Mahagonny* (both 1929). These works are deliberately 'popular' and jazz-inspired in idiom, and in them Weill shows himself as much a political and social satirist as a musician. In 1933 he was obliged to flee Nazi Germany, settling (1935) in the U.S.A., where he produced music for plays and a folk opera, *Down in the Valley* (1948).

Weil, Simone (1909–43). French social philosopher and mystic, born in Paris. Daughter of a rich Jewish (but agnostic) physician, she was a youthful prodigy and studied philosophy, literature and science. She taught philosophy in provincial *lycées*, worked for a year in the Renault factory (1934–35) and as a cook for an Anarchist group in the Spanish Civil War (1936–7), also writing for socialist journals. She was severely burnt in Spain, suffered from acute migraine and contracted tuberculosis. In 1938 she had a series of mystical experiences, became absorbed in Catholicism and, although she did not enter the Church, was instrumental in converting others. She left France in 1942 and starved herself to death in England. The posthumous publication of her books aroused intense critical interest: they include *Waiting for God* (1951), *The Need for Roots* (1952) and *Notebooks* (2 volumes: 1956).

Weinberg, Steven (1933–). US astrophysicist. Educated at Cornell, Copenhagen and Princeton Universities, he held chairs in physics at the University of California (Berkeley) 1964–73, Harvard 1973– and Texas 1982– . He wrote the best-seller *The First Three Minutes* (1977) and won the Nobel Prize for Physics 1979.

Weinberger, Caspar Willard (1917–). U.S. administrator. He served as U.S. secretary of health, education and welfare 1973–75, became general counsel to the Bechtel Corporation and was secretary of defence 1981– .

Weinberger, Jaromir (1896–1967). Czech composer. Chiefly remembered for his opera *Schwanda the Bagpiper* (1927), in 1938 he left Czechoslovakia and eventually settled in the U.S.A.

Weingartner, (Paul) Felix von (1863–1942). Austrian conductor, composer and critic. He studied at Leipzig and then under Liszt. As conductor he held posts in Berlin, Munich, Vienna – where he was Mahler's successor at the Imperial Opera (1907–11) – and elsewhere, and became well known by his foreign tours. His compositions, which include operas, symphonies and chamber music, lack individuality. He wrote books on, e.g., Beethoven's symphonies and his own art of conducting.

Weismann, August Friedrich Leopold (1834–1914). German geneticist, born at Frankfurt-am-Main. He studied medicine at Göttingen, and practised at Rostock and then in Frankfurt. He became professor of zoology at Freiburg in 1873. During the 1860s he carried out detailed microscopical investigations into insects, crustaceans and embryology, though difficulties with his eyes eventually put a stop to this work. Weismann is best remembered for his chromosome theory of heredity. Within evolutionary theory there was deep disagreement as to how constant features and variations were passed on by inheritance. * Darwin had early favoured 'pangenesis', the theory that all characters were coded together in the genetic material. Other biologists had stressed the inheritance of acquired characteristics. Weismann launched a full-scale attack on this latter theory. His own experimentation had convinced him of the totally separate existence of genetic cells (germ cells) from body cells. He believed in the reality of an unbroken line of descent between the germ cells of successive generations, punctuated only by mutations in those cells (whereby evolution occurred). He argued that the hereditary material is contained in 'chromosomes'. Fertilization takes place by the bringing gether of chromosomes from two individuals; variation resulted from the combinations of different chromosomes that occurred. Weismann's essentially genetic theory of the action of evolution was erroneous in detail, but essentially underlies modern genetic theory.

Weiss, Peter Ulrich (1916–1982). Swedish-German writer, born in Germany to a Czech-Jewish family. A painter, documentary film-maker and Marxist social critic, he lived in Sweden from 1939. His best known work was *Marat/Sade* (1964) which was staged in many countries and made into a powerful film (1967) by Peter * Brook.

Weizmann, Chaim (1874–1952). First president of Israel (1948–52). Born in Motol, Byelorussia, he was educated in Berlin and Freiburg, lectured at Geneva (1900–04) and was a reader in biochemistry at Manchester (1904–16), becoming director of the Admiralty laboratories (1916–19). He pioneered biotechnology by using bio-organisms to extract acetone from maize: this was of enormous importance in making explosives during World War I and attracted the interest and friendship of A.J. * Balfour. The Balfour Declaration (1917) promised the Jews a 'national home' in Palestine. Weizmann was president of the World Zionist Organisation (1921–31; 1935–46), of the Hebrew University, Jerusalem (1932–50), and first director of the Sieff Research Institute (later named for Weizmann) in Rehovot (1934–48).

Weizmann, C., *Trial and Error*. 1949

Welensky, Sir Roy (1907–). Rhodesian politician. At 18 he became heavyweight boxing champion of Rhodesia. He worked as a barman and engine driver, and having gained a reputation as a forthright and belligerent trade union leader first entered the legislature of Northern Rhodesia (Zambia) in 1937; he became a member of the Executive Council (1940) and founded (1941) the Northern Rhodesian Labour party. He took part in the discussions (1950–51) which led to the formation of the federation of Northern and Southern Rhodesia with Nyasaland. He joined the new federal government as minister of transport (1953) and succeeded (1956) Lord Malvern (Sir Godfrey Huggins) as prime minister; he was bitterly disappointed when the federation ended in 1963.
Welensky, R., *Welensky's 4000 Days*. 1964

Welles, (George) Orson (1915–1985). American film and theatre director, producer, writer and actor, born in Kenosha, Wisconsin. The son of a successful inventor and a concert pianist, he was orphaned at 12 and had a peripatetic childhood punctuated by short bursts of education. At 16 he made his debut as an actor with the Gate Theatre, Dublin. After some years in touring companies, he founded the Mercury Theatre, in New York (1937) with **John Houseman** (1902–) and this led to innovative stage, radio and film productions. His realistic radio production (1938) of H. G. Wells's *War of the Worlds* caused a sensation and even some panic. His masterpiece, the film *Citizen Kane* (1941), which he wrote directed and acted in, was a thinly disguised and controversial biography of W. R. * Hearst, the newspaper proprietor (with some elements of R. R. McCormick). Many film historians regard this as the greatest American film: Welles was 25 when he made it. His second feature *The Magnificent Ambersons* (1942) also used the Mercury stock cast, but not Welles himself. He directed and acted in the films *Macbeth* (1947), *Othello* (1952), *Touch of Evil* (1958), *The Trial* (1962) and *Chimes at Midnight/Falstaff* (1966). None of his later films made money so major production houses were unwilling to back him. Welles' influence on European and American film makers has been enormous. He acted in many films—*Jane Eyre*, *The Third Man* (as Harry Lime), *Moby Dick* and *Catch 22*. His semi-documentary *F is for Fake* (1975) was highly regarded.
Kael, P., *The Citizen Kane Book*. 1971

Welles, Sumner (1892–1961). American diplomat. He began his career (1915) as secretary to the U.S. embassy in Tokyo and later specialized in Latin American affairs. He supported Franklin Roosevelt politically, became assistant secretary of state (1933) and under-secretary (1937). During World War II he played a leading part in the negotiations which led to the signing of the Atlantic Charter (1941). Differences of opinion with Cordell Hull caused his resignation (1943).

Wellesley, Richard Colley Wellesley, 1st Marquess (1760–1842). British politician and administrator. He was the eldest son of the 1st Earl of Mornington, whose Irish title he inherited (1781): his younger brother, Arthur, became the Duke of * Wellington. Wellesley, who had been a member of the Indian Board of Control 1793–97, served as governor-general and commander-in-chief in Bengal and India 1797–1805. He pursued a forward policy aimed at destroying French influence and extending British rule. He first dealt with the Nizam of Hyderabad, whose French-trained forces he contrived, by diplomacy and a display of force, to disarm without firing a shot. Next he turned against * Tippoo, sultan of Mysore, who was killed at the storming of Seringapatam (1799); Mysore was virtually brought under British rule. For the remaining years of his rule Wellesley was engaged in a prolonged struggle with the Mahratta confederacy, in which the victories of his brother played a decisive part. Before a final settlement was reached, however, Wellesley, whose annexationist policy alarmed some of the Company's directors, was recalled. During his tenure of office the small strips of British-held territory had been enlarged to become the foundations of an empire. He later served as foreign secretary 1809–12 and Lord Lieutenant of Ireland 1821–28 and 1833–34.
Martin, M., *Wellesley Papers: Life and Correspondence*. 1914

Wellington, Arthur Wellesley, 1st Duke of (1769–1852). English soldier and politician. He was a son of the 1st Earl of Mornington and a younger brother of the 1st Marquess * Wellesley. He first gained an army commission in 1789 but did no regimental service until war with France broke out (1793). He served in a futile Dutch campaign (1794) but his first opportunity for distinction came when he was serving in India, where his brother was governor general. He successfully restored order after the fall of Seringapatam and held an independent command in the Mahratta wars. His greatest triumph was at Assaye (1803), where the Mahratta army was shattered. He returned to England (1805), married Lady Katharine Pakenham (1806) and after a brief interlude in politics commanded the expedition sent (1808) for the relief of Portugal. Despite early successes, including the Battle of Vimiero, he was superseded, and was not therefore responsible for the much criticized Convention of Cintra by which the French were allowed to withdraw rather than surrender. In 1809 he resumed his command in Portugal, which the French were again invading. He gained a victory at Talavera, which earned him the title Viscount Wellington and enable him to take up a secure position in the prepared lines of Torres Vedras. Here after checking the French at Busaco (1810) he stood firm against Massen's advance. In 1811 he was strong enough to advance in turn, but had to await the fall of Ciudad Rodrigo (January 1812) and Badajoz (May). Though he then captured Madrid he had to retire and winter in Portugal once more. In 1813, with the French forces depleted to replace Napoleon's losses in the Russian campaign, he advanced across Spain and after the victory of Victoria (July) forced the enemy to retire to France; Wellington followed and after winning the last victory of the Peninsular War at Toulouse (April 1814) heard that Napoleon had abdicated four days before. The title of duke bestowed in that year marked his achievement. He was discussing peace terms at the Congress of Vienna (1815) when he heard of Napoleon's escape from Elba. Wellington was placed in command of the allied army of the Netherlands and, though Napoleon succeeded in dividing his opponents, defeating the Prussians at Ligny and checking the British at Quatre Bras, it did not prevent Wellington, with the help of Blücher's Prussians in the later stages, gaining his final victory at Waterloo (18 June 1815). Wellington retained his position as commander-in-chief in France until 1818, when he returned to England to take part in political life. For this he was temperamentally ill-equipped and there was constant friction with * Castlereagh and * Canning until he resigned in 1827. He was prime minister (1828–30), his term of office made memorable by the passage of the Roman Catholic Emancipation Act (1829). Wellington's opposition to the Reform Bill made him increasingly unpopular and brought about the fall of his government. He was again briefly prime minister (1834) and served under Peel (1841–46). Though he then retired from public life he retained his position as commander-in-chief. His burial at St Paul's Cathedral marked the English nation's ceremonial farewell to one of its greatest military leaders. The nickname 'the Iron Duke' indicated an austere nature but he had a gentler, more humane side to his character and was a man of complete integrity who, though little loved, commanded universal respect.

Longford, E., *Wellington – the Years of the Sword*. 1969; *The Pillar of State*. 1972

Wells, Herbert George (1866–1946). English writer. Son of a professional cricketer, he worked first as a draper's assistant, then took to teaching and with the aid of scholarships graduated in science (1888). He joined the Fabian Society (founded 1884), but though he reached a theoretical belief in scientific planning he was too much the born novelist to be bound by dogma. He disdained the stylistic graces of his contemporary Henry James nd professed to regard writing as a utilitarian means of expressing his ideas. But his character, like those of Dickens (with whom he had affinities), came to life beneath his pen, and Wells the novelist and Wells the social theorist tended to go their separate ways. The world in which his characters for the most part moved was that of the lower middle class, a world whose boundaries were quickly changing: new opportunities, new hopes, new challenges, were appearing. The reaction of men and women to these changes Wells watched with an observant and understanding eye; the new trends and new problems were the themes in which he took most delight.

But before he embarked upon them there was a phase of fantasy and 'science fiction', as it came to be called. To this period belong *The Time Machine* and *The Wonderful Visit* (both 1895), *The Invisible Man* (1897) and *The War of the Worlds* (1898). In the same vein, written much later in the shadow of coming events, was *The Shape of Things to Come* (1933). The great novels of Wells's maturity were introduced by *Love and Mr Lewisham* (1900); then followed *Kipps* (1905), *Tono-Bungay* (1909),

Anne Veronica (1909) and the *History of Mr Polly* (1910). *Mr Britling Sees it Through* (1916) recalls World War I, but on the whole the later novels show a decline. Much the most influential of his post-war books was *An Outline of History* (1920), 'an attempt to reform history teaching by replacing narrow nationalist history by a general review of the human record'. He also wrote *Experiment in Autobiography* (1934), as well as a number of social and political works.
Dickson, L., *H. G. Wells, His Turbulent Life and Times*.

Wenceslas (died 929). Patron saint and Duke of Bohemia. He was the grandson of Borivoj, a Czech chieftain who had been converted to Christianity by the Byzantine missionary Methodius. The memory of his enlightened rule, a reputation for sanctity and the fact that he was murdered during a heathen rebellion ensured him an honoured place in national history, and mention as the hero of the familiar carol.

Wentworth, William Charles (1790–1872). Australian politician, born near Norfolk Island. His father D'Arcy Wentworth was assistant surgeon in New South Wales and his mother, Catherine Crowley, a convict. Educated at Greenwich, he crossed the Blue Mountains in 1813 in the first major inland exploration, then studied at Cambridge and in 1819 published *A Statistical, Historical and Political Description of the Colony of New South Wales*, the first book written by a native-born Australian. Called to the English bar in 1822, he returned to establish *The Australian* (1824), a newspaper in which he espoused the cause of convict emancipation. He was one of the most powerful speakers in the New South Wales Legislative Council and took a prominent part in the negotiations (1852–53) by which the colony gained responsible government. He lived in England from 1855, died there but was buried in Sydney.

Werfel, Franz (1890–1945). Austrian poet, novelist and dramatist, of Jewish parentage. His poetry, mostly written in early life, is characterized by a deep compassion for mankind; the themes of his plays were both historical and modern. He married Alma * Mahler in 1929. He is most widely known for his novels, especially *The Song of Bernadette* (1941), concerned with the origins of the Lourdes miracles, and *Jacobowsky and the Colonel* (1945), a comedy filmed as *Me and the Colonel*. From France, where he had taken refuge after the German occupation of Austria, he escaped on foot (1940) over the Pyrenees during World War II and eventually reached the U.S.A.

Werner, Abraham Gottlob (1749–1817). German geologist. He proposed a general succession of the creation of rocks, beginning with Primary Rocks (precipitated from the water of a Universal Ocean), then passing through Transition, Flötz (sedimentary) and finally Recent and Volcanic. The oldest rocks were chemically deposited, crystalline and fossil-less. Later rocks were mechanically deposited and contained fossils. Werner's approach was particularly important for linking the order of the strata to the history of the earth and relating the study of mineralogy and geology.
Abraham Gottlob Werner Gedenkschrift. 1967

Werner, Alfred (1866–1919). Swiss chemist. Professor of chemistry at Zurich (1893–1919), his studies on complex metal-ammonia compounds and other inorganic salts led him to formulate (1893) his co-ordination theory of valency. His postulation of 'co-ordination numbers' led to the discovery that inorganic as well as organic compounds have spatial structures. He thus laid the foundations of modern inorganic chemistry. He won the Nobel Prize for Chemistry (1913).

Wesker, Arnold (1932–). British playwright. Born in the East End of London of Jewish parentage, he found there a setting for his play *Chicken Soup with Barley* (1958), part of a trilogy completed by *Roots* (1959) and *I'm Talking about Jerusalem* (1960). Among a variety of occupations he was employed in a hotel, which provided a setting for *The Kitchen* (1961) and as a clerk in the RAF, *Chips with Everything* (1962). From 1961 until its ultimate failure in 1970 he devoted himself to running Centre 42, a TUC project for introducing workers to mainstream culture. Later plays included *The Journalists* (1975) and *Caritas* (1981).
Taylor, J. R., *Anger and After. rev. ed.* 1969; Leeming, G., *Wesker the Playwright*. 1982

Wesley, Charles (1707–1788). English hymnwriter. The brother and devoted adherent of

John * Wesley, he wrote over 600 hymns, including *Jesu, Lover of my Soul, Hark The Herald Angels Sing* and *Love Divine, all Loves Excelling*.
Gill, F. C., *Charles Wesley*. 1964

Wesley, John (1703–1791). English religious leader, founder of Methodism. A member of an old family linked with that of the Duke of Wellington, he was educated at Charterhouse and Oxford, was ordained deacon (1725) and priest (1728). Elected a fellow of Lincoln College he remained in Oxford to teach, and there he, his brother Charles, George * Whitefield and other religiously earnest young men began to be known as Methodists, pledged to live according to the 'method laid down in the New Testament'. In 1735, when he crossed the Atlantic to go to Georgia under the auspices of the Society for the Propagation of the Gospel, he was still a high-church man but he became an admirer of the work of the Moravian Brethren and on his return to England made friends with their missionary Peter Bohler, who convinced him that to be a Christian it was not enough to believe in a body of orthodox doctrine but that a positive act of acceptance was necessary, resulting in living in union with and under the direct guidance of Christ. Such an instant conversion was experienced by Wesley himself at a meeting in London (24 May 1738): 'I felt my heart strangely warmed. I felt I did trust in Christ alone for salvation, and an assurance was given me that He had taken away my sins . . . '. This change meant an actual if not a formal breach with Anglicanism. As pulpits were refused John and Charles Wesley held vast open-air meetings, the first at Bristol, which some 3,000 attended. The rest of his life was a prolonged pilgrimage, during which time he rode 60–70 miles a day and is said to have delivered over 40,000 sermons. Most of his converts were people of the working classes, miners, labourers, artisans, for whom the ancient parish system, a formalized ritual and a clergy grown languid and genteel provided little comfort. In these circumstances the Methodist movement grew in strength and as it did so doctrinal differences increased: ecclesiastical traditions could not survive the move into the open air; the apostolic succession was rejected; separate chapels came to be built. The year 1784, when despite the strongest protests from Charles Wesley John ordained a bishop for America, is regarded as a turning point. Ministers in Scotland first, then in overseas territories and finally in England were also freely ordained by John.

From a vast literary output his *Journal* stands out as an impressive witness to his character and observation. Such a man had little time for private life, but a lack of tolerance and tact in dealing with women may explain his unhappy marriage.

Wessel, Horst (1907–1930). German Nazi agitator. Severely injured in a street brawl, he died after refusing attention from Jewish doctors. His senseless death was commemorated in the Nazi anthem *The Horst Wessel Song*.

West, Benjamin (1738–1820). Anglo-American painter, born in Pennsylvania. He went to Italy to study (1759) and in 1763 reached England. He soon became known for classical, religious and especially historical paintings, such as the *Death of Wolfe* (1770), remarkable at the time for the use of contemporary clothing. He also did illustrations for the Boydell Shakespeare. A foundation member of the Royal Academy (1768), he succeeded * Reynolds as president (1792–1820).

West, Mae (1892–1980). American actress. She specialised in glamorous but witty and earthy 'sex-bomb' roles and was noted for a voluptuous figure: the 'Mae West' naval life-jacket was so named because, when inflated, it produced a similar effect.

West, Nathaniel (Nathan Wallenstein Weinstein) (1903–1940). American novelist, born in New York City. Before he was killed in a car crash at the age of 37, West had written four novels which, taken together, are a picture of disillusionment and an indictment of the American Dream. In his 'black comedy' vision of society, the common pursuits of happiness and liberty are inverted and seen as the paths of boredom, nightmare, neurosis and failure. His novels are *The Dream Life of Balso Snell* (1931), *Miss Lonelyhearts* (1933), *A Cool Million* (1934) and *The Day of The Locust* (1939).
Reid, R., *The Fiction of Nathaniel West*. 1968

West, Dame Rebecca (real name Cicely Isabel Andrews, née Fairfield) (1892–1983). British novelist, critic and journalist, born in Ireland.

Trained as an actress, she adopted her pen-name from an * Ibsen character and wrote a long series of original and penetrating books, including studies of Henry James (1916), D. H. Lawrence (1930) and St Augustine (1933), *Black Lamb and Grey Falcon* (about Yugoslavia: 1942), and several volumes reporting notable trials.

Westermarck, Edward Alexander (1862–1939). Finnish sociologist. Professor of sociology at London University (1907–30), his many books included *History of Human Marriage* (1891), *Origin and Development of the Moral Ideas* (2 volumes, 1906–08), *Ritual and Belief in Morocco* (2 volumes, 1926) and *Ethical Relativity* (1932).

Westinghouse, George (1846–1914). American inventor. He had no academic training as an engineer but after taking part in the Civil War he went to work on the railways. He invented (1867) an automatic brake worked by air pressure and formed a company to manufacture it. Later he applied the same principles of air pressure to the movement of signals and points. He also devised gas and water meters and a system for safely transporting gases over long distances. He took out over 400 patents. Nikola * Tesla worked for him (1885–88) and in 1888 Westinghouse bought all his patents for the alternating current (AC) electric motor. At his workshops in Pittsburgh he also manufactured electrical equipment including generators to utilize power from the Niagara Falls. His campaign for the use of alternating current for the distribution of electricity was ultimately successful.

Wettin. A German dynasty which was first heard of in the 10th century in Thuringia. The conferment of the electorate of Saxony on the Margrave Frederick (1423) confirmed the family's supremacy in that area. It was weakened, however, by a territorial partition between his grandsons: Ernest, founder of the Ernestine line, obtained the electorate and the larger part of the territory, while the Albertine line, stemming from his brother, was given the rest. The position was reversed during the Reformation. The Ernestine line, which provided * Luther's strongest princely supporters, was deposed by Charles V and the Albertine line substituted. Its members were also kings of Poland (1697–1763). After the fall of the Holy Roman Empire during the Napoleonic period the elector of Saxony took the title of king. Meanwhile the Ernestine line had split into a number of branches, one of them that of Saxe-Coburg, from which sprang Leopold I of the Belgians, Albert, the British Queen Victoria's Prince Consort, and the kings of Bulgaria.

Weyden, Rogier van der (*c*. 1399–1464). Flemish artist. He was appointed city painter of Brussels in 1436. Whether or not he actually visited Italy in 1450 (as supposed) is uncertain but his *Entombment* (Uffizi) certainly has affinities with Italian art. For the most part he worked in the Gothic tradition of the van Eycks, but the figures, with the folds of the garments emphasized and characters of the subjects more boldly defined by expression and gesture, give a more dramatic effect, sometimes at the expense of observed detail. Among his most characteristic paintings is the *Adoration of the Magi* at Munich.
Beenken, H., *Rogier van der Weyden*. 1951

Weygand, Maxime (1867–1965). French soldier of Belgian birth, probably son of the Mexican Emperor Maximilian. As chief of staff to * Foch (1914–23) he made a great impression with his clear mind and quiet competence. He led the 'allied armies of intervention' (mostly French) in Poland 1919–20 and forced the Red Army back to the boundaries agreed on at Brest-Litovsk. He was elected to the Academie Française in 1931. Commander-in-chief of the French Army 1931–35, in 1939 he was recalled to service as commander-in-chief in the Levant. He replaced * Gamelin as allied generalissimo (May–June 1940) after the German breakthrough but was too late to retrieve the situation. He served as * Petain's minister for defence (1940–41) and governor-general of Algeria (1941–42). He was imprisoned 1942–46, first by Germans, then by the French.
Weygand, M., *Recalled to Service*. 1952

Wharton, Edith Newbold Jones (1862–1937). American novelist. She came of a family well known in New York society, a fact which both helped and limited her literary achievement. Henry * James was an early influence and like him she was concerned with the lives of the rich, leisured, cosmopolitan Americans of her own class. Wit, irony and satire characterize her novels; her themes are ethical as well as social, and sometimes, especially when writing of the position of women, she achieves tragic intensity. Among her best known novels are *The House of Mirth* (1905), *The Age of Innocence* (1920), and the more realistic *Ethan Frome* (1911).

Whately, Richard (1787–1863). English scholar and churchman. At Oxford, where he obtained a fellowship (1811) he associated with Keble, Newman and Pusey but held no extreme religious views. He became archbishop of Dublin (1831). He wrote much but is remembered by *Historic Doubts Relative to Napoleon Buonaparte* (1819), a satire on rationalist criticism of the Scriptures.

Wheatstone, Sir Charles (1802–1875). English physicist. He had no formal education in science, but while apprenticed to his uncle, an instrument-maker, became absorbed in experiments in physics. This led to his becoming (1834) professor of experimental philosophy at King's College, London, an appointment which he held for the rest of his life. He was elected F.R.S. in 1837, the year in which he patented with W. F. Cooke the first electric telegraph. Another invention of his was a clock for which polarized light was ingeniously used to measure time, but curiously enough he did not invent the so-called 'Wheatstone bridge' for measuring electrical resistance. The many other products of his inventive mind included the 'concertina'. He was knighted in 1868.

Wheeler, Sir (Robert Eric) Mortimer (1890–1976). English archaeologist. After being keeper of the London Museum (1926–44), he held an archaeological professorship at London University. His most notable work was on Roman Britain (e.g. at Verulamium near St Albans) and on the Indus Valley civilization of ancient India. He did much to popularize archaeology by writing, broadcasting and television appearances.
Wheeler, M., *Still Digging*. 1955

Whewell, William (1794–1866). English scientist. The son of a carpenter, in 1841 he became Master of Trinity College, Cambridge, and held the post till his death (which resulted from a riding accident). He was a polymath whose main interests tended to the field of the sciences, and he was an omnipresent figure in all scientific movements in England in the first half of the nineteenth century. He coined many terms in the field, including 'scientist', 'ion', 'cathode', 'Eocene', 'Miocene' etc. His own active scientific interests spanned many fields. As Professor of Mineralogy at Cambridge he was interested in the angles of refraction of crystals. Over a period of twenty years he collected tide data in order to build up maps of cotidal times. But he is chiefly remembered for his writings on the *History* and the *Philosophy of the Inductive Sciences* (1840 and 1838), the most substantial accounts of the subject yet to have appeared in English. In these Whewell advanced an 'idealist' view of scientific progress: it was not more facts that caused advance, but better theories.
Douglas, Mrs S., *Life and . . . Correspondence of William Whewell*. 1881

Whistler, James Abbot McNeill (1834–1903). American-born artist. After a brief incursion into military life at West Point academy and a short period with the Coastal Survey Department (where he learned to etch) he went to Paris (1855) to study art. From the 1860s he lived mostly in London, and the Thames near his Chelsea home inspired some of his finest work. Courbet's work in Paris impressed him most, but a later and stronger influence was that of the Japanese artist Hokusai. In his famous *Nocturnes*, for example, he was more concerned with tone values than with the direct reproduction of nature's effects attempted by the Impressionists. Even his well known portraits of his mother and of Thomas Carlyle are studies in black and grey. A similar preoccupation with tone is seen in his *Little White Girl* hung at the Salon des Refusés in Paris (1863). Some of his best work is to be seen in his etchings of London and Venice. Whistler was slow to gain recognition, partly because of an angularity of character. Being extremely resentful at Ruskin's criticism, he embarked on the famous libel suit (1878) in which he obtained a farthing damages. The trial is documented in *The Gentle Art of Making Enemies* (1890).

Whitaker, Joseph (1820–1895). English publisher. He founded *The Bookseller* (1858) and the *Almanack* that bears his name (1869).

White, E(lwyn) B(rooks) (1899–1985) American author. Educated at Cornell, he joined *The New Yorker* as a staff writer (1926), published volumes of essays, the children's books *Stuart Little* (1945) and *Charlotte's*

Web (1952), and revised and enlarged *The Elements of Style* by William Strunk, Jr. (1959).
Elledge, S., *E. B. White: A Biography*. 1984

White, Gilbert (1720–1793). English clergyman and naturalist, born at Selborne, Hampshire where from 1751 he lived as curate. His *Natural History and Antiquities of Selborne* (1789) records in prose of great charm his observations of nature. In 1885 the Selborne Society was founded in his memory.
Scott, W. S., *Gilbert White*. 1950

White, Patrick Victor Martindale (1912–). Australian novelist, born in London. He lived in Australia as a child but was educated at Cheltenham and Cambridge. He served in the RAF during World War II and returned to Australia in 1947. His books include *The Tree of Man* (1954), *Voss* (1957), *The Vivisector* (1970), *The Eye of the Storm* (1973), *The Twyborn Affair* (1979), and an autobiography, *Flaws in the Glass* (1981). He is also a playwright. In 1973 he received the Nobel Prize for Literature.

White, T(erence) H(anbury) (1906–1964). English author. He is chiefly known for a series of Arthurian fantasies which reflect his love of the Middle Ages and of traditional sports such as falconry taken up while he was a schoolmaster at Stowe (until 1936). These tales, of which *The Sword in the Stone* (1939) was the first, were published as the trilogy *The Once and Future King* (1958).

White, William Hale *see* **Rutherford, Mark**

Whitefield, George (1714–1770). English preacher. One of a large family left early fatherless, he was servant at Pembroke College, Oxford, where he first came under Methodist influence and worked devotedly among prisoners and the sick. Ordained as deacon (1736), he immediately attracted attention as a preacher. He followed John * Wesley to Georgia and on his return to collect funds moved from place to place, preaching wherever he halted and attracting a huge following by his eloquence and sincerity. His Calvinistic doctrines on predestination led to a breach with Wesley and though a personal reconciliation took place each took a separate religious path. For Whitefield his followers built a large church at Moorfields, London, known as the Tabernacle.
Dallimore, A., *George Whitefield*. 1970

Whitehead, Alfred North (1861–1947). English mathematician and philosopher. He studied and taught mathematics at Cambridge (1880–1910) and in 1898 published *A Treatise in Universal Algebra*. A collaboration with Bertrand * Russell in writing *Principia Mathematica* followed. From 1910, when he left Cambridge for London University – he was professor of the Imperial College of Science and Technology (1914–24) – he became increasingly interested in philosophy and wrote several books in which he tried to link facts learned through physics into a philosophical scheme. In *The Principle of Relativity* (1922) he propounds an alternative to Einstein's theory. A move to Harvard University (1924) coincided with the inclusion of metaphysics in his wide range of thought. The best known of his books in this field was *Science and the Modern World* (1926); others include *Process and Reality* (1929), the highly important *Adventures of Ideas* (1933) and *Nature and Life* (1934). Whitehead was awarded the O.M. in 1945.
Lowe, V., *Understanding Whitehead*. 1962

Whitehouse, Mary (1910–). English moral reformer. A former schoolteacher, she became a journalist and broadcaster working for 'cleaning up' the media, particularly television. Her publications include *Whatever Happened to Sex?* (1977) and the autobiographical *Who Does She Think She Is?*

Whitelaw, William Stephen Ian, 1st Viscount Whitelaw (1918–). English Conservative politician. A guards officer who won the MC, he became a farmer and MP 1955–83, serving as a minister under Edward * Heath 1970–74 and deputy prime minister 1979– to Margaret * Thatcher. In 1983 he was made the first hereditary peer since 1964.

Whiteman, Paul (1890–1967). American dance band leader. He was a close friend of George * Gershwin and stimulated interest in 'symphonic jazz', in which the performers did not improvise but played from written parts.

Whitlam, (Edward) Gough (1916–). Australian Labor politician, born in Melbourne. He became a barrister, member of the Australian parliament 1952–78, deputy leader of the Australian Labor Party 1960–67, and succeeded A. A. * Calwell as leader of the party 1967–77. In December 1972 the Australian Labor Party regained office after 23 years but without a majority in the Senate, and Whitlam served as prime minister to November 1975. In 1974 the Senate forced a double dissolution of the two houses and Labor won the House of Representatives again but failed to win the Senate. Much Labor legislation was rejected in the Senate and party support fell due to high levels of unemployment and inflation. Following deferral of supply by the Liberal-dominated Senate, Whitlam was dismissed by the Governor-General Sir John * Kerr (November 1975) and lost the ensuing election. He became ambassador to UNESCO, Paris, 1983–

Whitman, Walt (1819–1892). American poet. He grew up in Brooklyn and worked briefly as an office boy, printer, journalist and teacher. Among other journals he edited (1846–1848) the *Brooklyn Eagle* which he made a platform from which to voice his anti-slavery views. At loggerheads with his proprietors, he left to enlarge his knowledge of America by a trip to New Orleans, from which he returned by the Mississippi and the Great Lakes. There followed a period of avid but unsystematic reading, from the Bible, Homer and the classics to Shakespeare and writers such as Scott, Carlyle, Coleridge and Emerson. Apart from a vein of mysticism in his poems, attributable to his philosophic readings, the main result was an attempt to shed European influences and introduce a national literature suited to the free, robust, democratic American. He began the realization of this purpose with the first publication of *Leaves of Grass* (1855), an attempt 'to put a *Person*, a human being (myself, in the latter half of the nineteenth century in America) freely, fully and truly on record' and 'to loosen the mind of still-to-be-formed America from the folds, the superstitions and all the long, tenacious and stifling anti-democratic authorities of Asiatic and European past'. At first a volume of twelve poems, *Leaves of Grass* grew with successive editions to many times its original size. His poems are marked by irregular measures, long verse lines, strong rhythms and an incantatory manner. His themes were social, political, moral; beauty, death, war, sex. The language was free, frank and natural. Sometimes in his portrayal of himself he shows an unpleasing arrogance; sometimes there are passages which caused his works to be held immoral and led to his dismissal from a clerkship after the Civil War.

In 1873 he had a paralytic stroke but gradually recovered from complete invalidism. From 1884 he lived in retirement in Camden, New Jersey, where he died. In addition to his poems Whitman wrote several prose works including *Democratic Vistas* (1871) and the random jottings in e.g. *Specimen Days in America* (1887). Whitman was the first great poet to be distinctively American, but it is ironic that it has always been to the intellectual that his work has appealed rather than to the 'common man' for whom he wrote.

Allen, G. W., *The Solitary Singer*. Rev. ed. 1967

Whitney, Eli (1765–1825). American inventor. He graduated at Yale University, and had been a tutor when a chance conversation turned his mind to the problem of separating seed and dirt from the cotton fibre. The result was the 'cotton gin' (1792), a machine consisting of a wire-toothed drum which tore the fibre from the seeds, the fibre being in turn removed from the wires by revolving brushes. The use of a single machine to do the work of some 200 men revolutionized the cotton industry but owing to patent difficulties he got more prestige than money. The former, however, led to his being granted a government contract for the manufacture of firearms, which brought him a fortune. One of the greatest figures of the Industrial Revolution, his major achievement was the theory of standardized interchangeable parts.

Green, C. M., *Eli Whitney and the Birth of American Technology*. 1956

Whittier, John Greenleaf (1807–1892). American Quaker poet, born in Massachusetts. He worked untiringly for the abolition of slavery, as politician and journalist, writing pamphlets and editing abolitionist journals. His numerous volumes of poetry, especially those depicting New England life and legends, gave him great contemporary popularity and some poems are still recalled. Among them are *Snowbound, The Barefoot Boy*, and the ballad *Barbara Frietchie*.

Whittington, Richard (*c.* 1358–1423). English mercer. The son of a Gloucestershire knight, he acquired great wealth in London, which enabled him to lend money to Henry IV and Henry V, and since he was childless to bestow many benefactions on the city of London both before his death and by bequest; he was mayor of London 1397–98, 1406–07 and 1419–20. The legend of Dick Whittington and his cat was first given currency in a play and a ballad in 1605. The only similarity between history and fiction seems to be that both Richard and Dick married an Alice Fitzwaryn (Fitzwarren).

Whittle, Sir Frank (1907–). British aircraft engineer. He joined the RAF (1923) and his mind soon turned to the problems of jet propulsion for aircraft. Having striven hard and long for official support, he at last found himself with a small team of craftsmen, fired by his own enthusiasm, installed in a small, ill-equipped workshop and using every spare hour to turn his idea into a reality. At last (1937) the first successful gas turbine engine was made. In 1941 a Gloster plane fitted with one of Whittle's engines flew and achieved excellent results, but owing to the time required for manufacture the jet-propelled aircraft played no effective part in World War II. In 1948 Whittle was awarded £100,000 for his work, but, a natural individualist, he kept aloof from the great firms concerned with later developments.

Whittle, F., *Jet*. 1953

Whitworth, Sir Joseph, 1st Bart. (1803–1887). British engineer and inventor. Founder of the Whitworth scholarships in engineering science, he is best known for his invention of a gun-barrel with a revolutionary type of bore, and for the now standard screw thread named after him. He was made a baronet in 1869.

Whymper, Edward (1840–1911). English mountaineer. A wood-engraver and book illustrator by profession, he is better known for his travels in Greenland (1867 and 1872) and for his mountaineering feats, including the first ascents of the Matterhorn (1865) – when three of his companions lost their lives – and of Chimborazo in the Andes (1879).

Smythe, F. S., *Edward Whymper*. 1940

Wicliffe *see* **Wyclif, John**

Wieland, Christoph Martin (1733–1813). German writer. The son of a pastor, he first wrote pious and religious poems but after contact with the literary and social world he began to produce a variety of elegant and witty works. From 1762 he produced the first German translations of Shakespeare (all in prose except *A Midsummer Night's Dream*). Of his original works the narrative poem *Oberon* (1780) is of particular charm; it is based on a medieval *chanson de geste* which relates the fantastic adventures of Huon of Bordeaux at the court of Babylon. More important, perhaps, is the novel *Agathon* (1766), the classical setting of which does little to disguise its autobiographical theme of a young man's reaction to the impact of experience and philosophy. In 1772 Wieland went to be tutor to the future Duke Karl August of Saxe-Weimar and remained at Weimar until his death. While there he translated many classical texts and wrote opera libretti.

Wien, Wilhelm (1864–1928). German physicist. As professor of physics at Giessen, Würzburg and Munich, he carried out important studies on cathode rays, canal rays, and black-body radiation. He discovered (1893) the 'displacement law' (Wien's law) which shows how the intensity maximum in the spectrum moves to shorter wavelengths with increase in temperature, so that the product of the wavelength at maximum intensity and the absolute temperature is constant. This law made it possible to determine the temperature of bodies such as the sun and stars by observing the distribution of spectral intensity. He won the 1911 Nobel Prize for Physics.

Wiener, Norbert (1894–1964). American mathematician, a child prodigy who had enrolled by the age of fifteen at Harvard Graduate School. He spent his late teens and early twenties trying out various approaches in mathematics, philosophy and zoology, before moving to the Massachusetts Institute of Technology (assistant professor, 1924, associate 1929, full professor 1932). He remained there till his retirement. Much of his early career was devoted to pure mathematics; he was concerned with harmonic analysis, and did work on Lebesgue integration and the Brownian motion. The mathematical consequences of the laws of thermodynamics were worked out by Wiener. His most original work

came after 1940 when he became absorbed in the development of computing machines. His penetrating analysis of feedback control in artificial intelligence systems led to interest in human intelligence, and to creative work in the general field of systems analysis. The science of communication and information opened up as a result of Wiener's probings: his *Cybernetics* was published in 1948.
'Norbert Wiener' in *Bulletin of the American Mathematical Society*, 72; 1966

Wieniawski, Henryk (1835–1880). Polish composer and violinist. He ranked immediately after * Paganini and * Sarasate as a great virtuoso and wrote many works to show off his prodigious technique, including two concertos, *Legende, Scherzo-Tarantelle* and *Fantasy on Gounod's Faust*.

Wiggin, Kate Douglas (née Smith) (1865–1923). American author. She was a pioneer of kindergarten teaching before becoming a writer. The best known of her novels, *Rebecca of Sunnybrook Farm* (1903), gives a charming picture of New England life.

Wilberforce, William (1759–1833). English politician and philanthropist. He was born of a wealthy Yorkshire family; after leaving Cambridge University he entered politics. He was first elected M.P. in 1780 and became a friend and supporter of Pitt, but having been converted to Evangelicism (1784–85) he devoted himself to philanthropic causes, e.g. the abolition of the slave trade, a bill for which he finally carried (1807) after twenty years' struggle. His next objective was the abolition of slavery itself. He helped to found the Anti-Slavery Society (1825) but as his health failed leadership of the movement passed to T. F. Buxton. A month before the measure was passed Wilberforce died. He helped to found the Church Missionary Society (1798) and the Bible Society (1803); he wrote *A Practical View of Christianity* (1797).

His son, **Samuel Wilberforce** (1805–1873), was a high-church man who rose to be bishop of Oxford (1845) and of Winchester (1869). Though he opposed * Newman and * Pusey he did much to invigorate the Anglican church, supported retreats and religious communities, Cowley (for men) and others for women, and founded Cuddenson Theological College. His nickname 'Soapy Sam' referred to his unpopular role in the controversy over Bishop * Colenso. He was killed by a fall from his horse.
Wilberforce, A. M., ed., *Private Papers of William Wilberforce*. 1898

Wilbye, John (1574–1638). English composer. One of the leading masters of the English madrigal, among the longer and best known examples are *Draw on Sweet Night* and *Sweet Honey-Sucking Bees*.

Wilcox, Ella Wheeler (née Ella Wheeler) (1850–1919). American verse writer. Extremely prolific, she was described by the London *Times* as 'the most popular poet of either sex and of any age'. Sentimentality was the key to her success.

Wild, Jonathan (1682?–1725). English criminal. Having gone to London (*c.* 1706) from Birmingham, where he was a buckle-maker's apprentice, he controlled a gang of thieves, whose loot he 'recovered' for its owners for a fee which he shared with his accomplices. Eventually he was hanged at Tyburn. Defoe related his exploits, which Fielding elaborated to provide a plot for his satirical romance, *Jonathan Wild the Great* (1743).

Wilde, Oscar Fingall O'Flahertie Wills (1854–1900). Irish writer and wit, born in Dublin. He showed his brilliance at Trinity College, Dublin, and then at Oxford, where he was regarded as the founder of the aesthetic movement which cultivated 'art for art's sake'; Wilde, notorious for his eccentricities of manner and dress, was satirized as 'Bunthorne' in Gilbert and Sullivan's *Patience* (1881). His first book of poems was published in 1881 and in 1882–83 he lectured in the U.S.A. On returning to London he married (1884). Of his two sons, the younger, later known as Vyvyan Holland, did much by his writings to vindicate his father's reputation. In 1888 Wilde published *The Happy Prince*, a collection of children's stories and in 1891 a novel *The Picture of Dorian Gray*, an arresting study in the macabre. Meanwhile he had established himself as the most brilliant conversationalist of his day, coining epigrams and paradoxes which provided the main substance of his highly successful comedies: *Lady Windermere's Fan* (1892), *A Woman of No Importance* (1893), *An Ideal Husband* and *The Importance of Being Earnest* (both 1895). His *Salome*, written in French, was refused a

licence in London and subsequently became the libretto of an opera by Richard Strauss. In 1895 the Marquess of Queensberry, who objected to Wilde's close friendship with his son Lord Alfred Douglas, accused him of homosexuality. Wilde sued, but the action revealed evidence which resulted in his own trial and a two-year sentence. From his experiences of prison life came his long poem *The Ballad of Reading Gaol* (1898) and the bitter *De Profundis* (published posthumously in 1905). After his release he lived in France under the name of Sebastian Melmoth, dogged by ill health and poverty.
Wilde, Oscar, ed. Foreman, J. B., *Complete Works*. 1966

Wilder, Thornton (1897–1975). American novelist and playwright. His novels include *The Bridge of San Luis Rey*, which won the Pulitzer Prize (1927), and *The Ides of March* (1940). His first successful play was *Our Town* (1938), followed by *The Skin of our Teeth* (1942). Later he wrote *The Matchmaker* (1954) and *A Life in the Sun* (1955), a version of the Oedipus legend.

Wilhelmina (1880–1962). Queen of the Netherlands (1890–1948). She was a daughter of King William III by the king's second wife Emma of Waldeck-Pyrmont, who acted as regent for her daughter until she came of age (1898). In 1901 Queen Wilhelmina married Prince Henry of Mecklenburg-Schwerin. In World War II, when her country was overrun by the Germans, she headed the government in exile and did everything in her power to encourage resistance. She abdicated in favour of her daughter, * Juliana.
Wilhelmina, *Lonely but not Alone*. 1960

Wilkes, Charles (1798–1877). American naval officer. He led an exploring expedition to the Antarctic (1838–42) but did not land: Wilkes Land, in the Australian territory, is named for him. During the US Civil War, he provoked a diplomatic incident with the British by arresting the British mail steamer *Trent* (1861) and removing Confederate officials.

Wilkes, John (1727–1797). English politician. He was the son of a wealthy distiller and as a young man was prominent among the members of the Hell-fire Club who celebrated their orgies at Sir Francis Dashwood's residence, Medmenham Abbey. In 1757 he was elected M.P. for Aylesbury but in 1761 became a violent opponent of Lord * Bute, chief minister of the young George III. To this end he established a weekly newspaper *The North Briton*, in No. 45 of which he asserted that the speech from the throne contained lies put into the king's mouth by his ministers. He was arrested under a general warrant (soon held to be illegal) against authors, printers and publishers, but was acquitted on the grounds of parliamentary privilege. The government's next step was to obtain a copy of his privately printed *Essay on Woman*. Obscene extracts read out in the House of Lords caused its condemnation, and after a duel Wilkes took refuge in France. During his absence he was expelled from parliament for his 'No. 45' and outlawed. On his return (1768), though elected four times in succession for Middlesex, he was imprisoned for twenty-two months and not allowed to take his seat. 'Wilkes and Liberty' became the Radical catchwords. Wilkes, however, was not born to be a martyr; he was elected sheriff of Middlesex (1771), lord mayor of London (1774) and in the same year he took his seat in parliament without opposition. Meanwhile he had made his peace with the court and in 1780 was to play a prominent part in the suppression of the Gordon Riots. None the less by his stands for the freedom of the press, and against arbitrary governmental action he earned the epitaph of his own composing, 'a friend of liberty'.
Bleakley, H. W., *John Wilkes*. 1917

Wilkie, Sir David (1785–1841). Scottish painter. He came to London in 1805, and won fame with his genre pictures such as *Village Politicians* (1806) and *Penny Wedding*, notable for their imaginative colour and sense of character. He was elected A.R.A. (1809) and R.A. (1811). Later he turned (less happily) to historical pictures, e.g. *The Preaching of John Knox*. He suceeded * Lawrence as court painter (1830) and was knighted in 1836.
Cunningham, A., *The Life of Sir David Wilkie*. 1843

Wilkins, Sir (George) Hubert (1888–1958). Australian explorer. After being a war correspondent in the Balkan Wars (1912–13) he accompanied Stefansson's expedition to the Arctic before joining the Australian Flying Corps in World War I. He was with the *Quest* during * Shackleton's last Antarctic voyage

(1921–22); he was knighted (1928) for a flight from Alaska to Spitsbergen, one of several exploratory flights he made in the Arctic at this time; and in the Antarctic (1928) he led an expedition to Grahamsland. In 1931 he tried unsuccessfully to navigate the submarine *Nautilus* under the North Pole.

Wilkins, John (1614–1672). English scientist. The son of a goldsmith, he studied at Oxford, graduating in 1631, entered the Church, and became warden of Wadham College in 1648. In 1659 he was made Master of Trinity College, Cambridge. Though a supporter of Oliver Cromwell (he married a sister of Cromwell's) he was made Bishop of Chester in 1668. Wilkins took an early interest in science and was one of the founder members of the Royal Society, a member of the Council and one of the secretaries. He took great interest in machines and technological improvements. He speculated about the Moon possibly being inhabited. His *Mathematical Magick* (1648) analyses the principles of machines; *Mercury, or the Secret and Swift Messenger* suggests telegraphic communication. Perhaps his most important interest lay in attempts to construct a universal, rational language, spelt out in his *An Essay towards a Real Character and Philosophical Language* (1688).
Shapiro, B. J., *John Wilkins*. 1969

Wilkins, Maurice Hugh Frederick (1916–). Irish biophysicist, born in New Zealand. His work on X-ray diffraction, assisted by Rose Franklin, suggested that molecules of DNA (deoxyribonucleic acid) had a helical structure. This led to the conclusive work on DNA by F. H. C. * Crick and J. D. * Watson and in 1962 they shared the Nobel Prize for Medicine.

Willard, Frances Elizabeth (1839–1898). American social reformer. She was secretary of the Women's Christian Temperance Union and for a time editor of the Chicago *Daily Post*. She wrote extensively in social issues.

William (known as 'the Lion') (1143–1214). King of Scotland (from 1165). He was the grandson of David I and brother of Malcolm IV, whom he succeeded. Angered by the refusal of Henry II of England to restore the disputed territories of Northumberland and Cumberland he allied himself with Henry's rebellious sons but was captured at the siege of Alnwick; by the humiliating Treaty of Falkirk (1174) he was forced to do homage for his kingdom. From this obligation Richard I's monetary needs for the 3rd Crusade enabled him to escape, but renewed war with King John compelled him to make another large payment to obtain peace. Before he died he had brought the Scottish lords under firm control.

William (known as 'the Silent') (1533–1584). Prince of Orange. He was a descendant of the Counts of Nassau and inherited (1554) their estates in the Netherlands and Burgundy as well as the principality of Orange (in Provence). His parents were Protestant but at the insistence of the emperor Charles V, who was then holding court at Brussels, and whose page he became, he was educated as a Catholic. In 1559 he was made stadholder of Holland, Zeeland and Utrecht by the emperor's son, Philip II of Spain, whom he served ably as a diplomat. He was horrified, however, by the persecutions of the Protestants in the Netherlands. Failure to obtain an agreement which would secure toleration for all was followed (1567) by the arrival of * Alba and the execution of Counts * Egmont and Horn. William, who had left the Netherlands in 1567, realized that the time for compromise had gone and made plans for a rising against Spain. His first invasion (1568) failed but in 1572 he returned, aided by an alliance with the Sea Beggars (*Gueux*), a group of rebels who had taken to the sea and who in 1572 captured Briel (Brielle), a port on the Maas. For the next few years William maintained the struggle and in 1576, by the pacification of Ghent, even managed to unite the northern and southern provinces against the Spaniards. Under Alba's more conciliatory successor, the Duke of Parma, however, the Catholic provinces were regained for Spain, but by the Union of Utrecht (1579) the northern alliance was confirmed and strengthened. Anxious for French help William induced the Duke of Anjou, the King's brother, to come with a view to sovereignty. When this plan failed William himself was chosen as Count of Holland and Zeeland but before he could be installed he was assassinated at Delft by Balthasar Gerard, a Catholic fanatic. His family continued as a dominant force in Dutch politics.
Wedgwood, C. V., *William the Silent*. 1944

William I (known as 'the Conqueror') (1027–1087). King of England (from 1066). Illegitimate son of Robert 'the Devil', Duke of Normandy, he succeeded his father as Duke (1035); but twelve years of fighting followed before he fully established himself. He married (1053) Matilda, daughter of Baldwin, Count of Flanders. His claim to the English throne rested upon a promise said to have been made (with no legal authority) by his cousin, Edward the Confessor, while William was paying him a visit. He also seems to have obtained under duress an oath of fealty from * Harold, who was in his power after being shipwrecked on the Normandy coast. As soon, therefore, as he heard that Harold had become king, he prepared to invade and on 14 October 1066 he won the decisive Battle of Hastings, in which Harold was killed. William himself was crowned at Westminster on Christmas Day but the conquest was not complete until 1070. There was little devastation except in the north where resistance was strongest. * Malcolm of Scotland submitted in 1072, and for a time * Hereward the Wake maintained a pocket of resistance in the East Anglian fens. Once in control of the country William proved himself a wise, just and resourceful ruler. The form of feudalism which he introduced was intended to curb the tyranny of the local barons and concentrate power in royal hands. By replacing Stigand, archbishop of Canterbury, by * Lanfranc he brought the English church into closer touch with that of the continent, but he strongly resisted the authoritarian claims of papacy. In 1086 he ordered the compiling of the Domesday Book, which recorded the value of royal, baronial and church lands and the distribution of the population. In his later years he had to contend with the intrigues of his half-brother Odo, bishop of Bayeux, and the disloyalty of his own eldest son Robert. He died after a fall from his horse in Mantes, captured by him while fighting the French.
Douglas, D. C., *William the Conqueror*. 1964

William I (1797–1888). German emperor (from 1871), and king of Prussia (from 1861). He went to England during the revolution of 1848 but returned in 1849 to lead the army which crushed the insurgents. He was regent for his brother, Frederick William IV of Prussia (by then insane), from 1858 until he succeeded him. When he became king he quarrelled with the Diet over the reorganization of the army, and even thought of abdicating; but in 1862 he appointed * Bismarck as his chief minister, and thereafter he gave continuous, though not uncritical, support to his minister's triumphant policy by which, through wars against Denmark, Austria and France, Prussia was given a dominating position in Europe and became the hard core round which the new empire was built (1871). William, a good soldier and, though a reactionary ruler, an honourable man, disliked the new-fangled imperial dignity thrust upon him as well as many of the means by which it was obtained, but he had neither the will nor power to quarrel with * Bismarck to whom he owed so much.

William II (known as William Rufus) (*c.* 1056–1100). King of England (from 1087). Called Rufus because of his red hair, he was the second surviving son of William the Conqueror, whom he succeeded as king. Normandy had passed to the elder son Robert, on which account the two brothers were in constant feud until the duchy finally fell into William's hands (1096), Robert having been forced to 'pawn' it to enable him to go on the 1st Crusade. William was ruthless and brutal; he quarrelled with his great archbishop of Canterbury, * Anselm, but was an able soldier, held the barons in check and maintained firm if extortionate rule through his chief minister Rannulf Flambard. He was accidentally shot while hunting in the New Forest by his companion Walter Tirel.
Slocombe, G., *Sons of the Conqueror*. 1960

William II (1859–1941). German emperor and king of Prussia (1888–1918). The grandson of William I and the son and successor of the emperor Frederick, he was the 'Kaiser' of World War II. Unlike his liberal-minded father, he gloried in the traditions of the Prussian army and indulged in dreams of leading it to new triumphs. Though * Bismarck had been the hero of his youth he could not submit to the tutelage of anyone, however great. In 1890 he 'dropped the pilot' and thereafter Germany's destiny lay in the hands of its able but impetuous and unpredictable ruler. At home he chose ministers for pliability rather than wisdom; abroad he stirred antagonism as though intentionally. He even managed to bring Britain, France and Russia together by truculent interference in

their concerns. To Britain, for example, his telegram of congratulation to President * Kruger on the suppression of the Jameson Raid was a deliberate provocation, while his vast naval construction could have only one purpose. Thus, when the murder of the Austrian archduke (1914) proved to be the match that fired World War I, Germany and Austria stood alone; even Italy, the third member of the Triple Alliance, joined her enemies (1915). The German army fought at first with all its old brilliance and success but it was the generals not the emperor who gained the plaudits; and when the tide turned it was remembered whose policy had brought disaster. William fled to Holland when defeated Germany became a republic and lived quietly at Doorn, near Arnhem, for the rest of his life. His first wife, by whom he had several children including the Crown Prince ('Little Willie' of the cartoonists during the war), died in 1921, and he married Princess Hermine of Reuss (died 1947).
Cowles, W. S., *The Kaiser*. 1963

William III (1650–1702). King of Great Britain (from 1689). A posthumous son of William II of Orange and Mary, daughter of Charles I of Great Britain, he was chosen stadholder of the United Provinces after the murder (1672) of * de Witt. He brought the long struggle with Louis XIV of France to an end by the honourable Peace of Nijmegen (1678), having meanwhile strengthened his position by marriage (1677) with the British princess Mary, daughter of the future James II. He formed (1686) the Grand Alliance to combat Louis's renewed aggression and, seeking fresh allies, was glad, therefore, to accept an invitation from England to intervene on behalf of 'English liberties' endangered by his father-in-law James II. He landed at Torbay (November 1688) with an army of 15,000 and quickly gained almost universal support. James fled to France; a convention parliament declared the throne vacant and in February 1689 William and Mary were proclaimed joint sovereigns. Resistance in Scotland was all but ended by the death of 'Bonnie * Dundee' at the Battle of Killicrankie (1689) and in Ireland by the surrender of Limerick (1691). The continental war was ended by the Treaty of Ryswick (1697). William, his power limited by the Bill of Rights (1689), neither liked nor was liked by his new subjects and his popularity waned further after the death of Mary (1694). He refused to commit himself to a single party and his administration included politicians from both Whigs and Tories. The foundation of the Bank of England and the start of the National Debt were of more interest to future generations than to his own. Another continental war (of the Spanish Succession) was about to start when he died. His final illness was complicated by a fall when his horse stumbled on a molehill. (Jacobites toasted the mole: 'The little gentleman in black velvet'.)
Baxter, S. B., *William III*. 1966

William IV (1767–1837). King of Great Britain and Ireland (from 1830). He was the third son of George III and in 1789 became Duke of Clarence. His early career in the navy earned him the nick-name of 'the sailor king'. He became titular admiral of the fleet (1811) and the office of 'lord high admiral' was revived for him (1827–28). He parted from his mistress, the actress Mrs Jordan, with whom he had lived from 1790 to 1811 and who had borne him ten children. In 1818 he married Adelaide, daughter of the Duke of Saxe-Meiningen, but both their daughters died in infancy. On the death of the Duke of York (1827) he became heir presumptive and in 1830 succeeded George IV. As king he objected strongly to the parliamentary Reform Bill of 1832 but eventually promised to create as many peers as might be necessary to secure its passage through the House of Lords. His outspokenness and eccentric remarks were often an embarrassment to his ministers but he strictly observed the constitutional proprieties. He was succeeded by his niece, Victoria.

William of Malmesbury (*c.* 1095–*c.* 1143). English historian. He was a monk who compiled accurate and impartial histories, notably the *Gesta regum Anglorum*, the story of the English kings to 1128, continued in *Historia novella* (up to 1142). He also wrote accounts of the bishops and monasteries and a life of St Dunstan.

William of Occam (or Ockham) *see* **Occam**

William of Wayneflete *see* **Waynflete**

William of Wykeham *see* **Wykeham**

Williams, Fred(erick Ronald) (1927–1982). Australian painter and graphic artist. He trained in London, evolving a spare, almost calligraphic, style which captured the strangeness and isolation of the Australian landscape.

Williams, (George) Emlyn (1905–). Welsh actor and playwright. His successful plays include *Night Must Fall* (1935) and *The Corn Is Green* (1941). He has acted in his own and other plays including those of Shakespeare; later his dramatized readings of Dickens and Dylan Thomas were widely acclaimed. His sensitive autobiography, *George*, 1961, relates the stages by which he emerged from a poor home in Wales to Oxford University and success on the stage.

Williams, Roger (*c.* 1603–1683). American colonist. He emigrated (1630) from England to Massachusetts, but was expelled through the intolerance of its Puritan rulers. He then established the new colony (charted 1644) of Rhode Island with complete religious freedom. He epitomized his views in *The Bloudy Tenent of Persecution* (1644) and many pamphlets, and also wrote *A Key into the Language of America* (1643), a remarkable grammar of Indian languages.

Williams, Shirley Vivien Teresa Brittain (1930–). British politician and daughter of the novelist Vera Brittain. She was secretary of the Fabian Society (1960–64) and was elected a Labour MP in 1964. From 1966 she held a number of junior ministerial posts and in 1974 became secretary of state for prices and consumer protection, following which she became secretary of state for education and science in 1976. She lost her seat in Parliament at the 1979 general election. She was a co-founder of the Social Democrats, and was re-elected as MP (November 1981) in a by-election, losing in 1983.

Williams, Tennessee (Thomas Lanier Williams) (1914–1983). American playwright. He first came into prominence with *The Glass Menagerie* (1945). This was followed by a series of major successes, most of them set in sordid surroundings in the Deep South in an atmosphere of impending tragedy with sex as a dominating theme. Among the best known are *A Streetcar Named Desire* (1947), *The Rose Tattoo* (1951), *Camino Real* (1953), *Cat on a Hot Tin Roof* (1955), and *Sweet Bird of Youth* (1958). He also wrote screen plays, short stories and novels.
Spoto, D., *The Kindness of Strangers*. 1985

Williams-Ellis, Sir Clough (1883–1978). Welsh architect and environmentalist. An innovative designer, conservationist and town planner, he was a prolific writer and propagandist who created the model resort village of Portmeirion, North Wales.

Williamson, Henry (1897–1977). English author and naturalist. He wrote successful books over a long period but it was by *Tarka the Otter* (1927) that he became renowned and is still best remembered.

Willingdon, Freeman Freeman-Thomas, 1st Marquess of (1866–1941). English Liberal politician. He served as governor-general of Canada 1926–31 and viceroy of India 1931–36 at the time of* Gandhi's civil disobedience campaigns.

Willis, Thomas (1621–1675). English physician. One of the leading anatomists of the seventeenth century, and a pioneer student of the nerves and brain, he graduated B.A. at Christ Church Oxford in 1636, and turned to medicine, getting his M.B. in 1646. Willis practised medicine in Oxford, and in 1660 became Sedleian Professor of Natural Philosophy. He was an early member of the Royal Society; in the 1660s he moved his medical practice to London. His most important work was the *Cerebri Anatome* (1664), the best anatomical account of the brain yet published. He offered new descriptions of the cranial nerves and described cerebral circulation. Willis also pioneered the clinical and pathological analysis of diabetes. He produced accurate descriptions of many fevers, such as typhus and typhoid, and puerperal fever, making considerable contributions to epidemiology.
Singer, C., and Underwood, E. A., *A Short History of Medicine*. 1962

Willkie, Wendell Lewis (1892–1944). American politician. He was a successful corporation lawyer before entering politics. Originally a Democrat, he opposed some aspects of Roosevelt's New Deal and in 1940 was adopted, almost as a forlorn hope, as Republican candidate for the presidency. Roosevelt used his services for several missions during World War II.

Wills, Helen (Helen Wills Moody, née Roark) (1905–). American lawn tennis player. With Suzanne * Lenglen she could claim to have brought lawn tennis for women up to modern championship standards, but unlike her rival she showed a 'poker face' whatever the fortunes or incidents of the game. She dominated the tournaments of America, England and France from 1923 to 1938.

Wilson, Sir Angus Frank Johnstone (1913–). British author, known for short stories and for satirical novels, e.g. *Hemlock and After* (1952) and *Anglo-Saxon Attitudes* (1956). He also wrote literary biographies: *The World of Charles Dickens* (1970) and *The Strange Ride of Rudyard Kipling* (1977).

Wilson, Charles Thomson Rees (1869–1959). Scottish physicist. From 1895 he worked in the Cavendish Laboratory at Cambridge and then held a professorship at that university (1925–34). He invented the 'cloud chamber' in which the behaviour of ionized particles can be observed and photographed by the tracks they make in supersaturated air. He shared the Nobel Prize for Physics (1927) with * Compton. Other honours included the Hughes Medal (1911), a Royal Medal (1922), the Copley Medal (1935) of the Royal Society and a C.H. (1937).

Wilson, Edmund (1895–1972). American literary critic. Recognised as the best of his time, he began as a journalist; he worked as Associate Editor of *New Republic* (1926–31), and was book reviewer on *The New Yorker*. He wrote *To the Finland Station: a study in the writing and acting of history* (1940, a historical study of socialism), *Memoirs of Hecate Country* (1946, a novel), *The Scrolls from the Dead Sea* (1955) and *Patriotic Gore* (1962, civil war literature). His literary criticism included *Axel's Castle* (1931), a definitive analysis of the Symbolists, *The Wound and the Bow* (1941) and an anthology, *The Shock of Recognition* (1943).

Wilson, Edmund Beecher (1856–1939). American naturalist. He made huge contributions to the observational and analytical understanding of the cell, which he published above all in his *The Cell in Development and Inheritance* (1896). Born of rich parents, Wilson was educated at various places before obtaining his Ph.D. at Johns Hopkins in 1881. He began to embark upon zoological research. After teaching at Bryn Mawr he moved in 1891 to Columbia University where he remained for the rest of his career. The study of cells preoccupied Wilson, gradually leading him to concentrate upon the problems of genetics and heredity. He was an enthusiastic supporter of Mendelian theory, and carried out extensive experimental research to work out the chromosomal theory of sex determination in detail. T. H. Morgan built his experiments on fruit flies upon these foundations. Wilson was concerned to depict the cell as a flexible, developing entity, and to chart the emergence of the cell as part of evolutionary descent. He was not however a wholehearted Darwinian, believing that * Darwin had overstressed the role played by natural selection.

Muller, H. J., 'Edmund B. Wilson' in *American Naturalist*, 77, 1943

Wilson, E(dward) O(sborne) (1929–). American biologist. Professor of biology at Harvard (1956–), he carried out work on social insects. His book *Sociobiology: the New Synthesis* (1975) proposed a unified, but intensely controversial, science of social behaviour which applied to all species (including humans).

Wilson, (James) Harold, Baron Wilson (1916–). British Labour politician. Born in Yorkshire, he was educated at Wirral Grammar School and Oxford University, where he later lectured on economics. He served in the ministry of fuel during World War II and entered parliament (1945) as a Labour MP. He served in Attlee's post-war governments, but while president of the Board of Trade resigned (1951) in protest against the governments's armaments policy. After Attlee's retirement and Gaitskell's succession to the parliamentary leadership of the party, which was then in opposition, Wilson was the principal spokesman on financial matters; he was regarded also as leader of the party's left-wing faction. When Gaitskell died (1963) Wilson was chosen to succeed him as opposition leader and when Labour won (by the smallest possible margin) the 1964 election he became prime minister. After he had weathered the financial crisis of the first difficult year, parliament was dissolved and the ensuing election (1965) gave him a majority of nearly 100. He was defeated by the conservatives in 1970 but again became prime minister after the elections of 1974. He resigned as prime minister in 1976 and in the same year was made a KG.

Wilson, H., *The Governance of Britain*. 1976

Wilson, Sir Henry Hughes (1864–1922). British soldier, born in Ireland. He was trained in the Staff College, of which he was later commandant (1907–10), and held a series of administrative and staff appointments throughout his career. As director of military operations at the War Office, he had to concert plans for cooperating with the French in case of a German war. When World War I broke out he was sub-chief of the general staff with the BEF and subsequently did valuable liaison work with the French. In February 1918 he was chosen by Lloyd George to succeed Robertson as chief of the imperial staff, and thus filled an important role during the final operations. He became MP for North Down in 1922 and in the same year, as an ardent Ulster sympathizer and friend of Lloyd George, was assassinated. As a 'political' soldier he was viewed with distrust by many of his army colleagues.

Wilson, Henry Maitland Wilson, 1st Baron (1881–1964). British soldier. After serving in the Boer War and World War I, 'Jumbo' Wilson (as he was called because of his size) was in command of British troops in Egypt at the beginning of World War II. He commanded the British troops in Greece, Syria and Iraq (1941–42). He succeeded * Alexander in the Middle East command (1943) and from 1944 was in control of all Allied operations in the Mediterranean area. He became a field-marshal in 1944.

Wilson, (Thomas) Woodrow (1856–1924). 28th president of the U.S. (1913–21). He was born at Staunton, Virginia, the son of a Presbyterian minister of Ulster and Scottish ancestry. After graduating at Princeton University, he briefly practised law and studied further at Johns Hopkins University. He became increasingly prominent in the academic world during the next twenty-five years. After being professor of jurisprudence and political economy at Princeton (from 1890) he became its president in 1902. He instituted many reforms in the teaching system but his more general plans met with rebuffs. He resigned from Princeton (1910) and accepted the Democratic nomination for the governorship of New Jersey. When elected, he soon dispelled any idea that he would be tractable and conservative and instituted a full liberal programme including Corrupt Practices and Employers' Liability Acts. Progressives of his party rallied to his side and he was chosen as Democratic candidate for the presidency in 1912, his success aided by the split in the normal Republican vote between Taft and Theodore Roosevelt. In office Wilson continued his policy of reform (the 'New Freedom') with such measures as Workers' Compensation and Child Welfare Acts, but the real challenge to his qualities came with the opening of World War I. He began by being a convinced neutralist and his 1916 re-election was his reward for keeping his country at peace. But Germany's disregard for common humanity and neutral rights shown by the torpedoing of the *Lusitania* (1915) and the subsequent sinking of many American ships forced him at last (1917) to lead his country into war. His moral ascendancy was so great that almost at once he represented the collective conscience of the Allied powers. In pursuance of the aim to make a world 'safe for democracy' he enunciated his famous 'Fourteen Points', which outlined the pattern of a just and lasting peace. At the Paris Peace Conference (1919), which he attended, he was often at a disadvantage in confrontation with the astute Allied negotiators with their nationalistic aims, but nevertheless some of his idealism filtered through into the Treaty of Versailles. But the traditional isolationism of America proved too much for him. Too late he realized the need to train public opinion to accept such a revolutionary change of political thought as participation in the complex series of obligations that the treaty demanded. On his return from Paris he made a great speech-making tour in defence of the Treaty but the Senate failed to ratify it. A tragic consequence was that the League of Nations, that great conception for the inclusion of which in the treaty Wilson had fought so hard, was launched without American participation. The exertions of his propaganda campaign proved too great for his health: he had a stroke from the effects of which he never fully recovered. For the last part of his term as president (until 1920), Wilson stood aloof and resentful. With his many qualities and weaknesses (at least in

practical political terms) he remains one of the most influential of American presidents.
Walworth, A. C., *Woodrow Wilson.* 1958

Wincklemann, Johann Joachim (1717–1768). German writer on ancient art. The son of a cobbler, he had to struggle to obtain an education and it was only after fifteen years as tutor and schoolmaster and much study that he was able to realize his ambition of going to Rome (1755). Here in the congenial service of the great collector Cardinal Alessandro Albani, he was able to combine the judgements of eye and mind, and, in language of singular felicity, give historical and aesthetic verdicts upon the works of art which he considered. His *History of Ancient Art* (1764), his best known work, established new criteria of genuineness and attribution which placed all future art historians in his debt. He was stabbed to death by a thief in Trieste.
Leppman, W., *Wincklemann.* 1970

Windsor. The dynastic name adopted (1917) by the British royal house when George V gave up his German titles. (The previous name was * Wettin.) In 1960 it was announced that descendants of Queen Elizabeth II and Prince Philip, other than those styled princes and princesses, should bear the surname Mountbatten-Windsor.

Windsor, Duke of *see* **Edward VIII**

Wingate, Orde Charles (1903–1944). British soldier. He served as an officer in British army intelligence in Palestine (1936–39) but was repatriated for his pro-Zionist activities. In Palestine he met and impressed * Wavell who sent him first to Ethiopia (1940) to organise guerrillas against the Italians and in 1942 to India to conduct similar operations behind the Japanese lines in Burma. After careful training and practice the first raid of Wingate and his 'Chindits' was made early in 1943; when Wingate with some 60 per cent of his original force returned in May he had proved that a force could live and fight for several weeks sustained only by supplies hazardously brought by air. Now hailed as a hero, Wingate persuaded Churchill and Roosevelt to allow him to command a large force of more than twenty battalions, British, Gurkhas and Nigerians, which should be dropped from the air to form an enclave behind the Japanese lines. The drop successfully took place, but, while Wingate was returning from a conference to discuss subsequent difficulties and delays, his aircraft crashed into a hill and he was killed. A man of great courage and imagination, he was intolerant of opposition but gifted with the qualities that won and sustained the enthusiasm of political leaders as well as troops.
Sykes, C., *Orde Wingate.* 1959

Wingate, Sir (Francis) Reginald, 1st Bart. (1861–1953). British general and administrator. He served in India and Aden before being posted to the Egyptian army; his record there led to his appointment as Governor General of the Sudan in 1899, a post which he filled with notable success for seventeen years. He was High Commissioner for Egypt at his retirement in 1922.
Wingate, F. R., *Wingate of the Sudan.* 1955

Wint, Peter de (1784–1849). English watercolourist. Of Dutch descent, he illustrated many aspects of English landscape and rural life. Among his paintings are *The Hay Harvest, Nottingham, Richmond Hill* and *Cows in Water.*

Winterhalter, Franz Xavier (1806–1873). German painter. He became famous for his royal portraits, e.g. of Louis Philippe of France, Napoleon III, Leopold I of the Belgians and above all of Queen Victoria, Prince Albert and the British royal family.

Winthrop, John (1588–1649). American colonist. An Englishman by birth, a Puritan by religion, prosperous both as lawyer and Suffolk landowner, he sponsored the Massachusetts emigration scheme and went there as its first governor in 1630, an office which he held until 1633 and from 1637 until his death. Many of the social and political institutions of Massachusetts preserved his memory but the rigid Puritanism of the administration caused many to leave the colony. Winthrop's diary is an important authority for the early period of American history. His son, **John Winthrop** (1606–1676), a chemist and first American member of the Royal Society, established the first iron furnaces in Massachusetts. He became governor of Connecticut (1660–76).
Morgan, E. S., *The Puritan Dilemma.* 1958

Wiseman, Nicholas (1802–1865). British cardinal. Of Irish descent, he was born in Seville and educated for the priesthood at the English College in Rome, of which he became rector in 1828. Realizing the way for a revival in England had been prepared by the Tractarian movement in the Church of England (* Keble, * Newman, * Pusey) he went there in 1840, became vicar-apostolic in London (1848) and in 1850 was made a cardinal. When the Roman Catholic hierarchy was re-established in England in the same year, he was given primacy by his appointment as first archbishop of Westminster.

Withering, William (1741–1799). British botanist. The son of a Wellington apothecary, he trained in medicine at Edinburgh University, graduating M.D. in 1766. Withering practised first in Stafford and then in Birmingham. He became an active member of the Lunar Society alongside Erasmus Darwin, Joseph Priestley, Josiah Wedgwood etc. Withering is important in the history of botany for his *A Botanical Arrangement of all the Vegetables Naturally Growing in Great Britain* (1776), which made early use of the Linnaean method of classification. He also performed useful chemical and mineralogical analysis, and translated Torbern Bergman's *Mineralogy*. His most original scientific work was his championing of digitalis, derived from foxglove, as a specific for diseases ranging from dropsy to heart trouble. A slightly querulous man, Withering spent the last years of his life in bitter controversy with Erasmus Darwin and his son.
Peck, T. W. and Wilkinson, K. D., *William Withering*. 1950

Witt, Jan de *see* **de Witt, Jan**

Witte, Count Sergei Yulievich (1849–1915). Russian statesman. At first an official in the railway administration he was appointed minister of finance (1892). He introduced various financial reforms, sponsored the building of the Trans-Siberian Railway and promoted industrial development. He lost favour and was dismissed (1903), but was recalled to negotiate peace with Japan (1905); the terms he secured in the Treaty of Portsmouth (1905) were more favourable than had been expected, and his reputation was enhanced. He was created a count in recognition and he persuaded the Tsar to sign the Manifesto of 1905 promising to set up a Duma (parliament) which had elements of constitutional government. He became premier (1905) but resigned almost immediately when he failed to obtain the support of the Duma. He was followed shortly by the more conservative Stolypin.
von Lane, T., *Sergei Witte and the Industrialisation of Russia*. 1963

Wittelsbach. German dynasty. It enters history in the 11th century, taking its name from a castle in west Bavaria. Later there were numerous branches, the most important of which ruled in the Palatinate and (eventually as kings) in Bavaria. From the former branch, through * Elizabeth, daughter of James I, stem the present British royal house and (after the failure of the royal Stuart line) the later Jacobite pretenders.

Wittgenstein, Ludwig Josef Johann (1889–1951). Austrian philosopher, a British subject from 1938. After studying engineering in Berlin he became interested in mathematics and at Cambridge came under the influence of Bertrand * Russell. He served as an Austrian officer in World War I but in 1929 he returned to Cambridge, where he succeeded (1939) G. E. * Moore as professor of philosophy; he resigned his chair in 1949. His *Tractatus Logico-Philosophicus* (1921) presents a system usually described as logical atomism, comprising a theory of language and a closely related physical view of the world. Language is seen as basically made up of simple propositions, which are immediately meaningful because they picture (or have the same structure as) simple or ultimate facts. The *Tractatus*, notoriously difficult to interpret, also contains among other doctrines the view that the only meaningful assertions are either factual or strictly logical ones; it thus anticipates the central meaning of the theory of logical positivism. Wittgenstein's later work, published posthumously, is contained in *The Blue and Brown Books* (1958) and *Philosophical Investigations* (1953). It includes a rejection of his earlier view of language, eschews metaphysical speculation about ultimate facts and offers reflections on the nature of philosophy. Language is now seen to have a large number of functions, including promise-making and giving orders, for example. It is absurd, Wittgenstein argues, to assimilate all these to the business of stating facts; they are like games, which overlap in various ways but have no common character. Philosophy, he suggests, should be an attempt to clear up puzzles that have arisen, at least in part,

through linguistic confusions. The concern of recent British philosophers with the clarification of concepts owes much to Wittgenstein's inspiration.
Fann, K. T., *Wittgenstein's conception of Philosophy*. 1969

Wladislaw *see* **Ladislaus**

Wodehouse, Sir P(elham) G(renville) (1881–1975). English humorist, born in Guildford. After working as a bank-clerk, he began writing boys stories. He moved to New York in 1909 and became successful as a musical comedy librettist (with Cole Porter, George Gershwin, Irving Berlin and Jerome Kern) and author of humorous serials for magazines, featuring such characters as Psmith, Ukridge, Mr Mulliner and the Earl of Emsworth. He wrote more than 100 books and developed a highly distinctive prose style. By weaving his consummately stylish humorous fancies round a few brilliantly conceived characters – caricatures even when they first appeared – and by never seriously altering the character of his dialogue, he maintained an almost unparalleled popularity for more than half a century. His Bertie Wooster and his omniscient manservant Jeeves have been acclaimed as warmly on the television screen as in his books. Wodehouse was interned by the Germans in France (1940–45) and incurred criticism for broadcasts made at that time. From 1945 he lived in the U.S.A.
Usborne, R., *Working with Wodehouse*. 1961; Jasen, D. A., *P. G. Wodehouse: A Portrait of a Master*. 1975

Wöhler, Friedrich (1800–1882). German chemist. He was trained in medicine but turned to chemistry, of which he was professor at Göttingen from 1836 until his death. He was the first (1827) to isolate aluminium by reduction of its anhydrous chloride with potassium; he used similar means to isolate beryllium (1829). He was the first to make calcium carbide, from which he prepared acetylene, and he also improved the method of manufacturing sulphur. His synthesis of urea from ammonium cyanate by intermolecular rearrangement (1828) disproved the theory that organic compounds could be produced only by living organisms. Many other examples of such synthesis followed, opening a new era in organic chemistry.

Wolf, Hugo (1860–1903). Austrian composer. His dismissal for insubordination while a student at the Vienna Conservatoire was followed by a period of precarious living. In the many songs he then wrote the influence of * Schumann is especially evident. As music critic of the *Wiener Salonblatt* (1884–87) he made many enemies by his savage attacks on * Brahms and his circle and by his wholehearted support of * Wagner. His best known works are song collections: fifty-three settings of Mörike (1888), twenty of Eichendorff (1880–88), and fifty-one of Goethe (1888–89), the *Spanisches Liederbuch* (1889–90) and *Italienisches Liederbuch* (1890–91, 1896). He also wrote an opera, *The Corregidor* (1895) and the *Italian Serenade* for string quartet (1887). In 1897 he became insane and after a brief period of recovery he ended his life in an asylum. His songs, among the greatest written, represent a unique blend of poetry and music into an organic whole, achieved by a close interdependence of the voice and piano parts and his own imaginative response to the written word.

Wolfe, Humbert (1885–1940). English poet and civil servant. After leaving Oxford he entered the civil service (1908). His poetry, e.g. *London Sonnets* (1920), *Requiem* (1927) and the verse play *X at Oberammergau* (1938), was both romantic and satirical. He also wrote works of criticism and autobiography.
Wolfe, H., *The Upward Anguish*. 1938

Wolfe, James (1727–1759). British soldier. He was born at Westerham, Kent, and while still a boy adopted his father's profession of soldier; he was only 17 when he took part in the Battle of Dettingen as a regimental adjutant. He fought at Falkirk and Culloden (against the Jacobites) and on the continent. After the opening of the Seven Years War (1756) he was chosen by Pitt to command a brigade in Amherst's expedition against Cape Breton in Nova Scotia. Hailed for the skill and heroism which led to the fall of Louisburg (1758) he was given command of the expedition sent to capture Quebec and end French rule in Canada. He finally achieved success (September 1759) by the discovery of a steep unguarded path which enabled him to land his troops and scale the cliffs of the St Lawrence River unobserved. The armies met on the Plains of Abraham outside the city. Both commanders, the French general

Montcalm and Wolfe himself, were killed in battle but Wolfe lived long enough to hear of his complete victory. He was only 32, one of the youngest and most famous of British generals.
Grinnell-Milne, D., *Mad is he?* 1963

Wolfe, Thomas (1900–1938). American novelist, born in Ashville, North Carolina. *Look Homeward, Angel* (1929) was the first of his mainly autobiographical novels, giving portrayals of life in a small Southern town. *Of Time and the River* was published in 1935; *The Web and the Rock, You Can't Go Home Again* and *The Hills Beyond* appeared posthumously.
Johnson, P. H., *Thomas Wolfe*. 1947

Wolfe, Tom (Thomas Kennerly, Jr) (1931–). American journalist. One of the originators of 'new journalism', he wrote biting studies of contemporary American culture. His books included *The Kandy-Kolored Tangerine-Flake Streamline Baby* (1965), *Radical Chic and Mau-mauing the Flak Catchers* (1970) and *The Right Stuff* (1975).

Wolff, Kaspar Friedrich (1733–1794). German physiologist. One of the 18th century pioneers of embryology, having studied at Berlin and Halle, he graduated in 1759. He served for a time as an army surgeon and developed a Berlin private practice. In 1767 he moved to St Petersburg as an Academician in Anatomy and Physiology. He researched there continuously until his death. Wolff's work in embryology challenged the 'preformationist' hypothesis (which held that the embryo contained in miniature all the parts of the adult-to-be, ready formed). Wolff adopted the counter position that the embryo contained as-yet-undifferentiated tissue. He tried to show that the growing tips of plants contain undifferentiated tissue which only gradually unfolds into the distinct parts, such as leaf and flower. This more 'evolutionist' account came to dominate the field over the next half century.
Oppenheimer, J., *Essays in the history of embryology and biology*. 1967

Wolfit, Sir Donald (1902–1968). British actor-manager. He made his debut in 1920 and his first London appearance in 1924. In 1937 he formed his own touring company and, through provincial tours and the lunch-time performances he gave in war-time, presented Shakespeare's plays and other classical drama to audiences which would otherwise never have seen them. His acting style was romantic and emotional. He was knighted in 1957.
Wolfit, D., *First Interval*. 1954

Wollaston, William Hyde (1766–1828). English physician and chemist. He developed a method of making platinum malleable for conversion into wire and vessels, and the income from this enabled him to retire from medical practice and take up scientific research. He discovered palladium (1803) and rhodium (1804), drew up a table of equivalents, showed that static and current electricity are similar, devised a lens combination which eliminated aberration, and invented the camera lucida and the reflecting goniometer used to measure the angles of crystals. The mineral Wollastonite, a compound of calcium, silicon and oxygen, was named after him.

Wolseley, Garnet Joseph Wolseley, 1st Viscount (1833–1913). British soldier. He held his first independent command in Canada where his administrative skill enabled him to suppress the Red River rebellion (1870) without bloodshed (* Riel, Louis). His great victory at Tel el Kebir (1882), by which he completely crushed the rebellion of Arabi Pasha in Egypt, added still further to his fame and though in 1885 he arrived at Khartoum too late to save * Gordon the blame was not his. Between his campaigns he had taken a prominent part in carrying out and extending Caldwell's army reforms.
Wolseley, G. J., *Story of a Soldier's Life* 1903

Wolsey, Thomas (1471–1530). English prelate and statesman. The son of a butcher (or grazier and innkeeper) at Ipswich, he was educated for the priesthood at Oxford; he became chaplain to the archbishop of Canterbury (1501) and, a few years later, chaplain to the king. Under Henry VIII, who liked and admired him and found him useful for diplomatic missions, Wolsey advanced quickly; he was made bishop of Lincoln and then archbishop of York (1514). When he succeeded (1515) Warham as lord chancellor he became Henry's chief minister. The pope created him cardinal in 1517. Henry's foreign policy aimed at maintaining a balance between the young Francis I of France and the emperor Charles V, who also became king of

Spain. In Wolsey he found a skilful agent who was obsessed with the idea of making his master Europe's arbiter; at home too he aimed at making Henry supreme, only once summoning parliament and when he did so addressing the members in the most arrogant terms; a strengthened court of the Star Chamber kept the nobles in check. Thus his unpopularity grew and he depended entirely on royal favour. This was at first lavish and enabled Wolsey to build the magnificent palace of Hampton Court (which he later found it expedient to hand over to his royal master), but Henry began to have misgivings about his minister's growing power and did not support unreservedly his attempts to be elected pope. The crisis in their relations arose through Henry's domestic affairs. Queen Catherine had borne Henry many children but only one girl had survived; he needed a son and planned to annul his marriage on the grounds that, despite papal dispensation, it was an infraction of church law to marry his dead brother's widow. With the agreement of Henry, Wolsey as papal legate summoned the king to appear before an ecclesiastical court. But these and subsequent proceedings were drawn out and indecisive and Henry, blaming Wolsey for the delays, began negotiations with the papacy behind his back. The situation was abruptly changed when the troops of Charles V seized and sacked Rome (1527) and the pope was a virtual prisoner of Charles, Queen Catherine's nephew. Henry now realized that he could only gain his purpose – doubly urgent now owing to his infatuation for Anne * Boleyn – by a breach with the papacy in which Cardinal Wolsey would be unwilling to assist. Wolsey, therefore, retired in disgrace to his see at York (1529). But his enemies at court were not to be appeased. Charges were made against him and eventually one of treason, which he was summoned to London to answer. On the way he fell ill at Leicester Abbey and there died. Wolsey was a great patron of education and Cardinal College (now Christ Church) which he founded at Oxford remains his finest memorial.
Ridley, J., *The Statesman and the Fanatic: Thomas Wolsey and Thomas More*. 1982

Wood, Mrs Henry (née Ellen Price) (1814–1887). English novelist. Widowed early, she took to writing novels; of her thirty or more books she is mainly remembered for *East Lynne* (1861), equally popular as novel, play and eventually film. She successfully combined melodramatic plots with some skill in character drawing. Her other books include *The Channings* (1862) and the *Johnny Ludlow* series (1874–89).

Wood, Sir Henry Joseph (1869–1944). English conductor. Until the year of his death he conducted annually the famous Promenade Concerts in London, of which with Robert Newman he was co-founder (1895), originally given at the Queen's Hall (until it was bombed in World War II) and then at the Albert Hall.
Wood, Sir H. J., *My Life of Music*. 1938

Wood, John (1704–1754). English architect and planner, born in Yorkshire. He is famous for his plans for Bath (from 1727), where he designed Queen's Square, North and South Parades and the Circus. His work, unfinished at his death, was carried on by his son, **John Wood** (1728–1781), who also built Royal Crescent and the Assembly Rooms.

Woodcock, George (1904–1979). English trade union leader. He started work as a boy in a Lancashire cotton mill and in 1929 went to Ruskin College, Oxford. After winning a scholarship to New College, he obtained a first-class degree. From being secretary of the research and economic department of the T.U.C. he rose to become assistant general secretary in 1947 and in 1960 was appointed general secretary: he retired in 1969. His moderation and wisdom added much to the authority of this office. He then became Chairman of the Commission on Industrial Relations but resigned in 1971 in protest at the Conservative Government's Industrial Relations Act. He was created a C.B.E. in 1953.

Woodward, John (1665–1728). English geologist, born in Derbyshire. He was apprenticed to a linen draper in London, and subsequently studied medicine, becoming Professor of Physic at Gresham College, London, in 1692. He was a pioneer geologist, who set up the Woodwardian Chair of geology at Cambridge in 1728. He was a theorist of the earth, a pioneer of stratigraphy, and an important collector of minerals and fossils. In his theory, *An Essay Toward a Natural History of the Earth* (1695) he asserted that the strata lay in regular order throughout the globe and that fossils were organic remains. Both phenomena

he attributed to the effects of the Biblical Deluge, which he explained by the action and suspension of the Newtonian force of gravity. In his other major works, such as the *Attempt towards a Natural History of the Fossils of England* (1728–29), he sought to order all the British fossils into a collection and to provide a classification of mineral objects. Woodward had wide interests, and made important contributions to plant physiology and to Roman antiquities.
Porter, R., 'John Woodward' *Geological magazine*. 116, 1979, 335–43

Woodward, Robert Burns (1917–1979). American chemist. Educated at the Massachusetts Institute of Technology, he was a chemistry professor at Harvard (1950–79) and became known as the father of synthetic organic chemistry. He succeeded in synthesising penicillin, terramycin, chlorophyll, strychnine, quinine, reserpine, vitamin B 12 and many other substances. He received the 1965 Nobel Prize for Chemistry, was a Fellow of the Royal Society and a Davy Medallist.

Woolf, Virginia (1882–1941). English writer. She was a daughter of Sir Leslie* Stephen and sister of Vanessa (wife of Clive * Bell). She married (1912) Leonard Woolf, printer, publisher and political writer. They established (1915) the Hogarth Press in Richmond; it was moved to Bloomsbury in the early 1920s and Virginia Woolf became a leading figure in the literary coterie known as the Bloomsbury set. Meanwhile she had begun her career as a novelist with the publication of *The Voyage Out* (1915). Her novels are difficult but rewarding: she seldom uses direct narrative but is most concerned with the inner consciousness of her characters expressed by internal monologue, while the emotional intensity and symbolism of her language are more typical of poetry than prose. But she is not over-serious and sometimes, e.g. in the fantasy *Orlando* (1928), shows an impish sense of humour. Among the most characteristic of her novels are *Jacob's Room* (1922), *Mrs Dalloway* (1925), *To The Lighthouse* (1927) and *The Waves* (1931). She was also a distinguished essayist and showed her interest in social changes affecting women in, e.g., *A Room of One's Own* (1929). Another aspect of her talent was shown by her biography of the artist and critic Roger Fry. Under the stresses of World War II she drowned herself.
Daiches, D., *Virginia Woolf*. 1945

Woollcott, Alexander (1887–1943). American journalist. He became a famous dramatic critic respected and feared for his reputation of being able to make or break plays. Later he won renown as a broadcaster and essayist. Sheridan Whiteside, the central character in the play (and film) *The Man who Came to Dinner* by George S. Kaufman and Moss Hart was based on him.

Woolley, Sir (Charles) Leonard (1880–1960). English archaeologist, famed for his excavations of the site of the biblical 'Ur of the Chaldees' in Mesopotamia. After being assistant curator at the Ashmolean Museum, Oxford, he gained practical experience of excavation in Egypt, Syria, Nubia and at Carchemish in Turkey (where he had the assistance of T. E.* Lawrence). After being a prisoner of war in Turkey in World War I he spent twelve years from 1922 excavating at Ur (by then in Iraq); at the royal cemetery evidence of human sacrifice at the burials of the nobles was found and rich accumulations of artistic treasures were uncovered. These are described in *The Royal Cemetery* (1934); his other works include *Digging up the Past* (1930).
Woolley, C. L., *Spadework*. 1953

Woolman, John (1720–1772). American Quaker preacher. A farmer's son born in New Jersey, he preached and wrote against slavery and published several religious works, as well as his *Journal* (1774, often reprinted).
Whitney, J., *John Woolman*. 1943

Woolton, Frederick James Marquis, 1st Earl of (1882–1964). British businessman and Conservative politician. As minister of food (1940–43) he devised an efficient rationing scheme in World War II. He was minister of reconstruction (1943–45) and as chairman of the party was largely responsible for bringing the Conservatives back to office in 1951.
Woolton, F., *Memoirs*. 1959

Woolworth, Frank Winfield (1852–1919). American retailer. He was a farm worker until becoming a shop assistant in 1873. His first 5-cent store, opened (1879) in Utica, N.Y., failed, but a 5- and 10-cent store started in

Lancaster, Pennsylvania, in the same year became the nucleus of the vast international chain of shops that bears his name. The giant New York skyscraper, the Woolworth Building, for a time the world's tallest building, was constructed (1913) to house his central offices.

Wootton, Barbara Frances, Baroness Wootton of Abinger (1897–). English social scientist and economist. Educated at Cambridge, she lectured in economics at Girton College 1920–22, did research work for the Labour Party 1922–26 and was principal of Morley College 1926–27. She was director of studies at London University 1927–44 and professor of social studies 1948–52. She was made a life peeress in 1958 and wrote many books.
Wootton, B. F., *Testament for Social Science*. 1950

Worde, Wynkyn de (*fl.* 1480–1535?). English printer, born in Alsace. He was a pupil of * Caxton, who in 1491 succeeded to his business. He made great improvements in printing and typecutting, and printed many books, including *The Golden Legend* (1493), *Morte D'Arthur* (1498) and the third edition of the *Canterbury Tales*.
Plomer, H. R., *Wynkyn de Worde*. 1925

Wordsworth, Dorothy (1771–1855). English writer. Only sister and close companion of William * Wordsworth, her *Journals* show that she shared his poetic sensibility and his response to nature; her own delight in natural beauty and her sharp observation of it is said to have been a continuous inspiration to him. She had a nervous breakdown in 1829 and never fully recovered; by the time of her death she had become simple-minded.
de Selincourt, E., ed., *Letters of William and Dorothy Wordsworth*. 1935–39

Wordsworth, William (1770–1850). English poet, born at Cockermouth, Cumberland. After leaving Cambridge University he went to France (1791–92), then approaching the height of the Revolution, and there fell in love with Annette Villon, who bore him a daughter. At first he supported the Revolutionary cause, but after his return to England the Jacobin excesses and the entry of England into war with France horrified him and confused his mind. From this condition his sister * Dorothy, by reinvigorating his love of nature, and his friend * Coleridge, by his philosophy, restored him to his vocation as a poet. A legacy enabled them to move first to Dorset, then to Somerset, and in 1799 brother and sister went to Grasmere in the Lake District, in the neighbourhood of which they made their permanent home. Jointly with Coleridge he had already published *Lyrical Ballads* (1798), which marked a revolt from the highly-wrought 'Augustan' style of Pope and his successors and the return to nature for inspiration. It thus heralded the Romantic revival which dominated English poetry for so long. He married (1802) Mary Hutchinson, a friend from childhood, and they lived with Dorothy in the Lake District, the centre of a group of writers and friends who made Lakeland their home.

Wordsworth rejected the artificiality of 'poetic' language, and the careful, apposite simplicity of his diction in the *Lyrical Ballads* of 1801, shown in *Michael, Ruth* and the *Lucy* poems, is most effective.

He used the sonnet form finely to express a stirring patriotism:

We must be free or die, who speak the tongue
That Shakespeare spoke; the faith and morals hold
Which Milton held . . .

or meditatively as in the early-morning soliloquy on Westminster Bridge with its famous last lines:

Dear God! the very houses seem asleep,
And all that mighty heart is lying still!

His nature poems show the acuteness of his inner vision – 'the raindrop lingering on the pointed thorn' – but Wordsworth's final enthusiasm was for humanity itself, humanity in its natural setting, the ploughman, the girl reaper, the shepherd and also – for he was not censorious – the lover and even the drunkard and thief. Less appealing to the modern reader than his shorter pieces is the great, unfinished philosophic poem, *The Recluse*, on which Wordsworth was engaged from 1798 to 1814. The introductory *The Prelude*, finished in 1805 but only published after his death, is autobiographical in the sense that it relates the poet's mental development; *The Excursion* (9 books, 1814), the only other part to appear, was intended as the middle portion. It contains long philosophic discussions illustrated by poetic tales, e.g. the beautiful *Story of Margaret*.

Wordsworth became Poet Laureate in 1843. His last years were clouded by the death (1847) of his daughter Dora.

Wordsworth, W., (eds. de Selincourt, E., and Darbishire, H.), *Poetical Works*. 5 vols. 1940–49

Wotton, Sir Henry (1568–1639). English diplomat and writer. After leaving Oxford, where he became a close friend of John * Donne he became secretary to the Earl of * Essex, whom he accompanied on several expeditions. Later he was sent by the Grand Duke of Tuscany to warn James VI of Scotland of a Roman Catholic plot against his life, which entailed a journey in disguise through Germany and Denmark and led to his being made ambassador to Venice when James came to the English throne as James I. This and other diplomatic posts he held with distinction. Finally returning in 1623, he was provost of Eton from 1624 until his death. He was responsible for the definition of an ambassador as 'an honest man sent to lie abroad for the good of his country'. His *The Elements of Architecture* (1624), suggested adaptations of the Palladian style for English country houses; he also wrote many charming lyrics (Izaak * Walton).

Wouk, Herman (1915–). American novelist. Among his most popular successes were *The Caine Mutiny* (1951), *Marjorie Morningstar* (1955) and *Youngblood Hawke* (1962). *The Caine Mutiny* was also a successful play and film.

Wouverman, Philips (1619–1668). Dutch painter. He is known for his numerous hunting and battle scenes, the latter often distinguished by a conspicuous white horse in the foreground. He spent his life at Haarlem, where he is believed to have studied under Frans * Hals.

Wrangel, Baron Peter Nikolayevich (1878–1928). Russian soldier. Having served with distinction in the Russo-Japanese War and become a young major-general in World War I he succeeded * Denikin in command of the anti-Bolshevik forces in south Russia. He held out in the Crimea until November 1920, when he evacuated troops and refugees to the Balkans.

Wren, Sir Christopher (1632–1723). English architect and scientist. His father was dean of Windsor; after graduating at Oxford, where his scientific attainments earned him the reputation of a prodigy, he taught mathematics at Gresham's College, London, was a co-founder of the Royal Society and in 1660 became a professor of astronomy at Oxford. There his active interest in architecture developed and it was the originality of his design (exhibited as a model in 1663 and carried out in 1669) for the Sheldonian Theatre there that ensured his fame. He was on a commission considering the restoration of the old St Paul's Cathedral when the Great Fire (1666) destroyed about two-thirds of the city. Though his grandiose plans for rebuilding the city were not accepted he was given the task of redesigning St Paul's and the city churches. St Paul's was finally completed in 1711. His secular work is almost equally famous; the new buildings of Hampton Court for all their magnificence conform to the domestic charm of the old. To the same decade (the 1690s) belong to the Royal Hospital, Chelsea, Kensington Palace and the start of work on Greenwich Hospital. Earlier the perfect proportions of Trinity College Library in Cambridge had given promise of what he could achieve. A visit to Paris (1665) had resulted in French influence throughout but his later work, especially the western towers of St Paul's, shows familiarity (probably through engravings) with Roman baroque.

Wren was knighted in 1673, was president of the Royal Society (1681–83) and was twice briefly M.P. (1685–87 and 1701–02). He was twice married and a son by each marriage survived him.

Whinney, M., *Wren*. 1971

Wright, Sir Almroth Edward (1861–1947). English pathologist, professor of experimental pathology at London University. He developed the first successful anti-typhoid serum and investigated parasitic diseases. He was the teacher of Sir Alexander * Fleming.

Wright, Frank Lloyd (1869–1959). American architect, born in Wisconsin. He was apprenticed to Louis * Sullivan in Chicago. He pioneered a highly original style which was arrived at by integrating engineering methods into architectural expression, by understanding use of materials, and by stressing the importance of a harmonious relationship be-

tween building and landscape. His domestic buildings, emphasized low, horizontal proportions (the 'prairie style') and were the prototypes of the open-planned house. His public buildings include the Imperial Hotel, Tokyo (1916), one of the few major buildings to survive the 1923 earthquake, and the Guggenheim Museum, New York (1949).
Wright, F. L., *A Testament*. 1957

Wright, Thomas (1711–1786). English astronomer. He became one of the most original cosmological and astronomical thinkers in eighteenth century England. Born in County Durham and largely self-taught, Wright set himself up as a teacher of navigation and pursued astronomical research. In 1750 he published his most important work, the *Original Theory, or New Hypothesis of the Universe*. This was primarily an attempt to fuse his own heterodox religious views with physical truth. Wright believed that the universe had a divine and gravitational centre, which was the abode of light. He saw the Milky Way as a thin shell of stars, and proposed the existence of a multiplicity of star systems, each with its own supernatural centre. Wright later published his *Second Thoughts* in which he suggested that the universe rather consisted of an infinite sequence of concentric shells surrounding the divine centre. The sky is one of those opaque shells. Stars he saw as pinpricks, letting light pass through from within.
Hoskin, M. A., 'The cosmology of Thomas Wright of Durham', *Journal for the history of astronomy*, i (1970), 44–52

Wright, Wilbur (1867–1912) and **Orville** (1871–1948). American aircraft pioneers. The brothers had a bicycle-repair shop in Dayton, Ohio, when they were attracted to aviation (1892). They studied Otto Lilienthal's gliding experiments, but when they began to think of aircraft construction found themselves frustrated by a lack of scientific data. To overcome this they built (1901) a small wind tunnel to determine the effect of air pressure on wing surfaces. They invented 'ailerons' or wing flaps as controls; finally they designed and built their first aircraft, a machine weighing 750 lb. and powered by a 12 h.p. petrol motor. On 17 December 1903 they made what are generally regarded as the first powered, sustained and controlled flights at Kitty Hawk, North Carolina. The first flight lasted for only 12 seconds but on the fourth the machine travelled 852 ft in 59 seconds – a speed of 30 m.p.h. By 1905 Wilbur had remained aloft for 38 minutes and in 1908 Orville increased this to 75 minutes, during which he covered 77 miles. They formed the Wright Aeroplane Company in 1909. (R. W. * Pearse.)
McFarland, M. W., ed., *The Papers of Wilbur and Orville Wright*. 2 vols. 1953

Wriothesley, Henry *see* **Southampton, 3rd Earl of**

Wunderlich, Carl Reinhold August (1815–1877). German physician. He practised in Leipzig where he became professor. Among the earliest to recognize that fever was not a disease *per se*, but a symptom, he introduced the regular taking of temperatures and their recording on a chart. (The clinical thermometer he used was a clumsy instrument a foot long, which took over a quarter of an hour to register.)

Wundt, Wilhelm (1832–1930). German experimental psychologist. The son of a Lutheran pastor, he pursued a career in medicine, attending university at Tübingen, Heidelberg and Berlin, where he worked under * du Bois-Reymond. He taught at Heidelberg till 1871, moving first to Zürich and then to Leipzig. After a generation in the shadows, his career blossomed. His laboratory became one of the great centres of psychological research. Wundt's approach to psychology was always physiological. He was concerned with response and reaction, with the speed of nerve impulses, and with the understanding of electrical impulses in the brain. His approach was frequently described as 'psychology without a soul', though he himself denied that his outlook was reductionist and materialist. Many of the distinguished figures in experimental psychology of the early twentieth century took their training from him.
Boring, E. G., *A History of Experimental Psychology*. 1950

Wyatt, James (1746–1813). English architect. He was the son of a builder and after studying in Italy returned to England and worked in the style made fashionable by the * Adam brothers. From about 1780 he became a leader of the Gothic revival. The eccentric William * Beckford gave him a wonderful opportunity when he commissioned (1796) Fonthill

Abbey, and Wyatt escaped blame when the 276-ft tower fell down (1820). Wyatt did much unfortunate restoration of churches and was chosen by George III to work for him at Windsor Castle. The present appearance of the castle is due to his nephew **Jeffry Wyatt** (1766–1840), later Sir Jeffry Wyatville (thus titled to lessen the confusion caused by the fact that nine members of the Wyatt family were architects).

Robinson, J. W., *The Wyatts: An Architectural Dynasty*. 1980

Wyatt, Sir Thomas (1503–1542). English poet and diplomat. He was sent on diplomatic missions to France and the papal court, after which he privately visited many Italian cities, where he admired and absorbed their literary culture. His further career was interrupted by Henry VIII's suspicions about his relationship with Anne Boleyn and he spent two brief periods in the Tower of London. He translated much of Petrarch and is credited with introducing the Petrarchan sonnet into English literature. His own lyrics were published after his death, in *Tottel's Miscellany* (1557). In the twentieth century he has been recognized as a good and even great poet after a long period of critical neglect.

His son **Sir Thomas Wyatt the Younger** (1521?–1554), proved his worth as a soldier, but raised a rebellion to prevent Queen Mary's marriage to Philip of Spain. He was executed when his plan failed.

Lewis, C. S., *English Literature in the Sixteenth Century*. 1954

Wycherley, William (1640–1716). English playwright. After some years in France and attending Oxford University he went to London, where he lived a somewhat dissipated life while nominally studying the law. His first play, *Love in a Wood* (1671), was dedicated to the king's mistress, the Duchess of Cleveland, whose patronage he won with that of the Duke of Buckingham and of the king himself. *The Gentleman Dancing Master* (1672) was less successful, but his third play, *The Country Wife* (1675), was one of the most entertaining Restoration comedies; it was adapted by Garrick and has been revived in modern times. *The Plain Dealer*, written earlier but produced in 1676, was the last of his plays. He married the Countess of Drogheda (1679) but was reduced to poverty by lawsuits which followed her death (1681); James II came to his rescue with a pension. In later life Wycherley became a friend of Pope. His plays have been condemned for their bawdiness (a reflection of the taste of the period) but his wit and satire are indisputably brilliant.

Zimbardo, R., *Wycherley's Drama*. 1965

Wyclif (Wyclif, Wiclife), **John** (*c*. 1320–1384). English ecclesiastical reformer. He is first mentioned in 1360, when, already renowned for scholarship, he was master of Balliol College, Oxford; but he soon left to work in near-by parishes, which allowed him to maintain his links with Oxford. By this time he was known at court and had come under the powerful patronage of John of Gaunt. In 1374, the same year that he was presented with the living of Lutterworth, he was sent on an embassy to confer with the papal envoys at Bruges. The removal of the papacy to Avignon and its close connexions with the French crown had increased English resentment at papal exactions. Thus Wyclif, taking his stand on the authority of the New Testament, was voicing the popular view in denouncing the church's right to interfere in secular affairs and in maintaining the state's right to withdraw ecclesiastical endowments. Supported by John of Gaunt, who wanted the church's wealth for the French wars, Wyclif, whose aim was a return to apostolic simplicity, was able to evade episcopal and papal attempts to secure his condemnation. The scandal of two popes (1378) – Urban VII (supported by England) at Rome and Clement VII at Avignon – persuaded Wyclif to go further. He not only attacked the church's corruption and the Pope's temporal power, he also rejected the system of priestly absolution, penances and indulgences. To convince his followers that these lacked scriptural authority he organized, with the help of the Oxford scholars, a complete translation of the Bible for which he himself contributed a rendering of the Gospels and probably most of the New Testament. So far his support had been widespread even in the church itself, but when he attacked the dogma of transubstantiation and assailed the whole hierarchy the attitude changed. Condemned by a synod (1382) he had to retire to Lutterworth, where he died. His followers, contemptuously called 'Lollards' after a Dutch word meaning 'mumblers', were generally stamped out. Wyclif's teaching strongly influenced John Huss, the great Bohemian reformer, and the doctrines

of both were condemned by the Council of Constance (1414–18).
MacFarlane, K. B., *John Wyclif and the Beginnings of English Noncomformity*. 1952

Wyeth, Andrew (1917–). American painter. His spare, sometimes unnerving, landscapes were extremely popular and widely reproduced. In 1963 President * Kennedy awarded him the Medal of Freedom for work 'which in the great humanist tradition illuminated and clarified the verities of life'.

Wykeham, William of (1324–1404). English prelate and patron of learning. He entered royal service (*c.* 1347) and eventually as lord privy seal and lord chancellor (1363–71) became the virtual head of the administration. Meanwhile his ecclesiastical progress continued and in 1367 he was appointed bishop of Winchester. During Edward III's closing years he fell into disfavour for supporting the parliamentary opposition but with the accession of Richard II he was back in office and was again lord chancellor (1389–91). During his long career he had amassed a great fortune with which he founded a grammar school at Winchester (Winchester College), and New College, Oxford. He also bore the expense of rebuilding the nave of Winchester Cathedral in the new Perpendicular style.
Heseltine, G. C., *William of Wykeham*. 1932

Wyndham, Sir Charles (1837–1919). English actor-manager. After serving as a doctor in the American Civil War he quickly made a name in light comedy parts, partnered on stage from 1876 by his wife Mary Moore. From the profits of their management Wyndham's and the New theatres were built. He was particularly successful in the plays of Henry Arthur * Jones. He was knighted in 1901.

Wynkyn de Worde *see* **Worde**

Wyss, Johann Rudolf (1781–1830). Swiss writer. He wrote the Swiss national anthem and finished and published *The Swiss Family Robinson* (English translation 1814), which, originally written by his father for his children, quickly became a world-wide classic.

Wyszynski, Stefan (1901–1981). Polish cardinal. After being bishop of Lublin from 1946 he became archbishop of Warsaw and primate of Poland; he was made cardinal in 1953. Throughout the period of Communist rule he maintained the church's position with the greatest courage. He was imprisoned (1953–56) but by co-operating with the government where co-operation did not offend the church's dignity and conscience he saved it from still greater interference.

X

Xavier, St Francis (1506–1552). Spanish Jesuit. The name by which he is known indicates his birthplace in Navarre. He first met * Loyola in 1529 and was among the first members of the Society of Jesus. He was ordained in 1537 and in 1541 made his first missionary journey to Goa in Portuguese India. Thence (1545–49) he visited many parts of the East Indies including Ceylon, where he converted the King of Kandy. A mission which he established in Japan (1549–51) endured for a century and attained great influence. He returned to Goa (1552) to organize a similar mission to China but on his way there died of fever on the island of Changchwen (St John) near Macao. One of the greatest Christian missionaries, he fully merited the title of 'apostle of the Indies' by which he became known; he was canonized in 1622. As well as many interesting letters his writings include treatises on asceticism.

Brodrick, J., *St. Francis Xavier, 1506–1552.* 1952

Xenakis, Yannis (1922–). Greek composer, architect and mathematician, born in Romania, living in France. He fought in the Greek Resistance, then worked as an architect for 12 years with * Le Corbusier, while studying composition with * Honegger and * Messaien. He was the originator of 'stochastic' (i.e. dependent on random variables) music, in which pieces were programmed with the aid of a computer.

Xenophon (*c.* 430–*c.* 355 B.C.). Greek soldier and writer. He was a pupil of Socrates at Athens and wrote several books about him, e.g. *Memorabilia*, which reveal a much more ordinary personality than that portrayed in Plato's works. Xenophon's greatest experience as a man of action took place when (401 B.C.) he joined the arm of the Persian prince Cyrus in revolt against his brother King Artaxerxes. The death of Cyrus (400) left 10,000 Greeks marooned in Persia; Xenophon placed himself at their head and led them on the long and hazardous march across Asia Minor made famous by his *Anabasis*. Next he joined the army of the Spartan king Agesilaus, an act regarded as treasonable by the Athenians, who decreed his banishment. During his exile he lived in retirement at Scillus in Elis, where he devoted much time to writing, and at Corinth. It is known that the banishment decree was eventually repealed but the exact date and manner of his death are uncertain. His other works include *Cyropaedia*, a kind of political romance in which Cyrus I of Persia fills the role of a model ruler; and *Hellenica*, a continuation of the work of Thucydides from 411 to 362 B.C. All Xenophon's books are written in a clear, straightforward style and his historical works reveal a gift for narrative and an objective search for truth.

Miller, W., et al. (eds.), *The Complete Works of Xenophon*. 1960–1968

Xerxes I (*c.* 519–464 B.C.). King of Persia (from 485), son and successor of * Darius I. Having crushed revolts in Egypt and Babylon he continued his father's preparations for an invasion of Greece. In the spring of 480 his great army began to cross the Hellespont (the Dardanelles) by a bridge of boats, an operation said to have taken a full week. No resistance was encountered during the march through Thrace until the Spartan king Leonidas and his famous 'Three Hundred' made their heroic stand at the Pass of Thermopylae. When Xerxes reached Athens he found that the population had taken to the sea; seated on his throne above the straits between Salamis and the mainland he had the humiliation of watching the destruction or dispersion of his ships. Fighting in Greece ended with the defeat and death of the Persian general Mardonius at Plataea (479). Xerxes spent the rest of his reign in peace until his murder by the traitor Artabanus.

Ximenes (Jimenes) **de Cisneros, Francisco** (1436–1517). Spanish prelate and statesman. He was born in Castile and completed his education for the priesthood in Rome, but though he received a papal nomination as archpriest for the Spanish diocese of Toledo, the archbishop refused to admit him and held him in prison for six years. After his release he retired to a Franciscan monastery where he gained such a reputation for learning and the austerity of his life that Queen Isabella of Castile appointed him her confessor (1492); three years later he became archbishop of Toledo and in this dual capacity exercised his great talent for affairs of state. Eventually, Isabella having died (1504), and with her husband and co-ruler Ferdinand of Aragon often absent in Italy, her daughter and heiress Juana mad and her son-in-law Philip of Burgundy dying in 1507, the influence of Ximenes (cardinal from 1507) became almost paramount. Much of what he did, and especially the centralizing of monarchic rule and his financial management, was beneficial; the capture of Oran in Africa by an expedition (1509) financed and led by himself reduced piracy; but his continued persecution of the Moors (in defiance of the promise of religious tolerance which led to the capitulation of Granada) did irretrievable harm. After the death of Ferdinand (1516) Ximenes became regent and fully maintained the royal authority, but on his way to meet his new sovereign, Charles (afterwards the emperor * Charles V), the great minister died. Apart from his political achievements Ximenes was a great patron of literature and the arts; he refounded the university of Alcala de Henares and published at his own expense the great work of Spanish scholarship known (from Complutium, the Latin name for Alcala) as the Complutensian Polyglot Bible.

Y

Yale, Elihu (1649–1721). British merchant, born in Boston, Massachusetts. He was educated in England, joined the East India Company and by 1687 was governor of Madras. When the collegiate school of Saybrook, Connecticut, was moved to New Haven it was named after Yale (1718) in gratitude for a generous benefaction. In 1887 it was renamed Yale University. It is regarded as the third oldest university of the U.S.A.

Yale, Linus (1821–1868). American inventor and industrial manufacturer. He invented various types of locks including those named after him.

Yamagata Aritomo, Prince (1838–1922). Japanese soldier and politician. One of the emperor's most influential counsellors, he became War Minister in 1873 and chief of staff in 1878. He was responsible for modernising the organisation and equipment of Japanese forces. He served as Prime Minister 1889–91 and 1898–1900 and continued the policy of modernisation which ultimately brought Japan to a position of influence. He became an honorary O.M. in 1906.
Hackett, R. F., *Yamagata Aritomo in the Rise of Modern Japan, 1838–1922.* 1971

Yamamoto Isoroku (1884–1943). Japanese admiral. Trained in naval aviation, he studied at Harvard, was a naval attaché in Washington and rose to be commander-in-chief of the Japanese combined fleet (1939–43). Although pessimistic about the outcome of war, he planned the Pearl Harbor strategy (1941) to strike a knock-out blow against U.S. naval forces. He directed the Battle of Midway (1942) and died when his plane was shot down in the South Pacific.

Yamashita Tomoyuki (1885–1946). Japanese general who led the conquest of Singapore in 1942 and conducted the Philippines campaign. His success was ended by a counter-attack of US forces under General MacArthur, by whom he was captured and hanged (for authorising atrocities) in Manila.

Yeats, William Butler (1865–1939). Irish poet and dramatist. With the example of his father before him – later followed by his younger brother **Jack Butler Yeats** (1873–1958) – he studied art for a time but by 1889 he had published his first book of poems and thereafter was one of the leaders of the Irish literary movement. He was closely associated with Lionel Johnson, Katherine Tynan, and G. W. Russell (A.E.), and took part with Lady Gregory in the various dramatic ventures which led to the opening of the Abbey Theatre, Dublin (1904). To this result Yeats's plays *The Countess Cathleen* (1892, staged 1899) and *Cathleen ni Houlihan* (1902) contributed. Other plays included *The Land of Heart's Desire* (1894) and *Deirdre* (1907). Meanwhile volumes of his poetry were appearing in steady sequence. His early work was much concerned with Irish myth and folk lore; there were delicate romantic lyrics, e.g. *The Lake Isle of Innisfree*. Prose works, e.g. *The Celtic Twilight* (1893), evoked similar themes. In 1893 Yeats published an edition of Blake, and the influence of mysticism, both the occult mysticism of the east and that of Maeterlinck and the French symbolists, becomes apparent. *A Vision* (1925) shows a remarkable insight into the sources of poetic inspiration. The publication of a second collection of poems (1910) marked the beginning of what is known as Yeats's middle period; the twilight mists begin to disperse, imagination is tempered by reality, heroes of that violent phase in Irish history join those of myth. This period, at the end of which he was a senator (1922–28) of the Irish Free State, was marked by his own emergence as a public character. In his later works, e.g. *The Tower* (1928), *The Winding Stair* (1933) and the last collections, there is greater simplicity but at the same time greater violence – violence of ecstasy, but also of bitterness at the inevitable consequences of old age. But it is probable that despite his great output of plays, poems, essays, critical and philosophical works it is by the lilt and melody of his gentler lyrics that he will be best remembered:

I have spread my dreams under your feet;
Tread softly, because you tread on my dreams.

Yeats edited *The Oxford Book of Modern Verse* (1936); he won the Nobel Prize for Literature (1923).
Donoghue, D., *Yeats*. 1971

Yersin, Alexandre Émile John (1863–1943). Swiss bacteriologist. He studied under Pasteur and worked at the Pasteur Institute in Paris, where, with Pierre Roux, he did research on diphtheria serum. In Hong Kong he isolated (1894) the plague bacillus and prepared an effective serum for it (1895). He lived in Indochina from 1910 and set up branches of the Pasteur Institute in China.

Yevtushenko, Yevgeny Alexandrovich (1933–). Russian poet. His poems first appeared in the U.S.S.R. in 1952. He quickly became the most prominent of the young writers who rejected 'socialist realism' in literature. He incurred much criticism for his poem 'Babiy Yar', which pilloried Soviet hypocrisy and antisemitism. He continued courageously to maintain his critical attitude in his autobiography, which was published in Paris (1963).

Yonge, Charlotte Mary (1823–1901). English novelist. She wrote historical novels which were moderately popular, but her best-sellers were romantic chronicles of contemporary family life, with a strong Anglican flavour. Two of her most famous books are *The Heir of Redclyffe* and *The Daisy Chain*; she gave the proceeds of both to the Church of England for missionary work.
Battiscombe, G., *Charlotte M. Yonge*. 1943

York, Henry Benedict Maria Clement Stuart, Duke of (known as Cardinal York) (1725–1807). British prelate. He was the younger son of James Edward * Stuart and the last male in direct descent from the Stuart kings. On the death of his elder brother Charles Edward * Stuart he was hailed by the Jacobites as Henry IX. He was created cardinal as a young man and spent most of his life in Rome. He was impoverished in the French Revolutionary period but in 1800 George III granted him a pension of £4,000.

York, House of. That branch of the Plantagenet dynasty descended, through * Richard, Duke of York, from Lionel, Duke of Clarence, second son of Edward III. Yorkist kings were Edward IV, Edward V and Richard III. Later the Duke of York became a common title in the British royal family, e.g. the kings James II, George V and George VI before accession and George III's second son, Frederick Augustus (1763–1827), whose military career culminated in his appointment (1798) as commander-in-chief, the office he held (except for the years 1809–11) until his death.
Green, V. H. H., *The Later Plantagenets*. 1955

Yoshida Shigeru (1878–1967). Japanese Liberal politician. A diplomat, he was ambassador to Great Britain (1936–39), opposed extremist policies during World War II and was imprisoned (1945) until the Americans released him. He was foreign minister (1945–46) and twice premier (1946–47 and 1948–54), largely setting the pattern of post-war Japanese politics.

Young, Arthur (1741–1820). English agriculturist and writer. His father, a clergyman, owned an estate at Bradfield, Suffolk, which his son began to farm in 1763. As a farmer he was a failure, but he gradually gained success as an agricultural writer, basing his work on information gathered during a series of tours (from 1767) through the agricultural districts of England. In 1776 he went to Ireland where as estate factor to Lord Kingsborough he renewed his practical experience. Meanwhile he had begun to publish his observations, which, e.g. in *Political Arithmetic* (1774), extended to social and political comment. He edited (1784–1809) a periodical called *Annals of Agriculture*. As well as being elected F.R.S. he received recognition from abroad which encouraged him to make journeys in France and Italy. His *Travels in France* (1792–94) is a most valuable account of that country on the eve of the Revolution. From 1793 he was secretary to the newly formed Board of Agriculture. Larger farms, enclosures of unfarmed land, the use of fertilizers, improvement of stock and secure tenure were among the things he advocated, supporting his arguments with statistics and surveys. The 'agricultural revolution' was in fact largely of his making. From 1811 his old age was saddened by blindness.

Betham-Edwards, M. (ed.), *The Autobiography of Arthur Young*. 1898

Young, Brigham (1801–1877). American Mormon leader. He was a carpenter, painter and glazier by trade but his life was completely changed when in 1830 he saw the Book of Mormon and was subsequently converted by a brother of the prophet Joseph * Smith. In 1835 he became one of the 'twelve apostles' of the Mormon church and after Smith's murder (1844) – the result of his claim of divine sanction for polygamy – he led his people to Utah where founded Salt Lake City. As president of the church he was made territorial governor (1849). Though deposed by the U.S. government for adhering to polygamy he retained his hold over his co-religionists who under his guidance became a self-contained and prosperous community. He was survived by twenty-seven wives and fifty-six children, to whom he bequeathed $2,500,000. The Mormons (Church of Latter Day Saints) renounced polygamy in 1890.

Young, Francis Brett (1884–1954). English novelist. Trained as a doctor, he won the James Tait Black Memorial Prize with *Portrait of Clare* in 1927, but did not afterwards attain the same quality. His books were charming chronicles of life in his native rural Worcestershire, which he described with great affection.

Young, Thomas (1773–1829). English physicist and egyptologist. He was trained in medicine but became interested mainly in physics. He was elected F.R.S. in 1794 and was later professor of physics at the Royal Institution (1801–03) and secretary of the Royal Society (1803–29). From 1801 he did much to establish the wave theory of light, particularly in attributing phenomena such as 'Newton's rays' to 'interference' between trains of light waves; he also put forward a theory of colour vision which was later improved by * Helmholtz. He first used the term 'modulus of elasticity' in its modern sense, and introduced what is now known as 'Young's modulus'. He was also an outstanding linguist and helped to decipher the inscriptions on the Rosetta Stone.

Younghusband, Sir Francis Edward (1863–1942). British soldier and explorer. As the culmination of a long period of difficult relationships and unsatisfactory negotiations, Colonel Younghusband accompanied by an armed escort advanced into Tibet (1904) and after being attacked reached Lhasa, the capital. An agreement resulted which marked the opening of Tibet to British trade. He explored and wrote about many parts of Central Asia and vainly tried to reach the summit of Everest.

Seaver, G., *Francis Younghusband*. 1952

Yourcenar, Marguerite (de Crayencour) (1903–). French author, born in Brussels, and a US citizen from 1947. Her *Memoirs of Hadrian* (1951) were a critical and popular success, and in 1980 she became the first woman elected to the Academie Française.

Ypres, John (Denton Pinkstone) French, 1st Earl of (1852–1925). British soldier. He commanded the cavalry in the Boer War (1899–1901) with * Haig as his chief of staff. He was made field marshal in 1913; he was chief of the imperial general staff (1912–14), resigning because of the policy of coercing Ulster. Despite this he was chosen to command the British Expeditionary Force on the outbreak of World War I. He was in command during the retreat from Mons, the subsequent counter-attack at the Marne and the first two battles of Ypres, and the Battle of Loos (autumn) which he mishandled, leading to his recall and replacement by Haig. He became Lord-Lieutenant of Ireland (1918–21). He was rewarded after every failure: the OM when he resigned over Ulster (1914), made Viscount French after his defeats in Flanders (1916), £50,000 when the war ended and he was commanding the home forces, culminating in the earldom of Ypres (1922) after his disastrous term in Ireland.

Yüan Shih-kai (1859–1916). President of China (1912–1916). As a soldier he gained the highest honours under the dowager empress * Tz'u Hsi in her last years but fell from favour after her death (1908). On the outbreak of the revolution he was hastily given supreme command, gained some success over the revolutionaries, but, backed by the only fully trained troops in the country, was soon playing a double game. He persuaded the imperialists to accept the necessity for the young emperor's abdication and at the same time induced * Sun Yat-sen, who had already been elected president, to stand down in his favour. The next step to supreme power was the abolishing of parliament, but he over-reached himself when he followed this (1915) by a plan to make himself emperor. Confronted with the anger of the people and the defection of his own commanders he was forced to withdraw, a decision causing so much 'loss of face' as to bring about his death, the exact details of which are not known.
Ch'en, J., *Yüan Shih-K'ai: Brutus assumes the Purple*. 2nd ed. 1972

Yukawa Hideki (1907–1981). Japanese physicist. While a lecturer at Osaka University, he evolved a theory of nuclear forces and predicted (1935) the existence of a particle (the meson) having a mass 200-300 times that of the electron. Mesons were observed in cosmic rays in 1936, but in 1947 these were found to be of a different type from those predicted by Yukawa, which were then observed. He became the first Japanese Nobel Prize winner when he was awarded the Prize for Physics (1949). In 1953 he was made director of the new Research Institute for Fundamental Physics in Kyoto, retiring in 1970.

Z

Zabarella, Jacopo (1533–1589). Italian scientist and philosopher. One of the major figures in the revival of Aristotelian studies, he helped purify, by humanist methods, Aristotelian texts of medieval glosses and inaccuracies. He recognized the fruitfulness of Aristotelian theological and organic approaches to the study of the living body and the practice of medicine. Zabarella wrote extensively on the methodology of science. He tried to show that logic was not so much a system complete in itself but rather a tool for investigation. In this respect he was probably instrumental in reorienting Aristotelianism away from rationalist metaphysics and in the direction of a more experimental approach.

Zaghlul, Sa'ad (1860–1927). Egyptian politician. He was leader of the nationalist party (the *Wafd*) in its demands for independence from Britain. He played a principal part in the various negotiations and was deported more than once. After winning an overwhelming majority in the elections of 1924 he was forced by Britain to resign when a few months later Sir Lee Stack, the sirdar, was murdered. Zaghlul never resumed office as premier.

Zaharoff, Sir Basil (1850–1936). Greek financier, born in Anatolia (Turkey). His wide interest and many deals in oil, shipbuilding and especially armaments involved movements and activities where secrecy was essential and so made him into something of a 'mystery man'. During and after World War I his international connexions and great wealth made his help and advice useful to such great political figures as Lloyd George, Clemenceau, Briand and Venizelos. He became a British subject and received the G.B.E. (1918) and the G.C.B. (1919) for his services. He gave generously to post-war relief and reconstruction and endowed chairs of aviation and language at universities in England, France and Russia.

Zahir Shah, Mohammed (1914–). King of Afghanistan (1933–1973). He succeeded to the throne after the assassination of his father Nadir Shah and continued a policy of orderly progress. He showed considerable astuteness in using the rivalry between the U.S.A. and Russia after World War II to secure aid from both for his country. He was deposed in a *coup* organized by his cousin.

Zamenhof, Lazarus Ludovic (1859–1917). Polish–Jewish philologist. He spent most of his life in Warsaw where he practised as an oculist: he is remembered as the inventor of Esperanto, best known of the artificial languages.

Zamora y Torres, Niceto Alcalá (1877–1949). Spanish politician. A lawyer by profession, he had already held ministerial office when he came into international prominence as leader of the revolutionary committee which forced Alfonso XIII to abandon the throne. Zamora served as first president of the Spanish republic 1931–36, when his political opponents forced him to resign.

Zangwill, Israel (1864–1926). Anglo-Jewish writer. The best known of his novels and plays of Jewish life was *Children of the Ghetto* (1892, dramatized 1899). He was a philanthropist and also a keen Zionist; he organised the Jewish Territorial Organisation, which was however a failure.

Zanuck, Darryl Francis (1902–1979). American film producer. He began his film career in the 1920s, writing scenarios first for the Fox Film Company and later for Warner Brothers, becoming an associate producer there. In 1933 he and Joseph M. Schenk founded 20th Century, and in 1935 they combined with the Fox Film Company to become 20th Century Fox. As head of production Zanuck was noted for his direct involvement with actual filming and for his talent in picking good directors and letting them think for themselves. He moved to his own independent company in 1957, and retired in 1971. He was the last of the tycoons of Hollywood, and his main concern was to tell a strong story and make money from it. His very varied productions included some of the best-known Hollywood films: *The Jazz Singer; 42nd Street; Little Caesar; The Grapes of Wrath; 12 o'clock High; Cleopatra; The Sound of Music.*

Zapata, Emiliano (1879–1919). Mexican revolutionary. He led the first major agrarian revolution of the 20th century against * Carranza, became a guerrilla and died in an ambush. He has been a folk legend ever since.

Zappa, Frank (1940–). U.S. rock musician, leader of The Mothers of Invention, flourishing mainly in the '60s and early '70s. Major records include *Lumpy Gravy; We're Only In It For The Money; Grand Wazoo* and *Bongo Fury.*

Zatopek, Emil (1922–). Czech athlete noted as a long-distance runner. Between the Olympic Games of 1948 and those of 1952 he broke thirteen world records in the 5,000 metres, 10,000 metres and Marathon. He was considered the best of his time.

Zeeman, Pieter (1865–1943). Dutch physicist, professor of physics at Amsterdam (1900–1935). He discovered (1896) the 'Zeeman effect', the splitting of spectral lines when a beam of light passes through a magnetic field. The effect was explained by Lorentz and led to the development of magneto-optics. Zeeman also demonstrated the existence of magnetic fields around the sun and the stars. He shared the Nobel Prize for Physics (1902) with Lorentz.

Zeffirelli, Franco (1923–). Italian theatre and film director. He began his career in the theatre, as an actor and designer, in 1945. He produced his first opera (*La Cenerentola*) at La Scala, Milan, in 1953 and worked subsequently at Covent Garden and the New York Metropolitan. His notable stage productions included *Hamlet* and *Romeo and Juliet*, both marked by keen perception of the author's intentions and vivid clarity in interpreting them. His films include *Romeo and Juliet* and *The Taming of the Shrew.*

Zeiss, Carl (1816–1888). German optical-instrument manufacturer. He founded the famous firm at Jena, renowned for the precision with which lenses for telescopes, microscopes, field-glasses, cameras etc. were made. He was a pioneer of co-partnership.

Zeno of Citium (334?–262 B.C.). Philosopher, born in Cyprus. He founded the Stoic system of philosophy, called after the *Stoa Poikite* ('painted colonnade') in Athens where he taught.

Zeno of Elea (fl. *c.* 450 B.C.). Greek philosopher. He was born in the Greek colony in southern Italy after which he was named, and came to Athens with * Parmenides, of whom he was a disciple. According to Aristotle he introduced the form of argument known as 'reduction to absurdity'. A famous example of his method is his 'proof' that a hare can never overtake a tortoise, because by the time that the hare has covered the distance between them the tortoise will have made some small advance. When this distance, too, has been covered by the hare, another advance, however small, will have been made by the tortoise and so on indefinitely; there will always be a fractional gap between them.

Zenobia (fl. *c.* 260–270). Queen of Palmyra in Syria. After the death of her husband Odenathus, Rome's ally against Persia, she ruled as regent for her son, established a brilliant court at Palmyra and increased her realm until she exercised power from the Egyptian frontier to the Black Sea. In 272 she revolted from Rome; her armies were defeated and her capital destroyed. Zenobia herself, in chains of gold, was led in the emperor Aurelian's triumphal procession through Rome. She died in a villa at Tivoli.

Zeppelin, Count Ferdinand von (1838–1917). German airship designer. He served in the Union army in the American Civil War and later reached the rank of general in his own country. He retired (1891) to fulfil a long-held ambition to construct a rigid and dirigible airship. This he first accomplished in 1900; in 1912 he made a 12-hour flight which stirred such enthusiasm in Germany that 6,000,000 marks were raised for him to start a Zeppelin Institute for their manufacture. In World War I they carried out several raids on England but their hydrogen-filled containers made them very vulnerable and they played only a restricted role. After the war Zeppelins were used commercially on flights between Germany and North and South America, but the superiority of aeroplanes and a series of disastrous accidents led to their abandonment.

Zernike, Fritz (1888–1966). Dutch physicist. Professor at Groningen University (1920–58), he won the Nobel Prize for Physics (1953) for his work from 1932 on the phase-contrast principle in microscopy, which made it possible to observe transparent, colourless microorganisms in the living state.

Zetterling, Mai (1925–). Swedish stage and film actress and film director. Her most notable roles include Hedvig in *The Wild Duck* and Nora in *The Doll's House* (film). She directed *Night Games* (1966) and *Vincent the Dutchman* (1973).

Zhao Ziyang (1919–). Chinese Communist politician. After serving as a party official in Guandong province 1965–67, he was purged in the Cultural Revolution, rehabilitated and became first secretary in Sichuan province 1975–80. A protégé of * Deng Xiaoping, he was premier of China 1980–

Zhdanov, Andrei Alexandrovich (1896–1948). Russian politician. The son of a teacher, he became Communist party chief of Leningrad, succeeding * Kirov (1934–44) and was a Politburo member 1939–48. He organized the defence of Leningrad during the war, then emerged as * Stalin's favourite, chief party ideologist and promoter of the 'Zhdanov line', which chastised composers and writers for deviating from party orthodoxy.

Zhou Enlai (also Chou En-lai) (1898–1976). Chinese Communist politician. Son of a bankrupt mandarin, he studied in Tianjin and Tokyo, was jailed in 1920, then went to Europe until 1924, mostly living in Paris (where he worked at a Renault plant). He joined the Chinese Communist Youth League (1921) and became a student organiser in France and Germany. He returned as CCP Secretary in Guangzhou (Canton), working closely with the Guomintang and their Russian military advisers, then taught at the Huangpu Military Academy and was a political commissar with Chiang Kai-shek's 1st Army (1926). In 1927 he broke with Chiang, led an abortive rising in Shanghai, escaped with a price on his head and became a member of the CCP Politburo (1927–76), a record term. He worked in Moscow in 1928, then shared party leadership with * Li Lisan until another unsuccessful rising at Nangchan (1930) led to direct Russian political intervention in the CCP. He retreated to Jiangxi (Kiangsi) in 1931 and was a rival of Mao's until the 'Long March' began: he then deferred to Mao (1935), accepted his 'peasant strategy' and was a leader in the March. When the Japanese war began, he was the CCP's liaison officer with Chiang's HQ at Chongqing (Chungking) 1937–45. After the revolution, he was first premier of the Peoples' Republic 1949–76 and foreign minister 1949–58. Fluent in English and French, he was the best known figure of the regime overseas. He favoured greater technological change and closer links with the US to counterbalance Soviet influence in Asia. His position was strengthened by the 1973 Party Congress, then weakened by his own illness.
Wilson, D., *Chou*. 1984.

Zhu De (Chu Teh) (1886–1976). Chinese marshal and politician, born in Sichuan province. The son of a rich peasant, he took part in the 1911 Revolution against the Manchu dynasty. He joined the army, rising to the rank of brigadier in 1916. He became an opium addict but, after breaking himself of the habit, was sent to Germany to study engineering in 1921. He joined the Communist Party in Berlin in 1922 and was expelled from Germany in 1926. He led the Nanchang rising against * Chiang Kai-shek (1927) and in 1928 organised an army with * Mao Ze-dong. He became commander in chief of the 4th Red Army from 1931. With Mao he led the celebrated 'Long March' from Jiangxi to Yan'an (1934–36). He commanded the 8th Route Army against the

Japanese until 1945, was commander in chief of the People's Liberation Army 1945–54 and, after Chiang's defeat, became Vice President of the Peoples' Republic 1949–59. He served as Acting Head of the State 1968–76.

Zhukov, Georgi Konstantinovich (1896–1974). Russian soldier. The son of a peasant, he served uncommissioned in World War I, joined the Red Army (1919) and rose steadily in rank until in World War II he became a marshal. When the Germans invaded Russia (1941) he commanded the central front and became prominent in the defence of Moscow and later in the operations at Leningrad and Stalingrad. He commanded the successful Ukraine offensive (1943) but it was in command of the great central offensive which brought the Russians from White Russia to Berlin that his talents were seen to the full. He received the German surrender (1945), commanded the Russian occupation forces (1945–46), was deputy minister for defence (1953–55) and defence minister (1955–57).

Zia ul-Haq (1924–). Pakistani general. He rose to the rank of lieutenant-general and was appointed army chief of staff by Z. A. * Bhutto in 1976. In July 1977, Zia took power as president and martial law administrator, and Bhutto was executed on a murder charge in 1979.

Ziegfeld, Florenz (1869–1932). American impresario. He won renown as a showman with the lavish production (1907) of the Ziegfeld Follies, from whose ranks many girls, subsequently well known, started their stage or matrimonial careers. *Showboat* (1927) was among his many successes.

Ziegler, Karl Waldemar (1898–1973). German chemist. He was best known for his observation of the Ziegler Catalysts (e.g. titanium trichloride) which produce stereospecific polymers which led to greatly improved industrial plastics. He shared the 1963 Nobel Prize for Chemistry.

Zieten, Hans Joachim von (1699–1786). Prussian soldier. He was a brilliant trainer and leader of cavalry, whose exploits in the War of the Austrian Succession and the Seven Years War made him a national hero. In the latter he was made a cavalry general on the battlefield of Liegnitz (1760) and by his dash won acclaim at Prague, Leuthen and Torgau. In his old age he was in high favour with Frederick the Great.

Zinoviev, Grigory Evseyevich (original name Ovsel Radomylsky) (1883–1936). Russian revolutionary politician. He left Russia (1908) and lived abroad with * Lenin, as a Bolshevik propagandist. He was a foundation member of the CPSU Politburo (1917–26), president of the Third International (1919–26) and party chief in Leningrad (1921–26). After Lenin died (1924), party leadership was held by a triumvirate of Stalin, Kamenev and Zinoviev. As Stalin moved towards one-man rule, Zinoviev allied himself with Trotsky and was expelled from the party in 1926. Readmission followed recantation but he was never again secure and was executed after condemnation in the 1936 treason trials. Kirovograd was named Zinoviesk after him between 1924–1936. He had become notorious in British politics when the publication (1924) of a letter, allegedly by him, urging the supporters in Britain to prepare for violent insurrection, contributed materially to Ramsay MacDonald's electoral defeat.

Zinzendorf, Count Nicolaus Ludwig von (1700–1760). German religious leader. By sheltering the persecuted Moravian Brethren on his estates, he enabled a revival to take place. His visits to England (where he came to know Wesley), America and elsewhere greatly extended their influence.

Zoffany, John (*c.* 1734–1810). German painter, resident in England from *c.* 1758. Among his early patrons was David Garrick for whom he painted *Garrick in 'The Farmer's Return'* (1762) and similar works. From 1766 George III commissioned royal portraits and conversation pieces; in 1768 he became a founder member of the R.A. During a visit to India (1783–90) he found exotic subjects to extend his range. Though Zoffany was not, perhaps, a great painter his works attract by their liveliness and glitter.
Millar, O., *Zoffany and his Tribuna.* 1967

Zog I (Ahmed Bey Zogu) (1895–1961). King of Albania (1928–39). Before becoming king he had been premier (1922–24) and president (1925–28). As king he was forced to rely on Italian support but he became irked by his dependence. As soon, however, as he tried to assert himself, Mussolini ordered the invasion of his country. Zog took refuge abroad and was never able to return.

Zola, Émile (Édouard Charles Antoine) (1840–1902). French writer. Born in Paris, after his father's death (1847) he was brought up in poverty at Aix-en-Provence, where at the Collège de Bourbon he became a great friend of * Cézanne. His first novel, *Thérèse Raquin* (1867), a psychological crime story, established a new trend in fiction. Soon, however, he became deeply concerned about social evils and planned a series of novels relating the effects of environment on a single family (*Les Rougon-Macquart*) and intended to be an indictment of Napoleon III's régime. The empire had, however, collapsed years before the novels began to appear. This resulted in serious anachronisms as in *Germinal* (1885), where child labour in the coalfields, long abolished, was assailed as though it were one of the contemporary evils with which the novel was concerned. Other well known novels of this series include *L'Assommoir* (1877) on drunkenness and *Nana* (1880) on prostitution. His works lack humour, but their realism is impressive and few have evoked more convincingly the sordidness and stresses that accompanied the growth of industrialism. An exception was *La Débâcle*, a vivid story of the catastrophe of the Franco-Prussian War. Zola also made a name for himself in critical journalism and in 1898 made a sensational incursion into public affairs with *J'accuse*, an open letter to the French president which forced reconsideration of the celebrated * Dreyfus case. He accidentally gassed himself.
Wilson, A., *Émile Zola: An introductory study of his novels*. 2nd ed. 1965

Zoroaster (*c.* 630–*c.* 553 B.C.). Persian prophet. Little is known about him except that in middle life he appears to have converted a King Wishtaspa (Hystaspes) and to have lived and preached under his protection. His teaching postulates a contest between Good, personified as Ormuzd, and Evil, unmentionable by name but represented by the evil spirit Ahriman and Asmodeus (wrath). The tradition of Zoroastrianism is maintained by the Parsees and their sacred writings, the *Ayesta*. These include the *Gathas*, philosophic poems almost certainly attributable to Zoroaster himself. In *Thus Spake Zarathustra* * Nietzsche makes Zoroaster the spokesman of his own ideas.

Zuckerman, Solly Zuckerman, Baron (1904–). British anatomist, born in South Africa. Educated at Cape Town University, he carried out scientific research on monkeys and apes, and became professor of anatomy at Birmingham 1943–68. He advised the RAF during World War II and was chief scientific advisor to the British Government 1964–71. He received the OM in 1968.

Zurbarán, Francisco de (1598–*c.* 1664). Spanish painter. He worked mostly in Seville and in Madrid, but though he painted at the court of Philip IV, his best work is found in his religious works and especially in pictures of single figures – saints and ascetic monks – at their devotions. The naturalism of his Spanish contemporary Velazquez and the chiaroscuro of Caravaggio are clear influences. His *Still-life with Lemons, Oranges and a Rose* (1633; Norton Simon Museum, Pasadena) has an extraordinary ecstatic quality and is his most reproduced work.
Sona, M. S., *The Paintings of Zurbarán*. 1953

Zweig, Arnold (1887–1968). German writer, born in Silesia. His most famous work was the war novel *The Case of Sergeant Grischa* (1927). He left Germany to live in Israel in 1934, returning to East Germany in 1948.

Zweig, Stefan (1881–1942). Austrian writer. Having gained an early reputation by his translations from English and French, he wrote a number of biographical essays, published in groups of three, e.g. Balzac, Dostoyevsky and Dickens (1910); Casanova, Stendhal and Tolstoy (1928). He also wrote plays, short stories, essays and memoirs, e.g. *The World of Yesterday* (1943). He left Austria in 1934 and after some years in England reached Brazil, where, in despair at the condition of the world, he committed suicide.

Zwingli, Ulrich (1484–1531). Swiss religious reformer. After graduating at Basle University he became a parish priest at Glarus, and having served as military chaplain in Italy he denounced the mercenary system. In 1516 he moved to Einsiedeln, and denounced the superstitions connected with that place of pilgrimage: but his influence, other than local, began only with his appointment (1518) as preacher at the Great Minster in Zurich.

Having persuaded the civil council to forbid the entry of indulgence sellers and the enlistment of mercenaries, he went on to preach that only those acts definitely forbidden in the scriptures need be regarded as sinful. Thus it was decided by the council that meat could be eaten in Lent, and other changes, e.g. the removal of images from church, were made after public discussion and debate; eventually (1528) after a great disputation at Berne the *Ten Theses* of the reformed church were adopted. Meanwhile monasteries had been secularized and a communion service substituted for the mass. In 1524 Zwingli's own marriage was announced. An attempt by Philip of Hesse to bring German and Swiss Protestantism into accord failed at the Colloquy of Marburg (1529), Zwingli's belief that the Communion should be merely commemorative being in conflict with Luther's sacramental doctrines. But it was the Roman Catholic cantons of his native Switzerland that were the immediate threat. Despite the fact that a treaty between Romanist and Protestant cantons had been signed in 1529, the Catholics attacked Zurich territory and at the Battle of Kappel (October 1531) Zwingli, once more a chaplain with the troops, was killed. He was the least dogmatic of the great reformers; his urge to reform the church sprang not from striking religious experiences but from his studies of the scriptures.

Potter, G., *Zwingli*. 1978

Zworykin, Vladimir Kosma (1889–1982). American electronics engineer, born in Russia. He migrated to the U.S. in 1919, investigated the photoelectric effect and while working for the Westinghouse Electric Corp. developed (1924) a primitive electronic television camera, the kinescope, based on the cathode ray tube. Westinghouse showed little interest and in 1929 he joined RCA. By 1938 he had perfected his 'Iconoscope' which superseded the method of mechanical scanning devised by * Baird. He also worked on an electronic microscope with far greater magnifying power than optical instruments. Zworykin was called 'the father of modern television'.

Notes

Notes

Notes

Notes

Notes